ENCYCLOPAEDIA
JUDAICA

ENCYCLOPAEDIA JUDAICA

SECOND EDITION

VOLUME 14
Mel–Nas

Fred Skolnik, *Editor in Chief*
Michael Berenbaum, *Executive Editor*

MACMILLAN REFERENCE USA
An imprint of Thomson Gale, a part of The Thomson Corporation

IN ASSOCIATION WITH
KETER PUBLISHING HOUSE LTD., JERUSALEM

Detroit • New York • San Francisco • New Haven, Conn. • Waterville, Maine • London

ENCYCLOPAEDIA JUDAICA, Second Edition

For more information, contact
Macmillan Reference USA
An imprint of Thomson Gale
27500 Drake Rd.
Farmington Hills, MI 48331-3535
Or you can visit our internet site at
http://www.gale.com

LIBRARY OF CONGRESS CATALOGING-IN-PUBLICATION DATA

Encyclopaedia Judaica / Fred Skolnik, editor-in-chief ; Michael Berenbaum, executive editor. -- 2nd ed.
v. cm.
Includes bibliographical references and index.
Contents: v.1. Aa-Alp.
ISBN 0-02-865928-7 (set hardcover : alk. paper) -- ISBN 0-02-865929-5 (vol. 1 hardcover : alk. paper) -- ISBN 0-02-865930-9 (vol. 2 hardcover : alk. paper) -- ISBN 0-02-865931-7 (vol. 3 hardcover : alk. paper) -- ISBN 0-02-865932-5 (vol. 4 hardcover : alk. paper) -- ISBN 0-02-865933-3 (vol. 5 hardcover : alk. paper) -- ISBN 0-02-865934-1 (vol. 6 hardcover : alk. paper) -- ISBN 0-02-865935-X (vol. 7 hardcover : alk. paper) -- ISBN 0-02-865936-8 (vol. 8 hardcover : alk. paper) -- ISBN 0-02-865937-6 (vol. 9 hardcover : alk. paper) -- ISBN 0-02-865938-4 (vol. 10 hardcover : alk. paper) -- ISBN 0-02-865939-2 (vol. 11 hardcover : alk. paper) -- ISBN 0-02-865940-6 (vol. 12 hardcover : alk. paper) -- ISBN 0-02-865941-4 (vol. 13 hardcover : alk. paper) -- ISBN 0-02-865942-2 (vol. 14 hardcover : alk. paper) -- ISBN 0-02-865943-0 (vol. 15: alk. paper) -- ISBN 0-02-865944-9 (vol. 16: alk. paper) -- ISBN 0-02-865945-7 (vol. 17: alk. paper) -- ISBN 0-02-865946-5 (vol. 18: alk. paper) -- ISBN 0-02-865947-3 (vol. 19: alk. paper) -- ISBN 0-02-865948-1 (vol. 20: alk. paper) -- ISBN 0-02-865949-X (vol. 21: alk. paper) -- ISBN 0-02-865950-3 (vol. 22: alk. paper)
1. Jews -- Encyclopedias. I. Skolnik, Fred. II. Berenbaum, Michael, 1945-
DS102.8.E496 2007
909'.04924 -- dc22

2006020426

ISBN-13:

978-0-02-865928-2 (set)
978-0-02-865929-9 (vol. 1)
978-0-02-865930-5 (vol. 2)
978-0-02-865931-2 (vol. 3)
978-0-02-865932-9 (vol. 4)
978-0-02-865933-6 (vol. 5)
978-0-02-865934-3 (vol. 6)
978-0-02-865935-0 (vol. 7)
978-0-02-865936-7 (vol. 8)
978-0-02-865937-4 (vol. 9)
978-0-02-865938-1 (vol. 10)
978-0-02-865939-8 (vol. 11)
978-0-02-865940-4 (vol. 12)
978-0-02-865941-1 (vol. 13)
978-0-02-865942-8 (vol. 14)
978-0-02-865943-5 (vol. 15)
978-0-02-865944-2 (vol. 16)
978-0-02-865945-9 (vol. 17)
978-0-02-865946-6 (vol. 18)
978-0-02-865947-3 (vol. 19)
978-0-02-865948-0 (vol. 20)
978-0-02-865949-7 (vol. 21)
978-0-02-865950-3 (vol. 22)

This title is also available as an e-book
ISBN-10: 0-02-866097-8
ISBN-13: 978-0-02-866097-4
Contact your Thomson Gale representative for ordering information.
Printed in the United States of America

10 9 8 7 6 5 4 3

TABLE OF CONTENTS

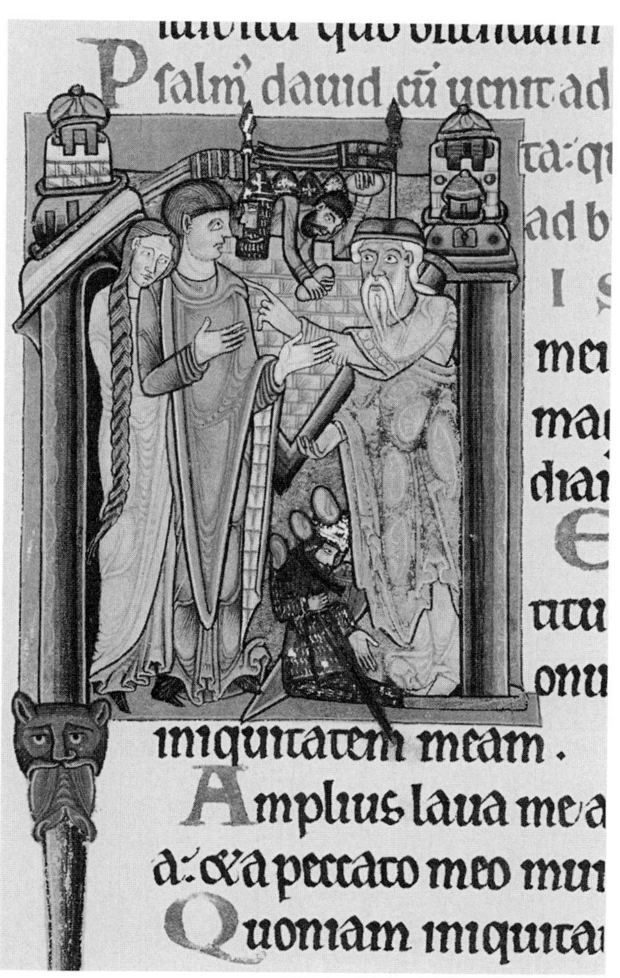

Initial letter for the word Miserere mei, *"Have mercy upon me," at the beginning of Psalm 51 (Vulgate Ps. 50) from the 12th-century* Psalter of York. *Seen here are David, with Bath-Sheba behind him, being admonished by Nathan. Uriah the Hittite lies dead, stoned by an Ammonite. Copenhagen, Royal Library, Thott, 143, fol. 68r.*

MEL-MZ

MELAMED, EZRA ZION (1903–1994), Israel talmudic scholar and philologist. Born in Shiraz, Persia, Melamed was taken to Palestine by his father, R.R. *Melamed, when he was two. He worked at the Ministry of Education (1952–56), and was appointed professor of Bible at the Hebrew University (1964) and of Talmud at Bar Ilan (1961) and at Tel Aviv (1964) universities. He was elected to the Hebrew Language Academy in 1956 and to the Higher Archaeological Council in 1963. He was awarded the Israel Prize in 1987 for Torah literature and commentary on the sources. Melamed's major works are in the fields of talmudic literature: *Midreshei Halakhah shel ha-Tanna'im be-Talmud Bavli* (1943), in which he collected *beraitot* in the Babylonian Talmud based on verses from the Pentateuch, and *Ha-Yaḥas she-Bein Midreshei Halakhah la-Mishnah ve-la-Tosefta* ("Relations Between Halakhic Midrashim and Mishnah and Tosefta," 1967). Two related works were published posthumously: *Midreshei Halakhah shel ha-Tanna'im be-Talmud Yerushalmi* (2001) and *Midreshei Halakhah shel ha-Amoraim be-Talmud Yerushalmi* (2004). Melamed devoted much labor to editing the scientific legacy of his teacher Jacob Nahum *Epstein, including *Mekhilta de-Rabbi Simeon bar Yoḥai* (1955), *Mevo'ot le-Sifrut ha-Tanna'im* (1957), *Mevo'ot le-Sifrut ha-Amora'im* (1962), and *Dikduk Aramit Bavlit* (1960). He also edited B. de Vries' *Meḥkarim be-Sifrut ha-Talmud* (1968). He composed a special work in which he summarized the most significant achievements of modern Talmud scholarship: *Pirkei Mavo le-Sifrut ha-Talmud* (1973). He prepared textbooks and popular works, including *Pirkei Minhag ve-Halakhah* ("Chapters of Custom and *Halakhah*," 1955), and *Parashiyyot me-Aggadot ha-Tanna'im* ("Chapters of Tannaitic *Aggadot*," 1955). Among his other writings are *Tafsir Tehillim bi-Leshon Yehudei Paras* ("Psalms in Judeo-Persian," 1968), *Millon Arami-Ivri le-Talmud Bavli le-Mathilim* ("Aramaic-Hebrew Dictionary of the Babylonian Talmud for Beginners," 1969), and a comprehensive glossary to the entire Babylonian Talmud (*Millon Arami-Ivri shel ha-Talmud ha-Bavli*, 1992), as well as articles in scientific journals. Of special significance is his edition of Eusebius' geographical work *Onomastikon*, which he translated from the original (1938). Because of his involvement with the Persian and other Oriental communities (whom he served as honorary rabbi) and his familiarity with their traditions of custom and language, Melamed served as an important source on such community traditions.

[Menahem Zevi Kaddari / Stephen G. Wald (2nd ed.)]

MELAMED, MEIR (second half of 15th century), financier in Spain during the period of the expulsion. A Hebrew author of the period calls him the "king's secretary," apparently because he held office in one of the royal accounting departments. In official documents he is referred to as "Rabbi" and not "Don," as were most of the other Jewish tax farmers, which indicates that he was a scholar. He lived mainly in Segovia. In 1487 he succeeded his aged father-in-law Abraham *Seneor as chief administrator of tax farming in the kingdom. On June 15, 1492, he and Abraham Seneor were baptized with great ceremony at Guadalupe, Ferdinand and Isabella acting as godparents. As a Christian he adopted the name Fernándo Núñez Coronel. On June 23, 1492, he was appointed chief accountant (*contador mayor*). He also became a permanent member of the royal council and was town councillor (*regidor*) in Segovia.

BIBLIOGRAPHY: Baer, Spain, index, s.v. *Meir Melamed* Baer, Urkunden, index; Suárez Fernández, Documentos, index. **ADD. BIBLIOGRAPHY:** C. Carrete Parrondo, in: *Sefarad*, 37 (1977), 339–49.

MELAMED, RAḤAMIM REUVEN (1854–1938), Persian rabbi and preacher. Born in Shiraz, he moved to Jerusalem in 1906, established a yeshivah in his own home, and served as rabbi to the Persian Jews. He wrote many commentaries in both Hebrew and *Judeo-Persian to the Pentateuch, the Scrolls, *Avot*, and portions of the Zohar: among them *Kisse Raḥamim* (1911), *Yeshu'ah ve-Raḥamim* (1912), *Ẓedakah ve-Raḥamim* (1926), *Ḥayyei Raḥamim* (1929), *Zikhron Raḥamim* (1930), and *Seder Leil Pesaḥ* (in Hebrew and Persian, 1930), all published in Jerusalem. Some of his works were republished by his son, Ezra Zion *Melamed.

BIBLIOGRAPHY: M.D. Gaon, *Yehudei ha-Mizraḥ be-Ereẓ Yisrael*, 2 (1937), 437–8.

[Walter Joseph Fischel]

MELAMED, SIMAN TOV (d. c. 1780), spiritual leader of the Jewish community in *Meshed. A poet, philosopher, and author of many treatises in Hebrew and *Judeo-Persian, he composed **azharot* (1896) in Judeo-Persian (portions of which were written in Persian, as well as Aramaic and Hebrew). A manuscript of his commentary to *Pirkei Avot* is in the possession of Hebrew Union College, Cincinnati, together with other of his writings. His major work is his philosophical-religious *Sefer Ḥayyat al-Rukh* (published 1898), which combines a commentary on Maimonides' teachings on the 13 articles of faith and a treatise on Israel's existence in the Diaspora and ultimate salvation. The work shows a strong influence of the Sufic ideas of *Baḥya ibn Paquda's *Ḥovot ha-Levavot* and other Jewish and Muslim medieval thinkers. In the tradition of Meshed's Jews, Siman Tov Melamed is also remembered as a staunch defender of Judaism in theological disputations which the Shiʿa clergy arranged between him, Muslims, and Jewish converts.

BIBLIOGRAPHY: W. Bacher, in: ZHB, 14 (1910), 51ff.; A. Yaari, *Sifrei Yehudei Bukharah* (1942), nos. 33, 39, 161; E. Neumark, *Massaʿ be-Ereẓ ha-Kedem*, ed. by A. Yaari (1947), 95; W.J. Fischel, in: L. Finkelstein (ed.), *The Jews*, 2 (1960^3), 1174, 1177; E. Spicehandler, in: SBB, 8 (1968), 114–36.

[Walter Joseph Fischel]

°MELANCHTHON (Schwarzerd), PHILIPP (1497–1560), German reformer and theologian. Born at Bretten in Baden, Melanchthon was a great-nephew of the Hebraist and Christian kabbalist Johann *Reuchlin, who taught him Hebrew and supervised his education at Pforzheim. In 1518, at the age of 21, Melanchthon was appointed professor of Greek at Wittenberg but within a year he had sided with Martin *Luther in the struggle with Rome, thus alienating Reuchlin, who later disinherited him. Melanchthon was Luther's principal assistant in translating the Old Testament into German (1523–34). Widely respected as a humanist and theologian, he favored study of the Kabbalah, but condemned its later accretions. One of his addresses on the importance of Hebrew, *De studio linguae Ebraeae*, appeared in 1549. Although Melanchthon was influenced by Luther's antisemitism, he avoided its cruder excesses and in 1539, at the Frankfurt religious assembly, publicly denounced the blood libel that had resulted in the martyrdom of 38 Brandenburg Jews in 1510.

BIBLIOGRAPHY: K. Hartfelder, *P. Melanchthon als Praeceptor Germaniae* (1889); G. Ellinger, *Philipp Melanchthon* (Ger., 1902); F. Hildebrandt, *Melanchthon: Alien or Ally?* (1946); C.L. Manschreck, *Melanchthon, the Quiet Reformer* (1958); H. Sick, *Melanchthon als Ausleger des Alten Testaments* (1959); G. Kisch, *Melanchthons Rechtsund Soziallehre* (1967); Baron, Social[2], 13, 229ff.

MELAVVEH MALKAH (Heb. מְלַוֵּה מַלְכָּה; "escorting the queen"), term used to describe the meal and festivities at the end of the Sabbath. This gesture of farewell to the "queen" (Sabbath) is designed as the counterpart of the festivities which greeted her arrival. The origin of the custom has been traced to the Talmud. R. Ḥanina asserted that the table should be (festively) laid at the termination of the Sabbath, although only a small amount of food would be eaten (Shab. 119b). The *melavveh malkah* was later seen by both *Jacob b. Asher and Joseph *Caro to be the fulfillment of R. Ḥidka's injunction to celebrate four meals on the Sabbath (Shab. 117b). It was in the context of this injunction that the *melavveh malkah* later assumed the image of a virtually voluntary extension of the Sabbath. Isaac *Luria, for example, believed that not until the *melavveh malkah* was over did the sinful dead return to hell from their Sabbath rest, and the kabbalists and Ḥasidim were so reluctant to relinquish the honored Sabbath guest, that they used the *melavveh malkah* as a means of prolonging the Sabbath day as long as possible. They used the occasion to chant special *zemirot and to relate ḥasidic tales. The *melavveh malkah* is also known as *se'udat David* ("King David's banquet"). As such, it serves as a reminder of the legend that King David, having been told by God that he would die on the Sabbath (Shab. 30a), celebrated his survival each new week with special joy (*Ta'amei Minhagim*).

One of the favorite *melavveh malkah* hymns is *Eliyahu ha-Navi* ("Elijah the Prophet"), attributed by some authorities to *Meir of Rothenburg. It welcomes the prophet as the herald of the Messiah. According to legend, Elijah is expected to announce the salvation of Israel at the first opportunity after the termination of the Sabbath. Medieval *paytanim* devoted several other *zemirot* to the *melavveh malkah* festivities. Among the most notable are *Be-Moẓa'ei Yom Menuḥah* by Jacob Menea (14th century); *Addir Ayom ve-Nora, Ish Ḥasid* by Jesse b. Mordecai (13th century); and *Amar Adonai le-Ya'akov*.

BIBLIOGRAPHY: Eisenstein, Dinim, 227; H. Schauss, *Guide to Jewish Holy Days* (1962), 27, 30, 35.

[Harry Rabinowicz]

MELBOURNE, capital of Victoria, Australia. The 15 Port Phillip Association members who founded Melbourne in 1835 included two Jews. Melbourne is today the only Jewish community of any size in the State of Victoria. During the 19th century however a considerable number of Jews settled in other centers in the State, but the country communities practically disappeared. The Melbourne Jewish community was established in 1841.

Early Metropolitan Settlement

Jews clustered around shops and businesses in the center of the city in Collins, Bourke, and Elizabeth streets and in 1847 opened the first synagogue (Melbourne Hebrew Congregation) in that area. The influx in the 1850s and 1860s led to settlement in working-class districts in the suburbs adjoining the city – Fitzroy, Carlton, Richmond, and East Melbourne. The East Melbourne Congregation was founded in 1857 with Moses Rintel as minister, most of the congregants being immigrants from Germany and Austria. At the turn of the century this congregation was led by the patriarchal figure, Rev. Jacob Lenzer.

There were continuous movements of Jews from their first areas of settlement to new areas. In the wake of such a group movement the St. Kilda Synagogue was opened in 1872. In the period before compulsory education the Melbourne Hebrew School was established as a day school in 1874 and continued until 1886, when it was closed because of financial difficulties. In 1888 the three congregations (Melbourne, East Melbourne, and St. Kilda) established the United Jewish Education Board, which conducted part-time Hebrew schools in various centers. As they moved from area to area, the Jews ascended in the social and occupational ladder and by 1900 the most popular occupations were textile manufacturing, general dealing, and skilled trades such as tailoring, watchmaking, and cabinetmaking. Small draper shop-owners were beginning to acquire large retail stores. Carpenters were opening furniture factories. Less than 3% were in the professions. During the first decades of the 20th century there gradually developed a struggle for communal supremacy between the earlier immigrants who lived south of the Yarra River, and who were more prosperous and assimilated, and the more recent immigrants, mostly from Eastern Europe, who were concentrated north of the river, and who were Yiddish-speaking, with an Orthodox background, Yiddish culture, and strong Zionist leanings.

Concurrently, a change took place in the centers of Jewish activity. Whereas until the first decades of the 20th century life centered around the synagogues, in the next decades a shift took place, non-synagogal bodies being organized and gradually taking a more prominent place in communal leadership. The synagogues in the first decades of the 20th century were the Melbourne Hebrew Congregation (first at Bourke St. in the city; after 1930 at Toorak Road) and the St. Kilda Synagogue south of the Yarra, and the East Melbourne Synagogue and the Carlton Synagogue (established 1927), north of the Yarra. Some smaller *minyanim* had also been formed, notably the Woolf Davis Chevra, run by the family of J.E. Stone, and the Talmud Torah Hascola at North Carlton. A number of societies mainly in the hands of the south of the Yarra element were already in existence – the Philanthropic Society, Aid Society, Welfare Society, Sick Visiting Society, the Chevra Kadisha (founded 1910), the United Shechita Board, and the Beth Din. A number of bodies began to spring up north of the Yarra. In 1912 new immigrants had helped to form a center of Yiddish culture, the "Jewish National Library-Kadimah," which apart from its book collection held regular cultural meetings including Yiddish lectures and plays.

The Judean League of Victoria was founded in 1921 as a roof-organization for non-synagogal activity, sports, literary, cultural, social, and Zionist activity. Its headquarters in its heyday at Monash House, Carlton, was a vibrant center of Jewish activity every night of the week for three decades. Its founder and leading spirit was Maurice *Ashkanasy. The struggle between the two elements ended in 1948 with a democratic representation unifying the whole community and putting an end to the era of Anglo-Jewish patrician control and of the congregational dictatorship in communal affairs. The place of Melbourne (later Victorian) Jewish Advisory Board (established in 1921), a strictly synagogal body, was taken by the Victorian Jewish Board of Deputies (in 1948) which gave a new direction to communal activities, and brought about the formulation of a community viewpoint on all matters affecting both local Jewry, such as public relations, immigration, and a deepening of Jewish cultural values, and wider Jewish issues such as Zionism and antisemitism. There was also a move from voluntary philanthropy to organized professional social services. It operated through the following committees: education, social welfare, immigration, public relations, appeals coordination, youth, organization and statistics, and congregational. The struggle was fought out on a number of points, including the question of the *kashrut* of frozen meat exported to Palestine, prepared under the supervision of the United Shechita Board and its chief *shoḥet* Rabbi I.J. Super (who served the community as *shoḥet, mohel*, and teacher for more than half a century), which was challenged by Rabbi J.L. Gurewicz, disciple of Chaim Ozer *Grodzinsky of Vilna and the respected leader of the Orthodox Carlton Synagogue in its heyday. The main issues however were the battle against anti-Zionist elements in the mid-1940s, the struggle for the establishment of a Jewish day school, the continuing cleavage between the Orthodox and the Liberals, a stubborn but losing battle for the greater use of Yiddish, the attitude to antisemitism, and the problem of public relations.

The Transformation of the Community

Between the late 1930s and the mid-1950s the Melbourne Jewish community was transformed, as were the other centers of Australian Jewish life, by a number of important interrelated events. Some of this change occurred before, when the traditional synagogues, mainly Anglo-Jewish in orientation, such as the Melbourne Hebrew Congregation and the St. Kilda Hebrew Congregation, which had provided communal leadership, were challenged by new synagogues representing either a stricter European Orthodoxy or the Reform congregation founded in 1930. A Yiddish-speaking component already existed, centered in Carlton, just north of central Melbourne, rather than in the traditional middle-class Jewish area of St. Kilda, south of the inner city. Institutions like the Jewish National Library–Kadimah, founded in 1912, and the Judean League, a center of cultural life and pro-Zionist activity, founded in 1921, emerged in Yiddish Carlton, whose inhabitants demonstrated the range of Jewish orientations and ideologies of troubled Europe.

There was no secular communal representative body until the foundation of the Victorian Jewish Advisory Board in 1938, an organization which changed its name in May 1947 to the Victorian Jewish Board of Deputies (VJBD), and, in October 1988, to the Jewish Community Council of Victoria. Although all local synagogues which wished to affiliate to the Board could do so, it also included a plethora of secular bodies, including Zionist and Yiddish groups. These representative bodies took a much more visible and direct role in lobbying on behalf of Jewish interests to the government and the media than was previously the case.

While (with many exceptions) the old Anglo-Jewish-dominated Melbourne community had been notably lukewarm on Zionism, the new community was, by and large, enthusiastically pro-Zionist, and, in the decade before the establishment of Israel, defended the creation of a Jewish state against influential local Jewish non-Zionists such as Rabbi Jacob *Danglow and Sir Isaac *Isaacs. Perhaps the most important manifestation of the new Jewish assertiveness in Melbourne was the foundation of Mt. Scopus College, the first Jewish day school, in 1949. Mt. Scopus was coeducational, and moderately Orthodox and Zionist in its orientation. By the 1980s eight full-time Jewish day schools, representing various trends in the Jewish community, had been founded. The relatively large-scale migration to Melbourne of perhaps 35,000 Holocaust refugees and survivors, especially from Poland, dramatically changed the nature of the community, adding not merely to its pro-Zionist and Orthodox strength, but to its secular Yiddish and leftist elements. This in turn produced a number of major cleavages within the community, especially between the mainstream community and an allegedly pro-Communist communal defense body, the Jewish Council to Combat Fascism and Antisemitism, which resulted in the Council's expulsion from the VJBD in 1952, and notably bad relations between the Orthodox synagogues and the Reform movement (which included significant numbers of German and Austrian refugees). As well, Yiddish persisted as a significant Jewish *lingua franca* in Melbourne for decades after the War. By the mid-1950s, however – and certainly by the 1967 War – the Melbourne Jewish community had been transformed into one which was enthusiastically pro-Zionist, religiously pluralistic but with a large Orthodox majority, outspoken in defense of its interests, and keen to deter assimilation through the creation of a large Jewish day school movement. A number of individual activists responsible for these developments, such as Maurice *Ashkanasy, Alex Masel, and Benzion Patkin (1902–1984), the chief founder of Mt. Scopus College, should to be mentioned here. Visitors to Melbourne were often amazed at the breadth and vigor of its institutions and it was often known as the "*shtetl* on the Yarra" – Melbourne's river – for its extraordinary preservation of many of the cultural, linguistic, and ideological matrices of prewar Europe. Melbourne was also often contrasted with Sydney, which had fewer Polish Holocaust refugees but more from Britain and Hungary, and was widely seen as less assertively Jewish than Melbourne, at least down to the 1990s. The rivalry between Melbourne and Sydney was found in many aspects of Australian life, and, in the case of the two Jewish communities, probably owed something to the more extreme nature of Victoria's left-wing, often anti-Israel, stance which emerged in the 1950s from local political developments.

The Contemporary Community

DEMOGRAPHY. Melbourne has experienced considerable and continuing growth during the postwar period. The number of declared Jews in Melbourne, according to the optional religious question in the Australian census, rose from about 22,000 in 1954 to 26,409 in 1971 and then to 35,383 in 1996 and 37,779 in 2001. Since this is based on responses to an optional question of religious affiliation (rather than ethnic identity), the actual number is certainly much higher, probably in the range of 50–55,000, just under 2% of Melbourne's population of about 2.9 million. Most Melbourne Jews tend to live in a small number of well-defined Jewish neighborhoods. Among the 17 postal code areas (equivalent to zip codes in the United States, but somewhat smaller in size) in Australia with the highest number of Jews in the 2001 census, nine were in Melbourne, including three of the top five. The largest and most obviously Jewish areas of concentration are the Caulfield–St. Kilda East–Elsternwick districts, about five miles south of central Melbourne, where 18,216 Jews were identified in the 2001 census. This area contains many Jewish synagogues, institutions, and shops, and a large and visible Strictly Orthodox community. The other significant areas of Jewish concentration were adjacent to this core area: Bentleigh (2,667 Jews in 2001), to the east; the wealthy neighborhood of Toorak (1,611 Jews) to its north; and East Brighton (1,316 Jews) to its south. These neighborhoods became heavily Jewish just after World War II and have remained very stable ever since. There is little or no sign of Jewish suburbanization, as in many other Diaspora societies, nor any equivalent of "white flight," as in the United States, away from decaying neighborhoods. The only major change in Melbourne's Jewish demographic pattern since 1945 has been the decline to the vanishing point of the former area of East European Jewish settlement in Carlton, immediately north of central Melbourne, which, until the 1960s, contained many Yiddish-based institutions such as the Kadimah, the leading Yiddish cultural and social center. The Melbourne Jewish community has grown chiefly by immigration, welcoming successive waves of German Holocaust refugees and a very large flow of postwar Holocaust survivors, especially from Poland, and then more recent groups of South African and ex-Soviet immigrants, as well as a continuing settlement of Jews from the English-speaking world and elsewhere for normal professional purposes. Nevertheless, the stability of Melbourne Jewry, and other social characteristics, have given it some very favorable features. A 1991 random sample survey of the community, for example, found that the Melbourne Jewish fertility rate was apparently above the replacement level, a notable accomplishment for a middle-class Diaspora Jewish community.

CONGREGATIONS. In terms of congregational affiliation, Melbourne had about 50 synagogues in the early 21st century, of which four were Liberal (Reform) and one Masorti (Conservative), one Independent, and all the others Orthodox of various strands ranging from moderate Anglo-Orthodoxy to Strict Orthodoxy. The postwar era has seen a vast expansion in the range of congregational affiliation beyond the Anglo-Orthodoxy predominant before 1939, especially at the religious extremes. Relations between the Orthodox and Reform components of the community have been notably bad, as have, to a lesser extent, relations between different strands in Orthodoxy. In part for this reason, no postwar Melbourne rabbi has been able to act as recognized spokesman for the whole community, in the manner of Rabbi Jacob Danglow before the war. A number of rabbis, such as the Orthodox *Gutnicks, Yitzhak *Groner, and John S. *Levi from the Liberals, have been viewed by many as notable leaders, but none has been regarded as a consensual leader.

COMMUNAL LEADERSHIP. Instead, the leadership of the community has been vested in its representative body, known (1938–47) as the Victorian Jewish Advisory Board, then (1947–88) as the Victorian Jewish Board of Deputies (VJBD); and since 1988 as the Jewish Community Council of Victoria (JCCV). Its president (elected annually, and normally serving a two-year term) and other office-holders are regarded as the community's spokesmen to the media and government. The JCCV is composed of representatives of many Jewish organizations in Melbourne, including most synagogues, Zionist bodies, fraternal, women's, and youth groups. There is no provision to elect individuals on a personal basis. The JCCV has at all times represented a consensual position in the community, strongly supportive of Israel as well as multiculturalism and the Jewish day school system. It monitors and combats antisemitism and extreme anti-Zionism. By its constitution, no religious question can be discussed, since any debating of religious issues is likely to be divisive. The JCCV, which meets on a monthly basis, works closely with the Executive Council of Australian Jewry (ECAJ), the national representative body of the community, and the Zionist Federation.

EDUCATION. Probably the major reason for the relative success of the Jewish community in Melbourne has been the Jewish day school system. Since 1949, nine full-time Jewish day schools have been established in Melbourne. (See *Australia for list.) In 1962, 1,480 students attended these schools, a total which rose to 4,840 in 1982, 5,492 in 1989, and about 6,000 in 2004. The experience of Melbourne has clearly been that education there strongly discourages assimilation and intermarriage. One of the major challenges confronting the Melbourne Jewish community is the ever-increasing cost of education at Jewish schools (which are private and fee-paying, although they receive some state funding). No long-term solution to this problem is yet in sight. Jewish interest courses exist at Monash University, but the underfunding of the tertiary and research sectors compared with the Jewish school system is also a notable and unfortunate feature of the community.

There are a number of Jewish museums in Melbourne which would be of interest to tourists. The Jewish Museum of Australia (26 Alma Road, St. Kilda) contains exhibits on Australian Jewry history. The Jewish Holocaust Museum and Research Centre (13 Selwyn Street, Elsternwick) has used Holocaust survivors as tour guides. Melbourne's most prominent Jewish landmark is certainly the magnificent Melbourne Hebrew Congregation's synagogue at Toorak Road and Domain Road, South Yarra.

COMMUNAL RELATIONS. Relations between the Melbourne Jewish community and the local state government of Victoria have generally been very good. Only very occasionally have difficulties arisen, for instance in the late 1970s when a strongly anti-Zionist and radical segment of the local Australian Labor Party supported a radical radio station, 3RC, whose license to broadcast to the Jewish community was questioned at a series of public hearings. By and large, however, relations between the Jewish community and successive Victoria governments have been harmonious. Relations with the local media are also good, although the community has protested many times when Israel is unfairly criticized, as has become common, especially in the liberal media and on "talk-back" radio. Relations with other groups in the wider community are normally also harmonious, despite the existence of antisemitic and anti-Zionist activists and the threat of terrorism, especially from extremist sections of Melbourne's growing Muslim community.

BIBLIOGRAPHY: P.Y. Medding, *From Assimilation to Group Survival* (1958), incl. bibl.; L.M. Goldman, *Jews in Victoria in the 19th Century* (1954), incl. bibl.; I. Solomon, in: *Journal of the Australian Jewish Historical Society*, 2 (1946), 332–48; N. Spielvogel, *ibid.*, 2 (1946), 356–8; R. Apple, *ibid.*, 4 (1955), 61. **ADD. BIBLIOGRAPHY:** W.D. Rubinstein, "Jews in the 1966 Australian Census," in: *Australian Jewish Historical Society Journal*, 14, Part 3 (1998), 495–508; idem, "Jews in the 2001 Australian Census," *ibid.*, 17, Part 1 (2003), 74–83; P. Maclean and M. Turnbull, "The Jews [of Carlton]," in: P. Yule (ed.), *Carlton: A History* (2004). See also *Australia.

Israel Porush and Yitzhak Rischin / William D. Rubinstein (2nd ed.)]

MELCHIOR, family prominent in Denmark since the mid-18th century. Originally from Hamburg, where the family had lived since the 18th century, MOSES MELCHIOR (1736–1817) arrived in Copenhagen in 1750. He became a successful dealer in leather and tobacco and in 1795 founded the import-export firm of Moses and Son G. Melchior, which is still in existence. His son GERSON (1771–1845) took over the business on his father's death, and enlarged it by importing sugar, rum, and tea. He was one of the leaders of the Copenhagen Jewish community. One of his sons, NATHAN GERSON (1811–1872), was a prominent ophthalmologist. He lectured at Copenhagen University and in 1857 became a director of the Ophthalmological Institute in Copenhagen. Another son, MORITZ GERSON (1816–1884), succeeded his father as head of the firm in 1845, establishing branches in the Danish West Indies and in Melbourne, Australia. Melchior was a member of the *landsting* (upper house of the Danish parliament) from 1866 to 1874 and was the first Jew to belong to the Danish Chamber of Commerce, becoming its president in 1873. Active also in the Jewish community, he served as a trustee and was made president in 1852. The writer Hans Christian Andersen was a friend and frequent guest in his house. His brother MOSES (1825–1912) succeeded him in 1884, opening a New York office in 1898. He was well known for his philanthropy, contributing to many Jewish and general causes. CARL HENRIQUES (1855–1931) took over the business after his brother's death and expanded it. He organized many athletic associations and sports clubs in Denmark and became their patron. Like his brother, he was the president of the Copenhagen community (1911–29). His son HARALD RAPHAEL (1896–1973) succeeded him in the firm, which dealt in the import of coffee, tea, rice, cocoa, and vanilla.

BIBLIOGRAPHY: *Moses og søn G. Melchior, Et dansk handelshus gennem 6 generationer* (1961), Eng. summary 53–56; *Dansk Biografisk Haandleksikon*, s.v.; *Dansk Biografisk Leksikon*, s.v.

MELCHIOR, CARL (1871–1933), German banker. Melchior, who was born in Hamburg, studied law and later became a judge there. In 1900 he was appointed legal counsel to the bank M.M. Warburg and Co. and in 1917 became a partner in the bank. During World War I, he served as a captain in the German Army and was badly wounded. After his recuperation, he worked for the German government's Zentraleinkaufsgesellschaft (ZEG), which was charged during the war with importing foodstuffs. Melchior always considered himself a patriot. From 1918 to 1919, together with Max M. Warburg, he took part as a German delegate in the financial and economic negotiations following the armistice. Melchior subsequently played a prominent role in the lengthy negotiations which eventually paved the way for Germany's reacceptance into the community of nations and displayed a mastery of financial and legal issues, diplomatic tact, and attention to detail. As a Jew he was afraid to arouse antisemitism by holding official positions, so he tried to act more in the background. At the international conference in Spa in 1920 as an expert for the German government, together with Walther *Rathenau and Moritz Julius *Bonn Melchior created the "policy of fulfillment" as a strategy of how Germany should pay its reparations. After Germany's admission to the League of Nations, Melchior became the only German member of the League's finance committee and in 1928–29 its chairman. In 1929 he was one of the German delegates discussing the revision of the Dawes Plan, under which German reparation payments were scheduled. He also served as a member of the board of the Bank for International Settlements in Basle and in other political or economic functions concerning international financial affairs. In the early 1930s he hoped that integrating the NSDAP, which he detested, into the government would placate the Nazis. After the Nazis took power in 1933, he lost his positions on several company boards. Melchior became active in the preparation for the formation of the *Reichsvertretung der deutschen Juden. In November 1933 he died.

BIBLIOGRAPHY: *Carl Melchior, Ein Buch des Gedenkens und der Freundschaft* (1967). **ADD. BIBLIOGRAPHY:** J.M. Keynes, *Two Memoirs: Dr. Melchior: A Defeated Enemy and My Early Beliefs* (1949), German translation: *Freund und Feind* (2004); Verein fuer Hamburgische Geschichte (ed.), E. Rosenbaum et al., *Das Bankhaus M.M. Warburg & Co. 1798–1938* (1976); S. Philipson, *Von Versailles nach Jerusalem: Dr. Carl Melchior und sein Werk* (1985).

[Joachim O. Ronall / Christian Schoelzel (2nd ed.)]

MELCHIOR, MARCUS (1897–1969), chief rabbi of Denmark. Born in Fredericia of an old Danish family, Melchior received his rabbinical diploma in 1921 from the Hildesheimer Seminary. He served as rabbi in Tarnowice, Poland (1921–23), in Beuthen, Germany (1925–34), and as rabbi of the Danish refugees in Sweden (1943–45). From 1947 he was the chief rabbi of Denmark. Melchior endeavored to promote understanding between all the religious trends in Judaism, while personally advocating the modern Orthodox one. He supported Zionism short of advocating *aliyah*. The main spokesman of Danish Jewry before the gentile community, Melchior was considered one of the prominent orators in Denmark. He supported the establishment of relations and furthering of understanding with West Germany. Among his books are *Jødedommen i vor tid* (1966[2]); *En jødedommens historie* (1962); *Levet og oplevet* (1965; *A Rabbi Remembers*, 1968; also Ger. tr.); and *Tænkt og Talt* (1967). He translated into Danish (1961) Shalom Aleichem's *Tevye de Milkhiger*. He was succeeded in the chief rabbinate by his son Bent.

MELCHIOR, MICHAEL (1954–), rabbi and Israeli politician. Born in Copenhagen, the son of Chief Rabbi Bent Melchior, Melchior studied in Israel at Yeshivat ha-Kotel after high school. He was ordained in 1980 and in the same year became the first chief rabbi of Oslo and was largely responsible for the community's renaissance (see *Norway; *Oslo). After six years he returned to Israel but continued to serve Norwegian Jewry. In Israel he entered politics and was elected to the Knesset in 1999 as a representative of Meimad, a moderate religious party aligned with the Labor Party. In the government he served as minister without portfolio, minister for Diaspora affairs, and deputy minister for foreign affairs.

MELCHIZEDEK (Heb.: מַלְכִּי צֶדֶק; "legitimate/righteous king"; the English spelling follows LXX Melxisedek as opposed to MT Malkizedek), king of Salem (or Jerusalem; cf. Ps. 76:3) according to Genesis 14:18–20. He welcomed *Abraham after he had defeated the four kings who had captured his nephew, Lot. Melchizedek brought out bread and wine and blessed Abraham. Finally, it is related that "he gave him a tithe of everything" although who gave the tithe to whom became a subject of considerable dispute (see below). The biblical account states that "he (Melchizedek) was priest of God Most High" (וְהוּא כֹהֵן לְאֵל עֶלְיוֹן). Melchizedek's priesthood was a source of numerous post-biblical speculations, which were intensified by the difficult verse Psalms 110:4: "The Lord has sworn/and will not repent/Thou art priest for ever/after the manner of Melchizedek" (אַתָּה כֹהֵן לְעוֹלָם עַל־דִּבְרָתִי מַלְכִּי צֶדֶק). It is generally believed that the Melchizedek mentioned here and the one in Genesis are the same. Some interpreters, however, maintain that the Melchizedek of Psalms is not a person but a title, "my righteous king," presumably because the name is written as two separate words (מַלְכִּי צֶדֶק).

The first post-biblical documents mentioning Melchizedek in various contexts appear from around the beginning of the Christian era. The earliest is probably the fragmentary scroll discovered in cave 11 at Qumran (11Q Melch or 11Q 13) and published by A.S. Van der Woude (in OTS, 14, 1965) and again with certain corrections by M. de Jonge and A.S. Van der Woude (in NTS, 12, 1966) and much studied since (bibliography in Brooke). Although this text "is a midrashic development which is independent of the classic Old Testament loci" (J.A. Fitzmyer, JBL, 86, 1967), it is clear that the eschatological and soteriological functions it attributes to Melchizedek draw on the perplexing figure of the biblical Melchizedek. In the Qumran text, Melchizedek is described as passing judgment, in the time of the tenth or last Jubilee, on Belial and those of his sort. The judgment takes place in heaven, and immediately there follows the "day of slaughter" prophecied by Isaiah. Here, Melchizedek is both judge and executor of his own decree, and in all likelihood he is to be identified with the Angel of Light, who figures in the dualistic doctrine of the Qumran sect (I. Gruenwald, in: *Maḥanayim*, 124 (1970), 94). He has also been identified with the Archangel Michael. Melchizedek is also mentioned in another Qumran text, the Genesis Apocryphon (22: 13–17), where the biblical story of the meeting between Abraham and Melchizedek is retold. Here it is Abraham who offers the tithe to Melchizedek: "And he [i.e., Abraham] gave him a tithe of all the goods of the king of Elam and his companions" (cf. Heb. 7:2 followed by the Christian translations of Genesis where, however, Melchizedek, not Abraham, is the subject of the verse). The question of who gave the tithe to whom was of considerable importance in rabbinical literature. In several places Melchizedek is stated to be a descendant of Noah, and is even identified with Shem the son of Noah. The same sources maintain that his priesthood was taken away from him and bestowed upon Abraham because he blessed Abraham first and only afterward blessed God (Gen. 14:19–20; cf. Ned. 32b; Lev. R. 25:6). Abraham's priesthood is also mentioned in connection with Psalms 110 (Gen. R., 55:6). In other rabbinical sources Melchizedek is mentioned among the four messianic figures allegorically implied by the "four smiths" of Zechariah 2:3. Melchizedek's messianic functions are also elaborated in two other literary documents. At the end of several manuscripts of the Slavonic Book of Enoch appears the story of the miraculous birth of Melchizedek as the son of Nir, Noah's brother. He is transported to heaven and becomes the head of a line of priests leading down to messianic days. There will presumably be another eschatological Melchizedek who will function as both priest and king. In symbolizing Mechizedek as Jesus in his three functions as messiah, king, and high priest (see below) the author's ingenuity combines all the motives singled out in the above-mentioned sources. A gnostic sect whose particular theological position is unknown called itself after Melchizedek.

[Ithamar Gruenwald]

In Christian Tradition

The two brief and somewhat enigmatic references to Melchizedek in the Bible provided the New Testament with a subject for typological interpretation. In the Epistle to the Hebrews (7:1–7), Melchizedek (king of justice – Zedek; of peace – Salem) is described as unique, being both a priest and a king, and because he is "without father, without mother, without genealogy"; he is eternal, "having neither beginning of days nor end of life." In this respect Melchizedek resembles Jesus, the son of God, and thus is a type of the savior.

Abraham, and therefore Levi "in the loins of his father" (*ibid.* 9–10), paid the tithe in submission to Melchizedek. Since in Christian tradition Jesus is high priest "after the order of Melchizedek" and "not after the order of Aaron" (*ibid.* 7:11, 17–21), Jesus' priesthood is excellent, superior to that of

Abraham's descent, and transcends all human, imperfect orders (Heb. 7:23–28; 8:1–6). To Christians the objection that Jesus, like Aaron, was "in the loins" of the patriarch, and consequently paid the tithe was met by the Church Fathers with the argument that Jesus, though descended from Abraham, had no human father.

[Ilana Shapira]

BIBLIOGRAPHY: H.L. Strack and P. Billerbeck, *Kommentar zum Neuen Testament*, 4 (1928), 452–65; Rowley, in: *Festschrift Bertholet* (1950), 461ff.; A. Vaillant, *Le livre des secrets d'Hénoch* (1952); Yadin, in: *Scripta Hierosolymitana*, 4 (1958), 36–55; idem, in: IEJ, 15 (1965), 152–4; Panikkar, *Kairos*, 1 (1959), 5–17; J. Maier, *Vom Kultus zur Gnosis* (1964), 37ff.; Flusser, in: *Christian News from Israel* (1966), 23ff.; J.A. Fitzmyer, in: JBL, 86 (1967), 25–41; A.R. Johnson, *Sacral Kingship in Ancient Israel* (1967^2), 35–53; S. Paul, in: JAOS, 88 (1968), 182. IN CHRISTIAN TRADITION: Friedlaender, in REJ, 5 (1882), 1–26, 188–98; 6 (1883), 187–99; Barody, in: RB, 35 (1926), 496–509; (1927), 25–45. **ADD. BIBLIOGRAPHY:** M. Astour, in: ABD, 4:684–86; G. Brooke, ibid, 687–88; ibid, B. Pearson, 688; J. Reiling, in: DDD, 560–63.

MELDOLA, Sephardi family of rabbis and scholars. The family originated in the 15th century in Meldola, northern Italy; the legend that they descended from Spanish exiles cannot be substantiated. The first of the family to attain prominence was JACOB MELDOLA, rabbi in Mantua in the 16th century. His son SAMUEL MELDOLA or MENDOLA was both a rabbinic scholar and physician to the Mantuan court. In the next generation members of the family settled in Leghorn, entering thus into the tradition of Sephardi life. For the next 200 years they provided rabbis, printers, and leaders to the Sephardi communities in Holland, Italy, France, and England.

BIBLIOGRAPHY: E. Castelli, *I banchi feneratizi ebraici nel Mantovano*... (1959), index; Mortara, Indice, 38; Ghirondi-Neppi, 79, 311, 355–7.

[Cecil Roth]

MELDOLA, RAPHAEL (1754–1828), British rabbi; son of Moses Hezekiah Meldola (1725–1791), professor of Oriental languages in Paris. Raphael was born in Leghorn, received rabbinical ordination there from Ḥ.J.D. *Azulai in 1796, became a *dayyan* in 1803, and in 1804/05 was appointed haham of the Sephardi community in London – an office vacant since the death of Moses Cohen d'*Azevedo in 1784. Energetic and capable, he helped to reform the educational institutions of his community in the face of missionary activities, introduced a choir into the synagogue, and cooperated cordially with Solomon *Hirschel, the Ashkenazi chief rabbi. On the other hand, his belligerent nature was responsible for periodic friction with the members of his community. Notwithstanding his imperfect knowledge of English he corresponded extensively with Christian scholars. Before leaving Leghorn, he had published there *Ḥuppat Ḥatanim* (1797), a handbook on the laws of marital life. He also published sermons and memorial poems: part of his catechism *Derekh Emunah (The Way of Faith)* appeared with his English translation after his death (1848). His son DAVID (1797–1853), who succeeded him as presiding rabbi though not as haham of the Sephardi community in London, was one of the founders of the **Jewish Chronicle*, and ineffectively opposed the movement for religious reform among London Jewry in 1840. A grandson of Raphael's was the British scientist, Raphael *Meldola.

BIBLIOGRAPHY: DNB, s.v.; Roth, Mag Bibl, index; M. Gaster, *History of the Ancient Synagogue ... Bevis Marks* (1901), 159–64; A.M. Hyamson, *Sephardim of England* (1951), index; Barnett, in: JHSET, 21 (1968), 1–38 (bibl. of Meldola's publications 13–14).

[Vivian David Lipman]

MELDOLA, RAPHAEL (1849–1915), British chemist and naturalist. Meldola was the grandson of Raphael *Meldola, the haham of the London Sephardi community. He worked at the Royal Mint (1868–71), with a firm of color manufacturers, and at the Royal College of Science. In 1875 he led a Royal Society expedition to the Nicobar Islands to observe a total eclipse of the sun. He spent several years as a schoolteacher and in industry and in 1885 became professor of chemistry at Finsbury Technical College, a position he held for over 30 years. Meldola's early investigations were in the fields of natural history and entomology as well as astronomy, but his main interest was dyestuffs. "Meldola's Blue" was the first oxazine dye, and he also discovered the first alkali green. In 1904 he published *Chemical Synthesis of Vital Products*. Meldola played an important role in the British chemical profession and was president of the Chemical Society and of the Institute of Chemistry, as well as a fellow and vice president of the Royal Society. After his death the Society of *Maccabeans, of which he had been president, instituted the Meldola Medal of the Royal Institute of Chemistry in his memory.

BIBLIOGRAPHY: J. Marchant (ed.), *Raphael Meldola* (Eng., 1916); A. Findlay and W.H. Mills, *British Chemists* (1947), 96–125.

[Samuel Aaron Miller]

°**MELEAGER OF GADARA** (c. 140–70 B.C.E.) was of Syrian parentage and grew up in Tyre. The *Palatine Anthology*, which includes 130 of his love epigrams (vii. 419, 7–8), exhibits his knowledge of Eastern languages: "If you are a Syrian, Salam! If you are a Phoenician, Naidius! If you are a Greek, Chaire!" His Menippean satires, Cynic sermons in prose mingled with verse (a Semitic form called "maqāma" by the Arabs) are lost. In one of his epigrams (A.P. 5. 160), Meleager sighs for his sweetheart Demo who is naked in another's arms, and disparagingly concludes: "If thy lover is some Sabbath-keeper, no great wonder! Love burns hot even on cold Sabbaths," an allusion (cf. *Rutilius Namatianus*) probably to the fact that from a pagan point of view the Sabbath, with its numerous prohibitions, was "cold," i.e., "dull."

°**MELITO OF SARDIS** (c. 120–185 C.E.), bishop of Sardis (Asia Minor), Christian author, and the earliest known pilgrim to the Holy Land. Scholars found his description of the crucifixion of Jesus "in the *middle* of the city [of Jerusalem]" confusing. Clearly Melito was referring to the site in the context of the layout of Aelia Capitolina and not of the city from the time of Jesus. Together with other bishops of Asia Minor, Melito continued to celebrate Easter on the 14th of Nisan, the eve of Passover. He visited Palestine in an effort to establish an accurate canon (Greek διαυήκη) of the Old Testament (from which he excerpted passages pertaining in some way to Jesus). His list of books (Eusebius, Hist. Eccles. IV, 26:13 f.) corresponds to the Hebrew canon (excluding Esther). Only brief quotations from Melito's works were known until the mid-20th century, when two papyrus copies of his homily on the Passion (*On Pascha*) were published. As a result of this discovery, Latin, Coptic, Georgian, and two Syriac translations of this treatise could be identified. The bishop delivered the treatise as a sermon after the biblical account of the Exodus was read on Easter, precisely the time when the Jews observed the Passover feast. The coincidence of observances and Melito's animosity toward Judaism caused his sermon, which was written between 160 and 170 C.E., to become one of the most important documents of early Christian anti-Judaism. After a theological introduction, Melito gives a dramatic description of Egypt's sufferings at the time of the Exodus. Influenced by the Midrash on Exodus 10:21, the darkness that engulfed Egypt is described as tangible. However, the events surrounding the Exodus were only a prefiguration of the Passion of Christ, the true Passover lamb. The earlier model no longer had validity and usefulness, because the prefigurations of the Old Testament had become a reality in the New Testament. The second part of the sermon is the oldest and one of the strongest accusations of deicide made against the Jews in early Christian literature. Jews are, among other things, described as having themselves crucified Jesus; and the murder is clearly defined as deicide: "God has been murdered, the King of Israel has been slain by an Israelite hand" (§96). In view of the tragic events suffered by the Jews of this period – the destruction of the Temple and the defeat of Bar Kokhba – Melito could say that, in consequence of the deicide, "Israel lay dead," while Christianity, "the broad grace," was conquering the whole earth. The sermon, nevertheless, attests the antiquity of the Passover *Haggadah*. Paragraph 68 of the sermon contains a Greek version of part of the introduction to *Hallel* in the *Haggadah*; and paragraphs 84–85 and 88 derive from the famous Passover litany "*Dayyeinu*."

BIBLIOGRAPHY: Eusebius Pamphili, *Ecclesiastical History*, 2 vols. (1926–32), index; T. Otto, *Corpus Apologetarum Christianorum*, 9 (1872), 374–478, 497–512; E.J. Goodspeed, *Aelteste Apologeten* (1914), 306–13; C. Bonner, *Homily on the Passion* (1914); M. Testuz (ed. and tr.), *Papyrus Bodmer XIII, Méliton de Sardes, Homélie sur la Pâque* (1960); O. Perler, *Méliton de Sardes sur la Pâque, sources Chrétiennes* (1966); J. Blank, *Meliton von Sardes vom Passa* (1963); E. Werner, in: HUCA, 37 (1966), 191–210. **ADD. BIBLIOGRAPHY:** S.G. Hall (ed.), *On Pascha* (1979); E.D. Hunt, *Holy Land Pilgrimage in the Later Roman Empire AD 312–460* (1984), 3; J.E. Taylor, *Christians and the Holy Places* (1993), 116ff.

[David Flusser / Shimon Gibson (2nd ed.)]

MELITOPOL, city in Zaporozhe district, Ukraine. Jews started to settle in Melitopol when it was proclaimed a town in 1842. In 1886 there were 2,021 Jews, and in 1897 6,563 Jews and 454 *Karaites in Melitopol (45.7% of the total population). At the turn of the 19th century, Melitopol turned into an important city of metallurgical industries. Part of them, as well as other industries, belonged to Jews, and many Jewish workers were employed in them. On April 19, 1905, a mob attacked Jewish houses, but a Jewish *self-defense group of 300 Jewish and Christian youngsters managed to minimize the pogrom; 15 were wounded and 45 shops (Jewish and Christian) were robbed. In 1910 Melitopol had a *talmud torah* and two private schools for boys and two for girls. Joseph *Trumpeldor was active in the town and the first *ḥaluẓim* he organized left from there for Palestine. During World War I 2,043 refugees arrived in Melitopol, and were helped by a local aid committee. By 1926 the Jewish population had risen to 8,583 (33.6% of the total), then dropped to 6,040 (8% of the total population). In the 1920s there was a Yiddish school with 63 pupils, which was probably closed later in the 1930s. The ex-bourgeoisie who were denied state rights tried to learn trades and join artisan cooperatives, or went to farm in Birobidzhan or to established kolkhozes in the vicinity of the town. In 1938–40 a clandestine yeshivah operated, but when it was discovered, it moved to Kutaisi (Georgia). Melitopol was occupied by the Germans on October 5, 1941. On October 8 the Jews, about 1,800 families, were concentrated in a ghetto in the flourmill. Intermarried Jews and children from mixed marriage were freed. On October 10 and 15, the *Sonderkommando* 10a murdered 75 Jewish prisoners of war, and on October 11, 3,000 local Jews. The killings of Jews continued for a year, and on October 9, 1942, the Jewish spouses and children of mixed marriages were brutally killed. About 8,000 Jews, including those from nearby towns, and a few hundred Karaites were murdered. Melitopol was liberated on October 23, 1943. There were 2,500 Jews in 1959, and 1,800 in 1979. There was no synagogue. Most remaining Jews left in the 1990s.

BIBLIOGRAPHY: *Voskhod*, nos. 17, 18, 19 (1905); Dubnow, Hist. Russ., 3 (1920), 115.

[Shmuel Spector (2nd ed.)]

MELNIKOFF, AVRAHAM (1892–1960), Israeli sculptor. Born in Russia, Melnikoff studied in Vienna and the U.S. He came to Ereẓ Israel in 1918 and left for England in 1934, returning in 1960. Melnikoff was one of the pioneers of sculpture in modern Israel. His best-known work is his lion erected between Tel Ḥai and Kefar Giladi in memory of the defenders of Tel Hai (1926). This work, inspired by the sculpture of the ancient East, was the first modern monument in the country.

MELOKHIM-BUKH (*Sefer Melokhim*), anonymous 16th-century Yiddish epic. The epic's narrative material derives from the biblical book of Kings and its midrashic traditions (especially those concerning Solomon), while its poetic form and conception derive from the medieval German epic. It focuses less on battle scenes and more on ethical and didactic matters than the related *Shmuel-Bukh* (1544). Both authors were well versed in both the broad sacred text tradition of Judaism and non-Jewish secular epic literature. Composed in four-line stanzas of two rhyming couplets (AABB), each line divided rhythmically into two half-lines of three primary accents each, the form derives from the stanza characteristic of the Middle High German *Nibelungenlied*. With its 2,262 stanzas, it is the longest poem in Old Yiddish literature. The basis of the entire extant text tradition is the edition of Augsburg, 1543.

BIBLIOGRAPHY: L. Fuks (ed.), *Das altjiddische Epos Melokîm-Bûk*, 2 vols. (1965; facsimile of Augsburg, 1543); Ch. Shmeruk, *Prokim fun der Yidisher Literatur-Geshikhte* (1988), 114–16, 192–99; M. Wolf, in: *Tarbiz*, 51 (1992), 131–34; J.C. Frakes (ed.), *Early Yiddish Texts: 1100–1750* (2005), 193–213; J. Baumgarten, *Introduction to Old Yiddish Literature* (2005), 140–42, 151–55.

[Jerold C. Frakes (2nd ed.)]

MELON, two plant species belonging to different botanical genera: the watermelon and the muskmelon.

(1) The watermelon (Heb. אֲבַטִּיחַ, *avati'aḥ*) is the *Citrullus vulgaris*. The Bible mentions it among the vegetables eaten by the Israelites in Egypt, for which they hankered in the wilderness (Num. 11:5). The Hebrew name may possibly be connected with the verb בטט (*btt*) meaning to swell or grow. Watermelons were a familiar plant in Egypt, and a papyrus from the 21st dynasty preserves a pictorial representation of one. The *avati'aḥ* is frequently mentioned in rabbinical literature. It was comparatively cheap (Ma'as. 2:6) and was usually eaten when ripe, though some ate it as a vegetable while still unripe (Ma'as. 1:5).

(2) The muskmelon, *Cucumis melo*, is called in the Mishnah *melafefon* (מְלָפְפוֹן), a name of Greek origin. It is not known if it was grown in biblical times and no Hebrew name exists for it. The Palestinian Targum identifies the biblical *avati'aḥ* with *melafefonya*, i.e., the muskmelon, but this does not appear likely, since in a number of places in the Tosefta and Talmud they are mentioned together (Tosef., Kil. 1:1). Some held that these two species do not constitute a mixed species (**kilayim; ibid.*) for "a man takes a seed from the upper part of the *avati'aḥ* and plants it – and it becomes a *melafefon*" (TJ, Kil. 1:2, 27a), i.e., these species may be interchangeable. This view was taken over from Greek and Roman agricultural folklore which assumed that the characteristics of species were subject to change. An echo of this view is found in the Palestinian Targum in the philological explanation of the name *melafefon* given by R. Judah: "A man takes one seed from the upper part of an *avati'aḥ* and one seed from the upper part of an apple and puts them into the same hole, they grow together and become a hybrid species, that is why in Greek it is called *melafefon*." The Greek μηλοπέπον and the Latin *melopepo* both mean "apple-watermelon" probably because the taste of the muskmelon is reminiscent of both the apple and the watermelon. According to Pliny the *melopepo* originated in Campania from a species of cucumber which looked like a quince (Natural History 19:67). There is certainly no substance for these views, which are based on the polymorphism of the family Cucurbitaceae. The plant *Cucumis melo* var. *Chate*, identified with the *kishut, kishu'im* (see *Cucumber), that belongs to the same botanical genus (and apparently even to the same species) as the muskmelon, is especially polymorphic. It could be that pollination between these two species gives rise to hybrids and is the reason for the *halakhah* that the *kishut* (*Chate* melon or cucumber) and the *melafefon* do not constitute *kilayim* (Kil. 1:2). Despite the ruling of the Academy for the Hebrew Language, modern Hebrew has adopted the name *melafefon* for cucumber.

BIBLIOGRAPHY: Loew, Flora, 1 (1928), 528–54; B. Chizik, *Ẓimḥei ha-Delu'im be-Ereẓ Yisrael*, 1 (1937); H.N. and A.L. Moldenke, *Plants of the Bible* (1952), 315 (index), s.v.; J. Feliks, *Kilei Zera'im ve-Harkavah* (1967), 44–53; idem, *Olam ha-Ẓome'aḥ ha-Mikra'i* (1968²), 164f. **ADD. BIBLIOGRAPHY:** Feliks, Ha-Ẓome'aḥ, 101, 144.

[Jehuda Feliks]

MELTON, FLORENCE (1911–), U.S. community leader and philanthropic supporter of a variety of Jewish causes. Melton is best known for envisioning and establishing a highly successful program of serious adult Jewish learning called the Florence Melton Adult Mini-School. She was born in Philadelphia, Penn., and raised under the influence of her grandmother, whom she credited for much of her commitment to Jewish education and Jewish values. In 1930 she married Aaron Zacks, with whom she had two sons. In 1946 she and her husband founded the R.G. Barry Corporation, one of the world's largest manufacturers of soled slippers. She invented the first use of foam in footwear and revolutionized the industry. Zacks died in 1965 and in 1968 she married Samuel Mendel Melton of Columbus, Ohio, a successful businessman and philanthropist. Samuel Melton had endowed the Melton Research Center at the Jewish Theological Seminary of America and the Melton Centre at the Hebrew University of Jerusalem, and Florence Melton became an active partner in his philanthropic projects as she pursued her own parallel interests.

In the early 1980s Melton became convinced that although many Jews were accomplished in their careers, they lacked basic knowledge about Jewish history, philosophy, and religious practices. Hence she began to advocate for the creation of a program of study to help adults attain "Jewish literacy." She envisioned a well-designed curriculum, taught by engaging and interactive teachers, open to students from across the various Jewish denominations. Adult students, in her view, would need to commit to two years of weekly study. Her ideas were met by skepticism; few people believed that contemporary adults were either interested in Jewish study or would want to view Jewish learning as seriously as her program proposed. Eventually she turned to the Melton Centre for Jewish Education at the Hebrew University, which agreed to recruit sites and develop the curriculum for the project. Melton's idea turned out to be prescient. Proving the skeptics wrong, Mini-Schools were established in more than 60 cities and thousands of adult students participated in the program. Through its carefully designed organizational structure and its commitment to a serious learning curriculum the Mini-

School became a model for adult education throughout the Jewish community.

In recognition of her communal leadership Melton received a number of awards, including honorary doctorates from the Hebrew University of Jerusalem and the Jewish Theological Seminary of America, the Scopus Award from the American Friends of the Hebrew University, and the Ohio State University Distinguished Service Award. She was inducted into the Ohio Women's Hall of Fame in October 1994.

[Barry W. Holtz (2nd ed.)]

MELTON, SAMUEL MENDEL (1900–1993), U.S. industrialist and philanthropist. Melton was born in Saros, Austro-Hungary. His family immigrated in 1904 to Toledo, Ohio. He established the Capitol Manufacturing and Supply Company in Columbus, as well as several pipe and nipple companies, which later merged with the Harsco Corporation (1968) and became a leader in the metals industry. Melton extended the Capitol Company to Israel in 1949 and deeded it to various Israeli institutions in 1955. Active in numerous communal and national Jewish organizations, he was a member of the UJA "cabinet" and the board of the Jewish Theological Seminary (JTS), where he founded the Melton Research Center in New York (1959) to develop Jewish educational materials. He established the Samuel Mendel Melton Foundation (1951); professorships in Judaica at Ohio State University and the Hebrew University in Jerusalem (1965); a vocational school in Bat Yam, Israel (1968); the Melton Center for Jewish Education in the Diaspora at the Hebrew University (1968); the Melton Building at the Hebrew University; the *Melton Journal* of the JTS; the Melton Fellowship; the Jewish History and Studies Center at Ohio State University (1976); and the Melton Coalition for Creative Interaction at the JTS, devoted to Jewish arts education (1993).

[Edward L. Greenstein / Ruth Beloff (2nd ed.)]

MELTZER, ISSER ZALMAN (1870–1953), talmudic scholar and yeshivah head. Born in Lithuania, Meltzer studied in Volozhin under Ḥayyim Soloveichik and Naphtali Ẓevi Judah Berlin, and later under the Ḥafeẓ Ḥayyim in Radin. All of these exercised a profound influence upon him, Soleveichik by his talmudic methodology, Berlin by his love for Ereẓ Israel, and the Ḥafeẓ Ḥayyim by his humility and his ethical approach. In 1892 he married Beila Hinda, daughter of R. Faivel Frank of Ilukste. His wife possessed considerable scholarly abilities and throughout his life assisted him in transcribing his works and in arranging them for publication. In 1894 he was appointed by R. Nathan Ẓevi *Finkel one of the principals of the *Slobodka yeshivah and in 1897 the head of a yeshivah for advanced students in Slutsk, where Jacob David *Willowski was the rabbi. Hundreds of students flocked to the yeshivah, and when Willowski immigrated to Ereẓ Israel in 1903 Meltzer succeeded him as rabbi of Slutsk. After the Bolshevik Revolution in 1917 the yeshivah moved to Kletsk in Poland. Meltzer, however, refused to leave his community in Slutsk, despite his suffering at the hands of the Bolsheviks, including imprisonment for teaching Torah. In 1923 he left Russia for Kletsk and in the same year participated in the founding conference of the *Agudat Israel in Vienna, at which he was elected to the Mo'eẓet Gedolei ha-Torah. In 1925 he became head of the Eẓ Ḥayyim Yeshivah in Jerusalem. In Ereẓ Israel, he devoted himself almost entirely to the dissemination of Torah and the strengthening of yeshivot. As a fervent Zionist, he exercised a moderating influence in the councils of the Agudah. In 1935 his first work appeared, *Even ha-Ezel* on the *Mishneh Torah* of *Maimonides which is regarded as a fundamental work of its kind. Seven volumes appeared during his lifetime, the other posthumously. He also edited and wrote commentary to the novellae of Naḥmanides (1928/29).

BIBLIOGRAPHY: S. Zevin, *Ishim ve-Shitot* (1966³), 337–60; D. Katz, *Tenu'at ha-Musar*, 3 (1957), 37–42 and passim; *Yahadut Lita* (1960), index; A. Rothkoff, in: *Jewish Life* (March 1971), 51–57.

[Mordechai Hacohen]

MELTZER, SHIMSHON (1909–2000), Hebrew poet. Born in Tluste (eastern Galicia; present-day Tolstoye), Meltzer immigrated to Palestine in 1933, after having taught in Horodenka (Gorodenka), Galicia. For a time he taught secondary school in Tel Aviv, but from 1937 he engaged in editorial work; first in the daily **Davar*, and later in the Am Oved publishing house and in the children's magazine *Davar li-Yladim*. From 1959 he was on the editorial staff of the Zionist Library publications of the Jewish Agency.

His first poems were published in *Ba-Derekh*, the magazine of the teachers' seminary in Lvov where he studied. After his arrival in Ereẓ Israel his poetry appeared mainly in *Davar*, but also in various literary journals. He published a number of volumes of poems and ballads, including *Be-Shiv'ah Meitarim* (1939); *Me'ir ha-Keleizemar Na'asah Komisar* (1940); *Asarah She'arim* (1943); *Alef* (1945, 1963²), memoirs of the *ḥeder; Sefer ha-Shirot ve-ha-Balladot* (1950); and *Or Zaru'a* (1966). Meltzer attempted to capture the folk flavor of Eastern European Jewry by using ḥasidic tales and motifs in his ballads. His collection of essays on literature is entitled *Devarim al Ofnam* ("Words and their Forms," 1962). Meltzer translated extensively from Polish-Jewish writers, especially from Yiddish writers, dramatists, and poets. For English translations of his works, see Goell, Bibliography, 1033–38.

BIBLIOGRAPHY: D. Zakkai, *Keẓarot* (1956), 470–1; A. Cohen, *Soferim Ivriyyim Benei Zemannenu* (1964), 195–8; I. Cohen, *Sha'ar ha-Soferim* (1962), 355–8; J. Lichtenbaum, *Bi-Teḥumah shel Sifrut* (1963), 105–9; D. Sadan, *Bein Din le-Ḥeshbon* (1963), 105–11. **ADD. BIBLIOGRAPHY:** Y. Ben, "*Okyanus shel Yidish*," in: *Davar* (August 12, 1977); K.A. Bertini, "*S. Melzer Kefi Shehu*," in: *Al ha-Mishmar* (April 29, 1977); D. Sadan, "*Bein ha-Aspaklariyot: Sh. Melzer*," in: *Moznayim*, 49:1 (1979), 10–13; E. Tarsi-Gai, "*Tivam u-Mekomam shel Shirei ha-Zahav le-Miryam bi-Yẓirato shel S. Melzer*," in: *Gazit*, 33, 7–8 (1980), 391–392.

[Getzel Kressel]

MELUN, capital of the department of Seine-et-Marne, 26 mi. (42 km.) S. of Paris. The first explicit reference to Jews in Melun dates from the middle of the 12th century: in his will, Simon of Beaugency mentions a Jew of Melun among his creditors. From the beginning of the 13th century, there is evidence of a Rue des Juifs and an "*escole des Juis*" (the synagogue). There is no record of a medieval Jewish community after the expulsion of the Jews from the Kingdom of France in 1306. Scholars of Melun took part in the *synod convened by *Samuel b. Meir (Rashbam) and Jacob b. Meir *Tam. Meshullam b. Nathan of Melun, previously from Narbonne, lived in Melun from 1150. During the second half of the 12th century, Jedidiah of Melun also lived in the town. Judah b. David of Melun was one of the four rabbis who confronted Nicholas *Donin at the famous *disputation organized by *Louis IX (St. Louis) in 1240. Preserved in the municipal library of Melun is a *maḥzor* of the 14th century for the New Year and Day of Atonement according to the French rite (Ms. No. 14): it had previously been in the possession of the Carmelite monastery of Melun and is possibly of local origin. On the eve of World War II there was a very small community in Melun. It increased in the postwar period, mainly as a result of the arrival of Jews from North Africa, and numbered over 500 in 1969.

BIBLIOGRAPHY: S. Rouillard, *Histoire de Melun* (1628), 352f.; M. Schwab in: REJ, 13 (1886), 296–300; G. Leroy, *Histoire de la ville de Melun* (1887), 126, 167: Gross, Gal Jud, 351–5; J. Thillier and E. Jarr, *Cartulaire de Ste-Croix d'Orléans…* (1906), 13.

[Bernhard Blumenkranz]

MELVILLE, LEWIS (pen name of **Lewis Saul Benjamin**; 1874–1932), biographer. A prolific writer, he was best known for his books about the English novelist Thackeray, whose works he also edited (1901–07). *Farmer George* (1907) was an important account of the private life and character of George III. Lewis' other works include scholarly, yet good-humored, studies of figures such as John Gay (1921), Nell Gwyn (1923), and Beau Brummell (1924); and several anthologies.

MEM (Heb. מ, ם; מֵם), the 13th letter of the Hebrew alphabet; its numerical value is 40. In Proto-Sinaitic and early Proto-Canaanite inscriptions the *mem* was drawn as a pictograph representing water (*mayim*) 〰 or ⦚. In the later Proto-Canaanite script the vertical zigzag prevailed, which turned into 𐤌 in the tenth-century B.C.E. Phoenician script. Later, the *mem* consisted of a zigzag-shaped head and a downstroke 𐤌. The Hebrew forms were: 𐤌 → 𐤌 (cursive) and 𐤌 (formal); hence the Samaritan ࠌ. From the eighth and seventh centuries B.C.E., the Phoenician *mem* was written 𐤌, which in the Aramaic became 𐡌. In the late fifth century B.C.E. and later Aramaic cursive the downstrokes were bent leftward. Thus the medial מ and final ם variations evolved. These are prototypes of the Jewish medial מ and final ם *mem* forms. The Nabatean *mem* was drawn without lifting the pen 𐢖 and this led to the Arabic م. The ancestor of the Latin "M," the Archaic Greek Μ developed from the early Phoenician *mem*. See *Alphabet, Hebrew.

[Joseph Naveh]

MEMEL (Lith. **Klaipėda**), a Baltic port in W. Lithuania. The town was founded in the 13th century; the earliest existing document in which Jews are mentioned is dated April 20, 1567, and refers to an edict expelling the Jews from the city. In 1664 the elector of Brandenburg permitted a Jewish merchant from the Netherlands, Moses Jacobson de Jong, to settle in Memel, and eventually Jews were allowed to visit the city for the annual trade fairs. Only after the emancipation of Jews in Prussia (1812) were they able to settle freely in Memel.

In the 19th century the community consisted of Eastern European and Prussian Jews. The former had settled in the port in connection with their trans-Baltic business and formed the majority of the Jewish population (in 1880 they accounted for 80% of the total number of Jews). In later years there was an increased influx of Jews from Germany. The number of Jews grew from 887 in 1867, to 1,214 in 1900, and to over 2,000 in 1910. Each group had its own synagogue and communal institutions, but the official community administration was run by German Jews. Israel *Lipkin (Salanter), founder of the Musar movement, lived and taught in Memel 1860–80, founding a *bet midrash* and societies for Torah study, and publishing here the short-lived periodical *Ha-Tevunah* (1861). Isaac *Ruelf, one of the spiritual leaders of German Jewry, was rabbi of Memel from 1865 to 1898 and devoted much effort to alleviating the plight of Russian Jews. Ruelf was succeeded by Emanuel Carlebach (until 1904), M. Stein (until 1915), L. Lazarus (until 1932), and S. Schlesinger (until 1939).

After World War I, the League of Nations adopted the Memel Convention (1924), whereby it became an autonomous region under Lithuanian rule. As the country's only port, it played an important role in the economic life of Lithuania, and there was a steady influx of Jews into the city in the interwar period. In March 1939 it had a Jewish population of approximately 9,000 (17% of the total). Most of the Jews were engaged in commerce but there were also a few industrialists. The Memel district also had a few Jewish-owned estates, some of which were made available for *hakhsharah*. On March 22, 1939, the Germans occupied Memel and incorporated it into the Reich. Most of the Jews managed to flee to *Lithuania, where they later shared the fate of their coreligionists. In 1970 the estimated Jewish population was less than 1,000. There was no synagogue, cemetery, or organized religious life.

BIBLIOGRAPHY: I. Ruelf, *Zur Geschichte der Juden in Memel* (1900); Gringauz, in: *Lite*, 1 (1951), 1427–38; Shulman, in: *Yahadut Lita*, 3 (1967), 281–3; A. Carlebach, *Adass Jeshurun of Cologne* (1964), 25–28; L. Scheinhaus, in: *Memeler Dampfboot* (Aug. 15, 1928).

[Joseph Gar]

MEMMI, ALBERT (1920–), French author and sociologist. Memmi, a native of Tunis, fought with the Free French during World War II. After completing his studies he returned to Tunis, where he became head of a psychological institute. In 1959, he joined the Centre National de la Recherche Scientifique in Paris, and became a teacher at the Ecole Pratique des Hautes Etudes where he was appointed a professor in 1966.

He specialized in the social effects of colonization, finding a similarity between the situation of the Jew and that of colonized peoples. Though an advocate of independence for the countries of the Maghreb, he was well aware that one of its consequences would be the mass exodus of North African Jewry. Memmi's first two books were novels, both largely autobiographical. *La statue de sel* (1953; *Pillar of Salt*, 1955), is the story of a North African Jew's emergence from a narrow Jewish society through the discovery of French culture, and his eventual disillusionment with an idealized Western humanism. *Agar* (1955; *Strangers*, 1958) describes the isolation of a Tunisian Jew, rejected by both Frenchmen and Arabs. Memmi was still dealing with the same problem a decade later in essays such as *Portrait d'un Juif* (1962; *Portrait of a Jew*, 1963) and its sequel, *La libération du Juif* (1966; *The Liberation of the Jew*, 1966). He portrays the Jew as a "shadow figure," neither wholly assimilated nor anxious to lose his distinctiveness, concluding that "Israel is our only solution, our one trump card, our last historical opportunity." Memmi's sociological studies appeared in various journals and in *Le Français et le racisme* (1965). He published an *Anthologie des écrivains nord-africains* (1964) and a *Bibliographie de la littérature nord-africaine d'expression française 1945–1962* (1965). He also wrote essays on Jewish subjects for *L'Arche, Evidences*, and *Commentary*. His later works include *Dictionnaire critique à l'usage des incrédules* (2002) and a conversation volume with Catherine Pont-Humbert, *L'individu face à ses dépendances* (2005).

BIBLIOGRAPHY: Sartre, in: *Les Temps Modernes*, 137–8 (1957), 289–92; Camus, in: A. Memmi, *La statue de sel* (1953), preface; A. Khatibi, *Le Roman Maghrébin* (1968); Di-Nour, in: *Dispersion et Unité*, 8 (1967), 81–92.

[Jacqueline Kahanoff]

MEMMINGEN, city in Bavaria, Germany. Jews were present in Memmingen by the second half of the 13th century, since the city statutes of 1270 contain references to Jewish money-lending activities. In 1344 the bishop of Augsburg excommunicated the city for nonpayment of its debts to a Jew; the burghers thereupon threatened to bury their dead in the Jewish cemetery. The Jews made their living in the city in 1373. By 1500, however, there were no *Judengasse*. The community was destroyed during the *Black Death persecutions of 1348, but Jews were again living in the city in 1373. By 1500, however, there were no longer Jews there. The privilege of *Judenfreiheit* ("freedom from Jews"), granted in 1541, was renewed in 1559. Many Jews who had formerly lived in Memmingen concentrated in Fellheim, a nearby village, and maintained a settlement there numbering 379 persons (63% of the population) in 1810 (during World War II it again served as a center for refugees). Jews from Fellheim often visited Memmingen for trading purposes during the 17th and 18th centuries. In 1862 the first Jew received citizenship in Memmingen. A community comprising 100 members was formed in 1875, and 20 years later it had grown to 231. A synagogue was dedicated in 1909. The community subsequently declined: from 194 in 1900, to 161 in 1933, and 104 on Jan. 1, 1939. The Jews, who were mainly textile manufacturers and livestock merchants, were severely hit by the Nazi boycott of Jewish business establishments, and considerable numbers emigrated despite the many obstacles they encountered. In 1938 the synagogue and Jewish homes were looted and destroyed, and in the spring of 1942 the community was liquidated. In 1947 some 125 Jews lived in Memmingen, but they later emigrated. In 1968 there were two Jews in the city. There are memorials to commemorate the former synagogue, the former Jewish community, and the Jewish citizens of Memmingen who were killed by the Nazis. In 2000 the museum of Memmingen set up a permanent exhibition on Jewish life in Memmingen.

BIBLIOGRAPHY: J. Miedel, *Die Juden in Memmingen* (1909); FJW (1932–33), 304; W. Rapp, *Geschichte des Dorfes Fellheim* (1960); D. Linn, *Das Schicksal der juedischen Bevoelkerung in Memmingen, 1933–1945* (1962); Germ Jud, 2 (1968), 534–6; PK. **ADD. BIBLIOGRAPHY:** A. Maimon, M. Breuer, Y. Guggenheim (eds.), *Germania Judaica*, vol. 3, 1350–1514 (1987), 858–60; C. Engelhard, *Erinnerung stiftet Erloesung. Gedenkheft fuer die juedischen Frauen, Maenner und Kinder aus Memmingen, die zwischen 1941 und 1945 verfolgt, verschleppt und ermordet wurden* (Materialien zur Memminger Stadtgeschichte, Reihe B, Materialien, vol. 3 (1999)); P. Hoser, *Die Geschichte der Stadt Memmingen*, vol. 2: Vom Neubeginn im Koenigreich Bayern bis 1945 (2001), 203–40, 339–46. **WEBSITE:** www.alemannia-judaica.de.

[Larissa Daemmig (2nd ed.)]

MEMORBUCH, a community prayer book once common in Jewish communities throughout Central Europe. It consisted of three major parts:

(1) a collection of prayers usually intoned by the reader while standing at the *almemar* (see *Bimah) such as the order of blowing the *shofar* and reading the Scroll of Esther, different forms of the *Mi She-Berakh* prayer, etc;

(2) a necrology of distinguished persons, either of local or of general Jewish importance;

(3) a martyrology of persons and places.

The last has been subjected to minute research by scholars, particularly by S. *Salfeld. According to one view the *Memorbuch* received its name from being placed, for the convenience of the reader, on the *almemar*, while another holds that it is derived from the Latin *memoria*.

The custom of reading the names developed after the massacres of the *Rhine communities during the First Crusade; to this list were added the names of the martyrs of the *Rindfleisch massacres and other catastrophes. The list of martyrs who perished during the *Black Death persecutions (1348–49) was of such magnitude that mainly names of places were recorded. It became the custom to read off the list of thousands of names in ceremony on the Sabbath before Shavuot (when the massacres of the First Crusade took place); at a later date it was also read off on the Sabbath before the Ninth of Av although the author probably intended it to be read in part each Sabbath. Rabbi Jacob b. Moses Levi of Mainz (see *Moellin), the codifier of the Ashkenazi *minhag*, made the reading of the full list obligatory for Rhenish communities while non-Rhenish ones were to read only the list of places. The *Memorbuch* of the Mainz community, begun by Isaac b. Samuel of Meiningen in 1296, was supplemented and became the complete and authoritative version for all other copies. (Salfeld considered the early version to be that of the Nuremberg community, a view not accepted by M. Weinberg, a later authority.) It was updated by mention of the catastrophes of 1492 in *Mecklenburg, and 1510 in *Brandenburg, and by the names of communities which perished in the *Chmielnicki massacres (1648). As no community could be complete without the *Memorbuch*, it was frequently copied in the 17th and 18th centuries.

The *Memorbuch* was expanded in the different localities to include names of esteemed local personages, lists of deceased, as well as prayers of purely local use and origin. It was therefore never printed and gradually fell into disuse in the mid-19th century, through the unification and standardization of services and ritual.

The earliest *Memorbuecher* (excluding that of Mainz) appeared in about 1600, but between 1650 and 1750 a large number were commenced (based on that of Mainz), for many communities were established in this period. The *Memorbuch* reflected the religious life of the community and accompanied it in its tribulations and migrations; refugees from Vienna (1670) continued using their *Memorbuch* in Fuerth; refugees from Fulda (1671) took theirs with them to Amsterdam and subsequently back to Fulda. Some communities had more than one *Memorbuch* (Fuerth Jewry had five complementary ones). *Memorbuecher* were particularly common among communities in rural areas; it is estimated that there were about 150 in Bavaria alone and a few hundred more in *Baden, *Wuerttemberg, *Hesse, *Alsace, and *Switzerland. The *Memorbuch* continues to serve the historian as an important source for the social and religious history of the Jews and is frequently cited.

BIBLIOGRAPHY: M. Weinberg. *Die Memorbuecher der juedischen Gemeinden in Bayern* (1938); idem, in: JJLG, 16 (1924), 253–320; 18 (1926), 203–16; C. Duschinsky, *Gedenkbuecher "Memorbuecher" von Offenbach a. M. und anderen deutschen Gemeinden* (1924): A. Neubauer, in: REJ, 4 (1882), 1–30; Salfeld, Martyrol; W.H. Lowe, *The Memorbuch of Nuremberg* (1881); L. Loewenstein, in: ZGJD, 1 (1887), 195–8; 2 (1888), 86–99. **ADD. BIBLIOGRAPHY:** B. Purin (ed.), *Buch der Erinnerung* (1999); A. Pomerance, in: *Erinnerung als Gegenwart* (2000), 33–53.

MEMORIAL FOUNDATION FOR JEWISH CULTURE. The Memorial Foundation was established with German reparations funds by Nahum Goldmann in 1965 with the mandate to raise up a new generation of scholars, intellectuals, rabbis, and cultural and communal leaders to replace the Jewish cultural elite annihilated in Europe during the Shoah.

The Foundation awards scholarships and fellowships to scholars, academicians, writers, artists, rabbis, educators, and communal workers. Funds are also provided to academic and scholarly institutions for research and publication. For the first few decades after its founding, special attention was paid to the Jewish communities in the former Soviet Union countries where Jewish life had been suppressed for seven decades under Communist rule. The list of individuals and institutions who received the Foundation's support since its inception can be found on its Website, www.mfjc.org.

In addition to its support of communities and institutions, the Foundation has developed innovative programs to address needs not adequately met by the Jewish community globally. These include the International Nahum Goldmann Fellowship, which prepares communal, cultural, and professional leadership for Jewish communities around the world; reaching the Jewish unaffiliated; Jewish family education; and utilization of new technologies for Jewish culture and education. Currently the Foundation's programs extend to Jewish communities on six continents, reaching both individuals and institutions at the core of the Jewish community as well as Jews affiliated only marginally with Jewish life.

The Memorial Foundation for Jewish Culture is committed to the creation, intensification, and dissemination of Jewish culture worldwide, the development of creative programs to meet the emerging needs of the Jewish communities as they enter the 21st century, and service as a central forum for identifying and supporting innovative programs to ensure the continuation of creative Jewish life wherever Jewish communities exist. Its headquarters are in New York.

[Jerome Hochbaum (2nd ed.)]

MEMORIAL LIGHT (Heb. נֵר נְשָׁמָה; "the light of the soul"), a light kindled on the anniversary of the death of a relative. It is lit on the eve of the anniversary, according to the Hebrew calendar, and should burn without interruption for 24 hours. A memorial candle is also kindled when a person dies (it is placed near his head until the burial) and during the seven-day mourning period, or according to some customs during the *sheloshim* ("30 days") after the death. In some communities, it is customary to kindle memorial lights on the eve of the *Day of Atonement.

It is generally believed that the custom of memorial lights, as well as that of **yahrzeit*, originated in Germany in the Middle Ages and spread from there to other Jewish centers. The medieval custom easily linked up with earlier notions of light as a symbol for the soul as found, e.g., in Proverbs 20:27, "The spirit of man is the lamp of the Lord" or in the story about R. *Judah ha-Nasi who asked on his deathbed that a light be kindled in his room after his death (Ket. 103a). In some synagogues memorial lights are lit on the anniversary of departed members of the congregation who have bequeathed money for that purpose. Near the lights (electrical bulbs are used nowadays), nameplates indicate the persons who are being commemorated.

BIBLIOGRAPHY: I. Abrahams, *Jewish Life in the Middle Ages* (1932[2]), 156 and n. 2; Eisenstein, Dinim, 274; H. Rabinowicz, *Guide to Life* (1964), 106.

MEMPHIS (from the Greek Menophreos which in turn was derived from the late Old Kingdom Egyptian *Mn-nfr*, meaning "established and beautiful"), ancient city in Lower Egypt, on the west bank of the Nile, approximately 12 mi. (c. 19 km.) south of Cairo, lying partly under the site of the modern village Mit Riheina. According to tradition, Memphis was founded by the legendary Egyptian king Menes (probably the same as King Aha) in about 3100 B.C.E. The Egyptian name *Mn-nfr* originally designated the pyramid of King Pepi I (c. 2300 B.C.E.) at Saqqara, and was eventually extended to include also the town that grew up around it. By the end of the second millennium the name was probably vocalized "Menufi," although a papyrus from the late 20th Dynasty (c. 1184–1087 B.C.E.), gives the variant reading *Mnf*, from which the Coptic *Menfi*, Arabic *Menf*, and Hebrew *Mof* were derived.

Until the founding of Alexandria, Memphis played a paramount role in Egypt. As the administrative capital of the Old Kingdom, it had many palaces and temples, particularly that of Ptah, the city's creator god (with the Apis bull sacred to Ptah being venerated at Memphis); the remains of these structures can still be seen on the site. Literary texts, lavish in their praise and descriptions of the city, indicate that it was a cosmopolitan metropolis with a large, resident foreign population which included Jews (cf. Jer. 44:1); this has been confirmed by archaeological excavation. Foreign divinities worshiped at Memphis include Resheph, Baal, Astarte, and Qudshu. The eventual destruction of Memphis is predicted in Isaiah 19:13; Jeremiah 2:16; 46:14, 19; and Ezekiel 30:13. The city was not in fact destroyed, although it was besieged and taken by the Persians. Memphis was also the place where it was said Antiochus IV Epiphanes received the crown of Egypt. Archaeological excavations have brought to light the large Ptah temple, the palace of Apries, another large ceremonial palace, shrines of Seti I and Rameses II, an embalming house of the Apis bulls, tombs of the high priests, and various settlement remains. A project to record the scattered remains of Memphis through excavation and survey has been undertaken by D. Jeffreys and H.S. Smith for the Egypt Exploration Society since 1982.

BIBLIOGRAPHY: W.F. Petrie, *Memphis*, 1 (1909); idem, *The Palace of Apries* (1909); idem, *Meydum and Memphis* (1910), 38–46; W.F. Petrie et al., *Tarkhan I and Memphis V* (1913); A.H. Gardiner, *Ancient Egyptian Onomastica*, 2 (1947), 122–6. **ADD. BIBLIOGRAPHY:** J. Kamil, "Ancient Memphis: Archaeologists Revive Interest in a Famous Egyptian Site," in: *Archaeology*, 38:4 (1985), 25–32.

[Alan Richard Schulman / Shimon Gibson (2nd ed.)]

MEMPHIS, city in Tennessee, U.S., with a Jewish population of 9,500 (.08 percent of the general population) in 2005.

Memphis was first settled in 1818 and the first known Jewish settler, David Hart, arrived in 1838. In the 1840s Jews began to settle in larger numbers, and they acquired land for a cemetery in 1848. In 1850 a Hebrew Benevolent Society was formed, and by 1853 the Jews were "regularly organized" for purposes of worship. In 1935 the Society changed its name to the Jewish Welfare Fund, and in 1977 it became the Memphis Jewish Federation. In 1853, B'nai Israel Congregation (Children of Israel), with 36 members, was granted a charter by the state legislature. The congregation worshiped in rented halls until 1857, and in 1858 converted a bank building into a place of worship. The building was dedicated by Rabbi Isaac Mayer *Wise, the founder of American Reform Judaism, and would later be known as Temple Israel. Rev. Jacob J. Peres, a native of Holland, was the first spiritual leader. In 1860 the relationship between the congregation and Rev. Peres was severed and a new congregation, Beth El Emeth, was organized. From 1860 to 1870 R. Simon Tuska was rabbi of Congregation Children of Israel.

At this time, the city's Jews, some 400 people, worked in banking, barbering, and auctioneering (including slaves); they even operated a racetrack. A good number ran several businesses simultaneously. A few entered the professions; most were small storekeepers who dealt in clothing and dry-goods, groceries and hardware. Memphis suffered little or no damage during the Civil War. Some Memphis Jews served in the army of the Confederacy. From 1863 to 1866 Congregation Children of Israel sponsored a nonsectarian school – Hebrew Educational Institute. The school was to provide educational opportunities during the disruption caused by the war. Following the death of Rabbi Tuska in 1870, Rabbi Max Samfield was elected rabbi of the congregation in 1871 and served until 1915. In addition to serving the congregation, Samfield published *The Jewish Spectator* from 1885 until his death. This paper served the Jews of Memphis and the mid-South.

In 1884 the Orthodox Baron Hirsch Congregation was organized and in 1891 converted a church as a place of worship. The first rabbi was Benjamin Mayerowitz. It became the largest synagogue in the United States. In recent years it moved to a new, smaller sanctuary to be within the area with the highest concentration of Jews in East Memphis. Congregation Anshei Sphard was organized in 1898. Beth Sholom, a Conservative congregation, was established in 1950 and in 1967 dedicated its new synagogue. Like many Jews in the Memphis community, Beth Sholom's rabbi at that time, Rabbi Arie Becker, was well known for his involvement in the civil rights movement. Long-time Rabbi Zalman Posner was a *ḥasid* of the *rebbe*, but he served in a congregational role. Official Chabad Lubavitch of Tennessee was founded in Memphis in 1994. Under the leadership of Rabbi Levi Klein, Chabad quickly became an active part of Memphis Jewish life.

A B'nai B'rith Lodge was organized in 1856 and in 1927 the B'nai B'rith Home was established to serve the Jews of Memphis and the mid-South. It was completely rebuilt in the 1960s and dedicated in 1968 as the B'nai B'rith Home and Hospital. The Jewish Community Center was organized in 1949 and in 1968 dedicated a $2,000,000 edifice, and the Jewish Historical Society of Memphis and the Mid-South was established in 1986.

Jews have been active in the economic, political, and civic life of the community. The Goldsmith family, leading merchants, were known as benefactors of the community for three generations. The Jewish community was so well accepted in Memphis that in the 1920s, it chose not to build a Jewish hospital, fearing that it might alienate the non-Jewish medical community and lead to a restriction of their hospital privileges. Abe Plough, a native of Tupelo, Mississippi, was generally regarded as one of the foremost citizens of the community by virtue of his philanthropy. His company was bought out by Schering to form Schering-Plough, a pharmaceutical giant. He played an important role in settling the famous sanitation strike of 1968 that brought Martin Luther King, Jr., to town, the site of his assassination in April 1968, contributing money anonymously to offset the costs to the city of pay raises. Other families who generously supported the entire Memphis community include the Fogelman, Lipman, Lowenstein, Lemsky, and Belz families. The Jews have also served as presidents of the bar association and the medical society.

The Jewish population has remained relatively stable for more than 80 years. It has received 200 Holocaust survivors and 300 Russians. The community's hub shifted to East Memphis, the heart of Jewish life today.

The community boasts the Bornblum Judaic Studies Program, established in 1985 at the University of Memphis through the generosity of David Bornblum and Bert Bornblum. The program brings numerous scholars and lecturers to the community. As in many college towns, the town-gown gap is bridged by the Judaic Studies Program. There are two Jewish days schools: the Bornblum Solomon Schechter Conservative day school, and the Orthodox Margolin Hebrew Academy Feinstone Yeshiva of the South, which honors Harry Feinstone.

The Orthodox community of Memphis was described by Tova Mirvis in her highly acclaimed novel *The Ladies Auxiliary* (1999).

BIBLIOGRAPHY: R. Musleah, "The Jewish Traveler: Memphis," in: *Hadassah* (Dec. 2000).

[James A. Wax / Michael Berenbaum (2nd ed.)]

MENAHEM (Heb. מְנַחֵם; "comforter"; in Assyrian inscriptions Me-ni-ḫi-im-me, Mi-in-ḫi-im-mu), king of Israel, c. 746/6–737/6 B.C.E., son of Gadi (II Kings 15:17). Menahem seized the throne after assassinating *Shallum son of Jabesh (15:14). Shallum and Menahem may possibly have competed for the throne during the decline of the house of *Jehu. It is widely believed that both were among the officers from Gilead, a group which had been influential from the beginning of Jehu's reign (of. II Kings 9:1ff.; 15:25). Both Jabesh (the name of the principal city of Gilead) and Gadi (the name of a tribe) are designations pointing to the fact that both Menahem and Shallum were of Transjordanian origin. The struggle between the two was conducted with great cruelty. II Kings 15:16 states: "At that time Menahem sacked Tiphsah and all who were in it and its territory." Tiphsah is Thapsacus which is on the River Euphrates, east of Aleppo. From this statement it appears that Menahem's campaign extended to the Euphrates. However, most scholars maintain that in light of the political-military situation of the Kingdom of Israel since the end of the reign of *Jeroboam II, it is not possible that Menahem ruled over such a large kingdom, and they therefore accept the Lucian version of the Septuagint, where Tappuah appears instead of Tiphsah (cf. Josh. 16:8; 17:8). In view of the biblical chronological data with regard to Menahem and *Pekah, several scholars concluded that Menahem ruled only in the mountain of Ephraim, while at the same time Pekah ruled in eastern Transjordan. It appears that Pekah first served as Menahem's military commander, but later rebelled with the help of Aram, and became an independent ruler in Gilead, although nominally he was still considered the military commander of Menahem and Pekahiah.

According to the biblical account, during Menahem's reign, Pul, the king of Assyria (i.e., Pulu, the name given to *Tiglath-Pileser III when he became king of Babylon in the latter part of his reign), extended his campaign into Israel; Menahem paid him 1,000 talents of silver in order to retain his throne (II Kings 15:19). The annals of Tiglath-Pileser III mention "Menahem of Samaria" (the city; this designation may be considered as attesting the limited area of his administration) among the kings who paid tribute to Assyria in 738 B.C.E., immediately after the defeat inflicted by the Assyrian king on *Uzziah, King of Judah. It is questionable whether the biblical account of Menahem's tax and the account of Menahem's tax in the Assyrian source refer to the same event. It is Y. Yadin's opinion that the *Samaria ostraca belong to the last years of Menahem's reign and bear some relation to the tribute paid to the king of Assyria, to which every "mighty man" of wealth was required to contribute 50 shekels (II Kings 15:20). Apparently the Assyrian recognition of Menahem as the vassal king of Israel strengthened his status and helped stabilize his regime. Menahem needed Assyrian support both against rebel bases within his domain and against neighboring states, including the state of Judah (cf. Hos. 5:8–11). It is possible that most of the prophecies of Hosea 4–14 reflect the period of Menahem (H. Tadmor).

BIBLIOGRAPHY: Bright, Hist, 252–4; Kittel, Gesch, 2 (1923), 351ff., 516; E.R. Thiele, *The Mysterious Numbers of the Hebrew Kings* (1951), 73ff.; Y. Yadin, in: *Scripta Hierosolymitana*, 8 (1961), 19–25; H. Tadmor, *ibid.*, 248–66; M. Haran, in: *Zion*, 31 (1966), 18–38; idem, in: *Fourth World Congress of Jewish Studies*, 1 (1967), 33–35 (Heb. pt.), 252 (Eng. summ.); H.L. Ginsberg, *ibid.*, 92–93 (Eng. pt.); EM, 5 (1968), 30–33 (includes bibliography). **ADD. BIBLIOGRAPHY:** M. Cogan and H. Tadmor, *II Kings* (1988), 169–79; T. Hobbs, in: ABD, 4, 692–93; H. Tadmor, *The Inscriptions of Tiglath-Pileser III King of Assyria* (1994), 291, index, s.v. Menihimme.

[Jacob Licht and Bustanay Oded]

MENAHEM BEN AARON IBN ZERAḤ (c. 1310–1385), codifier. Menahem was born in Estella, Navarre, where his father had settled after leaving his native France, on the expulsion of the Jews in 1306. In 1328 riots broke out against the Jews of Navarre and the Estella community suffered severely. All of Menahem's family, including his parents and four brothers, were killed, and he himself was severely wounded, but his life was saved by a Christian friend of the family. When he recovered, he went to Toledo and studied in the yeshivot there. Among his teachers were Joseph b. Shuʿayb and Judah the son of *Asher b. Jehiel (the Rosh). From Toledo he went to Alcalá and studied under Joseph b. al-ʿAysh, succeeding him on his death in 1361. In Alcalá also, there were troubles and suffering. Fratricidal war had broken out in Spain between the two aspirants to the throne, Henry of Trastamara and Pedro the Cruel, and many Jewish communities suffered as a result. Menahem escaped to safety through the help of the royal courtier Don Samuel *Abrabanel, and Menahem praises him in the introduction to his *Ẓeidah la-Derekh*.

In Toledo Menahem compiled his *Ẓeidah la-Derekh*, a code of laws dealing in the main with the laws concerning the daily way of life. The work has an added importance on account of the introduction, which contains valuable historical material, including important details of the method of study in the yeshivot of France and Germany, as well as contemporary incidents in the history of the Jews in Spain. The book was designed as an abridged code for the upper classes who, because of their preoccupation with material concerns, had no time to refer to the sources. He writes reprovingly of those Jews who, because of the demands of the times, began to disregard the observance of the precepts. Although he shows great erudition in his knowledge of the Talmud and codes and was acquainted with the teachings of the earlier Spanish, French, and German scholars, he relies mainly for his halakhic rulings on those of Asher b. Jehiel.

Menahem gives much information about the different customs of the Jews of Spain, France, and Germany, as well as of various communities (see pp. 71, 82, 88, 104, 110, 116 in the Warsaw edition of 1880). He had some knowledge of medicine, and in the code he includes the need to preserve one's bodily health (see pp. 28–33; et al.). He also knew astronomy and believed in astrology (pp. 98–120). Although he criticized philosophy, he appears to have engaged in its study to some extent (104–48). In these sciences, however, Menahem merely gleaned from the works of others. His work reflects contemporary conditions. He complains that many of the youth, particularly children of the wealthy, were careless in the observance of the precepts and scoffed at the words of the sages, and some were even licentious in matters of sex (pp. 68–81). The book is divided into five *maʾamarim* ("articles"), which are divided into *kelalim* ("principles"), which are subdivided into chapters. The first *maʾamar* discusses prayer and the blessings; the second, the *halakhot* of **issur ve-hetter*; the third, laws of marriage; the fourth, the festivals; and the fifth, fasting and mourning, the Messiah, and the resurrection. It was first published in Ferrara in the printing press of Abraham Usque in 1554. In addition to his major work, three small works by Menahem are extant in manuscript – an abridgment of Baḥya ibn Paquda's *Ḥovot ha-Levavot, Hilkhot Sheḥitah u-Vedikah*, and *Menaḥem Avelim* – it is possible however, that they are simply abridgments from his *Ẓeidah la-Derekh* (see A. Freimann, in: *Annuario di Studi Ebraici* (1934), 166ff.).

BIBLIOGRAPHY: Weiss, Dor, 5 (1904[4]), 126–8, 210; A. Freimann, in: *Annuario di Studi Ebraici*, 1 (1935), 147–67; H. Tchernowitz, *Toledot ha-Posekim*, 2 (1947), 191–8; Urbach, Tosafot, 15, 210, 454, 465; Baer, Spain, 1 (1966), 373, 378, 419, 450f.

[Shlomo Eidelberg]

MENAHEM BEN ḤELBO (11th century), one of the first commentators on the Bible in northern France. Little is known of his life. He was the uncle of Joseph *Kara, who transmitted Menahem's comments to *Rashi. Apparently he lived for some time in Provence, and it is his influence which accounts for the presence of Arabic words as well as some Provençal forms of French in Rashi. Menahem was also called "Kara," which shows that his principal occupation was biblical commentary. He also wrote comments on the *piyyutim*. Menahem collected his commentaries in book form which he called *pitronim* ("solutions"). They covered all the Prophets and the Hagiographa, but not the Pentateuch upon which, apparently, he did not attempt to comment. His books are no longer extant as they were apparently superseded by Rashi's commentaries. Fragments, however, were collected by S.A. Poznański from quotations, especially by Joseph Kara, and also from the works of commentators in Germany (published by Poznański in *Festschrift N. Sokolow* (1904), 389–439 with Menahem's commentary on the *piyyutim*, and also separately).

Menahem was the first commentator in France to interpret the Bible according to the simple meaning of the text, although he also gave homiletical interpretations. He often limited himself to explaining difficult words and phrases, relying extensively on the Targum (e.g., Isa. 1:8). He employed many French words and terms in his commentary and had little recourse to grammar. Zunz is of the opinion that Menahem did not commit his comments on the *piyyutim* to writing, but transmitted his explanations of *Kallir's *piyyutim* orally. There is now evidence that he also wrote commentaries to other *piyyutim*.

BIBLIOGRAPHY: Abraham b. Azriel, *Sefer Arugat ha-Bosem*, ed. by E.E. Urbach, 4 (1963), 3–6.

[Avraham Grossman]

MENAHEM BEN JACOB (also known as **R. Menahem of Worms**; 1120?–1203), rabbi and liturgical poet in Worms. Menahem, whose tombstone bore the inscription *posek, darshan* ("preacher"), and *paytan*, was a member of the *bet din* of *Eleazar b. Judah, the author of *Rokeʾaḥ*, and Kalonymus b. Gershom. His relatives included Gershom *ha-Gozer and *Eliezer b. Joel ha-Levi. From the words of the latter, it appears that Menahem was influential in ruling circles. None of his teachings has been preserved, but 33 of his *piyyutim* are known. These include *yoẓerot, kinot*, and *seliḥot*, some of which were published in various places. Among them is the *kinah, Alelai Li Ki Vaʾu Rega Almon ve-Shakhol*, on the martyrs of Boppard of 1179 and of the islands of the sea (i.e., Britain) of 1190; the *piyyut Maẓor Batah ha-Ir* refers to the siege of Worms by Emperor Otto IV in 1201. Some of his *piyyutim* are signed "Ẓemaḥ," which in *gematria* is equal to "Menahem." In one manuscript he is mentioned as R. Menahem b. Jacob of Lutra (which is Bavarian Kaiserslautern in the Rhenish Palatinate); Zunz assumed that he was identical with Menahem b. Jacob, the *paytan* of Worms. If so, then Menahem was born in Lutra.

BIBLIOGRAPHY: Davidson, Oẓar, 4 (1933), 434; Zunz, Lit Poesie, 294–8; Berliner, in: *Kobez al-Jad*, 3 (1887), 3–9 (2nd pagination); Schechter, in: JHSET, 1 (1893–94), 8–14; Germ Jud, 1 (1934), index; V. Aptowitzer, *Mavo le-Sefer Ravyah* (1938), 382–4; A.M. Habermann, *Sefer Gezerot Ashkenaz ve-Ẓarefat* (1946), 147–51, 239f., 260.

MENAHEM BEN JACOB IBN SARUQ (**Saruk**; tenth century), Spanish author and lexicographer. Born in Tortosa, he moved at an early age to Cordova, where Isaac, the father of *Ḥisdai ibn Shaprut, became his patron. After Isaac's death, Menahem went back to his native town for a short interlude, and then returned to Cordova, where he lived under the patronage of Ḥisdai and worked as his secretary. Besides eulogies on Ḥisdai's parents, Menahem composed Ḥisdai's famous letter to the king of the *Khazars. Ḥisdai encouraged him to compile his *Maḥberet*, a biblical dictionary in Hebrew. However, Menahem endured poverty because Ḥisdai was not a very generous patron. Later, when Menahem fell into disgrace, Ḥisdai even persecuted his former protégé and forced him to return to Tortosa. Here Menahem wrote a touching letter of complaint to Ḥisdai, a gem of epistolary style and an important historical document concerning its author's life.

Menahem's most important work, intrinsically and historically, is the *Maḥberet*, whose original name was probably *The Book of Solutions*. Because Menahem's dictionary was originally written in Hebrew, its style surpasses that of biblical dictionaries of greater quality translated into Hebrew from Arabic, such as Judah ibn *Tibbon's translation of *Ibn Janaḥ's *Book of Roots*. More importantly, because the dictionary was in Hebrew, it was also understood by Jews in Christian countries where it exerted great influence. For example, in France, the *Maḥberet* was used extensively by *Rashi. Menahem carefully refrained from linguistic comparisons between Hebrew and Arabic, presumably as Hebrew was considered a holy language. Menahem's theological concern is further reflected in his attempt to show that *ehyeh* which is referred to as a name for God in Exodus 3:14 is not derived from the verb *hayah* ("to be").

Often original in terminology, the dictionary attempts, without reference to its predecessors, a systematic summation of the lexicographical and grammatical knowledge of the time. Menahem shows awareness of ellipses and pleonasms occurring in the Bible, and brings into relief poetic parallelism, or constructions in which, as he put it, "one half instructs us in the meaning of the other." However, he did not have a systematic knowledge of grammar, and his approach tended to the empirical. Although Menahem carried out the investigation of the Hebrew roots systematically and built his dictionary accordingly, he thought that letters of the root that disappear in conjugation are not radical, and therefore established, on the synchronic level, biliteral and even uniliteral roots, e.g., *náṭâh*, root ṭ; *hikkâh*, root k. Thus, the *Maḥberet* can only be regarded as a summary of past achievements and it was, according to some authorities, reserved to Menahem's pupils to initiate the new period of linguistic research. Shortly after the *Maḥberet* appeared, it was vehemently attacked by *Dunash b. Labrat who claimed that certain definitions were likely to lead the reader to erroneous interpretations of *halakhah* and belief. The expectation that the dictionary would therefore become a source of heresy explains the bitterness of the attack. Menahem himself did not reply to Dunash's criticisms, but three of Menahem's pupils took it upon themselves to defend their master. One of the pupils was Judah ibn Daud whom some scholars think is identical with Judah b. David *Ḥayyuj, the great initiator of the theory of the triliterality of Hebrew roots, while other scholars consider this identification doubtful. However, Isaac ibn *Gikatilla, another of the three, was the teacher of Ibn Janaḥ, the greatest medieval Jewish lexicographer and philologist. The controversy between the two camps continued; Yehudi b. Sheshet defended his master Dunash against the attacks of Menahem's pupils, and the famous tosafist Jacob b. Meir *Tam in his *Book of Decisions* (appended to the Filipowski ed. of the *Maḥberet*) tried to prove that Menahem's definitions were valid. Several decades later, Rabbi Joseph *Kimḥi, the first of the philologists of the Kimḥi family, wrote *Sefer ha-Galu'i* in his own effort to settle the disputes, this time in light of Ḥayyuj's theory. A modern scholar, D. *Yellin, demonstrated that, from the scientific point of view, Dunash's criticisms were generally well founded (*Sefer Zikkaron le-A. Gulak ve-S. Klein* (1942), 105–14; *Leshonenu*, 11 (1941–43), 202–15).

BIBLIOGRAPHY: W. Bacher, in: ZDMG, 49 (1895), 342–67; idem, in: J. Winter and A. Wuensche (eds.), *Die juedische Litteratur*, 2 (1894), 145–9; H. Hirschfeld, *Literary History of Hebrew Grammarians and Lexicographers* (1926), 24–31; Ashtor, Korot, 1 (1966²), 160–170, cf. also 310f. as to the identification of Judah ibn Daud with Judah Ḥayyuj; the *Maḥberet* was edited by Z. Filipowski (1854) from five manuscripts; for additions from a Berne Ms. see D. Kaufmann, ZDMG, 40 (1886), 367–409; the response of Menahem's pupils, *Liber Responsonuim*, was edited by S.G. Stern (1870; where introd. 23–37 Menahem's epistle to Ḥisdai first edited by S.D. Luzzatto, in: *Beit ha-Oẓar*, 1 (1847), 26a–33a is reprinted. It was re-edited by Schirmann, in: *Sefarad*, 1 (1955), 8–30). **ADD. BIBLIOGRAPHY:** A. Sáenz-Badillos, *Menahem Ben Saruq, Maḥberet* (1986). On this edition see I. Eldar, "*Askolat ha-Dikduk ha-Andalusit: Tekufat ha-Reshit*," in: *Pe'amim*, 38, 2 (1989), 24; idem, "Early Hebraists in Spain: Menahem ben Saruq and Dunash ben Labrat," in: M. Saboe (ed.), *Hebrew Bible – Old Testament: The History of its Interpretation* 1/2: *The Middle Ages* (2000), chapter 25.5, 96–109; A. Maman, *Comparative Semitic Philology in the Middle Ages from Saadia Gaon to Ibn Barun (10th–12th cent.)* (2004), 276–283; idem, "Menaḥem ben Saruq's *Maḥberet* – The First Hebrew–Hebrew Dictionary," in: *Kernerman Dictionary News*, 13 (2005), 5–10.

[Joshua Blau]

MENAHEM BEN MICHAEL BEN JOSEPH, medieval Karaite scholar. He was author of a Hebrew polemical epistle in verse addressed to "Akylas the Proselyte, in care of Saadiah the Rabbanite," dealing with the laws of slaughtering. S.P. *Pinsker, who first published the poem, assumed that it was directed against *Saadiah Gaon and that therefore the author must have lived in the first half of the tenth century. His vocabulary, however, is that of a Byzantine Karaite of a later date, presumably the 12th century, and he is very likely identical with Menahem b. Michael, the author of several hymns included in the Karaite liturgy.

BIBLIOGRAPHY: S. Pinsker, *Likkutei Kadmoniyyot* (1860), index, s.v. *Menaḥem Giẓani ha-Goleh*; S. Poznański, *Karaite Literary Opponents of Saadiah Gaon* (1908), 11–12.

[Leon Nemoy]

MENAHEM BEN MOSES HA-BAVLI (d. 1571), rabbi and author in Ereẓ Israel. Despite his surname ("the Babylonian"), Menahem appears to have come from Italy; his ancestors probably lived in Babylon. Until 1525 Menahem served as *dayyan* in Trikkola, Greece. In 1527 he was living with his family in Safed, among whose scholars his name is included. There, with his brother Reuben, he engaged in business connected with the wool-dyeing industry. After 1546 he moved to Hebron, apparently being among the Safed rabbis who renewed the Jewish settlement in that city in the middle of the 16th century. Menahem achieved renown through his *Ta'amei ha-Mitzvot* (Lublin, 1571), in which he briefly sets forth the reasons for the precepts. In the introduction Menahem refers to a lengthy work he had written called *Ta'amei Mitzvot ha-Arukot*. One of his responsa on divorce was published among those of Joseph *Caro to *Even ha-Ezer* (Salonika, 1598, 80a, *Dinei Gittin ve-Gerushin*, no. 10).

BIBLIOGRAPHY: Ben-Yaakov, in: *Ḥemdat Yisrael, Koveẓ le-Zikhro shel … Ḥ.Ḥ. Medini* (1946), 89–97; M. Benayahu, in: KS, 29 (1953/54), 173f.; 31 (1955/56), 399f.; Roth, *ibid.*, 399; Dimitrovsky, in: *Sefunot*, 7 (1963), 67.

MENAHEM BEN SOLOMON (first half of 12th century), author of the midrashic work *Sekhel Tov*. Menahem's country of origin is unknown. The foreign words in his book are Italian, but it is difficult to establish on this basis that he lived in Italy since he does not mention the *Arukh* of *Nathan b. Jehiel of Rome though it was written about 50 years earlier. Similarly, all that is known of Menahem is that two halakhic responsa were addressed to him apparently by Solomon b. Abraham, the nephew of Nathan of Rome (included in the *Shibbolei ha-Leket*, pt. 2, still in manuscript). Menahem's fame rests on his *Sekhel Tov*, an aggadic-halakhic midrashic anthology arranged according to the weekly scriptural readings. Only the first two parts of the book, to Genesis and Exodus, have been preserved and published by S. Buber (*Sekhel Tov*, 1900), who added a detailed introduction. However, many early scholars possessed complete manuscripts from which they frequently quote, particularly the author of the *Asufot* (in manuscript) who lived in Germany at the beginning of the 13th century. The *Sekhel Tov* was written, according to its author, in 1139, with the aim of explaining the verses in accordance with the Midrashim and Hebrew philology. Apart from the talmudic and midrashic sources, the only works he quotes are the *She'iltot* of *Aḥa of Shabḥa, the *Halakhot Gedolot*, *Hananel b. Ḥushi'el, Isaac *Alfasi, and the Midrash *Lekaḥ Tov* of Tobias b. Eliezer. Menahem's comprehensive knowledge of *halakhah* is evident from his work; in some places he actually assembles collections of *halakhot* on specific subjects, such as the laws of the Sabbath, **eruv*, Passover (in the weekly portion *Yitro*), etc. Still more marked is his great interest in linguistic topics and Hebrew grammar, which in fact constitute the underlying basis of the whole work. Indeed, Menahem devoted another work to this subject, *Even Boḥan*; only a minor part, of which fragments alone have been published, is extant in manuscript. This work was completed in 1143. It was divided into 50 *she'arim* ("gates"), constructed on a most complicated system. Only five of these "gates" remain, all of which deal with the study of the roots of Hebrew verbs, and they are of considerable importance for scriptural exegesis. The work mentions by name only the Targums of Onkelos and of Jonathan b. Uzziel, and also Eliezer *ha-Kallir, but it is based on the works of *Menahem ibn Saruq and *Dunash b. Labrat, although they are not mentioned by name. Menahem's knowledge of grammar did not exceed theirs; like them he too assumed the existence of verbal roots of two and even of one letter, and his table of the conjugations is far from perfect. Besides these authors, he also used Saadiah Gaon's translation of the Scriptures. Some regard the book as the first attempt at a treatise on the Hebrew language.

BIBLIOGRAPHY: Bacher, in: *Jubelschrift … H. Graetz* (1887), 94–115; idem, in: *Oẓar ha-Sifrut*, 5 (1895), 257–63.

[Israel Moses Ta-Shma]

MENAHEM THE ESSENE (first century B.C.E.), a contemporary of *Herod, to whom prophetic powers were attributed. Josephus relates how Menahem "had once observed Herod, then still a boy, going to his teacher, and greeted him as 'king of the Jews.'" The pious Essene added, however, that Herod would abandon justice and piety and thus bring upon himself the wrath of God. When Herod had reached the height of his power, he sent for Menahem and questioned him about the length of his reign. Menahem succeeded in satisfying the king, albeit with an ambiguous answer, and hence (according to Josephus) Herod continued to hold all Essenes in honor. L. Ginzberg suggests that Menahem is to be identified with the Menahem mentioned in the Mishnah (Ḥag. 2:2). This Menahem was, together with *Hillel, one of the heads of the Sanhedrin, who left his post (presumably to join the Essenes) and was succeeded by *Shammai. There is little evidence, however, to support his view. Talmudic discussions of the Mishnah tend to describe the mishnaic Menahem in terms far more fitting to *Menahem son of Judah the Galilean, a patriot leader during the uprising of 66–70 C.E.

BIBLIOGRAPHY: Jos., Ant., 15:373–8; Klausner, Bayit Sheni, 3 (1950^2), 115; 4 (1950^2), 148; A. Schalit, *Koenig Herodes* (1969), 459; L. Ginzberg, *On Jewish Law and Lore* (1955), 101.

[Isaiah Gafni]

MENAḤEMIYYAH (Heb. מְנַחֲמִיָּה), moshav in northern Israel with municipal council status, southwest of Lake Kinneret, affiliated with Ha-Iḥud ha-Ḥakla'i. Menaḥemiyyah was founded as a moshavah by the Jewish Colonization Association (ICA) in 1902, as part of the *ICA enterprise to establish villages in Galilee based on grain production. Its name is based both on the previous Arabic name of the site – Milḥamiyya – and the first name of Herbert *Samuel's father.

Menaḥemiyyah's progress was slow, and it suffered from the frequent attacks by Bedouins in the vicinity. In the 1920s, a gypsum quarry was opened nearby to supply the Haifa "Nesher" cement works. Later, World War II veterans ("Ya'el") joined the first settlers. Following the Israel *War of Independence (1948), new immigrants, mainly from North Africa and Romania, settled in Menaḥemiyyah. In 1969 the moshav had 585 inhabitants; in the mid-1990s – 1,240; and in 2002 – 1,100 on an area of 2.3 sq. mi. (6 sq. km.).

[Efraim Orni / Shaked Gilboa (2nd ed.)]

MENAHEM MENDEL BEN ISAAC (second half of 16th century), tax collector, architect, and builder in Kazimierz, near *Cracow. Menahem Mendel was born in Brest-Litovsk, and from 1560 to 1568 was the king's tax farmer in the Zhmud (Zemaitkiemis) region of Lithuania. In 1572 he moved to Kazimierz, and by 1581 he had become one of the elders of the *kahal*. From the early 1570s, he constructed flour mills and city walls, and was noted as a designer and builder of bridges. During the Polish campaign against Russia (1579–82), King Stephen Báthory was accompanied by Menahem Mendel, who built bridges over the Dvina and military installations for the sieges of Polotsk, Velizh, and Pskov. In 1587, since he had supported the defeated Austrian archduke Maximilian, he was compelled to leave Poland. Upon his arrival in Vienna, he was given a modest allowance by the court. On July 4, 1589, he proposed that Emperor Rudolph II finance the building of a bridge over the Danube, between Vienna and Nussdorf, at an estimated outlay of 30,000 *Rheingulden*. Menahem Mendel was to levy tolls to repay the investment. After two years of deliberations the project was deferred indefinitely and Menahem Mendel returned to Kazimierz. In 1592 King Sigismund III Vasa of Poland deputed him to arrange a match between the king's aunt, Ann Jagellon, and an Austrian archduke. All trace of Menahem Mendel vanishes after this point.

BIBLIOGRAPHY: M. Balaban, in: *Nowy Dziennik* (Nov. 15, 1919); idem, *Dzieje Żydów w Krakowie i na Kazimierzu*, 1 (1931), 139, 159, 162; M. Bersohn, *Dyplomataryusz dotycrący Żydów w dawnej Polsce* (1910), 108 no. 171; Schwarz, in: *Jahrbuch fuer Landeskunde von Niederoesterreich* (1913), suppl. 1.

[Arthur Cygielman]

MENAHEM MENDEL OF PEREMYSHLANY (b. 1728), ḥasidic leader. In his youth he joined the group of *Israel b. Eliezer, the Ba'al Shem Tov, and in the late 1750s is mentioned as a participant at a "third Sabbath meal" gathering (Israel *Loebel, *Sefer Vikku'aḥ* (Warsaw, 1798), 9b). In 1764, he went to Ereẓ Israel together with R. *Naḥman of Horodenko (Gorodenka) and settled in Tiberias. Before his emigration, he visited Cekinowka and Soroki, townlets on both banks of the Dniester, where he occupied himself in the "redemption of captives" (*pidyon shevuyyim*). He is identical with R. Mendel of Cekinowka mentioned in *Shivḥei ha-Besht* (Kapust, 1815), 19. As for the reason for his emigration, one of his intimates has written: "He emigrated to the Holy Land because emissaries started traveling to him urging that he occupy himself with community affairs" (A. Rubinstein, in: *Tarbiz*, 35 (1965/66), 177), which probably signifies that they came to him as a *ẓaddik* and miracle-worker (*Ba'al Shem) and he refused to assume such a role.

R. Mendel represents the extreme enthusiast among the first generations of the ḥasidic movement. His teachings abound in radical expressions which aroused violent opposition, such as: "One should not be exceedingly meticulous in every act performed, because this is the intent of the evil inclination; even if, Heaven forbid, one has sinned – one should not be overtaken by melancholy" (*Darkhei Yesharim* (Zhitomir, 1805), 4b, 5a). Like other disciples of the Ba'al Shem Tov, he considered devotion to God the pivot of ḥasidic doctrine and conduct. In contrast to others, however, he thought that Torah study and the practice of devotion were not compatible; study was therefore to be restricted so as not to restrain the process of approximation to the Creator. "If we divert our thoughts from devotion to God, and study excessively, we will forget the fear of Heaven … study should therefore be reduced and one should always meditate on the greatness of the Creator." R. Mendel considered prayer the most suitable manner in which to achieve devotion, and that prayer must be restrained and not, as was the opinion of Ḥasidim of other schools, vociferous. In general, it was his view that devotional conduct should be based on contemplative concentration attainable by seclusion from society and cessation of all occupation. His principal teachings were published in his booklet *Darkhei Yesharim ve-hu Hanhagot Yesharot* (Zhitomir, 1805); in *Likkutei Yekarim* (Lvov, 1792); and in *Yosher Divrei Emet* (1905), of R. Meshullam Feivush of Zbarazh.

BIBLIOGRAPHY: Dubnow, Ḥasidut, index; A. Rubinstein, in: *Tarbiz*, 35 (1965/66); J. Weiss, in: *Tiferet Yisrael – I. Brodie Jubilee Volume* (1967), 158–62.

[Avraham Rubinstein]

MENAHEM MENDEL OF SHKLOV (d. 1827), rebuilder of the Ashkenazi community of Jerusalem at the beginning of the 19th century; he was born in Shklov. His father was R. Baruch Bendet, who was a *Maggid*. Menahem Mendel was one of the outstanding pupils of R. *Elijah b. Solomon the Gaon of Vilna. He himself recounts: "I did not withdraw from his presence; I held onto him and did not leave him; I remained in his tent day and night; I went where he went, slept where he slept, and my hand never left his hand." After the death of his teacher in 1794 he worked with R. Elijah's sons on the arrangement and publication of his works. Through his initiative the following of Elijah's works were published in the course of nine years: R. Elijah's commentary on Proverbs; his annotation on *Seder Olam Rabbah* and *Seder Olam Zuta*; his interpretation of the Shulḥan Arukh, *Oraḥ Ḥayyim*; his commentary on *Avot*, and others.

In 1808 Menahem Mendel immigrated to Ereẓ Israel and settled in Safed where he established *battei midrash* for study and prayer and became the leader of the community of Ashkenazim-Perushim (followers of the Vilna Gaon), which then numbered around 150 persons. From Safed he maintained a correspondence with his friend R. *Israel of Shklov and entreated him to act on behalf of the economic consolidation of the community and even encouraged him to immigrate to Palestine. As a result of philosophical and traditional conflicts with the ḥasidic community of Safed, Menahem Mendel drew close to the Sephardi rabbis and their *bet midrash*.

When a plague broke out in Safed in 1812, he fled with others to Jerusalem. He probably reached the decision at that time to remain there permanently, but he set up his home in the city only in 1816. At the same time he rented the courtyard of the yeshivah of R. Ḥayyim ibn *Attar as a place for Torah study and prayer. This action should be seen as the renewal of the Ashkenazi community of Jerusalem, after a lapse of about 100 years. In his letters abroad he requested that **ḥalukkah* funds be transferred to the new community. Here, too, however, he maintained friendly relations with the *rishon le-Zion* R. Solomon Moses Suzin who aided him in consolidating his community. Despite the numerous difficulties – resulting from the non-legalization of the residence of the Ashkenazim in the city – the Ashkenazim under Mendel's leadership continued to live in Jerusalem. After his death, his son Nathan Nata was appointed in his place. Mendel was a prolific author and wrote about ten books dealing mainly with the teachings of Kabbalah and mysticism.

BIBLIOGRAPHY: Frumkin-Rivlin, 3 (1929), 138ff.; *Yerushalayim*, ed. by A.M. Luncz, 13 (1919), 223ff.

[Joshua Kaniel (Mershine)]

MENAHEM MENDEL OF VITEBSK (1730–1788), ḥasidic leader active in Belorussia, Lithuania, and Ereẓ Israel. He was a disciple of *Dov Baer the Maggid of Mezhirech, and headed a congregation in Minsk during the lifetime of his teacher; in *Zemir Ariẓim ve-Ḥarvot Ẓurim* (Warsaw, Bialystok, 1798), a pamphlet written by one of the **Mitnaggedim*, he is mentioned by the name of Mendel of Minsk. When the first wave of opposition to *Ḥasidism erupted (1772), he visited Vilna on two occasions – on the second occasion, accompanied by his disciple *Shneur Zalman of Lyady and attempted to meet *Elijah b. Solomon the Gaon of Vilna in order to point out to him the merits of Ḥasidism, but the Gaon refused to receive him and "he closed the door upon us twice." Ḥasidic tradition also regards him as one of the leading spokesmen at the meeting which was convened in Rovno in the house of Dov Baer after the imposition of the *ḥerem* on the Ḥasidim in 1772. The persecutions of the *Mitnaggedim* made him leave Minsk, and in 1773 he settled in Gorodok, from where he spread Ḥasidism in the Vitebsk and Mogilev provinces (assisted by *Israel of Polotsk, *Abraham b. Alexander Katz of Kalisk, and *Shneur Zalman of Lyady).

In 1777 Menahem Mendel went to Ereẓ Israel, accompanied by Abraham of Kalisk and Israel of Polotsk, at the head of a group of 300 persons, of whom only some were Ḥasidim. He became the leader of the ḥasidic *yishuv*, and sent emissaries to Russia in order to raise funds for its support. In Ereẓ Israel ḥasidic immigrants also encountered hostility among the Jewish community, as a result of the initiative of some *Mitnaggedim*, who addressed special letters on the subject to Ereẓ Israel. In the wake of the disputes which broke out, Menahem Mendel moved to Tiberias, where he erected a ḥasidic synagogue. He became related by marriage to one of the prominent Sephardim of Jerusalem. After his arrival in Ereẓ Israel Menahem Mendel remained the spiritual leader of the Ḥasidim of Belorussia, who maintained a correspondence with him. He continued to guide them in their conduct and interpreted the principles of Ḥasidism to them. Menahem Mendel did not consider himself to be a *ẓaddik* who could bless his Ḥasidim with the bounties of Heaven. He regarded his function of *ẓaddik* as being restricted to teaching and guidance in divine worship and not as that of a "practical" *ẓaddik*.

Teachings

In his teachings, Menahem Mendel remained faithful to those of the Maggid. Following him, he regarded the *ẓimẓum* (contraction) of divine emanation and its restriction as a condition for revelation, because that which is not limited cannot be conceived, just as thought is conceived by restriction and contraction into letters. The worlds were created by divine will as an act of mercy, by the contraction of the divine emanation, because of the deficiency of the recipients. "When one teaches a small child, he must be instructed in accordance with his young intelligence … in accordance with the ability of reception of his mind" (*Likkutei Amarim* (1911), 17a). Divinity is restricted in every place (the world is not His abode, but He is the abode of the world). It is the duty of man to adhere to the Divinity in the material creation and to redeem the Divine Presence from its exile in the material world. This can be achieved by various methods:

(1) By widening the conception of man as the wisest and most capable of understanding, "when he has attained wisdom and studies the Torah, he then creates new heavens and a new earth" (*ibid.*).

(2) By *devekut* (devotion) to God. Man is a part of the Celestial Divinity. The root of his soul is to be found in the world of **Aẓilut* (emanation) and he is therefore able to commune with God without the obstruction of any interruption or barrier. Menahem Mendel emphasizes prayer with devotion and *kavvanah* (intention). "With his prayer, he is a groomsman who brings the Divine Presence before God" (*ibid.*, 31b). In order to attain the virtue of *devekut*: (a) "He must consecrate his person and his meditation to wisdom to the extent

that he, so to say, has no further existence," i.e., spiritual self-denial. (b) By self-abnegation in the moral aspect and by the cultivation of other ethical values, such as humility, compassion, etc. With the consciousness of his own worthlessness, he is to regard himself as naught so that he become enwrapped with awe (as a result of which he will rise to speculative contemplation), which is the gateway to love. This degree of love will attach him to all men and his spiritual elevation will be followed by the uplifting of all of them in perfect contact and *devekut*. His occupation in secular affairs is to resemble the coming and goings of a man who immediately returns to his home (i.e., to his condition of *devekut*).

(3) By the observation of the precepts it is within the power of man to knit together the whole of the world, to control it and exert his influence in the heavenly spheres; he should therefore accustom all his limbs to the precepts. When observing a precept, he must realize that the reward of the precept is the actual observance of the precept itself (the observance of the precept for its own sake). Similarly, he emphasizes that there must be fear of sin and not fear of punishment. The perfect fear is a sublime degree which surpasses *ẓimẓum*; it is the fear of God's majesty, a constant fear before which all the other fears are contracted and "happy is the man that feareth always" (Prov. 28:14). He stresses the importance of faith even beyond logic and rational reason.

On worship through corporeality, he argues that one must not follow "the heretics who say that a man must be at a lower degree so that he may ascend from there, a drop which must needs precede a rise; may there not be such a thought in Israel" (*Likkutei Amarim*, 25b–26a).

His main works were *Peri ha-Areẓ* (Kopys, 1814); *Peri ha-Eẓ* (Zhitomir, 1874); *Eẓ Peri* (Lvov, 1880); *Likkutei Amarim* (Lvov, 1911). His letters appeared in *Nefesh Menaḥem* (Lvov, 1930).

BIBLIOGRAPHY: A.S. Heilman, *Beit Rabbi*, 1 (1903), 11–22; A. Yaari, *Iggerot Ereẓ Yisrael* (1943), 308–24; W. Rabinowitsch, *Lithuanian Ḥasidism* (1970), index; R. Mahler, *Divrei Yemei Yisrael*, vol. 1, book 3 (1955), 246–8; Dubnow, Ḥasidut, index; Horodezky, Ḥasidut, vol. 2, 13–35; H. Liberman, in: KS, 36 (1960), 127–8; L.I. Newman, *The Hasidic Anthology* (1934), index; M. Buber, *Tales of the Hasidim*, 1 (1968[4]), 175–81; B.D. Kahana, *Ḥibbat ha-Areẓ* (1968); M. Wilensky, *Ḥasidim u-Mitnaggedim* (1970), index.

MENAHEM OF MERSEBURG (first half of the 14th century), one of the leading scholars of Saxony, Germany. Menahem was a pupil of Isaac b. Ḥayyim of Oppenheim (apparently to be identified with the son of *Ḥayyim b. Isaac Or Zaru'a, who was a pupil of *Meir b. Baruch of Rothenburg). Menahem was renowned in his time as a talmudic scholar, and was particularly well known for his *takkanot* which determined relations between the individual and the community in all matters affecting the communal life of the Jew – especially in the subjects of taxation, personal injuries, and fines. Especially important was the *takkanah* in which he abolished the right of *me'un* (see *child marriage; responsa Judah Mintz (Venice, 1553) no. 13), which had been a cause of great tragedies in Jewish family life, particularly as a result of the widespread custom of child marriage. Some 150 years later his *takkanah* gave rise to violent controversy when some wanted to explain it as having been instituted only in cases where the child had been influenced to exercise it (see Jacob *Falk). Solomon *Luria writes in the *Yam shel Shelomo* to *Yevamot* (13: 17): "It has become customary during recent years not to permit *me'un*, this having originated with Menahem, author of *Me'il Ẓedek*, who carefully weighed up and enacted many restrictive and preventive measures and was a great expert and scholar, and his *takkanot* and restrictions spread throughout the whole of Germany." Here the name of Menahem's book is mentioned; only fragments of it have been preserved. Quotations from it are found in talmudic works of the 15th and 16th centuries, particularly in those of Jacob *Weil and Solomon *Luria, as well as in the glosses of Moses Ḥazzan to the *Minhagim le-Kol ha-Shanah* of *Isaac of Tyrnau, and in the *Shitah Mekubbeẓet* of Bezalel *Ashkenazi. Jacob Weil describes Menahem of Merseburg as an eminent scholar in his generation living in Saxony. "He laid down many laws and decisions which he collected, and from them compiled an extensive work. That book is to be found in Saxony and the *minhag* of Saxony completely follows it. Many of these rulings have been extracted from his book and are in my possession…" (Resp. Maharyu 133). These words were written in reply to questioners who were unaware of Menahem's identity and turned to Weil for information. In fact, at the end of the printed editions of the responsa of Jacob Weil there is a small collection, extracted from the *Me'il Ẓedek*, entitled *Nimmukei Menaḥem Merseburg*. It is entirely devoted to the judicial relations between individuals and communities. Among Menahem's pupils was Yom Tov Lipmann *Muelhausen, author of *Seder Tikkun ha-Get* which was based on his tradition (*Yam shel Shelomo*, Git. 2:5).

BIBLIOGRAPHY: Joseph b. Moses, *Leket Yosher*, ed. by J. Freimann, 2 (1904), xiiv.

[Israel Moses Ta-Shma]

MENAHEM SON OF JUDAH, patriot leader at the outset of the Roman War (66–70 C.E.). He was the son of Judah of Galilee, leader of the insurgents against the census of *Quirinus in 6 C.E. and must therefore have been well on in years at the time of the outbreak of the war. His most successful exploit was the capture of *Masada in the early stages of the war and his subsequent distribution of the contents of the armory to his followers. Menahem now led his forces to Jerusalem where the insurgents were besieging the royal palace and forced the Romans to surrender. Convinced that he could act as the leader of the rebels, he proceeded with a purge of the army, putting to death the former high priest *Ananias and his brother *Hezekiah. His assumption of power, however, was unacceptable to the Jerusalem insurgents (headed by Eleazar son of *Ananias) who, according to Josephus, were unwilling to fight for their freedom against the Romans only to become enslaved under a despot of lowly origin. When Menahem came to pray in the Temple Court, dressed in royal garb and accompanied by an armed guard, Eleazar and his men attacked him. Menahem was killed, and his followers forced to flee (Jos., Wars 2:443ff.). They regrouped themselves at Masada under *Eleazar son of Jair, a relative of Menahem, where they held out even after the fall of Jerusalem. The opposition of the Jerusalemites to Menahem and his followers was apparently due to a number of factors, among them the opposition of the Jerusalemites to revolutionary social changes and to the alleged messianic pretensions of Menahem. Geiger identifies Menahem with the Menahem mentioned in talmudic sources (TJ, Ḥag. 2:277d; Ḥag. 16b) and with the Menahem b. Hezekiah mentioned in the *aggadah* as the Messiah, born on the date of the destruction of the Temple (TJ, Ber. 2:4, 5a). Following the publication of the Dead Sea Scrolls, attempts have been made to identify the *Teacher of Righteousness mentioned there with Menahem the insurgent leader or his relative Eleazar son of Jair. These suggestions must be treated with reserve, pending further research.

BIBLIOGRAPHY: Graetz, Hist, 2 (1949), 260–1; Klausner, Bayit Sheni, 4 (1950²), 149, 175; 5 (1951²), 145–8; M. Hengel, *Die Zeloten* (1961), 365ff.; M. Stern, in: *Ha-Ishiyyut ve-Dorah* (1964), 70–78; G.R. Driver, *The Judean Scrolls* (1965), 276f.; 366f.; C. Roth, *The Dead Sea Scrolls* (1965), index.

[Lea Roth]

MENAHEM ẒIYYONI (late 14th–early 15th century), kabbalist and exegete who lived in Cologne, where he signed a document in 1382, probably as rabbi of the community. His father was R. Meir Ẓiyyoni. Nothing else definite is known about his life, his career, or his teachers. He is known only through his major work, *Ẓiyyoni*, a homiletical commentary on the Torah (first printed in Cremona in 1559 and again there in the following year after the first impression had been destroyed by fire), and by the treatise *Ẓefunei Ẓiyyoni* (partly preserved in Ms.), one of the major early kabbalistic books dealing in detail with the powers of evil and demonology. Menahem Ẓiyyoni was one of the few kabbalists in 14th-century Germany, and his work demonstrates that he was heir to two different esoteric traditions: the Spanish Kabbalah, including the Zohar, the *Sefer ha-Bahir*, and the exegetical works of Naḥmanides; and the esoteric theology of the 12th–13th-century movement of the Ḥasidei Ashkenaz. He quotes frequently from Eleazar b. Judah of Worm's *Sodei Razayya*, referring to him as *"ish sodi"* ("my esoteric authority"). These two traditions are also reflected in his subject matter: the customary kabbalistic questions on the emanation of the *Sefirot* alongside the Ashkenazi-ḥasidic conception of the *Kavod* ("divine glory") and its relationship to the prophets. He composed a *kinah* for the Ninth of Av which was incorporated in the Ashkenazi liturgy.

BIBLIOGRAPHY: Davidson, Oẓar, 4 (1933), 435; A. Kober, *Cologne* (1940), 358; Y. Dan, *Torat ha-Sod shel Ḥasidut Ashkenaz* (1968), 259f.

[Joseph Dan]

MENAḤOT (Heb. מְנָחוֹת; "meal-offerings"), second tractate in the order *Kodashim*, in the Mishnah, Tosefta, and Babylonian Talmud (there is no Jerusalem Talmud to this tractate). *Menaḥot* has 13 chapters and deals, as its name indicates, with the various meal-offerings in the Temple. Chapters 1–3 discuss in great detail the defects in the sacrificial act, especially wrongful intent and omission, which render the offering unfit (*pasul* or *piggul*). Chapter 4 continues with the same subject, listing instances of omissions which do not invalidate the offering; the last part deals with the meal-offering of the high priest (Lev. 6:13–16). Chapters 5 and 6 are mainly concerned with the preparation of the meal-offering. Chapter 7 deals with the loaves of the thanksgiving-offering (Lev. 7:12), of the consecration-offering (Lev. 8:26), and of the Nazirite-offering (Num. 6:15). Chapter 8 gives the ingredients of the meal-offering (flour, oil, wine, etc.) and the manner in which they were processed and prepared. Chapter 9 gives valuable information on the liquid and dry measures used in the Temple. Chapter 10 deals with the offering of the *Omer* ("sheaf of the waving"; Lev. 23:15–22), and Chapter 11 with the meal-offering of the barley of the new harvest (Lev. 23:16) and the shewbread (Lev. 24:5–9). Chapter 12 is mainly on vows concerning meal-offerings and drink-offerings. Chapter 13 discusses the problem arising out of sacrificial vows which were inaccurately defined. It also mentions, incidentally, the temple of *Onias. The Mishnah ends with a homily on the fact that the Bible employs the phrase "a sweet savor unto the Lord" equally with regard to offerings of cattle (Lev. 1:9), fowl (Lev. 1:17), and meal (Lev. 2:2) in order to emphasize that "it matters not whether one offers much or little, provided one's heart is directed towards heaven." The Tosefta, also 13 chapters, ends with a homily on the causes of the destruction of the Temple, and, quoting Isaiah 2:2–3, visualizes the future Temple as a universal one.

The first three chapters of the tractate have language patterns similar to the first four chapters of *Zevaḥim*. The similarity between Mishnah 3:1 and *Zevaḥim* 3:3 is especially striking. Epstein (Tannaim, 156f.) points to various strata in the Mishnah: *mishnayot* 3:5–4:4 end are from the Mishnah of R. Simeon, while *mishnayot* 1:3–4 belong to Judah b. Ilai (cf. Zev. 1:2; 6:7). Mishnah 3:4, quoted in the name of Simeon, appears in the Tosefta in the name of his son Eleazar. Apparently Eleazar had recorded his father's sayings together with his own, and thus the editor of the Tosefta attributed it to Eleazar. The Tosefta includes several groups of *beraitot*. Thus 1:2–4 contrasts the laws of *sheḥitah* ("slaughtering"), *kemiẓah* ("scooping out" with the hand), and *melikah* ("nipping" the neck of a bird). In the group 4:9–14 each of the passages starts with the word *kamaẓ* ("he scooped"), and the group 12:11–13:12 consists of laws concerning the dedication of offerings to the Temple. The Tosefta includes some aggadic material: Moses' blessing of the nation after the erection of the Tabernacle (7:8); God's evaluation of the sacrifices (7:9); an account of the golden tables, and candelabra, and of the shewbread of the Temple (11:6–18); and the corruption of the priests (13:18–21) and the sins that brought about the destruction of Shiloh and of the First and Second Temples: "Why was the First Temple destroyed? Because of the idolatry, incest, and shedding of blood that prevailed. But at the Second Temple we know that they toiled in the study of Torah and were heedful of the tithes: why then were they exiled? Because they loved money and hated one another. This teaches that hatred of man for his fellow is heinous before the Omnipresent and is regarded as being as grave as idolatry, incest, and murder" (13:22). The Babylonian *Gemara* has some interesting aggadic passages. There is a remarkable story to demonstrate the merits of wearing *ẓiẓit* as a safeguard against immorality (44a); a most interesting homily of R. Ezra (53a); and passages on the Jewish attitude toward Greek culture (64b, 99b) and on the origin of the Temple of Onias (109b). Several of the *aggadot* in *Menaḥot* emphasize the spiritual implications of sacrificing. A poignant *aggadah* by R. Isaac states that when the poor offer God a meal-offering, in spite of its negligible value, God honors the giver as though he had offered up his soul (104b). Regarding its *halakhot*, large portions of the text are taken up by extraneous material; e.g., 28a–44b deal mainly with the *menorah, mezuzah, tefillin*, and *ẓiẓit*. In the printed editions the sequence of the chapters in the Babylonian Talmud differs from that of the separate Mishnah edition; the 10th Mishnah chapter is 6th, and consequently the mishnaic 6th, 7th, 8th, and 9th chapters become the 7th, 8th, 9th, and 10th respectively. *Menaḥot* was translated into English and published by the Soncino Press, London (1948).

BIBLIOGRAPHY: Ḥ. Albeck, *Shishah Sidrei Mishnah-Kodashim* (1959), 59–62; Epstein, Amora'im.

[Arnost Zvi Ehrman]

°**MENANDER OF EPHESUS** (possibly second century B.C.E.) is probably identical with Menander of Pergamum quoted by Clement of Alexandria (*Stromateis* 1:114) as stating that "Hiram gave his daughter in marriage to Solomon at the time when Menelaus visited Phoenicia after the capture of Troy" (cf. *Laetus). He wrote a history of Phoenicia (in Ant. 8:144, Josephus says that Menander translated the Tyrian records from Phoenician into Greek) which included an account of *Hiram of Tyre, in whose reign "lived Abdemon, a young lad, who always succeeded in mastering the problems set by Solomon, king of Jerusalem" (Jos., Apion, 1:120; Ant. 8:146; cf. *Dios). Hiram also dedicated the golden pillar in the temple of Zeus, which, according to *Eupolemus (Eusebius, *Praeparatio Evangelica*, 9:34), was a present from Solomon. According to Josephus (Ant. 8:324), Menander also alluded to the drought which occurred during King Ahab's reign.

°**MENANDER OF LAODICEA** (third century C.E.), author of rhetorical works. He mentions that Jews from all over the world flock to Palestine for their festal assembly (*panegyris*).

MENASCE, DE, Egyptian family which went to *Egypt from Spain, by way of Ereẓ Israel and *Morocco. The members of the De Menasce family played a significant role in the economic development of Egypt in the second half of the 19th century.

JACOB DAVID DE MENASCE (1802–1885) was president of the *Cairo Jewish community and leader of the Austrian subjects in Egypt. He received the hereditary title of baron from the emperor Francis Joseph. In 1871 he settled in Alexandria, where he established the Menasce synagogue in 1873 and a large Jewish school (1881). He was the **sarraf* (banker) of the Giza quarter and before he settled in Alexandria was employed by Hasan Pasha Al-Manstrali as administrator of his large estates. Later, he founded an import-export company and opened branches of the company in Marseilles and Liverpool. His son BAKHOR DE MENASCE (1830–1884) was president of the *Alexandria community and active in Jewish philanthropy. Three of his sons became well-known: JACQUES (1850–1916), banker and head of the local community from 1889 to 1914, helped to found the Menasce hospital, financed jointly by his family and the community. In 1885 he opened in Alexandria a private secular school for boys and girls, in which the majority of the teachers were Catholic. FELIX (1865–1943) was president of the community of Alexandria from 1926 to 1933. In 1918 he founded the Zionist Pro-Palestine Society and aided pioneers traveling to Ereẓ Israel through Alexandria. He was a baron and in 1938 was honorary president of the Alexandria community. Alfred (1867–1927) was a member of the Alexandria municipal council for many years and honorary consul of Hungary. In 1925, after a teacher in a Christian school had repeated stories of the *blood libel before Jewish pupils, he reacted by becoming the principal benefactor in the establishment of a Jewish vocational school in the city. He married a member of the Suarez family. Felix's son GEORGES (b. 1900) was known in Egypt for his art collection and generosity, especially on behalf of Jewish causes. He settled in England. Another son, JEAN (b. 1910), who became a Jesuit priest in France, wrote a book on Ḥasidism (*Quand Israël aime Dieu*, 1931), following a visit to Poland. Members of the De Menasce family competed with the Aghion and Rollo families for leadership of the Alexandria community, which was divided into two parties, one of which was headed by the De Menasce family. In 1885 the family helped the Jewish hospital. Other members of the family were known especially as philanthropists: Abramino founded in 1917 a Jewish hospital in Cairo; Elie in 1920 made an important donation to the De Menasce school in Alexandria; Jacque Elie in 1930 founded the Society "Amelei Tora."

ADD. BIBLIOGRAPHY: J.M. Landau, *Jews in Nineteenth-Century Egypt* (1969), index; S. Stambouli, in: J.M. Landau (ed.), *Toledot ha-Yehudim be-Miẓraim ba-Tekufah ha-Otmanit* (1988), 119–22; S. Raafat, in: *Egyptian Mail* (Nov. 16, 1996), 1–4; M. Fargeon, *Les Juifs en Egypte depuis l'origine jusqu'à ce jour* (1938).

[Haim J. Cohen / Leah Bornstein-Makovetsky (2nd ed.)]

MENDA, ELIEZER (1887–1978), journalist. Born in *Edirne, he studied between 1905–10 in the Ecole Normale Orientale, Paris. He was a teacher at the *Alliance Israélite Universelle schools in Edirne, Tetouan, and Tatarpazarcik. Between 1910–1925 he taught French and German in various lycées in Mersin, Adana, Konya, and İzmit. He contributed to different Ladino newspapers such as *El Judio, El Jugeton, El Telegrafo,*

La Boz de Oriente, and to French newspapers such *L'Aurore* and *Le Journal D'Orient.* In December 1950 he started publishing the Ladino newspaper *La Luz* with a partner, Robert Balli. Later on Balli left and started to publish his own newspaper, *La Luz de Türkiye,* while Menda continued with *La Luz* until 1972.

BIBLIOGRAPHY: N. Benbanaste, *Örneklerle Türk Musevi Basının Tarihçesi* (1988); A. Elmaleh, "Türkiye'de Yahudice-Ispanyolca Basınının Emektarı: Eliezer Menda," in: *La Vera Luz* (Dec. 17, 1964–Jan. 21, 1965); "Homenaje a los Dekanos de la Prensa Judia Turka don Eliezer Menda i don Eliya Gayus," in: *La Vera Luz* (Feb. 9, 1967).

[Rifat Bali (2nd ed.)]

MENDEL, wealthy family prominent in Hungary in the late 15th and early 16th centuries. It appears that the family went there from Germany and they seem to have been in Buda from 1470. On the suggestion of the royal treasurer, the apostate János Ernuszt, King Matthias Corvinus (1458–90) granted to members of the Mendel family the office of **Praefectus Judaeorum.* Probably the family was friendly with Ernuszt or may even had been related to him. First to hold the office was JUDAH (c. 1470). He was succeeded by his son JACOB (1493–1522), who was particularly respected. A record of his seal, inscribed with his initials, still exists. Next in office was ISRAEL (1523–26), who was followed by ISAAC (1527–39). With the expulsion of the Jews from Buda to Turkey (1526; see *Budapest) and the conquest of the town the family declined; the office of *Praefectus Judaeorum* also ceased to exist at that time. A prominent member of the family was MENDEL SCHWARTZ, one of the most important financiers of the Hungarian capital. He is mentioned for the last time in 1526. Members of the Mendel family were also to be found in other Hungarian towns, such as in Sopron, but those mentioned in Pressburg were almost certainly identical with the Buda branch, who also owned houses in Pressburg.

BIBLIOGRAPHY: S. Kohn, *A zsidók története Magyarországon* (1884), 220–2; S. Bschler, *A zsidók története Budapesten* (1901), 48–51; Sz. Balog, *A magyarországi zsidók kamaraszolgasága* (1907), 68–69; B. Mandl, in: *Mult és Jövő,* 5 (1915), 304–5; *Magyar Zsido Lexikon* (1929), 586; P. Gruenwald, in: *N.M. Gelber Jubilee Volume* (1963).

[Andreas Kubinyi]

MENDEL, ARTHUR (1905–1979), musicologist, critic, and conductor. Born in Boston, Mendel studied music theory and composition with Nadia Boulanger (1925–27) at the Ecole Normale de Musique in Paris. He was music critic of the *Nation* (1930–33), literary editor for G. Schirmer, Inc. (1930–38), editor of the American Musicological Society's journal (1940–43), associate editor of the *Musical Quarterly,* and editor of Associated Music Publishers (1941–47). From 1936 to 1953 he conducted the Cantata Singers, a small choir performing baroque music. He held lectureships at Columbia University (1949) and the University of California, Berkeley (1951), became chairman of the music department at Princeton (1952–67), and held the Henry Putnam University Professorship from 1969 to 1973. He was a member of the editorial boards of the Neue Bach-Ausgabe and of the new Josquin edition. His editions of the *St John Passion* brought him recognition as the foremost American Bach scholar of his generation. In his later years he investigated the possible applications of computer technology to musicological problems.

ADD. BIBLIOGRAPHY: Grove online; R.L. Marshall (ed.), *Studies in Renaissance and Baroque Music in Honor of Arthur Mendel* (1974), incl. R.L. Marshall, "Arthur Mendel: A Portrait in Outline," 9–11; and list of writings, 377–84.

[Israela Stein (2nd ed.)]

MENDEL, HERMANN (1834–1876), music publisher and lexicographer. Born in Halle, Germany, Mendel edited a music journal, a series of operatic librettos with commentaries, and a book of folk songs. His chief work was his *Musikalisches Conversations-Lexikon* (1870–83), a music encyclopedia in 12 volumes, the last five of which were edited by August Reissmann after Mendel's death. He also published two books on *Meyerbeer (1868, 1869).

MENDEL, LAFAYETTE BENEDICT (1872–1935), U.S. physiological chemist and pioneer in nutrition. Born in Delhi, New York, Mendel became professor at the Yale Sheffield Science School, and in 1921 professor of physiological chemistry at Yale University. He was the first person to study vitamin A, and first president of the American Institute of Nutrition. His contributions to scientific literature were concerned with proteins, nutrition, growth, and accessory factors.

MENDELS, MAURITS (1868–1944), Dutch Socialist politician. Born in The Hague to an Orthodox family, Mendels worked as a journalist, and from 1909 practiced as a lawyer in Amsterdam. As a member of the Dutch Social Democrat Party (SDAP) since 1899, he always operated on its left, Marxist wing. In Parliament (1913–19) and in the Senate (1919–37), Mendels specialized in legal affairs. He was known for his witty and astute speeches. Mendels sympathized with the Zionist cause. During Nazi occupation he did not go into hiding and he was deported to Theresienstadt. One day before his death on June 3, 1944, he noted down: "I would rather die as an old courageous lion than live as a vile and pitiable dog."

MENDELSOHN, ERIC (1887–1953), architect. He was born in Allenstein, Germany and was a member of the revivalist movement in European architecture from the 1920s onward. His early works, especially his sketches made during World War I and the buildings designed in the early twenties (such as the observatory near Berlin, 1920), are of an expressionist character. His later buildings are noteworthy, against the background of the contemporary style, for the originality of their shapes and their monumental nature. He built a large number of business-houses and large office blocks in Berlin and in other towns in Germany, as well as factories and dwelling-houses. When Hitler seized power in 1933, Mendelsohn left

Germany and worked in Britain and Palestine until the outbreak of World War II. Between 1934 and 1939, he built in Palestine the villa and library of Zalman Schocken in Jerusalem, the Anglo-Palestine Bank in Jerusalem, the Hadassah hospital on Mount Scopus, Chaim Weizmann's villa in Reḥovot, part of the Hebrew University's Faculty of Agriculture at Reḥovot, and the Haifa government hospital. When World War II broke out, he went to the United States, and from 1945 onward, built in various places. His works include the Maimonides Health Center in San Francisco, and many synagogues, in which he tried to achieve a monumental impression without adherence to any traditional style. These include synagogues in St. Paul, Minnesota; Washington, D.C.; Baltimore, Maryland; Dallas, Texas; Saint Louis, Missouri. He wrote the autobiographical *Letters of an Architect* (1967).

BIBLIOGRAPHY: A. Whittick, *Eric Mendelsohn* (Eng., 1956^2); W. Eckardt, *Eric Mendelsohn* (Eng., 1960).

[Abraham Erlik]

MENDELSOHN, FRANKFURT MOSES (Moses ben Mendel Frankfurt; 1782–1861), Hebrew scholar and writer. Born in Hamburg, he received a traditional education but, under the influence of N.H. *Wessely, became attracted to Haskalah. He engaged mainly in literary work, writing in both German and in Hebrew. His main work is *Penei Tevel* (published posthumously in Amsterdam in 1872), a collection of poetry and prose in the style of the *maqāmāt* of Al-*Ḥarizi. The book contains satire, polemics, epic poems on biblical themes, and a history of the Hebrew Haskalah movement at the turn of the 18th century. He was an uncle of S.R. *Hirsch.

BIBLIOGRAPHY: E. Duckesz, *Ḥakhmei Ahav* (1908), 120–1; G. Kressel, *Ivrit ba-Ma'arav* (1941), 36–41; Ḥ.N. Shapira, *Toledot ha-Sifrut ha-Ivrit ha-Ḥadashah* (1967^2), 503–10.

[Getzel Kressel]

MENDELSOHN, SHELOMO (1896–1948), Yiddish critic. Born in Warsaw, he early showed his brilliance in talmudic studies. While enrolled at Warsaw University, he taught Jewish history and literature at Polish secondary schools. From 1917 he was coeditor of *Dos Folk* and a leader of the Folk Party. In 1928 he joined the Bund and eight years later was elected to the Jewish *kehillah*. He immigrated to the United States in 1941 and joined the editorial board of *Undzer Tsayt*. In 1947 the Bund sent him to Europe, where he organized Jewish educational, cultural, and communal organizations. His articles on literature were published in various Yiddish journals. His literary criticism includes works on Solomon *Ettinger, H.D. *Nomberg, and J.J. *Trunk.

BIBLIOGRAPHY: H.S. Kashdan, *Shloyme Mendelson* (1949). **ADD. BIBLIOGRAPHY:** G. Pickhan, "Gegen den Strom," in: *Der Allgemeiner Juedische Arbeiterbund "Bund" in Polen* (2001), index.

[Israel Ch. Biletzky]

MENDELSON, JACOB BEN-ZION (1946–), *ḥazzan*. Jacob Ben-Zion Mendelson was born in New York to a well-known family of cantors. He is the brother of the cantor Solomon *Mendelson, a former president of the Cantors' Assembly. He was a student of the Etz Haim Yeshiva in Brooklyn. He studied cantorial music with the cantors Moshe and David *Koussevitzky, William Bougcester, and especially Moshe *Ganchoff. He served as cantor in Riverdale, New York, at the Beth Torah Synagogue in Miami, Florida, in the Shaarai Tefila congregation in Flushing, New York, and from 1986 at Temple Israel in White Plains, New York. He appeared in concerts and in prayer services throughout the United States, and also at the Jerusalem congress of the Cantors' Assembly in honor of the 20th anniversary of the unification of Jerusalem. Cantor Mendelson was called mentor by an entire generation of cantors, having taught at the Hebrew Union College-School of Sacred Music, the H.L. Miller Cantorial School at the Jewish Theological Seminary, and the Academy of Jewish Religion. It is true to say that he was one of the most sought-after teachers in the world of *ḥazzanut*. He produced record selections from the prayer service in the style of the cantors Alter, *Ganchoff, and Rappaport. A documentary film dealing with the entire spectrum of cantorial music today, from the prism of Cantor Mendelson's career, was made for PBS and other venues. From 2002 he was president of the Cantors' Assembly.

[Akiva Zimmerman / Raymond Goldstein (2nd ed.)]

MENDELSON, JOSÉ (Yoysef; 1891–1969), Argentine Yiddish editor and writer. Born in Cherkassy (Ukraine), Mendelson had a traditional education from his father and was early recognized as a talmudic genius. His first publication was an article on Peretz *Smolenskin in 1912 in the Russian-Zionist monthly, *Di Yidishe Hofenung*. In the same year, he immigrated to Argentina, where he taught Hebrew. With Z. Brokhes he co-edited the fortnightly, *Der Kolonist*, in which he also published articles on Yiddish and Spanish writers. He began writing for *Di Yidishe Tsaytung* in 1917 and later edited the publication (1923–29); with Y. Helfman he edited the Yiddish monthly *Argentine* (1921). He also edited the anthologies *Oyf di Bregn fun La-Plata* ("On the Banks of La Plata," 1919), *50 Yor Yidishe Kolonizatsye in Argentine* ("50 Years of Colonization in Argentina," 1939), and *Rashi-Bukh* ("Rashi-Book," 1940). A collection of his writings, *Amol in a Halbn Yoyvl* ("Once in Half a Lifetime"), was published in 1943. He translated many Russian, Spanish, French, and English novels into Yiddish. Among his other works were plays and writings about artists, sculptors, etc. From 1943, he directed the Hebrew-Yiddish Teachers Seminary in Buenos Aires.

BIBLIOGRAPHY: LNYL, 6 (1965), 39–41.

[Israel Ch. Biletzky / Jerold C. Frakes (2nd ed.)]

MENDELSON, SOLOMON (1933–), *ḥazzan*. Solomon Mendelson was born in New York to a well-known family of cantors. Since 1954 he has been cantor of the Beth Shalom Synagogue in Long Beach, New York. At the Jerusalem congress of the Cantors' Assembly he was elected president of the assembly, which is the largest organization of cantors in the world. He was a member of the administration of the Cantorial School of the Jewish Theological Seminary and a teacher of the traditional style of the prayer services. He served in the U.S. Army with the rank of captain. Mendelson initiated and organized concerts of cantorial music. He assisted in the writing of new compositions in the areas of Jewish and cantorial music and was president of the Cantors' Assembly (1987–89). In 1994 the Jewish Theological Seminary awarded him the degree of Doctor of Music *honoris causa.* His brother is the cantor Jacob Ben-Zion *Mendelson.

[Akiva Zimmerman]

MENDELSSOHN, family of scholars, bankers and artists. The founder of the family was MOSES *MENDELSSOHN (1729–1786). His wife, FROMET (1737–1812), was a great-granddaughter of the Viennese Court Jew, Samuel *Oppenheimer. (See Chart: Mendelssohn Family).

Moses' eldest son, JOSEPH (1770–1848), had a banking business, at times in partnership with his brother ABRAHAM (1776–1835). The bank helped transfer the French indemnity after Napoleon's defeat, and was later active mainly in German and foreign railway issues and state loans, particularly Russian. Mendelssohn and Co. were bankers and correspondents for many foreign commercial banks, central banks, and governments, but did not launch any industrial ventures of their own. After World War I the bank opened an issuing house in Amsterdam. The Berlin house was absorbed by the Deutsche Bank in 1939. Joseph was the friend and patron of Alexander von *Humboldt, the naturalist, and for many years chairman of the corporation of Berlin merchants. He and his brother Abraham were co-sponsors of the enlightened circle of Jewish notables, Gesellschaft der Freunde. His nephew, Abraham's son, the composer FELIX MENDELSSOHN BARTHOLDY (for the Bartholdy see Felix *Mendelssohn) urged him to go through with his old project of an edition of his father's collected works, on the suggestion of F.A. Brockhaus, the noted publisher; in this he was aided by his son, GEORG BENJAMIN (1794–1874), professor of geography at Bonn University. Joseph himself contributed to this project, for which he wrote his father's biography. Of Joseph's sons, Georg Benjamin was baptized; ALEXANDER (1798–1871), head of the bank, remained a Jew. Through social contacts with the *Hohenzollerns, Joseph's grandson FRANZ (1829–1889) and Abraham's grandson ERNST (1846–1909) were elevated to the hereditary nobility.

In 1804, Abraham married Leah Salomon, granddaughter of Daniel *Itzig, and thereby became a naturalized Prussian citizen, ahead of the bulk of his coreligionists. He served for many years as municipal councilor without pay. A deist and rationalist by conviction he brought up his children as Protestants in order to improve their social opportunities. He and his wife embraced Christianity in 1822 "because it is the religious form acceptable to the majority of civilized human beings" (in a letter to his daughter Fanny). This decision to convert was influenced by the current *Hep! Hep! riots (1819).

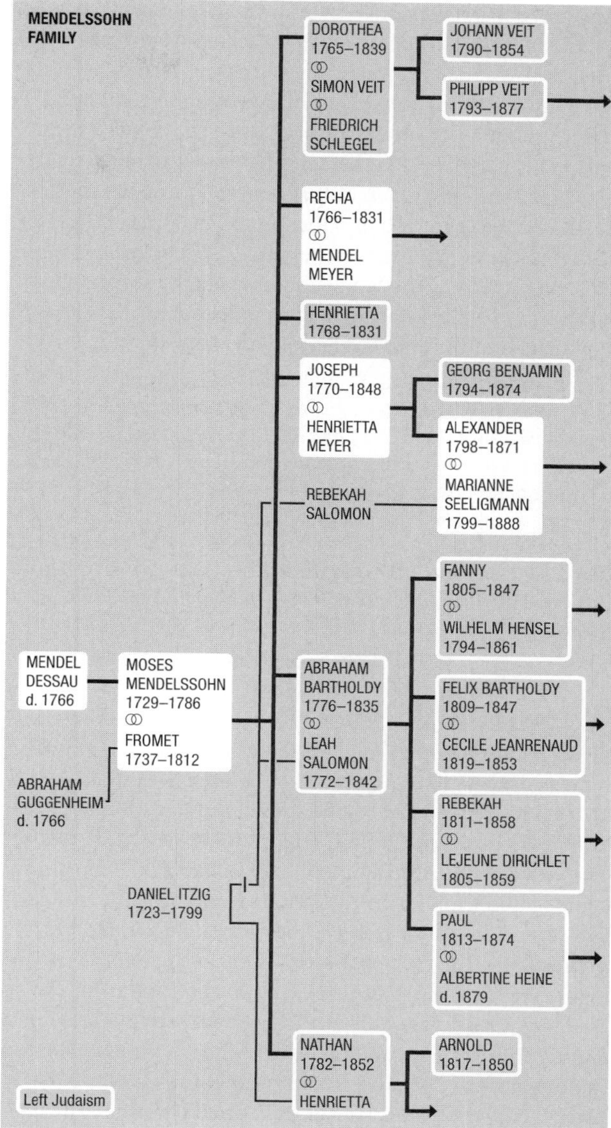

Later Mendelssohn-Bartholdy descendants include ALBRECHT MENDELSSOHN-BARTHOLDY, editor of the *Europaische Gesprache* in Hamburg, who died in exile in England. Felix *Gilbert, a historian, at the Institute of Advanced Study, Princeton, New Jersey; the philosopher Leonhard *Nelson (1882–1927); KURT HENSEL, a West German diplomat posted to Tel Aviv in 1968. CARL MENDELSSOHN-BARTHOLDY (1838–1897), assisted by his uncle PAUL (1813–1874), wrote the first biography of his father Felix. Felix's nephew SEBASTIAN HENSEL (1830–1898) was the first family chronicler.

Moses' eldest daughter, Dorothea *Mendelssohn-Veit-Schlegel (Brendel, 1765–1839), was married twice: to the banker Simon Veit (see *Veit family) and to Friedrich Schlegel, man of letters. Her sons, Johannes *Veit (1790–1854) and Philipp Veit (1793–1877), were painters of the Romantic "Nazarene" school. HENRIETTE (Sorel; 1768–1831), Moses' youngest daughter, resembled her father in character. She never married, having his deformity. She served as governess and teacher in Vienna and Paris, where she was head of a boarding school. The intellectual luminaries of the age, Madame de Staël, Spontini, Benjamin Constant, and the Schlegels formed part of her salon. In 1812 she became tutor to the French general Sebastiani's daughter. In that year, following her mother's death, she was baptized into the Catholic Church, taking the name Marie (a few years earlier she had rebuked her sister Dorothea for doing the same). Moses' youngest son, NATHAN, had a son, the physician Arnold Mendelssohn (1817–1850), a supporter and confidant of Ferdinand *Lassalle.

BIBLIOGRAPHY: S. Hensel, *Mendelssohn Family…*, 2 vols. (1882; tr. of *Die Familie Mendelssohn*, 3 vols., 1879); E. Werner, *Mendelssohn; a New Image of the Composer…* (1963); idem, in: HUCA, 26 (1955), 543–65; M.A. Meyer, *Origins of the Modern Jew* (1967), index; J. Jacobson, in: YLBI, 5 (1960), 251–61; 7 (1962), 279–82; H.G. Reissner, *ibid.*, 4 (1959), 93–110; A. Altmann, in: BLBI, 11 (1968), 73–116; E. Achterberg and M. Mller-Jabusch, *Lebensbilder deutscher Bankiers…* (1963); M. Peez, *Henriette Mendelssohn* (Ger., 1888). **ADD. BIBLIOGRAPHY:** H.J. Klein, *Die Mendelssohns im Bildnis* (2004); H.J. Klein, *Die Familie Mendelssohn* (2004).

[Hanns G. Reissner / Andreas Kennecke 2nd ed.)]

MENDELSSOHN, ARNOLD (1855–1933), composer and organist. Born in Ratibor, Germany, a collateral descendant of Felix *Mendelssohn, Arnold Mendelssohn studied law at Tübingen (1877) and pursued a musical education at the Institut für Kirchenmusik in Berlin (1877–80), where he studied organ with Karl August Haupt, the piano with Loeschhorn, and composition with Grell, Friedrich Kiel, and Taubert. Mendelssohn was organist of Bonn University (1880–82), conductor at Bielefeld (1882–85), professor at the conservatories of Cologne (1885–90) and Darmstadt (1890–1912) and from 1912 of the Hoch Conservatory at Frankfurt, where Paul Hindemith and K. Thomas were his students. Mendelssohn contributed to the renewal of interest in Lutheran church music both by his promotion of the works of Bach and Schütz and through his own compositions, rejecting the romanticized style of his contemporaries and evolving a purer and more appropriate polyphonic liturgical idiom. His compositions include the sacred choral works *Abendkantate* (1881) and *Geistliche Chormusik* (1926); operas, symphonies, chamber music, and songs. He edited Heinrich Schütz's oratorios, some of Monteverdi's madrigals, and wrote essays such as *Gott, Welt und Kunst* (ed. by W. Ewald, 1949).

ADD. BIBLIOGRAPHY: Grove online; W. Nagel, *Arnold Mendelssohn* (1906); A. Werner-Jensen, *Arnold Mendelssohn als Liederkomponist* (1976); E. Weber-Ansat, *Arnold Mendelssohn (1855–1933) und seine Verdienste um die Erneuerung der evangelischen Kirchenmusik* (1981).

[Israela Stein (2nd ed.)]

MENDELSSOHN, FELIX (Jakob Ludwig Felix; 1809–1847), composer. Born in Hamburg, Felix was the grandson of Moses *Mendelssohn and the son of Abraham Mendelssohn, a successful banker first in Hamburg and later in Berlin, and Lea Mendelssohn, the granddaughter of Daniel *Itzig (see *Mendelssohn family). His parents had their children baptized and later converted to Christianity themselves. Felix grew up in an intellectual, cultivated atmosphere. The Sunday morning concerts at his parents' Berlin home were notable occasions attended by many celebrities, and most of Mendelssohn's early music was written for these gatherings. Abraham Mendelssohn added the name Bartholdy (after a property that had belonged to his wife's brother) to the family name, stating that "A Christian Mendelssohn is an impossibility." He wished his son to go by the professional name of Felix M. Bartholdy, but he refused to comply and in 1829 conducted under the name Felix Mendelssohn. (His sister Rebecca often signed her letters Rebecca Mendelssohn Meden (the latter meaning "never" in Greek) Bartholdy.)

Mendelssohn advanced rapidly as a composer and pianist. His String Octet, completed in 1825, is a major work of chamber music. Two years later the first public performance of his overture to *A Midsummer Night's Dream* took place, and in 1829, Mendelssohn performed what some believe to be his greatest achievement: the revival of J.S. Bach's *St. Matthew Passion* (at the Singakademie in Berlin), which initiated the renewed popularity of Bach's works. That same year, he made the first of many journeys to England, where his popularity grew. This trip was the first episode in a three-year grand tour that included Scotland, Italy, Switzerland, and France. Some important works of this time, reflecting impressions of his travels, are the *Hebrides Overture* and the *Italian* and *Scotch* symphonies.

In 1833, Mendelssohn was appointed musical director of the Dusseldorf Music and Theater Society; he also supervised the city's church music and directed the subscription concerts of the Society's orchestra. Far more to his liking was his appointment as director of the Gewandhaus concerts in Leipzig in 1835. He continued to be identified with this city for the rest of his life. In 1835 he completed his oratorio *St. Paul* for the Lower Rhine Festival in Duesseldorf (May 1836). Then he traveled to Frankfurt to direct the Caecilien-Verein.

In 1840 Mendelssohn was the most famous living composer in Central Europe. It was therefore inevitable that Frederick William IV, who wished to ensure Prussia's cultural and political supremacy, would summon him to court. In spite of the frustrations of bureaucracy, Mendelssohn did accomplish some good work there, notably the complete incidental music to *A Midsummer Night's Dream*. During this period he also continued writing his many *Songs Without Words*, the most popular piano pieces of their genre. In 1843 he returned to Leipzig and founded the conservatory which became the most renowned institution of its kind in Germany in the 19th century. Mendelssohn's last years saw many triumphs, the greatest of which was the première of *Elijah* in Birmingham (1846). But his strenuous existence as pianist, conductor, composer, and pedagogue had worn him out prematurely. His sister Fanny's sudden death in May 1847 was a shock to his already weakened system, and he died six months later in Leipzig.

Fanny Caecile (Zipporah) *Mendelssohn (1805–1847) was unusually close to her brother Felix, and her marriage to the painter Wilhelm Hensel in 1829 did not weaken this bond. Felix relied upon her musical taste and advice, and six of her songs which were published along with his (without identification) are stylistically indistinguishable from his work. Under her own name, she published four books of piano pieces, two books of solo songs, and one book of part-songs. After her death, a few more piano pieces, some songs, and a piano trio in D major were published.

BIBLIOGRAPHY: G. Grove, *Beethoven, Schubert, Mendelssohn* (Eng., 1951); S. Hensel, *Mendelssohn Family 1729–1847*, 2 vols. (1882); J. Horton, *Chamber Music of Mendelssohn* (1946); F. Mendelssohn, *Letters*, ed. by G. Selden-Goth (1945); J. Petitpierre, *Romance of the Mendelssohns* (1948); P. Radcliffe, *Mendelssohn* (Eng., 1954, 1967[2]); E. Werner, *Mendelssohn: A New Image of the Composer and his Age* (1963); J. Werner, *Felix and Fanny Mendelssohn*, in: *Music and Letters*, 28 (Oct. 1947), 303–38; P. Young, *Introduction to the Music of Mendelssohn* (1949); Grove, Dict, s.v.; MGG, s.v.; Riemann-Gurlitt, s.v.; Baker, Biog Dict, s.v.

[Dika Newlin]

MENDELSSOHN, HEINRICH (1910–2002), Israeli zoologist. Mendelssohn was born in Berlin and studied zoology there at the Humboldt University. He immigrated to Ereẓ Israel in 1933, continuing his studies at the Hebrew University. From 1947 to 1956 he served as director of the Biological and Pedagogical Institute of Tel Aviv, which became the department of zoology of Tel Aviv University. In 1961 he was appointed professor. Mendelssohn devoted most of his activity to nature conservation. He served as a member of the Nature Conservation Authority and chairman of the Israel Committee for Nature Preservation in Israel of the International Biological Program. He represented Israel on the International Conference of Ecology. He was awarded the Israel Prize in science in 1973.

MENDELSSOHN, KURT ALFRED GEORG (1906–1980), British physicist. Mendelssohn was born in Berlin and educated at Berlin University. Forced to leave Germany, he came to Oxford to work at Clarendon Laboratory in 1933 and was the first person to liquefy helium in Britain. Subsequently F.E. Simon, N. Kurti, and H. London came to Oxford and contributed with Mendelssohn to the establishment of the Clarendon Laboratory as an important center of low temperature research. With the advent of World War II the low-temperature apparatus had to be dismantled and Mendelssohn turned to various collaborative projects in medical physics. After the war he resumed his work on low temperatures in collaboration with a succession of gifted research students, many of whom built up graduate schools of their own after leaving the Clarendon, thus making their mark in low-temperature centers all over the world. In addition to his laboratory work Mendelssohn was closely involved with other low-temperature scientists at the international level. He was chairman and founding member of the International Cryogenic Engineering Committee and president of Commission A2 of the International Institute of Refrigeration. He was the founder and editor of the journal *Cryogenics*, an international journal of low-temperature engineering and research (1961–65). He was elected fellow of the Royal Society in 1951. As "extramural" activities he was especially interested in China and in the sociological and engineering backgrounds of the Egyptian and Mexican pyramids, publishing and lecturing widely on these topics.

[Bracha Rager (2nd ed.)]

MENDELSSOHN, MOSES (**Moses ben Menahem**, acronym **RaMbeMaN**, or **Moses of Dessau**; 1729–1786), philosopher of the German Enlightenment in the pre-Kantian period, early Maskil, and a renowned Jewish figure in the 18th century. Born in Dessau, son of a Torah scribe, Mendelssohn received a traditional Jewish education under the influence of David *Fraenkel, who was then rabbi of Dessau. When the latter was appointed rabbi of Berlin in 1743, Mendelssohn followed him there in order to pursue his religious studies and to acquire a general education. He earned his livelihood with difficulty while simultaneously studying Talmud diligently and acquiring a broad education in literature and philosophy. In addition to his fluent knowledge of German and Hebrew, he acquired knowledge of Latin, Greek, English, French, and Italian. His teachers were young, broadly educated Jews, such as the Galician immigrant Israel M. Zamosc, who taught him medieval Jewish philosophy, the medical student Abraham Kisch, who taught him Latin, and the well-born Berlin Jew, A.S. Gumpertz, who taught him French and English and in general served as a model of a pious Jew immersed in the larger intellectual world. During this period he met the writer and dramatist G.E. *Lessing (1754) and a deep and lifelong friendship developed between them. In 1750 he became a teacher in the house of Isaac Bernhard, owner of a silk factory; in 1754, he was entrusted with the bookkeeping of the factory and eventually he became a partner in the enterprise. Throughout his life he worked as a merchant, while carrying out his literary activities and widespread correspondence in his free time. Only in 1763 was he granted the "right of residence" in Berlin by the king. In 1762, he married Fromet Guggenheim of Hamburg, and they had six children (see *Mendelssohn family). In 1754 Mendelssohn began to publish – at first with the assistance of Lessing – philosophical writings and later also literary reviews. He also started a few literary projects (for example, the short-lived periodical *Kohelet Musar*) in order to enrich and change Jewish culture and took part in the early Haskalah. In 1763, he was awarded the first prize of the Prussian Royal Academy of Sciences for his work *Abhandlung über die Evidenz in metaphysischen Wissenschaften* ("Treatise on Evidence in Metaphysical Knowledge"). However, when the academy elected him as a member in 1771, King Frederick II refused to ratify its decision. In 1769, he became embroiled in a dispute on the Jewish religion, and from then on, he confined most of his literary activity to the sphere of Judaism. His most notable and enduring works in this area included the translation into

German and commentary on the Pentateuch, *Sefer Netivot ha-Shalom* ("Book of the Paths of Peace," 1780–83) and his *Jerusalem: oder, Ueber religiöse Macht und Judenthum* ("Jerusalem, or On Religious Power and Judaism," 1783), the first polemical defense of Judaism in the German language and one of the pioneering works of modern Jewish philosophy. An active intermediary on behalf of his own people in difficult times and a participant in their struggle for equal rights, he was at the same time a forceful defender of the Enlightenment against the opposition to it which gained strength toward the end of his life. In the midst of a literary battle against one of the leading figures of the counter-Enlightenment, he died in 1786.

Philosophy

Mendelssohn made virtually no claim to be an original thinker in the realm of philosophy. He considered himself to be little more than an exponent of the teachings of the Leibniz/Wolffian school, perhaps contributing a more felicitous and contemporary expression to the demonstrations of God's existence and providence and human immortality that had been propounded by Leibniz and Wolff and their other disciples. Here and there, however, he modestly acknowledged that he was providing a new version of an old argument or even saying something that had not been said before. Mendelssohn first acquired a wide reputation for philosophical acumen with the publication of his prize essay in 1763. The Berlin Academy's question was whether "the truths of metaphysics, in general, and the first principles of natural theology and morality, in particular," can be shown to be as securely established as those of mathematics. Mendelssohn answered that such principles "are capable of the same certainty" but are by no means as easily grasped. After discussing the obstacles to such comprehension, he went on to offer cosmological and ontological proofs for the existence of God. He sought to give the ontological argument an "easier turn" by reversing its usual course and arguing first for the impossibility of God's nonexistence and then against the notion that the most perfect being would enjoy a merely possible existence. In his later works, Mendelssohn continued to reformulate and refine these very same arguments. Following Leibniz, Mendelssohn argued in a number of writings that the combination of divine goodness and greatness known as providence brings into being "the best of all possible worlds." Like his mentor, he could maintain this position only by adducing the evidence of the afterlife. He first examined this question in his most celebrated philosophical work, *Phädon, oder ueber die Unsterblichkeit der Seele* (*Phaedo, or on the Immortality of the Soul*, 1767; Eng tr., 1784), which borrows its form but not its substance from Plato's dialogue of the same name. Mendelssohn was encouraged in this project by his correspondence with Thomas Abbt (1738–1760), a professor at the University of Frankfurt, about the destiny of man and the fate of the soul after death. He placed in the mouth of his Socrates arguments that he had admittedly derived from his own recent predecessors, including such thinkers as the natural theologian Hermann Samuel Reimarus and the liberal Protestant theologian Johann Joachim Spalding. Mendelssohn developed his thesis along Leibnizian lines: things that perish do not cease to exist; they are dissolved into their elements. The soul must be such an element or substance, rather than a compound, since it is the soul that imposes a unifying pattern on the diverse and changing elements of the body. Hence it is neither weakened by age nor destroyed by death. However, this line of argument demonstrates only that the soul is imperishable and not that it will retain its consciousness in a future state. This is guaranteed by the goodness of God, who could not conceivably have created rational beings only to deprive them after a brief interval "of the capacity for contemplation and happiness." Nor would God ever have aroused his rational creatures to desire eternal life had He not allotted it to them. It is, moreover, impossible to vindicate divine providence without reference to a future life. In Mendelssohn's later *Sache Gottes*, his reworking of the *Causa Dei*, Leibniz's abridgement of his Theodicy, he spelled out most clearly his principal difference with his philosophical mentor's conception of the afterlife. Unlike Leibniz, who had sought to show how most human souls were destined for eternal damnation even in the best of all possible worlds, Mendelssohn maintained that all posthumous punishments would be both corrective and temporary. Divine goodness guaranteed that every human being was destined ultimately to enjoy "the degree of happiness appropriate for him." Following Wolff, Mendelssohn affirmed that the fundamental moral imperative is a natural law obliging all rational beings to promote their own perfection and that of others. Unlike Wolff, he did not elaborate all the ramifications of this natural law. But he clearly saw perfection in much the same terms as Wolff, as an unending process of physical, moral, and intellectual development, leading naturally to the increase of human happiness. In sharp contrast to Wolff, Mendelssohn regarded liberty as an indispensable precondition of the pursuit of moral and intellectual perfection. Only a free person, he argued, can achieve moral perfection. For virtue is the result of struggle, self-overcoming, and sacrifice, and these must be freely chosen. Intellectual perfection, too, can be attained only by one who is free to err. So, in place of Wolff's tutelary state, Mendelssohn developed a contractarian political philosophy that left individuals largely free to define their own goals. Insisting above all on the inalienable liberty of conscience, he decried any state attempt to impose specific religious behavior or to discriminate against members of any minority faith.

In time Mendelssohn himself came to see weaknesses in the philosophical structure that he had once upheld unquestioningly. Confronted, toward the end of his life, by the irrationalism of F.H. Jacobi and by the new critical philosophy of Immanuel Kant, whom he called the "all-crusher," he felt compelled to acknowledge the insufficiency of rationalist metaphysics. In his fullest exposition of the philosophy to which he owed his allegiance, *Morgenstunden, oder Vorlesungen ueber das Dasein Gottes* ("Morning Hours, or Lectures on the Existence of God," 1785), he sorrowfully ceased to reaffirm its irrefutable truth. Yet, whatever speculative reason might seem to teach, he now argued, common sense still sufficed to orient people and guide them along the path to the most important truths. Just what Mendelssohn meant by common sense has been a subject of much dispute, both among his contemporaries such as Thomas Wizenmann and Kant himself and among modern scholars. But, however he conceived of this faculty, it is clear that he did not believe that it would necessarily remain humanity's last resort. For, in the "cyclical course of things," providence would no doubt cause new thinkers to arise who would restore metaphysics to its former glory.

Critic of German Literature

During the period in which his first philosophical writings appeared, Mendelssohn also began to publish critical articles in the *Bibliothek der schönen Wissenschaften und der freien Künste* (1757–60), a periodical edited by the bookseller and publisher Friedrich Nicolai (1733–1811), his closest friend after Lessing. While his first reviews were mainly concerned with philosophical works, he also took up literary criticism which was published in Nicolai's second periodical *Briefe die neueste Literatur betreffend*, behind which Mendelssohn was a moving spirit. At this time German literature, which was still in an early stage of its development, was struggling for recognition and a position in the cultural life of Germany which was dominated by Latin and French. Nicolai, Lessing, J.G. Herder, and others accomplished a kind of cultural revolution by adopting German as the language in which to express their innovative ideas. Mendelssohn became a natural ally of these writers, who did not identify with the academic and intellectual establishment, which, in turn, looked upon them, "Nicolai's sect," with contempt and suspicion. Like them, Mendelssohn was not a member of the establishment; like them, he sought to renovate his spiritual world and was distinguished for his universal humanist aspirations, which, like them, he chose to express in German. Mendelssohn found himself so much at ease in this cultural milieu that he embarked upon an offensive war in support of the use of the German language, even venturing to criticize King Frederick II himself for the publication of a book of poems in French. "Will the Germans never be aware of their own value? Will they forever exchange their gold (i.e., their basic thinking) for their neighbors' tinsel?" (i.e., French literature). The aesthetic writings of Mendelssohn attest to the supreme value which he attributed to beauty and above all to poetry. Mendelssohn's philosophic style in German was recognized by all, including Lessing, Herder, and Kant, as one of the best of his time, but his talent for poetic expression was limited, a fact which he admitted himself.

The Dispute with Lavater

Mendelssohn's longstanding effort to keep his Jewishness out of the public eye was brought to an end by Johann Caspar Lavater (1741–1801), a Swiss scholar and Lutheran clergyman renowned for his writings on human physiognomy, who challenged him to clarify his religious position. As a young man, Lavater had met Mendelssohn in Berlin (1763) and had been deeply impressed by his tolerant attitude toward Christianity, his appreciation of its moral value, and his general philosophic approach. In the summer of 1769, he translated into German a section of *La Palingénésie philosophique* by the Calvinist Charles Bonnet (1720–1793), professor of philosophy and psychology in Geneva, which to his mind had satisfactorily proved the truth of Christianity. Activated by his strong millenarian belief in the necessity of the Jews' conversion, Lavater dedicated this translation to Mendelssohn. He called upon him either to refute it publicly or "to do what wisdom, love of truth, and honor require, and what Socrates would have done had he read the treatise and found it irrefutable." Profoundly distressed by this challenge, Mendelssohn felt compelled to respond to Lavater in public, which he did in a polite and restrained but forceful manner (*Schreiben an den Herrn Diaconus Lavater zu Zürich*, 1770). Eschewing the two alternatives presented to him by his adversary, Mendelssohn instead explained why his religion and his philosophy as well as his marginal position in the world militated against his participation in interreligious polemics. The Torah, he maintained, was given solely to the people of Israel, who are therefore the only ones bound by it; all other men are only obliged to abide by the law of nature and the religion of the patriarchs embodied in the "*Noachide Laws." A religion that does not conceive of itself as the exclusive path to salvation, Judaism is devoid of any missionary tendencies, discouraging even those who seek to convert. In general, said Mendelssohn, one should not challenge other people's fundamental religious conceptions, even if they are based on error, as long as they serve as the basis for social morality and do not undermine natural law. Finally, as a Jew in a country like Prussia where the Jews enjoyed only a limited amount of freedom, Mendelssohn felt that it was advisable to abstain from religious disputes with the dominant creed. "I am a member of an oppressed people," he said. Mendelssohn thus avoided dealing with the fundamental questions posed by Lavater; he did not publicly attack Christianity nor did he provide a comprehensive philosophical rationale for his adherence to Judaism.

Far from putting an immediate end to the matter, Mendelssohn's missive evoked a new response from Lavater, in which he simultaneously apologized for his intrusiveness and persisted in his conversionary efforts. Mendelssohn, however, once again refused to take the bait and did his best to bring the dispute to an amicable conclusion. Only in his *Gegenbetrachtungen über Bonnets Palingénésie* ("Counter-reflections on Bonnet's Palingénésie"), which remained unpublished until the middle of the 19th century, and in private letters, some of which were addressed to Bonnet himself, did he lay bare his objections to Christianity and articulate a defense of Judaism. The general debate that swirled around the controversy between Lavater and Mendelssohn continued until the beginning of 1771 and resulted in the publication of a large number of booklets and pamphlets, most of them sympathetic to Mendelssohn. This confrontation nevertheless upset Mendelssohn to such an extent that for over seven years he suffered from a disease that prevented him from pursuing his philosophic studies.

Activities in the Realm of Jewish Culture

In the middle 1750s, at around the same time that his first German-language publications were seeing the light of day, Mendelssohn produced his earliest writings in Hebrew. They consisted of anonymous contributions to *Kohelet Musar* ("Preacher of Morals"), a periodical he co-edited with Tobias Bock. Although the two men managed to publish only two eight-page issues, their effort nevertheless constituted a revolutionary turning point in the development of Jewish culture. It marked the first occasion on which Jewish intellectuals attempted to introduce into their own culture an innovative form of publication then quite popular and influential in Germany, England, and elsewhere, the "moral weekly." Here some of the ideas of the moderate Enlightenment were first presented to Jewish readers in the Hebrew language known to the community's educated elite and couched in terms familiar to them. Above all, the publication by two laymen of a periodical aimed at the moral improvement of the Jewish population amounted to an unprecedented subversive measure in a world in which the rabbinical elite was acknowledged to be the absolute authority in such matters. The weekly called on the Jews to fill their lungs with the air of natural life, to observe freely the beauty of nature, to nurture their sense of aesthetics and harmony. It proclaimed their right to delight in a world that is, as Leibniz taught, the best of all possible worlds created by God. Man, "God's finest creature," is at the center of nature, and it is unthinkable that the Jew, of all people, should repress his humanistic traits. Man can discover the majesty of the Almighty and His powers by observing the creation of the great architect of the world. *Kohelet Musar's* transmission of such messages appear to have made no significant impression on the Jewish society of the 1750s but it did pave the way for the publication, decades later, of a much more influential successor, the maskilic journal *Ha-*Me'assef.*

In the decades following this abortive effort Mendelssohn's writings in the Hebrew language were limited in number. In 1761 he published a commentary on Maimonides' *Millot ha-Higgayon* ("Logical Terms") and in 1769 or 1770 he published a commentary on the biblical book of Ecclesiastes. The former volume consisted of a republication of Maimonides' introduction to logic and philosophical primer together with an introduction and commentary designed not only to clarify Maimonides' work but to bridge the distance between medieval Jewish philosophy and the regnant philosophy of Mendelssohn's own day. The latter utilized the text of Ecclesiastes to expound in a popular form an essentially Wolffian teaching with regard to two principal tenets of natural religion, providence and immortality of the soul. At the end of the introduction to this commentary, Mendelssohn announced that if it were well received he would attempt to write similar works on Job, Proverbs, and Psalms but he never carried this plan to completion.

What Mendelssohn did instead was to translate books of the Bible into German. As early as 1770, in a letter to Michaelis, he had mentioned the publication of a German translation of Psalms, which would act as a counterbalance to the translations and commentaries written in the spirit of Christianity. After laboring on this work for 13 years, he finally published it in 1783. The principal work among his biblical translations was, however, the version of the Pentateuch that accompanied the *Bi'ur*, a commentary that he and a group of his associates, including Naphtali Herz *Wessely and Herz *Homberg, collectively composed (*Bi'ur*, 1780–83; see *Bible: Translations, German). This translation began, by Mendelssohn's own account, as a project for the instruction of his sons, yet he soon recognized its general utility. In his overall introduction to it he explained that it was designed to provide the younger generation of Jewish students with an alternative to the extant Yiddish translations, which failed to do justice to the beauties of the original, and the available Christian translations, which strayed too far from the Masoretic text and traditional rabbinic interpretations of it. Elsewhere, in a private letter to his non-Jewish friend August Hennings, Mendelssohn described the translation as a "first step toward culture" for his nation. The German text of the translation was written, in accordance with the custom that prevailed among German Jews, in Hebrew characters, and the commentary, *Bi'ur*, in Hebrew. In addition to serving, as David Sorkin has put it, as "a usable digest of the medieval literalist tradition," the commentary provided Mendelssohn with a venue for the articulation of the theological views that he was soon to spell out more systematically in Jerusalem.

Despite its declared conservative aims, the translation project faced opposition from the very moment that Mendelssohn and his collaborator Solomon Dubno published a sample of their work, entitled *Alim li-Terufah* (1778). Rumors of the protestations of R. Ezekiel *Landau of Prague and actual reports of the opposition of R. Raphael Kohen of Altona soon reached Mendelssohn along with the news of a plan to excommunicate him and a campaign to organize a united rabbinical front against the *Bi'ur.* Averse to any direct confrontation with his adversaries and fully committed to the principle of free speech, Mendelssohn sought to deter any action by Rabbi Kohen not by silencing him but through behind-the-scenes maneuvers. He prevailed upon his friend August Hennings to arrange for subscriptions to the *Bi'ur* to be taken out in the name of the Danish king, Christian VII, Rabbi Kohen's sovereign. Hennings' success in this endeavor greatly enhanced the prestige of the maskilic literary project and earned it a measure of immunity from its opponents' machinations.

Immediately after its publication the *Bi'ur* was adopted as a textbook for biblical instruction at the Freischule (free school) co-founded by the brothers-in-law David *Friedlaender and Daniel Itzig. While Mendelssohn was not directly involved in the founding of this school, he nevertheless supported it and also contributed to its revolutionary new textbook, the *Lesebuch fuer jüdische Kinder* ("Reader for Jewish

Children"), in which he published a translation of Maimonides' 13 Articles of Faith. The last of Mendelssohn's biblical translations to appear in print was his translation of the Song of Songs with commentary, which was published posthumously (1788).

Activities for the Improvement of the Civic Status of the Jews

Prior to the controversy with Lavater, Mendelssohn had not campaigned for the improvement of the civic status of the Jews, but from the 1770s onward he became something of an activist on their behalf. He willingly replied to anyone who came to him for counsel or guidance, endeavoring to assist within the limits of his means any Jew who had been overtaken by misfortune or who had become embroiled in difficulties with the authorities. He also came to the aid of beleaguered Jewish communities, taking advantage of his reputation in order to request help from various renowned personages whom he had befriended. After receiving an appeal for help from the tiny Jewish community of Switzerland in 1775, he enlisted none other than Lavater in a successful effort to forestall imminent anti-Jewish measures. When the community of Dresden was threatened by an expulsion order in 1777, he prevailed upon one of the leading officials of Saxony, who ranked among his admirers, to prevent any action against it. In the same year his brief on behalf of the community of Königsberg enabled it to refute the accusation that the *Aleinu* prayer was anti-Christian and led to the abrogation of the royal edict requiring the presence of a government-appointed "supervisor" in the city's synagogue during the recitation of prayers. Yet Mendelssohn did not always see eye to eye with the people who requested his assistance. In 1772, when the duke of Mecklenburg-Schwerin issued an order to his Jewish subjects prohibiting the religious custom of immediate burial and requiring a three-day waiting period before interment, the local community called upon Mendelssohn to intercede on its behalf. He dutifully composed a memorandum to the duke in which he recommended that the Jews be permitted to maintain their existing custom as long as they obtained medical certification of death prior to burial. At the same time, he maintained in his correspondence with the Jews of Mecklenburg-Schwerin that their resistance to the duke was unwarranted, since the three-day waiting period was reasonable, prudent, and not without ancient precedent and talmudic justification. While his memorandum inspired the duke to replace his earlier edict with a regulation along the lines of his suggestion, his letter to the community met with the disapproval of the local rabbi. More importantly, it also aroused the ire of Jacob *Emden, who accused Mendelssohn of being too ready to relinquish the requirements of Jewish law and to adopt the ways of the Gentiles. Even in the face of Emden's dire warnings that he was increasingly being regarded as someone who was edging toward heresy, however, Mendelssohn did not retreat from his position on this matter.

Mendelssohn's involvement in the public debate on the civic status of the Jews commenced with a request emanating from France. Cerf Berr, the leading figure in Alsatian Jewry, asked Mendelssohn in 1780 to write a memorandum on the question of the rights of the Jews to be submitted to the French Council of State. Believing that it was Gentiles – enlightened Christians who sought an improved society – who should raise this question, Mendelssohn turned to Ch.W. von *Dohm, who participated in the composition of the memorandum and shortly thereafter wrote his *Ueber die buergerliche Verbesserung der Juden* (*Concerning the Amelioration of the Civil Status of the Jews*, 1781), which became the classic work in the struggle for Jewish emancipation. Despite his broad sympathy with the aims of this volume, Mendelssohn was not completely satisfied with it in every aspect. He expressed his reservations in his introduction to a German translation of the apologetic tract composed a century earlier by *Manasseh Ben Israel, *Vindiciae Judaeorum* (1782). Contesting Dohm's negative appraisal of the Jews' economic role, Mendelssohn insisted upon the productivity and usefulness of Jewish merchants and middlemen. He rejected Dohm's recommendation to preserve a limited judicial autonomy for the Jewish community and especially his argument that the community ought to retain the right of excommunication. According to Mendelssohn, the exercise of religious coercion of any kind was utterly unwarranted and incompatible with the spirit of "true, divine religion."

The views of Dohm and Mendelssohn aroused criticism and controversies. Among the critics was J.D. Michaelis (1717–1791), a theologian and professor of Semitic languages, who decades earlier, in his review of Lessing's play *The Jews* (1754), had denied that a Jew could exemplify a noble person. Now Michaelis argued that the Jews' anticipation of the arrival of the messiah and their return to Zion together with their burdensome laws made it impossible for them to identify completely with their host country or to fulfill civic obligations, such as military service. Mendelssohn retorted that the Jews' messianic hopes would have no influence whatsoever on their conduct as citizens and that they had in any event been expressly forbidden by the Talmud even to think of returning to Palestine on their own initiative. He brushed off concerns that the Jews would be unable to serve in the military by noting that they, no less than the Christians before them, would know "how to modify their convictions and to adjust them to their civic duty."

Mendelssohn's Jerusalem

Among the reactions to Mendelssohn's introduction was a pamphlet, published anonymously in 1782, entitled *Das Forschen nach Licht und Recht in einem Schreiben an Herrn Moses Mendelssohn auf Veranlassung seiner merkwürdigen Vorrede zu Menasseh Ben Israel* (*The Search for Light and Right, an Epistle to Moses Mendelssohn occasioned by his Remarkable Preface to Menasseh ben Israel*). Now known to have been authored by a minor writer by the name of August Friedrich Cranz, the pamphlet accused Mendelssohn of having undermined the authority of Judaism with his blanket denial of the legitimacy of any form of religious coercion. "Clearly," Cranz wrote, "ecclesiastical law armed with coercive power has always been one of the cornerstones of the Jewish religion of your fathers… How then can you, good Mr. Mendelssohn, profess attachment to the religion of your forefathers, while you are shaking its fabric, by impugning the ecclesiastical code established by Moses in consequence of divine revelation?" On this occasion, Mendelssohn felt that it was his duty to answer his critic and wrote his *Jerusalem* primarily in order to do so. But the book ranged far beyond an answer to Cranz to articulate a full-blown philosophy of Judaism, the first to be developed in modern times.

STATE AND RELIGION. In the first part of *Jerusalem* Mendelssohn expounded a political theory clarifying the grounds for his opposition to religious coercion. His account of "the origin of the rights of coercion" belonging to the state restricted such rights to the sphere of transferable goods. This does not encompass convictions, inalienable by their very nature. Hence the state can never acquire the right to make any religious demands upon its citizens, and its grant of even the smallest privilege or exclusive right to members of any particular religion is entirely devoid of legitimacy. Mendelssohn nevertheless advised the state not to intervene directly but to "see to it from afar" that such subversive doctrines as "atheism and Epicureanism" are not propagated in its midst. And he declared churches no more entitled than states to resort to coercion in matters of faith, since "a religious action is religious only to the degree to which it is performed voluntarily and with proper intent." Only after having thus reiterated and amplified his opposition to religious coercion of any kind did Mendelssohn refer to the claim of *The Search for Light and Right* that his own adherence to Judaism was incompatible with his liberal principles. Once he had restated Cranz's argument, he acknowledged that it cut him to the heart but did not hasten to refute it. He first explained more systematically and in greater detail than ever before why he remained convinced of the veracity of Judaism and what he considered to be its nature and purpose.

JUDAISM. Drawing a fundamental distinction between the supernatural revelation of a religion and supernatural legislation, Mendelssohn identified Judaism exclusively with the latter. The former, he argued, does not truly exist, since God makes known the basic truths of religion – the existence and unity of God, divine providence, and the immortality of the soul – not by disclosing them miraculously to any particular group of people but by granting all men the degree of reason required to grasp them. Revelation could not, in any case, convince any man of the validity of something his reason could not understand. Nor would a just God ever have vouchsafed the truths indispensable to human happiness to some peoples and not to others. What distinguished the people of Israel was not their religion, with which they had presumably been imbued already prior to the Sinaitic revelation, but the unique laws, statutes and commandments that were given to them on that occasion. That God spoke at Sinai is for Mendelssohn a *vérité de fait*, an established historical fact, because it was indubitably witnessed by the entire people of Israel. The best statement of the quintessence of the legislation He then revealed, according to Mendelssohn, was the one uttered by Hillel the Elder: "Love thy neighbor as thyself. This is the text of the law; all the rest is commentary." But in *Jerusalem* Mendelssohn devoted his energies much less to an elucidation of the humanitarian dimension of biblical law than to a somewhat tentative explanation of the purpose for the rituals it prescribed.

Although humankind possessed from the outset the capacity to grasp on its own the fundamental truths of natural religion, Mendelssohn wrote, it eventually descended into idolatry. To account for this corruption of religion he resorted to what was, in Alexander Altmann's opinion, "the least substantiated of all theories he ever advanced." The primary cause of the religious deterioration of humankind was, according to this theory, hieroglyphic script. Men initially employed hieroglyphic signs derived from images of animals to symbolize the deity. In the course of time, however, they fell victim to their own misunderstanding and the manipulations of unscrupulous priestly hypocrites and came to regard these signs themselves as deities, to worship them and even to offer human sacrifices to them. In response to this debasement of humankind, Mendelssohn maintained, God ordained the ceremonial law of the Pentateuch. Through its eschewal of all imagery and its concentration on actions this law avoided the hazards of hieroglyphic script. Its main purpose, however, was not prophylactic but positive – to connect vital knowledge with required practices. The ceremonial laws "guide the inquiring intelligence to divine truths, partly to eternal and partly to historical truths" upon which Judaism is founded. God gave the commandments only to Israel, but He did not do so, according to Mendelssohn, for its sake alone. Israel was to be a priestly nation, a nation that "through its laws, actions, vicissitudes, and changes was continually to call attention to sound and unadulterated ideas of God and His attributes. It was incessantly to teach, to proclaim, and to endeavor to preserve these ideas among the nations, by means of its mere existence, as it were."

At the conclusion of *Jerusalem* Mendelssohn indicated how his account of Judaism was meant to dispel the objections raised by "the Searcher after Light and Right." Composed of religious doctrines acquired by purely rational means and a revealed legislation designed to remind its practitioners of these truths as well as their own people's historical record, Judaism cannot be conceived as a religion authorizing temporal punishments for unbelievers or those who adhere to false doctrines. While it is true that the original constitution of Israel provided for a polity in which religion and state were identical and in which a "religious villain" was a criminal, this "Mosaic constitution" existed only once and has disappeared from the face of the earth. Since the destruction of the Temple in Jerusalem, religious offenses have ceased to be offenses against the state and the Jewish religion "knows of no punishment, no other penalty than the one the remorseful sinner voluntarily imposes on himself." Contemporary Judaism could thus be seen to be fully in accord with Mendelssohn's own liberal principles, even if the original "Mosaic constitution" was not.

Jerusalem evoked little response in the Jewish community. Rabbis and maskilim alike paid only very limited attention to it. In the years following its publication Mendelssohn learned to his dismay that he would find few supporters for the positions he took in *Jerusalem*. Enlightened thinkers who shared his appreciation of natural religion were alienated by his reaffirmation of revelation and his insistence on the obligatory character of the ceremonial law. The orthodox rejected his absolute denial of the right of religious institutions to wield coercive authority, and the earliest representatives of what Isaiah Berlin called the "Counter-Enlightenment" assailed the very rationalism in which his arguments were rooted.

The "Pantheism Controversy"

Mendelssohn's most consequential brush with the Counter-Enlightenment resulted not from the publication of *Jerusalem* but from his plan to produce an essay on the character of his lifelong friend, G.E. Lessing, who had died in 1781. Lessing, whose early support had been so crucial to Mendelssohn, had always been an interlocutor whom he cherished, even when they disagreed over matters of great importance, such as the views he had expressed in his *Die Erziehung des Menschengeschlechts* (*The Education of the Human Race*) on the nature of revelation and human progress. Lessing, for his part, had composed shortly before his death his famous play in support of religious toleration, *Nathan the Wise*, whose eponymous hero was unmistakably patterned after Mendelssohn himself. Upon learning in 1783 from one of his friends, Elise Reimarus, that Mendelssohn was on the brink of returning Lessing's literary favor by writing an essay extolling his deceased friend's character, Friedrich Jacobi, one of the avatars of the Counter-Enlightenment, claimed that Lessing had admitted to him during the last years of his life that he had been a Spinozist. What Jacobi wished to do was not so much to expose Lessing's clandestine heresy as to point to Lessing's intellectual evolution as evidence supporting his own general thesis that reason necessarily leads to nihilism. What he succeeded in doing was to deflect Mendelssohn from his original purpose and to force him to interpret Lessing's alleged Spinozism in a way that warded off any distressingly close association between the thought of the Enlightenment and the philosophy of a man reviled almost everywhere as an atheist. Mendelssohn's arduous efforts to do this in the face of Jacobi's relentless attacks sapped his remaining strength. A few days after he sent to his publisher his last work on this subject, *An die Freunde Lessings* ("To Lessing's Friends," 1786), he died.

Appreciation and Influence

The Leibniz/Wolffian philosophy that Mendelssohn spent a lifetime defending did not long survive his own demise. Its foundations were undermined by Immanuel Kant – a fact that Mendelssohn recognized toward the end of his life. Nor did the philosophy of Judaism that Mendelssohn outlined in the *Bi'ur*, *Jerusalem*, and elsewhere provide a satisfactory understanding of their religion for more than a few of the inquiring minds of the coming generations. Nor, finally, did Mendelssohn's efforts to win equal rights for European Jews yield any immediate results. On the other hand, there is no doubt that Mendelssohn's contribution to Jewish thought served as a reference point, focus, and challenge to later thinkers. From the standpoint of the history of modern Jewish philosophy, or the history of biblical translation and exegesis, Mendelssohn's thinking with regard to the age of emancipation and secularization are of great importance. Thus on topics such as the place of the Jewish community in the modern state, the validity of *halakhah*, the belief in divine revelation, the relations between religion and community, the question of coercion in religious matters, and the status of the commandments, Mendelssohn not only asked questions, but also proposed answers that were of great significance for modern Jewish thought. Finally, his *Bi'ur* played an incalculably large role in fostering the development of the Haskalah in Eastern Europe.

Already in his own time Mendelssohn became a legend and in the centuries after his death he became a symbolic hero or villain to Jews of very different stripes. In the 19th century Jewish historians in Germany proudly placed Mendelssohn at the threshold of a new era in the history of the Jews, cementing his image as the founding father of the Haskalah and the patron saint of Germany Jewry. They placed special emphasis on his role as the first harbinger of a favorable turning point in Gentile-Jewish relations in the European states. The deep ties of friendship between Mendelssohn and Lessing were represented as the ideal model of the longed-for future, a symbol of the respectable status and legal equality finally obtained by German Jewry nearly a century after Mendelssohn's death. Above all, this friendship represented in the eyes of German Jewish historians and thinkers the beginnings of a moderate integration of the Jews into German life, a social absorption that stopped short of complete assimilation. For Mendelssohn, as the chroniclers of his life and times correctly noted, knew how to parry all attempts to bring him over to Christianity. The writings of these historians and thinkers, for whom Mendelssohn was a cultural hero of enormous proportions, reflected the predominant image of Mendelssohn in the cultural memory of German Jewry. Mendelssohn was the Jew with whom it was easy to identify, the Jew who brought honor to Judaism, who proved that a modern Jew can simultaneously be a loyal German citizen at home in the German language and German culture and maintain his ties to the Jewish community and Jewish culture. In the eyes of many he was the prototype of the age of Jewish emancipation and integration into the middle class and served as a kind of entrance ticket into the state and society. Thus the historical Mendelssohn became a very precious resource to German Jews, who for many years had again and again to prove in the public arena their fitness to be accepted and to be treated no differently from members of the majority. Mendelssohn became the ideal representative of those who dreamed of German-Jewish relations in far-reaching terms of "symbiosis."

At the very same time that this Mendelssohn myth grew and flourished, the spokesmen of the more conservative camp in modern Jewish society developed a counter-myth. The members of this camp vigorously repudiated the ideas of change and transition in the fate of the Jews that were linked to the historical Mendelssohn and denied the necessity for breaking out of the confines of the traditional, religious Jewish way of life. They looked with alarm on the processes of modernization and dreaded a general collapse of the structure of Jewish life. The increasing focus on studies outside the realm of Torah, particularly philosophy, seemed to them to be the gateway to apostasy. In these people's eyes Mendelssohn loomed as a demonic historical figure, a destructive force responsible for all the crises of the modern era: assimilation, the demolition of the traditional community, the loss of faith, religious permissiveness, and the weakening of the authority of the rabbinical elite. They painted a picture of the past diametrically opposed to that of enlightened, liberal Jewry.

Over the years, both Mendelssohn's admirers and detractors have seen him through a similar lens: both the myth and the counter-myth assigned him the proportions of a giant possessing enormous power to set the wheels of Jewish history in motion. They identified him for better or worse as the man who represented, symbolized, and sparked all the forces of change of the modern era: Haskalah, religious reform, secularization, assimilation, and integration and the rest of the terms that generally describe the processes of modernization that have influenced the Jews over the course of the past two and a half centuries. In recent decades, however, modern scholarship on Mendelssohn has taken a more objective, balanced, and nuanced approach that has consisted of efforts to demythologize him without overlooking his importance. Mendelssohn is no longer considered to have been the founder of the Haskalah movement, which was actually initiated by the members of a younger generation, the most prominent among them being Isaac *Euchel. Scholars now view him less in emblematic terms than as a man whose life was highly complex and full of frustrations, conflicts, dreams, and disappointments.

Collected Works and Translations of Works

The Jubiläumsausgabe of Mendelssohn's collected works (Stuttgart, 1971–2004) now includes 24 volumes. English translations include *Jerusalem and other Jewish Writings* (by A. Jospe, 1969), *Moses Mendelssohn: Selections from his Writings* (E. Jospe, 1975), *Jerusalem* (by A. Arkush, 1983), *Philosophical Writings* (D. Dahlstrom, 1997).

BIBLIOGRAPHY: H.M.Z. Meyer, *Moses Mendelssohn Bibliographie* (1965); Shunami, Bibl., no. 5, 3953–57; A. Altmann, *Moses Mendelssohn: A Biographical Study* (1973); A. Arkush, *Moses Mendelssohn and the Enlightenment* (1994); E. Breuer, *The Limits of the Enlightenment: Jews, Germans and the Enlightenment Study of Scripture* (1996); S. Feiner, *The Jewish Enlightenment* (2004); S. Feiner, *Moses Mendelssohn* (Heb., 2005); J. Hess, *Germans Jews and the Claims of Modernity* (2002); D. Sorkin, *Moses Mendelssohn and the Religious Enlightenment* (1996).

[Alfred Jospe and Leni Yahil / Allan Arkush and Shmuel Feiner (2nd ed.)]

MENDELSSOHN HENSEL, FANNY CAECILIE (1805–1847), pianist and composer. Born in Hamburg, the eldest of four children of Lea and Abraham Mendelssohn, she was part of a close family circle that included many intellectuals, including her grandfather, Moses *Mendelssohn. Along with her siblings, Fanny was secretly converted to Christianity by her father, Abraham, in 1816. He and his wife were baptized in 1822. The name "Bartholdy," which came from a family real estate holding, was then added to their surname to establish them as Christian and distinct from their Jewish extended family. The Mendelssohn Bartholdys distanced themselves from Judaism, but continued relationships with Jewish relatives. For them, Protestant Christianity reflected the highest levels of civilization, morality, enlightenment ideals, and toleration. Despite their conversions and dedication to German culture, the family experienced antisemitism at many levels.

Fanny was well educated. In 1820 she and her brother Felix *Mendelssohn, also a child prodigy, were admitted to the Sing-Akademie in Berlin under C.F. Zelter. While Fanny Mendelssohn displayed extraordinary musical talents, her professional ambitions were not encouraged. Although she and Felix both studied composition with Zelter, Fanny was always told that her future was to be a wife and mother. Felix, with whom she had a complex relationship, delighted in her musical compositions but discouraged their publication. Fanny advised Felix on his compositions and greatly aided him on various projects. The siblings had an important musical collaboration throughout their lives that has only recently been recognized.

Fanny met the artist Wilhem Hensel, the son of a Lutheran pastor, when she was 15. Despite her mother's objections, they married in 1829 and had one child, Sebastian, in 1832. Her husband encouraged not only her piano playing but her composition and conducting.

Fanny composed lieder, cantatas, and instrumental works for her own family and friends' entertainment. According to the fashion in Berlin, she held musical salons, *Sonntagsmusik*, at her family home, where she performed, conducted, and gave life to some of her own music. Over the years, her series grew in reputation and Berlin society, nobility, and famous personalities such as Franz Liszt attended and admired the skills of Frau Hensel.

In 1846, Mendelssohn composed her masterpiece, the *Trio in D Minor for Piano, Violin and Cello,* and in that same year, with Felix's blessing, she published *Sechs Lieder,* Opus 1 (1846) and *Vier Lieder fuer das Pianoforte*, Opus 2 (1846). The following year she continued to release compositions, some of her *Gartenlieder: Sechs Gesange fuer Sopran, Alto, Tenor und Bass,* Opus 3 (1847), *Six Melodies for Piano,* Opus 4, no. 1–3 and Opus 5, no. 4–6 (1847). Additional works were published posthumously but most of Mendelssohn's over 500 compositions remain unpublished. Those that were encountered skepticism, as it was then considered impossible for a woman to have the creative power to compose music with any depth. Fanny Mendelssohn died suddenly of a stroke while rehearsing for a concert. She had completed her last composition, *Bergeslust* (Mountain Pleasure), just the day before.

[Judith S. Pinnolis (2nd ed.)]

MENDELSSOHN-VEIT-SCHLEGEL, DOROTHEA (1764–1839), woman of letters and convert to Christianity. Born in Berlin, as Brendel, Dorothea was the eldest daughter of Fromet and Moses *Mendelssohn. She was taught German, French, music, and drawing, but seems not to have received a thorough Jewish education. Her friendship circle of Jewish girls included the future *salon hosts Rahel Levin *Varnhagen and Henriette de Lemos *Herz. Dorothea's parents arranged her engagement with Simon Veit, son of a prominent Berlin family, when she was 14 and the couple married in 1783. Two of their four children, Jonas and Philipp, survived to adulthood. Moses Mendelssohn died in 1786 believing his daughter was happily married.

During the 1790s, Brendel began to call herself Dorothea; she socialized with Christian intellectuals, hosting a reading club and joining a secret society. In 1797, Dorothea fell in love with Friedrich Schlegel (1772–1829), an up-and-coming literary critic, and after much introspection, she left her husband. When they were officially divorced in 1799, she received custody of Philipp. With her divorce Dorothea forfeited her right to live in Berlin; she became estranged from her Mendelssohn siblings, and lost many of her Christian friends. For years she led a peripatetic life with Schlegel, roaming from Jena to Paris to Vienna to Rome and back again to Vienna, where their home became a social and intellectual center.

In 1804, Dorothea became a Protestant and the couple married; four years later both she and Friedrich became Catholics. Although Dorothea's exit from Judaism was particularly stormy, ultimately four of the six Mendelssohn siblings became Christians, two of them Catholics and two of them Protestants. Neither of the siblings who remained Jewish was involved in Jewish institutions or causes.

Dorothea and Friedrich were often impoverished, and she did her part to support them by editing his work, publishing a novel, *Florentin* (1801), and editing and translating medieval texts. All of her work was published under her husband's name. Her novel has been edited by L. Weissberg (*Florentin. Roman, Fragmente, Varianten* (1987)). The Schlegels' letters have been edited by E. Behler (*Briefe von und an Friedrich und Dorothea Schlegel* [1980]). Schlegel's two sons with Veit also became committed Catholics and flourished in Rome as painters in the Nazarene style. After Friedrich died in 1829, Dorothea made peace with her Mendelssohn siblings and they provided financial support during her decade as a widow.

Scholars continue to ponder the significance of Dorothea Mendelssohn-Veit-Schlegel's life, trying to understand her attitude to Judaism and the motives for her two conversions. Her dramatic life journey demonstrates that Moses Mendelssohn's important Enlightenment legacy did not pass easily to his own children in a time and a place when baptism offered many attractions for bright and ambitious young Jews.

BIBLIOGRAPHY: H. Frank, "*...Disharmonie, die mit mir geboren ward, und mich nie verlassen wird...*" *Das Leben der Brendel/Dorothea Mendelssohn-Veit-Schlegel* (1988); C. Stern, "*Ich möchte mir Flügel wünschen.*" *Das leben der Dorothea Schlegel.* (1990).

[Deborah Hertz (2nd ed.)]

MENDES (Mendiz), family of rabbis and merchants in *Morocco and *Algeria of Spanish-Portuguese origin. JOSEPH MENDES (mid-16th century) was rabbi of the community of Spanish exiles (Heb., *megorashim*) in *Fez and a signatory of its *takkanot*. GIDEON (late 17–early 18th century), a merchant of *Amsterdam, served as consul of the Netherlands in Salé from 1703 and was active in promoting commerce and negotiating treaties with Morocco. His son JOSHUA was a merchant in Salé and in Amsterdam. A contemporary R. ISAAC was a rabbi and an international merchant in *Agadir and spent time in London trading with European countries. His son JACOB remained in Agadir and one of his daughters married the rabbi and thinker Khalifa b. *Malca.

BIBLIOGRAPHY: Hirschberg, Afrikah, 2 (1965), 268–72; J. Ben-Naim, *Malkhei Rabbanan* (1931), 107; SIHM, index.

MENDES (Mendez), family in England of Marrano origin. FERNANDO MOSES MENDES (1647–1724), a Marrano physician, arrived in London in 1669 and practiced there, in 1678 becoming court physician to Queen Catherine (the story that he arrived as physician to Catherine of Braganza, wife of Charles II, is due to a confusion with Antonio Mendes, who attended her on her return to Portugal in 1692 (see JHSET, 16 (1952), 226–7)). His wife was a professing Jew, but his reluctance to declare himself a Jew caused anger and distress among his wealthy relatives. He attended Charles II during his last illness and was highly respected. He remained a Catholic, although he was close to London's Sephardi community. His daughter CATHERINE (Rachel) (1679–1756), who married her cousin Anthony (Moses) da Costa, was the first known Anglo-Jewish portrait painter. Fernando's grandson, MOSES MENDES (c. 1690–1758), amassed a fortune as a stockjobber. Baptized and married to a gentile, he acquired a reputation as a successful dramatist and wit. His musical entertainment *The Chaplet* (London 1749, 1753, 1756) was the earliest published contribution of a Jew to English belles lettres, while his farce *The Double Disappointment* was presented at Covent Garden theater in 1760. His sons took their mother's name, Head, and the family passed out of Anglo-Jewish history, though achieving some prominence in English life; Moses' grandson, SIR FRANCIS BOND HEAD (1793–1875), for example, became lieutenant governor of Upper Canada. A kinsman of Moses, SOLOMON MENDES (d. 1762), was a patron and associate of writers.

BIBLIOGRAPHY: L. Wolf, in: JHSET, 5 (1902–05), 5–33; A. Rubens, *ibid.*, 14 (1935–39), 95–97; A.M. Hyamson, *Sephardim of England* (1951), index; J. Picciotto, *Sketches of Anglo-Jewish History* (1956^2), index; Roth, England, index; Roth, Mag Bibl., 137, 409 ff.; idem, *Anglo-Jewish Letters (1158–1917)* (1938), 99–114, 121–6, 133–40, 144–7; *Gentleman's Magazine* (Jan. 1812), 21–24. **ADD. BIBLIOGRAPHY:** ODNB online; A. Ruben, "Early Anglo-Jewish Artists," in: JHSET, 14 (1935–39), 91–129; Katz, England, index.

[Vivian David Lipman]

MENDES, U.S. Sephardi family of rabbis. FREDERIC DE SOLA MENDES (1850–1927) was born in Montego Bay, Jamaica, where his father, ABRAHAM PEREIRA MENDES (1825–1893), was at that time rabbi. Frederic became preacher at the New Synagogue, London, in 1873 but in the same year was appointed to Congregation Shaarey Tefillah, New York. He served there for 47 years, as assistant to S.M. *Isaacs (to 1877) and then as rabbi (to 1920). Mendes led his congregation within the orbit of Reform and became a member of the Central Conference of American Rabbis. He was one of the founders of the *American Hebrew* (1879) and served as a member of the original editorial board of the Jewish Publication Society's English translation of the Bible. For a period he was an editor of the *Jewish Encyclopedia*. Frederic's brother HENRY PEREIRA MENDES (1852–1937) was born in Birmingham, England. In his early youth he was educated at Northwick College, a boarding school founded by his father in London which offered a combination of religious and secular education. Henry studied at University College, London, and took the medical degree at the University of the City of New York. Henry served as rabbi to the new Sephardi congregation of Manchester from 1874 to 1877 and then immigrated to New York to take up his post as *ḥazzan* and rabbi at Shearith Israel congregation, serving there until 1923. Championing an enlightened modern Orthodoxy, Mendes used his privileged position as rabbi at Shearith Israel to work closely with all sectarian and social elements in Jewish life. In facing the problems affecting Jewry, he followed his belief in *kelal Yisrael* ("the totality of Israel"). He was one of the founders and leaders of the Union of Orthodox Congregations of America, the Jewish Theological Seminary, the New York Board of Jewish Ministers, and – at the personal request of Theodor Herzl –the Federation of American Zionists. He was a prolific writer on Jewish and general themes for the *American Hebrew*, which he and his brother helped establish, and wrote scores of books and pamphlets. Some of his better-known books are *Looking Ahead* (1899), *Bar Mitzvah* (1938), *Esther and Harbonah* (1917), *Jewish Religion Ethically Presented* (1905), *Jewish History Ethically Presented* (1898), *Mekor Ḥayyim: Mourners Handbook* (1915), and *Derekh Ḥayyim: Way of life* (1934).

BIBLIOGRAPHY: D. de S. Pool, *H. Pereira Mendes…* (1938); E. Markovitz, *Henry Pereira Mendes* (Eng., 1962), incl. bibl.; idem, in: AJHSQ, 55 (1965/66), 364–84.

[Sefton D. Temkin and Eugene Markovitz]

°**MENDES, ARISTIDES DE SOUSA** (1895–1964), Portuguese diplomat and Righteous Among the Nations. Born into an aristocratic Portuguese family, Mendes chose a diplomatic career for himself. After filling posts in various capitals (including the United States and Europe), he was posted to Bordeaux, France, as the Portuguese consul-general. In May 1940, with the onset of the German invasion of France and the Low Countries, thousands of refugees, among them many Jews, headed for Bordeaux, hoping to cross into Spain in advance of the conquering German army and continue via Portugal to lands across the Atlantic Ocean. At this critical juncture, the Portuguese government, headed by dictator Antonio Salazar (who also filled in as foreign minister), forbade the issuance of Portuguese transit visas to all refugees, and particularly to Jews. This virtually also closed the Spanish border to the refugees. Against the grim background of France on the verge of collapse, and with the Germans within striking distance of Bordeaux, in mid-June 1940 Consul-General Mendes came face to face with Rabbi Haim Kruger, one of the fleeing Jews, who pressured him to urgently issue Portuguese transit visas. Rabbi Kruger rejected Mendes' initial offer to issue visas only to the rabbi and his family, insisting that visas also be issued to the thousands of Jews stranded on the streets of the city. After several days of further reflection, Mendes reversed himself and decided to grant visas to all persons requesting them. "I sat with him a full day without food and sleep and helped him stamp thousands of passports with Portuguese visas," Rabbi Kruger related. To his staff, Mendes explained: "My government has denied all applications for visas to any refugees. But I cannot allow these people to die. Many are Jews and our constitution says that the religion, or politics, of a foreigner shall not be used to deny him refuge in Portugal. I have decided to follow this principle. I am going to issue a visa to anyone who asks for it – regardless of whether or not he can pay…. Even if I am dismissed, I can only act as a Christian, as my conscience tells me." The Portuguese government dispatched two emissaries to bring the insubordinate diplomat home. On their way to the Spanish border, the entourage stopped at the Portuguese consulate in Bayonne. Here too, Mendes, still the official representative of his country for this region, issued visas to fleeing Jewish refugees, again in violation of instructions from Lisbon. It is estimated that the number of visas issued by Mendes ran into the thousands. To his aides, he said: "My desire is to be with God against man, rather than with man against God." Upon his return to Portugal, Mendes was summarily dismissed from the diplomatic service and a disciplinary board also ordered the suspension of all retirement and severance benefits. He countered with appeals to the government, the Supreme Court, and the National Assembly for a new hearing of his case – but to no avail. After his dismissal, Mendes reportedly told Rabbi Kruger (whom he met again in Lisbon): "If thousands of Jews can suffer because of one Catholic (i.e., Hitler), then surely it is permitted for one Catholic to suffer for so many Jews." He added: "I could not have acted otherwise, and I therefore accept all that has befallen me with love." Bereft of any income, and with a family of 13 children to feed, Mendes was forced to sell his estate in Cabanas de Viriato. When he died in 1954, he had been reduced to poverty. Two of his children were helped by the Jewish welfare organization HIAS to relocate to the United States. In 1966, Mendes was posthumously awarded the title of Righteous Among the Nations by Yad Vashem. After much pressure from private individuals and organizations, in March 1988 Aristides de Sousa Mendes was officially restored to the diplomatic corps by the unanimous vote of the Portuguese National Assembly, and the government thereafter ordered damages to be paid to his family.

BIBLIOGRAPHY: J. Fralon, *A Good Man in Evil Times* (2001); Yad Vashem Archives M31–264; M. Paldiel, *The Path of the Righteous* (1993), 59–62.

[Mordecai Paldiel (2nd ed.)]

MENDÈS, CATULLE (1841–1909), French poet. Mendès was born in Bordeaux. His father was a banker of Sephardi origin and his mother a Catholic. At the age of 18 he went to Paris, where in 1861 he founded *La Revue fantaisiste* – the first of several journals issued by the French Parnassian poets. It stressed their anti-utilitarianism and their devotion to art. He also contributed to the serialized anthology *Le Parnasse contemporain* (1866–76), which he later described in *La Légende du Parnasse contemporain* (1884). A versatile, "decadent" poet, Mendès had a prolific output – some 150 volumes over four decades. They include verse collections – *Poésies* (3 vols., 1892), *Poésies nouvelles* (1893), and *Choix de poésies* (1925); neo-Romantic plays such as *La Femme de Tabarin* (1887), *Médée* (1898), and *La Reine Fiammette* (1899); and several novels, notably *Monstres parisiens* (1882), *Les Folies amoureuses* (1877), and *Zohar* (1886). Mendès also wrote short stories; a study of Richard *Wagner, of whose music he was the French champion; and, in collaboration with the lyric poet Ephraïm *Mikhaël, the dramatic poem *Briséis* (1899). The *Rapport sur le mouvement poétique français 1867–1900* (1902) reveals considerable critical insight. Mendès, who married the daughter of the poet Théophile Gautier (1811–1872), was killed in a railroad accident.

BIBLIOGRAPHY: A. Bertrand, *Catulle Mendès, biographie critique* (1908); A. Schaffer, *Parnassus in France* (1929), 46–71; M. Souriau, *Histoire du Parnasse* (1929); J.F. Herlihy, *Catulle Mendès, critique dramatique et musical* (1936).

[Sidney D. Braun]

MENDES, DIOGO (b. before 1492–D.C. 1542), Marrano merchant, born in Spain, and descended from the *Benveniste family. With his brother Francisco (d. 1536), he established a business in spices and precious stones. He settled in *Antwerp, and on his brother's death was joined there by the latter's widow, later Gracia *Nasi. Mendes became a magnate in the spice trade and made large-scale loans to the governments of the Low Countries, Portugal, and England. Taking advantage of a network of factors and agents throughout Europe, he organized an "underground railway" to facilitate the flight of Marranos from Portugal, via the Low Countries (and sometimes England) to Italy and Turkey. In 1535, he and his sister-in-law, Gracia Nasi, headed the group of *New Christians who sought the help of the papal nuncio to stop the activity of the *Inquisition in Portugal. Arrested in 1532 on a charge of Judaizing, Mendes managed to exculpate himself, but after his death in Antwerp, the same charge led to the sequestration of his property.

BIBLIOGRAPHY: L. Wolf, *Essays in Jewish History* (1934), 75–81; J. Vroman, *L'Affaire Diego Mendez* (1937); C. Roth, *House of Nasi: Doña Gracia* (1947); J.A. Goris, *Les Colonies marchandes méridionales à Anvers* (1925); P. Grunebaum-Ballin, *Joseph Naci, duc de Naxos* (1968).

[Cecil Roth]

MENDES, SAM (1965–), U.S. stage and film director. Samuel Alexander Mendes was born in Reading, Berkshire, England, the son of Sephardic Jewish parents born on the Caribbean island nation of Trinidad. His father was the son of the writer Alfred Mendes, author of the novel *Black Fauns*, and part of the group around C.L.R. James and Albert Gomes which produced the literary magazine *Beacon* in the early 1930s. Mendes' secondary education was at Magdalen College School, Oxford, and he later earned a degree from the University of Cambridge.

As a stage director, Mendes became known for his 1998 production of *Cabaret* starring Alan Cumming, in which he boldly reinvented the noirish musical, achieving a long-running hit in London and on Broadway. The Broadway production garnered four Tony awards, three Drama Desk awards, and other honors. As a film director he is best known for his debut film, *American Beauty*, for which he won an Academy Award for best director in 2000 and awards as best director from virtually every professional film organization.

Mendes got his start in the theater following his graduation from Cambridge in 1987 when he joined the Chichester Festival Theater. Soon after he directed Dame Judi Dench in *The Cherry Orchard*, which brought him a Critics' Circle award for best newcomer. He joined the Royal Shakespeare Company in 1990, where he directed such productions as *Troilus and Cressida* with Ralph Fiennes, *Richard III*, and *The Tempest*. In 1992 Mendes became artistic director of the reopened Donmar Warehouse in London, where he directed many award-winning productions. During his tenure he won Olivier awards for best director for *Cabaret, The Glass Menagerie,* and *Company.* He also directed *The Sea* and *The Plough and the Stars*, both with Judi Dench, *The Birthday Party,* and *Othello*, for which he received another Olivier award. In 1998 he directed Nicole Kidman on Broadway in *The Blue Room.*

Among his other films are *The Road to Perdition* (2002), *Jarhead* (2005), and *The Kite Runner* (2006).

In 2000 Mendes was named a Commander of the British Empire.

[Stewart Kampel (2nd ed.)]

MENDÈS-FRANCE, PIERRE (1907–1982), French statesman. Born and educated in Paris, his university thesis *Le Redressement Financier Francais en 1926 et 1927* (1928) attracted considerable attention and his later study, *L'Oeuvre financière du gouvernement Poincaré* (1928) was used as propaganda by the left-wing parties and made Mendès-France one of the leading financial experts of the Radical party.

At the age of 16 Mendès-France joined the Radical Socialist Party and in 1932 was elected to the National Assembly, being its youngest member. In the same year he outlined an economic program for the party which was accepted at its conference at Toulouse. He supported the Popular Front government of 1936–38 and in 1938 was an undersecretary to the treasury. An advocate of resistance to the Nazis even before World War II, Mendès-France organized an opposition to the Vichy government after the fall of France and was imprisoned by the Pétain government. He escaped to England in 1941 and joined the Free Fench under General De Gaulle who later made him finance commissioner of Algeria. From 1944 to 1945 he was minister of economic affairs and in 1946 he was appointed French governor of the Bank for Reconstruction and Development. In the same year he returned to parliament and in 1954, after a series of cabinet crises, became prime minister with a huge majority of 419 out of 617 deputies.

As premier, Mendès-France offered France a "new deal," promising to end the Indochina war, tackle the problems of European defense, and enact wide-reaching economic reforms. His prestige rose considerably when he ended the war and introduced the plan for a Western European Defense Community with a British military commitment for the defense of Europe. In February 1955 he was defeated over his North Africa policy to grant independence to Morocco and Tunisia and resigned. From January to May 1956 Mendès-France was minister without portfolio but resigned following disagreement with the prime minister, Guy Mollet, on the Algerian policy. He remained an important figure in French politics and frequently opposed De Gaulle's policies. In 1968, he formed a new party, the Parti Socialiste Unifié, which he headed. Mendès-France was a consistent supporter of Zionism and outspoken in his championship of the cause of Israel. He was an ascetic in his private life and once aroused controversy when he urged Frenchmen to abandon their wine drinking for milk, his favorite beverage. He wrote extensively on politics and finance. His books are widely read and some have been translated into other languages. They include: *La Banque Internationale* (1930); *Liberté, Liberté Chérie* (1943; *The Pursuit of Freedom*, 1956); *Gouverner c'est choisir* (3 vols., 1953–58); and *La République moderne* (1962; *A Modern French Republic*, 1963).

[Moshe Rosetti]

MENDLOWITZ, SHRAGA FEIVEL (1886–1948), *rosh yeshivah*, U.S. educator, and Orthodox Jewish leader. Mendlowitz was born in Vilag, Austria-Hungary, on the Polish border. His mother died when he was 10, and he and his father moved to Rimanov. By the time he was 12, he was studying with Reb Aaron, *dayyan* of Mezo-Laboretz, who considered him his top pupil. At 16 he studied with the rabbi of Chust, Moses Greenwald, and at 17 he moved to Unsdorf to study with Rabbi Samuel Rosenberg, author of the *Be'er Shemuel*, who became his role model. He then transferred to the yeshivah in Pressburg, where he studied with R. Simḥah Bunem Schreiber, a grandson of the Ḥatam Sofer.

In 1913, he left his family behind and moved to the United States. Known as a man who inspired his students, he served as a teacher-principal in the *talmud torah* of Scranton, Pennsylvania, for seven years. He returned to Europe after World War I to bring his family to Scranton. In 1920, he moved his family to Williamsburg, Brooklyn, in New York City. In 1921, he was engaged as the principal of Yeshiva Torah Vodaath (founded in 1917), one of only four yeshivahs in the city. He switched from Hebrew to Yiddish as the language of instruction and in 1926 opened a high school.

In 1923, Mendlowitz and the *ḥazzan* Yossele *Rosenblatt produced *Dos Yiddishe Licht*. Filled with comments and inspiring articles, it started as a weekly, became a daily, and folded in 1927. Mendlowitz was also one of the first people to insist on *meḥiẓot* at Jewish weddings in America, and spoke out against dancing and mixed swimming, which were all accepted practices in those days.

He later organized a high school for secular studies under the auspices of the yeshivah, the second such school in the United States, after consulting with leading European rabbis. Mendlowitz also was happy to send Torah Vodaath students to other institutions of higher Jewish learning. In 1941, he set up a school in Spring Valley, New York, which was later to serve as a *kolel* for the graduates of Yeshiva Torah Vodaath. A committed member of the Agudat Israel World Organization, he became vice president in 1938 and personally raised large sums of money for the Ẓe'irei Agudah's rescue programs during the war. In 1944, he founded *Torah Umesorah, a national society for Orthodox Hebrew day schools with Rabbi Reuven Grozovsky. His son-in-law, Rabbi Alexander Linchner, founded Boy's Town Jerusalem and Merom Zion Institute as a result of Mendlowitz's dying wish that something be done for Ereẓ Israel.

[Jeanette Friedman (2nd ed.)]

MENDOZA, province in Argentina and capital city of the province.

The Province

According to data of Vaad Hakehilot as of 2005 there were some 550 families in the capital city of Mendoza and some 30–40 families in San Rafael, out of a total population in the province of about 1,579,651 (2001). Jews had settled in the province as agriculturists and plantation owners by the end of the 1880s. In 1904–05 Jews from Yekaterinoslav attempted to settle in Palmira, but after a short time found they could not meet the difficult terms of their settlement contract and were compelled to leave. A similar attempt to settle there in 1913 likewise failed. In 1943 there were Jews in 24 out of the 123 towns and villages in the province. In 1964 only San Martín, San Rafael, and the capital city of the province, Mendoza, had organized Jewish communities affiliated with the Va'ad ha-Kehillot (see *Argentina). The province is well known for its grapevines and since 1952 there has been industrial production of strictly kosher wine.

The City

In 1909 there were some 600 Jews in the city – approximately 500 from Eastern Europe and the remainder from France and Sephardim. The first community organization, Sociedad Israelita de Beneficencia, was established in 1910, and continues to function. Its membership in 1968 was 577 families. The Sociedad, which comprises the Ashkenazim of Mendoza, owns a large community building, a synagogue, and a cemetery, and plays an important role in the operation of all Jewish institutions in the city. In 1918 a Sephardi community – the Sociedad Israelita de Socorros Mutuos – was established. In 1943 it comprised about 60 families and has come to maintain its own synagogue and cemetery. The Sephardi and Ashkenazi organizations, however, cooperate in running the school, the Maccabi Social Club, and the country club (purchased in 1954).

Various welfare institutions were established in the city but they became superfluous and no longer exist. The financial institution Asociación Israelita de Crédito Mutual has become the Jewish bank Crédito de Cuyo with branches in other provinces. The bank and the Ashkenazi community cooperated in financing the erection of the Max Nordau Jewish School, which in 1968 had an enrollment of 277 students in kindergarten, elementary school, and high school. Local committees of the Jewish National Fund and of the United Jewish Appeal are active in Mendoza as well as the local committee of *DAIA, the umbrella organization of Argentinean Jewry. There formerly existed in Mendoza a pro-Communist group whose number was estimated in 1966 at 80 families; it maintained its own committee and a school, "I.L. Peretz." The majority of Jews in Mendoza are engaged in business and some own vineyards and fruit plantations. Jewish participation in the liberal professions and in the local university has been increasing.

[Daniel Benito Rubinstein Novick]

MENDOZA, DANIEL (1764–1836), English boxing champion. Born in Aldgate, London, Mendoza learned at a young age to defend himself with his fists. In 1780 he won his first professional fight. A natural middleweight, Mendoza became the father of scientific boxing by devising defensive moves that enabled him to fight against much heavier opponents. His ring success brought him to the attention of the Prince of Wales and he became the first boxer to receive royal patronage. Mendoza's ascendancy to boxing heights, and his acceptance by royalty, helped ease the position of the Jew in the English community. He proudly billed himself as "Mendoza the Jew." He opened his own boxing academy and became a teacher. He went on tour and gave boxing exhibitions in England, Wales, Scotland, and Ireland. Mendoza lost the title of English Champion to John Jackson on a ninth-round knockout on April 15, 1795. He wrote *The Art of Boxing* (London, 1789) and *The Memoirs of the Life of Daniel Mendoza* (London, 1816). In 1954 Mendoza was one of the inaugural group chosen for the Boxing Hall of Fame in the United States.

BIBLIOGRAPHY: H.D. Miles, *Pugilistica*, 1 (1880); H.U. Ribalow, *Fighter from Whitechapel* (1962).

[Jesse Harold Silver]

MENE, MENE, TEKEL, U-FARSIN, enigmatic inscription referred to in *Daniel 5:25, which appeared on a wall, written by a detached hand. The narrative in Daniel 5:1ff. relates that King *Belshazzar of Babylonia made a feast for 1,000 of his lords, wives, and concubines. During the feast, wine was drunk from the vessels which had been taken out of the Temple in Jerusalem, and the guests at the feast praised (or perhaps sang to – the Aramaic *shabbaḥ le-* can mean either) the gods of gold and silver, bronze, iron, wood, and stone. Suddenly, the fingers of a man's hand appeared and were seen writing something on the wall of the king's palace. The king became alarmed and summoned all his wise men, but they were unable to read or interpret the writing. The queen then suggested that Daniel, a sage whom Nebuchadnezzar used to consult and found matchless, be brought before the king. Daniel was summoned to Belshazzar. After rebuking the king for his arrogance toward the Lord, for drinking wine from the holy Temple's vessels, and for worshiping man-made gods, Daniel read and interpreted the writing as follows: *mene, mene, tekel* (*teqel*), and *parsin*. *Mene*: God has numbered (*menah*) the days of your kingdom and will bring it to an end; *tekel*: you have been weighed (*teqilta*) in the balance and found wanting; *parsin*: your kingdom has been divided (*prisat*) and given over to the Medes and Persians (*Paras*).

The narrative presents four basic problems. The first question concerns the actual designation of the words *mene, mene, tekel*, and *parsin*. C. Clermont-Ganneau was the first to suggest that the words refer to weights of monetary units. Thus, *mene* (Aramaic *mene*; Heb. *maneh*) is a mina; *tekel* (Aram. *teqel*; Heb. *shekel*) is the shekel; and *u-farsin* (of which the *u* is simply the copulative) is two half-minas. The word פרש has been found on half-mina weights in bilingual Aramaic-Akkadian inscriptions and also occurs in the Talmud (Aramaic *peras*) in the sense of a half-mina. Most scholars have accepted Clermont-Ganneau's explanation of the words and at most add that the first *mene*, unlike the second (5:15), is the Aramaic passive participle (equivalent to the Heb. *manui*, "counted") and is to be read as, "it was counted: *mene, tekel* and *parsin*."

The second question to be asked is why the characters of the inscription baffled the Chaldeans, who should have been able to read easily a few simple Aramaic words. The narrative clearly indicates that the wise men could not decipher the writing, as the king promised a great reward for the man who read the writing (5:7). Daniel solved the riddle by first reading the script; only afterward did he explain it (5:25ff.). Talmudic sages suggest that the letters of the inscription were written in reverse order or in accordance with the *Atbash* (see **Gematria*) sequence (Sanh. 22a). A. Alt proposes that only the initials and not the whole words were written, and he bases his view on the premise that it can be corroborated from archaeological evidence that names of weights were often designated by initials only; Aramaic contracts from the fifth century B.C.E. attest to this practice. Alt, therefore, assumes that what was written were the initials *MMTPP* (ממתפ"פ). H.L. Ginsberg points out that in the Aramaic contracts the word *tekel* is generally written *shkl* and abbreviated as *sh*, and it is possible that even after the more modern spelling *tkl* was adopted, the abbreviation *sh* was retained. Therefore the legend on the wall may have been not *MMTPP* but *MM Sh. PP*, which made it harder for the king's regular sages to recognize it as a series of abbreviations. Daniel, however, realized that the letter *shin* was the initial of the obsolete spelling *shkl*, for *tekel*, and so he read for the two *mem's* – *mene mene*, for the *shin* – *tekel*, and for the two *pe's* – *parsin*.

A third problem is the variance between the written version on the wall (5:25): *mene, mene, tekel*, and *parsin* and the words in Daniel's version: *mene, mene, tekel* and *peras* (5:26ff.). Most ancient versions (Vulg., Theod., and Jos., Ant., 10:239ff.) give the written version (verse 25) also as *mene, tekel, peras*. Since, however, Daniel interprets the last expression as meaning both *perisat* and *paras*, the Masoretic Text's version of verse 25 can be upheld, and the reading in verses 26 and 28 could be the result of haplography. The doubling of the word *mene* at the beginning, Ginsberg believes, was suggested by the doubling of *nafelah*, "fallen," in Isaiah 21:9, "Fallen, fallen is Babylon."

The fourth and last problem is concerned with what the words actually refer to. These words were probably used not only to indicate monetary values but also to express estimates of character. Thus, these words presumably referred to a situation of degeneration. God has weighed the kings of Babylon and has found them to be steadily decreasing in weight. P. Haupt and J.D. Prince hold that the phrase refers to Nebuchadnezzar (*mene*), Belshazzar (*tekel*), the Medes (*peres*, a half-*mene*, i.e., half the greatness of Nebuchadnezzar) and the Persians (*peres*, a half-*mene*, i.e.; half the greatness of Nebuchadnezzar). E.G. Kraeling believes that the phrase was applied to the occupants of the neo-Babylonian throne after Nebuchadnezzar: Awêl-Marduk (Evil-Merodach), Labâshi-Marduk, Nabonidus, and Belshazzar.

BIBLIOGRAPHY: C. Clermont-Ganneau, in: JA, 8 (1886), 36ff.; idem, *Recueil d'archéologie orientale*, 1 (1888), 136–59; J.D. Prince, *Mene Mene Tekel Upharsin* (1893); A. Kamphausen, *Daniel* (Ger., 1896), 28; H. Bauer, *Vierter deutscher Muenzforschertag zu Halle, Festgabe den Teilnehmern gewidmet* (1925), 27–30; J.A. Montgomery, *Daniel* (ICC, 1927), 262ff.; E.G. Kraeling, in: JBL, 63 (1944), 11–18; O. Eissfeldt, in: ZAW, 63 (1951), 105; A. Alt, in: VT, 4 (1954), 303–5; H.L. Ginsberg, in: EM, 5 (1968), 10–13.

[Daniel Boyarin and Moshe Zeidner]

MENELAUS (d. c. 162 B.C.E.), high priest in the time of Antiochus Epiphanes. Menelaus was the brother of Simeon and Lysimachus, both mentioned in II Maccabees. According to II Maccabees 3:4, Simeon and Menelaus belonged to the tribe of Benjamin, and Simeon did not therefore belong to a priestly family. This raises a difficulty and attempts have been made to amend the text, or to suggest that he belonged to a priestly family named Benjamin or Miamin (cf. I Chron. 4:24). It seems preferable to accept the reading found in some Latin manuscripts which reads "Bilgah" instead of Benjamin. Bilgah was the name of one of the priestly divisions (I Chron. 24:14) and probably Menelaus and his brothers belonged to it. The statement of Josephus (Ant., 12:238–9) that Menelaus was a brother of *Jason and a son of *Onias III, is certainly erroneous. Merelaus was one of the leaders of the Hellenists and one of the extremists among them. When sent by the high priest Jason to Antiochus Epiphanes, he intrigued against his principal, bribed Antiochus and received from him appointment as high priest (II Macc. 4:23–24). At the beginning of his tenure of office he plundered the Temple of its gold vessels (*ibid.*, 4:32). He also instigated the murder of Onias III (*ibid.*, 4:34). His appointment and policy aroused the opposition of the people and caused uprisings and disturbances. Jason attempted to seize the high priesthood back from him, but Menelaus succeeded in retaining power, chiefly with the assistance of the Syrians. He remained loyal to Antiochus and sent him large amounts of money. As leader of the Hellenists he must be considered responsible to a great extent for the persecution of Antiochus (see Bickermann in bibl.; cf. II Macc. 13:4). It seems, however, that later, when it became clear that this policy brought no advantage to the Hellenists, he was partly responsible for the more conciliatory policy of Antiochus Epiphanes (164 B.C.E.; II Macc. 11:29). Later he lost favor in the court of the Seleucids and on the advice of Lysias was put to death (apparently in 162 B.C.E.).

BIBLIOGRAPHY: F.M. Abel, in: *Miscellanea Giovanni Mercati*, 1 (1946), 52–58; Rowley, in: *Studia Orientalia loanni Pedersen… Dicata* (Eng. 1953), 303–15; V. Tcherikover, *Hellenistic Civilization and the Jews* (1959), 70–74, 216–20, and index; E. Bickermann, *From Ezra to the Last of the Maccabees* (1962), 106f.

[Uriel Rappaport]

MENES, ABRAM (1897–1969), historian. Born in Grodno, Poland, Menes became engrossed in the problems of socialism early in his youth; at the age of 20 he founded an illegal *Bund branch in Grodno, which engaged in educational work and the distribution of illegal socialist literature. After World War I he devoted himself to public affairs, becoming the vice chairman of the Grodno Jewish community. After moving to Berlin in 1920, where he studied Jewish history and Bible, Menes, together with Nahum *Shtif and E. *Tcherikower, laid the foundations of *YIVO (the Institute of Jewish Research). In 1933 he moved to Paris, and became one of the leading contributors to the *Yiddish Encyclopedia*, writing on a wide range of historical subjects. He continued his work on the editorial board of the encyclopedia even after settling in the U.S. (1940), where he also joined the staff of the Yiddish daily *Forward*.

Menes' main area of interest in Jewish history was its economic and social aspects. Articles on these subjects, covering the talmudic period as well as late 19th-century Russian Jewry, appeared in YIVO's historical publications. Together with Raphael *Abramowitz, Menes wrote *Leyenbukh tsu der Geshikhte fun Yisroel* ("A Layman's History of Israel," 1923). Another favorite topic of his was the history of the Jewish Workers Movement and of socialism: *Der Onhoyb fun der Yidisher Arbeter-Bavegung un ir Shoyresh in Yidishen Folks Lebn*, published in the *Zukunft* (40 (1935), 539–44), is an investigation into the problems of socialism, in general, and in particular among the Jews. His essays on significant events in Jewish history, in both the preexilic and postexilic periods, were published in *Oyfn Sheydveg*, an independent publication of Jewish culture, art and literature, and cultural philosophy, edited by E. Tcherikower and I. Efroikin. These essays mark a turning point in Menes' approach to Jewish history: "The time has come to amend Heine's youthful error and to replace 'le credit' with 'la religion' – the belief in man with the belief in God." Mention should also be made of his contribution, "Jewish History," to the volume "Jews" in the *Yiddish Encyclopedia*, in which he wrote on the biblical and talmudic periods. His articles in the *Forward* dealt to a large extent with Jewish holidays. His writings on the problems of methodology in Jewish history are of significance to scholars in the field.

Menes' writings on Jewish ethics, sociology, and philosophy continued to be based on the principle that "there can be no faith in man without a feeling of sanctity." Jacob Glatstein described Menes as a historian "who has introduced a new evaluation of Jewish history."

BIBLIOGRAPHY: LNYL, 6 (1965), 72–78.

[Israel Ch. Biletzky]

°**MENGELE, JOSEF** (1911–1978), doctor of the Auschwitz extermination camp. Born in Guenzburg, Germany, he studied medicine and anthropology at the University of Munich, the University of Vienna, and the University of Bonn. At Munich he obtained a doctorate in anthropology (Ph.D.) with a dissertation in 1935 on racial differences in the structure of the lower jaw, supervised by Prof. Theodor Mollison. After his exams he went to Frankfurt, working as an assistant to Otmar von Verschuer at the Frankfurt University Institute of Hereditary Biology and Racial Hygiene. In 1938 he obtained a doctorate in medicine (M.D.) with a dissertation called "Familial Research on Cleft Lip, Palate and Jaw." (He was deprived of both academic degrees in 1961 and 1964, respectively.) Declared medically unfit to serve at the front in World War II, he was, at his own request, appointed doctor of the Auschwitz camp where, from 1943 to 1945, he initiated a series of cruel "medical" experiments which caused the death of many Jewish inmates. To perfect the master race he studied twins to see if the breeding of the German people could be improved and two members of the race could be obtained in a single pregnancy. He studied dwarfs and other abnormalities, in his mind to protect the German people and improve the species. And while he was experimenting, he could be kind and generous to those who were specimens for his lab. He dreamed of scholarly prominence. He participated in the selection of tens of thousands of prisoners in the Birkenau camp (see *Auschwitz), whom he consigned to die in the gas chambers. The figure of Mengele decreeing life or death by a flick of his finger has become one of the symbols of the Holocaust; he was called by the camp inmates "the Angel of Death." But not all survivor recollections of Mengele are accurate. He could not have done all that he was credited with doing. Mengele did work with a "scientific team" recruited from among arriving physicians who faced the choice of *Selektion* or working with him. Several of these inmate physicians have written memoirs, and they are among the most important recollections of life inside Auschwitz. At one moment Mengele could be gracious, but not for long. He was unpredictable and everyone around him lived in constant fear. Thus, Dr. Olga Lengyel reveals that Mengele supervised the birth of a child with meticulous care. Within an hour mother and child were sent to the gas chamber. Dr. Gisella Perl, a Hungarian Jewish gynecologist, described the aftermath of one brutal killing by Mengele. "He took a piece of perfumed soap out of his bag and whistling gaily with a smile of deep satisfaction on his face, he began to wash his hands." Vera Alexander described brutal "scientific" experiments in which inmates were sewn back to back, wrist to wrist. And Dr. Miklos Nyiszli depicts the murder of 14 twins killed during one night.

When Mengele fled Auschwitz, according to Raul *Hilberg, he brought with him the records of his medical experiments, still believing that they might hold the key to his postwar prominence. According to one source, he also took these potentially incriminating records with him when he left for Argentina.

Until 1951 Mengele lived under his own name in various places in Bavaria, Germany. The name Mengele is proudly seen on farm equipment. It is a symbol of quality in Germany and elsewhere. Throughout the years the Mengele family funneled enough money to Josef to permit his survival, enough to elude capture but not quite enough to achieve comfort. Mengele was forced to move from Argentina to Paraguay and later to Brazil, where he lived his final years in seclusion, perhaps even in loneliness. He met his only biological son, Rolf Mengele, on two occasions after the war, once when he was introduced as "Uncle Fritz" and the second time when his son sought to understand his father, to comprehend his deeds, to come to terms with his motivations. Rolf had rejected his father and his politics.

Mengele was divorced from his first wife, Irene. They grew apart in the postwar separation. After his divorce he married his beautiful sister-in-law, Martha Mengele, the wife of his late brother, Karl, in what seemed like a merger to protect the family assets as well as a marriage. He raised his nephew Karl Heinz, the son of his brother, as his stepson and a surrogate son.

The search for him started only in 1953, after he escaped from Germany. It is known that in 1954 he was granted Argentinean citizenship. In Argentina he represented the Karl Mengele and Sons factory for agricultural machinery, a firm managed by his brother in Guenzburg. Mengele was traced by organizations of former Nazi victims, both Jewish and non-Jewish. His extradition was demanded by the government of West Germany, but Mengele escaped from Argentina. His disappearance was also, apparently, connected with the apprehension of *Eichmann. Various conflicting news items subsequently appeared in the world press concerning the whereabouts of Mengele. Mengele's name was often mentioned by witnesses at the Eichmann trial in Jerusalem and at numerous trials in West Germany, in particular at the *Auschwitz trials held in Frankfurt on the Main in 1963–65. He figures in Rolf Hochhut's play *The Deputy* (1963). He died in an apparent drowning in Brazil in 1978. Efforts were made to ascertain that indeed the corpse discovered was that of Mengele. Some suspected that the drowning was staged. But forensic evidence and dental records confirmed his death.

BIBLIOGRAPHY: M. Nyiszli, *Auschwitz: A Doctor's Eyewitness Account* (1960); O. Kraus and E. Kulka, *Death Factory* (1966). ADD. BIBLIOGRAPHY: G. Perl, *I Was a Doctor in Auschwitz* (1988).

[Emmanuel Brand / Michael Berenbaum (2nd ed.)]

MENINSKY, BERNARD (1891–1950), English artist. Meninsky was born in Liverpool, the son of immigrants from the Ukraine. He studied at the Liverpool School of Art and the Slade School. In 1913 he became a founder member of the London Group. During World War I Meninsky served as an official war artist. In 1920 he became teacher of life drawing at the Westminster School of Art and the City of Oxford Art School. Retrospective exhibitions of his work were held in London in 1951 and 1958 and several of his paintings are held by the Tate Gallery.

ADD. BIBLIOGRAPHY: J. Russell Taylor, *Bernard Meninsky* (1990).

MENKEN, U.S. family. SOLOMON MENKEN (1787–1853), who was born in Westphalia, Prussia, arrived in the U.S. from Holland in 1820 and soon established a wholesale drygoods business in Cincinnati, where he was one of the first Jewish settlers. His eldest son, JULES MENKEN (1836–1890), was a lieutenant in the Cincinnati Home Guards during the Civil War. NATHAN DAVIS MENKEN (1837–1878), his second son, was a merchant and soldier. During the Civil War, he held the rank of cavalry captain and was cited for bravery. He later joined his younger brother's Memphis business. He died assisting victims of yellow fever during an 1878 epidemic. JACOB STANWOOD MENKEN (1838–c. 1900), Solomon's third son, was born in Cincinnati. A merchant and philanthropist, he founded the large Menken and Co. department store in Memphis in 1863, and was active in organizing the Children's Christmas Club and the first Southern kindergarten for blacks. S. STANWOOD MENKEN (1870–1954), Nathan's son and great-great-grandson of Haym *Solomon, was born in Memphis, Tenn. A lawyer and publicist, he was educated at Cornell and Columbia Law School and admitted to the New York bar in 1894. Active in New York City politics, he organized the Hall of Records Association in 1896, the Democratic League (1908), and the National Security League of America (1915).

MENKEN (née **Theodore**), **ADAH ISAACS** (1835–1868), U.S. actress, known mainly for her flamboyant way of life. The first of her four husbands was a musician, Alexander Isaac Menken, whose name she kept after he divorced her. Her stage career began in 1856 in New Orleans. Probably not a great actress, she had an arresting stage personality, and displayed her dark, slim beauty with a boldness that created a sensation wherever she appeared. The first American actress to wear flesh-colored tights, she made her most spectacular appearance in the play *Mazeppa* (adapted from Byron's poem) in which she rode up a steep ramp strapped to a fiery horse. She mixed in the circle of American literary bohemians that included Walt Whitman, Bret Harte, and Mark Twain. In London in 1864 her *Mazeppa* angered the press, but she won the literati with her poems. Dickens, Charles Reade, and Rossetti were her friends. Swinburne described her as the world's delight and claimed she was his mistress. She enjoyed triumph in Paris in 1866, won over Gautier and George Sand, and became the mistress of the elder Dumas. Though she invented fanciful accounts of her origin, which was obscure, she took a militant pride in her Jewishness. In 1857 she led a protest against the exclusion of Jews from the House of Commons. She never performed on the Day of Atonement and kept a Hebrew Bible under her pillow. Her two books of poems, *Memoirs* (1856) and *Infelicia* (1868), teem with biblical allusions. She died in Paris, and Baron Lionel de *Rothschild erected a memorial on her grave in Montparnasse.

BIBLIOGRAPHY: A. Lesser, *Enchanting Rebel* (1947); B. Falk, *Naked Lady* (1934); P. Lewis, *Queen of the Plaza* (1964).

MENKEN, ALAN (1949–), U.S. composer. Born and raised in New Rochelle, New York, Menken was extremely musical as a child, learning to play the piano, violin, guitar, and accordion. However, it was not until he had graduated from New York University with a liberal arts degree that he decided to pursue a career in music. While attending the Lehman Engel Musical Theater Workshop, Menken first discovered and nurtured his passion for musical theater. As he unsuccessfully attempted to get his first musicals produced, Menken supported himself by writing and singing commercial jingles. His career changed forever when he met lyricist Howard Ashman, with whom he first collaborated on the WPA production of *God Bless You, Mr. Rosewater* (1979) and with whom he went on to create the score for the Broadway production of *Little Shop of Horrors*. Since his first Oscar nomination for best song for "Mean Green Mother from Outer Space" from the film version of *Little Shop of Horrors* (1986), Menken has won a series of awards almost too long to count, including Tony, Emmy, Grammy, and Oscar Awards. In fact, Menken is tied with legendary costume designer Edith *Head for most Oscar Awards won – they both have eight. Menken has produced some of his best-known work since the late 1980s, composing the scores for such Disney films as *The Little Mermaid* (1989), *Beauty and the Beast* (1991), *Aladdin* (1992), and *Pocahontas* (1995).

[Casey Schwartz (2nd ed.)]

MENKES, ZYGMUNT (1896–1986), U.S. painter. Menkes was born in Lvov, Galicia. The artist's subjects included nudes, still-lifes, portraits, and landscapes. While restoring rural churches, he studied art at the Industrial School in Lvov and the Academy of Fine Art, Cracow, beginning in 1912. He established a reputation as an artist in Poland before leaving that country. In 1922 he studied in Berlin with the Constructivist artist Alexander Archipenko. He arrived in Paris in 1923, where he joined the École de Paris, a circle of Central and East European ex-patriots which included Marc *Chagall, Amedeo *Modigliani, Jules *Pascin, and Chaim *Soutine. After finally setting in Paris, Menkes participated in such exhibitions as the Salon d'Automne (1924, 1925, 1927) and the Salon des Independants (1925–28) as well as exhibiting his work in a number of Parisian, British, and Canadian galleries. Menkes was well traveled, returning to Poland on a number of occasions, as well as visiting the United States in 1930 and Spain in 1925. In Poland, he exhibited with the New Generation and Keystone groups, while having solo shows in Lvov and Warsaw in 1930 and 1931. He moved to the United States in 1935, enjoying his first American one-man show a year later at the Sullivan Gallery in New York. Menkes eventually settled in Riverdale, New York. He also taught at the Art Students League in New York. Many New York galleries exhibited and sold Menkes' work: the Associated American Artists' Gallery (1936–54), Durand-Ruel Gallery (1941), and the Georgette Passedoit Gallery (1942). Like many other artists of his generation, his work was greatly influenced by that of Henri Matisse: Menkes often painted women in lushly decorated interior spaces animated by expressive line. Menkes' pictures, cheerful still lifes, especially of flowers, introspective portraits, and vivid landscapes have a decidedly French accent. He resisted the trend toward abstract art and never veered from recognizable subject matter. Primarily a colorist who often used rich, sensuous tones, his work showed an increasing tendency toward flatness and two-dimensionality later in his career. Menkes frequently used Jewish themes in his earlier work, depicting his memories of Poland with poignancy and nostalgia. One of his best-known canvasses is *The Uplifting of the Torah* (1928), in which a group of East European Jews are shown excitedly raising up a partly unrolled Torah scroll. Menkes considered this painting an homage to his family and upbringing. In the manner of Rembrandt, the figures in the composition are dramatically lit. Broad brushstrokes, distinctive in texture, reveal the ecstatic expressions of the worshippers, who gather in a circle around the sacred scroll. In 1943, he bore witness to the sufferings of the Jews of Europe, especially those in his native Poland, in *Uprising of Ghetto Warsaw*. Menkes' work is represented in the collections of the Brooklyn Museum of Art, the Whitney Museum, the Hirschhorn Museum, Washington, D.C., the Pennsylvania Academy of Fine Arts, and the Walker Art Center, among others.

BIBLIOGRAPHY: *École de Paris: le Groupe des Quatre* (2000); A. Kampf, *Jewish Experience in the Art of the Twentieth Century* (1984).

[Nancy Buchwald (2nd ed.)]

MENORAH (Heb. מְנוֹרָה; "candelabrum"), the name given to the seven-branched candelabrum which, according to the Bible, was a prominent feature of the *Tabernacle erected by the people of Israel in the wilderness, as well as in the Jerusalem Temple. In archaeological finds in Ereẓ Israel and Syria dating from the Middle Bronze Period onward, lamps have been uncovered in the form of a deep bowl, with seven spouts on the rim for inserting wicks. At the high place (*bamah*) discovered at Nahariyyah, several bowls, similar to those of the Middle Bronze Period, have been found. Some lamp bowls have a clay, stone, or metal stand, thereby transforming them into *menorot*. At Taanach such a *menorah* has been unearthed, consisting of a small bowl with seven spouts, set on a stand whose circumference, narrowing in the middle to form a grip, broadens out at the bottom into a base for placing it on the ground.

The Tabernacle

Among the vessels of the Tabernacle mentioned in the Priestly Code, reference is made to a *menorah* of gold, whose form is given in two parallel passages (Ex. 25:31–40; 37:17–24). A pattern of this *menorah* was, it is related, shown by God to Moses at Mount Sinai (Ex. 25:40), as He also showed him the pattern of the Tabernacle and all its furniture (Ex. 25:9). Six branches, three on each side, curved upward from the *menorah's* central shaft, which stood on a base (Ex. 25:31; Num. 8:4) whose precise shape cannot be determined. The shaft and each of the branches were ornamented respectively with four and three carvings of cups made like almond-blossoms, each subdivided into a knop and a flower. Under every two branches that were of one piece a knop was carved on the central shaft, making a total of three knops "for the six branches going out of the *menorah*" (Ex. 25:35). These three knops were probably an integral part of the cups on the central shaft and not, as some (A.R.S. Kennedy, S.R. Driver, and others) hold, in addition to its four cups. The fourth cup was at the top of the central shaft, above the places where the branches joined it. The uppermost cups of the branches were similarly at their top, with all of them – as well as that of the central shaft – ending at the same height. The flowers on these uppermost cups served as receptacles for the seven lamps.

The entire *menorah* was carved from one ingot of gold, "beaten work" (Ex. 25:31), and its vessels, also of gold and including the lamps, were carved separately (Ex. 25:37–38). The *menorah* was placed in front of the veil (*parokhet*) "on the side of the Tabernacle toward the south ... over against the table" (Ex. 26:35; 40:24). When the lamps burnt they gave "light over against it" (Ex. 25:37) "in front of the *menorah*" (Num.

8:2–3), that is, the spouts of the lamps and the wicks faced northward, so that their shadow was cast on to the wall. The measurements of the *menorah* are not given in the Bible but the Talmud stated that its height was 18 handbreadths, which are three short cubits (Men. 28b; Rashi to Ex. 25:35). The use to which the Tabernacle *menorah* was put is described in the Priestly Code. The lamps (*nerot*) are said to have burned from evening to morning (Lev. 24:3), were lit at dusk and trimmed in the morning by the high priest (Ex. 30:7–8), and hence are called *ner tamid* (a perpetual lamp; Ex. 27:20; Lev. 24:2), that is, they were lit according to a fixed routine and for the nighttime only. This is specifically mentioned in connection with the lamp in the sanctuary at Shiloh (I Sam. 3:3). However, in the Second Temple (see below) three of the lamps burned throughout the day, the rest being lit in the evening (Jos., Ant., 3:199).

The First Temple

In the Temple built by Solomon there were ten *menorot* of gold, five along the northern and five along the southern wall of the *Heikhal* (the hall; I Kings 7:49; II Chron. 4:7). These were ornamented with carvings of flowers and furnished with appliances of gold for tending the lamps (I Kings 7:49–50), the number of which on each *menorah* is not stated. Some scholars hold that the passage listing the golden vessels made by Solomon for the house of the Lord (I Kings 7:48–50) is a later addition; but this view should be rejected. All the vessels of gold in Solomon's Temple, including the ten *menorot*, were cut in pieces at the end of Jehoiachin's reign by the Chaldeans who entered the *Heikhal* during their siege of Jerusalem (II Kings 24:13). Hence neither vessels of the *Heikhal* nor *menorot* are mentioned in the description of the Temple in Ezekiel's vision (Ezek. 41:1–4), for this description is apparently based largely on the actual appearance of the Temple in Jerusalem after the exile of Jehoiachin.

The *menorot* in Solomon's Temple may have had branches, and these may have numbered seven on each *menorah*. For the *Heikhal*, which Solomon built and which measured 40 by 20 cubits (I Kings 6:2, 17), was too large for only ten lamps to give it adequate illumination. Hence it is probable that each of the ten *menorot* had not one but several lamps, arranged on a central shaft and on branches, and that they numbered seven. Further support for the similarity between the *menorot* of Solomon and the one in the Tabernacle is to be found in the fact that the former, too, were ornamented with carvings of flowers (7:49), resembling the latter which had "cups made like almond-blossoms" and flowers. Moreover, the *menorot* in Solomon's Temple were made of pure gold (*ibid.*, loc. cit. *zahav sagur*, apparently the equivalent expression for *zahav tahor* used in the Priestly Code; see Ex. 25:31, 39; et al.; see *Metals). The vessels of the *menorah* in the Tabernacle consisted of lamps, tongs, snuff-dishes, and oil vessels (Ex. 25:37–39; Num. 4:9); the first three are among those mentioned in connection with the *menorot* in Solomon's Temple (I Kings 7:49–50).

In addition to the vessels in the *Heikhal*, there were others in Solomon's Temple treasuries whose collection was started already in the days of David (II Sam. 8:10–11), and which were left as objects consecrated to God but not used in worship. The passage in the Book of Chronicles enumerating the gifts prepared for the Temple by David before his death refers to the *menorot* of gold and silver in the Temple treasuries (I Chron. 28:15; and cf. 28:12). When the First Temple was destroyed the Chaldeans removed from it all these vessels, among which *menorot* are again included (Jer. 52:19), but they were not those of the *Heikhal*. No actual specimen of the *menorah* in the Tabernacle nor of one with a different number of branches has up to the present been uncovered in archaeological finds. Only reproductions of the *menorah* of the Second Temple are extant (see below).

Although according to the critical views the Priestly Code's account of the subject is legendary tradition, the artistic and architectonic elements of its description are undoubtedly based on an actual art style and derived from reality. Many scholars of the Wellhausen school held that the Tabernacle *menorah* was a literary projection of the one in the Second Temple. Their theory proceeds from that school's basic view that the Priestly Code was compiled at the beginning of Second Temple times, and hence its need to explain the entire Tabernacle as an imaginary reflection of the Second Temple. If, however, it is maintained that the Priestly Code was committed to writing earlier and is the production of the Jerusalem pre-Exilic priesthood, it must necessarily be held that the *menorah* described in it reflects a historic situation preceding the Second Temple. That the *menorot* in Solomon's Temple provided the pattern for the *menorah* in the Tabernacle is, indeed, not impossible.

The Second Temple

According to rabbinic legend, when the Temple was about to be destroyed the *menorah* was hidden away and it was later brought back by the exiles (see L. Ginzberg, *Legends of the Jews*, 4 (1913), 321; 6 (1928), 410–1). In reality, however, the *menorah* of the Tabernacle, as a hallowed emblem mentioned in the Pentateuch, had an influence on the interior of the Second Temple, in which from the outset one *menorah* as in the Tabernacle, and not ten, as in the Temple of Solomon, was placed. The *menorah* in the Temple of necessity had to conform to that in the Pentateuch, which became its archetype. The force that the *menorah* of the Tabernacle had in Second Temple times as a hallowed and binding emblem can be seen from the claim, incorporated by the Chronicler in Abijah's speech, that the people of Judah, keeping the commandments of the Lord, every night lit the lamps of the *menorah* of gold (II Chron. 13:11). Elsewhere, however, the Chronicler repeats the evidence of the Book of Kings by stating specifically that in the First Temple there were ten *menorot* and not one (see above). This contradiction between the enduring and binding validity of the *menorah* mentioned in the Pentateuch and the ten *menorot* in Solomon's Temple was met by the Sages with the above-mentioned statement that the *menorah* made by Moses was used during the entire existence of the First Temple, where all the *menorot* were placed on the south side, five on its right side and five on its left, and that of Moses in the middle (Men. 98b).

The golden *menorah* which stood in the Second Temple in the early stage of its history (it is referred to by Ben Sira – 26:17) was removed in 169 B.C.E. by Antiochus Epiphanes IV (I Macc. 1:21). Judah Maccabee made new Temple vessels, including the *menorah*, after the cleansing of the Temple (I Macc. 4:49–50; II Macc. 10:3). According to the Talmud the first one was made of iron overlaid with tin (or with wood): "When they grew richer they made it of silver; when they grew still richer, they made it of gold" (RH 24b, Av. Zar. 43b); according to Josephus (Ant., 12:238), however, it was made of gold from the outset. It was seen by Pompey and his men when they entered the Temple (*ibid.*, 14:7) and remained in Herod's Temple until its destruction (Jos. Wars, 5:216–7). After the destruction of the Temple it was borne by the Romans in Titus' triumphal procession (*ibid.*, 7:148–9) and depicted with the other vessels on the wall of the triumphal arch called after him (see below). Elsewhere, however (*ibid.*, 6:387–8), Josephus relates that during the siege of Jerusalem by Titus one of the priests went out and handed over to him two lamps of gold similar to the lamp in the Temple. On the erroneous assumption that the reference is to the *menorah*, some maintain that there were in the Second Temple several copies of the *menorah* of the *Heikhal*, one of which was carried in the triumphal procession (see below). In the Second Temple three of the lamps of the *menorah* burned throughout the day, the rest being lit in the evening (Jos., Ant., 3:199). The Talmud states that the priest who entered used to clean and trim the lamps except its two eastern ones which he found burning, and that its western lamp burnt continuously, and from it the priest relit the *menorah* at dusk (Tam. 3, 9; 6, 1; Sifra, Emor, 13, 7; Sif. Num. 59; Yoma 33a; et al.). If the western lamp was extinguished it was interpreted as boding ill for the future (Yoma 39b). Josephus (Apion, 1:22) similarly reports in the name of Hecataeus that on the Temple *menorah* there was a light which was never extinguished by night or by day. According to some, the western lamp mentioned by the sages refers to the second of the two easterly lamps, according to others, to the middle lamp, designated as "western" because its spout faced westward, that is, toward the inner sanctum, the Holy of Holies (see Rashi to Shab. 22b, and to Men. 98b; Maim. Yad, Beit ha-Beḥirah, 3, 8). According to the latter interpretation the tradition of the sages accords with Josephus' statement (Ant., 3:199) that three lamps burnt throughout the day, that is, the two eastern and the western lamps.

[Menahem Haran]

Menorah on the Arch of Titus

The most important testimony for the form of the Temple *menorah* is the candelabrum on the Arch of Titus in Rome, which ought to be considered in conjunction with Josephus' description. Only three sides of each octagon of the arch are visible. They show reliefs within a threefold frame: in the middle shield of the upper cone two eagles face each other and hold a garland in their beaks; the other shields have different types of sea-monsters. The upper part of the *menorah* is, by and large, in accordance with biblical tradition and archaeological evidence. The hanging leaf-ornament of the middle shaft shows the Oriental (Persian) origin (cf. the pillars of Persepolis). The problem of the Arch of Titus *menorah* is, however, its pedestal, which consists of two octagonal casings, a smaller above the larger, giving a cone-shaped form. Though its proportions are rather large, it does not necessarily cast doubt on the fidelity of the sculptor, since this was a peculiarity of Roman – and later Christian – artists. What does make this representation of the pedestal suspect is that according to all Jewish sources (cf. Men. 28b) and archaeological finds the Menorah stood on three legs, usually lion's paws. These paws are particularly distinct in the Nirim Mosaic (see below). The Bible speaks of the *yerekh* of the candelabrum (Ex. 25:31), which Rashi explains as a plate with three legs (see S. Shefer (ed.), *Enẓiklopedyah le-Inyenei ha-Mishkan…*, 1 (1965), 126ff.), and so it appears in the wall painting of *Dura-Europos and perhaps on the coin of Mattathias Antigonus, the only ancient coin depicting a *menorah*. The few extant specimens of this coin are, however, badly preserved, one only showing, besides the plate, a rudimentary foot.

This divergence between the Arch of Titus and the sources has given rise to a lively controversy beginning with Relandus' *De Spoliis…* (1716) which maintained, on the basis of the biblical prohibition of depicting animals, that the pedestal of the *menorah* on the Arch of Titus could not be an authentic reproduction. In point of fact, as E. Cohn-Wiener pointed out, there is a difference in style between the lower and upper parts of the *menorah*. The upper part, dating from the time of the later Hasmonean kings (see above), shows characteristics of late Hellenistic style, whereas the pedestal is typical of a later Roman style. Important too, is the evidence of Josephus, who must have seen the *menorah* often, both in Jerusalem and in Rome, and who has proved reliable in matters such as these, e.g., the Masada excavations. Whether his description supports or contradicts the authenticity of the Arch of Titus *menorah* depends on the interpretation of the relevant words used by him. According to W. Eltester (in bibl. cf. Michel-Bauernfeind's edition of Josephus, Wars, 2, 2, 1969), the words translated from Greek, "the central shaft arose firmly from the pedestal," seems to confirm the Arch of Titus representation which indeed gives this impression of weight and firmness. Another interpretation would be that the central shaft "stretched" out of its pedestal, that it was of one piece with it. This would not only be in accordance with the biblical injunction of Numbers 8:4 (cf. Ex. 25:31, 36; 37:17, 22), but also with Josephus' statement preceding the above quotation that the *menorah* was different from those in general use. These were put together from separate parts (cf. Pliny, Nat. Hist. 34, 6, 11).

Various suggestions have been made to solve the difficulty. Chief Rabbi Isaac Herzog, after summing up all other proposals, suggested that the original pedestal had been broken in the transport from Jerusalem to Rome and was replaced by the work of a Roman artist. Another hypothesis is that of W. Wirgin (IEJ 11, 1961, no. 3) who suggests that in order to carry the *menorah* in the triumphal procession without mishap, a Roman artist built a box-shaped covering from relief plates – well known from Roman censers – around the base to give it greater stability. A third suggestion is that the *menorah* on the Arch of Titus had as its model another *menorah*, perhaps one given as a gift to Rome by Herod. In fact Josephus (Wars, 6:388) relates that after the capture of Jerusalem, a priest handed to Titus "two lampstands similar to those deposited in the Temple." The Talmud (Ḥag. 26b, 27a) also mentions duplicates and triplicates of all Temple vessels in case the original ones were defiled. The Jerusalem Talmud (Ḥag. 3:8; 79d) and the Tosefta (Ḥag. 3:35) report the cleansing of the *menorah* on the Sabbath which provoked the derision of the Sadducees. This would not have been done had there been a duplicate but in any case it does not solve the problem of the Arch of Titus, since the duplicate would have been an exact replica of the original.

Reproductions of the Temple Menorah

Though the *menorah* of the Arch of Titus was widely known – the medieval pilgrims' guide *Mirabilis Urbis Romae* mentions the *arcus septem lucernarum* – it was not copied in late antiquity or the Middle Ages. While church candelabra and manuscript illustrations have animal feet, only one example of the Arch of Titus type is known: the Gothic candelabrum in Sta. Maria i Vulturella near Rome (see bibl. P. Bloch).

Several sketches of the *menorah* have been preserved from the time of the Second Temple in Jason's Tomb, Jerusalem (see Rahmani, in: *Atiqot*, 1964, Plate XII no. l and 2), and in the two pieces of plaster excavated in the Jewish Quarter of the Old City of Jerusalem in 1969, an artisan's sketch; three feet or triangle-basis are visible, but with knobs on them, a feature not corroborated by any other ancient literary or archaeological source (see the publication of this find by Li-hi Habas from 2003).

The Later History of the Menorah

Vespasian deposited the *menorah* together with the other booty in the special Peace Temple which he erected after the Jewish War (Jos. Wars 7:148–50; ARN[1] 41, 133). The subsequent fate of the candelabrum is uncertain. Procopius of Caesarea, the sixth-century Byzantine historian, in his introduction to the history of the Gothic War, reports that the "treasures of the Jews" were carried in Belisarius' triumphal procession in Constantinople (Byzantium) after his victory over the Vandals, who had taken them to Carthage after their sack of Rome in 455. Procopius goes on to relate that a Jew had warned a high official at Justinian's court not to keep the sacred vessels in Byzantium, as they had manifestly brought ill luck to Rome and Carthage, whereupon the Emperor had sent them hurriedly to Jerusalem, where they were deposited in one of the churches. As the result of the Persian and Arab invasions of the seventh century, their fate once more became unknown. This story has little credibility; no other source, such as the reports of the pilgrims, can be adduced in its support, nor is the *menorah* mentioned explicitly in this story.

On the other hand, medieval sources speak of the presence of the candelabrum in Constantinople. The seventh-century apocalypse *Milḥemet Melekh ha-Mashi'aḥ* ("War of the King Messiah") mentions Temple vessels deposited in the palace library of Emperor Julian. The learned emperor Constantine Porphyrogenitus (905–59) reports that a Heptalychnos, i.e., a seven-branched candelabrum, was lit for solemn processions. The imperial palace is said to have included a "Dome of the Seven-branch Candelabrum" It is not clear whether all these reports refer to the original *menorah* or a later copy. If the one or the other was really in Constantinople during the Middle Ages, it must have shared the fate of other ancient masterpieces when the town was sacked in 1204 in the course of the Fourth Crusade. It may appear odd that no reference to it is found in later medieval chronicles.

[Heinrich Strauss]

In Kabbalah

From the early days of Kabbalah, the *menorah* appears as a symbol of the structure of the *Sefirot*. As far as is known, it was *Asher b. David, in his *Perush Shem ha-Meforash* (published in *Ha-Segullah* (1932) pamphlet 2 ff.), who first explained the *menorah* in kabbalistic symbolic terms as reflecting the world of the *Sefirot*. He was followed by *Baḥya b. Asher and especially by Menaḥem *Recanati and others. There is little difference between the interpretations of Recanati and Asher b. David. The basic idea is that the *menorah*, despite the fact it is composed of branches, bowls, etc., is not a combination of parts but is one solid whole made from "one bar." Similarly, the world of the *Sefirot*, despite its multiplicity, is a unity. The seven branches symbolize the seven lower *Sefirot*. Asher b. David and, following him, Recanati, placed special emphasis on the middle branch, which is equal to the *Sefirah Tiferet* ("glory"), which is called the "middle line." This *Sefirah* is directed toward the "attraction of the body" of man, in contrast to the other lower *Sefirot* which are directed toward the arms and legs. The middle branch, which stands on the *menorah* itself, toward which all the other branches face, therefore naturally stands for the "middle line." This *Sefirah* is imbued with abundance flowing from above which is transferred from it to the others. The oil which is put in the branches and is the force for the light of the *menorah* signifies the dynamic stream influenced by the **Ein-Sof*. This stream is the inner soul of all the *Sefirot* which operate within every *Sefirah*. For the same reason – these kabbalists maintain – the Torah calls the seven lower *Sefirot* "lights" and days of the week according to Genesis. The oil as a symbol of the streaming of abundance from above is a commonplace idea in kabbalistic literature. There were kabbalists who explained that the oil and the light indicate the three higher *Sefirot*.

According to the view of several kabbalists that Divine Providence is exercised through the *Sefirot*. Recanati interprets the saying of Zechariah (4:10): "These seven are the eyes of God," to mean that God governs by means of the seven *Sefirot* symbolized by the seven branches of the *menorah*.

The *Zohar itself gives no details of the symbolic significance of the parts of the *menorah*. In the *Tikkunei Zohar* the symbolism differs from that of the kabbalists mentioned above. In one place the *menorah* symbolizes an angelic power outside that of the *Sefirot*. The wick stands for the last *Sefirah, Malkhut*, equated with the *Shekhinah*; the oil is the *Sefirah Yesod* ("foundation"); and the light is the *Sefirah Tiferet* (*Tikkunei Zohar*, Introd., 146, ed. R. Margulies).

In a 14th-century kabbalistic manuscript Psalm 67 is interpreted as signifying the *menorah* and the counting of the *Omer* (Vatican Ms. no. 214). A reproduction of the text of the psalm in the form of a *menorah* has since become widespread among Oriental Jews and appears both in prayer books and in the form of amulets on walls in homes and, especially, synagogues.

[Efraim Gottlieb]

THE MENORAH IN ART

After the destruction of the Temple the *menorah* became "the most important Jewish pictorial motif, and from an implement it became an emblem." Out of 1,207 reproductions in the third volume of Goodenough's standard work, *Jewish Symbolism in the Greco-Roman World* (see bibliography), no less than 182 are representations of the *menorah*. This number has considerably increased through later findings. Here only a short review of the various kinds of archaeological remnants together with the most important examples can be given (the numbers refer to Goodenough).

Synagogues

ACTUAL MENORAH. Upper part of brass menorah from En-Gedi (Barag-Porat, in Qadmoniot 3, 1970, 97–100, back-cover; see below).

STONE FRAGMENTS AND CAPITALS. Stone screen from Ashkelon (575, 576), from El Ḥamma (629), stones from Eshtemoa and Naveh (615, 618); Capitals in Capernaum (478), Beit Jibrin (542), and Caesarea (997, 998); on a column in Gaza mosque Djami-el-Kebir (584); and on stones in Pergamon (877), Priene (878), and Ostia.

MOSAIC FLOORS. In Beth Alpha (639); Hammath-Tiberias (in both these and many others are two *menorot* right and left of the Ark); and Maon (Nirim, see above; the Nirim *menorah* is reproduced on the Israel 50 lira banknote).

PAINTINGS. The only preserved example is in Dura-Europos, and it is a conical base with three feet near Ark (602). It appears twice in narrative paintings: Aaron in the Temple (Goodenough vol. 11, color-plate x), and Moses giving water to the tribes (color-plate XII).

On Tombs

SCULPTURES. In Bet She'arim, a menorah on the head of a warrior (56).

ON DOORS OF TOMBS. Ibelin: YMHEY 17 (1953), nos. 3 and 4; Kefar Yassif (44); Kefar Tamra, near Shefar Am (Haifa Municipal Museum), which shows the *menorah* on the top of a date tree.

FRESCO AND SARCOPHAGUS IN THE TORLONIA CATACOMB, ROME (817, 818). In the catacombs the *menorah* is often the only indication of Jewishness.

SARCOPHAGI IN VIGNA RANDANINI CATACOMB, ROME (789). Now in the Museo di Terme, the *menorah* is in a medallion, borne by two winged Victorias; on gentile sarcophagi such medallions show the head of the buried person or a Medusa. Here the *menorah* is the distinctive emblem of Judaism on an artifact common to other religions as well.

LEAD SARCOPHAGI IN THE ISRAEL MUSEUM, JERUSALEM. The same type as made for pagans, Christians, and Jews. On the Jewish sarcophagi (from Bet She'arim) *menorot* – in contradistinction to the ornaments – are pressed on the three sarcophagi (see bibl. Katz reproductions nos. 104, 120).

TOMBSTONES. Frequently in catacombs (e.g. Randanini and Monteverde in Rome: 33 example in Goodenough).

OSSUARIES. Ossuaries (rare): *menorah* (220, not certain): Ḥanukkah lamp (198).

Varia

GLASS-BOTTLES. Glass-Bottles: 391, 411, 424, 428, 961.

GOLD-GLASSES. From catacombs (963–974), with peculiar techniques: between two layers of glass is the golden design (mostly ritual objects, Ark, lions).

LAMPS. Bronze. K. Katz, *From the Beginning*, pl. 109, p. 126: Reifenberg Collection, now on loan to Israel Museum; ceramic lamps: with various numbers of holders for oil lamps, but very frequently with a *menorah* design (more than 40 reproductions in Goodenough).

AMULETS, SEALS, RINGS, CORNELIANS. On these small artifacts too, the *menorah* is the most frequent symbol indicating the Jewishness of the owner (1012–1027). A good example is a glass amulet (third–sixth centuries) showing a *menorah* among other ritualia (Hechal Shlomo Museum).

The Middle Ages

Representations of the *menorah* are found frequently in medieval manuscripts, Jewish and Christian, of both Spanish and Franco-German origin, depicted alongside other Temple vessels. Earlier even, and of particular importance in this context, is the one in the *Codex Amiatinus* (Italy, c. 500, see bibl. H. Strauss and P. Bloch), which no doubt still reflects an older, classical-Oriental tradition (cf. Strauss, in *Ereẓ Yisrael*, 6, 1960, 126/7; Roth, *Warburg-Courtauld 16*, 1953, 37–38). B. Narkiss, *Hebrew Illuminated Manuscripts* (1969), reproduces (and describes in detail) five medieval manuscripts with *menorah* representations: Plate 1: Bible (Leningrad), probably from Egypt (Introduction, 23); Plate 6: Cervera Bible (Portugal, *ibid.*, and note 53); Plate 16: Farḥi Bible (Spain-Provence, Introduction, 23); Plate 23: British Museum (11639, Franco-German, *ibid.*, 28, note 95); and Plate 24: Pentateuch (French, *ibid.*, 26; note 96). In the British Museum plate, Aaron is twice depicted lighting the *menorah* (*ibid.*, 114a and 122b), the differences in style suggesting two artists. The frequency of this representation may be connected with the fact that it is based on Numbers 8:2–3 and with its ample treatment by the Midrash. All five examples reflect faithfully and impressively their local background: the first three, the influence of the iconoclastic Islamic art, including the playful one of the *Reconquista* in no. 2: the burning lights turned toward the center and the variant of the oil flowing in the same direction; while the last two show the influence of the late Gothic French environment with their wealth of figures and drolleries. Numerous seven-branched candelabra may also be found in medieval French, German, and Italian churches.

A hitherto unpublished *menorah* with its appurtenances (Ex. 25, 38) painted in gold and color, is contained in a Spanish 14th-century Bible-manuscript on parchment, which was shown in an exhibition of the Jewish National and University Library (Jerusalem April–May 1970, Catalogue No. 6). This *menorah* has three feet with rather rare knobs (as in the recently excavated piece of plaster from the Old City of Jerusalem, see above), and snuff dishes like goblets with coats of arms: the tongs hang from the outer branches of the candelabrum and are shown in perspective before and behind the branches. It is apparently the work of an artist of the late Middle Ages, already accustomed to perspective. It frequently appears as an emblem also on book plates showing *Ḥanukkah lamps, printers' marks, and community seals.

Modern Times

In modern times the *menorah* has continued to be used as a religious symbol, particularly in synagogue art: wall-paintings, stained glass windows, mosaics, and – in spite of the talmudic prohibition (see below) – as a seven-branched metal candelabrum. In imitation of the ancient mosaics, some synagogues place a *menorah* to the right and the left of the Ark. The *menorah* representations in modern American synagogues reveal the problem of expressing ancient symbols in terms of modern art. In many cases little is left of the original tree-and-branches motive, but in some this has been preserved, in spite of modern simplicity. Independently of the synagogue, Benno *Elkan created several tree-shaped bronze *menorot*, of which one stands in Westminster Abbey, London, and another in the vicinity of the Knesset building in Jerusalem. Marc *Chagall incorporated a lighted *menorah* and olive leaves (Deut. 33:24) in his Tribe of Asher window (Hadassah Synagogue, Jerusalem). The Warsaw Ghetto memorial (1963) embodies two outsize *menorot* flanked by lions. The U.S. Jewish artist Ben *Shahn, who is responsible for the mosaic in the Ohev Shalom synagogue in Nashville, Tenn. (Kampf, *ibid.*, 134–6), has produced as its sketch a *menorah* (with *shofar*) in tempera (Ben Shahn, 1966, no. 116) and another one as the colored frontispiece of a Passover *Haggadah* illustrated by him (1965). Jankel *Adler has a *menorah* – together with several ritualia – in his "Jewish Still-Life" painted in the 1930s. In literature Stefan *Zweig devoted his short story *Der begrabene Leuchter* ("The Buried Candelabrum; 1937) to the saga of the *menorah*. The Arch of Titus *menorah* was adopted as the official symbol of the State of Israel, expressing the idea of Judaea Resurrecta, 2,000 years after the last Hasmonean prince had used the same symbol on his coins.

According to the Talmud it was forbidden to make an exact copy of the seven-branched candelabrum (RH 24b; Av. Zar. 43b; Men. 28b), and this prohibition is largely observed to the present day. On the other hand, the discovery of the upper part of a small bronze *menorah* during the excavations of a synagogue of the Byzantine period at En-Gedi (see above) shows that this prohibition was not always observed. It is possible that the bar of brass connecting the seven branches on their upper end which is also found in mosaic, stone-and-oil-lamp-representations of the same time (Bet Alfa, Ashkelon, oil lamp from Syria: Good-enough 3, p. 941) may have invalidated the above prohibition. J. Gutmann suggests that since the prohibition is found in a *baraita* in the Babylonian Talmud only, it was not accepted in Palestine. Gregorovius reports (*History of the City of Rome…* 2, 2, 3) that in the time of King Theodoric (c. 500) the Jews of Rome used to assemble in their synagogue on Sabbaths and festivals to the light of a gilded seven-branched candelabrum. The Ḥanukkah lamp, having eight branches, did not violate the talmudic law.

[Heinrich Strauss]

BIBLIOGRAPHY: A.R.S. Kennedy, in: *Hastings Dictionary of the Bible*, 4 (1914), 663–4; K. Galling, in: ZDPV, 46 (1923), 23–29; Galling, Reallexikon, 348–9; Gressman, Bilder, 134. fig. 467; E. Cohn-Wiener, *Die juedische Kunst* (1929), 73–75; M. Kon, in: PEQ, 82 (1950), 25–30; G. Widengren, *The King and the Tree of Life in Ancient Near Eastern Religion* (1951), 64–67; S.R. Driver, *Exodus* (1953, Cambridge), 275–8; Goodenough, 4 (1954), 71–98; Y. Herzog, in: *Sinai*, 36 (1955); M. Dothan, in: IEJ, 6 (1956), 19; Ḥ. Albeck, *Seder Kodashim* (1957), 427, 429; W. Eltester, *New Testament Studies*, 3 (1957), 102–4; Y. Levi, *Olamot Nifgashim* (1960), 255–8; E. Peterson, *Judentum und Gnosis* (1959), 31ff.; W. Wirgin, in: IEJ, 11 (1961), 151–3; M. Haran, in: *Scripta Hierosolymitana*, 8 (1961), 277–8; idem, in: IEJ, 13 (1963), 54–55, 57; A. Negev, in *Eretz-Israel*, 8 (1967), 193–210; L. Yarden, *Tree of Light* (1971). IN KABBALAH: I. Weinstock, *Be-Ma'gelei ha-Nigleh ve-ha-Nistar* (1970), index; G. Scholem, *Ursprung und Anfaenge der Kabbala* (1962), 348; idem, in: *Judaica*, 19 (1963), 97–98; *Lu'aḥ ha-Areẓ 5708* (1947–48). IN ART: K. Katz et al. (eds.), *From the Beginning* (1968); P. Bloch, in: *Wallraf-Richartz Jahrbuch*, 23 (1961), 55–190; idem, in: *Monumenta Judaica* (1963), 21–25 and plates 76–88, 97, 100, 102; C. Roth, in: PEQ, 87 (1955), 151–64; H. Strauss, in: *Warburg and Courtauld Institute Journal…*, 12 (1959), 6–16; idem, in: *Muenster am Hellweg*, 15 (1962), no. 4, 60–63; S.S. Kayser and G. Schoenberger (eds.), *Jewish Ceremonial Art* (19592), 14–15, 120ff.; D. Sperber, in: JJS, 16 (1966), 135–59; J, Gutmann, in: ZNTW, 60 (1969), 289–91; M. Simon, *Recherches d'histoire judéo-chrétienne* (1962); A. Kampf, *Contemporary Synagogue Art* (1966), index; Roth, Art, index; J. Zwarts, *De zevenarmige Kandelaar* (1935); Schuerer, Gesch 1 (1901), 636–7; 2 (1898), 342–4; 3 (1898), 717. **ADD. BIBLIOGRAPHY:** J. Guttman, "A Note on the Temple Menorah," in: J. Guttman (ed.), *No Graven Images. Studies in Art and the Hebrew Bible*. (1971), 36–38; V.A. Klagsbald, "The Menorah as Symbol: Its Meaning and Origin in Early Jewish Art," in: *Jewish Art*, 12–13 (1986–87), 126–34; L.Y. Rahmani, "Representations of the Menorah on Ossuaries," in: H. Geva (ed.), *Ancient Jerusalem Revealed* (1994), 239–43; A. Amar, "The Menorah of Zechariah's Vision: Olive Trees and Grapevines," in: B. Kűhnel (ed.), *The Real and Ideal Jerusalem in Jewish, Christian and Islamic Art: Studies in Honor of Bezalel Narkiss…* (1998), 79–88; Y. Yisraeli (ed.), *In the Light of the Menorah: Story of a Symbol* (1998); L.I. Levine, "The History and Significance of the Menorah in Antiquity," in: L.I. Levine and Z. Weiss (eds.), *From Dura to Sepphoris: Studies in Jewish Art and Society in Late Antiquity* (2000), 131–53; R. Hachlili, *The Menorah, the Ancient Seven-Armed Candelabrum. Origin, Form and Significance* (2001): L. Habas, "An Incised Depiction of the Temple Menorah and Other Cult Objects of the Second Temple Period," in: H. Geva (ed.), *Jewish Quarter Excavations in the Old City of Jerusalem*, vol. 2 (2003), 329–42.

MENORAH (Illustrated Monthly for the Jewish Home), a German-language family journal for science, art, and literature, founded in Vienna in July 1923 by Paul J. Diamant. In his preface, Diamant defined the paper's aims "in the first place to advance the efforts directed towards bridging the various, often conflicting tendencies within Jewry, hoping, on a cultural basis, to bring about the necessary harmony. We intend carefully to cherish the spiritual and artistic traditions, to look back to those times when Judaism was deeply rooted in genuine soil, unsophisticated by sickly questionings. We intend to cooperate – a lofty aspiration – in creating a homogeneous Jewish cultural atmosphere." As a liberal-conservative Jewish paper, *Menorah* was primarily directed towards acculturated and educated bourgeois circles, including women and the younger generation, presenting the Jewish family as "the bulwark and prop of Judaism" at all times. While the journal sought to publish articles on all aspects of Jewish life (its main interest, however, lay in fields of Jewish religion and East European Jewish culture), it consistently maintained a high level of scholarship and of literary and artistic quality. Though "not tied to any party," *Menorah* tended to support the Zionist *Revisionist movement and published articles by its leader, Vladimir *Jabotinsky. During the first year, some contributions even appeared in Hebrew and in English, thus facilitating the paper's intended circulation throughout Western and Eastern Europe, the United States, and Palestine. However, the periodical does not seem to have been widely read.

In July 1924, *Menorah* passed into the hands of Norbert Hoffmann. He reorganized the paper, dropped its English subtitle (the Hebrew was kept until December 1925), and appointed new permanent staff members such as Nathan Birnbaum (Hamburg), Friedrich Matzner, and Robert Weiss (Vienna), Hoffmann's wife, Fine, the composer Rudolf *Réti, the chess champion Richard *Réti, and W. Loewinger. Moreover, from July 1924, *Menorah* was jointly edited in Vienna and Frankfurt/Main, and from Oct. 1928 in Vienna and Berlin, then mostly as double issues every two months (until January 1929 together with the publisher Abraham *Horodisch). From January 1926, *Menorah* was reduced in size and its German subtitle "Illustrierte Monatsschrift fuer die juedische Familie" changed to "Juedisches Familienblatt fuer Wissenschaft / Kunst und Literatur." Frequently, artwork was included or special editions issued, such as on the Jews in Vienna (March 1926) and Silesia (May 1926), on Jewish hygiene (June/July 1926) and folklore (Oct. 1926), on the Jews in Poland (June/July 1927), on the artist Max *Liebermann (August 1927), on Mainz and the Maharil (December 1927), on the Jewish section (JSOP) of the International Press Exhibition "Pressa" in Cologne (June/July 1928), or on the Jews in Bavaria (Nov./Dec. 1928). In December 1932, *Menorah* ceased publication. Norbert Hoffmann, together with his wife, immigrated to Palestine in 1938. He died in 1977.

BIBLIOGRAPHY: S. Federbush (ed.), *Ḥokhmat Yisrael be-Ma'arav Eropah*, 2 (1963), 403–6; I. Gartner, "Menorah. Juedisches Familienblatt fuer Wissenschaft / Kunst und Literatur (1923–1932), Geschichte einer Wiener Zeitschrift – mit einer deskriptiv-analytischen Bibliographie" (Ph.D. dissertation, Innsbruck University, 1997).

[Johannes Valentin Schwarz (2nd ed.)]

MENORAH ASSOCIATION AND MENORAH JOURNAL, U.S. Jewish campus organization and periodical. Both grew out of the Harvard Menorah Society, a Jewish campus group formed in 1906 by Henry *Hurwitz, at the time an undergraduate at the university. Influenced by the "new humanism" then being propounded in Cambridge by such figures as William James and George Santayana, the society sought to pursue the study of humanistic values in Judaism and to develop a positive intellectual relationship to Jewish tradition and belief. Similar groups soon formed on other American campuses, and in 1913 an intercollegiate Menorah Association was established which eventually numbered some 80 chapters. The association became largely defunct in the 1930s, but as the first attempt to establish an intercollegiate Jewish body of its kind it helped pave the way for such later organizations as the *B'nai B'rith Hillel societies.

The *Menorah Journal*, first published in 1915, was similarly dedicated to the promotion of a "Jewish humanism." Appearing bimonthly from 1915 through 1927, monthly from 1928 to 1930, and irregularly thereafter until 1962 for a total of 157 issues in all, it featured articles and fiction by leading Jewish scholars, intellectuals, and writers, and reproductions of contemporary Jewish art. It served for several decades as a center for lively controversy in American Jewish life. The *Journal* lost much of its prominence in the years after World War II, but like the Menorah Association, it was in many ways the prototype of the successors that displaced it.

BIBLIOGRAPHY: L.W. Schwartz (ed.), *The Menorah Treasury* (1964); H.M. Kallen, in: *Menorah Journal*, 49 (1962), 9–16; R. Alter, in: *Commentary*, 39:5 (1965), 51–55.

[Hillel Halkin]

MENTAL ILLNESS. Man has been subject to mental illness from the earliest known times. The Bible makes frequent reference to it among Jews, and describes recognizable types of mental disturbances. The reference in Leviticus 20:27, "A man also or a woman that divineth by a ghost or a familiar spirit…," apparently included the mentally ill and, almost definitely, people subject to hysterical conditions. In Saul's personality, a brooding homicidal paranoia was overlaid by suicidal depression. Some of the prophets seem to have experienced states of ecstasy, and there are indications of neuroses among them.

The legal tenets of the Talmud regarding mental illness indicate the existence of conditions ranging from grave types of psychoses to those which develop out of physical states. The writings of the noted Jewish physicians of the medieval period, which were generally based on their practice among Jewish patients, reveal that mental illnesses were frequently encountered. They included melancholia, mania, and other serious psychotic states, states of anxiety, and psychosomatic conditions. The "wonder" cures of the 18th-century folk healers (*ba'alei shem*) provide evidence of the hysterical nature of the emotional disturbances they treated. In dealing with possession by a dybbuk, which was of the same nature, they were carrying on the practice of the Kabbalists in Safed, in Ereẓ Israel.

Toward the end of the 19th century mental disturbances were clearly classified into two major categories. The first is psychosis, where there is profound disturbance of perception (e.g., hallucination), thought (e.g., delusion), and mood (e.g., depression), and accompanying vagaries of behavior, but the patient does not understand that he is disturbed. The second category is neurosis (and deviations of personality), where the disturbance is less profound and the individual retains his perception of reality and knows that he is disturbed, but suffers from worry and guilt, or anxiety, or medically unexplained physical symptoms. Psychotic, neurotic, and "normal" personalities shade imperceptibly into each other and have more in common than appears from these categories. Thus agreement about diagnosis is not constant. Theories of the causes of mental illness fall into three main groups: physical (including genetic); psychological (which has to do with the control of instinct and the personal development of the child within the family); and social (which has to do with the effect of general social influence or stresses and deprivations). Modern theory seeks an explanation for many cases in a varying combination of all three factors.

In the study of mental illness, the analysis of large numbers by statistical methods (epidemiology), and comparison between groups, may provide clues to understanding its nature and causation and the mental health situation and needs of a particular group. The most important epidemiological method is the comparison of the incidence (frequency) of new cases. Incidence is measured as a rate: the number of new cases occurring per year in a given number of the population. In this article, incidence and all other rates are noted per 100,000 of the population concerned. A rough but fairly reliable incidence may be determined by calculating the rate of new cases hospitalized per year. More reliable information is obtained by noting all the cases which appear at both mental hospitals and clinics. Prevalence of illness refers to all the cases – old and new – that exist at any given moment, either in an institution or at home. Prevalence is obtained by a total survey of the community.

Knowledge about mental illness among Jews at the present time is confined mainly to those in the United States and Israel, since by and large it is only in these countries that specific reference to Jews is made in hospital statistics. In Israel, statistics of mental illness are provided by the Mental Health Services of the Ministry of Health. The statistics available on the rates of mental disturbances among Jews and other significant observations about them through 1970 are presented here under three headings: psychoses; neuroses; and other indicators of mental ill health.

Psychoses

DEPRESSION. Depression (manic-depressive, affective psychosis – including involutional melancholia in the aging) is a relatively significant mental illness among Jews. The U.S. statistics of the 1920s for manic-depressive and involutional illnesses from hospitals in New York City, Illinois, and Massachusetts, showed Jews to have had slightly lower first-admission rates than non-Jews (including blacks). However, the painstaking work of Benjamin *Malzberg reveals that in 1949–51, Jews in New York State had a notably higher rate of first admission to private and public hospitals than white non-Jews (27 *v.* 15). These rates are crude, i.e., per 100,000 of the total population of all ages. The crude rate for Jews in Israel in 1958 was about the same (24) as for New York Jews. However, Jews in Israel born in Central and Eastern Europe had in 1958 twice the rates (50, 46) as for New York Jews of the same origin and descent. As usual, the rate is about twice as high in women as in men. On the other hand, in Israel in 1958, Asian-African-born Jews showed only half the rate of European-born Jews and Israel-born Jews even less. The Oriental-born rates were somewhat lower than that for New York Jews and probably only of a slightly higher order than for white non-Jews in New York. Israel-born Jews seem to have had the lowest rates of all these groups, despite the higher proportion among them of those of European rather than Oriental descent.

The Israel rates of first admission for psychotic depressive conditions in 1966 seem to bear out all these conclusions and show that (1) European-born Jews in Israel have a notably higher rate (45) than their non-Jewish European counterparts (Sweden: 21); (2) Asian-African-born Jews in Israel have a markedly lower hospital rate (23) than those born in Europe, lower than the known rate for Jews in New York, and resembling that for European non-Jews; (3) Israel-born Jews of both European and Afro-Asian descent show an even lower rate (16) than the Afro-Asian-born and, *a fortiori*, a lower rate than European-born immigrants. Israel-born Jews have a lower rate than those known for Jews and even non-Jews in New York State. Israel-born Jews in 1966 had a clearly lower crude rate than Swedes (1964) and New Zealanders (1967), the ratio being 6:21:27. The rate for Israel-born over the age of 15 was only 17. The age-specific rate for the population over 15 is a finer measure than the crude rate, since mental illness usually manifests itself after that age. To these conclusions must be added Malzberg's proof of the higher incidence of depressive psychosis in New York State among Jews of European birth and descent than among non-Jews.

The hypothetical reasons for the higher incidence of depressive psychoses in Jews of European birth in Israel and those of European birth and descent in the U.S. may well include the family and social tensions accompanying their profound, achievement-oriented ethical system. This has been incorporated in their personality as a sense of individual conscience and responsibility, the control of aggression, and sobriety. This psychosocial system does not allow for easy solutions and the camouflage of problems by the use of alcohol and other reality-denying behaviors. Furthermore, it is known that closed Orthodox societies in the West tend to produce more depression. The very high incidence of depression among European-born Jews in Israel is undoubtedly the result of persecution and concentration-camp experiences, underlain by tendency to depression and exacerbated by migrational upheavals.

The hypothesis that there is a hereditary element in the Jewish tendency to depression is probably not tenable in the light of the moderate rate among Asian-African-born Jews. The apparent generational change manifested as a lower incidence of this psychosis in Israel-born Jews also argues against genetic causes. The speculation that the higher incidence is the result of the known readiness of Jews to seek psychiatric help cannot hold much water. The high rates for European-born Jews as compared to Asian-African-born Jews in Israel, where all psychotics have an almost equal chance of hospitalization, rule out that factor. It is certain, therefore, that European Jews have a higher rate of psychotic depression than non-Jews. Research in Israel has proved that Jewish women, like all women, have a depression rate about 100 percent higher than men. In 1966, the rate for Israel-born women (27), because of the particularly low rate for Israel-born men (7), was four times as high as for men.

SCHIZOPHRENIA. This form of insanity is characterized by profound disturbances such as hallucinations, delusions, and social withdrawal. In this universally found psychosis, the crude rates of first hospitalizations were approximately the same for Israel Jews in 1958 (39) as those given by Malzberg for New York Jews in 1949–51 (36). However, closer examination reveals marked differences in the Israel Jewish population. In 1958, Asian-African-born immigrants of 15-plus showed a considerably higher incidence of first admissions for schizophrenia (57–80) than Central-European-born (44) and East-European-born (34), Israel-born (81) had the highest incidence. Among the Asian-African-born, Yemenite immigrants had the lowest rate and Turkish the highest.

The high rate of schizophrenia in the Israel born is difficult to explain and may have something to do with the intergenerational adjustment between them and their foreign-born parents, and with the pressures of mass immigration. However, in 1966 the Israel-born rate in the population over the age of 15, while it had declined, was still the highest (67). In that year the incidence in the Asian-African-born had fallen to 51, indicating that their former high rates were due to transient stresses of immigration and sociocultural change. In 1966 the Asian-African rates were only slightly higher than the European-American, and definitely lower than the Israel-born ones. The total European-American-born crude rate in Israel in 1966 stood at 45, which is about the same as the European-born rate for 1958, but appreciably higher than the earlier-known rate for New York Jews. In every case the schizophrenic rate in Israel Jews still appears to be higher than earlier rates for non-Jews. The general urban crude rate in the U.S. in 1929–31 was 27. In New York in 1949–51 it was 32 for non-Jews. In New Zealand in 1963–67 the general crude rate was 21, while the figures for Jews in Israel in 1958 and 1966 were 39 and 37, and higher if "psychotic episodes" are included. In Israel, among the Asian-African-born the male rate predominates, while among the European-American-born the female rate is in excess of the male.

PARANOIA. This generally rather firm diagnostic category has often been said to be more common in Jews than in non-Jews. Malzberg's work in New York did not bear this out. However, in Israel in 1958, higher first admission rates were diagnosed among European-born Jews (10) and among the Asian-African-born (8–20). The latter was probably a reaction to migration and change, and not always true paranoia. The Israel-born had the same rate in 1958 as Jews and white non-Jews in New York (0.7). In New Zealand in 1967 the rate was 1.0. More recent information indicates no abatement, but rather an increase, in the rates of paranoia diagnosed and treated among the foreign-born Israelis. It was especially marked in women of European-American origin (21 for the 15-plus age group).

It should be noted that among Jews in Israel in 1966 the incidence of all psychoses of a functional, or non-organic nature (schizophrenic, effective, psychotic episode, paranoiac) was approximately the same for the Israel and Asian-African-born (107 and 100 respectively for the 15-plus) and for European-American-born (121). As elsewhere, foreign-born immigrants in Israel in the 15-plus group have higher total rates of first admission to hospital than the native-born, but the differences are not very significant (1966: Israel 188, Asian-Africa 218, European-American 226).

Malzberg showed that Jews have about the same total rate of first admissions as white non-Jews. The Israel rate was later discovered to be about 12 per cent higher than both. In the Midtown Manhattan study, *Mental Health in the Metropolis* (1962), Leo Srole and Thomas Langner found that Jews showed a far higher prevalence of all treated disorders than Protestants and Catholics, but for cases normally treated in hospital approximately the same rate as Protestants and less than Catholics. Jews generally had the lowest rate for serious impairment of mental health. Because Jews were found less frequently in the lower socioeconomic strata, their seriously impaired rates were lower. This leads to the conclusion that the rate of the more severe conditions for which treatment was sought in the U.S. was not greater among Jews than among non-Jews. In Israel, European-American-born Jews had a definitely higher rate for all psychoses (including organic conditions) than Jews of other origins.

Neuroses and Allied Conditions

The available hospital statistics in New York City (Bellevue Hospital, 1938) and in New York State (Malzberg's study, 1949–51) indicate a higher rate of neuroses in Jews than in non-Jews. A higher rate of neuroses for Jews was reported among military selectees in Boston in 1941–42. The rate for first admissions to Illinois State mental hospitals, however, was lower for Jews.

Leo Srole notes that in the early 1950s the prevalence rate of treated neuroses for Jews was twice that of Catholics and Protestants. In the Manhattan study, Jews also yielded considerably higher patient rates for disorders usually treated in an ambulatory facility. While in the community survey they showed the lowest seriously impaired rate, their mental health was generally not as satisfactory as that of Catholics and Protestants, from which it is to be concluded that neurosis rates in New York are higher among Jews than among non-Jews.

In Israel in 1958 Jews had a hospital first admission rate which was definitely higher for neuroses than Jews in New York (1949–51, 21 *v.* 12). Furthermore, the Asian-African-born had generally twice the rate (15-plus) of the European- and Israel-born. The highest rate (65) was among those born in Iran, who had particular adjustment problems and also showed an apparently greater tendency to paranoid reactions. In 1966 the general Israel rate for neuroses was even higher than in 1958 (30), but the two groups of immigrants had approximately the same rate (±40). This is accounted for by the steep rise in the first admission rate for neurosis among European immigrants and some subsidence in the rate among Oriental immigrants.

Concentration-camp survivors, while generally known to have made a good social adjustment in Israel, were in a large proportion of cases deeply affected by the trauma they had suffered. Their emotional reactions often included anxiety, depression, and difficulty in reestablishing relations. Kibbutz-born Israelis appear to have the usual emotional disturbances, and in average proportions. They do not, however, manifest homosexuality or delinquency.

For personality (character, behavior disorders), Malzberg's study of hospitalization showed a crude rate slightly less for Jews in New York (1.5) than for white non-Jews. Israel Jews in 1958 showed a very much higher hospital incidence rate. The Asian-African-born in Israel showed remarkably high rates in the population over the age of 15 (36–48), as did the Israel-born (50), when compared to the European-born (15–25). This accords with their rates for schizophrenia, and like these they decreased in 1966 (Asian-African-born 25, Israel-born 23). This indicates that these reactions were the product of immigration and social upset and that they were reduced after social adaptation. In 1958 and 1966 the rates for personality disorders among the European-American-born were the lowest in Israel (9).

Other Indicators of Mental Ill Health

ALCOHOLISM. Jews are traditionally known for their sobriety. In the 1920s their rate for arrests for drunkenness in Warsaw was 30 *v.* 1,920 for Christians. In 1925 the rate of admission to public and private mental hospitals in New York City was 0.1 for Jews and 5.9 for non-Jews. A similar picture held in Massachusetts and Illinois State hospitals. In the Boston examination of military selectees, Jews had the lowest incidence of alcoholic psychosis of all ethnic groups. Malzberg found only two cases during a three-year period (1950–52) in Canada, where the Jewish population was 240,000. He also states that he found an intemperate employment of alcohol in 2.2 percent of Jewish first admissions in New York as against 18 percent of non-Jewish first admissions. In the New Haven psychiatric census of 1950, no alcoholic Jews were found among the patients at any treatment site.

In a census in Israel in 1964 analyzing cases found in mental hospitals, only 21 (0.3 percent) presented alcoholic problems. In 1966, however, a total of 152 alcoholic cases were admitted to the hospital (2 percent of all cases admitted). This was the total crude rate of 6.6 (for men 12.5), which resembles the earlier rates for non-Jews in the U.S. (urban total rate 7, males 12). However, this rate constituted about one in ten of which only four were Israel-born; 26 were from Europe-America (rate 3) and 44 from Asia-Africa (rate 7). It is evident, therefore that alcoholism in Israel is a problem relating almost entirely to male immigrants, especially those from Asia and Africa. However, social changes in the country and the growing consumption of alcohol may conceivably increase its incidence, in spite of the intense social cohesion in Israel.

It is possible that a part of the real incidence of neurosis and depression in many non-Jewish populations is masked by or expressed through alcoholic overindulgence. In Jews it may well be that emotional difficulty is expressed through neurosis and depression rather than through the escape into and physical self-destruction of alcoholism (see *Drunkenness).

DRUG ADDICTION. Drug addiction is relatively speaking not new or uncommon among Jews in Israel. In 1966 and 1967 91 Jews with a primary diagnosis of addiction were admitted to hospital for treatment. Thirty-two of these cases were admitted for the first time (23 males, 9 females). They were composed equally of immigrants from Europe-America and Afro-Asia, with only five or six Israel-born. In 1970 there were probably somewhat more than 400 hard-core addicts in Israel. Drug addiction is known to be associated in the underworld with criminality and with pimping and prostitution, but a few of the cases were related to medical treatment. The New Haven study of 1950 revealed no drug addicts among Jews. A comparison of half-year figures for 1966 with 1970 shows a rise of first admissions related to drugs (from 20 to 39) with an especial increase of the number of younger Israel-born Jews. In 1970, despite the absence of statistical study, the abuse of drugs was known to have spread to groups of Jewish youth in the U.S. A few who visited Israel after the Six-Day War required treatment. Some of the older immigrants to Israel from North Africa and the Middle East had been in the habit of smoking marijuana, but it became much less evident among them in Israel and was not used by their children except among delinquents and small marginal groups. Following the Six-Day War, with the occupation of the West Bank and the flood of volunteers and students from North America, the use of marijuana increased in marginal groups. The occasional and apparently temporary use of a small amount of marijuana even appeared among groups of pupils at secondary schools.

Suicide

Emile *Durkheim demonstrated at the end of the 19th century that Jews had a lower suicide rate than Protestants and Catholics. It was estimated that in 1925 the suicide rate for Jews in New York was ten as compared to a similar general average yearly rate for the period 1950–59 in the U.S., a rate of three in Ireland, and one of 23 in Denmark. In Israel in 1952–58 the general rate was ten (and 15 for the population above 15 years of age in 1949–59). While the suicide rate in Israel represents a mid-point between extremes in other nations, it has special characteristics. The female rate relative to the male rate is unusually high. In European countries males usually have a suicide rate three or four times that of females. In Israel in the years 1949–59, female rates were never less than half that of males and in two of those years equaled that of males. This has been explained as a result of the social equality and shared burdens of the sexes in Israel. A slackening of religious Orthodoxy may be a factor, but high female ratios are not found in other egalitarian societies. It is more probably a result of the high incidence of depression, especially among older Western women in Israel. Since 1949 at least 70 percent of female suicides have occurred in women over the age of 31, which is also the age associated with the onset of depression.

The high ratio of suicides in women as compared to men among Jews in Europe can be seen from a report by Arthur *Ruppin in 1940. Of the suicides of Jews in Warsaw between 1927 and 1932, 49.4 percent were women. Ruppin ascribes this to the difficult psychological situation of Jewish girls who, in the secular environment of the Polish capital, had lost touch with their Orthodox parents. Another striking fact is the very low suicide rate in Israel among the Asian-African- and Israel-born. However, attempted suicide is becoming more frequent among young women from Oriental homes in Israel. This is probably related to the psychological conflict described by Ruppin, who ascribes rising rates of suicide among Jews generally to growing secularity. Where Durkheim quotes a rate of 18 for Jews in Prussia in 1890, Ruppin gives a rate of 50 for 1926. Since 1956 the suicide rate in Israel has gradually declined. In 1964 it was 12 for the population above the age of 15, while the rate for the general population was 7.6. This decrease may also be related to the general readaptation which followed the absorption of the mass immigration of the early 1950s.

Criminality and Delinquency

While no statistics exist, criminality was known to be rare among Jewish communities in the Diaspora and has generally been so in Ereẓ Israel as well. However, delinquency has been found, especially among the less privileged Oriental, near-slum groups in Israel's cities. Striking evidence of the stress which followed the mass immigration is seen in the high rates of crimes of violence (murder, attempted murder, and manslaughter) and causing death by negligence from 1949 until about 1956–57. The rate for murder dropped from 45 in 1949 to one in 1962. The total rate of these crimes of violence decreased from 20 in 1950 to five in 1960. This again indicates adaptation after the tensions caused by mass immigration (but see below).

The percentage of juvenile delinquency rose from 0.7 in 1949 to 1.0 in 1957. The proportion was higher for Oriental groups. In 1957 children of all groups of immigrants constituted 69 percent of the delinquents. Delinquency and criminality are not encountered among kibbutz-born children. The incidence of juvenile delinquency among Oriental groups indicates problems which at times arise out of cultural and social changes in their families. On the other hand, the palpable increase in delinquency among children from a "good" socioeconomic background highlights the difficulties being encountered by some developed city families in the modern, technologically advanced society of Israel.

[Louis Miller]

Later Figures

At the end of 2002, 5,439 psychiatric patients were occupying hospital beds in Israel and during the year around 58,000 outpatients had been treated in government clinics. Hospitalization resulting from drug and alcohol abuse reached 19,528. In this regard the estimate of 400 addicts in the country in 1970 cited above, reflecting even then the gradual introduction of drugs into the country after the Six-Day War, underscores the extent to which Israel in the early 21st century had evolved a drug and alcohol culture. Hundreds of thousands can be said to be users of illegal drugs of one kind or another. Similarly the sharp rise in criminality and delinquency (see *Crime) are further indications of Israel's new realities.

BIBLIOGRAPHY: L. Miller, in: N. Petrilowitsch (ed.), *Contributions to Comparative Psychiatry* (1967), 96–137; idem, in: A. Jarus et al. (eds.), *The Child and the Family in Israel* (1970); B. Malzberg, *Mental Health of Jews in New York State, 1949–1957* (1963); L. Srole and Th. Langner, in: *Mental Health in the Metropolis*, 1 (1962), 300–24; M. Mandel, J. Gampel, and L. Miller, *Admission to Mental Hospital in Israel – 1966* (1971); L. Eitinger, *Concentration Camp Survivors in Norway and Israel* (1964). **WEBSITE:** www.health.gov.il.

MENUHIN, HEPHZIBAH (1920–1981), pianist. Born in San Francisco, Menuhin began to study piano at an early age, giving her first recital in 1928. She continued her studies in Paris with Marcel Ciampi. There, in 1934 she made her debut with her brother Yehudi *Menuhin, thus starting a long partnership in sonata recitals. She toured widely as a recitalist in most of the major cities of Europe and America, visiting Israel with her brother in 1950. Her playing had a clean, clear approach abjuring frills.

Among her recordings are works by Schubert, Mendelssohn, Bach, Beethoven, and Bartók. In 1938 she married and settled in Australia. In 1954 she moved to Sydney, where she gave concerts and opened her home to anyone in need. Three years later she settled in London. With her second husband, Richard Hauser, she set up the Center for Human Rights and Responsibilities. After her death, a Hephzibah Menuhin Memorial Scholarship fund for young pianists was established in conjunction with the NSW State Conservatorium of Music.

BIBLIOGRAPHY: Grove online; *Baker's Biographical Dictionary* (1997); L.M. Rolfe, *The Menuhins: A Family Odyssey* (1978); T. Palmer, *Menuhin: A Family Portrait* (1991).

[Naama Ramot (2nd ed.)]

MENUHIN, SIR YEHUDI (1916–1999), violinist and conductor. Menuhin was born in New York, the son of parents who had left Palestine to settle in the U.S. He himself spoke Hebrew in his early years. He started to learn the violin at the age of five and appeared as soloist with the San Francisco Orchestra when he was seven. He was taken to Europe in 1927, and continued his studies with Georges Enesco and with Adolf Busch. By 1929, he captivated Paris, London, and New York, and made his first gramophone records. He had played the Bach, Beethoven, and Brahms violin concertos under Bruno *Walter in Berlin, and performed 75-year old Elgar's violin concerto under the composer's baton in London and Paris. In 1935 he retired for almost two years to California. During World War II Menuhin gave an estimated 500 performances for U.S. and Allied Forces. In 1944 he was the first Allied soloist to play in liberated Paris and in 1945 he was invited to play in Moscow. He paid the first of several visits to Israel in 1950.

Menuhin had increased the scope of his musical involvement. His second career, as a conductor, was initiated with the Dallas SO in 1947 and became a regular feature of his activities. He established and directed music festivals in Switzerland (1957) and later in England (Bath and Windsor). He established a school for musically gifted children. Menuhin's admiration for Indian music prompted an important musical friendship with Ravi Shankar. He became an active member of UNESCO's International Musical Council of which he served as president. In 1970 he was awarded the Jawaharlal Nehru Prize for International Understanding. He received degrees, doctorates, and fellowships from universities around the world and state honors from 17 countries. After adopting British citizenship in 1985 he was knighted, and in 1987 he was awarded the Order of Merit. Among the many composers who wrote specially for him were Ernst *Bloch, Béla Bartók, Paul *Ben-Haim, and Sir William Walton. He published several books including the autobiography *Unfinished Journey* (1977), *Life Class of an Itinerant Violinist* (1986), and *The Violin* (1996). Yehudi Menuhin's sisters, Hephzibah *Menuhin (1920–1981) and YALTA (1921–2001), both gifted pianists, appeared with him in chamber music recitals and in concert tours.

BIBLIOGRAPHY: H.O. Spingel, *Yehudi Menuhin* (Ger., 1964). **ADD. BIBLIOGRAPHY:** Grove online; *Baker's Biographical Dictionary* (1997).

[Uri (Erich) Toeplitz / Naama Ramot (2nd ed.)]

ME'OT ḤITTIM (Heb. מְעוֹת חִטִּים; "wheat money"), collection made before *Passover to ensure a supply of flour for unleavened bread (*maẓẓot*) for the poor. Residence in a town for 12 months obliged one to contribute to or entitled one to receive communal funds known as *Kimḥa de-Fisḥa* ("flour for Passover"; TJ, BB 1:6, 12d). In medieval Europe it was customary for the communal rabbi and seven notables to draw up a list of those eligible to donate and to receive the tax, at the beginning of the month of Nisan. The custom was codified by *Isserles (OḤ 429:1). In modern times, the term has been broadened to include all the holiday needs of the poor at Passover (e.g., wine, fish, meat).

BIBLIOGRAPHY: E. Ki-Tov, *Sefer ha-Toda'ah*, 1 pt. 2 (1960), 22f.; Eisenstein, Dinim, 342.

MEPHIBOSHETH (Heb. מְפִיבֹשֶׁת), a son of Jonathan and a grandson of Saul; called Merib-Baal (מְרִיב־בַּעַל) or Meribaal (מְרִיבַעַל) in the genealogy of the house of Saul (I Chron. 8:34; 9:40) where the name is parallel to Eshbaal (see *Ish-Bosheth). The original form in I Chronicles is obviously, *boshet*, "shame" having deliberately been substituted for *ba'al*, "lord," which later generations objected to because it was the name of the pagan god Baal. Mephibosheth, the sole heir of the house of Saul (cf. II Sam. 9:1ff.), became lame at the age of five as the result of a fall from the hands of his nurse when she hurriedly picked him up in order to flee after receiving the news of the death of Saul and Jonathan (II Sam. 4:4). David treated Mephibosheth compassionately, refusing to deliver him over to the Gibeonites to be hanged with the other descendants of Saul (21:7), inviting him to eat at the royal table, and restoring him to the fields of Saul (9:1ff.). These kindnesses toward Mephibosheth can be explained as the fulfillment of David's oath to Jonathan (I Sam. 20:15, 42; II Sam. 21:7) and perhaps even of his oath to Saul (I Sam. 24:22). The story telling of David's generosity, however, makes no mention of the oaths, perhaps thereby implying that David's magnanimity was motivated not only by his oath but also by a plan to keep the descendants of the preceding dynasty under observation and to impress upon his own monarchy the stamp of continuity and legitimacy. Reasons of state become particularly evident in David's attempts to draw closer to the Benjamites and those who had been allied with Saul (II Sam. 3:19; 9:4–5; 17:27; 19:17, 18, 21; I Chron. 12:1–9). During Absalom's revolt Mephibosheth did not take any action and apparently remained loyal to David (II Sam. 19:25–32). *Ziba failed in his attempt to impute to Mephibosheth the ambition of receiving the monarchy from the people (II Sam. 16:1–4; 19:25–30).

[Samuel Abramsky]

In the *Aggadah*

Mephibosheth was an outstanding scholar. David called him "My teacher," and consulted him on all matters (Ber. 4a), and in the Talmud his name, used metaphorically to denote a noted scholar (Erub. 53b; "out of my mouth, humiliation"), indicated that he humiliated even David by his learning (*ibid.*). Nevertheless, David saved his life (cf. II Sam. 21:7) by praying that Mephibosheth should not be made to pass before the Ark and thus risk being condemned to death as were the rest of Saul's sons (Yev. 79a). Because David gave ear to Ziba's slander against Mephibosheth, the Temple was destroyed TJ, Yev. 4a). The later division of the kingdom was a punishment for David's decision that Mephibosheth and Ziba were to divide the land (II Sam. 19:29; Shab. 56b).

BIBLIOGRAPHY: H.P. Smith, *The Books of Samuel* (ICC, 1912), 310–3, 374–6; W. Caspari, *Die Samuelbuecher* (1926), 579–80; Noth, Personennamen, 119, 143; M.Z. Segal, *Sifrei Shemuel* (1956), 255, 293, 332, 352–3; J. Lewy, in: HUCA, 32 (1961), 36–37; H.W. Hertzberg, *Samuel* (Ger., 1960²), 298–301. IN THE AGGADAH: Ginzberg, Legends, 4 (1954), 76; I. Ḥasida, *Ishei ha-Tanakh* (1964), 265.

MER, GIDEON (1894–1961), Israeli expert on malaria and epidemiologist. Mer was born in Ponevez (Panevezys), Lithuania, and gave up the study of medicine in 1913 to immigrate to Palestine. On the outbreak of World War I he was expelled by the Turkish authorities as an enemy alien and went to Egypt, where he responded to *Trumpeldor's call for volunteers to found a Jewish brigade. He was one of the first to join the Mule Corps and served with distinction at Gallipoli. After the war, Mer obtained work in the anti-malaria service under Professor *Kligler, who persuaded him to return to Europe to complete his medical studies. In 1928, at the invitation of the Hebrew University of Jerusalem, he rejoined Kligler on the staff of the malaria research station at Rosh Pinnah, and in 1935 was appointed professor.

In World War II, Mer served as an expert on malaria first with the Australian army in the Middle East and then with the British forces in Iraq, Persia, and Burma. In Burma he carried out the first large-scale experiments on the use of DDT. After the war he returned to Rosh Pinnah and in 1948 served as brigade medical officer in the Palmaḥ. With the founding of the State of Israel Mer was appointed head of the department of preventive medicine of the Israeli army, but returned to his research station at Rosh Pinnah in 1951. Mer's work in the field of malaria control earned international recognition. His greatest contribution to the study of the bionomics of anopheles was his method of age grouping of the female anopheles by the size of the ampulla of the ovary.

BIBLIOGRAPHY: L. Dror et al. (eds.), *Gideon G. Mer…* (Heb., 1962 = *Beri'ut ha-Ẓibbur*, 5 (1962), 149–219).

MERAB (Heb. מֵרַב; probably from the root *rbb*), the eldest daughter of King *Saul (I Sam. 14:49). Saul promised Merab as a wife for *David, upon the condition that David fight Saul's wars against the Philistines (18:17–18). Saul did not fulfill his part of the bargain (18:19). Instead he gave Merab to *Adriel the Meholathite, and *Michal, her younger sister, became the wife of David. The conditional promise of marriage is similar to I Samuel 17:25, where Saul promises his daughter to the person who defeats Goliath. II Samuel 21:8 mentions the five sons of Michal and Adriel. The text should, however, read Merab instead of Michal on the basis of the Lucianic version of the Septuagint, the Peshita, and two masoretic texts.

BIBLIOGRAPHY: de Vaux, Anc Isr, 32.

MERANO, town in the province of Bolzano, N.E. Italy, near the Austrian border. Only around the middle of the 19th century did a few Jewish families, mainly from Central Europe, settle in Merano, the area having been under *ḥerem* since 1475 (see *Trent). In 1905, a community was constituted in Merano, encompassing the communities of Trent and Bolzano. In 1918 Merano passed from Austrian to Italian rule. In 1931, 780 Jews lived there, many of whom were foreign citizens. During World War II the Jews in Merano had to face the hostility of the German-speaking population, as well as the Nazi occupation: 25 Italian Jews from Merano are known to have died in the extermination camps; many more were executed or disappeared. There were 64 Jews in Merano in 1945, and about 30 in 1970.

[Sergio Della Pergola]

MÉRAY, TIBOR (1924–), author and journalist. At first a dedicated supporter of the Rákosi regime after World War II, Méray later joined Imre Nagy's revisionists and, when the 1956 revolution collapsed, fled to Paris. There he edited the radical newspaper *Irodalmi Ujság* and, during the Six-Day War of 1967, wrote in support of Israel. *The Enemy* (1958), confessions of a party hack, was a satire on Stalinism. *Thirteen Days That Shook the Kremlin* (1958) described the Hungarian Revolution. *The Revolt of the Mind: A Case History of Intellectual Resistance behind the Iron Curtain* appeared in English in 1975.

MERCHANT, LARRY (1931–), U.S. sports broadcaster and writer, known for his acerbic style of commentary. Merchant was born in Brooklyn, New York. His father ran a laundry and dry-cleaning business; his mother was a legal secretary. Merchant received a journalism degree from the University of Oklahoma in 1951, and after serving as a reporter for *Stars and Stripes* while in the Army, he began his journalism career in 1954 as sports editor of the *Wilmington News* in North Carolina. He was named sports editor of the *Philadelphia Daily News* at 26, and moved to the *New York Post* as a sports columnist in 1965. He left the *Post* a decade later and moved into television, becoming the HBO boxing commentator in 1978. HBO officials said they wanted Merchant to become another Howard *Cosell, himself an outspoken sportscaster. In a 2003 interview, Merchant said: "It's not my job to be a cheerleader. I'm skeptical of hype." He covered many of the top boxing events of the late 20th century, including Sugar Ray Leonard vs. Thomas Hearns, and Mike Tyson vs. Michael Spinks. In 1985, Merchant received the Sam Taub Memorial Award for Excellence in Boxing Broadcast Journalism. He was inducted into the World Boxing Hall of Fame in 2002. He wrote the award-winning HBO documentary series "Legendary Nights," which focused on famous boxing matches. Merchant played himself in two movies that featured boxing scenes, the 2001 remake of *Ocean's 11* and *I Spy* in 2002. He is the author of three books on sports: *… And Every Day You Take Another Bite* (1971), *The National Football Lottery* (1973), and *Ringside Seat at the Circus* (1976).

[Alan D. Abbey (2nd ed.)]

°**MERCIER, JEAN** (**Joannes Mercerus**; d. 1570), French Hebraist. Born in Uzès, near Nîmes, Mercier was a pupil of François Vatable, whom he succeeded as professor of Hebrew at the Collège Royal, Paris, in 1546. Unlike his master, Mercier was a prolific writer, publishing works on Hebrew and Semitic grammar, Latin translations and editions of the Targums, Bible commentaries, and other books of Jewish interest. Owing to his sympathy with the Reformers during the French religious wars, Mercier was obliged to take refuge in Venice in 1567 and, after returning to France, he died of the plague. One of his best-known works was the *Libellus de abbreviaturis Hebraeorum, tam Talmudicorum quam Masoritarum et aliorum rabbinorum* (Paris, 1561), later exploited by Guy *Le Fèvre de la Boderie, which reveals Mercier's interest in the Kabbalah and cites scholars such as *Reuchlin and *Galatinus. However, from remarks in his commentary on Genesis (Geneva, 1598), published after his death by Théodore de Bèze, his enthusiasm for later kabbalistic literature clearly waned. Mercier translated almost the whole of Targum Jonathan b. Uzziel on the Prophets; and he wrote annotations to Santes *Pagnini's *Thesaurus* (*Ozar Leshon ha-Kodesh*; Lyons, 1575, etc.). His other works include *Besorat Mattei* (1955), a Hebrew version of the gospel of Matthew; *Luḥei Dikduka Kasda'ah o Arama'ah: Tabulae in grammaticen linguae Chaldaeae* (Paris, 1560); *Aseret ha-Devarim: Decalogus*, with the commentary of Abraham Ibn Ezra, in Hebrew and Latin (Lyons, 1566–68); and the posthumous *De notis Hebraeorum liber* (1582), revised by another French Hebraist, Jean Cinqarbres (Quinquarboreus; d. 1587). Among those who studied under Mercier was the Huguenot leader and author Philippe de Mornay (Du Plessis-Mornay, 1549–1623).

BIBLIOGRAPHY: F. Secret, *Les Kabbalistes Chrétiens de la Renaissance* (1964), 208–9; Steinschneider, Cat. Bod., 1748.

[Godfrey Edmond Silverman]

MERCURY (**Mercurius**; in talmudic literature מֶרְקוּלִיס, **Merkulis**), Roman god of merchants and wayfarers, identical with the Greek god Hermes. The rabbis of the Talmud discussed Mercury more than any other pagan deity and apparently considered him almost synonymous with idolatry. Thus, where one *baraita* states, "He who sees Mercurius should recite 'Blessed (be God) who has patience with those who transgress His will'" (Ber. 57b), the parallel source reads simply, "He who sees idolatry…" (Tosef., *ibid.* 7[6]:2). Similarly, the Midrash interpreted the general prohibition against erecting statues or pagan monuments (Lev. 26:1) as referring to statues of Mercury on the roads (Sifra, Be-Har 9:5). The rabbis were also aware of certain modes of worship connected with Mercury, and thus the Mishnah proclaims: "He that throws a stone at a Mercurius is to be stoned, because this is how it is worshiped" (Sanh. 7:6). The trilithon, or three stones erected as part of the Mercurius, was also known, and therefore "R. Ishmael says: Three stones beside a Mercurius, one beside the other, are forbidden, but two are permitted" (Av. Zar. 4:1). So well known, in fact, was Mercurius worship in Palestine that it is mentioned even in popular proverbs: "As one who throws a stone at Mercurius is guilty of idolatry, so one who teaches a wicked pupil is guilty of idolatry" (Tosef., Av. Zar. 6[7]:18). Rabbis were constantly confronted with Mercury, and according to one talmudic account, a Mercurius was erected in the field of R. Simeon, son of Judah the Patriarch, but he succeeded in having it dismantled by the local authorities (TJ, Av. Zar. 4:1, 43d).

BIBLIOGRAPHY: S. Lieberman, in: JIR, 36 (1945/46), 366–8; 37 (1946/47), 42–54.

[Isaiah Gafni]

MERCY (Heb. רַחֲמִים), a feeling of compassion tempered with love, which engenders forgiveness and forbearance in man and which stimulates him to deeds of charity and kindness. This quality, inherent in man's attitude toward his loved ones, is an essential characteristic of God who "pitieth like a father" (Ps. 103:13; Isa. 49:15; Ex. 20:6; 34:6; Micah 7:8), and of the descendants of Abraham, renowned for their compassion. As God is known as *Raḥamanah* ("the Merciful"), so are the people of Israel distinguished as "merciful sons of merciful fathers" (Yev. 79a). In accordance with the tradition of the *imitation of God – "as He is merciful so be you merciful" (Shab. 133b) – mercy transcends familial bounds to encompass the entire range of human relationships (Ecclus. 18:13; Gen. R. 33: 1). Just as God is bound by His covenant of mercy with His people (Deut. 13:17; 30:3; II Kings 13:23), so is the Jew bound by specific commandments to act mercifully toward the oppressed, the alien, the orphan, the widow, indeed, every living creature (Deut. 22:6; 25:4; Prov. 19:17; Git. 61a; Moses Cordovero, *Tomer Devorah*, ch. 3). The exercise of mercy is the fulfillment of a covenantal obligation, and, in turn, enhances moral sensibility (Suk. 49b; BB 9b). The stress placed upon maintaining charitable institutions in Jewish communal life is an outgrowth of this view of mercy. Man's recognition of God as "the Merciful One" finds its verbal expression in his prayers (Num. 19:19; Ps. 106:1), wherein he implores God to deal compassionately even with the undeserving man (Ex. 34:7; Sot. 14a; Ber. 7a). Because of the imperfection of every mortal, even such righteous men as Abraham are dependent on God's mercy. Recognizing human frailty, God forgives transgressors, especially those who themselves are forgiving (Ecclus. 28:2; Shab. 151b; BM 85a; Ex. R. 12:1). The firm belief that "it is because of the Lord's mercies that we are not consumed, because His compassions fail not" (Lam. 3:22) has sustained the Jewish people through many periods of travail (Hos. 12:7). God's mercifulness does not negate the principle of divine justice, but rather complements it and reinforces its efficacy (see *God, Justice and Mercy of). In analyzing the 13 attributes by which God manifests Himself, the rabbis point to the positive interaction of mercy and justice in God's relation to the world (RH 17a, b; Lev. R. 29:3). This combination of justice and mercy in God is denoted in the two names of God, *Elohim*, and YHWH, the first of which designates justice, the second, mercy. God resolves the tension between strict judgment and mercy in favor of the latter (Ps. 89:3; Prov. 20:28). Philo expresses this in his statement: "God's pity is older than his justice" (Deus, 16). Judaism can thus demand of its judges the seemingly contradictory qualities of impartiality and compassion (Ex. 23:3; Ket. 9:2: Sanh. 6b). The principle of mercy assumes an overriding significance in the administration of Jewish law, where rules of equity qualify strict legalism: "… execute the judgment and show mercy and compassion every man to his brother" (Zech. 7:9).

BIBLIOGRAPHY: G.F. Moore, *Judaism*, 2 (1946), 154 and 169; C.G. Montefiore and H. Loewe, *A Rabbinic Anthology*, index; Orḥot *Ẓaddikim* (Prague, 1581); I. Heinemann, *Ta'amei ha-Mitzvot be-Sifrut Yisrael*, 2 (1956), index s.v. *ḥemlah*.

[Zvi H. Szubin]

MERECINA OF GERONA, 15th century author of a Hebrew liturgical poem, rich in biblical allusions, that begins, "Blessed, Majestic, and Terrible," discovered by A.M. Habermann in the manuscript of a medieval Spanish *maḥzor*. She is described in the manuscript as "'a woman of virtue' – the lady Merecina, the Rabbiness from Gerona." Merecina's plea for divine redemption for the faithful of Israel is also an acrostic: the first word of each of the five verses starts with a letter of her name. Since the Jewish community of Gerona disappeared after the expulsion of 1492, the poem was evidently written before that date. Merecina is one of only two known female Hebrew poets in medieval Spain; her predecessor was the tenth-century wife of *Dunash ben Labrat.

BIBLIOGRAPHY: A. Habermann, *Iyyunim ba-Shirah u-va-Piyyut shel Yemei ha-Beinayim* (1972), 265–67; Merecina of Gerona, "Blessed, Majestic and Terrible," in: S. Kaufman, G. Hasan-Rokem, and T. Hess (eds), *The Defiant Muse: Hebrew Feminist Poems from Antiquity to the Present. A Bilingual Anthology* (1999), 64–65; K. Hellerstein, "The Name in the Poem: Women Yiddish Poets," in: *Shofar*, 20:3 (2002), 34; Y. Levine, "*Nashim Yehudiyot she-Ḥibru Tefillot le-Kelal Yisrael – Iyyun Histori*," in: *Kenishta*, 2 (2003), 91.

[Cheryl Tallan (2nd ed.)]

MEREMAR (d. 432), Babylonian *amora* of the end of the fourth and beginning of the fifth centuries. According to the *Sefer Kabbalah* of Abraham *Ibn Daud, Meremar succeeded Ashi as head of the academy of Sura (427–32). He was a pupil of the elder Ravina (Yev. 75b) and transmitted to the younger Ravina in the name of the latter's father the teachings of Joseph (Ned. 60b) and of Papi (Ned. 90a). He transmitted a statement once in the name of R. Dimi (Git. 19b), but he could hardly have known him personally, since Dimi lived in the first half of the fourth century. Among his colleagues were Mar Zutra (Suk. 45a) and Ashi (Ber. 30a). His pupil the younger Ravina, who visited him later in Sura (Pes. 117b), is mentioned frequently (Shab. 81b; Git. 19b; BM 72b, 104a; et al.), and Aḥa of Difti (Ber. 45b; Ḥul. 47a) is also apparently a pupil of Meremar. He was succeeded as head of the academy by Idi b. Avin. Meremar had a son Judah who was a colleague of Mar b. Rav Ashi and the above-mentioned Aḥa (Ber. 45b).

BIBLIOGRAPHY: Hyman, Toledot, 908–10; Ḥ. Albeck, *Mavo la-Talmudim* (1969), 438f.

[David Joseph Bornstein]

MERETZ, Israeli parliamentary group and political party. Meretz first emerged as a ten-member parliamentary group on March 9, 1992, through the merger of the Citizens Rights Movement, *Mapam, and *Shinui. The three parties were united on the issues of peace, religion and state, and human rights issues, but differed on social and economic issues, with Mapam and the CRM following a socialist line, and Shinui a liberal one.

Meretz ran in the elections to the Thirteenth Knesset, under the leadership of Shulamit *Aloni, receiving 12 seats, and emerged as the third largest party in the Knesset. It joined the government formed by Yitzhak *Rabin, and received three ministerial posts, increased to four after Shas left the government on the eve of the signing of the Oslo Accords in 1993. As long as Shas remained in the government, there was constant pressure on its part that Aloni be removed from the Ministry of Education and Culture, to which she had been appointed minister, owing to what Shas considered lack of sensitivity to the religious sector. As a result Aloni was replaced in the ministry by Amnon *Rubinstein, and received a portfolio that combined Communications, Science, and the Arts. As a staunch supporter of an agreement between Israel and the PLO, Meretz supported the Oslo Accords, but was only marginally involved in their formulation. In addition to attending to the portfolios that were in its hands, Meretz continued throughout the Thirteenth Knesset to be active in the field of civil and human rights, within Israel proper and in the territories, and even before Rabin's assassination warned against the growing strength of the religious extreme right-wing movements. Following Rabin's assassination, Meretz blocked an attempt by Prime Minister Shimon *Peres to bring the NRP into the coalition and thus give it an effective veto on any future peace moves. Meretz joined Haim *Ramon when he established the list Ḥayyim Ḥadashim ba-Histadrut, in the Histadrut elections, and some of its members played an active role in the reorganization of the Histadrut after those elections. In the elections to the Fourteenth Knesset in 1996, Meretz, led by

Yossi *Sarid, received nine seats, and remained in the opposition. In February 1997 it registered as a party, and its three bodies ceased to exist as separate parties. In the elections to the Fifteenth Knesset Meretz received ten seats, and entered the government formed by Ehud *Barak, receiving three portfolios, but it left the government in June 2000, because Sarid was displeased by Barak's efforts to pacify Shas, and went into opposition. In the elections to the Sixteenth Knesset Meretz received only six seats, despite the fact that Yossi *Beilin and Yael *Dayan, who had failed to enter the *Israel Labor Party list for the elections to the Sixteenth Knesset in a realistic place, joined the Meretz list. This failure led to Sarid's resigning the party leadership. In the elections for the party's leadership held in February 2004, Yossi *Beilin beat MK Ran Cohen, and the party changed its name to "Yaḥad and the Democratic Choice." In the summer of 2005 "Meretz" was brought back into the party's name. In the 2006 elections it won five seats.

[Susan Hattis Rolef (2nd ed.)]

MERGENTHEIM (Bad Mergentheim), city in Wuerttemberg, Germany. Jews settled in Mergentheim in the first half of the 13th century; 16 Jews were murdered during the *Rindfleisch massacres of 1298. Jews are mentioned again in 1312; they suffered during persecutions in 1336 and again during those of the *Black Death in 1349 when a number of Jews were martyred. They reappeared in the city, however, in 1355, and during the next century prospered, in large part through moneylending. The Jewish population remained small throughout the 14th and 15th centuries. In 1516 there was only one Jew in the city, but by the end of the century the population rose again. In 1590 a cemetery plot was put to use in Unterbalbach for the Jews of that town as well as those of surrounding communities, including Mergentheim. This cemetery was enlarged in 1702 and remained in continuous use throughout the modern period. During the early 17th century, only **Schutzjuden* were permitted in the city; all other Jews were restricted to an eight-day stay. Throughout the century, every attempt was made by the municipal authorities to restrict Jewish economic activities. Nonetheless, the Jewish families managed to build a synagogue in 1658; this was enlarged in 1762. By 1700 there were 40 Jewish residents, among them the Court *Jews Calman Model and Hirsch Manasses. At this time Jewish commercial interests included trade in horses, livestock, corn, and wine. By the end of the century these had expanded into wholesale trade and banking. In 1728 Mergentheim became the seat of the **Landrabbiner*, an office filled with distinction between 1742 and 1763 by Naphtali Hirsch Katzenellenbogen (see *Katzenellenbogen Family). In 1799 there were 90 Jews; 110 in 1830; 176 in 1869; 250 in 1886; and 276 in 1900. In 1933 there were 196 Jews.

On November 9/10, 1938, Jewish stores and homes were demolished; the rabbi, M. Kahn, was physically assaulted and the interior of the synagogue destroyed. By 1939 there were only 87 Jews left in the city. In 1941 and 1942, 41 Jews were deported to concentration camps. The community's Torah scrolls and sacred objects were saved from destruction and turned over to an American army chaplain after the war. In 1946 the synagogue was renovated but shortly thereafter was closed again and subsequently demolished. All that remained of the Mergentheim Jewish community in 1990 was the cemetery in Unterbalbach. There is a memorial to commemorate the former synagogue.

BIBLIOGRAPHY: *Germania Judaica*, 2 (1968), 538–9, incl. bibl.; P. Sauer, *Die juedischen Gemeinden in Wuerttemberg und Hohenzollern* (1966), 37–43, incl. bibl.; FJW, 338. **ADD. BIBLIOGRAPHY:** A. Maimon, M. Breuer, Y. Guggenheim (eds.), *Germania Judaica*, 3, 1350–1514 (1987), 861–66; J. Hahn, *Erinnerungen und Zeugnisse juedischer Geschichte in Baden-Wuerttemberg* (1988), 331–33; H. Fechenbach, *Die letzten Mergentheimer Juden und die Geschichte der Familien Fechenbach* (1997; reprint of 1972 edition).

[Alexander Shapiro]

MERḤAVYAH (Heb. מֶרְחַבְיָה; "God's Wide Space"), (1) kibbutz in the Jezreel (Ḥarod) Valley, Israel, E. of Afulah and at the foot of Givat ha-Moreh, affiliated with Kibbutz Arẓi Ha-Shomer Ha-Ẓa'ir. In 1909, the first holding in the Jezreel Valley was acquired at Merḥavyah by Jews through the efforts of Yehoshua *Hankin on behalf of the Palestine Land Development Company. Initially, a group of *Ha-Shomer established a farm there (1911). They persevered in spite of the malaria and the attempts of the Turkish authorities and their Arab neighbors to make them leave the place. Merḥavyah soon became a workers' cooperative according to Franz *Oppenheimer's ideas. During World War I, German pilots set up a temporary camp there. The cooperative dispersed after the war and another group founded a settlement, joined by veterans of the *Jewish Legion, which, however, did not succeed. In 1929 a group of Ha-Shomer ha-Ẓa'ir pioneers from Poland established its kibbutz on the site. It became the movement's organizational center, including the Kibbutz Arẓi secretariat, archives, printing press, and the Sifriat Poalim publishing house. In 1969, the kibbutz, with 550 inhabitants, based its economy on intensive farming, and also had a factory for plastic pipes and a metal workshop. In the mid-1990s, the population of the kibbutz was approximately 620, growing further to 675 in 2002. In the 2000s the kibbutz economy was based on two industries, plastics and wood, and a resort with an amusement park and events garden. Farming included field crops, citrus groves, and dairy cattle. The "Big Yard" featured restored houses built between 1912 and 1916, a visitors center, and a museum in memory of Meir *Yaari, one of the Kibbutz Arẓi Ha-Shomer ha-Ẓa'ir's leaders. (2) Moshav founded on part of the Merḥavyah lands in 1922 by a group of Third Aliyah pioneers from Eastern Europe. Merḥavyah, affiliated with Tenu'at ha-Moshavim in 1969, engaged in intensive agriculture with field and garden crops, dairy cattle, and poultry as prominent branches. In 1968 its population was 42, jumping to 285 in the mid-1990s and 630 in 2002 after expansion.

WEBSITE: www.merchavyard.org.il.

[Efram Orni / Shaked Gilboa (2nd ed.)]

MÉRIDA, city in W. Spain, capital of the ancient Lusitania. Located at an important road junction, it had one of the oldest communities in Spain. A folk legend relates that the Jewish settlement there dated from the arrival of captives brought by Titus after the destruction of the Second Temple; the exiles were "the nobles of Jerusalem ... among them there was a maker of curtains [for synagogue arks] by the name of Baruch who was also skilled in silk-work. These people remained in Mérida where they raised families ..." (Ibn Daud, *Sefer ha-Qabbalah*, ed. by G. Cohen (1967), 79). There was a Jewish settlement in Mérida in the late Roman and Visigothic periods. A Jewish tombstone inscription in Latin, probably dating from not later than the fourth century, embodies Latin translations of Hebrew formulas commonly found on Jewish tombstones of the period. After the Arab conquest, there was an important Jewish community in Mérida. Its prominent families included those of Ibn Avitur and Ibn al-Balia.

During Christian rule the Jewish quarter was situated near the Church of Santa Catalina, formerly the synagogue. From 1283 the tax paid by the community was 4,000 maravedis. The Jews in Mérida suffered during the 1391 persecutions, and a *Converso group existed there during the 15th century. However the amount of tax paid by the community in 1439 (2,250 maravedis) shows that it was relatively flourishing. Because of its proximity to the Portuguese border, the exiles from Mérida went to Portugal when the Jews were expelled from Spain in 1492.

BIBLIOGRAPHY: Ashtor, Korot, 1 (19662), 230–2; Baer, Urkunden, 2 (1936), index; J.M. Millás, in: *Sefarad*, 5 (1945), 301ff. (cf. plate between 300–1); C. Roth, *ibid.*, 8 (1948), 391–6; J. Ma. Navascués, *ibid.*, 19 (1959), 78–91; Cantera-Mlliás, Inscripciones, 410ff.; H. Beinart, in: *Estudios*, 3 (1962), 9f., 14, 27–30; Suárez Fernández, Documentos, 69, 81, 257–7; A. Marcos Pon, in: *Rivista di Archeologia Cristiana*, 32 (1956), 249–52 (It.). **ADD. BIBLIOGRAPHY:** L. García Iglesias, in: *Revista de estudios extremeños*, 32 (1976), 79–98.

[Haim Beinart]

MERIDOR, DAN (1947–), Israeli politician and lawyer, member of the Eleventh to Fifteenth Knessets. Meridor was born in Jerusalem, son of Eliahu Meridor, who served in the Fourth to Sixth Knessets on the *Ḥerut Movement and *Gaḥal lists. Dan Meridor went to school in Jerusalem and finished the Hebrew Gymnasium High School in 1965. He served in the army in the Armored Division and then studied law at the Hebrew University of Jerusalem. After completing his degree he went into private law practice in Jerusalem. In 1973 he joined the Ḥerut Movement Executive, where he was viewed as one of the "Ḥerut princes" – sons of the movement's founders. He failed to get onto the *Likud list to the Ninth Knesset in 1977. After the elections he was offered several positions in the government but rejected them all. During Operation Peace for Galilee, after the resignation of Arie Na'or as government secretary, Meridor was appointed in his place, serving in this position until being elected to the Eleventh Knesset in 1984. He referred to the Sabra and Shatilla massacre in Lebanon as "the ugly accident." In the government formed by Yitzhak *Shamir after the elections to the Twelfth Knesset in 1988 Meridor was appointed minister of justice. In that position Meridor took a clear liberal line on issues of human rights and the rule of law, actively promoting the passing of Basic Law: Human Dignity and Freedom, and Basic Law: Freedom of Occupation, which were viewed as the first stage in the passing of a complete bill of human rights. Meridor also insisted that human rights and the rule of law be preserved with regards to the Palestinians in the West Bank and the Gaza Strip in the difficult period of the first Intifada. As a result he gained many political enemies in the extreme right. He continued to push for the passing of additional basic laws in the field of human rights, and promoted Basic Law: Legislation in the Thirteenth Knesset, when the Likud was in opposition. In the primaries in the Likud for a new leader after the 1992 electoral defeat, Meridor supported the candidature of his friend Ze'ev Binyamin *Begin opposite Binyamin *Netanyahu, despite Begin's more right-wing positions. In the government formed by Netanyahu after the elections to the Fourteenth Knesset in 1996, Meridor was appointed minister of finance in which role he advocated a further liberalization of the economy, and the privatization of government-owned companies, the banks whose shares were held by the government since the 1983 bank crisis, and state lands. Meridor resigned from the government in June 1997 after expressing his dissatisfaction with the appointment of Ronnie Bar-On as attorney general, and Netanyahu's treatment of the issue, and owing to growing tension with the governor of the Bank of Israel, Prof. Ya'akov *Frankel, on his interest rate and foreign exchange policies. In February 1999, Meridor was one of several leading members of the Likud, including Yitzhak Mordechai and Roni *Milo, who left the party to form the new Center Party. The new party gained six seats in the elections to the Fifteenth Knesset. Meridor was not appointed as a minister in the government formed by Ehud *Barak in 1999, which was joined by the Center Party, and was appointed chairman of the Foreign Affairs and Defense Committee, until he joined the government formed by Ariel *Sharon in 2001 as minister without portfolio. The Center Party began to disintegrate after the elections for prime minister of February 2001, and though Meridor had decided to return to the Likud, he formally remained part of the Center Party parliamentary group.

Throughout his political career Meridor was known for his honesty, mild temper, and gentlemanly demeanor, which while gaining for him a good deal of respect, also led to his being presented by satirists as a weak figure, and made it very difficult for him to contend with the new atmosphere that developed in the Likud Conference before and after the elections to the Sixteenth Knesset. As a result he decided not to run for a place on the Likud list to the Sixteenth Knesset, and to return to his private law practice.

Dan Meridor's brother, Salai, was chairman of the Jewish Agency.

BIBLIOGRAPHY: S. Ben-Porat, *Siḥot Im Dan Meridor* (1997).

[Susan Hattis Rolef (2nd ed.)]

MERINIDS (Banu-Marin), Berber dynasty ruling over Morocco and parts of Algeria from the mid-13th century to 1472. Their capital and center of operations was the city of *Fez. From the 1390s, the Jewish population under the dynasty increased significantly as a result of the flow of Jewish refugees from areas re-conquered by the Christians in Spain from the Muslims. Important Jewish communities expanded in Fez and Taza. The King Abd al-Haqq (murdered by Muslim fanatics in 1465) appointed Harun, a Jewish physician, as vizier (minister). Members of the Jewish elite served as vital trade and diplomatic intermediaries between the Merinid court and Portugal, then a key military and commercial power with strategic interests inside Morocco. Although several Merinid kings manifested compassion and even generosity toward the Jews, the same was not true of all of them, and it most certainly was not the case with ordinary Muslims, who resented the growing Jewish political and economic influence. Jews were periodically harassed and beaten by Muslims and were prohibited from residing anywhere near Muslim holy sites.

ADD. BIBLIOGRAPHY: H.Z. Hirschberg, *A History of the Jews in North Africa*, 1 (1974); C.-A. Julien, *History of North Africa: From the Arab Conquest to 1830*, ed. and rev. by R. Le Tourneau (1970); N.A. Stillman, *The Jews of Arab Lands* (1979).

[Michael M. Laskier (2nd ed.)]

MERKABAH MYSTICISM or **MA'ASEH MERKAVAH** (Heb. מַעֲשֵׂה מֶרְכָּבָה), the name given to the first chapter of Ezekiel in Mishnah *Ḥagigah*, 2:1. The term was used by the rabbis to designate the complex of speculations, homilies, and visions connected with the Throne of Glory and the chariot (*merkavah*) which bears it and all that is embodied in this divine world. The term, which does not appear in Ezekiel, is derived from I Chronicles 28:18 and is first found with the meaning of Merkabah mysticism at the end of Ben Sira 49:8: "Ezekiel saw a vision, and described the different orders of the chariot." The Hebrew expression *zanei merkavah* should possibly be interpreted as the different sights of the vision of the chariot in Ezekiel, chapters 1, 8, and 10 (according to S. Spiegel, in: HTR, 24 (1931), 289), or as the different parts of the chariot, which later came to be called "the chambers of the chariot" (*ḥadrei merkavah*). It has been suggested (by Israel Lévi in his commentary on Ben Sira, *L'Ecclesiastique*, 1 (1898), and 2 (1901)) that the text be corrected to *razei merkavah* ("secrets of the chariot"). The divine chariot also engrossed the Qumran sect; one fragment speaks of the angels praising "the pattern of the Throne of the chariot" (Strugnell, in: VT, 7 supplement (1960), 336). In Pharisaic and tannaitic circles Merkabah mysticism became an esoteric tradition (see *Kabbalah) of which different fragments were scattered in the Talmud and the Midrash, interpreting *Ḥagigah* 2:1. This was a study surrounded by a special holiness and a special danger. A *baraita* in *Ḥagigah* 13a, which is ascribed to the first century C.E., relates the story of "A child who was reading at his teacher's home the Book of Ezekiel and he apprehended what *Ḥashmal* was [see Ezek. 1:27, JPS "electrum"], whereupon a fire went forth from *Ḥashmal* and consumed him." Therefore the rabbis sought to conceal the Book of Ezekiel.

Many traditions relate to the involvement of Johanan b. *Zakkai, and later of *Akiva in this study. In the main, details about the conduct of the rabbis in the study of Merkabah are found in the Jerusalem Talmud *Ḥagigah* 2 and the Babylonian Talmud, *Shabbat* 80b. According to the manuscript of the latter source the prohibition on lecturing to a group was not always observed and the tradition adds that a transgressor, a Galilean who came to Babylonia, was punished for this and died. In the Babylonian Talmud, *Sukkah* 28a, Merkabah mysticism was put forward as a major subject (*davar gadol*) in contrast to the relatively minor subject of rabbinic casuistry. Traditions of this type are found, for example, in *Berakhot* 7a, *Ḥullin* 91b, *Megillah* 24b, and at the beginning of *Genesis Rabbah, Tanḥuma, Midrash Tehillim, Midrash Rabbah* to Leviticus, Song of Songs, and Ecclesiastes. Several traditions are preserved in *Seder Eliyahu Rabbah* and in small tractates, such as *Avot de-Rabbi Nathan* and *Massekhet Derekh Ereẓ*. In contrast with the scattered fragments of these traditions in exoteric sources, books, and treatises collecting and developing *Ma'aseh Merkavah* according to the trends prevailing in different mystic circles were written at the latest from the fourth century on. Many of the treatises include early material but numerous additions reflect later stages. *Re'iyyot Yeḥezkiel*, the major part of which was found in the Cairo *Genizah* (published in S.A. Wertheimer, *Battei Midrashot*, 2 (1953²), 127–34), depicts historical personalities and the context is that of a fourth-century Midrash. Scraps of a second-or third-century Midrash on the *Ma'aseh Merkavah* were found in pages of the *Genizah* fragments. These sources do not yet show any sign of the pseudepigraphy prevailing in most surviving sources; in these the majority is formalized, and most of the statements are attributed to Akiva or to Ishmael. Several of the texts are written in Aramaic, but most are in Mishnaic Hebrew. A great deal of material of this type has been published (mostly from manuscripts) in collections of minor Midrashim such as A. Jellinek's *Beit ha-Midrash* (1853–78), S.A. Wertheimer's *Battei Midrashot*, E. Gruenhut's *Sefer ha-Likkutim* (1898–1904), and H.M. Horowitz' *Beit Eked ha-Aggadot* (1881–84). *Sefer Merkavah Shelemah* (1921) includes important material from the manuscript collection of Solomon Musajoff. Some of the texts included in these anthologies are identical, and many are corrupt.

The most important are:

(1) *Heikhalot Zutrati* ("Lesser *Heikhalot*") or *Heikhalot R. Akiva*, of which only fragments have been published, mostly without being recognized as belonging to the text. The bulk of it is in a very difficult Aramaic, and part of it is included in *Merkavah Shelemah* as "*Tefillat Keter Nora*."

(2) *Heikhalot Rabbati* ("Greater *Heikhalot*," in *Battei Midrashot*, 1 (1950²), 135–63), i.e., the *Heikhalot* of Rabbi Ishmael, in Hebrew. In medieval sources and ancient manuscripts the two books are at times called *Hilkhot Heikhalot*. The division of *Heikhalot Rabbati* into *halakhot* ("laws") is still preserved in several manuscripts, most of which are divided into 30 chap-

ters. Chapters 27–30 include a special tract, found in several manuscripts under the title *Sar Torah*, which was composed much later than the bulk of the work. In the Middle Ages the book was widely known as *Pirkei Heikhalot*. The edition published by Wertheimer includes later additions, some of them Shabbatean (see G. Scholem, in *Zion*, 7 (1942), 184f.). Jellinek's version (in *Beit ha-Midrash*, 3, 1938²) is free of additions but suffers from many corruptions.

(3) *Merkavah Rabbah*, part of which is found in *Merkavah Shelemah*, mostly attributed to Ishmael, and partly to Akiva. Perhaps this work contained the most ancient formulation of *Shi'ur Komah* ("the measurement of the body of God"), which later was copied in manuscripts as a separate work that developed into *Sefer ha-Komah*, popular in the Middle Ages (see G. Scholem, *Jewish Gnosticism…* (1965), 36–42).

(4) A version of *Heikhalot* which has no name and was referred to in the Middle Ages as *Ma'aseh Merkavah* (G. Scholem, *ibid.*, 103–17). Here statements of Ishmael and Akiva alternate.

(5) Another elaborate treatise on the pattern of *Heikhalot Rabbati*, but with differing and partly unknown new details; fragments have been published from the Cairo *Genizah* by I. Greenwald, *Tarbiz*, 38 (1969), 354–72 (additions *ibid.*, 39 (1970), 216–7);

(6) *Hekhalot*, published by Jellinek (in *Beit ha-Midrash* (vol. 1, 1938²), and later as *III Enoch or the Hebrew Book of Enoch* (ed. and trans. by H. Odeberg, 1928). Unfortunately Odeberg chose a later and very corrupt text as a basis for his book, which he intended as a critical edition. The speaker is R. Ishmael and the work is largely made up of revelations about Enoch, who became the angel Metatron, and the host of heavenly angels. This book represents a very different trend from those in *Heikhalot Rabbati* and *Heikhalot Zutrati*.

(7) The tractate of *Heikhalot* or *Ma'aseh Merkavah* in *Battei Midrashot* (1 (1950²), 51–62) is a relatively late elaboration, in seven chapters, of the descriptions of the throne and the chariot. In the last three works a literary adaptation was deliberately made in order to eradicate the magical elements, common in the other sources listed above. Apparently they were intended more to be read for edification rather than for practical use by those who delved into the Merkabah.

(8) The Tosefta to the Targum of the first chapter of Ezekiel (*Battei Midrashot*, 2 (1953²), 135–40) also belongs to this literature.

A mixture of material on the chariot and creation is found in several additional sources, mainly in *Baraita de-Ma'aseh Bereshit* and in *Otiyyot de-Rabbi Akiva*, both of which appear in several versions. The *Seder Rabbah de-Bereshit* was published in *Battei Midrashot* (1 (1950²), 3–48), and in another version by N. Séd, with a French translation (in REJ, 3–4 (1964), 23–123, 259–305). Here the doctrine of the Merkabah is connected with cosmology and with the doctrine of the seven heavens and the depths. This link is also noticeable in *Otiyyot de-Rabbi Akiva*, but only the longer version contains the traditions on creation and the Merkavah mysticism. Both extant versions, with an important supplement entitled *Midrash Alfa-Betot*, were published in *Battei Midrashot* (2 (1953²), 333–465). M. Margaliot discovered additional and lengthy sections of *Midrash Alfa-Betot* in several unpublished manuscripts. Again, these works were arranged more for the purposes of speculation and reading than for practical use by the mystics. The doctrine of the seven heavens and their angelic hosts, as was developed in Merkabah mysticism and in cosmology, has also definite magical contexts, which are elaborated in the complete version of Sefer *ha-Razim (ed. by M. Margalioth, 1967), whose date is still a matter of controversy.

In the second century Jewish converts to Christianity apparently conveyed different aspects of Merkabah mysticism to Christian Gnostics. In the Gnostic literature there were many corruptions of such elements, yet the Jewish character of this material is still evident, especially among the Ophites, in the school of Valentinus, and in several of the Gnostic and Coptic texts discovered within the last 50 years. In the Middle Ages the term *Ma'aseh Merkabah* was used by both philosophers and kabbalists to designate the contents of their teachings but with completely different meanings – metaphysics for the former and mysticism for the latter.

BIBLIOGRAPHY: Scholem, Mysticism, 40–70; idem, *Jewish Gnosticism, Merkabah Mysticism and Talmudic Tradition* (1965); P. Bloch, in: MGWJ, 37 (1893); idem, in: *Festschrift J. Guttmann* (1915), 113–24; Néher, in: RHR, 140 (1951), 59–82; J. Neusner, *Life of Rabban Yohanan ben Zakkai* (1962), 97–105; M. Smith, in: A. Altmann (ed.), *Biblical and Other Studies* (1963), 142–60; B. Bokser, in: PAAJR, 31 (1965), 1–32; J. Maier, *Vom Kultus zur Gnosis* (1964), 112–48; E.E. Urbach, in: *Studies in Mysticism and Religion presented to G.G. Scholem* (1968), 1–28 (Heb. section).

[Gershom Scholem]

MERNEPTAH (Egyptian, Mr-n-Pth; "the beloved of Ptah"), king of Egypt (reigned c. 1224–1214 B.C.E.). Most scholars believed that Merneptah was the pharaoh of the *Exodus until the discovery of the "Israel" stela at Thebes in 1896. This stela, dated to the fifth year of Merneptah's reign, states in the second line that "Israel is laid waste, his seed is not." Since in this part of the stela "Israel" is the only name containing the Egyptian determinitive sign of a people and not of a land, many scholars have presumed that at this time Israel was a nomadic people located somewhere in or near Palestine. However, others think that this may be merely due to a scribal error. Although the major historical texts of Merneptah deal with the repulsion of a Libyan invasion of the Egyptian Delta in the fifth year of his reign, the concluding lines of the "Israel" stela and his use of the epithet "reducer of Gezer" in a Nubian inscription may attest to the crushing of a revolt in Palestine early in his reign. A few other miscellaneous texts of the period (notably *Papyrus Anastasi I*) show that the Egyptians had a thorough geographic, topographic, and toponymic knowledge of Palestine and Syria, particularly along the main arteries of traffic.

BIBLIOGRAPHY: Pritchard, Texts, 376–8, 475–9; A.H. Gardiner, *Egypt of the Pharaohs* (1961), 271ff.; R.O. Faulkner, in: CAH², 2 (1966), ch. 23.

[Alan Richard Schulman]

MERODACH (Heb. מְרֹדַךְ), a Babylonian god (Jer. 50:2), whose name also enters into the composition of the personal names *Merodach-Baladan (= Berodach-Baladan; II Kings 20:12; Isa. 39:1), *Evil-Merodach (II Kings 25:27; Jer. 52:31), and *Mordecai.

See *Marduk.

MERODACH-BALADAN (Heb. מְרֹדַךְ בַּלְאֲדָן; Akk. dMarduk-ap-la-iddin; "Marduk has given a son"), Babylonian king (722–710 B.C.E.). Assyrian inscriptions place the origin of Merodach-Baladan in the land of Bît-Iakin, a Chaldean kingdom near the coast of the Persian Gulf ("Sealands"). This is more probable than Merodach-Baladan's claim that he was the son and legal heir of the Babylonian king Erība-Marduk. In 731 B.C.E., Ukin-zer of Bît Amukkani, a Chaldean, wrested the kingship of Babylonia from the pro-Assyrian king Nabunadin-zer. Merodach-Baladan, who also had designs on the kingship, supported the Assyrian king Tiglath-Pileser III, against Ukin-zer. He was thus able to strengthen his position among the Chaldean tribes, increase his influence in Babylonia, and forge an alliance with Elam, without interference from Tiglath-Pileser III or Shalmaneser V, both of whom exercised sovereignty over Babylonia (729–722 B.C.E.).

With the death of Shalmaneser V, Merodach-Baladan seized the Babylonian throne (722/721 B.C.E.). This marked the beginning of violent struggles between Merodach-Baladan and the Assyrians. By 720, Sargon II was preparing for war against Merodach-Baladan, who had the support of the Elamites. Conflicting reports have been preserved of this battle, which took place in the plain of Dêr, east of the Tigris. Merodach-Baladan ruled Babylonia until 710, when, through neglect and economic exploitation, he incurred the enmity of the native Babylonian population in the large urban centers which had been loyal to him, although he enjoyed the support of the Chaldean and Babylonian tribes which were largely concentrated in the southern part of the country.

Therefore, it is not surprising that when Sargon II waged war against Merodach-Baladan in 710, he was warmly received by the urban population. Sargon defeated Merodach-Baladan's armies and conquered his fortresses, causing Merodach-Baladan to flee south to Bît-Iakin, where he waited for an opportunity to regain the throne. Seeing in the widespread disturbances that arose after the death of Sargon (705) the opportunity to resume his rule over Babylonia, Merodach-Baladan, in 703, with the support of the Elamites and much of the Babylonian population, reestablished his rule there. He found an ally in *Hezekiah, who was at that time planning a revolt against Assyria, exploiting the latter's political goals for his own benefit. Hezekiah could help Merodach-Baladan by distracting the attention of the Assyrians to the west. This appears to be the background of the biblical narrative concerning the goodwill delegation sent by Merodach-Baladan to Hezekiah of Judah in 701 B.C.E. after Sennacherib's campaign there (II Kings 20:12–19; Isa. 39:1–8; II Chron. 32:31). However, it is doubtful that political conditions in Palestine after the Assyrian campaign were favorable for Merodach-Baladan and Hezekiah to form an alliance.

In 703 B.C.E. Sennacherib conducted a campaign against Merodach-Baladan, defeating the Elamite and Babylonian armies surrounding Kish. Merodach-Baladan fled to the "Sealands," and from there continued to rule over Bît-Iakin and the southernmost part of Babylonia. After Sennacherib returned from his campaign in the west in 701, he waged war against Merodach-Baladan (700). The Chaldeans were no match for the Assyrians, and Merodach-Baladan fled further along the Persian Gulf to the region bordering on Elam, dying there in 694.

[Bustanay Oded]

In the ***Aggadah***

Merodach-Baladan is praised for honoring his father. He added his father's name Baladan to his own when acting as regent during the incapacity of his father, and signed documents in the name of both his father and himself (Sanh. 96a). When told that the sun had reversed its course on the day that Hezekiah miraculously recovered from his illness, he acknowledged the superiority of God, though previously he had been a sun worshiper. He thereupon addressed a letter to Hezekiah the original introduction of which was "Peace to Hezekiah, Peace to the God of Hezekiah, and Peace to Jerusalem." Realizing, however, that he had been disrespectful in not placing God first, he took steps and recalled his messengers in order to change the wording. As a reward he was told: "You took three steps for the honor of My name … I will therefore raise up from thee three kings [Nebuchadnezzar, Evil-Merodach, and Belshazzar], who shall rule from one end of the world to the other" (Est. R. 3:1).

BIBLIOGRAPHY: H.W.F. Saggs, *The Greatness that was Babylon* (1962), 109–20; J.A. Brinkman, in: *Studies Presented to A. Leo Oppenheim* (1964), 6–53; idem, in: JNES, 24 (1965), 161–6; P. Artzi, in: EM, 5 (1968), 445–9; Ginzberg, *Legends*, 4 (1913), 275, 300; 6 (1928), 368, 430; I.Y. Ḥasida, *Ishei ha-Tanakh* (1964), 269.

MERON, city located just north of the Wadi Meirun on one of the eastern spurs of Mt. Meron (map ref. 191/265) at an elevation of 2,450 ft. (750 m.) above sea level around the ancient synagogue. It is not to be confused with Merom, as in the "waters of Merom" in the Hebrew Bible (Josh 11:5, 7), near where Joshua defeated Jabin, King of Hazor, or the city which appears in the list of Caananite cities conquered by Thutmosis III, Meron is also frequently confused with the site of Meroth (map ref. 199/270), which is most likely the one mentioned in Josephus as being fortified in 66 C.E. on the eve of the great revolt against Rome (*Wars* 3: 573; *Life* 188) and excavated in the 1980s by Z. Ilan.

Meron may be identified with the rabbinic town of that name which is associated with Rabbi *Simeon bar Yoḥai (Tosef. Dem. 4.13) and his son Eleazar, who are believed to be buried there. It is also listed as one of the towns or villages of the priestly courses (I Chron. 24; Mish. Ta'an. 4.2, etc.) where the family of Jehoiarib was located. By medieval times Meron was an important pilgrimage site associated with the festival of *Lag ba-Omer and influenced by the mystical traditions that emerged in nearby Safed, just 6 miles (9 km.) away. R. Moses Basola mentions the festival as early as 1522. The name Meron also appears in this connection in the various poems of Kalir and other liturgical authors.

The synagogue site was first surveyed and documented in the important work of Kohl and Watzinger published in 1916, though 19th century explorers and travelers knew the ruin as well. The site was excavated between 1971 and 1977 by Eric M. Meyers and an American team and their finds were published in 1981. A subsequent Israeli salvage excavation was carried out by N. Feig and published in 2002. One of the most important observations to be made is that there was a very modest settlement in the late Hellenistic period, ca. 200–63 B.C.E., and the Early Roman period represented even less in scant remains. No evidence for Josephus' fortification was uncovered in any excavation, which has led the excavators to abandon the idea that Meron and Meroth of Josephus were one and the same place. The heyday of occupations was the rabbinic period, or the Middle-Late Roman era, from ca. 135–363 C.E., the latter date the year of the great earthquake that contributed to the abandonment of the site; and significant remains of domestic buildings and structures survive from this period as do important agricultural installations. The main building identified with this period is the great synagogue on the summit, which is a long basilical structure with the familiar triple doorway on the Jerusalem-facing wall. A shallow portico with six columns was attached to the southern façade wall. The interior of the synagogue has two rows of eight columns, making it the longest of the Galilean synagogues, and while no trace of a Torah Shrine was found it is likely that one stood on the interior of the southern wall. Most of the remains of the building had been robbed in antiquity, and only a small attached room along the southeastern corner has survived. In its rubble foundations were found materials from the third century, allowing the excavators to posit a date for the construction of the building in the third century C.E. It may be assumed that its final period of use came in ca. 363, when the rest of the town was abandoned.

Remains from the lower city show a vibrant town with shops and living complexes that reflect the indigenous life style of the Land of Israel in late antiquity, with many industrial and agricultural installations dotting the interior spaces of the town in the rabbinic period. Olive oil production was very common in the region and its importance is reflected in the material culture of Meron. A room full of charred foodstuffs, possibly intended as *hekdesh*, was found in one of the more upscale homes in the lower city, as was a *mikveh* in another, pointing to a community that observed Jewish laws.

After the abandonment of the site in the second half of the fourth century the site was reoccupied in the 13th–14th century, while some evidence for the 15th century also exists along with the evidence of pilgrim travelers such as Rabbi Obadiah of *Bertinoro (1495). In the 16th century Meron was a Muslim village with approximately 500 souls with an economy similar to the ancient one and based on the cultivation of wheat, fruit, and olives. In early modern times cotton was also raised, and there were some 60 known olive presses known to have been in operation at this time.

[Eric M. Meyers (2nd ed.)]

The modern moshav Meron, at the foot of Mt. Meron, affiliated with the Ha-Po'el ha-Mizrachi Moshavim Association. Founded in 1949, near the yeshivah and remnants of the ancient Meron synagogue, by immigrants from Hungary and Czechoslovakia, it specialized in hill farming, with deciduous fruit orchards, dairy cattle, and poultry as major branches. In the mid-1990s, the population was approximately 605, increasing to 805 in 2002.

[Efraim Orni]

BIBLIOGRAPHY: H. Kohl, and C. Watzinger, *Antike Synagogen in Galilaea* (1916); E.M. Meyers, J.F. Strange, and C.L Meyers, *Excavations at Ancient Meiron, Upper Galilee, Israel* (1981); N. Feig, "Salvage Excavations at Meron," in: *Atiqot*, 43 (2002), 87–107.

MERON (originally **Maierzuk**), **HANNA** (1923–), Israeli actress and star of the *Cameri Theater in Tel Aviv. Born in Berlin, she appeared on the German stage and in Fritz Lang's movie "M" as a child before going to Palestine in 1933. She trained at the Habimah Studio, served in a British army entertainment unit during World War II, and in 1945 joined the newly founded Cameri Theater. She was subsequently responsible for some of the company's greatest successes. Her realistic portrayal of the title role in *Pick-Up Girl* shocked some and delighted others. Possessing incisive style and vitality, she was particularly successful in modern, sophisticated comedy. She also distinguished herself in a wide range of parts that included Micka in Moshe Shamir's *He Walked in the Fields*, Eliza in *Pygmalion*, Rosalind in *As You Like It*, Elizabeth in Schiller's *Mary Stuart*, and the title role in Ibsen's *Hedda Gabler*. She was active in the management of the Cameri Theater and helped to shape its policy. In 1968, she played the lead in the musical *Hello Dolly*. In 1970, she lost a leg as a result of an Arab attack in Munich airport on Israeli passengers. However, on her recovery she resumed her performances on the Israeli stage, giving many striking performances, among them her role in *Medea* and as the ultimate slattern in *The Effect of Gamma Rays on Man-in-the-Moon Marigolds*. A recording of her beautiful reading of poetry accompanied a ballet of the *Batsheva Dance Company. She was awarded the Israel Prize for arts (theater) in 1973. She also appeared in a popular TV sitcom ("Relatives, Relatives") and has directed plays at Tel Aviv University and the Beit-Zvi acting school. In December 2003 she was honored on her 80th birthday by the Herzliyyah Theater, where she served as a founder-director. She was married to the late Ya'akov *Rechter, who received the Israel Prize for arts (architecture) in 1972.

BIBLIOGRAPHY: M. Kohansky, *The Hebrew Theater* (1969), index. **WEBSITE:** www.habama.co.il.

[Mendel Kohansky]

MEROZ (Heb. מֵרוֹז), an unidentified locality, which is cursed in the Song of Deborah (Judg. 5:23) because the inhabitants refused to help the prophetess and Barak in their war against Siserah. Suggested identifications for Meroz are Mazar on Mt. Gilboa or al-Ruz near al-Lajjūn.

BIBLIOGRAPHY: J.J. Garstang, *Joshua-Judges* (1931), 396; Abel, Geog, 2 (1938), 385; A. Alt, in: ZAW, 58 (1941), 244ff.

[Michael Avi-Yonah]

MERRICK, DAVID (1911–2000), Broadway producer. Merrick was born in St. Louis, Mo., as David Margulois, the youngest child of a salesman. His parents were divorced when he was seven and he bounced among relatives through adolescence. A good student, he won a scholarship to Washington University in St. Louis, then went to St. Louis University, where he studied law, a trade that would help him in his tough theatrical contract negotiations. His marriage to Leonore Beck, whom he had met in school, and who had a modest inheritance, allowed the couple to leave St. Louis for New York in 1939. A year later, he invested $5,000 in a forthcoming comedy, *The Male Animal*. The play was a hit, and David Merrick, taking a new name inspired by the 18th-century English actor David Garrick, was born.

For a quarter of a century that ended with his last blockbuster, the musical *42nd Street* in 1980, Merrick was the dominant showman in the Broadway theater. In a typical season during the 1960s he produced a half-dozen or more plays and musicals. His productivity and profitability were unmatched by any single impresario in the history of New York's commercial theater. Among his successes were some of the most popular musicals of his era, including *Gypsy, Hello, Dolly!,* and *Promises, Promises* as well as *42nd Street*, one of the longest-running productions in Broadway history. He introduced Woody *Allen to Broadway as a playwright (*Don't Drink the Water*) and actor (*Play It Again, Sam*) and produced the 1962 musical *I Can Get It for You Wholesale*, which catapulted the 19-year-old singer Barbra *Streisand to stardom. His productions also gave signature roles to Ethel Merman (Mama Rose in *Gypsy*) and Carol Channing (Dolly Levi in *Hello, Dolly!*) and he worked with nearly every major songwriter of the Broadway musical's heyday. Merrick presented Laurence Olivier in his most celebrated postwar performance (as Archie Rice in *The Entertainer*), the breakthrough dramas of John Osborne (*Look Back in Anger*), Brian Friel (*Philadelphia, Here I Come!*), and Tom Stoppard (*Rosencrantz and Guildenstern Are Dead*), as well as two pivotal Royal Shakespeare Company productions directed by Peter Brook, *Marat/Sade* and *A Midsummer's Night Dream*.

Merrick became famous for baiting critics, his own stars, and his fellow producers, all to promote his wares. He gloried in his image as "the abominable showman." When Al *Hirschfeld drew a "particularly unflattering caricature of him as a Grinch-like Santa Claus," Merrick reproduced the image on his annual Christmas card.

Merrick was famous for masterstrokes of publicity. In 1967, when the audiences for *Hello, Dolly!* began to decline, he successfully replaced the entire cast with an all-black company headed by Pearl Bailey and Cab Calloway. When the musical *Subways Are for Sleeping* got poor reviews in 1961, he turned to the phone book, found men with the same names as the seven daily newspaper critics, invited them to see the show, and then got them to endorse it with such raves as "the best musical of the century." When Gower Champion, the musical director and choreographer of *42nd Street*, died early the day of the opening, Merrick kept the news secret so he could announce it from the stage at the curtain call, to the screams and tears of a devastated cast and first-night audience. Again, Merrick assured the show's notoriety and success.

[Stewart Kampel (2nd ed.)]

MERRICK, LEONARD (1864–1939), English novelist, and short-story writer. Born of a London family named Miller, Merrick at first tried to make a career on the stage. His first novel, *Violet Moses* (1891), crude in technique, especially in its portrayal of Jewish types, was not included in his collected works. He won attention in 1898 with *The Actor-Manager*, followed by *The Quaint Companions* (1903), the story of a black tenor and his white wife; he also wrote *Conrad in Quest of his Youth* (1903), and *The Position of Peggy Harper* (1911). Merrick's best achievement was his three volumes of short stories, *The Man Who Understood Women* (1908), *A Chair on the Boulevard* (1921), and *While Paris Laughed* (1918), where he excelled in the delineation of French Bohemian types as seen through English eyes. Merrick developed a humorous and satiric style, but his stories were later criticized as too contrived. He never won popularity, but was highly regarded by his fellow writers, a number of whom, including Wells, Hewlett, Barrie, and Pinero, wrote prefaces to the collected edition of his works, issued in 1918. In 1945 George Orwell wrote an introduction to a never published reprint of Merrick's *The Position of Peggy Harper*. Merrick still attracts interest because of his willingness to deal with unusual themes, such as the issue of miscegenation in *Peggy Harper*.

ADD. BIBLIOGRAPHY: E.W. McDiarmid, *Leonard Merrick, 1864–1939* (1980); ODNB online.

[Lewis Sowden]

MERRILL, ROBERT (1917–2004), U.S. baritone singer. Born in New York City, Merrill studied with his mother, Lillian Miller Merrill, then, from 1936, with Samuel Margolies. His professional career began in popular music, at the Radio City Music Hall (1943); but he made his operatic début in 1944, in *Aida*. The following year, having won an audition contest sponsored by the Metropolitan Opera Company, he made his début there as Germont in *La Traviata*, and remained one of its leading singers, except for the season 1951–52, owing to his appearance in a Hollywood film, of which the Metropolitan's general manager, Rudolph Bing, disapproved. Merrill was a Verdi and Puccini singer of great power and richness and a favorite performer of Arturo Toscanini's last years. Among his recordings are famous arias from *Carmen, The Barber of Seville, La Traviata, Hamlet,* and *L'Africaine*, and songs.

[Max Loppert]

MERSEBURG, city in Germany. The Jewish community of Merseburg was one of the oldest in Germany. As early as 973 Emperor Otto II granted Bishop Gisiler authority over "the Jews, the merchants, and the mint in the city." King Henry II renewed this privilege in 1004. In 1234 three Jews lent 80 silver marks to the burgrave of Merseburg. In 1269 the convent of Pegau sold properties to repay debts to Merseburg Jews. In this period R. Ezekiel of Merseburg addressed a number of halakhic queries to Meir b. Baruch of *Rothenburg. Another scholar of the period was R. Samuel of Merseburg. The cemetery of the community dated at least from 1362. The assertion that there was a persecution in 1349–50 rests on a confusion between similar names of localities. In a Hebrew source *Menahem of Merseburg, author of *Nimmukim*, was a leading German rabbi in the second half of the 14th century. In 1434 the Jews of the Merseburg bishopric paid 100 gilders coronation tax to King Sigismund II; in 1438 a 3% income tax to King Albert II; and in 1440 a coronation tax again. At an unknown time thereafter the Jews left the city, which underwent economic decline and internal tension. In 1556 the Saxon historian Ernst Brotuff wrote, "Formerly many Jews lived in Merseburg who had their own synagogue with a courtyard in the small street west of the Cathedral chapter." In 1565 Merseburg came under the rule of Saxon, where no Jews were tolerated, and in 1815 under Prussia, which lifted the restrictions in the new territories only in 1847. By 1849, some 34 Jews lived in Merseburg; there were 23 in 1871; 16 in 1880; 20 in 1903; 29 in 1905; 20 in 1913 (five families); and 40 in 1925. They were affiliated with the Jewish community in Weissenfels. Records for the years 1933–45 are missing. No Jews settled in Merseburg after 1945.

BIBLIOGRAPHY: Salfeld, Martyrol, 78, n. 4; FWJ (1928–9), 293; *Deutsche Reichstagsakten*, publ. by Hist. Kommiss. Bayer, Ak. d. Wissenschaften (1867–1961), 11, 305–7; 13, 465; 14, 671; G. Kisch, *Forschungen zur Rechts-und Sozialgeschichte der Juden…* (1955), 54; Baron, Social², 4 (1957), 65–66; T. Oelsner, in: YIVOA, 2 (1958–9), 193; idem, in YLBI, 7 (1962), 189; S. Neumann, *Zur Statistik der Juden in Preussen* (1884), 47; H.L. Mursek, *Merseburg* (1963), passim; *Germania Judaica*, 1 (1963), 226–28; 2 (1968), 539–40. **ADD. BIBLIOGRAPHY:** A. Maimon, M. Breuer, Y. Guggenheim (eds.), *Germania Judaica*, vol. 3, 1350–1514 (1987), 867–69.

[Toni Oelsner]

MERSIN, city in *Turkey, on the Mediterranean coast in Cilicia, capital of the province of Icel; population (2004), 587,800. In ancient times there was a Jewish community in the town. In 107 B.C.E., some of its Jewish inhabitants were transferred to the Bosphorus region by Mithridates IV, king of Pontus. No information is available on the existence of a Jewish community during the Middle Ages. From the 19th century, however, there were a number of Jews in the town who had come from various Turkish towns (especially *Salonika) and were engaged in commerce. In 1909, there was a *blood libel, in which one of the heads of the local Gatenyo family was accused of using Greek blood for the baking of *matzah*. The accusation was withdrawn after the intervention of the Greek patriarch of *Istanbul. During the late 1930s the community consisted of about 35 families, some of which were newcomers from such inland towns as Urfa, Maras, Antep, and Kilis. With the establishment of the State of Israel most Jews left to settle there. In 1977 there were still 43 Jews in Mersin, divided into groups according to origin (Ladino or Arabic as a second language). Most of them were merchants. There was a synagogue but no rabbi.

BIBLIOGRAPHY: A. Galanté, *Histoire des Juifs d'Anatolie*, 2 (1939), 303f. **ADD. BIBLIOGRAPHY:** EIS², 6 (1991), 1023; S. Tuval, "*Ha-Kehillot be-Turkiyah ka-Yom*," in: *Pe'amim*, 12 (1982), 135–36.

[Abraham Haim / David Kushner (2nd ed.)]

MERTON, family of British and German industrialists and philanthropists. ABRAHAM LYONS MOSES (1775–1854), whose sons later dropped the name Moses and called themselves Merton, shared in the founding of the Jews' Orphan Asylum and with Henry Solomon endowed a number of almshouses in 1838. RALPH MERTON (1815–1883), his son, settled in Frankfurt and joined the metal firm of his father-in-law, Philip Abraham Cohen, after whose death Merton expanded the company and renamed it Metallgesellschaft. It became one of the most important metal and metallurgical concerns in Germany. He maintained close business relations with his brother, HENRY R. MERTON (1848–1929), who headed Henry R. Merton and Co. of London, which held a dominant place in England parallel to that of Metallgesellschaft in Germany. Both firms had strong associations with the American Metal Company in New York. Because of its connections with the German firm, the British Merton company was liquidated during World War I and reorganized as two separate firms under the names of H. Gardener and Co. Ltd. and the British Metal Corporation. Both H. Gardener and Co. and the British Metal Corporation were later incorporated into a new company, the Amalgamated Metal Corporation Ltd. Ralph Merton's son, WILLIAM (WILHELM) MERTON (1848–1916), who was born in Frankfurt, became the head of the Metallgesellschaft in Frankfurt. A generous philanthropist, he founded the Academy for Social and Commercial Sciences which later formed the basis of the University of Frankfurt in Frankfurt and supported the institution for many years. Under Hitler, the Merton family lost control of the Metallgesellschaft and took refuge in England. A relative, SIR THOMAS RALPH MERTON (1888–1969), was professor of spectroscopy at Oxford University. He made notable contributions to the development of the spectroscope, and, significantly, to the modern radar screen, the latter credited with helping Britain win the Battle of Britain in 1940. He was treasurer of the Royal Society from 1939 to 1956 and was knighted in 1944. In 1958 he was awarded the Rumford Medal of the Royal Society.

BIBLIOGRAPHY: P.H. Emden, *Jews of Britain* (1943), index; P. Stein, *Wilhelm Merton* (1917); C. Fuerstenberg, *Lebensgeschichte eines deutschen Bankiers* (1931). **ADD. BIBLIOGRAPHY:** ODNB online for Sir Thomas Ralph Merton.

[Morton Mayer Berman]

MERTON, ROBERT C. (1944–), U.S. economist and educator; co-recipient of the 1997 Nobel Memorial Prize for economics. A New York City native, raised in Hastings-on-Hudson, N.Y., Merton was the middle child of renowned sociologist Robert K. *Merton and Suzanne Carhart. In 1966 Merton received his B.S. in engineering mathematics from Columbia University and an M.S. in 1967 from Caltech for applied mathematics. He switched his focus to economics and transferred to the Massachusetts Institute of Technology (MIT) on a full fellowship and completed his Ph.D. in 1970; subsequently, he began his teaching career at MIT's Sloan School of Management where he taught through 1988. Upon leaving MIT he moved to the Harvard Business School where, in 1998, he was named its first John and Natty McArthur University Professor.

As a youth, mathematics was his favorite school subject and the love of both numbers and baseball led him to memorize all the big-leaguers' statistics. While his mother provided him with his practical life knowledge, his father served as his enduring intellectual adviser despite his choice of a starkly divergent academic path.

Searching for real-life applications of mathematics is what lured Merton to the field of economics. His research while a member of MIT's faculty led to his 1973 paper "The Theory of Rational Option Pricing" (appearing in the *Bell Journal of Economics*) not long after Myron Scholes and Fischer Black advanced their landmark option-pricing formula in the *Journal of Political Economy*. Together, the men successfully tested the system in the live market with their mutual fund, Money Market/Options Investment, Inc., activated in 1976. The ramification on Wall Street of their mutually supporting theories on valuing stock options was considerable and served as the backbone to the formation of enormous "derivatives" markets. This watershed in economics was finally honored in 1997 when Merton and Scholes were bestowed with the Nobel Memorial Prize in economic sciences.

Merton's success was tempered by the 1998 collapse of his and Scholes' Long-Term Capital Management (LTCM), the Greenwich, Conn.-based hedge fund of which they were two of several founders in 1993. Undeterred, he co-founded Integrated Finance Limited (IFL), an international investment firm based in New York City in 2003, and also serves as its Chief Science Officer; in that same year, Dimensional Fund Advisors, an investment management company, chose Merton as a member of its board of directors/trustees. He served on numerous corporate boards, held the presidency of the American Finance Association in 1986, and was awarded many honorary degrees from various universities. Along with the scores of articles appearing in professional journals during his three decades in academia, Merton wrote several books including *Continuous-Time Finance* (1990) and *Finance* (1998), co-authored with Zvi Bodie. In 2004 Merton donated his MIT and Harvard lecture notes on finance theory to the Professional Risk Managers' International Association (PRMIA) for the purpose of training financial risk managers.

[Dawn Des Jardins (2nd ed.)]

MERTON, ROBERT KING (**Meyer Schkolnick**; 1910–2003), U.S. sociologist. Born in Philadelphia, Merton received his B.A. from Temple University in 1931 and his M.A. (1932) and Ph.D. (1936) from Harvard. A student of George R. Simpson, Pitirim Sorokin, and Talcott Parsons, he taught at Harvard and Tulane universities. From 1941 he taught at Columbia University, where for 35 years he collaborated with Paul Lazarsfeld, with whom he co-developed the Bureau of Applied Social Research. Merton was president of the American Sociological Association and a member of the board of the Center for Advanced Study in the Behavioral Sciences at Stanford University.

Merton, whose thinking was influenced by Marx, Durkheim, Simmel, and Weber, was one of the leading American theorists in the social sciences. Merton studied the sociology of science itself; in 1942 he developed an "ethos of science," which challenged the prevailing public perception that scientists were eccentric geniuses who were not bound by normal social constraints. Essentially, he interpreted the task of sociology as the understanding of the ways in which social structures shape and channel the values, attitudes, and actions of persons. Among the numerous concepts first formulated or felicitously reformulated by Merton are "theories in the middle range" (as against sweeping theories in the grand style); "manifest and latent functions"; "self-fulfilling prophecy," elaborating a theorem of W.I. Thomas; "role model"; "deviant behavior"; and focus groups. His most significant contributions can be located in four areas. First, he provided an objective analysis of various kinds of deviant behavior, which has been widely used in research on delinquency, criminality, and social movements. Second, he made significant contributions to the sociology of science, especially about the impact of religion on science, about multiple discoveries in science, rivalry among scientists, and unintended consequences of scientific discoveries. Third, he was interested in the study of bureaucracy, partly refining Durkheim's concept of "anomie," partly complementing Max Weber's structural approach with an analysis of the psychological consequences of bureaucratic organization. Fourth, he advanced the study of adult socialization, focusing especially on the activation of attitudes by key personalities and on the concept of the reference group. Generally, he emphasized the interdependence of theory and research; the collection of essays that he published under the title *Social Theory and Social Structure* (1957²) is one of the most influential books in American sociology.

In 1994 Merton was awarded the National Medal of Science by President Bill Clinton, becoming the first sociologist to receive that honor.

Other significant publications of Merton include *Science, Technology, and Society in Seventeenth Century England* (1938); "The Sociology of Knowledge," in Gurvitch and Moore, *Twentieth Century Sociology* (1945); *Mass Persuasion* (1946); *Continuities in Social Research* (1950); *Focused Interview* (with M. Fiske and P. Kendall, 1952²); *Social Theory and Social Structure* (1957); *On the Shoulders of Giants* (1965); *Con-*

temporary Social Problems (with R. Nisbet, 1966²); *On Theoretic Sociology* (1967); and *The Sociology of Science* (1973). He was one of the editors of *Reader in Bureaucracy* (1952) and wrote numerous papers, chiefly dealing with topics of the sociology of knowledge.

ADD. BIBLIOGRAPHY: C. Mongardini and S. Tabboni (eds.), *Robert K. Merton and Contemporary Society* (1997); J. Clark et al. (eds.), *Robert Merton: Consensus and Controversy* (1990); P. Sztompka, *Robert K. Merton, an Intellectual Profile* (1986); R. Hill, *Merton's Role Types and Paradigm of Deviance* (1980); L. Coser (ed.), *The Idea of Social Structure: Papers in Honor of Robert K. Merton* (1975).

[Werner J. Cahnman / Ruth Beloff (2nd ed.)]

MERV (modern **Baīram Alī**), ancient city in Turkmenistan. According to a tradition reported by the 12th-century Muslim historian al-Bayhaqī, Ezra the scribe is said to have traveled from Palestine to Merv, building a synagogue which was still in existence in the 11th century. In connection with tax reforms carried out in the time of the caliph Omar II (717–20), a certain Akiva the Jew, of Merv, is mentioned as being responsible for the collection of taxes from the Jews there. That a Jewish community continued in existence is attested by a disputation held in Merv in 1336 between Christian monks and one of the leaders of the community, and by a *Judeo-Persian dictionary composed there in 1473. Nineteenth-century European travelers (J. *Wolff, E.N. *Adler, etc.) refer to the numbers and occupations of the Jews in Merv. After the forced conversion of the Jewish community in *Meshed (1839), many *jadīd al-Islām* converts found refuge in Merv. No recent information is available.

BIBLIOGRAPHY: W.J. Fischel, in: *Zion*, 1 (1935), 49–74; idem, in: HJ, 7 (1945), 29–50.

[Walter Joseph Fischel]

MERZBACHER, family of numismatists. ABRAHAM MERZBACHER (1812–1885), rabbi, banker, numismatist, and bibliophile, was born in Baiersdorf (near Erlangen), Bavaria. His education at the yeshivah in Fuerth and the universities of Erlangen and Munich was followed by a short career as rabbi of Ansbach. Although running a business in antique books and prints in Baiersdorf, Merzbacher lived in Munich from 1833. In 1846 he became an associate of the banking firm J.N. Oberndoerffer, owned by his father-in-law at Munich, which was also the leading German coin dealer, and later the house of Rollin et Feuardent in Paris – Rollin was a foremost European expert in numismatics. He exposed the "Becker Counterfeits," a famous case of counterfeiting of ancient coins. He became an expert on Polish medals, and also took a special interest in Jewish coins and medals, building up a valuable collection. In 1873 he retired from business and turned to collecting rare Jewish manuscripts and prints to assist R.N.N. *Rabbinovicz in his monumental *Dikdukei Soferim* (*Variae Lectiones in Mischnam et in Talmud Babylonicum*, 1876ff.), also financing its publication. His library grew to over 4,000 volumes, including 156 manuscripts and 43 incunabula, and eventually became part of the city library of Frankfurt (see *Libraries). Merzbacher was also active in the Jewish community, becoming a member of the central committee of the Alliance Israélite Universelle. He held several leading positions in the Munich Jewish community and used to practice – gratis – as a *mohel*. Merzbacher's son EUGEN (1845–1903) also became a numismatist. Born in Munich, he took the *shekel as subject for his thesis (*De Siclis…* 1873). Merzbacher had a vast knowledge of classical and modern coins, but his main interest was in Jewish numismatics. He started a successful business in coins and numismatic books in Munich in 1881.

BIBLIOGRAPHY: *Mitteilungen der Bayerischen Numismatischen Gesellschaft* (1885), fasc. 4., on Abraham; *ibid.* (1903), on Eugen; J. Perles, *Trauerrede… A. Merzbacher* (1885); R.N.N. Rabbinovicz, *Ohel Avraham* (1888), catalog of A. Merzbacher's library; L.A. Mayer, *Bibliography of Jewish Numismatics* (1966), nos. 457–60.

[Arie Kindler]

MERZBACHER, GOTTFRIED (1843–1926), German explorer. Born in Baiersdorf, Bavaria, Merzbacher grew up in a family of highly respected businessmen and bankers. He founded a successful fur business in Munich in 1868. He retired and sold his business in 1888 at the age of 45 which allowed him to concentrate on his true passion: the scientific research of mountain areas. Merzbacher, an accomplished mountaineer explored in Africa, North America, the Caucasus, and from 1892 climbed mountains in Arabia, Persia, and India. He published the reports of these expeditions in scientific journals. From 1902 to 1908 he climbed the Central Tien Shan range of Asia and his findings were published by the Bavarian Academy of Sciences. His book *Aus den Hochregionen des Kaukasus* (1901) became a classic. One of his last trips led him to the Bogdo-Ola mountain range. There a ridge was named after him in 1927. In 1901 Merzbacher received an honorary doctorate from the University of Munich. In 1907 he was appointed Royal Professor.

BIBLIOGRAPHY: Y. Gleibs, *Juden im kulturellen und wissenschaftlichen Leben Münchens in der zweiten Hälfte des 19. Jahrhunderts* (1981), 196–200).

[Andreas Heusler (2nd ed.)]

MERZBACHER, LEO (1810–1856), first U.S. Reform rabbi. Merzbacher, who was born in Fuerth, Bavaria, studied rabbinics under R. Moses Sofer. He went to the United States in 1841 and took up a teaching position with Congregation Rodeph Shalom in New York. In 1843 Congregation Anshe Chesed, New York, appointed him preacher and teacher at a monthly salary of six dollars. A sermon critical of the practice of married women covering their hair led to nonrenewal of his appointment, whereupon his partisans in the congregation united with the recently formed Cultus Verein to establish Congregation Emanuel with Merzbacher as its rabbi (1845). The reforms made by the new congregation were minimal in character. Confirmation was introduced in 1848 and Merzbacher compiled a shortened prayer book in 1855. He was one of the founders of the Independent Order of True Sisters. Sickness limited Merzbacher's activities, and he seems to have had little impact either on his own congregation or on the New York Jewish community.

[Sefton D. Temkin]

MERZER, ARIEH (1905–1966), Israeli artist specializing in repoussé reliefs, mainly in copper and silver. Born in a small town near Warsaw, Merzer studied art in Warsaw and began his career as an artist there. From 1930 he lived and worked in Paris. After the occupation of France he was detained in a concentration camp, but in 1943 managed to escape and made his way to Switzerland. At the end of 1945 he immigrated to Ereẓ Israel where he lived alternately in Holon and Safed. He was one of the founders of the Safed artists' colony.

Merzer revitalized the ancient technique of hammered metal which has a long tradition in the Jewish creative arts, especially in the decoration of ceremonial objects. His style reflects the Jewish popular art of Eastern Europe, and his subjects were drawn from the Jewish lore of the past: the ghettos and *shtetls* of Poland whose culture he knew from his youth. His work includes scenes of Jewish feasts and religious ceremonies, daily life, genre and figures of craftsmen, as well as illustrations of folksongs and of stories by the great Yiddish writers.

In Safed he found an atmosphere not unlike that of the small towns of the Diaspora. The Ashkenazi and Sefardi inhabitants of Safed are depicted in their traditional garb, their earthly simplicity strongly recalling the Jews of the ghetto. Many of his works reflect everyday scenes of Safed, its Old City, its famous synagogues, narrow lanes, and ancient stone houses with wrought-iron railings. He also depicted stories of the Bible as he saw them in his imagination when he first studied them as a child in the *ḥeder*. Biblical heroes are shown as real characters from the Eastern European Jewish world, those very Jews whom he had encountered in his childhood flavored with Oriental elements with which he was impressed after his arrival in Ereẓ Israel. Occasionally he also addressed himself to contemporary Israeli subject matter, but the bulk of his work is a testament of love to a way of life that has disappeared.

Ornamental elements are emphasized in his reliefs by the frequent use of symmetry especially notable in the decorative effects of the backgrounds, in details and elaborated patterns. He frequently designed animals, plants, and ornamental motifs taken from the rich resources of Jewish folk art. He combined tactile values of the figures, which are the main components of his depictions, with pictorial effects in the backgrounds and landscapes. His work, deeply rooted in Jewish folklore, has a charming simplicity and a naive air and represents a direct continuation of the traditional Jewish folk art.

[Mira Friedman]

MESELSON, MATTHEW (1930–), U.S. biologist. Born in Denver, Colorado, he was educated at the University of Chicago, the University of California at Berkeley, and the California Institute of Technology, where he was research fellow in chemical biology (1957–60). He moved to Harvard University (1960) where he became professor of biology (1964–76) and Thomas Dudley Cabot Professor of the Natural Sciences and Principal Investigator from 1976. He also directed a laboratory program at the Josephine Bay Paul Center in Woods Hole. His research concerned the relationship between DNA structure and the control of gene function and replication, the repair of defective DNA, and related regulatory mechanisms in molecular genetics. He studied the microscopic animal bdelloid rotifer, with the part objective of elucidating the evolutionary disadvantages of asexual reproduction. His paper with Franklin Stahl (1958) described the first experiments confirming the Watson-Crick model of DNA replication and is a classic landmark in the history of molecular biology. Later he collaborated with Sydney Brenner and Francois Jacob (1961) in identifying transfer RNA, a crucially important molecule in protein synthesis. His experimental example and teaching skills continue to influence the development of modern biology. From the Vietnam War Meselson worked to prohibit chemical and biological weapons. In 1990 he co-founded with Julian Robinson and directed the Harvard Sussex program based mainly at Harvard University and the University of Sussex dedicated to arms limitation. In 1994 he and his collaborators revealed that the anthrax epidemic in Sverdlovsk in the former U.S.S.R. originated in a military facility. His many honors include membership in the U.S. National Academy of Sciences, foreign membership of the Royal Society of London, the Linus Pauling Prize, the Leo Szilard Award of the American Physical Society, the Scientific Freedom and Responsibility Award of the American Association for the Advancement of Science, and the Lasker Award for Special Achievement in Medical Science (2004). He served on many national and international councils concerned with scientific policy and education.

[Michael Denman (2nd ed.)]

MESENE, the land of southern Mesopotamia extending from about 24 mi. (40 km.) below Kut al-Amāra to the Persian Gulf. This area was also called Characene, a term giving political identification derived from Charax Spasinu, name of the fortified capital city of the district. During the late Middle Ages the name was replaced by that of the new capital and port of the district, Basra. The economy of Charax depended on her role as the main port and relay point for east-west trade on the upper Persian Gulf. During the first and second centuries C.E. overland trade developed via Mesene with the Nabatean city of *Petra and with the Syrian desert emporium of Palmyra (Tadmor), and through these centers with the rich Roman west.

A Jewish community existed in Mesene from at least the late Parthian period. During the reign of Artabanus V (209–27 C.E.) a Jewish merchant of Meshān converted Izates, prince of Adiabene, to Judaism. At this time a second Jewish merchant of Meshān similarly converted a number of women of that city (Jos., Ant. 20: 2, 4).

In talmudic sources of the third century C.E. the Jews of Babylonia refer to Mesenean Jews as imprudent (Kid. 49b), unfit and of tainted descent (Kid. 71b), since "whosoever did not know his family and his tribe made his way there" (Yev. 17a). Marriage between Babylonian Jews and the Jews of the northern Mesenean city of *Apamea was forbidden (Kid. 71b). The city of Meshan (Charax) is described as being lower than hell, and Harpania, a second city of Mesene (perhaps a variant spelling of Apamea), as being lower still than Meshan (Yev. 17a). This hostility shown by Babylonian Jews may have been caused, in part, by the adoption of elements of Mandeanism by the Jews of Mesene. It has also been noted that the practice of allowing the Jewish dead of Harpania to lie while the shroud was woven (Sanh. 48b) would indicate an adaptation by the Jews of that city of the Zoroastrian practice of exposing a corpse before burial (see Obermeyer, 197). A possible preference by Mesenean Jews for the Jerusalem Talmud may have further contributed to their being disliked by the Jews of Babylonia.

BIBLIOGRAPHY: Neubauer, Géogr, 325, 329, 382; E. Peterson, in: ZNW, 27 (1928), 55–98; J. Obermeyer, *Die Landschaft Babylonien...* (1929), index; S. Nodelman, in: *Berytus*, 13 (1960); J. Hansman, in: *Iranica Antiqua*, 8 (1967).

MESHA (Heb. מֵישַׁע), king of Moab in the ninth century B.C.E. (see *Moab). The name is formed from the root *yšʿ*, "to deliver, save." In II Kings 3:4 it is stated that Mesha was a sheep breeder. He was subjugated by *Ahab and paid him tribute. After Ahab's death, the king of Moab, most likely Mesha, revolted and ceased paying tribute (II Kings 3:4–5; cf. II Kings 1:1). *Jehoram son of Ahab conducted a military campaign against Moab to subjugate it (II Kings 3:6ff.).

Most of the information on Mesha is contained in the stele which he erected at Dibon (see *Mesha Stele). The first three lines of the inscription mention that Mesha's father Chemoshyat, whose name is known from a stele found in Kerak (Kir of Moab; W.L. Reed and F.V. Winnett, in: BASOR, 172 (1963), 6), ruled over Moab for 30 years, and that Mesha succeeded him. Mesha resided at Dibon, situated north of Arnon, and called himself "King of Moab, the Dibonite." The stele then relates how *Omri, king of Israel, took possession of the land of Medeba in the northern part of the plain, and subjugated Moab "his days and a part of the days of his son, forty years." The phrase "his son" obviously refers to Ahab. However, all the days of Omri and Ahab together are considerably fewer than 40 years. Moreover, the Bible relates that the king of Moab revolted after Ahab's death, rather than during his lifetime. Among the many attempts to explain the discrepancy between what is recorded in the Bible and in the Mesha Inscription, the most acceptable theory is that the number 40 is not to be taken literally, but is the conventional length of a generation (cf. Num. 32:13; Ps. 95:10). Mesha apparently revolted twice, once during the reign of Omri's son Ahab, as is related in the stele, and once after Ahab's death, as is stated in the Bible. If this theory is correct, the following sequence of events can be proposed: Moab revolted against Israel following the division of Solomon's kingdom, or at the latest in the days of Baasha. The Moabites even reached north of the Arnon and captured the plateau, including the land of Medeba. The king's residence was established at Dibon, at the latest in the days of Mesha's father. Omri waged war against Moab, recapturing Medeba and several cities in the plateau. For various reasons, the Israelite king preferred to leave Dibon in Moabite hands and was content to receive yearly tribute as a token of subjugation. In Ahab's time, Mesha revolted against Israel. It is not clear if Ahab fought against Mesha, since the stele contains the expression "king of Israel" (lines 10–11, 18), which may refer to either Omri or Ahab. It is more likely that the reference is to Omri (cf. line 7), since Ahab was occupied with wars against the Arameans (but see *Ben-Hadad). Mesha first concentrated upon preparing fortifications for a confrontation with Israel. He secured communications between Dibon and Moab proper by building roads across the Arnon (line 26). He fortified Aroer, strengthened the acropolis (*qarḥoh*) of Dibon, and prepared the city for withstanding a siege by digging ditches and building a cistern (*ʾswḥ*; vocalization uncertain) inside the city. Upon the death of Ahab, Mesha exploited Israel's defeat at Ramoth-Gilead and the weakness of *Ahaziah son of Ahab; he erupted northward, capturing all the cities of the plain. He reached Nebo, which he destroyed, killing its population of 7,000 people, "because I consecrated it to Ashtar-Chemosh." Jehoram, king of Israel, combined forces with *Jehoshaphat, king of Judah, and the king of Edom and invaded Moab from the south, through Edom (II Kings 3:20), reaching the city of Kir-Hareseth in the heart of Moab. The battle in the city of Horonaim in southern Moab and its capture by Mesha, which is related at the end of the inscription, should be connected with this campaign. The biblical account agrees, stating that Jehoram's campaign ended in failure and that he was forced to withdraw without conquering Moab. The Bible attributes the failure to a ritual act performed by the king of Moab: "Then he took his eldest son that should have reigned in his stead and offered him for a burnt offering upon the wall. And there came great wrath upon Israel; and they departed from him, and returned to their own land" (II Kings 3:27).

BIBLIOGRAPHY: Y. Liver, in: PEQ, 99 (1967), 14–31.

[Bustanay Oded]

MESHA STELE, an inscribed basalt stele, measuring about 40 inches (one meter) high and about 28 inches (70 centimeters) wide, erected by *Mesha, king of Moab, at Dibon (today, Dhībân), probably in the third quarter of the ninth century, B.C.E. The shape of the stele, with a flat base and rounded top, is characteristic of those erected by kings of that period. Unlike many other memorial inscriptions, the Mesha stele has no relief on the upper part. It was found at Dibon in 1868 by F.A. Klein, a Prussian missionary. Prior to its acquisition by the Louvre, it was smashed by Bedouins, who, observing the great interest it aroused among Europeans, assumed that it contained a treasure or ghost. The inscription was deciphered with the aid of a squeeze made by Clermont-Ganneau of all but the last few lines. The language of the inscription is Moabite, which is closely related to Hebrew, though it diverges from it in several grammatical features. The alphabetic Canaanite-Hebrew script is well shaped and clear; the words are separated from each other by dots, and the sentences by vertical lines. Mesha dedicated the stele to his deity Chemosh out of gratitude for the latter's deliverance of the Moabites from Israelite rule, and for his help in the conquest of the plain. The stele (lines 4–9) relates, "As for Omri, king of Israel, he humbled Moab many years [lit. days], for Chemosh was angry with his land. And his son followed him and he also said 'I will humble Moab.' In my time he spoke [thus], but I have triumphed over him and over his house, while Israel hath perished forever" (cf. II Kings 1:1; 3:4–5). However, by describing the events in the first person, Mesha's real intention was probably to perpetuate his own victories over Israel.

BIBLIOGRAPHY: A.H. Van Zyl, *The Moabites* (1960), 247ff., incl. bibl.; W.F. Albright, in: JQR, 35 (1944/45), 247–70; EM, 4 (1962), 925–9, incl. bibl.; Pritchard, Texts, 320–1; H. Donner and W. Roellig, *Kanaanaeische und aramaeische Inschriften*, 1 (1962), 33; 2 (1964), 168–79.

[Bustanay Oded]

MESHECH (Heb. מֶשֶׁךְ), a nation from Asia Minor, identified today with Muški of Assyrian sources (beginning about the 12th century B.C.E.) and with Μόσχοι of classical sources. In the table of nations (Gen. 10:2; I Chron. 1:5) Meshech appears after Javan and Tubal as one of the sons of Japheth. Meshech, again with Javan and Tubal, is mentioned in Ezekiel 17:13 as slave traders and merchants of copperware. This description appears to be historically accurate. The mention of Meshech together with Tubal and *Gog (Ezek. 38:2–3; 39:1), derives from the legend about Gog which gained currency in the time of Ezekiel.

BIBLIOGRAPHY: E.A. Speiser, *Genesis* (1964), 66; R.D. Barnett, in: CAH², vol. 2, ch. 30 (1966), incl. bibl.; EM, 5 (1968), 531–2, incl. bibl.

MESHED (pronounced and written **Mashhad** in Persian), a city situated in northeast *Iran, capital of the province *Khurasan. This is one of the few cities in Iran where the beginning of its Jewish settlement is documented. It is also one of the two holy Muslim cities in Iran where Ali-Reza, the eighth Imam of the Shi'ites, is buried (818 C.E.). (The other one is Qomm (the burial place of his sister, Fatimah)). Nāder Shah was unintentionally the cause of Jewish settlement in Meshed. It is well documented that two kings, Shah *'Abbās I and Nāder Shah, transferred people from one region to the other, mostly for economic and security reasons. After his famous war with India, Nāder Shah brought over a large amount of treasures and housed them in Kalāt-e Nāderi (1741), about 100 km. north of Meshed. Being a Sunni, he did not trust the Shi'ites to guard his house of treasures. He ordered that Jews be brought to Kalāt-e Nāderi to guard the house. Consequently, Jews were uprooted from their native towns and villages in *Gilān, Deylamān, and *Kazvin areas to be transferred to Kalāt-e Nāderi. They marched in several groups, one of which reached the Kalāt, while the two others, on their way to Kalāt, arrived in Meshed and the city of Sabzvār. Actually Jews were on the march to Kalāt when Nāder Shah was murdered (June 1747) and they were thus left alone at their temporary stations. Therefore, it is probable that by sheer accident a group of Jews was compelled to settle in Meshed some time before the king's murder. Jews were not allowed to settle inside the holy city; they were given a piece of land outside the wall. The place, which formerly belonged to the Zoroastrians, was called 'Id-gāh. In their new home the Jews prospered, especially in trading with neighboring cities and settlements. Joseph Wolff, a Christian missionary, reported in 1831 that Jews mingled too much with the Muslims and that among them one could also find Jewish Sufis who possessed the *Koran and Sufi books of poetry (pp. 133ff.). Some of the leaders of the Jewish community of Meshed, according to certain official documents, collaborated with the British authorities in the areas of Khurasan, *Afghanistan, and *Bukhara.

On March 27, 1839, Muslims attacked the Jewish quarter where about 2,000 Jews lived. They killed some 35 and wounded many more, insisting that they embrace Islam (see document concerning this event: ms 948 in Netzer, 1985, p. 89; Ben-Zvi, plate 10). Soon afterwards ritual arrangements were made and the Jews performed the necessary procedures for conversion. The converts were known as *Jadīd al-Islām* (in short: *Jadīd*) meaning New Muslims. They were ordered to close their synagogues and schools, and to abandon all Jewish practices. They were to change their Jewish names to Muslim ones, attend mosques regularly, participate in all Muslim rituals, and perform the pilgrimage to the holy Muslim sites in Karbala and Mecca. They were also very cautious not to engage in intermarriage. As *anusim*, almost all of them lived a double life: they continued to keep all the Jewish laws and customs such as *kashrut*, prayers, observance of the Sabbath, Passover, Day of Atonement, and other Jewish holidays. Some families left Meshed to live as Jews in Herat and other nearby cities. Some found their way to India, the Land of Israel, South Africa, London, and New York. Many of these immigrants prospered and became rich. In *Jerusalem, they settled in the Bukharan Quarter, where they contributed to its construction and also built two synagogues there.

Reporting in 1850 and 1884, respectively, both Benjamin II and Neumark, tell us about the difficult life of the 400 *anusim* families of Meshed. From time to time their cryptic life was noticed by the Muslim authorities, which led to pogroms in the Jewish quarter. The severest of these occurred in 1891 and in 1902. Immigration to the Land of Israel increased year by year. Though the *Pahlavi regime (1925–79) brought some degree of peace and freedom to the Jews of Meshed, and officially they were not obliged to remain Muslims, the Muslim inhabitants of Meshed still continued to call them *Jadīd al-Islām* and expected them to remain loyal to their new religion. However, during the Pahlavi regime, they built their own synagogues in *Teheran and Meshed. They especially benefited from the protection granted them by the Red Army during World War II, when Meshed and Khurasan were occupied by Russia (1941–46). On Passover 1946, while the Russian army was leaving the city, the Jewish quarter was once again attacked by Muslims, who this time intended not only to kill and injure the Jews but, equipped with fuel, to burn all the Jewish houses. Thanks to the protection they received from the local officials and some Tudeh members of Meshed, the disaster was averted. According to Landshut in 1948 2,500 Jews lived in Meshed. This number was reduced to 30 persons by 1973. The major cities where the Jews of Meshed now conduct community life with their own synagogues are Jerusalem, Tel Aviv, Milan, London, and New York.

BIBLIOGRAPHY: Benjamin II, *Eight Years in Asia and Africa from 1846 to 1855* (1863); I. Ben-Zvi, *Meḥkarim u-Mekorot* (1969); S. Landshut, *Jewish Communities in the Muslim Countries of the Middle East* (1950), 61–66; A. Levi, "*Eduyot u-Te'udot le-Toledot Yehudei Mashhad*," in: *Pe'amim*, 6 (1980), 57–73; A. Netzer, "*Korot Anusei Mashahd lefi Ya'akov Dilmanian*," in: *ibid*., 42 (1990), 127–156; idem, "*Toledot Anusei Mashhad*," in: *Pe`amim*, 94–95 (2003), 262–268; E. Neumark, *Massa be-Ereẓ ha-Kedem*, ed. by A. Ya'ari (1947); R. Patai, *Jadid al-Islam: The Jewish New Muslims of Meshhed* (1997); J.B. Schechtman, *On Wings of Eagles* (1961); Y. Benzion and Y. Raz, *Mi-Nidḥei Yisrael be-Afganistan le-Anusei Mashhad be-Iran* (1992).

[Amnon Netzer (2nd ed.)]

MESHEL, YERUHAM (1912–2002), Israeli trade union leader, member of the Ninth and Tenth Knessets. Meshel was born in Pinsk in Belorussia. He went to a reformed *ḥeder*, and later studied at the Tarbut Hebrew gymnasium in Pinsk. As a youth he joined the Ha-Shomer ha-Ẓa'ir movement. He settled in Palestine in 1933, and worked as an agricultural laborer, and in construction. During World War II Meshel was the representative of the Histadrut in British army camps. In 1943–47 he was head of the Metal Workers Union, in 1947–61 head of the Factory Workers Department of the Histadrut, and in 1961–69 head of the Histadrut's Trade Union Department. In 1969 Meshel was elected deputy secretary general of the Histadrut responsible for Social Security, and in 1973 was elected secretary general, succeeding Yitzhak *Ben-Aharon. He remained in this position until 1984. He became head of the Institute for the Study of the Labor Movement named after Pinhas *Lavon in 1987. He wrote *Sheliḥut ve-Derekh* (1980).

[Susan Hattis Rolef (2nd ed.)]

MESHULLAM BEN JACOB OF LUNEL (12th century), Provençal scholar. A master of *halakhah*, Meshullam also occupied himself with secular studies. He was a wealthy man and philanthropist, and together with his sons provided for the support and maintenance of the disciples and scholars who flocked to his *bet ha-midrash*. Benjamin of Tudela describes him and his five sons as being "great and wealthy scholars, Joseph, Isaac, Jacob, Aaron, and Asher the ascetic, who had no concern with worldly matters, but devoted himself to study day and night, fasting and refraining from eating meat, and an outstanding talmudist, together with their brother-in-law Moses" (*The Itinerary of Benjamin of Tudela*, ed. by E.N. Adler (1907), 3). Around them there gathered an outstanding group of talmudic scholars and seekers after knowledge, who became known as "the company of Lunel." In consequence *Lunel became famous as an important center of study. Many of them and their disciples were among the great scholars of that generation, including Samuel b. Moses, "the lion of the group," who apparently was head of the *bet din*, *Abraham b. Isaac of Narbonne, author of *Ha-Eshkol*, his son-in-law *Abraham b. David of Posquières, and *Samuel b. David. This center even attracted scholars from Spain. As Judah ibn *Tibbon notes, Meshullam was distinguished in fields of study other than Talmud. This was in contrast to Jewish scholars before him in Christian countries, who occupied themselves essentially with the Talmud, either because they regarded it as their sole avocation or because of lack of books on general sciences (which were then written in Arabic). Meshullam sponsored the translation of books on grammar, theology, rhetoric, ethics, and parables (cf. introduction to the *Ḥovot ha-Levavot* of *Baḥya b. Joseph ibn Paquda, translated by Ibn Tibbon on the instruction of Meshullam). Meshullam himself also composed halakhic works, as well as books on "parables of wisdom and ethics" that are no longer extant. He is known to have written a book called *Issur Mashehu*, on minute quantities of forbidden foods, mentioned by Solomon b. Abraham *Adret in his novellae to *Ḥullin* (93b, Jerusalem, 1 (1963), ed. 227). From a fragment of the *Issur Mashehu* of Abraham b. David of Posquières published by S. Assaf (*Sifran shel Rishonim* (1935), 185–98) "which I wrote before my teacher Meshullam" it is clear that Abraham b. David wrote it in answer to a work of the same title by Meshullam so as to discuss critically the latter's views. It was recently discovered and published by Y. Kafaḥ in the responsa of the Rabad which he edited (1964, 241ff. no. 207). According to Solomon ibn Verga (in *Shevet Yehudah*), Meshullam died in 1170, but the date is not certain.

BIBLIOGRAPHY: Meshullam b. Moses of Béziers, *Sefer ha-Hashlamah le-Seder Nezikin*, ed. by J. Lubetzki, 1 (1885), introd., VI; Abraham b. Isaac of Narbonne, *Sefer ha-Eshkol*, ed. by S. Albeck, 1 (1935), introd., 10; Benedikt, in: *Tarbiz*, 22 (1950/51), 100f.; S. Assaf, *Sifran shel Rishonim* (1935), 185f.; I. Twersky, *Rabad of Posquières* (1962), index.

[Shlomoh Zalman Havlin]

MESHULLAM BEN KALONYMUS (10th–11th century), rabbi and *paytan*. Born into a rabbinical family from *Lucca, his grandfather was R. Moses the Elder who was taught by Abu Aaron the secrets of the Kabbalah. Meshullam's father (see *Kalonymus family) was a well-known talmudic scholar and *paytan*. His teacher was *Solomon b. Judah ha-Bavli. Meshullam himself was a famous talmudist and liturgical poet, often called "the Great." His works include a commentary on *Ethics of the Fathers*, of which only one extract is extant; responsa, dealing with explanations of talmudic passages and with matrimonial, legal, and ritual matters and including a responsum against the Karaites; and liturgical poems, of which the best known are a composition for the morning service of the Day of Atonement and "*Ammiẓ Ko'aḥ*," the version of the **Avodah* adopted in the Ashkenazi rite. His responsa, apart from their intrinsic value, are important sources of information for the social and economic history of the Jewish communities of pre-Crusade Europe. He is the first author in Europe to mention the commercial law of Ma'arufya. His answers are usually brief and concise, and devoid of argumentation. His decisions are based mainly on the Babylonian Talmud but also refer to the writings of the *geonim*. Both *Gershom Me'or ha-Golah and *Rashi held Meshullam in high regard. The center of Meshullam's activity is uncertain. Responsa by *Sherira and *Hai Gaon point to Italy as does the title "of Rome" sometimes given him. Later he settled in Mainz where his tombstone was discovered. His works helped to establish Rhineland scholarship and stimulated the development in France and Germany of a powerful poetical tradition.

BIBLIOGRAPHY: Rapoport, in: *Bikkurei ha-Ittim*, 10 (1829), 40–41, 111; 11 (1830), 100; Carmoly, in: *Israelitische Annalen*, 1 (1839), 222; Schirmann, Italyah, 27–36; Roth, Dark Ages, index; Zunz, Vortraege, 378; Zunz, Lit Poesie, 107; Wiener, in: MGWJ, 3 (1854), 236–7; Gross, *ibid.*, 27 (1878), 249–50; Davidson, Oẓar, 4 (1933), 451 (index); *Ginzei Schechter*, 2 (1929), 194–235, 279–87.

[Yonah David]

MESHULLAM BEN MOSES (c. 1175–c. 1250), scholar of Béziers and one of the most prominent scholars of Provence in the 13th century. Meshullam, born in Lunel into one of the distinguished families of Provençal Jewry, went to Béziers with his father, Moses b. Judah, one of the leaders of the community and friend of *Abraham b. David of Posquières and *Zerahiah ha-Levi Gerondi. Meshullam's maternal grandfather was *Meshullam b. Jacob of Lunel. His sister's son was *Meir b. Simeon ha-Me'ili of Narbonne, author of *Ha-Me'orot*. Among Meshullam's grandsons were the renowned 14th-century talmudists and scholars of the *Lattes family. Meshullam typifies the remarkable Provençal blending of Torah and general culture. He is known to have taken a definite stand against the new trend favoring the study of Kabbalah, then making inroads among the Jews of Provence, and supported his sister's son, Meir, in his opposition to the *Sefer ha-*Bahir*. Meshullam was highly regarded in France and Spain, and even *Naḥmanides, when he complained to Meshullam of the baseless aspersions emanating from Béziers against the family of Jonah *Gerondi, couched his remarks in highly respectful terms (*Kitvei ha-Ramban*, ed. by C.B. Chavel (1963), 360–4). There is a reference to correspondence between them in Naḥmanides' novellae to the tractate *Eruvin* (still in manuscripts). *Jedaiah ha-Penini, who studied in Meshullam's yeshivah at the age of 15, has left an account of his master's eminence and wisdom, along with a very detailed and impressive description of the program of study in the yeshivah which closed with Meshullam's death.

Meshullam is chiefly renowned for his *Sefer ha-Hashlamah*, designed to complete the *halakhot* of Isaac *Alfasi, explaining its difficult passages, adding *halakhot* that do not appear in it, updating it with the Provençal tradition of scholarship, and dealing with criticisms of the work, including those of Zerahiah ha-Levi Gerondi in his *Ha-Ma'or* – all this in order to give it uncontested authority. Indeed, Menahem *Meiri, who wrote more than 50 years later, refers to Alfasi in the same breath as the *Sefer ha-Hashlamah*, thus showing it to be the standard version of Alfasi in his locality (see introduction to Meiri's commentary on *Avot* ed. by B.Z. Prag, 1964). Meshullam based his work chiefly upon the teachings of the earlier scholars of Provence, and shows especially high regard for Abraham b. David of Posquières, though he does not hesitate to disagree with him on occasion.

Publication of *Sefer ha-Hashlamah* was begun during the last century and the greater part of it, comprising the orders *Mo'ed* and *Nezikin*, and the tractate *Ḥullin*, has already appeared. Those chiefly responsible for its publication were Judah *Lubetzky – *Nezikin* (Paris, 1885–87; Warsaw, 1907), with an extensive commentary, *Torat ha-Hashlamah*; Moses Herschler in the series *Ginzei Rishonim* (1962–); and Abraham Ḥaputa, who also added an extensive commentary, *Reshit ha-Hashlamah* (1961–). The *Sefer ha-Hashlamah Yevamot* was published in the Vilna (Romm) edition of the Talmud under the title *Tosafot Ḥad mi-Kamai*. Some of Meshullam's *hassagot* on Maimonides to *Shabbat, Eruvin*, and *Shevu'ot* (in J. Lubetzky, *Bidkei Battim*, 1896), show he was apparently unaware of Abraham b. David's *hassagot* on Maimonides.

BIBLIOGRAPHY: Meshullam b. Moses of Béziers, *Sefer ha-Hashlamah le-Seder Nezikin*, ed. by J. Lubetsky, 1 (1885), introd.; idem, *Bidkei Battim* (1896); Neubauer, in REJ, 20 (1890), 244–8; I. Twersky, *Rabad of Posquières* (1965), 252f.

[Israel Moses Ta-Shma]

MESHULLAM BEN NATHAN OF MELUN (12th century), talmudist in northern France. Meshullam was born in Narbonne, where he eventually became a member of the *bet din* of *Abraham b. Isaac of Narbonne. From there he went to head the community of Melun. Meshullam became involved in a long and bitter dispute with Jacob *Tam, who accused him of abrogating ancient customs and replacing them with new ones; of introducing many lenient rulings; of exaggerated emendment of the text of the Talmud; of slighting *Rashi and French scholars in general; and of unwarranted independence in *halakhah*. Tam cited, among other instances, permitting a gentile to touch wine-vinegar, permitting ritual immersion for women in the daytime because of the danger from attacks by gentiles at night (an accusation denied by Meshullam), and abrogating the blessing over the Sabbath candles. Tam's complaint to the community of Melun resulted in a lengthy correspondence between the two men, which has in part been preserved (*Sefer ha-Yashar le-Rabbenu Tam*, Responsa vol. ed. by F. Rosenthal (1898), nos. 43–50). Meshullam defended himself vigorously against all the accusations of Tam, accusing him (though in much milder language) of essentially the same things and refusing to accept the slightest external interference in matters of Torah. The fact that Meshullam could base himself on existing halakhic traditions which differed in origin from those held by Tam, and his mastery of the Talmud, stood him in good stead in his dispute with Tam, the greatest scholar of his generation. Meshullam is frequently mentioned in the printed *tosafot*. Meshullam's son, Nathan, and his descendants after him (with the family name of Official) were renowned as the family of the *Mekanne'im* ("Zealots") because of its many noted polemists, who, for several generations, engaged in disputes with high church dignitaries.

BIBLIOGRAPHY: Kahn, in: REJ, 1 (1880), 222–46; 3 (1881), 1–38; Urbach, *ibid.*, 100 (1935), 49–77; Urbach, Tosafot, 62–71 and index; Z. Malter, in: *Mi-Mizraḥ u-mi-Ma'arav*, 4 (1899), 9–16; J. Rosenthal, in: *Aresheth*, 2 (1960), 142–3.

[Israel Moses Ta-Shma]

MESHULLAM FEIVUSH HELLER OF ZBARAZH (d. c. 1795), Galician ḥasidic author, descendant of Yom Tov Lippmann Heller, disciple of Jehiel Michel of Zloczow. Though there are numerous ḥasidic legends about Heller, few authentic biographical details are available. In his youth he ministered to the early ḥasidic masters Menahem Mendel of Peremyshlany and Dov Ber, the Maggid of Mezhirech, to both of whom he refers in his writings. A fellow disciple of Jehiel Michel, Ḥayyim of Czernowitz, records teachings in his name. Heller's importance in the history of ḥasidic thought is due to his little booklet *Yosher Divrei Emet*, first published as part of the anthology of ḥasidic teachings entitled *Likkutei Yekarim* (1792, 1974; published separately 1905, by Samson Heller of Kolymyja, Heller's descendant). It is possible that Heller is to be identified, in fact, with the anonymous editor of the *Likkutei Yekarim. Yosher Divrei Emet* is in the form of two epistles to a friend, describing in detail the ḥasidic way as taught by the Ba'al Shem Tov and his disciples.

In Heller's view, the main thrust of Ḥasidism focuses on the need for complete attachment to God (*devekut*) as the aim of the religious life, to which all else must be subordinated. This involves the "stripping off of corporeality" (*hitpashtut ha-gashmiyyut*), which means not so much the living of an ascetic life, but a thorough detachment from worldly delights, even when engaging in the things of the world. Eating, drinking, earning a living, the marital act, should all be engaged in, but as a duty, under compulsion, as it were, with the mind not on the physical enjoyment but on God as the source of all. In Heller's bold illustration, the man in love with a woman, when he sees her dress, has no thoughts for the dress itself but only of the reminder which it provides of his passion for his beloved. *A fortiori*, when a man studies the Torah and offers his prayers, there should be no trace of self-interest. Hence Scripture says: "Say unto wisdom: 'Thou art my sister'" (Prov. 7:4). Man's attitude to the Torah should be one of pure disinterested love, like that of brother and sister, not like that of man and wife. Heller's novel interpretation of *Torah li-Shmah* ("Torah for its own sake") is: "Torah as its name implies," i.e., Torah means "that which shows forth"; the aim of all Torah study is for man to come near to God, who is shown forth through the Torah. Consequently, the distinction between *nigleh* ("the revealed things") and *nistar* ("the secrets") must not be understood in the conventional sense as referring, respectively, to the Talmud and Codes and the Kabbalah. A "secret" for Heller is that which cannot be communicated. It is a religious experience. Therefore one who studies the Kabbalah merely as an intellectual endeavor has to his credit only the *nigleh* aspect of study, whereas one who studies the Talmud and Codes as a means of experiencing the Divine attains to the far higher stage of *nistar*. The distinction between *nigleh* and *nistar* is not between two different types of subject matter but between different approaches to the study of the same material. Heller is severely critical of the rabbinic scholars of his day, whom he accuses of being immersed in worldly lusts and ambitions. They fondly imagine that the study of the Torah constitutes in itself the love of God and fail to appreciate that without loss of selfhood and complete detachment from the world there can be no love of God, the true aim of Torah study.

On the other hand, the ḥasidic *ẓaddik* can, for Heller, do no wrong. The ḥasidic master, Ẓevi Elimelech of Dynow (*Igra De-Pirka*, No. 15) reports that Heller's disciples told him of their master's saying that one who scrutinizes too closely the deeds of a *ẓaddik* is like one who gazes too closely at the sun, and he will suffer the same fate in that his eyes will become dim.

With Heller there begins the rejection of the early ḥasidic doctrine of the elevation of extraneous thoughts, i.e., the idea that when a wayward or sinful thought enters the mind during prayer, it should not be pushed away but raised to its source in God. Heller considers this to be a dangerous doctrine, but is unable to deny it completely, since it was taught by the early masters; he consequently adopts the rationalization that the practice was never intended for ordinary folk but only for the greatest of saints. By a similar rationalization, Heller urges the abandonment of the Lurianic *kavvanot* in prayer, except in rare instances. Luria was thinking of himself and his great contemporaries; for the modern man, the *kavvanot* would frustrate the aim of *devekut*.

BIBLIOGRAPHY: M. Bodek, *Seder ha-Dorot*, Ch. 3, 56; A. Walden, *Shem ha-Gedolim he-Ḥadash* (1879), 114; S.A. Horodezky, *Ha-Ḥasidut ve-ha-Ḥasidim* (1951), II, 123–45; S. Dubnow, *Toledot ha-Ḥasidut* (1967), No. 45, 323–4; J.G. Weiss, in: JJS, IX (1958), 163–92.

[Louis Jacobs]

MESHULLAM PHOEBUS BEN ISRAEL SAMUEL (1547–1617), Polish rabbi. Meshullam's exact birthplace is unknown. Before becoming *av bet din* in Cracow, he held a similar position in Brest-Litovsk. It appears that in 1590, while in Brest-Litovsk, he introduced regulations to prevent work being done on the Sabbath. These regulations afford an insight into the economic situation of the Jews of Poland and Lithuania in the 16th and 17th centuries. They were first published in an abbreviated form in *Kevod Ḥakhamim* (Venice, 1700) by Judah Leib Poḥovitz, and then more fully by I. Sonne (see bibliography). Although the year of Meshullam's arrival in Cracow is not certain, his presence there is recorded in 1609, when he gave a ruling as to which *haftarah* should be recited when the New Moon of Av falls on a Sabbath. While in Cracow, he participated in the meetings of the *Council of Four Lands, and it is possible that even the aforementioned regulations gained the approval of the council. A recognized and respected halakhic authority, Meshullam gave numerous rulings on synagogue customs. The most famous of his disciples was Joel *Sirkes. Meshullam had a wide knowledge of languages other than Hebrew and was well versed in medical matters, as is evident in his responsa on these subjects. Nothing is known of his family and children except that he had two sons: SAMUEL, who became *av bet din* in Przemysl, and JOSEPH (d. 1648), who was *av bet din* in Cracow. Meshullam died in Cracow.

Few of his works remain but his responsa are found in contemporary works, including those of *Meir b. Gedaliah of Lublin, in *Turei Zahav* by *David b. Samuel ha-Levi, and in *Bayit Ḥadash* by Joel Sirkes. Meshullam's work, *Sefer Shemot Gittin*, on the names used in bills of divorce, is mentioned by Abraham *Rapaport in his *Eitan ha-Ezraḥi*. Meshullam also edited responsa by Moses b. Isaac *Mintz from manuscripts in his possession.

BIBLIOGRAPHY: J.M. Zunz, *Ir ha-Ẓedek* (1874), 49–52; Sonne, in: *Horeb*, 2 (1935), 237–46; Halpern, Pinkas, 22, 63, 456, 483–8; Ben-Sasson, in: *Zion*, 21 (1956), 183–206; Feldman, *ibid.*, 34 (1969), 90–97; Lewin, in: *Sinai*, 65 (1969), 109.

MESHULLAM ZALMAN HA-KOHEN (late 18th and early 19th century), preacher and moralist in Fuerth, Bavaria. His first work, *Bigdei Kehunnah* ("Priestly Garments," Fuerth, 1807), contains responsa on various laws in the Shulḥan Arukh and *novellae on the talmudic tractates *Gittin* and *Bava Meẓia*. *Naḥalat Avot* ("Heritage of our Fathers," Fuerth, 1811), his second work, was written when the author was 70 years old. Utilizing the form of the ethical will, the book was intended to educate both the author's children and pupils. After an introduction in rhymed prose, the work comprises sermons on ethical subjects – both personal and social – the commandments, and devotion to God.

MESHWI (or **Mishawayh**, a form of Moses) **AL-ʿUKBARĪ** (second half of the ninth century), Jewish sectarian of Ukbara, near Baghdad. Later *Karaites refer to him as Meshwi Ba'albaki, since his followers emigrated from Babylonia to Syria in the tenth century. No details are known of the life of Meshwi, founder of a sectarian movement whose members are known as Misḥawayhites. No writings of his are known, and his opinions and teachings have been preserved only in the writings of his opponents. His teachings differed in many ways from Rabbinic and Karaite Judaism. This is particularly evident in his calendar computations. According to Meshwi, the first day of Passover must always fall on a Thursday, Shavuot on a Sunday, and the Day of Atonement on a Saturday. As he claimed that the day spanned from dawn to dawn, his followers observed the Sabbath from the dawn of Saturday to the dawn of Sunday. He also claimed that no sacrifices were offered at the Tabernacle on Saturdays, interpreting Numbers 28:10 to mean that the burnt-offering must be sacrificed on Friday for Saturday. Many deviations from tradition were ascribed to him by his opponents: in his commentary on Leviticus Saadiah Gaon refers to Meshwi's permitting the fat of animals which were not sacrificed at the altar to be eaten. The 11th-century Karaite scholar, Tobias b. Moses, attacked him as a heretic for declaring many pentateuchal laws void. Meshwi may have been influenced by his contemporary, the heretic Hiwi al-Balkhī. Remnants of the Misḥawayhites survived until the 12th century; *Benjamin of Tudela, who met them in Cyprus, relates their heretical manner of observing the Sabbath, and Abraham *Ibn Ezra, in his commentary on Exodus 16:24 and in his epistle on the Sabbath, refers to their interpretation of Genesis 1:5 and their observance of the Sabbath. It is striking that the interpretation of *Samuel ben Meir (Rashbam) of Gen. 1:5 corresponds to that of Meshwi.

BIBLIOGRAPHY: Ankori, *Karaites in Byzantium* (1959), 372–417 and index; S.A. Poznański, in: REJ, 34 (1897), 161–91; L. Nemoy, in: HUCA, 7 (1930), 330, 389–90; Y. Rosenthal, in: *YIVO-Bleter*, 21 (1943), 79.

[Judah M. Rosenthal]

MESILLAT ZION (Heb. מְסִלַּת צִיּוֹן; "Roadway to Zion"), moshav affiliated with Tenu'at ha-Moshavim in the foothills of Judea on the highway leading to Jerusalem, near the entrance to the Sha'ar ha-Gai gorge (the moshav's initial name was Sha'ar ha-Gai). Mesillat Zion was founded in 1950 initially as a "work village" whose inhabitants were employed in land reclamation and in planting the nearby Martyrs' Forest and other woodlands. Its inhabitants originated from Cochin, India. The moshav's economy was based on vineyards, deciduous fruit orchards, poultry, and flowers. In the mid-1990s, the population was approximately 350, increasing to 585 in 2002 after expansion.

[Efraim Orni]

MESILLOT (Heb. מְסִלּוֹת; "Roadways"), kibbutz in central Israel, at the foot of Mt. Gilboa, affiliated with Kibbutz Arẓi Ha-Shomer ha-Ẓa'ir. It was founded in 1938 as a tower and stockade village by pioneers from Bulgaria who had participated in establishing *Ma'oz Ḥayyim and worked there. The kibbutz' economy was based on intensive field crops, fruit orchards, citrus groves, dairy cattle, carp ponds, poultry, a plant nursery, and guest rooms. In 2002 the population was 423.

[Efram Orni / Shaked Gilboa (2nd ed.)]

MESKIN, AHARON (1898–1974), Israel actor, a founding member of *Habimah. Meskin was a Russian government official, when in 1917, he heard of the establishment of the Habimah studio in Moscow and applied for admission. He played his first major role in 1924 as *The Golem* in H. Leivick's play of that name and from that time ranked as a leading member of the company. He subsequently played many leading roles, both in Israel and on tour abroad, among his most effective being Othello and Shylock. A tall man with a rough-hewn face and a striking deep voice, Meskin endowed his roles with dignity and humanity. In 1960 he was awarded the Israel Prize. He was the first chairman of the Israel section of the International Theater Institute.

BIBLIOGRAPHY: D. Lazar, *Rashim be-Yisrael*, 2 (1955), 297–301.

[Mendel Kohansky]

MESOPOTAMIA. The original article in the first edition of the *Encyclopaedia Judaica* traced Mesopotamian history to its earliest beginnings and provided a detailed survey of Mesopotamian literature and institutions. With the availability of such tools as J. Sasson et al. (eds.), *Civilizations of the Ancient Near East* (CANE, 1995), the ETANA website, and A. Kuhrt, *The Ancient Near East c. 3000–330 B.C.* (2 vols., 1995) the need for such comprehensive coverage in this Encyclopaedia is less acute. Accordingly, the present revision concentrates on those elements of Mesopotamian history and culture most relevant to understanding the Bible and ancient Israel and Judah.

HISTORY

THE AMORITE PERIOD C. 2000–1800 B.C.E.

Within the limits imposed by the nature of the evidence, the beginning of the second millennium may be characterized as the era of the *Amorites. Amurru (or Amaru) was, in its earliest cuneiform attestations, simply a geographic name for the west, or for the deserts bordering the right bank of the Euphrates. This area, which stretched without apparent limit into the Syrian and Arabian Deserts, was traditionally the home of nomadic tribes of Semitic speech who were drawn to the civilized river valley as if by a magnet and invaded or infiltrated it whenever opportunity beckoned. In the process they became progressively acculturated – first as semi-nomads who spent part of the year as settled agriculturalists in an uneasy symbiosis with the urban society of the irrigation civilizations, and ultimately as fully integrated members of that society, retaining at most the linguistic traces of their origins. It was thus that, perhaps as early as about 2900 B.C.E., the first major wave of westerners had entered the Mesopotamian amalgam, and under the kings of Kish and Akkad became full partners in the Sumero-Akkadian civilization that resulted. When, however, the Akkadian sources themselves spoke of Amorites, as they did beginning with Shar-kali-sharri about 2150, they were alluding to a new wave of invaders from the desert, not yet acclimated to Mesopotamian ways. Such references multiply in the neo-Sumerian texts of the 21st century, and correlate with growing linguistic evidence based chiefly on the recorded personal names of persons identified as Amorites which shows that the new group spoke a variety of Semitic, ancestral to

Map 1. The ancient East in the second millennium B.C.E. Borders of modern states are in gray.

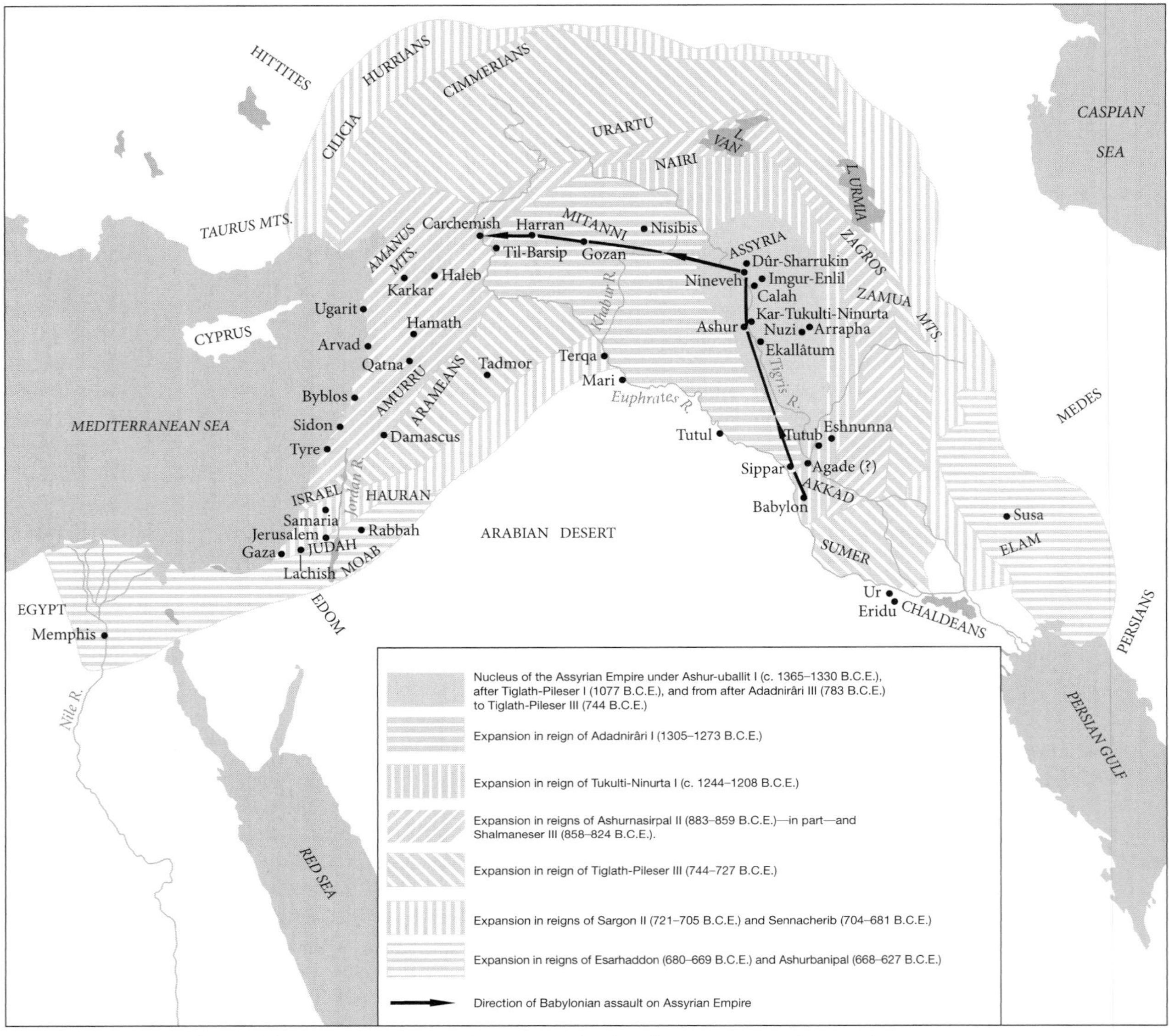

Map 2. Expansions and decline of the Assyrian Empire. Based on M. A. Beek, Atlas of Mesopotamia, *Nelson, London, 1962.*

later Hebrew, Aramaic, and Phoenician. All these languages (and some other dialects) are therefore called West Semitic (or Northwest Semitic) by modern linguists, to distinguish them from the East Semitic, or Akkadian, language spoken in Mesopotamia. The latter, used side by side with the non-Semitic Sumerian, and often by one and the same speaker, was heavily influenced by Sumerian and developed along lines of its own; but it also reacted to the Amorite impact and split into two fairly distinct dialects: Babylonian in the south and Assyrian in the north.

Amorite influence was not, however, confined to the linguistic level. Many cultural innovations of the second millennium, notably in religion and art, can be traced to the new immigration. Since the migrations moved in the direction of Syria-Palestine as well as of Mesopotamia, it is not surprising that numerous common traditions – linguistic, legal, and literary – crop up at both ends of the Asiatic Near East hereafter. Among these common traditions, those of the semi-nomadic wanderings preserved in the patriarchal narratives in Genesis, and elsewhere in the Hebrew Bible, deserve special notice. The glimpses they provide of tribal organization, onomastic practices, kinship patterns, rules of inheritance and land tenure, genealogical schemes, and other vestiges of nomadic life find analogies in cuneiform records. Yet they are preserved within the framework of a polished literary narrative too far removed from the times it presumes to describe to command uncritical confidence. Nonetheless, it is in this period, that it can be said, that the Levant (that is, the area of Syria-Palestine) begins at this time to emerge from prehistory into history.

The pattern established by the Amorites was to characterize Near Eastern history down to the present: it was only when the natural arenas of centralized political power in Mesopotamia and Egypt were in eclipse that the intervening area, destined by geography for division into petty states, enjoyed an opportunity to make its influence felt in unison. The simultaneous collapse of the Sargonic empire of Akkad and the Old Kingdom in Egypt provided such an opportunity, and already Shulgi of Ur had to construct a defensive wall, presumably at the point where the Tigris and Euphrates flow closest together, to deflect unwanted barbarians from the cities that lay to the south. Shulgi was succeeded by two of his many sons, Amar-Sin and Shu-Sin, each of whom reigned for nine years. Like him, these conducted most of their military campaigns in the east, across the Tigris, but Shu-Sin greatly strengthened the wall, calling it "The one which keeps Didanum at bay" in a direct reference to the Amorite threat. He managed thereby to postpone the final reckoning, and even enjoyed divine honors in his lifetime beyond those of his predecessors. His son Ibbi-Sin, however, was less fortunate, and in native Mesopotamian traditions was remembered as the model of the ill-fated ruler. Unable to withstand the simultaneous onslaughts of Elamites and Subarians from the east and Amorites from the west, he appealed for help to Ishbi-Irra of Mari only to end up with Ishbi-Irra extorting ever more powers for himself until he was able to found a dynasty of his own at Isin, and subsequently allowing the capital city of Ur to be sacked and Ibbi-Sin to be carried off to exile and ultimate death and burial in Elam.

The fall of Ur about 2000 B.C.E. did not mark so clear a break in the historical continuum as has sometimes been assumed. Ishbi-Irra paid homage to the Sumero-Akkadian traditions of the Ur III dynasty, reigning as king of Ur and perpetuating such time-honored practices as the cult of the deified king, the patronage of the priesthood and scribal schools of Nippur, and the installation of royal princes and princesses as priests and priestesses at the principal national shrines and of loyal officials as governors of the principal provinces. However, whether with his consent or not, these governors were now increasingly of Amorite stock, and wherever possible aspired to royal status for themselves and independence for their city. The latter course particularly characterized the situation beyond the immediate range of his control, notably at Ashur, Eshnunna, Dêr, and Susa beyond the Tigris, as well as upstream on the Euphrates and its tributaries. From Ashur and northern Mesopotamia, a lively trade soon car-

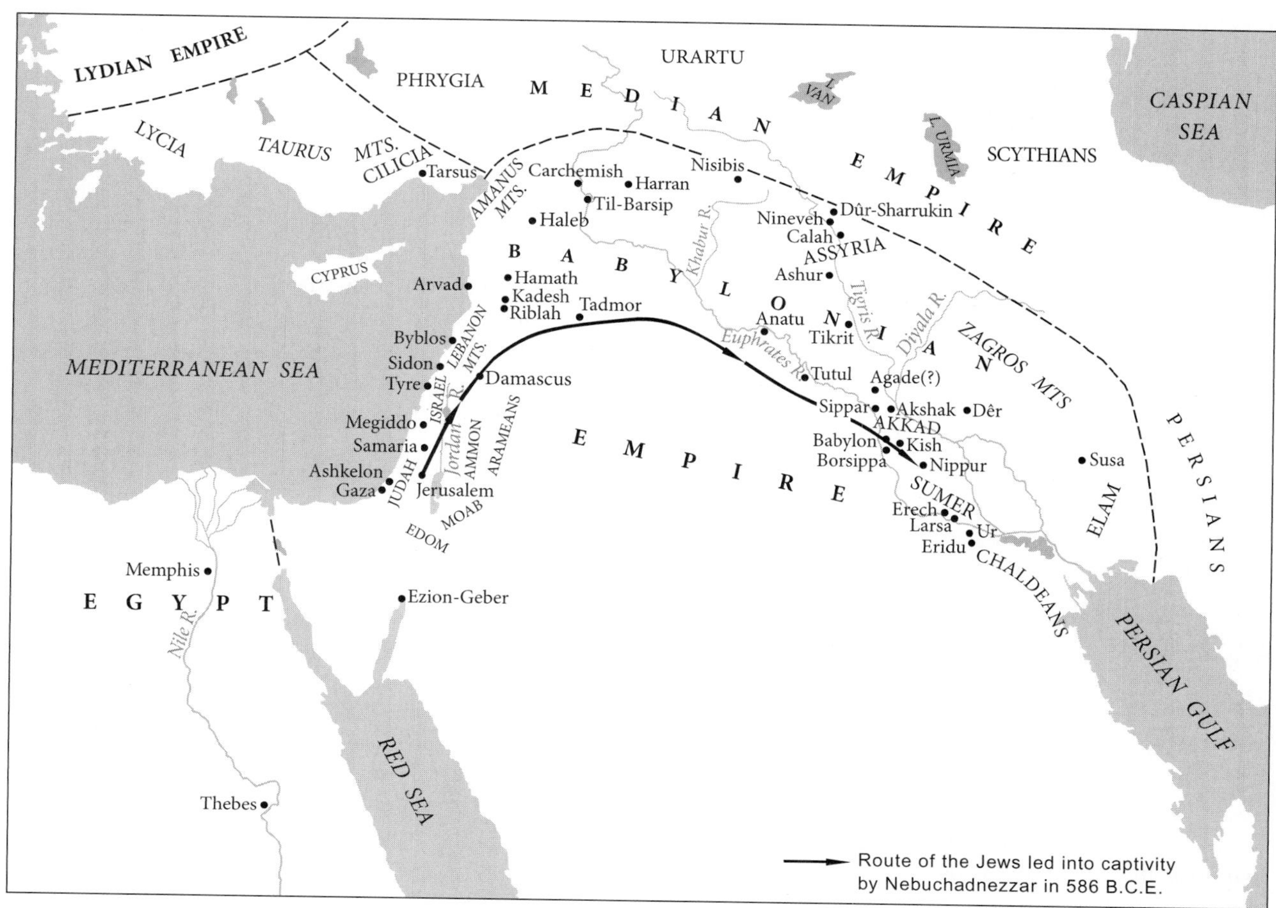

Map 3. The Empire of Nebuchadnezzar II (604–562 B.C.E.). Based on M.A. Beek, Atlas of Mesopotamia, *Nelson, London, 1962.*

ried Amorite and Akkadian influence even further afield, into Cappadocia.

Closer to home, the traditional central control was at first maintained, but even here the loyalty of the provinces was shortlived. For most of the 20th century, Ishbi-Irra's descendants at Isin were unchallenged as the successors of the kings of Ur, but before it was over, the Amorite governors of the southeast, probably based at the ancient city of Lagash, asserted their independence in order to protect the dwindling water resources of that region. Under Gungunum, they established a rival kingdom at Larsa which soon wrested Ur from Isin. In short succession, other Amorite chieftains established independent dynasties at Uruk, Babylon, Kish and nearly all the former provinces of the united kingdom, until Isin effectively controlled little more than its own city and Nippur. With the more distant marshes long since under Amorite rule, the 19th century was thus characterized by political fragmentation, with a concomitant outburst of warfare and diplomacy that embroiled all the separate petty states at one time or another.

The "staging area" for the Amorite expansion was probably the Jabel Bishri (Mt. Basar) which divides or, if one prefers, links the Euphrates River and the Syrian Desert. From here it was a comparatively short and easy march down the river to Babylonia or across the river to Assyria. The way to Egypt was not only longer but led through more hilly and intractable land. This may be one reason that the Amorite wave was somewhat longer in reaching the Egyptian border. When it did reach it, it confronted just such a wall as Shu-Sin (c. 2036–2028) had built "to keep Didanum at bay": in one of those curious parallels that punctuate Ancient Near Eastern history, they met the "Wall-of-the-Ruler, made to oppose the Asiatics and crush the Sand-Crossers," and attributed to the founder of the 12th Dynasty. But the extraordinary revitalization of the Egyptian monarchy by this dynasty (c. 1990–1780) was the real reason that the Amorite wave broke harmlessly at the Egyptian border and the characteristic petty statism that it brought in its train was deferred for two centuries.

THE ERA OF HAMMURAPI (1800–1600 B.C.E.)

With the beginning of the 18th century B.C.E., the political geography of the Asiatic Near East can for the first time be rendered with reasonable accuracy, and many previously blank spots filled in. This was a period of intense commercial and diplomatic activity, punctuated by military campaigns and sieges conducted at considerable distances from home. The fortuitous recovery of archives from many diverse sites reveals a host of geographic names, and many of these can be approximately located, or even identified with archaeological sites, with the help of occasional itineraries. Such itineraries were guides to travelers or, more often, records of their journeys or of campaigns, comparable to the "War of the four kings against the five" in Genesis 14, by marauding armies, and come closest to maps in the absence of any real cartography.

No small-scale map can, of course, show all the minor vassal and petty states in all their complexity. Even the larger kingdoms and city-states add up to a bewildering number. However, certain patterns can be detected. The Syrian desert was populated by loosely organized tribal groupings still maintaining a largely nomadic way of life; the mountainous border regions beyond the Tigris and the Upper Euphrates were being organized under various non-Semitic peoples who came under varying degrees of Mesopotamian cultural influence; the "Fertile Crescent" itself (that is, the valley of the two rivers together with the eastern Mediterranean littoral) was firmly in the hands of urbanized Amorite rulers. Within this great arc, the largest and most central position was occupied by the kingdom of Shamshi-Adad I (c. 1813–1783), and, at the turn of the century, his seemed the most commanding position. From his capital at Shubat-Enlil, he kept a close eye on his two sons, who ruled their provinces from Mari and Ekallâtum, respectively. The vast archives of *Mari have revealed the intricacies of administration, diplomacy, and warfare of the time as well as the highly personal character of Shamshi-Adad's rule. The crown prince at Ekallâtum, whom he held up to his younger brother as a model, had inherited much of the wealth of nearby Ashur, amassed in the profitable trade with Anatolia in the previous century. Nonetheless, it is misleading to call Shamshi-Adad's realm, as is sometimes done, the first Assyrian empire, for his empire was not based on Ashur, and the petty kingdom of Ashur that survived his death was in no sense an empire.

The main challenge came from the south. The way had been paved by the kingdoms of Warium and Larsa. Warium, with its capital at Eshnunna in the valley of the Diyala River, included the ancient center of the Akkadian empire (and perhaps even preserved its Sumerian name, Uri, in Akkadianized form), while Larsa controlled the ancient Sumerian cities. These two Amorite kingdoms had succeeded in subjecting most of the independent city-states of Sumer and Akkad, and thus turned the tide of particularism that had followed the collapse of the Ur III empire. They directed their expansionist policies into separate spheres of influence: Eshnunna north and west into Assyria and upper Mesopotamia, Larsa eastward to the ancestral lands of its last dynasty in Emutbal and beyond that toward Elam. That they avoided an open clash was, however, due even more to the existence, between the two, of a relatively small state that nonetheless maintained its independence from both and was destined shortly to succeed and surpass them as well as Shamshi-Adad.

The city of Babylon was a relative newcomer among the members of the old Sumero-Akkadian amphictyony, though later, to match its subsequent importance, it claimed a fictitious antiquity reaching back to antediluvian times. It was strategically located near the narrow waist of the Tigris-Euphrates valley where the two rivers come closest together and whence the capitals of successive Mesopotamian empires have ruled the civilized world from Kish and Akkad down to Ctesiphon and Baghdad. Throughout the 19th century, it was the seat of an independent dynasty which shared (or claimed) a common ancestry with Shamshi-Adad and whose rulers enjoyed long reigns and an unbroken succession passing smoothly from father to son. In 1793, the succession of this first dynasty of Babylon (also known simply as the Amorite Dynasty) passed to *Hammurapi (1792–1750). Hammurapi was one of the great rulers of history, a man of personal genius and vision who left an indelible impress on all his heirs.

At first Hammurapi's prospects seemed anything but favorable. A celebrated Mari letter phrased his situation in classic terms: "There is no king who is all-powerful by himself: ten or 15 kings follow in the train of Hammurapi of Babylon, as many follow Rîm-Sin of Larsa, as many follow Ibal-pî-El of Eshnunna, as many follow Amut-pî-El of Qatna, and 20 kings follow in the train of Yarim-lim of Yamḥad" (G. Dossin, Syria 19 [1938], 105–26). A lesser personality would have fallen victim to the struggles between these and other major powers of the time, but by an adroit alternation of warfare and diplomacy, Hammurapi succeeded where others had failed. He maintained the friendship of Rîm-Sin until his 30th year, when, in defeating him, he fell heir as well to all that Larsa had conquered. He avoided challenging Shamshi-Adad, another older contemporary, but defeated his successor two years after disposing of Rîm-Sin. Three years later, he conquered Mari, where Zimri-Lim had reestablished a native dynasty after the Assyrian defeat. Eshnunna and the lesser states across the Tigris fell to Hammurapi's armies before the end of his reign, and only the powerful kingdoms beyond the Euphrates-notably Yamḥad and Qatna – escaped his clutches. He was a zealous administrator, and his concern for every detail of domestic policy is well documented in his surviving correspondence. He is most famous for his collection of laws which, in the manner initiated by Ur-Namma of Ur, and elaborated in the interval at Isin ("Code of Lipit-Ishtar") and Eshnunna, collected instructive legal precedents as a monument to "The King of Justice." That was the name he gave to the stelae inscribed with the laws which were erected in Babylon and, no doubt, in other cities of his kingdom. Fragments of several, including a well-preserved one, were carried off centuries later as booty to Susa, where they were rediscovered in modern times; some of the missing portions can be restored from later copies prepared in the scribal schools, where the laws of Hammurapi, recognized as classic, were copied and studied for over a thousand years more. Framed in a hymnic prologue that catalogued his conquests, and an epilogue that stressed his concern for justice, the laws do not constitute a real code. They are not noticeably adhered to in the innumerable contracts and records of litigation from this and subsequent reigns. However, they remain the starting point for the understanding of Babylonian and all Near Eastern legal ideals. Many of their individual formulations, as well as their overall arrangement, are paralleled by the casuistic legislation of Exodus and Deuteronomy.

It is important, in spite of all this, to see Hammurapi's achievement in its proper perspective. His reunification of Mesopotamia, consummated at the end of his reign, survived him by only a few years. His son and successor had to surrender much of the new empire before he had ruled more than a decade. The extreme south was lost to a new dynasty, sometimes called the First Sealand Dynasty; across the Tigris, Emutbal and Elam regained their independence; and the Middle Euphrates was soon occupied by Hanean nomads from the desert and by Kassites (see below). The enduring legacy of Hammurapi lies rather in the legal, literary, and artistic realms, where his reign marked both the preservation and canonization of what was best in the received traditions and a flowering of creative innovations.

THE SACK OF BABYLON AND THE DARK AGE (1600–1500 B.C.E.)

As the fall of Akkad ushered in the end of the Early Bronze Age, so the end of the Middle Bronze Age was marked by the capture of Babylon and Memphis. The two great capitals fell to different captors, but a common source may have set in motion the train of events that culminated in their defeat, for to the north of both the high civilizations, an entirely new ethnic element had made its entry onto the stage of history early in the Middle Bronze Age: the *Hittites. These first-attested bearers of Indo-European names played a minor role in the 19th and early 18th centuries, when Hattic princes ruled Anatolia and Assyrian traders crisscrossed the highlands. But, the last Assyrian caravan is attested about 1770 (under Zimri-Lim of Mari); the centers of their trade were destroyed, and by about 1740, the Hittites were able to forge a united kingdom out of the remains of the Hattic principalities. Hattusilis I (c. 1650 – 1620) felt strong enough to rebuild the city of Hattusas (from which he took his throne name) in spite of the curse laid on it a century earlier by its Hattic conqueror, and to rule a growing Anatolian kingdom from this relatively remote northern base inside the great bend of the Halys River. Soon his ambitions extended beyond the Anatolian highlands southward to the fertile plains that beckoned from across the Taurus Mountains. Cilicia fell into his power first, and the Cilician gates opened the way through the Amanus Mountains, the last natural barrier on the way south. However, the Mediterranean coastal route was barred by the Amorite kingdom of Yamḥad, centered on Haleb (Aleppo) and still retaining some of its vigor. After neutralizing this threat, Hattusilis, and more particularly his adopted son Mursilis I, therefore directed their principal efforts against the Hurrian kingdom of Carchemish which controlled the Euphrates. After a long and apparently successful siege of the Hurrian stronghold at Urshu, the Hittites found that they could march unopposed down the rest of the Euphrates all the way to Babylon itself. Here they put an end to the rule of Samsu-ditana (c. 1625–1595), last of the descendants of Hammurapi, and to the Amorite dynasty (or First Dynasty) of Babylon. The great city was sacked and its humiliation completed when the cult statues of its god Marduk and his consort Sarpanitum were carried into captivity.

The Hittites themselves did not press their advantage: 750 miles in a straight line away from Hattusas, Mursilis had overextended himself, and hastened home only to meet his death at the hands of a palace conspiracy that plunged the

Hittite kingdom into several generations of turmoil and weakness. The immediate beneficiaries of the sack of Babylon were rather the rulers of the Sealand, who moved north from their independent stronghold in the old Sumerian south and, in the wake of the withdrawing Hittites, seized Babylon for themselves and thus qualified for inclusion in the Babylonian King List as the Second Dynasty of Babylon. However, their occupation, too, was destined to be transitory: within a couple of years the city was occupied by the Kassites, who moved downstream from their foothold in the Kingdom of Hana on the Middle Euphrates. With their arrival in Babylonia proper, a curtain of silence descended over the documentation from that area; for the first time since the invention of writing, there is a nearly total eclipse of cuneiform textual evidence, and for the rest of the 16th century, the Asiatic Near East was plunged into a true dark age.

In the meantime the Amorite kingdoms of the Mediterranean littoral also reacted to the stirrings set in motion by the Hittites. Cut off from their kinsmen in the east, they evolved distinct variations of the common cultural traditions. In the north, these crystallized around *Ugarit, a strategically located center of commerce and industry which was also a seat of learning. It devised an alphabet with an order of letters ancestral to, and essentially identical with, the order of the letters of the Hebrew and Western alphabets. Using this script, Ugarit produced a rich religious and mythological literature, with many features that show up later in biblical poetry. Further south, the biblical corpus itself enshrined much of the common heritage in the distinctive medium of the Hebrew language and Israelite conceptions.

THE FEUDAL ERA (1500–1400 B.C.E.)

The map of the Near East presented a very different appearance in 1500 than it had 300 years earlier. In place of numerous small and medium-sized Amorite states, a few large non-Semitic royal houses now ruled the Fertile Crescent with the help of a nobility based on the ability to maintain horses, equipment, and retainers. The indigenous Semitic population was, at least for the time being, reduced either to the status of a semi-free peasantry or to that of roving mercenaries. A parallel may nonetheless be drawn with the earlier situation, for just as geography seemed to favor Shamshi-Adad I at the beginning of the 18th century, so now it served to favor a kingdom similarly centered in the triangle formed by the tributaries of the Khabur River in Upper Mesopotamia. Somewhere in this Khabur Triangle, at a site still not rediscovered, lay the city of Washukkanni, capital of an empire which stretched clear across northern Mesopotamia from the Mediterranean in the west to beyond the Tigris in the east. The empire, called Mitanni, was headed by a small aristocratic ruling class whose names identify them as Indo-Aryans, i.e., as the western branch of a migration that was at the same time overflowing India. They invoked "Indian" deities and perfected the raising of horses and horse racing, employing in part an Indo-Aryan terminology. (For hesitations about the Indo-European dominance see Kuhrt, 296–98). However, the kingdom which they ruled was primarily a Hurrian state, for it was the Hurrian stratum of the population that made up the bulk of its chariot-nobility.

The Hurrians had begun to settle, and even rule, on the northern and eastern frontiers of Mesopotamia even before the end of the Akkadian empire (to whose fall they may have contributed). They began to enter Mesopotamia proper in increasing numbers in the neo-Sumerian and Old Babylonian periods. They ruled minor localities like Shushara (Shashrum) under Shamshi-Adad I and left their mark at Mari in the form of Hurrian incantations. However, it was only now, with the creation of the Mitanni state, that they took advantage of their strategic location to assume a commanding position. The center of their power in the Khabur region was known as Hanigalbat. To the east they claimed sovereignty over the client kingdoms of Assyria and Arrapha, to the west over those of Mukish and Yamḥad. Most of the documentation comes from these client states rather than from the center of the empire. In particular the archives of *Nuzi and *Alalakh have yielded vast numbers of texts from the realms of family law and public administration respectively. Together they throw valuable light on the newly emerging institutions of a society thought (by some scholars) to have had a direct impact on the institutions of pre-monarchical Israel. The cultural unity of the extensive Mitanni domain is also attested archaeologically: an elegant pottery style designated variously as Khabur, Mitanni, or Nuzi ware characterizes the ceramic remains of sites of this period throughout the area.

A separate Hurrian state grew up at the same time northwest of Mitanni: in the fertile plain later known as Cilicia, the kingdom of Kizzuwatna united the areas lying between Mitanni and the Hittite lands of Anatolia. It served both as a buffer between them in political and military terms and as a bridge in cultural terms. It was, at least in part, by this road that Hurrian literary and religious influences reached Asia Minor, where they were soon to play a major role. The Hurrians, however, were important beyond that as transmitters and transmuters of the older traditions of Babylonia, many of which, according to one theory, reached the West – that is, Hittites and Phoenicians, and via these ultimately also Greeks and Hebrews, respectively – in Hurrian guise.

The prestige of Babylonian culture at this time was in marked contrast to its political eclipse. The country was now securely in the hands of the Kassites, who had already controlled the Middle Euphrates for over a century (c. 1735–1595) before they seized Babylon, and who went on to rule Babylonia proper (which they gave the name of Kar-Duniash) for over four centuries thereafter (c. 1595–1157) – longer than any other dynasty. However, these were centuries of political stagnation for Babylonia. The Kassites were foreign invaders of uncertain ethnic affiliation who eagerly adopted, and adapted themselves to, the literary and artistic heritage of the ancient civilization to which they had fallen heir. They conquered the Sealand in the south about the beginning of the 15th century, thus probably recovering the surviving remnants of Sumerian learning (both scholars and texts) that had found refuge there at the time of the sack of Babylon. Under Kurigalzu I they built a great new administrative capital named Fortress of Kurigalzu (Dur-Kurigalzu) in the strategic narrow waist of the valley, dominated by a traditional stepped tower (ziggurat), the best preserved example of its kind from within Mesopotamia. They adjusted their northern frontiers with varying fortunes in occasional battles with the emerging Assyrians, and one of their 15th-century kings even met on friendly terms with Pharaoh Thutmose III on the Euphrates. They evolved an essentially feudal society, which secured, while at the same time diluting, the royal power through grants of land and remission of taxes to favored retainers. But by and large they were content to depend on their inherited Babylonian prestige in order to seek a place for themselves in the shifting kaleidoscope of Late Bronze international relations.

This prestige had, in some sense, never been higher. Throughout the Near East, the cuneiform script was being put to use in one form or another, and Akkadian was becoming the language of international diplomacy. In order to master the Akkadian script and language, scribal schools arose as far away as Anatolia and Egypt, and their curriculum followed to some degree the Babylonian model. A fragment of the Gilgamesh Epic, found at *Megiddo, indicates that this was true also of Palestine. Many of the great scribal families of later Babylonia traced their ancestry to Kassite times, and it was probably at this time that the major works of cuneiform literature were put into their canonical form. Thus it was through the patronage of Kassite overlords, and the mediating role of the Hurrians (see above), that traditional Sumero-Akkadian literature and learning spread far and wide from its ancestral home.

In the West, meantime, military and political hegemony was also passing out of the hands of Semitic-speaking peoples. A new dynasty of Theban rulers, the 18th, had succeeded by the middle of the 16th century in driving the *Hyksos (largely consisting of Amorite elements) from Egypt and reuniting the country. Thutmose III (1490–1436) carried Egyptian arms as far as the Euphrates and reduced all the intervening city-states to vassalage. His greatest victory was won on the very first campaign, when he defeated the armies of the Asiatics, combined, if not exactly united, under the prince of Kadesh (better; Kedesh), at the great battle of Megiddo, the first "Armageddon" (the graecized form of Har Megiddo, "hill of Megiddo"). With Retenu, as the Egyptians called Palestine and Southern Syria, firmly in his grasp, Thutmose III even challenged the armies of Mitanni and eventually extracted a treaty that recognized a common frontier running between Hama and Qatna (c. 1448). His successors continued to maintain the Asiatic empire by repeated incursions into Palestine and Syria to receive the submission of loyal vassal princes and secure that of the recalcitrant ones. Sporadic finds of cuneiform tablets from Palestine (Taanach, Gezer) seem to include royal exhortations to this effect.

Thus the subjection of the indigenous Amorites was completed before the end of the 15th century throughout the Near East. There was, however, one exception to this rule. Since the emergence of the Amorites, cuneiform texts from very diverse regions had begun to make mention of a group of people called *Ḥabiru with ever increasing frequency until, by the 15th century, they appear in texts from all over the Near East. On philological grounds, these Ḥabiru can be conclusively equated with the ʿApiru of the Egyptian texts and less likely, with the Hebrews of the Bible. Their name was explained, tellingly if not scientifically, as meaning "robbers," "dusty ones," or "migrants," respectively. These Ḥabiru were thus not an ethnic but a social entity: though largely of Amorite stock, they constituted that portion of the population unwilling to submit to Amorite rule or, subsequently and more particularly, to that of their nonsemitic conquerors. Instead they chose to serve as roving mercenaries under successive masters, or, alternatively, to band together in order to impose their own rule in areas beyond the reach of the various imperial armies. The latter was particularly true of the wooded hill country of Syria and Palestine.

There they maintained a tenacious and much maligned independence even while the great powers were dividing up the cleared lowlands.

THE EMERGENCE OF ASSYRIA (C. 1400–1200 B.C.E.)

The last two centuries of the Near Eastern Bronze Age witnessed a new cosmopolitanism which flowered under courtly patronage in the 14th century only to disintegrate under the rude assaults of mass migrations in the 13th. The pace of international diplomacy quickened dramatically in the "Amarna Age" (see *El-Amarna); Akkadian became the lingua franca of the Near East (see above) as attested by school texts, correspondence, and treaties from Amarna itself and elsewhere; dynastic marriages were the subject of protracted negotiations and reflected not only the raised status of women (or at least of princesses) but also the international outlook of the ruling strata. This outlook was no doubt fostered by the common practice of educating vassal princes at the great courts – Egyptian, Hittite, or Babylonian – where they served at the same time as hostages for their fathers' loyalty. The delicate balance of power thus constructed on the novel ideas of international negotiation and accommodation survived even the ambitions of particularly strong rulers, such as Suppiluliumas of the Hittites (c. 1375–1335). However, it was not equal to the threat from below: in the end it succumbed to the tidal waves of diverse new ethnic groups which broke on all the shores of the Near East and destroyed the last vestiges of the age of diplomacy. The momentous events that characterized the waning Bronze Age involved Mesopotamia in general, and in particular set the stage for the emergence of Assyria, the only Asiatic power that survived intact into the Iron Age.

The emergence of Assyria as a major Near Eastern power can best be dated to the accession of Ashur-uballiṭ I (c. 1365–1330), who first claimed the title "king of the land of

Ashur." Ashur was the name of the god held in special reverence by the Assyrians, and of the ancient city built by his worshipers on the Tigris. For a thousand years before Ashur-uballiṭ's accession, the city had been ruled by a long succession of foreign masters as a minor province, in succession, of the great empires of Akkad, Ur, Eshnunna, Shubat-Enlil, and Washukkanni.

In all this millennium, Ashur had enjoyed the status of an independent city-state only once, in the brief interlude following the fall of Ur (c. 2000–1850). At that time its citizens displayed their vitality by their extensive and sophisticated trading operations deep into Anatolia; many thousands of "Cappadocian" tablets, inscribed in the Old Assyrian dialect, have left an enduring record of this trade. However, even in periods of political subservience, the Assyrians maintained a clear sense of their own identity. Foreign rulers were given native genealogies or, by an equally pious fiction, local governors were elevated to royal status by the later historiography. The Assyrian historians should not, however, be accused of willful distortion; rather, they were giving formal expression to a very real sense of continuity which centered on the worship of Ashur, the deity from whom their city took its name. They thus provide an instructive parallel to the Israelite experience as canonized in the Bible. In both instances, it was the reality of an unbroken religious tradition which permitted an ethnic group to lay claim to the memories or monuments surviving from the Middle Bronze Age and to link them to later political institutions.

In Assyria, these institutions got their chance when Mitannian power began to collapse in the middle of the 14th century, under the combined impact of Hittite pressure and the progressive disengagement from Asiatic affairs by the Egyptian pharaohs of the Amarna period, since Egypt, as the principal ally of Mitanni, was the only effective counterweight to Suppiluliumas' ambitions. Ashur-uballiṭ took advantage of the situation to throw off the Hurrian overlordship of Mitanni. Disdaining that of Kassite Babylonia which claimed to have inherited it, he began to negotiate on a footing of equality with all the great powers of his time, as well as to show the Assyrian mettle in battle, chiefly with the Kassites. Indeed, the fortunes of Assyria and Babylonia were henceforth closely linked; dynastic intermarriages and treaties alternated with breaches of peace and adjustments of the common border in favor of the victor. A synchronistic king list recorded these contacts in the first systematic attempt to correlate the histories of two discrete states before the Book of Kings (which made the same attempt for the Divided Monarchy). This synchronistic style was cultivated by the Assyrian historians along with other historical genres, while the court poets created a whole cycle of epics celebrating the triumphs over the Kassites. The Assyrian kings, portrayed in heroic proportions, figured as peerless protagonists of the latter, and generally claimed the upper hand in these encounters. However, a deep-seated respect for the older culture and religion of Babylonia, which they regarded as ancestral to their own, constrained them from following up on their advantage at first.

This restraint was dropped by Tukulti-Ninurta I (c. 1244–1208), one of the few intriguing personalities in the long line of Assyrian kings who were more often so true to form that they are barely distinguishable one from another. So far from respecting the sanctity of Babylon, he took its defeated king into Assyrian captivity together with the statue of Marduk its god, razed the walls of the city, and assumed the rule of all of Babylonia in his own person. At home, he claimed almost divine honors and, not content with an extensive building program at Ashur, he moved across the Tigris to found a whole new capital, which he named after himself. But in all this he aroused increasing enmity, both for the sacrilege against Babylon and for the heavy exactions of his military and building programs. A reaction set in and, led by the king's own son and successor, the more conservative party imprisoned the king in his new capital and set fire to it. The fame of Tukulti-Ninurta was such that garbled features of his reign are thought to be preserved in both biblical and Greek literature. Thus he is supposed (by some scholars; but cf. above, on Narâm-Sin) to have suggested the figure of Nimrod, the conqueror and hunter of Genesis 10; the "King Ninos" who built "the city of Ninos," according to one Greek legend; and the Sardanapalos who died a fiery death in his own city, according to another. Separating fact from legend, it is clear that his death ushered in a temporary eclipse of the newly emergent Assyrian power that was destined to last for almost a century.

The Assyrian eclipse starting about 1200 was only one phase, and a relatively mild one at that, of the upheaval that marked the end of the Bronze Age throughout the Near East, and whose principal cause was the wave of mass migrations that engulfed the entire area. If there was any one event that may be said to have unleashed these movements, it may conceivably have been the sack of Troy, about 1250 B.C.E., and the subsequent fall of the Mycenean cities of the Greek mainland. The survivors of these catastrophes fled by sea and are collectively known as Sea Peoples. They came, however, not across the open water, but along the coasts, seeking new lands to conquer and settle wherever the established powers were too weak to withstand them, and leaving their names scattered across the Mediterranean littorals and islands to this day, from Cilicia and Philistia (Palestine) in the east to Sicily, Etruria (Tuscany), and Sardinia in the west. The populations displaced by their arrival fled elsewhere to spread the process in a chain-like reaction, until confronted by corresponding migrations from an opposite direction. Thus the Hurrians of Cilicia fled northeast into Hittite Anatolia, putting an end to the Hittite empire there; the Hittite refugees in turn moved southeast into the former Mitanni area of northern Syria. Here they encountered a wave of Semitic-speaking seminomads now moving north from the Syrian desert. These were the *Arameans, with whom the Hittites reached an accommodation resulting in an Arameo-Hittite symbiosis in the petty Syrian city-states of the early Iron Age, who probably spoke Aramaic but used a dialect of Hittite (probably Luwian, written in "hieroglyphic Hittite") for many of their monuments.

Further south, the Canaanite (or Amorite) population of Canaan displaced by the *Philistines meanwhile encountered the Israelites, while further to the east, the waning dynasty of the Kassites finally succumbed to Aramean and other pressures by 1157 B.C.E. Thus in the short span of a century, the Near East took on a wholly new aspect, and new protagonists were to rule its destinies in the Iron Age.

THE EARLY IRON AGE (C. 1200–750 B.C.E.)

For several centuries, the political history of Babylonia and Assyria after 1200 had little noticeable impact beyond the borders of Mesopotamia, and cannot, therefore, claim the attention of historians in the same measure as earlier periods, some of which contribute in crucial ways to our understanding of all history. The international power vacuum of the time enabled the rise and consolidation of the smaller Levantine polities including Israel and Judah. Occasional royal figures stand out for specific achievements; their names, in consequence, were copied by later kings and thus in some cases passed into the Bible. *Merodach-Baladan I (1173–1161), for example, was the last Kassite king who still exercised effective control over Babylonia; a considerable number of boundary stones (*kudurru*'s) attest to the vitality of the land which characterized this dynasty's relations to its feudal retainers. Nebuchadnezzar I (1124–03) was the outstanding ruler of the Second Dynasty of Isin which succeeded the Kassites in Babylonia. He is generally thought to have retrieved the statue of Marduk from captivity (see above), elevated Marduk to his role as undisputed head of the Babylonian pantheon, and commissioned the so-called Epic of Creation (*Enuma eliš*), actually a hymnic exaltation of Marduk, often cited for its parallels to the biblical versions of creation, though in fact more nearly relevant to the exaltation of the God of Israel in the Song of the Sea (Ex. 15).

His younger Assyrian contemporary, Tiglath-Pileser I (c. 1115–1077), was a worthy adversary who reestablished Assyria's military reputation and, while respecting the common frontier with Babylonia in the south, and holding off the warlike mountaineers on Assyria's eastern and northern borders, laid the foundations for her "manifest destiny" – expansion to the west. An Assyrian campaign down the Tigris to the Babylonian frontier and then up the Euphrates and Khabur rivers to rejoin the Tigris north of Ashur had become an annual event by the time of Tukulti-Ninurta II (890–884); the petty chieftains of the Arameo-Hittite lands west of Assyria learned to expect swift retribution if they did not pay the tribute exacted on these expeditions. The "calculated frightfulness" of Ashurnaṣirpal II (883–859) was graphically impressed on his visiting vassals by the reliefs he carved on the walls of his new palace at Kalhu (biblical Calah).

Under Shalmaneser III (858–824), the Assyrian policy took on all the earmarks of a grand design. The repeated hammer blows of his armies were directed with an almost single-minded dedication and persistence against Assyria's western neighbors and brought about the first direct contact between Assyria and Israel. The battle of *Karkar in 853 pitted Shalmaneser against a grand coalition of Western states, including Israelites, Arameans, Cilicians, Egyptians, Arabians, Ammorites, and Phoenicians. King *Ahab of Israel contributed significantly to the infantry and more especially the chariotry on the allied side, which held the Assyrians to a draw if it did not actually defeat them. Ahab died within the year, but the coalition survived with minor changes, and met Shalmaneser four more times (849, 848, 845, and 841). Only after the last of these encounters could the Assyrian king truthfully claim the submission of the western states, and the triumphal march across the now prostrate westland by "Shalman" (i.e., Shalmaneser) was recalled more than a century later in the first explicit, if elliptic, biblical reference to an Assyrian king (Hos. 10:14) other than the legendary Nimrod. The extinction of the Israelite house of Omri ensued in the same year, together with the accession of *Jehu in Israel, the Omride Queen *Athaliah in Judah, and *Hazael in Damascus. The prompt submission of Jehu and other kings is graphically depicted on Shalmaneser's Black Obelisk which conceivably preserves not only the first but the only contemporary pictorial representation of an Israelite figure known from the Bible.

Shalmaneser's reign nevertheless ended in disaster. His last six years (827–822) were marked by revolts at home and the loss of all his western conquests abroad, and not until 805 did Assyria reassert itself there. It was Adadnirâri III (810–783) who, by relieving the Aramean pressure, was regarded as a veritable deliverer in Israel (II Kings 13:5), and his stele from Tell al-Rimah records the grateful tribute of *Jehoash of Israel (797–82) among others. However, Assyria was not yet strong enough to reclaim its western conquests. Urartu (biblical *Ararat), a state based around Lake Van in the later Armenia, rallied the remnants of the Hurrian populations who had fled upper Mesopotamia in the wake of the mass migrations at the end of the Bronze Age, and now sought to restore its influence in Northern Syria. Throughout the first half of the eighth century, Assyrians, Arameans, and Urartians thus fought each other to a standstill in Syria while the Divided Monarchy briefly regained the economic strength and territorial extent of the Solomonic kingdom. Israelite tradition reflected the memory of these four decades of her resurgence and Assyrian weakness by attaching the legend of the near-collapse of Nineveh to *Jonah, a prophetic contemporary of Jeroboam II (793–753; sole rule 781–53) or, conversely, by assigning the Jonah of legend to the reign of Jeroboam (II Kings 14:25).

THE LATE IRON AGE (C. 750–540 B.C.E.)

The last two centuries of Mesopotamian independence under Akkadian-speaking rulers restored first Assyria and then Babylonia briefly to a preeminent position in the Near East, and brought these lands into almost constant contact with the West. They left an indelible impress on both Hebrew and Greek sources which, until the decipherment of cuneiform were, in fact, virtually the only materials for the recovery of Mesopotamian history. The accession of Nabunasir (Nabonassar) in Babylonia in 747 seems to have been regarded by the native sources themselves as ushering in the Mesopotamian revival. The scribes of Babylon inaugurated a reform of the calendar which systematized the intercalation of a 13th month, on the basis of astronomical calculation rather than observation, seven times in every 19 years, according to the so-called Metonic cycle; taken over later by the Jews, it continues as the basis of the Jewish lunisolar calendar to the present. Babylonia was by now divided largely between urbanized Chaldeans and still mainly rural Arameans, and since the Chaldeans soon became the principal experts of Babylonian astronomy, the very word *Chaldean came to be equated with "astronomer, sage" in Hebrew (Dan. 2:2), Aramaic (Dan. passim), and Greek. These astronomers now began to keep monthly diaries listing celestial observations together with fluctuations in such matters as commodity prices, river levels, and the weather, as well as occasional political events. Perhaps on the basis of the last, they also created a valuable new historiographic record, the Babylonian Chronicle, into which they entered the outstanding events of each year. In the Ptolemaic Canon, the "Nabonassar Era" was recognized as a turning point in the history of science by Hellenistic astronomy. Nonetheless, Nabonassar himself was but a minor figure. When he enlisted the help of his greater Assyrian contemporary Tiglath-Pileser III (744–727) in his struggles against both Chaldeans and Arameans, the step proved as fateful as did that of *Ahaz of Judah (735–716; sole ruler 731–716) against the Syro-Ephraimite coalition. Tiglath-Pileser III was a usurper, the beneficiary of still another palace revolt that had unseated his weak predecessor. He and his first two successors changed the whole balance of power in the Near East, destroying Israel among many other states, and reducing the rest, including Judah, to vassalage. They found Assyria in a difficult, even desperate, military and economic situation, but during the next 40 years they recovered and consolidated its control of all its old territories and reestablished it firmly as the preeminent military and economic power in the Near East. Only the outlines of the process can be given here.

Tiglath-Pileser's first great campaign against the West (743–738) involved organizing the nearer Syrian provinces under Assyrian administration, regulating the succession to the king's liking in a middle tier of states, and waging war against the more distant ones. The semiautonomous Assyrian proconsulates were broken up into smaller administrative units, and their governors thereby deprived of the virtually sovereign power which the interval of royal weakness had allowed them to assume. The Urartians were conclusively driven out of northern Syria, and the northern and eastern frontiers were pacified (737–735). The second great campaign to the west (734–732) was in response to Judah's call for help according to II Kings 16:7 (cf. II Chron. 28:16) and reduced Israel to a mere fraction of its former size as more and more of the coastal and Transjordanian lands were incorporated in the growing empire or reduced to vassalage. If Israel was allowed to remain a vassal for now, it was because the king's attention was briefly diverted by the rebellion of Nabu-mukin-zeri (Mukin-zeri) in Babylonia (731–729). When this was crushed, Tiglath-Pileser himself "seized the hands of Bel," that is, he led the statue of Bel (Marduk) in procession in the gesture of legitimation and ostensible submission to the Marduk priesthood that was traditionally demanded of Babylonian kings. As the first Assyrian king who ventured to take this step since the ill-fated Tukulti-Ninurta I, he was duly enrolled in the Babylonian King List (see above) under his nickname of Pulu, a name that passed, more or less intact, also into the later biblical and Greek accounts of his reign (II Kings 15:19; I Chron. 5:26).

His short-lived successor, Shalmaneser V (726–722), followed this example, reigning in Babylon as Ululaia, but left few records of his reign in Assyria. His greatest achievement was the capture of Samaria in 722 and the final incorporation of the Northern Kingdom into the Assyrian empire, but the event is better attested in the Babylonian Chronicle and the Bible (cf. especially II Kings 17:6; 18:10) than in the Assyrian annals. He is thoroughly overshadowed by his successor. Sargon II of Assyria (721–705) took the name of the great founder of the Akkadian empire and lived up to it. He founded the last royal house of Assyria, called Sargonid after him. Perhaps the most militant of all the neo-Assyrian kings, he conducted a major campaign every single year of his reign (or had his annals edited to this effect); he frequently led the army in person and commissioned elaborate reports of his exploits en route in the form of "open letters" to the god Ashur; he even died in battle on his last campaign, a fate unknown for Mesopotamian kings since Ur-Namma of Ur. His major opponents were Merodach-Baladan II, the Chaldean who tenaciously fought for Babylonian independence; the Elamites, allied with Babylon at the great battle of Dêr before the Iranian foothills (720); the supposedly impregnable island fortress of Tyre, which he finally reduced to submission; and Egypt, which for the first time was defeated by an Assyrian army and forced to pay tribute. The rump kingdom of Judah was no match against a figure of this stature, and *Ahaz wisely heeded Isaiah's counsels of caution. When the accession of *Hezekiah (715–687) restored the anti-Assyrian party in Judah, retribution was not slow in coming. In 712, Sargon dispatched his commander in chief (*turtānu*; cf. the *tartan* of Isa. 20:1) against Ashdod, a city allied with Judah, which was captured. The recent discovery of steles of Sargon at Ashdod, on the one hand, and in western Iran (Godin Tepe) on the other, typify the monarch's far-flung exploits, as does his death on the northern frontier.

The accession of Sennacherib (704–681) marked a new phase in Assyrian imperialism. No longer did the Assyrian army march annually towards new conquests. Only eight campaigns occupied the 24 years of the new monarch, besides two conducted by his generals. Assyrian power was approaching the natural limits of which it was capable, and new thrusts into distant border regions were probably defensive in inspiration. Although the warlike ideals of their forebears continued to color the records of the later Sargonid kings, the impression of sustained militarism that they create is an exaggerated one. The real spirit of the time is revealed, on the one hand, by such marvels of civil engineering as Sennacherib's aqueduct at Jerwan and, on the other, by the greatly increased attention to administrative matters reflected in the growing amount of royal correspondence. Literature and learning too came into their own, and the vast library assembled by Ashurbanipal at Nineveh is only the most dramatic expression of the new leisure.

The new *Pax Assyriaca* was, of course, not unbroken by military campaigns. Sennacherib's unsuccessful siege of Jerusalem in 701 is well known from both the Assyrian and biblical accounts (II Kings 18:13–19:37; Isa. 36–37). His generals campaigned against Cilicia and Anatolia (696–695), while his successor Esarhaddon (680–669) is perhaps most famous for his conquest of Egypt. Esarhaddon had succeeded to the throne in the troubled times following his father's assassination (cf. II Kings 19:37; Isa. 37:38), and was determined to secure a smoother succession for his own sons. The vassals of the empire were therefore forced to swear to abide by his arrangements, and the treaties to this effect, excavated at Calah, have proved a new key to the understanding of Deuteronomy. The king's planning at first bore fruit, and for 17 years his designated successors ruled the empire side by side, Ashurbanipal from Nineveh and Shamash-shum-uk-îm from Babylon. However, in 652, war broke out between the two brothers. After four years of bloody warfare, Ashurbanipal emerged victorious, but at a heavy price. The *Pax Assyriaca* had been irreparably broken, and the period of Assyrian greatness was over. The last 40 years of Assyrian history were marked by constant warfare in which Assyria, in spite of occasional successes, was on the defensive. At the same time the basis for a Babylonian resurgence was being laid even before the final Assyrian demise.

Ashurbanipal had installed a certain Kandalanu as loyal ruler in Babylon after crushing his brother's rebellion. When this regent died in 627, however, Babylonia was without any recognized ruler for a year. Then the throne was seized by Nabopolassar (625–605), who established a new dynasty, generally known as the neo-Babylonian, or Chaldean dynasty. Although the Assyrian military machine continued to be a highly effective instrument for almost 20 years, Nabopolassar successfully defended Babylonia's newly won independence and, with the help of the Medes and of *Josiah of Judah (639–609), finally eliminated Assyria itself. The complete annihilation of the Assyrian capitals – Nineveh, Calah, Ashur, Dur-Sharrukin – between 615 and 612 is attested in part by the Babylonian Chronicle and even more tellingly in the contemporaneous world can still be measured in the prophecies of *Nahum, and possibly of *Zephaniah. Only Egypt remained loyal to Assyria, and Pharaoh Neco's efforts to aid the last remnants of Assyrian power at Haran under Ashur-uballiṭ II (611–609) were seriously impaired by Josiah at Megiddo in 609. The last Assyrian king fled Haran in the same year, and Assyrian history came to a sudden end.

Four years later, the Battle of *Carchemish (605) consolidated the Babylonian success with a defeat of the Egyptians by the crown prince, who presently succeeded to the throne as Nebuchadnezzar II (604–562) (see Map 3). The Chaldean empire fell heir to most of Assyria's conquests and briefly regained for Babylonia the position of leading power in the ancient world. Nebuchadnezzar's conquest of Jerusalem and Judah, with the exile of the Judean aristocracy to Babylonia, is the most famous of his many triumphs, but his own inscriptions prefer to stress his more peaceful achievements. These certainly matched his foreign conquests. He reconstructed Babylon in its entirety, filling it with magnificent temples and palaces and turning the city into one of the wonders of the ancient world. Its fame traveled far and wide with those who had seen it, and even after its destruction by Xerxes in 478, its ruins fired the imagination of later ages. Even Nebuchadnezzar's contemporaries were moved by his achievements to catalog the topography of the restored capital in all its details, thus providing an unrivaled description of an ancient city. Among its more noteworthy sights were the ziggurat (*ziqqurratu*), the famous hanging gardens, and the museum attached to Nebuchadnezzar's new palace. Here the king and his successors brought together statues, stelae, and other inscribed relics of the then already long antiquity of Mesopotamia. This neo-Babylonian interest in the monuments of the past thus complemented the neo-Assyrian efforts to collect the literary heritage of Babylonia that climaxed in the creation of the library of Ashurbanipal.

The same antiquarian interest characterized the rule of Nabonidus (555–539), who succeeded to the throne of Babylon after the three brief reigns of Nebuchadnezzar's son, son-in-law, and grandson. He was not related to the royal Chaldean house, although he was the namesake of a son of Nebuchadnezzar, whom he had served as a high diplomatic official as early as 585. The biography of his mother, Adad-guppi, is preserved on inscriptions from Haran, from which we learn that she lived for 104 years (650–547). Her long devotion to Haran and its deity may help to explain her son's similar, but more fateful, preoccupation. Virtually alone among the former Assyrian strongholds, Haran recovered some of its old glory under the neo-Babylonians and survived for many centuries thereafter as the center of successive forms of the worship of the moon-god Sin. According to Adad-guppi's biography, Haran lay desolate (that is, in the possession of the Medes) for 54 years (610–556) until, at the very beginning of the reign of Nabonidus (555–539), a vision informed him, in words strangely reminiscent of Isaiah 44:28–45:1, that Marduk would raise up "his younger servant" Cyrus to scatter the Medes. In obedience to the divine injunction, Nabonidus presently rebuilt the great temple of Haran, and reconsecrated it to Sin. At the same time, he singled out the other centers of moon worship, at Ur in Babylonia and at the oasis of Temâ in Arabia, for special attention. The latter move, which carried Babylonian arms for the first time all the way to Yatrib (modern Medina), was particularly fateful. Though it may have been inspired by reasonable strategic or even commercial considerations, it was regarded as an act of outright madness by the Babylonians and as a self-imposed exile of the king by later legend. The Book of *Daniel associates this sojourn of seven years (or, in the cuneiform sources, ten years) in the desert with Nabonidus' more famous predecessor, Nebuchadnezzar, but new finds from Qumran show that other Jewish traditions linked it with the correct king. In any case, his sojourn in Arabia was resented by the population of Babylon, and the veneration of Sin there and at Haran and Ur was regarded as a veritable betrayal of Marduk, the national deity. Led by the Marduk priesthood, Babylon turned against Belshazzar, the son whom Nabonidus had left behind at the capital, and delivered the city into the waiting hands of Cyrus the Persian. In a bloodless conquest (539), he assumed control of all of Babylonia and rang down the curtain on the last native Akkadian state.

ASSYRIOLOGY

Assyriology in its widest sense is the scientific study of all those civilizations which employed one or another of the cuneiform scripts; defined more narrowly, it is the study of the languages, literature, and history of ancient Babylonia and Assyria. Because the earliest documents were found in excavations in Assyria (northern Iraq), the discipline received the name "Assyriology." The native language of both Assyria and Babylonia (southern Iraq) was Akkadian, with "Assyrian" and "Babylonian" referring to the respective dialects.

EARLY EXPLORATIONS OF CUNEIFORM SITES

The collapse of the Assyrian and Babylonian civilization was so complete that its cities and remains were either wiped off the earth or buried under it, and its peoples, art, languages, and writings were erased from the memory of history. The very names of its cities, rulers, and gods were forgotten except in sundry local traditions, in the neglected works of Arab geographers, and in scattered and garbled allusions in the Bible and in Greek literature. Only the finds of modern archaeology have been able to reveal the character, achievements, and enormous contribution of this civilization and its great contribution to the civilizations that came after it.

EARLY EXCAVATIONS IN ASSYRIA

In 1842, the first English and French expeditions began a determined search for the lost cities and treasures of Mesopotamia that occupied the next four decades. Its most conspicuous successes were scored in the northeastern part of the country, ancient Assyria, and the whole field of study thus newly opened soon acquired the name of Assyriology. The first spectacular discoveries were made at Khorsabad, where Paul-Emile Botta excavated D-r-Sharrukin, the great capital city built by *Sargon II of Assyria at the end of the eighth century B.C.E. (1843–44) The paintings and drawings made in situ by E. Flandin for Botta's five magnificent volumes (1849–50), and the original sculptures with which the Louvre opened its Assyrian Gallery in 1847 opened Western eyes to the grandeurs of Assyrian archaeology. From 1852 to 1855, Victor Place resumed the French efforts at Dur-Sharrukin. In the meantime an Englishman, Austen Henry Layard, had already begun to excavate the other great Assyrian capitals, beginning with Kalah (Nimrud) in 1845, Nineveh (the twin mounds of Kuyunjik and Nebi Yunus) in 1846, and Ashur (Qalʿat Sherqat) in 1847. The seven seasons of excavation by Layard were crowned with very impressive discoveries of the palaces of *Sennacherib and Ashurbanipal at Nineveh and the palace of Ashurnaṣirpal at Kalah, of the many stone reliefs and colossal statues which stood at their gates; the great majority of these were transfered to the British Museum and elicited wide public response. Layard was succeeded in 1851 by his assistant Hormuzd Rassam, a native of Mosul. By 1854, the latter had succeeded in recovering the bulk of the great library of Ashurbanipal at Nineveh, which to this day remains the most important single source of Akkadian literature. Thereafter, the Crimean War brought all excavation in the area to a temporary halt. In 1872, George Smith, who examined cuneiform texts for the British Museum, discovered a version of the flood narrative which was recognized later as the 11th tablet of the Gilgamesh Epic, and interest in further excavations was renewed. For four years Smith continued to mine the vast treasures of the library at Nineveh until an early death overtook him on the way back to Aleppo (1876). From 1878 to 1882, H. Rassam renewed his activities in Nineveh, but interest in Assyria was for the time being exhausted as attention was directed instead to Babylonia.

THE RECOVERY OF THE SUMERIANS

Until the 1870s, impressive results were not had from the archaeological investigation of the southern half of Mesopotamia. However, in 1877 Ernest de Sarzec began to unearth Lagash (Tellōh) "The mound of the tablets," and by 1900 he had laid bare a whole new civilization whose very existence, adumbrated by the Assyrian tablets, had until then been a matter of dispute: the Sumerian civilization. These excavations and those which succeeded them helped to bring to light a whole new millennium in human history. American excavations at Nippur, meanwhile (1889–1900), uncovered the religious capital and center of learning of the Sumerians, with a library rivaling that of Ashurbanipal in importance, and antedating it by more than a thousand years. The origin of the Sumerians is unknown, and their non-Semitic language seems to have no affinities with other known languages. Other Babylonian expeditions before World War I identified numerous other ancient sites apart from Babylon, such as Sippar, Borsippa, Shuruppak, Adab, and Kish. Improvements in stratigraphic techniques in the field and the cumulative evidence of the inscriptional finds permitted the gradual construction of a chronological sequence and the recognition of certain significant cultural epochs. The extensive French excavations at Susa in Elam, begun in 1897, also proved significant, for this ancient capital of Elam was for millennia a faithful mirror of Mesopotamian influences, and the repository of some of its most precious booty, notably the "Stele of *Hammurapi," inscribed with his laws. The American-led invasion of Iraq in 2003 led to widespread looting, illegal sale of antiquities, and the destruction of significant elements of the archaeological record.

TRENDS AND PROSPECTS

New centers and new names have contributed their share to postwar Assyriology. American influence has been strongest in the lexical field, with Benno *Landsberger and the Oriental Institute at Chicago leading the way (*Materialien zum sumerischen Lexicon*, and *The Assyrian Dictionary* (almost complete in 2005), and the recovery of Sumerian Literature by S.N. Kramer and Thorkild Jacobsen. Vigorous studies are also being pursued in the homelands of the cuneiform sources, notably Turkey and Iraq. There are very active centers in Germany, France, and Italy, and also in Austria, Holland, Finland, and Israel.

Substantial syntheses of the materials already recovered are likely to occupy the attention of most Assyriologists for some time to come. In textual terms, such syntheses include (1) critical editions of literary or "canonical" compositions; (2) tabular compendia of the data contained in economic or "archival" tablets, using computer technology where necessary to cope with the large numbers of texts and entries; (3) new editions of the historical, religious, and votive texts of all periods and areas, together with the monuments on which they are found, to serve as a sound basis for the chronological outline on which all other historical judgments must rest. When these three fundamental syntheses have been achieved, the way will be open for the modern interpretation of the cuneiform evidence and its full integration into the record of human achievement.

[William W. Hallo]

The comprehension of the Bible has greatly benefited from the utilization of the results of Assyriological investigations. The following survey serves only as a collection of examples of contributions of Assyriology to biblical studies, as well as discussing Mesopotamian culture in more general terms.

HISTORY AND CHRONOLOGY

A great deal of historical information concerning the Near East during the period 626–594 B.C.E. is derived from a group of tablets known as the Babylonian Chronicle. Of immediate value is the chronological data provided by these tablets. According to the chronicle, the battle of Carchemish which is mentioned in Jeremiah 46 as taking place in the 5 fourth year of *Jehoiakim of Judah, was fought in the spring of the year 605 B.C.E. The month of Elul in the same year marks the accession of Nebuchadnezzar to the throne of Babylon. According to the Babylonian method of reckoning regnal years, Nebuchadnezzar's first year started in April 604 B.C.E. It is also learned from these tablets that on the second day of Adar in the seventh year of the reign of Nebuchadnezzar, which corresponds to March 15/16, 597 B.C.E. according to the Gregorian calendar, King *Jehoiachin of Judah surrendered the city or Jerusalem to the Babylonians, after ruling for only three months (II Kings 24:8–20). These dates serve as fixed points for those scholars who wish to calculate the chronology of the last years of the Kingdom of Judah. Among other features of interest to Bible scholars found in the Babylonian Chronicle is the tablet that covers the events of the years 616–608 B.C.E., during which time the Assyrian capital of *Nineveh fell to the Medes and Babylonians, and so provides us with background information to the prophetic book of *Nahum. Another feature of interest is the description of the defeat and flight of the Egyptian army after the battle of Carchemish, which is remarkably similar to the description of the same event in Jeremiah 46. It should not be assumed that a reference in cuneiform sources to a person or event recorded in the Bible will automatically amplify or clarify the biblical notice. It is entirely possible that such evidence may only complicate an already complex problem. Nevertheless, any discussion of a particular problem must take into account any evidence available from Mesopotamian sources.

A great deal of effort has been expended in order to establish the chronology of the mid-monarchial period in Israel. *Ahab, king of Israel, is the earliest biblical personage mentioned in cuneiform historical sources. According to a stele of Shalmaneser III, king of Assyria, Ahab was alive in the year 853 B.C.E. He was in fact one of the major participants in the battle of Karkar which was fought in that year. This battle which temporarily checked the Assyrian invasion of Syria is, curiously enough, not mentioned in the Bible (see *Karkar). An important synchronism between Assyria and Israel is to be found in the stele of Nergal-ereš (L. Page, in: *Iraq*, 30 (1968), 139ff.). According to this stele Joash, king of Israel was on the throne of Israel in the year 802 B.C.E. According to the Masoretic Text of the Bible, 57 years elapsed from the death of Ahab until Joash ascended the throne. The Assyrian evidence points to a period of 51 years between the two kings. In order to solve this problem, some scholars resorted to various Greek versions and the Assyrian sources. A similar situation surrounds that event whose shadow looms large in the prophetic literature of the last century of the existence of the Judahite kingdom, namely, the defeat of *Sennacherib before the gates of Jerusalem in 701 B.C.E. The biblical account of this event is to be found in II Kings 18–19 as well as in Isaiah 36–37. Sennacherib's own record of this event is also available. The biblical account of the siege appears to be inconsistent. According to II Kings 18:13–16, *Hezekiah, king of Judah, surrendered to Sennacherib and paid tribute to him. The Assyrian account in the main agrees with this account, though it differs on the amount of the tribute paid by Hezekiah.

[Aaron Skaist]

LAW

CUNEIFORM LAW

The term cuneiform law has usually been understood to denote the legal practice, and the records bearing on that practice, in those cultures or political entities in the Ancient Near East that used Sumerian or Akkadian cuneiform as their written medium. Taken in this sense, the realm of cuneiform law embraces not only the heartland of the cuneiform world, that is, ancient Sumer, Babylonia, and Assyria, but also the Elamite territory to the east of the Mesopotamian plain, the Syrian coast, and its immediate hinterlands from northern Syria down to Palestine, and especially the Hittite Empire which included practically all of Asia Minor. It must not be thought that these territories together constituted a homogeneous area in which a fairly uniform type of legal structure was in force. The homogeneity consists rather of the uniformity, or near uniformity, of a literary tradition that began in the scribal schools of southern Mesopotamia and spread with time to all the territories which are included in the definition of cuneiform culture. In all the areas thus named, cuneiform was employed as the regular written medium, at least for some period of time between 3000 and 300 B.C.E.

In the Ancient Near East the notion of "law" was inseparable and virtually indistinguishable from "justice" and the judicial process, and the idea of "law" suggested to the Mesopotamian mind- and, more or less, to the consciousness of all the peoples of the Ancient Near East – violations of existing obligations, including obligations to the state and society as well as private (i.e., civil) ones, but not the obligations themselves, insofar as the Mesopotamians did not think in terms of "law" in the context of specific regulatory institutions. The documentary sources from which knowledge of cuneiform law may be derived are to be divided into a number of categories. Primary among them are the large number of private records of judicial cases which were heard in, and adjudicated by, the courts. These cover many kinds of incidents and situations, most of which fall within the realm of property law. Litigations, as far as they are preserved, deal primarily with the disposition of family property and suits which may arise among members of a family or between two families over rightful ownership of certain real estate or other property. Contracts between individuals concerning sale, rental, and marriage and adoption agreements also constitute an important category for knowledge of cuneiform law. Here, too, the topic for the most part is property. A lesser number of documents fall into the category of private legal records, such as litigations concerned with matters that may be designated as private torts or crimes, which ought preferably to be subsumed under the more generic name, wrongs. For the present purpose, wrongs may be understood as invasions against persons or property by someone who held no prior claim or right against the victim or the object of this action. Punishments for such acts are not distinguished in terms of the category of the act itself, but rather in terms of the degree of seriousness of the offense or the amount of aggravating circumstances involved in it and could vary all the way from the requirement of simple restitution or pecuniary fine to the capital penalty.

Cuneiform private and public correspondence includes references to judicial or quasi-judicial acts that have a bearing on the practice of law in ancient Mesopotamia. The correspondence of private persons very often contains reports about dispositions of property in accordance with established customs, or possibly some references to legal action, which usually concerned questions of property. The correspondence of officials, including that of rulers, naturally concerned every area of political and economic administration, as well as other subjects, and occasionally mention materials directly pertinent to the subject of law. Among these are to be found the relatively scarce references to situations which would fall under the rubric of criminal law, as opposed to civil matters, with which all the other categories of private documents are almost exclusively concerned. Thus among the letters of Hammurapi of Babylon and of his older contemporary Rîm-Sin of Larsa there are references to official corruption and how the king dealt with it, and a royal order for the execution of an individual charged with homicide.

The category of material that may be defined as literature provides still another source of information about the legal institutions of the area. From sources such as proverbs, didactic compositions of various kinds, wisdom literature, and even from epics and legends, may be culled a not inconsiderable amount of information about legal behavior in ancient Mesopotamia.

Although these categories of documents constitute the only body of evidence for the actual practice of law in the cuneiform civilizations, the private documents must be utilized in a systematic way for the reconstruction of the real legal institutions of these societies themselves. It is often difficult also to assess the degree to which usages and procedures observed in the private documents represent true and fast "rules" or at least established custom; they may represent nothing more than the momentary whims of kings and officials without having the status of fixed rules or precedents. This condition contrasts with the formal legal corpora, which at least pretend to represent rules designed for application in all like cases and conditions, and which certainly represent the consensus on ideal moral and legal practice within the societies for which they were propounded.

By far the largest source of information, and the one which has usually been considered the primary source for knowledge of the legal institutions of ancient Mesopotamia, has been that formed by the so-called legal codes, most famous of which is the document known as the "Code of Hammurapi." Many fundamental questions may be raised as to the propriety of construing these legal codes as a reflection of the true legal institutions they purport to represent. There is sufficient evidence to indicate that these documents are more appropriately to be viewed not as legal codes in the strict sense but as representing a very special genre of literature of the oldest that were cultivated in Mesopotamian civilization. This view is based on both internal analysis of the documents themselves and external evidence. We cannot enter here into a detailed presentation of the case for our position; it will be sufficient to indicate that these so-called codes bore little relation, if any, to the ongoing legal practice in the very areas where they were formerly assumed, to have been in force.

Nevertheless, this article will be concerned with these codes more than with any other genre of text bearing on Mesopotamian legal institutions, for the simple reason that they are fairly straightforward, have for the most part been carefully edited, and are readily accessible to layman and scholar alike. Moreover, despite our reservations about their reliability as indicators of legal conduct in ancient Mesopotamia, they do form an important clue to the legal thinking that prevailed in that civilization at different times. In addition, inasmuch as we have almost no actual case law surviving from ancient Israel (there is a judicial plea from Mesad Hashavyahu and documents from the Jewish colony at Elephantine in Egypt of the fifth century B.C.E.), it makes sense to compare the two theoretical corpora, the Mesopotamian law codes and the Bible.

The major bodies of legal rules are listed below, in chronological order. The "middle chronology," which sets Hammurapi's reign at 1792–1750 B.C.E. will be followed; the "high" chronology sets these dates about 60 years earlier, the "low" about 60 years later; the letters enclosed in brackets are the abbreviations which will be used to refer to individual corpora in the ensuing discussion:

The Laws of Ur-Nammu of Ur [LU] (21st century B.C.E.)
The Laws of Lipit-Ishtar of Isin[LL] (c. 1950 B.C.E.)
The Laws of the Kingdom of Eshnunna [LE] (c. 1800 B.C.E.)
The Laws of Hammurapi of Babylon [LH]
(c. 1792–1750 B.C.E.)
The Assyrian Laws [AL] (c. 1400–1100 B.C.E.)
The Hittite Laws [HL] (c. 1400–1300 B.C.E.)

There are in addition lesser groups of laws of diverse dates and origins, such as a very fragmentary group from Cappadocia of the Old Assyrian period (c. 1900 B.C.E.), scattered groups of Sumerian laws, and a small group of laws from the Neo-Babylonian period.

The legal corpora exhibit many similarities both in style and content. There is a remarkable unanimity of expression throughout, whether the language of the individual corpus be Sumerian – as are LU and LL – Akkadian, or Hittite. This unanimity, which can be traced to the traditions of the scribal schools, manifests itself in duplications of thought and verbal formulation. Most of the rules are presented as sets of postulated acts or circumstances viewed as having occurred in the past or constituting an existing condition, followed by the prescribed sanction for each respective set of circumstances, which is to be viewed as the "decision." Depending on the type of case at hand, the sanction may be penal, civil, or simply in procedural prescription for a case which consists of some "unusual" circumstances not involving any "wrongs". Sometimes the judgment consists only of a denunciatory characterization of the offense without specification of the penalty to be imposed, a phenomenon largely restricted to the Hittite code. Variations in the circumstances of what may be essentially a single situation are treated for the most part as separate "cases" since they entail appropriate variations in their respective rulings.

The usual arrangement of the rules in the corpora is by groups dealing with the same general topic. There appears to be no discernible rationale, however, for the order in which these larger groups or topics are taken up. In some cases, after a subject has been treated in a number of rules presumably considered adequate by the authors or editors of a legal corpus, the transition to the next topic is effected by some suggestive similarity or common element between the first rule of the new subject and the preceding rule. It may be noted that LH, of all the cuneiform law corpora, appears to be the most rationally organized. The arrangement there is by topical, rather than by legal principles, but even this rationale is not uniformly followed. In the other corpora the arrangement seems to be much more arbitrary both as to the order of the topics treated and the order of the individual rules comprising a given topic.

The division of the different corpora into legal "clauses," "laws," or "paragraphs" is in some cases dictated by ruled lines inscribed on the original tablets, as in the case of AL, HL, and the excerpt tablets of LL, while the division into separate "laws" of LE and LH is the work of the first modern scholars who edited these texts, no indication for such divisions being given in the originals. Generally speaking, a single set of circumstances and the ruling that applies to it are treated as a separate "law" or "paragraph." AL, however, often combines sets of varying circumstances of a single basic situation, together with their appropriate rulings, into a single "paragraph." Thus Tablet A of AL, ruled off into some 60 sections in the original text, contains in fact many more separate rules or "laws" than that. HL, on the other hand, sometimes divides into two "paragraphs" what is essentially a single rule, and sometimes two unrelated rules are combined into a single paragraph. The numbering of the laws or "paragraphs" in the separate law corpora must therefore not be taken as more than a rough approximation of the actual number of distinct rules contained in each corpus; the standard numbering is best viewed as an aid to facilitate modern reference, with the actual number of separate rules to be determined by closer textual analysis in each case.

Apart from the agreement among the various corpora on the classes of subjects chosen for inclusion in their texts, and the more specific literary relationship among the corpora of Lower Mesopotamia, there is also substantial agreement among the corpora with respect to the sanctions that apply in the individual cases. Especially noteworthy in this connection are those cases where the sanctions are pecuniary, the damages often being identical or very close in amount among the several corpora. Such points of agreement constitute a more reliable index of the degree of uniformity of legal custom and usage in the Ancient Near East than those cases and fields in which penal sanctions apply, e.g., the sexual offences, such as rape (only of women who are married or preempted for marriage ["engaged"] by payment of a bride-price), adultery, and incest, all of which involve the death penalty; for these latter are acts which in almost any civilized society would be treated as the gravest of offenses, warranting the summary death of the offender. In all the codes, including the Bible, the death penalty is most often meted out for sexual offenses (E. Good, *Stanford Law Review* 19 (1967), 947–77).

Wherever the law corpora treat homicide and bodily injuries in any detail, it is evident that they distinguished between premeditated acts, non-intentional acts, accident, and negligence, the penalties increasing in direct proportion to the degree of guilt, with injuries or deaths which are the result of negligence regarded as more serious than accidental or even non-intentional acts. Homicide resulting from negligence such as faulty house-building that caused the death of an occupant, was treated as a serious offense, and could bring the death penalty to the builder or a member of his family. However, the owner of a dangerous animal such as a goring ox was subject only to pecuniary damages. Talionic punishments ("an eye for an eye") appear to have been an innovation in the Laws of Hammurapi, since the earlier corpora prescribe only pecuniary damages for injuries resulting from assault and battery. Even in LH the talionic penalty was limited to assaults upon the upper classes, which is an indication that such actions were viewed more gravely than similar acts against the lower classes. However, it should be stressed that talionic punishments and penalties of physical mutilation are rarely attested in documents referring to actual cases, and very likely were hardly ever resorted to. The victim of an eye gouging would have in most cases preferred monetary compensation. The talionic rules in the biblical law collections are probably equally to be viewed as an ideal principle of justice and equity. The non-talionic laws of Ur-Namma 18–22 (M. Roth, *Law Collections from Mesopotamia and Asia Minor* (1995), 19) permit a rich man to maim anyone so long as he pays the stipulated fines. The talionic punishments subject the offender to physical punishment.

An offense may be termed "criminal" when it is viewed as inimical to the well-being of the society as a whole and when the sanction is imposed by the public authority and not necessarily in the interest of any private party who may have been directly injured by the offending act. A "religious" offense, if subject to regular and predictable sanction, was thus a criminal offense. According to these criteria, sorcery is a criminal offense. It is already so treated in LH, which prescribes the penalty of death by drowning (i.e., through the river ordeal) and can be traced through LH, AL, HL, and finally in biblical law. Blasphemy and sedition, and insurrection appear to constitute another group of offenses treated early as criminal, e.g., AL 2 (blasphemy and sedition by a woman), and HL 2:173 (opposing the decision of the crown and the elders). The character of the offense in the example from HL is clearly indicated by the inclusion in the same paragraph of the case of the slave who rebels against his master. This, in turn, indicates that the offense of the wife in LH 143, for which she was to be cast into the water, involved some overt act of disloyalty to her husband in addition to profligacy, and from this it may be assumed a fortiori that similar acts of disloyalty or sedition against the crown or the religious order were dealt with in Babylonia with at least equal severity.

It is often noted that the legal corpora of the Ancient Near East are almost exclusively concerned with "secular" or "civil" law, in contrast to the biblical corpora in which "civil" and "cultic," or religious, rules are intermingled without apparent differentiation. HL, however, includes a number of cultic rules organized as a consecutive group, which indicates that the compiler of the corpus was conscious of the distinctive character of this group of rules. All the offenses in this group deal with violations, in one way or another, of real property, but the interesting feature of all of these rules is that there is no mention of any pecuniary or related form of penalty for these acts (apart from restitution wherever applicable); the expiation of these wrongs consists solely of ritual purification and sacrificial offerings. The conclusion is therefore inevitable that in Hittite society the institution of private real property was invested with the aura of religious sanctity, transgressions against which constituted a ritual defilement as well as a civil injury.

It may be said that the reason the law corpora of the cuneiform civilizations of the Ancient Near East appear to us to deal almost exclusively with "civil" or secular" law is not that the compilers of these corpora deliberately excluded religious subjects from their interest, but that "religious" laws were almost totally irrelevant for the general public; the public was rarely in a position to commit purely "religious" offences. Because the Torah in its final form is the product of the theocracy of the period of the Second Temple, we find the intermingling of "religious" and "secular" laws. The Torah makes no distinction between "religious" and "civil" offenses, nor, in terms of its own ideological orientation, would it have been meaningful for its writers to have introduced such distinctions into their legal structure.

The most common Akkadian term relating to the sphere of law is *dīnum*. The often-expressed notion that this term denoted statutory law is in error. The term *dīnum* denotes a case which is actually or hypothetically before the court. It comprises the statement of the facts of a given case, the court proceedings in its adjudication, and the verdict or decision of the real or hypothetical judge. The rules which comprise the Laws or Code of Hammurapi, for example, are nothing but a collection of hypothetical cases and their respective rulings as propounded by Hammurapi in his role of the supreme judge. They do not constitute law in that they cannot, and probably were not even intended to, serve as binding precedents for similar cases.

Another term which had wide currency in the Old Babylonian period, particularly during the dynasty of Hammurapi, is *ṣimdatum*, which in the older literature on the subject has been taken to mean "statutory laws." It occurs most often in the expression "according to the royal *ṣimdatum*" or simply "according to the *ṣimdatum*." The two phrases may be used interchangeably, and must have the general sense of "according to the regular, or established, procedures [governing the specific situation]." The *ṣimdatum* is, therefore, to be understood as the entire established body of legal tradition, of which some aspect is to be invoked in the particular instance where the *ṣimdatum* is alluded to. When a text refers to the "*ṣimdatum* of the king" the phrase is to be understood in the broad sense as, e.g., "the laws of the crown, of the realm" of which the particular reigning monarch is only the guardian, not the author.

Finally, there occurs frequently in legal contexts the term *mīšarum* or *mēšarum*; it denotes the quality of "equity" or "balance," "equilibrium" and, hence, "justice." The achievement and maintenance of this "balance" is viewed as the primary function and duty of the king. The periodic royal decrees and edicts which are sometimes referred to as *mīšarum* acts are specific measures directed towards this end. In different periods and different reigns the content of these measures would vary in accordance with the immediate situation. Hence the name *mīšarum* edict does not describe a measure of a specific or fixed content, but is something of an epithet attached to measures announced by the king, usually early in his reign, which are designed to remedy particular economic imbalances, and which thereby seek to assure the populace that the new ruler has truly dedicated himself to the advancement and maintenance of justice. These measures entailed cancellation of certain types of debts, release from certain kinds of tenant obligations, and freedom from servitude for debt. Not all obligations were cancelled for all the people on such occasions, but the edict specified the classes of persons, cities, and types of obligations which were to be affected by each act. References to such acts are found in the year-dates of the rulers of the Old Babylonian period, but to date only two texts are known which are devoted to the specific measures that such royal pronouncements entailed. These are the edicts of Samsu-iluna (c. 1750 B.C.E.), Hammurapi's son and successor, and of Ammi-ṣaduqa (c. 1650 B.C.E.), the fourth successor to the throne in Babylon after Hammurapi, and next-to-the-last of the line. It must be kept in mind that such edicts were directed by the promulgating authority to the immediate situation only, and were in no way intended to become the permanent "law of the land." Nor was there any rule which dictated the issue of such decrees at regular intervals, or for having the provisions contained in them take effect automatically at such times, as was the case of the biblical rules for the *Sabbatical year and the Jubilee.

One might conclude by characterizing law in ancient Mesopotamia as being essentially a congeries of local customary systems, which kings periodically attempted to make uniform or "reform" for administrative efficiency. These attempts, however, were at best of limited effectiveness even at the time of their promulgation. Doubt may even be raised concerning the degree to which the so-called lawgiver intended to have his precepts enforced and whether he disposed of a bureaucracy that was really capable of assuring such enforcement. These law codes, however, remain of prime historical value as an index to the morals, ethical notions, and institutions prevailing at the time of their publication.

[Jacob Finkelstein]

The centrality of law in life is a theme common to both Israel and Mesopotamia. There are, in fact, laws that are common to both societies, even in their wording. Thus, the Laws of Eshnunna paragraph 54 reads: "If an ox is known to gore habitually and the ward authorities have had the fact made known to its owner, but he does not have his ox dehorned [?] it gores a man and causes [his] death, then the owner of the ox shall pay two-thirds of a mina of silver" (trans. by A. Goetze, in: AASOR, 31 [1956];. Roth, *Law Collections*, 67), and the code of Hammurapi paragraph 251 reads, "If a man's ox is a gorer and his ward authorities had informed him that it is a gorer but he did not cover its horns or tie up his ox and that ox gores a free man and causes his death he shall pay one half mina of silver." A parallel law is to be found in Exodus 21:29: "If, however, that ox has been in the habit of goring, and its owner, though warned, has failed to guard it, and it kills a man or a woman – the ox shall be stoned and its owner, too, shall be put to death." Mesopotamian law, apart from the monetary penalty that the owner must pay, contains no penalty provision as far as the ox is concerned. Hebrew law requires that the owner of the ox be executed (according to Ex. 21:30 he can redeem himself), and that the ox likewise be executed. Moreover, the ox is to be killed by being stoned, and its flesh is not to be eaten.

Yet these laws, as similar as they may appear to be, reflect the basic difference between the Israelite and Mesopotamian legal systems. The codes of Mesopotamia are essentially secular codes in that they treat only matters concerning the conduct of one human being towards another. The relationship between the human and the divine is not regulated, nor are religious sanctions used to back up the essentially secular laws. In Israelite legal theory as articulated in the Bible, religion and law are intertwined. All law ultimately derives from God. Violations of religious law are punishable by human courts, and religious sanctions are applied as well as secular sanctions. Mesopotamian law contains no provisions regarding the goring ox itself. Israelite law requires that the ox be stoned, and its flesh is not to be eaten. The underlying principle of biblical law derives from the concept of the sanctity of human life connected with a certain concept of divinity as expressed in Genesis 9:5–6, "For your own life-blood I will require a reckoning: I will require it of every beast; of humans too, will I require a reckoning for human life, of every human for that of his fellow-human! Whoever sheds the blood of a human, by a human shall his blood be shed; for in His image did God make the human." In the law of the goring ox this concept finds full expression in the penalty meted out to the ox.

[Aaron Skaist]

LITERATURE

Ancient Mesopotamian literature commonly refers to the vast – and as yet far from complete – body of writings in cuneiform script which has come down from Ancient Mesopotamia. It is mostly found on clay tablets on which the writing was impressed when the clay was still moist. The writing reads, as does the writing on a printed English page, from left to right on the line, the lines running from the top of the page downwards. There are indications, however, that cuneiform writing once read from top to bottom and then, column for column, from right to left. The tablets when inscribed were usually allowed to dry naturally, occasionally, if durability was of the essence, they were baked at a high temperature to hard ceramic.

Except for a few excerpts in ancient classical writers from a book by the Babylonian priest Berossus, nothing at all was known either about cuneiform or the literature written in it until explorations and excavations – beginning shortly before 1800 C.E. – focused attention on the cultural treasures that lay hidden in the ruined city mounds of Mesopotamia. Mesopotamia, which corresponds to present-day Iraq, was in antiquity divided into a northern part, Assyria, and a southern part, Babylonia, also called Karduniash or Chaldea. The border between them ran approximately east-west a little above modern Baghdad. In still earlier times, Babylonia too was divided into a northern part, Akkad, and a southern part, Sumer, the dividing line running east-west a little above Nippur. Reliable copies of cuneiform inscriptions had been brought back by Carsten Niebuhr, only survivor of a Danish expedition in 1767 C.E. In 1802 C.E. a young German teacher, Grotefend, made the first substantial advance in decipherment of the difficult script. He was followed by the Englishman Rawlinson, who independently had reached conclusions similar to Grotefend's. With Rawlinson, the Irish scholar Hincks should be mentioned. Around 1860 C.E. the decipherment was essentially achieved.

Of the greatest importance, both for the help it proved in the decipherment and for the interest it created in wider circles, was the fortunate fact that English excavations at Nineveh came upon the remnants of a great library collected around 600 C.E. by one of the last Assyrian kings, Ashurbanipal. Historical texts from this library, as well as inscriptions found in other Assyrian palaces, threw new light upon personages and events dealt with in the Bible: occasionally Assyrian words would help the understanding of a difficult biblical idiom and, most striking of all, a story about the Deluge, remarkably similar to the biblical account, was among the finds.

Unfortunately, the importance of the tablet find did not immediately dawn on the excavators, so no efforts were made to keep together fragments that were found together; rather everything was simply dumped in baskets. As a result, scholars to this day are hard at work piecing fragments of Ashurbanipal's library together, and the finding of a new "join" is a source of great joy and satisfaction.

The content of the library was rich and varied, ranging from literary works in the strict sense of belles-lettres, to handbook literature codifying the knowledge of the times in various arts, sciences, and pseudo-sciences. Of particular importance for the decipherment were the lexical texts found. They gave precious information about how the multi-value cuneiform signs could be read. They also contained grammatical and lexical works dealing with a new and unheard of language, ancient Sumerian. This language, which preceded Akkadian (that is Assyrian and Babylonian) as vehicle of ancient Mesopotamian culture, has no relative among known languages and would almost certainly have proved impenetrable had not the Library of Ashurbanipal provided ancient grammars, dictionaries, and – most important of all – excellent and precise translations from Sumerian to Akkadian, its many bilingual texts.

Comparable in many ways to the find of the Library of Ashurbanipal was the find to the south, in Nippur, of what was at first believed to be a temple library belonging to Enlil's famous temple there, Ekur. Further exploration has shown, however, that the tablets in question come from private houses, and it seems probable that they represent the "wastepaper baskets" of scribal schools carted over and used simply as fill in the rebuilding of private houses.

The content of these – also mostly broken and fragmentary – tablets is the early Sumerian literature as it survived in the schools, during the period when Sumerian culture was coming to an end in the first centuries of the second millennium B.C.E. Here too, a great task of reconstructing the works involved from fragments awaited the scholars, a task still far from complete. Besides the two large finds here described, mention should also be made of important discoveries of texts in smaller libraries in Ashur found by the German excavation there, and a later, surprising find of tablets in the mound of Sultan Tepe by an English expedition.

SUMERIAN LITERATURE

General Character

The earliest evidence of writing from Mesopotamia – or indeed from anywhere – dates back to around the middle of the fourth millennium B.C.E. to the period known variously as the Protoliterate period or Uruk IV. Before this, however, literature doubtlessly existed in Mesopotamia in oral form, and as such it probably continued alongside written literature for long spans of time. The uses of writing were from the beginning those of aiding memory and of organizing complex data, as is well illustrated by the two genres that comprise the earliest written materials: sign lists and accounts. In time, new genres evolved from these genres: lexical texts, derived from sign lists; contracts and boundary stones, derived from accounts of gifts that accompanied a legal agreement to serve as a testimony to it; and, as a new departure, monumental inscriptions: votive and building inscriptions; and the letter, originally, as shown by its form, an aide-mémoire for the messenger delivering it as an oral message.

The use of writing as a means to organize and remember data underlies such genres as date lists and king lists. However, it is quite late that this power to organize complex data is fully utilized, with the creation of canonical series and handbooks, a development which begins in Old Babylonian Times and culminates in the Kassite period around the middle of the second millennium B.C.E.

The oral literature, in the meantime, while continuing in its own medium, must gradually have explored the possibilities of using writing as an aid in memorizing. While the innately written genres were, as has been seen, in general oriented toward serving as reminders and organizing data, the genres which originated as oral genres, and only secondarily took written form, had as a whole a different aim. A magical aspect may be distinguished in oral literature, retained in its pure form in the genre of incantation, where the spoken word is meant to call into actual existence that which it expresses; the more vivid the incantation, the more effective it is, a fact which accounts for its being cast in literary, or even poetic, language and form. The incantation was the province of a professional performer, the incantation priest (Sum. *mašmaš*, Akk. *ašipu*). A very similar magical purpose also seems to underlie other genres rooted in oral tradition. Myth, epic, and hymns to gods, temples, and kings, all had the purpose of praising somebody or something, and in so doing – as in a blessing – of enhancing or calling into being in the object of the praise, the virtues ascribed to it. This magical dimension of praise can still be seen to be very much alive in the short hymns of praise or blessings spoken by the incantation priest to the various materials he uses in his magical ritual, the so-called *Kultmittelgebete*, blessings intended to call up in these materials the powers and virtues attributed to them in the blessing. The praise takes in myths and epics the form of narrative presentations of great deeds of gods and heroes, originally, seemingly, to achieve by presenting them a vitalizing of the power to which they testify. In hymns, the praise usually takes the more static form of description of great qualities.

The praise genres were the province of a professional performer, the bard, Sumerian *nar*, Akkadian *nāru*, who sang to the accompaniment of a small lyre-like instrument held in the hand. The basic character of the myths, epics, and hymns he recited is indicated by the standard ending for them found over and over again; *zag-mì* NN, "Praise be NN" where NN is the name of the god, hero, or temple sung about. On the basis of the praise it offered up, the lyre was also called *zag-mì*, "praise." The bard (*nar*) was a cherished member of the court of the Sumerian ruler and is depicted reciting at royal banquets, on monuments from around the middle of the Early Dynastic Period.

A praise of a special kind was the lament, the praise of values lost. The lament genre may plausibly be assumed to have originated as lament for human dead and from there to have been extended to use in the rituals marking the death of the god of fertility in his various forms, and to rituals seeking the rebuilding of a destroyed temple. Actually, however, only very few elegies for human dead have come down to us, and on the whole, examples of laments of any kind do not antedate the Third Dynasty of Ur. The genre of laments was the province of a professional performer, the elegist (*gala*). He was, like his colleague the bard, a fixture at the Sumerian rulers' courts, ready to soothe the dark moments for his master by his elegies. He played, as the texts show, a major role at funerals.

Besides the genres mentioned, there were a number of others which made their way from oral into written form, most of them, as far as one can judge, of a popular and informal character with no professional performers in charge of them, but presented as occasion arose by whoever felt like it. Among these were love songs, generally placed in the mouth of women and dealing with gods and kings; wisdom texts, including proverbs and disputation texts pitting different evaluations against one another; didactic compositions such as the so-called Farmer's Almanac; letters to gods with prayer for personal misfortune; and copies of royal diplomatic correspondence, of royal inscriptions of various periods, of legal decisions by courts, and others not lending itself easily to literary classification.

The Agade period (ca. 2340–2159) in which rulers of Semitic origin adopted Sumerian culture, introduced a distinctive type of votive inscription detailing military achievements. From later copies two works credited to the daughter of Sargon of Akkad, Enheduanna, the first named author in history, who served as high priestess of the moon-god Nanna in Ur, are known. One is a series of short hymns to each of the major temples of Sumer and Akkad, the other is a long, impassioned plea to the goddess Inanna. The short Gutian period that followed the Agade period is notable mainly for works produced when it ended. A vivid account by Utu-hegal of Uruk of his war of liberation against the Gutians to "return the kingship of Sumer into its own hands" survives in later copies. To Utu-hegal's reign may also be assigned the composition of the great Sumerian King List, though other scholars prefer a slightly later date. To the end of the Gutian domination belong, furthermore, the famous cylinders A and B of Gudea, inscribed with a hymn to the temple of Ningirsu in Girsu as rebuilt by Gudea. They recount in wonderfully pregnant classical language the divine command to build, the building itself, and lastly the organization of the divine staff serving the needs of Ningirsu and the feast marking the completion of the work.

The perfection and ease of style in the Gudea cylinders show that Gudea's reign was a golden age of literature. In fact under him and in the following period of Ur III, may be placed the main burst of creativity that created Sumerian literature as now known and as it was preserved and handed on in the schools of the Isin-Larsa and Old Babylonian periods which followed Ur III.

The Standard Body of Sumerian Literature

An outline of the content of Sumerian literature as it took form around the period of the Third Dynasty of Ur (c. 2113–2000 B.C.E.) and was added to and transmitted in the schools of the following Isin-Larsa Period (c. 2000–1763 B.C.E.) can most conveniently be given in terms of the genres discussed in the general section above.

MYTHS, EPICS, AND HYMNS. *Myths.* The Sumerian myths seem to be devoted to a relatively small number of major deities only; Enlil, Ninurta, Enki, Inanna, and Dumuzi are the central figures in most of them. The myths about Enlil include the following:

(1) "Enlil and Ninlil: The Birth of the Moon-god," which tells how Enlil when he was young took Ninlil by force, was banned from Nippur by the assembly of the gods and set out for the Netherworld. Ninlil, who had become pregnant with the moon-god, followed him and on the road, in various disguises, Enlil persuaded her to lie with him to conceive another child to take the moon-god's place in the Netherworld. Thus three further divine children were engendered, all chthonic in character.

(2) "Enlil's wooing of Ninlil," a second, more conventional version of Enlil's wooing of Ninlil when she was yet a young girl in her mother's house in Eresh. Even in this tale Enlil is depicted as impetuous, but here he commits no wrong.

(3) "The Creation of the Pickax," a short tale relating how in the beginning Enlil forced Heaven apart from Earth to make room for things to grow, fashioned the pickax with which he broke the crust of the earth in *Uzumua*, "Where Flesh was grown," a sacred spot in Nippur, to uncover the heads of the first men growing out of the earth like plants, and how he then let the other gods share in the use of the pickax and the human workers.

The myths about Enlil's son Ninurta, god of the plow, of the thunderstorms in spring, and of the yearly floods, are mainly two.

(1) *Lugal-e*, a myth telling how Ninurta went to war in the mountains to the east against the *Asakku*, a demonic being engendered on Earth by Heaven, whom the plants had elected king. After a pitched battle Ninurta was victorious. He then built the near ranges, the *ḥursag*, as a dam, directed the waters from the mountains into the Tigris to provide irrigation water for Sumer, presented the *ḥursag* as a gift to his mother Ninlil when she came to see him, and gave her the name Ninhursaga(k), "Queen of the *ḥursag*." After that Ninurta sat in judgment on the stones, some of which had opposed him viciously in the war. His judgments on them determined the character and qualities they now have. The section about the dolerite, a stone imported by Gudea for his statues, suggests that the myth was written, or perhaps added to, in his reign.

(2) A second myth about Ninurta known as *An-gim-dim4-ma* tells how Ninurta, as he nears Nippur in full panoply of war, is met by Enlil's vizier Nusku, who bids him lessen his clamor and not disturb Enlil. Ninurta answers huffily with a long boastful speech, but is calmed down and is made to enter Nippur peacefully by his barber, Ninkarnunna.

(3) A third myth "Ninurta's Pride and Punishment" seems to tell that Ningirsu, at Enki's behest, captured the thunderbird Ansud who had stolen the tablets of fate from Enki. He had obviously hoped thus to obtain the tablets for himself, but when Ansud released them from its claw they returned to Enki in Apsu. Ninurta then, by bringing on a flood, sought to take over from Enki by force, but was outwitted and imprisoned in a pit dug by the tortoise, where Enki severely chided him for his ambitions.

It may be questioned whether the myth just told is best considered a Ninurta or an Enki myth. Clearly its sympathies are with the latter. Clever Enki, the god of the fresh waters in rivers and pools, was one of the most beloved subjects of the mythmakers. Among tales about him may be mentioned the following:

(1) "Enki and Ninhursaga" in which Enki presented the city on the island of Tilmun (modern Bahrain) to Ninhursaga, provided it with water and made it an emporium. He then united with Ninhursaga, engendering a daughter with whom in time he united, again engendering a daughter, and so forth. At last, when he has lain with Uttu, the spider, goddess of weaving, Ninhursaga removes his semen from Uttu's body and throws it on the ground. Seven plants grow up and Enki in time appears, names, and eats the plants. This makes him very ill, but eventually Ninhursaga is mollified and helps him give birth to the seven goddesses which have grown in his body from the plants. The myth ends with their being married off.

(2) "Enki and Ninmah" tells how the gods complained about having to do the hard work of irrigation agriculture, how Enki had his mother Namma give birth to man to relieve them, and how at the party to celebrate Namma's delivery Ninmah, another name for Ninhursaga, boasted that she could alter man's shape for good or bad at will. Enki accepted the challenge, saying that he could find a living for anything she might make, and then fashioned five freaks of various kinds, for all of whom Enki provided a job. When the roles were reversed, however, and Enki tried his hand at mischief, the being he created was afflicted with all the ills of old age, which thus came into the world, Ninmah being unable to do anything to help.

(3) As organizer of the world, Enki appears in "Enki and World Order" in which at Enlil's behest he organized the world much as one would organize an estate, determining first the character of the major cities in Sumer, then arranging for the sea, the rivers, clouds, and rain, then instituting economies such as agriculture, herding, etc., placing appropriate gods in charge, and lastly having to pacify the goddess Inanna, who did not think she had been given enough offices.

(4) The text which would be called the "Eridu Prehistory," which deals with the creation and settling of humans, creation of animals, the antediluvian cities, and the flood, is probably to be classed as an Enki myth since he is the hero of the Flood story. It is he who warns his worshiper Ziusudra against Enlil's wrath afterward.

As popular with the mythmakers as Enki, or even more so, was his granddaughter Inanna, city goddess or Uruk and one of the most complex figures in the Mesopotamian pantheon. She seems to combine features of a goddess of stores, a rain-goddess, and a goddess of the morning and evening star. The myths picture her as a young unmarried girl of the aristocracy, proud, willful, jealous, and power-hungry.

(1) In one of the myths about Inanna, "Inanna and the Powers of Office," she is pitted against her wily grandfather Enki. Arriving on a visit to him in Eridu, she is properly feasted

and Enki, drinking deep, confers in his expansive mood one important office after another upon her. When he wakes up sober next morning he rues his prodigality, but Inanna is gone. He still tries to stop her boat and get the offices back but in vain, and Inanna triumphantly brings them into Uruk.

(2) The myth of "Inanna and Ebeh" tells of the victory of Inanna over the mountain Ebeh (modern Jabel Hamrin) and consists mainly of a series of speeches glorifying her prowess in one form or another.

(3) Another myth, "Inanna and Bilulu," tells how Inanna hears about the killing of her young husband, Dumuzi, composes a paean in his honor, and then sets about avenging him on his killers Bilulu and her son Girgire.

(4) The longest of the myths about Inanna is the one called "Inanna's Descent." It tells how Inanna took it into her heart to descend to the Netherworld to wrest control of it from her elder sister Ereshkigal. The venture ended in disaster and Inanna was killed and changed into a cut of meat gone bad. Her loyal handmaid, Ninshubur, seeking help for her, finally obtained it from Enki, who fashioned two beings who were to win Ereshkigal's favor by expressing compassion for her. They did so, and when in return she granted them a wish, they asked for the meat that was Inanna and brought her back to life with food and water of life that Enki had given them. Still Inanna was not permitted to leave the Netherworld unless she could provide a substitute for herself, and so a posse of Netherworld deputies were sent along with her. As they met persons close to Inanna on their way – all dressed in mourning for her – she balked at giving them over to the demons. Only when in Uruk they found her young husband Dumuzi festively dressed and enjoying himself, did hurt and jealousy make her turn him over to the deputies. He, terrified, appealed to the sun-god, Utu, Inanna's brother and Dumuzi's brother-in law, to change him into a gazelle that he might escape his pursuers. Utu did so, and Dumuzi escaped but was again captured. This repeated itself three times, but in the end there was no way out for Dumuzi, who was taken to the Netherword. His sister, Geshtinanna, seeking him, found him there with the help of the Fly, and the myth ends by Inanna rewarding or punishing the Fly – it is not clear which – and dividing the stay in the Netherworld between Dumuzi and his sister so that they alternate, each of them spending half a year only in the Netherworld, the other half they are up with the living.

The myth about Dumuzi's repeated flights and captures, which forms the second half of "Inanna's Descent" exists also, with only slight modification, as a separate tale,

(1) "Dumuzi's Dream," which relates how Dumuzi had an ominous dream, and sent for his sister Geshtinanna, who interpreted it as foreboding his death. Attempting to hide from the deputies who came to carry him off, Dumuzi was betrayed by a colleague and caught. His subsequent appeal to Utu, his escape, etc., runs parallel to the story in "Inanna's Descent." A more cheerful myth is

(2) "Dumuzi's Wedding," which begins by relating how Inanna sends messages to her bridal attendants, including the bridegroom, Dumuzi, inviting them to bring their gifts. They do so, and the story goes through all the stages of a Sumerian wedding: the bridegroom arriving with his gifts, the bride having her bath and dressing in all her finery before opening the door to him, which is the symbolic act concluding the marriage, Dumuzi leading his bride to his own home, stopping on the way to visit his own tutelary god, and his reassuring of his nervous young bride that she will not be asked to work hard or do any tiring tasks in her new house.

Epics. The epics, which deal with great and memorable deeds of men rather than of gods, are more immediately accessible than the myths, which often presuppose a knowledge of what the gods stand for, which is not easily come by. Most of the epics that have come down to us center around rulers of the First Dynasty of Uruk. This was the dynasty from which the kings of the Third Dynasty of Ur thought themselves descended, and it seems likely that what has been transmitted is in effect a choice aimed at the taste of that court, perhaps as it changed with time from one king to the next.

Closest to the effect of primary epic with its emphasis on martial valor and honor is perhaps the following:

(1) The epic tale "Gilgamesh and Agga (Akka; COS I, 550–52)." It tells how Gilgamesh, vassal ruler of Uruk under Agga of Kish, persuades him to resist performing its corvée duties with weapon in hand. Agga and his longboats soon appear before Uruk's walls. Only Gilgamesh himself is valiant enough to make a successful sortie. He cuts his way to Agga's boat and takes Agga captive. Having thus proved himself, however, he grandly sets Agga free and even reaffirms his overlordship, all in gratitude for the fact that on an earlier occasion Agga had taken Gilgamesh in when the latter sought his protection as a fugitive.

(2) Also in some degree warlike in spirit, but with distinct romantic overtones of the strange and the far away, is the tale of "Gilgamesh and Huwawa," which tells how Gilgamesh, to win fame, undertakes an expedition against the terrible Huwawa in the cedar mountains in the west. The adventure nearly ends in disaster, but by deceit Gilgamesh gets Huwawa in his power and, when he is nobly inclined to spare him, Huwawa rouses the anger of Enkidu, Gilgamesh's servant, who promptly kills him.

(3) A mythical element enters into the tale of "Gilgamesh and the Bull of Heaven." The city goddess of Uruk, Inanna, has offered Gilgamesh marriage and has been rudely refused. To avenge herself, she asks the loan of the fierce "bull of heaven" from her father Anu. Anu reluctantly grants her wish. Contrary to expectations, however, the bull does not manage to kill Gilgamesh, but is itself slain by him and Enkidu.

(4) Gilgamesh exhibits a quite different friendly, attitude toward Inanna in another story, "Gilgamesh, Enkidu, and the Netherworld". In this tale, Inanna finds a tree drifting on the river, pulls it in, and plants it, in the hope of making a bed and a chair from its wood when it is fully grown. By that time, however, the tree has been taken over by the Ansud bird, the

demoness Lilith, and a great serpent. In her disappointment she turns to Gilgamesh, who scares off the unwelcome guests, fells the tree, and gives her wood for her bed and chair. From the tree stub and the branches he makes what seems to be a puck and stick for some hockey-like game, and celebrates the victory with a feast. At the feast, however, a waif, who has no one to take care of her, utters a cry of protest to the god of justice and fairness, Utu, and Gilgamesh's puck and stick fall into the Netherworld. Enkidu offers to go down and bring them up and Gilgamesh instructs him in how to behave so as not to be held back down there. Enkidu, however, disregards the instructions and so must remain in the Netherworld. All Gilgamesh can do is to obtain permission for Enkidu's ghost to come up to see him. Enkidu's ghost then ascends through a hole in the earth, the two embrace, and in answer to Gilgamesh's questions Enkidu tells him in detail how people are treated in the hereafter.

(5) A badly damaged tale called "The Death of Gilgamesh" will be dealt with later when the genre of elegiac epic is discussed.

To the romantic epic with its penchant for the strange and fantastic belongs also the "Lugalbanda Epic," the hero of which is listed in the Sumerian King List as the successor of Enmerkar and predecessor of Gilgamesh, separated from the latter by one Dumuzi, a fisherman from Kuar. According to other traditions, Lugalbanda was the father of Gilgamesh.

In the epic called after him Lugalbanda is still a young man. It relates how Enmerkar calls up his army for a campaign against the city of Aratta in the eastern highlands. On the march, Lugalbanda falls seriously ill and is left to die in a cave (*ḫurrum*) in the mountains by his fellows. He partly recovers, however, and begins fervently to pray to the gods for help. The gods hear his prayers and as he roams the mountains he comes upon the nest of the thunderbird, Ansud, gains its favor, and is granted, at his own wish, supreme powers of speed and endurance. The bird also helps him find his way back to the army, and there, among his comrades, Lugalbanda completely recovers. The army reaches Aratta and begins a long siege of it. However, after a while Enmerkar's zest for the task wanes and he wishes to send a message back to Uruk to Inanna, upbraiding her for no longer caring enough for him; she must choose between him and her city Aratta. There is, however, no messenger who dares undertake the hazardous journey. At last Lugalbanda volunteers, and successfully carries the message to Inanna. She receives him well, hears Enmerkar's message, and advises Enmerkar to catch a certain fish on which Aratta's life depends. Thus he will put an end to the city. Its craftsmen, handiwork, copper and moulds for casting, he can then take as spoil.

There are two other epics of which Enmerkar is the hero: "Enmerkar and Suhkesdanna" and "Enmerkar and the Lord of Aratta." The first of these is a romantic epic verging on fairy tale. It tells how Ensuhkesdanna of Aratta sent messengers to Enmerkar in Uruk, demanding that he submit to Aratta since Ensuhkesdanna could provide a temple of lapis lazuli and a richly adorned couch for the rite of the sacred marriage with Inanna, while Enmerkar had but a temple of mud brick and a bed of wood to offer. The demand is, as could be expected, proudly refused, and Ensuhkesdanna then wishes to obtain his demands by force of arms. The assembly in Aratta is not willing to support him in this, however, and so he is temporarily at an impasse. Then an incantation priest (*mašmaš*) and magician at his court offers to use his powers to have a canal dug to Uruk and to have the inhabitants load their possessions on boats and haul them to Aratta. Ensuhkesdanna is delighted and rewards him richly. The magician then sets out from Aratta, and arriving on his way at Nidaba's city Eresh near Uruk he persuades – since he can speak the language of animals – the cows and goats there to stop giving milk, thus interrupting the cult of Nidaba. At the complaint of the herders, a learned amazon goes up against him in a sorcerer's contest in which both cast fish spawn into the river and pull out animals: the magician, a fish, and the amazon, a bird, which flies off with the fish; the magician, an ewe and its lamb, the amazon, a wolf that runs off with them, and so forth. After the fifth try the magician is exhausted, it becomes dark before his eyes, and he is all confused. The amazon chides him, saying that while his wizardry is plentiful, his judgment is sadly lacking in that he has tried his wizardry against the holy city of Nidaba. So saying, the amazon seized his tongue in her hand and, denying his plea for mercy on the grounds that his crime was sacrilegious, killed. Word of his fate reached Aratta, and Ensuhkesdanna, much sobered, acknowledged the preeminence of Enmerkar.

The other epic about Enmerkar makes of the rivalry between Enmerkar and the lord of Aratta a battle of wits, a test of which of them is most competent as ruler. In its scale of values, peaceful compromise seems to win out over military solutions. It begins by telling how Enmerkar appealed to Inanna to make her other city, Aratta, subject to Uruk, so that its people would bring down stone and other precious building materials as tribute to Uruk for Enmerkar's temple building. Inanna grants his wish, tells him to send a messenger to Aratta to demand submission, and withholds rain from Aratta, in order to put pressure on it to submit. The ruler of Aratta at first rejects the demand, but when he is told that Inanna sides with Enmerkar he accedes pro forma: he will submit if Enmerkar will send grain to relieve the famine caused by the drought, but this grain must not be sent in sacks, it must be loaded into the carrying nets of donkeys. Enmerkar complies with this seemingly impossible demand by sending sprouted grain and malt, but is set a new similar, seemingly impossible condition. After he had complied with that and still another, he loses patience, however, and threatens to destroy Aratta. His angry message is too long for the messenger to remember, and so to help him Enmerkar invents the letter. When the messenger arrives in Aratta with the written letter and the lord of Aratta is pondering it to think of a new subterfuge, the god of rainstorms, Ishkur, apparently knowing nothing about what is going on, drenches the region around Aratta, producing a bumper crop.

At this point, unfortunately, the text is incompletely preserved. From what we have, however, it is possible to gather that the conflict was resolved by the invention of trade and a peaceful exchange of goods follows. Thus Enmerkar is able to obtain his coveted building materials through peaceful means.

The later Dynasty of Agade, with its heroic figures Sargon and Narâm-Sin, formed a second, minor focus for the epic tradition. Sargon, the founder of the dynasty, figures in an unfortunately very fragmentary text in which he seems to have made the wife of his Sumerian opponent Lugal-zagge-si his concubine, but under what circumstances is not clear. Another, as yet unpublished, story tells how he was protected by Inanna at the court of Ur-Zababa of Kish when he was serving there as cupbearer. The figure of Narâm-Sin seems to have become the type of the self-willed human ruler challenging the gods in his hubris. The epic tale called "The Fall of Agade" tells, after describing the might and prosperity of Agade, how Narâm-Sin, wishing to rebuild Enlil's temple Ekur in Nippur, failed to obtain favorable omens that would allow him to do so. Yet, against Enlil's will, Narâm-Sin mustered his forces and began demolishing Ekur. Enlil in his anger called in the wild Gutian mountaineers, who disrupted all communication in the country and produced dire famine. Lest the whole country be destroyed, the major deities of Sumer then appealed to Enlil and succeeded in having the punishment focused on Agade as the actual offender. It was thoroughly cursed by the gods so that it would never again be inhabited.

Hymns to Gods. Praise, with its attendant effects of enhancement and expression of allegiance to persons and to values, can take descriptive as well as narrative form and becomes then hymnal rather than mythical or epic. Mesopotamian literature focused such hymnal praise particularly on three subjects: gods, temples, and kings. The resultant genres are not, however, kept rigidly apart, and sections of a hymn to a god may well be devoted to praise of his temple, just as hymning a temple generally includes praise of its divine owner. The royal hymns abound in addresses to the gods to assist and protect the king hymned.

Among major hymns directed to gods, there is reason to mention first the great hymn to Enlil of Nippur called *Enlil suraše*. It tells how Enlil chose Nippur as his abode, describes its sacred character so fiercely intolerant of all evil, moves on to Enlil's temple in it, Ekur, describes the latter's rituals and sacred personnel, and then Enlil himself as the key figure in the administration of the universe, planning for the maintenance and well-being of all creatures; it ends with a brief acknowledgement also of Enlil's spouse, Ninlil, who shares his powers with him.

Another remarkable hymn is a hymn to the sun-god Utu, which praises him as maintainer of justice and equity in the universe and the last recourse of those who have no-one else to turn to. Utu's sister, Inanna, is hymned as the evening star in a hymn of ten sections. It describes her role in judging human conduct, and ends with a description of her rite of the holy marriage as performed under Iddin-Dagan of Isin with the king embodying her divine bridegroom, Dumuzi. Other hymns dealing with this rite may be considered actual cult texts. Most likely they accompanied a performance of the ritual acts, for often they furnished a running account of what is done in the rite as seen by an observer at close quarters.

A very remarkable and ancient hymn to Inanna (COS I, 518–22) was written, according to Sumerian tradition, by a daughter of king Sargon of Agade, Enheduanna, who was high priestess of the moon-god Nanna in Ur. In the hymn, she has been driven out by enemies, feels abandoned by her divine husband Nanna, and turns in her distress to Inanna, the divine protector of her father and her family – and also, at that time, holder of the kingship of the gods. The description of Inanna in this hymn is that of a goddess of rains and thunderstorms.

Other hymns to goddesses of notable literary qualities are a long hymn to the goddess Nanshe in Nina emphasizing her role as upholder of morals and ethics, a long hymn to the goddess Nininsina praising her powers to heal and to drive out demons of disease, and a hymn to the goddess Nungal in Nippur, a prison goddess with strong Netherworld affinities. The hymn to her describes in detail the features of her temple, which serves as a place of ordeal and place where she judges and imprisons evildoers. It then moves into a self-praise by the goddess in which she lists her various functions and those of her husband Birtum. Many more such hymns could be mentioned, but these may suffice as examples of the genre and of the variety of treatment it allows.

A particular group of hymns to gods deserves, however, special mention: the "processional hymns." These are hymns meant to be sung as accompaniment on the occasion of ritual processions of the gods and on ritual journeys to visit other deities in other cities. Occasionally, as in the case of the composition called "The Journey of Nanna to Nippur," they approach narrative form, describing the stages of the journey by boat and Nanna's cordial reception by Enlil in Nippur before launching into a long catalog of the blessings bestowed upon him by Enlil to take along home to Ur. Somewhat similar hymns celebrate, respectively, Inanna's and Ninurta's journeys to Eridu, and a hymn of this kind, verging on both the myth and the hymn to temples in "Enki Builds Eengurra," which tells how Enki built his temple in Eridu, then traveled by boat to Nippur, where he invited the gods to a party to celebrate the completion of his new home, and where his father Enlil spoke the praise of it.

Hymns to Temples. Praise of temples looms large, as we have mentioned, in many of the hymns to gods. It may also be the main theme of a hymn. Such hymns to temples would seem to have been represented already in the Fara and Abu Salabikh materials. A particularly noteworthy example of the genre is a cycle of hymns to all the major temples in Sumer and Akkad composed by the already mentioned Enheduanna and faithfully copied in the schools for centuries afterwards. Even older, is the much copied "Hymn to the Temple of Kesh," which is already represented in the Abu Salabikh materials. The finest example of the genre is, however, a hymn which never entered the standard body of school literature: the great hymn to the temple of Ningirsu in Girsu, E-ninnu, written on the occasion of its rebuilding by Gudea. The hymn was originally written on three large clay cylinders, of which the second and third are preserved. It describes in detail the communication of Ningirsu's wishes to Gudea in a dream, the care taken to check that the god's message was correctly understood and to carry out the task correctly, the bringing of building materials from afar, the actual building process step for step, and finally the occupation of the new temple by Ningirsu, the appointment of its divine staff, and the concluding "housewarming party" for the gods.

Hymns to Kings. A suitable subject for hymning was also the king, and a great many royal hymns are extant. The oldest examples of the genre deal with Ur-Namma, the first king of the Third Dynasty of Ur. A high point of productivity was reached with his successor, Shulgi, who figures in more than 20 hymnal compositions, and the genre continues to be productive through the first half of the succeeding Isin Dynasty, at which point it begins to peter out. The last example is a hymn to Abi-eshuh of the First Dynasty of Babylon. The content of the genre is varied in the extreme. Many of the hymns deal with the election of the king by the assembly of the gods, or with divine favors showered upon him. Some contain appeals to the gods on the kin's behalf, and some – the royal hymns in the narrower sense – contain a sustained praise of the king, his abilities, e.g., as warrior or as scholar, his virtues, e.g., his sense of justice and fairness, and the prosperity he brought to the country. Frequently these hymns take the form of self-praise and are put in the mouth of the king himself.

Love Songs. Love songs, of which Sumerian literature has quite a few, may perhaps also be considered hymns of praise, albeit of a special distinctive character. Some of these are put in the mouth of the divine lovers, Dumuzi and Inanna, or deal with episodes of their courtship, in some the beloved is the king, particularly Shu-Sin of the Third Dynasty of Ur. These songs praise his physical attractions and express the longing and love of the girl who sings of him. It seems not unlikely that a considerable number of these songs were the work of a poetess in the circle around Shu-Sin; one would guess the *lukur* priestess Kubatum.

ELEGIACS. Whereas the praise in myths, epics, and hymns is directed toward extant values, in the elegiac genres it is focused on values lost and longed for. In elegiacs corresponding to the myth are narrative accounts of the death of gods; in those corresponding to the epic, accounts of the death of kings and heroes; and in those corresponding to the hymn, dirges for gods, temples, and kings, and in very rare cases for ordinary human dead.

Elegiac Myth. A number of works whose central theme is the death and loss of gods may be characterized as elegiac myths. Among these are first of all a number of cult texts from the cult of the dying gods such as Dumuzi and Damu, apparently meant to be sung as accompaniment to ritual acts such as, e.g., processions into the desert to Dumuzi's deserted fold. An example of such an elegiac is "The Wild Bull Who Has Lain Down," in which Inanna seeks her dead husband, killed by the men of the Bison in the mountains. Another example is "The Bitter Cry For Her Husband," which tells of the attack on Dumuzi's fold, his escape, and his death as he tries to swim to safety across the swollen Euphrates in its flood. Many others could be quoted. Perhaps the longest such composition is *Edinna u saga*, "In the Desert in the Early Grass," a Dumuzi text with long insertions of related Damu materials. It tells of the disappearance of the god, and follows his mother and sister as they search for him. It relates how the rough deputies of the Netherworld tore him away from his mother in Girsu on the Euphrates, how she is determined to stand in the gate of their superior claiming her son back, how she asks the canebrake about him, and how she finally takes the road of no return to the Netherworld. Eventually, it seems, it is his sister rather than his mother who reaches him there. A somewhat similar narrative dealing with Damu describes how his sisters wish to board the boat on which he is taken captive and bound to the Netherworld by a deputy from there, and how on arrival there the deputy's superior frees Damu. While these and other compositions seem to have been used in the cult, purely literary accounts of the attack on Dumuzi and his death are also found. One such is "Dumuzi's Dream" of which we spoke above under myths.

Elegiac Epic. Elegiac epic may be defined as epic tales centering around the death of a king or hero, which do not, however, treat that death as heroic, but rather as pure loss. Such tales are "The Death of Gilgamesh," which we mentioned earlier. It treats of the death and burial of Gilgamesh and contains a long address to him by Enlil, in which Enlil tries to reconcile Gilgamesh to his mortality. Of particular interest in that it shows how old the traditions on which the epic genres build are, is the fact that this text has preserved memories of the ancient custom of having the servants of a ruler follow their master also in death. This custom, which existed in the times of Gilgamesh, is also attested to by the finds in the royal graves of Ur excavated by L. Woolley but must have been abandoned long before the times of the Third Dynasty of Ur. Another work in this genre is "The Death of Ur-Namma," which tells of the death and burial of Ur-Namma, of the honored role he is given in the Netherworld, and, in spite of this, his unhappiness about all he left behind him unfinished.

Laments for Gods. Lament for the dead god was a central part of the cult of most dying gods and many such laments are preserved. To the Dumuzi cult belongs the moving lament by his mother in "A Reed-Pipe – My Heart Plays a Reed-Pipe

(Instrument) of Dirges for Him in the Desert" and many others. Most often there is an element of narrative, reflecting the fact that these laments were part of the ritual of going to the god's destroyed fold in the desert. The Damu laments likewise tend to alternate with narrative sections, but the lament of Aruru for her lost son, and the lament of Lisin are examples of pure laments.

Laments for Temples. As the loss of gods and kings was mourned, so were the great public disasters: destruction of cities and their temples at the hand of enemies. The lament was intended to soothe the emotions of the bereaved god and channel them, and thus prepare the way for divine will to restoration. To the genre of lament for destroyed temples belongs what is perhaps the highest achievement of Sumerian poetry, the magnificent and deeply moving "Lament for the Destruction of Ur," which deals with the capture and destruction of the city by the Elamites and the Sua people that ended the Third Dynasty of Ur. The vivid and very detailed, but much less powerful, "Lament for Ur and Sumer" (COS I: 535–39) deals with the same event. Among later laments there is the long "Lament for Nippur and Ekur" connected with the restoration of Ekur by Ishme-Dagan, which ends with a long section in which Enlil promises to restore the temple. Other laments for Ekur and for Inanna's temple in Uruk, EAnna, popular in later times, go back to the end of the Isin-Larsa period. As in the Dumuzi laments, so in the laments for temples, narrative and lyrical sections alternate, the dramatic events around the day of destruction being told in all their stark detail.

Dirges. Laments for kings and heroes in non-narrative lyric form have not so far been found, but two examples of dirges for ordinary mortals succeeded in entering the standard body of literature. They were written by a certain Ludingirra, one in honor of his father, the other on occasion of his wife's death.

WISDOM LITERATURE. Wisdom literature is not committed from the outset as are, each in its way, the encomiastic and elegiac works, but is rather discriminating and evaluative.

Disputes. One of the most popular forms of entertainment and humorous examination of standard values was the dispute or logomachy, which seems to have flourished particularly under the rulers of the Third Dynasty of Ur, several of whom are referred to by name in these works. The usual pattern is a mythological introduction setting the action in the beginning of time, which is then followed by a lengthy dispute about their respective merits by the two contestants. Sometimes the end of the tale is a judgment by a god or the king, but other settings occur, and the text may launch directly into the debate. Examples of works in this genre are "Summer and Winter," "Silver and Copper," "Ewe and Grain," "Plow and Hoe," "Shepherd and Farmer," and others. As a rule, the more lowly contestant carries the day. A special group of such disputes have the school or the life of a scribe as a setting. Among these are "A Scribe and His Disappointing Son," in which a father details the many failings of his son – one senses that he has spared the rod too much – as also "The Overseer and the Scribe," in which the scribe lists the numerous services a scribe performs in a large household, "Enkimansum and Girniisag," a dispute between an obstreperous student and his tutor, and "The Dispute between Enkita and Enkihegal," which, as the disputants get more and more heated, deteriorates into a mere slanging match. It would seem that the ancient listeners must have derived a good deal of vicarious enjoyment from hearing of quarreling and listening to the unrestrained flow of bad language, for in this genre such things are frequent. Another example of it, perhaps the worst, is a vitriolic slanging match known as "Debate Between Two Women." The most interesting evaluative work of Sumerian wisdom literature is, however, probably the one called "Man and His God," in which a man complains about his god's neglecting him and the bad luck dogging him as a consequence. It is a Sumerian precursor, in some sense, of later treatments of the motif of the just sufferer and the earliest indication of awareness of the problem we have.

Apodictic and Didactic Wisdom Texts. Apodictic statements of do's and don'ts characterize the extensive proverb genre, which comprises actual proverbs, as well as all kinds of saws, turns of phrase, etc. and also includes short fables with pointed morals. A large collection of such saws was attributed to Shuruppak, father of the Sumerian hero of the Flood, Ziudsudra, and appear in the composition "The Instructions of Shuruppak"as this wise father's counsels to his son. This composition was, as mentioned, already in existence in the Abu Salabikh materials. The composition commonly called the "Farmer's Almanac," which is cast in the form of a father's – the plow-god Ninurta's – advice to his son, and describes in order all the standard activities to be carried out by a good farmer during the year, is apodictic and didactic insofar as it presents a norm for the activities of the farmer. Formally similar in many ways is the composition called "Schooldays," in which a schoolboy takes time out on his way to school to tell a questioner where he is going so early in the morning, and what he usually does in school.

INCANTATIONS. The genre of incantations continues, and substantial collections of individual incantations begin to be made. There are three major types of incantation: (1) The first is the legitimation type, in which the incantation serves to identify the incantation-priest as the messenger and agent of a god-usually Enki – and as under his protection. It ends with a formula conjuring the demons in the name of heaven and earth. A similar type of incantation is (2) the so-called prophylactic type, which first describes the evil doings of the demons, then orders them to depart. Lastly (3) the Marduk-Ea type describes first the evil done by the demons, then how Asalluhe/Marduk sees it and asks his father Enki's/Ea's advice. Enki then states what ritual acts will serve as cure.

VARIA. A variety of other types of writings, not easily classifiable, are found with works of the genres here listed. Mention may be made of such things as copies of royal inscriptions, of royal diplomatic correspondence, of noteworthy letters of various kinds – among them appeals to deities for help in illness and misfortune – riddles, copies of legal deliberations and decisions in the assembly of Nippur, lists of medical prescriptions, of legal formulas, and copies of law codes, among them those of Ur-Nammu and Lipit-Ishtar. In general these various memorabilia are examples of specific utilization of the organizing and mnemotechnical powers in writing. Not infrequently they stand at the beginning of new handbook genres developing in the second and first millennia.

OLD-BABYLONIAN LITERATURE

Cuneiform writing seems to have been used to write Akkadian very early, perhaps already toward the end of the Protoliterate period. Apart from votive inscriptions and royal monumental inscriptions, however, there is little evidence of Akkadian literary activity. Economic texts, contracts, deeds, letters, a few incantations with perhaps a fragment of a royal hymn, seem to be all. It is not until Old-Babylonian times, around 1700 B.C.E., that more substantial literary activity in Akkadian is attested; quite possibly sparked by a tradition of, and an appreciation for, oral literature among the West Semitic Amorites, who by that time had entered Mesopotamia in large numbers and had furnished such a key ruling dynasty as the First Dynasty of Babylon.

Old-Babylonian literature is, however, clearly written in the country and builds in large measure on Sumerian materials. However, it treats these materials freshly, with notable originality and literary power.

The genres represented are first myths, with works such as the "Poem of Agushaya" which tells how Ea created the goddess Saltu, "Strife," to challenge the warlike goddess Ishtar (Agushaya) and the "Myth of Anzu" about the thunderbird which stole the tablets of fate from Enlil, and with them his powers of office. More impressive than these, though, is the remarkable "Myth of Atrahasis," which deals both with the creation of humans and their near destruction by flood (COS I, 450–53). The gods in those early days had to toil themselves as agricultural workers. After a while, in the first record in history of a strike, they rebelled and rioted in front of Enlil's temple in Nippur. Eventually a compromise was worked out by Enki: a god – presumably the ringleader in the rebellion – was to be killed, and from his flesh and blood man was to be created to take upon himself the toil of the gods. After a while, however, mankind grew so numerous and made so much noise that Enlil found it impossible to sleep. He tried various means to diminish their number and noise, but without lasting effect. Eventually he persuaded the other gods to bring on the Flood and thus to wipe out humanity entirely. Enki, however, as might have been expected, warned his protégé Atrahasis and had him save himself and his family and all species of animals in a big boat. Enlil's anger when he found that a human being had survived was appeased by Enki, who instituted a variety of measures – orders of nuns who were not to conceive and give birth, barren women, and demons killing newborn children – which would serve to hold man's numbers permanently within bounds. Man, the myth seems to say, must know his limitations. He has his place and his useful function in the Universe and will be tolerated by the powers that rule existence, as long as he does not make himself obnoxious to them. The genre of epics is represented by a fragment of the "Epic of Etana" (COS I, 453–57). Etana was the first king, and was carried up to heaven on the back of an eagle he had helped and befriended in order to fetch the plant of birth-giving so that his son could be born. Of special interest are a number of fragments dealing with Gilgamesh.

Hymns to gods and goddesses are well represented. One may mention the Papulegarra Hymn and a hymn to Ishtar with a prayer for Ammi-ṣaduqa. Examples of a new genre, the penitential psalm, which has parallels and perhaps antecedents in the Sumerian "Letters to Gods," makes its appearance. To the genre of love songs, or possibly that of disputes, may be counted a humorous dialogue between a girl and her somewhat naive young man. The dispute genre shows a debate between the tamarisk and the palm. Among the handbook genres mention may be made of the Akkadian "Laws of Eshnunna" and the famous "Code of Hammurapi." They continued – and show distinct influences of – the earlier Sumerian codes of Ur-Nammu and Lipit-Ishtar. Completely new is the prolific genre of omina, which clearly shows work of considerable length and advanced organization of the materials; also the genre of "Mathematical Problem Texts" with the famous Plimpton Tablet, which shows understanding of the laws governing the so-called Pythagorean Theorem, and the Sumerian grammatical texts, which operate with a most ingenious organization scheme, the one column grammatical paradigm.

STANDARD BABYLONIAN LITERATURE

The Old-Babylonian period was followed by a dark age, concerning which little evidence is available. What happened to literature at this time is therefore in some measure a matter for surmise only, but it would seem that a process of selection took place. Only certain works and certain kinds of works survived; others, whether by accident or for reasons of changing taste, were dropped. At the same time there are indications of considerable literary activity during the later half of the Kassite period, from about 1400 B.C.E. onward. The nature of this activity was to a great extent ordering and canonizing, utilizing more fully the possibilities for organizing and preserving large and complex bodies of data. At this time, therefore, major series were put together and a standard text established for genre after genre. The result was an emphasis on the informational and utilitarian aspects of literature, rather than on its aesthetic qualities, which is evident not only in the relative number and length of texts in the belletristic and the more practically oriented genres and the vigor and productivity of the latter, but also in the fact that genre like hymns, laments, and prayers through the setting of the texts in instructional framework appear to move toward what have been called the handbook genres. In the belletristic genres proper the spirit of the age leads toward the establishing of relatively large epic cycles such as, e.g., the 12-tablet Gilgamesh epic, trend which was already discernible in the standard body of Sumerian literature. The standard Babylonian Gilgamesh Epic, for instance, will, with its 12 tablets have covered well over 3,000 lines when complete. Similarly, the appreciation of repetition and ornate description seems to grow. In the genre of laments, for instance, a composition can often be followed from its concise form in the time of standard Sumerian literature to a vastly enlarged, interminably repetitious form which almost makes such narrative elements as it has impossible to follow, in standard Babylonian literature. In part, perhaps such treatment is explicable from the use of the text for recitation in which the music is the main concern. Improved organization, greater length, and less terse language are noticeable also in the genres which specifically grew out of the use of writing to make lasting records: royal memorial inscriptions, legal deeds and contracts, and so on, and which are thus essentially evidential in character. A feature of considerable interest is the occurrence of a tradition about individual authorship of literary works at this time. The works of the standard Babylonian literature may, then, conveniently be considered under the headings of belletristic, handbook, and evidential genres.

Belles Lettres

MYTH. A certain number of Sumerian myths were translated into Akkadian, seemingly already in Old-Babylonian times, and continued to be copied. Among these were the two Ninurta compositions, *Lugal-e*, which as has been mentioned, seem to date back to Gudea or earlier, and *An-gim-dim4-ma*; a bilingual creation myth.

Among Akkadian works, such myths as the one about Anzu and the Atrahasis myth continued to be copied. New additions were the "Dynasty of Dunnum," a tale about the earliest generations of gods, who cheerfully murdered their fathers to take over rule of the world, and then married their mothers or sisters; the myth of "Nergal and Ereshkigal" (COS I, 384–90), which relates how Nergal became lord of the Netherworld and subdued and married its queen, Ereshkigal; and the "Erra Epic" (COS I, 404–16), which describes how Erra tricked Marduk into letting him take over rule of the universe and then embarked upon a veritable orgy of rioting and killing. He was finally pacified by his vizier Ishum, but still had the gall to pride himself on having left "a remnant" and not wiped out everybody. The "Myth of Adapa" (COS I, 449) also deserves mention. Adapa refused, at his master Ea's clever advice, the food of life and water of life offered to him in heaven when he was called to account there before Anu for having broken the wing of the south wind with a spell. Ea, clearly, did not want his clever servant to be other than mortal.

The most substantial and impressive literary work that should be mentioned here is, however, the Babylonian epic of creation *Enuma eliš* (COS I, 390–402). Scholars differ considerably in their dating of it and estimates range from Old-Babylonian times down to shortly after 1000 B.C.E. It can be assumed that in essentials it is a creation of late Old-Babylonian times, but that what has been preserved is a late redaction from approximately the beginning of the first millennium B.C.E. It tells how in the beginning there was only Tiamat, the Sea, and Apsu, the sweet waters under the earth. As their waters mingled the gods were born of them. The gods, as embodiments of activity, found themselves in basic conflict with their first parents. Provoked beyond endurance by the gods, Apsu, at the first, determined to destroy them, but was subdued by Ea with a spell and killed. Ea's son Marduk, playing with the winds which his grandfather Anu had given him, further provoked Tiamat and her brood, and she was brought to attack the gods. She raised an army and placed her second husband, Kingu, in command. Marduk, chosen champion, "king," by the gods, met her in battle and defeated her. Out of her carcass he then created the present universe. Kingu, after he had been indicated as fomenter of the rebellion, was killed, and Marduk had Ea create man from his blood to take over the hard menial work and leave the gods free. Marduk then pardoned those gods who had sided with Tiamat and distributed all the gods as administrators in heaven and on earth. To show their gratitude, the gods then for the last time took tools in hand and built Babylon, the city Marduk had asked for. Here in his temple Esagil they all gathered for a feast and assembly to appoint him permanent king and to celebrate his powers and virtues in 50 names by which they named him, one after the other. The postscript to *Enuma eliš* suggests that it be read to princes, and it is in fact a paean in praise of the ideal absolute monarch as personified in Marduk. When later in the first millennium the benevolent despot became a rarity in Babylonia, the despot pure and simple seems, in the figure of Erra, to have been a more believable symbol of the power ruling existence. In fact, the Erra Epic looks almost like a deliberate attack on *Enuma eliš* and its political optimism.

EPIC. Of older Sumerian epics that of Lugalbanda – at least its second half – survived as a bilingual. An Akkadian translation of the end of "Gilgamesh, Engidu and the Netherworld" was appended mechanically to the late version of the Gilgamesh Epic as its 12th tablet, probably by a copyist rather than by the author of the version. Of Akkadian epics the Etana Epic and the Narâ m-Sin Epic survived. An epic about Sargon's campaign into Asia Minor, *Šar tamḫari*, "The King of Battle," would seem to have been first composed in Old-Babylonian times. The Gilgamesh Epic, which may have existed as an epic in Old-Babylonian times and which in part builds on Sumerian materials, was reworked traditionally by one Sin-liqi-unninni into the standard later version which has been preserved from Ashurbanipal's library. A completely new epic of this time is a warlike epic about Tukulti-Ninurta's wars with Babylonia.

WISDOM LITERATURE. New and notable contributions to the genre of wisdom literature are two long poems, *Ludlul bel nêmeqi*, "Let me Praise the Expert" (COS I, 492), which treats the theme of the righteous sufferer, and the Theodicy (COS I, 492–95), which deals with the problem of the worldly success of the wicked. The proverb tradition continues, and new material is added, especially, it appears, fables. The genres of disputes also continued with new compositions such as a "Dispute between the Horse and the Bull." A new creation – based on the omen form – is a text warning rulers against mistreating Babylon and its citizens. It dates most likely from early in Sennacherib's reign. Humor seems to be represented – outside of the proverb literature – by the so-called "Dialogue of Pessimism" (COS I, 495–96), an ironical dialogue between a fickle master and his slave, and by the story of a poor man getting his revenge on an abusive official called "The Poor Man of Nippur."

Handbook Literature

INCANTATIONS AND PRAYERS. Numerous large series of incantations belong to the collections recording the lore that a capable incantation-pries (*ašipu*) ought to control. Of the better known of those which have come down may be mentioned *Utukke limnuti*, "The Evil Demons," against demons of diseases; *Bit rimki*, "The Bath House," containing ritual and incantations for purifying the king by means of lustrations; the series "Mouthwashing"; and the series *Maqlu* and *Šurpu*, devoted to the burning of witches in effigy and other white magic; and many more. Individual prayers were sorted under the incantation priest: various new types of prayer, with hymns to gods as their introductory part, developments of the penitential psalm, and prayers classed as incantations. To a large extent treatment of illness that was considered to be caused by evil demons was the task of the *ašipu*, who thus overlaps in function with the physician or *asu*, who worked mainly with medicaments of various kinds. It is often difficult to distinguish between his handbooks and those of the *ašipu*.

LAMENT. The lament genre with its laments for great public disasters continued to be in the hands of the *kal-* (Sumerian *gala*) or "elegist." As mentioned, the laments tended to grow in length and to become more and more repetitious. They also tended to be held in more general terms and lost the close connection with identifiable historical events which characterized the older laments for destroyed cities…

OMEN. A new Akkadian genre was in Old-Babylonian times the omen. In the following centuries the collections of omens, their systematization, and the systematic extension of possible ominous data, grew. The handbooks for the use of the *barû*, the "seer," were numerous. There were series dealing with omens from the shape of the liver of sacrificial animals, from dreams, from monstrous births, from ominous happenings of all kinds in city and country, astronomical omens, omens from wind and weather, and so on.

PHILOLOGY. To the *dupšarru* (Sumerian *dubsar*), the "scribe," may be ascribed particularly the continuing tradition and development of the lexical texts, which began back at the very beginning of writing as sign lists. This genre grows considerably both in new works and in the sophistication of lexical treatment. One may mention the large series arranged according to sign-form *ea-A-nâqu* and its expanded version *-A-nâqu* and the great series of realia organized in terms of logical classification: *Urra-ḫubullu*. Noteworthy are also the Akkadian synonym list and the examples of lexical and grammatical commentaries to individual works. With the lexical texts go the grammatical treatises. Here the older type of paradigm texts is replaced with a more radical analysis into grammatical elements in so far as such could be represented in a syllabic script.

SOCIAL INSTITUTIONS

Like present-day governments, governments in the ancient world, whether Mesopotamia or Canaan, placed a great deal of emphasis on the need for statistical, especially demographic, information. One of the best ways of obtaining such information was by means of a *census. Scholars have been bothered by certain aspects of the census as noted in the Bible (Ex. 30:11–16; Num. 1:1 19), and questioned the need on the part of the participants in the census for ritual expiation (Heb. *kippurim*; see **Kipper*).

Documents discovered in the royal archives of *Mari in northern Mesopotamia have greatly helped to clarify the problem. In one letter discovered in the archives the following order is given: "Let the troops be recorded by name" (G. Dossin, *Archives royales de Mari*, 1 (1950), no. 42, lines 22–24; cf. Num. 1:2). In other words, a list of names was to be prepared. Such lists are also available from many other sites in the Ancient Near East. The technical term for a census at Mari was *tēbibtum*, "purification" (according to other scholars, "expert counting"). At Mari as in the Bible there appears to be a connection between census and purification. It is known that in Mesopotamia there existed a definite fear among the people of having their names put on lists. The similarity between the census and the books of life and death caused a feeling of discomfort about a census. There is much in common between the institution of the census in Mari and in Israel. The purposes of the censuses were similar: they served as military lists and for the division of property. So too, some of the technical terms associated with the census are similar: Hebrew *pqd* and Akkadian *paqādum*, "to count"; Hebrew *kippurim* and Akkadian *ubbubum* "purification." Censuses in Israel, as in Mari, were taken by writing down the names, as noted in Numbers 1:2: *be-mispar shemot*, "according to the number of the names." It is likely then that the reason for the expiation connected with the census in Israel was the same as in Mari. There is a reference to a *book of life in the Bible (Ex. 32:32–33), when Moses, pleading for Israel after they sinned with the golden calf, says "Erase me from the book that You have written." The concept of a book of life and death is well known among Jews in the mishnaic period. Its antecedents go back to the biblical period (S. Paul, *JANES* 5 [1973], 345–53).

RELIGION

It has sometimes been claimed that the religion of Mesopotamia was based on premises totally different from those underlying the religion of Israel. But we must distinguish between the religious ideals of the Bible and the practices of ancient Israel. The biblical prophets portray themselves as a minority who tolerate the worship of no god other than Yahweh, whereas their opponents worship other gods alongside Yahweh (e.g. Jer. 7:8–11). Depending on who controlled the Yahweh temples it was possible for Yahweh to entertain visiting gods in his temple just as Marduk might do in Babylon (II Kings. 21:4–5). In the area of religious institutions it is likely that materials from Mesopotamia will be helpful. A case in point is the temple. In Mesopotamia the temple was conceived as a house of the god, comparable to the house of a noble or king. The temple housed the statue of the god, thought to contain the essence of the god. The temple building itself, and its symbolism, was considered a reflection of the cosmic abode of the god. The rites of worship consisted mainly in ministering to the physical needs of the gods. The Israelite temple is in many ways similar to the Mesopotamian temple at least in its external aspects. The Hebrew language employs vocabulary similar to that of its neighbors. Thus the temple is a "house" or "palace," while to worship is "to serve" or "to work." Like its Mesopotamian counterparts, the Israelite temple made use of cosmic symbolism. Scholars in recent years have begun to question the axiom that the cult of Yahweh was aniconic. The fact that Deuteronomy 4:12–19 fulminates against making an image of Yahweh (see already Hazzekuni a.l.) suggests strongly that the practice was known. Judges 17–18 indicates the presence of an image of Yahweh in the temple of Dan (especially Judg. 17:1–6). As such, the role of the cult statue in Mesopotamia may yet illuminate a similar phenomenon in ancient Israel. Apostolic prophecy once considered unique to ancient Israel is now known from *Mari as well as from Neo-Assyrian sources (SAA IX) proximately closer to the days of the Hebrew monarchy. The use of blood sacrifices in the Israelite cults differentiates from the Mesopotamian cults in which the gods were fed a diet that was vegetarian in the main.

The culture of Mesopotamia pervaded the ancient Near East. Ancient Israel and Judah spent centuries in the shadow of Mesopotamia. Biblical law, language, literature and religion were all influenced by Mesopotamian civilization. Through the intermediacy of Aramaic, the Akkadian language continued to make an impact on the Jews of Babylonia. As such, Assyriology is significant, not just for its own sake, but for the study of the Bible and Judaism.

[Aaron Skaist / S.David Sperling (2nd ed.)]

BIBLIOGRAPHY: HISTORY: H.W.F. Saggs, *The Greatness that was Babylon* (1962); S.N. Kramer, *The Sumerians: their History, Culture and Character* (1963); J. Hawkes and Sir L. Woolley, *Prehistory and the Beginnings of Civilization* (1963); A.L. Oppenheim, *Ancient Mesopotamia: Portrait of a Dead Civilization* (1964); G. Roux, *Ancient Iraq* (1964); L. Pareti et al., *The Ancient World*, 2 (1965); T. Jacobsen, in: W.L. Moran (ed.), *Toward the Image of Tammuz and other Essays on Mesopotamian History and Culture* (1970); W.W. Hallo and W.K. Simpson, *The Ancient Near East: a History* (1971); For further bibl. see CAH2, 1–2 (1961ff.). GOVERNMENT: T. Jacobsen, in: *Zeitschrift für Assyriologie*, 52 (1957), 91–140; idem, in: W.L. Moran (ed.), *Toward the Image of Tammuz…* (1970), 132–56, 157–243, 366–96, 396–430; N. Bailkey, in: *American Historical Review*, 72/74 (1967), 1211–36. LAW: Pritchard, Texts (19693), 159 (Lipit-Ishtar), 161 (Eshnunna), 163 (Hammurapi), 180 (Assyrian Laws), 188 (Hittite Laws), 523 (Ur-Nammu/a), 525 (Sumerian Laws), 526 (Ammisaduqa); G.R. Driver and J. Miles, *The Assyrian Laws* (1935); idem, *The Babylonian Laws*, 2 (1952–55); F.J. Steele, in: *American Journal of Archaeology*, 52 (1948), 425–50; A. Goetze, *The Laws of Eshnunna* (1956); F.R. Kraus, *Ein Edikt des Königs Ammsaduqa von Babylon* (1958); J. Friedrich, *Die hethitischen Gesetze* (1959); J.J. Finkelstein, in: JCS, 22 (1969), 66–82. LITERATURE: SOURCES IN TRANSLATION: Pritchard, Texts3; A. Heidel, *The Babylonian Genesis* (1942); A. Schott and W. von Soden, *Das Gilgamesch Epos* (1970); W.G. Lambert and A.R. Millard, *Atra-Hasis – The Babylonian Story of the Flood* (1969); A. Falkenstein and W. von Soden, *Sumerische und akkadische Hymnen und Gebete* (1953); T. Jacobsen and J. Wilson, *Most Ancient Verse* (1960); W.G. Lambert, *Babylonian Wisdom Literature* (1960); Luckenbill, Records. TREATMENTS: S.N. Kramer, *Sumerian Mythology* (1944); idem, *From the Tablets of Sumer* (1956); idem, *The Sumerians* (1963); B. Meissner, *Babylonien und Assyrien*, 2 (1925); A.L. Oppenheim, *Ancient Mesopotamia* (1964; rev. E. Reiner, 1977); T. Jacobsen, in: W.L. Moran (ed.), *Toward the Image of Tammuz…* (1970). RELIGION: GENERAL: J. Bottéro, *La religion Babylonienne* (1952); E. Dhorme, *Les Religions de Babylonie et d'Assyrie* (1945²); D. Edzard, in: H.W. Haussig (ed.), *Wörterbuch der Mythologie*, 1 (1965); T. Jacobsen, in: H. Frankfort et al. (eds.), *The Intellectual Adventure of Ancient Man* (1946 = *Before Philosophy*, 1949); S.N. Kramer, *The Sumerians* (1963); B. Meissner, *Babylonien und Assyrien*, 2 vols. (1920–25). SPECIAL STUDIES: H. Frankfort, *Kingship and the Gods* (1948); C.J. Gadd, *Ideas of Divine Rule in the Ancient Near East* (1948); T. Jacobsen, in: W.L. Moran (ed.), *Toward the Image of Tammuz…* (1970); S.N. Kramer, *Sumerian Mythology* (1944); idem, *From the Tablets of Sumer* (1956); idem. *The Sacred Marriage Rite* (1969); R. Labat, *Le caractère religieux de la royauté assyrobabylonienne* (1939); S.A. Pallis, *The Babylonian Akitu Festival* (1926). SOURCES IN TRANSLATION: Pritchard, Texts³; Luckenbill, Records. ASSYRIOLOGY: E.A.W. Budge, *The Rise and Progress of Assyriology* (1925); A. Deimel, *Orientalia, Uebersicht ueber die Keilschrift-Literatur; Reallexikon der Assyriologie* (1928ff.); A. Pohl et al., *Orientalia, Keilschriftbibliographie*, 9 (1940); A. Parrot, *Archéologie Mésopotamienne*, 1 (1946); S. Lloyd, *Foundations in the Dust* (1955); S.A. Pallis, *The Antiquity of Iraq: A Handbook of Assyriology* (1956); J. Friedrich, *Extinct Languages* (1957); A.L. Oppenheim, in: *Current Anthropology*, 1 (1960), 409–23; idem, *Ancient Mesopotamia* (1964); P. Garelli, *L'Assyriologie* (1964); B. Meissner, *Die Keilschrift* (1967); R. Borger, *Handbuch der Keilschrifliteratur* (1967–1975). **ADD. BIBLIOGRAPHY:** GENERAL: M. Chavalas and K. Younger (eds.), *Mesopotamia and the Bible* (1992); D. Snell (ed.), *A Companion to the Ancient Near East* (2005). HISTORY: P. Steinkeller, ABD, 4:724–32; A.K. Grayson (ibid), 732–77; R. Drews, *The End of the Bronze Age* (1993); *Cambridge Ancient History*, I; II; III:1; III/2; IV; VI (revised; 1972–1994); A. Kuhrt, *The Ancient Near East c. 3000–330 B.C.* (2 vols., extensive bibliography; 1995); CANE, 2, 807–979; LANGUAGE AND LITERATURE: Translations in COS; Studies in CANE IV, part 9. LAW: S. Geengus, in: ABD, 4, 242–52; M. Roth, *Law Collections from Mesopotamia and Asia Minor* (Akkadian and Sumerian in transliteration and translation. Hittite laws in translation by H. Hoffner; 1995); RELIGION: T. Jacobsen, *The Treasures of Darkness* (1976); J. Black, *Gods, Demons and Symbols of Ancient Mesopotamia an Illustrated Dictionary* (1992); S. Dalley, *Myths from Mesopotamia* (2000); K. van der Toorn, *Family Religion in Babylonia, Syria and Israel* (1996); idem, (ed.), *The Image and the Book* (1997).

MESQUITA, family name of prominent American and European Sephardim of Marrano descent. The merchant LUIS DE MESQUITA (or Amesquita), of Segovia, Castile, took up residence in Mexico and was reconciled at an *auto-da-fé there in 1646. BENJAMIN BUENO DE MESQUITA, who went to Jamaica from Portugal in the 1660s, petitioned the English authorities for the right to trade with the crown, which foreign merchants could not ordinarily do. Permission was granted in 1664, but soon thereafter he and two sons were banished from Jamaica on an extraneous charge. He then went to New York where he died in 1683 (the earliest date on any tombstone in New York's Jewish cemeteries). JOSEPH BUENO DE MESQUITA, one of these sons, became prominent in New York and around 1700 had important financial dealings with Lord Bellamont, the colonial governor. On behalf of Congregation Shearith Israel he purchased a burial ground, the Chattam Square cemetery, from William Merett. Joseph's will gives the name of the other brother, ABRAHAM BUENO DE MESQUITA who was then living at Nevis in the British West Indies. The name Mesquita appears also in Europe. MOSES GOMEZ DE MESQUITA (1688–1751) was haham of London's Spanish-Portuguese Jews from 1744.

BIBLIOGRAPHY: A.M. Hyamson, *Sephardim of England* (1951), index s.v. *Bueno de Mesquita and Gomez de Mesquita*; J. Picciotto, *Sketches of Anglo-Jewish History* (1956), 465; M. Gaster, *History of the Ancient Synagogue…* (1901), passim; I.S. Emmanuel, *Precious Stones of the Jews of Curaçao* (1957), index; J.R. Rosenbloom, *Biographical Dictionary of Early American Jews* (1960), 112.

MESSEL, German family. AARON MESSEL (1784–1848) founded the banking house of A. Messel & Co. in Darmstadt which his son SIMON BENJAMIN MESSEL (1817–1859) continued. Simon's son L.E.W.L. MESSEL (1847–1915) apparently left Judaism. He settled in England, and his granddaughter ANNE was mother of Anthony Armstrong-Jones, Earl of Snowden, who in 1960 married Princess Margaret, sister of Queen Elizabeth II of England. RUDOLPH MESSEL (1848–1920) also settled in England where he was a successful chemist and engineer. ALFRED MESSEL (1853–1909) distinguished himself as an architect in Germany. He renounced Judaism in the 1890s. OLIVER MESSEL (1904–1978), a grandson of L.E.W.L. Messel, achieved distinction in England as a theatrical producer, stage designer, and painter.

ADD. BIBLIOGRAPHY: C.W. Behrendt, *Alfred Messel*, 1997; R. Pingham, *Oliver Messel*, 1983; C. Castle, *Oliver Messel*, 1986.

[Sefton D. Temkin]

MESSEL, ALFRED (1853–1909), German architect, born in Darmstadt. He built apartments, public buildings, banks, the Pergamon Museum, and the villa of Eduard Simon. His most famous work, the Wertheim department store in Berlin, built in 1897, was the first store to be constructed entirely of stone, steel, and glass. An extension made in 1904 is overlaid with neo-Gothic decoration, but the basic design of repeated verticals proved to be a prototype of the modern store.

MESSERER, ASAF MIKHAILOVICH (1903–1992), dancer and teacher of the Bolshoi Ballet, Moscow. Messerer, who was born in Vilna, graduated from the Bolshoi School in 1921 and was soon dancing important roles, including Siegfried in *Swan Lake*. He had a brilliant technique, performing feats of virtuosity seldom accomplished by men. He revolted against traditional mime, which he replaced with expressive acting, and was equally brilliant in *danseur-noble* parts, and in demi-character roles. His first choreographic work, in collaboration with Igor Moiseyev, was a new production of *La fille mal gardée* (1930). He restaged the last act of *Swan Lake* in 1936, and his later works include *Sulla* (1952) and *Ballet School* (1962). Messerer retired from dancing in 1954, but remained with the Bolshoi company as a teacher and principal choreographer. SULAMITH MESSERER (1908–2004), Asaf's sister, was also a dancer and teacher for the Bolshoi Ballet. She entered the company from the Bolshoi School in 1926. Her first important role was that of Lise in *La fille mal gardée* (1929). Other outstanding roles were those of Swanilda in *Coppélia* and Kitri in *Don Quixote*. She was an athletic dancer more suited to demi-character than classical roles. She became a teacher in the Bolshoi School in 1938, and continued as a principal instructor after retiring from dancing in 1950. Asaf Mikhailovich and Sulamith Messerer received the title of People's Artist of the U.S.S.R. The ballerina Maya *Plisetskaya was their niece. In 1980 Sulamith Messerer defected to England, continuing to coach there.

BIBLIOGRAPHY: M. Abrahamski (ed.), *Bol'shoy Teatr SSSR* (Russ., 1958), 398–403.

[Marcia B. Siegel]

MESSIAH, an anglicization of the Latin *Messias*, which is borrowed from the Greek Μεσσιας, an adaptation of the Aramaic *meshiḥa* (Aram. מְשִׁיחָא), a translation of the Hebrew (*ha-melekh*) *ha-mashi'aḥ* (Heb. [הַמֶּלֶךְ] הַמָּשִׁיחַ), "the Anointed [King]"; a charismatically endowed descendant of David who the Jews of the Roman period believed would be raised up by God to break the yoke of the heathen and to reign over a restored kingdom of Israel to which all the Jews of the Exile would return. This is a strictly postbiblical concept. Even *Haggai and *Zechariah, who expected the Davidic kingdom to be renewed with a specific individual, *Zerubbabel, at its head, thought of him only as a feature of the new age, not as the author or even agent of its establishment. One can, therefore, only speak of the biblical pre-history of messianism. It may be summarized as follows: *Stage I*. At the height of David's power there appears the doctrine that the Lord had chosen David and his descendants to reign over Israel to the end of time (II Sam. 7; 23:1–3, 5) and had also given him dominion over alien peoples (II Sam. 22:44–51 = Ps. 18:44–51; Ps. 2). To quote II Samuel 22:50–51 (= Psalm 18:50–51; all the arguments against dating this composition later than the age of David seem forced):

(50) For this I sing Your praise, O Lord among the nations/and hymn Your name://

(51) "He who grants wondrous victories to his king/and deals graciously with his anointed (*mashi'aḥ*), with David,

and with his offspring, evermore."//David is here, as Saul was before him (I Sam. 24:6; 26:9; II Sam. 1:14, 16), and as he expects descendants of his to be after him, the Lord's anointed in the sense that he was anointed as a sign of consecration to the Lord (see *Kingship, *Oil), not, of course, in the sense of "the Messiah" described at the beginning of this article. Because anointing is an act of consecration, Deutero-*Isaiah speaks of Cyrus as the Lord's "anointed" in the purely derived sense of a non-Israelite-king chosen by the Lord for a great destiny and a great mission (Isa. 45:1). Thus "Stage I" of the prehistory of messianism is the doctrine that David's present position of power will endure throughout his lifetime and be inherited by an endless chain of succeeding links in his dynasty. Stage II began with the collapse of David's empire after the death of Solomon. There arose the doctrine, or hope, that the House of David would again reign over Israel as well as Judah and again exercise dominion over neighboring nations. This hope was expressed

(a) probably by reinterpretation of compositions like Psalm 18 in a prophetic sense and

(b) in so many words in prophecies like Amos 9:11–12; Isaiah 11:10; Hosea 3:5 (the phrase – a Judahite interpolation – "and (the Israelites will seek) their king David"); Ezekiel 37:15 ff., especially verses 24 ff. (and see *Isaiah A, Panel 3, Field A, on Isa. 9:1–6 [2–7]). *Stage III.* Isaiah's shifting of the emphasis from the perpetuity of the dynasty to the qualities of the future king: the foundation of his throne will be justice, he will be distinguished by his zeal for justice, and, finally, he will be charismatically endowed for sensing the rights and wrongs of a case and for executing justice. (See not only the passage in *Isaiah just cited on Isa. 9:1–6 [2–7], but also Isaiah B I, 4 on Isa. 16:4–5 and, in particular, *Isaiah A, Panel 3, Field B on Isa. 11:1 ff., where the origins of this idea are discussed). The "*Immanuel prophecy" in Isaiah is completely irrelevant, so far as one can see and the echoes of ancient Canaanite-Ugaritic mythology that have been "discovered" there are as dubious as those in the figure of the Ancient of *Days in Daniel 7. Without "stage III" in its biblical prehistory, the development of the postbiblical idea of "the Messiah" would not have been possible.

[Harold Louis Ginsberg]

Second Temple Period

The title "Messiah" (Heb. משיח) as a designation of the eschatological personality does not exist in the Old Testament; it occurs only from the time of the Second Temple after the Old Testament period. However for ancient Judaism the idea of eschatological salvation was more important than the concept of Messiah. Hence there are books from the Second Temple period where the Messiah does not occur, even if they refer to eschatological salvation. Such a book, for instance, is the Book of *Tobit, in which the salvation of Jerusalem, the return of the Diaspora, and the conversion of nations to the God of Israel is described but a personal Messiah is lacking. The same also applies to the Book (Wisdom) of Ben *Sira and probably the Book of Daniel. In the latter, the messianic figure of the son of *man is explained as a symbol for the holy ones (or saints) of the Most High (chap. 7). In the Assumption of *Moses (chap. 10) the eschatological figure is the angel of God but a human agent of the salvation is not mentioned. It seems also that in the more ancient form of the *Amidah* a personal messiah was not mentioned, but only the hope of the return from the Diaspora and the building of the eschatological Jerusalem and the Temple. Even in such ancient Jewish prayers where the concept of Messiah occurs the word *mashi'aḥ* is lacking.

In the time of the Second Temple there was a greater variety of messianic figures than later. The Old Testament Book of Zechariah already makes mention of two messianic figures, the high priest and the messianic king. This idea did not disappear from the rabbinic literature where the priest of righteousness (*Kohen ẓedek*) is sometimes mentioned together with the Davidic king Messiah. These two figures, the priest and the king, are important for the eschatology of the Dead Sea *Sect, the eschatological high priest being more important than the scion of David. The third figure occurring in the Dead Sea *Scrolls with the two messiahs is the prophet of the Last Days. Thus in the Dead Sea Scrolls there are three messianic figures which correspond to the three main functions of the ideal Jewish state, in which kingdom, priesthood, and prophecy shall exist (see I Macc. 14:41). The three eschatological figures of the Dead Sea Scrolls are therefore based upon a broader ideological concept. These three figures are reflected later in the theological concept of the ancient Jewish sect of the Ebionites (see Jewish Christian *sects) according to which Jesus united in himself the function of king, priest, and prophet. The importance of the Davidic Messiah in Judaism who weakened or caused the disappearance of the other messianic figures was the outcome especially of the Old Testament heritage because the eschatological king is hinted at in the Hebrew Bible.

The oldest description of the eschatological king is in the third book of the Sibylline Oracles (c. 140 B.C.E.) and in the Vision of Seventy *Shepherds in the Book of Enoch which was written approximately a decade earlier. However the prevalence of the Davidic Messiah in the apocryphal literature became common from the time when the Maccabean Aristobulus I accepted the title of a king. This was seen as a usurpation of the rights of the family of David; hence as a reaction, the Davidic Messiah received his central importance as can be seen from the Psalms of Solomon written approximately in 63 B.C.E. (especially in the 17th Psalm). The other component of the political messianic hope in Judaism was caused by the Roman occupation, and so in later books the Davidic Messiah is the only figure which occurs. He thus appears in IV Ezra and in the Syrian Apocalypse of Baruch. A further proof of the expectation of the Davidic Messiah can be found in the New Testament where Jesus is identified with the Davidic Messiah. Even the name "Christians" and the word "Christos" are Greek translations of the word "Messiah" (Christos = the anointed one). This hope was not only an abstract one: from the first century C.E. there were messianic *movements centered on messianic pretenders. Such a list of messianic pretenders occurs in Acts 5:36–37. One of the names there is Judas the Galilean, who was the founder of the *Zealots. Thus this movement was centered on a family with messianic pretensions. Josephus (Wars 2:444–448) states that Judas' son, Menahem, was murdered in the Temple, being "arrayed in royal robes." Apparently after Judas' death his partisans transferred the status of pretender to the kingship to his son.

The most important historical messianic figure was surely Bar *Kokhba, though he himself did not sign as king and names himself only *nasi*. He was already seen by others as the messiah, and it is important that on his coins his name also occurs with that of a priest Eleazar. Both Josephus and the Talmud also mention other messianic pretenders from the first and beginning of the second centuries C.E. The first messianic interpretation of a biblical verse occurs in the Greek translation of the Pentateuch (Num. 24:17) where the word "scepter" is translated in the Greek by "man" (see also the Greek translation of Num. 24:7). The Greek translation of the Pentateuch dates back to the third century B.C.E. Possibly the designation of the Messiah as "man" is a proof that the special concept of son of man already existed in the early third century B.C.E. Philo, who did not like to refer explicitly to the eschatological hopes of Israel, mentions the hope of the coming of the Messiah in connection with this Greek interpretation of the biblical verse. The above shows that messianic concepts were manifold in the time of the Second Temple, and there were even numerous aspects to the function of the Messiah. All depended upon the spiritual and theological approach of the various Jewish trends, but the Messiah or messiahs were always human beings, even if sometimes supernatural qualities were connected with them. The political aspect, if it prevailed, did not always eliminate the supernatural. However, the Messiah was always an agent of God and never a savior in the Christian meaning. The Davidic origin of the kingly Messiah was supposed; but, as it seems, the messianic pretender had to prove his authenticity by his deeds – in the period of the Second Temple Davidic descendants were not traceable.

[David Flusser]

Messiah in Rabbinic Thought

In rabbinic thought, the Messiah is the king who will redeem and rule Israel at the climax of human history and the instrument by which the kingdom of God will be established. While the Bible stresses the nature of the age called the "end of days," the rabbis focus as well on the person of their regent, who gives the messianic age (*yemot ha-mashi'aḥ*) its very name. "Messiah" (*Mashi'aḥ*) means "anointed" and in the Bible can refer either to a king or a priest. The *aggadah* restricts the term to the eschatological king, who is also called *malka meshiḥa* ("king messiah") in the Targums, *ben David* ("son of David"), and *mashi'aḥ ben David* ("Messiah, son of David"). The Messiah was expected to attain for Israel the idyllic blessings of the prophets; he was to defeat the enemies of Israel, restore the people to the Land, reconcile them with God, and introduce a period of spiritual and physical bliss. He was to be prophet, warrior, judge, king, and teacher of Torah.

A secondary messianic figure is the Messiah, son of (i.e., of the tribe of) Joseph (or Ephraim), whose coming precedes that of the Messiah, son of David, and who will die in combat with the enemies of God and Israel. Though some (e.g., Torrey, Segal) claim that this figure is described in pre-Christian apocalyptic and apocryphal works, most scholars note that the first unambiguous mentions of this doctrine occur in tannaitic passages of uncertain date (Suk. 52a) and in the Targums (Pseudo-Jon., Ex. 40:11; Pesh., Song 4:5). The genetic function of the doctrine is similarly unclear: Messiah ben Joseph has been seen as the symbolic embodiment of the reunification with the ten tribes of Israel, as the Samaritan Messiah, and as a figure whose martial character and death testify to the impact of the abortive revolt under Bar *Kokhba upon the Jewish imagination.

There are a number of developmental accounts of the messianic idea. Klausner argues that the nationalist-naturalist base of the idea was "spiritualized" after the political and military debacle of the Bar Kokhba revolt; Mowinckel claims virtually the same results due to the acceptance of apocalyptic and spiritualizing elements. It is true, on the whole, that the later Midrash is more extravagant and inventive than the earlier sources in the elaboration of many messianic motifs; the relative sobriety of the earlier sources contrasts markedly with the portrait drawn in the apocalyptic literature. The earliest sources speak little of messianic origins. Subsequently there is the belief that he was born at Beth-Lehem (cf. Micah 5:1) or Jerusalem on the day of the Temple's destruction. He is then hidden – either in Rome or (in the later Midrash) in heaven, where he pines over the agony of people and his own impotence – to come forth at the time of the Redemption. Some have him present at the creation of the world; for some the "name" (i.e., concept) of the Messiah existed before creation; in yet others (assumed late), the Messiah himself exists before the world (PR 36:161).

The prophetic books do not all assume a personal messiah, nor do they identify him. The rabbis agree he is of Davidic lineage (based on Hos. 3:5 and Jer. 30:9), nor is this idea necessarily post-Bar Kokhba. Some expected a resurrected David, and others a messiah named David. Hezekiah, king of Judah, was a potential messiah: Johanan b. Zakkai announced the "coming" of Hezekiah in what some take to be a messianically oriented deathbed declaration. The name Menahem b. Hezekiah, which may refer to an anti-Roman patriot rebel or may simply be symbolic of "comfort," is also found. Various *amoraim* derive the name of the Messiah from the names of their masters; there is also a puzzling identification of the Messiah and Judah *ha-Nasi (Sanh. 98b). The messianic "name" is sometimes meant descriptively, as when Yose ha-Gelili said that the Messiah's name is *Shalom* ("peace"). The early sources do not mention a "suffering Messiah." In the Targum to Isaiah 53:3–6 suffering is the historical lot of the people, who are reconciled to God by the prayers of Messiah; the toils of Messiah are those of constructive achievement. Third-century sources speak of a suffering Messiah, or a leprous Messiah; still later, his suffering atones for Israel (Sanh. 98b; PR 37:162b). The vicarious atonement of all righteous for the wicked is a general aggadic theme, however.

The Messiah is generally assumed to be man, though writ large. As such, he can come either riding a donkey, in subdued fashion (cf. Zech. 9:9), or triumphantly riding the clouds (Dan. 7:13). That the Messiah is fully human is dramatically shown by Akiva's knowledgement of the rebel leader, Bar Kokhba, as the Messiah. (Yet Akiva also declared that the Messiah would occupy a throne alongside God). One talmudic source does apparently attribute immortality to Messiah (Suk. 52a), and the Midrash (mostly later) singles him out among the immortals of Paradise. The Messiah does not displace either God or Torah in rabbinic thought. Thus, Hillel (fourth century) can deny the coming of Messiah (for which he is rebuked), though he doubtless expected Israel's redemption. So too, the Midrash can declare that the ultimate author of redemption is not Messiah but God, and His kingship is stressed in the liturgy as well (Mid. Ps. to 31:1; 36:1; 107:1).

[Gerald J. Blidstein]

The Doctrine of the Messiah in the Middle Ages

Jewish ideology in the Middle Ages did not receive from the ancient period a coherent, unified concept of the Messiah, messianic times, and the signs of the messianic age. Apocalyptic literature of the Second Temple period (see above) differed greatly from the biblical concept of the Messiah and his times, and talmudic literature and the various Midrashim included many contrasting views about this problem. In the Middle Ages messianic ideas were a product of medieval thought and experience, based on some ancient sources, but developed within medieval Hebrew literature and thought. During the last decades of Byzantine rule in Palestine, in the last years of the sixth century and the beginning of the seventh century, the political upheavals in the Middle East – especially the continuous wars between the Byzantines and the Persians – gave rise to a body of messianic literature, which was destined to play a major role in shaping the image of the messianic age in the eyes of medieval Jewry. The most important work which was written at that time was the Book of *Zerubbabel. In this pseudepigraphical work Zerubbabel, the last ruler of Judea from the House of David, tells his visions concerning the happenings at the end of days and the time of the Messiah. According to this work, the appearance of the Messiah will be preceded by the appearance of a satanic king of Rome, who will be the son of Satan and a stone sculpture of a woman; his name will be *Armilus (= Romulus, the first king of Rome who will also be the last). Armilus will conquer the whole world, vanquish all the traditional enemies of Rome, especially Persia, and will unify the whole world under his religion. He will be a spiritual Satan as well as an emperor. According to the descriptions, the writer seems to see in him a new incarnation, or a new appearance, of Jesus. The whole world will believe in him and see him as god and emperor, except the Jews. The war of the Jews against this monster will be conducted, at first, by the Messiah son of Joseph, assisted by a woman named Hephzibah. The Messiah son of Joseph will gather all the Jews to Palestine and Jerusalem, but Armilus will overcome him and kill him; Jerusalem will be saved by Hephzibah. Then Hephzibah's son, the Messiah son of David, will arise, overcome Armilus, and the messianic age will begin.

It is possible that this story, which is rich in detailed descriptions of the persons and the wars, and contains detailed dates for all the occurrences included in it, was written under the influence of the great victories achieved by the Byzantine emperor, Heraclius, against the Persians; for a Jew living in Palestine at that time it seemed that the emperor was about to conquer the whole world and reunite the empire with the Christian religion. The author believed that the Messiah was not going to overcome an enfeebled, divided Roman-Christian empire, but that his victory should be against an empire which would be physically and spiritually as strong as possible. Only after such unity is achieved by a Christian "messiah" can the Jewish Messiah appear and overcome the enemy.

A vast literature developed around the Book of Zerubbabel – apocalyptic literature describing the end of the Diaspora, the wars of the Messiah, and the final victory. It is difficult to date the various works in this literature; some of them may even be earlier than the Book of Zerubbabel. One of the most important works in this apocalyptic literature is the "*Otot Mashi'aḥ*" ("The Signs of the Messianic Age"), in which ten occurrences are described as foreshadowing the imminent appearance of the Messiah. This literature had an enormous impact upon medieval Jewry.

One of the main characteristics of this apocalyptic literature is the complete absence from it of any doctrinal religious or ideological elements. In these works the future is described as an inevitable end of the world as known and the beginning of a new one. In none of these works is there any explanation as to why anything is going to happen, or what a Jew should do in order to help in the great task of bringing about the redemption. The apocalyptic future is given as a story, not as a theological doctrine. This fact became very meaningful in the Middle Ages, when Judaism was divided between conflicting ideologies and theologies; there was nothing in this apocalyptic description which could make it unacceptable to any Jewish ideology. A philosopher, an Ashkenazi Ḥasid, a kabbalist, or a rabbinic traditionalist, could accept the apocalyptic future as described in the Book of Zerubbabel and related works. Thus the appeal of this body of literature became universal to all Jews, in all countries, in both medieval and early modern times. Another characteristic which helped these ideas to be accepted and believed by all Jews is that this literature contained many elements taken from biblical and talmudic sayings about the messianic age. There was no conflict between the texts from ancient times and the apocalyptic literature of the early Middle Ages; what was fragmentary and incomplete in the ancient texts was developed in the latter into a complete, coherent picture, in which it was as easy to believe as if it sprang directly from the traditional sources.

This does not mean that other, non-apocalyptical concepts of the messianic age did not exist in the Middle Ages among Jewish thinkers. Thus, for instance, whereas Eleazar *Kallir, in describing the messianic age, used images similar to those in the apocalyptic literature, his predecessor and probable teacher, the *paytan* *Yannai, used more quiet, non-apocalyptical images in referring to the redemption. Most of the philosophers did not accept the apocalyptic picture, even though Saadiah *Gaon, the first systematic Jewish philosopher, included in his *Book of Beliefs and Opinions* a paraphrase of the Book of Zerubbabel when describing the messianic age. *Maimonides and his followers regarded the coming of the Messiah as a political deliverance of the Jews from the rule of the gentiles, without any upheaval in the order of the world and without any apocalyptic elements. Maimonides also opposed messianic speculation, and rejected rumors from Yemen and other places that a Messiah had come (see Messianic *Movements). However, other philosophers held different opinions. Abraham bar Ḥiyya, a rationalist philosopher with neoplatonic tendencies, wrote a major work, *Megillat ha-Megalleh*, attempting to establish, by astrological calculations, the date of the coming of the Messiah.

Messianic speculation and attempts to find such dates were a constant feature of Jewish culture in the Middle Ages and early modern times. Dozens of dates were proposed as the dates of the beginning of the redemption, which was divided into many stages; sometimes different dates for different stages were also given. Sometimes the dates set for redemption coincided with great upheavals in the world and terrible persecutions of the Jews – like the beginning of the persecutions by the crusaders (1096), the years of the Black Death in Europe, the Expulsion from Spain (1492), or the persecutions in Poland and the Ukraine (1648). But, even though one date after the other was refuted, the explanation was that the Jews were not sufficiently righteous to accept the Messiah, and a new date was set. The generations preceding and following the Expulsion from Spain were especially rich in such speculations, but in fact every age engaged in such speculations, with very little differences in method and ideological concepts.

Among the theological movements in the Middle Ages the ideas of apocalyptical eschatology clashed with the ideas of personal eschatology, the personal reward that a devout person will receive upon his death in the next world. Evidently, when emphasis was put upon personal redemption in the Garden of Eden the descriptions of national deliverance upon the coming of the Messiah tended to be somewhat blunted. This may have been one of the reasons why Maimonides and his school de-emphasized the apocalyptic nature of the redemption. However, among the masses of the people, belief in the apocalyptic redemption did not diminish.

A good example for this conflict can be found in the movement of the Ḥasidei *Ashkenaz in the late 12th and early 13th centuries. In their popular works the teachers of Ashkenazi Ḥasidism, Judah he-Ḥasid and Eleazar b. Judah of *Worms, explained the dangers of engaging in messianic speculation and in the belief in false messiahs. Several passages in the *Sefer Ḥasidim* are dedicated to this question. However, from other sources, esoteric works, and contemporary documents, a different picture is obtained. It was believed that Judah he-Ḥasid knew when the Messiah was to come, but he died before he could reveal it to his disciples. Judah himself explained in one of his esoteric works that there are a few righteous people in every generation who know this date, but they have to keep it a secret; there is no doubt that he included himself among them. A passage describing the appearance of the Messiah was deleted from the *Sefer Ḥasidim*, but is found in manuscripts. There is a document from the Cairo *Genizah* from which it can be learned that when a person appeared claiming to be the Messiah, the community appealed to Eleazar of Worms for advice, and he seemed to believe in the veracity of the miracles worked by that person. Even though Ashkenazi Ḥasidism put the main emphasis on personal redemption, belief in messianic speculation and the imminent appearance of the Messiah was still very strong even among their leaders.

From the 13th century on, especially after the publication of the *Zohar*, messianic speculation and messianic belief was centered in kabbalistic literature, and culminated in the great kabbalistic-messianic movement, Shabbateanism.

[Joseph Dan]

In Modern Jewish Thought

Classical Reform in the 19th century reinterpreted the doctrine of the Messiah in two ways. First, it substituted the belief in a messianic age for the belief in a personal Messiah. Secondly, the messianic hope was severed from its traditional associations with a return of the exiles to Zion, these associations being viewed as too particularistic. The destruction of the Temple and the exile of the Jewish people were seen not as calamities but as affording greater opportunities for the fulfillment of Judaism's "mission" to all mankind. The whole world would become perfected and, through the example of Judaism, monotheism would be the religion of all men. Progress in the Western world, in terms of greater liberalism, Jewish emancipation, social reforms, and better educational facilities, was hailed as the dawn of the messianic age of which the prophets had dreamed. References to a return to Zion were erased from the prayer book. The principles regarding the Messiah in the Reform "Pittsburgh Platform" (1885) read: "We recognize in the modern era of universal culture of heart and intellect the approaching of the realization of Israel's great messianic hope for the establishment of the kingdom of truth, justice, and peace among all men. We consider ourselves no longer a nation, but a religious community, and therefore expect neither a return to Palestine, nor a sacrificial worship under the sons of Aaron, nor the restoration of any of the laws concerning the Jewish state."

The Reform vision of messianism as a perfect world just around the corner and of the Jews as the brave carriers of a universalistic message ready to be heeded by all was rendered hollow by the rise of Zionism with its stress on the Jews as a nation and its emphasis on a physical return to Palestine, culminating in the emergence of the State of Israel; the threat of antisemitism and the Holocaust in which six million Jews were murdered; and the disillusionment that set in after the two world wars. Even as early as 1937 the "Pittsburgh Platform" was considerably modified by a conference of Reform rabbis in Columbus, Ohio. A statement by the conference dealing with the messianic question reads: "In all lands where our people live, they assume and seek to share loyally the full duties and responsibilities of citizenship and to create seats of Jewish knowledge and religion. In the rehabilitation of Palestine, the land hallowed by memories and hopes, we behold the promise of renewed life for many of our brethren. We affirm the obligation of all Jewry to aid in its upbuilding as a Jewish homeland by endeavoring to make it not only a haven or refuge for the oppressed but also a center of Jewish culture and spiritual life. Throughout the ages it has been Israel's mission to witness to the Divine in the face of every paganism and materialism. We regard it as our historic task to co-operate with all men in the establishment of the kingdom of God, of universal brotherhood, justice, truth and peace on earth. This is our messianic goal."

There is a tendency among some modern Jewish thinkers to invoke once again the traditional idea of messianism as a direct, divine intervention, in which a "new heart" will be created for men, rather than as automatic human progress towards an ideal state. Even a determined non-supernaturalist like Mordecai Kaplan can write (*Questions Jews Ask* (1956), 183): "We can no longer believe that any person or semi-divine being, is divinely destined to rule as the Messiah and usher in the millennium. Nevertheless, the idea of the Messiah can still figure symbolically to express the valid belief in the coming of a higher type of man than this world has yet known." Will Herberg (*Judaism and Modern Man* (1951), 227–35) is typical of the new school of thought. History cannot redeem itself. It proceeds and ends in catastrophe from which it must be redeemed by God. Even the most perfect world state could do no more than enforce peace throughout the world, but the hatred and conflicts among men would remain. The "peace" in the messianic age dreamed of by the prophets is, on the other hand, an inner harmony that needs no external sanctions. To attempt to reduce the prophetic vision of perfection to the level of perfectionist utopianism is to throw confusion into both practical politics and the ultimate insights of religion. It is not surprising, therefore, to find voices raised, also outside the Orthodox camp, in favor of retaining the doctrine of the personal Messiah sent by God.

Orthodoxy retains unimpaired the traditional doctrine. The Messiah is a scion of the House of David. He will reign in Jerusalem, will rebuild the Temple, and will reinstitute the sacrificial system. Many Orthodox rabbis were at first opposed to Zionism in that it seemed to substitute a purely human redemption for the redeemer sent by God. But with the establishment of the State of Israel the widely held Orthodox view was to see the events in Israel as *athalta de-geulla*, "the beginning of the redemption," i.e., the foundations laid by humans, under God's guidance, ready to receive the building to be erected by God's direct act. Among Orthodox rabbis there is no lack of speculation on the meaning of contemporary events in the light of the messianic hope. Thus M. Kasher (*No'am*, 13 (1970), end) has tried to read: "Then the moon shall be confounded, and the sun ashamed; for the Lord of hosts will reign in Mount Zion, and in Jerusalem, and before His elders shall be glory" (Isa. 24:23) as a prophetic vision in which the moon landings coincide with the establishment of the State of Israel. In the writings of A.I. Kook the argument is advanced that the Jewish people had become too "spiritual," too remote from the world. To pave the way for the Messiah the concrete realities of a modern state based on Jewish principles of justice and compassion are essential. Kook accepted the theory of evolution even in the moral sphere in that it is evidence of the movement of the whole of creation toward its ultimate fulfillment, as in the messianic hope (*Orot ha-Kodesh* (1938) v, 19–22).

[Louis Jacobs]

BIBLIOGRAPHY: GENERAL: J. Klausner, *The Messianic Idea in Israel* (1955); A.H. Silver, *A History of Messianic Speculations in Israel* (1927); S. Mowinckel, *He That Cometh* (1956); Kaufmann Y., Toledot, 3 (1960), 626–56; G. von Rad, *Old Testament Theology*, 1 (1962), 306–24; 2 (1965), 165–79; H.L. Ginsberg, in: *Conservative Judaism*, 22 no. 1 (1967), 2–11. SECOND TEMPLE PERIOD: D. Flusser, in: IEJ, 9 (1959), 99–109; M. Hengel, *Die Zeloten* (1961); J. Liver, *Toledot Beit David* (1959); E. Sjöberg, *Der Menschensohn im aethiopischen Henochbuch* (1946); P. Volz, *Die Eschatologie der juedischen Gemeinde im neutestamentlichen Zeitalter* (1934); M. Zobel, *Gottesgesalbter; der Messias und die messianische Zeit in Talmud und Midrasch* (1938); F. Hahn, *Christologische Hoheitstitel* (1964); IN THE AGGADAH: Ginzberg, Legends, 7 (1938), 306–9 (index); J. Even-Shemuel, *Midreshei Ge'ullah* (1954[2]); G.F. Moore, *Judaism*, 2 (1927), 323–76; W.D. Davies, *Torah in the Messsianic Age* (1952), 50–85; Baron, Social[2], (1952), 351f.; 5 (1957), 138ff.; Kaufman, in: *Molad*, 16 (1958), 197–203; E.E. Urbach, *Ḥazal, Pirkei Emunot ve-De'ot* (1969), 639 (index): J. Liver, *Toledot Beit David* (1959). DOCTRINE OF THE MESSIAH IN THE MIDDLE AGES: J. Even-Shemuel, *Midreshei Ge'ullah* (1954[2]); A.Z. Aešcoly, *Ha-Tenu'ot ha Meshiḥiyyiot be-Yisrael* (1956); B.Z. Dinur, *Yisrael ba-Golah*, 2/3 (1968). 358–453; J. Dan, *Torat ha-Sod shel Ḥasidei Ashkenaz* (1968), 241ff.; idem, in: *Ha-Ummah*, 30 (1970), 237–55; G. Scholem, *The Messianic Idea in Judaism* (1971); IN MODERN JEWISH THOUGHT: J.H. Greenstone, *The Messiah Idea in Jewish History* (1943); S.S. Schwarzschild, in: *Judaism*, 5 (1956, 123–35; L. Jacobs, *Principles of the Jewish Faith* (1964). 368–97.

MESSIANIC MOVEMENTS.

Basic Elements

The pattern on which Jewish messianic movements were based crystallized in the late Second Temple period and furnished Jews in following generations with certain basic elements. These, when confronted by certain typical challenges, culminated in messianic movements of varying scope. The term "messianic movement" in Jewish history applies to a movement centered around or expressing the yearning for a king or leader of the house of David and for a new ideal political existence for the Jewish people that would serve as a reassertion of independence and cause their return to Ereẓ Israel, as well as acting as a model and focus for a united and better mankind. Experiencing the miracle of Jewish redemption, mankind would attain an ideal world where true faith and real harmony would prevail. Jewish prayers for redemption, while seeking the advent of the king and the kingdom, also ask "may they all blend into one brotherhood to do Thy will with a perfect heart," and express the hope that with this change of heart, "Thou shalt reign over all whom Thou hast made, Thou alone" (in evening service (*Arvit*) for Rosh Ha-Shanah). This formulates the abiding hope of the Jew while in the **galut*. The basis of the movements is intense longing for the messianic era. Up to the 18th century it was both an article of faith and an emotional necessity among Jews to hope constantly for the immediate advent of the Messiah. Yet this persistent element did not of itself necessarily lead to the emergence of such movements. Jewish messianic history includes periods and religious trends in which people experienced intense and wholehearted hopes for the Messiah while being lukewarm toward active messianic movements. Thus the *Karaites throughout the Middle Ages had a deep-seated feeling of being in exile; Karaite settlers in Jerusalem in the tenth century called themselves *Avelei Zion ("Mourners for Zion"), organizing their life and patterning their thought on the basis of this attachment to Zion. Yet only one Karaite messianic movement is known for certain. The Rabbanite *Ḥasidei Ashkenaz longed for the Messiah, yet only rarely is any active striving for a Messiah mentioned in their relatively extensive writings. Indeed, some of the expressions they use appear to satirize computations of the date of the coming of the Messiah (J. Wistinetzki (ed.), *Sefer Ḥasidim* (1924), 461, no. 1706). They even warned their readers: "If you see that a man has prophesied the advent of the Messiah, know that he is engaged either in sorcery or in dealings with devils; or that he uses the power of the Divine Name.... One has to say to such a man: 'Do not talk in this manner'..., eventually he will be the laughingstock of the whole world ... they teach him calculations and secrets to bring shame on him and on those who believe him" (*ibid.*, 76–77, no. 212).

This attitude displayed by mystics and ascetics in opposing activist messianism finds even sharper expression in the views of the 13th-century mystic, Naḥmanides. In his disputations with the representatives of Christianity, Naḥmanides told the Spanish king at *Barcelona in 1263:

> Our Law and Truth and Justice are not dependent upon a Messiah. Indeed, you yourself are more important to me than a Messiah. You are a king and he is a king. You are a gentile sovereign and he is a king of Israel. The Messiah is but a king of flesh and blood like yourself. When I serve my Creator under your jurisdiction, in exile, torment, and subjection, exposed constantly to universal contempt, I merit great reward; for I offer of my own flesh a sacrifice to God, and my reward in afterlife will be so much the greater (*Kitvei Rabbenu Moshe ben Naḥman*, ed. by H.D. Chavel, 1 (1963), 310).

The basic consideration put forward here is that the greatness of the individual suffering under alien rule can be as rewarding as redemption. In a work addressed to Jews Naḥmanides wrote:

> Even if we thought that it is the will and purpose of God to afflict us with political enslavement on this earth [forever], this would in no way weaken our adherence to the precepts of the Torah, for the sole rewards which we anticipate are those of the world to come – the beatitude of the soul which, having escaped hell's torments, enjoys the bliss of paradise.

He continues that he believes in the Messiah and redemption because it is true and because it gives him comfort to face the adversities suffered by the Jewish people; but this is not a necessary or sustaining element of his Jewish faith (*Sefer ha-Ge'ullah*, pt. 2; *ibid.*, 279–80).

The extreme wing of modern *Orthodoxy in Judaism and most of the adherents of *Neo-Orthodoxy – in particular *Agudat Israel in the period before the Holocaust and, later, *Neturei Karta – continued, under changed and secularized conditions, old attitudes of messianism which were halfhearted toward a messianic movement. Messianic-prompted efforts have been made toward an ingathering of the Jews without an express connection with either Ereẓ Israel or political independence (see Anan b. David, *Sefer ha-Mitzvot*, ed. by A. Harkavy (1903), 6–7). Jacob *Frank in the 18th century had a savage desire for armed Jewish power and a Jewish settlement on the land – but all this was to be achieved on the soil of Poland. Thus, the modern movement of *territorialists can claim some ancient though rare precedents in traditional Jewish messianic trends.

Within this ideological framework and set of attitudes, the emergence of an active messianic movement required a challenge that would break through the tranquility of the regular messianic hope to turn it into fervent and directed effort, and create a revolutionary constellation. There were elements in Jewish historical consciousness encouraging such active responses to various and widely differing challenges. One element basic to Jewish messianism is anticipation of the "birth pangs of the Messiah" (*ḥevlei Mashi'aḥ*) – the time of troubles and turbulence that precedes his coming. Hence, periods in which terrible massacres of Jews occurred (e.g., during the *Crusades or the *Chmielnicki massacres) have also been periods of fervent messianic expectations and movements. Jewish historical conception – and for that matter Christian also – interpreted Daniel's apocalyptic vision of the four evil beasts (7:2ff.) as denoting four successive evil empires. The fourth will be succeeded by the everlasting dominion of "one like unto a son of man." He will be given "dominion and glory and a kingdom that all the peoples, nations, and languages should serve Him." This conception enabled Jews to view great historical and political transformations – the fall and rise of empires and kingdoms, or revolutions and counterrevolutions –

as the death throes of the fourth and last beast-kingdom and the harbingers of the messianic eternal kingdom.

The person to lead the messianic movement – the Messiah himself – was viewed from two different angles. Jews – in particular since the parting of the ways with Christianity – saw the Messiah as a man and not God; in the first place, as a national king. But here the agreement ends. Some, like *Maimonides in the 12th century, stressed that the Messiah will himself die even though his life will be a long one. He will first be tested as the successful warrior-king of Israel and proved its lawful ruler by devotion to Torah. Mankind will follow this new exemplary Jewish state. Nature will not change its laws, though society will become perfect (Yad, Melakhim (1962), 417). Along with this rationalistic conception of the Messiah, there is also a miraculous one, in which the person of the Messiah sometimes attains semi-divine heights. The 17th-century pseudo-Messiah, *Shabbetai Ẓevi, concluded a letter:

> I will have to give full reward to all those who believe truly, men, women, and children – from the Lord of Peace and from me, Israel your Father, the bridegroom coming out from under the marriage canopy, the husband of the dear and virtuous Torah, this beautiful and virtuous matron, the man set on high, the Messiah of God, the lion of the upper regions and the deer of the high regions, Shabbetai Ẓevi (his letter to Venice, in: J. Sasportas, *Ẓiẓat Novel Ẓevi*, ed. by I. Tishby (1954), 129).

The rationalistic attitude sometimes reached the extreme of conceiving a Messiah-like political leader. The 14th-century rationalist, Joseph b. Abba Mari ibn *Kaspi, theorizes about:

> The imminent actual possibility of our coming out from this *galut*, becoming free to rule ourselves, without a Lord. Thus, while being confined as slaves in Egypt, God took us out from there with a high hand. Now why should not this be even easier for Him in these days? Is there no longer any material available with which this Creator may create a man like Moses, or even of smaller stature, who shall come before the kings and they will give in to him, as Pharaoh gave in the end, though in the beginning Pharaoh hardened his heart to him (*Tam ha-Kesef*, ed. by Last (1913), 44ff., sermon 8).

The miraculous conception of the Messiah evolved a complex of superhuman traits, anticipated actions, and achievements; the Messiah is to take the crown from the head of the alien sovereign by his virtue of appearance alone and redeem and avenge the Jews by miraculous means.

According to the rationalistic image of the Messiah, he should be "a very eminent prophet, more illustrious than all the prophets after Moses" (Maim., *Iggeret Teiman*, ed. A.S. Halkin (1952), 87). In Maimonides' view prophecy necessitated the highest intellectuality. These criteria were not accepted by most of the messianic movements, whose leadership was largely charismatic. It is related of a pseudo-Messiah who appeared around the end of the seventh century, *Abu ʿIsā (Isaac b. Jacob al-Iṣfahanī), that, "the most wonderful thing about him in the opinion of his followers is the fact that although he was, as they say, an illiterate tailor and could neither read nor write, he produced books and pamphlets without having been instructed by anyone" (Jacob al-Kirkisānī's account of the Jewish sects, ed. by L. Nemoy, in: HUCA, 7 (1930), 328). Not many of the messianic claimants had such humble intellectual beginnings, but practically none of them was regarded by his contemporaries as preeminent among scholars of his day, though some were known as considerable scholars. The most widespread of the messianic movements, that of Shabbetai Ẓevi, had for its leader a man of less than 40 years old, while its great prophet, *Nathan of Gaza, was 21 when he announced the Messiah and died at the age of 36. It is hardly surprising that men of rationalistic bent rarely saw the embodiment of their ideal in the actual messianic claimants who arose, whereas those inclined to follow a Messiah seldom found a man to rouse them in the Maimonidean ideal. This generally created a situation in which the supporters and opponents of the movement were driven into two opposing camps.

The messianic movements envisioned the coming of the Messiah as an historic breakthrough, a new lease of divine grace, and, according to some theories, as a basic change in the cosmos and divine relationships. Hence a phenomenon accompanying many messianic movements was some proposed change in the way of life of Jews. This ranged from the extreme innovations introduced by the New Testament of early Christianity, through minor variations in the law introduced by early medieval messianic movements, up to the orgiastic tendencies and activities of the Shabbatean movement and even more of the Frankists.

The Movements

EARLY MANIFESTATIONS. Some consider the events surrounding *Zerubbabel of the house of David and his mysterious disappearance (c. 519/518 B.C.E.) as the first messianic movement. The charismatic leadership of the first *Hasmoneans and the devotion they inspired is by rights part of the messianic movement cycle, but for the open question of the claims of this house as opposed to the claims of the house of David. The political and moral ferment created with the rise of *Herod and his house, and even more so with the advent of undisguised Roman rule in Judea, led to the emergence of many messianic leaders and influenced new concepts concerning their aims and leadership. *Jesus of Nazareth was one of many Jews who in this turbulent period claimed to be bringing redemption to the people and who were eventually crucified for announcing their message. *Judah the Galilean told Jews about ten years before the birth of Jesus that it was shameful for them to be "consenting to pay tribute to the Romans and tolerating mortal masters after having God for their Lord" (Jos., Wars, 2:118). Judah and his comrade, "the Pharisee Saddok," were regarded by the hostile *Josephus as the founders of the Zealots. They had "a passion for liberty that is almost unconquerable since they are convinced that God alone is their leader and master" (Jos., Ant., 18:23). With these men there began a heroic and tragic line of short-lived kings, martyred leaders, and brave fighters for freedom. Combating both the Romans and the Herodians, they developed the concept of inaugurating the reign of the "Kingdom of Heaven" for God's elected people here and now. There were many such leaders; it is almost certain that not all of them are mentioned in the extant sources. It is difficult to be certain about their ideas and types of leadership, for the accounts of their activities are subject to distortion either by uncritical admirers or by tendentious enemies. In the case of some of them, not only Jesus, miraculous elements enter the conduct of their leadership. Of *Theudas it is related that he influenced "the majority of the masses to take up their possessions and to follow him to the Jordan River." He stated that he was a prophet and that at his command the river would be parted and would provide them an easy passage (Jos., Ant., 20:97ff.; see also Acts 5:35–39). For this, he and many of his followers paid with their lives, about 45 C.E. Also mentioned is a Jew from Egypt, "who had gained for himself the reputation of a prophet"; followed by "about thirty thousand" Jews, he went to "the Mount of Olives. From there he proposed to force an entrance into Jerusalem" and to free it from the Romans. Many of his followers were killed in battle (Jos., Wars, 2:261ff.). How he was regarded by the Romans appears clearly from the fact that the Christian apostle *Paul was mistaken for him (Acts 21:37–38). It is almost certain that *Menahem b. Judah was considered a Messiah by the Zealots, as possibly was *Simeon Bar Giora.

The unflinching heroism displayed by the warriors in the great revolt against the Romans (66–70/73 C.E.) is comprehensible only in the context of a messianic movement. Some consider that the reason why the Jews did not despair when their messianic leaders had fallen in battle was because of their belief in the Messiah in the person of the son of Joseph (see *Messiah), who is destined to fight and die before the coming of the Messiah in the person of the son of David. Even Josephus – who tried to conceal the messianic motives of the great revolt – once had to reveal that "what more than all else incited them to the war was an ambiguous oracle, likewise found in the sacred Scriptures, to the effect that at that time one from their country would become ruler of the world" (Wars, 6:312; cf. Tacitus, *Historiae*, 5:13, and Suetonius, *Lives of the Caesars*, Vespasian, 4). The *Qumran scrolls also point to messianic hopes and suffering as activating factors in the life and thoughts of this sect, though lacking the Davidic element.

As the great revolt, the precedent of many types of messianic leadership and activity, lay crushed, many new concepts of messianic challenge and response entered the Jewish mind and imagination as the legacy of this period. One trend of Jewish messianism which left the national fold was destined "to conquer the conquerors" – by the gradual Christianization of the masses throughout the Roman Empire. Through Christianity, Jewish messianism became an institution and an article of faith of many nations. Within the Jewish fold, the memory of glorious resistance, of the fight for freedom, of martyred messiahs, prophets, and miracle workers remained to nourish future messianic movements.

Jewish messianic revolt against the Roman Empire did not cease with the severe defeat of 70 C.E. The Jewish revolt against Emperor *Trajan in 115–17, which spread like wildfire through Egypt, Cyrenaica, and Libya, had a messianic king-figure at its head. *Simeon Bar Kokhba was at first only one of several messianic figures, though he became the dominating one in the uprising of 132–35 C.E. It is related that the great *tanna*, *Akiva, "when he saw [him] would say: 'This is the king Messiah'" (TJ, Ta'an. 4:8, 68d). It was only after the death of this semi-legendary figure that the messianic movements began to aim at redeeming the Jews and carrying them back to renewed greatness. Symptomatic of this change is the story about the Jew who appeared in 448, approximately, in Crete and, "said that he is Moses and promised the many Jews on this island to bring them through the sea without ships to Judea." He fixed a certain date for this miracle, and ordered them to jump into the sea; several of them drowned (Socrates Scholasticus, *Historia Ecclesiae*, 12:33).

Early Middle Ages

The challenge of the appearance of the victorious Arabs and the Muslim caliphate on the world scene gave rise to a new upsurge of Jewish messianic movements. They again assumed a warlike temper, while utilizing social tensions within the Jewish community and some of the military tactics used among Muslims to attain their aims. About 645 there is mention of a Jew who "asserted that the Messiah had come. He gathered around him weavers, carpet makers, and launderers, some 400 men. They burned down three [Christian] sanctuaries and killed the chief of that locality." The leader of these craftsmen was crucified, after his followers and their families had been massacred (Nestorian Chronicle, as quoted in: Baron, Social[2], 5 (1957), 184). Similar movements relying on miracles are recorded in Muslim Spain and its vicinity in the eighth to ninth centuries.

Much more significant was the movement led by the above-mentioned Abu ʿĪsā. His teachings include many significant halakhic variations. According to the Karaite sources, he followed the Rabbanite rite and laws in many matters for tactical reasons so that the Rabbanites did not persecute his followers. Abu ʿĪsā acknowledged the prophecy of Jesus and Muhammad, regarding them as prophets for their own followers only. This practical motivation and tendency to temporize was belied by the direction his movements took: Abu ʿĪsā led a battle and fell in the fighting, though some of his followers later believed "that he was not killed, but entered a hole in a mountain and was never heard of [again]" (Kirkisānī, ed. by L. Nemoy, in: HUCA, 7 (1930), 328, 382–3). Those who followed him in the Islamic lands in the eighth to ninth centuries, like *Yudghan and Mushka, resembled him in inaugurating changes in aspects of religion and in their warlike spirit.

The Later Middle Ages

With the *Crusades, certain new features in messianism appeared. In the Balkans a general movement of repentance was induced by crusader violence. At *Salonika, in 1096, Jews and Christians reported "that Elijah… had revealed himself openly, and not in a dream, to certain men of standing." People saw "many signs and miracles." There was widespread excited anticipation. It was reported that, under the impression that the redemption was at hand, "the Jews were idly neglecting their work." They sent letters to Constantinople to appraise them of the good news. Other communities sent to inquire about it. There was also a rumor "that all the Byzantine congregations were together in Salonika, and would leave from there" for Ereẓ Israel (J. Starr, *The Jews in the Byzantine Empire 641–1204* (1939), 203–6 no. 153). This was apparently a messianic movement without a Messiah. Jews were united by general feelings of excitation, rumors, and indeterminate tidings.

Maimonides heard that a miracle-working Messiah had appeared – at Lyons in France or Leon in Spain – about 1060. He also heard a tradition that in approximately 1100 a man had been influenced by a dream to proclaim himself Messiah. The man, Ibn Aryeh, was flogged and excommunicated by the community leaders, and with this the affair ended. In the first half of the 12th century messianic ferment was strong in Jewish communities everywhere. About 1121, *Obadiah, the Norman proselyte, met a Karaite *Kohen*, Solomon, who prophesied that within two-and-a half months all the Jews would be gathered together in Jerusalem, "for I am the man whom Israel is waiting for." The proselyte was amazed that a man of Aaronide descent should claim messiahship: "It is 19 years since I entered the Covenant and I never heard that Israel is looking for redemption at the hands of a son of the tribe of Levi – only at the hands of the prophet Elijah and the King Messiah of the seed of King David" (J. Mann, in: *Ha-Tekufah*, 24 (1928), 336–7). This encounter in the Near East reveals how deep-rooted, even in the case of a proselyte, was the concept that the Messiah should be of Davidic descent, whereas in sectarian circles the ancient sectarian concept of an Aaronide Messiah (as shown in the *Dead Sea Scrolls) still persisted.

More or less about the same time, in 1120/21, there was messianic excitation in Baghdad centered around a young prophetess (see S.D. Goitein, in: JQR, 43 (1952/53), 57–76). In 1127 approximately the same occurred in Fez, Morocco, where the man, Moses Al-Dar'i, a great scholar – and admired by Maimonides even after he proclaimed his messiahship – announced the coming of the Messiah.

> He told them that the Messiah was about to appear on the first night of Passover. He advised them to sell all their property and to become indebted as much as possible to the Muslims, to buy from them a thing worth a dinar for ten dinars, and thus to fulfill the words of the Torah [Ex. 12:36], for after Passover they would never see them. As Passover came and went and nothing happened, these people perished for they had sold all their property and their debts overwhelmed them (*Iggeret Teiman*, 103).

Nevertheless, Maimonides expressed satisfaction that this Moses managed to escape to Ereẓ Israel:

> There he died, may his memory be blessed. As has been told to me by those who have seen him when he left, he prophesied all that happened later on to the Maghreb Jews, the main outlines as well as the details (*ibid.*, 103).

The story is not only remarkable in demonstrating the influence wielded by the Messiah on large groups of Jews, and their obedience to his instructions, but also instructive since this movement occurred soon after the visit to Fez of Muhammad ibn Tumar, the founder of the *Almohads, and the public discussions he held there with the leaders of the Muslim establishment. Maimonides' attitude to Moses, his blessing him after his death, and his statement that his prophecies were true, reveal that even such a consistent rationalist could be inconsistent with regard to messianic movements.

The first half of the 12th century also saw the remarkable messianic movement led by David *Alroy. Though the dates and personalities are very confused in the sources mentioning this event, they all indicate that it occurred in the first half of the 12th century, and in the remote eastern districts of the Muslim Empire. Most traditions indicate his great and widespread influence and an extensive campaign of written and oral propaganda. All of them agree about the military character of the movement. The apostate to Islam, *Samuel al-Maghribi, relates that Alroy attempted to take the fortress of Amadiyah, in the mountains of Azerbaijan, by the stratagem of having masses of his believers enter the fortress with hidden weapons (tactics resembling those used by the earlier Muslim founder of the Assassins, Hasan ibn al-Sabbah, with regard to the fortress of Alamut). The apostate adds that:

> When the report about him reached Baghdad two Jewish tricksters, cunning elders, decided to forge letters by Menahem to the Jews of Baghdad bringing them the good tidings which they had been expecting since of yore; that he would appoint for them a certain night in which all of them would fly to Jerusalem. The Jews of Baghdad, their claim to sagacity and pride in craftiness notwithstanding, were all led to believe it. Their women brought their moneys and jewels in order that it all might be distributed on their behalf, as charity to those whom the two elders considered deserving. In this manner the Jews spent the bulk of their wealth. They donned green garments and on the night gathered on the roofs expecting, he asserted, to fly to Jerusalem on the wings of angels. Women began to weep over their nursing infants; what if the mothers should fly before their children or the children before their mothers? The children might suffer because of the delay in feeding (*Ifḥām al-Yahūd: Silencing the Jews*, ed. and trans. by M. Perlmann (1964), 73).

Despite its obvious intention to ridicule, this tale cannot be dismissed out of hand, for this readiness among Jews to believe in miracles is also found in Maimonides' story about the movement in North Africa.

About 1172 a Messiah appeared in the Yemen. Maimonides' hostile reaction to him shows that he had a clear and proclaimed revolutionary social aim, incomprehensible to Maimonides:

> He told them that each man shall distribute all his money and give to the poor. All those who obey him are fools and he is a sinner; for he acts against the Torah. For according to our Torah a man should give as charity only part of his money and not all of it.... No doubt his heart and mind that have misled him to say that he is a Messiah have also brought him to tell the peo-

ple to leave all their property and give it to the poor. Thus they will become poor and the poor rich, and according to his law they [the former poor] will have to return to them [the now impoverished rich] their money. In this fashion money will go back and forth between rich and poor unceasingly (*Iggeret Teiman*, 89).

Maimonides advised the communities to proclaim him a madman or put him to death (*ibid.*, 93, 95). Later on, in a letter to the scholar of Marseilles, Maimonides related further details about the movement and its end. By this time he knew that the man in the Yemen was only:

saying that he is a messenger to smooth the path for the King Messiah. He told them that the Messiah [is] in the Yemen. Many people gathered [around him] Jews and Arabs and he was wandering in the mountains.... He gave them new prayers.... After a year he was caught and all who were with him fled." Asked by his Arab captor for proof of the divine source of his message, the Yemen Messiah "answered him: 'Cut off my head and I will come back to life immediately,'" and so he was killed. Maimonides heard that there were still many foolish people in the Yemen who believed that he would arise and lead them yet (A. Marx, in: HUCA, 3 (1926), 356).

In the 1240s a new source of messianic excitation accompanied the rumors and hopes centering around the news of the Mongol advance into European countries. Meshullam da Pierra in a poem was certain that:

in our days the kingdom shall be renewed for the lost nation and the scattered communities. Tribute will be brought to the son of David, and gifts to my counts and dukes. My Temple will be rebuilt.... There are tribes that have been exiled and now they have left the land of the living. Proof that God has sent them is that many rulers have come to harm.... Babylonia, Aleppo, and Damascus were taken [by the Mongols in 1260].... My Savior has broken through the mountainous wall.

To about the same time should be ascribed the information that "women in the land of Canaan [i.e., Bohemia] were reciting the entire Book of Isaiah by heart and ignorant people knew by heart all the prophecies of consolation" (J. Wistinetzki (ed.), *Sefer Ḥasidim* (1924), 77 no. 212).

Spain and the Marranos

At the end of the 13th century the kabbalist Abraham b. Samuel *Abulafia saw himself as the Messiah or the harbinger of the Messiah and tried to spread the word through apocalyptic writings. Solomon b. Abraham *Adret had to oppose the "prophet of Avila" who prophesied the coming of the Messiah in 1295 and had a large following in Avila. There is some information that there was an upsurge of messianic excitation around 1350 (see *Shemariah of Negroponte). The catastrophe of the persecutions of 1391 in Christian Spain led to widespread messianic ferment. In the vicinity of Burgos there appeared a prophet who foretold the imminent coming of the Messiah. At the Disputation of *Tortosa the Christian protagonist claimed that "in our day R. Ḥasdai *Crescas has announced a report and preached to congregations in the synagogues that the Messiah had been born in Cisneros, in the kingdom of Castile." Crescas entertained, it would seem, even more earthly hopes. He imagined the realities of the Second Temple period "as if the king of Egypt, who now reigns over the land of Israel, were to grant permission to Jews living elsewhere in his empire to go and rebuild the sanctuary, on the condition that they submit to his rule" (in his *Or Adonai*). In a letter of that time from which all proper names have been carefully deleted, it is related that a certain teacher taught that the calamities of the period should be seen as the birth pangs of the Messiah; there was a proliferation of confused messianic tidings:

This one writes about the Lord's Messiah, that he shall surely come by Passover time, and that one says: 'Behold, he stands already at our walls....' Another declares that if the Feast of Tabernacles should arrive and there is yet no Messiah, then surely it is God's will to have us die and to harden our hearts from his fear. But before he has done talking, yet another comes and says: 'It is rumored that a prophet has arisen in Israel who has seen a vision of the Almighty.... The Lord revealed himself in a dream at night and assured him of great amelioration: misery and grief shall flee the years wherein we have seen evil shall be no more; lo, this presages good, this proclaims salvation' (Baer, Spain, 2 (1966), 158–62).

As the position of the Jews in Christian Spain steadily deteriorated, messianic hopes were kept alive. The fall of Constantinople in 1453 awakened great messianic hopes and speculations both in the communities of Spain and among Ashkenazi Jewry. Among the forced converts (**anusim*) men and women prophesied the coming of the Messiah. Letters from the Constantinople community related tales about the birth of the Messiah, the place of his activity, and mode of living. A mother and daughter told their Converso friends: "The gentiles do not see us [do not understand us], for they are blind and know not that the Lord our God hath decreed that for a time we should be subject to them, but that we shall now surpass them [have the upper hand], for God hath promised us that after we go to those lands [overseas], we shall ride on horses and pass them by" (*ibid.*, 292–5). Even on the eve of the expulsion of the Jews from Spain, both Jews and *anusim* actively harbored these hopes. About 1481 a Converso told a Jew, when at his request the latter read the messianic prophecies to him: "Have no fear! Until the appearance of the Messiah, whom all of us wait for, you must disperse in the mountains. And I – I swear it by my life – when I hear that you are banished to separate quarters or endure some other hardship, I rejoice; for as soon as the measure of your torments and oppression is full, the Messiah, whom we all await, will speedily appear. Happy the man who will see him!" One Marrano was certain that the Messiah would possess the philosopher's stone and be able to turn iron into silver. He also hoped that "in 1489 there will be only one religion" in the world. Even after the expulsion many Marranos expressed these hopes and were punished for them by the Inquisition (*ibid.*, 350ff.).

Ferment in the 16th to 18th Centuries

In the 16th century there were numerous expressions of messianic expectation. In 1500–02 Asher *Lemlein (Lammlin) preached repentance and the imminent coming of the Messiah. He had great influence. The grandfather of the chronicler David *Gans "broke up the oven that he had for baking *mazzot*, being sure that next year he would be baking *mazzot* in the Holy Land" (*Ẓemaḥ David*). From the end of the 15th century tales originating in and letters from Jerusalem show messianic hopes centering around the *Ten Lost Tribes of Israel. Joseph *Ḥayyun commenting on the verse "In his days Judah shall be redeemed and Israel will live secure" (Jer. 23:6) wrote:

> He [Jeremiah] said that Judah shall be redeemed and not that Israel shall be redeemed, for Israel need no redemption for they are not in *Galut*. I mean the Ten Tribes, for they are a great people and they have kings – according to what has been told about them – but Judah needs redemption, whereas [the people of] Israel will then live secure in Ereẓ Israel, for now they are not living so secure as they are abroad. What is more, they fight continuously with the gentiles around them (his commentary to Jeremiah, British Museum, Add. Ms. v 27, 560, fol. 106).

The great Mishnah commentator Obadiah of *Bertinoro wrote in 1489 from Jerusalem to his brother in Italy:

> Jews have told us that it is well known, as related by reliable Muslim merchants, that far away, a journey of 50 days through the desert, there lies the famous *Sambatyon River; it surrounds the whole country where the Children of Israel live like a thread. It throws up stones and sand, resting only on the Sabbath. The reason why no Jew goes to this country is because they avoid desecrating the Sabbath. According to their tradition all of them – the descendants of Moses – are saintly and pure like angels; there are no sinners among them. On the outer side of the Sambatyon River there are Children of Israel as numerous as the sands of the seashore, kings and lords, but they are not as saintly and pure as those living on the inner side of the river (A. Yaari, *Iggerot Ereẓ Yisrael* (1943), 140).

Obadiah believed in the existence of a Jewish realm beyond and around the miraculous river which was not only independent and strong but also consisted of two circles of life – an inner, more holy one, and an open, less holy one. Messianic expectations in this period centered actively around these images and fantasies as shown, for example, in the writings of *Abraham b. Eliezer ha-Levi from Jerusalem.

With the advent of David *Reuveni and Solomon *Molcho many Jews were convinced that they were seeing and hearing a prince of those tribes and one of his devoted companions. About the same time many Jews pinned their hopes on Martin *Luther as a man who had come to pave the way for the Messiah through gradually educating the Christians away from their idolatrous customs and beliefs. In Safed, messianic hopes were strong in the circles around Isaac b. Solomon Ashkenazi *Luria and Ḥayyim b. Joseph *Vital. The latter once dreamed:

> I stood on the peak of the great mountain to the west of Safed … over Meron village; I heard a voice announcing and saying, 'The Messiah is coming and the Messiah stands before me.' He blew the horn and thousands and tens of thousands from Israel were gathering to him. He said to us, 'Come with me and you shall see the avenging of the destruction of the Temple.' We went there; he fought there and defeated all the Christians there. He entered the Temple and slew also those who were in it. He commanded all the Jews and told them, 'Brethren, cleanse yourselves and our Temple of the defilement of the blood of the corpses of these uncircumcised ones and of the defilement of the idolatry that was in it.' We cleansed the Temple and reconstructed it as it was, the daily burnt offering was brought by the arch-priest who looked exactly like my neighbor Rabbi Israel (his *Sefer ha-Ḥezyonot* (1954), pt. 2, no. 2, p. 41).

This blend of the Safed reality and messianic visions of war and glory expresses the intensity of messianic hopes in kabbalistic circles that found expression in Shabbetai Ẓevi in the 17th century. Most communities became involved with Shabbetai Ẓevi and the messianic movement he led in the 1660s. In it many aspects of the messianic movements reached their highest expression, to be faced by crisis: his followers fervently believed that the Messiah would achieve a miraculous victory and were cruelly disappointed when Shabbetai Ẓevi collapsed before the terror of punishment; the masses of his followers repented, but repentance proved of no avail. The movement stimulated Jews to feelings of liberation, but they remained subjugated; orgiastic aspects developed which discredited the movement. The movement led by Jacob Frank in the 18th century introduced the elements of nihilism, licentiousness, and severance of the connection between messianism and Ereẓ Israel.

Scholars are divided as to whether in its origins Ḥasidism bore traits of a messianic movement or whether it was on the contrary a kind of sublimation of messianism.

The Modern Period

In modern times the *Haskalah (Enlightenment) and *Reform wings of Judaism increasingly tended to regard their activity in spreading pure and rational monotheism as a kind of collective movement of messianic "mission." In his letters Leopold *Zunz referred many times to the European revolution of 1848 as "the Messiah." Even many Jews who left the faith tended to invest secular liberation movements with a messianic glow. Martin *Buber expressed the opinion that the widespread Jewish activity in modern revolutionary movements stemmed both from the involvement of the Jew with the state and his criticism of it through his messianic legacy (see *disputations).

Zionism and the creation of the State of Israel are to a large extent secularized phenomena of the messianic movements. The ideology of the Zionist religious parties, *Mizrachi and *Ha-Po'el ha-Mizrachi, tends to regard them – in particular the achievements of the State of Israel – as an *atḥalta di-ge'ulla* ("anticipation and beginning of redemption"), thus retaining the traditional concepts held by messianic movements in conjunction with the new secularized aspects of the State and its achievements.

Jewish messianism, though appearing in many shapes and permutations, has been and continues to be an activist element in world culture. For Jews it has retained, through the leaders and movements to which it has given rise, the life-force of charisma, and the binding spell of Jewish statehood and kingship to be realized immediately through God's will, through the passion and devotion of His people. Some have spoken of "the price" that Jews and Judaism have had to pay for disappointment and disenchantment after every failure of the messianic movements. Against this are to be set the benefits that these visionary movements gave to a suppressed people – in inspiring them to activity, revitalization, and a sense of sacrifice.

For a late 20th century manifestation of this phenomenon, see *Chabad and *Schneersohn, Menahem Mendel.

BIBLIOGRAPHY: J. Klausner, *The Messianic Idea in Israel* (1955); A.H. Silver, *A History of Messianic Speculation in Israel* (1959²); A.Z. Aescoly, *Ha-Tenu'ot ha-Meshiḥiyyot be-Yisrael* (1956); Y. Baer, *Yisrael ba-Ammim* (1955); M. Hengel, *Die Zeloten* (1961); Baron, Social², index; S. Yeivin, *Milḥemet Bar Kokhva* (1946); Scholem, Shabbetai Ẓevi; J. Liver, in: HTR, 52 (1959), 149–85; H.H. Ben-Sasson (ed.), *Toledot Am Yisrael*, 3 (1969), s.v. *Meshiḥim*; idem, *The Reformation in Contemporary Jewish Eyes* (1970).

[Haim Hillel Ben-Sasson]

MESSINA, seaport in Sicily. Around the year 1171, Benjamin of *Tudela found 200 (families of?) Jews in Messina. Between 1279 and 1282 the community received the famous kabbalist Abraham *Abulafia, who gave instruction there to two disciples, Abraham and Nathan. In 1347 some Jews of Messina were accused of the ritual murder (see Blood *Libel) of a Christian boy and consequently sentenced to death, an event which was commemorated by a marble inscription in the cathedral. At that time, the Jews lived in a separate quarter called the Paraporto or Giudecca. Although the various communities in Sicily were under the jurisdiction of the *dienchelele, at one stage the Jews of Messina were exempt from it. Their community was administered by councillors (*proti*), who, with the assent of the elders, had the authority to excommunicate offenders against Jewish law. When he was *dienchelele*, Moses *Bonavoglia (Ḥefeẓ) of Messina intervened with Alfonso v in 1428 on behalf of the Sicilian Jews and succeeded in having the order concerning conversionist sermons revoked: in 1440 he constructed an assembly hall for the synagogue. In 1487–88 Obadiah of *Bertinoro was in Messina for some months. He gives a vivacious account of the conditions of the community in a letter to his father in Città di Castello. A manuscript of *Naḥmanides' commentary on the Pentateuch, revised and corrected by the scholars of Messina, formed the basis of the 1490 Naples edition. There were 180 Jewish families in the city in 1453. When the Jews were expelled from Sicily in 1492, some 2,400 of them left Messina. In 1728, permission was given for the return of Jews to Messina and the reestablishment of a synagogue, but the experiment was unsuccessful.

BIBLIOGRAPHY: Elbogen, in: RI, 1 (1904), 108–11; G. De Giovanni, *L'ebraismo della Sicilia…* (Palermo, 1748), index; B. and G. Lagumina, *Codice diplomatico dei giudei di Sicilia*, 3 vols. (1884–1909), passim; E.N. Adler, *Jewish Travellers* (1930), 214; Roth, Italy, index; idem, *Gleanings* (1967), 291–7; Milano, Bibliotheca, index; Milano, Italia, index.

[Sergio Joseph Sierra]

MESSING, SHEP (1949–), U.S. soccer goalie. Messing was born in the Bronx, the third of five children of Elias, a lawyer, and Anne, a teacher. The family moved when Messing was two to Roslyn, Long Island, where he was a wrestling, soccer, and track & field star at Wheatley High School, setting a county record in the pole vault at 13 ft. 6 in. and winning the county championship in soccer his senior year in 1967. He spent two years at New York University, being named to the All-American soccer team his second year. After tasting his first international competition as goalie for the U.S. Maccabiah team in 1969, Messing transferred to Harvard College, graduating in 1972. After playing for the U.S. Pan American team in 1971, Messing was the starting goalie on the U.S. Olympic team at the 1972 Munich Games. He signed with the New York Cosmos, playing one game in 1973 and eight games in 1974 before leaving for the Boston Minutemen for the 1975 season. He led the league that year with six shutouts. The following season Messing returned to the New York Cosmos, helping to lead them to the championship in the Soccer Bowl in 1977. A flamboyant goalie who once posed for *Playgirl* magazine, Messing was in the forefront of the late 1970s soccer boom in the United States. He played with the Oakland Stompers in 1978 and with the Rochester Lancers in 1979 before retiring from the North American Soccer League after appearing in 120 games for four teams. He then played six seasons for the New York Arrows of the Major Indoor Soccer League, leading the team to the championship in the league's first four seasons of existence. Messing rejoined the Cosmos in 1985 when the team switched to the MISL, his last season playing professionally. After retiring, Messing began a career in broadcasting. He is the author of *The Education of an American Soccer Player* (1978).

[Elli Wohlgelernter (2nd ed.)]

MESSINGER, RUTH WYLER (1940–), U.S. political leader, activist, and organizational philanthropist. The daughter of Wilfred and Majorie Goldwasser Wyler, Messinger was a third-generation New Yorker who received university degrees from Radcliffe College and the University of Oklahoma. In her early career she worked as a teacher, social worker, and administrator. She was married to Eli C. Messinger (from whom she was later divorced), and had three children.

Messinger served 20 years in New York City government, beginning in 1977, including 12 years on the City Council advocating for children, public education, campaign financing reform, gay rights, and small businesses. In 1990 she began eight years of service as Manhattan Borough president. Messinger became the first woman to be selected as the Democratic Party's candidate for mayor in 1997 and ran a campaign focused on improving public education. Throughout her 20 years in public service she worked extensively on issues of foster care, domestic and other violence against women, campaign finance, waterfront development, and tax policy. Messinger also founded the first non-profit facility in New York serving women with AIDS and their children.

In 1998, Messinger assumed the role of president and executive director of the American Jewish World Service, a humanitarian organization providing non-sectarian grassroots development and emergency relief to people in developing nations. Under Messinger's leadership, AJWS expanded its scope and visibility, creating new programs in the areas of education, outreach, and service. In 2000, Messinger also launched the Women's Empowerment Fund (WEF) through the AJWS, supporting projects in 18 countries that provide funds to grassroots women's groups in the developing world. Messinger is an active member of the Society for the Advancement of Judaism and has worked in an advisory capacity with the Jewish Fund for Justice. She served as national chair of the advisory council of the National League of Cities and president of Women in Municipal Government. Messinger has also been a board member of the Jewish Foundation for Education for Women, a board member of Project Enterprise, and a member and president of the board of Surprise Lake Camp, a Federation of Jewish Philanthropies camp for New York City area children.

BIBLIOGRAPHY: E.I. Perry and R. Holub, "Messinger, Ruth." in: P.E. Hyman and D.D. Moore (eds.), *Jewish Women in America*, vol. 2 (1997), 917–18.

[Marla Brettschneider (2nd ed.)]

MESTEL, JACOB (1884–1958), Yiddish poet, actor, journalist, playwright, and theater director. Born in Zlochev, Galicia, his first lyrics appeared in the Lemberg (Lvov) *Togblat* and were collected in the booklet *Ferkholemte Shoen* ("Dream Hours," 1909). He gained his first professional theatrical experience in Vienna (1910–14), and after serving as an officer during World War I, he directed the Freie Juedische Folksbuehne (1918–20). Immigrating to the United States in 1920, he joined Maurice *Schwartz's Yiddish Art Theater in 1923, and then directed his own group Artef, where he experimented with bold theatrical innovations. From 1926 he and Jacob *Ben-Ami produced Yiddish plays in New York and on tours which included South America. Author of *Literatur un Teater* ("Literature and Theater," 1962), he co-edited the leftist monthly *Yidishe Kultur* and the first three volumes of Zalman Zylbercweig's *Leksikon fun Yidishn Teater.* From 1950 to 1958 he was editor of the IKUF publishing house.

BIBLIOGRAPHY: Rejzen, Leksikon, 2 (1929), 458–61; LNYL, 6 (1965), 78–81; Z. Zylbercweig, *Leksikon fun Yidishn Teater*, 2 (1934), 1369–74; M. Neugroeschel, in: *Fun Noenten Over* (1955), 298–305; D.S. Lifson, *Yiddish Theater in America* (1965), 116–25, 436–51. **ADD. BIBLIOGRAPHY:** Sh. Rozhansky, *Dos Yidishe Gedrukte Vort in Argentine* (1941), 201–20; Z. Weinper, *Shrayber un Kinstler* (1958), 222–31.

[Sol Liptzin]

METALS AND MINING.

In the Bible

Six metals are mentioned in the Bible and in many passages they are listed in the same order: gold, silver, copper, iron, tin, and lead. Antimony is also mentioned. The metals are referred to in various contexts, including methods of mining, metallurgical processes of extracting the metal, and preparing finished products. The strategic and economic importance of metals and of metal craftsmen is stressed. The prophets employ figures of speech based on the properties of metals and the stages of their treatment. These metals have been uncovered in excavations in Ereẓ Israel in the form of vessels and slag. At Tell Jemmeh, Tell Kasila, Timnah, and other sites, furnaces for smelting iron and copper have been found dating from different periods. The only explicit biblical reference to a foundry is to that of King Solomon "in the plain of Jordan … in the clay ground" where Temple vessels were produced (I Kings 7:46). Utensils for smelting are mentioned mainly as metaphors – "But you the Lord took and brought out of Egypt, that iron blast furnace" (Deut. 4:20). Isaiah speaks of refining silver in a furnace (Isa. 48:10); while Proverbs (27:21) describes the refining of gold and silver in a furnace. Ezekiel compares Israel with the process of refining metals: "The house of Israel has become dross unto Me; all of them, silver and bronze and tin and iron and lead in the furnace, have become dross" (Ezek. 22:18). The prophet was apparently well acquainted with the technical process of refining and smelting silver, and describes how silver is extracted from its ores by means of bellows, leaving slag behind. The working of metals was executed by special smiths and craftsmen, the first of whom was "… Tubal-Cain, who forged all implements of copper and iron" (Gen. 4:22). The Bible speaks of the high qualifications necessary for the specialized metalwork of the Tabernacle: "I have endowed him with a divine spirit of skill, ability, and knowledge … to make designs for work, in gold, silver, and copper" (Ex. 31:3–5). Solomon was forced to bring the craftsman Hiram from Tyre to work in copper (I Kings 7:13–14). The Bible describes the Philistine monopoly of metalsmiths and their strategic importance: "Now there was no smith to be found throughout all the land of Israel; for the Philistines said, 'Lest the Hebrews make themselves swords or spears'" (I Sam. 13:19). The great importance attributed by Nebuchadnezzar to craftsmen and smiths is evident in his deporting them from Jerusalem together with Jehoiachin's army to prevent a possible revolt (II Kings 24:15–16). The methods of working metal after its extraction varied according to the type of metal and the use to which it was put: casting, hammering, gilding, preparing metal, wires, etc.

GOLD (Heb. *zahav*). Gold is one of the rare metals found as an element in nature. It is extracted from the earth by a process of collecting and washing. Specialized goldsmiths employed two methods in working gold. The first consisted of beating it with a hammer into very thin sheets which was possible because of the gold's softness. The sheets were used for, among other things, gilding, and also for making gold wire: "They hammered out sheets of gold and cut threads…" (Ex. 39:3). The second method consisted of melting the gold and then casting it (Ex. 25:12). In the process of melting, the gold was also refined; refined gold, which was necessary for certain purposes (I Chron. 28:18), is apparently identical with "pure gold" (Ex. 25:17).

In various biblical passages words are mentioned that are explained as synonyms of gold: *segor* (Job 28:15); *paz* (Ps. 21:4; Lam. 4:2); *ketem* (Prov. 25:12); *ḥaruẓ* (Ps. 68:14; Prov. 3:14); and *baẓer* (Job 22:24; sometimes understood as "gold ore" or "ingots"). In addition, there are adjectives describing gold, some of which may designate types of gold. The various kinds of gold mentioned in the Bible are summarized in the Talmud (Yoma 44b–45a): "There are seven kinds of gold: gold; good gold (Gen. 2:12); gold of Ophir (I Kings 10:11); fine gold (*ibid.* 10:18); beaten gold (*ibid.* 10:17); pure gold (*ibid.* 6:20); gold of Parvaim (II Chron. 3:6)." In the talmudic discussion concerning the different types of gold, Ophir gold is said to be derived from the place name *Ophir, whereas the other adjectives are said to designate metallic or commercial qualities of gold: *zahav mufaz*, "fine gold," because it resembles *paz* ("a shining jewel"); *zahav shaḥuṭ*, "beaten gold," because it is spun like thread (Heb. *ḥuṭ*); *zahav sagur*, "pure (lit. "locked") gold," indicates such fine quality that when its sale begins all the other shops lock up; *zahav parvaim*, "gold of Parvaim," is said to look like the blood of a bullock (Heb. *par*), but it may also designate a place-name.

The Bible mentions various places from which gold was brought into Ereẓ Israel. Scholars do not agree as to the identification of most of these places but in all probability they include the countries in which gold mines were located in the biblical period: Egypt, Sudan, Saudi Arabia, and India. Among the places cited is the "land of *Havilah" (Gen. 2:11–12), which scholars locate either in southeast Sudan, northwest Ethiopia, or in the southern Sinai Peninsula. The location of Sheba (I Kings 10:6–10) is also disputed (see *Sabea); some scholars place it in Ethiopia and others consider it the name of one of the regions or tribes in southern Arabia. Ophir, which was reached by ships from Ezion-Geber (I Kings 9:26–28; 10–11; 22:49), is identified by *Josephus with India, but, like Havilah and Sheba, it has also been located in Saudi Arabia. Uphaz has not been identified (Jer. 10:9). Parvaim (II Chron. 3:6) is either a place in Arabia or an adjective describing gold as in the talmudic explanation mentioned above.

As early as the patriarchal period, gold was used for manufacturing jewelry and fine vessels (Gen. 24:22) whose value was measured by the amount of gold they contained. Gold was a symbol of wealth and position and served as capital but not as a means of payment. Silver served as currency, but gold bullion as payment is mentioned only once in the Bible: "So David paid Ornan 600 shekels of gold by weight for the site" (I Chron. 21:25; but cf. Num. 22:18; 24:13; II Sam. 21:4; I Kings 15:19; Ezra 8:25f.). The Mishnah explains that "Gold acquires silver, but silver does not acquire gold" (BM 4:1), i.e., gold is valuable as property while silver is a means of payment. At the time of the Exodus from Egypt, the Israelite women borrowed from their neighbors "objects of silver, and gold, and clothing" (Ex. 12:35). Aaron broke off golden earrings to make the golden calf (*ibid.* 32:3). The fullest descriptions of the use of gold are found in the accounts of the building of the Tabernacle in the desert and of Solomon's Temple. In the Tabernacle, gold leaf and gold casts were used, for which the gold was contributed by the Israelites: "And these are the gifts that you shall accept from them: gold, silver, and copper" (Ex. 25:3). The finest craftsmen executed the work (*ibid.* 31:4). Solomon obtained gold for the Temple and his palace from the booty taken in King David's wars (II Sam. 8:7; 12:30) and from trade with Ophir on Hiram's ships (I Kings 9:28). Gold vessels of all kinds denoted wealth and nobility and were also important in ritual. At the same time, the principal idols were made of gold and silver and the prophets inveighed against the worship of these graven images (Isa. 30:22). The wealth and prestige of silver and gold in the form of property and of idols were used as symbols by the prophets: "Neither their silver nor their gold shall be able to deliver them…" (Zeph. 1:18). Wealth and gifts of splendor were associated with gold: the Queen of Sheba brought Solomon "… very much gold" (I Kings 10:2); "and the whole earth sought the presence of Solomon to hear his wisdom … every one of them brought articles of … gold" (*ibid.* 10:24–25). The shields of Solomon's guard were made of gold (*ibid.* 14:26), and when Ahasuerus made a great banquet for the nobility of his court, he served them from "golden goblets" (Esth. 1:7).

SILVER (Heb. *kesef*). The main minerals in which silver appears in nature are natural silver and silver sulfides. Silver is commonly found in association with gold and copper, and sometimes with lead. Silver was known to man in earliest antiquity; articles of silver have been found in Ereẓ Israel from as early as the Middle Bronze Age. Silver mines in ancient times were located in Spain, Egypt, and Anatolia. According to the Bible, silver, like other metals, was brought by Solomon from *Tarshish (II Chron. 9:21) and Arabia (9:14). Silver was extracted from its ore by smelting, with the use of bellows, and the slag containing lead was separated from the silver (Jer. 6:29–30). Job was acquainted with the technical process of extracting silver: "Surely there is a mine for silver, and a place for gold which they refine" (Job 28:1). Ezekiel also describes the method of extracting silver and mentions slag containing bronze, iron, lead, and tin (Ezek. 22:20–22).

Because of the high value of silver, it was used as a means of payment from earliest times, in preference to gold which was extremely soft. Payment in silver took the form of bullion ("400 shekels of silver," Gen. 23:15) or was weighed on scales. The biblical verse "Here, I have with me the fourth part of a shekel of silver" (I Sam. 9:8) clearly indicates the use of coins. The Temple tax was also paid in silver coins ("a half-shekel," Ex. 30:13). In the Bible the shekel designates a unit of weight (Heb. *mishkal*), from which the term *shekel is apparently derived. Weighing the silver was replaced by standard units of weight, which became *coins; later the coins were counted, as, for example, "I herewith give your brother 1,000 pieces of silver" (Gen. 20:16).

Silver was also used for making vessels for the Tabernacle and the Temple. It was a symbol of wealth and position as in the description of the palace of Ahasuerus "… silver rings and marble pillars, and also couches of gold and silver…" (Esth. 1:6). When "all the kings of the earth" came to hear Solomon, they brought him gifts of gold and silver (II Chron. 9:23–24). The most outstanding description of a king's wealth is the chariot bought in Egypt by Solomon for 600 shekels of silver (I Kings 10:29). Job describes kings and counselors "who filled their houses with silver" (Job. 3:15). Among biblical figures of speech and similes based on silver is: "Your silver is become dross" (Isa. 1:22), i.e., the very valuable metal is transformed into something worthless like the slag formed during its reduction. The smelting and refining of silver are used as symbols of the Israelites: "For Thou, O God, hast tested us; Thou hast tried us as silver is tried" (Ps. 66:10). Trade in silver becomes a symbol of trade in general; although it is an honest trade, it is transcended by the acquisition of wisdom "For the gain from it is better than gain of silver" (Prov. 3:14).

COPPER (Heb. *neḥoshet*). The copper referred to in the Bible is not pure copper but an alloy of copper and tin. This alloy – bronze – was the most useful and important metal from the beginning of the third millennium B.C.E. to the 13th century B.C.E. when it began to be replaced by iron. Copper mines in the ancient Near East were located in Cyprus (from which the name copper is apparently derived), Sinai, and Egypt. It was the main metal extracted in Ereẓ Israel in antiquity and is the only one mined there today. Copper is usually extracted from sulfide minerals, and partly from silicates, and carbonates; very small amounts of native copper are also found.

The Arabah contains copper mines in three main centers: (1) Faynān (biblical Punon, Num. 33:42), around 25–30 mi. (40–50 km.) south of the Dead Sea in the eastern Arabah; (2) the area of Wadi Abu Khushayba, around 8 mi. (13 km.) southwest of Petra; (3) and in the Timnah-Amram region which also extends southwest of Elath. The copper deposits appear in the form of concentrates in the white Nubian sandstone with a base of *Evronah* complex formation of the Lower Cretaceous period. The concentrates are connected with the layer of fossilized trees in the sandstone and are composed mainly of sulfides, carbonates, silicates, and copper oxides. They have a high copper content which reaches as much as 30–40%. N. Glueck, the first to describe these deposits in detail, attributes the beginning of copper mining and smelting activities to the Kenites, Kenizzites, and Kadmonites (Gen. 115:19), who inhabited the area and were related to Tubal-Cain (i.e., the Kenite), the first metalsmith (*ibid.* 4:22). In Glueck's opinion they were nomadic tribes who wandered in the Arabah and were metallurgical specialists. He also associates the Edomites with the metal industry and its trade through the Arabah and the Red Sea. The area was conquered by David, and Solomon continued to work the mines and develop international trade, mainly by way of Ezion-Geber; his metallurgical industry was located in the plain of the Jordan "in the clay ground between Succoth and Zarethan" (I Kings 7:46). Glueck suggests that copper was even exported from the Arabah by Solomon, and also that the protracted wars between Judah and Edom during the period of the Kingdom of Judah were over control of the copper mines in the Arabah.

Excavations carried out between 1959 and 1969 by the Arabah Expedition headed by B. Rothenberg concluded that the copper mines in the Timnah area are not to be attributed to the time of Solomon. Rothenberg distinguished three periods at the site: the Chalcolithic period (fourth millennium B.C.E.), the Early Iron Age, and the Byzantine period (third–fourth centuries C.E.). Rothenberg suggests that Egyptian kings in the 14th–12th centuries B.C.E., and not the kings of Israel and Judah, sent mining expeditions to the Arabah, and that the copper mines and the smelting installations were operated by the Egyptians together with the Midianites, Kenites, and Amalekites. Among the finds in an Egyptian temple discovered in Timnah was a copper snake which dates it to the time of the Exodus. According to the excavator, the Kenites and the Midianites employed highly developed methods of copper production that ceased with the Israelite Conquest; only commercial activities, and not production, were undertaken in the period of the Monarchy by way of Ezion-Geber and the Red Sea to Ophir and Sheba. Rothenberg also emphasizes that a metallurgical center was located in the Succoth-Zarethan area where imported raw copper was made into finished products (I Kings 7:46). The copper was extracted from its ore by smelting in an oven and then cast. Heat was produced by charcoal from acacia trees which grow in the Arabah.

Much copper was used in manufacturing vessels for the Temple and especially for the Tabernacle: clasps, sockets, rings, posts of the enclosure, lavers, etc. (Ex. 26–36). The biblical description of copper weapons indicates a highly developed military culture, e.g., the description of Goliath: "He had a helmet of bronze on his head, and he was armed with a coat of mail, and the weight of the coat was 5,000 shekels of bronze" (I Sam. 17:5–7). Copper was fashioned into a symbol for the Israelites in the desert in the form of a serpent of copper made by Moses (Num. 21:9; see *Copper Serpent); it was preserved by the Israelites up to the time of Hezekiah who destroyed it, calling it *Nehushtan (II Kings 18:4). The destruction of the Temple is emphasized by the removal of the copper; after the Temple was burnt, the Babylonians destroyed all the objects in it and carried away a great many copper objects to Babylonia and "the bronze of all these vessels was beyond weight" (II Kings 25:13, 16). In its use in vessels for the Tabernacle and Temple and for weapons, copper symbolized strength and rigidity – "The skies above your head shall be copper" (Deut. 28:23). It also denoted drought – "I will make your skies like iron and your earth like copper" (Lev. 26:19). The word for chains (*neḥushtayim*) is also derived from copper. Not only the heaven and earth but also the Israelites are compared with rigid copper: "your forehead copper" (Isa. 48:4).

IRON (Heb. *barzel*). Job was acquainted with the technical process of extracting iron from iron ore: "iron is taken out of the earth" (Job. 28:2). Isaiah described the smith's technique of working iron with the help of charcoal to produce steel suitable for making vessels (Isa. 54:16). The Bible speaks of Tubal-Cain as the first metalsmith (Gen. 4:22; see above discussion of copper). Some scholars identify the family of Japheth, to whom Tubal-Cain was related, with peoples who inhabited the coast of the Black Sea. Iron was first exploited by the Hittites in Asia Minor and it was brought to Syria and Ereẓ Israel by Phoenician merchants. Another source of iron was Tarshish, and "massive iron" was brought from Vedan and Javan (Ezek. 27:12–13, 19).

The Early Iron Age in Ereẓ Israel corresponds roughly with the period of the Philistines (from c. 1200 B.C.E.). The iron in the hands of the Philistines may have been connected with their maritime trade and with imports by merchants from the north. Iron mines were apparently located in the mountains of iron in the hill region of Edom (Josephus mentions an "Iron Mountain" near Gerasha) and also in southern Lebanon, but these were probably of little importance. Iron was used primarily for weapons, and ironsmiths were thus of prime importance in the military organization. The Philistines succeeded in securing control of all the smiths – apparently ironsmiths: "Now there was no smith to be found throughout the land of Israel" (I Sam. 13:19). Whoever needed the services of ironsmiths for sharpening everyday tools, such as agricultural implements, was forced to go to the Philistines. Iron implements (a plow and a spade) have been found at Tell Jamma and also furnaces for smelting iron; the earliest finds come from Tell al-ʿAjūl where a dagger with an iron blade and copper handle were also discovered. As early as the biblical period, iron was employed extensively in everyday life: war, agriculture, building, religion, trade, and household utensils. Iron weapons included chariots (Josh. 17:16); horns (I Kings 22:11); swords and spears (I Sam. 13:19; II Sam. 23:7); "iron objects" (Num. 35:16); and fetters (Ps. 105:18); while iron agricultural tools included sledges (Amos 1:3) and yokes (Jer. 28:14). In building, iron was used in door bars (Isa. 45:3), nails for doors of gates (I Chron. 22:3), and hammers and axes (I Kings 6:7); in religion, it was used for statues of gods (Dan. 5:4); and in trade, for weights (I Sam. 17:7). Household utensils made of iron included bedsteads (Deut. 3:11) and pens (Job 19:24).

Iron often appears in figures of speech in the Bible, but it mainly symbolizes the material from which instruments of war were made. Its use was prohibited in building an altar (Ex. 20:25): "an altar of unhewn stones, upon which no man has lifted an iron tool" (Josh. 8:31). The Mishnah elaborates: "for iron was created to shorten man's days, while the altar was created to lengthen man's days; what shortens may not rightly be lifted up against what lengthens" (Mid. 3:4). Solomon carried the ban against using stones hewn with iron in building the altar even further when he built the Temple, "so that neither hammer nor axe nor any tool of iron was heard in the Temple," while it was being built (I Kings 6:7). In the Talmud a discussion is held on whether the prohibition against the use of iron tools applied only to the Temple site or to the quarry as well (Sot. 48b), for Solomon built three rows of hewn stone in the inner court (I Kings 6:36). In the description of David's battle with Goliath, spiritual values are contrasted with iron weapons symbolizing war, as Goliath appears with a sword, spear, and javelin, opposite David's faith in God (I Sam. 17:45, 47). Iron also denotes strength: "iron yoke" (Deut. 28:48), "your neck is an iron sinew" (Isa. 48:4), and has a special meaning in Psalms 107:10.

TIN (Heb. *bedil*). Tin was known to, and utilized by, the ancient Egyptians. There was an extensive international trade in tin that was alloyed with copper to make bronze – the copper of the Bible. Tin was mentioned by Ezekiel as one of the products imported by the Phoenicians from Tarshish (27:12). It appears in the Bible together with the other metals, gold, silver, copper, iron, and lead, for example, in connection with the laws of their purification after being captured as booty (Num. 31:22). Tin is mentioned by Ezekiel as one of the components of the slag obtained by reducing silver from its ore (22:18–22) and by Isaiah: "smelt away your dross as with lye, and remove all your tin" (1:25). No specific tin vessels are mentioned in the Bible.

LEAD (Heb. *ʿoferet*). The ancient sources of lead were Asia Minor and Syria, and it was included among the metals brought by the Phoenicians from Tarshish (Ezek. 27:12). Lead galena is found today at the foot of Mount Hermon; however, nothing is known of its extraction in antiquity. Because of its high specific gravity, it served as weights for fishermen's nets – "they sank like lead in the majestic waters" (Ex. 15:10), from which the simile "to sink in water like lead" is derived. The plumb line may also have been made of lead (Amos 7:7). Lead served also as a cover of utensils because of its high specific gravity (Zech. 5:7–8). The verse, "… that with an iron pen and lead they were graven in the rock for ever!" (Job. 19:24), seems to indicate that as early as biblical times, lead was used for writing; because of the softness of lead, writing implements were made of stone filled with lead. Lead is mentioned several times in the Bible together with the other metals (e.g., Num. 31:22). Lead, or lead minerals, may have been used for cosmetics and dyes.

ANTIMONY (Heb. *pukh*). No objects made of antimony are known, but it appears in copper alloys. Unlike the other metals, the Bible does not mention antimony as a metal but only its use as a mineral – as eye shadow. Kohl for painting the eyes (II Kings 9:30; cf. Ezek. 23:40) is translated in the Vulgate as stibium.

[Uri Shraga Wurzburger]

In Rabbinic Literature

Rabbinic literature – the Talmuds in particular – contains a wealth of information on metals and metallurgy (though not on their primary production by mining), on the use of the various metals in manufacture, on metal artifacts, and so on. The growth of terminology as well as the use of terms borrowed from Greek, Latin, and even Persian is an indication on the progress from biblical times in the refining process and in the use of metals, though the basic metals remained more or less the same. As distinct from the Bible, rabbinic literature has generic terms for metals, generally *mattekhet* from the biblical root (*ntk*, "to smelt"), and in the Middle Ages also *metilin* or *metil* from the Greek μέταλλον or Latin *metallum*. Metals mentioned in rabbinic literature are gold, silver, copper (brass and bronze), iron, tin, lead, and antimony or stibium. A number of terms exist for metal sheets, bars, or lumps: *eshet* or *ashashit niska* ("cast metal"), particularly a bar of silver or gold; *ḥarakhah* ("lumps of metal [iron ore]"), before smelting; *milela* for gold ore as broken in the mine; *peitalon* (Gr. πέταλον; "metal or gold leaf"), for which there is also a Hebrew word (*tas*); and also the more general term *golem* (pl. *gelamim*), meaning any raw, unfinished material. There is also a whole range of terms for old and broken metal which could be used again, the most general of which is *gerutei* (pl. *geruta'ot*) or *gerumei* (in Gr. γρύτη), "junk iron" still used in modern Hebrew for junk, rubbish, but other derivations have been suggested (see S. Krauss in JE, 8, 515 and Kohut, *Arukh ha-Shalem*, s.v.). *Asimon* (Gr. ασημος) is uncoined bullion or coins on which the stamping has worn off.

The social standing of metalworkers was high, but they maintained fine distinctions between them, with the gold- and silversmith (*zehavim, kassafim*) ranking higher than the ordinary smith (*nappaḥ*); see the description of the separate seats occupied by different craftsmen in the great synagogue of Alexandria in *Sukkah* 51b. The metalworker is called *nappaḥ* as he has to blow (*nafaḥ*) the fire with the *mappu'aḥ* ("bellows") in order to soften the metal. The gold- and silversmith is also called *meẓaref*, though this is occasionally applied to the coppersmith as well. For fuel, the smith used *peḥam* (charcoal), which he had to make himself, and the *peḥami* is therefore both the charcoal burner and the blacksmith (see the story of R. Gamaliel's visit to the home of R. Joshua b. Hananiah, who was a needle maker; Ber. 28a). For the smelting of gold, straw was used as fuel. When taken from the fire with *ẓevat* ("tongs," see Avot 5, 6), the metal was beaten with the *pattish* ("hammer") or *kurnas* (Gr. κέαρνον) on the *saddan* ("anvil") made by the *sadna'ah*. The term "beat with the hammer" became typical for every kind of manufacture. Rabbinic literature contains many further details on the various activities of the blacksmith and other instruments which he uses (see Krauss, Tal Arch, 2 (1911), 299ff.). There is an equally great variety of implements and vessels, which were made from the various metals. Metals were used in every kind of manufacturing process, in agriculture, for domestic and personal needs, for weapons and armaments, for coins, and Temple use. Gold and silver were the main raw material of women's ornaments (*ibid.*, 307ff.).

GOLD. Both Talmuds and some Midrashim have slightly differing lists of seven varieties of gold, most of which occur already in the Bible (TJ, Yoma 4:4, 41d; Yoma 44b; Num. R. 12:4; Song R. 3:10, no. 3; for the talmudic discussion on the various names for gold see above, in the biblical section). Various information is given on the smelting of the gold used for the making of the **menorah* by Moses (TJ, Shekalim 6:4, 50b), Solomon, and in the Second Temple (Song R. 3:10, no. 3). According to the Midrash, gold had, in any event, been created for its use in the Temple (Ex. R. 35:1). It does not deteriorate (Me'il. 5:1, 19a). In Solomon's time, weights were made of gold (PDRK 169a). The gold (and silver), which the Israelites carried away from Egypt, is a frequent subject of *aggadah* (see Ber. 32a). So are the golden tables of the rich (Shab. 119a; Ta'an. 25a; Tam. 32a). The members of the Sanhedrin of Alexandria sat on golden chairs in the famous basilica (Suk. *ibid.*, and parallels). Famous, too, is the golden ornament (*Yerushalayim shel zahav*) which R. Akiva gave to his wife (Shab. 59a). His colleague R. Ishmael had a bride fitted with a golden tooth to make her more attractive (Ned. 66b; cf. Shab. 6, 5). Rich men in Jerusalem would tie their *lulavim* with threads of gold (Suk. 3, 8) and offer their first fruits in baskets of silver or of gold (Bik. 3, 8).

SILVER (Heb. *kesef*). The term *argentariyya* and similar forms (Gr. ἀργεντάριος, Lat. *argentarium*) is used in TJ, *Peah* 8:9, 21b and the Midrash (PdRK 106b) for table silver (and gold) and *martekha* for silver slag (Git. 69b).

COPPER, BRASS, BRONZE (Heb. *Nehoshet*).The word *beronza* ("bronze") is found in medieval rabbinic literature (Heilprin, *Seder Dorot*, 1 (1905), 104). The Greek word χαλκός which like *neḥoshet* means copper as well as the alloys brass and bronze, though later the latter only, is used in the Babylonian Talmud (BK 100b) for copper caldron (so also in Gr.; see Jastrow, Dict., s.v.); in the Jerusalem Talmud (BB 4:6, 14c) for the copper (caldron) room in a bathhouse; the Targum often used the form *karkoma* (χαλκωμα), Greek for anything made of copper, etc. (see S. Krauss, *Griechische und lateinische Lehnwoerter* (1898), 299). The term *peliza* (a kind of bronze, see JE, 8, 516) is used in *Bava Kama* (113b, Ms., see Rabbinowicz, Dik Sof, BK 140). According to the Midrash (Lev. R. 7:5; Tanḥ., Terumah 11), the copper covering on the altar of the Tabernacle would miraculously not melt in spite of the perpetual fire. Bronze tablets were used to inscribe international treaties, such as the one between Judah Maccabee and Rome (I Macc. 8:22; Jos., Ant., 12:416) and his brother Simeon and Sparta (I Macc. 14:18). Mishnah *Parah* (12:5) mentions a "hyssop of brass." Nathan b. Jehiel's *Arukh* quotes from the lost *Midrash Yelammedenu* the term *konekhi* (Gr. κόγχη), a copper shell or bowl (for oil). Corinthian bronze (*kelinteya*), famous for its quality and shine, was used for the Nicanor gates of the Herodian Temple (Eliezer b. Jacob, Yoma 38a; Tosef. *ibid.* 2:4).

IRON (Heb. *barzel, parzel, parzela*). As to the sources of iron ore, the Palestinian Targum translates the place names Kadesh and Wilderness of Zin (Sinai) as "Mountain of Iron" (Num. 33:36; 34:4). The Mishnah (Suk. 3:1) and Josephus (War, 4:454) mention an Iron Mountain near Gerasa in Transjordan (Avi-Yonah, Geog., 162). Indian iron was used for making weapons (Av. Zar. 16a), and Indian swords were the very best available

(Tanḥ., Va-Etḥannan 6). *Parzelayyah* is used as a generic term for iron tools (Lev. R. 24:3; TJ, Nid. 2:6, 50b, as a simile for a sharp mind). He who bathes in hot water without showering himself afterward with cold water is like iron that has been treated in the fire without being put into cold water afterward (Shab. 41a). According to R. Eliezer, it is permitted on the Sabbath to cut wood on which to burn coal to forge a knife for a circumcision which is to occur on that day (*ibid.* 19:1, 130a). The Talmud speaks of *even sho'evet*, a magnetic stone which attracts iron (Sot. 47a).

TIN. The terms used for this metal are either *ba'aẓ* or *avaẓ, kassitera, kassiteron*, and *gassiteron* (Gr. κασσίτερος). Both *ba'aẓ* and *kassitera* are used in the same passages (Men. 28b and elsewhere), which implies that they were two different metals or kinds of the same metal. The Temple *menorah* was not to be made of them, but when the Hasmoneans cleansed the Temple and needed a new *menorah* (the golden one having been carried off by Antiochus IV), they made it of seven spears plated with tin (*ibid.*). It was forbidden to make weights out of metal – tin and lead being mentioned specially – because metal wears away (BB 89b and Tos. ad loc.; Tosef., *ibid.* 5:9). The traveler Pethahiah of Regensburg (12th century) reports that in Babylonia people were summoned to synagogue by a tin instrument. In the later Middle Ages up to modern times tin was used extensively for artistic *ritual objects such as Ḥanukkah *menorot, seder, Kiddush*, and *Havdalah* plates, etc.

LEAD. Lead is called *avar* in rabbinic literature, also *karkemisha* in the Palestine Targum (Num 31:22; Job 19:24). *Ḥullin* 8a (cf. Neg. 9:1) mentions "lead from its source" as a naturally hot substance causing injury. The water reservoirs below the Temple Mount were said to be lined with lead (Letter of Aristeas 90). Lead was also used as a writing material (Shab. 104b, see Rashi). A wick of hot lead was used to carry out the death sentence by burning (Sanh. 52a), and water pipes were made of lead (Mik. 6:8). The term *alsefidag* (of Persian origin) is used in geonic literature for white lead (Kohut, Arukh, 4 (1926), 82).

ANTIMONY OR STIBIUM. Antimony or stibium, called *koḥal*, was used in the form of a powder for painting the eyelids (verb *kaḥol*). From the word *koḥal* the modern Hebrew word for blue (*kaḥol*) is derived. Both the noun and the verb are used in many talmudic passages (e.g., Shab. 8:3; 10:6, 80a; Ket. 17a). A species of hyssop is called *ezov koḥalit* (Neg. 14:6 and elsewhere), probably after a district (Kid. 66a) in Transjordan (see Jastrow, Dict., s.v.), which may, in turn, have derived its name from the metal; cf. the "hyssop of brass" in *Parah* 12:5, mentioned above.

ḤASHMAL. The mysterious *ḥashmal* (Ezek. 1:4; 8:2) is interpreted in *Ḥagigah* (13a–b) as fire-spouting dragons. Translators called it amber or galena (lead-ore), while in modern Hebrew it has become the word for electricity (cf. S. Munk (ed.), *Guide des égarés*, 2 (1961), 229 n. 4).

VALUE OF METALS. The relative value attached to metals can be seen from the pages concerning the Temple *menorah* (Men. 28b), where they are listed either in descending order – gold, silver, tin, lead – or ascending order – iron, tin, silver, gold. The relative value of metals depended on the currency situation, the coins made of less valuable metal being considered currency in relation to those of the more valuable one, which is then considered commodity but not currency (see BM 4:1; Mishnah lists gold, silver, and copper in descending order, whereas the same Mishnah in the Jerusalem Talmud (BM 4:1, 9c) puts silver before gold).

SYMBOLISM OF METALS. The symbolism of metals representing the Four Kingdoms in Daniel 2 and 3 is expanded in *Exodus Rabbah* (35:5), "Gold is Babylon; silver is Media; copper is Greece; iron is Edom (Rome); etc." A symbolic meaning is found by *Midrash Tadshe* 11 in the fact that of the two altars in the Tabernacle and Temple one was overlaid with gold (the soul) the other with copper (the body). On account of the Golden Calf, gold became a symbol of sin, and therefore a *shofar* mouthpiece was not to be overlaid with gold (RH 27a; cf. Maharil, *Hilkhot Rosh Ha-Shanah*), nor did the high priest officiate on the Day of Atonement in the Holy of Holies in his golden vestments but in white linen ones (*ibid.* 26a). At the same time, the gold plate on the incense altar of the Tabernacle and Temple was to atone for the sin of the Golden Calf (Yal., Ex. 368). Iron is also a metaphor for strength of character, and a scholar who is not as hard as iron is no scholar (Ta'an. 4a; cf. Men. 95b concerning Rav Sheshet). Similarly the Evil Inclination may be as hard as iron, but the Torah, which is likened to an (iron) hammer (Jer. 23:29), will smash it (Suk. 52b; see Tos. ad loc.). Some students may find their studies as hard as iron (Ta'an. 8a), but two scholars studying together sharpen each other's mind as one piece of iron sharpens the other (*ibid.* 7a). As wine cannot be preserved in golden or silver vessels but only in the humblest of vessels (earthen ones), so the words of the Torah will not be preserved in one who is in his own eyes like a gold or silver vessel but only in one, who is like the lowliest of vessels (Sif. Deut. 48).

Jews as Metalworkers and Miners

A study of the part played by Jews in the mining and metal industries proves that there has been too great a tendency to minimize their participation in the promotion and development of these branches. It is true that the objective restrictions which kept the Jews off the land and prevented their ownership of it, especially in medieval society, contributed in no small measure to limiting their opportunities of exploiting natural resources in general and various metals in particular. Yet despite all this the Jews succeeded, at different times and in various countries, in penetrating several branches connected with the mining of metals, their contribution to the advance of the industry being at times of great significance.

PRE-MODERN PERIOD. Very little information on the exploitation of the earth's resources has come down to us from the mishnaic and talmudic periods. Until the end of the fourth century there were copper mines at Punon, at the south of the Dead Sea, and *Jerome (340?–420) testifies that mining was discontinued there during his lifetime. The literature of these periods frequently mentions coal and copper refiners; it may be assumed that the "refiner" mentioned in the Mishnah (Ket. 7:10) is merely a copper smelter. As mentioned, the separation of Jews from the land in the Middle Ages had implications for the mining industry. In those times mining was frequently connected with agricultural labor, and thus in Germany, for instance, there were farmers who were engaged in extracting iron ore in their free time. It is therefore evident that since the Jews were cut off from agriculture their opportunities for extracting metals were limited. Added to this, in Christian Europe minerals were considered crown property, so that private ownership of mines was impossible. Yet in spite of all these restrictions Jews were to be found in various branches of the mining industry, as lessees and managers, traders in metals, and even miners. As for precious metals, there can be no doubt that their employment as minters of coins, especially in absolutist Europe at the time when *Court Jews flourished, brought them into direct contact with gold and silver mining (see *Mintmasters and Moneyers). A similar state of affairs prevailed with regard to the extraction of precious stones (see *Diamond Industry and Trade), since the Jews were prominent in the international trade in luxury goods and in purveying them to royal courts, at least from the days of the Carolingian kingdom up to the time of the absolutist states in modern Europe. In such countries as Spain and Poland, where Jews played an outstanding part as colonizers, they were prominent as lessees of salt mines (see *Salt Production).

There were also Jews in different countries throughout the Middle Ages who were engaged in extracting both heavy and light metals of various kinds. In England, for instance, Jews had worked in tin mining in Cornwall in 1198. Joachim *Gaunse appeared in 1581 and suggested to the English government new methods for processing copper. When it became known that he was a Jew from Prague, he was arrested by the authorities and his fate is unknown. In Sicily, there was a long tradition of Jewish activity in the mines from the times of the emperor Tiberius, who sent 4,000 Jewish youths as slaves to the mines. Jews were commonly engaged there not only in the manufacture of metalware but also in mining silver and iron. In spite of the opposition of the local authorities, a royal decree of 1327 ordered Sicilian officials to support Jewish mine prospectors and miners. At the beginning of the 15th century two Jews of *Alghero received special authorization to exploit the resources of the region, on condition that half the output be handed over to the crown. Attempts by Jews to extract metals in Germany are also known: in 1625 Duke Frederick Ulrich of Brunswick asked the theologians of the University of Helmstedt if he might be allowed to hand over the lead trade to two Jews and authorize them to move freely through his state for that purpose. After the members of the faculty had agreed, these Jews mined lead from the Harz Mountains.

MODERN PERIOD. In modern times the part played by Jews in the mining and metal industries of Germany reached considerable dimensions. After Aron Hirsch (1783–1842) had established a firm for buying and selling copper in 1805, Halberstadt became the cradle of the modern German nonferrous metal trade. In 1820 he became a partner in founding copper enterprises in Werne and Ilsenburg. When his son Joseph (1809–1871) joined the business, its name was changed to Aron Hirsch and Son. In 1863 they acquired the copper works of Heegermuehle, near Eberswalde. A branch was established in New York in 1894 and the firm began to take an interest in the metal enterprises of France, Belgium, and England and the mines of Australia, America, and Eastern Asia. At the close of the 19th century Aaron Siegmund Hirsch initiated the establishment of the zinc enterprises of *Vladivostok. The firm of Hirsch Kupferund Messingwerke A.G. was founded in 1906; World War I and the economic crisis of 1929–32 caused it to be liquidated in 1932. Dr. Emil Hirsch (1870–1938) then founded a new enterprise in Berlin, the Erze und Metalle Hirsch A.G., with a branch in Amsterdam, but the firm was liquidated when the Nazis came to power. Philipp Abraham Cohen, a descendant of the Hanover banking family, transferred the family business to Frankfurt in 1821. In Hanover they had been connected with the mining enterprises in the Harz Mountains. Philipp Abraham Cohen's son-in-law established the metal-trading firm of Henry R. Merton and Co. in London. In the meantime the Frankfurt firm extended its scope and traded in American copper and tin from the Dutch Indies. This enterprise was also involved in the nickel and aluminum trades, and until 1873, when the Deutsche Gold und Silber-Scheideanstalt was established, in the silver trade too. In 1881 the branches in England and Frankfurt established the Metallgesellschaft, Frankfurt on the Main, which became the leading German firm in the metal trade. Among other enterprises, they established the Usine de Désargentation (de-silverizing plant) in Hoboken, near Antwerp. In 1896, together with the firms of Hirsch and Beer, and Sondheimer and Co., they undertook zinc and lead mining. The Metallurgische Gesellschaft (Lurgi) was established in 1897; together with the Metallgesellschaft, it founded the Berg und Metallbank A.G. in 1906. Once the firm had successfully overcome the post-World War I crisis, branches were established in Amsterdam, Basle, Brussels, Copenhagen, Madrid, Milan, Prague, Stockholm, and Vienna. It was liquidated as a Jewish firm when Hitler came to power.

The Jews of Russia, too, had considerable achievements to their credit in the mining of certain metals and in associated industries. In 1807 there were 253 Jewish copper and tin workers in Minsk, Kiev, and Yekaterinoslav, that is, 6.8% of the Jewish craftsmen in these towns. ICA (*Jewish Colonization Association) statistics of 1897 reveal that there were then 15,669 Jewish smiths and 11,801 Jewish craftsmen in the various branches of the metal industry. The Jews were also well represented in the development of the industry: in Moscow four metal factories were established by Jews between 1869 and 1878, and a further two factories in the Moscow area between 1878 and 1880. Of the 96 large iron and tin plants in Odessa in 1910, 88 belonged to Jews. The laws of 1882 and 1887 excluded the Jews from the mines, but in spite of this they played a considerable role in the gold mines. Descendants of exiles and Jewish settlers in Siberia were among the pioneers of gold mining there. The director of the largest gold-mining enterprise in Russia in 1913, Lena Goldfields Co., was Baron Alfred Guenzburg; Jews were represented in the Gold Mining Co., and also in the platinum mines: of the five directors of the A.G. Platinum enterprise in 1912, two were Jews.

In the U.S. there were several prominent Jewish firms engaged in copper extraction. In 1813 Harmon *Hendricks established in Belleville, New Jersey, the Soho Copper Rolling Mills, later known as the Belleville Copper Mills. His descendants were prominent in the metal trade. In 1891 Meyer *Guggenheim (1828–1905), formerly a peddler and dry-goods merchant, acquired copper mines and then established an enterprise in Aguas Calientes, Mexico. Together with his sons he founded the mining company of M. Guggenheim's Sons. In 1901 they merged with the American Smelting and Refining Co. and the Guggenheim sons directed the enterprise. The firm initiated the acquisition and development of a copper mine in Alaska, developed copper mines in Mexico, and even extended its activities to Australia, Canada, and Africa.

Coal, which had been practically unknown in medieval Europe, was introduced into various branches of industry in England at the beginning of the 17th century because of the rise in the price of firewood. The Industrial Revolution increased the importance of coal, which came into use in the other countries of Europe during the 18th and the beginning of the 19th centuries. In Eastern and Central Europe the Jews were pioneers in developing coal mines. In Poland, prospecting by Solomon Isaac of *Bytom led to the establishment of two large coal mining enterprises in 1790: the Krol mine near Chorzow and the Królowa Ludwika mine near Zabrze, which were worked for about 50 years. Between 1874 and 1879 many Jews studied at the mining school of Tarnowskie Gory; they were later employed as miners and engineers in Upper Silesia. Jews participated in the wholesale coal and iron trade until World War II. The large coal concern of *Katowice was a development of the important coal firm of Emmanuel Friedlander and Co. Their activity in the coal mines led them to develop an interest in mining other metals and brought them into various branches of the metal industry. In 1805 there were three copper foundries in Podolia employing 42 Jewish workers; in Warsaw a Jewish iron factory, which employed 200 Jewish workers, was established in 1848. Until 1938, when the cartel organizations introduced their policy of ousting all factories not connected with international concerns, the iron foundry of Cracow belonged to Jews. In the wholesale iron trade, the old-established Warsaw firms of Priwess, and Freilach and Carmel were prominent; both prospered between the two world wars. According to the census of 1931, 1,462 Jews were employed in the mines (including 853 miners), 33,318 Jews were employed in metal foundries and in the metal and machinery industries (9,185 manual workers), and 4,209 Jews in the minerals industry (1,440 manual workers). The great majority of the Jews employed in the metal branch (73.9%) were craftsmen.

The Jews of Germany, too, were active in the coal industry in that country; many of them entered it via the coal trade or real estate business. Fritz Friedlaender-Fuld (1858–1917), an apostate, extracted coal in the Rybnik region. Eduard Arnhold (1849–1925), who had been director of the Caesar Wollheim coal firm, supervised a considerable part of the mining industry of Upper Silesia. Paul Silberberg succeeded his father as director of a lignite mine (Fortuna) in 1903.

In various parts of Czechoslovakia the Jews were the first to extract coal. The first person to exploit the coal mines of Ostrava-Karvina (Moravia), in 1840, was David Gutmann of Lipnik nad Becvu (see Wilhelm von *Gutmann). After obtaining the support of the Rothschild family, who owned iron works in Vitkovice, they established joint iron and mining enterprises there. At the beginning of the 20th century some of the coal mines of Kladno were owned by Jews, among them Leopold Sachs. The *Petschek family was active in the development of the lignite coal mines, particularly in northern Bohemia. Their competitor and former employer was Jakob *Weinmann.

[Jacob Kaplan]

In South Africa Jews were among the pioneers in the exploitation of South Africa's mineral resources. They were early in the field when industrial development started during the second half of the 19th century, and they remained prominent in the opening up of the country's coal, diamond, gold, and base metal mines. Jews like Barney *Barnato, the *Joel brothers, Lionel *Phillips, the *Beit brothers, and the *Albu brothers were among the prospectors, explorers, diggers, and financiers who flocked to the diamond fields at Kimberley in the 1870s. Sammy *Marks began coal mining on a large scale in the Transvaal and laid the foundations of the steelworks at Vereeniging. When the industrial focus moved to Johannesburg with the discovery of gold there in 1886, the Kimberley Jews played a foremost role in the creation of the great mining groups which developed the Witwatersrand. Here Sir Ernest *Oppenheimer created the powerful Anglo-American Corporation, headed the De Beers group, and stabilized the diamond market through the Diamond Corporation. Oppenheimer also pioneered the copper industry in Northern Rhodesia (now Zambia) and after World War II led the development of the new goldfields in the Orange Free State and in the Eastern Transvaal. During this period A.S. Hersov and S.G. Menell created the Anglo-Vaal mining and industrial group. Jewish financiers also promoted the exploitation of platinum, manganese, and asbestos deposits.

As for the oil industry (see *Petroleum), which was first developed in the second half of the 19th century, not only did the Jews participate in it (especially in Central and Eastern Europe) but Jewish industrialists were among the first to engage in the commercial exploitation of petroleum products.

From the above it is clear that the notion that Jews succeeded in forming part of the metal industry in the Diaspora only in secondary branches, close to the consumer, ignores the specific part they played in developing the primary branches. Even if this part was not quantitatively significant, there is no doubt that it was qualitatively important. It would appear that in those times and countries in which Jews were able to enter these branches of industry they engaged in them with great success.

Jewish Craftsmen in the Metal Trades. Many successive generations of Jews were engaged in various crafts connected with the metal industries. This continuity of occupation could be preserved chiefly in Muslim countries, where the Jews were enabled to conduct a more varied economic life than in Christian Europe. This was also true of such countries as Spain and Sicily which, although conquered by the Christians, still preserved modes of life from the days of Muslim domination. Jews were especially noted for arms manufacture. Jewish armorers are mentioned in the Mishnah (Av. Zar. 1:6), and Josephus describes the preparation of arms during the Jewish War (see, e.g., Jos., Wars, 3:22). *Dio Cassius, the historian of the second to third centuries C.E., relates that before the *Bar Kokhba War Jewish smiths deliberately manufactured defective weapons so that they would be rejected by the Romans and could later be used by Bar Kokhba's soldiers. From this account it can also be deduced that the Romans conscripted Jewish craftsmen to manufacture their arms. When *Muhammad gained control of *Medina, in southern Arabia, many of the weapons he obtained for his army were manufactured by local Jewish artisans. The "coats of mail of David" (probably named after a Jewish smith) were then famous in Arabia. The Jews of Portugal, too, excelled in this craft; their expulsion in 1496 brought a considerable number of them to Turkey, where they made a significant contribution to strengthening the military might of the Ottoman Empire.

The agent of the king of France in Constantinople during the first half of the 16th century tells of the numerous Marranos who revealed to the Turks the secrets of manufacturing cannons, guns, warships, and war machines. Obadiah of *Bertinoro found many Jewish copper and ironsmiths in *Palermo in 1487. When an expulsion decree was issued against the Jews of Sicily, in the wake of the expulsion from Spain, the local authorities complained that tremendous loss would result "because almost all the craftsmen" in Sicily were Jews; their expulsion would deprive the Christians of "workers who manufacture metal utensils, arms, and ironware." A similar complaint was heard in Portugal as a result of the expulsion order of 1496.

Many Jewish craftsmen and artisans were engaged in the metal industry in Christian Spain. In 1365 three Jewish smithies are mentioned in Toledo, and there were also Jewish workshops in Avila, Valladolid, Valdeolivas near Cuenca, and Talavera de la Reina; a Jewish tinsmith, Solomon (Çuleman) b. Abraham Toledano of Avila, is mentioned in a document of 1375; at the close of the 14th century Jewish smiths were called upon to repair the copper fountain of Burgos. Before 1391 many Jewish smiths, engravers, and goldsmiths lived in Barcelona. From a Saragossa register of 1401 we learn that there were many Jewish engravers and artisans in copper and iron. The local engraver's synagogue was used for the meetings of the community administration.

Jewish metalworkers continued to pursue their crafts along traditional medieval lines in various Muslim lands, where manual occupations were often despised and therefore pursued by religious minorities, particularly Jews. The report of the French consul on the condition of the Jews in Morocco at the close of the 18th century speaks of Jewish armorers there. The traveler *Benjamin II relates that Jews were employed in the iron industry in Libya in the middle of the 19th century. There are also reports on Jewish smiths who manufactured horseshoes there at the beginning of the 20th century. R. Ḥayyim *Habshush, who guided the researchers Joseph *Halevy and Eduard *Glaser in their search for ancient manuscripts in Yemen during the second half of the 19th century, was a coppersmith. Visiting that country in the late 1850s, R. Jacob *Saphir found many Jewish smiths. Yom Tov Ẓemaḥ reports that in 1910 the three remaining Jewish smiths of San'a were compelled to move to the provincial towns because of unemployment.

[Jacob Kaplan]

BIBLIOGRAPHY: IN THE BIBLE: M. Narkiss, *Metal Crafts in Ancient Palestine…* (1937), 113–25; N. Glueck, *Copper and Iron Mines in Ancient Edom* (1937), 51–60; idem, *The Other Side of the Jordan* (1954), 150–89; Albright, Arch; R.W. Forbes, *Studies in Ancient Technology*, 7 (1966); B. Rothenberg, in: PEQ, 94 (1962), 5–71; idem and A. Lupu, in: *Archaeologia Austriaca*, 47 (1970), 91–130; S. Abramsky, in: EM, 5 (1968), 644–61 (incl. bibl.). IN THE TALMUD: Krauss, Tal Arch, 2 (1911), 219–315; 3 (1912), 371; idem, in: JE, s.v.; M.D. Gross, *Oẓar ha-Aggadah*, 1 (1954), 223–5 (gold and silver). JEWS AS METALWORKERS AND MINERS: Baer, Urkunden, index; I. Abrahams, *Jewish Life in the Middle Ages* (1917, repr. 1960), 221, 226ff.; G. Caro, *Sozial und Wirtschaftsgeschichte der Juden im Mittelalter und in der Neuzeit*, 2 (1920), index, s.v. *Metall*; Baron, Social², 273; L. Hermann, *A History of the Jews in South Africa* (1935), 226–40; L. Berger, in: I. Halpern (ed.), *Beit Yisrael be-Polin*, 1 (1948), 211–3; A. Marcus, in: YIVOA, 7 (1952), 176–81; M. Hendel, *Melakhah u-Va'alei Melakhah be-Am Yisrael* (1955); M. Wischnitzer, *A History of Jewish Crafts and Guilds* (1965), index, s.v. *blacksmiths, coppersmiths*, etc.; I.M. Dijur, in: J.G. Frumkin et al. (eds.), *Russian Jewry* (1966), 140ff.; G. Saron and L. Hotz (eds.), *The Jews in South Africa* (1955), passim; *The Jews of Czechoslovakia*, 1 (1968), 371–7; S.M. Auerbach, in: YLBI, 10 (1965), 188–203; J. Jaros, in: BZIH, 35 (1960), 87–99.

METAPHYSICS, the philosophic discipline that deals with ontology and cosmology. The Jews through the end of the medieval period did little original work in metaphysics, drawing mainly on other, primarily secular, authorities. The major systems employed were *Platonism, *Kalam, *Neoplatonism, and *Aristotelianism, which appear in Jewish works largely in mixed form, containing elements borrowed from one another as well as from other philosophies, such as *Stoicism.

Moreover, the Kalam only constitutes a metaphysics in the broadest sense. While there was no one period in which any one of these metaphysical systems was exclusively subscribed to by the Jews, the periods of dominance for each were: Platonism, the first centuries before and after the Common Era; Kalam, the tenth century; Neoplatonism, the 11th and 12th centuries; and Aristotelianism, the 12th century through the end of medieval times. The foremost representatives respectively among the Jews employing these systems were *Philo, *Saadiah, Solomon ibn *Gabirol, and *Maimonides. The Jewish philosophers were primarily interested in meeting the challenges that various metaphysics presented to their Judaism and their understanding of revelation. Metaphysics, pursued scientifically through reason, produced ostensibly different conclusions about God, the universe, and salvation from those conveyed by the literal meaning of Scriptures. The religious thinker who valued human reason and did not wish to repudiate what was considered its profoundest activity met the challenge by reconciling and synthesizing metaphysics with Scripture. This was usually accomplished by partially limiting the validity of metaphysics, and partially by interpreting the literal meaning of Scriptures. Philo, in his great works of metaphysical and scriptural synthesis, formulated the basic methods for reconciling reason and revelation, which were employed throughout medieval philosophy not only by the Jews, but by the Muslims and Christians as well. It may be noted that not all Jews acquainted with metaphysics found its claims to truth convincing. Thinkers such as *Judah Halevi and Ḥasdai *Crescas met the challenge of metaphysics, not by reconciliation, but with trenchant critiques of its conclusions. As the validity of metaphysical knowledge in post-Cartesian thought came increasingly under attack from within philosophy itself, which concentrated primarily on the problems of epistemology, there existed little need for Jewish thinkers to meet speculative claims in the grand medieval style. However, in modern thought new challenges arose from rationalism and idealism, the scientific and empirical philosophies, and from existentialism which required the continued involvement of Jewish thinkers in philosophic thought.

BIBLIOGRAPHY: Guttmann, Philosophies; Husik, Philosophy; H.A. Wolfson, *Philo, Foundations of Religious Philosophy…*, 2 vols. (1947).

[Alvin J. Reines]

METATRON (Matatron), angel accorded a special position in esoteric doctrine from the tannaitic period on. The angelology of *apocalyptic literature mentions a group of angels who behold the face of their king and are called "Princes of the Countenance" (Ethiopic *Book of Enoch*, ch. 40, et al.). Once Metatron's personality takes a more definitive form in the literature, he is referred to simply as "the Prince of the Countenance."

In the Babylonian Talmud Metatron is mentioned in three places only (Ḥag. 15a; Sanh. 38b; and Av. Zar. 3b). The first two references are important because of their connection with the polemics conducted against heretics. In *Ḥagigah* it is said that the *tanna* *Elisha b. Avuyah saw Metatron seated and said, "perhaps there are two powers," as though indicating Metatron himself as a second deity. The Talmud explains that Metatron was given permission to be seated only because he was the heavenly scribe recording the good deeds of Israel. Apart from this, the Talmud states, it was proved to Elisha that Metatron could not be a second deity by the fact that Metatron received 60 blows with fiery rods to demonstrate that Metatron was not a god, but an angel, and could be punished. This imagery recurs frequently in different contexts in Gnostic literature and is associated with various figures of the heavenly realm. It is however thought that the appearance of Metatron to Elisha b. Avuyah led him to a belief in *dualism.

The story in tractate *Sanhedrin* also confers on Metatron a supernatural status. He is the angel of the Lord mentioned in Exodus 23:21 of whom it is said "… and hearken unto his voice; be not rebellious against him… for My name is in him." When one of the heretics asked R. *Idi why it is written in Exodus 24:1 "And unto Moses He said 'Come up unto the Lord,'" instead of "Come up unto Me," the *amora* answered that the verse refers to Metatron "whose name is like that of his Master." When the heretic argued that, if that were so, Metatron should be worshiped as a deity, R. Idi explained that the verse "be not rebellious against (תמר) him" should be understood to mean "do not exchange (תמירני) Me for him." R. Idi added that Metatron was not to be accepted in this sense even in his capacity as the heavenly messenger. Underlying these disputations is the fear that speculations about Metatron might lead to dangerous ground. The Karaite *Kirkisānī read in his text of the Talmud an even more extreme version: "This is Metatron, who is the lesser YHWH." It is quite probable that this version was purposely rejected in the manuscripts.

The epithet "lesser YHWH" is undoubtedly puzzling, and it is hardly surprising that the Karaites found ample grounds for attacking the Rabbanites over its frequent appearance in the literature they had inherited. The Karaites viewed it as a sign of heresy and deviation from monotheism. The use of such an epithet was almost certainly current before the figure of Metatron crystallized. The explanations given in the latter phases of the *Heikhalot* literature (Hebrew *Book of Enoch*, ch. 12) are far from satisfactory, and it is obvious that they are an attempt to clarify an earlier tradition, then no longer properly understood. This tradition was connected with the angel Jahoel, mentioned in the *Apocalypse of Abraham* (dating from the beginning of the second century), where it is stated (ch. 10) that the Divine Name (Tetragrammaton) of the deity is to be found in him. All the attributes relating to Jahoel here were afterward transferred to Metatron. Of Jahoel it is indeed appropriate to say, without contrived explanations, that his name is like that of his Master: the name Jahoel contains the letters of the Divine Name, and this therefore signifies that Jahoel possesses a power exceeding that of all other similar beings. Apparently, the designation "the lesser YHWH" (יהוה הקטן) or "the lesser Lord" (אדני הקטן) was first applied to Jahoel. Even before Jahoel was identified with Metatron, designations such as "the greater Jaho" or "the lesser Jaho" passed into Gnostic use and are mentioned in various contexts in Gnostic, Coptic, and also in Mandean literature, none of which mentions Metatron. The name *Yorba* (יורבא) in Mandean in fact means "the greater Jaho" but he has there been given an inferior status as is characteristic of this literature in its treatment of Jewish traditional concepts.

Two different traditions have been combined in the figure of Metatron. One relates to a heavenly angel who was created with the creation of the world, or even before, and makes him responsible for performing the most exalted tasks in the heavenly kingdom. This tradition continued to apply after Jahoel was identified with Metatron. According to this tradition, the new figure took over many of the specific duties of the angel *Michael, an idea retained in certain sections of the *Heikhalot* literature up to and including the Kabbalah. The primordial Metatron is referred to as Metatron Rabba.

A different tradition associates Metatron with Enoch, who "walked with God" (Gen. 5:22) and who ascended to heaven and was changed from a human being into an angel – in addition he also became the great scribe who recorded men's deeds. This role was also already delegated to Enoch in the Book of Jubilees (4:23). His transmutation and ascent to heaven were discussed by the circles who followed this tradition and elaborated it. The association with Enoch can be seen particularly in the *Book of Heikhalot*, sometimes also called the *Book of Enoch*, of R. Ishmael Kohen ha-Gadol, or the Hebrew *Book of Enoch* (H. Odeberg's edition (see bibl.) includes an English translation and a detailed introduction). The author links the two traditions and attempts to reconcile them. But it is clear that chapters 9–13 allude to the primordial Metatron, as Odeberg points out.

The absence of the second tradition in the Talmud or the most important Midrashim is evidently connected with the reluctance of the talmudists to regard Enoch in a favorable light in general, and in particular the story of his ascent to heaven, a reluctance still given prominence in the Midrash *Genesis Rabbah*. The Palestinian Targum (Gen. 5:24) and other Midrashim have retained allusions to Metatron in this tradition. Instead of his role of heavenly scribe, he sometimes appears as the heavenly advocate defending Israel in the celestial court. This transposition of his functions is very characteristic (Lam. R. 24; Tanḥ. *Va-Etḥannen*; Num. R. 12, 15). A number of sayings of the sages, in particular in *Sifrei, Parashah Ha'azinu*, 338, and Gen. R. 5:2, were explained by medieval commentators as referring to Metatron on the grounds of a corrupt reading of Metraton instead of *metator* ("guide").

In certain places in Merkabah literature, Metatron completely disappears and is mentioned only in the addenda that do not form part of the original exposition, such as in *Heikhalot Rabbati*. The descriptions of the heavenly hierarchy in *Massekhet Heikhalot* and Sefer ha-*Razim also make no mention of Metatron. On the other hand, Metatron is a conspicuous figure in the *Book of the Visions of Ezekiel* (fourth century) although he is mentioned without any reference to the Enoch tradition. This source mentions a number of the other secret names of Metatron, lists of which later appear in special commentaries or were added to the Hebrew *Book of Enoch* (ch. 48). Explanations of these names in accordance with ḥasidic tradition are given in the *Sefer Beit Din* of Abraham Ḥamoy (1858), 196ff., and in another version in the *Sefer ha-Ḥeshek* (1865). According to the traditions of certain Merkabah mystics, Metatron takes the place of Michael as the high priest who serves in the heavenly Temple, as emphasized particularly in the second part of *Shi'ur Komah (*Sefer Merkavah Shelemah* (1921), 39ff.).

One can, thus, detect different aspects of Metatron's functions. In one place he is described as serving before the heavenly throne and ministering to its needs, while in another he appears as the servitor (*na'ar*, "youth") in his own special tabernacle or in the heavenly Temple. In the tannaitic period, the duty of the "prince of the world" formerly held by Michael was transferred to him (Yev. 16b). This conception of Metatron's role as the prince of the world since its creation contradicts the concept of Metatron as Enoch who was taken up to heaven only after the creation of the world.

It is already observed in *Shi'ur Komah* that the name Metatron has two forms, "written with six letters and with seven letters," i.e., מטטרון and מיטטרון. The original reason for this distinction is not known. In the early manuscripts the name is almost always written with the letter *yod*. The kabbalists regarded the different forms as signifying two prototypes for Metatron. They again distinguished between the various components that had been combined in the Hebrew *Book of Enoch* in their possession. They identified the seven-lettered Metatron with the Supreme emanation from the *Shekhinah*, dwelling since then in the heavenly world, while the six-lettered Metatron was Enoch, who ascended later to heaven and possesses only some of the splendor and power of the primordial Metatron. This distinction already underlies the explanation given by R. *Asher b. David to *Berakhot* (see G. Scholem, *Reshit ha-Kabbalah* (1948), 74–77; and idem, *Les Origines de la Kabbale* (1966), 225–31).

The origin of the name Metatron is obscure, and it is doubtful whether an etymological explanation can be given. It is possible that the name was intended to be a secret and has no real meaning, perhaps stemming from subconscious meditations, or as a result of glossolalia. To support the latter supposition are a number of similar examples of names with the suffix – on: *Sandalfon (סנדלפון), Adiriron (אדירירון), etc., while the doubling of the letter *t* (טט) is characteristic of names found in the Merkabah literature, e.g., in an addition to *Heikhalot Rabbati*, 26:8. Among numerous etymological derivations given (see Odeberg, 125–42) three should be mentioned: from *matara* (מטרא), keeper of the watch; from *metator* (מיטטור), a guide or messenger (mentioned in *Sefer he-Arukh* and the writings of many kabbalists); from the combination of the two Greek words *meta* and *thronos*, such as *metathronios* (μεταθρόνιος), in the sense of "one who serves behind the throne." However, the duty to serve the heavenly throne was associated with Metatron only at a later stage and does not agree with the earlier traditions. It is highly doubtful whether the "angel of the Countenance" entering "to exalt and arrange the throne in a befitting manner" mentioned in *Heikhalot Rabbati* (ch. 12) can in fact be Metatron, who is not mentioned at all in this context. The Greek word *thronos* does not appear in talmudic literature. The origin of the word, therefore, remains unknown.

In contrast to the lengthy description of Metatron found in the Hebrew *Book of Enoch*, in later literature the material relating to him is scattered, while there is hardly a duty in the heavenly realm and within the dominion of one angel among the other angels that is not associated with Metatron. This applies particularly to kabbalistic literature (Odeberg, 111–25). Extensive material from the Zohar and kabbalistic literature has been collected by R. Margalioth in his work *Malakhei Elyon* (1945, 73–108). In books dealing with practical Kabbalah there are no incantations of Metatron, although his name is frequently mentioned in other incantations.

BIBLIOGRAPHY: H. Odebeg, *III Enoch or the Hebrew Book of Enoch* (1928); Scholem, Mysticism, 67–70; idem, *Jewish Gnosticism* (1965), 43–55; idem, *Les Origines de la Kabbale* (1966), 132–5, 225–31, 263.

[Gershom Scholem]

METCHNIKOFF, ELIE (1845–1916), Russian biologist, born at Ivanovka, near Kharkov. Metchnikoff's father was an officer of the Imperial Guard; his mother was Jewish (her family name was Neakovich). After graduating from the University of Kharkov he went to Germany for further training in biology. A succession of important discoveries in embryology earned Metchnikoff a reputation for originality and acuteness of observation, and in 1870 he was appointed professor extraordinarius at the University of Odessa.

The political upheavals and persecution of the Jews that followed the assassination of Czar Alexander II led Metchnikoff to leave Odessa in 1882. He went to Messina, a place especially favorable for the study of marine organisms. Here, during the course of studies on jellyfish and sponges, he began to turn his attention to the remarkable behavior of certain amoeba-like cells that ingest and destroy foreign particles in the body. Metchnikoff developed the theory that these cells, which he named "phagocytes," served to engulf and digest bacterial invaders of the organism. He set forth this thesis in an essay "The Struggle of the Organism Against Microbes" (1884).

In 1888 Pasteur invited him to Paris and gave him a laboratory at the Ecole Normale. When the Pasteur Institute was established, Metchnikoff became its subdirector. To this laboratory Metchnikoff attracted large numbers of investigators, whose research established the validity of the phagocytosis theory.

Metchnikoff later became interested in the problems of biological aging. In *Etudes sur la nature humaine* (1903; *The Nature of Man*, 1904) he advanced the idea that senile changes result from toxins produced by bacteria in the intestine. To prevent these "unhealthy fermentations," Metchnikoff advocated the inclusion of sour milk in the diet. In 1908 Metchnikoff shared the Nobel Prize for medicine with Ehrlich for his work on immunity.

BIBLIOGRAPHY: O. Metchnikoff, *Life of Elie Metchnikoff, 1845–1916* (1921), incl. bibl.; H. Zeiss, *Elias Metschnikow, Leben und Werk* (1932), incl. bibl.; A. Besredka, *Histoire d'une idée* (1921); T. Levitan, *Laureates, Jewish Winners of the Nobel Prize* (1960), 111–5.

[Mordecai L. Gabriel]

METHUSELAH (Heb. מְתוּשֶׁלַח), patriarch of mankind, son of *Enoch, father of *Lamech, and grandfather of *Noah (Gen. 5:21–25). The name has been variously explained as meaning "man of the weapon" or "man [worshiper] of [the deity] Salah." Methuselah in the genealogy of Seth (Gen. 5:2–21, P) is the counterpart of Methusael in that of Cain (4:18, J). The parallel is even more exact in the Septuagint which transcribes "Methuselah" in both instances. Methuselah according to the Bible lived 969 years, longer than any of the pre-Abrahamic fathers of the human race. Babylonian tradition attributes exaggerated longevity – tens of thousands of years – to its heroes. U. Cassuto believes that the Bible wishes to negate the fantastic figures which attribute to kings a longevity that is unnatural to human beings and that makes them godlike. Not even Methuselah attained the age of 1,000 years, a single day of the Almighty (Ps. 90:4). If the biblical story be compared with the prevailing Babylonian tradition, the many years of Methuselah seem a modest, even a short life-span. The Bible diminished the exaggerated ages attributed to people in the Ancient Near East, but still preserved the tradition of assigning extraordinary longevity to great men.

BIBLIOGRAPHY: K. Budde, *Die biblische Urgeschichte* (1883), 93–103; A. Ehrenzweig, in: ZAW, 38 (1919/20), 84; E.G. Kraeling, *ibid.*, 40 (1922), 154–5; M. Tsevat, in: VT, 4 (1954), 41–49, 322; U. Cassuto, *A Commentary of the Book of Exodus 1* (1961), 287.

METMAN-COHEN, YEHUDAH LEIB (1869–1939), educator in Ereẓ Israel. Born in Ostiya, a village in Ukraine, Metman-Cohen was ordained as a rabbi. He joined *Benei Moshe, and in 1904 settled in Ereẓ Israel, where he became headmaster of the school in *Rishon le-Zion. In 1906, he founded the first Hebrew high school in Jaffa, the Herzlia Gymnasium with 17 pupils and four teachers, and directed it until 1912; he was its headmaster again during World War I. Metman-Cohen was one of the founders of Tel Aviv (1909) and one of the initiators of Ir Gannim (1913), which eventually became *Ramat Gan. His publications included textbooks on the teaching of technical subjects in Hebrew and works on Hebrew language.

His wife, FANIA (1874–?), was one of the first teachers at the Hebrew high school in Jaffa and was active in the Women's Federation for Equal Rights.

[Abraham Aharoni]

°**METTERNICH, PRINCE KLEMENS WENZEL VON** (1773–1859), Austrian statesman. A supporter of Jewish rights in the German Confederation and abroad – although in Austria itself he did little for the Jews – at the Congress of Vienna he consistently supported the liberal policy of Karl August von *Hardenberg and Wilhelm *Humboldt (see Congress of *Vienna). He repeatedly warned the senate of *Frankfurt on the Main not to infringe upon the rights of its Jewish community and sent letters of protest to *Hamburg, *Luebeck, and *Bremen when they deprived their Jewish citizens of their civil rights. During the 1819 *Hep! Hep! riots he cautioned the Frankfurt authorities against letting matters get out of control. Metternich ordered his diplomatic agents to reveal France's complicity in the 1840 Damascus *blood libel affair. A frequenter of the sophisticated Jewish salons of Vienna, he associated, for business and pleasure, with the patrician Jewish banking families to such a degree that the *Rothschilds were suspected of aiding his escape from revolutionary *Vienna in 1848. His right-hand man, Friedrich von Gentz, was also sympathetic to Jewish causes.

BIBLIOGRAPHY: M.J. Kohler, *Jewish Rights at the Vienna Congress* (1918), index; S. Baron, *Die Judenfrage auf dem Wiener Kongress* (1920), index; N.M. Gelber, *Aktenstuecke zur Judenfrage am Wiener Kongress* (1920); idem, in: JJLG, 18 (1926), 217–64; I. Kracauer, *Geschichte der Juden in Frankfurt a. M.*, 2 (1927), 498–521; M. Gruenwald, *Vienna* (1936), index. **ADD. BIBLIOGRAPHY:** E. Timms, in: YLBI 46 (2001), 3–18; N. Ferguson, *ibid.*, 19–54.

METULLAH (**Metulah**; Heb. מְטוּלָּה, מְטֻלָּה), northernmost Israel village (moshavah). It stands on the Israel-Lebanese border, on the hill chain connecting the Naphtali Ridge with the *Hermon Massif and separating the *Ḥuleh Valley from the Iyyon Valley in Lebanon. Metullah was founded in 1896, on Baron Edmond de *Rothschild's initiative, by young settlers specially chosen for their ability to defend the isolated site. The name Metullah is derived from the Arabic.

Metullah progressed slowly until the 1950s, when water and electricity were supplied to the village, and new immigrants settled there. The village's economy was based on deciduous fruit orchards, vineyards, field crops, and cattle, but it also served as a summer resort. From 1977 until the Israeli withdrawal from Lebanon in 2000, the moshavah served as a transit point for Christian Lebanese citizens working in northern Israel. The population at the end of 1969 numbered 350, rising to 950 in the mid-1990s and 1,480 in 2002, with a new neighborhood constructed to accommodate newcomers. The settlement has municipal council status and an area of 0.8 sq. mi. (2 sq. km.). Income still derives mainly from the orchards (apples, pears, apricots, cherries, plums, and nectarines) and tourism, featuring a big sports center with an ice-skating rink.

WEBSITE: www.metulla.muni.il.

[Efraim Orni / Shaked Gilboa (2nd ed.)]

METZ (Heb. מיץ), capital of the Moselle department, in the northeast of France. Even if Simon, bishop of Metz in 350, was really of Jewish origin (as a later source claims), it does not prove that Jews were present in the town during that period. However, their presence is confirmed from at least 888; a *Church Council held in Metz at that date forbade Christians to take meals in the company of Jews. There is a reference that predates the 11th century to a Jew called David perhaps renting a vineyard. It was in Metz that the series of anti-Jewish persecutions accompanying the First Crusade began, claiming 22 victims in the town in 1096. Foremost among the local scholars in the early Middle Ages was *Gershom b. Judah ("Light of the Exile"). Although he lived mainly in Mainz, he was born in Metz, as was his disciple Eliezer b. Samuel. Another local scholar was the tosafist David of Metz. The medieval Jewish community occupied its own separate quarter, the *Vicus Judaeorum*, whose memory is perpetuated in the street named "Jurue." In 1237, every Jew who passed through Metz was compelled to pay 30 deniers to the town, but was not permitted to remain there. In the 15th century successive bishops, whose residence had been transferred to Vic, tolerated the Jews under their jurisdiction and granted them privileges (1442). In Metz itself, however, the Jews were allowed to stay only three days.

After the French occupation (1552), the first three Jewish families were admitted to reside there as pawnbrokers (1565/67). They were soon followed by others, and in 1595, 120 persons established a community that Henry IV and his successors took under their protection. Thanks to the influx of Jews from the Rhine areas, the community increased to 480 families in 1718 and almost 3,000 persons in 1748. Assigned to the Rhimport quarter, it established a self-governing body with elected trustees. Community officials levied numerous taxes that grew more burdensome after the introduction of the Brancas tax (1715), which had originated as gifts given by the community mainly to the duke of Brancas. The debts of the community became enormous, reaching 500,000 livres at the time of the French Revolution. With the consent of the king, community leaders chose a chief rabbi who was often renowned for his erudition. Among the rabbis invited to lead the community were Jonah Teomin-Fraenkel of Prague (1660–69), Gabriel b. Judah Loew *Eskeles of Cracow (1694–1703), and Jonathan Eybeschuetz (1742–50) – chosen from abroad. The chief rabbi judged lawsuits between Jews but from the 18th century the parliament sought to assume this right. To this end, it ordered a compendium of Jewish customs to be deposited in its record office (1743).

From the beginning of the 17th century the community owned a cemetery, a synagogue, and a poorhouse. In 1689 free and compulsory elementary schooling was introduced, and in 1764 a Hebrew press began publishing. The Jews were restricted in their economic activities by legal disabilities, however. While an oligarchy developed that achieved great wealth, the masses remained mired in poverty. Hostility toward the Jews reached its peak at the time of the execution of Raphael *Lévy (1670) for alleged ritual murder. Nevertheless, before the Revolution the jurists Pierre Louis Lacretelle (1751–1824) and Pierre Louis *Roederer of Metz, future members of the National Assembly, called for granting Jews full rights. The latter organized the famous concourse of the academy of Metz on this subject Jewish emancipation (1785). In 1792 Marquis de Lafayette, who commanded the army at Metz, proclaimed the religious freedom of the Jews. The proclamation was later suspended during the Reign of Terror (1794). The *consistory created in Metz in 1808, which included Moselle and Ardennes, served 6,517 Jews. The yeshivah (Ecole Centrale Rabbinique), which became the Rabbinical Seminary of France in 1829, was transferred to Paris in 1859. The synagogue, which had been destroyed earlier, was rebuilt in 1850, as was the almshouse in 1867. After the German annexation of Alsace-Lorraine (1871) about 600 Jews immigrated to France. Immigrants soon arrived from other parts of Germany as well. After 1918, when the region reverted to France, there was a massive influx of immigrants from Eastern Europe and from the Saar region. The Jewish population of the city numbered about 2,000 in 1866; 1,407 in 1875; 1,900 in 1910; and 4,150 in 1931.

[Gilbert Cahen / David Weinberg (2nd ed.)]

Hebrew Printing

In 1764 Moses May set up a Hebrew printing press in Metz. In association with the royal printer Joseph Antoine, May published a Yiddish translation of Daniel Defoe's *Robinson Crusoe* (1764) and the first edition of Bezalel *Ashkenazi's *Asefat Zekenim* (*Shitah Mekubbeẓet*, to tractate *Beẓah*, 1765). These works were followed by a large number of rabbinic and liturgical works, including the outstanding rabbis of Metz, such as Aryeh Leib b. Asher's novellae *Turei Even* (1781). May's effort to publish a small-scale edition of various talmudic tractates from 1768 onward led to his financial ruin. His son-in-law and successor Godechau-Spire printed several volumes of "enlightened" literature in Hebrew, such as a volume of riddles by Moses Ensheim (1787). May and his successors were active until 1793. Other Hebrew printers in Metz were Ephraim Hadamar and Seligmann Wiedersheim and successors. The Wiedersheim press continued to publish until 1870, when the German annexation of Alsace-Lorraine led to its closure.

Holocaust Period and After

Under German occupation in World War II, Metz, like the rest of Moselle and Alsace, was made judenrein following the flight of the population and the particularly brutal expulsions carried out by German troops. About 1,500 Jews died after being deported, among them rabbis Bloch and Kahlenberg. German soldiers plundered and defiled the two synagogues and destroyed the workhouse. The great synagogue was used as a military warehouse. After the liberation, the reorganized Jewish community began a slow process of reconstruction. In 1970 Metz had about 3,500 Jews (including some 40 families recently arrived from North Africa) and a well-organized communal body. Metz was the seat of the consistory of Moselle, which comprised 24 communities with a total of about 5,500 Jews; the largest communities were Thionville with 450; Sarreguemines with 270; Sarrebourg with 180; and Forbach with 300. In Metz itself, in addition to the great synagogue (Ashkenazi rite) with a seating capacity of 700, there are four smaller places of worship, including one Polish and one Sephardi. The community also ran a Talmud Torah, a kindergarten with a kosher canteen, a workhouse, a mikveh, and a ḥevra kaddisha. In 1987, the Jewish population of Metz was estimated to be about 4,000.

BIBLIOGRAPHY: Gross, Gal Jud, 346ff.; R. Anchel, *Juifs de France* (1946), 153–212; N. Netter, *Vingt siècles d'histoire…* (1938); J. Schneider, *La ville de Metz…* (1950), 288f.; R. Clement, *Condition des juifs de Metz…* (1903); A. Cahen, in: REJ, 7 (1883), 103–15; 204–26; 8 (1884), 255–74; 12 (1886), 283–97; 13 (1886), 105–26; Germ Jud, 2 pt. 2 (1968), 228ff.; H. Contamine, *Metz et la Moselle…*, 1 (1932), 44–46; 2 (1932), 352–9; A. Hertzberg, *French Enlightenment and the Jews* (1968), index, **ADD. BIBLIOGRAPHY:** Guide du judaîsme français (1987), 39.

METZGER, ARNOLD (1892–?), German scholar and author. Metzger was born in Landau in the Palatinate and began his career at the Hochshule fuer die Wissenschaft des Judentums in Berlin, where he taught from 1934 to 1937. In the face of rising Nazism he escaped to England, and then spent time in the United States where he became associated with Simmons College, Boston. After the war he returned to Germany, accepting a professorship in philosophy at the University of Munich. Much of his writing treats those areas of philosophy that touch on psychology; his contributions center on the phenomenology of recollection, perception, and the longing for death. His early books include *Phaenomenologie und Metaphysik* (1933); better known are his works on free will and determinism, *Freiheit und Tod* (1955), on transcendentalism, *Daemonie und Transzendenz* (1964), and on the ramifications of technology for the human personality, *Automation und Autonomie* (1964). His later interests include existentialism, social philosophy, and the American pragmatic school in juxtaposition to the German metaphysical schools. In this connection he wrote "William James and the Crisis of Philosophy" (*In Commemoration of William James*, 1942).

ADD. BIBLIOGRAPHY: K. Bloch, *Wir arbeiten im gleichen Bergwerk – Briefwechsel 1942–1972 Ernst Bloch und Arnold Metzger*, 1987.

METZGER (Metzger-Lattermann), OTTILIE (1878–1943), contralto. Born in Frankfurt, Metzger was a student of Selma Nicklass-Kempner in Berlin and made her debut at Halle in 1898. She sang and was the leading contralto at the Hamburg Stadttheater (1903–14) and appeared in Wagner operas at Bayreuth, gaining a reputation as a singer of dramatic parts. Her great roles there where Erda and Waltraute in *Götterdaemmerung*. Between 1916 and 1921 she sang with the Dresden Staatsoper. She toured in Austria, England (at Covent Garden she made her debut in 1902, singing in Wagner's *Die Meistersinger*, *Siegfried*, and *Tristan*), and the United States (1914–15), and appeared with the German Opera Company at the Manhattan Opera House, New York, in 1922–23. She taught in Berlin until the Nazi rise to power, took refuge in Brussels, and was deported to Auschwitz in 1942, where she met her death.

ADD. BIBLIOGRAPHY: Grove online.

MEUNITES (Heb. מְעוּנִים), an Arab tribe which lived on the border of the kingdom of Judah. Along with "the Philistines … and the Arabians that dwelt in Gur-Baal" (II Chron. 26:7), the Meunites paid a tax to *Uzziah king of Judah. At about the time of Hezekiah, the Meunites were attacked by the tribe of Simeon, which reached "to the entrance of Gedor, even unto the east side of the valley" (I Chron. 4:39–41). An inscription of the Assyrian king Tiglath-Pileser III indicates that at about this time (eighth century B.C.E.) the Meunites lived near the Egyptian border, which extended to the "Brook of Egypt" (Wadi el-Arish). There is no basis for J.A. Montgomery's identification of the Meunites of Chronicles with the Mineans, one of the south Arabian kingdoms whose economic activities and settlements reached as far as the oases in northern Arabia, or for A. Musil's location of them in the region of Ma'an in southern Transjordan. These theories are based upon references to the M(ε)ιναῖοι in the Septuagint and in works of the classical historiographers of the third century B.C.E. and later; the conditions reflected in these sources are later and do not conform to those of the eighth century B.C.E.

[Israel Eph'al]

MEVASSERET ZION (Heb. מְבַשֶּׂרֶת צִיּוֹן "Herald of Zion"), Israel urban settlement with municipal council status, 5 mi. (8 km.) W. of Jerusalem. The settlement's area extends over 2.2 sq. mi. (5.6 sq. km.). On a 2,600 ft. (799 m.) high hilltop the Romans erected a fortress, Castellum, to secure the road to Jerusalem. The Crusaders renewed it, calling it Castellum Belveer. This strategic spot became a small Arab village which preserved the ancient name (al-Qastal). During the Israel *War of Independence (1948), it changed hands in heavy battles, but finally (April 9) fell into Jewish hands. In 1951 the settlement Ma'oz Zion ("Stronghold of Zion") was established at the foot of Qastal Hill to house immigrants from Iraqi Kurdistan who worked in the nearby *Solel Boneh stone quarry, reactivated after the War of Independence. They developed fruit gardens and auxiliary farms. In 1956 a laborers' garden suburb, Mevasseret Yerushalayim, was established east of Ma'oz Zion, on a ridge close to the armistice lines of the time and north of *Moẓa. Its inhabitants found employment partly in the fruit orchards, in the Arazim Valley stretching south and east of Mevasseret Yerushalayim, and partly in Jerusalem. In 1963 Ma'oz Zion and Mevasseret Yerushalayim merged into one municipal unit, Mevasseret Zion, which in 1969 had 4,160 inhabitants. In the mid-1990s, the population was approximately 14,400, increasing to 20,800 in 2002. From 1978, 11 new neighborhoods were created there under the settlement's continual expansion. It attracts many Jerusalem residents, mainly secular, as an upscale location. It also has the largest immigrant absorption center in Israel, hosting 1,100 *olim*.

[Efraim Orni / Shaked Gilboa (2nd ed.)]

MEVORAKH BEN SAADIAH (11th century), **nagid* and leader of the Jewish community in Egypt. Mevorakh was a descendant of a family of scholars and physicians, and was himself a distinguished scholar; therefore, he is referred to in letters as *Sanhedra Rabba* ("member of the Sanhedrin"). His fame as a physician was such as to gain him an appointment at the Egyptian royal court. He succeeded his brother Judah as *nagid* in about 1080. At that time *David b. Daniel b. Azariah arrived in Egypt to wrest the leadership from the heads of the Egyptian community. He instigated others to bring false accusations against Mevorakh and forced the latter's banishment from the Egyptian capital to Fayyum and later to Alexandria. After some time Mevorakh succeeded in proving his innocence, and was reinstated as court physician and *nagid*. His triumph over David b. Daniel was complete by 1094. He wielded much influence with al-Malik al-Afḍal, the *Fatimid regent, and remained in his position until the beginning of the 12th century.

BIBLIOGRAPHY: Mann, Egypt, 1 (1920), 169, 188ff.; 2 (1922), 249ff.

[Eliyahu Ashtor]

MEVORAKH HA-BAVLI (11th century), *paytan* and poet. Although his family was Babylonian, Mevorakh lived in Ereẓ Israel or its surroundings. In the Cairo **Genizah*, parts of his *divan* were found, including both religious and secular poems, some of which have been published by various scholars. He was one of the first poets in the Oriental countries supported by philanthropic contributions, and, in his poems, explicitly appeals for support, adding praise for those who furnish it. In one of his poems, he mentions the philanthropist Abraham b. Samuel, from whom he requested a "night shroud" (i.e., a sheet), and, in another, one of his friends, R. *Abiathar b. Elijah ha-Kohen, the author of *Megillat Evyatar*. An acrostic bearing the name of the recipient, Yasa (?) ha-Kohen, appears in still another poem.

BIBLIOGRAPHY: S. Abramson, in: *Tarbiz*, 15 (1944), 216; M. Zulay, in: *Haaretz* (Oct. 3, 1948); A.M. Habermann, in: *Maḥanayim*, 36 (1958), 112f.; J. Schirmann, *Shirim Ḥadashim min ha-Genizah* (1965), 79–86. **ADD. BIBLIOGRAPHY:** A. Scheiber, in: AOB, 31:2 (1977), 237–45.

MEXICO, federal republic situated south of the United States of America with a population of 97,483,412 (2000) inhabitants and a Jewish community of about 40,000 (2000), most of whom live in Mexico City.

Colonial Period

The Jewish presence in Mexico began with the Spanish conquest led by Hernán Cortés in 1521. Many secret Jews and "Conversos" sought refuge in the newly conquered lands, and in this way a significant movement toward "La Nueva España" (New Spain – the name of Mexico in the colonial period) was initiated. There were two kinds of Conversos arriving in the "New World," first, the Crypto-Jews (also called disrespectfully "Marranos") who had been forced to convert and continued their traditions in secret and were looking for a better economic situation and a way to evade the persecution of the Inquisition's Tribunal. Many of those belonging to this group were accused before the Tribunal and their records were kept at the "Archivo General de la Nación" (Mexican National Archive), so that their history can be tracked. Also, there were those who were truly converted and integrated who hid their origin and their blood "impurity." The latter were the ones that most frequently gave away the Crypto-Jews and were incorporated to the Church structure; remarkable examples, among many others, were Fray Bartolomé de las Casas, Fray Alonso de la Veracruz, and Fray Bernardino de Sahagún.

Following the arrival of the Conversos in the New World, we can divide their history into three periods: from the discovery to the conquest (1492–1519); from 1519 until the establishment of the Inquisition Tribunal in New Spain in 1571; and from 1571 to 1810 during which the Tribunal functioned. The first stage was initially characterized by the abandonment of Spain, owing to the expulsion decree. Many Crypto-Jews and New Christians decided to sail with Columbus and other expeditions in order to discover new routes; they even financed these trips. Some remained in the newly discovered islands, while some returned and motivated others they knew into joining this adventure. Until 1502 the migratory restrictions were minimal. From then on, however, the Crown allowed access to the newly discovered lands only to the descendents of Christians who counted no converts among their ancestors or, in other terms, were "pure blooded" (*limpios de sangre*), meaning that the children of the Jews, the Moorish, the newly converted, and those processed by the Inquisition were not able to sail in official missions such as that of Nicolás de Ovando in 1502. Yet, beginning in 1511 restrictions became flexible owing to the need to populate the new lands with craftsmen, leading to an increase of the number of Conversos with a professional license as well as of businessmen. The commerce in false documents attesting to "pure blood" increased as well, allowing the sailing of a large number of Crypto-Jews heading toward the "Indias."

In the second period many Crypto-Jews participated with Hernán Cortés in the conquest of the mainland and in the defeat of the Aztec Empire situated in Tenochtitlan. We know about them because of the process against four of them that took place in 1528: two of the Morales brothers, Hernando Alonzo and Diego de Ocaña, were burnt at the stake and the other two received minor punishments. During this stage a significant arrival of Conversos took place, mainly from Madrid and Seville. They arrived as soldiers, conquerors, and colonizers. There is information that by 1536 there were in New Spain Crypto-Jewish communities in Tlaxcala and Mérida and there are files and records of the procedure against Francisco Millán, a bartender who sold Sabbath wine to the community and informed on a large amount of correligionists. Along with the development of the mining districts, the Crypto-Jews' settlements became diversified as well, such as in Taxco, Zacualpan, Zumpango del Rio, Espíritu Santo, and Tlalpujahua (1532), Los Reales del Monte in Pachuca, Atotonilco (1544), Zacatecas (1547), and Guanajuato (1554). By the end of the 16th century some small communities were known in Guadalajara, Puebla, Querétaro, Oaxaca, Veracruz, Michoacán, and elsewhere.

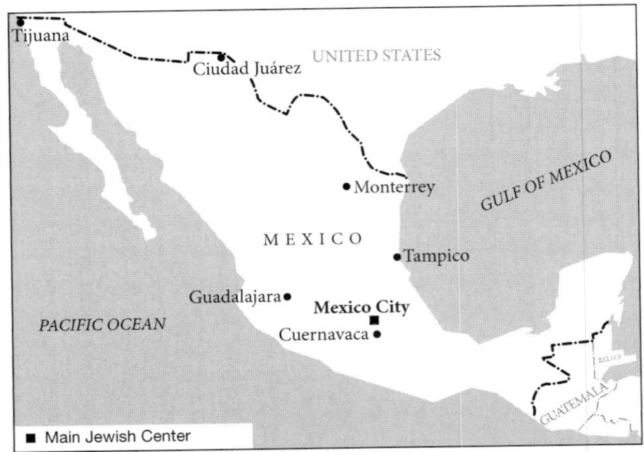

Main Jewish communities of Mexico in 2005.

The Conversos lived in specific neighborhoods and on certain streets; some dedicated themselves to the local trade, but they traded also with foreign countries, especially with Manila and the Philippines; these last ones ascended the social scale and married with "old" Christian Spaniards.

The third stage was initiated in 1571, a time by which the Crypto-Jewish communities were already consolidated. By the funding of the "Nuevo Reino de Leon," created in the northeast of Mexico by a New Christian called Luis de Carvajal y de la Cueva (who went by the nickname of "El Viejo" (The Elder)), and due to a concession of the Crown and as a reward to him for his pacifying the Chichimecas, a hundred Spanish families arrived there, most of them from a Crypto-Jewish origin.

During these years of economic progress, some Conversos from Portugal arrived; they were descendants of the Jews who had been expelled from Spain. Despite the fact that they had come to Mexico only ten years earlier, in 1589, one of their spiritual leaders, García González Bermejo, was discovered, judged, and condemned to death. In the same period there were some "autos-da-fé," capable of shocking the whole community of New Christians in Mexico. In 1590 a large number of Crypto-Jews were prosecuted, especially those coming from Portugal and Seville; among them were Hernando Rodríguez de Herrera and Tomás de Fonseca Castellanos. In 1596, 46 Conversos were prosecuted, and as a result a few from the Carvajal family were sent to the stake, among them Luis de Carvajal "El Mozo" (The Young) who had become one of the spiritual leaders of the community. In 1601, 45 Crypto-Jews were sent to trial and between 1574 and 1603, 115 "judaizantes" were prosecuted. Also Indians were prosecuted, accused of being adepts in Judaism, quite possibly converted by their Crypto-Jewish masters so they would not give them away. The proceedings present a clear view of the Conversos' everyday life, their meetings, the way they practiced their traditions, their occupations, and their active participation within the colonial society. Among their crafts particular notice may be given to the shoemakers, tailors, silver craftsmen, engravers, barbers, doctors, painters, wagon riders, musicians, lawyers, and solicitors.

From 1625 to the end of the 17th century, the migration of the Conversos and their descendants from Spain and Portugal diminished, and the persecution of the wealthy Crypto-Jews increased – actions that benefited the wealth of the Inquisition, which confiscated their assets. The inquisitors prosecuted over 200 people between 1620 and 1650 and from 1672 to 1676 a hundred more. Most of the accused came from Portugal, owing to the separation of the two kingdoms in 1640, which provoked increased persecution of Portuguese by Spain. Typical cases were those of Domingo Márquez, deputy major of Tepeaca in 1644, and Diego Muñoz de Alvarado, who was chief magistrate in Puebla de Los Angeles and accumulated a large fortune to the extent of having his own commercial ships.

The Faith Prosecutions did not stop. In 1646, 46 Conversos were prosecuted and were obliged to make a public "reconciliation" with the Church; in 1647 there were 21; 40 in 1648; and finally, on April 11, 1649, 35 were prosecuted out of which eight were executed by burning. From that moment the reconciliated were deported to the Iberian Peninsula to prevent them from reinitiating their Jewish practices for lack of surveillance. Among the deported were Captain Macías Pereira Lobo, sent to trial in 1662; Teresa Aguilera y Roche, wife of New Mexico's governor; Bernardo López de Mendizábal, judged in 1662; Captain Agustín Muñoz de Sandoval, sentenced in 1695; and a Crypto-Jewish monk tried in 1706 called Fray José de San Ignacio.

From the beginning of the 18th century through to the achievement of Independence (1821), migration disappeared and religious persecution diminished. The Crown and authorities of New Spain took care to prohibit the reading of books from European encyclopedia writers that had liberal and democratic ideas. By then the assimilation of Crypto-Jews into the society was much greater, causing the loss of Jewish customs and traditions due to the lack of contacts with outside political allies. Oral tradition survived in some cases, albeit deformed, and some objects went from generation to generation without a link to their ritual meaning. Some families did not forget their origins, and such was the case of a university professor, Francisco Rivas, who, by the end of the 19th century, published a journal called *El Sábado Secreto* ("The Secret Saturday"), in which he declared himself to be a descendant of Conversos from the Colonial period.

Despite the fact that the Inquisition ended symbolically as well as physically regarding Judaism, there are still some groups in Mexico that define themselves as Jews descending from the Crypto-Jews. The main congregations identified as such are the ones at Venta Prieta in Pachuca, Hidalgo, and Vallejo – a northern neighborhood of Mexico City. The members of those communities at Venta Prieta and Vallejo, named *Kahal Kadosh Bnei Elohim* (the leader of the latter in 2005 was Dr. Benjamín Laureano Luna), who have "mixed blood" and Indian features, claim that their genealogy comes from the colonial period. However, there are scholars like Loewe and Hoffmanthat who conclude that they are not Crypto-Jews but descendants of a protestant Evangelical church called "Iglesia de Dios" (Church of God). When the modern Jewish community got in touch with them in the 1940s, the problem of their inclusion or exclusion into the community arose. On the basis of anthropological studies by Rafael Patai, this community received attention from foreign Jews, who made several trips in order to support and teach them normative Jewish practices. The ambiguity in the relations remains, and the attitudes from the different community sectors are varied, from the religious and cultural acceptance to open rejection.

19th Century: From the Independence to 1900

When Mexico started its independent life in 1821, the decrees and legislation of the new Republic maintained Catholicism as the sole and official religion, despite the abolition of the Inquisition. Religious prejudices promoted by the church did not disappear and Catholics kept blaming Jews of "deicide" (God killers). The Mexican governments during the first 50 years of autonomy reached commercial and political agreements with some European companies that belonged to Jews, and it is possible that some of the latter lived temporarily or permanently in the country, though there was no community lifestyle. Religious freedom was proposed by a generation of liberals by the middle of the 19th century, under the leadership of Benito Juárez. His political and economic modernization project was established in articles 5 and 130 of the 1857 Constitution, which neither affirm religious freedom explicitly nor deny it.

At the time of the arrival of Maximilian of Austria as Emperor of Mexico (1864–67), some Jews from Belgium, France, Austria, and Alsace came with his court; they even talked about the possibility of building a synagogue, but the project was not accomplished, so religious services were held in private homes. One of the most outstanding personalities was Samuel Basch, chief surgeon at the Military Hospital at Puebla and personal doctor to the emperor in 1866. It was Basch who took Maximilian's remains to Vienna and after that published "Mis recuerdos de México" ("My memories of Mexico"). With the end of the empire most of these Jews returned to their countries.

During the "dictadura Porfirista" (dictatorship of President Porfirio Díaz, 1876–1911), the country was peaceful and foreign investors saw Mexico as a business option. Some foreign companies' representatives were Jews from France, Austria, Germany, Italy, Belgium, the United States, and Canada; however they did not identify themselves publicly as Jews. Assimilation prevailed among these Jews, manifested in intermarriage and integration into aristocratic society, with nationality as the most important aspect of their identity.

By the end of the 19th century, Jews from Russia and Galicia arrived in Mexico, and they were associated by the European Jewish press with colonization projects. In 1891, when the *Baron Maurice de Hirsch Fund was established in New York and the *Jewish Colonization Association (ICA) in London, several plans for the establishment of extensive Jewish farming settlements in Mexico were proposed. However, this was not accomplished due to the negative reports that were given by the experts who were sent to evaluate this possibility. They thought that the potential settlers would not be able to compete with the cheap local labor work. In 1899, when the first immigrants from Syria reached Mexico, the above-mentioned Francisco Rivas Puigcerver started with his weekly journal *El Sábado Secreto* (later called *La Luz del Sábado* – "Shabbat Light"), dedicated to Sephardi history and language.

Immigration and Community Organization (1900–50)
The deterioration in the quality of life of the Jews in the Turkish-Ottoman Empire, caused by political instability and the frequent wars with which they had to contend on their borders, forced the different Jewish communities to look for more appropriate geographical and economic arenas. Sephardi Jews from the Middle East, the Balkans, and Turkey (Ladino speakers), as well as Jews from Syria and Lebanon (Arab speakers), were the first interested in recreating a Jewish life in Mexican grounds.

Jews coming from Damascus and Aleppo maintained daily prayers and rituals inside private homes, owing to the fact that families had known each other previously and kinship was the basis for their strong union. Parallel to the informal gathering among the Syrian Jews, scattered Ashkenazim living in Mexico tried to organize a community. In 1904 a group called "El Comité" (The Committee) organized the Rosh Ha-Shanah services on the premises of a Masonic Lodge. After this event, there were several attempts at community organization, but it was not until 1908 in which the Union of American Hebrew Congregations, which was interested in establishing a Jewish community in Mexico to avoid illegal immigration to the United States, sent Rabbi Martin Zielonka to organize a congregation in Mexico. "The Committee" was then summoned and with the 20 attendees the "Sociedad de Beneficencia Monte Sinai" was established. However, the activities of this group were not fruitful, because many of them left the country with the outburst of the Mexican Revolution in 1910.

In 1912 the Alianza Monte Sinai – AMS re-constituted itself under Isaac Capon's initiative. Born in Turkey, he was aware of the need to have a Jewish cemetery, since upon the death of his mother she had to be buried in a Catholic graveyard. All of the Jewish residents in Mexico, including the Syrians, participated in the initiative, and thanks to the good relationship between one of its members, Jacobo Granat, with the president at that moment, Francisco I. Madero, the AMS received permission from the authorities for the acquisition of the first Jewish cemetery. In 1918 AMS bought a house on Jesus Maria Street in the center of Mexico City where they decided to build a synagogue. The day when President Venustiano Carranza gave his authorization signature became a memorable one, because it was the first time the existence of a Jewish community was recognized by law. AMS kept itself united with ups and downs for a decade, during which religious services and financial and social assistance were given to the new immigrants, including Hebrew classes, kosher meat, a *mikveh*, and the services of a *mohel*.

Between 1913 and 1917 the revolutionary conflict caused a decrease in the Jewish population. The victorious Carranza's regime, however, adopted liberal policies guided by the secular principle of religious freedom and, within this context, the formal recognition of the Jewish community, as well as other religions, meant the reconfirmation of modern ideology. After World War I, Jewish immigration continued, Sephardim as well as Ashkenazim, mainly from Eastern Europe. Their number in 1921 was estimated at around 12,000 persons, about 0.1% in a country of 12 million inhabitants. Many of these Jews used Mexico only as a stopover on their way to the United States. With the establishment of immigration quotas in the United States in 1921, which became stricter in 1924, many Jews decided to stay in Mexico.

The first Jewish immigrants from Europe arrived in Mexico in 1917 through the United States. They were young men who spoke Russian and Yiddish, who had evaded their military service and sustained political ideologies such as Zionism, Jewish Nationalism, and Socialism. They founded the first Jewish cultural organization in Mexico: the Young Men's Hebrew Association (YMHA), working as a club dedicated to the promotion of culture, sports, and society. This model was followed by some Jewish communities in the province, and during the 1950s also by the "Centro Deportivo Israelita" (CDI; Jewish Sport Center). In the 1920s the YMHA, with its headquarters at Tacuba street no. 15, in the center of the city, became a place for social gatherings and for economic assistance to the new Ashkenazi immigrants.

Prayer in the synagogue and religious services for the Jewish residents in Mexico City started in 1922. At that time over half of the Jewish population came from Turkey, Syria, Lebanon, and the Balkans. Nevertheless, Jews from Eastern Europe started to arrive by the thousands from Russia, Poland, Lithuania, Austria, Germany, Hungary, and Czechoslovakia, encouraged by the effects of World War I, the Russian revolution, and the economic depression in the area. In the 1920s alone approximately 9,000 Ashkenazim and 6,000 Sephardim increased the Jewish population to 21,000 persons.

An organizational readjustment occurred in this decade, characterized by the diversity in cultural patterns brought by the immigrants from their respective countries of origin. The differences in languages, in religious rituals, and in daily habits were obvious, especially among those who came from Europe and the Middle East. The Ashkenazi separation from the AMS was completed in 1922 when they decided to hold their religious services by themselves and to create their own organizations. The religious, ideological, and cultural plurality expressed in the welfare organizations, periodic publications, and artistic and cultural expressions show the dynamism of a community in the process of formation. In 1922 Nidhei Israel was created in order to take care of the religious needs (such as prayer, *talmud torah, kashrut, ḥevrah kaddisha,* and others). This institution became the Kehilá nucleus that was established with official recognition in 1957. After some attempts begun in 1923, the Zionist Federation was established in 1925, with the different ideological trends of the Zionist Ashkenazi Jews. In the 1920s and the 1930s there were also active Bundist and Communist organizations. The Sephardim formed their own Zionist organization, Bnei Kedem, in 1925, because they did not feel comfortable in meetings where the predominant language was mostly Yiddish. In 1924 the Yiddishe Shul – Colegio Israelita de Mexico was founded, the first of a wide network of Jewish day schools still in operation.

In 1924 Jews from Turkey, Greece, and the Balkans – Ladino speakers – decided to separate from the AMS and establish their own community and welfare association "La Fraternidad" in order to help their fellow countrymen with economic, medical, and social aspects. In 1940 the "Union Sefaradí" was founded, with the fusion of "La Fraternidad," the women's mutual aid society "Buena Voluntad," and the youth organization "Unión y Progreso." Since then, this community has had a day school (founded in 1943), two synagogues, and a cemetery as well as a formal administrative structure.

The AMS was left actually in the hands of the Syrian Jews. Those who came from Aleppo (halebies), however, did not actively take part, because they had their own places of prayer and their own *talmud torah*, so that their economic participation was very limited. They even built their own synagogue, "Rodfe Sedek," in 1931, and in fact were separated from the AMS. Problems arose when they wanted to make use of the cemetery and they were required to update the payment of their membership fees. The halebies founded their own communal and administrative institutions and bought their own grounds for a cemetery. In 1938 Sedaká uMarpé was founded, a charity society that grouped together the diverse institutions of men, women, and youth, as well as the observant groups that were in charge of the religious services, assistance, and social activities. On the other hand, the AMS, managed by the Damascenes since the second half of the 1920s, changed its statutes in 1935 and became an exclusive organization for this sector. By the end of the 1930s, the limits of the community structures were defined, so that community affairs administration would be taken care of by institutions organized according to their origin, and the original culture would be recreated within them, preserving the identity of the first immigrants.

ECONOMY AND SOCIAL STRATIFICATION. Since their arrival, Jewish immigrants dedicated themselves to commerce, mainly as peddlers. Before 1940 the Mexican population was basically rural, so that salesmen had to carry the goods to the smaller towns and not only to the urban centers. For this reason there were Jews who preferred to stay in the provinces and prospered as itinerant salesmen or with fixed or semi-fixed shops in the markets, even though most of them lived in the capital. Along with other foreign merchants, they introduced the credit system sales, which made it easier for their customers to enhance their lifestyle and acquire goods which otherwise would have been impossible to get. They sold shoes, socks, ties, fabrics, thread, stockings, ribbons, and some other consumer goods necessary for domestic use. In the second half of the 1920s, the B'nai B'rith contributed economically, together with the Ashkenazi associations, to incorporate immigrants; it gave them credit to start as merchants, taught them Spanish, and organized their social life.

In the 1930s, and as a result of the unemployment caused by the economic effects of the Great Depression of 1929, antisemitic and xenophobic movements promoted attacks against the vendors at "La Lagunilla" market. Antisemitism forced the small Jewish merchants to install their own commercial spaces as well as to establish small manufacturing workshops in order to protect themselves from the attacks of ultra-right nationalist groups, in the long run resulting in their economical ascendance. During this process the Banco Mercantil, founded by Jews in 1929 on the basis of a loan fund, financed the acquisition of machinery for the textile industry and industrial input assets. In 1931 the Cámara Israelita de Industria y Comercio (Jewish Industry and Commerce Chamber) was created in order to coordinate the economic efforts of the Jews and to serve as a representative organ of the Jews vis-à-vis the Mexican authorities and the society at large.

IMMIGRATION AND ANTISEMITISM. Mexican migratory policy turned from an open attitude to a restrictive one based on racial selection. Before the Mexican revolution there were practically no regulatory laws. In the 1920s, presidents Obregón and then Calles, in their national reconstruction goal, invited the Jews to move to Mexico with the purpose of promoting the economic development of the country. However, in 1927, the Mexican Congress approved new legislation on immigration according to racial criteria, considering the assimilation capacity of the immigrants into the *mestizo* (mixture of Indian and Spanish) races of the country as well as the country's economic absorption capacity and the immigrants' contribution toward its productive development. In 1929 the entrance of workers was prohibited and in 1936, the Population Law established differential quotas according to the national interest (racial assimilation and economic potential), elaborating tables with restrictions to the admission of certain foreign groups. German and Austrian Jews, who fled the racial laws of the Nazi government, had difficulties in entering the country, despite the intensive efforts made by the Jews on the local and international levels. For the Polish and Romanians only ten visas per year were available, clearly insufficient facing the scope of the European problem. Throughout the period of Nazi persecution (1933–45) Mexico accepted only 1,850 Jews.

The increase of antisemitism, expressed in the attacks of fascist groups, such as the "Camisas Doradas" (Golden Shirts), reinforced the unity of the Jewish community to resist the situation. The result of this union was the creation of the Comité Central Israelita de México (Central Jewish Committee of Mexico) in 1938 as an umbrella institution of all the existing Jewish organizations, becoming the only representative body recognized as the legitimate Jewish representative by the government, as well as by international Jewish institutions the world over, such as the *Joint Distribution Committee and the *World Jewish Congress. In 1944, the Anti-Defamation League was created within the Comité Central, becoming better known by the name of its journal *Tribuna Israelita*, with the objective of preventing antisemitism. The tumultuous antisemitic attacks from the ultra-right were silenced in 1942 when Mexico declared war on the Axis powers.

The 1940s in Mexico were outstanding, because it was the starting point for a sustained economic growth that lasted for over 30 years. World War II promoted the export of food and basic goods into the United States as well as the strengthening of the Mexican internal market. The imports substitution program, launched by the government, stimulated the creation of industries in a protected economic environment. The Jews saw in this project the opportunity for improvement, so they established manufacturing factories, especially in the textile field. Their economic status improved and the occupational areas that participated were also diversified. A survey performed in 1950, among the Ashkenazi sector, found 52 occupations in different fields, especially commerce and industry and also professions such as medicine, engineering, and the sciences.

Jewish Education

In many cases the community institutions organized schools of Jewish studies for the children of their members. They established *talmudei torah* and *Kutabim* (complementary traditional schools), and also day schools in which general studies were imparted together with subjects of Jewish culture. At the beginning the Jewish studies were learned in Yiddish, Arabic, or Spanish, together with rudimentary knowledge of Hebrew. The first day school was the Yiddishe Shul – Colegio Israelita de Mexico, established in 1924 by Meir Berger. During the first decade Jewish studies were taught in Yiddish. In the 1930s a few attempts were made to teach in Hebrew but they failed. Since then the school has defended Yiddish as a fundamental cultural current of Judaism. In the 1940s many new schools were established, according to the ideology of the founders and the parents, and also according to the community of origin of the families. Two schools were established in 1942: the Hebraist school Tarbut by Avner Aliphaz and Yeshaiahu Austridan, and the Ashkenazi religious school Yavneh. They were followed by the Hebraist schools of the Sephardi community (1943) and that of the AMS (1944). All these schools adhered to the Zionist movement or sympathized with it, and after 1948 they were among the most important vehicles for the linking of the communal identity with Israel. In 1946 a Teacher's Seminary was established in the Yiddishe Shul by its new principal, Avraham Golomb. In 1947 the day school Sedaká uMarpé of the Aleppan community was founded and functioned until 1951 without a curriculum in Jewish studies. In 1950 Avraham Golomb left his former school and established a new Ashkenazi school – the Naye Yiddishe Shul I.L. Peretz – Nuevo Colegio Israelita with a Yiddishist trend and inclination towards the Bund. The Sephardi School, the Monte Sinaí School, and the Teacher's Seminary adhered to the Zionists and adopted the educational politics sent from Israel to the Diaspora. The schools were connected to the Vaad haHinuch (educational council), that was linked with the Jewish Agency and the State of Israel. The Jewish Agency assigned to the schools in the 1950s, 1960s, and 1970s Israeli *sheliḥim* – teachers and principals – to teach Hebrew, Yiddish, and Jewish culture, and to bring the schools closer to the Jewish state. Since then the schools have employed Israeli educators on their own.

ZIONISM. The events that marked world Jewish history in the middle of the 20th century, the Holocaust and the creation of the State of Israel, were present in the life of the Jewish Mexican community and its leaders. Zionism was the flag identifying Mexican Jews vis-à-vis the national society. The Jewish efforts to achieve the legitimation of the national Jewish aspirations and the obtaining of a favorable vote from Mexico on the partition of Palestine in the United Nations in November 1947, was the main challenge for the Zionist sector. The coordination, unification, and efforts were manifested in the creation of the Zionist Emergency Committee and the Emergency pro-Palestine Jewish Committee, representative organizations of the Jewish community before the Mexican society. The legitimate demands that accompanied the Zionist ideals as a national liberation movement, gave a positive image of Judaism, compensating for the impact of previous anti-Jewish expressions and demonstrations, despite the abstention of Mexico in the United Nations in 1947.

The creation of the State of Israel in 1948 had concrete effects within the internal dynamic of the Ashkenazi sector; the organized unification of the Zionist parties and groups became a reality in 1950. The Zionist Federation of Mexico became the framework in which the different sectors coordinated their efforts thanks to the links established with Israel. The new state replaced the Zionist party organizations with government institutions, a process that the Zionists in Mexico also followed as they developed community institutions. Since then, Israel became the central issue for the secular Jewish solidarity and identification. Within the Sephardi community, the Zionist youth organizations were very active. In the case of Sedaká uMarpé and AMS, Zionism introduced a new element of identity and Jewish pride, and gave meaning to their work on behalf of the State of Israel.

Consolidation of the Jewish Community in Mexico 1950–2000

During the first half of the 1950s the Club Deportivo Israelita (CDI) was created, becoming the largest organization of Mexican Jewry, with the affiliation of Jews from all the community's sectors, becoming one of its most inclusive institutions. The objective of the CDI was to stimulate physical and cultural activities allowing the association of children, youngsters, and adults. Around 15,000 Jewish families are members of the CDI, including some non-affiliated.

The two main communities that consolidated outside Mexico City and its metropolitan area since the 1930s are Monterrey and Guadalajara, consisting of approximately 150 families each. Having created institutions that include synagogues, schools, recreational facilities, and their own cemetery, both maintain religious institutions and organizations for women and men, where Ashkenazim and Sephardim gather in the same community space. In Tijuana there is also a community of 70 families that since 1943 had been closely linked to the U.S. community of San Diego. Some Jewish families also live in Veracruz, Puebla, and Cuernavaca, however, with no representative institutions. In the 1990s, in Cancún, community life has been promoted among the 70 families that moved to that city.

In the 1950s and the 1960s the Jewish institutions were consolidated. The fast economic ascent of the Jewish families, made possible the change of residential neighborhoods in Mexico City: from the downtown area and "Colonia Roma" to "Condesa" and "Polanco"; for this reason some new community facilities were built, such as large and elegant synagogues, new school buildings, new community centers, and places for the youth movements. These were the years in which the religious attachment diminished because the Jewish core identity remained linked to Zionism, coinciding with the secularization process with which Mexican society was experimenting along with its fast growing urban modernization. It is quite significant that during this period there emerged the only two Conservative synagogues that exist in Mexico City: Bet Israel created in 1953 by American Jews, and Bet El founded in 1963 by Ashkenazi Jews who were not able to find in the religious legacy of their parents a meaningful Judaism, and decided to be separated from the Kehilá in order to practice more modern religious forms that were closer to their reality. However, in the Ashkenazi sector as well as among the Sephardim, there remained vigorous nuclei of religious Orthodox families who continued the rites and practices preserving the different modalities according to the original tradition of the immigrants.

SOCIAL INTEGRATION AND IDENTITY. The socioeconomic improvement placed the Jews in the upper levels of the Mexican society and their cultural practices resembled those of the elite. Many sent their children to American schools to learn English, intermingled with Mexican entrepreneurs to do business, and made frequent trips to the United States. The Jews learned how to adapt themselves into the Mexican political system; they registered their institutions according to the national schemes, e.g., the welfare societies were registered in the Secretaría de Salubridad y Asistencia (Health and Welfare Ministry). However, an asymmetric relationship with the government prevailed, since it recognized the Jews as citizens, but did not consider them as a distinct group, although in fact it did treat them as such. This situation was reproduced in the next generations, which were perceived as foreign as their parents had been, despite the cultural synthesis with which they were experimenting, and they remained suspect of maintaining dual loyalty, to the Jewish people and to the Mexican nation, which in a way took away their credit as legitimate Mexicans. This constant questioning led the Jewish community to live as an enclave, at the margins of the political and social life of the country. The isolation of the Jews was the result of an internal attitude of wanting to preserve the social community living space, and an external one due to the rejection of the general society to admit differences.

By the 1970s the anti-Zionist government policy was expressed in the international arena, when in 1975 the president of Mexico, Luis Echeverría, proposed, before the United Nations General Assembly, that Zionism was a form of racism. The Mexican-Jewish community had very little influence on trying to alter this proposal, which was approved by the majority with the support of the Arab nations and their allies of the Third World. Diplomatic relations between Mexico and Israel became tense and the tourism boycott of the American Jews against Mexico had an influence on the change of the Mexican position towards Zionism. This change came in 1992 when another Mexican president, Carlos Salinas de Gortari, proposed at the United Nations General Assembly to abrogate this resolution, a proposal that was approved.

The third Jewish generation in Mexico lived in a hard national economic context, marked by a crisis that returns every six year, which means they have to confront a constant challenge to the maintenance of the social status acquired by their parents. In the 1980s and 1990s, Mexico and the world were facing changes in the economic model toward an open economy. Not all the Jews adapted themselves successfully. Just like other small- and middle-sized merchants and industrialists in the country, they suffered from the consequences of the international competition for which they were not prepared. The opening of the Mexican markets provoked a strong readjustment in the textile industry and a great recession in the construction field, areas in which a large number of Jewish entrepreneurs were involved. The collapse of enterprises and the consequent loss of jobs among the Jews led to more employees and professionals and fewer company owners. Facing this situation, all the community organizations started a program known as "Fundación Activa" which gives training and tutorial assistance for self-employment and for the creation of micro-enterprises that do not require large investments. This and other assistance programs contributed to the stability and cohesion of the Mexican Jewish community and helped to maintain its institutional diversity and its demographic and socioeconomic level, preventing poverty and/or migration.

From the 1990s Mexican Jewry experienced an increase of religiosity in some of the community's sectors, that may be associated with this economic, political, and cultural trend in the global and national environment. The number of synagogues and especially of *midrashim* and *kolelim* (religious adults' study centers for bachelors and married men respectively) rose, in particular in the most Orthodox sector, the Maguén David Community, formerly the Aleppan Sedaká uMarpé. This trend is a new development in the religious life in Mexico, since it is linked to the ultra-Orthodox movements from Israel, in which there is a kind of synthesis of the religious tradition of the communities of Middle Eastern origin with the Ashkenazi tradition.

A significant change in the relations between the Jewish community and the Mexican State was felt after the creation of the "Ley de Asociaciones Religiosas y Culto Publico" (Religious Associations and Public Cult Law) in 1992. Until the 1990s, the Jewish minority had adapted to the limited space given by the State, registering itself as civil associations. Since the 1940s, the relations between State and Church were based on the agreement, according to which the government did not interfere in the affairs of the Church in exchange for the recognition of the Church in the sociopolitical hegemony of the State. This relation was also applied to the Jewish case. This was illustrated in the increase in Jewish schools during the 1940s, which besides the official program taught Jewish history, Bible, and tradition which could be interpreted as religion. The State tolerated this kind of expression even though it was forbidden by law.

The reforms of 1992 in the Constitution, related to the legal recognition of the religious institutions and their public activities, attempted to normalize the common practices. This kind of legality recognizes the legitimacy of group consolidation through the religious identification. The religious associations became another channel of collective expression. The religious and ideological diversity in the society increased in correlation with a greater democratization of political and cultural life. Gradually the participation of the Jews in these areas is becoming wider and less questioned everyday, and the presence of Jews in senior official posts is becoming more frequent.

In the Beginning of the 21st Century

As we have seen, the Jewish community in Mexico is highly organized within well-defined communities according to the origin of the first immigrants; each of these groups is represented at the Comité Central de la Comunidad Judía de México (Central Committee of the Jewish Community of Mexico) which is in charge of maintaining the relations with government authorities as well as with the social and cultural organizations in the country. Tribuna Israelita is the executive arm of the Comité Central in anti-defamation duties, preventing and denouncing antisemitism and violence against Jews.

DEMOGRAPHY. According to a socio-demographic study of the Jewish community in Mexico, performed by request of the Comité Central in 2000, the number of families and their percentage per sector is as follows: Maguén David: 2,630 families (25.8%), Monte Sinaí: 2,350 (23.0%), Kehilá Ashkenazí: 1,870 (18.4%), Sephardi Community: 1,150 (11.3%), Bet El: 1,080 families (10.6%), CDI: 340 families not affiliated to other sectors (3.3%); Bet Israel: 260 (2.6%), Guadalajara: 250 (2.5%), and Monterrey: 250 families (2.5%), which gives us a total of 10,180 families.

Demographic tendencies show a larger growth in the non-Ashkenazi sectors that became the majority of the Jewish population in Mexico. Almost all the Jews marry Jewish spouses. According to the socio-demographic study of the Jewish population performed by DellaPergola and Lerner in 1991, between 5% to 10% of the marriages are exogamic. Marriages within the community of origin are the most frequent, even though every day there are more inter-communal marriages. The main Jewish residential neighborhoods are located in the northeast of the Metropolitan area: 28.6% live in Las Lomas, 21.8% in Tecamachalco, 21.6% in Polanco, 16% in La Herradura, and the rest in Hipodromo-Condesa, Narvarte, Satélite, and other neighborhoods.

The occupational structure is as follows, according to the data of 1991: 53% of the economically active people are in the managerial sector as owners of businesses and directors, 27% professionals, 11% office employees, 5% merchants, and 4% handcraft workers. The analysis of this data by age groups confirms the well-known upward economic mobility of the Jewish population as well as the tendency toward a larger professional sector in the new generations. The total of the work force is divided into three groups according to the branch of production: industry (35%), commerce (29%), and services (28%) and two groups with minor incidence, which are construction (3.5%) and personal services (4%). The family and social networks have an important influence in the integration pattern of the working force in economic activity and represents 75% of the work location grounds.

JEWISH EDUCATION AND JEWISH CULTURE. The Jewish education network, with over a dozen schools in Mexico City, has professional educators and shows high academic levels. It is estimated that more than 80% of the Jewish children attend Jewish day schools from kindergarten to secondary school. Some of these day schools have Jewish religious studies as in a yeshivah. The Jewish curricula of these day schools include Hebrew language and literature, Jewish history, Bible, tradition, and in some of them Yiddish language and literature. There is a Jewish pedagogic college – Universidad Hebraica – which prepares new professionals for Jewish education. The Universidad Iberoamericana (a private university) offers a study program on Jewish Culture linked to disciplinary studies in the Humanities. The educational level in the Jewish community has increased considerably: in 1991, 57% of the Jews in the 30 to 64 age group were university graduates, as compared with 8.5% for those older than 65. Most frequently, people with graduate and postgraduate studies are found among the members of the Bet El and Bet Israel congregations (49%) and in a slightly lower proportion in the Kehilá Ashkenazí (38%). Conversely, the presence of people with university studies is lower in the Maguén David and Monte Sinaí communities (18 and 10% respectively). However these differences tend to diminish in the younger generations. In addition to education, community life dynamics are expressed in a variety of social and cultural activities. Besides the activities performed by each of the community sectors, there are also inter-communal organizations, such as the women's associations WIZO, Na'amat, and the Mexican Federation of Jewish Women or the Mexican "Friend Associations" of the Israeli universities.

There are around 16 youth movements with approximately 2,000 members, most of them identified with the State of Israel. Each year several hundred Mexican Jewish youngsters visit Israel in groups organized by the schools. The Federación Mexicana de Universitarios Judíos (FEMUJ) and the Federación de Universitarios Sionistas de Latinoamérica (FUSELA) have a significant presence in the community. Since 1948, nearly 4,000 Mexican Jews have made *aliyah*.

The Jewish press is diverse but mainly dedicated to inner community matters. The news or ideological publications typical of the 1940s and the 1950s, mainly in Yiddish, no longer exist. Each community sector has its own bulletins and periodic magazines. There are some independent organs such as *Foro* magazine distributed through subscriptions or *Kesher* with free distribution in all the communities and the Centro Deportivo Israelita. The Jewish journalists and writers association meet and express themselves through the community press.

The Jewish museum named Tuvia Maize is dedicated to the history of the Jewish community in Mexico and to the Holocaust. At the Ashkenazi Kehilá there was established a Centro de Documentación e Investigación (Center for Documentation and Research); it preserves historical documents of the Jewish Community in Mexico, as well as books in several languages, that were part of private libraries of the first immigrants, and promotes the publication of documentary books and researches.

Another important cultural site is the Centro Deportivo Israelita (CDI), which besides having excellent sports facilities, has an art gallery, a theater, and a banquet hall. This is the location of the most important Annual Jewish Dance and Music Festival in Latin America.

RELIGIOUS LIFE. In Mexico City there are around 25 synagogues and an equal number of small places for prayer and study that belong to the most Orthodox sectors in the community. Two of the synagogues are Conservative, and all the others are Orthodox. The level of religious observance has increased by 4% from 6.7% Orthodox Jews, according to the results of the socio-demographic study of 1991, to 10.7% according to that of 2000. Most of the Mexican Jews consider themselves as traditionalists (76.8%) while the non-observant, secular, and atheist Jews comprise 12.5%, according to the data of 2000. When analyzing figures per community, Maguén David presents the lower index of traditionalists (66%) and an equal number of Orthodox (17%) and non-observants (17%), which shows a tendency toward polarization of the religious and the non-religious. In contrast, 86% of those affiliated to Bet El considered themselves traditionalist. The most popular ritual practice is the Passover *seder* celebrated by 93% of the population within the family. In second place is the Yom Kippur fast observed by 89%, and after that, Hanukkah festivities in which 71% perform the ritual of candle lighting, while the frequency of other religious practices is reduced to half or less. In relation to the regular observance of Shabbat, 12% rest, 49% eat kosher meat, and 19% separate their dishes.

RELATIONS WITH ISRAEL. Mexico abstained in the vote of November 29, 1947, on the Partition of Palestine. On April 4, 1952, Mexico recognized the State of Israel, and shortly afterwards the two countries established diplomatic relations, opening embassies in both countries. At the beginning, Mexico adopted a policy of neutrality, abstaining from voting at the international forums where Middle East affairs were dealt with. However, since the Six-Day War in 1967, this position changed and Mexico frequently votes against Israel. The most delicate moment was the above-mentioned equation of Zionism with racism in the 1970s abrogated in the 1990s.

Commercial exchange between the two countries was very low until the end of the 1970s (with an annual average of under $2 million). In the 1980s its scope started to increase, with an average of $25 million annually (14.8 exports from Israel and 11.3 imports). In the 1990s, bilateral relations improved: cultural agreements were signed, and there were visits from ministries and functionaries of both countries. Israel has provided technical and scientific counseling to certain areas of agriculture and industry in Mexico, and Israel also buys manufactured products, food, and Mexican oil. Nevertheless, the volume of trade remained close to the same level. In 2000 a Free Trade Agreement was signed between both countries when President Ernesto Zedillo visited Israel, and ever since, economic exchange has increased. Exports from Israel jumped to $212 million and imports grew to 17 million. This unbalanced relation between exports and imports has continued since then. The total volume of commerce in 2001 was over $169 million (155.6 exports and 13.5 imports), in 2002 close to $212 million (191.6 and 20.2), in 2003 over $246 million (228.7 and 17.6), and in 2004 more than $362 million (340.5 and 22.1).

[Liz Hamui (2nd ed.)]

ADD. BIBLIOGRAPHY: P. Bibelnik, "*Olamam ha-Dati shel ha-Mityaḥadim be-Mexico ba-Me'ah ha-Sheva-Esreh*," in: *Pe'amim*, 76 (1998), 69–102; idem, "*Mishpetei ha-Inkvizizyah neged ha-Mityaḥadim be-Mexico (1642–1659)*," in: D. Gutwein and M. Mautner (ed.), *Law and History* (1999), 127–45 (Heb.); J. Bokser-Liwerant (ed.), *Imágenes de un Encuentro. La presencia judía en México durante la primera mitad del siglo XX* (1992); I. Dabbah, *Esperanza y realidad. Raíces de la Comunidad Judía de Alepo en México* (1982); S. DellaPergola and S. Lerner, *La población judía en México: perfil demográfico, social y cultural* (1995); D. Gleiser Salzman, *México frente a la inmigración de refugiados judíos, 1934–1940* (2000); A. Gojman Goldberg, *Los Conversos en la Nueva España* (1984); A. Gojman de Backal, "Los Conversos en el México Colonial," in: *Jornadas Culturales. La presencia judía en México* (1987); idem, *Generaciones Judías en México. La Kehilá Ashkenazí (1922–1992)* (1993); idem, *Camisas, escudos y desfiles militares. Los Dorados y el antisemitismo en México (1934–1940)* (2000); N. Gurvich Peretzman, *La memoria rescatada. La izquierda judía en México y la Liga Popular Israelita 1942–1946* (2004); C. Gutiérrez Zúñoga, *La Comunidad Israelita de Guadalajara* (1995); L. Hamui de Halabe (ed.), *Los Judíos de Alepo en México* (1989); L. Hamui de Halabe, *Identidad Colectiva. Rasgos culturales de los inmigrantes judeoalepinos en México* (1997); idem, *Transformaciones en la religiosidad de los judíos en México* (2004); C. Krause, *Los judíos en México. Una historia con énfasis especial en el período 1857 a 1930* (1987); S. Liebman, *Los judíos en México y América Central (Fe, llamas e Inquisición)* (1971); A. Toro, *La Familia Carvajal* (1944); M. Unikel Fasja, *Sinagogas de México* (2003); E. Zadoff, "La disputa en torno al idioma nacional en los colegios judíos ashkenazíes de México a partir de la década de 1930," in: *Judaica Latinoamericana*, 4 (2001), 135–55; G. Zárate, *México y la diáspora judía* (1986).

MEYER, ANNIE NATHAN (1867–1951), U.S. educator, activist, and writer. Born in New York City to a family of early colonial stock (see *Nathan family), Meyer was an autodidact. Dissatisfied with the lack of serious educational opportunities for women in New York, Meyer determined to found a college for women within Columbia University, advocating her cause on the speaker's platform and in the press. When she had obtained substantial financial contributions, she negotiated with the trustees of Columbia University, and, in just two years, her efforts were realized. In 1889, two years after her marriage to ALFRED MEYER, a prominent New York physician, Barnard College opened, and Meyer became its lifelong trustee. The Meyers had one daughter who died tragically in 1924.

Although Annie Meyer considered herself a feminist, she opposed the women's suffrage movement. Decrying unintelligent use of the vote, she called for the inclusion of an educational clause in the suffrage bill. Meyer was the prolific author of plays, novels, social studies, magazine articles, and art reviews, including *Barnard's Beginnings* (1935) and *Women's Work in America* (1891; rep. 1972). Her first novel, *Helen Brent, M.D.* (1892), celebrated a woman who chose medicine over marriage. However, Meyer idealized motherhood and expressed her opposition to mothers who worked for self-fulfillment in two plays dealing with that theme, *The Dominant Sex* (1911) and *The Advertising of Kate* (produced on Broadway in 1921). Another play, *Black Souls* (produced and published in 1932), dealt with hypocrisy and race relations in the American South. Her autobiography, *It's Been Fun*, appeared in 1951.

Meyer was an active lecturer and publicist who spoke to both Jews and African Americans about the "challenge of prejudice" and the need for pride in one's heritage. True to her principles, she sponsored and supported several Jewish and African-American students at Barnard, including writer Zora Neale Hurston. Early in the 1930s, she recognized the dangers of Nazism and clashed publicly with several prominent New Yorkers whom she accused of antisemitism. Though she was not acknowledged in her lifetime as Barnard College's founder, she never lost her enthusiasm for the school, even as she devoted her energies to literature and social justice causes.

BIBLIOGRAPHY: D. Askowith, *Three Outstanding Women* (1941); M. Goldenberg, "Annie Nathan Meyer," in: JWA, 2, 918–21.

[Myrna Goldenberg (2nd ed.)]

MEYER, BARON DE HIRSCH (1900–1974), lawyer, banker, and philanthropist. Born in Wisconsin, he lived in Miami from 1925.

In 1933, with Harry Lipton, he established the Miami Beach Federal Savings and Loan, known later as Financial and Federal, as well as the Dade Federal, which Lipton took over. These federally backed firms were an important factor in revitalizing Florida's economy. Meyer and his business associate Leonard Abess controlled the City National Bank Corporation and held real estate interests all over the state.

In addition to his successful business involvements, Baron de Hirsch Meyer was active in general communal activity and in almost all Jewish organizations and institutions. He was among the founders of Mount Sinai Hospital on Miami Beach, which he served as president, then as board chairman and chief fundraiser for many years.

[Gladys Rosen]

°MEYER, EDUARD (1855–1930), German Bible critic and historian. Born in Hamburg, Meyer was professor of ancient history at the universities of Breslau (from 1885), Halle (from 1889), and Berlin (1902–22). While he supported *Wellhausen's critical views on Pentateuchal composition, in his *Die Entstehung des Judenthums* (1896, 1965²) he opposed Welhausen's position concerning the authority of the documents mentioned in Ezra and the list of names referred to in Nehemiah, suggesting that a late date for Ezra does not allow for the development of Judaism as is known from the sources. In writing his classic *Geschichte des Altertums* (5 vols., 1884–1902; 1925–58²) he examined all available documentary evidence but failed to appreciate the contributions of archaeologists in regard to early Phoenician and Israelite history. He wrote, among other things, on the culture and history of the Sumerians (*Sumerier und Semiten in Babylonien*, 1906) and the Hittites (*Reich und Kultur der Chetiter*, 1914). He was one of the first to interpret the papyrus finds from Elephantine, and his *Die aeltere Chronologie Babyloniens, Assyriens, und Aegyptiens* (1925) reached very sound conclusions which are still widely referred to by students of the chronology of the ancient world. His *Ursprung und Anfaenge des Christentums* (3 vols., 1921–23) dealt with the history of Judaism and early Christianity, and it reflected the bias of classical biblical criticism, which respected prophetic Judaism, but saw talmudic Judaism as a fossil of rabbinic casuistry.

[Zev Garber]

MEYER, ERNST HERMANN (1905–1988), musicologist and composer. Born in Berlin, Meyer studied musicology in Berlin and Heidelberg, and composition with Paul Hindemith and

Hanns *Eisler. He immigrated to England in 1933 and returned to Germany in 1948 to become professor of music sociology at the Humboldt University in East Berlin. An authority on the music of the 16th and 17th centuries, he wrote *English Chamber Music* (1946), *Musik im Zeitgeschehen* (1952), and *Aufsaetze ueber Musik* (1957). He composed ballet and chamber music, and a cantata, *Das Tor von Buchenwald* (1959). His teachings and compositions followed the principles of socialist ideology.

MEYER, EUGENE (1875–1959), U.S. banker, government official, and newspaper editor and publisher. Born in California, he formed the banking firm of Eugene Meyer, Jr., and Co. in 1901. For 16 years he played a leading role in developing oil, copper, and automotive industries. During World War I he entered government service as an adviser on nonferrous metals to the War Industries Board. In 1918 he was named managing director of the War Finance Corporation, and under President Hoover he served as governor of the Federal Reserve Board and organized the Reconstruction Finance Corporation (1932). He was also the first chairman of the Reconstruction Finance Corporation. In 1933, he bought the then moribund *Washington Post* at a public auction, pumped new life into it, absorbed the Washington *Times-Herald*, and raised the *Washington Post* daily circulation to 400,000. After World War II, Meyer accepted an appointment by President Truman to become first president of the International Bank for Reconstruction and Development, and continued to serve on various commissions under President Eisenhower. The Washington Post Company, owner also of *Newsweek* magazine and a number of radio stations, was later headed by Meyer's daughter, Katherine *Graham.

BIBLIOGRAPHY: *Current Biography*, 20 (Oct. 1959), 30.

[Irving Rosenthal]

MEYER, HANS JOHANNES LEOPOLD (1871–1944), Austrian organic chemist. Meyer was born in Vienna and worked at German University of Prague (1897–1933) where from 1911 he was professor of chemistry. His books include *Anleitung zur quantitiven Bestimmung der organischen Atomgruppen* (1897), *Analyse und Konstitution* (1908, 1938[6]), *Boehmisches Porzellan und Steingut* (1927), and *Lehrbuch der organischen chemischen Methodik* (4 vols., 1933–40). Meyer died in Theresienstadt.

MEYER, JONAS DANIEL (1780–1834), Dutch jurist and public figure. Meyer was a grandson of Benjamin *Cohen, a prominent Dutch Jew and friend of William V of Orange. A child prodigy, Meyer was awarded the LL.D. at the age of 16 for a thesis on the American revolutionary Thomas Payne, whom he attacked for the latter's disapproval of religious ceremonies, particularly those of the Jews. Meyer was the first Jew in Holland to be admitted as a lawyer. In 1808, Louis Napoleon – then king of Holland – appointed Meyer director of the *Royal Gazette*, a member of the Institute of Sciences, and a court magistrate in Amsterdam. Within the Jewish community Meyer was a member and from 1809 president of the High Consistory (1806–10), and subsequently after the annexation of Holland to France member of the Amsterdam consistory. In 1813 Meyer was elected as a member to the Amsterdam municipal council.

Meyer retained most of his positions under King William I of Orange until he resigned from all public and Jewish functions in 1817. In 1815 the king appointed him secretary of a government committee for the drafting of a new Dutch constitution, but antisemitic prejudice prevented him from being appointed to higher positions and he returned to private practice. He appeared in 1820 on behalf of Louis Napoleon in a lawsuit against William I. In 1827 Meyer returned to public life as secretary of a royal commission to prepare a new Dutch history. He was given the Order of the Netherlands Lion – the first Jew to receive this award.

In 1808 Meyer was largely instrumental in reuniting the old Ashkenazi congregation of Amsterdam and the dissident liberal congregation of Adath Yeshurun. He was chairman of a commission for drafting a program for Jewish schools in Amsterdam and together with his friend Carel *Asser, Meyer drew up a report disclosing the appalling social and educational situation of the Jews of Amsterdam. In 1873, a square separating the Sephardi and the main Ashkenazi synagogues in the center of the Jewish quarter of Amsterdam was named after him. Meyer's legal works include *Principes sur les questions transitoires* (Amsterdam, 1813) on legal problems which arose from the introduction of the Code Napoléon in Holland, and *Esprit, origine et progrès des institutions judicaires des principaux pays de l'Europe* (6 vols., 1819–23), a history of legal institutions in England, France, Holland, and Germany. He was a member of the French Academy, the Royal Academy in London, of the academies of Brussels, Göttingen, Batavia, and Torino, and of the Dutch Society for Literature.

BIBLIOGRAPHY: N. de Benedittу, *Leven en Werken van J.D. Meyer* (1925). **ADD. BIBLIOGRAPHY:** N. Mayer-Hirsch, in: *Misjpoge*, 8 (1995), 123–34; J. Michman, *Dutch Jewry during the Emancipation Period. Gothic Turrets on a Corinthian Building* (1995).

[Henriette Boas / Bart Wallet (2nd ed.)]

MEYER, LEON (1868–1957), French politician. Born in Le Havre, Meyer was a cousin of the Jewish anti-Dreyfusard journalist, Arthur Meyer. Having established a position for himself as a coffee merchant, he was elected to the city council in 1912 and as mayor of Le Havre in 1919. In 1921 Meyer became a radical-socialist member of the Chamber of Deputies and served as undersecretary of state in two administrations, first in 1925 and again in 1929. In 1932 he became minister of mercantile marine, in which post he made a substantial contribution to France's shipbuilding industry and to the development of the port of Le Havre. An outspoken critic of the Popular Front coalition of 1936, in which the radical socialists participated, Meyer fell out of favor with his own party. He devoted himself entirely to local politics until the fall of France in 1940, after which he took no further part in public affairs.

[Shulamith Catane]

MEYER, LUDWIG BEATUS (1780–1854), Danish lexicographer. Born in Germany, Meyer was a teacher in Stockholm before he settled in Copenhagen in 1803. He retired from a high civil service post in 1821 and turned to scholarly pursuits, publishing a guide to German poetry (1823). His *Lexicon* (1837) of foreign words and phrases in Danish became a standard work and, under the title *Meyers Fremmedordbog*, was often reprinted.

MEYER, MARSHALL T. (1930–1993), rabbi, educator, social activist. Meyer was born in New York City, grew up in Norwich, Connecticut, and attended Dartmouth College and the Jewish Theological Seminary, where he was ordained in 1958 and served as secretary of Rabbi Abraham Joshua Heschel. With his wife, Naomi, Meyer left for Argentina in 1959 to become the assistant rabbi at Buenos Aires's Congregación Israelita de la República Argentina. Meyer's sharp intellect, his outreach to youth, and his social activism quickly earned him distinction. In 1963 he founded Comunidad Bet-El, which within a few years became the leading Conservative synagogue in Argentina and the model upon which future Conservative synagogues would be built throughout Latin America.

Anticipating the Conservative movement's emergence and expansion throughout Latin America, Meyer founded the Seminario Rabínico Latinoamericano in 1962, the first non-Orthodox Latin American institution of higher Jewish studies. Meyer also supervised the translation into Spanish of a *siddur* for weekdays and Shabbat, and of the *maḥzor* for the High Holy Days. In addition, he undertook the translation into Spanish of dozens of important volumes on theology and works by important Jewish authors. Meyer published the journal *Maj'shavot* which contained original articles by Latin American authors. He was committed to interfaith dialogue and was a member of a group that included several leading liberation theologians.

During the years 1976–83, when Argentina was ruled by a military junta, Meyer became one of the foremost critics of the junta's violation of human rights. Meyer visited detainees in jails and made himself available to relatives of the *desaparecidos*, those who had been kidnapped by the security forces and held in clandestine jails throughout the country. Shabbat services at Bet El were overflowing with worshippers who came to hear Meyer's reality-revealing sermons at a time when the junta severely controlled the media, with families of *desaparecidos* who came in search of comfort. Meyer was member of the Asamblea Permanente por los Derechos Humanos and part of a small network of human rights defenders and foreign ambassadors who worked to save the lives of hundreds by arranging hiding places for them and ensuring their safe passage out of the country. Meyer's own home was, on more than one occasion, such a place of refuge.

Meyer was awarded the Medal of San Martin, the highest Argentine honor upon the nation's return to democracy in 1983. During 1984, Meyer participated in the Comisión Nacional Sobre la Desaparición de Personas – CONADEP, the national commission which documented thousands of human rights abuse cases to be utilized at the courts and to be disseminated through the book *Nunca más* ("Never Again").

In 1985, Meyer was invited to instill new life into Congregation Bnai Jeshurun (BJ), an Ashkenazi synagogue in New York City. Through a combination of lively religious services and a dynamic social action program BJ grew dramatically in numbers and in prominence. At the time of his death in 1993, BJ had become a model for many other synagogues throughout the U.S. Meyer's disciples and graduates of the Seminario Rabínico Latinoamericano, renamed in his memory in 1994, occupy pulpits and Jewish communal positions throughout Latin America, in Israel, and in the U.S. He received honorary doctorates from the Jewish Theological Seminary, Kalamazoo College, Dartmouth College, the University of Buenos Aires, and HUC-JIR.

BIBLIOGRAPHY: J. Isay, *You Are My Witness: The Living Words of Rabbi Marshall T. Meyer* (2004); J. Timerman, *Prisoner Without a Name, Cell Without a Number* (1981); E. Zadoff (ed.), Comisión Israelí por los Desaparecidos Judíos en Argentina – website: www.mfa.gov.il/desaparecidos.

[J. Rolando Matalon (2nd ed.)]

MEYER, MARTIN ABRAHAM (1879–1923), U.S. Reform rabbi and scholar. Meyer, who was born in San Francisco, California, was ordained by the Hebrew Union College in 1901. Meyer served as rabbi of Congregation Beth Emeth, Albany, New York (1902–06); Temple Israel, Brooklyn, New York (1906–10); and Temple Emanu-el, San Francisco (1910–23). From 1911 to 1923 he was lecturer in Semitics at the University of California. During World War I, Meyer became a supporter of both Zionism and the movement for an American Jewish Congress. In 1918–19 he served with the Red Cross in France. Meyer, who was associated with several social service organizations in San Francisco, served as president of the Big Brothers movement and the California Conference on Social Work, and as a member of the California Commission of Charities and Corrections (1911–20). He helped to organize small Jewish communities in the area, was director of the Jewish Education Society of San Francisco and of the Pacific Coast branch of the Jewish Chatauqua Society, and was a board member of several national Jewish organizations. Meyer's publications include several articles on the condition of the Jews in Palestine; *History of the City of Gaza from the Earliest Times to the Present Day* (1907); and the two-volume *Methods of Teaching Post-Biblical History and Literature* (1915).

BIBLIOGRAPHY: AJYB, 27 (1925/26), 246–59.

[Sefton D. Temkin]

MEYER, MICHAEL A. (1937–), U.S. historian. Born in Berlin and brought to the United States in 1941, Meyer was educated at the Hebrew University of Jerusalem, the University of California, Los Angeles (B.A. 1959), Hebrew Union College-Jewish Institute of Religion (HUC-JIR), Los Angeles (B.H.L. 1960), and HUC-JIR, Cincinnati (Ph.D. 1964). He taught at HUC-JIR, Los Angeles, 1964–67, and from 1968 at HUC-JIR, Cincinnati, where he was named Adolf S. Ochs Professor of Jewish History. He also taught regularly at HUC-JIR in Jerusalem and was a visiting professor at UCLA, Antioch College, the University of Haifa, Ben-Gurion University, and the Hebrew University. Meyer served as chairman of the International Association of Historical Societies for the Study of Jewish History and was one of the founders of the (American) Association for Jewish Studies and its president in 1978–80. He was also the international president of the Leo Baeck Institute.

Meyer has been called "the dean of German-Jewish historians," and he has said that "my awareness of being one of the *nizzolei ha-Shoah* – those saved from the Holocaust – has deepened my commitment to things Jewish and to the study of German-Jewish history." He was considered perhaps the leading authority on Reform Judaism, about whose future he expressed optimism. His major work is *Response to Modernity* (1988), a history of the Reform movement through the 1970s, which won the National Jewish Book Award; it has become a standard work and has influenced all subsequent scholars on the subject. He has also edited (with Michael Brenner) a comprehensive four-volume history of modern German Jewry, sponsored by the Leo Baeck Institute, which is also recognized as a landmark work (its first volume won the National Jewish Book Award in 1997). In 1996 Meyer was awarded the Zeltzer Scholarship Award in Historical Studies by the National Foundation for Jewish Culture, in recognition of his stature and influence.

Meyer published many scholarly articles and edited a volume of the papers of Leo Baeck. His books include *The Origins of the Modern Jew: Jewish Identity and European Culture in Germany, 1749–1824* (1967), *Response to Modernity: A History of the Reform Movement in Judaism* (1988), *Jewish Identity in the Modern World* (1990), *Ideas of Jewish History* (edited, 1974), *German-Jewish History in Modern Times*, 4 vols. (edited with Michael Brenner, 1996–98), *The Reform Judaism Reader: North American Documents* (edited, with W. Gunther Plaut, 2001), and *Judaism within Modernity: Essays on Jewish History and Religion* (2001).

[Drew Silver (2nd ed.)]

MEYER, PAULUS (alias **Pawly**; originally **Kremenetzki, Eliezer Baruch Ashkenazi**; 1862–?), renegade who published testimony claiming that he had witnessed a ritual murder. Meyer, a native of Ostrow (Poland), acted during the 1880s as a Protestant missionary among the Jews in Germany. He came into conflict with the *Judenmission* there and published pamphlets against it, attacking H.L. *Strack and others. In 1892 missionary periodicals identified him as an impostor and swindler and he was expelled by the police from Prussia and Saxony. Meyer went to Vienna in 1893 and contacted Joseph *Deckert. On August *Rohling's recommendation, Deckert suggested to Meyer that he write a "scientific" book on the *blood libel. On May 11, 1893 the *Vaterland* published a letter by Meyer in which he claimed to have been present at a ritual murder in his native town in 1875, naming several participants. Joseph Samuel *Bloch took up the case. With the assistance of Nahum *Sokolow and Ḥayyim Selig *Slonimski, he discovered the persons accused by Meyer and, in some cases, their heirs. Joseph Kopp, who had represented Bloch in the Rohling controversy, persuaded them to sue for defamation of character. Throughout the trial Meyer denied having written or signed the letter or been responsible for its contents, although he admitted that the handwriting was that of his fiancée. The jury found him, Deckert, and the *Vaterland* guilty and they received a nominal sentence. The outcome, however, was symbolically important in the context of the antisemitic agitation of the 1890s.

BIBLIOGRAPHY: J.S. Bloch, *My Reminiscences* (1923), 385–570; H.L. Strack, *Das Blut im Glauben und Aberglauben der Menschheit* (900), index.

[Meir Lamed]

MEYER, RICHARD JOSEPH (1865–1942), German inorganic chemist. Meyer was born in Berlin. In 1896 he joined the Pharmacological Institute of University of Berlin and was professor of chemistry there until 1933. He was a member of international commissions on nomenclature and atomic weights and wrote *Bibliographie der seltenen Erden* (1905), *Analyse der seltenen Erden und der Erdsaeuren* (1912), and sections of Ullmann's *Encyclopaedie der Chemie* (1914). He edited several editions of the standard Gmelin-Kraut *Handbuch der anorganischen Chemie.*

MEYER, RICHARD MORITZ (1860–1914), German literary historian. Born and educated in Berlin, Meyer became professor (without salary) of literature at Berlin University in 1901. His books enjoyed a remarkable popularity extending far beyond his immediate scholarly circle. His prizewinning biography of Goethe in three volumes was published in 1895. He wrote a monograph on Nietzsche, *Nietzsche. Sein Leben und sein Werk* (1913). Meyer's outstanding achievements were his *Die deutsche Literatur des 19. Jahrhunderts* (1900; popular edition, 1912) and *Die deutsche Literatur bis zum Beginn des 19. Jahrhunderts* (ed. O. Pniower, 1916; enlarged edition ed. by Hugo *Bieber, 1923).

ADD. BIBLIOGRAPHY: R. Berbig, "'Poesieprofessor' und 'literarischer Ehrabschneider'. Der Berliner Literaturhistoriker Richard M. Meyer; mit Dokumenten," in: *Berliner Hefte zur Geschichte des literarischen Lebens*, 1 (1996), 37–99; H.H. Mueller, "'Ich habe nie etwas anderes sein wollen, als ein deutscher Philolog aus Scherers Schule.' Hinweise auf Richard Moritz Meyer," in: W. Barner and C. König (eds.), *Juedische Intellektuelle und die Philologien in Deutschland 187 –1933* (2001), 93–102; idem, T. Kindt and H.H. Mueller, in: C. Koenig (ed.), *Internationales Germanistenlexikon*, 2 (2003), 1218–1230.

[Rudolf Kayser]

MEYER, SELIGMANN (1853–1926), German rabbi and communal worker. Meyer was born in Reichelheim, Hesse and studied at the University of Giessen. In 1876 he moved to Berlin where he attended the Orthodox rabbinical seminary established by Azriel *Hildesheimer, at the same time working on the staff of the Orthodox Jewish weekly, *Juedische Presse*.

He received his doctorate in 1878, was ordained rabbi in 1881, and a year later was appointed rabbi of *Regensburg where he remained until his death. As a result of his communal activities Regensburg became a center of Orthodoxy. Meyer devoted himself particularly to the *Deutsche Israelitische Zeitung*, a religious monthly family journal, which he founded in 1884 and which he edited until his death.

[Henry Wasserman]

MEYER, TORBEN LOUIS (1909–2005), Danish journalist and author. Born in Copenhagen, Meyer joined the *Berlingske Tidende* daily in 1930 and after World War II edited Jewish journals, notably *Jodisk Samfund* (from 1947) and later *Jodisk Orientering*. He wrote *Flugten over Øresund* (1945), a vivid account of the escape of Danish Jews to Sweden in October 1943. Other books include a two-volume study of the Danish composer Carl Nielsen (1947–48) and *Musikalske selvportraetter* (1966). He also translated works of Bernard *Malamud into Danish.

MEYER, VICTOR (1848–1897), German organic chemist. Meyer, the son of a Berlin textile printer, obtained his doctorate at Heidelberg *magna cum laude* before he was 19. He worked with Bunsen at Heidelberg and Baeyer in Berlin, and in 1872, despite his youth, was appointed professor of general chemistry at the Zurich Polytechnic. He was professor at Goettingen University from 1885 to 1889 and at Heidelberg from 1889 until his death. Meyer invented the term "stereochemistry" and made basic contributions in the field of organic compounds. As well as being one of the foremost organic chemists of his generation and an outstanding lecturer and speaker, he was an accomplished musician, but he was dogged by ill-health and committed suicide. Meyer's biography was written by his brother, RICHARD EMIL MEYER (1846–1926), who was also an organic chemist of distinction. He held professorships at the Technische Hochschule of Braunschweig and at Heidelberg and was editor of the *Jahrbuch der Chemie* from 1891 to 1918.

[Samuel Aaron Miller]

MEYERBEER, GIACOMO (Jacob Liebmann-Beer; 1791–1864), German composer, remembered mainly for his spectacular operas. Meyerbeer was born in Berlin, where his father Jacob Herz Beer was a prominent banker; his brothers were Wilhelm *Beer and Michael *Beer. His musical gifts appeared early, and his grandfather Liebman Meyer Wulf was so impressed with the boy's genius that he made him his sole heir on condition that he added "Meyer" to his name. After studying with the composer Clementi, he went to live and work with the Abbé Vogler in Darmstadt. There he composed his first opera, *Jephthas Geluebde*, which was performed at Munich in 1813 with moderate success. His next dramatic work, *Die beiden Kalifen*, was a failure when produced in Vienna in 1814. Discouraged, Meyerbeer went to Italy. Between 1818 and 1824 he composed a series of successful Italian operas, among the most popular being *Romilda e Costanza, Semiramide riconosciuta, Emma di Resburgo*, and *Il crociato in Egitto*. His change of name from Jacob to Giacomo symbolized his "conversion" to the new Italian style.

In 1826, Meyerbeer was invited to the first performance of *Il crociato* in Paris. Its favorable reception led to his later career as a composer of French grand opera. His first in a series of brilliant successes in this genre, *Robert le Diable*, was produced in 1831, and within a year it was being presented in many European cities. Meyerbeer, aided by his librettist Eugène Scribe, gave the public what it wanted: a sensational story, novel stage effects, showy singing, and colorful orchestration. This formula was repeated many times, most notably in *Les Huguenots* (1836), *Le Prophète* (1843), and *L'Africaine* (*Vasco da Gama*; 1838–64), first produced in French and English a year after the composer's death. While vigorously promoting his own career, Meyerbeer was always ready to help other composers. For example, he warmly recommended Wagner's *Rienzi* for production in Dresden, and during his period as royal director of opera in Berlin (1842–47) he introduced the *Flying Dutchman* to the repertoire there. Wagner, however, violently attacked the music and personality of his one-time friend. Meyerbeer remained faithful to Judaism. Meyerbeer's popularity continued for some years after his death – in 1895 *Le Prophète* attained its 150th performance in London – but his reputation declined in the 20th century.

BIBLIOGRAPHY: M. Cooper, *Fanfare for Ernest Newman* (1959), 38–57; W.L. Crosten, *French Grand Opera: An Art and a Business* (1948), passim; H. Becker, *Der Fall Heine-Meyerbeer* (1958); B. Van Dieren, *Down Among the Dead Men* (1935), 142–74; *Giacomo Meyerbeer, 1791–1864, exposition…* (Fr. and Heb., Jerusalem, Jewish National Library, 1964); Istel, in: *Musical Quarterly*, 12 (1926), 72–109; J. Kapp, *Meyerbeer* (1920); A. Hervey, *Giacomo Meyerbeer* (1913); MGG, s.v.; G. Meyerbeer, *Briefwechsel und Tagebuecher*, ed. by H. Becker, 2 vols. (1960–70).

[Dika Newlin]

MEYERHOF, MAX (1874–1945), ophthalmologist and medical historian. He was born in Hildesheim, Germany. In 1903 he went to Egypt and served as chief of the Khedivial Ophthalmic Clinic. He returned to Germany in 1914 to serve as a medical officer in the German army and after the war settled in Hanover as a practicing oculist. He returned to Cairo in 1923 and stayed there until his death. During his lifetime, Meyerhof published over 300 books, monographs, and treatises on ophthalmology and medical history. He made special studies of the various eye diseases endemic in Egypt and North Africa, especially of trachoma and its complications, of glaucoma, lepra of the eye, etc. His book *Ueber die ansteckenden Augenleiden Aegyptens* appeared in 1909. He also wrote on the history of ophthalmology and pharmacology among Spanish Muslims and Jews and did research on medieval Arab medicine from unpublished documents in Cairo and other libraries. He edited and translated the Arabic text of the famous medieval ophthalmologist Ḥunain ibn Isḥāq, *The Book of the Ten Treatises on the Eye* (1928), and was one of the first to study Maimonides as a physician; he translated and published for the first time Maimonides' glossary of drugs *L'Explication des noms de drogues* (1940). In recognition of his many services as an oculist and medical historian, Meyerhof received many honors and decorations from medical societies all over the world. Meyerhof also contributed to the organization of medical care for the poor in Egypt.

BIBLIOGRAPHY: S.R. Kagan, *Jewish Medicine* (1952), 527f.; I. Fischer (ed.), *Biographisches Lexikon der hervorragenden Aerzte*, 2 (1933), s.v.; *Works of Max Meyerhof* (1944), compiled by U. ben Ḥorin.

[Suessmann Muntner]

MEYERHOF, OTTO (1884–1951), German biochemist and Nobel Prize winner. Meyerhof, who was born in Hanover, was first concerned with psychology (he wrote a book *Contributions to a Psychological Theory of Mental Diseases*) and philosophy (he edited a journal *Abhandlungen der Friesschen Schule*, mainly for neo-Kantian philosophers), and worked in Krehl's clinic and at the Marine Zoological Laboratory in Naples. In 1913 he joined the University of Kiel, where he became professor of physiological chemistry (1918–24). In 1923 Meyerhof was awarded the Nobel Prize in physiology and medicine (shared with A.V. Hill) "for his discovery of the fixed relationship between the consumption of oxygen and the metabolism of lactic acid in the muscle." An associated phenomenon is known as the Pasteur-Meyerhof effect. In 1924 Meyerhof became head of a division in the Kaiser Wilhelm Institute of Biology in Berlin-Dahlem, and in 1929 head of the department of physiology in the Institute for Medical Research in Heidelberg. He elucidated the roll played by ATP (adenosine triphosphate) in energy transfer in biological systems and introduced the term "energy coupling." He was forced to leave Germany in 1938, and became director of research at the Institut de Biologie Physicochimique in Paris. When the Germans conquered France, he escaped, first to southern France, and then to America. He then became research professor of physiological chemistry at the University of Pennsylvania's medical school.

BIBLIOGRAPHY: Nachmansohn, in: *Science*, 115 (1952), 365–8; idem, in: *Biochimica et Biophysica Acta*, 4 (1950), 1–3; T.N. Levitan, *Laureates: Jewish Winners of the Nobel Prize* (1960), 124–7.

[Samuel Aaron Miller]

MEYERHOFF, HANS (1914–1965), U.S. philosopher. He was born in Brunswick, Germany, and went to the U.S. in 1934. From 1943 to 1948 he worked for the U.S. government. From 1949 on he taught philosophy at the University of California at Los Angeles. He wrote *Time in Literature* (1955), an analysis of scientific and literary renderings of time. He edited *The Philosophy of History in Our Time* (1959), and translated works by Max Scheler and Paul Friedlander. His publications include articles on philosophy, literature, psychology, and politics. He died in an automobile accident. A free speech plaza at the Los Angeles campus of the University of California is named after him.

[Myriam M. Malinovich]

MEYERHOFF, HARVEY (1927–), U.S. businessman, communal leader, philanthropist. The middle child and only son of Joseph and Rebecca Witten Meyerhoff, Harvey "Bud" Meyerhoff was born in Baltimore, Maryland. He attended Baltimore public schools and the University of Wisconsin at Madison. He settled in Baltimore and joined his father in the family-owned firm known as the Property Sales Company (later the Joseph Meyerhoff Corporation). As a partner, Meyerhoff led the firm to focus on developing shopping centers and apartment buildings, and oversaw the merger of the Meyerhoff Corporation with Monumental Life Insurance Company, which became Monumental Properties, Inc. in 1969.

In 1987 Meyerhoff was appointed by President Ronald Reagan to succeed Elie Wiesel as chairperson of the United States Holocaust Memorial Council (USHMM). When he assumed office, expectations were high but little had been achieved with regard to constructing a building, developing the permanent exhibition, and raising the requisite funds. Meyerhoff strengthened the organization's fund-raising efforts and met its fiscal goals, pushed for distinctive architectural treatment of the museum building, and navigated complex matters of exhibition content.

Meyerhoff's leadership of the USHMM came in the midst of a long career of service to his native city of Baltimore and its Jewish community as well as national causes. He served as chairman of the Johns Hopkins Hospital (1987), the Central Maryland United Way Campaign (1975), and the Associated Jewish Charities Campaign. He was president of the board of trustees of Baltimore's Park School, a non-sectarian, private elementary and high school, from 1972 to 1975. He played a leadership role in such diverse organizations as the National Conference of Christians and Jews, Maryland Region; the United Jewish Appeal; the Baltimore County Advisory Committee on Mass Transportation; the Baltimore Convention Bureau; the Baltimore League for the Handicapped (president, 1961–64); the National Association of Homebuilders Research Foundation (president, 1965–66); and the United States Rent Advisory Board.

Meyerhoff's wife, LYN (1927–1988), was also a prominent community leader. Long active in Maryland and national Republican politics, she was appointed by President Reagan in 1983 as a United States public delegate to the United Nations 38th General Assembly. She was also very active in many philanthropic initiatives including the National Aquarium, the Digestive Disease Center at Johns Hopkins Hospital, and the Baltimore Symphony Orchestra. Harvey and Lyn Meyerhoff were following in Joseph Meyerhoff's footsteps when they established a charitable foundation, The Harvey M. and Lyn P. Meyerhoff Fund, in 1972. Seven years later, they broke new philanthropic ground by setting up a separate fund to be administered jointly by their four children, who named their fund The Children of Harvey M. and Lyn P. Meyerhoff Philanthropic Fund. It was joined in 1999 by an additional fund known as The Grandchildren of Harvey M. and Lyn P. Meyerhoff Philanthropic Fund.

BIBLIOGRAPHY: E.T. Linenthal, *Preserving Memory: The Struggle to Create America's Holocaust Museum* (1995); K.L. Falk, *If I Ran the World: A Biography of Lyn P. Meyerhoff* (2006).

[Karen L. Falk (2nd ed.)]

MEYERHOFF, JOSEPH (1899–1985), U.S. businessman, communal worker, and philanthropist. Meyerhoff was born in a small town near Poltava, Russia, and was taken to the United States in 1906, settling with his family in Baltimore, Maryland. From 1921 he headed his own building and real estate firm, which developed new communities, especially in the Baltimore area, and shopping centers in many cities. Meyerhoff was associated with the United Jewish Appeal (UJA), of which he was general chairman (1961–64) and a member of the executive committee thereafter. In 1961, while serving with the UJA, Meyerhoff established the Israel Education Fund, in conjunction with the government of Israel and the Jewish Agency.

He also served with the PEC Israel Economic Corporation, of which he was president (1957–63), and later as chairman of the board and the executive committee. He also was chairman of the Israel Education Fund of the UJA (1965–67). He served on the board of directors of many national and international Jewish organizations and institutions, including the Hebrew University in Jerusalem (1961–67). A philanthropic leader in his local Baltimore Jewish community, his local interests included the Sinai Hospital of Baltimore, of which he served as vice president and chairman of the board (1943–59), and Associated Jewish Charities and Welfare Fund Campaign of Baltimore, of which he was general chairman (1951–52). Meyerhoff served the state of Maryland as chairman of the State Planning Commission (1956–63), as member of the State Board of Public Welfare (1953–57), and in other capacities.

Many organizations and facilities in Israel and the United States bear the benefits of his benevolence. Some of those that bear his name include the Joseph Meyerhoff Family Charitable Funds; the Joseph Meyerhoff Library at Baltimore Hebrew University; and Hillel's Joseph Meyerhoff Center for Jewish Learning.

MEYER-LÉVY, CLAUDE (1908–?), French architect. Born in Paris, Meyer-Lévy established his reputation with his Yachting Pavilion at the Paris World Fair of 1937, and the French National Pavilion at the San Francisco Golden Gate Exposition of 1939 which he designed with E.T. Spencer. His synagogue at Strasbourg (1958), seating 1,700 people, was the largest to be built in Europe after World War II. It is a reinforced concrete structure containing a rectangular hall with an apse and galleries. The building takes the traditional form of the classical basilica.

MEYEROWITZ, HERBERT VLADIMIR (1900–1945), South African artist. Born in St. Petersburg (Leningrad), Meyerowitz specialized in decorative sculpture. His main work was done in South Africa, where he pioneered in wood-carving and architectural decoration, such as the memorial doorway (1930) at the South African National Gallery in Cape Town. In 1943 he established the West African Institute of Arts, Industries, and Social Sciences in Accra with funds from the colonial government, and became the acting director.

MEYEROWITZ, JOEL (1938–), U.S. photographer. Born in the Bronx, New York, Meyerowitz was working as an advertising director when one day in 1962 he quit his job to go out shooting on Fifth Avenue in Manhattan. In most of his early work, as a street photographer, he worked exclusively in color, treating the street as theater rather than as a landscape. Meyerowitz was instrumental in changing the attitude toward the use of color photography from one of resistance to nearly universal acceptance. Meyerowitz first exhibited at the Museum of Modern Art in 1963 in a show on which John Szarkowski's "The Photographer's Eye" was based, and he showed there, or under the Modern's auspices, in 1968, 1971, and 1978.

At first Meyerowitz focused on incidents like that in "Fallen Man, Paris, 1967," in which a young man lies supine on the street as passers-by stare or step around him. By the early 1970s Meyerowitz was shifting his view of the street to one in which people, buildings, and the flow of energy among them became the subject. "Woman in Red Coat, NYC" from 1975 depicts a flow of passers-by before a bland architectural façade. A woman in a bright red coat and long black gloves looms at the left of the picture. His first book, *Cape Light*, in 1978, is considered a classic, with more than 100,000 copies sold over a 25-year period. Photographs in the book, of Provincetown and Cape Cod, Mass., convey the look and delight of the areas. In 1980, with the support of public and private fellowships and grants, he published *St. Louis & the Arch*, a collection of more than 100 color plates with several foldouts and a minimum of text, focusing on the play of light and color on Eero Saarinen's Gateway Arch. He is the author of a dozen other books, including *Bystander: The History of Street Photography.*

In 1988 Meyerowitz produced and directed his first film, *Pop*, an intimate diary of a three-week road trip he made with his son, Sasha, and his father, Hy, who was suffering from Alzheimer's disease. The odyssey has as its central character an unpredictable, street-wise, and witty 87-year-old man with a failing memory. It is both an open-eyed look at aging and a meditation on the significance of memory, Meyerowitz said.

Within a few days of the attacks on the World Trade Center on September 11, 2001, Meyerowitz began to create an archive of the destruction and recovery at Ground Zero and the immediate neighborhood. "I walked and photographed nearly every inch of it," he said, "as it was transformed from an awesome pile to a vast and empty pit. Like an accordion, the 16-acre site was capable of appearing compressed and encircled one moment and then vast and beyond measure a second later. It breathed, as cities and nature do, when they draw us toward wonder and contemplation." The archive numbers more than 8,000 images and is available for research, exhibition, and publication at museums in New York and Washington. The State Department asked Meyerowitz and the Museum of the City of New York to create a special exhibition of images from the archive to send around the world. The only photographer granted unimpeded access to Ground Zero, Meyerowitz takes a meditative stance toward the work and the workers there. His color photos, presented in a 30 inch × 40 inch format, convey the magnitude of the destruction and loss and the heroic nature of the response.

His book *Tuscany – Inside the Light* was conceived as an antidote to the events of 9/11. During 2002, he and his wife, Maggie Barrett, collaborating author, returned to Tuscany, where they had taught photography and writing workshops. The tranquility of life, the enduring values, the deep familial bonds, the land itself and its 2,000 years of cultivation, Meyerowitz said, stand "inside this bowl of light" as nowhere else.

[Stewart Kampel (2nd ed.)]

MEYERS, NANCY JANE (1949–), U.S. director, producer, and writer. A Philadelphia native, Meyers earned a B.A. in journalism from American University in 1971. She moved to Los Angeles in 1972, where she started off supporting herself as a screenwriter by selling homemade cheesecakes. Meyers met her husband, screenwriter Charles Richard Shyer (1941–), on a date with his best friend, Harvey Miller. Meyers and Shyer were a couple by 1976. Shyer was already established in Hollywood, having written for the TV series *The Odd Couple* and *All in the Family* as well as the films *Smokey and the Bandit* (1977) and *Goin' South* (1978), starring Jack Nicholson. In 1976, Meyers and Shyer began collaborating on projects, joining Miller to pen a hit for fellow American University alumna Goldie *Hawn, in *Private Benjamin* (1980). The script earned an Academy Award nomination. Next, the two co-wrote *Irreconcilable Differences*, with Meyers as executive producer and Shyer as director. Their 1987 movie *Baby Boom* spawned an NBC TV series (1988–89) that the two produced. In 1991, the Meyers-Shyer remake of the 1950 film *Father of the Bride* was a success. The couple finally married in 1995 and also formed the Meyers/Shyer Company that year. The pair signed a development deal with Walt Disney Pictures in 1996 and remade the 1961 movie *Parent Trap* in 1998. It marked Meyers' directorial debut. The film's twin girls were named after Meyers and Shyer's daughters, Annie and Hallie. By that year, Meyers and Shyer's relationship had begun to dissolve and the two separated, personally and professionally. Meyers went on to direct *What Women Want* (2000) and *Something's Gotta Give* (2003), which she also wrote. Shyer directed *The Affair of the Necklace* (2001) and the 2004 remake of *Alfie*.

[Susannah Howland (2nd ed.)]

MEYERSON, EMILE (1859–1933), French chemist, historian, and philosopher of science; son of Malvina Meyerson, Polish novelist. Born in Lublin, Poland, Meyerson studied in Germany, mainly in Heidelberg with the noted chemist R.W. Bunsen. He later immigrated to Paris where he worked as an industrial chemist, editor, and administrator of the Jewish colonization association (ICA). Although never appointed to a university post, Meyerson came to be recognized as an unusually erudite scholar of the interrelationships among the natural sciences, the history of philosophy, and cultural developments, particularly since the rise of modern science in the 16th century. His knowledge embraced the most recent work on Einstein's theory of relativity and the early quantum theory of Max Planck and Niels Bohr. Meyerson wished to understand the nature of explanation both in the natural sciences and elsewhere. He believed that the philosopher of science has to have a thorough knowledge of the history of science, and of how scientists themselves conceived of their own work. His own philosophy, though abstract, was based on vast scholarly research which led him to conclude that rational understanding consisted of the discovery of those factors of permanence underlying processes of change, and the search for those identities found within the evident flux of experience or the incompletely rationalized world of most scientific work. Reality nevertheless seemed to Meyerson to be only partially open to rational understanding. Its sensual factors, for instance, which are so important for epistemological theory, remain unexplained. A complete understanding of nature thus seems to elude the grasp of a reasoned science. Meyerson's works include *Identité et Réalité* (1908; *Identity and Reality*, 1930), *De l'explication dans les Sciences* (2 vols., 1921), and various essays.

BIBLIOGRAPHY: T.R. Kely, *Explanation and Reality in the Philosophy of Emile Meyerson* (1937), incl. bibl.; G. Boas, *A Critical Analysis of the Philosophy of Emile Meyerson* (1930); L. de Broglie et al., in: *Bulletin de la Société francaise de Philosophie*, 55:2 (1961), 55–105, issue devoted to Meyerson and Milhaud.

[Robert S. Cohen]

MEYERSTEIN, EDWARD HARRY WILLIAM (1889–1952), English poet and novelist. The son of a well-known philanthropist, Meyerstein was educated at Harrow and Oxford. He worked for some years in the manuscripts department of the British Museum. Though a noted scholar, especially in Greek and Roman literature, Meyerstein was mainly drawn to poetry. He published a number of volumes of verse elaborate in diction and reminiscent of the fashions of the 1890s. They included *The Door* (1911); *New Odes* (1936); *Briancourt* (1937); *Sonnets* (1939); *The Visionary* (1941); *In Time of War* (1942); *Three Sonatas* (1948); and *The Delphic Character* (1951). *The Unseen Beloved* was published posthumously in 1953. Meyerstein also wrote several novels, outstanding among which was the trilogy *Terence Duke* (1935), a study in viciousness. Few of his works retained their popularity, but his careful and detailed life of Thomas Chatterton (1930) is one of the best extant studies of that romantic poet. A melancholy and eccentric bachelor who kept an "extraordinary collection of whips" in a box under his bed, Meyerstein is unsympathetically portrayed in the character of Brunstein in Arnold Lunn's novel, *The Harrovians* (1913). His own account of his youth appears in *Of My Early Life* (1958). *Some Letters of E.H. Meyerstein* (ed. Rowland Watson, 1959) is valuable in disclosing his strange life and views.

BIBLIOGRAPHY: Wain, in: *Encounter*, 19 (Aug. 1962), 27–42. **ADD. BIBLIOGRAPHY:** W.D. Rubinstein, *Great Britain*, 129–30, 454.

[Philip D. Hobsbaum]

MEYERSTEIN, EDWARD WILLIAM (1863–1942), British philanthropist. Meyerstein was a highly successful member of the London Stock Exchange, who was renowned as "the great benefactor of hospitals." He had a very special interest in the Middlesex Hospital in London, which received his gift of £350,000 to make possible its expansion. Other institutions which were beneficiaries of his generosity were the Queen Victoria College Hospital, Tonbridge, the Kent County Ophthalmic Hospital at Maidstone, and the Westminster, St. Mary's, and Princess Elizabeth of York hospitals in London. From 1937 to 1938 and from 1941 to 1942 he served as the high sheriff of Kent. He was knighted in 1938 for his benefactions to health services. His son, Edward Harry William *Meyerstein, was a writer of prose and poetry.

BIBLIOGRAPHY: JC (Feb. 6, 1942), 18.

MEYUḤAS, ABRAHAM BEN SAMUEL (d. 1767), rabbi and kabbalist in *Jerusalem, his birthplace. Abraham studied under Israel Meir Mizraḥi in the Yeshivah Bet Ya'akov founded by Jacob Israel Pereira, and married the daughter of Tobias *Cohn. His life was one of suffering and affliction. He was orphaned as a child and lost his sight at the age of 30. Abraham was the author of *Sedeh ha-Arez;* homilies on the Torah, in three parts (pts. 1 and 2, Salonika, 1784, 1798; pt. 3, Leghorn, 1788); *Diglo Ahavah*, a commentary on the *Derekh Eẓ ha-Ḥayyim* of Isaac *Luria: it was arranged by Meir *Poppers and included the latter's own work, *Or Zaru'a; Ha-Ma'or ha-Katan*, on the *Eẓ Ḥayyim* by Ḥayyim *Vital; and *Si'aḥ ha-Sadeh*, on the *Kavvanot* ("Meditations") of Isaac Luria, together with homilies and notes. Raphael *Meyuḥas was his brother. One of Abraham's sons, Benjamin Moses (d. 1804), was responsible for publishing part 1 of *Sedeh ha-Areẓ*, and another, Joseph Jacob, an emissary of the *Hebron community, published the other two parts while engaged on his missions.

BIBLIOGRAPHY: Michael, Or, 121, no. 253; Frumkin-Rivlin, 2 (1928), 118; 3 (1929), 86, 90–91; Yaari, Sheluḥei, 556–7, 598; idem, *Meḥkerei Sefer* (1958), 138–9.

[Abraham David]

MEYUḤAS, MOSES JOSEPH MORDECAI BEN RAPHAEL MEYUḤAS (1738–1805), chief rabbi of *Jerusalem. Moses studied in the *bet midrash* Bet Ya'akov. When only 15 years of age he answered questions on *halakhah*. After 1778 he was one of the members of the *bet midrash* Keneset Israel founded by Ḥayyim ibn *Attar. After the death of his father-in-law Yom Tov *Algazi, Moses succeeded him as Sephardi chief rabbi (*rishon le-Zion*) in 1802. He was on friendly terms with Ḥ.J.D. *Azulai. The titles of all his works include the word *mayim* from the initials of his name (he even signed his responsa "Mayim Meyuḥas"). They are *Sha'ar ha-Mayim* (Salonika, 1768), novellae on the laws of *terefot* in *Yoreh De'ah*, on tractate *Ḥullin* and responsa; *Berekhot Mayim* (*ibid.*, 1789), novellae to the Shulḥan Arukh; *Mayim Sha'al* (*ibid.*, 1799), responsa, including the work *Mayim Rishonim*, novellae written in his youth, to the *Mishneh Torah* of *Maimonides. Many of his novellae and responsa, among them *Penei ha-Mayim* and *Ein ha-Mayim*, remain unpublished.

BIBLIOGRAPHY: Frumkin-Rivlin, 3 (1929), 183–6; M.D. Gaon, *Yehudei ha-Mizraḥ be-Ereẓ Yisrael*, 2 (1938), 401f.; M. Benayahu, *Rabbi Ḥayyim Yosef David Azulai* (Heb., 1959), 350f.

[Abraham David]

MEYUḤAS, RAPHAEL MEYUḤAS BEN SAMUEL (1695?–1771), chief rabbi (*rishon le-Zion*) of *Jerusalem. Meyuḥas was born in Jerusalem and studied in the yeshivah Bet Ya'akov, which he subsequently headed. In 1723 when the troubles of the Jewish community of Jerusalem were aggravated because of the harsh rule of its governor, Yussuf Pasha, Raphael was sent by Abraham *Yiẓḥaki, the *rishon le-Zion*, to Constantinople to plead for the governor's removal. Meyuḥas served as *av bet din* in Jerusalem, his colleagues including Isaac Zerahiah *Azulai and, much later, his son Ḥ.J.D. *Azulai. In 1756 on the death of Israel Jacob *Algazi, he was appointed *rishon le-Zion*. In one of his rulings Raphael endeavored to bring about a rapprochement between the *Karaites and the Rabbanites, permitting the Karaites to send their children to the *talmud torah*. Tradition has it, however, that Raphael later recanted his ruling. He was the author of *Minḥat Bikkurim* (Salonika, 1752) on the Talmud; *Peri ha-Adamah* in 4 parts (*ibid.*, 1752–57 (64?)), novellae on *Maimonides' *Mishneh Torah* with responsa – appended to the fourth part are homilies called *Penei ha-Adamah; Mizbaḥ Adamah* (*ibid.*, 1777) on the Shulḥan Arukh. Raphael was the brother of Abraham b. Samuel *Meyuḥas and the father of Moses Joseph Mordecai *Meyuḥas.

BIBLIOGRAPHY: Frumkin-Rivlin, 3 (1929), 85–90; S. Assaf, *Be-Oholei Ya'akov* (1943), 203; Yaari, Sheluḥei, index, s.v. *Meyuḥas Meyuḥas*; M. Benayahu, *Rabbi Ḥayyim Yosef David Azulai* (Heb., 1959), index; idem (ed.), *Sefer ha-Ḥida* (1959), 28–31.

[Abraham David]

MEYUḤAS, YOSEF BARAN (ben Rahamim Nathan; 1868–1942), leader of the Sephardi community in Ereẓ Israel, writer, and educator. Born in *Jerusalem, from 1884 Meyuḥas taught in various schools, including the Evelina de Rothschild School, and was headmaster of the Ezra Teachers Seminary and the municipal school for boys. In 1888 he was one of the founders of the lodge of "Jerusalem" *B'nai B'rith – the first in Ereẓ Israel – and a founder of the Sha'arei Ẓedek quarter of

Jerusalem. Meyuḥas was also a leader of the Ḥibbat ha-Areẓ Society, which founded *Moẓa, near Jerusalem. One of the first Ereẓ Israel Sephardim to take an Ashkenazi wife, he married Margalit, the daughter of Y.M. *Pines. His was among the first families to follow Eliezer *Ben-Yehuda's example of speaking Hebrew. Meyuḥas was among the founders of the Ginzei Yosef u-Midrash Abrabanel Library, which formed the nucleus of the *Jewish National and University Library. From 1920 to 1931 he was president of the city council of Jews in Jerusalem. From his youth, he contributed to the Hebrew and Ladino press on matters of culture, education, and literature and became a specialist on Sephardi folklore, Oriental communities, the Arabs of Palestine, and the history of the Jews of the Orient and of the *yishuv*. He published a number of works and some have remained in manuscript.

[Abraham Aharoni]

MEZAḤ (Segal), JOSHUA HA-LEVI (1834–1917), Hebrew and Yiddish author. Born in Lithuania in the Kovno region, near Zagare, Mezaḥ (whose pen name derives from the initials of "Mi-Zager Ḥadash") lived in many different Jewish settlements in Russia and Romania, and for the last 25 years of his life in Vilna. From 1861 he wrote for most of the Hebrew and Yiddish newspapers existing at the time. His first book was *Ha-Emunah ve-ha-Haskalah* ("Faith and the Enlightenment," 1874). A collection of articles containing descriptions of the social shortcomings of various Jewish communities was published as *Mikhtavim mi-Sar shel Ya-M* ("Letters from Yehoshu'a Mezaḥ," 5 vols., 1884–88). *Tefaḥ Megulleh* (1886), for the greater part written by Judah Leib *Gordon, was an attack upon Alexander *Zederbaum, the editor of *Ha-Meliẓ*. In *Bamat Yiẓḥak* (1890), Mezaḥ wrote about the Yiddish theater, and *Ha-Eshel* (2 pts., 1893–94) contains selections from his tales, poems, and essays. He also wrote two plays, *Tummat Ivriyyah* (1904) and *Alilat Shav* (1908). He edited *Gan ha-Perahim* (1891), and, together with Reuben Asher *Braudes, the short-lived biweekly *Ha-Yahadut* (1885). After the 1890s Mezaḥ wrote almost nothing in Hebrew; but he published many popular short stories and popular booklets in Yiddish which were circulated in hundreds of thousands of copies, sometimes anonymously and often without receiving remuneration. Mezaḥ spent the end of his life in poverty. A bibliography of his works in Yiddish was compiled by A.J. Goldschmidt, in Ẓ. Shabad (ed.), *Vilner Zamlbukh*, 1 (1917), 192–201.

BIBLIOGRAPHY: Rejzen, Leksikon, 2 (1927), 366–74: Kressel, Leksikon, 2 (1967), 335–6.

[Yehuda Arye Klausner]

MEZEI, MÓR (1836–1925), Hungarian lawyer and politician. Graduating from law school in 1864, Mezei was admitted to the bar by special royal permission, since Jews were excluded from the legal profession until 1867. While still a student he joined the movement for Jewish emancipation. From 1861 he was secretary of the Izraelita Magyar Egylet ("Union of Hungarian Israelites"), and later editor of the union's official journal, *Magyar Izraelita*. In 1868–69 he was secretary of the General Congress of Hungarian Jews. It was largely through his efforts that the Jewish religion was officially recognized in Hungary (1895). From 1905 through 1925 he was president of the National Bureau of Hungarian Israelites, and was also active in general public affairs. He was a member of parliament (1893–1901) as a representative of the Liberal Party. His brother ERNŐ (1851–1932), a journalist and politician, also studied law at Budapest University. From 1874 to 1910 he was the political leader-writer of *Egyetértés* ("Concord"), the mouthpiece of the opposition Independence Party. In 1881 Mezei was elected member of parliament for Miskolc, but his parliamentary career was cut short when he submitted embarrassing questions in parliament in connection with the *Tiszaeszlar blood libel. Previously, Mezei had written several pamphlets against the policy of the Liberal Party leader Kálmán Tisza, who pursued a conciliatory policy toward the Hapsburg regime, *Tisza Kálmán a miniszterelnök* ("K. Tisza the Premier," 1875), *Tisza Kálmán 1877-ben* ("Tisza in 1877," 1877). His other works include a book describing his travels in Italy, *Bolyongások az olasz ég alatt* ("Roaming under Italian Skies"). At the beginning of the 20th century, Mezei, who was opposed to Zionism, corresponded with Theodor *Herzl. In a letter that later became famous, Herzl warned him of the fate in store for the assimilationist Jewry of Hungary.

BIBLIOGRAPHY: Zs. Groszmann, in: IMIT, 58 (1936), 197–208; J. Rákosi, in: *Zsidó Evkönyv*, 2 (1928–29), 111–2.

[Jeno Zsoldos]

MEZEY, FERENC (1860–1927), Hungarian lawyer and communal worker. Mezey studied law at the university of Budapest and took an interest in Jewish affairs from his student days. In the *Tiszaeszlar blood-libel case, he assisted the counsel for the defense, K. Eötvös. During the 1890s Mezey was one of the founders of the movement seeking institutional equality for the Jewish religion (granted in 1895). From 1902 he was the secretary of the national bureau of the Hungarian Jews, and its president in the last year of his life. Between 1889 and 1916 he was also secretary of the *ḥevra kaddisha* of Pest (see *Budapest), and was instrumental in establishing social welfare institutions. Mezey was also president of the administrative council of the rabbinical seminary. He founded the Jewish Museum of Budapest (1916), and was editor of the periodical **Magyar Zsidó Szemle*. An extreme assimilationist and anti-Zionist, Mezey sought to foster religious life organized within the religious institutions in order to repair the breach between the two factions of Hungarian Jewry, and helped to promote the influence of *Neologism.

BIBLIOGRAPHY: L. Blau, in: *Magyar Zsidó Szemle*, 45 (1928), 97–100; idem, in: IMIT, 44 (1929), 11–25; Ö. Kálmán, *M.F. élete és működése* (1929).

[Jeno Zsoldos]

MEZHIRECH (Pol. **Miedzyrzec Korecki**; Ukrainian **Mezhirichi**), a town in Rovno district, Ukraine. In Jewish sources Mezhirech is called *Mezrits Gadol* to distinguish it from

Miedzyrzec Podlaski in the province of Lublin and Miedzyrzec in the province of Poznan. An organized Jewish community existed there from the 1570s. In 1700 the economic situation of the Jews was satisfactory, and they were obliged to pay a poll tax (together with Kilikiev) of 1,550 zloty, which was a considerable sum on the Volhynian tax list. The community struggled to free itself from the dependency on Ostrog. During the liquidation of the *Council of Four Lands, Mezhirech is mentioned as an independent community. In 1707 there were no Jews due to the total destruction of the city by Ataman Mazepa. In 1784 there were 295 Jews. Among the celebrated Jewish personalities who lived there were the kabbalist R. *Jacob Koppel b. Moses Lipschuetz and R. *Dov Baer of Mezhirech; as a result of the latter's presence the town became a center of the ḥasidic movement. In 1847 the Jewish community numbered 1,808 persons. At the close of the 19th century the Jews of Mezhirech established and developed a factory producing brushes, which became known throughout Russia. During 1910–12 the annual turnover of this firm amounted to over 50,000 rubles. There were 2,107 Jews (67% of the total population) living in the town in 1897 and 1,743 (73%) in 1921. A Tarbut school and nursery operated in the town, and from 1930 a religious school. In 1937 Beitar established a farm to train agricultural workers for Ereẓ Israel, and served also as a base for the *Irgun Ẓeva'i Le'ummi. The town was occupied by the Soviet army in September 1939, and, on July 6, 1941, by the Germans, who murdered, robbed, and conscripted the Jews into forced labor, with the assistance of the local Ukrainians. Of the 160 young Jews sent to work in Kiev, almost all were murdered there, with only two who had joined Soviet partisans surviving. On the first day of Shavuot (May 22, 1942) most of the town's Jews were murdered at prepared pits outside the settlement. The remaining 950 were confined in a ghetto. On September 26, 1942, about 900 of them were executed, and others fled, but only part of them managed to survive by joining Soviet partisan units. On January 14, 1944, the town was liberated, and 30 Jews came out of the forests and from hiding, and another 50 from the interior of the U.S.S.R. They soon left for Israel and the West.

BIBLIOGRAPHY: Halpern, Pinkas, index; B. Wasiutyński, *Ludność żydowska w Polsce w wiekach XIX i XX* (1930), 85; I. Schiper, *Dzieje handlu żydowskiego na żiemiach polskich* (1937), index; H. Tenenbaum, *Bilans handlowy Królestwa Polskiego* (1916), 161; B. Brutzkus, in: *Sozialwissenschaft und Sozialpolitik*, 61 (1929), 275. **ADD. BIBLIOGRAPHY:** S. Spector, PK, Poland, vol. 5: Volhynia and Polesie (1990).

[*Encyclopaedia Hebraica* / Shmuel Spector (2nd ed.)]

MEZŐFI, VILMOS (1870–1947), Hungarian politician and journalist, leader of the socialist agrarian movement. Born in Debrecen, Mezőfi was a watchmaker's apprentice who became a journalist and columnist in liberal newspapers. He joined the Social Democratic Party and edited their daily newspaper, *Népszava*. He also edited the workers' literary magazine, *Népolvasótár*.

Mezőfi played a leading role in the Social Democrats' attempt to organize agricultural workers. He was elected to the Hungarian parliament in 1905 where he advocated universal suffrage and pressed for immediate land reform. He left the party in 1910 when he found that it was not applying itself to this question. After World War I Mezőfi joined the newly formed small landowners' party and edited its journal *Szabad Szó* ("Free Word"). He continued to be active in Hungarian politics after the counterrevolution of 1920. In 1938 legislation was introduced to deprive Jews of their civic rights. Mezőfi vigorously fought the proposals and helped to organize the defense of the Jewish community. He was elected president of the 14th synagogue district of Pest in 1941.

Among Mezőfi's many writings are *A szociáldemokrácia evangéliuma* ("Gospel of Social Democracy") and *A munkabérek Magyarországon az 1896–1898 években* ("Wages in Hungary During the Years 1896–1898," 1899). In 1937 he published a pamphlet, *Irás a żsidókról* ("Script on the Jews"), directed to the agricultural population to combat the antisemitic Nazi propaganda which was being distributed among them.

BIBLIOGRAPHY: *Magyar Irodalmi Lexikon*, 2 (1965), 226; *Magyar Életrajzi Lexikon*, 2 (1969), s.v.

[Baruch Yaron]

MEZUZAH (Heb. מְזוּזָה), parchment scroll affixed to the doorpost of rooms in the Jewish home. The original meaning of the word *mezuzah* is "doorpost" (cf. Ex. 12:7). Its etymology is obscure; it has been suggested that it is derived from the Assyrian *manzazu*, but this is by no means certain. The Bible twice enjoins (Deut. 6:9 and 11:20) "and ye shall write them (the words of God) upon the *mezuzot* of thy house and in thy gates"; by transference, the word was made to apply not to the doorpost, but to the passages which were affixed to the doorpost in accordance with this injunction. The *mezuzah* consists of a piece of parchment, made from the skin of a clean animal, upon which the two passages in which the above-mentioned verses occur (Deut. 6:4–9 and 11:13–21) are written in square (Assyrian) characters, traditionally in 22 lines. The parchment is rolled up and inserted in a case with a small aperture. On the back of the parchment the word שַׁדַּי ("Almighty," but also the initial letters of שׁוֹמֵר דְּלָתוֹת יִשְׂרָאֵל "Guardian of the doors of Israel" (Kol Bo 90, 101:4)) is written, and the parchment is so inserted that the word is visible through the aperture. It is affixed to the right hand doorpost of the room, or house, or gate, where it is obligatory (see below), in the top third of the doorpost and slanting inward. A blessing "Who hast commanded us to fix the *mezuzah*" is recited when affixing it. The earliest evidence for the fulfillment of the commandments of the *mezuzah* dates from the Second Temple period. A *mezuzah* parchment (6.5 cm. × 16 cm.) has been found at Qumran (Cave 8) in which are written some sentences from Deuteronomy (10:12–11:21) but not from the *Shema* (*Discoveries in the Judean Desert of Jordan* (1962), 158–61). The Samaritans make their *mezuzot* out of large stones and attach them to the lintel of the main door of their houses or place them near the doorway. They carve on them the Ten Commandments or the "ten categories by which the world was created." Sometimes they use abbreviations and initial letters of the ten or single verses in praise of God. *Mezuzah* stones of this sort are found in Israel dating from the early Arab and perhaps even Byzantine era. The Karaites do not make the *mezuzah* obligatory. Nevertheless, the *mezuzot* that they do attach are made of a tablet of blank plate in the form of the two tablets of the law but without writing on them and they fix them to the doorways of their public buildings and sometimes to their dwelling places.

In the Middle Ages the custom obtained of making kabbalistic additions, usually the names of angels, as well as symbols (such as the **magen david*) to the text. The custom was vigorously opposed by Maimonides. He declared that those who did so "will have no share in the world to come." With their "foolish hearts" "they turn a commandment" whose purpose is to emphasize the love of God "into an amulet" (Yad, Tefillin 5:4). Despite this, there is one clear reference in the Talmud to the efficacy of the *mezuzah* as an amulet, though from the context it need not be regarded as doctrine. In return for a material gift sent by *Ardavan to *Rav, the latter sent him a *mezuzah*, and in answer to his surprised query replied that it would "guard him" (TJ, Pe'ah 1:1, 15d; Gen. R. 35:3). To a similar context belongs the story of the explanation of the *mezuzah* given by *Onkelos the proselyte to the Roman soldiers who came to arrest him: "In the case of the Holy One, blessed be He, His servants dwell within, while He keeps guard on them from without" (Av. Zar. 11a).

Maimonides' decision prevailed, and the *mezuzah* today contains only the two biblical passages. However, at the bottom of the obverse side there is written the formula כולו במוכסל כולו, a cryptogram formed by substituting the next letter of the alphabet for the original, it thus being the equivalent of יהוה אלהינו יהוה ("the Lord, God, the Lord"). This is already mentioned by *Asher b. Jehiel in the 13th century in his commentary to the *Hilkhot Mezuzah* of Alfasi (Romm-Vilna ed. p. 6b).

The *mezuzah* must be affixed to the entrance of every home and to the door of every living room of a house, thus excluding storerooms, stables, lavatories, and bathrooms, and must be inspected periodically (twice in seven years) to ensure that the writing is still readable. The custom has become widespread and almost universal at the present day to affix the *mezuzah* to the entrance to public buildings (including all government offices in Israel) and synagogues. There is no authority for this, unless the building or room is also used for residential purposes (Levi ibn Ḥabib, Resp. no. 101), and the Midrash (Deut. R. 7:2) actually asks the rhetorical question, "Is then a *mezuzah* affixed to synagogues?" As the scriptural verse states, it is also to be affixed to "thy gates." It is thus obligatory for the entrances to apartment houses. On the gates of the suburb Yemin Moshe in Jerusalem, which stand since their erection in 1860, the *mezuzot* are still to be seen. After the Six-Day War *mezuzot* were affixed to the gates of the Old City of Jerusalem. In the responsa *Sha'ali Ẓiyyon* of D. Eliezrov (1962, pt. 2, nos. 9–10), who served as rabbi to the Jewish political prisoners at Latrun during the British Mandate, there are two responsa from him and Rabbi Ouziel, Sephardi chief rabbi of Israel, as to whether *mezuzot* were obligatory for the rooms and cells of the camp.

In the Diaspora the *mezuzot* must be affixed after the householder has resided in the home for 30 days; in Israel, immediately on occupation. If the house is sold or let to a Jew the previous occupier must leave the *mezuzah*. It is customary, among the pious, on entering or leaving to kiss the *mezuzah* or touch it and kiss the fingers (Maharil, based on the passage from Av. Zar. 11a quoted above).

The Talmud enumerates the *mezuzah* as one of the seven precepts with which God surrounded Israel because of His love for them. Of the same seven (the *ẓiẓit* being regarded as four) R. *Eliezer b. Jacob stated, "Whosoever has the **tefillin* on his head, the *tefillin* on his arm, the *ẓiẓit* on his garment, and the *mezuzah* on his doorpost is fortified against sinning" (Men. 43b). The *mezuzah* is one of the most widely observed ceremonial commandments of Judaism. In modern times the practice developed of wearing a *mezuzah* around the neck as a charm. Some of the cases in which the *mezuzah* is enclosed are choice examples of Jewish art, and the artistic *mezuzah* case has been developed to a considerable extent in modern Israel.

BIBLIOGRAPHY: Eisenstein, Dinim, 214f.; F. Landsberger, in: HUCA, 31 (1960), 149–66; J. Trachtenberg, *Jewish Magic and Superstition* (1939), 146ff.; V. Aptowitzer, in: REJ, 60 (1910), 38–52.

[Louis Isaac Rabinowitz]

MEZZROW, MILTON (Mesirow, Mezz; 1899–1972), jazz clarinetist. Born in Chicago, Mezzrow became one of the outstanding representatives of the Chicago style. In the mid-1920s he played occasionally with the Austin High School Gang in Chicago and recorded with the Chicago Rhythm Kings, the Louisiana Rhythm Kings, and Eddie Condon. During the 1930s and 1940s he was among the first white jazz musicians to perform with African American musicians, such as Tommy Ladnier and Sidney Bechet, with whom he appeared in New York and Paris. In 1937 he founded one of the earliest interracial jazz bands, led a band at Kelly's Stable (1943), and worked with Art Hodes (1943–44). In 1945 he became a co-founder and the president of the King jazz label. During the early 1950s Mezzrow moved to France, where he worked as an entrepreneur, organizing all-star touring bands, and appeared in the films *Vedettes en pantoufles* (1953) and *Premier festival Européen de jazz* (1954). His recordings include *Really the Blues* (1938); *Royal Garden Blues* (1938); *Comin' On with the Come On* (1938); *Revolutionary Blues* (1938); *Gone Away Blues* (1945); *Out of the Gallion* (1945); *Really the Blues* (1947); and *Mezz Mezzrow à la Schola Cantorum* (1955).

ADD. BIBLIOGRAPHY: Grove online; M. Mezzrow and B. Wolf, *Really the Blues* (1946); J. Simmen, "L'importante contribution de Mezz Mezzrow au jazz," in: BHcF, 342 (1986), 7.

[Israela Stein (2nd ed.)]

MIAMI-DADE COUNTY, located on the southeast coast of Florida. Miami-Dade County is comprised of 32 cities with Miami as the county seat and largest and oldest city. Miami, founded in 1896, was difficult to reach until the railroad was extended southward. The stereotyped image as the destination of Jews settling in Florida has been "Miami." In reality, Miami was among the state's latest communities to develop a Jewish population at all, with the Jews coming from other places in the United States (either New York or Key West); they were mostly immigrants from Russia and Romania. Romanian Jews had come to Key West in the 1880s and 1890s and left either as a result of a peddler's tax in 1891, the decline of the cigar industry, or the general decline of that city as the railroad arrived in Miami. Russian Jews who had come to New York began to come south with the railroad, first to Ft. Pierce, West Palm Beach, then Miami. This was true of the earliest Jews to settle in Miami. The first Jew to arrive in Miami in 1895 was either Sam Singer or Jake Schneidman. The earliest permanent Jewish settler was Isidor Cohen, who was a signatory of the city's charter in 1896 and helped found many Jewish and civic organizations. About 25 of these pioneer Jews had religious services beginning in 1896. There was no synagogue at the time but a rabbi was brought from West Palm Beach to conduct High Holy Day services. After the great fire that destroyed most of the businesses and took the life of Jewish merchant Julius Frank on December 26, 1896, and a yellow fever epidemic in 1899, the Jewish population declined by 1900 to three people: Isidor Cohen and Jake and Ida Schneidman; then Jake soon died. Cohen said that Jews owned 12 of Miami's first 16 retail stores. Miami remained a hostile environment for would-be settlers. Nonetheless, aided by the railroad and a fledgling tourist industry, Miami didn't give up. In 1905 Cohen married widow Ida Schneidman and the first *brit* was celebrated in 1907 for their son, Eddie, the first Jewish birth in the city. A girl, Nell Lehrman, was born in 1914. The death of a Jewish tourist in 1913 forced the small Jewish community to gather to discuss creating an organization and a cemetery. Meeting at the home of Mendel Rippa, the group of 35 Jews established the first congregation in Miami. They called it B'nai Zion, in tribute to its first president, Morris Zion. Later, the name was changed to Beth David. By 1915, there were 55 Jews in Miami. In the 1920s there was a Zionist Society; the United Jewish Aid Association (that eventually became Jewish Family Service); a B'nai B'rith lodge; chapters of the National Council of Jewish Women and Hadassah; Workmen's Circle *The New Jewish Unity* newspaper (1926–35); and then the *Jewish Floridian* (1928–90). Tremendous advertising combined with abundant land, new roads, and the availability of the automobile and commercial aviation, created a tourist and real estate boom. A population of 30,000 (that included 100 Jewish families) exploded to more than 130,000 with 3,500 Jews by 1925. Jews founded Temple Israel, the first Reform congregation, in 1922, and were among those who chartered the University of Miami in 1925. The hurricane that swept Miami just as *Kol Nidre* services on Yom Kippur ended on September 18, 1926, brought the real estate boom to an abrupt halt. From 1926 to 1931, the city suffered a boom and bust, two hurricanes, the failure of five banks, and finally the stock market crash. Headlines screamed, "Miami is Wiped Out."

But the headlines were wrong. By the mid-1930s, Miami began a gradual recovery. New residents arrived by air, train, and the Mallory Steamship Line. Streetcars were introduced in the city. Tourists were lured to boating, fishing, and tropical gardens attractions. Miami began to gain a reputation as the "gateway to Latin America" – a reputation that would increase dramatically as the century wore on. During the 1930s, approximately 4,500 Jews lived among a Miami population of more than 110,000. Satellite communities emerged. The hotel, building, and banking industries escalated with greater participation by Jews. Jews helped start and continue to support Miami-Dade College, the University of Miami, which has a Center for Contemporary Jewish Studies and Hillel, and Florida International University with a Judaic Studies Program. The perilous situation of European Jews evoked a response in Miami's small but active Jewish community, which founded the Greater Miami Jewish Federation in 1938. The first president was Stanley C. Myers. Ida Cohen founded the Jewish Home for the Aged with a $10,000 donation from a non-Jew in 1940; today it is a leader in the field of all levels of care for the Jewish frail and elderly.

When the Japanese bombed Pearl Harbor, local leaders, seeking to expand business and visibility, convinced the government that Miami was the ideal location for training military personnel. As a result, funding and soldiers poured into the area, particularly Miami Beach. Many of these soldiers were Jews, who returned after the war, when South Florida's image as a year-round resort reemerged. The tourist industry was revitalized with the widespread use of air conditioning, mosquito control, the development of Miami International Airport, and Israeli businessman Ted Arison's expansion of the cruise ship business. The post-war economic boom brought additional tourists and settlers to Miami. Many were Jews, attracted by the new jobs created from tourism. In 1950, Dade County had a population of 495,000 people of which 55,000 were Jewish. For the next five years, approximately 650 Jews arrived each month. A new house was built every seven minutes during this period – and many of the builders were Jews. In 1952 Abe Aronovitz became the first (and to date, the *only*) Jewish mayor of Miami. Many Jews, horrified by news of the Holocaust, began to challenge antisemitism at home. The Miami branch of the Anti-Defamation League had been founded in 1940. During the McCarthy era, bombings and desecration of area synagogues were prevalent. Following the communist takeover of Cuba in 1959, 10–12,000 Cuban Jews immediately fled the country, finding refuge in Miami and its environs. In Miami, the presence of middle-class Cubans with business acumen helped revitalize the city.

In the post-war period until the mid-1960s, most jobs were related to the tourist and building industries or real estate. Most Jews were involved in the services and retail trades, but by the 1960s, many were moving into medical and legal professions. In 1963 the first two Jews from South Florida were elected to the state legislature – Murray Dubbin and Louis Wolfson II. William Lehman was Florida's second Jew to serve in the U.S. Congress (after David Levy Yulee in the 19th century) when he began his 20 years of service in the House of Representatives in 1973. Lehman was a powerful force on transportation legislation, responsible for bringing mass transit to South Florida. In this period, Jews began to move north to North Miami and North Miami Beach. Cuban Jews started their own congregations.

From a shipping family, Israeli Ted *Arison, in 1972, acquired his own ship, the Mardi Gras, which was the start of Carnival Cruise Lines, today the largest cruise company in the world. Arison headed the campaign to bring professional basketball to South Florida (Miami Heat) and was the chief benefactor of the New World Symphony, founded by Michael Tilson *Thomas. The 1973 Arab oil embargo plunged Miami into the worst recession since the 1930s. Yet Jewish Miami continued to grow. By 1980 the Greater Miami Jewish population reached its all time peak of 230,000, with a full array of Jewish organizations, including Jewish Federation TV and the *Miami Jewish Tribune* (1986–93). The *Miami Herald* published an insert, the *Jewish Star Times* (2000–02).

In the 1980s, Miami became the new Ellis Island for people fleeing troubled countries like Haiti and the Dominican Republic. The influx of Caribbean immigrants, as well as the growing Spanish-speaking Cuban population, alienated some people and many Jews moved north to Broward and Palm Beach counties. By 1985 the Jewish population had declined to 209,000. As well, many of the old Jews, who had lived on Miami Beach, had died. But the greater Miami Jewish community was reinvigorated by the arrival of Jews from Latin America, Russia, and Israel. In 2005 the Jewish population of the county has decreased but stabilized at about 121,000 with a high percentage of retired and elderly persons (but less than in Broward and Palm Beach counties). There are more than 60 congregations, 34 Jewish educational institutions, and three Jewish community centers. The highest percentage and increase in Jewish population is in North Dade, especially in Aventura. Miami-Dade County hosts Florida's third largest Jewish population and the nation's tenth largest.

Miami Beach and Antisemitism

From the early 20th century, people visited the southern tip of Florida to picnic on its sandy beaches or bathe in the warm waters of the Atlantic Ocean. In 1913 the Collins Bridge opened, joining the beach to the mainland. That same year, New York Jews Joe and Jenny Weiss, and their son Jesse, relocated to Miami Beach. Joe and Jennie operated a snack bar at a popular bathing spot at the tip of the beach, the only place Jews could settle. Several years later, the Weiss family opened Joe's Stone Crab Restaurant in a small, wooden frame house, which they continued to expand and today remains the site of this world famous restaurant. It is still run by descendants of the Weiss family. Developers placed restrictive covenants in their land deeds that prohibited the sale of Miami Beach lots to Jews: "No lot shall be sold, conveyed, leased to anyone not a member of the Caucasian race, nor to anyone having more than one quarter Hebrew or Syrian blood." A letter, written in 1920, stated, "We don't want Miami Beach to ever become a Jewish outfit – it would not only ruin the Hotel but ruin the property." However, the Lummus Brothers who owned properties at the southern end of Miami Beach, did not bar Jews from ownership. Several modest Jewish-owned hotels and apartments arose on property sold to Jews south of Fifth Street. These early Beach Jews owned and lived in apartments and rented units to others. This was their chief source of income. Sam Magid and Joseph and Harry Goodkowsky moved to Miami Beach and in 1921 built the Nemo Hotel on Collins Avenue and First Street, the first hotel to cater to kosher Jewish winter tourists. Shortly thereafter, the Seabreeze Hotel, also kosher, opened nearby at Collins and Second Street. Rose and Jeremiah Weiss and their children moved to Miami Beach in 1919 because of Rose's health problems. They bought the Royal Apartments, which had dwellings for 15 families. Rose Weiss, known as "the Mother of Miami Beach," attended every city commission meeting for nearly 40 years and created the city's flag. In the mid-1920s, the Jacobs family opened the first of three hotels. The Blackstone opened in 1929 on Washington Avenue and Eighth Street. Built by Nathan Stone, the grandfather of future U.S. Senator Richard Stone, this hostelry became one of South Beach's most imposing buildings, as well as a haven for Jewish visitors. George Gershwin reportedly wrote portions of *Porgy and Bess* while reposing in the hotel's rooftop solarium.

Despite this activity, the Jewish population of Miami Beach grew slowly in the first half of the 1920s. It was confined to an area from Fifth Street south to the tip of the peninsula. Malvina Weiss Gutschmidt, the daughter of Rose Weiss, noted that there were no Jewish residences north of Fifth Street until 1925. From 1925 until the end of the decade a rapidly growing Jewish neighborhood moved north all the way to Lincoln Road at 16th Street. A fantastic real estate boom, which overtook all of South Florida and much of the rest of the state in the mid-1920s, prompted this growth. The boom led to the creation of hundreds of new subdivisions and communities in Greater Miami and to a sharp increase in the area's population. This speculative era lured many "bigger than life" Jews: bankers Leonard Abess and Baron de Hirsch *Meyer and attorney, businessman, Zionist, and community builder Max Orovitz. Henri Levy, a French-born Jew, migrated with his family to Miami Beach, an area he characterized as "a lush tropical paradise." In 1922 Levy developed the smart boom-era communities of Normandy Isle and Normandy Beach North, which later became Surfside. The boom collapsed in 1926, when a hurricane smashed into South Beach and other parts of the county. But many "boomers," whose ranks included a considerable number of Jews, remained in the area. In the 1930s, Miami Beach's Jewish population grew significantly, reaching at least several thousand (out of an overall population for Miami Beach of 28,012) by decade's end, as Miami-Dade County, formerly called Greater Miami, replaced Jacksonville as the center of Florida Jewry.

Many of the new arrivals to Miami Beach came initially as tourists. Most came from the northeast United States. Most hotels and apartments continued to exhibit "Gentile Only" signs. Jewish builders erected many of the finest hotels on South Beach during the 1930s. Many bore the Streamline or Nautical Modern style of architecture designed by Henry Hohauser, who moved to Miami Beach in 1936. His initial project was to design a new sanctuary for Miami Beach's first congregation – the building that now houses the Jewish Museum of Florida. For the next ten years, this brilliant architect was responsible for the design of more than 100 hotels, apartments, and buildings on Miami Beach. The Art Deco buildings of the 1930s and 1940s on Miami Beach are architectural treasures known throughout the world. The square-mile district is bounded by Fifth Street to 23rd Street, Lenox Avenue to Ocean Drive. In the 1980s, Barbara Baer Capitman, a Jew, launched the campaign that established the Art Deco District, the largest collection of 1930s Art Deco and Art Moderne buildings in the nation. Jews operated many of the hotels. The 1930s also marked the dismantling of restrictive barriers to Jewish ownership of real estate throughout the Beach, as large numbers of Jews purchased commercial properties from debt-ridden owners only too happy to sell them. Jews also began buying residential lots whose restrictive covenants proved impossible to enforce after the property had changed owners a couple of times. While discrimination had by no means vanished, conditions were improving. But it was not until 1949 that a law was passed by Florida's legislature that ended discrimination in real estate and hotels. The Jewish retail, institutional, and residential presence was most strongly felt at the southern portion of the island, especially along Washington Avenue and Collins Avenue and Ocean Drive, stretching from the tip more than one mile north to, and even beyond, Lincoln Road. Small Jewish businesses dotted Miami Beach streets and Jewish tenants filled apartments. In 1925, Jews began meeting for services in apartments. Several very observant Canadian Jewish visitors lobbied for a synagogue. As a result of their efforts, Orthodox Beth Jacob Congregation was organized in 1927. In the 1930s, as the Jewish population moved into areas north of Fifth Street, many members of Beth Jacob broke away and organized a Conservative congregation. Jacob Joseph of Miami Beach subsequently became the Miami Beach Community Center in the 1940s, and, finally, in 1954, Temple Emanu-El. Rabbi Irving *Lehrman served as the powerful spiritual leader for 50 years. As the Jewish population continued to move north, and many Jewish soldiers poured into the area for wartime training, Jews founded the Beth Sholom Center in a storefront on 41st Street in 1942 (it was renamed Temple Beth Sholom in 1945), where Rabbi Leon *Kronish served for nearly 50 years. Today there are more than 20 congregations on the Beach. Jewish education is abundant: the Hebrew Academy since 1947, Lehrman Day School since 1960, and Talmudic Academy since 1974. There has been a *mikveh* since 1945 and an *eruv* since 1982. Commensurate with their increase in numbers, Jews began to play increasingly more important civic roles. Baron de Hirsch *Meyer, who came to the area during the boom after earning a law degree from Harvard, served as president of numerous Jewish organizations and was the first Jew to sit on the Miami Beach City Council (1934). Mitchell Wolfson, who migrated to Miami with his family around 1915 from Key West, became Miami Beach's second Jewish councilman. Like de Hirsch Meyer, Wolfson was a stellar businessman, civic leader, and visionary. In 1943 he was elected mayor, the first of 15 Jews who have served as mayor of Miami Beach (as of 2005). Mitchell Wolfson was very important to business in Miami. With his brother-in-law Sidney Meyer, Wolfson formed WOMETCO (Wolfson Meyer Theater Company) in 1949. WOMETCO became the first television station in Florida, WTVJ. Wolfson also built the Seaquarium and left an endowment to create the Wolfson campus of Miami-Dade College. By the mid-1940s, the Greater Miami Jewish Federation placed the number of Jews in Dade County at 29,325 in a county nearing 400,000 in population. Nearly one-half of these Jews lived on Miami Beach.

Less civic-minded Jews also embraced Miami Beach. Most prominent of these was Meyer *Lansky, the reputed boss of South Florida crime in the middle decades of the 20th century. Less "prominent" than Lansky nationally but quite active on the Beach was the S&G Syndicate, founded and operated by five Jews. From its office on Washington Avenue, the S&G controlled bookmaking in a couple of hundred hotels on Miami Beach and elsewhere in the area in the 1940s, grossing millions of dollars annually. A U.S. Senate crime investigating committee, chaired by Estes Kefauver, put the syndicate out of business in the early 1950s.

The tragedy of the Holocaust caused many Jews to turn to Zionism. In 1944, more than 8,000 persons gathered in Miami's Bayfront Park to hear Dr. Stephen S. Wise, a renowned scholar and leader, present the case for the Jewish people and for a homeland in Palestine. Some South Florida Jews, led by Shepard Broad (Broad Causeway honors him), helped outfit boats and planes to transport Jews from Displaced Persons (DPS) camps in Europe to Palestine. Inspired by first-hand experience in financing boatloads of Holocaust survivors and DPS to arrive in Palestine, Max Orovitz formed "the Miami Group" with fellow Jewish businessmen and created the Dan Hotel chain in Israel following statehood. Following World War II, Jewish doctors could not get staff privileges at any area hospitals. In response, Jewish leaders in the community formed Mount Sinai Hospital on Miami Beach; Max Orovitz was the founding chairman for 30 years. Today, the 55-acre hospital, the largest employer in that city, is renowned for its leadership in medicine, especially cardiac care.

As the social and cultural fabric of Miami Beach changed following the end of World War II, so did the Beach's physical appearance. Hotels were built rapidly to satiate the desire of tourists for fancy new hotels. The hotel industry was greatly bolstered by Jews, including Ben Novack who, with Harry Mufson, built the Fontainebleau Hotel (1954). Designed by Morris *Lapidus, the elegant hotel quickly became a trademark property. A year later, Mufson commissioned Lapidus to design the equally grandiose Eden Roc Hotel next door.

Larry *King began his live talk show on Miami Beach in 1956. Sophie *Tucker belted her songs in Yiddish during the 1950s and 1960s in Miami Beach hotels. In 1967 Judy Drucker organized the first concert at Temple Beth Sholom and began bringing world famous performers to Miami Beach. Fifteen years later Drucker formed the Concert Association of Florida. From Yiddish theater in the 1930s to Pavarotti on the beach in the 1990s, from the Miss Universe Beauty Pageant at the Fontainebleau Hotel in 1960 to the opening of the Jewish Museum of Florida in 1995, Jews have played an active role in developing the arts and entertainment scene of Miami Beach to what it is today, and they continue to nurture it. Jews started the other museums, Bass Museum of Art and Wolfsonian, as well as the Miami City Ballet. In 1990 Kenneth Treister designed the Holocaust Memorial, a 50-foot outstretched arm with 135 life-sized bronze sculptures.

In the 1970s, about 80% of the population was Jewish. In 2004 it was 20% (about 20,000). There is a resurgence of Orthodoxy (17% of the Beach population), especially among younger families. The elderly Jews have passed away and Latin American and Israeli Jews have arrived. The increasing popularity of Miami Beach, rising real estate values, and a declining Jewish population have forced more synagogues to close their doors and become nightclubs and retail stores. The skyline of Miami Beach has changed from the day the first "skyscraper" went up in 1940. It continues to change, as some buildings come down and new higher ones go up. Jews have been involved in every aspect of these developments, as architects, developers, and contractors. Through their contributions to the physical appearance of Miami Beach, their roles in building the Beach are apparent and perpetual.

(Current demographics (2004) were provided by Ira M. Sheskin, Ph.D., for the Greater Miami Jewish Federation.)

[Marcia Jo Zerivitz (2nd ed.)]

Cuban Jewish Community

The Jews of Cuba form a special group among the Jews of Greater Miami. Despite their small number, 2,500 households (2001), they stand out as a link between the large Cuban exile population and the large Jewish population. Unlike other Jews from Latin America, who tend to use Miami as a temporary stopover, the Cubans made Miami their permanent home.

Following the Castro revolution, Cuban Jews started to migrate to South Florida, most of them to Miami Beach. Like other middle-class Cubans, their exodus was motivated by the complete change in the social and economic system under Castro, and particularly by the nationalization of private businesses. Between 1960 and 1963, more than 9,000 Jews, out of the 12,000 that had resided in Cuba prior to the revolution, left the island. Assisted by HIAS, which tried to relocate them in other parts of the United States, they favored Miami, which became their substitute for Havana. They found there a similar landscape and climate and a large Spanish-speaking population.

Though arriving with practically no property, the Cuban Jews were equipped with the experience and education to facilitate their economic integration and eventually their remarkable success. Like other Cuban exiles of the early 1960s they became owners and general managers of large business firms, senior bank executives, and professionals.

The Cuban Jews felt rejected by the resident Jewish population, which was indifferent to their presence and problems. The only congregation that was hospitable to the Cubans was Temple Menorah, which with time became an important social and religious center of Cuban Jews. In 1961 they founded the Círculo Cubano Hebreo, which became the Cuban Hebrew Congregation at the Ashkenazi Beth Shmuel synagogue. In 1969 the Sephardim founded the Cuban Sephardi Hebrew Congregation, and in 1980 they inaugurated their synagogue, Temple Moses (today Torat Moshe).

The two Cuban congregations were founded in Miami Beach, the center of the early immigrants, many of whom were born in Europe, migrated to Cuba, and finally settled in Miami. The younger generation, of Cuban-born Jews, tended to leave the Beaches and concentrate in South Dade. A study by I.M. Sheskin (see Bibliography) showed in 1982 that out of 3,213 Cuban-born Jews, 40% lived in the Beaches, 50% in South Dade, and 10% in North Dade. With time, however, the population of the Beaches decreased considerably, though most Cuban Jews still live within the boundaries of Dade County.

The Cuban-born Jews preserved the social and cultural patterns that they brought over from Cuba: they were very active in Zionist circles, they sent their children to Jewish day schools, and were less influenced by assimilation. With time, however, the Cuban identity tends to diminish. The third generation, born in the United States, is less affected by the Cuban heritage of their parents' community. They are integrated in an English-speaking environment and gradually lose their Cuban characteristics.

[Margalit Bejarano (2nd ed.)]

ADD. BIBLIOGRAPHY: M. Bejarano, "From Havana to Miami, The Cuban Jewish Community," in: *Judaica Latinoamericana*, 3 (1997); I.M. Sheskin, *Population Study of Greater Miami Jewish Community* (1982): B. Heisler-Samuels, "Forced to Leave Homes, Cuban Jews Thrive in Miami," in: the *Miami Herald* Internet Edition (Jan. 17, 2001).

MICA (Heb. מִיכָא; "who is like [El]"), son of *Mephi-Bosheth, son of Jonathan, son of Saul (II Sam. 9:12). In the genealogical list of the tribe of Benjamin (I Chron. 8:34, 35; 9:40, 41) he is called Micah (Heb. מִיכָה). Thanks to *Jonathan, his grandfather, and Mephi-Bosheth, his father, Mica no doubt benefited from David's generosity (II Sam. 9:12; cf. 19:24–29).

For his descendants, see *Benjamin.

MICAH (Heb. מִיכָה), the sixth book in the collection known as the Twelve Minor Prophets within the subdivision "Later Prophets" of the second division of the Hebrew Bible (the Prophets). In the Septuagint translation, where the order varies, Micah usually comes immediately after Hosea and Amos. It is possible that the prophet's name is a hypocoristic of a name formulated as a rhetorical question. Mi-ka-yahu, "who is like YHW(H)" or Mi-ka-El, "Who is like God / El." An ostracon from Jerusalem from the late eighth or early seventh century attests the name *Mk*[*y*]*hw* (Ahituv, 23).

The Content of the Book

The title (1:1) specifies the name, country, and date (in the days of Jotham, Ahaz, and Hezekiah, kings of Judah in the eighth century) of Micah's prophecy "concerning Jerusalem and Samaria." This is followed by a diatribe against Israel and Samaria (1:2–7). Critics have suggested that verse 1:5b, dealing with the "cult places" (*bamot*) of Judah – which are hardly a concern of Micah – is a gloss inspired by 3:12. Others emend *bamot* to *ḥattot*, "sins." In the succeeding lamentation (1:8–16), over the birthplace of the prophet and the neighboring towns, misfortune strikes at the gates of Jerusalem (12) but does not pass beyond them. The prophetic "I" makes its first appearance in verse 15. In verse 16, as the form of the Hebrew verb shows, a female person is addressed; no doubt Daughter-Zion of verse 13, or, following the reading of some manuscripts of the Septuagint, "Fair Israel." In fact the "kings of Israel" did suffer a reverse at Achzib, as verse 14 indicates.

In 2:1 the threat is no longer directed against cities but against those who, having dispossessed others and defrauded them of their holdings, shall themselves be dispossessed. This section of chapter 2 may be dealing with social injustices (8–12) or, like Hosea 5:9–11, with a territorial dispute between tribes. Note that it is a clan (*mishpaḥah*, 2:3), which has angered the Lord and it is a stranger who reaps the benefit of the vengeful spoliation, without right of repurchase. The key phrase is in verse 7: the Lord does not abandon Israel. The sense of the passage becomes clearer if the prophet is assumed to be warning the ministers of Judah, who wish to expand at the expense of Israel. From this the conclusion can be drawn that the Lord, the sole King, steps into the breach and gathers His people together despite Judah's policy. In a new soliloquy (3:1) the prophet personally attacks the "leaders" and "magistrates" of Israel (without any mention of kings) who ignore the law and devour each other in quarrels, which the prophet depicts figuratively as cannibalism, through which the people suffer. The prophets for their part mislead the people. In punishment, the Lord no longer provides them visions. Chapter 3 culminates in a prediction of the destruction of Jerusalem, corresponding to that of Samaria in 1:6. According to Jeremiah 26:18, this text had great repercussions, reaching the ear of Hezekiah and perhaps precipitating his reforms.

The allusion to Jerusalem and Zion is followed by the insertion of the famous passage, "from Zion shall come forth Torah/ teaching/ law and the word of the Lord from Jerusalem," which appears also in Isaiah (2:2–4). The passage predicts the universal reign of peace, with the Lord issuing instructions on Mount Zion and settling disputes so that war will be unnecessary. (On the relation between the Micah and Isaiah oracles, Andersen and Freedman (413–25) cite no fewer than seven options.) After the profession of faith in 4:5 ("We walk in the name of the Lord, our God"), a new oracle announces the reign of the Lord, who assembles the crippled. Daughter-Zion regains her former sovereignty (vs. 8). Her present pangs are pangs of birth that augur well for the future when YHWH will redeem her. The section (5:1–5:5) on Beth-Lehem-Ephrathah appears to be a unity. Though the area is too small to be a fighting unit, from there the leader (*moshel*, the term "king" is avoided) of Israel will arise (cf. the Christian reading of this passage in Matt. 2:5–6). The allusion to a Davidide is clear, inasmuch as his wellsprings, or origins, can be traced from ancient times (5:1). The schism between Israel and Judah is compared to the abandonment of the Israelites by this Davidide until the day when she, presumably Daughter-Zion (4:10), who is destined to give birth does so. The leader presides over the ingathering, but here this is presented as a return of Judah to Israel (cf. Deut. 33:7). This shepherd is capable of organizing a coalition against Assyria of seven shepherds and eight *nesikhim* ("princes") and of assuring peace. This passage is therefore linked with the preceding one, as B. Renaud pointed out. It likewise is connected with the following verses: 6–8, where the remnant of Israel is seen as present in the midst of the nations as a sign of the Lord's blessing or curse.

In contrast, chapter 5:9–14 returns to the theme of the extermination of idols (as in 1:7 against Samaria; cf. Isa. 2:6–22) with an allusion to the cities of the country (as in 1:10–15). This passage is linked associatively with chapter 6 by the repetition of the verb *shama*, "hear" (cf. 5:14) in 6:1. Here the presentation is in the form of a complaint (*riv*). The Lord recalls his acts of salvation, citing the exodus from Egypt led by Moses, Aaron, and Miriam (the only non-genealogical reference to Miriam outside the Pentateuch), and the plot of Balak and Balaam, which YHWH foiled. No response of the people has survived. The verses that follow are arguably among the most famous in the Bible. In vss. 6–7 we have a question modeled on the liturgy of entrance: "With what shall I come before YHWH, bow down to the god on high? Shall I come before him with burnt offerings, with calves sons of a year? Will YHWH be pleased with thousands of rams, with myriads of streams of oil? Shall I give my first born for my transgression, the fruit of my belly for my own sin?" Verse 8 replies that it has already been revealed to humans what is required of them: justice, mercy, and humility before the Lord. Chapter 6:9–16 is a new soliloquy to an unnamed town, and probably to a tribe. The resemblance to Amos 8:4–5 and the allusion in verse 16 to Omri and the house of Ahab make it probable that the passage alluded (at least originally) to Samaria. The tribe may be Ephraim, since in the oracles of Hosea and Isaiah the kingdom of the North dismembered by *Tiglath-Pileser III is called Ephraim (Isa. 9:7 (8)).

The prophetic "I" again appears in 7:1 in a lamentation on civil discord (cf. 3:3; Isa. 10:17ff.). This "I" reappears from verse 7 onward where the prophet speaks in the name of Israel, which reproaches its "enemy" for having rejoiced at its downfall. It is probable that (as in 2:8) the enemy is in this case Judah, since the question raised by the "enemy": "Where is your God?" is the reproach of the Judahites against the Israelites who did not recognize the choice of the sanctuary at Zion. Verse 10b is reminiscent of 3:12 on the ruin of Jerusalem. Chapter 7:14–20 is a prayer imploring the Lord to become the shepherd of His people once again (the geographical terms are of the North, Carmel, Bashan, and Gilead, alienated in 733 B.C.E.) as He promised to Jacob and Abraham. This rare reference probably aimed at encompassing both Judah and Israel in the same gathering.

Composition

The book is composed of independent but more or less connected sections. Ordinarily, these sections are re-divided into three: chapters 1–3 speak of condemnation, 4–5 of consolation, and 6–7 of a mixture of condemnation and consolation. The visions of consolation are generally attributed to the years following the Exile and are assumed to have been added to the original oracles of Micah at the time when the book was put together (Renaud). There are two objections to this view:

(1) It disregards the importance of the kingdom of the North and its downfall in 722 in the religious thought of Israel. This strain in Micah was given great emphasis by F.C. Burkitt, O. Eissfeldt, and J.T. Willis;

(2) It neglects the influence of the cultural traditions in the sanctuaries (including Jerusalem) on the prophetic oracles. E. Hammershaimb and B. Reicke have stressed this fact. In the ancient Orient, as at the beginning of the monarchy, prophecy announced good tidings rather than misfortune.

But as Willis' survey of the numerous theories about Micah demonstrates, the history of the book's composition is far from settled. The unity, coherence, and attribution to the prophet are all debated. Where some scholars see artful redactional unity, others (e.g., Hillers) find no meaningful structure. Willis himself enumerates areas that need to be addressed. Among these are the text, which swarms with philological difficulties, and the criteria for the dating of passages. It is impossible to speak meaningfully about the theology of the book, if indeed it has one or several, apart from the questions of composition, arrangement, and redaction. There is general agreement though that the present book has a historical core in the eighth century, and that at least some of the prophecies are those of the prophet Micah referred to in Jeremiah 26:16–19, and confused with Michaiah son of Imlah in I Kings. 22–28.

The Prophet and His Time

R. Weil emphasized the importance of historical events known from II Kings 20–22 for an understanding of Micah. His birthplace, Moresheth-Gath, near Lachish, is known as far back as the El-Amarna period (tablet 335:7). This region had suffered since the days of the Syro-Ephraimite war against Judah, which commenced under *Jotham (II Kings 15:37; cf. Micah 1:1 and probably 1:13) and continued up to the time of the Assyrian campaign against Gath and Ashdod in 733, 720 (the five *nesikim* of Micah 5:4 are reminiscent of the five Aramean "sheikhs" (Akkadian: *nāsikāti*) mentioned by the Assyrian king Sargon II (Fuchs, 147)), and 712 (cf. Isa. 20). Meanwhile Samaria had fallen. Hezekiah, who had probably been associated in the kingship from 729/7, became in any case the sole king after 716/5. He shared the views of Micah (Jer. 26:18), who attacked the leaders of Jerusalem (but never the king), and his political activities disturbed Sargon. Perhaps it was at this time that the mission of Merodach-Baladan took place and the oracles on the deliverance of daughter- Zion were delivered, but this mission probably dates from 703, the time of the general revolt against Sennacherib which was to end in 701 with a new occupation of Lachish and the region. The rabbis held that Micah's prophecies were redacted and canonized by the Men of the Great Assembly (BB 15a; see *Great Synagogue).

The Theological Problem

Micah 5 regards it as the will of YHWH that all Israel unite around the dynasty that issued from Beth-Lehem, where David was born. There are similarities in the theological teachings found in Micah and Isaiah: the fidelity of the Lord endures despite his "wrath" (Micah 7:9; Isa. 9:11, 16); He remains the light of the faithful (Micah 7:8; Isa. 10:17); He is King of Israel (Micah 4:7; Isa. 6:1); and He has chosen the Davidic dynasty for the salvation of the people (Micah 5:1; Isa. 7:1–9; 9:6). Finally, the theology of the book of Micah shares points in common with that of Hosea and *Deuteronomy when speaking of *ḥesed* ("mercy"; 7:18, 20), "the love of *ḥesed*" (6:8), and when it places mercy and humble submission to God above sacrifices (6:8; cf. Hos. 6:6). This prophet who, unlike the others, reveals himself as "full of strength, the spirit of YHWH, and justice and valor" takes on his shoulders the burden that the descendants of David should have assumed (Isa. 11:2–3).

There are numerous word plays in the book: *be-gat al taggidu ... be-bet le-aprah apar ...* (1:10); *akziv le-akzav* (1:14); *ha-yoresh ... moreshah; ad adullam* (1:15); *titgodedi bat-gedud* (4:14). The text of the book has not been well-preserved, with some passages unintelligible (e.g., 1:10–16; 2:6–11; 7:11–12).

[Henri Cazelles / S. David Sperling (2nd ed.)]

In the Aggadah

According to one opinion, Micah was a contemporary of Isaiah (SOR 20; and Pes. 87b); according to another, he was one of the post-Exilic prophets (PdRK 16, 128b). The verse: "He hath shewed thee, O man, what is good; and what doth the Lord require of thee, but to do justly, and to love mercy, and to walk humbly with thy God?" (Micah 6:8) is a quintessence of the 613 commandments of the Bible (Mak. 24a).

BIBLIOGRAPHY: F.C. Burkitt, in: JBL, 45 (1926), 159–61; K. Elliger, in: ZDPV, 57 (1934), 81–152; R. Weil, in: RHR (1940), 146–61; H.L. Ginsberg, in: *Eretz Israel*, 3 (1954), 84; idem, in: JAOS, 88 (1968), 47–49; Pritchard, Texts, 286–7; H. Tadmor, in: *Journal of Cuneiform*

Studies, 12 (1958), 80–83; O. Eissfeldt, in: ZDMG, 112 (1962), 259–68; idem, *Einleitung in das Alte Testament* (19643, rev. ed.); B. Renaud, *Structure et attaches littéraires de Michée IV–V* (1964); E. Hammershaimb, *Some Aspects of Old Testament Prophecy* (1966); B. Reicke, in: HTR, 60 (1967), 349–67; C. Cazelles, in: *Fourth World Congress of Jewish Studies*, 1 (1967), 87–89; J.T. Willis, in: VT, 18 (1968), 529–41; Kaufmann Y., Religion, 395–8. IN THE AGGADAH: Ginzberg, Legends, index; I. Ḥasida, *Ishei ha-Tanakh* (1964), 260. **ADD. BIBLIOGRAPHY:** H. Woolf, *Micah: A Commentary* (1981); R. Smith, *Micah-Malachi* (Word; 1984), 1–60; D. Hillers, *Micah* (Hermeneia; 984); idem, in: ADB, 4:817–10; P. King, Amos, *Hosea, Micah – An Archaeological Commentary* (1988); S. Ahituv, *Handbook of Ancient Hebrew Inscriptions* (1992); A. Fuchs, *Die Inschriften Sargons II. aus Khorsabad* (1993); J.Willis, in: DBI, 2:150–52; F. Andersen and D. Freedman, *Micah* (AB; 2000), 33–99, extensive bibl.

MICAIAH (**Micah**; Heb. מִיכָיְהוּ, מִיכָה), an Ephraimite in whose house was a shrine. Micaiah lived in the hill country of Ephraim though the exact location of his dwelling is not known. According to the Talmud (Sanh. 103b), his house was in Gareb, 3 mi. (5 km.) from Shiloh, which is perhaps Khirbet Arabah, about 2½ mi. (4 km.) west of Shiloh. The Bible relates that Micaiah took 1,100 pieces of silver from his mother but returned them because of her curse (Judg. 17–18). The mother consecrated the money to God: she gave 200 pieces of silver to a silversmith to make a graven image and a molten image and the rest she apparently consecrated to the shrine of God in her house. In the shrine were placed the graven and molten images, and an *ephod and teraphim. It is difficult to ascertain their significance: the images were apparently cultic symbols while the ephod and teraphim were used for asking counsel of God (Judg. 17:3–5; 18:3–7, 14–15, 18–21). At first one of Micaiah's sons served as a priest but later a young levite who had come to the hill country of Ephraim from Beth-Lehem in Judah was hired as a "father and priest." The men of the tribe of Dan, passing through Ephraim on their way to capture Laish, forced the young levite to accompany them and take the graven image. Henceforth the image stood in the sanctuary of the city of Dan and the young levite, whose name was Jonathan the son of Gershom, son of Moses (or son of Manasseh), served there as a priest; and his sons continued to serve "until the day of the captivity of the land" (18:30). This ancient story, which is connected with the description of the capture of Laish in the north, may possibly reflect cultic customs during the period of the Judges when affluent men set up their own houses of God and used the cultic objects to inquire of God. Along with local attendants (or in their place) they installed levites who worked for wages and whose merit as inquirers of God was greatly valued as "father and priest." The purpose of the story of Micaiah is to explain how the sanctuary was established in Dan and how a body of priests – perhaps descendants of Moses – came to be based there after having had their beginning in a private house of God in the hill country of Ephraim. The Bible stresses the greater importance of priestly service "unto a tribe and a family in Israel" as against serving "the house of one man" (18:19) and draws a parallel between the end of the sanctuary at Dan and that at Shiloh, perhaps as a result of some unknown historical event. From Judges 18:30–31 it can be concluded that the worship of Micaiah's graven image at Dan did not continue after the destruction of Shiloh.

BIBLIOGRAPHY: Ha-Ḥevrah le-Ḥeker ha-Mikra be-Yisrael, *Iyyunim be-Sefer Shofetim* (1957), 184–208, 547–84; Y. Kaufmann, *Sefer Shofetim* (1964), 8–9, 56–57, 267–77; Noth, Personennamen, 107, 144; G.F. Moore, *Judges* (ICC, 1949), 365–402.

[Samuel Abramsky]

MICAIAH (Heb. מִיכָיְהוּ; in II Chron. 18:14, **Micah**, Heb. מִיכָה), son of Imlah, prophet who foretold the death of *Ahab (I Kings 22:7–28). Before embarking on the campaign of Ramoth-Gilead, Ahab and his ally *Jehosaphat king of Judah consulted prophets who unanimously prophesied: "Go up; for the Lord will give it into the hand of the king" (22:6; cf. 22:12). When Micaiah was called, he at first expressed the view of the other prophets, but only in an ironic mockery, and when the king adjured him to speak "nothing but the truth in the name of the Lord," he described two visions he had had: one, of the Israelites scattered over the hills like sheep without a shepherd, which the Lord explained to mean, "these have no master, let every one of them return to his house in peace"; and one, of a meeting of the heavenly council at which it was decided that Ahab should be lured to his death in battle at Ramoth-Gilead by a spirit of falsehood in the mouths of his prophets. Micaiah, who firmly repeated the prediction that the king would not return home alive, was then imprisoned for the duration of the campaign.

It appears that Micaiah was known as a prophet even before this, and the king of Israel says of him "I detest him, for he does not prophesy good concerning me, but evil" (22:8). It thus appears that Micaiah was not one of the court prophets, who as a rule acquiesced and encouraged the king. However, he did not bear animosity toward the king and tried, in his prophecy, to prevent his death and the defeat of Israel. His personality was distinguished by prophetic independence and a firm, uncompromising stand not only against the king and his ministers but against all the 400 prophets gathered in the king's court, who in his opinion were not merely false prophets, but became messengers of falsehood through a divine temptation. He was not a rebuking prophet and was not eager to prophesy as were the messenger-prophets. Nor is there any proof that he was one of the prophets who advised the people, like Elisha. His prophecy was similar to that of the classical prophets in his obdurate and unusual stand and his readiness to suffer and be tortured for the sake of truth.

From a political point of view, too, Micaiah differed from the other prophets who in their extreme nationalism were violently anti-Aramean and urged the king to fight against Aram without compromise (I Kings 20:22).

[Samuel Abramsky]

In the Aggadah

In the Aggadah, Micaiah is identified with the anonymous prophet who "came near unto Ahab" and foretold the destruction of the Aramean army (I Kings 20:13; SOR 20, p. 52). Later, when he predicted the death of Ahab in battle, the false prophet Zedekiah b. Chenaanah challenged his prophecy, claiming that Elijah had previously prophesied that the dogs would lick Ahab's blood in the field of Naboth, and he would not therefore be slain on a battlefield three days' journey from there. However, both prophecies were fulfilled. Ahab fell in Ramoth-Gilead, but his blood was licked by the dogs in Samaria, when they washed the slain king's chariot there (I Kings 22:28; Jos., Ant. 8:15, 4).

BIBLIOGRAPHY: J.A. Montgomery, *The Book of Kings* (ICC, 1951), 335–41; B. Oppenheimer, in: *Sefer Urbach* (1955), 89–93. IN THE AGGADAH: Ginzberg, Legends, index; for further bibliography see *Prophecy.

°**MICHAEL II**, Byzantine emperor (820–29) to whom strong Judaizing leanings were ascribed, partly because of his iconoclasm. A tenth-century chronicler states that Michael relieved Jews of financial burdens and that he "loved Jews above all mortals" since he was himself half Jewish and had been brought up by Jews. It is possible that Michael may have come under Jewish influence as a native of Amorium in Phrygia, a province noted for Judeo-Christian syncretism, including sects which kept the whole of Jewish law except circumcision and had close contact with Jews. However, the main impetus for imputing pro-Jewish sentiments to Michael came from the desire of the succeeding dynasty, the Macedonian, to discredit the founder of the Amorian dynasty.

BIBLIOGRAPHY: J. Starr, *Jews in the Byzantine Empire 641–1204* (1939), index; idem, in: HTR, 29 (1936), 93–106; G. Caro, in: MGWJ, 53 (1909), 576–80; F. Doelger, *Regesten der Kaiserurkunden des Ostroemischen Reiches von 565–1453*, 1 (1924), no. 414; Baron Social², 3 (1957), 178.

[Andrew Sharf]

°**MICHAEL VIII PALAEOLOGUS**, Byzantine emperor (1259–82). In 1261 Michael recaptured Constantinople from the Latins, who had held it from 1204, and restored an independent if greatly reduced empire. Unlike his predecessors in Nicaea, he had no reason to suspect his Jewish subjects of having contact with Jews in hostile territory and was anxious to gain their support. Therefore as recorded by Jacob ben Elijah, the only contemporary Hebrew source, he called together the leaders of the Jewish communities and promised them religious tolerance as well as thus ending a series of nearly 40 years of persecutions (see *Epirus). Michael also persuaded his son and co-emperor Andronicus II Palaeologus (1282–1328) to continue and expand this policy, so that the Jews of Constantinople – as distinct from Jewish merchants of hostile Venice living in Constantinople – were allowed to live and build synagogues wherever they wished – to the displeasure of Patriarch Athanasius I.

BIBLIOGRAPHY: J. Starr, *Romania* (1949), 20–23; J. Mann, in: REJ, 82 (1926), 372–3; P. Charanis, in: *Speculum*, 22 (1947), 75–76.

[Andrew Sharf]

MICHAEL, HEIMANN JOSEPH ḤAYYIM (1792–1846), German merchant and bibliophile. Michael was born in Hamburg and lived there all his life. He assembled one of the finest collections of Hebrew manuscripts and books, a library containing 5,471 printed books and 862 manuscripts, of which 60 were autographs and 110 were written between 1240 and 1450. He maintained a lively correspondence, partly in German in Hebrew letters and partly in an attractive Hebrew, with L. *Zunz (in the years 1832–46), S.J. *Rapoport, and S.D. *Luzzatto. This correspondence is a treasury of bibliographical information.

A detailed catalog of Michael's collection, *Oẓerot Ḥayyim*, with notes by Moritz Steinschneider and an introduction by L. Zunz, appeared in 1848. After Michael's death his friend M. Isler appealed to all friends of Jewish scholarship, wealthy German Jewry in particular, to preserve the priceless collection in Jewish hands and to save it from being sold abroad. The appeal was in vain, and Michael's library was dispersed, the books going to the British Museum in London and the manuscripts, over 860 pieces, to the Bodleian at Oxford (see *Libraries) for a little over £1,000.

Michael's encyclopedic work, *Or ha-Ḥayyim* (1891; repr. Jerusalem, 1965, with additional notes by N. Ben-Menahem), based on his very rich collection, contains the biographies and bibliographies of medieval Jewish scholars.

BIBLIOGRAPHY: A. Berliner, in: JJLG, 4 (1906), 269–74; A. Marx, *Studies in Jewish History and Booklore* (1944), 221–4 and passim; H. Michael, *Or ha-Ḥayyim* (1965²). **ADD. BIBLIOGRAPHY:** ADB, vol. 21, 673.

[Naphtali Ben-Menahem]

MICHAEL, JAKOB (1894–1979), U.S. financier and philanthropist. Born in Frankfurt, he began his business career in 1910 with his father-in-law's metal-trading firm, Beer Sondheimer. Demobilized from the German army in 1917, he became active in trade and industry, but in 1933 left Germany for Holland, and in 1939 moved to the United States where he continued his activities in various industrial enterprises. He was prominent in many Jewish philanthropic, educational, and scientific institutions. He financed a high school and a children's home in Pardes Hannah, Israel; an institute of biomedical research at the Einstein College of Medicine, New York; the institute of nuclear science at the Weizmann Institute in Israel; and a college of Hebraic studies at Yeshiva University, New York. Much of his attention was devoted to religious institutions, and his special interests included the collecting of Jewish ceremonial objects and Jewish music. He donated a collection of 25,000 items of Jewish music to the Hebrew University and many valuable books and ceremonial objects to the Israel Museum (including a complete synagogue taken from Vittorio Veneto in Italy).

[Joachim O. Ronall]

MICHAEL (Michaes, Michall), MOSES (Moshe bar Jehiel; 1675–1740), ship owner and international trader, born in Harzfeld, Germany. Michael immigrated to New York, and from 1717 shipped large quantities of foodstuffs, sometimes lumber and candles, to Curaçao, and supplied its garrison with flour and other foodstuffs. Michael usually traveled with his cargo on board his schooner *Abigail*. From 1721 to 1722 he was in partnership with Michael Asser of Boston; from 1731 to 1732, with his son Michael Michaels (d. 1736). In 1729 he paid for the privilege of placing the first cornerstone of New York's Mill Street Synagogue. He died in Curaçao.

BIBLIOGRAPHY: H.A. Alexander, *Notes on the Alexander Family of South Carolina and Georgia* (1954), 98–105; I.S. Emmanuel, *Precious Stones of the Jews of Curaçao* (1957), 260–5.

[Isaac Samuel Emmanuel]

MICHAEL, SAMI (1926–), Israeli writer. Born in Baghdad, Iraq, to a middle-class family, Michael attended Jewish primary and secondary schools. After the pogroms in 1941 (the Farhoud), he joined the Communist underground. Years later, he explained that it was both as a Jew and as an Iraqi patriot that he chose to struggle for seven years in the underground, in the belief that only Communism had the potential to bring about a liberal society in Iraq which would, among other things, support the advancement of its Jewish citizens ("Unbounded Ideas," 2000). With the outbreak of the War of Independence in Israel, the situation of the Jews in Iraq worsened. Michael, targeted both as a Jew and as a Communist, fled to Iran, from where, with the help of the Jewish Agency in Teheran, he arrived in Israel in April 1949. "I belong to Israel out of love, not out of ideology," is how Michael describes his identity as an Israeli, eschewing a Zionist as well as an anti-Zionist definition. Michael sees himself first and foremost as a Jew, heir to the 2,500-year-old cultural tradition of the Babylonian Jews, which was unbroken until persecution and wanderings finally caught up with them after 1948. In other words, Michael does not consider Israel to be the ultimate, ideal home for all Jews. He believes that the Diaspora is another appropriate dynamic form of Jewish life. His own personal decision in favor of Israel was the result of his emotional bond, and he therefore defines himself as an "Israeli patriot" only in the sense of his attachment to the milieu and scenery of the place.

This nonconsensual view is a guiding force in Michael's life, expressing itself in both his civic and his creative activities. He arrived in Israel in a crucial period, during which the newly established state had to absorb hundreds of thousands of new immigrants from east and west. Michael did not accept the monolithic, culturally coercive attitude of the so-called "melting-pot" policy, and he sought instead to assert himself by remaining, as it were, on the seam. He served in the Israel Defense Forces (1950–52), lived through the trials and tribulations of his parents in a transit camp (1951–56), and made his living as a journalist for the Arabic newspaper *Al-Ittihad* in Haifa. Michael served it as an itinerant correspondent, covering the lives of the new immigrants in the transit camps as well as those of Arabs living in villages under the military regime that Israel imposed on them in the early years of the state. At the same time, he began writing prose in Arabic.

Throughout this period he was active in the Israeli Communist Party, but in 1955, with knowledge of the shocking details of Stalin's reign of terror, he left the party for good. He worked for 27 years (1955–82) as a hydrologist at the Department of Agriculture, studying hydrology in his free time at the British Institutes as well as psychology and Arabic literature at the University of Haifa.

For 15 years (1955–70), Michael swore himself to literary silence. Only at the beginning of the 1970s, did he turn back to writing – this time only in the Hebrew tongue. Michael's writing is distinguished by its humane and social sensitivity. He is among the prime movers of the literary sea-change that has been occurring in Israel since the mid-1970s. This trend shifted social representation from the central current to the margins, broadening the boundaries of the consensual culture toward a multiculturalism inclusive of ethnic communities and minorities, and stirring voices within a public discourse driven by sectorality and social divisions. Sami Michael deals primarily with "the Other," "the stranger," "the outsider," granting these figures a presence of their own: the immigrant facing the arrogance of the veteran citizen (in *Shavim ve-Shavim Yoter*, "All Men Are Equal, but Some Are More So," 1974); the Israeli Arab coping with the animosity of the Jewish-Israeli regime (in *Ḥasut*, 1977; *Refuge*, 1988; *Ḥaẓoẓrah ba-Vadi*, *A Trumpet in the Wadi*, 2003); the woman silenced by patriarchy, in both family and communal frameworks (in *Viktoria*, 1993; *Victoria*, 1995; and "The Third Wing," 2000). Of all these figures, the dominant one is that of the immigrant from an Arabic-speaking country, struggling with diverse versions of Israeliness. As might be expected, Michael's depiction draws upon biographical materials and his own experience of *aliyah*, tossed as he was between a loved, familiar past and a new, alien present, in which he struggled to forge his own Israeli identity. Thus, David in "All Men Are Equal, but Some Are More So," for all his efforts to shake off the past and hold fast to the Israeli present, is constantly made to feel like a second-class citizen; beginning as a penniless child of the transit camps, he emerges as a "hero" of the Six-Day-War, yet his erudition, professional skills, and his prowess as a fighter will never make him an equal among equals.

In contrast to David's angry protest, Mordokh, in *Refuge*, has spent years languishing in an Iraqi jail for his activity in the Communist underground and is grateful to the State of Israel for giving him asylum. Nevertheless, he finds it hard to reconcile himself to Israel's social reality, in which the class gap is continually widening, resulting in injustice and discrimination against both Jewish and Arab communities. Unable to withstand the tension, Mordokh flees to the past. In *Mayim Noshkim le-Mayim* ("Water Kissing Water," 2001), a sense of reconciliation with life in Israel begins to make itself felt. Joseph, who, like the other figures, came to Israel in the mass immigration during the 1950s, arrives only many years later at an alternative Israeli identity of his own, one that even now incorporates a wrenching internal oscillation between past and present and is repulsed by the communal rifts between Jews and Arabs, religious and secular Jews, and Jews of Ashkenazi (European) and Mizraḥi (Middle Eastern or North African) origin. Now, however, these dilemmas are played out in a context of pride, self-esteem, and a sense of belonging.

Along with his concern with the Israeli present, Michael devotes a large part of his *oeuvre* to the past – that is, to Jewish life in Baghdad in the 1930s and 1940s. Here too, he sets out to subvert the stereotypical image of the "*galut* Jew" by depicting episodes of a colorful, tempestuous past, unfolding a heterogeneous community of traditionalists, secularists, and intellectuals. These themes underlie *Ḥofen shel Arafel* ("A Handful of Fog," 1979) and *Victoria*, as well as two of Michael's novels for young people, *Ahavah bein ha-Dekalim* ("Love among the Palms," 1990) and *Sufah bein ha-Dekalim* ("Storm over the Palms," 1975).

The poetic fabric of Michael's writing is engaging for its plots and characters, but also for the play of his texts with multiple languages and cultures. The overt level is that of the Hebrew language, with the variety of styles which it embraces; implicitly, however, Michael continues to "flirt" lovingly and longingly with the Arabic (and Judeo-Arabic) language and culture, which emerges in a wealth of sayings and customs.

Michael's other works include novels for young people: "Tin Shacks and Dreams" (1979), "Brown Devils" (1993); plays: "Demons in the Basement" (1983), "Twins" (1988); and collected interviews: *Eleh Shivtei Yisrael* ("These Are the Tribes of Israel: Twelve Interviews about Social Integration in Israel," 1984), "The Israeli Experience" (2001). Michael also translated Naguib Mahfouz's *Cairo Trilogy* into Hebrew. His books have received many awards and have been translated into many languages, including Arabic. Information concerning translations is available at the ITHL website at www.ithl.org.il.

BIBLIOGRAPHY: D. Meirovitz, "*Meẓi'ut Murkevet, Ketivah Funkẓiyonalit: Al Ḥasut*," in: *Siman Keriah*, 8 (1978), 414–417; Y. Oren, "*Viktoriyah – Dugma le-Roman Etni*," in: *Dimui*, 10 (1995), 42–50; D. Ben-Shitrit (director), *Samir, a Documentary Film about S. Michael* (1996); N.E. Berg, "'*Sifrut ha-Ma'abarah*': Transit Camp Literature, Literature of Transition," in: *Critical Essays on Israeli Society, Religion and Government* (1997), 187–207; H. Hever, "*Lo Banu min ha-Yam: Kavim le-Geografiyah Sifrutit Mizraḥit*," in: *Teoriyah u-Bikkoret*, 16 (2000), 181–195; D. Ben-Habib, "*Margalit, Moladeti: Migdar ve-Edah be-Sifrei ha-Ma'abarah shel S. Michael*," in: *Teoriyah u-Bikkoret*, 20 (2002), 243–258; N.E. Berg, *More and More Equal: The Literary Works of Sami Michael* (2004).

[Yaffah Berlovitz (2nd ed.)]

MICHAEL AND GABRIEL, two *angels named in Daniel 10:13, 21; 12:1 and Daniel 8:16; 9:21 respectively.

The Attributions of Proper Names to Angels

Michael and Gabriel are usually cited as the earliest instance of the practice of attributing proper names to angels; and it is just the contrast between the anonymity of the seraphim in Isaiah 6:2, 6 on the one hand and the explicit naming of Gabriel in Daniel 9:21 and of Michael in Daniel 10:21 on the other that is cited by R. Simeon b. Lakish as proof that the names of the angels were something that the returning exiles brought with them from Babylonia (TJ, RH 1:2, 56d). But these are not strictly the oldest examples. According to the critical view, the Book of *Daniel is of later authorship than those of *Zechariah and *Job; yet "the Satan [Accuser]," Zechariah 3:1–2; Job 1:6–12; 2:2–7 is a virtual proper name, and it is retained as the name of the angel in question throughout Jewish literature; but these passages too are post-Exilic. A special early instance is Beth-El (Jer. 48:13), a real proper name shortened from (Ha) El-Beth-El, Genesis 31:13; 35:7, "The Numen of Beth-El," who was the special tutelary genius of Jacob and of the nation Israel (see the Book of *Hosea B-b; H.L. Ginsberg, in: JBL, 80 (1961), 339–47). Already the E document of the Pentateuch has made an angel of this being (Gen. 31:11), and Deutero-Hosea, who in Hosea 12:3–5, 13 palpably draws on the E story of Jacob embedded in Genesis 25 and 27–35 (and modifies it for his own purposes), refers to the being alternately as *e'lohim*, "a divine being" (Hos. 12:4) and *mal'akh*, "an angel" (Hos. 12:5).

Michael

Michael (*Mikha'el*, מִיכָאֵל "Who is like God?" – in ten passages the name of as many men: Num. 13:13; I Chron. 5:13, 14; 6:25; 7:3; 8:16; 12:21; 27:18; II Chron. 21:2; Ezra 8:8). Daniel 10:2–11 states that Daniel practiced asceticism for three full weeks in his endeavor to move Heaven to reveal to him what he wanted to know. At the end of that period a frightening figure appeared to him. He fell on his face in terror, but the being helped him to his feet and told him that he had been sent to deliver a message to him. In 10:12–21 he then explains that Daniel's petition had been received favorably on the very first day, but the speaker was unable to leave his post for 21 days because he was holding in check "the prince [*sar*, שַׂר] of the kingdom of Persia"; at the end of that period, however, he was relieved in this task by "Michael, one of the chief princes [*sarim*]," whom he left there "with the kings of Persia." He himself will only stay with Daniel long enough to inform him "what will befall your people at the end of the days" (verse 14), for he will have to "return to fight with the prince of Persia and when he retires – there comes the prince of Greece … and there is none who shares my efforts against all these but your (pl., i.e., the Jews') prince, Michael." At the climax of history, it is "Michael, the great prince who stands guard over your fellow countrymen," who will arise and save them (12:1). It will be seen that *sar* – properly "dignitary," "official," or "minister," but here better "prince" in view of the designation of God in 8:25 as "the *sar* of *sarim*" – means "angel," that every nation is conceived of as having an angelic representative, and that the author conceives of these representatives as engaging in clashes with each other which prefigure clashes between the respective nations. Obviously, the germ of this idea is Deuteronomy 32:8, which reads, according to the text of the Septuagint and a fragment from Qumran: "When the Most High gave nations their countries,/ When he set the divisions of man,// He established peoples' homelands/to the number of the divine beings."// For "the divine beings" (*bene'el*, lit. "children of God"), the Masoretic Text reads "the Israelites" (*bene Yisra'el*, lit. "the children of Israel"). The latter, however, is a conflation of the Septuagint-Qumran reading בני אל and a variant שרי אל which is presupposed by the above Daniel passages (H.L. Ginsberg, in: *Eretz-Israel*, 9 (1969), 45, n. 4). On the other hand the writer in Daniel diverges from his source in one important respect. The next verse in Deuteronomy 32, namely verse 9, specifically makes an exception of Israel: the latter is not apportioned to any *ben'el* or *sar'el* ("But YHWH's people is his own portion,/ Jacob is his own allotment.") All the passages cited above from Daniel 10–12 are from the pen of Apoc III (see *Daniel, Book of, B).

Gabriel

Gabriel (*Gavri'el*, גַּבְרִיאֵל). This angel is the creation of Apoc IV, the author of Daniel 9 and of sundry interpolations in chapters 7, 8, 11, and 12 (see *Daniel B). In chapter 9 itself, Gabriel appears to the apocalyptist (9:21) in the first year of Darius the Mede (9:1, see *Daniel B) in answer to his prayer for enlightenment on the subject of the 70 years of Jeremiah (Jer. 25:11–12; 29:10). Gabriel explains that those 70 years are in reality 70 weeks of years (*septennia*), and proceeds to sketch the course that history will take during those 70 hebdomads. This is closely analogous to the role that is played in Apoc III (chs. 10–12) by an angel who is not named but merely described, who appears to Daniel in the third year of Cyrus in response to three weeks of mourning, and tells him in astonishing detail what is destined to take place from that date until the horrors of Antiochus IV. Apoc IV wished to imply that his Gabriel was identical with this informant of Apoc III, and this he did in a subtle way. Apoc III's informant explains to him in 10:12–13 that Daniel's petition for enlightenment was favorably received at the very beginning of his quasi-fast, and the delay was only due to the informant's being tied down with keeping the prince of Persia at bay (see above). Then in 10:20–21 he goes on to say that he has barely enough time at his disposal to impart to Daniel "that which is written in the book of truth [or, that which is written in the book, truly]" because he must presently go back to the combat with the prince of Persia, and after that with the prince of Greece, "and there is none who shares my efforts against these but your [i.e., the Jews'] prince Michael," after which Apoc IV interpolates (11:1) "and ever since the first year of Darius the Mede [the date of 9:1, on which Gabriel appeared to the seer] I have been standing by him to strengthen and support him." The implication is clearly this: "The same cause that prevented me from coming to you during the past three weeks also explains why I have not appeared to you for such a long time since my last visit." In other words, the unnamed linen-clad one of chapters 10–12 is identical with the Gabriel of chapter 9. Apoc IV has also taken steps to identify with the latter the originally unnamed being of Apoc II (ch. 8). Daniel 8:15 reads. "And when I, Daniel, beheld the vision [*ḥazon*] I asked [prayed] for an explanation, and lo, there was standing before me one having the appearance of a man [*gaver*]." Inspired by this last word, Apoc IV interpolated here, "(16) And I heard somebody's voice between [the banks of?] Ulai. He called out, 'Gabriel [*Gavri'el*]! Explain the statement [*mar'eh*] to him.'" *Mar'eh* must mean "statement," and the reference must be to the statement about the evenings and mornings in verse 14, in view of verse 26; and verses 13–14 and 26a – also, by the way, verse 27b – are, just like verse 16, interpolations of Apoc IV in the text of Apoc II (the original text of ch. 8), so that they may be described as II-d. In 9:21b, then, when Apoc IV tells how he was visited by "the man [here the Hebrew has *ha-'ish*, but the Aramaic original doubtless had *gavra* here as well as *gevar* in 8:15] Gabriel who had appeared to me before in the vision," he is referring back to chapter 8 as interpolated by himself.

[Harold Louis Ginsberg]

In the Aggadah

Michael and Gabriel, along with Uriel and Raphael, are the four angels who surround the throne of the Almighty (Num. R. 2:10; cf. Enoch 9:1). Michael, as the constant defender of the Jewish people (PR, 46), is considered greater than Gabriel (Ber. 4b). The *aggadah* consistently identifies Michael and Gabriel with the anonymous divine messengers or angels mentioned in the Bible. Thus, they were two of the three angels who visited Abraham after his circumcision (Gen. R. 48:9), Michael's task being to announce the future birth of Isaac while Gabriel's was to destroy Sodom (Gen. R. 50:2). It is Michael who called to Abraham at the **Akedah*, telling him not to offer up Isaac (*Midrash Va-Yosha* in A. Jellinek, *Beit ha-Midrash*, 1:38). It was either Michael or Gabriel who wrestled with Jacob (Gen. R. 78:1) and appeared to Moses at Horeb (Ex. R. 2:5). It was Michael who rescued Abraham from the fiery furnace (Gen. R. 44:13) and also informed him of the capture of Lot (PdRE, 27). He also accompanied the servant of Abraham in his mission to find a wife for Isaac (Gen. R. 59:10). Michael and Gabriel were called upon to record that the birthright was sold to Jacob by Esau (Gen. R. 63:14). They were both among the angels who accompanied God when He came down on Mount Sinai (Deut. R. 2:34). Although they were considered the kings of the angels, they were afraid of Moses (Eccles. R. 9:11, 2), and they refused to take his soul, so that God himself had to do so. Michael and Gabriel then stood at either side of Moses' bier (Deut. R. 11:10). On the day that Solomon married the daughter of Pharaoh-Neco, Michael came down from heaven and stuck a reed in the sea, round which matter settled, and upon this Rome, the future destroyer of Israel, was built (Song R. 1:6, 4). Michael smote Sennacherib and his army, and Gabriel delivered Hananiah, Mishael, and Azariah (Ex. R. 18:5) from the fiery furnace. Michael acted as the defender of the Jews against every charge which Haman brought against them (Esth. R. 7:12). It was Michael who pushed Haman against Esther to make it appear as if Haman intended to violate her (Esth. R. 10:9). Both Michael and Gabriel will be among those who will accompany the Messiah, and they will then contend with the wicked (*Otiyyot de-Rabbi Akiva Shin*).

Michael is made up entirely of snow and Gabriel of fire, and though they stand near one another they do not injure one another, thus indicating the power of God to "make peace in His high places" (Job 25:2; Deut. R. 5:12). Michael also occupies an important place in the interpretation of biblical stories in later Midrashim, e.g., *Exodus Rabbah, Midrash Avkir,* and *Midrash Konen.*

[Aaron Rothkoff]

In the Kabbalah

The motifs of Michael and Gabriel as found in the *aggadah* are in general repeated in the Kabbalah, but Michael is given an added importance.

In the *Heikhalot* and Merkabah literature of the late talmudic period and the period of the *geonim*, Michael plays a central role in the realm of the Chariot. He is the guardian of the south side, the figure of the lion in the Chariot, and so on (the descriptions vary in the different versions of this literature). In any case he is one of the four archangels, despite the interchange of names in the list. G. Scholem has deduced, from a statement in *Perek Re'iyyot Yeḥezkel* (Wertheimer, *Battei Midrashot*, 2 (1955), 132–3) and from other sources, that at first Michael and *Metatron were identical – the guardian of the interior and the highest figure in the domain of the angels in the Merkabah literature and in the Kabbalah which succeeded it – and that some of the descriptions of Michael in talmudic and midrashic literature were later transferred to the figure of Metatron. He is outstanding as guardian and protector of Israel in Merkabah literature and in the European mystical literature of the Ḥasidei Ashkenaz and early kabbalistic circles. A central role in bringing about the redemption was attributed to him in midrashic and Merkabah literature. Such descriptions of the role of Michael relied mainly on sayings in the Book of Zerubbabel and other apocalyptic works dating from the end of the ancient era and the beginning of the Middle Ages, in which Michael was assigned the role of revealer and bringer of tidings. (As there is in the various versions an interchange between Michael and Metatron, it does indeed seem that the two figures are basically identical.)

In kabbalistic literature Michael is allotted the role of grace in the Merkabah, angel of the right, representing the *Sefirah Ḥesed* ("grace"). In several places in the *Zohar Michael symbolizes the *Sefirah Ḥesed* itself (Zohar 1:98b–99a, *Sitrei Torah*; 2:147, et al.). All the symbols of grace (the right side, silver, water, etc.) are to be found in the descriptions of the angel Michael. He is frequently described as a high priest, and the Zohar and later kabbalists (e.g., Moses Cordovero) portray him as bringing the souls of the righteous before the Almighty, an act which led to their inclusion in the world of emanation (*aẓilut*).

[Joseph Dan]

BIBLIOGRAPHY: H.L. Ginsberg, *Studies in Daniel* (1948). IN THE AGGADAH AND IN KABBALAH: J. Kaufman (Ibn Shemuel), *Midreshei Ge'ullah* (1954), 73ff.; R. Margulies, *Malakhei Elyon* (1945), 87–89, 108–35; I. Tishby, *Mishnat ha-Zohar*, 1 (1949), 463–9; Ginzberg, Legends, 7 (1967[3]), 311–2 and index; G. Scholem, *Jewish Gnosticism…* (1960), 43–45.

MICHAELIS, SIR ARCHIE (1889–1975), Australian politician. Born in Melbourne, Archie Michaelis worked in his successful family firm of leather goods merchants before entering state politics in Victoria, Australia. Michaelis became one of the best-known politicians in Melbourne and the state of Victoria. Always a member of the right-of-center party (which changed its name several times during his career), Michaelis sat in the Victorian Legislative Assembly as member for St. Kilda from 1932 to 1952. He served as minister without portfolio in 1945 and was speaker of the Victorian Legislative Assembly from 1950 to 1952. He was president of the St. Kilda Hebrew Congregation, a leading Orthodox synagogue in Melbourne. Originally typical of Jews of his background in opposing "political Zionism," by the end of his life he had become a strong supporter of Israel.

BIBLIOGRAPHY: W.D. Rubinstein, Australia II, 304–6.

[William D. Rubinstein (2nd ed.)]

°MICHAELIS, JOHANN DAVID (1717–1791), German Bible scholar. Born in Halle, Michaelis was the son of the theologian and Orientalist Ch. B. Michaelis. In 1746 he was appointed professor of Oriental languages in Goettingen. While he was at first a pietist of the Halle school, after a stay in England (1741–42) he advocated, somewhat inconsistently, a moderately rationalistic orthodoxy. His *Einleitung in die goettlichen Schriften des Neuen Bundes* (1750; 1787–884) was the first textbook on the historical-critical approach to the New Testament. His early works included a Hebrew grammar textbook (Halle, 1745) and a compendium of Jewish marriage laws *Ehegesetze Moses* (Goettingen, 1755). In his *Gruendliche Erklaerung des mosaischen Rechts* (Frankfurt, 6 vols., 1770–75) he interpreted the laws of the Pentateuch as the work of the statesmanlike wisdom of Moses, whose aim was the separation of Israel from the heathens. He popularized the conclusions of biblical scholarship in a translation of the Bible with notes (13 vols., 1769–83). He also wrote an introduction to the Old Testament, *Einleitung in die Schriften des Alten Bundes* (1787). In 1761 he suggested to the king of Denmark that a scientific expedition be sent to Arabia. Through his extremely diverse academic and literary activities he enjoyed a worldwide reputation; however, in his later years, as a result of weaknesses of character and of scholarship, he became progressively isolated.

BIBLIOGRAPHY: J.M. Hassencamp, *Leben des Herrn J.D. Michaelis, von ihm selbst beschrieben* (1793); R. Smend, *Johann David Michaelis* (Ger. 1898); R. Kittel, in: *Realencyklopaedie fuer protestantische Theologie und Kirche*, 13 (1903), 54ff.; E. Kutsch, in: RGG[3], 4 (1960), 934–5 (incl. bibl.). **ADD. BIBLIOGRAPHY:** A.-R. Loewenbrueck, *Judenfeindschaft im Zeitalter der Aufklaerung* (1995).

[Rudolf Smend]

MICHAELIS, LEONOR (1875–1949), German biochemist. Born in Berlin, he worked with Paul *Ehrlich at the City Hospital where he directed the bacteriology department from 1906 to 1922. In 1908 he was appointed professor of medicine at the University of Berlin, and from 1920, professor of physical chemistry. From 1922 to 1926 he was professor of biochemistry in Nagoya, Japan. In 1926 he went to the Johns Hopkins University in the U.S. and then to the Rockefeller Institute for Medical Research in New York. He contributed many scientific papers on topics concerned with casein, blood pH in biological systems, the behavior of dyestuffs in biological media, and respiration. His books included *Hydrogen Ion Concentration* (1926), *Praktikum der physikalischen Chemie inbesondere der Kolloidchemie fuer Mediziner und Biologen* (1930[4]; *Practical, Physical and Colloid Chemistry for Students of Medicine and Biology*, 1925), and *Oxydations-Reduktion Potential* (1929; *Oxidation Reduction Potentials*, 1930).

[Samuel Aaron Miller]

MICHAELIS, SIR MAX (1860–1932), South African mining magnate and philanthropist. Born in Eisfeld, Germany, Michaelis worked in a Frankfurt banking house before immigrating to South Africa in 1876. He settled in Kimberley where he formed a diamond-buying company which was later taken over by De Beers. Michaelis is best known for his interest in and benefactions to art and education. He established scholarships in South Africa and England, including the Jewish War Memorial Scholarship at Oxford. He donated funds to the University of Cape Town for a school of fine arts which was named after him. In 1912 he bought the Hugh Lane collection of Dutch masters, which he presented to the South African nation as the nucleus of the Michaelis Art Gallery in Cape Town. Michaelis contributed to the Johannesburg Art Gallery, City Library, and to hospitals. He was knighted in 1924.

BIBLIOGRAPHY: P.H. Emden, *Randlords* (1935), index. **ADD. BIBLIOGRAPHY:** G. Wheatcroft, *The Randlords*, 135–36, index.

[Louis Hotz]

MICHAELS, ALAN RICHARD ("Al"; 1944–), U.S. sports broadcaster. The Brooklyn, New York-born TV sports broadcaster was raised near Ebbets Field, fabled home of the Brooklyn Dodgers, which inspired his future award-winning career. Michaels graduated from Arizona State University in 1966, and almost immediately went into sports broadcasting, starting with a Hawaii team in the baseball minor leagues. He broadcast a World Series on radio in 1972, meeting his childhood goal of doing such a broadcast before he turned 30. He broadcast many prominent sports events of the late 20th century, including the U.S. upset of the U.S.S.R. hockey team at the 1980 Winter Olympics. As the game ended, he shouted, "Do you believe in miracles," one of the most famous calls in sports history, and has twice since then played himself in film and TV recreations of that event. Michaels was the lead broadcaster for Monday Night Football from 1986, and won an Emmy award for his broadcast of the third game of the 1989 World Series, which was interrupted by an earthquake. In 2004, Michaels broadcast his first National Basketball Association finals, making him the only sportscaster to have announced a World Series, a Super Bowl, a Stanley Cup final, and the NBA championship. Michaels received a star on the Hollywood Walk of Fame in 2004, and is a member of the National Sportscasters and Sportswriters Association Hall of Fame. He appeared as himself in the 1996 film, *Jerry Maguire*. Unlike Howard *Cosell and Larry *Merchant, Michaels is more of a reporter than a commentator. In a 2004 interview, he said: "I look at sports as drama.... Let the drama play out."

[Alan D. Abbey (2nd ed.)]

MICHAELS, ANNE (1958–) Canadian poet, novelist. The youngest of four children, Michaels was born in Toronto, where she continued to live. In 1980, she earned a B.A. in English from the University of Toronto, and taught creative writing courses there as well. Musically accomplished, she composed music for the theater. *The Weight of Oranges* (1986), her first collection of poetry, won the Commonwealth Prize for the Americas. A second poetry collection, *Miner's Pond* (1991), won the Canadian Authors' Association Award for Poetry and was short-listed for both the Governor General's Literary Award (Canada's most prestigious literary prize) and the Trillium Award. A single volume containing both books was published in 1997. A third poetry collection, *Skin Divers*, was published in 1999.

Michaels's first novel, *Fugitive Pieces*, quickly established her national and international reputation. The work is a Jewish Canadian artist parable, a bipartite intergenerational book which juxtaposes two first-person autobiographical memoirs. The longer first section presents the journals (subdivided into seven titled sections) composed retrospectively by Jakob Beer, a Jewish poet, translator, and orphaned child survivor of the Holocaust, who is rescued from the mud of a Polish town and raised on a Greek island by Athos Roussos, an archaeologist, scientist, and righteous gentile. The second section records the narrative of Ben, the child of Holocaust survivors, who grows up in Weston, Ontario (then a separate municipality, and, in the present of his life, a suburb of Toronto), and who eventually finds on the Greek island of Idhra the two journal volumes which form the first part of the novel. Although their individual histories differ, the lives of Jakob and Ben have been profoundly shaped and distorted by the Shoah. In language which is luminous, evocative, and poignant, the novel explores the nature of identity and the relation between personal, historical, genealogical, and geological memory. It highlights the acts of reading and writing and the power of language and love to heal, to redeem, and to provide meaning in a post-Holocaust world.

Fugitive Pieces was a Canadian literary phenomenon. It remained at, or near, the top of the Canadian bestseller list for over two years, and the rights to the novel were sold to 21 publishers around the world. The work has been awarded many prizes, both in Canada and abroad. These include the Trillium Prize and the Chapters / *Books in Canada* First Novel Award Canada; the Orange Prize for Fiction by female writers, and the *Guardian* Fiction Prize in Great Britain; the Lannan Literary Award in the United States and the Giuseppe Acerbi Literary Award in 2001.

[Alexander Hart (2nd ed.)]

MICHAELS, LORNE (1944–), Canadian writer-producer. Born Lorne David Lipowitz to successful furrier Abraham and Florence (née Becker) Lipowitz in the affluent Forest Hill area of Toronto, Ontario, Michaels got involved with a theater group and began working on sketch comedy and satires while studying in the English program at the University of Toronto. After graduating college, Michaels left for England, where he worked briefly as a car salesman. Upon his return to Canada in 1966, Michaels and Hart Pomerantz began performing as a popular comedy duo on the CBC. In November 1967, he married comedy writer Rosie Schuster. Michaels and Pomerantz went to Hollywood to write for *The Beautiful Phyllis Diller Show* (1968), but the show only lasted six weeks. The duo picked up work with *Rowan and Martin's Laugh-In*, writing the opening monologues for the hosts from 1968 to 1969; however, their material was often rewritten by senior writers or dismissed altogether. Disillusioned with the experience of writing for *Laugh-In*, Michaels and Pomerantz returned to Canada to create their own television programs. In 1970, the pair inked a deal with the CBC to create such specials as *The Hart and Lorne Terrific Hour* and *Today Makes Me Nervous*. Over the next four years Michaels continued to pitch ideas for TV shows in Hollywood, and in 1975 NBC agreed to launch a live sketch comedy program called *Saturday Night*. (The show was retitled *Saturday Night Live* in 1977 after *Saturday Night Live With Howard Cosell* was cancelled in 1976.) The show launched the careers of such *SNL* players as Chevy Chase, John Belushi, Dan Aykroyd, Gilda *Radner, Laraine Newman, Eddie Murphy, Billy *Crystal, Mike Myers, Adam *Sandler, and Will Ferrell in its more than 30-year history and has won 18 Emmy Awards and nabbed 60 nominations. Over the years Michaels also produced a film version of Gilda Radner's Broadway show *Gilda Live* (1980), *Simon and Garfunkel: The Concert in Central Park* (1982), *Nothing Lasts Forever* (1984), and the TV series *Kids in the Hall* (1988–94). By the early 1990s, a reinvigorated *Saturday Night Live* served as the springboard for a variety of successful comedy features, including *Wayne's World* (1992), *Coneheads* (1993), and *Tommy Boy* (1994). Michaels became executive producer of NBC's *Late Night with Conan O'Brien* in 1993 and *The Colin Quinn Show* in 2002. He was inducted into the Order of Canada and the Television Academy's Hall of Fame, and received a star on the Canadian Walk of Fame. In 2004, Michaels produced the hit comedy *Mean Girls* and received an honorary award from the Producers Guild of America.

[Adam Wills (2nd ed.)]

MICHAELSON, EZEKIEL ZEVI BEN ABRAHAM HAYYIM (1863–1942), Polish rabbi, biographer, and bibliographer. He was a child prodigy, and in one of his works he cites responsa which he claims to have written at the age of 12. Orphaned in his early youth, he was forced to move from one place to another. In 1884 he was invited to become rabbi of the important community of Zamosc, but he refused. In the same year, he was elected rabbi of Karsinbrod. There he was harassed by enemies and was even arraigned in court as a result of a false accusation. In 1893 he became rabbi of Plonsk and from then on was known as "the rabbi of Plonsk." At the outbreak of World War I he was on a visit to Carlsbad and was unable to return home. In 1922 he was elected a member of the rabbinical council of Warsaw, and engaged in many communal activities. When the German forces entered Warsaw he was working in the community archives and in 1942 he was taken to *Treblinka where he died.

An exceptionally prolific writer whose knowledge of family lineages was unequaled, Michaelson published many books in such diverse fields as *halakhah, aggadah*, history, biography, and bibliography.

His best-known works are *Degan Shamayim* on tractates *Berakhot* and *Rosh ha-Shanah* (appended to Israel Jonah Landau, *Ein ha-Bedolah*, 1901); responsa *Beit Yehezkel*, (1924); *Pinnot ha-Bayit*, novellae (1925); *Siddur Beit ha-Ozar* (1931 (1929)); responsa *Tirosh ve-Yizhar* (1936). His most famous biographies are those of R. Israel Jonah of Kempen, R. Meshullam Zalman Ashkenazi, R. Joseph *Te'omim, R. Shabbetai *Bass, R. *Phinehas of Korets, the Margolioth family, R. Solomon *Ganzfried, R. Zevi Hirsh Zemah, and R. Jacob Aryeh of Radzymin, all appended to his editions of their works. During the Holocaust, three large chests containing his manuscripts were lost. They included *Imrei Yehezkel* on the Pentateuch and *Me'at Zevi* on the other books of the Bible.

BIBLIOGRAPHY: N. Shemen, *Di Biografie fun a Varshever Rov ha-Rov Zevi Yehezkel Michaelson* (1948); *Elleh Ezkerah*, 2 (1957), 195–202.

[Itzhak Alfassi]

MICHAELSON, ISAAC CHESAR (1903–1982), Israeli ophthalmologist. Born in Scotland, he taught at Glasgow University and served with the Royal Army Medical Corps in World War II. During Israel's War of Independence in 1948, he was specialist adviser to the Israel government and from 1953 served as professor of ophthalmology at the Hebrew University-Hadassah Medical School in Jerusalem. He set up eye clinics in Liberia, Malawi, Tanzania, and Rwanda and trained local doctors and medical assistants to run them. The Ophthalmology Research Laboratories administered by Michaelson and his colleagues from Hadassah Hospital in Jerusalem served an estimated patient-population of 20 million in Africa.

A specialist on the diseases of the inner eye, Michaelson is the author of *Circulation of the Inner Eye in Man and Animals* (1952) and, with Ballantyne, of *Textbook of Diseases of the Eye* (1970²). Michaelson was awarded the 1960 Israel Prize for medicine.

[Lucien Harris]

MICHAL (Heb. מִיכַל), the youngest daughter of King *Saul (Sam. 14:49), who loved *David and was given to him in marriage after he had killed 200 Philistines (in the Septuagint – 100). Michal's father had insisted on this as the condition for the marriage contract – "a hundred Philistines' foreskins," instead of a dowry (18:27–29), hoping of course that David would lose his life in the attempt to collect them. Michal, who loved David, was given to him instead of *Merab the elder, who had been promised to him but had been given to *Adriel the Meholathite (17:15; 18:17–20).

Michal demonstrated her loyalty to David in deceiving her father's messengers, who had been sent to murder David in his own home (19:17ff.). By the time Saul's messengers discovered the deceit, David had had time to escape. Later Saul gave Michal to *Paltiel son of Laish from Gallim (25:44). When David reigned in Hebron, he asked Ish-Bosheth, the son of Saul, to bring Michal back apparently under pressure from Abner, who was about to defect to David. He did in fact take her from her husband and restore her to David (II Sam. 3:12–16). No doubt the demand was politically motivated, at least in part. David was trying to induce Israel (the northern tribes) to follow the example of Judah and accept him as its king (II Sam. 2:5–7), and his marriage to a daughter of Saul who might become the mother of his successor would be an added inducement to the men of Israel to act upon his suggestion. When David leaped and danced in front of the Ark as it was brought to Jerusalem, Michal jeered that he had exposed himself "as one of the vain fellows shamelessly uncovers himself." David answered her in anger, referring to his being chosen as king, "above thy father, and above all his house" (6:16, 20–23). Michal remained childless (6:23). The masoretic text of II Samuel 21:8 mentions five children of Michal by *Adriel of Meholah, but the latter was in fact the husband of Merab (see above). Some versions (LXX, the Syriac; cf. Sanh. 19b) have Merab here instead of Michal.

[Samuel Abramsky]

In the Aggadah

Michal's love for David is compared to that of Jonathan; whereas the latter saved David from Saul outside the palace, Michal did so inside the palace (Mid. Ps. 59:1). She is identical with Eglah (mentioned in II Sam. 3:5 as David's wife), and was so called because like a heifer (*eglah*) she refused to accept the yoke of her father (Mid. Ps. 59:4). This love was returned. Although David married Merab after Michal's death he continued to refer to "My wife, Michal" (II Sam. 3:14; Sanh. 19b). Michal's marriage to Palti (I Sam. 25:44) was illegal, since she was already bethrothed to David (Sanh. *ibid.*), and she had no marital relations with him (*ibid.*). She is stated to have worn *tefillin* (Er. 96a).

When rebuking David (II Sam. 6:20), Michal made a forceful comparison between the modesty which Saul displayed when covering his feet (I Sam. 24:4), and David's behavior (Num. R. 4:20); it was on account of this criticism that she was punished with childlessness (Sanh. 21a).

BIBLIOGRAPHY: Bright, Hist, 172, 176–7, 186; de Vaux, Anc Isr, index, s.v. *Mikal*; Morgenstern, in: ZAW, 49 (1931), 54–55; Stoebe, in: ZAWB, 77 (1958), 224–43; EM, s.v. incl. bibl.

MICHALI, BINYAMIN YIẒḤAK (1910–1989), Hebrew writer, literary critic, and editor. Born in Bessarabia, Michali lived in Bucharest from 1933 to 1939, where he was active in Zionist circles. He went to Ereẓ Israel in 1939 and joined the staff of the *Histadrut archives. He was a leading member of the Israel Writers' Association for many years and one of the chief editors of its journal, *Moznayim*. His first articles in Yiddish as well as Hebrew appeared in the Labor Zionist press. He published several books on modern Hebrew writers dealing in particular with the younger schools (*Olamam shel Benei ha-Areẓ*, 1951, and *Peri ha-Areẓ*, 1966, and *Ḥayyim Hazaz, Iyyunim bi-Yẓirato*, 1968) and edited several anthologies and journals of contemporary Hebrew literature. Other works include *Ya'akov Fichman* (1952), a study of the Yiddish poet Avraham Suzkever (1989), and a collection of literary essays *Mishbeẓot Bikkoret* (1981).

BIBLIOGRAPHY: I. Cohen, *Sha'ar ha-Te'amim* (1962), 197–9; Kressel, Leksikon, 2 (1967), 348. **ADD. BIBLIOGRAPHY:** Y. Cohen, "*B.Y. Michali ha-Mevaker*," in: *Yedioth Aharonoth* (November 28, 1980); A. Ekroni, "*Iyyunei Bikkoret*," in: *Yedioth Aharonoth* (May 29, 1981).

[Getzel Kressel]

MICHALOVCE (Hung. **Nagymihály**; Ger. **Grossmichel**), town in N.E. Slovakia. The first Jews settled there during the Ottoman occupation of Greater Hungary (1526–1699) and remained after the Turks left. A 1724 census attests to a Jewish presence. The aim of the census was to prevent Jews from owning real estate. The number of Jews at that time was small. Jews lived in the neighboring villages, such as Stranany and Pozdisovce, where they attended services. The first synagogue was constructed on the property of the Gueck family. In 1732, the number of Jews rose to 400. They also owned a *mikveh*. Most of the Jews lived on Silk Street ("Hodvabna ulica"). When it could no longer accommodate all the potential inhabitants, New Street ("Nova ulica") was added. The cemetery was in Stranany. In 1792 the *ḥevra kaddisha* was established. In 1865, a convention of Orthodox rabbis of greater Hungary was held in Michalovce, which affirmed the Conservative spirit of Hungarian Jewry. Fearing Jewish assimilation, the conveners codified several regulations to preserve accepted norms. It established the rule of use of only Hebrew and Yiddish in religious activity. After the Congress of Hungarian Jewry in 1868, the Michalovce congregation confirmed the Orthodox path it had followed in the past. The community was formally founded in 1867; in 1888 they built a large synagogue. A group of ḥasidim following *nusaḥ sefarad* split from the congregation. The synagogue was replaced with another edifice in 1905. In 1970 it was torn down.

In 1840 there were 170 Jews in Michalovce (excluding Pozdisovce and Stranany); in 1844 there were 311; in 1857 they increased to 445. In 1880 the community had 1,079 (27.6% of all inhabitants), and in 1910 there were 2,200 Jews. Immigration from Galicia caused rapid expansion of the community. The Jews in neighboring villages moved to the city, and the railway created even further expansion of the Jewish population. The second Czechoslovak census of 1930 recorded 3,386 Jews in Michalovce. On the eve of the deportations in 1940, there were 4,197.

During the last 20 years of the 19th century a *bet midrash*, a *mikveh*, and a *talmud torah* were constructed. In the 1930s a Beth Jacob school for girls and another Jewish school were established. In 1926 the ḥasidim consecrated a synagogue of their own. There was a main yeshivah and there was a ḥasidic yeshivah.

Zionist activity began in Michalovce before World War I, and all shades of political views were represented. The Jewish party was strong and was regularly elected to the municipal council. While the Jews were doing well economically, there was a poor segment among the population. The Po'alei Zion party had some support among them.

On October 6, 1918, autonomy was proclaimed in Slovakia, and on March 15, 1939, Slovakia proclaimed independence, under the aegis of the Third Reich. In Michalovce this latter act was accompanied by antisemitic disturbances. In 1919 Jewish children were expelled from schools, and the Jewish school founded shortly before the crisis took on the responsibility of educating them.

Antisemitism peaked in 1942 with the deportation of Slovakian Jews to Poland. Many tried to escape to Hungary. On May 4, 1942, the first transport of Michalovce Jews was sent to Poland. Four transports followed to the Lublin region, to ghettos in Lukow, Medzirieczie, and Podleske. Survivors in the community tried to help the deportees by smuggling money and medicine to them. Ultimately, they were all sent to the extermination camps at Sobibor and Treblinka.

In the spring of 1944, all eastern Slovakian survivors were ordered to move westward for fear of the advancing front. Indeed, in November 1944 Soviet troops entered Michalovce. In 1945 the surviving Jews organized a congregation and repaired the synagogue, the *mikveh*, and the cemetery. In 1947 there were 614 Jews in Michalovce. In 1948–49 most of the Jews emigrated, particularly to Israel. The community continued to function. In 1967 there were 200 to 250 Jews in Michalovce. In 1989, at the time of the Velvet Revolution, only a handful remained and religious life no longer existed. In 1995 there were a few dozen Jews.

BIBLIOGRAPHY: M. Ben-Zeev (ed.), *Sefer Michalovce ve-ha-Sevivah* (1969), Heb., Eng., and Hung.; R. Iltis (ed.), *Die aussaeen unter Traenen…* (1959), 165–7; M. Lányi and H. Propperné Békefi, *A szlovenszkói zsidó hitközségek története* (1933), 246ff. **ADD. BIBLIOGRAPHY:** E. Bàrkàny and L. Dojč, *Židovské náboženské obce na Slovensku* (1991), 405–8.

[Meir Lamed / Yeshayahu Jelinek (2nd ed.)]

MICHEL, JUD (d. 1549), also known as "the rich Michel," financier and soldier of fortune. According to legend Michel was an illegitimate son of one of the dukes of Regenstein, who were his benefactors at the beginning of his career but later became his bitter enemies. His loans to rulers of *Hesse, the Palatinate, and lesser principalities are first recorded in the early 1530s. Michel, who had no official title (see *Court Jew), stood in the relationship of vassal to Philip the Magnanimous of Hesse, for whom he had to muster five horsemen, as well as to the elector of the Palatinate and the margrave of Ansbach. When the duke of Regenstein repudiated a promissory note, Michel first warned and challenged him and then instigated acts of arson against his property. Called before the imperial court, he fled to Silesia where he organized effective support from nobility and *Ferdinand I, to whom he had once loaned 2,000 gold gulden. Michel subsequently entered the service of Joachim II, elector of *Brandenburg, with whom he conducted intricate economic transactions against the dukes of Regenstein, vassals of the elector. He owned two houses in *Berlin and one in *Frankfurt on the Oder, although the latter town objected to his presence there. In 1544 his wife, Merle, was accused of attempting to poison the wells and in 1546 he was accused of illegal slaughtering; in both cases Joachim intervened on his protégé's behalf. He was kidnapped while on a mission in 1549; his abductors were arrested and brought to Saxony and Michel was released on Joachim's command. Shortly after Michel died in dubious circumstances as the result of a fall down stairs. Michel made a singular impression on his contemporaries, including Martin *Luther, who reported having heard of a rich Jew who traveled throughout Germany, drawn by 12 horses. In dress and manners he conducted himself like a rich nobleman, surrounded by Jewish servants, and thus attended the Diets of the empire.

BIBLIOGRAPHY: H. Schnee, *Die Hoffinanz und der moderne Staat*, 1 (1955), 23–38; 5 (1965), 194, no. 80.

MICHEL-LÉVY, AUGUSTE (1844–1911), French petrologist and mining engineer. Michel-Lévy, who was born in Paris, was appointed director of the French geological survey and national inspector of mines in 1874. He was also a professor at the Collège de France. The most distinguished petrologist of his time, he was the first scientist to use the polarizing microscope to examine magmatic rocks and minerals. He extended this work by laboratory experiments in melting and crystallization, and with his collaborator F. Fouqué, was the pioneer of experimental petrology. He formulated fundamental queries which continue to pose major problems in the discussion of magmatic process as, for example, the role of volatiles (1875) and the mode of emplacement of granitic magmas through the assimilation of country rocks and bed-by-bed injection. The Fouqué-Lévy system became the standard one in the French teaching of petrography. Together with Fouqué, Michel-Lévy wrote *Minéralogie micrographique* (1879), *Synthèse des minéraux et des roches* (1882), and *Structure et classification des roches éruptives* (1889). He was a member of the French Academy.

This distinction was also conferred on his son, ALBERT-VICTOR (1877–1955), also a petrographer. He was born in Autun. Albert-Victor's main research was on the composition of the Vosges mountain range. He succeeded in producing artificial metamorphism in rocks by using pressure at high temperatures.

MICHELSON, ALBERT ABRAHAM (1852–1931), U.S. physicist; the first American to be awarded a Nobel Prize for science.

He was born in Strelno, Prussia, and was taken by his family to the United States at the age of two. Michelson graduated from the naval academy at Annapolis in 1873. However, after spending two years at sea he resigned to become an instructor in physics at the naval academy (1875–79). He spent a year in Washington and then two years studying in Germany. He returned to the U.S. in 1883 to become professor at the Case School of Applied Science in Cleveland until 1889. From 1889 to 1892 he was at Clark University and finally he was professor at the University of Chicago (1892–1929). He was awarded the Nobel Prize in physics in 1907. Michelson was a remarkable experimentalist able to secure astonishing accuracies with the simplest apparatus. His lifelong interest was the velocity of light, and this was the subject of his first experiment even in his mid-20s when he was an instructor at the U.S. naval academy at Annapolis. At that time physicists believed in the existence of an ether that filled all space, was at absolute rest, and through which light traveled in waves. There was then no way of measuring the motion of any body relative to the ether and leading scientists doubted whether this could be done. If it could be measured, two beams of light should show interference fringes denoting the difference. By measuring the width of the fringes it should be possible to show the earth's exact velocity when compared with the ether. Not only would the earth's absolute motion be determined, but also that of all bodies in the planetary system whose motions relative to the earth were known. For his experiment Michelson developed the interferometer, an instrument now used to measure wavelengths of light and other wavelengths of the radiation spectrum. He carried out his first experiments in Berlin in 1881 in Helmholtz' laboratory. In 1887, together with Edward Williams Morley, he performed one of the most important experiments in the history of science, which provided a new starting point for the great theoretical developments in 20th-century physics. The conclusion of the experiment indicated that light travels with the same velocity in any direction under any circumstances, and the implication was that the ether did not exist. This became one of the basic concepts which led *Einstein in 1905 to his special theory of relativity. The proving of this revolutionary theory of the absolute speed of light under any conditions has become the underlying principle of modern physics, astronomy, and cosmology and is considered to be, perhaps, the one absolute natural law in the universe. As a great experimentalist, Michelson established in 1892/93 the meter in terms of the wavelength of cadmium. He also determined the diameter of Jupiter's satellites and was the first person to measure the dimension of a star, Alpha Orion. Michelson wrote *Velocity of Light* (1902), *Light Waves and Their Uses* (1903), and *Studies in Optics* (1927).

BIBLIOGRAPHY: B. Jaffe, *Michelson and the Speed of Light* (1961), incl. bibl.

[Maurice Goldsmith]

MICHELSON, CHARLES (1869–1948), U.S. editor, journalist, and political publicist. Michelson, who was born in Virginia City, Nevada, ran away from home at the age of 13. He worked as a sheepherder, miner, and teamster, before going to work for the Virginia City *Chronicle* as a reporter. He subsequently worked for San Francisco newspapers, before going to Cuba as a correspondent for Hearst's New York *Journal* in 1896. Soon after his arrival Michelson was imprisoned briefly in Morro Castle, but was released in time to cover the Spanish-American War. After the war, Michelson worked for several other newspapers. From 1917 to 1929 he was chief of the Washington bureau of the New York *World*. In 1929 the Democratic National Committee hired Michelson as the first full-time publicity director, the first ever employed by a political party. Within two years of his appointment, Michelson was the ghostwriter of hundreds of press releases attacking the Hoover administration. After Roosevelt's election, Michelson also did publicity work for the Treasury Department and the Civilian Conservation Corps and was public relations director of the National Recovery Administration (NRA). His weekly column, "Dispelling the Fog," was distributed free to newspapers throughout the country. The Republican Party considered Michelson a key factor in the electoral successes of the Democratic Party. Michelson retired in 1942, returning briefly as associate director of publicity in 1944. He wrote his memoirs, *The Ghost Talks* (1944).

MICHELSTAEDTER, CARLO (1887–1910), Italian philosopher and poet. Michelstaedter was born at Gorizia, then part of the Austro-Hungarian Empire, into a well-known family. His mother was a descendant of Abraham *Reggio, chief rabbi of Gorizia in 1830, and Isacco Samuel *Reggio, who held the same office some years later, and who, together with Samuel David Luzzatto, co-founded the Rabbinical Institute of Padua. His father, Alberto, who came from a family of German origin, was an important part of the intellectual and social life of the city.

The young Michelstaedter strongly opposed his father's 19th-century positivist views, but politically, he did not disagree with him on the Irredentist cause. Michelstaedter undertook classical studies at the University of Florence. There he was greatly influenced by the writings of Schopenhauer, Nietzsche, and Ibsen and based his philosophy on the assumption that all human endeavor, spiritual or physical, is merely an illusion. Moreover Michelstaedter's Jewish origins gave his thought an original twist. Jewish Diaspora themes of the loss of self, exclusion from the fullness of life, the inability to enter deeply into existence, reflect a strong drive toward completeness. His ideas, as well as his Jewish identity, were reflected in his interest in the Kabbalah. On the other hand, Michelstaedter dissociated himself from the Zionist movement.

Michelstaedter's fundamental pessimism is expressed in his *Dialogo della Salute* (1912) and, in a more poetic fashion, in his *Poesie* (1912). He spent the last years of his short life in his native Gorizia preparing a thesis on "The Concept of Persuasion and Rhetoric in the Writings of Plato and Aristotle." After completing the second volume of this work (*La persua-*

sione e la retorica, 1913) Michelstaedter committed suicide. In this last book he anticipated the main doctrines of European existentialism. Michelstaedter's philosophical outlook led him to the extreme step of taking his own life out of inner conviction. His works, all posthumously published, were widely circulated and greatly influenced Italian philosophy and literature after World War II. A critical edition of Michelstaedter's complete works, including the first collection of his letters, was published in 1959.

His mother and sister, Emma and Elda Michelstaedter, perished in the Shoah.

BIBLIOGRAPHY: C. Pellizzi, *Gli spiriti della vigilia* (1924), 13–73; G. Chiavacci, in: *Giornale critico dela filosofia italiana*, 5 (1924), nos. 1–2; T. Moretti-Costanzi, in: L. Pelloux (ed.), *Esistenzialismo, saggi e studi* (1943); E. Garin, in: *Cronache di filosofia italiana* (1955), 36–41; A. Piromalli, in: *Saggi critici di storia letteraria* (1967), 165–81; G. Chiavacci et al., in: *La fiera letteraria* (July 13, 1952); L. Soperchi, in: *Rivista di Psicologia*, 28 (1932), 26ff., 280ff., incl. bibl. **ADD. BIBLIOGRAPHY:** O. Altieri, "La famiglia Michaelstaedter e l'ebraismo goriziano," in: *Dialoghi intorno a Michaelstaedter* (1987), 35–41; A. Neiger, "Michaelstaedter e la sindrome ebraica," in: *ibid.*, 43–57; P. Pieri, *La differenza ebraica, Ebraismo e grecita' in Michaelstaedter* (1984).

[Giorgio Romano]

MICHIGAN, one of the N. central states of the U.S. In 2001 there were an estimated 110,000 Jews among the 9,952,000 citizens of Michigan.

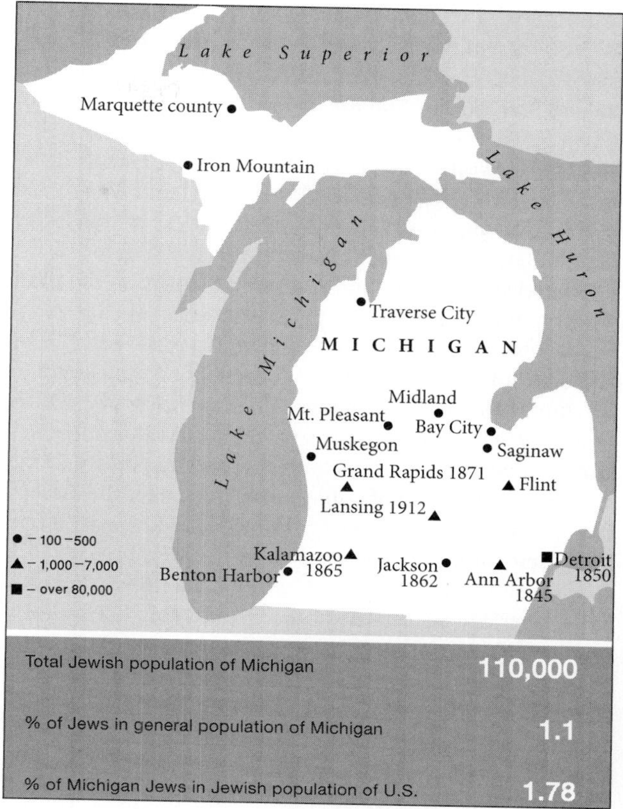

Jewish communities in Michigan and dates of establishment. Population figures for 2001.

Michigan has been home to Jews since 1761, when the first Jewish settler, Ezekiel Solomon, came as a fur trader and supplier to the British troops in the strategic wilderness outpost at Fort Michilimackinac.

Chapman Abraham, one of Solomon's partners, is the first known Jewish resident in Fort Detroit, held by the British. By 1762 he was bringing furs and needed goods in flotillas of voyageur canoes back and forth on the hazardous water route from Montreal. While residing most of the year in Michigan, both Solomon and Abraham remained members of the Montreal congregation, Shearith Israel. During Chief Pontiac's 1763 native uprising against the British, they each were captured and imprisoned, but eventually released. These two pioneer Jewish fur traders are recognized by Michigan Historical Markers placed by the Jewish Historical Society of Michigan.

Years before the American Revolution, Ezekiel Solomon, Chapman Abraham, and their other Jewish trading partners, Gershon Levi, Benjamin Lyon, and Levi Solomons, are credited with helping to "push back the wilderness of the Great Lakes country," and open up the continent for settlement. The British did not leave Michigan until 1796.

The completion of the Erie Canal in 1825, the laying of the railroads by 1848, and boat traffic on the Great Lakes opened up the route to Michigan. Moreover, the early promise of freedom of religion in the Northwest Ordinance of 1787 and free public education attracted Jewish immigrants. As the fur trade had brought Jews to Michigan in the 18th century, Michigan's prosperous lumber and mining industries offered economic opportunities during the late 19th and early 20th centuries. Jewish immigrant entrepreneurs fanned out to peddle needed supplies to the lumber and mining camps and farms in the wilderness of both the upper and lower peninsulas. These peddlers provided a needed alternative to the lumber barons' "company store." They became active citizens of their new communities and established Jewish cemeteries and synagogues in order to maintain their Jewish heritage. Their beginnings as peddlers often developed into prosperous mercantile businesses.

Michigan was declared a state in 1837. Ann Arbor was the first Michigan community where a colony of Jews settled in the 1840s, during the German-Jewish immigration. The five Weil brothers and their parents arrived in 1845; they conducted Sabbath and holiday services in their home. Michigan's first Jewish cemetery was established in 1848/9. The site is on the east lawn of University of Michigan's Rackham Building, noted with a historical plaque.

Starting out as farmers and peddlers, the Weil brothers later operated a prosperous tannery with over 100 employees. Jacob Weil, educated in European universities and a rabbi, was elected alderman in Ann Arbor and invited to the faculty of the University of Michigan, which he declined in order to continue as president of the family tannery firm. By 1873 the Weils had moved to Chicago to expand their business, J. Weil and Bros.

Jewish immigrant families followed the route of the railroad across southern Michigan to Chicago, establishing themselves in the mid-19th century not only in Ann Arbor, but also in Ypsilanti, Jackson, and Kalamazoo. Maurice Heuman was elected mayor of Jackson, Samuel Folz in Kalamazoo.

A Historical Marker in Kalamazoo honors arctic pioneer Edward Israel, a University of Michigan graduate, who served in 1881 as scientist on the nation's first polar expedition led by Lt. A.W. Greely. Along with 18 of the 25 expedition members, Israel perished of starvation after severe storms in the third winter of the expedition.

By 1845 the families of German immigrants Samuel Leopold and Julian Austrian, sailing their one-masted sloop to Mackinac, established a pioneer fishing business – which soon shipped as much as 1,000 barrels of salted fish to cities around the Great Lakes, including Cleveland. They became owners of a large fleet of sailing vessels, and after the discovery of copper in the Upper Peninsula, opened shops in five towns across the peninsula.

Jake Steinberg, Gustave Rosenthal, and Moses Winkleman operated successful stores in different "U.P." towns, supplying the many lumberjacks and miners and their families. "Winkleman's" grew to a large chain of shops for women's apparel.

An observant Jew who closed his store on the High Holidays, William Saulson operated the prosperous "People's Store" in St. Ignace. In 1888, he was elected Mayor of St. Ignace. In an ad published in 1884, Saulson proposed the building of the Mackinac Bridge, which opened 75 years later, in 1958. The five-mile-long suspension bridge linking the two peninsulas was designed by engineering genius David Steinman; Lawrence Rubin was the executive secretary of the Mackinac Bridge Authority.

Bavarian-born Dr. Frederick L. Hirschman, an 1873 graduate of one of the first classes of the Detroit College of Medicine, went to the Upper Peninsula to combat the smallpox epidemic there, and remained a doctor to the Republic Mines until his early death at the age of 38.

By 1903, at the far western end of the Upper Peninsula, Russian Polish immigrants Harry and Sam Cohodas first opened fruit markets in Houghton, Hancock, and Calumet. These developed into the nation's third largest wholesale produce business. The Cohodas family became nationally known for its philanthropy and support of civic and Jewish causes. Temple Jacob opened in Hancock in 1912, named for merchant Jacob Gartner, and still serves the Jewish students and faculty of Michigan Technological University.

Supplying five million board feet annually for the building of the nation's homes and factories, "white pine was king" in Michigan until about 1910, when the valuable forests had been stripped. In the late 18th and early 19th centuries, Jews followed the centers of lumbering, from Bay City and Saginaw on the state's eastern side to Grand Rapids, Traverse City, and Muskegon on the western shore, and, as mentioned, crossing over to the Upper Peninsula. A successful work shirt manufacturer, immigrant Julius Houseman first was elected mayor of Grand Rapids, then to the Michigan State Legislature, and in 1883 to the U.S. House of Representatives. He was the only Michigan Jew to serve as United States Congressman until a century later, with the elections of Howard Wolpe and Sander Levin.

Peddler Julius Steinberg from Souvalk, Poland, settled in Traverse City, where he soon built a prosperous clothing and dry goods store, and in 1894 opened an elegant two-story Grand Opera House on top of his store – known as "the finest opera house north of Chicago."

"The oldest synagogue building in continuous use," according to the Michigan Historical Commission, opened in Traverse City in 1885. A second synagogue was founded in 1896 in nearby Petoskey. Both continue in active use, serving local Jews as well as summer and winter vacationers.

A port on Lake Michigan, Muskegon survived the decline of lumbering by building foundries and factories to supply the emerging auto industry of the early 20th century. The Muskegon Scrap Metal Co. was run by Henry, Harry, and Isadore Rubinsky. In nearby Holland, Padnos Iron and Steel grew into an essential supplier to industry; the Padnoses are prominent philanthropists in the state. Later, in 1933, World War I veterans Harold and Leo Rosen opened the American Grease Stick Company, a major supplier of solid lubricants to the auto industry. The Muskegon Jewish House of Worship was dedicated in 1948.

In the 1890s, Russian Polish Jewish immigrants established a "Palestine Colony" at Bad Axe in Michigan's "Thumb" area, which unfortunately did not survive the economic "Panic" of that decade. Later, the Sunrise Cooperative Farm Community, of close to 100 families, supplied mint to Parke Davis pharmaceutical, but only lasted from 1933 to 1938. In the fruit belt of southwestern Michigan, a number of Jews established farms; the Ben Rosenberg family remained as successful farmers and community leaders for three generations. Nearby South Haven, on the shores of Lake Michigan, became known as the "Catskills of the Midwest." For three decades before World War II, Jewish immigrant families ran more than 60 resorts there, attracting thousands from Chicago and the Midwest.

By 1850 in Detroit, 12 Orthodox men formed Detroit's first Jewish congregation, the Beth El Society. In a characteristic pattern, they hired a rabbi, Rabbi Samuel Marcus, who for $200 a year also served as the *mohel*, the *shoḥet*, the cantor, the teacher of the children, and the judge to settle community disputes. They rented a room in which to meet, set up a school, bought land for a cemetery, arranged for traditional burials, and formed societies to care for the sick, the poor, and the widows and orphans. Rabbi Marcus died in the cholera epidemic of 1854.

When the Beth El Society adopted the Reform ritual advocated by Cincinnati's Rabbi Isaac Mayer Wise, in 1861 17 traditionalists withdrew to form the Shaarey Zedek Society. Today these two congregations are among the country's largest and most active, and both are recognized with Michigan Historical Markers.

In the time before the Civil War, Beth El's Rabbi Leibman Adler was preaching vigorous abolitionist sermons. Ernestine Rose, a Jewish woman who belonged to the national coalition of social reformers, had visited Detroit in 1846 to speak out against slavery as well as child labor, and for women's rights. Temple members Emil Heineman and Mark Sloman were active participants in the Underground Railroad. From the 151 Jewish families in Michigan, 181 men and boys served in the Union Armies; 38 lost their lives in the conflict.

To meet the needs of the growing wave of immigrants, in 1899 Detroit established the United Jewish Charities, under the leadership of Rabbi Leo M. Franklin. This included the Hebrew Free Loan Association, which since 1895 had been helping peddlers with loans of $5 to get them started.

By the early 1900s, an emerging automobile industry was providing additional economic opportunities. Engineer Max Grabowsky and his brother Morris, along with Bernard Ginsburg, formed the Grabowsky Power Wagon Company to manufacture the world's first gasoline-powered truck. Their successful four-story business in Detroit was bought by Will Durant to make up the new General Motors Company. Durant also hired bookkeeper Meyer Prentis who became treasurer of General Motors in 1919. Robert Janeway headed an engineering group for Chrysler for 30 years; A.E. Barit served as president of the Hudson Motor Car Company from 1936 to 1954. Participating in the wave of American inventiveness, in 1903 Rabbi Judah L. Levin received United States patents, and later British and Japanese patents, for his adding and subtracting machine which now is in the collection of the Smithsonian Institute.

However, since Jews were substantially excluded from the executive ranks of the automotive corporations, many Jewish entrepreneurs became suppliers to the industry. Jewish shops, which eventually grew into thriving businesses, supplied manufactured parts, glass, paint, chemicals, textiles, slag, and coveralls and operated laundries for factory uniforms. Max Fisher's Marathon Oil Company recycled and refined used oil. The Industrial Removal Office in New York City sent Jews to Detroit for industrial jobs and for work at the Ford Motor Company for "$5 a day."

Providing a needed voice for the rights of workers, Jews were prominent in the labor movement. Samuel Goldwater was elected president of Detroit's Cigarmakers Union in the 1890s. Later Myra Wolfgang organized the waitresses' union. Many Jewish leaders worked with Walter Reuther in the UAW, including Sam Fishman, Bernard Firestone, and Irving Bluestone, who later served as professor of labor studies in the Economics Department chaired by Professor Samuel Levin at Wayne University. Prominent labor lawyer Maurice Sugar's papers are collected at the Reuther Library at Wayne University.

In 1912, Henry Ford, who was actively antisemitic a decade later, hired architect Albert Kahn to design the first factory to house a continuously moving assembly line to manufacture the Model T. Kahn continued to design Ford factories. Henry Butzel served as chief justice of the Michigan Supreme Court, while his attorney brother Fred became known as "Detroit's Most Valuable Citizen." Charles Simons was appointed justice to the United States Sixth Circuit Court of Appeals; while his brother David was elected to Detroit's first nine-man city council in 1914.

In the 1990s, with a total Michigan population of 9,478,000, there were 107,000 Jews statewide, with a Jewish population of 96,000 in metropolitan Detroit, the greater majority in the nearby Oakland County suburbs. It is anticipated that more current studies will show a greater degree of spread to additional nearby communities as well as a decline in the Metro Detroit Jewish population.

An estimated 200,000 Muslims live in Metro Detroit, many concentrated in Dearborn. The local American Jewish Committee, the Anti-Defamation League, and the Jewish Community Council are each involved in outreach activities between local Muslims and Jews.

Carl *Levin served as United States Senator, elected four times from 1978.

His brother, Sander, was re-elected to the House of Representatives from 1982. A leader of the statewide Democratic ticket, Kathleen Straus was elected to the Michigan Board of Education and served as president. Community activist David Hermelin was appointed by President Bill Clinton as ambassador to Norway, where he served until his untimely death. Florine Mark, founder of Weight Watchers in Michigan and a philanthropic leader, is in the Michigan Women's Hall of Fame. William *Davidson, a third generation Detroiter, is the owner of the Detroit Pistons, the Detroit Shock, and the Tampa Bay Lightning; chairman of glass manufacturer Guardian Industries, Inc; he is a major philanthropist taking a special interest in Jewish education. The patriarch of the Jewish community, Max *Fisher, who passed away in 2004, was recognized as the "dean of American Jewry" and was acknowledged by United States presidents as a "world citizen."

BIBLIOGRAPHY: J.L. Cantor, *Jews in Michigan* (2001); I.I. Katz, *The Beth El Story* (1955). **WEBSITE:** MICHIGAN JEWISH HISTORY: www.michjewishhistory.com. See complete texts: Jewish Historical Society of Michigan, vol. 10, 1970, Graff, George, "Michigan's Jewish Settlers"; vol. 23, #1, #2, 1983. Aminoff, Helen "First Jews of Ann Arbor"; vol. 30, 1989. "Historical Markers"; vol. 38, 1998. Elstein, Rochelle. "Jews of Houghton-Hancock…"; vol. 42, 2002. Teasdle, Holly. "Jewish Farming in Michigan"; vol. 42, 2002. Wamsley, Douglas. "Michigan's Arctic Pioneer: Edward Israel and the Greeley Expedition"; vol. 44, 2004. Rose, Emily. "Ann Arbor…"

[Judith L. Cantor (2nd ed.)]

MICHMASH or **MICHMAS** (Heb. מִכְמָשׂ, מִכְמָס, מִכְמָשׁ), city of the tribe of Judah, originally belonging to the tribe of Benjamin, situated between Jerusalem and Beth-El in a strong strategic position north of the deep Wadi al-Suwaynīṭ. Saul gathered part of his army there (I Sam. 13:2) and the main part of the Philistine forces later encamped in the city prior to the battle of Michmash, fleeing by way of Aijalon after their defeat (I Sam. 13–14). It is mentioned in Isaiah's description of the advance of the Assyrian army, where it is placed between Aiath and Geba (Isa. 10:28), and in the lists of those returning from the Babylonian Exile (Ezra 2:27; Neh. 7:31). Jonathan the Hasmonean resided there (until 152 B.C.E.) before assuming the high priesthood (I Macc. 9:73; cf. Jos., Ant., 13:34). In the Mishnah, the wheat of the place is highly praised (Men. 8:1). Eusebius calls it a very big village, 9 mi. (c. 14 km.) from Jerusalem and in its territory (Onom. 132:3–4). Michmash is identified with Mukhmās, close to Rama, approximately 6 mi. (c. 10 km.) northeast of Jerusalem. A first-century C.E. ossuary is known from a local tomb bearing the names "Shimon" and "Levi." A Byzantine church with an inscription was found in the village. The Byzantine monastic laura of Firminus is situated in the vicinity of Mukhmās.

BIBLIOGRAPHY: Abel, Geog, 2 (1938), 386; Aharoni, Land, index; EM, 4 (1962), 961–2. **ADD. BIBLIOGRAPHY:** Y. Tsafrir, L. Di Segni, and J. Green, *Tabula Imperii Romani. Iudaea – Palaestina. Maps and Gazetteer* (1994), 173, s.v. "*Machmas*"; J. Patrich, *The Judean Desert Monasticism in the Byzantine Period: The Institutions of Sabas and his Disciples* (1995); B. Bagatti, *Ancient Christian Villages of Samaria* (2002), 22; G.S.P. Grenville, R.L. Chapman, and J.E. Taylor, *Palestine in the Fourth Century. The Onomasticon by Eusebius of Caesarea* (2003), 143.

[Michael Avi-Yonah / Shimon Gibson (2nd ed.)]

°**MICKIEWICZ, ADAM** (1798–1855), Polish poet. Born in Lithuania, Mickiewicz became involved in student nationalist politics at Vilna University and in 1826 was expelled from the country and ordered to live in Russia. In 1829 he was given permission to go abroad, and started the journeying from one European city to another that was to last for the rest of his life. It was during the period 1823–32 that he wrote his great drama *Dziady* (3 vols. (Paris, 1832); partial trans. *Forefathers' Eve*, 1928), in which he drew a picture of the future savior of Poland which has been interpreted as referring to himself. According to the vision of one of the characters, this savior would be "a son of an alien mother; his blood, the blood of ancient heroes; and his name – forty-and-four." Mickiewicz's mother, descended from a converted Frankist family, was an "alien"; and his own name, Adam (אדם), omitting the unvoiced "A" (א), has the numerical value of 44. Such kabbalistic notions were gleaned from the writings of the French mystic, Louis-Claude de Saint-Martin. Although Mickiewicz at first occasionally referred slightingly to the Jews, even in his biblically-influenced *Księgi narodu polskiego i pielgrzymstwa polskiego* ("Books of the Polish Nation and the Polish Pilgrimage," Paris, 1832), he soon revised his attitude. In this he was influenced by the mystical philosopher Andrzej Towiański, who considered the Jews, together with the French and Poles, to be a "chosen nation" and whose Messianic nationalism drew inspiration from Mesmer, Swedenborg, and the Kabbalah. Thus the idealized Jew, Jankiel, in Mickiewicz's masterpiece, the great epic *Pan Tadeusz* (1834), is an ardent Polish patriot. In the lectures he gave as professor of Slavonic languages and literatures at the Collège de France in Paris (1840–44), Mickiewicz was at pains to praise the Jews and defend them against their detractors. In a sermon delivered in a Paris synagogue on the Fast of the Ninth of Av, 1845, he expressed his sympathy for Jewish suffering and yearning for Ereẓ Israel. Although he dreamed for years of the conversion of the Jews to Christianity, he was greatly disappointed at the assimilationist tendencies of French Jews. In one of the statutes of the Polish legion which he organized in Italy in 1848 to fight against Russia Mickiewicz wrote: "To Israel, our elder brother: honor, fraternity, and help in striving towards his eternal and temporal goal. Equal rights in all things." When the Crimean War broke out in 1853, Mickiewicz went to Constantinople to help raise a Polish regiment to fight against the Russians. He hoped to include Jewish units, and was prepared to assure them the right to observe the Sabbath and all other religious obligations. His chief assistant, a French medical officer named Armand Lévy, was a Jewish nationalist, and it is possible that the two men believed that the creation of Jewish units would be a first step towards the revival of the Jewish nation in its own land. Mickiewicz died suddenly before his mission in Constantinople was completed.

BIBLIOGRAPHY: A.G. Duker, in: M. Kridl (ed.), *Adam Mickiewicz, Poet of Poland* (1951), 108–25; S. Scheps, *Adam Mickiewicz: ses affinités juives* (1964); R. Brandstaetter, *Legjon żydoswki Adama Mickiewicza* (1932=*Miesięcznik żydowski*, 2 (1932), 20–45, 112–32, 225–48); W. Feldman, *Stosunek Adama Mickiewicza do Żydów* (1890); P. Kon, in: *Źródłamocy*, 1 (1924), bibl. of Heb. and Yid. trans.; R.A. Braudes (Broydes), *Adam Mickiewicz* (Heb., 1890); F. Kupfer and S. Strelcyn, *Mickiewicz w przekładach hebrajskich* (1955).

[Yehuda Arye Klausner]

MICROCOSM (from Gr. *mikros kosmos*; "small world"), term in the Western philosophical tradition referring to man as an epitome of the universe (the macrocos) in his parts and structure. The Arabic (*ʿālam ṣaghīr*), Hebrew (*olam katan*), and Latin (*mundis minor*) terms are literal equivalents of the Greek. The term is said to be first attested in Aristotle (*Physics*, 8:2, 252b, 26–27), though the motif is older; indeed, the notion that some aspect of reality (the city, sanctuary, man) reflects the cosmos is both ancient and widespread. Though the broad diffusion of the microcosm motif in late antiquity (in Gnostic, Hermetic, neoplatonic, neopythagorean, Orphic, and stoic writings) complicates the study of original sources, its occurrence in medieval Arabic and Hebrew texts is mainly the result of neoplatonic influence. The analogy was frequently invoked to argue for the existence of a world soul or mind which directs and orders the physical universe as the soul does the body. The idea that man exemplifies all being was also used to buttress the theme of man's superiority, dignity, or freedom: as *nodus et vinculum mundi*, he epitomizes the entire scale of being (spiritual and material) and determines his own place, unlike angels and beasts whose nature is fixed. The elaboration of the neoplatonic hypostases was, in effect, a projection of human psychology to the supersensible world.

Furthermore, the neoplatonic notion that the human mind is potentially a κόσμος νοητός ("intelligible world") implies that by knowing the intelligibles man becomes identical with all being. Microcosmic speculation tended to combine with astrology (correspondence between heavenly bodies and parts of the human body), medicine (universal and human nature, parallel between the four elements and the four humors), and magical practice (universal sympathy). Philo frequently compares man as microcosm βραχὺς κόσμο to the universe (Conger, in bibl., 16–18; H.A. Wolfson, *Philo*, 1 (1948), 424, n.), stressing the parallel between the human and cosmic minds (*logoi*; e.g., Op. 69–71). He is said to have drawn his theory of the microcosm from Greek and rabbinic sources (A. Altmann in bibl., 20). Among the latter is found a long list of gross analogies between parts of the world and parts of man in *Avot de-Rabbi Nathan* (ARN² 31, 92). (For other rabbinic sources, see Altmann, 21, n.) In medieval Jewish philosophy the motif is frequently cited, being part of the common stock of popular philosophy found in such works as the Epistles of the *Brethren of Sincerity. It is mentioned, for example, by *Saadiah Gaon in his commentary on the *Sefer Yeẓirah* (ed. by M. Lambert (1891), 67ff., 91), where he compares God to life and intelligence and sets forth a series of analogues between the universe, the sanctuary, and man (followed by Abraham Ibn Ezra in his commentary on Ex. 25:40; see Altmann, in bibl., 25–26); by *Baḥya ibn Paquda (*Ḥovot ha-Levavot*, 2:4); and by *Judah Halevi in his *Kuzari* (4:3), where he quotes "the philosophers" who compared the world to a *macranthropos* ("large man") and man to a microcosm, implying that God is the spirit, soul, mind, and life of the world. (For other citations of the microcosm motif by medieval Jewish philosophers, see Conger, in bibl., 37ff., and Altmann, in bibl., 27–28.)

The microcosm theme was productive in *Israeli, Ibn *Gabirol, and Joseph ibn *Ẓaddik. Israeli links it to his definition of philosophy as self-knowledge: "This being so, it is clear that man, if he knows himself in both his spirituality and corporeality, comprises knowledge of all, and knows both the spiritual and the corporeal substance, and also knows the first substance which is created from the power of the Creator without mediator … " (A. Altmann and S.M. Stern (eds.), *Isaac Israeli* (1959), 27; see comments, *ibid.*, 28–30, 203–8, and Altmann, in bibl., 22–23). The same combination of philosophy as self-knowledge and the consequent knowledge of all is found in Ibn Ẓaddik's *Sefer ha-Olam ha-Katan* (Introd.). Ibn Ẓaddik adds that this knowledge leads to knowledge of the Creator. (See also *Sefer ha-Olam ha-Katan*, pt. 2, Introd., where Job 19:26 is cited as a proof verse – "And from my flesh I shall behold God"; cf. Altmann-Stern, 208; Altmann, in bibl., 23, 25; and Vajda, in bibl., 97 and n. 3, who cites the similar combination of the microcosm and γνῶθι σεαυτόν ("know yourself") themes by Abraham ibn Ezra.) In a more primitive vein, reminiscent of *Avot de-Rabbi Nathan* and the microcosm passage in the Iranian *Greater Bundahišhn* (trans. by B.T. Anklesaria (1956), 245), Ibn Ẓaddik (pt. 2, ch. 1), referring to "the ancients," compares the members of the human organism to the heavenly bodies (head to the outer sphere, nostrils to Venus, mouth to Mars, tongue to Mercury, vertebrae to the signs of the zodiac, eyes to the sun and moon, ears to Saturn and Jupiter), while the arteries are compared to the seas and rivers, the bones to the mountains, the hair to the plants, and the four humors to the four elements (see Altmann, in bibl., 24; and Vajda, in bibl., 113, who brands this a "*néoplationisme vulgarisé*"). Nothing so gross appears in Ibn Gabirol's *Mekor Ḥayyim*. Though the term for microcosm (*ʿālam ṣaghir = mundis minor*) appears but once (3:2, 10; see S. Pines, in *Tarbiz*, 27 (1958), 220), Ibn Gabirol makes ample use of the motif. Following the general principle that the inferior is an exemplar of the superior, man as microcosm is said to exemplify the macrocosm. The correspondence is utilized to demonstrate, for example, that the most simple substance is not in contact with the substance that bears the nine categories (3:2, 10, see also 3:58). The action of the particular will is invoked in order to explain that of the universal will (5:37).

Maimonides had little use for the popular philosophy of the Brethren of Sincerity and says he never read Ibn Ẓaddik's *Sefer ha-Olam ha-Katan* (in his letter to Ibn Tibbon; A. Marx (ed.), in: JQR, 25 (1934–35), 378–9), but in a central chapter of the *Guide* (1:72) he sets forth an elaborate analogy (with qualifications) between the whole of being and man, the parallel par excellence, being that between God vis-à-vis the universe and the rational intellect vis-à-vis man. It is on the basis of this parallel that man is called a microcosm. In his structure man exemplifies the unity within diversity and the hierarchical ordering of the universe (an idea which appears frequently in the writings of al-Fārābī). With this analogy in the *Guide* microcosmic speculation in Jewish philosophy reaches its peak, from which it ebbs with the decline of Jewish neoplatonism occasioned by the rise of Jewish Aristotelianism in the post-Maimonidean era. A notable exception is Judah *Abrabanel (Leone Ebreo), the Renaissance neoplatonist, who set forth analogies between the heavens and parts of the body (astrological microcosm; cf. Ibn Ẓaddik) in the second dialogue of his *Dialoghi d'amore* (ed. Carmella (1929), 84f.; trans. by F. Friedberg-Seeley and J.H. Barnes (1937), 93ff.).

BIBLIOGRAPHY: A. Altmann, *Studies in Religious Philosophy and Mysticism* (1969); G. Vajda, in: *Archives d'histoire doctrinale et littéraire du moyen âge*, 24 (1949), 93–181; D. Levy, in: *The Encyclopedia of Philosophy*, 5 (1967), 121–5 (with good bibl.); G.P. Conger, *Theories of Macrocosms and Microcosms in the History of Philosophy* (1922); M. Doctor, *Die Philosophic des Josef (Ibn) Ẓaddik* (1895); H. Schipperges, in: P. Wilpert (ed.), *Antike und Orient im Mittelalter* (1962), 129–53 (with extensive bibliography); R. Allers, in: *Tradition*, 2 (1944), 319–407; A. Goetze, in: *Zeitschrift fuer Indologie und Iranistik*, 2 (1923), 60–98.

[Joel Kraemer]

°**MICZYŃSKI, SEBASTIAN** (late 16th–early 17th century), anti-Jewish agitator and professor of philosophy at Cracow University. In 1618 Miczyński published a venomous antisemitic lampoon entitled *Zwierciadło korony polskiej* ("The Mirror of the Polish Crown"). It is a catalog of demagogic denunciations accusing the Jews of all the misfortunes that had befallen the kingdom of Poland and its people. Through reports of *blood libels and accusations that they had desecrated icons and profaned Catholic festivals, the Jews are presented as the implacable enemies of Christians. Miczyński also presents the Jews as traitors and spies in the pay of Turkey, and lays special emphasis on the wealth of the Jewish merchants and craftsmen who compete with their Christian neighbors, driving the guilds and towns to ruin. The pamphlet seriously disturbed the Jews of *Cracow. When riots broke out in the town, the *parnasim* of the community appealed to King Sigismund III Vasa. The king promptly prohibited the circulation of the pamphlet, but in spite of his order it was reprinted in a second and enlarged edition during the same year; it was published for a third time in 1648. Miczyński's work is an important link in the chain of Polish antisemitic literature.

BIBLIOGRAPHY: K. Bartoszewicz, *Antysemityzm w literaturze polskiej 15–17 wieków* (1914); M. Bałaban, *Historja Żydów w Krakowie i na Kazimierzu*, 1 (1931), 171–7.

[Arthur Cygielman]

MIDDLESEX COUNTY, county on the eastern coast of New Jersey, southwest of New York City, U.S.; estimated total Jewish population of 55,000 in 2005. The majority of Jewish settlers in Middlesex County were traders and peddlers. Most of the information about Jewish immigrants comes from court and land records. Aaron and Jacob Lozada owned a grocery and hardware store in Bound Brook, on the border between Middlesex County and Somerset County, as early as 1718, and helped form a synagogue ten years later. The next mention of a synagogue, Congregation Anshe Emeth of New Brunswick, is found in an 1861 land record. A court record from 1722 lists Daniel Nunez as town clerk and tax collector of Piscataway Township and justice of the peace for Middlesex County. Perth Amboy was an important Jewish center for Jewish merchants from the time that it was named capital of East Jersey in 1685. The first Jewish religious service was held here in 1890 in the home of a local Jewish resident. A *mikveh* was constructed shortly thereafter and Rosh ha-Shanah and Day of Atonement services were held at the Perth Amboy Savings Bank. When the size of the Jewish community increased, a building was purchased in about 1900 under the name of the Hebrew Mutual Aid Society. This subsequently became Congregation Shaarey Tefiloh which was dedicated on October 29, 1903. In 1904 a burial ground was purchased and a free Hebrew school was organized. The founders of the second congregation came from Perth Amboy, Metuchen, and South Amboy. It was incorporated on August 2, 1895. The first meeting places were in homes. In 1897 a synagogue was built and called Temple Beth Mordecai after a deceased son of Henry Wolff, one of the founders. In April 1927 the temple was dedicated. The Perth Amboy YMHA was formed in 1908 and was the first YMHA built in the state to have its own building rather than a rented one.

Middlesex County's prominent political figures included David T. Wilentz of Perth Amboy, the first Jewish New Jersey attorney general (1934–44), prosecutor in the Lindbergh kidnapping trial, and New Jersey national Democratic committeeman (1964–70); his son Robert Wilentz, also of Perth Amboy, state assemblyman from 1966 to 1970; Arthur J. Sills of Metuchen, state attorney general from 1962 to 1970; Donald Wernik, mayor of Metuchen in 1970; and Norman Tanzman of Woodbridge, who was elected state senator in 1962. By the 1970s the Jews of Middlesex County were mainly engaged in the professions and as business executives. Meryl Harris was the mayor of Highland Park and Brian Levine the mayor of Franklin Township. Linda Greenstein and Amy Handlin were members of the State Assembly and Barbara Buono was the State Senator.

The Federation of Middlesex County sponsors the Jewish Community Relations Committee, a Professional Networking Group, a Joint Chaplaincy Program, as well as a Missions program. It also supports a Jewish Home for the Aged, Jewish Family and Vocational Services, two Jewish community centers, a Solomon Schechter School in East Brunswick, the Rabbi Jacob Joseph School in Edison, as well as the Rabbi Pesach Raymond Yeshiva also in Edison. There is also an I.L. Peretz Community Jewish School, one of the few remaining secular humanist schools of its kind. Synagogues have been established in East Brunswick, New Brunswick, Perth Amboy, Highland Park, Edison, Monroe Township, South River, Carteret, Woodbridge, Metuchen, Old Bridge, Somerset. The Orthodox community established an *eruv* in Highland Park and in East Brunswick. The Hillel House at Rutgers University is quite active, along with the Allen and Joan Bildner Center. There is also a Chabad House on campus.

[Barry Dov Schwartz / Jeff Schekner (2nd ed.)]

MIDDOT (Heb. מִדּוֹת; "measures"), tenth tractate of the order *Kodashim* (in some codices and early editions it is ninth; in current Talmud editions the 11th and last). It is found in the Mishnah only. This tractate gives, in five chapters, exact details and measurements of the building of the Temple and of its component parts, intended perhaps to serve as a guide for the rebuilding of the Temple. The description is of the Temple of Herod. It is not based on a plan drawn up in Temple times, but depends on the memory of sages who saw the Temple and who after its destruction gave an oral description of it to their disciples. The main reporter seems to have been *Eliezer b. Jacob I, who figures prominently in this tractate. He is thought to have seen the Temple while it was still standing, but he may also have learned much about its inner arrangements from his uncle who actually served in it (1:2). That the descriptions are based on memory is evident from the controversies on factual points (1:9; 2:6; 3:4, 6; et al.); moreover, Eliezer b. Jacob is repeatedly reported to have "forgotten" certain details (2:5; 5:4). In fact this tractate was considered the original *mishnah* ("teaching") of Eliezer b. Jacob; the final redaction of Judah ha-Nasi contains, of course, the variant traditions of the other authorities as well (see Yoma 16a–17a; TJ, Yoma 2:3, 39d).

BIBLIOGRAPHY: Ḥ. Albeck, *Shishah Sidrei Mishnah*, 5 (1959), 313–5.

[Arnost Zvi Ehrman]

MIDIAN, MIDIANITES (Heb. מִדְיָן, מִדְיָנִים Gen. 37:28, מְדָנִים), name of a people or a group of (semi-) nomadic peoples in the Bible (LXX, Madian, or Madiam; 1QIsᵃ 60:6, מדים). The Midianites are among the sons of Abraham and Keturah who were sent to "the land of the East" (Gen. 25:1–6). "Midianite traders" are mentioned in the episode about the sale of Joseph (Gen. 37:28). *Jethro, Moses' father-in-law, was a Midianite priest living in the land of Midian (Ex. 2:15–3:1); he met Moses in the wilderness of Sinai (Ex. 18: 1–5), and the members of his family accompanied the Israelites in their wanderings in the desert (Num. 10:29–32). The elders of Midian displayed hostility toward the Israelites on the plains of Moab (22:7) and the Israelites fought the Midianites, killing many of them (31:1–20).

This episode was connected with the attempt to entice the Israelites to worship Baal-Peor, in which the daughters of Midian participated (25:6–18). In the period of the Judges, the Midianites exerted harsh pressure on Israel (Judg. 6:1–7), and Gideon defeated them far from the borders of Ereẓ Israel, in Karkor (8:10), which was probably in Wadi Sirḥān in Transjordan, on the border of the desert. After this war, the Midianites ceased to be a political or military factor.

The range of the Midianites' wanderings was very broad: from the neighborhood of Moab (Gen. 36:35; Num. 22:4, 7; 25:1, 5, 15) and the kingdom of Sihon the Amorite (Josh. 13:21) in the border region of Transjordan, along the border of the Arabian desert (cf. Judg. 8:21, 24) west of Edom (I Kings 11:18), to the Sinai Desert and the trade route between Ereẓ Israel and Egypt (Gen. 37:28). In Greek-Roman and Arabic sources Midian is mentioned in Arabia, as well as on the shore of the Red Sea, and, according to Josephus (Ant., 2:257), this is the biblical Midian (cf. Eusebius, Onom. 124:6). This Midian is identified, according to the tradition of the Arabic geographers, with modern Maghāyir Shuʿayb (= the caves near Akaba). It appears that the Midianites' settlement in Arabia occurred in a later time, when their living area was reduced, but it is possible that the settlement in North Arabia during the Hellenistic-Roman period was a continuation of the biblical settlement. Among the sons of Keturah are mentioned tribes which inhabited North Arabia – Ephah and Dedan (Gen. 25:3–4) – and it is also possible that from there the Midianites spread to the north, the east, and the west. In the Bible the Midianites are also designated by the inclusive typological title "Ishmaelites" (Judg. 8:24). Some scholars discern a connection between the Midianites and the Kushu tribes mentioned in the Egyptian Execration Texts from the 18th century B.C.E., who wandered in the southern deserts of Ereẓ Israel (cf. Cushan, Hab. 3:7). This may be hinted at in the story of the "Cushite woman" whom Moses married (Num. 12:1).

The name Midian is attributed to groups of tribes or peoples (cf. Gen. 25:4), as is attested by the nature of the monarchy in Midian. The Bible mentions "the five kings of Midian" during the war in the wilderness (Num. 31:8) and Zebah and Zalmunna in the war of Gideon (Judg. 8:1ff.). The Midianite kings are called "chieftains" (*nesi'im*) and "princes" (*nesikhim*; Josh. 13:21; Ps. 83:12), very fitting titles for a tribal organization united in groups; Zur, a prince of Midian, is explicitly called "the tribal head of an ancestral house in Midian" (Num. 25:15). Their typically (semi- and eventually complete) nomadic character made them close to other similar tribes – Amalekites and Kedemites. The Midianites in Transjordan followed the cult of the Moabite Baal-Peor, while those who inhabited the Negev and the Sinai became close to the Kenites or even identified with them (cf. Num. 10:29; Judg. 1:16; 4:11) and the Hebrews. The Midianites were known as shepherds (Ex. 2:17) and traders (Gen. 37:28, 36). From time to time, they, together with neighboring tribes, broke into the permanent settlements around them. The Bible describes them as robbers (Judg. 6:5). During the Monarchy the Midianites lived within the confines of their place of origin, North Arabia, and they were known as middlemen in the frankincense (*levonah*) and gold export from Sheba in South Arabia (cf. Isa. 60:6). During the Hellenistic period the Nabateans mined much gold in the land of Midian and exported it via the port of Macna (Strabo, *Geographica*, 17:784). There has been no systematic scientific research of Midian in North Arabia.

[Samuel Abramsky]

In the *Aggadah*

Midian and Moab had always been enemies but, fearing that Israel would subdue them, they composed their differences and entered into an alliance (Sanh. 105a). They succeeded in inducing the Israelites to commit fornication with the daughters of Midian only by first making them drunk. For this reason, Phinehas forbade the drinking of gentile wine (PdRE 47). The hatred of the Midianites for Israel was solely on account of the observance of the Torah by Israel (Num. R. 22:2). The Midianites are sometimes identified with the Moabites, who lost their claim to special consideration as descendants of Lot (Deut. 2:9), the nephew of Abraham, because they tried to induce Israel to sin (*Yelammedenu* in Yal. 1, 875). The command to Moses to make war upon the Midianites before his death was because, having no reason for their hatred against Israel, they nevertheless joined the Moabites and outdid them in their enmity. Moses did not lead the war in person because he had found refuge in Midian when he was a fugitive from Egypt. He delegated the command to Phinehas as he had been the first to take action against them by slaying the Midianite princess, Cozbi (Num. R. 22:4).

BIBLIOGRAPHY: R.F. Burton, *The Gold Mines of Midian* (1897); idem, *The Land of Midian* (1898); E. Glaser, *Skizze der Geschichte und Geographie Arabiens*, 2 (1890), 261ff.; E. Meyer, *Die Israeliten und ihre Nachbarstaemme* (1906), 326ff., 381–2; H. Grimme, in: OLZ, 13 (1910), 54–59; H. Gressmann, *Mose und seine Zeit* (1913), 416ff.; A. Musil, *The Northern Hegâz* (1926), 109ff., 267ff., 278–98, 321ff.; W.J. Phythian-Adams, in: PEFQS (1930), 193ff.; L.E. Binns, in: JTS, 31 (1930), 337–59; A. Reuveni, *Shem, Ḥam, ve-Yafet* (1932), 16–18, 68–69; Albright, Stone, 195–6; idem, in: BASOR, 83 (1941), 36, n. 8; M. Noth, in: ZAW, 60 (1944), 23ff.; B. Mazar, in: Eretz-Israel, 3 (1954), 20; S.

Abramsky, *ibid.*, 118–9; Y. Kutscher, *Ha-Lashon ve-ha-Reka ha-Leshoni shel Megillat Yeshayahu* (1959), 82; G.W. van Beer, in: BA, 23 (1960), 3, 70–95; A. Grohman, *Arabien* (1963), 21, 38–92. IN THE AGGADAH: Ginzberg, Legends, 7 (1938), 313; A. Rosmarin, *Moses im Lichte der Aggadah* (1932), index.

MIDLER, BETTE (1945–), U.S. singer, entertainer, and actress. Born in Honolulu, Midler entered show business as a member of the *Fiddler on the Roof* cast on Broadway in 1964. She gained notoriety as a popular performer in the Continental Baths cabaret, a meeting place for homosexuals, and then scored a hit single with the frequently recorded "Do You Wanna Dance?" (1974). She followed this success with her top-selling album *The Divine Miss M.* and a popular film of her live act called *Divine Madness* (1979). Midler turned actress in a movie loosely based on the life of Janis Joplin, *The Rose* (1981), which earned her an Academy Award nomination for Best Actress. Midler, who was named after legendary film icon Bette Davis, starred in subsequent films such as *Down and Out in Beverly Hills* (1986), *Ruthless People* (1986), *For the Boys* (Oscar nomination for Best Actress, 1991), *The First Wives Club* (1996), *Drowning Mona* (2000), *Isn't She Great* (2000), and *The Stepford Wives* (2004).

Over the years, among other TV guest spots, Midler appeared on Johnny Carson's *Tonight Show* 24 times, starting in 1970 and including the final program in May 1992. She also appeared in the TV movie *Gypsy* (1993) and produced and starred in the sitcom *Bette* (2000–1).

On the Broadway stage, Midler appeared in *Fiddler on the Roof* (1964–72), *Bette Midler Special Concert* (1973), *Bette Midler's Clams on the Half Shell Revue* (1975), *Bette! Divine Madness* (1979), and *Short Talks on the Universe* (2002).

For her multiple talents as an actress, writer, singer, and performer, Midler won a host of awards. In 1974 she received a special Tony Award "for adding luster to the Broadway season." She won four Grammy awards, including the 1973 Best New Artist and the prestigious Record of the Year in 1989 for her rendition of her #1 hit "Wind Beneath My Wings" from the movie *Beaches*. She won three Emmy awards and was nominated for another four. In 1987 she received the American Comedy Awards' Lifetime Achievement Award in Comedy, as well as the American Comedy Award in 1988, 1989, 1993, 1996, and 1998. Her writings include *A View from a Broad* (1980) and the fable *The Saga of Baby Divine* (1983).

BIBLIOGRAPHY: M. Bego, *Bette Midler: Still Divine* (2003); A. Waldman, *The Bette Midler Scrapbook* (1997); G. Mair, *Bette: An Intimate Biography of Bette Midler* (1995); A. Collins, *Bette Midler* (1989); M. Bego, *Bette Midler: Outrageously Divine* (1987); J. Spada, *The Divine Bette Midler* (1984).

[Jonathan Licht / Ruth Beloff (2nd ed.)]

MIDRASH (Heb. מִדְרָשׁ), the designation of a particular genre of rabbinic literature containing anthologies and compilations of homilies, including both biblical exegesis (see *Hermeneutics) and sermons delivered in public (see *Homiletics) as well as *aggadot* (see **Aggadah*) and sometimes even *halakhot* (cf. **Midreshei Halakhah*), usually forming a running commentary on specific books of the Bible.

The term Midrash itself derives from the root *drsh* (דרש) which in the Bible means mainly "to search," "to seek," "to examine," and "to investigate" (cf. Lev. 10:16; Deut. 13:15; Isa. 55:6; et al.). This meaning is also found in rabbinic Hebrew (cf. BM 2:7: "until thou examine [*tidrosh*] thy brother if he be a cheat or not"). The noun "*Midrash*" occurs only twice in the Bible (II Chron. 13:22 and 24:27); it is translated in the Septuagint by βίβλος, γράφη i.e., "book" or "writing," and it seems probable that it means "an account," "the result of inquiry (examination, study, or search) of the events of the times," i.e., what is today called "history" (the word history is also derived from the Greek root ἱστορὲω which has a similar meaning). In Jewish literature of the Second Temple period the word Midrash was first employed in the sense of education and learning generally (Ecclus. 51:23), "Turn unto me, ye unlearned, and lodge in my house of Midrash," which the author's grandson translated into Greek, "house of instruction or of study"; compare the similar development of the Latin *studium* which originated in the verb *studeo* which means "to become enthusiastic," "to make an effort," "to be diligent," etc. and only in a secondary sense, in the post-Augustan era, in the sense of learning (with diligence and the noun *studium* passed through the same stages of meaning; cf. Ger. *studium*; Fr. *étude*, etc.).

Darosh both in its nominal and verbal forms is sometimes found in the literature of the *Dead Sea sect as the designation for a certain method, a special technique of learning things – in *halakhah* and in *aggadah* – through rigorous study and painstaking, searching inquiry into the verses of the Bible. This method of Midrash was both ideologically and halakhically one of the fundamentals of the life of the sect: "and that his deeds appear in accordance with the Midrash of the Torah as followed by the holy upright men" (Damascus Covenant 8:29–30; cf. the Manual of Discipline 8:25–26: "If his way is perfect in company, in Midrash, and in counsel"; cf. also *ibid.* 6:24 and 6:6). The nature of this Midrash is testified to by the explicit words: "When these become a community in Israel with such characteristics they separate themselves from the company of the wicked men to go thither to the wilderness to make clear there the way of the Lord, as is written [Isa. 40:3], 'and in the wilderness clear ye the way… make plain in the desert a highway for our God,' that being the Midrash of the Torah [which] he commanded through Moses, to do in accordance with all that is revealed in every era and as the prophets revealed through his holy spirit" (Manual of Discipline 8:12–16); i.e., the Midrash of the Torah is the lesson derived from the verse (4:21–5 5:11). A different method of interpretation is the **pesher*, although the Midrash could also contain *pesharim* (see 4Q 174 Florilegium, 1–2, I 14–19, in: J.M. Allegro, *Discoveries in the Judean Desert*, V: Qumran Cave 4, I (1968), p. 53f.). This technique of biblical exegesis which is largely similar to that customary among the Greek grammarians, the students of the classical texts of Homer, and among the Roman rhetoricians, the exponents of Roman law, is found among the Jews for the first time in the Dead Sea sect (see particularly Book of *Jubilees). Nevertheless these earlier forms of exegesis must be distinguished from rabbinic midrash as a fully developed literary form (cf. **Midreshei Halakhah*: Literary Nature and Relation to Early Midrash). Suggestions to the effect that the *Liber Antiquitatum Biblicarum* (pseudo-Philo) is a Midrash are without foundation.

Midrashic Literature

It is very possible that the earliest Midrash to come down is the Passover **Haggadah*, the earliest and chief element of which is a Midrash to Deuteronomy 26:5–8 (cf. Sif. Deut. 301). A great part of the midrashic *aggadah* of the tannaitic period is included side by side with the midrashic *halakhah* in the halakhic Midrashim (cf. **Midreshei Halakhah*: The Aggadic Material). On the other hand there are no independent works devoted only to midrash *aggadah* from the tannaitic era (see however **Seder Olam Rabbah* and the **Baraita de-Melekhet ha-Mishkan*). All the extant literary works devoted primarily to midrash *aggadah* were apparently compiled originally in Ereẓ Israel during the amoraic and post-amoraic periods. While the Babylonian Talmud contains a vast amount of aggadic midrash (cf. the Midrash on the Book of Esther in Meg. 10b–17a, and on Lamentations in Sanh. 104a–b), it's literary structure follows the earlier tannaitic model, including both *midrash halakhah* and *aggadah* (as in the *midreshei halakhah*), and integrating both of them into an appropriate context following the order of the tractates of the Mishnah, as was done in both the Mishnah and the Tosefta (see *Mishnah: *Aggadah* in the Mishnah).

From the point of view of the period of their arrangement and collection the aggadic Midrashim can be divided into three groups: early, middle, and late. The determination of the time of the editing and arranging of the various Midrashim is by no means a simple matter. It is nearly impossible to determine with even approximate certainty the period when a Midrash or aggadic work was compiled (see *Pirkei de-R. Eliezer). However, it is possible to arrive at a relative date, that is, to determine the relation of a particular Midrash to others (see Table: *Midreshei Aggadah*). To do this one cannot rely on the historical allusions alone or merely on the names of the sages mentioned in the Midrash, nor can one rely on the first mentions of the Midrash and its first citations, since all the Midrashim contain much material from different and extended eras. The lack of historical allusions after a definite period do not suffice to testify to its compilation immediately after that period, just as the lack of mention of a Midrash and of its citation until a certain period does not prove that it was edited at the date nearest to the beginning of that period. In neither case can one rely on the *argumentum a silentio*. A more reliable method for determining priority and lateness among Midrashim is the relationship between the various Midrashim – the use one makes of another – as well as their relationship to other sources. This procedure, however, involves a number of very complex issues, and no consensus has yet been reached on how it should be applied in practice (see **Genesis Rabbah*: The Redaction of the Midrash). Moreover, even after one arrives by use of this method at a provisional determination regarding precedence, other additional factors must be taken into account (literary forms, language, style, etc.).

The Early Midrashim (the Classical Amoraic Midrashim)

This period, from which it seems only seven Midrashim have come down, is the golden age of the aggadic Midrashim. The most developed and perfect literary forms and constructions are already found in the oldest aggadic Midrash, *Genesis Rabbah*, proving that many generations of development preceded the literary crystallization. Since in general such perfect and developed literary constructions and forms are found neither in the halakhic Midrashim nor in their aggadic section (although here and there mere beginnings can be found), it is probable that the main development of the literary forms came in the amoraic era. Toward the close of this period the assembling, collecting, and editing was begun.

Among its most perfect forms, one should mention the classical proem at the beginning of a complete Midrash or of a chapter, which served fundamentally as the introduction to a homily delivered in public. The classical proem is a prelude to a homily on a certain verse by citing a verse from another source (in most cases from another book, or even from a different section of the Bible, usually the Hagiographa) and connecting it with the chief verse of the homily, the proem concluding with the verse with which the homily itself begins. Thus, for example, the proem to Lamentations 1:1 begins with a verse from the Pentateuch, while the proems to the Pentateuch Midrashim open with a verse usually from the Hagiographa. The proem, scarcely found in the tannaitic literature, was greatly developed and perfected in the time of the *amoraim*, in order to attract, stimulate, and rouse the curiosity of the audience and to emphasize the unity of the biblical books. When gathering and assembling the material the compilers and editors of the Midrashim followed the method of the actual preachers of the homilies and placed the proems at the beginning of the Midrashim and of the various sections. They did not always have proems readily available and in consequence created artificial proems themselves (combining different sayings and a number of homilies together). Sometimes they greatly enlarged the proems so that a simple proem became compound, i.e., it included a number of homilies independent in themselves. Classical proems in their pure form are almost wholly confined to the early Midrashim: *Genesis Rabbah; Leviticus Rabbah; Lamentations Rabbah; Esther Rabbah I; *Pesikta de-Rav Kahana; Song of Songs Rabbah*; and *Ruth Rabbah*. These Midrashim all consist of a collection of homilies, sayings, and *aggadot* of the *amoraim* (and also of the *tannaim*) in Galilean Aramaic and rabbinical Hebrew, but they also include many Greek words.

It seems that all these Midrashim were edited in Ereẓ Israel in the fifth and sixth centuries C.E. Two types can be distinguished: exegetical and homiletical. The exegetical Midrash (*Genesis Rabbah, Lamentations Rabbah*, et al.) is a Midrash to one of the books of the Bible, containing comments on the whole book – on each chapter, on every verse, and at times even on every word in the verse. The homiletical Midrash is either a Midrash to a book of the Pentateuch in which only the first verse (or verses) of the weekly portion is expounded (in accordance with the early *Triennial cycle that was current in Ereẓ Israel, e.g., **Leviticus Rabbah*), or a Midrash that is based only on the biblical and prophetic reading of special Sabbaths and festivals, in which, also, only the first verses are expounded (eg., *Pesikta de-Rav Kahana*). In both cases, in contrast to the exegetical Midrashim, the homiletical Midrashim contain almost no short homilies or dicta on variegated topics, but each chapter (or section) constitutes a collection of homilies and sayings on one topic that seem to combine into one long homily on the specific topic.

Midreshei Aggadah According to Types and Periods

Aggadic Works	Midrashim	Date C.E.	The Era
	Genesis Rabbah	400–500	Classical Amoraic
	Leviticus Rabbah		Midrashim of the
	Lamentations Rabbah		Early Period
	Esther Rabbah I		(400–600)
Apocalyptic and Eschatological Midrashim	*Pesikta de-Rav Kahana*	500–640	
	Songs Rabbah		
	Ruth Rabbah		
Megillat Antiochus	Targum Sheni	640–900	The Middle Period (640–1000)
Midrash Petirat Moshe ("Death of Moses")	Midrash Esfah		
Tanna de-Vei Eliyahu ("Seder Eliyahu")	Midrash Proverbs		
Pirkei de-R. Eliezer	Midrash Samuel		
Midrash Agur (Called "Mishnat R. Eliezer")	Ecclesiastes Rabbah		
Midrash Yonah	Midrash Ḥaserot vi-Yterot		
Midrash Petirat Aharon	*Deuteronomy Rabbah*[1]	(775–900)	
Divrei ha-Yamim shel Moshe	*Tanḥuma*[1]		
Otiyyot de-R. Akiva	*Tanḥuma (Buber)*[1]		
Midrash Sheloshah ve-Arba'ah	*Numbers Rabbah II*[1]		
Midrash Eser Galuyyot	*Pesikta Rabbati*[1]		
Midrash va-Yissa'u	*Exodus Rabbah II*[1]		
	Va-Yeḥi Rabbah[1]		
	The Manuscripts of the Tanḥuma		
	Yelammedenu Midrashim[1]		
Throne and Hippodromes of Solomon	Midrash Tehillim I	900–1000	
Midreshei Ḥanukkah	Exodus Rabbah I		
Midreshei Yehudith	*Aggadat Bereshit*		
Midrash Hallel	Aggadat Shir ha-Shirim (Zuta)		
Midrash Tadshe	Ruth Zuta		
	Ecclesiastes Zuta		
	Lamentations Zuta		
Midrash Aseret ha-Dibberot	Midrash Shir Hashirim	1000–1100	The Late Period
Midrash Konen	Abba Guryon		(1000–1200)
Midrash Avkir	Esther Rabbah II		
Alphabet of Ben Sira	Midrash Tehilim II		
Midrash va-Yosha			
Sefer ha-Yashar			
Pesikta Ḥadta	Panim Aḥerim le-Esther (version 1)	1100–1200	
Midrash Temurah	Lekaḥ Tov (c. 1110)[3]		
	Midrash Aggadah[2]		
	Genesis Rabbati[2]		
	Numbers Rabbah[2]		
	Yalkut Shimoni[3]	1200–1300	The Period of the Yalkutim
	Midrash ha-Gadol[3]	1300–1400	(anthologies)
	Yalkut Makhiri[3]		1200–1500
	Ein Ya'akov[3]	1400–1500	
	Haggadot ha-Talmud[3]		

1. Tanḥuma Midrash (Yelammedenu). 2. All based on the work of Moshe ha-Darshan. 3. These are anthologies
Note: Names in Italics are homiletical Midrashim; the rest are exegetical.

The Difference Between the Early Midrashim and Later Midrashim

In the Midrashim of the middle period a decline is already discernible in the developed literary constructions and forms, especially in the proem, which is not the classical proem but merely an inferior and artificial imitation. After the Muslim conquest there is a gradual strengthening in the influence of the pseudepigraphic and the apocalyptic literature of the Second Temple era (see *Apocrypha and Pseudepigrapha), which had been disregarded by the talmudic rabbis (particularly because of the controversy with Christianity; see *Church Fathers). This influence is apparent both in content and form. In content, there is an increase not only in homilies which refer to angels and demons, the garden of Eden and hell, but even complete topics from apocalyptic literature. In form, there is an increase in the type of aggadic work which does not belong to the genre of Midrash at all. This type is not a compilation but a unified work impressed with the seal of the author, who is a narrator but chooses to attribute his words to the ancients and to ascribe to them statements which they never made (see **Tanna de-Vei Eliyahu*). The increase of pseudepigraphic matter can also be seen in authentic Midrashim. In contrast to the early Midrashim there was also an increase of Midrashim and aggadic works in which the *aggadah* is connected with *halakhah* in a variety of forms, some of which are merely transferred from Second Temple literature (e.g., *Pirkei de-R. Eliezer*) and some are the result of internal development by the sages (e.g., *Tanḥuma Yelammedenu*). In addition there is also a difference in language. The Galilean Aramaic of the early Midrashim progressively disappears, as does rabbinical Hebrew. Instead there is progressive use of artificial Hebrew, apparently pure and polished and becoming freer from the influences of Aramaic or the admixture of Greek words.

The Middle Period

To the period from the Muslim conquest (c. 640 C.E.) to the end of the tenth century belong many variegated midrashic and aggadic works. In addition to the exegetical and homiletical types of Midrash, the above-mentioned composition by a single person belongs to this period. The most important group of Midrashim of this period – all of which are homiletical – are those of the *Tanḥuma Midrash* (**Tanḥuma Yelammedenu*) group in which the old and the new are used indiscriminately. Of the exegetical Midrashim, particular mention may be made of *Ecclesiastes Rabbah, Midrash Samuel, Midrash Proverbs* (greatly influenced by the apocalyptic and *Heikhalot* literatures), *Midrash Tehillim I, Exodus Rabbah I*, and the series of smaller *Midrashim (*Midreshei Zuta*) to four of the five *scrolls. In all these too, marks of the old and the new, both in content and in form, appear together. Among the aggadic works the most important are: *Seder Eliyahu Rabbah* and *Seder Eliyahu Zuta; Pirkei de-R. Eliezer* (compiled apparently close to 750); *Midrash Agur*, also called *Mishnat R. Eliezer*; and a further series of smaller compositions. In most of them external influences from the Muslim (*Pirkei de-R. Eliezer*) or Byzantine (*The Throne and Hippodrome of Solomon*, etc.) eras can be seen.

The Late Period

To the period of the 11th and 12th centuries belong the very latest Midrashim. Of these special mention should be made of *Midrash Abba Guryon, Esther Rabbah II, Midrash Tehillim II*, and the series from the school of *Moses ha-Darshan that already border on the anthologies with regard to their period of composition as well as to content. In these Midrashim there is hardly a trace of even an imitation of the classical proem, the Hebrew is completely medieval, and the pseudepigraphic influence both in content and form is still more pronounced. Among the aggadic works of this period particular mention must be made of the *Sefer ha-Yashar* (see *Midrashim, Smaller in supplementary entries, vol. 16) where the Muslim influence is most recognizable.

The Yalkutim (Anthologies)

From the beginning of the 12th century, scholars in various countries assembled anthologies from various Midrashim and aggadic works. To these belong such works as the **Midrash Lekaḥ Tov* (or the *Pesikta Zutarta*) to the Pentateuch and the five *scrolls (of Tobiah b. Eliezer); the **Yalkut Shimoni* to the whole of the Bible (assembled in Germany at the beginning of the 13th century); **Midrash ha-Gadol* to the Pentateuch and scrolls; and the **Yalkut Makhiri* to various biblical books. Anthologies of the *aggadot* in the Babylonian and Jerusalem Talmuds were also collected, especially close to the beginning of the age of printing. Most of the anthologies quote their sources with the original wording and indicate them (an exception being the *Midrash ha-Gadol*).

BIBLIOGRAPHY: Zunz-Albeck, Derashot; H.L. Strack, *Introduction to the Talmud and Midrash* (1945), pt. 2; A.G. Wright, *The Literary Genre Midrash* (1967); J. Bowker, *The Targums and Rabbinic Literature, and introduction to Jewish interpretations of Scripture* (1969); G. Vermes, *Scripture and Tradition in Judaism* (1961); Ginzberg, Legends; S.M. Lehrman, *The World of the Midrash* (1961). **ADD. BIBLIOGRAPHY:** J. Fraenkel, *Darkhei ha-Aggadah ve-ha-Midrash*. (Heb.; 1996); idem, *Midrash ve-Aggadah* (1996); idem, *Sippur ha-Aggadah – Aḥdut shel Tokhen ve-Ẓurah* (Heb.; 2001); Stemberger, *Introduction* (1996), 233–46, 276–325; M. Bregman, *The Tanḥuma-Yelammedenu Literature* (Heb.; 2003).

[Moshe David Herr]

MIDRASH ASERET HA-DIBBEROT (Heb. מִדְרַשׁ עֲשֶׂרֶת הַדִּבְּרוֹת; "Midrash of the Ten Commandments"), a collection of stories, occasionally connected by short homiletic passages, from the geonic period. Various scholars have ascribed different dates to it, ranging from the seventh century to the 11th. The collection cannot be dated later than the 11th century because in that century both Rabbi *Nissim of Kairouan and later the anonymous collector of the legends published by M. Gaster as *Sefer ha-Ma'asiyyot, The Ancient Collections of Agadoth. The Sefer ha-Ma'asiyyot and Two Facsimiles* (1894) made use of stories included in it. The work was apparently composed at the beginning of the geonic period, but later stories were added and have created confusion regarding both the number of stories included and the structure of the book as it appears in the several printed versions and the 20 extant manuscripts.

The collection was called a "Midrash" although its contents do not justify the name. It is basically a narrative work, one of the first medieval Hebrew works in the field of fiction. Its treatment of the midrashic material can be described as revolutionary: whereas traditional Midrashim place primary importance on homiletic material with only occasional use of stories, this work is primarily composed of stories, with the homiletic passages relegated to secondary importance. This stress on the fictional element is one of the characteristics of the new attitude toward the story introduced in medieval times (see *Fiction).

The work, which is based on the Ten Commandments, is correspondingly divided into ten parts. However, there is not always a close connection between the midrashic story and the commandment on which it is supposed to be based. This explains the material occasionally introduced into a story to create the impression of such a connection. In some versions the work is called *Midrash shel Shavu'ot* or *Haggadah le-Shavu'ot*, leading one to believe that it was used on Shavuot, the festival on which the receiving of the Ten Commandments is celebrated. However, there is no proof that any Jewish community ever used this work during Shavuot. Noy (see bibl.) concludes plausibly that the arbitrary connection between the *Midrash Aseret ha-Dibberot* and the commandments and Shavuot is merely an attempt to give a religious veneer to a collection of essentially secular stories which had no other purpose than to entertain.

Some of the stories in the collection are originally found in the Talmud and represent a medieval retelling of the talmudic *aggadah*. Others are derived from more ancient sources, like the Apocrypha and Pseudepigrapha: the story of Judith is told in a different version (without mentioning her name), and the story of the woman and her seven sons from the Book of Maccabees is also retold. However, most of the stories are folktales, either Jewish in origin or Jewish versions of international folktales found in a variety of versions in many languages (Noy lists among them the international types Aarne-Thompson 976, 670, 899, 2040, and others). Some of these stories are still current today among oral storytellers.

The number of stories composing the collection differs from version to version, some containing no more than 17 and others nearly 30. One manuscript (Parma 473) has 44 stories. As there are some which appear in only one version, the total number of stories connected with this work is over 50. A large number of stories (12) are concerned with the commandment "Thou shalt not commit adultery"; an erotic element is also found in stories related to other commandments. Women, frequently courageous and devout, are the heroines of many of the stories. From the religious point of view, the stories seem to imply an extreme devotion to the observance of the commandments, far beyond that required by the *halakhah*. The collection can also be described, therefore, as one of the earliest ethical works written in the Middle Ages.

BIBLIOGRAPHY: D. Noy, in: *Fourth World Congress of Jewish Studies, Papers*, 2 (1968), 353–5 (Heb.); A. Jellinek, *Beit ha-Midrash*, 1 (1938), 62–92; M.M. Kasher (ed.), *Torah Shelemah*, 16 (1954), 189–99; J.L. Maimon (Fishman), *Haggadah shel Shavu'ot* (1924); M. Gaster, *The Exempla of the Rabbis* (1924), 142–8.

[Joseph Dan]

MIDRASH HA-GADOL (Heb. מִדְרָשׁ הַגָּדוֹל), a 13th-century rabbinic work on the Pentateuch, emanating from Yemen and consisting mainly of excerpts of older rabbinic texts of the talmudic period. The Midrash is anonymous, but it is now certain that it was written by a native of Aden, David b. Amram *Adani. Adani writes in clear, limpid Hebrew prose, introducing each weekly portion with a proem in rhymed verse. His work is of importance not only because of the author's original contributions to the literature of *halakhah* and *aggadah*, but also because of the multitude of extracts which he incorporates from ancient tannaitic Midrashim either unknown, or only partially known, from other sources. Thus, for instance, the *Midrash ha-Gadol* has enabled scholars to reconstruct large portions of the lost **Mekhilta of R. Simeon b. Yoḥai*, the **Sifrei Zuta*, and the *Mekhilta of R. Ishmael* on Deuteronomy. In addition, the *Midrash ha-Gadol* is valuable for the accuracy of its quotations from known sources, such as the Talmud and the Midrashim. Its readings have made it possible to correct the texts of older works which have survived in garbled form. The *Midrash ha-Gadol* is also notable for its contribution to the study of the code of *Maimonides, as it preserves many sources available to Maimonides but otherwise unknown. Not only does Adani frequently quote the code on which the Yemenites largely, if not exclusively, base their religious rulings, but his work enables students to reconstruct the older authorities on whom Maimonides had based his rulings. As a result, many difficulties which had puzzled students of Maimonides over the generations have been solved. The *Midrash ha-Gadol* first came to the notice of European scholars in the 19th century. The text was brought to Europe in manuscript in 1878 and sold to the Royal Library in Berlin by M.W. Shapira, whose name is associated with the alleged forgery known as the *Shapira fragments. Since then, other manuscripts have been acquired by the major libraries in the western world. Solomon Schechter in his edition of the *Avot de-Rabbi Nathan* (1887) was the first to make extensive use of this Midrash and he edited the first part (on Genesis) in 1902. Different parts of the Midrash have been edited by other scholars: Exodus by D.W. Hoffmann (1913–21), Leviticus by Nahum E. Rabinowitz (1932), and Numbers by Solomon Fisch (partial edition, 1940; reissued in complete form with Hebrew commentary and introduction, 2 vols., 1957–63). Genesis and Exodus were re-edited by M. Margulies (*Margalioth; 1947, 1956), and Numbers by Z.M. Rabinowitz (1967). There exist two Yemenite commentaries on the Midrash, one titled *Segullat Yisrael* ("The Treasure of Israel"), dated 5440 (i.e., 1680) by R. Israel b. Solomon ha-Kohen, containing only a few interpretations and these of only slight value, and the other (anon.), the *Sefer ha-Margalit* ("Book of the Pearl"), containing explanations in Hebrew and Arabic of difficult words. The *Midrash ha-Gadol* is still a standard work of rabbinic homily for the Yemenite community and circulates widely in manuscript.

BIBLIOGRAPHY: J. Riqueti, *Ḥokhmat ha-Mishkan* (Mantua, 1676), 5, 6, 13; S.A. Poznański, in: HHY, 3 (1886), 1–22; S. Schechter, *Avot de-Rabbi Nathan* (1887), introd.; D.Z. Hoffman (ed.), *Mekhilta de-Rabbi Shimon ben Yoḥai* (1905); idem, *Midrash Tanna'im*, 2 vols. (1908–09); S. Liebermann, *Midreshei Teiman* (1940); S. Fisch, *Midrash ha-Gadol* (1940), 1–136; M. Kasher, *Ha-Rambam ve-ha-Mekhilta de-Rashbi* (1943), introd.; M. Margulies, *Midrash ha-Gadol, Shemot* (1956), 5–15; Y.L. Nahum, *Mi-Ẓefunot Yehudei Teiman* (1962), 181–205; Y. Ratzaby, in: *Tarbiz*, 34 (1965), 263–71; Z.M. Rabinowitz, *Midrash ha-Gadol, Ba-Midbar* (1967), 5–16.

[Solomon Fisch]

MIDRASHIM, SMALLER. This entry covers those aggadic and midrashic works which are not treated in separate articles.

(1) MIDRASH AGUR, also known as *Mishnat R. Eliezer*, or *Midrash Sheloshim u-Shetayim Middot*. Belonging to some extent to the category of aggadic works, this Midrash is an exposition on Proverbs 30:1–3 ("The words of Agur the son of Jakeh …"), and begins by quoting R. *Eliezer b. Yose haGelili's Baraita of 32 Rules. It used the Babylonian Talmud. Though written in a pure Hebrew, it contains Arabic words and refers to the "kingdom of Ishmael." Therefore it was probably composed in Ereẓ Israel, more or less contemporaneously with **Pirkei de-R. Eliezer* about the middle of the eighth century C.E. It was apparently used by *Saadiah Gaon, and was first printed by Menahem de Lonzano at Safed in 1626, but not a single copy of this edition has been preserved. An excerpt from the Midrash was published from a manuscript by L. Ginzberg in *Tarbiz*, 4 (1933), 297–342 (and see J.N. Epstein, *ibid.*, 343–53; S. Lieberman, in: *Ginzei Kedem*, 5 (1934), 186–90). A scholarly edition, with an introduction in English, was published by H.G. Enelow (1933).

(2) AGGADAT SHIR HA-SHIRIM (*"Aggadah* of Song of Songs") or *Shir ha-Shirim Zuta* ("Minor Song of Songs"), a collection of extracts from various Midrashim. The redactor made extensive use of a Midrash, no longer extant, which was also much used by the *Yelammedenu-Tanḥuma* Midrashim, especially **Pesikta Rabbati*. It has no proems. This Midrash in its present form was undoubtedly used by R. *Judah b. Kalonymus, the 12th-century author of *Yiḥusei Tanna'im ve-Amora'im*. The date of its redaction is apparently not earlier than the tenth century. Alongside later material it also contains much of an earlier date, unknown from other sources. It was published in scholarly editions (from Parma Ms. 541) by S. Buber (1894) and S. Schechter (1896).

(3) MIDRASH SHIR HA-SHIRIM ("Midrash Song of Songs"), also a collection of extracts from various Midrashim. The redactor used tannaitic literature, the Jerusalem and Babylonian Talmuds, and **Genesis Rabbah*, as well as sources used by the *Yelammedenu-Tanḥuma* Midrashim. This Midrash, which likewise has no proems and contains many *aggadot* of a later type, is also quoted by Judah b. Kalonymus. It was apparently redacted in the 11th century. A scholarly edition was published from a Cairo *Genizah* manuscript, dated 1197, by L. Gruenhut (1897).

(4) RUTH ZUTA ("Minor Ruth"), or *Midrash Megillat Ruth be-Fanim Aḥerim* ("Other Aspects of the Midrash on the Scroll of Ruth"), a late Midrash compiled from **Ruth Rabbah*, the Babylonian Talmud, and other sources. It begins with a proem which is not of the classical type. As the author of **Midrash Lekaḥ Tov* at the end of the 11th century used this Midrash it was apparently compiled in the tenth century. It was published (from Parma Ms. 541) by S. Buber (1894).

(5) KOHELET ZUTA ("Minor Ecclesiastes"), an abbreviated version of **Ecclesiastes Rabbah*, and much more popular than it. Since it was quoted by *Nathan b. Jehiel of Rome, the author of the *Arukh*, it was apparently redacted in the tenth century. This Midrash too was published by S. Buber (1894, from Parma Ms. 541).

(6) EIKHAH ZUTA ("Minor Lamentations"), an exposition of the first three verses of Lamentations, consisting mainly of *aggadot* on the destruction of the Temple. One version (A), which contains addenda from the Babylonian Talmud and **Pesikta de-Rav Kahana*, was used as a source by the compiler of the **Yalkut Shimoni*, and was published from Parma Ms. 541 by S. Buber (1894). A second, much shorter, version (B), which is defective at the beginning, contains addenda from **Lamentations Rabbah* and *Pesikta de-Rav Kahana* but not those in version A. It was published from Parma Ms. 261 by S. Buber (1894). Probably comprising excerpts from a complete Midrash on the Book of Lamentations in a manuscript as yet unexamined or no longer extant, the two versions were redacted not earlier than the tenth century.

(7) MIDRASH PANIM AḤERIM LE-ESTHER, NOSAḤ ALEF ("Other Aspects of the Midrash to the Scroll of Esther": Version A), a short collection of *aggadot* and homilies on the Book of Esther compiled from various sources, including *Esther Rabbah II*, *Midrash Abba Guryon*, the Babylonian Midrash on Esther (see Babylonian *Talmud; and **Megillah*), *Pirkei de-R. Eliezer*, and others. It was redacted not earlier than the 12th century. S. Buber published the Midrash from a manuscript in the *Sifrei… Esther* (as above).

(8) MIDRASH YONAH, a late aggadic work on the Book of Jonah. Its author, drawing mainly on *Pirkei de-R. Eliezer* and the Babylonian Talmud, worked his sources into a fluent account told in his own words (a pure but artificial Hebrew). It was written not earlier than the end of the eighth century. First published in Prague (1595), it was subsequently republished, notably by H.M. Horowitz in an edition from a manuscript in *Aguddat Aggadot* (1881), 11ff.

(9) MIDRASH HALLEL, a late midrashic work on the **Hallel* chapters in the Book of Psalms. The author used mainly **Midrash Tehillim* as well as the *Heikhalot* literature. Redacted not earlier than the tenth century, the work was published from a manuscript by A. Jellinek, *Beit ha-Midrash*, 5 (1938), 87–110.

(10) MIDRASH ESFAH, named from its introductory words: "Gather [*esfah*] unto Me seventy men of the elders of Israel" (Num. 11:16). This is a midrashic work on the Book of Numbers, most of which is no longer extant. Excerpts from it are quoted in *Yalkut Shimoni* and some have been published from manuscripts (*Abraham b. Elijah of Vilna, *Rav Pe'alim*, ed. by S.M. Chones (1894), 147–53; S.A. Wertheimer, *Battei Midrashot*, 1 (1950), 211–4). Unpublished fragments are also in existence. Known to the Babylonian *geonim* in the ninth century, apparently the work was edited not earlier than the end of the seventh century.

(11) MIDRASH ESER GALUYYOT ("Midrash on the Ten Expulsions"), found in different versions in several manuscripts, some of which have been published (Basle, 1578 [on which is based L. Gruenhut's *Sefer ha-Likkutim*, 3 (1889)], 1–22 (second pagination); Carmoly, Brussels (1842); A. Jellinek, *Beit ha-Midrash*, 4 (1938), 133–6; 5 (1938), 113–6; M. Ish-Shalom in *Sinai*, 43 (1958), 195–211). The date of the work, for which the author used Midrashim of tannaitic and amoraic times, is not earlier than the ninth century.

(12) MIDRASH SHELOSHAH VE-ARBA'AH ("Midrash Three and Four"; also called *Pirkei Rabbenu ha-Kadosh*, *Ma'aseh Torah*, and *Ḥuppat Eliyahu*), also extant in different versions in many manuscripts, only some of which have been published (S.A. Wertheimer, *Battei Midrashot*, 2 (1953), 45–73; S. Schoenblum, in the collection *Sheloshah Sefarim Niftaḥim* (1877); L. Gruenhut, *Sefer ha-Likkutim*, 3 (1899), 33–90 (second pagination); *Kol Bo*, para. 118; A. Jellinek, *Beit ha-Midrash*, 2 (1938), 92–101; H.M. Horowitz, in the collection *Kevod Ḥuppah* (1888), 45–56). However, most of the manuscripts remain unpublished. Enumerating various themes grouped in numbers from three onward, the work used various ancient sources and was redacted not earlier than the ninth century.

(13) OTIYYOT DE-R. AKIVA ("Letters of Rabbi Akiva"), or *Alef Bet de-R. Akiva* ("Alphabet of Rabbi Akiva"), an aggadic work likewise extant in different versions and in many manuscripts, only some of which have been published (Constantinople (1516), version A; Cracow (1579), version B; Wertheimer, *Battei Midrashot*, 2 (1953), 333–465, four versions), but most of them (including Mss. of the 13th and 14th centuries) have not yet appeared in print. This late Midrash on the alphabet contains many mystic and eschatological discussions. As it was quoted in the tenth century, the work was apparently compiled in the ninth century.

(14) MIDRASH ḤASEROT VI-YTEROT, a homiletic exposition on the reasons for the defective and plene writing in the Bible. It is also extant in many versions in numerous manuscripts, only some of which have been published (a critical edition including variant readings of the different versions was issued by Wertheimer, *Battei Midrashot*, 2 (1953), 203–332). The work shows the influence of the masoretic period. Since different versions are already cited in the responsa of *Hai Gaon, the date of its redaction has therefore to be fixed in the ninth century.

(15) MIDRASH AVKIR, so called after the initial letters of the formula אָמֵן בְּיָמֵינוּ כֵּן יְהִי רָצוֹן (*Amen be-Yameinu Ken Yehi Raẓon*) which concludes each homily. The Midrash is no longer extant but many excerpts from it have been preserved in *Yalkut Shimoni*; hence it was probably a Midrash on Genesis and Exodus, written in an artificial Hebrew. Both the style and contents of the excerpts are reminiscent of late aggadic and midrashic works, such as **Tanna de-Vei Eliyahu, Pesikta de-R. Eliezer*, and the additional *Midrash Va-Yeḥi of Genesis Rabbah*. It was first definitely quoted by German Jewish authors of the beginning of the 13th century. Since it is doubtful whether the author of *Lekaḥ Tov* used the work, its redaction should be dated to the beginning of the 11th century. Extracts from quotations of it were published by S. Buber (in *Ha-Shaḥar*, 11 (1883), 338–45, 409–18, 453–61), and from manuscripts by A. Neubauer (in REJ, 14 (1887), 109f.) and by A. Epstein (in *Ha-Eshkol*, 6 (1909), 204–7). It is doubtful if the extracts published by A. Marmorstein (in *Devir*, 1 (1923), 113–44) are from *Midrash Avkir*.

(16) MIDRASH TADSHE or *Baraita de-R. Pinḥas b. Ya'ir* derives its names from its introductory sentence: "It is written [Gen. 1:11]: 'And God said: Let the earth put forth [*tadshe*] grass…' R. *Phinehas b. Jair asked…" In both content and method, this pseudepigraphical Midrash resembles works of the Second Temple period, on which it drew (such as the Book of Jubilees, *Philo, etc.). Despite all the internal indications pointing to its late composition, its date is to be assigned to not later than 1000 C.E., since *Moses ha-Darshan used the work. It was first published from a manuscript by A. Jellinek (*Beit ha-Midrash*, 3 (1928), 164–93).

(17) KISSE VE-IPPODROMIN SHEL SHELOMO HA-MELEKH, an aggadic tale dating from the Byzantine period. The first half, an adaptation of a description found in **Targum Sheni*, was written apparently in the 11th century (see E. Ville-Patlagean, in REJ, 121 (1962), 9–33). In it Solomon figures as a Byzantine emperor who holds horse races in the hippodrome, the colors of the different factions in the circus (blue, white, red, and green) being those of the courtiers' clothes. The work was published from a manuscript by A. Jellinek (*Beit ha-Midrash*, 5 (1938), 34–39).

(18) SEFER HA-YASHAR ("Book of Jashar"), a late aggadic work corresponding to the narrative parts of the Pentateuch (in particular Gen. and Ex. 1:1–2:21, comprising more than three-quarters of the work), Joshua, and Judges 1:1–2:10. The style is fluent and the language a pure but artificial, pseudo-biblical Hebrew. The author used *Genesis Rabbah*, the Babylonian Talmud, *Pirkei de-R. Eliezer*, **Midrash va-Yissa'u*, *Josippon, *Midrash Avkir* (no. 15) as well as ancient sources from the literature of the Second Temple period (its structure is reminiscent of *Liber Antiquitatum Biblicarum*). Connecting the biblical events with later ones in Jewish history, the author at times used his imagination freely and was greatly influenced by Muslim legends. The work contains many Arabic names and a Latin one, as well as the medieval philosophical definition that man is a living soul endowed with speech. It is first quoted by *Yalkut Shimoni*. Hence the work was written

apparently at the end of the 11th century, perhaps in southern Spain. First published in Venice in 1625, it has since been republished many times.

(19) MIDRASH KONEN, or *Adonai be-Ḥokhmah Yasad Areẓ*, dealing with the Creation, the heavens, paradise, and hell. This Midrash was influenced by apocalyptic sources of the Second Temple period, and by the mystic literature of the beginning of the Middle Ages. Composed not earlier than about the 11th century, it was first published in Venice in 1601. Another version was published from manuscript by A. Jellinek (*Beit haMidrash*, 5 (1938), 63–69) and excerpts from similar Midrashim, *Seder Rabbah di-Vereshit*, were published by S.A. Wertheimer (*Battei Midrashot*, 1 (1950), 1–48). Yet another version, *Zeh Ma'aseh Bereshit*, appeared in *Sefer Razi'el ha-Malakh*, and still another version was published from a manuscript by L. Ginzberg (*Ginzei Schechter*, 1 (1928), 182–7).

(20) MIDRASH VA-YEKHULLU (RABBATI), called after its opening sentence (Gen. 2:1): "And the heaven and the earth were finished [*va-yekhullu*]…" This Midrash, which is no longer extant, was quoted from the middle of the 12th century onward. The various quotations that have been preserved (they have been collected by L. Gruenhut, *Sefer ha-Likkutim*, 2 (1898), 16b–20a) show that the redactor used the Jerusalem Talmud and *Yelammedenu-Tanḥuma*. It is difficult to fix the date of its redaction but it was apparently not before the end of the tenth century.

(21) MIDRASH VA-YOSHA, a late aggadic work on the song at the Red Sea, which used, among others, *Pirkei de-R. Eliezer* and *Pesikta Rabbati*. The name is derived from the opening sentence (Ex. 14:30): "Thus the Lord saved [*vayosha*]…" The Midrash mentions *Armilus as a well-known figure. Apparently redacted at the end of the 11th century, it was first published at Constantinople in 1519 and again in the collection *Divrei Ḥakhamim* (1849).

(22) MIDRASH AGGADAH, an exegetical Midrash on the Pentateuch consisting mainly of excerpts from the work of Moses ha-Darshan. This is evident from the many parallel passages between, on the one hand, *Midrash Aggadah* and, on the other, **Genesis Rabbati, Numbers Rabbah I*, and the quotations from Moses ha-Darshan's work cited in Rashi's commentary on the Pentateuch. It is further evident from the extensive use both of *Midrash Tadshe* (no. 16) and of apocryphal and pseudepigraphical works of the Second Temple period (in particular, the Book of Jubilees). *Midrash Aggadah*, compiled apparently in the 12th century, was published from the Aleppo manuscript by S. Buber (1894).

(23) MIDRESHEI ḤANUKKAH. Some of these Midrashim were published by A. Jellinek (*Beit ha-Midrash*, 1 (1938), 132–6; 6 (1938), 1–3), the rest being extant in manuscript. They are all late aggadic works, the oldest of them having been written apparently not earlier than the tenth century, and comprise various *aggadot* on the *Hasmonean revolt into which have been woven the story of *Judith and Holofernes as well as the theme of *ius primae noctis*.

(24) PESIKTA ḤADTA, or *Midrash Mah Rabbu* ("How manifold [*mah rabbu*] are Thy works, O Lord!"; Ps. 104:24), a compilation of homilies, of various dates and from different sources, on the festivals. It used, among others, late works (*Pesikta Rabbati, Sefer *Yeẓirah, Pirkei de-R. Eliezer, Midrash Konen* (no. 19), *Midreshei Ḥanukkah* (no. 23)). The date of its redaction is to be assigned to not earlier than the 12th century. It was first published from a manuscript by A. Jellinek (*Beit ha-Midrash*, 1 (1938), 137–41; 6 (1932), 36–70).

(25) MIDRASH TEMURAH, a pseudepigraphic aggadic work (ascribed to R. *Ishmael and R. *Akiva) dealing with the changes (*temurot*) in the world and in the life of man. The author was apparently acquainted with the commentary of Abraham *Ibn Ezra. The work was first mentioned by Menahem ha-*Meiri. According to all indications its redaction is not earlier than the end of the 12th century. It was first published at the end of H.J.D. Azulai's *Shem ha-Gedolim* (1786), then from another manuscript at the end of *Aggadat Bereshit* (Vilna, 1802), and frequently afterward. It was also issued in a critical edition, based on several manuscripts and on all the earlier published versions, by S.A. Wertheimer (*Battei Midrashot*, 2 (1953), 187–201).

(26) BERESHIT ZUTA ("Minor Genesis"). Extracted from many different sources this Midrash was compiled by R. Samuel b. Nissim *Masnut of Aleppo, who lived at the beginning of the 13th century, and published from manuscript by M. Hakohen (1962).

Many other small Midrashim, to which no individual articles have been assigned and which are not mentioned in this one, were published in various compilations containing collections of Midrashim. Such compilations, together with an introduction, notes, and a commentary, were published especially from the second half of the 19th century onward. Among these the most important are A. Jellinek, *Beit ha-Midrash* (with introductions in German), 6 vols. (1853–77, 1938²); H.M. Horowitz, *Aguddat Aggadot* (1881; repr. 1967); idem, *Beit Eked ha-Aggadot*, 2 pts. (1881–82; repr. 1967); idem, *Tosefta Attikta* (1890); S.A. Wertheimer, *Battei Midrashot*, 4 vols. (1893–97; 1950–53², in 2 vols.); idem, *Leket Midrashim* (1903); idem, *Oẓar Midrashim*, 2 vols. (1913–14); idem, *Midrashim Kitvei Yad* (1923); L. Gruenhut, *Sefer ha-Likkutim*, 6 vols. (1898–1903); J.D. Eisenstein, *Oẓar Midrashim*, 2 vols. (1915); L. Ginzberg, *Ginzei Schechter*, 1 (1928); J. Mann, *The Bible as Read and Preached in the Old Synagogue*, 1 (1940); 2 (1966), by J. Mann and I. Sonne.

For *Midrash Esther ha-Bavli* and *Midrash Eikhah ha-Bavli* see *Midrash; Babylonian *Talmud; and **Megillah*. For *Aggadat Esther* see **Midrash ha-Gadol*. For *Tefillat Mordekhai ve-Esther* see *Esther and *Mordecai. For *Midrash Petirat Aharon* see *Aaron. For *Midrash Petirat Moshe* and for *Midrash Divrei ha-Yamim shel Moshe* see *Moses, Chronicles of. For *Midreshei Yehudit* see *Judith. For *Midrash Birkat Ya'akov* see *Jacob. For *Midreshei Elleh Ezkerah va-Aseret Harugei Malkhut* see **Heikhalot*; *Merkabah; and *Ten Martyrs. For *Midrash Hashkem* see **Ve-Hizhir*. For *Midrash David ha-Nagid* see *David ha-

Nagid. For *Midreshei Teiman* see *Yemen. For *Haggadot ha-Talmud* and *Ein Ya'akov* see Babylonian *Talmud.

BIBLIOGRAPHY: H.L. Strack, *Introduction to the Talmud and Midrash* (1931, repr. 1959); Zunz-Albeck, Derashot.

[Moshe David Herr]

MIDRASH LEKAḤ TOV (Heb. מִדְרָשׁ לֶקַח טוֹב), a late 11th-century Midrash on the Pentateuch and Five Scrolls by Tobias b. Eliezer. The author called it *Lekaḥ Tov* ("good doctrine") on the basis of its opening verse (Prov. 4:2): "For I give you good doctrine" which he chose with allusion to his name (for the same reason he begins his interpretations of the weekly portions of Scripture and of the Scrolls with a verse containing the word *tov*, "good"). The book was called *Pesikta* by later scholars, and also, in error, *Pesikta Zutarta*. Tobias lived in the Balkans (Buber), and his Midrash contains allusions to contemporary historical events and specific reference to the martyrs of the First Crusade of 1096 (in the portion *Emor* and in his commentary on the verse "Therefore do the maidens love thee," Song 1:3). Zunz defined the Midrash as a composition which is "half exegesis and half *aggadah*," but even in the "half *aggadah*" the exegetical commentary aspect is conspicuous. Tobias took the ideas he needed from the Babylonian Talmud, the halakhic Midrashim, and the early aggadic Midrashim (including some no longer extant), as well as from the early mystical literature and used them as the basis of his Midrash. He did not however quote them literally nor as a rule did he mention their authors. He translated Aramaic passages as well as Greek and Latin terms into Hebrew; abridged the language of the early authors; and even combined their sayings and refashioned them. He tended to quote scriptural verses from memory, which explains the many variations from the standard text.

The work also contains hundreds of explanations by Tobias himself, some in the style of the midrashic literature and some giving the literal meaning. He expounds the *keri* and the *ketiv*, the **masorah*, **gematriot*, and **notarikon* and also gives many mnemotechnical devices in the manner of the rabbis. His literal explanations are based on the rules of grammar, vocalization, accentuation, etc. It is noteworthy that he explains anthropomorphic verses and statements as parables and frequently repeats: "The Torah speaks in the language of men." This tendency is without doubt an aspect of his violent struggle with the Karaites which finds expression in the Midrash in many places. His practical aim is also conspicuous when he deals with certain *halakhot* whose performance was apparently neglected in his time. Tobias' Midrash was frequently quoted soon after it was written, but until the end of the last century only the *Lekaḥ Tov* to Leviticus, Numbers, and Deuteronomy had been published (first edition, Venice, 1746). It was published in full, Genesis and Exodus by S. Buber (1884); Leviticus, Numbers, and Deuteronomy by Meir Katzenellenbogen of Padua (1884) from the Venice edition with corrections; the Song of Songs was published by A.W. Greenup (1909); Ruth by I. Bamberger (1887); Lamentations by J. Nacht (1895), and again by Greenup (1908); Ecclesiastes by G. Finberg (1904); Esther by Buber in the *Sifrei de-Aggadata al Megillat Esther* (1886).

BIBLIOGRAPHY: S. Buber, *Midrash Lekaḥ Tov* (1884), introd.; Zunz-Albeck, Derashot, 145f., 441–3; L. Ginzberg, *Ginzei Schechter*, 1 (1928), 253–97.

[Jacob Elbaum]

MIDRASH PROVERBS or **AGGADAT PROVERBS** (Heb. מִדְרָשׁ מִשְׁלֵי; cf. Arukh, s.v. *nakad* 3), Midrash on the Book of Proverbs, also frequently but wrongly referred to as Midrash *Shoḥer Tov*. The Midrash is distinguished by an exegetical style demonstrated both in the choice of its contents and the manner in which they are quoted. The compiler selected passages which largely explained the texts of Proverbs according to the literal meaning, and very frequently reworded them. As a result several of the characteristics of the early Midrash disappear and the exegetical method prevails. There are few proems, introductory words are rare, the few statements depend upon abstruse allusions, and the discussions in general are brief. A departure from the method of the early Midrashim is further conspicuous in two respects: in the formulation of disputes, and in the ascription of dicta to early scholars. The sources of the Midrash are the Mishnah, Tosefta, *Mekhilta*, and *Sifrei*. A phenomenon worthy of mention is the compiler's use of *Heikhalot* literature (to which Zunz drew attention; see *Merkabah Mysticism). The editor also made use of amoraic Midrashim, *Genesis Rabbah*, *Leviticus Rabbah*, *Pesikta de-Rav Kahana*, *Songs Rabbah*, and *Ecclesiastes Rabbah*, and he also knew the two versions of *Avot de-Rabbi Nathan*. He had no acquaintance with the Jerusalem Talmud, although there are numerous quotations from the Babylonian Talmud. From this, Buber concluded that it was compiled in Babylon, and not in Italy as claimed by Zunz, and conjectured from this and the quotations from it in geonic works of the eighth century, that it was edited after the final editing of the Babylonian Talmud. Although the quotations in the geonic writings are doubtful (Albeck) it is nevertheless certain that it cannot be as late as the end of the geonic period, despite the contrary view of Zunz.

The Midrash in its present state is incomplete. Parts of sections and whole sections are missing. The last third is particularly fragmentary, though the discussion of the last chapter (31) is given in detail. More Midrashim to this chapter are extant, namely *Midrash Eshet Ḥayil* (in S.A. Wertheimer, *Battei Midrashot*, 2 (1953²), 146–50); *Midrash Eshet Ḥayil* in the *Midrash ha-Gadol* to Genesis (ed. by M. Margulies (1947), 368–74); and L. Ginsberg published a fragment from a new edition of *Midrash Proverbs* (*Ginzei Schechter*, 1 (1928), 163–8). These apparently reflect different editions of the Midrash. Another version of the *Midrash Eshet Ḥayil*, which was collated in 1512 by Moses b. Joseph Albiladah of Yemen, is based upon ancient sources, and shows affinities in some details with the Ginsberg version (published in J.L. Nahum, *Mi-Ẓefunot Yehudei Teiman* (1962), 209–22). The most important printed editions of the Midrash are Constantinople, 1517, Venice, 1547, and

Prague, 1613. Subsequently the printers relied chiefly upon the Prague edition, which relied upon the Venice edition (whose reading is doubtful, as Buber has shown), and added to it the glosses, *Ot Emet*, of Meir b. Samuel Benveniste. In 1893 S. Buber published a new edition of great value based upon three manuscripts, as well as the Constantinople edition. Additional manuscripts of the Midrash are now available.

BIBLIOGRAPHY: Zunz-Albeck, Derashot, 133, 412f.; S. Buber (ed.), *Midrash Mishlei* (1893), introd.

[Jacob Elbaum]

MIDRASH SAMUEL (Heb. מִדְרַשׁ שְׁמוּאֵל, *Midrash Shemu'el*), the only Midrash to a book of the early prophets. It contains 32 chapters – 24 on I Samuel and eight on II Samuel – which appear to be the contents original to the time of composition. The Midrash, a compilation chiefly from early works, contains tannaitic material from the Mishnah, Tosefta, *Mekhilta*, and *Sifrei*, as well as amoraic material from the early aggadic Midrashim: *Genesis Rabbah*, *Leviticus Rabbah*, *Lamentations Rabbah*, and the *Pesikta de-Rav Kahana*. The author also included material from later Midrashim: *Song of Songs Rabbah*, *Ecclesiastes Rabbah*, *Ruth Rabbah*, *Esther Rabbah*, *Pesikta Rabbati*, and the *Tanḥuma* Midrashim (the question of whether he made use of the *Midrash Tehillim* is still unresolved). The Midrash also contains original material, however, both early, dating from the *tannaim* and the first *amoraim*, and late. The state of the Midrash seems to indicate that it is based upon an earlier Midrash on Samuel, with additions by the editor, mostly from existing material but also some of his original interpretation. Among indications of the editing are the interlacing of exegetical and homiletical matter, which is uncommon in early Midrashim. The Midrash however is, in the main, homiletical. Other evidence of later editing is to be seen in the artificial character of most of its 14 proems, as well as the incorporation of homilies which are irrelevant to the scriptural verse or the subject matter under discussion – apparently resulting from routine copying of the sources (Albeck).

Nothing is known of the author. Zunz's assumption that the work is to be dated no earlier than the 11th century appears probable. There is overwhelming evidence, however, that it was edited in Palestine. Its sources, as has been stated, are Palestinian, as are all the *amoraim* mentioned in it. It contains no passages from the Babylonian Talmud. The language contains elements from the Palestinian Midrashim and it contains many Greek words such as are found in the Palestinian Midrashim. Both the conditions reflected by the Midrash and the problems dealt with point clearly to a Palestinian background. Rashi was the first to mention and quote the Midrash, and it is frequently mentioned by later authorities (Buber, introd., p. 28). It is referred to by many names: *Midrash Samuel, Aggadat Samuel, Midrash Et La'asot* (from its opening words, Ps. 119:126). It is also sometimes erroneously referred to as *Shoḥer Tov*, the name of *Midrash Tehillim*, together with which it was published (Venice, 1546). The book was first published in Constantinople in 1517, the Venice edition being the second. It was published a third time in Prague in 1613 with the commentary of Isaac b. Samson Katz, son-in-law of *Judah Loew b. Bezalel of Prague, and has been frequently reprinted since. The best edition is that of S. Buber (Cracow, 1893) based on the printed editions of the Parma manuscript. For a commentary to *Avot* of the same name see Samuel ben Isaac *Uceda.

BIBLIOGRAPHY: Zunz-Albeck, Derashot, 133, 413–4; S. Buber, *Midrash Shemu'el* (1893), 7–40.

[Jacob Elbaum]

MIDRASH TEHILLIM (Heb. מִדְרַשׁ תְּהִלִּים; **Midrash Psalms**), an aggadic Midrash on the Psalms, called also *Aggadat Tehillim*, and *Shoḥer Tov* because of its opening verse, Proverbs 11:27. The Midrash embraces most of the Psalms. Despite the fact that most manuscripts and printed editions, as well as the copy that was before the author of the *Yalkut Shimoni*, lack homilies for Psalms 96, 97, and 98, they are included in the glosses of Abraham Provençal and in some manuscripts (see Jellinek and Buber). In several manuscripts and printed editions there is no Midrash to Psalm 15 but the Midrash to it is added to that of Psalm 14. The only psalms to which there is definitely no Midrash are 123 and 131. Zunz rightly conjectured that the Midrash on Psalms 119–50 differs from that to the preceding Psalms. From the differences of language and subject matter, the definite omission of the names of the authors, and the expository character of this section, he came to the conclusion that it was of later date than the earlier portion.

Zunz's claim was verified through the research of Buber. In six manuscripts and in the edition printed in Constantinople (1512), the Midrash concludes with Psalm 118. Only two manuscripts and those before Provençal contain a short fragment of a homily on Psalm 119. Buber also showed that the homilies of Psalms 122–137 were copied from the *Yalkut*, and since the latter contains no homilies to Psalms 123 and 131, these are also wanting in the Midrash. Zunz concluded from an examination of the sources, the methods employed, linguistic usages, and details of its contents (see especially Mid. Ps. 63:2; 6:2) that the first part is also late and that it was edited in Italy in the last centuries of the geonic period. From his examination of the manuscripts, Buber claimed that the original work had been added to by later copyists, and that its "youthfulness" is the result of these interpolations. According to him, Zunz erred in his identification of historical allusions in the work and was misled by errors in the names of persons and places (see his notes to Mid. Ps. 9:8). In his opinion the language of the original portions of the Midrash, its style, the manner of its homilies, and the *amoraim* mentioned in it, as well as the sources upon which it draws, are evidence of its antiquity and its Palestinian origin.

Buber, however, was mistaken, as has been shown by Ḥ. Albeck, who proved that the author of this Midrash also drew upon late Ereẓ Israel Midrashim. Albeck also bases his argument for late dating on an examination of the form of the proems and points to the signs of deterioration in them: the connection with the verses being interpreted is faulty, the terminology is inconsistent, the proems are mainly anonymous, and their formulation is at times defective. Albeck claims, furthermore, on the basis of the many differences between the manuscripts, the many additions in several of them, the errors in their arrangement, and the significant differences in the repetition of the same homily, that the present *Midrash Tehillim* consists of groups of Midrashim to the Psalms. This too is the reason, in his view, for the lack of uniformity in the methods of interpreting the Psalms: some are interpreted at length, every single verse being discussed, while in others homilies are found for only a few verses. It may be concluded, therefore, that the period of composition of the Midrash extended over some centuries. Obviously it is not identical with the *Midrash Tehillim* which Simeon b. Judah ha-Nasi taught Ḥiyya (Kid. 33a; and see also Av. Zar. 19a), even though it apparently contains material from as early as this period (third century). Its concluding section is definitely from the 13th century, and not as Mann suggested, that parts of it derive from an early "short" Midrash to Psalms.

Despite the lack of uniformity in this Midrash, its fragmentary nature on the one hand and the many additions to it on the other, it has retained many fine qualities and is one of the most beautiful in aggadic literature: it has exalted language and colorful themes, cites many stories and parables, and makes extensive and tasteful use of the hermeneutics of aggadic interpretation. L. Rabinowitz, adapting the main theory of Mann in his "The Bible as Read and Preached in the Old Synagogue," claims that one could assume a triennial reading of the Psalms paralleling that of the Torah, and from this it is possible to understand the contents of its homilies. This claim, however, is still far from being proved.

The Midrash has been frequently published: Constantinople, 1512, Venice, 1546, Prague, 1613, etc. Of great value are the Warsaw editions of 1873 and 1875, with the commentary of Aaron Moses Padua; the 1891 Vilna edition of Buber, for which he utilized eight manuscripts and the glosses of Abraham Provençal; and the English edition of Braude (1959). Important fragments of the *Midrash Tehillim* were published by A. Jellinek, *Beit ha-Midrash*, 5 (1873), 70–86 (glosses by A. Provençal); J. Mann, in: HUCA, 14 (1939), 303–32; and M. Arzt, in: *Alexander Marx Jubilee Volume* (1950), Hebrew section, 49–73.

BIBLIOGRAPHY: S. Buber (ed.), *Midrash Tehillim* (1891), introd.; Zunz-Albeck, Derashot, 131f., 407–12; L. Rabinowitz, in: JQR, 26 (1935–36), 349–68; W.G. Braude (trans.), *The Midrash on Psalms*, 1 (1959), introd.

[Jacob Elbaum]

MIDRASH VA-YISSA'U (Heb. מִדְרַשׁ וַיִּסָּעוּ), a medieval Midrash in Hebrew about the legendary wars of Jacob and his sons. The name derives from the first word of Genesis 35:5, with which the Midrash opens. The original name of the work is probably "The Book of Wars of the Sons of Jacob," a name which is preserved in Naḥmanides' commentary on the Book of Genesis (to Gen. 34:13), the earliest reference to the existence of the legend. The small book contains three chapters. The first describes a war of Jacob and his sons against the army of Ninevites, who came to Palestine to subdue the whole world. Characteristic of this chapter are exaggerations which are lacking in the two other chapters, a style possibly influenced by the Book of Josippon. This chapter does not appear in some manuscripts, although two of them consist of it only, which indicates that it was possibly a later addition to the Midrash. The second chapter describes the wars of the sons of Jacob against the Amorite kings seven years after Jacob and his family withdrew from Shechem (Gen. 35:5) because of the defilement of Dinah and the events which followed. The story of the victory over the Amorite kings is opposed to that of the biblical narrative, where Jacob fears that he will be outnumbered and destroyed. However, the story of the victory is hinted at in Genesis 48:22, a verse which is quoted to this effect in the Midrash. The third chapter describes the war between Jacob and his sons and Esau and his sons, in which Esau is killed by Jacob and Esau's descendants become tributary to Jacob's family.

The medieval Hebrew book (with the exception of the first chapter) is a free translation from Greek (or Latin) of an old Jewish (Hebrew or Aramaic) text from the time of the Second Temple, a text which was also used by the authors of the Book of Jubilees and the Testaments of the Patriarchs: the wars against the Amorites are narrated in the Testament of Judah, chapters 3–7, and in an abbreviated form in Jubilees 34:1–9; and a parallel narrative to the war against Esau and his sons is preserved in Jubilees 37 and 38:1–14, and in an abbreviated form, in the Testament of Judah, chapter 9. The medieval *Midrash Va-Yissa'u* is of great importance for a reconstruction of the original ancient Jewish text. The ancient text, which was used by the Book of Jubilees and the extant Testament of Judah, and is the basis of chapters 2–3 of *Midrash Va-Yissa'u*, could have been a separate work. It seems more probable, however, that the common source of all three works, in their description of the war of Jacob and his sons against the Amorite kings and against Esau, was an older and more expanded form of the Testament of Judah than its extant form in the Testament of the Patriarchs, a situation similar to that of the Testament of *Levi and the Testament of *Naphtali. Some scholars see in the description of the wars against the Amorites and Esau a tendentious projection into the biblical past of the wars of John Hyrcanus against the Samaritans and Edomites, the descendants of Esau, and a historical justification of these wars. *Midrash Va-Yissa'u* was used, expanded, and rewritten in the medieval *Sefer ha-Yashar* ("Book of Jashar"). A critical edition was published with an introduction by J.Z. Lauterbach in *Abhandlungen zur Erinnerung an H.P. Chajes* (1933, Heb. pt. 205–22).

BIBLIOGRAPHY: S. Klein, in: ZDPV, 57 (1934), 7–27; A. Jellinek, *Beit ha-Midrash*, 3 (1938²), ix–xiv, 1–5; R.H. Charles (ed.), *The Greek Versions of the Testaments of the Twelve Patriarchs* (1908), li, 235–8; idem (ed.), *The Testaments of the Twelve Patriarchs* (1908), lxv, 69–79; idem (ed.), *The Book of Jubilees* (1902), 200–4, 214–21; Ginzberg, Legends, 5 (1925), 315f., 321f.; Y.M. Grintz, *Perakim be-Toledot Bayit Sheni* (1969), 105f., n. 2.

[David Flusser]

MIDRESHEI HALAKHAH (Heb. מִדְרְשֵׁי הֲלָכָה; "Halakhic Midrashim"), the appellation given to a group of tannaitic expositions on four books of the Pentateuch. This body of tannaitic literature will be discussed below under the following headings: (1) Characteristics of Halakhic Midrash: (a) The Collections; (b) The Term Halakhic Midrash; (c) Literary Nature and Relation to Early Midrash; (d) Authority of the Bible; (e) Development of Exegetical Methods. (2) The Schools of R. Ishmael and of R. Akiva: (a) Distinct Exegetical Methods; (b) The Division into Schools; (c) Redaction of the Material from the Schools. (3) The Aggadic Material. (4) Traces of Early *Halakhah.* (5) Relation to Other Works: (a) Aramaic Targumim on the Torah; (b) Mishnah; (c) Tosefta; (d) Talmuds. (6) Time and Place of Redaction. (7) History of Research and Future Challenges.

1. Characteristics of Halakhic Midrash

(A) THE COLLECTIONS. Halakhic Midrashim (ḤM) contain both halakhic and aggadic (i.e., nonlegal) material from the tannaitic period, arranged according to the order of verses in the Torah, in contrast with other major compositions of this period – Mishnah and Tosefta – in which the material is arranged by subject. (See: *Mishnah: The Mishnah as a Literary Work; *Halakhah* in the Mishnah; *Aggadah* in the Mishnah.) ḤM were composed on four of the five books of the Torah: Exodus, Leviticus, Numbers, and Deuteronomy. There is only a single whole extant ḤM on each of these four books: **Mekhilta de-Rabbi Ishmael* on Exodus (MY), **Sifra* on Leviticus, **Sifrei* on Numbers (SN), and **Sifrei* on Deuteronomy (SD). Three other midrashim have been partially reconstructed from *Genizah* fragments, and from citations by *rishonim* (medieval authorities): **Mekhilta de-Rabbi Simeon ben Yoḥai* on Exodus (MS), **Sifrei Zuta* on Numbers (SZN), and **Mekhilta* on Deuteronomy (MD). Passages from an additional tannaitic midrash on the book of Deuteronomy, known as **Sifrei Zuta* on Deuteronomy (SZD), were recently discovered.

In his fundamental study of ḤM, Hoffmann drew a clear and persuasive distinction between the midrashic schools of R. *Akiva and R. *Ishmael, that differ from one other in their homiletical methods, midrashic terminology, the names of the major sages mentioned in them, and in the body of the exegeses. Hoffmann similarly demonstrated that the midrashim on each of the Pentateuchal books that have come down to us represent, in fact, these two schools, with one midrash from the school of R. Akiva and a second, from the school of R. Ishmael, extant for each of the books of the Torah (except for Genesis). MS, the major portion of Sifra, SZN, and SD belong to the school of R. Akiva, while the school of R. Ishmael is represented by MY, several additions that were appended to Sifra, SN, and MD. Other scholars, the most prominent of whom was J.N. Epstein, developed and expanded upon the distinctions between these two schools, while at the same time defining the unique character of each of the specific tannaitic ḤM.

A reexamination of the ḤM, taking into consideration additional passages from the three lost ḤM that were discovered in the *Genizah* and the new passages from SZD, teaches that, alongside the common elements of the midrashim belonging to each school, the differences between the midrashim are to be afforded greater prominence. The four midrashim from the school of R. Ishmael are marked by a relatively high degree of uniformity. Those from the school of R. Akiva, in contrast, are not homogeneous, and are to be divided into two subcategories that differ from each other in many realms: (a) MS, Sifra, and SD represent the classic midrashic school of R. Akiva, and bear a marked proximity to the Mishnah; (b) SZN and SZD exhibit a number of unique characteristics, both linguistically and with regard to their content, and have only very tenuous ties to the Mishnah of R. Judah ha-Nasi. This division, by itself, raises the possibility that the two groups of ḤM from the school of R. Akiva are merely representatives of the literary product of two academies, that originally included two parallel midrashic redactions for each of the Pentateuchal books from Exodus to Deuteronomy. Aside from the unlikelihood that the redactors of a school for the exegesis of the Torah would begin their activity with the Book of Numbers, or would be satisfied with midrashim on the Books of Exodus, Leviticus, and Deuteronomy, support for the existence of additional ḤM that have not been preserved may be brought from exegeses that were transferred verbatim from one midrash to another. Thus, for example, SZN and SZD contain exegeses that have their source in midrashim from the school of *Sifrei Zuta* on the books of Exodus and Leviticus. Remnants from other homiletical redactions of the tannaitic ḤM can also be discerned in many ḤM *baraitot* that are preserved in other compositions, most importantly, the Tosefta and the two Talmuds.

The above evidence teaches that the literature of the tannaitic Midrashim was originally much more extensive and richer than the extant written works. Such a perception requires us to beware of the drawing of unequivocal conclusions on the basis of the partial data that we possess, that are merely the tip of the iceberg. However, an awareness of our limitations does not exempt us from attempting to evaluate in considered fashion the body of data known to us regarding the details and rules of the ḤM.

Division of Midreshei Halakhah According to Types

	Type A ("*de-vei* R. Ishmael")	Type B ("*de-vei* R. Akiva")
Exodus	†*Mekhilta* (of *R. Ishmael*)	*Mekhilta* of *R. Simeon ben Yoḥai*
Leviticus	(fragments?)	† *Sifra*
Numbers	† *Sifrei* on Numbers	*Sifrei Zuta*
Deuteronomy	Deuteronomy = *Midrash Tannaim*	† *Sifrei Deuteronomy*

The Midrashim that were known in the middle of the 19th century are marked with a †.

(B) THE TERM HALAKHIC MIDRASH. The accepted name in scholarly literature for the tannaitic midrashim on the Torah, "*midrashei ha-halakhah*," is somewhat misleading, since these midrashim also contain aggadic material, a fact that is especially striking in MY and in SD, half of whose exegeses are of an aggadic nature. Nonetheless, the name "*midrashei ha-halakhah*" is defensible, since almost all the legal material mentioned in the Torah is included in ḤM, while only scant non-halakhic material, such as narratives, genealogical lists, ethical exhortations, and the like, are the subject of orderly midrashic exegesis in ḤM. Criteria have not been formulated that would explain why certain aggadic passages were included in ḤM, while others are not subject to such exegetical treatment. The clear linkage of the tannaitic midrashim to the halakhic material, specifically, can be learned from the fact that three out of the eight extant ḤM (MY, SN, and SZN) start with the first halakhic topic appearing in the appropriate biblical book, and not with the beginning of the book itself. This also explains the absence of any tannaitic midrash on the Book of Genesis, that is mostly concerned with nonlegal topics. It is worth noting in this context that a majority of the aggadic material incorporated in the ḤM seems to reflect an independent common source, and may not originally have derived from the two schools of halakhic exegesis. This strongly suggests that the midrashic material that was redacted by the sages from each of the two schools primarily contained passages that were fundamentally halakhic (see 3. The Aggadic Material below).

(C) LITERARY NATURE AND RELATION TO EARLY MIDRASH. ḤM literature draws a sharp distinction between the biblical text, on the one hand, and its interpretation by the rabbis, on the other. Every passage opens with a lemma consisting of the quotation of one or more words from the biblical verse, followed by a presentation of the exegetic interpretation of the words quoted. The quote and its interpretation comprise an independent literary unit known as a *midrash*. Generally, the order of the interpreted biblical passages precisely follows the order of the verses in the Bible, and only on rare occasions do the midrashim diverge from the biblical order.

The midrashim are written in Mishnahic Hebrew, and are formulated concisely, in a reserved and focused style. These works occasionally contain fairly simple and straightforward interpretations of the language of the Bible, that are formulated in accordance with the vocabulary and terminology of rabbinic language and paraphrases of the language of Scripture. Generally speaking, however, the midrashim go far beyond the simple interpretation of the biblical passage to derive laws and ideas from Scripture, or find support in it for them, employing exegetical methodology. Additionally, at times the midrashim tend to append to the narrow interpretation of the verse expanded and extensive discussion of halakhic matters and aggadic topics that only indirectly bear on the verse.

Most of the midrashic interpretations are unattributed, but the name of the rabbinic author of the midrash is often mentioned at its beginning or end. Frequently, a number of anonymous midrashic interpretations are offered for a single biblical expression, or are presented with an explicit tannaitic disagreement regarding the meaning of a verse. In many instances, reasons and proofs are appended to the exegetical interpretation to reinforce the rabbis' understanding of the passage. Some of the reasoning is formulated as a dialectic dialogue, during the course of which several alternative interpretations are suggested, and explanations are presented as to why a certain interpretation is to be accepted, and not others. Other verses are frequently cited as proof texts in the course of the midrashic interpretation of the specific verse under discussion. At times, these proofs are themselves based on the midrashic understanding of the proof text as it was interpreted elsewhere, and not on its simple meaning. Other verses are brought to resolve contradictions between different verses or to clarify some new teaching that is understood to be implied by the repetition of verses and expressions that are mentioned in the Bible more than once. The midrashic interpretations are usually founded on fine distinctions drawn with regard to the general content of the biblical text, its individual words, and, at times, even its letters. All this is rooted in certain fundamental assumptions regarding the absolute authority of the Bible and its sacred text as a divine source, and in a profound belief in the exclusive legitimacy of the interpretation of Scripture that accords with rabbinic *halakhah*.

The above literary qualities are unique to the tannaitic midrashim. The earlier exigetical literature contains glimmerings and beginnings of this sort of midrashic method, but such a consistent and developed body of work appears for the first time in ḤM. Signs of the attempt to resolve the seeming conflict between the authority of the Torah, on the one hand, and its actualization and harmonization, on the other, can already be found in the Bible itself, especially in Chronicles, where these attempts were made by a paraphrastic reformulation of the verses of the biblical verses themselves. The same is true of the *Temple Scroll*, in which the passages that discuss the same topic in a number of places in the Torah are concentrated, along with their interpretation and completion in the spirit of the laws and views prevalent among the Judean Desert sect. All this, however, was done in a rewriting of the Torah's words, as the direct, first-person, command of God, in sharp contrast with the differentiation in the tannaitic literature between the quoted verses and their interpretation. The Qumran *Pesher* literature provides an example of quoted verses in lemmas alongside their interpretation, but this is only for subjects pertaining to philosophic, ethical, or political actualization of the books of the prophets, and not of *halakhic* topics that appear in the *Torah*, as it is in the ḤM. A rare trace of an early rabbinic midrash, that apparently consists solely of quoted verses and their adjoining interpretation, by means of other verses, can be found in the homiletical expansion of "My father was a fugitive Aramean" (Deut. 26:5) in the Passover *Haggadah*. A few instances of the quotation of a verse and the presentation of its halakhic interpretation-exposition, along with the mention of alternative interpretations and their rejection, exist in the New Testament, but, obviously, these could hardly be compared with the systematic exegeses of the Torah in ḤM literature.

In comparison with the literature of the Judean Desert sect, ḤM literature exhibits a distinctly independent nature, that fundamentally differs from biblical literature: (1) unlike the Judean Desert scrolls, it does not present its interpretation as the absolute and unequivocal word of God, but rather as reasoned human interpretation of the verses of the Torah, that exposes the philological and theological difficulties that emerge from Scripture; (2) in contrast with those scrolls, that offer a consistent and uniform conception, the ḤM openly presents differing views and disagreements by rabbis from various generations, that are concentrated in a collective redaction; (3) the ḤM are written in pithy rabbinic language, while the Judean Desert scrolls employ language that more closely resembles that of the Bible, both in its grammar and in its lofty and dramatic style; (4) the great halakhic detailing of the ḤM, in comparison with the Bible, is vastly more developed than that in the scrolls; (5) in many instances the content of the *halakhot* set forth in the tannaitic literature is more removed from the simple meaning of the biblical *halakhah* than that of the Judean Desert scrolls. It is noteworthy, in this context, that in the second branch of the tannaitic literature, the Mishnah and the Tosefta, the *halakhah* is ordered in a completely new structure, that does not follow the sequence of the corresponding passages in the Torah.

The literary independence of the writings by the tannaim, in comparison with those of the Judean Desert sect, may be explained both by the relative lateness of the former, and by the overall worldview of the Sages regarding their own authority and power. We have not as yet uncovered written halakhic documents of proto-rabbinic orientation from the earlier period in which the Judean Desert scrolls were composed, thereby impeding our search for the main reason for these differences. Whatever the cause, it seems that the literary formulation of the ḤM in the tannaitic period was the result of several factors: (1) the canonization of the biblical literature and the conception that no books were to be added to the biblical canon bolstered the need to produce other compositions that clearly distinguished between the Bible per se, on the one hand, and its interpretation by the rabbis, on the other; (2) the consolidation of a more uniform version of the Bible and its sanctification, specifically, constituted a necessary condition for the composition of the exegetical interpretation of this text that would be based, inter alia, on a close reading of details in the accepted version; (3) the multiplicity of halakhic details that had no basis in the simple readings of Scripture, and the increasing gap between the early biblical law and the later rabbinic *halakhah*, furthered the need to create an updated compilation of *halakhot* and halakhic biblical exegesis; (4) the external polemics directed against the legitimacy of rabbinic *halakhah*, and the argument that it was only a human interpretation, led to an elaboration of the exegetical methods that had the potential for weakening these claims, while at the same time reinforcing the necessity of presenting the close link between the *halakhot* and the verses in independent compositions; (5) the internal debate between the different exegetical schools of the tannaim themselves also intensified the need for the redaction of midrashim by each of these schools. Another possibility is that external governmental prohibitions against Torah study, and the fear that this would result in the Torah being forgotten, spurred the process of a new summation of the *halakhot*, whether redacted by subject, as in the Mishnah, or in the order of the verses in the Torah, as in the ḤM. The general explanations cited above are applicable to a relatively long period; better knowledge of the time of the redaction of the ḤM might possibly enable us to gain a more correct understanding of the circumstances surrounding their redaction.

(D) AUTHORITY OF THE BIBLE. The Pentateuch, including all its verses, is perceived in ḤM as the authoritative and obligatory word of God. The belief in the divine source of the Pentateuch, and in the reliability of its transmitted and accepted version, constituted the necessary pre-conditions for the composition of ḤM, that in many instances are based on close readings of the minutest details of the words and even letters of the biblical text. The sages of ḤM openly do battle with the argument that Moses forged the Torah, or that he wrote certain verses of his own volition, while the *tannaim* concurrently reject the Samaritan version of the Torah on the grounds that it is a corruption of the original.

In no instance in ḤM or in other talmudic sources do we find the rabbis arguing among themselves as to the version of the Bible that is the subject of their exegesis, with one rabbi upholding a certain version, and another authority championing a different wording. Despite, however, the absence of overt disagreements between the rabbis concerning the versions of the Bible, ḤM contain indirect echoes of the awareness by the *tannaim* of more than a single version for some Scriptural passages, both in a number of explicit testimonies, and in several expositions that instruct: "Do not read x but y," when the second version does in fact exist in another textual tradition (and this is therefore not to be viewed as mere wordplay); and possibly also in midrashim that incorporate two alternative versions.

The (apparently intentional) absence of open disagreements on this issue is all the more striking given the clear indications of rabbinic cognizance of the existence of biblical textual variants brought above. This should come as no surprise, because controversies regarding the text of the Bible were liable to have undercut the very basis of the tannaitic exegetes. It should be emphasized, as regards the biblical text underlying ḤM, that it is not absolutely identical with Masoretic Text, the details of which were finally formulated only in the medieval period. Here and there ḤM cite verses in a version that differs from Masoretic Text and that, at times, accords with other versions, such as LXX, the Samaritan Torah, or the Peshitta. We also find interpretations based on the non-Masoretic Text version, that prove that this was the commonly accepted text of the Bible possessed by the *tannaim*-exegetes. An awareness of this phenomenon is of importance, both for an examination of the textual versions of the Bible, and for a proper understanding of the midrashic interpretations themselves.

(E) DEVELOPMENT OF EXEGETICAL METHODS. The first testimony in the tannaitic sources relating to the methods by which the Torah is expounded (*middot*) describes the principles employed by Hillel (Sifra, chap. 1, p. 9). These rules comprise, in practice, seven simple exegetical principles for the clarification of a given verse aided by an examination of other verses that contain (1) a law either more of less severe than that in the verse under discussion ("*kal va-ḥomer* [*a minori ad majus*]"); (2) a law equivalent to that in this verse (*gezerah shavah* [comparison of similar expressions]"); (3) a law that is specified in another place, but may be utilized elsewhere ("*binyan av* [prototype]"); (4) two verses that contradict one another ("*shenei ketuvim*"); (5) a verse that includes a general formulation along with one or more individual cases ("*kelal u-ferat* [general and particular]"); (6) a rare word or phenomenon that is explicated by other instances in other places ("*ka-yoẓe bo be-makom aḥer* [similarly, in another place]"); (7) a verse that is understood by its context ("*davar lamad me-inyano*").

A later list of 13 exegetical methods by which the Torah is expounded appears in the beginning of *Sifra*, in the name of R. Ishmael. In addition to their greater number, the methods of R. Ishmael are characterized by their extended explanation, their detail, and their distance from the relatively simple and straightforward principles of Hillel. For example: Hillel's "*shenei ketuvim*" is given an interpretation: "Two texts that refute one another, until a third text comes and decides between them"; *davar lamad me-inyano*, the method of "understanding from context," was supplemented: "*ve-davar ha-lamed mi-sofo* [and something that is learned from a later reference in the same passage]." Additional methods were specified, such as Hillel's "*binyan av*," that R. Ishmael developed into "*binyan av mi-katuv eḥad, u-binyan av mi-shenei ketuvim* [a prototypical inference from a single verse, and a prototypical inference from two verses]." The method of "*kelal u-ferat*" was the subject of especially extensive development, as it was divided into subsections, with an accompanying explanation of their meanings: "*kelal u-ferat; perat u-khelal* [particular and general]; *kelal u-ferat u-khelal* [general, particular, and general] – [the law] is discussed only in accordance with the subject of the particular case; [...] everything that was in the general statement that is specified, that does so to teach [a law], is not specified only to teach of itself [i.e., the specific case], but rather to teach of all that is encompassed by the general statement," and many more.

Furthermore, at times we witness a development of the meaning of exegetical methods that were formulated in the same fashion in the lists of Hillel and R. Ishmael. An outstanding example of this phenomenon is the method of "*gezerah shavah* [analogy]," whose primary meaning, as proposed by Lieberman, is a comparison between two identical matters. It was already related of Hillel himself that he learned out a *gezerah shavah* before the elders of Bathyra, based on a single word that appeared in two similar matters, with this word bearing directly upon the law learned from it (T. Pesaḥim 4:13, p. 165 and parallels). Later on, in the tannaitic period, the *gezerah shavah* became an almost arbitrary comparison between *halakhot* taught on two different matters, based on the same or proximate word that appeared in both laws – for the most part, without any relation to the literal meaning of these words. By means of the new transformation of this method, it was now possible in effect to prove anything, therefore compelling the rabbis to employ various measures to limit its possible uses.

An additional *baraita* containing specific midrashic interpretations illustrating the use of each method was appended to the *baraita* in the beginning of *Sifra* of R. Ishmael's 13 exegetical methods. Most of the traditional interpreters of the methods based their clarifications on this explanatory *baraita*. It would seem, however, that the explanations given in this *baraita* for several of the methods were elucidated in a manner at variance with their original meaning in the first *baraita* of R. Ishmael, one that reflects more fully developed methods, as they were formulated in the late tannaitic period. The method of "*kelal u-ferat*" is an outstanding example of this change. According to the initial meaning of this *baraita*, "*ke-ein ha-perat* [similar to the particular statement]" is to be employed for diverse instances of generalizations and specifications, without regard for their order of appearance in the verse: a generalization followed by a specification; and a specification followed by a generalization; and a generalization followed by a specification once again followed by a generalization. In contrast with this understanding, reflections of which can be found in a number of locations throughout the talmudic literature, the explanatory *baraita* in *Sifra* regards each of these three possibilities to be a different rule, as is more common in the talmudic literature: "*kelal u-ferat* – when there is a general and a particular statement, the general statement includes only what is specified in the particular statement"; "*perat u-khelal* – the general statement is made an addition to the particular statement"; "*kelal u-ferat u-khelal* – you discuss only similar to the particular statement." This explanation facilitates an almost certain reconstruction of the original count of the 13 methods, that the explanatory *baraita* sets at fifteen or sixteen. The development of the exegetical methods was paralleled by the formation of a school headed by R. Akiva, who preferred to base midrashic interpretation on close readings of certain words and letters in the verse under examination itself, and not to rely upon general exegetical rules, thus resulting in a widening of the gap between the exegeses and the simple meaning of Scripture.

This gradual process of the formulation of complicated and developed hermeneutical methods that were ever more distant from the initial interpretive rules that were characteristic of the early exegetical methods, continued in the amoraic period. For example, in most of their exegeses, the *amoraim* applied the *kelal u-ferat* method to verses in which the "*kelal*" no longer represents a biblical word of general content, and the "*perat*" does not denote a word that details the generalization. The main reason for this apparently can be traced to the ongoing attempt to find biblical proof texts for increasing numbers of laws, even though these *halakhot* had not initially been derived from Scripture, specifically. This tendency, of finding support in biblical verses for many diverse *halakhot* that had developed over the course of long periods of time, therefore gave rise to the need for a parallel development of the methods by which the Torah is expounded, and of the other exegetical methods.

(2)The Schools of R. Ishmael and of R. Akiva

(A) DISTINCT EXEGETICAL METHODS. One of the important achievements of ḤM research consists of the delineation of the methodological disagreement between R. Ishmael and R. Akiva concerning hermeneutical methods, and in its wake, the drawing of a distinction between the two chief types of ḤM: the midrashim that belong to the school of R. Ishmael, on the one hand, and those from the school of R. Akiva, on the other.

Some of the methodological differences between these two rabbis are already mentioned in tannaitic sources, and their consistent disagreement on a number of topics is also mentioned in amoraic sources. Only modern scholars, however, methodically collected the disagreements between these two rabbis concerning hermeneutical methods that are dispersed throughout the talmudic literature. The reconstruction of the differences between R. Ishmael and R. Akiva and their schools was made on the basis of four types of testimonies: (1) testimonies concerning dicta transmitted in the name of R. Ishmael or R. Akiva; (2) testimonies regarding views attributed by the talmudic sources to the schools of the two tannaim, such as "*tanna de-vei Ishmael*" or "*tanni R. Simeon bar Yoḥai*" of the school of R. Akiva; (3) disagreements implicit from an analysis of the differences between ḤM belonging to each school: (4) reconstructions of disagreements between R. Ishmael and R. Akiva proposed by the Talmuds. These different types of testimony generally complement one another. Based on a careful analysis and comparison of these various testimonies, scholars have reached well-founded conclusions. At times, however, the evidence concerning the disagreements between R. Ishmael and R. Akiva that emerge from the different types of testimony are inconsistent, and we should be cautious regarding generalizations and harmonizations, some of which were voiced by the talmudic sources themselves.

R. Ishmael's exegetic method is generally more moderate than that of R. Akiva, and the expositions by the former are less distant from the simple meaning of the biblical text than the far-reaching exegeses of R. Akiva. R. Ishmael also relies upon more *middot*, interpretive rules, and comparisons between different verses, in contrast with R. Akiva, who tends to focus upon the individual verse and draw conclusions regarding its exegetical meanings from its specific words and letters. These two *tannaim* frequently employ different exegetical methods to reach identical halakhic conclusions, while in some instances they differ regarding both the hermeneutical method and its halakhic significance. The following few examples will aid us in clarifying the differing approaches of R. Ishmael and R. Akiva to the exposition of "superfluous" words and particles, and the duplication of verbs, nouns, verses, and even of entire passages.

In one instance (TB Sanhedrin 51b) R. Akiva learns out a *halakhah* from the exposition of a letter *vav* that he considers to be superfluous, a legal conclusion that is vigorously opposed by R. Ishmael. As regards another exposition based on a seemingly unnecessary *vav*, according to R. Eliezer (Sifra, *Negaim*, chap. 13:2, 68b): "R. Ishmael said to him, 'My master, why, you tell Scripture to be silent until I expound(!).' R. Eliezer replied: 'Ishmael, you are a mountain palm,'" i.e., just as the palm that grows in the mountains bears no fruit, you, too, do not have the ability to expound. R. Akiva, in the footsteps of his teachers, also consistently expounded the particles "*akh*" (but) and "*rak*" (only) as exclusionary, on the one hand, and "*et*" and "*gam*" (also) as inclusory, on the other; R. Ishmael, as well, esteemed R. Akiva's erudition in these expositions (See Gen. R. 1, ed. Theodor-Albeck, p. 12). At times R. Akiva was even more adept at this than his teachers (See TB Pesahim 22b and the parallels).

R. Ishmael and R. Akiva similarly dissented regarding the interpretation of the combination of a finite verb with its infinitive, a standard grammatical form that commonly occurs in the Bible. R. Akiva expounds this literally, as referring to a specific and distinct *halakhah*, while R. Ishmael, in contrast, argues that "the Torah spoke in the language of man" (See, e.g., SN, *piska* 112, p. 121). It should be stressed that the expression "the Torah spoke in the language of man" appears in the tannaitic and amoraic sources only in relation to the rejection of exegeses based on verb-infinitive repetition, and on the repetition of the biblical phrase "man man" at the beginning of a topic. A similar situation is created by the concluding verses that come at the end of biblical passages, which R. Ishmael regards as literary repetitions, that are not to be expounded (See his view in SN, *piska* 152, p. 197; *piska* 157, p. 212). He also adopted a similar approach, in contrast to R. Akiva, regarding the repetition of entire passages.

R. Akiva's extreme methodology in his far-reaching expositions might possibly also explain the assertion by the Mishnah (mSot 9:15): "When R. Akiva died, the exegetes ceased." Noteworthy in this context is the aggadic tradition in TB *Menahot* 29b that the Holy One, blessed be He, said to Moses: "At the end of a number of generations there will be a man, Akiva son of Joseph by name, who will derive from every tip [of the letters in the Torah] mounds and mounds of laws." In practice, we do not know of any laws that R. Akiva derived from the tips of the letters, and this was most likely an extreme characterization of his hermeneutical method.

R. Ishmael, who opposed the overly precise exposition of biblical verses practiced by R. Akiva, based his own exegeses primarily on general hermeneutical rules and the comparison of different verses, as is demonstrated by his use of the 13 *middot* by which the Torah is explained, as described above. In addition to these rules, additional principles also were prevalent in the school of R. Ishmael, one of which relates to topics that are repeated in the Torah: "This is a rule for expounding the Torah: Every passage that was stated in one place but lacks one element, and was taught again in another place, was repeated only for the element that was omitted. R. Akiva says, Every place in which "*le-'emor* [saying]" is stated must be expounded" (SN *piska* 2, p. 4). This apparently indicates that the school of R. Ishmael maintained that expositions are not to be founded on the duplication caused by the repetition of the other similar verses in the two passages. The problem with this is that on occasion the ḤM of R. Ishmael, as well, employ such repetitions as the basis for exegeses, and it may reasonably be assumed that there was no unanimity within the school of R. Ishmael regarding this hermeneutical rule. At any rate, the incompleteness of our information regarding the opinions of both R. Ishmael and R. Akiva on this cardinal issue graphically illustrates the extent to which our knowledge regarding the conceptions of the *tannaim* are partial and imprecise.

Another hermeneutical rule of R. Ishmael relates to the tension between the simple meaning of the biblical text and what seemed logical and correct to the rabbis. R. Akiva resolves the contradiction by means of an extreme exegesis that removes the verses from their literal meaning and interprets them in accord with an opinion that seemed fitting to the *tannaim*. R. Ishmael, in contrast, candidly presents the inconsistency between the interpretation of the verse in accordance with his regular hermeneutical rules, on the one hand, and logic, on the other, and presents a compromise that allows both to coexist (See SN, *piska* 8, p. 14–15).

The tension between the simple meaning of Scripture and the *halakhah* is the subject of a similar disagreement between R. Ishmael and R. Akiva. The latter, as is his wont, explains the Torah in a manner that conforms with the *halakhah*. R. Ishmael, in contrast, pointedly indicates the instances in which there is a disparity between the two and says: "In three places the *halakhah* supersedes the biblical text" (*Midrash Tannaim* on Deut. 24:1, p. 154, and parallels). It nonetheless should be stressed that in many instances R. Ishmael, as well, uses his hermeneutical method to expound the Torah and harmonize it with the *halakhah*.

Another area in which we find a significant difference between R. Ishmael and R. Akiva relates to the bounds of the applicability of the *middot*, which R. Ishmael limits, while R. Akiva expands. A few examples: R. Ishmael permits the use of the *gezerah shavah* rule only if one of the two words on which it is based is free, i.e., it has not been used in other expositions. R. Akiva, in contrast, maintains that this hermeneutical method may also be used for two words that have already been put to other exegetical use. According to R. Ishmael, everything that is not specified in the Torah, but rather is learned by exegesis, cannot serve as the basis for an additional exposition. R. Akiva, on the other hand, permits founding a new exposition on a previous one; R. Ishmael is of the opinion that "punishments are not derived from logic" (in other words, a person is not punished for violating a law that is learned by a *kal va-ḥomer*), while other rabbis, including R. Akiva, according to one tradition, assert that punishments may be so derived.

R. Ishmael and R. Akiva also differ regarding the permissibility of expounding certain topics in public. R. Ba, in the name of Rav Yehuda (TJ *Hagigah* 2:1, 77a), attributes the law in *M. Hagigah* 2:1: "The forbidden sexual relationships may not be expounded before three persons" solely to R. Akiva, and as opposed to the opinion of R. Ishmael. Sifra (from the school of R. Akiva) accordingly did not include expositions regarding the forbidden sexual relationships in the portions of *Aḥarei Mot* (Lev. 18:7–23) and *Kedoshim* (Lev. 20:10–21), while the second midrash on Leviticus (from the school of R. Ishmael) does contain in these portions expositions of this subject, some of which were artificially included in several manuscripts of *Sifra*. Several explanations were offered for the reason behind this disagreement. I maintain that R. Akiva's position is to be understood in light of his extreme exegesis and his fear that the publicizing of such expositions on the subject of forbidden sexual relationships, that human nature craves, was liable to result in licentious behavior "and may come to permit that which is prohibited," in the words of TB (*Hagigah* 11b) on this mishnah. In contrast, R. Ishmael, who adopted a more moderate exegetical method, did not fear publicly expounding the passage of forbidden sexual relationships, presenting its prohibitions and concessions based on his hermeneutical rules. The *halakhah* in *M. Hagigah* loc. cit that "the Story of Creation is not expounded before two" is similarly attributed by R. Ba in the name of Rav Yehuda in TJ idem as following the view of R. Akiva exclusively, in opposition to the opinion of R. Ishmael. This dispute is reflected in the disagreement between the two *tannaim* concerning the legitimacy of the exposition in *Gen. R.*, p. 12, of the word "*et*" in Gen. 1:1. R. Akiva explains his position that the word is intended to prevent an erroneous Gnostic interpretation, that "we would say that the heaven and earth also are divinities," and therefore nothing can be derived from it, while R. Ishmael has no qualms in expounding the word *et* in this problematic verse of the act of Creation. *Gen. R.* p. 206 and p. 574 also contains a similar disagreement between these *tannaim* concerning the exposition of the word "*et*" in two other verses that are likely to be understood as supporting the view of the heretics; here as well, the dispute between R. Akiva and R. Ishmael is based in the different nature of the hermeneutical method of each Tanna. R. Ishmael was not wary of expounding these verses, while R. Akiva was apprehensive that the public exegesis of such sensitive verses in accordance with his extreme expositional method would be liable to serve as justification for the extreme interpretations of the heretics, following their methodology, and he therefore refrained from expounding them in public. In light of the above, we cannot accept the opinion of

Heschel that R. Ishmael was a rationalist who vigorously opposed esoteric expositions of the Torah and matters that cannot be attained by the intellect. More generally, the drawing of unnecessary connections between simple and literal interpretation and religious rationalism should be avoided.

(B) THE DIVISION INTO SCHOOLS. The discovery of the differing exegetical methods of R. Ishmael and of R. Akiva led scholars to divide ḤM into two schools: that of R. Ishmael and that of R. Akiva. This classification was based on the differences between the midrashim in the following areas: (1) The use of the exegetical *middot* that are prevalent in the midrashim from the school of R. Ishmael: Both midrashic schools make frequent use of several of the straightforward hermeneutical methods, such as *kal va-ḥomer* and *gezerah shavah* (although the emphasis that the word of the *gezerah shavah* is "free," as we could expect, appears only in the school of R. Ishmael). Other methods, such as *kelal u-ferat, perat u-kelal*, and *kelal u-ferat u-kelal*, appear only in midrashim from the school of R. Ishmael. (2) The terminology of the midrash: Some of the terms and introductory formulas that appear in ḤM are shared by all the midrashim, while additional midrashic terms are specific to each of the two schools. Some of these special terms are essentially related to the differing hermeneutical methods of the two schools, while others are merely alternative terms in which the redactors of each of the schools apparently were accustomed to use. (3) The names of the central rabbis: The midrashim from the school of R. Ishmael cite many dicta by R. Ishmael himself and by students from his school, headed by R. Joshia, R. Jonatan, R. Nathan, and R. Isaac, who receive scant mention in ḤM of R. Akiva and in the Mishnah, that also belongs to the sources of the school of R. Akiva. Conversely, ḤM of the school of R. Akiva make particular mention of R. Akiva himself and his students, headed by R. Judah and R. Simeon. In other instances, the midrashim are distinguished by the name each gives to the same rabbi (The most outstanding example of this practice is the use by ḤM of the school of R. Akiva of the name "R. Simeon," while the midrashim from the school of R. Ishmael cite "R. Simeon ben Yohai."). (4) Parallel expositions, appearing in a number of places in each school, whose content is virtually identical, or whose exposition employs a similar interpretive principle that is characteristic of each of the two schools. (5) Anonymous dicta whose attribution to the heads of the two schools is indicated by the parallels in the talmudic literature (Although this criterion was considerably amplified by Hoffmann, and after him, by Epstein, we should register a reservation, since ḤM also contain unattributed midrashim that the parallels ascribe to the rabbis of the opposing school. Scholars have not compiled orderly lists of this phenomenon, thus impeding an assessment of the relative weight of the unattributed dicta.). As was noted above, the fundamental division by early scholars, based on these criteria, between the schools of R. Akiva and R. Ishmael remains valid. A comprehensive and more precise examination, however, of the material based on these criteria themselves indicates that the midrashim from the school of R. Akiva are to be further divided into two subgroups, that are distinct from each other as regards their terminology, the names of the central rabbis who are cited, and their internal parallels.

(C) REDACTION OF THE MATERIAL FROM THE SCHOOLS. The redactors of ḤM did not limit their works to the teachings by the rabbis clearly identified with their respective school, and they frequently cited the views of rabbis from the other school. The redactors generally first included the material belonging to their own school, to be followed, in dialectical fashion, by the opinions of rabbis from the other school, adding the name of the author of the exposition, or without attribution, as "another interpretation [*davar aher*]," thus, precedence was given, for the most part, to the material from the school of R. Ishmael in ḤM of this school, to be followed by the teachings from the school of R. Akiva, while ḤM from the school of R. Akiva first present the dicta from their own school, and only afterwards the dicta from the school of R. Ishmael. The opinions of rabbis from the other school are usually presented in the terminology of the school to which the redactors belonged, and only in very rare instances is the terminology of the other school employed. Furthermore, at times we discern the tendentious redaction of the material in ḤM, with the redactors of each midrash presenting the views of the rabbis from the other school in a partial and fragmentary manner, in order to tip the scales toward the position that they favor. In conclusion, the redactors of ḤM are not to be considered "objective" editors of the sources they possessed. These redactors most likely belonged to the schools themselves, as can be learned from the exegetical methodology employed in their works; from the midrashic terms that they use, some of which are intrinsically linked to their exegetical methodology; from their system of ordering the material, with precedence given to the rabbis belonging to their own school; and from their tendentious adaptations of exegeses from the other school.

(3) The Aggadic Material

The major differences described above between ḤM belonging to the school of R. Ishmael and those from the school of R. Akiva find marked expression in the halakhic material that forms the core of this literature. The differences, however, between the midrashim from the two schools are considerably narrower in their aggadic passages, and the latter apparently originate in shared early material. The two parallel midrashim frequently contain aggadic expositions of extremely similar order, content, and style. Notwithstanding this, the differences between the two midrashim clearly indicate that these are two different redactions of early material, and not a division resulting from copying by different scribes. The two midrashic schools often differ in their specific interpretations of expressions and words, they sometimes adopt differing approaches to a certain biblical passage, and more comprehensive differences of opinion between the two are not unknown.

Despite the high degree of similarity in the aggadic material in the midrashim of both schools, most scholars have sought to apply to this material as well the accepted division of midrashim into the schools of R. Ishmael and R. Akiva. Although various signs supporting such a division appear at times, clear-cut differences between the schools in hermeneutical methods, exegetical terms, and names of rabbis are usually to be found only in the halakhic portions of the midrashim, and are hardly discernible in the aggadic sections. Accordingly, the common aggadic material of ḤM was quite probably not produced in the schools of R. Ishmael or of R. Akiva, but it is highly plausible that during the course of the appending of this material to the various ḤM, the later redactors of the two schools occasionally left their mark on this material, as well.

As regards the relation between the midrashim, concerning their shared aggadic material, the aggadic material appended to MY and MD (from the school of R. Ishmael) is notably lengthier than the parallel material that was added to MS and SD (from the school of R. Akiva). Additionally, the aggadic material incorporated in the former two midrashim, from the school of R. Ishmael, is frequently superior in style and content to the parallel material in ḤM from the school of R. Akiva. On the other hand, the reader is struck by the considered thought invested in the aggadic material by the redactors of SD, and especially of MS, who sought to reformulate the deficient material that they apparently received. The two ḤM on the Book of Numbers contain similar aggadic material, but there are no extant direct textual witnesses from *Genizah* fragments of SZN, thus hindering the conducting of any reliable comparison between them. A preliminary examination of the fragmentary aggadic citations from SZN in *Yalkut Shimoni* and in *Midrash ha-Gadol* indicates a relatively major distinction between them and the aggadot of SN, and the characteristic features marking the relationship between them differ from the common features exhibited by the dual midrashim on Exodus and Deuteronomy. The aggadic material appended to SZN (from the school of R. Akiva) is often more detailed than its parallels in SN (from the school of R. Ishmael). These initial findings are therefore not surprising, because SZN represents an independent midrashic branch of the school of R. Akiva, and it is only natural that the aggadic material appended to it possesses unique features, that do not necessarily resemble the aggadic fragments added to MS and SD, that represent the other branch of this school.

Finally, it should be noted that our characterization of the aggadic material in ḤM relates solely to the large units of entire Torah portions that are of an aggadic nature, and not to aggadic expositions of a certain verse that are incorporated within the halakhic sections, that are an integral part of the classical midrashim from both schools.

(4) Traces of Early Halakhah

The decisive majority of the halakhic material cited in ḤM resembles parallel tannaitic material in the Mishnah, Tosefta, and *baraitot* in the Talmuds. Moreover, ḤM quote more dicta from later *tannaim* than does the Mishnah. At the same time, ḤM also preserve opinions from, or allusions to, *halakhot* that differ from the prevalent rabbinic *halakhot*, as the latter were transmitted in most of the talmudic sources. Some of these opinions reflect the views of *tannaim* that, for whatever reason, have not come down to us in the other traditions, while another portion is representative of early or rejected *halakhot* that were observed in the Second Temple period.

The reasons for the preservation of these early *halakhot* in ḤM are to be found mainly in the following elements: (1) the highly developed dialectic deliberations in ḤM, including methodical discussions of several possible interpretations of the Bible, including a reasoned acceptance of one interpretation over another, with this alternative (rejected) interpretation occasionally representing the early *halakhah*; (2) the diverse sources used by the redactors of ḤM, some of which, such as the Mishnah that was used by the school of R. Ishmael or that used by the subschool of *Sifrei Zuta*, have not reached us in an orderly form through other transmission channels; (3) the incorporation of early interpretations and midrashim in ḤM, at times as part of the attempt by the later redactors to adapt them to the accepted *halakhah* of their time; (4) the inferior standing of ḤM in comparison with the Mishnah, a fact that paradoxically led to the more faithful preservation of their original versions and traditions. On the other hand, the halakhic authority of the Mishnah and its orderly interpretation by the *amoraim* and later authorities often resulted in the emendation and adaptation of its versions and traditions, under the influence of the reigning *halakhah* in a later period.

The traditional commentators of ḤM generally sought to obscure the remnants of non-normative *halakhah* in ḤM, in order to adapt it to the more common and well-known *halakhah* brought in the Mishnah and the Talmuds. A. Geiger was the first scholar to systematically reveal the early *halakhah* in ḤM. L. Finkelstein devoted discussions in a number of studies of this topic, in the attempt to prove that Sifra contains many remnants of an early, Second Temple period, midrash on Leviticus, and that many early *halakhot* following Beit Shammai are retained in SD, along with more ancient fragments from the Second Temple period, and possibly even from the time of the Prophets(!). While Geiger and Finkelstein have certainly made significant contributions to the scholarly research in this field, both by raising the proper questions and by providing many fertile insights into these difficult issues, a not inconsiderable portion of their brilliant and far-reaching conclusions are not sufficiently based on a literal interpretation of the language of the midrash, nor are they supported by the direct evidence of the Dead Sea Scrolls that was published only recently.

(5) Relation to Other Works

(A) ARAMAIC TARGUMIM ON THE TORAH. The Aramaic Targumim on the Torah, which were read in public, incorporated a considerable amount of midrashic material that corresponds to the teachings included in ḤM. At times the Targumim assist in the interpretation of the midrashim, both for the literal interpretation of the midrashim, and for an understanding of content of passages in which the exegesis alludes to a subject that is explicated in the Targumim.

Each Targum must be examined separately in order to answer the question of which came first, ḤM or the Aramaic Targumim. Early material that influences the language of the exegeses in ḤM is sometimes embedded in the Targum in MS. Neofiti, the Fragmentary Targum, and Onkelos. On the other hand, the Neofiti and the Fragmentary Targum occasionally contain homiletical expansions that would clearly seem to originate in ḤM. Although Pseudo-Jonathan is closely and consistently linked to ḤM, it would appear that the author of this Targum did not possess early midrashic material (as maintained by Geiger and other scholars), but rather made use of several of the currently extant ḤM, in order to complete the foundation of the Neofiti and the Fragmentary Targum, that, as is known, were available to him. Proofs of this use of ḤM by Pseudo-Jonathan can be brought from a number of corruptions in Pseudo-Jonathan that most likely were due to the errors made by the redactor of the Targum during the course of the rendition of ḤM. We would be hard-pressed to find a strong connection to ḤM and the other ancient Bible translations, such as the Septuagint, the Peshitta, and the Vulgate, and their primary contribution to the study of the midrashim lies in the versions of the Bible that they present, that are equivalent here and there to the accepted Bible text of ḤM.

(B) MISHNAH. The order of the *halakhot* of ḤM follows that of the biblical citations, which serve to demonstrate the close connection between the tannaitic *halakhah* and the verses. In addition, ḤM also interpret many aggadic passages. The Mishnah, in contrast, orders the tannaitic *halakhah* by subject, with the connection of the latter to the Bible generally not presented; moreover, the aggadic material in the Mishnah is very limited, in comparison to that in ḤM. Notwithstanding these differences, there is a clearly mutual relationship between ḤM and Mishnahic literatures; along with exegesis, ḤM contain a not inconsiderable number of quotations from mishnahyot and *baraitot*, that are frequently cited in ḤM after set terms such as "מיכן אמרו [From here they said]," "מיכן אתה אומר [From here you say]," "אמרו [They said]," and other such introductory formulas. In other instances, however, this material is brought in ḤM without a prefatory expression. On the other hand, every so often midrashic reasoning for laws is incorporated in the Mishnah, as well as short midrashic units that are characteristic of the school of R. Akiva. In other instances, the abstract halakhic formulation of the Mishnah is adapted from early midrashic material.

An examination of the mishnahyot and *baraitot* in ḤM teaches of an important distinction between MS, Sifra, and SD (from the central school of R. Akiva), on the one hand, and the midrashim from the school of R. Ishmael, on the other. The former make frequent use of the extant Mishnah: they often seek to link the verses and their exegeses with the Mishnah, and they generally cite our Mishnah verbatim. In MY and SN (from the school of R. Ishmael), on the other hand, the term "From here they said" is not so common, and when the Mishnah is cited, it is not brought in its actual language, but rather paraphrased and in abbreviated form; nor do these midrashim contain many instances of "from here they said" from *baraitot* and the Tosefta. This difference emerges quite strongly from a comparison of SN and SD, both of which are represented in the same important manuscript, Vatican 32. The abbreviation "וכולה מתניתין [etc. from the Mishnah]" is quite prevalent in SD, in which the Mishnah is quite frequently cited verbatim, but is totally absent from SN, in which the Mishnah is generally not cited in its original language. The disparity between the midrashim from the school of R. Ishmael and the Mishnah is also pronounced regarding the names of the rabbis who are clearly identified with this school, who are not mentioned in the Mishnah. To these indicators we should perhaps add the interesting finding that the term "*mishnah*" itself appears only in ḤM from the school of R. Akiva, and is totally absent from those of the school of R. Ishmael. It would therefore appear that the redactors of MS, Sifra, and SD (from the school of R. Akiva) related to the extant Mishnah, that also is founded in this school, as an authoritative source, while the editors of MY and SN (from the school of R. Ishmael), did not recognize the supreme authority of our Mishnah. An exception is the branch of SZ, that belongs to the school of R. Akiva, but is notedly singular in a number of realms: the decisive majority of the *mishnahyot* that it cites are considerably different from our Mishnah, and it has already been suggested that this is to be viewed as reflective of opposition by its redactors to Rabbi's court and teachings.

(C) TOSEFTA. The Tosefta, that was redacted following the Mishnah, also was based in great measure on halakhic sources from the school of R. Akiva. It contains a bit more midrashic material on halakhic and aggadic topics than the Mishnah, and a portion of it was even taken from midrashic sources from the school of R. Ishmael (Such as two large fragments in *T. Shevuot*). In contrast with the Mishnah, the Tosefta occasionally mentions rabbis who are prominent representatives of the school of R. Ishmael (R. Nathan, R. Josiah, R. Isaac and R. Jonathan). Additional study of each of the separate ḤM is required to determine whether all ḤM that we possess had knowledge of the extant Tosefta, or whether they made use of other collections that included similar *baraitot*.

(D) TALMUDS. The *amoraim* drew upon collections of tannaitic ḤM on the Torah, as we learn from thousands of quotations from the latter in TB and TJ (see their listing, by their order in the Pentateuch, in Melamed, *ḤM in the Babylonian/Palestian Talmud*). Most of the citations in the Babylonian Talmud are from the school of R. Akiva, but there are also a large number of passages from the school of R. Ishmael, and additional sources. About forty percent of the quotations in the Talmud are of new material that does not appear in the extant ḤM, some of which was unquestionably taken from other collections of the schools of R. Ishmael and R. Akiva and additional nonextant sources. The remaining 60 percent of the citations that are common to the Talmuds and ḤM apparently indicate that the *amoraim* possessed collections akin to the extant ḤM. The parallels for this material are not completely congruent, with the dissimilarity between the ḤM and TJ smaller than the difference between ḤM and TB Exceptional in this respect are *Sifra*, which is frequently cited by TB in its original language, and MS, with a not inconsiderable number of its expositions cited by TB Some of the differences between the otherwise similar parallels in ḤM and the Talmuds ensue from differing traditions and transmissions of the same basic or raw material, while in other instances various interpretive glosses and additions, along with numerous abridgements and adaptations, were attached to the *baraitot* in the Talmuds, notably in TB, but also in TJ We nonetheless may conclude with certainty that the *baraitot* in ḤM generally reflect the teachings of the *tannaim* in a manner better and more faithful to the original than their parallels in the Talmuds.

The *amoraim* often appended their explanations and clarifications to the *baraitot* of ḤM; needless to say, these ancient interpretations are of incalculable value for a full understanding of the tannaitic dicta. The midrashim were not, however, always given a literal interpretation by the *amoraim*, and several of the general perceptions in the Talmuds concerning the methods of the schools of R. Ishmael, R. Akiva, and other rabbis are inconsistent with the original views held by these *tannaim* themselves. In addition to the various concrete interpretive and halakhic considerations, that frequently influenced the nonliteral interpretation of the midrashic *baraitot* in the talmudic discussions, the *amoraim* also disagree with ḤM regarding several general principles concerning hermeneutical methods. This is especially true concerning the common tendency of redactors from both schools to base various *halakhot* on a single biblical expression, on the one hand, while, on the other, they find support for a single *halakhah* in a number of verses. One of the central assumptions prevalent in the Talmuds, in contrast, is that each biblical expression contains the foundation for a single halakhic derivation, and that the same *halakhah* is not to be derived from more than one biblical expression. The consistent application of this exegetical assumption in both Talmuds (which the Talmuds also ascribed to the *tannaim* themselves) led to the interpretation of many tannaitic midrashim in the Talmud in a manner which is not consistent with their literal or original sense. In addition to the growing belief in the unique halakhic significance of each and every biblical expression, the biblical exegesis of the *amoraim* themselves also represents a new direction in the development of midrashic methodology. Generally speaking, the latter took another step forward in developing the exegetical method of R. Akiva and his school, with increasing focus upon the details of the verse, and by basing ever-growing numbers of laws and their particulars on Scripture, while at the same time further distancing them from the simple meaning of the biblical text.

(6) Time and Place of Redaction

We probably should accept the predominant scholarly view that the final redaction of ḤM was conducted in the Land of Israel, in the first or second generation following the redaction of the Mishnah, that is, by the middle of the third century CE. An earlier dating cannot be proposed, because the latest rabbis mentioned in a majority of ḤM are from these generations. Nor, however, should a significantly later date be assigned to this editorial activity, placing it at the end of the amoraic period sometime in the fifth century, as has been suggested by several scholars, on the basis of quite weak evidence, and we certainly should reject the thesis of Wacholder that dates the redaction of several ḤM to the eighth century. The Mishnahic language of ḤM closely resembles that of the Mishnah, without influences of the Galilean Aramaic that was the predominant language of the *bet midrash* in the fifth century, at least in Galilee. The internal character of ḤM reinforces the theory that regards them as a transitional period between the Mishnah (that several quote verbatim) and the Talmuds. This transitional aspect is especially pronounced in the element of dialectic reasoning that is more fully developed in ḤM than in the Mishnah, but had still not reached the peak of its development that would come in the Talmud (even in the PT). Furthermore, the better preservation of tannaitic views in ḤM, in a form closer to the original, than in their emended and adapted parallels in the Talmuds, poses a very major obstacle for the conjecture that ḤM were redacted close to the redaction of the PT, after a lengthy period of "hibernation," in which they underwent no change. This same conclusion is also indicated by the fact that the more developed hermeneutical method of the *amoraim* is not discernible in ḤM.

Nor is it to be assumed, and this should be stressed, that the various ḤM were redacted at the same time, rather, a separate discussion must be devoted to the time of each individual midrash's redaction. For example, we should probably assign a slightly earlier date to the redaction of SN, which makes no mention of sixth-generation *tannaim*, except for a single narrative that speaks of R. Hiyya. Such a hypothesis is somewhat strengthened by the brevity and relative scarcity of associative expositions, in comparison with the other ḤM. It would appear, though, that after its initial redaction an additional stratum, from the "school of Rabbi," was incorporated in SN. On the other hand, while most scholars maintained that MS is the latest of ḤM, basing this estimate on its expansions, the use that it, in their opinion, made of other ḤM, and the developed nature that they found its *halakhot* and exegeses to possess, such a conclusion seems to lack a firm basis.

Most scholars properly think that all of the tannaitic ḤM were redacted in the Land of Israel, a conclusion that is supported by the similarity of the language of ḤM to that of the Mishnah and Tosefta, which were also redacted in the Land of Israel; and by the stronger affinity between the *baraitot* in ḤM and their parallels in the PT and the Palestinian *midrashei aggadah*, as compared to the frequent differences between them and the *baraitot* in the TB. Even more compelling evidence is provided by internal indicators, such as the phenomenon of transferring literary units from one place to another, usually unaccompanied by any attempt to adapt them to their new position, corresponding to the common strategy of the literary redactors of the tannaitic and amoraic literature in the Land of Israel. The redactors of the TB, in contrast, frequently sought to have their displaced *sugyot* conform to their new position. The division of the Pentateuch into portions following Land of Israel practice is also noticeable in the redaction of ḤM.

All this also applies to the midrashim belonging to the school of R. Ishmael, that some scholars thought were redacted in Babylonia, an opinion resting on the assumption that most of the leading *tannaim* from this school, headed by R. Josiah, R. Jonathan, R. Natan, and R. Isaac were Babylonians. A re-examination of the subject revealed that several of these rabbis, such as R. Josiah, were not Babylonians at all, and that some of them seemingly immigrated to the Land of Israel. Especially impressive is the statement in MD by R. Jonathan – who was (unjustifiably) considered in the past to be a Babylonian *tanna* – that is incorporated in a passage that extols the importance of the obligation to reside in the Land of Israel, and vehemently opposes leaving the Land, even for the purpose of Torah study: "I vow [*noder*] never to leave the Land [of Israel]" (MS Oxford Heb. c 18.5). All the above evidence therefore points in the direction of the Palestinian redaction of all ḤM.

At present we do not possess sufficient data for a more precise determination of the location within the Land of Israel of the *batei midrash* of R. Ishmael and R. Akiva, nor of settlements or regions in which the various ḤM were redacted. This question is obviously related to the difficulties involved in the identification of the last redactors of each of the midrashim, a subject to which most scholars have devoted lengthy inquiries, without reaching convincing or commonly accepted conclusions. It is to be hoped that new archaeological and future literary finds will aid in solving these knotty questions.

(7) History of Research and Future Challenges

The first steps in the systematic research of ḤM were taken in the late eighteenth and early the nineteenth centuries by scholars of the Wissenschaft des Judentums: A. Geiger, L. Zunz, Z. Frankel, J.H. Weiss, M. Friedmann, and others. They focused on three main areas: (1) a historical description of the development of the talmudic and midrashic literature as a whole; (2) the manner in which *halakhah* and midrash were learned in antiquity and developed; and (3) a reinterpretation of the various ḤM.

In the late 19th and early 20th centuries the study of ḤM intensified, with works by I. Lewy, D. Hoffmann, S. Schechter, H.S. Horovitz, and others, who focused on three other spheres: (1) the schools of R. Ishmael and R. Akiva and the classification of ḤM by this criterion; (2) the publication of critical editions of the major ḤM based on mss.; (3) the reconstruction of lost ḤM, based on **Yalkut Shimoni, *Midrash ha-Gadol, *Genizah* fragments, and other sources.

Modern ḤM scholars, the most prominent of whom were J.N. Epstein, Ch. Albeck, S. Lieberman, and L. Finkelstein, continued the publication of ḤM while conducting up-to-date studies in a diverse range of related subjects. Except for Finkelstein, however, these scholars devoted most of their energy in the study of tannaitic literature to the Mishnah and Tosefta, causing them to somewhat neglect the ḤM.

Continued progress in ḤM research depends, first and foremost, on vigorous effort to discover their lost portions in the libraries throughout the world, accompanied by the publication of new critical editions of all ḤM. Since the publication of the first editions, scholars have uncovered new manuscripts for most of the midrashim, *Yalkutim* and additional midrashim that quote passages from ḤM, and several previously unknown commentaries by *rishonim* and *aḥaronim*, whose versions and interpretations cast further light upon the subject of our scholarly inquiries. Eastern textual versions are of especial importance, primarily the many fragments from the Cairo *Genizah*, whose existence was not known to the editors of the early editions. The methodology of the critical editing of the talmudic sources has also advanced by great strides in determining the text and presenting textual variants.

Based on more authoritative editions of ḤM, a detailed commentary should be composed for each collection. New editions accompanied by critical interpretation will provide the foundation for a renewed discussion of all the basic issues pertaining to these midrashim. They will also facilitate an overall clarification of the formal and substantial character of ḤM and the meaning of the specific *halakhot* and ideas they contain, in comparison with the other strata of the talmudic literature, on the one hand, and other works, spanning a broad range of periods, both Jewish and non-Jewish.

Preparatory work in several of these realms has been undertaken in recent years, such as the production of a CD-ROM of tannaitic literature by the Historical Dictionary Project of the Academy of the Hebrew Language in Jerusalem; the systematic collection of extant ḤM fragments in libraries throughout the world, most importantly, substantial fragments from the *Genizah*; the publication of transcriptions of all the *Genizah* fragments (apart from the *Sifra*); preparations for the new scientific publication of several midrashim; the linguistic examination of good ḤM mss.; the development of a literary approach that will aid in the analysis of the halakhic and aggadic passages in ḤM; and an orderly and detailed commentary of several passages from ḤM. It is to be hoped that these will yield fruits that will continue to meet the scholarly challenges that we have listed.

BIBLIOGRAPHY: Ch. Albeck, *Introduction to the Talmud Babli and Yerushalmi* (Heb.; 1969), 79–143; idem, *Untersuchungen uber die Halakischen Midraschim* (1927); W. Bacher, *Die exegetische Terminologie der judischen Traditionsliteratur* (1905); D. Boyarin, "On the Status of the Tannaitic Midrashim," in: JAOS, 112 (1992), 455–65; D. Daube, "Methods of Interpretation and Hellenistic Rhetoric," in: HUCA, 22 (1949), 239–63; J.N. Epstein, *Introduction to the Mishnahic Text* (1948), 728–51 (Heb.); idem, *Prolegomena ad Litteras Tannaiticas* (Heb.) (1957), 499–544; L. Finkelstein, *Sifra on Leviticus* (Heb.), vol.

1 (1989), 21–71, 120–91; vol. 5, (1992), 49–60, 100–144, 151*–254*; S.D. Fraade, *From Tradition to Commentary: Torah and Its Interpretation in the Midrash Sifre to Deuteronomy* (1991), 1–23; idem, "Interpreting Midrash 2: Midrash and Its Literary Contents," in: *Prooftexts, 7* (1987), 284–99; idem, "Looking for Legal Midrash at Qumran," in: M.E. Stone and E. G, Chazon, *Biblical Perspective: Early Use and Interpretation of the Bible in Light of the Dead Sea Scrolls, Studies on the Texts of the Desert of Judah*, 28 (1998), 59–79; I. Gafni, *The Jews of Babylonia in the Talmudic Era* (Heb.; 1990), 81–86; A. Geiger, *Kevuẓat Ma'amarim* (Heb.; 1885); idem, *Urschrift und Ubersetzungen der Bibel* (1928²); A. Goldberg, "The Early and the Late Midrash," in: *Tarbiz*, 50 (1981), 94–106 (Heb.); idem, "Chanokh Albek: Introduction to the Talmuds," in; *Kiryath Sepher*, 47 (1972), 9–19 (Heb.); idem, "The Wordings of '*Davar Aher*' in the Midrashei ha-Halakhah," in: Gilat, et al., *Studies in Rabbinic Literature*, 99–107 (Heb.); idem, "The School of Rabbi Akiva and the School of Rabbi Ishmael in Sifre Deuteronomy, Pericopes 1–54," in: *Te'uda*, 3 (1983), 9–16 (Heb.); D Weiss Halivni, *Midrash, Mishnah and Gemara* (1986), 1–65; D. Henshke, "On the Relationship between Targum Pseudo-Jonathan and the Halakhic Midrashim," in: *Tarbiz*, 68 (1999), 187–210 (Heb.); idem, "The Rabbis' Approach to Biblical Contradictions," in: *Sidra*, 10 (1994), 39–55 (Heb.); A.J. Heschel, *Theology of Ancient Judaism* (Heb.), vols. 1–2 (1962–1965); D. Hoffmann, "Zur Einleitung in die Halachischen Midraschim," in: *Jahresbericht des Rabbiner-Seminars* (1888), 1–92; M. Kahana, "The Biblical Text as Reflected in MS Vatican 32 of the Sifre," in: *Talmudic Studies* (Heb.), 1, (1990), 1–10; idem, "The Development of the Hermeneutical Principle of *Kelal u-Ferat* in the Tannaitic Period," in: *Studies in Talmudic and Midrash Literature in Memory of Tirza Lifshitz* (Heb.; (2005), 173–216; idem, *The Genizah Fragments of the Halakhic Midrashim* (Heb.), 1 (2005); idem, "Halakhic Midrash Collections," *The Literature of the Sages*, vol. 3b (2006); idem, "The Importance of Dwelling in the Land of Israel according to the Deuteronomy Mekhilta," in: *Tarbiz*, 62 (1993), 501–13 (Heb.); idem, *Manuscripts of the Halakhic Midrashim: An Annotated Catalogue* (Heb.; 1995); idem, *The Two Mekhiltot on the Amalek Portion* (Heb.; 1999); idem, *Sifre Zuta on Deuteronomy* (Heb.; 2002); idem, "The Tannaitic Midrashim," in: *The Cambridge Genizah Collections: their Contents and Significance* (2002), 59–73; S. Lieberman, *Hellenism in Jewish Palestine* (1950); idem, *Siphre Zutta: The Midrash of Lydda* (Heb.; 1968); E.Z. Melamed, *Halachic Midrashim of the Tannaim in the Babylonian Talmud* (Heb.; 19882); idem, *Halachic Midrashim of the Tannaim in the Palestinian Talmud* (Heb.; 2000); idem, *An Introduction to Talmudic Literature* (Heb.; 1973), 165–317; idem, *The Relationship between the Halakhic Midrashim and the Mishnah & Tosefta* (Heb.; 1967); S. Naeh, "Did the Tannaim Interpret the Script of the Torah Differently from the Authorized Reading?," in: *Tarbiz*, 61 (1992), 401–48 (Heb.); E.S. Rosenthal, "*Ha-Moreh*," in: PAAJR, 31 (1963), 1–71 (Heb.); I.L. Seeligmann, "The Beginnings of the Midrash in the Book of Chronicles," in: *Tarbiz*, 49 (1980), 14–32 (Heb.); M. Zucker, "For the Resolution of the Problem of the 32 Middot and *Mishnat R. Eliezer*," in: PAAJR, 23 (1954), 1–39 (Heb.); L. Zunz, *Die gottesdientlichen Vorträge der Juden historisch entwickelt* (1892).

[Menahem I. Kahana (2nd ed.)]

MIDSTREAM, U.S. Jewish monthly. *Midstream* was founded as a quarterly in 1955 by the Theodor Herzl Foundation with the object of creating a serious Zionist periodical that would have an intellectual impact upon American Jewish life. Under the editorship of Shlomo Katz, the magazine published articles and fiction of merit on various aspects of U.S. Jewry and Israel. In 1965 it became a monthly.

Billing itself as "the leading intellectual Zionist magazine in the world," it then became an opinion magazine covering political, social, and religious topics that are relevant to Jewish communities around the world. In 2004, *Midstream* had a subscription list of 6,500 readers.

[Ruth Beloff (2nd ed.)]

MIEDZYRZEC PODLASK (Pol. **Międzyrzec Podlaski**; called **Mezhirech** or **Mezrich** by the Jews), town in Lublin province, E. Poland. An organized Jewish community existed in the town from the middle of the 17th century. Between 1689 and 1692, the *parnasim* of the community of Miedzyrzec Podlaski waged a stubborn struggle against the leaders of the community of *Tykocin (Tiktin) for the hegemony over the Jewish communities in the vicinity of *Mielec. A magnificent synagogue, which was still standing in 1970, was erected in Miedzyrzec Podlaski at the beginning of the 18th century. The owners of the town during the 18th century, the Czartoryski family (see Adam *Czartoryski), encouraged Jews to settle in order to develop the town. At the fair held twice a year in the town, local Jewish merchants, as well as those from other towns, played an important role. In 1714 the community of Miedzyrzec Podlaski and the Jews of the surrounding villages which were under its jurisdiction paid 1,000 zlotys as poll tax. In 1759 a compromise was reached between the communities of Miedzyrzec Podlaski and *Lukow: the Jews living in the surrounding villages and townlets would pray in Miedzyrzec on the High Holidays and would also bury their dead there; they would pay their taxes one year to one community and the next year to the other. In the 19th century, during the period of Russian rule, there were no residence restrictions in Miedzyrzec Podlaski. Around the middle of the 19th century, the influence of Ḥasidism spread among the Jews there. At the time of the political agitation in Poland (1861), a Hebrew manifesto on the contemporary problems was circulated among the Jews of the town. In 1863 a number of the local Jewish craftsmen assisted the Polish rebels supplying them with equipment and food. During the second half of the 19th century, a Jewish working class emerged which found employment in the sawmills, the tanneries, the production of ready-made clothing, and hauling. The organized Jewish proletariat and youth participated in the 1905 revolution. At the end of 1918, a Jewish self-defense group was active in the town. Between the two world wars, branches of all the Jewish parties were established, as well as Jewish educational institutions (*Tarbut, CYSHO, Beth Jacob). During the 1920s a weekly, *Podlashier Lebn*, was published.

[Arthur Cygielman]

Holocaust Period

Before the outbreak of World War II, there were about 12,000 Jews in the town and they constituted 75% of the total population. During the first year of Nazi occupation, about 4,000 Jews from other places were forced to settle there. In December 1939, 2,300 Jews from Nasielsk, Pultusk, Rupiń, and Serock were deported to Miedzyrzec Podlaski. In April 1940 over 1,000 Jews from Slovakia were deported there, followed by 600 Jews from Cracow, Mlama, and Mielec. In June 1940 about 2,300 men were deported to six forced labor camps organized in the vicinity of the town. Almost all of them perished. On Aug. 25–26, 1942, the first deportation to the *Treblinka death camp took place. Other deportations followed on Oct. 6–9, 1942, and Oct. 27 of that year. Over 11,000 Jews perished in these deportations, but hundreds succeeded in fleeing into the surrounding forests. Some of them organized small guerrilla units that operated in the vicinity.

In October 1942 the Germans issued a decree about the establishment of a ghetto in Miedzyrzec Podlaski. Jews who fled into the forests were encouraged to return and promised that no more deportations would take place. The Germans managed to concentrate over 4,000 Jews in the ghetto. In December 1942 about 500 of them were deported to the Trawniki concentration camp, where all of them perished. On May 2, 1943, the ghetto was liquidated and all its inmates were deported to the Treblinka death camp and exterminated there. Only about 200 Jews were left in a forced labor camp, but they too were executed on July 18, 1943, when the town was declared *judenrein*. After the liberation of the town in July 1944, 129 Jewish survivors settled there, but after a short time they left because of the inimical attitude of the local Polish population. Organizations of former residents of Miedzyrzec Podlaski are active in Israel, the United States, and Argentina.

[Stefan Krakowski]

BIBLIOGRAPHY: Halpern, Pinkas, index; Cracow, Archiwum PAN, 3795 (= CAHJP, ḤM 6739); B. Wasiutyński, *Ludność żydowska w Polsce w wiekach xix i xx* (1930), 35; A. Eisenbach et al. (1963), index. HOLOCAUST: J. Horn (ed.), *Mezrich Zamlung: Isum* (comps.), *Żydzi a powstanie styczniowe, materiały i dokumenty 10 Yortsayt* (1952). **ADD. BIBLIOGRAPHY:** J. Horn, *Mayn khoruve haym* (1946).

MIELEC, town in Rzeszow province, S.E. Poland. The Jewish community of Mielec was first organized in the middle of the 17th century. The *Council of Four Lands decided in 1757 that the Mielec community should pay an annual tax of 1,200 zlotys to the *Opatow *kahal*. In 1765 there were 585 Jewish poll tax payers in Mielec and 326 in the surrounding villages; among the former were 12 tailors, three hatters, three bakers, two goldsmiths, five butchers, three *shoḥatim*, four musicians (*klezmer*), and three jesters (*badḥanim*). In the 19th century Mielec came under the influence of the Ḥasidim of *Chortkov and *Ropczyce and descendents of the *ẓaddik* of Ropczyce were rabbis there. The few wealthy Jews exported timber, dealt in grain, livestock, feathers, and building materials, and ran sawmills, but the majority engaged in petty trade, tailoring, shoemaking, smithery, and building. There were also some Jewish farmers in the nearby villages. An elementary school was established by the *Baron de Hirsch fund in 1900, as well as a Beth Jacob school for girls. In 1907 the Zionist association, Benei Yehudah, was founded. During the elections of 1907 and 1913 there were anti-Jewish riots in the town. In 1917 a "Borochov circle" was organized, as well as a Jewish library and sports clubs. The Jewish population of the town remained relatively static, increasing from 2,766 (56% of the total population) in 1880 to 2,819 (57%) in 1900 and 3,280 (53%) in 1910, then falling to 2,807 (50%) in 1920. Zionist parties, *He-Ḥalutz and *Agudat Israel, were active in Mielec between the two world wars.

[Arthur Cygielman]

Holocaust Period

By September 1939 the population had reached 4,000. On Sept. 13, 1939, the eve of Rosh Ha-Shanah, the Germans set a synagogue aflame and pushed 20 persons into the burning building. Those who tried to escape were shot. German soldiers sent some Jews into the slaughterhouse and set it aflame. Then the soldiers entered the *mikveh* and murdered the Jews present. On Sept. 15, 1939 (second day of Rosh Ha-Shanah), a second synagogue was set aflame. Jews suffered from administrative and economic restrictions, from the local Germans living at Czermin, and from forced labor at the camp near the Berdechow airport.

Early in January 1942 the General Government decided on the deportation of the Mielec Jews. Orders were given to deport 2,000 persons, and on March 7–9, 1942, the order was executed in greater dimensions. The sick and old were shot on the spot; others were transferred to the Berdechow airport, where a *Selektion* was made. A group of youths was sent to the labor camp at Pustkow; the remaining population was sent to Parczew, Wlodawa, Hrubieszow, Miedzyrzec, Susiec, and other towns in the Lublin district. The Jewish population there eased the suffering of the Mielec refugees by providing lodgings and public kitchens. Some months later, the Mielec refugees and these Jewish communities were exterminated.

Mielec was among the first cities that the General Government made *judenrein*. Near the workshops of the Heinkel airplane company, Mielec had a labor camp under the direct auspices of the SS. At first the camp employed 250 forced laborers, 80 of whom were from Mielec and others from Wielopole Skrzynskie. The population at the camp increased with the deportation of Mielec Jews in the winter of 1942. By the summer the population reached 1,000, including Jews from Tarnobrzeg and Huta Komarowska. The mortality rate at the camp reached more than 15 per day, excluding the sick who were shot. The camp was liquidated on Aug. 24, 1944. Some of the prisoners were transferred to Wieliczka and the rest to the camp at Flossenburg. Some 200 persons of the Mielec community survived.

[Aharon Weiss]

BIBLIOGRAPHY: Halpern, Pinkas, index; R. Mahler, *Yidn in Amolikn Poyln in Likht fun Tsifern* (1958), index; B. Wasiutyński, *Ludność żydowska w Polsce w wiekach xix i xx* (1930), 111, 146, 150, 156; M. Balaban, *Historja żydów Krakowie i na Kazimierzu*, 1 (1931), 351, 540; Y. Keitelman, in: *Fun Noentn Over* (1955), 401–51.

MIELZINER, MOSES (1828–1903), rabbi, professor. Mielziner was born and educated in Germany, where he began his rabbinic career. He headed a Jewish school in Copenhagen, Denmark, while earning his Ph.D. from the University of Giessen (1859). Immigrating to the United States, Mielziner served as a congregational rabbi and educator in New York City until 1879, when Isaac Mayer *Wise appointed him professor of Talmud at Hebrew Union College in Cincinnati. Upon Wise's death, Mielziner was chosen interim president of the seminary, a position he held for three years, from 1900 until his death.

Mielziner was a charter member of the Central Conference of American Rabbis (CCAR), and his scholarly input on relevant subjects had an important influence on early discussions of CCAR policy. He published several treatises on Jewish law – including a volume on *halakhah* and divorce and marriage, as well as an overview of rabbinic civil and criminal law – but is best known for his classic work *Introduction to the Talmud*, published originally in 1894 and reissued three times since; the most recent edition, which appeared in 1968, contains an updated bibliography compiled by Alexander *Guttmann. Mielziner's exposition of talmudic methodology – featuring a skillful dissection of the Talmud's distinctive system of technical terms and phrases adapted to its unique methods of investigation and demonstration – has been an indispensable handbook for the serious student of the Talmud for more than a century.

BIBLIOGRAPHY: K.M. Olitzky, L.J. Sussman, M.H. Stern, *Reform Judaism in America: A Biographical Dictionary and Sourcebook* (1993).

[Bezalel Gordon (2nd ed.)]

MIESES, FABIUS (1824–1898), Hebrew writer and scholar. Born in Brody (Galicia), Mieses moved to Cracow in 1840. Subsequently he lived in Brody (1846–54), Breslau (1854–67), and Leipzig (from 1867). Mieses wrote extensively in the Hebrew journals of his day, publishing poems as well as articles on Judaism, philosophy, and topical subjects. His major work, the first of its kind in Hebrew, is *Korot ha-Filosofyah ha-Ḥadashah* ("History of Modern Philosophy," 1887), of which only the first volume appeared in print. He also wrote in German, contributing regularly to *Orient*.

BIBLIOGRAPHY: I.A. Guenzig, *Elleh Toledot ha-Rav Fabius Mieses* (1890), first published in *Oẓar ha-Sifrut*, 3 (1890); Kressel, Leksikon, 2 (1967), 345.

[Getzel Kressel]

MIESES, JACQUES (Jacob; 1865–1954), German-British chess master and journalist. Mieses was born in Germany and went to England in 1938. He was famed for his collection of brilliancy prizes in the tournaments which he won, the best being in Vienna, 1907. Mieses was the doyen of German chess writers. He was known for his old-fashioned attacking style, which resulted in many brilliant games but few first prizes in major tournaments. From the 1920s, he was also the editor of many standard chess textbooks. In 1948, when the International Chess Federation began officially to award titles to leading players, Mieses was the first British player to be given the title of Grandmaster.

ADD. BIBLIOGRAPHY: D. Hooper and K. Whyld, *The Oxford Companion to Chess* (1996), 258–59.

[William D. Rubinstein (2nd ed.)]

MIESES, MATTHIAS (1885–1945), Yiddish philologist. Born in Galicia, he was a prolific writer in Hebrew, Polish, and German. His main interest, however, was Yiddish, about which he wrote much, although little in the language itself. His Hebrew articles in defense of Yiddish against its detractors involved him in a controversy with Nahum *Sokolow. At the *Czernowitz Yiddish Conference of 1908, he created a sensation with his well-reasoned, scholarly espousal of Yiddish. I.L. *Peretz asked for the widest possible distribution of Mieses' speech. In his German study on the origin of Yiddish, *Die Entstehungsursache der juedischen Dialekte* (1915), a pioneer work in Yiddish philology, Mieses fought for the emancipation of the so-called Jewish "jargon" and its recognition as a language on a par with other European national languages. Another work on Yiddish was *Die jiddische Sprache* (1924). Mieses spent his last years in Cracow and was sent to Auschwitz with all remaining Jews as the Russian troops approached that city. He died on the way at the Glewitz station.

BIBLIOGRAPHY: Z. Rejzen, Leksikon, 2 (1927), 375–9; LNYL, 6 (1965), 566–9; M. Ravitch, *Mayn Leksikon*, 2 (1947), 42–44; Kressel, Leksikon, 2 (1967), 344.

[Sol Liptzin]

MIESIS, JUDAH LEIB (1798–1831), leading member of the Galician Haskalah movement in the early 19th century. Born in Lvov, to a wealthy, prominent family, Miesis received a broad general education as well as a traditional Jewish one. His home was a meeting place for young *maskilim*, whom he encouraged and helped, and to whom he made available his large library. His first literary effort was the publication of a new edition of David *Caro's *Tekhunat ha-Rabbanim* (1822). Miesis' main work is *Kinat ha-Emet* ("The Zeal for Truth," 1823; 2nd ed. Lemberg, 1879), written in the form of a dialogue between Maimonides and Solomon Ḥelma (author of a commentary on Maimonides, *Mirkevet ha-Mishneh*). In the body of the work, as well as in an appendix containing quotations from Jewish scholars down through the ages, Miesis attacks the obscurantist beliefs in spirits, demons, mystical powers, and all the superstitious views fostered by the Orthodox rabbis. His highly rationalistic approach and his outspoken criticism of traditional beliefs were so extreme that even a number of *maskilim*, including his colleague and friend S.J. Rapoport, felt that he had gone too far and dissociated themselves from his views. Miesis also published a number of articles in the Hebrew journals (*Ha-Ẓefirah, Bikkurei ha-Ittim, Kerem Ḥemed*). He died of cholera in 1831.

BIBLIOGRAPHY: Waxman, Literature, 3 (1960^2), 165; R. Mahler, *Ha-Ḥasidut ve-ha-Haskalah* (1961), s.v.; Zinberg, Sifrut, 6 (1960), 29–35; Klausner, Sifrut, 2 (1960^3), 267–82; Kressel, Leksikon, 2 (1967), 343f. **ADD. BIBLIOGRAPHY:** Sh. Werses, *Megamot ve-Ẓurot be-Sifrut ha-Haskalah* (1990), index.

[Getzel Kressel]

MIGDAL (Heb. מִגְדָּל; "Tower"), moshavah in the Ginnosar Valley, N.W. of Lake Kinneret, established in 1910 by Jews from Moscow who hired laborers to work their land. In 1921 it became a camp for Third *Aliyah pioneers working on the construction of the Tiberias–Rosh Pinnah road. These laborers founded *Gedud ha-Avodah, the "Labor Battalion," at Migdal. From 1924 Jews from England and America acquired parcels of land at Migdal and some of them went to settle. Lord *Melchett's farm was among those established at the time. After 1948 the moshavah was enlarged as new immigrants settled. In 1949 it received municipal council status. Banana, date palm, and other fruit orchards, out-of-season vegetable gardens, and dairy cattle constituted its principal farming branches. It also had resort facilities. The population numbered 535 in 1970 and 1,390 in 2002, occupying an area of 4.6 sq. mi. (12 sq. km.). The historical name of the site is *Magdala.

[Efraim Orni / Shaked Gilboa (2nd ed.)]

MIGDAL HA-EMEK (Heb. מִגְדַּל הָעֵמֶק; "Tower of the Valley"), town with municipal council status in Lower Galilee, 4 mi. (7 km.) S.W. of Nazareth, founded in 1952 with the aim of absorbing inhabitants of transitory immigrant camps in the vicinity. Real progress started at the end of the 1950s, when industrial enterprises opened there. The population increased from 1,650 in 1955 to 8,200 in 1968 when 67% of the inhabitants were from Morocco and other North African countries, 19% from Romania, and 7.5% from Iraq, while 1% were veteran Israelis and the rest from different countries. Approximately half of the town's gainfully employed worked in local factories, the largest of which were leather and cosmetic plants and produce mainly for export. In 1969 it was said to have the highest "export-dollar" income per capita in the country. Its educational network comprised 2,700 pupils in 1968, and maintained two comprehensive high schools. In 1988 Migdal ha-Emek received city status and in 2002 its population was 24,500 – a third new immigrants – with an area of 2.8 sq. mi. (7.3 sq. km.). The city expanded its industry to include a number of hi-tech firms but income remained well below the national average. The city overlooks a beautiful landscape, with a wide view over the Jezreel Valley in the south, and is surrounded by extensive woodlands, among them the *Balfour Forest.

WEBSITE: www.migdal-haemeq.muni.il.

[Efraim Orni / Shaked Gilboa (2nd ed.)]

MIGDOL (Heb. מִגְדֹּל).

(1) Canaanite city, mentioned in the list of cities conquered by Thutmosis III (no. 71) with Socoh (Ra's al-Shuwayka) and Yaham (Khirbat Yamma). It is identified with Khirbat Majdal southeast of *Ḥaderah. Sherds of the Late Bronze Age were found on the site.

(2) Egyptian border fortress near Baal-Zephon (Ex. 14:2; Num. 33:7), inhabited by Jews in Jeremiah's time (Jer. 44:1; Ezek. 29:10). It is the Greek Magdolos and the Migdol of Baalsephon in the demotic Cairo papyrus (31.169). It is present-day Tell al-Khayrī near Pelusium.

[Michael Avi-Yonah]

MIGRATIONS. Jewish migrations have a history of thousands of years: the wanderings of the Patriarchs; the Exodus from Egypt; the Babylonian Exile; the existence of Jewish groups outside Ereẓ Israel in the Second Temple period; the dispersion of the Jewish people in the Roman and Near Eastern empires after the destruction of the Second Temple; the spread of the Jews to many countries of the Christian and Islamic world; the attraction of Jews to places with favorable conditions, and, on the other hand, departures from countries as a consequence of persecutions and expulsions – culminating in the scattering of the Jews of the Iberian Peninsula and the settlement of some Jews (and Marranos) in the New World since the early stages of the European colonization. In small numbers, Jews made their way to the Holy Land throughout the ages of the Diaspora. From the second third of the 19th century, a noticeable stream of Jewish migration flowed from Europe to the United States.

The modern period of intensive Jewish migration began in 1881. Since then, migrations have completely changed the world map of the geographical distribution of the Jews. In the demographic history of mankind, this period is generally characterized by the relative frequency of intercontinental migrations, especially from Europe; the Jews, however, exceeded by far other peoples of similar or superior size in the relative volume of long-distance migration. The world Jewish population at the beginning of the 1880s, which is estimated to have been more than 7½ million, is almost equaled by the number of Jews who have taken part in international migrations since then (c. 6 million in intercontinental migrations). Another feature characterizing Jewish migrations is the motivation behind them. Whereas individuals from other nations migrated over great distances primarily for economic motives, the great majority of Jews also tried to escape discrimination and were in fact refugees, especially since the 1930s; on the other hand, *aliyah* to Ereẓ Israel was often based on idealistic motives. Consequently, whereas a considerable portion of the economically motivated migrants from other nations eventually returned to their countries of origin, remigration was much rarer among Jews.

When a substantial number of Jewish migrants had reached a country, further Jewish immigration was thereby facilitated (except for instances of worsening of the political or economic situation in the country or of the immigration regulations). The established Jews tended to assist – whether individually or through organizations – in the arrival and establishment of their fellow Jews. The changes in environmental influences produced by migration have strongly contributed to profound alterations in the economic, social, and demographic characteristics of the Jews in recent generations. Moreover, migrations have removed, before it became too late, large numbers of Jews from areas where they would otherwise have been faced with the danger of physical destruction. The Nazi persecutions might have come much closer to their aim of a genocidal "final solution" had it not been for the preceding large-scale emigration from Europe. The period of intensive Jewish migration since 1881 can be divided into three main parts, with several subdivisions.

1881–1914

This period is characterized by a large flow of Jewish migration from Eastern Europe overseas and by the virtual absence of administrative restrictions on free entry into the main immigration recipient – the United States of America. The total volume of Jewish intercontinental migrations during 1840–80 has been estimated at little above 200,000, but for the years 1881–1914 at about 2,400,000. The overwhelming majority of these Jewish migrants came from Eastern Europe: the czarist empire, the eastern regions of Austria-Hungary (especially Galicia), and Romania. They were escaping the hardships inflicted by poverty, antisemitic discrimination, or political oppression. Since East European Jewry experienced a strong natural increase at the time, emigration also served as a regulator drawing away the Jewish population surplus for which there were not enough opportunities for a livelihood in those backward and inhospitable surroundings. About 85% of the Jewish intercontinental migrants turned to the U.S. Conspicuous among the other destinations were (in descending order of numbers) Canada, Argentina, Ereẓ Israel, and South Africa.

The overseas movement of East European Jews started in 1881, after a series of pogroms in Russia. Its intensity increased in the first half of the 1890s, subsequently ebbed somewhat, but rose sharply after the great 1905 wave of pogroms in Russia, which came in the wake of the abortive revolution of that year. From mid-1905 to mid-1906, a peak figure of 154,000 Jews arrived in the U.S., and the total volume of Jewish international migrations in the same year has been estimated at 200–250,000. Similar figures were reached in the following year and again directly before the outbreak of World War I.

In most immigration countries, the statistics on Jewish arrivals were markedly higher during the second part of the period (1901–14) than during its first part (1881–1900). The outbreak of World War I put an abrupt stop to this vast movement while it was still gathering momentum. The absolute and relative size of intercontinental migration, by countries of destination, is seen in Table 1: Intercontinental Migrations, 1881–1914.

In the U.S. (see Table 2: Jewish Immigration to the U.S., 1899–1914), those registered as Hebrews accounted for nearly 11% of all migrants during 1899–1914 (the total share of the Jews may have even been somewhat greater as it is not certain that every Jew was actually registered under "Hebrews"). The number of Jews was second largest of all the immigrant national groups that came to the U.S. during that period; if, however, remigration is deducted and only net migration is considered, the difference between the Jews and the top group – the Italians – almost disappears. The Jews differed from other immigrant groups in the U.S. by their low proportion of remigration – seven remigrants per 100 immigrants during 1908–14, as compared to an overall average of 31 per hundred (among some national groups, remigration exceeded half the volume of immigration). Because of the permanent nature of their immigration, the Jews often brought their entire families with them and thus had higher proportions of women and children than other immigrant groups (see Table 3: Immigrant Characteristics, U.S.).

The Jewish immigrants to the U.S. were also distinguished by the high proportion registered as industrial workers: 66 per 100 wage earners. In the U.S. immigration statistics of 1899–1914, Jews thus accounted for 31% of all industrial workers, and in some branches, especially clothing manufacture, they were a clear majority. During 1899–1914, the distribution by previous country of residence of the close to 1,500,000 Jews who immigrated to the U.S. was as follows: Russia, 71.7%; Austria-Hungary, 16.2%; Romania, 4.2%; Great Britain, 4.0%; Canada, 1.2%; Germany, 0.7%; other countries,

Table 1: Jewish Intercontinental Migrations, 1881–1914 (rough estimates)

Country of destination	1881–1914 Total		1881–1900		1901–1914	
	Percent	Absolute Numbers (thousands)	Percent	Absolute Numbers (thousands)	Percent	Absolute Numbers (thousands)
Total	100.0	2,400	100.0	770	100.0	1,630
United States	85.0	2,040	88.0	675	84.0	1,365
Canada	4.0	105	1.0	10	6.0	95
Argentina	5.0	113	3.0	25	6.0	88
Other Latin American countries	0.5	14	0.5	2	0.5	12
South Africa	2.0	43	3.0	23	1.0	20
Ereẓ Israel	3.0	70	4.0	30	2.0	40
Other	0.5	15	0.5	5	0.5	10
Yearly average of migrants, absolute numbers (thousands)		70.0		38.0		116.0
Per 1,000 of Jewish population in whole world		6.8		4.2		9.7

Table 2: Jewish Immigration to the United States, 1899–1914

Year[2]	Number[1]	Year[2]	Number[1]
1899	37,415	1907	149,182
1900	60,764	1908	103,387
1901	58,098	1909	57,551
1902	57,688	1910	84,260
1903	76,203	1911	91,223
1904	106,236	1912	80,595
1905	129,910	1913	101,330
1906	153,748	1914	138,051

1 The category Hebrew was first introduced into official migration statistics in 1899.

2 Fiscal year, i.e., the 12 months ending in June of the year indicated.

Table 3: Immigrant Characteristics, U.S. – Differential Characteristics of Jewish and Total Immigrants to the United States, 1899–1914

	Jewish Immigrants	Total Immigrants
	Percent	
Females	44.0	31.7
Age distribution		
0–13	24.4	12.4
14–44	69.8	82.4
45 and over	5.8	5.2
Dependents	43.3	26.3
Occupational distribution of earners		
Agriculture	2.6	28.1
Clothing manufacture	39.6	} 17.8
Other industry	26.0	
Commerce and transport	9.2	4.7
Liberal professions	1.3	1.5
Unskilled labor	21.3	47.9

2.0% (but among the Jews arriving in the U.S. from countries outside Eastern Europe, particularly Great Britain and Canada, many were actually of East European origin).

Immigration to Ereẓ Israel during the same period fell immensely short of the mighty stream that turned to the U.S. In the history of modern Ereẓ Israel it is usual to distinguish between the First Aliyah (1882–1903) and the Second Aliyah (1904–14). Altogether about 70,000 Jews migrated to the country, but a considerable number of them left again, mainly because of economic difficulties. Due to the overwhelming attraction of the U.S. and of other economically promising overseas countries, the arrivals in Ereẓ Israel accounted for only 3% of Jewish intercontinental migrants.

During 1881–1914 there was also considerable international migration of Jews within Europe – generally from east to west and, particularly, from Russia and Romania to Central and Western European countries. This movement has been estimated to include 350,000 persons so that the total of Jewish international migrants over that period amounted to about 2,750,000. There were also large-scale streams of Jewish migration within the extended empires of Europe of that time: from east (Galicia, Bukovina, Poznan) to west in the Austro-Hungarian and German empires; in a southern direction (Odessa) within Russia. In addition, Jews in many countries participated with relative intensity in the movement from smaller localities to large cities. Within cities, the socio-economic rise of many Jews enabled them to move to more well-to-do residential quarters.

1915–May 1948

In some ways, this is an intermediate period between the intensive migration movements preceding and following it that turned to the U.S. and to the new State of Israel, respectively. It was also the period in which the *Holocaust occurred, profoundly changing the entire demographic makeup of the Jewish people. This period can be broken down into several subdivisions; common to most of them was the existence of restrictions to the free movement of Jewish migrants. The main statistical data on the period are concentrated in Table 4: Jewish Intercontinental Migrations, 1915–May 1948, and Table 5: Jewish Immigration to the United States and Ereẓ Israel, 1915–May 1948.

During and immediately after World War I, intercontinental migrations of Jews dwindled, but there were large movements of Jewish refugees in Europe to escape from the areas of the hostilities and from some of the subsequent political upheavals. Then the volume of overseas migrations swelled again, comprising more than 400,000 Jews during 1921–25; 280,000 went to the U.S. of whom nearly 120,000 arrived during the year ending in mid-1921. In the same year, Jews accounted for 15% of all immigrants to the U.S., and in the following year the figure rose to 17%. On the other hand, during 1921–24 the number of Jewish emigrants from the U.S. amounted to less than 1% of the number of Jewish immigrants. In Palestine, newly under British Mandatory rule, increased Jewish immigration came in response to the promise of a Jewish National Home. During 1919–26 (Third Aliyah and major part of the Fourth Aliyah), nearly 100,000 Jews immigrated to Ereẓ Israel. Other streams of Jewish migrants found their way to South America.

In Europe, the tendency continued for Jews to move from countries in the east to Central and Western Europe. The post-World War I migration impetus, which continued, as it were, the prewar trend, was soon halted by a combination of factors, among which the following were outstanding:

RESTRICTIONS ON IMMIGRATION. In the U.S., the previously almost unfettered influx of overseas migrants was curbed by two laws, enacted in 1921 and 1924. The limitations imposed by the second law – annual quotas for each country of origin, amounting to no more than 2% of the respective immigrant population already in the country at the comparatively early date of 1890 – affected with particular intensity prospective migrants from Eastern Europe, i.e., from the main area of Jewish emigration. The number of Jewish immigrants to the U.S. was thus forced down drastically: it declined to little more than 10,000 per annum during 1925–30. The other main immigration countries for Jews also increasingly curbed immigration,

Table 4: Jewish Intercontinental Migrations[1], 1915–May 1948 (rough estimates)

Country of destination	1915–May 1948 Total		1915–1931		1932–1939		1940–May 1948	
	Absolute Numbers	Percent	Absolute Numbers	Percent	Absolute Numbers	Percent	Absolute Numbers	Percent
Total	1,600	100	760	100	540	100	300	100
United States	650	41	415	55	110	20	125	42
Canada	60	4	45	6	5	1	10	3
Argentina	115	7	80	10	25	5	10	3
Other Latin American countries	140	9	65	9	60	11	15	5
South Africa	25	1	15	2	10	2	0	0
Ereẓ Israel	485	30	115	15	250	46	120	40
Other	125	8	25	3	80	15	20	7
Yearly average of migrants								
Absolute numbers (thousands)	48.0		45.0		68.0		37.0	
Per 1,000 of Jewish population in whole world	3.3		3.1		4.2		2.6	
Per 1,000 of Jewish population in main emigration regions[2]	7.8		6.3		10.2		8.7	

1 Includes migrants from Asian countries to Ereẓ Israel; excludes internal migration between the European and Asian parts of the U.S.S.R. and remigration to region of origin.
2 Up to 1931: Eastern Europe (inc. U.S.S.R.); 1932–May 1948; total Europe (excl. U.S.S.R.).

through legislation and administrative practice, by reducing the overall number of immigrants permitted and/or by insisting on financial and other requirements for their admission. Restrictions were created both in overseas countries – e.g., Canada, Argentina, Brazil, South Africa, Australia, Palestine (quotas based on economic "absorptive capacity") – and in Western Europe.

OBSTACLES TO EMIGRATION. After the first few years of the Communist regime, the Soviet Union began to frown on emigration and soon brought it virtually to a standstill.

POLITICAL AND ECONOMIC CONDITIONS. After the political and economic dislocations in Europe in the wake of World War I, which had also adversely affected many Jews, a stabilization occurred there. In Palestine, on the other hand, there were absorption difficulties and unemployment, leading to relatively considerable emigration in the later part of the 1920s. In the second half of the 1920s a majority of the then comparatively infrequent Jewish overseas migrants went to countries other than either the U.S. or Palestine – especially to Latin America.

In the 1930s, the objective motivation for Jewish emigration from Central and Eastern Europe increased tragically, but the would-be migrants encountered ever growing difficulties in gaining admission to other countries. The special motivation for departure arose from the accession of Hitler to power in Germany, the spread of authoritarian and more-or-less overtly antisemitic regimes in other states of Europe, and the great economic depression, which affected the livelihood of many Jews and provided further incentive to antisemitic agitation. However, with cruel irony, the very factors which made Jews wish to leave rendered prospective immigration countries unwilling to admit considerable numbers of Jews, so as to avoid aggravating their own international and internal problems. The more desperate the need to escape became for large numbers of Jews, the more tightly most prospective immigration countries shut the gates of entrance.

Whereas prior to World War I Jewish long-distance migration was strongly determined by economic considerations, from the 1930s until quite recently it has been predominantly a movement of refugees trying to escape oppression and unable to return to their former land for political, racial, or religious reasons. As opportunity allowed, Jews escaped from Nazi horrors, from antisemitism and Communist regimes in Eastern Europe and, especially after 1948, from the outbursts of intolerance and fanaticism in Arab lands. International efforts in the Nazi period to mitigate the plight of the Jewish refugees and find them new homes – e.g., through appointment of a special high commissioner for refugees by the League of Nations as early as in the autumn of 1933 and through the *Evian Conference of 1938 – led to few tangible results.

In the history of Jewish migration, the 1930s are characterized by the following traits: the prominence of emigrants from Central Europe – Germany and, toward the end of the decade, Austria and Czechoslovakia (about 350,000 Jews are estimated to have left Germany, Austria, and Czechoslovakia before the outbreak of World War II); the continuation of departures from Eastern Europe (except for the U.S.S.R., where exit was barred); and the growth in importance of Palestine as a major destination for Jewish refugees (in addition to the continuing idealistic motives for *aliyah*). During the period 1932–39, nearly one half of all intercontinental Jewish migrants turned to Palestine (Fifth Aliyah). In the years 1934–36, Palestine attracted even a strong majority of the intercontinental Jewish migrants. Then the protracted Arab riots (1936–39) led to a deterioration of the British authorities' immigration

Table 5: Jewish Immigrants to the United States and Ereẓ Israel, 1915–May 1948[1]

Year	United States[2]	Ereẓ Israel[3]
1915	26,497	
1916	15,108	
1917	17,342	
1918	3,672	
1919	3,055	1,806
1920	14,292	8,223
1921	119,036	8,294
1922	53,524	8,685
1923	49,719	8,175
1924	49,989	13,892
1925	10,292	34,386
1926	10,267	13,855
1927	11,483	3,034
1928	11,639	2,178
1929	12,479	5,249
1930	11,526	4,944
1931	5,692	4,075
1932	2,755	12,553
1933	2,372	37,337
1934	4,134	45,267
1935	4,837	66,472
1936	6,252	29,595
1937	11,352	10,629
1938	19,736	14,675
1939	43,450	31,195
1940	36,945	10,643
1941	23,737	4,592
1942	10,608	4,206
1943	4,705	10,063
1944		15,552
1945		15,259
1946		18,760
1947		22,098
Jan–May 1948	..	17,165

1 Official immigration statistics from Ereẓ Israel are available as from 1919; in the United States, the category "Hebrew" was included in official migration statistics only between 1899–1943.

2 In the United States, fiscal year, i.e., the 12 months ending in June of year indicated.

3 Includes tourists settling.

policy toward the Jews. Under the shadow of the impending world war, the British promulgated the White Paper of May 1939, which severely curtailed Jewish immigration for the following five years and virtually provided for its cessation at the close of that period. A consequence of this policy were organized and partly successful attempts at *"Illegal" immigration to Palestine.

During 1932–39 the U.S. and Canada together received only a fifth of the total intercontinental Jewish migrants. It was only when the above-mentioned restrictions on Jewish entry into Palestine were applied and World War II broke out (the U.S. did not join in the hostilities until the end of 1941) that Jewish immigration to the U.S. rose to more than 120,000 during 1938–42. In some of those years, Jewish immigration to the U.S. constituted a majority of both total Jewish intercontinental migration and of general immigration to the U.S. The 1930s also witnessed a considerable amount of international migration of Jews within Europe, from the central and eastern parts of the area (outside U.S.S.R.) to countries of Western Europe.

As the German armies swept over most of continental Europe, there were tragically few opportunities for the Jews to leave Nazi dominated areas. The most notable exception was in the east, where many Soviet Jews, together with Jews from Poland and other neighboring countries, managed to retreat before the invaders. Many joined the armed struggle against the common enemy; a large proportion of the Jewish civilians who were thus saved spent the remaining war years in Soviet Siberia and Central Asia. Sweden gave refuge to the Jews of occupied Denmark. On the whole, however, millions of European Jews remained confined under Nazi sway, left to their fate by an indifferent world engrossed in war. No more than 45,000 Jews were allowed to reach Palestine during the five years 1940–44. Among the "illegal" immigrants who were turned back from the shores of Palestine by the British, hundreds of lives were lost in tragic events such as the explosion on board the *Patria* in 1940 and the sinking of the *Struma* in the Black Sea in 1942. On the other hand, among the seven to eight million Jews caught in Nazi-dominated areas of Europe, the intensity of movement from one place to another reached fantastic heights. Most of the Jews were driven from their homes to be deported and crammed into ghettos, concentration camps, labor camps, and extermination camps or transferred from one to another of those places of horror. Only a small minority could join the partisans, go into hiding, escape into Soviet or neutral territory, etc. Except for those executed forthwith in their locality of residence, nearly all Jews in Nazi-occupied Europe "migrated" before the eventual doom overcame most of them.

After the war there was a reverse movement – back to previous places of residence, on a much smaller numerical scale, due to the paucity of survivors. This return migration took place within the areas previously occupied by the Nazis and as a repatriation movement of Polish and other Eastern European Jews from the Soviet Union. Jews also participated in some of the new population transfers in Eastern Europe from territories newly incorporated into the Soviet Union (eastern Poland, Bessarabia, Carpatho-Ruthenia) to other territories, some of which had been vacated by former German inhabitants (Silesia). The Jewish repatriates to places in Eastern Europe, however, found themselves haunted not only by the memory of their families and fellow Jews who had been maltreated and killed there, but also by fresh outbursts of antisemitism and active hostility toward the repatriates (e.g., the pogrom in *Kielce, Poland, in 1946). Many therefore moved to *Displaced Persons camps in Germany, Austria, and Italy, which accommodated about a quarter of a million Jews at the end of 1946. Most of them fervently wished to go to Ereẓ Israel and start a new life there. But the British authorities admitted little more than 70,000 Jews from 1945 to May 1948, turning back many "illegal" immigrants (e.g., the passengers of the *Exodus* in 1947) or interning them in Cyprus; the DP camps were emptied only after the establishment of the State of Israel. A smaller stream of DPs went to the U.S., where emergency legislation granted admission above the usual quotas. The following international organizations and Jewish bodies played a prominent part in the care, transportation, and resettlement of the DPs: UNRRA (United Nations Relief and Rehabilitation Administration), IRO (International Refugee Organization), the American Jewish *Joint Distribution Committee, the *Jewish Agency for Palestine, HIAS (Hebrew Sheltering and Immigrant Aid Society), the *World Jewish Congress, etc.

There was a high proportion of young adults among the migrants to Palestine throughout the Mandatory period (1919–May 1948) in keeping with the pioneering character of many of the newcomers (*ḥalutzim*), part of whom had received agricultural training prior to leaving their countries of origin. The proportion of young adults was particularly high among the "illegal" immigrants. Although the adjustment of Jewish overseas migrants to their new surroundings was universally necessary, a special situation existed in Palestine because of the emphasis of Zionist ideology on manual, and especially agricultural, work and the dynamic process of creating a new nation consisting of all economic and social strata. On the other hand, the age composition and occupational structure of the Jewish immigrants to the U.S. in the Nazi period reflected the "aging," as well as the considerable proportion of liberal professions and commerce, characteristic of Central European Jews at that time.

Throughout the period 1915–48 there was also a large volume of Jewish migration within countries. The case of the vast Soviet Union is of particular importance in discussing interregional migrations. After the abolition of the *Pale of Settlement following the Revolution (1917), hundreds of thousands of Jews moved into the central and southern parts of the country. Subsequent transfers of Jews to Siberia – not only to *Birobidzhan with its ill-starred experiment of Jewish territorial autonomy focusing on agriculture, but especially to new industrial centers that were set up in Siberia – became increasingly important. In addition, in most countries of the world, the urbanization of the Jews was accentuated by residential changes from smaller to larger localities, and especially to the biggest population centers of each country. In most cases Jewish overseas migrants turned directly to the main urban centers of their new country. Compared with this predominant trend, the movement to Jewish agricultural settlement – in Palestine, Argentina, Crimea – was of minor numerical importance.

[Usiel Oscar Schmelz]

Demographic and Economic Dimensions of International Migration: World Jewry and Israel (1948–2005)

INTRODUCTION. The study of international migration concerning the State of Israel revolves around five main issues that have attracted extremely unequal amounts of attention among researchers: (a) Jewish immigration (*aliyah*); (b) the Palestinian exodus of 1948–49; (c) Jewish emigration (*yeridah*); (d) labor immigration (legal or illegal), largely of a temporary character; and (e) family reunions (mostly of Palestinians into Israel). The terms *aliyah* (ascent) for immigration and *yeridah* (descent) for emigration indicate widespread value judgments toward these sociodemographic processes in Israeli society. Most of past research on Israel's migrations has focused on *aliyah* and longer-term immigrant absorption. This exposition attempts to briefly review each of the main aspects though it is naturally influenced by the diverse amount and quality of available data.

THE DIASPORA AND WORLD JEWISH MIGRATION. Israel is the successor country of the Jewish state established together with the Arab state by the UN General Assembly in its November 29, 1947, Resolution 181 decreeing the end of British Mandate and the partition of Palestine. In its Declaration of Independence in May 1948, the State of Israel affirmed its aim to serve both as the focal point for Jews worldwide and a democratic society offering equal civil and cultural rights to all citizens, irrespective of religious and ethnic origin. The demographic, socioeconomic, and cultural development of Israel cannot be understood without considering the key role played by immigration. It is therefore necessary to examine immigration first, and to analyze migration to, and from, Israel in the framework of a broader world Jewish migration system.

The call for mass immigration through the "ingathering of the exiles" and the "fusion of the diasporas" constituted basic tenets of the new society, legally sanctioned through the Law of Return (*Ḥok ha-Shevut*). Adopted in 1950, this law was the founding instrument of immigration policy. It established a broad definitional framework granting virtually unlimited immigration rights and Israeli citizenship to Jews, their children, grandchildren, and the respective spouses, irrespective of their religious or national affiliation. This entailed the related concepts of *core* Jewish population, and *enlarged* Jewish population, including persons of Jewish origin but currently of another denomination and other non-Jewish household members (see Table 6: Jewish Intercontinental Migration, May 1948–1964).

During the late stages of the Ottoman Empire, and to a larger extent under the post-World War I British Mandate, migration to Palestine led to the growth of the Jewish community (*yishuv*) from 43,000 in 1890 to half a million in 1945. During the 19th century and the first half of the 20th century, when the entire territory of Palestine hosted a large majority of Arabs, Jewish immigration significantly contributed to create the modern socio-economic and logistical infrastructure in the country. Rapid economic development in areas of heavier Jewish settlement along the Mediterranean coast and in Upper and Lower Galilee also stimulated internal migration from other parts of Palestine.

During the 1948–49 War of Independence, a large part of the Arab population of the territories allocated to the Jewish state by the UN fled the area, leading to what has since become the Palestinian refugee problem. According to Israeli sources, the number of Arabs who left the territory under Israeli control was estimated at between 625,000 and 650,000. Higher estimates exist and reflect conflicting views of the same history, namely competing evaluations of the size of the Arab population in the Jewish areas in 1948, and the permanent status as residents of some of those who fled, or who were cut off from their main sources of economic support there.

At the time of independence in 1948 the population of Israel comprised 630,000 Jews. An estimated 156,000 Arabs remained in Israel at the end of 1949. Between 1948 and the end of 2003, Israel's total net migration balance amounted to 2,385,800 individuals (excluding the exodus of Palestinian refugees). This resulted from 2,990,800 new immigrants and immigrant citizens and 605,000 emigrants, or a ratio of about five immigrants per single emigrant. Of the total international migration net balance in 1948–2003, 2,153,200 were Jewish, 158,000 were non-Jewish family members of the latter, 40,200 were Arabs (Muslims, Christians, and Druze), and another 34,400 otherwise unaccounted for probably reflected reclassification of group identifications and other data corrections.

In early 2005, Israel's population totaled 6,864,000, excluding the Palestinian population of West Bank and Gaza areas occupied and administered by Israel since the 1967 war, and partly transferred to the Palestinian Authority following the 1993 Oslo agreements. Of the total Israeli population, 5,234,800 were Jewish and 290,300 were non-Jewish members of Jewish households, making a total of 5,525,100. Of Israel's ethnically Arab population of 1,338,900, the vast majority (82%) were Palestinian Muslims, the rest being nearly equally split between Christian Arabs of various denominations (primarily Greek Orthodox) and Druze. These figures include about 240,000 Arabs residents of the area of East Jerusalem annexed by Israel in 1967, about 15,000 Druze residents of the Golan Heights, as well as 237,000 Israeli residents of the West Bank and Gaza. In addition, the number of Jewish residents in East Jerusalem neighborhoods is estimated at 185,000.

The changing structure and feedback of modern Jewish international migration fit a systemic perspective. The number, direction, and characteristics of Jewish migrants at any time were significantly determined by the existing worldwide distribution of Jews (see Table 7: Jewish Population Estimates, by Major Religions, 1900–2005) – which was in turn largely the product of previous migration. Between 1880 and 2004, over nine million Jews migrated between countries (see Table 8: Jewish International Migration, 1969–2002). Of these, about 2.4 million moved between 1880 and 1918, 1.6 million between 1919 and 1948, 1.9 million between 1948 and 1968, and about 3 million between 1969 and 2004. These figures do not include another several hundred thousand Jews who migrated between neighboring countries within the same continent (in addition to Israel and the United States), nor do they provide a full account of return migration. What they do include is the significant migration of Jews from North Africa to Western Europe, particularly from Morocco, Algeria, and Tunisia to France, and from Libya and Egypt to Italy between the late 1940s and the late 1960s. The departure to Europe and in part to North and Latin America of these over 300,000 Jewish mi-

Table 6: Jewish Intercontinental Migrations[1], May 1948–1964 (rough estimates)

Country of destination		Total May 1948–1964	May 1948–1951	1952–1954	1955–1957	1958–1960	1961–1964
					Absolute Numbers (thousands)		
Total		1,780	840	100	245	145	450
United States, Canada		240	105	30	30	30	45
Israel		1,210	685	55	165	75	230
Other		330	50	15	50	40	175
thereof: Europe		255	30 (1948–1954)		35	190 (1958–1964)	
						Percent	
Total		100	100	100	100	100	100
United States, Canada		14	12	30	12	21	10
Israel		68	82	55	68	52	51
Other		18	6	15	20	27	39
Yearly average of migrants							
Absolute numbers (thousands)		106	233	33	81	48	112
Per 1,000 of Jewish population	in whole world	8.6	19.9		6.6	3.8	8.6
	in main emigrations regions[2]	82.5	92.8		72.8	47.8	144.9

1 Includes migrants from Asian countries to Ereẓ Israel; excludes internal migration between the European and Asian parts of the U.S.S.R. and remigration to region of origin.

2 May 1948–1951: total Europe (excluding U.S.S.R.), Asia (excluding Israel and U.S.S.R.), North Africa. 1952–1964: Eastern Europe (excluding U.S.S.R.), Asia (excluding Israel and U.S.S.R.), North Africa.

Table 7: Jewish Population Estimates, by Major Regions, 1900–2005

Region	1900	1939	1948	1970	2005
Total (thousands)	10,600	16,500	11,185	12,633	13,033
Total (%)	100.0	100.0	100.0	100.0	100.0
Palestine/Israel[a]	0.5	2.7	5.8	20.4	40.2
East Europe[b]	71.6	49.4	23.8	15.6	2.9[c]
West Europe	11.1	8.2	9.3	8.9	8.8[c]
Other Asia[b,d]	3.6	3.4	4.2	3.9	0.3
North Africa[e]	2.9	3.0	5.3	0.6	0.0
North America[f]	9.7	30.0	45.6	45.0	43.4
Latin America	0.2	2.6	4.7	4.1	3.0
Southern Africa[g], Oceania[h]	0.4	0.7	1.3	1.5	1.4

a Palestine until 14 May 1948; Israel since 15 May, 1948.
b The Asian regions of Russia and Turkey are included in Europe.
c Population of seven countries formerly in East Europe which joined the EU in 2004 was included in West Europe.
d Including the republics of the former Soviet Union in Asia.
e Including Ethiopia.
f USA and Canada.
g South Africa, Zimbabwe, and other sub-Saharan countries.
h Australia, New Zealand.

Table 8: Jewish International Migration, by Major Areas of Origin and Destination – Absolute Numbers, Percent Distribution, Yearly Rates per 1000 Jewish Population in Countries of Origin, 1969–2002

Areas of origin and destination	1969-1976	1977-1988	1989-1996	1997-2002	Total
Absolute numbers (thousands)					
Grand total	451	589	1,240	535	2,815
Yearly average	56	49	155	89	83
Percent					
Grand total	100	100	100	100	100
From Eastern Europe	39	41	64	62	55
To Western countries	8	29	23	25	22
To Israel[a]	32	12	41	36	33
From Asia-Africa[b]	14	14	19	10	16
To Western countries	5	7	1	1	3
To Israel[a]	9	8	18	9	13
From Israel to Western countries	20	24	11	17	16
From Western countries to Israel[a]	27	20	5	12	13
Regional subtotals					
To Western countries	33	60	35	43	41
To Israel[a]	67	40	65	57	59
Percent to Israel					
Out of total Eastern Europe	80	71	64	59	60
Out of total Asia-Africa	64	53	95	90	81
Yearly emigration per 1000 Jews in country of origin					
Grand total	4	4	12	7	6
From Eastern Europe	10	12	110	97	51
To Western countries	2	8	38	40	20
To Israel[a]	8	3	72	57	31
From Asia-Africa[b]	44	73	146	134	97
To Western countries	14	32	42	13	27
To Israel	30	40	94	121	70
From Israel to Western countries[c]	4	3	4	3	4
From Western countries to Israel[a]	2	1	1	1	1

Source: Adapted from DellaPergola, "The Global Context of Migration to Israel" (1998), 58. Based on data from Israel Central Bureau of Statistics; HIAS; and various other sources.
a Since 1970 includes immigrant citizens (from West).
b Since 1990, Asian regions of FSU included in Asia-Africa.
c All emigration from Israel included here.

grants, along with the larger contingents that moved to Israel, virtually put an end to the bi-millenarian Jewish presence in North Africa, and substantially strengthened the Jewish communities in Europe.

Of all Jewish international migrants, Palestine – and since 1948 Israel – was the country of destination of 3% in 1880–1918, 30% in 1919–48, 69% in 1948–68, 52% in 1969–88, and 61% in 1989–2004. Between 1948 and 2003, Israel attracted 73% of the total Jewish emigration from North Africa and the Middle East, and 65% of the total from Eastern Europe. Since 1969, the percent of Jewish migrants choosing Israel from each main region reached 81% and 60%, respectively (Table 8).

Table 9: Jewish Immigrants to Israel[1] by Origin, May 1948–1967

Year	Number	Percent born in Europe, America, or Oceania
May–Dec. 1948	101,828	87.3
1949	239,576	53.7
1950	170,249	50.9
1951	175,249	29.2
1952	24,369	29.6
1953	11,326	28.4
1964	18,370	13.9
1955	37,478	8.6
1956	56,234	13.8
1957	71,224	57.6
1958	27,082	55.3
1959	23,895	66.3
1960	24,510	70.5
1961	47,638	52.9
1962	61,328	22.6
1963	64,364	31.8
1964	54,716	58.3
1965	30,736	53.6
1966	15,730	57.7
1967	14,327	38.2

1 Including tourists settling.

Jewish emigration propensities relative to local Jewish population size were consistently the highest from countries in North Africa and the Middle East, substantially high from Eastern Europe and the Balkans though reflecting highly variable opportunities to exit, comparatively low from Israel, and the lowest from the aggregate of Western countries. More recently (1969–2002), rates of emigration of Jews to any destination per 1,000 Jewish residents in each area were 97, 51, 4, and 1, respectively (Table 8).

The continuous wave-like pattern of Jewish international migration demonstrates recurrent crises involving discrimination and violence which negatively affected the position of Jewish communities in different parts of the world. The consequent need for prompt and large-scale relocation, and recurring limitations in the volume of migrants allowed to leave their countries of origin or to enter new countries of destination, greatly affected the total number of migrants. The Jewish Diaspora has been highly dependent on changing political, socioeconomic, and cultural circumstances in the respective countries of residence. In this respect, the virtual disappearance of sizeable Jewish communities in Muslim countries, the marked decline in Eastern Europe, and the growing concentration in North America and Israel were particularly evident (Table 9).

EXTERNAL MIGRATION OF PALESTINIANS. Besides the already noted question of Palestinian refugees, since 1967 Israel has been in total or partial control of the West Bank and Gaza, particularly concerning points of access to and from the outside. The Israeli border authorities have regularly collected data on Palestinian population movements across the border. These data are not fully comparable with data collected on Israeli population movements, and should only be taken as roughly indicative. However, major changes that appear over time do reflect real migration trends – whether temporary or definitive.

Over the extended period September 1967–2003, the total external migration balance of the West Bank and Gaza was 356,000, of which 88,000 was since 1995. A surplus of 29,000 immigrants and return migrants was only recorded (see Table 10: External Migration of Palestinians, 1967–2003) in 1990–94, after the 1991 Gulf War, and especially after the Oslo agreements. The generally negative migration balance significantly spread to Jordan and across the Gulf States.

Table 10: External Migration of Palestinians, 1967–2003

Year	Total
Total	-356,000
1967–1969	-74,900
1970–1974	-27,100
1975–1979	-81,800
1980–1984	-68,700
1985–1989	-45,300
1990–1994	29,400
1995–1999	-52,900
2000–2003	-34,700

Source: Israeli Border Authority and Israel Central Bureau of Statistics.

Migration between the West Bank and Gaza, and Israel was not systematically recorded. According to reports from Israel's Ministry of the Interior Population Register, about 130,000 Palestinians obtained a residence permit in Israel on the grounds of family reunion. However, population updates by Israel's Central Bureau of Statistics do not support this assumption. During prolonged periods since 1967, large numbers of Palestinians worked on a regular basis as commuters or temporary residents within Israel. Following the Palestinian Intifada (uprising) of the late 1980s and early 1990s the numbers declined significantly. After a short recovery, the second Intifada, which started in September 2000, virtually put an end to this form of economic migration.

IMMIGRATION INTO ISRAEL. *Current Flows, Including Return Migration.* Israel's Ministry of the Interior's file of Border Check Post provides basic information on the number and characteristics of new immigrants and of departing and returning residents. The data are processed by Israel's Central Bureau of Statistics. In addition, periodic census data provide information about population characteristics of immigrant stocks.

Immigration to Israel reflected the changing balance of circumstances in the Jewish Diaspora as well as in Israeli society. Between the various determinants, by far the most dominant were *push* (negative) and *hold* (positive) factors in the countries of origin of migrants. The intensity of *pull* (positive) and *repel* (negative) factors operating in Israel, while not negligible, played a complementary role. However, we cannot ignore the fact that the choice of Israel as a destination country reflected not only socio-economic processes that usually govern international migration, but also the powerful historical and cultural grounds for migration decisions. Indeed, Israel's economic ranking improved from being a poor country in 1948 to 24th worldwide in 1975 and to 22nd in 2002, but other countries in North America and Western Europe continued to offer a better standard of living.

Immigration occurred in waves, each dominated by a particular sub-set of countries of origin (see Figure 1 and Table 11: Jewish Immigrants to Israel, 1948–2004). The initial wave of immigration brought in 688,000 people, thus doubling Israel's population within the first three years of its existence through annual immigration impacts above 25% of the absorbing population in the country of destination. Subsequent waves of immigration in Israel were progressively weaker until the major influx of 1990–91 that accompanied the collapse of the Soviet Union. While the annual numbers of immigrants were comparable, the relative impact fell on a much larger veteran population and could be absorbed with fewer traumas.

The first major wave of migration to Israel (1948–51) included survivors of the destroyed Jewish communities in Eastern, Central, and Balkan Europe, as well as the transfer of the substantial majority of Jewish populations of Muslim countries such as Iraq, Yemen, Turkey, Egypt, Iran, and Bulgaria. Subsequent waves included large contingents from Romania, Hungary, and the Maghreb (1953–64), the United States and Western Europe (1968–72), and then predominantly the Soviet Union (1967–77), Ethiopia (the 1980s), and since the end of 1989 the major wave from the Former Soviet Union (FSU).

Figure 1: Migration to and from Israel 1947–2004

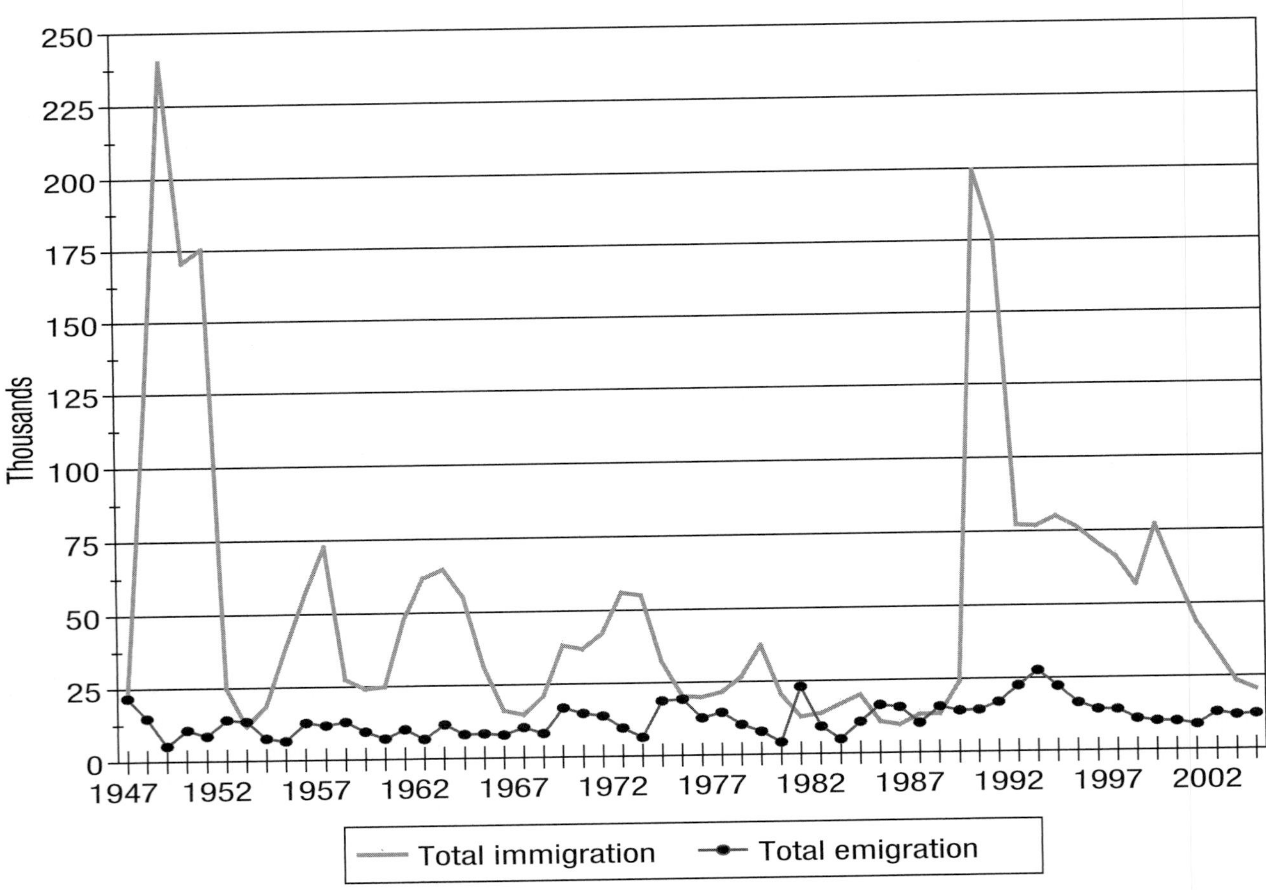

Source: Israel Central Bureau of Statistics.

Table 11: Jewish Immigrants[a] to Israel, by Continent of Last Residence and Period of Immigration, 1948[b]–2004

Period of Immigration	Total in Period (1,000s)	Annual Average	%				
			Total	Asia	Africa	Europe	America-Oceania
1948[b]–2004	2,971.8[c]	52.5	100.0	14.3	16.5	61.3	7.9
1948[b]–1951	686.7	189.2	100.0	35.8	14.2	49.3	0.7
1952–1954	54.1	18.0	100.0	24.6	51.8	18.1	5.5
1955–1957	164.9	55.0	100.0	5.3	63.0	29.5	2.2
1958–1960	75.5	25.2	100.0	17.6	18.5	59.2	4.8
1961–1964	228.0	57.0	100.0	8.6	50.9	34.0	6.5
1965–1968	81.3	20.3	100.0	18.5	31.2	38.9	11.4
1969–1971	116.5	38.8	100.0	17.0	10.4	43.3	29.1
1972–1974	142.8	47.6	100.0	4.4	4.8	72.0	18.8
1975–1979	124.8	25.0	100.0	9.5	4.8	62.1	23.6
1980–1984	83.6	16.7	100.0	8.3	18.8	42.6	30.3
1985–1989	70.2	14.0	100.0	9.3	11.0	51.9	27.5
1990–1991	375.6	187.8	100.0	0.4	6.6	91.0	2.0
1992–1999	580.7	72.6	100.0	7.4	3.4	83.9	5.1
2000–2004	181.5	36.3	100.0	12.2	8.9	65.9	13.0

a As from 1970 including non-Jewish family members of immigrants.
b As of 15 May.
c Including country not reported. Not including immigrant citizens.

The Foreign-Born Israeli Population. As a consequence of steady immigration, a high proportion of the Israeli population was foreign-born, but fairly high birthrates have progressively reduced the rate of foreign-born to native-born Israelis. Out of the total Jewish population, the share of foreign-born steadily declined from 65% in 1948 to 36% in 2004. Accounting for Israel's Arab population (excluding the territories), and assuming all of the latter was local-born, the share of foreign-born fell from 53% in 1948, to 29% in 2004.

Composition. The demographic, socio-economic, and socio-cultural characteristics of the Jewish population worldwide significantly affected the differential probability of deciding to emigrate, and the choice of destination country.

Demographic Characteristics. Because of its political-cultural – rather than merely economic – background, immigration to Israel tended to be more permanent, and less likely to be followed by return migration, than in other major countries of immigration. It was also less structurally selective than other migration streams. Entire families moved, including men and women across the age range rather than mostly young single males. This involved comparatively high dependency ratios and a high absorption burden. Wide socio-demographic gaps separated Jewish Diaspora communities that had undergone modernization to different degrees, particularly Jewish populations in Europe versus North Africa and the Middle East. Jewish migration to Israel included more children and elderly dependents than did Jewish migration from similar countries of origin to Western countries such as the United States or France.

Socio-Economic Characteristics. Jews abroad usually had a higher than average level of education and tended to concentrate in trade, selected branches of industry, and the liberal professions. The probability of emigrating was higher at the upper and lower extremes of the social spectrum in Jewish society. Israel absorbed a comparatively higher share of migrants previously employed in trade and blue-collar occupations. Structural differences were especially notable in the case of Jewish migration from North Africa to France and to Israel during the 1950s and 1960s. Immigration from Western countries and the more recent wave of immigration from the FSU contributed high proportions of university graduates and improved the quality of Israel's labor force. Different levels of modernization and socio-economic development attained by Jewish communities in the respective countries of origin generated internal social gaps within the new framework of Israeli society. Programs to ensure equal access to higher education have gradually reduced the gaps which, however, still persist in the second generation of immigrants.

Ethno-Religious Identification. The Law of Return was designed to promote Jewish immigration, but immigrants who arrived as families or as communities included a growing minority of non-Jews. The growing assimilation of Jews in the Diaspora in recent decades translated into a high percentage of mixed marriages. On the other hand, some communities had maintained intensive links to traditional Jewish religion and culture (including separate religious school systems). This entailed wide variations among types of immigrant and helped generate the diversified socio-cultural nature of Israeli society, and internal ideological tensions mostly stemming from the relation between the state and religion.

Economic, Legal, or Illegal Migrants, Refugees. The mechanisms of mass immigration to Israel also underlie the – often irreversible – nature of such migration. Emigration to Israel often means loss of citizenship and civil rights in the country of origin, making it impossible to return there. Most Israeli immigration from North Africa, the Middle East, and Eastern Europe thus corresponds to *ex post facto* refugee movements.

Since the 1990s, with Israel's rapidly growing economy, and following the halt on Palestinian labor in connection with the first and second Intifadas, there has been a significant increase in the influx of foreign labor. Many of these (non-Jewish) workers from Asia, Africa, Latin America, and the Balkans tend to remain after their working permits have expired. The numbers of actual – i.e., legal and illegal – foreign workers are not accurately documented. Estimates for 2004 ranged around 190,000, but the government's policy of forced expulsion attempts to significantly reduce this number.

ISRAELI EMIGRATION. *Definitions and Data.* While immigration and the absorption of immigrants lie at the core of societal and research focus in Israel, emigration remains both a sensitive and comparatively little researched subject. The very definition of an emigrant is beset with difficulties. In the past, data were collected on the reasons for leaving the country, including emigration. However, the information proved highly unreliable and data collection was discontinued in the early 1960s. Given the lack of precise data on numbers of emigrants, indirect estimates can be obtained on the basis of different operational criteria. Long-term absentees, i.e., people leaving and not returning for a period of several years, provided the customary basis for emigration estimates. Another measure compares the known number of new immigrants and returning residents with the annual international migration balance which also reflects permanent residents who traveled abroad and did not return within a period of 12 months. The latter is a measure of actual absence rather than of permanent emigration.

Major Trends and Differentials. The absolute number of annual emigrants including return migration increased over time, but reflecting more rapid population growth emigration rates per 1,000 resident population consistently declined from the late Ottoman period, the British Mandate, and after Israel's independence. Over the period 1949–2004, based on any of the mentioned measures, the annual number of emigrants never fell below 5,000 or exceeded 28,000. The number of emigrants from Israel regularly fell short of the number of new immigrants, with the exception of 1953, 1981, 1985, 1986, and 1988 in which the Israeli economy was especially under stress.

Between 1948 and the end of 2003 over 700,000 Israeli residents left the country and did not return. This figure includes over 100,000 Israeli residents who had been abroad for less than a year in 2003 and, based on the experience of previous years, could be expected to return in the short term. The total number of Israeli residents settled or planning to settle abroad for a period of four years or more at the end of 2003 could thus be estimated at about 600,000, but the number of those returning after a longer absence was not negligible. If one adds the estimated number of children born abroad to these persons, we arrive at a total pool of over 750,000 former Israeli residents and descendants living abroad or about 11% of the total Israeli population. These figures should be evaluated in the light of the marked increase in the numbers of Israelis who travel abroad. The annual number of departures grew from 30,000 in 1950 to 3,530,000 in 2000. The proportion of Arabs was generally smaller among emigrants than among residents in Israel.

Emigrants from Israel belong to one of three distinct groups: former immigrants returning to their country of origin; former immigrants emigrating to a third country; and emigrants born and raised in Israel. The propensities of emigrating differ according to specific socio-demographic characteristics; thus emigration was more frequent among young adults (aged 20–39), single people, and the better educated. Among former immigrants, there was a greater concentration of emigrants among persons entering Israel with a visa of "potential immigrant" (as compared to "immigrant"), who had lived in Israel for a relatively short period, or who had been born in Western Europe or North America.

The main countries of destination for Israeli emigrants were the United States, France, Canada, and Western countries in general. The largest pool of former Israelis is located in the United States, where it is estimated at over 200,000. The much higher figures sometimes circulated are not confirmed by research. In Europe, too, census figures of the respective countries reveal a much lower total than that commonly reported. Around 2004 the total officially reported number of Israeli citizens in Europe approached 40,000. Since 1991, a modest amount of re-emigration to the FSU has been recorded. The opportunity to enter a country, and the presence there of relatives, constituted a significant factor in the volume of emigration and in the choice of destination country.

Determinants and Consequences. Explanations of emigration from Israel have tended to focus on three factors. First, levels of immigration in the immediately preceding period, insofar as the early stages of immigrant absorption in the new country tend to be characterized by instability, but the probability of remaining (not re-emigrating) tend to increase the longer they remain. Major waves of immigration usually generate a minor wave of emigration with a few years' lag. Second, changing economic circumstances in Israel have an impact on emigration insofar as the latter tends to increase in years with diminishing levels of public investment, declining income, rising inflation, and unemployment. Third, albeit to a lesser extent, the security situation as expressed by major events such as wars or by the cumulative burden of military service (including reserve duty) impacts indirectly on the choice to emigrate or re-emigrate.

Therefore emigration is more strongly related to push factors in Israeli society than to pull factors abroad. Emigration from Israel resembles that for other countries with similar levels of development. Rates of emigration per 1,000 population closely match the levels of immigration to Israel per 1,000 Jews in countries with a level of development similar to that of Israel. Emigration from Israel differs markedly from large-scale Jewish migrations driven by the objective of permanent resettlement in new countries. The tendency towards further return migration to Israel is quite high.

At the same time, further attention should be paid to the longer-term picture of Israeli emigration. While Israeli immigration was long influenced by a commitment to building a new society by enhancing Jewish cultural, religious, and national values, emigration indicates a diminishing salience of these factors. Partial evidence indicates that the probability of emigrating is likely to be higher among those whose feelings of Jewishness and Israeli identity are weaker.

A little studied aspect of Israeli emigration concerns the economic impact of emigrants on the Israeli economy. It is not possible to provide a direct evaluation of the amounts of capital transferred by emigrants. However, total individual remittances (excluding personal payments from Germany) can be compiled from data on the balance of payments. Clearly, such transfers do not concern Israeli emigrants only, but rather the whole Jewish Diaspora which – while viewed by the Law of Return as a virtual target for future immigration – comprises a vastly large population. During the late 1990s and early 2000s the yearly amount transferred fluctuated around $ 1 billion and represented roughly 1 percent of the total Gross National Product (see Table 12: Net Personal Remittances, and Percent of GNP, 1995–2004).

Table 12: Net Personal Remittances, and Percent of GNP, 1995–2004

Year	Personal remittances (net) $ millions[a]	GNP[b] $ millions	Personal remittances (net) as % of GNP
1995	1,039	95,790	1.08
1998	826	111,011	0.74
1999	960	109,263	0.88
2000	949	122,475	0.77
2001	1,227	118,851	1.03
2002	1,179	109,195	1.08
2003	1,093	121,091	0.90

a. Other than personal restitutions from Germany. Source: Central Bureau of Statistics, Statistical Abstract of Israel, 2005, Table 15.2.

b. GDP plus total net transfers. Computed from GDP at current NIS value (Table 14.2) and NIS-$ rate of exchange (Table 17.3).

CONCLUDING REMARKS. There is a strong linkage between the country of residence and the probability of emigrating. Given the fact that most of the Jewish Diaspora currently resides in the more developed Western countries, further waves of large-scale immigration to Israel are unlikely in the near future, and only significant dislocations would reverse this situation. On the other hand, emigration from Israel is significantly determined by economic forecasts which in turn respond to broader geopolitical factors, namely security and the outcome of the peace process. Developments in the latter dimensions, both locally and internationally, will indeed determine the future migration balance of the State of Israel.

[Sergio DellaPergola (2nd ed.)]

ADD. BIBLIOGRAPHY: R. Bachi, *The Population of Israel* (1977); Council of Europe, *Recent Demographic Developments in Europe* (2004); S. DellaPergola, "The Global Context of Migration to Israel," in: E. Leshem and J.T. Shuval (eds.), *Immigration to Israel: Sociological Perspectives, Studies of Israeli Society,* 8 (1998), 51–92; S. DellaPergola, "World Jewish Population," in: *American Jewish Year Book,* The American Jewish Committee, yearly publication; S. DellaPergola, U. Rebhun, M. Tolts, "Contemporary Jewish Diaspora in Global Context: Human Development Correlates of Population Trends," in: *Israel Studies,* 10:1 (2005), 61–95; S.N. Eisenstadt, *The Absorption of Immigrants* (1954); D. Friedlander and C. Goldscheider, *The Population of Israel* (1979); S.J. Gold, *The Israeli Diaspora* (2002); HIAS – Hebrew Immigrant Aid Society, *Statistical Report,* New York, yearly publication; Israel Central Bureau of Statistics, *Statistical Abstract of Israel,* Jerusalem, yearly publication; idem, *Immigration to Israel,* Jerusalem, yearly publication; Jewish Agency for Israel, *Statistical Report,* Jerusalem, yearly publication; U.O. Schmelz, S. DellaPergola, U. Avner, *Ethnic Differences among Israeli Jews: A New Look* (1991); J.T. Shuval, E. Leshem, "The Sociology of Migration in Israel: A Critical View," in: E. Leshem, J.T. Shuval (eds.), *Immigration to Israel: Sociological Perspectives, Studies of Israeli Society,* 8 (1998), 3–50; M. Sicron, *Immigration to Israel 1948–1953* (1957); M. Sicron and E. Leshem, *The Absorption Process of Immigrants from the Former Soviet Union, 1990–1995* (Heb., 1998); United Nations Development Programme, *Human Development Report* (2004).

MIHAILENI (Rom. **Mihţileni**), town in Moldavia, N.E. Romania. When the town was founded in 1792 only Jews from the other side of the border were permitted to settle in the locality. The prayer house of the Jews and their ritual bathhouse were exempted from taxes, and during the first year Jewish merchants did not have to pay taxes. In 1834 the town became the property of the prince of Moldavia, Michael Sturdza. Eager to develop the town, he granted Jewish craftsmen special privileges, exempting them from taxes for five years. He also encouraged merchants to settle there by granting loans. From a population of 516 in 1820 the number of Jews reached 2,472 (67.6% of the total population), in 1859. In 1903 there were 248 Jewish and 58 Christian merchants in the town. The majority of the Jews were engaged in commerce, especially the fur trade. Jewish carriers plied their trade throughout the whole area; they had their own prayer house. An organized community dates from 1897. A Jewish primary school was founded in 1899. After World War I, with the Romanian annexation of Bessarabia and Bukovina, Mihaileni lost its position as a frontier town. In 1930 only 1,490 Jews (32%) remained in the town. In the same year, the Jewish Party obtained the majority of votes in the local council elections. The peasants preferred it to the other parties, asserting that the Jews were more capable administrators. The election, however, was canceled by the authorities. On the eve of World War II there were nine prayer houses, a ritual bath, a primary school, and a cemetery in Mihaileni. The Hebrew author of the Haskalah period Marcus *Strelisker lived and died in Mihaileni. The Yiddish poet Jacob *Groper (1890–1966) was born there.

In World War II the Jews of Mihaileni were deported to *Transnistria. Few returned to Mihaileni after the war; the majority emigrated. The Jewish population numbered 680 in 1947, 400 in 1950, and about ten families in 1969.

BIBLIOGRAPHY: PK Romaniya 180–1; E. Schwarzfeld, *Impopularea, reîmpopularea şi întemeierea tîrgurilor şi tîrguşoarelorîm Noldova* (1914), 26–33, 43, 82–83, 101–3; M. Schwarzfeld, in: *Analele Societăţś istorice Juliu Barasch*, 2 (1888), 28–29, 117; *Fraternitatea*, 4 (1882), 345.

[Theodor Lavi]

MIHALY, EUGENE (1918–2002), rabbi, professor, and college administrator. Mihaly was born in Hungary and immigrated to the United States in 1930. He received his B.A. from *Yeshiva University in 1940 and dual ordination from Rabbi Isaac Elchanan Theological Seminary (Orthodox, 1941) and *Hebrew Union College (Reform, 1949), where he also earned a Ph.D. in 1952. Invited to join the HUC faculty, Mihaly became professor of rabbinic literature and homiletics and Deutsch Professor of Jewish Jurisprudence and Social Justice (emeritus in 1989). He added high-level administration to his lecturing duties when he was named executive dean for academic affairs of all four HUC-JIR schools in 1976, becoming academic vice president in 1985. After his retirement in 1990, he continued to contribute to the *Encyclopedia Britannica* and the *Encyclopedia Judaica*.

Mihaly, a radical reformer in the mold of classical Reform, wrote responsa sanctioning such controversial practices as rabbinic officiation at mixed marriages and holding weddings on the Sabbath. In response to the Reform movement's perceived drift toward Orthodox and Conservative stances on such issues as the importance of Zionism and Israel, the vital role of Hebrew and the embracing of ritual and tradition, Mihaly wrote the articles "Reform Judaism and Halacha" and "Halakhah Is Absolute and Passé," which articulated the need for Reform Judaism to return to its original rejection of Jewish law. In 1974, he was unanimously elected president of the newly formed (and ultimately short-lived) Association for a Progressive Reform Judaism, established by a group of approximately 100 Reform rabbis who shared concerns about what they claimed to be the subordination of the freedom of individual rabbis to positions adopted by the *Central Conference of American Rabbis, the alienation of the institutions of Reform Judaism from Reform laity, and undue emphasis on the ethnic and national aspects of Judaism at the expense of pure religion. In addition to numerous articles, responsa, and monographs, Mihaly wrote the books *Religious Experience in Judaism* (1957) and *A Song to Creation* (1975).

[Bezalel Gordon (2nd ed.)]

MI'ILYA, Christian-Arab village in northern Israel, in western Upper Galilee, west of *Ma'alot. Mi'ilya constitutes an important center in Israel for the Greek-Catholic faith, to which almost all its inhabitants belong. Tobacco, deciduous fruit, vineyards, and olive groves, on land reclaimed from rocky slopes, formed the base of the village's economy. In 1957 Mi'ilya received municipal council status. In 1969 its population was 1,390, rising to 2,550 in 2002, on an area of 0.07 sq. mi. (1.8 sq. km.). According to archaeological evidence, Mi'ilya has been inhabited since the second millennium B.C.E. Although few remains from the earlier periods have been preserved, the crusader fortress built by German knights in the 13th century C.E. (Chasteau du Roi or Castrum Regis) has remained almost intact and still forms the village's nucleus. Another crusader fortress, Montfort (Burg Starkenberg), lies nearby in the Chezib River gorge.

[Efraim Orni]

MIKARDO, IAN (1908–1993), British politician. One of the most important leaders of the British Labour Party's left wing from the 1940s through the 1980s, Mikardo was born in Portsmouth, Hampshire, the son of a tailor for the Royal Navy who had recently emigrated from a town near Warsaw. Mikardo spoke Yiddish at home and was educated at Aria College, a Jewish school in Portsmouth. In the 1930s he acted as a management consultant and was long associated with the Supervisory Staffs Association. Mikardo was elected to Parliament in the Labour landslide of 1945, becoming one of the driving forces of its left wing and working hard for further extensive nationalization and other left-wing goals. He was one of the closest associates of Labour's left-wing leader Aneuran Bevan and of other left-wing figures like Michael Foot. Mikardo lost his seat in 1959, but again became a Member of Parliament in 1964, serving until 1987. While out of Parliament he developed a business trading with the Soviet Union and became a fierce opponent of the Vietnam War. His left-wing views kept him out of any ministerial post, although he was always an influential figure in the Labour Party's internal machinery, serving as chairman of the Parliamentary Labour Party in 1974. Mikardo was also a supporter of the Israeli Labor Party. In his last years, ironically he was criticized by Labour's militants as too moderate. Mikardo wrote an autobiography, *Back-bencher* (1988).

BIBLIOGRAPHY: ODNB online.

[William D. Rubinstein (2nd ed.)]

MIKES, GEORGE (1912–1987), Hungarian-born humorist. After working for the BBC during World War II, he wrote many lighthearted books on politics, social customs, and national foibles. These works include *How to Be an Alien: England* (1946), *Ueber Alles: Germany* (1953), and *How to Scrape Skies: United States* (1948). Mikes also poked fun at Japan (*The Land of the Rising Yen*, 1970), the UN (*How to Unite Nations*, 1963), and Britain again (*How To Be Inimitable*, 1966; *How To Be a Brit*, 1984; *How To Be Decadent*, 1986). Though converted as a boy, Mikes retained a keen interest in Jewish affairs, writing two incisive books on Israel, *Milk and Honey* (1950) and *The Prophet Motive: Israel Today and Tomorrow* (1969).

MIKHAËL, EPHRAÏM (1866–1890), French author. Georges Michel (his real name) was born in Toulouse of an Alsatian father and a Provençal mother. There were strong links and intermarriage with families from Montpellier and Nîmes, for example with the Bernards from Nîmes, whose eldest son Lazare was and remained Georges Michel's dearest "brother" in every sense, personal and intellectual. When both became budding writers in Paris, they changed their neutral-sounding French names for Jewish-sounding pen names – a gesture of Jewish self-assertion. Around 1884 Georges Michel became Ephraïm Mikhaël and Lazare Bernard became Bernard *Lazare. E. Mikhaël's other Jewish "brother" was Camille Bloch, from an Alsatian rabbinical family, who became a leading historian.

E. Mikhaël moved to Paris as a schoolboy with his family. He began his literary career at age 17, while a pupil at the prestigious "lycée Fontanes," where, in a spirit of fraternal poetic exaltation, small literary groups sprang up, fed by intellectual pursuits and love of beauty.

E. Mikhaël's student years (1884–88) were spent at the Sorbonne and exclusive École des Chartes, specializing in Latin and medieval studies, graduating as archivist-paleographer, which won him an appointment at the Bibliothèque Nationale, a post he held until his untimely death.

Mikhaël was a fine scholar, ever broadening his knowledge in the realms of Greek and Oriental studies, philosophy, and comparative religion. His vast fund of knowledge served both his theoretical speculations and his poetic inspiration and the thematic background for his literary creation. He was a prolific and intensive writer in the six years of his student and professional careers and regarded as the most gifted of his generation by Victor Hugo and Mallarmé among others.

Although he is remembered primarily as a poet and quoted in the leading anthologies, he also excelled in poetic prose (tales, prose poems, parables), composed fine dramatic works (see *La Fiancée de Corinthe*, 1988), and important theoretical essays. Except for one small volume of poems, *L'Automne* (1886), he published primarily in literary journals, particularly *La Pléiade*, launched by his own little group and destined to become the famed and long-lived *Mercure de France*. The bulk of his writings appeared in a fine volume of verse and prose, published shortly after his death.

Though he remained famous for his melancholy poems ("Crépuscule pluvieux," "Tristesse de septembre," et al.), he had a dual personality: on the one hand he had a sad, pessimistic bent and on the other an innate love of life, whimsical and ironic, as in his satirical poems and some tales. He progressed from an idle reverie on the theme of the fatal burden of solitude and self-concern (exemplified in "La dame en deuil" and "La captive" among others) towards an active meditation, no longer severed from real life and commitment. In his last major critical text, he stakes a claim for a "new art," which rejects both the formal luxuriousness of the Parnasse school of poetry in favor of renewed freer expression and the flatly naturalistic novel in favor of a type of literature that would stimulate philosophical reflection. This was to be the program of the "symbolists" for the next 15 years or so.

A similar evolution is noticeable in E. Mikhaël's overtly Jewish works. The author goes from allusive, ambiguous references to meaningful messages. Such poems as "La reine de Saba," "Le mage," "L'automne" remain ambiguous. For example "L'automne" makes a fairly clear allusion to the High Holy Days, but stresses the sadness of the season, the death of the old year, and an uncertain word of pardon rather than the opportunity for the soul's renewal. A comparison between two parables, playing on the similar subject of the messianic messenger, is instructive. In an early tale, "Miracles," a noble stranger arrives in a timeless city, filled with anonymous rabbis and sages, full of "ridiculous common sense" and blind to higher insights. They ignore the stranger (maybe a "divine messenger"). The poet Azahel, a sort of philosopher and seer, remains torn between faith and reason. He retreats in superstitious fear of the unknown. A much later tale, "L'imposteur," takes up the same theme, but in a precise setting in time (month of Elul, ten years after the fall of Jerusalem) and space (Galilee, Tiberias). The story presents a group of authentic pious priests and rabbis, all with Hebrew names, prepared to seek and greet the messianic figure announced in Scriptures. But the unfinished story and the ironic behavior of the supposed messiah warn against deceptive prophecy (cf. the title "L'imposteur"). This is in keeping with the author's evolution toward a rational philosophical outlook, a sane moralistic attitude, and love of life, as an antidote against superstition and esoteric doctrines. In his major tales ("Halyartès," "Le Solitaire," et al.) he presents a series of beautiful adolescent heroes, outstanding for their perfect purity of soul, thus condemned to solitude in a crude, vicious, and hypocritical world. The frequent theme of purity is balanced by a stinging satire of spurious mysticism in the midst of an evil society.

[Denise R. Goitein]

MĪKHĀ'ĪL, MURAD (1906–1986), Iraqi poet and educator. A *Baghdad lawyer, he was headmaster of the Shammāsh Jewish high school in Baghdad (1941–47). Some of his Arabic verse appeared in the Jewish press and a collection of love poems was published in 1931. Mīkhā'īl also wrote prose works in favor of women's rights and the peasants, and attacking superstition. After immigrating to Israel in 1949, he specialized in Arab education and wrote several textbooks.

[Shmuel Moreh]

MIKHALEVICH, BEINISH (pseudonym of **Joseph Izbitski**; 1876–1928), leader of the *Bund in Russia and Poland. Mikhalevich was born at Brest-Litovsk into a working-class family and at the age of 18 he joined a socialist circle. On the establishment of the Bund, he was active in Bialystok and Warsaw, set up its local organs there, and also wrote in its central newspaper *Arbeter Shtime*. After a period of arrest by the czarist police, he took part in the establishment of the Garber Bund and edited its organ *Der Kemfer*. In the following years – between repeated arrests, exile, and flight – he was an organizer, speaker, publicist, and propagandist of the Bund. In the internal struggles he belonged to the "soft" group that supported the Bund's return to the Russian Social Democratic party (1906), and during the period of reaction, after the short-lived constitutional aftermath of the revolution, he belonged to the "anti-liquidators," who demanded to continue illegal activities. Mikhalevich was the first to discuss the problem of the relationship between the Bund and the Jewish *kehillah* (the organized Jewish community) (1907). In 1912 he became a member of the central committee of the Bund and edited its weekly *Tsayt* in St. Petersburg. During World War I he was active in welfare and educational institutions in Vilna until his imprisonment by the German occupation forces for a leaflet he wrote against forced labor.

The leftward turn of the Bund in independent Poland decreased Mikhalevich's political standing and he devoted himself mainly to writing and to social and cultural work. He wrote in the Bund organ *Folkstsaytung*, and gave a historical-biographical description of the Jewish workers' movement in three volumes: *Zikhroynes fun a Yidishn Sotsialist* (1921–23). He took part in the founding of the Central Yiddish School Organization (CYSHO) and until his death served as its chairman, visiting the U.S. in 1923–24 as its emissary and promoting the establishment of the Society for Helping Children's Institutions Overseas. He was also a member of the Jewish community council in Warsaw (1925–28). One of the outstanding polemicists against Zionism, Mikhalevich was popular even among his opponents because of his honesty and attachment to Jewish values.

BIBLIOGRAPHY: LNYL, 5 (1963), 608–12; I. Cohen, *War's Tribulations and Aftermath* (1943), 361; idem, in: *Beinush Mikhalevich Gedenk Bukh* (1951), incl. bibl.; A. Litvak, *Mah she-Hayah* (1945), 237–45; A.S. Stein, *Ḥaver Artur* (1953), index; J.S. Hertz et al. (eds.), *Geshikhte fun Bund*, 3 vols. (1960–66), indexes.

[Moshe Mishkinsky]

MIKHMORET (Heb. מִכְמֹרֶת; "Fishing Net"), moshav village, and vocational school in central Israel, near *Kefar Vitkin, founded in 1945 by World War II veterans, some of whom had learned fishing in Holland. The moshav is affiliated with Tenu'at ha-Moshavim. Its economy is based on citrus groves, dairy cattle, and carp ponds. The village Mikhmoret Bet has developed the neighboring beach, one of the finest in the country, as a seaside resort. The fishery and seafaring school Mevo'ot Yam ("Approaches to the Sea") constituted a central maritime training institute. In 1970 the three sections of Mikhmoret had a population of 720. In 2002 it was 1,050.

[Efraim Orni]

MIKHOELS, SOLOMON (stage and public name of **Solomon Vovsi**; 1890–1948), Yiddish actor; head of the Moscow State Jewish Theater; chairman of the Jewish *Anti-Fascist Committee. Born in Dvinsk (today Daugavpils, Latvia), Mikhoels studied law at St. Petersburg. In 1918 he joined Alexander *Granovsky's Jewish drama studio, the next year following Granovsky to Moscow, where the group became the State Jewish Theater (GOSET). He was Granovsky's chief actor, and succeeded him to the directorship in 1928 when he did not returned from abroad. In 1931 he opened a studio affiliated with the theater, which trained actors for all Jewish theaters in the U.S.S.R. Mikhoels, whose distinction lay in his command of both tragic and tragicomic roles, first attracted attention in 1921 in a performance of *Shalom Aleichem's *Agents*. He was soon playing such famous Yiddish roles as Shimele Soroker in *Two Hundred Thousand*, Hotsmakh in Goldfaden's *The Witch*, Benjamin in *The Travels of Benjamin the Third* by Mendele Mokher Seforim (S.Y. *Abramovitsh), and Shalom Aleichem's Tevye. One of his most notable performances was King Lear in the production by Sergei Radlov in 1935. From August 1941, Mikhoels, as chairman of the Jewish Anti-Fascist Committee, launched fervent appeals to "our Jewish brethren" in the West to help the Soviet war effort against Nazi Germany. In 1943 he and the poet Itzik *Fefer traveled on behalf of the Anti-Fascist Committee to the U.S., Canada, Mexico, and England, where they were enthusiastically received by the Jewish public. At the end of World War II, when survivors of the Holocaust and Jews returning from evacuation in Soviet Asia tried to resettle in their old homes, Mikhoels gradually became their spokesman and protector, interceding for them with the Soviet authorities. He apparently was also connected with the "Crimean project" which aimed at the settlement of homeless Jews in the Crimea. On Jan. 13, 1948, while on an official mission in Minsk on behalf of the State Committee for Theater Prizes, Mikhoels was brutally killed, ostensibly in an alleged car accident, but in reality executed by the Soviet secret police, on the order of Stalin. (Svetlana Alliluyeva, Stalin's daughter, testified (in her book *Only One Year*) that her father was personally involved in covering up Mikhoels' assassination and presenting it as an accident.) On January 16, Mikhoels was eulogized at his state funeral in Moscow in which many thousands of Jews participated. Mikhoels' assassination was the first step in the process of the liquidation of all Jewish cultural institutions and of most outstanding Yiddish writers, artists, and actors which took place during the last years of Stalin's rule. In 1952, four years after his death, Mikhoels was claimed as a Jewish nationalist, a "Joint agent," and a contact man with the U.S. intelligence in the "Doctors' Trials." During the de-Stalinization in the mid-1950s Mikhoels was de facto rehabilitated. In Tel Aviv a square was named in his honor in 1962, on the tenth anniversary of the execution of Jewish writers in the U.S.S.R.

BIBLIOGRAPHY: B.Z. Goldberg, *The Jewish Problem in the Soviet Union* (1961), index; K.L. Rudnitskiy (ed.), *Mikhoels'* (Rus., 1965); Sutskever, in: *Di Goldene Keyt*, no. 43 (1962); I. Ionasovich, *Mit Yidishe Shrayber in Rusland* (1959), passim. **ADD. BIBLIOGRAPHY:** N. Vovsi-Mikhoels, *My Father Solomon Mikhoels* (Russian, 1984); G. Kostyrchenko, *In the Captivity of the Red Pharaon* (Russian, 1994).

[Binyamin Eliav and Joseph Leftwich]

MIKULOV (Ger. **Nikolsburg**), town in S. Moravia, Czech Republic. The Mikulov community was the largest and most important in Moravia, and was the seat of the *Landesrabbiner* ("chief rabbi") from apparently as early as 1574 until 1851. A Jew from Mikulov, a moneylender, is mentioned in a document of 1369, but there is no mention of Jews in the oldest known city record of 1414. An inscription in the synagogue (burned down in 1719) was dated 1450. The community was probably founded by expellees from Austria (1420), reinforced in 1454 by those from *Brno (Bruenn) and *Znojmo (Znaim). The charter granted the Jews in 1591 guaranteed a self-elected communal administration (the revised charter of 1612 (renewed in 1708) removed the Jews from the jurisdiction of the town to that of the lord). In 1593 the Jews were permitted to trade in textiles. On the conquest of the town by the Swedes (1642), the Jews raised a quarter of the town's contribution. Refugees from the *Chmielnicki massacres came to Mikulov in 1648. In 1653 the **ḥevra kaddisha* was founded. In 1657 there were 145 families in the town. Their number was augmented in 1670 by expellees from Vienna, who at first kept apart from the local community, maintaining their own institutions and endeavoring to return to Vienna. A hospital for infectious diseases was built in 1680. Jews who were captured on the conquest of *Belgrade were ransomed in 1688 and settled in Mikulov. Almost the entire Jewish quarter, including the old synagogue and all records, was destroyed in a fire in 1719. The concomitant plunder led to a conflict between the central authorities and the local lord over military intervention. Under the leadership of Samson *Wertheimer, communities throughout Europe offered assistance to the Jews of Mikulov. The municipality bought up building sites to avoid the enlargement of the Jewish quarter, whose boundaries were fixed by an imperial commission in 1720.

The prosperity of the community depended on its connection with the cultivation of wines and the wine trade and on the town's position on the main road between Brno and Vienna. Many of the Jews were carters. The Jewish wine merchants leased vineyards, vats, and cellars or bought up the grape crops, paying in advance of the harvest. Jews also distilled spirits and produced the special Moravian plum jam (*povidl*). In the 17th century, the Jews undertook to supply the whole town with candles, and in the 18th century the purveyors of gold and silver to the imperial mint lived in Mikulov. The community *takkanot* from the 18th century are preserved in the National Library in Jerusalem. The Jewish tailors, shoemakers, and butchers were organized into guilds, with their own synagogues. However, most members of the community earned their livelihood in peddling, mainly in the villages of Austria.

Mikulov, the center of all activities of Moravian Jewry, was especially prominent when Samson Raphael *Hirsch held office as chief rabbi (1846–51). A German-language school, connected with a textile workshop, was opened in 1839. Joel Deutsch founded the Jewish institute for the deaf and dumb in 1844 (transferred to Vienna in 1852). Mikulov became a political community (**Politische Gemeinde*) after 1848. After the economic importance of the community had declined when the Vienna-Brno railroad line bypassed Mikulov, many of its members left (after 1848), moving mainly to Brno and Vienna, where a "Verein der Nikolsburger" ("association of Nikolsburgers") grew up. The rapid decline in the community was reflected in the number of synagogues: 12 until 1868, five until the beginning of the 20th century, and then only two. The number of permitted families allotted under the *Familiants Laws was 620. From 3,020 persons in 1793, the community increased to 3,237 in 1830 and 3,680 in 1857, then fell sharply to 1,500 in 1869; 1,213 in 1880; 1,061 in 1890; 900 in 1900; 778 in 1913; 573 in 1921; and 437 in 1930 (5.6% of the total population).

The yeshivah of Mikulov was renowned, and many well-known rabbis held office in the town; nearly all of them were simultaneously chief rabbis of Moravia (see *Moravia). For a short period the town served as the seat of Hungarian chief rabbi and was a vital spiritual link between West Slovakian and Moravian Jewry. Until the mid-19th century Mikulov had the second largest Jewish community in the Czech-speaking lands. During World War I, Jewish refugees from Poland were concentrated in Mikulov, where they had their own school and prayer room. The scholar Abraham *Trebitsch lived in Mikulov and Aloys and Joseph von Sonnenfels were natives of the town.

In 1936 a Moravian Jewish museum was founded in Mikulov; it was transferred to Brno at the time of the Sudeten crisis, and from there to the Central Jewish Museum in Prague. The community dispersed at this time; many of its members were deported to the Nazi extermination camps from Brno in 1941. The community was revived for a short period after World War II. In 1948 members of the Czechoslovak volunteer brigade (the so-called Sochor brigade) were concentrated in Mikulov before leaving for Israel – 120 soldiers and about 700 family members. The old synagogue (Altschul) was thoroughly restored in the years 1990–92. Other Jewish buildings were all pulled down during the Communist regime in 1950–75. The ancient cemetery is well preserved and also serves as a repository for tombstones from other liquidated cemeteries. It contains the graves of numerous famous rabbis of Moravia and Hungary. The mass grave of 21 prisoners from the local labor camp murdered by the Nazis in April 1945 is located in the cemetery. The Jewish surname Naach/Nash is derived from the Yiddish abbreviation of the town's name.

BIBLIOGRAPHY: B.M. Trapp and V.R. Koenig, in: H. Gold (ed.), *Juden und Judengemeinden Maehrens* (1929), 417–50; A. Willmann and H. Flesch, *ibid.*, 45–52; I. Herrisch, *ibid.*, 193–7 (on Lednice); Y.Z. Kahane, in: *Arim ve-Immahot be-Yisrael*, 4 (1950), 210–310 (bibl. 310–3); E.N.C. Roth, *Takkanot Nikolsburg* (1961); A. Engel (ed.), *Gedenkbuch… Kuratoriums…* (Ger., Czech, and Heb., 1936); D. Feuchtwang, in: *Kaufmann Gedenkbuch* (1900), 369–84; idem, in: *Juedisches Archiv*, 1 (1928), nos. 3–4, 1–3; L. Loew, *Gesammelte Schriften*, 2 (1890), 165–218; B. Brilling, in: *Zeitschrift fuer die Geschichte der Juden in der Tschechoslowakei…*, 2 (1931/32), 243–7; L. Moses, *ibid.*, 5 (1938), 85–108; A.Z. Schwarz, in: *Studies… in Memory of A.S. Freidus* (1929),

170–81; A. Scheiber, in: *Yeda-Am*, 5 (1958/59), 71–73; M. Freudenthal, in: MGWJ, 46 (1902), 268–70; W. Mueller, *Urkundliche Beitraege* (1903), passim; Baron, Community, 3 (1942), index; S. Simonsohn, *Ha-Yehudim be-Dukkasut Mantovah*, 2 (1965), index, s.v. *Nikolsburg*; M.H. Friedlaender, *Kore ha-Dorot* (Ger., 1876); G. Deutsch, in: *Die Deborah*, 2 (1902), 354–62; Y. Heilperin, *Takkanot Kehillot Mehrin* (1952), index; A. Freimann, in: ZHB, 20 (1917), 36f.; M. Steinschneider, in: HB, 5 (1862), 128. **ADD. BIBLIOGRAPHY:** J. Fiedler, *Jewish Sights of Bohemia and Moravia* (1991), 114–16.

[Meir Lamed / Yeshayahu Jelinek (2nd ed.)]

MIKVA, ABNER J. (1926–), judge, legislator, special counsel to U.S. President Bill Clinton. Born in Milwaukee, Wisconsin, Mikva attended public schools there. He served in the U.S. Army Air Corps during World War II, and graduated from the University of Chicago Law School in 1951. Mikva was law clerk to Supreme Court Justice Sherman Minton from 1951 to 1952, then entered private practice in Chicago.

In 1956 Mikva was elected to the Illinois state legislature, running as a Democrat but against the Democratic machine. He served in the state legislature for ten years, writing reforms of the state criminal code and state mental health facilities; he gained a reputation as an opponent of corruption in the state welfare system and apparently earned the enmity of Chicago Mayor Richard Daley. In 1968 he was elected to the U.S. House of Representatives. He lost his bid for reelection in 1972 when Chicago's legislative districts were remapped, and he returned to Chicago, practicing law and teaching at Northwestern University School of Law.

In 1974 Mikva was reelected to Congress; he served there as a member of key committees until 1979, when President Jimmy Carter nominated him for the U.S. Court of Appeals in the District of Columbia. Mikva's nomination was opposed by the National Rifle Association, and conservative opponents unsuccessfully challenged his appointment with a lawsuit. He served in the Court of Appeals from 1979, becoming chief judge in 1991. During his judicial career, Mikva wrote over 300 opinions, many concerning free speech and consumer rights. In one noteworthy case, he ordered that a gay student be reinstated at the U.S. Naval Academy. He did not uphold the right of an air force captain to wear a yarmulke while on duty, though throughout the hearing whenever a skullcap was mentioned, he felt for the back of his head.

In 1994 he gave up his judicial appointment to become White House counsel to President Bill Clinton. With this new appointment within the executive branch, Mikva had served in all three branches of the federal government. In 1995 he returned to teaching, writing frequently on political and judicial issues. He continued to be known as an advocate of free speech, in 2001 speaking out against acts of racial profiling and wrongful imprisonment of Muslim immigrants in the United States.

[Dorothy Bauhoff (2nd ed.)]

MIKVA'OT (Heb. מִקְוָאוֹת; "Ritual Baths"), the sixth tractate in the order of *Tohorot* in the Mishnah and the Tosefta. The tractate consists of ten chapters and deals wholly with the details of the **mikveh*. Chapter 1 classifies *mikva'ot* according to the grade of their purity and purifying effect, from ponds or ditches containing less than 40 *se'ah* (c. 750 liters; see *Weights and Measures) and therefore invalid, to those of the highest grade, consisting of *mayim ḥayyim* ("pure spring water"). Chapter 2 discusses cases of "doubtful impurity" (e.g., if a person is not sure whether he has immersed properly or whether the *mikveh* was ritually fit), and then deals with the problem of *mayim she'uvim* ("drawn water"). Chapters 3 and 4 continue with various aspects of *mayim she'uvim*, e.g., how a *mikveh* invalidated by *mayim she'uvim* can be made ritually fit, or how to direct rainwater from a roof into a *mikveh* without letting the water pass through a "vessel" in order to prevent the water's becoming *mayim she'uvim*. Chapter 5 deals mainly with the fitness of springs, rivers, and seas as *mikva'ot*. Chapter 6 is concerned with the question of a body of water linked with a *mikveh*, or two *mikva'ot* connected so that the water of the one "touches" the water of the other (*hashakah*), which is of great significance in the construction of the modern *mikveh*. Chapter 7 discusses the minimal requirement of 40 *se'ah*, especially whether snow, ice, etc. may complete that measure. Chapter 8 first deals with the halakhic difference between *mikva'ot* of the Holy Land and those of other countries; it then discusses problems touching on seminal issue and menstruation. Chapter 9 discusses the problem of *haẓiẓah* ("interposition"). Chapter 10 deals with vessels or any other artifact requiring purification in a *mikveh*.

The Vienna manuscript of Tosefta *Mikva'ot* contains seven chapters (and is missing one page, containing the end of the third chapter through the beginning of the sixth chapter), while the printed edition contains eight chapters. The Tosefta quotes traditions about queries raised by the inhabitants of "Assia" with the scholars of Jabneh during the three pilgrim festivals (4:6); about R. Gamaliel and Onkelos the Proselyte bathing in the sea at Ashkelon (6:3); and about discussions which took place among 32 scholars in Lydda (7 (8):11). Although there is no Babylonian or Jerusalem Talmud on *Mikva'ot*, several of its Mishnayot are explained in the Babylonian Talmud; for example, Mishnah 4:1 is explained in *Shabbat* 16b, Mishnah 7:2 in *Yevamot* 82b and *Zevaḥim* 22a, Mishnah 7:4 in *Shabbat* 144b, Mishnah 8:4 in *Ḥullin* 24b, Mishnah 9:1 in *Shabbat* 57a, and Mishnah 9:5 and 6 in *Shabbat* 114a. The Mishnah of this tractate was translated into English by H. Danby (1933) and the Soncino Press (1948), while J. Neusner has recently published a translation of both the Mishnah (1991) and the Tosefta (2002).

BIBLIOGRAPHY: Ḥ. Albeck, *Shishah Sidrei Mishnah, Seder Tohorot* (1959), 337–9. **ADD. BIBLIOGRAPHY:** Epstein, *The Gaonic Commentary on the Order Toharot* (Heb.) (1982); S. Lieberman, *Tosefet Rishonim*, vol. 4 (1939); J. Neusner, *A History of the Mishnaic Laws of Purities* (1974–77), vols. 13–14; idem, *From Mishnah to Scripture* (1984), 73–79; idem, *The Mishnah Before 70* (1987), 181–94; idem, *The Philosophical Mishnah*, 2 (1989), 281–93; idem, *Purity in Rabbinic Judaism* (1994), 145–54.

[Arnost Zvi Ehrman]

MIKVEH (Heb. מִקְוֶה; pl. *mikva'ot*; Hebrew for a "collection" or "gathering" [of water]), a pool or bath of clear water, immersion in which renders ritually clean a person who has become ritually unclean through contact with the dead (Num. 19) or any other defiling object, or through an unclean flux from the body (Lev. 15) and especially a menstruant or postpartum woman (see *Ablution; *Niddah*; *Purity and Impurity, *Ritual; **Taharat ha-Mishpaḥah*). It is similarly used for vessels (Num. 31:22–23). Today the chief use of the *mikveh* is for women, prior to marriage, following *niddut*, and following the birth of a child, since the laws of ritual impurity no longer apply after the destruction of the Temple. *Mikveh* immersion is also obligatory for proselytes, as part of the ceremony of conversion. In addition immersion in the *mikveh* is still practiced by various groups as an aid to spirituality, particularly on the eve of the Sabbath and festivals, especially the Day of Atonement (see *Ablution) and the custom still obtains, in accordance with Numbers 31: 22–23 to immerse new vessels and utensils purchased from non-Jews. At the beginning of the 21st century, *mikveh* immersion also frequently constituted a symbolic expression of a new spiritual beginning for both women and men, in all branches of Jewish practice. In addition to conversion to Judaism, rituals have developed incorporating *mikveh* immersion as part of bar mitzvah and bat mitzvah (coming of age); prior to marriage for men as well as women; in cases of miscarriage, infertility, and illness; and following divorce, sexual assault, or other life-altering events. An indication of the probable long-term impact of this trend is the increased construction of *mikva'ot* by non-Orthodox Jewish communities in North America.

It is emphasized that the purpose of immersion is not physical, but spiritual, cleanliness. Maimonides concludes his codification of the laws of the *mikveh* with the following statement: It is plain that the laws about immersion as a means of freeing oneself from uncleanness are decrees laid down by Scripture and not matters about which human understanding is capable of forming a judgment; for behold, they are included among the divine statutes. Now 'uncleanness' is not mud or filth which water can remove, but is a matter of scriptural decree and dependent on the intention of the heart. Therefore the Sages have said, 'If a man immerses himself, but without special intention, it is as though he has not immersed himself at all.'

Nevertheless we may find some indication [for the moral basis] of this: Just as one who sets his heart on becoming clean becomes clean as soon as he has immersed himself, although nothing new has befallen his body, so, too, one who sets his heart on cleansing himself from the uncleannesses that beset men's souls – namely, wrongful thoughts and false convictions – becomes clean as soon as he consents in his heart to shun those counsels and brings his soul into the waters of pure reason. Behold, Scriptures say, 'And I will sprinkle clean water upon you and ye shall be clean; from all your uncleannesses and from all your idols will I cleanse you [Ezek. 36: 25]' (Yad, Mikva'ot 11:12).

Although Maimonides in this passage states that lack of intention invalidates the act under all circumstances, a view which is found in the Tosefta (Ḥag. 3:2), the *halakhah*, as in fact codified by him (Yad, *ibid.* 1:8), is that the need for intention applies only for the purpose of eating holy things, such as **ma'aser and terumah*. For a menstruant, and before eating ordinary food, though intention is desirable in the first instance, its lack does not invalidate the immersion. The importance of intention in the laws of ritual impurity is further illustrated by the fact that the rabbis permitted fig cakes which had been hidden in water – an action that would normally make the food susceptible to uncleanness – because they had been put there in order to hide them and not in order to wet them (Makhsh. 1:6). This stress on intention passed from Judaism into Islam. "Purity is the half of faith" is a saying attributed to Muhammad himself and in general the laws of uncleanness in Islam bear a striking resemblance to those of Judaism (*Encyclopedia of Islam*, s.v. *Tahara*).

According to biblical law any collection of water, drawn or otherwise, is suitable for a *mikveh* as long as it contains enough for a person to immerse himself (Yad, *ibid.* 4:1). The rabbis, however, enacted that only water which has not been drawn, i.e., has not been in a vessel or receptacle, may be used; and they further established that the minimum quantity for immersion is that which is contained in a square cubit to the height of three cubits. A *mikveh* containing less than this amount (which they estimated to be a volume of 40 *se'ah*, being between 250–1,000 liters according to various calculations) becomes invalid should three *log* of drawn water fall into it or be added. However, if the *mikveh* contains more than this amount it can never become invalid no matter how much drawn water is added. These laws are the basis for the various ways of constructing the *mikveh* (see below). To them a whole talmudic tractate, **Mikva'ot*, is devoted, and Maimonides assigns them a whole treatise of the same name. The laws can be conveniently divided into two parts, the construction of the *mikveh* itself, and the water which renders it valid or invalid.

The *mikveh* is valid, however built, providing that it has not been prefabricated and brought and installed on the site, since in that case it constitutes a "vessel" which renders the water in it "drawn water" ("*mayim she'uvim*"; Mik. 4:1). It may be hewn out of the rock or built in or put on the ground, and any material is suitable. It must be watertight, since leakage invalidates it. It must contain a minimum of 40 *se'ah* of valid water, and, although it was originally laid down that its height must be 47 in. (120 cm.) to enable a person standing in it to be completely immersed (Sifra 6:3), even though he has to bend his knees (Sifra 6:3) it was later laid down that providing there is the necessary minimum quantity of water, immersion is valid while lying down.

The Water

All natural spring water, providing it is clean and has not been discolored by any admixtures is valid for a *mikveh*. With regard to rainwater, which is ideal for a *mikveh*, and melted snow and ice (even if manufactured from "drawn" water) which are also valid, care must be taken to ensure that the water flows freely and is not rendered invalid by the flow into it being stopped, thus turning it into "drawn water." In addition the water must not reach the *mikveh* through vessels made of metal or other materials which are susceptible to ritual uncleanness. This is avoided by attaching the pipes and other accessories to the ground, by virtue of which they cease to have the status of "vessels." Similarly the *mikveh* is emptied from above by hand, by vacuum, or by electric or automatic pumps. The emptying through a hole in the bottom is forbidden since the plug may be regarded as a "vessel" as well as giving rise to the possibility of a leakage.

There is, however, one regulation with regard to the *mikveh* which considerably eases the problems of assuring a supply of valid water. Once it possesses the minimum quantity of 40 *se'ah* of valid water even though "someone draws water in a jug and throws it into the *mikveh* all day long, all the water is valid." In addition "if there is an upper *mikveh* containing 40 *se'ah* of valid water, and someone puts drawn water in the upper *mikveh*, thus increasing its volume, and 40 *se'ah* of it flows into the lower pool, that lower pool is a valid *mikveh*" (Yad, Mikva'ot 4:6). It is thus possible to exploit limitless quantities of valid water.

Various Forms of Mikveh

The above regulations determine the various kinds of *mikveh* which are in use. In rare cases where there is a plentiful supply of valid water, spring or rain- (or sea-) water which can constantly replenish the *mikveh*, the only desiderata which have to be complied with are to ensure that the water does not become invalidated by the construction of the *mikveh*, rendering it a "vessel" or by going through metal pipes which are not sunk in the ground, as detailed above.

Since, however, *mikva'ot* are usually constructed in urban and other settlements where such supplies are not freely available, the technological and halakhic solution of the valid *mikveh* depends essentially upon constructing a *mikveh* with valid water and replenishing it with invalid water, taking advantage of the fact that the addition of this water to an originally valid one does not invalidate it.

The following are among the systems used:

1. The basic *mikveh* consists of the minimum valid amount of 40 *se'ah* of rainwater. To this rainwater, ordinary water may subsequently be added through a trough which is absorbent, dug in the ground, or one made of lean concrete at least three handbreadths (c. 30 cm.) long, and one wide. Through this device the added water is regarded as coming from the ground and not through a "vessel." The resultant mixture of both types of water passes into the *mikveh* through a hole in the dividing wall. Since the added water is regarded as "seeding" the original valid water, it is called the *oẓar zeri'ah* ("store for seeding").

2. In a second system the added drawn water is not previously mixed with the rainwater, as in the previous case, but flows directly onto the basic rainwater *mikveh* through an aperture in the wall of the *mikveh*, the diameter of which must be "the size of the spout of a water bottle" (c. 2 in.; 5–6 cm., Mik. 6:7). This method is called *oẓar hasnakah* ("the store produced by contact"). Both the above methods, though they answer the halakhic needs, have their disadvantages in operation and in maintenance, particularly through the exhaustion of the rainwater and the stagnation of the standing water. The other systems are aimed at overcoming these drawbacks.

3. The *"dut"* is a cistern or tank built into the ground to store rainwater. When changing the water in the *mikveh*, it is filled each time with at least 21 *se'ah* of rainwater from the cistern and water is then added from the "store for seeding" by conduction. The water in the *mikveh* is brought into contact with the "contact store" by the method mentioned above. Though indeed this method overcomes the many shortcomings and halakhic problems, it nevertheless requires an extensive area for the cistern, and large areas of roof and pipes for filling with considerable amounts of rainwater in the winter.

4. Both a "store for seeding" and a "contact store" are built on each side of the *mikveh*. Each store has an aperture connecting its water with that of the *mikveh*.

5. A single "store" consisting of both "seeding" and "contacting."

6. A "store" upon a "store." A "contact store" is built on two stories joined by an aperture with the diameter of "the spout of a bottle." The water of the *mikveh* is validated by means of the hole in the party wall between the *mikveh* and the upper "store."

7. A "contact store" under the floor of the *mikveh*, connected by means of a hole the size of "the spout of a water bottle."

The *mikva'ot* of Jerusalem as well as the oldest *mikva'ot* in other towns of Ereẓ Israel are built in general by the method of the "contact store" as well as by the "store of seeding." In the new settlements and elsewhere the *mikva'ot* are built in the main only by the method of the "store of seeding" (a system approved by Rabbi A.I. Karelitz, the "Ḥazon Ish"). Latterly *mikva'ot* have been built by the method of two "stores."

In recent years vast improvements have been made in the hygienic and other aspects of the *mikveh*. An early enactment, attributed to Ezra, that a woman must wash her hair before immersing herself (BK 82a) may be provided for by the now universal custom of having baths as an adjunct to *mikva'ot*, the use of which is an essential preliminary to entering the *mikveh*, and especially in the United States they are provided with hairdressing salons and even beauty parlors.

The regulations for constructing the *mikveh* are complicated and its construction requires a considerable knowledge of technology combined with strict adherence to the *halakhah*, and it should be built only after consultation with, and under the supervision of, accepted rabbinic authorities. Nevertheless in order to increase the use of this essential requirement of traditional Judaism, a book has been published which consists almost entirely of instructions for making a valid "Do it yourself" *mikveh* (see D. Miller in bibl.).

[David Kotlar / Judith Baskin (2nd ed.)]

History and Archaeology

During the Second Temple period (roughly from 100 B.C.E. to 70 C.E.), the Jewish population in Palestine had a very distinctive practice of purification within water installations known as *mikva'ot*. Large numbers of stepped-and-plastered *mikva'ot* have been found in excavations in Jerusalem, in outlying villages, as well as at various rural locations. Most of the installations in Jerusalem were in basements of private dwellings and therefore must have served the specific domestic needs of the city inhabitants. Numerous examples are known from the area of the "Upper City" of Second Temple period Jerusalem (the present-day Jewish Quarter and Mount Zion), with smaller numbers in the "City of David" and the "Bezetha Hill." A few slightly larger *mikva'ot* are known in the immediate area of the Temple Mount, but these installations could not have met the needs of tens of thousands of Jewish pilgrims from outside the city attending the festivities at the Temple on an annual basis. It would appear that the Bethesda and Siloam Pools – to the north and south of the Temple Mount – were designed at the time of Herod the Great to accommodate almost all of the ritual purification needs of the large numbers of Jewish pilgrims who flocked to Jerusalem for the festivals. In addition to this, those precluded from admission to the Temple, owing to disabilities and bodily defects, would have sought miraculous healing at these pools and this is the background for the healing accounts in the Gospel of John (5: 1–13; 9: 7, 11).

Although water purification is referred to in the Old Testament, in regard to rituals and the Jewish Temple in Jerusalem, with washing, sprinkling, and dipping in water, we do not hear of specific places or installations that people would constantly frequent for the purpose of ritually cleansing their flesh. The term *mikveh* was used in a very general sense in the Old Testament to refer to a body of water of indeterminate extent (cf. Gen. 1:10; Ex. 7:19), or more specifically to waters gathered from a spring or within a cistern (Lev. 11: 36) or waters designated for a large reservoir situated in Jerusalem (Isa. 22: 11). None of these places are mentioned as having been used for ritual purification in any way. Hence, the concept of the *mikveh* as a hewn cave or constructed purification pool attached to one's dwelling or place of work is undoubtedly a later one. A distinction must be made therefore between the purification practices as they are represented in biblical sources, with Jewish water immersion rituals of the Second Temple period, as well as with later customs of *mikva'ot* prevailing from medieval times and to the present day (see below).

The basis for our information about what was or was not permitted in regard to *mikva'ot* appears in rabbinic sources: the tractate Mikva'ot in the Mishnah and Tosefta. One must take into consideration, however, that this information might very well be idealized, at least in part, and that the reality of purification practices in Second Temple times may have been much more flexible than one would suppose from these sources. Josephus Flavius is silent in his writings about the purification installations of his time, and the few references in Dead Sea Scroll manuscripts are definitely not to be relied upon to generalize about the common Jewish purification practices current in Second Temple period Palestine. The Mishnah (Mik. 1:1–8, ed. Danby) indicates that there were at least six grades of *mikva'ot*, listed from the worst to the best: (1) ponds; (2) ponds during the rainy season; (3) immersion pools containing more than 40 *se'ah* of water; (4) wells with natural groundwater; (5) salty water from the sea and hot springs; and (6) natural flowing "living" waters from springs and in rivers. Clearly the ubiquitous stepped-and-plastered installation known to scholars from archaeological excavations since the 1960s and now commonly referred to as the *mikveh* (referred to under No. 3, above) was not the best or the worst of the six grades of *mikva'ot* as set forth in the Mishnah. It is referred to as follows: "More excellent is a pool of water containing forty *se'ah*; for in them men may immerse themselves and immerse other things [e.g., vessels]" (Mik. 1:7). The validity of *mikva'ot* was apparently one of the subjects occasionally debated in the "Chamber of Hewn Stone" in Jerusalem (Ed. 7:4).

Stringent religious regulations (*halakhot*) are referred to in regard to certain constructional details and how the installations were to be used. A *mikveh* had to be supplied with "pure" water derived from natural sources (rivers, springs or rain) throughout the year and even during the long dry season, and it had to contain a minimum of 40 *se'ah* of water (the equivalent of less than one cubic meter of water) so that a person might be properly immersed (if not standing, then lying down). Once the natural flow of water into a *mikveh* had been stopped, it became "drawn" water (*mayim she'uvim*). Water could not be added mechanically, but there was a possibility of increasing the volume by allowing drawn water to enter from an adjacent container, according to the sources, so long as the original amount of water did not decrease to below the minimum requirement of water. Hence, an additional body of water, known since medieval times as the *oẓar* (the "treasury"), could be connected to the *mikveh*, and linked by pipe or channel. There was, of course, the problem of the water becoming dirty or stagnant (though not impure), but the *mikveh* was not used for daily ablutions for the purpose of keeping clean. Indeed, people appear to have washed themselves (or parts of their bodies, notably the feet and hands) before entering the ritual bath (Mik. 9:2). Basins for cleansing feet and legs have been found in front of the *mikva'ot* of Herodian dwellings in Jerusalem.

The *mikveh* was required, according to the rabbinical sources, to be sunk into the ground, either through construction or by the process of hewing into the rock, and into it natural water would flow derived from a spring or from surface rainwater in the winter seasons. There was, of course, the problem of silting (Mik. 2:6). The phenomenon of silts gathering within a *mikveh* was referred to quite clearly in rabbinic texts. For instance, in reference to the minimum quantity of water required in a *mikveh* for it to be ritually permissible, we hear that: "if the mud was scraped up [from the pool and heaped] by the sides, and three *logs* [a measure] of water drained down therein, it remains valid [for cleansing purposes]; but if the mud was removed away [from the pool] and three *logs* rained down therefrom [into the pool] it becomes invalid" (Mik. 2:6). Elsewhere, we are told about certain damming operations made inside the *mikveh*: "if the water of an immersion pool was too shallow it may be dammed [to one side] even with bundles of sticks or reeds, that the level of water may be raised, and so he may go down and immerse himself" (Mik. 7:7).

The walls and floors of the *mikveh* chambers were plastered (frequently made of slaked quicklime mixed with numerous charcoal inclusions); ceilings were either natural rock or barrel-vaulted with masonry. These installations are distinguished by flights of steps leading down into them and extending across the entire breadth of the chamber; such ubiquitous steps, however, were not referred to in the sources. The riser of the lowest step tended to be deeper than the rest of the steps, presumably to facilitate the immersion procedures when the level of water had dropped to a minimum. Some of these steps had a low raised (and plastered) partition which is thought to have separated the descending impure person (on the right) from the pure person leaving the *mikveh* (on the left). Similarly there were *mikva'ot* with double entrances and these may indicate that the activities carried out inside them resembled those undertaken in installations with the partitioned steps. This arrangement of steps and/or double entrances is known mainly from Jerusalem, but also from sites in the vicinity, as well in the Hebron Hills and at Qumran. The installations from Jerusalem and the Hebron Hills with the single partitions fit well the double lane theory, that it was constructed to facilitate the separation of the impure from the pure, but at Qumran, installations were found with three or more of these partitions, which is odd. According to one suggestion (Regev) maintaining the utmost in purity *inside* the *mikveh*, reflected by the addition of features such as the partitions, would have been a concern mainly for priests, but little support for this hypothesis has been forthcoming from the archaeological evidence itself. Indeed, Galor rightly points out that the partitions are at best symbolic rather than functional, and that in some of the installations at Qumran they were not even practical, providing in one installation a stepped lane which was only 6 in. (15 cm.) wide!

The *mikveh* was also used for the purifying of contaminated vessels (e.g. Mik. 2:9–10, 5:6, 6:1, 10:1; cf. Mark 7:4). It is not surprising, therefore, that in the excavation of *mikva'ot* at Jericho and Jerusalem, some were found to contain quantities of ceramic vessels. Alternatively, it is quite possible that such *mikva'ot* were intended specifically for the purpose of cleaning vessels and were never used for the immersion of people. At Jericho, in one *mikveh*, located in the northern sector of the main Hasmonean palace, hundreds of intact ceramic vessels (mainly bowls) of the first century B.C.E. were found in a silt layer on the floor of one installation. It is quite possible that these vessels were abandoned at one stage of the cleansing process because there was too much silt inside the installation, a phenomenon referred to in the Mishnah (see Mik. 2:10). A large concentration of pottery was also found trapped beneath a collapse of ashlars in the lower part of a *mikveh*, dating to the first century B.C.E., which was uncovered in the Jewish Quarter excavations in the Old City of Jerusalem. The concentration of pottery found there mainly consisted of an unspecified number of small bowls, mostly intact.

The date of the first appearance of stepped-and-plastered *mikva'ot* is a matter still debated by scholars, but the general consensus of opinion is that this occurred in the Late Hellenistic (Hasmonean) period, at some point during the end of the second century B.C.E. or very early in the first century B.C.E. One thing is certain: only a handful of *mikva'ot* are known from the time of the Hasmoneans, whereas by contrast large numbers of *mikva'ot* are known dating from the time of Herod the Great (late first century B.C.E.) and up to the destruction of Jerusalem (70 C.E.). This, therefore, led Berlin to conclude that the appearance of *mikva'ot* cannot predate the mid-first century B.C.E., but there is sufficient evidence at Jerusalem, Jericho, Gezer, and elsewhere to support an earlier date than that. What there can be no doubt about is that the *floruit* in the use of *mikva'ot* was in the first century C.E.

To sum up what we know about the use of the household *mikveh* in the first century based on the rabbinic texts and archaeological finds: the average size of the *mikveh* suggests that ritual bathing was ordinarily practiced individually (no more than one person would enter the installation at a time) and the location of *mikva'ot* within the basements of private dwellings suggests this purification was done regularly and whenever deemed necessary. The purpose of the immersion was to ritually cleanse the flesh of the contaminated person in pure water, but it may also have been undertaken within households before eating or as an aid to spirituality, before reading the Torah or praying. It was neither used for the cleansing of the soul nor for the redemption of sins (as with the purification procedures of John the Baptist), or any other rituals (except for the conversion of proselytes following their acceptance of the Torah and circumcision; Pes. 8:8). One assumes that disrobing took place before the immersion and that new garments were put on immediately afterwards. Ritual bathing could be conducted in the comfort of a person's dwelling, but there were also more public *mikva'ot* such as those used by peasants and other workers (such as quarrymen, potters, and lime burners) who would cleanse themselves at various locations in the landscape. A few *mikva'ot* are known in the immediate vicinity of tombs, but they are quite rare indicating that ritual purification following entrance into tombs was not common. The *mikveh* was not used for general cleaning and ablution purposes: this was done in alternative installations located within the house, or in public bathhouses instead.

The fact that so many *mikva'ot* are known from greater Jerusalem, from within the city itself as well as from the villages and farms in its hinterland, is a very clear reflection of the preoccupation Jerusalemites had in the first century with the concept of separating and fixing the boundary between the pure and the impure. A general concern about purity was common to all Jews at that time and especially in the city that contained the House of God – the Jewish Temple. There are definitely no grounds for linking the phenomenon of *mikva'ot* in Jerusalem to any one specific group within Judaism, as some have done. In the eyes of the inhabitants of the city, a clear separation would have been made between the use of *natural* and *built* places for purification. While rabbinical sources may have extolled the higher sanctity of immersing in natural sources of water, the ease with which immersion could be made in a specifically designed installation situated in the basement of a house, made it far more convenient than having to set forth into the countryside in search of a natural source of water in which one might seek to purify oneself. Natural sources of water were either situated at a distance from the city (e.g., the Jordan River), or were difficult to access (e.g., a spring used for irrigation for agriculture), or were only available at the right season in the year (e.g., pools in rocky depressions that filled up after the winter rains). Above all, it would appear that convenience counted as the most important consideration when a *mikveh* came to be built in the first century. A stepped-and-plastered installation in the basement of a house satisfied all those who wished to immerse themselves on a regular basis for purification. To that end the installation had to have had a satisfactory incoming source of pure water, and in most instances rainwater sufficed. Everything else was done for reasons of fashion and personal preference, and one should include such things as footbaths outside the *mikveh*, double entrances, and lane partitions on the steps. The idea that the construction of *mikva'ot* was done in strict accordance and adherence to religious rules and stipulations (such as those debated in the "Chamber of Hewn Stone"; Ed. 7:4) is highly unlikely and finds no support in the archaeological evidence itself. Hence, the information about *mikva'ot* as it appears in the tractates of the Mishna and Tosefta should probably be regarded as representing a certain degree of rabbinical idealism rather than the complete reality of empirical practice of *mikveh* construction that was supposedly passed down through the generations following the destruction of Jerusalem in 70 C.E.

The important and obvious conclusion, however, is that the rise in the popularity of this installation during the first century C.E. no doubt reflects changing attitudes that were coming to the fore in regard to the perception of everyday purity and possible sources of ritual contamination. In a way, we may regard the later rabbinical writings on the subject of *mikva'ot* as the reflected culmination of a heightened process of Jewish awareness regarding purity that began to intensify particularly in the mid-first century C.E. An unprecedented number of *mikva'ot* ultimately came to be built, sometimes with more than one or two installations per household, and not just in the city of Jerusalem but in the outlying villages and farms as well. This development may also be paralleled with the sudden upsurge seen in the manufacturing of stone vessels in the mid-first century C.E. (from c. 50 C.E. or perhaps 60) onwards. Such vessels were perceived of as being able to maintain purity and as such were extremely popular in the "household Judaism" assemblage of that time (see Berlin 2005), with small mugs and large (*kalal*) jars serving a particularly useful task during hand-washing purification procedures. Perhaps we should regard *mikva'ot* and stone vessels as two sides of the same coin representing the overall "explosion" of purity that took place within Judaism in the first century C.E. ("purity broke out among the Jews"; Tosef. Shab. 1:14), stemming from changing religious sensibilities on the one hand and perhaps serving on the other as a form of passive Jewish resistance against encroaching features of Roman culture in the critical decade or so preceding the Great Revolt.

[Shimon Gibson (2nd ed.)]

The Mikveh in Medieval and Modern Times

From Israel the *halakhot* of the *mikveh* and its construction spread to Europe, first and foremost to Italy. Eleazar b. Yose taught a *halakhah* on the topic of cleanness in Rome and his colleagues agreed with it (Tosef., Nid. 7:1). The close connection between Italy and Germany through the medium of the scholars of Alsace and the communities of Spires, Worms, and Mainz brought the spread of the *halakhot* of Ereẓ Israel and their *mikva'ot* were built according to the traditional format. In the Middle Ages the *mikveh* constituted civically an integral part of the Jewish center and synagogue, not merely in Byzantine Israel (Huldah, Maon-Nirim, etc.) but also in Italy, Germany, Bohemia, Lithuania, Poland, and other places. The most ancient remnants of *mikva'ot* in Germany have been uncovered in Cologne from 1170, Spires 1200, Friedberg 1260, Offburg 1351, and in Andernach, too, in the 14th century. The most typical is in Worms – a subterranean building with 19 steps descending to the entrance hall and then another 11 steps to the *mikveh* itself. A similar *mikveh* exists in Cairo and in the vault of the Tiferet Israel synagogue in Jerusalem. In Europe the architectural lines were influenced by the environment and by the builders who were generally not Jews (who had no entry to the trade guilds). The architectural and other details of their construction are remarkable by their precision – the outer and inner ornamentation, the capitals of the pillars, beautiful inscriptions, etc.; a mixture of Oriental and European elements created architectural solutions for the special problems of building the *mikveh*. In place of Roman modes, the Gothic and Baroque left their mark on the outer and inner style.

In many instances the *mikva'ot* of the Middle Ages served as bathhouses because of the order forbidding Jews to wash in the rivers together with Christians.

The views of the halakhic authorities in all generations differed with reference to many details of the *mikveh*. From this stemmed the great difference in the ways of building and in the systems of installation. Modern technology demands solutions of many problems, such as the permissibility of the use of reinforced concrete, porous concrete for the trough of validation, floor tiles to prevent leaking of the water. In every generation the authorities of each generation have delved deeply into the sources of the *halakhah* and its reasons, and from them have come to clear decisions for the planner and builder, leaving extensive scope for his imagination and his ability to coordinate *halakhah* with technology.

[David Kotlar]

BIBLIOGRAPHY: GENERAL: N. Telushkin, *Tohorat Mayim* (1964); D. Muenzberg, *Mivneh Mikva'ot ve-Hekhsheram* (1963); Krauss, Tal Arch, 1 (1910), 209ff.; ET, 11 (1965), 189–222; E. Roth (ed.), *Die alte Synagoge zu Worms* (1961), 46–51, 65, illus. nos. 25–27; R. Krautheimer, *Mittelalterliche Synagogen* (1927); D. Kotlar, in: *Miscellanea di Studi in memoria di Dario Disegni* (1969); C.M. Bassols, in: *Sefarad*, 28 (1968); J. Millás-Vallicrosa, *ibid.*, 25 (1965). **ADD. BIBLIOGRAPHY:** G. Heuberger (ed.), *Mikwe: Geschichte und Architektur juedischer Ritualbaeder in Deutschland* (1992); R. Slonim (ed.), *Total Immersion: A Mikvah Anthology* (1996); R. Wasserfall (ed.), *Women and Water: Menstruation in Jewish Life and Law* (1999). HISTORY: R. Reich, "Miqwa'ot (Jewish Ritual Baths) in the Second Temple Period and the Period of Mishnah and Talmud" (unpublished Ph.D. Thesis, Hebrew University, Jerusalem, 1991 (Heb.)); D. Amit, "Ritual Pools from the Second Temple Period in the Hebron Hills" (unpublished M.A. Thesis, Hebrew University, Jerusalem, 1996 (Heb.)). See also R. Reich, "Domestic Installations in Jerusalem of the Second Temple (= Early Roman) Period," in: G. Garbrecht (ed.), *Vortraege der Tagung Historische Wassernutzungsanlagen im oestlichen Mittelmeerraum, Jerusalem*, 21/22 (Maerz 1983), 1984, 1–9 (note alternate page numbers in the same volume); R. Reich, "A *Miqweh* at 'Isawiya near Jerusalem," in: IEJ, 34, 1984, 220–23; idem, "The Hot Bath-House (*balneum*), the Miqweh and the Jewish Community in the Second Temple Period," in: *Journal of Jewish Studies*, 39, 1988, 102–7; idem, "Ritual Baths," in: E.M. Meyers (ed.), *The Oxford Encyclopedia of Archaeology in the Near East*, vol. 4 (1997), 430–1; D. Amit, "Jerusalem-Style Ritual Baths from the Time of the Second Temple in the Mt. Hevron," in: Y. Friedman, Z. Safrai, and J. Schwartz (eds.), *Hikrei Eretz: Studies in the History of the Land of Israel Dedicated to Prof. Yehuda Feliks* (Heb., 1997), 35–48; A. Grossberg, "Ritual Baths in Second Temple Period Jerusalem and How They Were Ritually Prepared," in: *Cathedra*, 83 (1997), 151–68 (Heb.); idem, "How Were the Mikva'ot of Masada Made Ritually Fit?," in: *Cathedra*, 85 (1997), 33–44 (Heb.); E. Regev, "More on Ritual Baths of Jewish Groups and Sects: On Research Methods and Archaeological Evidence – A Reply to A. Grossberg," in: *Cathedra*, 83 (1987), 169–76 (Heb.); D. Amit, "A Miqveh Complex near Alon Shevut," in: *Atiqot*, 38 (1999), 75–84; R. Reich, "Miqwa'ot at Qumran and the Jerusalem Connection," in: L.H. Schiffman, E. Tov, and J.C. VanderKam (eds.), *The Dead Sea Scrolls: Fifty Years After Their Discovery* (2000), 728–33; A. Grossberg, "Ritual Pools for the Immersion of Hands at Masada," *Cathedra*, 95 (2000), 165–71 (Heb.); idem, "A Mikveh in the Bathhouse," *Cathedra*, 99 (2001), 171–84 (Heb.); R. Reich, "They *Are* Ritual Pool," in: BAR, 28:2 (2002), 50–55; K. Galor, "Qumran's Plastered Pools: A New Perspective," in: J.-B. Humbert and J. Gunneweg (eds.), *Science and Archaeology at Khirbet Qumran and 'Ain Feshkha. Studies in Archaeometry and Anthropology*, vol. 2 (2003); S. Gibson, "The Pool of Bethesda in Jerusalem and Jewish Purification Practices of the Second Temple Period," in: *Proche-Orient Chrétien* (2006); A.M. Berlin, "Jewish Life Before the Revolt: The Archaeological Evidence," in: *Journal for the Study of Judaism in the Persian, Hellenistic and Roman Periods*, 36 (2005), 452, note 92; L.H. Schiffman, "Proselytism in the Writings of Josephus: Izates of Adiabene in Light of the Halakhah," in: U. Rappaport (ed.), *Josephus Flavius: Historian of Eretz-Israel in the Hellenistic-Roman Period* (Heb., 1982); M. Samet, "Conversion in the First Centuries C.E.," in: I. Gafni, A. Oppenheimer, and M. Stern (eds.), *Jews and Judaism in the Second Temple, Mishna and Talmud Periods* (Heb., 1993); E. Regev, "Non-Priestly Purity and Its Religious Aspects According to Historical Sources and Archaeological Findings," in: M.J.H.M. Poorthuis and J. Schwartz (eds.), *Purity and Holiness: The Heritage of Leviticus* (2000); R. Reich, "Mishnah, Sheqalim 8:2 and the Archaeological Evidence., in: A. Oppenheimer, U. Rappaport, and M. Stern (eds.), *Jerusalem in the Second Temple. Avraham Schalit Memorial Volume* (1980), 225–56, J. Magness, *The Archaeology of Qumran and the Dead Sea Scrolls* (2002); C. Milikowsky, "Reflections on Hand-Washing, Hand-Purity and Holy Scripture in Rabbinic Literature," in: M.J.H.M. Poorthuis and J. Schwartz (eds.), *Purity and Holiness: The Heritage of Leviticus* (2000), 149–62.

MIKVEH ISRAEL (Heb. מִקְוֵה יִשְׂרָאֵל), Israel agricultural school, E. of Tel Aviv-Jaffa. Established in 1870, it is the oldest Jewish rural community in Ereẓ Israel. The school was founded by the *Alliance Israélite Universelle on the initiative of Charles *Netter, who visited the country for the first time in 1868. He then visualized such a school as the beginning of a future network of Jewish villages. In 1870 Netter obtained a lease of 650 acres (2,600 dunams) of land from the Turkish government, personally receiving the firman from the sultan in Constantinople. In the summer of 1870 he opened the school, which he directed until 1873, gaining support from the *Anglo-Jewish Association and from individuals and interesting Baron Edmond de *Rothschild in the enterprise. In 1882 the first *Bilu pioneers found work and were trained at Mikveh Israel immediately upon their arrival in the country. During his visit to Ereẓ Israel in 1898, Theodor *Herzl greeted Kaiser William II at the entrance of Mikveh Israel. Joseph *Niego directed the school from 1891 and Eliyahu *Krause from 1914 to 1955. Numerous species of fruit and forest trees were tried out there in the early years, and under Krause, Mikveh Israel became a pioneering ground for the introduction and improvement of new farm branches. Hebrew became the language of instruction soon after Krause had taken over. In the Israel *War of Independence (1948), the school was attacked several times. Since the 1930s Mikveh Israel has become an important education center for *Youth Aliyah. In 1968 it had 940 inhabitants (pupils, teachers, instructors, and other personnel). In the mid-1990s, the population was approximately 1,545, declining to 749 in 2002. Mikveh Israel has been instrumental in developing novel techniques in citrus and other farm branches, introducing avocado cultivation and the acclimatization of many livestock strains, and while it operated the Mikveh Israel wine cellars produced select wines and liqueurs. At the turn of the 20th century, the campus housed a state and state-religious agricultural high school and a school for agriculture technicians. It occupied 1.2 sq. mi. (3.2 sq. km.) and included a cultural center, a library named after Krause, experiment stations, and a botanical garden featuring over 1,000 species. Agriculture included field crops, fruit orchards, citrus groves, greenhouse crops, sheep, poultry, and bees. The name is taken from Jeremiah 14:8 and 17:13 and means "Israel's Hope."

[Efraim Orni / Shaked Gilboa (2nd ed.)]

MILAN, city in Lombardy, N. Italy. The presence of Jews in Milan in the Late Roman period is attested by three Jewish inscriptions, two of which refer to the "father of the community." In 388, *Ambrose, bishop of Milan, expressed regret for failing to lead his congregation in burning down the synagogue which instead had been destroyed "by act of God." It was soon rebuilt, but about 507 was sacked by the Christian mob, whose action was condemned by the Ostrogothic ruler Theodoric. The community presumably continued in existence, though there is little evidence in succeeding centuries except for vague references to Jewish merchants and farmers in the tenth century. With the spread of Jewish communities through northern Italy in the 13th century that of Milan was also revived, but in 1320 the *podestà* issued a decree expelling the Jews. In 1387 Duke Gian Galeazzo Visconti granted privileges to the Jews in the whole of *Lombardy; these were confirmed by Francesco Sforza and his successors. An important court Jew was Elia di Sabato da Fermo, who in 1435 became the personal physician of the duke Filippo Maria Visconti. When in 1452 Pope Nicholas v approved the Jewish right of residence in the duchy, he specifically authorized the construction of a synagogue in Milan. Pope Pius ii demanded a levy of one-fifth on the possessions of the Jews to subsidize a Crusade (1459), but was opposed by Duke Francesco Sforza. In 1489, under Ludovico il Moro, the Jews were expelled from the entire Duchy. They were soon readmitted, except to Milan itself where a Jew could only stay for three days. Similar conditions continued under the last Sforza dukes and after 1535, when the Duchy of Milan came under Spanish rule. In 1541 Emperor Charles v confirmed that Jews were allowed to live in various towns of the territory, but not in Milan. Thus, when the Jews were finally expelled in 1597, there were none in Milan itself.

Jews began to return to Milan at the beginning of the 19th century, when Milan was the capital of the Napoleonic Kingdom of Italy. An area for a Jewish cemetery was bought already before 1808. In 1820 around seven families lived in Milan; in 1840, there were already 200 Jews there. Jews came to Milan from the neighboring Kingdom of Sardinia to study at the university, as the learning centers were open to Jews. In 1848 some Jews were active in the rebellion against Austrian rule. In 1859 Milan became a part of the new Italian kingdom and the Jews received full rights. In 1870 there were more than 700 Jews in the city.

The first synagogue was built in 1840 in Via Stampa. In 1892 the synagogue of Via Guastalla was erected, designed by the architect Luca Beltrami.

Because of the great commercial and industrial development around Milan which now followed, the city became a center of attraction for new immigrants. In 1920, 4,500 Jews resided in Milano. In the same year the Jewish school was founded.

[Attilio Milano / Samuel Rocca (2nd ed.)]

Holocaust Period

Already after World War i, Jews from Central and Eastern Europe established themselves in Milan. However, only after Hitler assumed power did many refugees arrive from Central Europe; this flow continued illegally during the first years of war. In 1938 no fewer than 12,000 Jews were living in Milan. Between 1939 and 1941 around 5,000 Jews escaped to Palestine or the United States. During the autumn of 1943, the Germans carried out an anti-Jewish raid in the course of which the community synagogue was completely destroyed, after it was damaged during a bombardment. Many Jews were captured and killed by the Germans in the towns and villages where they had taken refuge. In all, 896 Jews were deported between 1943 and 1945. The biggest massacre took place at Meina on the shores of the Lake Maggiore, where 16 Jews were murdered at the end of September 1943.

Contemporary Period

At the end of the war, 4,484 Jews were living in Milan and were joined temporarily by many refugees from camps in Lombardy. The soldiers of the Jewish Brigade with the help of such members of the community as Raffaele *Cantoni, operated a refugee center at Via Unione 5. Most of the refugees continued on illegally to Palestine under the British Mandate. A number of Jewish immigrants came to Italy after 1949 from Egypt and, to a lesser degree, from other Arab countries; 4% came from Israel. The Jewish population of Milan in 1965 numbered 8,488 persons out of a total of 1,670,000 inhabitants, with the Sephardi and Oriental element predominating. In the 1950s and 1960s assimilation was widespread, especially among the Italian element, with the proportion of mixed marriages fluctuating around 50%. Still Milan emerged in this period as one of the leading and most prosperous communities in Europe. The most dominant and important figure of this period was the philanthropist Sally *Mayer, who was the president of the community from 1946 to his death in 1953. His son, Astorre Mayer, who for years presided over the Italian Zionist Federation and was honorary consul general of Israel, succeeded his father as president of the community. After the *Six-Day War (1967), some 3,000 Jews, who fled persecution in Egypt, and above all in Libya, sought refuge in Italy. In 1967 there were 8,700 Jews in Milan. Jews from Iran and Lebanon arrived in Milan in the 1970s.

[Sergio DellaPergola / Samuel Rocca (2nd ed.)]

On January 27, 1993, the Contemporary Jewish Documentation Center (CDEC) inaugurated in Milan the largest Jewish videotheque in Europe with 700 titles including *Holocaust documentaries found through research in East European archives. The CDEC archives and research facilities will be totally renovated thanks to donations by Eliot Malki, an Egyptian Jewish businessman who came to Milan in the 1970s. It included a modern conference center. The synagogue on Via Guastalla was restored and celebrated its 100th anniversary. Jewish silver ceremonial objects stolen during World War ii were returned to the synagogue by the Milan Fine Arts and History Department.

[Lisa Palmieri-Billig]

At the outset of the 21st century the community numbered around 6,500 Jews. The main school, sponsored by the community, is named after Sally Mayer. Besides the synagogue in Via Guastalla, which follows the Italian rite, there are seven other synagogues and houses of prayer of the Italian, Persian, Lebanese, and Ashkenazi communities, as well as a rest home for elderly people. The journal of the Jewish Community is *Il Bollettino della Comunita' di Milano.*

BIBLIOGRAPHY: Milano, Bibliotheca, index; Kaufmann, in: REJ, 20 (1890), 34–72; Ferorelli, in: *Vessillo Israelitico*, 63 (1925), 227–38, 337–39; A. Sarano, *Sette anni di vita e di opere della communita' israelitica di Milano (1945–52)* (1952). **ADD. BIBLIOGRAPHY:** O. Meron, "The Decline of Jewish Banking in Milan and the Establishment of the S. Ambrogio Bank (1593) – Were the Two Interrelated?" in: *Nuova Rivista Storica*, 74 (1990), 369–85; idem, "Demographic and Spacial Aspects of Jewish Life in the Duchy of Milan during the Spanish Period," in: WCJS, 10 (1993), 37–47; D. Noy, *Jewish Inscriptions of Western Europe* I (1993); J.N. Pavoncello, "Le origini della comunità di Milano," in: *Israel* (Feb. 22, 1968), 3; L. Picciotto-Fargion, *Gli ebrei in provincia di Milano 1943/45 – Persecuzione e deportazione* (1992); S., Simonsohn, *History of the Jews in the Duchy of Milan* I–IV (1982–86); A. Tedeschi Falco, *Lombardia, Itinerari ebraici* (1993), 55–71. See also bibliography to *Lombardy.

MILANO, ATTILIO (1907–1969), historian of Italian Judaism. Milano was born in Rome, where he studied law and economics. He immigrated to Israel in 1939 with the inception of the racist laws in Italy, settling in Ramat ha-Sharon, where he worked as a manufacturer. Milano's historical studies deal mostly with the economic and social conditions of various Italian Jewish groups, particularly stressing the study of the causes and consequences of usury and relations with the Roman Catholic Church. His *Bibliotheca Historica Italo-Judaica* (1954, 1964, and RMI, 1966) is an indispensable bibliographical tool for the study of Italian Jewry; it includes articles published in various periodicals by Milano himself. Among his important works are *Storia degli Ebrei Italiani nel Levante* (1949), *Storia degli Ebrei in Italia* (1963), and *Il Ghetto di Roma* (1964). He was editor of the department for Italian Jewish history of the *Encyclopaedia Judaica.*

His *Storia degli Ebrei in Italia*, originally published in 1963 (reprinted in Torino, 1992), has become a "classic" for the history of the Jews in Italy, and it is quoted very frequently. His fine collection of books, periodicals, articles and documents on the history and traditions of the Jews in Italy was donated to the Research Center for Italian Jewish Studies in Jerusalem.

BIBLIOGRAPHY: E.S. Artom, in: RMI, 29 (1963), 227–30; G. Romano, *ibid.*, 35 (1969), 369–73; idem, in: *Quaderni della labronica*, n. 3 (1969), 5–12; idem, et al., in *Scritti in memoria di Attilio Milano*, RMI, 36 (1970), 13–47. **ADD. BIBLIOGRAPHY:** G. Romano, "Attilio Milano 'ebreo letterato,'" in: *Rassegna Mensile di Israel*, 36:7–9 (1970), 13–20; R. Bachi, "Il primo lavoro storico di Attilio, Milano," in: *Rassegna Mensile di Israel,* 36:7–9 (1970), 31–34.

[Alfredo Mordechai Rabello (2nd ed.)]

MILBAUER, JOSEPH (1898–1968), poet. Born in Warsaw, Milbauer was raised in Brussels where, in 1914, he met Shalom *Aleichem, some of whose works he later translated. He went to Paris in 1921. Milbauer's early verse collections were well received. During the 1930s he was for a time editor of the *Univers Israelite*, but his outspoken Zionist opinions brought him into conflict with the paper's directors, and he resigned. Milbauer fought in both world wars and was a prisoner of war but after some harrowing experiences arrived in Ereẓ Israel as an illegal immigrant in 1944. He headed the French desk at the *Keren Ha-Yesod, and was a co-founder of a French literary circle which developed into the Association des Amitiés Israël-France. Milbauer published several more volumes of poetry, often inspired by the landscape of Israel. His other works include translations of S.Y. *Agnon, Ḥ.N. *Bialik, and S. *Tchernichowsky and the anthology *Poètes yiddisch d'aujourd'hui* (1936).

BIBLIOGRAPHY: C. Vigée, in: *L'Arche*, 134 (1968), 63–64.

[Pascal Themanlys]

MILETUS, city in Asia Minor captured by Alexander the Great in 334 B.C.E. According to a document cited by Josephus (Ant. 14:244–6), the inhabitants of Miletus during the Roman period attacked the Jews, "forbidding them to observe their Sabbaths, perform their native rites or manage their produce [tithes] in accordance with their custom." The Roman proconsul, Publius Servilius Galba, the author of the aforementioned document, was informed at Tralles of the inhabitants' actions by Prytanis, the son of Hermas and a citizen of Miletus. The proconsul subsequently ruled in favor of restoring the rights of the Jewish population. An inscription from the Roman theater refers to "the place of the Jews who are also called God-fearing." A ruined building dating from the late Roman-Byzantine period has been surmised by some to have been a synagogue.

BIBLIOGRAPHY: Schuerer, Gesch, 3 (1909^4), 16, 110, 125, 174; Juster, Juifs, 1 (1914), 252 n. 3; Frey, Corpus, 2 (1952), 14–15; E.L. Sukenik, *Ancient Synagogues in Palestine and Greece* (1934), 40–42; Mayer, Art, nos. 816–7.

[Isaiah Gafni]

MILEVSKY, AHARÓN (1904–1986), rabbi of the Jewish Ashkenazi community in Montevideo, Uruguay. He was born in Lithuania and studied at the yeshivot of Grodno and Slobodka, and in 1924–29 in the yeshivah in Hebron. In 1930–37 he was rabbi in Lithuania. In 1937 Rabbi Milevsky was invited to serve as community rabbi in Montevideo. He published two books with exegesis of Maimonides' writings: *Minḥat Aharon* (1941) and *Naḥalat Aharon* (1951). A third book, *Ḥelkat Aharon*, was published posthumously (1991). In 1970 he settled in Jerusalem.

MILEYKOWSKY, NATHAN (**Netanyahu**; 1879–1935), Zionist preacher. Born near Kovno, Lithuania, Mileykowsky was educated in the Volozhin yeshivah and ordained in the rabbinate. While in Volozhin he displayed talent as a preacher and speaker and spent two years with the preacher J.L. Yevzerow. At the age of 20, he was sent by Y. *Tschlenow on a propaganda tour of Siberia, and from that time he became a preacher and speaker on behalf of Zionism. In 1908 he settled in Poland, taught in the Hebrew high school of M. Krinski in Warsaw, and participated in its management. He continued his propaganda tours in the cities and towns of Poland. During World War I he was a preacher in the Ohel Ya'akov synagogue in Lodz. In 1920 Mileykowsky settled in Palestine, where he served as the principal of a school in Safed. From 1924 to 1929 he was sent to England, Carpatho-Russia (then part of Czechoslovakia), and the United States on a mission for the Jewish National Fund and the Keren Hayesod. Toward the end of his life, he settled in Herzliyyah and was active in the Farmers' Association. During the *Arlosoroff murder trial (1933–34), he set up a committee for the defense of the accused. Some of his speeches are included in his anthologies *Ha-Nevi'im ve-ha-Am* ("The Prophets and the People," 1913) and *Folk un Land* (1928).

BIBLIOGRAPHY: Tidhar, 1 (1947), 186–7; EẒD, 3 (1965) 417–9; LNYL, 5 (1963), 621.

[Yehuda Slutsky]

MILGRAM, STANLEY (1933–1984), U.S. social psychologist. Born in New York City, Milgram attended public schools in the Bronx, then earned a bachelor's degree in political science at Queens College in 1954. Convinced by an advisor to change his field of study to psychology, Milgram entered Harvard University, where he studied under Solomon Asch and Gordon Allport, receiving his doctoral degree in social psychology in 1960.

That year Milgram joined the faculty of Yale University as an assistant professor, and in 1961 he began his experiments on obedience to authority. He found, in studies conducted at Linsly-Chittenden Hall, that 65 percent of the subjects (ordinary citizens of New Haven) followed instructions to administer what they believed were harmful, even potentially fatal, electric shocks to an unwilling stranger – simply because they were directed to do so by an authority figure dressed in a lab coat. At the end of the experiment, the subjects were told that the victim did not actually receive shocks. Milgram's findings, released in 1963, were considered alarming; critics, including the American Psychiatric Association, initially questioned the ethics of the experiment. In time, however, Milgram's experiment was considered a milestone in the study of the social aspects of obedience and the primary documentation of what came to be called "situationism," whereby external situations override internal perceptions and moral standards. It is widely regarded as the most powerful experiment ever conducted in social psychology. Milgram, in his work *Obedience to Authority* (1974), used his findings to explain a range of shocking behavior, from guards in Nazi concentration camps to American soldiers at the My Lai massacre.

Milgram taught at Harvard from 1963 to 1967, where he conducted other noteworthy research, including the lost-letter technique and the "small world" problem, which both concerned the degrees of separation between randomly selected people. The studies gave rise to the popular expression "six degrees of separation."

In 1967 Milgram was named the head of the social psychology doctoral program at the City University of New York. In 1980 he was appointed a distinguished professor at the City University Graduate Center, where he continued to teach until his death in 1984. His research in the 1970s and early 1980s is considered to have established the subfield of urban psychology. Milgram's work continues to be widely cited in psychology textbooks, and its influence on popular culture has extended to a television movie, *The Tenth Level* (1976), and a Broadway play, *Six Degrees of Separation*, which was adapted for film in 1993.

[Dorothy Bauhoff (2nd ed.)]

MILGROM, JACOB (1923–), U.S. Bible scholar. Born in New York City and educated at Brooklyn College (B.A. 1943) and the Jewish Theological Seminary (B.H.L. 1943, M.H.L. 1946, D.H.L 1953, D.D. 1973), Milgrom was a rabbi at Conservative synagogues in Orange, New Jersey (1948–51) and Richmond, Virginia (1951–65). He taught at Virginia Union University, Graduate School of Religion (1955–65); the University of California, Berkeley; Graduate Theological Union (1965–72), where he directed the Jewish Studies Program; and the UCB study center at the Hebrew University, and he was named emeritus professor of Hebrew and Bible studies. Milgrom was a Guggenheim Fellow, a Fulbright Fellow, a fellow of the Institute for Advanced Studies and of the Albright Institute of Archaeological Research, both in Jerusalem, and a fellow of the American Academy for Jewish Research. In 1994 he and his wife, also an academic, moved to Jerusalem, where he began teaching at the Hebrew University and the Jewish Theological Seminary.

An outstanding Bible scholar, Milgrom is recognized as one of the leading authorities on Leviticus, as a result of his commentary on that book, his best-known work. Milgrom believes that "theology is what Leviticus is all about," and his massive commentary, according to critics, is distinguished by its comprehensiveness and thoroughness in its examination not only of the sources, authorship, meaning, and significance of the text, but of the ancient and modern commentary and scholarship on it. He has been praised, in particular, for his generosity in discussing theories and interpretations other than his own, even going so far as to cite his own students by name and arguing respectfully with them. Milgrom's interpretations have not met with universal agreement, but his commentary has established itself as the modern standard.

Milgrom's books include *Studies in Levitical Terminology* (1970), *Cult and Conscience: The Asham and the Priestly Doctrine of Repentance* (1976), *Studies in Cultic Theology and Terminology* (1983), *The JPS Torah Commentary: Numbers* (1990), and *Leviticus: A New Translation With Introduction and Commentary* (1–16, 1991; 17–22, 2000; 23–27, 2001). He also published over 200 scholarly articles.

[Drew Silver (2nd ed.)]

MILHAUD, DARIUS (1892–1974), French composer. Milhaud was born in Aix-en-Provence and was descended from an old Jewish family that claimed to have been among the first settlers in southern France after the fall of Jerusalem. He entered the Paris Conservatory at the age of 17, was soon attracted by the theater, and between 1910 and 1916 composed *La Brebis egarée*, *Agamemnon*, and *Le pauvre matelot*. He became acquainted with the composer Eric Satie and the writers Paul Claudel and Jean Cocteau and, when Claudel was appointed French minister to Brazil, he asked Milhaud to become his secretary. Milhaud spent almost two years (1917–18) in Rio de Janeiro, and his musical impressions of Brazil echo in many of his compositions. After his return to Paris, he joined a circle of progressive artists, the musicians of which formed an inner circle later known as "Les Six." A versatile and prolific composer, Milhaud wrote music for concert, stage, and screen, and for voice and orchestra. South American rhythms, U.S. jazz, Jewish synagogal traditions (especially those of his native region, the *Comtat Venaissin), 12-tone music, and trends and styles of great divergence merge in his works. Yet the mixture is always unmistakably his own.

Milhaud's most important contributions to 20th-century music are to be found in some of his operas: *Les Choëphores* (1915); *Esther de Carpentras* (1925, with text by Armand *Lunel); *Christophe Colomb* (1928); *Bolivar* (1943); and the biblical opera *David* which Milhaud composed with Lunel for the Jerusalem Festival of 1954. Milhaud wrote concertos for almost every orchestral instrument, ballets, short and full-scale symphonies, chamber music, songs, piano music, and cantatas. Among the best known of his compositions on Jewish themes are his *Service Sacré* (1947), and two song cycles with piano accompaniment: *Poèmes juifs* (1916) and *Chants populaires hébraïques* (1925). He also wrote musical settings of Psalms for solo voices and chorus; the ballet *La Création du Monde* (1923); a piano suite, *Le Candélabre à sept branches* (1951); and music for various festival prayers.

When France collapsed in 1940 Milhaud immigrated to the U.S. and became a professor at Mills College, Oakland, California. After 1947 he divided his time between the U.S. and Paris, where he became a professor of composition at the Conservatory. The story of his life and musical beliefs was told in *Notes sans musique* (1949; *Notes Without Music*, 1953), which also appeared in Hebrew, and in *Entretiens avec Claude Rostand* (1952). During his later years Milhaud suffered from rheumatoid arthritis which confined him to a wheelchair for long periods of time.

BIBLIOGRAPHY: P. Collaer, *Darius Milhaud* (Fr., 1947); H.H. Stuckenschmidt, *Schoepfer der neuen Musik* (1958), 204–16; P. Claudel, *Correspondence Paul Claudel and Darius Milhaud 1912–1953* (1961); Grove, Dict.; Riemann-Gurlitt; MGG.

[Peter Emanuel Gradenwitz]

MILIAN, MAXIMIN (**Mendel Gruenberg**; 1885–1953), Romanian journalist and short-story writer. Born in Ploeşti, Milian wrote for various papers and was editorial secretary of *Lupta* ("The Fight") until the antisemitic regime of Octavian Goga in 1937. He devoted himself to Jewish problems and contributed to *Curierul Israelit* ("Jewish Courier"). His volumes of short stories included *Pạcatul iubirii* ("Sin of Love," 1910) and *Puternicul* ("The Strong," 1910). In 1933 he gave warning of the dangers of Nazism in the book, *15 zile în imperiul lui Hitler* ("15 Days in Hitler's Empire").

MILIBAND, RALPH (1924–1994), British academic and socialist theorist. Born in Brussels, Miliband was a member of *Ha-Shomer ha-Ẓa'ir before fleeing to England with his father in 1940 just before the German invasion of Belgium. He was educated at the London School of Economics and came under the influence of Harold *Laski. An independent socialist, in the 1950s, Miliband was associated with E.P. Thompson, John Saville, and other active intellectuals of the British "New Left." Miliband taught at the London School of Economics before moving to Leeds University as professor of politics from 1972 to 1978. He was best known for his influential political works such as *Parliamentary Socialism* (1961), which argued that the British Labour Party, heavily weighed down by constitutional niceties, could never enact true socialism, and by works such as *The State in Capitalist Society* (1969) and *Capitalist Democracy in Britain* (1982), all written from an independent Marxist position. In his later *Socialism for a Skeptical Age* (1994), Miliband admitted the previous failures of socialism, but remained an independent, pro-democracy Marxist to the end. His son DAVID (1965–), who was educated at Oxford and MIT, was a leading figure on the moderate Labour left. He edited *Reinventing the Left* (1994) and became a Labour member of parliament in 2001. He was made minister for schools by Tony Blair in 2002 and entered the cabinet as cabinet secretary in 2004. Unlike his father, David Miliband was a moderate center-leftist, and headed Tony Blair's Policy Unit after Blair became prime minister in 1997.

BIBLIOGRAPHY: ODNB online; M. Newman, *Ralph Miliband and the Politics of the New Left* (2002).

[William D. Rubinstein (2nd ed.)]

MILICH, ADOLPHE (1884–1964), French painter, born in Tyszowce, Poland; a member of the school of Paris. He originally worked as a sign painter, finally settling in Paris in 1920. During the German occupation he lived in Switzerland. Milich worked in oils and watercolors, and painted landscapes, still lifes, large compositions of women bathing, and portraits. He particularly loved the Mediterranean landscape of Provence and of the area around Lugano. His painting owes much to his long study of the old masters. Among modern painters, the strongest influence is that of Cézanne. Milich cultivated his own idiom regardless of fashion. His work is well thought out and serene, and is characterized by its joyful color harmonies.

BIBLIOGRAPHY: G. Huisman, *Milich* (Fr., 1949); Roth, Art, 665.

MILITARY LAW.

Morality and War in Judaism

The prophetic view of the end of days is expressed in the words: "and they shall beat their swords into plowshares, and their spears into pruning hooks; nation shall not lift up sword against nation, neither shall they learn war any more" (Isa. 2:4). But until those days arrive, there may be times when war is required. In such circumstances, *halakhah* views war as a necessity, and participation therein as an obligation under certain circumstances.

A soldier acting in accordance with *halakhah* may not indulge in the naked exercise of force, brutality, or vandalism, but rather must be guided by the recognition of an obligation imposed by an exigency brought about by reality. The Torah establishes the boundaries of what is permitted and forbidden in war for both individual and for society, with the view of achieving the military objective while striking a balance between recognition of the nature of soldiers in war – who must, at times, be permitted to behave in ways that would be forbidden in peacetime – and the need to imbue those soldiers with the qualities of compassion and holiness, even during times of war. It is instructive that the laws of prayer and of the sanctity of the synagogue are derived from the laws governing a military camp (Ber. 25a). Although under certain circumstances the Torah views war as an obligation incumbent upon every man in Israel, King David was not allowed to build the Temple because he had fought many wars (I Chron. 22:7–10). This exemplifies the potentially problematic nature of war, and the need to strike an appropriate balance between single-minded combat against the enemy and preserving the moral standards of the combatants.

In this entry, we shall briefly consider the salient issues of military law in Jewish law. We shall examine the classic commandments related to war as they appear in the Bible, in Talmudic literature, and in halakhic decisions, and consider the contemporary ramifications of some of them and their expression in modern society.

The Sanctity of the Camp in Time of War

The Torah states (Deut. 23:10): "When you go forth against your enemies and are in camp, then you shall keep yourself from every evil thing." In the tannaitic Midrash, the Sages interpreted this verse as implying a special warning in time of war to be careful regarding matters of defilement and purity, tithes, incest, idolatry, bloodshed, and slander (Sif. Deut. 254, ed. Finkelstein). In his commentary to Deuteronomy 23:10, Naḥmanides explains that human nature is such that moral restraints are loosened at time of war, and we shed the sense of shame felt in normal human society, with regard to such acts as licentiousness and theft. This is a by-product of the cruelty that envelops soldiers when they go to war. The Torah therefore saw need for reinforcement of these matters through a special proscription. In the ensuing verses, the Torah cautions about purity and physical cleanliness in the military camp. The section concludes with a general explanation that these commandments are required so that the Divine presence not abandon the Israelite camp: "Because the Lord your God walks in the midst of your camp, to save you and to give up your enemies before you; therefore your camp must be holy, that He may not see anything indecent among you, and turn away from you" (Deut. 23:15).

Discretionary War and Obligatory War

The Mishnah (Sot. 8:7) distinguishes between two types of war: discretionary war and obligatory war. According to Maimonides, an obligatory war is like that fought by Joshua to liberate the land of Israel from the Seven Nations, the war to eradicate Amalek, or a war "to defend Israel against an enemy that attacks them." A discretionary war is one undertaken to extend the borders of the state, such as the wars fought by King David (Yad, Melakhim 5:1; Sot. 44b; TJ, Sot. 8:10). Later rabbinical authorities differed on the interpretation of the term "to defend Israel against an enemy that attacks them." Some explained that this refers to a situation in which Israel is attacked by her enemies, constituting a defensive war (obligatory). This is as opposed to a preventive war in which a preemptive strike is made against an enemy before it is able to realize its intention to attack, which constitutes a discretionary war (*Leḥem Mishnah* ad loc.). Others extended the scope of the term "to defend Israel against an enemy" (and hence of an obligatory war) to include a preventive war, inasmuch as a defensive war – i.e., once Israel is actually under attack – is clearly obligatory, just as one is always obligated to rescue a victim from an assailant (*Sheyarei Korban* commentary to TJ, Sot. loc. cit.).

The decision to embark upon a discretionary war requires the approval of a court of 71 (Mish., Sanh. 1:5; Yad, Melakhim 5:2). However, the court cannot initiate the war. The initiative must come from the king, who must then seek the court's approval (*Tosefot Yom Tov* on Mish. Sanh. loc. cit.). According to Naḥmanides (*Hassagot Ramban*, on *Sefer ha-Mitzvot*, gloss no. 17), the Urim and Thummim must also be consulted, as going to war must be done at the behest of the priest who wears them.

The Obligation to Serve, Fear, and Conscientious Objection

According to the Torah, the minimum age for military service is 20 (Num. 1:3, and Rashi and Naḥmanides ad loc.). The Torah does not expressly establish a maximum age. Some hold that the maximum age for military service is 60 (Sforno, Num. 1:45), while others suggest that it was 40 (according to certain versions of Sif. Deut., ed. Finkelstein, 197).

The book of Deuteronomy provides guidelines for exemption from military service. The Torah (Deut. 20) provides that, before venturing into battle, the priest– referred to in the Mishnah as the "Anointed for Battle" (Sot. 8:1) – must speak to the people and encourage them so that they not fear the enemy and to place their trust in God, as the Torah expressly forbids fear of the enemy in war (Maim., *Sefer ha-Mitzvot*, negative precept 58; *Sefer ha-Ḥinnukh*, 525). Following the priest's speech, the officers address the people and exempt the following four categories of people: (a) one who has built a home and not dedicated it; (b) one who has planted a vineyard but not yet enjoyed its fruit (the fruit can only be used after the fourth year); (c) one who has betrothed a woman but not yet married her (see *Marriage); (d) one who is afraid and fainthearted, "lest he cause his comrades to be afraid." Later sources explain the application of these exemptions in practice. Thus, prior to the battle with the Midianites, God commands Gideon to tell the fearful to return home; more than one third of the force leaves (Judges 7:3). The Book of Maccabees (I Maccabees 3:55) relates that soldiers were exempted for the same reasons. There is some disagreement among the *tannaim* regarding the nature of the fear that exempts a person from going to war (Mish. Sot. 8:5; Sot. 44a). In Rabbi Akiva's view, this alludes to fear of war. According to the mishnaic citation of R. Akiva, his concern was fear of the dangers of war, whereas according to the Tosefta (Sot. 7:24), R. Akiva's concern was not the fear of war per se, but rather the fear that his sense of mercy would affect his ability to fight, and even a stony and mighty warrior was commanded to return home in the event of his feelings of mercy being likely to impair his ability to fight. According to R. Yose the Galilean, this exemption also refers to a person who is fearful because he knows himself to be a sinner, his feelings of guilt leading him to fear that he will be punished for his sins by death in battle. Although these four categories of people are exempted from battle, they are commanded to contribute to the war effort by providing food and water for the troops, and by repairing the roads (Mish., Sot. 8; Yad, Melakhim 7:9).

In addition to the above, a man is exempt from going to war during the first year of his marriage, in order to make his wife happy (Deut. 24:5). The Sages extended this one-year exemption to building a house and harvesting a vineyard, as well (TJ, Sot. 8:8; Yad, Melakhim 7:9). Unlike the other exemptions, a person exempt for these reasons is not required to contribute to the war effort, but simply stays home (Deut. 24:5; Sot. 44a).

All these exemptions apply exclusively to a discretionary war; in the case of an obligatory war, "all go forth, even the bridegroom out of his chamber and the bride from her bridal pavilion" (Mish., Sot. 8:8).

The Israel Supreme Court discussed these issues at length in its decision in the *Schein* case (HC 734/83 *Shein v. Minister of Defense*, 38 (III) PD 393, per M. Elon). The petitioner in that case was a reserve soldier who refused a call-up order to serve in southern Lebanon, on grounds of conscience. He argued that he opposed the Israeli army's presence in Lebanon, and believed that presence to be illegal. The petitioner had already been tried for a previous refusal, and the petition related to a new call-up order and to the sentence that he had served. In denying the petition, Justice Elon surveyed philosophical and legal positions accepted by various states in regard to conscientious objection, and addressed the distinction between general conscientious objection and selective conscientious objection, that only relates to a specific type of military service. Justice Elon went on to examine the view of Jewish law. "In principle, the issue before us was addressed by Jewish law in its earliest days, as a matter related to the subject of exemption from the obligation of military service" (p. 403). After reviewing the above-mentioned sources and the opinions expressed by the *tannaim*, he concluded: "The foregoing quotations reflect the various opinions in Jewish law concerning an issue essentially comparable to the question of exemption from military service for reasons of conscience. The reasons for exemption are general and inclusive, and they concern the character of the person and his attitude to violence. They are not selective. They do not pertain to a particular time and place, and they are not based on ideological-social outlooks. Finally, even the general and inclusive reasons are applicable only to a "discretionary" war, but not to an obligatory war in a time of emergency (p. 405).

Participation of Women in War

From the Mishnah's statement that "all go forth, even the bridegroom out of his chamber and the bride from her bridal pavilion," one may conclude that both men and women are required to serve in an obligatory war. Certain later rabbinical authorities sought to limit this rule by saying that women are only required to help provision the troops (Rashash on Sot. 44b), while others opined that only the bridegroom goes to war, whereas the bride merely cancels her wedding (Radbaz on Maimonides, Melakhim 7:4).

The verse that forbids a woman from wearing a man's garments (Deut. 22:5) has been interpreted as prohibiting a woman from carrying arms, and thus prohibiting her going to war (Ibn Ezra). Others saw the verse as limited to matters of modesty, and therefore not to be taken as forbidding the participation of women in war (Rabbenu Perez, in *Shitat Kadmonim le-Nazir*, 1972). The subject assumed practical significance in the State of Israel with regard to the question of the conscription of women. Some authorities, relying upon some of the above-mentioned sources, argued that it is prohibited, while others expressed the view that it is not, so long as modesty is preserved. Under Section 39(c) of the Defense Service Law [Consolidated Version], 5746 – 1986, a woman may be exempted from service if she shows that it would be incompatible with "her family's religious way of life."

The Commandment to Sue for Peace

"When you draw near to a city to fight against it, offer terms of peace to it" (Deut. 20:10). Before launching war against a city or placing it under siege, the Torah requires an offer of peace. There is dispute as to whether this duty *also* applies to an obligatory war, as held by Maimonides (Melakhim 6:1), or only applies to a discretionary war, as is the view of Rashi (Deut. 20:10, based upon Sif. Deut., ed. Finkelstein, 199, and Rabad, on Maimonides ad loc.). Maimonides interprets the offer of peace as the granting of an opportunity to surrender and to accept subjugation to Israel and the obligation to pay tribute. Some commentators suggest that, practically speaking, this approach sees the purpose of the offer of peace as a means for achieving the objectives of war in an easier, more efficient manner, while avoiding the loss of life. Under this approach, the call for peace applies to an obligatory war as well, inasmuch as it is clearly preferable to achieve the objectives of an obligatory war without resort to combat. Another approach sees the call for peace as an end in itself, which prevents war and teaches compassion (*Sefer ha-Ḥinnukh*, Mitzvah 527). Therefore, it is not required in an obligatory war.

This *mitzvah* led the Sages to the midrashic statement regarding the importance of peace in Judaism: "Great is peace, for Israel requires it even in war" (Sif. Deut., loc. cit.).

The Laws of Siege

THE DUTY TO LEAVE ONE DIRECTION OPEN FOR ESCAPE. The Midrash (Sif. Num., ed. Horowitz, 157) cites the opinion of the *tanna* Rabbi Nathan, that when Israel laid siege in its war with Midian (Num. 31), one side was left open so that the Midianites could flee. Naḥmanides (*Hassagot al Sefer ha-Mitzvot la-Rambam*, 5), suggests two reasons for this. The first is educational, namely, to encourage compassion even for an enemy in time of war. The second reason is tactical: to avoid emboldening the enemy by putting it in a position from which there can be no escape, and in which it has nothing to lose. In his opinion, this rule only applies to a discretionary war. As opposed to this, Maimonides sees it as a duty in every war. Rabbi Meir Simḥah ha-Kohen of Dvinsk (*Meshekh Ḥokhmah*, at Num. 31:6) explains that the source of the disagreement between Naḥmanides and Maimonides is that Maimonides views this primarily as a matter of military tactics. Therefore it is not an obligation, but rather a recommendation applying even to an obligatory war. Naḥmanides sees the underlying reason as that of compassion, which applies only to a discretionary war.

This dispute has practical ramifications to this day. Is there a halakhic obligation to allow the enemy an avenue of escape? Contemporary halakhic authorities disagreed as to whether the *halakhah* required the Israeli army to allow PLO terrorists to escape during the 1982 siege of Beirut. Rabbi S. Goren rejected the distinction of the *Meshekh Ḥokhmah*, and ruled that according to Maimonides there was a duty to allow them to escape, even in an obligatory war. Rabbi S. Yisraeli accepted the distinction and ruled that according to Maimonides there was no such duty in an obligatory war, and the matter was subject to the discretion of the military commanders and the government (see Bibliography).

DESTRUCTION OF TREES DURING A SIEGE. A special provision of the rules of siege concerns the status of trees in and around the besieged city: "When you besiege a city for a long time, making war against it in order to take it, you shall not destroy its trees by wielding an axe against them; for you may eat of them, but you shall not cut them down. For is the tree of the field man that it should be besieged by you?" (Deut. 20:19). This rule applies only to a discretionary war (Sif. Deut., ed. Finkelstein, 203).

It should be noted that this verse constitutes the basis for the general prohibition upon destroying fruit trees, and of the destruction of property in general, independent of the rules of war (Maim., *Sefer ha-Mitzvot*, negative commandments, 57; Yad, Melakhim 6:8).

The prohibition only applies to unnecessary destruction. Felling trees for the purpose of constructing the siege, or to deprive the besieged enemy of wood for its own use, or to prevent the enemy from using the trees as cover, is permitted (*Hassagot ha-Ramban al Sefer ha-Mitzvot la-Rambam*, 6). Although the language of the Torah only prohibits the destruction of fruit trees, according to a *baraita* (BK 91b), the prohibition applies to all trees, and where there is need for wood, non-fruit bearing trees must be used first (BK 91b).

In his Torah commentary (Deut. 20:19–20), Naḥmanides explains that the reason for this special prohibition is that once the city is captured its property will fall into the hands of Israel, and the soldiers must have faith in God that they will be victorious and that they will inherit the spoils. Thus, the prohibition derives from the rule that a person may not destroy his own property. According to Naḥmanides, when the purpose of the war is not conquest but the destruction of the city, all the trees may be destroyed.

The closing expression, "Are the trees in the field man that it should be besieged by you?" has been variously interpreted by biblical commentators. Rashi understood it as a rhetorical question, expressing the idea that trees are not the enemy, and hence their destruction is not justified. Ibn Ezra explained: "For the tree is man's life"; therefore, in harming the trees we harm ourselves.

During Israel's war with Moab, the prophet Elisha expressly commanded that the army "fell every good tree, and stop up all springs of water, and ruin every good piece of land with stones" (II Kings 3:19). The explanation given for this deviation from the language of the Torah is that it was an emergency measure (Radak).

Spoils and Looting

From the Torah, it would appear that the taking of spoils was common, and was viewed as an integral part of war (Genesis 11:24; I Samuel 30:24). This conclusion can also be reached on the basis of the prohibition against destroying trees, discussed above. In Deuteronomy, following the command to sue for peace, we are told that Israel shall enjoy the spoils of a city that refuses the offer of peace (Deut. 20:14). In the Midrash, the Sages emphasized that it was not only permissible to plunder, but that the spoils could be taken for the personal use of the soldiers (Sif. Deut., ed. Finkelstein, 200). According to Maimonides, the spoils were intended solely for the soldiers, and might be described as their payment (Maimonides, Melakhim 4:9). In accordance with David's instruction that the spoils be divided equally between the front-line soldiers and those in the rear who stay "on the baggage" (I Samuel 30:24), Maimonides ruled that the spoils must be equally apportioned.

Although permitted, it would seem to be considered inappropriate to take more than the costs of war. This is concluded from Abraham's decision to take from the king of Sodom "nothing but what the young men have eaten, and the share of the men who went with me" (Gen. 14:24; Radak and Sforno, loc. cit.). In the Scroll of Esther we find that the Jews were permitted to plunder the property of their enemies, yet the text emphasizes "but they laid no hands on the plunder" (Esther 8:11; 9:15).

Taking spoils can bring about the undesirable result of lowered moral standards in war, such as occurred at the time of King Saul (I Samuel 14:31–32), when the people, in their excitement over the spoils, transgressed the prohibition of "eating with the blood." As earlier noted, the Torah considers maintaining the moral standards of the army to be an exalted goal and this is another argument against taking spoils. In view of this, some are of the opinion that taking spoils is permitted only for the army as a whole, in accordance with the instructions of the relevant authorities, but is not permitted to individual soldiers.

Harming Innocent Civilians

The language of the Torah leads to the conclusion that if, in a discretionary war, the enemy does not accept the terms of surrender offered by the Israelite army, then all the men are to be killed: "But if it makes no peace with you… you shall put all its males to the sword" (Deut. 20:12–13). This is the conclusion drawn by Maimonides (Melakhim 6:4), who emphasizes the corollary that women and children are not to be killed. Maimonides does not distinguish between combatants and noncombatants. This should perhaps be viewed in its historical and cultural context. In the ancient world, the enemy army comprised the entire male population, whether as direct participants in the fighting or as support. The correct translation of this rule to contemporary law might be that only combatants may be targeted, and that the innocent civilian population must not be harmed.

Over the last few generations, since the beginning of the Zionist enterprise, and particularly since the establishment of the State of Israel, contemporary halakhic authorities have addressed these issues. Rabbi S. Yisraeli (see Bibliography) was of the opinion that there is justification for harming a civilian population that supports the enemy forces and voluntarily assists them, even under the doctrine of the "pursuer" (*rodef*) (see *Penal Law). However, when the enemy forces compel that assistance from the civilian population, there is no justification for harming non-combatant civilians.

The biblical story of Simeon and Levi and the city of Shechem (Gen. 34) is germane to this discussion. After Shechem ben Hamor, son of the city's king, rapes Jacob's daughter Dinah, Simeon and Levi kill all of the males of the city. Some commentators (Naḥmanides, at Gen. 34:13) take a dim view of what they see as their immoral conduct, and argue that this is why Simeon and Levi were reprimanded by their father Jacob (Gen. 49:5–7). Others justify the act, arguing that it is of the nature of war that the acts of one *obligate* all (*Maharal, Gur Aryeh al ha-Torah*, Gen. 34:13), or that it was justifiable from a formal halakhic point of view (Yad, Melakhim 9:14). Some have responded that, even if it were halakhically permitted, it must nevertheless be morally condemned, as we should be strict in capital matters (Rabbi S. Goren, Bibliography, 1:28).

Rabbi S. Yisraeli addressed the question of the relationship between the international law of armed conflicts and Torah law (see Bibliography), expressing the view that the rule that the law of the country is binding (see entry **Dina de-Malkhuta Dina*) may apply not only to the spheres of civil and criminal law, but to international law, as well. According to this approach, international conventions on what is permitted and forbidden in war are halakhically valid (except, of course, in regard to what constitutes an "obligatory war").

BIBLIOGRAPHY: M. Elon, *Ha-Mishpat ha-Ivri* (1988), 1:454; idem, *Jewish Law* (1994), 2:554; idem, *Jewish Law* (*Cases and Materials*) (1999), 539–44; G. Garman, *Melekh Yisrael*, 297–313; S. Goren, *Meshiv Milḥamah*, 3 vols. (1983–86); I.Y. Herzog, S. Yisraeli, D. Lishinsky, S. Cohen, Y. Gershuni, S. Min-Ha-Har, Y. Shaviv, M. Ushpizai, in: *Teḥumin*, 4 (1983), 13–96; S. Rosenfeld, "*Ḥalukat Shalal u-Bizzah be-Milḥamot Yamenu*," in: *Teḥumin*, 23 (2003), 52–59; N.D. Shapira, "*Ha-Kri'ah le-Shalom*," in: *Torah she-be-al Peh*, 39 (1998), 82–90; A. Sharir, "*Etika Ẓeva'it al pi ha-Halakhah*," in: *Teḥumin*, 25 (2005), 426; E. Shochetman, "*Sikkun Ḥayyalei Ẓahal le-shem Meni'at Pegi'ah be-Ezraḥei ha-Oyev*," in: *Netiv*, 2 (2003), 25; 3 (2003), 28; Y. Unger and M. Finkelstein, *Parashot Lekh Lekha, Va-Yishlah*, in: *Parshat ha-Shavu'a* (2006); S. Yisraeli, *Amud ha-Yemini* (1992).

[Ariel Ehrlich (2nd ed.)]

MILITARY SERVICE. Jews served in the national armies of most countries in which they settled. However, in many states they were denied the right to bear arms before the 20th century since they were considered to be second-class citizens, not fit to fight for their country. A major consideration motivating the Jewish desire to fight in the armed forces of the countries of their adoption was that they hoped that the acceptance of this obligation would entitle them to civic rights. For this very reason, states which denied Jews civil rights frequently restricted their service in their armies. In the 20th century, however, Jews participated fully in modern warfare as the Table: Jewish Participation in World War I and Table: Jewish Participation in World War II show.

The figures in the table for the world wars were published by the United Nations and do not include Jewish partisans who fought against Nazi Germany. Jews served in all the services and a few became army commanders, for example the Italian general, Giorgio *Liuzzi. In the early years of Israeli statehood, the military achievements of the Israel Defense Forces during the *War of Independence (1948–49), the *Sinai Campaign of 1956, and the *Six-Day War (1967) focused attention on the quality of the Jewish soldier.

United States of America

Jews first did military service early in the colonial period in the form of militia duty. Asser *Levy insisted on his right to

Jewish Participation in World War I (by country)

U.S.	250,000
Great Britain	50,000
British Commonwealth	8,000
Czarist Russia	450,000
Austria-Hungary	275,000
Italy	8,000
France	35,000
Germany	90,000
Bulgaria	6,000
TOTAL	**1,172,000**

Jewish Participation in World War II (by country).

U.S.	550,000
Great Britain	62,000
Canada	16,000
South Africa	10,000
Australia and New Zealand	3,000
Palestinian Units in British army	35,000
Bulgaria	7,000
Holland	7,000
U.S.S.R.	500,000
Greece	13,000
France	35,000
Poland	140,000
Czechoslovakia	8,000
TOTAL	**1,397,000**

be allowed to stand guard duty against attack by Indians, and other early members of the community of New Amsterdam demanded the right of helping to defend the settlement and, when necessary, sprang to arms in a common effort to repel hostile assaults, earning full admission as citizens of the colony (1657). Later, in the 1750s, Jews served in the conquest of Canada in which Aaron *Hart led a battalion against the French in Canada, and Judah Hays commanded a 16-ton privateer, the *Duke of Cumberland*. During the American War of Independence (1775–83), a considerable number of Jews volunteered for the colonialist armies and several acquired considerable distinction, among them: Isaac Franks, David Salisbury *Franks, Lewis Bush, and Solomon Bush. In this war some U.S. companies included a considerable number of Jewish soldiers, such as that commanded by Major Benjamin Nones (d. 1826), a French Jew who served under the command of Lafayette and George Washington. During the second war between the United States and Great Britain from 1812 to 1814, there were a small number of Jews in the U.S. army most of whom were volunteers or members of militia companies. Aaron Levy (d. 1829) became a lieutenant colonel. Two naval officers achieved fame in this war. Captain John Ordraonaux (1778–1841) seized nine British prize vessels and later captured a British frigate and Uriah Phillips *Levy volunteered for the U.S. Navy in 1812 and rose to become commodore nearly half a century later. Levy's ship was captured by the British after sinking 21 merchant vessels and he spent the last 16 months of the war in a British prison. His subsequent career in the face of antisemitic opposition opened the way for future generations of U.S. Jewish sailors, among whom Claude C. *Bloch rose to become admiral of the U.S. fleet over a century later. In the following decades many Jews held senior posts in the U.S. forces; in the Nones family there were four naval officers who rose to the rank of captain. During the Mexican War (1846–48) the Jews of Baltimore formed a volunteer corps and Jonas Phillips Levy, brother of Uriah Phillips Levy, was promoted to naval captain. In the American Civil War (1861–65) Jews flocked to the colors of both Union and Confederacy armies. About 6,000 Jews fought on the Union side and a smaller number in the Confederate forces, though the exact figures are in dispute. The Confederate forces contained many prominent Jews, including Judah Phillip *Benjamin, the secretary of war, David de Leon (1813–1872), the first surgeon general, and 23 staff officers. The naval captain, Levi Myers Harby, distinguished himself in the defense of Galveston and commanded a fleet of gunboats on the Sabine River. On the Union side seven Jews were awarded the Congressional Medal of Honor: Leopold Karpeles, Benjamin Levy, Abraham Cohn, David Obranski, Henry Heller, Abraham Grunwalt, and Isaac Gans. Several Jews rose to the rank of general during the war including: Frederick Knefler (1833–1901), a Hungarian by birth, who volunteered for the Union army on the outbreak of war as a private and was the first Jewish brevet major general; Edward S. Salomon (1836–1913), who was made governor of Washington Territory in recognition of his military feats at the battles of Fredericktown, Munfordville, and Gettysburg; and Leopold C. Newman (1815–1863), who was killed in action. Max Einstein and Phillip J. Joachimson (1817–1890), who organized the 59th New York volunteer regiment, were made brigadier generals in the Union army. Jews played no conspicuous part in the Spanish-American War of 1898. Nevertheless, it is noteworthy that hostilities broke out following the sinking of the U.S.S. *Maine*, commanded until shortly before then by the Jewish officer Adolph Marix, and over 100 of nearly 5,000 Jews who fought in the U.S. army were killed. A few Jews were active in various Latin American armies including Jacob Baiz who was a brigadier general in the army of Honduras and Sam Dreben known as the "fighting Jew" who fought in Nicaragua in 1910, and was subsequently a colonel in the armies of Honduras and Mexico. In World War I a quarter of a million Jews fought in the armies of the United States, representing 5% of the total Jewish population of the United States, whereas only 3% of the total U.S. population served in World War I. Over 15,000 Jews were killed or wounded in the 18-month campaign. Nearly half of the 77th Division, the National Army unit from New York, consisted of Jews and there were approximately 10,000 Jewish officers, including three generals, Milton J. Foreman (1863–1935), Charles Laucheimer (1859–1920) and Abel Davis (1878–1937). Three Jews also rose to high rank in the navy during World War I: Rear Admiral Joseph Strauss (1861–1948) who commanded the battleship *Nevada* and was later responsible for placing a barrage of mines across the English Channel, Commander Walter F. Jacobs, who commanded a flotilla of minesweepers, and Captain Joseph K. *Taussig who was responsible for the safe escort of convoys against submarine attacks. Six Jews won the Congressional Medal of Honor: William Sawelson, Benjamin Kaufman (1894–1981), Sydney G. Gumpertz (1879–1953), Charles W. Hoffman, Samuel Sampler, and Philip C. Katz. In addition over 200 Jews were awarded the Distinguished Service Cross. The Jewish contribution to the U.S. fighting force in World War II was no less impressive. Over half a million U.S. Jews fought in the Allied armies, many of whom crossed the Canadian border early in the war to volunteer for the Canadian army before the United States entered the fighting. More than 50,000 Jewish servicemen were killed or wounded and two Jewish soldiers were awarded the Congressional Medal of Honor, one of whom was Lieutenant Raymond Lussman who single-handedly killed 17 German soldiers and captured another 32. An outstanding army officer who fell in battle was Major General Maurice Rose (1899–1945) who commanded the U.S. third armored division in the final offensive against Germany in 1945 and who was killed at Paderborn only a few weeks before the end of the war. In addition Lewis *Strauss was promoted to rear admiral during World War II. In 1953 Hyman *Rickover, a naval captain in World War II, was promoted to rear admiral and retired in 1958 with the rank of vice admiral. Jews also played an important part in the United States armies in Korea and in Vietnam; 150,000 Jews saw service in the Korean War and nearly 30,000 Jews fought in Vietnam, where Ben Sternberg (1914–) served as major general.

Great Britain

Until the repeal of the 1673 Test Act in 1828, professing Jews were debarred by religious tests from serving as officers in the regular armed forces of the crown. English Jews were, however, like their counterparts, the Continental Court Jews, prominent as army contractors for pay and supplies in the 18th century: the most famous were Sir Solomon de *Medina, the associate of Marlborough, and Abraham Prado (the diary and letter-book of the latter's subordinate, David Mendes da Costa, have survived). Aaron *Hart was commissary officer at the taking of Montreal and settled in Canada. Professing Jews could serve in the ranks and a number served especially in the navy, among them Barnett Abraham Simmons (later minister in the Penzance synagogue) and Isaac Vallentine, founder of the *Jewish Chronicle*. When invasion threatened, volunteers were enlisted and many professing Jews served, particularly in the London Volunteers. Jews could hold nonregular commissions and Sir Moses *Montefiore served as an officer in the Kent Militia; Daniel *Mendoza, the boxer, was a sergeant in the Fifeshire, then Aberdeenshire, Fencibles. There were a number of officers of Jewish origin before 1828 – Wellington said 15 served under him at Waterloo in 1815 – but they were presumably converts or at least not professing Jews: the most famous were the descendants of Meyer Low Schomberg, physician to the Great Synagogue; among his sons were Captain Sir Alexander Schomberg RN (Royal Navy), founder of a naval and military dynasty still flourishing, and Lieutenant Colonel Henry Schomberg, probably the first Anglo-Jewish army officer.

After the repeal of the Test and Corporation Acts, some professing Jews entered the army and became regular officers, particularly in the Indian army (e.g., Captain Lionel Gomez da Costa, who died of wounds at Lucknow in 1857, and Ensign Edmund Helbert Ellis, who died in 1851 at the age of 22), in which Indian native Jews had previously served. The most distinguished soldier in the community was Col. Albert E.W. *Goldsmid. An increasing number of professing Jews served in the ranks, including veterans of the Crimean War. Judaism was not, however, recognized in the British army as a separate denomination until 1886, partly owing to the efforts of Trooper Woolf Cohen of the 5th Lancers. In the South African War (1899–1902), between 3,000 and 4,000 Jews served, with 127 killed in action; many of those serving were South African "colonials" and "outlanders," notably Colonel Sir David *Harris who commanded the Kimberley Town Guard during the siege. During World War I the number of Jews in the British army rose to 50,000. Several Anglo-Jewish families provided large numbers of Jewish soldiers. The *Rothschild family contributed five officers, the *Sassoon family 14 officers, and five sons of Arthur *Sebag-Montefiore held commissions, while 41 descendants of Sir Isidore *Spielmann were said to have served as officers. Five Jewish soldiers won the Victoria Cross: Captain Robert Gee, Lieutenant Frank Alexander De Pass, Sergeant Issy Smith (Shmulevitsch), and Privates J. White and Leonard Keysor; 50 Jewish soldiers received the Distinguished Service Order. In addition the Jews formed their own unit, the Zion Mule Corps, which fought at Gallipoli and in the Dardanelles in 1915. Later, three Jewish units, the 38th, 39th, and 40th battalions of the Royal Fusiliers participated in the conquest of Palestine in 1918 under General Allenby (see *Jewish Legion). The regiments were disbanded after World War I. In World War II over 60,000 Jews fought in the British army. Jewish soldiers included volunteers from Central and Eastern Europe who were not British subjects and Palestinian volunteers who enlisted after the German advance across North Africa threatened the *yishuv* in Palestine. Two Jewish soldiers won the Victoria Cross in World War II: Captain David Hirsch, and naval lieutenant T. Gould. Several others rose to high military rank including Major General William Beddington (1893–?), Brigadier Sir Edward Beddington (1884–1966), who was deputy director of military intelligence at the War Office, Brigadier Barnard Goldstone (1896–?), Brigadier Fredrick Morris (1888–1941), Brigadier Bernard Schlesinger (1896–1945), and Brigadier Frederick *Kisch, who was killed in action. In addition, Irish-born Abraham Briscoe (1892–?) was the first Jew to reach the rank of air-commodore in the Royal Air Force. Jewish soldiers also fought in the British army in Korea and in Egypt where Brigadier Edmund Meyers (1906–?) was chief engineer to the British forces at the Suez

Canal. Major General James A. *D'Avigdor-Goldsmid became colonel of the 4/7th Dragoon Guards and director-general of the Territorial army.

British Commonwealth

No discrimination existed against Jews serving in the armed forces of Canada, Australia, and South Africa and a number of Jewish officers rose to high rank. In World War I Lieutenant General Sir John *Monash commanded the Australian army corps in France from June 1918 and was responsible for the breach of the German lines on August 8 which led to the collapse of German resistance. He was considered the outstanding army commander of World War I and in 1930 was promoted to full general. Major General Sir Charles Rosenthal also achieved prominence in the Australian army during World War I, commanding the ANZAC artillery and later the second Australian army division under Monash's supreme command. Another Australian, Private Leonard Keysor, was awarded the Victoria Cross during the Gallipoli campaign of 1915. In World War II 16,000 Jews fought in the Canadian army in Europe and North Africa, and one of them, Colonel Phinias Rothschild (1914–), was later promoted to major general and quartermaster-general of the Canadian army. 10,000 Jews fought in the South African army in which Major General Alexander Ohrenstein was director-general of the medical services.

[Vivian David Lipman]

Czarist Russia

Before 1827 Jews were exempted from military service on payment of a money tax. In that year, however, on the accession of Nicholas I, Jews were conscripted into the Russian army for periods of up to 25 years. Ten Jews for every thousand males were conscripted, recruitment being of boys aged between 12 and 25 while those under 18 were placed in special schools (see *Cantonists). Jewish soldiers were subjected to persistent pressure to convert, young Jewish children were seized and pressed into military service for 25-year periods, and Jews were excluded from the ranks of officers. Not unnaturally Jews sought every opportunity to evade military service in Russia under these conditions. These conscription laws did not apply to Jews in Polish territories annexed by Russia at the end of the Napoleonic wars. Thousands of Jews fought in the czarist army in the Crimean War (1854–56) and about 500 were killed. In 1864 a monument was erected to the Jewish soldiers who fell in the siege of Sebastopol and one Jewish soldier, Chaim Zaitchikoff, was congratulated by Prince Gortchakoff for his valor. Following the accession of Alexander II the condition of the Jews improved slightly and they were given the right to be promoted to sergeant while demobilized Jewish soldiers were allowed to live outside the *Pale of Settlement. The seizure of Jewish children for military service was abolished and the maximum period of service was reduced to 15 years. In 1874 a law was enacted introducing universal military service obliging all Russian citizens to report for military service at the age of 21. The effect of the new law was to grant Jews equality with the rest of the population but half a century of enforced service in the Russian army had already conditioned them to avoid enlistment wherever possible. Nevertheless, many thousands of Jews fought in the Russo-Turkish War of 1877. They were not allowed to become officers though as an exception to the rule Captain Zvi Hertz *Zam was permitted to enter the officers' school in 1874 after eight years of service; however, he was promoted to captain only after more than 40 years of service in the Russian army. Another exception was Joseph *Trumpeldor, who refused to be discharged from service after he lost his right arm in action. The acute shortage of doctors in the Czarist army also led to Jews being admitted as surgeon officers. On the outbreak of World War I nearly 400,000 Jews were drafted into the Russian army and the number increased to nearly half a million by 1917. Several thousands won awards for bravery on the battlefield.

Austro-Hungary

The Austro-Hungarian Empire generally adopted an enlightened policy toward its Jews. In 1782 Joseph II granted civic rights to the Jews and six years later Jews were declared fit for military service, though the right was at first restricted to serving in the supply corps in the province of Galicia where most Jews lived. Later Jews were allowed to serve in all branches of the Hapsburg army. During the Revolutionary and Napoleonic wars (1792–1813) many Jews served in the Austro-Hungarian army. Some were allowed to become officers. In 1818 Jews were officially accepted as officers even in the conservative cavalry regiments. Nevertheless, several professing Jews rose to the rank of general in the Hapsburg army, among them Field Marshal-Lieutenant Joseph *Singer who was chief of staff of the Third Army, and Major General Alexander von *Eis and Field Marshal-Lieutenant Eduard von *Schweitzer, both of whom commanded major Austrian army units. The comparatively generous treatment of Jews in the Austro-Hungarian army led many Jews to take up a military career, especially as certain other professions were closed to them. In 1855 there were 157 Jewish officers in the Hapsburg army and by 1893 this number had risen to 2,179 or 8% of all the officers in the Hapsburg army. A number of Jews also became prominent in the navy, including Tobias von Oesterreicher, who was the first Austrian Jew to be promoted to rear admiral, and two battleship commanders (sea captains), Friedrich Pick (1839–1908) and Moritz von Funk (1831–1905). Nearly 300,000 Jews fought in the Austro-Hungarian army during World War I. Among 2,500 officers were three field marshal-lieutenants, Eduard von Schweitzer, Adolph Kornhaber (1856–1925), and Hazai *Samu, and five major generals, Simon *Vogel, Johann Mestitz, Leopold Austerlitz, Emil von *Sommer, and Márton Zöld. Nearly 30,000 Jewish soldiers were killed during the four years of war, including 600 Austrian Jewish officers. After the collapse of the Hapsburg Empire Jews played an increasingly smaller part in the armed forces of both Austria and Hungary, and following the advent of Fascist and pro-Nazi regimes in the 1930s they ceased to serve in the armed forces altogether. One outstanding figure of the post-World War I period was General Vilmos Böhm (1880–1947) who was commander in chief of the Hungarian army during the four-month Soviet dictatorship of Béla *Kun in 1919.

U.S.S.R.

Following the Revolution of February 1917, Jews were granted equal rights and for the first time were allowed to become army officers. Many were transferred to officers' schools and on graduating received the rank of sub-officer (*praporshchik*). When the Bolsheviks seized power in November 1917, many Jewish soldiers fought in the Red Army organized by Leon *Trotsky, aided by Skliansky and Jacob Sverdlov. Four divisional commanders were Jews and a few units consisted solely of Jews such as the brigade commanded by Joseph Furman. After the civil war J.B. Goldberg became commander of a reserve army. Among Jews who obtained senior army commands were Grigori Stern, Jan Gamarnik, and Feldman. Most of them were executed during Stalin's purges, a notable exception being Stern, who was sent to the Far East (1935), where he routed the Japanese army which had invaded Soviet territory. He later commanded the Soviet Far Eastern Forces with the rank of full general and drove the Japanese from Mongolian territory. Stern's army was assisted by air force units under Yaacov *Shmushkevich, appointed commander in chief of the Soviet air force in 1940.

WORLD WAR II. Following the outbreak of World War II, the Soviet Union annexed the Baltic state and territories in eastern Poland and Belorussia thus incorporating a large number of Jews within its borders. After the German invasion of Russia, Polish and Belorussian soldiers in the Soviet army were considered of suspect loyalty and were transferred to labor battalions. In December 1941, however, the order was revoked and Jews from the Baltic states were permitted to serve in all units of the Soviet army. Subsequently four Lithuanian Jews were made Heroes of the Soviet Union. The Soviet Jewish historian Jacob Kantor estimated that almost half a million Jews fought in the Soviet army in World War II of whom at least 140 were awarded the title Hero of the Soviet Union (the official Soviet figure is 107). Jews constituted a disproportionately large number of senior officers, largely because the percentage of Jews having a university education was higher than that of other nationalities. More than 100 Jews held the rank of general (see the partial Table: Jewish Generals in the Soviet Army).

Number of Jewish Generals in the Soviet Army during World War II, by Corps

No. of Jewish Generals	Corps
13	Engineering and Mechanical
13	Artillery
10	Tank
10	Medical
6	Infantry
5	Air Force Engineering
4	Air Force
4	Quartermaster Service
2	Veterinary
2	Navy
2	Cavalry
1	Communications

Jewish generals were particularly prominent as field commanders, notably General Jacob *Kreiser. Other Jewish commanders at the battle of Stalingrad included Lt. Gen. I.S. Beskin and Major Gen. (later Lt. Gen.) Matvey Weinrub. Jewish generals also held key commands during the final assault on Berlin. Lieutenant General Hirsh Plaskov was artillery commander of the Second Guards Army, Lieutenant General Semion Krivoshein commanded one of the first corps to break into Berlin in the spring of 1945, and Lieutenant General Weinrub was artillery commander of the Eighth Guards Army. Special mention should also be made of the Jewish Cossack commander, Major General Lev Dovator, who was killed during the first Soviet offensive in December 1941, Lieutenant General David Dragunski, who was twice made a Hero of the Soviet Union, and Major Caesar Konikov, whose courageous defense of the fishing village of Stanichka for seven months led to the village being renamed Kunikovo after his death. In addition Colonel General Leonti Kotlyar was commander of the engineering corps and six Jews held the rank of major general in the medical services (where there were a large number of Jewish doctors and nurses): Vovsy, Levitt, David Entin, Reingold, Gurvich, and Slavin. A number of Jews were given the award Hero of the Soviet Union in the Soviet air force, among them Michael Plotkin, who flew in the first Soviet bombing raid on Berlin in August 1941, Henryk Hofman, and four women: Polina Gelman, Zina Hofman, Lila Litvak, and Rachel Zlotina, who belonged to a women's air regiment. Two Jewish Soviet submarine commanders became Heroes of the Soviet Union – Israel Fisanovich and Isaac Kabar – as did Abraham Sverdlov who commanded a flotilla of torpedo boats. Jews were also prominent among the partisans, constituting more than 20,000 men in separate units in the Polish-Russian border areas. The official Soviet history of the war mentions the names of several Jewish partisan heroes, among them N.S. Kagan, one of seven Moscow Komsomol members hanged by the Germans while on a mission behind enemy lines, L.E. Bernstein, commander of the Pozharski unit which joined the Slovak rising against the Germans, and Vladimir Epstein, who escaped from Auschwitz to form a partisan unit in Poland. (See also *Partisans.)

AFTER WORLD WAR II. Although famous Jewish generals such as Dragunski and Kreiser retained their popularity after World War II, Soviet policy toward the Jewish soldier changed for the worse, in accordance with general Soviet policy toward the Jews. It is believed that nearly all the Jewish generals of World War II were retired by 1953 as were nearly 300 Jewish colonels and lieutenant colonels. By 1970 the number of Jewish senior officers on active service in the Soviet army had declined drastically.

Italy

Before the beginning of the 19th century Jews were forbidden to bear arms in any of the Italian states or to be a member of any military organization. The French Revolution, however, led to the demand for equal rights in Italy as elsewhere and the Jews were among the beneficiaries of progressive legislation. Following the conquest of north Italy by Napoleon, Italian Jews even established their own units and fought with the emperor all over Europe. However, during the reactionary period in north Italy following the final defeat of Napoleon in 1815, Jews were debarred from military service. After the decree of March 1848 granting Jews full equality in Piedmont, 235 Jews volunteered for the Piedmontese army in the war against Austria. Enrico *Guastalla was among the Italian soldiers who captured Rome in 1849, and among the Piedmontese troops fighting on the allied side in the Crimean War (1854–56) was Colonel Cesare Rovighi who later became aide-de-camp to King Victor Emanuel I. In the war against Austria, 1859–60, 260 Jews volunteered for the Piedmontese armies and several were awarded medals. There were 11 Jews among the 1,000 led by Garibaldi who captured southern Italy and Sicily from the Bourbons and Enrico Guastalla later became one of Garibaldi's chief lieutenants. In 1870, 236 Jews were among the victorious Italian army which conquered Rome. Jewish soldiers were subject to no restrictions in the army of united Italy and the percentage of Jewish officers was disproportionately large. Many Jews held the rank of general in the Italian army. They included Lieutenant General Achille Coen (1851–1925), Lieutenant General Emanuele *Pugliese, Lieutenant General Roberto *Segre, Lieutenant General Angelo *Arbib (Arbid), Lieutenant General Angelo Modena, and others. Other Jewish soldiers rose to high military rank, among them Lieutenant General Giuseppe *Ottolenghi who was minister of war from 1902 to 1904. In all, several thousand Jewish officers and men fought in the Italian army in World War I.

Other Jewish officers included four major generals: Carlo Archivolti (1873–1944), Armando *Bachi, Adolfo Olivetti (1878–1944), and Giacomo Almagia (1876–1947), and 12 brigadier generals. Five Jews became admirals in the Italian navy. Augusto Capon, Franco Nunes (1868–1943), and Guido Segre (1871–1942) were full admirals, and Vice Admiral Paolo Marani (1884–1950) and Rear Admiral Aldo Ascoli (1882–1956) commanded ships in the invasion of Abyssinia in 1935. In November 1938 a new law was promulgated prohibiting Jews from serving in the armed forces and all the Jewish generals and admirals were forced to retire. During World War II no Jews fought in the army of Benito Mussolini, and some joined the partisan underground movement. Nevertheless two Jews were specially recalled to service because of particular skills: these were Rear Admiral Pontremoli and Major General Umberto Pugliese (1880–1961). The latter was given the task of raising Italian naval vessels sunk by the British at Taranto. After World War II Giorgio *Liuzzi who was one of the senior officers retired in 1938 was recalled to active service and was chief of staff of the Italian army from 1956 to 1958 with the rank of lieutenant general.

Germany

In the early Middle Ages, Jews were accorded the right to bear arms. Later on, however, with the deterioration in their social and political standing after the upheavals of the *Crusades, this right was gradually withdrawn until by the middle of the 13th century Jews, numbered with women, children, and clerics, as being forbidden to bear arms. Exceptions to this rule were rare during the following centuries (see Jud *Michel), though Jews were very prominent as military *contractors (purveyors of livestock, fodder, food, uniforms, etc.) in the 17th and 18th centuries.

The first German Jews conscripted in modern times were from the left bank of the Rhine occupied by revolutionary and Napoleonic France. German states under French influence followed suit (*Westphalia). In 1812 Prussia decreed that Jews were liable to military service and when the War of Liberation broke out a year later many hundreds volunteered, 82 of them receiving decorations. Nevertheless, Frederick William II repudiated his promise that war veterans could receive positions, irrespective of religion, and even wounded veterans suffered discrimination. The sole Jewish officer in the army during his reign was Major Meno Burg (1787–1853), who owed his position to the influence of the king's brother, the commander of the artillery. It was commonly accepted that Jews were inferior soldiers and that their service was mainly of educational and assimilatory value.

In 1845 the first Jewish officers were commissioned into the Prussian reserve forces, the *Landwehr*. Until about 1885, Jewish officers, primarily university graduates, were commissioned by co-option; but after this date virtually none became officers, despite their exemplary service in the Austro-Prussian (1866) and Franco-Prussian (1870–71) wars, because of growing antisemitism. An exception was Walther von *Mossner, the sole senior Jewish officer in the Prussian army, and he owed his position to personal connections with the king and converted to Christianity during his career. Most German states followed Prussia's discriminatory policy (particularly Hanover) while others were more liberal, Bavaria permitting Jewish officers to rise to the upper ranks in the standing army. During the 1848 Revolution Jews enlisted in the National Guard, where they were reluctantly accepted. That year the first Jewish doctor was commissioned in Prussia, and subsequently, due to the lack of physicians, the medical corps harbored Jewish officers in large numbers without permitting them to become senior officers.

Many thousands of Jews fought in the German army in World War I. About 2,000 Jewish officers were commissioned and 12,000 Jews were killed in battle. Nevertheless, during and after the war there was an ugly upsurge of accusations that Jews had either not enlisted or shirked front-line service. To combat this propaganda the Reichsbund juedischer Frontsoldaten, an association of Jewish war veterans, was founded. In 1917 the War Ministry ordered a thorough survey conducted to find the number and proportion of Jews serving in front-line units. The results and the dubious manner in which they had been obtained became the subject of a bitter public controversy. In fact, the percentage of Jews was almost equal to that of Christians; that it was not higher is explained by the diminishing birthrate among German Jewry (between 1880 and 1930) which resulted in a lower proportion of those of military age relative to the non-Jewish population. After World War I the small professional army of the Weimar Republic contained few Jews, who were all removed in 1933.

[Henry Wasserman]

France

During the Middle Ages Jews were generally excluded from military service except in times of emergency. Their position remained unchanged until 1789 when, following the outbreak of the French Revolution, all Frenchmen, including Jews, were made liable for military service. Many Jews served in Napoleon's armies, among them Brigadier General Marc-Jean-Jerome Wolffe (1776–1848) who commanded the first cavalry brigade of the Grande Armée and Captain Alexandre Marcquefoy who was awarded the Legion of Honor by Napoleon himself; 800 Jews were estimated to be serving under Napoleon in 1808, among them a number of Italians and Poles. Berek (Berko) *Joselewicz, the Polish patriot, commanded a regiment in Napoleon's Polish Legion. The outstanding Jewish soldier in Napoleon's army was Henri *Rottenbourg who was made major general in 1814. Nevertheless, conditions of the Jewish soldiers were made difficult by the refusal of many commanding officers to allow Jews into their ranks and the restrictions on the rights of promotion.

During the early part of the 19th century an increasing number of Jews fought in the French army and a few achieved considerable prominence, among them Colonel Martin Cerfbeer, Captain Abraham Lévy, Captain M. Vormess, and Captain Benoît Lévy who were all awarded the Legion of Honor. No exact details are available as to the number of Jews who fought in the Crimean War (1854–56) but several won awards for gallantry, among them Leopold *See and Colonel Abraham Lévy. In the Italian war of 1859 See and Lévy were again decorated as was Major Adolph Abraham, and in the Franco-Prussian War (1870–71), Colonel Jules Moch and Captain Halphen broke through the Prussian lines after the French army had been surrounded at Metz. In that war Major Franchetti was posthumously decorated having fallen during the siege of Paris. During the Third Republic (1870–1940), Jews entered the French army in unprecedented numbers and 23 rose to the rank of general. Although subject to no official restrictions, Jews were frequently the target of antisemitic attacks, the most notable occasion being the *Dreyfus case. The outstanding Jewish officers of the period before World War I were: Major Generals Leopold See, Aimé *Lambert, Abraham Lévy, and Naquet-Laroque (1843–1921), and Brigadier Generals Edgar Wolffe (c. 1840–1901), Gabriel Gustave Brisac (1817–c. 1890), Adolphe Hinstin (c. 1820–c. 1890), Bernard Abraham (1824–c. 1900), and Adolphe Aron (c. 1840–c. 1910). On the outbreak of World War I, several hundred Jews volunteered for the French army, among them captains Charles Lehmann and René Frank, both of whom had fought in the Franco-Prussian War 44 years earlier. About 50,000 French Jews, over 20% of the total Jewish population, fought in the French army between 1914 and 1918, and an additional 4,000 Jewish refugees from Eastern Europe volunteered. Twelve French Jews held the rank of general, among them Lieutenant General Valabrègue, Major Generals Naquet-Laroque and Justin Dennery (1847–1928), who were recalled from retirement, Major Generals Camille Baruch Levi (1860–1933) and Jules Heymann (1850–1928) and Brigadier Generals René Alexandre (1864–1931), Lucien Lévi (1859–1932), Paul Emile Grumbach (1861–1931), Gédéon Geismar (1863–1931), and André Weiller (1865–c. 1940). Of 39 French Jewish airmen who fought in World War I, all but four were killed in battle and the total number of French Jews killed in action exceeded 8,000. Several Jews rose to the rank of general after World War I, among them Major General Pierre Boris, Major General Raymond Laroque and Brigadier General Albert Baumann (1869–1945).

Before the French collapse in June 1940 General Boris was made general inspector of the French artillery. Major General Charles Huntzinger and Major General Pierre Brisac were all permitted by the Vichy régime to retain their rank despite the racial laws against Jews. Similarly the Vichy régime gave Samuel Meyer the award of the Legion of Honor for bravery while André Gutman received the award of the Croix de Guerre for bravery in action. The French army included one regiment almost entirely made up of Polish Jews. Following the French defeat in June 1940 many French and East European Jews joined the Free French under Charles de Gaulle in London, among them Ingénieur-Général Louis *Kahn who was director of naval construction. Jews were also prominent in the French resistance, among them Roger Carcassonne who led the resistance movement in North Africa. In 1944, following the liberation of France, General Boris was one of several Jewish officers reinstated in the French army, and in 1945 General *Dassault commanded the French artillery. After World War II a small number of Jews served in the French army in Indo-China.

Poland

Jewish settlement had begun in Poland by the 12th century and Jews were conscripted principally to reinforce the local militia and help build fortifications. They were not expected to take any important part in the Polish army until the Tatar attacks on eastern Poland at the end of the 16th century. Jews were recruited into defense units and some were taken prisoner, a fact recorded in the orders of the Russian czar Michael (1613–1645). A Jewish unit was formed under the command of one Mozko and in some cities the general mobilization of Jews was ordered. Jews were also prominent in the wars against Sweden (1655–60). During the 18th century, Catholic pressure was brought to bear against Jews fighting in the Polish army and the number of Jews serving fell from over 2,000 to a few hundred. During the uprising in the year following the second partition of Poland of 1793, numbers of Jews joined the revolutionary army along with other Poles and many Jews fought in the Polish force which drove the Russians out of Warsaw. Later in 1794, a Jewish cavalry legion was formed under the command of Berek Joselewicz, initially numbering 500 men and later nearly 2,000. The Jewish legion distinguished itself in the defense of Warsaw but was completely wiped out in the Russian massacre in the suburb of Praga after the collapse of the rebellion. At the turn of the 19th century a number of Jews joined Napoleon's army and fought for France in Italy and Eastern Europe. Joselewicz himself commanded a regiment of Polish cavalry, and another Polish Jew, Caspar Junghof, was awarded the Legion of Honor. Similarly Jews volunteered for the army of the Grand Duchy of Warsaw established by Napoleon in 1807. Among them was Josef *Berkowicz, the son of Joselewicz, who fought with other Poles in the French army which invaded Russia in 1812.

After the defeat of Napoleon in 1814, Jews in the area of Poland under czarist rule played an active part in the Polish uprisings of 1830, 1848, and 1863. During World War I, Polish Jews fought in units of both the armies of the Allies and the central powers. A number of Polish Jews in the Russian Austro-Hungarian and French armies were decorated. After the war thousands of Jews fought in the Polish army against Russia, among them Colonel Goldman, Colonel Karaffa-Kreutenkraft, and Colonel Floyar-Reichman. Nevertheless, Polish antisemitism permeated the army and all the other organs of state, and although there were never less than 20,000 Jews in the Polish army between the wars, very few Jewish soldiers held high military rank. An outstanding exception was Bernhard *Mond who was promoted to colonel in 1924 and on the outbreak of World War II commanded the Fifth Infantry Division with the rank of major general. The condition of the Jewish soldier improved during the nine-year rule of Joseph Pilsudski (1926–35) but deteriorated after his death. Nevertheless, 400,000 Jews were recruited into the Polish army on the outbreak of World War II and many thousands were killed in battle during the four weeks of fighting. A large number of Jewish soldiers were taken prisoner by the Russians and interned in the Soviet Union. In 1942 an agreement between the U.S.S.R. and the Polish government in exile resulted in the formation of a Polish army in Russia under General Anders. Although Jews were generally excluded from this army, usually on the pretext that they were unsuitable for military service, 4,000 fought in General Anders' army in Western Europe while over 5,000 Jews fought in a second Polish army in Russia, a large number of them holding officer's rank. In addition many more Jews fought in Polish units serving in the armies of other Allied states.

Despite the fact that the Jewish population of Poland was decimated by the Holocaust, a large number of Jews joined the Polish army and after World War II many held senior ranks. Following the Six-Day *War in 1967, however, nearly all of them were removed from their posts.

Romania

Romania became an independent kingdom in 1881. Restrictions were subsequently placed upon the right of Jews to serve in the armed forces despite the fact that nearly 1,000 Romanian Jews had fought against the Turks in the Balkan War of 1877. An outstanding Jewish soldier in the Romanian army was Colonel Maurice Brociner (1855–1942) who was decorated for gallantry in 1877 and in 1882 was made secretary to Charles I, king of Romania. In 1896 a law was enacted prohibiting Jews from volunteering for the Romanian army but in 1913, following the involvement of Romania in the Balkan Wars, the law was rescinded. During World War I, 20,000 Jews fought in the Romanian army, including several hundred officers. Thirty-seven Jewish officers and 845 men were known to have died. After World War I a large number of Jews served in the Romanian army, and some rose to the rank of officer. During World War II, however, Nazi pressure led the Romanian government to remove all the Jews from the Romanian army. Few Jews served in the army of Communist Romania after 1945.

Bulgaria

Following Bulgarian independence in 1878 Jews were given equal rights with the rest of the population. Bulgarian Jews fought in the Turkish army when Bulgaria was under Turkish rule, and after independence they joined the Bulgarian army in the thousands. Many Jewish soldiers distinguished themselves during the Serbo-Bulgarian war of 1885 and were described by Prince Alexander of Bulgaria as "true descendants of the ancient Maccabeans." Despite growing antisemitism, no restrictions were placed on Jews entering the army or even the officers' training schools. Five thousand Jews fought in the Bulgarian army in the Balkan Wars (1912–13) and several hundreds of them were killed. In World War I a number of Jews reached senior army ranks, among them three Jewish colonels Graziani, Tajar, and Mushanov. Over 700 Jews were killed in the war, among them 28 officers. Between the wars, Jewish soldiers continued to enjoy equal rights in the Bulgarian army until 1940 when Bulgaria allied herself with Nazi Germany. All Jews were removed from the Bulgarian army and organized into labor units to perform manual work. Many of them were later sent to concentration camps but some succeeded in joining the partisans headed by the Fatherland Front. After the war most of Bulgaria's surviving Jews emigrated to Israel and hardly any joined the army of Communist Bulgaria.

Greece

Greek Jews were subject to continual persecution for many years after Greek independence in 1821. Very few Jews joined the army until the outbreak of the Greco-Turkish War of 1897 in which 200 Jews fought in the Greek army. Abraham Matalon rose to the rank of colonel during World War I and was one of several Jewish soldiers to have been decorated. The total number of Greek Jews fighting in World War I was estimated at 500. Many Jews fought in the Greek army against Italy in 1940 and by 1942, when the Germans invaded Greece, over 13,000 Jews had been recruited, many of them from Salonika and Macedonia where there were large concentrations of Jews. Five hundred and thirteen Jews were known to have been killed in action, among them Colonel Mordechai Parisi, who was killed after holding off an entire Italian brigade for nine days. A monument was erected in his memory in his native town of Chalcis and 25 Greek towns have streets named after him. Following the German conquest of Greece, many Jews were deported to concentration camps. Among the Greek Jews deported to Auschwitz was Colonel Baruch who set fire to part of the gas chambers and was later killed by the Nazis. A few Greek Jews joined the partisan movement in the mountains of northern Greece and some fought in the Allied armies in North Africa.

Switzerland

Before 1850 Jews were exempted from military service upon payment of a tax. In 1866 Jews were granted equal rights including the obligation of military service but even before the law of 1866 certain cantons permitted Jews to bear arms, the first of them being Aargau where the civil authorities acceded to a request of Marcus Dreyfus, head of the Jewish community. In 1855 Moritz Meyer from Aargau was made an officer and several other Jews became officers during the latter part of the 19th century. Several hundred Jews were recruited into the Swiss army for border defense during the two world wars and two Jewish soldiers rose to the rank of colonel: A. Nordman and his son, Jean Nordman.

Holland

Jews were allowed to bear arms in Holland from the 17th century when the country became an independent state under the House of Orange. In 1808, during Napoleonic rule, Jews were granted equal rights and were therefore obliged to do military service along with the rest of the population. The number of Jews serving in the Dutch army grew steadily during the 19th century and a few Jewish soldiers were singled out for merit, one of them, Michael Kohen (b. 1877), being decorated for outstanding bravery in the fighting in Surinam. Thousands of Jews fought against the Nazi invasion of Holland in May 1940 and a small number of them succeeded in escaping to Britain to continue fighting from there. After World War II, hardly any Jews served in the Dutch armed forces.

Other Countries

A small number of Jewish soldiers rose to fame in India, the Middle East, and North Africa, some of them serving as soldiers of fortune. Some of the Jewish soldiers of fortune achieved fame in the Turkish army in which several thousand Jews fought during the Balkan wars of the 19th century. Fischel-Freind (1885–1928), a Polish Jew, became a colonel in the Turkish army and was later governor of Syria with the title Magyar Mahmud Pasha. An English Jew, Stephen Lakeman (1812–1897), was briefly a Turkish general with the title, Mazar Pasha. In addition David Effendi Molcho, a Jew from Salonika, was made head of the Turkish navy's medical services with the rank of vice admiral. Another Jewish soldier of fortune was Rubino *Ventura who held military commands both in Persia and in India during the 19th century. A small number of Indian Jews reached high military rank in the British army, among them Subadar Major Haskelji Israel Kolatkar who was killed during the Burmese campaign of 1887 and Subadar Major Shalom Moses Penkar of the 15th Bombay Infantry unit. Indian Jews fought in the two world wars and after Indian independence, some became senior officers, and one of them, Colonel Joseph Ephraim Jhirad, was killed in the 1965 war against Pakistan. North African Jews were prominent in World War II both in the French and British regular armies and in the French underground. Thus Maurice Guedj (1913–1945), a Tunisian lawyer, joined the Free French air force and won numerous decorations. He was killed in action in January 1945. Leaders of the underground included José *Abulker, Pierre Smadja, and Raoul and Edgar Bensoussan. Jews were not prominent in the Algerian war against the French after 1955 or in the armies of the Arab North African states after independence.

Women in Military Service

There is no record of Jewish women serving in the army of any modern state until 1813 when Louise Grafemus (Esther Manuel; 1785–1852), in search of her husband in the Russian army, joined the Prussian infantry disguised as a man. She was twice wounded and rose to become a sergeant major before her sex was discovered. Louise Grafemus was awarded the Iron Cross and returned to her home in Hanau with great honor. During the 19th century women played an increasing part in the conduct of wars in auxiliary capacities such as nurses. Thus nurse Woolf was decorated by King George V for her services in the British army in World War I and several Jewish women became nursing officers in the Allied forces in World War II. During World War II women went into active service for the first time as auxiliary troops; in Russia they served with men in the front lines during the initial invasion by Germany and afterward. A number of Soviet Jewish women became famous through their bravery in action, among them Lyudmila Kravetz who was made a Hero of the Soviet Union when as a medical sergeant she took command of her unit when all the officers were killed and advanced against the enemy. Riva Steinberg (d. 1944), who was killed trying to rescue a Russian soldier from a burning aircraft, was posthumously decorated. Mary Ykhnovich, a senior battalion commander, Sarah Meisel, Klara Gross, and Lea Kantorovich, a nurse, were all cited for bravery under fire. Another Russian Jewess, Gitta Schenker, a telephone operator, took command of an infantry battalion during the battle of Stalingrad. However, the most famous Jewish heroine of World War II was Hannah *Szenes who was parachuted into Yugoslavia to organize Jewish resistance and was captured and killed.

See also *Israel, State of: Defense Forces.

Conclusion

In most states Jews were not called upon to do military service until well into the 19th century since the obligation to take up arms was considered a privilege to which Jews were not entitled. Even where they did fight they were usually restricted in their right to hold officer's rank (as in Prussia and Russia) or were excluded from certain branches of the army such as the general staff in Austria-Hungary. In the 20th century most restrictions on Jews as soldiers were removed but only in France, Italy, and Austria-Hungary was the number of Jewish senior officers relatively high. Vilmos Böhm and Giorgio Liuzzi were the only Jews to become commanders in chief of an army, the former when he held this post in the short-lived regime of Bela Kun in Hungary, the latter in Italy. Three other Jews reached the rank of full general: John *Monash, Grigori Stern, and Jacob *Kreyzer; and three Jews the rank of full admiral: Ben Moreel (1892–?), Augusto *Capon, and Roberto Segre (1872–1942). One Jew, Yaacov *Shmushkevich, was commander of an air force.

Jewish Chaplaincy

In most countries of Europe where Jews have volunteered or been enlisted into the armed forces, provision has been made for the appointment of chaplains to look after the religious needs of servicemen and women in times of war and peace. One can generally say that from the middle of the 19th century, following the political emancipation of the Jews, Judaism became a recognized denomination having more or less the same privileges and obligations as those of other denominations. Commissioned chaplains were given relative military rank, senior chaplains having the relative rank of colonel, lieutenant colonel, or major. This was the case in Austria, France, Prussia, Britain, Belgium, Italy, Holland, and Poland. In Britain in 1889 Judaism was recognized as a denomination for the purpose of chaplaincy in the forces. The first Jewish chaplain was Rabbi Francis L. Cohen who was appointed in 1892. In European countries, such as Italy and Belgium, chaplains were first commissioned during World War I when the number of Jews serving in the various national armies increased considerably. In World War I Jewish chaplains, with the approval, and sometimes at the request of the superior commanding officer, rendered service to the Jews in occupied territories. Thus German Jewish chaplains acted as intermediaries between the German army authorities and Jewish civilians in Poland and in northern France. They also provided religious appurtenances and Passover requirements (such as *maẓẓot* and *haggadot*). British chaplains performed similar services for Jewish civilians in northern France and Belgium. They were supported by chaplains attached to the forces of Australia, New Zealand, Canada, and South Africa, and chaplains also served with the Jewish units serving in Palestine and Egypt. A number of chaplains in both the Allied and central armies were decorated for bravery. An outstanding example of bravery was that of Rabbi A. Bloch of the French army who was killed by a shell in 1914 after seeking a crucifix for a severely wounded Frenchman when there was no priest available. During World War II there was a further increase in the number of chaplains in the Allied forces. On the other hand the Dutch government in exile, for the first time, appointed a Jewish chaplain, Chief Rabbi S. Rodrigues Pereira, to look after the religious requirements of Dutch Jews serving with the Allies. In the Polish army Rabbi J. Mieses was senior chaplain to be succeeded by Rabbi B. Steinberg who was killed during the Katyn massacre in 1943. Jewish chaplains served with the Polish army in Russia, the Middle East, and Europe. The last senior chaplain in the Polish army was Rabbi David Kahana who served from 1945 to 1952. Jewish chaplains were also attached to the Jewish infantry group made up of Palestinians and Jews from other British army units who served in the western desert, in Italy, and with the army of the Rhine. As in World War I, a number of Jewish chaplains were decorated for gallantry in the Allied armies, among them Grand Rabbi Jacob Kaplan of the French army who was awarded the Croix de Guerre. The duties of chaplains during the two world wars were extensive and involved a considerable amount of travel. They were required to organize religious services whenever possible, particularly during the festivals and High Holy Days, to distribute service prayer books and religious literature, visit the sick and wounded in hospitals and casualty clearing stations, and bury the dead. They were also required to assist observant soldiers in following the religious requirements of their faith without detriment to their army duties and to deal with the many welfare and social problems affecting the domestic life of the soldier. At the end of World War II chaplains were additionally required to help bury Jews who had died in concentration camps and to help those who survived as far as possible. As in the case of chaplains of other denominations, Jewish chaplains were requested to use their influence in maintaining the morale and fighting spirit of the troops. They were encouraged to participate in educational and recreational programs designed to improve the mind and outlook of the serviceman. In the Royal Air Force a scheme of moral leadership courses was devised to guide and train officers and men who had shown a talent for leadership to apply their potential in the groups to which they were attached.

[Sir Israel Brodie]

IN THE UNITED STATES. The Jewish military chaplaincy in the United States began in 1862 during the U.S. Civil War. Before then army chaplains had to be ordained Christian clergymen, selected by the officers of the regiments to which they were assigned. By an Act of Congress of 1862, a regularly ordained minister of any religious denomination could be commissioned as a chaplain. Three rabbis were commissioned as chaplains in the Union forces: Rabbi Jacob Frankel of Philadelphia, who served the six Philadelphia military hospitals; Rabbi Bernhard Gotthelf, of Louisville, Kentucky, who served 18 army hospitals in Kentucky and Indiana; and Rabbi Ferdinand L. Sarner of Brith Kodesh Congregation, Rochester, New York, who was elected chaplain of the 54th New York Volunteer Regiment and was wounded at Gettysburg.

No Jewish chaplains served in the Spanish-American War (1898), although Rabbi Emil G. *Hirsch and Rabbi J.

Leonard Levy of Philadelphia were commissioned. Rabbi Joseph *Krauskopf of Philadelphia spent the summer of 1898 at military camps in the United States and in Cuba as a field commissioner for the National Relief Commission, and conducted religious services for Jewish personnel. A number of other rabbis also conducted services at camps adjacent to the communities in which their congregations were located.

In 1917 the *National Jewish Welfare Board (JWB) was organized to serve the religious and morale needs of Jewish soldiers and sailors in the U.S. armed forces during World War I. One of the duties assigned to the JWB by the government was the recruiting and endorsing of Jewish military chaplains. In October 1917 Congress authorized the appointment of chaplains-at-large of "faiths not now represented in the body of Chaplains of the Army." As a result, 149 of the 400 English-speaking rabbis in the United States volunteered, and 34 received the ecclesiastical endorsement of the JWB's Chaplains Committee. Of these, 26 received commissions. The first Jewish chaplain commissioned was Rabbi Elkan C. Voorsanger of St. Louis, who earned two decorations for gallantry under fire, and became senior chaplain of the 77th Division.

After World War I, some chaplains maintained reserve commissions, and a number of younger rabbis enlisted in the reserves between 1918 and 1940. As World War II approached, the chaplaincy underwent a major reorganization. Cyrus *Adler was succeeded by Rabbi David de Sola *Pool as chairman of the JWB Chaplaincy Committee, and the committee was renamed Committee on Army and Navy Religious Activities (CANRA) of the JWB. Rabbi Phillip S. *Bernstein was named executive director. By the time the United States entered World War II, 24 Jewish chaplains were on active duty. By the end of the war 311 rabbis had been commissioned and served in the armed forces; seven died in service, among them Alexander Goode who was one of four chaplains who lost their lives on the military transport, S.S. *Dorchester*. CANRA provided the chaplains with vast supplies of religious literature, equipment, and kosher foods in a supply line that reached around the world. Two tasks of special importance performed by Jewish chaplains were their work as leaders in the first penetration of areas cut off from Jewish contacts during the Nazi occupation, and their aid to concentration camp survivors. After World War II the chaplaincy became a career for some, and a way for the promotion of senior Jewish chaplains to key administrative chaplaincy posts. Many of those who did not choose a career in the chaplaincy retained their reserve commission. Only 18 Jewish chaplains remained on active duty at the outbreak of war in Korea in 1950. Twelve Jewish chaplains were decorated in that war.

After World War II CANRA was renamed to emphasize its function within the JWB organization, which finances it, first as the Division of Religious Activities and, after the outbreak of the Korean War, as the Commission on Jewish Chaplaincy of the JWB Reform, Conservative, and Orthodox rabbis rotated as commission chairmen for three-year terms. The commission instituted a draft to supply 100 Jewish chaplains; it drew from all rabbis and newly-ordained students eligible for military service who had not already served in the forces, and required a two-year tour of duty. From 1950 to 1968 the draft brought 485 rabbis into the chaplaincy, about a third of all the rabbis ordained by the major Jewish seminaries of the United States during the period. The commission also used civilian rabbis who had their own congregations to provide chaplaincy services at military bases, academies, and hospitals and nonmilitary federal installations where no full-time Jewish chaplain was assigned. About 800 rabbis were involved in this program up to 1970. In 1969, reacting to anti-Vietnam sentiment among rabbinical students, the commission substituted a voluntary system for the drafting of newly-ordained rabbis. When the Vietnam War led to a new military buildup, four Jewish chaplains were assigned to duty in that country. From 1966 to 1970, 11 chaplains were decorated. In 1970 Jewish chaplains were serving 611 domestic installations and hospitals, as well as in more than 40 foreign countries. Jewish chaplains were active in the later military actions in Iraq. By 2005, in the renamed Jewish Chaplains Council, approximately 40 full-time military and Veterans Administration chaplains, 55 chaplain reservists, more than 88 military lay leaders, and thousands of Jews were serving at more than 500 military installations and VA medical centers.

PUBLICATIONS AND CHILD EDUCATION. In the 1950s and 1960s, religious-lay cooperation and interdenominational harmony were strikingly evident in the work of the Jewish Chaplaincy Commission's responsa and publication committees. The former formulated mutually acceptable answers to questions of religious practices under military conditions. The latter published prayer books, *Haggadot*, hymnals, and a library of pamphlets on the Sabbath, holy days, festivals, Jewish ethics, and Jewish history, all widely distributed and serving as excellent expositions of Judaism to non-Jews in the military. In 1954 the commission published the first standardized religious school curriculum for the children of servicemen, rewritten in 1965 as "Unified Jewish Religious Education Curriculum." It is particularly important because of the growing number of service children who live far from civilian synagogues and Jewish schools. Religious education for service children has become a prime task of the Jewish chaplains, who prepare many youngsters for bar and bat mitzvah as part of an organized program of elementary Jewish training.

[Bernard Postal]

BIBLIOGRAPHY: M. Kaplan, *Ha-Loḥem ha-Yehudi bi-Ẓeva'ot ha-Olam* (1967), incl. bibl.; J. Ben Hirsch, *Jewish General Officers* (1967), incl. bibl.; G. Loewenthal, *Bewaehrung im Untergang* (1966); J. Lazarus, *Juifs au combat* (1947); F. Servi, *Israeliti italiani nella guerra 1915–18* (1921); J.G. Fredman and L.A. Falk, *Jews in American Wars* (1963); A.L. Lebeson, *Pilgrim People* (1950); S. Wolf, *The American Jew as Patriot, Soldier, and Citizen* (1895); P.S. Foner, *Jews in American History 1654–1865* (1945), 16–27, 36–42, 63–78, incl. bibl.; P. Wiernik, *History of the Jews in America* (1931), 87–97, 229–41, 417–20; W. Ziff, in: D. Runes (ed.), *Hebrew Impact on Western Civilization* (1951), 240–312; Z. Szajkowski, in: PAAJR, 26 (1957), 139–60, incl. bibl.; Comite zur Abwehr Anti-semitischer Angriffe in Berlin, *Juden als Soldaten* (1896); M. Fruehling, *Biographisches Handbuch* (1911); Wiener Library, *German Jewry* (1958), 201–4; H. Fischer, *Judentum, Staat und Heer in Preussen* (1968); R. Ainsztein, in: L. Kochan (ed.), *Jews in Soviet Russia* (1970), 269–87. JEWISH CHAPLAINCY OUTSIDE THE U.S.: I. Brodie, in: AJYB, 48 (1946/47), 58ff.; *Ha-Gedudim ha Ivriyyim be-Milḥemet ha-Olam ha-Rishonah* (1968); A. Tabian, *Australian Jewish Historical Society Transactions*, 6 (1965), 344; *South African Jewry in World War II* (1950); *Illustrierte Neue Welt* (June 1970), 26; *L'Aumznerie militaire belge* (1966), 88; Redier et Honesque, *L'Aumznerie militaire française* (1960). IN THE U.S.: L. Barish (ed.), *Rabbis in Uniform* (1962); O.I. Janowsky et al., *Change and Challenge: A History of Fifty Years of JWB* (1966), 80–83; *JWB Circle*, 1 (1946–), index. **ADD. BIBLIOGRAPHY:** A.I. Slomovitz, *The Fighting Rabbis: Jewish Military Chaplains and American History* (1998).

MILK. The milk most commonly mentioned in the Bible is that of sheep and goats (Prov. 27:27; Deut. 32:14), but cows' milk was also known and was consumed at least in the form of curds (Isa. 7:21–22). Milk is considered among the finest of foods (Deut. 32:14; Isa. 55:1) and is used as a term of abundance (Joel 4:18; Isa. 60:16), as the standard of whiteness (Lam. 4:7) and, with honey, of sweetness (Song 4:11). A "land flowing with milk and honey" refers to the abundant fertility of Canaan (e.g., Ex. 3:8, 17; Num. 13:27; Deut. 6:3; Jer. 11:5) and of Egypt (Num. 16:13). The prohibition against boiling a kid in its mother's milk (Ex. 23:19; 34:26; Deut. 14:21) most probably refers to a Canaanite sacrificial custom. Some scholars believe that this practice is referred to in Ugaritic text 52, line 14, but the textual restoration is uncertain. Boiling in milk – called "its mother's milk" – is a common way of preparing a kid or a lamb among modern Arabs, but it has no ritual significance for them.

[Tikva S. Frymer]

In Halakhah

The milk of clean animals such as cows, sheep, and goats, etc., although it comes "from the living" (*min ha-ḥai*, Bek. 6b), is permitted for consumption, but not the milk of unclean animals or of those suffering from visible disease which causes the animal to be ritually unfit for consumption (*terefah*), or that or an animal which after ritual slaughtering is found to have suffered from such a disease. In the latter case, all milk which the animal produced during the three days before it was slaughtered is forbidden to be used (Sh. Ar., YD 81:2). Milk bought from a non-Jew is forbidden for consumption out of fear that he may have mixed it, either through carelessness or in order to improve it, with milk of unclean animals. If a Jew was present at the milking, the milk may be used (*ibid.*, 115:1). There are, however, opinions that nowadays, even if the Jews did not supervise the milking, the milk is permitted since the law of the land forbids adulterating the milk. By many authorities butter made by gentiles is permitted for consumption on the grounds that butter cannot be produced from the milk of unclean animals (Av. Zar. 35b, Maim. Yad, Ma'akhalot Asurot, 3:12, 15, 16).

BIBLIOGRAPHY: C.H. Gordon, *Ugaritic Text-Book* (1966), 174; Eisenstein, Dinim, 68: ET, 5 (1953), 84–91: S. Lieberman, *Ha-Yerushalmi ki-Feshuto* (1934), 39–42.

MILKEN, MICHAEL R. (1946–), U.S. investor, philanthropist. Nicknamed "the junk bond king," Milken, by using a little-noticed financial tool, transformed corporate takeovers and financing in the 1970s and 1980s, amassing great personal wealth – $200 million to $550 million a year – through what some considered questionable financial dealings. In 1989 a federal grand jury indicted Milken for violations of federal securities and racketeering laws. He pleaded guilty to securities fraud and related charges in 1990, and the government dropped the more serious charges of insider trading and racketeering. Milken was fined and sentenced to 10 years in prison but in 1991 his sentence was reduced to two years plus three years probation. Barred from the securities business for life, Milken worked as a strategic business consultant after his release from prison. The Securities and Exchange Commission charged that this work was a violation of his probation, and in 1998 Milken settled with the SEC and paid the government $42 million in fees that he had earned plus interest.

Michael Robert Milken grew up in Encino, Calif. His paternal grandparents were Jewish immigrants from Poland. He attended the University of California at Berkeley during the height of protest movements in the mid-1960s and graduated as a business major with highest honors. He began his financial career at the university, when he invested money for his fraternity brothers in return for 50 percent of the profits. With no returns to his clients on losses, Milken had virtual assurance of profitability. At that time he developed a theory about low-grade "junk" bonds. Milken believed that under a revised rating system, one that also factored the potentials for return on investment, cash flow, business plans, personnel and corporate vision, junk bonds might pose a worthwhile risk. In 1970, after earning a master's degree from the Wharton School at the University of Pennsylvania, Milken went to work for the Drexel Corporation as assistant to the chairman and later became head of bond research. When Drexel merged with Burnham & Co. in 1973, Milken headed the noninvestment-grade bond-trading department, an operation that earned 100 percent return on investment. In 1977 Milken returned to California and moved his High-Yield Bond Department to Los Angeles. Milken's younger brother Lowell joined him. In the early 1980s Drexel-Burnham began using the "highly confident" letter, a correspondence designed to convince commercial banks to finance corporate takeovers. The letters stated that Drexel was "highly confident" the funds could be raised to finance the deal. In the company's first attempt at this scheme, Milken raised $1.5 billion in 48 hours. In 1982, Drexel-Burnham took on a new client, the financier Ivan *Boesky. Milken's dealings with him violated the securities law. In June 1989 Milken resigned from Drexel to form his own company, International Capital Access Group. The new venture was unsuccessful largely because Milken was fighting the SEC charges in a 98-count indictment. Eventually, he issued an apology and admitted that he cheated clients and plotted with Boesky to accomplish a corporate raid.

Milken completed his prison term in 1993. He co-founded a company called Education Entertainment Network, which produces business videos. In 1996 he and Larry *Ellison founded Knowledge Universe, a company dealing in a diverse variety of goods and services, including day care, executive education, corporate training, and toys. The SEC came after him again. He admitted no wrongdoing but paid a fine of $47 million in response to accusations that he served as a broker.

Milken used his personal fortune and high-level contacts to become an influential voice in economics, education, and medical research. In 1982 he co-founded the Milken Family Foundation to support medical education and research. In 1991 he founded the Milken Institute, a kind of think tank that sponsors prestigious international conferences. In 1993, after he was diagnosed with prostate cancer, he founded the Prostate Cancer Foundation, the world's largest philanthropic source of funds for prostate cancer research. The Milken Family Foundation, through the Milken National Educator Awards, founded in 1985, awarded $52 million to honor more than 2,000 teachers and principals, with each educator receiving an unrestricted $25,000 prize.

Milken's philanthropy – some critics questioned his motives – was widespread. In 1995 he donated $5 million to a large Jewish secondary school in Los Angeles. In gratitude the school was to be renamed Milken Community High School of Stephen Wise Temple until parents and students objected. However, a number of Milken grants to Jewish causes endure. The Skirball Cultural Center, one of the most prominent cultural venues in the United States, has a Milken Gallery, for which the Milken Family Foundation was the lead benefactor. It contains exhibits that explore the connections between the 4,000 years of Jewish heritage and the vitality of American democratic ideals. The Milken Archive of American Jewish Music is an international undertaking to record, preserve, and distribute a vast cross-section of American Jewish music covering 350 years. The archive comprises 50 CD's and 600 works on the Naxos American Classical label, the largest collection of American Jewish music ever assembled. The archive has also videotaped more than 100 oral histories of composers, conductors and performers and commissioned a comprehensive history of American Jewish music. The Milken Family Foundation is also a major supporter of American Friends of the Hebrew University, and the foundation for many years has supported the College of Judea and Samaria, the largest public college in Israel. It has a Milken Family Campus, embodying its teaching and research laboratories as well as its library, main administration building and computer center.

[Stewart Kampel (2nd ed.)]

MILKWEED, plant of the Euphorbiaceae family. Many genera comprising scores of species are found in Israel. Attempts have been made to identify them with plants mentioned in the Bible, but such attempts are without foundation. One plant mentioned in the Mishnah belongs to the Asclepiadaceae family: the *Calotropis procera*, the mishnaic *Petilat ha-Midbar* ("desert wick," Shab. 2:1). It is a shrub growing in the salt Jordan valley and the Arabah. It has large leaves and its fruit is like a big lemon, but instead of juice it contains many seeds enveloped in shining silky fibers. These are used for making cushions, and wicks too can be prepared from them, but since the oil does not rise well in the fiber its use for the Sabbath lamp is forbidden (Shab. *ibid.*). The popular name of the fruit is "Sodom apple," which has no connection with "the vine of Sodom" (Deut. 32:32). Milkweed is mentioned by Josephus (Wars, 4:484) who points out that this fruit of Sodom appears edible but on being opened turns to dust. The reference is to the seeds, which have hairy adhesions by which they are broadcast.

BIBLIOGRAPHY: Loew, Flora, 1 (1928), 282f.; J. Feliks, *Olam ha-Ẓome'aḥ ha-Mikra'i* (1968³), 82. **ADD. BIBLIOGRAPHY:** Feliks, Ha-Tzome'aḥ, 131.

[Jehuda Feliks]

MILL, JOSEPH SOLOMON (**John**; 1870–1952), pioneer of the *Bund. Born in Panevezys, Lithuania, Mill was left on his own when his family immigrated to the United States. From an early age he established close relations with Polish families, acquainting himself with the complex nationality problems of the region. He joined revolutionary circles under the influence of Z. *Kopelson. From 1890 he was a most active member of the Jewish Social Democratic organization in Vilna, except for intervals of imprisonment (1892), military service, and studies at the University of Zurich. He established ties with the leaders of the Polish Social Democrats, Rosa *Luxemburg, and L. *Jogiches, who led the Social Democratic "circles" in Vilna at the end of the 1880s. In 1895 Mill went to Warsaw as the head of a group interested in laying a foundation for a Jewish workers' society that later became a branch of the Bund there. He fought the Polish Socialist Party and its group of Jewish members and succeeded in uniting Lithuanian and local workers into one Jewish association. After the arrest of Bund members in 1898, Mill fled the country, and together with Kopelson initiated the establishment of the Bund "committee abroad." He was the editor of its organ *Der Yidisher Arbeter* (nos. 6–11) and initiated the setting up of the Bund archives. At the third congress of the Bund (1899) Mill was the first to demand that the claim to national autonomy be included in its program. For many years he headed the organizational affairs of the Bund and its "committee abroad" until he imigrated to Chicago in 1915. In the United States he worked at his profession of dental technician, and was active in the *Jewish Socialist Verband and the Socialist Party, holding the position of Jewish secretary and translator. He wrote for Jewish socialist periodicals and published important memoirs entitled *Pionern un Boyer* (2 vols., 1943–46).

BIBLIOGRAPHY: LNYL, 5 (1963), 624–6, incl. bibl.; J.S. Hertz et al. (eds.), *Geshikhte fun Bund*, 3 vols. (1960–66), indexes; M. Mishkinsky, in: *Asufot*, 14 (1970), 81–131.

[Moshe Mishkinsky]

°**MILLÁS VALLICROSA, JOSÉ MARIÁ** (1897–1970), Spanish scholar and historian. Millás Vallicrosa was born in Santa Coloma de Farnés, Spain. From 1925 onward he was professor of Hebrew studies at the University of Barcelona, having also taught at the University of Madrid. Millás Vallicrosa did research into the history of Spanish Jewry, medieval Hebrew poetry, the Bible, and the history of the sciences. He also translated medieval works from Hebrew and Arabic into Spanish. One of his important studies on Spanish Jewry is *Documents hebraics de jueus catalans* (1927), in which he compiled and explained Hebrew documents of the Catalonian Jews in the 11th–12th centuries. Another work of his is *Assaig d'histúria de les idees fisiques i matemàtiques a la Catalunya medieval* (1931), on the history of the development of science in Catalonia. In the field of the history of science, Millás Vallicrosa's studies on Abraham ibn Ezra and *Abraham bar Ḥiyya are notable, while in the research into Hebrew poetry and literature a special place is occupied by his work, *La poesía sagrada hebraicoespañola* (1940). He suggested that antecedents of poetic forms in medieval Hebrew poetry in Spain can be traced to biblical poetry (in *Sefarad*, 1 (1941), 45–87). In this field he also published the studies, *Yehuda ha-Leví, como poeta y apologista* (1947), and *Šĕlomō ibn Gabirol, como poeta y filósofo* (1945). Millás Vallicrosa published scores of articles in scholarly journals, including *Al-Andalus, Sefarad, Revue Internationale de l'Histoire des Sciences*, and *Osiris: Archeion*. Many of his pupils earned scholarly reputations, among them his own sons. His wife, FRANCISCA VENDRELL, also a scholar, studied the history of medieval Spanish Jewry. A two-volume *Homenaje…* containing scholarly articles by Jewish and non-Jewish scholars was published in honor of Millás Vallicrosa in 1954–56. A list of his works was published under the title *Títulos y Trabajos de Profesor D. José M. Millás Vallicrosa* (1950).

ADD. BIBLIOGRAPHY: T.F. Glick, in: *Isis*, 68 (1977), 276–83.

[Haim Beinart]

MILLER, ARTHUR (1915–2005), U.S. playwright. In his work, Miller wrestled with the primal issues of modern society. Because he came of age in New York City during the Great Depression, he embraced the themes of personal integrity and social responsibility, themes writ large in his immediate surroundings and his own family. Relationships, typically between one and one's family and society, were at the heart of nearly all his work. Theater director Robert Whitehead has been quoted as saying Miller had a "rabbinical righteousness," that his plays "sought to be a light unto the world." For Miller, theater was not mere entertainment, but an opportunity for consciousness raising, to change or broaden the minds of the audience. Writing and producing plays was a politically engaging experience for him. However, while he acknowledged that a given work might reflect a creator's political and social ideology, he rejected the notion that a play could encapsulate one's entire philosophy. He felt that real life was far too complex to be fully explained in a work of art or in a political methodology. He repeatedly tried to illustrate this ultimately unknowable complexity in his work. Very often the motivations of his characters are vague and mysterious. He offered no succinct answers to the problems he presented; indeed he may have believed there were none.

He acquired an international reputation after World War II, following the publication of two plays and of *Focus* (1945), a novel about antisemitism. In it, a pair of glasses allows a man to see better as it encourages others to see him differently. A meek gentile, who, as part of his job, identifies Jewish job applicants, is mistaken to be Jewish when he begins wearing a pair of glasses. He loses his job and can only find employment in the office of Jewish businessmen. He passively participates in the antisemitism in his initial job, in his neighborhood, where hatred of Jews reaches a virulent level, and at home. Ultimately he redeems himself by trying to stop vandals from destroying the store of a Jewish shopkeeper.

The play *All My Sons* (1947) revealed his ability to portray characters involved in emotional conflicts. It is a realistic play, intended for the general public. The dialogue is of common speech. The plot involves an overwhelming crisis growing out of smaller crises. The play has symbolic overtones despite the realistic characters and plot, which combine to help Miller focus on his themes of mutual responsibility and survivor guilt.

His reputation was really established with *Death of a Salesman* (1949), which won the Pulitzer Prize for drama. The play, later made into a motion picture, owed its success to the delineation of Willy Loman, the unsuccessful traveling salesman, and was regarded as an indictment of the false sense of values of American life. Miller has stated his initial idea for the play came from one notion: that the main character would kill himself. Loman's is a realistic portrayal of decline, of never quite giving up on the American dream, despite all evidence to the contrary. His sacrifice is a hopeless attempt to preserve some personal dignity and to help his family. The audience is never told if the insurance from his death properly provides for his family, but there are hints in the play that his death is in vain, that his plan does not work. Because of his drastic and self-destructive behavior for what may be an ideological misconception, Willy Loman is one of the great tragic characters of American drama.

In 1951, engaged by the problem of freedom of speech, Miller wrote an adaptation of Henrik Ibsen's *An Enemy of the People*, and in 1953, in his own play *The Crucible*, he turned to the Salem witch trials of 1692, and spoke for freedom of conscience during the period of Senator McCarthy's anti-communist campaign. Miller hoped the play "would be seen as an affirmation of the struggle for liberty, for keeping one's own conscience." John Proctor is a strong protagonist, flawed, but with no misplaced idealism. With Proctor at the center, Miller plays with the theme of retaining one's sense of morality in the face of public pressure. The witch-hunt mentality (reminiscent of the antisemitic hysteria in *Focus*) has both rational and irrational origins: some, like those causing the fuss, are conscious of the social and economic power it brings, while others are merely swept up in the supernatural paranoia. Miller adeptly portrays the act of ruination by accusation. When one character is accused of witchcraft, he has two choices: to confess and lose his land, or deny and lose his land. When he remains silent, even to his death, his land at least stays with his family. During the political climate of the McCarthy Red Scare, this proved to be a profoundly important lesson in social and individual responsibility. In an odd case of life imitating art, Miller played Proctor for real. Summoned before McCarthy's House Un-American Activities Committee, Miller was asked about Communist meetings he had attended. He did not refuse to answer, telling the committee everything they wanted to know about him, while denying he was a Communist. But he stopped short of implicating others. As Proctor refused to speak about people already known to his questioners, so did Miller. He was found guilty of contempt of court, but that charge was later reversed. This play was screened as the *Witches of Salem* (1957).

A View from the Bridge (1955) again won a Pulitzer Prize. It showed Miller still striving for significant realistic drama and imaginative dramatic form. In the play he continued his practice of trying to mythologize the ordinary and everyday. Falling short of being entirely uplifting, the play has a positive message: that life goes on despite any tragedy.

The film script *The Misfits* (1961), written after his marriage to the screen star Marilyn Monroe, and acted in by her and Clark Gable, was an unusually sensitive, though commercially unsuccessful, study of loneliness and divorce.

Miller returned to the theater with an autobiographical drama, *After the Fall* (1964), based largely on his life with Marilyn Monroe, whom he had divorced in 1962, and relating his own conflicts in love and friendship to the state of the world. This expressionistic drama concerns the various crises of Quentin, one of which is his sense of guilt at not experiencing the Nazi death camps. His proximity to Holga, a woman who has escaped Auschwitz, exacerbates this feeling in him. He laments his inability to atone for what he feels are sins, because they are sins of omission, that is, he is guilty, not for things he has done, but for things he has not done.

Incident at Vichy (1965) deals with the arrest of a number of Frenchmen, including some Jews, during the Nazi occupation. Each prisoner separates himself from the others while trying to understand why the Nazis want to destroy them. The gypsy, the Communist, the Catholic, and the Jew are unable to come together even as fellow prisoners, even in their hatred of the Nazis. There is no sense of union, that each is responsible for the others. One Nazi officer is shown having feelings of guilt, but he ultimately does nothing about it. Miller stresses that guilt is not enough, that action is necessary. To deny one's connection to humanity is to deny one's own humanity.

The Price (1968), depicting a dramatic conflict between two brothers, had as a central character an old Jew who acted as a wise commentator.

Miller stated his intention as a dramatist as being to "bring to the stage the thickness, awareness, and complexity of the novel." He endeavored to give postwar American drama depth of purpose and content, and a sense of tragic conflict in terms of contemporary American life. Widely regarded in the 1950s as America's leading dramatist, his reputation faded somewhat in the 1960s as realistic drama itself passed out of critical fashion. The 1980s, however, saw a return to appreciation of Miller's contribution to 20th-century theater. Other plays include *The American Clock* (1983), *The Archbishop's Ceiling* (1984), *Danger: Memory* (1986), *Two-Way Mirror* (1989), *The Ride Down Mount Morgan* (1991), *The Last Yankee* (1991), and *Broken Glass* (1994). For the collected edition of his plays published in 1958, he wrote a 50-page introduction, which clarified his purpose and explained his methods of work. Translated into many languages, the plays were internationally popular. Miller was elected president of the International PEN Club in 1965, in which position he strove vigorously to organize protests against literary censorship and repression all over the world.

BIBLIOGRAPHY: D. Welland, *Arthur Miller* (1961); B. Nelson, *Arthur Miller* (1970); L. Moss, *Arthur Miller* (1967); S. Huftel, *Arthur Miller, The Burning Glass* (1965); R. Hogen, *Arthur Miller* (University of Minnesota Pamphlets on American Writers, no. 40, 1964); J. Gassner, *Theater at the Crossroads* (1960); *Contemporary Authors*, first rev. (1967), incl. bibl. **ADD. BIBLIOGRAPHY:** M. Gottfried, *Arthur Miller: His Life and Work* (2003); A. Miller, *Timebends: A Life* (1987); H. Bloom (ed. & intro.), *Arthur Miller* (2003); E. Brater (ed.), *Arthur Miller's America: Theater & Culture in a Time of Change* (2005); C.W.E. Bigsby, *Arthur Miller: A Critical Study* (2005); M. Berger, "Arthur Miller, Moral Voice of American Stage, Dies at 89," in: *New York Times* (Feb. 12, 2005), A1, A14.

[Joseph Mersand and Jonathan Licht / Robert L. DelBane (2nd ed.)]

MILLER, BEN-ZION (1947–), *ḥazzan*. Miller was born in Germany where his father, Rabbi Aharon Miller, was serving as *ḥazzan* to the Klausenburger rebbe in a German refugee camp. He studied at the Bobov yeshivah in Israel, becoming a *ḥazzan* and *shoḥet*. He also came under the tutelage of the well-known cantor Samuel Baruch *Taube. Thereafter he served as *ḥazzan* in New Jersey, New York, and Canada, before becoming, in 1981, *ḥazzan* of the Beth-El synagogue of Boro Park in Brooklyn, New York. He has also appeared in concert in Europe, the United States, Australia, and Israel. He is one of the few Orthodox cantors dedicated to perpetuating the great virtuoso cantorial styles and tradition of the 19th and early 20th centuries. A tremendous recording and performing artist, Miller has many varied recordings to his credit, including the Milken Archive releases issued by Naxos.

[Akiva Zimmerman / Raymond Goldstein (2nd ed.)]

MILLER, EMANUEL (1893–1970), English psychiatrist. Born in London, Miller studied medicine at Cambridge University and the London Hospital and lectured in psychology at Cambridge for a brief period after 1924. He became a psychiatric specialist in 1940 and in 1946 was made a Fellow of the Royal College of Physicians. One of the foremost psychiatrists in Britain, Miller was founder and honorary director of the East

London Child Guidance Clinic and chairman and honorary president of the Association of Child Psychiatry. He showed a keen interest in the development of medicine in Israel and in 1953 was elected president of the British Friends of Magen David Adom. His publications include *Modern Psychotherapy* (1930) and *Neurosis in War* (1940). His wife, BETTY MILLER (née Spiro; 1910–1965), born in Cork, Ireland, was the author of various novels including *Farewell Leicester Square* (1940), *A Room in Regent's Park* (1942), *On the Side of the Angels* (1945), and *The Death of the Nightingale* (1949). She also wrote a biographical study, *Robert Browning: A Portrait* (1952), and was elected a Fellow of the Royal Society of Literature. Their son JONATHAN MILLER (1934–) was educated at St. Paul's school and Cambridge and qualified as a doctor but established his reputation as an actor in the revue *Beyond the Fringe*, a satire on various aspects of British life from Shakespeare to the Royal Family, which played in London and New York. Later he directed many successful theatrical and television productions, frequently winning acclaim for his originality. His television series on the history of medicine, *The Body in Question*, became internationally known.

ADD. BIBLIOGRAPHY: ODNB online.

MILLER, IRVING (1903–1980), U.S. rabbi and Zionist leader. Rabbi Miller, who was born in Kovno, Lithuania, was taken to the U.S. in 1912. Ordained a rabbi at Yeshivath Rabbi Isaac Elhanan in 1926, he served congregations in Youngstown, Ohio (1926–28), Chelsea, Mass. (1928–30), and Far Rockaway, N.Y. (1930–46), before becoming rabbi of Congregation Sons of Israel, Woodmere, N.Y. (1946–63). Extremely active in Jewish affairs, Miller's posts included secretary-general of the World Jewish Congress (1942–45); president of the American Jewish Congress (1949–52); president of the Zionist Organization of America (1952–54); president of the American Zionist Council (1954–63); chairman of the Conference of Presidents of Major American Jewish Organizations (1961–63); and member of both the national cabinet of the United Jewish Appeal and the Actions Committee of the World Zionist Organization.

MILLER, ISRAEL (1918–2002), U.S. Orthodox rabbi, communal leader, and university administrator. Miller was born in Baltimore and educated in New York, where he earned his B.A. from *Yeshiva College in 1938 and his ordination from the Rabbi Isaac Elchanan Theological Seminary of Yeshiva University in 1941. He received an M.A. from Columbia University in 1949 and a D.D. from Yeshiva University in 1967. Immediately after ordination, Miller became rabbi of the Kingsbridge Heights Jewish Center in the Bronx, New York, becoming emeritus in 1968, with a brief interruption to serve as a United States Air Force chaplain (1945–46). In 1968 Miller began a second career at Yeshiva University, as a professor, vice president, senior vice president, and senior vice president emeritus, until his *aliyah* to Israel in 2000.

Miller was president or chairman of nearly every major Orthodox or American national Jewish organization; in fact, he was one of the founders of several of them, including the American Jewish Conference on Soviet Jewry, serving as its first chairman (1965–67); the American Zionist Federation (successor to the *American Zionist Council, of which he was chairman from 1967–70, and precursor to the *American Zionist Movement), serving as its first president and then honorary president (beginning 1970 and 1974, respectively); and the New York Jewish Community Relations Council, serving as its first vice president (1976). Miller was elected president of the *Rabbinical Council of America in 1964, and led the RCA's first mission to the Soviet Union and the Moscow Great Synagogue under KGB scrutiny in 1965.

From 1969 to 1976, Miller was vice chairman and chairman of the *Conference of Presidents of Major American Jewish Organizations. He was an advisor to presidents of both Democratic and Republican administrations: President Johnson appointed him to the National Citizens Committee for Community Relations to help implement civil rights legislation; he received a citation from President Ford; and President Reagan consulted him prior to his Geneva summit with Mikhail Gorbachev and dispatched him on a fact-finding mission to South Africa.

For the last 20 years of his life, Miller was president of the *Conference on Jewish Material Claims against Germany (and the Claims Conference against Austria), overseeing the disbursement of $2 billion to 400,000 Holocaust survivors and $500 million in institutional allocations. In this capacity, he negotiated with world leaders, including German Chancellor Helmut Kohl, and visited thousands of survivors personally to ensure that they were living their final years with dignity. In addition to serving as president of the Association of Jewish Chaplains of the Armed Forces, honorary chairman of the Jewish National Fund, and vice president of the Religious Zionists of America, Miller sat on the executive committees or boards of directors of many organizations, including the World Zionist Organization, National Jewish Welfare Board, and American Israel Public Affairs Committee.

Miller received numerous awards, not only from the organizations he led, but also, for instance, from Yeshiva University and the Boy Scouts of America. The greatest honor, however, came from the accolades and votes of confidence of his colleagues, who elected him repeatedly to the highest leadership positions on account of his gentility, grace, integrity, and wisdom, rather than as a result of vigorous campaigning for office.

[Bezalel Gordon (2nd ed.)]

MILLER, LOUIS (1917–1988), Israeli psychiatrist. Born in Somerset West, South Africa, he went to Israel in 1948 and established psychiatric and psychological services in the Israeli army and air force. In 1949 Miller became director of psychiatry in Israel's Ministry of Health, where he planned and initiated its regional hospital and community services. In 1954 he entered the field of public health and developed a family health and community organization program for the Jerusalem region. In 1959 he returned to his post of director of Mental Health Services, and in 1970 became chief national psychiatrist. In 1966–67, as visiting professor at Northwestern University, he planned and initiated a community mental health program in Chicago for the State of Illinois. His contributions to mental health theory, research, and practice were concerned particularly with the effects of socio-cultural and community influences on mental health and ill health and its treatment. He integrated this approach with the biological and psychological interpretations of personality. His publications include studies concerning the incidence of psychiatric conditions in various cultures in Israel, immigration and mental health, child rearing on the kibbutz and among Tripolitanian Jews, aging, urbanization, and social change. He was chairman of the National Committee for the Study of Drug Abuse and the *Encyclopaedia Judaica* (first edition) departmental editor for Jews in psychiatry.

MILLER, LOUIS E. (pseudonym of **Louis E. Bandes**; 1866–1927), Yiddish editor and labor leader. Miller was born in Vilna and became involved in socialist and revolutionary activities in his boyhood. He fled from Russia at 14 and participated in émigré revolutionary circles in Berlin, Switzerland, Paris, and, after 1886, in New York. In the U.S. Miller worked in a shirt factory, and helped found the first shirtmakers union among Jewish workers. Miller was also deeply involved in the political life of socialist and other labor organizations. In his early years he remained close to organizations which used Russian as their language, but in 1889 he represented the Yiddish-language-oriented United Hebrew Trades at the Second International in Paris.

Miller was most influential as editor and writer in Yiddish. In 1890, with Philip *Krantz, Morris *Hillquit, and Abraham *Cahan, he founded the Yiddish-socialist *Die Arbeiter Zeitung* (1890). In 1897 he joined Cahan in launching the daily *Forward* (1897). In 1905 he broke with Cahan, the editor in chief of this daily, and founded his own paper *Die Wahrheit* (1905) which stressed Jewish national aspirations no less than socialism. When World War I broke out, he espoused the cause of the Allies, while most of his daily's 100,000 readers favored Germany as against czarist Russia. The paper continued to lose circulation, and he preferred to resign rather than to keep silent. He attempted several journalistic ventures after 1917, but never regained his earlier influence with the Yiddish reading masses.

BIBLIOGRAPHY: Rejzen, Leksikon, 2 (1927), 409–14; LNYL, 5 (1963), 628–31.

[Alexander Tobias]

MILLER, MARTIN RUDOLF (1899–1969), Czech actor, who from 1939 worked in England. Miller (né Rudolf Muller) was born in Kremsier, Czechoslovakia, started his career in Vienna, and made his last appearance in Berlin at the Jewish Culture Theater in 1939. In London he appeared in *Awake and Sing* (1942) and in 1,000 performances of *The Mousetrap* (1952). In New York he was in *The Mad Woman of Chaillot* (1949) and *The Magnolia Street Story* (1951). Miller was noted for his portrayal of elderly Jews.

MILLER, MARVIN JULIAN (1917–), one of the most influential figures in American sports history, baseball's first labor leader who served as executive director of the Major League Baseball Players' Association (MLBPA) from 1966 to 1982. Miller was born in the Bronx and raised in Brooklyn, New York, by his father Alexander, a salesman of women's coats on the Lower East Side and a member of the wholesale clothing workers union, and by his mother Gertrude (Wald), an elementary-school teacher in New York's public schools who became one of the early members of the city's teachers' union. Miller studied first at the University of Miami and then at New York University, where he graduated in 1938. He worked at the National War Labor Relations Board, the Machinist Union, the United Auto Workers, and the United Steelworkers union, where he was assistant to the president and its leading economist and negotiator. On March 5, 1966, the baseball player representatives elected him executive director of the MLB Players' Association. Through his innovative thinking and keen negotiating skills, Miller united a loosely organized association and transformed it into one of the strongest unions in the United States, thereby revolutionizing baseball. As a pioneer in the unionization of professional athletes, Miller was instrumental in its development into a powerful labor union that transformed the economics and labor relations of baseball, which led ultimately to profound changes in the nature of U.S. professional sports and their place in society. He led the baseball union to two strikes, the first on April 1, 1972, which lasted 13 days and was the first successful strike in the history of professional sports, and again in 1981, which lasted 50 days.

Among Miller's accomplishments were the recognition of the players' union; the right to bargain collectively; the use of agents to negotiate individual contracts; an end to the reserve clause, with free movement from team to team through free agency; arbitration in labor disputes; the right for veteran players to veto trades; and a vastly improved pension plan funded largely through percentages of television revenue. During Miller's tenure, major league players saw their minimum salary jump from $6,000 to $33,500, while the average salary rose from $19,000 to over $240,000. Miller also instituted changes to make the game safer, successfully bargaining for improved scheduling and padded outfield walls, better-defined warning tracks, and safer locker rooms. Journalist Red Barber called Miller "one of the three most important men in baseball history," along with Babe Ruth and Jackie Robinson, and author Studs Terkel said Miller was "the most effective union organizer since John L. Lewis." In 2000, *The Sporting News* ranked Miller fifth on its list of the "100 Most Powerful People in Sports for the 20th Century." Miller was the author of *A Whole Different Ball Game: The Sport and Business of Baseball* (1991).

[Elli Wohlgelernter (2nd ed.)]

MILLER, MITCH (**Mitchell William**; 1911–), U.S. oboist, record producer, arranger, and conductor. Miller studied piano and oboe and later attended Rochester's Eastman School of Music (B. Mus., 1932). Miller played oboe with the Rochester Philharmonic (1930–33) and the CBS symphony orchestra (1935–47). In the 1950s he became a major force in the recording industry. Miller was appointed director of artists and repertoire for the classical division of Mercury Records (1947–50) and produced a series of major hits, including Frankie Laine's "That Lucky Old Sun." When he was in charge of the popular division of Columbia Records (1950–61), he recorded Guy Mitchell and Tony Bennett, and signed artists like Mahalia Jackson and Rosemary Clooney. He got Laine to record "High Noon," the title song from the Gary Cooper western, and played an important role in fostering the 1950s folk revival. Miller's own recording career, mostly credited to "Mitch Miller and His Gang," began with his adaptation of the Israeli folk song "Tzena, Tzena," "The Civil War Marching Song," "The Yellow Rose of Texas," and the "Colonel Bogey March" from *The Bridge on the River Kwai*. His series of "Sing Along With Mitch" albums, in which he led an all-male chorus in spirited versions of mostly older tunes, led to his own television program *Sing Along with Mitch* (1960–65), which became extremely popular. By 1965 Miller's influence had waned. He appeared as guest conductor of pop concerts and light classical recordings with orchestras in and outside the U.S. Miller and Freedman edited his *Mitch Miller Community Song Book: A Collection for Group Singing for All Occasions* (1999).

BIBLIOGRAPHY: *Baker's Biographical Dictionary of Musicians* (1997); "The *Audio* Interview – Mitch Miller: A Hidden Classic," in: *Audio*, 69 (Nov 1985), 40–51, (Dec 1985), 42–53.

[Naama Ramot (2nd ed.)]

MILLER, SHAYE (1895–1958), Yiddish novelist, editor, and translator. Born in Filpovitch, Ukraine, he immigrated to the U.S. at age 17 and lived in New York and Cleveland before settling in Los Angeles ten years later. He began to publish Yiddish short stories at the age of 22, translated Maeterlinck, Tagore, and Wedekind, and published ten volumes of impressionistic stories. Miller published in the leading Yiddish periodicals of his day, including the *Forverts*, *Der Yidisher Kemfer*, *Tsukunft*, and *Der Tog*. His novel *Dor Hafloge* ("The Lost Generation," 1948) deals with the decay, in the new American environment, of an Eastern European Jewish family which symbolizes the pre-World War I generation of transition. The stories of *Nekhtn* ("Yesterday," 1956) deal largely with Los Angeles Jews: Miller gives a panoramic view of the charlatans, the noble characters, and the ordinary men and women who were caught up in California's boom-psychosis of the 1920s and ended their lives tragically during the Great Depression of the early 1930s. He stresses the nostalgia for old-fashioned Jewishness that assailed the Jews who had wrested themselves loose from their Jewish roots and who found their materially successful life empty of meaning in later years. Miller is a master of dialogue, accurately reproducing the speech, intonations, and gestures of his marginal, semi-assimilated Jews. His posthumously published essays *Skeptishe Makhshoves* ("Sceptical Thoughts," 1959) deal with basic questions of American-Jewish cultural survival and cast light upon his own personality and approach to literary craftsmanship.

BIBLIOGRAPHY: Rejzen, Leksikon, 2 (1927), 417ff.; LNYL, 5 (1963), 631–4; J. Glatstein, *In Tokh Genumen* (1960), 328–33; S. Bickel, *Shrayber fun Mayn Dor* (1958), 327–34. **ADD. BIBLIOGRAPHY:** Sh. Niger, *Dertseylers un Romanistn* (1946), 133; Y. Botoshansky, *Pshat* (1952), 355–99.

[Sol Liptzin]

MILLET, the *Panicum miliaceum*, a summer plant of the Gramineae family, whose small seeds are utilized as fodder or are sometimes ground to produce a poor quality flour. It is regarded by some as identical with *doḥan*, one of the ingredients of the flour mixture that Ezekiel was commanded to eat for 390 days (Ezek. 4:9). The probability is, however, that *doḥan* is *sorghum. *Doḥan* is mentioned a number of times in rabbinic literature together with *orez* ("rice"), *peragim*, and *shumshemin* ("sesame"; Shev. 2:7), as summer plants from which occasionally bread is made (Ḥal. 1:4). *Peragim* cannot therefore be poppy as is stated in the *Arukh* of Nathan b. Jehiel (and as the word is used in modern Hebrew), since the poppy is a winter plant and is used only as a spice. From Syrian Aramaic it would seem that *peragim* is to be identified with millet, an identification compatible with the talmudic sources.

BIBLIOGRAPHY: Loew, Flora, 1 (1928), 738–40; H.N. and A.L. Moldenke, *Plants of the Bible* (1952), index; J. Feliks, *Olam ha-Ẓome'aḥ ha-Mikra'i* (1968²), 154f. **ADD. BIBLIOGRAPHY:** Feliks, Ha-Ẓome'aḥ, 46.

[Jehuda Feliks]

MILLET, name for the religious communal organization of non-Muslims in the Ottoman Empire. The Koran uses *milla* for religion or rite, e.g., religion of the Jews and Christians (2:114), and the religion of Abraham (2:124; 3:89). It is assumed that a Jewish communal organization was already in existence for some time in the areas occupied by the Ottoman Turks in the 14th and early 15th centuries. Even before the capture of Constantinople in 1453 the Ottoman conquerors of the Balkans had granted the Christian population religious, juridical, and administrative autonomy. Mehmed II the Conqueror (1451–81) organized all non-Muslim communities and recognized their religious leaders as heads of the respective millets. Each head had jurisdiction over and responsibility for the members of his millet, and even in matters of taxation, the apportionment of the whole amount was left to him. R. Moses *Capsali was the first to be appointed (1461?) head of the Jews in Constantinople (see also *ḥakham bashi). The powers of the second head, R. Elijah b. Abraham Mizraḥi (1485?–1526), were in fact restricted to religious matters of the Jews in Constantinople. Mizraḥi clearly had nothing to do with the collection of taxes and the representation of the Jews with the various authorities. That the collection of taxes was not the concern of the official representatives of the millet is confirmed by many sources. In fact, the opposite is true: the various tax collectors, toll farmers, cashiers, and bankers of the pashas, in so far as they were non-Muslims, were the natural spokesmen of their communities by virtue of their functions and influence at court. In his time *Kakhya Shealtiel was the official spokesman who represented the Jews of the city – especially in the matter of tax collection – before the authorities. Mizraḥi's judgment in the case of Kakhya Shealtiel repeatedly mentions the representatives of the congregations in Constantinople. The representative's title of *memunneh* (lit. "appointee") is one of the titles designating the persons elected by the congregation to manage its affairs; other titles are *parnas, barur, kaẓin*, and the ancient collective designation, *tovei ha-ir*. The powers, number, manner of election, and period of tenure of these functionaries varied greatly. Their main task was the collection of communal taxes (especially the *gabella*), which were used to maintain the children of the needy at school and to finance charitable purposes. The mode of imposition and amount of the taxes were also different; as a rule, the consent of the whole congregation or at least of the taxpayers was required. The congregations of expellees and immigrants from Europe usually retained the practices they had followed in their countries of origin. The veteran residents likewise maintained their ancestral tradition according to which public affairs were looked after by the elders, who were the heads of prominent and influential families.

In connection with the reforms in the Ottoman Empire in the 19th century, the structure of the millet organization underwent many changes. The regulations of the Greek community (*Rum milleti*) were finally drafted and approved in 1862 and those of the Armenian community (*Ermeni milleti*) in 1863. The submission of proposals for the reorganization of the Jewish community (*Yahudi milleti*), as required by the *Khaṭṭi humayun* (imperial decree) of 1856, was delayed due to internal dissension. The "Organizational Regulations of the Rabbinate" (*ḥakham Khane niẓamnamesi*) was approved finally in 1865 (see *community and *ḥakham bashi*). The tenor of the regulations reveals a desire to limit the powers of the *ḥakham bashi*, and they remained in force so long as the Ottoman Empire existed; only under the republic did they lapse de facto – without being officially replaced.

BIBLIOGRAPHY: R. Gibb and H. Bowen, *Islamic Society and the West*, 1 pt. 2 (1957), index and 219–26; G. Young, *Corps de Droit Ottoman*, 2 (1905), 148–55; A. Galanté, *Documents Officiels turcs concernant les Juifs de Turquie* (1931), 10–27; H.Z. Hirschberg, in: A.J. Arberry (ed.), *Religion in the Middle East*, 1 (1969), 185f., 200–2; B. Lewis, *Emergence of Modern Turkey* (1961), 329–30. **ADD. BIBLIOGRAPHY:** B. Braude and B. Lewis (eds.), *Christians and Jews in the Ottoman Empire*, 1–2 (1982), esp. vol. 1, 69–88; EIS², 7 (1993), 61–4 (includes bibliography).

[Haïm Z'ew Hirschberg]

MILLETT, SIR PETER, BARON (1932–), British barrister and judge. Born in London and educated at Harrow and Cambridge, Millett was called to the bar at the Middle Temple and became a QC in 1973, having served (1967–73) as standing junior counsel to the Department of Trade and Industry. From 1986 to 1994 he served as a judge of the High Court (Chancery Division), and then became a judge of the Court of Appeal (1994–98), and a lord of appeal in Ordinary from 1998 to 2004. Lord Millett was one of the most prominent senior Freemasons in the British judiciary and wrote widely on aspects of the law. He was knighted in 1986 and made a life peer in 1998.

[William D. Rubinstein (2nd ed.)]

MILLGRAM, ABRAHAM EZRA (1901–1998), U.S. rabbi, Jewish educator. Millgram was born in Russia and immigrated with his family to the United States where he was educated at the City College of New York (B.S., 1924) and at Columbia University (M.A. in 1927), the year he was ordained by the Jewish Theological Seminary where he also received his D.H.L. in 1959. While serving as the rabbi of Temple Beth Israel in Philadelphia (1930–40), Millgram attended Dropsie College for Cognate Learning where he received his Ph.D. in 1942. He went to work for the then new organization for Jewish college youth, Hillel, at the University of Minnesota from 1940 to 1945. (In the first generation of rabbis who served Hillel were many men who would have preferred an academic career but Judaic studies had not yet developed as a field so they joined Hillel to be close to the university environment.) He then came back to New York as the educational director of the United Synagogue of America, where he was responsible for their widespread educational activities at a time when it was most influential and respected. He retired to Jerusalem where he continued to write. Among his publications were *Sabbath: Day of Delight* (1944); *Handbook for the Congregational School Board Member*, United Synagogue Commission on Jewish Education (1953); *Concepts That Distinguish Judaism* (1985); *Jerusalem Curiosities* (1990); and *A Short History of Jerusalem*, published in the year of his death. He was also the editor of *An Anthology of Medieval Hebrew Literature* (1961), *Great Jewish Ideas* (1964), and *Jewish Worship* (Jewish Publication Society, 1971).

[Michael Berenbaum (2nd ed.)]

MILLIN, PHILIP (1888–1952), South African Supreme Court judge. Millin began his career as a journalist in Johannesburg and Cape Town, studying law at the same time. On graduation in 1913 he began to practice in Johannesburg. He became a King's Counsel in 1927, and was chairman of the Bar Council for several years. He was appointed to the Supreme Court in 1937. As chairman of the Company Law Amendment Inquiry Commission he drafted the "Millin Report," which led to important changes in company law. He was also the coauthor of *Mercantile Law of South Africa* (1917 and several other editions), a standard work. For some years Millin was vice president of the South African Friends of the Hebrew University. His wife was the novelist, Sarah Gertrude *Millin.

BIBLIOGRAPHY: S.G. Millin, *The Measure of My Days* (1955).

[Lewis Sowden]

MILLIN, SARAH GERTRUDE (born **Liebson**; 1889–1968), South African novelist. Born in Lithuania, she grew up near Kimberley and married Philip *Millin. After publishing several novels, she made her name with *God's Step-Children* (1924), a story of the colored people of Cape Province. None of her subsequent novels had the same popular impact, though at least one of them, *Mary Glenn* (1925), a rural tragedy, showed great power of projecting atmosphere and passion. Turning to biography, she published a life of Cecil Rhodes (1933) and *General Smuts* (2 vols., 1936). A prolific writer on South African and world affairs, Sarah Gertrude Millin produced among other works short stories of South Africa, and during World War II she wrote her war diaries in six volumes (published 1944–48), in which she devoted much attention to Palestine. Returning to fiction, she broadened her scope in *King of the Bastards* (1949) and *The Burning Man* (1952). She wrote two volumes of autobiography, *The Night is Long* (1941) and *The Measure of My Days* (1955).

Sarah Gertrude Millin's style was terse and her objectivity in fiction carried to the point where it often seemed that she disliked the people she wrote about. In her later years she often expressed conservative and controversial views on South Africa's race relations and color policies (apartheid). In 1966 she edited and contributed to a volume of essays, *White Africans are Also People*, in defense of Rhodesia and South Africa. Sarah Gertrude Millin, although interested in Jewish affairs, took no part in Jewish life. She occasionally introduced Jews in her stories, as in *The Coming of the Lord* (1928).

ADD. BIBLIOGRAPHY: M. Rubin, *Sarah Gertrude Millin: A South African Life* (1977).

[Lewis Sowden]

MILLMAN, JACOB (1911–), U.S. electrical engineer. Millman was born in Russia and taken to the U.S. in 1913. He was a faculty member of City College, New York from 1936 to 1951, and from 1952 professor of electrical engineering at Columbia University. He wrote *Electronics* (1941), *Pulse and Digital Circuits* (1956), and *Vacuum-Tube and Semiconductor Electronics* (1958).

MILLO (Pasovsky), JOSEF (1916–1996), Israeli theatrical producer and actor. Born in Prague, Millo was taken to Israel in 1921 but received his theatrical training in Prague and Vienna. On returning to Israel he worked with a marionette troupe (1937–41), acted for two years with the satirical theater "Ha-Matate," and in 1942 founded the Cameri Theater, which he directed until 1959. In 1961 he founded and became director of the Haifa Municipal Theater. Millo inaugurated a naturalistic school of Israel drama and strongly influenced the younger generation of actors and writers. He directed about 100 plays, including works by Bertolt Brecht and Shakespeare, himself playing many leading roles. He was considered to have shown new trends in modern Hebrew drama with N. Shaham's *They Will Return Tomorrow* and M. Shamir's *He Walked Through the Fields*. He was also responsible for the film version of the latter (1967). Millo translated into Hebrew Goldoni's *The Servant of Two Masters* and Čapek's *The World We Live In*. He directed plays at drama festivals in Paris (1956), Venice (1965), and other European cities. In 1968 he was awarded the Israel Prize for theater.

BIBLIOGRAPHY: Ohad, in: *Teatron* (Heb., June–Aug. 1963), 23–26.

MILLSTONE (Heb. רֵחַיִם), an instrument used for grinding grain. The word has a dual ending, indicating an instrument composed of two parts: an upper millstone (Heb. *rekhev*, Deut. 24:6) and a lower millstone (talmudic Heb. *shekhev*), which, however, was called *reḥayim* as well (*ibid.*). Other terms for both millstones are *pelaḥ* (Judg. 9:53, in combination with *rekhev* for upper millstone; Job 41:16, in combination with *taḥtit*, lower millstone), and *taḥanah* (Eccles. 12:34). The mill was worked by slaves (Ex. 11:5; Judg. 16:21 – Samson; Isa. 47:2; Lam. 5:13). The manna too was ground by millstones (Num. 11:8). Abimelech was killed with an upper millstone by the woman of Thebez (Judg. 9:53). Grain would be spread out between the upper and lower millstones, and the friction and pressure of one stone upon the other would break the kernels and grind them into flour. The desired friction was achieved by passing the upper stone back and forth over the lower one, as is illustrated in early Egyptian pictures. Millstones of this type have been found in abundance in excavations in Ereẓ Israel, for example at Gezer, Megiddo, and Hazor. This type of millstone was in use until the end of the Israelite period. Only at the end of the Persian period did another type of millstone come into use, in which the desired friction was achieved by means of the circular motion of the upper stone – which turned on an axle – upon the stationary lower stone. Millstones were essential household items, and it was forbidden to remove them from their owner's possession, for example, as a pledge for a loan (Deut. 24:6). In talmudic times a distinction was made between "hand mills" or "human mills," usually worked by the housewife and standing in a special room or place, and a mill operated by a donkey, which was both larger and of a more complicated construction. Water mills are mentioned but were rare.

BIBLIOGRAPHY: J.A. Wilson and T.G. Allen, *Megiddo*, 1 (1939), pl. 114, no. 11; C.C. McCown, *Tell En-Naẓbeh*, 1 (1947), pl. 91, nos. 1, 2, 4; R. Amiran, in: *Eretz Israel*, 4 (1956), 46–49; Y. Yadin et. al., *Hazor*, 3–4 (1961), pl. 233, nos. 20, 21; Krauss, Tal Arch, 1 (1910), 95–97.

[Ze'ev Yeivin]

MILNER, MOSES MICHAEL (**Mikhail Arnoldovich**; 1886–1953), composer, born in Rokitno, Ukraine. As a child he sang in the choirs of several famous *ḥazzanim*, including J.S. *Morogovski (Zeidel Rovner), and then studied at the Kiev and St. Petersburg conservatories. From 1912 to 1919 he was conductor of the choir of the Great Synagogue in St. Petersburg, and then worked as singing teacher and choral conductor in various posts. From 1924 to 1931 he was musical director and conductor of the Yiddish Theater in Moscow and Kharkov, musical director of the Jewish Voice Ensemble in Leningrad (1931–41), and coach of the choir of the Leningrad Bolshoi Theater from 1941 until his death.

Milner's renown began with the publication of his songs in 1914 by the *Society for Jewish Folk Music which he had helped to found. His works indicated new possibilities for the harmonization of traditional melodic material in the dramatic style of Moussorgsky. Until the mid-1930s he wrote many works on Jewish themes, mainly for the stage. The opera, *Die Himlen Brenen*, based on S. *An-Ski's *Dibbuk* and adapted by M. Rivesman, performed in 1923, was later denounced as reactionary and its performance was forbidden. Among his other works are *Der Najer Veg* (1933); *Josephus Flavius* (1935), based on L. *Feuchtwanger's novel; stage music for the Habimah performances of H. Leivik's *Golem* and R. *Beer-Hoffmann's *Jaakobs Traum*; and a ballet, *Ashmedai*. In addition, he also wrote settings of Jewish folk songs and liturgical texts. After the repression of Jewish art, Milner turned to more general subjects and wrote a symphony (1937); a symphonic poem, *The Partisans* (1944); and a piano concerto.

BIBLIOGRAPHY: I. Heskes and A. Wolfson (eds.), *Historic Contribution of Russian Jewry to Jewish Music* (1967), 74–79 (= *Jewish Music Festival*, 23rd, New York, 1966); Sendrey, Music, index; L. Saminsky, *Music of the Ghetto and the Bible* (1934), index; I. Rabinovitch, *Of Jewish Music* (1952), index; B.C. Steinpress (ed.), *Entsiklopedicheskiy muzykalny slovar* (1959); G. Bernandt, *Slovar Oper* (1962).

[Haim Bar-Dayan]

MILO (Milkovsky), RONI (1949–), politician, lawyer, and businessman; member of the Ninth to Thirteenth and Fifteenth Knessets. Milo was born in Tel Aviv. As a pupil in the leftist-oriented Tikhon Ḥadash high school, Milo sought to introduce the mention of Ze'ev *Jabotinsky in the curriculum, and argued in favor of the cancelation of the matriculation exams. In 1966 he was elected mayor of Ir ha-No'ar (Youth City), and got Menaḥem *Begin to help him write his inauguration speech. He studied law at Tel Aviv University and served as assistant to constitutional law professor Amnon *Rubinstein, who served at the time as dean of the Law Faculty, and like Milo was elected to the Ninth Knesset. From his student days Milo was an active member of the Ḥerut Movement. He served as chairman of the Israeli Students' Association and was one of the organizers of a students' general strike over differential tuition. He also initiated the establishment of a bureau for free legal advice for the needy and received a budget from Minister of Education Yigal *Allon to finance private lessons for needy students. After the Yom Kippur War he supported the "Temurah – Yisra'el Shelanu" Movement, which called for the resignation of the government of Golda Meir. Because of health reasons he was not mobilized for regular military service but after completing his law studies served in the army in the military attorney's office as a justice officer and military prosecutor. Following his army service he worked as an independent lawyer.

Milo was elected to the Ninth Knesset on the Likud list. In his early years in politics he was considered a firebrand and an extremist. After returning from a visit to the United States in 1978, he claimed that the *Peace Now Movement was being funded by the CIA, even though its leaders might not have been aware of the fact. He nevertheless supported the peace agreement with Egypt.

In the Tenth Knesset Milo served as chairman of the Likud parliamentary group as well as chairman of the Ḥerut Movement section. He fell out with Begin after supporting the appointment of David *Levy as deputy prime minister in the government formed by him in 1981. When Begin decided to resign the premiership in October 1983, Milo supported Yitzhak *Shamir as his successor. In the National Unity governments of 1984–88, he served as deputy to Shamir, first in the Ministry for Foreign Affairs and then in the Prime Minister's Office. In the National Unity government formed in 1988 he served as minister for the environment, after the new ministry was tailor-made for him. Between the fall of the government in March 1990 and the establishment of the new narrow government by Shamir in June 1990 he served as minister of labor and welfare, and in the new government was appointed minister of police, and served in the narrow cabinet. In this period he started to advocate a unilateral Israeli withdrawal from the Gaza Strip, but the idea was rejected by Shamir. He also supported the idea of granting the Palestinians in the West Bank and Gaza autonomy, but not a state. On the eve of the German reunification, Milo demanded that Israel express its opposition to this development. When Milo was minister of police an investigation was opened against MK Aryeh *Deri, and tension developed between the two. Before the elections to the Thirteenth Knesset, his name was raised as a candidate for the post of treasurer of the Jewish Agency and World Zionist Organization, but he decided not to run. Soon after the Likud's defeat he was elected chairman of the World Likud. In September 1993 Milo was one of several Likud MKs who abstained in the vote on the Declaration of Principles with the Palestinians. Soon after that vote he resigned from the Knesset to be mayor of Tel Aviv-Jaffa, and served in that post until 1999. In September 1996 Milo met with Abu-Ma'azen, and in November with the chairman of the Palestinian Authority, Yasser *Arafat. He backed Prime Minister Binyamin *Netanyahu in the Likud Central Committee after he had met Arafat and was booed by its members. In January 1997, after the fiasco around the appointment of Ronnie Bar-On as attorney general (Bar-On resigned after one day), Netanyahu offered Milo the Justice portfolio in his government, but Milo declined. He became progressively more critical of Netanyahu's leadership, and at the end of 1997, when it was generally believed that Netanyahu would fall, registered a "shelf party" (a passive party, which could be activated at short notice). In this period he started talking to Labor politician Haim *Ramon about the possibility of establishing a new center party. In 1998 he considered running for the premiership at the head of an independent party and started to discuss the establishment of such a party with Dan *Meridor and former Chief of Staff Amnon *Lipkin-Shahak. By the end of 1998 he started to talk about the eventual establishment of a Palestinian State.

In the elections to the Fifteenth Knesset Milo was elected to the Knesset on the list of the Central Party, of which he was one of the founders. Until he joined the government formed by Ehud *Barak as minister of health in August 2000, he served on the Finance Committee, the House Committee, and the Economics Committee, and chaired the lobby for Tel Aviv-Jaffa in the Knesset. Milo joined the government formed by Ariel *Sharon in August 2001 on behalf of the Center Party as minister for regional cooperation, returning to the Likud in November 2002, after establishing a parliamentary group by the name of Ha-Lev. Milo was not elected to the Sixteenth Knesset. From November 2003 he served as chairman of the board of Azorim Investment Co. Ltd., in the IDB group.

[Susan Hattis Rolef (2nd ed.)]

MILOSZ, OSCAR (originally **Oscar Venceslas De Lubicz-Milosz**, 1877–1939), French poet, mystical writer, and diplomat. Milosz, who was born in Chereya, Belorussia to a Lithuanian nobleman and the baptized daughter of a Warsaw Hebrew teacher, was raised as a Catholic. He nevertheless retained a warm regard for his Jewish heritage and developed a keen interest in the Kabbalah. At the age of 12 he was taken to Paris, where he later studied Hebrew and Assyrian at the Ecole des Langues Orientales. He was Lithuania's minister resident in Paris (1919–26) but, despite his eventual assumption of French citizenship, remained attached to his ancestral land, which inspired his *Contes et fabliaux de la vieille Lithuanie* (1930) and *Contes lithuan iennes de ma Mère L'Oye* (1933). In his poetry Milosz progressed from erotic mysticism to spiritual and metaphysical speculation. Among his early works were *L'Amoureuse initiation* (1910), a novel in the form of a poetic monologue, and two plays, *Miguel Mañara* (1912; Eng. tr. in *Poet Lore*, 1919) and *Méphiboseth* (1914), the second of which dealt with David and Bathsheba. His mystical experiences inspired two metaphysical works, *Ars magna* (1924) and *Le Poème des Arcanes* (1927). These mingle Catholic theology with mystical and kabbalistic doctrine, stressing the belief that man possesses the ability to perceive reality as it is seen by God and that this faculty, at present hidden, will one day be recovered. In his *Arcanes*, Milosz glorified the Jewish people as the servant of humanity who "preserved the sacred treasure of the original Revelation in all its purity through a thousand vicissitudes for the sole purpose of the world's future regeneration." *Les origines ibériques du peuple juif* (1932), a product of Milosz' last, kabbalistic, and eschatological period, attempted to prove, by comparing Andalusian and biblical place-names and Basque and Hebrew etymology, that the Hebrews emigrated to Canaan from southern Spain.

BIBLIOGRAPHY: A. Richter, *Milosz* (Fr., 1965); J. Buge, *Milosz en quête du divin* (1963); A. Godoy, *Milosz, le Poète de l'Amour* (1961); G.I. Židonis, *O.V. de L. Milosz* (Fr., 1951); J. Rousselot, *O.V. de L. Milosz* (Fr., 1949).

MILSTEIN, U.S. family with vast interests in real estate, banking, and philanthropy. SEYMOUR MILSTEIN (1920–2001) was born in New York City and graduated from New York University. His father, Morris, had founded Circle Floor Company, which installed the floors at Rockefeller Center, the World Trade Center, and other buildings. Shortly after World War II, Milstein joined a second company founded by his father, Mastic Tile Company. Both companies flourished in the postwar housing boom in the United States and in 1955 Seymour Milstein became Mastic's president. Four years later, the company was sold to Ruberoid, a building products company, for $24 million. Seymour became a Ruberoid director and vice president, but when it was bought by GAF in 1967, he was not offered a top job. Milstein and his brother tried and failed to take control of GAF. In 1970 the family took control of United Brands, a large food company, and Starrett Housing Corporation. They later sold the companies. In 1986 they took over the failing Emigrant Savings Bank and pumped $90 million into it.

In the early 1960s PAUL MILSTEIN (1923–), who was born in New York City and graduated from NYU's School of Architecture, built the family's first apartment house, the Dorchester Tower near Lincoln Center. It was the first luxury building in that area since World War II. He also developed two other Manhattan landmarks, 1 Lincoln Plaza in 1972 and 30 Lincoln Plaza in 1978. Two of the buildings overlook a plaza that is one of Lincoln Center's most popular thoroughfares, and it was renamed in Milstein's honor in 1992. In the 1980s the Milsteins built tens of thousands of apartment, office, and hotel units in New York. The Milsteins were also responsible for buying and refurbishing the Milford Plaza Hotel in the Broadway area.

During their partnership, Seymour Milstein handled the financial details and was in charge of dealing with banks. Paul was more boisterous, and they were classic risk takers. Then they became more famous for litigation than for development. In 1981 they promised city officials that they would protect the famous and fabled gilded clock and Palm Court lounge of the Biltmore Hotel, and then demolished both. For nearly five decades the brothers presided over a multibillion-dollar real estate and banking empire with three million square feet of office space, 8,000 apartments, and one of New York's oldest financial institutions, Emigrant Savings Bank, which in 2003 had 36 branches in the New York area. The brothers lunched together daily and took family vacations together, but in later years, as succession issues loomed, the rivalry between their sons escalated into a legal battle of operatic intensity. By the end, the brothers were no longer speaking. In 2003, the family ended a decade-long feud and withdrew several lawsuits against one another.

The Milsteins gave widely to medical, educational, and Jewish causes. Among Seymour Milstein's beneficiaries was New York Presbyterian Hospital, where he was chairman from 1989 to 1996. His family's $25 million gift, in 1989, made possible the construction of the Milstein Hospital Building, a ten-story addition above the Hudson River in Washington Heights. The donation was in the name of Seymour and Paul Milstein and their sister, Gloria Milstein Flanzer. Eight children of the three donors were born at Presbyterian. Seymour also supported research on interferon, the hepatitis and cancer drug. From 1964 to 1973, Seymour was chairman of Bronx Lebanon Hospital Center. He was also a founder of the United States Holocaust Memorial Museum and a contributor to many Jewish philanthropies.

In 1994 the family of Paul Milstein gave $10 million to Cornell University for its Architecture, Art, and Planning College. The New York Public Library was also a beneficiary of the Milsteins, establishing the Irma and Paul Milstein Division of United States History, Local History, and Genealogy, in 2000 with a $5 million gift. The division brought together microfilm and other research materials long scattered in other parts of the library and a specialized staff to handle public inquiries, particularly on genealogical research.

[Stewart Kampel (2nd ed.)]

MILSTEIN, CESAR (1927–2002), immunologist and Nobel Prize laureate in medicine. Milstein was born in Bahia Blanca, Argentina. He studied at the University of Buenos Aires and received his doctorate from Cambridge University in 1960. From 1961 to 1963, when he emigrated from Argentina to England, he was affiliated with the National Institute of Microbiology in Buenos Aires. From 1963 he was with Cambridge University and in 1981–93 the joint head of the division of protein and nucleic acid chemistry. In 1980 he became head of the molecular immunobiology subdivision. He was the recipient of many awards, including the Wolf Prize in medicine. In 1984 he was a co-recipient of the Nobel Prize in medicine with George Koehler and Niels Jerne for their research into the body's immunological system and their development of a revolutionary method for producing antibodies, a technique which gave rise to new fields of endeavor for theoretical and applied biomedical research. From 1995 until his retirement in 2002 he was deputy director of the MRC Laboratory of Molecular Biology.

MILSTEIN, NATHAN (1904–1992), U.S. violinist. Born in Odessa, Russia, he was a child prodigy and studied with L. *Auer and E. Ysaye, making his debut in 1914. He toured Russia after the revolution with Vladimir *Horovitz and Gregor *Piatigorsky but left for Paris in 1925 where he soon became famous as a soloist. He went to the United States in 1929 and first appeared there with the Philadelphia Symphony Orchestra under Stokowski. He made his home in the United States but toured widely and gained a reputation as one of the great virtuosos of his time. He wrote arrangements and cadenzas for the violin.

BIBLIOGRAPHY: B. Gavoty, *Nathan Milstein* (Fr., 1956, Eng. tr., 1956); *The International Who Is Who in Music* (1951).

[Uri (Erich) Toeplitz]

MILTON, ERNEST (1890–1974), British actor. Born in San Francisco of partly Jewish origin, Milton acted in New York before making his London debut in *Potash and Perlmutter* in 1914. Of his many roles of Jewish interest, Ferdinand de Levis in Galsworthy's *Loyalties* (1922) gave him his first London success. Others were *Daniel Deronda* (1927), Ḥanan in *The Dybbuk*, Disraeli in Laurence Housman's *Victoria Regina* (1927), and *The King of Schnorrers* (1950). With the London Old Vic Company he acted in Shakespeare, Shaw, Ibsen, Pinero, and Pirandello. His own plays included *Christopher Marlowe* (1924), *Paganini* (1935), and *Mary of Magdala* (1945). He also appeared in a number of films, including *Alice in Wonderland* (1950). Milton was a Roman Catholic.

°**MILTON, JOHN** (1608–1674), English Puritan poet, whose works contain an unusual concentration of biblical and Judaic sentiments. Milton may have learned Hebrew while he was at Cambridge from the Semitic scholar, Joseph Mede (1586–1638). His knowledge of Hebrew and Aramaic was sufficient to enable him in later years to read the Hebrew Bible and probably also the classical Hebrew commentators. On the other hand, it seems certain that he had no first hand knowledge of Talmud or Kabbalah, although he read the works of Maimonides and other post-biblical texts in the Latin translations of Johannes *Buxtorf. The result of these studies is apparent in two tracts, *Doctrine and Discipline of Divorce* (1643) and *Tetrachordon* (1645), obviously prompted by his own unhappy marriage. In pleading for more liberal divorce laws, Milton tends to view the Hebrew legislation on the subject in Deuteronomy as the normative code for Christians. He was attacked as a flagrant heretic by many fellow Presbyterians, including William Prynne (1600–1669), who was later to oppose the reentry of the Jews into England. In 1659 he became Cromwell's Latin secretary, and continued to maintain his covenant faith in the God who had chosen England as the messiah-nation and himself as the prophet-poet of Reformation. The end of the Commonwealth in 1660 found him a blind, abandoned, and aging revolutionary.

Milton's great epic poem, *Paradise Lost* (1667), which seeks to "justify the ways of God to men," frames the biblical account of the Creation and the fall of Man in the Christian tradition, relating the battles in the fall of the angels; however, its fundamental emphasis is on human freedom and responsibility. This indicates Milton's relative proximity to Hebraic norms and his remoteness from the deterministic views of the more orthodox Puritans. *Paradise Lost* also reflects in part Milton's early acquaintance with Sylvester's English translation (1605) of *Du Bartas' epic *On the Creation*. In *Samson Agonistes* (1671), he clearly identifies himself with his hero, the Hebrew judge, "Eyeless in Gaza at the mill with slaves," whom God had nevertheless chosen for special tasks and revelations. Biblical and Judaic elements are also prominent in the sonnets *On His Blindness* (1651?–5) and *On the Late Massacre in Piedmont* (1655), and in the pamphlet *Areopagitica* (1644).

Milton's most heretical work, the *De Doctrina Christiana* (written c. 1658–60, but published in 1825), which rejects the orthodox view of the Trinity, indicates his virulent Puritan objection to the Jewish priesthood and ritual code. His theological and philosophical position was marked by considerable internal conflict as he sought to resolve the tensions set up between the Hellenic, Hebraic, and Christian elements of his cultural inheritance. Milton's biblical verse had a considerable influence on the romantic poets Blake, Wordsworth, and Coleridge.

BIBLIOGRAPHY: D. Saurat, *Milton, Man and Thinker* (1924); H.F. Fletcher, *Milton's Semitic Studies…* (1926); W.B. Selbie, in: E.R. Bevan and C. Singer (eds.), *Legacy of Israel* (1927), 407–31; M. Kelley, *This Great Argument…* (1941); D. Daiches, *Milton* (1957); Wolfe, in: *Journal of English and Germanic Philology*, 60 (1961), 834–46; H. Fisch, *Jerusalem and Albion…* (1964); idem, in: R.D. Emma and J.T. Shawcross (eds.), *Language and Style in Milton* (1967); H.F. Fletcher, *Milton's Rabbinical Readings* (1967). **ADD. BIBLIOGRAPHY:** ODNB online; W.R. Parker and G. Campbell, *Milton: A Biography* (1996); L. Ilfrah, *De Shylock à Samson: Juifs et Judaïsme en Angleterre au Temps de Shakespeare et Milton* (1992).

[Harold Harel Fisch]

MILWAUKEE, Wisconsin's largest city, located on the southeast tip of the shores of Lake Michigan. A few Jews are known to have lived in the area in the latter part of the 18th and early 19th centuries. Ezekial Solomon, perceived to be Jewish, was one of 14 fur traders permitted by the British to come to the area in 1770. An 1820 newspaper account refers to a "Jew peddler who was a victim of murder by three Indians who committed the deed to obtain the goods he carried on his back, going on foot from place to place" – an incident in Kaukauna. Gabriel Shoyer arrived in 1836, followed shortly by his brothers, Charles, Gabriel, Emanuel, Meyer, Samuel, and William. Several of the brothers opened a clothing store, Emanuel Shoyer a tailor shop, and in 1851 Charles began to practice medicine.

Early settlers, in 1842, were the families of Solomon Adler, Isaac Neustadt, and Moses Weil. Other immigrants arrived shortly afterwards from Germany, Bohemia, Hungary, Austria. From 70 families in 1850, the population grew to 200 in 1856 and to an estimated 2,074 in 1875. Intensive czarist persecutions in 1882 generated a flow of immigrants from Russia. By 1895, Russian Jews represented 39 percent of the Jewish population, then 7,000 people. The population grew to an estimated 22,000 by 1925. Several thousand Jewish refugees fleeing Nazi Germany and World War II came from 1938 on. The Jewish population was estimated at 23,900 in 1968 and 21,000 in 2001.

The earliest settlers from Western Europe settled on the near east side. Those settlers were soon vastly outnumbered by immigrants from Eastern Europe who settled on the near north side. There were two centers of Jewish population by the mid-1940s, the largest on the northwest side; the older east side settlers increased in number and moved northward into suburbs along Lake Michigan. By 1990, the majority of northwest side Jews had also moved to those suburbs; now a diminished northwest side community consists essentially of families desiring proximity to an Orthodox synagogue because of connections to its ḥasidic rabbi Michel Twerski.

The earliest Jewish settlers from Western Europe were involved in clothing manufacturing, grain, meatpacking, and had a substantial presence in the Great Lakes transportation business. Those who followed from Eastern Europe had less financial resources, working for their livelihoods as country peddlers, grocers, and clothiers. From 1895 into the 1920s Jews owned many clothing factories and retail shops. Wholesale dry goods, knitting goods, and yarn mills were developed with Jewish initiative. Jews had a substantial presence in flour milling, soap, and tobacco manufacturing and department store enterprises. Immigrants from Eastern Europe advanced from their roles as small tradesmen into larger retail and wholesale fields. In the 1920s, Jews became clerical workers and began to enter the arts and professions. By the early 1960s, the number of small storekeepers had substantially diminished; the peddler and small junk dealer virtually vanished; many of their sons were prominent in professions and in the business world.

A number of manufacturing, industrial, and commercial companies of national note were created and operated by Milwaukee Jews. The Master Lock Company, the world's largest padlock manufacturer, was founded by Harry E. Soref, an inventor, Samuel Stahl, and P.E. Yolles in 1921. The most extensive food store chain in Wisconsin was begun by Max Kohl in 1927. Kohl and his sons also founded the Kohl's Department Store chain, which by 2000 had grown to be one of the largest chains in the United States. Elmer L. Winter and Aaron Scheinfeld established Manpower in 1948; the company became the largest of its kind in the world with branches on all continents. In 1956, Max H. Karl founded the world's largest private mortgage insurer, Mortgage Guarantee Insurance Company. Clothing manufacturers of national note included Jack Winter & Company, Junior House, founded by William Feldstein and Sol Rosenberg, later becoming J.H. Collectibles.

Responding to the social, financial, welfare, and health needs of Jewish people, a number of communal agencies were created, the first of which was the Hebrew Relief Society (1867), now the Jewish Family Service. The Settlement, predecessor of the Abraham Lincoln House, now the Jewish Community Center, was begun in 1900. A Jewish-sponsored hospital, Mount Sinai, was organized in 1902. By the 1990s, it had become a non-sectarian institution in sponsorship as well as in service – the Aurora-Sinai Medical Center. The Jewish Vocational Service (1938) was created to help Jews find employment during the Great Depression, a time when substantial numbers fleeing from Nazism were coming as refugees. The Jewish Vocational Service became the largest organization of its kind in the United States outside of New York, financing coming from the state and federal governments and a variety of Jewish and non-Jewish sources with primary support from the Milwaukee Jewish Federation. In the early 1990s, it became non-sectarian in sponsorship as well as in service.

The Milwaukee Jewish Council, organized initially to combat antisemitism, and then xenophobia in all forms, was created in 1938. A Bureau of Jewish Education was organized by the Jewish Federation in 1944 to develop, strengthen, and coordinate Jewish education activity. The Milwaukee Jewish Home for Jewish elderly (1904) and the Jewish Convalescent Hospital (1950) merged in the late 1990s into one entity, which provides a variety of forms of assisted living, including intensive nursing home care.

All communal agencies came together in 1902 to create the Federated Jewish Charities in order to unify fundraising efforts and to help strengthen the work of all communal agencies. During the Depression, the organization foundered and discontinued operations. The pressing need to aid refugees in the 1930s resulted in the creation of a successor organization, the Milwaukee Jewish Welfare Fund, with a name change to Milwaukee Jewish Federation in 1972 to reflect its functions as a central communal organization for planning of services and centralized fundraising to meet needs deemed to be the responsibility of the total Jewish community. To coordinate work with refugees, the Federation created the Milwaukee Committee for Jewish Refugees in 1938 and in 1948 developed the Central Planning Committee for Jewish Services, its community-planning arm to avoid duplication and waste in efforts, etc. Orderliness in fundraising was served by the Committee on Unified and Coordinated Fund Raising beginning in 1957.

Major community buildings include the Max and Anita Karl Campus, which houses the Jewish Community Center, the B'nai B'rith Youth Organization, the Coalition for Jewish Learning (previously the Board of Jewish Education), the Milwaukee Jewish Day School, the Hillel Academy, and the Children's Lubavitch Living and Learning Center. The Helfaer Community Services building houses the Federation, the Milwaukee Jewish Council, and the *Wisconsin Jewish Chronicle*. The Milwaukee Jewish Home, which is adjacent to the Helfaer Building, and a new additional campus of the Jewish Home created in the suburb of Mequon in 2004 serve the elderly. The Jewish Community Center runs a summer overnight camp situated in Eagle River, 300 miles north of Milwaukee, and a summer day camp.

The first Jew elected to the state legislature was Bernard Schlesinger Weil in 1851. Henry M. Benjamin, one of eight Jewish aldermen before 1900, also was acting mayor of Milwaukee in 1875. Three Jews sat on the Common Council after 1920: Arthur Shutkin until 1928, Samuel Soref until 1940, and Fred P. Meyers after that. Charles L. Aarons served as a county judge from 1926 to 1950; Max Raskin, a city attorney from 1932 to 1936, later was a circuit court judge. Maurice M. Spracker served in a similar capacity for many years, beginning in 1968. Charles Schudson served as a circuit court judge until 2004. Myron L. Gordon, who had served as a justice on the Wisconsin State Supreme Court, became a federal judge for the Wisconsin Eastern District beginning in 1967.

Milwaukee Jews were in positions of note nationally and internationally. Marcus *Otterbourg was U.S. minister to Mexico in 1857. Newton *Minow, who was born in Milwaukee, but later lived in Chicago, was appointed by President John F. Kennedy to be Chairman of the Federal Communications Commission. His description of television programming as a "vast wasteland" resulted in legislation enabling oversight by the government of television and radio advertising.

Joseph A. *Padway, who served as a State senator and then as a civil court judge, became the first general counsel of the American Federation of Labor. In that capacity, he successfully defended the constitutionality of the National Labor Relations (Wagner) Act before the United States Supreme Court.

Among those who became prominent nationally was Wilbur J. *Cohen, who served as secretary of health, education, and welfare beginning in 1968. Earlier, he had helped write the Social Security Act in 1935. Victor L. *Berger, principle founder of the Social Democratic Party, was the first socialist elected to the House of Representatives of the United States (1911–13 and 1919–29). From 1992 onward both United States senators, democrats from Wisconsin, were Jewish: Herbert *Kohl, who served continuously from 1988 and Russ *Feingold of Madison, first elected in 1992.

William *Haber was advisor on Jewish affairs to General Lucius Clay, commander and chief of all Allied forces in Europe after World War II. Haber also served as an economic advisor for several U.S. presidents and as dean of the College of Literature, Science, and the Arts at the University of Michigan. Prominent in Jewish organizational life, he was chairman of several national and international Jewish organizations.

The best known of all Jewish Milwaukeeans was Golda *Meir (Myerson), who emigrated to Israel from Milwaukee and became Israel's prime minister in 1969, leading the country through the 1973 Yom Kippur War, which threatened the very existence of the state. Her life has been the subject of numerous books, biographies, and her own autobiography. Baseball fans may dispute Meir's primacy and think of Bud *Selig, the long-reigning first Jewish commissioner of baseball, who was also an owner of the Milwaukee Brewers team.

The community's oldest synagogue, Congregation Emanu-el B'ne Jeshurun, organized in 1856, grew out of a merger of Congregation Emanu-el (1850), Ahabath Emuno (1854), and Anshe Emeth (1855). Its membership was of German and West European extraction. Synagogues organized by immigrants of Eastern Europe followed, e.g., Beth Israel, initially Orthodox – now Conservative (1886); Anshe Sfard (1889); Agudas Achim (1904); Anshe Lubavitch (1906); and Beth Jehudah (1929). Additional reform congregations are Sholom (1951) and Sinai (1955). Conservative Temple Menorah was organized in 1957. Orthodox Anshe Sfard Kehillat Torah was organized in 1988; Agudas Achim merged with North Shore Chabad in 1993; Lake Park Synagogue in 1983; a Reconstructionist Congregation Shir Hadash was begun in 1990.

The primary public media instrument in Milwaukee is the *Wisconsin Jewish Chronicle*, established in 1921 by Nathan J. Gould and Irving R. Rhodes. Rhodes published the paper as sole proprietor after Gould's death in 1941. There had been several predecessor Jewish newspapers; the first, The *Zeitgeist*, was published in German by a Milwaukee rabbi for a few years, beginning in 1880. In 1914, a Yiddish newspaper, The *Wochenblat*, was created, published until it folded in 1932. Another Yiddish language paper, The *Yidishe Shtimme*, lasted for just one year, beginning in September 1930. Rhodes saw the paper as an advocate for the concept of community and consensus building. He simultaneously served as a board member of a number of agencies and was the only Federation General Campaign Chair to serve for three successive years. When Rhodes found publication burdensome, the Milwaukee Jewish Federation purchased the *Chronicle* to assure continuity of the publication and the Federation continues to publish the newspaper.

BIBLIOGRAPHY: L.J. Swichkow and L.P. Gartner, *The History of the Jews of Milwaukee* (1963); *American Jewish Year Book* (1900–1, 1928–29, 1939–39); *Jewish Community Blue Book of Milwaukee and Wisconsin*, compiled by the *Wisconsin Jewish Chronicle* (1924); L.J. Swichkow, "The Jewish Agricultural Colony of Arpin, Wisconsin," in: *American Jewish Quarterly* (1964).

[Melvin S. Zaret (2nd ed.)]

MIN (Heb. מִין, pl. מִינִים, *minim*; "heretic," "sectarian"). The term *min* for which no truly convincing etymology has yet been found (see Talmudic Dictionaries; G.F. Moore, *Judaism*, 3 (1930), 68f.; S. Krauss, *Griechische und Lateinische Lehnwoerter*, 1 (1898), introd. 15, n. 2, etc.), occurs frequently in rabbinic literature, though in the printed texts, due to the censors, the terms *ẓedoki* and *kuti* ("Samaritan") have often been substituted. The term was widely applied to cover many different types of "heretics" or sectarians. From some halakhic definitions in the Talmud, it would appear the *min* was used to refer only to a Jewish sectarian (Ḥul. 13b; cf. Tosef., Shab. 13:5). Thus, for example, *Horayot* 11a states that a Jew who eats forbidden fat in a flaunting and defiant manner or (according to another opinion) worships idols is a *min*. The *minim* who ridiculed aggadic descriptions given by the rabbis (Git. 57a; BB 75a) were probably Jewish. However, there is also abundant evidence to show that the term was applied to non-Jews as well, as in *Pesaḥim* 87b where a Roman nationalist is called a *min* (see Ḥul. 13b; see also S. Lieberman, *Greek in Jewish Palestine* (1942), 141, n. 196; idem, *Hellenism in Jewish Palestine* (1950), 135, n. 69).

Any attempt to identify *minim* with one single sectarian group is thus doomed to failure. H. Hirschberg's discussion (in JBL, 67 (1948), 305–18) in which he defends his own earlier thesis that in talmudic literature the term denotes Pauline Christians is a case in point, since at various historical periods, the word *min* was applied to different kinds of "heretics." Thus the *min* who according to (the printed editions of) *Leviticus Rabbah* 13:5 upbraided Alexander the Great for standing up before Simeon the Just was probably a Samaritan, or even a member of Alexander's own retinue (cf. Mss. readings in M. Margalioth ed., 2 (1954), 294). The *minim* mentioned in *Berakhot* 9:5 (variant Sadducee, JQR, 6 (1915–16), 314, n. 86) who taught that there was but one world and who apparently had considerable influence in the Temple were undoubtedly Sadducees, who among other things, as is well-known, denied the existence of an afterlife. According to Johanan, the people of Israel did not go into exile until they had become 24 different groups of *minim* (TJ, Sanh. 10:6, 29c), i.e., Jewish schismatics. Johanan was probably referring to the situation in his own time, when there appears to have been a proliferation of Jewish schismatic groups, and there were numerous *minim* in most Galilean towns, with reference to whom the verse (Ps. 14:1) could be cited, "The fool hath said in his heart there is no God" (Sif. Deut. 320).

Sometimes the term *min* may apply to more than one kind of sectarian even within one text. Thus, in *Ḥullin* 87a, two *minim* are mentioned: The first puts forward a proof (from a biblical verse) for the existence of two deities, and was therefore in all probability either a heathen Christian (believing in God the Father and God the Son) or a Gnostic; but the second *min* was invited by Rabbi (Judah ha-Nasi) to pronounce the blessing over food, and must therefore have been a Jew. *Minim* appear as wonder-workers (TJ, Sanh. 7:19, 25d), but again it is not clear whether they were Gnostics (Ebionites?) or (Judeo-) Christians, such as the well-known Jacob of Kefar Sekhanya (fl. c. 80–110), the wonder healer (Av. Zar. 17a, 27b; Tosef., Ḥul. 2:22, 24; et al.). In some passages, however, it is fairly certain that Gnostics are being referred to. Thus, the *minim* who (according to Tanḥ. B., Num. 30, 41) believe that God does not revive the dead nor receive penitents, etc., were probably Marcionite Gnostics (A. Buechler, *Studies in Jewish History* (1956), 271). Similarly, those of *Megillah* 29b were, according to Lieberman, Gnostics believing in the demiurge (S. Lieberman, in *Biblical and Other Studies*, ed. by A. Altmann (1963), 140f.). However, it is very often difficult to know for certain whether heathen Christians or Gnostics are meant (e.g., Sanh. 4:5 and Gen. R. 8:8, where the plurality of gods may be either a Gnostic or a Christian notion; see Scholem, Mysticism, 359, n. 24). Now, though it is true that the term *min* had a wide and ambiguous range of application, and that consequently in individual passages it is generally difficult to pinpoint exactly the schismatic group to which a *min* belongs, nonetheless, it is possible to distinguish historically two semantic phases in the use of the term. Thus according to Buechler (op. cit., 247, 271 etc.), until the early second century C.E. "it denoted heretic Jews," whereas "in Galilee in the second and third centuries *min* denoted in the first instance non-Jewish sectaries… Bible-reading heathens who oppose Judaism and its basic doctrines, antinomian Gnostics, or, in a few cases, heathen Christians who agree with them."

According to *Berakhot* 28b, Samuel ha-Katan (fl. c. 80–110), at the invitation of Gamaliel II of Jabneh, composed the "benediction against the *minim*," included in the *Amidah* as the twelfth benediction (see E.J. Bickerman, in HTR, 55 (1962), 171, n. 35). This was directed primarily against Judeo-Christians (specifically mentioned in one old text – see Schechter, JQR 10 (1897/98)), either to keep them out of the synagogue or to proclaim a definite breach between the two religions. This undoubtedly "represented the formal recognition by official Judaism of the severance of all ties between the Christian and other schismatic bodies, and the national body of Judaism" (Baron, Social², 2 (1952), 135, 381, n. 8, incl. bibl.). This severance of the *minim* from the national body of Judaism had obvious halakhic implications. Thus, meat slaughtered by a *min* was forbidden to a Jew (Ḥul. 13a). Likewise Torah scrolls, *tefillin*, and *mezuzot* written by him are barred from use (Git. 45b; cf. Tosef., Ḥul. 2:20). For Maimonides' five-fold classification of *minim* see *Mishneh Torah*, Teshuvah, 3:7. On the books of the *minim*, see *Sifrei ha-Minim.

BIBLIOGRAPHY: A. Buechler, *Studies in Jewish History* (1956), 245–74; G.F. Moore, *Judaism*, 3 (1930), 68f.; H. Hirschberg, in: JBL, 62 (1943), 73–87; 67 (1948), 305–18; Neusner, Babylonia, 3 (1968), 12–16; Allon, Meḥkarim, 1 (1957), 203–5.

[Daniel Sperber]

MINC, HILARY (1905–1974), Polish Communist politician. Born in Kazimierz Dolny into an assimilated family, Minc joined the Communist youth movement in 1921. From 1925 to 1928, studying economics in France, he was a member of the French Communist Party. After his return to Poland, he worked in the chief statistical office in Warsaw and at the same time joined the illegal Communist Party, becoming secretary of its central editorial staff. During World War II Minc lived in the Soviet Union, and was one of the chief organizers of the Soviet-sponsored Union of Polish Patriots. He was also prominent in the formation of the Polish Army units organized in Russia. Following the liberation of Poland from the Germans (1945), Minc became minister for industry and commerce. He was made a vice premier in 1949 and in the same year was appointed chairman of the State Planning Commission. In this capacity he was the chief author of Poland's economic policy; but in 1956, when Wladyslaw Gomulka came to power, he was removed from all his posts in the party and government, both as a Stalinist and as a Jew.

ADD. BIBLIOGRAPHY: I. Gutman, *Ha-Yehudim be-Polin aḥarei Milḥemet Olam ha-Sheniyah* (1985), index; K. Nusbaum, *Ve-Hafakh la-Hem le-Ro'eẓ, Ha-Yehudim be-Ẓava ha-Amami ha-Polani be-Verit ha-Mo'eẓot* (1984), index.

[Abraham Wein]

MINCO, MARGA (1920–), Dutch author, born in Ginneken (near Breda), who lived in Amsterdam. Her first book, the short novel *Het bittere kruid* (1957; *The Bitter Herb*, 1960), describes the deportation of her family and her own survival in hiding during World War II. It was translated into many languages. The book, like the ones that were to follow, was praised for its sparing yet impressive style. Marga Minco was one of the first Dutch writers to deal with "survivor's guilt." Most of her books are partly autobiographical; they often relate to the persecution of Jews during World War II and the lack of understanding of the non-Jewish world after the war. After *Het bittere kruid* Minco wrote the collection of stories *De andere kant* ("The Other Side," 1959), the short novels *Een leeg huis* ("An Empty House," 1966), *De val* ("The Fall," 1983), *De glazen brug* ("The Glass Bridge," 1986), *Nagelaten dagen* ("Posthumous Days," 1997), the collection of short stories *Storing* ("Breakdown," 2004), and several short stories, collected in *Verzamelde verhalen 1951–1981* ("Collected Stories, 1951–1981," 1982). *Het bittere kruid* and *Een leeg huis* were adapted for the stage several times; *Het bittere kruid* was filmed, not very successfully, by Kees van Oostrum in 1985. Marga Minco also wrote children's stories, notably *Kijk 'ns in een la* ("Look into a Drawer," 1963) and *De verdwenen bladzij en andere kinderverhalen* ("The Missing Page and Other Children's Stories," 1994).

BIBLIOGRAPHY: Daphne Meijer, *Joodse tradities in de literatuur* (1998); Johan P. Snapper, *De wegen van Marga Minco* (1999).

[Hilde Pach]

MINDA, ALBERT GREENBERG (1895–1977), U.S. Reform rabbi. Minda was born in Holton, Kansas, and earned his B.A. from the University of Cincinnati in 1918 and his ordination from Hebrew Union College in 1919. He received a doctor of divinity degree (honoris causa) from HUC-JIR in 1947. Following pulpits at Temple Beth El of South Bend, Indiana, and in Lingonier, Indiana (1919–22), he became rabbi of Temple Israel in Minneapolis, Minnesota, where he remained for the rest of his career, becoming emeritus in 1963. During his tenure, the congregation grew from 275 members in 1922 to more than 1,400 in the 1960s. An innovator, Minda pioneered the establishing of a Jewish Art Gallery and Museum on the premises of an expanded temple.

In the greater community, Minda was one of the founders and first presidents of the Minneapolis Federation for Jewish Service, as well as a founder of the Minneapolis Urban League and the Minneapolis Round Table of Christians and Jews. He was also the first president of the Minnesota Rabbinical Association and a member of the executive board of the United Fund of Greater Minneapolis and of the faculty of Hamlin University in St. Paul, Minnesota.

Nationally and internationally, Minda served Reform Judaism as a member of the executive board of the Central Conference of American Rabbis in three different decades and chairman of the organization's Church and State Committee (1939–46). Following a term as vice president, he was elected president of the Central Conference of American Rabbis (1961–63), concurrently with holding the position of vice president of the World Union for Progressive Judaism.

Minda was also a prolific author, whose writings include *Over the Years*, vols. 1 and 2 (1957–63); *The Sanctuary of the Home* (1945); *The Fire on the Altar* (1948); *Speak to the Heart* (1956); and *And Thou Shalt Write Them* (1967).

[Bezalel Gordon (2nd ed.)]

MINDEN, town in Germany. Jews are mentioned for the first time in 1270 as being under the bishop's protection. After 1336 the town agreed to recognize the bishop's prerogatives over the Jews provided that they paid municipal taxes as well as protection money to the bishop. Moneylending was the only authorized Jewish occupation at the time. The small community numbered no more than 12 families in 1318 and ten in 1340. They were expelled in 1350 following the *Black Death persecutions.

Jews did not settle in Minden again until the 16th century. In 1571 the council granted them residence permits of 12 years' duration and allowed them to engage in commerce and moneylending and to hold religious services. From that time Jewish settlement was continuous, even after the town had come under the rule of Brandenburg, whose authorities claimed all prerogatives over the Jews. After 1652 no Jew was permitted to settle in Minden without permission from the elector; the numbers of "tolerated" Jews were ten in 1682 and 12 in 1700. In Prussian Minden, the Jews engaged not only in moneylending but also in commerce and the slaughtering and sale of meat. Between 1806 and 1810 Minden belonged to the kingdom of *Westphalia, where the Jews received equal civil rights. After emancipation, when Minden reverted to Prussia, the small community grew steadily, from 65 in 1787 to 81 in 1810; 193 in 1840; and 267 in 1880. Their numbers later decreased to 192 in 1933 and 107 in 1939, when there were 228 Jews in the district of Minden. In October of 1939, there were 54 Jews in Minden. During World War II, 179 Jews were deported from the town and district. The *Memorbuch of the synagogue from the 17th and 18th centuries has been preserved. The synagogue built in 1867 was destroyed in 1938. After World War II a small community was reconstituted, which had 44 members in 1962. A new synagogue was consecrated on June 15, 1958. The ethnologist Franz *Boas and the astronomer Philip S. Wolfers were born in Minden. The Jewish community numbered 43 in 1989 and 113 in 2005. The increase is explained by the immigration of Jews from the former Soviet Union.

BIBLIOGRAPHY: *Germania Judaica*, 2 (1968), 542–3; B. Brilling and H. Richtering (eds.), *Westfalia Judaica* (1967), s.v.; M. Krieg, in: *Westfaelische Zeitschrift*, 93 (1937), 113ff.; L. Loewenstein, in: ZGJD, 1 (1887), 195ff. **ADD. BIBLIOGRAPHY:** K. Rueter and C. Hampel, *Die Judenpolitik in Deutschland 1933–1945 unter besonderer Beruecksichtigung von Einzelschicksalen juedischer Buerger der Gemeinden Minden, Petershagen und Luebbecke* (1986); *Germania Judaica*, vol. 3, 1350–1514 (1987), 874–76; H. Nordsiek, *Juden in Minden. Dokumente und Bilder juedischen Lebens vom Mittelalter bis zum 20. Jahrhundert* (1988); B-W Linnemeier, *Juedisches Leben im Alten Reich. Stadt und Fuerstentum Minden in der Fruehen Neuzeit* (Studien zur Regionalgeschichte, vol. 15 (2002)).

[Bernhard Brilling]

MINDLIN, HENRIQUE (1911–1971), Brazilian architect who contributed to the flowering of modern Brazilian architecture after World War II. Mindlin helped to introduce the modern style of American skyscraper design, with its glass curtain walling, into Brazil. In 1960, he built the synagogue and Cultural Center of the Congregação Israelita de São Paulo (Jewish Community of São Paulo).

MINHAG (Heb. מִנְהָג; "custom," "usage") from the verb "to lead."

DEFINITION

The word is found in the Bible (II Kings 9:2) meaning "the driving" (of a chariot) but it was taken by the rabbis to refer to "usage." As such, it is used in a wide variety of senses. It refers primarily:

(1) to customs which, having been accepted in practice, became binding and assume the force of **halakhah* in all areas of Jewish law and practice (see below);

(2) to local custom (*minhag ha-makom*) which obtains in one locality, whether a whole country or a single community, but not in another, and is binding upon the local community. The question of the extent to which the *minhag* is binding upon those who come from a place where it does not obtain is exhaustively debated in the Talmud and codes. The Mishnah already takes notice of this difference of local custom and its binding force (Pes. 4). These local *minhagim* have been collected in special **minhagim* books;

(3) The word *minhag* is also employed to designate the various liturgical rites which have developed, e.g., *minhag Romania, minhag Polin, minhag Ashkenaz* (see *Liturgy).

GENERAL

Custom is one of the most important foundations of the *halakhah*. It can be assumed that the Written Law (cf. *Oral Law) already takes for granted the continuation of some customs that were common practice before the giving of the law. This is probably the reason why the Torah makes no mention of laws which are fundamental in some domains, in spite of their importance and central position in life (such as the detailed laws of *betrothal and *marriage, modes of acquisition, *buying and selling). On the other hand, external customs entered the world of the precepts during later periods as a result of prevailing conditions, and were either temporarily integrated or remained permanently. An instructive example is that of the *New Moon, which the Torah only mentions with regard to the additional sacrifice and the blowing of the trumpets (and this too was probably only intended against those who believed it to be a festival to the god of the *Moon as was common in the ancient Middle East). During the days of the First Temple, however, as a result of Canaanite-Phoenician influence, the day became an accepted and important festival in Israel to such a degree that work and commerce were interrupted (with the difference that with the Jewish people the New Moon lost its pagan character and assumed a purified Jewish value of "a statute for Israel – a law of the God of Jacob" (Ps. 81:5)). Frequently, a particular matter of the *halakhah* is nothing but the consolidation of customs created among the people over the generations (e.g., see *Mourning, *Fasts). There are some customs which are as binding as legal regulations (see Tosef., Nid. 9:17) while others are no more than a consensus (ʾajmāʿ with Muslims) which is accepted in cases where there is no fixed and decided *halakhah* ("Go out and see what the custom of the public is and act likewise" (TJ, Pe'ah 7:5, 20c); cf. "Go out and see how the people act" or "the people are accustomed" (TB, many times)). There are also individual customs in situations where there is no existing *halakhah*; these may be a local custom ("the custom of the country" (Suk. 3:11; Ket. 6:4; BM 7:1, 9:1; et al.); "in a place where the custom has been" (Pes. 4:1–5; Suk. 3:11; Av. Zar. 1:6; et al.); "the custom in Jerusalem" (BB 93b; Sof. 18:7)), or a custom of a section of the public ("the custom of those traveling with a caravan" (Tosef., BM 7:13); "the custom of the sailors" (*ibid.*), "the custom of women" (TJ, Pes. 4:1; 30c–d); "the custom of landlords" (Tosef., Pe'ah 2:21); "the custom of the priests" (*ibid.* 4:3)), and even from one of these "there must be no deviation" (Tosef., BK 11:18; et al.). There are, however, also customs which are in opposition to the *halakhah*, and of these the sages said: "The custom annuls the *halakhah*" (TJ, Yev. 12:1, 12c; and cf.: "R. Judah said, the *halakhah* is according to the opinion of Bet Shammai, but the majority acts according to the opinion of Bet Hillel"; Tosef., Ter. 3:12). It is obvious that "just as punishment is inflicted for transgression of the *halakhah*, so it is inflicted for transgression of a custom" (TJ, Pes. 4:3, 30d) and "permitted things [or actions] which the custom of others considers as prohibited, you are not authorized to permit them in their presence" (Pes. 50b–51a). It has also been prescribed many times that a man should deviate "neither from the custom of the place nor from that of his ancestors" (see TJ, Pes. 4:1, 30d; etc.), even though the reason for the custom has become obsolete. The following saying indicates the importance of the custom as a basis of the *halakhah*: "It has become accepted by the people that the *halakhah* cannot be fixed until a custom exists; and the saying, that a custom annuls the *halakhah*, applies to a custom of the earnest, while a custom for which there is no proof from the Torah is nothing but an error in reasoning" (Sof. 14:16).

Indeed, to prevent vain and foolish customs superseding the *halakhah*, the rabbis opposed following stupid customs which had their origin in error or even in periods of persecution. *Yehudai Gaon, who wrote to the population of Palestine in order to abolish the "custom of the persecution era" which they respected "against the *halakhah*" was unsuccessful. He received the reply that "A custom annuls the *halakhah*" (*Pirkoi b. Baboi*, L. Ginzberg, *Genizah Studies*, 2 (1929), 559–60). Maimonides violently attacked erroneous customs (see, e.g., Yad, Issurei Bi'ah 11:14–15, even in opposition to the opinion of the *geonim*; cf. responsa of Maimonides, ed. A.H. Freimann, §98–99), but even he stressed that there are certain cases which "depend on the custom" (see, e.g., Yad, Issurei Bi'ah 11:5–7). Customs arising from ignorance, however, and even those of which it was evident, not only from their origin but by their very nature, that they belonged to the "ways of the Amorites" and were to be suspected as idolatrous, often penetrated within the limits of the *halakhah* and secured a permanent place. It is significant that such customs often became so popular with the public, in spite of the opposition of the rabbis, that more importance was attached to them than to some of the strictest precepts of the Torah. There were instances where strange and doubtful customs became sanctified with the masses only because of the superstitious beliefs attaching to them. Such customs penetrated not only the text of the prayers but also the field of the prohibited and the permitted (see **Issur ve-Hetter*). They were especially tenacious in critical periods of human life (birth, marriage, death) or in the calendar (Day of Atonement, New Year). Thus, for example, some consider that the essentials of repentance and expiation can be found in the customs of **Kapparot* (expiation ceremony) and **Tashlikh*, and throughout the whole year do not visit the synagogue except for the *Kol Nidrei* ceremony. One common denominator of all these customs is their foreign origin and nature. However, they became so popular with the masses that even some of the rabbis attempted to find grounds to permit them, even through some kind of compromise. This was naturally even more true of customs which did not stem from a foreign origin, such as the recitation of *piyyutim* in the morning benedictions of *Shema* and during the repetition of the *Amidah* prayer by the *ḥazzan*, which became the accepted practice in many countries in spite of the opposition of many authorities. The same also applies to the foreign custom of addressing prayers to angels or mentioning their names in the *mezuzah*. This situation, whereby nonsensical customs found a home in Jewish life, still remains and has possibly even been strengthened in modern times. It is sufficient to mention the demonological customs connected with birth and circumcision (the night of vigil before the circumcision) or with death and burial, such as the strange custom current among Ashkenazim that a person whose parents are alive leaves the synagogue when the souls of the dead are remembered, or the "prohibition" of the sons from entering the cemetery during their fathers' funeral, which is widespread among the Ashkenazim of Jerusalem. Thus it can be said that the custom has been the most important channel through which external influences, even odd and unwanted ones, penetrated and still penetrate into the domain of *halakhah*. The general importance of customs is also reflected in literature.

[Moshe David Herr]

IN JEWISH LAW

Minhag as a Source of Law

Three possible meanings may be attributed to the term "source of law": a historical source of the law, i.e., a source which factually and historically speaking constitutes the origin of a particular legal norm; a legal source of the law, i.e., the source which lends the particular normative direction legal recognition and validity as part of the entire body of legal rules comprising the relevant legal system; and a literary source of the law, i.e., the informative source constituting the authentic repository for purposes of ascertaining the content of a particular legal direction (see **Mishpat Ivri*). *Minhag*, as does custom in other legal systems, sometimes serves as the historical source of a particular legal norm and sometimes as the legal source.

AS A HISTORICAL SOURCE. A study of the formative stages of any legal system will reveal that to some extent its directions originated from customs evolved in the practical life of the society concerned, and that only at a later stage was legal recognition conferred on such customs – by way of legislation or decision on the part of the legislator or judge. This phenomenon is also evidenced in Jewish law. Thus, for instance, certain legal usages which had been prevalent in pre-Mosaic Hebrew society later came to be affirmed in the Torah, as, for example, the law of the bailees' liability (see *Shomerim), and sometimes also with material modifications, as with regard to the laws of *yibbum* (see *Levirate Marriage and *Ḥaliẓah*). The historical source of such directions is the pre-Mosaic usage, but their legal source is the Written Law, which gave them recognition and validity. Custom has fulfilled this historical function in all stages of the development of Jewish law, by serving to prepare a particular normative direction for acceptance into this legal system.

AS A LEGAL SOURCE. In Jewish law *minhag*, like custom in any other legal system, has also fulfilled an important function as a legal source, and it is with custom in this capacity that this article is concerned. Custom constitutes a legal source when the legal system, in certain circumstances and upon fulfillment of certain requirements, recognizes a consistently followed course of conduct as a binding legal norm. When custom serves merely as a historical source, it is only capable of preparing the normative course of conduct toward acquisition of legal recognition by means of a law-creating source, such as *takkanah*; however, when custom is a legal source, the normative usage already has legal force by virtue of such usage alone, without the affirmation of any law-creating source. As a legal source, the primary purpose of custom is like that of legislation (see *Takkanot ha-Kahal*), namely to fill a void in the existing *halakhah* when the latter offers no solution to new problems that arise, or in order to rectify or vary existing legal rules if and when the need arises. There is, however, a formal difference – which, as will be seen below, is also of substantive importance – between these two legal sources: legislation functions demonstratively and directly, at the direction of the competent authority, such as the halakhic scholars or the leaders of the people and of the community; custom, on the other hand, functions without preconceived intent and anonymously – at the hands of all or part of the people at large – and in order to ascertain it, it is necessary to "go and see what is the practice of the people" (Ber. 45a; Pes. 54a; in the TJ the version is, "go and see what is the practice of the public, and follow it" (TJ, Pe'ah 7:6, 20c; Ma'as. Sh. 5:3, 56b; Yev. 7:2, 8a). It is true that even in the case of a normative direction originating from custom there is the indirect influence of the halakhic scholars, by virtue of a certain control which they exercise over it (see below; see also Yad, Mamrim 1:2–3); nevertheless it is the public as a whole that is the direct creative source of the legal direction. The public is invested with such creative authority on the presumption that, since its conduct is founded on the Torah, its creative authority will be directed in the spirit of the Torah, in accordance with the statement of Hillel the Elder made in affirmation of the binding force of a public custom in determining the *halakhah*: "Leave it to Israel. If they are not prophets, they are still the children of prophets" (Pes. 66a).

SUBSTANTIATING THE VALIDITY OF MINHAG AS A LEGAL SOURCE. Some of the scholars apparently sought to explain the validity of a custom by saying that it had to be assumed that the earliest source of such a norm – now appearing in the form of custom – was ancient *halakhah* founded on transmitted tradition, *takkanah*, or other legal sources, but that the latter had become forgotten in the course of time, leaving the norm in the form of a custom only. This opinion finds expression in the Jerusalem Talmud: "Any Torah which has no source (*bet av*) is no Torah" (TJ, Shab. 19:1, 17a stated in relation to the *baraita* (Pes. 66a) in which Hillel recalls that the custom followed by the people concerning the paschal sacrifice on a Sabbath day he had heard mentioned by Shemaiah and Avtalyon (see below); the term *torah* is here used in the sense of custom). Elsewhere it is stated: "A custom which has no support in the Torah, is like the erroneous exercise of discretion" (Sof. 14:18; see also Mordekhai BM 366). According to this view custom has no independent creative force, but merely offers testimony to the existence of a rule created by one of the legal sources of the *halakhah*. In post-talmudic times some halakhic scholars expressly adopted this attitude toward custom (Resp. Rif no. 13; Nov. Ramban BB 144b, s.v. *Ha de-Amrinan*). Some scholars explained the decisive power of custom, even when this was called forth only to decide between disputing scholarly opinions (see below), on the basis that a custom proves the existence of an ancient, deliberate determination of the law which has become forgotten, being preserved in this form only (Resp. Rosh 55:10). The source of authority of custom remained a matter of dispute among the *aḥaronim* (for particulars, see Pitḥei Teshuvah ḤM, 163, n. 16).

Certainly there are customs which have their source in ancient *halakhah*, as is evidenced by the Jerusalem Talmud in the matter of the paschal sacrifice on a Sabbath day (see above) and in other instances (see, e.g., Tosef., MK 2:14–15; see also Pes. 51a and TJ, Pes. 4:1, 30d). However, it transpires that the distinguishing feature of custom as a legal source lies not in its probative efficacy but in the law-creating authority of the public, whether the custom serves to decide between disputing opinions or to add to the existing *halakhah*. This is undoubtedly so as regards the validity of custom in matters of the civil law (*dinei mamonot*), where it is within the power of custom to operate even contrary to the existing law, in terms of the general principle of Jewish law which permits the parties to a transaction – and all the more so the public as a whole – to contract out of the Law of the Torah (see below). This is accepted by the majority of halakhic scholars as the explanation for the rule that custom overrides the law in matters of the civil law, which is certainly a classic illustration of the creative activity of custom.

Elucidation of Terms

At times, a particular halakhic direction which has its source in custom is also called *dat* (Bez. 25b and Rashi thereto) or *dat yehudit* (Ket 7:6 and Rashi to Ket. 72a; Tosef., Ket. 7:7). At other times the term *minhag* is used by the halakhic scholars to describe a normative direction having its source in *takkanah* (e.g., TJ, Ket. 1:5, 25c; Mid. Prov. to 22:28) and even the verb הנהיג is sometimes used to describe the enactment of a *takkanah* (cf. Tosef., RH 4:3 with RH 4:1 and Suk. 3:12). The use of a common term to describe both *takkanah* and custom (cf. further Yad, Mamrim 1:2–3; Resp. Rashba, vol. 2, no. 268) is attributable to their common function, namely legislative activity (each in its own different way, as already mentioned). Sometimes the term *minhag* is also used to describe *halakhah* which has its source in the Bible itself (see Sifra, Emor 17:8, the law concerning habitation of a *sukkah* etc., described as *minhag le-dorot*; in Suk. 43a/b, the phrase is *mitzvah le-dorot*). Contrariwise, a normative direction having its source in custom is sometimes called *halakhah* (BM 7:8; Kid. 38b; and see Samuel's interpretation, in TJ, Or. 3:8, 63b of the term *halakhah* appearing in Or. 3:9). Such use of common labels of *minhag, takkanah*, and *halakhah* for differing concepts not only calls for the exercise of great care in distinguishing the correct identity of each law appearing under such a name, but also offers proof of the legal efficacy of normative directions which have their source in custom and are integrated into the general halakhic system as a substantive part of it (even though there is a variance at times between the force of a direction originating from *takkanah* and one originating from custom; see below). Transgression against a direction decreed by custom is punishable by sanction: "Just as a fine is imposed in matters of *halakhah*, so a fine is imposed in matters of *minhag*" (TJ, Pes. 4:3, 30d) and R. Abbahu even sought to have punishment by flogging imposed on a person who transgressed a prohibition decreed by custom (TJ, Kid. 4:6, 66b; see also Kid. 77a).

At the same time, the scholars occasionally distinguished, primarily in the field of the ritual law, between a rule originating from custom and one originating from another legal source. Such distinctions, particularly from the amoraic period onward, are illustrated by the following examples: the majority of the *amoraim* held that the prohibition of *orlah (eating the fruit of young trees) outside of Ereẓ Israel had its source in custom, and therefore they sought various legal ways in which to permit the fruit of *orlah* outside of Ereẓ Israel – something they would not have done had the prohibition belonged to the category of *halakhah le-Moshe mi-Sinai* (Kid. 38b–39a and see above). Similarly, there is recorded the talmudic dispute between R. Johanan and R. Joshua b. Levi as to whether the rite of taking the willow-branch on Sukkot (the branch that is raised and beaten on Hoshana Rabba) was an enactment of the prophets or a custom of the latter – i.e., a usage of the prophets but not enacted as a *takkanah* (Suk. 44a and Rashi ad loc.; see also *Sha'arei Teshuvah* no. 307); the answer to this question was relevant to the need (i.e., if it was an enactment) or otherwise (if it was a custom) for recital of a benediction at the time of beating the willow-branch (see Suk. 44a and see *takkanot* concerning benedictions in respect of matters instituted by the halakhic scholars). Even as regards deciding the *halakhah* in a matter under dispute, the *amoraim* distinguished between *halakhah* determined by way of open and deliberate decision, *halakhah* determined by custom introduced by the scholars, and *halakhah* determined by mere anonymous undirected custom (see TJ, Shek. 1:1, 46a; Meg. 1:6, 70d; Nid. 3:1, 50c; and Pes. 4:6, 31a; Av. Zar. 14b; Yev. 13b; Nid. 66a; et al.). Some of the Babylonian *amoraim* even laid down a further distinction, one relating to the nature of the custom. Thus three possibilities are distinguished: *nahagu ha-am* ("the practice followed by the people") was apparently interpreted by the Babylonian *amoraim* as referring to a usage not yet fully crystallized into an established custom, and therefore "we do not teach in this way initially, but should a person have done so, we allow the matter to stand"; *minhag*, to a crystallized custom which, although it has sufficient authority for the people to be taught to act from the start in accordance with it, nevertheless does not have the same force as a rule openly and expressly decided by the halakhic scholars – "we do not teach to act in this way in public, but we may teach (those who ask, to act according to the rule embodied in the custom)"; and that which is decided as *halakhah*, which must be published and made known to the public (Ta'an. 26b and see also Er. 62b and 72a). These distinctions relate primarily to the field of ritual law and not to the creative function of custom in civil law matters (see below, "Custom Overrides the Law").

Scriptural Support for the Validity of *Minhag* as a Legal Source

Halakhic scholars sought to rely on various scriptural passages as the source of the validity of custom. Simeon b. Yoḥai's statement, "Change not the custom set by your fathers!" is supported in the Midrash (Mid. Prov. 22:28, and see annotation there), by allusion to the scriptural injunction, "Remove not the ancient landmark, which thy fathers have set" (Prov. 22:28). R. Johanan found support for the validity of custom in another passage from the Book of Proverbs (1:8), "Hear, my son, the instruction of thy father, and forsake not the teaching of thy mother" (see Pes. 50b; Ḥul. 93b; cf. also *She'iltot*, Va-Yakhel, Sh. 67; *Halakhot Gedolot* end of Hil. Megillah). Sherira Gaon quotes the following tradition, which is not extant in the Talmuds: "Whence is it said that custom obliges? As it is said, 'Thou shalt not remove thy neighbor's landmark, which they of old time have set'" (Deut. 19:14; *Sha'arei Ẓedek*, 1:4, 20; Tur, ḤM 368). The discussion concerns an article stolen from its owner and sold to another; in law, if the owner has "despaired" (see *Ownership), the purchaser will not be required to return the article to him, but Sherira Gaon decided that there was in operation a custom to restore the article in such circumstance, from which there could be no departure. The factor which is common to all legal sources is that a norm which has been followed for some considerable time (see below) acquires for itself a fixed place in the *halakhah* and may not be overlooked nor "trespassed" upon (cf. the comment of Philo on the above scriptural passage, Spec. 4:149).

Functions and Categories of *Minhag*

Just as *takkanah* – the directed legislation of the halakhic scholars – has functioned in all fields of the *halakhah*, so custom – anonymous legislation – has also functioned in all its fields, although in some of them the measure of authority of custom is limited as compared with that of *takkanah*. Custom fulfills a number of functions in *halakhah* and is also divisible into several further categories.

FUNCTIONS. Custom serves three possible functions:

(1) as the decisive factor in the case of disputing opinions as to a particular halakhic rule; in this event the custom operates even where the *halakhah*, but for such a custom, would be decided differently in accordance with the accepted rules of decision;

(2) as adding to the existing *halakhah*, whenever the practical realities give rise to new problems to which the former has no available answer;

(3) as establishing new norms which stand in contradiction to the existing *halakhah*, i.e., norms which serve to vary the latter, or derogate therefrom.

The latter two functions of custom parallel that of legislation (see *takkanot*), save that the last one (abrogation of an existing law) is of lesser efficacy than is the case with legislation (see below).

CATEGORIES OF MINHAG. *Custom (Minhag) and Usage (Nohag)*. At times minhag functions of its own inherent power, independently and directly, just as does a direction by express *takkanah*; at other times it functions by way of an inference that the parties to a particular matter acted as they did on the assumption that the decree of the *minhag* concerned would determine their relationship. This distinction is developed in other legal systems too, and in English law *minhag* of the first kind is termed "legal custom" or simply "custom," and *minhag* of the second kind "conventional custom" or "usage." In current Hebrew the latter is customarily termed *nohag*.

General Custom and Local Custom. A custom may be general in the sense of obliging the whole of the people or the public, or it may be local and obligatory only for the people of a particular place, in which case it is termed local custom, *mores civitatis* in Roman law. In the same way the operation of a custom may be confined to people of a particular class, occupation, etc., and further like subdivisions of custom may be made (see below).

Minhag as Deciding the *Halakhah*

In case of dispute between halakhic scholars as to the law, custom decides the issue – whether in circumstances where there are no established rules of decision concerning the particular matter, or in circumstances where the custom stands in contradiction to the accepted rules of decision. The matter is illustrated by the following examples: It is recorded that R. Tarfon differed from the majority opinion of the scholars with regard to the blessing to be recited over water (Ber. 6:8) and the *amoraim*, when asked how to decide the *halakhah*, replied: "go and see what is the practice of the people" (Ber. 45a; Eruv. 14b); this was also stated with regard to a similar question concerning the eating of **terumah* (TJ, Pe'ah 7:6, 20c; Ma'as. Sh. 5:3, 56b; and Yev. 7:2, 8a). In another case R. Judah and R. Yose held the view that just as the priests generally did not lift their hands when reciting the priestly benediction at the *Minḥah* (afternoon) service – because of the proximity of the service to the meal and the apprehension that a priest might lift his hands while intoxicated – so this was forbidden at the *Minḥah* service on the Day of Atonement (even though the above apprehension would not exist) lest this lead the priests to the erroneous practice of lifting their hands during weekday *Minḥah* services; however, R. Meir differed, holding that such lifting of the hands was permissible at the *Minḥah* service on the Day of Atonement (Ta'an. 26b). Although the accepted rules of decision required that the *halakhah* on the matter be decided according to R. Yose (see Eruv. 46b) – who in this case represented the stringent view – it was nevertheless decided according to the view of R. Meir – representing in this case the lenient view – for the reason that "the people followed the view of R. Meir" (Ta'an. 26b; see also Resp. Maharik no. 171).

According to some of the Babylonian *amoraim*, the power of determining the *halakhah* contrary to the accepted rules of decision was to be withheld from custom in matters concerning the ritual law (*dinei hetter ve-issur*). Thus in response to R. Johanan's statement, "In regard to carob trees, it has become the custom of the people to follow the rule of R. Nehemiah" (RH 15b) – i.e., contrary to the majority of the scholars – the question is asked: "In a matter of prohibition, shall it be permitted to follow a custom?" (*ibid.*). On the other hand, the *amoraim* of Ereẓ Israel – along with some Babylonian *amoraim* – conferred on custom the power of deciding the law in any case of dispute, even in matters of ritual law and even when it was contrary to the accepted rules of decision, for instance when decreeing in favor of an individual opinion against the majority opinion (TJ, Shev. 5:1, the opinion of R. Johanan quoted in RH 15b; cf. the statement of Rava, "The custom accords with the view of R. Meir" Ta'an. 26b; see also Pes. 103a and Ber. 52b, contrary to the unqualified statement of the law in the Mishnah).

In the 13th century, *Meir b. Baruch of Rothenburg stated, "For in all matters on which the great halakhic scholars are in dispute, I hold that a stringent approach must be followed, save … when the permissibility of a matter has spread in accordance with the custom of the scholars by whom we have been preceded" (Resp. Maharam of Rothenburg, ed. Berlin, no. 386). At this time too the dispute concerning the extent to which it was within the power of custom to determine the *halakhah* was continued. Thus Jacob *Moellin justified the custom of lending the money of orphans at fixed interest (*ribbit kezuzah*, see *Usury), contrary to the opinion of the majority of scholars, who held this to be prohibited; Moellin based his view on a solitary opinion (Resp. Maharil no. 37), which in fact only permitted such interest in respect of loans given from charitable funds (*Or Zaru'a*, Hil. Ẓedakah, no. 30), but Moellin extended the opinion to embrace also money lent by orphans, "for all matters concerning orphans are deemed to be matters of *mitzvah*, and this is truly so because they are alone and meek" (Maharil, loc. cit.). Other scholars contested this view: "There are places where it is customary for an *apotropos* [guardian] to lend orphans' money at fixed interest, but this is an erroneous custom and should not be followed" (Rema to YD 160:18; see also *Siftei Kohen* thereto, n. 27).

Minhag as Adding to Existing *Halakhah*

In its previously described function, custom serves to decide between two existing disputing opinions rather than to create a new rule. The latter effect is achieved by custom in fulfillment of its second function, namely that of establishing a new rule in relation to a question to which the existing *halakhah* offers no solution. For instance, as regards the paschal sacrifice, it is enjoined that it shall be brought on the 14th day of the month of Nisan (Num. 9:3), even when this falls on a Sabbath day (Pes. 6:1); when Hillel the Elder was asked what the law was in the event that it had been forgotten to prepare the knife on the eve of the Sabbath – i.e., whether it was also permissible to have the knife fetched on the Sabbath – he replied: "Leave it to Israel! If they are not prophets, they are still the children of prophets" (i.e., to await the morrow and see how the people would act); on the morrow, "he whose sacrifice was a lamb, stuck it [the knife] in its wool, and he whose sacrifice was a goat, stuck it between its horns; he [Hillel] saw the act and recalled the *halakhah*, saying, 'thus have I received the tradition from Shemaiah and Avtalyon'" (Pes. 66a). Hillel thus left the solution to the custom of the people, only later recalling that this custom had its source in ancient *halakhah*. A further illustration is to be found in the reply given in the Jerusalem Talmud to the question whether it was necessary or not to set aside tithes from the fruit of trees in their fourth year: "when there is no clearly established *halakhah* on any matter before the court and you do not know what its true nature is – go and ascertain the custom of the public and act accordingly, and we see that the public does not set aside tithes in this case" (TJ, Pe'ah 7:6, 20c and see Ma'as. Sh. 5:3, 56b). In this way custom served to decide the *halakhah* in a lenient manner (in TJ, Yev. 7:2, 8a – the above rule is quoted in connection with the function of custom as deciding between disputing opinions; see also Resp. Rosh 55:10).

"Custom Overrides the Law" – *Minhag Mevattel Halakhah*

Many halakhic scholars devoted a great deal of attention and research to the question whether it was within the power of custom, "concealed legislation," not only to add to existing *halakhah* but also to vary the latter and set aside any of its rules in certain circumstances – as it was within the power of *takkanah*, "open legislation," to do. This function, which in talmudic sources is termed *minhag mevattel halakhah* ("custom overrides the law"), has been the subject of much dispute – as in other legal systems in which custom is a recognized legal source. In Roman law, for instance, disputing opinions are found on the question whether custom (*mores, consuetudo*) has the power to create also a rule that is contrary to existing law (*contra legem*, see J. Salmond, *Jurisprudence* (1966[12]), 189–212; C.K. Allen, *Law in the Making* (1964[7]), 82f.).

DISTINCTION BETWEEN CIVIL AND RITUAL LAW. Jewish law distinguishes between civil and ritual law for purposes of the instant function of custom, recognizing the power of the latter to set aside the law in civil law matters but not in matters of the ritual law, where it cannot operate contrary to existing law in permitting that which has been prohibited. The explanation for this distinction lies in one of the substantive differences between these two fields of the law – one that relates to the freedom of stipulation (see *Contract; **Mishpat Ivri*). In matters of the civil law the rule is, "a person may contract out of the law of the Torah" – i.e., the law is *jus dispositivum*, since the premise is that halakhic rules of the civil law are laid down as a binding arrangement only as long as the parties do not disclose their preference for an alternative arrangement. On the other hand, the directions of the ritual law are *jus cogens*, obligatory and not variable at the will of the parties concerned. The logical conclusion is that just as the order in civil law matters is variable at the instance of the parties to a particular transaction, so it may be varied by the public as a whole, which, as it were, stipulates in advance that such and such an order, contrary to that laid down in the Torah, is convenient and desirable for each and every one of its members (see Resp. Rosh 64:4; Resp. Rashbash no. 562; Resp. Maharashdam ḤM no. 380). Thus custom, in expressing the collective will of the public, functions with power to change the halakhah in the civil law field – where the will to change the law has recognized authority – but not in the field of ritual law, in which a prohibition is obligatory and unchangeable whether at the will of the instant parties or of the public as a whole. In this function there is accordingly an important distinction between open legislation by way of *takkanah* and concealed legislation by way of custom. The Torah, in all fields, was entrusted to the authority of the halakhic scholars (see *Authority, Rabbinical), authority being delegated to them in the Torah itself to make legislation, whether to add to or derogate from the existing *halakhah* (see **Takkanot*). This is not the case as regards the authority of the public in relation to concealed legislation; the public may decide, by way of *minhag*, between disputing opinions of the halakhic scholars within the existing *halakhah*, may add to the *halakhah*, but may not set aside any rule of the existing *halakhah* – except when the abrogation of such a rule is rendered possible at the hands of individual members of that public by way of express stipulation, i.e., in the field of civil law.

COINAGE OF THE PHRASE MINHAG MEVATTEL HALAKHAH. The essential principle that in the field of civil law custom overrides the law is mentioned in various parts of talmudic and post-talmudic halakhic literature (see below). However, the characteristic phrase for this principle, *minhag mevattel halakhah*, is quoted in the Jerusalem Talmud in connection with the following two matters: The first relates to the determination in the Mishnah (BM 7:1) of the laborer's working hours in two different ways: one whereby he goes to work early in the morning and returns home late, these being the hours of work according to law (BM 83a–b); the other, whereby the laborer goes to work at a later hour and returns home earlier. The Mishnah lays down that local custom determines the hours of work even if this is contrary to the hours laid down by law; the comment of R. Hoshaiah is, "that is to say the custom overrides the *halakhah*" (TJ, BM 7:1, 11b), so that the employer may not withhold the wages of the worker by requiring that he abide by the legally prescribed working hours, but will himself have to abide by the working-hours decreed by custom – this without need for any proof that the parties had so intended (TJ, *ibid.*). The second matter in which the phrase is quoted relates to the laws of *ḥaliẓah* (see *Levirate Marriage); the fact that this forms part of ritual law does not affect the premise that in the latter field of the law the doctrine of *minhag mevattel halakhah* does not operate. In the Mishnah (Yev. 12:1) it is stated that the *ḥaliẓah* rite may be performed with a shoe or sandal (both of leather) but not with *anpilya* (sock or shoe made of cloth) since only the first two are included in the Pentateuchal term *na'al* (Deut. 25:9). In the Jerusalem Talmud (Yev. 12:1, 12c) it is stated: "If Elijah should come and state that *ḥaliẓah* may be performed with a shoe he would be obeyed; that *ḥaliẓah* may not be performed with a sandal he would not be obeyed, for it has been the practice of the public to perform *ḥaliẓah* with a sandal, and custom overrides the law." In this particular case custom supports the existing *halakhah*, since the Mishnah permits *ḥaliẓah* with a sandal and this is not prohibited by any extant talmudic source; accordingly, if Elijah were to come and forbid performance of *ḥaliẓah* with a sandal he would be determining a new rule, contradicting the existing *halakhah*, and in such an event custom – in supporting the existing *halakhah* – would serve to override the new *halakhah* being laid down by Elijah, a function of custom effective in the field of the ritual law. (It is also possible that the phrase *minhag mevattel halakhah* was originally stated in relation to the laborer's hours of work and its application extended to the case of *ḥaliẓah* by the redactor of the talmudic discussion. It may be noted that the above version of the doctrine does not occur in Yev. 102a, where the rule, "if Elijah should come…" is also found, nor in BM 83a–b; see also Men. 31b–32a.)

The rule that it is not within the power of custom to render permissible an undisputed prohibition is stressed by the use, on several occasions, of the phrase, "Does the matter then depend on custom?" (Ḥul. 63a; BM 69b–70a). On the other hand, custom does have the power, even in the field of the ritual law, to render prohibited something that has been permitted, since the law is not abrogated thereby but only rendered more stringent: "Custom cannot set aside a prohibition, it can only prohibit that which has been permitted" (Yad, Shevitat Asor 3:3; see also Resp. Rosh 55:10). According to some scholars, custom – even in civil law matters – only overrides *halakhah* when it has been accepted by way of a communal enactment (see **Takkanot ha-Kahal*; and see *Nimmukei Yosef* BB 144b; Nov. Ritba to Ket. 100a and *Shittah Mekubbeẓet* ad loc.; *Bedek ha-Bayit* ḤM 368:6, commentary on the statement of Sherira Gaon). This view seems to be in conflict with the plain meaning of a number of talmudic discussions, particularly as regards the rule of *sitomta* (affixing of a mark; see below), and was not accepted by the majority of the scholars. The matter was succinctly summarized by Solomon b. Simeon *Duran – after a detailed discussion of the two relevant talmudic references – as follows: "It will be seen that the doctrine of 'custom overrides *halakhah*' is true in matters of civil law, but erroneous when applied to a matter in which it has been the practice to permit something that is prohibited, for custom only has the power to prohibit something that has been permitted, and not to render permissible something that has been prohibited" (Resp. Rashbash no. 562).

MINHAG AS VARYING THE LAW IN VARIOUS FIELDS. The facility of custom to override the law in civil matters has lent Jewish law great flexibility in adapting to changing economic realities, and many rules – sometimes even entire branches of the law – have come to be based on the legal source of custom.

In the Talmudic Period. The following are some of the rules that were laid down: deeds that are not signed as required by law are valid if prepared in accordance with local custom (BB 10:1; BB 165a; Kid. 49a); debts which according to law may only be recovered from the debtor's immovable property (Ket. 51a, 69b) may also be recovered from his movable property when it is local custom to recover them in this way (TJ, Git. 5:3, 46d; in geonic times a special *takkanah* was enacted permitting the recovery of debts from the debtor's movable property since at that time most Jews had ceased to be landowners (see *Execution, Civil); this is an illustration of *halakhah* received first by way of custom and later by expressly enacted *takkanah*). Similarly, many illustrations of the rule that custom overrides the law are to be found in matters of the financial relationship between *husband and wife (see Ket. 6:3–4; Tosef., Ket. 6:5–6; see also *Beit ha-Beḥirah*, Nov. Rashba, and *Shitah Mekubbeẓet* to Ket. 68b).

In the Post-Talmudic Period. In this period too custom actively fulfilled the far-reaching function of changing the law, this phenomenon sometimes leading to sharp dispute – even in the case of one specific matter only – and at other times accepted by all scholars in relation to an entire branch of the law. Thus, as regards the authentication of deeds (see *Shetar) – which according to law must be done by three judges and is ineffective if done by a single judge (Ket. 22a) – it was stated in the 15th century: "For the scholars of the yeshivot it is the accepted custom for deeds to be authenticated by the signature of one [judge], and this is a possible application of the doctrine that custom overrides the law in matters of the civil law" (*Terumat ha-Deshen*, Resp. no. 332). This custom was accepted by Moses Isserles (*Rema* ḤM 46:4), but others differed (see *Yam shel Shelomo*, BK 10:11; *Siftei Kohen* ḤM 46, n. 8). On the other hand, it is generally accepted that the extensive field of tax law is largely founded on the legal source of custom. This is due to the fact that halakhic principles stated in the Talmud in this field (including also the rule of *dina de-malkhuta dina* and the laws of *partnership) were unable to offer adequate solutions to the multiple legal problem that had arisen – commencing from the tenth century onward – in this field of the law (see *Taxation). At first a certain hesitation was expressed concerning the extent to which it was within the power of custom to create an obligation even when it was contrary to "established and known *halakhah*" of the Talmud concerning tax law matters (see statement of Baruch of Mainz, 12th-century author of the *Sefer ha-Ḥokhmah*, quoted in *Mordekhai* BB no. 477); later, however, this hesitation gave way to full recognition of the validity of any legal rule or usage sanctioned by custom, even when it was contrary to the existing *halakhah*.

Nowhere are the tax laws founded on talmudic sanctity and everywhere there are to be found variations of such laws deriving from local usage and the consent of earlier scholars; and the town residents are entitled to establish fixed *takkanot* and uphold recognized customs as they please, even if these are not according to *halakhah*, this being a matter of civil law. Therefore if in this matter they have an established custom, it should be followed, since custom overrides the *halakhah* in matters of this kind (Resp. Rashba, vol. 4, nos. 177, 260 and see *Taxation for further particulars).

The preference for flexible custom above rule of *halakhah* as regards the legal order in all public matters was emphasized by Israel *Isserlein:

> In all matters affecting the public, their custom shall be followed in accordance with the order they set for themselves as dictated by their needs and the matter under consideration, for if they be required to follow the strict law in every matter, there will always be strife among themselves; furthermore, at the outset they allow each other to waive the strict law and make up their minds to follow the decree of their own custom (*Terumat ha-Deshen*, Resp. no. 342).

At the same time, the halakhic scholars made every effort to integrate the legal norm originating from custom into the pattern and spirit of the rules within the Jewish legal system, and in this regard Isserlein adds (*ibid.*):

> Even though it has been said that in tax matters custom overrides the law, it is at any rate desirable and proper to examine carefully whether we can reconcile all customs with the strict law and even if not entirely so, it is yet preferable that we find support and authority in the statements of the scholars and substantiate them with the aid of reason and legal logic (*ibid.*).

In this and in other ways – for instance by means of the control exercised by the halakhic scholars to ensure that rules originating from custom should not depart from the Jewish law principles of justice and equity – the rules of tax law, largely derived from custom, became an integral part of the Jewish legal system.

In Jewish Law in the State of Israel. The stated power of custom continues even in present times actively to assert itself in Jewish law, a fact that finds expression particularly in the decisions of the rabbinical courts in Israel. A notable example concerns the matter of severance pay, payable to the employee on his dismissal. The rabbinical courts have sought various legal ways of conferring binding legal force on the employer's duty to pay this (see *Ha'anakah*), and one of the principal ways has been reliance on the legal source of custom. Thus it was held, "since in our times there has spread this custom of paying compensation to employees … we have to enforce this as an obligation according to the law of the Torah, in terms of the rule stated in regard to the hire of workers: 'all in accordance with local custom'" (PDR, 1:330); moreover, by virtue of custom the claim for severance pay "is not a matter of grace, but a claim founded on law," for which the employer, even if a charitable institution, is liable (PDR, 3:286 f.). Particular importance was held to attach to custom in this case, since "we have found support for it in the Torah and *halakhah* … this custom being based on the Pentateuchal law of the grant payable by the master to his Hebrew bound servant" (*ha'anakat eved Ivri*, PDR, 4:129; *Yam ha-Gadol* no. 22), and as such represented "a proper and just custom" (PDR, 1:330 f.; cf. *Terumat ha-Deshen*, Resp. no. 342 concerning reliance on the Pentateuchal law on tax matters).

MINHAG IN THE DEVELOPMENT OF THE MODES OF ACQUISITION AND OF ESTABLISHING OBLIGATION. In the above field – one that is particularly sensitive to changing trends in commercial life, the nature and scope of which is subject to constant fluctuation – custom was destined to exercise a decisive influence. A transaction executed in a verbal manner alone attains no legal validity in Jewish law, which provides for the transfer of ownership and establishment of an obligation in prescribed ways, generally requiring much formality, as by way of *kinyan meshikhah* or *hagbahah*, etc. ("acquisition by pulling or lifting," etc.; see *Contract; *Acquisition). Such formality was not in keeping with the demands of developing commerce, which called for more convenient and flexible modes of acquisition. Custom, in the form of mercantile or trade usage, was instrumental in providing a large part of the forthcoming answer to the stated demands.

As early as talmudic times (BM 74a), it was laid down that where it was the custom of the merchants for a sale of wine to be concluded by the purchaser affixing a mark (*sitomta*, Rashi ad loc. and Targ. Jon., Gen. 38:18) on the barrel of wine, this action would complete the sale even though the purchaser had not yet "pulled" the barrel and it remained in the seller's possession. This is an illustration of law overridden by custom, since in law acquisition was not complete until the purchaser had "pulled" the barrel, and until then both the seller and the purchaser remained free to retract; thus, in law the barrel would still have remained in the ownership of the seller but custom decreed that ownership of the chattel would pass to the purchaser after it was marked in the customary manner and after this the parties might no longer retract. From this *halakhah* Solomon b. Abraham *Adret concluded: "From this we learn that custom overrides the law in all matters of the civil law, in which everything is acquired and transferred in accordance with custom; hence the merchants effect *kinyan* in any mode according with their own usage" (Nov. Rashba BM 73b; see also *Nimmukei Yosef* BM, loc. cit.; *Maggid Mishneh* Mekhirah 7:6; *Sma* ḤM 201, n. 2). In the course of time and on the basis of this principle, Jewish law came to recognize new modes of acquisition and of establishing obligation. Thus the fact that it was the trade custom to conclude a transaction by shaking hands, by making an advance on the purchase price (*Piskei ha-Rosh*, BM 5:72), or by delivering a key to the place where the goods were stored was held to be sufficient to confer full legal validity on a transaction concluded in any of these ways (Sh. Ar., ḤM 201:2).

The extent of the creative power of custom in relation to the modes of acquisition has been the subject of much discussion founded on halakhic and economic considerations. R. Joel *Sirkes held that custom served to create new modes of acquisition in respect of transactions of movables only, "as there is much trade in these and he [the purchaser] has not the time to pull all the goods into his possession" (*Baḥ* ḤM 201:2), but the majority of scholars took the view that custom also served to do so as regards various transactions of immovable property (*Yam shel Shelomo*, BK 5:36; *Sma* ḤM 201, n. 6; *Siftei Kohen* thereto, n. 1). Similarly, many scholars held that custom served to lend full legal validity to an acquisition of something not yet in existence (see *Acquisition, Modes of; *Contract; Resp. Rosh 13:20; other scholars differed – see *Keẓot ha-Ḥoshen* 201, n. 1; *Netivot ha-Mishpat, Mishpat ha-Urim*, 201, n. 1). At times custom operated with such far-reaching effect that not only were new modes of acquisition added to those halakhically recognized but even certain substantive elements of the existing acquisitory modes as determined by the halakhic scholars were changed (see, e.g., Resp. Ribash no. 345 on the custom concerning acquisition incidental to four cubits of land (*kinyan aggav arba ammot karka*), without specification of the land, contrary to the opinion of Maimonides, when locally the latter's statement of the law was otherwise followed; similarly, in Resp. Rosh 79:4).

In the 13th century a question of principle arose whose answer was to be of great significance as regards the measure of the creative power attaching to custom in general. The fundamental idea underlying the need in Jewish law for acquisitory formalities in the formation of legal transaction is that in a such manner the parties demonstrate their absolute *gemirut ha-da'at* ("making up of their minds") to close the transaction (see *Contract). The modes of acquisition that came to be decreed by custom also served to demonstrate such *gemirut ha-da'at*, since these represented accepted trade customs; however, the question arose whether local custom to close a transaction in a verbal manner alone was capable, from the standpoint of Jewish law, of conferring full legal validity on such transaction. *Asher b. Jehiel took the view that no affirmative conclusion could be drawn from the rule of *sitomta* (see above), except with regard to the validity of a custom requiring the performance of some act such as those mentioned above (handshake, etc.), "but never by mere speech alone, and even when this is the practice it is a bad custom which is not to be followed" (Resp. Rosh 12:3). This view denied custom the power of contraverting the basic requirement of Jewish law for the performance of some act indicating the absolute *gemirut ha-da'at*; a custom of this kind was therefore not proper except when it served only to change the substance of the act, but when it was aimed at eliminating the need for any act at all it was a "bad custom" from which the scholars would withhold validity (see below).

Another view was that whenever custom decreed mere speech alone as sufficient for the conclusion of a legal transaction it had to be assumed that absolute *gemirut ha-da'at* would come about in such a way too (opinion of Meir of Rothenburg and of R. Jehiel, quoted in *Mordekhai*, Shab. nos. 472–3), and this was the opinion accepted by the majority of the *posekim*. Thus it was decided that a person who had promised his neighbor to be the *ba'al berit* ("sandek"; see *Circumcision) at a circumcision ceremony was not free to retract from such an undertaking and assign it to another "since it has long been the practice among all Israelites for the privilege of performing such a *mitzvah* to be conferred in mere verbal manner and it is already established that custom is an important tenet in all matters of this kind" (Resp. Radbaz no. 278). This is also the position as regards the formation of partnership. According to talmudic law a partnership is formed by performance on the part of each partner of an act of acquisition in relation to the share of the other partners (Ket. 10:4; Yad, Sheluḥin 4:1; and see *Partnership). However, it was held that "where it is local custom to become a partner even by speech alone – there will be a partnership; such is the custom in this country too ... and so we decide in every case, for custom is an important matter in the field of the civil law" (Resp. Radbaz no. 380). This opinion came to be accepted as *halakhah* by the later *posekim*, "reason inclines to the view that whenever it is the custom to rely on speech alone, it is like the custom of *sitomta*" (*Kesef ha-Kedoshim* ḤM 201:1), in terms of which full recognition according to Jewish law was given to public sales (*Mishpat u-Ẓedakah be-Ya'akov*, no. 33), to sales on the exchanges (Resp. Maharsham, pt. 3, no. 18), and to like legal transactions customarily concluded in mere verbal manner (see *Ohel Moshe* pt. 2, no. 138).

In cases before the rabbinical courts in the State of Israel reliance on custom (see above) is particularly evident in the field of the modes of *kinyan*. In several cases acquisition by way of registration in the registry in accordance with the state law is recognized as a valid *kinyan* according to Jewish law, by the force of custom (see, e.g., PDR 4:81). In another leading decision it was laid down that "in our times a signed contract between purchaser and seller constitutes a *kinyan* by virtue of the rule of *sitomta*, whether relating to immovable or to movable property, since this is a trade custom" (PDR 6:216, and see also the distinction drawn with regard to the text of the contract).

THE RULE OF MINHAG MEVATTEL HALAKHAH – IN THE CASE OF LOCAL CUSTOM. Custom overrides the law even when it is not general but customary with part of the public only. Thus in talmudic law it is laid down that when a desert caravan is attacked by robbers who demand a price for the release of the travelers, each must pay according to the amount of the property he carries and not on a per capita basis; in the case where a guide is taken to avert danger to life, payment of the guide is made according to a calculation based both on the amount of property carried by each and per capita; however, "the custom of caravan travelers must not be departed from" (i.e., if the custom decrees that the participation always be according to property and not per capita, it must be followed, Tosef., BM 7:13–14; see also BK 116b; TJ, BM 6:4, 11a). Similarly, it is laid down that "a shippers' custom [minhag *sappanin*] must not be departed from" in the case where cargo has to be jettisoned to lighten the load (Tosef., loc. cit.). Hence it follows that a local custom or trade usage overrides the *halakhah* for the people governed by such custom: "In matters of the civil law custom is followed, even the custom of ass drivers and shippers, for even if the strict law requires that participation must be according to money and the load carried, nevertheless the custom of ass drivers and of shippers overrides the law" (Resp. Maharik, no. 102).

Proof of the Existence of a Custom

Jewish law sets three requirements for the validity of a custom:

(1) It must be widespread over the whole country, or in the whole of a particular locality, or amidst the whole of a particular class of people, according to its purported field of operation: "In all such matters [of the financial relationship between spouses] custom is an important tenet and must be followed in deciding the law, provided, however, that the custom be widespread (*pashut*) over the whole country" (Yad, Ishut 23:12 and cf. with the matter of *takkanah, ibid.* 16:7–9). A custom which exists in most parts of a particular district must be presumed to exist in the whole of such a district (Resp. Rosh 79:4; *Beit Yosef* ḤM 42:21).

(2) A custom must be of frequent application: "It must be known that the custom is established and widespread, that the townspeople have followed it at least three times, for often the public adopt for themselves a practice to suit their immediate needs [i.e., in regard to a particular matter only] without intending to establish a custom at all" (*Terumat ha-Deshen*, Resp. no. 342; Resp. Maharashdam, ḤM no. 436). The time required for the evolution of a custom depends on the nature of the matter in each case: "This matter [whether or not there was a custom to exempt the communal cantor from tax payment] is not like a custom relating to the hire of workers, which happens every day so that everyone can see what the custom is; but as regards the cantor's tax immunity, since there is only one cantor in the town, how shall the fact that tax was not demanded from one or two cantors be called a custom unless it be public knowledge in the town that cantors had been exempted there on account of local custom to exempt them" (Resp. Ribash no. 475).

(3) The custom must be clear: "The custom must be clear to exempt" (Resp. Ribash, loc. cit.). In another matter Samuel b. Moses *Medina held that the rule of custom overrides *halakhah* was applicable to that case, provided only that the instant custom was sufficiently clear, "there are two approaches to this matter: one according to the law of our holy Torah, the other according to the trade custom; for there is no doubt that in such matters custom is decisive, provided that the import of the custom be clear, but if there be any doubt about this then we have to revert to what is decreed by the law of the Torah" (Resp. Maharashdam, ḤM no. 33).

Jewish law dispenses with the formality of the laws of evidence for purposes of proving the establishment of a custom – a fact that has provided custom with wide creative opportunity. Thus hearsay evidence suffices and the testimony of normally disqualified witnesses is admitted (*Terumat ha-Deshen*, Resp. no. 342). The wide latitude which Jewish law allows to the creative power of custom is evidenced in a decision given by the rabbinical court in the State of Israel concerning the matter of severance pay due to an employee upon his dismissal (see above). In 1945 R. Ouziel (in a responsum quoted in M. Findling, *Teḥukat ha-Avodah*, p. 133f.) refrained from basing the law of severance pay on the legal source of custom (relying instead on an ethical-halakhic principle: see *Ha'anakah*), for the reason that a custom had no validity unless it was widespread, of frequent application, and clear: "and as far as I am aware this custom [of severance pay] is not widespread in the whole country nor of common application, but only followed in certain specific cases, and therefore the court is not ordering severance pay to be paid in terms thereof" (*ibid.*). A mere ten years later the rabbinical court – seeking a full legal justification for the obligation of severance pay – held: "Now that this custom has spread and become accepted in the whole country, and is popular and of common, daily application, it must be followed and the statements mentioned above (i.e., of R. Ouziel), made in the year 1945, are no longer applicable or valid because the custom has become widespread and established." Recognition of such an accelerated spread of a custom within the short period of ten years is indicative of the special readiness of Jewish law to enrich itself by means of the legal source of custom.

Custom (*Minhag*) and Usage (Nohag)

The customs so far discussed belong mainly to those in the category of a legal norm functioning of its own power and independently of the consent of the parties to a particular transaction. Thus, for instance, the validity of a mode of acquisition sanctioned by custom is not to be explained on the ground that the parties to a particular transaction intended, by implication, to confer legal validity thereon – since it is beyond the authority of the parties to pass on the validity of a *kinyan* even if they should expressly say so. In this case the new mode of acquisition draws its validity from the efficacy of custom to create new legal norms of selfstanding force. On the other hand, many customs operate in the *halakhah* – as in other legal systems – not from their own independent force but by virtue of a presumption that the parties intended, by implication, to introduce a particular usage as part of the transaction between themselves. An agreement between two parties is generally composed of two kinds of terms, those expressly stipulated and those imported by implication as an integral part of the agreement. Such implied terms may be inferred in two ways: either because they are decreed by factors of logic and reasonableness, or because they are usual and customary, since it may be presumed that the parties intended to include in the terms of their agreement the dictates of all the former factors (see J. Salmond, *Jurisprudence* (1966[12]), 193–7). The matter may be illustrated as follows: The Mishnah (BM 9:1) lays down that a transaction of *arisut* or *ḥakhirah* (land tenancy and cultivation in return for a share of the crop, see *Lease and Hire) includes implied terms concerning cultivation of the land in accordance with local usage – *keminhag ha-medinah* – and that neither party to the transaction may contend, for instance, that he intended the crop to be reaped by scythe when it was local custom to reap by hand (BM 9:1). The Talmud adds that a party's plea that he had not intended to abide by local custom will not be accepted even if it is supported by circumstantial evidence, such as higher or lower rental than usual (see BM 103b), because in the absence of any express stipulation to the contrary it will be presumed that both parties intended to embrace local custom in their agreement (see also Yad, Sekhirut 8:6; Sh. Ar., ḤM 320:4–5). Talmudic *halakhah* offers abundant examples, in most branches of the civil law, of usages which are imported by implication as part of the terms agreed upon between the parties to a transaction, e.g., in the laws of joint ownership (BB 1:1 and 4a; TJ, BB 1:2, 12b) and partnership (BM 68b; 69b; Tosef., BM 5:6–7; TJ, BM 5:6, 10b; see also Yad, Sheluḥin 5:1 and 8:4; and see Partnership); in the laws of *pledge (e.g., BM 67b–68a; Yad, Malveh 7:2–3); in the laws of master and servant (BM 7:1; BM 83a concerning the hours of work; 86a concerning the worker's sustenance; 87a concerning the worker's wages; and see *Labor Law); in the laws concerning the pecuniary relationship between spouses (see above; see also *Husband and Wife), etc. Usages of the above kind also fulfill an important role as regards the interpretation of various deeds and documents, in which local usage in the particular matter is of decisive importance (BB 166b; Yad, Malveh 27:15; and see *Interpretation).

The Rule of Doreshin Lashon Hedyot. This rule (Tosef., Ket. 4:9ff.; TJ, Ket. 4:8, 28d; TJ, Yev. 15:3, 14d; BM 104a) is of application in the interpretation of documents (for details, see *Interpretation). Many halakhic scholars regarded this rule as serving to give recognition to the implicit importation into the terms of a document of a usage followed by the people, on the presumption that the parties intended their transaction to be subject to such usage: "For whatever is customarily written by the people is deemed to have been written by the parties, even if they have not done so … and this is as if provided by an enactment" (*tenai bet din*; Resp. Rashba vol. 1, no. 662; vol. 3, nos. 17,433, et al.; this is also the view of Hai Gaon and Ramban, in Nov. Ramban, Tos., *Beit ha-Beḥirah* Nov. Ritba and *Shitah Mekubbeẓet* BM 104a; Resp. Ran no. 54; Resp. Ritba no. 53). Just as scholars saw the need in matters of marriage and *ketubbah* to enact essential conditions for the good of all, these being applicable, *setaman ke-ferushan*, i.e., binding even if not expressly stipulated between the parties – so there are matters "which the scholars did not enact and which have not been accepted by all, but are usages which have been followed by the people in certain places, simply of their own accord without [communal] enactment, and this too is a matter of *setaman ke-ferushan*, which the scholars refer to as *derishat hedyotot*" (Resp. Rashba, vol. 4, no. 186). In this sense the rule of *derishat leshon hedyot* served the halakhic scholars as a means of solving many legal problems relating to the laws of marriage, property, and obligations (see Resp. Rashba, Ritba, and Ran as cited above; for an interesting example in the field of obligations see Resp. Rashba, vol. 4, no. 125).

General and Local Custom

A general custom is created at the hands of the public as a whole and as such applies to the whole of that public, whereas a local custom is created at the hands of the people of a certain place, class, or some other group, and as such its application and validity is confined to the people of that place or group. Already mentioned above are the customs of various trade associations like those of shippers and caravan drivers, and the talmudic sources also mention customs relating to priests (Kid. 78b; TJ, Bik. 1:5, 64a; and TJ, Kid. 4:6, 66b), women (Pes. 48b; TJ, Pes. 4:1, 30c), *ḥavurot* in Jerusalem (Tosef., Meg. 4:10, 25c), the fair-minded (*nekiyyei ha-da'at*) of Jerusalem (Sanh. 30a), etc. Often a custom is referred to as *minhag ha-medinah* (i.e., custom of a particular area or district: BM 7:1 and 9:1; BB 1:1 and 10:1; Suk. 3:11, et al.). Sometimes a custom is quoted as followed in Judea (Tosef. Ket. 1:4, 1:5 and 4:12; BB 100b, et al.), in Galilee (Tosef. and Mishnah, *ibid.*), or in particular settlements, e.g., Tiberias, Acre, Kabul (TJ, Pes. 4:1, 30d; TJ, Ta'an. 1:6, 64c), also Jabneh, Sepphoris, etc. Such local or group customs relate to diverse fields of the *halakhah*, both the civil and the ritual law.

Many local customs render the law more severe by prohibiting matters which are permitted (see, e.g., Pes. 4:1–4).

Thus although the law permitted the performance of all labor on the 14th day of Nisan – i.e., on the eve of Passover – it became the general custom to refrain from labor from noon onward, since from that time the paschal sacrifice could properly be brought, so that the rest of the day was treated as a festival day; the Mishnah records that there were places where it was customary to perform labor until noon, and other places where it was customary not to do so lest the need for burning the leaven and other requirements of the festival be forgotten, and the Mishnah prescribes that the local inhabitants should follow their own custom. The halakhic validity of a custom that prohibited what was legally permissible was justified by regarding this as a form of vow undertaken by the public, and the sanction against breaking such a custom as akin to that of the prohibition against breaking a vow: "Matters which are permitted [in law] but prohibited by others by virtue of their custom may not be rendered permissible to the latter, as it is said (Num. 30:3), 'he shall not break his word'" (Ned. 15a; see also Ḥ. Albeck, *Shishah Sidrei Mishnah*, Nashim, p. 137f.). It seems however that the Babylonian *amoraim* restricted the operation of the prohibition deriving from the above rule, holding it as applicable only to a custom of the Cuthites (non-Jews), or of Jews amidst whom there were no scholars – out of apprehension that if the latter persons were permitted matters which their own custom prohibited, even though these were permissible in law, they would make light also of other prohibitions stemming from the law itself (Pes. 50b–51a).

These local customs were also discussed in relation to the biblical injunction, "you shall not cut yourselves" (Deut. 14:1), interpreted by the halakhic scholars as a stringent prohibition against the formation of separate "societies" in relation to the rules of *halakhah*, so that the Torah "should not become like several Torot." In R. Johanan's opinion this prohibition only applied in circumstances where in one place a decision is given according to one opinion – for instance according to Bet Hillel, and in another place according to another opinion – for instance according to Bet Shammai, for in this way the *halakhah* itself would be divided; however, if from the standpoint of the law all decide according to the same opinion but part of the public renders the law additionally stringent for itself, this does not amount to a division of the *halakhah*, and it is permissible in the same way as any individual may take a vow and render prohibited for himself that which is permissible in law (TJ, Pes. 4:1, 30d; Yev. 13b; see also L. Ginzberg, *Perushim ve-Ḥiddushim ba-Yerushalmi*, 1 (1941), 152–60). Despite this theoretical distinction, the halakhic scholars maintained that in practice the diversity of customs might lead to division and strife and therefore laid down that a person should follow no custom but that of the place where he finds himself at any given time, if to do otherwise might lead to dispute (Pes. 4:1 and 51a; Yad, Yom Tov 8:20; see also in detail *Peri Hadash*, OH 468 and 496).

Minhag and the Conflict of Laws (within Jewish Law)

The multiplicity of customs, particularly local customs, inevitably gave rise to the phenomenon of varying laws on the same legal subject. At times it transpired that the law on the same subject differed in different places, and in this event – when the different stages of a legal obligation required performance in different places, in each of which there prevailed a different law concerning such an obligation – there arose the question of whether to apply the customary law at the time and place of establishment of the obligation, or the customary law at the time and place of its performance, or some other law. This and like questions, relating to the field of the conflict of laws, frequently arose in many fields of Jewish law against the background of differing customs on the same subject: e.g., as regards the laws of marriage, divorce, labor, partnership, and land tenancy. The result was the evolution of a proliferous body of case law on the subject of the *conflict of laws, constituting one of the important contributions made by custom to the development and creativity of Jewish law.

Control over *Minhag* by the Halakhic Scholars

Custom, because of its spontaneous and undirected nature, sometimes calls for a measure of supervision and control. At times a custom may be founded on error, or develop unreasonably or illogically in a certain direction, or may even be in conflict with substantive and fundamental principles of Jewish law in a manner leaving no room for its integration into this system. From time to time the halakhic scholars exercised such control in order to contain or discredit entirely a particular custom.

CUSTOM FOUNDED ON ERROR. The Mishnah (Er. 10:10) mentions the case of a certain usage observed in Tiberias until the scholars came and set it aside; according to one opinion the usage of the people of Tiberias involved a prohibition which the scholars later permitted; according to another opinion, it involved a permission which the scholars later forbade (*ibid.*). Some commentators held that the usage was set aside because it was based on error (Tos. to Eruv. 101b, s.v. "*R. Yose Omer*"; for a further illustration, see Ḥul. 6b concerning Rabbi's permissiveness regarding the eating of untithed fruit from Beth-Shean). In the Jerusalem Talmud a rule is laid down by R. Abun that a custom founded on error may be set aside: if the custom prohibits when it is clearly known that the relevant matter is permitted in law, the custom is valid and the matter must not be rendered permissible; however, if the custom prohibits as an outcome of an erroneous belief that the relevant matter is prohibited in law, when the error is discovered, the matter may be rendered permissible and the custom discredited (TJ, Pes. 4:1, 30d).

In post-talmudic literature frequent reference is made to customs discredited by the halakhic scholars on the ground of error. Thus Rabbenu Tam censured those who counted a minor as helping to make up a *minyan* as long as he held a Pentateuch in his hand: "This is a nonsensical custom … is a Pentateuch to be regarded as a man?" (Tos. to Ber. 48a). In another case Asher b. Jehiel examined the source of a custom concerning the testamentary disposition of property by a woman, concluding that "this is certainly an erroneous custom" and even if widespread, "it is not a custom that may properly be relied upon for purposes of the disposition of property … the custom is wrong and it must be invalidated" (Resp. Rosh 55:10). Similarly Mordecai *Jaffe opposed the custom of not reciting *birkat ha-mazon* (*Grace after Meals) in the home of a gentile, holding that the spread of "this nonsensical custom" originated from an erroneous understanding of a talmudic statement completely unconnected with such a custom (*Levush ha-Tekhelet*, 193:6). In another instance it became customary to take a stringent view and regard a woman as married in circumstances where – in the opinion of all scholars – there was no *kiddushin* at all in law; Simeon Duran strongly condemned this custom: "In circumstances where the whole world holds that there is no *kiddushin*, some people wish to impose on themselves such a stringent rendering of the law – this is a custom born in ignorance which the public must not be compelled to uphold" (*Tashbeẓ*, 1:154).

UNREASONABLE OR ILLOGICAL CUSTOM. At times the scholars examined a custom from the aspect of its reasonableness. Thus it was determined that a custom of the women not to do any work during the whole of the evening following the Sabbath was unreasonable and of no validity except insofar as it was restricted to the time of prayer on that evening (TJ, Pes. 4:1, 30d; Ta'an. 1:6, 64c); similarly invalid was a custom of the women not to do any work on Mondays and Thursdays, but their custom to do no work on a public fast-day or on Rosh Ḥodesh was reasonable and proper (*ibid.*). Some customs were condemned as imposing hardship on the public and contrary to the purpose of the actual law concerned. Thus the custom of those who prepared grits in Sepphoris and of the crushers of wheat in Acre not to work on *ḥol ha-mo'ed* was held to be a good custom since it was not likely to detract from the joy of the festival; however, the custom of the fishermen of Tiberias not to work on *ḥol ha-mo'ed* was opposed by the scholars, since it was impossible to prepare in advance fresh fish for the whole festival, and the custom was therefore likely to detract from the joy of the festival (TJ, *ibid.*).

BAD CUSTOM. In post-talmudic times there was disputed the question of the extent to which a custom concerning a matter of civil law had to be accepted even when it appeared to be a "bad custom." On the dispute over a custom concerning the erection of a partition between two joint holders so that one might not observe the other (see below), Rabbenu Tam held that a custom of erecting a partition which fell short of the talmudic requirements was a bad custom and was not to be followed: "it may be concluded that some customs are not to be relied upon, even though it has been said, 'all in accordance with custom'" (Tos. to BB 2a). This opinion was followed by many scholars but others held that in civil law matters even a custom of this kind had to be followed when locally accepted (see Piskei ha-Rosh BB 1:1 and 5; Tur, ḤM 157:3–4, 16; Sh. Ar., ḤM 157:1 and commentaries; Haggahot Maimuniyyot, Shekhenim 2:20; Mordekhai, BM no. 366). Even those who took the former view conceded that in certain matters even a bad custom had to be followed – for instance in tax matters – if it was necessary for the good order of the public (Terumat ha-Deshen, Resp. no. 342; Sh. Ar., ḤM 163:3, *Rema* and commentaries).

CUSTOM CONTRARY TO FUNDAMENTAL RULES AND THE PRINCIPLES OF EQUITY AND JUSTICE. The halakhic scholars were also at pains to ensure that custom did not controvert basic general rules as well as the principles of equity and justice in Jewish law. In so doing they rendered possible the integration of legal norms originating from custom into the general framework of the law, in the same way as their similar close control over communal enactments (see *Takkanot ha-Kahal*) rendered possible their integration. The matter is illustrated by the following examples:

(1) When Asher b. Jehiel decided that the custom of closing a transaction by verbal agreement alone controverted the basic rule requiring demonstration of the absolute *gemirut ha-da'at* of the parties to a transaction, he laid down that this amounted to a bad custom which was not to be followed (see above).

(2) In law, on division of a courtyard between joint owners, "a partition must be built by both of them in the middle, so that neither may observe his neighbor in the enjoyment of his portions, since the injury of being observed is a real injury" (Yad, Shekhenim 2:14, based on BB 3a); the width of the partition is determined by local custom "even when the custom is to build the partition of reeds and palm fronds" (BB 4a; Yad, Shekhenim 2:15). In this regard, Rashba decided that a custom not to erect any partition at all – leaving each neighbor free to observe the other – was of no legal validity, so that either partner could oblige the other to erect the partition: "If it has been the custom, as regards houses and courtyards, not to pay heed at all to the injury of observing one's neighbor, the custom is a bad one and no custom at all; for waiver may only be made in matters of civil law in which event a person may give of his own or tolerate damage to his property, but he is not free to breach the fences of Israel and to act immodestly in a manner causing the Divine Presence *[Shekhinah]* to depart from this people, as it is said, 'a person shall not make his windows to open onto his joint owner's courtyard' (BB 3:7) … Scripture relates, 'And Balaam lifted up his eyes, and he saw Israel abiding in his tents according to their tribes' (Num. 24:2). What did he see? That the openings to their tents were not made to face each other, and he said, 'These are worthy that the Divine Presence abide with them'" (BB 60a; Resp. Rashba, vol. 2, no. 268). Thus the custom in question stood in conflict with a material tract of the *halakhah* and could be given no legal recognition.

(3) A custom may not conflict with the Jewish law principles of justice and equity. Hence even in cases where a bad custom is given legal recognition, as in tax matters (see above), some way must be found for anchoring it within the general

spirit of the *halakhah*. Hence a tax custom which did not adequately distinguish between rich and poor was held to have no legal validity: "The contention of the rich has no justification, for certainly according to the law of the Torah taxes must be shared according to financial means and there can be no greater injustice than to make the rich and the poor bear the tax burden in virtually equal measure, and even if the custom has been in existence for some years it must not be upheld" (Moses Rothenburg, quoted in *Pitḥei Teshuvah*, ḤM 163, n. 16).

[Menachem Elon]

BIBLIOGRAPHY: GENERAL: S. Eisenstadt, *Ein Mishpat* (1931), 45–49; M. Higger, *Massekhet Soferim* (1937), 270–1; Weiss, Dor, index, s.v. *Minhag*; Guedemann, Gesch Erz, index, s.v.; Urbach, in: *Tarbiz*, 27 (1957/58), 169; B. De Vries, *Toledot ha-Halakhah ha-Talmudit* (1966²), 157–68; Dinary, in: *Benjamin De Vries Memorial Volume* (1968), 168–98. JEWISH LAW: *Naḥalat Shivah* no. 27, notes 6–16; S.A. Horodezky, in: *Ha-Shilo'aḥ*, 6 (1899), 417–20; Weiss, Dor, 2 (1904⁴), 62–65; Ha-Toseftai, in: *Ha-Shilo'ah*, 25 (1911), 600–8; A. Perls, in: *Festschrift… Israel Lewy* (1911), 66–75; J. Unna, in: *Jeschurun*, 10 (1923), 463–78; J. Carlebach, *ibid.*, 14 (1927), 329–51; Ch. Tchernowitz, *Toledot ha-Halakhah*, 1 pt. 1 (1934), 144–50; A. Guttmann, in: MGWJ, 83 (1939, repr. 1963), 226–38; J.L. Fischmann, in: *Sefer ha-Yovel…B.M. Lewin* (1939), 132–59; M. Vogelmann, in: *Ha-Zikkaron… le-ha-Rav… Cook* (1945), 366–77; Z.H. Chajes, *Darkhei ha-Hora'ah*, in his collected works: *Kol Sifrei Maharitz Ḥayyot*, 1 (1958), 207–80; T.Z. Kahana, in: *Mazkeret Kovez Torani… la-Rav Herzog* (1962), 554–64; M. Havatzelet, in: *Sinai*, 54 (1963/64), 155–63; idem, in: *Talpioth*, 9 (1964), 261–76; B.Z. Katz, *Mi-Zekenim Etbonen* (1964); Elon, Mafte'aḥ, 131f., 418–24; idem, in: ILR, 2 (1967), 547f.

MINHAGIM BOOKS. Variations in usage between various sections of Palestine are already recorded in the period of the *tannaim* and *amoraim*. Thus, customs of Jerusalem (Ket. 4b, 12b; BB 93b; TJ, Suk. 4:14; Sem. 3:6), variations between Judah and Galilee (TJ, Pes. 4:5; Ket. 12b), and differences between Sura and Pumbedita (Ḥul. 110a) are mentioned. Also mentioned are usages established by individual sages in certain localities (Shab. 130a; Yev. 14a; Ḥul. 116a). A tolerant attitude was obtained toward these variations but it was insisted that once established, the observance of the usage is obligatory (Pes. 4:1; Ket. 6:4; BM 86b), sometimes even when it was contrary to a normative rule (TJ, Yev. 12:1; BM 7:1). De facto, the *minhag* assumed the force of law consisting of popular halakhic works, whose chief purpose was to record differences in religious custom as reflected in the daily life of their authors, in contrast to other *likkutim* ("anthologies"), which recorded similar – or at times the very same – differences culled from books or from the statements of rabbis but without personal acquaintance with them. By definition, a *minhag* is a prevalent religious practice or usage not enjoined by normative regulations, in contradistinction to *din*, which is a normative prescription. Often, however, such usages assumed the status of normative regulations (see **Minhag*).

The first book of this nature to survive is the *Sefer ha-Ḥillukim bein Mizraḥ ve-Erez Yisrael* ("Variations in Customs Between the People of the East and of Israel"; Jerusalem, 1938), which was apparently compiled in Erez Israel in the eighth century. This early work summarizes some scores of major differences between the customs of Erez Israel and Babylon actually in force, and seems to refer to the customs of Babylonian Jews living in Erez Israel who preserved the customs of their country of origin. Many and varied suggestions have been made to explain the nature and purpose of this early work, but it is still not clear. Another work, *Ḥilluf Minhagim*, from the same period, of which not even a fragment has survived, gave the differences in custom between the academies of Sura and Pumbedita. It is certain, however, that such lists were in the possession of early scholars even though they may have been merely a collection from a variety of sources.

Minhagim books differ from one another in content, structure, purpose, and literary standard. Some describe the totality of customs peculiar to a certain area either on one topic only or covering a broader range – with the purpose of presenting "local custom" in its purity in order to preserve its existence and secure its uninterrupted continuation against penetration by external influences.

Middle Ages

Sefer ha-Minhagot of *Asher b. Saul of Lunel, which describes the customs of southern France over a very wide range of subjects and is apparently the earliest *minhagim* book to come down to us from Europe, belongs to this category. To this period also belongs *Ha-Manhig* of *Abraham b. Nathan ha-Yarḥi which is, however, of a different character. It limits itself mainly to the laws of prayer, Sabbath, and festival, but in it are described Spanish, Provençal, French, and German customs which the author himself saw while traveling in these countries. Consequently the aim of the two books also differs. While Asher of Lunel explicitly states that his purpose is to indicate the sources in rabbinical literature of the customs in order to prove their authenticity and prevent the disrespect for them which stems from lack of knowledge, the aim of *Ha-Manhig* was to show that all customs, even when contradicting one another, have a halakhic source, and that none of them should be rejected, but each locality should maintain its *minhag*. These two books were of great importance and played a prominent role in molding the *halakhah* in succeeding generations. A book, unique of its kind, though of the same type as the *Ha-Manhig*, discusses a collection of 25 variant customs between Catalonia and Provence. It was written by Menahem b. Solomon with the aim of proving that despite the great halakhic authority of *Naḥmanides, the ancient customs of Provence were not to be undermined because of him, and Menahem exerted himself to show their sources in the *halakhah* (see *Magen Avot*, London, 1909). In 12th-century Germany, halakhic compilations were known of the type of "*Minhagei Spira*," "*Kunteres Magenza*," and the like, which are mentioned for example in *Ha-Roke'aḥ* of *Eleazar b. Judah of Worms and the works of the school of Rashi. There are already allusions to it in *Sefer Rabban* of *Eliezer b. Nathan which was the first Hebrew book written in Germany. From the quotations it is recognizable that although these were not actually complete "books," like the Provençal and Spanish *minhag* books of the 13th century, they were nevertheless the first *minhag* books in this region, and some 300 years later they were to serve as the main source for the growth of a ramified and developed *minhagim* literature. These early Ashkenazi compilations committed to writing for the first time the great fragmentation in the sphere of custom that prevailed in Germany, each city, including even adjacent cities, having different customs.

Another type, much more rare, confines itself to the customs appertaining to one single theme, in most cases an actual professional sphere, like the book of Jacob *Hagozer which describes the comprehensive customs applying to the laws of circumcision, and was intended to serve as a handbook for those performing the ceremony. Despite the rarity of this type, it is of great importance, since through it the close connection which exists between *minhagim* literature and "professional" literature is well recognized, an affinity which became blurred in the course of time, but which is still apparent in one sphere of *halakhah*, **Issur ve-Hetter*. The various types of works of *Issur ve-Hetter* are in fact merely *minhagim* books intended to ease the burden of giving decisions from rabbis, and to a large extent they transmit different local customs in accordance with the different evidence they adduced, including visual evidence.

During the period of the *rishonim*, *minhagim* literature dealt mainly with the description of the customs of distinguished rabbis, with the avowed aim of establishing as the accepted norm their personal customs down to their last detail. The beginnings of this category are connected with the personality of *Meir b. Baruch of Rothenburg, who was the central figure in Germany in the 13th century and whose disciples created a complete *minhagim* literature, known as that "of the school of Maharam of Rothenburg," basing themselves on his customs and rulings. The first apparently was Ḥayyim *Paltiel, whose *minhagim* served as the foundation for the *Sefer ha-Minhagim* of Abraham *Klausner, regarded as "the father of the *minhag* Ashkenaz." In contrast to Ḥayyim Paltiel, who does not mention Meir of Rothenburg by name in his work, the *Ha-Parnes*, also compiled in conformity with the views and practices of Meir by his pupil Moses Parnes, in most cases refers to him by name. The personality of Meir is especially recognizable in the *Tashbeẓ* of his pupil Samson b. Zadok, and in the anonymous *minhagim* book published by I. Eifenbein (New York, 1938). A century later this type of literature received powerful stimulus, chiefly in the Rhine region, and the description of the customs of outstanding rabbis became a widespread activity, in great demand by the public. It was engaged in by disciple-attendants who were in close personal contact with a certain scholar – at times living with him for decades – and these included in their descriptions the actual minute-by-minute practice of their master, including the very smallest details even of the most intimate and private kind. They saw in each such detail a model worthy of emulation by every pious Jew. The best-known writers in this field are *Joseph b. Moses of Hochstadt who in his *Leket Yosher* described the customs of his distinguished teacher Israel *Isserlein, and Zalman of St. Goar who recorded the customs of his teacher Jacob *Moellin ha-Levi. In this connection it is worth mentioning the *minhagim* book of Isaac *Tyrnau – incidentally the first rabbinic work to be written in Hungary – who in point of fact recorded the customs of his teachers, Abraham Klausner and R. Sar Shalom of Vienna; but in contrast to the other two, who were not distinguished scholars, he was himself a renowned scholar who also devoted his energy to compiling a book of his teacher's customs. Together, these books constitute the well-known "*minhag* of Austria," and from them all important Ashkenazi customs developed – in particular the order of prayer and the festivals – down to the latest periods. Also deserving mention is the importance of the *Mordekhai* of *Mordecai b. Hillel which served as a primary work to which various Ashkenazi scholars, particularly in the 15th century, added their local customs, thus creating many different texts of the *Mordekhai*.

From the 15th century *minhagim* literature in Germany held an important place, without precedent in the world of *halakhah* and rabbinical literature. Moreover during this period the status of the *minhag* was raised to such a high level that great scholars and leading personalities of the period speak with great respect even about the customs of women and children and ascribe to custom a degree of authority exceeding that of the normative *halakhah* which is independent of custom. In opposition to the view of 19th-century Jewish historians, that the inordinate devotion to the writing of *minhagim* books in Germany in the 15th century testifies to the deterioration of intellectual creativity occasioned by the many persecutions with which this period was marked, it should be stressed that this tendency is evidence of a completely different process; namely, to a drawing near of the contemporary rabbis and leaders to the masses and their effort to transmit the practices of Judaism to the masses as a whole instead of to a mere handful of students. From the scholarly point of view, research into *minhagim* literature is very difficult, because these works have frequently been copied from one manuscript to another, and in the process sections of the halakhic discussions have been omitted, and glosses, supplements, **hassagot*, and corrections have been added by the various copyists, who tried to adjust the work to the local prevailing custom as it was known to them, or at least to interweave this custom into the earlier work. This feature is especially noticeable in the *minhag* book of Abraham Klausner, as it has been preserved in the printed edition (Riva di Trento, 1558) and in the manuscripts which are so completely surrounded by glosses and comments that it is no longer possible to distinguish the actual text from the additions.

[Israel Moses Ta-Shma]

Modern Period

In more recent times, the *minhagim* literature was enriched by works that sought to give reasons for each *minhag*. Among the more popular were *Ta'amei ha-Minhagim* (1896), by A.I. Sperling and *Oẓar kol Minhagei Yeshurun* (1917), by A.E. Hirshovitz. The reasons given are often far fetched and jarring to the modern ear. More recent works describe the *minhagim* lucidly and give reasons based on research and scholarship. Two examples are *Ziv ha-Minhagim* by J.D. Singer (1965), and *Sefer ha-Toda'ah* by Eliyahu Kitov, 2 vols. (1958–60; *Book of our Heritage*, 3 vols., 1968). Both follow the traditional pattern of the calendar.

The establishment of the State of Israel and the ingathering of the exiles has added impetus to the study of the *minhagim* of the various communities of the Diaspora, particularly of the Oriental communities. The latter is pursued particularly by the Ben Zvi Institute in Jerusalem, which has already published a number of studies. Of the *minhagim* of other communities the following have been republished: *Sefer Ereẓ Ḥayyim*, by Ḥayyim Sithon (1968), and *Sefer Ereẓ Yisrael*, by Y.M. Tukazinsky (1966). Of special note is the exhaustive study of Jacob Gellis on *Minhagei Ereẓ Israel* (1968).

[Isaac Klein]

Illustrations on *Minhagim* Books

A different kind of *minhagim* books were written for popular use, and, since they were designed also for women, many were written in Yiddish. They were usually arranged according to the order of the religious year and it was customary to add to their interest by the inclusion of illustrations. The antisemitic publications of the apostate J. *Pfefferkorn (*Judenbeichte*, 1508) contain illustrations of Jewish observances which may be based on an authentic prototype.

The Prague *Birkat ha-Mazon* ("Grace after Meals"), of which one copy has survived, is the first Hebrew work of the type known to contain such illustrations. The earliest published illustrated *minhagim* book is that of Venice of 1593. Its text was based on a similar work edited by one Simeon Ashkenazi in 1590. The 1593 edition, though printed in Italy, is in Yiddish. It was no doubt published partly for export and partly for the use of the Ashkenazi Jews then living in the north of Italy. It was accompanied by a series of woodcuts illustrating various observances and customs of Jewish religious life throughout the year, the participants dressed in the unmistakable German style. These illustrations became very popular. They were repeated but with growing indistinction in all manner of editions produced in Amsterdam and northern Europe from the second half of the 17th century onward. The same woodcut sometimes serves to illustrate two different subjects in different editions. Thus the Sabbath before Passover and the Day of Atonement is illustrated by a scene showing the delivery of the special sermon on that occasion. They are still reproduced to illustrate Dutch Jewish social life of the 17th–18th centuries, whereas they in fact belong to a much earlier period and in great part to another environment. In 1601 another *minhagim* book appeared in Venice with a series of remarkable woodcuts, far superior to the earlier edition and clearly illustrating the Italian Jewish environment.

A *minhagim* book produced in 1693 for the Sephardi community of Amsterdam but with illustrations in some cases showing typical Ashkenazi costume has some independent interest and attraction. Unfortunately this one was not imitated later. The imitative editions of Prague of 1665, of Frankfurt c. 1674, and of Hamburg 1729 deserve cursory mention. That of Dyhernfurth of 1692, edited by S. Bass, has certain independent elements but like the earlier ones is poorly executed. The Frankfurt edition of 1717 has half a dozen badly executed cuts (most of them repeated in the 1729 edition) reflecting tenth-century German Jewish customs and usages. The *minhagim* books as a whole, but particularly the hitherto neglected Venice edition of 1601, are of considerable importance for the study of Jewish social life. Of particular significance are the female costumes, the ritual details (e.g., the form of the Sabbath lamp and the *Havdalah appurtenances), the interior of the synagogue and the separation of the sexes, the wedding ceremony, the Purim mummers, and even the barber's shop included to illustrate Lag ba-Omer.

[Cecil Roth]

BIBLIOGRAPHY: Guedemann, Gesch Erz, 3 (1888), 12ff.; Weiss, Dor, 5 (1904[4]), index; Elbogen, Gottesdienst, 368ff., 565f.; S. Assaf, *Sifran shel Rishonim* (1935); I. Elfenbein (ed.), *Sefer Minhagim de-Rabbi Maharam b. Barukh mi-Rothenburg* (1938), 7–8; M.J. Sachs, *Kunteres Minhagei Ereẓ Yisrael* (1951); Baron, Social[2], 6 (1958), 129–30, 391–2; Zinberg, Sifrut, 3 (1958), 194ff.; D. Cassel, in: *Jubelschrift… Zunz* (1884), 122–37. ILLUSTRATIONS: Mayer, Art, nos. 60, 452; A.M. Habermann, in: Roth, Art, 478.

MINḤAH (Heb. מִנְחָה), the afternoon prayer service, one of the three daily services of the Jewish liturgy. The name of this prayer is derived from Elijah's devotions "at the time of the offering of the evening (*minḥah*) offering" (I Kings 18:36). One tradition ascribes the institution of this service to Isaac, who "went out to meditate in the field at eventide" (Gen. 24:63), while another attributes the formalization of the three daily prayer services to the men of the *Great Synagogue as substitutes for the daily sacrifices, with the *Minḥah* prayer taking the place of the lamb sacrificed in the Temple at dusk (Num. 28:8; Ber. 26b). The custom of three daily prayers is also implied by Daniel 6:11. The *Minḥah* prayer consists of **Ashrei* (Ps. 145, preceded by Ps. 84:5 and 144:15 and closed by Ps. 115:18), the **Amidah*, **Taḥanun*, and concludes with the **Aleinu*. On Sabbaths and fast days, a portion of the Torah is read before the *Amidah* (see *Torah, Reading of). In some rites, portions dealing with the daily sacrifices are read before *Ashrei*. The time for the recitation of the *Minḥah* prayer begins at the conclusion of six and one-half hours of the day. In calculating this time, an "hour" is one-twelfth of the length of the day. *Minḥah* prayed at this time is known as *Minḥah Gedolah* ("major"). *Minḥah* recited after nine and one-half hours of the day is called *Minḥah Ketannah* ("minor"). R. Judah set the final time for the *Minḥah* prayer until midway (*pelag*) through the time designated for the *Minḥah Ketannah*, or until one and one-quarter hours before sunset. The law is, however, in accordance with the opinion that the *Minḥah* may be recited until sunset, which is calculated to occur at the conclusion of the 12th hour of the day (Ber. 4:1; Ber. 26b–27a). As a precaution lest people forget to pray the afternoon prayer, the rabbis ruled that it is forbidden to commence a large business transaction or sit down to a banquet once the time has begun for the *Minḥah Gedolah*, without having previously recited the prayer. Likewise, it is forbidden to begin a minor transaction or partake of an ordinary meal after the time for the *Minḥah Ketannah* (Shab. 1:2; Shab. 9b). It seems that some made it a practice to pray both at *Minḥah Gedolah* and *Minḥah Ketannah*. However, *Asher b. Jehiel ruled that it is forbidden to do so (resp. 4:13). According to the Shulḥan Arukh (OḤ 234), it is permitted to recite the *Minḥah* prayer twice, provided one is recited as an obligatory prayer (*ḥovah*) and the other as a voluntary act (*reshut*). This, however, is only allowed for the extremely pious who are certain that both their prayers will be recited with true devotion. Otherwise, the additional prayer will be considered an unwelcome addition in accordance with the exhortation of Isaiah: "To what purpose is the multitude of your sacrifices unto Me?" (Isa. 1:11). The third meal on the Sabbath (see **Se'udah Shelishit*) is usually eaten between *Minḥah* and *Ma'ariv*. During daily worship, the *Minḥah* prayer in the synagogue is usually delayed until near sunset in order that the congregation may assemble to pray *Ma'ariv* shortly after the *Minḥah* service is completed (see *Magen Avraham* to Sh. Ar., OḤ 233:1).

BIBLIOGRAPHY: Idelsohn, Liturgy, 118, 145; Elbogen, Gottesdienst, 98f., 117–20.

[Aaron Rothkoff]

MINIS, family of original settlers of Savannah, Georgia. ABRAHAM MINIS (1694?–1757) arrived in Savannah with his wife ABIGAIL (1701–1794), two daughters, LEAH and ESTHER, and brother SIMON in 1733. Four sons and three daughters were born in Savannah. When fear of Florida's Spaniards drove Sephardi Jews from Georgia by 1741, only the Minis and Sheftall families, Ashkenazi in origin, remained. After trying farming unsuccessfully, Abraham began trading and shipping, and soon became an official supplier for General Oglethorpe. Upon Abraham's death, his widow Abigail, aided by her sons, continued his import business, and expanded their land holdings in Georgia to more than 2,500 acres. At the outbreak of the revolution, PHILIP MINIS (1734–1789), Abraham's only surviving son, was made acting paymaster and commissary general for Georgia, subsequently advancing $11,000 of his own funds to Virginia and North Carolina troops in Georgia. In 1779 he and Levi Sheftall guided Count d'Estaing and General Franklin in their unsuccessful attempt to recapture Savannah. The entire Minis family moved to Charleston, but Abigail secured agreement from the royal governor not to confiscate her property, and when the British left Savannah the family returned. Upon the reorganization of Savannah's Congregation Mikveh Israel in 1786, Philip was elected president. The following year he became a warden of the city, holding both posts until his death.

BIBLIOGRAPHY: M.H. Stern, in: AJHSQ, 52 (1963), 169–99; 54 (1965), 243–77; J.R. Marcus, *Early-American Jewry*, 2 (1953), passim; Rosenbloom, Biogr Dict, 113f., incl. bibl.

[Malcolm H. Stern]

MINKIN, JACOB SAMUEL (1885–1962), U.S. Conservative rabbi and author. Minkin was born in Russian Poland and received his education in Prague. He immigrated to the United States in 1904, earned a B.A. from Columbia University in 1908, and was ordained at the *Jewish Theological Seminary in 1910, where he earned his D.H.L. in 1935. Minkin's first pulpit was with Congregation Anshe Shalom in Hamilton, Ontario, Canada (1910–17), where he organized Jewish education classes and an evening school teaching English to Jewish immigrants. The program was so successful that the city's Board of Education adopted the school and appointed Minkin superintendent of Hamilton night schools. In 1919, he was appointed rabbi of Temple Beth El in Rochester, New York, a newly established Reform congregation that Minkin led into the Conservative movement. In 1922, he began writing a syndicated column, *News of the Jewish World*, which appeared in more than 50 newspapers for eight years. In 1929, he became rabbi of Inwood Hebrew Congregation in New York City (1929–33), before leaving the congregational rabbinate to devote more time to scholarly research and writing. He took a part-time position as Jewish chaplain of Fordham Hospital in New York, where he remained for 25 years. Minkin wrote biographies of outstanding Jewish men of the ancient and medieval worlds, a study of the contribution of Jewish thought to modern philosophy, and one of the first books in English on the history and founders of the Ḥasidic movement. His works include *The Romance of Hassidism* (1935); *Herod: A Biography* (1936); *Abarbanel and the Expulsion of the Jews from Spain* (1938); *The World of Moses Maimonides* (1957); posthumously, *The Shaping of the Modern Mind: The Life and Thought of the Great Jewish Philosophers* (1963); and *Gabriel da Costa* (1969).

BIBLIOGRAPHY: P.S. Nadell, *Conservative Judaism in America: A Biographical Dictionary and Sourcebook* (1988).

[Bezalel Gordon (2nd ed)]

MINKOFF, NAHUM BARUCH (1893–1958), Yiddish poet, critic, literary historian. Born in Warsaw, he immigrated to the U.S. in 1914 and graduated from New York University's Law School in 1921. But instead of practicing law, he taught at Jewish schools, the Jewish Teachers' Seminary, the New School for Social Research, and edited the Yiddish literary monthly *Tsukunft*. Together with the poets A. *Glantz-Leyeles and Jacob *Glatstein, he issued the first manifesto of the *In-Zikh group, emphasizing modernism, cosmopolitanism, and individualism. In his five collections of poetry published between 1924 and 1952, Minkoff tried to analyze emotions and moods intellectually. He succeeded in his poems on the Holocaust, *Baym Rand* ("At the Edge," 1945). As a trained musician, he had an impeccable ear for tonal effects and for verse melodies. His critical essays and studies in literary history strengthened his position in Yiddish literature. He wrote studies of Elijah *Levita (1950), *Glueckel of Hameln (1952), and a monumental work in three volumes, *Pionern fun Yidisher Poezye in Amerike* ("Pioneers of Yiddish Poetry in America," 1956). Regarding literary criticism as a scientific discipline, he attempted an intellectual, objective evaluation and classification of writers and their works – an approach which had found embodiment in his earlier works of criticism in the books *Yidishe Klasiker Poetn* ("Yiddish Classic Poets," 1939), *Zeks Yidishe Kritiker* ("Six Yiddish Critics," 1954), and *Literarishe Vegn* ("Literary Ways," 1955).

BIBLIOGRAPHY: Rejzen, Leksikon, 2 (1927), 425ff.; LNYL, 5 (1963), 656–62; *N.B. Minkoff 1893–1958* (1959); A. Glantz-Leyeles, *Velt un Vort* (1958), 110–35; S. Bickel, *Shrayber fun Mayn Dor* (1958), 222–30; J. Glatstein, *In Tokh Genumen* (1960), 301–5.

[Shlomo Bickel]

MINKOWSKI, EUGÈNE (1885–1972), French existentialist psychiatrist. Eugène Minkowski, born in St. Petersburg, studied medicine and was appointed psychiatrist at the Henri Rousselle Hospital in Paris from 1925. He had already come under the influence of the Zurich school of psychiatry led by Eugen Bleuler, which included Ludwig Binswanger the existentialist psychiatrist whom he met in 1922. In 1921 he wrote an analysis of Bleuler's conception of schizophrenia, "*La schizophrénie et la notion de la maladie mentale.*" This was a precursor of his book, *La Schizophrénie* (1927), in which Minkowski maintained that insanity was nothing more than an exaggeration of the individual's habitual character. The influence of Henri *Bergson is seen in his belief that the patient's impetus toward integration with reality was reduced and he existed in a world of his own. In the case of the schizophrenic, the dynamic functions of mental life were impaired and contact with reality lost. From Edmund *Husserl, he took his views on "phenomenology" as the study of immediate experiences in a living and concrete fashion of reality. Minkowski's existentialist views are in evidence generally in his writings. In *Les notions de distance vecue et d'ampleur de la vie* (*Journal de Psychologie*, 1930), he stated that the patient affirms his relation to a "becoming" around himself in which relationship he is able to grow and which contains all the vital dynamics of the human personality. In 1933 he published *Le Temps Vécu* and in 1936, *Vers une Cosmologie*. His many shorter works appeared regularly each year from 1921, except for the war years, in various medical journals. He served on the executive of the French *ORT and was honorary president of the world *OSE union. His wife FRANCOISE MINKOWSKI, a psychologist, carried out clinical work with the Rorschach test in the area of epilepsy, the typology of personality, and the rapport or detachment of the schizophrenic. In her book *Le Rorschach* (1956), she developed the Rorschach test as a clinical instrument analyzing specific dynamic factors rather than providing only a diagnosis. Her study of Van Gogh, *Van Gogh, sa vie, sa maladie et son oeuvre* (1963), confirmed her findings that the sensory type lives in the abstract and her work on childrens' drawings is set out in *De van Gogh et Seurat aux dessins d'enfants*. MIECZYSLAW MINKOWSKI (1884–1972), Swiss neurologist and brother of Eugene, was a research worker in the Pavlov Physiological Laboratory in St. Petersburg from 1907 to 1908 and worked in a neuropsychiatric clinic in Berlin from 1909 to 1911. In 1928 he became a professor of neurology at Zurich University and the president of the Swiss Neurological Society (1943–46). He wrote a number of neurological research papers beginning in 1925 with "Zum gegenwaertigen Stand der Lehre von den Reflexen." His work on the foetus included "Prenatal neuropathologic changes leading to neurological or mental disturbances" and his integrative views are expressed in "Neurobiologie, Moral und Religion" (1963). He was the president of the Swiss friends of the Hebrew University, Jerusalem from 1932 to 1947.

BIBLIOGRAPHY: *Cahiers du Groupe Françoise Minkowska* (1965), 169–75; *Bulletin du Groupement Français du Rorschach* (July 1952); *Mieczyslaw Minkowski zum 70. Geburtstag* (1954), 23–33.

[Louis Miller]

MINKOWSKI, HERMANN (1864–1909), German mathematician. Minkowski, who was born in Alexoten, Lithuania, was taken to Koenigsberg, Germany, by his parents when he was eight years old. He held chairs of mathematics at Koenigsberg in 1895, Zurich in 1896, and in Goettingen (where a special chair was created for him) in 1902. In 1881 the Paris Academy of Science offered their prize for an investigation of the representation of integers as sums of squares. Although only a freshman, he produced a brilliant paper which went far beyond his terms of reference. The Academy overlooked his writing in German, a language not permitted by the prize regulations, and awarded him a prize. Minkowski's early work was on the theory of numbers. Apart from some work of *Eisenstein and others, Minkowski is entitled to nearly all the credit for creating the geometry of numbers. He was one of the earliest mathematicians to realize the significance of *Cantor's theory of sets at a time when this theory was not appreciated by most mathematicians. The later work of Minkowski was inspired by *Einstein's special theory of relativity which was first published in 1905. He produced the four-dimensional formulation of relativity which has given rise to the term "Minkowski space." He also made contributions to the theories of electrodynamics and hydrodynamics. The collected works of Minkowski were edited by D. Hilbert in two volumes and published in 1911 in Leipzig. The first volume contains a biographical article by Hilbert. In addition to his papers, he published the book *Diophantische Approximationen* (1907).

BIBLIOGRAPHY: J.C. Poggendorff, *Biographisch-literarisches Handwoerterbuch...der exakten Wissenschaften*, 5 (1926), s.v.

[Barry Spain]

MINKOWSKI, PINCHAS ("**Pinie**"; 1859–1924), Russian cantor and composer. He was born in Belaya Tserkov, Ukraine, where his father was the town cantor. Minkowski received his basic training from his father, and joined the choir of Nissan

*Spivak ("Belzer") in Kishinev. At the age of 18, he was appointed Spivak's successor and three years later became chief cantor of the Choral Synagogue ("Chor-Schul") in Kishinev. After further study in Vienna, he sang in Kherson, Lemberg, and Odessa, and spent three years at the Kahal Adas Yeshurun Synagogue in New York, but was recalled to Odessa in 1892 as chief cantor of the Brody Synagogue, an office he held for 30 years. Minkowski had a tenor voice of natural sweetness though lacking in power. He avoided extraneous effects such as word repetition, falsetto, and needless coloraturas. A prominent member of the intellectual group which flourished in Odessa, headed by *Bialik, he lectured at the Jewish Conservatory, was chairman of the Ha-Zamir ("The Nightingale") musical society, and published many articles on *ḥazzanut* and Jewish music, in Hebrew, Yiddish, and German. After the Russian Revolution he left for the United States, where he continued to sing and lecture.

Many of Minkowski's compositions remained in manuscript and are preserved, with his papers, in the Jewish National and University Library, Jerusalem. His setting of Bialik's poem *Shabbat ha-Malkah* ("Sabbath the Queen"), to a chorale-like melody, became a much-loved song for Friday evening in Israel and in many communities and synagogues abroad.

BIBLIOGRAPHY: Sendrey, Music, indexes; Friedmann, Lebensbilder, 3 (1927), 55; idem, *Dem Andenken Eduard Birnbaums*, 1 (1922), 131ff.; *Di Khazonim Velt* (Dec. 1933); Jewish Ministers-Cantors Association of America and Canada, *Di Geshikhte fun Khazones* (1924), 88.

[Joshua Leib Ne'eman]

MINNEAPOLIS-ST. PAUL. The Twin Cities of Minneapolis and St. Paul in *Minnesota consist of a metropolitan area of 2.7 million inhabitants, well over half of the state's population. Although settled earlier, St. Paul was smaller, which is reflected in the fact that St. Paul's Jewish population in 2004 was estimated to be almost 11,000, while Minneapolis' was a bit over 29,000. The cities are arranged like beads on a necklace, with the Mississippi River running through both. Settled at different times, the towns have different personalities: St. Paul is sometimes compared to Boston, while Minneapolis is a brash prairie town. St. Paul developed as a river port and later as a wholesaling center, while Minneapolis gained ascendancy as a railroad center as well as for its role in lumber and grain milling. They even differ in ethnic makeup: St. Paul has a high proportion of Irish Catholics while Minneapolis' is Scandinavian. The cities' Jewish development also took different trajectories. Today the cities' industrial drivers are high technology, manufacture of scientific instruments and products, industrial machinery, printing, publishing, and food product processing.

St. Paul

Jews were among the earliest settlers in the city, which was incorporated in 1849. By 1856 there were enough Jews to establish Mount Zion Hebrew Congregation. Despite internal rancor, the congregation endured and hired their first rabbi in 1871. The congregation moved toward Reform during his stay, evidenced by the fact that in 1871 the women's auxiliary suggested purchasing an organ. Members were both American-born and of German origin who became wholesale and retail merchants. Some took part in civic affairs as well: Jacob J. Noah, son of Mordecai Manuel Noah, was appointed clerk of the Dakota County District Court and elected as the first clerk of the state Supreme Court in 1857. Isaac Cardozo was appointed a deputy of the United States District Court in 1858. He was among the founders of Mount Zion and the first president of B'nai B'rith in Minnesota. St. Paul Jews from German-speaking lands also felt a kinship with the growing German population of the city, joining their singing societies and social clubs.

After the Civil War, Jewish migration from Eastern Europe began. The first group arrived with both funds and skills but with different modes of worship. They established Sons of Jacob, incorporated in 1875, but often lived in the same neighborhood as the German Jews. The year 1882 began with the arrival by train of some 200 desperate refugees fleeing from the Russian Empire, who overwhelmed the resources of the Mount Zion Congregation. The city of St. Paul helped feed, clothe, and shelter them, and even the Archbishop of St. Paul and Minneapolis donated funds for their welfare. The population grew chiefly through chain migration as those newly settled sent back funds for their relatives. It was augmented through select migration through Galveston and aided by efforts of B'nai Brith members to find jobs for them. They found jobs as peddlers, craftsmen, shopkeepers, and tailors.

Immigrants settled in two neighborhoods near downtown, the West Side and Capitol City areas. Each had numerous Orthodox synagogues, European-style *Talmud Torahs*, and Socialist clubhouses, and each had a settlement house. In both cases, the houses were either founded or supported by women who were members of Mount Zion. St. Paul German Jews, in general, practiced benevolence at arm's length. Beginning in the 1910s, movement to middle class neighborhoods occurred. Here within a four block radius could be found a Jewish Community Center, a modern *Talmud Torah*, and the Reform and Conservative synagogues (Temple of Aaron, the city's first Conservative synagogue, was founded in 1912). A nearby commercial street supported kosher butcher shops and other ethnic commerce.

Although antisemitism was certainly not unknown, particularly in the 1920s and 1930s, St. Paul's large Catholic community has generally accommodated Jewish participation in civic affairs. Housing restrictions and employment discrimination were not as severe as in Minneapolis.

The city's Jewish population did not truly unite until World War II. It settled about 400 Displaced Persons after the war. Movement toward the western section of the city began in the 1940s and toward suburbs south of the Mississippi River in the 1960s. Voluntarism was strong during this era: St. Paul Section of National Council of Jewish Women (NCJW) 1964 project at McKinley School served as a model for the Headstart program. Russian-speaking immigrants began arriving in the 1970s and were well looked after by the community. During the 1960s, the Lubavitchers established a synagogue and later a day school. They also maintain Bais Chanah, established in 1971, which draws women from all over the world. The community founded a Jewish day school in 1982. Beth Jacob, a newer Conservative synagogue, was founded in 1985. Norman Coleman was the mayor of St. Paul before his election to the Senate.

Minneapolis

Minneapolis's Jews did not establish a synagogue until 1878 although the city was incorporated in 1866. Shaarei Tov (later Temple Israel) was founded by German Jews who lived south of the downtown area near a chain of lakes. They evinced Reform practices as early as the 1880s. Although south Minneapolis had a Romanian Jewish neighborhood until the early 1950s, Eastern European Jews tended to settle on the north side of downtown. The area housed Jews from the 1880s through the 1950s. Interestingly, the same area contained public housing near the downtown section, built in the 1930s and one quarter of which was reserved for Jews, as well as mansions near the opposite end bordering the city limits. Jews of every economic stratum mixed in the public schools, *Talmud Torah*, and in neighborhood businesses.

The city's civic structure was tightly controlled by a group who had arrived from New England and who developed the city's industries, particularly that of flour milling. They were not hospitable to sharing power with the enormous Scandinavian population and certainly not with Jews. A few women of intellect were spared this treatment: Nina Morais Cohen, daughter of Rabbi Sabato Morais and wife of attorney Emanuel Cohen, was a founding member of the Women's City Club. She also founded the Minneapolis chapter of NCJW in 1894 and educated a cadre of women, even those of Eastern European origin.

It may be a result of this exclusion, or the long-term effects of a community unifier such as Rabbi Samuel Deinard, Lithuanian-born rabbi of Temple Israel, who attended services at Orthodox synagogues on the second day of Jewish holidays and preached in Yiddish, but the German and Eastern European Jews of Minneapolis coalesced more rapidly and created a strong infrastructure with the full panoply of Jewish institutions

Chief among these was the community-sponsored Minneapolis Talmud Torah, founded in 1894 and renowned for its early embrace of teaching *Ivrit be-Ivrit* and the number of students who became rabbis. Beth El (Conservative) Synagogue, founded in 1921 is also an offshoot of the Talmud Torah. The community also supported an orphanage for the temporary placement of children in need, a community center, Zionist and Socialist meeting halls, numerous synagogues, loan societies, and a Hachnosses Orchim. An Orthodox day school was founded in 1944 and a non-denominational day school in the 1980s. A number of these institutions were beneficiaries of the Minneapolis Jewish Federation, founded in 1930 and representing all persuasions within the community.

Synagogues were established as well. Kenesseth Israel, founded in 1891 was the first Orthodox place of worship, and Adath Jeshurun became the first Conservative one in 1907. The city had at least seven other Orthodox synagogues.

It took a massive exposé in 1946 by journalist Cary McWilliams called, "Minneapolis: The Curious Twin" to call attention to the fact that while St. Paul Jews felt they were full civic participants, Minneapolis Jews endured many sorts of discrimination. Entire neighborhoods were "off limits" to Jewish home ownership; the city's major businesses did not hire Jews; organizations such as the Minneapolis Automobile and the Minneapolis Athletic Clubs, the Elks, Rotary, and Lions Clubs excluded Jews. Even the city's hospitals denied admitting privileges to Jewish physicians. One result was the building of Mount Sinai Hospital, which opened its doors in 1951. The election of Hubert Humphrey in 1945 and the formation of the Mayor's Council on Human Relations did effect a change when ordinances to ensure civil rights and discourage housing and job discrimination were passed.

The Jewish community settled about 800 Displaced Persons after World War II. It was always hospitable to Zionism, and a number of Minneapolitans settled on Kibbutz Kefar Blum. The city has the distinction of being home to two national presidents of the National Council of Jewish Women. Fanny Brin served from 1932 to 1938 and throughout her life devoted herself to world disarmament issues. Viola Hymes was president during the early 1960s and also served on the President's Commission on the Status of Women.

The movement to the suburbs began earlier than in St. Paul. During the 1950s young families began purchasing homes in nearby St. Louis Park. Synagogues and a Jewish Community Center soon followed. The torching of North Side businesses during the late 1960s hastened Jewish flight. Since that time, Jews have continued to move both north and west of the city. Two new Reform congregations have also been founded, while the Lubavitch sect also gained adherents. The community has resettled between 4,000 and 6,000 Jews from the Former Soviet Union (FSU), who in 2004 made up 17 per cent of the Jewish population.

While the Jewish community is still vibrant, the 2004 Jewish population study found some worrisome features centered on integration of members of the FSU and intermarried couples.

Although the rivalry between the cities has abated, they still have separate Federation structures and accompanying beneficiary agencies, a mystery to outsiders. They jointly support institutions such as a middle school, Hillel on the University of Minnesota campus, the Jewish Community Relations Council, and the Jewish Historical Society of the Upper Midwest. Rudy *Boschwitz was a U.S. senator and later an ambassador. He was defeated in the 1990 and 1996 Senate races by another Jew, Paul *Wellstone, who died in 2002 in a plane crash as he was running for reelection.

BIBLIOGRAPHY: H. Berman and L.M. Schloff, *Jews in Minnesota,* (2002); L.M. Schloff, *"And Prairie Dogs Weren't Kosher": Jewish Women in the Upper Midwest Since 1854* (1997); W.G. Plaut, *The Jews in Minnesota-the First Seventy-Five Years* (1959); A.I. Gordon, *Jews in Transition,* Twin Cities Jewish Population Study (2004).

[Linda M. Schloff (2nd ed.)]

MINNESOTA, U.S. state in the north central tier with about 4.9 million inhabitants of which the Jewish population is roughly 42,000. (The 2004 Twin Cities' Jewish Population Study found 10,900 Jews in St. Paul and 29,100 in Minneapolis. It is estimated that about 1,000 Jews live in outstate towns, chiefly Duluth and Rochester). While they make up less than 1% of the state's population, Jews comprise about 1.7% of the Twin Cities metropolitan area.

While isolated Jewish fur traders were not rare, the first Jewish community was established in St. Paul, the northernmost steamboat landing on the Mississippi. They found little prejudice in a frontier town and by 1856 formed Mount Zion Hebrew Congregation. Minneapolis just upriver did not grow until the advent of the railroad system. Its pioneer synagogue, Shaarei Tov (later Temple Israel), was not founded until 1878.

These Jewish pioneers arrived from the eastern and southern United States and from Germanic lands with some capital. They became clothing and dry goods merchants, fur traders and cigar makers. Some took part in civic affairs. Impoverished Eastern Europeans arrived beginning in 1882. The population grew chiefly through chain migration as those newly settled sent back funds for their relatives. It was augmented through select migration through Galveston. The newly arrived worked as craftsmen and on railroads, they peddled, collected scrap metal, and sewed in factories. Jews tended not to be employed in the giant state industries, such as lumber, flour milling, and iron mining.

Jews filtered into market towns, such as Austin, Albert Lea, and Mankato, serving as clothing and dry goods purveyors, hide and fur merchants, and scrap metal dealers. After iron ore was discovered nearby, Duluth's Jewish population soared, reaching a peak of about 4,000. This discovery provided the impetus for Duluth's Jews to move inland to newly created towns, such as Virginia, Hibbing, Chisholm, and Eveleth, where they became merchants. Each town once supported a synagogue between about 1905 and the 1950s. The most famous Iron Ranger is undoubtedly Bob Dylan (Robert Zimmerman), who was born and raised in Hibbing. Rochester, renowned for its Mayo Clinic, also has maintained a synagogue. Its population is more transient due to the high proportion of physicians in training at the Mayo Clinic. The state had a peak Jewish population of about 44,000 in 1937. While there has been migration to Sun Cities, it received a modest influx of displaced persons after World War II and a large number of Jews from the Former Soviet Union (FSU). In 2004, this group comprised 17% of the Twin Cities' Jewish population.

By the 1930s, Minneapolis, St. Paul, and Duluth all had established Federations, which supported social service, educational, and defense institutions. Religious institutions and social clubs flourished as well, and Herzl Camp with its Zionist orientation attracted Jewish youth from all over the Upper Midwest. The weekly *American Jewish World*, established in 1912, is still published.

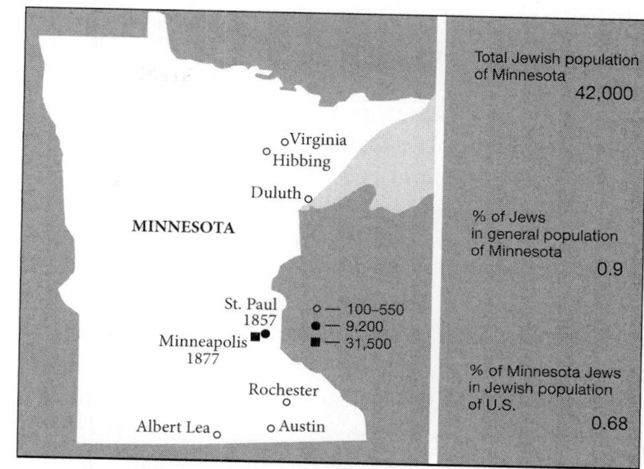

Jewish communities in Minnesota and dates of establishment. Population figures for 2001.

The gubernatorial election of 1938 between Harold Stassen and Elmer Benson used vicious antisemitic cartoons to vilify several of Benson's Jewish supporters. The Minnesota Jewish Council (now called the Jewish Community Relations Council) was created soon after to counter organized antisemitism. The situation changed dramatically after Hubert Humphrey was elected mayor of Minneapolis in 1945 and instituted reforms that were repeated at the state level. Since then, Jews have actively engaged in running for political office. In 1961, Arthur Naftalin was elected mayor of Minneapolis. St. Paul elected Larry Cohen mayor in 1972, a position that hitherto was an Irish Catholic stronghold. Rudy *Boschwitz, elected in 1978, was the state's first Jewish senator. Ironically, he was defeated by another Jew, Paul *Wellstone, in 1990 in a race in which the Jewish identity of Wellstone, who was married to a non-Jewish woman became an issue. The tactic (a nasty letter campaign) backfired against Boschwitz, and Wellstone went to the Senate. Wellstone triumphed over Boschwitz a second time in 1996. Norm Coleman won in 2002 over the successor to Wellstone, who had died during the campaign. So in a state where Jews make up less than 1% of the population, Jewish candidates for U.S. Senate faced each other three times in a dozen years.

Today, the Minnesota Jewish community can be characterized as generally prosperous with great population stability, and a high level of support for communal institutions. The University of Minnesota has a Center for Jewish Studies. The Jay Phillips Center for Jewish-Christian Learning at the University of St. Thomas and St. John's College promote interfaith understanding. The Jewish Historical Society of the Upper Midwest interprets the region's Jewish history for Jews and non-Jews alike.

Nevertheless, there are major challenges such as integrating the Jews from the FSU into the general Jewish community and devising ways of embracing the intermarried and their children. Only by inculcating both with a sense of allegiance to Jewish communal institutions will the Minnesota Jewish community remain healthy in the 21st century.

BIBLIOGRAPHY: H. Berman & L.M. Schloff, *Jews in Minnesota* (2002); L.M. Schloff, *"And Prairie Dogs Weren't Kosher": Jewish Women in the Upper Midwest Since 1854* (1997); W.G. Plaut, *The Jews in Minnesota-the First Seventy-Five Years* (1959); Twin Cities Jewish Population Study (2004).

[Linda M. Schloff (2nd ed.)]

MINNITH (Heb. מִנִּית), one of the farthest limits of the area in which Jephthah smote the Ammonites (Judg. 11:33). The wheat of Minnith was traded in exchange for goods from Tyre (Ezek. 27:17). Eusebius (Onom. 132:2) locates the place at the fourth Roman mile on the road from Heshbon to Philadelphia (Rabbath-Ammon). It has accordingly been placed at Khirbat el-Ḥanūttiyya in the fertile Heshbon plain, 6 mi. (c. 9½ km.) north-northeast of Ḥisbān. The earlier identification with Umm al-Ḥanāfish has generally been abandoned.

BIBLIOGRAPHY: C.R. Conder, *Survey of Eastern Palestine* (1889), 246ff.; Schultze, in: PJB, 28 (1932), 75; Abel, Geog, 2 (1938), 388; Glueck, in: AASOR, 18/19 (1939), 161–62; Hentschke, in: ZDPV, 76 (1960), 122; Press, Ereẓ, s.v.; EM, s.v. (incl. bibl.).

[Michael Avi-Yonah]

MINOR, OSIP S. (**Joseph**; 1861–1932), Russian revolutionary and a leader of the Social Revolutionary Party. Born in Minsk, he was the son of Rabbi S.Z. *Minor. While still a student at the University of Moscow, he joined the "People's Will" (Narodnaya Volya) Society. In 1883 he was arrested for the first time, and in 1887 he was exiled to Siberia. After participating in a rebellion of exiles in Yakutsk, he was sentenced to forced labor for life (1889). Freed in 1896, he was banned from living in European Russia. In 1900 he nevertheless returned to Russia and settled in Vilna. He resumed his revolutionary activities, traveled abroad, and was one of the organizers of the Social Revolutionary Party. In 1909 he was again arrested as a result of the intervention of the czarist agent Y.F. *Azeff and was sentenced to ten years' forced labor. He was freed at the time of the Revolution of 1917 and was briefly mayor of Moscow. Minor left Russia in 1919 after the Bolshevik victory and settled in France, where he became chairman of the Society for Assistance to Exiles and Political Prisoners in Russia. He died in Paris. His book *Eto bylo davno* ("It Was Long Ago") appeared posthumously in 1933.

BIBLIOGRAPHY: *Sotsialisticheskiy Vestnik*, 19 (1932), 16; V. Chernov, *Yidishe Tuer in der Partey Sotsial Revolutsionern* (1948), 246–58.

[Yehuda Slutsky]

MINOR, SOLOMON ZALMAN (**Zalkind**; 1826–1900), writer and scholar, one of the pioneers of the Russian-Jewish intelligentsia. As a youth, he entered the newly opened government rabbinical seminary in Vilna and was one of its first two graduates – he was later a Talmud teacher in the seminary. Through the efforts of the *maskilim* he was elected **Kazyonny ravvin* ("government-appointed rabbi") of the Minsk community in 1859. There he opened a Saturday school and a public library. One of the first to preach in Russian in the synagogue, he became well known for his sermons, which were published in book form and served as models for other rabbis ("The Voice of Happiness," 1862, and "Speeches," 1895). Minor was active in the promotion of the *Haskalah in Minsk, and in 1869 he was invited to serve as rabbi in Moscow. In the early 1890s, when the Jews of Moscow were persecuted, he interceded with the authorities on behalf of his community and was consequently expelled from Moscow on the order of the governor of the city, the Grand Duke Sergei. He then returned to Vilna and continued his literary activity there. Minor published many articles in the Russian-Jewish and the Hebrew press, for the most part under the name "Remez." He conducted a debate with antisemites (including the priest *Lutostansky) and was a friend of Tolstoy and directed his studies in Hebrew and the Bible. He was one of the first Jewish scholars to work in the field of the history of Russian Jewry. His son LAZAR (ELIEZER) MINOR was a professor of nervous diseases and another son, Osip *Minor, was a leader of the Social Revolutionary Party.

BIBLIOGRAPHY: J. Slutsky in: *He-Avar*, 7 (1960), 29–48; S. Guenzburg, in: *Knizhki Voskhoda*, 2 (1901), 128–35; A. Katzenelson, in: *Yevreyskaya Starina*, 2 (1909), 175–88.

[Yehuda Slutsky]

MINORCA, Mediterranean island of the Balearic group. The earliest information about the Jews on the island dates from 418 C.E. when Severus, the bishop of Minorca, reports on the victory of Christianity in the island. The agitation he fomented led to the destruction of the synagogue. Many Jews, especially the women, died for their faith: a few succeeded in hiding in the forests and caves. According to Severus he gained 540 Jews for Christianity. While it existed, the community was organized as a national group under the leadership of a "defensor": the last, Theodore, acted as *archisynagogos. There is no information available on the Jews during the Byzantine and Muslim rule. When Minorca was reconquered by the Christians during the reign of James I of Aragon, he received help from the Jews to equip the expedition. Most of the later history of the Jews of Minorca is closely connected with that of their coreligionists in *Majorca. In 1319 King Sancho I declared that they and the Jews of the nearby island of Ibiza were to be included in all the levies imposed upon them by the communal leaders of Majorca. The Jews shared the sufferings of the general population when Minorca was almost depleted of its inhabitants during the *Black Death (1348). After the disorders which swept Spain in 1391, there were apparently no Jews on the island. Nevertheless, a number of Judaizers in Minorca were sentenced by the Inquisition of Majorca which maintained a commission at Mahón. A small Jewish community existed again in Minorca during the temporary English occupation in the 18th century (1720–56; 1762–81).

BIBLIOGRAPHY: Baer, Spain, 1 (1961), 17, 174, 381, 404; P.G. Segeni, *Carta encíclica del obispo Severo* (1937); C. Roth, in: B. Schindler (ed.), *Gaster Anniversary Volume* (1936), 492–7; B. Braunstein, *Chuetas of Majorca* (1936), 118 ff.; J. Parkes, *Conflict of the Church and the Synagogue* (1963), 204–5; López de Meneses, in: *Estudios de edad media de la Corona de Aragon*, 6 (1956), 255, 353, 388. **ADD. BIBLIOGRAPHY:** R. Moulinas, in: REJ, 132 (1973), 605–15; E.D. Hunt, in: *Journal of Theological Studies*, n. s. 33 (1982), 106–23; J. Mascaró Pasarius, in: *Revista de Menorca*, 74 (1983), 241–81; F. Lotter, in: *Proceedings of 9th World Congress of Jewish Studies* (1986), Division B, vol. 1, 23–30; R. Rosselló Vaquer, *Els jueus dins la societat menorquina del segle XIV* (1990).

[Haim Beinart]

MINORITY BLOC (1922–30), political alliance of representatives of the national minorities in Poland created with the aim of obtaining representation in the Sejm corresponding to their numbers in the population – up to 40%. The Bloc was formed in 1922 in reaction to the election regulations issued under the pressure of the extreme nationalist bloc led by the clergymen Lutoslawski, which sought to present to the world an artificial image of a monolithic national state. In the mapping of the constituencies there was blatant discrimination between the Polish ethnographic region and the mixed regions, as well as the intentional addition of rural and urban units to the disadvantage of scattered minorities such as the Jews and the Germans. The common objective of assuring their national rights enabled the parties to overcome the wide differences which prevailed among the various ethnic sections and to establish a countrywide bloc. Its initiator was the German Hasbach, and its executor and organizer was the Zionist leader Yiẓḥak *Gruenbaum. The Ukrainians of Galicia boycotted the elections because in theory they did not yet recognize the Polish government; the Zionists of Galicia therefore presented their own national list. On the other hand, in Congress Poland and in the Belorussian border regions ("Kresy") the overwhelming majority of the Jewish public, with the exception of the *Folkspartei, the *Bund, and the *Po'alei Zion, supported the Bloc. The Poles regarded this union as a hostile act because they suspected its partners of irredentist tendencies and anti-national aims. The elections brought an impressive victory for the Minority Bloc, which won 66 seats, including 17 Jewish ones. The drastic defeat of the Polish lists was most evident in the mixed border regions. In eastern Galicia 15 Jewish representatives were elected as a result of the Ukrainians' abstention and in western Galicia two, so that the "Jewish club" consisted of 34 seats in the Sejm and 12 in the Senate. During the parliamentary term of 1922–27 only loose links were maintained between the minority "clubs," because the policy of all the Polish factions was to achieve the dissolution of the Bloc either by fomenting disunion within its ranks or by promising to fulfill specific demands. In 1923 Premier Sikorski, who headed the Leftist coalition, attempted to win over the Ukrainians and the Belorussians, while in 1925 the *Grabski government endeavored to attract the Jews by means of an "agreement" which became known as the *Ugoda. In 1926 Marshal Pilsudski came to power in the wake of the May coup d'état. The new regime adopted the slogan of "moral improvement" (*sanacja*) and attempted to form a wide public front for constructive purposes. However, the hopes which had been aroused among the national minorities rapidly melted away when the weakening of parliamentary government became apparent and the promises to fulfill national aspirations in culture and education did not materialize. With the approach of the elections of March 1928 a second Minority Bloc was organized. On this occasion it was joined by the Ukrainians of Galicia, and their representative, Dmitri Levitsky, became the active colleague of Gruenbaum and Hasbach. In the meantime, however, conditions had changed. A split, arising out of social differences, had occurred within the minorities. This prevented the affiliation of the Radicals, and the Bloc thus became an association of political parties instead of whole national groupings. The representation of the Jews was also reduced as a result of the departure of all the Galician Zionists, who formed their own national list, and the pro-government bloc consisting of Agudat Israel, the Folkspartei, and a faction of the organization of merchants and craftsmen. In addition to this there were Orthodox and assimilationist Jewish circles that preferred to vote directly for the government list. These differences were responsible for a sharp decrease in the number of Jewish representatives: seven in the Minority Bloc; and six in the National List of Galicia. The other lists did not obtain a single seat.

After the third Sejm was unexpectedly dissolved by the president before the end of its term, new elections were held in 1930 in an atmosphere of growing political suppression. Internal frictions rendered the establishment of a countrywide Zionist list impossible. Among the Ukrainians radical nationalistic feelings were expressed in the thesis that since they constituted a majority in their regions, it was not in their interest to maintain a union with scattered minority groups. The Zionists of Congress Poland under the leadership of Gruenbaum joined forces in six regions with the German minority of central and western Poland – a substitute for the former comprehensive Minority Bloc. The economic businessmen list of Agudat Israel, the Folkspartei, and the merchants also increased their strength. The government employed harsh measures against the candidates of the reduced Minority Bloc, who did not secure more than two seats. The Zionists of Galicia only succeeded in obtaining four seats. Thus ended the attempt to unite the minorities in a common political campaign, and in the relations between the Jews and the other minority groups there were increasing differences, estrangement, and even hostility as a result of the economic and political suffocation of the masses.

BIBLIOGRAPHY: I. Schiper, *Żydzi w Polsce odrodzonej*, 2 (1930), 286–311; L. Halpern, *Polityka żydowska w Sejmie i Senacie Rzeczypospolitej, 1919–1933* (1933). **ADD. BIBLIOGRAPHY:** S. Netzer, *Ma'avak Yehudei Polin al Zekhuyoteihem ha-Ezraḥiyot ve-*

ha-Le'ummiyot (1980), 282–314; M. Landau, *Gush ha-Mi'utim* (1922); "*Makhshir Beḥirot o Etgar Medini*," in: *Galed*, 4–5 (1978), 365–96; P. Korzec, "Der Block der Nationalen Minderheiten im Parlamentarismus Polens des Jahres 1922," in: *Zeitschrift fuer Ostforschung*, 2 (1975); S. Rudnicki, *Zydzi w Parlamencie drugiej Rzecyzpospolitej* (2004), 126–74, 249–64, 307–26.

[Moshe Landau]

MINORITY RIGHTS, rights enjoyed by Jews and other ethnic minorities between the two world wars in some countries, mainly eastern and southeastern Europe, according to the provisions of the minorities treaties at the Versailles Peace Conference, 1919. In all the other states the treatment of minority nationals was regarded as an internal matter, subject only to the state's own laws and not to international law. In those states which were bound, between the two world wars, by the minorities treaties, Jews and other minority nationals were guaranteed certain minimal rights, and the *League of Nations created a machinery for supervising their implementation. These were rights granted in addition to civil, political, and religious freedoms. Whereas the *French Revolution and *Napoleon brought *emancipation of the individual in parts of Europe as an equal citizen of the state, the minority rights expanded the concept of equality to include ethnic and cultural distinctions within the territory of the state. These national rights differed from medieval *autonomy in that the latter presupposed a society that is subdivided into corporations, each of which lives according to its own distinct law. The minority rights, on the other hand, posited an egalitarian society, where the individual enjoyed individual rights plus his rights as a person belonging to an ethnic or religious minority. The proponents of the idea gave it widely differing interpretations. Minority rights tended to embrace largely secular, as opposed to religious, elements; therefore the terms cultural, national, ethnic, or linguistic are interchangeable with the term minority.

Development of the Idea

The idea originated at the beginning of the 20th century in the multi-national states of Eastern Europe where it was impossible to carve out territorial units to accommodate particular ethnic groups. Karl Renner, an Austrian socialist, published in 1902 his *Der Kampf der oesterreichischen Nationen um den Staat* in which he developed the proposition that national affiliation was primarily a personal and not a territorial matter. He therefore advocated that the state represent a federation of nationalities, without separation of state and nationality, similar to the separation of Church and state. Since the Jews represented an extraterritorial minority *par excellence* the idea that they constitute a distinct nationality and are therefore entitled to a special national existence appealed very strongly to East European Jewish intellectuals. Chaim *Zhitlowsky and Simon *Dubnow in Russia, and Nathan *Birnbaum in Austria, attracted at first only a small group of intellectuals to their ideas of national autonomy. Zhitlowsky, an émigré socialist revolutionary, sought to synthesize socialism with nationalism as early as 1883. He demanded for Jews "national equal rights with all peoples" and asserted that only through the Yiddish language could the social and national revival of the Jewish people be effected. He maintained that one could remain identified with the Jewish nationality even if abandoning the Jewish religion. He urged the Jewish masses to participate in the class struggle as a national unit. Alone among the cosmopolitan Jewish socialists he favored national socialism.

In 1897 he began publishing philosophical studies in Jewish history and a comprehensive program of action which later appeared in book form as *Pisma o starom i novom yevreystvie* ("Letters on Old and Modern Judaism," 1907). His main thesis was that national consciousness consists mainly of spiritual-cultural determinants and that these national characteristics can be maintained by the Jews in the future in the lands of their dispersion, just as they have survived the lack of territory or unity of language since the end of the second commonwealth. After emancipation of the individual the Jews as a group should be granted national self-government within the framework of the state along with other national minorities. His secularization of the national idea as opposed to those who saw the essence of Judaism in religion, and his optimistic view of the future of Judaism in the Diaspora, were the main underpinnings of his insistence on national cultural autonomy.

Popular Movement

These meager beginnings in academic speculation turned into a powerful popular movement during the 1905 revolution in Russia (1904–07), petered out from 1907 to 1914, and then gained in volume in both east and west during World War I. A number of middle-class parties and socialists tended toward "*assimilation"; i.e. they sought only civil and political rights, and shied away from nationalist identification. Before long, however, *autonomism developed into a mighty stream; most Jewish parties adopted Diaspora nationalist plans in their platforms. The League for Equal Rights for Jews, consisting of middle-class liberals and Zionists, met illegally in 1905 and declared in favor of "civil, political, and national rights… the freedom of national-cultural self-determination… a comprehensive *kehillah* autonomy, freedom of language and of school education." This was adopted despite the wishes of the top leadership which was anti-nationalistic. The Zionists, too, at their conference in *Helsingfors, Finland, in 1906, demanded "the recognition of the Jewish nationality with the right of self-government in all affairs of Jewish life." This was achieved although large segments of political Zionists clung to the doctrine that creative Jewish living was possible in Palestine only. In 1918 the Zionist headquarters issued the "Copenhagen Manifesto," which demanded a national home in Palestine, and in all other countries full equality of rights, including "national autonomy, cultural, social, and political, for the Jewish population of countries largely settled by Jews, as well as of all other countries whose Jewish population demands it"; and admission into the "League of Free Nations."

The followers of Dubnow's Diaspora nationalism formed the *Folkspartei (People's Party) in 1906, only to remain a mere handful. The *Bund in Russia, Poland, and Lithuania was organized in 1897. Though it initially had made the class struggle paramount in its program, it soon became a major protagonist of autonomism, with especial emphasis on Yiddish as the national language. The proletarian Zionist groups, the *Jewish Socialist Workers' Party (Sejmists), the *Jewish Social Democratic Party, *Po'alei Zion, and the *Zionist Socialist Workers' Party, more or less hesitantly, also came around to demand national self-determination. Similar agitation took place in Austrian Jewry and to a lesser extent in the Ottoman Empire and the United States. Thus in the space of less than two decades national autonomy grew from a mere theory into a mass movement. During World War I activity was transferred to the west. In the United States, after several years of numerous meetings, the *American Jewish Congress was organized in 1918 to present the Jewish case for Palestine and minority rights for the Jews of Europe at the Peace Conference. They adopted a "Jewish Bill of Rights" to be presented to the conference. In addition to guarantees of equal civil, political, religious, and national rights, it proposed autonomous management of communal institutions by minorities, respect for the languages of ethnic groups, and no discrimination against Sabbath observance. Whereas in the U.S. a modicum of accommodations was arrived at between the nationalists and the members of the non-nationalist *American Jewish Committee, no such rapprochement was achieved in England or France.

At the Peace Conference

At the Versailles Conference the Jews assumed leadership in the struggle for minority rights. Delegations and petitions from Jews in many countries began to arrive in Paris. Immediately an attempt was made to form a united front, and a Committee of Jewish Delegations (*Comité des Délégations Juives) was formed. Most of the erstwhile opponents bowed to the desires of the East European Jews who were directly concerned. The French and British delegations, who refused to join the Committee of Jewish Delegations, agreed not to oppose actively the efforts of the majority to attain national rights.

Minority Treaties

After prolonged and stubborn negotiations that lasted in some cases until 1923, minorities treaties were signed by the newly created states of Poland, Czechoslovakia, Romania, Yugoslavia, and Greece; and by the defeated states of Austria, Hungary, Bulgaria, and Turkey; declarations of willingness to abide by minority stipulations were secured from Lithuania, Latvia, Estonia, Albania, and several other localities. Iraq made its Minorities Declaration when it became independent in 1932. The Polish Minority Treaty became the model for all the rest. It had 12 articles. Some of them dealt with the basic civil, political, and religious rights of minorities. The specific rights of minority nations were dealt with in detail. Polish nationals were to have the free use "of any language in private intercourse, in commerce, in religion, in the press, or in publications of any kind, or at public meetings." Minority nationals were guaranteed "the use of their own language, either orally or in writing, before the courts." They were also authorized "to establish and control, at their own expense, charitable, educational, religious and social institutions, with the right to use their own language and to exercise their religion freely therein." Minorities were guaranteed the right to establish schools in their own language, and to obtain an equitable share of public funds for their "educational, religious, and charitable purposes." Finally, in view of the special position of the Jews in Poland, who were not concentrated in any one area in compact masses but were diffused over the entire country, and in view of Polish antisemitism, two special "Jewish articles" were inserted to safeguard their unique position. Article 10 read:

> Educational Committees appointed locally by the Jewish communities of Poland will, subject to the general control of the State, provide for the distribution of the proportional share of public funds allocated to Jewish schools in accordance with article 9, and for the organization and management of these schools.

Article 11 provided that: "Jews shall not be compelled to perform any act which constitutes a violation of their Sabbath," with specific reference to attendance at courts of law, and elections or registration for electoral or other purposes. Other articles dealt with enforcement. The minority obligations must be recognized as fundamental law of the country. Infractions were to be supervised by the League of Nations, and member-states of the League Council were entitled to appeal to a world court. Some of the other countries resolutely resisted the minorities provisions, but were forced to sign them. The "Jewish articles" were omitted in some treaties. There was general satisfaction among Jews with the provisions of the Minorities Treaties. Some were jubilant over the new era that had dawned to enable them to live their own lives and to develop their own culture.

Implementation of Treaty Provisions

The minorities system represented a remarkable experiment in international control that lasted some 20 years. With all its faults, substantive and procedural, it could have developed into a major force for minority protection. However, it crumbled along with the League of Nations that sponsored it. The system helped prevent serious disturbances by providing minorities an outlet in the international provisions for resolving grievances and by serving as a brake on oppressive chauvinism. In most minority states there were provisions for national education, and protection against undesirable assimilation, and some of them experimented, on their own initiative, in autonomous minority institutions on a considerable scale. The main weakness lay in the refusal of minority states to act on their international pledges in good faith. Some of the substantive provisions of the Minority Treaties lacked precision. The procedure in hearing complaints was faulty. The League itself did not pursue recalcitrant states with proper vigor. Only the Permanent Court of International Justice at The Hague tried valiantly, in two cases brought before it, to preserve decency and public order. All this was to no avail. In 1934 the world was stunned by the declaration of Col. Józef Beck (Polish minister of foreign affairs) renouncing minority obligations. The whole structure toppled along with the League of Nations. World War II put an abrupt end to the experiment.

Treatment of Jews by Countries

The Jews had been most instrumental in the promulgation of minority rights. They set out full of hope for a new deal. They were the ones to be most disappointed. Unlike other minorities they did not constitute a threat to the state by irredentist or restoration dreams. Except for three cases, they did not resort to petitioning Geneva on their grievances, as did other minorities; they feared antagonizing their governments. Only Estonia excelled in granting its minorities, including the Jews, complete autonomy. A chair of Jewish studies was established there at the University of Dorpat (*Tartu).

LATVIA. Although Latvia by a law of 1921 narrowed the grant of rights, including minority rights, to those who could prove residence over a period of 20 years, it provided liberal allowances for minority schools until 1934. The Education Law of 1919 provided for compulsory education in the language of the family. Central and local authorities were to establish such schools and to bear the necessary expense. Such a class was to be established if at least 30 pupils were enrolled. The minority section of the ministry of education had a Jewish division, its head nominated by the Jews, subject to the approval of the Council of Ministers. The Jewish educational system thrived. This autonomy, however, was limited to schools; Latvia never enacted laws regarding cultural, religious, and welfare organizations of minorities. In 1934, with the abolition of the democratic regime, school autonomy was virtually nullified by a new law which provided that paid officials of the state administer minorities school systems, that a child be instructed in his family's language provided he could express his thoughts in that language, and that state and local subventions to minority education not exceed their ratio in the population.

LITHUANIA. In Lithuania, too, there was at first a great surge of hope when the constitution in 1922 granted to minorities autonomy and the right to levy taxes. Autonomous Jewish communities, already recognized by law in 1920, were allowed to administer their own cultural, welfare, social, and educational affairs. These communities were united into a national council with a minister of state for Jewish affairs who could levy taxes for Jewish needs and exercised some authority in school affairs. The schools were under the ministry of education. The national and municipal authorities were charged with subventing the Jewish schools. They were entitled to employ Yiddish in government offices. All this exuberant activity in national self-determination came to a halt after only two years. In 1924 both the Jewish national council and the ministry of Jewish affairs were abolished. The following year the local communal organizations were disbanded. Only a modicum of school autonomy remained.

POLAND AND OTHER COUNTRIES. In Poland antisemitism was rampant, especially in the economic sphere. Almost all Polish parties obstinately opposed the granting of equal minority treatment for Jews. The government did not open public schools in Hebrew or Yiddish. The school system established by the Jews themselves was subsidized very grudgingly and in diminishing manner. Jewish religious communities were permitted to deal with cultural and social matters and to organize a council of all congregations. Such a council, however, never convened. Most odious was the limitation of the numbers of Jewish students at state universities by a **numerus clausus*. Despite all these restrictions and an endemic poverty, the Jews of Poland succeeded in maintaining a vibrant cultural life and a thriving network of schools in both Yiddish and Hebrew. In Romania the government disclaimed antisemitic tendencies, yet tolerated the most virulent attacks by Jew-baiting parties. The Romanian language was forced upon Jewish children in schools; the religious sensibilities of Jewish students were violated. In the higher schools of learning a tacit *numerus clausus* prevailed. Yugoslavia respected the rights of its Jewish minority. Apart from Nazi Germany, Hungary was the only state which introduced a *numerus clausus* for Jews not only in practice but by official legislation.

In Turkey the right not to appear in court or to transact legal business on their holidays was vouchsafed the Jews. The autonomy enjoyed by Jews for many centuries was gradually narrowed by the new nationalist regime. Turkish was made the language of instruction in schools. Schools could be directed only by Turkish nationals. In 1926 Turkey renounced its minority obligations. The office of the **ḥakham bashi*, the chief rabbi, was abolished and with it the unified organization of the Jewish communities. Iraq granted to religious congregations the right to form schools in the language of their members. Jewish and Armenian minorities were granted certain autonomous rights.

IN SOVIET RUSSIA. Due to unsettled conditions in Russia during the period of the Peace Conference no arrangements were made there for minorities protection. The country itself, however, experienced inordinate agitation for minority rights during the revolutions of 1917. Again the Jews were most active. Hundreds of meetings and conferences were held as if to celebrate the new-found freedom. On April 3, 1917, Alexander Kerensky, head of the Provisional Government, published a decree removing all restrictions based on "religion, sect, or nationality." All Jewish parties, middle-class or proletarian, gradually united on the question of autonomy. At the end of July 1917 a preliminary conference agreed upon a platform for a Russian Jewish congress to be convened soon. It proposed an elaboration of "the fundamentals of Jewish self-government in Russia; the determination of legal guarantees for the Jewish national minority," as well as the communal organization of Russian Jewry, and the civil and national rights of the Jews in Poland, Palestine, and Romania. The congress never took place due to the seizure of power by the Bolsheviks. On

Nov. 15, 1917, the new Soviet government issued the Declaration of the Rights of Peoples which proclaimed the principle of national self-determination, even to the point of secession. In the Ukraine the Jews were the leading spirits in a flurry of legislative plans designed to establish national-personal autonomy as a fundamental law. On Jan. 9, 1918, the Ukrainian parliament enacted into law a detailed set of articles prepared by the Jewish secretariat. It all came to naught, however, in the political turmoil that ensued with the occupation of the Ukraine by the Germans. It fell to Soviet Russia to launch an experiment in autonomy for minorities on a vast scale. The Soviet government departed from the personal principle of minority rights, namely, that they would apply to all members of a particular nationality throughout the country, and proclaimed, instead, the rights of territorial nationalities. A soviet or a region with a national majority could enjoy cultural autonomy. Since the Jews were scattered all over the country in the large cities, this privilege did not apply to them. Only in hamlets and villages or certain regions where they constituted a majority did they enjoy linguistic, judicial, and educational self-rule. Jews had 67 courts of their own where the official language was Yiddish. In the late 1930s they had five autonomous regions in the Ukraine and the Crimea and 224 local Jewish soviets. In 1931, 160,000 pupils attended Yiddish schools. The high point of this policy was reached in 1927 when *Birobidzhan, a territory in eastern Siberia, was proclaimed a Jewish autonomous region inviting Jewish settlers. None of these efforts, however, were directed at the perpetuation of Jewish identity. On the contrary, the stated purpose of the Soviet government and of the *yevsektsiya (the Jewish sections of the ruling Communist Party) was to eradicate Judaism in favor of atheism and Communism. The Yiddish courts aimed at weaning the Jews away from their accustomed rabbinic courts. The schools proscribed all religious and traditional Jewish content. They declined rapidly before World War II and were not reopened after the war. In the last years of the Stalin era all vestiges of Jewish national life were cruelly obliterated.

In the Western world the demand for minority rights was seldom heard. There the Jews were satisfied with civil rights and the freedom to foster their own religion and culture.

After World War II

In the *United Nations, which after World War II succeeded the League of Nations, no minority rights provisions survived. Instead, emphasis was put on human rights, concerning all men, including members of the majority nation. In 1966 an International Covenant on Civil and Political Rights was drawn up, which in its 27th paragraph stipulates that "in those States in which ethnic, religious, or linguistic minorities exist, persons belonging to such minorities shall not be denied the right, in community with the other members of their group, to enjoy their own culture, to profess and practice their own religion, or to use their own language." This provision is binding on member-states of the UN which sign and ratify the Covenant.

BIBLIOGRAPHY: I. Elbogen, *A Century of Jewish Life* (1960), 502ff., 507ff., 532ff.; O. Janowsky, The *Jews and Minority Rights 1918–1933* (1933); J. Robinson et al., *Were the Minorities Treaties a Failure?* (1943). **ADD. BIBLIOGRAPHY:** O. Janowsky, *Nationalities and National Minorities* (1945); E.Viefhaus, *Die Minderheitenfrage und die Entstehung der Minderheitensschutzverträte* (1960); J. Stone, *International Guaranties of Minority Rights* (1932); S. Netzer, *Ma'avak Yehudei Polin al Zekhuyoteihem ha-Ezraḥiyot ve- ha-Le'ummiyot* (1980), 146–67; N. Feinberg, *La Question des minorités à la conférence de la paix de 1919–1920 et L'action Juive enfaveur de la protection internationale des minorités*; F Brzezinski, *Prawa mniejszosci, komentarz do traktatu 28.6.1919 pomiedzy Polska a glownemi mocarstwami* (1920).

[Isaac Levitats]

MINOR PROPHETS, a collection of the books of 12 prophets: *Hosea, *Joel, *Amos, *Obadiah, *Jonah, *Micah, *Nahum, *Habbakuk, *Zephaniah, *Haggai, *Zechariah, and *Malachi. This collection counts as a single book (the last) of the second division – the Prophets (Heb. *Nevi'im*) – of the Palestinian Canon. In the Alexandrian Canon (according to the Septuagint), Minor Prophets, again as a single book, occurs in the fourth and last division, that of prophecy, and is the first of the ten books enumerated there, but the order of the first six of the 12 is there Hosea, Amos, Micah, Joel, Obadiah, and Jonah. The designation "Minor Prophets" alternates with the title "The Twelve" as the designation of this collection, the latter being the native Jewish one (Heb. שנים עשר; Aram. תרי עשר, BB 14b) and that of the Septuagint (*Dodekaprophe-ton*), while the former seems to be rooted in the Latin designation of the Vulgate (*Prophetae Minores*). The adjective "minor" in the title "Minor Prophets" does not reflect upon the relative importance of the 12 prophets in comparison to Isaiah, Jeremiah, and Ezekiel, but rather upon their much smaller size. This is implied by the observation about Hosea in *Bava Batra* 14b. The order of the prophets within the anthology is based on a combination of Midrash, the chronological understanding current at the time of compilation, and certain word associations. For example, Hosea is first because his book opens (1:2): "When God first spoke to Hosea" (cf. BB 14b). Amos is placed third after the Book of Joel because of the occurrence of two very similar verses, one at the end of Joel (4:16) and the second at the beginning of Amos (1:2). Finally, the last three books, Haggai, Zechariah, and Malachi, were put at the very end of the anthology because they were thought to be the only prophets of the 12 who belonged chronologically to the Second Temple period. The Minor Prophets could not have been compiled as an anthology any earlier than the fourth century B.C.E., the probable date of the Book of Jonah, the latest of the 12 books. Its compilation can be no later than the time of Ben Sira (c. 180 B.C.E.), however, since the latter, in praising the Israelite heroes in chronological order, mentions all the other prophets by name, each one in his own age, while the Minor Prophets are grouped together namelessly as "the twelve prophets" (Ecclus. 44–49).

BIBLIOGRAPHY: M.L. Margolis, *The Hebrew Scriptures in the Making* (1922), 18; M.Z. Segal, *Mevo ha-Mikra*, 4 (1964), 838; O. Eissfeldt, *The Old Testament, an Introduction* (1965), 382–4, incl. bibl.

[Chayim Cohen]

MINOR TRACTATES. In addition to the 63 regular tractates of the Mishnah and Talmud, there are appended at the end of the fourth order, **Nezikin*, 14 smaller or minor tractates which were first published together in their present format in the Romm-Vilna edition (1886). These tractates contain a wealth of legal and aggadic material. In manuscript and published form, these uncanonical treatises may also be found under different titles, arrangements, and order. Their appellation as minor or smaller tractates does not necessarily refer to their size, but rather to the fact that they were not canonized. **Avot de-Rabbi Nathan* for instance, consists of 41 chapters. **Soferim, Semaḥot* (*Evel Rabbati*), and *Kallah Rabbati* are also of considerable length. The other main tractates are **Kallah, *Derekh Ereẓ Rabbah*, and *Derekh Ereẓ Zuta*. For additional details see the articles on the individual tractates. Also included in this section, however, are seven more brief treaties which were compiled to give in a methodological form the rules of topics which were not dealt with in specific tractates of the Talmud. These are *Gerim*, about proselytes; *Kutim*, about Samaritans; *Avadim*, about Hebrew slaves; *Sefer Torah*, on the writing of a Torah scroll; *Tefillin*, on the precept of **tefillin*; *Ẓiẓit*, on the fringes (**ẓiẓit*); and *Mezuzah*, on the **mezuzah*; and it is sometimes only to them that the term minor tractates applies (see *Shem ha-Gedolim*, II, 161 and cf. Eccles. R. 5:8, 2). The time when these works were compiled remains uncertain. Some scholars assign them to the end of the geonic period, but recent scholarship favors a much earlier date. M. Higger, in the introduction to his critical edition of these seven minor tractates, judges them to be the "first post-mishnaic compendia regulating specific Jewish practices and usages." His opinion is that "most of the Minor Tractates are Palestinian in origin, but were later modified or elaborated in Babylonia." Thus it may be that the original composition of these codes was already completed by 400 C.E. Since they were of Palestinian origin, they were not included in the final redaction of the Babylonian Talmud.

The first medieval scholar to clearly cite one of these brief codes is *Naḥmanides. In his *Torat ha-Adam Inyan ha-Hoẓa'ah* (*Kitvei Rabbenu Moshe b. Naḥman*, ed. by C.D. Chavel, 2 (1964), 100) and in his *Milḥemet ha-Shem* to Alfasi (Alfasi; MK 16a), he cites the passage in *Ẓiẓit* which discusses whether the fringes in the *tallit* in which the deceased is buried should be untied. Menahem b. Solomon *Meiri likewise makes reference to this same passage in *Ẓiẓit* (*Beit ha-Beḥirah al Massekhet Berakhot*, ed. by S. Dikman (1965[2]), 61b). A similar passage, to be found in *Semaḥot* (ch. 12), is twice cited by *tosafot* (Pes. 40b and Av. Zar. 65b). Although a substantial portion of these tractates consists of material already in the Talmud, they occasionally contain items which are not found elsewhere, such as the above-cited text from *Ẓiẓit*. Another example of such new material is the concept that the main shortcoming of the Samaritans was that they denied the centrality of Jerusalem. *Kutim* concludes with the statement that when the Samaritans renounce Mount Gerizim and acknowledge Jerusalem and the resurrection of the dead, they will be accepted as Jews.

Gerim

Gerim consists of four chapters:

(1) the preliminary procedure for receiving proselytes is detailed;

(2) regulations are set forth regarding the circumcision, ritual bath, and sacrifice, of converts;

(3) the *ger toshav* is defined by Meir as one who has merely renounced idolatry, although according to Judah he is one who will only eat the meat of ritually slaughtered animals;

(4) Jews are exhorted to maintain a friendly attitude toward proselytes.

Kutim

Kutim regulates the relationship between *Samaritans, Jews, and gentiles, in two chapters:

(1) sales to and intermarriage with Samaritans are prohibited since they desecrate holy objects, but it is permitted to lend them money;

(2) buying meat, wine, cheese, and bread from the Samaritans is discussed.

Avadim

Avadim contains three chapters:

(1) the validity of the regulations concerning Hebrew slaves is limited to the period when the *Jubilee is observed, and the purchase and manumission of bondmen is detailed;

(2) the relationship between the master and his slave, the slave's family's obligation to redeem him, and his status after redemption are discussed;

(3) the details of the ceremony prescribed for a slave who does not wish to go free, and the acquiring of freedom by a slave when he is sold to a non-Jew or outside of Palestine are given.

Sefer Torah

Sefer Torah has five chapters:

(1) details of the writing material that may be utilized are given;

(2) the blank spaces that must be left between sections of the scroll are explained;

(3) laws for the reading and respect of the Torah are given;

(4) the names of God and the interdiction against erasing them are explained;

(5) the method for writing God's names is laid down.

These five chapters are almost identical with the first five chapters of *Soferim*.

Tefillin

Tefillin contains only one chapter, and it gives the rules for writing the biblical passages on the parchment of the *tefillin*, the manner and time of wearing them, and those persons who are obligated to wear them.

Ẓiẓit

Ẓiẓit consists of only one chapter which details the regulations of the fringes (Num. 15:38–40; Deut. 22:12). It discusses such topics as the persons who are obligated to obey this law, the garments which are exempt, the number of threads in each fringe, and the manner of dyeing the blue thread that is part of the fringes.

Mezuzah

Mezuzah has two chapters:

(1) details are given of the parchment to be used and the types of doorposts that require a *mezuzah*;

(2) the exact spot for the *mezuzah*, its case, and differences in regulations for houses within and outside of Palestine are discussed.

In the Romm edition of the Talmud, only *Gerim* has a detailed commentary, titled *Naḥalat Ya'akov*, by R. Jacob Neuberg of Offenbach. His commentary on the first five chapters of *Soferim* also serves as a commentary to *Sefer Torah*. More recent commentaries to these tractates were published by Samuel I. Hillman of London and R. Ḥayyim Kanievsky of Bene-Berak (1963–65). These seven tractates have been twice translated into English. Michael Higger published his edited text and translation in 1930. In 1965, the Soncino Press issued a new English translation.

BIBLIOGRAPHY: M. Higger (ed.), *Sheva Massekhtot Ketannot* (1930), introd.; idem (ed.), *Massekhet Semaḥot* (1931), introd.; J. Goldin, *The Fathers according to Rabbi Nathan* (1956), introd.; D. Zlotnick, *The Tractate Mourning* (1966), introd.

[Aaron Rothkoff]

MINOW, NEWTON NORMAN (1926–), U.S. lawyer and public official. Born in Milwaukee, Wisconsin, Minow served in the U.S. Army in 1944–46. He graduated from Northwestern Law School and was admitted to the Wisconsin and the Illinois Bar in 1950. He served as law clerk to U.S. Supreme Chief Justice Fred M. Vinson (1951–52), and as administrative assistant to Governor Adlai Stevenson of Illinois (1952–53). He was a member of Stevenson's campaign staff during the latter's two attempts for the presidency (1952 and 1956), and was also a partner in two Stevenson law firms (1955–57 and 1957–61). In 1961 President John F. Kennedy appointed Minow chairman of the Federal Communications Commission. Minow caused a furor within the television industry soon after becoming chairman by describing most of its programming as a "vast wasteland." His conception that the FCC should oversee the networks and protect the public interest brought industry charges of government censorship and interference, but resulted in congressional legislation to assist educational television, the passage of the Communications Satellite Bill (1962), and an attempt to vary and enlarge the area of television programming by enabling new channels to operate on the ultra-high frequency band. Under his direction, the FCC also attempted to supervise television and radio advertising closely. Although he served in that position for only two years, it was estimated that during that time, Minow and his ideas received more news coverage than any other federal official besides the president.

Minow resigned from the agency in 1963 to become executive vice president and general counsel to the *Encyclopaedia Britannica* (1963–65). He then became a partner in the communications law firm Sidley and Austin (1965–91), after which he took on the Of Counsel role. Minow took to teaching as well, serving from 1987 as professor of communications policy and law in the Annenberg Program of Northwestern University.

Active in Jewish affairs, Minow was a member of B'nai B'rith; a director of the Chicago chapter of the American Jewish Committee; and chair of the board of overseers of the Jewish Theological Seminary. He wrote *Equal Time: The Private Broadcasters and the Public Interest* (1964); *Presidential Television* (with J. Martin and L. Mitchell, 1973); *For Great Debates* (1987); *How Vast the Wasteland Now* (1995); and *Abandoned in the Wasteland* (with C. Lamay, 1995).

BIBLIOGRAPHY: L.J. Silver, *Profiles in Success* (1965), 303–13. **ADD. BIBLIOGRAPHY:** M. Curtin, *Redeeming the Wasteland* (1995); M. Watson, *The Expanding Vista: American Television in the Kennedy Years* (1990); R. Macneil, *The People Machine: The Influence of Television on American Politics* (1968).

[Ruth Beloff (2nd ed.)]

MINSK, capital of Belarus; in *Poland-Lithuania from the beginning of the 14th century until 1793; under czarist rule, the most important commercial center of Belorussia from the 15th century. Jews first leased the customs duties of Minsk in 1489, and after the expulsion of Jews from Lithuania in 1495 they started to settle in Minsk. In 1579 King Stephen Báthory granted the Jews of Minsk a charter, but in 1606 King Sigismund III prohibited Jews from opening shops there or engaging in commerce. In 1623 the community of Minsk was under the jurisdiction of Brest-Litovsk, but in 1631 the Lithuanian Land Council granted it a special regional status, which included the Russian hinterland. In 1633 King Ladislaus IV confirmed these rights and permitted the Jews of Minsk to acquire real estate on the market square or anywhere else, and to buy land for a new cemetery. During the *Chmielnicki revolt and the Russian-Polish War which followed it, the Jews of Minsk were among those who suffered. In 1679 King John III Sobieski confirmed their right to the ownership of houses and shops, their synagogue and cemetery, and restated their freedom to engage in commerce and crafts and their exemption from all jurisdiction excepting that of the king. These rights were confirmed in their entirety by King Augustus II in 1722. Hence the community of Minsk prospered during the 17th and 18th centuries in spite of the opposition of the townspeople. In 1766, 1,322 Jewish poll tax payers were registered in Minsk. Jews were prominent in the town's commercial life and at the fairs of nearby *Mir and Kapulia (see *Market Days and Fairs). The spiritual life of the community was also enriched. In 1685 a yeshivah was established by the local rabbi, Moses Mordecai. Among the rabbis and *rashei yeshivah* of Minsk during the 18th century were Jehiel b. Solomon *Heilprin, Aryeh Leib b. Asher *Gunzberg, and Raphael *Cohen.

During the 19th century, Minsk was one of the largest and most important communities in Russia. In 1847 the Jewish population numbered 12,976, rising to 47,562 (52.3% of the total population) in 1897, which made Minsk the fourth largest community in the *Pale of Settlement. Jewish life in the first half of the 19th century is reflected in the community records, which were published with a Russian translation by Jacob *Brafman. *Mitnaggedim* were influential in Minsk, and Ḥasidism was relatively weak. There were several yeshivot in the town, the largest of which was known as "Blumke's Kloyz." At the end of the 19th century Jeroham Judah Leib *Perelmann, who was known as "the *gadol* [the great scholar] of Minsk," officiated there as rabbi. A circle of *maskilim* also existed in the town, and in the 1840s several Jewish schools which included secular subjects in their curricula were opened there. Minsk was one of the places where the Jewish labor movement originated and developed. In the mid-1870s circles of Jewish Socialists were organized, which were very active during the 1880s and 1890s. The years 1893–94 also saw the birth of the "national opposition" to them, led by A. *Liessin. In 1895 a convention of Jewish Socialists was held in Minsk, which discussed the projected establishment of a Jewish Socialist Federation. The Jewish Socialists of Minsk sent delegates to the founding convention of the *Bund in 1897, and Minsk became one of the centers of the Bund's activities, being the first seat of the movement's central committee until 1898, when it was dispersed by the police. From 1901 to 1903, Minsk likewise became the center of the activities of the *Independent Jewish Workers' Party. Jews were predominant in the demonstrations and revolutionary meetings held in the town in 1905 and were also the principal victims of the riots directed against liberal elements in general which took place in October 1905. Groups of Ḥovevei Zion (see *Ḥibbat Zion) were first organized in Minsk in the early 1880s. In 1882 the Kibbutz Niddeḥei Israel association was founded there, and in 1890 the Agudat ha-Elef. Later, Zionism became very influential. In 1902, with the authorization of the government, the Second Convention of Russian Zionists was held in Minsk. In the communal elections of 1918, the Zionists and *Po'alei Zion won 33 seats, the Orthodox 25 seats, the Bund 17 seats, the nonaffiliated six seats, and the *Folkspartei and the *United Jewish Socialists Workers' Party two seats each.

After the establishment of the Soviet regime, Jewish communal and religious life was silenced at Minsk as elsewhere in the Soviet Union. The suppressed religious and national institutions were replaced by institutions of Jewish culture based on the Yiddish language and Communist ideology, and Minsk became an important center of Jewish-Communist cultural activity in the Soviet Union. Yiddish schools were established, and at the Institute of Belorussian Culture, founded in 1924, a Jewish section was organized. It published several scientific works, including *Tsaytshrift* (5 vols., 1926–31) devoted to Jewish history, literature, and folklore. A Jewish department was also established (1921) within the faculty of education of the University of Minsk. These institutions, however, were closed down in the mid-1930s. Various newspapers, periodicals, and other publications in Yiddish were issued in the town. These included the daily newspaper *Der Shtern* (1918–21), *Der Veker* (1917–25; until 1921 the organ of the Bund), *Oktyabr* (1925–41), and the literary monthly *Shtern* (1925–41). In 1926 the Belorussian Jewish State Theater was opened, presenting performances until June 1941. In 1926 there were 53,686 Jews in Minsk (40.8% of the population), increasing to 70,998 by 1939 (29.7% of the total population).

Hebrew Printing

In 1808 Simḥah Zimel set up in Minsk a Hebrew printing press which he had brought from *Grodno. Up to 1823, he had printed at least 12 books, mostly liturgical. Another press was established in 1820 by Gerson Blaustein, who by 1837 had also printed 12 books, again mostly liturgical, though including one volume of Hebrew poetry by M. *Letteris (1832). In the 20th century a Hebrew press once more operated in Minsk, printing books and newspapers mainly for local use. After the Russian Revolution, the studies in the history of Russian Jewry and Yiddish literature which were published in Yiddish by the Jewish section of the Institute of Belorussian Culture were printed in Minsk.

The Minsk Province

In czarist Russia, the province of Minsk was one of the "western" provinces of the Pale of Settlement. In 1797 its *gubernator* presented Czar Paul I with the resolutions of the meetings of the province noblemen, who alleged that the Jews were responsible for the sorry plight of the peasants of the province and for the famine which then raged. This statement was the forerunner of the program to expel the Jews from the villages, which later took the form of the "Jewish Statute" of 1804 (see *Russia). In 1847 there were 37 Jewish *kahal* administrations, in which 87,633 Jews were registered. In 1897 the Jews of the province numbered 345,015 (16% of its population); 37.5% of them lived in the towns, the same number in the townlets, and 25% in the villages. The largest communities of the province (with the exception of Minsk itself) were then *Pinsk (21,065 Jews), *Bobruisk (20,759), *Slutsk (10,264), *Borisov (7,722), *Mozyr (5,631), *Rechitsa (5,334), *Novogrudok (5,015), *Nesvizh (4,687), and Shchedrin (4,002); 41.5% of the province's Jews earned their livelihood in crafts and as hired labor, and 28.9% from commerce. About 21,000 Jews (6.1% of all those in the province) depended on agriculture, and over 6,000 of them lived in the mostly small Jewish agricultural settlements. In Minsk oblast there were 70,713 Jews (13.1% of the total population) in 1926; in the Minsk oblast as it had been organized in 1938 (with the exception of the town of Minsk itself), there were 9,054 Jews (0.61% of the population) in 1959.

[Yehuda Slutsky]

Holocaust Period

Some 100,000 inhabitants were left in the city when the German forces entered on June 28. The population rose to 150,000 as the front line moved farther east, and tens of thousands who had fled and had been overtaken by the speed of the German advance, turned back. About one-third of these were local Jews. Their number was increased by refugees from as far west as *Bialystok, as well as by survivors of mass executions carried out by the *Einsatzkommandos* (mobile killing squads) in the vicinity, so that another 30,000 Jews were added. Later, about 23,500 German, Austrian, and Czech Jews were deported to Minsk, and settled in a separate ghetto, so that despite the fact that a large number of Minsk Jews had been murdered before the establishment of the ghetto, at least 85,000 Jews were confined in it. Their choice of Minsk as a site for a large Jewish slave labor camp was dictated by military needs and the geographical position of the city in the rear of two German army groups advancing on Leningrad and Moscow.

Immediately following the occupation of Minsk, the German city commandant ordered all males between the ages of 15 and 45 to report for registration under the penalty of death. About 40,000 reported and, in a field at Drozdy outside Minsk, were segregated in three sections: Jews, Red Army men, and non-Jewish civilians. On the fifth day the non-Jewish civilians were released. All Jewish members of the intelligentsia were ordered to step forward; the several thousand who did so were marched off to the nearby woods and machine-gunned. The remaining Jews were moved to Minsk prison and released on Aug. 20, 1941. On the same day the city commandant issued an ordinance for the establishment of a ghetto in a suburb consisting mostly of wooden cottages, and ordered every Jew to wear the yellow badge. All Jews had to be inside the ghetto by July 25, but the Judenrat managed to delay the date until the middle of August by means of bribes. As there were no Jewish communal organizations to provide the Germans with officials to carry out their orders, a group of Jews was arrested. One of them, Ilya Mushkin, who knew a little German, was appointed head of a Judenrat and ordered to select the other officials.

Once inside the ghetto, the Jews were terrorized by nightly murders and kidnappings carried out by the Germans and their local henchmen. On the nights of August 14, 25, and 31, thousands were taken away and only a few appeared in the dreaded "labor" camp on Shirokaya Street, where in addition to Jews the Germans held non-Jewish Red Army men. On Nov. 7, 1941, 12,000 Jews were seized and taken to Tuchinka, where they were machine-gunned at the side of the newly dug pits. Some of the emptied streets were used to house 1,500 German Jews, most of them from *Hamburg. By means of barbed wire fences, the ghetto was henceforth divided into three sections: the main ghetto for "unskilled" Jews; a section for "skilled" workers and Judenrat employees, including the ghetto police; and a section housing the German, Austrian, and Czech Jews. On Nov. 20, 1941, 5,000 people were removed to Tuchinka, where they were murdered. Some of the emptied streets were used to house 6,500 Jews brought from Germany, Austria, and Czechoslovakia.

At the end of February 1942, the *Gestapo asked the Judenrat to turn over 5,000 Jews not employed in Wehrmacht enterprises. The resistance leaders ordered Serebryanskiy, the chief of the ghetto police and a member of the resistance organization, to use his trustworthy policemen to warn the Jews of the impending massacre and tell them to hide. On March 1 the Germans ordered the Judenrat to dig a pit in Ratomskaya Street, an unpaved ravine in the center of the ghetto. On the following morning, after the columns of workers had left the ghetto, Nazi officials arrived and demanded the 5,000 victims. Informed that the Judenrat had been unable to collect them, the Germans began a hunt for their victims. Dr. Chernis, the woman in charge of the ghetto orphanage, and Fleysher, the supervisor, were ordered to bring their charges in front of the Judenrat building. Unaware of what awaited their children, they led them, dressed and washed, and carrying the youngest in their arms, toward the building, but when they arrived in Ratomskaya Street, they were all thrown into the pit and buried alive. When the columns of workers returned at night, several thousand were taken to *Koidanovo and murdered there. Others were forced to join the people rounded up inside the ghetto and butchered in the Ratomskaya Street ravine.

Shortly after the March 2 massacre, the Germans discovered the existence of the underground organization in the "Aryan" part of Minsk in which several Jews, such as R.M. Bromberg and M.P. Malkevich, had played a prominent role, and its connection with a similar organization inside the ghetto. On the night of March 31, 1942, the Gestapo raided the ghetto and arrested several resistance leaders, but failed to capture the head of the resistance, Hersh *Smolar. The raid was followed by nightly massacres directed against relatives and neighbors of runaways, in an attempt to discourage Jews from fleeing to the forests to join the partisans. On July 28, 1942, after the labor columns left the ghetto, the Germans and their local collaborators invaded the ghetto and for three days murdered and tortured the inhabitants. Some 10,000 were murdered, including 3,500 German, Austrian, and Czech Jews, most of whom were old people, women, and children. Nine thousand Jews still survived. On Feb. 1, 1943, 1,500 Jews were rounded up and shot over open pits at Maly Trostenets. The number of survivors was systematically reduced by the shooting of smaller groups of men and the gassing of women and children in vans during the summer. To speed up the total annihilation, a transport of some 2,000 people, including a group of Jewish Red Army men held in the Shirokaya Street camp, was sent to *Sobibor on Sept. 18, 1943. This transport included Lt. Alexander *Pecherski and Shelomo Lejtman, the latter a Jewish Communist from Poland, who together led the revolt in the death camp on Oct. 14, 1943. On September 22, Generalkommissar Kube was killed by a bomb placed by his Belorussian maid, E.G. Mazanik. The assassination was organized by David Keymakh, the political commissar of the detachment commanded by G.M. Linkov, who as "Uncle Batya" became one of the most successful Soviet partisan leaders. This event speeded up the final liquidation of the ghetto, which took place on Oct. 21, 1943.

Resistance

The resistance record of the Jews imprisoned in Minsk ghetto is unique. One Sunday in 1941, within days of finding themselves inside the ghetto, a group of local Jews and Jewish Communists from Poland met and decided that it was the duty of the Minsk Jews to take an active part in the war against the German invaders. They rejected the possibility of armed resistance inside the ghetto and decided to devote all their efforts to effecting the escape of the largest possible number of Jews into the forests in order to become partisans. Four resistance groups arose in the "Aryan" part of the city in August and September 1941. However, it was only after the November 7 massacre that Hersh Smolar, the Polish-born leader of the Jewish resistance, met Isai Pavlovich Kozinets, known as Slavek, the leader of one of the four groups, who subsequently became the leader of the entire underground movement in Minsk. It was only in 1969 that it became known that Kozinets was a Jew born at Genichesk on the Azov Sea and that his first name was Joshua. A petroleum engineer by profession, Kozinets had been in charge of the installations in Bialystok at the outbreak of the war. The underground organization inside the ghetto then became an integral part of the city underground and was known as the "Ernst Thaelmann district," in recognition of the part played by the ghetto inhabitants in the struggle against the Nazis. The Judenrat itself, under Mushkin, took orders from the city-underground committee and played a unique part in diverting much of the production from the workshops and factories manned by Jews to the needs of the partisans. The Jewish organization provided the city underground with news of what was happening in the outside world by establishing a radio monitoring station. It also supplied a printing press and printers, while the ghetto hospital provided surgical and other treatment for wounded partisans. Moreover, Jews employed in the factories working for the Wehrmacht set an example to their Belorussian fellow workers in how to sabotage production. In 1942 the ghetto resistance was better organized and more efficient than the city organization, and the Jews, who ran incomparably greater risks than their Russian and Belorussian fellow citizens, contributed greatly in the common fight against the Germans. In return, the Jewish resistance leaders asked their "Aryan" comrades to help them save the maximum number of Jews from slaughter by making possible their escape into the forests to become partisans. As their assistance proved inadequate, the Jews also had to take the initiative in developing the partisan movement. They organized the nuclei of future partisan detachments inside the ghetto, while M. Gebelev and M. Pruslin, two of the Jewish resistance leaders, helped organize similar ten-man teams in the "Aryan" part of the city. Furthermore, when most of the "Aryan" resistance leaders fell into the hands of the Germans in the spring of 1942, Gebelev and other Jews played a decisive role in rebuilding the city organization. Gebelev was actually captured when preparing the escape of a group of Russian prisoners of war to the forests. The first organized group of Jewish partisans left the ghetto in December 1941 to join Captain Sergeyev-Bystrov's detachment, which in time grew into the Stalin Brigade. Many Jews escaped with the help of the railwaymen's resistance group headed by Kuznetsov; they formed a large proportion of the Narodny Mstitel ("People's Avenger") Brigade, which Kuznetsov later commanded. The Jews of Minsk created the 406, Kutuzov, Budyonny, Dzerzhinskiy, Sergei Lazo, and Parkhomenko Detachments, as well as the 106 Family Detachment commanded by Semion Zorin (who immigrated to Israel), which provided protection in the forests for over 600 Jewish women and children. Jews also formed a large percentage of the Frunze Detachment. The Kutuzov Detachment became the nucleus of the Second Minsk Brigade, while the Parkhomenko Detachment, formed mostly by Jews who had been helped to escape from the ghetto by boys and girls ranging in age from 11 to 15, served as the basis of the Chapayev Brigade. Hundreds of Minsk Jews were also active in other brigades. After the liberation about 5,000 Jews returned from the forests.

[Reuben Ainsztein]

Contemporary Jewry

A memorial to the Jewish victims of the Holocaust was erected in Minsk immediately after World War II – the only one in the U.S.S.R. – bearing a Yiddish inscription which explicitly mentions Jewish victims. On Jan. 13, 1948, Solomon *Mikhoels, the chairman of the Jewish *Anti-Fascist Committee and the director of the Jewish State Theater in Moscow, was murdered on Lodochnaya Street in Minsk while visiting the city on an official mission. Later the murder was acknowledged to have been the work of the secret police (on Stalin's orders). In the 1959 census 38,842 Jews were registered in Minsk, 5,716 of whom declared Yiddish to be their mother tongue. However, the population figure was estimated to be in fact between 50,000 and 60,000. The Great Synagogue of Minsk was closed down by the authorities in 1959, and in the same year private religious services were dispersed by the militia. A small synagogue was left, but in 1964 it was destroyed, as the site was earmarked for new apartment buildings. Eventually the Jewish congregation was allowed to open a small synagogue in a wooden house on the outskirts of the city. There is no Jewish cemetery in Minsk, but Jews are buried in a separate section in the general cemetery. Matzah baking was banned for several years, and on March 23, 1964, an article in the local newspaper, *Sovetskaya Belorussiya*, condemned the sending of packages of matzah to Minsk from Jewish communities abroad. Kosher poultry, however, was available. In 1968 several young Jews were arrested for Zionist activity. In the 1990s most Jews left for Israel and the West.

BIBLIOGRAPHY: S.A. Bershadski, *Russko-yevreyskiy Arkhiv*, 1 (1882), nos. 20, 53, 63, 109; 3 (1903), nos. 14, 41, 52, 60; A. Subbotin, *V cherte yevreyskoy osedlosti*, 1 (1888), 4–47; B. Eisenstadt, *Rabbanei*

Minsk va-Ḥakhameha (1898); *Regesty i nadpisi*, 3 vols. (1889–1913), indexes; Khorosh, in: *Voskhod*, 12 (1901), 100–10; A.H. Shabad, *Toledot ha-Yamim she-Averu al haḤevra Kaddisha "Shivah Keru'im" u-Veit ha-Midrash ha-Gadol ba-Ir Minsk*, 2 vols. (1904–12); *Die Judenpogrome in Russland*, 2 (1909), 458–65; S. Dubnow (ed.), *Pinkas ha-Medinah* (1925), index; Alexandrov, in: Institute of Belorussian Culture, *Tsaytshrift*, 1 (1926), 239–49; 2–3 (1928), 763–78; 4 (1930), 199–224; S. Agurski, *Revolyutsionnoye dvizheniye v Belorussii* (1928), 139–43 and passim (= *Di Revolutsionere Bavegung in Vaysrusland* (1931), 168–71); Levitats, in: *Zion*, 3 (1938), 170–8; A. Liessin, *Zikhronot ve-Ḥavayot* (1943), 1–78, 116–31; A. Yaari, in: KS, 20 (1943/44), 163–70; *Yahadut Lita*, 1 (1959), index; A. Greenbaum, *Jewish Scholarship in Soviet Russia* (1959), 22–27, 66–73, passim; J.S. Hertz (ed.), *Geshikhte fun Bund*, 3 vols. (1960–66), indexes; Goldstein, in: *He-Avar*, 14 (1967), 3–27. HOLOCAUST AND AFTER: H. Smolar, *Fun Minsker Geto* (1946); idem, *Resistance in Minsk* (1966); S. Schwarz, *Jews in the Soviet Union* (1951), index; J. Greenstein, in: *Sefer Pabianice* (1956), 349–73 (Yid.); *Sefer ha-Partizanim ha-Yehudim*, 1 (1958), 501–37; K. Loewenstein, *Minsk: im Lager der deutschen Juden* (1961).

MINSK CONFERENCE, the second conference of Russian Zionists, held publicly and with the government's permission in Minsk from Sept. 4 to Sept. 10, 1902. The number of representatives was estimated at 526. The Minsk Conference was in essence the "first all-Russian Zionist Congress," an assembly of a national minority in a state that had suppressed national minorities and denied them the right of assembly. Two organized factions were represented at the conference: *Mizrachi with 160 representatives and the *Democratic Fraction with about 60 representatives. The majority of representatives did not align with either group but organized a neutral faction. The main point of contention between Mizrachi and the Democratic Fraction was the cultural question. Mizrachi opposed the Zionist Organization's conducting cultural activities, demanding instead, practical work in Ereẓ Israel by means of the *Jewish National Fund (JNF) and the *Jewish Colonial Trust. Jehiel *Tschlenow was elected chairman. M. *Ussishkin proposed the establishment of a "Zionist Guard" composed of young men whose task would be to deliver public speeches on the Zionist idea, organize schools, write propaganda pamphlets, etc. This call for practical efforts enthused many delegates, especially among the youth. The focal point of the conference was the delivery of reports on cultural activities by N. *Sokolow and *Aḥad Ha-Am. The latter explained his outlook on the close relationship between the movement of national renaissance and cultural work; Sokolow proposed that Hebrew be the official language of the Zionist Organization. Isaac *Reines, the Mizrachi leader, expressed his objections to the Zionist Organization's conducting cultural activities. After a vehement debate, the conference's presidium summoned both Aḥad Ha-Am and Reines to a consultation, in which the latter accepted the proposal to choose two educational committees – a traditional one and a progressive one. This arrangement dissolved the crisis that threatened to split the Russian Zionist Movement. After the conference, there was a marked change for the worse in the government's attitude toward the Jews in general and the Zionist Organization in particular. During Passover 1903 the *Kishinev pogrom took place, and in June of the same year all Zionist activities were totally prohibited in Russia.

BIBLIOGRAPHY: M. Nurock, *Ve'idat Ẓiyyonei Rusyah* (1963), includes introduction by I. Klausner; A. Boehm, *Die Zionistische Bewegung*, 1 (1935), 200, 296, 517ff.; Ch. Weizmann, *Letters and Papers*, 1 (1968), index; M. Kleinman, in: *Lu'aḥ Aḥi'asaf* (1902), 454–70; *He-Avar*, 9 (1962), 94–106; A. Raphaeli (Zenziper), in: *Kaẓir*, 1 (1964), 60–75; *Die Welt*, nos 37, 38, 40 (1902); S. Eisenstadt (ed.), *Yeḥi'el Tschlenow* (Heb., 1937).

[Israel Klausner]

MINSKI, NIKOLAI MAXIMOVICH (pseudonym of **N.M. Vilenkin**; 1855–1937), Russian poet and essayist. Born in Glubokoye, near Vilna, Minski studied law at St. Petersburg. For a time he was influenced by P. *Smolenskin and the rising Jewish nationalism among young, educated Russian Jews. In 1879–80 he wrote a series of essays, under the pseudonym "Nord-Vest," in which he argued that the Jewish problem in Russia could be solved by the creation of a Jewish farming class which would "cleanse Judaism of its impurities." He also claimed that all Jewish groups were opposed to socialism. Minski later became alienated from Jewish affairs, and before the turn of the century converted to Christianity. In the 1870s he lived in Italy and Paris, where he taught the children of Baron G. Ginzburg. Due to the antisemitism of the journal "Novoye Vremia," he published in *Voskhod* (nr. 1, 2, 1888) the drama in verses "The Siege of Tulchin," where he compared the *Chmielnicki murders with the pogroms of 1881. He published his first poems in 1876. His early poetry, such as *Belyye nochi* ("White Nights," 1879), deals with socialist and folk themes, but his later writing betrays his disillusionment with socialism and an attraction to mysticism and Nietzschean philosophy. During the 1905 Revolution, Minski helped to publish *Novaya zhizn* ("New Life"), the organ of the Bolshevik wing of the Social Democrats. He translated the *Internationale* into Russian, but with the failure of the Revolution he was imprisoned and thereafter he was freed and left Russia and lived in Berlin, London, and Paris. During the 1917 Revolution he wrote anti-Bolshevik articles for the French press. Some of Minski's poetry, which Soviet critics have stigmatized as decadent, appeared in a Hebrew translation by Leah Goldberg (*Yalkut Shirat he-Ammim*, 1 (1942), 5–6). He translated into Russian Homer's *Iliad* and some poems of Yehuda Halevi, Byron, Shelley, and Verlaine.

BIBLIOGRAPHY: M. Slonim, *Modern Russian Literature* (1953), index.

[Yitzhak Maor]

MINSK MAZOWIECKI (Pol. **Mińsk Mazowiecki**), town in E. central Poland. Minsk Mazowiecki received urban status in the first half of the 15th century, but Jewish settlement did not develop there until the close of the 18th century. From the beginning, and particularly during the second half, of the 19th century, the number of Jews increased until they were the majority in the town. In 1827 there were 260 Jews in a general population of 770, while by 1864 they numbered 620 (46.3% of the total population). In 1897 there were 3,445 Jews (55.6%). During World War I the number of Jews decreased as a result of migration to Warsaw and other large centers. In 1921 the Jewish population numbered 4,130 (39.3%). During the period between the two world wars the Polish population increased considerably, while the Jewish population grew at a slower rate. On the eve of World War II, 5,845 Jews lived there.

The Jewish community was not at first independent; at the close of the 18th century the rabbi also served the Kaluszyn community. During the 19th century ḥasidic groups such as those of Gur (*Gora Kalwaria) and Parysow gained in strength, and the court of the *ẓaddik* of Minsk Mazowiecki was established by R. Jacob Perlov at the close of the 19th century. After World War I his successor, the *ẓaddik* Alter Israel Simeon, removed his seat to Warsaw. There were eight Jews among the 24 members of the municipal council elected in 1927. The Jewish population's political affiliations may be deduced from the 1931 elections to the community council, which included seven members of *Agudat Israel, four craftsmen, and one member of right *Po'alei Zion. The Jews of Minsk Mazowiecki earned their livelihood principally from small trade and crafts. During the 1930s they aroused the jealousy of the Polish tradesmen and craftsmen, who declared an economic war on them. As a result of this struggle, severe anti-Jewish riots broke out in May 1936, which were fomented by the antisemitic *Endecja party and destroyed the means of livelihood of the Jews. Antisemitic agitation was particularly violent in the town on the eve of World War II.

[Shimshon Leib Kirshenboim]

Holocaust Period

In 1940 about 2,000 Jews from Pabianice, Kalisz, and Lipno were forced to settle in Minsk Mazowiecki. In August 1940 a ghetto was established and on Aug. 21, 1942, the great *aktion* in Minsk Mazowiecki took place when about 1,000 were shot on the spot. Almost all of the rest of the Jewish population was transferred to the *Treblinka death camp and exterminated there. Only two groups of workers in the town were left: one, with about 150 men, was transferred to a camp in the Rudzki factory; and the second, with over 500 men, was placed in a camp in the Kopernik school building. Another several hundred succeeded in fleeing the town. Some of them organized small partisan units which became mixed Jewish-Russian units and operated for some time in the region. On Dec. 24, 1942, the Germans shot 218 workers from the Kopernik camp. On Jan. 10, 1943, this camp was liquidated. On the same day the Jewish prisoners offered armed resistance, during which a few Germans were killed or wounded. On June 5, 1943, the camp in the Rudzki factory was liquidated and all its inmates were shot. No Jewish community in Minsk Mazowiecki was reconstituted.

[Stefan Krakowski]

BIBLIOGRAPHY: T. Brustin-Berenstein, in: BŻIH, 1 (1952), 83–125, passim. **ADD. BIBLIOGRAPHY:** *Sefer Minsk Mazowiecki* (1977).

MINSKY, LOUIS (1909–1957), U.S. journalist. Born in England, Minsky went to the U.S. in his youth. He became a special writer on religious topics and in 1934 established the Religious News Service as an independent affiliate of the National Conference of Christians and Jews. It was dedicated to providing authoritative and bias-free news about religion and ethics to both the secular and religious press. Minsky remained head of this interfaith press agency, serving daily newspapers, religious periodicals, radio, and television.

Now the oldest secular news agency covering religion and ethics, RNS is owned by Newhouse News Service and its parent, Advance Publications, Inc. Its daily and weekly news wires are syndicated in hundreds of newspapers, reaching more than 20 million readers worldwide. In the past, it covered such stories as the civil rights movement, the persecution of the Jews during World War II, the rise of the evangelical movement, the Vietnam antiwar movement, and the founding of the State of Israel, as well as Pope John Paul II's visit to the Holy Land in 2000. Ever widening its scope, its coverage includes such topics as Islam, Asian religions, New Age, tribal beliefs, gay rights, and sexual harassment.

[Ruth Beloff (2nd ed.)]

MINTCHINE, ABRAHAM (1908–1931), painter. Mintchine was born in Kiev, Russia, where he became apprenticed to a goldsmith. He went to Berlin in 1923 but in the following year went to France and began to exhibit in the Salon des Indépendents. By the time of his premature death, Mintchine had established himself as one of the most gifted of the East European artists who settled in Paris and who constituted the Paris School of Art. He painted still-life, compositions, and landscapes, but the most striking part of his output was a series of superb self-portraits. Early influences of Cubism were soon abandoned for a broader style, closer to German Expressionism, but devoid of *angst* or nervous anxiety. René Gimpel, the distinguished French art dealer, was one of Mintchine's main patrons. He is represented in leading public museums throughout the world, including his native Kiev; his masterpiece, a self-portrait as a harlequin, is in the Tate Gallery, London.

[Charles Samuel Spencer]

MINTMASTERS AND MONEYERS. In the Middle Ages rulers tended to lease the right of minting coins to mintmasters or to grant and sell the right to their territorial vassals, who themselves employed such mintmasters. Jews carried out this prestigious and profitable enterprise mainly either as suppliers of precious metals for minting purposes or as distributors of coins; very rarely were they the actual craftsmen. In general, in the later Middle Ages, the Jewish master of the mint or purveyor was superseded by a Christian.

The Jew *Priscus was probably master of the mint for King Clotaire of the Franks and issued the royal coins at Chalon-sur-Saône around 555 C.E. Some Czech numismatists consider that Omeriz, Mizleta, and Nacub, moneyers for Duke

Boleslav II in Prague toward the end of the tenth century, were Jews. This is also true of Zanta and Noc, who worked at the Vysehrad mint (near Prague). Ladislaus II of Bohemia (1158–73) had a Jewish mintmaster in his province of Lusatia. In the 13th century a cleric complained that the Jews were still lessees of the mint and customs. For much of the 12th and 13th centuries the coinage of some Polish rulers was issued by Jewish mintmasters and often had Hebrew inscriptions on the coins. Boleslav IV (1146–73) used Jews to mint and distribute his currency. Shortly after, Casimir II (1177–94) allowed a Hebrew inscription to appear on state coins. Mieszko III (1173–77, 1195–1202) gave a life grant to the Jews to lease the state mint, and Polish currency in the last two decades of the 12th century was stamped solely in Hebrew. Most of the inscriptions were various dedications to Mieszko. Boleslav of Kujawy and Mieszko the Younger imitated their father. Boleslav permitted his own name to be stamped in Hebrew, while Mieszko the Younger allowed the names of Jewish mintmasters, such as Ben Jacob and Joseph ha-Kohen, to be inscribed; sometimes the names covered the entire face of the coin, as in the case of R. Abraham b. Isaac Nagid. Przemyslav I later continued this practice some 40 years, as did his son Przemyslav II; Menahem, Jacob, and Abraham were mintmasters whose names were stamped on coins.

In later Polish history, Jews continued to be mintmasters, although no Hebrew appeared on their coins. In 1360 the Cracow mint was transferred to *Lewko, an important Jewish financier. Under Sigismund I, between 1509 and 1518, Abraham *Ezofowitz was minister of the exchequer and in charge of minting coins. In 1555 Sigismund II leased the mint in his Lithuanian province of Poland for three years to a Jew in Vilna. He again gave the Vilna concession to the Jews Felix and *Borodavka in 1560. Because of their prominence in the fields of money changing, moneylending, and finance, Jews participated in minting activities in Poland almost without interruption from the early stages of the kingdom until its partition. From the 17th century, the Councils of the Lands, both in Poland and Lithuania, showed much concern and great reservation about coin minting and the coin trade.

Jews leased mints in Christian Spain as early as the 11th century. Bonnom (Shem Tov) made gold coins under the authority of Count Ramón Berenguer I of Barcelona. In 1066 the count's son sold the right to mint coinage to a syndicate which included David b. Jacob ha-Ivri. *Benveniste de Porta (d. 1268) leased the mint of Barcelona from James I of Aragon. Sancho IV of Castile gave a similar concession to Abraham el Barchilon in 1287. A century later, in 1331, Alfonso XI of Castile repeated this with Samuel *Ibn Waqar (Aben Huacar); Pedro IV of Aragon gave control of the royal mint to a Jewish company at about the same time.

As early as 1063 Queen Anastasia of Hungary permitted a Jew to mint his own coins at the royal mint. Hebrew appears on a coin of Andrew II in the early 13th century. Andrew's Golden Bull of 1222 excluded Jews and Muslims from the office of mintmaster, but the prohibition was disregarded, for the coins of his son Bela IV and his grandson Stephen V bear Hebrew letters, apparently standing for the initials or signs of Jewish mintmasters.

The first Jew recorded by name in Austria was *Shlom the mintmaster, massacred by crusaders in 1195. The nobility obtained a decree in 1222 specifically excluding Jews from the post, but Jews were again employed in this capacity some 40 years later. Jewish mintmasters were found in other German states and principalities, particularly in the 12th century, though their role was much less significant in the centuries that followed. In the Wetterau region, thin coins stamped on one side only, known as bracteates, were issued between 1170 and 1180, with the name David ha-Kohen imprinted in Hebrew. In this same period Otto the Rich, margrave of Meissen, employed Gershon, who also struck his name in Hebrew on bracteates. Nearby, at Lausitz and Pegau, Jews operated mints for the local nobility. Twelfth-century bracteates from Saxony, made under both Count von Mansfeld and Duke Bernhard I, show Hebrew letters. Similarly Jehiel, the name of a Jewish mintmaster at Wuerzburg in the early 13th century, is clearly marked in Hebrew on numerous bracteates. The question of whether a Jewish mintmaster might operate on the Sabbath appears twice in contemporary responsa; he might do so only if he had a Christian partner. The number of Jewish mintmasters was restricted, however, both by the appearance of Christian symbols and formulas on coins and by guild regulations.

The 16th and 17th centuries witnessed political and economic developments in central Europe which enabled Jews to play an unprecedented role in purveying. The growing independence of the many petty German states, the mercantilist theory of the supreme value of precious metals for state economy, as well as the readiness of the unprincipled rulers to issue debased coin, combined to create a need for expertise and initiative. The increased demand for currency was thwarted by the depletion of the silver mines; the metals had to be imported from the Americas or bought at the entrepôts of Amsterdam, London, and Hamburg, where Sephardi Jews were prominent in the bullion trade. In Poland, too, Jews were experts in all aspects of the coin trade. The princes and rulers of the petty and larger states of the Holy Roman Empire and elsewhere turned to them for purveying, minting, and distributing currency. This was done by means of contracts (see *contractors) between the ruler and his *Muenzjude* ("mint Jew"), who was to be found at virtually every court. The purveying of silver was conducted by a sophisticated network of contractors and subcontractors reaching down to the level of the peddler (see *peddling), entrusted with the task of buying up foreign coinage, silver and copper wares, and anything else suitable. The actual minting was supervised by Jews, contractors of the mint. The coin dies were often made by Jewish seal engravers, a profession which Jews tended to monopolize, by virtue of its being free of medieval guild restrictions. The distribution of the freshly minted, often inferior quality coinage was often entrusted to military contractors, frequently Jews.

While *Muenzjuden* were active throughout the 17th and 18th centuries, their activity increased even further during the unstable periods of intensive monetary activity, especially so from 1618 to 1623, the 1670s and 1680s, from 1756 to 1763, and at all times during war and turmoil. During these crucial phases the activity of the *Muenzjuden* brought them into a disrepute that aroused anti-Jewish feelings, reaching a peak during the Seven Years' War.

Among the more prominent Jewish mintmasters of the 16th century were Phybes of Hanover, a lessee of the mint at Wunstorf, Brunswick, in 1566, and Isaac Meir (Mayer) of Prague, who administered the mint from 1546 to 1549. The most famous was *Lippold, the mintmaster of Brandenburg, who ruled the electorate's Jewry with an iron hand. In the first decades of the 17th century, a number of Jewish mintmasters and contractors achieved fame, influence, and notoriety, such as Albertus *Denis (Alvaro Diniz), Jacob *Bassevi of Treuenberg, and Israel Wolf (Auerbacher) in Vienna. In Breslau Manasseh of Hotzenplotz gained a foothold to power through his services to the mint, and the number of Jewish silver purveyors in other minting centers in Austria and southern Germany was large. In 1627 they supplied 29% of the silver to the Breslau imperial mint and 50% in 1656. The dependence of the government on such purveyors increased in the 18th century to 78% in 1704, and to 94% in 1720. In the crisis of the 1670s and 1680s Jews were less prominent, although some *Court Jews were active in the precious metals and coin trades. Among such Court Jews was Jacob Mussaphia, of the duchy of Holstein-Gottorf. Jewish mintmasters reestablished communities in Saxony, from which Jews had been expelled. The nuclei of the Jewish communities of Leipzig and Dresden were formed by the *Muenzjuden*. Gerd Levi (1659–1739) received a license to buy and supply silver (1710) to the Leipzig mint; his son, Levi Gerd, continued in his father's footsteps.

The classical country of Jewish minting activity, however, was Prussia. Throughout most of the 17th and 18th centuries the *Muenzjuden* constituted the leadership of the Berlin community. Israel Aron, first head of the newly reconstituted (1671) community of Viennese exiles, was purveyor to the Berlin mint. His widow, Esther, married the court jeweler Jost *Liebmann and received (between 1700 and 1713) permission to mint large series of small coins as payment for the precious stones which she had supplied to the court. Levin Veit monopolized the purveying of silver in the years 1717 to 1721 and received permission to smelt and refine silver. In the 1750s two firms, that of Daniel *Itzig and members of the *Gomperz family, and that of V.H. *Ephraim and members of the *Fraenkel family, competed fiercely, one outbidding the other for the state minting contract. Frederick II's growing and urgent demands for funds during the war forced the competing firms into a partnership (in 1758), which leased all Prussian and Saxon mints. The Saxon mints of Leipzig and Dresden had been occupied by Frederick, who turned them over to his entrepreneurs, who then issued successive series of millions of more debased Saxon coins. These were known as "Ephraimiten" and gave rise to the bitter popular refrain: "Pretty on the outside, worthless within; on the outside Frederick, Ephraim within." Frederick instituted similar proceedings with the currency of Mecklenburg-Schwerin, Anhalt-Zerbst, and Anhalt-Dessau, and he was also forced to debase Prussian currency. The last Ephraim-Frederick contract was signed on Dec. 17, 1762. After the war *Muenzjuden* were employed in buying up the corrupt coinage and in supplying silver for the reconstituted currency. Ephraim and his sons were gradually overshadowed by the Itzig family, who were sole purveyors of precious metals between 1771 and 1786. One of Itzig's many agents was David *Friedlaender of Koenigsberg and his sons (David was the most talented). The last important mint entrepreneur was Liepmann Meyer Wulff of Berlin, who supplied the mint between 1799 and the Prussian debacle of 1806, after which thorough governmental reforms were introduced which abolished the need for the services of private silver and gold purveyors.

The tradition of Jewish moneyers and mintmasters in the Muslim world goes back to the Middle Ages. A certain Sumayr was die cutter and mintmaster for Abdalmalik (685–705), the Umayyad caliph at Damascus. Since the earliest Muslim coins were struck at this time, Sumayr was one of the technical founders of Islamic coinage. Jewish moneyers were known in Cairo from earliest times, possibly being successors to those previously operating in Alexandria. Japheth b. Abraham, in partnership with two other Jews, was administrator of the Fostat mint (see *Cairo) in about 1086. A brief mention is made in a document from the Cairo *Genizah* of two Jewish partners working the caliphate mint in the second half of the 12th century. The most noted Cairo mintmasters were Isaac *Sholal and Abraham Castro, who was appointed to the position after the conquest of Egypt by Sultan Selim (c. 1520). When the Egyptian viceroy, Ahmed Pasha, plotted independence, it was Castro who informed Constantinople. He was reinstated after Ahmed's defeat in 1524. In the 1660s this same position was held by the court banker Raphael Joseph, known as Chelebi. Under Murad III (1574–95) the director of the Turkish mint was a Jew, Hodja Nessimi (or Nissim). In this same period, Moses *Benveniste – known to the Turks as Hodja Moussahibi – was involved in the currency "reform" which led to a revolt of the janissaries against "Jews' Money" in 1589. Samuel b. Abraham, head of the Crimean Karaites, was moneyer to the last Tatar khan in the mid-18th century. As the treasury minister, he held the official title of Aga. His son Benjamin succeeded him in both position and title. When the Crimea was conquered by Russia in 1783, Benjamin was permitted to retain his title. Yaḥyā b. Judah *Badiḥi (1810–1888) was minter for the imam of Yemen in the mid-19th century.

See also *Banking; *Court Jews; *Moneylending; *Medalists; *Numismatics; *Coins and Currency.

BIBLIOGRAPHY: MEDIEVAL EUROPE: P. Grierson, *Bibliographie Numismatique* (1966); S. Stern, *Court Jew* (1950), 47, 157, 162–76, 211, 218; M. Hoffmann, *Geldhandel der deutschen Juden* (1910); S. Katz, *Jews in the Visigothic and Frankish Kingdoms of France and Gaul*

(1934), 122f.; d'Amecourt, in: *Annuaire de la Société française de Numismatique et d'Archéologie*, 4 (1873), 128–31; J. Cahn, in: *Zeitschrift fuer Numismatik*, 33 (1922); *Biographical Dictionary of Medalists*, 8 vols. (1902–30); Baer, Spain, 1 (1961), 146, 327, 131–2; 2 (1966), 29; Neuman, Spain, 2 (1942), 237, 245, 252; D.M. Friedenberg, in: *Numismatist*, 130 (1967), 1515–28; W. Gumowski, *Handbuch der polnischen Numismatik* (1960), 91–96; I. Schiper, *Di Virtshaft Geshikhte fun di Yidn in Poyln Beysn Mittelalter* (1929), 235ff.; A. Wolf, in: MGJV, 9 (1902), 24–25; L. Réthy and G. Probszt, *Corpus Nummorum Hungariae*, 71, 74, 77, 89. CENTRAL EUROPE AND MODERN ERA: H.I. Bloom, *Economic Activities of the Jews of Amsterdam* (1933); B. Brilling, *Geschichte der Juden in Breslau 1754–1802* (1960); idem, in: JGGJC, 7 (1935), 387–98; F. Redlich, in: *Explorations in Entrepreneurial History*, 3 (1951), 161–98; H. Kellenbenz, *Sephardim an der unteren Elbe* (1958), 210–44; H. Schnee, *Hoffinanz und der Moderne Staat*, 5 vols. (1953–67); A. Pribram, *Urkunden und Akten zur Geschichte der Juden in Wien* (1918), index, s.v. *Muenzjuden*; M. Koehler, *Juden in Halberstadt* (1927), 41–48; S. Stern, *Preussische Staat und die Juden*, 2 (1962), Akten: no. 46–71; no. 124–8; no. 144–69; no. 177; M. Grunwald, *Samuel Oppenheimer und sein Kreis* (1913), index. MUSLIM COUNTRIES: S.D. Goitein, *A Mediterranean Society*, 1 (1967), 362, 365; S. Poznański, *Babylonische Geonim* (1914), 133; S. Assaf, in: *Zion*, 1 (1937), 256f.; A.N. Pollak, *ibid.*, 24–30.

[Daniel M. Friedenberg and Henry Wasserman]

MINTZ, MOSES BEN ISAAC (15th century), German talmudist. Moses was born in Mainz sometime between 1420 and 1430. He studied under his father, Israel *Isserlein, and Jacob *Weil. During his extensive travels, he visited various towns, investigating their customs and communal regulations. His first rabbinate was at Wuerzburg where he served for a short time, until the expulsion of the Jews from the town in 1453. He proceeded to Mainz, where he stayed until the expulsion of 1462. From there he went to Landau and in 1464 to Ulm. In 1469 he was appointed rabbi of Bamberg. Four years later he went to Nuremberg and the following year to Posen. While there he decided to immigrate to Ereẓ Israel; he had already made all final preparations when for some reason he had to abandon his plan, and it appears that he remained in Posen until the end of his life. The year of his death is unknown.

Mintz's influence spread in Germany and beyond. He was involved in communal affairs and individuals, including outstanding scholars, as well as communities turned to him with their problems and disputes. Concern for the community and its general welfare was of paramount importance to him. He directed a yeshivah and engaged in discussions with his pupils. In 1456–57 R. Seligman Bing Oppenheim and R. Menahem Bachrach convened a council in *Bingen for the purpose of enacting *takkanot* that would be binding on other communities also – a step which did not meet with the approval of the rabbis of Germany. Despite his esteem for Seligman Bing, Mintz strongly opposed them and the *takkanot* were not adopted. Similarly, when he felt that Bing had been guilty of faulty judgment, he did not hesitate to criticize him, though there was nothing personal in his criticism. In another dispute in Italy, when Liva Landa placed a ban upon the rabbis of Padua, including Mintz's cousin Isaac Mintz, Moses agreed to place Landa under a ban although he was a venerable scholar and teacher, "unless he withdraw his ban and appease the rabbis of Padua," and at the same time he appealed to the rabbis of Padua "to waive their rights and show respect for a sage." Should Landa remain obdurate, however, "then the ban on him is to remain in force." Moses concludes: "I do this neither for my own honor nor for the honor of my family, but for the sake of Heaven to prevent the increase of strife in Israel." Moses was an accomplished *ḥazzan* and conducted the services on the high holidays. His best-known pupil is *Joseph b. Moses, author of the *Leket Yosher*.

Moses Mintz's fame rests on his responsa (Cracow, 1617); the 119 published, chiefly on civil and matrimonial law, abound in references to local customs and *takkanot*, ancient and new, including those ascribed to *Gershom b. Judah of Mainz and *takkanot* SHUM (Speyer, Worms, and Mainz). The index lists 120 responsa, but the last one has been omitted from all editions. This may be because of its subject, which the author describes as: "The stern words I wrote to the seven elders of the Regensburg community. It lays down that one who has a right of settlement in a community and leaves, subsequently to return, has not lost his previous right… And it explains that a scholar should not take advantage of his status to act haughtily." The main source for Moses' biography is the responsa, where it is related that his wife Minlan was "crowned with the crown of the Torah and piety." They also include many local *takkanot* introduced by Mintz, some of a social character, including rulings on the vestments a reader should don when conducting the service, how a man should conduct himself during prayer, etc.

Of special value are three responsa in manuscript entitled "The Three Branches," which are an important source for the history of the yeshivot of Germany in the 15th century. They depict the woeful condition of pupil-teacher relations, which had broken down as a result of the arrogance of the teachers and their exaggerated concern for their dignity, as well as because of the pupils' desire for greater freedom of activity and the acquisition of social status. The laymen, too, did not accept the authority of the rabbis and disregarded their rulings. The responsa reflect other aspects of the life of the Jews in Germany: their economic, social, family, and religious life, study, the attitude of the Jews to gentiles, persecutions, and expulsions, etc.

BIBLIOGRAPHY: Joseph b. Moses, *Leket Yosher*, ed. by J. Freimann, 2 (1904), 45 no. 103 (introd.); Guedemann, Gesch Erz, 3 (1888), index; M.A. Szulwas, *Die Juden in Wuerzburg* (1934), 77; Tal, in: *Sinai*, 40 (1957), 228–47, 278–92.

[Shlomo Tal]

MINTZ, PAUL (1870–after 1940), Latvian lawyer. Born in Dvinsk (Daugavpils), Mintz was one of the most prominent lawyers in Riga. After Latvia became an independent republic (1918), he was appointed professor of criminal law at the University of Riga. He was a member of the Latvian National Council and the Constituent Assembly, and was the only

Jewish member of the Latvian government, serving as state controller. He published various legal works and was chairman of the commission preparing the Latvian code of criminal law. He was also active in Jewish affairs as founder of the Ḥevrat Mefiẓei Haskalah (*Society for the Promotion of Culture Among the Jews of Russia), in Riga, chairman of the Jewish National-Democratic Party, chairman of the commission preparing a draft for the legal framework of Jewish national autonomy, a non-Zionist member of the *Jewish Agency for Palestine, and chairman of the Jewish Lawyers' Society in Latvia. In 1940, when Latvia was occupied by the Soviet forces, Mintz was arrested together with other Jewish and non-Jewish leaders and deported to Kansk, near Krasnoyarsk, and later to a Soviet labor camp, where he died.

BIBLIOGRAPHY: *Yahadut Latvia* (1953), index.

[Joseph Gar]

MINTZ, SHLOMO (1957–), Israeli violinist, violist, and conductor. Mintz was born in Moscow. The family immigrated to Israel in 1959. He was a student of Ilona Feher and gave his first recital in 1966, making his début with the Israel PO in 1968. With the support of Isaac Stern and the America Israel Cultural Foundation Mintz made his Carnegie Hall debut in 1973 and completed his training with Dorothy DeLay in Juilliard. He made a major European tour in 1977 and appeared regularly with the most celebrated orchestras and conductors. He was also heard in recital and chamber music concerts as well as playing the viola. Mintz is esteemed for his silvery beauty of tone, his command of the standard repertory, sensitive playing, and commanding technique. He gave recitals with the pianists Itamar Golan and Georges Pludermacher, and as a member of the Golan-Mintz-Haimovitz Trio. Among his recordings are works by Bach, Ravel, Sibelius, and Paganini. He was musical director of the Israel Chamber Orchestra in 1989–93 and also conducted the Israel PO and the Rotterdam PO. In 1994 he was appointed musical director of the Limburg SO in Maastricht. Mintz held master courses in many places, and was one of the founders and supporters of the Keshet Eilon International Violin Master Course for talented young musicians. He was a member of the jury of several important international competitions, such as the Tchaikovsky Competition in Moscow. He won many music prizes, including Sienna's Premio Accademia Musicale Chigiana and three times the Grand Prix du Disque.

BIBLIOGRAPHY: Grove online; *Baker's Biographical Dictionary* (1997).

[Naama Ramot (2nd ed.)]

MINYAN (Heb. מִנְיָן; "number"), designation for the quorum of ten male adults, aged 13 years or over, necessary for public synagogue service and certain other religious ceremonies. The Talmud (Ber. 21b; Meg. 23b) derives this number from the term *edah* ("community"), which in the Scriptures is applied to the ten spies (Num. 14:27). Thus ten men constitute a congregation. The Talmud (Ket. 7b) also mentions Ruth 4:2 and Psalm 68:27. Some relate the rule to Abraham's plea to God to save Sodom if at least ten righteous men were found there (Gen. 18:32). On the basis of Psalm 82:1: "God standeth in the congregation of God," the Talmud explains that if ten men pray together, the Divine Presence is with them (Ber. 6a). This quorum of ten adult males is necessary for the following sections of the public synagogue service: The repetition of the *Amidah* with *Kedushah*, the pentateuchal and *haftarah* reading, priestly benedictions (Meg. 4:3), and the *Kaddish*. Some also require a *minyan* for the recital of the *Barekhu* invocation; others permit this to be said even if only six or seven males are present (Sof. 10:6). The accepted custom in emergency cases is nine adults and a boy holding a Bible (based on PdRE, 8; see Tos. Ber. 48a and Sh. Ar., OH, 55:4). A quorum of ten is also necessary in the rites of comforting the mourners (*ma'amad u-moshav*; Meg. 4:3; Meg. 23b). The recital of the seven nuptial blessings at wedding ceremonies and the special invocation preceding grace there ("Let us bless our God of whose bounty we have eaten") also require a *minyan* (*ibid.*).

Ten male adults constitute a quorum in any place, and there is no need for a synagogue building or an officiating rabbi to hold divine services. In talmudic times, a community was regarded as "a city" if there were at least "ten idle men" (not occupied by work or other duties) who could come to each synagogue service to make up the *minyan* (Meg. 1:3). R. Johanan said, "when God comes to a synagogue and does not find a *minyan* there, He is angry, as it is written (Isa. 50:2). 'Wherefore, when I came, was there no man? When I called, was there none to answer?'" (Ber. 6b). In traditional congregations, especially in Eastern Europe, when it was difficult to hold daily services with a *minyan*, it was customary to pay a few old or idle men to be present twice a day at the services. These people were called "*minyan* men."

In Reform, Reconstructionist, and most Conservative practice at the beginning of the 21st century, women were counted in the minimum quorum of 10 persons required to constitute a public prayer service, since they had full religious equality with men.

BIBLIOGRAPHY: Eisenstein, Dinim, 239ff.; Elbogen, Gottesdienst, 493ff.; JE, 8 (1907), 603; JL, 4 (1930), 203ff. **ADD. BIBLIOGRAPHY:** R. Biale, *Women and Jewish Law* (1984), 21–24; S. Freehof, *Reform Jewish Practice*, 1 (1948), 49–52; D. Golinkin. *The Status of Women in Jewish Law: Responsa* (2001).

MINYAT ZIFTA, town in Lower *Egypt, on the eastern tributary of the Nile. In the *Fāṭimid period, there was an important Jewish community in this town. R. *Abraham b. Shabbetai, who wrote several works on *halakhah*, was rabbi (*ḥaver*) of the community at the beginning of the 12th century, and after him, his son Shabbetai held the same position for many years. In a list of contributions to a collection among the communities of Lower Egypt at the middle of the same century, Minyat Zifta is mentioned as the second largest contributor. From the **Genizah* documents it appears that the social status of the Jews was variegated; among them were craftsmen, merchants, and government officials. The Jewish population decreased over the generations and in the 19th century, Jacob *Saphir found only five families there: in 1897 there were 84 Jews, in 1907, 54, and in 1927 only 37. By 1924 the synagogue had already been sold, and in 1937 there was only one family living in the town.

BIBLIOGRAPHY: J. Saphir, *Even Sappir* (1866), 8b; Mann, Egypt, 2 (1922), 257–9, 287, 290; Mann, Texts, 1 (1931), 446ff.; Poznański, in: REJ, 65 (1913), 43; Goitein, in: JQR, 49 (1958/59), 41; J.M. Landau, *Ha-Yehudim be-Miẓrayim ba-Me'ah ha-Tesha-Esreh* (1967), 51–52. **ADD. BIBLIOGRAPHY:** J.M. Landau, *Jews in Nineteenth-Century Egypt* (1969), 47–8, 172.

[Eliyahu Ashtor]

MINZ, ABRAHAM BEN JUDAH HA-LEVI (d. 1525), Italian scholar and rabbi. Some time before 1509, acting on behalf of his father, Judah b. Eliezer ha-Levi *Minz of Padua, he insulted the famous rabbi, Jacob Margolis of Regensburg. Both father and son subsequently made public apology. In January 1509, after his father's death, Abraham was appointed to succeed him, but in July of the same year a decree of expulsion was issued against him by the Venetian authorities for having presented a gift in the name of the Padua community to the chief of the conquering imperial German army during the sack of Padua. The decree was apparently revoked some time thereafter, as Minz is known to have visited Padua about ten years later. After leaving Padua, Abraham spent 15 months in Ferrara, being supported there by the wealthy *parnas*, Norsa, whom he later sided with in the notorious *Finzi-Norsa controversy, at the height of which Jacob *Pollak, a partisan of Abraham Raphael Finzi, and Minz excommunicated each other. Abraham subsequently became rabbi in Mantua. His son-in-law, Meir *Katzenellenbogen, occupied the Padua rabbinate.

Abraham was the author of a number of responsa, which are printed together with those of his uncle by marriage, R. Liwa of Ferrara (Venice, 1511). He was the author, too, of *Seder Gittin va-Ḥaliẓah*, printed together with the responsa of his father and his son-in-law (Venice, 1553). He died in Padua.

BIBLIOGRAPHY: A. Marx, *Studies in Jewish History and Booklore* (1944), 107–54 (= *Abhandlungen… Chajes* (1933), 149–93); I.T. Eisenstadt and S. Wiener, *Da'at Kedoshim* (1897/98), 5–38, 88 (third pagination).

[Shlomo Eidelberg]

MINZ, BENJAMIN (1903–1961), leader of the *Po'alei Agudat Israel movement. Born in Lodz, Poland, Minz went to Palestine in 1925. A member of Agudat Israel from his youth, he persistently advocated cooperation with the Zionist Movement, despite the opposition of his leaders. At the Third Great Assembly of Agudat Israel (Marienbad, 1937), he was elected a member of the Central Council, and in 1938 was elected to the Po'alei Agudat Israel Executive. During World War II, he was active on the Va'ad ha-Haẓẓalah (rescue committee), and after the war he worked in DP camps in Germany (see *Displaced Persons). He initiated the founding of the World Union of Po'alei Agudat Israel at the Antwerp Conference (1946), and as its head led the movement into close cooperation with the institutions of the *yishuv*, in opposition to the policy of *Agudat Israel. Minz was a member of the Provisional State Council of Israel (1948) and later of the Knesset. He was elected deputy speaker of the Second Knesset and held the post until the Fourth Knesset. He overruled a decision of the Council of Torah Sages of Agudat Israel and joined the coalition government as minister of posts in 1960, thus causing a rift between his party and Agudat Israel. Minz wrote several books, mainly on ḥasidic topics.

[Menachem Friedman]

MINZ, JUDAH BEN ELIEZER HA-LEVI (c. 1408–1506), Italian rabbi. Judah, a first cousin of Moses *Mintz, was a member of a family of scholars and bankers which derived its name from the town of Mainz, where he was probably born. It is presumed that Minz left Mainz in 1462 during the expulsion of the Jews (see Graetz, Hist. 4 (1894), 294). He settled in Padua where he became rabbi and rector of the yeshivah and where he remained until his death. In Padua he was taught by R. Asher (Israel) Enschechin, a German talmudist, who lived in the city during his latter years (Resp. Judah Minz, nos. 2, 3; *Leket Yosher*, 2 (1904), xlvii, no. 113). Minz corresponded on halakhic matters with many famous rabbis of his time, including Elijah *Mizraḥi of Turkey (who supported Minz in a quarrel with Elijah Delmedigo, the cause of which is unknown), Israel Isserlein of Wiener-Neustadt, Israel *Bruna of Regensburg and Joseph *Colon of Mantua (see *Seder ha-Get* of Abraham Minz at the end of Judah's responsa and *Leket Yosher*, 2 (1904), xxxii, no. 54). His responsa are a valuable historical source and reveal his involvement in the problems of his time (see e.g., *Leket Yosher*, nos. 5, 6, 11). Ghirondi's assertion that Judah was a student of philosophy, and, subsequently, a professor of philosophy at the University of Padua (Ghirondi-Neppi 122ff.), is now held to be unfounded. In his ritual decisions Judah leaned heavily on his German predecessors (see, e.g., Resp. Judah Minz, nos. 7, 13, 15), but, rather uniquely, permitted men to masquerade as women on Purim (*ibid.* no. 16). Minz's library and most of his manuscripts were destroyed in the year of his death during the sack of Padua (see introd. to *Leket Yosher*). 16 of his responsa were discovered by his grandson Joseph b. Abraham Minz and were published in Venice in 1553 by the husband of Judah's granddaughter, Meir *Katzenellenbogen, together with his own responsa and the *Seder Gittin va-Ḥaliẓah* of Abraham b. Judah ha-Levi *Minz. Many later editions have been published, among them one with notes and a preface by Johanan Moses Preschel (1898).

BIBLIOGRAPHY: Benjacob, Oẓar, 557; Michael, Or, no. 1020; S. Eidelberg, *Jewish Life in Austria in the XVth Century* (1962), 86 n. 21, 103 n. 69; I.T. Eisenstadt and S. Wiener, *Da'at Kedoshim* (1898), Supplement, 63; Finkelstein, Middle Ages, 27, 306, 308; Guedemann, Gesch Erz, 3 (1888), 251 passim; Joseph b. Moses, *Leket Yosher*, ed. by J. Freimann, 2 (1904), xxxii, no. 54; Weiss, Dor, 5 (1924), 280–2; M.A. Shulwas, *Ḥayyei ha-Yehudim be-Italyah bi-Tekufat ha-Renaissance* (1955), 355, index s.v. *Yehudah Minz*; M.D. Cassuto, *Ha-Yehudim be-Firenze bi-Tekufat ha-Renaissance* (1967), 229.

[Shlomo Eidelberg]

MIR, town in Grodno district, Belarus. From 1569 until 1813 the town and the surrounding estates were the property of the Radziwill princes. Jews first settled in Mir at the beginning of the 17th century. To begin with they were under the jurisdiction of the community of *Nesvizh, but within a few years their numbers had rapidly increased, and it can be assumed that they then had their own communal organizations. The Jews became an important factor in local trade and at the two annual fairs held in Mir. Many of them also earned their livelihood as carters. Jewish merchants from every part of Lithuania and Poland were attracted to the fairs of Mir, where they carried on an extensive trade in furs (exporting them especially to Leipzig), horses, oxen, spices, grain, textiles, tobacco (from 1672), and wine. In the records of the Lithuanian council (see *Councils of the Lands) Mir is mentioned for the first time in 1662. The Council convened there four times: 1687, 1697, 1702, 1751. From 1673, the taxes owed by the Jews of Lithuania to state institutions and debts to other creditors were occasionally collected at the Mir fairs. In 1685, after complaints by the Jewish representatives, Catherine Sapieha of the Radziwill family instructed the administrator of the town to respect the rights of the Jews and to refrain from dispensing justice or arbitrating in their internal affairs.

During the early decades of the 18th century, the Jewish population of Mir increased considerably. The local Jewish contribution to the poll tax rose from 45 zlotys in 1673 to 1,160 zlotys in 1700 and 1,350 zlotys in 1720. During this period the merchants of Mir maintained fruitful commercial relations with *Leipzig, *Koenigsberg, *Memel, and Libau (*Liepaja). From the second half of the 18th century, the economic situation of the community declined. In 1760 the Jews of Mir paid 480 zlotys in poll tax; the census of 1765 recorded 607 Jews in the town and the vicinity who paid this tax.

Prominent rabbis officiated in Mir during the 18th century. The first *av bet din* known by name (in the late 1720s) was R. Meir b. Isaac *Eisenstadt, followed by R. Ẓevi Hirsch ha-Kohen Rappoport; during the middle of that century, R. Solomon Zalman b. Judah Mirkish, author of *Shulḥan Shelomo* (Frankfurt on the Oder, 1771), held rabbinical office for 15 years. He was succeeded by R. Ẓevi Hirsh Eisenstadt. During the rabbinate of R. Joseph David Ajzensztat (1776–1826), the famous yeshivah of Mir was founded, functioning there until the eve of WWII. At the beginning of the 19th century *Ḥabad Ḥasidism acquired considerable influence in the community.

In 1806 the Mir community numbered 807, including 106 tailors, five goldsmiths, six cord-makers, and about 30 merchants. In the 65 nearby villages, there were 494 Jews in 1818. The numbers in Mir itself rose to 2,273 in 1847 and 3,319 (about 62% of the total population) in 1897. From the second half of the 19th century, with the exception of the wood, grain, horse, and textile merchants who formed the upper class, the majority of the local Jews were craftsmen such as scribes, carters, butchers, and tailors. The wooden synagogue, which had been erected in the middle of the 18th century, was burnt down in 1901. With the threat of pogroms in 1904–05, Mir Jews organized a *self-defense organization. During this period, the *Bund and *Po'alei Zion movements won many adherents in the town. The Zionist movement was organized there in 1914. In 1921 there were 2,074 Jews (c. 55% of the population) living in the town. Their difficult economic situation deteriorated even further from the late 1920s. A Yiddish elementary school and kindergarten were founded in 1917; during the 1920s they were administered by CYSHO and during the 1930s by the Shul-Kult. During the same period, *Tarbut, Yavneh, and *Beth Jacob schools functioned in Mir. The Jewish library was founded in 1908.

The yeshivah of Mir, founded by Samuel b. Ḥayyim *Tiktinski in 1815 and directed by his son Abraham after his death, played a central role in the spiritual life of the community. From 1836 it was headed by Moses Abraham b. Joseph Ajzensztat and later by Ḥayyim Zalman Bresler, rabbi of the town, who resigned as the result of a dispute. From then on, the offices of town rabbi and *rosh yeshivah* were separated. From the 1880s, the rabbi was Yom Tov Lipman (R. Lipa). In 1903 he was succeeded by R. Elijah David *Rabinowitz-Teomim, who served until his *aliyah* to Ereẓ Israel. The last rabbi of Mir was Abraham Ẓevi Kamai (from 1917 until the Holocaust). During World War I, the yeshivah of Mir was transferred to Poltava but returned to the town in 1921, and was then headed by R. Eliezer Judah Finkel. Mir was the birthplace of Zalman *Shazar (Rubashov).

[Arthur Cygielman]

Holocaust Period

Under Soviet rule (1939–41) private enterprise was gradually stifled and factories, businesses, and even large buildings were taken over by the state. The yeshivah students and rabbis, headed by R. Eliezer Judah Finkel, moved to Vilna in still independent Lithuania (Finkel managed to reach Palestine and founded the Mir Yeshivah in Jerusalem). The Germans captured Mir on June 27, 1941. They immediately executed scores of Jews on charges of Soviet collaboration. On Nov. 9, 1941, 1,300 Jews were murdered on the outskirts of the town. The surviving 850 Jews were segregated into a ghetto and transferred in May 1942 to the ancient fortress in the city. A young Jew, Shemuel (Oswald) Rufeisen, born in the Cracow district, played a key role in the Mir resistance movement. He posed as a *Volksdeutscher*, Joseph Oswald. After the removal of the Jews to the Mirski fortress, a resistance movement of 80 members was organized to offer armed resistance to the imminent *Aktion* ("action") against the Jewish population. Working in groups of five, they acquired weapons and trained themselves. Their central command was made up of Ha-Shomer ha-Ẓa'ir, Deror, Bund, and Communists.

Early in August 1942 Rufeisen informed the underground that the Germans would begin their liquidation campaign on Aug. 13. On Aug. 9 about 300 young people left for the forests on the assumption that no effective resistance action against the Germans could be taken inside the ghetto. On August 13 the liquidation action began, and all those who had remained in the ghetto were murdered in Yablonoshchina and buried in mass graves. Those who had escaped to the forests were confronted with many difficulties. Russian partisan units often refused to accept Jews into their ranks, and many of the Mir Jews who came to the forests were killed by antisemitic Russian partisans. Despite all these difficulties, Mir Jews managed to join Soviet partisan units, mainly the Brothers Bielski brigade, and took part in sabotage activities. Following the arrival of the Soviet army, the Jewish partisans from Mir joined the Soviet forces to continue the fight against the Nazis up till the end of the war.

The student body of the yeshivah was saved during the war by escaping to *Shanghai. After the war (1947), the yeshivah was transferred to Brooklyn, New York (Mirrer Yeshivah Central Institute). Some of its scholars later joined the Mir Yeshivah in Jerusalem.

[Aharon Weiss]

BIBLIOGRAPHY: S. Dubnow, *Pinkas Medinat Lita* (1925), 197, 240–1, 257–9; Halpern, Pinkas, index; idem, *Tosafot u-Millu'im le-"Pinkas Medinat Lita"* (1935), 31–33, 40–44, 51–52, 66–67; *Regesty i nadpisi*, 2 (1899), nos. 1184, 1232, 1235, 1596; S. Maimon, *Autobiography*, ed. by M. Hadas (1967); I. Schiper, *Dzieje handlu żydowskiege na ziemiach polskich* (1937), index; R. Markgraf, *Zur Geschichte der Juden auf den Messen in Leipzig von 1664–1839* (1894), 29–30; N. Blumenthal (ed.), *Sefer Mir* (Heb. and Yid., 1962). **ADD. BIBLIOGRAPHY:** S. Spector (ed.), PK Polin, vol. 8, North-East (Vilna, Grodno, Bialystok) (2005).

°MIRABEAU, HONORE GABRIEL RIQUETI, COMTE DE (1749–91), statesman of the *French Revolution. Mirabeau became interested in the Jewish question during his visits to Holland in 1776, England in 1784, and Prussia in 1786. Influenced by the enlightened members of the Jewish communities in the capitals of these three countries, he was particularly attracted by the image of Moses *Mendelssohn. In the book resulting from this journey, *Sur Moses Mendelssohn, sur la réforme politique des Juifs* (London, 1787), he argued that the faults of the Jews were those of their circumstances. Although his main reason for admiring Mendelssohn was that "humanity and truth" seemed much clearer to him than "the dark phantoms of the Talmudists," Mirabeau did not consider Judaism an immoral faith, and he defended it against attacks both old and new. In the course of his argument, he repeated *Dohm's assertion that "the Jew is more of a man than he is a Jew." Quoting from Turgot and *Rousseau in support of his pro-Jewish arguments, Mirabeau affirms that history proves that "the Jews, considered as men and as citizens, were greatly corrupted only because they were denied their rights." Like Dohm he advocated preserving some measure of Jewish autonomy, a view he developed in his memorandum to *Frederick the Great of Prussia, *De la monarchie prussienne* (1788), p. 462, but he envisaged it as a transitory phenomenon; the organized Jewish community would wither away and die as the Jews entered fully into the economic and social life of the majority. Mirabeau continued to work for the emancipation of the Jews as he saw it. In the debate of Dec. 24, 1789, he denied Rewbell's assertion that "they [the Jews] do not regard themselves as citizens," and followed *Clermont-Tonnerre in stating that the very fact that the Jews were requesting equality was proof of their desire to cease being Jewish in any separatist way.

BIBLIOGRAPHY: L. Kahn, *Les juifs de Paris pendant la révolution* (1898); H. de Jouvenel, *Stormy Life of Mirabeau* (1929); A. Hertzberg, *French Enlightenment and the Jews* (1968), index.

[Emmanuel Beeri]

MIRACLE. Biblical Hebrew has no word corresponding to the English "miracle." Occasionally, the Bible mentions "wonders" (*pele'*, *nifla'ot*) meaning "miracles" (Ex. 3:20; Josh. 3:5; Ps. 78:11; etc.), but the meaning of "wonder" is much broader than "miracle." A particular class of miracles, however, can be considered as a definite biblical concept, since it is designated by terms of its own. These are the "signs" (*'otot, mofetim*), i.e., extraordinary and surprising events which God brought about in order to demonstrate His power and will in particular situations, when men had to be convinced. A sign can be given as proof of prophecy. Thus the altar of Beth-El collapsed as a sign that the prophecy of its future destruction was true (I Kings 13:1–6). The more important signs occurred in Egypt: the staff turned into a serpent to show that Moses was indeed sent by God (Ex. 4:1–7), and the ten plagues coerced Pharaoh to accept the divine command and let the people go. Deuteronomy 13 raises the problem of a sign given by a false prophet: it can be genuine, brought about by God to test the people, who must not obey under any circumstances a prophet summoning them to idolatry. The problem shows that "signs" as proofs of prophecy were regarded – at least among theologians – as regular (or indeed necessary) events.

Some biblical miracles are more than signs, i.e., their purpose goes beyond the mere proof of divine power. Israel was saved and Egypt's army destroyed by the parting of the Red Sea, the people were given water and food in the desert by means of miraculous acts, and so on. Both Samaria (II Kings 6:8–7:20) and Jerusalem (II Kings 19:35) miraculously escaped conquest by besieging armies. Such miracles can be viewed as direct divine intervention at critical moments of human history. Even in these incidents, the element of a "sign" is never wholly absent. Dathan and *Abiram and their followers were swallowed by the earth; it was a just punishment, whose suddenness was demanded by the situation. Moses' words (Num. 16:28–30), however, designate the event clearly as a sign. It is also stated that when Israel saw the mighty deed of Egypt's destruction in the sea, they believed in God and in Moses (Ex. 14:31). Evidently, the Bible makes no distinction between signs proper and miraculous divine intervention in human history. There is a third type of miracle in the Bible in which the sheer admiration of the wonder-worker seems more important than both elements discussed above. One cannot escape this impression when reading the stories about Elijah and, to an even greater degree, about Elisha. Such stories are a regular feature of popular religion of all times and in all places; in the Bible they are almost entirely confined to the figures of these two "nonliterary" prophets.

The problem of whether miracles are "natural" or "supernatural," which was of concern to scholars of later ages, does not bother Bible writers. In one case (Num. 16:30), a miracle is described as a "creation," which indicates an awareness of what moderns might call the "suspension of natural laws" (see also Ex. 34:10). On the other hand, the miracle of the descent of the quail (Num. 9:18–23) is quite plainly and clearly described as a "natural" – though unexpected – occurrence and yet is treated as a full-scale miracle. Bible writers simply do not question God's ability to do anything, by any means.

The intellectual's dislike of miracles has furnished the mainstream of Bible criticism with a yardstick: some "sources" contain more accounts of miracles than others, and are therefore deemed less "valuable." Scholars with apologetic tendencies tend to minimize the importance of Bible miracles, in their endeavor to make biblical religion less "crude" and more "pure." This case can be based on the preponderance of the "sign" concept in the Bible discussed above, but is nevertheless wrong. The Bible does not, as a rule, tell miracle stories for their own sake, but it does regard the "signs and wonders" of God as extremely important. Man has to know that God can do anything, whenever and wherever He chooses; that this has been demonstrated in history many times; and the sacred history of Israel has been shaped often enough by direct and quite evident divine intervention. Faith that can do without this notion of miracles is possible, but unthinkable in biblical terms.

[Jacob Licht]

In the Talmud

The almost universal word for a miracle in the talmudical literature is the term נֵס (*nes*), used in the Bible for a "sign" or "standard." The biblical miracles are unquestionably accepted by the sages of the Talmud. Insofar as their theological aspect is concerned, three main considerations exercised the minds of the sages: (1) the reversal of the order of creation with its corollary of an insufficiency in the act of creation; (2) the miracle as a testimony of the truth of religion; and (3) the "daily miracles" which do not involve a disturbance of the order of creation.

(1) According to the rabbis, the miracles were, so to speak, preordained and provided for in the act of creation. "R. Johanan said, God made a condition with the sea that it would part before the Children of Israel… R. Jeremiah b. Eleazar said, not with the sea alone, but with whatever God created on the six days of creation… God commanded heaven and earth that they should be silent before Moses; the sun and moon that they should stand still before Joshua; the ravens that they should feed Elijah; the fire that it should not harm Hananiah, Mishael, and Azariah; the lions that they injure not Daniel; the heavens that they should open to the voice of Ezekiel; and the fish that it should cast up Jonah'" (Gen. R. 5:45). Another passage emphasizes this idea even more strongly. When God commanded Moses to lift up his staff and part the Red Sea, Moses argued with God that it would involve a breach of his own act of creation, God answered him, "Thou hast not read the beginning of the Torah… I made a condition at the time"; and only then did Moses heed the divine behest (Ex. R. 21:6). In the same vein, the Mishnah (Avot 5:6) enumerates ten things which "were created on the eve of the Sabbath [of creation] at twilight," including the mouth of the earth which opened up to swallow Korah (Num. 16:32), the mouth of the ass of Balaam which spoke (Num. 22:28), the manna (Ex. 16:14), and the rod of Moses (Ex. 4:17). As Zangwill (quoted by J.H. Hertz, Comm. to Prayer Book) puts it, the Talmud sages "discovered the reign of universal law through exceptions, the miracles that had to be created specially and were still a part of the order of the world, bound to appear in due time."

(2) That miracles are not evidence of religious truth is clearly and explicitly stated in the Bible (Deut. 13:2–4). The rabbis emphasize this in a striking incident wherein R. Eliezer b. Hyrcanus called for, and achieved, a series of miracles for the purpose of proving that his halakhic ruling was correct, but R. Joshua disdainfully rejected them, quoting "the Torah is not in heaven" and his contrary view was accepted (BM 59a).

(3) The rabbis, however, almost go out of their way to emphasize the daily miracle of life which does not express itself in violations of the laws of nature. "Come and consider how many miracles the Holy One, blessed be He, performs for man, and he is unaware of it. If a man were to swallow unmasticated bread, it would descend into his bowels and scratch him, but God created a well in the throat of man which enables it to descend safely" (Ex. R. 24:1). This thought is expressed in the formula of thanksgiving prayer (*Modim*) which forms part of the daily *Amidah*, "for Thy miracles which are daily with us, and for Thy wonders and Thy benefits, which are wrought at all times, evening, morning, and night."

In this connection is it not without interest that the formula of thanksgiving "for the miracles… which Thou didst wage for our fathers" is confined to the two festivals of Ḥanukkah and Purim (Sof. 20:6; the formula is found in *Seder R. Amram*). It is true that the rabbis emphasize the miraculous aspect of the Ḥannukah legend of the pure oil which was sufficient for one day only but lasted for eight until new oil could be brought (Shab. 21b), to which there is no reference in the Book of Maccabees, and that many of the regulations of the festival are enjoined "in order to publicize the miracle" (Shab. 23b), but this miracle cannot compare with the biblical miracles, and there is no *deus ex machina* miracle in the story of Purim. On the whole they belong to the class of "natural miracles." The parting of the Red Sea is regarded as the greatest ("most difficult") of the biblical miracles (Pes. 118a).

Although the Talmud is replete with stories and legends of miracles wrought for its worthies (cf. especially Ta'an. 21–25), it is generally accepted that the age of miracles (probably for the benefit of the people as a whole) has ceased, because "they were performed for those who were willing to sacrifice themselves for the sanctification of the Name, and we are not worthy of having miracles performed for us" (Ber. 20a; Ta'an. 18b; Sanh. 94b).

Nevertheless ten minor miracles happened in the time of the Temple (Avot 5:5). They include such mundane miracles as that no person was ever bitten by a snake or scorpion in Jerusalem, that there was always accommodation to be found there (during the pilgrim festivals), and that rain never extinguished the altar fire.

It is forbidden to rely upon miracles (Pes. 64b). "One should never stand in a place of danger and say 'a miracle will happen to me' since perhaps it will not happen, and if it does, it will be deducted from his merits" (Ta'an. 20b). But "the recipient of a miracle does not recognize the miracle" (Nid. 31a). When coming to a place where miracles were wrought for the Jewish people, one must recite a special blessing (Ber. 9:1 and 54a).

[Louis Isaac Rabinowitz]

In Medieval Jewish Philosophy

The subject of miracles was one of the most important and problematic in the writings of medieval Jewish philosophy. The medieval philosopher found it difficult to accept the biblical notion of miracles, not only because it was difficult to explain the particular miracles described in the Bible in terms of contemporary science, but also because the acceptance of miracles entailed the belief in creation and divine providence – notions rejected by Greek philosophy.

The first of the medieval Jewish philosophers, Saadiah *Gaon, who, following the Mu'tazilites (see *Kalam), proved the existence of God from the temporal origin of the world (*Beliefs and Opinions* 1:2), and deduced the concept of divine omnipotence from the concept of creation (2:4), does not question the possibility of miracles. Since he accepted the concepts of creation and divine providence, it was consistent for him to maintain that God may see fit to alter His creation in order to preserve the faithful or in order to confirm His revelations to the prophets. The purpose of miracles, according to Saadiah, was to confirm the prophet as God's emissary whose word is truth (3:4, 5).

Saadiah believed that a perfect correlation exists between the content of revelation and the conclusions of rational investigation. Thus the miracle, insofar as it confirms revelation, confirms at the same time the conclusions of rational investigation – the existence of God, His unity, and the creation of the world. It might seem, therefore, that the miracle is superfluous. However, Saadiah maintained that while the intellectual verification of revealed doctrines is indeed an obligation, it is lengthy and accessible to few, and therefore revelation and miracles are required for the masses. Revelation and miracles are helpful even for those capable of speculation, insofar as they serve as guides in the search for the truth.

To distinguish between the true religion and a false one which lays claim to miracles, both the miraculous occurrence itself, as well as the doctrine it confirms, must be subjected to scientific scrutiny. One must examine the supposed miracle to discover whether it may not have been illusory (ch. 3), and also the tradition which reports it (introd.). Because there is a correlation between that which is revealed and that which is arrived at through rational speculation, nothing which clearly contradicts intellectual judgment may be accepted as prophecy (excluding, of course, phenomena which transcend intellectual understanding; 3:8).

Neoplatonism

Like Saadiah, the early Jewish Neoplatonists accepted the possibility of miracles without question. While they attributed the same function to miracles as Saadiah had, their conception of the phenomenon of the miracle itself was different. The Neoplatonists no longer viewed miracles as events which contradict the natural order thus serving as evidence of God's will, but rather as the interposition of a higher supranatural order amid the natural order below it. The Neoplatonists maintained that a miracle can take place only in the presence of a person who is worthy of the suprasensual order and attracts it in the form of a particular providence, that person being the prophet. The prophet plays an active role in the manifestation of the miracle. Miracles do not merely serve to confirm the content of the revelation; they are in themselves revelations in the sense that they represent the direct appearance of the divine order in the midst of the natural order (cf. Ibn Ezra, commentary on Ex. 3:15, and 6:3).

The Challenge of Aristotelianism

The problem of miracles grew more acute as the Aristotelian influence on Jewish philosophy became stronger. According to Aristotelianism, which conceives of the natural order as deriving necessarily from the rational Being of God, all that contradicts nature is, by definition, contradictory to reason. Thus a Jewish philosopher confronted by these Aristotelian teachings had two alternatives: if he rejected Aristotelian physics and metaphysics he was challenged by the intellectual demands that physics and metaphysics make, and if he accepted them, he had to account within their framework for the existence of revelation which is the basis of the Torah.

Judah *Halevi accepted the first alternative, Maimonides, the second. Judah Halevi set out from the premise that experience takes precedence over intellectual judgment. Although the intellect might deny the possibility of the occurrence of miracles, the fact of miracles is upheld by the immediate authenticity of the event and the authenticity of the tradition which recorded it (*Kuzari*, 1:5). Rejecting the idea that intellectual judgment must confirm the substance of revelation, and perceiving that the miracle *per se* is no evidence of the validity of the prophet's utterances, Judah Halevi does not, as did Saadiah, regard the miracle as an affirmation of the content of revelation, but views the miracle as itself a direct revelation of God. God's direct communication with a person or a nation is a miracle. The deviation from the natural order for the purpose of guiding a man or a nation to their religious destiny is a miracle. Both occurrences share the fact of God's immediate presence in the lives of men. The miracle, therefore, affirms nothing more than the possibility of its occurrence (1:13–25), and revelation can be verified only as an immediate experience. The authenticity of the revelation at Sinai was established by the fact that all of Israel were granted prophecy together with Moses and could bear witness to revelation out of their own experience. This fact confirmed the revelation for all time, and any prophecy which conflicts with it must be invalid even if it is supposedly supported by miracles (1:80–90).

Maimonides

While Maimonides adopted Aristotelian physics and metaphysics, he deviated from the Aristotelian view that the world is eternal. He upheld the assumption of the temporal origin of the world, although he maintained that it can be neither proved or disproved conclusively, as the only one which allows for miracles (Guide 2:25). Miracles, according to Maimonides, are necessary in order to sustain the authority of revelation for the masses, as well as to support the biblical assumption that God guides men by giving them the Law.

In his attempt to reconcile the concept of miracles with the Aristotelianism that he accepted, Maimonides maintained that the creation of the world as well as miracles are voluntary acts of God, and that in its essence and constitution the world reflects divine reason. Thus there is no conflict between divine wisdom and divine will, both of which were impressed upon the original mold of creation (3:25). According to Maimonides, miracles are predetermined at the time of creation and thus do not indicate a change in God's will or wisdom. The difference between the act of nature and the miracle is a difference between the regular and the unique, although the unique is also governed by its own laws. Indeed, the miracle, like creation, is a unique occurrence which establishes a reality or an order. For example, the miracles of the patriarchs and Moses established the existence of a nation with a particular role to play in the order of the world. The Sinaitic revelation established an ideal legislation for human conduct. Maimonides was careful not to define the miracle as an abrogation of the laws of nature. He explained that in the miracle of the crossing of the Red Sea (Sea of Reeds), for example, the nature of the water was not changed but was affected by another natural force, the wind. A miracle, such as the revelation at Mt. Sinai, was the manifestation of a particular act of creation, and thus may be considered an addition to nature rather than an abrogation thereof.

In sum, Maimonides concurred with Aristotle's position that reality derives from divine reason and therefore not everything imaginable is necessarily possible. While he did maintain that there are things which nature disallows, he differed with Aristotle on the limitation of the possible. Aristotle maintained that only that which exists is possible, whereas Maimonides posited the possibility of singular, constitutive occurrences as equally a necessary effect of divine wisdom (3:15). In accordance with his definition of miracles as constitutive events of general significance, Maimonides elevated the miracles of Moses above all others, while he interpreted allegorically many other biblical episodes which when understood literally are miraculous (2:46, 47).

Naḥmanides

Among Jewish philosophers after Maimonides there were those who repudiated the belief in the temporal origin of the world and in miracles, explaining biblical references to them as allegories. There were also renewed attempts to prove that miracles did take place, notably by Naḥmanides, who disputed Maimonides' conception of miracles from a kabbalistic viewpoint. In opposition to Maimonides' view of nature as a necessary effect of divine wisdom, Naḥmanides posited the miracle as preceding nature. The miracle is not a singular occurrence – it is an immutable supranatural reality. According to Naḥmanides, "nature and worldly order do not affect the ends of the Torah," and therefore the destiny of Israel is not natural but miraculous. However, miracles do not necessarily conflict with, or deviate from, the natural order. Naḥmanides postulated a distinction between self-evident miracles, i.e., those which deviate from the natural order thus serving to impart faith to unbelievers and the ignorant, and hidden miracles, which consist in the unusual coincidence of a number of natural events. The miraculous nature of the latter will be evident only to the believer (A. Jellinek (ed.), *Torat Adonai Temimah*, passim).

Ḥasdai Crescas

The most fully developed critique of Maimonides' position is found in Ḥasdai *Crescas' writings. Crescas held that the world was created *ex nihilo* but had no temporal beginning. The world is eternal and continually renewed by God, characterized by Crescas as infinite grace. As well as being infinitely good, God is omnipotent, and therefore miracles, which are instruments of good, are not merely within His power and in harmony with His wisdom but are a necessary effect of His being (Or Adonai, 2, proposition 3:1).

For Crescas, miracles were neither a deviation from nature nor in conflict with it, but an expression of a supranatural order. What distinguishes miracles from natural occurrences is not the fact of their deviation from the natural order, which is after all an external manifestation, but an intrinsic quality. Whereas the natural occurrence is brought about by God indirectly, expresses a limited force, occurs as part of a process, and has only a relative existence, the miracle is brought about directly by God, expresses unlimited power, is a singular event, is not part of a process, and has an absolute existence (*ibid.*, proposition 3:2). This conception of miracles fits in with Crescas' view that the world is continually recreated *ex nihilo* by the divine will: the world itself is actually a perpetual miracle which encompasses the natural order. Thus the miracle is not an aberration of nature, rather it precedes nature. The ultimate purpose of the miracle is to impart faith to unbelievers and to strengthen the faith of believers. However, he did not regard the miracle as an external verification of prophecy, but, along the lines of Judah Halevi, he believed that in every event in which the infinite power of God is revealed, God becomes present to man, and thus heresy and doubt are abolished (*ibid.*, 3, proposition

4:2). In Crescas' doctrine there is a strong universalistic orientation, although emphasis is placed on the particular supranatural providence of Israel: God's grace, being infinite, must reveal itself to everyone, and the miracle which will bring this about, the resurrection of the dead, will be superior even to the miracles performed by Moses (*ibid.*, 3, proposition 4:2).

An analysis of Crescas' doctrine illustrates the development of the concept of miracles through the confrontation with Platonism and Aristotelianism, in that it represents a critical synthesis of both. The miracle, which had been regarded as an external confirmation of revelation, came to be viewed not as a non-natural occurrence but as an immediate revelation of the truth of the Torah. In his critical synthetic doctrine, Crescas also anticipated ideas which were fully developed only by modern Jewish philosophers.

[Eliezer Schweid]

In Later Jewish Thought

S.D. *Luzzatto was against the rational approach to religion, which he dubbed "Hellenism," and claimed that Judaism based on love and mercy was superior. Attacking the Jewish philosophers of his day for trying to assimilate Judaism to the barren "Hellenism" of Western culture, he affirmed the historicity of the miracles in the Bible, including the miracle of prophecy, and he held that miracles were proof of divine providence.

Samuel *Hirsch, in his *Die Religionsphilosophie der Juden* (1842), also upheld the historicity of the miracles recorded in the Bible. However, for him it was not the miraculous incident itself that was important, but its educational value. In the biblical period, God revealed Himself to Israel by means of miracles in order to demonstrate that He was above nature and that nature was not omnipotent – an idea which the Israelites had acquired in Egypt. Once the idea of the omnipotence of nature had been uprooted, miracles were no longer necessary and, therefore, ceased to take place. According to Hirsch, however, there was one miracle that did not just take place in the past but has continued up to the present, namely, the existence of the Jewish people, which serves as an additional means of teaching the existence of God.

Moses *Mendelssohn maintained that the truth of any religion cannot be proved by appealing to miracles; it can be proved only on the basis of the rationality of its doctrine. Only after a religious faith has been upheld by reason is it possible to consider the miracles associated with that religion. While Mendelssohn did not reject the possibility of miracles, he stressed that Judaism did not appeal for belief to the authority of miracles but to that of direct revelation witnessed by the entire people.

Nachman *Krochmal felt that there were potent spiritual forces underlying the workings of nature. These forces can operate and cause events which defy the laws of nature and appear miraculous. However, not all miracles are of this type. There is another class of miracles in which God actually directly interferes in nature. However, Krochmal does not satisfactorily explain this class of miracles in terms of his general metaphysical system.

Contemporary Views

There have been two trends in modern Jewish thought concerning miracles. The first, represented by such thinkers as F. *Rosenzweig, M. *Buber, and A.J. *Heschel, has returned to an almost biblical conception of miracles, based upon the idea that the miracle is a "sign" of God's presence. The second trend, represented by M. *Kaplan, may be said to follow the rationalistic approach of the medieval philosophers. However, it goes beyond the medievals in denying the significance of miracles qua miracles. The first trend explains away the problem of the miracle being contrary to natural law by proposing a new definition of the miracle, according to which the essence of the miracle does not lie in its being contradictory to nature, but in its having a particular significance in history. The second trend, in a sense, chooses science over miracles, denying any validity to the miracle, insofar as it supposedly goes against natural law.

Rosenzweig holds, as does Maimonides, that the miracles of the Bible were built into the scheme of things from creation, hence, they were part of the natural order. These events were miracles because they played a significant role in history. Rosenzweig attempts to connect science and miracles, or what he called objectivity (idealism) and subjectivity (personal meaning), revelation being the point at which they are joined. The man who receives and lives a revelation carries both in him. The miracle of personal revelation is genuine. It infuses meaning into a particular moment, while its impact carries over into the future (see F. Rosenzweig, *Kokhav ha-Ge'ullah* (1970), 131–48).

Buber also stressed that no miracle is contrary to nature, maintaining that the miracle and nature are two different aspects of the same phenomenon – revelation. For Buber, man's attitude is the essential element in the miracle: the miracle is "our receptivity to the eternal revelation." Buber approaches biblical miracles by asking, "what human relation to real events this could have been… (which) grew into the written account we have read" (*Moses* (1958), 61ff.). A man today can experience the same relation to real events, the same miracle, that biblical man experienced. The attitude that a man has to events, the world, or other people is the raw material out of which experiences that are miracles arise. For a person properly attuned, any event may be considered a miracle, in terms of its meaning for him.

Heschel stresses the same points using various terms such as "the legacy of wonder" (*God in Search of Man* (1959), 43), or "radical amazement," terms that he gives to the sense of mystery and awe that he attributed to biblical figures. He writes that, "What stirred their souls was neither the hidden nor the apparent, but the hidden in the apparent; not the order but the mystery of the order that prevails in the universe" (*ibid.*, 56). He also speaks of the "ineffable," and of a sudden extraordinary and meaningful moment which he calls an "event" as distinguished from "process," the usual scientific way of looking at things.

M. Kaplan conceives of the accounts of miracles in Jewish literature as reflecting the attempt "of the ancient authors to prove and illustrate God's power and goodness" (*Judaism as a Civilization* (1934), 98). Kaplan maintained that these traditions concerning miracles were in conflict with modern thought, and that the belief in miracles that contravene natural law is a "psychological impossibility for most people" (*Questions Jews Ask* (1956), 155–6). The idea of God's exercising control and direction over the workings of the world is passé after modern physics. However, while Kaplan rejects the literalness of the miracle, he sees in the concept that God performs miracles for the sake of the righteous an important idea that has value for modern man, namely, the idea of responsibility and loyalty to what is right.

[Michael J. Graetz]

BIBLIOGRAPHY: O. Procksch, *Theologie des Alten Testaments* (1950), 454–8; C. Tresmontant, *Etudes de métaphysique biblique* (1955), 223–8; S.V. McCasland, in: JBL, 76 (1957), 149–52; W. Eichrodt, *Theology of the Old Testament*, 2 (1967), 162–7; G. Quell, in: *Verbannung und Heimkehr* (1961), 253–300. IN MEDIEVAL JEWISH PHILOSOPHY: Guttmann, Philosophies, index; Husik, Philosophy, 358ff.

MIRANDA, SALOMON RODRIGUES DE (1875–1942), Dutch social-democratic politician. Born in Amsterdam of poor parents, De Miranda became a diamond worker and one of the leading figures of the General Diamond Workers Trade Union (ANDB). The lack of support by the orthodox clergy for their social struggle caused a rupture with their faith and marked the beginning of a secular integration process. De Miranda was a prominent member of the Dutch Labour Party (SDAP) and represented the party as an Amsterdam municipal councilor after 1911. In 1919 he was made alderman for the distribution and price control of foodstuffs, public baths, housing, and public works. In this capacity he was both practitioner and theoretician of the main social-democratic policy at municipal level, which enabled the Labor Party to receive a mass base. He held his function for nearly 20 years and was responsible for the building of several workers' quarters, which were remarkable for their architectural design (the "Amsterdam School"). After the German invasion of the Netherlands, he was arrested and taken to Amersfoort concentration camp where he was beaten to death.

[Henriette Boas / Bob Reinalda (2nd ed.)]

MIRANDA DE EBRO, city in Castile, N. Spain. It had one of the oldest Jewish communities in Castile. The *fuero* ("municipal charter") granted to Miranda de Ebro in 1099 gave the Jews equal rights with the Christian and Moorish residents. In 1290 the community numbered 15 families who paid an annual tax of 3,312 maravedis and 744 maravedis in services. Jews from Miranda went to work in the fields of neighboring villages. In 1304 Ferdinand IV confirmed that the Jews, Moors, and Christians in Miranda had equal rights, in particular as regards financial liabilities. Ferdinand's ruling was reconfirmed by Alfonso XI in 1347 and by Pedro I in 1351. In 1360, at the beginning of the civil war between Pedro the Cruel and Henry of Trastamara, Henry's supporters in the city attacked the Jewish population and many were massacred. Pedro punished the ringleaders and the municipal authorities but, on finally gaining control of the city, Henry granted a moratorium on debts owed to Jews for a year. The privileges of Jews in Miranda, as enumerated to the authorities in Burgos in 1453, included the right to own synagogues, to participate in the tax apportionment, and to work on Sundays at home or in closed workshops, as well as exemption from paying dues to the cathedral. By the system of taxation introduced by Jacob ibn Nuñez in 1474, several neighboring communities were joined with Miranda and their joint tax was fixed at 2,000 maravedis. In 1485 they had to pay a levy of 107 castellanos for the war with Granada. On the expulsion of the Jews from Spain in 1492, the synagogue of Miranda was handed over to the municipal council. The remains of the synagogue in Miranda are preserved in a house in Calle de la Fuenta (no. 18). The Jewish quarter was located in and around the present Calle de la Independencia (formerly de los Judíos).

BIBLIOGRAPHY: Baer, Spain, 1 (1961), 423; Baer, Urkunden, index; F. Cantera, *Fuero de Miranda de Ebro* (1945); idem, *Sinagogas españolas* (1955), 246–51; idem, in: *Sefarad*, 1 (1941), 89–140; 2 (1942), 327–75; 22 (1962), 15–16; Suárez Fernández, Documentos, index.

[Haim Beinart]

MIRANSKY, PERETZ (1908–1993), Yiddish poet and fable-writer. Miransky was born in Vilnius (Vilna), Lithuania, where he attended *ḥeder* and then public high school. He made his literary debut in 1934 with two fables in the *Vilner Tog*. He joined the *Yung Vilne (Young Vilna) group of poets and artists, and contributed to its literary publications such as *Yung Vilne*. He was one of the group's last remaining members along with Abraham *Sutzkever. His fables appeared in Yiddish periodicals, including the Warsaw *Literarishe Bleter* and the Kovno (Kaunas) *Emes*, and newspapers in Bialystok, Grodno, and Gluboke (Hlybokaye, Belarus). His fables were used in pedagogical materials for the Yiddish schools. He wrote pieces that were performed in the Vilna ARRT revue theater and in the *Maydim* Yiddish puppet theater.

Miransky fled the Nazi invasion to Samarkand, Uzbekistan, and worked in an artel. After the war he lived in the Tempelhof DP camp in Berlin, where he was culturally active among the refugees and coedited the journal *Undzer Lebn*. He immigrated to Canada in 1949 and settled in Montreal. He moved permanently to Toronto in 1955 and greatly enriched the Toronto Yiddish cultural scene. His Yiddish poetry and fables were published widely in the Yiddish press and in literary journals including the *Keneder Odler*, *Yidisher Zhurnal*, *Goldene Keyt*, *Svive*, *Tsukunft*, *Afn Shvel*, *Yidishe Kultur*, and the *Forverts*. He published several volumes of his writing in Canada and Israel: *A Likht far a Groshn* (1951), *Shures Shire: Lider un Mesholim* (1974), *Tsvishn Shmeykhl un Trer: Mesho-*

lim Bukh (1979), *Nit Derzogt* (1983), and *A Zemer fun Demer* (1991). His writing, with its eternal themes and emphasis on issues of social justice, has been widely published in translation, most recently in a bilingual English-Yiddish edition: *Selected Poems and Fables: An English/Yiddish Collection* (ed. Anna Miransky, 2000). His poetry has also been set to music, found in Marilyn Lerner and David Wall's *Still Soft Voiced Heart: New Yiddish Lieder* (2002) and the Flying Bulgar Klezmer Band's *Sweet Return* (2003).

BIBLIOGRAPHY: C.L. Fuks, *Hundert Yor Yidishe un Hebreyishe Literatur in Kanade.* (1982) 164–65; S. Niger et al., (eds.), *Leksikon fun der Nayer Yidisher Literatur,* vol. 5 (1956–81), 669; "Peretz Miransky," in: M. Ravitch, *Mayn Leksikon: Yidishe Shraybers, Kintslers, Aktiorn, oykh Klal-tuers in di Amerikes un Andere Lender,* vol. 6, book 2 (1982), 108–10.

[Rebecca Margolis (2nd ed.)]

MIRELMAN, family of Argentine industrialists and Jewish leaders. SIMON (1894–1978) was born in London, moved to Russia and Switzerland, and settled in Buenos Aires in 1914. Three of his brothers, ROBERTO (1898–1991), JACOB (1900–1990), and JOSE (1902–1996), were born in Russia, educated in Switzerland, and eventually joined Simon in Buenos Aires at different stages after World War I. LEON (1907–2003) was born in Switzerland and moved to Buenos Aires in 1927. There the brothers founded a highly successful textile factory. Simon was president of the Hospital Israelita, B'nai B'rith, the Committee Against Antisemitism (later *DAIA), the Argentine-Israel Cultural Institute, the United Jewish Appeal, and the Israel Bond Drive. He also had a prominent role in the establishment of an office of the American Jewish Committee in Buenos Aires, and was a member if the Board of Governors of the Hebrew University. Roberto was president of the Congregacion Israelita and later among the founders of Bet El synagogue. Jose became a strong Zionist advocate and a leader of the Revisionists in Argentina. In 1949 he moved to Israel. Already in the 1960s he became an activist for the immigration of Russian Jews to Israel, and printed over a million Russian-Hebrew dictionaries, *haggadot* in Russian, and other educational materials, to be forwarded to Jewish communities in Russia. In the 1970s he supported the exchange of Russian Jews for hard currency, which enabled the exit of over 100,000 Jews. Leon was president of the board of the Seminario Rabinico Latinoamericano from its inception in 1962 until 1969, and for many years the president of the United Jewish Appeal.

The Mirelman brothers were benefactors of many Jewish causes, especially those connected with Israel. In the 1930s they founded Editorial Israel, a pioneering effort to publish books of Jewish content in Spanish. Over 100 titles were published.

Jose's son, DAVID (1938–), born in Argentina, emigrated to Israel in 1949 and became a biochemist at the Weizmann Institute of Science, known for his investigation of infectious and parasitic diseases in less developed countries, and in particular as an expert in the molecular biology of host-pathogen interactions.

Leon's son, VICTOR (1943–), born in Argentina, moved to the U.S., where he became a Conservative rabbi and professor of Jewish history, publishing in particular scholarly works on the Jews of Argentina.

BIBLIOGRAPHY: V. Mirelman, *Jewish Buenos Aires (1890–1930). In Search of an Identity* (1990).

[Victor A. Mirelman (2nd ed.)]

MIRIAM (Heb. מִרְיָם); the daughter of *Amram and Jochebed and sister of *Moses and *Aaron (Num.26:59; I Chron. 5:29. The name may mean "gift" (see von Soden, UF 2 (1970), 269–72). According to tradition, Miriam is the sister, mentioned in Exodus 2:2–8, who advised Pharaoh's daughter to call a Hebrew nurse for him. The critical view is that the representation of Moses, Aaron, and Miriam as "siblings" is secondary. In the earliest form of the tradition, Miriam was one of the leaders of the Exodus (Micah 6:4). The title "prophetess" was given to Miriam when she appeared, timbrel in hand, at the head of the singing and dancing women after the crossing of the Red Sea (Ex. 15:20–21). It was an Israelite custom for women to welcome the men with timbrels and dancing when they returned from the battlefield and at other celebrations (cf. Judg. 11:34; I Sam. 18:6–7; Ps. 68:26).

Miriam is also mentioned in the context of her and Aaron's attempt to challenge Moses' exclusive right to speak in the name of the Lord (Num. 12). Miriam is mentioned first, and according to G.B. Gray, the verb appearing in the feminine, *va-tedabber be-* ("she spoke against"), suggests that Miriam led this revolt. In any event, she alone was punished. The text preserves two traditions: one that the cause of the rebellion was Moses' marriage to a Kushite (black Sudanese) woman (Num. 12:1), while the other cause was a challenge to the unique authority of Moses, i.e., Miriam and Aaron objected to Moses' exclusive right to prophesy in God's name (cf. Num. 11:25–30). Miriam was smitten with a dread skin disease (see *Leprosy), and was healed only after Moses interceded on her behalf, and after she had been quarantined for seven days. Her punishment is recalled again (Deut. 24:9), as a warning against disobeying the laws against "leprosy." Miriam died in Kadesh and was buried there (Num. 20:1). It is likely that there were more traditions about Miriam that did not survive the canonization of the Bible.

[Ephraim Stern / S. David Sperling (2nd ed.)]

In the Aggadah:

Miriam was so called in reference to the bitterness of the bondage of Egypt (מר, "bitter"; Ex. R. 26:1). Although she is referred to as a prophetess in the Bible (Ex. 15:20), none of her prophecies is mentioned there. The *aggadah*, however, fills the lacuna. It explains that her father *Amram, unwilling to have children who would be doomed to death, divorced his wife after Pharaoh's decree. Miriam urged him to remarry *Jochebed, rebuking him for being even more cruel than Pharaoh since the latter had decreed only against the male children, and prophesying that a child would be born from them who would be the liberator of Israel. Amram acceded and Miriam sang and danced before her parents on the occasion of the remarriage (Sot. 12a–13a; BB 120a). Miriam is identified by some rabbis with Puah (from פעה, "to open the mouth": Ex. R. 1:13; Rashi, Sot. 11b), one of the midwives (Ex. 1:15), who was so called because she comforted the mother and cooed to the child to make it open its mouth. As a reward she was destined to have illustrious descendants. She is also identified with Azubah, the wife of Caleb (I Chron. 2:18); their son, Hur (Ex. R. 1:17) was the grandfather of Bezalel, who inherited the wisdom of his great-grandmother and was the architect of the Sanctuary. Some rabbis hold that even King David was descended from her (Sif. Num. 78; Ex. R. 48:3–4).

Miriam is portrayed as fearless in her rebukes. As a child, she reprimanded Pharaoh for his cruelty, and he refrained from putting her to death only as a result of her mother's plea that she was but a child (Ex. R. 1:13). She also saw fit to rebuke Moses when he separated from Zipporah, because she felt that he should procreate (Sif. Num. 99). Although Miriam was punished with leprosy, God honored her by Himself officiating as the kohen to declare her definitely a leper and subsequently to declare her cleansed (Zev. 102a). Because she had waited for Moses by the river, the Israelites waited for her to recover (Sot. 11a). A miraculous well, created during the twilight on the eve of the first Sabbath (Avot 5:6), accompanied the Children of Israel in the desert due to her merits (Ta'an. 9a). Like Moses and Aaron, she too died by the kiss of God since the angel of death had no power over her (BB 17a).

[Aaron Rothkoff]

In Islam

In his early prophecies Muhammad speaks about Miriam (Mary, Ar. Maryam) and her son Jesus, who was born of the Holy Spirit (Sura 19:20; 23:52; 66:12). It is, however, also said in Sura 19:29 that she was the sister of Aaron, while in the third Sura (3:31), known as the sura of the family of ʿImrān, she is described as the daughter of ʿImrān. In connection with the decrees of Firʿawn (*Pharaoh), Muhammad related that the mother of Mūsā (Moses) ordered his sister to watch over the ark in which Moses had been placed (20:41–42; 28:10–12) – without mentioning her name. On another occasion (66:11–12), he mentions the wife of Pharaoh and Miriam (the mother of Jesus) among the righteous women. According to Tabarī and Thaʿlabī, Miriam was married to Caleb, while in Kisāʾī's tale about Qārūn (*Korah), it is said that Miriam was his wife and that it was from her he had learned the science of alchemy, the reason for his attainment to wealth.

[Haïm Z'ew Hirschberg]

For Miriam in the arts, see *Moses, In the Arts.

BIBLIOGRAPHY: IN THE BIBLE: M.D. Cassuto, *Perush al Sefer Shemot* (1953[2]), 125–6; Haran, in: *Tarbiz*, 25 (1955), 13–14; M.Z. Segal, *Masoret u-Vikkoret* (1957), 89–90; O. Bardenhower, *Der Name Maria* (1895); Haupt, in: AJSLL, 20 (1903/4), 152; Zorell, in: *Zeitschrift für katholische Theologie*, 30 (1906), 356–60; G.B. Gray, *Numbers* (ICC, 1903), 120–8; H. Gressmann, *Moses und seine Zeit* (1913), 264–75, 351–52; Humbert, in: ZAW, 38 (1919–20), 86; Voelten, *ibid.*, 111–12; Noth, Personennamen, 60; Bauer, in: ZAW, 51 (1933), 87n. 2; 53 (1935), 59; Rozelaar, in: VT, 2 (1952), 226; CH Gordon, *Ugaritic Manual* (1955), 292, no. 1170. **ADD. BIBLIOGRAPHY:** S.D. Sperling, in: HUCA, 70–71 (2000–01), 39–55. IN THE AGGADAH: M. Haran, in: JSS, 5 (1960), 54–55; Ginzberg, Legends, index. IN ISLAM: Ṭabarī, *Taʾrīkh*, 1 (1357 A.H.), 307; Thaʿlabī *Qiṣaṣ* (1356 A.H.), 141, 203; Kisāʾī, *Qiṣaṣ*, ed. by Eisenberg (1922–23), 229–30; A. Geiger, *Was hat Mohammed aus dem Judenthume aufgenommen?* (1902), 154; H. Speyer, *Die biblischen Erzählungen im Qoran* (1931, repr. 1961), 242–3; "Maryam," in EIS[2], 6 (1991), 628–32 (includes bibliography).

MIRIAM BAT BENAYAH, scribe who lived in *San'a, *Yemen, during the late fifteenth and into the early sixteenth century and followed her family's profession. Her education, which included, at a minimum, the skills of reading and writing in Hebrew, as well as the special prayers and procedures required of a Torah scribe, was highly unusual for a woman of her time and place. Miriam worked with her father, *Safra* (scribe) Benayah ben Sa'adiah ben Zekhariah, and her two brothers David and Joseph. Together, the family is credited with copying 400 books, including prayer books and collections of *haftarot* as well as copies of the Torah. Only a few examples of their work are still in existence, and most may have represented joint efforts, because not all are signed by a single family member. However, one Torah scroll, whose existence was first reported to the wider world in 1859 by a Jewish traveler to Yemen, is unmistakably the work of Miriam. Its colophon reads: "Do not condemn me for any errors that you may find, as I am a nursing woman," an apparent indication that Miriam continued her scribal work after she married and had a family. No information about her husband or her offspring is known.

BIBLIOGRAPHY: S.D. Goitein, *Jews and Arabs: Their Contacts Through the Ages* (1994[3]), 86; E. Taitz, S. Henry, and C. Tallan, *The JPS Guide to Jewish Women: 600 B.C.E.–1900 C.E.* (2003).

[Emily Taitz (2nd ed.)]

MIRISCH BROTHERS, HAROLD (1907–1968), **MARVIN** (1918–2002), and **WALTER** (1921–), U.S. film producers. Born in New York, the Mirisch brothers became a team in 1952, when they joined Allied Artists as executives. They wanted to produce high-quality films by giving a free hand to independent filmmakers, but Allied dropped the plan after two productions, so in 1957 the brothers set up their own company. They envisioned the Mirisch Company as a haven for independent filmmakers who did not want to deal with the business aspect of an independent production company. The brothers signed a 12-picture deal with United Artists in 1957, which was extended to 20 films two years later. The Mirisch Company moved to the Samuel Goldwyn Studios, where they became the largest tenant. Many actors, directors, and other producers enjoyed stability and creative autonomy under the canopy of the Mirisch Company. In 1969 Walter Mirisch was named president and executive head of production of the Mirisch Corporation.

The Mirisch brothers scored an immediate success with their first film, Billy Wilder's *Some Like It Hot* (1959). The company' subsequent films included *The Apartment* (1960), *The Magnificent Seven* (1960), *By Love Possessed* (1961), *West Side Story* (1961), *The Children's Hour* (1962), *Two for the Seesaw* (1962), *The Great Escape* (1963), *Toys in the Attic* (1963), *The Pink Panther* (1964), *The Russians Are Coming* (1966), *Hawaii* (1966), *In the Heat of the Night* (Academy Award winner for Best Picture, 1967), *Fitzwilly* (1967), *They Call Me Mr. Tibbs* (1970), *The Organization* (1971), *Scorpio* (1973), *Mr. Majestyk* (1974), *Midway* (1976), *Gray Lady Down* (1977), *Same Time Next Year* (1978), *The Prisoner of Zenda* (1979), *Dracula* (1979), *Romantic Comedy* (1983), *Lily in Winter* (1994), and the TV series *The Magnificent Seven* (1998).

Walter Mirisch was president of the Academy of Motion Picture Arts and Sciences from 1973 through 1978. In 1978 the Academy awarded him the Irving Thalberg Memorial Award, and in 1983 he received the Academy's Jean Hersholt Humanitarian Award.

[Jonathan Licht / Ruth Beloff (2nd ed.)]

MIRON, DAN (1934–), scholar and critic of Hebrew and Yiddish Literature. Miron was born in Tel Aviv. He studied for his first two academic degrees at the Hebrew University of Jerusalem, and for his Ph.D. at Columbia University in New York. For more than 40 years he taught at the universities of Tel Aviv and Jerusalem and at Columbia University. Dan Miron's oeuvre constitutes one of the largest, most impressive, and significant achievements in the research and criticism of Jewish Literature in recent generations. His unique contribution to Jewish literary studies can be considered under the following parameters:

Quantity

Miron's scholarly output has been prodigious. He published his first article in 1951, when he was just 17, and from then not a year went by without a written or published work. His publications include some 30 original books, another 30 or so which he edited or translated, generally adding a substantial foreword or postscript, and hundreds of articles. In addition, he was responsible for two massive, long-term editorial projects: The complete definitive edition of the poems of Ḥ.N. Bialik, in three volumes (1983–2000) and the edition of the works of U.Ẓ. Greenberg, not yet complete, comprising over a dozen volumes by 2005.

Scope

Miron's opus is multifaceted and spans historical periods, genres and languages. In historical terms, his research projects span from the beginning of the Haskalah during the first half of the 19th century to the most avant-garde literary frontline of the end of the 20th century and the beginning of the 21st. Within this wide range he has researched most of the major writers, of both prose and verse, and many of the more marginal, both Hebrew and Yiddish.

Methodology

Although Miron's intellectual heritage derived from the related trends of Anglo-American New Criticism, Russian Formalism, and French Structuralism, he was never content to remain within the bounds of textual and semiotic analyses, or of an "internal" investigation of literary dynamics. At the same time he never abandoned them. His interpretations combine a subtle and sensitive recording of the finest nuances of a text, of its multiple levels of meaning, its poetics and its aesthetics with an awareness of the text's historical, biographical, social and cultural contexts. These contexts he describes in lively detail, mapping their reciprocal and cross-fertilizing links to a group of texts.

Form

Miron's critical work takes the form of brilliantly organized essays, possessing a high artistic quality of their own. Their organization is of a rigorously classical kind, which functions by way of discovering an ordering idea within a primordial mass of heterogeneous material, thus imposing a boldly contoured clarity upon diversity and confusion. The aesthetics of masterly ordering in the essays has an emotional effect, due to its narrative, even dramatic character. Miron's essays tell a story, and they employ intuitively the tactics and strategies of effective storytelling to arouse interest, to maintain suspense and to provide enough information to satisfy the reader's natural curiosity without quenching a desire to investigate further.

Miron's oeuvre, developing since the 1950s, is a profoundly searching multidimensional project, which delineates a richly detailed map of modern Jewish literature and culture. It uncovers hidden areas and throws new light upon well-known territory. It offers the student of contemporary Jewish literature a superb entry route to the many faces of the subject.

Among his works are *Shalom Aleikhem: Pirkei Masah* (1970); *Sholem Aleykhem: Person, Persona, Presence* (1972); *Arba Panim ba-Sifrut ha-Ivrit* (1975); *Bein Ḥazon le-Emet: Nizzanei ha-Roman ha-Ivri* (1979); *Kivvun Orot: Taḥanot ba-Sipporet ha-Ivrit ha-Modernit* (1979); *Der imazsh fun Shtetl: Dray literarishe Shtudyes* (1981); *Ha-Preidah min ha-Ani he-'Ani* (1986); *Mul ha-Aḥ ha-Shotek: Iyyunim be-Shirat Milḥemet ha-Azma'ut* (1992); *H.N. Bialik and the Prophetic Mode in Modern Hebrew Poetry* (2000); *Parpar min ha-Tola'at: Natan Alterman ha-Ẓa'ir* (2001); *Akdamot le-Aẓag* (= U.Z. Greenberg) (2002); *Ha-Ẓad ha-Afel bi-Ẓeḥoko shel Shalom Aleikhem* (2004).

[Gidi Nevo]

MIRON (Michrovsky), ISSACHAR (1920–), Israeli composer. Born in Poland, Miron studied composition and conducting at the Warsaw Conservatory. He settled in Ereẓ Israel in 1939. He served in the British Army's Jewish Brigade and during that period composed his most popular song "*Tzena, Tzena*" ("Come Out, Come Out"). This song was performed and recorded all over the world by singers such as Pete Seeger, Bing Crosby, Judy Garland, and Richard *Tucker. Following the establishment of the State of Israel, he served in the Israeli Army as the director of music and art programs. From 1957 to

1961 he edited *Zemirot*, the Jewish Agency folk music periodical. In 1959 he was awarded the Engel Prize for his compositions. In 1963 he went to the U.S. where he continued to compose music. Among his many compositions of instrumental and liturgical music are: *Kol Rinah be-Ohalei Yisrael*: A Sabbath Service of Israel for Cantor, Chorus (SATB) and Organ (1963), *Tripartiture Epigram* for violoncello and piano (1975), *Sephardic nocturno* for violoncello and piano (1975), *Klezmer Reflections* for oboe and piano (1980), and many popular songs. His archive is at the Music Department at the Jewish National University Library, Jerusalem.

[Israela Stein and Gila Flam (2nd ed.)]

MIROSLAV (Ger. **Misslitz**), town in S. Moravia, Czech Republic. Jews apparently settled there after their expulsion from the Moravian royal cities (1454). There is a record of a community during the Turkish wars; subsequently it diminished to only three families, but later absorbed refugees from the *Chmielnicki massacres (1648). In 1666, 20 Jews were put in chains and expelled from the town. Subsequently Jews from *Vienna settled in the town, bringing the total Jewish population to 18 families. The oldest legible tombstone in the Jewish cemetery dates from 1692. The *Familiants laws allotted 119 families to Miroslav, where in 1753, 64 families lived in 18 houses. Their number had risen to 448 persons (18% of the total population) in 1801 and remained the same in 1820. In 1831 Rafael Koenig (b. 1808) became the first Jewish locksmith in the Hapsburg Empire. A synagogue in the Reform style was erected in 1845. In 1867 a political community (see **politische Gemeinden*) was established, which was incorporated in the municipality in 1924. The Jewish population reached its peak in 1857, when it numbered 1,032, subsequently declining to 424 in 1869 and then rising slightly to 528 in 1900. During World War I some 350 refugees fled to Miroslav, but few of them settled. In 1930 the community numbered 291 (6.6% of the total). The remainder of the community was deported to Nazi extermination camps in 1942, and the synagogue equipment was sent to the Central Jewish Museum in Prague. Although the community was not revived after the war, the Jewish quarter was preserved in its original plan.

BIBLIOGRAPHY: E. Reich, in: H. Gold (ed.), *Die Juden und Judengemeinden Boehmens in Vergangenheit und Gegenwart* (1934), 387–405; D. Kaufmann, in: MWJ, 17 (1890), 289–301.

[Meir Lamed]

MIROWSKI, MICHEL (1924–1990), doctor and co-inventor of the implantable defibrillator. Born in Poland, Mirowski survived the Nazi Holocaust as a teenager and was left without family. He immigrated to Lyon, France, to study medicine. He completed his postdoctoral studies in Israel at Tel Hashomer Hospital and fellowships with Professor Demetrio Sodi Pallares in Mexico City and with Dr. Helen Taussig at Johns Hopkins in the U.S. In 1963, he returned to Israel and became the chief cardiologist at Asaf Harofe Hospital, where he focused his research on abnormal heart rhythms.

In the late 1960s, his former mentor at Tel Hashomer Hospital and chief of medicine, Dr. Harry Heller, died of recurrent tachyarrhythmias. This event marked a turning point in Mirowski's career. Realizing that patients like Heller cannot stay indefinitely in hospitals, and inspired by the recent development of the implantable pacemaker, Mirowski conceived of a small implantable device that would monitor the heart continuously and deliver an appropriate electrical shock to patients in response to life-threatening abnormal heart rhythms (ventricular tachyarrhythmias). Mirowski hoped that the hundreds of thousands of people who succumbed annually to abnormal heart rhythms could be saved by such a device. However, the technology of the time rendered the concept of miniaturizing a large table-top external defibrillator with no monitoring capabilities untenable.

Unable to find resources to pursue his idea in Israel, Mirowski returned to Baltimore in 1968 to direct the new Coronary Care Unit at Sinai Hospital. It was within a year that his team developed the first prototype, making him the pioneer cardiologist who invented the implantable defibrillator (ID). The first surgical implant of the defibrillator occurred in 1980 at the Johns Hopkins Hospital.

He led the way for the clinical use of the implantable defibrillator despite enormous obstacles from within the medical profession, and in defiance of many leading cardiologists in the field who said the implantable defibrillator had no clinical utility. It was his steadfast commitment to the concept of the implantable defibrillator and the goal of introducing it into clinical cardiology in his lifetime that allowed him to see some of the fruits of his vision and his labors before his premature death in 1990 from multiple myeloma.

Since the 1980s, many new generations of IDs have been developed, all based on Mirowski's original concept and work. Hundreds of thousands of lives have been saved by IDs worldwide, and they have revolutionized the therapy for malignant tachyarrhythmia and heart failure. Mirowski's life story demonstrates the importance of unfettered scientific inquiry in medical advance. His favorite quote was, "The bumps in the road are not bumps. They are the road."

[Ariella M. Rosengard and Dan Gilon (2nd ed.)]

MIRSKY, AARON (1914–2001), Hebrew writer. Born in Novogrodek, Poland, he was ordained as a rabbi and immigrated to Ereẓ Israel in 1935. He was an editor at the Mosad Bialik publishing house (1950–60), and from 1952 taught Hebrew literature at The Hebrew University (professor, 1965). He published studies on ancient and medieval Hebrew poetry and on the Hebrew language. His books include *Yalkut ha-Piyyutim* (1958), an annotated anthology of medieval Hebrew religious poetry; *Shirei Yiẓḥak Ibn Ḥalfon* (1961), with an introduction and textual variants; *Reshit ha-Piyyut* (1965); and volumes of his own poetry, *Alei Si'aḥ* (1966), *Sefer ha-Gai ve-ha-Kaddish* (1986), and *Din ha-Shir* (1994). Among his other works are *Ha-Pisuk shel ha-Signon ha-Ivri* (1978), a study of the *piyyut* tradition in the Diaspora and in Ereẓ Israel (1990) as well as a book on Hebrew style (*Signon Ivri*, 1999). A bibliography of his works was published in 1986.

[Getzel Kressel]

MIRSKY, SAMUEL KALMAN (1899–1967), rabbinic scholar, religious Zionist, and Hebraist. Born in Russia, Mirsky emigrated as a child with his parents to Palestine, where he received a thorough talmudic education and *semikhah* at 16. After teaching for some time at various yeshivot, he graduated from the Palestine Government Law School in 1924 and settled in the United States in 1926. He began teaching at Rabbi Isaac Elchanan Theological Seminary in 1936; in 1954 he became professor of rabbinics and director of the Israel Institute at Yeshiva University. In 1942 Mirsky was appointed rabbi of the Borough Park, New York, Young Israel Congregation. He took a leading part in the work of *Mizrachi and of *Histadrut Ivrit of America, serving as president of the latter in 1958 and founding its Hebrew Academy and its journal *Perakim*, which he edited (3 vols., 1957–63). He also edited the Hebrew quarterly *Talpioth* (9 vols., 1944–65), the annual of the Sura Research Publishing Foundation, *Sura* (4 vols., 1953–64), which he founded, and the *Morashah* book series. Mirsky's main scholarly achievement lay in the publication of medieval critical texts, such as Aḥai Gaon's *She'iltot* (4 vols., 1959–66) and two commentaries on Alfasi, *Perush Rabbi Yehudah ben Binyamin Anav* (1955) and *Perush Rabbi Yonatan ha-Kohen mi-Lunel al-Megillah u-Mo'ed Katan* (1956). Only the first part of his new edition of the 13th-century halakhic compendium by Zedekiah b. Abraham Anau, *Shibbolei ha-Leket* (1966), with an extensive introduction, appeared. Mirsky also published collections of his own articles and edited two books of essays on the leading figures and institutions of modern Jewish scholarship, *Mosedot Torah be-Eiropah* (1957) and *Ishim u-Demuyyot be-Ḥokhmat Yisrael be-Eiropah* (1959). He contributed many articles to periodicals, some in English, and some in Hebrew. Two of his originally written autobiographical articles for *Genazim* appeared in *Hadoar* (Nov. 3 and 10, 1967).

BIBLIOGRAPHY: S. Bernstein and G.A. Churgin (eds.), *Sefer Yovel… Mirsky* (1958), incl. bibl.; G. Appel (ed.), *S.K. Mirsky Memorial Volume* (Heb. and Eng., 1970), incl. bibl.

[Eisig Silberschlag]

MIRVISH, family of Canadian entrepreneurs and theatrical producers. EDWIN ("Honest Ed"; 1914–) was born in Virginia in 1914 and lived his early years in Washington, D.C. Ed Mirvish moved to Toronto with his family when he was nine years old. His father opened a grocery store in a heavily Jewish immigrant downtown residential neighborhood. After running a series of different businesses, including a cleaner's and a dress shop, Ed, a high school dropout, moved into bargain merchandising and quickly found success with his no-credit, no-frills model of doing business. In 1948 he opened Honest Ed's, a discount store located at Bloor and Bathurst, a key intersection in Toronto's busy downtown. The store with its huge billboard remains a landmark in the city. Between 1959 to 1963 he purchased a two-block area of houses on Markham Street adjacent to his store and converted the area into "Mirvish Village," a trendy area of art galleries, studios, stores and restaurants.

In 1963 Mirvish purchased the Royal Alexandra, a historic theater that was slated for demolition, and refurbished it, revitalizing the Toronto theater scene. Convinced that theaters and restaurants worked well together, he also opened a series of restaurants which drew crowds into the area. With his son DAVID (1944–), in 1982 he bought and refurbished London's legendary Old Vic Theatre, which they owned and operated until 2000, and also built the Princess of Wales Theatre in Toronto in 1993. Ed and David operate Mirvish Productions, which has staged productions of many Broadway hits such as *The Lion King, Mama Mia!, The Producers*, and *Hairspray*. In addition to their theater business, David Mirvish has operated an independent bookstore from the 1970s, which specializes in books on art, architecture, design, and photography.

A tradition since Ed's 75th birthday has been the large annual party adjacent to the flagship store, which attracts over 50,000 people for seven hours of free food, entertainment, and children's rides. Ed has been awarded honorary degrees from five Canadian universities and from Tel Aviv University and has been inducted into the Canadian and American Business Hall of Fame and honored with the Order of Canada.

[Randal F. Schnoor (2nd ed.)]

MISES, LUDWIG EDLER VON (1881–1973), economist, best known for his work on monetary theory and his criticism of interventionism and central planning. Born in Lemberg, the son of an Austrian railway engineer, von Mises was educated in Vienna. As professor of economics at the University of Vienna from 1913 to 1938, he represented the Austrian economic school of thought. He served as a consultant to the Austrian Chamber of Commerce and formed the Austrian Institute for Business Cycle Research in 1926. From 1934 Von Mises taught in Geneva and from 1940 in New York. Together with Luigi Einaudi, Jacques Rueff, and Wilhelm Roepke, he founded the Mont Pélerin Society, an influential international association of free-market economists and sociologists. His writings include: *The Theory of Money and Credit* (1912); *Kritik des Interventionismus* (1929); *Die Ursachen der Wirtschaftskrise* (1931); *The Ultimate Foundation of Economic Science* (1962); *Human Action: a Treatise on Economics* (1966[3]).

BIBLIOGRAPHY: H. Sennholz (ed.), *On Freedom and Free Enterprise* (1956).

[Joachim O. Ronall]

MISGAV AM (Heb. מִשְׂגַּב עָם; "Stronghold of the People"), kibbutz on the Naphtali Ridge, on the Israel-Lebanese-border, affiliated with Ha-Kibbutz ha-Me'uḥad. Its establishment in 1945 by a group of Ha-No'ar ha-Oved youth 2,770 ft. (840 m.) above sea level, and accessible only by steep footpaths, was a daring undertaking. In the Israel War of Independence (1948), Misgav Am was for many months completely isolated but served eventually as a base for Israel forces in Operation Ḥiram. In 1980 five terrorists infiltrated the kibbutz, killing the kibbutz secretary and an infant and wounding four more children before being stopped by the army. In 1969 the kibbutz cultivated the hilly terrain in its vicinity and also had fields and orchards in the Ḥuleh Valley below. Subsequently it manufactured surgical dressings. In the mid-1990s, the population was approximately 280, declining to 236 in 2002.

WEBSITE: www.misgav-am.com.

[Efraim Orni / Shaked Gilboa (2nd ed.)]

MISHCON, VICTOR, BARON (1915–), British solicitor and politician. Educated at the City of London school, in 1937 Mishcon founded a one-man firm of solicitors in Brixton, south London. From 1988, after growth and merger, it was known as Mishcon de Reya and had become one of the largest and most prestigious firms of solicitors in Britain. It represented Princess Diana in her divorce proceedings against Prince Charles and acted for American historian Deborah *Lipstadt in the libel suit brought against her in 2000 by David Irving. Victor Mishcon served as a Labour member on many public bodies and was chairman of the London County Council in 1954–55. In 1954–57 he served as a member of the controversial Departmental Committee of Inquiry into Homosexuality and Prostitution. Mishcon was made a life peer in 1978 and was Opposition spokesman in the House of Lords on Home Affairs in 1983–90. In 1990–92, most unusually for a solicitor, he served as shadow lord chancellor, a post normally reserved for a senior barrister, and in 1992 was the first practicing solicitor to be appointed an honorary Q.C. Mishcon was associated with many Jewish and Israeli causes. He was president of the Anglo-Jewish Association and served as vice president of the Board of Deputies of British Jews.

[William D. Rubinstein (2nd ed.)]

MI SHE-BERAKH (Heb. מִי שֶׁבֵּרַךְ; "He Who Blessed"), initial words of a prayer formula said on various occasions and invoking God's blessing on the community and on individuals.

During the Sabbath morning service after the Torah reading a blessing is invoked "May He who blessed our forefathers… bless this holy congregation…" The wording of this *Mi she-Berakh* varies in the various rites, but in its essence can be found in the oldest manuscripts. In different communities there are various additional *Mi she-Berakh* prayers, e.g., for one who does not interrupt his prayers from **Barukh she-Amar* through the **Amidah*, for one who always comes on time to the synagogue, etc. In Israel there is a *Mi she-Berakh* for the soldiers of the Israel Defense Forces. A personal *Mi she-Berakh* is generally recited for every person called to the reading of the law sometimes specifying the donation being made to the synagogue. If the person called to the Torah is celebrating a special occasion, such as his bar mitzvah, forthcoming marriage, or the birth of a child, the prayer is worded so as to make reference to the event. For a female child the name is usually given in the prayer. The usual *Mi she-Berakh* starts with the words "May He who blessed our fathers Abraham, Isaac, and Jacob bless…," however, when the blessing is invoked for a sick female or one recovering from childbirth, the names of the matriarchs, Sarah, Rebekah, Rachel, and Leah are added to the invocation. It is also customary to recite relevant versions of the prayer at banquets celebrating events of religious importance.

BIBLIOGRAPHY: Eisenstein, Dinim, s.v.

MISHMAR HA-EMEK (Heb. מִשְׁמַר הָעֵמֶק; "Guard of the Valley"), kibbutz on the southwest rim of the *Jezreel Valley, Israel, affiliated with Kibbutz Arẓi ha-Shomer ha-Ẓa'ir. It was founded in 1926 by pioneers from Poland (joined later by immigrants from other countries) as the first Jewish settlement in the area. It soon became a center of the Ha-Shomer ha-Ẓa'ir movement, particularly since the first regional school of the Kibbutz Arẓi network was set up there. In the Israel *War of Independence (1948), Mishmar ha-Emek successfully resisted the first large-scale attack of the Arab "Liberation Army," commanded by Fawzī al-Qāwuqjī, aimed at a breakthrough to Haifa. The attacking Arab forces were eventually thrown back toward *Megiddo and Jenin (April 1948). In 1969, the kibbutz had 700 inhabitants, increasing to 790 in the mid-1990s and 935 in 2002. Its economy was based on intensive and diverse farming, such as field crops, orchards, dairy cattle, and poultry. It also operated a plastics factory for electrical appliances and household goods in partnership with Kibbutz Galed. The Ha-Shomer ha-Ẓa'ir Forest which was planted in the hills near the kibbutz at the end of the 1920s has become part of the Menasheh Forest, the largest in the country. The kibbutz has a local museum.

[Efraim Orni]

MISHMAR HA-NEGEV (Heb. מִשְׁמַר הַנֶּגֶב; "Guard of the Negev"), kibbutz in southern Israel, 12 mi. (20 km.) N.W. of Beersheba, affiliated with Ha-Kibbutz ha-Me'uḥad. It was one of the eleven Jewish settlements established in one night (Oct. 6, 1946) in the south and Negev as a continuation of the "tower and stockade" principle. In the Israel *War of Independence (1948), the kibbutz constituted an important link with the isolated Negev settlements and served as a base for the Israel forces which captured Beersheba. Its members, numbering 462 in 1969, originated from Latin American countries, France, North Africa, Bulgaria, and other countries. In 1969 its economy was based on agriculture irrigated by the National Water Carrier, and on a plastics factory. In 2002 the population was 592, and it also operated an events center, shooting range, and gas station. The local archaeological museum displays artifacts from the vicinity where ancient *Gerar is supposed to have been located.

[Efram Orni / Shaked Gilboa (2nd ed.)]

MISHMAR HA-SHARON (Heb. מִשְׁמַר הַשָּׁרוֹן; "Guard of the Sharon"), kibbutz in central Israel, in the Ḥefer Plain, affiliated with Iḥud ha-Kevuẓot ve-ha-Kibbutzim, founded in 1933. Mishmar ha-Sharon developed intensive, irrigated farming, including citrus, and dairy cattle; it pioneered in raising flowers. The kibbutz also operated a bakery, one of the oldest and biggest in the country and the mainstay of its economy. After it burned down, many of the kibbutz members began to work outside the kibbutz, contributing their salaries to the common fund. In 1969 the population was 400; in 2002, 447.

WEBSITE: www.mhash.org.il.

[Efraim Orni / Shaked Gilboa (2nd ed.)]

MISHMAR HA-YARDEN (Heb. מִשְׁמַר הַיַּרְדֵּן; "Guard of the Jordan"), moshav in northern Israel, near the upper Jordan River course, affiliated with the *Ḥerut Movement. In 1884 a Jew living in the United States acquired the land, to establish a farm, Shoshannat ha-Yarden, but shortly after sold his holding to a Ḥovevei Zion group from Russia which founded the moshavah of Mishmar ha-Yarden (1890). Although it received aid from Baron Edmond de *Rothschild, the village, which was based mainly on extensive grain crops, did not make much headway. It suffered from isolation and the endemic malaria. In 1946 the village, reinforced with the settlement of Irgun Wedgwood, a group of World War II veterans, intensified its farming. In the Israel *War of Independence, the Syrian army crossed the Jordan River from the *Golan over the nearby *Benot Ya'akov Bridge, and established a bridgehead at Mishmar ha-Yarden, in an attempt to cut off the Ḥuleh Valley and penetrate into Galilee (May 1948). The attempt of Israel forces to encircle the Syrians from the east in "Operation Berosh" (July 1948) was unsuccessful, but the bridgehead was contained and its area reduced. When the Syrians evacuated the area as a result of the armistice terms (1949), hardly any traces remained of the moshavah. At the end of 1949, the moshav and a kibbutz, Gadot, were founded on the site. Until the Six-Day War (June 1967), Mishmar ha-Yarden was the frequent object of sniping and shelling from Syrian positions, just beyond the Jordan River. Most of the moshav's inhabitants originated from Morocco. Its farming was based on irrigated field and garden crops, deciduous fruit orchards, and dairy cattle. In 2002 its population was 364.

[Efraim Orni]

MISHMAROT (Heb. מִשְׁמָרוֹת; "Guard Posts"), kibbutz in central Israel, near *Pardes Ḥannah, affiliated with Iḥud ha-Kevuzot ve-ha-Kibbutzim, founded in 1933. Mishmarot developed citrus, and field crops, became a partner in a large plywood factory, and set up smaller plants for metal products and furniture parts. Its population in 1968 was 240; in 2002, 290. The kibbutz is known as the birthplace of such pop singers as Shalom *Hanoch, Hanan Yovel, and the late Meir Ariel.

[Efram Orni / Shaked Gilboa (2nd ed.)]

MISHMAROT AND MA'AMADOT, priestly and levitical divisions.

Historical

According to I Chronicles 24–26 and rabbinic tradition, the priests and the Levites were organized into courses or divisions. According to post-biblical evidence, these divisions used to serve in rotation. The term which is rendered as "course" (Heb. *mishmar, mishmarot*) is the one used in post-biblical sources (*The Scroll of the War of the Sons of Light Against the Sons of Darkness*, p. 2, 2ff.; Suk. 5:6–7; Ta'an. 2:6–7, et al.), whereas the Bible generally employs the term "division" (Heb. *maḥlakah, maḥlakot*).

According to I Chronicles 23:1ff., it was King David who divided all the priests and Levites according to their families and clans and assigned them their tasks in the *Temple. This arrangement is attributed to David also in the description of the dedication of the Temple by Solomon in II Chronicles 8:14. The text of Nehemiah 12:45–46 ascribes the assignment of tasks to the Levites and priests to both David and Solomon. There is no information about the working arrangements in the Temple anywhere else in the Bible; neither is there any allusion to courses among the detailed instructions for the priests and Levites in the Bible. It would appear that even the listing of the divisions of priests and singers and porters, as given in I Chronicles 24–26, dates from the Second Temple era, and that they reflect a Second Temple reality, a conclusion based on the comparison of the list in I Chronicles 24 with the lists of the priestly families in the Book of Ezra and Nehemiah and post-biblical sources.

In the list of returnees in Ezra 2:36–39 (Neh. 7:39–41) – apparently a record of a general census after the rebuilding of the Temple – only four priestly clans are listed: the sons of Jedaiah (of the house of Jeshua), the sons of Immer, the sons of Pashhur, and the sons of Harim. They totaled 4,289, which was a tenth of the number of returnees. This is a complete record of all the priests as of that date, and they belonged to only four families or clans. Of these four clans, three – Jedaiah, Immer, and Harim – appear again in the list of the 24 divisions of the priesthood in I Chronicles 24:7ff. Again, a detailed list of priests (as representatives of clans) leads the list of 22 names of those who signed the covenant in Nehemiah 10:2–9. Eight of these – Immer (Amariah), Malchijah, Shebaniah (Shecaniah), Harim, Abijah, Mijamin, Maaziah, and Bilgai (Bilgah) – recur in the list in I Chronicles 24. With minor differences, these names are the same as those of the priestly clans listed in Nehemiah 12:12–20, which is attributed to the time of Joiakim, the high priest and the father of the high priest Eliashib of the period of Nehemiah. Fifteen names in the latter list are identical with the names of the signers of the covenant, including the eight clans which figure in the list of divisions in Chronicles; and it includes two names which recur in the Chronicles list, including Jehoiarib (Joiarib), the division to which the Hasmoneans belonged. These two lists – of Nehemiah 10 and of Nehemiah 12 – also predate the list of 24 priestly divisions in the book of Chronicles.

It would appear, then, that the author of Chronicles ascribed to David certain later arrangements of divine service, and that the priestly courses were actually not established until the Second Temple era. On the other hand, it may be argued that, although the list of courses in I Chronicles 24–26 reflects reality at the time of the author, the fact that priestly tasks were performed by established divisions serving in rotation indicates a historical tradition. Indeed, the theory that some sort of courses existed in the First Temple is supported by the parallel with the system of divisions in Egyptian temples, despite the generally dissimilar natures of the two priesthoods. The four priestly families mentioned in the list of returnees in Ezra 2:36–39 may possibly have corresponded to the four priestly divisions of the First Temple, which also served in rotation. Comparison of the list of priests in the Book of Ezra and Nehemiah and the list of the 24 priestly courses in Chronicles illustrates the relationship between all these lists, on the one hand, and the priority of the lists in the Book of Ezra and Nehemiah, on the other. The earliest among them is the list of four priestly families, mentioned in Ezra 2, from the time of the Return, which is based on the divisions in the First Temple. According to this list, the number of priests was already very large (4,289 men), and even the number of priests in one family was so great that they could not serve in the Temple simultaneously. An arrangement whereby the groups of priests would serve in rotation was necessary. The families were divided into clans, and the clans into courses (cf. rabbinic tradition: "four divisions returned from Exile – Jedaiah, Harim, Pashhur, and Immer; and the prophets in Jerusalem organized them into four-and-twenty divisions", Tosef., Ta'an. 2:1; TJ, Ta'an. 4:2, 67d, et al.). Perhaps to be included in the same framework is the account given by Josephus (Apion, 2: 108) concerning four priestly tribes that rotated service in the Temple at regular intervals. Indeed, there are those who would amend the text to read "twenty-four" in this place as well (cf. Jos., Life, 2; Jos., Ant., 7:366). A tradition concerning the gradual consolidation of the 24 priestly courses appear also in Tosefta, *Ta'anit* 4:2, and TJ, *Ta'anit* 4:2, 67d.

The establishment of 24 priestly courses and the order of their service as described in I Chronicles 24 was meant to be a permanent arrangement. When this order was established and at what time the list was made is not known. In any event, it was a late development, at least one or two generations after the time of High Priest Joiakim, to which the list of priestly clans in Nehemiah 12 is attributed. Various scholars date this list at the beginning of the Hasmonean era, since Jehoiarib, the representative of the Hasmonean clan, heads the list (I Chron. 24), whereas in Nehemiah his name is 16th on the list. According to this theory, the family of Jehoiarib was primarily a provincial one, which did not achieve greatness until the Hasmonean period. However, according to I Maccabees 2:1, the house of Joiarib (Jehoiarib) was Jerusalemite; only Mattathias moved to Modin (Modi'in, presumably because of the perilous times.). Although he is mentioned 16th on the Nehemiah list, he appears before Jedaiah, whose family was important from the early days of the Return of Exiles (Neh. 12:6, 19). The date of the list of 24 priestly courses may therefore be set close to the period of Nehemiah, still during the Persian occupation. Possibly Nehemiah, who testifies that it was he himself who assigned the priests and the levites their various duties (Neh. 13: 30), also established the arrangement of the 24 priestly courses, despite his failure to specify it in the account of his activities.

[Jacob Liver]

Talmudic Data

As the priests were numerous and scattered throughout Palestine, it was impossible for all of them to officiate at the same time. An arrangement was therefore made whereby they were divided (in the final stage) regionally into 24 *mishmarot* (lit. "guards"; Ta'an. 4:2), which served in a regular weekly rotation. The *mishmarot* were further broken up into a varying number of *battei avot* ("houses" or "families"). Each division and subdivision was presided over by a head, called *rosh mishmar* and *rosh bet av* respectively (Tosef., Hor. 2: 10); there is also mention made of a *bet av* (Tam. 1:1; Mid. 1:8; cf. Yoma 1:5). The levites were similarly divided into 24 *mishmarot*, which replaced each other every week (I Chron. 25:8ff, et al.; Jos., Ant., 7:363ff.; Ta'an. 4:2). These were in turn subdivided into seven *battei avot*, and presided over by "heads." Finally, there was an analogous division of the Israelites themselves into 24 *mishmarot*, each of which had to take its turn in coming to Jerusalem for a week. They served to represent the whole body of the people while the daily (communal) offerings were sacrificed, for "how can a man's offering be offered while he does not stand by it?" (Ta'an. 4:2, et al.).

That part of the *mishmar* of priests, Levites, or Israelites actually engaged in the performance of its duty was called a *ma'amad* or *ammud* ("station") and was headed by a *rosh ma'amad* (Tam. 5:6). When the time for the service of a *mishmar* came round, all the priests and Levites belonging to it would go to Jerusalem. Not all the Israelites of that *mishmar*, however, proceeded to Jerusalem. A portion of them certainly did (Ta'an. 4:2; cf. Tosef., Ta'an. 4:3) but those who could not do so assembled in their own towns and read the story of creation, etc. Only those in Jerusalem who actually "stood by" while the sacrifice was being offered could, strictly speaking, be called a *ma'amad*, or *ammud* (see Sof. 17:5; but see Lieberman, *Tosefta ki-Feshutah* 5, 1962, 1104, who shows that according to a different opinion the *ma'amadot* were of Israelites alone).

Activities

These 24 *mishmarot* conducted the daily Temple service, each in turn officiating for one week. Every Sabbath they changed, the retiring *mishmar* offering the morning and *musaf* additional sacrifices, whereas the new *mishmar* offered the evening one, and laid the fresh shewbread on the table (Tosef., Suk. 4:24–25). On the three pilgrim festivals, all the 24 *mishmarot* officiated together (Suk. 5:7–8). Each priestly *mishmar* had in the Temple its own ring at which its members slaughtered their animals (Mid. 3:5) and its own niche in which their vestments were kept (Tam. 5:3). Bilga's niche was, however, permanently blocked up and its ring immovable (Suk. 5:8), a sign of disgrace, because one of its members had once acted shamefully (Suk. 56b). The weekly *mishmarot* of priests were broken up into between four and nine subdivisions (*battei avot*). If there were fewer than seven, some would officiate twice during the week. If, on the other hand, there were more than seven, then on some days two would have to serve together (Tosef., Ta'an. 2:2, et al.). Furthermore, as only a small part of a *bet av* was required to serve at any given time, lots were drawn to decide which individual priests should officiate each day (Yoma 2:2–4, et al.).

A number of restrictions were placed upon members of the *mishmar* and *bet av* during their week (or day) of office. Thus, members of the *mishmar* were permitted to drink wine by night but not by day, whereas those of the *bet av* could not drink wine either by day or night, as they might be called upon to assist in the Temple service at any conceivable hour. Members of the *mishmar* and of the (Israelite) *ma'amad* alike were forbidden to cut their hair or wash their clothes throughout the week – as this should have been done earlier – except on Thursday, so that due honor be accorded the Sabbath (Ta'an. 2:7). On certain communal fast days, members of the *mishmar* and the *bet av* were permitted to eat, or else to fast only partially, so as to have enough strength to carry out their Temple duties (Ta'an. 2:6). The men of the Israelite *ma'amad*, however, would fast from Monday to Thursday on their week of service, while from Sunday to Friday they read (in sections) the chapter of Creation (Gen. 1; Ta'an. 4:2–3). Members of the *mishmar* who were not engaged in actual service would pray that the sacrifices of their officiating brethren be acceptable; while those of the Israelite *ma'amad* who could not come to Jerusalem gathered in their local synagogues (or meeting places) and prayed for the welfare of sailors, wayfarers, children, pregnant women, etc. The *ma'amadot* were considered to be of such importance that it was said that without them heaven and earth could not have survived (Ta'an. 27b; cf. the reading in Sof. 17:15). The institution of the *ma'amadot*, which dates back to the beginning of the Second Temple (see sources cited below), seems to have formed the basis of what later became the synagogal system.

History

Concerning the origins of the *mishmar* system, there are three conflicting (tannaitic) traditions recorded in rabbinic literature:

(1) Moses established eight (priestly) *mishmarot*, to which David and Samuel added another eight. Finally, on the return from the Babylonian Exile, 24 were established (TJ, Ta'an. 4:2, 67);

(2) Moses established eight (priestly and levitical) *mishmarot*; David and Samuel increased them to 24, and on the return from the Exile 24 (Israelite) *ammudim* (*ma'amadot*) were established, parallel to the priestly and levitical *mishmarot* (Tosef., Ta'an. 4:2);

(3) Moses established 16 *mishmarot*, which were later increased to 24 (Ta'an. 27a). Relative unanimity of opinion is to be found only in the account of the restoration of the *mishmar* system after the Babylonian Exile. Four *mishmarot* are said to have returned from the Exile, Jedaiah, Harim, Pashchur, and Immer. "And the prophets among them [or "in Jerusalem", according to the Tosefta; i.e., Haggai, Zechariah, and Malachi] arose and made 24 lots, and put them into an urn." Then each of the four *mishmarot* drew five lots in addition to his own, making a total of six. Finally, the *rashei mishmarot* divided them into *battei avot* (TJ, Ta'an. 4:4, 68a, et al.). It would seem (from tradition (2) above) that only at this stage were the Israelite *ma'amadot* introduced.

Thus rabbinic sources trace the first origins of the *mishmarot* via David and Samuel back to Moses. However, these accounts do not appear to have the value of independent traditions but rather to be based upon inferences drawn from scriptural passages. Thus, "… whom David and Samuel the seer did ordain, in their set office …" (I Chron. 9:22) is said to refer to the priestly and levitical *mishmarot* (Tosef., *ibid.*; cf. TJ, *ibid.*, citing I Chron. 2:4). Nevertheless, the resultant picture presented by rabbinic sources probably has considerable historical validity. The system remained unchanged even till Josephus' time (Jos., Ant., 7:363ff.; Life, 1:2).

Long after the destruction of the Temple, memories of the *mishmarot* lingered on. In Ereẓ Israel their names were mentioned each Sabbath in the *piyyutim*. Tablets, fragments of which have survived, were fixed on synagogue walls, engraved with a list of *mishmarot* and their geographical provenance. Karaite liturgy preserved echoes of both the *mishmarot* and the *ma'amadot*. Even as late as 1034, it was still the custom in some communities to announce on each Sabbath: "Today is the holy Sabbath, holy to the Lord. Today is [the Sabbath of] which *mishmeret*? [That of] *mishmeret* … May the Merciful One restore the *mishmeret* to its place, speedily and in our days. Amen."

[Daniel Sperber]

BIBLIOGRAPHY: IN THE BIBLE: Schuerer, Gesch, 1 (1901), 286–97; S. Klein, *Meḥkarim Ereẓ-Yisre'eliyyim* (1924), 3–30; idem, *Ereẓ ha-Galil* (1945, 1967[2]), 62–68, 177–92; A.C. Welch, *The Work of the Chronicler* (1939), 8–96; H. Kees, *Das Priestertum im aegyptischen Staat* (1953), 300–8; Jepsen, in: ZAW, 66 (1954), 87–106; W. Rudolph, *Die Chronikbuecher* (1955), 152–78; Y. Kaufmann, Toledot, 4 (1956), 358–9; P. Winter, in: VT, 6 (1956), 215–7 (Eng.); J.T. Milik, in: VT. *Supplement*, 4 (1957), 24–26 (Fr.); S. Talmon, in: *Scripta Hierosolymitana*, 4 (1958), 168–76 (Eng.); Avi-Yonah, in: IEJ, 12 (1962), 137–42; L. Finkelstein, *New Light from the Prophets* (1969), 49–76, 101–22. IN THE TALMUD: M.L. Bloch, *Sha'arei Torat ha-Takkanot*, 1 (1879), 27–40, 87–94; J. Liver, *Perakim be-Toledot ha-Kehunnah ve-ha-Leviyyah* (1968), 33–52; EM, 5 (1968), 569–80.

MISHNAH (Heb. מִשְׁנָה). The term "mishnah" is used in a number of different ways (see below), but when used as a proper noun ("the Mishnah") it designates the collection of rabbinic traditions redacted by Rabbi *Judah ha-Nasi (usually called simply "Rabbi") at the beginning of the third century

CE. The Mishnah supplements, complements, clarifies and systematizes the commandments of the Torah. The Torah, for example, commands: "Remember the Sabbath day" (Ex. 20:8). The Mishnah provides this abstract commandment with a concrete form – the *kiddush* and *havdalah* rituals which mark the beginning and the ending of the Sabbath day. The Torah commands "Observe the Sabbath day" (Deut. 6:12). The Mishnah specifies 39 categories of forbidden labor which are prohibited by this commandment, subsuming dozens of other kinds of labor under these 39 headings. The Torah commands: "When you eat and are satisfied, give thanks to your God for the good land which He has given you" (Deut. 8:10). The Mishnah spells out specific blessings to be recited before and after each kind of food, and what to do if the wrong blessing is recited by mistake. It also extends the recitation of blessings to areas other than food, detailing blessings to be recited before and after the performance of commandments, blessings of praise and thanksgiving, even establishing a regular order of daily prayers. When the commandments seem chaotic or inconsistent, as in Lev. 13–14 ("leprosy"), the Mishnah organizes these rules into a consistent system. When they are already relatively detailed and systematic, as in Lev. 1–7 (sacrifices), the Mishnah deals with additional aspects of the halakhah, either ignored or mentioned only in passing in the Torah, such as the proper intentions which should accompany the sacrifices, and the consequences of improper intention.

The contents of the Mishnah are the product of an ongoing process of elaborating and explaining the foundations, the details and the significance of the Torah's commandments. This process began long before the redaction of the Mishnah, and continued throughout the talmudic period (1st to 6th centuries CE) and beyond. Nevertheless, the Mishnah has a unique place within the rabbinic tradition. It was the central literary document of the entire talmudic period, providing the framework for the redaction of its companion volume, the *Tosefta, and serving as the foundation for both the Jerusalem Talmud and the Babylonian Talmud. Through these works the Mishnah has shaped most of the actual practice of the Jewish religion down to the present day. In the post-talmudic period commentaries were composed to the Mishnah, and together with them the Mishnah came to serve as the authoritative epitome of the talmudic tradition as a whole. In these two roles – as the foundation underlying the talmudic tradition and as the authoritative epitome of that tradition – the Mishnah has played a decisive role in the religious life of the Jewish people.

Below we will examine the formal structure of the Mishnah as a literary work, and provide an overview of certain aspects of the Mishnah's content, focusing on its two primary components – halakhah and aggadah – including an analysis of the logical structure of mishnaic halakhah. We will then discuss the sources of the Mishnah, its redaction, and its dissemination and acceptance in the later talmudic academies. After a discussion of the contributions of traditional and academic scholarship to the understanding of the Mishnah, we will provide a brief survey of editions, translations, and other aids to Mishnah study.

The Mishnah as a Literary Work

Originally the term "mishnah" designated the entire content of traditional Torah study, with the exclusion of the 24 books of the Hebrew Bible – "mikra" in Hebrew. Mishnah Ned. 4:3 opposes the term "mikra" to "midrash, halakhot, and aggadot," which are themselves grouped together in Tosefta Ber. 2:12 under the general heading of "mishnah." The terms midrash and halakhot (sing. halakhah) mentioned in these passages designate the two most fundamental forms in which rabbinic tradition was studied and transmitted. In midrash, rabbinic tradition is intimately interconnected with the explication of the biblical text, and the overall literary structure of midrashic compilations follows the order of the biblical text. Halakhot contain the same rabbinic material as is found in the midrash, but without any reference to the biblical text. In the halakhot, rabbinic tradition stands on its own, the structure and order of halakhic compilations being determined solely by the content of rabbinic tradition itself.

Only two halakhic compilations have come down to us from the earliest period of rabbinic literature: Rabbi's Mishnah and the Tosefta, a supplementary halakhic work similar in arrangement to the Mishnah, and probably redacted by Rabbi's disciples. Both of these works are divided into six *sedarim* (sing. *seder* = "order"): *Zera'im, concerning agricultural matters; Mo'ed, concerning holy times and related issues; *Nashim, concerning family law; *Nezikin, concerning civil and criminal law; *Kodashim, concerning sacrifices and the Temple; *Toharot, concerning ritual purity and impurity.

These six sedarim are further subdivided into tractates (*masekhtot*, sing. *masekhet*), and the tractates into chapters (*perakim*, sing. *perek*). The further subdivision of chapters into smaller groups of halakhot varies from edition to edition and does not seem to be original. With the exception of Zera'im, the order of the masekhtot follows the number of chapters which they contain. A tractate with a larger number of chapters comes first, followed by tractates with fewer chapters. If a seder contains more than one tractate with the same number of chapters, their order may vary between different manuscripts and editions. In the past, chapters of the Mishnah were referenced by the opening words of their first halakhah. Today references are made to tractates by name, and to chapter and individual halakhah by number, according to the accepted division of the most recent editions.

The redaction and dissemination of the Mishnah in the early third century marked a turning point in the history of rabbinic literature. Scholars who were active up to the time of Rabbi and his immediate disciples were called "teachers of mishnah" – **tannaim* (sing. *tanna*) in Aramaic. The later talmudic scholars – called **amoraim* – accepted the traditions of the tannaim as authoritative, and as time went on they were increasingly unwilling to disagree with them. As a result, talmudic literature is divided into two periods – the earlier, tannaitic period and the later, amoraic period. The tannaitic literature consists primarily of the Mishnah, the Tosefta, and tannaitic midrashim – Sifra, Sifre, and Mekhilta, etc. Amoraic literature is included primarily in the Jerusalem Talmud, the Babylonian Talmud, and the classic midrashei aggadah – *Genesis R., *Lamentations R., *Leviticus R., *Pesikta de-Rav Kahana, etc.

Since Rabbi's Mishnah was the most important and authoritative work of halakhah to come down to us from antiquity, the term "mishnah" came to be equated with the term "halakhot," and was often used in opposition to the term "midrash." In a parallel development, the term "hilkhata" ("halakhot" in Aramaic), apparently referring to Rabbi's Mishnah, is listed in later talmudic sources (TB Shav. 41b) along with "sifra, sifre and tosefta" – apparently referring to compilations similar to the tannaitic works known by these names today.

Finally, the individual unit of tannaitic tradition was called "a mishnah" (pl. mishnayot), or *matnita* (pl. *matneyata*) in Aramaic. Here also, the unique status of Rabbi's Mishnah within tannaitic literature leads to the further distinction between *matnitin* ("our mishnah"), a tradition included in Rabbi's Mishnah, and *matnita baraita* ("an external mishnah"), or baraita (pl. baraitot) for short, a tannaitic tradition not included in Rabbi's Mishnah. The baraitot were preserved not only in the Tosefta, but were also included in and transmitted as part of the amoraic tradition in the two Talmudim.

Our discussions below of tannaitic halakhah and aggadah apply not only to Rabbi's Mishnah, but also to the Tosefta and to many of the talmudic baraitot. However, the discussions of the place of the Mishnah in the development of talmudic literature, in the history of Jewish tradition, its redaction, and so on, apply to Rabbi's Mishnah alone, but not to the Tosefta or to the talmudic baraitot.

Halakhah in the Mishnah

The Mishnah itself uses the term halakhah to designate ancient or authoritative traditions (Pe'ah 2:6, Or. 3:9, Yev. 8:3), as well as accepted religious practices (Naz. 7:4, BK 3:9, Edu. 1:5, Men. 4:3, Nid. 4:3). It is also used to refer to individual units of tradition, irrespective of their authoritative status (Avot 6:3), and even to incorrect traditions (Oha. 16:1). These traditions may involve no more than the simple restatement or brief elaboration of some custom or practice. But by far the most characteristic tendency of the individual tannaitic halakhah is the close examination of some dimension of ordinary human life or experience, and the careful categorization of certain aspects of that experience in line with a limited number of formal dichotomies.

The most obvious – and familiar – halakhic dichotomy is the one between "forbidden" (*asur*) and "permitted" (*mutar*). This dichotomy is most regularly applied to human behavior. For example, the Mishnah may categorize sexual relations between two individuals under certain circumstances as permitted, and under other circumstances as forbidden. While eating on the Day of Atonement is certainly forbidden, tannaitic halakhah lists certain exceptions to this rule and even requires children under a certain age to eat. Similarly, the halakhah permits heating food on the Sabbath under certain circumstances and forbids it under other circumstances.

A related dichotomy – applying also to a large extent to behavior – is the one between "liable" for punishment or some other formal sanction (*ḥayyav*) and 'exempt' from such sanctions (*patur*). This dichotomy is generally applicable to actions which have already been categorized as forbidden. For example, tannaitic halakhah forbids the carrying of an object in the public domain on the Sabbath. In order for the transgressor to be considered "liable" for sanctions, however, the act of carrying must conform to a number of different conditions. If any one of these conditions is not met, the transgressor is considered "exempt" from sanctions. Similarly, the halakhah forbids baking bread on a holiday for use the following day. One who transgresses this rule is, however, not necessarily liable for punishment. It is forbidden to steal. Under certain circumstances the thief will be liable to pay double indemnity, while under other circumstances he will be exempt from this additional payment. Although a person can be liable for the indirect or inadvertent consequences of his or her actions (or inaction), it is not always possible to categorize these actions as forbidden.

The dichotomy between *ḥayyav* and *patur* may also be applied to human behavior in another way – with regard to positive commandments, such as the eating of matzah on Passover. Here *ḥayyav* should be translated as "obligated [to fulfill the commandment]" and *patur* as "exempt [from fulfilling it]." The halakhah categorizes eating matzah on the first night of Passover as an "obligation" (*ḥovah*), and on the remaining days of Passover as "optional" (*reshut*). The Mishnah states that properly prepared matzah "may be used in order to fulfill one's obligation" (*yosin bo*). When prepared improperly, the Mishnah states: "it may not be used in order to fulfill the obligation" (*ein yosin bo*). The Mishnah uses the dichotomy between "fit" (*kasher*) and "unfit" (*pasul*) in a similar fashion, in order to determine whether various ritual objects – a shofar or a lulav, for example – may be used to fulfill one's obligation in performing these commandments.

Halakhic categorizations are, however, by no means limited to the field of human behavior. The Torah itself designated certain days as "holy" (*kodesh*), during which various forms of activity are forbidden. It also designated certain places as holy, such as the Temple and walled cities, from which various kinds of impurity must be excluded. The Mishnah systematically applies the dichotomy between the "holy" (*kodesh*) and the "profane" (*ḥol*) in order to constitute an elaborate hierarchy of holy times and holy places. The holiest times were defined by the most rigorous and most comprehensive set of prohibitions, and lesser degrees of holiness by more lenient and less comprehensive sets of prohibitions. Similarly, the Mishnah defines ten ascending levels of holy space (Kel. 1:6–9), each defined by stricter and stricter rules of purity.

The most highly developed area of tannaitic halakhah is to be found in its system of ritual purity. Seder Toharot applies the dichotomy between ritually pure (*tahor*) and ritually impure (*tame*) to virtually every aspect of ordinary life. These terms can signify either that an object is susceptible to becoming impure, or that it is actually impure and capable of transmitting this impurity to something else. Certain tractates define the purity or impurity of tools, garments, vessels, and places of residence. Others define the purity or impurity of foods and drinks. Others categorize certain individuals as themselves being sources of ritual impurity, and other individuals as impure as a result of contact with other sources of ritual impurity. This area of halakhah seems to have played a decisive role in the life of the tannaitic sages, even among non-priestly families, and with no obvious connection to the Temple (see Alon).

Tosefta Demai (2:2ff.) describes the procedure by which a candidate is accepted into the elite association called the *ḥavura*. It lists in detail the responsibilities which the candidate must freely accept upon himself or herself in order to be considered a *ḥaver* – including the responsibility to observe all the rules of ritual purity (cf. Demai 2:3). From these descriptions it seems fairly clear that many or most of the purity rules involved no formal obligation (*ḥova*) whatsoever, but were rather purely voluntary practices (*reshut*). This example of Toharot should serve as a warning against viewing tannaitic halakhah as a legal system consisting entirely of formal obligations enforceable by earthly courts. While true in part, other aspects of tannaitic halakhah could be more accurately described as a moral or a spiritual discipline which the initiate freely accepts in order to draw closer to the ideal of divine service.

Aggadah in the Mishnah

The other primary component of the Mishnah is the aggadah. This term is notoriously difficult to define, and it has become the custom among scholars to define aggadah by means of negation – as the non-halakhic component of rabbinic tradition (Frankel, *Midrash and Aggadah*, 20). While fair enough, we must be careful in adopting this approach not to define halakhah itself too narrowly. As we have seen, the halakhah of the Mishnah can be described in part as a system of laws, but not infrequently it also has the character of a personal moral and spiritual discipline. It can be expressed in the form of concrete judgments about specific cases, but also in rules involving varying degrees of abstraction and generality. The Mishnah may even use stories to express a halakhah. This is obviously so when the story reports an explicit legal precedent. But it may also be true when a story merely describes the behavior of a notable sage, if it is understood that this behavior is worthy of imitation.

Despite these differences in form, the rules, judgments and precedents included in the Mishnah all have one thing in common. They all categorize specific forms of behavior and well defined areas of concrete experience in line with formal dichotomies of the sort described in the previous section. Aggadah, on the other hand, investigates and interprets the *meaning*, the *values*, and the *ideas* which underlie the concrete forms of religious life – as opposed to the specific rules which actually govern that life. Continuing the tendency to define aggadah as 'that which is not halakhah', we could say that the relation between aggadah and halakhah is similar in many ways to the relations between theory and practice, between idea and application, and, in the area of ethics, between character and behavior.

Starting from the last distinction, it is clear that the Mishnah makes extraordinary demands upon the external behavior of the sages and their disciples. Along with these external demands, the Mishnah makes equally extraordinary "internal" demands on the character, the faith, and the understanding of the sages and their disciples. The Mishnah contains a tractate – Avot – devoted in its entirety to these principles of character, faith, divine providence, justice, etc. Moreover, the Mishnah introduces related aggadic elements into the context of specific halakhic discussions. For example, after defining the obligation to recite a blessing on hearing bad tidings, the Mishnah adds the aggadic statement that one's love for God should never falter, "even if He takes your life" (Ber. 9:5). Similarly tractate Pe'ah, which deals with specific obligatory gifts to the poor, opens with an aggadic description of the unlimited nature of acts of loving kindness and charity, and of the rewards that await those who show love, respect and kindness to others. After defining the specific sums one is obligated to pay in restitution for assault, the Mishnah declares that "one is not absolved [of the sin] until one asks [the victim for forgiveness]" (BK 8:7). The Mishnah then goes on to state that the victim "should not be cruel" but rather should be merciful and forgiving.

It is in this sense that we should understand the programmatic statement concerning the nature and the purpose of the aggadah, found in the tannaitic midrash, Sifre Deut. 49: "If you desire to know the One who spoke and the world came to be, then you should study the aggadah, for in this way you will come to know the One who spoke and the world came to be, and *you will cleave to his ways*." As is made clear there, God's ways are the aspects of justice, mercy, etc., which both define the holy character of the righteous individual and underlie those forms of normative behavior which constitute much of the halakhah.

The aggadah of the Mishnah also deals with classic theological issues such as divine providence, theodicy and the afterlife. These issues, however, are regularly integrated into some appropriate halakhic context. For example, one of the most highly developed aggadic themes running throughout tannaitic literature is the doctrine of "measure for measure." At its foundation lies an ancient saying – "The vessel which you use to measure out [for others], will itself be used to measure for you" – which is already quoted in the New Testament (Matt. 7:2) as a warning not to be judgmental of others, lest one suffer the same fate at their hands. The tannaitic literature develops it into a general theory of divine justice. More specifically, it is used to explain and to justify the details of divine retribution as described in various biblical passages. One of these passages concerns the sotah, a wife suspected of unfaithfulness (Num. 5). Since the oracular method the Torah gives for determining the sotah's innocence or guilt seems extraordinarily harsh and cruel, the Mishnah (Sot. 1:6) quotes the ancient saying itself, and then goes on to argue that every aspect of the biblically ordained procedure is in fact just and appropriate. In the following two mishnayot, the Mishnah summarizes the entire tannaitic doctrine of measure for measure, not only with regard to divine retribution, but also with regard to divine reward.

Another prominent aggadic theme is that of the afterlife – the "portion in the world to come." The first three mishnayot of Sanhedrin 10 present an almost halakhic categorization of actions, beliefs, and historical figures, dividing them into those who do, and those who do not "have a portion in the world to come." This discussion fits the general context in Sanhedrin – a description of the various forms of capital punishment – since the loss of one's portion in the world to come is a kind of otherworldly capital punishment. It also fits the immediate context, coming immediately after a dispute (9:6) whether a non-priest who served in the Temple is to be executed "by the hands of Heaven," and before a discussion of the inhabitants of an idolatrous Israelite city (10:4), who lose their portion in the world to come.

By a recent count there are more than 50 such aggadic passages in the Mishnah, not including Avot and those found at the ends of tractates or sub-divisions of tractates which are generally viewed as later scribal additions, and not as integral parts of the text of the Mishnah (Frankel, *The Aggadah in the Mishnah*, 655–656). While preliminary conclusions may be drawn concerning this phenomenon as a whole, there is still much room for detailed analysis of each individual case in its own particular halakhic context.

Finally, we should mention that, despite its overall literary character, the Mishnah does contain a number of midrashic passages. With regard to their content, these passages are quite unexceptional, and reflect the same kind of halakhic and aggadic content found in the overwhelming majority of non-midrashic mishnah traditions. They differ only with regard to their external form. This phenomenon has been addressed with regard to the question of possible literary dependence between the extant tannaitic halakhic and midrashic works (Melamed; Friedman, *Tosefta Atiqta*, 76). Recently the midrashic material found in the Mishnah has been used as a starting point for a general examination of early rabbinic hermeneutics (Samely). The question of the specific role which these midrashim play within the context of mishnaic halakhah has recently been addressed (Raviv), but no firm conclusions have yet been reached.

The Structure of Tannaitic Halakhah

The style of the Mishnah is deceptively simple. Most individual halakhot consist of little more than a description of some situation and a brief statement of the ruling which applies to that situation. To the undiscerning eye these halakhot seem to lack virtually all of the dialectical and conceptual elements which are so characteristic of the later forms of talmudic and rabbinic literature. If the analysis of tannaitic halakhah were to end here, we would be left with a rather difficult question: How could these tannaitic halakhot have served as the foundation for the highly dialectical and conceptually sophisticated discussions found in the later talmudic and post-talmudic halakhic literature? Yet they did, and so it would seem that the logical structure of tannaitic halakhah deserves further examination.

First it must be admitted that the Mishnah contains many halakhot of a descriptive and historical character which have little or no conceptual content. For example, tractate Middot describes in detail the physical structure of the Temple. The related tractate Tamid describes the daily Temple service in the form of a continuous narrative. The third chapter of Bikkurim describes the process of bringing and offering of the first fruits. The first seven chapters of Yoma relate in chronological order the events leading up to and culminating in the Temple service of the Day of Atonement. Certain court and priestly procedures are also related in narrative form, as in Sanh. 3:6–7, Neg. 12:5–7, and 14:1–3. Some reports of second Temple practice and restatements of biblical law may include elements of constructive reinterpretation (as in Neg. 13:1), but by and large the conceptual element in these mishnayot, if present at all, is relatively small.

These are however exceptions to the rule. The overwhelming majority of tannaitic halakhot are normative in nature, not historical. The connection between the case description and the ruling in a normative tannaitic halakhah will rarely be merely contingent or accidental. On the contrary, it will almost always reflect the judgment that in this particular case, and under these specific circumstances, the ruling given in the halakhah *must* apply.

The presumption that the connection between the case description and the ruling in a tannaitic halakhah is essential, not accidental, gives rise to a number of interpretive principles. We may illustrate this by means of an example. Mishnah BK 1:4 posits a halakhic dichotomy between two categories – *tam* (lit. "innocent") and *mu'ad*. In the Mishnah the term *mu'ad* – based on Ex. 21 29 – signifies strict liability for all damages caused by one's property. The distinction between *tam* and *mu'ad* in BK 1:4 builds upon the distinction already found in Ex. 21 35–36 between an ox which caused damage unexpectedly, as opposed to an ox that was known to have caused damage repeatedly in the past, and whose owner, despite having been warned, did nothing to prevent further damage. In the latter case, the owner is held strictly liable for all damages caused by his animal, while in the former his liability is limited to one half of the damages. The reasoning behind this distinction is quite transparent. Strict liability is associated with a situation where the owner was clearly negligent, and the Torah holds him strictly liable for full damages because of this negligence.

Continuing this line of thought, Mishnah BK 1:4 states that the owner of a domesticated animal is held strictly liable for full damages if "it ate something appropriate for it." From this one can infer that if the animal "ate something not appropriate for it," the owner would not be liable for full damages, but rather only for half-damages. This then gives rise to the following question: Why should this change in the object consumed – from "appropriate for it" to "inappropriate for it" – affect the degree of liability for the damages caused by one's animal? An answer to this question requires a determination of the extent of the owner's responsibility to anticipate possible damages. This in turn would involve a more precise definition of the exact boundary between "appropriate" and "inappropriate."

In BK 2:2 the Mishnah provides such a definition. First it quotes BK 1:4 and then explains it by means of the following two halakhot: "If the animal ate fruits and vegetables – the owner is fully liable; [if the animal ate] clothes or vessels – the owner is liable only for half-damages." The first halakhah defines the case where the animal ate "something appropriate for it." The second halakhah defines the alternative case, where the animal ate "something not appropriate for it." A naive reader of BK 1:4 would probably have understood the words "appropriate *for it*" – i.e., for the animal itself – to signify some kind of feed which the animal is accustomed to eating, and to exclude other foodstuffs, such as avocados, artichokes, etc., which are not appropriate "for it." BK 2:2 draws a very different distinction, between "fruits and vegetables," generally consumed only by humans, and "clothes or vessels," which are totally inedible. While the tanna of BK 2:2 may not have given us a very precise interpretation of the original language of BK 1:4, he has, nevertheless, expressed a very clear and unequivocal judgment regarding his understanding of the notions of responsibility, negligence, and liability which underlie that halakhah.

The procedure outlined above is very characteristic of talmudic analysis. Starting from one halakhah, taught explicitly in the Mishnah, the student infers another halakhah – parallel to the original halakhah, but differing in two ways. First, the case description of the second halakhah differs from the original with respect to one detail – e.g. "inappropriate" instead of "appropriate." Second, the ruling in the second halakhah is totally different from the original – "not liable for full damages" instead of "liable for full damages." This analysis presupposes that the difference in the rulings of these two halakhot follows necessarily from the change in their case descriptions. If we then explain *why* a certain change in the ruling follows from the change in the case description, we will, in effect, have grasped the legal principle which underlies the original halakhah. In fact, the only way we can ever understand the essential connection between the case description and the ruling in a tannaitic halakhah is by explaining why, if the case changed, the ruling would necessarily be different.

From this perspective, it becomes clear how tannaitic halakhah – even an individual tannaitic halakhah – can be considered both dialectical and conceptual. It is dialectical because the meaning of the individual tannaitic halakhah is determined only in its relation to another alternative halakhah. It is conceptual because the comparison of these two contrasting halakhot requires a conceptual distinction which can justify the difference between them.

We normally associate conceptual explanation with some form of abstract generalization. Tannaitic reasoning, however, concerns itself almost exclusively with uncovering the principles operative in particular cases. As we have seen, this involves a close comparison of two distinct but closely related halakhot. This tendency explains one of the most characteristic and widespread phenomena in tannaitic literature – the *halakhic couplet*. A mishnah of this sort contains, not one, but two distinct halakhot, parallel in form and clearly linked together by some literary device. The case descriptions of these two halakhot are very similar in form and content, and usually differ with respect to one element only. The rulings, on the other hand, are usually diametrically opposed, often reflecting alternative sides of the halakhic dichotomies described above (cf. example from BK 2:2 above). These parallel halakhot invite comparison, and their differences demand explanation.

By expressing its notions in the form of concrete distinctions, and not by means of finished and formal abstractions, the Mishnah invites the student to refine its unstated principles by means of further distinctions. These principles are implicitly conceptual, and so lead the student beyond their immediate context. Yet they are expressed in an external form which is both concrete and limited in scope. The resulting tension between these two aspects of tannaitic halakhah gives rise to an open-ended process of interpretation and analysis, reinterpretation, and renewed analysis. In this way, the cumulative body of tannaitic – and early amoraic – halakhic literature, which was the result of this process, provided fertile ground for the growth of the explicitly dialectical and conceptual discussions and analyses of later talmudic and post-talmudic literature.

The Sources of the Mishnah

When speaking of the sources of the Mishnah, we must distinguish between three senses in which the term is used. First, it is used to designate the multiplicity of fully formulated tannaitic halakhic and aggadic traditions which were accessible to Rabbi when he began to redact his Mishnah (see the following section below). The second sense in which we use the term is to designate earlier and more primitive forms of these halakhic and aggadic traditions, stemming perhaps from the first generations of tannaitic activity. The extant body of tannaitic literature often quotes and interprets such earlier traditions. An examination of the various forms in which these traditions have been preserved in the extant tannaitic works provides indirect evidence for their existence, and to a certain extent for their reconstruction. The third sense in which we speak of the 'sources' of the Mishnah is in regard to ancient pre-literary traditions, stemming from the Second Temple period, which may have served as the background for the formulation of the earliest level of tannaitic literary activity.

With regard to this third sense, it has been claimed that the roots of tannaitic halakhah extend backward, "long before the destruction of the Second Temple" (Albeck, *Unter.* 3). In support of this position, scholars have pointed out numerous parallels between certain assumptions of tannaitic halakhah and similar positions reflected in the books of Judith and Jubilees, the Septuagint, as well as Philo, Josephus, and the Dead Sea writings (Safrai, 134–146). As further testimony to the antiquity of tannaitic halakhah, scholars have pointed to "internal evidence" within the Mishnah itself (Hoffmann, *Die Erste Mischna;* Epstein, *Tannaim,* 18 ff.). This testimony, however, usually involves little more than descriptions of events or practices which supposedly took place in Second Temple times (*Tann.* 36, 57), without any concrete proof that the tannaitic formulations themselves actually derive from an earlier period. As impressive as these arguments are, they concern at best the cultural prehistory of tannaitic halakhah, but not the concrete history of the development of tannaitic literature itself. So long as this distinction remains clear, these investigations into the "roots" of tannaitic halakhah against the background of earlier periods can only contribute to our understanding of the Mishnah and its content.

We also speak (in the second sense mentioned above) of the sources of the Mishnah with regard to the earliest historical levels of tannaitic literature. Even the most conservative talmudic scholars admit that tannaitic *literature* (as opposed to tradition) is the product of a change which occurred, at the very earliest, around the end of the Second Temple period. "Our Mishnah collection is the result of the intellectual work of several generations, extending over hundreds of years, which served to preserve, transmit, and to develop the oral tradition which was transmitted along with the written teaching – the Torah. The halakhot, which up to that time remained undecided and to a certain extent fluid, received in our Mishnah a fixed form, and so were preserved and not forgotten" (Albeck, *Unter.* 3). Even the earliest strata of tannaitic sources possess a literary "form." These literary forms were capable of being repeated and memorized, and so "preserved and not forgotten." In this way "tradition" became "mishnah."

If this were the whole story, the historical study of the Mishnah would be quite simple. However, "the simple fact is that the Mishna found its final redaction only by the end of the second century C.E., and that much development had taken place in the Tannaitic period which preceded" (Safrai 133). At some point in the history of the tannaitic period, these early mishnaic sources became the object of intense study and analysis, and, as we saw in the previous section above, tannaitic analysis can result in radical reinterpretation of these earlier mishnaic sources.

Albeck described in detail (*Unter.* 5–13) many of the ways in which later tannaim interpreted and expanded earlier, relatively primitive halakhic sources. Sometimes, taking a relatively short and simple tradition as their starting point, they would posit a series of additional layers of interpretation and elaboration. Sometimes later scholars would analyze the words of an earlier Rabbi, concluding that his halakhah reflected a more general principle. They would then take his words from their original context and copy them over, virtually verbatim, in another context, in which, according to their understanding, they should equally apply. Sometimes they would "interpolate" the original halakhah, i.e., insert interpretive comments of various lengths into the language of the original source. Albeck showed that these interpretive additions were sometimes drawn from other mishnaic sources found nearby in the same tractate. Sometimes an identical source was preserved in different schools or in different tractates within the Mishnah itself. In this case, the same original source might be expanded and interpolated in different ways, resulting in divergent, and even in contradictory versions of the same original tradition.

Other scholars went further than Albeck, asserting that tannaitic interpolation could also involve the *elimination* of words or passages from an original source, or even the *reformulation* of the original language itself, in line with some interpretation accepted by a later Rabbi. Epstein, for example, held that even the most ancient traditions "were *reworked* by later tannaim, and passed through the channels of intermediate redactors, who added to them and *subtracted* from them" (*Tann.* 57). Albeck explicitly rejected both of these notions (*Unter.* 12), and the reasons for his position will be examined below in the following section. It is nevertheless quite clear that the extant tannaitic sources cannot be relied upon to preserve traditions in the original form in which they were studied by earlier generations of tannaim.

This reservation should be kept in mind, not only with regard to the earliest literary layers of the Mishnah, but also with regard to traditions ascribed to the intermediate and later generations of tannaim. The tannaim who were active from the destruction of the Temple and up to the time of Rabbi are usually divided into four generations. The earliest tannaitic traditions – ascribed to Bet Hillel and Bet Shammai – are often the subject of debate, not only regarding the correct interpretation of their words, but even with regard to the words themselves. Similar disputes, however, are also found concerning Rabbi Joshua, Rabbi Eliezer, as well as Rabbi Akiva and his disciples, Meir, Simeon, Judah, etc. The attempt, therefore, to analyze the text of Rabbi's Mishnah into four distinct literary levels, and then to assign each level to a particular historical period or personality – as attempted by A. Goldberg in his commentaries on the Mishnah – is suggestive, but remains somewhat problematic for the reasons outlined above.

The most promising method for recovering earlier forms of tannaitic tradition remains the exhaustive analysis of *particular cases,* based on the detailed reconstruction of the process of interpretation and interpolation which resulted in the various parallel versions of a given source which we possess today. Albeck, and most notably Epstein, provide solid models and many excellent examples of this kind of analysis.

In the short span of these four generations, the tannaim produced a considerable body of halakhic and aggadic traditions – traditions which served as the immediate literary sources (in the first sense mentioned above) for Rabbi's Mishnah. Much of the evidence for these literary sources is found in the other extant tannaitic works, the Tosefta and the tannaitic midrashim, which were edited in the Land of Israel in the generations immediately following Rabbi, and in part by his own disciples. These works preserve many parallel traditions to those included in the Mishnah, in forms which often seem to be more original than those found in Rabbi's Mishnah itself. The comparison of these parallel traditions, together with the results of the critical analysis of the Mishnah text itself, provides the basis for an examination of the redaction of the Mishnah.

The Redaction of the Mishnah

The question of the form and purpose of the final redaction of the Mishnah has long been a topic of scholarly debate. In the twentieth century this debate focused on the question whether the Mishnah should be seen as a code of relatively self-consistent and authoritative religious practice (Epstein), or as an anthology of frequently contradictory sources (Albeck). As so formulated, this dispute seems somewhat artificial. On the one hand, there is no reason to assume that the final redaction of the Mishnah was governed by one single overriding principle. On the other hand, the redaction of the Mishnah could reflect a preliminary, but as yet incomplete, effort to bring order and consistency to the body of tannaitic halakhah. Beneath the surface of this discussion, however, lies a far more fundamental and significant disagreement concerning the way in which Rabbi adapted and modified his source material in the redaction of the Mishnah.

Albeck's views on this issue are laid out in his German work, *Untersuchungen ueber die Redaktion der Mischna* (1923). This work, which is based almost exclusively on a critical examination of the Mishnah itself, describes a range of significant literary phenomena. From these phenomena Albeck drew a number of important conclusions, some of which are highly persuasive, others less so. Among the phenomena which Albeck described: (1) literary units including more than one topic, brought intact in more than one tractate, even though only part of the unit is relevant in each place; (2) parallel material found in more than one tractate, to which additions have been made in one tractate only, even though these additions seem equally relevant in the other tractate as well; (3) halakhot found in a given tractate, which do not belong to the subject matter of that tractate, and which are not found at all in the relevant tractate; (4) halakhot found in more than one tractate, which in one place contain conditions and alternative positions not found in the other tractate; (5) alternative versions of the same halakhah in different places in the Mishnah which present the same content in different language; (6) lists of phenomena with a common characteristic, which fail to include similar elements listed elsewhere in the Mishnah which seem to share the same characteristic. On the basis of these and many other similar phenomena, Albeck concluded that the final redaction of our Mishnah did not reflect a comprehensive and sustained effort to revise, adapt, and reorganize its source material into a consistent and unitary whole (*Unter.* 39). On the contrary, the evidence seems to show that the final redactor (Rabbi) preserved much material in the form and in the context in which he received it, even when this material did not wholly correspond, or was even contradictory, to material included elsewhere in the Mishnah.

This conclusion – as far as it goes – seems highly persuasive. However, on the basis of this evidence Albeck went on to conclude "that the Tannaitic schools, including the final redaction of the Mishnah, arranged the individual mishnayot in the context and in the form in which they were originally learned; that they did not allow themselves to interfere in any way with their internal composition, neither did they dare to separate elements which originally belonged together; but rather that they conscientiously and faithfully transmitted these mishnayot, and systematized them" (*Unter.* 12). Albeck here seems to move beyond his evidence in two respects. First, on the basis of extensive, but still limited, evidence, he posits a universal, rather than a limited rule. Second, on the basis of this general rule, which has at most the status of an empirical observation, he posits a *necessary* rule – telling us not only what the Rabbis did or did not do, but rather what they *would not allow* themselves, or *would not dare* to do.

While Albeck's view of the Mishnah as an anthology has been accepted by recent scholars (cf. A. Goldberg, Literature, 214), it would seem that the more fundamental position which underlies his view has remained largely unexamined. For example, it is unclear how Albeck would reconcile his description of Rabbi's ultra-conservative approach to the final redaction of the Mishnah, with his own description (see above) of the creative interpretive process which gave rise to the multiplicity of sources which were available to Rabbi. Did the earlier tannaim "dare" to modify traditional sources in a way which the later tannaim viewed as illegitimate? Alternatively, is there some fundamental difference between modifying the interpretation of an earlier tradition by means of addition, interpolation, and transfer from one context to another, on the one hand, and subtraction and restatement on the other? Epstein's rather brief discussion of the issue (*Tann.* 225–226) hardly does justice to the complexity of Albeck's work. Moreover, the recent surveys of Albeck's work seem to have neglected the extensive evidence brought in his early research written in German, and to have based their assessment of his work solely on his late, popular summaries, published in Hebrew (*Modern Study*, 209–224). The fundamental validity of the substance of Albeck's claims is not in question, but rather only the apodictic and universal form in which he expressed them. It is this aspect which must first be reexamined, in order to make room for alternative insights into other aspects of Rabbi's redactional activity. For this purpose, one clear counter-example will suffice.

Tosefta Ḥullin 8:6 transmits a tannaitic dispute about a case in which a drop of milk fell into a pot containing pieces of meat. Rabbi Judah adopted a strict position, while the sages adopted a more lenient position. The Tosefta then states: "Rabbi said: The position of Rabbi Judah seems reasonable in a case where he didn't stir or cover the pot, and the position of the sages in a case where he stirred and covered the pot." Rabbi's position in the Tosefta represents a compromise between the extreme positions of Judah and the sages. The parallel anonymous halakhah found in Mishnah Ḥullin 8:3 matches precisely the compromise position ascribed to Rabbi in the Tosefta. This case of Mishnah and Tosefta Ḥullin provides a somewhat unusual opportunity to observe all three stages in Rabbi's redaction of a tannaitic tradition: (1) "raw" source material received from the previous generation of tannaim (R. Judah and the sages); (2) Rabbi's own editorial comments upon this source (Tosef. Ḥul. 8:6, end); (3) the final result of the editorial process (Mishnah Ḥullin 8:3). It would stretch the limits of credulity to maintain that Rabbi did not "interfere in any way with the internal composition" of his sources in the redaction of Mishnah Ḥullin 8:3. On the contrary, it is quite clear that he adopted part of R. Judah's ruling, part of the sages' ruling, and applied them to new and modified case descriptions, introducing the distinction between a situation where he "stirred and covered the pot" and one where he "didn't stir or cover the pot" – a distinction which neither R. Judah or the sages ever entertained.

This example shows that Rabbi indeed "dared" and "allowed himself" to add, to subtract, and to reformulate his source material in the process of redacting the Mishnah. Epstein, in his various works, adduced many examples of this kind of creative redactional activity. Recently, S. Friedman has revisited this issue in an extended redactional study of the parallel traditions found in Mishnah and Tosefta Pesaḥim (*Tosefta Atiqta*). Nevertheless, the question still remains open as to the relative weight we should ascribe to these two competing redactional tendencies – the creative (Epstein, Friedman) and the conservative (Albeck) – within Rabbi's literary activity as a whole.

The Later Development of the Text of the Mishnah

In the generations following its redaction, Rabbi's Mishnah achieved an unparalleled prominence and authority in the religious life of the Jewish communities both in Ereẓ Israel and in Babylonia. To a large extent this story belongs to the history of later tannaitic and amoraic literature. In one regard, however, it is relevant to the history of the Mishnah itself. During – and as a result of – this gradual process of disseminaton and acceptance, the Mishnah changed. Instead of a single uniquely authoritative Mishnah as redacted by Rabbi, the amoraic period is characterized by a multiplicity of *different versions* of Rabbi's Mishnah. The Mishnah as studied and transmitted in the Babylonian rabbinic tradition differed significantly from the Mishnah as studied and transmitted in the Palestinian rabbinic tradition. Moreover, there are clear indications of considerable differences between different versions of the Mishnah as studied and transmitted in the various rabbinic academies within the Babylonian and the Palestinian communities themselves.

These different versions of the Mishnah are reflected in the divergent citations of individual Mishnah passages in the Talmud Yerushalmi and the Talmud Bavli, as well as in the variant readings of medieval manuscripts and early editions of the Mishnah. This multiplicity of versions of the Mishnah text presents difficulties, not only for the student of the Mishnah, but also for the scholar who wishes to understand the origin and significance of these variant texts. The classic analysis of these phenomena is found in Epstein's *Introduction to the Text of the Mishnah* (1948). For a preliminary survey of its contents, see Bokser, *The Modern Study of the Mishnah*, 13–36. For an evaluation of its continued importance and its impact on modern scholarship outside of Israel, see Neusner, *The Study of Ancient Judaism I*, 9–12.

While the opening pages of Epstein's book have been the object of intense analysis and debate, it is primarily the second (pp. 166–352) and third (pp. 353–404) sections of his work which concern us here. The question Epstein deals with in these sections is the attitude of the early generations of amoraim to the text of Rabbi's Mishnah, and the impact of their studies on the development of the Mishnah text itself. After an exhaustive analysis of the activity of the first several generations of amoraim, Epstein concluded that the most significant variants in the textual tradition of Rabbi's Mishnah were not the result of errors in transmission, but rather reflected the cumulative impact of an ongoing process of conscious emendation of the text of the Mishnah. He summarized these findings in the following words: "From here we learn to recognize the fundamental nature of the 'emendations' of the Amoraim (at least the early ones), that they – like the 'emendations' of the Tannaim – are never strictly speaking emendations as such, but rather *textual variants* – if one may speak in such a fashion – reflecting *editorial revision*, whose cause and source is a dissenting opinion" (p. 218).

For Epstein the term 'emendation' signified the attempt of a later scholar to restore a corrupt text to its earlier original form. "Editorial revision," on the other hand, signified the conscious modification of an historically correct original text, in order to bring it in line with some external standard of authority or truth. The "dissenting opinion" which could provide, according to Epstein, the justification for an "editorial emendation," was regularly to be found in a tannaitic *baraita* – an alternative authoritative halakhic tradition. One should not, however, exclude the possibility that the individual halakhic judgments of some of the leading scholars among the first generations of the amoraim could also provide sufficient grounds for "editorial emendations" of the text of the Mishnah. In general, the very notion of "editorial emendations," as developed by Epstein, seems to presuppose that Rabbi's Mishnah was accepted as a fundamental study text in the amoraic academies some time before it was finally accepted as a uniquely authoritative corpus of normative halakhah.

As the amoraic period went on, the text of Rabbi's Mishnah became more and more sanctified in the eyes of the talmudic scholars. As a result, emendations of the Mishnah text became rarer and rarer. When confronted with an apparent contradiction between the text of the Mishnah and an alternative halakhic position, found in a baraita or in the words of an early amora, the later talmudic tradition had recourse to various kinds of forced interpretation of the Mishnah. In this way it 'resolved' contradictions between these competing sources of halakhic authority. These forced interpretations of the Mishnah often bear a striking resemblance to the 'editorial emendations' of the earlier generations of amoraim. Epstein went to great lengths to distinguish between these phenomena, as well as to describe and to categorize the various forms in which they appear.

By providing a comprehensive analysis and categorization of both the real and the apparent textual variants of the Mishnah attested in talmudic sources and in medieval manuscripts, Epstein's work was supposed to provide the foundation for a critical edition of the Mishnah. After more than 50 years since the publication of his work, this critical edition is still "in preparation." Various other attempts have been made to produce modern scientific editions of different parts of the Mishnah, and in the meantime scholars are still involved in the analysis and assimilation of the ramifications of Epstein's groundbreaking research for the future study of the Mishnah.

Finally, we should note that Epstein's notion of 'editorial emendation' has far-reaching ramifications for the entire field of talmudic research: for the relation between Mishnah and Tosefta; for the relation between talmudic baraitot and parallel traditions in tannaitic works; for the relation between the various redactional levels of talmudic texts; for the understanding of the textual variants found in the manuscript traditions of the Babylonian Talmud. At the same time, it must be emphasized that this notion was unequivocally rejected by Albeck and by a number of his followers. The reasons for Albeck's position (and some reservations regarding it) were outlined in the previous section.

The Traditional Interpretation of the Mishnah

Evidence for the interpretation of Rabbi's Mishnah can be found in the statements of the earliest amoraim – their *memrot* – many of which take the form of comments and additions to the text of the Mishnah. Also, the talmudic *sugya* (discussion) as a literary whole often takes as its starting point the text of the Mishnah and its interpretation, and even when a sugya begins elsewhere, the text of the Mishnah and its interpretation usually come up at some point in discussion, playing a significant role in the development of the argument. The sugya may begin by asking for the scriptural source of the halakhah of the Mishnah, and then proceed to quote the relevant parallel text from the *midrash halakhah*. The sugya may ask about the identity of the tanna who taught an anonymous halakhah brought in the Mishnah. In answer, the sugya will often quote a parallel *baraita* which ascribes the halakhah of the Mishnah to a particular tanna by name, and then goes on to inform us of alternative halakhic positions held by this tanna's contemporaries, and passed over by Rabbi's Mishnah.

While these talmudic sugyot, together with the parallel traditions in the Tosefta and the tannaitic halakhic midrashim, provide the starting point for any informed commentary on the Mishnah, they can also frequently be misleading. The parallel tannaitic traditions may reflect positions similar to, but not identical with, those recorded in Rabbi's Mishnah. The talmudic sugya may take the text of the Mishnah and its interpretation as its starting point, but along the way it also entertains other positions, both tannaitic and amoraic. The synthetic bottom line of the sugya, therefore, will not necessarily correspond – in any simple sense – to any of these individual traditions taken in isolation.

While the post-talmudic period saw the composition of a number of important Mishnah commentaries, the lion's share of talmudic scholarship during this period (up to about the 15th century) focused on the exposition of the Babylonian Talmud as a whole – with the Mishnah playing a distinctly secondary role within that whole. From the earliest period we possess a commentary of the *geonim* to Seder Toharot (ed. J.N. Epstein), which consists primarily of the explanation of difficult words. From the 11th century we possess a commentary by R. Nathan Av ha-Yeshivah on the entire Mishnah, also providing explanations of difficult words, along with brief comments. From the 12th–14th centuries, the period of the **rishonim* (early commentators), we possess a number of more extensive – and more substantial – commentaries, focusing on those parts of the Mishnah which have no Babylonian Talmud, such as Zera'im (with the exception of Berakhot) and Toharot (with the exception of Niddah). Extended works of this sort were composed by R. Isaac ben Melchitzedek, R. Asher ben Jehiel, R. Samson ben Abraham, and shorter ones on individual tractates, like R. Abraham ben David on Eduyot.

By far the most important Mishnah commentary from this early period (12th century) is that of *Maimonides. It is the only extensive commentary on the entire Mishnah which has come down to us from the time of the *rishonim*. Maimonides states in his introduction that his commentary is based on the full range of Talmudic sources – Tosefta, midrashei halakhah, the Jerusalem Talmud and the Babylonian Talmud. His avowed aim in writing his commentary was not to explain the simple sense of the Mishnah text as it stands. On the contrary, he wished to clarify those points that 'could never be derived by analysis' of a given Mishnah (Kafih, Zera'im-Mo'ed, 25), by providing the student with supplementary information found only in other talmudic works. Maimonides' goal was pedagogical – to use the Mishnah as a starting point from which the novice could begin to master talmudic halakhah as a whole.

To this end, Maimonides included in his commentary a number of important introductory essays – treating both halakhic and aggadic issues – to the Mishnah as a whole, and to individual sedarim, such as Kodashim, and especially

Ṭoharot. Similarly, he composed introductions to individual tractates and chapters, and even to individual halakhot, outlining the general principles and specific premises necessary for the proper comprehension of the halakhot under discussion. On the other hand, Maimonides often seems uninterested in how these principles actually apply to the specific cases mentioned in the Mishnah. He sometimes indicates that the student should focus on the general rules, the analysis of the details being relegated to a secondary role.

Maimonides' commentary was originally composed in Arabic and was revised constantly during his own lifetime. A new edition and translation by Rabbi J. Kafih has made both the final version and the various stages of revision available in an accurate modern Hebrew translation. Recent scholars have continued to expand and improve our knowledge and understanding of his commentary (Blau and Scheiber, Hopkins).

Special note should be made of two other commentaries from the period of the *rishonim*. The first is the commentary of R. *Jonathan ha-Kohen of Lunel. Although included in his commentary on the halakhot of Isaac *Alfasi, R. Jonathan's interpretations of the Mishnah are treated with a degree of attention and independence unusual for Mishnah commentaries from this period (cf. Friedman, *R. Jonathan Ha-Kohen of Lunel*, 7–9). The second commentary is that of the Meiri. While also part of his commentary to the Talmud, he included within it the entire text of Maimonides' commentary to the Mishnah and provided an extensive super-commentary of his own. The Meiri incorporates many of the issues raised by the Talmud into his commentary on the Mishnah, as opposed to other *rishonim*, who, following Rashi, tend to incorporate their commentary on the Mishnah into their discussion of the Talmud.

From the 15th century onward, talmudic scholarship underwent a series of important changes which had an impact on the study of the Mishnah. The exposition of normative halakhah gradually became divorced from the interpretation of the Talmud and began to center on the interpretation of the *Arba'ah Turim* and the *Shulḥan Arukh*, forming a new and specialized halakhic literature. As a result, the study of the classical talmudic works became more autonomous and more academic. No longer subordinated to the exposition of normative halakhah, commentaries were composed on the Mishnah, on the Tosefta, on the Midrashei Halakhah, and on the Jerusalem Talmud. While these commentaries remained, at first, rooted in traditional Talmud interpretation, they nevertheless began to investigate texts and traditions which had no direct bearing on any practical halakhic issues.

The earliest of these commentaries was that of R. Obadiah *Bertinoro. This relatively brief commentary is largely derivative in character, drawing mainly on Rashi's interpretations of the Mishnah imbedded in his commentary to the Talmud. Bertinoro also drew upon the commentaries of R. Samson ben Abraham, Maimonides, and others. Next in time is the commentary of R. Yom Tov Lipman *Heller, *Tosefot Yom Tov*. This work takes Bertinoro's as its starting point but is far more ambitious, examining both the talmudic literature and the literature of the *rishonim*, with the goal of determining the range of Mishnah interpretations imbedded within them. R. Solomon *Adeni's *Melekhet Shelomo* was composed at about the same time but was not published until the early 20th century. This extensive and scholarly commentary includes numerous critical textual notes based on manuscript evidence, as well as references to citations of the Mishnah in the Babylonian and Jerusalem Talmud, and in the halakhic codes and commentaries. Another important commentary was composed somewhat later (19th century) by R. Israel Lipschuetz. His *Tiferet Yisrael* provides a brief exposition of the simple sense of the text, alongside more elaborate analyses of various obscure points of interpretation.

Deserving of special note are the commentaries of the "Gaon" R. Elijah of Vilna (18th century) to various parts of the Mishnah, of the Tosefta, and of the Jerusalem Talmud. They deserve mention not only for their brilliance and originality, but also because they often interpret these sources without attempting to harmonize them with the normative halakhic tradition, rooted in the Babilonian Talmud. In this way, R. Elijah's work laid much of the groundwork for the modern critical interpretation of the Mishnah.

The Modern Interpretation of the Mishnah

The terms "traditional" and "modern" interpretation do not designate different periods of time, but rather different approaches to the interpretation of the Mishnah. Traditional commentaries – as described above – continued to be written throughout the 20th century and up to the present day. By far the most successful example is that of Pinḥas Kahati, which provides the contemporary student with succinct and accurate summaries of the classical Mishnah commentaries. We should also include in this category commentaries which, while written by modern academic scholars, are nevertheless oriented toward a traditional audience and agenda, like those of H. Albeck, D. Hoffman, and others.

By "modern interpretation" we mean primarily *historical interpretation* of the Mishnah. The program of historical Mishnah interpretation as set out by J.N. Epstein (see above) involves: (1) the identification (or reconstruction) of the literary sources of each mishnaic passage; (2) an analysis of the tendencies and results of Rabbi's redaction of each particular mishnah passage against the background of these sources; (3) a description of the reciprocal influences of the text of this mishnah on the later history of talmudic tradition, and of later tradition on the text and interpretation of the mishnah itself. The raw materials for this kind of commentary includes (in part): the direct witnesses to the textual tradition of the Mishnah (medieval manuscripts and geniza fragments), as well as the indirect witnesses (citations in ancient talmudic sources); the parallel tannaitic sources and talmudic sugyot which document the history of the halakhic and aggadic traditions; lexicographical and archaeological research.

While Epstein's own works contain analyses of hundreds of individual mishnah passages, he himself composed no extended or continuous commentary to the Mishnah. Commentaries and editions of individual tractates have addressed various aspects of this critical agenda, but the attempts made so far at producing a critical edition of the Mishnah fall far short of this ideal (Stemberger, 139–144). To date, the works which come closest to realizing this critical ideal are the Mishnah commentaries of A. Goldberg (Ohalot, Shabbat, Eruvin, Bava Kamma) and S. Friedman's comparative study of Mishnah and Tosefta Pesaḥim, *Tosefta Atiqta*.

Starting in the 1970s, a new approach to the study of the Mishnah began to emerge, centered around the person of Jacob *Neusner, and reflecting the creation of autonomous Judaic study programs within the modern secular university. In keeping with the interests and agenda of the modern academic world, the Mishnah came to be viewed historically, not only in the context of the talmudic tradition, but also in the broader context of ancient Judaism as a whole, and as part of the general intellectual and spiritual trends of late antiquity. New questions were raised regarding the formal structure of tannaitic halakhah; the literary relations between Mishnah, Tosefta and tannaitic midrash; the historical reliability of attributions and biographical traditions; the changing agenda of the different tannaitic schools over time, and so on. The mere quantity of scholarly studies produced over a short period of time – both by Neusner himself, and by colleagues and students – make it difficult to assimilate all the innovations, regarding content as well as methodology, which this new approach has generated. For example, Neusner's monumental work on Seder Toharot, *A History of the Mishnaic Law of Purities* (22 vol., 1974–1977), has never been properly reviewed or evaluated, and Neusner found it necessary briefly to restate some of his more important conclusions (*From Mishnah to Scripture* (1984); *The Mishnah Before 70* (1987)) in order to make them available to the general scholarly community. For a brief outline of Neusner's contribution to the study of the Mishnah, see *The Study of Ancient Judaism I*, pp. 14–23, which must of course be supplemented by reference to his subsequent work, especially his four volumes on *The Philosophical Mishnah* (1988–89).

Editions, Translations, and Aids to Mishnah Study

The edition of the Mishnah printed in Naples in 1492 is usually regarded as the first edition of the Mishnah. It includes the complete text of the Mishnah and Maimonides' commentary in Hebrew translation. The edition published by Tom Tov Lipman Heller, printed in Prague 1614–17 along with his commentary *Tosefot Yom Tov*, has exerted significant influence on subsequent editions of the Mishnah (see: Goldberg, Literature, 247–248). The 13-volume Romm edition (Vilna, 1908ff.) included for the first time the *Melechet Shlomo* commentary, in addition to Bartenura, *Tosefot Yom Tov*, and *Tiferet Yisrael*. It also included references to citations of Mishnah passages in Talmudic and rabbinic literature, alternative readings, and more than "70 commentaries." Most of these consist of little more than collections of isolated comments on sporadic Mishnah passages, but some are quite significant, including the important commentaries of R. Efraim Yitzhak (*Mishnah Rishonah* and *Mishnah Aḥaronah*) and the commentaries of the Gaon R. Elijah of Vilna. The text of the Mishnah found in most editions currently available today varies little from that of the Romm Mishnah, a notable exception being the new edition of Maimonides' Commentary to the Mishnah, translated and published by J. Kafih (1963ff.), which includes Maimonides' own (12th century) text of the entire Mishnah. For a list of the many manuscripts of the Mishnah with Maimonides's Arabic commentary, see Krupp, 260–262.

Other works include important information relating to the text of the Mishnah. For example, a critical edition of Mishnah Zera'im, based on all known manuscripts and genizah fragments, including comprehensive references to all Mishnah citations in talmudic and rabbinic literature, was published in 1972–1975 by the Yad ha-Rav Herzog Institute for the Complete Israeli Talmud. They have also included similar material in their critical edition of the Babylonian Talmud of Seder Nashim (Yev., Ket., Ned., Sot., and part of Gittin). Critical editions of various individual tractates have also appeared (Stemberger, 143–144). For the manuscripts of the Mishnah, see Krupp, 252–257; Stemberger. 139–142, and it should be noted that digital images of many of the most important Mishnah manuscripts have been posted on the website of the Jewish National and University Library in Jerusalem, either directly (Kaufman A50, Parma de Rossi 138, Parma de Rossi 497, the original manuscript of Maimonides' Mishnah text and commentary) or through links to other libraries (Munich 95). Similarly, the Talmud Text Data Bank published by the Saul Lieberman Institute of Talmudic Research of the Jewish Theological Seminary of America (available on CD-ROM) includes all the Mishnah texts and all partial Mishnah citations found in the manuscripts of the Babylonian Talmud. For translations, see Goldberg, in Literature, 248–249 and Stemberger, 144–145, the most common English translations being those of Danby (1933), Blackman (1951–56), and Neusner (1988).

The language of the Mishnah – both its grammar and its vocabulary – represent a distinct phase in the history of the Hebrew language, and as such it has been the object of intense critical study over the past fifty years. E.Y. Kutscher, Z. Ben-Haim, H. Yalon, S. Morag and many others have examined many important aspects of Mishnaic Hebrew. Much of this work, however, has remained in the form of scholarly articles aimed at professional linguists, and the fruits of this labor have yet to be made available in a form which can be of help to the ordinary student of Mishnah. We still await a new synthetic grammar book comparable in size and scope to M.H. Segal's now outdated *Grammar of Mishnaic Hebrew* (1927). Similarly, the modern student of mishnaic Hebrew must still make use of the old talmudic dictionaries of J. Levy, A. Kohut, M. Jastrow; a notable exception to this rule is M. Moreshet's extremely useful *Lexicon of the New Verbs in Tannaitic Hebrew* (1980). The archaelogy and realia of the Mishnah have also been treated by many scholars (most notably D. Sperber), but again no comprehensive handbooks like S. Krauss' *Talmudische Archäologie* have been produced in almost a century. J. Feliks' small book, *The Plants and Animals of the Mishnah* (1983), provides simple and useful information on these topics. A regular survey of recent books and articles dealing with different facets of Mishnah study is provided by A. Walfish in the Hebrew language journal *Netuim*.

BIBLIOGRAPHY: *Iggeret Rav Sherira Ga'on*, ed. by B.M. Lewin (1921); Frankel, Mishnah; J. Bruell, *Mevo ha-Mishnah* (1876–85); I. Lewy, in: *Zweiter Bericht ueber die Hochschule fuer die Wissenschaft des Judenthums in Berlin* (1876); D. Hoffmann, *Die erste Mischna und die Controversen der Tannaim* (1881); L. Ginzberg, *Studies in the Origin of the Mishna* (1920); Epstein, Mishnah; Epstein, Tanna'im, 13–240; Ḥ. Albeck, *Untersuchungen ueber die Redaktion der Mischna* (1923); idem, *Mavo la-Mishnah* (1959); S. Lieberman, *Hellenism in Jewish Palestine* (1950), 83–99; H. Yalon, *Mavo le-Nikkud ha-Mishnah* (1964); A. Goldberg, *The Mishnah Treatise Ohalot Critically Edited* (1955); idem, *Commentary to the Mishna Shabbat, Critically Edited, and Provided with Introduction, Commentary and Notes* (1976); idem, *The Mishna Treatise Eruvin, Critically Edited, and Provided with Introduction, Commentary and Notes* (1986); idem, in: *The Literature of the Sages, Part One*, ed. S. Safrai (1987), 211–251; idem, *Tosefta Bava Kama: A Structural and Analytic Commentary with a Mishna-Tosefta Synopsis* (2001); M. Krupp, in: *The Literature of the Sages, Part One*, ed. S. Safrai (1987), 252–262; Strack-Stemberger, *Introduction to the Talmud and Midrash* (1996), 108–148; S. Safrai, in: *The Literature of the Sages, Part One*, ed. S. Safrai (1987), 35–209; Strack-Stemberger, *Introduction to the Talmud and Midrash* (1996), 108–148; *Kovez Ma'amarim be-Lashon Ḥazal*, ed. M. Bar Asher (1972, 1980); S. Morag, *Studies in Hebrew, Aramaic and Jewish Languages* (2003), 3–97; A. Samely, *Rabbinic Interpretation of Scripture in the Mishnah* (2002); D. Raviv, *Analysis of Midrashic Passages in Mishna Sanhedrin*, Ph.D. Thesis, Bar-Ilan University (1998); *Netuim, Journal of Mishnah Study* (1993ff.); G. Alon, *Jews, Judaism and the Classical World* (1977), 146–234; E.Z. Melamed, *The Relationship between the Halakhic Midrashim and the Mishna and Tosefta* (1967); S. Friedman, *Tosefta Atiqta* (2002); idem, *R. Jonathan Ha-Kohen of Lunel* (1969), 7–9; J. Neusner, *The Modern Study of the Mishnah* (1973), idem, *A History of the Mishnaic Law of Purities* (22 vol. 1974–1977); idem, *Judaism, The Evidence of the Mishnah* (1981); idem, *The Study of Ancient Judaism I* (1981); idem, *From Mishnah to Scripture* (1984); idem, *The Mishnah before 70* (1987); J. Blau and A. Scheiber, *An Autograph of Maimonides from the Adler Collection and the Leningrad Library: Draft of the Introduction to Seder Tohorot* (1981); S. Hopkins, *Maimonides' Commentary on Tractate Shabbat: The Draft Commentary According to the Autograph Fragments from the Cairo Geniza* (2001).

[Stephen G. Wald (2nd ed.)]

MISHNAT HA-MIDDOT (Heb. מִשְׁנַת הַמִּדּוֹת; "treatise of measures"), considered the earliest Hebrew geometry. *Mishnat ha-Middot* comprises various methods for determining the dimensions of various plane and solid geometric figures. Its five chapters include, among other matters, a discussion of triangles, quadrilaterals, and frusta. The Heronic formula for the area of a triangle in terms of the lengths of the sides is given. For π the value of $3\frac{1}{7}$ is used and this divergence from the biblical 3 is homiletically justified. One of the extant manuscripts has a sixth chapter dealing with the Tabernacle which is similar to sections of the *Baraita de-Melekhet ha-Mishkan. In spite of the similar names, there seems to be no connection between this work and the *Baraita de-49 Middot* which is frequently cited by medieval commentators. This treatise is written in a distinctive Hebrew that combines mishnaic style with a technical terminology that has affinities with Arabic, although it stands apart from the Hebrew mathematical terminology of the Hispano-Arabic period. In content, the *Mishnat ha-Middot* belongs to the stream of Oriental mathematics represented, e.g., by Heron, Greek mathematician (c. 100 C.E.) in the Hellenistic period, and al-Khwarizmi (c. 825 C.E.) in the Arabic period, to both of whose works it offers striking parallels. Some attribute it to R. *Nehemiah (c. 150 C.E.), and see it as a link between the Hellenistic and Arabic texts, while others assign it to an unknown author of the Arabic period.

BIBLIOGRAPHY: S. Gandz (ed.), *Mishnat ha-Middot* (Eng., trans. 1932); Ẓarefati, in: *Leshonenu*, 23 (1958/59), 156–71; 24 (1959/60), 73–94.

[Benjamin Weiss]

MISHOL, AGI (1947–), Hebrew poetess. Mishol was born in Hungary to Holocaust survivors who came to Israel in 1950. She earned her B.A. and M.A. in Hebrew Literature from the Hebrew University and published her first collection of poems *Nanny ve-Sheneinu* ("Nanny and Both of Us") in 1972. Nine further collections followed, including *Gallop* (1980) and *Re'eh Sham* ("Look, There," 1999). In 2003 appeared *Mivḥar ve-Ḥadashim* ("Selection and New Poems") with an essay by Dan Miron entitled "*Ha-Sibilah ha-Komit: Al Shiratah shel Agi Mishol*" (293–443). Mishol belongs to the great dynasty of Hebrew women poets, maintains Miron. He underlines her stylistic individualism and her humorous outlook on life and on the self as a necessary condition for personal and communal mental health. Mishol was awarded the Yehuda Amichai Prize (2002) and the Tel Aviv Foundation Award. She teaches poetry in the M.A. Program in Creative Writing at Ben-Gurion University, works as a translator and literary critic for radio and written media, and grows peach and persimmon trees in her village, Kefar Mordechai. A bilingual edition, *The Swimmers*, appeared in English (1998). For further information concerning translations see the ITHL website at www.ithl.org.il.

BIBLIOGRAPHY: M. Harel, in: *Haaretz Sefarim* (July 27, 2005).

[Anat Feinberg (2nd ed.)]

MISHPAT IVRI.

This article is arranged according to the following outline:

DEFINITION AND TERMINOLOGY

The term *mishpat Ivri* (מִשְׁפָּט עִבְרִי) is now generally accepted as embracing only those matters of the **halakhah* (Jewish law) whose equivalent is customarily dealt with in other present-day legal systems, that is, matters pertaining to relations between man and man and not the precepts governing the relationship between man and his Maker. This definition diverges from the original meaning of the Hebrew term *mishpat* or *mishpatim*. Used in the sense of a system of laws – like the English term "law," or the German term "*Recht*" – the term refers not only to matters between man and man (in the sense of *jus, ius humanum*) but also to the precepts between man and his Maker (in the sense of *fas, ius divinum*). Thus for instance in Exodus 21:1 the words *ve-elleh ha-mishpatim* are stated by way of introduction to chapters 21, 22, and 23, which deal not only with matters of civil and criminal law but also with the laws of the sabbatical year, the Sabbath, first fruits, and so on.

Another Hebrew term for law is the word *dinim* (sing. *din*), used to designate matters included in the fourth mishnaic order, *Nezikin* (see Deut. 17:8; Ḥag. 1:8; Naḥmanides, Gen. 34:13). The term comprises two main classes of laws, namely *dinei mamonot* and *dinei nefashot*. The concept of *dinei mamonot* corresponds to but is not identical with "civil law," since it is wider than the latter in some respects (see Sanh. 2:2 and see below) and narrower in others, excluding, for instance, that part of family law dealing with what is ritually permitted and prohibited, the laws of usury, and so on. (Subject to this qualification, the term civil law will be used below and in the other articles on Jewish law as the equivalent of *dinei mamonot*.) The concept *dinei nefashot* takes in that part of the criminal law dealing with matters that call for capital and certain other forms of corporal punishment. (The term *dinei kenasot* relates to matters which are part of *dinei mamonot*; see *Obligations, Law of.) However, even the term *dinim* does not exclude matters concerning the precepts between man and God, as is evident from the concept of *dinei issur ve-hetter* – ritual prohibitions and permissions.

The reason for the absence in Hebrew sources of an accepted term describing legal norms pertaining exclusively to relations between man and man – for instance in the sense of "English law" or "Swiss law" – lies in the basic fact that both the laws applicable between man and man and the precepts concerning man and God have a single and common source, namely the *Written and the *Oral Law. This fact further asserts itself in the phenomenon that all parts of the entire halakhic system share and are subject to common modes of creation, thought, and expression, as well as principles and rules (see below). This, however, constitutes no hindrance to the acceptance of the term *mishpat Ivri* in the sense here described. The term first came to be used in this sense around the beginning of the 20th century, when the Jewish national awakening – which to some extent stimulated also the desire for a return to Jewish law – prompted a search for a Hebrew term to designate that part of the *halakhah* whose subject matter paralleled that which normally comprises other legal systems. What was sought was a suitable term that would circumscribe the bounds of the legal research and preparatory work to be undertaken. Thus there was accepted the term *mishpat "Ivri,"* in the same way as *safah "Ivrit"* and later also *medinah "Ivrit."* Today the term *mishpat Ivri*, as defined above, is generally accepted in all fields of practical legal life and research in the sense here described. In the Knesset legislation use is made of the term *din Torah* (authorized English translation, "Jewish religious law": see, e.g., sec. 2, "Rabbinical Courts Jurisdiction (Marriage and Divorce) Law," 1953); this Hebrew term is inaccurate as far as the distinction between *de-oraita* and *de-rabbanan* (see *Mishpat Ivri: De-Oraita* and *De-Rabbanan*) is concerned.

"RELIGIOUS" HALAKHAH AND "LEGAL" HALAKHAH

Common Features

The "religious" and the "legal" norms of the *halakhah* share certain common features, a fact that finds expression in a number of ways (and accounts for our use of inverted commas since the *halakhah* does not recognize the concept of special "religious" law, which is used here in its modern sense). In the talmudic discussions the same theoretical argumentation, terminology, and modes of interpretation that are applied to a matter of civil law are applied also to matters concerning, for instance, the Sabbath, the sacrificial cult, and ritual purity and impurity. Many legal principles are common to both parts of the *halakhah*. Thus for instance the laws of *agency apply in the same way to matters of **hekdesh*, **terumah*, and the slaughter of the paschal sacrifice, as they do to matters of marriage, divorce, recovery of debt, and so on. Moreover, the essential legal principle underlying the principal-agent relationship – that "a person's agent is as himself" – was derived by the scholars from the scriptural passages dealing with matters of the paschal sacrifice and *terumah* (Kid. 41b, etc.), and it is in relation to the laws of prayer that the solitary mishnaic reference to the above principle is made (Ber. 5:5). "Religious" directives are often found to be based on "legal" directives. This is illustrated in the discussions on the question of whether a person who has acquired the right to no more than the fruits of his neighbor's field, may, when bringing the first fruit, read the *Bikkurim* portion which includes the passage, "And now, behold, I have brought the first fruit of the land, which Thou, O Lord, hast given me" (Deut. 26:10), since this involves a declaration that the land is his. The answer is made dependent on the elucidation of a question of legal principle, whether acquisition of the fruits (*kinyan perot*) is as acquisition of the body (*kinyan ha-guf*; Git. 47b) – an elucidation which has important consequences in all fields of Jewish law.

To their common origin must also be attributed a mutual interaction between the two parts of the *halakhah*, with directions pertaining to the "religious" field supplementing lacunae in the "legal" field. This is illustrated in the law concerning the father's duty to maintain his children. In the *takkanah* of Usha, as finally accepted, it was laid down that the duty extended to children until the age of six years. In practice it sometimes happened that a father failed to maintain his minor children above the age of six and in such an event the court compelled the father to do so by applying two rules pertaining to the laws of charity: first, that a person who has sufficient for his own needs may be compelled to give charity if there is a poor man in need; secondly, that as regards the giving of charity, "the poor of a person's own household take precedence over the poor of his town, and the poor of his town over those of another town," and of all the poor the father's children are the nearest to him (Ket. 49b; Sh. Ar., YD 251:3; EH 71:1). Another illustration is found in the post-talmudic development regarding the establishment of an obligation by way of the promisor's vow or oath or undertaking on pain of ban to give or do according to his promise – whose fulfillment is imposed on him as a religious duty. This method was employed especially in the case of obligations which were incapable of being established in terms of the "legal" rules of the *halakhah*, such as an obligation relating to something not yet in existence (*Rema*, ḤM 209:4), or one tainted with the defect of **asmakhta* (Sh. Ar., ḤM 207:19) and so on (see *Obligation, Law of).

Distinguishing between "Religious" and "Legal" *Halakhah* – Ritual and Civil Law

A study of the halakhic sources reveals that the *halakhah*, notwithstanding its overall unity, distinguishes materially between the two main fields of its subject matter, between "matters of *mamon*" or "*mamona*" and "matters not of *mamon*" or "*issura*" (lit. "prohibitions," i.e., ritual law). Although the concepts of *issura* and *mamona* are not coextensive with the modern concepts of "religious" and "legal" law (see above), the material distinction made between them exerted a decisive influence on the evolutionary path taken by that large part of the *halakhah* embraced in the term *mishpat Ivri*. The first manifestations of the distinction date back to the time of Bet Shammai and Bet Hillel (Yev. 15a–b; Eduy. 1:12 – "If you have permitted in a matter relating to the stringent prohibition of incest, shall you not permit in civil matters (*mamon*) which are less stringent?") and in the course of time it became entrenched in many fields of the *halakhah*, as illustrated in the following examples: As regards the freedom of stipulation, the principle was laid down that "when a person contracts out of the law contained in the Torah, a stipulation which relates to a matter of *mamon* is valid but one that relates to a matter not of *mamon* is invalid" (Tosef., Kid. 3:7–8). The explanation is that the legal order prescribed by the Torah in civil matters was not enjoined in the form of a binding obligation (i.e., *jus cogens*), but as conditional on the will of the parties (i.e., *jus dispositivum*; Naḥmanides, Nov. BB 126b) except in cases of a stipulation inimical to personal freedom or the public weal (for details see *Contract). In case of an illegal contract the rule is that a contract whose fulfillment involves the transgression of law shall not be enforced, but transgression of a "religious" prohibition does not deprive the contract of legal validity and it will be enforced by the court; hence, "if a person sells or gives on the Sabbath, and certainly on festivals, even though he should be flogged, his act is effective" and an obligation undertaken on the Sabbath is similarly valid, "and a *kinyan* performed on the Sabbath (i.e., *kinyan sudar*, see *Acquisition) is valid, and the writing and handing over take place after the Sabbath" (Yad, Mekhirah 30:7).

The distinction between *issura* and *mamona* also has an important bearing on the question of legislative authority in Jewish law. While such authority was to some extent limited in matters of *issura*, it remained fully effective in matters of *mamona* (see **Takkanot*). So far as the legislative authority conferred on the public and its leaders was concerned, this never extended beyond matters pertaining to the civil law and criminal-police offenses (see **Takkanot ha-Kahal*). The distinction is also an important factor in the binding force of custom, particularly as regards the basic principle that "custom overrides the law," which is applicable in matters of the civil law exclusively (see **Minhag*). Similarly, different rules and principles of decision were laid down for civil and for ritual matters. A basic principle is that matters of ritual law are not to be learned from matters of civil law and vice versa, for the reason that on the one hand ritual matters are by their very nature of greater stringency than matters of the civil law, while on the other hand the rule that "the burden of proof rests on the person seeking to recover from his fellow" applies to civil but not to ritual law. Flowing therefrom are a number of rules applicable to matters of the ritual law only (for instance, that in certain circumstances "the majority is not followed in civil law matters"; BK 46b). It was likewise accepted by all scholars that the rule of **dina de-malkhuta dina* has no application to matters of ritual law (*Tashbeẓ*, 1:158, and see below), since all the reasons given for the adoption of the doctrine are relevant only to matters of the civil law. Thus the *halakhah* represents a unitary system of law with both its "religious" precepts and "legal" directions sharing a common origin and theoretical propagation as well as mutual principles and rules, the one part supplementing the other. At the same time the *halakhah*, as crystallized during its different periods, evolved a clear distinction between matters of *issura* and those of *mamona*, the latter being the counterpart of a substantial part of the subject matter of modern legal systems. This material distinction lent the legal part of the *halakhah*, which was the more sensitive and subject to the influence of changing social and economic realities, a wide flexibility and capacity for development.

LAW AND MORALS

Jewish law, like other legal systems, distinguishes between legal norms enforced by sanction of the courts and moral and ethical norms lacking such sanction. However, Jewish law also recognizes the existence of a special reciprocal tie between law and morality, a tie that stems from the common origin of both concepts in Judaic sources. The Pentateuchal commands, "Thou shalt not kill" and "Thou shalt not steal" (Ex. 20:13), are enjoined with the same finality as "Thou shalt love thy neighbor as thyself: I am the Lord" (Lev. 19:18), and the common origin of the concepts of law and morality remained a guideline for Judaism in all periods and generations (see, e.g., *Bertinoro*, Avot 1:1). The stated tie finds expression in the fact that from time to time Jewish law, functioning as a legal system, itself impels recourse to a moral imperative for which there is no court sanction, and in so doing sometimes prepares the way to conversion of the moral imperative into a fully sanctioned norm. An illustration is to be found in the law of tort, where there are cases in which the tortfeasor is legally exempt from the payment of compensation – whether for lack of necessary causality between his act and the resultant damage, or because he acted with license, or for other reasons – yet with reference to many of these cases the rule was laid down that the person occasioning damage to another "is exempt according to the laws of man but liable according to the law of Heaven" (BK 6:4; BK 55b; and codes), or "he is exempt according to the law of man but his judgment is entrusted to Heaven" (Tosef., BK 6:6–17). Liability according to the law of Heaven means, according to some scholars, that although the court should not compel compliance by regular sanction it "should bring pressure to bear on him, verbally, without compulsion" (*Yam shel Shelomo*, BK 6:6); others held that the court should exercise no constraint – not even verbal – but should inform the individual: "We do not compel you, but you shall have to fulfill your duty to Heaven" (*ibid.*). Hence even the adjuration that the duty to Heaven must be fulfilled is addressed to the individual concerned by the court.

An instance of the conversion of a moral imperative into a legally sanctioned norm is to be found in the direction to act *li-fenim mi-shurat ha-din* (i.e., leniently, beyond the requirements of the law). In the Talmud this direction does not generally carry the import of a norm fortified by some form of sanction, and means only that it is fitting for the person who has a concern for his manner of conduct not to base his deeds on the strict letter of the law but to act leniently beyond the requirements of the law (as in the matter of restoring lost property or that of paying compensation for damage resulting from an erroneous opinion: BM 24b and 30b; BK 99b). As regards the talmudic matter concerning the exemption of workers from liability for damage caused by them – even though they are unable to prove the absence of negligence on their part – the *posekim* were divided on whether or not this involved an enforceable duty to act beyond the requirements of the law (*Mordekhai* and others; see *Baḥ*, ḤM 12:4). In the post-talmudic era the direction to act *li-fenim mi-shurat ha-din* became, according to the majority of scholars, a full fledged legal norm enforced in certain instances by the court (for instance in the case of a wealthy litigant; *Baḥ*, loc. cit. and *Rema*, ḤM 12:2). See also *Law and Morality.

DE-ORAITA AND DE-RABBANAN

Jewish law, in fact the entire *halakhah*, distinguishes between two categories of law, expressed in the two Aramaic terms *de-oraita* ("of the Torah") and *de-rabbanan* ("of the scholars"). The second category is sometimes also termed *mi-divrei soferim* (a term which has an additional meaning, see Sanh. 88b, but is normally used as the equivalent of *de-rabbanan*) or *takkanat ḥakhamim*.

Distinguishing between the Two Categories

Classification of the halakhic rules into these two categories is beset with many difficulties and has been the subject of much scholarly discussion and research (see Z.H. Ḥayyut (Chajes), *Torat ha-Nevi'im*, s.v. "*Torah she be-al peh*"; Ḥ. Albeck, *Mavo ha-Mishnah* (1959), 49–53). Certainly the rules expressly stated in the Pentateuch are *de-oraita*, while those clearly originating from the enactments or decrees of the scholars are *de-rabbanan*. More difficult is classification of the rules deriving from one of the different modes of Pentateuchal Midrash (exegesis, see *Interpretation). Maimonides held that any such rule was not to be considered *de-oraita* unless the interpretation accorded with a tradition from Moses at Sinai and the Talmud specifically lays down that the rule is *de-oraita* (*Sefer ha-Mitzvot*, rule no. 2). Naḥmanides held that such rules were *de-oraita* except when the Talmud specifically determines that the midrashic derivation of a particular rule amounts to no more than *asmakhta*, in which event the rule is *de-rabbanan* (*Hassagot ha-Ramban le-Sefer ha-Mitzvot*, ad loc.). Naḥmanides' opinion was accepted by a majority of the scholars (many of whom interpret Maimonides' view in a manner which tends to reconcile it with that of Naḥmanides). This, however, still does not constitute an adequate distinction, since there are *halakhot* which are regarded as *de-oraita* even though they are linked to particular scriptural passages by way of *asmakhta* alone, and there are also many *halakhot* which are regarded as *de-oraita* even though they do not originate from the legal source of Midrash (but from some other legal source, such as *sevarah*). Nor does classification of the *halakhah* into *de-oraita* and *de-rabbanan* necessarily have a bearing on the antiquity of a particular law, since it is possible that a law classified as *de-rabbanan* had its origin in a particularly ancient *takkanah*, whereas a later law may be classified as *de-oraita* because of its derivation from the interpretation of Pentateuchal passages. There are many institutions whose classification into one or other of the two stated categories occasioned doubt to the scholars of different periods, for instance, in the following matters: *ketubbah* (Ket. 10a; 110b); the husband's right to inherit his wife's property (Ket. 83a; Bek. 52b; and see *Succession); the husband's duty to maintain his wife (Ket. 47b; and see *Maintenance); *kinyan meshikhah* (BM 47b); and modes of acquisition deriving from trade custom (*Kesef ha-Kedoshim*, Sh. Ar., ḤM, 201:1) and other matters. There is accordingly no absolute and exhaustive classification of the *halakhah* into *de-oraita* and *de-rabbanan* and the only method of determining the class to which a particular law belongs is an examination of the Talmudic and post-talmudic literature to determine the manner in which such law was classified by the sages of the Talmud and scholars who decided and codified the *halakhah*.

Legal Consequences of the Classification

A basic divergence between the two categories of law occurs when there is doubt or dispute as to the applicability or scope of a particular rule in certain circumstances: in a *de-oraita* matter a stringent approach is required, whereas a lenient approach is indicated in a *de-rabbanan* matter (Beẓah 3b; Av. Zar. 7a). In some cases the scholars laid down alleviations of the law as regards a *de-rabbanan* legal obligation, even in the absence of any doubt as to the existence of such an obligation (for instance as regards recovery of the *ketubbah* money; Tosef.,

Ket. 13 (12):3 and Ket. 110b; see also *Conflict of Laws) when special circumstances justified such leniency (Ket. 86a; *Rashbam*, BB 132b). In general, however, the scholars "imparted to their enactments the force of rules of the Torah" (see Git. 64b–65a; Ket. 84a). When the scholars saw the need for introducing a basic legal institution into daily life, they sometimes even enforced a rule of the rabbinical law more restrictively than a rule of the Torah. For this reason it was laid down that the parties may not stipulate for the payment of a lesser **ketubbah* amount than that determined by the scholars, notwithstanding the rule of freedom of stipulation in civil matters, even those pertaining to the *de-oraita* law (Ket. 56a). The rule that a legal obligation classified as part of the rabbinical law has the same legal efficacy as a *de-oraita* obligation is of special importance in view of the fact that so many of the rules in all the different branches of Jewish law belong to the *de-rabbanan* category (particularly those concerning the modes of acquisition, and the laws of obligation and tort). Any diminished regard for the standing and validity of a rule of the rabbinical law would have entailed the possibility of a far-reaching effect on the manner of execution and enforcement of such rules (see detailed discussion in Radbaz, 1,503).

THE BASIC NORM AND THE SOURCES OF JEWISH LAW

Three Meanings of the Expression "Source of Law"

Every legal system gives occasion for inquiry into the sources of its law (*fontes juris, Die Quellen des Rechts*). The expression "source of law" has three principal meanings, which may be distinguished as literary, historical, and legal sources of law.

The literary sources of law (in German, *Die Erkenntnisquellen des Rechts*) are those sources which serve as the recognized and authentic literary repository of the various rules and directions of a particular legal system for purpose of ascertaining their content.

The historical sources are those sources which constitute the historical-factual origin of particular legal norms. Legal research is largely concerned with an investigation of the historical sources of the directions comprising a particular legal system, of the various influences of one legal system on another, and other similar questions. The historical sources of law, in the wide sense of the expression, may also include any economic, social, moral, or other factor that led to the creation of a particular legal norm and there are many instances of laws which were enacted in answer to particular economic or social needs.

The legal sources (in German *Die Entstehungsquellen des Rechts*) are the sources of law and means of creating law recognized by a legal system itself as conferring binding force on the norms of that system (see J.W. Salmond, *Jurisprudence* (1966), 109ff.).

The distinction between a legal and a historical source of law is of a material nature. The quest for the legal source of a particular norm is aimed at ascertaining the source from which the latter derives the force of law, that is, the principle within the relevant legal system which serves to confer binding validity on such a norm. Thus it is possible to ascertain that a norm has its legal source in statute or precedent and so on, without any need to be concerned with the factual background or historical origin of such a norm. Salmond states: "This is an important distinction which calls for careful consideration. In respect of its origin a rule of law is often of long descent. The immediate source of a rule of English law may be the decision of an English court of justice. But that court may have drawn the matter of its decision from the writings of some lawyer, let us say the celebrated Frenchman, Pothier; and Pothier in his turn may have taken it from the compilations of the emperor Justinian, who may have obtained it from the praetorian edict. In such a case all these things – the decision, the works of Pothier, the Corpus Juris Civilis, and the Edictum Perpetuum – are the successive material sources of the rule of English law. But there is a difference between them for the precedent is the legal source of the rule, and the others are merely its historical sources. The precedent is its source, not merely in fact, but in law also. The others are its sources in fact, but obtain no legal recognition as such" (op. cit., p. 109).

The historical sources of law play only an indirect role in the evolution of a legal system, as factors which either offer a possible course to follow by way of imitation (as in the absorption of a principle from a different legal system) or create a need for the further development of such a legal system (as in the case of particular economic or social conditions). On the other hand, the legal sources play a direct role in the evolution of a legal system, serving as the sole means to add to, subtract from, or vary in any other way the existing norms of that system. This division of the sources of law into three classes is valid also for the Jewish legal system.

The Literary Sources of Jewish Law

VARIOUS CLASSES OF INFORMATIVE SOURCES OF LAW. The literary sources of a legal system constitute, as already mentioned, authentic sources for the ascertainment of its legal norms. Thus, for instance, the laws of a country may be ascertained from its official Statute Books. Similarly, knowledge of the law may also be gathered from what is called "the literature of the law." This includes the literature in which the law is discussed or interpreted, although that literature itself is not recognized as an authoritative and authentic source from which binding legal norms may be ascertained (e.g., legal textbooks and articles: see Salmond, op. cit. 112, n. c). From a certain standpoint even general literature may contribute greatly toward a better knowledge of a legal system. Thus, if an author gives a historical-economic description of a particular period and mentions bankruptcies and the imprisonment of debtors, it may be possible to learn from this that it was customary at that time to imprison a debtor for the nonpayment of his debt; this may be deduced from the contents of a book even though the author dealt only incidentally with the legal aspects of that subject. In this regard, both the literature of the law and general literature must be approached with caution and the degree of the author's accuracy and objectivity carefully examined in each case. These informative sources avail also in Jewish law. While its authoritative literary sources are the most important informative class, both literature of the law and general literature serve the important function of filling in the social and economic background to many legal norms. They are of added importance – subject to the above cautionary remarks – in relation to those periods when there were few authoritative literary sources, as was the position in Jewish law until the literary redactions undertaken in the tannaitic period. The different literary sources of the *halakhah* are briefly reviewed below in a general manner. (These are separately discussed elsewhere in greater detail; see, e.g., *Mishnah; *Talmud.)

FROM THE WRITTEN LAW UNTIL THE PERIOD OF THE TANNAIM. The Bible is not only the source of authority of the whole of the Jewish legal system (see below), it is also its first and foremost authoritative literary source. It contains legal directions which date from patriarchal times onward and are dispersed in specific books and chapters of the Pentateuch (Gen. 23:3–20; 31:41–43; Ex. 20–23; Lev. 5; 18–21; 24–25; 27; Num. 27:35–36; Deut. 1; 4–5; 15–17; 19–25). The next authoritative literary source is represented by the Books of the Prophets and the Hagiographa. From these information may be gained on the laws concerning the modes of acquisition (Ruth 4; Jer. 32 and see TJ, Kid. 1:5; 60c), the monarchy (I Sam. 8; I Kings 21), suretyship (Prov. 6:1–5; 11–15, et al.), the laws confining criminal responsibility to the transgressor (II Kings 14:6), and so on. It may be noted that the Prophets and Hagiographa contain scant material of a legal nature. The attention of the prophets and chroniclers was mainly directed to the numerous internal and external wars of their times, to moral, social, and religious problems. Therefore the silence of these sources on different matters of the law cannot be interpreted as pointing to the absence of a legal order on such matters.

Much of the accumulated knowledge of Jewish law in the above period and for some time after can be found in the informative sources termed literature of the law and general literature. These include the *papyri (such as the Elephantine papyri of the fifth century B.C.E.), the *Septuagint (end of the third century B.C.E.), the writings of *Philo (first half of the first century), the writings of Josephus (the period of the Temple destruction), the *Apocrypha (from the fourth century B.C.E. until the year 200), and other works. This literature contains some *halakhot* which are identical to those quoted in talmudic literature and others which are sometimes contrary to it. This may indicate a possible development in certain norms of Jewish law or it may also be that this literature preserved *halakhot* that appeared in talmudic sources which are no longer extant. Great care is needed in deducing conclusions from this literature: sometimes it represents the viewpoint of small sects or even a single individual; sometimes it may show the influence of a surrounding legal system (as in the case of the Elephantine papyri); sometimes the particular author gathered a rule of Jewish law from a translation and not in its original form (as did Philo in making use of Greek translations); and sometimes the description of certain matters reveals a blatant tendentiousness (see, for instance, Jos., Ant., 4:279 (ed. Schalit) note 174; ed. Shor, note 3).

FROM THE TANNAITIC PERIOD UNTIL THE REDACTION OF THE TALMUD. This period, spanning the lives of the *tannaim* and *amoraim*, gave rise to literary creations which constitute the classical sources of Jewish law and the starting point, until this day, for the study or discussion of any matter in it. Extant from tannaitic times are the following: compilations of halakhic Midrashim (see *Midreshei Halakhah* and *Interpretation); the Mishnah – compiled by Judah ha-Nasi and constituting the post-Mosaic "Corpus Juris" of Jewish law – and the *Tosefta (see *Codification of Law); other authoritative tannaitic literary sources are the *Beraitot* included in the two Talmuds, and **Megillat Ta'anit* which includes, besides descriptions of political and military events, halakhic and legal material. Authoritative amoraic literary sources are the Jerusalem Talmud and the Babylonian Talmud, which include commentaries and expositions on the Mishnah, *memrot* (new *halakhot* of the *amoraim*), *ma'asim* (i.e., cases, see **Ma'aseh*), questions and answers, *takkanot*, and *gezerot* as well as rules of decision (see *Codification of Law).

THE POST-TALMUDIC PERIOD. The following are the three main branches of the post-talmudic literary sources of Jewish law commencing from the geonic period:

(1) The *Perushim* and *Ḥiddushim* – commentaries and novellae – to the Mishnah and Talmud (as well as the other talmudic literary sources). The commentary literature represents the efforts of the scholars to elucidate the earlier literary sources with a view to facilitating the study and understanding of them; the classic commentary is that of *Rashi on the Babylonian Talmud (11th century). The novellae literature is a product of the study and comparison by the scholars of different sources and their reconciliation of contradictory statements within the talmudic literature, in the course of which new interpretations and *halakhot* were derived; the classic novellae are those of the *tosafists to the Babylonian Talmud (12th and 13th centuries). Of these two literary branches the commentaries represent the earlier development, which reached its peak in the 11th century (i.e., as regards commentaries on the TB; the commentaries on the TJ date from the 16th century onward), only then to be followed by the novellae, which have continued to be written until the present day.

(2) *She'elot u-Teshuvot* – the *responsa prudentium* of Jewish law. The responsa literature represents the decisions and conclusions written down by halakhic scholars in answer to written questions submitted to them. For the major part of the post-talmudic period these questions came either from *dayyanim* who sat in judgment over the litigants in their own community and found it necessary to turn to the outstanding halakhic scholars in the area for the solution to difficult

problems, or they arose from disputes between the individual and the community, or between different communities, which came directly before the competent scholars of the particular area. The responsa represent legal decisions on concrete questions arising in daily life and served as the main vehicle for the creativity and evolution of Jewish law in post-talmudic times. This body of literature is the case law of the Jewish legal system, estimated to include a total of approximately 300,000 judgments and decisions (see also *Ma'aseh; *Responsa).

(3) The Codes (see in detail under *Codification of Law).

Besides these three main sources two other classes of literary sources belonging to this period may be mentioned: first, the collections of bonds and deeds (see **Shetarot*), i.e., forms of written documents in use at various times during this period and serving to order the legal relations between parties in different fields of the law – such as deeds of sale, indebtedness, lease, marriage, and *ketubbah*; secondly, the collections of *takkanot*, particularly the *takkanot* enacted by the community and its leadership, namely *takkanot ha-kahal*. In addition, there is the auxiliary literature of Jewish law consisting of various works of aid and reference, which may conveniently be classified into five categories: (1) works of introduction to the Talmud or to the *halakhah* in general (such as the *Iggeret R. *Sherira Ga'on*; the *Sefer ha-Keritot* of *Samson b. Isaac of Chinon; et al.); (2) encyclopedias of the *halakhah* (such as *Paḥad Yiẓhak* by Isaac *Lampronti and, more recently, the *Enẓiklopedyah Talmudit*, etc.); (3) biographies of the halakhic scholars (such as the *Sefer ha-Kabbalah* of Abraham ibn Daud; first part of *Shem ha-Gedolim* of Ḥ.J.D. Azulai); (4) bibliographies of halakhic works (such as the *Oẓar ha-Sefarim* by Benjacob, the second part of *Shem ha-Gedolim* by Ḥ.J.D. Azulai); and (5) lexicons and dictionaries (such as *He-Arukh* by Nathan b. Jehiel of Rome; the *Arukh Completum* by A. Kohut; Levi's *Wörterbuch*; and Jastrow's *Aramaic Dictionary of the Talmud*). The main literary source in the post-talmudic period, however, remained the Talmud while around it and in continuation thereof there grew up a vast and profound literature in the form of all the aforementioned branches, sources, and auxiliary works.

The Historical Sources of Jewish Law

It is possible to point to the historical background of many norms of Jewish law – to the economic, social, and moral conditions leading to their creation (particularly in the case of the norms originating from *takkanot*), or to the influence of a different legal system (see below) and similar historical influences. General research on such historical sources is to be found in various works dealing with the history of the *halakhah* and some special research has been done on this subject (latterly, for instance, Y. Baer, *Yisrael ba-Ammim*; idem, in: *Zion*, 17 (1951/52), 1–55; 27 (1961/62), 117–55). Ascertaining the precise historical sources of a particular legal norm is often a formidable task which offers no assurance that the correct answer will be found. Some proffered answers lie in the realm of mere conjecture and are unacceptable without adequate further investigation and proof (see for instance the strictures of G. Alon in his *Meḥkarim*, 2 (1958), 181–247).

The Legal Sources of Jewish Law

There are six legal sources of Jewish law (as regards the Written Law see below): (1) *kabbalah* ("tradition"), based on "tradition transmitted from person to person" back to Moses from God (Avot 1:1; ARN *ibid.*; Yad, Mamrim 1:2; Maim., Introd. to Comm. Mishnah); it is materially different from the other legal sources of Jewish law, since it is not subject to change or development but is, by its very nature, static and immutable, whereas the other legal sources are dynamic by nature and mainly serve as the means toward the continued creativity and evolution of Jewish law; (2) Midrash ("exegesis" and "interpretation"), embracing the norms derived from interpretation of the Written Law and of the *halakhah* in all periods, and to a certain extent also taking in other principles relating to interpretation of deeds, communal enactments, and so on; (3) *takkanah* and *gezerah*, representing the legislative activities of the competent halakhic authorities and public bodies in every generation; (4) *minhag*, representing the legal norms derived from custom in all its different forms; (5) *ma'aseh*, representing the legal norms derived from judicial decision or the conduct of a halakhic scholar in a particular concrete case; (6) *sevarah*, representing the legal norms originating directly from the legal-human logic of the halakhic scholars.

The last five of these are recognized in Jewish law as being capable of both solving new legal and social problems and changing existing legal norms, when this need arises from the prevailing economic, social, and moral realities. In making use of these legal sources the halakhic scholars continued to shape and develop the Jewish legal system, which gave direction to the daily realities of life while being itself directed by them. This task the halakhic scholars carried out with a constant concern for the continued creativity and evolution of the *halakhah*, tempered at the same time by the heavy responsibility of preserving its spirit, objective, and continuity. This twofold assignment is entrusted in Jewish law to the halakhic scholars in every generation: "the judge that shall be in those days" (Deut. 17:9 and Sif. Deut. 153), in accordance with the fundamental principle that "the court of Jephthah is as that of Samuel … for the contemporary judge is in his generation as the judge who was in earlier generations" (Eccles. R. 1:4, no. 4; Tosef., RH 2 (1):3; RH 25b). No supra-human power – such as a heavenly voice or the prophet acting as bearer of the divine vision – has ever had any authority or influence in the determination and decision of the *halakhah* (Sifra, Be-Ḥukkotai 13:7–8; BM 59b; TJ, MK 3:1, 81d; for further particulars see *Authority, Rabbinical).

The Basic Norm of Jewish Law

As already mentioned, by the legal sources of a legal system is meant those sources which that legal system itself recognizes as valid sources from which its legal norms derive their binding force. Whence do these legal sources themselves derive their authority and validity? How and by whom have they been recognized as having the efficacy to determine and introduce legal norms into the legal system concerned? Salmond (loc. cit.) states (111–2): "There must be found in every legal system certain ultimate principles, from which all others are derived, but which are themselves self-existent. Before there can be any talk of legal sources, there must be already in existence some law which establishes them and gives them their authority… These ultimate principles are the *Grundnorm* or basic rules of recognition of the legal system." Thus the direct legal source of a municipal bylaw is the authority of the municipality to make bylaws; the bylaw has legal validity because parliament has delegated power to the municipality to make bylaws, while there exists a further rule – the *Grundnorm* – which determines that an act of parliament has binding authority in the English legal system.

So in any legal system there is to be found a chain of delegation of power extending from the ultimate legal value – the *Grundnorm* – to lower ones. The source of authority of the ultimate legal principle must be sought beyond the concepts of law and within the confines of history, religious faith, and beliefs, and the like: "But whence comes the rule that acts of parliament have the force of law? This is legally ultimate; its source is historical only, not legal. The historians of the constitution know its origin, but lawyers must accept it as self-existent. It is the law because it is the law, and for no other reason than that it is possible for the law itself to take notice of" (Salmond, op. cit., p. 111).

In the above-mentioned sense the basic norm of the Jewish legal system is the rule that everything stated in the Written Law is of binding authority for the Jewish legal system. The basic norm of Jewish law therefore not only expresses the concept of the delegation of power, but it is actually woven into the substantive content of the Written Law, the latter constituting the eternal and immutable constitution of Jewish law. This norm is the fountain of authority and starting point for the entire halakhic system with all its changes and evolution throughout the generations, and it is this norm that delegates authority to the legal sources of Jewish law rendering them valid means toward the continuing creativity and evolution of the latter. The source of authority of this basic norm itself is the basic tenet of Judaism that the source of authority of the Torah is divine command. In considering the matter from the aspect of Judaism as a whole it has to be said that there cannot be seen in it a system of legal norms isolated from and independent of other constellations of norms. All these constellations of norms have a single and uniform ultimate value, namely divine command as expressed in the Torah given to Moses at Sinai. Hence even the pre-Mosaic laws mentioned in the Written Torah – for instance concerning circumcision and the prohibition on flesh torn from a living animal, robbery, incest and so on – have binding force "because the Holy One commanded us through Moses" (Maim., Comm. Ḥul. 7:6) and because at the time the Torah was given "Israel entered into a covenant to observe them" (*Rashbam*, Gen. 26:5).

The exclusive authority to interpret the Written Law and ensure its continuing evolution was found by the halakhic scholars to be delegated, in the Written Torah itself, to the halakhic scholars of every succeeding generation. Such authority they derived from a number of Pentateuchal passages, particularly Deuteronomy 17:8–11, in which the resolution of problems and disputes arising from time to time is entrusted to the teachers and judges in every generation (see also *Authority, Rabbinical). In this and in other passages the halakhic scholars found not only their general authority to resolve problems but also the appointed means, that is the legal sources, wherewith to reach this goal (see Yad, Mamrim 1:2; Maim., Introd. to Comm. Mishnah). Further particulars of Pentateuchal passages as a basis for the various legal sources of Jewish law are given elsewhere under the heading of each legal source.

THE DIFFERENT PERIODS OF JEWISH LAW

Jewish law has a history extending over a period of more than 3,000 years. For reasons of convenience and, to a certain extent, for historical and substantive reasons, this may be divided into two general periods, each with its own further sub-divisions; the first covering the time from the Written Law until the closing of the Talmud, the second from the post-talmudic period until the present day. This division between talmudic and post-talmudic *halakhah* has no bearing on the matter of the continuing creativity and evolution of Jewish law. Such creativity not only continued uninterruptedly after the closing of the Talmud but, as regards volume and literary output, even gathered momentum in certain fields of the law. The significance of the closing of the Talmud as a historic turning point in Jewish law finds expression in the degree of authenticity attributed to the talmudic *halakhah*, which was accepted in Judaism as the authoritative expression and rendering of the Oral Law: "All matters stated in the *Gemara* … must be followed … and have been agreed to by all Israel" (Maim., Introd. to *Mishneh Torah*). Until the redaction of the tannaitic literary sources – and to some extent even of the amoraic – the Written Law was the direct source according to which the law was applied by the *dayyan*. After the redaction of the talmudic literary sources the Written Law still remained the constitution of Jewish law, but the Mishnah, the halakhic Midrashim (*midreshei halakhah*), the two Talmuds, and the remaining talmudic literature became the direct sources according to which all matters of Jewish law were decided. The talmudic literature became the starting point for any study or discussion of Jewish law, and retained this status even after Jewish law was enriched – in the course of some 1,500 years – by many additional literary creations which, in comprehensiveness, orderly arrangement, and convenience of use, overtake the talmudic literature. The first great period of Jewish law is further distinguished by the fact that in this period Jewish law acquired its characteristic lines and forms of legal thought and expression, and the fact that in this period there were evolved and consolidated the legal sources which served as the vehicle for the creativity and development of Jewish law in this and in the post-talmudic period.

The first general period can be subdivided in six eras: (1) the biblical age (up to the time of Ezra and Nehemiah, about the middle of the fifth century B.C.E.); (2) the period from Ezra and Nehemiah until the age of the *zugot* (up to 160 B.C.E. approximately), the greater part of which is customarily described as the age of the *soferim* ("the scribes"; see N. Krochmal, *Moreh Nevukhei ha-Zeman*, ed. Rawidowicz, 56, 194), but latterly the use of the term as descriptive of the scholars of this period only has been criticized (see Kaufmann, Y., Toledot, 4 pt. 1 (1960), 481–5); (3) the age of the *zugot* ("the pairs"; from 160 B.C.E. up to the beginning of the Common Era), which takes its name from the five pairs of leading scholars who headed the *battei din* during this period (the names of the *zugot*, of whom the last pair were Hillel and Shammai, are given in Ḥag. 2 and Avot 1); (4) the age of the *tannaim* (up to 220 C.E.) which spans the activities of six generations of *tannaim*, from *Gamaliel the Elder (grandson of Hillel) and his contemporaries to *Judah ha-Nasi (redactor of the Mishnah). The generation succeeding R. Judah (that of R. *Ḥiyya Rabbah and his contemporaries) saw the transition from the tannaitic age to that of the *amoraim*. Besides the Mishnah, there are extant from the end of this period also collections of halakhic Midrashim, the Tosefta, and other tannaitic literary sources; (5) the age of the *amoraim* embracing the activities of five generations of *amoraim* in Ereẓ Israel (until the end of the fourth century C.E.) and eight generations of *amoraim* in Babylon (up to the end of the fifth century). Extant from this period are the Jerusalem and Babylonian Talmuds; (6) the age of the *savoraim* (up to the end of the sixth century or, according to some scholars, the middle of the seventh century). This age must be regarded as the closing part of the talmudic period since the *savoraim* were mainly occupied with completing the redaction of the Babylonian Talmud and determining rules of decision (see *Codification of Law).

In the second period there are two main subdivisions, the age of the *geonim* and the rabbinic age, but the latter may be subdivided into six further categories. (1) The age of the *geonim* (from the end of the age of the *savoraim* until approximately the middle of the 11th century). The name is derived from the official title by which the heads of the academies of *Sura and *Pumbedita were known during this period. For most of this period the Babylonian academies remained the spiritual center of Jewry as a whole and most Jewish communities assigned absolute legal validity to the decisions and responsa of the *geonim*. For internal Jewish and external political reasons, the ties of the Babylonian *geonim* with the centers of learning that had arisen in North Africa and Spain became loosened towards the end of this period and, commencing from the middle of the 11th century, the phenomenon of a single spiritual center for the various centers of Jewish life came to an end and each of the latter began to rely on its leaders and teachers. This new reality was to exercise a great deal of influence on the subsequent modes of development of Jewish law, evidenced, for instance, in the proliferation of local custom and legislation (see **Takkanot*; **Takkanot ha-Kahal;* *Conflict of Laws). The *geonim* were instrumental in converting the Babylonian Talmud into the source according to which the *halakhah* was decided for all Jewry. In addition, this period saw the first flowering of the division of the post-talmudic literary sources of Jewish law into its three branches which exist until the present day – namely the commentaries and novellae, the responsa, and the codes (see above). Among the better-known *geonim* are R. Yehudai, R. Amram, R. Saadiah, R. Samuel b. Hophni, R. Sherira, and Sherira's son, R. Hai. Of the well-known figures of this period who did not officially hold the title of *gaon*, mention may be made of R. Aḥa (Aḥai) of Shabḥa, author of the *Sefer ha-She'iltot*, and R. Simeon Kayyara, author of the *Halakhot Gedolot* (see *Codification of Law). (2) The rabbinic age, which followed, was itself divided into three periods: (a) The period of the *rishonim* (the "early" scholars), from the middle of the 11th century (the time of Isaac Alfasi) until the 16th century (the time of Joseph Caro and Moses Isserles). This was the golden period of the rabbinic age in which were compiled the classic creations in all three branches of the post-talmudic literary sources of Jewish law: Rashi's commentary on the Talmud and the novellae of the tosafists; the codes of Isaac Alfasi, Maimonides, Jacob b. Asher, Joseph Caro, Moses Isserles, and others; the responsa collections of Solomon b. Abraham Adret (Rashba), Meir (Maharam) of Rothenburg, Asher b. Jehiel (Rosh), Isaac b. Sheshet Perfet (Ribash), Simeon b. Ẓemah Duran (Tashbeẓ), Joseph b. Solomon Colon (Maharik), and others. This was also the period in which the main part of the communal enactments was produced. It embraces the rise and decline of Spanish Jewry, and its close saw the initial flowering of several other Jewish centers – particularly in Ereẓ Israel and Poland-Lithuania – whose outstanding scholars were to make a great contribution to Jewish law, especially to its codification and to its responsa literature.

(b) The period of the *aḥaronim* (the "later" scholars), from the time of Joseph Caro and Moses Isserles until the coming of emancipation around the end of the 18th century. The legal creativity reflected in the three above-mentioned literary sources of Jewish law was continued in this period, particularly in the field of the responsa, which reached a peak of activity. From this period there have also come down numerous collections of communal enactments (such as the *Pinkas Va'ad Arba Araẓot, Pinkas Medinat Lita, Takkanot Mehrin*, and others).

(c) The period of the abrogation of Jewish judicial autonomy. The era of emancipation, which brought in its train the abrogation of Jewish judicial autonomy, represents a turning point in the evolution of Jewish law. This period may be further subdivided: from the end of the 18th century until the beginning of the 20th century, i.e., until the period of Jewish national awakening; from the beginning of the 20th century until the establishment of the State of Israel in 1948; from the establishment of the State of Israel onward.

JEWISH LAW – A LAW OF LIFE AND PRACTICE

Introduction

For the greater part of its history of over 3,000 years, Jewish law has served the Jewish people while they not only lacked political independence but were for a considerable part of this period deprived of their own homeland – Ereẓ Israel – and dispersed throughout the various countries of the Diaspora. The legal systems of other ancient peoples went into decline as soon as they lost their political sovereignty, eventually ceasing to exist except in scattered archaeological remains. Even Roman law, which has left an imprint upon – and still nourishes – many other legal systems, ceased to exist as a creative law of life and practice after having reached its peak of development in Justinian's *Corpus Juris*, in the middle of the sixth century. In the case of Jewish law, the position is otherwise. Despite loss of political independence and lack of physical tie with the homeland, the Jewish people retained judicial autonomy and Jewish law not only did not decline, but it experienced most of its creativity and structural evolution – the Babylonian Talmud and all the other post-talmudic creativity – after the exile. Two factors explain this unique phenomenon: an internal one resting on the substance and nature of Jewish law and its place in the cultural life of the Jewish people, and an external one resting on the general juridical-political outlook that was common in the political history of the nations among whom the Jews lived up to the 18th century.

The Religious and National Character of Jewish Law

Of the two above factors, the internal one is the more important, based as it is on the character of Jewish law which is both religious and national. It is a basic tenet of the Jewish faith that the source of Jewish law – like that of the entire edifice of the *halakhah* – is divine revelation; in the same way as the Jew is commanded in the Written Law to uphold the "religious" precepts – those pertaining to man's relations with the Almighty, such as the laws of the Sabbath and the festivals, the laws of *kashrut* and the like – so he is commanded in the Torah itself to uphold the "legal" precepts – those pertaining to man's relations with his fellows, for instance in matters concerning the laws of labor, tort, property, and different matters of the criminal law. The Ten Commandments enjoin observance of the Sabbath and "Thou shalt not steal," or "Thou shalt not murder," equally – as it were in the same breath. Hence, just as the vitality of the "religious" life remained unaffected by the people's exile, so the "legal" life continued to have unabated validity, and questions arising in both fields were brought before the same court or halakhic scholar for decision.

In addition to its religious character Jewish law has also been the national law of the Jewish people and its entire development has been the creative invention of this people. In this regard Jewish law differs from other legal systems, such as the Canon law or Muslim law, which were created and developed by followers of the faith – Catholic or Muslim – among many different nations. Notwithstanding its dispersion, the Jewish people continued to exist as a nation – not only as a religious sect – and constantly sought recourse to Jewish law, which it regarded as a part of its national assets through which to give expression to its essential being and character in all fields of its internal social and economic life.

The Jewish Judicial System – the Scope of Its Jurisdiction

A precondition for the practical application of a legal system is the existence of an effective judicial machinery to administer and carry out the law. The Pentateuchal law provides express and detailed instructions for the maintenance of a judicial system (Ex. 18:21–27; Deut. 16:18; see also **Bet Din*) and a Jewish judicial system has always existed, even in the absence of Jewish political sovereignty and in all countries of the Diaspora. The Jewish court (*bet din*), alongside the various institutions of Jewish autonomy (the exilarch, the community, inter-communal organizations), provided the mainstay of Jewish internal autonomy from the destruction of the Temple until the period of emancipation. The scope of Jewish judicial autonomy underwent change from time to time depending mainly on the attitude of the ruling power under whose protection the Jews lived.

After the destruction of the Temple, Jewish judicial autonomy was restricted for a short period in Ereẓ Israel (according to talmudic tradition jurisdiction over capital punishment (*dinei nefashot*) was abolished 40 years before the destruction (Shab. 15a; TJ, Sanh. 1:1, 18a; 7:2, 24b), but in practice the Jewish courts apparently did deal with such cases at least until the destruction). Soon, however, autonomy was fully restored and the time of R. Gamaliel, R. Akiva, and their contemporaries was one of the most creative periods in the history of Jewish law. Later, with the decrees of Hadrian and the revolt of Bar Kokhba, Jewish judicial autonomy was faced with another crisis (TJ, Sanh. 7:2, 24b), but by the end of the second century C.E., autonomy had already been fully restored (see Alon, *Toledot*, 1 (1958³), 129f.). The Babylonian Jewish center enjoyed wide judicial autonomy from an early period, and one of its main institutions was the Jewish court. After the decline of the Babylonian center the Jewish courts in all other centers continued to exercise the judicial function in matters between Jews. The halakhic scholars and communal leaders sought to impose a strict internal discipline in order to insure that all disputes between Jews would be aired before the Jewish judicial institutions. At the same time, they made every effort to obtain charters of privileges from the various rulers under whom they lived in order to insure the independence of Jewish law and the grant of powers of compulsion to the Jewish courts and internal authorities (see below).

The jurisdiction of the Jewish courts extended first and foremost to most civil law matters such as property, obligations, tort, family and succession law, and also to matters concerning the administration of local Jewish government at the hands of the representative communal and intercommunal institutions – such as election to the latter bodies, tax imposition and collection, relations between the individual and the community, and the like (see below). This measure of judicial autonomy was generally extended (up to the 18th century), even in times and places of restriction of the rights of Jews. In many centers such autonomy extended even to criminal matters, varying from place to place in its scope and modes of execution. In certain places it also extended to capital offenses, particularly with reference to *informers (e.g., in Spain, see Resp. Rashba, 1:181; 5:290; Resp. Rosh, 17:1, 8; *Zikhron Yehudah*, 58 and 79; Resp. Ritba, 131; Resp. Ribash, 251; in Poland – see Resp. Maharam of Lublin, 138, etc.; see also *Capital Punishment); in other places it extended merely to religious offenses, offenses against property, and police administrative offenses.

The wide range of matters over which the Jews enjoyed autonomous jurisdiction may be gathered from a study of the responsa literature containing decisions given by the leading halakhic scholars of different periods on concrete questions arising from the daily realities. Thus, out of some 1,050 responsa of *Asher b. Jehiel – one of the leading scholars of German and Spanish Jewry in the second half of the 13th century and the beginning of the 14th – one-fifth (about 200) deal with precepts concerning man and God (such as the laws of prayer, festivals, forbidden food, and the like) and the remaining four-fifths with Jewish law (i.e., matters for the greater part included in Sh. Ar., EH and ḤM). Of the latter group, some 170 questions deal with matters of Jewish family law (marriage and divorce, parent and child, and the like) and the rest, more than 600, are concerned with all other "legal" branches of Jewish law (civil, criminal, and public-administrative; see Elon, Mafte'aḥ, introd. (Heb. and Eng.)). A similar ratio of subject matter is found to be more or less constant in all the responsa literature up to the 16th century, and slightly different in that of the 17th and 18th centuries, where the percentage of matters concerning religious law is somewhat higher. A material change can be detected in the responsa literature from the 18th century onward – following the era of emancipation, which saw the abrogation of Jewish judicial autonomy – and by far the greater part of these responsa deal with matters of religious precepts and family law, with a modest and minor place reserved for the remaining branches of Jewish law.

The Available Sanctions of the Jewish Judicial System

Within the framework of judicial autonomy described above the Jewish courts and competent authorities of the self-ruling bodies had the power to impose sanctions. These too varied from place to place and from period to period. The ordinary means of compulsion were attachment of property, monetary fines, and corporal punishment. In certain centers there were even Jewish prisons under the control of Jewish institutions and supervised by Jewish wardens (see *Imprisonment). At times the autonomous Jewish authorities had to seek the assistance of the central authorities in carrying out the sanctions imposed by the Jewish courts, especially so in case of the death sentence. A common and most effective sanction was the *ḥerem, the quality and severity of which varied from place to place and also according to the nature of the offense and the degree of compulsion required. The use of this sanction was essential in circumstances where the Jewish authorities lacked the normal attributes of sovereignty, and it served as a most effective deterrent and means of compulsion in view of the self-centered living and residential conditions of the Jewish collectivity as an autonomous group. A person on whom the ban was pronounced was to a greater or lesser extent removed from the religious and social life of the community, and the stringent consequences of this sanction induced many halakhic scholars to refrain from its imposition except in the most difficult and serious cases.

The Prohibition on Litigation in the Gentile Courts

A striking expression of the religious and national character of Jewish law is to be found in the prohibition on litigation in the gentile courts (*arka'ot shel goyim*), to which the halakhic scholars and communal leaders attached the utmost importance. The first mention of this prohibition was made soon after the destruction of the Temple, when Jewish judicial autonomy was for a short period restricted by the authority of Rome (see above). It was laid down that there was to be no resort to the gentile courts not only when the material law applied in the latter courts differed from Jewish law but even when their law on a particular matter was the same as that applied in the Jewish courts (Git. 88b). Resort to the gentile courts was regarded as prejudicial to the existence of Jewish judicial autonomy and the prohibition served as a protective shield insuring the uninterrupted existence of such autonomy throughout the period of Exile; any person transgressing the prohibition was "deemed to have reviled and blasphemed and rebelled against the Torah of Moses our teacher" (Yad, Sanhedrin 26:17, based on Tanḥ. *Mishpatim*, 3). Contrary to the general principle that every rule of the civil law (*mamonot*) is *jus dispositivum*, so that in respect of it a man may contract out of the law of the Torah, it was laid down by a majority of halakhic scholars that the parties to a transaction may not mutually agree to submit their dispute to the jurisdiction of a gentile court, and also that resort to the gentile courts is not justifiable on the principle of *dina de-malkhuta dina* ("the law of the land is law"; Naḥmanides on *Ex.* 21:1; Resp. Rashba, vol. 6, no. 254; Tur and Sh. Ar., ḤM 26:1, 3).

In the political and social realities of the different centers of the dispersion it was not always fully possible to enforce this prohibition. As early as the middle of the ninth century Paltoi Gaon laid down that it was permissible to institute proceedings in a gentile court against a party aggressively and obdurately refusing to appear in a Jewish court (B.M. Levin (ed.), *Oẓar ha-Ge'onim*, BK, Resp. no. 227). It was decided that in such a case the plaintiff, after first obtaining leave of the Jewish court, might prosecute his claim in the gentile court, "in order not to strengthen the hands of the powerful and violent who do not obey the law" (Yad, Sanhedrin 26:7 and *Radbaz* thereto; Tur and Sh. Ar., ḤM 16:2, 4). At times resort to the gentile courts was permitted in certain matters in which the central authorities had a special interest, such as disputes over land (Resp. *Rema*, no. 109), governmental taxes, and currency (Finkelstein, bibl., pp. 361f.). Some of the halakhic scholars permitted recourse to the gentile courts when this was agreed on by both parties (Resp. Maharam of Rothenburg, ed. Cremona, no. 78; Finkelstein, op. cit., pp. 153, 156 and n. 1; *Sma*, ḤM 26 n. 11 and *Taz* thereto; see also *Siftei Kohen*, ḤM 22, n. 15). In different periods there were communities and places where Jews scorned the prohibition, but in general the halakhic scholars and communal leaders firmly stood guard over the authority of the Jewish courts by enacting special *takkanot* and adopting sharp countervailing measures against those who thus undermined the autonomy of Jewish jurisdiction (see Assaf, *Battei ha-Din* …, 11, 17–18, 24, 109–13; Elon, in: ILR 2 (1967), 524–7; as regards recourse to the gentile courts from the period of the emancipation onwards see below).

Arbitration and the Jurisdiction of Lay Jewish Tribunals

The aim of preventing recourse to the gentile courts as a means of preserving Jewish judicial autonomy induced the halakhic scholars to maintain judicial institutions composed of Jewish judges, even if the judgments of the latter were not based on Jewish law, or were based on this law in slight measure only. Institutions of this kind were arbitral bodies and lay tribunals in their various forms.

The arbitral body had its origin in the second half of the second century (R. Meir and other *tannaim*: Sanh. 3:1–3), when Jewish judicial autonomy was restricted, as we have already noted, by the decrees of Roman imperial rule following the Bar Kokhba revolt. The courts were destroyed and those which remained were deprived of the power of compulsion. In these circumstances the scholars directed the people to the institution of *arbitration, in which *ro'ei bakar* ("herdsmen," simple folk untutored in the law) could also sit and adjudicate in accordance with their own good sense and understanding. In order to give such adjudication a Jewish form, the scholars laid down that the arbitral body should be composed of three arbitrators (Sanh. 3:1), like the Jewish court which was always composed of at least three *dayyanim* (*ibid.* 1:1; and see **Bet Din*) and unlike the position in Roman law where there was generally a single arbitrator. Even after the restoration of judicial autonomy, arbitration continued to fulfill an important function alongside the regular judicial institutions, and its rules and procedures were prescribed by the halakhic scholars (see also *Compromise).

Of interest is the evolution of the institution of adjudication by lay judges (*hedyotot*, i.e., persons untutored in Jewish law; the term also has the meaning of judges tutored in the *halakhah* but lacking **semikhah* ("ordination"; see, e.g., Git. 88b), a distinction that must be borne in mind). The precise origin of this institution is disputed by scholars; one opinion is that it dates from before the destruction of the Temple, while others hold that it too developed after the Bar Kokhba revolt and the withdrawal of autonomous jurisdiction from the Jewish courts (see Elon, op. cit., p. 529). Lay jurisdiction was likewise designed to ensure that the people would bring their disputes before Jewish judges – even if the latter were not versed in the law – rather than resort to the gentile courts. These tribunals were composed of three members, one of whom had to be *gamir* – i.e., to have acquired some knowledge of the *halakhah* – while the other two had to be persons fit at least to understand any matter explained to them (Sanh. 3a, Rashi and Nov. Ran ad loc.). The scholars bestowed on the lay tribunal authority to deal with all matters of civil law, to the exclusion of criminal matters (Sanh. 3a and *Piskei Rosh* thereto, 1) along with power to compel the appearance of the parties (*Piskei Rosh* thereto, 2; Tos. to Sanh. 5a; Tur, ḤM 3:3; Sh. Ar., ḤM 3:1). In order to prevent resort to the gentile courts at all costs in post-talmudic times the scholars laid down that in any community where not even one *gamir* was to be found, three laymen could make up the tribunal even if none of them possessed this minimal qualification, provided that they were "fit and God-fearing persons, spurning corruption and equipped with sense and understanding"; such tribunals could deal also with criminal matters, in cases of great need and after much prior forethought and consultation (Resp. Rashba, vol. 2, no. 290). The existence of tribunals composed entirely of lay judges is confirmed in other historical sources (see, e.g., the Valladolid *takkanot* of 1432, in Finkelstein, bibl., pp. 356–7), and the validity of such courts was halakhically recognized (*Rema*, ḤM 8:1).

In general, the major part of the legal hearings, in disputes between individual Jews and between the individual and the communal authorities, took place before a court composed of three *dayyanim* expert in Jewish law and deciding in accordance therewith (a court of this kind called simply, *bet din*; Resp. Rashba, vol. 1, no. 1010); however, in most Jewish centers there were also lay tribunals functioning alongside these courts as a permanent judicial institution (a court of this nature being referred to as *bet din shel hedyotot*; Rashba loc. cit.). Many factors – social, economic, standards of knowledge and education – determined the measure of resort to lay tribunals. Their judges (known by different names: *tovei ha-ir, berurei tevi'ot, berurei averot, piskei ba'alei battim, parnasim, zekenim*, etc.) generally based their decisions on communal enactments (see **Takkanot ha-Kahal*), trade usages (see **Minhag*), appraisal, justice, and equity (see, e.g., Resp. Rashba, vol. 2, no. 290; vol. 3, no. 393 et al.; Resp. Maharshal, no. 93; Resp. Rema, no. 33) and at times even upon a particular branch of a foreign legal system (*Beit ha-Beḥirah*, Sanh. 23a concerning "courts in Syria"; see also *takkanot* of the Leghorn community: S. Toaff, in: *Sefunot*, 9 (1964/65), 190f.). Sometimes lay tribunals turned to halakhic scholars for their opinion and advice (*Zikhron Yehudah*, no. 58). In some places the limits of their jurisdiction were clearly defined. Mention is made of a tribunal composed of *tovei ha-ir* which dealt with tax matters (Resp. Rosh, no. 7:11). At times there was a predetermined division of matters over which the different courts were to have jurisdiction; thus a *takkanah* of the Lithuanian community prescribed that the courts of the communal leaders were to deal with matters of monopolies as well as certain tax and penal matters, and the *dayyanim* of the community with matters of civil law (*Pinkas ha-Medinah* [*Lita*], no. 364); in a *takkanah* of the Leghorn community it was laid down that all matters of trade, insurance, and the like were to be dealt with by the communal leaders (*adonei ha-ma'amad*) judging in accordance with the general law as regards trade customs, but that matters of marriage and divorce, inheritance, mortgage, interest, and the like were to be dealt with according to Jewish law (Toaff, in: *Sefunot* loc. cit.).

The lay tribunals were originally and primarily instituted for the purpose of preventing resort to the gentile courts and also so as to enable certain matters of trade and the like, which were dependent on local custom, to come before a tribunal of merchants and professional experts. These tribunals tended, however, to gain in influence and to assume jurisdiction in additional matters, notwithstanding the existence of courts composed of *dayyanim* learned in the law. The halakhic scholars regarded this development as posing a threat to the ordered evolution of Jewish jurisdiction and application of Jewish law (see, e.g., Resp. Maharyu, no. 146). The fact that these tribunals tried matters according to appraisal and a subjective feel for justice, rather than according to any fixed legal rules, led the scholars to apprehend the danger of possible partiality and perversion of justice, especially since the tribunals were generally composed of the leaders and wealthy members of the community with the poorer and less influential members of society almost completely unrepresented. Strong criticism to this effect was often expressed by the scholars (see, e.g., *Keneh Ḥokhmah, Derush ha-Dayyanim*, pp. 25f.; *Derushei ha-Ẓelaḥ*, 3:12–4). However, such criticism never challenged the basic existence and positive merits of an institution which served as a vital additional means of preventing recourse to the gentile courts. For this reason adjudication by lay tribunals was also held to "accord with the Torah," even if it had not always the same merit as adjudication by the courts of *dayyanim*, and only "the practice in a few places to turn without hesitation to the gentile courts is actually contrary to the Torah and amounts to a public profanation of the Divine Name for which those who act in this way will have to account" (*Sefer ha-Zikhronot*, 10:3). To do so was to undermine Jewish judicial autonomy. (In Sh. Ar., ḤM the matter of lay tribunals (ch. 8) is clearly distinguished from the stringent prohibition on recourse to the gentile courts (ch. 26); see also M. Elon, in: ILR, 2 (1967), 529–37.)

The Judicial-Political Position and Social-Fiscal Relations

The national-religious character of Jewish law, and the profound awareness that a zealous watch over this inalienable asset would ensure the continued existence and unity of the Jewish people, thus constituted the primary element in the application of Jewish law in the daily life of the Jewish people even when dispersed in exile. Yet it may be asked how it proved possible for the Jews to maintain judicial autonomy under the political sovereignty of the governments under whose rule they lived, and what motivated the state authorities to respond to the demand of the Jewish collectivity for its own autonomy. The answer lies in the second of the two factors mentioned above, that is the judicial-political concepts of government and jurisdiction as these were common up to the 18th century, and the fiscal and social relations between the central authorities and the different strata, including foreigners, who dwelt under their rule. The judicial system was based on the individual's adherence to one of a number of distinctive groups with different legal systems which were recognized by the state. Unlike modern centralistic states, the medieval state was corporative in nature and comprised of a series of autonomous strata and bodies, such as the nobility, the burghers, the guilds, etc. The latter frequently competed with one another and some of them with the central authority, and the Jewish community was often the object of rivalry among these different strata, bodies, and the central authority. This political-legal reality rendered possible the existence of an autonomous Jewish group with its own judicial autonomy. The central authority, as well as the different strata and bodies amidst whom the Jews lived, regarded it as their "duty" and right to impose on the Jews heavy taxes in return for the privileges of settlement and residence. The collection of such taxation from each individual involved many difficulties, especially as the Jews were counted as members of a separate and foreign national group. The authorities accordingly found it convenient to impose an aggregate tax on the Jewish collectivity as a whole and for this purpose to enable the latter to be a unitary autonomous body, functioning in such manner that its leaders would bear the responsibility of producing the total amount of the tax apportioned and collected by each community from among its individual members. The existence of an autonomous public Jewish body also made it possible to give directions and conduct negotiations on other state rights and obligations through the recognized leaders of this body. Considerations of faith and religious opinions held by the Christian rulers may also have contributed to the grant of autonomous Jewish jurisdiction (see H.H. Ben-Sasson, *Perakim be-Toledot ha-Yehudim bi-Ymei ha-Beinayim* (196), 90–91).

In this manner a zealously pursued desire of the Jewish people coincided with the existence of external historical conditions and factors to enable this people to preserve its religious and national law as a law of life and practice, faithfully served and interpreted by Jewish courts throughout the dispersion. The preservation by the Jews of their national law has been the main factor in the preservation of Jewish national existence. In the words of Y. Kaufmann (*Golah ve-Nekhar*), "It was judicial autonomy which truly made of the Jewish nation in exile 'a state within a state'" (1 (1929), 518) and "This autonomy derived from the striving of the nation to embody in its life the ideal of the Torah to the utmost limits. It derived especially from the striving to uphold the Jewish legal system, the Law of the Torah, and to base thereon the order of internal life. For this reason the ancient autonomy was fundamentally a judicial autonomy" (*ibid.*, 2 (1930), 312).

THE EVOLUTION OF JEWISH LAW

A material feature of Jewish law is the fact of its ever-continuing evolution. This is the logical and necessary outcome of the fact of Jewish law's being a living and practical law, since constant evolution is a characteristic feature of every living thing whether it is discernible during the passage from one state to another or only clearly distinguishable in the perspective of history. It will be clear to anyone taking up the *halakhah* that he has before him one large unit in which the earlier and later, the basis and the construction, are all interwoven and arranged according to subject matter with no particular regard shown for historical-epochal distinctions. The halakhic scholars rightly considered that Jewish law was of a nature which required them to unite and integrate the various periods of the *halakhah* into a single, all-embracing epoch of unitary *halakhah*, and not to divide and differentiate between different stages and periods. This is a legitimate and accepted conception in any system of legal thought, especially in a legal system which, by its very nature, deems the existing body of laws to be the starting point for its own renewal and further development. This is also largely true, as regards, for instance, the development of most of English law. However, this conception does not in any way bar the scholar from examining each and every one of the institutions of Jewish law in historical perspective, with a view to determining the different stages of development they may have undergone. Moreover, an examination of such different stages of development and of the legal sources through which these stages were integrated into the fabric of Jewish law will reveal that the halakhic scholars themselves frequently emphasized the changes and development through which one or other institution of Jewish law had passed. This is evidenced in their resort not only to *takkanah* – a means of expressly adding to or changing the existing law – but also to Midrash and the other legal sources of Jewish law (see M. Elon, *Ḥerut ha-Perat…*, 12 (introd.), 261–4).

Submission to Jewish law and the Jewish courts brought in its wake an unending creative development of the Jewish legal system. Social realities and economic exigencies change from period to period, and among the special conditions of the Jewish people must be included the social and economic variations that marked the different centers of the dispersion. Even when the Jewish people had possessed a single political center – and later on a spiritual center – there had existed a various and widely scattered Diaspora; however, geographical dispersion really began to impress its mark more critically at the end of the tenth and the beginning of the 11th century when the one center, the Babylonian, which had until then held sway over the entire Diaspora, declined and a number of centers made their appearance side by side and successively in North Africa, in Spain and Germany, in France and Italy, in Turkey, Egypt, and the Balkan countries, in Poland-Lithuania, and elsewhere. It is certainly true that despite the geographical scattering, Jewish scholars everywhere dealt with the same talmudic and rabbinic sources and that very often contact, personal and by correspondence, was also maintained among the different centers. But the variations in the social, commercial, and economic life of the Jews in each center, their communal organization and representative institutions in each locality, their relationship with the gentile environment and the state authorities – all these from time to time gave rise to problems for some of which the existing Jewish law provided no express solution and for some of which it was necessary to find solutions which differed from those provided by the existing law. At times the influence of local conditions led to the absorption of undesirable legal principles which were contrary to the spirit of Jewish law and did not serve to advance the system of law as a whole. To the extent that such foreign principles deviated from the fundamental doctrines of Jewish law they generally came to be rejected in the course of time (see, e.g., *Imprisonment, *Imprisonment for Debt).

Thus Jewish law continued to evolve as a law of life and practice, giving direction to the daily realities while being itself directed thereby. The phenomenon of a legal system which demands that the determination of its law and its solutions to legal problems be founded on the past while answering the manifold needs of every succeeding generation is found to be true of Jewish law in all periods of its history, both in the time of Jewish political sovereignty and during the long period when this was absent but the Jewish people enjoyed judicial autonomy in Ereẓ Israel, in Babylonia, and in all the other countries of the dispersion. This demand was satisfied through the ever-continuing evolutionary development of the institutions of Jewish law and through preservation of the central concept of each institution which constituted the common factor of all the different stages and changes through which it passed. (For illustrations of such development, see Authority, *Rabbinical; *Capital Punishment; *Contract; **Ha'anakah*; **Hassagat Gevul*; *Imprisonment for Debt; *Lien; *Limitation of Actions; *Obligation, Law of; *Surety; *Taxation. See also *Interpretation; **Ma'aseh*; **Minhag*; **Sevarah*; **Takkanot*; **Takkanot ha-Kahal*; and see M. Elon, *Ḥerut ha-Perat …*, 12 (introd.), and 255ff.)

Since the development of Jewish law was the outcome of the practical application of the latter in daily life, it follows that in places where there was diminished submission to Jewish law and its courts system there was a corresponding falling off in the creative development of this legal system, as is evidenced, for instance, in the case of Italian Jewry in certain periods (Resp. Rambam (ed. Leipzig), pt. 1, no. 140, p. 26; *Sefer ha-Zikhronot*, 10:3). This was, however, an uncommon phenomenon until the 18th century and the era of emancipation. Thereafter, with the abrogation of Jewish judicial autonomy, Jewish law was to a far lesser extent a law of practice and this was to lead to a far-reaching diminution in the creativity of Jewish law (see below).

THE EVOLUTION OF JEWISH LAW REFLECTED IN ITS LITERARY SOURCES

Sefer ha-Zikhronot (loc. cit.) emphasizes that recourse to the Jewish courts is of importance not only for the continuance of the creative development of Jewish law itself but also for the enlargement of its literature. A study of the various matters with which halakhic literature has dealt at different times shows that the part of the *halakhah* which was of practical application came to occupy an increasingly and incomparably larger place than the part that was not of such application.

The Mishnah as compiled by Judah ha-Nasi contains six orders, each of which treats one basic branch of the *halakhah*, and together they embrace the whole halakhic system. In the two Talmuds, the literary creations following immediately upon the Mishnah, the following phenomenon is apparent: the Babylonian Talmud, unlike the Jerusalem Talmud, contains no Talmud on the order of *Zera'im* (apart from the tractate *Berakhot* dealing with prayers and benedictions). There is no doubt that the Babylonian *amoraim*, like those of Ereẓ Israel, studied all the six orders of the Mishnah and their deliberations on *Zera'im* are largely scattered throughout the tractates of the other orders. That no Babylonian Talmud was edited for this order is due to the fact that the rules therein stated – "precepts which are dependent on the land" (these being applicable only in Ereẓ Israel), such as the laws of *shevi'it* (the Sabbatical Year) and *pe'ah* (the corner of the field) – were not of practical concern in Babylonia, whereas in Ereẓ Israel itself, where these rules were actually applied, a Talmud on this order was compiled and edited. In the post-talmudic period the overwhelming part of the halakhic literary creativity was also concentrated on the "precepts contemporaneously in use," that is on the branches of the *halakhah* which were of everyday use and not on the laws connected with the "precepts dependent on the land," with the Temple, ritual purity, and the like. It is found that sometimes even theoretical study itself was centered around the practical orders – *Mo'ed, Nashim*, and *Nezikin* – and those tractates of the other orders containing precepts in contemporaneous use – such as *Berakhot, Ḥullin* (concerning the laws of ritual slaughter and *kashrut*), and *Niddah* (concerning ritual purity of women) – were arranged together with these three orders (see *Beit ha-Beḥirah* (ed. Jerusalem, 1965[2]), Introd. to Ber., p. 32). In geonic times many monographs were written on various halakhic subjects, most of them on strictly legal topics and part on matters of ritual law, the majority of both kinds dealing exclusively with the laws of everyday use. These monographs were primarily compiled for practical use in the *battei din*.

This phenomenon recurs in two branches of the post-talmudic literature – in the responsa and in the codifications – and to a certain extent also in the third branch, the commentaries and novellae. Thus Alfasi included in his code only those laws then operative and not, for instance, the laws of the order of *Kodashim* (except the tractate *Ḥullin* in which the topics discussed remained of contemporaneous significance). The only one to deviate from this path was Maimonides in his code, *Mishneh Torah*. He sought to restore the *halakhah* to its original dimensions by including in his code even matters of faith and belief, which he formulated in legal style. However, this undertaking was unique and in all subsequent codifications, such as *Piskei Rosh, Arba'ah Turim*, and Shulḥan Arukh, the example set by Alfasi was followed and only the rules in current application were included. The responsa literature also deals overwhelmingly with practical questions of the law and not with matters of ritual purity and defilement or sacrifices. This is obviously due to the fact that problems arose, and were referred to the leading halakhic scholars for solution, only in the area of the practical day-to-day application of the law. In the commentaries and novellae alone is there found any more extensive discussion of the "theoretical" branches of the *halakhah*, but even here the greater part is devoted to practical halakhic matters. This is one explanation for the fact that commentaries and novellae to the Jerusalem Talmud were written only from the 16th century onward, following the renewal of the Jewish settlement in Ereẓ Israel in this period. (It is noteworthy that in latter times – before and since the establishment of the State of Israel – there has been greatly increased creativity in the field of the laws pertaining to the order of *Zera'im*, in all three literary branches of the *halakhah*, clearly because these laws have once more come to be of practical significance.) While it is true that at all periods Jewish law was frequently studied in purely theoretical manner, as Torah for its own sake, and an appreciable literature was created to this end, yet such study and literary creativity represent no more than embellishments of the main core, aids to the knowledge of Jewish law for everyday use in practical life.

THE DIFFERENT BRANCHES OF JEWISH LAW

Illustrations of Development and Change in the Different Branches of Jewish Law

In the different periods of its history Jewish law has comprised all the branches of law customary in other legal systems although from time to time changes of a structural nature took place. The institutions of Jewish law in all its different branches underwent, as already mentioned, an ever-continuing process of creative development. In some fields – for instance property, family and inheritance, procedure and evidence – this process was of no material consequence as regards the framework or content of a particular branch of the law, notwithstanding any changes in its principles. In other fields the process had a more material effect as regards the content and classification of an entire branch of the law.

LAWS OF OBLIGATION. A change of this nature took place, for instance, in the field of the laws of obligation. The original Jewish law fundamentally and unequivocally rejected any form of enslavement of the debtor's person as a means towards realizing the creditor's rights (see *Execution, Civic). Consequently there arose the need to find a strong alternative means of ensuring the fulfillment of an obligation in the form of an encumbrance on the debtor's property, which found expression in a right of lien over the debtor's property automatically conferred on the creditor upon creation of the obligation. For this reason an obligation in Jewish law had essentially a real character because the creditor was afforded a right of a real nature in the debtor's property, and in consequence of this many rules belonging to the field of property law came to be applied also to the laws of obligation (see *Lien; *Obligation,

Law of). In the course of time, the nature of the contractual obligation in Jewish law underwent a substantive change, one that found expression in a series of basic innovations introduced and given recognition in successive stages; these included the possibility, contrary to the laws of property, of establishing an obligation with regard to something not yet in existence; the possibility of establishing an obligation whether or not the property in the debtor's possession at such a time was capable of satisfying the debt, and a long series of further developments (see *Contract). Such a substantive change in the subject matter of a legal institution is an important factor in its classification or reclassification as belonging, for instance, to the field of the laws of obligation rather than the laws of property.

ADMINISTRATIVE LAW. A different phenomenon is evidenced in the field of administrative law, for the central subjects of this branch changed almost completely in consequence of the material changes in the nature of public Jewish leadership and administration in different periods. Whereas in ancient times the institutions of public law determined relations between the individual leader – the king (see *King and Kingdom), the **nasi*, the exilarch – and the people, new social realities spurred the development of a pervasive system of administrative law based on collective leadership, elected or appointed. The representative and elective institutions of local Jewish government and intercommunal organization were built up on the principles of Jewish law, and the halakhic scholars as well as the communal leaders were called upon to resolve (the latter by way of communal enactments) the numerous problems arising in the field of administrative law. These related, among others, to the determination of relations between the individual and the public authority, between the latter and its servants; to the composition of the communal institutions and the methods of election and appointment to the latter and to other public positions (see *Public Authority); to the modes of legislation of the community and to the legal administration of its institutions (see **Hekdesh; *Takkanot ha-Kahal*); to the imposition and collection of taxes (see *Taxation), and to many additional problems concerning economic and fiscal relations in the community. This wide range of problems was dealt with in a very large number of responsa and communal enactments, in the course of which the halakhic scholars and public leaders developed a new and complete system of public law within the framework of the *halakhah*.

CONFLICT OF LAWS. In the field of the conflict of laws development came mainly in consequence of periodic migratory movements and social changes in the life of the Jewish people. The conflict of laws is not usually regarded as a distinct branch of Jewish law, because of the substantive nature of Jewish law as a personal law purporting to apply to each and every Jew wherever he may be – even beyond the territorial limits of Jewish sovereignty or autonomy. From this it naturally follows that in Jewish law no importance attaches to the fact, as such, that a contract between two Jews is scheduled to mature in a different country than that in which it was concluded – a fact that is normally the staple source of problems arising in the area of the conflict of laws. Nevertheless, the fact that for the greater part of their history, the Jews enjoyed their judicial autonomy under the political sovereignty of the foreign ruler with his own legal system, and especially the fact of the geographical dispersion of the various Jewish centers, inevitably caused the Jewish legal system to be confronted with many fundamental problems relating to the conflict of laws. There developed in Jewish law the phenomenon of a multiplicity of *takkanot* and customs relating to the same legal subject but varying in content from place to place. To some extent this phenomenon was also present in talmudic times, but it assumed significant proportions only from the tenth century onward when there ceased to be a single Jewish center exercising hegemony over the other centers of the Diaspora. The result of the rise of many centers was the proliferation of local *takkanot*, customs, and legal decisions, which brought in train the problem of the choice between different laws – not between Jewish law and any other law, but between the rules deriving from differing customs and *takkanot* within the Jewish legal system itself. Similarly, as a result of the close contact between Jewish law and the various legal systems of the nations amidst whom the Jewish collectivity lived, there evolved the principle of *dina de-malkhuta dina* and, flowing from this, various rules pertaining to the field of the conflict of laws.

CRIMINAL LAW. A different and completely opposite trend is evidenced in the field of criminal law. During those periods when the Jewish people enjoyed full judicial authority, it is possible to point to the existence of important principles and great creativity extending also to the criminal law (see *Penal Law; *Punishment). However, the scope of application of this branch of the law was already substantially narrowed around the time of the Temple destruction, and in consequence it reflects a diminished creative continuity and a smaller framework. It is true, as already mentioned, that in some places Jewish judicial jurisdiction extended even to capital offenses but in most centers the criminal jurisdiction of the Jewish courts was confined to offenses against property, administrative offenses, and the like. On the whole the lack of sovereignty deprived the Jewish people of the media required for the proper implementation of criminal jurisdiction and of suitable conditions for its organic development. All these factors therefore stunted the growth of the functional framework and content of this branch of Jewish law.

Classification of the Different Branches of Jewish Law

Like other legal systems, Jewish law has its own distinctive basic principles pertaining to each of the different branches of the system. Sometimes these principles are unique to Jewish law and characterize its approach to matters such as personal freedom and the rights of the individual, the substance and nature of legal and moral obligations, the concept of ownership of property, the essential nature of judicial jurisdiction, modes of proof, and other fundamental questions. In other cases the principles of Jewish law correspond to parallel principles in other legal systems. Such differences and similarities are dealt with elsewhere under the heading of the subject to which they pertain.

A full enumeration of the articles on Jewish law appearing in this Encyclopaedia is given below, some articles being repeated since they pertain to more than one branch of law:

THE SOURCES OF LAW. Authority, *Rabbinical; *Codification of Law; *Interpretation; *Ma'aseh; *Minhag; *Mishpat Ivri; *Sevarah; *Takkanot; *Takkanot ha-Kahal.

GENERAL. *Agency, Law of; *Asmakhta; *Conditions; *Ḥazakah (in part); *Law and Morals; *Legal Person; *Majority Rule; *Legal Maxims; *Mistake; *Noachide Laws; *Ones; *Shetar; *Slavery.

THE LAWS OF PROPERTY. *Acquisition; *Gifts; *Hazakah; *Hefker; *Hekdesh; *Lost Property, Finder of; *Maẓranut; *Ona'ah; *Ownership; *Property; *Sale; *Servitude; *Slavery; *Ye'ush.

THE LAWS OF OBLIGATION. *Antichresis; *Assignment; *Contract; *Gifts; *Ha'anakah; *Hassagat Gevul; *Labor Law; *Lease and Hire; *Lien; *Loans; *Maritime Law; *Meḥilah; *Obligation, Law of; *Partnership; *Pledge; *Sale; *Shalish; *Shi'buda de-Rabbi Nathan; *Shomerim; *Surety; Unjust *Enrichment; *Usury.

THE LAWS OF TORT. *Avot Nezikin; *Damages; *Gerama; *Nuisance; *Theft and Robbery (civil aspects); *Torts.

FAMILY LAW AND INHERITANCE. *Adoption; *Agunah; *Apostate (Family Law); *Apotropos; *Betrothal; *Bigamy; Child *Marriage; *Civil Marriage; *Concubine; *Divorce; *Dowry; *Embryo; *Firstborn; *Husband and Wife; *Ketubbah; *Levirate Marriage and Ḥaliẓah; *Maintenance; *Mamzer; *Marriage; *Marriage, Prohibited; *Mixed Marriage (Legal Aspects); *Orphan; *Parent and Child (legal aspects); *Rape; *Succession; *Widow; *Wills; *Yuḥasin.

CRIMINAL LAW. *Abduction; *Abortion; *Adultery; *Assault; *Blood-Avenger; *Bribery; *Capital Punishment; *City of Refuge; *Compounding Offenses; *Confiscation; *Crucifixion; *Expropriation and Forfeiture; *Contempt of Court; *Divine Punishment; *Extraordinary Remedies; *Fines; *Flogging; *Forgery; *Fraud; *Gambling; *Hafka'at She'arim; *Ḥerem; *Homicide; *Imprisonment; *Incest; *Informer (legal aspects); *Oppression; *Ordeal; *Penal Law; *Perjury; Police *Offenses; *Punishment; *Rape; Rebellious *Son; *Sexual Offenses; *Slander; *Sorcery; *Suicide; *Talion; *Theft and Robbery (criminal aspects); *Usury; *Weights and Measures (criminal aspects).

THE LAWS OF PROCEDURE AND EVIDENCE. *Admission; *Arbitration; *Attorney; *Bet Din; *Compromise; *Confession; *Evidence; *Execution (Civil); *Extraordinary Remedies; *Ḥerem; *Imprisonment for Debt; Limitation of Actions; *Oath; *Pleas; *Practice and Procedure (Civil and Penal Law); *Shetar; *Witness.

MERCANTILE LAW. *Acquisition; *Agency, Law of; *Contract; *Hafka'at She'arim; *Hassagat Gevul; *Imprisonment for Debt; *Labor Law; *Lease and Hire; *Legal Person; *Loans; *Maritime Law; *Minhag; *Obligations, Law of; *Ona'ah; *Partnership; *Sale; *Shalish; *Shetar; *Shomerim; *Takkanot; *Takkanot ha-Kahal; *Taxation; *Usury. (The articles enumerated above are all mentioned under other branches of the law, but are grouped together here because of the commercial elements they contain.)

PUBLIC AND ADMINISTRATIVE LAW. *Confiscation, Expropriation, and Forfeiture; *Dina de-Malkhuta Dina; *Hekdesh; Public *Authority; *Takkanot ha-Kahal; *Taxation.

CONFLICT OF LAWS. *Conflict of Laws; *Dina de-Malkhuta Dina; *Domicile.

It may be added that classification of the subjects comprising a legal system is a task beset with difficulties, particularly so in the case of the Jewish law, and calls for the exercise of much care. Thus, for instance, certain institutions of Jewish law are classified both under the laws of property and the laws of obligation because of the close connection between these two branches of the law. This is true also as regards the classification of criminal matters, which in Jewish law do not always conform to those customarily classified in other legal systems as part of criminal law. It is questionable whether the classification of subject matter in one legal system is appropriate for another and any automatic application to Jewish law of the classification adopted in another legal system is especially liable to be misleading. To a certain extent the special legal terminology of Jewish law also influences the manner of classification of its subject matter (see for instance the definitions above of the terms *mishpat Ivri, issura, mamona*, and others). The difficulties entailed in the classification of Jewish law into defined legal branches derive in part from the fact that during the periods when the foundations of the various rules of Jewish law were laid, the system knew only a classification of a most general nature. This is reflected in the Mishnah and in the remaining halakhic literature of the tannaitic period and also in the two Talmuds. A more definitive and detailed classification of Jewish law came only with the compilation of Maimonides' code, the *Mishneh Torah*, and some of the subsequent codes. A classification of the subject matter of Jewish law in keeping with the character and spirit of this legal system is possible only after deep and careful study of its different institutions. For these reasons the above classification is not to be regarded as final and absolute.

PUBLIC JEWISH LEADERSHIP IN THE DEVELOPMENT OF JEWISH LAW

Introduction

The halakhic scholars and the *battei din* filled the central role in the development of the Jewish legal system. In addition, an important creative role was filled by the public leadership and representation of the Jewish people in all the different institutional forms it assumed throughout the history of the Jews:

from the kings, the *nesi'im*, and exilarchs down to the elected or appointed representatives of the community.

The King's Law

The fundamentals of the laws concerning the king and his kingdom are enjoined in the Pentateuch (Deut. 17:14–20, dealing mainly with the duties of the king and his modes of conduct), in the first Book of Samuel (ch. 8, in which the prerogatives of the king and the duties owed him by the people are defined), and in other biblical passages (see for instance I Kings 21, concerning the matter of Naboth's vineyard). The scholars also learned about the powers of the king from certain biblical statements concerning leaders of the people other than the kings (see for instance Josh. 1:18 concerning rebellion against the kingdom; cf. Sanh. 49a). The king was vested with wide powers in the legislative (see **Takkanot*), judicial, and executive fields, with authority to deviate in various matters from the rules as laid down in the *halakhah*. His authority was not confined solely to fiscal and economic matters relating directly to the rule of the kingdom, such as taxation and the mobilization of manpower or property, but extended also to the field of criminal law. In the latter field he had authority, for instance, to impose the death sentence on a murderer, despite the existence of formal defects in the evidence against him, when this was required "for the sake of good order in accordance with the needs of the hour" (Yad, Melakhim 3:10; 5:1–3 *ibid.*, Roẓe'aḥ 2:4; and Sanhedrin 14:2, 18:6).

The king's law represents the earliest determination in Jewish law of a creative factor not directly attributable to halakhic scholars, and the *halakhah* conferred similar creative authority on the various other post-monarchic institutions of central Jewish government. Thus for instance it was said of the exilarchs who headed the internal Jewish government in the Babylonian exile that "they take the place of the king" (Yad, Sanhedrin 4:13, based on Sanh. 5a and *Rashi* ad loc.) and that the king's law applies "in every generation… in favor of the leaders of each generation" (*Beit ha-Beḥirah*, Sanh. 52b; see also *Mishpat Kohen*, no. 144). The question of the relationship between the regular law and the king's law is often the subject of discussion in halakhic literature, particularly of the post-talmudic period. R. Nissim b. Reuben *Gerondi explains the parallel existence of the two systems on the basis that justice administered according to law, while correct and ideal, does not always answer the social and other needs of the hour, and that this function is filled by administration of the king's law; for this reason Scripture enjoins the king to have the Torah with him always, "that his heart be not lifted up above his brethren" (Deut. 17:14–20), because inasmuch as he is not always subject to the law he must at all times, when making use of his powers, take particular care to ensure that he does not deviate from the general object of the Torah and its principles of justice and equity (*Derashot Ran*, Derush no. 11). All subsequent creative authority permitted in Jewish law to deviate, in certain cases, from the rules of the *halakhah* was subject to this above basic requirement (see *Minhag; Takkanot ha-Kahal*). In later periods different scholars found a legal basis for the authority of the king's law in the idea of an agreement between the king and the people in terms of which the latter allows the king his prerogatives in all matters falling within the king's law in return for his undertaking to guard and protect the people (see Z.H. Chajes, *Torat ha-Nevi'im*, ch. 7 "*Melekh Yisrael*"). This idea was apparently the influence of the commonly accepted medieval theory which based the validity of the king's law on a consensus of the people, a theory which different halakhic scholars also adopted as a basis for the doctrine of *dina de-malkhuta dina*.

Local Jewish Government

Creativity in the legislative field of Jewish law is also evidenced at the local governmental level. The halakhic sources relating to the early part of the Second Temple period already mention certain legislative powers entrusted to the townspeople (*Benei ha-Ir*, see Tosef., BM 11:23; BB 8b). From this modest beginning there developed, at a much later stage, a wide legislative creativity at the hands of the autonomous governmental institutions of the Jewish community and intercommunal organizations. This was expressed in the *takkanot ha-kahal*, enacted, particularly from the tenth century onward, in all fields of the civil, criminal, and administrative law. As in the case of the king's law, it was possible for these enactments to be contrary to a particular rule of the *halakhah*, and the scholars determined ways to ensure that such enactments remained an integral part of the overall Jewish legal system. One of their principal means was to check that the enactments did not conflict with the Jewish law principles of justice and equity. Another contribution to Jewish law, not directly attributable to the halakhic scholars, was that which resulted from participation of the public in some of the institutions of Jewish jurisdiction, such as arbitration and the lay tribunals (see above). Although at times these jurisdictional institutions were prejudicial to the orderly evolution of Jewish law, it may nevertheless be accepted that the generally harmonious cooperation that existed between these institutions and the halakhic scholars enabled the public leaders to make a significant contribution toward the forging of a stronger link between Jewish law and the realities and problems of everyday life. This in turn was a spur to the further development of Jewish law.

THE RELATIONSHIP BETWEEN JEWISH LAW AND FOREIGN LAW

Introduction

The question of the relationship between Jewish law and foreign law has two aspects. First, the extent – if any – of reciprocal relations and influence of the one on the other in a manner leading to the integration into the one legal system of legal directives deriving from the other; secondly, the extent of the recognition – if any – given to a directive of a foreign legal system, without such recognition involving any integration of the directive into the host system. These are two separate but related aspects, for recognition by the host system of the validity of a foreign legal principle entails, in certain cases, some measure of recognition – witting or unwitting – of the correctness of the foreign principle and of the possibility that the contents of the host legal system may be influenced in a manner leading to the integration of a foreign legal principle into its own framework.

Reciprocal Influences

From the 17th century onward a great deal of research in Jewish law has been devoted to the subject of mutual influence between Jewish law and other legal systems (latterly see B. Cohen, bibl., Introd. and ch. 1). More than any other, this field of research has been particularly conducive to the adoption of an apologetic approach – in the form of both an over-emphasis on the influence of foreign law on the Jewish legal system and exaggeration of the influence of Jewish law on other legal systems. Moreover, the influence of one legal system on another is no easy matter to prove because of the possibility that similar circumstances may have led to the evolution of like institutions in different legal systems, uninfluenced by each other. However, in general it may be said that there were reciprocal relations and influences between Jewish law and the surrounding legal systems or that of the nation under whose political sovereignty Jewish law functioned in any particular period of its history. The fact that the Jewish collectivity lived its social and economic life in accordance with its own law, yet all the while was under the patronage of many different nations with their own legal systems, inevitably left the mark of Jewish law on the other legal systems. The reverse process applied equally: the halakhic scholars were familiar with the law applied in the general courts of the land and sometimes even recommended the adoption of a foreign legal practice which commended itself to them (see, e.g., Elon, Mafte'aḥ 425; *Pesakim u-Khetavim*, no. 83; Resp. Israel of Bruna, no. 132). In certain cases the halakhic scholars recognized the particular social efficacy of certain aspects of the foreign law (see **Derashot Ran*, Derush no. 11) and sometimes they were not even deterred from lauding the gentile administration of justice when they found this superior to that of the Jews (*Sefer ha-Ḥasidim*, no. 1301). To some extent directives of the foreign law were absorbed by Jewish law by means of the legal source of custom (see **Minhag*). When absorption of a foreign principle did take place, such a principle underwent a process of internal "digestion" designed to accommodate it to the general principles and objectives of Jewish law. If in particular social circumstances a foreign principle was occasionally absorbed which conflicted with the fundamental doctrines of Jewish law, such a principle was usually rejected in the end by the Jewish legal system (see, e.g., M. Elon, *Ḥerut ha-Perat…*, pp. 238–54, 259 f.).

Recognition of Foreign Legal Rules

The much-discussed subject of the validity in Jewish law of the provisions of a foreign legal system centers on the doctrine of *dina de-malkhuta dina*, which holds that the law of the land is law and must be followed. The earliest formulation of the doctrine was made in the Babylonian Exile by the *amora* Samuel as appears from some of the legal explanations given for its entrenchment. An unqualified recognition of the provisions of the foreign law pertaining to civil matters – *dinei mamonot* (in matters of ritual law the doctrine of *dina de-malkhuta dina* never applied; *Tashbeẓ*, 1:158 and see above) – would have constituted a serious danger to the orderly evolution of the Jewish legal system and may well have rendered it of theoretical interest only. As the main means of averting this danger many halakhic scholars restricted the scope of the above doctrine – contrary to the plain meaning of some talmudic *halakhot* – by holding it applicable solely to certain matters falling within the sphere of relations between the central authorities and the public, such as taxation, expropriation of property for governmental purposes, and the like. Such restriction was expressly justified on the ground that extension of the doctrine to all matters of civil law would lead to "nullification of all the laws of Israel" (*Beit ha-Beḥirah*, BK 113b). Even the scholars who in principle extended the doctrine beyond matters concerning relations between the authorities and the public (see Resp. Rashba, vol. 1, no. 895; Nov. Naḥmanides, BB 55a; Nov. Ran and *Nimmukei Yosef ibid.*; *Sefer ha-Terumot* 46:8, 5), did not always carry this out in practice (see Resp. Rashba, vol. 6, no. 254) and some scholars restricted the scope of the doctrine in other ways (see *Teshuvot Ḥakhmei Provinẓyah* (ed. A. Sofer), pp. 426 f.; *Siftei Kohen*, ḤM 73, n. 39). The *halakhah* was decided according to the view that restricted the application of the doctrine solely to certain matters concerning relations between the authorities and the public (*Rema*, ḤM 369:11).

The proliferous and ever-continuing creativity evidenced in talmudic and post-talmudic Jewish law offers eloquent proof of the fact that the doctrine of *dina de-malkhuta dina* remained only a marginal aspect of the Jewish legal system. Indeed, by their judicious use of the doctrine, the scholars rendered it a contributory factor toward the preservation of Jewish judicial jurisdiction, since qualified recognition of certain matters of foreign law enabled the Jewish collectivity to adapt itself, in the required and necessary manner, to the conditions of the gentile environment. The attitude of Jewish law toward a different legal system is determined, first and foremost, by its basic objective of safeguarding its own continued existence and, flowing therefrom, autonomous Jewish jurisdiction with all that it entails. As long as the realization of this objective is not endangered, no obstacle presents itself in Jewish law to resorting in certain cases, as the need arises, to a rule deriving from foreign law. Even then, however, such recognition is given only to the extent that the rule of the foreign law is not in conflict with any of the fundamental Jewish law principles of justice and equity. For this reason Jewish law attributes no validity to the law of the land with regard to a directive which does not apply equally to all but discriminates between different citizens, since any directive of this nature "is robbery" (Yad, Gezelah 5:14). Similarly, Jewish law holds the imposition of a monetary fine on the whole public, on account of the transgression of a few individuals, to be "absolute robbery" because such conduct contraverts the principle which prohibits the imposition of a collective fine and vicarious criminal responsibility (Resp. Ribash Ha-Ḥadashot, no. 9; in support the following references are cited: Gen. 18:25; Num. 15:22; Pes. 113b; see also Deut. 24:15 and II Kings 14:6).

THE ERA OF EMANCIPATION

Inner Spiritual and External Political Changes

On the eve of emancipation and the end of Jewish autonomy, substantial changes began to manifest themselves in Jewish law which were crucial to its development. As already indicated, two basic factors account for the survival of Jewish law as an operative law, even when it was deprived of its single territorial center and political sovereignty: the first the internal discipline of traditional Jewish society which regarded itself enjoined from a national-religious point of view to preserve Jewish law as a living force, and the second the political circumstances of the corporative medieval state. Both these elements now underwent a decisive change. At the same time as the rise of pressures for equality of rights for all, including Jews, the governments of Europe in turn deprived the Jewish community of the mandatory jurisdictional rights of the Jewish courts, even in matters of civil law; the use of the *ḥerem* as well as other means of execution were forbidden. But the main factor for the progressive ending of the living practice of Jewish law was the social-spiritual change that began to assert itself among the Jewish people. The Jewish community, which had hitherto regarded the *halakhah* as the supreme value of its existence, split into a society part of which remained traditional while part no longer regarded itself as bound to the observance of the Torah and its precepts, and this decisively weakened the internal factor of a religious imperative to order daily practical life in accordance with Jewish law. This substantive change in the spiritual outlook of the Jewish world carried with it also a disregard for the national element in Jewish law and not only did the leaders of the community not oppose the abolition of Jewish judicial autonomy but a good number of them welcomed the ending of the "separation" between the Jewish and the general public, regarding it as promising achievement of the hoped-for freedoms and equality of rights as well as organic integration into the vibrant Europe of the emancipation era.

The Abrogation of Jewish Judicial Autonomy

With the beginning of this transformation relating to the continued existence of Jewish judicial autonomy, a number of the leading halakhic scholars gave voice to their concern and warned about the religious and national dangers inherent in yielding up this autonomy. Thus R. Ezekiel *Landau railed against the frequent recourse to the gentile courts, a practice so prevalent that "all three pillars of the world are shaken: the Law, Truth, and Peace" (*Derushei ha-Zelaḥ*, 8:14; 22:24). R. Raphael Cohn, spiritual leader of various communities in Poland-Lithuania and Germany in the 18th century, devoted much effort in the latter years of his life toward the preservation of an autonomous Jewish legal system and all it entailed. Acknowledging the new reality of a laxity in Torah observance by a section of the Jewish public, he emphasized that the neglect of recourse to Jewish judicial jurisdiction was the most serious defect in non-observance of the laws of the Torah, and he particularly criticized those members of the Jewish public who saw the abrogation of such Jewish jurisdiction as a step toward equality of rights and duties (see *Zekher Ẓaddik*, pp. 7, 8, 20).

These political and spiritual changes, which were increasingly manifest in the course of the 19th century, left their impress upon that part of Jewry that continued to preserve the religious tradition. As regards Western and Central European Jewry, recourse to the general courts rapidly became widespread and common to all Jewish circles. Traditional Jewry of Eastern Europe still preserved for some considerable time its connection with Jewish law and brought its disputes to the rabbi and his *bet din* for *din Torah*. However, the decisions of the rabbinical courts became more and more arbitral awards and compromise settlements, lacking the semblance of judgments under a living and organic law, and in the course of time, here also, resort to the general courts grew increasingly frequent. Even the halakhic scholars reconciled themselves with the new situation of the lack of judicial autonomy and justified it on the principle of *dina de-malkhuta dina* – quite contrary to the attitude taken by the scholars in earlier periods (see, e.g., *Kelei Ḥemdah*, Mishpatim, no. 1, and see above). The main and greater part of Jewish law in civil and criminal, administrative and public matters, came to be treated as if it were rules "not contemporaneously applied" and now studied merely theoretically. The only sphere of Jewish law that continued to be practiced was a part of family law, the arrangement of marriage and divorce in accordance therewith. In this field, involving the laws of prohibitions and permissions, a powerful internal discipline continued to govern traditional Jewry and to some extent also those who did not observe religious precepts. However, recognition by the central authorities of such marriage and divorce varied from country to country in the Diaspora.

Continuance of Judicial Autonomy in the Eastern Jewish Centers

An interesting phenomenon is the fact that to some extent Jewish law continued to develop as a living law among Oriental Jewish communities in Turkey, North Africa, and elsewhere. This phenomenon is partly explained by the different political circumstances of the Ottoman Empire in the 19th and 20th centuries, but was also an outcome of the determined struggle waged by Oriental Jewish communities, as in Algeria for instance, to retain their judicial independence in the face of efforts by the central authorities to impose on them the general law of the land. A demonstrative expression of this reality is the fact that even in the 19th century the responsa literature of this Jewry continued to occupy itself to a very large extent with matters of the *Ḥoshen Mishpat* arising from actual events in everyday life, while the responsa literature of European Jewry of this period is very poor in this respect and even then is more of a theoretical study than a consideration of practical problems.

Consequences of the Abrogation of Judicial Autonomy

The abrogation of Jewish judicial autonomy carried with it two far-reaching consequences with regard to the world of Jewish law. In the first place, Jewish law's dynamism as a living law of practice was greatly inhibited and its organic development suffered a marked curtailment. It was unfortunate for Jewish law that this development occurred in the course of the 19th century, a period which saw a revolution in social, economic, and industrial life that left a decisive imprint on different legal fields. The other consequence was the loss, by the greater part of the 19th-century Diaspora communities, of the former deep national and religious awareness that daily practical life, ordered in accordance with Jewish law, in all fields, became as an integral part of the way of life of the Jewish people. This consequence, as was later to become apparent, carried even more fateful implications for Jewish law than those stemming from the first-mentioned consequence.

THE PERIOD OF JEWISH NATIONAL AWAKENING

Ha-Mishpat ha-Ivri Society and Mishpat ha-Shalom ha-Ivri

The Jewish national awakening and the rise of Zionism also evoked a change in the mental attitude of the Jewish people toward Jewish law. Soon after the *Balfour Declaration the Ha-Mishpat ha-Ivri Society was founded in Moscow. Its members – drawn from all sections of the Jewish public – regarded the return of Jewish society to Jewish law as an aspect of national renaissance parallel to the building of the Jewish homeland and revival of the Hebrew language. Among the goals set by the society was the preparation of suitable literature on Jewish law and the establishment in Jerusalem of an institute – within the framework of a university – for research into that law preparatory to its adoption in the future Jewish state. In the editorial introduction to the first volume of the journal *Ha-Mishpat ha-Ivri* (Moscow, 1918) it is noted that "the 'legal' *halakhah* has been integrally bound up with the 'religious' *halakhah*… [yet]… over the last decades a process has begun of separating out our law from its religion and ethics, and we intend to continue this process in order to prepare our law for a secular existence." The pursuit of this object was and still is a controversial one and its desirability as well as manner of achievement remain central problems relating to the integration of Jewish law into the legal system of the State of Israel (see below).

In 1909–10, on the initiative of the head of the Palestine office of the Zionist Organization, Mishpat ha-Shalom ha-Ivri was established in Jaffa as a judicial institution for the adjudication of disputes between Jews in Ereẓ Israel. In the course of time district tribunals were established in a number of places and over them a supreme tribunal. Between the years 1918 and 1936 rules and regulations were issued containing directives as to judicial organs, procedure, evidence, and so on. The first head of Mishpat ha-Shalom ha-Ivri was Arthur *Ruppin and the writer S.Y. *Agnon served as its first secretary. Mishpat ha-Shalom ha-Ivri functioned as an arbitral body and its work was facilitated by the enactment of the Arbitration Ordinance in 1926, which recognized the submission of disputes not only to individual arbitrators but also to an existing "arbitration tribunal" (see *Arbitration). It worked alongside the official bodies, first of the Ottoman Imperial government and later of the Mandatory power, and alongside the rabbinical courts. Mishpat ha-Shalom ha-Ivri did not, however, achieve its goal. Its main activities were confined to the years 1920–30 and after this date the number of cases brought before it began to wane. All in all it cannot be said to have produced any real harvest of Jewish law in consequence of its deliberations and decisions. Some of the reasons for this were objective, such as the tribunal's lack of powers of compulsion and the fact that it provoked sharp criticism from the rabbinical courts, the leaders of national religious Jewry, and respected scholars such as S. *Assaf who were opposed to the existence of fixed judicial bodies outside the framework of the rabbinical courts and in opposition to them. Mainly, however, its lack of success was due to the fact that not only did it not assume to decide according to the existing *halakhah* as set out in the Shulḥan Arukh *Ḥoshen Mishpat* and the subsequent halakhic literature, but it possessed no system of norms, either of Jewish law or generally, upon which to act. In fact, proceedings before this tribunal were much like inquiries by laymen based on generally conceived principles of justice and equity, ethics and public good, since the judges were for the larger part persons of general education only, without any legal training or specific knowledge of law (see P. Daikan, *Toledot Mishpat ha-Shalom ha-Ivri*, and bibl. there cited; J. Yonovitz, Introd. to S. Assaf, *Ha-Onshin* … (1922), 5–6).

Jewish Law in the Rabbinical Courts

At the beginning of the 20th century the rabbinical courts in Ereẓ Israel displayed a total lack of central organization. With the establishment of the Chief Rabbinate in 1921, most of the rabbinical courts came to organize themselves within the framework of this institution. In matters of personal status, the rabbinical courts were assigned exclusive jurisdiction as regards marriage, divorce, and "probate" of wills, and concurrent jurisdiction as regards maintenance, succession, etc. (all other areas of the law remained within the jurisdiction of the general Mandatory courts). The task of this supreme halakhic institution was pictured by its first head, Rabbi *Kook. After outlining the important creative role played by the *battei din* in all periods, through the enactment of *takkanot*, he went on to add that "in our renewed national life in Ereẓ Israel there will certainly sometimes be great need to make important *takkanot* which, as long as they are consented to by the majority of the competent scholars and are then accepted by the community, will carry the force of a law of the Torah" (*Ha-Tor*, 1 (1921), nos. 18, 21–22). To some extent the rabbinical courts were equal to this important task in matters of procedure and personal status, but in all other areas of Jewish law almost nothing was achieved.

MATTERS OF PROCEDURE AND PERSONAL STATUS. An important *takkanah* enacted immediately in 1921 established the Rabbinical Supreme Court of Appeal, thus introducing a regular appellate tribunal which had not previously existed in Jewish law (see *Practice and Procedure). That this *takkanah* rendered the appellate court an integral part of the Jewish legal system was made clear in a judgment of the Rabbinical High Court of Appeal of Jerusalem which rejected the contention that no right of appeal existed in Jewish law, holding that "the right of appeal has been enacted by a rabbinical *takkanah*, the force of which is as that of a rule of our Holy Torah" (OPD, p. 71).

At first the rules of procedure in the rabbinical court left much to be desired, but improvement followed upon the publication in 1943 of procedural regulations by the Chief Rabbinate Council. These included detailed provisions on the initiation of proceedings, on procedure during the hearing, rules of evidence, modes of appeal, and on other matters. A series of forms were also appended, among them statements of claim, summonses of parties and witnesses, applications for appeal and so on. In part these regulations were based on Jewish law and in part they showed the influence of existing practice in the general legal system. An innovation in Jewish law was the detailed rules laid down concerning the payment of various court fees and the adoption of children. The most radical innovation introduced by the above regulations involved an engagement by the rabbinical courts to distribute the estate of a deceased person in accordance with the provisions of the Succession Ordinance of 1923, which prescribed an order of distribution treating husband and wife and son and daughter in terms of equality. In 1944 a number of *takkanot* were enacted introducing further important changes: the customary minimum sum of the *ketubbah* was increased; the levir refusing to grant the widow of his brother *ḥaliẓah* was rendered obliged to maintain her until releasing her (see *Levirate Marriage and *Ḥaliẓah*); an important *takkanah* imposed on the father the legal duty to maintain his sons and daughters up to the age of 15 years and not merely until the age of six years in accordance with talmudic law (see *Parent and Child; M. Elon, *Ḥakikah Datit…*, 157ff.).

After 1944, however, creativity by way of *takkanot* ceased almost entirely, except for three additional *takkanot* enacted by the Chief Rabbinate in 1950 (the principal one involving a prohibition on the marriage of children under the age of 16 years; see *Child Marriage). This may be regarded as a matter for great regret since a number of urgent problems in the area of personal status still await solution by way of *takkanah* (such as certain cases of hardship for the **agunah*, problems relating to the joint property of the spouses, and other matters). On the other hand, there has since the 1940s been halakhic creativity in the area of personal status by means of interpretation as applied in actual cases. In this manner, for instance, there was innovated the substantive principle giving a woman, upon divorce, the right to receive over and above her *ketubbah* a certain additional sum, called "compensation." The amount thereof varies with the circumstances, one of the important considerations in its determination being the need to award the woman part of the property acquired in the course of the marriage through the joint efforts of the spouses (see M. Elon, *Ḥakikah Datit…*, loc. cit.).

OTHER FIELDS OF THE LAW. In fields of the law other than personal status the rabbinical courts were assigned no jurisdiction under the general law of the land, and the bearers of the *halakhah* initiated no real effort toward adaptation of the Jewish legal system to the contemporary social and economic needs of Ereẓ Israel Jewry. The call to the people to submit their disputes in civil matters to the rabbinical courts by way of arbitration brought a very restricted response, even from the religious section of the community. Hence, except in a few exceptional cases, no evidence is to be found in the judgments of the rabbinical courts of any creative activity in the overwhelming part of the civil law. One notable exception is represented by a leading judgment given in 1946, in a matter concerning the laws of evidence, when a marriage was entered into before two witnesses in the absence of a rabbi. As violators of the Sabbath both witnesses were incompetent (Sh. Ar., ḤM 34:2, 24) and since they were the only witnesses the marriage stood to be regarded invalid according to Jewish law. On the man's death, this was the contention raised by the remaining heirs of the deceased in opposition to the woman's claim to the widow's share in the estate of the deceased. The court, however, recognized the validity of the marriage, holding the witnesses to have been competent: "For reasons of religious transgression… and bearing in mind the fact… that libertarianism has increasingly spread for general and universal reasons, transgressions of this kind are not likely to affect the credibility of witnesses… who act almost unwittingly. The disqualification of transgressors as witnesses arises from the fear that their evidence will be false… and therefore in such cases the credibility of a witness is largely determined by reasons of time and place. If it is clear to the court that the person is not one who is likely to lie for the sake of deriving a benefit, he is to be admitted as a competent witness" (OPD, p. 137). This decision of principle was essential to the proper administration of justice under present day social realities in which a substantial part of the public is not religiously observant, and it is carried out in practice by the rabbinical courts.

Jewish Law and the Hebrew Language

It is appropriate that the quest for the restoration of Jewish law as a law of practice be compared with the struggle for the revival of Hebrew as a spoken language. From one aspect the latter represented the more difficult task. Ever since the beginning of the Diaspora, Hebrew had served almost exclusively as a literary language, not spoken in the common pursuits of everyday life, and as a result of emancipation it came to be further and further removed from life – even the spiritual and cultural – of the Jewish people. Many of the faithful followers of the Zionist movement in its early stages entertained doubt about the possibility of using Hebrew in modern conditions: "Who among us knows sufficient Hebrew to ask for a train ticket in this language?" asked Herzl, who contemplated a Jewish state without Hebrew as its commonly spoken language (*The Jewish State*, ch. 5). Yet an inner awareness that the use of Hebrew in the social, economic, and cultural life of the people was a prime requisite without which there could be no complete national revival led eventually to Hebrew becoming not merely a holy tongue, but the national language, written and spoken, of the Jewish people returning to its homeland. As a result of the untiring efforts of individuals and public bodies expressions and terms were coined and style and forms created, largely drawn from the ancient treasure houses of the language, and in this manner there flowered a modern living language based on and preserving continuity with the ancient holy tongue.

In other respects the possibility of restoring Jewish law was more limited than the revival of Hebrew, which is not so dependent on political sovereignty or assistance from the ruling authorities and is more closely connected with individual inclination and the wishes of interested bodies; legal norms encroach more on the realm of philosophy and ideological outlook than do the byways of a language and the task of restoring Jewish law demanded more comprehensive study and preparation than did the revival of Hebrew. Yet it is conceivable that these obstacles to the restoration of Jewish law could have been overcome by a determined effort. To a large extent the political autonomy of the Jews in Ereẓ Israel in the pre-state period was similar to that enjoyed by the Jewish people in the Diaspora until emancipation, an autonomy which also allowed for judicial independence. Moreover, by far the greater part of the subject matter with which Jewish law deals – such as obligations, property, public administration, and so on – is free of fundamental religious or ideological dispute. However, emancipation had produced a weakened religious and national consciousness of the need for daily life to be ordered in accordance with Jewish law, and all sections of the population displayed an irresolute apathy toward the preparation of Jewish law for its historic task. It is true that research was undertaken and books were written by scholars such as A. *Gulak, S. *Assaf, and A. *Freimann, which were of importance for the scientific research of Jewish law. But the required auxiliary literature of the law, written in convenient form with the law phrased and classified in accordance with modern legal concepts and terminology, was not prepared, nor were possible solutions to modern legal problems for which Jewish law has no ready or adequate existing answer, although it allows for one to be found by way of *takkanah* or any other of its recognized creative legal sources.

The Legal System in Ereẓ Israel Preceding the Establishment of the State of Israel

The unique legal system in force in Ereẓ Israel under the British Mandatory regime was a factor which might have served as a strong stimulus toward the integration of Jewish law into the legal system of the state about to be established. The principles which governed the Mandatory legal system were set out in Article 46 of the Palestine Order in Council of 1922. In accordance with this, on the eve of the establishment of the State of Israel there was crystallized a legal system nourished by a number of legal systems: the *Mejelle*, based on Muslim religious law; various Ottoman laws embracing principles of French law and other legal systems; Mandatory ordinances based on English law; law based on the English common law and doctrines of equity introduced into the Mandatory legal system, in cases where the existing system provided no solutions to concrete problems. In addition, matters of personal status were to a considerable extent dealt with under the religious law of the different communities recognized by the general law. This was a legal system composed of a number of disparate elements and created a situation inviting its own replacement by a homogeneous legal system.

JEWISH LAW IN THE STATE OF ISRAEL

The Official Position Assigned to Jewish Law

On the establishment of the State of Israel, Jewish law continued to occupy the same official position in the legal structure of the state as it had done in the pre-state period. The Law and Administration Ordinance of 1948 prescribed that the law in existence on the eve of establishment of the state should remain in force (sec. 11), with the practical result that officially Jewish law was incorporated in the area of personal status only. At the same time the Hebrew language celebrated its final victory, even in a formal sense, and section 15b of the above ordinance repealed any provision in any law requiring the use of English, thus making Hebrew the language of the state, of its law, and of its everyday life.

MATTERS OF PERSONAL STATUS. The jurisdiction of the rabbinical courts was defined in a Knesset law of 1953 which, save for one or two changes, entailed no substantial departure from the existing situation. It gave the rabbinical courts exclusive jurisdiction in matters of *marriage, *divorce, and *ḥaliẓah*; as regards the wife's claim for maintenance, jurisdiction is given to the court to which the wife applies – the rabbinical or the district court. In this and in other laws there were also prescribed the circumstances in which the rabbinical courts have concurrent jurisdiction in other matters of personal status (see *Adoption; *Apotropos; *Maintenance; *Succession).

THE RABBINICAL COURTS. Matters entrusted to the jurisdiction of the rabbinical courts are naturally dealt with in accordance with Jewish law. In the course of their activities these courts have given decisions introducing a number of important innovations in Jewish law, such as a married woman's right to the income deriving from the pursuit of her own profession, and recognition of the existence of mutual pecuniary rights between spouses married abroad in a civil ceremony only, and so on (see M. Elon, *Ḥakikah Datit*…,

166–72). In certain matters the law prescribes that the rabbinical courts too must decide in accordance with the general law. In the Succession Ordinance of 1923 provision was made for the treatment of son and daughter, husband and wife, on terms of equality as regards the division of certain kinds of property on succession, and the Women's Equal Rights Law, 1951, extended the directive to all other property. Some of the other main provisions of this law are the following: men and women are equated as regards all legal acts; the father and mother are given natural guardianship of their children; a married woman is given full capacity of acquisition during marriage and retention of her rights to property acquired by her prior to the marriage. In addition this law allows the litigants, if they are above the age of 18 years, to consent to having their case tried according to the laws of their community. It also states that its provisions shall not affect any halakhic prohibition or permission relating to marriage or divorce. In the main its provisions accord with the position under Jewish law as it has evolved (for instance as regards equal rights on succession), a notable exception relating to the husband's right to the fruits of his wife's *melog* property (see *Husband and Wife). A law of 1955 prescribes the status and manner of appointment of rabbinical court *dayyanim* and, except for two variations, its provisions correspond closely to those laid down in the Judges Law, 1953. (As regards two variations see M. Elon, *Ḥakikah Datit…*, 47–49.)

THE GENERAL COURTS. In matters of personal status concerning Jewish parties the general courts are also required to decide according to Jewish law, except when a law of the state makes express provision on the matter. As already mentioned, the general courts have jurisdiction in all matters not entrusted to the exclusive jurisdiction of the rabbinical courts. Matters of marriage and divorce may also be pronounced on by the general courts, either when the problem arises incidentally to the matter before the court (for instance in a claim by the wife for maintenance there may arise incidentally thereto the question of the validity of her marriage), or in a matter brought before the Supreme Court sitting as a High Court of Justice. Possibly a rabbinical court and a general court, even though both apply Jewish law, may arrive at entirely different conclusions. Thus, for instance, the general courts first resort to the principles of private international law before applying Jewish law and therefore may recognize a marriage entered into abroad as valid in accordance with the law of the country concerned, even when it is invalid according to Jewish law. In addition the general courts apply only substantive Jewish law and not its laws of evidence and procedure, thus for instance admitting the testimony of the parties themselves and that of their relatives.

LEGISLATIVE PROVISIONS CONTRARY TO JEWISH LAW. Legislation in the area of personal status contrary to Jewish law is reflected in a number of provisions, scattered in various Knesset laws, which confer on the commonly reputed spouse ("wife" as well as "husband") numerous rights. These provisions relate to rights of a social-economic nature (pensions, tenants' protection, and so on), rights under the Succession Law, and include also the right conferred on a woman to give her child born of the man reputed to be her husband the latter's family name, even without his consent. These rights were held by the Supreme Court to extend to the commonly reputed spouse even though the latter (or even both parties) be validly married to another (except with regard to the right of succession, which is only available if, upon the death of one of the parties who have lived together as husband and wife in a common household, neither is then married to another). The explanation that the above enactments were made in order to alleviate the hardship which is sometimes suffered by a couple who are unable to marry on account of Jewish law prohibition (for instance in certain cases of the *agunah*) is indeed weighty and hope may be expressed that the Chief Rabbinate will speedily find solutions to these problems. Nevertheless, it does not seem to justify the institution of the reputed spouse with its threat to the orderly existence of the family unit. This institution is the subject of controversy in Israel society and there are recent indications of a tendency by the Supreme Court to limit its scope (see M. Elon, *Ḥakikah Datit…*, 119–54).

"WHO IS A JEW?" – ANSWERED ACCORDING TO JEWISH LAW. In March 1970 an amendment to the Law of Return of 1950 incorporated into this law a most material principle of Jewish law. This law, which ensures for every Jew the right to come to Israel as an *oleh* and automatic citizenship from the moment of his arrival, was amended to define the term "Jew" as a person born of a Jewish mother or converted to Judaism, who is not a member of a different religious faith. This definition, including the latter part, is entirely in accord with Jewish law. A Jew converted to a different faith remains a Jew as regards his personal status and all this entails – such as the need for him to grant a divorce to his Jewish wife – but he is deprived of various religio-social rights and is not numbered as a member of the Jewish community (i.e., he cannot be counted toward **minyan* and so on); for this reason he is also deprived of the rights of a Jew under the Law of Return. The stated definition applies also for purposes of registering an individual's Jewish nationality (*le'om*) in the population register and related documents, including the identity card (see also *Jew).

LEGISLATION CONFORMING WITH RITUAL LAW. In addition to the already mentioned cases, Israel law is also based on the *halakhah* – in the wide sense of the term – in a number of different matters. Thus in 1948 the Provisional Council of State enacted that the supply of *kasher* food be ensured to all Jewish soldiers of the Israel Defense Forces; a law of 1962 prohibits the raising, keeping, or slaughtering of pigs in Israel except in specified areas (populated mainly by non-Jews) and for certain other limited purposes; the provisions of the Law and Administration Ordinance of 1948 (as amended) lay down that the Sabbath and the Jewish festivals shall be prescribed days of rest in the state (but do not prohibit labor on such days, such matters being ordered in certain respects in the Hours of Work and Rest Law of 1951) and allows non-Jews the right to observe their own Sabbath and festivals as days of rest.

The "Unofficial" Application of Jewish Law in the State

INDEPENDENCE OF THE ISRAEL LEGAL SYSTEM. As already mentioned, Jewish law is reserved no official place in the Israeli legal system, except in matters of personal status. The proposal (made by P. Daikan on the eve of the state's establishment and subsequently raised again by others) that Israel law be freed from its dependence on the English common law and principles of equity and that Jewish law be resorted to in any case of lacuna in the law of the state (see above, Art. 46 of the Palestine Order in Council) was not accepted. Until the present time there is to be found in two Laws only, the Succession Law of 1965 and the Land Law of 1969, a provision (entitled "Autarky of this Law") which excludes the operation of the aforementioned article 46 in all matters with which the relevant law is concerned. None of the other laws so far passed by the Knesset proclaims its own independent operation. To some extent such independence has been established in the case law in consequence of decisions by the Supreme Court to the effect that the post-1948 English case law does not have binding force in Israel law as does that of the pre-1948 period, and even reliance on the pre-1948 English case law is also gradually diminishing.

LEGISLATION BASED ON JEWISH LAW PRINCIPLES. In some measure law in the State of Israel follows the principles of Jewish law even in areas where the latter system has not officially been rendered applicable. In the introduction to a draft bill for one of the early comprehensive laws there were set out the general legislative guidelines adopted for the entire area of the civil law. The legislative policy thus enunciated assigned to Jewish law the status of "the main but not the only or binding source" and enumerated the existing legal and factual position in Israel as well as the laws of other countries as additional sources (Draft Bill for a Succession Law, published by the Ministry of Justice in 1952). To some extent this policy has been adhered to in practice and some of the matters enacted in accordance with the principles of Jewish law are the following: the possibility of separate ownership of dwellings in a cooperative house (see *Ownership); the prohibition of delay in the payment of wages (see *Labor Law); the right of the dismissed employee to severance pay (see **Ha'anakah*); the legal arrangement concerning imprisonment for debt; the laws of bailment (see **Shomerim*), and so on. Particular reliance on Jewish law is to be found in the provisions of various Knesset laws in the area of family law, relating among others to the following matters: the duty of a person to maintain, besides his wife and children, also his other relatives (on the Jewish law principle of obliging a person to uphold the *mitzvah* of *ẓedakah*; see *Maintenance); in matters of guardianship that the minor's own good is the primary consideration and that "the court is the father of all orphans" and a complete departure – expressed in various provisions – from the Roman law concept of *patria potestas* (see *Apotropos); in matters of succession Jewish law is followed in the conferment of equal rights on all children of the deceased whether born in or out of wedlock, in the solution provided to the problem which arises in the case of commorientes (see *Succession), in acceptance of the Jewish law institution of a *shekhiv mera* will (see *Wills), and in the provision made for maintenance out of the estate of the deceased (see *Widow).

LEGISLATION CONTRARY TO JEWISH LAW. In contrast, there are Knesset laws containing provisions which are – without any real justification – contrary to the position taken by Jewish law. Some of the matters so enacted are the following: the right of the creditor to turn directly to the surety even without initial agreement to this effect (see *Surety); the right of a party to plead prescription of a claim along with an admission as to the existence of the debt (see *Limitation of Actions); the automatic administration of an oath to all witnesses whereas Jewish law leaves the matter to the discretion of the court (Resp. Ribash, no. 170; *Tashbeẓ*, 3:15; *Rema*, ḤM 28:2; for further illustrations see Elon, in: ILR, 4 (1969), 80–140).

JEWISH LAW IN THE CASE LAW OF THE GENERAL COURTS. The decisions of the courts, particularly of the Supreme Court, represent a further channel through which the influence of Jewish law is brought to bear on the Israel legal system. In numerous decisions of the Supreme Court diverse legal matters have been dealt with by way of a comparison between the position under the general law and Jewish law respectively, the two systems sometimes leading the judges to the same conclusion and sometimes otherwise. In some cases Jewish law has been quoted for the purpose of construing legal terms and definitions and on occasion Jewish law has constituted the primary legal source relied on by the Supreme Court, even in areas in which Jewish law is not expressly rendered applicable. This integration of Jewish law through the case law of the general courts is of great practical significance from the aspect of the confrontation between Jewish law and the legal problems that arose before the courts in the 1950s and 1960s.

JEWISH LAW IN THE CASE LAW OF THE RABBINICAL COURTS. A noteworthy phenomenon is the existence of a proliferous case law of the rabbinical courts, in diverse areas of the civil law, in matters coming before these courts as arbitral bodies. Some 30% of the judgments of these courts published since the middle of the 1960s deal with matters unrelated to personal status and concern, for instance, labor law, contracts, copyright, partnership, pledge, administrative law, and so on. These offer an instructive insight into the manner in which concrete questions of everyday life are dealt with in accordance with Jewish law and represent an important contribution to the solution of modern social and economic problems (see, e.g., *Contract; **Ha'anakah*; *Labor Law; *Public Authority).

Attitudes toward Jewish Law in the Law of the State

Integration of Jewish law into the legal system of Israel is sometimes opposed because it entails a "secularization" of the *halakhah* since the acceptance by the state of a Jewish law principle does not stem from recognition of the binding validity of such a principle from the religious point of view, but is dictated by purely human and national interests. The argument views that by such integration the Knesset's own binding authority substitutes itself as the source of authority of any Jewish law principle it has adopted, and that neither the Knesset nor the general courts possess the necessary qualifications postulated by the halakhic system for deciding any of its rules. This view is decried by a decisive majority of religious Jewry and its spiritual leaders, who consider that the *halakhah* does not become secularized for the mere reason that the theory of the general law may hold a change to have taken place as regards the basic norm of a particular halakhic rule. It is argued that neither the Knesset nor the courts purport – nor indeed is it possible for them to do so – to decide the *halakhah* within the religious meaning of such activity; that not only is the *halakhah* not prejudiced by its integration into the legal system of the state, but the halakhic system itself commends that the legal order in the Jewish state shall, even if not based on religious faith, correspond with the substance of Jewish law and its principles of justice and equity rather than be founded on other legal systems. For some generations now this middle path has been followed by a decisive majority of religious Jewry, also with regard to other fundamental Jewish values, as with the revived use of the holy tongue in everyday secular life and with the settlement of the holy land even without observance of the religious precepts. The declared attitude of non-observant Jewry also favors the assignment of first priority to the reception of Jewish law principles when these are in keeping with present-day social and economic needs (see, e.g., the statement made in the session of Nov. 29, 1965, by Knesset members belonging to almost all political parties with reference to the Gift Law and Pledge Law Bills (*Divrei ha-Keneset*, v. 44, pp. 24–36)). It should be borne in mind that except in the area of family law the subject matter of Jewish law is generally free of fundamental public dispute of a religious or ideological nature.

The integration of Jewish law into the legal system of Israel is of importance to the former since it has a vital need to contend with the problems of practical everyday life as the only means toward the restoration of its former, almost unbroken, creative and evolutionary function, and this in its natural environment – the Jewish state and its legal system. Such an integration of Jewish law is no less important for the legal system of the state. Israel legislation is of an eclectic nature, the legislator choosing as he sees fit from many different legal systems. There is well-founded apprehension that this must necessarily result in a lack of homogeneity and lead to contradictions in Israel law due to the absence of a common axis around which the entire legal structure may revolve. A legal system so constructed moreover lacks roots and a past. If, as the revival of Hebrew proved, a people's language has to lean on history and foundations, then a priori a people's legal system requires roots and a past on which to draw for sustenance and growth. The absence of these requisites in Israeli law accounts for the large number of Supreme Court decisions evidencing resort to numerous legal systems in a search for solutions to legal problems. The appointed way for the emerging legal system of the Jewish state to take root, to find the common denominator for its laws as well as the homogeneity it requires, is for it to become linked and integrated in the proper way with historical Jewish legal thinking and creativity.

Modes of Integration

Achievement of the desired integration of Jewish law with the Israel legal system demands strict observance of the rule that in all legislative activity preference be given to every principle of Jewish law which is in keeping with the existing social and economic exigencies. It is also necessary to ensure that all principles of Jewish law adopted in the laws of the state shall be construed within the spirit of the Jewish sources of law from which they were derived. Finally, it is necessary to lay down a "Jewish version" of the controversial Article 46, to the effect that the Jewish sources of law shall be resorted to in the event of any lacuna in the existing law. The decisions of the Supreme Court and of the rabbinical courts in matters involving Jewish law – not only in the area of personal status but in all its different fields – and a long series of varied research studies undertaken in recent years, point to the fact that it is within the power of Jewish law to contend successfully with the overall range of new problems that arise. In addition, Jewish law occupies a substantial part of the law faculty study curriculum at different universities in Israel and to the new generation of Israel lawyers and jurists Jewish law is no longer a remote and unfamiliar subject. Accelerated research activity in the different fields of Jewish law and the preparation of an auxiliary literature to facilitate study of and resort to the latter will be invaluable aids to the process of integrating the legal system of the State of Israel and Jewish law.

Legal Creativity

During various periods of its history Jewish law has experienced the reality of jurisdiction and legislation existing alongside the jurisdictional and legislative system of the halakhic authority itself – as illustrated by the king's law, jurisdiction of the public leadership, lay jurisdiction, and communal enactments. In numerous matters such jurisdiction and legislation of the Jewish leadership diverged from the rules of Jewish law, but the halakhic system evolved a series of rules and principles which ensured that such jurisdiction and legislation of the public leadership became an integral part of the overall system (see above *Takkanot ha-Kahal*). It is true that during all the above-mentioned periods the entire Jewish people looked upon Jewish law as the ultimate and binding value, whereas the same cannot be said of the present-day Jewish public, which, in the existing socio-cultural realities, finds itself divided on matters of religious faith and ideological outlook. Yet in this society there have developed certain cultural and social values – such as the restored language and homeland – which exist as the undisputed assets of all. Consequently the hope may be expressed that the acceptance of Jewish law principles into the legal system of Israel in a proper and consistent manner, along with the latter's formation of a tie with Jewish law for purposes of its own supplementation, will ensure that at some time in the future unity and integrity – and thereby continuity as well – will also be restored to this precious cultural and spiritual asset of the Jewish nation, that is, Jewish law.

[Menachem Elon]

Development in the Status of Jewish Law in the Israeli Legal System

Two significant and illuminating developments have occurred over the years in the status of Jewish law in the legal system of the State of Israel, whose common denominator is the entrenchment of the status of Jewish law in the legal system and the obligation to have recourse to and to rely upon it. The first development occurred in 1980, with the enactment of the Foundations of Law Act, 5740 – 1980, and the second with the enactment of the Basic Laws in 5752 – 1992.

THE FOUNDATIONS OF LAW ACT, 5740 – 1980. The Foundations of Law Act, 5740 – 1980, repealed Article 46 of the Palestine Order in Council, 1922–1947, thereby revoking the binding link between Israeli law and English law, and rendering complete the autonomy of the Israeli legal system. Instead of having recourse to English law, the Foundations of Law Act sets forth a different arrangement in cases involving a lacuna in the law, where the court is unable to find an answer to a legal question in the conventional sources of law: "Where the court, faced with a legal question requiring decision, finds no answer to it in statute law or case law or by analogy, it shall decide the issue in the light of the principles of freedom, justice, equity and peace of the Jewish heritage" (sec. 1). This was the first fundamental change wrought in the status of Jewish law in the State of Israel, as for the first time the legislator required the judge, in confronting questions to which no answer was available in the regular sources of law, to have recourse to Jewish law, and left no discretion to the judge in this regard.

Opinions are divided on two main issues regarding this section. First, in what cases must the court, pursuant to the provisions of the law, rule in accordance with "the principles of freedom, justice, equity and peace of the Jewish heritage"? Second, what is the nature and essence of these principles of "the Jewish heritage"?

Thus, in the case of Hendeles (CFH 13/80, *Hendeles et al. v. Kupat Am Bank Ltd.*, PD 35(2), 785), the Court discussed the meaning of the phrase "another person's domain" in the Lost Property Law, 5733 – 1973 (see at length *Lost Property). Justice Cohn stated that, when a statute incorporates a given term or phrase borrowed from Jewish law, it is clear that the court must resolve questions that arise in connection with that term by turning to Jewish law. However, while such a term or phrase is to be construed according to its meaning in Jewish law, this does not dictate the concurrent application of the substantive provisions of Jewish law as they relate to that term. This was true, Justice Cohn argued, before the enactment of the Foundations of Law Act, and remains true after its passage. The law establishes that the need to refer to the sources of the Jewish heritage does not arise at all so long as an answer can be found to any question requiring decision "in statute law or case law or by analogy." It is permitted to have recourse to Jewish law in such cases, for purposes of comparison or enrichment; however, such recourse remains optional, by way of obiter dicta, and not obligatory.

Regarding the interpretation of the phrase "the principles of freedom, justice, equity and peace of the Jewish heritage," Justice Cohn (see bibliography, H. Cohn, "Residuary Law," 295ff.) opined that the legislator specifically chose the specific principles enumerated in the section (i.e., freedom, justice, and equity), which have become a part of the Jewish heritage, while rejecting other principles, which the legislator did not include. Moreover, the term "Jewish heritage" implies all those cultural assets created by the Jewish nation, including not only Jewish law, but also extra-legal sources. Any heritage that may be called Jewish, whether on account of the identity of its author or the nature of the bequest, comes within the rubric of the Jewish heritage, even if it is not part of the Jewish religious heritage.

Justice Menachem Elon thought that, "In the event of a lacuna, the aforesaid principles of Jewish law assume the status of a supplementary legal source of the Israeli legal system, to which the court is duty bound to rely upon as a binding legal source" (p. 793). Where doubt exists as to the *construction* of an existing provision of law, one may turn to other legal systems as a source of inspiration and influence, but not as a binding source. But even in those cases the recourse to Jewish law is primary in importance, and the Foundations of Law Act, which confers a binding status on the principles of the Jewish heritage in the event of a lacuna, strengthens the priority of turning to Jewish law even in cases where a doubt exists as to the *construction* of an existing provision.

As to the definition of a lacuna, Justice Elon held that: "Legal terms and concepts, which originate in ethical systems and cultural values – such as justice, good faith, public policy and the like – and are found in the Israeli legal system, must be construed according to the basic outlook of Jewish law – an outlook rooted in that law's moral and cultural values… It appears to me that the fleshing out of these value-laden terms, which, apart from their nomenclature, do not refer to any specific, substantive content, involves the filling of a lacuna… Therefore, the aforesaid method of interpretation, adopted by these judges, now constitutes the filling of a lacuna and is not only a matter for construction, with everything that implies" (p. 793).

Justice Aharon Barak disagreed with Justice Elon over the question of how to define a lacuna: "Where Israeli legislation has recourse to such fundamental terms as 'justice,' 'good faith,' 'public policy' and other such value-laden concepts, the task of the court is to infuse them with concrete content according to the statutory purpose and with regard to the actual and ideal conditions of life in Israel. Here, the judge is not at all confronted with a 'lacuna,' since the legislature has stipulated the applicable norm. I therefore can see no possibility in such a case of applying the provisions of the Foundations of Law Act, which contemplates only the filling of a lacuna" (p. 797). Regarding the use of Jewish law as a source for interpretative inspiration in cases of doubt as to a term's interpretation, Justice Barak held one cannot say that such inspiration must come primarily from the principles of Jewish law. Rather, he held, a piece of legislation must be interpreted from within the legislation itself, and where it is influenced by a foreign system, we must turn to that system for interpretative inspiration.

Justice Moshe Landau held that, where a lacuna exists, the court must have recourse to the principles of the Jewish heritage contained in the Foundations of Law Act. However, the legislator avoided referring to Jewish law by name and instead selected the concept, thus far undefined in point of law, of "Israel's heritage." According to Justice Landau, similar to the opinion of Prof. Barak, the very idea that the interpreter must refer specifically to any particular source for answers in the event of a doubt as to the proper construction of a particular term conflicts with the rules of interpretation. Therefore, in his view, the recourse to Jewish law should be to enrich our legal thinking; however, there can be no obligation to turn primarily to Jewish legal sources in order to interpret a legal term the meaning of which is in doubt.

Justice Menachem Elon criticized Justice Barak's highly restrictive approach to the function of the Foundations of Law Act, to the extent of almost divesting it of all legal content:

> We take it for granted that one of the basic rules of interpretation is that the legislature does not waste words and that some content must be given to the words it chooses to use. This rule has particular force when an entirely novel law is involved, and utmost force when the statute is a basic statute that occupies an important place in the legal system of the State.... Even before this law became part of the Israeli legal system, the court was at liberty to engage in the worthy task of turning to Jewish Law for the purpose of "expanding the judge's horizons and field of vision, so as to produce additional depth of interpretive creativity." What change has then been generated with the adoption of the statute entitled the Foundations of Law Act? If the response is that Jewish Law will have its day in the event of a lacuna, and if we define lacuna as my distinguished colleague [i.e., Justice Barak] did in the Hendeles case... and if a lacuna does not include what he said it does not include, I would very much like to know when and how it will ever be possible to find a lacuna totally unaddressed in "legislation or judicial precedent or by means of analogy." Is it indeed possible to construe a statute so that the legislator's words are devoid of all legal meaning...? How many debates did the Knesset and lawyers generally have, and how many versions did they draft, before the enactment of this basic statute? Was this solely for the purpose of addressing the problem of a lacuna which has never yet nor will ever likely occur and which, if and when it does occur, will more than likely encounter the refusal of the majority of the court to acknowledge its existence? I wonder. (FH 40/80 *Koenig v. Cohen*, PD 36(3) 701, 742–743)

In accordance with his interpretation of the Foundations of Law Act, Justice Menachem Elon in many cases turned to Jewish law for the resolution of a variety of legal issues. Thus, for example, Justice Elon had recourse to Jewish law, pursuant to the Foundations of Law Act, for construing provisions of the Succession Law in cases where defects occurred in the writing of a will according to the provisions of that law (FH 40/80 *Koenig v. Cohen*, PD 36(3) 701, 742–743 – see *Will); to address the question of whether a political agreement between factions in the Knesset which was entered into in the aftermath of the composition of a new government had legal validity (HC 1635/90 *Schereschewsky v. Prime Minister*, PD 45(1) 749); in determining that the publication of a person's identity in connection with the claim that said person is collaborating with the authorities of the State of Israel is not to be regarded as defamation, even though the society in which that person lives disapproves of such collaboration (CA 466/83 *Ajiman v. Dardarian*, PD 39(4) 734; see *Slander); to emphasize the importance of pluralism of views in the world of *halakhah* on an appeal, which was accepted, concerning the decision to reject applications by two party lists from taking part in elections to the Knesset (EIA 2/84 *Neiman v. Chairman of Central Elections Committee*, PD 39(2) 225); and in many other cases. In general, the courts have tended to use the method of analogy whenever a claim can be made that a lacuna exists in a statute – at times relying upon the Foundations of Law Act, which directs the search for a solution by way of an analogy. It should be noted however that this method was not adopted by Israeli law with the passage of the Foundations of Law Act, and was used even before its enactment.

BASIC LAWS: HUMAN DIGNITY AND FREEDOM; FREEDOM OF OCCUPATION. In 1992, a highly significant development took place in the status of Jewish law in the State of Israel, with the enactment of two Basic Laws – "Basic Law: Human Dignity and Freedom" and "Basic Law: Freedom of Occupation." These laws have constitutional status, and protect a series of fundamental rights. Section 1A of the law states that: "The purpose of this Basic Law: Human Dignity and Freedom is to protect human dignity and freedom, in order to anchor in a Basic Law the values of the State of Israel as a Jewish and democratic state"; similar wording appears in section 2 of the Basic Law: Freedom of Occupation. These sections establish *the obligation* to turn to Jewish law in the framework of "the values of the State of Israel as a Jewish and democratic state" in order to interpret the values protected in the Basic Laws (see *Human Dignity and Freedom; *Rights, Human). This has been the most significant development in recent times in the status of Jewish law in the State of Israel, as until 1992 the obligation to have recourse to Jewish law applied, apart from matters of a personal status, only in cases of a lacuna, according to the Foundations of Law Act. With the enactment of the Basic Laws, Jewish law acquired constitutional status, with ramifications for the validity and construction of all the laws in the State of Israel. Jewish legal principles have accordingly been implemented on many occasions by the courts in the course of turning to the values of the State of Israel as a Jewish and democratic state. Thus, for example, the courts have ruled, on the basis of Israel's Jewish and democratic status, that there was no room for active euthanasia in the State of Israel (see Justice Menachem Elon's ruling in 506/88 *Shefer v. State of Israel*, PD 48 (1) 87; see entries: *Medicine and Law: Euthanasia; *Values of a Jewish and Democratic State). The court similarly ruled that the Execution Law, 5727 – 1967 must be construed so as to permit a debtor's imprisonment only in cases in which it is clear that the debtor is concealing his assets and refuses to pay (HC 5304/92 *Perach v. Justice Minister*, 47(4) 715, Justice Elon; see *Imprisonment for Debt). It similarly ruled that the severity of an offense of which an accused has been charged is not in itself sufficient to justify his imprisonment until the termination of legal proceedings against him (Cr.A. 2169/92 *Suissa v. State of Israel* PD 46(3) 388, Justice Menachem Elon; see *Detention).

The key phrase – "Jewish and democratic state" has merited a variety of interpretations. According to Justice Elon, the court is required to examine the principles of Jewish law and the principles of democracy, in order to create a synthesis between the two when interpreting the Basic Laws. Where a number of different approaches exist in respect of the "democracy" component, the approach which befits the "Jewish" component should be adopted (see, for example, the case of active euthanasia, which some democracies permit and others outlaw; in such a case, that approach which is compatible with the "Jewish" approach prevails and active euthanasia becomes outlawed (see the *Shefer* case, on pp. 167–168, and *Medicine and Law: Euthanasia)). According to Justice Barak: "The values of the State of Israel as a Jewish state are the same universal values that are common to democratic societies, which emerged from the Jewish tradition and history. These values are accompanied by the same values of the State of Israel and which spring from the democratic nature of the state. The combination and synthesis between the two are what has shaped the values of the State of Israel" (see Bibliography, A. Barak, *Ha-Mahapeikhah ha-Ḥukatit* …, p. 31). It should be noted that Justice Barak has recently attributed more weight to Jewish law in the framework of the relevant sources for interpreting the Basic Laws, and for the construction of legislation in general (see Bibliography, A. Barak, *Shofet be-Ḥevrah Demokratit*). For a detailed discussion of these Basic Laws, see entries: *Values of a Jewish and Democratic State; *Human Dignity and Freedom; *Rights, Human).

LEGISLATION CONSISTENT WITH JEWISH LAW. Many of the laws enacted in the State of Israel were inspired by the principles of Jewish law. Thus, for example, the Unjust Enrichment Law, 5739 – 1979, integrated its concepts and principles from Jewish law. The preamble to the law states: "The proposed law adopts the approach of Jewish Law in a number of respects: it entitles a person who improves another person's property to restitution, it adopts the principle that '*One* derives a *benefit* and the *other* sustains no loss as a factor in exempting the beneficiary from restitution' and it entitles a person who protects another person's property to indemnification for his expenses, with the aim of encouraging acts of rescue" (Draft Bill, 5739, p. 266 – see *Unjust Enrichment).

Another such statute is the Criminal Registry and Rehabilitation of Offenders Act, 5741 – 1981, whose name and provisions are based on the principle of Jewish law that an offender must be assisted to return to the proper and correct path, and not reminded of his previous offenses (see *Punishment).

Yet another law whose name and inspiration emanates from Jewish law is the Good Samaritan Law 5758 – 1998[5] (whose Hebrew title is taken from the biblical verse Lev 19:16, "You shalt not stand idly by the blood of thy neighbor"), which imposes a duty on any person to assist another person "in whose presence he finds himself, who is, as a result of a sudden incident, in severe and immediate danger to his life, bodily integrity or health, when he has the ability to extend assistance, without endangering himself or the other person" (section 1).

On the issue of the non-extension of the life of a terminally ill patient, the Terminally Ill Persons Act, 5766 – 2005, was enacted, in light of the Supreme Court judgment in the Shefer case, which was in turn based upon principles of Jewish law. Section 1(b) of the law expressly determines, similar to the above stated Basic Laws, that: "This Law is based on the values of the State of Israel as a Jewish and democratic state and on fundamental principles in the field of morality, ethics, and religion." (See *Medicine and Law: Euthanasia.)

The Rules of Evidence Amendment (Cautioning of Witnesses and Annulment of Oath) Law, 5740 – 1980, annulled the previously existing practices, whereby the court used to administer an oath to every witness that appeared before it, adopting instead the approach of Jewish law on this issue. The preamble to the draft bill states:

> According to Jewish Law, no person shall take an oath before giving testimony and no witness shall be sworn save in exceptional cases… It is true that we caution the witness to tell the truth… Maimonides, Yad, *Shevuot* 11:16, emphasizes the severity of the oath: "How do we intimidate him who takes the oath? [The judges] tell him: You must be aware that the entire world trembled when the Holy One blessed be He stated at Sinai: 'You shall not take the name of the Lord your God in vain' (Exod. 20:7). Moreover, for all [other] transgressions in the Torah retribution is exacted only from the violator, while here [in the case of a false oath, it is exacted] from him and from his family… Moreover, retribution is even exacted from the enemies of the Israel [i.e, a euphemism for the Jewish People as a whole], for all Jews are responsible for one another" (Draft Bill, 5740, p. 328).

According to Section 1 of the law: "Notwithstanding anything provided in any other law, a witness about to testify in any judicial or quasi judicial proceeding, shall not be sworn." In place of an oath, the law prescribes the administering of a warning, under which the witness is cautioned to tell the truth only, and is told that if he fails to do so he will be penalized in the manner prescribed by law. According to the law, the court is authorized to administer an oath to a witness if it has reasonable grounds to assume that an oath will assist in discovering the truth; notwithstanding, the witness is entitled to affirm by giving his word of honor in place of an oath – on the grounds of religion and conscience – unless the court is convinced that the witness's refusal to swear is not in good faith (see, at length, *Oath).

For numerous additional laws which are based on Jewish Law, see bibliography, M. Elon, *Ha-Mishpat ha-Ivri*, p. 1361ff.; idem, *Jewish Law* (1994), p. 1624ff.

JEWISH LAW IN THE CASE LAW OF GENERAL COURTS. The application of the principles of Jewish law to judicial decisions continues in our own time. Jewish law continues to leave its imprint in all areas of case law, as indicated in the above discussion of the Foundations of Law Act and the Basic Laws. For a detailed discussion of the principles of Jewish law in the judicial system in the State of Israel, cf. *Imprisonment. As stated, the integration of Jewish law into the Israeli legal system is of great and undisputed importance both for the benefit of Israeli law and for the benefit of the development of Jewish law itself. The best and most accessible means available to judges, attorneys, and law students is by way of judicial decisions of the various courts. It should be noted that judgments which incorporate Jewish law are now translated into the English language, and this project will contribute to the increasing accessibility of Jewish law in a great many countries. Indeed, in the course of the updates that have been made to this edition of the *Encyclopaedia Judaica*, most of the entries have been enriched by the addition of examples from case law, integrating principles of Jewish law, and these have been incorporated into the new entries. See, for example, *Majority Rule, *Legal Person, *Extradition, *Evidence, *Medicine and Law, *Slander.

Additional changes in the status of Jewish law in the State of Israel, beyond those which appear in the previous edition, shall be detailed below.

INFLUENCE OF ISRAELI LAW ON JEWISH LAW. In the relationship between Jewish law and Israeli law, there is also influence in the opposite direction, i.e., the influence of Israeli law on Jewish law. The Supreme Court first dealt with this matter in the *Wilozni* case (HC 323/81 *Wilozni v. Rabbinical Court of Appeals*, PD 36(2) 733). The petitioner requested the Court to annul the decision of the Rabbinical Court of Appeals, which ruled that the petitioner must leave the apartment in which he continued to reside alone after his wife had left it owing to the husband's violent behavior, following a judgment for divorce. According to the petitioner, the Rabbinical Court should have ruled that the apartment was regarded as property occupied by the husband, pursuant to the Tenants Protection Law (Consolidated Version), 5732 – 1972, and should therefore be sold as occupied property, and not as vacant property, as ruled by the Rabbinical Court of Appeals. The Rabbinical Court had determined that its ruling was consistent with the provisions of the above-mentioned tenant protection legislation, "which is given halakhic validity like any *sitomta* (i.e., customary practice) or *masi'in al kizatan* (i.e., communal enactment)." The Supreme Court (Justice Menachem Elon) relates to this point made by the Rabbinical Court and expands on the subject of the case law of the rabbinical courts and its tendency to adopt principles of law from the general legal system in many cases, and the various methods used for adopting such principles. The first method is based on the principle that "the law of the state is the law" (see: *Dina de-Malkhuta Dina), according to which the rabbinical courts have given effect to different kinds of legal transactions even where these would not be valid under Jewish law. When the principle of "*dina de-malkhuta dina*" is applied, a rule of the general legal system is given *binding force*, although the latter does not become part of Jewish law. Rules of other legal systems are incorporated into the Jewish legal system "by means of the legal source of custom; when the public acts in accordance with some legal norm, that norm is in certain circumstances recognized as part of the Jewish legal system, and it may be valid even if it is contrary to a particular regulation of Jewish civil law" (p. 741; see *Minhag). The second means for the absorption of the general law into Jewish law is by way of *takkanot ha-kahal* (communal enactments), according to which the community legislates, via its representatives, various enactments which become a part of Jewish law. The Talmud refers to this as "*masi'in al kizatan*" (i.e. communal enactment, lit: "the townspeople may impose penalties for breach of their enactments"; see: *Takkanot ha-Kahal). Justice Elon stresses that "there is a special, fundamental character to the relationship between the Jewish legal system and the general legal system of Israel, in accordance with the principle of *masi'in al kiẓatan*. Under this principle, various laws in the area of civil, criminal, and public law of the general legal system may actually become part and parcel of the Jewish legal system – in the broad sense of this concept – and not merely recognized by it, as was the case under the principle of *dina de-malkhuta dina*, nor simply absorbed by it, as was the case with custom" (p. 742). Justice Elon notes the uniqueness of this judgment, which ruled that the provisions of civil legislation (i.e., the Tenants Protection Law) are recognized *as part of the case law of the rabbinical courts*, not only by virtue of custom, but also under the rule of *masi'in al kiẓatan*. The implication, in this context, is that the Members of Knesset, elected by the public, who enact Knesset legislation, are capable of promulgating regulations for the benefit of the public, and that these regulations become part of Jewish law, and were even created as part of the Jewish legal system, "in the broad sense of this concept."

In addition to the aforementioned example from section 33 of the Tenants Protection Law, other laws as well have had an impact on Jewish law. Thus, for example, the arrangement in respect of cooperative houses appearing in the Land Law, 5729 – 1969, was recognized by the rabbinical courts. This, notwithstanding that this arrangement regulates the interrelationships between all the apartment owners, a subject already governed by detailed regulations in Jewish law which differ from those prescribed by the relevant sections in the Tenants Protection Law, which came to resolve a public problem of poor housing and does not contradict specific arrangements prescribed in this regard in Jewish law.

A further example is the recognition of the validity of the arrangement for the transfer of rights in land. According to section 7 of the Land Law, 5729 – 1969, *in rem* rights in immovable property are only transferred via registration in the Land Registry. By contrast, according to Jewish law such rights pass at the time of payment, and in a locale where it is conventional for property transactions to be executed solely via a written document, the rights pass under the terms of the deed. Notwithstanding this difference between Jewish law and Israeli law, many authorities have ruled, on the basis of the principle of "*dina de-malkhuta dina*" and "*minhag ha-medinah*" (custom of the state), that proprietary rights – *in rem* rights in land – pass, in general, upon their registration in the Land Registry, as prescribed by Israeli law. (On the differences between the halakhic authorities in this regard, see further the article of D. Frimer, bibliography, ad. loc.)

THE RABBINICAL COURTS. As stated earlier, the rabbinical courts must rule in accordance with Jewish law, and pursuant to the general provisions of the general law which expressly apply to them. According to Justice Aharon Barak in the *Bavli* case (HC 1000/92 *Bavli v. Rabbinical Court of Appeals*, PD 48(2) 221; see also HC 3914/92 *Lev v. Tel Aviv/Jaffa Regional Rabbinical Court*, PD 48(2) 491, Justice Aharon Barak), the rabbinical courts are also obligated to rule in accordance with the general law, *as interpreted in the rulings of the Supreme Court*, on all matters which are not related to personal status, in the narrow sense of this term. Pursuant to this principle, Justice Barak determined that the rabbinical courts are obligated to apply the "presumption of joint property," as developed by rulings of the Supreme Court, in respect of matrimonial property (see *Matrimonial Property). This approach was criticized by Justice Menachem Elon and by additional scholars, who held that no change should be made from the original law, which was that the rabbinical courts are obligated to rule in accordance with the Jewish law and in accordance with the principles of the general law that are expressly applied to them by the legislator. Elon held that the rabbinical courts must rule according to Jewish law, just as rabbinical courts have ruled in accordance with Jewish law throughout the generations. Intervention in the principle of adjudication in accordance with Jewish law is a power reserved for the legislator, after having obtained the consent of the representatives of the Jewish people, as occurred, for example, with the Women's Equal Rights Law and the Rabbinical Courts (Jurisdiction) Law. Generally, the rabbinical court is not called upon to rule according to the general law, nor is it able to do so, because its judges lack the requisite expertise. Justice Elon held that the Supreme Court's intervention in the rulings of the rabbinical courts stymies the development of Jewish law, as developed by the rabbinical courts throughout the generations, because according to this precedent the need to turn to the rabbinical courts is limited only to matters of personal status, and does not enable Jewish law to develop in other branches of law. In addition, Justice Elon held that this ruling creates needless tension between the civil courts and the rabbinical courts, who will find it difficult, and rightfully so, to accept such a broad encroachment upon their authority and freedom of action.

Regarding the presumption of joint property, Justice Elon opined that the rabbinical courts were under a duty to adopt this presumption as part of Jewish law, whether by way of regulation (see **Takkanot*) or whether by other means conventionally used in Jewish law, but not in accordance with the binding precedent of the Supreme Court (see Bibliography, M. Elon, "These Are Obiter Dicta…"). Opinions are divided among the judges of the rabbinical court as to the possibility of adopting the presumption of joint property as part of Jewish law (see *Dina de-Malkhuta Dina). With regard to a husband's right to enjoy the proceeds of his wife's usufruct property, the law has now been amended, entitling the court to take account of the wife's income from usufruct property, when determining the amount of maintenance which the husband owes to her (see *Husband and Wife).

[Menachem Elon (2nd ed.)]

BIBLIOGRAPHY: Gulak, Yesodei, 1 (1922), 3–31; 4 (1922), 3–45; S. Assaf, *Ha-Onshin Aḥarei Ḥatimat ha-Talmud* (1922); idem, *Battei ha-Din ve-Sidreihem Aḥarei Ḥatimat ha-Talmud* (1924); A.H. Freimann, in: *Lu'aḥ ha-Areẓ* (1945/46), 110–25; Ḥ. Cohen, in: *Ha-Peraklit*, 3 (1946), 38 ff.; Baron, Community; "Hebrew Law and the State of Israel: a Symposium," in: *Sura*, 3 (1957/58), 457–518; Alon, *Toledot*²; Alon, Meḥkarim; M. Silberg, *Kakh Darko shel Talmud* (1961), 66 ff.; M. Elon, *Ḥerut ha-Perat be-Darkhei Geviyyat Ḥov…* (1964), 11–14 (introd.), 255–69; idem, in: ILR, 2 (1967), 515–65; 3 (1968), 88–126; 416–57; 4 (1969), 80–140; idem, in: *Ha-Peraklit*, 25 (1968/69), 27–53; idem, *Ḥakikah Datit…* (1968); idem, *Mishpat Ivri* (Heb.; "Jewish Law, History Sources and Principles"; 1973), 3 vols. with the table of contents for the three volumes given in English at the end of Volume 1; B. Cohen, *Jewish and Roman Law*, 2 vols. (1966); J.I. England, in: ILR, 3 (1968), 254–78; Finkelstein, Middle Ages. **ADD. BIBLIOGRAPHY:** M. Elon, *Ha-Mishpat ha-Ivri*, vol. 3 (1988), index; idem, *Jewish Law*, vol. 4 (1994), index; idem, *Jewish Law (Cases and Materials)* (1999), index; idem, "These Are Obiter Dicta… Which Are Based on a False Premise, and Which Should Be Reversed," in: *Multi-Culturalism in a Jewish and Democratic State* (Heb., 1998), 361; idem, "More about the Foundations of Law Act," in: *Shenaton ha-Mishpat ha-Ivri*, 13 (1988), 227; A. Barak, "The Foundations of Law Act and the Heritage of Israel," in: *Shenaton ha-Mishpat ha-Ivri*, 13 (1988), 265 (Heb.); idem, "The Constitutional Revolution: Protected Basic Rights," in: *Mishpat u-Mimshal*, 1 (5753) 9, 30–31 (Heb.); idem, *Shofet be-Ḥevrah Demokratit* (2004), 156–58, 289–90; H. Ben Menachem, "The Foundations of Law Act, 5740 – 1980 – How Much of a Duty," in: *Shenaton ha-Mishpat ha-Ivri*, 13 (1988), 257; H.H. Cohn, "Residual Law," in: *Shenaton ha-Mishpat ha-Ivri*, 13 (1988), 285; M. Corinaldi, *Mafte'aḥ ha-Pesikah ha-Kolel be-Livvui Divrei Mavo shel Mikha'el Korinaldi*, in:

Mishpatim, 25 (5755), appendix; S. Deutsch, *"Ha-Mishpat ha-Ivri be-Pesikat Batei ha-Mishpat,"* in: *Meḥkarei Mishpat*, 6 (5748), 7; A. Edrei, *"Madu'a Lanu Mishpat Ivri?"* in: *Iyyunei Mishpat*, 25 (5762), 467; Y. Englard, *"Ma'amado shel ha-Din ha-Dati ba-Mishpat ha-Yisra'eli,"* in: *Mishpatim*, 2 (5731), 268 and 488; idem, *Mishpatim*, 4 (5732); idem, *Mishpatim*, 6 (5735), 5; D. Frimer, *"Hashpa'at ha-Mishpat ha-Ivri al ha-Misphat ha-Yisra'eli,"* in: *Mada'ei ha-Yahadut*, 39 (5759), 133; M. Hacohen, "Writings of Menachem Elon," in: *Shenaton ha-Mishpat ha-Ivri*, 13 (1988), 1; S. Lifshitz, *"Nissuin Ba'al Korḥam? Nitu'aḥ Liberali shel Mosad ha-Yedu'in be-Ẓibbur,"* in: *Iyyunei Mishpat*, 25:741; N. Rakover, *Ha-Mishpat ha-Ivri be-Ḥakikat ha-Keneset* (1988); idem, N. Rakover, *Ha-Mishpat ha-Ivri bi-Pesikat Batei ha-Mishpat be-Yisra'el* (1988); B.Z. Schereschewsky, "The Foundations of Law Act, 5740 – 1980," in: *Shenaton ha-Mishpat ha-Ivri*, 13 (1988), 379; P. Shifman, "Jewish Law in the Civil Courts Decisions of the Courts," in: *Shenaton ha-Mishpat ha-Ivri*, 13 (1988), 371; S. Shilo, "The Foundations of Law Act – Comments and Some New Light on the Foundations of Law Act," in: *Shenaton ha-Mishpat ha-Ivri*, 13 (1988), 351; E. Shochetman, *"Ha-Yesh Ḥashash Kiddushin be-Kisherei Ishut im Yedu'a be-Ẓibbur,"* in: *Meḥkarei Mishpat*, 10 (1993), 7.

MI-SINAI NIGGUNIM (Heb.-Yid. נִגּוּנִים, נִגּוּנֵי מִסִּינַי "Melodies from Mt. Sinai"), Hebrew term for a traditional group of cantorial melodies sung in the Ashkenazi synagogues of both East and West European rite and regarded as obligatory, and for which no other melody may be substituted. Located at those points in the service where the liturgical and emotional elements join in equal force, the *Mi-Sinai* tunes may be called the heart of Ashkenazi synagogue song.

Mi-Sinai is an abbreviated form of *Halakhah le-Moshe mi-Sinai, referring to an ordinance going back to Moses, who received it on Mt. Sinai. The term was connected with biblical chant in the 12th century (*Sefer Ḥasidim*, ed. Wistinezki-Freimann §3); its present application is due to A.Z. *Idelsohn. In cantorial circles, the *Mi-Sinai* melodies are called "Tunes of our Rabbi Maharil" (erroneously, also Maharal), or, in Eastern Europe, *skarbowe niggunim* (Polish: "official" tunes).

The family of *Mi-Sinai* tunes includes about ten solemn compositions that are associated mainly with prayers of the Penitential Days (see ex. 1–7). The exact scope cannot be determined precisely, since the tradition is not unanimous and was never codified authoritatively. The distinctive features of the melodies are as follows: they must belong to the common patrimony of the Eastern and Western Ashkenazi rites; must invariably be found in their proper liturgical place; and must exhibit a special musical structure (see below). Accordingly, ancient psalmodies such as **Akdamut Millin*, or the many melodies designated as "ancient" by the 19th century compilers, and well-known hymn melodies (e.g., *Eli Ẓiyyon) do not belong to this category. A close examination reveals that they do not entirely comply with the conditions, and no *ḥazzan* would count them among the *Mi-Sinai* tunes. However, there still remain some border cases which are classified differently by different writers.

The usual concept of "melody" as an indivisible unit is not applicable to the *Mi-Sinai niggunim*. They are real compositions built of several sections ("movements") of individual character. These are often fitted to the divisions of the text (e.g., the *Kaddish), but may also be constructed on an independent plan (e.g., the *Kol Nidrei tune). In general, the first section is individual and characteristic of the specific tune; the following ones may include motives or entire themes of other *niggunim*, thereby creating a "family likeness" among the members of this group. Every section contains one or more "themes," which are composed of short motives (see music examples of **Aleinu*; **Avodah*). The order of these themes is usually constant, distinguishing this music clearly from the *nusaḥ style. An important feature is the plasticity of themes and motives, which allows for their easy adaptation to a wide range of texts. Still more characteristic is the liberty granted to the performer to shape the music by himself; tradition prescribes only the approximate layout and motivic profile – an "idea" which the singer must realize in sounds. This challenge to creative improvisation recalls principles governing Oriental music and exceeds by far the freedom of embellishment in older European art. Therefore one should not expect to discover the archetype of any *Mi-Sinai* tune, for there exist only numerous "realizations" of a certain mental image (cf. *Maqām). Other Oriental features are the free rhythm, which cannot be fitted to regular bars without distortion, and the rich and fluent coloratura adorning it. Tonality is modal (today with a bias to major and minor); *Shtayger scales occur,

Mi-Sinai *tunes: inventory of initial motives. No. 2, cf.* *Amidah; *earliest notation, 1783 (Aaron Beer). No. 3, for full version see* *Music, example 30; *earliest evidence, c. 1800 (Jacob Goldstein). No. 4, cf.* *Aleinu le-Shabbe'aḥ; *earliest evidence, 1765 (A. Beer). No. 5, earliest notation, 1765 (A. Beer). No. 6, cf.* *Avodah; *earliest notation, 1791 (A. Beer). No. 7, earliest notation, 1744 (Judah Elias of Hanover). No. 8, earliest evidence, 1782 (A. Beer). Nos. 1 and 9, conventional form notated by H. Avenary.*

but are not maintained rigorously (ex. 1, no. 3; see full version in *Music, ex. 30).

In East Ashkenazi tradition, the bond between music and text has been loosened: entire sections may be sung without words. Certain themes, still found in the earlier Western notated documents, have become lost, and others changed their places in the established order. As a result those themes or sections which were preserved came to be repeated in order to provide for the full text. This regressive evolution in the East was apparently caused by the early displacement of these communities from the birthplace and centers of *Mi-Sinai* song. The Western *ḥazzanim*, on the other hand, developed extensive and elaborate compositions from the original tunes. Such "Fantasias" were in fashion from about 1750 to 1850.

That the musical ideas and outlines of the *Mi-Sinai niggunim* originated in the Middle Ages can be concluded from musical evidence, a few references in literature, and, above all, the fact that they are found in two Ashkenazi rites, which separated early in their history. It may be supposed that the sufferings during Crusader times made Ashkenazi Jewry ripe for expressing in music the deep feelings that emanate from these melodies. Their character and profound musicality also attracted gentile composers, such as Max Bruch (*Kol Nidrei*, op. 47) and Maurice Ravel (*Kaddish*, 1914); their confrontation with the idioms of contemporary music is demonstrated in A. *Schoenberg's *Kol Nidrei* (1938).

BIBLIOGRAPHY: A.Z. Idelsohn, in: *Zeitschrift fuer Musikwissenschaft*, 8 (1926), 449–72; H. Avenary, in: *Yuval*, 1 (1968), 65–85.

[Hanoch Avenary]

MISKOLC, town in N.E. Hungary. Jews attended the Miskolc fairs at the beginning of the 18th century, and the first Jewish settlers earned their livelihood from the sale of alcoholic beverages. In 1717 the municipal council sought to expel them but reconsidered its attitude in 1728 and granted them the right to sell at the market. The number of Jews gradually increased, supplanting the Greek merchants from Macedonia. In 1765 several Jews owned houses. They enjoyed judicial independence and were authorized to impose fines and corporal punishment. Early in the 19th century there were two rabbis in the community. Many Jews acquired houses and land, but the majority engaged in commerce and crafts. When the local guild excluded Jews from membership in the unions, the Jews organized their own guild. The cemetery, dating from 1759, was still in use in 1970. The first synagogue was erected in 1765. The Great Synagogue was built in 1861; it was here that a choir, which aroused violent reactions on the part of the Orthodox, appeared for the first time. In 1870 the community joined the Neologians (see *Neology), but in 1875 a single Orthodox community was formed.

The educational institutions were among the most developed and ramified throughout the country. There were three yeshivot, an elementary school, two sub-secondary schools, and the only seminary for female teachers in Hungary. The Ḥasidim established a separate elementary school. In the course of time the percentage of Jews of the general population became the highest in Hungary (around 20%), numbering 1,096 in 1840, 3,412 in 1857; 4,117 in 1880, 10,029 in 1910, and 11,300 in 1920.

Holocaust Period and After

In 1941, when there were 10,428 Jews in the town, 500 were deported to the German-occupied part of Poland for alleged irregularities in their nationality, and were murdered in *Kamenets-Podolski. Large numbers of youths, as well as elderly people, were conscripted into labor battalions and taken to the Ukrainian front, where most of them were exterminated. After the German occupation of Hungary (March 19, 1944) the Jews of the town, about 10,000 in number, were deported to *Auschwitz; only 400 of them survived.

After the liberation Miskolc became an important transit center for those who returned from the concentration camps. The elementary school was reopened and existed until the nationalization of elementary schools (1948). The reconstituted community had 2,353 members in 1946 but dropped to around 300 in the 1970s as most left for Israel.

BIBLIOGRAPHY: B. Halmay and A. Leszik, *Miskolc* (1929); *Miskolci zsidó élet*, 1 (1948); *Uj Élet*, 23 no. 7 (1968), 4; 24, no. 20 (1969), 1; E. László, in: R.L. Braham (ed.), *Hungarian Jewish Studies*, 2 (1969), 137–82.

[Laszlo Harsanyi]

MISREPHOTH-MAIM (Heb. מִשְׂרְפוֹת מַיִם), one of the farthest limits of the flight of the Canaanites after defeat by the waters of Merom (Josh. 11:8) and a boundary of the Sidonians (Josh. 13:6). Some scholars suggest reading Misrefot mi-Yam ("at the sea," i.e., on the west). It may be mentioned in the Egyptian Execration texts, dating to approximately 1800 B.C.E., as *ʾisrpʾi*, which appears beside Achsaph. Abel and others identified it with Khirbat al-Mushayrifa, near Rosh ha-Nikrah. This site was partly excavated in 1951 by Miriam Tadmor and M. Prausnitz, and remains dating to the early Bronze Age, including a wall of early Bronze II–III, and to middle Bronze Age I, were uncovered. However, the site did not yield remains of the late Bronze Age, which corresponds to the time of the biblical descriptions. Recently, Aharoni suggested that it is not the name of a city, but a definition of the border of Sidon, which may be identified with the outlet of the Litani River.

BIBLIOGRAPHY: Prausnitz, in: *Atiqot*, 1 (1955), 139ff.; Tadmor and Prausnitz, *ibid.*, 2 (1959), 72ff.; Abel, Géog, 2 (1938), 388; Aharoni, Land, index; M. Noth, *Das Buch Josua* (1938), 43.

[Michael Avi-Yonah]

MISSISSIPPI, southern state of the U.S. The 2001 Jewish population of Mississippi was 1,500 out of a total of 2,849,000, and has been in decline for several decades. Jews settled along the Gulf of Mexico from earliest times; they came via Mobile, Alabama, and New Orleans, Louisiana. There are extant records of their early presence in what is now Biloxi, on the Gulf Coast, and Natchez, on the Mississippi River. By the 1830s these com-

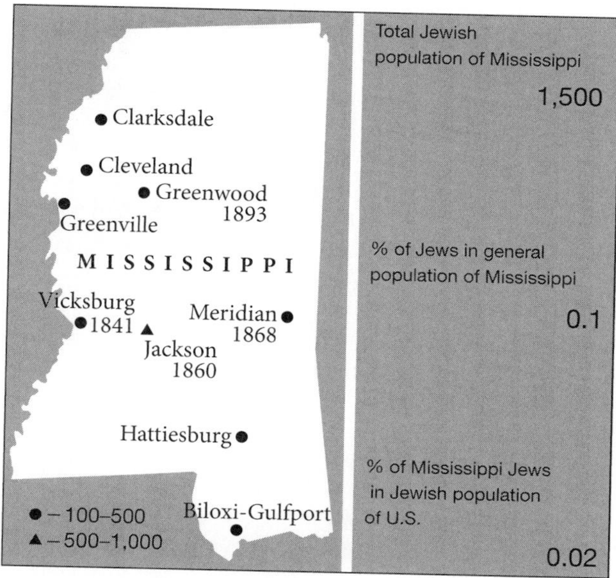

Jewish communities in Mississippi and dates of establishment. Population figures for 2001.

munities had Jewish cemeteries. High cotton prices, cheap land, and steamboat traffic stimulated population expansion, bringing a considerable number of Jews from Germany and Alsace who made a living as peddlers and small storekeepers. The first congregations formed in the state were in Natchez and Vicksburg in the early 1840s, both trading towns on the Mississippi River. Although their total number at the beginning of the Civil War (1861) is unknown, between 200 and 300 served in the Confederate armies. The later Eastern European Jewish migration increased the settlement in the state, particularly in the cotton-growing region of the Delta, where Jewish merchants settled in small towns throughout the region. In 1937, Jews lived in 46 different communities in the Mississippi Delta alone. In many of these towns, Jewish-owned stores dominated main street. The state's reforestation program and aggressive industrialization have brought in branch operations from the North, particularly in clothing and wood products. Many have absentee Jewish ownership. Since the mid-1950s there has been a steady decline in the Jewish population. The turmoil over civil rights slowed the pace of newcomers, while much of the state's Jewish youth left for higher education and did not return. The high-tech Sunbelt boom that has attracted many Jews to the South has largely passed over Mississippi. Chain store expansion into the state has led to the disappearance of family-owned enterprises and a consequent loss in Jewish numbers. The exception is Jackson, the capital city, which has become a regional center for education, law, and medicine providing employment for Jewish professionals.

Mississippi Jewish communities are synagogue oriented. Most of the Jews in isolated communities maintain membership in the nearest congregation. In 1936 the state's synagogues reported a total membership of 2,897, with six resident rabbis. In 1970 there were eight rabbis and 20 synagogue structures, several of the latter used infrequently or not at all. In 2005, there were 13 congregations, though most were small and in decline; only two, Jackson's Beth Israel and Hattiesburg's B'nai Israel, had a full-time rabbi. Despite this, the majority continued to hold regular Shabbat services with lay leaders, rabbinic students, or visiting retired rabbis. Reform congregations in the state include: Adath Israel in Cleveland; B'nai Israel, Natchez; Beth Israel, Jackson; Hebrew Union Congregation, Greenville; Beth Israel, Meridian; Anshe Chesed, Vicksburg; B'nai Israel, Columbus; B'nai Israel, Hattiesburg; and Beth El, Lexington. Unaffiliated congregations include B'nai Israel in Tupelo and Beth Shalom in Oxford. Congregation Beth Israel in Biloxi is Conservative while Ahavath Rayim in Greenwood is nominally Orthodox. The Mississippi Assembly of Jewish Congregations, founded in 1955 by the Jackson rabbi, dissolved about ten years later. Fewer than five Jews have been members of the state legislature in the 20th century, and no Jew has achieved statewide prominence in politics. Jews have had a greater impact on local politics, with 21 Jews serving as mayor of 16 different towns, including "Mayor for Life" William Sklar, who served as mayor of Louise for 25 years, and Sam Rosenthal, mayor of Rolling Fork for 40 years. Jews have held presidential offices in statewide business, professional, and welfare organizations. During the Civil Rights era, two of the state's rabbis, Charles Mantinband and Perry E. Nussbaum, achieved various degrees of prominence for their efforts on behalf of racial equality. They pioneered in the development of local and statewide organizations that sought a peaceful resolution to the civil rights struggle. Mantinband occupied Hattiesburg's B'nai Israel pulpit from 1952 to 1963, when he moved to Longview, Texas. Nussbaum served in Jackson from 1954 to 1973. He took on the unofficial role of "prison chaplain" to the "Freedom Riders" of all creeds and races by traveling to Parchman State Penitentiary each week and writing numerous letters to Northern Jewish parents letting them know that their children were okay. Nussbaum was also among the founders of the state's Committee of Concern, which raised funds to rebuild burned black churches. His newly dedicated fourth synagogue edifice was dynamited by members of the Ku Klux Klan in September 1967. Two months later his home was severely damaged by a similar device. The same group dynamited Meridian's new synagogue in May of 1968. Jews in Jackson and Meridian raised money to pay an FBI informant, who revealed a plot to bomb the home of Meyer Davidson, a prominent Jewish community leader in Meridian. After a police stakeout of Davidson's home, one of the assailants was killed while the other was captured. These bombings produced expressions of outrage from state officials and an outpouring of support for the Jewish communities of Jackson and Meridian. These attacks were a turning point of sorts as many whites came to realize that the violent tactics of "massive resistance" had gone too far. It was time for Mississippi to change, and Jews have been in the forefront in building a new integrated society.

Although they have always been a tiny minority of the state's population, Mississippi Jews have worked hard to preserve and pass on their traditions. In 1970, after years of effort, Jewish leaders of the region opened the Henry S. Jacobs Camp for Living Judaism in Utica. In 1986, camp director Macy B. Hart created the Museum of the Southern Jewish Experience, which now has branches in Utica and Natchez. In 2000, the museum became the Goldring/Woldenberg Institute of Southern Jewish Life, based in Jackson, which works to preserve and document the practice, culture, and legacy of Judaism in the South.

In August 2005 Hurricane Katrina badly damaged the Congregation Beth Israel Synagogue, two blocks from the Mississippi Gulf Coast in Biloxi. Other synagogues in Mississippi were also damaged.

BIBLIOGRAPHY: L.E. Turitz and E. Turitz, *Jews in Early Mississippi* (1983); J. Nelson, *Terror in the Night: The Klan's Campaign Against the Jews* (1993); United States, Work Projects Administration, The Mississippi Historical Records Survey Project, *Inventory of the Church and Synagogue Archives of Mississippi: Jewish Congregations and Organizations* (1940).

[Perry E. Nussbaum / Stuart Rockoff (2nd ed.)]

MISSOURI, state located in the central part of the United States. The Jewish population of Missouri in 2001 was 62,500, out of a general population of 5,603,000 with almost all Jews living in the *St. Louis (54,000) and *Kansas City (7,100 on the Missouri side) metropolitan areas. About 1,600 Jews live in at least 27 smaller towns, in eight of which there are congregations. There are communities in Columbia (400), Joplin (100), St. Joseph (265), and Springfield (300), and 12 synagogues in parts of the state other than the two major centers.

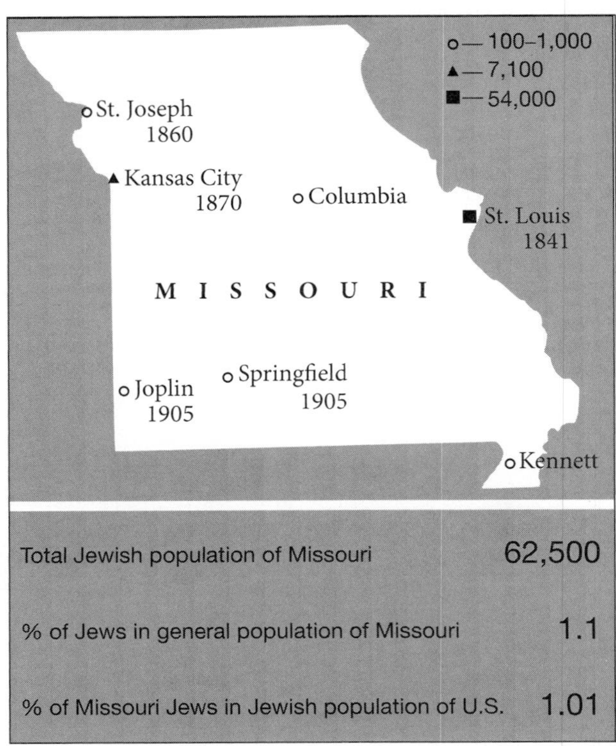

Jewish communities in Missouri and dates of establishment. Population figures for 2001.

Jews were legally admitted into the area of Missouri with the Louisiana Purchase in 1803. The first known Jewish Missourian was Ezekiel Block, a slave owner who was part of a traditionally oriented family which gradually left Schwihau, Bohemia, between 1796 and 1850. At least 23 family members settled in Troy, Perryville, and mainly Cape Girardeau, Louisiana, and St. Louis. They engaged primarily in merchandising, but one also became a lawyer and another became a mill owner and an insurance company resident. Most eventually married Christians. However, one married into the Philipson family of St. Louis, the first Jewish family in that town.

By 1837 St. Louis had a *minyan* and, although the city had less than 100 Jews, a cemetery was founded in 1840 and a congregation in 1841. By mid-century the Jewish population in St. Louis increased to between 600 and 700 due to the German immigration of 1848–53, which also led to a Jewish influx into St. Joseph and Kansas City where congregations were established in 1860 and 1870 respectively. Congregations were established in the mid-1880s in the state capital, Jefferson City, and by 1905 in both Springfield (south-central) and Joplin (southwest). By 1950 regular services were being held at University of Missouri Hillel in Columbia, Fort Leonard Wood, and in Cape Girardeau (southeast). In 1948 Eddie Jacobson, a once failed Missouri Jewish merchant, played a role – whose importance is a matter of dispute – when he approached his former partner Harry S Truman and pressed for the recognition of the State of Israel. By the early 1960s the Jews of Sedalia (west-central) had organized their own congregation. Two of the most popular organizations in outstate Missouri are B'nai B'rith and Anti-Defamation League. Washington University had a fine Judaic studies program. Steven Schwarczchild taught there for a generation and Hillel Kieval was the Gloria M. Goldstein Professor of Jewish Thought. The University of Missouri had an active Hillel program. The *St. Louis Jewish Light* was the Jewish publication for the St. Louis area. Kansas City, Missouri, was covered by the *Kansas City Jewish Chronicle*, which was based in Kansas.

BIBLIOGRAPHY: AJHSP (1914), index; D.I. Makovsky, *The Philipsons; the First Jewish Settlers in St. Louis 1807–1858* (1958); S. Bowman, *Tribute to Isidore Busch* (1920).

[Donald J. Makovsky]

MISTAKE. A legal transaction requires that the "making up of the mind" (or the conclusive intention of the parties to close the bargain – *gemirat ha-da'at*) be demonstrated (see *Acquisition, Modes of). When it is apparent that one of the parties lacked such conclusive intention, the transaction may be voided, but only at the instance of that party. One of the factors showing that the required conclusive intention was missing is mistake, whether caused by the mistaken party himself or by the other party, whether willfully or unintentionally or whether relating to the subject matter of the transaction, its price, or any other aspect of the transaction. In all these cases the mistaken party is allowed to withdraw from the transaction, provided that the mistake is outwardly and objectively revealed, and not of a subjective nature only, even if it can be proved.

The contracts of *sale and *marriage exemplify the rules of mistake in Jewish law. An error as to price is generally termed *ona'ah* (overreaching), but when relating to the subject matter or any other aspect of the transaction it is termed *mikkaḥ ta'ut* (mistake). If the mistake is common to both parties the contract is voidable at the instance of either of them, otherwise it is voidable only at the instance of the mistaken party (Maim., Yad, Mekhirah 17:1–2). If however the latter consented to the transaction as actually carried out, such consent being demonstrated by him either explicitly or by his subsequent use of the subject matter of the transaction with knowledge of the mistake (*ibid.* 15:3), he may not withdraw from the transaction, even though it does not accord with his original intention. Since the test for mistake is an objective one, the transaction will be voidable only if the majority of those of a particular place and time would consider it material, so that one would generally be expected to refuse to accept the property sold if the true position were made known (*ibid.* 15:5). Thus, if bad wheat is sold as good, i.e., a mistake as to quality, the purchaser may withdraw. Similarly the seller may withdraw if he purported to sell bad wheat, which is in fact found to be good. If the mistake concerns the nature of the object sold, e.g., when a person sells dark-colored wheat which is found to be white, or olive wood that turns out to be sycamore, both parties may withdraw since this is not what was agreed upon (*ibid.* 17:1–2). Similarly the discovery of a defect in the property sold entitles the purchaser to void the transaction, provided that he has not waived such right by his interim use of the property (*ibid.* 15:3). The purchaser retains the right even if the seller mentioned the defect at the time the transaction was negotiated, but did so in a manner that would not normally be taken as revealing the true existence of the defect. An example of this kind of mistake would be if the seller declares, "this cow is blind, lame, given to biting, and to lying down under a load," and it is found to have one or other of these latter two defects but is neither blind nor lame, since the purchaser naturally assumed that the latter defects were as nonexistent as the two former ones (*ibid.* 15:7–8).

[Shalom Albeck]

Unexpressed Intentions

The Talmud determines that for non-conformity with the parties' intentions to be regarded as a mistake, there must be an expression and disclosure of the intention; it is not sufficient for the error to arise as a result of unspoken intentions. The rule formulated by the *amoraim* was that: "*devarim she-ba-lev einam devarim*" (lit: "words of the heart" [unexpressed words], are not words" (Kid. 49b). The rationale for this rule is that when the mistake is the consequence of the person's misleading himself, by keeping his thoughts to himself and not sharing them with the other party, the misunderstanding is not considered a mistake (*Tosafot Rif ha-Zaken*, ad loc.). However, there is a category of facts that need not be expressed, where one can presume that the parties understood each other (*umdana mukhaḥat* = presumption of common sense; see: *Evidence; *Ḥazakah). In reliance on this principle, the court can determine which facts can be presumed [even when unexpressed], because they constitute "information known and understood by everyone" (Ran on Rif, Kid. 20b [Comm. on Rif]; Tos., Kid. 49b).

Mistake in Motivation for Performing Transaction

The Babylonian Talmud (Ket. 97a) records a discussion between *amoraim* concerning a person with a specific motive for a particular sale, and who after its completion found out that the grounds for his motivation did not exist. Can this person, under these circumstances, annul the sale? The Talmud concludes that he can: "If a man sold [a plot of land] and [on concluding the sale] was no longer in need of money the sale may be withdrawn." Nonetheless, according to halakhic rulings, this case of mistake, based on an unproven motive, is governed by the same rule that governs all other cases of mistake: namely that the transaction can only be voided if the seller formally stipulated that the transaction was conditional. Absent such an express stipulation, the seller's intention would be considered unexpressed, as explained above (Rif, Ket. 56a; Yad, Mekhirah 11:8).

Deceit

An error by one party caused by or under the influence of another constitutes deceit. If this deceit is intentional, it constitutes a fraud or *onaah* (see *Ona'ah; *Fraud; *Theft and Robbery). Such a deceit is considered a transgression of the biblical prohibition: "When you make a sale to your fellow or make a purchase from the hand of your fellow, you shall not wrong one another" (Lev. 25:14). This prohibition does not only refer to fraud regarding the value of a sale, but also to any form of swindle as proscribed by the Torah (R. Moses di Trani, *Kiryat Sefer*, Mekhirah, 18). There is yet another explicit prohibition regarding deceiving a purchaser in weights and measures: "You shall do no unrighteousness in judgment, in measure of length, weight, or volume. You shall have just scales, just weights, just dry measures, and just liquid measures" (Lev. 19:35–36); and: "You shall not have in your house diverse weights and measures, a great and a small… For an abomination to the Lord your God are all who do such things, all who act corruptly" (Deut. 25:13–16). Talmudic literature extends this ruling of the prohibition of willfully defrauding others with weights and measures, to include the merchant's duty to ensure that his weights and measures are accurate. Thus, the Mishnah states (BB 88a) that weights and measure must be regularly cleaned from the residue that tends to settle and congeal therein, and the Talmud states that weights must not be made of materials which corrode and wear away (*ibid.* 89b).

The validity of a fraudulent sale is the same as that of a mistaken sale, and as in the case of an intentional deceit, the sale may be rescinded, as explained above.

The laws of marriage provide an example of deceit which can result in the annulment of the transaction. The Rashba rules that where a person betrothed a woman using a cup (see *Marriage), but told her: "You are betrothed to me with this ring," and she accepted the cup, without noticing the object being handed to her – she is not betrothed, because he misled her, and even if the cup was worth more than the ring (Resp. Rashba, vol. 3, no. 1186).

A person causing deceit, including deceit by failure to disclose, e.g., the seller's silence when he knows that the buyer is making a mistake in a particular transaction (because the sale involves a defective item which was unnoticed by the buyer), is obligated to compensate the buyer. The Babylonian Talmud (BB 93b) records a dispute concerning a person who sold garden seeds that did not grow. In such a case, is the seller required to reimburse the buyer for the seeds alone, or also for the buyer's expenses incurred during the unsuccessful planting, such as plowing expenses, hiring laborers to sow the field, etc. (Rashbam, ad loc.)? The particular talmudic passage deals with a case where the seller was not aware that the seeds were defective. Yet, if the seller had been aware that they were defective and unable to sprout, the Talmud rules that he is also required to pay the buyer's expenses. Thus, the Tur (ḤM 232:20) cites the Rema's ruling that: "One who purchases an item which is defective… if the seller knew of the defect he is even obligated to pay the expenses the buyer incurred, because of the law of *garmi*" (see *Gerama and Garme); and the Shulḥan Arukh rules accordingly (ḤM 232:21).

Remedies Not Involving Rescission of Transaction

When the defect (mistake) can be repaired or compensated for, the deceived party can only recover the cost of the repair or addition but not cancel the agreement. In the Babylonian Talmud, the *amora*, Rava, rules that: "anything sold by measure, weight, or number… is returnable" (Kid. 42b). Maimonides rules as follows: "If a person sells a specific measure, weight, or number, and made an error, the aggrieved party may always void the sale … For example, if someone sold nuts at the rate of 100 nuts per dinar, and there were only 99 nuts, the sale is binding and even many years later the amount overcharged must be returned, … because the transaction was made in error…" (Yad, Mekhirah 15:1–2). Commenting on these words, the *Maggid Mishneh* cites Ri Migash's ruling – that such a sale is valid and not void, and the seller must merely compensate the buyer for the exact sum he paid. This ruling applies even when the margin of error is more than a sixth of the real value, the sale is still binding and the seller need only make good on the discrepancy. The law of *ona'ah* does not apply in this case because *ona'ah* only applies when the deceit relates to the essence of the intrinsic value and not to the quantities – their weight, size, or number (ad loc.).

Mistake in Knowledge of the Law

Where a person performs a legal act relying on a legal presumption stemming from his misunderstanding of the law, as in any case of a mistake, his act is revocable. This emerges from the opinion of the Sages cited in a *baraita* (Arakhin 5a), that states that a person who vows to give the fixed value of an infant less than a month old – for whom the Torah does not assign any value at all – "has said nothing" (i.e., the vow is meaningless). The Talmud clarifies that since his vow stems from an ignorance of the law there are no practical ramifications to the undertaking he assumed as a consequence of his mistake. This is in contrast with an act of waiver (see *Meḥilah) where a person's act is based on his misunderstanding of the law. Regarding a mistaken waiver the halakhic authorities are divided. Many contend that a mistaken waiver should be considered valid. This was the ruling when a minor gave land as a gift – an act which has no legal effect, i.e., since the one giving the gift is a minor, the gift is revoked and the land returned to the minor. The purchaser need not pay for usufruct he has enjoyed from the property, because by giving it, the minor waived his right thereto, in his belief that he had given the land. Notwithstanding that this waiver originates in a mistake in the knowledge of the law – it is nonetheless regarded a valid waiver (Resp. attributed to Naḥmanides, no. 2; Rashi, BM 66b; Resp. Rivash, 375). In contrast, other halakhic authorities rule that such a waiver, just like any other legal act which is invalid if performed as a result of a mistake of law, is not regarded as a waiver and has the status of any other legal act which is invalid if performed as a result of a mistake of law (*Maḥaneh Efrayim*, Zekhiyah, 35; *Shevut Ya'akov*, vol. 3, no. 173).

Errors in Formulation and Drafting of Documents and Regulations

The resolution of contradictions between an earlier part and a later part of the same deed is governed by two legal rules. The first – "one is always to be guided by the lower entry" (Mish., BB 10:2; Yad, Malveh ve-Loveh 27:14; Sh. Ar., ḤM 42:5) – determines that whatever appears at the end of the document is decisive and in cases of contradiction represents a retraction of what was previously stated in the document. Concurrently, when the application of this rule is not feasible, because it is obvious that what is stated at the end of the document is a mistake, and not a retraction, the guiding rule is that "holder of the deed is always at a disadvantage (i.e., weaker)" (Ket. 83b; Yad, Malveh ve-Loveh 27:16). Similarly, if the "mistake" indicates that the undertaking party misunderstood the law, here, too, as detailed above, the rule that "holder of a deed is always at a disadvantage" applies (Resp. Maharik, no. 94).

Similarly, when a mistake is found in the wording of a communal regulation (see *Takkanot ha-Kahal), manifesting itself in contradictory provisions concerning the manner in which public money is to be administered, the Rashba ruled that the latter sum is binding; this presumes that the latter sum constituted a retraction of the former sum (Resp. Rashba, vol. 3, no. 386). In another case of mistaken phraseology in a regulation affecting debts between two people, the Rashba ruled that "the claimant has the lower hand." This ruling relied both on the rule which states that "the burden of proof rests on the claimant" as well as on the fact that the regulation goes beyond the requirements of the law, and therefore in the case of doubt, the existing law is followed, and not the regulation (Resp. Rashba, vol. 3, no. 397). In yet another case the Rashba addressed the issue of an alleged error in the drafting of a regulation. The question was one of interpretation of a communal enactment concerning taxes, the objective of which was to enable a more extensive collection of taxes from the population. However, the wording of the enactment created a situation in which a particular citizen paid *less* than what he would have paid prior to the enactment. The community argued that the enactment should be interpreted in terms of its objective, i.e., its intent, even if this absolutely contradicts its explicit wording. The Rashba rejected their claim, ruling that the community's claims were unexpressed intentions and as such had no legal weight (lit. "words in the heart are not words"); thus, the clear language of the enactment was binding (Resp. Rashba, vol. 5, no. 282).

For a detailed discussion on this topic, see *Interpretation.

Customs Based on a Mistaken Premise

(See **Minhag*, for the essence of a custom, the manner of its acceptance, and its validity.) As early as mishnaic times, cases are recorded where it became apparent that a particular custom was based on a mistaken premise, and the custom was then annulled. The Mishnah describes a particular custom involving a matter concerning the Sabbath laws practiced in a synagogue in Tiberias, "until Rabban Gamaliel came with the Elders and forbade them to do so" (Er. 10:10). According to the explanation of *Tosafot* (Er. 101b), the reason for annulling the custom was that it was based on a mistaken premise. Elsewhere in the Talmud (Ḥul. 6b–7a), R. Judah ha-Nasi annulled the custom of separating tithes on fruits and vegetables grown in Beth She'an, after it became apparent to him – on the basis of testimony concerning R. Meir's practice to eat even untithed fruits grown in that area – that Beth She'an had not been conquered by the Jews who returned from the Babylonian exile and was not sanctified by Ezra, such that the origin of the custom was based on a mistaken premise.

In the third generation of *amoraim* of the Land of Israel, R. Avin set out a clear general ruling regarding the possibility of canceling a custom which is the result of a mistake of fact. According to this ruling, if a stringent custom – a prohibition – had been enacted despite the clear knowledge that by "the letter of the law" the matter is permitted, the custom is valid, and may not be annulled. However, if the origin of the custom is based on a mistaken premise, then once the mistake is discovered, the custom should be annulled and the prohibition undone (TJ, Pes. 4:1; 30:4).

In the post-talmudic period, the authorities discussed at length the annulment of a custom which originated in a mistake of fact. In certain cases, in addition to the sharp attacks against customs that are referred to as "foolish customs," if investigation into a custom's roots indicates its mistaken premise, even if the custom was extremely widespread it was annulled, and if "this is not a custom which ought to be relied upon in matters involving financial outlay… the custom is a mistake and needs to be cancelled" (Resp. Rosh 55:10).

The Law in the State of Israel

The Contracts (General Part) Law, 5733 – 1973, contains provisions concerning mistake and deceit. Section 14 provides that a party may rescind a contract which was entered into in consequence of a mistake, whether of fact or of law, when it may be assumed that – but for the mistake – he would not have entered into the contract, and the other party knew or should have known this. When the other party did not know or need not have known this, the court may exercise its discretion. As in Jewish law, if the contract can be maintained by rectifying the mistake, provided the other party is prepared to rectify the mistake, then this course should be followed.

Section 15 establishes that in a case of deceit, the contract may be rescinded, even if the deceit includes the non-disclosure of facts which the other party – by law, custom, or circumstances – should have disclosed.

The law emphasizes that a mistake as to the worthwhileness of a transaction does not constitute grounds for rescission of the contract.

[Menachem Elon (2nd ed.)]

BIBLIOGRAPHY: Gulak, Yesodei, 1 (1922), 63f.; 2 (1922), 156; Herzog, Instit, 2 (1939), 116–29. **ADD. BIBLIOGRAPHY:** M. Elon, *Ha-Mishpat ha-Ivri* (1988), 1:233, 359, 361, 373, 378, 383, 386, 498, 573, 647, 723, 727, 730, 760f., 774, 801f.; 2:978; 3:1381; idem, *Jewish Law* (1994), 1:263, 433f., 436, 452, 458, 464, 468; 2:607, 706, 801, 892, 896, 901, 936f., 952, 982f.; 3:1182; 4:1645; M. Elon and B. Lifshitz, *Mafte'aḥ ha-She'elot ve-ha-Teshuvot shel Ḥakhmei Sefarad u-Ẓefon Afrikah* (legal digest) (1986), 1:119; B. Lifshitz and E. Shochetman, *Mafte'aḥ ha-She'elot ve-ha-Teshuvot shel Ḥakhmei Ashkenaz, Ẓarefat ve-Italyah* (legal digest) (1997), 78; S. Warhaftig, *Dinei Ḥozim be-Mishpat ha-Ivri* (5734), 53–116; I. Warhaftig, "*'Devarim she-ba-Lev' ve-Ta'ut*," in: *Dinei Yisrael*, 3 (5732), 191–206; idem, "*Haganat ha-Ẓarkhan le-Or ha-Halakhah (Mekaḥ Ta'ut u-Geneivat Da'at)*," in: *Teḥumin*, 3 (5742), 335–82.

MITCHELL, YVONNE (1925–1979), British actress and writer. Born in London, Yvonne Mitchell made her adult debut in 1944 in *Cradle Song*, and subsequently acted in Shakespeare, Ibsen, Shaw, Turgenev, and Pirandello. Her own play, *The Same Sky*, won the Festival of Britain Prize in 1950. She made her New York debut in *The Wall* in 1960. Mitchell appeared in 11 films between 1949 and 1976, winning the BAFTA Best Actress award in 1955 for her role in *The Divided Heart*. Her best-known film was probably *Woman in a Dressing-Gown* (1963). Her novels include *A Year in Time* (1964) and *The Family* (1967).

MITHREDATH (Heb. מִתְרְדָת; LXX, **Mithradates**), a popular Persian name meaning "Given by Mithra," and borne by kings of Parthia and Pontus and a king of Armenia. The name Mithredath occurs in the Elephantine papyri (Cowley, Aramaic, 26:2, 7; E.G. Kraeling, *The Brooklyn Museum Aramaic Papyri* (1953), 3:23b) and designates two individuals in the Bible. One is the treasurer whom Cyrus ordered to deliver the Temple vessels to Sheshbazzar, for return to Jerusalem (Ezra 1:8). The other is an official who apparently wrote a letter to Artaxerxes I against Jerusalem (Ezra 4:7).

BIBLIOGRAPHY: R.A. Bowman, in: *The Interpreter's Bible*, 3 (1954), 574, 598–9; J.M. Myers, *Ezra-Nehemiah* (1965, Anchor Bible), 9, 32ff.

[Bezalel Porten]

MITHRIDATES, FLAVIUS, sobriquet of a 15th-century humanist and Orientalist (apparently Samuel b. Nissim Bulfarag) of Caltabellotta, Sicily. He became converted to Christianity around 1466, taking the name Guglielmo Raimondo de Moncada, probably conferred by Guglielmo Raimondo Moncada Esfanoller, count of Adernò, who may have acted as godfather at his baptism. He is also referred to as Guglielmus Siculus ("the Sicilian"). After his conversion, he studied at the University of Catania where he learned Latin. He later stayed for a time in Messina. In 1470 he left Sicily to study at the University of Naples. He had the financial support of several Sicilian cities and several private persons who financed his studies, which shows that he must have enjoyed the patronage of influential figures in Sicily. Between 1476 and 1478, he acquired ecclesiastical benefices in several Sicilian cities. In 1477 he was accused of heresy but he was able to refute the accusations. Notarial acts preserved in Sicily in the archives of Sciacca and Caltabellotta show that he maintained his connections with the Jews of Caltabellotta but Mithridates' attitudes toward his former coreligionists were for the most part antagonistic. While at the court of King John II of Aragon, around 1474, he took part in religious disputations with Jews and was praised for converting some of them to Christianity. Later in his life he disputed with Jewish scholars in Florence. In 1474 he appealed to Pope Sixtus IV to be granted the legacy left by the Jew Salomone Anello of Agrigento for the foundation and maintenance of a Jewish school confiscated and used to further the Christian faith rather than Judaism. The heirs of Anello contested the decision to close the school, and the litigation continued for several years, until a kind of compromise was reached and the Jews of Agrigento were ordered to provide Moncada/Mithridates with a house in Palermo instead of the school building in their city. Around 1478 he moved to Rome and came under the patronage of Giovanni Battista Cibo, bishop of Molfetta, later Pope Innocent VIII, and became a lecturer in theology at the Sapienza in Rome. In 1481, on Good Friday, he preached a sermon before Pope Sixtus IV and the College of Cardinals on the sufferings of Jesus (*Sermo de Passione Domini*, ed. by H. Wirszubski, 1963), offering Christological interpretations of Jewish texts. Wirszubski demonstrated that in his sermon he relied extensively on the *Pugio Fidei* ("Dagger of Faith"), the polemical work of the Dominican Raymundus Martini, without, however, giving credit to his source. Toward the end of his discourse, Mithridates quoted so-called secret Jewish doctrines, some of them outright forgeries, fabricated from rephrasings of rabbinical sayings. In 1483 Mithridates was accused of committing a serious offense (unspecified) and as a consequence was deprived of all benefices and forced to flee Rome. The offense could have been of a sexual nature, as in his writings Mithridates is very explicit about his homosexuality, including his relationship with a young boy, Lancilotto de Faenza.

Mithridates taught Arabic, Hebrew, and Aramaic in Italy, France, and Germany and was one of the teachers of the humanist, Giovanni *Pico della Mirandola. He translated works from Arabic, Hebrew, and Greek into Latin, including parts of the Koran for Federigo da Montefeltro, duke of Urbino, intending also to translate it into Hebrew and Syriac. For Pico he translated Menahem *Recanati's commentary on the Torah, *Levi b. Gershom's commentary on the Song of Songs, a treatise on resurrection by Maimonides, and a number of kabbalistic works, among them *Sitrei Torah* and *Sefer Ge'ulah* (translated into Latin as *Liber Redemptionis*) both by Abraham Abulafia, *Nefesh ha-Hakamah* by Moses de Leon and *Ha-Yeri'ah ha-Gedolah*, a 14th-century kabbalistic text by an unknown author. According to Giulio Busi in *The Great Parchment*, Mithridates proved to be a skilled translator, able to grasp the subtlest nuances of mystical speculations. The translations also serve as a valuable historical source as Mithridates often added his personal remarks that allude to contemporary events and figures, mostly regarding Pico himself and Mithridates' former patron, Giovanni Battista Cibo (by then Pope Innocent VIII), and the late Pope Sixtus IV. The translations also provide some biographical notes on the personality of their author such as his Hebrew name (Samuel), his homosexuality, and his personal relationship with Pico.

Mithridates' influence and his contribution to Renaissance culture went well beyond that of a skilled translator. Pico used some of his translations for writing his *900 Theses*, which had a wide impact on Renaissance thought. He also had a crucial role in the spread of Christian Kabbalah.

BIBLIOGRAPHY: Starrabba, in: *Archivio Storico Siciliano*, 2 (1878), 15–19; Secret, in: REJ, 106 (1957), 96–102; idem, *Les Kabbalistes Chrétiens de la Renaissance* (1964), index; Wirszubski, in: *Sefer Yovel. Y. Baer* (1960), 191–206; Cassuto, in: ZGJD, 5 (1934), 230–6; Baron, Social2, 13 (1969), 174–5, 401–2. **ADD. BIBLIOGRAPHY:** Ch. Wirszubski, *Sermo de Passione Domini* (1963); idem, *Pico della Mirandola's Encounter with Jewish Mysticism* (1989); idem, "Liber Redemptionis. An Early Version of Rabbi Abraham Abulafia's Kabbalistic Commentary on the Guide to the Perplexed," in: *Proceedings of the Israel Academy of Sciences*, 3:8 (1969), 135–49; S. Simonsohn, "Some Well-known Jewish Converts during the Renaissance," in: REJ, 148 (1989), 17–52; idem, "Giovanni Pico della Mirandola on Jews and Judaism," in: J. Cohen (ed.), *From Witness to Witchraft: Jews and Judaism in Medieval Christian Thought* (1996), 402–17; S. Campanini, "Pici Mirandulensis bibliotheca cabbalistica Latina," in: *Materia Ju-*

daica, 7:1 (2002), 90–95; *The Great Parchment: Flavius Mithridates' Latin Translation, the Hebrew Text, and an English Version*, eds. G. Busi et al. (2004); S. Simonsohn, *The Jews in Sicily*, 6 (2004), index; A. Scandaliato, "Le radici familiari e culturali di Guglielmo Raimondo Moncada. Ebreo convertito del rinascimento nell'isola dello specchio," in: *Una manna buona per Mantova. Studi in onore di Vittorio Colorni* (2004), 203–40.

[Menachem E. Artom / Nadia Zeldes (2nd ed.)]

MITIN, MARK BORISOVICH (1901–1987), Russian ideologist. Born in Zhitomir, he joined the Communist Party in 1919. Educated in Moscow, he held executive positions at the Krupskaya Communist Academy of Pedagogical Sciences, a training school for party theoreticians. At the same time he worked in the Institute of Philosophy of the U.S.S.R. Academy of Sciences. In 1939, he became director of the Marx-Engels-Lenin-Stalin Institute, and five years later he assumed the position of chief of the philosophy department of the Central Committee's higher party school. For his services to the party, Mitin was awarded two Orders of Lenin, two Orders of the Red Banner of Labor, and the Stalin Prize in 1949. Between 1939 and 1961, he served as a member of the Party Central Committee, one of the few Jews permitted to occupy such a high party post. Never deviating from Stalinism, and taking an active part in the anti-Jewish campaign during the "*Doctor's Plot," etc., Mitin's philosophical and historical books included *Dialekticheskiy i istoricheskiy materializm* (1934); *Istoricheskaya rol G.V. Plekhanova v russkom i mezhdunarodnom rabochem dvizhenii* (1957); *Filosofiya i sovremennost* (1960). He was coeditor of the massive five-volume *Istoriya filosofii* (1957–61), and was editor of the journal *Voprosy filosofii*.

[William Korey]

MITNAGGEDIM (Heb. מִתְנַגְּדִים; sing. *Mitnagged*; lit. "opponents"), a designation for the opponents of the *Ḥasidim. The name originally arose from the bitter opposition evinced to the rise, way of life, and leadership of the ḥasidic movement founded by *Israel b. Eliezer Ba'al Shem Tov, but in the course of time lost its connotation of actual strife, and became a positive description, representative of a way of life. Since it was the personality and genius of *Elijah b. Solomon Zalman the Gaon of Vilna (1720–1797) which gave the powerful impetus to the rise of the *Mitnaggedim*, this way of life became especially characteristic of Lithuanian Jewry (except for the Lithuanian Ḥasidim, particularly the *Karlin dynasty and the Ḥabad trend). His iron will and intellectual perseverance shaped, through an elect circle of pupils, both adamant opposition to Ḥasidism, as well as the patterning of institutions, tendencies of thought and expression, and a way of life which formed a specific culture. One of its characteristics, which derived from the opposition to the charismatic, miracleworking leadership of the ḥasidic rabbis, was a pronounced skepticism and a severe criticism of credulity and authoritarianism. After the death of Elijah the Gaon of Vilna the struggle between the Ḥasidim and the *Mitnaggedim* assumed even more bitter proportions than during his lifetime, with mutual recrimination, but by the second half of the 19th century the hostility began to subside. One of the causes of the cessation of hostilities was the common front which both formed against the Haskalah. The main differences between them today are in matters of rite, the Ḥasidim having adopted the prayer book of Isaac Luria (largely the Sephardi *minhag*), while the *Mitnaggedim* retained the Polish form of the Ashkenazi *minhag*, and in the greater stress laid by the *Mitnaggedim* on study of the Talmud, while the Ḥasidim emphasize the emotional side of Judaism. There are large groups of *Mitnaggedim*, most of Lithuanian origin, in the State of Israel, the United States, England, and South Africa. The term *Mitnagged*, however, is not confined to Jews of Lithuanian origin.

BIBLIOGRAPHY: M. Wilensky, *Ḥasidim u-Mitnaggedim* (1970).

MITTWOCH, EUGEN (1876–1942), German Orientalist. Born in Schrimm, Prussian province of Posen (now Poland), Mittwoch originally intended to be a rabbi and studied at the Rabbinical Seminary in Berlin. He made his first journey to the East with Moritz Sobernheim and thus became familiar with Palestine and the culture of the Near East. He returned to the Orient with Paul *Nathan in 1907 and helped him set up the *Hilfsverein's school system in Palestine. Mittwoch himself was one of the first German Jews to speak modern Hebrew. He taught at the University of Berlin (1915–16) and at the University of Greifswald (1917) and returned to Berlin in 1919 to serve as a professor at the Seminary for Oriental Languages, of which he became director in 1920. During World War I he was head of the Nachrichtenstelle fuer den Orient, which propagated pro-German feelings in the countries of the Near East. In 1933, having been dismissed from his position by the Nazis, Mittwoch first directed the office of the Joint Distribution Committee in Berlin and in 1939 moved to England, where he assisted the Ministry of Information on Arabian and Persian problems. Between 1910 and 1930 Mittwoch was active in educating young Falashas (Beta *Israel), and was a prominent member of the Hilfsverein der deutschen Juden. He also cooperated in the Jewish World Relief Conference and was a representative at HICEM (a relief organization) from its inception. He was the last president of the council of the Gesellschaft zur Foerderung der Wissenschaft des Judentums and transferred the scholarly material from its office to England in 1938. He served on the executive of the Zentralverein deutscher Staatsbuerger juedischen Glaubens, immigrated to London and died there in 1942.

Mittwoch's special scholarly interest was in the study of classical and modern Arabic as well as Ethiopian dialects and literature, such as *Die traditionelle Aussprache des Aethiopischen* (1926). In his *Zur Entstehungsgeschichte des islamischen Gebets und Kultus* (1913) he illustrated the influence of Jewish prayer and liturgy on Islam. He also contributed to Hebrew epigraphy as well as to that of South Arabian, Himyaritic, and Sabean inscriptions. Among his other works is *Die arabischen Lehrbuecher der Augenheilkunde* (with J. Hirschberg and J. Lippert, 1905). Mittwoch also wrote about Islamic art and modern Islamic politics. He was a coeditor of the jubilee edition of the works of Moses Mendelssohn (seven vols., 1929–38). In 1937 the Gesellschaft presented him with a *Festschrift* (see bibliography).

BIBLIOGRAPHY: I. Elbogen, *Eugen Mittwoch, zum 60. Geburtstag* (1937), 186–93, incl. bibl. (= MGWJ, 81 (1937), 243–50. **ADD. BIBLIOGRAPHY:** W. Gottschalk, *Die Schriften Eugen Mittwochs* (1937).

[Bjoern Siegel (2nd ed.)]

MITZVAH (Heb. מִצְוָה), a commandment, precept, or religious duty. The term is derived from the Hebrew root צוה which means "to command" or "to ordain." In common usage, *mitzvah* has taken on the meaning of a good deed. Already in the Talmud, this word was used for a meritorious act as distinct from a positive commandment. The rabbis for instance declared it "a *mitzvah* to hearken to the words of the sages" (Ḥul. 106a; cf. Git. 15a). Although many different terms such as *ḥukkah* ("statute," Ex. 27:21), *mishpat* ("ordinance," Deut. 4:5), *edut* ("testimony," Deut. 4:45), *mishmeret* ("observance," Lev. 8:35), and *torah* ("teaching," Ex. 16:28) are mentioned in the Pentateuch to indicate laws, only the word *mitzvah* is generally used to include all its commandments. There are traditionally 613 biblical *Commandments which are divided into 248 positive mandates and 365 prohibitions. With the increased ritual obligations imposed by the rabbis, the *mitzvot* were also separated into two main categories: *mitzvot de-oraita*, the biblical commandments, and *mitzvot de-rabbanan*, the rabbinic commandments (Pes. 10a; Suk. 44a). There are also instances when the *mitzvot* were classified as *mitzvot kallot*, less important *mitzvot*, and *mitzvot ḥamurot*, more important *mitzvot* (e.g., Ḥul. 12:5; Yev. 47b; Av. Zar. 3a). Nevertheless, the rabbis exhorted the people to be mindful of all the *mitzvot*, both light and grave, since the reward for the fulfillment of each precept is not known to man (Avot 2:1). The *mitzvot* were further divided into *sikhliyyot* (rational) and *shimiyyot* (revealed) by medieval Jewish philosophers (see *Commandments, Reasons for). Other distinctions have also been made, such as commandments performed with the external limbs of the body and those by the heart; commandments regulating conduct between man and his Maker and between man and his fellows; and commandments applicable only to Ereẓ Israel and those not dependent upon Ereẓ Israel. Responsibility for the *mitzvot* is formally assumed by boys at the age of 13 plus one day, and by girls at 12 plus one day (see *Bar Mitzvah, Bat Mitzvah, and *Puberty). Women are exempt from all affirmative precepts contingent upon a particular time or season, although the Talmud also makes those of the Sabbath, Ḥanukkah, Purim, and Passover obligatory on them. All negative precepts, whether limited to a certain time or not, are binding upon both men and women (Kid. 1:7). The performance of most *mitzvot* is preceded by a *benediction which is usually worded: "Who has sanctified us by His commandments and commanded us to…" The omission of the benediction, however, does not invalidate the performance of the *mitzvah*. The opposite of *mitzvah* is *averah, a transgression. A "precept fulfilled through a transgression" is considered as an *averah*, e.g., one does not discharge his obligation through a stolen *lulav* (Suk. 30a; see *Four Species). Although *mitzvot* were not meant to provide material enjoyment (RH 28a), and the final reward for their performance is in the hereafter (Kid. 39b), true joy and sanctity can be attained only through their observance (Shab. 30b; Sifra 9:2). Man should not anticipate any material recompense for performing the *mitzvot*, but one *mitzvah* brings another in its train (Avot 1:3; 4:2). "God desired to make Israel worthy, therefore He enlarged the Law and multiplied its *mitzvot*" (Mak. 3:16).

BIBLIOGRAPHY: M. Steckelmacher, in: *Festschrift… A. Schwartz* (1917), 259–68; J.M. Guttmann, in: *Bericht des juedisch-theologischen Seminars Fraenckel'scher Stiftung fuer das Jahr 1927* (1928); idem, *Beḥinat Kiyyum ha-Mitzvot*, in: *Bericht… 1930* (1931); J. Heinemann, *Ta'amei ha-Mitzvot be-Sifrut Yisrael*, 1 (1954³), 22–35; Alon, Meḥkarim, 2 (1958), 111–9; E.E. Urbach, *Ḥazal – Pirkei Emunot re-De'ot* (1967), 279–347.

[Aaron Rothkoff]

MIVḤAR HA-PENINIM (Heb. "A Choice of Pearls"), an ethical work consisting of a collection of epigrams, usually attributed to Solomon b. Judah ibn *Gabirol. It was believed that Gabirol made the collection in preparation for composing his small ethical work, *Tikkun Middot ha-Nefesh*. *Mivḥar ha-Peninim* (Soncino, 1484) is undoubtedly a translation from the Arabic; the material included in it was taken from Islamic ethical literature, much of it from Persian and Indian sources.

The book is divided into chapters ("Gates," *she'arim*). Some of them contain a long chain of instructions, epigrams, and parables relating to the subject of the chapter, as for example *Sha'ar ha-Ḥokhmah* ("The Gate of Wisdom"), *Sha'ar ha-Anavah* ("The Gate of Humility"), and *Sha'ar ha-Emunah* ("The Gate of Belief"). However, most of the chapters give no serious treatment of their ostensible subject and have a title for nothing but a single epigram or ethical paragraph. They deal with all aspects of religious and social life, from the unity of God (*Sha'ar ha-Yiḥud*) to the proper way to treat one's friends. One of the chapters is an ethical will – "*Sha'ar Ẓavva'at Av li-Veno*" ("Gate of the Will of a Father to his Son").

Mivḥar ha-Peninim was translated into Hebrew by Judah ibn *Tibbon, who translated most of the early Jewish works on philosophy from Arabic. It is not, however, a typical product of the genre, despite the clear influences of philosophical-ethical thinking found in it. Rather it is a popular collection of ethical epigrams and parables, collected from Arabic ethical literature. Its authorship has not been established, and there is no clear evidence that it was written by Gabirol. Some traditional editions attribute it to *Jedaiah b. Abraham Bedersi (ha-Penini), although there is no basis for this view either. The book has been very popular throughout the ages; it was used by the Ḥasidei Ashkenaz as well as by philosophers. It has been often printed and many commentaries have been written on it, even in modern times.

BIBLIOGRAPHY: A. Marx, in: HUCA, 4 (1927), 433–48.

[Joseph Dan]

MIX, RONALD JACK (Ron; "The Intellectual Assassin"; 1938–), U.S. football player, member of the Pro Football Hall of Fame and the American Football League Hall of Fame. Born and raised in Los Angeles, Mix attended the University of Southern California on a football scholarship. He entered the school as a 180-pound end but by the time he graduated was up to 250 pounds due to an intensive weight-training program. Mix was a starter for three years (1957–59), and co-captained the 1959 team that had a record of 8–2–0 and tied for first in the Pacific Coast Conference. Mix was named consensus All-America first team, AP All-Pacific Coast first team, All-Big Five first team, MVP USC Lineman Award, and won the Trojaneer Diamond Award as the senior athlete who did the most to further the reputation of USC. In 1960, Mix was drafted in the first round by the Baltimore Colts of the NFL and the Boston Patriots of the newly formed American Football League. The Patriots traded Mix to the Los Angeles/San Diego Chargers, for whom he played tackle from 1960 to 1969, and then with the Oakland Raiders for the 1971 season. Mix played in five of the first six AFL title games, winning the 1963 championship 51–10 over the New England Patriots. He was an All-AFL selection eight times as a tackle and once as a guard, and played in eight AFL All-Star games (1961–68). Mix was known for his excellent speed and strength, and for his quick charge and accomplished blocking on both passing and running plays. Mix, one of only 20 men who played the entire ten years of the AFL, played in 142 career games, with only two holding penalties assessed in his career. He was unanimously chosen for the AFL's all-time team in 1969. His coach with the San Diego Chargers, Sid *Gillman, said, "Ron Mix was one of the greats of all time ... I think he's the greatest tackle who ever lived." He was inducted into the Pro Football Hall of Fame in 1979.

[Elli Wohlgelernter (2nd ed.)]

MIXED MARRIAGE, INTERMARRIAGE. The terms intermarriage and mixed marriage are used interchangeably. Intermarriage in the present context is defined as a marriage where one partner professes a religion different from that of his spouse. Marriages in which a partner has converted to the faith of the other are not considered intermarriages. Therefore, marriages between *converts to Judaism and born Jews are not treated here.

Problems of Measurement

FORMATION DATA VERSUS STATUS DATA. Statistical data on the frequency of religious intermarriage are obtained from marriage licenses on which groom and bride state their religions, and from questionnaires connected with censuses or community surveys. Questionnaires reveal the religious composition of married couples and the status of heterogamy within a population. It is of the utmost importance to distinguish between intermarriage formation and heterogamy status data.

INDIVIDUAL RATES VERSUS COUPLE RATES. A number of methodological problems complicate the computation of intermarriage rates. Some researchers base their rates upon the number of individuals who marry out. However, since the couple is the basic unit in the marriage relationship and since the couple is expected to be homogamous, intermarriage rates are most meaningfully computed by determining the ratio of intermarried couples to the total number of couples in which one or both partners are Jewish.

SURVEYS OF THE ORGANIZED JEWISH COMMUNITY VERSUS COMPREHENSIVE SURVEYS. Surveys which produce intermarriage data should indicate whether the survey was limited to the organized Jewish community or encompassed the total population of a locality. As might be expected, the former type yields a significantly lower rate of intermarriage than the latter. Surveys of the former type sponsored by local Jewish organizations in the United States between 1930 and 1970 yielded an intermarriage status rate of about 6%. By contrast the Greater Washington survey which sampled the total population yielded a rate of 13.2%, more than double that of the organized Jewish community.

The Extent of Jewish Intermarriage

MAGNITUDE. In contrast to the period between World Wars I and II there are no data for Eastern and Southeastern Europe on intermarriage rates. Considerable variations exist from country to country and even within one country, namely the United States. In 1970 status rates ranged from a high of 26% for Switzerland and the Netherlands to a low of 7.2% for the United States; formation rates from a high of 80.6% in West Germany to a low of 16.8% in Canada. (See Table: World Jewish Population Distribution, by Frequency of Current Out-Marriages around 1930 and 2000.)

THE MEANING OF INTERMARRIAGE RATES: THE PROBLEM OF JEWISH SURVIVAL. There is a widespread belief that a high rate of Jewish intermarriage in a given locality leads to the disappearance of the Jewish community there. "How high is high?" The answer will be found in a comparison of what the intermarriage rate might be if random selection of partners would occur (expected random rate) with the actual (observed) intermarriage rate. A 1957 sample survey in the United States revealed that, compared to Catholics and Protestants, Jews are least likely to intermarry.

Social Factors Related to Intermarriage

ROMANTIC LOVE VERSUS GROUP COHESION. In the Western world the selection of marital partners is governed by two considerations. One is the romantic love ideal, which tends to override considerations of race, creed, cultural origin, or social class. The other consideration is group survival, the pressure to marry a member of one's own race, religion, or cultural group.

World Jewish Population Distribution, by Frequency of Current Out-Marriages around 1930 and 2000

Rate of Jews now marrying non-Jews[a]	1930			2000		
	Country[b]	Jewish pop. in thousands	%	Country[b]	Jewish pop. in thousands	%
	Total	16,600	100.0	Total	12,950	100.0
0–0.9%	Poland[1], Lithuania[1], Greece[2], Palestine[2], Iran[4], Yemen[4], Ethiopia[4]	4,130	24.9	West Bank-Gaza (Yesh"a)[1]	215	1.7
1–4.9%	Latvia[1], Canada[1], United States[2], Latin America[4], United Kingdom[4], Spain-Portugal[4], Other Asia[4], Maghreb[2], Egypt[1], Libya[4], Southern Africa[4]	6,700	40.4	Israel[1], Yemen[4]	4,879	37.7
5–14.9%	Switzerland[1], France[2], Austria[1], Luxembourg[1], Hungary[1], Romania[2], Czechoslovakia[1], USSR[1], Estonia[1], Belgium[4], Bulgaria[4], Yugoslavia[4]	5,340	32.1	Mexico[1], Gibraltar[4], China[4], Iran[4], Syria[4], North Africa[4]	60	0.4
15–24.9%	Italy[1], Germany[1], Netherlands[1]	385	2.3	Bahamas[4], Costa Rica[4], Guatemala[2], Venezuela[1], India[3], Japan[4], Singapore[4], South Africa[3]	101	0.8
25–34.9%	Australia[2], New Zealand[4], Scandinavia[3]	45	0.3	Canada[1], Chile[2], Latin America not otherwise stated[4], Turkey[2], Africa not else stated[4], Australia[1], New Zealand[3]	535	4.1
35–44.9%				Argentina[3], Brazil[2], Uruguay[2], France[1], United Kingdom[1], Western Europe not otherwise stated[3]	1,176	9.1
45–54.9%				United States[1], Italy[2], Netherlands[1], Switzerland[1], FSU in Asia[3]	5,400	41.7
55–74.9%				Austria[1], Germany[1], Eastern Europe (besides FSU)[3]	194	1.5
75% +				FSU in Europe[2], Cuba[3]	390	3.0
Average rate	World Diaspora	5.1% 5.2%		World Diaspora	30.8% 48.3%	

a Not Jewish at time of marriage. Out-marriage figures are countrywide or regional estimates. This table ignores variation in out-marriage frequencies within countries.
b Data quality rated as follows: 1 Recent and reliable data; 2 Partial or less recent data of sufficient quality; 3 Rather outdated or incomplete data; 4 Conjectural.

The effectiveness of this pressure is directly related to the value that adults place upon the survival of their group. Elopements can be considered an extreme case of romantic love, producing a maximum rate of intermarriage, while arranged marriages can be viewed as a most conscious effort to foster group survival generating a minimum of such marriages.

Size of the Jewish Community

DENSITY AND CONCENTRATION. It has been repeatedly observed that the rate of intermarriage is the result of density, the proportion that a subgroup constitutes of the total population in a given locality. However, density becomes relevant only when the will for group survival has been weakened or abandoned. Once group cohesion is weakened, however, the factor of density operates in the expected manner: the smaller the proportion that Jews constitute of the total population in a given locality, the larger the intermarriage rate becomes. This relationship has been observed in Canada, the United States, and Australia. For example, in the United States the intermarriage formation rate in the state of Indiana between 1960 and 1963 was 38.6% for the five large Jewish settlements and 63.5% for those counties where there was only a scattering of Jewish families. Jews are well aware of the fact that dispersal of Jewish families over a rural or urban area increases the likelihood of intermarriage. Therefore, in urban areas they have been eager to concentrate their residence in specific neighborhoods and to locate their institutions within them.

AGE OF JEWISH SETTLEMENT AND DEMOCRATIC SOCIAL PROCESSES. Jews more than any other religio-ethnic group have been involved in migrations from one country to another. As immigrants they have encountered economic, cultural, and social barriers. However, in democratic societies where equalizing processes between immigrants and older settlers and between different racial, ethnic, and religious groups are at least not discouraged and at best consciously fostered, these barriers will be lowered with increasing length of settlement. In time, then, Jews will become "acculturated," i.e., less distinguishable from older settlers and other immigrant groups.

The most significant break in cultural continuity, social distance, and personal identity occurs with the birth of each new generation. Therefore, intermarriage is likely to increase with increased length of Jewish settlement, as measured by generations, and in the absence of continued Jewish immigration. The Greater Washington survey found that intermarried families increased from 1.4% among the foreign born, the first generation, to 10.2% among the native born of foreign parentage, the second generation, to 17.9% among the native born of native parentage, the third generation. The readiness of Jewish individuals to intermarry is met by a corresponding frame of mind on the part of non-Jews, who, as members of the upper classes, are no longer conscious of previous status differentials or who, as members of other immigrant groups, have also been "acculturated." The fact that a new wave of immigrants can effectively lower earlier upward trends of intermarriage can best be demonstrated by Australia and to a lesser extent by Canada. In Australia, mainly because of the immigration of refugees from Nazi Europe, the Jewish population nearly doubled between 1933 and 1954. At the same time the percentage of intermarried families dropped drastically from a high of 29% for Jewish husbands and 16% for Jewish wives in 1921 to a low of 12% for Jewish husbands and 6% for Jewish wives in 1961.

OCCUPATION AND EMPLOYMENT STATUS. Occupation and employment status (independent owner versus employee) are factors significantly related to intermarriage. As long as occupational choice was limited by discriminatory practices, occupational homogeneity discouraged intermarriage. With virtually unlimited freedom of occupational choice in the United States, individuals who break away from traditional occupations are likely to have a higher intermarriage rate. The growth of corporate capitalism is also likely to generate a higher rate of intermarriage. Since large corporations demand from their executives considerable geographic and social mobility, local ties to the organized Jewish communities become attenuated. Surveys in the mid-50s revealed that roughly 80% of the heads of Jewish households in the United States were engaged in white-collar occupations while only 20% did blue-collar work. Within the white-collar group, managers, proprietors, and officials constituted the largest concentration, with 36% of all heads of Jewish households. It comes as no surprise, then, that the intermarriage formation rate for the latter group amounted to only 10% (for first marriages) in the state of Iowa. For the total white-collar group the rate was 27.2% and for blue-collar workers 46.8%. Thus the expectation that Jews who adhere to the traditional occupational pattern are less likely to intermarry was borne out.

SECULAR EDUCATION. Secular education in the Western world has two major functions. One is to ensure the continuity of cultural tradition and values, the acquisition of basic skills, and of occupational training. The other is to provide for cultural change, the production of new ideas, and technical innovation. Students who are oriented to or exposed to the first type of schooling should be less inclined to intermarry than students enrolled in the second type. The Greater Washington survey supports the expectation for the native-born of native parentage. The intermarriage rate of those who had enrolled in the first type was nearly one-third lower than of those who had attended the second type.

RELIGIOUS EDUCATION. There is a widespread belief that Jewish education, including a bar mitzvah ceremony, helps to keep young men from marrying outside the Jewish faith. The Greater Washington survey showed that this belief is well founded as far as the native-born of native parentage (the third and subsequent generation) is concerned. Religious education cut the intermarriage status rate in half. It was 16.4% for those husbands who had been exposed to religious school as compared to 30.2% who had not had such instruction. Since the ethnic bond – expressed in secular activities and in a common language – has been virtually dissolved in the third generation, exposure to religious instruction, which usually includes some learning of Jewish history and some identification with Israel, serves as a check to intermarriage.

SEX DISTRIBUTION AND INTERMARRIAGE. In the beginning of the last quarter of the 20th century Jewish men were more likely to intermarry than Jewish women. One reason for this differential was that men take the initiative in proposing marriage. This was especially significant in localities where Jewish families are sparsely settled. Jewish parents allowed their sons more freedom in dating across religious lines. However, the following years witnessed an increase in the proportion of Jewish women who intermarry, and it is likely that the sex differential will diminish in the future. The proportion of Jewish men who intermarry varied from country to country and within a country from place to place. In Canada only 10.2% of all bridegrooms intermarried between 1955 and 1960, as compared with 26.7% in Iowa between 1953 and 1959. In the Netherlands, the percentage of such bridegrooms rose from 36.4% in 1946 to 44% in 1958. In Indiana, only about half as many Jewish bridegrooms intermarried in the five relatively large Jewish communities of the state (30% versus 55.8%). Jewish brides exhibit similar variations in their propensity to intermarry.

PREVIOUS MARITAL STATUS. Data available for the United States and the Netherlands demonstrate that the previous marital status of a person affects his decision to intermarry. Previously widowed persons, upon remarriage, have a lower intermarriage rate than persons never before married. By contrast, persons who were previously divorced have a considerably higher intermarriage rate than the never married. For example, in Indiana one group of previously divorced couples had an intermarriage formation rate of 64.9% as compared with 33.2% for the never married before and 20% for the previously widowed.

The Prevention of Intermarriage

In societies where democracy and individualism are dominant values, intermarriage is bound to occur. Empirical observations have revealed that Jewish communities are trying to keep the frequency low with the help of a "survival" formula consisting of voluntary segregation, residence in a high-status area, a modicum of Jewish education, and Jewish group consciousness in the form of Zionism which is defined as supporting the State of Israel.

[Erich Rosenthal]

Legal Aspects

THE CONCEPT. A mixed marriage is a marriage of a non-Jew to a Jew, i.e., one born of Jewish parents, or whose mother alone was Jewish, or who has become a proselyte in accordance with Jewish law (see *Jew; **Yuḥasin*). Conversion from the Jewish religion, both in the case of a Jew by birth and of a proselyte who reverts to his "evil" ways, has no halakhic significance in respect of the law on mixed marriages. For "an Israelite, even if he has sinned, is still an Israelite" (Sanh. 44a; Rashi thereto; see *Apostasy).

MIXED MARRIAGES ARE PROHIBITED AND INVALID. From the biblical passage (Deut. 7:3) "neither shalt thou make marriages with them: thy daughter thou shalt not give unto his son, nor his daughter shalt thou take unto thy son," the sages inferred that marriage with a non-Jew is forbidden as a negative precept by the Torah (Av. Zar. 36b; Yad, Issurei Bi'ah 12:1–2; Sh. Ar., EH 16:1). As the passage cited refers to the "seven nations" ("The Hittite, and the Girgashite, and the Amorite, and the Canaanite, and the Perizzite, and the Hivite, and the Jebusite," Deut. 7:1), according to one opinion, the prohibition applies only to intermarriage with those seven nations. Others maintain, however, that the prohibition applies to all gentiles because after the prohibition "neither shalt thou make marriages" the biblical passage continues: "For he will turn away thy son from following after Me" (Deut. 7:4), which serves "to include all who would turn [their children] away" (Av. Zar. 36b; Yev. 77a; and codes). The prohibition against marrying a gentile is also explicitly stated in the period of the return to Zion: "And that we would not give our daughters unto the peoples of the land, nor take their daughters for our sons" (Neh. 10:31; see Maim., *ibid.*). It was also inferred from the passage in Deuteronomy that in a mixed marriage there is "no institution of marriage," i.e., mixed marriages are not legally valid and cause no change in personal status (Kid. 68b; Yev. 45a; and codes). Hence if the Jewish partner of such a marriage subsequently wishes to marry a Jew there is no need, according to the *halakhah*, for divorce from the previous "marriage." However, where one or even both of the parties to a marriage are apostate Jews who have married in a halakhically binding manner, neither can marry a Jew as long as the first marriage is not terminated by death or divorce, since a purported change of religion does not affect personal status (Yev. 47b; Bek. 30b; Sh. Ar., EH 44:9). Similarly if both parties (or only one of them) apostatize after a halakhically valid marriage and are then divorced by way of a civil divorce, neither party can marry a Jew until the previous marriage is terminated as above (Yad, Ishut 4:15; Rema, EH 154:23).

MIXED MARRIAGES HAVE NO LEGAL CONSEQUENCES. Since mixed marriages are not binding, such marriages entail no legal consequences (Yad, loc. cit.). Hence, the prohibitions of marriage (in respect of certain relations of the other spouse), which apply to a valid marriage, do not apply to the parties – even after the non-Jewish partner has become a proselyte (see *Marriage, Prohibited). Similarly the wife has no halakhic right to be maintained by her "husband," since this right arises only if a valid marriage exists between them. For the same reason, in a mixed marriage none of the inheritance rights that flow from a valid marriage, such as the husband's right to inherit his wife's estate (see *Succession), come into effect.

The State of Israel

It is impossible to contract a mixed marriage in the State of Israel, since according to section 2 of the Rabbinical Courts Jurisdiction (Marriage and Divorce) Law, 5713 – 1953, no marriages of Jews in Israel are valid unless contracted in accordance with the law of the Torah. However, the criminal code does not provide criminal punishment for contracting a mixed marriage in Israel. Where a mixed marriage is contracted in the Diaspora, proceedings regarding it cannot be brought directly before the Israel rabbinical courts inasmuch as such courts have jurisdiction only in the event of both parties being Jews. In 1969, however, a law was passed whereby such marriages can be dissolved at the discretion of the president of the Supreme Court. If a problem arises before the civil courts, such as a wife's claim for maintenance, the civil courts will act according to the general principles of private international law, and where such a marriage cannot be denied validity according to those principles, it will be sustained. The Succession Law, 5725 – 1965 provides that differences of religion do not affect rights of inheritance.

[Ben-Zion (Benno) Schereschewsky]

Reform and Conservative Practice

Through to the 1970s most Conservative and Reform rabbis requested conversion from the non-Jewish spouse before undertaking any action as regards marriage, although a small, though growing minority of Reform rabbis were prepared to officiate at mixed marriages (N. Mirsky, in: *Midstream*, 16 (Jan. 1970), 40–46). The practice of almost all Conservative rabbis was not to perform a marriage between a Jew and a non-Jew. Indeed those rabbis who do perform such marriages do so only in emergency cases. Another question which was debated by the Conservative Rabbinical Assembly was the status of an intermarried Jew as regards membership in a Conservative congregation. The practice until 1963 had been to exclude such an intermarried Jew from synagogue membership. In 1963 the law committee of the Rabbinical Assembly adopted a modified view of the former position and, while affirming their opposition to mixed marriages, allowed the Jewish partner of a non-Jewish marriage to become a member of their congregation, provided that there was a definite agreement to raise the children of the marriage as Jews. The privileges of membership did not extend to the non-Jewish spouse, and the Jewish partner was restricted from holding office in the synagogue. All restrictions were to be lifted when the non-Jewish partner accepted Judaism.

Reform practice on the other hand was to accept both members of the marriage as members of the congregation, and to urge that any children of the marriage be brought to the Jewish religious school so that they could have Jewish training. They felt that by this policy they would be able to influence the non-Jewish spouse to affiliate with Judaism.

IN THE UNITED STATES, 1970–1990

Introduction

Intermarriage has always been a danger to the Jewish People. Any group that lives as a minority has the potential of being absorbed by its host society. Some contact among the groups within a society is inevitable, but that contact can take many forms as relations among groups are played out – not always in consistent patterns – along several dimensions: cultural, institutional, residential, social, and familial. Because these dimensions can be independent of one another, acculturation, for example, need not lead to residential integration, nor does residential integration necessarily bring about socializing across group lines. Almost all kinds of acculturation and integration are compatible with continued group identity, at least theoretically. Integration at the familial level, on the other hand, is a sufficient condition for total assimilation by a subgroup into the larger society and its eventual disappearance as an identifiable group. Although most social identities are transmitted through families, Jewishness, going much further, explicitly defines itself in familial terms. Intermarriage thus is seen as the very antithesis of Jewish continuity. From the time that Abraham sent his servant to choose a wife for Isaac from among his own people through Ezra's expulsion of the non-Jewish wives of the Jews who returned to establish the Second Commonwealth to the recent practice of severing all ties with and sitting *shivah* for intermarried children, exogamy was one of the most energetically discouraged and forcefully condemned acts that a Jew could perform.

Most of the research on intermarriage has been done on American Jewry, which serves as the focus of this section, but much of the analysis can *mutatis mutandis* be extended to other Diaspora communities. Since the early 1960s intermarriage has changed dramatically in the United States – not only in quantity, but also in its meaning and in the reactions it engenders. Although a number of books and articles on intermarriage written before the 1960s viewed it with alarm as "an epidemic," intermarriage was not then generally seen as a serious communal threat, and the data on which those works rested pale in the perspective of the 1990s. Widespread communal concern with intermarriage followed the publication of Erich Rosenthal's "Studies of Jewish Intermarriage in the United States" in the 1963 *American Jewish Year Book* and a cover story on the "Vanishing American Jew" in *Look* magazine. These two articles left the Jews of the time shaken and less assured about the future of the American Jewish community. They had come to believe that, while the Jewishness of their children would not be the same as that of earlier generations, the changes that they had made in order to "modernize" Judaism would guarantee that future generations would maintain their Jewishness even as they acquired full economic, political, civic, and cultural equality as American citizens. They knew that some would intermarry and be lost, but not enough, they were convinced, to seriously weaken American Jewish life. Most Jews entering the 1960s felt themselves part of what had become the world's premier Jewish community, at least in the Diaspora, and, for all its problems, they felt secure in its future.

In the late 1960s and early 1970s many committees, commissions, and task forces were established by Jewish organizations to propose ways of reducing what was viewed as a dangerously high intermarriage rate. Despite those efforts, in the intervening years the rate increased.

The national study, undertaken by the Council of Jewish Federations in 1990, reported that 52% of the Jews who married between 1985 and 1990 married non-Jews (and another 5% married converts to Judaism). The exogamy rate climbed dramatically from decade to decade from the comparatively low and stable level characteristic of the periods before the 1960s. Another recent study, by the Center for Modern Jewish Studies at Brandeis University, also reported recent intermarriage rates for successive decades, in eight communities in various parts of the country. Although the figures are somewhat lower than in the CJF study, the increase over time is equally steep. (The overall lower rates may be due to a combination of factors: the communities chosen, the decade break points, and the way Jews become eligible for the sample.) Whatever the precise figures may be, it is clear that at this point exogamy is as common as endogamy among American Jews.

Characteristics of Those Most Likely to Intermarry

Which Jews are most likely to intermarry? Until the 1980s, men were twice as likely as women to marry non-Jews. In later years, however, the gap has narrowed considerably. It also used to be the case that intermarriage was most frequent among Jews with the highest educational and income levels, but recent studies call this pattern into question. Now, when such variables as age are controlled, Jews at the top of the socioeconomic scale turn out to be less likely to intermarry than those toward the middle, but the differences are small. It is also found that the older Jews are at the time of their first marriage, the more likely they are to be exogamous. This is probably due to the fact that older people are more independent, have a wider network of professional and business contacts including non-Jews, and face a shrinking pool of potential partners. Second marriages after divorce are also much more likely than first marriages to involve a non-Jewish partner. The higher tendency to exogamy among the divorced may be strengthened by their desire for a second spouse "different" from the first and by their greater independence from ties to family and community. Geographic variations are important. Generally, areas of high Jewish concentration have less intermarriage, but some cities with large Jewish populations have very high intermarriage rates (San Francisco, Denver, and Washington, DC, are examples). The less traditional the religious "movement" with which a Jew identifies, the more likely that Jew is to intermarry, with the highest rates of intermarriage among those who identify with no religious movement at all and claim to be "just Jewish."

During most of the 1980s it was generally believed that in about one-third of the marriages between Jews and partners born non-Jews, the originally non-Jewish partner converted to Judaism according to the norms and practices of one or another of American Judaism's religious movements, either before or after the marriage. (The phenomena led to the adoption of a more elaborate terminology in which "intermarriage" is often used to refer to any marriage between a Jew and someone born not Jewish, "conversionary marriage" refers to a marriage between a Jew and a non-Jew who converts to Judaism, and "mixed marriage" is the term reserved for marriages in which one partner is Jewish and the other is not.) The most recent studies show that a much smaller proportion of intermarriages is conversionary than had previously been thought to be the case.

Another terminological development is use of the phrase "Jews-by-choice" instead of "convert." Many feel that the former term is more positive. It is also seen as a way at least partly to get around some of the problems that arise from the different definitions of conversion held by various segments of the Jewish community. The latest statistical projection estimates that there are now approximately 185,000 "Jews-by-choice" in North America.

Trying to assess the demographic impact of intermarriage, optimistic analysts used to point out that if half of the children of intermarried couples are Jewish there should be no net loss in the size of the Jewish community. Recent studies show, however, that far fewer than half of the children of intermarriage identify as Jews, even by the most liberal criteria. Moreover, those who do consider themselves Jews have weaker Jewish identity on the whole than do born Jews, and they are themselves far more likely to intermarry in turn. The 1990 CJF study projects that there are about 415,000 adults in North America who are descended from Jews but were raised from birth in another religion and another 700,000 children under 18 years of age who are not identified as Jews but have a Jewish parent or grandparent.

The organized Jewish community in North America is now expressing renewed alarm over intermarriage. Not only has the rate risen dramatically over the last couple of decades, but the demographic impact is seen as more threatening than had been hoped. Many federations and other Jewish organizations have begun to address what they articulate as the problem in "Jewish continuity." Several inquiries have been undertaken into what can be done to bolster Jewish identity, Jewish organizations and agencies have been encouraged in a number of communities to strengthen those aspects of their programs that are seen as contributing to Jewish identity, and some funds are being allocated for activities designed to enhance Jewish continuity.

Meaning of Intermarriage in the Contemporary Jewish Community

In order to understand intermarriage in the contemporary Jewish community, it is essential to recognize that its very meaning has changed. In earlier periods intermarriage was often a rebellion against Jewishness or a quiet renunciation of Jewish identity – if not for oneself, then for one's children. There were several variations on that theme. Intermarriage could be a way of breaking free from what were felt as the constraints of Jewish life and the discrimination to which to which Jews were subjected. It could be an extreme means to declare independence from, perhaps even to punish, parents. For the upwardly mobile, it could provide entry into desired social circles. Whatever the motives, however, intermarriage was understood as sufficiently incompatible with Jewish identity to constitute a decisive break with Jewishness. It was in that context that Jewish parents and, reflecting their sentiments, Jewish organizations reacted so forcefully when the intermarriage statistics of the 1960s were published.

Jewish identity had been re-shaped in America in the 20th century, but most Jews were not assimilationists. The dominant belief in American Jewry in the first two-thirds of the 20th century was that while Jewishness should undergo some acculturation in order to fit comfortably into modern Western culture, it should survive as a separate identity. Indeed, most Jews believed that acculturation was precisely what would guarantee Jewish continuity. If Jewishness were not adjusted according to the norms of the larger society, they were convinced it would be too culturally deviant for coming generations, which would consequently reject it altogether. Most American Jews understood, however, that intermarriage was the ultimate vehicle of assimilation. They could accept, if with some regret, whatever other changes their children made in Jewish self-expression. Exogamy, by contrast, was the decisive indicator of a failure to perpetuate Jewishness. Ironically, the changes in Jewish identity that were made in order to preserve Jewishness can now be seen as having engendered the kind of Jewish identity which is not inconsistent with intermarriage. It is for that reason that many young Jews came to view intermarriage as compatible with continued Jewish identity and as an essentially unremarkable act.

The Jewish identity of 20th century American Jewry can best be understood as an outgrowth of "Emancipation." The fundamental change in the Jews' status that is denoted by the term "Emancipation" occurred in central and western Europe at the turn of the 19th century. The French Revolution was, of course, the threshold event which offered Jews citizenship as individuals. For the preceding two millennia Jews had had corporate status as part of the Jewish community. The shift to individual political status, generally and for the Jews, made its way across Europe, unevenly, during the 19th and 20th centuries.

To appreciate the cultural dynamics of Jews in contemporary America, however, it is necessary to remember that about nine-tenths of American Jewry is descended from the major wave of Jewish immigration to the United States from Eastern Europe between 1881 and 1924. In other words, most American Jews are only two or three generations removed from the kind of intensive and enclosed Jewish life that prevailed in the Pale of Settlement and other Jewish areas of eastern Europe. For the Jew who came to America in the 40 years around the turn of the 20th century, the trip was not a journey for political freedom and economic opportunity alone. It was, rather, a fundamental transition to a "new world" in every sense. For them, their voyage was the "Emancipation."

The marginal generation, those who carved out a new American identity (specifically, the children of older immigrants and the younger immigrants themselves), made two basic changes in Jewish identity. One concerned its scope; the other, its content. The marginal generation, welcoming America's offer of equal status, sought to specify the part of behavior that should appropriately be molded by Jewishness, leaving the rest to other elements in each person's overall identity. The most frequent position was that Jewishness was religion, defined narrowly as including some theological assertions, ethical injunctions, and ritual observances, none of which was thought (by most American Jews) to interfere with the larger society's normative expectations regarding occupational, political, recreational, social, or even familial patterns of behavior. For other Jews, Jewishness was manifested in a special enjoyment of Hebrew and/or Yiddish literature. Still others expressed Jewishness through philanthropic activity, giving their largest financial contributions to Jewish causes and devoting significant portions of their volunteer time to service in those causes. In another alternative, the focus of Jewish activity was participation in efforts to enhance intergroup amity and to diminish prejudice and discrimination. Finally, there were Jews whose Jewishness found expression in their choice of other Jews as friends, but whose activities with those friends had no particular Jewish content.

These five general approaches to the limitation of the scope of Jewishness were reflected in the organizations of American Jewry. Most Jewish organizations in the earlier part of the 20th century had closely defined purposes, and activity outside of an organization's prescribed scope was usually discouraged. Moreover, while Jews could, and did, belong to organizations in more than one category of Jewish self-expression, most Jews tended to express themselves primarily in one or another mode.

Distinctiveness of Jewish Identity

The second fundamental change which the marginal generation made in Jewish identity concerned the extent to which Jewishness is distinctive. During virtually all of Jewish history, Jews were different from their non-Jewish neighbors in ideologically important and personally profound ways. American Jews in the early 20th century tried to convey the idea that being Jewish did not make them different from non-Jews in any significant way. There were several reasons for their effort. They wanted to reassure other Americans that the offer of equal status for the Jews was appropriate. More generally, the underlying ideology of intergroup relations activities during that period was that emphasis on the commonness of all humanity would encourage tolerance. It was believed that if people could accept that all human beings are fundamentally the same, then mutual respect and amity would grow. The basis of the approach was the combination of individualism and universalism that reached its apex at that time and which also found expression in a downplaying of other dimensions of identity such as race, ethnicity, and even family. (Now the emphasis is on cultural differences and the need to recognize and respect them, but that approach began to gain strength only in the 1960s.)

In the context of the early 20th century, then, it is not surprising that American Jews tended to articulate a Jewishness whose differentiating impact was restricted to detail. Most Jews preferred to emphasize what they had in common with non-Jews and to insists that what they had in common mattered much more than what set them apart. It is hard to assess the extent to which they believed their own claim, but the fact that they made it had its impact.

The children of the marginal generation were effectively the first "post-Emancipation" generation, and their Jewish identity differed in a number of far-reaching ways from that of previous generations of Jews. First, while all identifies have both individual, and collective aspects, the relationship between those two aspects varies. Before Emancipation, a person's Jewishness was derived from his/her being part of the Jewish people. "Jewish" was understood primarily as the designation of a group, and a "Jew" was someone who belonged to that group. For American Jews of the mid-20th century, "Jewish" described an individual first. Its application to organizations and communities was derived from the Jewishness of their members. In America's political ideology Jewishness was the private business of individuals and of no official public relevance. Jewish organizations were understood as nothing more than voluntary associations of Jews who made them and could use them for whatever ends they wished. During this time, the phrase "Jewish people" was almost always used as the plural of Jewish person rather than to denote an entity with its own inherent meaning.

Jewishness in mid-20th century America was most often conceptualized as one role among the many roles that every person plays. A typical man would see himself in many roles – husband, father, son, brother, neighbor, friend, lawyer, golfer, Democrat, Jew, Chicogoan, tenant, investor, contributor, and so forth. Each role had its own institutionalized set of relationships, its own mandated behaviors, and, consequently, its own well-delineated sphere of relevance. Pre-Emancipation Jews also had multiple roles, of course, even though they were less likely to say it that way. The difference is that Jewishness cannot properly be viewed as one of their roles. It would be more correct to see it as the substance with which all role behaviors were specified and evaluated. Another way of saying the same thing is that, for most Jews, Jewishness was transformed from a diffuse characteristic into a very specific one.

Something can be of specific relevance, yet still be very important. However, most post-emancipation American Jews not only restricted the scope of Jewishness; they also greatly diminished its power. For the typical pre-Emancipation Jew, the fact that s/he was Jewish took priority over virtually every competing claim to time, energy, or normative prescription. By contrast, most Americans Jews in the mid-20th century made Jewish self-expression fit into the time, energy, and options left by almost the entire range of other claims – occupational, educational, recreational, civic, social.

The Jews growing up as a post-Emancipation generation heard from their parents that Jewishness did not make a Jew different in any major way. Young Jews learned that Judaism was one of the world's great monotheistic religions, and if there was pride to be found in the fact that it was the first, that, after all, was a matter of history and of little consequence. In Will Herberg's well-known formulation, a person could be a good American in any one of three ways, by being a Protestant, a Catholic, or a Jew. All were seen as acceptable variations on a common theme, and what mattered was the basic set of values and styles that constituted the American way of life, not the specific literature and symbolism with which the three religions were supposed to convey that way of life. In earlier periods, of course, Jewishness had made Jews different in many far-reaching and fundamental ways, as was fully recognized by Jews and non-Jews.

Because Jewishness was so narrowly restricted and made subordinate to external contexts of interpretation, most post-Emancipation Jews lost the kind of familiarity with Jewish behavior that people have with their own culture. It is probably a fair rule of thumb that the more internationalized an item of culture is, the fewer directions a person needs when performing it. Thus, the inability of post-Emancipation Jews to carry out Jewish acts without guidance says much about their level of estrangement from the content of Jewishness.

This description does not apply to all Jews in the mid-1900s. Some purposely assimilated altogether; others maintained Jewish identities that were far more comprehensive, primary, distinguishing, internalized, and rooted in Jewish peoplehood past and present. The vast middle group, however, molded a Jewish identity which, though generally positive, was not compelling. Although the Holocaust and the establishment of the State of Israel certainly affected Jewish identity, they did not alter its basic structure of place in the lives of most American Jews.

The key point is that the kind of Jewish identity described here is not a barrier to intermarriage, nor is intermarriage incompatible with that kind of Jewish identity. America is an open society, and the American ethos places overwhelming importance on individual choice in most things. While some group-based hurdles to individual choice remain, marriage across religious and ethnic lines is not discouraged. Rather, even in a period which has for the last two or three decades seen increasing emphasis placed on religion and on ethnic identity, interreligious and interethnic marriages are likely to be viewed as helping to demonstrate the compatibility of disparate traditions and the possibility of amity, even of love, across lines. Other factors encouraging intermarriage are improvement in the socioeconomic standing of Jews and increased acceptance of Jews as friends and potential marriage partners. As a result, most Jews have circles of colleagues, classmates, and friends that include non-Jewish peers. Inevitably, these relationships often lead to romance.

When subjective feelings of romance begin to grow between two people, they make judgments about whether their differences are numerous enough, large enough, or profound enough to be a barrier to marriage. If not, then the differences become the issues over which the compromises that are part of any marriage are worked out. Otherwise, one party or the other will end the relationship.

If Jewishness is seen to consist of some vague ideas about God's existence and providence, a number of almost universally endorsed ethical principles, two or three holiday dinners a year, a Ḥanukkah lamp in the house in December, brief attendance at synagogue services once or twice a year, the obligation to give some emphasis to Jewish causes among one's charitable donations, a somewhat higher and more consistent level of political support for Israel than other pro-Israel Americans offer, a political stance generally in the "liberal" camp, and pride in the Jewish achievements of the past, then Jewishness is compatible with intermarriage. No loving non-Jewish spouse is likely to find these behaviors and attitudes objectionable, and none of them requires the kind of joint participation by a spouse that a non-Jew cannot easily and readily provide. If we add some Jewish art and artifacts to the decorations of the home, a few hours of Jewish education for one's children for a few years, and some ceremonial recognition that those children are (at least "partly") Jewish, which is how ritual circumcision and Bar and Bat Mitzvah are sometimes conceptualized, exogamy still need not be an impediment to continued Jewishness. It is possible for a Jew to be proud of his/her Jewishness, enjoy it, consider it "important" and yet give it a form which is not pervasive enough and a content which is not distinguishing enough to interfere with a satisfying intermarriage. By contrast, when Jewishness orders one's priorities, locates a person in history and society, provides basic goals and norms, furnishes the cultural material for the expression of "self," and marks out life's rhythm, then marriage to a non-Jewish spouse is inconceivable without either a total transformation of self or a severe narrowing of the normal marital relationship.

The intermarriage rate has risen as it has, not because Jews want to escape their Jewishness, but because they see intermarriage as quite compatible with their Jewishness. As Marshall Sklare explained, young Jews who marry non-Jews are likely to see themselves not as intermarrying, but merely as marrying.

Responses to Intermarriage

In another sense, however, intermarriage is not that simple. Resistance is likely to arise from several quarters. Parents and other relatives, synagogues and rabbis, and Jewish communal institutions can all be expected to express some level of opposition to intermarriage. The desire to include Jewish elements in the wedding ceremony or to raise children as Jews can elicit concern from the non-Jewish partner and/or his/her family. The many compromises that need to be made can be harder to work out than was anticipated. Normally suppressed stereotypes and resentments can emerge. Perhaps most indicative of the current mood regarding exogamy is the appearance in the last decade of several books of advice on how to carry out a successful intermarriage. These books usually deal with reactions of parents and other relatives, planning the wedding ceremony, the raising of the children, and ways of handling Jewish and Christian institutions. While some set forth the advantage of religious homogeneity and clarity in the home, others offer guidance on how to maintain active links to both traditions.

The responses of the organized Jewish community to intermarriage fall into two broad categories – opposition and outreach. As the 1990 CJF study shows, many Jews do not oppose intermarriage at all. Only 22% of the respondents who were born Jews and list Judaism as their religion said that they would oppose the marriage of their child to a non-Jew. The corresponding statistic for secular Jews is 4%. Among those Jews who do oppose intermarriage, either in general or in specific cases when they arise, there are several positions about what form opposition should take. Some Jews, though decreasing in number, still break all relationships with relatives and friends who marry non-Jews. Others reduce their relationships with people in mixed marriages, but do not sever them altogether. Yet others express opposition to intermarriage and try, with varying degrees of determination, to urge the Jewish partner to withdraw from the planned marriage or to bring about the conversion of the non-Jewish partner, but accept the marriage once it is a *fait accompli*.

Most Jewish institutions take the position that intermarriage should be discouraged but the intermarried should not be rejected. While that position has a tone that seems resonant with both Jewish principle and the ideology of individual choice and universal human concern, it is hard to specify what coherent attitudes or concrete behaviors it implies.

Just as opposition takes many forms, so does outreach, and the two modes of response are usually in interplay with each other. Sometimes the effort to bring the non-Jewish partner to convert is explicit. Sometimes it is offered as one option. A frequently expressed view is that, where conversion does not seem immediately likely, it is important to maintain linkage to and positive feelings about the Jewish community in the hope that conversion may eventually ensue and that, even if it does not, there will be more readiness to transmit some Jewish identity to the children and a positive feeling toward the Jewish community by the children. In general, the more liberal the religious movement, the greater its emphasis on outreach relative to opposition as the proper response to intermarriage.

The religious movements deal with intermarriage and its consequences at four specific points. First, rabbis are often asked to officiate or co-officiate as intermarriages. The Orthodox and Conservative rabbinates refuse to participate in intermarriages. The Reform movement officially leaves the decision about participating in intermarriages to its individual rabbis, who are divided on this issue. Many liberal rabbis who will not take part in intermarriages themselves will, nevertheless, counsel interreligious couples or refer them to colleagues willing to be available.

The second issue that arises concerns the status of the children of intermarriage and of converts. Orthodoxy, following *halakhah*, defines Jewishness as acquired by being born to a Jewish mother or through conversion that meets the standards of traditional Jewish law. Since the Reform movement does not adhere to traditional Jewish law in conversion and Conservative rabbis are not uniformly careful in applying Jewish law, Orthodoxy generally does not accept conversions under non-Orthodox auspices. Those Conservative rabbis who do adhere to traditional law have similar problems with Reform conversions, but the Conservative movement's emphasis on pluralism makes it harder for them to be publicly explicit on this matter. The Reform movement's formal adoption of the principle of patrilineal descent, which it had practiced quietly for decades before declaring it officially, complicated the issue. By defining Jews differently from traditional Jewish law, it created a category of people who are Jewish by the standards of some Jews and not Jewish by the standards of others. Although there have long been such people, their number is growing and the resolution on patrilineality made the controversy over their status and the potential difficulty of their situation more severe. The reform rabbinate decided that its action was justified, nonetheless, as a way to compensate for demographic decline by broadening the definition of Jewry and by extending a welcome and a sense of legitimacy to people who, it felt, would otherwise most likely be lost to the Jewish community. The traditional view is that, since those people are not Jews, they are lost in any case.

The third specific issue with which synagogues must deal is the participation of non-Jewish spouses in synagogue activities. Membership in synagogues is normally a family matter, and members can, of course, hold positions of leadership and play a number of roles in the ritual. Many intermarried Jews wish to join synagogues, and many synagogues, for outreach and other reasons, are willing, even eager, to welcome interreligious families. The consequence is that synagogues, especially but not only the more liberal ones, must make decisions about which roles can be played in leadership [and in ritual] by intermarried members and by their non-Jewish spouses.

Admission of children of intermarried couples to religious school, especially when those children are not Jewish also poses difficulties. Their parents may want to enroll them in order to make Jewishness an option or simply to give them some information about part of their family background. However, the curricular challenges of simultaneously teaching children from Jewish homes and from mixed homes are formidable.

Other organizations in the Jewish community must also delineate which roles, as participants and as leaders, can appropriately be played by intermarried Jews and, what is more difficult, by their non-Jewish spouses. Jewish organizations which cut across "movement" lines also have the problem that their members do not agree on which other members are Jewish.

Beyond the concerns about the status and roles of individual members, there is the problem of program. It cannot be entirely comfortable for a Jewish organization to deliberate about and then adopt a program whose goal is to discourage intermarriage when a not insubstantial proportion of its members and leaders are themselves intermarried or have accepted intermarriage among their children.

There is controversy over the proper balance between opposition and outreach as responses to intermarriage. Advocates of opposition argue that efforts must be made to strengthen a more comprehensive, distinctive, and rewarding Jewish identity in Jews and that, in the meantime, Jewish institutions and organizations should unambiguously convey Judaism's position that only that kind of identity, in individuals and embodied in family life, is authentic and viable. Their acceptance of outreach is limited to attempts to bring non-Jewish spouses and prospective spouses to conversion. Advocates of outreach, by contrast, usually despair of changing the overall character of Jewish identity in America and predict that the intermarriage rate will not decline significantly as a result of any Jewish policy or program. Their approach to assuring Jewish continuity, therefore, rests on encouraging intermarried families to maintain positive links to the Jewish community and on increasing the number of people who are considered Jewish by expanding the lines of Jewish descent and broadening the criteria and methods by which people can be treated as Jews-by-choice. What balance between these two modes of response will ultimately be struck, and with what consequences, remains to be seen.

[Mervin F. Verbit]

JEWISH OUT-MARRIAGE: A GLOBAL PERSPECTIVE

The frequency, determinants, and consequences of marriages between Jews and non-Jews have long been a central topic of social-scientific research and community debate. Many observers consider the recent trends in Jewish family formation with great concern and a leading factor in the quantitative and identificational erosion of Jewish population. Others view the same trends as an opportunity for community growth and expansion. Both approaches may be using sophisticated theories, concepts, and analyses, and interestingly, the same data. The main debate revolves around the paradigms of Jewish assimilation and erosion versus resilience and revival. The main trends call for examination in broad comparative context, outlining the specifics of local situations.

HISTORY. In long-term historical perspective, Jewish marriage patterns underwent different stages. During the early formative periods, the ancient Hebrew tribes were small and geographically mobile, and may have frequently incorporated individuals from the proximate surrounding. With the codification of Jewish identification in late antiquity, Jewish society entered a long period of prevalent segregation – initially self-imposed, and much later forcefully imposed by others. Contemporary studies of population genetics point to the overall similar origins of Jews from disparate continents and countries, thus testifying to very limited marital interaction between Jews and others throughout the Middle Ages and early modern period.

From the 19th century but especially since the second half of the 20th, Jewish society underwent transformations which completely revolutionized cultural identities and socioeconomic structures. International migration, extensive urbanization, occupational mobility, and secularization were some of the main agents of change, generally evolving from traditionalism to modernity, and from segregation to openness, though counter-streams of search for more traditional cultural and social behaviors also appeared occasionally.

The transition, among many, of Jewish identity from mainly religious to ethnic-national was one of the main consequences of social change in the context of political emancipation of the Jews and general modernization. In the Europe of the 19th century, the quest for integration into general society led at least 200,000 Jews to opt out of Judaism into the prevalent Christian denominations. More recently, the *rites de passage* inherent in changing one's own religious allegiance ceased to be a prerequisite for acceptance by the public at large, and moving out of Jewishness tended to become an expression of the freedom of choice in growingly individualistic societies.

Since 1948, the composition of world Jewry was crucially altered with the establishment of the state of Israel and the rapid growth of its large and densely interacting Jewish population which constituted a majority of total society. In contrast, Diaspora communities typically comprised smaller Jewish minorities, well integrated in a non-Jewish societal context, and eventually shrinking. Historically and in contemporary times, the Israel and Diaspora contexts generated entirely different opportunities for Jewish community life and identity. The low frequency of out-marriage in Israel had a counterbalancing effect on the leading global trend to greater integration and assimilation among Jews and non-Jews. More recently, increasing globalization of society created growing opportunities for interaction among different social and cultural groups, including Jews in Israel.

CONCEPTS. *Determinants.* Marriage and out-marriage in particular, reflect three basic factors, each widely varying over time and across individuals and sub-groups within the same Jewish community: (a) *Desirability*: the normative centrality of the act of marrying, and the choice of a partner from within or outside the group of origin. (b) *Feasibility*: the economic means and resources available to form a new family, and more specifically an in-marriage or an out-marriage. (c) *Availability* of appropriate marital partners, where age, sex, and marital status composition determine the choice of relevant partners to choose from within and outside the group.

Terminology. Intermarriage is a broadly used term but a number of distinctions should be kept in mind. *Out-marriage* refers to marrying someone who was born in a different group; *conversionary out-marriage* and *conversionary in-marriage* apply if conversion happens out of or into the group studied. In case each partner keeps to his/her original group identity, *mixed-marriage* applies. In more technical language we speak of *homogamy* (sameness) versus *heterogamy* (otherness). *Endogamy* and *exogamy*, respectively, indicate the same concepts but in a normative, ideal rather than descriptive sense.

Sources. Retrospective information often stems from general sources such as population censuses and general surveys that were not designed specifically for the purpose of investigating out-marriage. *Vital statistics* provide information on current marriages. *Specialized surveys* may provide a richer array of variables on existing households. Each of these sources has advantages and disadvantages regarding representation, coverage, and depth of questioning. Sources tend to be different in each country, when they exist at all.

Measurement. One should distinguish between *individual* versus *couple* measurement. If there are three Jews, two married among themselves, and one married a non Jew, we have one individual Jewish among three that out-married (33%), and one Jewish couple out of two that is a mixed-marriage (50%). These are both valid statistics but they are often mistakenly mixed up. Another problem is that measurement may refer to *all existing couples* in a certain population, regardless of age, or only to the younger *couples married in recent years*. In the 20th century since the trend to out-marry has been on the increase, later rates of out-marriage are significantly higher than the former. Finally, measurement may focus on the current or past marital status of people who were *born Jewish*, or on those who are *Jewish now*, and the results may vary accordingly. This distinction was at the core of an intense discussion about the results and interpretation of the 1990 U.S. National Jewish Population Survey (NJPS).

MAIN TRENDS. At the beginning of the 20th century, rates of Jewish out-marriage were generally low or very low. In many countries with large Jewish communities out-marriage still was nearly nonexistent, portraying nearly complete socio-cultural segregation between Jews and the majority of society. Few exceptions appeared in highly acculturated and veteran communities such as Italy, Germany, or the Netherlands, or even more so in distant and relatively isolated outposts with small Jewish populations such as Australia and New Zealand.

Over time, growing differentiation in the propensity to out-marry emerged across Jewish communities. The table presented here reports a classification of Jewish populations, according to the frequency of individual out-marriage in each country around 1930 and around 2000. Countries tend to concentrate at certain levels based on the respective histories and general levels of modernization, and different types of legal regimes in the respective countries allowing or not the opportunity for marriage across religious lines. A steady trend appears outlining a move from lower to higher rates of out-marriage.

In 1930, most Jews in the world lived in countries where the rate of out-marriage was below 5% of individuals. These included most of the large communities in Eastern Europe, most communities in the Middle East and North Africa, including Palestine, but also large and modern communities in the United States, the U.K., Latin America, and South Africa. Jewish communities with an out-marriage rate between 5% and 15% included France, and the other large communities in Eastern Europe such as the Soviet Union. No community stood above an out-marriage rate of 35%.

In 2000, a majority of world Jewry lived in countries where the out-marriage rate was higher than the 35% threshold. Jews in Israel were virtually alone still below a 5% out-marriage rate. Jews living in the Judea, Samaria and Gaza territories were probably the only group with less than 1% out-marriage. The out-marriage rate of the main part of Israel within the pre-1967 "green line," approaching 5%, reflected the presence and social absorption of new immigrants mostly from the FSU lacking a formal Jewish status. Many of these actually performed their marriage ceremonies abroad. Mexico was the largest Diaspora Jewish community with an out-marriage rate estimated at less that 15%. Communities in Australia, Canada, and Turkey had an out-marriage rate of 25% to 35%. A rather large share of world Jewry, including France, the U.K., and the main Latin American countries experienced out-marriage rates between 35% and 45%. The Jewish community in the U.S., still the largest in the world, had moved to above 50%. Out-marriage rates for Jews in the European parts of the FSU were above 65%.

As a consequence of these trends, the worldwide average level out-marriage rate passed from 5% around 1930 to 31%

around 2000. The same average computed for Jews in the Diaspora only, without Palestine/Israel, passed from 5% in 1930 to 48% in 2000. While this quite dramatic increase underscores the nearly irreversible trend toward social integration and acceptance of Jews among general society, it should be stressed that the rising share of Israel and the parallel shrinking of the Diaspora in the world Jewish population tends to reduce significantly the world out-marriage average.

CORRELATES, DETERMINANTS, AND CONSEQUENCES. *Societal models.* At least in the past, ethnocentric and pluralistic societies coped quite differently with the issue of cultural and religious diversity, which in turn affected the amount of pressure to conform exerted on Jewish minorities. Out-marriage trends, in general and within Jewish society, was significantly associated with these different types of societal configurations.

Jewish community models. Some of these are more central and more comprehensive, while some others are quite dispersed. The amount of participation of Jews in Jewish community life is usually different across countries. This may reflect certain general assumptions in society but also reflects the specificities of the history of particular Jewish communities.

Sameness and otherness. Out-marriage in terms of religion or ethnic identity is also associated with other elements of otherness among the partners. Heterogeneous couples in terms of Jewish identification tend also to be more different in terms of other aspects of their socio-demographic profile, such as education or age.

Gender. Women in the past had lower rates of out-marriage, due probably to the more limited set of opportunities they had – less education, less participation in the labor force, more limited and confined leisure life. However, through the emancipation of women and their achieving education and jobs, the differentials narrowed very significantly. By the 1980s-1990s the gender gap was disappearing and the previously lower out-marriage rates of Jewish women converged to the higher rates of men.

Age. The structure of the marriage market – that is, how many available mates there may be – may sometimes be unbalanced, to the point that people may be left with the alternative not to marry at all, or to out-marry. Out-marriage tends to occur at a later age than in the case of in-marriage.

Socioeconomic differentials. In the past, out-marriage was strongly related to upward social mobility, and was more frequent among the better educated, wealthier, and more socially mobile. More recent data suggest that, on the contrary, out-marriage seems to be related to lower education, and lower social class – which indeed is quite infrequent among Jews. It is likely that the high cost of Jewish life causes some people to be marginalized vis-à-vis the opportunities of Jewish education, leisure, and culture. Those will consequently live mostly in a non-Jewish context.

Residence. Size and density of a Jewish community can be importantly correlated to marriage opportunities. The relation of out-marriage to place of residence reflects both the cause and the consequence. Internet and distance connections may have an impact on these relations in the future.

Jewish identification. This is the most important predictor of in- versus out-marriage. We have good evidence that Jewishness of the parental home is probably the most powerful factor, followed by formal Jewish education received. Patterns of socialization that begin very early in life appear to have a crucial effect on subsequent patterns of affiliation, social networks, and the subsequent opportunities for marital choice.

Marital stability. Out-marriages are more unstable than in-marriages. The reasons may be complex. The couple's assortment in re-marriages tends to be often of the opposite sign than in first marriages.

Acceptance. A circular relation emerges between frequencies of out-marriage and its social acceptance. Something that is more frequent is more acceptable, and something that is more acceptable becomes more frequent. Attitudes tend to be more open to intermarriage than actual behaviors.

Transmitted identity. Theoretically, if one half of the children of out-marriages are affiliated with one side and one half is affiliated with the other, there is no gain and no loss to either side. In reality, according to nearly all research evidence available, the Jewish side has received less than half of all the children of out-marriages. During the 1990s, less than 20% of the children of out-marriages were affiliated with the Jewish side both in the U.S. and in the Russian Republic. In the U.S., Canada, and other English-speaking countries, the mother is the dominant parent in transmitting a group identity to the children. If the mother is Jewish, the child tends to be Jewish, and if the mother is not Jewish the child tends to be non-Jewish. This conforms to the Jewish *halakhah*. In other societies, such as Latin American or Southern and Eastern European countries, where the father is the dominant parent in the allocation of the child's public identity, children mostly follow the father's identity.

IMPLICATIONS. Second and Third Generation. While the evidence is not massive, it points to a spectacular increase in the rate of out-marriage among the children of out-marriage, even if they have grown up as Jews. Possibly because of the model gauged from their parents, children may consider out-marriage a normal option. The children's social networks, too, tend to be more open to people of different backgrounds. Out-marriage in effect becomes very high in the 2nd generation.

Collective consequences. Broader implications affect the Jewish collective beyond individual experiences. What out-marriage does to the Jewish people needs to be considered in terms of the major actors and processes such as Israel-Diaspora relations, consensus on core values, polarization among the Jewish polity, and even Jewish theology. Inasmuch as it is perceived as contradicting prevailing norms, besides its likely erosive effects on population size and composition, out-marriage is a factor of internal tension and stress. This is a fundamental question for Jewish policy making, and one of the major challenges world Jewry faces at the beginning of the 21st century.

[Sergio DellaPergola (2nd ed.)]

BIBLIOGRAPHY: E. Mayer, *Jewish-Gentile Courtships* (1961); W.J. Cahnman (ed.), *Intermarriage and Jewish Life* (1963); JJSO, 3 (1961), 195–242; 4 (1962), 47–71; W.M. Lipman, *ibid.*, 8 (1966), 213–39; JSQS, index s.v. *Intermarriage*; E. Rosenthal, in: AJYB, 64 (1963), 3–53; idem, in: *Journal of Marriage and the Family*, 32, no. 3 (1970), 435–40; M. Sklare, in: *Commentary*, 37 (April 1964), 46–52; 49 (1970), 51–58; M. Davis,*Beit Yisrael ba-Amerikah* (1970), 276–342 (incl. bibl.); I. Ellman, in: *Dispersion and Unity*, 9 (1969), 111–42; N. Mirsky, in: *Midstream*, 16 (1970), 40–46; M. Altschuler, in: *Beḥinot*, 1 (1970), 56–58; A. Schwartz, in: AJYB, 71 (1970), 101–22. **ADD. BIBLIOGRAPHY:** S.B. Fishman, *Double or Nothing: Jewish Families and Mixed Marriage* (2004). LEGAL ASPECTS: ET, 5 (1953), 286–93, 295–300; B. Shereshevsky, *Dinei Mishpaḥah* (1967²), 80–87, 349–51; M. Elon, *Ḥakikah Datit* (1968), 77–79, 85–89. **ADD. BIBLIOGRAPHY:** M. Elon, *Ha-Mishpat ha-Ivri* (1988), 1:1496; idem, *Jewish Law* (1994), 1: 1782. DEMOGRAPHIC PERSPECTIVES: M. Altschuler, "Some Facts Regarding Mixed Marriage Among Soviet Russian Jewry," in: *Dispersion and Unity*, n. 11 (1970); AMIA, *La Communidad judia de Tucuman: Estudio estadistico* (1963); idem, *Censo de la Comunidad Judia de Quilmes* (1963)Austria, *Die Ehescheidung, in: Beiträge zur Österreischen Statistik*, vol. 33 (1959); M. Axelrod, F.J. Fowler Jr. and A. Gurin, *A Community Survey for Long Range Planning: A Study of the Jewish Population of Greater Boston* (1967); R. Bachi, "Aims and Ways of Comparative Research on the Demography of the Jews" in: *Sixth World Congress of Jewish Studies, Demographic Sessions* (1973); Baltimore, *The Jewish Community of Greater Baltimore: A Population Study* (1968); D. Bensimon and S. DellaPergola, "Sondage socio-démographique auprés des Juifs en France," in: *Archives Juives*, vol. 10, n. 1 (1973); D. Bensimon and F. Lautman, "Aspects religieux et culturels des mariages entre juifs et chrétiens en France," in: *Ethnies*, vol. 4, (1974); L.A. Berman, *Jews and Intermarriage* (1968); J. Blum, *Dansk og / eller jøde?* (1972); S. Bronsztein, "Badanie ankietowe ludnosci zydowskiej Dolnego Slaska: Problematyka Demograficzna," in: *Biuletyn Zydowskiego Instytutu Historycznego*, n. 47–48 (1963), n. 50 (1964); H. Carter and P. Glick, *Marriage and Divorce: A Social and Economic Study* (1970); M. Davis, "Mixed Marriage in Western Jewry: Historical background to the Jewish response," in: JJS, vol. 10, n. 2 (1968); S. DellaPergola, *Jewish and Mixed Marriages in Milan, 1901–1968* (1972); A.A. Dubb, "Retrospect and Prospect in the Growth of the Jewish Community in the Republic of South Africa," in: U.O. Schmelz, P. Glikson and S. DellaPergola (eds.), *Papers in Jewish Demography, 1969* (1973); I. Ellman, "Jewish Inter-Marriage in the United States of America," in: *Dispersion and Unity*, n. 9 (1969); L. Fein, "Some Consequences of Jewish Inter-marriage," in: JSS, n. 1 (1971); P. Glikson, "Selected Bibliography, 1969–1971," in: U.O. Schmelz, P. Glikson and S.J. Gould (eds.), *Studies in Jewish Demography, Survey for 1969–1971* (1975); N. Goldberg, "Intermarriage from a Sociological Perspective," *Intermarriage and the Future of the American Jew, Proceedings of a conference sponsored by the Commission on Synagogue Relations* (1964); S. Goldstein, *A Population Survey of the Greater Springfield Jewish Community* (1968); idem, "American Jewry, 1970: a Demographic Profile," in: AJYB, 72 (1971); S. Goldstein, and C. Goldscheider, "Social and Demographic Aspects of Jewish Intermarriages," in: *Social Problems*, vol. 13, n. 4 (1966); J.S. Heiss, "Premarital Characteristics of the Religiously Intermarried in an Urban Area," in: *American Sociological Review*, 25 (1960); E. Krausz, *Leeds Jewry: Its History and Social Structure* (1964); B. Lazerwitz, "Intermarriage and Conversion: A Guide for Future Research," in: JJS, vol. 13, n. 1 (1971); J.S. Levi, "Intermarriage in Melbourne: A 12 Months Survey," in: *Conference on Sociological Studies of Jews in Australia* (1969); Los Angeles, *A Report on the Jewish Population of Los Angeles* (1968); F. Massarik and A. Chenkin, "United States National Jewish Population Study: A First Report," in: AJYB, 74 (1973); J.A. Newth, "Statistical Study of Intermarriage among Jews in Vilnius (Vilna)," in: *Bulletin on Soviet Jewish Affairs* (1968); Ph. van Praag, *Demografie van de Joden in Nederland* (1971); S.J. Prais and M. Schmool, "Statistics of Jewish Marriages in Great Britain: 1901–1965," in: JJS, vol. 9, n. 2 (1967); H. Rattner, "Census and sociological research of the Jewish community in Sao Paulo, 1968," in: U.O. Schmelz, P. Glikson and S. DellaPergola (eds.), *Papers in Jewish Demography, 1969* (1973); Rochester, *The Jewish Population of Rochester, New York, 1961* (1964); E. Rosenthal, "Divorce and religious intermarriage: the effect of previous marital status upon subsequent marital behavior," in: *Journal of Marriage and the Family*, vol. 32, n. 3 (1970); idem, "Mixed marriage, Intermarriage," in: *Encyclopaedia Judaica*, vol. 12 (1971); A. Schwartz, "Intermarriage in the United States," in: AJYB 71 (1970); U. Schmelz, "*He'arot Aḥadot le-Demografia shel ha-Yehudim be-Amerika ha-Latinit*," in: *Gesher*, 68–69 (1971); U.O. Schmelz, "An overview of new findings and studies in the demography of the Jews, 1969–1971," in: U.O. Schmelz, P. Glikson and S.J. Gould (eds.), *Studies in Jewish Demography, Survey for 1969–1971* (1975); idem, "A Guide to Jewish Population Studies," in: U.O. Smelz and P. Glikson (eds.), *Jewish Population Studies,1961–1968* (1970); U.O. Schmelz and S. DellaPergola, *Ha-Demografia shel ha-Yehudim be-Argentina u-be-Araẓot Aḥerot shel Amerika ha-Latinit* (1974); M. Sicron and H. Jaimovich, *Mimẓa'im 'Ikarim mi-Seker Yehudei Cordoba* (1973); M. Sklare, "Intermarriage and Jewish Survival," in: *Commentary*, vol. 49, n. 7 (1970); idem, "The Conversion of the Jews," in: *Commentary*, vol. 56, n. 3 (1973); State of California, *Divorce in California: Initial Complaints for Divorce, Annulment and Separate Maintenance, 1966* (1967); F. de Tenenbaum, *La Comunidad Judia de Guatemala: estadisticas recopiladas del Censo de la Comunidad en 1963* (1964); United States, *Current Population Reports*, Series P. 20, n. 79 (1958); C.F. Westoff, *A Population Survey: The Greater Camden County Jewish Community* (1965); C. Zelenka (ed.), *La Comunidad de Panama: datos estadisticos compilados de censo de la Comunidad en 1960–1961* (1961).

MIXED SPECIES (Heb. כִּלְאַיִם; *kilayim*), prohibition mentioned twice in the Bible. Leviticus 19:19 states: "Ye shall keep my statutes. Thou shalt not let thy cattle gender with a diverse kind; thou shalt not sow thy field with two kinds of seed; neither shall there come upon thee a garment of two kinds of stuff mingled together." Deuteronomy 22:9–11 states: "Thou shalt not sow thy vineyard with two kinds of seed; lest the fulness of the seed which thou hast sown be forfeited together with the increase of the vineyard. Thou shalt not plow with an ox and an ass together. Thou shalt not wear a mingled stuff, wool and linen together." From these two passages the sages deduced six types of mixing of species which are forbidden: the mixing of seeds; the grafting of different species of trees and vegetables; the mixing of seed in a vineyard; the hybridization of domestic and wild animals; plowing or driving with domestic or non-domestic animals of different species; and the mixing of wool and linen (*sha'atnez).

The prohibitions against mixing species are defined in Mishnah *Kilayim* 8:1 "It is forbidden to sow diverse kinds in a vineyard or to suffer them to grow, and it is forbidden to have any benefit from them. It is forbidden to sow diverse kinds of seed or to suffer them to grow, but they may be eaten and certainly benefit may be derived from them. Mixed materials are permitted for all purposes, only the weaving of them being forbidden. Hybrid cattle may be reared and maintained; it is forbidden only to breed them." The many *halakhot* connected with the laws of mixed species are taught in the Mishnah, Tosefta, and Jerusalem Talmud of the tractate *Kilayim. The chief problems relating to those laws are detailed below.

The Mixing of Seeds

The prohibition applies to the sowing together of two kinds of grains if they are regarded as belonging to different species (see below), or of grain and legume, as well as of other edible plants. A lenient ruling was given regarding vegetables, which were customarily sown in small beds, and it was permitted to sow five species at specified distances from one another in a bed one cubit square and with variations even 13 species (Kil. 3:l). According to most authorities, it is obligatory to separate fields sown with different species by the space of a *rova* (104 square cubits) or of three furrows (two cubits). In the opinion of some commentators, including Solomon Sirillio and Elijah Gaon of Vilna, the measures mentioned in the Mishnah (Kil. 2:6–10) refer to the size of the plot near which a different kind may be sown (and not to the space by which they must be separated), since plots of this size and larger have the appearance of separate fields, and there is no fear that they may be thought to have been planted indiscriminately, nor is there any risk that the different species will derive sustenance from one another. The prohibition of mixed seeds applies only in Ereẓ Israel, while the prohibitions of the other mixed species are of universal application (Kid. 39a).

The Mixing of Trees

This is not mentioned explicitly in the Bible but is inferred from the juxtaposition of verses (Lev. 19:19), "Thou shalt not let thy cattle gender with a diverse kind; thou shalt not sow thy field with two kinds of seed," which were interpreted to mean, "Just as the prohibition of cattle refers to mating, so does that of the field to grafting" (Kid. 39a), i.e., it is forbidden to graft two plant species in the same way as it is forbidden to mate two animal species. Some inferred the prohibition of grafting plants of different species from the beginning of the verse (Lev. 19:19): "Ye shall keep my statutes"; *Sifra, Kedoshim* (Perek 4:17) and the Jerusalem Talmud (Kil. 1:7, 27b) explain that the word *ḥukkah* ("statute"), is connected with the root *ḥakok* ("to carve"), i.e., that it is forbidden to change by grafting the original form "carved out" by the Creator at Creation. The prohibition applies to grafting a tree onto a tree, a vegetable onto a tree, and a tree onto a vegetable (Kil. 1:7). However, it is permitted to plant different trees side by side and to sow vegetables or grain among trees.

Mixing in the Vineyard

The laws of mixed species in the vineyard are stringent and complex, and almost half of the tractate *Kilayim* is devoted to them. The Bible (Deut. 22:9) rules that the resulting vines and seed become forfeit, and it is forbidden either to eat them or to benefit from them. The prohibition applies to grain but not to any trees among the vines. Concerning vegetables and other plants there are differences of opinion in the Mishnah and Talmud as to which are forbidden by biblical law and which permitted. A distance of four cubits must be allowed between a vineyard and any species forbidden to be sown there. In the case of a single vine, however, it suffices to leave a distance of three or six handbreadths (Kil. 6:1).

Mixing of Cattle

According to the Mishnah (Kil. 8:1) "they may be reared and maintained, and it is only forbidden to breed them." "To rear and maintain" means that different species of cattle may be reared together without the fear that they will crossbreed. Some explain it to mean that the product of crossbreeding (e.g., a mule) may be reared. This prohibition applies to domestic and wild animals and to birds (BK 5:7).

Plowing and Driving with Two Species

The Bible forbids only plowing with an ox and an ass. The rabbis, however, explained that "Scripture spoke what was customary," i.e., people were accustomed to plow with an ox or an ass, but the prohibition applies equally to plowing with any two other species and to riding, leading, and driving with them (Kil. 8:2).

Problems of Definition

In the discussion of the laws of mixed species the problem of defining like and unlike species arises. Although criteria for determining whether a plant or animal belongs to one species or another are laid down, an examination of the pairs enumerated in the Mishnah that do or do not constitute mixed species shows that there is no identity between the term "species" used in the law of mixed species and the term as applied by the modern system of botanical and zoological classification. Mixed species were determined by a tradition crystallized in the course of many generations (cf. Tosef., Kil. 1:3–4). Indeed two plants which are now classified as belonging to different species or even to different genera are reckoned as the same species for the law of mixed species (e.g., wheat and tares; Kil. 1:1). In contrast, however, different strains of the same species are regarded as different species (Kil. 1:6). With regard to mixed seeds an *amora* in the Jerusalem Talmud (Kil. 1:5, 27a) summarizes: "in some cases [the form of] the fruit is the determinant, and in others the leaf," while another *amora* notes: "in some cases the taste of the fruit is the determinant."

One of the assumptions in the prohibitions of mixed trees is the possibility of crossbreeding by grafting the scion of one species onto the stock of a second. Thus it is pointed out in the Jerusalem Talmud that grafting the almond onto the terebinth produces the *pistachio, a fruit similar to that of both these species but systematically very far removed from the almond. It is almost certain that a graft of such a nature will not take, and it is certain that a species which has the median characteristics of the scion and the stock cannot be obtained by grafting. The early scholars saw an analogy between the grafting of plants and the crossbreeding of animals, but this latter could be compared to the cross-pollination of plants, a technique unknown to the ancients.

These views on grafting stem from the once-accepted assumption that environmental factors were liable to change the hereditary characteristics of the creature (see *Biology). The opinion that new species could be created by grafting belongs to agricultural folklore, and also to Greco-Roman "science," and from there entered into rabbinic literature. Because of the prohibition of mixed species, Jews were unable to test the truth of this notion. Many *halakhot* on the subject commence with the formula: "If a gentile grafted" species A with species B, then species C is produced. It should be stressed, however, that *halakhot* of this nature, common in the Tosefta and the Jerusalem Talmud, were not incorporated in the Mishnah (see *Kilayim).

Reasons for the Precept of Mixed Species

Some of the reasons given for the prohibition stemmed from the above-mentioned belief that the effects of environmental factors are hereditary. To the same category belongs the reason for forbidding change in the order of Creation. Naḥmanides gives this reason in his biblical commentary (to Lev. 19: 19), adding that if the crossbreeding of a horse and an ass produces a mule, which is a miserable creature that cannot beget, so too when mixed species of trees are grafted, "their fruit does not grow thereafter." Maimonides (*Guide* 3, 49) explains that the man who couples creatures of different species defies the laws of nature and of ethics, and similarly in the grafting and mixing of plants. It was part of the false beliefs of idolators that this served as a specific for fertility (*ibid.* 3, 37). That crossbreeding was unnatural was an early belief: Josephus (Ant., 4:229) explained that "nature delighteth not in the conjunction of things dissimilar." Rabbenu Nathan, *av ha-yeshivah* (Ereẓ Israel in the 11th century), gives an agricultural reason, that one species prevents the development of the adjacent one (commentary to Mishnah Kil. ch. 1). A similar reason for the prohibition of mixed seeds in the vineyard was given earlier by Philo: "since as a result of it too great a burden is put upon the earth" (Spec. 4:211). Some Greek and Roman agricultural writers laid down that summer plants which impoverish the soil should not be sown in the vineyard (Pliny, Naturalis 18, 101) and that it is forbidden to sow intermediate plantings in a vineyard (Geoponica 5, 11).

As against those who sought to rationalize the prohibition, Rashi concluded: "These statutes are a royal decree, for which there is no reason." In point of fact it is impossible to determine the reasons for the prohibition. Post factum, however, it seems that, as a result of the care taken by Jews in this matter, the fields were kept free of weeds and the purity of plant species was preserved. It is also possible that it was a contributory factor to the success of Jewish agriculture in Ereẓ Israel.

In the present, prohibitions of mixed species have raised a number of problems for farmers who adhere to these laws. Thus they are prevented from sowing vetch with grain as fodder in order to prevent the vetch from trailing on the ground. The problem was solved by the introduction of strains of vetch which do not trail. In connection with the prohibition against grafting trees of different species, experiments have taken place on stocks belonging to the same species as the scion, but so far no satisfactory solution to the matter has been found.

BIBLIOGRAPHY: Loew, Flora, 4 (1934), 291ff.; J. Feliks, *Ha-Ḥakla'ut be-Ereẓ Yisrael bi-Tekufat ha-Midrash ve-ha-Talmud* (1963); idem, *Kilei Zera'im ve-Harkavah* (1967).

[Jehuda Feliks]

MIZMOR LE-DAVID (Heb. מִזְמוֹר לְדָוִד; "A Psalm to David"), a frequently occurring superscription to a number of psalms whose authorship is ascribed to King *David. Many of them form part of the traditional liturgy. Among them are (1) Psalm 29 ("Ascribe unto the Lord, O ye sons of might"), the last of the six psalms chanted at the Sabbath eve service at which the Sabbath is welcomed; and on Sabbath mornings, after the conclusion of the *Torah reading, when the Torah scroll is carried back in solemn procession to the *Ark. (2) Psalm 23 ("The Lord is my shepherd, I shall not want"), which in the Sephardi ritual is sung prior to the *Kiddush on Sabbath morning, and in the Ashkenazi ritual, on Sabbath afternoon at the third meal (*Seudah Shelishit). According to one talmudic opinion (Pes. 118a), it was also sung as a festive hymn at the Passover *seder.

BIBLIOGRAPHY: JE, 8 (1904), 624–5; Elbogen, Gottesdienst, index s.v. Psalm 29.

MIZMOR SHIR LE-YOM HA-SHABBAT (Heb. מִזְמוֹר שִׁיר לְיוֹם הַשַּׁבָּת; "A Psalm, a Song for the Sabbath Day"), the superscription of Psalm 92 which, according to the Talmud (Tam. 7:4, RH 31a, Sof. 18:1) was the Sabbath hymn chanted by the levites in the Temple. The Psalm forms part of the Sabbath eve service in which the Sabbath (*Kabbalat Shabbat) is welcomed. It is also part of the *Pesukei de-Zimra and the daily hymn at the conclusion of the Sabbath morning service, as well as in the Sabbath *Minḥah* service in the Sephardi and some Ashkenazi rites. Some aggadic sources ascribe its authorship to Adam who pronounced it in his great joy for the gift of repentance. In the course of time, it was forgotten until Moses reintroduced it with ten other psalms (Gen. R. 22, end; Mid. Ps. 90:30).

BIBLIOGRAPHY: JE, 8 (1904), 625–7; Eisenstein, Dinim s.v.

MIẒPAH (Heb. מִצְפָּה; "lookout point"), moshavah in northern Israel, W. of Tiberias, founded in 1908 by Second *Aliyah pioneers from Russia, on *Jewish Colonization Association (ICA) land. For many years the small village, based on mixed farming, preserved its original layout of closely grouped farmsteads interconnected by a surrounding basalt wall. It only began to expand after it was connected to a water line in 1979, its population increasing from 39 in 1968 to 167 in 2002.

[Efram Orni / Shaked Gilboa (2nd ed.)]

MIZPEH or **MIZPAH** (Heb. מִצְפֶּה, מִצְפָּה, הַמִּצְפָּה; "lookout point"), the name of several places mentioned in the Bible.

(1) A city belonging to the tribe of Benjamin (Josh. 18:26), the best-known place with the name of Mizpeh. The Israelites gathered there to punish the tribe of Benjamin after the outrage committed by the men of Gibeah (Judg. 20–21). Samuel assembled the people to fight against the Philistines and judged them in Mizpah (I Sam. 7:5ff.; 10:17). Asa of Judah fortified the place (I Kings 15:22; II Chron. 16:6). Gedaliah, the son of Ahikam, established the capital of Judah in Mizpah after the fall of Jerusalem and was later assassinated there (II Kings 25:22ff.; Jer. 40–41). It was a district capital in the time of Nehemiah (Neh. 3:7, 15, 19). The place of origin of Simeon of Mizpeh (Pe'ah 2:6) is uncertain.

The ancient site is identified with Tell al-Naṣbeh about 8 mi. (13 km.) north of Jerusalem, following A. Raboisson (*Les Maspeh*, 1897). It was excavated from 1926 to 1936 by W.F. Badè on behalf of the Pacific Institute of Religion in Berkeley. The first settlement there dates to the Early Bronze Age. Its main period of occupation, however, belongs to the Iron Age. The excavations uncovered the main part of the city, which contained many four-room houses typical of the period, some unusually large and built with pillars. Outstanding is a ninth-century wall and gate, evidently built by Rehoboam, which had been preceded by a tenth-century casemate wall. The mound was occupied until the Hellenistic period. A number of tombs uncovered there date from the Canaanite to the Hellenistic periods and were very rich in finds.

Hebrew seals and seal impressions were particularly abundant on the site. A seal with the inscription "Jaazaniah servant of the king" is ascribed by some to the Jezaniah who met with Gedaliah at Mizpah (Jer. 40:8; 42:1). A special seal from the Persian period reading *mṣh* (Mozah?) is interpreted by various scholars as an abbreviation of Mizpeh (*mṣ[p]h*).

(2) The land of Mizpah (Josh. 11:3) or the valley of Miẓpeh (Josh. 11:8) in the north of the country below the Hermon, an area settled by the Hivites. It was probably located in the region of Marj al-ʿAyyūn (ʿIyyon), north of Metullah.

(3) A place in Gilead which marked the boundary between the territories of Laban and Jacob (Gen. 31:49). It is perhaps identical with Ramoth-Gilead, a border stronghold between Aram and Israel in northern Gilead (I Kings 22:3).

(4) The hometown of *Jephthah, also in Gilead, but farther south than (3) above. The Israelites gathered there before setting out for battle against the Ammonites (Judg. 10–11). It is identical with Ramath-Mizpeh in the vicinity of Mahanaim of Joshua 13:26. It has been tentatively identified with Khirbat Jalʿad south of the Jabbok.

(5) A city in the territory of the tribe of Judah in the vicinity of Lachish (Josh. 15:38). Eusebius (Onom. 130:2 – Masseba) describes it as a village near Eleutheropolis (Bet Guvrin).

(6) A Mizpeh of Moab (Rujm al-Mushayrifa?) is mentioned in I Samuel 22:3.

(7) A Mizpeh (Massepha) at which Judah Maccabee assembled his army against Gorgias (I Macc. 3:46) is probably identical with Nabi Samuîl northwest of Jerusalem.

BIBLIOGRAPHY: C.C. McCown et al., *Tell en Nasbeh*, 1 (1947); J.C. Wampler, *Tell en Nasbeh*, 2 (1947); Avigad, in: IEJ, 8 (1958), 113ff.; Albright, in: AASOR, 4 (1924), 90ff.; Abel, Geog, 2 (1938), 340ff.; Aharoni, Land, index; Diringer, in: D. Winton Thomas (ed.), *Archaeology and Old Testament Study* (1967), 329ff.; EM, s.v. incl. bibl.

[Michael Avi-Yonah]

MIẒPEH RAMON (Heb. מִצְפֵּה רָמוֹן), development town in S. Israel, in the Negev Hills, 54 mi. (87 km.) S. of Beersheba toward Eilat. Founded in 1954, initially as a labor camp of the workers employed in the construction of the highway, it became an "urban cooperative," and when this dispersed seven months later, it was turned into a development town. At the beginning conditions were extremely hard; water had to be brought in trucks from the north, and communications were frequently cut off when the highway to the north was blocked by floods. In spite of these difficulties the town absorbed new immigrants from North Africa and Europe and in 1968 had a population of 1,470. In 1964 Miẓpeh Ramon received municipal council status and in 2002 its population was 4,820, occupying an area of 33 sq. mi. (86 sq. km.).

Although servicing the central Negev, the opening of the Sedom-Eilat road increased its isolation and contributed to the town's high unemployment rate and low personal income, though efforts have been made to develop tourism. In recent years, artists from all over the country have established their residence there, and Israel's largest observatory, belonging to Tel Aviv University, is located in the town. The name means "Ramon Lookout" and refers to the town's site on the rim of the Ramon Crater, which affords a remarkable view of Negev desert landscape.

WEBSITE: www.mitzpe-ramon.muni.il.

[Shlomo Hasson / Shaked Gilboa (2nd ed.)]

MIZRA (Heb. מִזְרָע; "sown field"), kibbutz in northern Israel, north of Afulah, affiliated with Kibbutz Arẓi Ha-Shomer ha-Ẓa'ir. It was founded in 1923 by pioneers from Central Europe, who were later joined by others. Farming was highly intensive, including fruit orchards, citrus groves, field crops, and dairy cattle, and the kibbutz also ran a meat factory and a plant producing hydraulic presses. More recently, Mizra began to develop a tourist industry, including a hotel, restaurant, and small museum documenting the history of the kibbutz. In 1969 Mizra had 610 inhabitants; in 2002, 722.

WEBSITE: www.mizra.org.il.

[Efram Orni / Shaked Gilboa (2nd ed.)]

MIZRACHI (term coined from some of the letters of the Hebrew words *merkaz ruḥani*, spiritual center), religious Zionist movement whose aim was expressed in its motto: "The Land of Israel for the people of Israel according to the Torah of Israel" (coined by Rabbi Meir Berlin – Bar-Ilan). Mizrachi was founded in 1902 as a religious faction in the World Zionist Organization. The name was first used by Samuel *Mohilewer, an early leader of *Ḥibbat Zion, to express the idea that the Torah should be the spiritual center for Zionism.

The Beginning of Mizrachi

Many religious Jews, including famous rabbis, joined the movement of political Zionism, which worked toward the establishment of a Jewish state in the Land of Israel. Among the first to join was Rabbi Isaac *Reines, who responded to Theodor *Herzl's call and devoted his energies to spreading the idea of a national renaissance among Orthodox Jews. Reines believed that the Zionist movement must be dedicated exclusively to a political goal, and he led the fight against the inclusion of cultural activities in the Zionist program. After the Fifth Zionist Congress, however, when the strength of the "cultural" camp grew and official permission was granted to establish factions (federations) within the framework of the Zionist Organization. Reines decided to found a federation of religious Zionists. Toward this end, he convened the founding convention in Vilna on March 4–5, 1902, and it established the national-religious organization within the Zionist Organization. At the suggestion of Rabbi Abraham *Slutzky, the organization was called Mizrachi.

An outstanding participant at the founding convention was Rabbi Ze'ev *Jawitz, who was charged with composing the organization's first manifesto. Two groups clashed at the founding convention: the "political" faction, which called for the preservation of the purely political character of the Zionist movement and opposed the decision of the Fifth Zionist Congress (1901) obligating the Zionist Organization to include cultural activities in its program; and the "cultural" faction, which demanded that Mizrachi, as a "spiritual center," influence the Zionist movement and its work in the Land of Israel in its traditional-religious spirit. The Mizrachi program, which was accepted by the majority of the participants at the founding convention, stated that the Zionist Organization should not engage in activities that do not have a direct relationship to Zionism. and it was stated in the manifesto that Mizrachi should try "to gather around it all those Zionists who wish to purge practical Zionism of any alien element that is not directly related to political and practical Zionism." These decisions seem to reveal the victory of the "political" faction. Jawitz, however, who formulated the manifesto, succeeded in reflecting in it both viewpoints and thus satisfied both trends. An opening was thus created for cultural activities, albeit only in the framework of branches, "in line with local conditions and in the spirit of Orthodoxy."

A year after its establishment, Mizrachi's second conference was convened in Lida on March 22–24, 1903. During its first year, Mizrachi succeeded in building up 210 branches in Russia alone (which then included Poland, Lithuania, Courland, etc.). Mizrachi societies were also established in Galicia, Romania, Austria, Hungary, Germany, England, and Switzerland. First attempts were made to organize Mizrachi in Ereẓ Israel, and two-and-a-half years after it was founded, its branches also became active in Western Europe and in the United States. The first world conference of Mizrachi took place, with the participation of about 100 delegates, in Pressburg, Hungary (now Bratislava, Slovakia), on Aug. 21–23, 1904. The conference laid the foundation for the Mizrachi World Organization. Reines was the conference's chairman and delivered the opening address in Hebrew. Other speakers included Nehemiah *Nobel, among the great rabbis of Western Europe; Jawitz; Rabbi Nahum Grinhaus from Troki; and Rabbi Judah Leib Fishman (*Maimon). The movement's program was summed up at the conference as follows:

(1) Mizrachi is an organization of Zionists who follow the *Basle Program and desire to work for the perpetuation of Jewish national life. Mizrachi sees the perpetuation of the Jewish people in the observance of the Torah, Jewish tradition, and the *mitzvot* and the return to the land of its forefathers.

(2) Mizrachi will remain within the framework of the Zionist Organization, in which it will struggle for its opinions and views. However, it will create a special organization of its own for its religious and cultural activities.

(3) The purpose of Mizrachi is to realize its goals by employing all the legal means at its disposal to explain its ideas to all Orthodox circles, by creating and distributing national-religious literature, and by educating youth in the spirit of its ideals and programs.

From Crisis to Expansion

At the Tenth Zionist Congress, which took place in Basle in 1911, the question of cultural work was again raised, and a bitter battle ensued between its advocates and opponents. In order to establish its stand on the question, Mizrachi called a meeting before the congress and decided to light against the inclusion of cultural work in the Zionist program, but not by threatening secession. The majority at the congress, however, decided to include cultural work in the framework of the Zionist Organization's activities. Consequently, all the Mizrachi delegates walked out of the hall to demonstrate their opposition to the decision. The fifth world conference of Mizrachi was held in Berlin, immediately after the Zionist Congress, to formulate a stand on the decision of the Zionist Congress about cultural activities. The delegates from Russia and Poland were in favor of a struggle within the Zionist Organization using all possible means short of creating a split, for any schism would be a tragedy for the entire Jewish people and the national renaissance. On the other hand, representatives from the center in Frankfurt and some of the Swiss and Hungarian delegates were in favor of withdrawing from the Zionist Organization. The Berlin conference finally decided against leaving the Zionist Organization while conducting the struggle within its ranks. This decision brought about a rift in the ranks of Mizrachi, and a number of its leaders, including members of the head office in Frankfurt, left the organization. As a result the center of Mizrachi was moved to Altona, near Hamburg. Louis Frank was elected chairman and was later the second president of World Mizrachi.

During the term of the Hamburg executive, the central office of Mizrachi was established in the Land of Israel under the direction of Rabbi Fishman. Also during the Hamburg period, Rabbi Meir Berlin (Bar-Ilan) began working as the general secretary organizer of the Mizrachi World Organization. He left Lithuania for Berlin and there published the weekly *Ha-Ivri*. When Rabbi Berlin entered office, Mizrachi received a great impetus in its work and became a strong and influential factor both in the Zionist movement and among religious Jewry. Under his leadership, the first conference of Mizrachi to take place in the United States was convened in 1914, in Cincinnati, Ohio, and he succeeded in making the movement into an important factor in the lives of American Jewry and in the American Zionist movement. Rabbi Berlin was joined there by Rabbi Fishman, who had been expelled from Ereẓ Israel during World War I by the Turkish authorities and who added projects of his own and the atmosphere of Ereẓ Israel to the American movement. The first world conference of Mizrachi that took place after World War I (Amsterdam, Jan. 14–15, 1920) decided to transfer the seat of the world center to Jerusalem. Mizrachi was thus the first Zionist party to establish its center in Ereẓ Israel (and specifically in Jerusalem). In 1923 Rabbi Berlin, who was the leader of the movement and expanded its activities, settled in Ereẓ Israel. Some time later he was also elected president of the world organization and remained in this position until his death.

Mizrachi in Ereẓ Israel

After fundamental organizational preparation within circles of the old *yishuv* and organizational work that began in March 1918, including the foundation of branches in various areas of settlement in the country and the establishment of a "temporary center" in Jaffa, the foundations for Mizrachi were laid in Ereẓ Israel. Its first conference was held on Sept. 2, 1918, and since then Mizrachi has become a political and cultural force in the country. Among the founders of Mizrachi in Ereẓ Israel were Rabbi Ben-Zion *Ouziel, then the rabbi of Jaffa and afterward the Sephardi chief rabbi (*rishon le-Zion*), and Moshe *Ostrovsky (ha-Meiri), then the rabbi of the settlement of Ekron and afterward a member of the Va'ad Le'ummi. Rabbi Fishman participated at the second national conference (September 1919) after returning to the country from his absence during the war. Mizrachi reached the height of its development with the transfer of its world center to the country and especially after Rabbi Berlin settled there in 1923. During certain periods, Rabbi Berlin also served as the chairman of Mizrachi in the country.

As early as its first conference in Ereẓ Israel, Mizrachi raised the matter of establishing the offices of the rabbinate as one of the major points on the agenda. It subsequently devoted much effort to ensure the success of the conference to establish the chief rabbinate of Ereẓ Israel, which took place through the initiative of Rabbi Abraham Isaac *Kook in Jerusalem in February 1921. After great efforts, in December 1919 Mizrachi succeeded in acquiring the recognition of the Zionist institutions for its trend of religious education as a part of the educational system of the Zionist Organization.

With the end of World War I and the publication of the *Balfour Declaration, the Third Aliyah began to arrive in Palestine and brought with it members of Ẓe'irei Mizrachi, who strove to build up the land on the basis of pioneering labor and religious renewal. As young pioneers they called for "personal fulfillment," i.e., for religious Zionists to settle in Ereẓ Israel and build it in the spirit of the Torah. Their vision was expressed in the short motto "*Torah va-Avodah*," which became the basis for the religious labor movement and the establishment of *Ha-Po'el ha-Mizrachi in Ereẓ Israel. The idea struck roots in the Diaspora as well and became the slogan of the mass movement, called Torah va-Avodah, throughout the world. It was an active participant in the Jewish Agency prior to 1948 and was an active partner in Israel's government coalitions since the birth of the State (from 1956 as the National Religious Party; see below). Through the early 1980s it consistently polled about 10% of the total vote in Israel, but then dropped sharply to under 5% as less moderate parties to the right attracted many of its voters. (See *Israel, State of: Political Life and Parties.) The party was also active in the municipal level and was the main supporter of the chief rabbinate.

Educational Work

After the crisis that overcame Russian Jewry with the outbreak of the Russo-Japanese War, the revolution, and the pogroms that followed (1905), it was practically impossible to maintain the world center of Mizrachi in Russia. It was therefore decided to transfer the seat of its executive to Frankfurt, Germany. During the "Frankfurt period," Mizrachi activities became more systematic. Their most important aspect was the beginning of the educational work of Mizrachi in Ereẓ Israel. The world center decided to send Rabbi Fishman to study the situation of education in Ereẓ Israel and find ways to develop educational and cultural activities there. He laid the foundation for the establishment of the Taḥkemoni School in Jaffa, the first educational institution of Mizrachi in the country, which inaugurated Mizrachi's educational system based on a synthesis of "the people of Israel, the Torah, and Zion."

In 1920 an agreement was reached in the World Zionist Organization that ensured Mizrachi autonomy in the field of religious education in Ereẓ Israel. An educational program began to be designed, followed by the establishment of a network of Mizrachi schools, which included kindergartens, elementary schools, high schools, yeshivot, vocational schools, and teachers' seminaries. The educational network of Mizrachi continued to exist as a separate trend in Israel until the establishment of the State religious school system in the 1953/54 school year (see *Israel, State of: Education). The large majority of Mizrachi schools, which then encompassed more than 60,000 students and about 3,000 teachers, were integrated into the new framework of governmental religious education. The yeshivot have been the most outstanding achievement of Mizrachi education. In 16 high school-level yeshivot of *Bnei Akiva, students receive both a yeshivah and general education; in 12 girls' schools the educational program is parallel to that of the yeshivot. The network includes Midrashiat No'am in Pardes Ḥannah, "Torah and Melakhah" yeshivot, the agricultural yeshivah at Kefar ha-Ro'eh, and the yeshivah for higher studies at Kerem Yavneh. At *Bar-Ilan University in Ramat Gan, which was established by Mizrachi in the United States, there were more than 7,000 students in 1970, with extensions in Safed, Ashkelon, and the Jordan Valley. In 2005 it had over 30,000 students. After the 20th world conference of Mizrachi (1962), the educational work of the movement was administered by the Center for Religious Education in Israel, affiliated with the world center of Mizrachi-Ha-Po'el ha-Mizrachi and the movement in Israel. In 2005 the Center provided supplementary religious education in 255 secondary schools in Israel. The Emunah women's organization operated 120 day care centers throughout the country.

Structure of the World Movement

From 1955 the world movement of Mizrachi and Ha-Po'el ha-Mizrachi constituted one united organization. Before the merger of the two movements, however, they existed as separate world organizations – Mizrachi as the Mizrachi World Organization and Ha-Po'el ha-Mizrachi as Berit ha-Olamit shel Torah va-Avodah. The activities among women and youth had also been separate. The world center of Mizrachi and Ha-Po'el ha-Mizrachi is the highest body of the religious Zionist framework and constitutes a common executive of the two movements. It is elected by the world conference of the movement, which meets every few years. Rabbi Meir Berlin served as president of the world movement for many years. After his death (1949), Rabbi A.L. *Gellman was elected chairman of the world center. At the 21st world conference (1968), Ḥayyim Moshe *Shapira was elected president of the world center and the world movement and Rabbi Ẓemaḥ Zambrowski was elected chairman of the world center. The world movement's financial instrument is the Keren Ereẓ Israel shel Mizrachi.

When Mizrachi and Ha-Po'el ha-Mizrachi united throughout the world, a common conference of the two organizations in Israel was held in the summer of 1956 and decided to found a united party by the name of the *National Religious Party (Miflagah Datit Le'ummit, abbreviated to Mafdal). At the second conference of the NRP and the 13th conference of Ha-Po'el ha-Mizrachi in Israel (1963), the responsibilities and tasks of the NRP and Ha-Po'el ha-Mizrachi were divided as follows: the party will deal with matters of policy, municipal affairs, organization of the middle class, religion and rabbis, public relations and publication of the daily newspaper *Ha-Ẓofeh*; Ha-Po'el ha-Mizrachi with organization, fees, immigration and absorption, labor and vocational affairs, housing, settlement, culture, pension funds and economic affairs, matters concerning free professionals, and departments for elderly members and development towns.

Projects and Achievements

Mizrachi fought for the observance of the Sabbath in Israel and the preservation of the character of the Sabbath and Jewish holidays in the public life of the Jewish community. It initiated the establishment of the Ministry of Religions in the government of Israel and of covering the religious needs of the population from government funds and local authorities. Its efforts also led to the passage of the laws governing *kashrut* and Sabbath observance in the Israel Defense Forces, marriage and divorce, rabbinical judges, etc. Through the initiative of Rabbi Berlin, the Mifal ha-Torah Lema'an ha-Yeshivot be-Ereẓ Israel (Torah Fund for Yeshivot in the Land of Israel) was established whose publication of the Talmud and the *Encyclopedia Talmudica* is in progress. In the field of literature and journalism, the daily *Ha-Ẓofeh* and Mosad ha-Rav Kook, established by Rabbi Fishman and constituting the largest publishing house in the world for literature on the Torah and studies of Judaism, are worthy of mention. Since its foundation, more than 1,000 books have been published by the Mosad or with its aid.

Women's and youth organizations also hold an important place in the framework of the world movement. The women in the Mizrachi movement have taken part in the activities of Histadrut Nashim Mizrachi (Omen; Women's Mizrachi Federation in Ereẓ Israel) and Mo'eẓet ha-Po'alot shel Ha-Po'el ha-Mizrachi, which integrated into one movement called the National Religious Women's Movement in Ereẓ Israel, encompassing more than 50,000 members. This movement is active in the sphere of establishing kindergartens and day nurseries, the cultural absorption of new immigrants, the organization of agricultural and vocational training for its members, etc. Among the youth organizations centered around Mizrachi is *Bnei Akiva. Until the union of Mizrachi and Ha-Po'el ha-Mizrachi and the establishment of the NRP, the youth organization No'am (short for No'ar Mizrachi), which was founded on Ḥanukkah 1940 and established Midrashiat No'am in Pardes Ḥannah, existed separately. Other youth organizations are Ha-No'ar ha-Dati ha-Oved for working youth and Ha-Mishmeret ha-Ẓe'irah (The Young Guard), which encompassed thousands of students and army veterans. The world center of Mizrachi and Ha-Po'el ha-Mizrachi also established a special department for the young generation that centralized the activities of Ha-Mishmeret ha-Ẓe'irah around the world. Finally, there is the religious sports organization, Eliẓur.

The Mizrachi movement also established a series of financial and economic institutions including Bank ha-Mizrachi and Bank Ha-Po'el ha-Mizrachi, which united and established the United Mizrachi Bank, the fourth largest bank in the country; Mishhav, a company for construction and the establishment of religious quarters and suburbs; a center for the economic institutions and programs of the movement; the cooperative of Ha-Po'el ha-Mizrachi; pension funds; etc.

[Itzhak Goldshlag]

In the United States

Mizrachi of America was founded in 1911 with groups in New York and St. Louis. Rabbi D.B. Abramowitz was the first president. The organization did not become effective until 1913, when Rabbi Meir Berlin settled in New York and became the leader of the movement. Following a tour of the country by Rabbi Berlin, Mizrachi held its first annual convention in Cincinnati in 1914. The Mizrachi Palestine Fund was established in 1928, and in 1936 became part of the United Palestine Appeal. Its youth movement, Benei Akiva, was established in 1934. In 1951 Mizrachi merged with Ha-Po'el ha-Mizrachi, which had been established early in the 1920s. AMIT, the Mizrachi Women of America (AMIT), is involved in educational work, funding an educational network in Israel that includes 22 primary and secondary schools, four youth and family residential facilities, five youth technology centers, and seven technical training colleges.

[Louis Bernstein]

BIBLIOGRAPHY: M. Waxman, *Mizrachi, its Aims and Purposes* (1918); P. Churgin and L. Gellman (eds.), *Mizrachi Jubilee Publication of the Mizrachi Organization of America 1911–1936* (1936); J.L. Maimon, *History of the Mizrachi Movement* (1938); S.Z. Shragai, *Vision and Realization* (1945); S. Rosenblatt, *History of the Mizrachi Movement* (1951); Y. Tirosh, *Essence of Religious Zionism* (1964); idem, *Religion and State in Israel: The Religious Zionist Standpoint* (1965); Mizrachi-Ha-Po'el ha-Mizrachi, *The Length and Breadth of the Land* (1965); B. Cohen, *Religious Zionism – a Revaluation* (1966); M. Berlin, *Mi-Volozhin ad Yerushalayim*, 2 vols. (1939–40); idem, *Bi-Shevilei ha-Teḥiyyah* (1940); idem, *Kitvei…* (1940); M. Ostrovsky, *Toledot ha-Mizrachi be-Ereẓ-Yisrael* (1944); I. Goldschlag, *Mi-Vilna ad Yerushalayim* (1954); *Mizrachi Woman* (1933–); *Mizrachi Outlook* (1936–57); *Jewish Horizon* (1957–).

MIZRACHI, SHIMON (1940–), chairman of the Maccabi Tel Aviv basketball team. Mizrachi was born in Tel Aviv. In 1969 he joined the management of Maccabi Tel Aviv, when the team faced economic crisis. He initiated an economic plan to save the team, and began for the first time to sell tickets to the team's games. Mizrachi was also the first to understand that without foreign players the team would not succeed. His vision was fulfilled when Maccabi Tel Aviv won its first European championship in 1977 with a team that included former Illinois All-American Tal *Brody and a 6′10″ black center named Aulcie Perry. Maccabi went on to win European championships another four times, in 1981, 2001, 2004, and 2005, becoming a European powerhouse. Under Mizrachi's leadership, Maccabi Tel Aviv was seen to represent the country as a whole in international sports, though it was in fact only a local sports club with its own rivals on the Israeli sports scene. For Mizrachi, the team was his life, with his own family events being fitted in around the team's schedule. Perhaps his greatest triumph was to convince European Basketball Association officials not to pull the Final Four out of Tel Aviv in 2004 despite the security situation. In 2004 he was chosen as one of the torch bearers on Independence Day.

WEBSITE: www.hamaccabi.com.

[Shaked Gilboa (2nd ed.)]

MIZRAḤ (Heb. מִזְרָח; "east"), designation of the direction to be faced during prayer, of the wall of the synagogue where seats were reserved for the rabbi and other dignitaries, and of an ornamental wall plaque used to indicate the location of east. The custom of facing the Temple during prayer has biblical origins beginning with Solomon's prayer (I Kings 8:34, 44, 48; II Chron. 6:34). The Bible also relates that Daniel prayed three times daily in his chamber, the windows of which were opened toward Jerusalem (Dan. 6:11). The rule laid down in the Mishnah (Ber. 4:5) and amplified in the Talmud, is that if one prays in the Diaspora, he shall direct himself toward Ereẓ Israel; in Ereẓ Israel, toward Jerusalem; in Jerusalem, toward the Temple; and in the Temple, toward the Holy of Holies. If a man is east of the Temple, he should turn westward; if in the west, eastward; in the south, northward; and if in the north, southward. Thus all Jews direct their prayers toward one place (Ber. 30a; T.J. Ber. 4:5 8b–c; Tosef., Ber. 3:16). The term *mizraḥ*, therefore, applies properly to the cities and countries situated west of Jerusalem. Excavations of ancient synagogues generally bear this out, as those houses of worship found in Miletus, Priene, and Aegina, all west of Ereẓ Israel, show an eastern orientation, as has been recorded of Egyptian synagogues (Jos., Apion, 2:10). Those synagogues north of Jerusalem and west of the Jordan River, as *Bet Alfa, *Capernaum, *Hammath, and *Chorazin all face southward, whereas ancient sanctuaries east of the Jordan, such as Val-Dokkī Umm al-Qanātir, Jarash, and *Dura-Europos all face west. In the south, the synagogue excavated at *Masada faces northwest to Jerusalem. The directions frequently varied slightly due to the terrain. Exceptions have been found in the synagogues at Khirbat Summāqa, a village on Mt. Carmel, and at ʿUsifiyyā, where the orientations are not toward Jerusalem. There is no satisfactory explanation for this divergence from the norm. In the early Christian church it was also customary to pray facing toward the Holy Land. For Islam the original direction of prayer (*qibla*) was toward Jerusalem, but this was subsequently changed by Muhammad in favor of Mecca.

Excavations of ancient synagogues show that the earliest houses of worship had their entrances facing Jerusalem, and portals, therefore, indicated the sacred direction. The remains of the Dura-Europos synagogue on the Euphrates reveal that by the third century C.E. the doors were on the eastern side, and the opposite wall, in which a special niche had been made to place the scrolls during worship, faced Jerusalem. This niche was too small to have been the permanent location of the ark, which was obviously still portable at that time. In Ereẓ Israel the wall facing the Temple site was changed from the side of entrance to the side of the ark in the fifth or sixth century. This change is already found in synagogues at Naaran near Jericho and Bet Alfa. Worshipers came through the portals and immediately faced both the scrolls and Jerusalem. However, in those sanctuaries found in Hammath, Yafa in Galilee, and Eshtemoa in Judea, the sacred direction is properly south in the first two cases and north in the third, while the entrance is from the eastern side. This may be in imitation of the Tent of Meeting, which had its gates on the eastern side (Num. 2:2–3; 3:38), or of Solomon's Temple, the portals of which were to the east (Ezek. 43:1–4), although the precise reason is not known. Maimonides, quoting the second passage in Numbers, states that the doors of the synagogue should face east, while the Ark should be placed "in the direction in which people pray in that city," i.e., toward Jerusalem (Yad, Tefillah, 11:2). The Shulḥan Arukh records the same rule, but to avoid the semblance of worshiping the sun by facing east, it recommends that one turn toward the southeast (Isserles OḤ 94:2; also Suk. 5:4). If a person is unable to ascertain the points of the compass, he should direct his heart toward Jerusalem. This was also the opinion of R. Tarfon and R. Sheshet, who held that, since the Divine Presence is everywhere, the essential requirement is to direct one's heart to God (BB 25a). It is customary in traditional homes to mark the eastern wall to enable a person to recite his prayers in the proper direction. Artistic wall plaques inscribed with the word *mizraḥ* and scriptural passages like "From the rising (*mi-mizraḥ*) of the sun unto the going down thereof, the Lord's name is to be praised" (Ps. 113:3), kabbalistic inscriptions, or pictures of holy places are used for this purpose.

BIBLIOGRAPHY: Goodenough, Symbols, 1 (1953), 216; F. Landsberger, in: HUCA, 28 (1957), 181–203; L.A. Mayer, *Bibliography of Jewish Art* (1967), index; E.L. Sukenik, *The Ancient Synagogue of Beth Alpha* (1932), 11; idem, *The Ancient Synagogue of El-Ḥammeh* (1935), 78–81; idem, *Ancient Synagogues in Palestine and Greece* (1934), 27, 50–52; Y. Yadin, *Masada* (Eng., 1966), 180, 184.

MIZRAHI, ASHER (1890–1967), cantor, composer, and poet. Mizrahi was born in the old city of Jerusalem. He later moved to Yemin Moshe, the first quarter outside the walls. At this period of his life, he composed and performed religious and secular songs connected with the traditional Judeo-Spanish repertory, as well as in the style of Turkish and Arabic classical music, which mark an early mingling of Sephardi and Oriental styles. He thus achieved a kind of qualitative compromise between the religious and secular in his musical works.

In 1917, Mizrahi quit Jerusalem, clandestinely seeking to escape his recruitment by the Turkish army, and settled in Tunis. Except for short stays in Jerusalem in 1919 and 1929, he sojourned there until 1967. He then returned to Jerusalem, where he died the same year.

During the many years he stayed in Tunis, he became a central figure in the musical life of the Tunisian Jewish community, not only by promoting the cantorial tradition and considerably enriching its musical life, but also thanks to his great artistry in the realm of the new Egyptian art style that was at that time the subject of great favor among both Jewish and non-Jewish Tunisians. It is noteworty that Mizrahi, who was a great admirer of the Egyptian singer and composer Muhammad ʿAbd al-Wahhab, set many of his own Hebrew poems to his melodies. Thus, in addition to his essential role in developing the religious musical life of the community and the appropriate musical education he provided to the community's children and youth by means of the children's choir, he created *awlad al-Biyyut* ("the children of the *piyyut*"). He distinguished himself as an interpreter of Arab music and *ʿud* playing. In this latter activity he gained the favor of the Tunisian president, Habib Bourguiba.

In Tunisia, Mizrahi published an anthology of Hebrew poems for singing, the title of which is *Maʿadanei Melekh* ("The King's Delicacies," Sousse: Makhluf Najjar, 1945; republished in Israel in 1968).

In Tunis he established choirs that performed his songs.

Among his outstanding pupils were Rabbi Getz, the late rabbi of the Western Wall, and David Riyahi, who established a synagogue choir in Netanyah that accompanied the services and performed many of his *piyyutim*.

[Amnon Shiloah (2nd ed.)]

MIZRAḤI, DAVID BEN SHALOM (c. 1696–1771), one of the most prominent *halakhah* scholars in *Yemen. Mizraḥi propagated Torah studies and headed the synagogue of the *nagid* Sar Shalom Irāqi (al-Usta). When the need was felt for a commentary on the Shulḥan Arukh adapted to the requirements of Yemenite Jewry and its customs, David Mizraḥi undertook this task in his work *Shetilei Zeitim* (1886–91), on *Oraḥ Ḥayyim* (1886–91; 1895). He explains the Shulḥan Arukh with brevity and clarity, quoting the customs of Yemenite Jewry which are not mentioned by R. Moses *Isserles and the commentaries of the Shulḥan Arukh. He retained all the notes of R. Moses Isserles that are in agreement with the Shulḥan Arukh and omitted everything that was in contradiction to it, including customs. Mizraḥi adopted the same style in his work *Rashei Besamim* (1895) on the *Yoreh Deʿah*. His third work is *Revid ha-Zahav* (1955), responsa and novellas on the Shulḥan Arukh and R. Moses Isserles (some of which were written by his son Yiḥya). This work is the first of its kind in the responsa literature of Yemenite Jewry.

[Yehuda Ratzaby]

MIZRAḤI, ELIJAH (c. 1450–1526), rabbinical authority, the greatest of the rabbis of the *Ottoman Empire of his time. Mizraḥi was of Romaniot origin (the original Turkish Jews as distinct from the Spanish exiles) and was born and educated in Constantinople. Among his teachers he mentions Elijah ha-Levi in rabbinic studies and Mordecai Comitiano (see *Comtino) in general studies. Until the death of Moses *Capsali, Mizraḥi devoted himself to study and public instruction. As early as 1475 he is mentioned as heading a *keneset* (probably a school in addition to a synagogue) and as having students. During this period of his life he was involved in controversies with *Moses Esrim ve-Arba and Perez Colon, and despite his stormy and aggressive temperament he submitted to the intervention of Capsali in these disputes, an intervention which reveals a certain tension between them. Perhaps for this reason he took no part in the famous controversy between Capsali and Joseph Colon. After the death of Capsali in 1498, Mizraḥi became the foremost rabbinical authority in Constantinople and in fact throughout the whole Ottoman Empire. From far and near, problems of *halakhah* and procedure were addressed to him. There is reason to believe that he filled the position of head of the rabbis of Constantinople (though he did not have the title of *ḥakham bashi*, appointed by the sultan, since that office did not exist in that period). Nevertheless, it would seem that his authority derived not from any official position, but from the recognition of his personality and strength. He was considered both by his contemporaries and later generations as the greatest *posek* of his time in *Turkey. He was firm and unbending in his decisions, and even the great rabbis among the Spanish exiles accepted his authority.

In his responsa (56) he gives a description of his daily routine, which reveals the strain under which he worked. Fulfilling a number of functions simultaneously, he conducted the affairs of the community, gave decisions on all matters, headed a yeshivah, and taught not only Talmud but secular subjects. At the same time he wrote commentaries on both religious and scientific works, had an inner circle of select students whom he taught the codes, and wrote responsa in answer to queries addressed to him from afar. Like Moses Capsali, he was active in the problem of the absorption of the exiles from Spain and Portugal, collecting funds on their behalf, and forcing the wealthy members of the community to pay the amounts imposed on them (Resp. 66). Mizraḥi's attitude to these exiles was one of respect and high regard. He appreciated that their standards of culture and knowledge were higher than those of the native Turkish Jews, but nevertheless he came out firmly against attempts by some of them to impose their will on the old community. He resisted attempts on their part to impose customs and procedures to which they were accustomed, but which were contrary to those ruling in Turkey. Of special importance was his attitude toward the *Karaites. On the one hand he exerted himself to attract them to the Rabbanites, and, in opposition to Moses Capsali, to give them instruction in both secular subjects and even in the Oral Law, and in this context firmly resisted every attempt to isolate them. On the other hand he completely rejected on halakhic grounds the permissibility of intermarriage between Karaites and Rabbanites. Mizraḥi's halakhic method is distinctive and clear. He lays down fundamental principles and raises possible objections to his own statements, so that every topic is exhaustively examined and clarified. His responsa were accepted as authoritative by his and succeeding generations, despite the fact that some of the leading contemporary scholars opposed his views.

His best-known pupils and colleagues were Elijah ha-Levi, *Tam ibn Yaḥya, and Abraham ibn Yaish. Mizraḥi suffered greatly from ill health, financial strain, and family misfortunes. Three of his sons are known, Gershon, Israel, and Reuben, and a daughter. There are legends about his son-in-law's connections with the court of the sultan. Reuben died during his father's lifetime. Gershon was the victim of a libel that during a severe illness he had sought to be converted to *Islam. He had to abandon his family and, after paying heavy bribes, escaped to Naxos, but even there he suffered persecution and strife. These two incidents, as well as the death of his wife, affected Mizraḥi greatly. His third son, Israel, published his father's Rashi commentary and *Sefer ha-Mispar.* Mizraḥi died in Constantinople and Joseph *Taitaẓak eulogized his works.

Mizraḥi's personality and multi-faceted character emerge clearly from his works. His main activity was in the writing and teaching of both *halakhah* and general knowledge, but his main fame rests upon his crowning achievement, his supercommentary to Rashi (1st ed. Venice, 1527), a fact which he himself states. In this work he exhaustively discusses almost every word in Rashi, but does not refrain from disagreeing with him on numerous occasions. On the other hand he defends Rashi against the criticism of Naḥmanides. This work has given rise to a veritable literature. Later commentators answered his criticism and justified Rashi. The two works, Rashi's commentary and Mizraḥi's supercommentary, became a main subject of study of rabbinical commentators of the Bible from the 16th century onward. The work has an added importance as a result of the quotations it gives from the Romaniot scholars of the 14th and 15th centuries for which his work is the sole source, side by side with those of Ibn Ezra and the French and German scholars. Mizraḥi's responsa, published in two collections, number 140, but of them only 110 are his, although they undoubtedly represent only a fraction of his many responsa. More than 40 are still in various manuscripts. A comparison between the two reveals the many errors in the printed responsa, particularly in the Constantinople edition. An extant fragment (Resp. Const. 96) reveals the method of teaching in his yeshivah, consisting of notes made at the time by one of his pupils.

The only other rabbinic work of Mizraḥi published is his novellae on the *Sefer Mitzvot Gadol* of *Moses of Coucy (Constantinople, 1521), the only work of his published in his lifetime. His work on the *Halakhot* of Isaac Alfasi is not extant. In the field of secular knowledge his *Sefer ha-Mispar* (Constantinople, 1533) on mathematics is famous. It was highly thought of in its time and has been translated into Latin. He also wrote a commentary on Ptolemy's *Almagest* and on Euclid's *Elements.* R. Moses Almosnino possessed a commentary by Mizraḥi on the "Intentions of the Philosophers" of al-*Ghazālī. Mizraḥi took a negative attitude toward Kabbalah, particularly against relying on it for halakhic decisions, and the introduction of kabbalistic ideas into the prayer book.

BIBLIOGRAPHY: A. Geiger (ed.), *Melo Ḥofnayim* (1840), 12 (Heb. pt.); Conforte, Kore, index; E. Bashyazi, *Adderet Eliyahu* (1833); M. Almosnino, *Ma'amaẓ Ko'aḥ* (Venice, 1588), 138b.; *Me'ora'ot Olam* (Izmir, 1756); M. Lattes, *De Vita et Scriptis Eliae Kapsalii* (Padua, 1869); Michael, Or, nos. 161–4, 306; Rosanes, Togarmah, 1 (1930),

70–77; A. Freimann, in: *Zion*, 1 (1936), 188–91; *Ha-Segullah*, 5 no. 5 (1938); A. Ovadyah, *Ketavim Nivḥarim*, 1 (1942), 63–198; S. Assaf, *Be-Oholei Ya'akov* (1953), 145–96; Steinschneider, Uebersetzungen, 322, 508, 524; A. David, in: KS 45 (1970), 299.

[Joseph Hacker]

MIZRAHI, HANINAH (1886–1974), teacher. Born in Teheran in 1886, he immigrated to the Land of Israel in 1895 and died in Jerusalem. His father, Haim Elazar, was a *paytan*. Mizrahi began his studies at the Alliance school in Jerusalem, where he learned French. He also learned German by himself and could read the Judeo-Persian works by Wilhelm Bacher of Budapest. In 1907, he received his teaching certificate from the Ezra school in Jerusalem, where he also improved his German language. In 1911 he married Sarah, the daughter of R. Shalom Yehezqel. For 15 years, beginning in 1921, he taught at the *talmud torah* of the Sephardim in Old Jerusalem. After Israel's War of Independence, the school fell into the hands of Jordan, so Mizrahi continued to teach at Harel school in West Jerusalem until his retirement in 1951. He is regarded as one of the founders of the Bet ha-Kerem quarter in Jerusalem. Mizrahi published the following books on the Jews of Iran: *Yehudei Paras* (1959); *Toldot Yehudei Paras* (1966); *Bi-Yshishim Ḥokhmah* (1967). He was mainly a folklorist in his education and writings.

BIBLIOGRAPHY: A rather full account of Mizrahi's life and works can be found in A. Netzer, "*Yādi az yek shakhsiyat-e farhangi*," in: *Pādyāvand: Judeo-Iranian and Jewish Studies Series*, vol. 3 (1999), 361–70.

[Amnon Netzer (2nd ed.)]

MIẒRAYIM (Heb. מִצְרַיִם), Hebrew place-name. In the Septuagint it is rendered as Egypt. The Hebrew proper noun, however, has a broader range of meaning. As Aiguptos, the name of the country was derived from a name for the city of Memphis, *Ḥet-kau-ptaḥ* ("Castle of the *ka*-souls of Ptah"), so the name of Miẓrayim may have been derived from the name of a city of Lower Egypt, if not of Lower Egypt itself. This is based on the occurrences in the Bible of Miẓrayim in combination with Pathros (*pa to resy*; "the southern country," i.e., Upper Egypt), in which cases Miẓrayim seems to mean Lower Egypt (*To Mehy*). Secondarily, it came to mean both all of Egypt and Egyptians, and was – and still is – the common Hebrew word for Egypt.

[Alan Richard Schulman]

MLADA BOLESLAV (Czech **Mladá Boleslav**; Ger. **Jungbunzlau**), town in N. Bohemia, Czech Republic. One of the important communities in Bohemia, it is first mentioned in 1471 and is noted in a Hebrew document of 1556. Eleven families lived there in 1570, and a synagogue was recorded in 1579. The cemetery (well known mainly because of the tombstone of Jacob *Bassevi von Treuenberg) was consecrated in 1584 and still existed in 1970. The number of adult Jews in the town in 1615 was 120. In 1643 the community came under the protection of the Swedish king for a time. The community elders were forced to sign an agreement in 1661 which greatly limited their freedom of commerce. At the end of the century, Jews had a near monopoly of transportation. In 1710 a shopkeeper, David Brandeis, was accused of poisoning a Christian with plum jam; the day of his release was celebrated on the tenth of Adar as *Povidl* ("plum jam") *Purim*. After a fire in the late 17th century had destroyed part of the Jewish quarter and the synagogue, the community built a new synagogue on the model of the Meisl synagogue in Prague. It had to be demolished in 1960 because of decay. The Jewish population numbered 794 in 1834; 865 (9.1% of the total population) in 1880; 402 (2.8% of the total) in 1910; 419 in 1921; and 264 (1.3%) in 1930. In 1922 a local Jewish museum was founded; its treasures were later transferred to the Central Jewish Museum in Prague. In 1942 the Jews from Mlada Boleslav and the surrounding district were concentrated in the old castle. Of the 1,041 persons deported to *Theresienstadt in January 1943, only 40 were still alive in November 1944. After World War II a small congregation was reestablished, administered by the Prague community.

Among the outstanding rabbis of Mlada Boleslav were Moses Isaac Spira (until 1702), Ezekiel Glogau-Schlesinger (until 1821), and Isaac Spitz (1824–42). The house in which Sigfried *Kapper (1821–79) lived was marked by a memorial tablet. Jewish life in Mlada Boleslav at the beginning of the 19th century is described in Leopold *Kompert's *Die Kinder des Randars* ("The Randar Children"). Mlada Boleslav was considered a kind of a Bohemian *Chelm and many tales were told of "*Bumsler Shtiklekh*" ("pranks"). The Prague scholar Meir *Fischels (Bumsla) came from Mlada Boleslav. A **seliḥah*, printed in 1854 to commemorate a conflagration, was the last literary production of this kind published in Bohemia. Benjamin Isaac (d. 1750), "Jew merchant of extensive charity" in London, came from Mlada Boleslav, and he set up a foundation in his name in his native community.

BIBLIOGRAPHY: A.E. Goldmann and M. Gruenwald, in: H. Gold (ed.), *Juden und Judengemeinden Boehmens…* (1934), 204–21; M. Gruenwald, in: MWJ (1888), 192–6; idem, in: *Českožidovský kalendar*, 11 (1891/92), 138ff.; H. Volávkov, *Schicksal des Juedischen Museums in Prag* (1965); R. Iltis (ed.), *Die Aussaeen unter Traenen…* (1959), 99–101; Roth, England, 284.

[Jan Herman]

MLAWA (Pol. **Mława**; Rus. **Mlava**), town in the province of Warsaw, N.E. central Poland. The earliest documented information on the Jewish community is dated 1543. It is included in a report of a case of *blood libel, which mentions the name of the *parnas* of the community – Berechiah (Pol. Bogusław). In 1569 there were 23 Jewish families living in the town and in 1578 they had increased to 34. Their main sources of livelihood were the livestock trade and crafts. A charge of desecrating the *Host in 1670, and the fires which devastated Mlawa in 1659 and 1692, caused the number of Jews gradually to decrease. On the other hand, the Jewish population of the suburb of Zabrody, which was beyond the area of municipal jurisdiction, and the surrounding villages, increased.

Until 1753, the community of Mlawa was under the jurisdiction of that of *Ciechanow. The growth of economic activity in the region during the last third of the 18th century brought an increase in the Jewish population. The 1765 census showed 70 Jewish families numbering 487 poll tax payers in Mlawa and the neighboring villages. Fifteen houses in the town were owned by Jews. Sources of 1781 mention a Jewish population of 718. After the Prussian conquest (1793), the town was granted a *de non tolerandis Judaeis* privilege, and the Jews then moved to the suburb of Zabrody.

The Jews returned to Mlawa with the establishment of the grand duchy of Warsaw (1807). In 1808 they numbered 137, forming 15% of the population. Following restrictions on Jewish settlement, a special quarter was established in 1824, and only there (with some rare exceptions) were Jews permitted to live. In addition, the entry of Jews from other regions was almost completely prohibited, because of the location of the town in the border area. In 1827, there were 792 Jews (36% of the population) living in the town. The ghetto and the other restrictions on residence and ownership of real estate were abolished in 1862. Once the railway lines from Mlawa to Warsaw (1877) and Gdansk (1883) were opened, the trade in grain, livestock, wood, and army supplies, from which many Jews earned their livelihood, increased considerably. Between 1857 and 1897, the Jewish population of Mlawa grew from 1,650 to 4,845 (41% of the population).

The influence of Ḥasidism manifested itself among the Jews of Mlawa from the beginning of the 19th century. With the consolidation of their economic situation at the close of that century, the influence of *Mitnaggedim* circles gained in strength (in 1870, Wolf Lipszie was appointed rabbi of the town). The last rabbi of Mlawa, R. Jehiel Moses Segalowicz (appointed 1901), was known as one of the *Mitnaggedim*. In the late 1890s, a *Ḥovevei Zion circle was organized in the town. During the revolution and pogroms of 1905–06, the *Bund and the *Po'alei Zion wielded considerable influence among the Jewish workers, youth, and intelligentsia of Mlawa. The Jewish author Joseph *Opatoshu, the Hebrew author Jakir *Warshavsky, and the publicist and leader of the Bund in Poland, Victor *Alter, were born in Mlawa, where they also began their careers. Between 1921 and 1927 the Jewish population of Mlawa increased from 5,923 to 6,301. A newspaper, *Dos Mlauer Lebn*, was published; its editors included Bunim Warshavsky, Moses Lichtensztain, and Moses Laska.

Holocaust Period

At the outbreak of World War II there were about 6,500 Jews in Mlawa. At the beginning of November 1939 the Germans destroyed all the synagogues in Mlawa and vicinity. The first deportation took place on Dec. 6, 1940, when 300 Jews were deported to Miedzyrzec *Podlaski, *Lubartow, and *Lublin; they shared the fate of the Jews there. The ghetto was established on Dec. 7–8, 1940, and liquidated two years later on Nov. 24, 1942. The last deportations took place from Nov. 10, 1942, to Dec. 10, 1942; almost all the Jews were deported to *Treblinka death camp. The Jewish community of Mlawa was not reconstituted after the war. Organizations of former residents of Mlawa are active in Israel, the United States, and Mexico.

BIBLIOGRAPHY: Halpern, Pinkas, index; B. Wasiutyński, *Ludnoś żydowska w Polsce w wiekach XIX i XX* (1930), 23, 46f., 75, 78; S. Pazyra, *Geneza i rozwój miast mazowieckich* (1959), 398; Y. Trunk, *Geschikhte fun Yidn in Plotsk* (1939), 59, 62, 65; A.G. von Hoelske, *Geographie und Statistik von West-Sued-und Neu-Ostpreussen* (Berlin, 1800), 497; J. Shakky (ed.), *Pinkes Mlave* (1950); S. Zuchowski, *Odgłos processów kryminalnych na Żydach* (1700); Irgun Yoẓe'ei Mlawa be-Israel, *Yedi'on* (1967); *Pinkas Mlawa* (Yid., 1950).

[Arthur Cygielman]

MLOTEK, CHANA (1922–), U.S. musicologist, folklorist, researcher, archivist, and scholar of Yiddish song and culture. Born Eleanor Gordon in Brooklyn, New York, the daughter of Leo and Bessie Gordon, Mlotek grew up as a native Yiddish speaker in the Bronx. She attended the Yiddish elementary school associated with the Workman's Circle, the Sholem Aleichem Yiddish High School, and Hunter College, receiving a B.A. in French and music in 1946.

Chana became a secretary to Lucy *Davidowicz at YIVO in New York in 1944 and then worked for Max *Weinreich. She went to California as Weinreich's secretary and later served as his assistant. In 1948, she studied folklore and linguistics at UCLA on a YIVO scholarship. Her interest in collecting Yiddish songs began around that time, and between 1948 and 1961 she worked intensively in this area. Chana married Joseph Mlotek, a teacher and writer of Yiddish musical plays in 1949, and the couple had two sons. Between 1963 and 1966, Chana served as music director of Camp Boiberik, where she created and taught Yiddish musical material for children. In 1968, she and Malke Gottlieb, through the Workman's Circle, published *Finf un Tsvantsik Geto Lider* ("Twenty-Five Ghetto Songs"), in commemoration of the 25th anniversary of the Warsaw Ghetto Uprising. Later, she published *Mir Zaynen Do: Lider fun di getos un lagern* ("We are Here: Songs of the Holocaust," 1983).

In 1970, she and her husband started a column in the Yiddish *Forward* newspaper, "*Perl fun der Yidisher poezye*" (Pearls of Yiddish Poetry), about Yiddish songs and poetry. People sent them material and between 1970 and 2000 they published over 2,000 Yiddish songs in their column. In 1972, Chana published an anthology of these songs, *Mir Trogn A Gesang* ("*The New Book of Yiddish Songs*"), in which she constructed an organizational scheme based on the songs' function and genre. In 1974, she published *Perl fun der Yidisher poezye* ("Pearls of Yiddish Poetry") in Tel Aviv. After Joseph's death in 2000, she continued to edit the column. Other published anthologies include *Yontefdike teg* ("Song Book for the Jewish Holidays," 1972), *Perl fun Yidishn lid* ("Pearls of Yiddish Song," 1988), and *Lider fun dor tsu dor: naye perl fun Yidishn Lid* ("Songs of Generations: New Pearls of Yiddish Songs," 1990).

Chana Mlotek wrote over 20 articles on folk songs, folk poetry, and Yiddish literature in various journals. She contributed to the first two volumes of Uriel Weinreich's compendium, *The Field of Yiddish: Studies in Language, Folklore and Literature*, and served as co-editor of the magazine *Yidisher Folklor*. Beginning in 1978, she worked at YIVO as an archivist.

[Judith S. Pinnolis (2nd ed.)]

°**MNASEAS OF PATARA** (in Lycia; probably second century B.C.E.), a disciple of *Eratosthenes. He wrote a Periegesis, a geographical work covering Europe, Asia, and Libya. According to Josephus (Apion, 2:112–4), Apion attributes to Mnaseas a story of how an Idumean named Zabidus duped the Jews into believing that he intended to deliver his god Apollo and thus gained entrance into the Temple, from which he stole the golden head of the ass allegedly worshiped by the Jews (cf. *Damocritus) – the first occurrence in literature of the canard that the Jews worshiped an ass. Since Mnaseas' words are known only at third hand, little weight attaches to the story, but it does illustrate the credulity (cf. *Hecataeus, *Horace, etc.) widely ascribed to the Jews in antiquity.

MNEMONICS OR MEMORA TECHNICA (Heb. סִימָן, *siman*; "a sign"), devices based on the principle that the mind is able to recall relatively unfamiliar ideas by connecting, as some artificial whole, parts of them which are mutually suggestive. Mnemonics are widely used in the Talmud – as in post-talmudic literature – but their use in the former was rendered imperative by the fact that the Talmud was originally transmitted orally, and even after it was committed to writing, both the scarcity of the texts, and the custom of teaching the text orally which prevailed in the geonic academies (Weiss, Dor, 3 (1904[4]), 215ff.; Halevy, Dorot, 3 (1928), 227) made it necessary for mnemonic devices to be employed. The rabbis laid great store on the efficacy of mnemonics as an aid to study. R. Ḥisda in Babylon deduced that the Torah can be acquired only by the use of mnemonics, adducing as evidence the verse "Put it in their mouth" (Deut. 31:19) reading *simona* – mnemonic for *sima* ("put"); R. Taḥlifa in Palestine explained that in Palestine they deduced the same lesson from the verse "Set thee up waymarks" (Jer. 31:21), proving that the "waymarks" refer to mnemonics (Er. 54b). The fact that the scholars of Judah retained their learning while those of Galilee forgot it was ascribed to the fact that the former employed mnemonics while the latter did not (Er. 53a). The verse in Ecclesiastes 12:9, "and besides that Koheleth… taught the people knowledge" was explained that he taught them by mnemonics (Er. 21b). It has been suggested that the widespread use of the alphabetical *acrostic in the Bible (e.g., Lam. 1–4; Ps. 119 and 145) had a mnemonic purpose since it reminded the person who recited it of the letter with which the succeeding verse commenced, but this form of mnemonic, though widely used in medieval poetry and even in prayers (e.g., *El Barukh* in the morning service, *Tikkanta Shabbat* in the Sabbath *Musaf*) is not at all resorted to in the Talmud.

The mnemonic devices of the Talmud can be divided into two main categories, those in which the mnemonic is an integral part of the text, forming part of its body, and those in which a passage is preceded by the mnemonic as an aid to the memory of what is to follow. The former are usually designated as *simankha*, i.e., "your mnemonic," while for the latter the simple word *siman* is given. Since the essence of the mnemonic is to call to mind the unfamiliar by use of the familiar, it naturally follows that it consists of the use of a well-known phrase. These phrases can be divided into biblical verses, since knowledge of the text of the Bible was regarded as axiomatic, well-known talmudic phrases, popular proverbs, or readily remembered catchphrases.

Biblical Mnemonics

Examples of biblical verses used for this purpose are numerous. For the six orders into which the Mishnah is divided, Isaiah 33:6 was cited: "There shall be faith in thy times, strength, salvation, wisdom, and knowledge," each of the nouns indicating a specific order (Shab. 31a). That basilicas attached to royal buildings are forbidden because of idolatry, but those of baths and storehouses permitted, was to be remembered by the mnemonic "to bind [forbid] their kings with chains" (Ps. 149:8; Av. Zar. 16b). The law that if the lungs of animals are liver-colored they are permitted, but if flesh-colored forbidden, had the mnemonic "and if flesh in the field, it is *terefah*" (Ex. 22:30; Ḥul. 47b). The mnemonic to remember that one should not curse one's parents in the presence of one's children is the verse (Gen. 48:5), "Ephraim and Manasseh [the grandchildren] shall be mine even as Reuben and Simeon [the children]" (Ket. 72b).

Talmudic Phrases

The bird called the moor-cock is forbidden as food, but the moor-hen permitted; the mnemonic is the rabbinic interpretation of the prohibition of an Ammonite to enter the congregation (Deut. 23:4): "An Ammonite," but not an Ammonite woman. A bird called the wine-drinker is also forbidden, and the mnemonic is "a drunkard is forbidden to officiate" (cf. Sanh. 22b). These are two examples given from a list in *Ḥullin* 62b.

Catchphrases

By their nature these are pithy statements in which the element of apparent paradox is often used. Thus the fact that a fish called the "sea ass" is permitted while one termed "the sea bull" is forbidden produces the mnemonic "the unclean is clean, the clean unclean," since the ass is forbidden and the ox permitted for consumption. To remember that meditating on sin can be worse than its actual commission, the mnemonic was devised "the odor of meat" (i.e., the odor of the meat excites the appetite more than the meat itself).

Mnemonics are used as an easy way to remember different statements in the name of one authority. Thus three statements on charity by R. Eleazar (BB 9a) provide the mnemonic "great is the sanctuary of Moses." Three statements of R. Manasseh found in different parts of the tractate *Ḥullin* (4a, 31a, 51a) are mnemonically connected by the sentence,

"Inserting a blade into rams" (Ḥul. 4a). It is one of the characteristics of the methodology of the Talmud that a statement in the name of a sage which is relevant to the discussion is followed by a number of statements in the name of the same sage which have no connection with the subject under discussion. The need for mnemonics in these cases was obvious, and as far as possible they are made into a sentence. Thus three statements of Samuel b. Naḥamani in the name of R. Johanan (the first has Naḥamani in the texts) were to be remembered by the sentence "In truth money shall he see." An interesting example is provided in the same passage. Six anonymous popular epigrams are quoted, for all of which Samuel finds a biblical proof verse. They are combined in a mnemonic which (probably) means "Hear, Vashti, Seven Songs, (and) another" (Sanh. 7a). It is obvious, however, that any device which aided the memory was pressed into service. There was a difference of opinion between the scholars of Pumbedita and Sura as to the number of nails permitted in a shoe for walking on the Sabbath. R. Ḥiyya reported that the former said 24, the latter 22. The mnemonic was "Ḥiyya lost two nails in walking from Pumbedita to Sura" (Shab. 60b).

Popular Proverbs

The wealthy Simeon b. Judah ha-Nasi was of the opinion that a certain defect in an animal did not render the animal invalid and he ate its meat, while the poor R. Ḥiyya discarded it as invalid; they had a similar disagreement about the oil for the Temple. In both cases the mnemonic was the popular proverb, "the wealthy are parsimonious" (Ḥul. 46a; Men. 86a). Among the most frequent devisors of mnemonics are Rava, R. Papa, R. Safra, and especially R. Naḥman b. Isaac.

The second category of mnemonics (indicated by the word *siman* without the suffix) is usually merely a combination of words, each indicating a topic. Sometimes it is possible to make a sentence out of them (e.g., a mnemonic in *Ḥullin* 46b, "Date, Red, Dry Scabs" may be read as "A date, red and dry with scabs"), but sometimes this is quite impossible. These *simanim* appear to be post-talmudic and were often omitted from the text. In *Bava Batra* 113a the mnemonic has been omitted from the printed texts, but the word *siman* has been retained, giving rise to the erroneous view that it was the name of an *amora*. There was in fact a tendency to ignore the *simanim* even if they were printed, a practice of which Isaiah *Horowitz strongly disapproved, insisting that they had a mystic connotation (*Torah she-be-Al Peh, ayin, Shenei Luhot ha-Berit* (Amsterdam, 1698), 407b).

Another type of mnemonic consisted merely of the initial letters of words. The best known example is the mnemonic *DeẒa-KH ADa-SH Be-AḤa-B* for the ten plagues. The Midrash states that it was engraved on the staff of Moses and calls it a *notarikon (Ex. R. 5:6), but in the Passover Haggadah it is referred to as *simanim*. Another example is the word *Ma-NẒe-Pa-Kh* for the letters of the alphabet which have a final form. The Talmud makes a kind of mnemonic of this mnemonic, seeing in it a reference to the fact that "the prophets [seers] introduced them" (*ẓofim amarum*), i.e., *Mi-N Ẓo-Fayi-KH* ("from thy prophets"; Meg. 2b). The medieval grammarians similarly made the mnemonic *Ba-Ga-D Ke-Fa-T* for the six letters which take a *dagesh kal*. The six things in which Shemini Aẓeret is regarded as a festival independent of Sukkot are indicated by the words *Pa-Ze-R Ke-SHe-V*, each letter indicating one of the things. The six laws in which the opinion of Abbaye prevails over that of Rava are indicated by the mnemonic *Ya-AL Ka-Ga-M* (BM 22b). The difference of opinion as to the order of the festival blessings for wine (*yayin*), *Kiddush*, the festival (*zeman*), the candle (*ner*), and *Havdalah* is indicated by whether it should be *Ya-KZa-Na-H* or *Ya-KNe-Ha-Z* (Pes. 102b, 103a). For the order of biblical readings for the intermediate days of Passover a full sentence was used, "He dragged an ox, and sanctified it with money" (Meg. 31a).

The use of mnemonics did not end with the Talmud, and they are found in late rabbinic literature. The laws of *terefah* begin, "there are eight categories of *terefah* and their *siman* is *Da-N Ha-Na-K Ne-Fe-SH*" (YD 29:1). A remarkable calendrical mnemonic is provided by *atbash* (the cryptogram whereby the first letter of the alphabet, *alef*, is equated with the last, *tav*; the second, *bet*, with the penultimate *shin*, etc.) so as to determine the days of the week on which the festivals of a certain year fall. *Alef, bet*, etc. represent the eight days of Passover, and the rule is that *alef* = *tav* (Tishah be-Av); *bet* = *shin* (Shavuot); *gimmel* = *resh* (Rosh Ha-Shanah); *dalet* = *kaf* (*Keri'at ha-Torah*, i.e., Simḥat Torah in the Diaspora); *he* = *Ẓadi* (*Ẓom*, i.e., the Day of Atonement); *vav* = *peh* (Purim, but of the previous year). The list ends with *vav*. *Zayin*, however, corresponds to *ayin*, and the seventh day of Passover always falls on the same day of the week as Israel Independence Day. Another calendrical mnemonic is "*Lo ADU Rosh ve-lo Ba-DU Pesaḥ*," i.e., (the first day of) Rosh Ha-Shanah cannot fall on the first, fourth, or sixth day of the week (*alef, dalet, vav*), nor Passover on the second, fourth, or sixth (*bet, dalet, vav*).

Distinct from mnemonics, although they serve the same purpose, are such mnemonic aids as are frequent in the Mishnah, whereby *mishnayot* on completely unrelated topics are grouped together because of their identical opening formula, e.g., "the only difference between A and B is" (Meg. 1), and "that which is invalid in A is valid in B" (Ḥul. 1:4–6).

BIBLIOGRAPHY: J. Bruell, *Doresh le-Ẓiyyon* (1864); Bruell, *Jahrbuecher*, 2 (1876), 58–67; B. Epstein, *Torah Temimah* to Ex. 34:27 (n. 40) and Num. 21:18 (n. 18); P.J. Kohn, *Sefer ha-Simanim ha-Shalem* (1953).

[Louis Isaac Rabinowitz]

MNOUCHKINE, ALEXANDRE (1908–1993), French film producer. Mnouchkine was born in Petrograd, Russia. One of the most influential producers in France, his endeavors left their mark on French cinema from the 1930s through the 1980s. He produced films with most of the great artists of his time, and a number of his films are among the greatest box office successes of France. He founded Majestic Films which operated from 1935 to 1940, and from 1945 he was chairman of Ariane Films.

Among the films he produced were *Les parents terribles* (1948), *Fanfan la Tulipe* (1951), *Babette s'en va-t-en guerre* (1959), *Cartouche* (1961), *L'Homme de Rio* (1965), *Le Train* (1964), *Stavisky* (1974), *Garde a vue* (1981), and *La Balance* (1983).

His daughter ARIANE (1939–) is the founder and main director of the world-famous theater, Theatre du Soleil (established 1964). Mnouchkine and the actors in her company – most of whom come from academic backgrounds – live together in a kind of commune. Their creative activities take place in a former ammunition warehouse in a Paris suburb which was put at their disposal in 1972. They renovated the building and turned it into a theater setting, La Cartouche de Vincennes.

In 1960 Mnouchkine established the ATEP, the Paris University Theater. She studied the forms of Oriental theater in Cambodia and Japan in 1962. The Theatre du Soleil had its initial success with its presentation of *The Kitchen* by Arnold Wesker which was given in a Circus Medrano tent. The world-wide reputation of the theater was gained by its performance of *1789* in Milan in 1970 and of *1793* in Paris in 1972. The Mnouchkine formula for total theater includes physical expression and body language, the use of elements taken from the circus world, and audience participation. The performances also demonstrated a politically left-wing outlook on life.

A movie made by the Theatre du Soleil on the life of Molière was also a great success. In 1984 Mnouchkine participated very successfully in the Los Angeles international theater festival where the troupe presented three plays by Shakespeare, *Richard II*, *Henry IV*, and *Twelfth Night* in a Japanese-Oriental adaptation. In 1992 she presented her production of *Les Atrides* in England.

[Gideon Kouts]

MOAB (Heb. מוֹאָב), a land E. of the Jordan and the Dead Sea, one of Israel's neighbors in biblical times. The highland of Moab extends southward to the Zered River (Wādī al-Ḥasā'), eastward to the desert, and westward to the Dead Sea. Its northern boundary was much disputed; sometimes it was limited by the river Arnon and sometimes it extended north of the Dead Sea (cf. the "plains of Moab" in Num. 26:3). The area of Moab is mountainous in the south, with ridges up to 4,000 ft. (1,250 m.), leveling off to a plateau in the north (the biblical *mishor*, "tableland"). The decline to the desert is gradual; that to the Dead Sea steep. The area was traversed by the "King's Highway." Its economy was mainly pastoral (cf. II Kings 3:4).

The People and the Country

Archaeological surveys have established that after a period of pre-Moabite settlement in the last centuries of the third millennium, Moabite tribes settled the country in about the mid-14th century B.C.E., not long before the Exodus. They were of Semitic stock, closely akin to the Israelites.

[Michael Avi-Yonah]

According to the tradition in Genesis 19:30–38, Moab (LXX: Μωαβ) was born to Lot by his elder daughter in the vicinity of the town of Zoar, at the southeastern tip of the Dead Sea. The meaning of the name, according to Targum Jonathan and the Septuagint, is "from my father" (cf. Gen. 19:37). Other than this tradition, there is no further information on the origin of the Moabites and the process of their formation into a national kingdom in Transjordan. The story of the birth of Moab and Ammon to Lot, son of Haran, the brother of Abraham, was intended to explain, in a popular midrashic manner, the names Moab and Ammon. However, the tradition of ethnic kinship between the children of Lot and Israel, echoes of which occur elsewhere in the Bible, is not based merely on the geographical proximity of these peoples to Israel. Biblical tradition and especially the Moabite language and the conjectured time of their settlement in Transjordan suggest that the Moabites were among the tribes of the sons of Eber, who spread out from the Syrian-Arabian desert in the second millennium B.C.E., and established national kingdoms throughout the Fertile Crescent. The Moabites, like the *Ammonites and *Edomites, were not among the pre-Israelite inhabitants of the land of Canaan (Gen. 10:15–20; 15:18–21; et al.). According to Deuteronomy (2:10–11), the Emim formerly occupied the land of Moab – "a people great, and many, and tall, like the Anakim" (see *Rephaim) – but it does not indicate when and in what circumstances they were driven out by the Moabites. Egyptian lists of the Middle and New Kingdoms (until the end of the 14th century) do not mention Moab as a people, state or territorial region. The archaeological survey of N. Glueck has revealed an interruption in the continuity of settlement in the Transjordanian plateau from the 19th until the 14th centuries B.C.E. During this period central and southern Transjordan were occupied by nomadic tribes. The mention of the sons of Seth in Transjordan (Num. 24:17) almost certainly refers to the nomadic Shutu tribes mentioned in Egyptian and Akkadian sources of the second millennium B.C.E. Only a few well-fortified settlements, such as Ader, Balūʿa, Aroer, and Khirbat al-Madayyina, near Wādī al-Thamad, southeast of *Dibon, had the strength to withstand the raids from the east, while the other settlements were destroyed. It may be assumed, following Glueck, that the renewal of permanent settlement in Transjordan at the close of the 14th century, and the appearance of a new agricultural society, is connected with the penetration of West Semitic tribes, including the Moabites, from the east. After the Moabites were in possession of Transjordan, they founded a state that embraced regions on both sides of the Arnon (Wādī al-Mawjib). North of the Arnon, Moab extended to "the tableland" (Deut. 4:43; Josh. 13:9; Jer. 48:21), to the valley of Heshbon (Wādī Ḥisbān) and to "the plains of Moab" opposite Jericho (Num. 22:1). The "tableland" is a plateau rising to approximately 2,400 ft. (800 m.) above sea level.

It is rich in pasturage and fertile farmland (cf. Num. 32:1–4). South of the Arnon, the land of Moab extended over a mountainous plateau, which is suitable for cattle raising; it rises to approximately 3,750 ft. (1,250 m.) above sea level. The Zered River (Wādī al-Ḥasā') marked the border between Moab and *Edom. Moab was bounded on the west by the Dead Sea and the southernmost part of the Jordan up to the Nimrin Valley. "The mountains of Abarim" and "the slopes of Pisgah" (Num. 27:12; Deut. 3:17) refer to the steep slopes of the Moabite plateau which descend to the Dead Sea. The Moabite plateau terminates on the east in shelving slopes which descend to the desert that marked the eastern border of Moab.

Throughout the entire area of Moab, there have been discovered the remains of numerous settlements which existed from the 13th to the sixth centuries B.C.E. The capital of Moab was Kir-Hareseth or Kir of Moab (II Kings 3:25; Isa. 15:1, 16:11; Jer. 48:31, 36), modern Karak, in the heart of Moabite territory south of the Arnon. However, most of the large settlements were situated in the fertile tableland (Num. 32; Josh. 13:16–27). Prominent in their importance were: Aroer (Khirbat ʿArāʿir), overlooking the fords of the Arnon, Dibon (Dhībān), Ataroth (Khirbat ʿAṭṭārūs), Medeba (Mādabā), and Nebo (Muḥayyiṭ). The topographical conformation of Moab does not favor easy communications. The many wadis flowing into the Dead Sea have sawed deep ravines that make passage difficult. Only in the northern plateau region, in the territory of Medeba, was there a wide, convenient road, which connected the regions on both sides of the Jordan. Great importance was attached to the "King's Highway," the international route which connected Arabia and Egypt with Syria and Mesopotamia, and of which a section passed through the Moabite plateau.

The geographical and economic conditions of Moab made it easy for the Moabites to achieve a suitable blend of their desert heritage with the values of an urban and rural society; this is to be attributed to Moab's position on the border of the desert and to its economy, which was based, on the one hand, upon agriculture, and on the other, upon cattle raising and trade conducted along the desert routes. Living in a border country, the Moabites, like the Edomites and Ammonites, were in need of effective defense against sudden attacks by raiders from the desert, as well as against invasion by the regular armies of neighboring countries. For this reason, the Moabites organized themselves into a national kingdom administered from a single center at the beginning of their settlement in Moab; only a permanent and strong leadership was capable of establishing a system of border fortresses, of setting up a permanent force able to match itself against external dangers, and of organizing guards for protection of the section of the "King's Highway" which passed through Moab. The archaeological survey of Moab and the excavations at Aroer and Dibon, as well as the epigraphic material, have revealed the technical skill of the Moabites in the building of strongholds, watchtowers, walled cities, and installations for collecting water. They built fortresses along the borders. On the eastern border, along the edge of the desert, strong and impressive forts have been discovered; the most prominent are Khirbat al-Madayyina, overlooking the Zered River, Maḥāy, Mudaybīʿ, al-Madyyina, overlooking one of the southern tributaries of the Arnon, Qaṣr Abu al Kharaq, and Qaṣr al-ʿĀl, overlooking the fords of the Arnon on the south. These are only some of the fortresses which guarded entry into Moab from the east. In the service of the king of Moab were garrisons stationed in fortresses and troops trained for field combat and siege. He was assisted by a staff of officers who held various positions, such as that of scribe; one of the Moabite seals carries the name of "Chemosʿam [son of] Chemoshʾel ha-sofer."

Most of the Moabite population obtained its livelihood from agriculture and cattle raising. *Mesha, king of Moab, was called a sheep-master (II Kings 3:4). In areas unsuitable for agriculture, chiefly in the easternmost part of the country, the settlers lived in temporary dwellings (huts or tents), and continued to lead a seminomadic way of life, either as shepherds or as escorts of the merchant caravans that made their way along the nearby desert routes. Moabite culture, to the extent that it is revealed by the finds, most of which are from the Middle Iron Age, was influenced by various other cultures, chiefly by Aram in the north and Arabia in the south. Despite the eclectic character of Moabite culture, the Moabites developed a style of their own, which is particularly conspicuous in the pottery. Pottery sherds defined as Moabite have been discovered in large quantities in many settlements in the land of Moab proper and in localities north of the Arnon.

Moabite religion was essentially idolatrous and was national in character. *Chemosh was the national god of Moab (I Kings 11:7, et al.), and was worshiped on high places and in temples. The god's name was used as a theophoric component in Moabite personal names. Proscription (*ḥerem*, Mesha stele, line 17), burnt offerings – either of an animal or, in special circumstances, of a human being (Num. 23:1, 14, 29; II Kings 3:27) – and circumcision (Jer. 9:24–25) were features of Moabite cultic practices. The polytheism of Moabite religion is attested by the names "ʿAshtar-Chemosh" (Mesha stele, line 17), "Beth-Baal-Peor" (cf. Num. 25), "Bamoth-Baal", and apparently also by the noun *ʾariʾel* ("altar hearths"; II Sam. 23:20; in Mesha stele, line 12, it is the name of an Israelite person or object), as well as by the many clay figurines found at various Moabite settlements, especially at Khirbet al-Madayyina near Wādī al-Thamad.

The language and script of the Moabites is known first and foremost from the *Mesha Stele, found in Mesha's native Dibon in 1868, as well as from two stele fragments (one found at Dibon and the other at Karak), from seals and from Moabite personal names. The language belongs to the northwest Semitic family and is close to the northern dialect of Hebrew. The Moabite script does not differ essentially from the Canaanite-Hebrew alphabetic script and, by the middle of the ninth century B.C.E., it had already attained a fine form. The length of the Mesha inscription and its content, style and form testify to a developed tradition of writing.

The History of Moab and its Relation with Israel

The first period of Moabite history bears the marks of Egyptian influence, as expressed in the stele found at Khirbat Balūʿa in Moab. Its estimated date is approximately 1200 B.C.E. The relief on the monument depicts a figure, perhaps of the local ruler, in the presence of a god and goddess. Above the relief can be seen traces of several lines of writing in a script as yet undeciphered. Both the relief and the inscription contain clearly Egyptian characteristics. (According to some scholars, the Balūʿa stele may be regarded as one of the earliest monuments of a Moabite tradition of writing.)

The land of Moab (*m-ʾ-b*) is mentioned in the geographical list of Ramses II (13th century B.C.E.). Ramses II undertook an expedition to Transjordan and captured cities in Moab, including Dibon. In the days of the first king of Moab, in the 13th century B.C.E., the Moabites were driven from the region north of the river Arnon by the Amorite king *Sihon, who ruled in Heshbon (Num. 21:27–35; cf. Isa. 15–16; Jer. 48). A short time later, Sihon's entire kingdom, from Wadi Jabbok to the Arnon, fell into the hands of the Israelites (Num. 21:13, 15, 24; 22:36; 33:44, et al.), who had reached the tableland by way of the desert east of Moab, because the king of Moab refused to allow them passage through his country. Fearing that they would now attack his land from the north, *Balak son of Zippor, the king of Moab, hired *Balaam to curse them but, on YHWH's order so goes the tradition, Balaam blessed them instead. Their inhospitality and their spite made the reasons for a prohibition against admitting Moabites and Ammonites "into the assembly of the Lord forever" (Deut. 23:4–8; Neh. 13:1). However, the enmity between Israel and Moab, echoes of which are also found in prophecies about the nations, was not the result of a single incident but grew out of a bitter and protracted struggle over disputed areas in Transjordan. With the conquest of the land of Sihon, the tribes of Reuben and Gad were settled in the tableland (Num. 32; Josh. 13), and the Arnon marked the border between Israel and Moab (Deut. 2:36, 3:8; Judg. 11:20, et al.). However, it is clear that a Moabite population remained north of the Arnon even after the conquest of the tableland from Sihon by the Israelites. An echo of the relations between the Moabites and Israelites in the tableland is the story of the affair of Baal-Peor in Shittim in the plains of Moab (Num. 25). The course of events following the Israelite conquest clearly shows that the Moabites did not surrender the tableland, and the region became a focus of strife between Israel and Moab as the border moved northward to the plains of Moab or southward to the Arnon, in accordance with the balance of power between Israel and Moab. The first attempt by Moab to reconquer the areas it had lost is the aforementioned incident of Balak and Balaam (Num. 22; cf. Micah 6:5). Numbers 22:6 and Joshua 24:9 suggest that Balak, with the support of the Midianites, waged war against the Israelites in an attempt to drive them from the tableland (but cf. Judg. 11:25–26). In the time of *Eglon, king of Moab (Judg. 3), the Moabites succeeded in thrusting northward across the Arnon. They imposed their rule on the tribes of Reuben and Gad, and perhaps also upon the Ammonites, and even penetrated by way of the plains of Moab and Jericho to the center of the country on the western side of the Jordan, within the bounds of the territory of Ephraim and Benjamin. The Israelites were obliged to pay tribute and to bring a gift to the king of Moab. *Ehud son of Gera of the tribe of Benjamin saved Israel from the Moabites. In the time of *Jephthah the tableland was in the possession of Israel (Judg. 11:26). The datum in Genesis 36:35 according to which Hadad son of Bedad king of Edom smote Midian in the field of Moab (c. 1100 B.C.E.), is explained by some commentators as evidence of Edomite or, more plausibly, Midianite rule over Moab. The narrative in the Book of Ruth concerning the immigration of a Judean family to Moab when a severe drought struck Judah indicates that the history of relations between Israel and Moab included periods of tranquility and peace (cf. also I Chron. 4:22, 8:8).

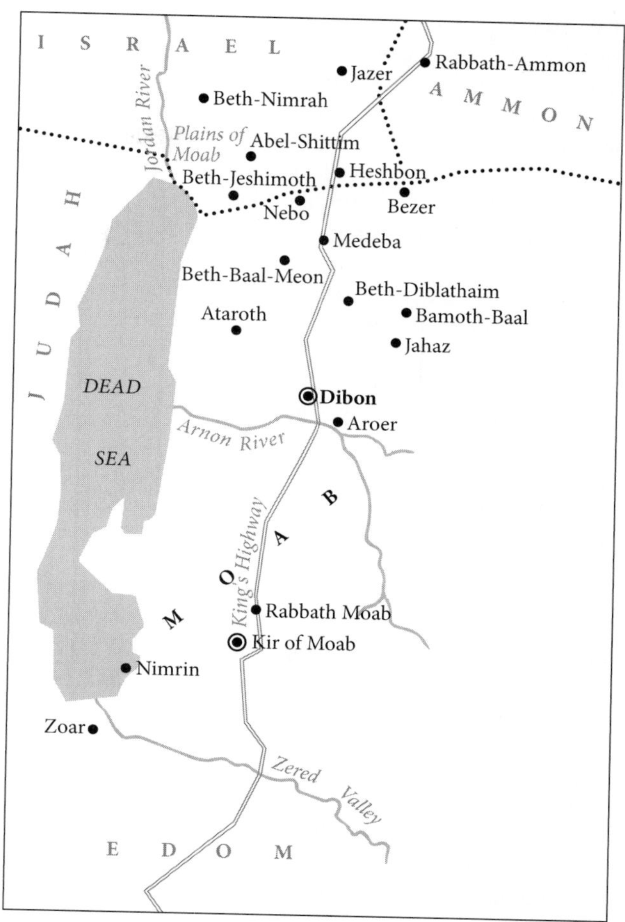

Moab in the time of Mesha (9th century B.C.E.). Based on Y. Aharoni, Carta's Atlas of the Bible, *Jerusalem, 1964.*

The attacks by Moab on Israel at the end of the period of the Judges and in the time of Saul (Ps. 83:7, 9; I Sam. 14:47), and perhaps in the time of his son Eshbaal as well, served as a justification for David to wage war against Moab and to subdue it (II Sam. 8:2; 23:20; cf. Num. 24:17), despite the friendly ties that had developed between David, a descendant of Ruth the Moabite, and the king of Moab (I Sam. 22:3–5). The actions taken by David against Moab after he had subjugated them (II Sam. 8:2, I Chron. 18:2), although not sufficiently clarified, are indicative of the intense enmity that prevailed between Israel and Moab. David did not abolish the monarchy in Moab but contented himself with its subjection (II Sam. 8:2; I Chron. 18:2). After the division of Solomon's kingdom, Moab came under the domination of the Northern Kingdom of Israel. As indicated by the stele of Mesha, king of Moab, it is probable that a long time before the death of Ahab, the Moabites threw off the rule of Israel and seized control over areas north of the Arnon (cf. II Kings 1:1, 3:5). The rise to power of Aram-Damascus immediately after the death of Solomon and its pressure on Israel (I Kings 15:16–20), the expedition of *Shishak against the kingdoms of Israel and Judah, and the intense struggle between the house of Jeroboam son of Nebat and the house of David, especially in the time of Baasha and Asa, presented an opportunity to throw off the domination of Israel. The Moabites seized control of the tableland up to Medeba. Since Mesha called himself "king of Moab, the Dibonite," it is possible that his father, whose name, as far as can be seen, was Chemoshyatti (?), had already established Dibon as the royal capital. The period of Moab's independence came to an end when the political and military situation of Israel improved under the rule of Omri. Omri "took possession" of the land of Medeba, but out of political and military considerations did not conquer the region of Dibon from Moab. Instead, he imposed his authority on the king of Moab, who resided in Dibon. The subjection continued throughout the days of Omri "and part of the days of his son," apparently Ahab. When the pressure of the Arameans on Israel in the time of Ahab increased, Mesha withheld tribute from Ahab. The king of Moab took steps to strengthen his kingdom against the expected attack by the king of Israel. Mesha first secured communications between the region of Moab south of the Arnon and the region of Dibon by fortifying Aroer and building roads along the Arnon. He strengthened his city of residence, built an acropolis in it and prepared the city to withstand a protracted siege. Ahab did not turn his attention to Moab but satisfied himself with fortifying Jericho (I Kings 16:34), which commanded the fords of the Jordan. Mesha, who had rebelled against Israel, chose not to participate in the joint campaign of Aram and Israel against Shalmaneser III in the year 853 B.C.E. (battle of *Karkar). Only after the death of Ahab did Mesha find the time ripe to begin the conquest of the entire tableland. He conquered Ataroth and the land of Ataroth, inhabited by the tribe of *Gad, Beth-Diblathaim, and the strong fortress of Jahaz on the border of the desert. He then continued northward, conquering Medeba and the land of Medeba, together with the large fortress of Bezer. The capture of Medeba opened the road to the plains of Moab for the Moabites; Mesha continued in a northwesterly direction to the plains of Moab by way of Wādī al-Harī, and seized control of the largest Israelite city of *Nebo, which he consecrated to ʿAshtar-Chemosh. Toward the end of the inscription, Mesha mentions an expedition to Horonaim in southern Moab, close to Zoar (cf. Isa. 15:5; Jer. 48:5, 34). Thus Mesha succeeded in restoring the borders of the Moabite kingdom from the tip of the Dead Sea in the south to the vicinity of the plains of Moab in the north. He rebuilt cities in the tableland and settled Moabites in them. Some scholars hold that the expedition of Mesha to Horonaim is connected with the narrative in II Kings 3 of the joint campaign of *Jehoram, king of Israel, *Jehoshaphat, king of Judah, and the king of *Edom. The campaign of the three kings was carried out by way of Edom in order to attack Moab from the south, since the way to Moab from the plains of Moab was held by Mesha and was well defended by Moabite garrisons. In the battle that took place on the southern border of Moab, Jehoram and his allies defeated the Moabite army (II Kings 3:20–24). Subsequently the allied armies penetrated into the heart of Moab and besieged the capital Kir-Hareseth (3:24–26). From the biblical description, it appears that the armies of Israel and Judah withdrew from Moab without succeeding in conquering the capital. According to II Kings 3:27, the king of Moab, in an act of despair, sacrificed his firstborn son upon the wall as a burnt offering, an act that brought "great wrath upon Israel." Despite this, the great destruction caused to the cities of Moab in the campaign of the three kings weakened Moab and undermined Moabite rule in the tableland. Although Moabite bands were still able to make raids into Israel west of the Jordan (II Kings 13:20), almost all of the tableland returned to Israelite possession, as is suggested by II Kings 10:32–33, which is concerned with Hazael's seizure of Transjordan down to the Arnon. Still later, in the time of Jeroboam, son of Jehoash king of Israel, Israelite rule in the tableland was consolidated (II Kings 14:25; Amos 6:14), and Moab may have recognized the rule of Israel. Moab apparently never again attained full independence. Before it could benefit from the decline and fall of the kingdom of Israel, it was forced to recognize the sovereignty of the Assyrian empire.

The Moabites under Assyrian and Babylonian Rule and the End of their Kingdom

The expedition of *Tiglath-Pileser III to Israel in 734–733 B.C.E. brought the states of Transjordan under the rule of the Assyrian Empire. In one of his inscriptions, Tiglath-Pileser III mentions Salaman the Moabite (*Sa-la-ma-nu* KUR *Ma-ʾ-ba-ai*) among the kings of Syria and Israel who brought him tribute, apparently in 732 B.C.E. The paying of tribute was an expression of recognition of Assyrian rule. Acceptance of Assyrian sovereignty was generally bound up with the payment of tribute at fixed times, the offering of a gift on appointed occasions, bond service, and military aid to the Assyrian king for his expeditions. The Assyrians usually appointed an inspector (*qēpu*) to work alongside the local ruler and placed Assyrian garrison troops in fortresses and citadels, both in the provinces and in the domain of the vassal king. Aianūr of the land of Tabeel, who reported the raid of the men of Gidir into Moab to the Assyrian king, was apparently responsible to the latter for the state of affairs in Moab. An Assyrian letter from Nimrud of the last third of the eighth century B.C.E. mentions a delegation from Moab which came to the city of Calah (Nimrud) to present a gift of horses to the Assyrian king. The king of Moab did not heed the words of incitement of Iamani, king of Ashdod, to rebel against Sargon II in 713 B.C.E. When Sennacherib conducted a military campaign against Ḥezekiah in 701 B.C.E., Chemosh-nadab the Moabite (*Kam-mu-su-na-ad-bi* KUR *Ma-ʾ-ba-ai*) came to meet him, bearing many gifts. In approximately 677 B.C.E., Esarhaddon, king of Assyria, ordered "the 22 kings of Ḥatti, the sea coast and within the sea" to drag cedar and pine beams from the mountains of Lebanon and Sirion to the capital Nineveh in order to build his palace. Included among these kings is Muṣuri, the king of Moab (*Mu-ṣur-i šar* KUR *Ma-ʾa-ab*). Ashurbanipal also relates that "22 kings of the seacoast, of the islands of the sea and of the mainland, servants subject to me" brought him numerous gifts and accompanied him with their troops on his first expedition to Egypt in 667 B.C.E. It is highly probable that Muṣuri the Moabite was among these kings. An Assyrian list of tribute from the time of Esarhaddon or Ashurbanipal states that the Moabites tendered "one gold mina" as tribute to Assyria. The kings of Transjordan bore Assyrian sovereignty without attempting to throw it off because they were aware that the Assyrian government, in the prevailing circumstances, was of greater benefit than harm. The Assyrian government usually defended loyal vassal kings from neighboring enemies. Danger to the peace of the countries of Transjordan came chiefly from the inhabitants of the desert, whose pressure on the border countries increased, beginning in the eighth century B.C.E. From the description of the wars of Ashurbanipal against the Arabs, it is clear that the Assyrians stationed garrisons along the border of the desert in order to prevent attempts by the nomadic tribes to penetrate into the cultivated areas. The Assyrians were interested in strengthening the border countries against the desert raiders and consequently the former were included in the defense system of the empire. The defeat of Amuladi, king of Kedar, by Chemosh-halta, king of Moab (*Ka-ma-as-ḫal-ta-a šar* KUR *Ma-ʾa-ab*), is merely one episode in a chain of similar events that are no different from that which occurred 500 years previously, when Hadad son of Bedad the Edomite defeated the tribes of Midian in the field of Moab (Gen. 36:35). Furthermore, under the Assyrian rule, the peoples of Transjordan extended the borders of their kingdoms into areas with an Israelite population, and they enjoyed economic prosperity. The Assyrians managed the defense of the desert caravan routes that connected Egypt and Arabia with Syria and Mesopotamia. Echoes of Moab's economic prosperity and of the extent of its territory appear in the prophecies about Moab (Isa. 25:10–12; Jer. 48, chiefly verses 7 and 29; Ezek. 25:9; Zeph. 2:8).

The passage from Assyrian to Babylonian rule did not involve a great change in the status of the kingdom of Moab. The king of Moab was apparently numbered with "all the kings of the land of Ḥeth [Ḥatti]" who brought tribute to Nebuchadnezzar when the Chaldean king campaigned against Ashkelon (c. 604/3 B.C.E.). Moabite and Ammonite troops were in the service of the king of Babylon when the revolt of Jehoiakim was crushed (II Kings 24:1–2; cf. Ezek. 25:6–8). However, a few years later a change in the policy of Moab toward Babylon is noticeable. In the fourth year of Zedekiah of Judah (594 B.C.E.), the king of Moab participated in a scheme to form a conspiracy against Babylon (Jer. 27:3). While there is no explicit information about the fate of the conspiracy, Moab apparently did not come to the aid of Zedekiah but stood aside when the Chaldean army drew near. A Babylonian punitive expedition against the countries of Transjordan was undertaken in the fifth year of the destruction of Jerusalem, i.e., the 23rd year of Nebuchadnezzar's reign. Josephus states that in that year, the Chaldean king proceeded against the army of Syria and defeated it, and that he also fought against the Ammonites and Moabites (Jos., Ant., 10:181; cf. Jer. 40:11; 48:7). Although there is no certain information that it was the Babylonian empire which brought about the end of the kingdom of Moab and turned it into a Babylonian province, the lack of information about Moab as an independent or semi-independent kingdom after the period of Babylonian rule, as well as a reference to the province of Moab (Ezra 2:6) during the first period of Persian rule in Israel, indicate that Moab was made a Babylonian province in the time of Nebuchadnezzar or a short time after his death. Glueck's archaeological survey testifies to a decline of settlement in Transjordan which ended with complete destruction in the sixth century B.C.E. The destruction was apparently a result of the collapse of the defense system on the desert front, which desert nomads broke through in order to raid Transjordan (e.g., the sons of Kedar and Nebaioth), damaging cultivated lands and destroying permanent settlements. Many Moabites were driven from the region south of the Arnon. Some of them concentrated in the region of the plateau, a region that was later known as Moabitis, and some dispersed to near and distant countries. The Moabite population remaining in Moab was assimilated among the Arabian tribes who took possession of the land. The punishment of the kingdoms of Transjordan cited by Ezekiel (25:4–10, 35:15) faithfully reflects the disaster that befell the settlements in Transjordan, and points to the settling in of nomads and shepherds from the east. The lament on the destruction of Moab in Numbers 21:27–35, which is echoed in Isaiah 15–16 and Jeremiah 48, is an old fragment of Moabite poetry. Moab achieved an additional period of prosperity in the Hellenistic-Roman period, but by then it had already been taken over by the Nabatean tribes, and was included in the Nabatean kingdom. In Hasmonean times, Alexander Yannai conquered the area, which was returned to the Nabateans by Hyrcanus II. It was later incorporated into Provincia Arabia.

[Bustanay Oded]

BIBLIOGRAPHY: H. Tristram, *The Land of Moab* (1873); A.H. Van Zyl, *The Moabites* (1960); A. Musil, *Arabia Petraea*, 1 (1907); Aharoni, Land, index; EM, s.v. (incl. bibl.); N. Glueck, in: AASOR, 14 (1934), 1–114; 15 (1935), 1–202; 18–19 (1939), 1–288; 25–28 (1951), 1–423;

H.L. Ginsberg, in: *Alexander Marx Jubilee Volume* (1950), 347–68; R.E. Murphy, in: CBQ, 15 (1953), 409–17; W.L. Reed and F.V. Winnett, in: BASOR, 172 (1963), 1–9; F.V. Winnett and W.L. Reed, in: AASOR, 36–37 (1964), 1–79; W.H. Ward and M.F. Martin, in: ADAJ, 8–9 (1964), 5–29; J. Liver, in: PEQ, 99 (1967), 14–31.

MOATI, SERGE (1946–), French television director. Moati was born in Tunis. From 1982 to 1986 he was the head of the state-owned channel 3 of French television (FR3), where he had been director of programming in 1981–1982. In addition to his work in television, he directed a number of feature films and was a film critic. He was awarded several prizes for his television programs, among them a prize for a documentary film (Prague, 1970), a prize for the best French-language film (1970), television critics award (1973), and the International Critics Award at the Monte Carlo festival in 1980.

[Gideon Kouts (2nd ed.)]

MOCATTA, English family of Marrano origin. MOSES MOCATTA (d. 1693), who came from Amsterdam, appears in a Bevis Marks (London) synagogue list in 1671. He was a diamond broker and merchant. His granddaughter REBECCA married as her second husband Moses Lumbrozo de Mattos. Their son ABRAHAM (d. 1751), (who added the name Mocatta and later dropped Lumbrozo de Mattos) joined with Asher Goldsmid to found Mocatta and *Goldsmid, later bullion brokers to the Bank of England, engaging in enormous transactions. Abraham Mocatta had 11 children (including Rachel, mother of Sir Moses *Montefiore). His son MOSES (1768–1857) retired early from business to devote himself to scholarship. He published *Faith Strengthened* (1851), a translation of Isaac b. Abraham *Troki's *Ḥizzuk Emunah*, and *The Inquisition and Judaism* (1845), a translation of a Portuguese inquisitorial sermon and the reply to it. In communal life, he was especially concerned with education and the reorganization of the Sephardi schools, "Sha'arei Tikvah."

Moses' children included DAVID (1806–1882), an architect, a pupil of Sir John Soane, and best-known for his railway stations on the London to Brighton line. As architect for his cousin Sir Moses Montefiore at Ramsgate, he was the first Jew to design an English synagogue. Another son, ISAAC LINDO (1818–1879), wrote tracts on Jewish moral teachings and social questions. Nine of the 24 founders of the Reform Congregation were Mocattas, including Moses and his nephew Abraham, father of FREDERICK DAVID MOCATTA (1828–1905). Philanthropist, scholar, and communal leader, Frederick was the representative ideal of late Victorian Anglo-Jewry. Active in both the Charity Organization Society and the Jewish Board of Guardians, he campaigned for the reform of voting charities. Widely traveled, he lectured on contemporary Jewish communities and wrote on Jewish history, publishing *The Jews and the Inquisition* in 1887. A munificent patron of scholarship, he was a correspondent and supporter of *Zunz. Sympathetic to most Jewish causes (although disapproving of nascent Zionism), he was an observant Jew and member of two Orthodox synagogues as well as his family's Reform congregation. He left his library (now known as the Mocattta Library) to University College, London, and the Jewish Historical Society of England. EDGAR MOCATTA (1879–1957) continued to head the family business, Mocatta and Goldsmid, and was known as the "silver king" for his specialist knowledge of dealings in silver as a currency. The family firm was sold to Hambros Bank in 1957.

One branch of the Mocatta family remained within the Orthodox community: a descendant of this was SIR ALAN ABRAHAM MOCATTA (1907–1990), a judge of the High Court from 1961, also active in Anglo-Jewish communal and historical affairs (president of the Board of Elders of the Spanish and Portuguese Synagogue, and chairman of the Council of Jews' College, 1945–62). He was the joint editor of *Scrutton on Charter Parties* (14th–17th editions).

BIBLIOGRAPHY: J.W. Scott, in: J.M. Shaftesley (ed.), *Remember the Days* (1966), 323–31; R.P. Lehmann, *Nova Bibliotheca Anglo-Judaica* (1961), 74, 171, 207; A.M. Hyamson, *Sephardim of England* (1951), index; J. Picciotto, *Sketches of Anglo-Jewish History* (1956^2), index; Roth, Mag Bibl, index; Roth, Art, 724, 781; V.D. Lipman, *Century of Social Service 1859–1959* (1959), index; E. Jamilly, in: JHSET, 18 (1953–55), 134. **ADD. BIBLIOGRAPHY:** ODNB online for the Mocatta family, Frederick David Mocatta, Edgar Mocatta; T. Endelman, *Jews of Georgian England*, index; C. Bermant, *The Cousinhood* (1961), index; T. Green, *Precious Heritage: Three Hundred Years of Mocatta and Goldsmid* (1984).

[Vivian David Lipman / William D. Rubinstein (2nd ed.)]

MOCH, JULES (1829–1881), French colonel, one of the first Jews to reach this rank in the French army. Moch fought with distinction in the Crimean War in 1854–55, and in the conquest of Rome in 1859, as well as in the Franco-Prussian War of 1870–71. He was the first Jew to be an instructor and examiner at the Military Academy of Saint-Cyr. Moch, proud of his Jewishness, was one of the founders of the Club Militaire which after his death became the moving spirit behind the incitement against Captain *Dreyfus.

MOCH, JULES SALVADOR (1893–1985), French socialist leader. Born in Paris, Moch worked as an engineer and industrial manager from 1920 to 1927. From 1928 to 1940 he sat as a socialist deputy in the National Assembly and in 1936 was made secretary-general of the prime minister's office under Leon *Blum, who held him in high esteem for his wide scientific and managerial experience. He was later under-secretary of state (1937) and minister of public works (1938).

During World War II, Moch served in the French navy; in 1940, after the fall of France, he was imprisoned for voting in the National Assembly against the granting of constitutional powers to Marshal Pétain. He escaped and joined the Free French Navy in 1943. In the following year he became a member of the Consultative Assembly and, on the termination of the war, a member of the National Assembly. From

1945 to 1947 Moch was minister of public works and between 1946 and 1951 be held important posts in 11 successive cabinets, serving as minister of the interior, vice premier, and minister of defense. In 1949 he was nominated premier but failed to secure a majority. Between 1953 and 1960 he served as French representative at the Geneva disarmament conference. He returned to the Ministry of the Interior in 1958 for a short period but resigned when General De Gaulle came to power.

Moch was one of the most respected figures in the French socialist movement. As a member of the French government he gave considerable assistance to Jewish refugees, as he took a keen interest in Zionism. He was an enthusiastic supporter of Israel, paying several visits, and closely following the development of the Israel labor movement. Among Moch's many publications were *Restitutions et réparations* (1921) and *La Russie des Soviets* (1925). He also wrote a number of books on financial questions including *Le Parti Socialiste et la politique financière* (1928), which were issued as handbooks by the French Socialist Party to demonstrate their ability to handle economic affairs.

[Moshe Rosetti]

MOCHA (Ar. **al-Mukhā**), a port city on the Red Sea coast of *Yemen. It is famous for being the major marketplace for coffee from the 15th to the 17th centuries, when the Dutch managed to obtain some seeds from the coffee tree – seeds which the Arab traders had guarded zealously – and soon enough were cultivating coffee in their colony of Indonesia. According to a sketch plan compiled by Brouwer (p. 143), the population of Mocha may have reached 20,000 permanent residents including a Jewish community (p. 228). It was the principal port for Yemen's capital, *San'a, until it was eclipsed in the 19th century by *Aden and Ḥudayadah as Yemen's main port. That, along with the fact that the Arabs no longer had an exclusive hold on the coffee trade, eventually pushed the city of Mocha into obscurity.

The earliest information about a Jewish community in Yemen can be derived from al-Ẓāhirī's *Sefer ha-Musar* from the 16th century. Since then we have a flow of information about Jews entering Yemen through Mocha, such as the emissary and book-printer from *Tiberias, Abraham b. Isaac Ashkenazi (1578). As can be judged from the main source of this information – responsa collections of Jewish rabbis outside of Yemen, mostly from *Egypt – the Jewish community in Mocha consisted not of Yemenite Jews but of non-Yemenite Jewish merchants who settled there for their business and others who came for a limited time only. In about 1770 there were some 400 Jewish families in the town, including some wealthy merchants, craftsmen, goldsmiths, weavers, and builders of smelting furnaces. R. Aaron Iraqi ha-Kohen, the president of the Jewish community in *San'a, lived there for some years as a ruler and judge (early 18th century), and his son Shalom, who also acted as president, built a magnificent synagogue there. After the British occupation of Aden in 1839 and its economic development, most Jews moved there from Mocha. In 1859 Jacob *Saphir found in Mocha only eight Jewish families living in a derelict quarter outside the city walls in wooden and reed constructions, as was the case in many other Yemenite towns. There were not enough members to form a *minyan* for Rosh Ha-Shanah services. One of the plagues common in this region caused the Jews to abandon the town and they dispersed in the mountain villages. The number of Jews gradually dwindled and by the 20th century no Jews remained in Mocha.

BIBLIOGRAPHY: Zechariah al-Ẓāhirī, *Sefer ha-Musar*, ed. by Y. Ratzaby (1965), 39–40, 285, 424–6; J. Saphir, *Even Sappir*, 1 (1886), 100–1, 110b. **ADD. BIBLIOGRAPHY:** Y. Tobi, in: *Shevet va-Am* 7 (1973), 272–91; C.G. Brouwer, *Al-Mukha, Profile of a Yemeni Seaport Sketched by Servants of the Dutch East India Company (VOC) 1614–1640* (1997).

[Haïm Z'ew Hirschberg / Yosef Tobi (2nd ed.)]

MODAI, ḤAYYIM (d. 1794), Safed scholar. In 1749 Modai journeyed to Europe as an emissary of the Safed community. Passing through Egypt, he came across a manuscript of geonic responsa which he published 43 years later under the title *Sha'arei Ẓedek* (Salonika, 1792). In 1755 he was appointed a member of the *bet din* in Constantinople as well as one of the *pekidim* ("commissioners") of Safed in the town. Following the earthquake in Safed in 1760, he was again sent to Europe in 1762 as an emissary for the town by the Constantinople commissioners, who published four letters on the subject of his mission in order to give it full publicity. After visiting various Italian towns (Mantua, Turin, and Venice in 1763), he went to Holland and England (Amsterdam and London) in 1765, and Germany. In 1766 he was in Prague where he had halakhic discussions with Ezekiel *Landau, who refers to him in respectful terms (responsa *Ḥayyim le-Olam*, YD no. 2; *Noda bi-Yhudah, Mahadura Kamma*, YD no. 87–88). Four years later he returned to Constantinople where he stayed until the death of Ḥayyim b. David Abulafia, when he was invited to succeed him as the rabbi of Smyrna. There he remained until 1793. At the end of his commendation to *Sha'arei Ẓedek*, Modai expresses his longing to return to Safed. His wish was fulfilled and he returned to Safed in 1793. His works include *Tiv Gittin* (1875), containing the bills of divorce arranged by him between 1737 and 1775 with the glosses of Yom Tov Israel; and *Ḥayyim le-Olam* (1878–79), responsa in two parts, including many written while on his travels; it also contains the responsa of his grandson, Nissim Ḥayyim Modai, entitled *Meimar Ḥayyim*. His glosses on the Shulḥan Arukh, *Oraḥ Ḥayyim* and *Yoreh De'ah*, and the *Peri Hadash* appear in the *Berakh Moshe* (Leghorn, 1809) of Moses b. Mordecai Galante (pp. 151–69); a responsum by him in the *Ma'amar ha-Melekh* (Salonika, 1806), of Raphael Abraham Maẓli'aḥ; and an alphabetical poem on the smoking of tobacco (*toton*) at the beginning of the *Avodah Tammah* (1903) of Joshua Raphael Benveniste. From 1767 Modai was on friendly terms with Ḥ.J.D. Azulai; on one ruling – in connection with reading from an invalid

Sefer Torah – they expressed opposing views; the correspondence between them continued until 1787.

BIBLIOGRAPHY: S. Ḥazan, *Ha-Ma'alot li-Shelomo* (1894), 31a–32a, 39b; M. Benayahu, *R. Ḥayyim Yosef David Azulai*, 1 (Heb., 1959), 362–6; 2 (1959), 412–3; I. Ben Zvi, in: *Sefunot*, 6 (1962), 360, 381–3; S. Emmanuel, *ibid.*, 406–7, 411, 419; S. Simonsohn, *ibid.*, 334, 348–9: Yaari, Sheluḥei, 130–1, 451–5.

[Josef Horovitz]

MODAI (Madzovitch), YITZHAK (1926–1998), Israeli politician and businessman, member of the Eighth to Twelfth Knessets. Modai was born in Tel Aviv. He studied at the Ge'ulah High School in Tel Aviv, and as a high-school student joined the Haganah in 1941. He joined the British mandatory police in 1943. He served in the IDF in 1948–50 as a field officer and as a staff officer, reaching the rank of lieutenant colonel. In 1951–53 he served as military attaché in London, and in 1953 headed the Israeli-Syrian and Israeli-Lebanese Mixed Armistice Commissions. Modai completed his studies in the Technion in Haifa as a chemical engineer in 1957 and received a law degree from the Tel Aviv branch of the Hebrew University in 1959. After that he entered the business world, and in 1961–77 was director general of the Revlon cosmetics company in Israel.

Modai joined the *Israel Liberal Party in 1961 and was appointed chairman of its Young Guard in 1962. He was a staunch supporter of the establishment of *Gaḥal, and as member of the Liberal Party executive consistently advocated full unity with the *Ḥerut Movement. In the course of the Six-Day War he was appointed military governor of Gaza. In 1969–73 he served as member of the Herzliyyah city council. Modai was elected to the Eighth Knesset in 1973, on the Likud list. Even though he objected to Israeli withdrawal from the territories, he expressed support for concessions on the Egyptian front, as long as Western Ereẓ Israel would not be redivided. In the government formed by Menaḥem *Begin in June 1977 he was appointed minister of energy and infrastructures, serving also as minister of communications from January 1979 to December 1980. In May 1980 Modai was elected chairman of the Liberal Party presidium. In the second government formed by Begin in August 1981, he was appointed minister without portfolio, and in October 1982 returned to the Ministry of Energy and Infrastructures. In the National Unity government formed in September 1984, Modai was appointed minister of finance. At first he worked in harmony with Prime Minister Shimon *Peres, and together they passed the Economic Stabilization Plan of 1985 that was designed to deal with a three-digit inflation rate and balance of payments difficulties. However, due to growing tensions in the government, Peres decided to switch him with Minister of Justice Moshe Nissim. As minister of justice Modai dealt with the GSS Affair, following the scandal over the killing of a terrorist that had been taken prisoner. In July 1986 Modai was forced to resign from the government after insulting the prime minister. Following the rotation in the premiership in October, Modai returned to the government as minister without portfolio. In 1984 he was elected chairman of the Liberal Party presidium, in which capacity he served until the Liberal Party and the *Ḥerut Movement finally merged into a single party in 1988. After the elections to the Twelfth Knesset in 1988 he was appointed minister of economics and planning. After the government approved the Shamir-Rabin initiative in May 1989 for holding elections in the West Bank and Gaza Strip, Modai joined Ariel *Sharon, and David *Levy in opposition to the initiative. On the day of the vote on a motion of no-confidence in the government on March 15, 1990, Modai and four additional members of the Likud parliamentary group broke away from the group and established a parliamentary group by the name of the Party for Advancing the Zionist Idea. In the narrow government formed by Yitzhak *Shamir in June, he was once again appointed minister of finance, after demanding a vast financial guarantee to back up the agreement he signed to join the coalition. Modai objected to the American conditioning of the grant of financial guarantees to Israel in return for stopping the Jewish settlement activities in the West Bank and Gaza Strip. He ran in the elections to the Thirteenth Knesset at the head of a new party called the New Liberal Party, but it failed to pass the qualifying threshold, and Modai returned to private business. He wrote *Meḥikat Afassim* (1988).

[Susan Hattis Rolef (2nd ed.)]

MODEH ANI (Heb. מוֹדֶה אֲנִי; "I give thanks"), initial words of a prayer said immediately upon waking in the morning. The short prayer ("I give thanks unto Thee, O living and eternal King, who hast restored my soul unto me in mercy; great is Thy faithfulness") does not mention any of the Divine Names and may therefore be said while still in bed and before performing the prescribed morning ablutions; hence it was preferred to the traditional *Elohai Neshamah* prayer (which was transferred to the morning benedictions).

Modeh Ani, possibly a shortened version of the *Elohai Neshamah* prayer (Ber. 60b), is of late origin and seems to have been composed about the 17th century; it was printed for the first time in the addenda to the prayer book *Seder ha-Yom* (1695). Because of its shortness and simplicity it became a favorite morning prayer for very small children before they are capable of reciting the ordinary daily morning service.

BIBLIOGRAPHY: Hertz, Prayer, 1116ff.

MODEL, MARX (d. 1709), *Court Jew of *Ansbach. The Model family originated in *Oettingen in the 16th century and subsequently spread throughout *Bavaria. It included a number of rabbis and Court Jews, foremost of whom was Marx Model, who in 1676 inherited his father's position as military and court purveyor at the court of the Margrave of Ansbach. One of the earliest Court Jews to engage in economic ventures, Marx acquired a number of estates and farms, a paper mill, and a workshop making roof tiles. In 1691 he was freed from custom duties and was granted the right to be sole publisher of the Talmud in Ansbach. His eldest daughter married Wolf, son of Samuel *Oppenheimer, the influential Austrian Court

Jew; Model served the latter as agent and supplier of silver for the mint and aided him in revoking an expulsion order against the Jews of Rothenburg. Model maintained his own synagogue and cantor in Ansbach. His unsuccessful attempt to unite the rival Jewish communities of *Fuerth was utilized by his rival Elkan *Fraenkel, who undermined his position at court and subjected the Jews to a harsher rule. However, Fraenkel's triumph was short-lived; Model's sons inherited their father's position and intrigued to bring about the eventual fall of the Fraenkels.

BIBLIOGRAPHY: S. Haenle, *Geschichte der Juden im ehemaligen Fuerstenthum Ansbach* (1867); L. Loewenstein, in: JJLG, 8 (1910), 131–4; L. Lamm, *ibid.*, 22 (1932), 152–9: M. Grunwald, *Samuel Oppenheimer* (1913), 305; S. Stern, *The Court Jew* (1950), 100, 193; H. Schnee, *Die Hoffinanz und der moderne Staat*, 4 (1963), 27–28; D.J. Cohen, in: *Kovez al Yad*, 6 pt. 2 (1966), 470, 514–5.

MODELL, ARTHUR B. (**Art**; 1925–), U.S. football team owner who was instrumental in transforming the NFL into the most popular TV sport in American history. Born and raised in Brooklyn, New York, Modell grew up destitute during the Depression and dropped out of high school at 15 to support his mother and two sisters after his father died. During World War II, he served stateside in the Air Force and then enrolled in television school under the GI Bill. He produced *Market Melodies*, one of the first regular television shows in the nation, and worked in advertising, public relations and television production in New York in the 1940s and 1950s. Modell was 35, living with and caring for his mother, when he purchased the Cleveland Browns on March 22, 1961 for $4 million – a sixfold increase from the previous franchise sale. He invested $250,000 of his own money, borrowed $2.7 million and found partners for the rest. Modell owned the Browns for 34 seasons but his near bankruptcy forced him to move the team to Baltimore in 1996, provoking the lasting wrath of Browns fans. Soon after moving the team to Baltimore, he sold a minority interest and eventually the controlling interest in the team, and left the game in 2004 after 44 seasons in the NFL. During his time as owner, the Browns won the NFL championship in 1964, reached NFL and AFC league title games in 1964, '65, '68, '69, '86, '87, '89. His Baltimore Ravens won the Super Bowl in 2000.

Modell, an influential visionary, helped popularize the NFL through the league's increasingly lucrative television contracts, which he negotiated as chairman of the league's TV committee for 31 years. Along with Pete Rozelle and Roone Arledge, Modell also created Monday Night Football on ABC; was instrumental in pushing the owners in the 1960s to share revenues equally; in bringing about the merger of the NFL and the AFL by agreeing to move the Browns to the less-established AFL for the good of the league; played an essential role in the creation of NFL Films, which became a financial success and one of America's premier production companies, and was instrumental in helping the league raise its profile; and, as chairman of the owners' labor committee, completed the first collective bargaining agreement in NFL history in 1968. Modell was also a leader on diversity by promoting minorities to key positions in his front office, including naming the first black general manager in NFL history. He wrote his autobiography *Owning Up: the Art Modell Story*, in 2005.

[Elli Wohlgelernter (2nd ed.)]

MODENA, city in N. central Italy. The first document relating to Jews in Modena may date back to 1025, but the existence of a stable Jewish community, formed by loan-bankers who originated from *Perugia, *Rimini, and Fermo, was not recorded until 1393. For many years the Jews of Modena enjoyed the protection of the house of Este, which ruled Modena as well as Ferrara. After the expulsion from Bologna (1569) and the devolution of Ferrara (1598) when Modena became the capital city of the Duchy of Estense a number of Jews moved there; also in the 17th and 18th centuries the duchy of Modena attracted a large Jewish settlement. Generally, the dukes considered favoring Jewish settlement and development as beneficial to the state, mainly for economical reasons, but this did not prevent the establishment of the ghetto (1638–1859), Inquisitional controls, and the activity of the Opera Pia dei Catecumeni, founded in 1700. When the ghetto was established in 1638 the Jews in Modena numbered 750; in 1767 they were 1,262; in 1847, 1,538 lived in the entire province of Modena.

Modena was long a principal center of scholarship for Italian Jewry and was distinguished as a seat of kabbalistic study. Among its scholars were the kabbalist *Aaron Berechiah of Modena, author of *Ma'avar Yabbok* (Mantua, 1626); the scholars Leone Poggetti, Natanel Trabotti, and Yedidià Carmi; the remarkable bibliophile Abraham Joseph Solomon *Graziani; Abraham *Rovigo; and Ishmael *Cohen (Laudadio Sacerdote). During the first half of the 16th century the Hevrot Ghemilut Chassdim and the Talmud Torà were founded; in 1614 Aharon Berechiah of Modena founded the Hevrat Machshivim for kabbalistic studies. The cultural and economic activities of Modenese Jewry were central to the Duchy of Este. Although they were confined to the ghetto in 1638, the Jews of Modena were allowed to carry on their business activities. The Jews of the Este Dukedom in fact were involved in a variety of entrepreneurial, commercial, and cultural activities – among other things, the manufacture and trading of precious silks, silver, and diamonds. These activities were handled by large-scale entrepreneurs, and there were also a number of ordinary workers. Jews played important cultural roles – as ducal librarians, court silversmiths, printers, etc. – in the city, and often it was Jews who imported new cultural ideas from abroad. From 1638 to 1721, the Jews of Modena opened nine synagogues with women's galleries and two schools. The *ḥevrot* in Modena at the end of 18th century numbered 15. In 1735 the Hevra Soked Holim for women was established. There was also a renowned yeshivah in the city. In 1796 Modena was occupied by the French and became part of the Cisalpine Republic. Moisé Formiggini was the first Italian Jew to be elected to office in the government of the Repubblica Cisalpina (1797).

He took part in the Lyon consultation in 1802 and in the Great Sanhedrin of Paris in 1806. In 1796 he moved to Milan, where he expanded his entrepreneurial activities and became a public figure, uniting the Jewish communities of Northern Italy. At the same time, with his brother Salomone, the merchant Angelo Sanguinetti and the rabbis Buonaventura Modena and Ishmael Cohen he continued to lead the Modena community. During the Restoration, the ghetto restrictions were renewed, but the Jews of Modena contributed effectively to the Italian Risorgimento, collaborating with the Carbonari, the secret revolutionary movement. Angelo and Emilio Usiglio in particular were among the supporters of Giuseppe Mazzini. With the arrival of the Piedmontese troupes of the Savoy in 1859 the Jews of Modena were granted full equality with the other citizens. Yet the community, which up to the middle of the 19th century still consisted of about 1,000 Jews, then began to diminish numerically because of immigration, mostly to Milan. Devotion to Ereẓ Israel was particularly strong in Modena in the ghetto period, and later on Zionism obtained an early foothold there: the monthly *L'Idea Sionnista* was published in Modena from 1900 to 1910, founded by Professor Carlo Conegliano, of the Faculty of Economics. Moreover in the 1930s, thanks the educational activity of Angelo da Fano, the Jewish community contributed greatly to the Italian Zionism movement.

In 1931 the community of Modena had a membership of 474 Jews. During the Holocaust 70 Jews were deported to the death camps from the province of Modena, and over 15 Modenese Jews died. Many Jews of Modena participated in antifascist activities and the Resistenza movement. Angelo Donati organized the escape of thousands of Jews from Nice to Palestine; the president of the community, Gino Freidman, was one of the organizers of the rescue of young refugees at Villa Emma. After the war 185 Jews remained in the community; by 1959 their number had decreased to 150 and by 2005 to 100, though the main synagogue remained open and there were regular Sabbath services. In the last quarter of the 20th century the community president Massimiliano Eckert (1908–2004) and Rabbi Adolfo *Lattes (1910–1995) did encourage the immigration to Israel of young people and the maintenance of religious life. In spite of its small number the Jewish community of Modena is very active in promoting cultural activities on Jewish and Israeli themes and Jewish education at the primary and secondary levels.

BIBLIOGRAPHY: Milano, Bibliotheca, index; Milano, Italia, index; Roth, Italy, index; A. Balletti, *Gli ebrei e gli estensi* (1930²), passim; C. Bernheimer, *Catalogo dei manuscritti orientali della Biblioteca Estense* (1960); J. Vaccari, *Villa Emma: un episodio agli albori della Resistenza modenese nel quadro delle persecuzioni razziste* (1960); Levi Minzi, in: *Israel* (Feb. 19, 1931); C. Levi, in: *Riforma sociale*, 4 (1897), 962–69; Milano, in: RMI, 11 (1936/37), 450–55; Artom, *ibid.*, 44–49. **ADD. BIBLIOGRAPHY:** F. Francesconi, "A Network of Families from Modena: Italian Jewish Life between the Renaissance and Modernity (1600–1810)," (Ph.D. thesis, University of Haifa, 2006).

[Ariel Toaff / Federica Francesconi (2nd ed.)]

MODENA, ANGELO (1867–1938), Italian general. Born in Reggio Emilia on January 28, 1867, he was appointed second lieutenant of the Alpine troops in 1887. He took part in the Italian-Turkish war of 1911–12; promoted to major (he was a captain from 1907), he was decorated with the bronze medal for military valor. In 1915, he was appointed colonel; during World War I, he was also decorated with the silver medal for military valor. In 1927, he was appointed general.

BIBLIOGRAPHY: A. Rovighi, *I Militari di Origine Ebraica nel Primo Secolo di Vita dello Stato Italiano*, Stato Maggiore dell'Esercito, Ufficio Storico, Roma (1999), 92.

[Massimo Longo Adorno (2nd ed.)]

MODENA, AVTALYON (da; 1529–1611), Italian scholar, and son of Mordecai (Angelo da) Modena, the eminent physician. After studying in Padua, Avtalyon settled in Ferrara, where he became noted as a talmudist and scholar; Azariah dei *Rossi mentions him with deference in his *Me'or Einayim*. He took part in the famous controversy on the ritual propriety of the *mikveh* constructed at *Rovigo. When the papal attack on Jewish literature was renewed in 1581, he went to Rome as delegate of the Italian Jewish communities and is said to have made a two-hour oration in Latin before the assembled Curia, as the result of which the edict was modified. He was known also as a writer of verse. Letters addressed to him are preserved among the correspondence of his nephew, Leone *Modena.

BIBLIOGRAPHY: L. Blau, *Leo Modenas Briefe und Schriftstuecke*… (1905), 41, 81 (Heb.); Ghirondi-Neppi, 26–29.

[Cecil Roth]

MODENA, FIORETTA (**Bat Sheva**; 16th century), wife of Solomon Modena (1522 or 1524–1580) and very learned in Torah, Mishnah, Talmud, Midrash, Jewish law, especially Maimonides, and kabbalistic literature, including the Zohar. Fioretta's sister, Diana Rieti of Mantua, was equally well versed. Fioretta spared no expense or effort to find the best teachers for her grandson, *Aaron Berechiah (d. 1639), later a rabbi and kabbalist in Modena. Nor was she unique in this respect; Italian Jewish women regularly supervised the educations of their sons and grandsons, especially when fathers and grandfathers were preoccupied. At the age of 75, after the death of her husband, Fioretta set out to Palestine to live in Safed, the Jewish equivalent of monastic retirement. According to her Venetian nephew Leon *Modena (1571–1648), who met Fioretta and witnessed her signal learning when she passed through Venice, she died just before reaching her destination.

BIBLIOGRAPHY: Aaron Berachiah of Modena, *Ma'avar Yabbok* (Vilna, 1860). fol. 7a; L. Modena, *The Autobiography of a Seventeenth Century Venetian Rabbi: Leon Modena's Life of Judah* (ed. and tr., Mark R. Cohen (1988)), 79.

[Howard Tzvi Adelman (2nd ed.)]

MODENA, LEON (**Judah Areyeh mi-Modena**; 1571–1648), Venetian rabbi, cantor, preacher, teacher, author, and polemicist. His father, Isaac, came from an old French Jewish family which settled in Modena and, after they moved to Bologna and later Ferrara, retained the surname Modena. His mother, named Rachel, but renamed Diana by his father, came from an Ashkenazi family that had resettled in Italy. Leon Modena was born in Venice but spent his youth in Ferrara, Cologna, and Montagnana. He studied Bible, rabbinics, Hebrew language, poetry, letter writing, voice, music, dancing, Italian, and Latin. At the age of 13, he composed *Kinah Shemor*, a macaronic poem, sounding and meaning the same in Hebrew and Italian; translated sections of Ludovico Ariosto's *Orlando furioso*; and wrote a pastoral dialogue on gambling (1595/6).

In 1590, at the age of 19 after the death of his fiancée, his cousin Esther Simḥah, Modena married her sister Rachel and received the title of *ḥaver*. He wished to embark on a rabbinic career, so in 1592 he returned to Venice, but the Jewish lay leaders raised the age of ordination to 35 and then 40. Modena, therefore, had to create his own opportunities for income and recognition until he was ordained in 1609.

Modena used his skills to serve as a legal clerk for the leading rabbis of Venice; a teacher of Hebrew and rabbinics for students of all ages; a popular preacher; a proofreader, expediter, and author of dedicatory poems in the Venetian Hebrew publishing industry; author of many Hebrew tombstone epitaphs, including his own; and a letter writer for his students. He also turned to gambling, a popular form of entertainment in Venice. Indeed, due to both emotional and financial distress, he gambled intermittently, despite his own better judgment, with both Christians and Jews, for the rest of his life.

Unable to earn a living in Venice, Modena moved to Ferrara from 1604 to 1607 where he functioned as a rabbi and taught for a wealthy family. During these years Modena made a successful presentation concerning Jewish moneylending before the papal legate, sided with most of the rabbis of northern Italy against the rabbis of Venice in a continuing controversy over a ritual bath in Rovigo, and supported a major musical performance in Ferrara that took place in the synagogue on Friday evening, Tu be-Av. He spent another year abroad in Florence (1609–10).

Modena met with and taught Hebrew to many English and French Christians. One offered him a chair in Oriental languages in Paris which he refused, probably because he would have had to convert. Another commissioned him to write for James I a description of Judaism, the *Riti Ebraica*, the first vernacular description of Judaism written by a Jew for a non-Jewish audience, first published in Paris in 1637 and subsequently republished and translated many times.

In his published books, Modena demonstrated his skills as an author, teacher, and popularizer of rabbinic teachings. In *Sod Yesharim* (1594/5), he prefaced magic tricks, folk remedies, and Jewish riddles to a curriculum of biblical and rabbinic studies to make it attractive to young students. In *Ẓemaḥ Ẓaddik* (1600), he embellished a Hebrew translation of the most popular Italian book of the period, *Fior di Virtù*, removing Christian references and adding citations from traditional Jewish sources. In *Midbar Yehudah* (1602), he translated some of his Italian sermons into Hebrew. In *Ẓeli Esh* he made the first Italian translation of the Passover *Haggadah* (1609). In *Galut Yehudah* (1612), he tried to overcome Church laws against translating the Bible by providing a translation of difficult words, to which he later added a rabbinic glossary as well (1640). In *Lev Aryeh* (1612), he presented a Hebrew system of memory improvement, based on those popular in Venice, as a preface to a work on the 613 commandments of Judaism. In his play, *L'Ester* (1619) he combined the current dramatic standards with traditional rabbinic sources. To the anthology *Ein Yaakov*, the major source for rabbinic materials in Italy where the Talmud was banned, Modena contributed an index, *Beit Leḥem Yehudah* (1625); a supplementary collection, *Beit Yehudah* (1635); and a commentary (*Ha-Boneh*, 1635). Modena's devotion to rabbinic learning and his educational program found expression in these books.

During his early years as a rabbi in Venice, Modena wrote some interesting responsa on contemporary Jewish cultural and legal issues, such as going about bareheaded and playing tennis or traveling by boat on the Sabbath. From his ordination until his death, Modena served as the chief Hebrew translator for the government and secretary for several organizations, including the Italian synagogue, where he also was elected cantor. In 1622 he prepared for press the first book of Hebrew music, *Ha-Shirim asher li-Shelomo*, by Salamone Rossi. He ordained candidates for the degrees of *ḥaver* and rabbi, including medical students in Padua, approved the decisions of other rabbis, and authorized books for publication, with the result that by 1618 he was referred to as a *gaon*, and an excellent, well-known, honored and brilliant preacher. By 1627 Modena signed his name first in order among the Venetian rabbis. In 1628 he was maestro di cappella for a Jewish academy of music, Accademia degli Impediti, which was popular both inside and outside the ghetto..

In 1630, when the leaders of the Jewish community tried to ban gambling, he published a Hebrew pamphlet in the form of a rabbinic responsum in which he questioned whether gambling was a sin according to Jewish belief and challenged the lay leaders' authority to issue such a ban without rabbinic approval. But even the rabbis of Venice, on whose behalf he argued, opposed his views.

Modena's most important writings remained unpublished during his lifetime. These included his defenses of rabbinic Judaism against Jewish critics, Christianity, and Jewish mysticism. He wrote *Sha'agat Aryeh* (1622) against *Kol Sakhal*, an anti-rabbinic work; *Magen ve-Ẓinnah* (c. 1618), a response against attacks on rabbinic Judaism; and *Diffesa* (1626), a defense of the Talmud against the apostate Sixtus of Sienna, whose appeal was based in part on his use of Kabbalah.

His critique of recent trends in Jewish mysticism, especially the spread of the new school of Lurianic Kabbalah and the impact of Christian utilization of Kabbalah on Jewish apostasy, included a trilogy of works: a tract against reincarnation, *Ben David* (1636); a text challenging the authenticity of the Kabbalah, *Ari Noḥem* (1639); an attack on Christian Kabbalah, *Magen va-Ḥerev* (1645, incomplete).

In *Ḥayyei Yehudah*, the first full-length Hebrew autobiography, Modena recorded many of the details of his unhappy but productive life. His difficult family life included, in addition to the death of two infants, the loss of his three adult sons: Mordecai, who died by inhaling fumes during alchemy experiments; Zebulun, who was murdered by a Jewish gang over a Jewish woman; and Isaac, whom he banished to the Levant and who traveled as far as South America. His main source of solace remained his two daughters: Diana, who would become the executrix of his estate, and Esther or Sterella, married to Jacob of La Motta. Modena's intellectual and spiritual heirs were Diana's first husband, Jacob Halevi, and Jacob's son, Isaac min Haleviim. After his beloved son-in-law died in the plague of 1629, Diana soon remarried Moses Saltaro Fano, with whom Modena did not get along, and who moved away, leaving her father to raise her son. Modena and his wife, Rachel, quarreled a great deal, especially after all the family moved out and their health deteriorated. According to the Venetian Ministry of Health she died on March 7, 1648, and he two weeks later. After his death the Italian congregation made extensive plans for his burial, and he was eulogized by the Jewish community and by Christian writers abroad.

As Modena's manuscripts were discovered during the 19th century, they were viewed as attacks on traditional Judaism. The early proponents of Reform Judaism looked to Modena as a precursor and, in the same tendentious spirit, those who wished to undermine the Reform appropriation presented him as a gambler, a heretic, a hypocrite, or someone racked by contradictions. Trying to make sense of these complexities, some have sought to identify him as the personification of the Renaissance Jew or the "first modern rabbi." The fact is, however, that in Italy the Renaissance was over by the time he lived and to see him as modern is to miss the fact that he spent much of his life defending traditional medieval rabbinic authority against attempts by the Jewish laity to limit their coercive power. Indeed, it may be more apt to view Modena as one of the last medieval rabbis and to see the period in which he lived as the earliest beginnings of the modern period for the Jews.

Leon Modena's life, however, is not only an important example of the struggles of early-modern rabbinic authority but also of social history. His candid and extensive writings provide details about the social and economic conditions of the family, women, and children and about daily life, community, and religion, including the occult, magic amulets, and especially, Jewish-Christian relations.

BIBLIOGRAPHY: R. Davis and B. Ravid (eds). *The Jews of Early Modern Venice* (2001); T. Fishman, *Shaking the Pillars of Exile: "Voice of a Fool," an Early Modern Jewish Critique of Rabbinic Culture* (1997); D. Malkiel (ed.), *The Lion Shall Roar: Leon Modena and His World* (2003); L. Modena, *The Autobiography of a Seventeenth-Century Venetian Rabbi: Leon Modena's Life of Judah*, ed. and tr. Mark R. Cohen (1988); B. Richler, "Ketavim bilti Yedu'im shel Rabbi Yehudah Aryeh mi-Modena," in: *Asufot*, 7 (1992/3), 157–72.

[Howard Tzvi Adelman (2nd ed.)]

MODERN, JUDAH (1819–1893), Hungarian rabbi. Modern was born in Pressburg where he became one of the outstanding pupils of Moses Sofer, Meir Asch, and Moses Teitelbaum. In 1837 he married the daughter of Samuel Zanvil ha-Kohen of Sziget and remained in Sziget for the rest of his life, refusing to accept offers of rabbinic office. On the title page of his *Zikhron Shemu'el* it states: "Neither rabbi nor *av bet din*, despising honor and praise, engaged in Torah by day and by night." In Sziget he became attracted to *Ḥasidism and, to the displeasure of his teacher, Moses Sofer, paid visits to the ḥasidic rabbis. He was one of the leaders of the community which in 1886 broke with the Orthodox community of Sziget and established the separatist community which was called Ha-Kehillah ha-Sefaradit.

Modern was the author of *Zikhron Shemu'el* (1867), a detailed commentary on tractate *Gittin*, and *Peri ha-Eẓ* (1885–87), on the Pentateuch. He published Judah Kahana's *Terumat ha-Keri* (1858), on the Tur and Shulḥan Arukh, *Ḥoshen Mishpat*, with his own glosses and novellae. Individual responsa by him have appeared in various works.

BIBLIOGRAPHY: J.J. (L.) Greenwald (Grunwald), *Zikkaron la-Rishonim* (1909), 38–45; idem, *Maẓẓevat Kodesh* (1952), 36–39; N. Ben-Menahem, in: *Sinai*, 63 (1968), 172–6.

[Naphtali Ben-Menahem]

MODIANO, PATRICK (1945–), French writer. Modiano's first book, *La Place de l'Etoile* (1968), gained him immediate fame and recognition. It is the story of a young French Jew caught in the turmoil of the war years in occupied Paris. Though Modiano was born after World War II, that period appears to fascinate him, and he goes back to it time and again in search of inspiration. Antisemitism and collaboration, black market and Resistance, spies and doubtful heroes: these are his most regular themes. His other works include *La ronde de nuit* ("Night Round," 1969), *Les boulevards de ceinture* ("Circle Line Boulevards," 1972). In *Lacombe Lucien* (1974), made into a successful film by Louis Malle, Modiano caused a furor by delving into the murky relationship between a young French Nazi and a Jewish girl. Memory becomes increasingly obsessive in his work, as shown in *Villa triste* ("Sad Villa," 1975), *Livret de famille* ("Family Record Book," 1977), and *Rue des boutiques obscures* ("Dark Shops Street"), in which an amnesiac detective is inextricably tied to the period of German Occupation. For the latter, Modiano was the winner of the 1978 Goncourt Prize. Also of note are *Remise de peine* ("Reduction," 1988), "*Voyage de noce*" ("Honeymoon Trip," 1990), and *Dora Bruder* (1997), in which Modiano tells of the last months of a young Jewish girl in Paris before being arrested and deported. His later works include *Ephéméride* ("Block Calendar," 2002), *Accident nocturne* ("Night Accident," 2003), and *Un pedigree*

("A Pedigree," 2005), in which Modiano evokes his conflict-laden relationship with his father.

Modiano also wrote children's books. They include *Catherine Certitude* (1988) and *28 Paradis* (2005), illustrated by his wife, Dominique Zehrfuss.

[Gideon Kouts / Anny Dayan Rosenman (2nd ed.)]

MODIGLIANI, AMEDEO (1884–1920), painter. Modigliani was born in Leghorn, the son of a small businessman. One of his brothers, Vittorio Emanuele *Modigliani, was an active Socialist leader. Amedeo studied art in Florence and Venice. In 1905 he went to Paris. While there, though leading a life of dissipation, he learned a great deal from Cézanne, Gauguin, Toulouse-Lautrec and from African sculpture. He greatly admired the last and his own sculpture was in a similar simplified abstract style. Despite his many love affairs, his excesses of drunkenness and frequent lapses into illness aggravated by poverty, he managed to produce a substantial body of work within his relatively short career. More than 20 of his sculptures, some 500 paintings, and thousands of watercolors and drawings have survived. Modigliani usually painted single figures with backgrounds only vaguely defined. There are portraits of his fellow artists and of the two women who played leading roles in his life, the English poet, Beatrice Hastings, with whom he lived from 1914 to 1916, and later his wife, Jeanne Hébuterne. His sitters included the streetwalkers of the Left Bank whom Modigliani never made pretty but who always evoke pity. His portraits look as if he had caught the sitter in a moment of utter fatigue, lonely and devoid of glamor or gaiety. Their energy has been drained and their hands dangle limply on their laps. Their heads are inclined and their eyes look listlessly and unseeing, as though staring from another world. His women seem to be constructed of almond shapes connected by cylindrical necks to larger ovoids formed by the rounded shoulders of the upper body.

Modigliani was a superb draftsman and his color sense was fascinating. His sensuous nudes are painted in broad planes of vivid ochre, orange, and earthy hues, surrounded by strong lines. His iridescent tones are achieved by covering thin layers of color with many coats of varnish. In 1917 his only one-man show was a complete fiasco. The police ordered the five canvases of nudes to be removed and this led to a scandal. It was soon after his death that the greatness of his work was discovered and his paintings and sculpture were acquired by leading museums and collectors all over the world.

BIBLIOGRAPHY: F. Russoli, *Modigliani* (Eng., 1959); A. Werner, *Modigliani the Sculptor* (1962, 1965); J. Modigliani, *Modigliani* (Eng., 1958). **ADD. BIBLIOGRAPHY:** D. Krystof, *Modigliani* (Taschen, 2000); A. Kruszinski, *Amadeo Modigliani: Portraits and Nudes* (2005); J. Meyers, *Modigliani: A Life* (2006).

[Alfred Werner]

MODIGLIANI, FRANCO (1918–2003), economist and Nobel Prize laureate. Modigliani was born in Rome. After earning a law degree at the University of Rome, he escaped the Fascist regime in Italy and moved to the United States in 1939. In New York he studied at the New School for Social Research, obtaining his Ph.D. in social sciences in 1944. Modigliani taught at the New School from 1944 to 1949 and was a research consultant to the Cowles Commission at the University of Chicago from 1949 to 1952. He was a professor at Carnegie Institute of Technology from 1952 to 1960 and at Northwestern University from 1960 to 1962. He was on the faculty of the Massachusetts Institute of Technology from 1962, becoming professor emeritus in 1988. He served as president of the American Economic Association in 1976.

Modigliani's research work focused on the analysis of household savings, wherein he determined that people save towards retirement rather than amass money to be left as inheritance for the next generation, and on the different types of national pension programs and their effects. He also was highly influential in the area of corporate finance by directing attention to the fact that future earnings of a company serve to determine stock market values. The Nobel Prize in economic science for 1985 was awarded to him for "his pioneering analyses of saving and financial markets," for work that he published in the second half of the 1950s.

Modigliani's autobiography is entitled *Adventures of an Economist* (2001). His other publications include *The Debate over Stabilization Policy* (1986); *Capital Markets* (with F. Fabozzi, 1992); *Foundations of Financial Markets and Institutions* (with F. Fabozzi and M. Ferri, 1994); and *Rethinking Pension Reform* (with A. Muralidhar, 2004).

[Ruth Beloff (2nd ed.)]

MODIGLIANI, VITTORIO EMANUELE (1872–1947), Italian lawyer and politician; brother of the artist Amedeo *Modigliani. Born in Leghorn, Modigliani joined the Socialist party as a student. From 1913 to 1924 he sat as a Socialist in the Italian parliament. He opposed Italian participation in World War I and supported the formula of a peace without victor or vanquished. In 1924 Modigliani joined the rest of his party in abstaining from all parliamentary activity, in protest against the new Fascist law making parliamentary opposition ineffective. He appeared for the prosecution in the Giacomo Matteotti trial in 1923–24 in which leading Fascists were accused of complicity in Matteotti's assassination. Soon afterward he left Italy in protest against the Fascist regime and lived in Austria and France, where he was a virulent opponent of Fascism. Modigliani participated in the formation of a socialist pro-Palestine committee formed in Brussels. He returned to Italy in 1945 and was elected a deputy to the constituent assembly and chairman of the Italian Socialist Party.

[Giorgio Romano]

MODI'IN (Heb. מוֹדִיעִין, מוֹדִיעִים, or Modi'im), town or village in the toparchy of Lydda, the family home of Mattathias the Maccabean and of his Hasmonean descendants; here the Maccabean revolt broke out (I Macc. 2:1, 15, 23; cf. Jos., Ant. 12–13). Nothing much is said in the sources about the place, its size and situation. Although the rebels were soon forced to evacuate the village, they were able to bury their dead there (I Macc. 2:70, 9:18–21, 13:25–30). Simeon the Hasmonean eventually built a splendid mausoleum at Modi'in, which was adorned with seven pyramids and high columns with sculptures of ships that were said to be visible from the sea (I Macc. 13:25–30; Jos., Ant. 13:210–11). In the time of Jonathan, Modi'in passed into Jewish possession with the rest of the toparchy of Lydda. An important battle was undertaken against the Seleucid Kendebaois from a camp situated close to Modi'in. Judas Maccabaeus is mentioned as having marched out of Modi'in in order to fight Seleucid forces sent against him by Antiochus V (II Macc. 13:14ff.), suggesting that the town was unfortified (but some historians, notably Longstaff, have cast doubt on the veracity of this story). John and Judah, the sons of Simeon, camped close to Modi'in before the battle of Kidron (I Macc. 16:4). In the Mishnah, it is described as a town on the border of Judah (Pes. 9:2; Ḥag. 3:5). It was the home town of R. Eleazar of Modi'in, a close relative of Bar Kokhba and perhaps identical with Eleazar the high priest, who appears on coins of the Second Jewish War. R. *Eleazar was put to death in 135 C.E. on grounds of treason. Another teacher associated with Modi'in is Rabbi Yossi, but details regarding this person and his teachings are sparse. In the *Onomasticon* (132:16) of *Eusebius Pamphili (c. 260–339 C.E.) and on the Madaba mosaic map (mid-sixth century), it is located east of Lydda. The whereabouts of Modi'in the village/town and burial-place of the Maccabean family is a subject that has intrigued pilgrims and travelers since the 12th century when the Crusaders identified it at the site of Belmont, next to present-day kibbutz Ẓova, west of Jerusalem, a mistake that was maintained until the 19th century by visitors to the region. E. Robinson (1852), however, suggested that Modi'in should be identified at Latrun on the grounds of its position and elevation. In the mid-19th century, considerable efforts were made by scholars (notably E. Forner, Ch. Sandreckzi, V. Guérin, C.R. Conder and Ch. Clermont-Ganneau) to identify Modi'in at Khirbet el-Midya and Sheikh al-Gharbāwī, about 7½ mi. (12 km.) east of Lydda in the northern Shephelah, but the famous "Tombs of the Maccabees" seen there today are mostly of Byzantine date. During an archaeological project conducted by S. Gibson and E. Lass in the area of the modern city of Modi'in from 1995 to 1999, a proposal was put forward to identify ancient Modi'in at Horvat Titora (Khirbet el-Burj) as a result of the finds made there from the Iron Age, Hellenistic and Early Roman periods, including large numbers of subterranean hideaways from the Bar Kokhba period. More recently, Khirbet Umm el-'Umdan, which is the site of an Early-Roman period village with a public building (perhaps a synagogue), excavated by S. Weksler-Bdolach and A. Onn, has also been proposed as the site of Modi'in. To sum up: unless an inscription were to be found at one of these sites, the exact location of Modi'in will apparently always remain a mystery.

[Michael Avi-Yonah / Shimon Gibson (2nd ed.)]

Modi'im and Modi'im Region

In the Israel *War of Independence, the area west of the Naḥal Modi'im gorge was occupied by Israel forces in July 1948, while the village al-Midya remained beyond the 1949 armistice line in Jordanian territory. In the 1950s and 1960s, the Herzl Forest of *Ben Shemen was gradually enlarged eastward to become the Modi'im Forest, and an observation tower and amphitheater were built there. In 1964, the Modi'im region development project was started, providing for further afforestation and land reclamation; the area's northern section was set aside as an ultimate reserve for the expansion of the Tel Aviv conurbation, with plans laid out for the construction of a future city to be named Makkabit. In 1965, a *Naḥal outpost settlement, Mevo Modi'im (מְבוֹא מוֹדִיעִים), was established less than a mile (1 km.) from the armistice line by a group affiliated with *Po'alei Agudat Israel. After the *Six-Day War, these settlers moved southeastward to set up a new village in the Aijalon Valley, at the foot of the *Beth-Ḥoron ascent, while the site of Mevo Modi'im, which has poor and rocky soil, was earmarked for a village to be based on industry and a Po'alei Agudat Israel seminary. Forest planting continued after 1967 on both sides of the former armistice line, carried out in the west by Jewish laborers and in the east by Arabs.

[Efraim Orni]

The City of Modi'in

The modern city of Modi'in was officially established in 1993 in a ceremony attended by late Prime Minister Yitzḥak Rabin. Plans for the city were drawn up in the mid-1980s by the architect Moshe *Safdie and approved in the beginning of the 1990s by Ariel *Sharon, then minister of housing. In 1996 the first residents moved in and its rapid expansion earned it city status in 2001. It is located in a former army firing zone between the Judean Plain and the Jerusalem Hills, midway between Jerusalem and Tel Aviv. The city's convenient location has served to attract residents from both the Jerusalem and Tel Aviv areas. Its jurisdiction extends over 18 sq. mi. (46 sq. km.), 50% of which are green areas.

In 2003 the municipality was united with *Makkabim-Re'ut. The population of Modi'in at the time was 34,700 while Makkabim-Re'ut had 10,700 residents. The population was well educated, with 60% holding academic degrees, and the majority were young families with an average of two children. Most residents commuted to work but an industrial park was planned for the outskirts of the city.

[Shaked Gilboa (2nd ed.)]

BIBLIOGRAPHY: Guérin, in: *PEFQS*, 2 (1870), 390; F.M. Abel, *Les Livres des Maceabées* (1949); idem, in: *RB*, 32 (1923), 496ff.; Beyer, in: *ZDPV*, 56 (1933), 223. **ADD. BIBLIOGRAPHY:** A. Negev and S. Gibson (eds.), *Archaeological Encyclopedia of the Holy Land* (2001), 341, s.v. "Modi'in"; S. Weksler-Bdolach, A. Onn and Y. Rapuano, "Identifying the Hasmonean Village of Modi'in," in: *Cathedra* (2003), 69–86.

MODON (now **Methone**), port city in S.W. Peloponnesus, Greece. Benjamin of Tudela found a Jewish community in Modon, and it became of importance during the Venetian rule. Four travelers in the late 15th century recorded details about this Jewish community ruled by the Venetians (1206–1500). In 1481 Meshullam of Volterra found 300 Jewish families in Modon in a ghetto "on the outskirts of the city" engaged in trade and handicrafts. Jews were engaged in the silk and tanning industries, as well as the maritime trade. Jews were excluded from citizenship and obliged to provide an executioner, as in other Venetian colonies. Jewish men and women had to perform forced labor. Modon fell to the Turks in 1501, whereupon many exiles from Spain settled there. Venice demanded an exorbitant sum from its Jewish population. In the assault on the town in 1531 by the Knights of Malta, Jewish captives were presumed to have been among those non-Christians carried off by the invaders. The Jewish community ceased to exist after the Venetian-Turkish war of 1646.

BIBLIOGRAPHY: J. Starr, *Romania* (1949), 63–72.

[Simon Marcus]

MODZHITZ, ḥasidic dynasty in Poland (family name: Taub). Its founder was Israel of Modzhitz (d. 1921), son of Samuel Elijah of Zwole. He emphasized the value of music in Ḥasidism and is regarded as the creator of the ḥasidic melody as an art form. Israel composed hundreds of melodies, of which the best known are those to *Ezkerah Elohim ve-Ehemayah*, consisting of over 30 stanzas composed at a time of physical suffering, and to *Le-Mizmor Todah* (also called *Niggun li-Meḥusserei Bayit* ("A Tune for the Homeless"), expressing the distress of Jewish refugees during World War I. Much of his teachings are devoted to the praise of music. His son, SAUL JEDIDIAH ELEAZAR (d. 1947), was *av bet din* in Rakov and Karzow. In 1929 he moved to Otwock near Warsaw and after his father's death headed the Modzhitz Ḥasidim. He combined Torah with music, and popularized the Modzhitz melodies throughout the Jewish world, composing hundreds of tunes. He edited and published his father's sermons with his own in *Divrei Yisrael* (Lublin, 1901–04; Warsaw, 1912; Warsaw, 1930; New York, 1931) and in the Passover *Haggadah, Ishei Yisrael* (Warsaw, 1938); he also edited and published the booklets *Tiferet Yisrael – Kunteres Ma'amarim* (Warsaw, 1936–38; Brooklyn, 1941–47). He died in Tel Aviv.

BIBLIOGRAPHY: M.S. Geshuri (ed.), *La-Ḥasidim Mizmor* (1936); idem, *Neginah va-Ḥasidut be-Veit Kuzmir u-Venoteha* (1952).

[Avraham Rubinstein]

MO'ED (Heb. מוֹעֵד), the second of the six orders of the Mishnah according to the accepted order established by *Simeon b. Lakish. He interpreted the verse (Isa. 33:6), "and the stability of thy times shall be a hoard of salvation, wisdom, and knowledge …" such that "stability" refers to the order *Zera'im*, "thy times" to the order *Mo'ed* … (Shab. 31a, et al.). In the order given by R. Tanḥum, however, it is the fourth (Num. R. 13:15). *Mo'ed* treats comprehensively of the Sabbath and the festivals of the Jewish calendar, but it includes tractates **Eruvin*, which is a kind of appendix to *Shabbat*, **Shekalim*, because of the fixed appointed time for the collection of the half-*shekel* (see Shek. 1:1–3), and **Ta'anit*, dealing with congregational fasts, since to some extent its subject matter is similar to that of the festivals. *Mo'ed* comprises 12 tractates arranged, as are all the orders, in descending order according to the number of chapters. They are (1) **Shabbat*, with 24 chapters; (2) *Eruvim*, 10; (3) **Pesaḥim*, 10; (4) *Shekalim*, 8; (5) **Yoma*, 8; (6) **Sukkah*, 5; (7) **Beẓah* or *Yom Tov*, 5; (8) **Rosh Ha-Shanah*, 4; (9) *Ta'anit*, 4; (10) **Megillah*, 4; (11) **Mo'ed Katan* or *Mashkin*, 3; (12) **Ḥagigah*, 3; in all, 88 chapters.

In the Tosefta of *Mo'ed, Shabbat* has 17 (or 18) chapters; *Eruvin* 8 (or 11), *Pesaḥim* 10, *Shekalim* 3, *Kippurim* 4 (or 5). *Sukkah* 4, *Yom Tov* 4, *Rosh Ha-Shanah* 2 (or 4), *Ta'aniyyot* 3 (or 4), *Megillah* 3 (or 4), *Mo'ed Katan* 2, and *Ḥagigah* 3. There is no *Gemara* to *Shekalim* in the Babylonian Talmud but there is in the Jerusalem Talmud. In contrast to all the other orders which have plural names, the name of *Mo'ed* is in the singular. The reason is apparently that the concept *Mo'ed* has two meanings, one in the sense of a festival and the other in that of a fixed time, as for example, "the season [*mo'ed*] that thou camest forth out of Egypt" (Deut. 16:6), or, "therefore will I take back My corn in the time thereof, and My wine in the season thereof [*be-mo'ado*]" (Hos. 2:11). In this sense the Bible uses the term *Mo'ed* in the singular, and this is apparently the implication of the use of the singular for the name of the order, since it treats not only of the festivals, but also of other topics that nevertheless have a fixed time, such as *Shekalim*, *Ta'anit* and the readings of the Law. It seems that the tractate *Shabbat* alone was once called *Mo'ed*.

BIBLIOGRAPHY: Epstein, Mishnah, 980ff.; Albeck, *Shishah Sidrei Mishnah, Seder Mo'ed* (1952).

[Abraham Arzi]

MO'ED KATAN (Heb. מוֹעֵד קָטָן; "small festival"), 11th tractate in the Mishnah order of *Mo'ed*, concerned mainly with **ḥol ha-mo'ed* ("the intermediate days of the festivals of *Passover and *Sukkot"). The original name of this tractate seems to have been *Mo'ed* (TJ, MK, 2:5, 81b), and in fact, throughout this tractate, the intermediate days are referred to as *Mo'ed* and not as *ḥol ha-mo'ed*. To distinguish the tractate **Mo'ed* from the mishnaic order of that name, the former was sometimes referred to as *Mashkin* (Lev. R. 34:4), its opening word. The present designation, *Mo'ed Katan*, prevailed to distinguish the tractate from its order.

While the Scripture does not explicitly forbid work on *ḥol ha-mo'ed*, Leviticus 23:37, speaking of the daily festival sacrifices, includes the intermediate days of the festival in the term "holy convocation" and on account of this *ḥol ha-mo'ed* is considered as semi-festival, days on which certain kinds of work (and as a rule all unnecessary work) are forbidden. Chapter 1 of the tractate discusses a great variety of activities (e.g., agriculture, burial, marriage, sowing, repairs) which in certain circumstances may be allowed on *ḥol ha-mo'ed*.

Chapter 2 speaks of further kinds of work (e.g., pressing olives, or finishing the manufacture of wine, and gathering fruits, etc.) which are allowed if they are urgent; the general rule is that no work which should have been done before the festival or could be postponed until after the festival may be done on *ḥol ha-mo'ed*. Chapter 3 speaks of the conditions under which shaving, washing clothes, drawing up of documents and other scribal activity are allowed; it then discusses the manner in which mourning customs are observed on Sabbath and festivals, including New Moon, Ḥanukkah, and Purim. The tractate ends on a note of comfort by quoting Isaiah 25:8: "He will swallow up death for ever, and the Lord will wipe away tears from all faces." The *Gemara* in Chapter 3 explains the connection between the laws of the intermediate days and those of mourning. In that context, the Babylonian *Gemara* discusses details or burial and mourning customs and records several interesting funeral orations and dirges, and deals with the laws of excommunication. There is also a *Gemara* in the Jerusalem Talmud. In the Tosefta the material of the tractate is divided into two chapters, and like the Mishnah contains many details which reflect life and conditions during the tannaitic period. An English translation and introduction by H.M. Lazarus is to be found in the Soncino Talmud translation (1938).

BIBLIOGRAPHY: H.M. Reinhold, *Tal Ḥayyim… al Massekhet Mo'ed Katan…* (Lvov, 1866); Ḥ. Albeck, *Shishah Sidrei Mishnah*, 2 (1958), 371–3.

[Arnost Zvi Ehrman]

MOELLIN, JACOB BEN MOSES (1360?–1427), usually referred to as Maharil (Morenu ha-Rav Jacob ha-Levi) and also as Mahari Segal and Mahari Molin), the foremost talmudist of his generation and head of the Jewish communities of Germany, Austria, and Bohemia. Born in Mainz, Jacob was taught by his father, one of its leading rabbis, and then proceeded to Austria, where he studied under Meir ha-Levi and Shalom b. Isaac, who ordained him rabbi with the title *morenu*. Summoned to Mainz while still young to succeed his father who had died in 1387, Jacob founded a yeshivah there to which many students streamed. The students lived in his house and were supported by "the means provided for him by the leaders of the country" (*Sefer Maharil*). From this yeshivah came the greatest rabbis of Germany and Austria of the next generation, among them Jacob *Weil.

Moellin became famous throughout Europe. While he was still young, halakhic problems were addressed to him "since from your mouth Torah goes forth to all Israel" (Maharil, resp. no. 148). He was also regarded as the leader of the people in that troubled period. During the Hussite wars and the strengthening of Catholic reaction various communities turned to him for help. On this occasion he decreed a three-day fast upon the whole community, "even upon sucklings," and also took the matter up with the government, with successful results. His rulings, together with those of Israel *Isserlein, serve as the foundation of all the traditions which were kept in German Jewry. In his decisions Moellin took prevailing conditions into consideration, and when a matter which affected the economic position of the community came before him, he assembled the scholars and "investigated the matter until he found a favorable solution." When he felt he had been too strict, he excused himself saying, "I have been very strict with you because you are without a rabbi" (resp. no. 26). He attacked rabbis who "bought" rabbinical positions which they were unqualified to fill (Jacob Weil, *Dinim ve-Halakhot*, no. 68, Kapust ed. (1834), 59b), and protested against the neglect of Torah study and against the widespread practice of giving decisions based on abridged halakhic works. In his sermons he placed particular emphasis upon the *mitzvah* of charity, and he was keenly solicitous of the honor of the poor.

Moellin also occupied himself with astronomy and applied himself to the solution of astronomical problems with the aid of instruments, and the study of the astronomical work *Shesh Kenafayim* of Immanuel b. Jacob *Bonfils. Jacob was well-versed in the different German dialects and composed Hebrew rhymed verse (in Ms.) and *piyyutim* (Joseph b. Moses, *Leket Yosher*, ed. by J. Freimann, 1 (1903), 50). Though, like all the rabbis of Germany, he shunned philosophy, he acted with a degree of tolerance toward those who, attracted by it, had strayed in matters of belief. He declared valid the *sheḥitah* of one who "accepted resurrection only as a traditional belief, but denied that there was a biblical basis for it," even declaring that "though his sin is too great to be tolerated, he is not under suspicion of deliberately transgressing the Torah" (resp. no. 194, p. 64a–b).

Moellin was renowned as a *ḥazzan* and his activities left a lasting influence on the Ashkenazi tradition. His opinion that traditional tunes should not be changed was a constantly stabilizing factor. The so-called "*Niggunei Maharil*," attributed to him (or at least thought to have been sanctioned by him) were in use in the Mainz community until modern times (see Idelsohn, Music, 170, 177, 206, 456, and see *Mi-Sinai melodies).

His known works are (1) *Minhagei Maharil* (*Sefer Maharil*, first published in Sabionetta, 1556), compiled by his pupil Zalman of St. Goar who for many years noted down his halakhic statements, customs and, in particular, the explanations he heard from him. Through the efforts of various copyists, the work enjoyed wide circulation. Most of the customs noted in it were included by Moses Isserles in his glosses to the Shulḥan Arukh; (2) Responsa, some copied and arranged by Eleazar b. Jacob and published for the first time in Venice in 1549. A far more complete collection has been preserved in manuscript (Margoliouth, Cat. No. 575). The printed editions of the *Maharil* are full of errors, apparently having been published from a corrupt copy. Moellin died in Worms.

BIBLIOGRAPHY: G. Steiman, *Custom and Survival – A Study of the Life and Work of R. Jacob Molin* (1963); G. Polak, *Halikhot Kedem* (1846), 79–86; Guedemann, Gesch Erz, 3 (1888), 17–20; D. Kaufmann, in: MGWJ, 42 (1898), 223–9; Weiss, Dor, 5 (1904[4]), 81f., 239–42; Joseph b. Moses, *Leket Yosher*, ed. by J. Freimann, 2 (1904), XXXV, 132; Fin-

Restored family houses from the talmudic era (3rd–5th centuries C.E.) found at Kaẓerin in the Golan Heights. *Photo: Z. Radovan, Jerusalem.*

The Land of Israel offers a fascinating variety of archaeological findings that illuminate the attachment of the Jewish people to its ancient homeland from the birth of the nation in the biblical period through the period of the Second Temple and beyond. They are a part of the Israeli landscape as much as its flora and fauna.

ARCHAEOLOGY

(opposite page): **Masada—Backdrop of the aerial view of Herod's reconstructed palace.** *Photo: Albatross Aerial Photography.*

(this page): **A mosaic of the "Galilean" Mona Lisa, found at Zippori, early 3rd century C.E.** *Photo: Dinu Mendrea.*

Bas relief of a *menorah* from the 3rd century C.E., Bet She'arim, which became a center of Jewish learning as attested in rabbinic literature. *Photo: Hanan Isachar.*

A capital from the synagogue in Kaẓerin with symbols of the *menorah* and the four species, from the talmudic era (3rd–5th centuries C.E.) *Photo © Katzerin Museum, Israel.*

Interior of the Shrine of the Book housing the Dead Sea Scrolls, at the Israel Museum, Jerusalem, designed by American architects Armand Bartos and Frederick Kiesler. *Photo: Hanan Isachar.*

Isaiah scroll, 1st c. B.C.E.–1st c. C.E., one of the Dead Sea scrolls found in Cave 1 at Qumran. The Shrine of the Book at the Israel Museum, Jerusalem. *Photo © The Israel Museum, Jerusalem, by David Harris.*

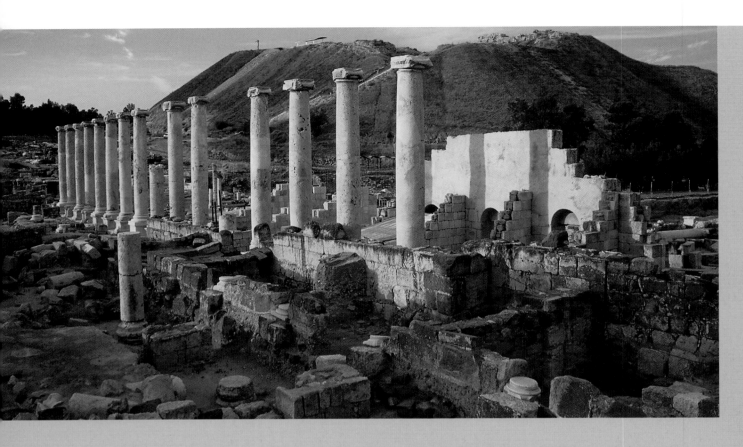

The ruins of Kazerin, a talmudic village in the Golan Heights. *Photo: Hanan Isachar.*

Remains of the Ḅar'am Synagogue in the Golan Heights, 3rd century C.E. *Photo: Dinu Mendrea.*

(opposite page) TOP: Street lined by Roman columns in the Amphitheater of Bet She'an, destroyed in 749 C.E. and restored by archaeologists. *Photo: Dinu Mendrea.*

(this page): Remains of the ancient Nabatean city of Shivta, which flourished mainly in the 4th to 6th centuries C.E. Shivta was declared a World Heritage Site by UNESCO in June 2005. *Photo: Hanan Isachar.*

Central medallion of the synagogue pavement (5th–6th century C.E.). The birds are depicted in the new, more orthodox abstract approach of Jewish art in the Byzantine period, breaking away from the naturalistic forms of the earlier Hellenistic period. *Photo: Z. Radovan, Jerusalem.*

kelstein, Middle Ages, index, s.v. *Maharil*; L. Rosenthal, in: MGWJ, 71 (1927), 364–7; J.J. (L.) Greenwald (Grunwald), *Maharil u-Zemanno* (1944); M.S. Geshuri, in: *Sinai*, 13 (1943/44), 317–49; Hacohen, *ibid.*, 57 (1965), 133–7.

[Ephraim Kupfer]

MO'EẒET HA-PO'ALOT, the General Council of Women Workers of Israel, founded in 1922 as a part of the *Histadrut (the General Federation of Labor). Its roots go back to the pioneering movement of the Second *Aliyah, when girls, as well as young men, went to build Ereẓ Israel "by the sweat of their brow." Masculine prejudices continued to exist even in an idealistic society. For women to work, especially in the open field, was considered not only unfair competition but a fall from grace. The handful of *ḥalutzot* (pioneer women) banded together, proclaiming the slogan: "Women demand the right to be partners in the revival of our People and to fulfill themselves … as women and as human beings." In 1968 the membership of Mo'eẓet ha-Po'alot totaled 486,000, composed of three categories: wage-earners – 177,000; women members of cooperative villages (kibbutzim or moshavim) – 33,000; and wives of Histadrut members, known as Immahot Ovedot (working mothers) – 276,000.

Since women are now accepted as full-fledged members of the trade unions, Mo'eẓot ha-Po'alot is preoccupied mainly with social services and the special problems of working women, such as retirement age, maternity benefits, vocational training, and career advancement. Branches of Immahot Ovedot exist in every town and village, providing social services and education for housewives. Assisted by *Pioneer Women organizations in 12 countries, it maintains some 500 social and educational institutions, such as day-nurseries, children's residential homes, kindergartens, youth clubs, and summer camps, catering in 1968 to some 20,000 children. In 2005 Mo'eẓet ha-Po'alot operated 75 day care centers, kindergartens, nurseries, and boarding schools. Special attention is given to children of immigrants and culturally deprived families, who are generally referred to these institutions by social workers. It also supports four residential agricultural high schools (two in cooperation with WIZO, which in 2005 included 1,250 pupils), four workshops for immigrants, several community centers (the largest of which is Bet Elisheva in Jerusalem), girls' vocational high schools (including a school for baby nurses), women's hostels, and special training courses, that in 1968 trained 7,500 women and girls and in 2005 2,850. In scores of women's clubs, immigrants are taught Hebrew, home economics, and social responsibility. In 2005 Mo'eẓet ha-Po'alot offered professional training to 2,400 immigrant women. It operated 35 social and cultural centers for Arab women and 36 community centers. In developing towns, Mo'eẓet ha-Po'alot ran the Education for Family Living project, counseling teenage girls in 50 centers and mothers of large families in 65 training groups. Residential seminars, study days, field trips, and lectures are organized. An advisory bureau on legal and psychological problems assists widows and orphans.

The executive of Mo'eẓet ha-Po'alot is elected by general ballot every four years (simultaneously with the Histadrut elections). Mo'eẓet ha-Po'alot is affiliated with many women's international movements and, through the Histadrut, with the International Labor Office (ILO), participating particularly in committees pertaining to women workers. Among the best-known members of Mo'eẓet ha-Po'alot were Golda *Meir, Raḥel Yanait *Ben-Zvi, and Raḥel Shazar (*Katznelson).

BIBLIOGRAPHY: Pioneer Women's Organization, *Pioneer Woman* (1926–); A. Maimon (Fishman), *Ḥamishim Shenot Tenu'at ha-Po'alot 1904–1954* (1955²); R. Katznelson-Shazar, *Im Pa'amei ha-Dor*, 2 vols. (1963).

[Shoshana Hareli / Shaked Gilboa (2nd ed.)]

MOFAZ, SHAUL (1948–), 16th chief of staff of the IDF (1998–2002). Mofaz was born in Iran and immigrated to Israel in 1957. In 1966 he joined the paratroops and in the Six-Day War fought under the command of Rafael *Eitan. During the Yom Kippur War he was the commander of the paratroop commando unit, and subsequently deputy commander of the special General Staff commando unit. In this post he participated in the Entebbe operation. Afterwards he took a break to study business administration at Bar-Ilan University for two years. In the Lebanon War he commanded a brigade and after the war went to study at the Command and Staff College of the U.S. Marine Corps in the U.S. On his return he was named head of the Officers' School and, in 1986, commander of the paratroop brigade. Afterwards he received a tank division and in 1993 was promoted to brigadier general and given command of Israeli forces in Judea and Samaria. A year later, in 1994, he became GOC Southern Command and in 1996 he was made chief of the IDF planning branch. In 1997 he became deputy chief of staff and in 1998 he was chosen as chief of staff, a position he held until 2002. Under his command, the IDF withdrew from Lebanon and the second Intifada commenced. After his retirement he was chosen by Prime Minister Sharon as defense minister, a position he continued to hold after the 2003 elections. At the end of 2005 he left the Likud for Sharon's new Kadimah Party, and after the 2006 elections he became minister of transport in Ehud *Olmert's government.

[Shaked Gilboa (2nd ed.)]

MOGADOR, now known as **Essaouira**, an Atlantic seaport in western *Morocco, midway between the towns of *Safi and *Agadir. The word Mogador is a corruption of the Berber term for "self-anchorage." The city was occupied by the Phoenicians and Carthaginians in the 5th century B.C.E. From the Middle Ages to the 17th century there were sugar-cane refineries in the vicinity of Mogador whose operation was brought to a halt in the latter half of the 18th century. The town became a bustling seaport in 1764 under the Alawite Sultan Sidi Muhammad ibn Abdullah, who sought to transform it into a rival port to Agadir and have it serve as his main port for international commerce. The most important Moroccan Jewish merchant families from *Tangier, Agadir, *Marrakesh, and parts of northern Morocco were recruited by the sultan to take charge of developing trade activity and relations in Mogador *vis-à-vis* Europe.

The sultan chose 10 or 12 of them, especially from the Corcos, Afriat, Coriat, Knafo, Pinto, and Elmaleh families, for the task and granted them the status of *tujjār al-sultān* (the "king's merchants"). In sharp contrast to ordinary Jews who dwelt in the cramped Jewish *ghetto (**mellah*), the sultanate offered them the most luxurious dwellings of Mogador within the more prestigious *casbah* quarter. They not only became the leading merchants of the sultan's court – parallel to a tiny elite of Muslim *tujjār* – but were entrusted with the role of mediation and diplomacy with European consuls and entrepreneurs. Not only were they influential in Moroccan economic affairs, but their functions extended to include the leadership of the local Jewish community. From their ranks the Jews chose the *tujjār* as presidents, vice presidents, and treasurers. The extraordinary and privileged Jewish *tujjār* elite controlled all of the major imports of Mogador and other Moroccan trade centers where their influence was gradually extended. These included sugar, tea, metals, gunpowder, and tobacco. The *tujjār* also managed such vital exports as wheat, hides, cereals, and wool, items which became government monopolies at the time, resulting from the *makhzan*'s fears of the political and social consequences of European penetration. Some *tujjār* were in fact dispatched by the Palace to European trade centers as economic attachés and were given interest-free loans to undertake major trade transactions and augment the sultan's profits. Unlike the rest of the Jews, they were not required to pay the traditional poll-tax (*jizya*) commonly imposed on non-Muslim minorities throughout the Muslim world, and they received full protection – legal and political – from the *makhzan* (Moroccan government) from those in Muslim society who sought to harass or undermine them. The *tujjār* declined in influence after the 1890s with the aggressive penetration of the European powers into the Sharifian Empire of Morocco. By the early part of the 20th century, and certainly following the formation of the French protectorate (1912), they disappeared from the scene. A new elite of Jewish entrepreneurs, recruited by the French, Spaniards, Italians, and British commercial houses replaced them, as did foreign merchants who settled in Mogador and other parts of the country, controlling commerce until Moroccan independence in 1956.

Spiritually and religiously, the Mogador community was led over the years by the old established rabbis and **dayyanim* such as Abraham Coriat, Abraham b. Attar, Mas'ud Knafo, and Haim Pinto. Mogador Jewry was relatively well educated. Their musicians were renowned throughout Morocco. The town had exceptionally beautiful synagogues, with the community being dotted by numerous *battei midrash* and yeshivot. As British influence in Mogador became particularly dominant from the 18th century, English schools flourished there, including those of the London-based Anglo-Jewish Association and the Board of Deputies for British Jewry. The schools helped spread the English language and culture among the Jews. The French-based *Alliance Israélite Universelle also opened schools for boys and girls in Mogador. As British influence declined in the town after 1912, the Alliance schools and those of the Protectorate, which propagated French influences, emerged supreme and oriented local Jews toward new cultural currents. By the mid-1950s, on the eve of large-scale Jewish immigration to Israel and the West, most young men and women spoke French in addition to the Moroccan Judeo-Arabic dialect.

During the 19th century the Jewish population grew from 4,000 in the 1830s and 1840s to approximately 12,000 in 1912, only to decline to 6,150 in 1936 and to once again rise slightly to 6,500 in 1951. This is attributed to the decline of commerce and other economic activity during the French Protectorate era in Mogador (and other inland or coastal cities which in the past enjoyed prosperity) in favor of Casablanca and Agadir. The immigration trends of the 1950s and 1960s caused the Mogador community to dwindle. Once Morocco's most important commercial seaport, a phenomenon largely attributed to Jewish initiatives, Mogador became a sleepy and relatively unimportant town. In the early 1970s most of its Jewish community members resided in the Americas, Europe, and Israel. By 2005, the community had all but disappeared.

BIBLIOGRAPHY: M. Abitbol, *Témoins et acteurs: les Corcos et l'histoire du Maroc contemporain* (1977); A. Chouraqui; *Between East and West* (1968); D. Corcos, *Studies in the History of the Jews of Morocco* (1976); M.M. Laskier, *The Alliance Israélite Universelle and the Jewish Communities of Morocco: 1862–1962* (1983); J.L. Miège, *Le Maroc et l'Europe: 1830–1894*, 4 vols. (1961–63); C.R. Pennell, *Morocco since 1830: A History* (2000); D.J. Schroeter, *Merchants of Essaouria: Urban Society and Imperialism in Southwestern Morocco, 1844–1886* (1988); idem, *The Sultan's Jews: Morocco and the Sephardi World* (2002).

[Michael M. Laskier (2nd ed.)]

MOGILEV, capital of Mogilev district, Belarus; from the middle of the 14th century until 1772 Mogilev was part of Poland-Lithuania. One of the largest and most important in Belarus, the Mogilev community was founded during the 16th century by Jews who leased the collection of customs duties; the first of these was Michael *Jozefowicz (1522). During the 1580s one of the most prominent Jewish merchants of Lithuania, Ephraim b. Jeraḥmeel (Afrash Rakhmaelovich) lived in Mogilev and leased the customs duties. In 1585 the Christian population requested King Stephen Báthory to prohibit the settlement of Jews in Mogilev. Although the king agreed, the order was not carried out and Jews continued to live in the town. A synagogue existed from the beginning of the 17th century. The struggle between the townspeople and the Jews of Mogilev continued throughout the 17th and 18th centuries. In 1626 King Sigismund III Vasa granted letters patent to the town (confirmed by King Ladislaus IV in 1633) in which it was stipulated that all the Jews must move into the street where the synagogue stood, beyond the city walls. On Rosh Ha-Shanah 5406 (1645) the townspeople, led by the mayor, attacked the Jews. In 1646 the municipality decided to forbid the Jews to live in lodgings rented from the townspeople or to acquire these lodgings. This too was confirmed by King Ladislaus IV. When Mogilev was occupied by the invading Russian armies in 1654, on the request of the townspeople Czar Alexis Mikhailovich ordered the expulsion of the Jews. Their houses were to be shared equally between the municipality and the Russians. The order was not immediately carried out, but as the Polish army approached Mogilev in 1655, the Russian commander drove the Jews out of the town and ordered their massacre. Those Jews who remained became apostates. After the end of the war the community was renewed and most of the apostates returned to Judaism. In 1656 John II Casimir granted letters patent to the town, according to which the Jews were forbidden to live within the walls of the city and to build houses or maintain shops there. There was a *blood libel in Mogilev in 1692. In 1736 King Augustus III confirmed the earlier letters patent of John II Casimir, adding further anti-Jewish restrictions. Restrictive orders on settlement and occupations were later reissued, but were not applied in practice.

In spite of opposition, the community continued to develop. By 1692 there were two synagogues. In 1748 the municipality reprimanded the townspeople because they themselves had helped the Jews to settle in the center of the town and to engage in commerce. In 1766, 642 poll tax paying Jews were registered within the community of Mogilev and the surrounding villages. In the *Councils of the Lands Mogilev was subordinated to *Brest-Litovsk, and a few gatherings of the Council were held in Mogilev. The community developed to a considerable extent after Mogilev was annexed by Russia. The Jews of the annexed region were granted judicial autonomy, and the community of Mogilev was designated as the central community of the whole province, its *bet din* being given authority to hear appeals against the legal decisions of the province's communities. The Jews played a principal role in Mogilev's extensive trade with Riga, Memel, Koenigsberg, and Danzig (*Gdansk), and later with southern Russia. In 1847 there were 7,897 Jews registered in Mogilev. The Jews were greatly influenced by *Chabad Ḥasidism, but by the end of the 18th century there were several *maskilim* among the wealthy merchants. In 1783 one of them, Jacob Hirsch, addressed a memorandum to the Russian government in which he suggested that the *ḥadarim* and *talmud torah* schools in both the district of Mogilev and the town itself be converted into schools where secular studies would also be taught. During the 1860s and early 1870s Pavel (Pesaḥ) *Axelrod, who had studied at the local secondary school and later spread the ideas of the Haskalah among Jewish youth, lived in Mogilev. In 1870 the *Malbim (Meir Leib b. Jehiel Michael) was invited to become rabbi of Mogilev, but was soon compelled to leave the town after the *maskilim* denounced him to the authorities as disloyal to Russia. In 1897 there were 21,539 Jews in Mogilev (about 50% of the total population). In October 1904 pogroms were initiated by soldiers mobilized for the war against Japan. Mogilev was one of the important centers of the *Bund and of the Zionist Movement. Jews owned 219 small factories, where 667 workers were engaged, and also the 93 distilleries (except for one). There were 400 small merchants and wholesalers, and most of the Jewish artisans, 244, were tailors. Following World War I and the establishment of the Communist regime, the number of Jews decreased and by 1926 only 17,105 (34.1% of the population) remained, increasing to 19,715 (20% of the total population) in 1939. During the 1920s a violent struggle occurred between the religious circles and the Zionists on the one hand, and the *Yevsektsiya on the other, which terminated with the liquidation of Jewish communal life in the town. In 1924, 432 Jews were artisans, and many city Jews worked the 2,000 acres allocated by the government. Two seven-grade schools and one with four grades existed in Mogilev. In 1927 Jewish sections were opened in the local law courts. Mogilev was the birthplace of Mordecai b. Hillel *Hakohen, Nachman *Syrkin, and Jacob *Mazeh, the writers David Pinski and Eliezer Zwiefel, and the actor Aharon Meskin.

The Germans occupied the town on July 26, 1941. In August 80 Jews were shot, a Judenrat and a ghetto were established, and the Jews from the surroundings were concentrated there. In September another 337 were killed and the ghetto was moved to another place; 113 Jews who refused to move were murdered. On October 2–3, 2,208 children, women, and older persons were executed. On October 19, 3,600 were killed, and in November another 3,726 Jews were murdered. The 315 skilled laborers who were put into a labor camp were killed in December 1941. Most of those who were in hiding were discovered and murdered or later sent to Shiroka camp in Minsk. It was estimated that there were about 7,000 to 10,000 Jews in Mogilev in 1959. The last synagogue was closed down by the authorities in 1959 and turned into a sports gymnasium. There was a Jewish cemetery.

The Province of Mogilev

Together with the province of Vitebsk, it was the first region with a large Jewish population to be annexed by Russia, later comprising the core of the *Pale of Settlement as one of the "western" provinces in which most of Russian Jewry was concentrated. The province of Mogilev was one of the two provinces where the prohibition concerning the settlement of Jews in the villages, included in the "Jewish Constitution" of 1804, was fully applied (in 1823). In 1847, 87,739 Jews were registered in the communities of the province. By 1897 the number had risen to 203,947 (12.1% of the total population), 37.9% living in the towns, 38.9% in the townlets, and 23.06% in the villages. The large communities of the province included (in addition to Mogilev): *Gomel (20,385 Jews), *Orsha (7,383 Jews), *Shklov (5,422 Jews), *Mstislavl (5,076 Jews), and *Rogachev (5,047 Jews). In 1897, 38.95% of the province's Jews earned their livelihood from commerce and 36.90% in crafts; 9,517 Jews (4.7% of the total Jewish population) depended on agriculture. There were about 70 small Jewish agricultural settlements in the province. Under the Soviet regime, most of the territory of the province was incorporated into the oblasts of Mogilev, Vitebsk, and Gomel. In 1926 there were 48,900 Jews in the oblast of Mogilev.

BIBLIOGRAPHY: Belkind, in: *Keneset Yisrael*, 1 (1886), 699–704; Dubnow, in: *Pardes*, 3 (1896), 94–100; Darin-Drabkin, in: *Haaretz* (Dec. 6, 1963); Mstislavskiy, in: *Voskhod* (Sept. 1–10, Oct. 1–16, Dec. 1–8, 1886); P.B. Axelrod, *Perezhitoye i peredumanoye* (1923), 33–67.

[Yehuda Slutsky]

MOGILEV-PODOLSKI, city in Vinnitsa district, Ukraine; in Poland until 1795; under czarist rule it was a district town of Podolia. Mogilev-Podolski was an important station on the commercial route between Moldavia and Ukraine. Jews are first mentioned in the town in 1713. In 1765 there were 957 Jews in Mogilev and the vicinity. The number had grown to 5,411 in 1847, and by 1897 there were 12,344 (55.3% of the total population) Jews in the town itself. In 1808 H.Z. Stein and his father, David, transferred their Hebrew press from Slopkovicz to Mogilev and operated there until 1819, producing 24 books. Jews traded in farm products and lumber, exporting them through the Dniester river to the Odessa port. In October 1905 and in December 1919 the community suffered in the wave of pogroms. With the establishment of the Soviet regime, the Jewish communal organization and its institutions were liquidated. In 1926 the Jewish population had fallen to 9,622 (41.8% of the total) and to 8,703 (40% of the total population) by 1939.There were two Yiddish primary schools, and Jewish sections in the local law courts. Two Jewish kolkhozes operated near the city. The Germans occupied Mogilev-Podolski on July 19, 1941. They murdered about 1,000 Jews until the city was included in Romanian Transnistria, The Romanians created a ghetto, a Judenrat, and a Jewish police. In December the ghetto numbered 3,700 locals and 15,000 expelled from Bessarabia and Bucovina. By June 1942 some 1,200 had died of typhoid; to control the epidemic, the Romanians expelled thousands to other towns, but most perished. In 1946 there were 3,000 Jews in the town. According to the 1959 census, there were about 4,700 Jews in Mogilev (22.5% of the population). The last synagogue was closed down by the authorities in the mid-1960s.

BIBLIOGRAPHY: Berman, in: *Reshumot*, 1 (1925), 411–3; Ya'ari, in: KS, 23 (1946/47), 309–27; *Die Judenpogrome in Russland*, 2 (1909), 443–6; M. Carp, *Cartea neagră*, 3 vols. (1946–48), index; PK Romanyah (1969), 461–73.

[Yehuda Slutsky / Shmuel Spector (2nd ed.)]

MOGULESKO, SIGMUND (**Zelig**; 1858–1914), Yiddish actor. As a boy he sang in a synagogue choir in Bessarabia. Discovered by Abraham Goldfaden, he became a successful comedian. In 1880 he led a company in Odessa and in 1881 published a collection of verse, *Kupleten Komishe un Humoristishe*. Arriving in New York in 1886, he sang in Offenbach's *Bluebeard*, acted in Thomashefsky's productions, and was in Jacob P. Adler's presentation of *Siberia* (1892). He wrote the music for M.H. Hurwitz' *The Sacrifice* and for Jacob Gordin's only operetta, *The Fair Miriam*.

MOHÁCSI, JENÖ (1886–1944), Hungarian author and translator. Born in Mohács, Mohácsi studied law and began his writing career as a literary journalist. A man of great versatility who wrote poetry and Hungarian and German prose, he was outstanding as a translator and was instrumental in gaining a world public for Hungarian literature. His best work was a literary biography of Imre Madách (1823–64), author of the dramatic poem *Az ember tragédiája* ("The Tragedy of Man"), of which Mohácsi also made a complete German translation (1904[4]). He translated such classics of Hungarian drama as *Bánk Bán*, a historical play by József Katona (1791–1830), and *Csongor és Tünde*, a fairy tale by Mihály Vörösmarty (1800–1855). His original works include *Hegedű és koldusbot* ("A Violin and a Beggar's Staff," 1942); *Madách* (1935), a playlet; and *Gemma, Dante Hitvese* ("Gemma, Dante's Wife," 1944). Mohácsi was secretary of the Judah Halevi Society for the dissemination of Hebrew literature and wrote a book about the poet (1941). Together with many other Jewish journalists he was arrested by the Nazis in 1944 and scheduled for deportation. His exemption certificate, signed by the regent of Hungary, Admiral Horthy, never reached him, and he died during transport.

BIBLIOGRAPHY: *Magyar Irodalmi Lexikon*, 2 (1965), 259.

[Baruch Yaron]

MOHILEWER, SAMUEL (1824–1898), rabbi, early member of Ḥovevei Zion (*Ḥibbat Zion) in Russia, and a founder of religious Zionism. Born in Glebokie (now Glubokoye), Vilna district, the son of a rabbinical family, Mohilewer was ordained a rabbi by the Volozhin yeshivah (1842) and took up the post of rabbi in his native city from 1848, in Szaki from 1854, in Suwalki from 1860, and in Radom from 1868. In each place he was active in community affairs, especially during the Polish rebellion (1863), toward which he asked the Jews to maintain a neutral attitude. In his articles, which were published in *Ha-Levanon*, he stressed the need for cooperation with the *maskilim* for the welfare of the people and demanded that the rabbis "combine the Torah and wisdom as the time is appropriate." In 1873 he participated in the St. Petersburg gathering of rabbis, and the leading moderate *maskilim* and tried to bring the two sides closer together. He was attracted to the idea of settling Ereẓ Israel even before the 1881 pogroms, but immediately after they took place he went to Brody and Lvov in order to encourage the masses of refugees who fled Russia and to influence the philanthropists and workers who came to their aid to divert the stream of migration to Ereẓ Israel. Afterward, together with two other rabbis, he appealed to the Russian rabbis to found an organization for *aliyah* to Ereẓ Israel and to settle there. Even after many rabbis withdrew their support of Ḥibbat Zion because the movement was headed by *maskilim* and "students," Mohilewer remained faithful to the concept and supported the efforts of L. *Pinsker and M.L. *Lilienblum to organize the various Ḥovevei Zion into one organization.

Mohilewer was among those who influenced Edmond de *Rothschild to extend aid to the first settlements in Ereẓ Israel and induced him to establish a settlement for Jewish farmers coming from Russia (*Ekron). He then influenced Jews in Bialystok and its surroundings to settle in *Petaḥ Tikvah. In 1883 he was chosen as rabbi of Bialystok under an agreement with the members of the community that he be allowed to devote himself to his public activities several months a year. Mohilewer was the honorary president of the *Kattowitz Conference of Ḥovevei Zion (1884). His speech at the closing session of the conference on the "Dry Bones" (Ezek. 37) served as a foundation for the sermons of the preachers of Ḥibbat Zion and of Zionism for the following years. In 1888 he joined I.E. *Spektor, M. *Eliasberg, and others who allowed the farmers to work the fields during the *shemittah* year in the Jewish settlements in Ereẓ Israel. He chaired the Ḥovevei Zion conferences in Druskininkai (1887) and in Vilna (1889) and struggled for the influence of the Orthodox circles in the movement. Through his influence a board of rabbis was chosen to ensure that the settlement work in Ereẓ Israel was carried out in a traditional Jewish spirit.

In 1890 Mohilewer was among the first speakers at the Odessa founding assembly of The Society in Support of Jewish Farmers and Artisans in Syria and Palestine (the official name of the Odessa Committee of Ḥovevei Zion). After the meeting he headed a Ḥovevei Zion group on a tour of Ereẓ Israel and, upon his return, published his open letter titled "The Purpose of My Trip to the Holy Land," in which he called upon Ḥovevei Zion "to work physically and financially for the sake of Ereẓ Israel." At a gathering of Ḥovevei Zion in Druskininkai (1893), it was decided, at Mohilewer's initiative, to establish a Spiritual Center (Merkaz Ruḥani – *Mizrachi) for the movement to direct public relations activities and explain ideas connected with the settlement of Ereẓ Israel. It was also decided to plant a citron orchard on land adjoining Ḥaderah and to name it Gan Shemu'el, in honor of Mohilewer's 70th birthday. Mohilewer and his close associates continued in their propaganda work, especially among the Orthodox Jews, and the Mizrachi became the foundation for the development of the religious Zionist movement, which four years after Mohilewer's death became a faction in the Zionist Organization (assuming officially the name Mizrachi).

Mohilewer joined the World Zionist Organization when it was founded by *Herzl, but because of his physical weakness he was not able to participate in the First Congress in 1897. His letter was read to the delegates, however, and created a great impression upon them. He was chosen as one of the four leaders who were charged with directing the work of the Zionist Movement in Russia and as the head of its "spiritual center" which disseminated directives to the members in their work. In his last letter before his death, Mohilewer called upon the Jews of Russia to support the *Jewish Colonial Trust. The basic goals in his public relations work were the attainment of a deep attachment to the commandment to settle Ereẓ Israel, "which is the foundation of the existence of our people"; and tolerance toward the *maskilim* as a prerequisite to the unity of the Jewish people, which was necessary for the rebuilding of the Jewish homeland.

Mohilewer wrote many short works, including responsa, talmudic and rabbinical novellae, homilies, and scholarly works. Most of these writings were lost in the Bialystok pogrom (1906). Some of those that survived were published under the name *Ḥikrei Halakhah u-She'elot u-Teshuvot* (1944).

[Yehuda Slutsky]

His grandson, JOSEF MOHILEWER (1872–1943), was a Zionist leader and educator in Russia and Ereẓ Israel. Born in Radom, Poland, he received a traditional Jewish education from his grandfather. He was active in various Zionist groups, and from 1902 was a government-appointed rabbi in Bialystok. Mohilewer was active in the fields of Jewish education and community affairs in Odessa. In 1920 he moved to Palestine, where he became deputy headmaster of the Jerusalem Teachers' Seminary and, from 1923, headmaster of the Hebrew High School in Jerusalem. He published articles in the Russian, German, and Hebrew press.

[Abraham Aharoni]

BIBLIOGRAPHY: N. Sokolow, *Hibbath Zion* (Eng., 1935), index; idem, *History of Zionism*, 2 (1919), index; M. Ben-Zvi (comp.), *Rabbi Samuel Mohilewer* (Eng., 1945); I. Nissenbaum, *Ha-Rav Shemu'el Mohilewer* (1930): idem, *Ha-Dat ve-ha-Teḥiyyah ha-Le'ummit* (1920), 92–118; A. Druyanow, *Ketavim le-Toledot Ḥibbat Ẓiyyon ve-Yishuv Ereẓ-Yisrael* (1932), index; Y.L. Fishman, *Sefer Shemu'el* (1923); S. Federbush, *Ḥazon Torah ve-Ẓiyyon* (1960), 99–117; I. Trivaks and E. Steinman, *Sefer Me'ah Shanah* (1938), 365–86; Tidhar, 1 (1947), 291–2; A. Hertzberg, *Zionist Idea* (1960), 398–404; L. Jung (ed.), *Men of the Spirit* (1964), 415–35.

MOHOLY-NAGY, LÁSZLÓ (1895–1946), painter, sculptor, graphic designer, photographer, filmmaker, educator. Born in Bàcs-Borsod, Hungary, Moholy-Nagy studied law at the University of Budapest, a field in which he received his degree after his military service in World War I. Afterwards, he became active in Budapest artistic circles, starting an artists' group and founding a literary magazine. He fled the city's political unrest in 1919 for Vienna. After traveling to Berlin the following year, Moholy-Nagy made the acquaintance of such Dada practitioners as Kurt Schwitters, Hannah Hoech, and Raoul Hausmann. As early as 1919, he was influenced by the ideas of the Russian artists Kasimir Malevich and El *Lissitsky and brought their work to the attention of the European, and especially German, art worlds. While in Berlin in 1921, both Moholy-Nagy and Man *Ray produced Dada-influenced Rayographs and photograms by placing objects, including gears and machine components, on light sensitive paper, thereby creating complex compositions in which the objects' silhouettes created bright spots on a dark surface. Moholy-Nagy elicited a variety of different gradations of light-suffused abstract shapes by arraying transparent or translucent objects, like glass, veils, and nets, on the photographic paper. Moholy-Nagy believed, as did many other artists of the opening decades of the 20th century, that an art of universal geometric shapes and forms possessed the capability to order and revolutionize society.

In the 1920s, Moholy-Nagy wrote for several influential art periodicals and edited with Ludwig Kassák a book of poetry and essays on art. The artist met El Lissitsky in 1921 and emerged as an important figure in the promulgation of Constructivism, a non-objective art movement based on geometrical forms associated with the work of Lissitsky, Naum Gabo, Antoine Pevsner, and Aleksandr Rodchenko, among others. Moholy-Nagy had his first show in 1922 at Der Sturm gallery, Berlin, and took part in the Congress of Constructivists and Dadaists. In 1923, he joined the famous Bauhaus school and for five years conducted the preliminary course together with Joseph Albers. During this period, Moholy-Nagy involved himself in book and stage design. He later became Walter Gropius' assistant. While teaching at the Bauhaus, Moholy-Nagy made the acquaintance of a number of seminal figures in the German art community, including Herbert Bayer, Marcel Breuer, Lyonel Feininger, Wassily Kandinsky, and Paul Klee. In 1924–25, Gropius and Moholy-Nagy edited and designed a 14-volume set of books. The eighth volume, Moholy-Nagy's *Malerei, Fotographie, Film* (*Painting, Photography, and Film*) of 1925 posited that the camera functioned as an instrument whose powers enhanced that of the human eye. The book included photographs and photograms by Moholy-Nagy and others, scientific imagery, and novel photographic techniques, including multiple exposures and photomontages. In 1928, Moholy-Nagy resigned from his position at the Bauhaus and settled in Berlin, where he remained active in numerous artistic fields, notably film, theater, and photography. In 1929, he published *Von Material zu Architektur* (translated as *The New Vision: From Material to Architecture*), which further codified his conception of the idea and practice of art-making within the context of Constructivist principles. In 1934 he went to Amsterdam, but with the rise of the Nazi threat he traveled the following year to England. Between 1935 and 1937, Moholy-Nagy worked in London as a designer and filmmaker. He finally settled in Chicago in 1937, where he founded the New Bauhaus. However, the Chicago school shut its doors within one year because of financial problems and amidst objections to Moholy-Nagy's utopian and collectivist ideals. In 1939, Moholy-Nagy and other former faculty re-organized the institution as the Chicago School of Design, renamed the Institute of Design in 1944. The artist's work continued to blossom in technique with his interest in the properties of Plexiglass, a durable resin available starting in 1937, which he molded, painted, and incised. In 1941, Moholy-Nagy became a member of the American Abstract Artists group. He attained American citizenship in 1944. Despite his international reputation in Europe, his first solo show was organized in the United States by the Modern Art Society of Cincinnati only in 1946, a year after his death from leukemia.

Moholy-Nagy's work is owned by private collectors and by numerous museums, including the Bauhaus-Archiv Museum of Design, Berlin; the Guggenheim Museum; the J. Paul Getty Museum; the Kunstmuseum, Basel; the Museum of Modern Art; the National Gallery of Art, Washington, D.C.; and the Tate Gallery.

BIBLIOGRAPHY: S. Barron, *Exiles & Emigrés: The Flight of European Artists from Hitler* (1997); V.D. Coke, *Photography: A Facet of Modernism: Photographs from the San Francisco Museum of Modern Art* (1986); D. Mrázková, *Masters of Photography: A Thematic History*, tr. Š. Pellar (1987); K. Passuth, *Moholy-Nagy* (1985).

[Nancy Buchwald (2nd ed.)]

MOHR, ABRAHAM MENAHEM MENDEL (1815–1868), Hebrew scholar. Born in Lemberg, he was a *maskil* who wrote in Hebrew and Yiddish. His fecund literary work commenced in 1834 when he published *Magen ha-Ḥokhmah*, in which he defended science and philosophy. Together with N.I. Fischmann, Jacob Bodek, and Jacob Mentsch, he issued the two volume *Ha-Ro'eh u-Mevakker Sifrei Meḥaberei Zemannenu* (1837, 1839), in which famous scholars were harshly criticized. The book aroused the anger of his contemporaries. His publication *Yerushalayim*, which appeared for three issues (1844–45), was more moderate. In 1848–49 he published a Yiddish newspaper, *Tsaytung*, which at the time was the only Yiddish newspaper in the world. Mohr wrote about the Rothschilds (*Tiferet Yisrael*, 1843), Columbus (1846), and Napoleon III (*Ḥut ha-Meshullash*, 1853). His works also included *Mevasseret Ẓiyyon*, (1847), a geography of Palestine and its Jewish inhabitants, and his Purim parodies *Kol Bo le-Purim* (1855) and *Shulḥan Arukh Even ha-Shetiyyah* (1861). He published editions of *Mikveh Yisrael* by Manasseh Ben Israel (1847) and *La-Yesharim Tehillah* by M.Ḥ. Luzzatto (1859).

BIBLIOGRAPHY: Zeitlin, Bibliotheca, 242–4; Kressel, Leksikon, 2 (1967), 320–2.

[Getzel Kressel]

MOHR (Mohar), MEIR (1888–1967), Hebrew writer. Born in Rozwadow, Galicia, Mohr left for the U.S. in 1908, where be worked as a tailor and a part-time teacher. After returning to Galicia he taught in Jaslo. Recruited for the Austrian army during World War I, in which he served until 1918, Mohr afterward taught in Tarnow and in various German cities, including Berlin (from 1923). From 1939, when he left Berlin for Palestine, he taught Hebrew to children and to adults.

Mohr's publication, under the pen name R. Simla'i, of light, humorous verse in G. Rosenzweig's *Ha-Devorah* (1912) was followed by poems, articles, and essays in the majority of Hebrew newspapers and literary periodicals of this period. In his later years, he regularly published articles and poems in *Ha-Po'el ha-Ẓa'ir*. His books are *Ayin be-Ayin* (1950), a selection of his poetry, and *Ḥeret Enosh* (1959), a selection of his essays on poetry and prose. Mohr translated exclusively into Hebrew.

His son, JEHIEL MAR (MOHAR; 1921–1969), also a Hebrew poet, was born in Tarnow, and went to Ereẓ Israel in 1937. He was a founding member of kibbutz Dovrat. Mar published five volumes of poetry, of which the first, *Mi-Lev va-Nof*, appeared in 1951. His verse aimed at a simple conversational idiom often achieved by irony. One of Israel's most skillful writers of lyrics for popular songs, he published these lyrics under the name Mohar.

BIBLIOGRAPHY: Y. Keshet, *Maskiyyot* (1954), 221–8; *Kol Kitvei G. Schoffmann*, 4 (1960), 250–1; 5 (1960), 166; A. Cohen, *Soferim Ivriyyim Benei Zemannenu* (1964), 247–9.

[Getzel Kressel]

MOINESTI (Rom. **Moineşti**), town in Moldavia, E. central Romania. Tombstones from 1740 and 1748 prove the existence of a Jewish settlement predating the foundation of the town (1781) and dating back to the discovery of oil in the vicinity. There were 42 Jewish taxpayers in 1820, 500 families in 1885, and 2,398 individuals in 1899 (50.6% of the total population). The community was organized in 1885 and had five prayer houses, a ritual bath, and a primary school for boys (founded in 1893) as well as one for girls (1900). The locality played a prominent role in the history of the colonization of Ereẓ Israel. Jews from Moinesti were the founders of Rosh *Pinnah. In 1881 a group of 50 families was organized which sent David *Schub as a delegate to Ereẓ Israel. He purchased the plots of land where 22 families settled in the summer of 1882, together with several families from other Moldavian cities. The Moinesti Jews addressed a call to all the Romanian Jews; the pre-Zionist movement Yishuv Ereẓ Israel was subsequently established. Between the two world wars the number of the Jews decreased to 1,761 (26.6% of the total). After emancipation (1919), there were Jewish members on the municipal council and in 1930 Moinesti even elected a Jew as deputy mayor. Tristan *Tzara (Sami Rosenstein), a founder of the Dadaist movement, was born in Moinesti.

In World War II the Jews of Moinesti were expelled to Botoşani. About 80 families returned after the war. The Jewish population numbered 480 in 1947, 400 in 1950, and about 15 families in 1969.

BIBLIOGRAPHY: PK Romanyah, 177–9; E. Schwarzfeld, *Impopularea, reîmpopularea si întemeierea tîrgurilor si tîrguşoarelor în Moldova* (1914), 40, 44, 85; I. Klausner, *Ḥibbat Ẓiyyon be-Rumanyah* (1958).

[Theodor Lavi]

MOÏSE, ABRAHAM (c. 1736–1809), progenitor of the Moïse family of South Carolina. Born in Strasbourg in Alsace, France, Moïse immigrated to the West Indies and was living at Cape François, Santo Domingo, when a black slave insurrection broke out in 1791. He and his family were forced to flee and made their way to Charleston, South Carolina, reputedly leaving their wealth behind. Aged 56, he started anew as a small shopkeeper and later became a vendue master (auctioneer). His descendants achieved distinction in various fields.

BIBLIOGRAPHY: H. Moïse, *The Moïse Family of South Carolina*, (1961).

[Thomas J. Tobias]

MOÏSE, PENINA (1797–1880), U.S. poet, hymnist, and teacher; daughter of Abraham *Moïse. Penina Moïse left school at the age of 12 – when her father died – to help support her large family, which had been left without means, by doing needlework. On her own, she continued to study and read avidly, showing a literary talent at an early age and becoming a prolific writer of verse. She frequently contributed poems to the Charleston *Courier* which were on a variety of subjects, many on current events. She also wrote for the leading papers and periodicals of her day. In 1833 she published a small volume of her poems, *Fancy's Sketch Book*. She was admired by Charleston's antebellum writers. A devout Jew, she was superintendent of Beth Elohim Congregation's Sunday school and was the author of the first American Jewish hymnal. When the congregation installed the first American synagogue organ in 1841, she composed hymns for the organ service. A book of her hymns was published by Beth Elohim; later editions were used by other Reform temples. Many are still found in the *Union Hymnal* of the Union of American Hebrew Congregations. They are notable for a spirit of submission to the will of God. In her sixties Penina Moïse gradually became blind, but, with rare courage, she continued to write, using her niece as an amanuensis. She was widely known as Charleston's "blind poetess." Reduced to poverty after the Civil War, she, her sister, and niece eked out a modest living with a small private girls' school, in which she gave oral instruction by drawing on her remarkable memory. Her warmth and sympathy made her a favorite confidante of youth. Her hymns and poetry were published, as *Secular and Religious Works* (1911). She never married.

BIBLIOGRAPHY: B.A. Elzas, *Jews of South Carolina* (1905), 181–4; S.A. Dinkins, in: *American Jews' Annual, 5646* (1885/86), ch. 5.

[Thomas J. Tobias]

MOÏSE, THEODORE SYDNEY (1808–1883), U.S. painter; grandson of Abraham *Moïse. Born in Charleston, South Carolina, he received instruction in painting from his aunt, Penina *Moïse, a part-time artist. Nothing is known about his further education. In 1835, Moïse opened a studio in Charleston, advertising his services as a portrait painter, animal painter, picture restorer, and ornamental draftsman. Moïse moved to New Orleans in 1842–43, where he gained a reputation as an accomplished portrait painter and maintained a studio from 1850 until his death. Members of his studio included Benjamin Franklin Reinhart, Paul Poincy, and the portrait and genre painter Trevor Thomas Fowler. During and after 1842, Moïse traveled with Fowler in the pre-Civil War and then Reconstruction South. Fowler sometimes collaborated with Moïse in the execution of portraits of members of wealthy Southerners. So closely did Moïse and Fowler work that art historians find it impossible in some instances to differentiate Moïse's work from that of Fowler's. Moïse's subjects often included wealthy landowners, their families, servants, horses, and dogs. The latter images might have been commissioned on the strength of Moïse's reputation as a portrait painter and as a master of making expressive likenesses of horses. Moïse's portraits demonstrate a Neoclassical style which shares characteristics of the work of the French 18th century artists Jean-Auguste-Dominique Ingres and Jacques-Louis David, as well as the American 19th century painter Rembrandt Peale. John Freeland commissioned the artist to paint a portrait of the senator and orator Henry Clay the year of Moïse's arrival in New Orleans. Moïse's painting of General Jackson on horseback (1815, City Hall, New Orleans) took a $1,000 prize for its accurate likeness of the general. When the portrait was cleaned in 1844, the signature "Amans and Moïse" was revealed; historians speculate that Moïse painted the horse, while Amans depicted General Jackson. Other portraits by Moïse include Mordecai Cohen and Governor Herbert (State Library, New Orleans). The Court House of New Orleans contains many portraits of judges by Moïse, as well as *Life on the Metairie*, which he completed in collaboration with Victor Pierson. Depicting portraits of 44 distinguished citizens of New Orleans at the last meeting of the old Metairie Race Track, this painting won Grand State-Fair First Prize in 1868 for best historical painting. The New Orleans Court House also houses a massive painting by Moïse which depicts portraits of 64 members of the Volunteer Fire Brigade marching in the city's Canal Street. Moïse attained the rank of major in the Confederate Army. He participated in the defense of the lower Mississippi during the Civil War by helping to deploy floating fire rafts to repel the Federal fleet. Works by Moïse are owned by private collectors, as well as by the Filson Historical Society in Louisville, Kentucky, the Louisiana State Museum, the Metropolitan Museum of Art, the Ogden Museum of Southern Art, and the S.J. Schwartz Historical Collection in Maison Blanche, Louisiana, among other museums and public buildings.

BIBLIOGRAPHY: H. Moïse, *The Moise Family of South Carolina and Their Descendants* (1961); C. Roth, (ed.), *Jewish Art: An Illustrated History* (rev. ed. by Bezalel Narkiss, 1971); P.B. Schmit (ed.), *Encyclopaedia of New Orleans Artists, 1718–1918* (1987).

[Nancy Buchwald (2nd ed.)]

MOISEIWITSCH, BENNO (1890–1963), pianist. Born in Odessa, Moiseiwitsch won the Anton Rubinstein Prize at the Odessa Academy at the age of nine, and later studied with Theodor Leschetizky in Vienna. He was regarded by many as the finest Chopin interpreter of his time. His London debut took place in 1909. He settled in England during World War I and thereafter played frequently in Britain and on concert tours abroad. His repertoire was extremely wide, but in his later years he tended to confine his programs to the standard favorites. His daughter, TANYA MOISEIWITSCH (1914–2003), became a theatrical designer. She designed 50 productions in Dublin, and from 1940 worked in London, Stratford, and Edinburgh. She also designed productions at Stratford, Ontario, at the New York Metropolitan Opera, the Habimah, Tel Aviv, etc.

BIBLIOGRAPHY: M. Moiseiwitsch, *Moiseiwitsch* (Eng., 1965); R. Newqvist, *Showcase* (1966), 277–86 (on Tanya).

[Dora Leah Sowden]

MOISSAN, HENRI (1852–1907), French inorganic chemist and Nobel Prize winner. Moissan was born in Paris of a non-Jewish father and a Jewish mother. He joined the Ecole Supérieure de Pharmacie, where in 1886 he became professor of toxicology and in 1899 professor of inorganic chemistry. From 1900 he was professor of inorganic chemistry at the Sorbonne. Moissan's main work was on metal oxides and inorganic and organic fluorine compounds. He developed a laboratory electric furnace which he used to make artificial (black) diamonds. He was awarded the Nobel Prize for chemistry in 1906 for his investigation and isolation of the element fluorine, and for the adoption in the service of science of the electric furnace called after him.

Moissan published his work in scientific journals and in his books, *Le Four Electrique* (1897) and *Le Fluor et ses composés* (1900); he also wrote an inorganic chemistry textbook in five volumes, *Traité de chimie minérale* (1904–06).

BIBLIOGRAPHY: W.R., in: *Proceedings of the Royal Society*, A80 suppl. (1908), xxx–xxxvii; Ramsey, in: *Journal of the Chemical Society*, 101 (1912), 477–88; Lebeau, in: *Bulletin de la Société Chimique de France* (1935), 135–8; T.N. Levitan, *Laureates: Jewish Winners of the Nobel Prize* (1960), 30–33.

[Samuel Aaron Miller]

MOISSIS, ASHER (1899–1975), Greek author, translator, and Jewish communal leader. Born in Trikkala, Moissis became a lawyer but soon began to take an active part in Jewish communal and Zionist affairs. In 1917 he founded the Zionist monthly *Israel* which he edited for the two years of its existence. In the early 1930s he began to publish books on Jewish subjects, particularly concerned with Greco-Jewish relations through the ages. Before World War II he wrote *Dheka pende imere ana tin Evraikyin Palestinin* ("Fifteen Days Across Jewish Palestine," 1933), *Isaghoyi is to Oikoyeniakon Dhikyeon ton en Elldi Israiliton* ("Introductory Study of the Civil Laws of the Jewish Family in Greece," 1934), and a translation of the *Autoemancipation* of J.L. *Pinsker (1933). He was president of the Jewish National Fund (1930–38), of the Salonika Jewish community (1934–36), and of the Greek Zionist Federation (1936–38). Following the liberation of Greece, Moissis resumed his communal and literary activities. He was president of the Central Council of Jewish Communities in Greece (1944–49) and, from 1948, honorary consul of Israel in Athens. He translated parts of the diaries of Theodor Herzl (1952) and the *History of Modern Hebrew Literature* by Joseph Klausner (1968). His postwar books include *I Filia Ellinon kye Evreon ana tous Eonas* ("The Friendship of Jews and Greeks Through the Centuries," 1953), *Ellenoioudhaikye Melete* ("Helleno-Judaic Studies," 1958), and *Pion "Ellinismon" Katepolemisan i Makkavei* ("The Hellenism that the Maccabees Fought," 1962). After the Six-Day War of 1967, he wrote *Istoria kye Thrili yiro apo to Tikhos ton Dhakrion* ("History and Legend Concerning the Wailing Wall," 1968), which was translated into Italian and English, the latter by Rae Dalven. Moissis also translated into Greek verse the *Haggadah* (1970). Moissis was probably the most committed and prolific Jewish writer in modern Greece.

[Rachel Dalven]

°**MOJECKI, PRZECLAW** (second half of 16th and early 17th century), Polish Catholic priest and antisemitic author. His principle work, *O zydowskich okrucieństwach, mordach y zabobonach* ("The Cruelty, Murders, and Superstitions of the Jews"), was the first outright attack on the Jews and Judaism in Polish political writings. The pamphlet, which first appeared in Cracow in 1589 and was later printed in 1598 (Cracow) and in 1636 (Lvov), was dedicated to Prince Janusz Ostrogski – a newly converted Catholic – in the hope of convincing him to support the expulsion of the Jews from Poland. The author gives 25 stories of *blood libels from various countries and nine from Poland. Mojecki complains that Jewish trade finally results in the depletion of the country's resources in waste and corruption because of the encouragement of luxury, and that the Jews are not under the jurisdiction of the authorities of the towns in which they live. Moreover, Mojecki is of the opinion that the Jews are traitors to Poland and spy for the Turks, the Tatars, and the rulers of Moscow. The author attempts to convince his readers that God rewards those who persecute and expel the Jews and commends the measures adopted by the kingdoms of France, Spain, and Germany toward the Jews. This work, which was influenced by German and Italian antisemitic literature, was influential in the propagation of antisemitic ideas in Polish literature of the 17th century.

BIBLIOGRAPHY: K. Bartoszewicz, *Antysemityzm w literaturze polskiej XV–XVII w.* (1914), 40–50; S. Dubnow, *Divrei Yemei Am Olam*, 6 (1958[6]), 161–2.

[Arthur Cygielman]

MOKADY, MOSHE (1902–1975), Israeli painter. Born Moshe Brandshtat in Tarnow, Galizca, Mokady was sent to study at a high school in Zurich during World War I. Among other things he studied music and painting there. In 1920 the family decided to immigrate to Ereẓ Israel in spite of their comfortable life. The family built a home in Haifa. Subsequently Mokady lived in many places in Israel and also abroad for short periods. In the 1950s he was one of the founders of the Ein Hod artists' village and later he moved there. In those years he was chosen to represent Israel in the Venice Biennale (1952) and the Sao Paulo Biennale (1955).

Mokady's artistic style was characterized by his individualistic approach and variety. The connection between his private life and his art was clear and can be identified through the style of the paintings. In the beginning his style was a mixture of Cubism and Naive art. His penchant for painting portraits began then (*Sitting Boy – Portrait of Daniel Sharshavsky*, 1925, Israel Museum, Jerusalem). When Mokady dealt with the local landscape, he would describe figures in it.

His style changed after his Paris period. His meeting with the Jewish artists who lived there like *Chagall and *Soutine directed him toward the Expressionist style and his colors became darker and melancholic. The monochromatic painting that was one of his typical styles began to appear during this period.

At the end of the 1940s Mokady reached the abstract style. His interest in the music world and his awareness of the New York Abstract lay in the background of his return to this art style. Mokady's abstract paintings show a clear influence of Israel's landscapes. The paintings were assembled from stains of color placed near the middle of the canvas. Many abstracts were done monochromatically and some were colorful and full of light.

After the death of his elder son, Raphi, in the Six-Day War, Mokady's paintings became darker and the black and white contrast returned again and again.

A significant part of Mokady's artistic corpus belongs to his stage design. He worked for most of the theaters operating in Israel, and was in great demand.

BIBLIOGRAPHY: J. Shen-Dar, *Mokady Moshe 1902–1975* (1986); Y. Fisher and I. Hadar, *Moshe Mokady* (1999).

[Ronit Steinberg (2nd ed.)]

MOLADAH (Heb. מוֹלָדָה), city in the Negev of Judah, described in Joshua 19:2 and I Chronicles 4:28 as a town of the tribe of Simeon, and in Joshua 15:26 as a town of the tribe of Judah in the Negev, near Beer-Sheba. It is among the cities listed in Nehemiah 11:26, apparently settlements which endured through the Babylonian Exile. The commonly proposed identification with the Malatha of Josephus (Ant., 18:147) and the Malaatha of Eusebius (Onom. 14:3; 88:4; 108:3) is baseless. Khirbat al-Waṭan, approximately 8 mi. (13 km.) east of Beersheba, has been suggested as a possible identification. Pottery found on the site dates from the Iron Age. The Arabic name may be a translation of the Hebrew (both Ar. *waṭen* and Heb. *moladah*; "birthplace").

BIBLIOGRAPHY: Abel, Geog, 2 (1938), 391–2; EM, s.v. (incl. bibl.); Press, Ereẓ, s.v.; Avi-Yonah, Geog, index.

[Michael Avi-Yonah]

MOLCHO, DAVID EFFENDI ISAAC PASHA (1839–1909), vice admiral of the Ottoman navy. Born in *Salonika, he was descended from an established family of Salonika rabbis. Molcho entered the College of Military Medicine and, upon graduation, joined the Turkish armed forces as a surgeon. He was promoted to lieutenant colonel in 1877 and was later appointed inspector general of the health services. He was appointed a vice admiral in 1902. He served also as the chief translator of the *Divan-i Humayun* and as the head of the communal council of the Jewish community of *Istanbul in the years 1892 and 1905. Previously, in 1883, 1885, and 1890, he had been a member in this institution.

BIBLIOGRAPHY: A. Levy, in: M. Rozen (ed.), *Yemei ha-Sahar* (1996), 259–61.

[Leah Bornstein-Makovetsky (2nd ed.)]

MOLCHO, SOLOMON (c. 1500–1532), kabbalist and pseudomessiah. Born in Lisbon of Marrano parents, he was originally called Diogo Pires. Though details on his early life are scarce, it is clear that he received a secular education and, at the age of 21, was appointed secretary to the king's council and recorder at the court of appeals. It is probable that Molcho secretly studied the Kabbalah. On meeting David *Reuveni after the latter's arrival in Portugal in 1525, he asked to be circumcised. Reuveni dissuaded him but, undeterred, Molcho circumcised himself and took a Hebrew name. While the symbolic meaning of the name is obscure, some scholarly opinion takes it as referring to Molcho's spiritual kinship with Reuveni (the name Molcho deriving from the Hebrew *melekh* = "king"). Reuveni suggested to Molcho that he flee, while he himself was forced to leave Portugal because of the suspicion that he had had a part in Molcho's conversion. The details of Molcho's flight are uncertain. Reuveni later claimed that he had sent him on a mysterious diplomatic mission to *Turkey; Molcho himself stated that a divine command had directed his departure. His destination is also somewhat obscure. There are those who claim that he spent some time in Italy, *Jerusalem, *Safed, *Damascus, and even Constantinople. All authorities agree, however, that he settled for a period in *Salonika where he studied Kabbalah in the *bet ha-midrash* of Joseph *Taitaẓak. There he probably met R. Joseph b. Ephraim *Caro, whose writings reflect his admiration for Molcho. In Salonika Molcho gathered disciples and students who prevailed upon him to publish a collection of his sermons which are filled with expectation of coming redemption, *Derashot* (Salonika, 1529). In later editions the work is entitled *Sefer ha-Mefo'ar*. In the sack of Rome in 1527 he saw the signs of the coming redemption, and returned to Italy in 1529 and began to preach about it in Ancona. His sermons attracted many people, including Christians. The accusations of an informer that he was a Marrano who had reverted to Judaism caused him to flee to Pesaro and eventually to Rome. By then Molcho had become convinced that he was indeed the Messiah. In fulfillment of the talmudic legend (Sanh. 98a) that recounted the suffering of the Messiah, Molcho, dressed as a beggar, sat for 30 days, tasting no meat or wine, among the sick and the infirm on a bridge over the Tiber by the pope's palace.

Molcho succeeded in gaining the confidence of Pope *Clement VII, who granted him protection (1530). His standing was further strengthened when his prophecies of a flood in Rome (1530) and an earthquake in Portugal (January 1531) came true. He preached widely and was successful in preventing the spread of the Inquisition to Portugal. He left Rome for Venice at the end of 1530 for an unsuccessful meeting with Reuveni. Attempting to mediate in a dispute between Jacob *Mantino, the pope's physician, and Elijah Ḥalfon, kabbalist and physician, Molcho succeeded only in arousing the enmity of Mantino. Molcho fled to Rome and a friendlier atmosphere, but Mantino, seeing danger in Molcho's activities, followed him and intrigued against him. Molcho was accused by an inquisitional court of judaizing and was condemned to be burned at the stake. He was saved by the personal intervention of the pope, and another man was burned in his place. In 1532 Molcho left for northern Italy, where he again met with Reuveni. Together they went on a mission to Emperor Charles V who was then at Regensburg. Although the nature of their mission to Charles is somewhat speculative, R. *Joseph (Joselmann) of Rosheim records in his memoirs that Molcho came in order to rouse the emperor to call upon the Jews to fight against the Turks. However, Charles brought Molcho to Mantua, where he was tried and burned at the stake in late 1532 after refusing to recant and convert to Christianity. Many Jews and Marranos in Italy, however, did not accept that Molcho had died, but believed that he had been saved once more.

The influence of Molcho was considerable both during his lifetime and after his death. R. Joseph of Orly took note of Molcho in his messianic prophecies. Already in 1531 an important messianic movement had spread under his influence and had reached Poland. Some of his belongings were saved by the Jews of Prague and displayed long after his death; his influence on Shabbateanism (see *Shabbetai Ẓevi) was not insignificant. In addition to his *Sefer ha-Mefo'ar*, Molcho left a number of letters incorporated by R. Joseph ha-Kohen in his historical writings and in *Ḥayyat Kaneh* edited by Abraham Rothenberg in 1648, and some poetry. His life and that of Reuveni were the subject of much fictional writing, such as M. Brod's *Reuveni Fuerst der Juden* (1925); E. Fleg's *Le Juif du pape* (1925), and A.A. Kabak's *Shelomoh Molkho* (1928–29).

BIBLIOGRAPHY: A.Z. Aescoly (ed.), *Ḥayyat Kaneh* (1938); idem, *Sippur David ha-Re'uveni* (1940), 27–64, 140–83; idem, *Ha-Tenu'ot ha-Meshiḥiyyot be-Yisrael* (1956), 266–78; 365–412; R.J.Z. Werblowsky, *Joseph Caro: Lawyer and Mystic* (1962), 97–99; Scholem, Shabbetai Zevi, index: R. Joseph Caro, *Maggid Yesharim* (Amsterdam, 1644); A.H. Silver, *A History of Messianic Speculation in Israel* (1927), 133–5, 147–50; D. Kaufmann, in REJ, 24 (1897), 121–7; Vogelstein-Rieger, 2 (1895), 53–58; S. Stern, *Josel of Rosheim* (1965), 133–7; J.H. Greenstone, *The Messiah Idea in Jewish History* (1906), 195–202.

[Joseph Shochetman]

MOLDOVA (formerly Moldavia), independent democratic republic belonging to the CIS, which proclaimed its independence in May 1990. In 1979 it had 80,100 Jews and in 1989–65,800 (of whom 35,700 lived in Kishinev). Emigration in 1989 was 4,304 (3,702 from Kishinev). Immigration to Israel in 1990 amounted to 12,080 (7,578 from Kishinev); the corresponding figures the following year were 17,305 and 9,487.The estimated Jewish population at the end of 1991 was 28,500.

The first Jewish organizations in Moldova included the Moldova-Israel Friendship Association (established in November 1991), the Moldova-Israel Foreign Trade Association, and the Jewish Museum. The monthly Jewish newspaper *Nash golos* began appearing in March 1990. In June of that year the paper printed an interview with Prime Minister Mircea Druk, who stated that he had never concealed his revulsion for antisemitism and stressed the need to normalize relations between Moldovans and Jews. The prime minister also came out in favor of education in Hebrew for Jews in the republic.

Moldovan Jews appeared to be concerned about their future. Not a single Jew was elected to the Supreme Soviet in

1990. A law was passed making knowledge of the Moldovian language mandatory: this created difficulties for the basically Russian-speaking Moldovan Jews. Intensive Jewish emigration was renewed in mid-1992 in the wake of fighting in Transnistria. Both the Joint Distribution Committee and the Jewish Agency began operating in Kishinev. Direct flights from Moldova to Israel started in January 1992.

At the end of 1993 there were an estimated 15,000 Jews in the Republic of Moldova, and by 2000 their number had dropped to 5,200. In an effort to revive Jewish life, a Chabad-run synagogue opened its doors to the community.

In March 1994 the old Jewish cemetery was desecrated in Kishinev. There were several instances of anti-Jewish violence.

BIBLIOGRAPHY: U.O. Schmelz and S. DellaPergola in AJYB, 1995, 478; *Supplement to the Monthly Bulletin of Statistics*, 2, 1995, Jerusalem; M. Beizer and I. Klimenko, in *Jews in Eastern Europe*, 1 (24) 1995, 25–33; *Antisemitism World Report 1995*, London: Institute of Jewish Affairs, 167.

[Michael Beizer/ Dan Rom (2nd ed.)]

MOLE, rodent. The only mole found in Israel is the mole rat (*Spalax ehrenbergi*), a small mammal belonging to the order Rodentia. It is blind, its rudimentary eyes being covered with a membrane. Inhabiting subterranean burrows which it digs, it throws up the ground in a continuous series of mounds. Sometimes it builds a nest in a small mound. Into these burrows, Isaiah prophesied (2:20) a man would cast away "his idols of silver, and his idols of gold… to the moles and to the bats," the biblical word here for "moles," *ḥafor perot*, denoting a burrower in Aramaic (*pina*, i.e., "burrower"). According to another opinion *ḥafor perot* refers to an animal which digs up fruits in the ground. In talmudic literature the mole rat is called *eishut* which, because of the damage it causes to crops, may be hunted also on the intermediate days of a festival (MK 1:4). The word *eshet*, which occurs in Psalms (58:9) in a reference to those "that have not seen the sun," has been identified by some with *eishut*, i.e., mole rats "which do not see the sun but burrow in the ground and live there" (Mid. Ps. to 58:9). In modern Hebrew the mole rat is called *ḥoled*, mentioned among the unclean creeping things (Lev. 11:29). The biblical *ḥoled*, however, is the *rat.

The identification of *ḥafor perot* with the mole rat is most plausible. However, some scholars believe that it is a kind of bat (cf. Tur-Sinai, in: *Leshonenu*, no. 26, 77ff.), and S. Lieberman holds that it is the "flying fox" (which is not found in Israel) or the fruit bat (cf. *Leshonenu*, no. 29, 132f.).

BIBLIOGRAPHY: Lewysohn, Zool, 101, no. 135; J. Feliks, *The Animal World of the Bible* (1962), 43; M. Dor, *Leksikon Zoʾologi* (1965), 121.

[Jehuda Feliks]

MOLEDET (Heb. (בְּנֵי בְּרִית) מוֹלֶדֶת B'nai B'rith; "Homeland"), moshav shittufi in northern Israel in S.E. Lower Galilee, affiliated with Tenu'at ha-Moshavim. Moledet was founded in 1937 by pioneers from Germany as a tower and stockade settlement, its construction being aided by the *B'nai B'rith. In its initial years Moledet had to defend itself against frequent attacks by Arabs, and in 1939 was for the most part destroyed in a conflagration. Subsequently the moshav shittufi recovered, basing its economy on field crops, orchards, cattle, and a metal factory. Its population was 340 in 1968, growing to 520 in the mid-1990s and 622 in 2002. In recent years, like many other rural settlements, the moshav underwent major changes, including the distribution of collective property among members and the absorption of newcomers

[Efram Orni / Shaked Gilboa (2nd ed.)]

MOLHO, ISAAC RAPHAEL (1894–1976), Greek journalist and Zionist. Molho was born in Salonika, a descendant of Rabbi Joseph Molho, author of *Shulḥan Gaviyyah*, and Rabbi Abraham di *Boton, author of *Leḥem Rav*. He studied at the *talmud torah*, the Alliance Israélite Universelle, and the Beit Yosef Rabbinical Seminary in Salonika. In Salonika he was active in commerce and journalism becoming a partner in the Recanati firm and founding the newspapers *Pro-Israel* (French) and *La Renaissanca* (Judeo-Spanish). *Pro-Israel* was the organ of the Zionist league, B'nai Moshe, which Molho started with Yitzhak David Cohen and Yitzhak Samuel Amarilio. He also served as librarian and secretary of the *Kadima* society, which disseminated the Hebrew language and culture. While a student at Beit Yosef, he worked as a reporter for the French daily newspaper *La Liberte*.

Molho worked to win the support of the French and the Italian governments as well as the Greek Parliament and government for the Balfour Declaration. In 1918 he met with the king of Greece, Alexandros, at the time Allenby conquered Jerusalem, and afterward in Salonika he organized a Jewish Legion to fight in Ereẓ Israel. In 1919 he emigrated to Jerusalem.

In Jerusalem he worked as an agent and representative of several film companies. He was manager of the Rainois film company and the Gaumont and Metro Goldwyn Mayer movie theaters for the entire region from Jerusalem to Teheran. Molho brought cinema to Baghdad and was elected chairman of the Film Distributors Union in Ereẓ Israel. He also helped organize the mass immigration of more than 15,000 Salonikan Jews to Ereẓ Israel, many of whom worked in fishing or as port workers. In 1924 he met with King Hussein Abu-Ali in Amman.

In Jerusalem, he was one of the founders of the Rehavia neighborhood, and also served as its chairman and "mukhtar." Also as a member of the Bayit ve-Gan neighborhood committee, he helped found its commercial center.

In Sephardi affairs, he was chairman of the Union of Sephardi Communities in Israel, and in 1938 he was elected by the World Zionist Organization executive and Jerusalem Sephardi Council as the Jerusalem delegate to the Amsterdam gathering of the World Union of Sephardi Communities and was later elected to the Union's Central Committee in Paris.

He was an active in the Jerusalem Municipality, was responsible for supervising apartment rental, and served as chairman of the property assessment committee. He was also was a member of the Council for General Education of the Va'ad ha-Le'ummi.

By befriending the Italian consul in Jerusalem he was able to get immigration certificates for some Rhodian Jews facing expulsion or help them reach Palestine clandestinely. In 1939, at the outset of World War II, the British imprisoned him for 20 days because of his amicable relations with the Italian consul. During World War II, he was an active member of the rescue committee for European Jewry, Al-Dami (Don't Keep Silent!).

He was an active member with Judah Leib *Magnes and Martin *Buber in *Berit Shalom. He also assisted in the founding of the *Iḥud movement and Kedmah Mizraḥah in the interest of making peace with the Arabs of Ereẓ Israel.

Molho edited the journal *Oẓar Yehudei Sepharad* and was also one of the founders of *Ha-Hed* ("The Echo"). He wrote in the Hebrew dailies *Davar*, *Ha-Ẓofeh*, and *Do'ar ha-Yom* in Ereẓ Israel, the French Sephardi press of Egypt and France, and the Judeo-Spanish press in Salonika until the Holocaust.

He compiled several volumes of the *Enẓikopedyah Le-Ẓiyyonut* under the editorship of Moshe Kleinman. His books include *Be-Ha'ir ha-Mizraḥ*; *Los Diversas Tintativas de Reconstituir la Nationalidad Judiya*; *Rav Moshe Almosnino, Ḥayav ve-Sefarav*; *Yosef Marko Barukh*; and *Tur Ha-Zahav be-Toledot Saloniki be-Dorot ha-Aḥaronim*.

BIBLIOGRAPHY: J. Heller, *From Brit Shalom to Ichud, Judah Leib Magnes and the Struggle for a Binational State in Palestine* (2003), 146; Yad Ben Zvi Archives, files 6–4–5–4, 6–4–5–8; *Davar* (June 24, 1966); M.D. Gaon, *Yehudei Mizraḥ be-Ereẓ Yisrael*, part 2 (1938), 382, 733–34; D.A. Recanati (ed.), *Zikhron Saloniki*, 2 (1986), 512; D. Tidhar, *Enẓiklopedyah le-Ḥaluẓei ha-Yishuv u-Vonav*, vol. 4 (1950), 1984–85; H.A. Toledano et. al. (eds.), *Avraham ha-Ivri*, 7–17.

[Yitzchak Kerem (2nd ed.)]

°**MOLITOR, FRANZ JOSEPH** (1779–1860), Christian philosopher and kabbalist. Born into a Catholic family at Oberursel, near Frankfurt, Molitor at first studied law. Later he concentrated on research into the philosophy of history and was deeply influenced by *Schelling. His first book, *Ideen zu einer kuenftigen Dynamik der Geschichte* (Frankfurt, 1805), was an evaluation of the various books of idealistic philosophy. He pursued this inquiry in his next two books, in which he established Schelling's central position, although he criticized the latter's *Philosophy and Religion*. Molitor moved in liberal intellectual circles and consequently came into contact with Jews. He advocated the establishment of the Jewish school at Frankfurt, later known as the Philanthropin, and was one of its first teachers. Full of enthusiasm, he joined the *Freemasons and in 1808 he became a member of their "Jewish" lodge, Zur aufgehenden Morgenroethe, which he fought to have recognized. He headed this lodge in 1812, but finally succumbed to the opposition of the Masonic leaders and closed it in 1816. From the start of his activity in Jewish and Masonic circles he befriended Ephraim Joseph *Hirschfeld and was influenced by his campaign for Jewish-Christian brotherhood. Unlike Molitor's other Jewish acquaintances, who favored the *Haskalah, Hirschfeld was the first to direct Molitor's attention to *Kabbalah as a way of attaining this brotherhood. Schelling's espousal of theosophy in 1809 also influenced Molitor to explore Jewish theosophy, although he never compromised his faith in liberal Catholicism and Masonry.

Molitor's ascetic life weakened his body, and he was almost completely paralyzed for over 40 years. From 1816 he concentrated on the study of Judaism and the Kabbalah, but his Jewish guides, other than Hirschfeld, are unknown. He considered the Kabbalah to be that part of Jewish tradition which had preserved, in relative purity, those ultimate truths of primeval religion which tend to become more and more revealed with the progress of history. Learning Hebrew and Aramaic, he explored in depth both talmudic and kabbalistic literature. With the aim of describing kabbalistic teaching in all its depth and breadth, he devoted 40 years to this task. The four volumes of his great anonymous work, *Philosophie der Geschichte oder ueber die Tradition*, were actually intended as an introduction to the main bulk of the work, which remained uncompleted. After the appearance of the first volume (1827) he became acquainted with the philosophy of Franz von Baader, whose influence is marked in the succeeding volumes and in the second, much enlarged, edition of the first volume (part 2, 1834; part 3, 1839; part 4, 1853; part 1, in a second edition, 1857). The first volumes of his work are devoted to the principles of Judaism in the light of Kabbalah, with special emphasis, in the third volume, on purity and impurity. The fourth volume emphasizes the importance of Kabbalah for Christianity.

Despite his Christian theosophic leanings, Molitor's work remains unsurpassed by any previous attempt, both in speculative depth and familiarity with Jewish sources. His influence can be discerned in the work of all Christian theologians who were inspired by Baader. Molitor died in Frankfurt on March 23, 1860. His admiration for the Kabbalah was ignored by Jewish researchers in the 19th century, but it may well be that the weaknesses in the historical chapters of his book led the researchers to dismiss him completely.

BIBLIOGRAPHY: J. Katz, *Freemasons and Jews* (1970), 33–37, 58–63; R. Rocholl, *Beitraege zu einer Geschichte deutscher Theosophie mit besonderer Ruecksicht auf Molitor's Philosophie der Geschichte* (1856); C. Frankenstein, *Molitor's metaphysische Geschichtsphilosophie* (1928); G. Scholem, *Bibliographia Kabbalistica* (1927), 108–9; G. Van Rijnberk, *Episodes de la Vie Ésotérique 1780–1824* (1948), 174–91 (portrait).

[Gershom Scholem]

MOLLER, HANS (1896–1962) and his cousin **ERICH** (1895–), textile industrialists in Ereẓ Israel. Born in Vienna and Ostrava, respectively, Hans and Erich were the fourth generation of textile industrialists. The Moller family owned the cotton-spinning mill, founded in 1865 by their great-grandfather, Simon Katzau in Babi (Bohemia). They both went to Palestine in 1933 and in 1934 founded Ata Textile Company at Kefar Ata. They finally settled in Palestine in 1938. This was the first integrated cotton, spinning, weaving, dyeing, and finishing plant in the country, manufacturing and retailing ready-to-wear clothing and supplying the Allied forces in the Middle East during World War II. Originally a family business, Ata became a public company. In 1967 it had 1,861 employees. In 1948 a subsidiary company, Kurdaneh Textile Works Ltd., was founded. Erich left Ata in 1949 to build Moller Textile Ltd., a spinning, twisting, and dyeing plant in Nahariyyah. Both plants made major contributions to Israel export.

[Kurt Gruenberger]

MOLNÁR, ÁKOS (1895–1945), Hungarian author. An outstanding storyteller, Molnár wrote many books including *A császár dajkája* ("The Emperor's Nurse," 1935) and *Az égő csipkebokor* ("The Burning Bush," 1940). He also wrote *A hitehagyott* ("The Apostate," 1937), the biography of Imre *Szerencses (Fortunatus), a baptized court Jew. Molnar was murdered by the Nazis.

MOLNÁR, FERENC (originally **Neumann**, 1878–1952), Hungarian playwright and novelist. Born in Budapest, Molnár's first novel, *Az éhes város* ("The Hungry City," 1900) was a historical picture of Budapest, and particularly of its Jewish quarter. The children's story, *A Pál utcai fiúk* (1907; *The Paul Street Boys*, 1927), was Molnár's outstanding work. Another of his social novels, *Andor* (1918[2]), symbolized the young Jewish intellectual destroyed by the defects of his own character. During World War I Molnár was a war correspondent, and some of his experiences appeared in his *Egy haditudósíto emlekei* ("Memoirs of a War Correspondent," 1916). In Molnár's books, which brilliantly expose contemporary Hungarian social problems, the central figure is always a weak-willed Jew who makes himself ridiculous by trying to imitate his surroundings.

It was as a dramatist that Molnár was most distinguished. His witty dialogue owes much to Oscar Wilde. His ideas are sometimes fantastic, but never ridiculous. His first play was *A doktor úr* ("The Lawyer," 1902). He achieved world fame with *Az ördög* (1907; *The Devil*, 1908); the tragicomedy *Liliom* (1909; Eng. vers., 1921), *A testör* (1910; *The Guardsman*, 1924); and *A farkas* (1912; *The Tale of the Wolf*, 1914). All these characters deal with the problems of a changing society, and the characters are, almost without exception, Jews fighting to improve their image, sometimes turning into caricatures in the process. *The Guardsman* inspired Oscar *Strauss' musical comedy *The Chocolate Soldier; Liliom* became the musical *Carousel* (1945), by Richard *Rodgers and Oscar *Hammerstein. Molnár also wrote lyrical, symbolic dramas. Most of his plays have been translated into English. There are two anthologies of his stage works, *Plays* (1927) and *The Plays of Ferenc Molnár* (1929, 1937[2]); and a prose anthology, *Husbands and Lovers* (1924). During the end of the 1930s, antisemitism drove Molnár from Hungary, and he lived in France and Switzerland, but immigrated to the U.S. in 1940. His last major work was the autobiographical *Útitárs a számúzetéshen* (1958; appeared in English as *Companion in Exile*, 1950).

BIBLIOGRAPHY: B. Halmi, *Molnár Ferenc…* (Hung., 1929); *Magyar Irodalmi Lexicon*, 2 (1965), 263–6; S.J. Kunitz and H. Haycroft (eds.), *Twentieth Century Authors* (1942), 970f.

[Baruch Yaron]

MOLOCH, CULT OF. Evidence concerning Moloch worship in ancient Israel is found in the legal, as well as in the historical and prophetic literature of the Bible. In the Pentateuch, the laws of the *Holiness Code speak about giving or passing children (lit. "seed") to Moloch (Lev. 18:21, 20:2–4) and the law in *Deuteronomy speaks of "passing [one's] son or daughter through fire" (18:10). Although Moloch is not named in the Deuteronomy passage, it is likely that his cult was the object of the prohibition. The author of the Book of Kings speaks about "passing [one's] son and daughter through fire" (II Kings 16:3 [son], 17:17, 21:6 [son]). II Kings 23:10 speaks about "passing [one's] son or daughter through fire to Moloch." Some scholars interpret the phrase *lə-haʿavir ba-esh*, as a reference to a divinatory or protective rite in which children were passed through a fire but not physically harmed. However, the same phrase *lə-haʿavir ba-esh* is found in an unmistakable context of burning in Numbers 31:23. Other biblical texts refer to the sacrifice of children. Psalms 106:37–38 speaks of child sacrifice to the unnamed idols of Canaan. In prophetic sources, Jeremiah 7:31 and Ezekiel 20:25–6 speak disapprovingly of sacrificing children to Yahweh (for the "bad statutes" referred to by Ezekiel, see Ex. 22:28–29; but see Friebel); Jeremiah 19:5 speaks of sacrificing children to Baal; Ezekiel 16:21, 20:31, 23:37, 39 of sacrificing children to unnamed divinities; as does Isaiah 57:5. In none of these is there a mention of Moloch. Only in Jeremiah 32:35 is Moloch mentioned by name and there he is associated with Baal (see below). Distinction should be made between human sacrifice as a sporadic deed at a time of crisis and distress, such as the holocaust of the son of Mesha king of Moab (II Kings 3:27), or as an act which serves to express an unusual degree of religious devotion as the binding of Isaac (cf. Micah 6:7), on the one hand, and the Moloch cult which was an established institution with a fixed location (the Topheth), on the other. As the classical sources have it, the sacrifices of children at Carthage, a colony founded by Phoenicians on the coast of Northeast Tunisia, usually came after a defeat and a great disaster – a religious practice based upon an ancient mythological tradition. Thus Phoenician tradition ascribed to Sanchuniaton relates that the god Elos (= El) sacrificed his son following a war which brought disaster upon the state. If the classical reports are accurate, it could be maintained that there is no real connection therefore between the Phoenician-Punic child sacrifices which are sporadic and conditioned by crisis and the Moloch worship which was an institution or cult. In contrast though to the classical reports, the archaeological discoveries at Carthage, which attest some 20,000 burials of infant bones along with animal bones in what are evidently not instances of natural death appear to conflict with the classical reports. There is as yet no evidence of child sacrifice in the Carthaginian homeland, the cities of Phoenicia (Lebanon) proper, where far less excavation has been done.

The Name

The accepted view since A. *Geiger is that Moloch is a tendentious mis-vocalization of the word *melekh*, "king," the original vowels being changed and patterned after the vocalization of *boshet*, "shame," which was often used as an intentional substitute for Baal (see *Euphemism and Dysphemism). It is true that the names Moloch (I Kings 11:7) and Milcom occur in the Bible in reference to an Ammonite god, and that deities by the name Malik/Muluk are attested to from the 18th century B.C.E. onward. However, the laws and warnings against the worship of the Moloch could hardly refer to these particular deities. It is unlikely that one particular god who is not especially famous would be singled out for mention, while other prominent gods, e.g., Baal, are not mentioned by name in the Torah even once. That the original vocalization was *melekh* may be learned from Isaiah 30:33, which undoubtedly alludes to the fiery ceremony of the Moloch rites. The fact that the Septuagint of the Pentateuch (which was the first to be translated by the Greek translators) translates *molekh* as "king" (*archon*) seems also to indicate that at the time of the translation of the Torah, the reading *molekh* instead of *melekh* was as yet unknown.

A new dimension was added to the problem of the name Moloch with the discovery of some Latin dedicatory inscriptions in North Africa. In these inscriptions the term *molchomor* – which has been equated with מלכ אמר in the Punic inscriptions, the meaning of which was also unclear – occurs in the context of a lamb offering. The context has provided a clue to the meaning of both *molchomor* and מלכ אמר. *Molchomor* has been interpreted as *molech immer*, i.e., *molech*, "sacrifice" (see below) and *ommor*, "a lamb." This interpretation, however, is beset by difficulties. First, it is hard to explain how *immer* (Aram. and Akk. "lamb") became *ommor*; no less difficult is the interpretation of *molech* as sacrifice. O. Eissfeldt argued (on the basis of Syriac) that *molech* means "vow," but this can hardly be reconciled with the biblical text. It would be futile to translate *li-znot ʾaḥare ha-molekh* (לזנות אחרי המלך) in Leviticus 20:5: "to go astray after the vow." Besides, it is methodologically unsound to explain a Hebrew word in the Bible on the sole basis of a late Aramaic word. Another expression occurring in the Punic inscriptions מלכאדם, turned out to be even more crucial for the understanding of the Hebrew *molekh*. Here again some scholars understood the term as human sacrifice. However, as in the case of מלכ אמר, no objective evidence has been found for this interpretation of מלכאדם. The most plausible explanation is, as has already been suggested, that the term means "king of humankind," and is the epithet of the god to whom the inscription is dedicated. The word "king" was indeed a common attribute of the deities in the Phoenician-Punic sphere, e.g., Melkart ("king of the city," i.e., Tyre), מלכבעל, etc. El, the head of the Canaanite pantheon, later identified with Kronos, was named Malkandros (Plutarch, *De Iside et Osiride*, 16) which means "king of man" (Greek *aner* [gen. *andros*], "man"), in other words מלכאדם. This is corroborated by evidence from the Assyrian-Aramean sphere where the epithet "King" is applied to the god Adad/Hadad, who is identified with the Canaanite-Phoenician Baal – was also called "King," cf. מלכבעל – "Baal is king." The identification of Hadad-Baal with Moloch provides the background to Jeremiah 32:35, which fulminates against the *bamot*-altars of Baal in the valley of Ben-Hinnom where male and female children were burnt to Moloch, i.e., Baal-Hadad. Furthermore, a series of Assyrian-Aramean documents analyzed by K. Deller showed that Adadmilki or Adadšarru ("Adad the king") was actually the god to whom children, sometimes firstborn, were burned (see below). The Assyrian material sheds new light on II Kings 17 where Adadmelech (to be read instead of Adrammelech) is the god to whom the Sepharvites burn/dedicate their children (verse 31). Adadmelech in this verse stands next to Anammelech who has been correctly related by scholars to Anath who bears the title "Queen of Heaven," the standard term for Ishtar in Akkadian (*šarrat šamê*; cf. Sum. *nin.anna.ak* = Inanna). The pair Adad and Ishtar, or the "king" and the "queen," are the ones to whom children are dedicated in the Assyrian-Aramean documents quoted above. Adad and ʿAshtart were actually the dominant gods in Syro-Palestine until the beginning of the common era, as may be deduced from the passage preserved by Philo of Byblos (ascribed to Sanchuniaton): "Ashtart the great and Zeus Demarus who is Hadad, the king of the gods, were enthroned on the earth" (Eusebius, *Praeparatio Evangelica* 1:10, 31; cf. O. Eissfeldt, *Kleine Schriften*, 3 (1966), 335–9). Another instructive example is the second century B.C.E. Greek inscription, found in Acre, that is dedicated to Hadad and Atargatis (= combination of Ishtar and Anath) who listen to prayer (M. Avi-Yonah, in: IEJ, 9 (1959), 1–2). As will be shown below, the introduction of the Moloch coincided with the introduction of the worship of the "queen of the heaven," although the latter persisted after the reform of Josiah whereas the Moloch cult seems to have perished following the reform. The worship of the Moloch along with the worship of the "queen of the heaven" are therefore to be seen against the background of the widespread worship in the Assyro-Aramean culture of Adad/Hadad, the king, and Ishtar Ashtarth/Anath, the queen, that began in the ninth-eighth century B.C.E. This sheds new light on the controversial passage Amos 5:26: "… You carried the canopy [Heb. *sikkut* is a deliberate misvocalization of *sukkat* or *sukkot* to make it resemble to שִׁקּוּץ; *shikkuẓ*, "abhorrence," cf. LXX and 6QD 14–17] of your king and the *kaiwanu* [changed deliberately into *kiyyun*, as *skikkuẓ*] of your image[s] the star of your god[s] which you made for yourselves." The *kamānu*/*kawānu*, found in Jeremiah 7:18, and 44:19, is a cultic cake in the form of a star which is the image of Ishtar, who is called in Akkadian *kakkab šamê*, "the star of the Heaven." The image of Ishtar צלמיכם כוכב אלהיכם, is depicted here as having been carried under a canopy in a procession, a procedure attested in the Assyrian documents (cf. L. Waterman, Royal Correspondence of the Assyrian Empire, 1 (1930), no. 1212, rev. 1–10 = SAA XIII: 192; for corrected reading see A.L. Oppenheim, in: BASOR, 107 (1947), 8, n. 4), but unrecognized until now. "Your king" in this verse is none other than her consort, Adad the king, sometimes identical with the sun-god Shamash.

The Nature of the Worship

As already indicated above, the legal and historical sources speak about passing children to Moloch in fire. According to the rabbinic interpretation, this prohibition is against passing children through fire and then delivering them to the pagan priests. In other words, according to this interpretation, this refers to an initiation rite. This kind of initiation or consecration is actually attested to in various cultures (see T.H. Gaster, in bibl.) and the Septuagint interprets Deuteronomy 18:10 in a similar manner. This is a Midrash of the rabbis likewise attested by the Septuagint. A similar non-sacrificial tradition, perhaps more ancient, is found in the Book of Jubilees. The Book of Jubilees 30:7ff. connects intermarrriage or rather the marrying off of one's children to pagans with the sin of Moloch. This tradition seems to be echoed in the dissenting opinion of R. Ishmael (cf. Meg. 4:9) in *Sifrei Deuteronomy* 18, who explains the prohibition of Moloch as the impregnation of a pagan woman, an interpretation lying behind the Syriac translation in Leviticus 18 and 20. The common denominator of all these traditions is the understanding of Moloch worship as the transfer of Jewish children to paganism either by delivering them directly to pagan priests or by procreation through intercourse with a pagan woman. This tradition is in keeping with the general rabbinic tendency to make biblical texts relevant to their audiences, who were more likely to be attracted to Greco-Roman cults and to intercourse with pagan women than to the sacrifice of humans to a long-forgotten god.

In the framework of the penalty clauses of some neo-Assyrian contracts, there is the threat that if one of the parties violates the contract, he will burn his son to Adad the king and give his daughter to Ishtar, or Belet-ṣēri. Some of these documents showed that Adadmilki or Adadšarru ("Adad the king") was actually the god to whom children, sometimes firstborn, were burned. Ch.W. Johns, who first published these documents, contended that burning is used here in the figurative sense, meaning dedication (*Assyrian Deeds and Documents*, 3 (1923), 345–6). This figurative interpretation was accepted by Deller and Weinfeld, but context indicates that they are to be taken literally (see CAD š/II, 53; SAA VI: 102). From the fact that Ahaz, who opened the door to Assyria and Assyrian culture and religion (see e.g., II Kings 16:6ff.), was the first king to indulge in the worship of Moloch, it may be deduced that this was introduced through Assyrian influence, along with other practices such as the burning of incense on the roofs (II Kings 23:12), the sun chariots (23:11), and the tents for the Asherah (23:7). There is no reason to suppose that the Moloch was introduced as a result of Phoenician influence, as is commonly supposed. Were this true, one would expect to find the Moloch worship in Northern Israel, which was overwhelmed by Phoenician influence, especially at the period of the Omri dynasty. No allusion, however, to this practice in the Northern Kingdom has been found. The worship of Moloch, which was practiced at a special site (outside the walls of Jerusalem in the valley of Ben-Hinnom) called Topheth, became firmly established in the time of King Manasseh, his son Amon, and at the beginning of Josiah's reign. If it was completely eradicated by Josiah within the framework of his reform activities (II Kings 23:10), then Jeremiah's references to this worship (7:31, 19:1ff., 32:35) might apply to the days of Manasseh and also to the time of Josiah before the reform (see Y. Kaufmann, Toledot, 3 (1960), 382–90).

BIBLIOGRAPHY: Ḥ. Albeck, *Das Buch der Jubiläen und die Halacha* (1930), 26ff.; O. Eissfeldt, *Molk als Opferbegriff im Punischen und Hebräischen…* (1935), 46ff.; N.H. Tur-Sinai, *Ha-Lashon ve-ha-Sefer*, 1 (1954²). 81ff.; H. Cazelles, in: DBI Supplément, 5 (1957), 1337–46; R. de Vaux, *Studies in Old Testament Sacrifice* (1964), 52–90; M. Buber, *Malkhut Shamayim* (1965), 99–100; K. Deller, in; *Orientalia*, 34 (1965), 382–6; T.H. Gaster, *Myth, Legend and Custom in the Old Testament* (1969), 586–8. **ADD. BIBLIOGRAPHY:** M. Weinfeld, in: UF, 4 (1972), 133–54; M. Smith, in: JAOS, 95 (1975), 477–79; M. Held, in: *ErIsr*, 16 (1982), 76–77; B. Levine, *JPS Torah Commentary Leviticus* (1989), 258–60; R. Clifford, in: BASOR, 279 (1990), 55–64; A. Millard, in: DDD, 34–35; G. Heider, in: DDD, 581–85, incl. bibl.; K. Friebel, in: R. Troxel et al. (eds.), *Seeking Out the Wisdom of Ancients..Essays … M. Fox* (2005), 21–36.

[Moshe Weinfeld / S. David Sperling (2nd ed.)]

MOLODECHNO, town in Molodechno district, W. Belarus; during the interwar period it was within Poland. The Jewish community in Molodechno started in the early 18th century and numbered 251 in 1847, increasing to 1,105 (46 percent of the total population) in 1897. After improvement in the economic situation resulting from the construction of a railroad in 1905, the Great Synagogue was erected in 1906. Later a prayer house was built by the Ḥasidim. A government school for Jewish boys, with a special vocational department and boarding facilities, was erected but was destroyed at the time of the Polish annexation. In 1925 the Jews numbered 950. Under Polish rule Jewish children received their education in the Hebrew *Tarbut elementary school. The Jews were mainly engaged in trade and crafts. During World War II Molodechno was annexed from September 1939 to July 1941, liquidating Jewish economy and public life. The Germans entered Molodechno in July and immediately killed 50 Jews. In October they murdered another 400 to 800, and the remaining 350–600 were herded in a barn and burned alive in December 1941.

[Zeev Elyashiv / Shmuel Spector (2nd ed.)]

MOLODOWSKY, KADIA (1894–1975). Yiddish poet and novelist. Born in Bereze (Bereza Kartuska) in Belorussia, Molodowsky was educated by her father, grandmother, and tutors. After passing the gymnasium exams, she departed for

Warsaw and Odessa to prepare for a teaching career. Following the 1917 Revolution, she participated in the publications of the Kiev Yiddish Group before returning to Warsaw to teach in the CYSHO Yiddish secular schools; she also taught Hebrew to workers in a Jewish community night school. For her pupils she wrote playful verses, ballads, and poetic tales, some of which were set to music and sung in Yiddish schools throughout the world. In 1935 she settled in New York and founded and edited the journal, *Svive* (1943–4 and 1960–74). Her many volumes of poetry reflect her experiences in Europe, the U.S., and Israel, displaying her concerns for women, the oppressed poor, the tragedy of war, and the Holocaust. After the establishment of the State of Israel in 1948, a new joyous tone appeared in her lyrics, many of which were publicly sung and broadcast in Israel. A book of her children's poems translated into Hebrew, *Pitḥu et ha-Sha'ar* ("Open the Gate," 1945), was taught in Israeli schools. Her drama *Nokhn Got fun Midber* ("Toward the God of the Desert," 1949) was staged by Israel's Ohel Theater in 1956, and her novel *Baym Toyer* ("At the Gate," 1967) described the fate of new immigrants, life in the kibbutz, and the forging of a nation. Other works of fiction include a novel, *Fun Lublin biz Nyu York* ("From Lublin to New York," 1942), and a short story collection, *A Shtub mit Zibn Fentster* ("A House with Seven Windows," 1957). Among her volumes of poetry are *Kheshvendike Nekht* ("Nights of Kheshvan," 1927); *Dzshike Gas* ("Dszhike Street," 1933), *Freydke* (1935), *In Land fun Mayn Gebeyn* ("In the Country of My Bones," 1937), *Der Melekh Dovid Aleyn iz Geblibn* ("Only King David Remained," 1946) and *Likht fun Dornboym* ("Light of the Thorn Bush," 1965).

BIBLIOGRAPHY: M. Ravitch, *Mayn Leksikon* (1945), 122–4; E. Auerbach, in: JBA, 24 (1966–7), 97–106; C. Madison, *Yiddish Literature* (1968), 319–20. **ADD. BIBLIOGRAPHY:** K. Hellerstein, *Paper Bridges: Selected Poems of Kadya Molodowsky* (1999).

[Sol Liptzin / Kathryn Hellerstein (2nd ed.)]

MOMBERT, ALFRED (1872–1942), German poet. Descended from a family of Jewish merchants that had settled in Karlsruhe, Mombert studied law in Heidelberg, where he later went into practice as a lawyer. In 1894, he published his first volume of poetry, *Tag und Nacht*. Despite the clear stylistic influence of naturalist and impressionist poetics, it nonetheless maintained a unique tone. From the start, it is an ostentatious "cosmological" focus that gives Mombert's early poem cycles – *Der Gluehende* (1896), *Die Schoepfung* (1897), *Die Bluete des Chaos*, and *Der Sonne-Geist* (both 1905) – their characteristic setting, necessitating a new language on which Mombert continued to work throughout his career. Only marginally integrated into contemporary artistic and intellectual circles (Martin Buber, Hans Carossa, and Richard Dehmel were his only partners in spiritual exchange), Mombert adopted a 19th-century aesthetic of monism and neo-romanticism. Impressed by the totalizing view of his poetry and its mythic and religious allusions, contemporaries likened Mombert to William Blake; the German poet Richard Dehmel detected in him the fervor of the ancient Hebrew prophets. Abandoning the practice of law, Mombert turned toward cosmic verse-drama of epic scope. The trilogy *Aeon* (1907–11) established an imagery and dramatic figures to which Mombert would cling in all his further works, such as in *Der Held der Erde* (1919) and in *Atair* (1925).

In 1933, Mombert, with other Jewish members, was expelled from the German Academy of Arts. His last publication during his lifetime, *Sfaira der Alte*, was printed – at Buber's insistence – by the Schocken Verlag in 1936. Four years later, Mombert, already seriously ill, was arrested by the Gestapo in Heidelberg and deported to the Gurs concentration camp. With the intercession of non-Jewish friends and admirers (among them Hans Carossa and Mombert's biographer, Richard Benz), he was allowed to leave for Switzerland in 1941, where he died in Winterthur only a few months later.

BIBLIOGRAPHY: R. Benz, *Der Dichter Alfred Mombert* (1947); M. Buber, in: G. Krojanker (ed.), *Juden in der deutschen Literatur* (1922), 113–20. **ADD. BIBLIOGRAPHY:** R. Haehling von Lanzenauer, *Alfred Mombert. Dichter und Jurist* (2001); S. Himmelheber (ed.), *Alfred Mombert (1872–1942)* (1993); F.A. Schmitt, *Alfred Mombert* (1967).

[Sol Liptzin / Philipp Theisohn (2nd ed.)]

MOMENT, DER, Yiddish daily newspaper in Poland. The paper was founded in Warsaw in November 1910 by Ẓevi Hirsch *Prylucki. Working with him were his son, Noah *Prylucki, and Hillel *Zeitlin. *Der Moment* became one of the most influential of the Jewish dailies of Poland, with a circulation of about 30,000, although that figure was far exceeded in times of tension: during the *Beilis blood libel proceedings, 1911–13, it reached a circulation of 150,000, and shortly before World War II it printed 60,000 copies daily.

In 1914 *Der Moment* published its first dispatches from Ereẓ Israel; its contributor was Izhak *Ben-Zvi. The Russians suspended the paper in July 1915, but 18 days later the invading Germans allowed it to continue under censorship. During the Warsaw municipal elections of 1916, the paper backed the *Folkspartei. Prominent among the paper's contributors after the war were Hirsh David *Nomberg, Julius Schwalbe, Ignacy *Schiper, and from 1925 Isaac *Schwarzbart. In 1936 the paper became a cooperative and two years later was taken over by a syndicate which adopted a Revisionist policy. It printed Vladimir Jabotinsky's article "The Eleventh Hour" in 1938 and also his series "*Fun Mayn Tagebukh*." The publication of *Der Moment* was discontinued in September 1939 with the Nazi invasion of Poland.

ADD. BIBLIOGRAPHY: M. Mozes, "Der Moment," in: *Fun Noenten Over II, Yidishe Presse in Varshe* (1956), 241–99; J. Gothelf (ed.), *Ittonut Yehudit she-Hayeta* (1973), 95–125; M. Fuks, *Prasa zydowska w Warszawie 1923–1939* (1979), index.

[Artur Fiszer]

MOMIGLIANO, ARNALDO DANTE (1908–1987), historian of antiquity; born in Caraglio (Cuneo), Italy. After the Italian antisemitic legislation of 1938 he settled in England, where from 1951 to 1975 he was professor of ancient history at University College, London. Momigliano wrote, in Italian, books on Thucydides, Claudius, Philip of Macedon, as well as works on classical historiography. His best-known English books are *Conflict Between Paganism and Christianity in the Fourth Century* (1963), and *Studies in Historiography* (1966). One of his earlier works, *Prime Linee di Storia della Tradizione Maccabaica* (1930, 3d ed. 1968), was an impressive contribution to Jewish history of the Hellenistic and Roman periods. Also notable were his *Ricerche sull' organizzazione della Giudea sotte il dominio romano* (1934, 1967) and his chapters on the Second Temple period in the *Cambridge Ancient History*. A comprehensive bibliography of Momigliano's works is included in his *Quarto contributo alia storia depli studi classici e del mondo antico* (pp. 669–719). He was renowned for his deep learning and erudition.

ADD. BIBLIOGRAPHY: ODNB online.

[Bernard Semmel]

MOMIGLIANO, ATTILIO (1883–1952), Italian literary critic, and historian. Momigliano was born in Asti to observant Jewish parents; he studied literature at the University of Torino, under the direction of the critic and writer Arturo Graf, and was professor of Italian literature at the universities of Catania, Pisa and Florence. After 1938 he was forced out of academic life by Mussolini's racist legislation and settled in Florence, where he continued to write under the pen name of Giorgio Flores. In 1943–44, during the German occupation of Italy, he took shelter in a hospital in Borgo San Sepolcro, where he was accepted as a patient by a cooperative doctor; he made use of this period to write a commentary to Torquato Tasso's *Gerusalemme Liberata*. He returned to his teaching post, but only as substitute, following the liberation. Momigliano has been called "an attentive and subtle impressionist of criticism." He was remarkably alive to the most delicate vibrations of poetry, reconstructing character motivation and presenting the results of his diligent reading in a calm and lucid prose. He was particularly skillful in bringing out detail in texts ranging from Dante's *Divina Commedia* to Tasso's *Gerusalemme Liberata*. The critic Luigi Russo found in Momigliano's Jewish origin an explanation for his isolation and historical detachment. A prolific writer, Momigliano published short literary essays and textual commentaries in the Italian press, all of unusual interest. His works include: *Impressioni di un lettore contemporaneo* (1925), *Introduzione ai poeti* (1946), *Studi di poesia* (1938; 1948^2), and *Elzeviri* (1945). He also wrote valuable monographs such as *L'indole e il riso di L. Pulci* (1907), *Carlo Porta* (1910), and *Dante, Manzoni e Verga* (1944), but his best books were perhaps those based on his knowledge and analysis of Manzoni's works: *L'Innominato* (1913) and *La vita e le opere del Manzoni* (1933^3). His *Storia della letteratura italiana* (1932), was reprinted several times after the author's death, and was studied by generations of high-school and university students.

BIBLIOGRAPHY: G. Trombatore, *Saggi critici* (1950), 266–75; G. Getto, *Poeti…* (1953), 138–61; L. Russo, *La critica letteraria contemporanea* (1967), index; N. Libertini, in: *Annuario dell'Istituto tecnico-statale G. Galilei di Firenze* (1966), 3–33. **ADD. BIBLIOGRAPHY:** G. Di Pino, in: G. Grana (ed.), *Letteratura italiana. I critici*, vol. 3 (1973), 2091–111; A. Biondi (ed.), *Attilio Momigliano. Atti del Convegno di studi nel centenario della nascita* (1990); R. Bonavita, in: *Storia e problemi contemporanei*, 32 (2003), 45–52.

[Louisa Cuomo / Alessandro Guetta (2nd ed.)]

MOMIGLIANO, FELICE (1866–1924), Italian philosopher and historian. Born in the ghetto of the small town of Mondovì, in Piedmont, Italy, Momigliano gave up a possible rabbinical career and embraced instead the life of teacher and journalist. A socialist militant and at the same time an admirer of Mazzini, Momigliano saw himself as the son of both the Italian and the Jewish cultures, which he tried to reconciliate: in his thought patriotism, socialism, and prophetic faith were three sides of the same question. Among his works are *G. Mazzini e le idealità moderne* (1895), *Gli Ebrei e la civiltà moderna* (1912), *Il giudaismo di ieri e di domani* (1916), and *Ebraismo e Cristianesimo* (1922).

ADD. BIBLIOGRAPHY: A. Cavaglion, *Felice Momigliano, Una biografia* (1988).

[Alessandro Guetta (2nd ed.)]

°**MOMMSEN, THEODOR** (1817–1903), German classical scholar and historian; a vigorous opponent of antisemitism. A staunch liberal member of the Prussian and German parliaments and a luminary of Berlin University, Mommsen was active on behalf of Russian Jewry and consistently opposed all antisemitic manifestations, from the appearance of Adolf *Stoecker, the court preacher (1878), to the electoral success of Hermann *Ahlwardt (1902). He was also a prominent member of the *Verein zur Abwehr des Anti-semitismus and signed the public declaration of German notables against antisemitism (1880). Mommsen was the most renowned Christian to attack his colleague, Heinrich *Treitschke, the nationalist historian and antisemite. Paradoxically, a passage in his *History of Rome*, in which he described the Jews as one of the elements leading to the breakdown of the Roman state and the growth of cosmopolitanism, was repeatedly utilized by antisemites. Whereas Mommsen took a positive attitude to the Jewish role in furthering universalism, antisemites viewed the passage in a contemporary, ultra-nationalist setting. Despite his liberalism, Mommsen had no sympathy with the Jews' wish to preserve their cultural inheritance and religious independence. He called upon them to abandon their separateness and assimilate in a more thorough fashion; thus he shared the theoretical assumptions and principles of some conservative German leaders.

BIBLIOGRAPHY: H. Liebeschuetz, *Judentum im deutschen Geschichtsbild* (1967), index. **ADD. BIBLIOGRAPHY:** A. Heuss, *Theodor Mommsen und das 19. Jahrhundert* (1956, 1996); L. Wickert, *Theodor Mommsen*, 4 vols. (1959–80); C. Hoffmann, *Juden und Judentum im Werk deutscher Althistoriker…* (1988), index; St. Rebenich, *Theodor Mommsen* (2002); K. Krieger (ed.), *Berliner Antisemitismusstreit*, 2 vols. (2003), index..

[Michael J. Graetz]

MONASH, SIR JOHN (1865–1931), Australian engineer and soldier who commanded the Australian forces in the Allied armies during World War I. Monash was born in Melbourne into an immigrant family who had been printers of Hebrew books in Krotoszyn. He was related to Heinrich *Graetz. At the university, he displayed exceptional versatility. Besides a doctorate in engineering, he graduated in arts and law, and also studied medicine. After 1900 he specialized in reinforced concrete construction, introducing this engineering technique into Victoria, Tasmania, and South Australia. Between 1913 and 1915 he was president of the Victorian Institute of Engineers. Perhaps uniquely for a senior commander in World War I, Monash was never a professional soldier; his background in civil engineering might well have assisted him in avoiding much of the pointless slaughter, the result of poorly conceived attacks, notorious among the British and French armies in the 1914–18 War. He volunteered for the Victoria militia in 1884 and was commissioned three years later. In 1900 he won a gold medal for military articles in the *Commonwealth Journal*, and on the outbreak of World War I, he had already risen to the rank of colonel in the militia. In April 1915 Monash commanded the Fourth Infantry Brigade at Gallipoli. Although the campaign was unsuccessful, the Australian and New Zealand troops under his command distinguished themselves, and "Monash Valley" there was so named in commemoration of his service. He was sent to France in the following year and in April 1917 participated with the Canadian forces in the capture of Vimy Ridge. In May 1918, as lieutenant general, he was appointed to lead the entire Australian and New Zealand Army Corps (ANZACS) on the western front, and his troops played a decisive part in breaking the German lines on the Amiens front in the summer of 1918. The Allied offensive brought about the end of World War I and gained Monash a reputation as the most resourceful leader in the British army. The British prime minister, Lloyd George, described him as the only soldier of World War I with the necessary qualities of leadership. Besides numerous military decorations, he received honorary degrees from the universities of Oxford, Cambridge, and London. After the Armistice, he led his ANZACS through the streets of London and received a tumultuous welcome. He returned to Australia and resumed his engineering practice. He replanned the electricity supply in Victoria, basing it on the exploitation of huge brown coal deposits at the open cast mine fields of Yallourn, in Victoria. He was made vice chancellor of Melbourne University. In 1930, shortly before his death, he was made a full general, the first Jew to attain that rank in any army. He wrote of his campaigns in *Australian Victories in France in 1918* (1920). Monash remained a practicing Jew all his life. He took an active part in Jewish affairs in Australia and was president of the Zionist Federation in 1928. A village in Israel, Kefar Monash, bears his name. In the 1950s the second university established in the State of Victoria was named Monash University in his honor.

Sir John Monash held an arguably unique position among Diaspora Jews of his time, being regarded as an authentic and universally popular national hero. When he died, one-third of Melbourne's population lined the route of the funeral procession, the sense of loss being, as one observer put it, "as if the king had died." *John Monash: A Biography* by Geoffrey Serle (1982) is the authoritative account of his life.

BIBLIOGRAPHY: I.A. Isaacs, *Australia's Greatest Military Genius* (1937); E. Rubin, *140 Jewish Marshals, Generals and Admirals* (1952), 41–57; J. Ben Hirsch, *Jewish General Officers*, 1 (1967), 5–7; P.H. Emden, *Jews of Britain* (1943), 453–7, index; F.M. Cutlack (ed.), *War Letters of General Monash* (1934²); *The Australian* (Oct. 17, 1931); Gordon, in: *Australian Jewish Historical Society*, 6, no. 2 (1966), 69–80. **ADD. BIBLIOGRAPHY:** ADB; B. Callinan, *Sir John Monash* (1981); P.A. Pedersen, *Monash as Military Commander* (1985).

MONASTIR (Serbo-Croat, **Bitolj**; Macedonian, **Bitola**), town in Yugoslav Macedonia 1918–1992, now in the F.Y.R. of Macedonia, near the Greek border. Monastir was situated on one of the ancient and main trade routes of the Balkans (the Roman "Via Egnatia") which went from the Albanian port of Durazzo to Salonika and Constantinople. It is therefore not surprising that Jews lived there already in Roman times. Direct evidence of Jewish settlement in this region was discovered in 1930 by a Yugoslav archeologist, Joso Petrović, who found at nearby Stobi a column from a third-century C.E. synagogue donated by one Claudius Tiberius Polycharmos, *pater synagogae* ("father of the Synagogue") – the chief *parnas* Marmorstein presumes that the ancestors of Polycharmos were freemen of the Emperor Claudius who had left Rome for Macedonia around the middle of the first century.

Nothing is known about Jewish settlement in Monastir in the Byzantine period. In the 12th century there were Greek-speaking (*Romaniote) Jewish artisans and traders in the town. More Jews arrived after the expulsion from Hungary in the 14th century. At the end of the 15th century refugees from Asia Minor, and during the first half of the 16th century many Spanish exiles who came by the sea or through Salonika, settled in Monastir. Throughout the Ottoman period (1382–1913) Monastir was a lively commercial center. Trade was mainly in Jewish hands (export of liquor, olive oil, salt and salted fish, and import of wool, silk and woven cloth, copper, etc.); many Jews were tanners, silversmiths, cheesemakers, etc. In the 16th century R. Joseph b. Lev was head of the yeshiva. In the 18th century Abraham b. Judah di Buton was a rabbi of Monastir. A fire which swept through the town in 1863 destroyed over 1,000 Jewish homes and shops. A blood libel accusation was leveled against the Jews in 1900.

In 1884 there were 4,000 Jews in Monastir and in 1910, 7,000. After World War I the economic situation deteriorated considerably and many Jews left the town, mainly for the United States and Chile, while others settled in Jerusalem. The remaining Jews were impoverished, and there were many unemployed and poor people who were workers, porters, and peddlers. Between the two world wars community activity was varied and intense, with growing Zionist consciousness and endeavor; the leader was Leon Kamhi. In the 1930s, the central Jewish bodies became aware of the acute social problems in this community and introduced vocational training courses, encouraged *ḥalutz* youth movements and other activities, but the time was too short. This old community with its several synagogues, diverse social and cultural institutions, as well as a rich and original Judeo-Spanish folklore with some Turkish admixtures, was wiped out during the Holocaust. The approximately 3,500 Jews were deported by the Bulgarian occupation authorities, for the most part to Treblinka on April 5, 1943. In 1952 there were only one or two Jews in the town, and none at the outset of the 21st century. The Jewish cemetery was renovated by volunteers from Israel.

BIBLIOGRAPHY: Marmorstein, in: JQR. 27 (1936/37); Rosanes, Togarmah, 1 (1930), 152–3; 2 (1938), 41, 59; M. Luria, *Study of the Monastir Dialect of Judeo-Spanish* (1930), 1–9; *Jevrejski Kalendar za godinu 5713* (1952), 189–95. **ADD. BIBLIOGRAPHY:** J. Lebl, *Ge'ut va-Shever* (1986; Serbian version, 1990).

[Zvi Loker]

MONASTYRISKA (Pol. **Monasterzyska**), city in Tarnopol district, Ukraine. Until 1772 the city was part of the Red Russia province in the kingdom of Poland, and from 1772 until 1918 in eastern Galicia under Austrian rule. First Jews are recorded in 1625. The Jewish community numbered 2,450 (56 percent of the total population) in 1890 and 2,041 (49 percent) in 1910. They comprised the majority of artisans, and some of them worked in a home-based toy industry organized by relief organizations from Vienna in 1902. Until World War I the community had four synagogues and an elementary school administered by the *Baron de Hirsch Fund. Owing to pogroms by Russian soldiers, Ukrainians, and Petlyura gangs during WWI, the number of Jews decreased to 1,168 (39 percent of the total) in 1921, and 1,488 in 1931). A Jew served as town mayor.

Holocaust Period

By 1939 the number of Jews had grown again and was close to 3,000. During the period of Soviet rule (1939–41), the activities of the Jewish community were stopped. The Jewish social services were also liquidated. The Jews tried to adjust to the new conditions and some of the youth moved to the large cities. With the outbreak of war between Germany and the U.S.S.R. (June 22, 1941), the Ukrainian nationalists began to attack the Jews. These attacks intensified after the Soviets withdrew from the city on July 4. On July 13 hundreds of Jews deported from Hungary were brought to the city. In March 1942 the Jews of Kopyczynce and Koropiec were brought to the city. At the beginning of October 1942 an *Aktion* was carried out and 800 were sent to the *Belzec death camp. At the end of October, the Jews of Monastyriska were transported to Buczacz, where they perished together with the Jews of this city. Jewish life in the town was not revived after the war.

BIBLIOGRAPHY: B. Wasiutyński, *Ludność żydowska w Polsce w wiekach XIX i XX* (1930), 120, 130.

[Aharon Weiss]

MONATSSCHRIFT FUER GESCHICHTE UND WISSENSCHAFT DES JUDENTUMS, learned monthly publication which appeared in Germany for 83 years between 1851 and 1939. The *Monatsschrift* was founded by Z. *Frankel, while he was still rabbi at Dresden, to serve as the organ of what was called the "positive-historical school" in Jewish life and scholarship, which took up a middle position between Reform as represented by A. *Geiger, and Orthodoxy as interpreted by S.R. *Hirsch and A. *Hildesheimer. This type of Judaism, conservative in its approach to Jewish observance and ritual but undogmatic in matters of scholarship and research, was taught at the Jewish Theological Seminary at Breslau, founded in 1854 with Frankel as head; the *Monatsschrift* was intimately though not formally connected with this Seminary and drew its editors and contributors mainly from the ranks of its lecturers and alumni. Frankel remained the editor of the *Monatsschrift* until 1868. In the post-revolutionary years after 1848, Frankel had hoped to stem the growing indifference of the younger generation to Jewish values by spreading the scientific knowledge of the Jewish past, thus reviving Jewish consciousness and self-respect. Frankel hoped, in particular, to influence the younger generation of rabbis who had turned their back on traditional learning. In time, the *Monatsschrift* became the Jewish world's leading journal. Frankel himself wrote about a quarter of the material published under his editorship, dealing with such subjects as the Septuagint, Jewish Hellenism, history of *halakhah*, and religious disputations in antiquity; he also wrote many painstaking book reviews. In 1869 H. *Graetz took over the editorship, assisted from 1882 to 1886 by P.F. Frankl of the Berlin *Hochschule. Graetz himself wrote mainly on Jewish history, Bible, and the language of the Mishnah. In 1887, when Graetz was 70, publication ceased for five years until M. *Brann revived it in 1892, sharing the editorship with D. *Kaufmann until his death in 1899, upon which Brann continued as sole editor. In 1903 the *Monatsschrift* found a new financial backer in the *Gesellschaft zur Foerderung der Wissenschaft des Judentums. At Brann's death in 1920, I. *Heinemann took over until his immigration to Palestine in 1938. The last volume was prepared by L. *Baeck. From Frankel to the last, the *Monatsschrift* steered, more or less, an even course. Articles ranged over the entire gamut of Jewish scholarship. The editors generally tended to avoid systematic theology and purely religious problems. Most of the nearly 500 contributors were rabbis and seminary or university lecturers from Germany, Austria, and Hungary; but there were some from other European countries, the U.S., and Ereẓ Israel. The last volume (83, 1939) of the *Monatsschrift*, a tragic and heroic monument to German-Jewish scholarship in its death throes, was confiscated and destroyed by the Nazis and only a few copies were saved; it was reprinted in 1963. Previously A. Posner had published a general index for volumes 1–75 (1938, repr. 1966, including an update of the last 8 volumes).

BIBLIOGRAPHY: D.S. Loewinger, in: S. Federbush (ed.), *Ḥokhmat Yisrael be-Ma'arav Eiropah*, 1 (1959), 529ff.; K. Wilhelm, in: G. Kisch (ed.), *The Breslau Seminary* (1963), 325ff.; L. Baerwald, *ibid.*,

351ff. **ADD. BIBLIOGRAPHY:** A. Brämer, in: M. Nagel (ed.), *Zwischen Selbstbehauptung und Verfolgung* (2002), 139ff.

[Nahum N. Glatzer]

MONCALVO, small town in Piedmont, northern Italy. The first Jewish settlers in Moncalvo arrived presumably after the expulsions from France, as it was one of the only three communities following the *Apam (= Asti, *Fossano, Moncalvo) liturgy, which was of French origin (see *Liturgy). The first documents attesting to the presence of Jews in Moncalvo date only from the 1570s. When Moncalvo passed to the dukes of Savoy, the situation of the Jews deteriorated. They were confined to a ghetto in 1723 and forbidden to own real estate. At that time 176 Jews lived in Moncalvo. By 1836 there were 233 and in 1860 a new synagogue was dedicated, but toward the end of the 19th century the community declined. On the eve of World War II the community ceased to exist.

BIBLIOGRAPHY: Roth, Italy, index; Milano, Italia, index; Milano, Bibliotheca, index; Foà, in: *Scritti... Ríccardo Bacchi* (1950), 188–201; idem, in: *Israel* (May 12, 1932); Servi, in: *Corriere Israelitico*, 4 (1865/66), 315–6; Disegni, in: *Scritti... Sally Mayer* (1956), 78–81 (Italian section). **ADD. BIBLIOGRAPHY:** D. Colombo, "Il ghetto di Moncalvo e una sua poesia," in: RMI, 36 (1970) 436–41; M.R. Lehman, "*Massa al penei Kehillot Apam u-Sevivoteihem*," in: *Sinai* (101), 1989; P. De Benedetti, *"La gran battaja"; una poesia sul ghetto di Moncalvo, Scritti sull'ebraismo in memoria di Emanuele Menachem Artom* (1996), 137–51.

[Daniel Carpi]

MONCORVO (Torre de Moncorvo), town in N. Portugal, district of Bragança. Early a center of Jewish life, Moncorvo was one of the seven provincial centers with an official rabbinical seat. Its rabbi was authorized by the crown to adjudicate all civil, criminal, and religious questions concerning the Jews of the Bragança district. Once a year the *arraby moor ("chief rabbi") visited Moncorvo to hear appeals. During the Peninsular War of 1803–13, a large number of Conversos – who were referred to simply as Jews by the Old Christians – entered Moncorvo as refugees from the neighboring town of Vila Nova de Fozcoa, where they were persecuted for alleged sympathy with the French. Mutual recriminations between the two towns eventually developed into armed battles. The descendants of these *New Christians were still in Moncorvo in 1917, when the Polish engineer Samuel *Schwarz made contact with the remnants of Portuguese Jewry. In 1927, when A.C. de *Barros Basto proselytized among the Conversos of the Bragança district, a special community was established in Moncorvo.

BIBLIOGRAPHY: Graetz, Hist, 4 (1967), 159; R. Way, *A Geography of Spain and Portugal* (1962), 160; M. Kayserling, *Geschichte der Juden in Portugal* (1867), 13; N. Slouschz, *Ha-Anusim be-Portugal* (1932), 68–69.

MOND (Melchett), British family of chemists and industrialists, of German origin. Ludwig Mond (1839–1909) was born in Cassel, Germany. In 1859, while working at a small soda works, he patented a method for the recovery of the sulfur otherwise wasted in the process. Mond went to England where he tried to sell his patent. His process was not economical under British conditions, however, and he left for Holland. In 1867 Mond returned to England where he met Ernest Solvay (1838–1922), a Belgian chemist who had devised a process for making soda based on the use of ammonia. Mond put this process into operation when he joined Sir John Brunner (1842–1919) in founding the firm of Brunner, Mond and Company in 1873. In 1884 he developed a new process for the recovery of nickel and formed the Mond Nickel Company, which is still in operation. He was a noted art collector and most of his paintings were donated to the National Gallery in London. Of his two sons, the elder, Sir Robert Ludwig Mond (1867–1938), a scientist in his own right, was also a notable archaeologist, associated with the discovery of the *Elephantine papyri, and treasurer of the Palestine Exploration Fund. He was vice president of the Friends of the *Hebrew University and leader of the British Empire's anti-Nazi boycott.

The younger son, Alfred Moritz Mond (1868–1930), later the first Baron Melchett, entered his father's firm. During his lifetime Brunner, Mond and Co. greatly expanded and, after merging with other companies, became Imperial Chemical Industries (ICI) in 1926. Mond entered Parliament as a Liberal in 1906. He was made commissioner of works in the cabinet of Lloyd George (1916–21) and later became minister of health (1921–22). In 1924 Mond opened a debate in Parliament on the respective merits of the capitalist system and socialism, and his address was considered an outstanding defense of private enterprise. In 1926, in disagreement over land policy, he transferred his allegiance to the Conservative Party. He initiated a conference between leaders of commerce and industry on the one hand, and the workers organized in the Trades Union Congress headed by Sir Ben Turner on the other (1928). Out of this conference emerged the Mond-Turner agreement for industrial relations. In the same year he was raised to the peerage, as Baron Melchett.

Alfred Mond was not brought up as a Jew. His sole connection with Judaism in the earlier stage of his public life was that he helped to support the synagogue of Swansea, his parliamentary constituency, in order to present a more favorable picture there of the Jews and Judaism. Nevertheless, he was the butt of antisemitic attacks, and in consequence was won over to Zionism after the Balfour Declaration. He then became a dedicated Zionist and contributor to Zionist causes. Mond was one of the founders of the enlarged Jewish *Agency in 1929 and the chairman of its council. He acquired an estate in Ereẓ Israel in Migdal overlooking the Sea of Galilee, and a township in central Israel, Tel Mond, bears his name. Alfred Mond was married to a non-Jew and his two children, Eva Violet (1895–1973), who married the second Marquis of *Reading, and Henry (1898–1949), second Baron Melchett, were brought up in the Christian faith but converted to Judaism after the rise of Hitler. Lady Reading was an active Zionist and president of the British section of the *World Jewish Congress. Henry, also an ardent Zionist, succeeded his father as chairman of the council of the Jewish Agency and was president of the *World Union of Maccabi. Henry's son, Julian Edward Alfred (1925–1973), third Baron Melchett, was appointed chairman of the nationalized steel industry in 1967.

BIBLIOGRAPHY: H.H. Bolitho, *Alfred Mond, First Lord Melchett* (1933); J.M. Cohen, *Life of Ludwig Mond* (1956); P. Emden, *Jews of Britain* (1943), index; W.J. Reader, *Imperial Chemical Industries; A History*, vol. 1 *The Forerunners* (1970). **ADD. BIBLIOGRAPHY:** J.R. Lischka, *Ludwig Mond and the British Alkali Industry*, 1985; J. Goodman, *The Mond Legacy*, 1982.

[Moshe Rosetti]

MOND, BERNHARD STANISLAW (1887–1944), Polish general. Born in Stanislav, Galicia, he fought in the Austro-Hungarian army during World War I. In 1916 he was taken prisoner by the Russians and released in February 1918 following the peace of Brest-Litovsk. At the end of World War I Mond joined the army of newly independent Poland and fought in the defense of Lvov against the invading Ukrainian forces. In 1920 he commanded an infantry regiment against the Bolsheviks in Russia. Subsequently, Mond became commander of Vilna. At the outbreak of World War II, he commanded an army corps with the rank of major-general. After the fall of Poland Mond was taken prisoner by the Germans and died in a prisoner-of-war camp.

MONDA (Moscovici), **VIRGILIU** (1898–1991), Romanian novelist. Beginning as a poet in 1923, Monda soon changed to prose and published novels reflecting his interests as a practicing physician. In his works he displayed great ingenuity and a sense of atmosphere. Monda's novels include *Urechea lui Dionys* ("The Ear of Dionysius," 1934), *Hora paiatelor* ("Dance of the Clowns," 1935), *Trubendal* (1946), and *Statuia* ("The Statue," 1969).

MONDAY AND THURSDAY (in Heb. *Sheni va-Ḥamishi*, "the second and fifth [day of the week]"), those days on which the liturgy of the morning service includes additional penitential and supplicatory prayers (among them the long *Taḥanun). On these days, in ancient times, villagers came to town for marketing and attending law courts. Pious Jews also fast on Monday, Thursday, and again on the Monday following the first Sabbath of the new month after *Passover and *Sukkot. These three days are known as *"Behab"* (see *Fast Days, and *Shovavim Tat). Some ultra-pietists make voluntary fasts every week on these days. The morning service on Mondays and Thursdays also includes a reading from the Pentateuch. Three persons are called up to the reading, but only the first part of the weekly portion of the following Sabbath is covered in the reading (see *Torah, Reading of).

BIBLIOGRAPHY: Elbogen, Gottesdienst, 76–77, 155–7, 207–25; Eisenstein, Dinim, 428.

MONDOLFO, RODOLFO (1877–1976), Italian historian of philosophy. Born in Senigalia, Mondolfo began teaching at Padua (1904). He was appointed professor at Turin in 1910, and at Bologna in 1913. Because of the racial laws he lost his post in 1938 (reinstated 1944), and moved to Argentina where he was professor at Córdoba (1940) and Tucumán (1948). Mondolfo's first studies were on psychology in the 17th and 18th centuries. Next he turned to studies of Hobbes, Helvétius, and Rousseau. After his work on Lassalle (*La filosofia della storia di Ferdinand Lassalle*, 1909), Engels (*Il materialisma storico di Federico Engels*, 1912), Feuerbach and Marx (*Feuerbach e Marx*, 1919), he devoted himself to the study of Marxism, emphasizing the activistic, humanistic side as opposed to the materialistic one, as in *Sulle orme di Marx* (1919, 1948[4]) and *Intorno a Gramsci e alla filosofia della prassi* (1955). After the rise of Mussolini and the suppression of his *Biblioteca di studi sociali* in 1925, he turned to Greek philosophy and made many original contributions, especially in *L'Infinito nel pensiero dei Greci* (1934), his edition of Zeller (*La filosofia dei Greci*, 2 vols, 1932–38), and *Problemi del pensiero antico* (1936, 1961[3]). In Argentina he wrote other works on Greek thought, one on Bruno, Galileo, and Campanella, and *Problemas y métodos de la investigación en historia de la filosofia* (1949).

BIBLIOGRAPHY: G. Morra, in: *Enciclopedia filosofia*, 3 (1957), 677–8, incl. bibl.; *Enciclopedia Italiana*, appendix, 2 (1949), s.v. *R. Mondolfo; R. Mondolfo,, 1877–1976: In Memoriam* / Amigos de Rodolfo Mondolfo (1977).

[Richard H. Popkin]

MONDZAIN, SIMON (1890–1979), French painter. Born in Lublin, Poland, Mondzain came to Paris in 1909. He painted figures of men and women with musical instruments, as well as portraits, interiors and still lifes, but became known largely through his sensitive studies of villages in France, Algiers, and Morocco. His style was post-impressionist, with elements of expressionism.

MONEY CHANGERS. Money changing was very common in the Roman Near East, where there was a proliferation of currency systems and standards. In Palestine, as in Egypt, each district had its *basilikai trapezai* ("royal bank") retained from Hellenistic times (Jos., Life 38), and probably each village had its own money changer (cf. Sif. Deut., 306).

In the period of the Second Temple vast numbers of Jews streamed to Palestine and Jerusalem "out or every nation under heaven" (Acts 2:5), taking with them considerable sums of money in foreign currencies. This is referred to in the famous instance of Jesus' driving the money changers out of the Temple (Matt. 21:12). Not only did these foreign coins have to be changed but also ordinary deposits were often handed over to the Temple authorities for safe deposit in the Temple treasury (Jos., Wars 6:281–2). Thus Jerusalem became a sort of central bourse and exchange mart, and the Temple vaults served as "safe deposits" in which every type of coin was represented (TJ, Ma'as. Sh. 1:2, 52d, and parallels). The business of money exchange was carried out by the *shulḥani* ("exchange banker"), who would change foreign coins into local currency and vice versa (Tosef., Shek. 2:13; Matt. 21:12). People coming from distant countries would bring their money in large denominations rather than in cumbersome small coins. The provision of small change was a further function of the *shulḥani* (cf. Sif. Deut., 306; Ma'as Sh., 2:9). For both of these kinds of transactions the *shulḥani* charged a small fee (agio), called in rabbinic literature a *kolbon* (a word of doubtful etymology but perhaps from the Greek κόλλυβος "small coin"; TJ, Shek. 1:6, 46b). This premium seems to have varied from 4 percent to 8 percent (Shek. 1:6, et al.). The *shulḥani* served also as a banker, and would receive money on deposit for investment and pay out an interest at a fixed rate (Matt. 25:27), although this was contrary to Jewish law (see below; *Moneylending).

Thus the *shulḥani* fulfilled three major functions: (a) foreign exchange, (b) the changing of large denominations into small ones, and vice versa, and (c) banking. Three terms for "money-changer" are found in the New Testament: (a) *kermatistēs* (John 2:14), (b) *kollybistēs* (Matt. 21:12), and (c) *trapezitēs* (literally, *shulḥani*; Matt. 25:27, et al.) It seems probable that these three terms correspond to the three functions of the *shulḥani* outlined above. Thus *kermatistēs*, from *kermatizō*. "to cut small," is one who gives small change; *kollybistēs*, from *kollybos*, changed foreign currency; while the *trapezitēs* was a banker (from *trapeza*, "table").

The *shulḥanim* in Jerusalem used to set up their "tables" in the outer court of the Temple for the convenience of the numerous worshipers, especially those from foreign countries (Matt. 21:12–13). Excavations around the Temple walls have uncovered stores or kiosks, some of which, it has been surmised, were occupied by money changers. The Mishnah states that on the 15th of Adar, every year, "tables" were set up in the provinces (or in Jerusalem) for the collection of the statutory annual half-shekel, and on the 25th of Adar they were set up in the Temple itself (Shek. 1:3). The activity of the Jewish banker, *shulḥani*, was of a closely defined nature, as his transactions had to be in accordance with the biblical prohibition against taking interest (*ribit*). The Talmud records much information relating to his activities. An additional and interesting feature of his business was the payment on request of sums deposited with him for that purpose (BM 9:12).

See also: Ṣarrāf.

BIBLIOGRAPHY: F. Heichelheim, in: T. Frank, *An Economic Survey of Ancient Rome*, 4 (1938), 224–7, 247–8, 256–7 (bibl.); F. Madden, in: *Numismatic Chronicle* (1876), 290–7; A. Gulak, in: *Tarbiz*, 2 (1931), 154–71. **ADD. BIBLIOGRAPHY:** D. Sperber, *Roman Palestine, 200–400. Money and Prices* (1974).

[Daniel Sperber]

MONEYLENDING.

The Religious Context

BIBLICAL PERIOD. Deuteronomy 23:20–21 states: "You shall not lend on interest to your brother, interest of food or money or anything on which interest can be charged. You may charge interest to a foreigner, but not to your brother that the Lord, your God, may bless you in all you put your hand to in the land into which you are going, to possess it." This text has become the subject of much discussion and controversy for nearly two millennia. Within the framework of the so-called Book of the Covenant, another law on moneylending is to be found, in Exodus 23:24: "If you lend money to my people, to the poor with you, you shall not act toward him like a creditor. You must not lay interest [*neshekh*] upon him." In this verse, *nosheh* ("creditor") is philologically and semantically equivalent to the Assyrian *rašu* ("creditor"), the professional moneylender. A third pentateuchal law on interest-bearing loans occurs in Leviticus 25:35–38, in a context usually referred to as the Holiness Code: "If your brother has become poor and cannot support himself with you, you shall assist him [as] a resident alien [*ger ve-toshav*], and he shall live with you. You shall not give him your money on interest [*be-neshekh*], nor give him your food for increase [*be-marbit*]. I am the Lord, your God, who brought you forth out of the land of Egypt, to give you the land of Canaan, to be your God." Usually the difference between *neshekh* and *tarbit* or *marbit* is explained as a difference between interest on capital and interest on food. The passage in Deuteronomy, however, also refers to interest on food (*neshekh okhel*) and it is possible that the two codes employ a slightly different terminology.

Many attempts have been made to answer questions on the literary form and the dates of these pentateuchal laws, but during the last decades detailed study of the various Ancient Near Eastern codes from the 19th to the 12th centuries B.C.E. has enabled scholars to substantiate their opinions on the *Sitz im Leben* of the Hebrew law collections more accurately than hitherto possible. The Book of the Covenant is generally considered the oldest of the pentateuchal codes, because of the social and economic structure it presupposes. No urban life or king is referred to, and there is no organized state or priesthood. There is, moreover, ethnological evidence of many similarly primitive units, among whom all loans of money and food were given free of interest, usually up to the time of the next harvest when they could be paid back by the debtor. Such legislation could not, of course, apply to the alien (*nokhri*), who was not a permanent resident.

In comparison, there are some similarities but also major differences between the pentateuchal law codes and their Ancient Near Eastern antecedents. The latter mirror a society much more fully developed than that of the still half-sedentary Hebrews. Thus, the *tamkarum* appears as a professional moneylender in various sections of the Code of Hammurapi, where rates of interest are specified for food as well as for money loans. Even in relatively late strata of the Bible, it is the Canaanite rather than the Israelite or the Hebrew, who is represented as the merchant or the trader. Had the nucleus of the Hebrew Codes been compiled at the time of the monarchy, they would have reflected quite different socio-economic conditions. Their literary form is of equal importance. In his *Urspruenge des israelitischen Rechts* (1934), 69ff., A. Alt distinguishes between casuistic law, characteristic of the Ancient Near Eastern codes, and apodictic law, more frequently, although by no means exclusively, found in comparable Israelitic source material. Exodus 22:24 is a mixture of both. The casuistic beginning, "If you lend money to my people…," which would logically be followed by a reference to the rate of interest or to the punishment to be meted out to a defaulting debtor, concludes apodictically with: "You shall not act as a creditor."

The Holiness and the Deuteronomic Codes are normally assigned to a much later date than that of the Book of the Covenant. The problem of their editing and ultimate incorporation into the Pentateuch is a difficult one, but as far as the laws on interest are concerned, all of them have elements in common, which stress, directly or indirectly, a special covenant between God and Israel and the consequent obligations of brotherhood between the members of the community. Just as biblical history with its predominantly theological tendencies has been described as *Heilsgeschichte*, much of biblical law may be classified as *Heilsgesetz*, addressing itself to the pre-state sacred institution of the 12 tribes. Moreover, Ancient Near Eastern codes do not claim divine inspiration, while all Hebrew laws are presented as having been revealed by God to Moses, even if, as in the case of the prohibitions against taking interest from a brother, no guidance is given as to judicial procedures against ruthless exploitation of the poor. The few other passages in the Bible which refer to money-lending confirm the impression that the relevant pentateuchal ordinances were interpreted by the prophets, psalmists, wisdom-writers, and chroniclers more as moral exhortations than as laws (cf. Hab. 2:6; Ezek. 18; Ps. 15:5; Prov. 28:8; II Kings 4:1–2; and Neh. 5:1–11; for apocryphal and pseudepigraphical literature, see Ecclus. 20:15;29 and IV Macc. 2:8). Neither indignation nor pious hopes could replace the jurisdiction of established courts.

Documentary evidence of the nonobservance of these pentateuchal admonitions comes only from the Diaspora, but affords an even clearer picture of prevailing conditions. Thus, the Aramaic Papyri show that the Jews of the military colony in Elephantine lent each other money on interest at the rate of 60 percent per annum in the fifth century (cf. Cowley, Aramaic nos. 10 and 11). In the Tebtunis Papyri, numbers 815, 817, and 818, loans at interest between Jews are also referred to. These documents belong to the third and second centuries respectively, and reflect typical Hellenistic usage in their formulation (cf. Tcherikover, Corpus, 1 (1957)). In the talmudic period such documents would be invalid. Aristotle had expressed contempt for the taking of interest in a well-known utterance in his *Ethics* (4:3), basing his opinion on the nature of money which is in itself not subject to physical growth. In addition, on several occasions during the last few pre-Christian centuries, popular resentment against impoverishment through usury forced Greek and Roman legislators to forbid the taking of interest altogether, although enactments of this sort did not remain in force for long. Among Jewish Hellenistic writers, Philo appears to have been the first to add his own comment to Deuteronomy 23:20, by extending the prohibition about taking interest from the brother to anyone of the same citizenship (*astos*), or nation (*homofulos*) in *De Virtutibus*, 82. He is, however, not quite consistent and keeps himself closer to the biblical text in *De Specialibus Legibus* (II, 73ff. and 122).

THE TALMUDIC PERIOD. After the destruction of the Temple, halakhists and aggadists determined the development of Jewish religious law proper, at least until the 17th century. The tannaitic Midrash *Sifrei Deuteronomy* 23:20f. understands *la-nokhri tashikh* as a positive commandment; i.e., you shall lend at interest to a foreigner. Although this is possible on philological grounds, heavy oppression under Roman rule in the first part of the second century may have led to such an interpretation, particularly since R. Akiva was closely connected with the revolt of Bar Kokhba and with the editing of the *Sifrei*. The contemporary *Mekhilta of R. Ishmael* offers a different explanation on the related passage in Exodus 22:24. Interest-free money should be lent to Jews and gentiles alike, although a Jew should be given preference. In addition, one commentator states that it is only toward the poor that one should not act as a professional moneylender, but one may do so toward the rich. From the third century onward, the prohibition against taking interest had been accepted as applicable to every Jew, rich or poor. The *Mekhilta* on Exodus 22:24, ends with a homiletic statement by R. Meir: "He who lends on interest… has no share in Him who decreed against taking interest." Similar denunciations occur frequently in halakhic and aggadic Midrashim, in Mishnah, Tosefta, *baraita*, and the Babylonian and Jerusalem Talmuds. Transgressors against the ever growing injunctions are called robbers and murderers. They are likened to those who rear pigs, described as denying the fundamental tenets of the Jewish faith and declared to be unfit as witnesses. The frequency of such utterances implies the frequency of the offenses. It is to be stressed, however, against apologetic tendencies that still prevail in the relevant literature, that views of this kind refer to inter-Jewish transactions only, unless the gentile is explicitly included in the prohibition. The expression "even interest from a non-Jew" (*afillu ribbit de-goi*) implies that the difference between them is still clearly felt.

As to inter-Jewish transactions, discussions continue as to whether paid interest, fixed or unfixed, can be taken back for the debtor by the judges. Also proposed are the relinquishment of the principal and the rescinding of written contracts or *shetarot* on which interest was specified. The Mishnah (BM 5:6) says quite plainly that one may lend to and borrow from gentiles at interest. In the course of the debate in the *Gemara* (ad loc.) R. Naḥman transmits Rav Huna's objection to taking interest from anybody, but it is, apparently again for apologetic reasons, generally overlooked that his view is challenged by Rava on the basis of the Deuteronomic law and the Mishnah which precedes the *Gemara*. R. Ḥiyya replies that money may only be lent on interest to the non-Jew, as far as it is necessary for the sustenance of the Jew (*bi-khedei ḥayyav*). Ravina maintains that the reason for this restriction is based on religious self-protection. The lender should reduce his contact with the alien to a minimum, lest he learn from the debtor's deeds (*shema yilmad mi-ma'asav*; see also Rashi on Mak. 24a, s.v. *afillu le-akkum*). The Jewish scholar, on the other hand, is allowed to take interest from non-Jews, even where there is no economic necessity, because he would not be influenced by the practices of the latter.

There is one further aspect regarding money-lending at interest in talmudic literature which calls for attention – the regulations against the employment of a non-Jewish intermediary, a device sometimes resorted to in order to make illegal inter-Jewish loan transactions possible. A number of tannaitic traditions have a bearing on the subject (cf. BM 71bf. and TJ, BM 10c; Tos., BM 5:15). This convention has a prehistory in Roman law. Livy mentions that at the beginning of the second century B.C.E., Roman creditors had found a device (*fraus*) for collecting interest by transferring the ownership of accounts to citizens of allied states, who thus became the real or fictitious lenders without being subject to internal Roman legislation (ed. by E.T. Sage (1935), 10:18). That such evasive tactics were current among Jews of the talmudic period is evident not only from the various *halakhot*, but also from the following homiletic statement in *Bava Mezia* 61b: "Why did the All-Merciful mention the Exodus from Egypt in connection with the law on interest?… The Holy One, blessed be He, answered: 'I, who distinguished between the firstborn and those who were not firstborn in Egypt, shall in future punish him who hangs his money on a gentile and lends it on interest to a Jew.'"

THE GEONIC PERIOD. This period lasted from about the seventh to the 11th centuries. During that time, the main autonomous center of Jewish life was in Babylonia, although the decisions of the *geonim* were considered binding in the remotest communities of Europe and Africa. The Jews were active as artisans, builders, merchants, and as experts in agriculture and horticulture in many parts of the new Islamic world. Yet the Koran (4:160) is the first source to accuse them of usury. Contemporary halakhic compendia offer little original material on the subject. Only one responsum of the ninth century, by Amram Gaon (*Sha'arei Ẓedek*, 1792, p. 40a), forbids any money-lending on interest, permitting only such as would come about in a credit transaction involving the exchange of money and fruit. He adds that Muslims, too, allow this according to their law. The strong anti-usury legislation of Islam as well as the almost unrestricted professional facilities then open to Jews prompted him to be stricter than the traditional rulings on Jewish-gentile money transactions. In an anonymous responsum of the tenth century, biblical and talmudic ordinances are stressed again, and it is left to the discretion of the pious to refrain from money-lending altogether.

THE EARLY RABBINIC PERIOD. The center of Jewish life shifted toward Europe. The academies of Babylonia were gradually replaced by famous schools in France, Germany, and Spain. Monographs on the various European countries contain detailed accounts of the general and specific in their history. Two factors, however, stand out: growing anti-Jewish legislation and the development of the feudal system with its demand for a Christian oath on the acquisition of land. As a result, Jews were increasingly cut off from landownership. Yet even in countries like Spain and Italy, where Jewish urbanization took place less rapidly than in England and Germany, the Jews themselves no longer desired close contact with the soil, although they complained more and more about the shrinking opportunities to support themselves. An often quoted responsum by the French 11th-century scholar, Joseph b. Samuel Tov Elem *Bonfils, illustrates the change. Leah, the questioner, expresses dissatisfaction with the fact that taxes for which the community was responsible to the government were evenly distributed among the Jewish owners of fields and among merchants and traders. She is assessed for the ground she holds and for the crops it yields. In addition, the rulers of the land take their share from it. In contrast, money lent on interest is profitable, because the pledge remains in the hand of the creditor, and the principal increases without effort or expense. Joseph Tov Elem agrees with Leah's arguments against those who wish to assess her (cf. Responsa of Meir of Rothenburg, 1895, no. 941). Generally it must be said that early medieval rabbinic legislation cleared the path for a great variety of gentile-Jewish and inter-Jewish money transactions. Especially the authority of Jacob b. Meir Tam, Rashi's grandson, carried great weight with his contemporaries and successors. He summarizes the reasons for a number of his decisions in the following way: "Today people usually lend money on interest to gentiles… because we have to pay taxes to the king and princes and everything serves to sustain ourselves [*kedei ḥayyenu*]. We live among the nations and it is impossible for us to earn a living unless we deal with them. It is, therefore, no more forbidden to lend at interest because 'one might learn from their deeds' than it is to engage in any other business" (cf., e.g., Tos., BM 70b, 71b and Av. Zar. 2a).

Menahem b. Solomon Meiri, an eminent 13th-century scholar, gives an account of the position in Provence: "In our days nobody cares about refraining from business dealings with and loans to gentiles, even on their festivals – not a *Gaon*, not a rabbi, not a scholar, not a pupil, not a *ḥasid* ["pious man"], and not one who pretends to be a *ḥasid*. All these laws refer only to idolators and their images, but all transactions with Christians are perfectly legal." Meiri coined a special phrase for this group: "nations who are restrained by the paths of their religion" (cf. J. Katz, in: *Zion*, 18 (1953), 18ff.). He thus differs implicitly or explicitly, with most of his predecessors, including Maimonides. Only the Ḥasidei Ashkenaz, German-Jewish pietists and some Spanish kabbalists of the beginning of the 13th century, viewed the new development with anxiety and disfavor. According to them, interest should not be charged to gentiles if a living could be made from the fields, although they no longer ventured to state this in terms of a legal prohibition. Contemporary Jewish commentators on the Bible follow the same distinctions as halakhic literature. In addition, they reflect full awareness of Christian polemics against the ever increasing number of Jewish moneylenders.

David *Kimḥi of Narbonne says the following about Psalms 15:5: "…the Hebrew must not overreach or rob the alien or steal from him, but interest which he takes by full agreement [with a non-Jewish lender] is permitted… If the gentile is kind to the Jew, the Jew must certainly be kind and good to him…" He adds explicitly that his views should serve as an answer to those Christians who maintain that David did not distinguish between the Israelite and the gentile.

Meir b. Simeon's only partly edited manuscript (Parma 2749) *Milḥemet Mitzvah* ("Obligatory War") contains by far the richest source material on Jewish-gentile moneylending transactions. His attempts to defend old and established practices show greater knowledge of former privileges granted by popes, emperors, and feudal lords than that of any of his predecessors, and he makes the widest possible and often ingenious use of practically all biblical and talmudic data on the subject. One or two generations older than David Kimḥi and also from Narbonne, he had frequent discussions with the lower and higher clergy, including two archbishops, the second of whom was probably Guido Fulcodi, who later became Pope Clement IV.

It was on this occasion that Meir was confronted with the same accusations about gentile disadvantages in Jewish law as those which had been made in the famous Paris disputation in 1240 at the palace of Louis IX. No Latin record of his disputation appears to be extant, and it is doubtful whether he could have said all he wrote down in the diary of his public activities. The whole historical background of his time is unfolded in his work – anti-Jewish legislation, persecutions, expulsions, and his able and often successful efforts to counter them. His sharp criticism of the release of interest and sometimes even of the principal, owed to Jews by the Crusaders, is of special significance. Fearless defense and daring attack are often juxtaposed. Thus, Joseph b. Nathan ha-Mekanne *Official, a contemporary and fellow-citizen of Meir b. Simeon, refutes the attacks against Jewish money-lending with the by now usual arguments, and subsequently adds: "You lend money at high rates… of 100%… and take reward for delayed payment" (Z. Kahn, in: *Birkhat Avraham… Berliner* (1903), 89).

Jewish moneylenders in England acted, as far as one can judge from their documents, in exactly the same way as those on the continent – i.e., in accordance with the ordinances of the sages (*ke-tikkun ḥakhamin*), even if there are certain peculiarities which seem to be influenced by non-Jewish legal practice. Thus, *ribbit* ("interest"), unless used in connection with *ribbit al yedei goi* ("inter-Jewish interest charges, made possible through a gentile proxy"), occurs only four out of about 30 times in M.D. Davis' *Hebrew Deeds* (1888). Instead of *ribbit, shevaḥ* ("profit") is used. In some inter-gentile promissory notes, too, the expression *lucrum* ("gain") is found for *fenus* ("usury"). There is also the sudden emergence of the formula "if the stipulated time for repayment of the loan is over" (*im ya'avor zeman*) in Hebrew *shetarot* ("promissory notes" see *Shetar) of English provenance. According to talmudic law, there is no justification for this, but contemporary regulations of civil and canon law had adopted the Roman concepts of *lucrum cessans* and *damnum emergens*. They may well have found their way into inter-Jewish transactions, although still under the proviso that creditor A allow creditor B to borrow from a gentile, to indemnify the lender against damage or loss of gain.

In Spain, too, similar practices, perhaps even without the gentile intermediary, seem to have become customary during the 13th century, as is known from a responsum by Solomon b. Abraham Adret (ed. Hanau, 1600, 172b). He declares such convention to be forbidden, but adds that, strictly speaking, we have in this case to deal with a penalty (*kenas*) and not with interest. Officially, at least, Max Weber's distinction between *Binnen* and *Aussen-Moral* retained its validity in talmudic and rabbinic law. Similar Christian differentiations between the "brother" and the "other" can be traced back to the Church Father Ambrose of the fourth century. According to him, the Jew must be loaded with such a burden of usury that by the very punishment of the charges imposed upon him, he is compelled to move more quickly toward righteousness (*De Tobia*, 1, Migne, P.L. 14 (1845), 799; and T.P. Mc-Laughlin, *Medieval Studies*, 1 (1939), 92, 137).

THE LATE RABBINIC PERIOD. The Jewish analogue of this position was expressed by the 14th-century French philosopher and exegete, *Levi b. Gershom, who also holds that it is a positive commandment to lend money to an alien on interest, "if he needs it…, because one should not benefit an idolator… and cause him as much damage as possible without deviating from righteousness," i.e., without demanding from him exorbitant rates of interest (see his commentary on Deut. 23:21). Such sentiments are extreme, though not isolated (cf. R. Tam on BM 70b and Maimonides' uncensored comment on Av. Zar. chs. 3 and 4). Sometimes the passion of the spirit gave way to the demands of economic necessity, and periods of quasi-normal business relationships between believers and non-believers interrupted the cold or actual war between them. More often the force of faith, never quite unconnected with the relatively high proportion of Jewish moneylenders, broke through and led to their persecution and expulsion. An ultimate judgment on the priority of powers which determine political and ideological reality remains difficult, if not impossible. The situation differed from country to country, from province to province, and even from town to town. Yet an analysis of the uneven and widely dispersed Jewish and Christian source material, ranging from the 14th to the 17th centuries, reveals an astounding development from unyielding medieval thought patterns to their integration with new economic theories, and leads almost to a breakdown of denominational barriers.

In his *Ikkarim*, the Spanish philosopher Joseph *Albo declares that the "brother" in the Deuteronomic law refers to everyone who is not an idolator. Interest is, therefore, only to be taken from one who belongs to the "seven nations of old" – for instance, from an Amorite or Amalekite: "If it is permitted to take his life, surely one may take his property" (*Im gufo mut-*

tar mamono kol she-ken; ed. Husik, 3 (1946), 237). Albo's words are an almost literal translation of Ambrose's "*ubi enim jus est belli, ibi est usurae*" (cf. also Plato's Laws, 10:909). In a position of defense vis-à-vis the archbishop of Narbonne, Meir b. Simeon had advanced a similar argument. Albo's statement is not part of the public disputation in Tortosa (1413) in which he was one of the Jewish spokesmen, but a record of another encounter with a Christian opponent. It is clear, however, that he did not refer to current halakhic practices, although some talmudic proof texts can be found in their support. Other Jewish writings, not concerned with interdenominational altercations, do not question the legality of charging interest from gentiles. Thus, Joseph Colon, who came from France and held a distinguished position in the Italian rabbinate during the second part of the 15th century, states casually that the Jews of both countries hardly engaged in any other business (Resp. Maharik 118, 132). Abraham b. Mordecai Farissol (1451–1526) confirms Colon's assessment of circumstances prevailing in Italy. Conditions of this kind were bound to bring about irregularities, but they were not restricted to Jews. Early propaganda of the Franciscans was, in fact, not specifically directed against the Jews. *Hebraei et Christiani usurarii* were the target of Bernardino da Feltre.

The establishment of Jewish loan banks was subject to a license of the papal administration or of the local rulers or of both. The stipulations of these *condotte* varied from time to time and from place to place. They were often changed unexpectedly, and as a result the insecurity of the Jewish moneylender increased, however much he might have profited from an occasional boom. Matters came to a climax through the propaganda for the establishment of Christian loan-banks, the *montes pietatis*, which were originally meant to work on a nonprofit basis. Particularly during the Lenten period "the friars [*ha-doreshim*] are a strap of castigation for Israel and preach every day to destroy us… Their hand is heavy upon us… and the situation reaches a point when both body and property are endangered" (Colon, ed. princeps, no. 192).

Isaac Abrabanel's view on interest-bearing loans to gentiles is laid down in his commentary on Deuteronomy 23:21, and forms part of his elaborate exegesis of the whole book, which was completed in Monopoli in 1496 and published in uncensored form in Sabbioneta in 1551. He expounded his theories "before Christian scholars and the masters of the land." The first three of his arguments offer nothing new; only the fourth is straightforward and assailable on philological and historical grounds. At the same time, it foreshadows the general development toward capitalism, so characteristic of the 16th century: "There is nothing unworthy about interest… because it is proper that people should make profit out of their money, wine, and corn, and if someone wants money from someone else… why should a farmer… who received wheat to sow his field not give the lender 10% if he is successful, as he usually should be? This is an ordinary business transaction and correct…. Interest-free loans should only be given to the coreligionist, to whom we owe special kindness." Abrabanel sums up with an assurance to his readers that what he had said in the first three paragraphs was only meant "to promote peace. What a Jew should really believe is laid down in the tradition of the sages."

Shortly before the completion of Abrabanel's commentary on Deuteronomy, Abraham b. Mordecai Farissol had a disputation in Ferrara at the famous Palace of Ercole d'Este I, again attended by many prominent people (cf. *Magen Avraham*, ch. 73, ed. by D.S. Loewinger in: HHY, 12 (1928), 290ff.). Some of Farissol's answers also represent a definite opposition to medieval economic concepts. His formulations might well be borrowed from the views of contemporary civil lawyers. In contrast to the opinion of the canonists and of Levi b. Gershom who, like Aristotle, considered money as barren metal, a distinction is now drawn between primitive and advanced society: "After society had expanded and people began to be distinguished from one another by their views… there followed a new Nature and another Order. The custom of giving another person something for nothing ceased unless the person was poor. Thus, the law has developed to pay rent for houses… and to make loans… All comes for a price… Sometimes credit is even more important than lending an animal or a house. Hence… it is appropriate to give some compensation for a loan. A proof for this argument is that even the *ba'alei ha-datot* [canonists] have agreed that one may pay up to 5% for the lending of money." Farissol seems to refer especially to the *montes pietatis*, which were forced to charge a small amount for the maintenance of their administration. As to the rates of interest charged, "one need not ponder over them, because they are agreed upon by the communities who require money from the Jews. They fluctuate according… to the availability or scarcity of silver and gold and the demand for it."

In 1588 the physician David de Pomis published his *De Medico Hebraeo Enarratio Apologetica*, in which he set himself the task of putting on record the devoted services of distinguished Jewish doctors in the past. The book, written in Latin, also contains his views on money-lending to gentiles. His effusive flattery about the relationship between Christianity and Judaism makes it unnecessary to refer to the first part of his arguments. Only in the last paragraph of the relevant section does he return to the practical aspects of the problem: "If the Jews do sometimes take interest from Christians, it can either be maintained that they abuse the law or…" and here his statements are almost identical with those of Farissol, "… their transactions represent an official agreement between the parties concerned… A Jew could effect the same transaction with another Jew according to recent rabbinic authorities." One form is technically called *tarsha* and the other *hetter iska* (cf. Sh. Ar., YD 167, 177). Both concessions represent developments dictated by the general change of economic conditions. In practice, de Pomis' labored defense came late. It was Calvin who challenged the Deuteronomic differentiation between the "brother" and the "alien" on principle. According to him, interest is forbidden only insofar as it is contrary to equity and charity. Otherwise, "*nous sommes frères sans aucune distinc-*

tion." The enunciation of his program became the decisive formula for the new spirit of capitalism.

FROM OTHERHOOD TO BROTHERHOOD? From the 17th century onward, the collapse of the traditional Christian exegesis of Deuteronomy 23 is apparent in Europe and in the U.S. On the Jewish side, too, responsa on the subject become less frequent; even the records of the Council of the Four Lands have relatively little to say on the matter. The *hetter iska* (see *Usury) had opened the path to a mercantilistic interpretation of talmudic law. Nevertheless, on the readmission of the Jews to England, Manasseh Ben Israel, in his *Humble Address to His Highness the Lord Protector of the Commonwealth of England*, did not deem it necessary to revoke the ancient distinction: "For to lay out the money without any profit was commanded only toward their brethren of the same nation of the Jews, but not to any other nation" (cf. B.N. Nelson, *Idea of Usury* (1949), 73–109). In spite of occasional regressions, a gradual improvement of the position of the Jews in Western Europe became noticeable. Money-lending still remained one of their main occupations, but they also traded, sometimes simultaneously, in all kinds of merchandise, or they earned their living as craftsmen and artisans. Above all, there was the ascendancy of the Court Jew who, in spite of his fluctuating fortunes, played an important part in the economic administration of the estate of many a duke and king in peace and war (cf. H. Schnee, *Die Hoffinanz und der moderne Staat*, 6 vols., 1953–67). The Age of Reason further contributed to the disappearance of barriers between the various denominations. Although Leopold I expelled the Jews from Vienna and Lower Austria in 1670, Joseph II issued his *Toleranzpatent* only about 100 years later.

In 1807, the ecclesiastical and lay representatives of French, Italian, and German Jewry assembled in Paris to attend a meeting that had been convened by Napoleon. Bearing the proud title, "Grand Sanhedrin," it concluded a development of 2,000 years and to many of those who had come seemed to open a new era. Two of the 12 questions they were asked concerned the problem of inter-Jewish and Jewish-gentile loan transactions. Although eminent rabbinic scholars of personal integrity were present, the answers, *Décisions Doctrinales* or, in their Hebrew version, *takkanot*, reveal neither any depth of historical understanding nor sincerity on the part of those who were responsible for their formulation. *Neshekh*, for example, is defined as a rate of interest to be determined by the *Code Civil* (*Code Napoleon*) of France. Such interest may be charged by one Jew from another, provided that the lender share the risk of loss and the chance of gain, and that the debtor give indemnification to the creditor in the case of *damnum emergens*. Only the poor Jew must be charged no interest at all. Gentiles, particularly those living in France or Italy, are to be considered as brothers of the Jews, and there must not be any difference between them if charity is required. Those who disregard this ordinance will be called sinners and transgressors of the law of the holy Torah. All this may, to a degree, be defensible from the standpoint of the *halakhah*, but a complete renunciation of Jewish autonomy is implied. Jews have become Frenchmen of the Israelite persuasion. The law of the State (*ḥok ha-medinah*) sets the tone and the "Grand Sanhedrin" decides accordingly (*Takkanot ha-Sanhedrin shel Paris* (1958), 56–67). Ishmael b. Abraham Isaac ha-Kohen of Modena, who also received an invitation to the Paris Sanhedrin, was too old to make the journey, but gave his answers to each question in writing. Although gentle and dignified in his reply, he disassociates himself from the views expressed in the *Décisions Doctrinales*: "To deny permission to lend money on interest to gentiles is against all exegetes, against the *Gemara*, and against the literal understanding of the Bible" (cf. J. Rosenthal, in: *Talpioth*, 4 (1950), 583).

Events of the last 150 years belied the identification of the "brother" and the "other," and in all probability the reaction of the old rabbi of Modena and those who thought like him, even at the beginning of the 19th century has not disappeared from Jewish life. The full awareness of covenantal relationship between God and Israel and Jew and Jew is still strongly felt. Until this day many Jewish banks both in and outside Israel display a notice to the effect that it is understood that business and loan transactions between Jews will be conducted according to *hetter iska* regulations.

[Siegfried Stein]

The Historical Context

The biblical injunctions against usury relate neither exclusively nor mainly to money-lending on interest. Their spirit reflects a nomadic and village society where the borrowing of goods is the norm, and moneylending the exception. Yet the so-called archives of the *Murashu house discovered at Nippur show Jews in Babylonian regions engaged in extensive financial operations. The Talmud largely treats the problem of usury and interest from the point of view of product loans, though financial operations are also dealt with in this connection. There is evidence that as Jews moved in the city life of the Roman Empire, some of them gave loans on interest.

With the development of an urban economy in the caliphate of the ninth century, the financing of the ever-growing needs of trade, of crafts, and of the state, became a pressing need. Jews financed the business of their coreligionists through participating in various ways as partners, both in financing and in profits. While some of these means of participation were actual, others were formal only, devised to evade the prohibitions on usury. In the tenth century, large-scale Jewish financiers appear, like the *Netira family, who loaned large sums to the state on interest, against the collateral of state incomes. These loans were evidently the accumulated savings of middle- and small-scale Jewish merchants, deposited with Jewish state bankers for greater income and security. When (up to the 15th century) the majority of the Jewish people lived in Islamic lands and in Christian Spain, money-lending was one of the occupations of Jews, as of other city dwellers. While in Northwestern Europe Jews first came mainly as international traders, when some of them later turned to local trade (1000 C.E.), they engaged in credit operations. The impact of the First Crusade (1096–99) on the status and livelihood of the Jews in France, Germany, and England drove them out of trade through the lack of security arising from the inimical attitude of society in general; at the same time, Jewish merchants and craftsmen were denied any share in the Christian towns and *guilds which were rapidly evolving as the only social framework for trade and crafts in those countries. This crystallized at a time when European trade, agriculture, and building were expanding and in need of financing. Ready cash – which then meant precious metals – was scarce. Available means in Christian hands were channeled into credit for merchant ventures and other relatively creative loans, in which it was also easier to formulate partnerships that evaded the stigma of usury. Under such circumstances the Church found it easy to act in accordance with the agricultural ethos of its upper strata, and to insist on the prohibition of usury. There remained the field of loans for consumption – the need for which arose in cases of illness, litigation, and unforeseen expenses – for which Christian capital was not readily available and where usury was least avoidable. Deprived of its former uses, Jewish capital entered this field, as well as granting any other possible loan. Hence among the Jews of the region between the Pyrenees and Scotland, between the Atlantic and the Elbe, usury became the main source of livelihood from about the 12th to the 15th centuries. They were not the only people to lend money on interest in that region: there were also the Cahorsins of southern France, the Catalans, and the Lombards. But religious enmity, the social separateness of the Jews, and their hateful image, combined to identify Jew with usurer in the western Christian imagination. In those countries Jews sometimes lent on a debt deed only, without surety. Medieval Hebrew sources from those regions described this kind of loan as *be-emunah* ("on trust"), a practice usually reserved for established and proved clients. Most loans were given on the double surety of a written deed and a collateral (Heb. *mashkon*). Since repayment of a loan for consumption was often difficult, the needy debtor came to hate the infidel Jewish creditor who, out of his own need, had helped him. Many anti-Jewish persecutions hence acquired an economic as well as a religious character, the instigators being no less anxious to destroy incriminating bonds than to eliminate accursed infidels.

In England the extent as well as the problems of Jewish money-lending were seen at their clearest. The most common interest rate was two pence in the pound a week (43 1/3 annually), though half and twice as much were also common. There were many partnerships, often between members of the same family; this form was utilized by the extremely wealthy *Aaron of Lincoln. To supervise Jewish lending, to insure maximum tax exactions from the Jewish lenders, and to make certain that debt deeds would not be lost even in times of massacres, the *Archa system was introduced. In the 13th century Jewish money-lending was conducted through tenants of the commons and of the middle class, whose bonds were bought up, on default, by the nobility and ecclesiastical institutions. This too, aroused the enmity of the commoners toward the Jews. In 1275 Edward III passed severe anti-usury laws, at the same time exacting extremely high tallages and calling in Italian moneylenders to replace the Jews. Some of the latter turned to coin-clipping, which led in part to the total expulsion in 1290.

Though in the heterogeneous Holy Roman Empire money-lending practices varied greatly according to time and place, the history of Jewish money-lending in *Regensburg may be typical of Rhenish and south German cities. Until about 1250 the municipality was the chief beneficiary of Jewish loans; until about 1400 the nobility and clergy were the main recipients; while after 1400 knights, burghers, and artisans pawned objects for short terms, and borrowed small sums at high rates of interest. This latter situation eventually became the focus of lower-class enmity toward the Jews and contributed to their expulsion in 1519.

Interest rates in Germany fluctuated greatly in practice and even in their legal norms. Frederick II of Austria fixed the Jews' maximum interest rate at 173⅓% in 1244; in the more developed cities of the Rhineland and south Germany 43⅓% was more common, though this rate did not apply in the case of foreigners or peasants; 86⅔% was also common and acceptable. An investigation in 1676, motivated by anti-Jewish feeling, in the electoral Palatinate in western Germany, showed that an interest rate of 14.5% was honored there by the Jewish moneylenders. The Christian rulers who exploited Jews as their agents for usury – and then extorted from them a large part of their usurious gains, especially when the Jews became impoverished – used to proclaim moratoriums on the individual, partial, or total debts to Jews. The respective treasuries all profited by such measures, the best known being those of Emperor Wenceslaus in 1385 and 1390, which utterly impoverished the Jews while barely alleviating the burdens of the treasury. Likewise, total and bare-faced confiscation was often resorted to, as was expulsion, which left the field open to the Jews' remaining competitors. Because of the collateral in their hands Jewish moneylenders frequently engaged in related occupations, such as the repair and upkeep of clothes, armor, and precious objects, and in their sale when pledges were not redeemed, a frequent occurrence. Hence the rudiments of certain crafts, as well as the sale of *secondhand goods, were an integral part of this occupation. Articles regulating money-lending constituted the core of all charters issued to Jews in medieval Germany from the 12th century. They determined not only the rates of interest, but also ensured the rights of the creditor to the collateral, even if it had been stolen. The moneylender had to take an oath that he had received it in good faith and in daylight whereupon the legal owner of the collateral had to repay him the amount loaned on the pledge. This right clashed with Germanic legal conceptions, which demanded the return of the object to the rightful owner without any payment; hence the misconception that the charters allowed the Jews to act as fences.

When it became apparent in Italy that the citizens had need of cash loans, the activities of Jewish moneylenders were regulated by means of the *condotta*, conditions set out in charter treaties between municipalities or rulers and Jewish moneylenders, first signed in the late 13th century in Umbria. The interest rate varied between 15% and 25% and was never to exceed the value of the pledge. The profit of the loan-banks in 15th-century Florence was approximately 4% (see also *Monti di Pietá*).

The first privilege granted to Jews in Poland in 1264 regarded them mainly as moneylenders. However, under favorable conditions, Jews soon took part in other economic activities, so that within a century money-lending became only one of their many-sided economic functions in the Polish cities and countryside. The **arenda* system, for example, stems from a change from lending to leasing. By the end of the 16th century, Jewish trade demanded more capital than the Jews themselves possessed, so that many Jewish traders became indebted to Christians. Lending on interest between Jews was explicitly initiated and legalized there, in the institution *hetter iska*, a legal device which created a formal partnership between creditor and debtor. Interest rates inside the Jewish business community in the latter half of the 17th century were between 25% and 33⅓%, whereas the Christians loaned at 6%–10%, and interest rates between Jews and Christians ranged between these two figures. Jews also developed their own system of credit bonds – the *mamran* (*membranum*) – used mainly at the great fairs of Poland-Lithuania. With the rise of modern *banking, Jewish money-lending of the conventional type gradually decreased in importance, though in Western Germany and in *Alsace-Lorraine it was sufficiently widespread to be detrimental to *emancipation of the Jews during the French Revolution, and later on to influence the attitude of Napoleon *Bonaparte to Jewish emancipation. It likewise was one of the causes of the anti-Jewish *Hep! Hep! disturbances of 1819, as well as 1830 and 1848.

When Jews moved to western countries in the late 19th-early 20th centuries, moneylending was a frequent occupation, especially in the first and second generation, and the Jewish moneylender became a familiar stereotype.

BIBLIOGRAPHY: S. Stein, in: *Essays… J.H. Hertz* (1942), 403f.; idem, in: JTS, 4 (1953), 161–70; idem, in: HJ, 17 (1955), 3–40; idem, in: JSS, 1 (1956), 141–64; 2 (1957), 94; idem, in: JJS, 10 (1959), 45–61; idem, *Jewish-Christian Disputations in 13th Century Narbonne* (Inaugural Lecture, University College, London, 1969), 1–27; D. Tama, *Transactions of the Parisian Sanhedrin* (1807); W. Sombart, *Die Juden und das Wirtschaftsleben* (1911); Roth, Italy; J.T. Noonan, Jr., *Scholastic Analysis of Usury* (1957); R.W. Emery, *Jews of Perpignan in the 13th Century* (1959); J. Katz, *Exclusiveness and Tolerance* (1961); Baer, Spain; S. Stern, *Der preussische Staat und die Juden*, 2 vols. (1962); J. Parkes, *Jew in the Medieval Community* (1938), index, s.v. *usury*; B.N. Nelson, *Idea of Usury* (1949), index, s.v. *Jews*; L. Poliakov, *Les banchieri juifs et le Saint-Siège* (1965); M. Neumann, *Geschichte des Wuchers in Deutschland* (1865), 292–347; J.E. Scherer, *Die Rechtsverhaeltnisse der Juden in den deutsch-oesterreichischen Laendern* (1901), 185–96; G. Caro, *Sozial-und Wirtschaftsgeschichte der Juden im Mittelalter*, 2 vols. (1908–20), index, s.v. *Wucher*; M. Hoffmann, *Der Geldhandel der deutschen Juden waehrend des Mittelalters* (1910); R. Straus, *Die Judengemeinde Regensburg* (1932); idem, *Regensburg und Augsburg* (1939); idem, *Die Juden in Wirtschaft und Gesellschaft* (1964); Kisch, Germany, index; M. Breger, *Zur Handelsgeschichte der Juden in Polen im 17. Jahrhundert* (1932); W.J. Fischel, *Jews in the Economic and Political Life of Medieval Islam* (1937); Z. Szajkowski, *Agricultural Credit and Napoleon's Anti-Jewish Decrees* (1953); idem, *Economic Status of the Jews in Alsace, Metz and Lorraine* (1954); H.H. Ben-Sasson, *Hagut ve-Hanhagah* (1959); idem, *Toledot Am Yisrael*, 2 (1969), 92–98; S. Simonsohn, *Toledot ha-Yehudim be-Dukkasut Mantovah*, 2 vols. (1962–64), index, s.v. *Halva'ah u-Malvim be-Ribbit*; H.G. Richardson, *English Jewry under Angevin Kings* (1960), index, s.v. *usury*; S. Grayzel, *The Church and the Jews in the XIIIth Century* (1966²), index; S.D. Goitein, *Mediterranean Society*, 1 (1967), index, s.v. *loans on interest*; F.R. Salter, in: *Cambridge Historical Journal*, 5 (1935–37), 193–211; P. Elman, in: *Economic History Review*, 7 (1936–37), 145–54.

MONGOLIA, region of E. central Asia, which gained fame originally due to the *Mongols under Genghis Khan, who established an enormous empire in the early 13th century that eventually encompassed most of Asia. By the 17th century, Mongolia was firmly under Chinese control. Outer Mongolia became the Mongolian People's Republic in 1924 and Inner Mongolia remained under Chinese rule. At the end of the 19th century Jewish families from Siberia traded with Mongolia and a few settled there as a result of their businesses. Between 1918 and 1920 Russian Jews, fleeing from the civil war atrocities, crossed Lake Baikal to settle in Outer Mongolia. Most of them were wiped out in 1921 by the White Russian units under Baron Ungern-Sternberg which were retreating before the advancing Soviet forces. In 1925–26, a Russian-Jewish journalist discovered 50 newly settled Jewish families in a deserted area of Outer Mongolia, some 200 miles from the Manchurian border. Ulaan Bataar (or Ulan Bator, formerly Urga), the capital of the Mongolian People's Republic, had a community of 600 Russian Jews in 1926, including watchmakers, jewelers, barbers, furriers, and construction workers. The increasing Soviet influence in the area induced most of them to leave Outer Mongolia for *Manchuria and elsewhere. Those who remained were employees of state enterprises. Jews visited Outer Mongolia from the Manchurian town of Hailar during the 1920s only seasonally in order to buy furs and other domestic products, but they did not take up permanent residence. Over the years of Communist rule, Jewish civilian and military specialists from the Soviet Union spent time in Mongolia. The contact of Jews with Mongols led to some mixed marriages, a phenomenon strengthened by the many Mongols who traveled to the Soviet Union for study and other activities. With the end of Communism in both the Soviet Union and Mongolia around 1991, several of the children resulting from these marriages immigrated to Israel.

BIBLIOGRAPHY: M. Wischnitzer, *Juden in der Welt* (1935), 305–7; A. Druyanow in: *Reshumot*, 3 (1923), 549–51. **ADD. BIBLIOGRAPHY:** C.R. Bawden, *The Modern History of Mongolia* (1989).

[Rudolf Loewenthal / Reuven Amitai (2nd ed.)]

MONGOLS, a group of tribes from the eastern Eurasian steppe, north of China, which were welded by Genghis

(Chinggis) Khan in the late 12th and early 13th centuries into a state that created the largest land-based empire in history. Mongol successor states ruled much of Eurasia well into the 14th century, and smaller states of Mongol provenance ruled more restricted areas even longer. In contemporary sources, the Mongols are often referred to as Tatars/Tartars, and modern day Tatars, although speaking Turkic languages, are of at least partial Mongol descent. The Mongols touched upon and influenced the history of the Jews in Central and Eastern Europe as well as the Islamic world.

At the beginning of 1260 Mongol forces invaded *Syria, and their raiders reached as far as *Jerusalem, *Hebron, and *Gaza. A report of the arrival of the Mongols in Jerusalem and their depredations in the area is found in the famous letter of *Naḥmanides to his son from 1267. Mongol advanced forces, however, were defeated by the *Mamluks at the battle of ʿAyn Jalut in northern *Palestine in August 1260, and the Euphrates River became the frontier between the two hostile states. Mongol raiders again reached Palestine, including Jerusalem, in 1300 after their defeat of the Mamluks near Homs at the end of 1299. In Western Asia, including the Middle East, Central Asia, and Eastern Europe the Mongols eventually underwent a double process of Islamization and Turkification, i.e., conversion to Islam and the replacement of Mongolian by Turkish, the language of many of their soldiers and officers.

The Mongols played an important role in world history, not the least in facilitating cultural contact between east and west Asia, as well as creating the conditions by which western Europe learned about China and East Asia, thereby contributing to European seaborne expansion. Latin Christian writers, such as Matthew of Paris, saw them as descendants of the Ten Tribes. Some Jews themselves in Central and Eastern Europe appear to have harbored messianic expectations of the Mongol advance, which combined with a desire for revenge against the Christians. Again, Matthew of Paris saw the Jews as encouraging and abetting the Mongols. This perceived "cooperation," together with a more concrete understanding of a contemporary messianic upsurge among the Jews, may have contributed to increased antisemitic feelings among Christians.

The situation of the Jews in the Islamic countries conquered and ruled by the Mongols appears to have dramatically improved. Jews, as well as Christians, enjoyed relative religious freedom and the restrictive laws derived from the so-called Covenant of *Omar were abolished for several decades. The activity of the free-thinking Jewish philosopher and scholar of comparative religion *Ibn Kammūna (d. 1285) in *Baghdad can be attributed to some degree to the relatively tolerant atmosphere in the realm of religion introduced by the Mongols. One prominent Jewish personality was Saʿd al-Dawla, who rose to become the wazir of the Ilkhan Arghun in 1289. His efficiency in raising funds is noted in the sources, as are the many enemies that he made. His being a Jew certainly exacerbated the dissatisfaction with him. He was removed and executed in 1291 when his patron was on his deathbed. Another important individual of Jewish origin, albeit one who converted to Islam, was *Rashīd al-Dīn (al-Dawla) al-Hamadānī, who served as the co-wazir to three Ilkhans until his final dismissal and execution in 1318. Besides his success as a senior bureaucrat, Rashīd al-Dīn has gained fame as the author of the great historical work, *Jāmiʿ al-Tawārīkh* ("Collection of Chronicles") written in Persian, although some parts have come down to us in Arabic. Not only is this the most important extant source on Mongol history, it is perhaps the earliest attempt at writing a comprehensive history of humankind. This may reflect the open atmosphere prevalent under the Mongols, the communication between all of Asia, and the fact that Rashīd al-Dīn himself was living on a frontier of two cultures. In any event, his Jewish origins were not forgotten. After his death, his head was paraded around, and common people shouted: "This is the head of the Jew who abused the name of God; may God's curse be upon him." In spite of these outbursts, there was much to commend Mongol rule to the Jews who came under their control, compared to many contemporary rulers in both the Muslim and Christian countries.

BIBLIOGRAPHY: R. Amitai, "Mongol Raids into Palestine (A.D. 1260 and 1300)," in: *Journal of the Royal Asiatic Society* (1987), 236–55; J.A. Boyle (ed.), *The Cambridge History of Iran*, vol. 5: *The Saljuq and Mongol Periods* (1968); W.J. Fischel, *The Jews in the Economic and Political Life of Mediaeval Islam* (1937); S.D. Goitein, "Glimpses from the Cairo Geniza on Naval Warfare in the Mediterranean and on the Old Mongol Invasion," in: *Studi orientalistici in onore di Giorgio Levi della Vida* (Rome, 1956), vol. 2, 393–408; P. Jackson, "Medieval Christendom's Encounter with the Alien," in: *Historical Research*, 74 (2001), 347–69; D.D. Leslie, "The Mongol Attitude to Jews in China," in: *Central Asiatic Journal*, 39 (1995), 234–46; S. Menache, "Tartars, Jews, Saracens and the Jewish-Mongol 'Plot' of 1241," in: *History*, 81 (1996), 319–42; D.O. Morgan, *The Mongols* (1986); J.J. Saunders, *The History of the Mongol Conquests* (1971).

[Reuven Amitai (2nd ed.)]

MONIS, JUDAH (1683–1764), Colonial American Hebraist. Monis, who was born in Algiers or Italy, was educated in Leghorn and Amsterdam. Very little is known about his career before he went to America. On Feb. 28, 1715/16, he was admitted as a freeman of New York, his occupation being that of merchant, although at a later period he was described as having been a rabbi in Jamaica and in New York. Much of his erudition may have been secondhand. He appears in the Boston area in 1720, and on March 27, 1722 was publicly baptized in the College Hall at Cambridge, at which time the Reverend Benjamin Colman delivered *A Discourse… Before the Baptism of R. Judah Monis, to which were added Three Discourses, Written by Mr. Monis himself, The Truth, The Whole Truth, Nothing but the Truth. One of which was deliver'd by him at his Baptism* (Boston, 1722). Monis' essays are an apology and defense of his new faith, and in support of the doctrine of the Trinity drawn from "the Old Testament, and with the Authority of the Cabalistical Rabbies, Ancient and Modern." Shortly after his conversion, on April 30, 1722, he was appointed instructor of Hebrew at Harvard College, a position he held until his resignation in 1760. Monis received the degree of Master of Arts from Harvard in 1723. His instructorship, marriage, and academic degree came after his conversion to Protestant Christianity.

The study of Hebrew was a required subject at Harvard College, and Monis' Hebrew grammar, *Dickdook Leshon Gnebreet: A Grammar of the Hebrew Tongue* was published in Cambridge in 1735, sponsored by the Harvard Corporation. It was published in English: "to Facilitate the Instruction of all those that are desirous of acquiring a clear Idea of this Primitive Tongue by their own Studies; In order to their more distinct Acquaintance with the Sacred Oracles of the Old Testament, according to the Original, And Published more especially for the Use of the Students of Harvard College."

Monis insisted on the use of the Hebrew vowel points in this grammar as being essential for the correct pronunciation of the Hebrew. Monis also owned a manuscript volume of Kabbalistic tracts and excerpts (372 pages), some transcribed by him, and some in the handwriting of others. His brother-in-law, the Rev. John Martyn, presented his books and manuscripts to Harvard College Library in 1767. Monis also left a small fund for the needy widows of Christian ministers.

BIBLIOGRAPHY: L.M. Friedman, in: AJHSP, 22 (1914), 1–24; I.S. Meyer, *Proceedings of the Massachusetts Historical Society*, 52 (1919), I.S. Meyer, *ibid.*, 35 (1939), 145–70; G.F. Moore, in: *Proceedings of the Massachusetts Historical Society*, 52 (1919), 285–312; C.K. Shipton (ed.), *Sibley's Harvard Graduates*, 7 (1945), 380–1, 626, 639–46.

[Isidore S. Meyer]

MONITOR (Heb. כֹּחַ; lit. "strength"; AV "chameleon"; JPS: "land crocodile"), reptile included in the Pentateuch among the creeping things which are prohibited as food and whose dead bodies defile by contact (Lev. 11:30–39). The reference is to the *Varanus griseus*. It is the largest reptile found in Israel, with a length, including its long tail, of up to 4 ft. (1.20 m.). Feeding on reptiles and rodents, it is frequently found in the southern coastal belt, in the Negev, and in the Arabah. Alone of the reptiles in the country, it hibernates for six months in a burrow in the ground, and it is then that the Bedouin catch it, using it for medicinal purposes and eating its flesh, which the Greeks, who called it a land crocodile, believed granted immunization from poisoned arrows. It is usually hunted while in a torpid state, for when awake it is aggressive, defending itself by biting and lashing out with its powerful tail. The Septuagint and Vulgate identified the biblical *ko'aḥ* with the *chameleon.

BIBLIOGRAPHY: Lewysohn, Zool, 223–4, no. 274; J. Feliks, *The Animal World of the Bible* (1962), 99. **ADD. BIBLIOGRAPHY:** Feliks, Ha-Tzome'aḥ, 241.

[Jehuda Feliks]

MONMOUTH COUNTY, county in central New Jersey, lying along the Atlantic Ocean about 40 miles southwest of New York City. About 500 square miles in area, it is divided into 52 municipalities of various sizes. Monmouth's approximately 72,500 Jewish residents in 2005 (11.5% of the county's total population) make it one of the fastest growing Jewish communities in the Metropolitan region.

The county's Jewish history is long and varied. Evidence shows Sephardi peddlers from New York traveling through the county in the early 1700s. The first resident, Isaac Emanuel, a Freehold merchant, appears in a series of court cases in the early 1720s. By the 1750s Jonas Solomon and Levy Hart, both married to local Protestant sisters, were well known as Jewish merchants and tavern keepers. Solomon lived in Freehold and Hart in a small settlement further east that was to be labeled "Jewstown" by his colonial neighbors and by the British during the ensuing Revolutionary War. The original Freehold home and tavern owned by Jonas and Hannah Solomon was burned by the British during the Battle of Monmouth in 1778. The barn, circa 1800, owned by their son, Levi Solomon, who farmed nearby, is still in existence and was designated as the site for the newly established Monmouth County Jewish History Museum in 2005.

No permanent Jewish communities in the county developed, however, until the arrival of sizable numbers of German Jews just prior to and after the Civil War. Monmouth's 33-mile coastline became the destination of wealthy vacationers escaping the summer heat of New York City. By 1861 Aaron Cristaler had build and was operating the kosher Atlantic Hotel in Long Branch, which accommodated 500 persons. Denied acceptance at Christian resorts in New York and Rhode Island, more and more wealthy German Jews came to what was called the "Jewish Newport" at the Jersey Shore. Families with illustrious names such as Seligman, Guggenheim, Schiff, Loeb, Warburg, Sachs, Baruch, Mandel, Rothschild, Lewisohn, Lehman, Wimpfjeimer, and Oppenheim built magnificent summer mansions from Rumson to Long Branch. By the late 1880s the need for a permanent synagogue resulted in the establishment of Temple Beth Miriam in Long Branch. Many of the supporters of this synagogue of Reform Judaism were also instrumental in 1887 in establishing the nearby hospital that is now known as Monmouth Medical Center.

In addition to their more wealthy compatriots, Monmouth attracted many German Jews who sought commercial opportunity in small trades and services. Such a close-knit community of Jews was already present in the northern Monmouth Bayshore town of Keyport in the 1860s. In 1880 they organized themselves as the United Hebrew Congregation and within a decade established a synagogue. By the last decades of the 19th century, Red Bank was also emerging as a commercial center, its growth synonymous with the career of Sigmund Eisner. Starting off with the family sewing machine Eisner developed a prosperous business producing military uniforms for the Spanish-American War. By World War I he had factories in Red Bank, Freehold, and Keansburg. One of Eisner's neighbors was summer resident Judge Abram I. Elkus, who served as U.S. ambassador to Turkey in 1916. His daughter Katherine Elkus White became mayor of Red Bank in 1950 and U.S. ambassador to Denmark in 1964.

Several other German Jewish entrepreneurs stand out: John Steinbach, proprietor of large department stores in Long Branch and Asbury Park; Frank Marx of Shrewsbury, cattle dealer and meat supplier; Joseph Goldstein, dry goods department store owner; Clarence Steiner and his sleepware factories in Long Branch and Freehold, Manasquan and Keyport; Walter Rosenberg founder of the Walter Reade Theater chain; Berthold Sussman and Siegfried Hirschfield and their hotels. Political acceptance followed; William Levy served as mayor of Deal in 1916, Clarence Housman was elected mayor of Long Branch in 1920, and Aaron J. Bach, mayor of Deal in 1922.

A wave of Eastern European immigration also hit Monmouth at the turn of the 19th century. Most of these poor Yiddish-speaking newcomers settled in the more established communities along the shore and to the south, working in factories and the retail trades. Finding that the existing summer German Jewish Temple Beth Miriam did not meet their year-round needs, the Orthodox residents of Long Branch formed their own synagogue, Congregation Brothers of Israel, in 1898. A larger building was completed in 1920. A YMHA and YHWA was organized, followed by the Ladies Independent Hebrew Sick Benefit Association, the Gemilath Chesed, the Hebrew Ladies Hospital Auxiliary, and the Workmen's Circle. Kosher hotels and boarding houses catering to wealthy and moderate income East European Jews proliferated.

In 1904 the Orthodox Jewish community in Asbury Park incorporated as the Sons of Israel and were in their own building the following year replete with Hebrew school and *mikveh*. The new Conservative Temple Beth El was dedicated in 1927. Soon Asbury Park could boast its own community center providing a meeting place for the YMHA, Jewish War Veterans, and other organizations. Similar activity occurred around the same period in Red Bank, Keyport, Bradley Beach, Belmar, and Manasquan. Belmar became a summer gathering place of the New York intelligentsia attracting such luminaries as the world renowned Yiddish writer Sholem Aleichem and Morris Hillquit, the Social-Labor Party leader and author. Ira Gershwin, the famed lyricist, courted and married one of the daughters of the Strunsky family, owners of the local hotel.

A smaller number of East European immigrants moved westward into the more rural areas surrounding Freehold, Englishtown, Perrineville, and Farmingdale.

The Jewish Agricultural Society, which provided loans, training and assistance to Jewish farmers, most often in Yiddish, described them as growers of vegetables, potatoes, and general farm crops with a cow or two and some chickens. A few, like Jacob Zlotkin, were horse and cattle dealers. In 1910 Jacob Grudin led a group of Millstone Township Jewish farm families in setting up a congregation named the First Hebrew Farmers Association of Perrineville. In 1913 the Perrineville Co-operative Credit Union was organized, one of the first farm credit unions in New Jersey. Local Jewish farmers were also largely responsible for the formation of the Central Jersey Farmers Cooperative Association in 1930. Maurice Wolf of Perrineville played an important role in the national Jewish farmers movement, serving on the board of the Federation of Jewish Farmers of America.

The largest concentration of Jewish farm life in the county, however, was to develop in the Farmingdale-Howell area. Starting out in 1919 Benjamin Peskin found he had to take in summer boarders to supplement his meager potato and dairy farming earnings. By 1928 he and 12 other families joined to build a Jewish Community Center and in a few years a Yiddish school affiliated with the Sholem Aleichem Folk Institute was in operation. Other organizations took root; a Ladies Auxiliary, a Jewish reading circle, a Jewish farmers' chorus, two farmers' cooperative associations, a unit of the International Workers Organization, the Zionist Pioneer Women, and a chapter of the Rural Youth of America. At the advice of the Jewish Agricultural Society the farmers started raising poultry. By the late 1920s the fields around Farmingdale and Freehold were dotted with chicken coops as New Jersey was on its way to becoming the egg basket of the East. Jewish farmers soon accounted for about 75% of the state's egg production and by 1935 Monmouth County contained more Jewish farmers than any other county in the state.

It was at this time that, under the direction of the idealistic social planner and organizer Benjamin Brown, one of America's unique experiments in cooperative farming and industry was instituted in Jersey Homesteads (renamed Roosevelt after the president's death) in rural Millstone Township. Brown secured a $500,000 federal government subsistence loan for the creation of a colony of 200 Jewish needle workers from New York who were to become self-sufficient through seasonal farming combined with seasonal employment in a cooperative garment factory. Individual homestead plots were to be supplemented by a community truck garden, a dairy and poultry plant, and cooperative store. The factory was opened in 1936 and from the start was a failure. Conflict between Brown and the International Ladies Garment Workers Union and other political and economic factors led to a federal government takeover of the cooperative in 1940. After World War II the houses were sold to individuals. Although Jersey Homesteads failed as a cooperative enterprise in many ways it succeeded as a community. Surrounded by a hostile rural Christian township the Jewish residents formed their own elementary school which became the cultural and social center of the town. Attracted by the intellectual and cultural atmosphere of the town, the famous artist Ben Shahn and many other painters and sculptors moved in and soon Roosevelt was hailed as an artists' colony as well.

By the late 1950s though, Monmouth's Jewish farm communities were in decline owing to a combination of economic, political, and social reasons. Another wave of immigration was to change the county's landscape as large numbers of families from New York City and northern New Jersey moved to the suburbs.

With America's entry into World War II, the U.S. Signal Corps located at Fort Monmouth in Eatontown underwent a tremendous growth of both military and civilian personnel. A majority of the scientists, engineers, physicians, and dentists were Jewish men, and many of these stayed on at Ft. Monmouth blending into the great postwar movement from New York City to the Monmouth suburbs that was about to begin. The completion of the Garden State Parkway is 1955 facilitated the construction of massive industrial parks and residential subdivisions. Research organizations such as Bell Telephone Laboratories in Holmdel brought in thousands of new employees as did other corporations that were part of Monmouth's burgeoning electronic industry. Older citizens also found attractive homes in Monmouth, in high rises and garden apartments along the shore and in massive adult communities such as Covered Bridge in the western part of the county.

In addition, the postwar exodus to Monmouth's suburbs included a large contingent of Sephardi families with their own distinct religious and cultural practices. Many originally emigrated from Syria, settled in New York, and summered in Monmouth's shore communities before moving year round into the Deal and Ocean Township area. The number of Sephardi Jews increased so dramatically that three new Sephardi synagogues opened within a short period in the late 1970s.

From a prewar figure of 7,000 Monmouth's total Jewish population grew to 50,000 by 1977. Most of this growth was in the western part of the county. Mayor Arthur Goldwizweig estimated that in 1977 30% of Marlboro's residents were Jewish; Mayor Stanley Kruschick put the figure in neighboring Manalapan as 50%.

This growth has continued into the 21st century. The median age for Monmouth's 72,500 Jewish residents (divided into 26,000 households) is 41.1 years. They are well educated (55% of the adults have a college degree) and well off (median income is almost double that of all U.S. Jewish households); 54% live in western Monmouth, 32% in eastern Monmouth and about 14% in northern Monmouth. Summer vacationers number about 5,000. Of employed Jews, 52% work in Monmouth County, the rest commute to New York City or North Jersey. Of households surveyed by the Jewish Federation of Greater Monmouth 37% consider themselves Conservative, 26% Reform, 9% Orthodox, and 28% "just Jewish." There are 9 Conservative synagogues in the county, 6 Reform, 18 Orthodox, and 2 Traditional.

Four separate Jewish day schools exist in the county: The Hillel Yeshiva in Oakhurst, the Solomon Schechter Academy in Howell, the Shore Hebrew High School in Oakhurst, and the Solomon Schechter Day School in Marlboro.

An intense organizational life accompanied each stage of Monmouth's population growth. Local units of national Jewish organizations with a wide range of aims and purposes developed alongside synagogue religious and social clubs. The Monmouth Jewish Community Council (MJCC) was formed in 1969 to coordinate county-wide rallies for Jews overseas and in Israel. In 1971 several organizations in the shore area affiliated with the Jewish Federation movement and by 1976 most communities within the western and northern areas of the county joined them to create the Jewish Federation of Greater Monmouth County, which eventually incorporated the MJCC as well. Federation also fostered the formation of the Jewish Family and Children's Service. A similar history of consolidation among YMHAS and YWHAS led to the completion in 1971 of the Ruth Hyman Jewish Community Center in Deal, which also houses the 500-seat Axelrod Auditorium. Western Monmouth has set up its own Jewish Community Center office and a building drive is underway.

Due to the efforts of Professors Albert Zager and Jack Needle the Center for Holocaust Studies at Brookdale Community Collage in Lincroft was established in 1979. The center, which is the first of its kind in the state, provides educational materials and programs about the Holocaust, genocide, racism, and antisemitism.

[Jean Klerman (2nd ed.)]

MONOBAZ I AND II, two kings of *Adiabene in the first century, C.E. Monobaz I was both brother and husband of Queen *Helena. His attitude to Judaism is unknown, but in view of the fact that his sister-wife and their son Izates both became converts to Judaism, it is highly probable that he was sympathetic to it. Monobaz I and Helena had a son, Monobaz, who was older than his brother Izates, but when Monobaz I died, Helena, in accordance with the king's testament, placed Izates upon the throne. Monobaz II was loyal to his younger brother and like him embraced Judaism. He succeeded Izates to the throne. Little is known of Monobaz II. Josephus, who is the main source, relates that he sent the remains of his mother and brother to Jerusalem for burial, and that he erected a palace in Jerusalem, which was called by his name (Wars 5:252). Many of his kinsmen took part with distinction in the war against the Romans (Wars 2:520). Though Josephus features Izates as the chief figure among the converts to Judaism of the Adiabene royal dynasty, the account of Monobaz II in the talmudic literature makes a deeper impression, highlighting his generosity to the people of Jerusalem and the Temple, his righteousness, and his wisdom. His circumcision and that of his brother are also mentioned.

BIBLIOGRAPHY: Yoma 3:10; BB 11a; Tosef., Yoma 2:3; Gen. R. 46:10; Jos., Ant. 20:17–96; Derenbourg, Hist, 224–7; Schuerer, Gesch, 3 (1909⁴), 169–72; Klausner, Bayit Sheni, 5 (1951²), 44–49.

[Uriel Rappaport]

MONOGAMY, the custom and social or religious institution, often sanctioned by law, according to which a person can be married to only one single mate at a time. The discussion in this article is restricted to polygamy and monogamy in Jewish practice, since polyandry was absolutely forbidden by biblical law.

The Bible does not limit the right of a man to have more than one wife. Indeed, many instances are cited where a man has several wives (and *concubines) – a prevalent custom in the Ancient Near East. It seems, however, that due to economic conditions, most of the people did not practice polygamy or even bigamy. Indeed, practice was more monogamous than theory. The ethos underlying the creation story (Gen. 2), and the last chapter of Proverbs, is essentially monogamous. The situation changed during the Second Temple period. In addition to the economic factors which gave justifiable grounds to monogamy – factors applicable even more than in the First Temple period – the concept of mutual fidelity between husband and wife took root. Some men refrained from taking more than one wife because of an explicit agreement they had made with their first wife. Such agreements, preserved in Babylonian and Assyrian documents, are also to be found in the *Elephantine (Yeb) documents (Cowley, Aramaic, 44ff., no. 15, line 31ff. Bigamy and polygamy, while on the decrease, were mainly practiced among Hellenistic Jews (Joseph the *Tobiad, Herod, the administrator of Agrippa (Suk. 27a)), but they are also mentioned in the *halakhah* (Yev. 1:1–4; Ket. 10:1–6; Git. 2:7; Kid. 2:6–7; cf. Justin Martyr, *Dialogue with Tryphon*, 134:1; 141:4), and occurred even in the families of sages (Yev. 15a). Bigamy took place sometimes because of a *levirate marriage or the sterility of the first wife. Yet despite the rare occurrence of polygamy, its explicit prohibition in the *halakhah* of the Dead Sea Sect that saw polygamy as a Pentateuchal prohibition (Damascus Document 4:20–5:5) was a complete innovation. Christianity adopted a similar attitude, which was in conformity with Jesus' approach to marriage and to divorce (Tit. 1:6; 1 Tim. 3:2, 12).

But even the Mishnah and the *baraitot* clearly reflect a situation which was almost completely monogamist (Yev. 2:10; etc.). Some sages preferred *ḥaliẓah ("levirate divorce") to *yibbum* ("levirate marriage"; Bek. 1:7); others violently condemned marriage to two wives even for the purpose of procreation (Ket. 62b). According to R. Ammi a Palestinian *amora*, "Whoever takes a second wife in addition to his first one shall divorce the first and pay her *ketubbah*" (Yev. 65a). Such statements possibly reflect the influence of Roman custom which prohibited polygamy, especially since all the Jews of the empire became Roman citizens after 212 C.E. The Roman emperor *Theodosius issued a prohibition against the practice of bigamy and polygamy among Jews, but it did not disappear completely.

The Jews of Babylonia also practiced bigamy and polygamy, despite the Persian monogamistic background, and Rava said: "A man may marry several women in addition to his wife, on condition that he can provide for them" (Yev. 65a; cf. Ket. 80b; Pes. 113a). The sages however advised that one should not take more than four wives (and this would appear to be the source of the Muslim law which permits only four wives). Under the influence of the Muslim custom during the Babylonian geonic period, polygamous marriage became even more common (see Lewin, Oẓar, Yevamot (1936), 148–54). With the *Karaites, polygamy was a controversial issue. Bigamy was practiced among North African and Spanish Jews. There were women, however, who demanded that it be explicitly written in the document of marriage or in the *ketubbah* that the husband would not take a second wife.

In Germany and northern France polygamy was rare, mainly due to the economic conditions and to the influence of the Christian environment. It seems that at the beginning of the 12th century, the Jewish communities issued a regulation which forbade polygamy. Later, this regulation became a *ḥerem* (ban), attributed to R. *Gershom b. Judah. In the case of a levirate marriage, or the sterility of the first wife, the regulation was disregarded, while in cases where the wife had become insane (and could not therefore be divorced, see *Divorce) a regulation was introduced whereby the *ḥerem* could be lifted by 100 rabbis from three countries (or three communities). By the 13th century, however, it had already been decided that levirate marriage was to be abolished and *ḥaliẓah* performed instead. The ban on bigamous marriage however did not include a clause annulling the offender's second marriage (see Yev. 110a; BB 48b): For example, although the man had disregarded the *ḥerem*, broken the law, and married a second woman, his second marriage remained valid; but he could be compelled to divorce his second wife. The prohibition on bigamy became widespread in most countries of the Ashkenazi Diaspora, but not in Provence, Spain, North Africa, and among the Oriental communities, and it was accepted only by Ashkenazi halakhic authorities. Bigamy was however not common even in those localities where it had not been prohibited, including the Islamic countries.

In the Palestinian *yishuv*, bigamy was extremely rare, and in the State of Israel it is prohibited by law (the 1951 law on equal rights to women), although immigrants coming with more than one wife are allowed to maintain that status. In 1950 the Chief Rabbinate of Israel unanimously decided that *ḥaliẓah* was preferred to *yibbum* (Herzog, *Heikhal Yiẓḥak, Even ha-Ezer*, 1 (1960), 51n). See *Bigamy; *Marriage.

BIBLIOGRAPHY: Z. Falk, *Jewish Matrimonial Law in Middle Ages* (1966), 1–34 (esp. 1 n.1, 34 n.3; exhaustive bibl.); P. Tishby, in: *Tarbiz*, 34 (1964/65), 49–55; Eidelberg, *ibid.*, 287f.

[Moshe David Herr]

MONOTHEISM, in its literal meaning, oneness of the godhead (i.e., one God). The concept of monotheism is embedded in the domain of religious discourse, and its full and relevant significance must be derived from the connotation which it carries within this domain. Monotheism is usually attributed to biblical faith as its unique and distinct contribution to the history of religious thought. The significance of the word monotheism in its biblical context is taken to lie in the "mono," in the godhead's being one. As such, it is contrasted with paganism, the fundamental religious alternative to biblical faith, whose distinctive religious concept is taken to be polytheism, i.e., the plurality of the godhead (many gods). The difference between the biblical and pagan orientation is thus constituted here as a mere arithmetical difference, a difference between one and many gods. On this basis, biblical monotheism is seen by modern biblical scholars as emerging gradually and in a continuous line from the polytheistic thought of paganism. The mediating stage in such a development is found in monolatry, where the godhead is reduced to one only as far as worship is concerned, while ontologically there is a plurality of gods. It is a mediating stage inasmuch as the arithmetical reduction to oneness is partial. The full reduction of the godhead in all its aspects to oneness emerges from monolatry only later in biblical classical prophecy, when God is claimed not only as the one God of Israel but as the one God of universal history. Here, by drawing the arithmetical reduction to oneness in all the aspects of the godhead, biblical faith achieves ultimately its distinctive, unique character. It is observed, however, that an ontological arithmetical unity of the godhead is achieved also in paganism, even with a remarkable degree of purity (e.g., Plotinus). It must be concluded, therefore, that paganism too has a monotheistic formulation. Yet it is generally felt that a fundamental difference between biblical faith and paganism does exist, and that this difference is expressed in the respective concepts of monotheism. This difference, however, cannot be accounted for on the basis of monotheism understood as the arithmetical oneness of the godhead.

Theistic Monotheism

Consequently, it has been suggested that the difference between biblical and pagan monotheism lies in the fact that the former is theistic while the latter is pantheistic. While it is true that biblical monotheism is exclusively theistic and that pagan monotheism has a definite tendency toward pantheism, to formulate the difference between biblical and pagan monotheism on this basis is to formulate the difference with regard to a totally different aspect of the godhead from that to which the concept of monotheism refers. Monotheism refers to the being of the godhead as such, while theism and pantheism refer to the relation subsisting between the godhead and the world. Thus, while this attempt locates a difference which may follow from the fundamental difference within the concept of monotheism, it does not locate that fundamental difference itself.

Ethical Monotheism

The same point can be made regarding yet another attempt to locate the difference between biblical and pagan monotheism, according to which biblical monotheism is ethical while pagan monotheism is purely philosophical-ontological. Correlated to this is the suggestion that, while paganism arrives at the oneness of its godhead through philosophical reasoning and because of ontological-metaphysical considerations, biblical faith arrives at the oneness of its godhead because of ethical considerations and through a direct insight into the absolute character of the moral law. Thus, biblical monotheism can be distinguished from pagan monotheism in that it alone is ethical monotheism. Here again, however, the distinction is located in an aspect to which the concept of monotheism as such does not refer; the concept of monotheism as such conveys no ethical connotation. It may be that this distinction follows from the proper understanding of the difference between the meaning of monotheism in the biblical context and its use in the context of paganism, but this distinction as such does not capture this difference. In attempting to define the difference, it is interesting first to note that the two formulations above have already shifted the aspect where the difference is to be located from the "mono" to the "theos" part of the concept of monotheism; the theistic-pantheistic distinction refers to the relation of the "theos" to the world, while the ethical-metaphysical distinction refers to what kind of a "theos" is involved. This means that the difference between biblical faith and paganism is no longer seen as a quantitative difference, i.e., how many gods are involved, but as a qualitative difference, i.e., what kind of a god is involved. This shift is essential to a proper understanding of the difference and must form the basis of the attempted formulation.

Ultimate Being

On this basis it can be asserted that the minimal necessary connotation of the term "theos" in the concept of monotheism is that of ultimate being. As such, the arithmetical comparison between biblical monotheism and pagan polytheism is clearly seen to be illegitimate. The "theos" in pagan polytheism is not ultimate. It is superhuman, or "man writ large," but still it remains finite and non-absolute. In polytheism a plurality of ultimate beings is untenable and self-contradictory. Consequently, the "theos" in biblical monotheism and the "theos" in pagan polytheism connote two different kinds of being, for the difference between ultimate and non-ultimate being is not merely quantitative but qualitative. It is not legitimate, however, to compare quantitatively entities which belong to different orders of being. In order to locate the difference meaningfully it must be determined with reference to the same kind of entity, i.e., to the ultimate being which is connoted by the concept of monotheism. As such, however, it is not correct to speak of the development of the concept of monotheism in paganism. Paganism always had a conception of ultimate being transcending its gods and, as indicated above, ultimate being necessitates oneness. There can be no development from many to one with regard to ultimate being. Thus, if the "theos" in monotheism signifies ultimate being, paganism always had a conception of monotheism. The only development that can be pointed to is a development in its articulation, i.e., a development from the cultic-mythological to the speculative-philosophical expression. If the "theos" in monotheism, however, signifies only ultimate being, then it would not be possible to locate any difference between biblical and pagan monotheism, for then the "mono" conveys no additional information which is not already conveyed by the "theos" in itself. In order for the concept of monotheism to have a distinct meaning, the "theos" has to stand for something more than ultimate being. It is here that the real, fundamental difference between pagan and biblical monotheism becomes evident.

Personal Monotheism

In biblical monotheism the "theos" stands for a god who is personal. The "mono" connotes essentially not arithmetical oneness but oneness in the sense of uniqueness. Ultimate being is uniquely one in that it excludes the existence of any other qualitatively similar being. Thus, the authentic meaning of biblical monotheism is the assertion that the "mono," i.e., the unique, the ultimate, is "theos," i.e., a personal being, and this is the distinctive and unique feature of biblical faith and its monotheistic formulation. Paganism, while it too always had a conception of ultimate being and thus a conception of a unitary being, never asserted that ultimate being as personal. It follows from this analysis that the development of biblical monotheism from paganism cannot be envisioned as a linear, continuous development, but must be seen as a "jump" from one orbit to another, for the change that biblical monotheism introduced is qualitative and not quantitative. There is no continuous line of development either from non-personal to personal being or from relative being to ultimate being. This development involves a shift in perspective. While the above articulates the distinctive and essential content of the monotheistic conception of Judaism, it does not preclude or invalidate the fact that the monotheistic conception in Judaism may convey also the arithmetical oneness and the ontological uniqueness of God. Indeed, in post-biblical Judaism (and even in some biblical instances) it is these notions that come to the fore and become the main expressions of the Jewish monotheistic conception. It would seem, however, that the notion of the arithmetical unity of God arises mainly as a reaction against pluralistic formulations found in other religions, such as the *dualism of the Zoroastrian, Manichean, or Gnostic formulation and the trinitarianism of Christianity. The notion of the ontological uniqueness of the godhead arises mainly when Judaism conceives and expresses itself in the philosophical-metaphysical domain, i.e., when its God becomes the god of the philosophers.

Monotheism in Jewish Sources

Thus, Deutero-Isaiah, in response to Persian dualism, stresses the oneness of God in the sense that He alone is God, the one and only creator and ultimate cause of all phenomena: "I form light and create darkness; I make peace and create evil" (Isa. 45:7). This assertion is repeated frequently in rabbinic literature: "He who brought all things into being and who is their first cause is one" (Maimonides, *Sefer ha-Mitzvot*, positive commandment 2); "I have created all things in pairs. Heaven and earth, man and woman,… but my glory is one and unique" (Deut. R. 2:31). Likewise, the specific use of this assertion polemically against dualism and trinitarianism is extensive: "'I am the first' for I have no father, 'and I am the last' for I have no son, 'and beside me there is no God' for I have no brother" (Ex. R. 29:5); "The Lord, both in His role as our God [who loves us and extends His providence to us, i.e., the second person of the trinity] and the Lord [as He is in Himself, i.e., the first person of the trinity] is one from every aspect" (Leon de Modena, *Magen va-Ḥerev*, 2:7, 31–32). Furthermore, a number of the basic tenets of Judaism follow logically from this assertion of the arithmetical oneness of God, and rabbinic literature derives them from it. Thus, all forms of idolatry are rejected: God's absolute sovereignty and glory is proclaimed; both love and judgment, mercy and justice are attributed to one and the same God; God's infinity in time as the one God in the past, present, and future is declared. Although the concept of arithmetical oneness is involved also in the assertion of God's unity, the latter is distinct in that God is here distinguished qualitatively rather than merely quantitatively. This assertion finds its expression mainly in philosophical speculation, where the uniqueness of God is understood as essentially conveying the non-composite, non-divisible nature of His being (see Attributes of *God). This is expressed by Maimonides when he says that God is "not one of a genus nor of a species and not as one human being who is a compound divisible into many unities; not a unity like the ordinary material body which is one in number but takes on endless divisions and parts" (*Guide of the Perplexed*, 1:51ff.). This means that "God is one in perfect simplicity" (Ḥasdai *Crescas, *Or Adonai*, 1:1, 1), that He is wholly other (Saadiah Gaon, *Book of Beliefs and Opinions*, 2:1), and unique (Baḥya ibn Paquda, *Ḥovot ha-Levavot*, "*Sha'ar ha-Yiḥud*"). Even in rabbinic Judaism, although the emphasis is clearly placed on the two aspects of the monotheistic idea, i.e., the arithmetical oneness and the ontological uniqueness of God, the fundamental underlying assertion is that God is first and foremost a personal being. Thus, though shifting the emphasis, rabbinic Judaism remains fully bound to that aspect of the monotheistic idea where Judaism makes its fundamental and distinctive contribution to the history of religions.

BIBLIOGRAPHY: Y. Kaufmann, *The Religion of Israel* (1960), index; Guttmann, Philosophies, index; A. Altmann, in: *Tarbiz*, 27 (1958), 301–9; G. Vajda, in: A. Altmann (ed.), *Jewish Medieval and Renaissance Studies* (1966), 49–74.

[Manfred H. Vogel]

MONROE, MARILYN (1926–1962), U.S. actress. Monroe was born Norma Jean Mortensen in Los Angeles, California, to mechanic Edward Mortensen and RKO film technician Gladys Monroe. Her father abandoned the family before her birth, her mother was frequently institutionalized because of paranoid schizophrenia, and Monroe was raised in a series of foster homes. After a failed youthful marriage to James Dougherty and a few modeling jobs she changed her name to Marilyn Monroe. Contracts with Columbia and Fox resulted in small parts in John Huston's *Asphalt Jungle* (1950), *All About Eve* (1950), *Let's Make It Legal* (1951), *Niagara* (1952), and *Monkey Business* (1952). In 1953, she appeared nude in the first issue of *Playboy*, certifying her role as the All-American sex symbol. In 1954, she married baseball player Joe DiMaggio; however, the stormy marriage was brief and the couple divorced the same year. After making Billy Wilder's *Seven Year Itch* (1954) she broke her contract with Fox and moved to New York City to study with Lee and Paula *Strasberg at the Actors Studio. Introduced to playwright Arthur *Miller by Elia *Kazan, she converted to Judaism in a ceremony officiated by Rabbi Robert Goldberg two days after they married. She went on to appear in a string of successful films, including *Bus Stop* (1956), *Some Like It Hot* (1959), and *Let's Make Love* (1960). In 1961, she starred in *The Misfits*, which featured a script written by Arthur Miller. The Huston film was a difficult shoot, and was followed by the death of star Clark Gable 12 days after it was completed. Monroe divorced Miller in 1961, and entered a New York psychiatric clinic later that year. She returned to Fox in 1962 to finish her part in the film *Something's Got to Give*, but was found dead in her Brentwood, California, home on Aug. 5; an autopsy found a lethal dose of barbiturates.

[Adam Wills (2nd ed.)]

MONSKY, HENRY (**Ẓevi**; 1890–1947), U.S. communal leader, organization executive, and lawyer. Monsky was born in Russia and taken as an infant to Omaha, Nebraska. Of Orthodox background, as a matter of principle he belonged to Reform, Conservative, and Orthodox synagogues. In 1921 he founded the Omaha Community Chest and Welfare Federation, serving as its first vice president and later as president (1929); he was a trustee of Boys' Town, a member of the National Board of Community Chests and Council, Inc., president of the Nebraska Council of Social Work, and chairman of the Executive Committee of the National Conference of Prevention and Control of Juvenile Delinquency. Monsky was elected president of the Omaha lodge of B'nai B'rith in 1912 and eventually served as national president of the organization (1938–47). In 1941 he was invited by President Franklin D. Roosevelt to plan for the Office of Civilian Defense.

A lifelong Zionist, Monsky succeeded in enlisting the support of non-Zionists in protests against the British White Paper, Cyprus internment, and restrictions of immigration to Palestine. On Dec. 8, 1942, he led a delegation of representatives of Jewish organizations to the White House to call Roosevelt's attention to the plight of the Jews of Europe and to request firm action against the Nazis. Monsky collaborated with Zionists as the principal organizer of the all-inclusive *American Jewish Conference of 1943 in Pittsburgh, Pennsylvania, at which the U.S. Jewish community endorsed the Zionist program of a Jewish commonwealth. In April 1945, as consultant to the U.S. delegation to the United Nations Organizing Conference in San Francisco, he effectively helped influence the UN leaders to guarantee the rights of any states or peoples living under international bodies such as the Palestine British Mandate. He testified before the 1946 Anglo-American Commission of Inquiry in favor of this demand and also served as a member of U.S. Attorney General Tom Clark's Juvenile Delinquency Board. Monsky's Jewish communal interests included leadership positions in the Council of Jewish Federation and Welfare Funds, the Joint Distribution Committee, the National Conference of Christians and Jews, the Jewish Welfare Board, the American Friends of the Hebrew University, and the United Palestine Appeal. A moshav in Israel, Ramat Ẓevi, is named in his memory.

[Benjamin Kahn]

MONTAGU, English banking family, prominent in politics and public life. SIR SAMUEL MONTAGU, FIRST BARON SWAYTHLING (1832–1911), banker, communal worker, and philanthropist, was born in Liverpool as Montagu Samuel, but in his boyhood the names were reversed. In 1853 he founded the merchant bankers, Samuel Montagu and Company. By securing a larger proportion of the exchange business, he helped make London the chief clearing house of the international money market. He was Liberal member of Parliament for Whitechapel from 1885 to 1900, and a benefactor to its poor, Jewish and non-Jewish. An advocate of, and writer on, decimalization of the currency and adoption of the metric system, he was consulted by successive chancellors of the exchequer on financial matters and in 1894 persuaded the government to exempt from death duties works of art and gifts to universities, museums, and art galleries. In 1894 he was made a baronet and in 1907 a baron. A strictly observant Jew, he assumed leadership of the Orthodox Russo-Jewish immigrants, founding in 1887 the Federation of Synagogues to unite the small congregations. More theologically "right-wing" than the mainstream United Synagogue, it continues to be a force in the Anglo-Jewish religious spectrum. He, however, worshiped at the fashionable New West End Synagogue and was a life member of the United Synagogue Council, though because of disagreements with its president, the first Lord Rothschild, he was inactive there. A masterful personality, he traveled to Palestine, Russia, and the United States on behalf of Jewry, but vigorously opposed Zionism.

His eldest son, LOUIS SAMUEL (1869–1927), SECOND BARON SWAYTHLING, was president of the Federation of Synagogues. Also an anti-Zionist, he declared, "Judaism is to me only a religion." He married Gladys, daughter of Colonel A.E.W. *Goldsmid. Their second son, EWEN EDWARD (1901–1985) was president of the United Synagogue (1954–62). As part of his wartime role in naval intelligence he originated and oversaw the famous scheme (known as "Operation Mincemeat") to fool the Germans into thinking that an Allied landing at Sardinia, rather than Sicily, was imminent in 1943. He did this by planting cleverly forged papers and documents on the corpse of a dead British vagrant, which was placed in such a way that it was certain to be found by the Germans. It was one of the greatest examples of successful wartime deception; Montagu's best-selling account, *The Man Who Never Was* (1953), was later made into a well-known film. After the War, he became judge advocate of the fleet and chairman of Middlesex Quarter Sessions (a leading London judicial post). Samuel Montagu's second son, EDWIN SAMUEL (1879–1924), a Liberal politician, was elected to parliament in 1906, becoming private secretary to Herbert Asquith (later prime minister). As parliamentary undersecretary of state for India from 1910 to 1914, he championed Indian aspirations to independence. In 1914 he became financial secretary to the Treasury, in 1915, chancellor of the duchy of Lancaster, and in 1916, minister of munitions. Secretary of state for India in Lloyd George's administration (1917–22), he was responsible for the Government of India Act (1919), devolving wide powers of self-government. He resigned in 1922, because of his opposition to government policy which was offensive to Indian Muslims, and lost his parliamentary seat the same year. In Jewish affairs, he was best known as an uncompromising opponent of Zionism and of the Balfour Declaration, being largely responsible for the modification of the original text. In 1915 he married (Beatrice) Venetia Stanley (1887–1948), the daughter of the fourth Lord Sheffield, who had been the (probably non-sexual) confidante of Prime Minister Herbert Asquith. As a result of her marriage she converted to Judaism, but without enthusiasm. Samuel Montagu's daughter, Lillian (Lilly) Helen *Montagu (1873–1963), a social worker and magistrate, was a pioneer of Liberal Judaism in Britain, and thus father and daughter have the possibly unique distinction of founding significant religious movements on opposite ends of the Jewish religious spectrum.

BIBLIOGRAPHY: S.D. Waley, *Edwin Montagu…* (1964); Ch. Weizmann, *Trial and Error* (1950), index; L. Stein, *Balfour Declaration* (1961), index; E.M.L. Umansky, *Lily Montagu and the Advancement of Liberal Judaism: From Vision to Vocation* (1983); R.P. Lehmann, *Nova Bibliotheca Anglo-Judaica* (1961), index; Roth, Mag Bibl, index; DNB, s.v.; JC (June 17, 1927), 11–12; (Jan. 25, 1963), 1, 7, 35; *The Times* (June 6, 1927; Jan. 24, 1963). **ADD. BIBLIOGRAPHY:** ODNB online; W.D. Rubinstein, *Jews in Great Britain,* index; G. Alderman, *Modern British Jewry,* index; idem., *The Federation of Synagogues, 1887–1987* (1987); C. Bermant, *The Cousinhood* (1961), index; M. Brock and E. Brock (eds.), *H.H. Asquith: Letters to Venetia Stanley* (1982); N.B. Levine, *Politics, Religion, and Love: The Story of H.H. Asquith, Venetia Stanley, and Edwin Montagu* (1991); S. Bayme, "Claude Montefiore, Lily Montagu and the Origins of the Jewish Religious Union," in: JHSET, XXVII (1978–80), 61–71; E.C. Black, "Edwin Montagu," in: JHSET, 30 (1987–88), 199–218.

[Vivian David Lipman / William D. Rubinstein (2nd ed.)]

MONTAGU, LILY (1873–1963), social worker, magistrate in the London juvenile courts, suffragist, writer, religious organizer, and spiritual leader. Born Lilian Helen Montagu in London, the sixth of ten children of Ellen Cohen Montagu and Samuel Montagu (né Montagu Samuel, later First Baron Swaythling), Lily Montagu founded and long remained the driving force behind the Liberal Jewish movement in England.

In 1893, Montagu established the West Central Jewish Girls' Club with her sister, Marion, and their cousin, Beatrice Franklin, to give working-class Jewish girls social, intellectual and spiritual opportunities. Montagu led brief Sabbath services in English, and addressed contemporary issues and concerns through sermons and selected traditional prayers. From 1890 until 1909, Montagu led similar services for children at the New West End Synagogue. Their success among women led her to envision ways of religiously revivifying the Anglo-Jewish community as a whole.

In 1899, in "The Spiritual Possibilities of Judaism Today," she asked all religiously committed Jews, traditional and liberal, to help her form an association aimed at strengthening the religious life of Anglo-Jewry through Liberal Jewish teachings. Influenced by Claude *Montefiore, scholar and proponent of Liberal Judaism, and inspired by the growth of Reform Judaism in Germany, Montagu established the Jewish Religious Union (JRU) in February 1902. The Union instituted Sabbath afternoon worship services conducted along Liberal Jewish lines and held "propaganda meetings," led by Montagu, to clarify and spread its teachings. Montefiore agreed to serve as the group's official leader, thus strengthening its credibility, but Montagu assumed responsibility for daily affairs and major activities.

During the next few decades, Montagu helped form Liberal Jewish congregations throughout Great Britain, frequently serving as their chairman or president. She became lay minister of the West Central Liberal Jewish Congregation in 1928, a position to which she was formally inducted in November 1944, and which she held until her death in 1963. Following Montefiore's death in 1938, she became president of the JRU, a position she held for 23 years. Montagu also helped found and eventually became president of the World Union for Progressive Judaism, administering the organization's daily affairs from 1926 through 1959. At the first WUPJ conference in Berlin, in 1928, Montagu delivered a sermon in German, on "Personal Religion," at a worship service held in Berlin's Reform Temple; she was the first Jewish woman to occupy a German pulpit. Through her efforts, the number of World Union constituencies steadily increased and new Liberal Jewish congregations were created in Europe, South America, Israel, South Africa and Australia. In 1959, when the World Union's headquarters were transferred to the U.S., she was named honorary life president and elected to chair the Union's newly-established European Board. Many of her writings appear in *Lily Montagu: Sermons, Addresses, Letters, and Prayers* (ed. E.M. Umansky, 1985).

While most British Jews continued to maintain at least a formal attachment to Orthodoxy, Montagu succeeded in establishing Liberal Judaism as an important religious force in Anglo-Jewish life. A Lily Montagu Centre of Living Judaism, housing the West Central Liberal Jewish Congregation, the European Board of the World Union, and the offices of the Union of Liberal and Progressive Synagogues (formerly the JRU), was named in Montagu's honor following her death in 1963.

BIBLIOGRAPHY: E.M. Umansky, *Lily Montagu and the Advancement of Liberal Judaism: From Vision to Vocation* (1983); idem, "Liberal Judaism in England: The Contribution of Lily H. Montagu," in: HUCA, 55 (1985), 309–22; L.G. Kuzmack, *Women's Cause: The Jewish Women's Movement in England and the United States: 1881–1933* (1990); M.A. Meyer, *A Response to Modernity: A History of the Reform Movement in Judaism* (1988).

[Ellen M. Umansky (2nd ed.)]

MONTAGU, MONTAGUE FRANCIS ASHLEY (1905–1999), physical and cultural anthropologist. Born in London, Montagu served as research associate in the British Museum of Natural History (1926–27) and as curator of physical anthropology at the Wellcome Historical Museum, London (1929–30). He emigrated to the U.S. and taught anatomy at New York University (1931–38) and Hahnemann Medical College and Hospital (1938–49), and was chairman of the anthropology department at Rutgers University (1945–55). An expert in physical anthropology and evolutionary theory, he served as rapporteur of the UNESCO committee of experts which formulated the 1950 UNESCO *Statement on Race* (1951, 1952[2]), and was a member of the second UNESCO committee of experts of geneticists and physical anthropologists. Convinced that the idea of race was not only fallacious but antihuman and socially destructive, he dedicated his rhetorical and literary gifts to the production of a number of popular books on this question and on anthropological themes of large humanistic interest. Among his best-known works are *Coming into Being among the Australian Aborigines* (1937, 1938[2]), *Man's Most Dangerous Myth: The Fallacy of Race* (1942, 1998[6]), *The Natural Superiority of Women* (1953, 1991[4]), *Human Heredity* (1959, 1964[2]), *Man in Process* (1961), and *The Direction of Human Evolution* (1955, 1959[3]), *Touching: The Human Significance of the Skin* (1971, 1985[3]), and *The Elephant Man* (1971, 1996[3]).

BIBLIOGRAPHY: *Current Biography Yearbook*, 1967 (1968), 294–7.

[Ephraim Fischoff]

MONTAIGNE, MICHEL DE (1533–1592), French writer and philosopher. His mother, Antoinette de Louppes de Villanueva, came from a Spanish Jewish family. One of her ancestors, Mayer Pacagon of Catalayud was forcibly converted to Catholicism and took the name of Lopez de Villanueva. His descendants, however, remained secretly faithful to Judaism, and several of them were persecuted by the Inquisition. One of them, Juan de Villanueva, from whom Montaigne's mother was descended, fled to Toulouse, France, where he settled. She later married the Catholic Eyquem de Montaigne, her uncle's business partner. Montaigne studied at the College de Guyenne run by Portuguese New Christians and, later, at Toulouse University, a center of New Christian ferment and heterodoxy. From 1557 to 1570 Montaigne held a post at the Bordeaux Parliament and at the Court of France. He began his literary career in the late 1560s by translating the *Natural Theology* of Raimond Sebon, a Spanish theologian, and editing the works of his deceased friend, La Böetie, a gifted young writer and thinker. In 1571 Montaigne retired from public life and wrote his *Essais* but, after a journey through Italy (1580–81), he was elected mayor of Bordeaux. In spite of his return to public office, Montaigne devoted much of his time to the continuation of the *Essais*. His humanistic skeptical philosophy, which had an enormous impact on later writers, undermined thinkers' acceptance of received theories. Philosophers such as Bacon, Descartes, Gassendi, and Pascal tried to overcome Montaigne's skepticism by finding new or different bases for knowledge. Montaigne also had a deep influence on English literature. Shakespeare cited him in a number of plays, notably in *The Tempest*, and he also inspired Dryden. The essay, as a literary form, is Montaigne's creation, and admirably suits the freedom of thought and open-mindedness he wished to attain.

It is difficult to know what Montaigne actually thought of the Jews, for this was a dangerous subject in those days of religious intolerance. Almost all his references to the Jews, however, show a sympathetic attitude. In the *Essais* he mentions disapprovingly the persecutions in Portugal, as well as the Jews' stubborn loyalty to their religion (Book I, chap. 14). But it is in the Travel Diary (*Journal de Voyage*), not intended for publication (it saw the light for the first time in 1774), that numerous references are found to Jewish life and customs, as Montaigne saw them at first hand during his Italian journey. There is no doubt that he went out of his way to visit synagogues, attend Jewish ceremonies, and converse with Jews. Montaigne gives a detailed, accurate and sympathetic account of Sabbath services and a circumcision ceremony. He comments on the communal participation in prayer, study, and discussion, and on the widespread knowledge of Hebrew, even among children. On February 6, 1581, he witnessed a pre-Lent "entertainment": burlesque races on the Corso, in which half-naked Jews had to take part. He also attended a conversion sermon, given by a famous preacher, himself a converted Jew, who used his talmudic knowledge to convince his brethren to convert. In all these instances his tone is objective, detached, and completely free from the accepted prejudices of the time. But two facts remain puzzling: Montaigne's obvious interest in Jewish life and his refraining from any mention of his mother in the *Essais*, a largely autobiographical work. Some critics interpret this as proof that Montaigne was deeply preoccupied with his Jewish identity and, for reasons of caution, deliberately avoided any reference to it. This may be so, but one basic fact is unknown, whether Montaigne even knew of his mother's Jewish ancestry. It seems doubtful, as her ancestors had been Christian for several generations, and no one, in those intolerant days, would have gone out of his way to unearth his Jewish ancestry. Montaigne may have had other reasons for emphasizing his father's influence and ignoring his mother's. His education, which partially determined his philosophical direction, was shaped by his father. Furthermore his mother, like his siblings who are absent from the *Essais*, converted to Protestantism and this, for a public figure such as Montaigne, was not an asset in the midst of the religious wars. As to his display of interest in Jewish life in Italy, it could well be that of a liberal humanistic non-Jew, keen as he was on heterodox, free, original ways of living and thinking, as manifested in various groups of outsiders, and unaffected by the current oppressive Church restrictions. Unless other manuscripts come to light, which is unlikely, the question remains open.

BIBLIOGRAPHY: Th. Malvezin, *Michel de Montaigne, son origine, sa famille* (1875); H. Friedrich, *Montaigne* (1949); D. Frame, *Montaigne, a biography* (1965); A. Thibaudet, in: NRF (1922); C. Roth, in: *Revue des Cours et Conférences* (1937); H. Friedenwald, in: JQR 31 (1940); A. Lunel, in: *Bulletin des Amis de Montaigne*, no. 19 (1956); M. Catalane, in: *Sixth World Congress of Jewish Studies* (Jerusalem, 1973).

[Denise R. Goitein]

MONTANA, one of the Rocky Mountain states of the United States. In 1969 it had a Jewish population of 615 out of a total

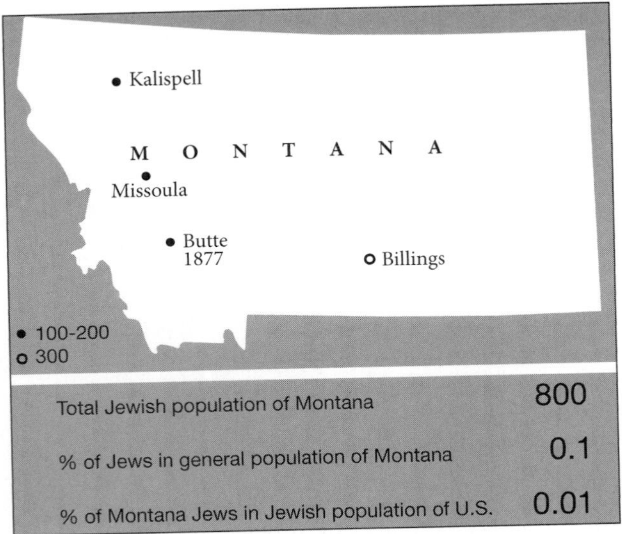

Jewish communities in Montana and dates of establishment. Population figures for 2001.

of 710,000. By 2001 Montana has a Jewish population of some 800 among 903,000.

According to one observer, Montana's Jews tend to fall into three categories: remnants of the pioneer community still in Helena or Butte; out-of-state professionals who mass in university towns such as Bozeman or Missoula; the lone Jew who lives in Townsend or Ennis or Miles City. The community is united by the Montana Association of Jewish Communities (MAJCO).

Member communities include Aitz Chaim (Great Falls Jewish Community), Bet Harim (Flathead Valley Jewish Community), Beth Aaron (Billings Jewish Community), Beth Shalom (Bozeman Jewish Community), Har Shalom (Missoula Jewish Community), and B'nai Israel (Butte Jewish Community). MAJCO regularly holds a shabbaton in the spring of each year. Chabad has sent summer rabbis to work with the community and is planning a full-time rabbinic presence in Bozeman, perhaps the liveliest of the Jewish communities.

The first Jews, who arrived in 1862 during the gold rush at Bannock and Virginia City, were miners, wagon drivers, merchants, freighters, hotel and saloon keepers, lawyers, and journalists, many of whom became solid citizens in the raucous mining camps. Ben Ezekiel was chief clerk of the first territorial legislature and Jacob Feldberg was a member of Virginia City's first town council. Jews were also among the leaders of the vigilantes who suppressed outlawry. The oldest Jewish settlement dates from 1864, with the arrival of Jewish merchants in Helena. One of the pioneers was Gumpertz Goldberg, for whose wife Helena is said to have been named. The First Hebrew Benevolent Society, organized in 1865, became the nucleus for Temple Emanu-El, founded in 1887; their synagogue, the state's first synagogue, was built in 1891. When the Jewish community declined in the 1920s, the synagogue was deeded to the state, and it now houses the State Department of Public Welfare. When Butte became the biggest city in the state following the silver and gold booms around Anaconda in the 1870s, most of the early Jewish settlers and the later arrivals settled there. There was a Jewish congregation, Beth Israel, in Butte in 1877. It split over ritual in 1897 and a second one came into being, but today there is only one congregation with a synagogue dating from 1904. Long before Montana became a state in 1889, its Jewish residents were counted among its leading citizens. Henry Jacobs was Butte's first mayor in 1879, and Henry Lupin held that office from 1885 to 1889. Charles S. Cohan, editor of *The Butte Miner*, wrote the words for the state song. One of the early cattlemen was Louis Kaufman, who employed the cowboy artist Charlie Russell. Between 1873 and 1906 four Jews were grand masters of the State Masonic Grand Lodge: Sol Star, Moses Morris, H. Sol Hepner, and Henry I. Frank, a former mayor of Butte. Livingston, Great Falls, and Havre also had Jewish mayors before 1900. Among the colorful figures in the early days of the state were Daniel Bandman, a Shakespearean actor who brought theater to the mining camps (Bandman's Bridge outside Missoula is named for him); Moses Solomon, a Buffalo hunter and Indian fighter; and Philip Deidesheimer, a mining superintendent, who invented the square set system of mining timbers and for whom Philipsburg is named. The Bob Marshall Wilderness Area of 950,000 acres in the Flathead National Forest is named for the son of Louis *Marshall, who was chief of the division of recreation in the U.S. Forest Service.

The story of Billings, Montana, tells much about the paradox of Jewish life in Montana. In 1993 Billings had a population of 48 Jewish families among 81,000 residents. Hate literature appeared in mailboxes; the synagogue was painted with a swastika along with a picture of a Jew being shot by *Einsatzgruppen*, tombstones were overturned, Holocaust denial literature was circulated, and the homes of two Jewish families including the symphony conductor, which had been adorned with menorahs, had their windows broken. A cinder block was thrown through a Jewish child's window. The local Church Council and the senior minister of the First Congregational Church passed out menorahs to his congregation. He put a menorah in his own window. The newspaper printed a full page cutout of a menorah. The chief of police characterized the response: "It became physically impossible for the hate group to harass and intimidate thousands and thousand of Billings' citizens … We have spoken one very loud voice." In this case, the response to hatred was a united chorus of solidarity. The specific motif of the Holocaust, which was the threat of the hate groups, was embraced by the community to say, "We will behave differently." Hatred will not triumph. The Jews will not be isolated but embraced. It was a hopeful moment for all concerned.

BIBLIOGRAPHY: B. Kelson, "The Jews of Montana" (thesis, University of Montana, 1950); B. Postal and L. Koppman, *A Jewish Tourist's Guide to the U.S.* (1954), 281–9. **ADD. BIBLIOGRAPHY:** E. Linenthal, *Preserving Memory: the Struggle to Create America's Holocaust Museum* (1995)

[Bernard Postal / Michael Berenbaum (2nd ed.)]

MONTCLUS (Heb. מונטקלוס, מונטקלוש, הר סגור), former town and fortress at the foot of the Pyrenees, in Aragon, western Spain. Jews apparently lived in the fortress of Montclus and the adjacent area from the beginning of the 11th century. The annual tax paid by the community in the 13th century was reduced by the king from 800 to 500 solidos in 1271, increased to 707 solidos and 3½ denarii in Jaca coin in 1304, and again reduced to 450 solidos in 1315. In 1298 James II ordered an investigation on the rate of interest charged by Jews on loans.

The Montclus community helped to rehabilitate Jews expelled from France in 1306. In 1307 the king authorized the community to absorb four families, including those of the physician Maestre Boninfante and Vitalis de Boulogne. However, between the end of June and the beginning of July 1320, the community was annihilated in the *Pastoureaux (Shepherds) massacres. On July 22, James II ordered that assistance should be given to the survivors, but that Jewish children who had been forcibly baptized were to remain in Christian households. In 1321 the king freed the remnant of the community from paying taxes and ordered that the walls of the fortress should be rebuilt, but by 1323 the Jews of Montclus had to pay taxes like the other Jews of the kingdom to finance the royal expedition to Sardinia. His successor, Alfonso IV, in 1335 freed the community from paying taxes, as did Pedro IV in 1341–42. Nevertheless, when disorders broke out in 1333, the commander of the fortress, Garcia Bardaxi, did nothing to prevent the rioters from massacring the Jews and was pardoned.

With the expulsion of the Jews from Spain in 1492, Montclus began to decline. In the 17th century it was completely abandoned.

BIBLIOGRAPHY: Baer, Studien, 149; Baer, Urkunden, 1 (1929), index; Baer, Spain, 1 (1961), 42; 2 (1966), 15; S. ibn Verga, *Shevet Yehudah*, A. Shochat (ed.), (1947), 25; Miret y Sans, in: REJ, 53 (1907), 255ff.; Cardoner and Vendre, in: *Sefarad*, 7 (1947), 311, 328; Ashtor, Korot, 2 (1966), 153.

[Haim Beinart]

MONTEFIORE, CLAUDE JOSEPH GOLDSMID (1858–1938), theologian and leader of Liberal Judaism in England. Montefiore was a great-nephew of Sir Moses *Montefiore and a grandson of Isaac Lyon *Goldsmid. He studied at Balliol College, Oxford, where he came under the influence of the master of Balliol, Benjamin Jowett, the famous liberal Christian thinker. Later he studied Judaism at the *Hochschule (Lehranstalt) fuer die Wissenschaft des Judentums in Berlin, and under Solomon *Schechter, whom he had taken to England as his private tutor. A man of means, Montefiore did not serve as a professional scholar or man of religion but nevertheless frequently preached eloquent sermons.

In 1888 he founded the *Jewish Quarterly Review*, which he financed and edited, with Israel *Abrahams, as coeditor, until 1908. He was the founder in England of a radical Reform movement (Jewish Religious Union, 1902), which led in 1911 to the establishment of the Liberal Jewish Synagogue; he served as its president. In 1926 Montefiore was elected president of the World Union for Progressive Judaism, an office which he held until his death. Together with the Catholic theologian Baron von Hugel, he founded the London Society for the Study of Religion, a select group of Jewish and Christian thinkers which met regularly to read and discuss papers on the philosophy of religion. A generous philanthropist, he assisted many Jewish and general good causes. He was a determined opponent of Zionism, and as president of the *Anglo-Jewish Association (1895–1921) tried to prevent the signing of the Balfour Declaration. He was president of the Jewish Religious Union and of the Jewish Historical Society of England (1899–1900). He also played a major part in the educational life of the Jewish community and beyond, and University College, Southampton, presented him with a volume of essays on his 70th birthday (*Speculum Religionis*, 1929).

Works

Montefiore was a prolific writer. In addition to numerous articles in periodicals, he wrote: *Aspects of Judaism* (1895²), sermons, together with Israel Abrahams; *Bible for Home Reading* (2 vols., 1897–1899²); *The Synoptic Gospels* (2 vols.; 1909; 1927²; repr. 1968), a commentary on the Gospels primarily for the Jewish reader; *Liberal Judaism* (1903); *Some Elements of the Religious Teaching of Jesus* (1910); *Outlines of Liberal Judaism* (1912, 1923²); *Judaism and St. Paul* (1914); *Liberal Judaism and Hellenism* (1918); *The Old Testament and After* (1923); *Rabbinic Literature and Gospel Teaching* (1930); and *A Short Devotional Introduction to the Hebrew Bible for the Use of Jews and Jewesses* (1936). Together with Herbert *Loewe, Montefiore published: *A Rabbinic Anthology* (1938; repr. 1960, 1963), a collection of rabbinic teachings with remarkable notes by the two editors, one Liberal and the other Orthodox. Montefiore delivered the Hibbert Lectures (1892) on *Origin and Growth of Religion as Illustrated by the Religion of the Ancient Hebrews.*

Thought

At the center of Montefiore's thought was his complete conviction of the truth of Jewish theism. He acknowledged that the Jewish conception of God and His relation to man and that of the relation of religion to morality are akin to but not identical with Christian conceptions dealing with these themes. The distinctiveness of Jewish theism lies in its insistence on both the transcendence and immanence of God. Montefiore holds that modern Biblical scholarship has demonstrated conclusively that the Pentateuchal Code is not Mosaic, homogeneous, and perfect. Yet this does not mean that the conception of law in religion should be abandoned. Man discovers the Law within him but it is also revealed to him.

Montefiore was very suspicious of Jewish nationalism because of its "narrowness" and its betrayal, in his view, of Jewish universalism. He was so much at home in England that his affinities were much closer to his native land than to the community of Israel throughout the world.

The greatest cause of offense to traditionalists was Montefiore's leaning toward Christianity. He viewed Christianity entirely sympathetically, and seemed to look forward to the religion of the future as embracing all that is good in both Judaism and Christianity as well as in other religions.

Montefiore's main contention is that in some respects but not in others the Christian ethic is more admirable than the Jewish, and that there is a mystical, appealing note sounded in the Gospels not sounded in quite the same way in the Bible. Jesus, for Montefiore, was a great teacher but not divine as Christians have it. He was opposed to any attempt at placing the New Testament on a par with the Hebrew Scriptures or at having readings from the New Testament in any act of Jewish worship. He, nevertheless, felt that the time had come for Jews to read and understand the New Testament and even allow it to occupy an honored place in present-day Judaism. Soon after the publication of *The Synoptic Gospels*, Aḥad Ha-Am launched a vigorous attack against it (*Al Parashat Derakhim*, 4 (1921), 38–58). Aḥad Ha-Am argued that Jewish ethic, based on justice, is incompatible with the Christian ethic based on love, so that it is impossible for the same man to embrace both of them at the same time. In his very last years, when the Nazi regime was systematically persecuting German Jewry, Montefiore may have been moving away from his adamant stance on the issues of Jewish nationalism and Zionism, but died before the full impact of the Holocaust and, later, the creation of Israel, might have necessitated a full-scale revision of his views.

BIBLIOGRAPHY: V.E. Reichert, in: CCARY, 38 (1928), 499–520; F.C. Burkitt, in: *Speculum Religionis* (1929), 1–17; J. Wolf, in: *La Question d'Israel (bulletin catholique)*, 17 (1939), 503–16; 561–72; L. Cohen, *Some Recollections…* (1940), incl. bibl.; W.R. Matthews, *Claude Montefiore, the Man and his Thought* (1956); F.C. Schwartz, in: JQR, 55 (1964/65), 23–52; A. Montefiore, in: *Quest*, 1 (London, 1965), 73–75; N. Bentwich, *C.M. and his Tutor in Rabbinics* (1966), incl. bibl.; W. Jacob, in: *Judaism*, 19 no. 3 (1970), 328–43. **ADD. BIBLIOGRAPHY:** ODNB online; C. Bermant, *The Cousinhood* (1961), index; D. Langton, *Claude Montefiore: His Life and Thought* (2002); E. Kessler, "Claude Montefiore: Defender of Rabbinic Judaism," in: JHSET, XXXV (1998), 231–38.

[Louis Jacobs]

MONTEFIORE, JOSEPH BARROW (1803–1893), Australian pioneer. A cousin of Sir Moses *Montefiore, Joseph Barrow Montefiore was born in London. At the age of 23, he bought a seat on the London Stock Exchange and became one of the 12 "Jew brokers" in the city. He immigrated to Australia in 1829 with considerable means at his disposal and was granted 5,000 acres of land. In Melbourne, Sydney, and later in South Australia, he acquired extensive parcels of land. In 1838 he was invited to give evidence to the House of Lords on the state of the islands of New Zealand. He and his elder brother Jacob, who was one of the 11 commissioners appointed by King William IV to organize the administration of South Australia, helped to establish the Bank of Australasia. Montefiore, who had ultimately made his home in Adelaide, became one of its most prominent commercial and industrial figures. When in Sydney, he was South Australia's agent in New South Wales, and one of the original trustees of the State Savings Bank of South Australia. In 1832 Montefiore helped to organize Australia's first congregation, the Sydney Synagogue, the predecessor of the Great Synagogue, and was its first president. He was a trustee of the Jewish cemetery, for which he had secured a land grant from the government. The township of Montefiore in New South Wales and Montefiore Hill in Adelaide are tributes to the pioneering work of Montefiore and his family. He spent the last years of his life in England.

ADD. BIBLIOGRAPHY: J.S. Levi and G.F.J. Bergman, *Australian Genesis: Jewish Convicts and Settlers, 1788–1860* (2002), 171–74, index; ADB; H.L. Rubinstein, Australia I, index.

[Israel Porush]

MONTEFIORE, JOSHUA (1762–1843), British-born lawyer and author. Montefiore, an uncle of Sir Moses *Montefiore, was born in London. Most unusually, he attended Oxford University and was admitted to practice as a solicitor in 1784. In 1787 he was in Jamaica, where discriminatory precedent prevented his admission as an attorney and notary. He participated in an unsuccessful expedition in 1791 to establish a British colony without slave labor off the west coast of Africa, near Sierra Leone, an adventure he described in *An Authentic Account of the Late Expedition to Bulam* (1794). Montefiore allegedly declined a knighthood and was the first Jew to hold the rank of captain in the British army. Around 1810 he went to the United States, pursued the practice of law, and for a time edited a New York weekly political journal, *Men and Measures*, said to have been subsidized by the British government. Montefiore compiled a number of useful lay guides to commercial law which sold briskly in England and the U.S., including *Law of Copyright* (1802), *Commercial Dictionary* (1803; first U.S., ed., 1811), *Traders and Manufacturers Compendium* (1804), *American Traders Compendium* (1811), and *Commercial and Notarial Precedents* (1804). Montefiore's second wife was a Catholic, but his eight children were raised as Protestants. At his request, he was buried on the farm on the outskirts of St. Albans, Vermont, where he had settled in 1835.

BIBLIOGRAPHY: M.J. Kohler, in: AJHSP, 19 (1910), 179–80; L.M. Friedman, *ibid.*, 40 (1950), 119–34. **ADD. BIBLIOGRAPHY:** "Joshua Montefiore," in: *Appleton's Encyclopedia.*

[Isidore S. Meyer]

MONTEFIORE, JUDITH (1784–1862), daughter of Levi Barent *Cohen and wife of Sir Moses *Montefiore, whom she married in 1812. Her influence on her husband was profound. She left a diary of their first visit to Palestine in 1827 and described their second visit in 1838 in her *Notes from a Private Journal* (1844). She was the author, or coauthor, of the first Anglo-Jewish cookbook, the *Jewish Manual* by "A Lady" (1846). She was commemorated by her husband in the foundation of the Judith Lady Montefiore College. Originally lax in observance, she later returned to strict Orthodox practice.

BIBLIOGRAPHY: See Sir Moses *Montefiore; Lipman, in: JHSET, 21 (1962–67), 287–303.

[Sonia L. Lipman]

MONTEFIORE, SIR MOSES (1784–1885), most famous Anglo-Jew of the 19th century. Montefiore was born in Leghorn while his parents were on a visit from London, where he was brought up, being taught elementary Hebrew by his maternal uncle Moses *Mocatta. First apprenticed to a firm of wholesale grocers and tea merchants, he left to become one of the 12 "Jew brokers" in the City of London. After initial setbacks, he went into partnership with his brother Abraham, and the firm acquired a high reputation. His marriage in 1812 to Judith Cohen (see Judith *Montefiore) made him brother-in-law of Nathan Mayer *Rothschild, for whom his firm acted as stockbrokers. After his retirement from regular business in 1824, though he retained various commercial directorships, he had the time and the fortune to undertake communal and civic responsibilities.

Contrary to accepted opinion, he was apparently somewhat lax in religious observance in earlier life; but from 1827, after his first visit to Ereẓ Israel, until the end of his life, he was a strictly observant Jew. Montefiore maintained his own synagogue on his estate at Ramsgate from 1833 and in later years traveled with his own *shoḥet*. His determined opposition checked the growth of the Reform movement in England. Though a patron of scholars, he had no pretensions to scholarship himself. He paid seven visits to Ereẓ Israel, the last in 1874. In 1838 his scheme for acquiring land to enable Jews in Ereẓ Israel to become self-supporting through agriculture was frustrated when Mehmet Ali, viceroy of Egypt, who had shown sympathy for the idea, was forced by the great powers to give up his conquests from the Turks. He later attempted to bring industry to the country, introducing a printing press and a textile factory, and inspired the founding of several agricultural colonies. The Yemin Moshe quarter outside the Old City of Jerusalem was due to his endeavors and named after him. In 1855, by the will of Judah *Touro, the U.S. philanthropist, he was appointed to administer a bequest of $50,000 for Jews of the Holy Land.

Montefiore was sheriff of London in 1837–38 and was knighted by Queen Victoria on her first visit to the City. He received a baronetcy in 1846 in recognition of his humanitarian efforts on behalf of his fellow Jews. Although president of the *Board of Deputies of British Jews from 1835 to 1874 (with only one brief interruption), he did not, after the early years, play a prominent part in the emancipation struggle but devoted himself to helping oppressed Jewries overseas. He has been described as the last of the *shtadlanim who by their personal standing with their governments were able to further the cause of Jews elsewhere. He was active as such from the time of the *Damascus Affair in 1840. In 1846, he visited Russia to persuade the authorities to alleviate persecution of the Jewish population, and went to *Morocco in 1863 and *Romania in 1867 for the same purpose. His intervention in the *Mortara Case in 1855, however, proved a failure. Some of his achievements appear in retrospect as transitory. Although in 1872, after representing the Board of Deputies at the bicentenary celebrations of Peter the Great, he reported that a new age had dawned for the Jews of Russia, persecution was renewed in 1881. Lover of Ereẓ Israel though he was and believer in the messianic restoration of a Jewish state, he did not conceive of large-scale, planned development of the country as a solution to the Jewish problem. This was largely because Montefiore (and his contemporaries) trusted absolutely in the inevitability of progress and with it worldwide emancipation for the Jews.

Nevertheless, both in his own lifetime and since, he enjoyed enormous prestige. Montefiore's physical presence (he was 6 ft. 3 in. tall), his commanding personality, his philanthropy, and his complete disinterestedness, made him highly respected and admired both in England and abroad. The support of the British government for his activities – consonant with British policies overseas – and the personal regard shown him by Queen Victoria added to his reputation. His 100th birthday was celebrated as a public holiday by Jewish communities the world over.

One of the most famous Jews of the 19th century, Moses Montefiore was important for many different reasons, for instance as an early, influential Zionist. His most significant role, however, might have been as arguably the template of a wealthy, influential, well-connected Jew in a Western democracy, who used his influence to ameliorate the condition of persecuted Jews in countries where antisemitism was rife. This model of Jewish leadership has persisted, perhaps as the norm, into our own times.

BIBLIOGRAPHY: Roth, Mag Bibl, 140–6; Lehmann, Nova Bibl, 109, 112, 117; L. Wolf, *Sir Moses Montefiore* (1885, Eng.); L. Loewe, *Diaries of Sir Moses and Lady Montefiore*, 2 vols. (1890); P. Goodman, *Moses Montefiore* (1925, Eng.); S.U. Nahon, *Sir Moses Montefiore* (Eng. 1965). **ADD. BIBLIOGRAPHY:** S. and V.D. Lipman (eds.), *The Century of Moses Montefiore* (1985); G. Alderman, *Modern British Jewry*, index; W.D. Rubinstein, *Jews in Great Britain*, index; D.S. Katz, *Jews in England*, 336–40, index; T. Endelman, *Jews of Britain*, index.

[Vivian David Lipman]

MONTEFIORE, SEBAG-MONTEFIORE, English family originating from Leghorn, Italy. (See Chart: Montefiore Family 1, 2, and 3). The first to come to England were the brothers MOSES VITA (1712–1789), who set up successfully as an importer of Italian straw hats, and JOSEPH (b. 1723). The former had 17 children who intermarried with the Anglo-Jewish families. His grandsons Joseph Barrow *Montefiore (1803–1893) and JACOB MONTEFIORE (1801–1895) were prominent in early Australian history; two other sons were Joshua *Montefiore and JOSEPH ELIAS (1759–1804) who married Rachel Mocatta and was the father of Sir Moses *Montefiore. Sir Moses' brother and business partner, ABRAHAM (1788–1824), married as his second wife Henrietta Rothschild. Their two sons were JOSEPH MAYER (1816–1880) and NATHANIEL (1819–1883), the father of Claude Goldsmid *Montefiore. Joseph Mayer succeeded Sir Moses as president of the Board of Deputies in 1874, after having been the first vice president since 1857. Under his presidency the Board and the Anglo-Jewish Asso-

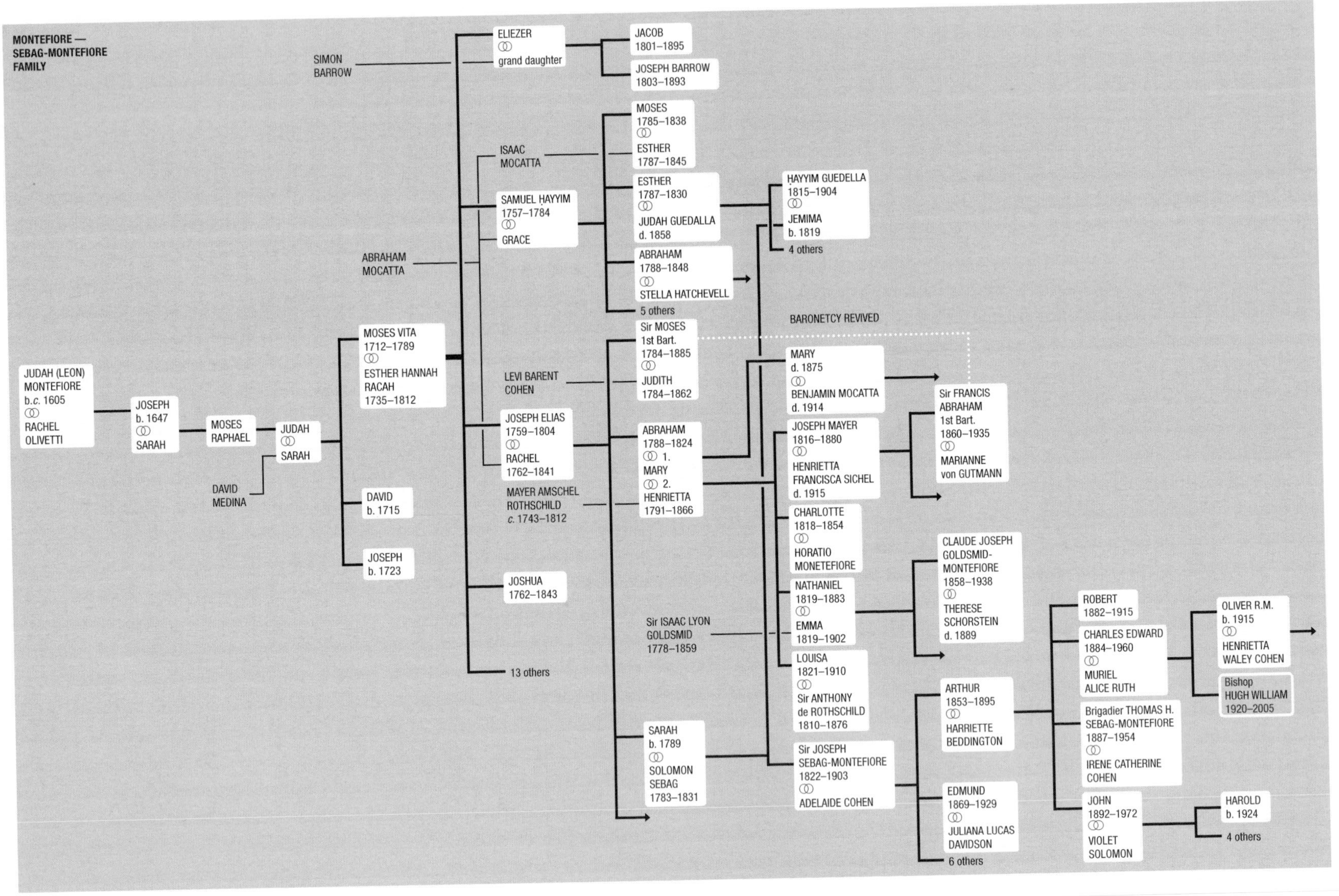
MONTEFIORE — SEBAG-MONTEFIORE FAMILY
JUDAH (LEON) MONTEFIORE b.c. 1605 ⚭ RACHEL OLIVETTI
JOSEPH b. 1647 ⚭ SARAH
MOSES RAPHAEL
JUDAH ⚭ SARAH
DAVID MEDINA
MOSES VITA 1712–1789 ⚭ ESTHER HANNAH RACAH 1735–1812
DAVID b. 1715
JOSEPH b. 1723
SIMON BARROW
ABRAHAM MOCATTA
ELIEZER ⚭ grand daughter
ISAAC MOCATTA
SAMUEL ḤAYYIM 1757–1784 ⚭ GRACE
LEVI BARENT COHEN
JOSEPH ELIAS 1759–1804 ⚭ RACHEL 1762–1841
MAYER AMSCHEL ROTHSCHILD c. 1743–1812
JOSHUA 1762–1843
13 others
JACOB 1801–1895
JOSEPH BARROW 1803–1893
MOSES 1785–1838 ⚭ ESTHER 1787–1845
ESTHER 1787–1830 ⚭ JUDAH GUEDALLA d. 1858
ABRAHAM 1788–1848 ⚭ STELLA HATCHEVELL
5 others
Sir MOSES 1st Bart. 1784–1885 ⚭ JUDITH 1784–1862
ABRAHAM 1788–1824 ⚭ 1. MARY ⚭ 2. HENRIETTA 1791–1866
Sir ISAAC LYON GOLDSMID 1778–1859
SARAH b. 1789 ⚭ SOLOMON SEBAG 1783–1831
ḤAYYIM GUEDELLA 1815–1904 ⚭ JEMIMA b. 1819
4 others
BARONETCY REVIVED
MARY d. 1875 ⚭ BENJAMIN MOCATTA d. 1914
JOSEPH MAYER 1816–1880 ⚭ HENRIETTA FRANCISCA SICHEL d. 1915
CHARLOTTE 1818–1854 ⚭ HORATIO MONETEFIORE
NATHANIEL 1819–1883 ⚭ EMMA 1819–1902
LOUISA 1821–1910 ⚭ Sir ANTHONY de ROTHSCHILD 1810–1876
Sir JOSEPH SEBAG-MONTEFIORE 1822–1903 ⚭ ADELAIDE COHEN
Sir FRANCIS ABRAHAM 1st Bart. 1860–1935 ⚭ MARIANNE von GUTMANN
CLAUDE JOSEPH GOLDSMID-MONTEFIORE 1858–1938 ⚭ THERESE SCHORSTEIN d. 1889
ARTHUR 1853–1895 ⚭ HARRIETTE BEDDINGTON
EDMUND 1869–1929 ⚭ JULIANA LUCAS DAVIDSON
6 others
ROBERT 1882–1915
CHARLES EDWARD 1884–1960 ⚭ MURIEL ALICE RUTH
Brigadier THOMAS H. SEBAG-MONTEFIORE 1887–1954 ⚭ IRENE CATHERINE COHEN
JOHN 1892–1972 ⚭ VIOLET SOLOMON
OLIVER R.M. b. 1915 ⚭ HENRIETTA WALEY COHEN
Bishop HUGH WILLIAM 1920–2005
HAROLD b. 1924
4 others

ciation cooperated to form the Conjoint Foreign Committee. Joseph Mayer's eldest son, Sir Francis Abraham Montefiore, succeeded to Sir Moses' baronetcy in 1886, when the title, which had become extinct, was revived in his favor. With his death, the title became extinct.

Sir Moses' sister SARAH (b. 1789) married Solomon Sebag (1783–1831). Their son JOSEPH (1822–1903), a stockbroker who amassed a fortune, was the closest associate of Sir Moses in his last years and heir to his Ramsgate estate. In 1885 he added the name of Montefiore to his own by royal license, the family name henceforward being Sebag-Montefiore. He was a justice of the peace, high sheriff of Kent in 1889, and was knighted in 1896. Joseph, who had accompanied Sir Moses to Ereẓ Israel in 1866, remained concerned with the welfare of the Jews there, administering on behalf of the Spanish and Portuguese synagogue the Holy Land Trust bequeathed by Sir Moses. In the 1890s he was a vice president of the Ḥovevei Zion (*Hibbat Zion). He was president of the Board of Deputies from 1895 until his death. His grandson ROBERT (1882–1915), a leading member of the London County Council and the Anglo-Jewish community, was killed in World War I. The London County Council named an East London school in his memory.

In the mid-20th century, some members of the family remained active both in public life and in the Sephardi community: BRIGADIER T.H. SEBAG-MONTEFIORE; OLIVER SEBAG-MONTEFIORE, a president of the London Jewish Welfare Board; and HAROLD SEBAG-MONTEFIORE (b. 1924), a Conservative member of the Greater London Council and president of the Anglo-Jewish Association. However, as with many of the older and wealthier Anglo-Jewish families, there has been considerable assimilation into English society, many of the members marrying non-Jews. An example was Sir Joseph's great-grandson, HUGH WILLIAM MONTEFIORE (1920–2005), converted to Christianity while still at Rugby school and entered the Anglican Church in 1949. He taught theology at Cambridge (1951–63), was appointed bishop suffragan of Kingston upon Thames, Surrey, and, in 1978–87, was Bishop of Birmingham, where he became nationally known. Montefiore was well aware of his Jewish origins. He is the author of *On Being a Christian Jew* (1999) and of an autobiography, *Oh God, What Next?* (1995), as well as dozens of other theological works.

BIBLIOGRAPHY: D.A.J. Cardozo and P. Goodman, *Think and Thank*, 2 vols. (1933); A.M. Hyamson, *Sephardim of England* (1951), index; Roth, England, index; J. Picciotto, *Sketches of Anglo-Jewish History* (1956²), index. **ADD. BIBLIOGRAPHY:** ODNB online; R. Sebag-Montefiore, *A Family Patchwork* (1987); C. Bermant, *The Cousinhood* (1961), index.

[Vivian David Lipman]

MONTÉLIMAR, town in the department of Drôme, S.E. France. The first explicit mention of the presence of Jews in Montélimar dates from 1222. The community attained considerable importance during the 14th and first half of the 15th centuries. The synagogue, remains of which still existed at the end of the 19th century, was situated in the Rue de Juiverie or the Rue Puits-Neuf; the school (or possibly another synagogue) was near the Porte Saint-Martin and the cemetery to the northwest of the present cemeteries. The community also maintained a special butcher's shop. As late as 1452, the dauphin granted the Jews of Montélimar, with Jews in several other localities of Dauphiné, some advantageous privileges; the municipal authorities, however, endeavored to render the lives of the Jews intolerable, for instance by compelling them to attend missionary sermons from 1453 onward. The same situation occurred at the end of the century: in 1476, King Louis XI had granted letters of protection to the Jews of Montélimar; however, in 1486, when only seven Jewish families remained there, the townsmen accused them of debauchery and shady practices and demanded their expulsion. From 1489, there no longer appear to have been Jews in Montélimar and the Jewish cemetery was closed. At the beginning of World War II, 150 Jewish families found refuge in Montélimar. There was no organized Jewish community in Montélimar in the 1960s.

BIBLIOGRAPHY: Gross, Gal Jud, 319; de Coston, *Histoire de Montélimar*, 1 (1878), 516ff., 4 (1891), 521; Z. Szajkowski, *Analytical Franco-Jewish Gazetteer 1939–1945* (1966), 186.

[Bernhard Blumenkranz]

MONTEREAU (Montereau-Faut-Yonne), town in the department of Seine-et-Marne, France. A Jewish community existed in Montereau by 1228 consisting of at least 12 families. In 1251, the Jews of Montereau are mentioned in the poll tax roster of the Jews of Champagne. A new community was constituted after the return of the Jews to France in 1359. The houses of two of its members, Benion of Salins and Sannset of Baumes, were looted during the riots of 1381. The memory of the medieval community was preserved until the 18th century in the name of a quay known as the Port-aux-Juifs.

BIBLIOGRAPHY: H. Stein, in: *Annales de la Société Historique et Archéologique du Gâtinais*, 17 (1899), 54ff.; A. Longnon, *Documents relatifs au comté de Champagne*, 2 (1904), 418; 3 (1904), 11, 299.

[Bernhard Blumenkranz]

°MONTESQUIEU, CHARLES LOUIS DE SECONDAT, BARON DE LA BREDE ET DE (1689–1755), French writer and political philosopher. Montesquieu inherited the humanistic French tradition of Jean *Bodin, with his vision of a society tolerant toward all religions, including Judaism. His earliest statement on the Jews was in the *Lettres Persanes* (1721), 50, where he described Judaism as "a mother who has given birth to two daughters [Christianity and Islam] who have struck her a thousand blows." In *L'Esprit des lois* (25:13), published in 1748, he reacted to the burning of a ten-year-old Jewish girl by the *Inquisition with an eloquent denunciation cast in the form of an argument written by a Jew: "You complain [he said to the inquisitors] that the emperor of Japan is having all the Christians in his domain burnt on a slow fire; but he could answer you: 'We treat you, who do not believe as we do, as you treat those who do not believe as you do'... If you do not want to be Christian, at least be human." Nevertheless, he was not entirely uncritical of the Jews. Also in the *Lettres persanes*, his traveler writes: "Know that wherever there is money there are Jews." In a passage from *Mélanges inédits*, which was published posthumously (1892), the rabbinic texts are considered to have fashioned the low taste and character of the Jews, for there was not "one among [the rabbis] of even a minor order of genius." But this private opinion of Montesquieu at his most Christian was unknown in the 18th century. His relativistic view, which ran counter to *Voltaire's absolute deism in favor of an appreciation of the Jew and Judaism as one of the many valid forms of culture and religion, was one that influenced history.

BIBLIOGRAPHY: J. Weill, in: REJ, 49 (1904), 150ff.; R.R. Lambert, in: *Univers Israélite*, 94 (1938/39), 421ff.; R. Shackleton, *Montesquieu...* (Eng., 1961), 354–5; A. Ages, in: *Romanische Forschungen*, 81 (1969), 214ff.; A. Hertzberg, *French Enlightenment and the Jews* (1968), index; L. Poliakov, *Histoire de l'antisémitisime*, 3 (1968), index.

[Arthur Hertzberg]

MONTEUX, PIERRE (1875–1964), conductor. Born in Paris, Monteux studied at the Paris Conservatoire where he won the first prize for violin in 1896. He played the viola in various orchestras and founded an orchestra of his own, the Concerts Berlioz. From 1911 to 1914 he conducted the Ballets Russes of Diaghilev, giving the first performances of Ravel's *Daphnis et Chloë*, Debussy's *Jeux*, and Stravinsky's *Petrouchka, Le Sacre du Printemps*, and *Le Rossignol*. He was conductor of the Metropolitan Opera in New York from 1917 to 1919 and then of the Boston Symphony Orchestra until 1924. From 1924 to 1934 he appeared as second conductor of the Concertgebouw in Amsterdam. He founded the Orchestre Symphonique de Paris (1929–38), and from 1936 to 1952 he was director of the San Francisco Symphony Orchestra. Monteux's conducting was faithful to the intentions of the composer and combined brilliant technique with profound musical culture. From 1961 until his death, Monteux was chief conductor of the London Symphony Orchestra.

BIBLIOGRAPHY: Baker, Biog. Dict; Riemann-Gurlitt; Grove, Dict.; MGG.

[Claude Abravanel]

MONTEVIDEO, capital of Uruguay with a population of 1,200,000, and a Jewish population of 23,500 in 2005 (90.78% of the Jewish population of the country). Some 13,000 former Uruguayan Jews live in Israel. The community was established before World War I by immigrants from Eastern Europe and the Middle East. The main representative body is the Comite Central Israelita (Jewish Central Committee), constituted of four *kehillot*: Jewish community of Montevideo (Ashkenazi), the Sephardi community, the New Jewish Congregation (German-speaking) and the Hungarian Jewish society. All of them together embrace the majority of the Jews except those of Communist ideology and affiliations. Another main body is the Zionist Organization of Uruguay (OSU), the roof organization and central authority of the local Zionist movement, its political factions, women organizations, and youth movements as well as both national funds – Keren Kayemet and Keren Hayesod–Hamagbit. For more details see *Uruguay.

[Nahum Schutz (2nd ed.)]

MONTEZINOS, ANTONIO DE (**Aaron Levi**; d. c. 1650), Marrano traveler. On a trip to South America during 1641–42, Montezinos discovered a group of natives in Ecuador who could recite the *Shema* and were acquainted with other Jewish rituals. He brought this news to Amsterdam in 1644, and the congregational authorities – *Manasseh Ben Israel among them – had him repeat his account under oath. The assumption was that these natives were a remnant of the *ten lost tribes, of the tribes of Reuben and Levi according to Montezinos. He then left for Brazil where he died, reasserting on his deathbed the truth of his report. Manasseh Ben Israel dwells on Montezinos' discovery in a booklet entitled *Esperança de Israel* ("The Hope of Israel," Amsterdam, 1650), which he dedicated to the British parliament, appending it to his petition for the readmittance of Jews to England. His thesis was that Montezinos' account points to an imminent fulfillment of the messianic prophecy of the lost tribes of Israel being reunited with Judah. The Montezinos report aroused literary interest even outside Jewish circles. In 1650 Thomas Thorowgood (1595–1669) published his *Iewes in America, or Probabilities that the Americans Are of that Race*. In reply Sir Hamon L'Estrange (1583–1654) wrote *Americans no Iewes, or Improbabilities that the Americans Are of that Race* (London, 1652). Thorowgood then retorted with *Jews in America, or Probabilities that those Indians are Judaical, Made More Probable by Some Additionals to the Former Conjectures* (London, 1660).

BIBLIOGRAPHY: C. Roth, *Life of Menasseh Ben Israel* (1934), 176–92, 330–1.

MONTEZINOS, DAVID (1828–1916), librarian and bibliophile in Amsterdam. His father, Raphael Montezinos, served as rabbi of the Portuguese community there from 1852 to 1866. David studied at the Eẓ Ḥayyim seminary where he obtained the title *Maggid*. An enthusiastic bibliophile, he acquired one of the largest private libraries of the time. In 1866 he was appointed librarian of the Eẓ Ḥayyim library. In 1889, after the death of his wife, he donated his private collection to the library of the seminary, including 20,000 books, pamphlets, manuscripts, and illustrations. It contained extensive material relating to the Jews in Holland, and in particular to the Spanish-Portuguese community. The library was named after Montezinos and was directed by him until his death. Montezinos wrote a number of bibliographic studies, published in *Letterbode*, as well as a monograph on David *Franco-Mendes, published in 1867 in *Joodsch-letterkundige bijdragen*.

BIBLIOGRAPHY: J.S. de Silva Rosa, *David Montezinos, de stichter der "Livraria D. Montezinos"* (1914); idem, *David Montezinos* (Dutch, 1917); idem, *Geschiedenis der Portugeesche Joden te Amsterdam* (1925), 153ff.

MONTI DI PIETÀ (Montes pietatis), savings and loan agencies originally formed in Italian cities in the mid-15th century; considered as the predecessors of the modern credit union. Historically, the word *mons* was used during the Middle Ages to designate funds collected for a specific purpose, *pietatis* being added to identify them as nonspeculative. The initial object of the *monti* was to provide loans at a relatively low rate of interest (4–15%) to small artisans and dealers and to the poor in general, on the pledge of various goods. The interest was used to defray administrative expenses and salaries of employees. The formation of the *monti* was the result of a combination of factors, both economic and theological. It arose from the decline of handicrafts and the ensuing impoverishment of the masses, and a scarcity of money; and from the desire to oust the Jews from the business of *moneylending, which they had successfully practiced as their principal profession. The growing prosperity of Jewish bankers aroused the wrath of the *Franciscans who, as some historians have pointed out, themselves often came from the ranks of the "new aristocracy," the merchant class.

Previously the progressive monopolization of moneylending by Jewish bankers had been justified both morally and theologically; on the one hand, it helped the poor, and on the other hand, it saved Christians from committing the sin of usury; but the founders of the *monti* advanced the argument that it was necessary to protect Christians from the voracity of Jewish usurers. The establishment of the first *monti* in *Perugia in 1462, after an earlier experiment eight years before at Ancona, came at the climax of a campaign against Jewish moneylenders waged by the Observant friars, the radical wing of the Franciscans. Its primary sponsor was Fra Michele da Milano, who protested vigorously against the arrangements then existing between the Jewish loan bankers and the city of Perugia. In subsequent years the Franciscans sought support for the expansion of the institution, preaching on its behalf throughout Italy, in opposition to the *Dominicans and the Augustinians, who condemned what they called the "*montes impietatis*" is a breach of the prohibition on usury proclaimed by Jesus (Luke 6:33). Foremost among those in favor of the institution was Bernardino of *Feltre, who bent all his charismatic talent for rabble-rousing to denouncing the Jewish moneylender. His sermons led to the establishment of the *monti* in many cities and were instrumental in the widespread persecution of Jews during the blood libel in *Trent in 1475 as well as in many other parts of the country. Pope Paul II approved (1467) the establishment of a *monte* in Perugia, despite theological opposition, and successive popes sanctioned *monti* in other Italian cities. By 1494 there were 30 *monti* in central and northern Italy. The controversy was finally settled by the papal bull, *Inter multiplicis* (May 1515), issued by Leo *X at the Fourth Lateran *Council, which declared the *monti* neither sinful nor illicit but, on the contrary, meritorious.

The institution of the *monti* did not, in itself, arouse the fears of the Jews. In some cases Jewish loan bankers, recognizing the charitable nature of the *monti*, actually gave them support. One such loan banker, Manuele da Camerino, bequeathed a considerable sum to the *monte* of Florence which had been set up by Girolamo Savonarola. At times Jewish loan bankers utilized the *monti* for their own purposes, depositing in it a pledge left with them, thereby raising capital for further operations. The *monti* were not in a position to meet the growing need for capital, and, as a result, there were times when Jewish loan bankers were allowed to reopen their *condotte* in the Italian cities, as occurred in Florence after the return of the Medici in 1512. Eventually, both *monti* and Jewish loan bankers found it possible to coexist and the first decades of the 16th century proved to be among the most prosperous for the Italian Jewish banker. By the mid-16th century, it was common practice for many *monti* to make loans to businessmen (at an interest rate of from 8 to 10%) as well as to the poor. The *Monti di Piet* remained an essentially urban feature, an outgrowth of conditions specific to Italy. The decision of the Lateran Council of 1515 to allow *urbi et orbi* the establishment of *monti* was the signal for setting up official lending institutions sponsored by governments in the Catholic countries of Europe.

BIBLIOGRAPHY: L. Poliakov, *Les Banquiers juifs et le Saint-Sige du XIIIue au XVIIue sicle* (1965), 169–98, passim; M. Weber, *Origines des Monts-de-Piet* (1920); A. Sapori, *History of the Principal Public Banks* (1934), 373–8; G. Fabiani, *Gli Ebrei e il Monte di Piet in Ascoli* (1942), 169–72; M. Ciardini, *I banchieri ebrei in Firenze nel secolo XV e il monte di piet fondato da Girolamo Savonarola* (1907); N. Mengozzi, *Il Monte dei Paschi e le sue azende* (1913); U. Cassuto, *Gli Ebrei a Firenze* (1918), 51–82; Roth, Italy, 166–77; S. Simonsohn, *Toledot ha-Yehudim be-Dukkasut Mantovah* (1963), 7–16; D. Carpi, *Ha-Yehudim be-Padovah bi-Tekufat ha-Renaissance* (1967), unpublished thesis Hebr. Univ., Jerusalem.

[Emmanuel Beeri]

MONTIEL, town in Castile, central Spain, in the frontier district of La Mancha. The small community there had close relations with the Order of Santiago, on whose lands it was situated. In 1273 the head of the Order, Pelayo Pérez, gave Don Samuel, Don Bono, and Don Jacob, all of them Jews under the jurisdiction of the Order, the right to settle their debts out of tax farming. They not only farmed the general taxes in Montiel but also in other lands belonging to the Order. At that time, tax farming produced considerable revenues. In 1290 the taxes paid to the king by the community of Montiel amounted to about 1,522 maravedis. The community probably suffered during the persecutions of 1391 when most of the La Mancha communities were destroyed. Nevertheless, a community may have existed in Montiel in the second half of the 15th century; Don Isaac Abudarham, a resident of Toledo, farmed the *alcabala* ("indirect taxes") there in 1462.

BIBLIOGRAPHY: Baer, Urkunden, 2 (1936), 62ff., 81, 310.

[Haim Beinart]

MONTOR, HENRY (1905–1982), U.S. organization executive and Zionist. Montor, born in Canada, was taken to the U.S. as a boy. He was active in Zionist affairs from his youth and assistant editor of *New Palestine* (1926–30). During his service with the United Palestine Appeal (1930–39) and as executive vice president of the United Jewish Appeal (1939–50), Montor directed the raising of previously unparalleled amounts from overseas Jewry for Israel. In 1939, as chief fundraiser for the United Palestine Appeal, he approached the prolific Zionist organizer Meyer *Weisgal about Jewish participation in the New York World's Fair. The Jewish Palestine Pavilion, which Weisgal claimed was "the first Palestine exhibit at an international exposition in the United States," attracted record-breaking crowds. The presence of Albert Einstein at the opening helped produce the largest single day's attendance in the history of the fair. In all, a total of more than two million people were estimated to have visited the pavilion.

Although Montor was an ardent Zionist, the prevailing Zionist aim at the time was for "selective" immigration to build a Jewish state, not the rescue of Jewish refugees. Therefore in 1940 Montor, as executive vice president of the United Jewish Appeal, refused to intervene for a shipload of Jewish refugees stranded on the Danube. He wrote a letter to a rabbi in Maryland stating that "Palestine cannot be flooded with … old people or with undesirables." He circulated thousands of copies of the letter, which asked Jews not to support illegal immigration to Palestine.

Yet for the UJA, Montor is credited with being the first man to have the conviction to set $100 million as a campaign goal – and attain it. As vice president and chief executive of the American Financial and Development Corporation for Israel (1951–55), Montor established the Israel Bonds campaigns and supervised the sale of approximately $190 million worth of bonds for Israel. He resigned his position as head of the State of Israel Bonds organization in 1955 to found his own brokerage firm.

[Ruth Beloff (2nd ed.)]

MÓNTORO, ANTÓN DE (1404–1480?), Spanish Converso poet who denounced the persecution of his fellow converts. He was born in Andalusia, probably in Montoro, and because he dealt in clothes he came to be known as the "tailor of Cordoba." He flourished during the reigns of Henry IV and Ferdinand and Isabella. Montoro was a noted writer of humorous and satirical verse which won him the esteem of the court poets but, despite his success, he never denied his humble origin or relinquished his trade. In a humorous poem addressed to his horse, he admitted that he had children, grandchildren, parents, and a sister who had not converted. Montoro was one of the few authentic and sincere voices of the age. He protested vigorously against the treatment of the Conversos and satirized the weak efforts of Alfonso de Aguilar, the governor of Cordoba, to stop the outrages. After the sack of Carmona in 1474, Montoro implored Ferdinand and Isabella to protect his people, whose sufferings he portrayed most movingly. He concluded his poem with a ferocious joke, saying that the killing should at least be postponed until Christmas, when the fire would be more welcome. Critics have therefore accused Montoro of cynicism, not realizing that the remark represents the black humor of despair. Despite his work on behalf of the Conversos, Montoro himself was apparently sincere in his Catholic beliefs and in a poem addressed to Queen Isabella toward the end of his life lamented that in 70 years he had been unable to lose the name of "old Jewish dog," despite the fact that he went to church and ate bacon. Montoro engaged in a poetic feud with another convert, *Juan (Poeta) de Valladolid. The two men exchanged mutual insults, much to the amusement of their contemporaries. Montoro also rebuked Rodrigo de *Cota de Maguaque for his thoughtless attacks on fellow Conversos; such criticism, he claimed, might eventually rebound on its author.

BIBLIOGRAPHY: E. Cotarelo y Mori (ed.), *Cancionero de Anti de Montoro* (1900); Roth, Marranos, 37; Baer, Spain, 2 (1966), 310ff. **ADD. BIBLIOGRAPHY:** Ch. V. Aubrun, in: *Filología* (Buenos Aires), 13 (1968–69), 59–63; M. Ciceri, in: *Codici della tragressività in area ispanica* (1980), 19–35; idem, in: *Rasegna iberistica*, 29 (1987), 3–13; R. Mai, *Die Dichtung Antón de Montoros, eines Cancionero-Dichters des 15. Jahrhunerts* (1983); A. de Montoro, *Cancionero*, F. Cantera Burgos and C. Carrete Parrondo (eds.), (1984); M. Costa, in: *Anuario medieval*, 1 (1989), 87–95.

[Kenneth R. Scholberg]

MONTPELLIER, capital of the Hérault department, southern France. The first direct evidence of the presence of Jews in the city is found in the will of Guilhem V, Lord of Montpellier, who forbade the investiture of a Jew as a bailiff. The Jewish traveler *Benjamin of Tudela, visited Montepellier in about 1165. Though he does not mention any figure for the Jewish population of the city, its importance can be deduced from the fact that he mentions the existence of several yeshivot. Until at least the end of the 12th century, the Jews of Montpellier appear to have been particularly active in commerce; they are explicitly mentioned in the trade agreement between Montpellier and *Agde; and they appear in the tariff of taxes due from the merchants of Montpellier in *Narbonne. Until the end of the 12th century, they do not appear to have practiced moneylending. In times of war, particularly when the town was besieged, the Jews helped in its defense by supplying weapons. (An agreement written at the beginning of the 13th century, for example, speaks of Jews providing 20,000 arrows.) From the middle of the 13th century, moneylending was regulated by the ordinances of James I, king of *Majorca, who also ruled over the duchy of Montpellier together with the bishop of Maguelonne. Before any contract could be drawn up, the Jewish lender was called upon to swear that it involved neither fraud nor usury. In addition, the consuls of the town prohibited loans to people under the age of 25 without the consent of their parents. James I's legislation concerning the Jews promulgated in 1267 was fairly favorable. Especially noteworthy was the clause prohibiting their prosecution on the basis of an anonymous denunciation. Those who accused or denounced Jews were to provide two guarantors and were threatened with being condemned themselves if they could not prove their accusation. Bail was to be granted to the accused Jew if he could provide a satisfactory guarantee.

During the 13th century, a Jewish quarter existed on the present site of the Rue Barralerie (until the 15th century it was named Sabatariè Neuve); in the first house on this street there are still some remains of the synagogue, and of the *mikveh* in the cellar. Although James I gave the old Jewish cemetery to the Cistercians of Valemagne in 1263, the latter were required to refund the cost of the exhumation and the transfer of the remains to the new cemetery. When the Jews were expelled from France in 1306, the king of Majorca opposed the measure. After considerable delay, the expulsion finally took place. It was little comfort to the Jews that the king of France was required to give to the king of Majorca two-thirds of the booty seized from "his Jews" and one-third of that taken from the other Jews of Montpellier.

In 1315, when the Jews were allowed to return to France, the Jews of Montpellier, like those elsewhere, were again placed under the authority of their former lords. In 1319 Sancho I, king of Majorca, permitted them to acquire a cemetery. It is not known in which quarter the Jews lived during this short stay, which lasted until 1322 (or 1323). In 1349 James III of Majorca sold his seigneury over Montpellier to Phillip VI of France. As a result, when the Jews resettled in the city in 1359 they found themselves under the direct sovereignty of the king of France, Charles V. Originally assigned to the Castelmoton quarter, they were forced to move to the Rue de la Vielle Intendance quarter after complaints from the Christian inhabitants. In their new settlement, they owned a synagogue and a school (after 1365). The Jews of Montpellier had to provide large financial contributions to the defense of the town, particularly in 1362 and 1363. In 1374 they were also obliged to participate in guarding the gates. The construction of a beautiful new synagogue in 1387 gave rise to a lawsuit with the bishop of Maguelonne, to whom the Jews paid the then enormous sum of 400 livres. In Montpellier the final expulsion of the Jews from France in 1394 was preceded by violent accusations against them in the municipal council.

Scholars

Even though the town had numerous Jewish physicians – who were subjected to a probative examination from 1272 – there is no valid evidence that the Jews had a part in founding and organizing the school of medicine there. Excluding those scholars who only lived temporarily in Montpellier, such as *Abraham b. David of Posquières, the foremost scholar in the town was *Solomon b. Abraham b. Samuel, who denounced the work of Moses Maimonides to the Inquisition. One of his leading followers was *Jonah b. Abraham Gerondi, who died in Toledo, Spain. The liturgical poet *Aryeh Judah Harari lived in Montpellier during the second half of the 13th century, as did *Aaron b. Joseph ha-Levi, the opponent of Solomon b. Abraham *Adret; and Isaac b. Jacob ha-Kohen *Alfasi. From 1303 to 1306 Montpellier was again the scene of a renewed polemic between the supporters and opponents of the study of philosophy. The latter were led by Jacob b. Machir ibn *Tibbon. In the later medieval community of Montpellier, the physician and philosopher Abraham *Avigdor was particularly distinguished.

Later Centuries

In the middle of the 16th century, the presence in Montpellier of *Conversos, who chiefly lived among the Protestant population, is vouched for by a Swiss traveler, a student named Platter. From the beginning of the 16th century, Jews from *Comtat Venaissin traded in the town. In 1653 the attorney general of the parliament of Toulouse directed the town magistrates to expel them. Similar orders were issued in 1679 and 1680. A special register was opened at the town record office for the Jews who entered Montpellier as a result of a general authorization granted from the end of the 17th century enabling them to trade for one month during each season. From 1714 nine Jews were allowed to settle in the town; others followed with the tacit consent of the magistrates in spite of complaints by the Christian merchants. In 1805, the Jewish community consisted of 105 persons and was headed by R. Moïse Milhau, who represented the department of Vaucluse at the great *Sanhedrin. Thirteen local Jews served in the armies of the revolution and of the empire, five as volunteers. The historian and physician Joseph *Salvador was born in Montpellier of an old Spanish-Jewish family that had fled the Inquisition. At the beginning of the 20th century there were about 35 Jewish families in Montpellier.

Holocaust and Contemporary Periods

After the 1940 armistice, Montpellier, which was in the "free" zone, became a center for Jewish refugees from the occupied part of France. After the North was occupied by the Germans in November 1942, Montpellier became an important transit stop for Jewish partisans. After the liberation, the community was reorganized and by 1960 had 600 members. The arrival of Jews from North Africa increased the number to 2,000 in 1969, and led to the construction of a communal center and a Sephardi synagogue with 300 seats. There were two kosher butchers and a *Talmud Torah.*

BIBLIOGRAPHY: Gross, Gal Jud, 322–35; C. d'Aigrefeuille, *Histoire de la ville de Montpellier*, 2 (1875²), 348 ff.; A. Germain, *Histoire du Commerce de Montpellier*, 2 vols. (1861), index s.v. *Juifs*, S. Kahn, in: REJ, 19 (1889), 259–81; 22 (1891), 264–79; 23 (1891), 265–78; 28 (1894), 118–41; 33 (1896), 283–303; G. Saige, *Les Juifs du Languedoc* (1881), index; L.H. Escuret, *Vieilles rues de Montpellier*, 2 (1964), 23 ff., 28–34; Z. Szajkowski, *Franco-Judaica* (1962), index.

[Bernhard Blumenkranz and David Weinberg (2nd ed.)]

MONTREAL, Canada's second largest city and home to the country's oldest and second largest Jewish community, one that is well known for the overall quality of its Jewish life. Until the 1970s the community was the largest and most dynamic in Canada, but it has declined in importance relative to Toronto's since then. The multicultural city is the metropolis of the overwhelmingly French-speaking province of Quebec. Most of the Jews are Ashkenazim, descended from immigrants who arrived during the first 60 years of the 20th century and assimilated into the English-language community, in part due to the more favorable educational and economic opportunities available in that sector. The Sephardim, largely French-speaking, have become increasingly important during the past 20 years. They are mainly the products of the post-1956 immigration from North Africa.

As Quebec nationalism, especially as manifested in demands to secede from Canada, became more assertive after the founding of the Parti Québécois (PQ) in 1968, minority ethnic groups, including Jews, felt less secure. PQ election victories and independence referenda between 1976 and 1995 sparked an exodus of thousands of Jews, mainly young adults, and left the remaining Jewish community on edge and apprehensive about its future. In the face of continuing threats of secession, the vast majority of Montreal Jews remains staunchly federalist and vigorously opposes the idea of an independent Quebec.

History

The community was founded by Sephardim from New York in 1768 but remained minuscule until the emigration from Eastern Europe began late in the 19th century. By 1901 there were about 7,000 Jews. During the 20th century there were rapid growth spurts connected with immigration spurred by antisemitism, the destruction of the two world wars, and later by upheavals in the Arab world after the creation of Israel. The community reached its peak population of nearly 120,000 during the 1970s but has been in decline since then due to out-migration, mainly to other cities in Canada. During much of the 20th century Montreal was the leading force in the countrywide community, with most of the major organizations, notably the *Canadian Jewish Congress, headquartered there.

The flow of immigrants, almost all European until the Sephardi immigration that began in 1956, gave the community a European character in many respects: religious, cultural, social, and linguistic. Montreal was home to numerous Yiddish writers and a lively cultural life. The Jewish Public Library and the Montreal Yiddish Theatre are two examples of institutions with deep roots in the community. The geographical concentration of Jews in particular neighborhoods also produced a sense of genuine community that had a positive effect on organizational life. One concrete manifestation was the Jewish Federation, now known as Federation CJA, formed in 1965. It is well known for effective fundraising and coordination of a range of services to meet community needs. Through its power to allocate the funds raised in the annual campaign to the various agencies, the Federation is able to dominate Jewish organizational life in the city. However, there are numerous organizations that operate outside the orbit of the Federation, including religious institutions, B'nai B'rith, and bodies with direct links to Israel.

Montreal's Jews have always been consigned to minority status politically, even those who speak French. The same was largely true in the business world as well. Opportunities have been severely limited in both fields. In politics, there have been a few Jews elected, usually to represent predominantly Jewish constituencies. Among the prominent examples since 1970 are the federal minister of justice and former president of the Canadian Jewish Congress Irwin *Cotler, the Quebec minister of revenue Lawrence Bergman, Victor Goldbloom, Gerry Weiner, Sheila *Finestone, Herbert Marx, and Robert Libman. Others, such as Norman *Spector and Stanley Hartt, have been top advisers to prime ministers. Morris Fish is the second Jew appointed to the Supreme Court of Canada.

In business, the largest success stories have been small businesses that eventually grew into large enterprises. Examples are the Seagram liquor empire under Samuel *Bronfman and Steinberg's supermarkets under Sam *Steinberg. In fact, traditionally Montreal Jews were more likely to be employed in Jewish rather than non-Jewish businesses.

By the early part of the 21st century the community faced a number of serious problems. The largest was demographic: a declining Jewish population with an age distribution skewed toward the elderly. Other key problems were the ongoing threat of Quebec independence, inadequate immigration levels, the difficulty of maintaining sufficient levels of community fundraising to support the demands generated by the aging population, and the challenge of supporting an elaborate day school system that educates over half of the Jewish children with only partial government subsidies.

Demography

Since the decennial Canadian Census asks questions about both religion and ethnicity, it is possible to generate accurate data about the Jewish population in the Montreal Census Metropolitan Area. According to Federation CJA demographer Charles Shahar, the population (using the "Jewish standard definition") stood at 92,970 in 2001, down from 101,405 in 1991, 103,765 in 1981, and 112,020 in 1971. Jews constituted 2.8 percent of the population of the metropolitan area in 2001, compared to 4.1 percent in 1971. Montreal's Jews were 25.1 percent of the countrywide Jewish population and had a higher median age (41.8 years) than Jews nationwide (40.2). In 1971, over 39 percent of Canada's Jews lived in Montreal. Jews constitute the seventh largest ethnic group in Montreal.

A comparison of Montreal's Jews with the non-Jewish population shows that there is a bulge in the over-65 category (21.6 versus 11.9 percent) and a shortfall in the 25–44 group (21.6 versus 32.0 percent). There are similar differences when compared to other Canadian Jews, though not as marked. In addition, the 15–24 cohort shrank dramatically between 1971 and 2001 (from 18.2 to 12.7 percent). The age distribution suggests that the growing social and health care demands of the elderly will be increasingly difficult for the community to meet because of the small size of the key productive age cohorts. As a result, the community actively seeks immigrants but has found that the supply is insufficient to maintain the population size.

The largest concentrations of Jews in the metropolitan area are found in the suburban areas of Côte St. Luc (19,785) and the West Island (13,030). Other areas with more than 7,000 Jews are St. Laurent, Côte des Neiges, and Snowdon. Hampstead and Côte St. Luc have Jewish populations in the 70–75 percent range. There are ḥasidic enclaves in Outremont (mainly *Belz, Skver, and *Satmar), Côte des Neiges (Lubavitch), and Boisbriand (Tosh), as well as an ultra-Orthodox community in Outremont and the Park Avenue area. There are 6,795 Holocaust survivors, constituting nearly one quarter of Jews over 55. About 18 percent of Montreal's Jews live below the poverty line.

Approximately one third of the Jewish population was born outside Canada. The largest numbers of immigrants came from North Africa and the Middle East (10 percent) and Eastern Europe and the former Soviet Union (11 percent). Smaller proportions came from Western Europe, Israel, and the United States. About two thirds of the Jews speak both English and French, with English the predominant mother tongue and language of home use. Another 26 percent speak English only and four percent speak French only. About 10 percent have Yiddish as their mother tongue, with about 56 percent English, 18 percent French, and three percent each for Russian and Hebrew. Some 70 percent now use English at home.

Religious Life

Jewish religious life in Montreal is extensive and quite varied. There are dozens of synagogues, the overwhelming majority Orthodox. There is one major Reform temple, several Conservative synagogues, and a Reconstructionist congregation. Even among the Orthodox there is a wide range, running from the various ḥasidic sects to yeshivah-oriented ultra-Orthodox to Modern Orthodox to Sephardi, each with its own type of synagogue. Finally, there are also quite a number of informal *minyanim* around the city, meeting in such venues as schools, homes, synagogue buildings, and even shopping centers. Some of these *minyanim* have been formally organized as congregations in order to enjoy certain legal advantages.

During the early years of the 21st century, *Chabad has energetically tried to extend its impact in the community beyond traditional Lubavitcher ḥasidim by establishing a major presence in both Hampstead and Côte St. Luc. Among the leading synagogues, the Shaar Hashomayim in suburban Westmount, while originally Orthodox, was affiliated with the Conservative movement through most of the 20th century. It is currently unaffiliated and has hired only Orthodox rabbis since the retirement of long-time Rabbi Wilfrid Shuchat. The Conservatives' decision to ordain women was the key precipitating factor.

In addition to regional bodies representing the various religious movements, there are community organizations whose purpose is to facilitate religious life. The Montreal Board of Rabbis and the Synagogue Council are inclusive. The Va'ad Ha'ir, styled as the Jewish Community Council of Montreal, is Orthodox and has traditionally been the sole body to offer *kashrut* supervision in the city. The long-time monopoly, while objectionable to some, did serve a unifying purpose because the Va'ad's authority was accepted by virtually the entire community. During the past decade that authority has come into question for two reasons. First of all, the Communauté Sépharade du Québec (CSQ) organized its own *kashrut* supervision operation, which amounted to a competing *hekhsher.* Some kosher eating establishments opted for CSQ supervision, thereby undermining those who wanted to preserve a single standard of *kashrut* in the community. Secondly, under the influence of ultra-Orthodox rabbis, the Va'ad became more stringent in its interpretation of *kashrut* requirements. Its various edicts elicited some complaints from within the Modern Orthodox group.

Personal status issues such as conversion and divorce have generally been handled discreetly through the Va'ad or associated institutions. Issues involving marriage are more open, with traditional norms generally prevailing except among the most liberal groups. Questions about gays and lesbians have not had a high profile, though again the Reform and Reconstructionist congregations have been the most open to those minorities.

In general, studies have shown a pattern of greater religious observance, particularly in terms of Sabbath, holidays, and *kashrut*, than in other communities on the continent. In addition, there is a considerable amount of tolerance. For example, although most congregations are Orthodox, many of those who attend such synagogues are not. Yet that fact does not seem to have caused significant problems.

Education

Education has been a major issue for the community for over a century. Originally the public school system was confessional, with parallel Catholic and Protestant schools. Ashkenazi immigrants found greater acceptance in the Protestant sector, which is a major reason for the fact that they became part of the English-speaking community. The Catholic schools, most of which operated in French, were not open to the Jews. By the 1960s and 1970s Jewish involvement in Protestant schools was protected as a right; they were no longer there on sufferance.

Due to the confessional character of the public schools, many Jews had opted for private Jewish day schools, of which there is a great variety in Montreal. In 1968, the provincial government agreed to provide partial funding for the general studies portion of the curriculum, a policy that is still in effect. During the 1970s increasing numbers of strings were attached to those grants, notably a requirement that the major proportion of the teaching hours be in French. The schools were also made subject to the eligibility requirements of the language law that limited admissions to schools classified as English (which included most of the main Jewish schools) to students who were officially certified as Anglophones. This condition limited choices for immigrants, including English-speakers. Meanwhile, the Sephardim developed their own day schools, which were classified as French, meaning that any student was eligible for admission.

The result of the government subsidy of tuition kept tuition charges relatively low in the North American context. That, plus the tradition of Jews attending their own schools, has resulted in over half the Jewish school age children enrolled in day schools at the elementary or high school level. Only about half of those who complete Jewish elementary schools remain in the Jewish system for high school. The schools offer a wide range of ideological options, including Religious Zionist-Modern Orthodox, Yiddishist, Conservative, community, and ultra-Orthodox (including ḥasidic). Most of the schools maintain a strong commitment to Hebrew language studies, and the community is known for its innovations in Hebrew language instruction.

There was an agreement with the Quebec government in 2004 to increase the public support to 100 percent of the amount allocated to the public schools (now non-confessional) for secular studies. However, the announcement triggered a political storm that included thinly disguised antisemitism. Within a month the government backtracked, leaving the schools at 60 percent funding. The result was most embarrassing for both the community and the government, especially because of the way that opponents succeeded in ridiculing the government for proposing to channel additional public funds to the affluent Jews.

Organizational and Institutional Structure

Ever since the early part of the 20th century, Montreal's Jews have created a host of organizations, largely to deliver services to the community. Many of these were in the health care, social welfare, recreation, cultural, or education areas. Eventually, in 1965, a federation structure, similar to those in existence in the United States, was established in order to bring more coherence to fundraising, allocations, community planning, and coordination of community affairs. What was originally known as Allied Jewish Community Services was renamed Federation CJA during the 1990s. It is one of the 16 large Jewish federations on the continent. The Federation has proven to be exceptionally successful in the annual Combined Jewish Appeal, giving the Montreal community the reputation of being one of the most generous in North America on a per capita basis. In 2005 the expenditures on programs were about $45 million. Of that, about 38 percent supported Israel and related activities, about 6 percent went to countrywide organizations and programs, and 56 percent was retained for local services. The local allocation is primarily for social services, education, and culture (including tuition assistance at the day schools), and various community initiatives.

The Canadian Jewish Congress, which had been the dominant representative body of Canadian Jewry for nearly a century, never established a solid fundraising base. Eventually it had to turn to the federations, including Federation CJA, for support. Its Quebec regional operation is now somewhat limited and is supported by the Federation. B'nai B'rith Canada is outside the federation structure. It has a national organization that raises money to fund its local activities, including a Quebec Region office in Montreal, with the main focus on community relations and antisemitism. Other national bodies, such as the *Canadian Jewish News*, National Jewish Campus Life, the Canada-Israel Committee, the Canadian Council of Israel and Jewish Advocacy, Canadian Jewish Congress, and JIAS (*Jewish Immigrant Aid Services) Canada, are funded by all the federations in the country through UIA Federations Canada.

The Quebec Issue

Ever since the Parti Québécois (PQ) became one of the two main provincial parties in 1970, the issue of secession has bedeviled the political scene. The raison d'être of the PQ is making Quebec an independent sovereign state, a goal that few in the Jewish community share. Montreal Jews clearly prefer that Quebec remain within Canada. In the 1980 and 1995 referendums on independence Jews overwhelmingly opposed the PQ's goal. Indeed some were quite outspoken. After 1995 Jews became particularly prominent in leadership roles within the Anglophone community.

After the PQ achieved power for the first time in 1976, many Jews began to contemplate leaving Quebec, despite their strong roots in Montreal. Among the factors that they considered were the deleterious effect of separatism on the economic climate, the accentuation of the minority status of anyone other than the French Québécois, the political uncertainty associated with the secession option, and a general fear of nationalism. It is difficult to be precise about how many Jews left from 1976 onwards, but an estimate of 20,000 is certainly reasonable. The departure of such a sizable portion of the community, especially younger people, is a major cause of the imbalance in the age structure of Montreal's Jews.

Future developments regarding separatism are likely to have a profound effect on the community's future. Although the issue became quiescent with the election of the provincial Liberals in 2003, the PQ remains the main opposition party. Should it regain power and hold a successful referendum, there would likely be a further exodus from the productive age cohorts. Consequently the future of the community is in some ways dependent on the vagaries of Quebec politics and nationalist sentiment.

Montreal's Jews have built a strong, cohesive, and thriving community that in many ways exemplifies the best that Jews can achieve in the North American context. Although it retains considerable energy and has been revitalized by the arrival of the Sephardim, its future is clouded by the political uncertainty. There is no doubt that it will persist, but its ability to maintain an elaborate structure remains to be determined.

[Harold M. Waller (2nd ed.)]

MONZÓN (**Monson, Montisson**), city in Aragon, N.E. Spain. The history of three communities, Monzón, Barbastro, and Lérida, was closely interconnected. Information on Jewish settlement in Monzón, which had many connections with the local Knights Templar, dates back to the second half of the 12th century. In 1232 the Monzón community joined the communities which pronounced a counter-ban against the scholars who banned the study of *Maimonides' writings. For taxation purposes, the community formed part of a collecta (tax administrative unit) with the neighboring communities of Albalate de Cinca, Alcoletge, Pomar, Estadilla, and Granadella. In 1271 the annual tax paid to the crown by the community of Monzón amounted to 4,000 sólidos. A ruling of Solomon b. Abraham ibn *Adret (Responsa, pt. 3, no. 242; cf. Responsa of Isaac b. Sheshet, no. 19) indicates how the tax was paid in Monzón. Anti-Jewish riots occurred in Monzón in 1260. During the persecutions at the time of the *Black Death (1348), the Jews of Monzón entrenched themselves inside their walled quarter and were thus saved. They suffered no harm during the 1391 persecutions, although a number of them subsequently became *Conversos. The community sent Don Joseph ha-Levi and R. Yom Tov Caracosa as its representatives to the disputation of *Tortosa in 1413–14, which had serious consequences for the Monzón community. In 1414 the antipope *Benedict XIII wrote to the bishop of Lérida authorizing him to turn the synagogue of Monzón into a church, since the majority of the community's members had become converted. He also ordered that property belonging to the burial society and the *Talmud Torah* should be given as *beneficium* to the chapel to be erected in the new church. However it seems that later the community revived. Forty-four names of Jewish householders are mentioned in the notarial records of 1465–78. No details are recorded regarding the departure of the Jews from Monzón on the expulsion of the Jews from Spain in 1492.

BIBLIOGRAPHY: Baer, Spain, index; Baer, Studien, 149; Baer, Urkunden, 1 (1929), index; Neuman, Spain, index: Ashtor, Korot, 2 (1966), 174; F. Cantera, *Sinagogas españolas* (1955), 251–2; Vendrell Gallostra, in: *Sefarad*, 3 (1943), 124; Romano, *ibid.*, 13 (1953), 72ff.; Lopez de Meneses, *ibid.*, 14 (1954), 108; Cabezudo Astrain, *ibid.*, 23 (1963), 266f., 274, 280, 282. **ADD. BIBLIOGRAPHY:** R. Pita Mercé, in: *Ilerda*, 44 (1983), 287–303; J.M. Viladés Castillo, in: *Boletín de la Asociación Espan~ola de Orientalistas*, 20 (1984), 307–15.

[Haim Beinart]

MONZON, ABRAHAM, the name of two scholars.

(1) (d. after 1603), halakhic authority and preacher, and apparently of North African origin. During his youth he lived in Egypt, where he studied under R. Bezalel *Ashkenazi. His pupils in Egypt included R. Abraham *Iskandari. He later went to Constantinople, where he died. He wrote halakhic decisions, and homiletical interpretations; some of his responsa are scattered in various manuscripts and in the works of contemporary scholars, such as Joseph di *Trani, Samuel de *Medina, Bezalel Ashkenazi, and Solomon b. Abraham ha-Kohen. *Azulai saw in manuscript a composition of his on the work *Imrei Emet*, by Menahem de *Lonzano, criticizing the kabbalistic system of R. Ḥayyim *Vital. Azulai also saw a collection of his sermons.

(2) (18th century), rabbi and author. He was born in Tetuan, Morocco, where he engaged unsuccessfully in commerce. He therefore wandered to Algiers and Oran and in about 1732 arrived in Egypt, where he was considered one of the most prominent rabbis. His works are extant in manuscript.

BIBLIOGRAPHY: J. Ayash, *Responsa Beit Yehudah* (Leghorn, 1746), *Ḥoshen Mishpat*, no. 4 (75a); Conforte, Kore, 39–43, 48–49; J.M.Toledano, *Ner ha-Ma'arav* (1911), 158–9, 230–1; J. Ben-Naim, *Malkhei Rabbanan* (1931), 13b; Rosanes, Togarmah, 5 (1938), 336–7; S. Assaf, *Mekorot u-Meḥkarim* (1946), 206–8; Hirschberg, Afrikah, 2 (1965), 115.

[Abraham David]

MOON (Heb. usually יָרֵחַ, *yare'aḥ*; poetical form לְבָנָה, *levanah*; Isa. 24:23, 30:26; Song 6:10). A deity for ancient Israel's neighbors, the moon is for Israel "the lesser light" created on the fourth day of creation "to rule the night" (Gen. 1:16). The calendar used in ancient Israel was probably lunisolar. At any rate, the month was based on the periodical recurrence of the moon's phases. (For full details, see *Calendar.) The New Moon, Rosh Ḥodesh, the beginning of a new period, was proclaimed by the Sanhedrin and marked by the blowing of trumpets and special offerings (Num. 10:10, et al.), and was a minor holiday of which liturgical traces have remained (see *New Moon). Two main festivals, Passover and Sukkot, begin at the full moon.

Cult

As a male deity, the moon (Nanna) was worshiped by the Sumerians and by the Semites in general. Known as Sin among the eastern Semites, the moon god was called Eraḥ in the "west." Sin was the patron god of Ur and Haran, which were connected with the origins of the Patriarchs. The popularity of the moon cult is attested by the frequency of theophoric names with the divine element Sin or Eraḥ. The Israelites were warned against worshiping the moon, and convicted transgressors were punished by stoning (Deut. 4:19, 17:3–5). The moon cult was, nevertheless, introduced into Judah by King Manasseh (II Kings 21:3) but was subsequently abolished by King Josiah (II Kings 23:5).

For fuller details see *Host of Heaven.

In the Aggadah

Rabbinic literature uses *levanah*, and not *yare'aḥ* for the moon. The moon and the sun were created on the 28th of Elul (PdRE 8), and were originally equal in size (both being referred to as "the two great lights" – Gen. 1:16), but jealousy between them caused dissensions, so that God decided to make one of them smaller. The moon was chosen to be degraded because it had unlawfully intruded into the sphere of the sun, and hence the difference between the sun, "the greater light." and the moon, "the lesser light," (*ibid.*). The unlawful intrusion is based on the phenomenon that the moon is sometimes visible during the day (PdRE 6; Gen. R. 6:3). The remarkable statement is made that the he-goat offered on the New Moon is a sin-offering brought by God; according to the Midrash this was for having permitted the moon to encroach upon the domain of the sun (Gen. R. 6:3), but the Talmud says it was for diminishing its size (Ḥul. 60b). God also appeased the moon by surrounding it with stars like a viceroy encircled by his assistants (Gen. R. 6:4). God's original intention was that the sun alone should furnish light to the earth, but foreseeing the future idolatrous worship of the heavenly objects, He decided that it would be better to have two large celestial bodies, thus minimizing the danger of one becoming a central deity (Gen. R. 6:l). For this reason the sun and moon stand in judgment daily before the Almighty, ashamed to go forth, and pleading, "People worship us and anger the Holy One, blessed be He!" (Mid. Ps. 19:11).

The moon was designated as Jacob's luminary, while the sun symbolized Esau. The Jewish nation bases its calendar on the lunar year, since they have a portion in this world and the world to come, like the moon which can be seen both by day and by night (Gen. R. 6:3). An eclipse of the moon is therefore considered an evil omen for Israel, and is attributed to four different sins: forgery, false testimony breeding small cattle in Ereẓ Israel (since they damage the crops of the field), and cutting down fruit trees (Suk. 29a). The rabbis declared that the countenance of Moses was like that of the sun, while that of Joshua was like that of the moon (BB 75a). Esther, who brought light to Israel after the evil decree of Ahasuerus, is likewise compared to the moon, which enables people to rejoice and walk about when it illuminates the darkness of the night (Ex. R. 15:6). In the future, seven companies of righteous men whose faces will shine like the sun and the moon will welcome the presence of God (Lev. R. 30:2). Moses did not comprehend exactly when the New Moon was to be sanctified until God showed him the form of the moon when it was beginning its monthly cycle and said to him. "When you see it like this, sanctify it" (Mekh. Pisḥa 1).

BIBLIOGRAPHY: Ginzberg, Legends, index s.v. *Moon.*

MOON, BLESSING OF THE, prayer of thanksgiving recited at the periodical reappearance of the moon's crescent. In Hebrew, the prayer is known by several names: *Birkat ha-Levanah* ("the blessing of the moon") or *Kiddush Levanah* ("sanctification of the moon"). It can be recited front the third evening after the appearance of the new moon until the 15th of the lunar month; after that day, the moon begins to diminish. The prayer is recited only if the moon is clearly visible (not when it is hidden by clouds), and it should preferably be said in the open air. According to the Talmud (Sanh. 42a), "Whoever pronounces the benediction over the new moon in its due time welcomes, as it were, the presence of the *Shekhinah*" ("Divine Presence") and hence it is recommended (Sof. 20:1) to pronounce the benediction, if possible, on the evening after the departure of the Sabbath when one is still in a festive mood and clad in one's best clothes. The blessing of the new moon in some rites is delayed in the month of Av until after the Ninth of *Av, in Tishri, until after the *Day of Atonement, and in Tevet until after the fast of the tenth of *Tevet. A mourner does not bless the moon until after *shivah ("the first week of mourning"); in the rainy season, however, when the moon is often hidden by clouds, he recites it whenever possible. The blessing of the moon is not recited on Sabbath and holiday eves, mainly because of the prohibition to carry prayer books outside the house or synagogue building when there is no *eruv. The basic text of the blessing is given in *Sanhedrin* 42a and in *Soferim* 2:1, but many addditions were subsequently made. In the present Ashkenazi ritual, the blessing is introduced by the recital of Psalms 148:1–6 (in the Sephardi rite also Ps. 8:4–5), after which a benediction praising God as the creator and master of nature is pronounced. In the mishnaic period, the proclamation of the new month by the rabbinical court was celebrated with dancing and rejoicing. It is still customary to rise on the tips of the toes in the direction of the moon while reciting three times "As I dance toward thee, but cannot touch thee, so shall none of my evil-inclined enemies be able to touch me." This is followed by "Long live David, King of Israel" (also pronounced three times) and by the greeting *Shalom aleikhem* ("Peace be to you") which is extended to those standing around who respond *Aleikhem shalom* ("to you be peace"). This part of the ceremony is reminiscent of the days of *Judah ha-Nasi when the Romans abrogated the authority of the rabbinical court to consecrate the new moon which therefore had to be carried out clandestinely. "Long live David, King of Israel" served as a password between Judah ha-Nasi and his emissary R. *Ḥiyya (RH 25a). It also voiced Israel's continuous hope for redemption by the Messiah, a descendant of David whose kingdom would be "established forever as the moon" (Ps. 89:38). The ceremony concludes with the recital of several scriptural verses, a quotation from the Talmud (Sanh. 42a) "In the school of R. Ishmael it was taught: Had Israel merited no other privilege than to greet the presence of their Heavenly Father once a month, it were sufficient," the plea that God readjust the deficiency of the light of the moon caused by the moon's complaint against the sun (Ḥul. 60b), and a prayer for the fulfillment of the promise of the restoration of the Kingdom of Israel when the Jews will "seek the Lord their God, and David their King" (Hos. 3:5). The blessing of the new moon and the festive character of Rosh Ḥodesh (New Month) originated in the time of the *Second Temple. Due to the significance of the moon in the Jewish *calendar (see Ex. 12:2), it may be of much older origin; in the course of time it has, however, undergone substantial changes. The rite takes the moon as a symbol of the renewal in nature, as well as of Israel's renewal and redemption. Various other elements, some of them of a superstitious nature, have become attached to the rite.

BIBLIOGRAPHY: Hertz, Prayer, 994–5; E. Levi, *Yesodot ha-Tefillah* (1952^2), 302–5; Idelsohn, Liturgy, 160–1; ET, s.v. *Birkat ha-Levanah*; E. Munk, *The World of Prayer*, 2 (1963), 94–101.

[Meir Ydit]

MOONMAN, ERIC (1929–), British politician and communal leader. Moonman was born in Liverpool and left school at 13, when he was apprenticed to a printer. He worked for the

Daily Mirror in Manchester and was involved in local politics in Stepney, London, before becoming the Labour member of Parliament for Billericay (1966–70) and Basildon (1974–79). More recently he was an executive in the radio industry and, despite leaving school at 13, a professor of management at the City University Business School. Moonman was one of the most visible and consistent pro-Israeli politicians in the British Labour Party, serving as chairman (1975–80) and president (2001–) of the Zionist Federation of Britain. He was vice president (1994–2000) of the Board of Deputies of British Jews and served on many other bodies fighting antisemitism.

[William D. Rubinstein (2nd ed.)]

MOONVES, LES (1949–), U.S. entertainment executive. Born in New York, Moonves is a distant relative of David Ben-Gurion through a marriage on his father's side. Although he once planned on becoming a doctor, after graduating Bucknell University in 1971 he decided to become an actor. Moonves lived in Greenwich Village for five years, studying acting at the Neighborhood Playhouse and working as a bartender at the renowned restaurant Tavern on the Green. In 1976, Moonves moved to Hollywood, where he bartended between minor roles on television shows like *The Six Million Dollar Man* and *Cannon*. He abandoned acting for an executive role at Columbia in 1979, and in 1981 he was hired by Twentieth Century Fox to produce made-for-television films. Joining Lorimar Television in 1984, he produced *The Two Mrs. Grenvilles* and *I Know My First Name Is Steven*. He was promoted to head of series production in 1986, overseeing shows like *Dallas*, *Knots Landing*, and *Falcon Crest*; head of public affairs in 1988; in 1989 he was made president of Lorimar, which was acquired by Warner in 1991, becoming Warner Bros. Television. Moonves oversaw a variety of hit television shows, and in 1995 he went to third-place CBS to take over as president of its entertainment division. Success came in the form of sitcom *Everybody Loves Raymond* (1996–2005), the reality-television show *Survivor* (2000–) and the drama *CSI: Crime Scene Investigation* (2000–). In 2002, CBS's parent company Viacom named Moonves to head its floundering network UPN, making him the first executive to run two networks simultaneously. That same year CBS ranked first in total viewership. In 2004, Moonves and MTV chairman Tom Freston were named co-presidents and co-chief operating officers of Viacom, Inc., taking over for Viacom chief executive officer Sumner Redstone. In 2004, Moonves married *The Early Show* anchor Julie Chen after divorcing actress Nancy Wiesenfeld, his wife of 26 years.

[Adam Wills (2nd ed.)]

°**MOORE, GEORGE FOOT** (1851–1931), U.S. teacher of religion. Moore graduated from Yale in 1872 and from Union Theological Seminary in 1877, was ordained to the Presbyterian ministry in 1878, and became professor of Hebrew at Andover Theological Seminary in 1883. In 1902 he went to Harvard and was made professor of the history of religion in 1904.

Moore's work was of importance in four fields – the shaping of U.S. scholarship, the reshaping of U.S. concepts of religion, the study of the Hebrew Bible, and the study of tannaitic Judaism. For scholarship, he helped introduce the "scientific" standards and concepts developed in Germany into the U.S. His influence was exercised through his own example, teaching, committee work, editorship of the *Andover Review* (1884–93), the *Harvard Theological Review* (1908–14, 1921–31), and *Harvard Theological Studies* (1916–31), innumerable book reviews, articles, and lectures, and participation in learned societies. He was president of the American Academy of Arts and Sciences, the Massachusetts Historical Society, and the Society of Biblical Literature. Thus he also did much to shape the concept of religion as a universal human activity of which the various religions are particular instances, and the study, one of the "humanities." This conception was important for the ecumenical movement, cooperation between Christians and Jews, reorientation of missions from conversion to social work, and introduction of courses on the history of religion into college curricula. The professor of history of religion appeared as a new social type, distinct from the chaplain and the professor of theology, and Moore's works – *Metempsychosis* (1914), *The Birth and Growth of Religion* (1923), *History of Religions* (2 vols., 1913–19, 1927–28) – were used in many courses.

In the study of the Hebrew Bible Moore not only introduced German methods, standards, and conclusions, but added his own common sense and enormous learning. Beside his many articles in the *Andover Review* and Cheyne's *Encyclopaedia Biblica*, his *Critical and Exegetical Commentary on Judges* (1895) remains most valuable. Finally, his *Judaism in the First Centuries of the Christian Era: The Age of the Tannaim* (3 vols., 1927–30, 1966²) is an outstanding study of rabbinic Judaism. Although it too much neglects the mystical, magical, and apocalyptic sides of Judaism, its apology for tannaitic teaching as a reasonable, humane, and pious working out of biblical tradition is conclusive and has been of great importance not only for Christians, but also for Jewish understanding of Judaism.

BIBLIOGRAPHY: DAB, 13 (1934), 124–5, incl. bibl.; M. Smith, in: *Harvard Library Bulletin*, 15 (1967), 169–79.

[Morton Smith]

MOPP (**Max Oppenheimer**; 1885–1954), painter and printmaker. Born in Vienna, he studied there from 1900 to 1903 at the Akademie der Bildenden Künste and at the Academy of Fine Arts in Prague from 1903 to 1906. He returned to Vienna in 1908. With the artists Oskar Kokoschka and Egon Schiele, Oppenheimer originated Austrian Expressionism, a style characterized by distorted form, exaggerated or unnatural color, and intensely expressive lines intended to signify turbulent emotion. Oppenheimer signed his name as Mopp beginning in 1910. Both Mopp's and Kokoschka's portraits, which share very similar visual characteristics, helped to establish Expressionism as the major Viennese visual style by 1909. Mopp was a masterly portraitist, with deep psychological insight. Among his many sitters were the writer Thomas Mann (1913), writer Arthur Schnitzler, composer Arnold Schönberg, and composer Anton Webern (1909). After travel and study in Holland, France, and Italy, Mopp moved to Berlin in 1911, where he contributed drawings to the Expressionist periodical *Die Aktion*. During the same year, the artist had his first solo exhibition at the Galerie Thannhauser in Munich. The poster for the exhibition created a scandal because of its adaptation of Mopp's painting *The Bleeding Man*, an image of the artist as a wounded, semi-nude Christ. Mopp often composed paintings with religious, specifically Christian themes. In addition to *The Bleeding Man*, among other works, the artist produced several etchings for the German edition of Gustave Flaubert's *Legend of St. Julian the Hospitable*. Mopp fled from the rising National Socialist movement in Germany to Berne in 1915 and then to Zurich a year later. During this period, Mopp composed still lifes in a Cubist and Futurist style and experimented with Dada. With artist Marcel *Janco, Mopp created decorations and the Dada dancers' masks for the Cabaret Voltaire, and exhibited pictures there for the Cabaret's 1916 opening night. In addition, Mopp, with Guillaume Apollinaire, Jean Arp, Wassily Kandinsky, Janco, and Pablo Picasso, contributed to Hugo Ball's 1916 pamphlet titled *Cabaret Voltaire*. A music-lover and an accomplished violinist, Mopp painted many group portraits of celebrated string quartets. For example, Mopp's painting *The Klinger Quartet* (1916) is a tondo or circular composition in which the repeated depiction of the musician's expressive hands seeks to visually communicate the quality and rhythm of the sound emanating from the instruments. Mopp's massive painting *The Symphony* (1920–40), a work upon which Thomas Mann commented in an essay, was intended as an homage to the late Gustav Mahler. In 1924, 200 of the artist's now well-known orchestra works were shown in an exhibition organized by the Viennese Hagenbund artists' association. Later, Mopp's work revealed the influence of the Neue Sachlichkeit. The artist relocated frequently in the years before and during World War II. Between 1917 and 1923, Mopp lived in Geneva and Vienna; he resided in Berlin in 1924 and 1925, but returned once again to Vienna in 1932. In the latter city, Mopp exhibited at the Wiener Künstlerhaus. After he was labeled by the National Socialists as a "degenerate artist," nine pieces of Mopp's work were removed from German museums in 1937. The following year, the artist fled to New York. At the end of his life, his work displayed an Impressionist style. In addition to Flaubert's book, Mopp illustrated several more publications, including stories by Heinrich *Heine and two works by the chess master, Emanuel *Lasker. Mopp's work is represented in numerous museums, including the Fine Arts Museum of San Francisco; the Los Angeles County Museum of Art; the Museum of Modern Art, New York; the National Gallery of Canada; the Jewish Museum, Prague; and the Leopold Museum, Vienna.

BIBLIOGRAPHY: *Mopp. Max Oppenheimer, 1885–1954: Juedisches Museum der Stadt Wien, 23. Juni bis 18. September 1994* (1994); M.-A. von Puttkamer, *Max Oppenheimer,* MOPP *(1885–1954): Leben und malerisches Werk mit einem Werkverzeichnis der Gemaelde* (1999).

[Nancy Buchwald (2nd ed.)]

MOPSIK, CHARLES (1956–2003), French scholar of Jewish mysticism. Mopsik was employed in the Centre national de la recherche scientifique (CRNS) and was instrumental in disseminating the serious study of Jewish mysticism in France in both academic and popular circles. He is best known for his translations of Zohar-related literature and central works of Castilian Kabbalah from the same period. He edited the series "Dix Paroles" (editions Verdier), establishing a library of annotated translations into French of classical Jewish texts. He also edited various Hebrew and Aramaic texts in their original, including works by Moses de León and Joseph Hamadan. Mopsik's scholarly career began with his dissertation on sexual symbolism and sexuality in Jewish sources, comprising a study and edition of the celebrated "Treatise on Holiness" (*Iggeret ha-Kodesh*). He further published numerous articles on sex and gender, including the posthumously issued collection of studies in English, *Sex of the Soul*. One of his unique contributions was to assert that in some kabbalistic works the category of sex applies to the soul even prior to its embodiment in the material world. Mopsik's field of inquiry ranged from ancient Jewish mysticism, including a volume on the so-called "III Enoch" of the Heikhalot Literature, to kabbalistic texts in the early modern period, Lurianic and ḥasidic texts, and some reflections on the Holocaust. His magnum opus is his lengthy study on theurgy in Judaism, showing how the various forms of Jewish practice are seen to effect changes within the divine.

His works include (1) *Lettre sur la sainteté*. Étude préliminaire, traduction et commentaire, suivi d'une étude de Moshé Idel. 1986/1994; (2) *Le Zohar*: Traduction de l'araméen, introduction et notes. Genèse: vols. 1 (1981), 2 (1984), 3 (1991), 4 (1996); *Le Livre de Ruth* (1987); *Cantique des Cantiques* (1999); *Lamentations* (2000); (3) *R. Joseph Gikatila, Le secret du mariage de David et Bethsabée*, édition critique, traduction, introduction et notes, 1994/2003; (4) *Les grands textes de la cabale: les rites qui font Dieu*, 1993; and (5) *Sex of the Soul: The Vicissitudes of Sexual Difference in Kabbalah*, 2005.

[Daniel Abrams (2nd ed.)]

MORAG (Mirkin), SHLOMO (1926–1999), Hebrew philologist. Morag was born in Petaḥ Tikvah. He graduated in Jewish and Oriental Studies at The Hebrew University, receiving his doctorate in 1955, and also studied at the School of Oriental Languages of the Sorbonne, Paris. From 1950 he taught at The Hebrew University, and in 1975 he was appointed professor of Hebrew and Semitic languages as well as professor of Hebrew philology at the Tel Aviv University. Morag was a member of the Hebrew Language Academy. He was awarded the Israel Prize for Jewish studies in 1966. He initiated and founded a research project in the language traditions of the Jewish communities, becoming later *The Jewish Oral Traditions Research*

Center, which is part of the Institute of Jewish Studies of The Hebrew University. He served as director of the project, which collected and studied the language traditions of the Jewish communities. Among his works are *The Vocalization Systems of Arabic, Hebrew, and Aramaic* (1962), *The Hebrew Language Traditions of the Yemenite Jews* (1963), and *The Book of Daniel,* – a Yemenite Babylonian MS (1973). A full list of his works and scientific studies was published in *Meḥkarim ba-Lashon ha-Ivrit u-vi-Leshonot ha-Yehudim Muggashim li-Shelomo Morag* (ed. M. Bar-Asher, 1996), 21–38; an autobiographical sketch, ibid., 7–20; and an assessment by the editor, ibid. 1–6. To this list should be added *Edah ve-Lashon,* vols. 21–25.

Morag's father, Moshe Aryeh Mirkin, published a long commentary on the *Midrash Rabbah.*

MORAIS, SABATO (1823–1897), U.S. minister-*ḥazzan* as his position was defined and founder of the *Jewish Theological Seminary. Morais, who was born in Leghorn, Italy, received his early Hebrew education from teachers in his community. At the age of 22, he applied for the position of assistant *ḥazzan* at the Spanish and Portuguese (Bevis Marks) congregation in London and in 1846 he became director of that congregation's orphan school. During his five years in England he learned much about Jewish life in an Anglo-Saxon environment, and established a friendship with Moses *Montefiore and the Italian patriot Mazzini. In 1851 he arrived in the U.S. to become *ḥazzan* of Mikveh Israel congregation, the oldest congregation in Philadelphia (and one that exists until this day), succeeding Isaac Leeser. He was a pioneer in introducing adult education classes and supplemental religious schooling. He had a discretionary fund for the distribution of money to the poor. He served in this position until his death, 47 years later. He opposed slavery during the pre-Civil War period, much to the consternation of some of this congregants. He strove to unite the Sephardi and the Ashkenazi elements in the congregation, and later to help the Russian Jewish immigrants. Morais influenced many young men who became leaders of American Jewry, including Cyrus *Adler, Mayer *Sulzberger, and Solomon *Solis-Cohen. He was, in the words of Pamela Nadel, "a founder or a supporter, of nearly every Philadelphia philanthropy and institution," at a time when Philadelphia was a source of enormous Jewish creativity.

He had a deep love for Jewish music and a great interest in Jewish scholarship, especially in Sephardi studies. He translated a work of S.D. Luzzatto and rendered the writings of other Italian Jewish scholars into English. He was involved in the revival of Hebrew and wrote prose and poetry and encouraged others to write in Hebrew. He published a commentary on the Book of Esther and translated Jeremiah that was the initial draft used in the 1917 Jewish Publication Society edition of the Bible. In 1887 he received an honorary LL.D. from the University of Pennsylvania, the first Jew to receive this distinction. He was a professor at Maimonides College, one of the early attempts to create a rabbinical seminary, from 1867–1873; many of its graduates later supported the Jewish Theological Seminary.

Morais was neither an original thinker nor an incisive expositor but his earnestness and breadth of outlook enabled him to rally the forces of tradition that defined itself as "other than Reform" at a time when the drift was predominantly in the direction of Reform. At one stage he showed a readiness to cooperate with I.M. *Wise in the work of Hebrew Union College, but the radical nature of the Pittsburgh Platform (1885) convinced him that a separate institution to train rabbis on Conservative lines was needed. He was the prime mover in the establishment of the Jewish Theological Seminary (1887) and was president of its faculty until his death, commuting from Philadelphia to New York. He helped shape the institution along the lines of the Breslau Seminary, meaning that candidates for the rabbinate would have both a secular and a religious education.

BIBLIOGRAPHY: M. Davis, in: AJHSP, 37 (1947), 55–93; idem, in: *Sefer ha-Shanah li-Yhudei Amerikah* (1945), 574–92; idem, *Emergence of Conservative Judaism* (1963), index; P. M Nadell, *Conservative Judaism in America: A Biographical Dictionary and Sourcebook* (1988).

[Jack Reimer / Michael Berenbaum (2nd ed.)]

MORAVIA (Czech **Morava**, Ger. **Maehren**, Heb. מרהרן, מערדין), historic region of the Czech Republic (formerly in *Czechoslovakia). A political unit from around 769, it formed the nucleus of the Great Moravian Empire (first half of the ninth century until 906). From 1029 it was under Bohemian rule; in 1182 it became a margravate and as such a direct fief of the empire. Together with *Bohemia it became part of the *Hapsburg Empire (1526–1918), and then part of Czechoslovakia, united with former Austrian Silesia after 1927. Between 1939 and 1945 it was part of the Nazi-occupied Protectorate of Bohemia-Moravia, after parts had been ceded to Germany as a result of the Munich Agreement of September 1938. It was replaced, in 1960, by the establishment of two provinces, southern and northern Moravia. Partly because of the region's location on the crossroads of Europe, throughout the centuries there was a considerable amount of reciprocal influence between Moravian Jewry and the Jewries of the surrounding countries. It had a thriving cultural life, promoted by the high degree of autonomy and communal organization it developed. Moravian Jews played a large part in the development of the communities in Vienna and northwestern Hungary.

From the Early Settlement to the 17th Century

Documentation of the first stages of Moravian Jewry is very scanty. In all probability Jews first came to Moravia as traders in the wake of the Roman legions. According to tradition, some communities (e.g., *Ivanice, *Jemnice, *Pohorelice, and *Trebic) were founded in the first millennium C.E., but such reports cannot be substantiated. Moravia is mentioned rarely in early medieval Jewish sources. However, it may well be that some authorities confused part of Bohemia with Moravia. As other authorities referred to all Slav countries as "Canaan," it is difficult to make any positive identification of a Jewish settlement in Moravia. It is likely that Jews lived in Moravia before the date of conclusive documentary evidence for their presence. In the biography of Bishop Clement of Bulgaria (d. 916) it is reported that, after the death of the Byzantine missionary Methodius (885), when the Frankish Church prevailed in the Byzantine Empire, about 200 Slav priests were sold to Jewish slave traders. The Raffelstaetten toll regulations (903–906), which fixed relations between the Great Moravian and the Carolingian empires, mention Jews as slave traders, but do not say whether they resided in Moravia. According to the Bohemian chronicler Cosmas of Prague (1039?–1125), a baptized Jew built the Podivin castle in southern Moravia in 1067; Cosmas also mentions a community in *Brno (Bruenn) in 1091. Isaac *Dorbelo, a student of R. Jacob b. Meir *Tam, speaks of observing the rite of the *Olomouc (Olmuetz) community around 1146 (*Maḥzor Vitry*, Hurwitz ed. (1923), 247, 388). The first extant document explicitly mentioning Jews in Moravia is the *Jihlava (Iglau) city law of 1249. In 1254 *Premysl Ottokar II issued his charter, an adaptation of one originally issued in 1244 by Duke Frederick II of Austria (1230–46). Among other provisions it forbade forced conversion and condemned the *blood libel. A gravestone excavated in *Znojmo (Znaim), dated 1256, is the oldest known Jewish tombstone from Moravia. In 1268 Premysl Ottokar II renewed his charter; at the time the Jews of Brno were expected to contribute a quarter of the cost of strengthening the city wall. In an undated document (probably from c. 1273–78), he exempted the Brno Jews from all their dues for one year since they had become impoverished. Writing to the pope in 1273, Bishop Bruno of Olomouc complained that the Jews of his diocese employed Christian wet nurses and accepted sacred objects as pledges, and that the interest they took during one year exceeded the initial loan. The first time a Jew, Nathan, is mentioned by name is in 1278, in connection with a lawsuit about church property. Solomon b. Abraham *Adret (d. 1310), responding to a question addressed to him from Moravia, mentions the *Austerlitz (Slavkov) and *Trest (Triesch) communities. Wenceslaus II confirmed Premysl Ottokar's charter (1283 and 1305) "at the request of the Jews of Moravia."

When Moravia passed under the rule of the Luxembourg dynasty in 1311, the Jewish community of Brno, carrying their Torah Scrolls, participated in the celebrations welcoming King John of Luxembourg to the city. In 1322 John permitted the bishop of Olomouc to settle one Jew in four of his towns (*Kromeriz (Kremsier), Mohelnice, Vyskov, and Svitavy (Zwittau)), and to benefit from their tax payments. At that time Jews earned their livelihood mainly as moneylenders, but gentile moneylenders could also be found. Several Moravian communities, such as Jemnice (Jamnitz), Trebic, and Znojmo, were affected by the wave of massacres evoked by the *Pulkau *Host desecration in 1338. A toll privilege granted in 1341 to the monastery of Vilimov, which was on the main road between Moravia and Bohemia, puts Jewish merchants on a par with their gentile counterparts and mentions a great variety of merchandise in which they dealt. *Charles IV granted the cities of Brno and Jihlava the right to admit Jews in 1345, making the Jihlava community independent of that in Brno. There was an influx of Jews fleeing from Germany into Moravia during the *Black Death massacres (1348–49). In 1349 the bishop of Olomouc complained to the city authorities that Jews did not wear special Jewish hats, as they were supposed to do. Between 1362 and 1415 Jews were free to accept real estate as security on loans.

Some of the Jews expelled from Austria in 1421 (the **Wiener Gesera*) settled in Moravia. Accused of supporting the *Hussites, the Jihlava community was expelled by Albert V, duke of Austria and margrave of Moravia, in 1426. As a result of John of *Capistrano's activities, the Jews were expelled from five of the six royal cities in 1454 (Jihlava, Brno, Olomouc, Znojmo, and Neustadt; the sixth royal city, Uherske Hradiste, expelled the Jews in 1514). The royal cities remained forbidden to them until after the 1848 revolution. The Jews who were expelled settled in the villages. During the 16th century, when there was no central power in Moravia ("in every castle a king"), the Jews were settled in small towns and villages under the protection of the local lords. The latter treated them well, not only because of the part they played in the economic development of their domains, which they shared initially with the Anabaptist communes, but also because some of the lords belonged to the Bohemian Brethren (see *Hussites) or were humanists; many therefore believed in religious tolerance. The importance of the Jews in the Moravian economic life (as military purveyors and *Court Jews) increased because of the constant threat of the Turkish wars. Since several Christian sects lived side by side, it became somewhat easier for the Jew to pursue his own interests without interference. When the Anabaptists were expelled (1622), and the country became depopulated during the Thirty Years' War (1618–48), the Jews took over new economic areas and were also permitted to acquire houses formerly occupied by "heretics." However, at the same time some communities suffered severely during the war (e.g., Kromeriz and *Hodonin (Goeding)). Moravia also absorbed refugees from Poland after the *Chmielnicki massacres (1648), among them scholars such as Gershon *Ashkenazi, author of *Avodat ha-Gershuni*, and Shabbetai Kohen, author of *Siftei Kohen*, the renowned commentary on the Shulḥan Arukh, who became rabbi of Holesov. Many Jews also arrived after the expulsion from Vienna (1670).

At this time an increasing number of Moravian Jews were engaged in crafts, a process that had already begun in the 16th century, and the cloth and wool merchants and tailors, who made goods to be sold at fairs, were laying the foundations of the textile and clothing industry for which Moravia was later known. In 1629 *Ferdinand II permitted the Jews to attend markets and fairs in the royal cities, on payment of a special body tax (*Leibmaut*; see *Leibzoll); in spite of protests from the guilds and merchants, the charter was renewed in 1657, 1658, and 1723. Jews also attended fairs outside Moravia, especially those in *Krems, *Linz, *Breslau (Wroczlaw), and *Leipzig. In

Jewish Communities in Moravia before World War I. After Th. Haas, Die Juden in Maehren, *1908.*

List of alternative names for places shown on map

Alstadt – Stare Mesto
Auspitz – Hustopece
Aussee – Usov
Austerlitz – Slavkov
Bajkowitz – Bojkovice
Battelau – Batelov
Bautsch – Budisov
Bielitz – Bielsko
Bisenz – Bzenec
Bistritz – Bystrice nad Pernstynem
Blansko
Boskowitz – Boskovice
Bruenn – Brno
Bruesau – Brezova
Butschowitz – Bucovice
Bystritz – Bystrice pod Hostynem
Damboritz – Damborice
Datschitz – Dacice
Eibenschitz – Ivancice
Eisgrub – Lednice
Eiwanowitz – Ivanovice na Hane
Frain – Vranov
Frankstadt – Frenstat pod Radhostem
Freiberg – Pribor
Freistadt – Karvina
Freiwaldau – Jesenik
Friedek – Frydek
Fulnek – Fulnek
Gaya – Kyjov
Gewitsch – Jevicko
Goeding – Hodonin
Gross Bitesch – Velka Bites
Gross Meseritsch – Velke Mezirici
Hof – Dvorce
Hohenstadt – Zabreh
Holleschau – Holesov
Hotzenplotz – Osoblaha
Hrottowitz – Hrotovice
Hullein – Hulin
Iglau – Jihlava
Ingrowitz – Jimramov
Jaegerndorf – Krnov
Jamnitz – Jemnice
Joslowitz – Jaroslavice
Kanitz – Dolni Kounice
Klobouk – Klobouky
Kojetein – Kojetin
Konitz – Konice
Koritischan – Korycany
Kostel – Podivin
Kosteletz – Kostelec
Kremsier – Kromeriz
Kromau – Moravsky Krumlov
Kunstadt – Kunstat
Kwassitz – Kvasice
Leipnik – Lipnik nad Becvou
Liebau – Libava
Littau – Litovel
Lomnitz – Lomnice
Loschitz – Lostice
Lundenburg – Breclav
Maehrisch Budwitz – Moravske Budejovice
Maehrisch Neustatd – Unicov
Maehrisch Ostrau – Moravska Ostrava
Maehrisch Truebau – Moravska Trebova
Misslitz – Miroslav
Mistek
Mueglitz – Mohelnice
Namest – Namest nad Oslavou
Napagedl – Napajedle
Neu Rausnitxz – Rousinov
Neustadtl – Nove Mesto na Morave
Neutitschein – Novy Jicin
Nikolsburg – Mikulov
Oderberg – Bohumin
Olmuetz – Olomouc
Pirnitz – Pirnice
Plumenau – Plumlov
Pohrlitz – Pohrelice
Prerau – Prerov
Prossnitz – Prostejov
Puklitz – Puklice
Pullitz – Police
Roemerstadt – Rymarov
Roznau – Roznov pod Radhostem
Saar – Zdar
Schaffa – Safov
Schoenberg – Sumperk
Seelowitz – Zidlochovice
Shildberg – Stity
Skotschau – Skoczow
Steinitz – Zdanice
Sernberg – Sternberk
Strassnitz – Straznice
Teltsch – Telc
Teschen – Cesky Tesin
Tischnowitz – Tisnov
Tobitschau – Tovacov
Trebitsch – Trebic
Triesch – Trest
Troppau – Opava
Ungarisch Brod – Uhersky Brod
Ungarisch Hradisch – Uherske Hradiste
Ungarish Ostra – Uhersky Ostroh
Wagstadt – Bilovec
Wallachisch Klobouk – Valasske Klobouky
Wallachisch Meseritsch – Valasske Mezirici
Weisskirchen – Hranice
Wessely – Veseli nad Moravou
Wischau – Vyskov
Wisowitz – Vizovice
Witowitz – Vitkovice
Woelking – Bolikov
Wsetin – Vsetin
Zdounek – Zdounky
Zlabings – Slavonice
Zlin – Gottwaldov
Znaim – Znojmo
Zwittau – Svitavy

1650 the Moravian Diet decided that Jews could reside only where they had been living before 1618, but the decision was not enforced. Later this was modified by the Diet of 1681 to permit Jews to dwell where they lived before 1657.

The Modern Era

On July 31, 1725, during the reign of Charles VI, an imperial order fixed the number of registered Jewish families at 5,106 and threatened any locality which accepted Jews where they had not been previously settled with a fine of 1,000 ducats. On September 20 of that year the same penalty was imposed on anyone who allowed Jews to come into possession of real estate, particularly customhouses, mills, wool-shearing sheds, and breweries. The first enactment was reinforced a year later by allowing only one son in a family to marry (see *Familiants Law); the second was never carried out, as it would have deprived noblemen of lucrative revenue and most Jews of their livelihood. Under Charles VI the geographical separation of the Jews was implemented in most Moravian towns.

*Maria Theresa threatened Moravian Jewry with expulsion (Jan. 2, 1745) but rescinded her order, permitting them to remain for another ten years. In 1748, however, she raised their toleration tax (*Schutzgeld*) from a total of 8,000 florins (since 1723) to 87,700 for the next five years and 76,700 in the following five; in 1752 the tax was fixed at 90,000 florins. Two years later the empress' definitive "General Police Law and Commercial Regulations for the Jewry of the Margravate of Moravia" appeared; as its name indicates it regulated all legal, religious, and commercial aspects of Jewish life in Moravia. The authority of the **Landesrabbiner* was defined and his election regulated, as were those of the other offices of the **Landesjudenschaft*. In essence the law was based on a translation by Aloys von *Sonnenfels of the resolutions and ordinances of the old Council of Moravian Jewry. Although the earliest recorded session of the council had taken place in 1651, it was at least a century older, for a Bendit Axelrod Levi was mentioned in 1519 as being "head of all Moravian communities." The names of most Moravian rabbis were recorded from the mid-16th century.

A clearer picture of the council emerges after the Thirty Years' War (1618–48): Moravia (*medinah*) was divided into three provinces (*galil*), in each of which two heads (*rashei galil*) officiated; at the same time, each one was a member of the governing body of Moravian Jewry (*rashei ha-medinah*). The chief authority was the *Landesrabbiner* (*rav medinah*), who had jurisdiction over both secular and religious matters. His seat was in *Mikulov (Nikolsburg). His presence at council sessions was obligatory and he was the authoritative interpreter of their decisions. There were two types of council: the governing "small" council of six heads of provinces, and the "large" legislative one, which was attended by representatives of the communities and met every three years at a different community. The franchise was very limited and the council oligarchic in spirit and practice. The last "large" council, that of 1748, was attended by 61 representatives elected by 367 house owners. Its main function was the election of small bodies of electors and legislators. The authority of the council was undermined by the absolutist state, which in 1728 defined its ordinances as "temporary"; from 1754 Maria Theresa limited the independence of the communities and their central council. The main function of the council and the *Landesrabbiner* was to divide the tax load justly among the communities. When *Landesrabbiner* Menahem *Krochmal was called upon to settle a dispute between the poor and the rich over the control of the communities, he claimed that the decisive voice belonged to those who contributed more to the community. Krochmal's tenure (1648–61) was vital in the formulation of the 311 ordinances (*shai takkanot*) of the Moravian council. Among his noted predecessors were R. *Judah Loew b. Bezalel (Maharal) and R. Yom Tov Lipmann *Heller. Among the more distinguished holders of the office were David *Oppenheim (from 1690 to 1704); Gabriel b. Judah Loew *Eskeles, nominated in 1690; and his son Issachar Berush (Bernard) *Eskeles, (d. 1753), who also became chief rabbi of Hungary and successfully averted the 1745 expulsion threat. His successor, R. Moses b. Aaron *Lemberger, ordained that henceforth at least 25 students should attend the Mikulov (Nikolsburg) yeshivah, and that each Moravian sub-province should support two yeshivot with ten students each. R. Gershon Pullitz and R. Gershon *Chajes (*Landesrabbiner* 1780–89) fought against the insidious influence of Shabbateanism and Frankism in Moravia: in 1773 Jacob *Frank resided in Brno, where the *Dobruschka family were among his adherents; members of the *Prostejov (Prossnitz) community were commonly called *Schebse* since so many of them were followers of Shabbetai Ẓevi.

In spite of the hostile attitude of Charles VI and Maria Theresa and the continuous curtailment of the authority of the council and the *Landesrabbiner*, there was a thriving communal life in Moravia. In the first half of the 19th century the *Landesrabbiner* Mordecai *Benet (d. 1829), Nehemiah (Menahem) Nahum *Trebitsch (d. 1842), and Samson Raphael *Hirsch (served from 1846 to 1851) wielded great influence. Besides the spiritual metropolis of Nikolsburg, there were important centers of learning in Boskowitz (*Boskovice), Ungarisch-Brod (*Uhersky Brod), Kremsier, Leipnik (*Lipnik nad Becvou), and Prossnitz.

The situation of Moravian Jews improved after Joseph II's **Toleranzpatent*, which abolished the body tax (see **Leibzoll*) and other special taxes and permitted some freedom of movement. But the limitation of the number of Jewish families remained, the number of licensed (*systematisiert*) Jewish families being kept at 5,106, later raised to 5,400. An edict of Francis II in 1798 limited their rights of settlement to an area of 52 Jewish communities (*Judengemeinden*), mostly in places where communities had existed from early times. The six royal cities remained closed to the Jews. Like most of the local Christian communities, the Jewish communities were subject to the authority of the feudal lord. At that time the largest communities were Mikulov with 620 families, Prostejov with 328, Boskovice with 326, and Holesov with 265. The total number of registered Jews increased from 20,327 in 1754 to 28,396 in 1803 (the actual numbers might have been from 10 to 20% higher). The revolutionary year of 1848 brought the abolition of most legal and economic restrictions, the right of free movement and settlement, and freedom of worship, but also gave rise to anti-Jewish disturbances: in Prostejov a Jewish national guard, 200 men strong, was organized. These measures of freedom were enacted by the Austrian parliament which convened in Kromeriz. *Landesrabbiner* S.R. Hirsch sent two messages to parliament. The process of legal emancipation was completed in the Austrian constitution of 1867. In conformity with the new municipal laws (passed temporarily in 1849 and definitively in 1867) 27 of the 52 Jewish communities were constituted as Jewish municipalities (*politische Gemeinden) with full municipal independence, and existed as such until the end of the Hapsburg monarchy, in striking contrast to the abolition of Jewish municipal autonomy in Prague in 1850 and in Galicia in 1866. The legalization of the Jewish religious autonomy, a longer process, was not completed until 1890, when 50 Jewish religious communities (*Kultusgemeinden*) were recognized, 39 in places where old communities existed and 11 in newly established Jewish centers.

The restrictions imposed on the Jews by Charles VI and Maria Theresa, most of which remained in force until the second half of the 19th century, led many Moravian Jews to leave the country, mainly for Hungary (Slovakia) and later for Austria. After equal rights and freedom of movement were granted, new communities were established in the big cities of Brno, Olomouc, Ostrava (Maehrisch Ostrau), and Jihlava, while others were set up in small places that previously Jews had only visited on market days. At the same time many Moravian Jews left for other parts of the Hapsburg Empire, particularly Vienna, and some emigrated. As a result, the Jewish population of Moravia remained relatively static at a time when the world Jewish population was rising, and even declined slightly from 1890. (See Table: Jewish Population in Moravia).

Jewish Population in Moravia

In 1787 Joseph II ordered that half of the main tax on Moravian Jewry (then 88,280 florins) be allowed to accumulate in a fund (known as *Landesmassafond*) for the payment of the *Landesrabbiner* and other officials. In 1831, when the fund was sealed, the capital was allocated for low-interest loans for needy communities. An assembly of 45 Moravian communities convened in 1862 in order to try to obtain control of the fund, which was managed by state officials. After protracted negotiations, *Francis Joseph I awarded the guardianship of the fund (almost 1,000,000 kronen) to an elected curatorium whose first chairman was Julius von Gomperz of Brno. This curatorium served in lieu of a central Jewish organization until the collapse of the Austrian regime and enabled Moravian Jewry to alleviate the lot of the declining small communities. Jews were mainly engaged in trade, but increasing numbers entered some industries and the free professions or became white-collar workers (mainly in undertakings owned by Jews). They were prominent in the wool industry of Brno, the silk industry of northern Moravia, the clothing industry in Prostejov, Boskovice, and some other towns, the leather industry, the sugar industry in central and southern Moravia, and the malt industry in Olomouc. The brothers Wilhelm and David von *Gutmann (orginally from Lipnik) developed jointly with the Rothschilds the coal mines of Ostrava and established the great iron and steel works there. The Rothschilds also built the Kaiser Ferdinand Nordbahn, a railway linking Vienna and Galicia via Moravia and Silesia. Consequently there was a substantial number of Jewish railway engineers, employees, engine drivers, licensees of railway restaurants, etc. In the late 19th and 20th centuries Jews were also prominent in the timber industry and trade, the glass industry, hat-making, hosiery, and even in the development of water power.

Jewish Population in Moravia, 1830–1921

Year	Number of Jews
1830	29,462
1840	37,316
1848	37,548
1857	42,611
1869	42,644
1880	44,175
1890	45,324
1900	44,255
1910	41,255
1921	37,989

The close ties between Moravian Jews and Vienna persisted until the end of the Austrian monarchy, and even increased after emancipation, since Moravia had no university under Austrian rule. Consequently, the great majority of Moravian Jews spoke German. In 1900, 77% of all Moravian Jews declared German as their mother tongue, 16% Czech, and 7% other languages (mainly foreigners), but this did not indicate any strong political assimilationist trend toward Germany or hostility toward Czech nationalism. Jews enthusiastically supported the candidacy of T.G. *Masaryk for the Austrian parliament in 1907 and 1911. Students from Moravian communities studying in Vienna were among the first followers of Theodor Herzl and many Zionist associations sprang up in Moravia, from the early days of Zionism.

After the Czechoslovak Republic had been established in 1918, Moravian Jews frequently constituted the bridge between the Jews in Bohemia on the one hand and those in Slovakia and Subcarpathian Ruthenia on the other, between traditionalists and modernists, Zionist and non-Zionists. Slovakian Jewry felt close to Moravian Jewry by ties of blood and tradition. The yeshivah of Mikulov was and remained the alma matter of many West Slovakian Orthodox Jews. Moravian Jews could perhaps not match West Slovakian Jews in religious feeling but surpassed their Bohemian brethren. Orthodoxy was not foreign to Moravian Jewry, and it was strengthened by the steady influx of Jews coming from Poland, often through the

Duchy of Tesin. Even ḥasidic *shtiblekh* were not an oddity. Jews from Carpatho-Russia, who migrated westward between the wars and who left their country after World War II in fear of Soviet domination, strengthened the religiosity of Moravian Jewry still further. However, after World War II there were only two communities in Moravia where religious observance was the rule – Brno and Ostrava. Between the wars, 60% of Moravian Jews declared themselves as being of Jewish nationality, far above the figure for Bohemia.

The first provincial union of Jewish communities was established in November 1918 under the leadership of Alois Hilf from Ostrava; this union became instrumental in the emergence and consolidation of the Jewish National Council, as well as in the setting up of the Supreme Council of the Jewish Religious Communities in Bohemia, Moravia, and Silesia. The Central Committee of the Zionist Organization in Czechoslovakia had its seat in Ostrava from 1921 to 1938, under the chairmanship of Joseph *Rufeisen; the center of *He-Halutz was also located in Ostrava and the main office of Keren Hayesod was in Brno for a long time. Brno had the only Jewish high school in the western part of Czechoslovakia and Ostrava had a fully equipped vocational school. Moravian Jews were represented by a Zionist in the provincial Diet. However, the number of Jews continued to decline, from 45,306 in Moravia and Silesia in 1921 to 41,250 in 1930, almost half of whom were concentrated in the three cities Brno, Ostrava, and Olomouc. The venerable communities dwindled or even disintegrated.

When the Germans occupied Austria in March 1938, several thousand Jews escaped to Moravia, mainly to Brno. They were followed in September and October of that year by a few thousand more from the areas detached from Czechoslovakia and incorporated in Germany by the Munich Agreement. The majority of Jews in the Teschen (Tesin; Cieszyn) district, ceded to Poland, did not flee. On March 15, 1939, the remaining parts of Moravia were occupied by Nazi Germany and became part of the Protectorate of Bohemia-Moravia. Immediately after the conquest, the lot of the Jews in northeast Moravia was especially disastrous. They constituted a high percentage of those expelled to the Nisko reservate in the Lublin area. Many perished there in the first winter of the war; others returned, only to join their fellows in *Theresienstadt and various extermination camps. After the war, very few survivors returned to Moravia, and the majority of them later emigrated to Israel and other countries. In 1970 barely 2,000 Jews remained in former Moravia, the largest community being in Brno. In Brno there also existed a center of Carpatho-Rus Jewry which was involved in communal problems such as indemnities from Czech authorities, Carpatho-Rus authorities, and German authorities. Brno was the seat of the chief rabbi of Moravia, Richard *Feder. The rabbi was the only leading Jewish figure who dared criticize the Communist regime for its treatment of the Jews. He also publicly expressed longing for Ereẓ Israel and interest in the State Israel. When he died in 1970, at the age of 95, the rabbinate remained vacant. In Brno and in Ostrava a prayer room, cemetery, and religious services were maintained. Purim and Hanukkah were celebrated, with the participation of the children of congregation members. The Jewish museum of Mikulov, established shortly before World War II, was restored as part of the state museum. The ancient synagogue was refurbished, as was the cemetery. The cemetery was also used as a repository for the tombstones of cemeteries liquidated elsewhere. Another Jewish museum was established by the state in *Holesov. For further details on the contemporary period, see *Czechoslovakia as well as *Czech Republic and Slovakia. For fuller details on the Holocaust period, see *Czechoslovakia under Protectorate of Bohemia-Moravia.

BIBLIOGRAPHY: H. Gold (ed.), *Die Juden und Judengemeinden Maehrens in Vergangenheit und Gegenwart* (1929); Th. Haas, *Die Juden in Maehren* (1908); B. Bretholz, *Geschichte der Juden im Mittelalter, I. Teil bis zum Jahre 1350* (1934); idem, *Quellen zur Geschichte der Juden in Maehren vom XI. bis zum XV. Jahrhundert (1067–1411)* (1935); I. Halpern, *Takkanot Medinat Mehrin* (1952); Baron, Community, index; L. Loew, *Gesammelte Schriften*, 2 (1892), 165–218; W. Mueller, *Urkundliche Beitraege zur Geschichte der maehrischen Judenschaft im 17. und 18. Jahrhundert* (1903); M. Lamed, in: BLBI, 8 (1965), 32, 302–14; G. Kisch, in: *The Jews of Czechoslovakia*, 1 (1968), 1–11; H. Kohn, *ibid.*, 12–20; R. Kestenberg-Gladstein, *ibid.*, 21–71; G. Fleischmann, *ibid.*, 267–329; H. Stransky, *ibid.*, 330–58; J.C. Pick, *ibid.*, 359–438, passim; R. Kestenberg-Gladstein, *Neuere Geschichte der Juden in den boehmischen Laendern. I. Das Zeitalter der Aufklaerung 1780–1830* (1969); idem, in: *Gesher*, 2–3 (1969), 11–82; F. Weltsch, *ibid.*, 207–12; idem, in: *Prag vi-Yrushalayim* (n.d.), 23–35; N.M. Gelber, *ibid.*, 36–51; A.F. Pribram, *Urkunden und Akten…*, 2 vols. (1918), index; Bondy-Dworský; M.H. Friedlaender, *Kore ha-Dorot. Beitraege zur Geschichte der Juden in Maehren* (1876); idem, *Tiferet Yisrael, Schilderungen aus dem inneren Leben der Juden in Maehren in vormaerzlichen Zeiten* (1878); R. Jakobson and M. Halle, in: *For Max Weinreich* (1964), 147–72; B. Bretholz and A. Glaser, in: *Zeitschrift fuer Geschichte der Juden in der Tschechoslowakei*, 3 (1932/33), 25–34; J. Bronner, *ibid.*, 1 (1930/31), 243–7; B. Brilling, *ibid.*, 2 (1931/32), 1–20, 237–56; T. Haas, *ibid.*, 32–38; L. Moses, *ibid.*, 4 (1934), 18–24; A. Engel, in: JGGJČ, 2 (1930), 50–97; B. Heilig, *ibid.*, 3 (1931), 307–448; 4 (1932), 7–62; W. Zacek, *ibid.*, 5 (1933), 175–98; A. Freud, in: BLBI, 2 (1959), 222–9; H.H. Ben-Sasson, *Hagut ve-Hanhagah* (1959), index; Y.L. Bialer, *Min ha-Genazim*, 2 (1968/69), 33–36; H. Flesch, in: MGWJ, 71 (1927), 71, 74; 74 (1930), 197–217; M. Wischnitzer, in: JSOS, 16 (1954), 335–60; S. Simonsohn, in: *Sefer Yovel… N.M. Gelber* (1963), 127–64; Y. Toury, *Mehumah u-Mevukhah be-Mahpekhat 1848* (1968), index; G. Horowitz, *The Spirit of Jewish Law* (1963²), 86–87; Germ Jud, 1 (1963), 171–3; 2 (1968), 510–2. **ADD. BIBLIOGRAPHY:** J. Fiedler, *Jewish Sights of Bohemia and Moravia* (1991).

[Meir Lamed / Yeshayahu Jelinek (2nd ed.)]

MORAVIA (Pincherle), ALBERTO (1907–1990), Italian novelist and critic. Born in Rome, Moravia took his pen name from his immigrant ancestors' country of origin. He made his reputation with works published after World War II, and in English-speaking lands was widely regarded as the outstanding Italian writer of his time. Moravia's first novel, *Gli Indifferenti* (1929; *The Indifferent Ones*, 1932; reissued as *The Time of Indifference*, 1953), was covertly critical of middle class society and its passive and cynical acceptance of the Fascist dictatorship. His violent hostility toward the bourgeoisie, into which he had himself been born, and the relentless psychological analysis of the characters in his works came to the fore in *Le ambizioni sbagliate* (1935; *Wheel of Fortune*, 1938) and dominated many later novels. Moravia's early writings made it clear that he had set out to combine the 19th-century narrative tradition of Dostoievski and Flaubert with the aesthetic principles of the realistic or naturalistic novel. Totally estranged from Judaism, Moravia served during World War II as a foreign correspondent in Germany and the Far East. His postwar works dealt largely with themes such as adolescence and relations between the sexes, and remained outside of any established literary current.

Moravia's artistry and skillful characterization are especially evident in the novels which he published after World War II: *Agostino* (1945, Eng. trans. 1947); *La Romana* (1947; *The Woman of Rome*, 1949); *La disubbidienza* (1948; *Disobedience*, 1950); *Il Conformista* (1951; *The Conformist*, 1952); and *Il disprezzo* (1954; *A Ghost at Noon*, 1955). However, some critics were sensitive to the writer's preoccupation with sex and to his disinclination to pass judgment on the amorality of his heroes. There is a warmer, more sympathetic tone to his stories about the lower strata of society in *Racconti romani* (1954; *Roman Tales*, 1956) and in *Il Paradiso* (1970). Moravia distinguished himself as a novelist most of all, perhaps, in *La Ciociara* (1957; *Two Women*, 1958), an acute study of two characters, contrasting intellect and sensuality, which was made into a successful motion picture. His later works include *La noia* (1960; *The Empty Canvas*, 1961); *L'attenzione* (1965; Fr. trans. *L'Attention*, 1966); and a volume of short stories, *Una cosa è una cosa* (1967). Moravia also published *L'uomo come fine* (1964; *Man as an End: A Defense of Humanism*, 1966), a collection of major essays published between the years 1941 and 1962, and a book of plays, *Teatro* (1958). The variety of his interests may be gauged from three other books – *Un mese in U.R.S.S.* (1958; Fr. trans. *Un Mois en U.R.S.S.*, 1954), *Un idea dell' India* (1962), and *La rivoluzione culturale in Cina* (1967; *The Red Book and the Great Wall*, 1968).

BIBLIOGRAPHY: A. Limentani, *Alberto Moravia tra esistenza e realtà* (1962); E. Sanguineti, *Alberto Moravia* (It. 1962); O. Del Buono, *Moravia* (Ital, 1962), incl. bibl.; M.F. Cimmino, *Lettura di Moravia* (1967); P. Pancrazi, *Scrittori italiani del Novecento* (19392), index; idem, *Scrittori d'oggi*, 1 (1942), index; G. De Robertis, *Scrittori del Novecento* (1958[2]), index; E. Kanduth, *Wesenszuege der modernen italienischen Erzaehlliteratur…* (1968), incl. Bibl. **ADD. BIBLIOGRAPHY:** G. Pandini, *Invito alla lettura di Alberto Moravia* (1990); F. Alfonsi, *Alberto Moravia in America: un quarantennio di critica (1929–1969)* (1984); idem, *Alberto Moravia in Italia: un quarantennio di critica (1929–1969)*, (1986); A. Elkann, *Vita di Moravia* (1991); R. Paris, *Alberto Moravia* (1991); M. Piccinonno, *Discorrendo di Alberto Moravia* (1992); T.E. Peterson, *Alberto Moravia* (1996); M. Procaccia, *'L'ebreo Pincherle; Moravia tra indifferenza e rimozione'*, *Appartenenza e differenza* (1998), 161–75.

[Giorgio Romano]

MORAVSKE BUDEJOVICE (Czech **Moravské Budějovice**; Ger. **Maehrisch-Budwitz**), small town in S. Moravia, Czech Republic. Its Jewish community is mentioned among those suffering from the wave of massacres following the Host desecration of *Pulkau in 1338. One Jew, Jacob, is mentioned in 1363 and in 1386 as a member of a consortium buying and selling a village. From 1528 transactions between Jews and gentiles, involving loans and the sale of houses, horses, and grain, are mentioned frequently in the town records. In 1562 the community numbered 47, and its members were not permitted to sell alcoholic beverages or to brew beer. The community was expelled in 1564. There were no Jews in the town until 1774, when a tobacco agent settled there, and in 1808 a Jew leased a distillery. Between 1794 and 1842, 120 Jewish merchants attended the local fairs. There were 19 Jews in Moravske Budejovice in 1848, 58 in 1869, 127 in 1890, and 97 in 1900. A congregation was founded in 1867 and recognized as a community in 1890. A cemetery was consecrated in 1908 and a synagogue in 1910. From 1926 the community was administered by the Safov (Schaffa) community. Its members numbered 77 in 1930 (1.8% of the total population). In 1942 those Jews remaining after the German occupation were deported to extermination camps, and the synagogue equipment was sent to the Central Jewish Museum in Prague. No community was reestablished after World War II.

BIBLIOGRAPHY: J. Fiser, in: H. Gold (ed.), *Juden und Judengemeinden Maehrens* (1929), 343–67; Bondy-Dworský, 1 (1906), nos. 673, 679; Germ Jud, 2 pt. 2 (1968), 512 s.v. *Maehrisch-Budwitz*.

[Meir Lamed]

MORAVSKY KRUMLOV (Czech. **Moravský Krumlov**; Ger. **Maehrisch-Kromau**; Heb. קרומענו), town in Moravia, Czech Republic. The community was in existence before 1437, the presence of Jews being mentioned in 1402. A synagogue was built in 1547. The number of families allotted by the *Familiants Laws was 49. In 1800, 43 houses were owned by Jews, a situation which was quite unusual in Moravia. With the 1848 revolution and the freedom of settlement, the Jewish population decreased steadily, from 356 persons in 1830, to 226 in 1869, 140 in 1880, and 116 in 1900. In 1930 it numbered only 34 persons (0.9% of the total population). The community had become a *politische Gemeinde after 1848 but gave up this privilege in 1869. From 1915 the community was under the guidance of Heinrich *Flesch, rabbi of nearby Dolni-Kounice. The community was liquidated under the Nazi occupation. Rabbi Samuel Baeck, father of Leo *Baeck (1873–1956), was born in the town.

BIBLIOGRAPHY: H. Flesch, in: JJLG, 17 (1926), 57–84; idem, in: H. Gold (ed.), *Juden und Judengemeinden Maehrens* (1929), 369–71. **ADD. BIBLIOGRAPHY:** J. Fiedler, *Jewish Sights of Bohemia and Moravia* (1991), 120.

[Meir Lamed]

MORAWETZ, OSKAR (1917–), Canadian composer. Morawetz was born in Svetla nad Sazavou, Czech Republic. Having studied piano and music theory in Prague and Vienna, he applied to enter Canada after the Nazis entered the Sudetenland (1938). Finally admitted in 1940, he continued music studies at the University of Toronto (D.Mus., 1953), where he taught theory and composition (1946–82).

A conservative throughout his career, Morawetz early gained attention for such expatriate works of Czech nationalism as *Carnival Overture* (1945) and *Overture to a Fairy Tale* (1957). Known especially as a symphonic composer, Morawetz had works performed on every continent by more than a hundred orchestras. Also representative of his output are *Fantasy on a Hebrew Theme* for piano (1951), his choral setting of *Who Has Allowed Us to Suffer?* with words by Anne Frank (1970), and his arrangement for voice of Psalm 22 (1979) whose words, "My God, why have you forsaken me?" Morawetz employed to comment on the Holocaust. Notable too are the orchestral *Passacaglia on a Bach Chorale* for John F. Kennedy (1964) and *Memorial to Martin Luther King, Jr.* for cello and orchestra (1968, commissioned by Mstislav Rostropovich).

The Canadian Performing Rights Commission honored Morawetz for two student works: *String Quartet no. 1* (1945) and *Sonata Tragica* (1946). The Segal Fund of Montreal provided a special award for the orchestral work *From the Diary of Anne Frank* – which focuses on Anne's fear for the survival of her former friend Lies – citing it as "the most important contribution to Jewish music" (1971). Morawetz's *Concerto for Harp and Orchestra* won a Juno award as best Canadian classical composition (1989). The Canada Council awarded Senior Fellowships (1960, 1967, 1974) for his contributions to Canadian music. Morawetz was the first composer to receive the Order of Ontario (1987) and became a Member of the Order of Canada in 1988.

[Jay Rahn (2nd ed.)]

MORAWITZ, KARL RITTER VON (1846–1914), Austrian banker. Born in Iglau (now Jihlava), Moravia, he was educated in Prague and began working as a bank clerk in small banking houses in Prague and Dresden. In 1860 he joined the Banque de Paris et des Pays-Bas in Paris, an establishment of Ludwig *Bamberger with whom Morawitz became closely associated. Subsequently he entered the Paris office of the Ottoman Bank, but, as a foreigner, had to leave that post in 1870 after the outbreak of the Franco-Prussian War. He then worked for Baron Maurice de *Hirsch and his railway enterprises. In 1906 he became president of the Anglo-Austrian Bank, a post he held until his death. Morawitz was an expert in international finance, and his experience and connections made him an influential adviser. Shortly before his death he was knighted by Emperor Franz Joseph. Morawitz frequently wrote and lectured, and his book, *Les Finances de la Turquie* (1902), is a standard work on the financial history of the Ottoman Empire. Other publications include: *Aus der Werkstatt eines Bankmannes, Aus Arbeitstagen und Mussestunden* (1907), and a history of the Anglo-Austrian Bank, *50 Jahre Geschichte einer Wiener Bank* (1913).

[Joachim O. Ronall]

MORDECAI (Heb. מָרְדֳּכַי, מָרְדְּכַי hypocoristic masculine proper name containing the theophoric element Marduk), name of two Biblical figures:

1) One of the 12 leaders who returned from Babylonia to Jerusalem at the time of Zerubbabel (Ezra 2:2; Neh. 7:7).

2) A Jew who lived in Shushan (Susa), the residence of the Persian King, Ahasuerus (Xerxes I), who reigned from 486 to 465 B.C.E. Mordecai was the great-grandson of a Benjamite of Jerusalem by the name of Kish who was a member of the group that was taken into exile by King Nebuchadnezzar of Babylon together with King Jehoiachin of Judah in 597 B.C.E. Since this group consisted mainly of the upper classes (II Kings 24:14), and since the name Kish is otherwise known only as that of the father of the Benjamite king Saul, the implication is doubtless that Mordecai's great-grandfather and, hence, he himself were descended from King Saul. Mordecai was foster father to his cousin *Esther (Esth. 2:5ff.).

When Esther was chosen for the harem of King Ahasuerus as a replacement for the deposed Queen Vashti, Mordecai charged her not to reveal her ancestry or nationality. Since he "sat in the king's gate" (Esth. 2:21), i.e., was one of the king's consultants (cf. Dan. 2:49), Mordecai was able to inquire daily about her welfare (Esth. 2:10–11); and when he discovered a plot by Bigthan and Teresh to assassinate the king, he informed her and she passed the information on to the king in Mordecai's name. The plotters were impaled; and the incident, with the part played in it by Mordecai, was recorded in the royal annals (Esth. 2:21ff.). For the time being, however, he was not rewarded, while Haman, a descendant of the Amalekite Agag, who was spared by Mordecai's ancestor Saul (I Sam. 15), was elevated by the king above all his other officials. Mordecai was the only one of these officials who refused to obey the king's command to bow down to Haman (Esth. 3:1ff.). This refusal has often been explained on religious grounds, but not only does Judaism not forbid, it actually enjoins, the showing of respect to highly placed persons, Jewish or otherwise. When Mordecai's colleagues asked him for the reason for his behavior he merely told them that he was a Jew, and the narrator evidently takes it for granted that everybody knew that there was a sacred, perpetual feud between Jews and Amalekites (Ex. 17:14ff.; Deut. 25:17ff.).

Haman for his part resolved to avenge himself not only on Mordecai but on the entire Jewish people, and persuaded the king to decree their extermination by a pogrom on a given day (Esth. 3:6ff.). Then Mordecai urged Esther to intercede on behalf of her people with Ahasuerus. Providence, he saw, had put her there for such an act. Failure to act would result in her own destruction but the Jews would still be delivered (Esth. 4). In an unexpected turn of events, Mordecai was rewarded for having saved the king's life by being dressed in royal garb and promenaded around the city on a royal steed by Haman (*ibid.* 6). As a result of Esther's intervention, Haman was hanged on the same gallows (7:10) he had prepared for Mordecai (5:13f.), who was further rewarded by receiving

Haman's property (8:1f.) and being appointed vizier (10:3). His fame spread abroad and all Persian officials aided the Jews in destroying their enemies. Mordecai recorded all these events and he and Esther wrote to all the Jews to commemorate the days of deliverance annually (14th and 15th day of Adar; Esth. 9). In Hasmonean times, the 14th of Adar was known as the "Day of Mordecai" (II Macc. 15:36).

A cuneiform tablet from the end of the reign of Darius I or the beginning of that of Xerxes (Ahasuerus) mentions an official named Marduka, whom some scholars have identified with the biblical Mordecai. It has further been suggested that the prominence of Jews in the Murashu tablets from the time of Xerxes' successors, Artaxerxes I and Darius II, and their absence from documents of earlier reigns, accords with the statement that Mordecai "sought [and achieved] the welfare of his people" (Esth. 10:3).

[Bezalel Porten]

In the Aggadah

The fact that Mordecai is referred to as both a Benjamite (Yemini) and a Judean (Yehudi) (Esth. 2:5) is explained in various ways: as a tribute to David, who belonged to the tribe of Judah, for saving the life of Shimei the Benjamite who is regarded as Mordecai's ancestor, or because his mother was of this tribe. His name is interpreted to mean "pure myrrh" (*mor*-myrrh, *decai*-pure) for he was as refined and noble as pure myrrh (Meg. 12a). Mordecai was a prophet and is sometimes identified with Malachi (*ibid.*). He prophesied in the second year of Darius (Meg. 15a). Mordecai fasted from the eve of Passover till its seventh day, supplicating God to mete out punishment to Ahasuerus for his desecration of the Temple vessels (Targ. Jon., Esth. 1:10).

Mordecai was appointed to the royal court at the request of Esther (Yal., Esth. 10:53). Thus it was while attending on the king that he discovered the plot of Bigthan and Teresh. They were Tarseans and spoke their native language in plotting to poison Ahasuerus, unaware that Mordecai knew 70 languages (Meg. 13b). It was on account of his ability as a linguist that he was called Bilshan (Men. 65a). When the court officials asked Mordecai why he refused to pay homage to Haman while his ancestor Jacob prostrated himself before Haman's ancestor Esau, Mordecai answered, "I am a descendant of Benjamin, who was not yet born when that took place" (Targ. Sheni, Esth. 3:4). The true reason for Haman's hatred of Mordecai and the Jews was that he had once sold himself as a slave to Mordecai and whenever they met his erstwhile master used to remind him of this fact (Meg. 15b).

After the fatal decree had been signed, Mordecai asked three school children to repeat to him the biblical verses they had just learned. The children recited three different biblical verses, each containing a prophecy that Israel should not fear the evil designs against them. Mordecai had been informed of the king's decree by Elijah. The prayer he and Esther prayed then unto God was the *Hallel*. The days Mordecai decided that Jews should fast were the first three days of Passover (Meg. 15a). When Mordecai saw Haman coming to him with the royal insignia, he thought his last moment had come. He therefore told his pupils to flee and leave him alone to his fate, but they refused. Mordecai spent what he thought were his last moments in prayer and Haman had to wait until he had finished. Since Mordecai had been fasting and mourning for several days he refused to don the king's apparel until he had bathed and trimmed his hair. But upon a decree of Esther, the baths and all the barber shops were closed on this day, so that Haman had to act as valet to Mordecai. Haman had also to offer him his back to enable Mordecai to mount the horse (Meg. 16a).

While Haman conducted Mordecai through the streets, 27,000 youths from the court marched before him, bearing golden cups and beakers (Targ. Sheni, Esth. 6:11). As he rode, Mordecai and his pupils gave praise to God (Lev. R. 28:6). As soon as the procession was over, Mordecai put off the royal attire and again covering himself with sackcloth, resumed his prayers and fasting (Meg. 16a). He did not stop praying until Ahasuerus charged him with the execution of Haman. In spite of Haman's pleas, Mordecai insisted upon hanging him like the commonest criminal (Targ. Sheni, Esth. 7:10). Mordecai became king of the Jews (Esth. R. 10:12). As such he had coins struck which bore sackcloth and ashes on one side and a golden crown on the other (Gen. R. 39:11). However in the measure in which Mordecai gained worldly power and consideration, he lost spiritually, because his high political function left him no time for study of the Torah. From first among the scholars of Israel, he had dropped to seventh place among them (Meg. 16b).

BIBLIOGRAPHY: S.H. Horn, in: BRE, 9 (1964), 14ff. IN THE AGGADAH: Ginzberg, Legends, index.

MORDECAI, ALFRED (1804–1887), U.S. soldier, engineer, and ordnance expert. Born in Warrenton, North Carolina, son of Jacob *Mordecai, Alfred was educated at the West Point Military Academy, passing out first in his class. He was commissioned in the Engineers, but transferred in 1832 to the Ordnance Department, where he remained until his retirement, with the rank of major, in 1861, on the eve of the Civil War. Mordecai served from 1839 to 1860 on the U.S. Ordnance Board, where he helped to develop and systematize weapons, ammunition, and equipment. His greatest contribution to American military technology was the introduction of scientific research and development to the military art. He was twice sent to Europe to study arms systems and production methods and commanded the arsenals at Frankford, Pennsylvania, Washington, D.C., and Watervliet, New York. He wrote several military works, notably *Second Report of Experiments in Gunpowder* (1849), and *Ordnance Manual for the Use of the Officers of the United States Army* (1841, 1850). His son ALFRED (1840–1920) was also an ordnance officer and rose to the rank of brigadier general.

BIBLIOGRAPHY: S.L. Falk, *Soldier-Technologist: Major Alfred Mordecai and the Beginnings of Science in the United States Army* (1959), incl. bibl.; idem, in: AJA, 10 (1958), 125–32; A. Mordecai, in:

North Carolina Historical Review, 22 (1945), 58–108; S.L. Falk, in: A.J. Karp (ed.), *The Jewish Experience in America*, 3 (1969), 300–22.

[Stanley L. Falk]

MORDECAI, JACOB (1762–1838), U.S. merchant and educator. Born in Philadelphia, Pennsylvania, his early formal education was slight, but he studied at home and in the synagogue and later earned a reputation as a scholar and biblical authority. He moved to Richmond, Virginia, in 1782 and became an independent businessman. In 1784 he was in New York, where he formed a brief partnership with Haym *Salomon, but after the death of the latter in 1785, Mordecai's business failed. He returned to Virginia, attempting various commercial ventures, and finally in 1792 moved to Warrenton, North Carolina, where he became a successful merchant. In 1807 Mordecai lost heavily in tobacco speculations and was forced to give up his business. In 1809, encouraged and backed by a group of townspeople, he opened the Warrenton Female Academy, which became famous throughout the South as a school for girls. Mordecai and his family ran the Academy successfully until 1819, when he sold it and moved to a farm near Richmond. He served as president of Beth Shalome, the first synagogue in the city, which he had helped found. He lived in Richmond from 1832.

BIBLIOGRAPHY: Mordecai, in: AJHSP, 6 (1897), 39–48; Falk, in: *North Carolina Historical Review*, 35 (1958), 281–98.

[Stanley L. Falk]

MORDECAI (Mokhi'aḥ) BEN ḤAYYIM OF EISENSTADT (1650–1729), wandering Shabbatean preacher – hence his cognomen *Mokhi'aḥ* ("reprover"). He propagated faith in *Shabbetai Ẓevi as the Messiah after the latter's conversion to Islam. An extreme ascetic, he wandered through Hungary, Moravia, Italy, and Poland spreading the doctrine, previously enunciated by *Nathan of Gaza, that for mystical reasons Shabbetai Ẓevi had to undergo conversion and that his death was merely an illusion. In three years, he insisted, the "Messiah" would reappear. Invited to Italy in 1682 by R. Issachar Behr *Perlhefter and R. Abraham *Rovigo of Modena – both secret Shabbatean adherents – he put forth the claim that, while Shabbetai Ẓevi had been the Messiah b. Ephraim, he, Mordecai, was the Messiah b. David. Apocalyptic writings stemming from Rovigo's circle and probably written by Perlhefter (1678–80) portray him as the forerunner of the Messiah. In the above-mentioned document reference is made to his plan to go to Rome in order to make certain "messianic" preparations. Upon meeting him in Modena, his host, R. Perlhefter, recognizing signs of madness in him, turned against him, apparently causing Mordecai's abrupt departure from Italy some time before 1682. He thereupon traveled through Bohemia and Poland, where, thanks to his prepossessing personality and fiery preaching, he won numerous adherents. Heinrich *Graetz dubbed him a "Jewish Vicente *Ferrer."

BIBLIOGRAPHY: Graetz, Gesch, 10 (1896), note 4, ii; J. Leveen, in: *Ignace Goldziher Memorial Volume*, 1 (1948), 393–9; G. Scholem, in: *Sefer Dinaburg* (1949), 240ff. (Heb.); I. Tishby, *Netivei Emunah u-Minut* (1964), s.v. *Eisenstadt, Mordecai.*

[Theodore Friedman]

MORDECAI BEN HILLEL HA-KOHEN (1240?–1298), author and rabbinic authority in Germany. The only biographical details known of him are that he was a descendant of *Eliezer b. Joel ha-Levi, a relative of *Asher b. Jehiel, and a brother-in-law of Meir ha-Kohen, author of the *Haggahot Maimoniyyot*, that he was an outstanding pupil of *Meir b. Baruch of Rothenburg, *Isaac b. Moses (author of *Or Zaru'a*), and *Perez b. Elijah of Corbeil. He appears to have spent some time in Goslar (Resp. Maharam of Rothenburg, ed. Lemberg, 476), from there moving to Nuremberg, where he died a martyr's death in the *Rindfleisch massacres, together with his wife and five children.

Mordecai's fame rests on the *Sefer Mordekhai*, always referred to as "the *Mordekhai*." This gigantic compendium consists of elaborations on talmudic problems in the style of the *tosafot*. However, it follows the arrangement of laws used by Isaac *Alfasi, its aim having been to spread the learning of the French and German scholars and of their predecessors by attaching them to the work of Alfasi, which had a wide circulation; but the *Mordekhai* does not refer at all to the content of Alfasi's book. Over 300 books and authors are cited in the *Mordekhai*, including whole pages from *Or Zaru'a* and dozens of responsa of Meir of Rothenburg in full. The absence of any of the writings which Meir of Rothenburg sent to his pupils while he was in prison proves that the book was completed before 1286, the year of Meir's incarceration. On the other hand, it is clear from the many references to "my master, Rabbi Mordecai" that the book was not edited by Mordecai himself but by his sons and pupils. If the *Sefer ha-Dinim* of Judah ha-Kohen and *Sefer ha-Ḥokhmah* of Baruch b. Samuel are still known today, it is almost entirely thanks to the *Mordekhai*. The history of the spread of the *Mordekhai* and the transmigrations of its many versions in manuscript and in print is one of the most complicated in all of rabbinic literature. Because of the book's tremendous scope, two main compilations of extracts, the "Austrian" and the "Rhenish," were made from it within a few decades, mainly reflecting regional laws and customs, and differing greatly from one another. The Rhenish version – which is the one extant – includes the views of many French and English scholars, and the customs of the German communities. These customs had spread eastward as far as Poland, but were not accepted west of Germany. The Austrian version reflects the *minhag* of southeastern Europe including the customs of Austria, Hungary, Bohemia, Saxony, and Moravia, and mentions many Austrian scholars. This version was in the possession of Israel *Isserlein.

In 1376 Samuel *Schlettstadt edited an abridgment of the *Mordekhai* (*Mordekhai ha-Katan*), adding glosses of his own (*Haggahot Mordekhai*). In print, these appeared independently at the end of the book, but sometimes they were confused with the text. This abridgment was based on the Rhenish version, and when Schlettstadt later obtained a copy of the Austrian version, he added some passages from it. The *Halakhot Ketannot* in the *Mordekhai* are also Schlettstadt's work. Many other abridgments have been made, both by copyists and by printers, this activity having begun, in fact, shortly after Mordecai's death. Apart from Schlettstadt's abridgment, there are extant two printed versions of the book (see below) and a larger number of versions in manuscript. Many manuscripts are extant in libraries in many parts of the world, but no two of them are identical, and all of them are different from *Mordekhai ha-Gadol* (the unabridged *Mordekhai*), also extant in manuscript, which was too long to be copied in full. In view of this situation, Judah Loew of Prague ruled that the *Mordekhai* should not be used as the basis for legal decisions. The *Mordekhai* was first printed together with the first edition of the Talmud (tractates *Berakhot* and *Beẓah*, by Soncino, 1483–84). While the amplifications on *Berakhot* are shorter than those in the regular printed editions, those on *Beẓah* are much longer. It was also published together with Alfasi's abridgment of the Talmud in Constantinople, 1508–09. The *Mordekhai* was published separately, and on the whole Talmud, in Riva di Trento, 1559–60, in an edition containing matter not found in the standard edition, which was published later from other manuscripts. Before printing a new edition, printers would generally compare the various editions already previously published, for the purpose of reconciling them, a practice which helped confuse matters even more. Following the ruling of Judah Loew, all passages that were lenient or permissive on points not stated in the Talmud were expunged from the printed editions (but not from the Mss.), causing the accuracy of the text to deteriorate still further.

The *Mordekhai* exerted a powerful influence in Germany on the manner of arriving at halakhic rulings until the time of Moses *Isserles, mainly through Israel Isserlein, who relied on it considerably in his *Terumat ha-Deshen*, and Joseph *Colon. The book was also most influential in the world of Sephardi *halakhah* – which it reached in its abridged form – and Mordecai b. Hillel ha-Kohen is one of the few Ashkenazi authorities cited by Joseph *Caro in his *Beit Yosef*. Many scholars wrote interpretations, amplifications, glosses, or corrections to the *Mordekhai*, including: Israel *Bruna, Israel Isserlein, *Joshua Boaz b. Simeon, Moses Isserles (who inserted the page references to the tractates of the Talmud), Menahem of Tiktin (who wrote *Ḥiddushei Anshei Shem* on it), Isaiah b. Abraham *Horowitz, and Mordecai *Benet. *Kiẓẓur Piskei ha-Mordekhai*, by Joseph *Ottolengo, which is generally published together with the *Mordekhai*, also deserves mention. Up to and including the time of Moses Isserles, small groups of Jews would get together for the regular and systematic study of the work. In addition to this book, Mordecai also composed a rhymed composition on the dietary laws (Venice, c. 1550), and a poem on the rules of vocalization. He also wrote a work on the laws pertaining to the Holy Land and the laws of *ḥallah* ("the priest's share of the dough") published in Z. Bindowitz, *Ḥut ha-Meshullash* (1940). Five of his *piyyutim* are extant including the *seliḥah Mah Rav Tuvekh*, a lament for Abraham the proselyte who died a martyr's death in 1264 at Augsburg.

[Israel Moses Ta-Shma]

Further Information

A study of the many manuscripts of *Sefer Mordekhai* reveals that there are "families" of manuscripts. Manuscripts belonging to a certain family are based on the same version and use the same linguistic expressions with the same additions as in the printed text of *Sefer Mordekhai* printed in different editions of the Talmud. The manuscripts of the *Mordekhai* make it possible to attempt to establish a text of the *Mordekhai* for the Talmud tractates that will include as many sections of the *Mordekhai* as possible, namely the text of the book as it is printed and, in addition, different parts not yet published and originating from the different manuscripts.

A. Halperin published a study called *The Complete Sefer Mordekhai for Tractate Bava Kamma* (1978): Part I, Introduction; Part II, a critical edition of the *Mordekhai* for *Bava Kamma* by Rabbi Samuel Schlettstadt. In addition, the complete *Mordekhai* for Tractate *Beiẓah* (edited by Yehoshua Horowitz and Yiẓḥak Kleinman) appeared in the Torat Ḥakhamei Ashkenaz series of the Jerusalem Institute (1983). This edition is based on 18 manuscripts and early printed editions and includes notes, sources and variant readings.

[Yehoshua Horowitz]

BIBLIOGRAPHY: S. Cohen, in: *Sinai*, 9–16 (1942/43–1946/47), passim; I.A. Agus, *Teshuvot Ba'alei ha-Tosafot* (1954), introd.; Bialer, in: *Genazim* (1967), 19–45; Urbach, Tosafot, index; Rosenthal, in: *Shanah be-Shanah* (1967/68), 234; Zulbach, in: JJLG, 3 (1905); 5 (1907); Zunz, Lit Poesie, 364; Germ Jud, 404; Davidson, Oẓar, 4 (1933), 436; E.E. Urbach, *Baalei ha-Tosafot*, vol.2 (1980), 556–60; A. Halperin, Introduction to *The Complete Sefer Mordekhai for tractate Bava Kamma* (1978); Y. Horowitz, "The Quality of the Texts of the *Mordekhai* for Tractates *Rosh ha-Shanah, Sukkah* and *Beiẓah*," in: *Proceedings of the 8th World Congress of Jewish Studies* (1982), 57–62; idem, Introduction to "The Complete *Sefer Mordekhai* for tractate *Beiẓah*" (1983), 10–15.

MORDECAI BEN JUDAH HA-LEVI (d. 1684), *posek* and rabbinical authority in *Egypt. Mordecai was the son-in-law of R. Abraham Tarikah. He served for over 40 years as rabbi, all or part of the time as *dayyan* of *Cairo and of *Rosetta, and moved to *Jerusalem in 1684, dying there in the same year. In 1678 a sharp dispute broke out between R. Gabriel Esperanza, one of the leading scholars of *Safed, and Mordecai ha-Levi over a *halakhic* ruling. The dispute was brought before R. Moses *Galante, the leading rabbi of Jerusalem, but he refused to become involved. His only published work was a collection of responsa, *Darkhei No'am* (Venice, 1697). It is a storehouse of information on the history of 17th-century Egyptian Jewry, which contains the responsa of many scholars of Mordecai's generation. The historian R. David *Conforte was among his friends. Other works written by him which were never published include: *Avodat ha-Kodesh*, a commentary on the Torah; *Mikra'ei Kodesh*, hermeneutics; *Toledot Adam*, concerning the education of children; and *Sof Adam*, collected eulogies. His son R. *Abraham b. Mordecai ha-Levi was the author of *Ginnat Veradim*.

BIBLIOGRAPHY: R.A. Ben-Simeon, *Tuv Miẓrayim* (1908), 24; Frumkin-Rivlin, 2 (1928), 96–98; M. Benayahu, in: *Sinai*, 43 (1958), 105–8.

[Abraham David]

MORDECAI BEN NAPHTALI HIRSCH OF KREMSIER (d. c. 1670), talmudic commentator and scribe. Mordecai came from Kremsier (Kromeriz), but lived in Cracow and died there. He was the pupil and friend of Shabbetai Sheftel *Horowitz, with whom he established friendship in Posen in 1648. He was famous as a preacher and was referred to as "the chief preacher." Among his works were *Ketoret ha-Mizbe'aḥ* (Amsterdam, 1660), expositions of the *aggadot* in the tractate *Berakhot*, and a study of the destruction of the Temple and the length of the exile; *Ketoret ha-Sammim* (*ibid.*, 1671), a commentary on the *Targum Jonathan and the Palestine Targum to the Pentateuch, to which was appended a kabbalistic commentary on *Berakhot*; and the elegy *Shema Eli Kol Bekhi ve-Kinah* (Lublin?, c. 1650, according to Steinschneider; see bibliography) on the 120,000 martyrs slain in the *Chmielnicki massacres, together with his own commentary to it.

BIBLIOGRAPHY: Steinschneider, Cat Bod, 1671f. no. 6253; Landshuth, Ammudei, 200; Gurland, in: *Oẓar ha-Sifrut*, 2 (1888), 161–3 (first pagination); Davidson, Oẓar, 3 (1930), 484 no. 1656.

[Josef Horovitz]

MORDECAI BEN NISAN (17th–18th centuries), Karaite scholar living in Kukizov, near Lvov (Lemberg), Poland. In answer to an inquiry by Jacob Trigland, professor at Leiden, Mordecai composed in 1699 an exposition of Karaism entitled *Dod Mordekhai* (Hamburg, 1714, with Latin translation; Hebrew text alone, Vienna, 1830, repr. 1966), in which he defends the antiquity of Karaism (reaching back into the Second Temple period) and its independence from Sadduceeism, and traces in brief the history of Karaite literature. His other works include *Ma'amar Mordekhai*, a supercommentary on the *Mivḥar* of *Aaron b. Joseph (unpublished); and *Levush Malkhut*, on the differences between the Karaites and the Rabbanites (published by Neubauer; see bibliography). Some hymns by him are included in the official Karaite prayer book.

BIBLIOGRAPHY: Fuerst, *Karaeertum*, 3 (1869), 87ff.; A. Neubauer, *Aus der Petersburger Bibliothek* (1866), 76ff.; S. Poznański, *The Karaite Literary Opponents of Saadiah Gaon* (1908), 87; Mann, Texts, 2 (1935), index.

[Leon Nemoy]

MORDECAI OF NESKHIZ (Rus. **Nesukhoyshe**; 1752–1800), ḥasidic *ẓaddik*, founder of the Neskhiz dynasty and one of the most famous "miracle-workers" of his generation. He was a disciple of *Jehiel Michael of Zloczow and became friendly with *Aryeh Leib of Shpola whom he met in Jehiel Michael's house. His name appears in the list of prominent *ẓaddikim* of 1798–1820 which mitnaggedic writers included in their works against Ḥasidism. After serving as rabbi in Leshnev (Leszniow), in the province of Brody, where a ḥasidic group flourished as early as 1772, he settled in Nesvizh, near Kovel in Volhynia, around 1790. There he became renowned as a "miracle-working" *ẓaddik* and "his miracles in heaven and earth were revealed to the world; raising the dead, healing the sick, and enabling deserted wives to remarry… and he became a great wonder" (*Zikkaron Tov* (1892), 99). According to another tradition "Mordecai of Neskhiz was familiar with the mysteries of creation… and wrought many miracles but he regretted his actions" (Uri of Strelisk, *Imrei Kodesh* (1871), 9). A wealthy man, Mordecai commissioned the scribe Moses of Przeworsk to copy a Torah scroll for him. The work took three years and he paid him 400 zlotys. He wrote a small pamphlet, later published under the title of *Rishpei Esh* (1869).

BIBLIOGRAPHY: Dubnow, Ḥasidut, index; M. Buber, *Tales of the Ḥasidim*, 1 (1968^4), 164–6; L.I. Newman, *The Ḥasidic Anthology* (1963), index s.v. *Neschizer.*

MORDELL, LOUIS JOEL (1888–1972), British mathematician. Mordell was professor of mathematics at Manchester from 1923 to 1945 and professor at Cambridge from 1945. He was elected a Fellow of the Royal Society in 1924, and president of the London Mathematical Society from 1943 until 1945. Mordell wrote many articles on the theory of numbers and allied topics. In addition he published *Three Lectures on Fermat's Last Theorem* (1921); *A Chapter on the Theory of Numbers* (1947); *Reflections of a Mathematician* (1958); and *Diophantine Equations* (1969).

[Barry Spain]

MORDELL, PHINEHAS (1861–1934), Hebrew grammarian and scholar. Mordell was born in Shat (Kovno province) and studied in Yelizavetgrad. In 1881, he went to the U.S. and settled in Philadelphia. During his first years there Mordell worked at various trades and was a beadle in a synagogue, at the same time industriously pursuing the study of Hebrew language and grammar. He was associated with the Wissenschaft scholars in the U.S., as well as with Hebrew writers. Finally, after achieving a wide reputation, he worked until 1903 partly as a teacher and partly as a night watchman in order to devote the day to his studies. He was among the pioneer proponents of Zionism and the Hebrew language movement in the U.S. Mordell spent much of his time on the study of Hebrew language and grammar and especially on the Sefer *Yeẓirah which he edited and to which he wrote a comprehensive commentary in English (1914). In 1895 he published, without commentary, the corrected text of *Sefer Yeẓirah*. He was greatly encouraged in his linguistic studies by Aḥad Ha-Am (Asher Ginsberg), who published some of Mordell's articles in *Ha-Shilo'aḥ* (vols. 3 (1898), 478–9; 5 (1899), 233–46; 10 (1902), 431–42; see *Iggerot Aḥad Ha-Am*, 2 (1957), 410–1). He continued publishing linguistic studies in *Ha-Toren*, 4 (1917/18), 8f.; *Ha-Ivri*, 9 (1919), no. 1, 3, 4, 5, 6, 9, 12, 17, 19, 21, 22, 24 (a series of articles on the reading of Hebrew which was also published separately); *Ha-Olam ha-Yehudi* (1924);

and *Leshonenu*, 3 (1930). His articles were also published in English (8 articles in JQR, 1912–34) and one was published in Yiddish. Mordell left an extensive Hebrew commentary to the *Sefer Yeẓirah* and chapters on grammar (unpublished). His son was Louis Joel *Mordell, the mathematician.

BIBLIOGRAPHY: J. Zausmer, *Be-Ikvei ha-Dor* (1957), 3–32.

[Getzel Kressel]

°**MORDOVTSEV, DANIIL LUKICH** (1830–1905), Russian and Ukrainian writer who preached the return of the Jews to Ereẓ Israel. Mordovtsev was a Ukrainian and one of the leaders of the Ukrainian nationalist movement throughout his life. Until 1866 he worked in various government offices, and afterward engaged in his historical and literary work. In his time he was one of the few liberals in Russia who openly sympathized with the Jews. In 1873 he began to publish articles refuting prevalent accusations by Russians, including liberals, against the Jews, and in particular attacked anti-Jewish instigators. In the summer of 1881 he visited Ereẓ Israel and in Jerusalem met a number of Jewish refugees who had fled from the pogrom in Odessa. In his series of stories and travel impressions he repeatedly expressed the demand that the nations of the world restore Ereẓ Israel to the Jews. His literary activity in this area increased especially after the pogroms of the early 1880s in Russia. In his historical stories, he censured the Ukrainian pogroms against the Jews. His stories on Jewish topics include *Za chto zhe?* ("Why?" 1884); *Mezhdu molotom i zakovalney* ("Between Hammer and Anvil," 1891), and *Irod* ("Herod"). These stories were translated into Hebrew and Yiddish (some by Z. *Shazar). His support for the Jewish national movement continued until his death and became especially strong from the time of the appearance of political Zionism.

BIBLIOGRAPHY: I. Maor, in: *Shivat Ẓiyyon*, 2–3 (1951/52) 69–82; M. Ben Hillel ha-Kohen, *In Mame Loshn* (1935), 237–55.

[Getzel Kressel]

°**MORDVINOV, NICOLAI SEMIONOVICH** (1754–1845), Russian statesman and admiral; president of the Department of Civil and Ecclesiastical Affairs of the Council of State. In 1802, as a member of the Council of State, he supported the proposal not to limit the commercial rights of the Jews in the *Pale of Settlement, but in the 1820s he insisted on the mass expulsion of the Jews from the villages and rural settlements. In the blood libel case at *Velizh, Mordvinov took a stand in favor of the Jewish community. Owner of an estate near Velizh and knowing many local Jews, he followed the case closely; when it reached its final stage and came to the attention of his department, he helped to establish the innocence of the Jews, settling the matter by a ukase issued in 1835.

BIBLIOGRAPHY: Gessen, in: *Voskhod*, 4 (1903), 3–34; 5 (1903), 3–28; idem, *Velizhskaya drama* (1905); Rivkin, in: *Perezhitoye*, 3 (1911), 60–102.

MOREEL, BEN (1892 –1978), U.S. admiral. Born in Salt Lake City, Utah, Moreel worked as an engineer and in 1917 joined the U.S. Navy engineer corps. In the 1930s he served as public works officer at Pearl Harbor, and in 1937 he was made chief of the Bureau of Yards and Docks. When World War II broke out, Moreel created the elite naval construction battalions known as the Seabees, starting with 3,000 men. His Seabees developed airfields, roads, and housing on undeveloped islands in the Pacific. After the Japanese attack on Pearl Harbor in 1941, Moreel recruited carpenters, machinists, electricians, and masons whose average age was 37. He valued work experience over youth. Eventually, more than 325,000 men signed on with the Seabees. On some 300 islands in the South Pacific, they went ashore shortly after the Marines had landed and began building hospitals, housing, and warehouses, in addition to the roads and airstrips. Proud of their reputation as fighters, the Seabees also became goodwill ambassadors who constructed orphanages, public utilities, and highways all over the world. In 1944 President Franklin D. Roosevelt made Moreel a vice admiral. Moreel retired as a full admiral in 1958, the first engineering officer and the first Jew to reach this rank. When he received his fourth star as admiral, he became the highest-ranking Jewish officer in Navy history.

In his honor, the U.S. Navy League created the Admiral Ben Moreel Award for logistics excellence.

Moreel's book *The Admiral's Log Vol. 1 and 2* was published in 1958.

BIBLIOGRAPHY: S. Howarth (ed.), *Men of War* (1993)

[Ruth Beloff (2nd ed.)]

MOREH, MORDECAI (1937–), Israeli printmaker and draftsman. Moreh was born in Baghdad, and immigrated to Israel in 1951. He studied at the Bezalel School of Arts and Crafts, Jerusalem, from 1955 to 1959, and from 1960 to 1962 studied on an Italian government scholarship at the Accademia di Belle Arti, Florence. In 1962 he was awarded a scholarship by the American-Israel Cultural Foundation to attend the Ecole Nationale Supérieure des Beaux-Arts, Paris.

Moreh mainly used the drypoint method in the technique of prints which revealed him to be a master draftsman. His subjects were traditional and, like Goya, Jean-Paul Sartre, and Pablo Picasso, he expresses a pessimistic and skeptical outlook. His philosophy about the human condition was revealed through his etchings, in which he employed symbols to convey his ideas – the illusions, the darkness of the unconscious, the violence and vanity of life. He differed from Goya and Picasso in his more moderate ironic attitude, and in his sense of humor and humanity. One of his favorite subjects was the woman through whom he portrays general human characteristics. In one of several drypoints titled "Monkey" (1970) he drew the profile of a woman whose backside is an untamed monkey in an open cage. Animals are another important subject in his work, forming part of his personal world of imagination.

Moreh used classical metaphors to indicate his philosophical research about the nature of reality. One of his famous metaphors is the mask – the mask of reality. For his masks he used directly the portraits of his earlier works. A Renaissance spirit is evident in his etchings. Moreh held a large number of one-man shows and his work was exhibited at the Israel prints exhibition held in 1961 at the Boston Public Library and at the fourth Biennale of Paris-Israel Prints in 1968. His work is displayed in many museums and private collections in Israel and abroad.

BIBLIOGRAPHY: M. Moreh, *Radierungen 1960–1972*, Heidelberg Kurpfaelzisches Museum (March–Apr., 1972).

[Judith Spitzer]

MOREH, SHMUEL (1933–), scholar of Arabic language and literature. Born in Baghdad, he immigrated to Israel April 1951. He received his B.A. and M.A. from The Hebrew University in Arabic literature and Islamic Studies and his Ph.D. in modern Arabic poetry (SOAS, London University) in 1965. He was a visiting professor at various universities in the U.S., U.K., Germany, Finland, and the Netherlands. Moreh became professor emeritus of Arabic language and literature at The Hebrew University of Jerusalem. He participated in conferences on Arabic and Islamic studies and on the Jews of Arab countries, especially of Iraq. He was awarded the Israel Prize in Oriental studies (1999) and the insignia of the Commander of the Order of the Lion of Finland (1986). He is the founder and chairman of the Association of Jewish Academics from Iraq in Israel (1980–) and chairman of the Academic Committee of the Babylonian Jewry Heritage Center, Or-Yehuda, Israel. He wrote *Modern Arabic Poetry 1800–1970* (1975), *Studies in Modern Arabic Prose and Poetry* (1988), *The Jewish Contribution to Nineteenth-Century Arabic Theatre* (with P.C. Sadgrove, 1996), *Live Theater and Dramatic Literature in the Medieval Arab World* (1992), *The Tree and the Branch, Studies in Modern Arabic Literature and Contributions of Iraqi-Jewish Writers* (Hebrew, 1977), and *Those Were the Days of Youth and Love, An Anthology of Poems in Arabic and English* (1998). He was also the translator and editor of al-Jabartī's *Chronicle of the First Seven Months of the French Occupation of Egypt* (1975) and of several collections of Arabic short stories as well as the compiler of bibliographies on Arabic literature.

MORENO, JACOB L. (1892–1974), U.S. social scientist. Born in Bucharest, he immigrated to the U.S. in 1927. He taught at New York University from 1952 to 1960 and was the founder of the Sociometric Institute and the Theater for Psychodrama. He edited the *International Journal of Sociometry, Group Psychiatry*, and *Group Psychotherapy and Sociodrama*. Moreno initiated the sociometric method in the social sciences. Sociometry assumes that societies have, besides a formal structure, an informal and emotionally based depth-structure of human relations, connecting the individual with other individuals. These relations can be made evident by appropriate methods. Among the techniques Moreno introduced for this purpose were the sociometric test, the sociogram, the interaction diagram, the locogram, and the sociomatrix. These techniques lead to group-therapeutic approaches, especially in "psychodrama" and "sociodrama." In these, the conventional doctor-patient relationship is replaced by acting in which the participants purge themselves through reliving and acting out their experience. These methods have been applied in a variety of situations, especially in schools, industries, and armies.

Major publications of Moreno, apart from a great many papers and monographs, are *Das Stegreiftheater* (1924; *The Theater of Spontaneity*, tr. by the author, 1947); *Who Shall Survive?* (1934, rev. ed. 1953); *Sociometry, Experimental Method and the Science of Society* (1951); *The First Psychodramatic Family* (1964); and *Discovery of Spontaneous Man* (1965).

[Werner J. Cahnman]

MORESHET, research and education center for Holocaust Studies.

The Founding of Moreshet

Moreshet was originally established by the Kibbutz Arẓi Ha-Shomer ha-Ẓa'ir in the early 1960s as a center for collecting testimonies of concentration camp survivors and resistance fighters from the ghettos. The moving spirits of the project were a group of former partisans and members of Jewish undergrounds which included: Abba *Kovner, Israel *Gutman, Chaike Grossman and a then young historian, Yehuda *Bauer. Their plan was adopted at a convention of the Kibbutz Arẓi Federation in 1961. Kovner explained to the delegates the significance of the name, which they had chosen:

> The project will be called *Moreshet*. Why? Because we are of the people. We intend to say that we have no political arrogance, but only an historical truth: that we are heirs to a great heritage of our people.

The primary incentive in all their activities was to make certain that future generations learn about the horrors of the Holocaust and to insure that it doesn't happen again.

As the years went by, Moreshet, expanded its field of work. In the early 21st century Moreshet had developed into a leading research and education center for Holocaust Studies. It carries out activities in various fields with a publishing house; *Yalkut Moreshet*, a journal; an educational Campus at Givat Ḥavivah; Holocaust Studies and Research Center: Moreshet Archives; an exhibition annex; journeys to Poland; and the Holocaust Remembrance Day Ceremony at Yad Mordechai.

Publications

MORESHET PUBLISHING HOUSE. The dozens of titles which have appeared over the years encompass central issues, such as personal testimonies, biographies, historical works, annals of communities and literature for children and youth. The books, covering important subjects of the Holocaust, are an important resource for pupils and researchers.

YALKUT MORESHET. The journal *Yalkut Moreshet* is a prestigious research periodical appearing twice annually. First issued in December 1963, it is the oldest and most significant of its kind in Israel and is dedicated to documentation, deliberation, and research of the Holocaust. The material that appears in *Yalkut Moreshet* has proven to be an invaluable source for courses in Holocaust Studies both in Israel and abroad.

As of 2003, an English edition of *Yalkut Moreshet* has begun appearing on an annual basis, containing articles from the current Hebrew edition, as well as articles from previous editions that have become classics in Holocaust research.

The Educational Campus at Givat Ḥavivah

The characteristic and unique guidelines of Moreshet's educational work are characterized by the participation of the pupils in the educational process, through various interdisciplinary activity workshops. Less emphasis is placed on lectures and more on discussions, stories and opportunity for self-expression. Major use is made of different means of illustration: films, pictures etc. Pupils are also given the opportunity to connect with the computerized archives for personal projects.

A significant portion of time is devoted to an encounter with Holocaust survivors. Since they were then the same age the pupils are now, it is easy for the youngsters to listen to them, ask questions and to identify.

Historical stress is placed on the role of youth, and especially graduates of the youth movements, in the resistance against Nazism. Historiography points out the place of youth as a leading element and stimulus to resistance, and at its head – graduates of the youth movements – owing to the education and values which they absorbed in their movements.

A central theoretical guideline is the exposure of the sources of racism and the roots of antisemitism and education towards universal humanistic values as a way of preventing it from happening again. Moreshet encourages participants to confront the complex dilemmas of one's own experience, to take a stand. and to make a moral choice.

Educational Programs

Among the educational programs carried out by Moreshet are (a) programs for the Israel Defense Forces, which enrich knowledge of moral struggles and values. Moreshet offers seminars dealing with the effects of military service in reinforcing Jewish and Israeli identity. Programs touch on obedience to authority, the role of civilians in war, heroism, human dignity. (b) Study days for pupils of all grades: the study units and means of illustration in the programs offered are designed with maximum consideration of the cognitive and emotional ability of the various age groups. During the course various activities take place, including creative activity to "work through" the experiences of the day. (c) A program on women Holocaust Resistance fighters, which deals with the role of women in fighting in the ghettoes and forests and as liaisons with the Aryan side. The seminar deals with conflicts stemming from the three components of women's identity – woman, Jew, and Holocaust fighter. Emphasis is placed on the education these women received in their youth, on the ways they overcame difficulties and obstacles, the dilemmas they faced, and the means they used to fulfill their missions. (d) A weekend seminar in Russian for new immigrants from the CIS, Antisemitism, Racism and the Holocaust as a Significant Element in Shaping the Collective Israeli Consciousness, has as its goal A weekend the clarification of the concepts connected with the Israeli collective identity; their significance to new immigrants and how they deal with these questions; antisemitism and the Holocaust as a significant element in shaping Israeli and Jewish collective consciousness. (e) Programs for visitors from abroad in the form of seminars on the Holocaust and its ramifications on Israeli society range from one to three days and include accommodations at Givat Ḥavivah, and are offered in English, Spanish, German, and other languages upon request. The schedule includes workshops, lectures and tours.

The Mordechai Anielevich Holocaust Studies and Research Center

MORESHET ARCHIVES. Founded in 1961, the task of the archives contain a collection of documents and testimonies from the period of the Holocaust, including important documents and files such as the Hannah Szenes, Abba Kovner, and Menachem Bader papers.

Moreshet has established a Reading and Research Center, including books of communities, of chronicles and documentation of the Holocaust period; personal memoirs and individual and group testimonies. Rooms for researchers are equipped with computers attached to the Moreshet computer network and research and information programs.

Exhibition Annex

Moreshet is in the process of developing an exhibition annex on the Givat Ḥavivah campus. The new annex will provide the basis for learning about the resistance to the Nazis in the ghettoes, in the concentration camps, and among the partisans. From there the visitors will go into the classrooms and the auditorium. The annex will also contain an area for temporary exhibitions, providing visual expressions of various events.

Journeys to Poland

The Kibbutz Arẓi high schools and the Ha-Shomer ha-Ẓa'ir youth movement were among the first to organize delegations to the sites of the Holocaust and have thus gained significant experience in organizing the journeys and preparing groups for the experience programs offered by Moreshet towards the journeys to Poland by high school students include detailed preparation for the journey; acquaintance with the Jewish world that perished; study of World War II in Europe; clarification on the forming of Jewish and Zionist identity as an aftermath of the Holocaust. Moreshet also provides experienced guides to accompany the groups as well as workshops for the participants upon their return home, to "work through" the experience.

There is a training program for guides and teachers accompanying the journey to Poland, which includes educational ways of dealing with the experience of the journey. The preparation course for accompanying teachers is a program aimed at expansion of knowledge on subjects related to the Holocaust, and the psychological and educational preparation for the role of accompanying teacher. It also trains teachers to deal with questions arising among young persons upon their return from Poland and develops the teachers' capabilities to cope with problems, difficulties and reactions by individuals and groups.

[Ariel Hurwitz (2nd ed.)]

MORESHETH-GATH (Heb. מוֹרֶשֶׁת גַּת), town of the tribe of Judah in the Shephelah, between Lachish and Achzib. It is mentioned by the prophet Micah, who was born there (Micah 1:1, 14; Jer. 26:18). Later sources (Eusebius, Onom. 134:10: Sozomenus, *Historia Ecclesiastica* 9:17; Jerome, *In Micam* 1:10) identify it with a village, which is also called Birat Satia or Kiryat Satia, in the territory of Eleutheropolis (Bet Guvrin). The *Madaba Map indicates a village called Morasthi to the north of Eleutheropolis, near a church of St. Micah. Some scholars have identified Birat Satia with Khirbat Saʿad or Khirbat al-Baṣal and Moresheth-Gath with nearby Tell al-Judayda; others have looked for it at Tell Khirbat al-Bayḍāʾ approximately 4 mi. (6 km.) northeast of Bet Guvrin. The Gath fortified by Rehoboam (II Chron. 11:8) has also been tentatively identified with Moresheth-Gath.

BIBLIOGRAPHY: A. Saarisalo, in: JPOS, 11 (1931), 98ff.; J. Jeremias, in: PJB, 29 (1933), 42–53; EM, 4 (1962), 741f.; Aharoni, Land, index.

[Michael Avi-Yonah]

MOREWSKI, ABRAHAM (Menaker; 1886–1964), Yiddish actor and producer. Born in Vilna, Morewski acted and studied in Russia, doing translations and research on Shakespeare which resulted in his study *Shylock and Shakespeare* (1917). He joined the *Vilna Troupe in 1920, played Mirapoler Tsadik in *An-Ski's *The Dybbuk* and the title role in Gutzkow's *Uriel Acosta*. He directed a four-act version of *The Dybbuk* reduced to three acts in 1920. He toured in Europe and the U.S. and during World War II in southern Russia. In Warsaw, from 1956, he wrote his memoirs, *Ahin un Aher*, four volumes published in 1963.

MORGENSTERN, JULIAN (1881–1977), U.S. Reform rabbi, Bible scholar, and president of the *Hebrew Union College. Born in St. Francisville, Illinois, Morgenstern graduated from the University of Cincinnati in 1901 and was ordained at the Hebrew Union College in 1902. He received his doctorate at Heidelberg in 1904; his dissertation was published as *Doctrine of Sin in the Babylonian Religion* (1905). After three years as rabbi in Lafayette, Indiana, he turned to academic life, teaching biblical and Semitic languages, concentrating on biblical studies, at Hebrew Union College.

In 1921 Morgenstern became acting president of the college and in 1922 was elected president; he was the first alumnus to hold this office. During his presidency the number of students and faculty and the scope of college activity grew markedly. Departments of education, social studies, and Jewish music were established; new buildings were erected; an endowment fund was created; the college, previously a department of the Union of American Hebrew Congregations, was independently chartered, and the Hebrew Union School of Religious Education was established in New York City. *Hebrew Union College Annual*, founded in 1924, at once became one of the world's outstanding publications in Jewish scholarship. During the Hitler period, a dozen European scholars found a haven at the college, chiefly as the result of Morgenstern's efforts. At first anti-Zionist, Morgenstern later modified his position on the creation of a Jewish state. After retiring as college president in 1947, Morgenstern continued to teach Bible. He served as president of the American Oriental Society and the Society of Biblical Literature; he was for many years recording secretary, and then honorary president, of the Central Conference of American Rabbis and one of the founders of the World Union for Progressive Judaism.

Biblical Studies

As a young professor Morgenstern immersed himself in biblical studies and published relatively little. As his views matured, the number and extent of his publications increased. Three works originally published in the *Annual* were later issued in book form: *Amos Studies* (1941); *Ark, the Aphod, and the "Tent of Meeting"* (1945); and *Message of Deutero-Isaiah* (1961). Among many other important essays in the *Annual* are "Oldest Document of the Hexateuch" (1927), which provided the first solid support for the so-called Kenite hypothesis (see *Kenites; *Pentateuch), and a series of studies on the calendars of ancient Israel (1924, 1926, 1935, 1947–48). Starting as a follower of the *Wellhausen school, Morgenstern became increasingly independent in his approach to Bible problems. In his analysis of documentary sources he relied chiefly on differences in economic, social, and political background rather than on differences of vocabulary and style. In his reconstruction of biblical history, he gave much weight to economic and social factors without minimizing the role of inspired thinkers and teachers. In his studies of the calendar, he showed that changes in the nomenclature of the months and the dating of the festivals reflected significant changes in the life of the people of Israel. He also found evidence that in the early post-Exilic period there was a strong universalist trend expressed in proselytizing activity, which came to a catastrophic end when a coalition of neighboring states destroyed Jerusalem and burned the Second Temple. (The Temple of Ezra-Nehemiah, later rebuilt by Herod, was thus actually the Third Temple; see "Jerusalem – 485 B.C.," in HUCA, 1956, 1957, 1960; see *Temple.) Morgenstern's continuing vigor in scholarly activity is evident in his *Fire on the Altar* (1963), *Some Significant Antecedents of Christianity* (1966), and *Rites of Birth, Marriage, Death, and Kindred Occasions among the Semites* (1966). More popular in character are *Jewish Interpretation of Genesis* (1919), *Book of Genesis: A Jewish Interpretation* (1965^2), and a collection of lectures and papers, *As a Mighty Stream* (1949).

Views on Reform

His historical research convinced him that what had been called "universalism" and "particularism" are not mutually antagonistic, but that both are necessary and each complements the other. Despite his official role within the Reform movement, Morgenstern was dissatisfied with the term "Reform Judaism," which he regarded as reflective of conditions in 19th-century Germany rather than in 20th-century America, and as carrying with it certain overtones of sectarian separatism. He preferred to speak (so far as the United States is concerned) of an emerging American Judaism, more pragmatic and less dogmatic than early Reform; and he envisioned an ultimate synthesis of the Reform and Conservative movements, in a pattern not yet evident.

BIBLIOGRAPHY: M. Lieberman, in: HUCA, 32 (1961), 1–9; B.J. Bamberger, in: CCAR *Journal* (April 1957); 1–4; L. Finkelstein (ed.), *Thirteen Americans: Their Spiritual Autobiographies* (1953), 253–372.

[Bernard J. Bamberger]

MORGENSTERN (née **Bauer**), **LINA** (1830–1909), German educational theorist, philanthropist, and author. Born in Breslau, she founded a society for supporting poor schoolchildren when she was only 18. In 1854, she married Theodor Morgenstern, a manufacturer, and they settled in Berlin.

From 1859 on, she devoted her life to education and philanthropy. She helped organize the first Froebel kindergartens, and in 1860 published *Das Paradies der Kindheit* (1904), a textbook based on Froebel's method. She established the first free kitchens for the needy in 1866, and in 1873 founded the *Berliner Hausfrauenverein*, a society which served to educate women and safeguard their welfare. The society conducted a cooking school, for which she wrote all the textbooks. In 1887, together with two nurses, she opened a school for nursing. In 1896, she convened the first International Women's Congress, in Berlin, where 1,800 delegates from all parts of the world heard her lectures on women's rights. She was active in peace movements and served as vice president of the Alliance des Femmes pour la Paix. She edited and wrote many books, including storybooks for children, novels, biographies, cookbooks, periodicals for women, and books on women's problems, such as *Die Frauen des 19. Jahrhunderts* or *Frauenarbeit in Deutschland.*

BIBLIOGRAPHY: Wininger, Biog, 4 (1925), 429–31. **ADD. BIBLIOGRAPHY:** NDB, Vol. 18 (1997). 1091–11.

[Shnayer Z. Leiman]

MORGENSTERN, OSKAR (1902–1977), U.S. economist. Born in Goerlitz, Germany, Morgenstern taught at the University of Vienna (1928–38) and served as a director of the Austrian Institute of Business Cycle Research (1931–38). From 1936 to 1938 he served concomitantly as an adviser to the Austrian Ministry of Commerce and from 1936 to 1946 as a member of the committee of statistical experts of the League of Nations. In 1938 he settled in the United States and taught at Princeton University, where he became a full professor in 1944, and in 1948 director of its econometric research program. From 1955 to 1957 he was a consultant to the U.S. Atomic Energy Commission, and from 1959 to 1960 the White House consultant on atomic energy matters. In addition to general economic theory, his principal interests were econometrics and business cycles. One of Morgenstern's major contributions to the field was the formal conception of "game theory" as part of economic theory, which he and John von Neumann first organized in the classic book *Theory of Games and Economic Behavior* (1944). Game theory was later expanded upon and refined by John Nash and others. Morgenstern retired from Princeton in 1970.

Morgenstern's other publications include *The Limits of Economics* (1937), *Economic Activity Analysis* (1954), *The Question of National Defense* (1959), *International Financial Transactions and Business Cycles* (1959), *On the Accuracy of Economic Observations* (1950, 1963[2]), *Predictability of Stock Market Prices* (with C.W.J. Granger, 1970), *Long-Term Projections of Power* (1973), and *Mathematical Theory of Expanding and Contracting Economies* (with G.L. Thompson, 1976).

BIBLIOGRAPHY: M. Shubik (ed.), *Essays in Mathematical Economics* (1967), incl. bibl.

[Joachim O. Ronall / Ruth Beloff (2nd ed.)]

MORGENSTERN, SOMA (1890–1976), novelist, journalist. Soma Morgenstern was born as Salomo in Budzanow, Galicia, and although reared in a ḥasidic environment and familiar with the languages of the multiethnic culture of the Habsburg monarchy, his father provided him with a tutor in German. He attended a gymnasium in Tarnopol and studied law and political science at the University of Vienna from 1912. Like his friend Joseph Roth, he served in the Austro-Hungarian Army during World War I and was commissioned. In 1921 he received his doctorate; however, did not work as a lawyer, deciding instead to become a writer. Attracted to the theater, he worked as an assistant to Max *Reinhardt and freelanced as a critic of drama, music and literature in Vienna and Berlin. In 1927 he joined the staff of the *Frankfurter Zeitung*, and from 1928 to 1933 was its cultural correspondent in Vienna. He later wrote for *Die Weltbuehne.* In 1932 he began work on his first novel, inspired not only by the music of Modest Mussorgski, as his friend Alban Berg noted, but also by the world congress of Agudat Israel in 1929 in Vienna, which he attended as a journalist for the *Frankfurter Zeitung*. He conceived an entire trilogy, *Funken im Abgrund*, the first part of which was printed in 1935 in Berlin under the title *Der Sohn des verlorenen Sohnes* and tells the story of the return of an assimilated Viennese Jew to East European Judaism. Morgenstern fled to Paris in 1938, escaped from a concentration camp in occupied France in 1940, and made his way via Morocco and Portugal to the United States in the summer of 1941. The English version of *The Son of the Lost Son*, translated by Joseph Leftwich and Peter Gross, and its sequels, *In My Father's Pastures* (1947), translated by Ludwig *Lewisohn and *The Testament of the Lost Son* (1950), completed the trilogy. *Funken im Abgrund* is a unique paean to the vanished Jewish life in rural Eastern Europe, revealing remarkable narrative power and with lengthy detailed description. It tells the story of the son of an apostate

Jew who returns to his father's native village, where he rediscovers the values of authentic Jewish life. In his later work *The Third Pillar*, translated by Lewisohn in 1955 (the German original, written between 1946 and 1953, was published under the title *Die Blutsaeule* in 1964, and a Hebrew translation appeared in 1976 under the title *Ammud ha-Damim*), he attempts to come to terms with the Holocaust; combining realistic and fantastic elements, it is set in the same locale as the trilogy, and told in biblical language. Abraham *Heschel called it "the only Midrash about the Holocaust." A passage from it has been incorporated in the liturgy of the Yom Kippur martyrology in the *Maḥzor for Rosh Ha-Shanah and Yom Kippur*, published by the Rabbinical Assembly of the Conservative Movement (1972). Morgenstern died in New York.

BIBLIOGRAPHY: A. Wholesale, in: *Midstream*, 23 (1977); M. Grossberg, *Oesterreiche Literarische Emigration in den Vereinigten Staten* (1970). **ADD. BIBLIOGRAPHY:** H. Altrichter, in: H.-J. Boemelburg (ed.), *Der Fremde im Dorf* (1988), 211–30; I. Schulte, in: *Exilforschung*, 13 (1993), 221–36; R. Kitzmantel, *Eine Ueberfuelle an Gegenwart. Soma Morgenstern* (2005).

[Wolfe Kelman / Andreas Kilcher (2nd ed.)]

MORGENTALER, HENRY (1923–), Canadian physician and abortion advocate. Henry Morgentaler was born in Lodz, Poland, the son of well-known members of the Jewish Socialist Labor Bund. His parents and sister were murdered by the Nazis, but Morgentaler and his brother survived incarceration in Auschwitz and Dachau. Following the war, Morgentaler accepted a UN scholarship offered to Jewish survivors and enrolled in medical school in Germany. He completed his first year at Marburg-Lahn University, and his second and third years at the Université de Bruxelles. In 1950 Morgentaler emigrated to Canada, where, despite quotas for Jewish medical students, he resumed his studies at the Université de Montréal and received his medical degree in 1953.

Convinced that women had a right to a safe medical abortion, Morgentaler appeared before the Canadian House of Commons Health and Welfare Committee as president of the Montreal Humanist Fellowship in 1967 and urged the federal government to repeal the Canadian law against abortion. Recognized as a leading advocate of abortion rights in Canada, he was inundated with requests for help from across the country and began performing abortions in his Montreal office. To deliberately challenge the law, he announced in 1973 that he had, in violation of the law, successfully carried out more than 5,000 abortions. Three times he was arrested, charged, tried by jury, and found not guilty of violating the Criminal Code. An unprecedented decision of the Quebec Court of Appeal overturned his first jury acquittal and sent Morgentaler to prison, prompting Parliament to pass a Criminal Code amendment – now known as the Morgentaler Amendment – denying appellate judges the power to strike down acquittals and order imprisonment.

In 1983 Morgentaler opened a clinic in Toronto. He was again charged and acquitted, and in early 1988 the Supreme Court of Canada finally struck down Canada's abortion law. Morgentaler, who had eight clinics across Canada, continued his campaign to provide abortion services and test federal and provincial law.

BIBLIOGRAPHY: C. Dumphy, *Morgentaler: A Difficult Hero* (2003).

[Andrea Knight (2nd ed.)]

MORGENTHAU, U.S. family of public officials. HENRY MORGENTHAU SR. (1856–1946), financier and diplomat, was born in Mannheim, Germany. His family immigrated to the United States in 1865, settling in New York City. He studied at the College of the City of New York and graduated from Columbia Law School in 1877. He specialized in real estate law and soon concentrated on several highly successful New York City real estate ventures. He relinquished his law practice in 1899 and served as president of the Central Realty Bond and Trust Company and, from 1905 to 1913, as president of Henry Morgenthau Company.

Retiring from active business affairs, Morgenthau entered national politics. He was chairman of the Democratic National Committee's finance committee during Woodrow Wilson's 1912 and 1916 presidential campaigns. In 1913 President Wilson appointed him U.S. ambassador to Turkey and told him: "Remember that anything you can do to improve the lot of your coreligionists is an act that will reflect credit upon America." Morgenthau faithfully followed this advice. He was not a Zionist and Zionism as a theory scarcely interested him, but he was deeply impressed by what he saw on a visit to Ereẓ Israel in April 1914: the pioneers appeared to him to be the personification of a new type of Jew.

Morgenthau's good will did much for Zionists during the war. In August 1914, he alerted the Jewish relief organizations in the United States and on October 6 Maurice Wertheim, his son-in-law, arrived in Jaffa on the American warship *North Carolina* to hand over 250,000 francs in gold ($25,000) for emergency purposes. As the war went on and conditions worsened, more warships and additional funds were sent. Once an entire ship, the S.S. *Vulcan*, arrived loaded with provisions; it was thanks to his help that the Jewish population in the country remained alive. *Persona grata* with the Ottoman government, Morgenthau used his influence to prevent the destruction of the *yishuv* by Jamal Pasha.

In 1916, Morgenthau returned to the United States and assisted Woodrow Wilson in his presidential election campaign. In June 1917, the president dispatched him on a secret mission to explore the possibilities of detaching Turkey from the Central Powers. The British government, for its part, learning about American objectives, dispatched Chaim Weizmann to counter the move. The latter met Morgenthau in Gibraltar (July 4–5) and managed to dissuade him from carrying out his mission. Outwitted, Morgenthau never forgave Weizmann for this maneuver and his attitude towards Zionism consequently soured.

He made his views known in a letter to the *New York Times* (December 12, 1917) in which he paid tribute to the settlement work in Palestine but branded Zionism a dangerous ideology which could undermine the hard-won civil rights of Jews in countries of their adoption; it provided no solution to the Jewish problem. This was the classic doctrine of the Reform movement, of which he was an adherent.

In 1919 Morgenthau was named by Wilson to head a U.S. commission investigating the treatment of Jews in Poland (see *Morgenthau Commission). A strong advocate of the League of Nations, Morgenthau was appointed chairman of its Refugee Settlement Commission in 1923 and implemented the complicated transfer of over a million Greeks from Turkish territory to Greece and of several hundred thousand Turks from Greece to Turkey. Morgenthau was one of the organizers of the International Red Cross and Near East Relief, Inc. He was a leader of the American Red Cross and a liberal patron of musical organizations. He was also active in Jewish religious and philanthropic work; he founded Bronx House in 1911 and served on the executive committee of B'nai B'rith. He was president of the Free Synagogue of New York, but resigned in 1919 because of his opposition to Stephen S. *Wise's Zionism.

Morgenthau was the author of *Ambassador Morgenthau's Story* (1918), an autobiography; *All in a Lifetime* (1922); *My Trip Around the World* (1928); and *I Was Sent to Athens* (1930).

His son HENRY MORGENTHAU JR. (1891–1967) was an agricultural expert and U.S. cabinet member. Henry Morgenthau Jr., who was born in New York City, studied agriculture at Cornell University. He purchased a large farm in Dutchess County, New York, modernized it, and operated it successfully. During World War I he worked to increase food production and also served as an officer in the navy. In 1922 Morgenthau purchased the *American Agriculturist* and used this journal to propagate his views on the state of American agriculture. Governor Franklin D. Roosevelt, a friend and Dutchess County neighbor, in 1928 appointed Morgenthau chairman of the Agricultural Advisory Commission and in 1930 appointed him state conservation commissioner. In response to the Depression, Morgenthau developed state work projects which were later used as models for national programs during Roosevelt's presidency.

Joining Roosevelt in Washington, Morgenthau served as head of the Federal Farm Board and the Farm Credit Administration, and in early 1934 was named secretary of the treasury. A skillful and dynamic administrator, he thoroughly reorganized the Treasury Department. U.S. national and international monetary policies instituted in the 1930s for the stabilization of the economy owed much to his initiative. In addition, he supported tax reforms emphasizing greater obligations of the wealthy. His humanitarian interests were consistently evident in his concern for relief activities. Morgenthau was one of the early champions of preparation for U.S. involvement in World War II and of support for the Allied nations early in the war; he promoted foreign purchases, industrial mobilization, and the huge wartime bond drives. In 1943 Morgenthau successfully intervened with Secretary of State Cordell Hull to obtain State Department approval of a plan of the World Jewish Congress to transfer private U.S. funds to Europe to rescue French and Romanian Jews. It was at Morgenthau's suggestion that Roosevelt established the *War Refugee Board as a presidential executive agency in January 1944.

As the end of the war approached, Morgenthau proposed a peace plan involving the partition of Germany and its conversion into an essentially agrarian area. The Morgenthau Plan, presented in his *Germany Is Our Problem* (1945), stirred much debate and Morgenthau resigned after Roosevelt's death.

While still at the Treasury, Morgenthau worked with such Jewish organizations as Mt. Sinai Hospital, B'nai B'rith, and the Jewish Welfare Board. In 1947–50 he served as general chairman and in 1950–53 as honorary chairman of the United Jewish Appeal; the unprecedented sums raised by the appeal during these crucial years significantly aided the new State of Israel. Morgenthau also served as chairman of the board of governors of the Hebrew University (1950–51) and of the American Financial and Development Corporation for Israel, and the Israel Bond drive (1951–54).

Henry Morgenthau Jr.'s son ROBERT MORRIS MORGENTHAU (1919–) was born in New York. He served in the Navy during World War II and engaged in private legal practice in New York (1948–61). In 1961 he was appointed U.S. attorney for the southern district of New York and served with distinction until 1970, winning a reputation for integrity and efficient prosecution. He was an unsuccessful candidate for governor of New York in 1962. In 1974 he was elected district attorney of New York County (i.e., Manhattan), serving for 30 years and being reelected unopposed in 2005. Among his Jewish communal affiliations were the Anti-Defamation League, the New York Federation of Jewish Philanthropies, and Brandeis University.

BIBLIOGRAPHY: Adler, in: *Herzl Year Book*, 5 (1963), 249–81; J.M. Blum, *From the Diaries of Henry Morgenthau Jr.*, 3 vols. (1959–67); idem, *Roosevelt and Morgenthau* (1970); A.D. Morse, *While Six Million Died* (1967), index; R.N. Lebow, in: JSOS, 32 (1970), 267–85. **ADD. BIBLIOGRAPHY:** I. Friedman, *Germany, Turkey and Zionism, 1897–1918* (1977, 1988[2]); idem, *The Question of Palestine, 1914–1918. British-Jewish-Arab Relations* (1973, 19922).

[Morton Rosenstock / Isaiah Friedman (2nd ed.)]

MORGENTHAU, HANS JOACHIM (1904–1980), political scientist. Born in Coburg, Germany, Morgenthau qualified as a lawyer and practiced in Munich from 1927 to 1930, when he became an assistant at the University of Frankfurt. He was acting president of the Frankfurt Labor Court from 1931 to 1933 and was professor of international law at the Madrid Institute of International and Economic Studies from 1935 to 1937, when he emigrated to the United States. From 1943 he taught international politics at the University of Chicago; in 1968 he was also appointed professor of political science at the City College of New York. He also served as consultant to the U.S. departments of State and Defense.

Morgenthau was the predominant figure in the post-World War II effort to refocus the study of international relations on the observed regularities of human conduct, rather than on the idealistic pursuit of abstract norms. This political realism gained wide influence with the publication of his *Scientific Man vs. Power Politics* (1947), and especially *Politics among Nations* (1949), which became the leading text in the field. Morgenthau was also active as a commentator on U.S. current affairs. His writings were published as *Politics in the Twentieth Century* (3 vols., 1962) and in 1970 as *Truth and Power.*

Morgenthau was a founder of the National Committee on American Foreign Policy and served as its first chairman in 1974. In his honor, in 1981 the committee established the Hans J. Morgenthau Award, which is presented to an individual whose efforts have contributed to the advancement of the national interests of the United States and to the achievement of U.S. foreign policy objectives within the framework of political realism.

As a founding proponent of political realism, Morgenthau was regarded as the central figure in international relations scholarship of the 20th century. Some of his other publications include *In Defense of the National Interest* (1951), *Dilemmas of Politics* (1958), *The Impasse of American Foreign Policy* (1962), *The Restoration of American Politics* (1962), *Crossroad Papers* (1965), *A New Foreign Policy for the United States* (1969), and *Science: Servant or Master?* (1972). Many of his writings were translated into foreign languages, and he served as editor of numerous philosophical, legal, and scientific journals.

ADD. BIBLIOGRAPHY: B. Mollov, *Power and Transcendence: Hans J. Morgenthau and the Jewish Experience* (2002); C. Frei, *Hans J. Morgenthau: An Intellectual Biography* (2001); S. Bucklin, *Realism and American Foreign Policy* (2001); M. Griffiths, *Realism, Idealism, and International Politics* (1995); G. Russell, *Hans J. Morgenthau and the Ethics of American Statecraft* (1990).

[Alan Dowty / Ruth Beloff (2nd ed.)]

MORGENTHAU COMMISSION (July–September 1919), U.S. commission, headed by Henry *Morgenthau Sr., to investigate the situation of the Polish Jews after the pogroms which took place in Poland at the end of World War I. The news of the pogroms set off stormy demonstrations in the important Jewish centers of the West. The representatives of the Polish National Committee in Paris were troubled by the extent of this reaction, and sought to improve their image with the public and among leading statesmen in order to strengthen their position at the forthcoming peace treaty negotiations. It was against this background that the Polish premier, Ignace Paderewski, suggested to President Wilson that an American commission be sent to Poland in order to carry out an objective investigation of the facts on the spot, and to prove that the rumors which had been circulated were maliciously exaggerated.

The mission, besides its chairman, included lieutenant general E. Jadwin, the lawyer H.G. Johnson, and the jurist Arthur L. *Goodhart as adviser. The commission considered that its task was not only to note facts but to uncover their causes and offer proposals for improving the situation. The activities of the commission in Poland lasted two months. The public and parliamentary debates on the ratification of the Treaty of Versailles and the Minority Treaty (see *Minority Rights) connected with it aroused exaggerated sensitivity among the Poles, some of whom were inclined to regard the commission as an expression of mistrust on the part of the Anglo-French Entente. The Morgenthau Commission met with the representatives of the various groups in Polish Jewry, paying special attention to the views of the parliament representatives and leaders of the political parties. Morgenthau did not conceal his sympathy for the assimilationists and was impressed by the *ẓaddik* of Gur (*Gora Kalwaria) as the spokesman of the ḥasidic masses. The commission visited the large urban centers and spent some time in disputed areas such as *Lvov and *Vilna, as well as in such towns as *Pinsk and *Kielce which had been the scene of pogroms. Morgenthau spoke to a considerable number of Polish leaders of various political parties. Morgenthau treated the unconventional figure of Marshal *Pilsudski with respect, the latter making no effort to hide his dissatisfaction with the whole idea of the commission, as a slur on the honor of Poland. Because of his delicate position as a Jew, Morgenthau made a point of appearing objective and was inclined to justify the Poles as much as possible.

The report of the commission was published in the *New York Times* on Oct. 3, 1919. It tended to minimize the outbreak of violence to a number of incidents occurring against a background of tension and hostile acts, perpetrated by the occupation armies and retreating forces. As for the future, the equality of all citizens, without any distinctions in their rights or obligations, was to be ensured. Endeavors were to be made to introduce changes in the lives of the Jews by diversifying the branches of economy in which they were engaged and by increased vocational training.

BIBLIOGRAPHY: H. Morgenthau, *All in a Lifetime* (1922); A.L. Goodhart, *Poland and the Minority Races* (1920); AJYB, 22 (1920/21), 255; H.M. Rabinowicz, *The Legacy of Polish Jewry* (1965), 38–41. **ADD. BIBLIOGRAPHY:** S. Netzer, *Ma'avak Yehudei Polin al Zekhuyoteihem ha-Ezraḥiyot ve-ha-Le'ummiyot* (1980), index; *Bulletin du Comité des Delegation Juive auprès de la Conférence de la Paix,* No.12 (March 16, 1920), 2.

[Moshe Landau]

MORGULIS, MANASSEH (Mikhail; 1837–1912), Russian writer and lawyer. Born in Berdichev, Ukraine, Morgulis was among the first to be educated in the government schools for Jews. In 1861 he completed his studies at the government rabbinical seminary in Zhitomir, and in 1864 he entered the University of Kiev, where he helped to create a Jewish students' circle working for the education of the masses and the propagation of information on Judaism in the Russian language. At the same time he contributed to the Hebrew and Russian Jewish press, as well as to the general press. In 1869 he graduated in law and settled in Odessa. He joined the group which published the *Den*, and in his "Impressions from Abroad," he presented a comparison between the situation of the Jews in Western Europe and in Russia. Attacking antisemitism in numerous essays, he sought to reform Jewish life from within. One of his longest essays dealt with the history of the education of the Jews (in *Yevreyskaya Biblioteka*, vols. 1–3).

Morgulis considered that Russian Jewry should accept Russian culture while remaining loyal to the religious-national values of Judaism. He therefore supported Yiddish literature, contributed to the Jewish press, and cooperated with the moderate *Ḥibbat Zion inasmuch as they minimized their projects for "the settlement of Palestine." Although initially he was a member of the committee of the Society for the Support of Agricultural Workers and Craftsmen of Syria and Ereẓ Israel, his violent opposition to political Zionism led him to abandon such activities; he also combated attempts to strengthen the Hebrew elements in the modern Jewish schools. A committee member of the Odessa branch of the *Society for the Promotion of Culture Among the Jews of Russia, he was also actively involved in the community's educational institutions, especially the vocational school, Trud, and the *talmud torah*, which were models for all the Russian communities. Morgulis' principal essays and studies were published in his *Voprosy yevreyskoy zhizni* ("Problems of Jewish Life," 1889), and his memoirs (in *Voskhod*, 1895–97 and in *Yevreyskiy Mir*, 1911) are of historical value.

BIBLIOGRAPHY: L.M. Bramson, *Obshchestvenno-kulturnaya deyatelnost M.G. Morgulisa* (1912).

[Yehuda Slutsky]

MORHANGE, town in the department of Moselle, N.E. France. Jews are first mentioned there in 1686. As a result of complaints by the townsmen about the increase in the number of Jewish families, Duke Leopold ordered the Jews not to attract new coreligionists to Morhange. In 1734 the townsmen demanded that Jewish residence be confined to a single street, and that the number of authorized Jewish families again be reduced. The Jews were compelled to conform to this order, despite their attempts to circumvent it with the connivance of some of the Christian inhabitants. Only five Jewish families remained in Morhange by 1739, the rest having moved away, mainly to Metz. Their numbers increased slightly after the French Revolution. The synagogue was destroyed by the Germans during World War II. Morhange has supplied the patronymic of several families of Lorraine.

BIBLIOGRAPHY: *Mémoires de la Société Archéologique de Lorraine*, 45 (1895), 284ff.; *Revue de Lorraine*, 6 (1930), 156ff.; 8 (1932), 82ff.; REJ, 49 (1904), 124; Z. Szajkowski, *Franco-Judaica* (1962), no. 727; idem, *Analytical Franco-Jewish Gazetteer* (1966), 230.

[Bernhard Blumenkranz]

MORHANGE, PIERRE (1901–1972), French poet. Born in Paris, Morhange gained his literary apprenticeship in the intellectual battles of the 1920s. He maintained that a special sensitivity identified the Jewish writer and that French culture had been enriched by the Jewish contribution. In *Blessé* (1951) he described Jewish suffering with violence and anguish. A prophetic tone dominates collections such as *La vie est unique* (1933), *Autocritique* (1951), and *La robe* (1954).

MORIAH (Heb. מוֹרִיָּה), an unidentified locality mentioned in the Bible. Abraham was ordered to offer Isaac as a burnt offering in the "land of Moriah," which was three days' distance from Beersheba and visible "[from] afar" (Gen. 22:2–4). Early tradition identifies "mount" Moriah with the place where Solomon built the Temple. Josephus also locates the sacrifice on the mountain where David [sic] later built the Temple (Ant., 1:226). Talmudic scholars explain the name Moriah as derived from the "the mountain of myrrh" (in Song 4:6; Mekh., Be-Shallaḥ 3; Gen. R. 50:7). The Septuagint, in translating "Amoria" (Amorite) for Moriah, offers another explanation. The assumption that Abraham intended to sacrifice Isaac on the threshing floor of Jebus (Jerusalem), in full view of the Canaanite city, is farfetched; nor is the Temple Mount visible from afar, as it is hidden by the higher mountains around it. It seems more probable that the biblical story left the location of Moriah deliberately vague; the importance of the sacrifice of Isaac in the series of covenants between God and Israel made it natural that at an early time this supreme act of faith was located on the site destined to become the most holy sanctuary of Israel, the Temple of Solomon, just as the Samaritans transferred the act to their holy mountain, Mt. Gerizim.

BIBLIOGRAPHY: Abel, Geog, 1 (1933), 374–5; EM, 4 (1962), 741–2.

[Michael Avi-Yonah]

MORIAH, Hebrew publishing house. In 1901 Ḥ.N. *Bialik, together with Y.H. *Rawnitzki, S. Ben-Zion, and others, founded the Moriah publishing house in Odessa, their primary intention being the printing of educational material for modern Hebrew schools. Up to 1914 they issued a large amount of such literature, including Bialik-Rawnitzki's famous anthology *Sefer ha-Aggadah*. Moriah's activities were expanded (under E.L. Lewinsky) to include the best in modern Hebrew literature, such as works by Mendele Mokher Seforim, Shalom Aleichem, I.L. Peretz, S. Asch, and D. Frischmann; poetry by Bialik, Tchernichowsky, and Z. Shneur; and scholarly works by M.L. Lilienblum, D. Neumark, and S. Krauss. Moriah became the leading house for modern Hebrew publishing, but World War I and the Russian Revolution caused the end of this remarkably successful enterprise. It was succeeded by the *Dvir publishing house, set up in Berlin after the war by some of the founders of Moriah.

BIBLIOGRAPHY: Ḥ.N. Bialik, *Devir u-Moriyyah* (1926).

MORIN, EDGAR (1921–), sociologist and one of France's leading contemporary thinkers. He was born in Paris to a family of Salonikan origin. His parents were Vidal and Luna Nahum. He adopted the name "Morin" during the period of his clandestine activities in the French Resistance during World War II. Formerly an active member of the Communist Party, he published his *Autocritique* in 1959. An emeritus researcher at the French National Center for Scientific Research (CNRS), Morin introduced the notion of inter-disciplinarity in his work, from his first book, *L'an zéro de l'Allemagne* (1946) until his last, *La violence du monde*, published with Jean Baudrillard (2003)). His interests covered an extensive range of themes, from cinema to modern biology, regardless of the current disciplinary boundaries. He became internationally famous – especially in Latin America – by attaching his name to the age of complexity. He was president of the European Agency for Culture (UNESCO), president of the Association for Complex Thought (APC), and a member of the council of the International Center for Transdisciplinary Research and Studies (CETSAP). His major work, on which he worked for over 20 years (1977–91), is the monumental six-volume series in which he aimed at reforming our way of thinking: *La méthode* – (1) *la nature de la nature*, 1981; (2) *La vie de la vie*, 1985; (3) *La connaissance de la connaissance*, 1986; (4) *Les idées, leur habitat, leur vie, leurs moeurs, leur organisation*, 1991; (5) *L'humanité de l'humanité: L'Identité humaine*, 2001; (6) *Éthique*, 2004. He also published his intellectual biography, *Mes démons* (1998). Several of his books were translated into English: *The Stars* (1960), *The Red and the White: Report from a French Village* (1970), *Method: Towards a Study of Mankind – The Nature of Nature* (1992), *Homeland Earth* (1998), *Seven Complex Lessons in Education for the Future* (1999), *Concept of Europe* (2006).

Acknowledging his Jewishness, he published his family's biography, *Vidal et les siens* (1989), and contributed a preface to Henry Méchoulan's *Les Juifs d'Espagne: histoire d'une diaspora: 1492–1992* (1992). Most of the following have been translated into Chinese, English, German, Greek, Italian, Japanese, Korean, Polish, Portuguese, Russian, Spanish, Swedish, and Turkish: *Rumour in Orleans* (1971); *Human Race, Preceded by an Homage to Robert Antelme* (1992); *Homeland Earth: A Manifesto for the New Millennium (Advances in Systems Theory, Complexity and the Human Sciences)* (1998).

BIBLIOGRAPHY: M. Kofman, E. Morin, *From Big Brother to Fraternity* (1996); R. Barbier, c. 2, "Morin et la connaissance,"in: *L'Approche Transversale. L'écoute sensible en sciences humaines* (1997); J.B. Fages, *Comprendre Edgar Morin (Pensée)* (1988), F. Bianchi, *Le Fil des idées: Une éco-biographie intellectuelle d'Edgar Morin* (2001); R. Fortin, *Comprendre la complexité. introduction à "La Méthode" d'Edgar Morin* (2002).

[Sylvie-Anne Goldberg (2nd ed.)]

MORNING BENEDICTIONS (Heb. בִּרְכּוֹת הַשַּׁחַר), designation of a series of benedictions (the number and sequence varying in the different rituals), which constitute the first part of the morning prayer (*Shaḥarit). After a number of preliminary hymns, the following blessings are recited: (1) for ablution; (2) for the wondrous harmony of the bodily functions; (3) the three Torah blessings (*Birkat ha-Torah), which in some versions appear in a different place; and (4) *Elohai Neshamah* (based upon Ber. 60b) closing with the formula: "Blessed art Thou, O Lord, Who restores the souls unto the dead." This is followed by a series of 15 benedictions (but this number varies in different versions) praising God who: (1) "endows the cock with the ability to distinguish between day and night"; (2) "has not made me a heathen" (the Conservative Sim Shalom siddur has "who has made me a Jew "); (3) "has not made me a slave" (Sim Shalom: "who has made me free"); (4) "has not made me a woman"; women say: "who has made me according to Thy will" (these last three blessings are near the end in the Sephardi rite and some ḥasidic rites; *Sin Shalom*: "who has made me in His image); (5) "enlightens the blind"; (6) "clothes the naked"; (7) "looses the bound"; (8) "raises them that are bowed down"; (9) "stretches out the earth upon the waters"; (10) "has provided me with all my necessities"; (11) "has ordained the steps of man"; (12) "girds Israel with might"; (13) "crowns Israel with glory"; (14) "gives strength to the weary" (this does not appear in all versions); and (15) "causes sleep to pass from my eyes." These blessings, most of which are mentioned in the Talmud (Ber. 60b), were recited originally at home during the various stages of a person's awakening: opening his eyes, standing up, getting dressed, etc. Maimonides opposed their recital at public worship (Yad, Tefillah, 7:9), but in the course of time they were incorporated into the morning service in the synagogue, probably because people did not remember by heart their wording or their order.

Several personal prayers of tannaitic and amoraic origin (quoted in Ber. 16b, 60b) are then recited. These are followed by the scriptural account of the *Akedah, by the confession of R. Johanan (Yoma 87b), by the *Shema, the order of sacrifices (*parashat ha-korbanot*), and in most rites, especially the Sephardi, *Pittum ha-Ketoret*, and by talmudic sections: *Zevaḥim* (Mishnah, chapter 5) and the *baraita* of R. Ishmael (Introd. to Sifra, Leviticus). The morning service proper then begins.

The Conservatives have introduced alternate passages after the Shema, omitting the *korbanot* and *Pittum ha-Ketoret* passages. These are: Avot de-Rabbi Natan 11a; Sukkah 49b; Sifrei Deut Ekev; and Sotah 14a. After the textual study paragraphs they have kaddish de-rabbanan, followed by Shir shel Yom, Psalm 27 for the month of Elul, Psalm 49 for a shiva house, then Anim Zemirot, Psalm 30, and the mourner's kaddish.

BIBLIOGRAPHY: E. Munk, *The World of Prayer*, 1 (1954), 18–56; Elbogen, Gottesdienst, s.v. *Birkhot ha-Shaḥar*; Eisenstein, Dinim., s.v. *Birkhot ha-Shaḥar*; J. Heinemann, *Ha-Tefillah bi-Tekufat ha-Tanna'im ve-ha-Amora'im* (19662), index s.v. *Birkhot ha-Shaḥar*; Freehof, in: HUCA, 23 pt. 2 (1950–51), 339–54; Abrahams, Companion, x–xix.

MORNING FREIHEIT (*Morgn-Frayhayt* – "Morning Freedom"), U.S. leftist Yiddish newspaper. In 1921, the U.S. group, the Jewish Socialist Federation (JSF), split from the Socialist Party. During the ferment of the Jewish labor movement at that time, the "independent" JSF was expelled from the building of the *Jewish Daily Forward*, located in the heart of Manhattan's Lower East Side; many of the federation's intellectual leaders worked as staff of the widely read Yiddish daily. The JSF, renamed the Jewish Federation, together with the just-formed Workers Party, founded the *Frayhayt* in April 1922 as a leftist daily afternoon newspaper. The *Frayhayt*, named for Germany's Independent Socialist Party's newspaper, initially tried to steer a "third course" between mainstream social democracy and proletarian communism. The *Frayhayt* managed for several years under the editorship of Moshe *Olgin to maintain high journalistic and linguistic standards and had a staff that included such first-rate writers as H. *Leivick, Moyshe-Leyb *Halpern, David *Ignatoff, Moses *Katz, and Moyshe *Nadir. In June 1927, the paper began appearing in the morning, from then on known as the *Morgn-Frayhayt*. As was the case with many Yiddish and radical newspapers of the day, the *Frayhayt* made available to a range of authors' works under the Farlag-Frayhayt imprint.

By the late 1920s, with the consolidation of different groups into what became known as the Communist Party, the *Morgn-Frayhayt* had become an unswerving Party organ, as was demonstrated by the reversal of its initial support of the *yishuv* (the Jewish community in Mandatory Palestine) to total support for the Arabs during the 1929 anti-Jewish riots. The paper's position alienated many of its readers and caused its circulation to slip sharply from its peak of 14,000. The *Morgn-Frayhayt* remained loyal to the Communist Party line through the Hitler-Stalin pact and the Cold War, undergoing a process of self-examination and eventual political and organizational independence beginning in late February 1956, with Nikita Khrushchev's de-Stalinization of the U.S.S.R. In 1967, the *Morgn-Frayhayt* supported Israel's right to defend itself during the Six-Day War, in direct opposition to the position of the Communist Party of the U.S. Two years later, the CPUSA attacked the *Morgn-Frayhayt* and its English-language sister publication, *Jewish Currents*, for their increasingly independent position regarding Soviet intervention in Poland and Czechoslovakia, although the *Morgn-Frayhayt* had not yet openly broken with the Communist Party. The *Morgn-Frayhayt*'s politics independently evolved to something akin to the "Eurocommunism" of the 1970s and 1980s. By 1970, the paper was appearing five times a week, with an estimated 8,000 circulation. Seven years later, it became a weekly, with an English-language supplement. The *Morgn-Frayhayt* folded in September 1988.

BIBLIOGRAPHY: M. Epstein, *Jew and Communism* (1959); J.L. Teller, *Strangers and Natives* (1968); G. Estraikh, "Metamorphoses of Morgn-frayhayt," in: G. Estraikh and M. Krutikov (eds.), *Yiddish and the Left; Papers of the Third Mendel Friedman International Conference on Yiddish* (2001); D. Hacker, *Jewish Currents – A History* (n.d.); T. Michels, "Socialism with a Jewish Face: The Origins of the Yiddish-Speaking Communist Movement in the United States, 1907–1923," in: *Yiddish and the Left; Papers of the Third Mendel Friedman International Conference on Yiddish, op. cit.*

[Arieh Lebowitz (2nd ed.)]

MOROCCO, westernmost country in North Africa. The first arrival of Jews in Morocco goes back to antiquity. There are numerous legends which claim that they settled in the country before the destruction of the First Temple. From the fifth to the third centuries B.C.E., the Carthaginian gold market was situated in Morocco. On this historical basis, an ancient legend relates that some five centuries before the Carthaginian expansion, in the days of Solomon and the Phoenicians, the Hebrews came to Sala (Chella) in the vicinity of Salé (Rabat) in order to purchase gold in large quantities. In another legend, it is related that Joab was sent to Morocco to fight the Philistines, who had been driven out of Canaan; an inscription describing this expedition is said to have existed near the present-day town of Zagora. Wadi Oued Draa and the region of Oufran (Ifran of the Anti-Atlas) are said to have been the sites of important Jewish settlements before the destruction of the Second Temple. The earliest epigraphic evidence on the presence of Jews in Morocco, however, comes from the second century C.E. It consists essentially of inscriptions on tombstones found in the ruins of the Roman town of Volubilis, between *Fez and *Meknès, and another inscription discovered in Salé. The latter is in Greek, while one of the inscriptions of Volubilis is in Hebrew.

Morocco, like the remainder of the Maghreb, was one of the favorite territories for Jewish missionary activities. The Jews, together with those whom they succeeded in converting, appear to have originally been numerous and particularly powerful. The great Arabic historian of the 14th century, Ibn Khaldūn, names a number of large Moroccan *Berber tribes who were converted to Judaism prior to the Arab conquest. These were the Fandalāwqa, Madyūna, Bahlūla, Ghiyāta, and Bazāz tribes. The capital of the last was also named Bazāz or Qulʿat-Mlahdī. It was completely inhabited by Jews and did not disappear until the 12th century. It was situated near the present-day town of Sefrou. Other tribes, such as the Barghwāṭa, were also heavily Judaized. Between 581 and 693 many Jews were compelled to leave *Spain as a result of the persecutions of the Visigoth kings who, while forcing them to accept baptism, also adopted draconian measures against them. According to later traditions, thousands of Spanish Jews had settled in Africa by 693. It is told that these Jews, together with their Moroccan coreligionists, plotted to conquer or deliver Spain into the hands of the more tolerant Muslims (694). Some historians maintain that there were Jews among the Berber-Muslim invaders of Spain in 711.

The Arab conquest of Morocco and its conversion to Islam did not bring about the elimination of the Jews or the Judaized Berbers. However, when Idris I seized power in 788, it was his intention to compel all the inhabitants of the country to embrace *Islam. After the death of Idris I, there remained some Jewish or Judaized tribes in the area of *Fez. When Idris II (791–828) decided to establish his capital in Fez, he authorized Jews of all origins to settle there. Their dispersion in all the regions was one of the principal reasons for their economic strength at the time. The story goes that the inhabit-

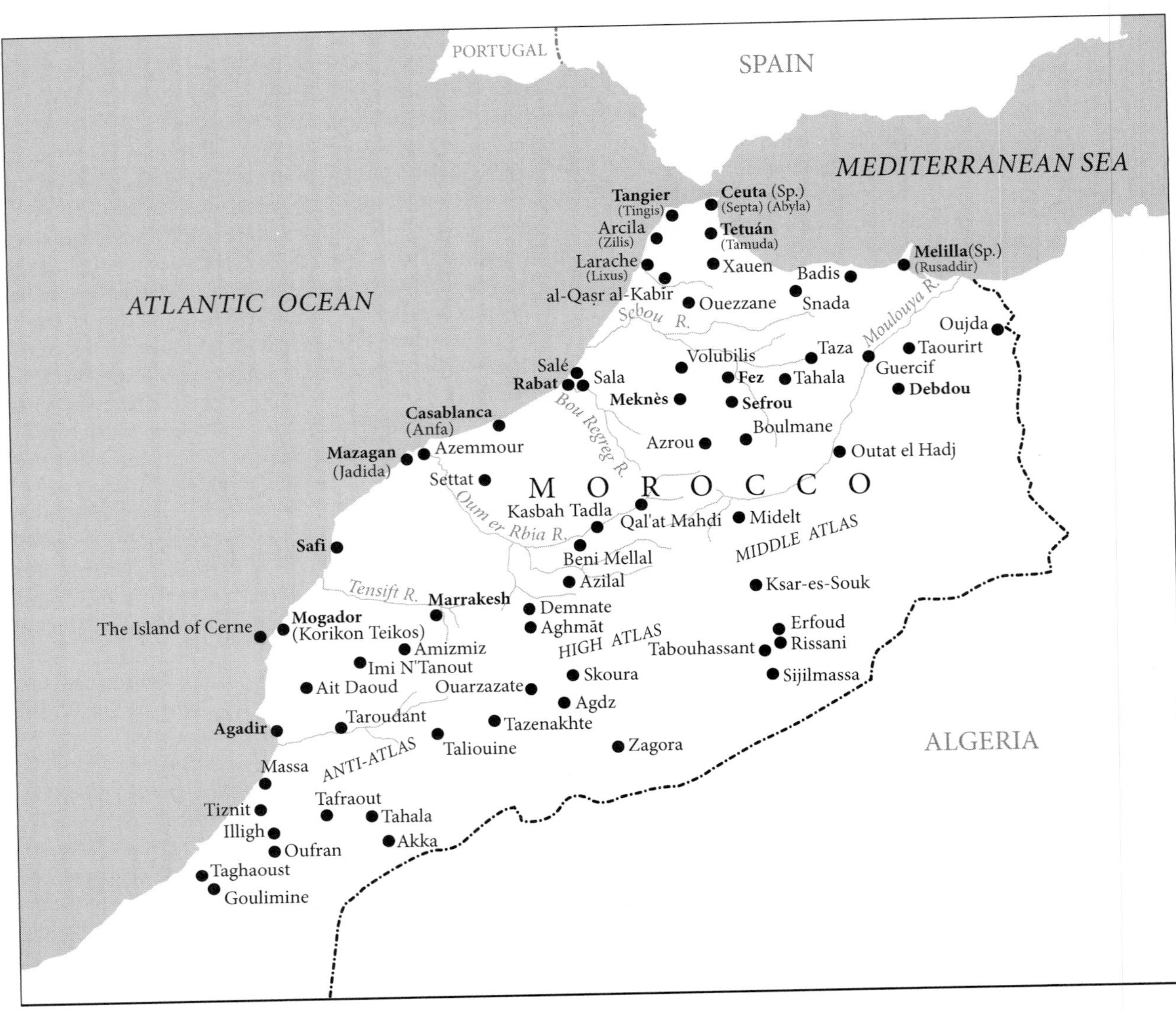

Jewish communities of Morocco. Names in boldface type indicate communities existing in 1971.

ants of Fez revolted against the ruler Yaḥya (860), who had violated the chastity of a Jewish girl. The pogrom in Fez in 1033 is to be seen as an isolated event due to the Jewish support for the Maghrawas, the rivals of the Ifrenids. At a later date, the *Almoravides prohibited the Jews to live in their capital *Marrakesh. The most brilliant period of the Jews of Morocco from the spiritual and intellectual point of view belongs to the reigns of the *Idrisids and their successors. The numerous departures for Spain drained neither the strength of Moroccan Jewry nor its intellectual activity. Even after the departure of R. Isaac *Alfasi from Fez for Cordoba (1088), Judaism in Morocco retained its vigor. Under the Almoravides there was even a trend in the opposite direction. Two of the physicians of the Almoravide sovereigns, Meir ibn *Kamniel and Solomon Abūab Muʿallim in Marrakesh, were of Spanish origin, one from Seville and the other from Saragossa. Both were distinguished Torah scholars. There were also scholars in *Ceuta, the native town of Joseph ibn Aknin, the disciple of Maimonides. There was also an important center of learning in *Sijilmassa (ancient capital of Tafilalet oasis). Scholars were to be found in the Atlas region, in Aghmāt; of these, there is information on the talmudist Zechariah b. Judah Aghmati. In Fez studies were carried on continuously; it was for this reason that *Maimonides and his family settled there after leaving Spain during the persecution of the Almohads.

The doctrine of the mahdi Ibn Tūmart, which inaugurated the *Almohad movement, did not tolerate the existence of non-Muslims. At the beginning, the latter were among the victims of the Almohad soldiers, who were highlanders in search of plunder. Indeed, many of the Jews were wealthy. By the time that ʿAbd al-Muʾmin (1128–63) had finally imposed Almohad domination in 1154, many Jews had already converted under the threat of the sword. After that, there was a short period of improvement in the situation of the Jews in

Fez. Those who had been spared from the massacres and the conversions were then able to resume a relatively normal life. This situation changed with the advent of Abu Yaʿqūb Yūsuf (1165–84). The recrudescence of fanaticism once more resulted in the forced conversion of Jews. The *dayyan* of Fez, R. Judah ha-Kohen ibn Shushan, who refused to submit to this, was burnt alive, and at that time Maimonides left Morocco. The situation deteriorated even further under al-Mansūr (1184–99) who imposed on the Jews, including those already converted, the wearing of a distinctive sign, the *Shikla*, because he did not believe in the sincerity of their conversion. The presence of Jews was authorized once more by al-Mʾamūn (1227–32), but their appearance drew the anger of the Muslims who massacred all of them in Marrakesh (1232). The Jews did not return in considerable numbers until the time of the dynasty of the *Merinids, who replaced the Almohads in 1269. During Almohad rule, many Moroccan Jews had left the country for the East, above all for Christian Spain. Large numbers of them settled in the territories of the kings of Aragon, in Catalonia and Majorca, where they were favorably received.

The Merinids proved themselves particularly friendly toward the Jews. When the still-fanatic mobs attacked them in 1275, the Merinid sultan intervened personally to save them. The sovereigns of this dynasty benevolently received the Jewish ambassadors of the Christian kings of Spain and admitted Jews among their closest courtiers. Of these Jews, Khalifa b. Waqqāsa (Ruqqasa) became steward of the household of the sultan Abu Yaʿqūb and his intimate counselor. A victim of palace intrigues, he was put to death in 1302. His nephew, who was also named Khalifa, held the same office and suffered the same fate (1310). However, there were no repercussions against the Moroccan Jews as a result of the execution of their powerful coreligionists. They were the principal factors in the prosperity of the country. The Sahara gold trade, which was of primary importance, and the exchange with the Christian countries were completely under their control. Their relatives and associates in the kingdom of Aragon financed, when necessary, the navies which defended the Moroccan ports. In addition to the **jizya* (poll tax), they paid enormous sums to the treasury in customs duties for their imports and exports. In the outlying areas, particularly in the Atlas region where there were large concentrations of Jews of early origin, the Jews wielded great influence in both the political and spiritual domains. Jewish physicians enjoyed well-deserved renown. The study of Kabbalah, as well as philosophy, was then in vogue. The last Moroccan philosopher of the Middle Ages was Judah b. Nissim ibn *Malkah, who was still alive in 1365.

From 1375 the Muslim world of the West clearly entered into its period of decline. The Jews of Morocco were all the more affected by this development because, unlike in *Algeria, there was no revival due to the arrival of important Jewish personalities fleeing from the Spanish persecutions of 1391. The Jews who came to Morocco during this period were mainly of average erudition; moreover, just like their native brothers, they encountered the fanaticism which had been introduced among the Muslim masses by the mystics who had then founded the Marabout movement. This movement eroded the authority of the last Merinid sovereigns, and a serious deterioration in the condition of the Jews ensued. In 1438 the Jews of Fez were enclosed within a special quarter, the first Moroccan *mellah.

The political and economic situation in Morocco during the 15th century was bad. The sultan ʿAbd al-Ḥaqq turned to the Jews in order to straighten out his finances. He chose the Jew Aaron ben Battas as his prime minister, but a short while later the Merinid dynasty was ended (1465) with the assassination of its last representative and his Jewish minister. A large number of Jews lost their lives in this revolution, and many others were forcibly converted. They were authorized, however, to return to Judaism when Muhammad al-Shaykh al-Waṭṭāsī came to power in 1471. According to local traditions, groups of Jews had in the meantime taken refuge in Spain. Among these were the family of the scholar and poet Saadiah *Ibn Danan, who settled in Granada, as well as Ḥayyim *Gagin, who became the leader of the native Jews upon his return to Morocco in 1492. The Jewish chroniclers are unanimous in their description of the welcome accorded by the sultan Muhammad al-Shaykh al-Waṭṭāsī to the Spanish and Portuguese refugees (*megorashim*) in 1492 and 1496. Bands of plunderers, however, attacked the numerous Jews on the roads to Fez, the town to which they had been attracted. Once they arrived there, they found a lack of accommodation and camped in the surrounding fields. About 20,000 of them died as a result of disasters, famine and diseases. Many of them returned to Spain. Under the influence of powerful religious personalities, a majority, both distinguished families and common people, permanently settled in the country. Among this new population there were such eminent men as Jacob Qénizal, Abraham *Saba, Abraham of Torrutiel, Joshua *Corcos, Naḥman Sunbal, and others. There was, however, also a trend for emigration to *Italy, *Turkey, and *Palestine. Among those who left Morocco at that time were Abraham *Zacuto, Jacob (1) *Berab, *David ibn Abi Zimra, and Judah Ḥayyat.

The newcomers were generally ill received by their native coreligionists (*toshavim*). In spite of the fact that the *megorashim* rapidly assumed the leadership in southern communities; such a possibility was for a long time withheld from them in the north. The *toshavim* feared their commercial rivalry and their technical superiority. Controversies broke out between the two elements. The former went so far as to question the faith of the *megorashim*. The latter, however, succeeded in strengthening their position and in due course dominated all the communities where they were represented. Fez became their spiritual center. Their rabbis issued a large number of *takkanot*, which were known by the name of "*takkanot* of the exiles of Castile." These dealt essentially with the laws of marriage, divorce and inheritance and were based on Spanish tradition. For 450 years they separated themselves in this manner from the *toshavim*. The descendants of the *megorashim* jealously adhered to their ways and customs. They worshiped in their own synagogues and sometimes had their own lots in the cemeteries. In such northern communities as *Tetuán and *Tangier, the native Jews were completely assimilated among the descendants of the *megorashim*. Oblivious to their own origin, they disdainfully referred to their brothers of the interior as *Forasteros* ("aliens," i.e., to the Castilian community). Until recently, most of these communities spoke Ḥakétia, a mixture of Spanish, Hebrew and an Arabic dialect. The ancient Castilian language, which differs from the Ladino spoken in the Orient, was, until the 19th century, in current usage among a large number of families of Spanish origin in both the north and south of the country.

At the beginning of the 16th century, Portugal occupied some of the Moroccan coast on the shores of the Atlantic. Communities of *megorashim* had settled in such ports as Azemmour and Safi. From the beginning, cordial relations were established between them and the Portuguese, who employed their members as official interpreters and negotiators. The political role of these men was of prime importance to the kings of *Portugal. Indeed, the latter granted the Jews of their Moroccan bases rights which may be considered as extraordinary for that period; they loaded such families as *Benzamero, Adibe and Dardeiro with favors. On the other hand, these Jews, as loyal subjects, did not hesitate in sacrificing their property or even their lives when this was required by Portuguese interests. The coreligionists who lived under the sharifs of Marrakesh or the *Wattasids of Fez were the principal factors in arranging the peace, always unstable, between the Portuguese and the Muslims. Jacob *Rosales and Jacob *Roti, talented ministers of the Wattasids, endeavored to create a lasting reconciliation between the Christians and the Muslims. Counselors of Muslim princes such as Menahem Sananes or Abraham Cordovi pursued similar objectives. These exiles from Spain and Portugal often traveled to the Portuguese kings as Moroccan ambassadors. During their stay in the Iberian Peninsula, they also induced the *Marranos to establish themselves in Morocco. During the 16th century, Morocco became a haven for Marranos who arrived from the Iberian Peninsula, the Madeira Islands, the Azores, the Canary Islands and even the Americas. In Tetuán, Fez, Meknès and Marrakesh, there were centers for reconversion to Judaism. Some Jews succeeded in transferring their fortunes there, while others, such as skillful craftsmen and especially the gunsmiths, found immediate employment. It was early Marranos who introduced a new process for the extracting of sugar from sugarcane. Due to their methods, Morocco became the leading producer of the world's best sugar during the 16th–17th centuries.

Until recent times, the Jews of Morocco engaged in a variety of professions. In some regions there were farmers and cattle breeders among them; in general, however, they were mostly craftsmen, small tradesmen, peddlers, and at times moneylenders. Some industries, such as that of beeswax, and the trading of rubber and ostrich feathers were exclusively concentrated in the hands of the Jews. For religious reasons, the Muslims ceded to them the craftsmanship and trade of precious metals as well as the making of wine and its sale. Until 1912, the overwhelming majority of the maritime trade was controlled by a closed society of Jewish merchants. Wealthy and influential from father to son, some of them were court bankers or high officials. They held the title of "merchants of the sultan," obtained for themselves or their protégés monopolies over a large number of products or foodstuffs, and held a monopoly over certain ports or took them in lease; the European countries entrusted them with their interests and they represented them before the sultan, officially or semi-officially. But the majority of the Jewish population, however, suffered in helpless poverty. The droughts which preceded famine and the exorbitant and arbitrary taxes which were temporarily levied on the communities from the 16th to the middle of the 18th century were the cause of their poverty. Nevertheless, the misfortunes which struck one community did not affect the others. It was thus, for example, a common occurrence that while Jews died of hunger in Fez or were persecuted in Meknès, prosperity reigned in the mellah of Marrakesh and Jews ruled the town of *Debdou.

When there was a weakening of the central authority of the sultan, Morocco was divided up into subordinated territory (*Bled al-Makhzen*) and unsubordinated territory (*Bled al-Sibā*), the latter of which was always that of the Berbers under whom the Jews generally suffered less in their capacity of tolerated "protected subjects" (**dhimmi*). Many of them were the serfs of the Muslim lord; however, until the 19th century there were also many Jews in the High Atlas Mountains, the Sūs (Sous), and the Rif, essentially Berber regions, who carried weapons, rode horses, and did not pay the *jizya*. Like the Berbers, the Jewish masses of Morocco were marked by their religiosity. But a sincere, profound, and intellectual piety also prevailed within Moroccan Judaism; its development was inspired by the writings of Maimonides. Over the last centuries this Judaism produced genuine scholars and a large number of authors, such as members of the families of Ibn Danān, Ibn Ḥayyim, *Abensur, *Almosnino, Assaban, Ben-Attar, *Berdugo, de *Avila, de Loya (*Delouga), *Elbaz, *Uzziel, *Serfaty, *Serero, *Toledano, and others. On given dates, thousands of Jews left on regular pilgrimages (*Ziyāra*) through the country to the tombs of saints whose origin was at times unknown and who were venerated by both Jews and Muslims.

In many educated circles, there was an inclination toward mysticism: its members devoted themselves almost exclusively to the study of Kabbalah. The Zohar, much esteemed in Morocco, was often the principal work in their curriculum. In several communities, particularly in Salé, Safi, and Marrakesh, teachers and disciples were grouped in closed circles from which emerged such personalities as: Joseph Gikatilla, author of *Ginnat Egoz*; Abraham ha-Levi Berukhim, author of *Tikkun Shabbat*; Joseph ibn Teboul, author of *Perush al Idra Rabba*; Abraham b. Mūsā; Ḥayyim b. Moses *Attar, author of *Or ha-Ḥayyim*; Raphael Moses Elbaz, author of *Kisse Melakhim*; Joseph Corcos, author of *Yosef Ḥen*; Solomon

Amar; and Abraham Azulai. Initiates of the Kabbalah have remained numerous in Morocco until the present day. Many others followed *Shabbetai Ẓevi. During the middle of the 17th century, the movement of this pseudo-Messiah achieved considerable success in Morocco. In the West, an important role in checking it was played by the Moroccan rabbis Jacob *Sasportas, Daniel Toledano and Aaron ha-*Siboni.

According to a tradition, a Jewish scholar of Wadi Draa forecast to the Saʿdian sharifs that they would accede to the throne of Morocco. Encouraged by this prediction, they set out to conquer the country and took Marrakesh in 1525 and Fez in 1549. In fact, the Jewish counselors of the sharifs were not strangers to their progress. Their coreligionists – administrators, merchants and bankers – supplied their financial requirements; other Jews, former Marranos who maintained close relations with Europe, supplied them with weapons in their capacity as armorers. When the Portuguese army was defeated by ʿAbd al-Malik at the Battle of al-Qaṣr al-Kabīr (or Battle of the Three Kings, 1578), the Jews commemorated the event by a joyful Purim (*Purim de los Cristianos*). On the other hand, the tens of thousands of Christian prisoners taken in this battle were fortunate enough to be ransomed by the descendants of the *megorashim*, who treated them with indulgence. The liberation of these prisoners against ransom by their families and the conquest of *Sudan in 1591 brought a considerable quantity of gold to Morocco. Many Jewish families, especially those in the retinue of Ahmad al-Mansūr, were among the beneficiaries of this exceptional prosperity. Of an enterprising nature, the Jews of Morocco traveled as far as India in the conduct of their trade; they also had gained a hold in the financial world, particularly in Tuscany, in one direction, and in northwestern Europe, in the other. This activity was in concert with the politics of the young Netherlands, which sought to strangle the economic power of Spain. In 1608 Samuel *Pallache arrived in the Netherlands and in 1610 he signed the first pact of alliance between Morocco and a Christian country. The Pallache family played an active role in the political and economic interests of Morocco in Europe over a long period. The sultan Zidah (1603–1628) and his successors (1628–1659) took many other Jews into their service. As in former times, every Muslim leader had his Jewish counselor. The latter were the natural protectors of the Jewish masses. As a result, these masses generally lived in superior conditions to those of the Muslim population, which resigned itself to its fate.

"Frankish" Jewish families from Leghorn and Holland settled in Morocco. Some were attracted by the pirate traffic which operated from Salé and Tetuán. In Tangier, which was under British domination, a small community of "Frankish" Jews existed from 1661; relations with the Muslims, however, were maintained through the mediation of the Jews of Tetuán: until the evacuation of the town in 1684, the Parienté and the Falcon families played an important political role in the relations between the English and the Muslims. Moroccan Jews had also inaugurated a migratory movement a long while before.

There was a fair amount of emigration in the direction of the Holy Land, *Turkey, *Egypt, Italy (especially Leghorn and Venice), Amsterdam, Hamburg, England, and the countries of the two Americas. Occasionally, in their old age and once they had made their fortune, emigrants returned to their communities of origin. In Tetuán and later in *Mogador, this was a frequent occurrence.

The Jews played a particularly important role in the rise to power of the *ʿAlawid (Alouite) dynasty of Hasanid descent, which still governed Morocco in the beginning of the third millennium. This role has been distorted by a legend which relates that at the time an extremely rich Jew, Aaron Ben-Meshal, governed the region of Taza and, as a tribute, demanded a young Muslim girl from Fez every year. By deceit, Mulay al-Rashid (1660–72) succeeded in assassinating this Jew and seizing his riches; the *ṭolba* ("students") assisted him in this exploit. He was thus able to become the first sultan of the ʿAlawid dynasty. To this day, this legendary event is celebrated with much pomp by the *ṭolba* of Fez. In reality, Mulay al-Rashid, who lacked financial means, was backed by the Jews of the Taza, which was then an important commercial center and the first place which he had dominated; he employed a faithful and wise Jewish counselor and banker, Aaron Carsinet. In order to gain control of Fez, where he was enthroned, he entered the city through the mellah, where in secret he spent the night in the house of a notable named Judah Monsano. Mulay al-Rashid subsequently adopted a favorable attitude toward the Jews. His reign was a most prosperous one.

The Jews also successfully contributed to the rise to power of the brother of Mulay al-Rashid, Mulay Ismail (1672–1727), one of the most outstanding Moroccan monarchs. Mulay Ismail was *khalifa* ("viceroy") in Meknès when, through one of his Jewish friends, Joseph *Maymeran, he learned of the death of his brother in Marrakesh. The speed with which he received this precious information and the large sum of money which Maymeran loaned him enabled Mulay Ismail to have himself proclaimed sultan immediately. It is also related that not wanting to be indebted to Joseph Maymeran, Mulay Ismail had him assassinated. In fact, he appointed him steward of the palace, a function of considerable importance which was later held by his son Abraham Maymeran, who had become the principal favorite of the sultan. The Toledanos, Ben-Attars, and Maymerans all enjoyed the favors of Mulay Ismail, who during various periods appointed one or the other as *shaykh al-Yahūd* with authority over all the Jews of the kingdom. Moses Ben Attar signed a treaty with England in his name; Joseph and Ḥayyim Toledano were his ambassadors to the Netherlands and London. Moreover, Jews who were close to Mulay Ismail wielded their influence over him. Thus, in spite of his cupidity, violence and cruelty, the Jews fared better under him than the Muslim masses. The greatest part of his long reign was marked by peace and security, and the Jewish communities were able to develop in every respect. However, during the last years of his reign, which were overshadowed by plagues and conflicts between his rival sons, the situation of the Jews began to deteriorate.

The 30 years of anarchy and plunder which followed upon the death of Mulay Ismail exhausted and impoverished the Jewish communities of the interior; they consequently transformed their social framework. The Middle Atlas region was literally drained of its Jews. The departure of the village Jews toward the urban centers changed the aspect of the mellahs of Fez and Meknès. These quarters, which had until then been well maintained, were converted into slums, with the exception of a few middle-class streets. Most of the ancient families were ruined and lost all power, only to be replaced by a few parvenus. Some Ben-Kikis and Mamans were sent on diplomatic missions to Europe; their rivalry with the former Jewish bourgeoisie caused controversies within the community; some members of the Levy-Yuly family became "confidants" of the sultans. Slowly, the towns of the interior were abandoned by their leading Jewish elements in favor of the ports, to which the new arrivals were already linked by ancient ties with the Jewish financial circles living there. Rabat, Safi and especially Marrakesh replaced Fez and Meknès as rabbinical centers.

Mulay Muhammad b. Abdallah (1757–1790) had formally been viceroy of southern Morocco from 1745. He had established security and, with the assistance of Jewish and Christian financial circles, an era of prosperity unknown in the north of the country reigned there. As under the Saʿdians, Marrakesh once more became the capital and royal residence. Its Jewish community flourished but then entered a period of decline as a result of the avariciousness of the sultan in his old age. The community of Safi took over the leading place in the foreign trade of Morocco, while that of Agadir acquired the monopoly over the trading with the Sahara. These roles later became the privilege of the community of Mogador (Essaouira), which was founded in 1764. The operations of the big Jewish merchants in Morocco began to expand. Sugar production and trade and maritime commerce were almost entirely concentrated in the hands of Jews. Commercial operations reached the ports of the eastern coast of the United States at the end of the 18th century. From the reign of Sidi Muhammad Ben-Abdallah (1757–90) down to the end of the 19th century, it was usually Jews who acted as agents for the European Powers in Morocco.

The wide-ranging activities of the Jews of this circle promoted the development of such communities as Sala, Asfi, Tetuan and Tangier and influenced the growth of new ones. These latter communities also gained economic supremacy over such older ones in the interior of the country as Fez and Meknès and the communities of the Marrakesh and Tapilalti regions. These Jews exploited their political and economic position to improve their legal and social status and improve the lot of the communities where they operated. In fact, beginning with the end of the 18th century, a circle of Jews arose in Morocco with rights protected by agreements under the aegis of the European Powers. Called "protégés," their number reached a few thousand. An example of the prosperity of the new type of community is Mogador in the last third of the 18th century. The beginnings of its accelerated development are linked to Sultan Sidi Muhammad Ben-Abdallah, who was interested in developing trade with Europe. He rebuilt the city and turned it into the chief port of Morocco. Ignoring the protests of the Muslim religious leaders, he levied taxes and customs duties on imports and exports and all the merchandise in the market place. He also brought to the city dozens of Jewish families, giving them special rights and exempting some of them from all the strictures (aside from the *jizya* tax) that applied to the Jews of Morocco. According to one source, there were around 6,000 Jews in Mogador in 1785. The city took on a Jewish character and the commercial center closed down on the Sabbath. The Jews of the city developed wide-ranging economic relations with Jewish communities outside Morocco, such as Amsterdam, London, Leghorn and *Algiers. The renewed desire of Morocco in the days of Mulai Abd Rahman (1822–59) to develop trade with Europe – a change caused partly by French pressure to open the gates of Morocco to European commerce – gave new impetus to the *'tjjar esltan* ("King's merchants"), who had gone into decline during the reign of Sultan Saliman (1792–1822).

Jewish merchants possessed various advantages: knowledge of Arabic and European languages, familiarity with local conditions, a good name and the confidence of the Sultan. The Sultan gave them greater freedom of movement in the country and custom discounts, and a number of them received the title of "King's merchants." Mogador served as a base for Jewish merchants operating in the south of Morocco and distributing European goods in Sous (the southern region of the country) and Sahara and exporting to Europe gold, ivory, ostrich feathers, almonds, olive oil, and goatskins. The familiarity of Jewish merchants with local business practices and their connections with the Sultan led European governments even to appoint local Jews as consuls (up to 1857). The condition of the Jews now improved throughout the country. Jews from abroad came to settle in Morocco. Among these were the Attals and Cardosos (Cordoza), who entered the service of the sovereign. Cardoso, however, drew the jealousy of the Attals upon himself and paid for this with his life. The leading favorite of the sultan was Samuel *Sunbal, a scholar, ambassador to Denmark, and the last "sheikh" of Moroccan Jewry. Certain Jewish personalities encouraged friendship with the United States, where their relatives had emigrated and with whom they had important commercial ties. Isaac Cordoza Nuñes, an interpreter of the sultan in Marrakesh, and Isaac Pinto, a Moroccan established in the United States, were largely responsible for the signing of a treaty between Morocco and the United States in 1787, whereby the U.S. Congress paid Morocco for the protection of U.S. shipping interests in the Mediterranean.

Mulay Muhammad entrusted the Jews with all his negotiations with the Christian countries. Those of the community of Tetuán, whose members included some wealthy merchants and who, as in Mogador, acted as consuls, refused the rebellious son of the sultan, Mulay al-Yazid, an important loan which he had requested from them. When he came to power,

Mulay al-Yazid (1790–92) wreaked cruel vengeance upon them and his hatred fell upon all the Jews of the kingdom. This was the greatest disaster which befell them after the period of the Almohads. In the first place, the community of Tetuán was handed over to the army, which plundered and perpetrated murder and rape. The communities of Larache, Arcila, al-Qaṣr al-Kabīr, Taza, Fez and Meknès then suffered the same fate. All the Jewish personalities who had been employed by the late sultan and upon whom Mulay al-Yazid could lay his hands were hanged by their feet at the gates of Meknès, where they remained for 15 days before they died. The treasurer Mordecai Chriqui, who refused to convert, was handed over to the executioner and Jacob Attal, who accepted such an offer, nevertheless died after being hanged by his heels. The notables and the Muslim masses then rose to intervene on behalf of the Jews. They hid many of them in their houses and saved a great many others. In Rabat, the governor Bargash saved the community from the worst. At the time Marrakesh had not been subordinated. Once it fell, the Jewish community was sacked, the men and children were massacred, and hundreds of women were taken into captivity. Mulay al-Yazid had the eyes of 300 Muslim notables of the town put out. Thousands of others were convened to the Great Mosque for prayers and massacred there. Shortly before he died as the result of a wound received in a battle near Marrakesh, Mulay al-Yazid ordered the drawing up of lengthy lists of Jewish and Muslim notables in Fez, Meknès and Mogador who were to be massacred. He died before the order was carried out, however.

The advent of Mulay Suleiman (1792–1822) came as a much needed respite. The new monarch was indeed opposed to violence but he proved to be a fanatic and the Jews felt the consequences. As he sought to seal off Morocco from foreign influence, he reduced trade with Europe to a considerable extent. He also decreed the establishment of ghettos in the wealthiest communities. In 1808 the Jews of Tetuán, Rabat, Salé and Mogador were for the first time enclosed within mellahs. The only exceptions were a few families in Mogador who continued to live in the residential quarter of the town. Since they were economically indispensable to the country, he restored to some of them their former prerogatives, notably to the Aflalos, the Corcos, the Guedallas, the Levy-Yulys, the Macnins, and the Sebags. He chose his diplomats, his bankers, and his counselors from these families. The terrible epidemics of 1799 and 1818 depopulated Morocco and wrought havoc with its social and economic conditions. As a result, some of these families emigrated to England, where they gained a prominent place within the Jewish society of London. One of the members of the Levy-Yuly family, Moses, emigrated to the United States, where his son David *Yulee became the first senator of Jewish origin.

The reigns of Mulay ʿAbd al-Raḥman (1822–59) and his successors Mulay Muhammad b. ʿAbd al-Raḥman (1859–73) and Mulay al-Ḥasan (1873–94) were marked by the pressure of the Christian powers on Morocco and an increased activity of the Jews in the economic and diplomatic fields. Meyer *Macnin was appointed ambassador in London (1827); Judah *Benoliel, consul in Gibraltar, successfully negotiated several treaties; Abraham *Corcos and Moses Aflalo were entrusted with several delicate missions; many other Jews, such as the families of *Altaras, *Benchimol, and *Abensur, played important roles in Moroccan affairs. Until 1875 consular representation in the Moroccan towns was almost entirely assumed by Jewish merchants, and many of them held such functions into the 20th century. The European powers, concerned with their economic interests, granted protection to a large number of Jews. By often exploiting the defense of their protégés as a pretext, they interfered within the internal affairs of Morocco. A Jewish consular agent, Victor *Darmon, was summarily executed on a trumped-up charge (1844). This became one of the causes of the Spanish-Moroccan War of 1860, when Jews were compelled to take refuge in Gibraltar, while those of Tetuán were the victims of a pogrom. Tangier and Mogador were bombarded by the French fleet. In Mogador the Jews, assailed by the tribes who came to plunder the town, defended themselves by force of arms. In Tangier, which only suffered some material damage, the Jews celebrated with a Purim (*Purim de las bombas*). Emigration nevertheless rose and the sultan reintroduced the exit tax which was to be paid by every individual who left the country. However, those who desired to settle in the Holy Land were exempted from this tax (1858). A number of families, many of them wealthy, then established themselves in Palestine.

The Moroccan people, already fanaticized by the French conquest of *Algeria, accused the Jews of being the agents of European influence in Morocco. In some of the regions populated by the Berbers, the situation of the Jews became quite precarious. Measures which even went beyond the restrictions of Muslim law were imposed against the Jewish masses of the interior, which were more vulnerable than those living along the coasts: Jews were often sentenced to bastinado for trifling reasons. This situation prompted a visit by Sir Moses *Montefiore to the court of Mulay Muhammad in Marrakesh; the later promulgated a *dahir* ("royal decree"; February 1864) which was marked by extreme benevolence toward the Jews and granted them equality of rights with all Moroccans. Nevertheless, this decree was never respected by the *qāʾids* and pashas. An energetic protest was then made by the consul general of the United States and other powers intervened on behalf of the Jews. France reinforced the system of consular protection and the other nations followed in her wake.

During the reign of Mulay al-Ḥasan and at the beginning of that of Mulay Abd al-Aziz (1894–1908), the Jews lived in tranquility. Mulay al-Ḥasan held a positive attitude toward his Jewish subjects, receiving their deepest respect in return. Upon the death of the sultan, the chamberlain (vizier) Ba Ahmad treated the Jews with justice and fairness. During the 19th century Moroccan Jewry, whose number has been variously evaluated as being between 200,000 and 400,000, produced many renowned rabbis, poets, and talmudists, as well as a number of legal authorities whose works continued to serve as the basis for the justice dispensed by Jewish tribunals under the French Protectorate. These scholars included: R. Abraham *Coriat and R. Masʿūd Knafo of Mogador, R. Masʿūd Ben-Moha and R. Mordecai Serfaty of Marrakesh, R. Joseph *Elmaleh of Rabat, R. Raphael Encaoua of Salé, R. Vidal Serfaty of Fez, R. Isaac Ben-Walīd of Tetuán and R. Mordecai Bengio of Tangier. Many of these leaders realized the importance of secular studies for the masses and they assisted the *Alliance Israélite Universelle of Paris in founding its first schools in Tetuán in 1862, in Tangier in 1865, in Mogador in 1867, and in other Moroccan towns from 1874. In contrast, other rabbis violently opposed the establishment of these schools, which they foresaw would encourage an estrangement from Judaism.

Upon the death of Ba Ahmad (1900), an epidemic of plague ravaged Morocco. In the mellah of Fez alone, there were more than 3,000 victims; the country then entered a period of anarchy during which the Jewish population suffered greatly. During the entire second half of the 19th century, thousands of impoverished Jews swelled the Jewish populations of the large urban centers. The overcrowding of the Jewish quarters became indescribable. This exodus went on uninterruptedly into the 20th century. *Casablanca, which underwent a tremendous expansion, was its final halting place. The misery which prevailed in the Jewish quarters and which was partly due to the inability of the ex-villagers to adapt to urban life, became one of the social stains of Morocco. Jewish economic activity reminiscent of years past was considerably curtailed, also, because of the creation of the French Protectorate in 1912 which brought competition from French firms and large banks (and later from other West European and American ones). But at the same time a new bourgeoisie of middle-class merchants, professionals and white-collar workers began to flourish.

In 1912 Morocco was divided into two colonial zones and protectorates: French Morocco that encompassed central Morocco, the key inland cities and towns, the Atlas Mountains to the south, and the Atlantic coastal areas; and Spanish Morocco (in the north and the Rif Mountains). In December 1923, Tangier in the north became an international zone. The establishment of the French Protectorate in March 1912 was marked in Fez by a pogrom which claimed over 100 victims (April 18–19, 1912). However, there were no incidents in the zone assigned to Spain or in Tangier, which was declared an international town. Under the French and Spanish domination, the Jews enjoyed complete freedom in all matters pertaining to their traditions, religion, occupations and movement. France and Spain did not interfere with the status of the Jews of Morocco, who remained subject to the sultan's protection – this proved to be advantageous for them when the anti-Jewish laws were latter issued by the *Vichy government. In a *dahir* of May 22, 1918, the French authorities contented themselves with granting official status to the existing organization of the Jewish communities, with a few modifications. These changes were more particularly emphasized by the *dahir* of 1931. During the 19th century, a council of notables appointed by the population was responsible for the administration of the community. A *gizbar* ("treasurer"), who was elected by the leading personalities of the town, was co-opted to the council. The council and the *gizbar* were responsible for the nomination of the rabbis-judges (*dayyanim*). After 1912, the nation which assured the protectorate, i.e., France, claimed for itself, directly or indirectly, most of the prerogatives emanating from this organization and more particularly the tutelage of the community committees, which then became mere benevolent institutions. These committees, the number of whose members varied with the numerical importance of the community, as well as their presidents, were appointed by the grand vizier, who in practice was dependent on the protectorate authorities. Moreover, the committees were supervised by a Jewish official of the government, who was chosen because of his devotion to French interests. By the maintenance of such a strict control over the Jewish elements of the country, the protectorate authorities revealed their distrust. Few Jews, however, were politically hostile toward France. It was the task of the community committees to bring relief to the numerous Jews living in miserable conditions. Their budget continued to be raised from the income derived from the sale of *kasher* wine and meat, the revenues from charitable trusts (*hekdesh*) which they administered, and the often generous contributions of the upper classes and Jews from overseas. The authorities did not grant them any subsidies.

With the exception of Tangier, where there were special circumstances, and a few other rare cases, the old Jewish upper class kept its distance from these community committees. They were constituted of new elements which came from a middle class that until then had been practically nonexistent in Morocco. The members of these committees were generally all loyal to the French authorities. The children of the long-time upper class were usually sent to the French primary or secondary schools. Their religious instruction was entrusted to private teachers. Living within a traditional environment which had withstood many a trial, they were sheltered from religious estrangement and unreserved assimilation. The westernization of the new class, which was accomplished by the Alliance Israélite Universelle, did not alienate this stratum from Jewish traditions and values. Their potential complete integration among the colonizers, however, was thwarted by the antisemitism of the middle-class Frenchmen of North Africa. A large number of Jews of this new social class amassed considerable wealth as a result of the accelerated development of the country. This new middle class formed an important section of the larger, as well as the smaller, communities. Moroccan Jewry was consequently transformed. Some Jews took up higher studies in Morocco itself or in French universities. At the same time, however, the French refused requests by educated Jews to grant them French citizenship and thus release them completely from Moroccan judicial jurisdiction. Unlike Algeria where the Jews were granted French citizenship collectively in the spirit of the Crémieux Decree of October 24, 1870, or Tunisian Jewry who were offered the same status on a more selective basis in the context of the 1923 Morinaud Law, the

Moroccan counterparts were denied this privilege. The French protectorate authorities, like the Spanish zone administration, did not wish to alienate Moroccan Muslims over this sensitive issue; they were equally concerned about the reactions of the European settlers who regarded the bestowal of any significant privilege on the Jews as a threat to their own status.

From 1912 Morocco attracted a large number of Jews from Algeria and Tunisia. Others arrived from Middle Eastern countries and Europe. In 1939 the Jewish population of Morocco, including foreign Jews, was estimated at 225,000. Until then, political Zionism had won only a few adherents in Morocco. Zionism, however, was often discussed in youth movements and organizations and regular lectures on the subject were given in Jewish circles. The philanthropist Raphael Benozérof was most active in the Zionist movement in Morocco, spreading its ideas among both the masses and the elite of the Jewish community. A periodical, *L'Avenir Illustré*, which was published in Casablanca from 1926, regarded itself as the organ of Moroccan Jewry, as well as the standard-bearer of Zionism. It actually became the unofficial voice of the Moroccan Zionist Federation that was then subordinate to the Zionist Federation of France and aroused the opposition of those who stood for the evolution of Moroccan Jewry and its assimilation into French culture. The French authorities, too, were unhappy with the orientation of the periodical. From 1932 elements opposing the Zionists published *L'Union Marocaine*. In 1939 World War II interrupted the publication of these two Jewish organs. Although Zionism gained momentum in the mid-1940s through the action of emissaries from Ereẓ Israel who came in contact with local Jews and helped them establish halutzic movements affiliated with Ha-Shomer ha-Ẓa'ir, Bnei Akiva, Dror, Habonim, Gordonia and Betar, while Zionist parties became part of the Moroccan Zionist associations and the federation (Mapai, Po'alei Ẓion, Ha-Po'el ha-Mizrachi, General Zionists and Ḥerut) starting in the late 1940s, Zionist activity between the two world wars still carried some symbolic weight.

[David Corcos / Michael M. Laskier (2nd ed.)]

Modern antisemitic tendencies, though prevalent among the European settlers, were practically nonexistent among Moroccan Muslims before the 1930s. The situation changed after 1933, when German and Italian fascist propaganda became widespread. European antisemitic elements in Morocco seized upon the Palestinian Arab Revolt of 1936–39. They presented "international Jewry" negatively before Muslims whose solidarity with the Palestinian Arabs was unquestioned. Furthermore, Moroccan nationalists were then unhappy with local Jewry's lack of enthusiasm for their cause. Some nationalists were moderates, but others identified with aspects of European fascism. Muslim-Jewish tensions emerged in several inland French Moroccan cities as a result of this atmosphere. In the Spanish zone anti-Jewish nationalist declarations disturbed Jews. When the secretary of the grand mufti of Jerusalem, Haj Amin al-Husseini, visited the zone in July 1939 to raise money, nationalists held conferences where they yelled, "Death to the Jews" and "Death to the British." The Spaniards did nothing to contain the unrest. Yet the outbreak of the Spanish Civil War in 1936 prompted the Spaniards to restrain pro-fascist youth gangs which harassed Jews.

The outbreak of World War II in 1939, the German occupation of France in 1940, and the establishment of the Vichy government rendered the Jews of French Morocco powerless. On October 3, 1940, the Vichy government enacted its first anti-Jewish law in France. Article 9 concerning the status of the Jews was introduced in the French zone by the Sultanic Decree (*zahir*) of October 31, 1940. It applied to all Jews by "race," which was defined as three Jewish grandparents, as well as all members of the Jewish faith. The law expressly authorized the exercise of rabbinic jurisdiction and allowed Jews to continue teaching at institutions intended solely for Jews. The Vichy Law of June 2, 1941, increased the hardships inflicted by the law of October 1940. It was implemented by the zahirs of August 5, 1941, which were issued separately for Moroccan Jews and the European Jews living in the zone. The decrees which followed were designed to deprive Jews from working in a wide array of professions, including real estate, moneylending, banking, non-Jewish journalism, and radio broadcasting. Jews were allowed to engage in crafts and wholesale trading. At the same time Vichy policy allowed only 2 percent of the total number of lawyers and physicians to be Jews. The Vichy Law of July 22, 1941 concerning the "Aryanization" of the economy was implemented in Algeria but was not introduced into French Morocco. In education, the policy of limiting the number of Jews in the protectorate's schools to 10 percent was enforced harshly though perhaps not completely. The French continued to subsidize the AIU schools because they did not wish to see Jewish children developing an aversion to French culture. Foreign Jews who sought sanctuary in Morocco were placed in labor or concentration camps, together with "undesirable" elements. Immediately after the U.S. landings, the Rabbi Eliahu Synagogue in Casablanca was desecrated and pogroms broke out all over the country. The landing of the allied forces in French Morocco on November 8, 1942, and its liberation did not result in the immediate obliteration of Vichy influence. This occurred only in the summer of 1943 when French Gen. Charles de Gaulle's supporters replaced the pro-Vichy elements.

While it is premature to assess the extent of the implementation of Vichy laws in French Morocco, not a single discriminatory law was issued against the Jews in the Spanish zone after Gen. Francisco Franco came to power in Spain. Spanish and local government officials foiled the efforts of German agents in the zone to foment anti-Jewish feelings. Jews in the International Zone of Tangier, however, faced certain problems related to immigration. During 1942–43 Tangier had 1,500 to 2,000 Jewish refugees, many of whom had arrived before the war. Approximately half were Sephardim originating from the Dodecanese Islands (then under fascist Italian occupation); some had left Rhodes for Italy and France even before Italy introduced anti-Jewish laws in 1938.

The Central Europeans had come mainly from Hungary and Poland via Italy. As long as Tangier remained an international zone, refugees were admitted without difficulty. After the fall of France and Spain's temporary occupation of Tangier, these people were deprived of various rights, including work. The indigenous Jewish elites of Tangier were far better off than their counterparts in French Morocco before and during the Spanish occupation. The small businessmen and lower middle class, however, were heavily taxed and they could not renew their import-export licenses. Politically, the Spanish occupiers dissolved the zone's legislative assembly, while the zahir of February 15, 1925, legalizing the Jewish community council, was abrogated. All community activity came under Spanish supervision. The Jewish community lost the subsidies that the government had hitherto allocated generously, as well as the right to elect a slate of community leaders from which the Spaniards would select appointees. All these restrictions were lifted with Spain's withdrawal in 1945 and the restoration of the international zone.

[Michael M. Laskier (2nd ed.)]

In 1948 about 238,000 Jews lived in French Morocco, 15,000 in Spanish Morocco, and 12,000 in the international zone of Tangier. The 1951 census in French Morocco indicated 199,156 Jews and, together with the Jewish population of Spanish Morocco, the total number of Moroccan Jews reached then about 222,000. The first census conducted in united Morocco in 1960 recorded 159,806 Jews, while in 1962 an estimated 130,000 Jews lived in the whole of Morocco, decreasing to 85,000 in 1964 and about 42,000 in 1968. The two censuses of 1951 and 1960 give valuable evidence of the demography of the Jewish population in Morocco. In 1951 over a third of the Jews lived in small towns and villages, but in 1961, as a result of the mass exodus to Israel, only about a quarter of them still lived there. The continued *aliyah* after 1960 reduced this number even further, so that the majority of Jews in the country in the late 1960s were concentrated in the major cities. Census data show that among the emigrants there were more young people than old; this is confirmed by the census conducted in Israel in 1961.

The dispersal of Moroccan Jews throughout scores of towns, townlets, and villages, which sometimes contained only a few dozen families, made it difficult to provide Jewish *education for all who wanted it, and up to the time of the mass exodus there were places in which there were no Jewish educational institutions. This is one of the reasons for the high percentage of illiteracy among Moroccan Jewry, even in 1960. In a sample of 2% of the overall Jewish population aged five and over, taken in Morocco in 1960, 43.2% were illiterate (i.e., could not read Arabic or French, for those who knew only Hebrew letters were counted as illiterate). However, the 10–14 age group had an illiteracy rate of only 18.1%, whereas the age group 60 years and older had a rate of 76.3%. The 52 schools of the Alliance Israélite Universelle had 21,823 pupils in 1948, and in 1956 28,702 pupils attended its 82 institutions. The number of its pupils subsequently dropped to 9,000 in 1965, of whom about 1,000 were non-Jewish. In October 1960, the Moroccan government nationalized a fourth of the schools run by the Alliance Israélite Universelle, turning them into government schools, to which hundreds of non-Jewish pupils enrolled. Apart from the Alliance Israélite Universelle institutions, there were also schools run by Oẓar ha-Torah, Em ha-Banim, and, from 1950, by the Lubavitcher ḥasidic movement. *Talmud Torah* schools and *ḥadarim* continued to exist, despite the fact that the opening of new *ḥadarim* was forbidden in 1953. The lack of a sufficient number of schools, along with the emigration of many educated Jews to France, resulted in a low number of university graduates in Morocco. In 1954 there were only 239 Jewish university students, of whom 151 had studied abroad. According to government statistics in 1964, of the 75,000 Jews who remained in the country there were only 60 physicians, 15 dentists, 50 pharmacists, and 44 lawyers. However, in proportion to the Muslim population, the Jews were better educated, for in that year the whole country contained only 232 lawyers.

Despite the fact that a few wealthy Jews lived in Morocco, most Moroccan Jews were considered to be poor. Many of them were peddlers or artisans or lived on social assistance. Since Jews lived in poverty and poor sanitary conditions in crowded homes of the mellah, where eight to ten people sometimes dwelt in one room, many Moroccan Jews suffered from diseases, especially trachoma. In fact, among the pupils attending Alliance Israélite Universelle institutions in Casablanca 30% suffered from trachoma, and the Alliance Israélite Universelle had to open a special school for them. This was also one of the reasons for the Israel government's adoption of a policy of health selectivity toward Moroccan immigrants. The Jewish Agency for Israel and *OSE worked in cooperation with many local doctors to treat Moroccan Jews before entry to Israel.

In the mid-20th century the legal status of Moroccan Jewry improved. With the exception of a few Casablanca Jews, they did not have the right to vote in local elections. Disputes between Jews and non-Jews had to be settled in Muslim courts, which judged according to Muslim religious and secular law. Jews were not allowed to elect their own representatives on the Jewish community councils, the members being appointed by the authorities. After the independence of Israel (1948), the Jews in Morocco, as in the East, suffered from severe attacks by the population. On June 7, 1948, 43 Jews were murdered and 155 injured at Jérada (Djérada) and Oujda, after nationalists incited the population. However, the government brought scores of guilty to trial, sentencing two of them to death and others to imprisonment. Beginning in August 1953, anti-colonial manifestations in French Morocco became widespread following the exile of the pro-nationalist Sultan Sidi Muhammad ben Yusuf to Madagascar. One year later and then again in 1955, pro-nationalist forces attacked Jews in Casablanca, Rabat, Mazagan and Petitjean. A number of Jews were murdered. Much Jewish property was looted in various places throughout the country; the Alliance Israélite

Universelle schools at Boujad, Mazagan and elsewhere were set on fire. Emigration subsequently increased. While between 1948 and 1953 about 30,000 Jews went to Israel, emigration figures in 1954–55 rose to 37,000 and in 1956, on the eve of Moroccan independence, to 36,301. Jews may have reached Israel in greater numbers at the time had the State of Israel and the Jewish Agency refrained from enforcing social and medical selection policies which deprived numerous elderly, sick, and economically disadvantaged elements from leaving Morocco. The Jews, however, feared that in an independent post-colonial Morocco their situation would worsen.

However, when Sultan Muhammad ben Yusuf (King Muhammad v since 1957) returned from exile in November 1955 and Morocco gained its independence in March 1956, the situation of the Jews improved temporarily. For the first time in their history, they were to enjoy greater equality with Muslims. A Jewish leader, Dr. Leon *Ben Zaqen, was appointed minister of posts in the first independent government. Other Jews began to gain important positions in the government administration as officials and in courts of law as judges. Jews were also appointed to the advisory council, the first being David Benazareff, shortly after his appointment to the presidency of the Casablanca community council. But on May 13, 1956, an order was issued forbidding Jews to leave for Israel. Then in June 1956 the offices of the Cadima organization – the name under which the Jewish Agency's Immigration Department functioned inside Morocco since 1949 – were closed. The Israeli *aliyah* emissaries, as well as envoys of other Jewish Agency departments dealing with Youth Aliyah, Zionist education and youth movements, were then compelled to leave the country. After long negotiations with the representative of the World Jewish Congress, the government permitted the emigration of the 6,325 Jews in the Mazagan camp who were ready to leave for Israel. At the same time, the Jewish Agency succeeded through channels and the bribing of senior Moroccan officials in smuggling several thousand additional Jews to Israel via Casablanca harbor and a "special route" through Tangier. However, vigilance on the Moroccan frontiers increased in 1957, after pressure from the opposition parties, and obstacles began to be placed in the way of those Jews requesting permission to travel legally for a short visit abroad, if it was suspected that their final destination was Israel. From that time on they had to show proof that they were able to support themselves abroad. Afterwards (1958–59), a number of Jews were tried and sentenced for smuggling their currency, or even for possessing an obsolete calendar issued by the Jewish National Fund. In 1958 when a new government was formed, Ben Zaqen was not included, and a number of Jewish officials were dismissed. In 1959 all Zionist activity was forbidden in Morocco and many Jewish organizations were forced to close their doors. That year, swastikas were daubed in Casablanca and Rabat. In September of that year Morocco severed postal ties with Israel, ties that were renewed only in 1994. All these measures were part and parcel of a Moroccan policy of avoiding conflicts with Egypt and Middle Eastern states in war with Israel. The Egyptians were quick to accuse the Maghrebi states of permitting Zionist activity and *aliyah*, which according to their argument, only strengthened the Jewish State. Moreover, Morocco did not desire to lose Jewish nationals as this could have been detrimental to the Moroccan economy.

As a result of this situation and despite the illegal exit, about 25,000 Jews went from Morocco illegally to Israel between 1956 and 1961. The groundwork for the illegal activity was laid in 1955, when Israel, fearing that Moroccan independence was imminent, formed a Zionist underground. The Mossad, Israel's secret service agency, created the Misgeret (Framework), which organized self-defense training for all of the Maghreb. Misgeret's operational headquarters were in Paris; Casablanca became its center in Morocco. Misgeret's Israeli emissaries arrived in the Maghreb between August 1955 and early 1956. In Algeria and Tunisia they engaged mostly in self-defense training but in Morocco they had five units in the urban centers: Gonen (self-defense), Ballet (recruiters of activists), Oref Ẓibburi (the channel for communicating with leaders of the Jewish community councils), Modi'in (intelligence gathering for missions), and Makhelah (illegal *aliyah*). The need to organize illegal immigration and to create the Makhelah unit stemmed from the Moroccan decision to dissolve Cadima; the Mossad understood that the Jewish Agency had erred in not evacuating more Jews when the opportunity existed under colonial rule. Between the end of 1956 and mid-1961 Misgeret smuggled out many of the 25,000 Jews who left Morocco, using various land and sea routes. Many Misgeret operations were successful because of services rendered by Spanish and Moroccan smugglers, who assisted Misgeret in evacuating Jews without travel documents. The underground falsified passports, bribed Moroccan officials in seaports, and enlisted the help of the authorities in the Spanish enclaves of Ceuta and Melilla, the British in Gibraltar, and the French who still controlled Algeria. The Moroccan government failed to destroy the underground, although many activists were arrested.

In January 1961, on the occasion of Egyptian President Gamal Abdel *Nasser's visit to Casablanca, Jews were beaten up and jailed. Several days later the *Egoz*, one of the Misgeret's smuggling ships, foundered at sea, and 42 Jewish immigrants drowned. The repercussions of these events prompted local Jewish leaders, Israel, and international Jewish organizations to pressure Morocco to liberalize immigration. King Muhammad v promised to tolerate immigration and instructed his minister of the interior to grant passports to all Jews who wanted to leave. But the king died in February 1961 and was succeeded by King Hassan II; these events prevented the policy from being implemented immediately. The intercession of two influential Jews close to the palace enabled Israel to enter into discreet negotiations with the Moroccans through a series of meetings held in Europe; the result of the negotiations between the Misgeret's top envoy in Morocco and a representative of King Hassan II was a plan. HIAS (Hebrew Immigrant Aid Society) would open offices in Morocco and, under its auspices, Israel could organize more semi-legal departures;

Morocco would then receive "indemnities" for the loss of the Jews. Known as "Operation Yakhin," between November 1961 and spring 1964 more than 90,000 Jews left for Israel by chartered planes and ships from Casablanca and Tangier via France and Italy. The secret negotiations leading to Yakhin also paved the way for Moroccan-Israeli negotiations over behind-the-scenes cooperation in intelligence and defense endeavors which yielded benefits in subsequent decades.

Until 1961, when the Moroccan authorities tightened restrictions on immigration, the remaining Jewish elite still held some privileges. In fact, the post-1956 elites were divided into three currents. The first, influenced by French and European schooling, emphasized the central importance of European culture. In general, the members of this group were not attracted to Zionism, and they eventually settled in France. The second group included those who, despite the education they had received at the Alliance Israélite Universelle schools, were still influenced by Zionism. The third group, which favored a Judeo-Muslim entente, emerged during the mid- and late 1950s and was by no means homogeneous. This group included about 400 activists with strong leftist tendencies and about 500 communists, as well as moderate leftists and conservatives. Several activists in the third group advocated Jewish-Muslim integration with Jews frequenting the same clubs as Muslims and attending the same schools, in order to bridge the political and intellectual gap between the two peoples. Others were more cautious, arguing that rapprochement should not compel Moroccan Jews to sever their ties with Israel or to embrace Arabic language and literature at the expense of French culture. To achieve national unity and engender reforms within the Jewish communities, the leftist integrationists affiliated with the Istiqlal party, and in 1956 the Union Marocaine de Travail, the Moroccan labor union, founded a pro-entente movement known as al-Wifāq (Agreement). During the late 1950s, leaders sharing their political orientation gained some prominence within the community councils, although eventually they either moderated their stance and remained in positions of authority or more moderate elements prevailed.

When Morocco gained its independence, a royal decree of January 1956 abolished rabbinical courts and turned them into state courts of law, with the exception of the Supreme Rabbinical Tribune in Rabat, which was abolished by government order in 1965. From 1945 the rabbinical court was headed by Chief Rabbi Saul D. ibn Danān, who went to Israel in 1966. From 1965, the other members of the rabbinical court were appointed judges in state courts. Jews who remained in Morocco were subject to military service.

Emigration continued to both Israel and other destinations. *Aliyah* reached a low point in the years 1965–67, but picked up its pace after the June 1967 war. Between 1967 and 1970 as many as 4,000 Jews left for Israel annually. Israel ceased to be attractive for most Moroccan Jewish immigrants afterwards. Those who left Morocco in the 1960s included wealthy and educated Jews, not only the lower socioeconomic stratum. In 1970, some 35,000 Jews were living in Morocco. Of those who had emigrated a considerable number, mainly the wealthy and more highly educated, settled in France and Canada. Among the immigrants were lawyers, engineers, and doctors who were marginalized in their place of work in favor of Muslims. The mass exodus caused the closing of most Jewish institutions, yeshivot, schools and many synagogues. The community in the 1960s lacked rabbis, *dayyanim* and even readers of the Law in synagogue. The charitable organizations that functioned throughout Morocco were liquidated; Jewish newspapers were closed. One of these, *La Voix des Communautés*, was an official communal organ. During this period anti-Jewish propaganda increased, organized mainly by the Istiqlāl Party, led by ʿAllāl al-Fasi, who at the time also served as minister of Islamic affairs. The party journal, *L'Opinion*, and the rest of the Moroccan press, with the exception of newspapers supported by the government party, published much incendiary material against Jews, and in 1965 the *al-Istiqlāl* newspaper published extracts from the *Protocols of the Elders of Zion*. During and after the June 1967 war, the Istiqlāl party encouraged Muslims to enforce an economic boycott of the Jews, but King Hassan adopted a firm policy so that Jews were not seriously harmed, and the economic boycott was implemented only partially.

In the 1970s, with a Jewish population of some 20,000 (1975), two-thirds of whom were concentrated in Casablanca and the remainder in Rabat, Marrakesh, Tangiers and Fez, Morocco had the largest organized Jewish community of any Arab country. But Moroccan Jewry was indeed moving slowly toward its self-liquidation. The school population was perhaps the best yardstick. Jewish day schools saw their enrollment drop by about 15 percent between October 1972 and October 1973, and they have noted subsequent drops of about 5 percent every year since. Yet the Arab-Israeli War of 1973 and later Middle East conflicts did not result in the end of Morocco's Jewish communities. Those who remained weathered the crises and expressed confidence in the monarchy's ability to safeguard their well-being. Despite the tolerant attitude of the authorities toward the Jews, difficulties were still placed in their way in respect to national organization or attempts to establish contact with Jewish organizations abroad, apart from philanthropic or religious organizations such as the American Jewish Joint Distribution Committee, the Alliance Israélite Universelle and the Lubavitch Ḥasidim.

Several communities of Jews delayed their complete departure in the 1970s through the 1990s, partly because they owned large pieces of communal property valued at many millions of dollars. These properties were registered with the Ministry of the Interior and could not be sold without the ministry's permission, while the proceeds of the sales had to be kept in cash in a bank or reinvested in other property. In the mid- and late 1990s, 6,000 Jews remained in Morocco. Influential Jewish leaders – among them Robert Assaraf, a noted entrepreneur and one of the most affluent Jews in Morocco, and Serge Berdugo, who served as a minister of tourism in the 1990s – have wielded influence, playing a cardinal role in politics. Their intimate ties to both the monarchy and opposition parties enabled them to promote diverse Moroccan-Israeli connections. While Berdugo was minister of tourism, Israeli-Moroccan tourist exchange gained considerable momentum. This came in the wake of the Israeli-Palestinian Oslo Accord of 1993 that led to the establishment of liaison offices in Rabat and Tel Aviv. The primary purpose of the liaison apparatus was to promote even greater tourist activity, particularly from Israel to Morocco. In October 1994 André Azoulay, a Jewish economist and one of King Hassan's confidants, was the driving force behind the first Middle East Economic Summit in Casablanca. The intermediary role played by the king in bringing Israel and the Arab states closer together, leading to the Egyptian-Israeli peace initiative back in 1977, also contributed to Muslim-Jewish coexistence at home.

After King Hassan's death on July 23, 1999, his son, Muhammad VI, ascended to the throne. In sharp contrast to his father's aspirations of involving Morocco in regional and international politics, Muhammad VI seemed – in the first years of his royal tenure, at least – to concentrate on domestic social reforms, greater equality for women, and democratizing the nation's political institutions. Thus far he has also demonstrated a belief in peaceful Muslim-Jewish coexistence. He retained Azoulay as the monarchy's chief adviser and facilitated the return from France of Abraham Sarfati, the exiled communist activist, whom the king appointed as his chief expert on sources of energy. The terrorist acts of the Moroccan al-Qai'da-affiliated Salafiyya Jihadiyya Islamist radical group in Casablanca (May 16, 2003) claimed many lives and also caused damage to Jewish institutions. This and other acts by Islamists may well hasten the departure of younger Moroccan Jews who will be followed to the West by their parents. Nevertheless, the king vowed to punish the perpetrators while the Moroccan press unanimously condemned the act. The latter argued that Morocco had always been a haven for Muslims and Jews, and no extremist forces would be allowed to sabotage the good relations between the two religions. Simultaneously, the outbreak of the second Palestinian uprising in 2000 compelled Morocco to shut down its liaison office in Tel Aviv and ask Israel to recall its representative from Rabat – a move that is seen as a temporary break in ties.

In 2005, some 3,000 Jews live in Casablanca and there were smaller communities in Rabat, Marrakesh, Meknès, Tangier, Fez and Tetuan. The major Jewish organization is the Conseil des Communautés Israélites in Casablanca. The welfare organization in Casablanca is responsible for medical aid to the needy and hot meals for underprivileged Jewish students. Most of the community are of the upper middle class and enjoy a comfortable economic position. Most Jewish schools are closed and only those in Casablanca – under the auspices of the Alliance Israélite Universelle, Ort, Chabad and Oẓar ha-Torah – remain active. Interestingly, the number of kosher restaurants in tourism-oriented cities is on the rise. The community has initiated historical research toward creating a Jewish museum documenting the Jewish presence in Morocco and has established a foundation for the Jewish Moroccan cultural heritage. In cooperation with UNESCO, the restoration of old synagogues has commenced.

[Hayyim J. Cohen / Michael M. Laskier (2nd ed.)]

Moroccan Jewish and Modern Education in the 20th Century: A Success Story

The history of the educational system represents the stabilization of a Jewish society under French rule that had preserved traditional values over a long period of time and now had to accommodate itself to new times and forms. Moreover, the importance of education grew because it served as a base for social mobility, particularly the growth of new elites: community leaders, merchants, officials and professionals achieved their positions through modern Western education. Some of them managed to combine education of this kind with values stemming from the Jewish heritage as it crystallized in Morocco.

Until the middle of the 19th century, public education was the responsibility of the Jewish community. In many places, no special buildings were set aside for the *Talmud Torah*, and elementary schools and often yeshivah studies as well were conducted in synagogues, this being the origin of the name *slla* ("synagogue" in Moroccan Arabic) as used for schools. The *sllas* were run by local teachers. The aim of elementary schooling in Jewish traditional education was to teach the child to read and write and prepare him to take part in the life of the synagogue. The yeshivot, which were post-elementary schools, were intended mainly for youngsters from rabbinical families. The status of the rabbi-teachers was shaky; they lived in dire economic straits, and were forced to take other jobs, as *ḥazzanim, shoḥatim*, etc., or abandon teaching when they found more remunerative occupations. Jewish girls generally remained ignorant, aside from what they learned from their mothers, which mainly concerned practical Jewish matters like *kashrut*, family purity, and the like.

From the beginning of reform in traditional education, Jewish institutions outside Morocco were involved – the Alliance Israélite Universelle and American institutions. The first school of the Alliance was founded in Tetuan in 1862. In conformity with its philanthropic-intellectual leanings, its institutions aimed at providing a secular education in French and in this way at achieving the Emancipation as understood by Western Jews, namely to abrogate the status of Jews as a tolerated minority and prepare them to take their place as useful citizens employed as craftsmen, merchants, and officials.

From the outset of Alliance activity, a major problem was the absence of teaching staff familiar with the new trends and a suitable pedagogic background. At first, out of political considerations, the Alliance, wishing to coexist with the communities and expand its activities, did employ teachers who had studied in traditional schools to teach Jewish subjects. But out of fear that the schools would become old-fashioned, the Alliance teachers, most of whom came from Alsace and different parts of the *Ottoman Empire, tried to get these other teachers dismissed. Filled with the zeal of pioneers in pursuit of their aims, the Alliance director and teachers entrenched themselves in the communities, particularly from around 1900 on. Not only did they assert their authority in educational matters but often settled disputes within the community and served as go-betweens for the community and the European consuls with the aim of protecting the Jews from the Muslims. In addition, once they had consolidated their position, they came out against *slla* education and its outdated methods. In the period from the mid-19th century to the early 1920s there were rabbis, mainly representing communities in the interior of the country less exposed to European influences, who regarded the Alliance schools as "centers of heresy." These rabbis clung to a policy of keeping their youngsters out of these schools so long as they had not completed their traditional educations. As a result many young people did not go to these schools.

The Alliance personnel at this time were not conciliatory. Nurtured on secular Western education in the rabbinical seminary of Paris, they lacked sensitivity to the values of Moroccan Jewry and their traditions. They sought to underscore the gap between the enlightened world and the tradition and experience of the parental generation and the *slla* schools, which they termed "centers of reaction." In fact their depiction of the *Talmud Torah* schools as lacking any value was an oversimplification. One of the problems that cropped up in the 1924–45 period in Alliance educational activities derived from its negative attitude to Jewish nationalism in the Land of Israel and to Hebrew as a living language. Other organizations took advantage of its difficulties to step in and operate in Morocco. First the Em ha-Banim *Talmud Torah* network, which had started operating through the efforts of Rabbi Zar Halperin, an East European Zionist who was in Morocco from 1914 to 1922, flourished. By 1935, it had important schools in the interior of the country, mainly in Fez, Sefrou, Meknès, and Marrakesh.

The stepped-up activities of the World Zionist Organization in the 1920s also constituted a challenge to the Alliance. At first the WZO tried to found societies for the renewal of Hebrew culture and language and to collect money for the development of Ereẓ Israel. Later it became a focus of local Zionist pressure exercised against the Alliance not only in the name of pedagogic advancement and the creation of new educational structures but also to adapt education to the needs of Zionism. The Alliance's problems did not only stem from its universalist ideology; it also had practical causes. The organization had received considerable financial support from the French government, a fact which the French used to put pressure on it to give priority to French and general studies over Hebrew and Jewish education. This pressure had a positive effect, as many parents wanted their children to receive an education that would prepare them for jobs in the modern bureaucracy of the Protectorate or in banks and business firms. However, they were uneasy about the cutback in Jewish studies. The arrangement also made life difficult for the pupils. They, as well as those who had studied first in a *slla* and then in an Alliance school, reached the fourth grade of elementary school at the age of 17.

The only way the Alliance could reconcile various circles by teaching Jewish subjects while instituting teaching reforms was by training a special staff of teachers. An attempt in this direction was made by supporting a local initiative on the part of the Torah and Ḥayyim Society of Tangier to set up a teachers' seminar. Teachers from within the community taught Jewish subjects while general subjects were taught by teachers from the French schools in the city and the Alliance faculty. Another change was in the encouragement given by the Alliance chief representative in Morocco, Yom Tov Sémach, to the teaching of modern, spoken Hebrew. Though not an adherent of political Zionism, but rather the opposite, Sémach argued that the teaching of living Hebrew was an expression of Jewish solidarity, the first and foremost means of communication in the Jewish world and part of the renascence of Jewish culture. The Alliance administration in Paris also did not heed the advice of the Tangier seminar's director to bring over teachers from Ereẓ Israel who had studied at the teacher training institute in Paris. Out of fear of the nationalistic reactions of Morocco's Arabs and the possibility that such a step would be interpreted as pro-Zionist, Hebrew studies were not allowed at the institute. But the pressure exerted by rabbis and parents did not abate. The parents sought a balanced curriculum in Alliance schools, with more Jewish studies than in the past.

The period after World War II, from 1946 until the 1960s, represented a major turning point in Jewish education in Morocco. The Zionist Organization contributed to the process by accelerating the acclimatization to modern Jewish thought and education in Jewish institutes. Another factor, after 1948, was the growing importance of aspects of Hebrew as a language representing the link between Moroccan Jewry and the State of Israel. Moreover, with increasing financial assistance from the Jews of America and Europe, the Alliance began to develop Jewish programs of study that were not totally subordinate to the French colonial administration in Morocco despite continued French aid to expand secular education.

Another factor contributing to the change was the disappointment of the Alliance leaders, who underwent bitter experiences during the war and witnessed the tragic failure of the ideology of "emancipation through assimilation" (which rather than being met with enthusiasm by colonial society provoked antisemitic propaganda). And indeed, from 1946 on, though the Alliance did not cooperate with the emissaries of the Jewish Agency, it did cooperate with influential local Zionists. An excellent example of this is the establishment of the Hebrew teachers seminar in Casablanca in cooperation with the Zionist Magen David Society. In 1956 almost all the teachers who were products of traditional education were replaced by graduates of the seminar. This produced big changes in the Jewish studies in schools, not to mention the fact that such an institute as the Hebrew University agreed to award graduates the "Jerusalem certificate," which exempted them from the University's entrance exam in the Hebrew language. The prestige of the seminar spread through the communities of Morocco and won for it rabbinical support. Graduates of the seminar began teaching in Alliance schools along the Mediterranean Basin and in Iran and, in the course of time, also in Israel, Latin America, Western Europe, and Canada. These graduates also played a part in the Arabization of the schools with the introduction of Arab studies after 1956. They also contributed to the creation of a social and economic elite among the Jews who remained, as the independent Moroccan government was not favorably inclined toward teachers educated in French (even if they were Moroccans). Moreover, while the number of admissions to French high schools before independence was relatively low because of the undeclared quota system, now after independence, admission became easier because of Moroccan policy. At the same time, the Alliance schools, which up to the mid-1950s had provided education up to junior high school only, now became full-fledged high schools. Thus the impetus of social and economic change that had its start in the 1940s and 1950s was not stopped with independence.

The 1946–60 period also represented a turning point in terms of the initiative shown by American Jewry on behalf of the Jews of Morocco in educational affairs. The outstanding American organization was Oẓar Hatorah, a society of Sephardi Jews believing in a combination of Jewish and general education and supported financially mainly by the Joint Distribution Committee. Oẓar Hatorah started operating in the large centers like Rabat and Mogador, and also in small villages in south Morocco. At first, relations between Oẓar Hatorah and the Alliance were tense. The representative and teachers of Oẓar Hatorah in Morocco (as opposed to the directorate in New York) regarded the Alliance teachers as confirmed secularists who had driven away the young Jews of Morocco from the Jewish heritage. But when they saw the Alliance's powerful popular support and the Hebrew teachers seminar was set up in Casablanca, they toned down their criticism. After Morocco received its independence they cooperated in such projects as preparing and printing Hebrew and Jewish texts in the face of Morocco's ban on the import of Hebrew books printed abroad. Not the least important of the Alliance's activities was its campaign to update traditional education. Together with Oẓar Hatorah, it succeeded in persuading a number of community leaders to institute reforms in curricula and methods in the old-fashioned *Talmud Torah* schools in the community. This influence continued to grow until in 1970 the number of students in reformed Jewish studies exceeded the number in Alliance schools: 7,800 compared with 7,100. This renascence of Jewish education made it possible to provide spiritual leaders for the North African communities in Western Europe and Canada. The change was also felt among the rabbis identified with this trend who reached Israel in the 1960s and 1970s. In the last three generations important work has also been done in Morocco by the Chabad educational system. The results of the work done by the Alliance and Oẓar Hatorah were impressive. On the eve of Moroccan independence in 1956 there were 83 Alliance schools with 33,000 students, representing 80% of all Jewish children of school age. The Oẓar Hatorah system had 6,564 students, or 16%, in 32 institutions. It is therefore correct to say that, in the 1940s and 1950s, the Jews of Morocco rapidly entered a new era in their history.

[Michael M. Laskier (2nd ed.)]

BIBLIOGRAPHY: H.Z. Hirschberg, Afrikah; André Chouraqui, *From East to West* (1968); M. Nahon, *Les Israëlites au Maroc* (1909); J.M. Toledano, *Ner ha-Ma'arav* (1911); M.L. Ortega, *Los Hebreos en Marruecos* (1919); M. Eisenbeth, *Les Juifs du Maroc* (1948); G. Vajda, *Un recueil de textes historiques Judéo-Marocains* (1951); I.D. Abbou, *Musulmans Andalous et Judéo-Espagnols* (1953); D. Corcos, *Les Juifs du Maroc et leurs Mellahs* (1971); D. Noy (ed.), *Moroccan Jewish Folk-Tales* (1966); J. Goulven, in: *Hesperis* (1921), 317–36; A. Laredo, *Bérberes y Hebreos en Marruecos* (1954); C. Monteil, in: *Hesperis*, (1951), 265–95; A. Halkin, in: *Joshua Starr Memorial Volume* (1953), 102–10; D. Corcos; *Studies in the History of the Jews of Morocco* (1976); idem, in: *Zion*, 32 (1967), 137–60; S.D. Goitein, *A Mediterranean Society*, 1 (1967), passim; H. de Mendoça, *Jornada de Africa* (1607), passim; H. Bentov, in: *Sefunot*, 10 (1966), 414–95; J. Braithwaite, *History of the Revolutions in the Empire of Morocco* (1729), passim; L. de Chenier, *Present State of the Empire of Morocco*, 2 vols. (1788), passim; S.M. Schiller-Szinessy, *Massa be-Arav, Romanelli's Travels in Morocco* (1886); J.-L. Miège, *Maroc*, passim; N. Leven, *Cinquante ans d'histoire*, 2 vols. (1914–20); D. Bensimon-Donath, *Evolution du judaïsme marocain sous le protectorat français 1912–1956* (1968); S. Romanelli, *Ketavim Nivḥarim, Massa ba-Arav*, H. Schirmann (ed.), (1968); N. Robinson, in: J. Freid (ed.), *Jews in the Modern World*, 1 (1962), 50–90; J.S. Gerber, *Jewish Society in Fez: Studies in Communal and Economic Life*; J.-L. Miège, *Le Maroc et L'Europe, 1830–1894*, 1, 86–98; 2, 560–561; A. Adam, *Casablanca: Essai sur la transformation de la société marocaine au contact de l'occident* (1968), 1, 183–204 (Ch. 3, La Population Israélite). **ADD. BIBLIOGRAPHY:** M.M. Laskier, *The Allliance Israélite Universelle and the Jewish Communities of Morocco: 1862–1962* (1983); idem, *North African Jewry in the Twentieth Century: The Jews of Morocco, Tunisia, and Algeria* (1994); idem, *Yehudei ha-Maghreb be-Ẓel Vichy u-Ẓelav ha-Keres* (1992); idem and E. Bashan, "Morocco," in: R. Spector Simon and M.M. Laskier (eds.), *The Jews of the Middle East and North Africa in Modern Times* (2003), 471–504; D.J. Schroeter, *Merchants of Essaouira: Urban Society and Imperialism in Southwestern Morocco, 1844–1886* (1988); idem, *The Sultan's Jews: Morocco and the Sephardi World* (2002); N.A. Stillman, *Jews of Arab Lands: A History and Source Book* (1979); idem, *The Jews of Arab Lands in Modern Times* (1991); Y. Tsur, *Kehillah Keru'ah: Yehudei Marokko ve-ha-Le'ummiyyut, 1943–1954* (2001); C.R. Pennell, *Morocco since 1830: A History* (2000); M. Orfali and E. Hazan, *Hitḥadeshut u-Massoret: Yeẓirah, Hanhagah ve-Tahalikhei Tarbut be-Yahadut Ẓefon Afrikah*; E. Bashan, *Yahadut Marokko: Avara ve-Tarbuta* (2000); S. Deshen, *The Mellah Society: Jewish Community in Sharifian Morocco* (1990).

[Michael M. Laskier (2nd ed.)]

MOROGOWSKI, JACOB SAMUEL ("Zaydl Rovner"; 1856–1942), *ḥazzan*, composer, and conductor. Born in Radomyshl, Ukraine, Morogowski in his youth worked as a flour merchant, at the same time serving as the "musician" of the Makarov Rabbi Twersky. His fame as a *ḥazzan* began to spread after the rabbi ordered him to officiate in the High Holy Day services of his *bet ha-midrash*. He then officiated as *ḥazzan* for five years in Kiev, where he studied music under the violinist Podhozer, and from 1881 to 1914 he officiated as *ḥazzan* in the communities of Zaslavl, Rovno (hence the name "Zaydl Rovner"), Kishinev (as the successor of Nisan *Belzer), Berdichev (as the successor of Yeruḥam ha-Katan *Blindman), London, and Lemberg, from where he returned to Rovno. In all these posts he was accompanied by a large choir, and for weekday services and festive occasions he also made use of an orchestra. His compositions enthralled his audiences and brought him worldwide fame. In 1914, Morogowski emigrated to the United States, where he remained until his death. He left a rich musical treasury of prayers for *ḥazzan*, choir and orchestra as well as marches. All his works were characterized by a true prayer style, fervent religious feeling, and ḥasidic melody. Hundreds of *ḥazzanim* considered themselves as his disciples. Some of his published compositions are *Halleluyah*, for choir and orchestra (1897); *Kinos* (Heb. text, 1922); *Uhawti*, for choir and orchestra (1899); and *Tisborach* (1874).

BIBLIOGRAPHY: Sendrey, Music, nos. 3530, 5689 – 91; *Di Shul un Khazonim Velt*, 3 (1939); Cantors' Association of the United States and Canada, *Di Geshikhte fun Khazones* (1924), 92; A. Zaludkowski, *Kultur-Treger fun der Idisher Liturgie* (1930), 310; A. Friedmann, *Lebensbilder beruehmter Kantoren*…, 3 (1927), 121; H. Harris, *Toledot ha-Neginah ve-ha-Ḥazzanut be-Yisrael* (1950), 433.

[Joshua Leib Ne'eman]

MOROSINI, GIULIO (Samuel ben David Nahmias; 1612–1683), apostate scholar, and polemicist. He was born in Salonika of a *Marrano family which had reverted to Judaism. His grandfather, Isaac, who had been a Christian in his youth, was referred to as "Paul Teshuvah" after his return to Judaism. When Morosini was a child, his family moved to Venice, where he studied under Leone *Modena. He at first engaged in commerce, traveling throughout the Ottoman Empire, and became converted to Christianity in Venice in 1649, when his family lost its fortune. In 1671 he became a clerk at the Collegium de Propaganda Fide. He completed the work, begun by the apostate Giovanni Battista Jonah, on textual variants in the Targums (Ms. Vat. Urb. 59; Ms. Oxford 2341). Morosini also engaged zealously in missionary activity among Jews, and wrote a work in three parts, *La Via della Fede* (Rome, 1683). In the first part, he attempts to show that it is the duty of the Jews to embrace Christianity. The second part contains important information on contemporary Jewish life and customs both in the home and in the synagogue. In the third part Morosini tries to demonstrate that the Jews do not observe the Ten Commandments, whereas the Christians do. A polemic against this work appears in Joshua *Segre's *Asham Talui*.

BIBLIOGRAPHY: Wolf, Bibliotheca, 3 (1727), 1126f.; G. Bartolocci, *Bibliotheca Magna Rabbinica*, 3 (1683), 755f.; 4 (1693), 404; Neubauer, Cat, 816f. n. 2341; M. Steinschneider, in: *Vessillo Israelitico*, 30 (1882), 372f.; idem, in: MGWJ, 43 (1899), 514f.; Vogelstein-Rieger, 2 (1896), 287; D. Simonsen, in: *Festschrift*… *A. Berliner* (1903), 337–44; C. Roth, in: RMI, 3 (1928), 156f.

[Umberto (Moses David) Cassuto]

MORPURGO, North Italian family of Austrian origin. Its earliest known member was Israel b. Pethahiah *Isserlein (1390–1460), who settled in Marburg, Styria, and became known also as R. Israel Marburg. In 1624 members of the Marburger or Marpurger family were appointed Court *Jews by Emperor Ferdinand II. About the mid-17th century, they were to be found in various parts of Europe, North Africa and the East, but mainly in northern Italy, at Trieste, Ancona, Venice and Padua. Arriving there from Gradisca d'Isonzo (Austria), they eventually changed their name to Morpurgo, and distinguished themselves in various fields. Members include the noted talmudist Samson *Morpurgo and ELIJAH MORPURGO (1740–1830), a Hebraist. GIUSEPPE LAZZARO MORPURGO (1759–1833) was a poet and financier. He wrote verses in Hebrew and Italian, was a supporter of Napoleon and founded the well-known insurance company, Assicurazioni Generali of Trieste. He also presided over the Jewish community there. MOSÉ MORPURGO visited Ereẓ Israel, where he met Ḥayyim Joseph David *Azulai (1764). Also of the family were Rachel *Morpurgo, poet, and EMILIO MORPURGO (1822–1882), who taught economics at Padua University and was undersecretary for agriculture in 1867. ABRAHAM VITA MORPURGO, a publicist from Gorizia, founded the *Corriere Israelitico* in 1867. He made a collection of prayers in Italian for the Jews of Trieste (1855), and translated the *Haggadah* into Italian (1864). Salomone *Morpurgo was a philologist and librarian. ELIO MORPURGO (1858–1943) was born at Udine, of which he was mayor in 1908. He served as undersecretary for posts in 1906 and 1908, and was made a senator for life in 1920. He was deported by the Germans in 1943. BENEDETTO MORPURGO (1861–1944), pathologist, member of the Lincei academy, held the chair of pathology at Turin University from 1900 to 1935. Following the Fascist discriminatory laws of 1938, he took refuge in Argentina, and died in Buenos Aires. GINO MORPURGO translated the Books of Ecclesiastes and Esther into Italian (1898–1904). GIULIO MORPURGO (1865–1931), of Gorizia, taught commercial technology at Trieste University and wrote numerous monographs on commercial subjects. EDGARDO MORPURGO (1866–1942), physician and Jewish historian, wrote *Psicologia e psicopatologia degli Ebrei* (1905); *Le origini del movimento Sionista* (1905); *La Famiglia Morpurgo di Gradisca sull' Isonzo, 1585–1885* (1909). Morpurgo donated to the library of Padua University the collection of Judaica belonging to his family, the *Raccolta Morpurgo di letteratura e storia dei popoli semitici*, whose catalog he published in 1924. LUCIANO MORPURGO (b. 1886), born in Spalato, publisher, wrote *Poesia della famiglia ebraica* (1948). Giuseppe *Morpurgo was an author and educator. VITTORIO MORPURGO (b. 1890), de Janeiro. MARCO MORPURGO (1920–1948) and EDGARDO an architect, designed buildings in Rome, Tirana, and Rio. Two grandsons of the historian Edgardo Morpurgo were Zionist pioneers. Both met their deaths during Israel's War of Independence, the first near Sedeh Eliyahu, and the second near Haifa.

BIBLIOGRAPHY: E. Morpurgo, *La Famiglia Morpurgo di Gradisca sull' Isonzo* (1909); I.M. Molho, in: *Oẓar Yehudei Sefarad*, 9 (1966), 102–3; G. Bedarida, *Ebrei d'Italia* (1950), index; M. Vardi, in: RMI, 15 (1949), 523–8; F. Luzzatto, *ibid.*, 17 (1951), 12–31; M.A. Szulwas, *Roma vi-Yrushalayim* (1944), 176.

[Emmanuel Beeri]

MORPURGO, GIUSEPPE (1887–1967), Italian author and educator. A secondary school teacher, Morpurgo was for some time after 1938 headmaster of the Jewish school in Turin. His writings on school education retain considerable value. He also edited popular literary anthologies, his subjects including Virgil, Petrarch, and Leopardi. His fiction includes the novels *Yom ha-Kippurim* (1925) and *Beati misericordes* (1930). The first deals with the problems of Jews loyal to their religious tradition but fascinated by humanist culture and liberal Western European society, in which they may nevertheless face suffocation. Morpurgo seems to visualize two possible outcomes of this conflict-complete assimilation through mixed marriage arising from a faulty education or emigration to Ereẓ Israel, the land of Jewish regeneration. The author's avowedly Zionist outlook is here quite explicit. In his second novel, Morpurgo examines a Catholic case of conscience, probing spiritual and theological questions with depth and learning.

[Louisa Cuomo]

MORPURGO, RACHEL LUZZATTO (1790–1871), Italian Hebraist and Hebrew poet. Morpurgo was born in Trieste and educated at home in Hebrew classics and secular subjects with her brother David and her younger cousin, Samuel David *Luzzatto (1800–1865), who became a prominent figure in modern Jewish thought and Hebrew literature, known as Shadal. Shadal credited Rachel with a major role in influencing his love for Jewish learning in general and Hebrew poetry in particular. In 1819, when she was 29 years old, Rachel married Jacob Morpurgo, a businessman from Gorzia, despite objections from her family. Devoted to serving her husband, who disapproved of her studies and literary efforts, and eventually the mother of three sons and a daughter, Morpurgo could only write late at night and on Rosh Ḥodesh. In 1847, 30 years after its inception, Shadal published their poetic exchange in *Kokhavei Yitzhak*, a journal devoted to modern Hebrew literature and enlightenment. Even her husband was proud of the recognition she now received for her talent. Some enlightened readers refused to accept that her Hebrew poems were actually written by a woman; others praised her for rising above women's ordinary activities and called her "Queen of the Hebrew Versifiers." Her letters and poems, in both Hebrew and Aramaic, invoke the matriarchs as well as the patriarchs, the hope for a return to Temple sacrifices in Jerusalem, a rare Hebrew description of a relationship between women, and the burdens of raising her own children. She also expresses her trepidation as a woman entering the literary realm of men. At the age of 65 she offered to work as a servant for Moses *Montefiore and his wife, Judith, passing through Italy on their way to Palestine. Morpurgo regularly signed herself as "The Worm," or "Rimah," the initials of Rachel Morpugo Ha-Ketanah (in Hebrew, "Little Rachel Morpurgo"), expressions of modesty often employed by prominent rabbis. Rachel Morpurgo's poetry, which was translated into several European languages, was included in a few anthologies of modern Hebrew poetry and is remembered in some of the histories of modern Hebrew literature. Critical emphasis is often on her novelty and uniqueness as the first female modern Hebrew poet. Rachel Morpurgo's Hebrew writings were published in *Ugav Raḥel: Shirim ve-Iggerot*, ed. Vittorio (Isaac Ḥayyim) Castiglione (Cracow: Yosef Fisher, 1891; ed. Y. Zemora, Tel Aviv: Mahberot Lesifrut, 1943); and in English in Nina Salaman, *Rahel Morpurgo and the Contemporary Hebrew Poets in Italy* (London: George Allen & Unwin Ltd., 1924).

BIBLIOGRAPHY: H. Adelman, "Finding Women's Voices in Italian Jewish Literature," in: J. Baskin (ed.), *Women of the Word: Jewish Women and Jewish Writing*. (1994), 50–69; Y. Levine-Katz, "Rachel Morpurgo," in: *Judaism* 49 (2000), 13–29.

[Howard Tzvi Adelman (2nd ed.)]

MORPURGO, SALOMONE (1860–1942), Italian philologist and librarian. While still a student, Morpurgo was an active member of the Italian nationalist movement. He was arrested by the Austrian authorities in his native Trieste and received a prison sentence. He then moved to Rome, where he became coeditor of the *Archivio storico per Trieste, l'Istria e il Trentino* (1881–95), which campaigned in favor of the Irredentist claim to Italy's Austrian-controlled territories. Best known for his literary work, Morpurgo was a coeditor of the *Rivista critica della letteratura italiana* (1884–91), director of the Riccardiana library in Rome (whose *Manoscritti italiani* he carefully described), and subsequently headed the Marciana library in Venice, which he transferred to the Palazzo della Zecca (*La Biblioteca Marciana nella sua nuova sede*, 1906). From 1905 to 1923 Morpurgo directed and reorganized the National Library in Florence. He investigated the medieval Italian version of the legend of the Wandering *Jew, publishing *L'ebreo errante in Italia* (1891), and edited the Italian manuscript of the story written in Florence by Antonio di Francesco d'Andrea early in the 15th century, which predates the well-known German edition of the legend. A pupil of the eminent writer Giosuè Carducci (1835–1907), Morpurgo specialized in the study of old Italian dialects and literary sources, and prepared editions of various manuscripts, analyzing their linguistic features and their relation to the figurative arts. The outcome of this work was his *Supplemento alle opere volgari a stampa dei secoli* XIII *e* XIV, *indicate e descritte da F. Zambrini* (1929; reissued 1961). A leading authority on Dante and Petrarch, Morpurgo later taught Italian literature at the University of Bologna.

BIBLIOGRAPHY: E. Battisti, in: *Studi Trentini*, 23 (1922), 135–6; *L'Osservatore Romano* (Feb. 18, 1942).

[Giorgio Romano]

MORPURGO, SAMSON BEN JOSHUA MOSES (1681–1740), Italian rabbi and physician. Samson was born in Gradisca d'Isonzo, Friuli. While still young he was taken by his parents to neighboring Gorizia, where he studied under Jacob Hai Gentili, the rabbi of the community, and his son, Manasseh. At the age of 12 or 13 he moved to Venice and there received a thorough education in the yeshivah of Samuel Aboab, as well as from his previous teacher Manasseh Gentili who had meanwhile moved to Venice. After some years he went to Padua to study medicine in the university there and in 1700 received the degree of doctor of philosophy and medicine. From then on he devoted himself to the study of Talmud, traveling between Padua and Venice, and between Gorizia and Mantua, where he studied under the outstanding scholar Briel, who in 1709 ordained him rabbi. In that year he was appointed a member of the *bet din* of the kabbalist Joseph Fiametta (Lehavah) whose daughter Rebecca he married. On the death of his wife in 1716, he married her sister, Judith. On the death of his father-in-law in 1721, Samson succeeded him as rabbi of the community, a post he held until his death. Morpurgo had connections with all the great scholars of his generation, who turned to him for counsel on complicated cases in the field of *halakhah*, among them Isaac Lampronti, who quotes Samson's rulings in his *Paḥad Yiẓḥak*, Moses Ḥagiz, and Benjamin ha-Kohen of Reggio. His skill as a doctor in Ancona, recognized by both Jews and Christians, and his profound compassion, particularly toward the suffering poor, won him the love and respect of all. In 1730 a devastating influenza plague swept Ancona, and, despite the Church ban against Jewish doctors' treating the Christian sick, Samson distinguished himself in the care he gave to all the town's inhabitants. In consequence, Cardinal Lambertini publicly presented him in 1731 with a document which expressed his gratitude and his esteem for Samson's devotion. Samson was involved in the polemics of the rabbis of the generation against Nehemiah Ḥiyya *Ḥayon, and was among those who took up a tolerant attitude toward him. There is extant correspondence between Morpurgo and Moses Ḥagiz on this subject from the end of 1711 to the beginning of 1715. The *Or Boker* (Venice, 1741) contains a prayer that was said at his grave on the anniversary of his death. The following of his works have been published: *Confutazioni alle Saette del Gionata del Benetelli* (Venice, 1703–04), a polemic against the Christian priest Luigi Maria Benetelli who wrote *Le Saette di Gionata scagliate a favor degli Ebrei* (1703), a book filled with hatred of the Jews and their religion; *Eẓ ha-Da'at* (*ibid.*, 1704), a philosophical commentary on the *Beḥinat Olam* of Jedaiah Bedersi; and *Shemesh Ẓedakah* (*ibid.*, 1743), a collection of responsa published posthumously by his son Moses Ḥayyim.

BIBLIOGRAPHY: E. Morpurgo, *La Famiglia Morpurgo…* (1909), 32–34, 65–69, 77, 104; I. Sonne, in: *Kobez al Jad*, 2 (1937), 157–96; B. Cohen, in: *Sefer ha-Yovel… A. Marx* (1943), 56; M. Wilensky, in: KS, 23 (1946/47), 199; idem, in: *Sinai*, 25 (1949), 68–75.

[Guiseppe Laras]

MORRIS, ERROL M. (1948–), U.S. director, producer, editor, and writer. Born in Hewlett, Long Island, Morris received a history degree from the University of Wisconsin and attended Princeton University and then the University of California at Berkeley to earn his Ph.D. in philosophy. Morris' first film, *Gates of Heaven* (1978), was created after German film director Werner Herzog said he would eat his shoes if Morris made a documentary about pet cemeteries. Morris won the bet and Herzog kept his end of the bargain, which is documented in Les Blank's *Werner Herzog Eats His Shoes* (1980). Morris' next documentary, *Vernon, Florida* (1981), recorded the eccentric lives of the small town residents. Morris worked as a private detective for two years, a profession that helped him direct and write *The Thin Blue Line* (1988), a documentary about a man wrongly accused of murder. The man was eventually released. In *Fast, Cheap, and Out of Control* (1997), Morris used his own invention, the Interrotron. A play-off of teleprompters, the Interrotron lets Morris project his image onto a screen in front of the camera, allowing the interviewee to look straight into the lens, not off to the side. It creates what Morris calls "the true first person." Morris used it in his TV series *First Person* (2000–1) and for his Academy Award winning documentary, *The Fog of War: Eleven Lessons from the Life of Robert S. McNamara* (2003). Other Morris films are *The Dark Wind* (1991), *A Brief History of Time* (1991), and *Mr. Death: The Rise and Fall of Fred A. Leuchter, Jr.* (1999), about an execution device inventor who testified on behalf of Holocaust denier Ernst Zundel. Beyond films, Morris makes commercials and won an Emmy in 2001 for a PBS ad.

[Susannah Howland (2nd ed.)]

MORRIS, HENRY HARRIS (1878–1954), South African lawyer, for 20 years the leading defense counsel and King's Counsel at the South African criminal bar. Henry Morris was the son of Hyman Morris, president of the first synagogue in Johannesburg. Morris had a reputation for grasping the human essentials in a situation and for his acute understanding of motives. He was at his best in cross-examination, when he could be forceful and caustic, but also urbane. Morris left a book of memoirs, *The First Forty Years* (1948).

[Lewis Sowden]

MORRIS, NATHAN (1890–1970), English Jewish educator. Born in Novogrudok, Russia, Morris went to England in 1909 and became a teacher in the Liverpool Hebrew Higher Grade School directed by J.S. *Fox, subsequently serving as headmaster of the institution (1912–20). Morris was founder and headmaster of the Glasgow Hebrew College, where he served from 1920 until 1929, when he was appointed education officer of the Jewish Religious Education Board of London, a post he held until 1940. When the ravages of war threatened Jewish schooling in Great Britain, he founded and directed the Joint Emergency Committee for Jewish Religious Education (1940–45), which set up classes for children in places far removed from the large population centers. At the end of the war, Morris was invited to take charge of the programs of the Central Council for Jewish Religious Education in the United

Kingdom and Eire and of the London Board for Jewish Religious Education (both 1945–48).

With Israel's independence, he helped to found the Jewish Agency's Department of Education and Culture and served as its director from 1949 until 1959, when he retired and returned to London. Morris wrote various Hebrew textbooks and educational manuals, but his most important work was the three-volume study on the history of Jewish education from the tannaitic period to the present, *Toledot ha-Ḥinnukh shel Am Yisrael* (1960–64). The study is a monumental work and the first of its kind in Jewish historiography.

[Judah Pilch]

MORRIS, NELSON (1839–1907), U.S. meat-packing executive. Morris, who was born in the Black Forest region of Germany, was taken to the U.S. at the age of 12. In 1854 he began working in the New York stockyards and two years later, he went into the meat-packing business for himself in Chicago. At the outbreak of the Civil War, Morris received a contract to supply meat to the Union armies. He subsequently supplied all the meat for the Army of the West later in the war, and filled meat-supply contracts for the governments of England, Germany, and France. His firm of Morris & Company was one of the largest in the U.S.

His son IRA NELSON MORRIS (1875–1942), who was born in Chicago, was a diplomat and author. Morris early severed his active connection with his father's firm. He served as commissioner-general to Italy (1913) and as U.S. minister to Sweden (1914–23). His books include: *With the Trade Winds* (1897); and *From an American Legation* (1926).

MORRIS, RICHARD BRANDON (1904–1989), U.S. historian. Born and educated in New York, Morris taught at City College, New York, from 1927 to 1949, and became professor of history at Columbia in 1949. Among his important books are *Studies in the History of American Law* (1930); *The Peacemakers* (1965); *Government and Labor in Early America* (1946); and *The American Revolution Reconsidered* (1967). He was coeditor of *The New American Nation* series (from 1953); *The Spirit of Seventy-Six* (1958); the *Encyclopedia of American History* (1953, 1963; 1970; 1982); and a *Documentary History of the United States* (from 1968). He also wrote *John Jay, The Nation and the Court* (1967); *The Emerging Nations and the American Revolution* (1970); *Seven Who Shaped Our Destiny* (1973); *Witnesses at the Creation* (1986); and *The Forging of the Union* (1987). He made noteworthy contributions in the field of archival preservation. He also served as chairman of the board of the editors of *Labor History*.

[Sidney I. Pomerantz / Ruth Beloff (2nd ed.)]

MORRIS, WILLIAM (1873–1932), U.S. talent agent. Born in Schwarzenau, Germany, Morris immigrated to America in 1898. He initially went to work for Marc Klaw and Abe Erlanger as a theatrical booking agent, and then as an independent vaudeville agent at a time when Keith-Albee United Booking Office was monopolizing bookings for vaudeville theaters. In 1907, Klaw and Erlanger joined with the Shubert Brothers to form the National Vaudeville Artists Association to compete with Keith-Albee, but they were acquired three months later and Klaw and Erlanger were forced out. Morris led a prolonged fight against Keith-Albee's monopoly with the aid of entertainment newspaper *Variety* and President Theodore Roosevelt. On January 31, 1918, a victorious Morris established the William Morris Agency with his son William, Jr. (born 1899 in New York) and office boy Abe Lastfogel. The agency's logo of four Xs actually represent William Morris' initials – a "W" superimposed on an "M." As silent film took hold, Morris pushed for clients like Al Jolson, Mae West, Charlie Chaplin, and the Marx Brothers to try out the new medium. By 1930, Morris had passed control of the agency to Lastfogel and his son, after 32 years in the business. Lastfogel managed the New York office, while William, Jr., took control of the Los Angeles office and later became president of the agency (1932–52). Morris died of a heart attack while playing cards at the Friar's Club in Manhattan.

[Adam Wills (2nd ed.)]

MORRIS AND SUSSEX COUNTIES, counties in New Jersey, U.S. The combined area of Morris and Sussex counties, located in western and northwestern New Jersey, is 1,000 sq. miles (2,700 sq. km.). In 2002, the Jewish population in Morris County was estimated at 33,000; Sussex County was estimated at 4,100. Morris-Sussex Federation merged with the Jewish Community Federation of Metropolitan New Jersey in 1983 to establish United Jewish Communities of MetroWest. A series of interstate highways, including Routes 280, 80, 78, 24, and 10, have made Morris County attractive to commuters. Hence, there is an active demographic shift of Jewish families from neighboring Essex County to portions of western New Jersey.

Sussex County Synagogues

There are three synagogues in Sussex County, located in the towns of Franklin, Newton, and Lake Hopatcong, and one "chavura," or social group, Congregation B'nai Emet, located in Sparta. The membership of Newton's Jewish Center of Sussex County (100 member families), and Franklin's Temple Shalom of Sussex County (150 member families) is predominantly intermarried. Lake Hopatcong Jewish Center has a scant 45 member families and has offered to sell its building to the MetroWest federation. There is one Chabad Center located in Sparta.

Morris County Synagogues

There are 19 synagogue communities in Morris County. The oldest congregation is Pine Brook Jewish Center (1896); the oldest Orthodox congregation is Shaya Ahavat Torah (1974); the oldest reform congregation is Temple B'nai Or (1954). There are three Chabad Centers and the Rabbinical College of America, which is located in Morristown.

Early Settlers and Synagogues Before World War II

There are six congregations over 100 years old located in Morris and Sussex Counties. The four in Morris County are Pine Brook Jewish Center (1896), Morristown Jewish Center-Beit Yisrael (1899), Dover Jewish Center (1917), and Mount Freedom Jewish Center (1923). Dover Jewish Center merged with Temple Shalom of Boonton in 1988 to form Adath Shalom, now located in Morris Plains. The two in Sussex County are Temple Shalom of Sussex County, formerly Congregation Sons of Israel (1909), and Jewish Center of Sussex County (1924), formerly Congregation Reuben Shimon.

The history of the Jews of Morris County dates back to the Civil War when Morristown's Henry and Rosena Sire owned the local stable and racetrack and sold remounts to the Union Army. The history of Dover's Jews, who referred to themselves as a "group of Israelites," is found on the pages of original minute ledgers dated October 4, 1882. Morristown's and Dover's Jews established Jewish business districts on Speedwell Avenue and Blackwell Street, respectively. At this time, Dover was located on the Morris Canal.

Newton was also a market town. Jewish merchants set up shop on Spring Street and from their stores went around the corner to attend services at the synagogue located on Washington Street. Franklin's Jews, never more than 25 Jewish families at one time, opened storefronts on Main Street, where they provided goods and services to the miners who worked for the New Jersey Zinc Company from the 1920s to 1955, when the mine closed. Sam Mindlin was Franklin's first Jewish settler in 1902.

Pine Brook and Mount Freedom were farming communities. Jews in both towns opened boarding houses and resort hotels as early as 1896 and 1903, respectively. Well known were Josef and Lena Konner's Sunrise Hotel in Pine Brook and Saltz's Hotel in Mount Freedom. Word-of-mouth and newspaper advertisements promoted the healthy air and virtues of New Jersey's countryside. Guests were primarily from Newark, New York City, and Brooklyn. Mount Freedom was home to nine kosher hotels and 45 bungalow colonies from 1920 to 1974. In both instances, local farmers were not enthusiastic about the influx of Jews to the area.

Synagogues and Lake Communities after World War II

A significant influx of Jews from New York City settled in and around the Morris and Sussex lake towns of Lake Hopatcong, Rockaway's White Meadow Lake, and Parsippany Troy-Hills' Lake Hiawatha immediately after World War II. Initially these were summer communities. Developer Benjamin Kline advertised affordable summer homes to New York City residents and Jews flocked to the New Jersey countryside. Residents winterized their summer homes, commuted to New York City by bus and train, and stayed year-round. Synagogues followed. Lake Hopatcong Jewish Center was founded in 1946, Lake Hiawatha Jewish Center (now merged with Pine Brook Jewish Center in 1995) was founded in 1945, and White Meadow Temple was founded in 1952. Other synagogues established after the war were Morristown's Temple B'nai Or in 1954 and Temple Shalom of Succasunna in 1965. Other synagogues located in Morris County include Congregation Beth Torah in Florham Park, Temple Hatikvah in Flanders, Congregation Ahavath Yisrael in Morristown, Temple Beth Am in Parsippany, and Congregation for Humanistic Judaism of Morris County.

Morris County's Alex Aidekman Jewish Community Campus

With the 1983 merger of Essex, Morris, and Sussex Counties into one umbrella federation, attention was paid to the demographic shift to western New Jersey. Hence, in 1990 the MetroWest community opened a second "Y" located in Whippany which moved Jewish services and agencies closer to Morris County. The Jewish Historical Society of MetroWest is located on this campus.

BIBLIOGRAPHY: L. Forgos, *The Jews of Morris and Sussex: A Brief History and Source Guide* (2003).

[Linda Forgosh (2nd ed.)]

MORSE, DAVID ABNER (1907–1990), U.S. labor executive and lawyer. Morse, who was born in New York, graduated from Rutgers University in 1929 and studied law at Harvard University; he was admitted to the New Jersey bar in 1933. Morse worked on the legal staff of the U.S. Department of the Interior (1933–34), as chief counsel for its Petroleum Labor Policy Board (1934–35), and as a regional attorney for the National Labor Relations Board in New York (1935–38), before entering private law practice. From 1940 to 1942 Morse was impartial chairman for the milk industry in the metropolitan New York area. On leaving the public service, he became a partner in the law firm of Coult, Satz, Tomlinson and Morse. He also lectured on labor relations, labor law, and administrative law at several educational institutions. From 1943 to 1944 he served in the U.S. army as head of the Labor Division of the Allied Military Government in Sicily and Italy, where he formulated and implemented labor policies and programs for the American and British liberators. From 1944 to 1945 he served as head of the Manpower Division of the United States Group Control Council for Germany, where he worked with representatives of Britain, France, the Soviet Union, and the United States to help coordinate the way they dealt with labor matters in occupied Germany. By the end of the war, he held the rank of lieutenant colonel and was awarded the Legion of Merit in 1946.

After serving with the military, Morse held the position of general counsel for the National Labor Relations Board (1945–47) until appointed assistant secretary of labor, in which capacity he created the department's Program of International Affairs. In 1948 he was elected director general of the International Labor Organization (ILO) based in Geneva, Switzerland, and remained in that position for an unprecedented 22 years. As ILO head, Morse directed its establishment of international labor standards and its training programs designed to assist underdeveloped countries, and particularly their workers, in raising their standards of living and bettering their job conditions. When the organization was awarded the Nobel Peace Prize in 1969, Morse accepted the award on behalf of the ILO. In 1970 he resigned as ILO director general and became the impartial chairman of the New York coat and suit industry.

[Ruth Beloff (2nd ed.)]

MORSE, LEOPOLD (1831–1892), U.S. congressman. Morse, who was born in Wachenheim, Bavaria, went to the U.S. in 1849. In 1850 he moved to Boston, Massachusetts, where he worked in a clothing store. In 1864 Morse and Ferdinand Strauss formed the Leopold Morse Company which specialized in the manufacture of men's clothing and soon became the largest of its kind in New England. After twice running unsuccessfully for Congress on the Democratic ticket (1870, 1872), Morse subsequently served five terms in Congress as Democratic representative from Massachusetts (1877–85, 1887–89). Morse was rumored to be a leading choice for the post of secretary of war in Grover Cleveland's cabinet, but religious prejudices were supposed to have ruled out his appointment. Active in Jewish affairs, Morse founded the Boston Home for Infirm Hebrews and Orphanage, renamed the Leopold Morse Home for Infirm Hebrews and Orphanage after his death.

MORTARA, LODOVICO (1855–1937), Italian jurist and statesman. Born in Mantua where his father Marco *Mortara was chief rabbi, he lectured from 1886 at the universities of Pisa and Naples. He became professor of law at Naples in 1903 and at the same time a magistrate in Rome. He was promoted to membership of the Supreme Court in Rome where he held the offices of attorney general, public prosecutor and eventually first president of the Supreme Court of Cassation. In 1919 Mortara became minister of justice and in the following year was appointed to the Senate. He was an outspoken critic of Fascism and opposed the constitutional changes introduced by Mussolini. His writings ran into many editions and strongly influenced the development of Italian jurisprudence. They include: *Lo Stato Moderno et la Giustizia* (1885); *Principii di Procedura Civile* (1922^7); *Manuale di Procedura Civile* (1921^3). Mortara also edited the review *La Giurisprudenza Italiana* (1891–), Italy's leading judicial publication.

BIBLIOGRAPHY: M. Rotundi, *L. Mortara* (1937); P. Calamandrei, *L. Mortara* (1937).

[Giorgio Romano]

MORTARA, MARCO (1815–1894), Italian rabbi and scholar. He attended the rabbinical seminary in Padua under Samuel David *Luzzatto, was ordained in 1836, and from 1842 officiated as rabbi of Mantua. Mortara represented the liberal trend in Judaism in Italy and argued that a distinction be made between the Jewish religion and Jewish nationality. He proposed a conference of Italian rabbis in 1866 in order to secure certain reforms in Jewish practices, but his suggestion did not materialize. In the sphere of biblical study, Mortara opposed the documentary hypothesis and argued for the unity and Mosaic authorship of the Pentateuch (1843). He considered that the task of Judaism was to spread monotheism and morality throughout the world and that this was facilitated by the Dispersion. Mortara published books on the principles of Judaism and a new edition of the prayer book whose translation into Italian was based on that by S.D. Luzzatto. His most important work was in the area of bibliography and includes a catalog of the manuscripts in the library of the Mantua community (1878), and *Mazkeret Ḥakhmei Italyah* (*Indice alfabetico dei rabbini e scrittori israeliti di cose giudaiche in Italia*; 1886), a list of approximately 2,000 Jewish scholars living in Italy from the first to the 19th centuries. He was a notable bibliophile, his collection of manuscripts being purchased after his death by David *Kaufmann.

BIBLIOGRAPHY: *Corriere Israelitico*, 22 (1884), 227–8; *Vessillo Israelitico*, 34 (1886), 188–9; 42 (1894), 59–62; Shunami, Bibl, nos. 3987–88.

[Menachem E. Artom]

MORTARA CASE, case of the abduction of a Jewish child by Catholic conversionists. On the night of June 23–24, 1858, Edgardo Mortara, aged six years and ten months, son of a Jewish family in Bologna, Italy, was abducted by the papal police and conveyed to Rome where he was taken to the House of *Catechumens. The boy had been secretly baptized five years before in an irregular fashion by a Christian domestic servant, who thought, as she said later, that he was about to die. The parents vainly attempted to get their child back. This flagrant abduction of a minor had many precedents in Italy. The church, moreover, had always maintained that the extemporized baptism of a child who was in danger of death was valid even if it had been carried out against the parents' will. The case caused a universal outcry. Napoleon III was among those who protested against the infringement of religious freedom and parental rights. Sir Moses *Montefiore went to Rome in 1859, in the hope of obtaining the child's release. The founding of the *Alliance Israélite Universelle in 1860, in order to "defend the civil rights and religious freedom of the Jews," was due partly to this case. Pope *Pius IX, however, rejected all petitions submitted to him. In 1860, after the annexation of Bologna to the Italian kingdom, the boy's parents took new steps, again in vain, for the return of the child. With the ending of the pope's secular power in 1870, Edgardo Mortara who had taken the name Pius and in the meantime was a novice in an Augustinian order – was free to return to his family and religion. However, he refused to do so. Mortara, who preached eloquently in six languages, was such an ardent conversionist that he received the title of "apostolic missionary" from Leo XIII. He became canon in Rome and professor of theology. He died at the Abbey of Bouhay near Liège in Belgium in 1940.

BIBLIOGRAPHY: G. Volli, *Il caso Mortara nel primo centenario* (1960); idem, in: *Bolletino del Museo del Risorgimento*, 5 (1960), 1087–1152; idem, in: *Scritti… Federico Luzzatto* (1962), 309–20; idem, in: RMI, 26 (1960), with illustrations; A.F. Day, *The Mortara Mystery* (1930); Meisl, in: MGWJ, 77 (1933), 321–8; B.W. Korn, *American Reaction to the Mortara Case: 1858–1859* (1957); J.L. Altholz, in: JSOS, 23 (1961), 111–8.

[Giorgio Romano]

MORTEIRA, SAUL LEVI (c. 1596–1660), rabbi and scholar in Amsterdam. Morteira was born in Venice and studied there under Leone *Modena. In 1611 he accompanied the physician Elijah Montalto to Paris, and on the latter's death in 1616 brought his body for burial to Amsterdam, where he himself subsequently settled. A few years after his arrival he was elected *ḥakham* of the Beit Ya'akov community. When three Sephardi communities merged to form the Talmud Torah congregation in 1638, Morteira was appointed one of its rabbis, taught Talmud and *tosafot* to advanced students, and preached in the synagogue three times a month. He founded the Keter Torah Yeshivah in Amsterdam and Baruch *Spinoza was among his students. Morteira was a member of the *bet din* that excommunicated Spinoza.

Morteira's works include *Givat Sha'ul* (Amsterdam, 1645), a collection of sermons arranged in the order of the weekly portions of the reading of the Law, and a work (no longer extant) on the immortality of the soul, both written in Hebrew. Only fragments of his responsa, mentioned in the introduction to his sermons, have survived. In addition, he wrote a number of apologetics for Judaism in Spanish; among them, *La Eternidad de la Ley de Mosseh* ("The Eternal Nature of the Law of Moses"); *Preguntas que hizo un clériqo de Roan alas quales respondí* ("Questions of a Priest from Rouen and My Answers to Them"); *Obstáculos y oposiciones contra la religión cristiana* ("Criticisms and Arguments Against the Christian Religion"); and a treatise against the 16th-century Italian apostate, *Sixtus of Siena. Also preserved in many copies is his *Providencia de Dios con Ysrael* ("The Providence of God with Israel") which contains an account of the vicissitudes of the founders of the New Amsterdam (New York) community on their escape from Brazil. None of these works was printed. Morteira's *Discursos Académicos* is printed in Reuel *Jusurun's *Dialogo dos Montes* (completed 1624; published in Amsterdam, 1767). His apologetic works circulated widely in manuscript and had a profound influence on the Sephardi communities in Western Europe.

BIBLIOGRAPHY: Kayserling, Bibl, 74–75; Steinschneider, Cat Bod, 2508–09; J.S. da Silva Rosa, *Gescheidenis der Portugeesche Joden te Amsterdam* (1925), index; C. Roth, *Life of Manasseh Ben Israel* (1934), index; F. Kupfer, in: *Przeglad Orientalistyczny* (1955), 97–99; A. Wiznitzer, in: HJ 20 (1958), 110ff.; I.S. Revah, *Spinoza et Juan de Prado* (1959), index.

[Joseph Kaplan]

MORTON, LOUIS C. (1913–), U.S. historian. Born in New York City, Morton received his M.A. from New York University in 1936 and his doctorate from Duke University in 1938 in the field of American colonial history. He taught at City College of New York from 1939 to 1941. He served in the U.S. Army (1942–46), and was deputy chief historian in the Office of the Chief of Military History, Washington, D.C. (1946–59). During that time, he also served as chief of the Pacific Section, responsible for the preparation of the 11-volume subseries on "The War in the Pacific," and was historical adviser for the post-World War II program. He served as consultant and lecturer at a number of military and civilian institutions, and from 1960 he was professor of history at Dartmouth College. In 1971–72 he served as provost. He was also president of the New England Historical Association (1968–69).

Morton's major scholarly interest was U.S. military history. Regarded as one of America's foremost experts on the history of World War II, he is best known for *The Fall of the Philippines* (1953); *The War in the Pacific: Strategy and Command* (1962); and *Writings on World War II* (1967). He was general editor of a 17-volume study, *Wars and Military Institutions of the United States* (1963).

[Ruth Beloff (2nd ed.)]

MORWITZ, EDWARD (1815–1893), U.S. physician and journalist. Morwitz, who was born in Danzig, studied Oriental languages in Halle and medicine at the University of Berlin. He participated in the revolutionary upheavals of 1848 and then fled to the U.S. Settling in Philadelphia, Morwitz first practiced medicine (1850) but swiftly moved to leadership in German-language journalism and publishing. He took an active role in the affairs of the Democratic Party but supported the Union cause during the Civil War. When the German Dispensary (now Lankenau Hospital) in Philadelphia was threatened with closure during the war, Morwitz himself took charge and served as its medical director. He organized the German Press Association of Pennsylvania in 1862, and through merger and expansion ultimately controlled a large number of German-language and English-language newspapers. Morwitz' primary interests and contributions were in the area of German immigrant cultural and political activities, but he did maintain ties with the Jewish community through his membership in Kenesseth Israel Congregation and his ownership of the Philadelphia *Jewish Record* from 1875 to 1886.

BIBLIOGRAPHY: DAB, 13 (1934), 271–2, incl. bibl.; H.S. Morais, *Jews of Philadelphia* (1894), 338–40; B.W. Korn, *Eventful Years and Experiences* (1954), passim.

[Bertram Wallace Korn]

MOSBACH, city in Baden, Germany. A Jewish community was in existence in Mosbach by the second half of the 13th century. In 1298 the *Rindfleisch massacres took 55 Jewish lives. Jews also suffered in 1343, when they were accused of desecrating the *Host, and during the *Black Death persecutions of 1349. By 1381 just one Jew lived in the city, and the number of the Jews there remained small throughout the following centuries. They traded in livestock, salt, and wine. The municipal authorities periodically sought to restrict Jewish commercial activity. In 1722 there were eight Jewish families in the city; the number had grown to 19 by 1773. A cemetery was consecrated in 1599 but no synagogue was built until 1860, and a Jewish school was established only in 1876. From 1827 the seat of the district rabbinate was in Mosbach. Leopold *Loewenstein (1843–1924), author of works on German Jewish history, served there as a rabbi from 1887 to 1924.

The 19th century saw a significant growth in the Jewish population. There were 100 persons in 1824, and 192 in 1884. By 1900 the numbers had declined to 161; 159 in 1925; 134 in 1933; and 18 in 1939. The Jews had been active in the commercial and industrial life of the city as merchants in grain and livestock, and owners of a cigar factory, liquor distillery, and numerous other businesses, which were all disrupted when the boycott of Jewish merchants began on April 1, 1933. On November 10, 1938, the synagogue was burned down and the cemetery desecrated. On October 22, 1940, 13 Jews were deported to *Gurs, only two of whom survived the war. The rabbi, Julius Greilsheimer, fled to Holland in 1939, only to be deported from there to Auschwitz, where he perished together with his family. In 1947 a grove of 100 trees was planted by the city in his memory and that of the Jewish community. In 1969 and, later, in 1985 a plaque was mounted to commemorate the desecrated synagogue.

BIBLIOGRAPHY: *Germania Judaica*, 2 (1968), 548; Salfeld, Martyrol, 54, 61, 66, 78, 80; F. Hundsnurscher and G. Taddey, *Die juedischen Gemeinden in Baden* (1968). **ADD. BIBLIOGRAPHY:** *Germania Judaica*, vol. 3, 1350–1514 (1987), 884–85; J. Hahn, *Erinnerungen und Zeugnisse juedischer Geschichte in Baden-Wuerttemberg* (1988), 387–89. **WEBSITE:** www-alemannia-judaica.de.

[Alexander Shapiro]

MOSBACHER, EMIL JR. (1922–1997), U.S. yachtsman and businessman. Born in Mt. Vernon, N.Y., Mosbacher won intercollegiate sailing titles for Dartmouth College and during World War II served as an officer in the U.S. navy. He returned to sailing in 1949, and from 1950 to 1957 defeated the nation's best yachtsmen in International One-Design Class competition. Mosbacher skippered his first 12-meter class sloop, the 19-year-old *Vim*, in 1958. He was at the helm of *Weatherly* in 1962, when she successfully defended yachting's most prized trophy (the America's Cup) against the Australian challenger, *Gretel*. He defeated the Australians again in the 1967 America's Cup races. A successful businessman, Mosbacher was chosen by President Richard Nixon to serve as the State Department's chief of protocol in 1969. He was converted to the Episcopal faith.

BIBLIOGRAPHY: *Time* (Aug. 18, 1967).

[Jesse Harold Silver]

MOSCATI, SABATINO (1922–), Italian semiticist and archaeologist. Moscati taught Hebrew, Semitic languages, and the history of religions at the universities of Florence, Naples, and Rome. He is a member of the Accademia dei Lincei and editor, the *Rivista di Studi Orientali*. His most important works deal with the origins of the Semites, the language and peoples of Palestine and Syria, and the history of the Arabs. Among them are *Le antiche civiltà semitiche* (1961; *Ancient Semitic Civilizations*, 1957); *L'epigrafia ebraica antica 1935–50* (1951); *I manoscritti ebraici del Deserto di Giuda* (1955); *I predecessori d'Israele* (1956); *Il profilo dell'Oriente mediterraneo* (1956; *The Face of the Ancient Orient*, 1960, repr. 1963); and *An Introduction to the Comparative Grammar of the Semitic Languages* (1964).

Moscati took part in the excavations of Ramat Raḥel in Israel in the years 1960, 1961, and 1962.

From the 1970s on Moscati dedicated his research to the Phoenicians and the Carthaginians and their impact on ancient Italy. He was the greatest expert on the Punic civilization in Italy. He published *I Cartaginesi in Italia* (1977), *Il mondo dei Fenici* (1979), *Il mondo punico* (1980), *I Cartaginesi* (1982), and *Italia punica* (1986).

BIBLIOGRAPHY: S. Moscati, *I Fenici* (1988).

[Alfredo Mordechai Rabello / Samuele Rocca (2nd ed.)]

MOSCATO, JUDAH BEN JOSEPH (c. 1530–c. 1593), one of the most important rabbis, authors, and preachers of the Italian Jewish Renaissance. He was forced to leave his native town Osimo when the Jews were expelled from the main places in the papal states by Pope Pius V in 1569. Moscato went to Mantua, at that time one of the great centers of Jewish culture and scholarship in Italy. It seems that, not long after his arrival in the city, he became the official preacher of the Mantua community and in 1587 was nominated to the post of chief rabbi.

Spheres of Interest

Moscato's range of learning and knowledge extended over all fields of cultural interest to Jews of the Renaissance, and he was better versed in them than most of his contemporaries. Besides being steeped in Jewish traditional culture, rabbinic literature, and *aggadah*, he was at home in Jewish medieval philosophy and was also familiar with classical philosophy; he was especially an advocate of Plato and of the medieval neoplatonists and Arab philosophies. Philosophic in his outlook, Moscato was, nevertheless, familiar with the Kabbalah which had become popular in the late 16th century and had begun to influence Italian Jewish intellectuals. His approach to a number of subjects, especially ethics and prayer, was distinctly mystical: he often quotes from the *Zohar, frequently using its ideas without mentioning the source. He also quotes Moses *Cordovero, mostly from his *Pardes Rimmonim*. Moscato's educational and cultural horizons extended to such secular sciences and disciplines as medicine, music, astronomy, and especially classical rhetoric. In all these fields, he quotes from the classical masters, as well as from medieval works. He was acquainted with a number of contemporary Italian non-Jewish writers, such as Pico della Mirandola, whom he quotes in his *Nefuẓot Yehudah* (sermon 8, fol. 23c), even supporting a number of obviously christological passages. Moscato, explaining his reliance on non-Jewish sources and his frequent reference to them, states that all the great philosophers had been disciples of ancient Jewish kings and prophets; that philosophy, a Jewish science which was part of Israel's ancient culture, had been lost during the long period of exile and was preserved only in the writings of the non-Jewish students of Jewish teachers. This idea, in vogue from the 13th century, came to explain the existence of non-Jewish philosophy in religious

Jewish works. Moscato used it effectively; in his sermon on music, for instance (*Nefuẓot Yehudah*, sermon 1), he argues in detail that the fundamental concepts of Renaissance music were based on the terms and formulas found in the Psalms, and concludes that King David was the inventor and teacher of the discipline of music, even though in Moscato's times the terms and forms were known in Latin and in Italian.

Moscato's Works

The spirit of the Jewish Renaissance is reflected in Moscato's two major works, *Kol Yehudah* and *Nefuẓot Yehudah*. The former (Venice, 1594) is a commentary on *Judah Halevi's *Kuzari*, which became one of the major influences in 16th-century Jewish ideology in Italy and elsewhere. Moscato's exegesis was a motivating factor in the process and reflected the new interest taken in this author. In his commentary, Moscato also based himself on the writings of other Jewish philosophers who were little read or studied at the time, such as *Philo.

Moscato's second major work, *Nefuẓot Yehudah* (Venice, 1589), is a collection of sermons preached in Mantua on the major holidays, on the special Sabbaths, at weddings, and at funerals. The sermons, 52 in number, correspond to the number of weeks in a year, signifying a full cycle, even though the sermons were not delivered weekly. Moscato's sermons may be described as a revolutionary innovation in Hebrew homiletic literature. None before him and very few, if any, after him achieved such a high degree of aestheticism in the genre. His sermons clearly reveal the influence of the Renaissance on the dialectic method of Hebrew homiletics. His main purpose was not to teach or educate, but to give aesthetic pleasure to his listeners – the actual congregation sitting before him. His sermons were, therefore, not written to be published as a book; it is rather their oral delivery which is reflected at every point. It is possible that Moscato preached both in Hebrew and in Italian, for it is known that many non-Jewish scholars came to listen to his sermons. However, the sermons collected in *Nefuẓot Yehudah* were undoubtedly delivered in Hebrew on special occasions; this fact is sometimes referred to directly, sometimes is reflected in the contents. Moscato's great achievement in the field of rhetoric and homiletics lies in the fact that, even though his primary aim was to please his listeners, he also succeeded in being instructive, and in developing some ideas, original either in content or in formulation. He drew on his vast knowledge of philosophy and of the Kabbalah in order to develop ethical ideas and to interpret them in a new way so that they might be acceptable to Jewish culture in Renaissance Italy (see *Preaching). Many of the great preachers in Italy who came after him, including Azariah *Figo (Picho) and Leone *Modena, applied Moscato's ideas and methods of preaching, creating thus a new school in homiletics.

Besides these two major works, Moscato also wrote some poetry: a prayer for rain to be recited in time of drought, composed in 1590; a dirge on the death of R. Joseph *Caro; a dirge on the death of the Duchess of Savoy; and a few other poems. Certain of his exegetical works, mentioned in his known works, have not survived.

BIBLIOGRAPHY: I. Bettan, *Studies in Jewish Preaching* (1939), 192–225; idem, in: HUCA, 6 (1929), 297–326; A. Apfelbaum, *Toledot ha-Ga'on Rabbi Yehudah Moscato* (1900); S. Simonsohn, *Toledot ha-Yehudim be-Dukkasut Mantovah*, 2 (1964), index; C. Roth, *Jews in the Renaissance* (1959), index.

[Joseph Dan]

MOSCHELES, IGNAZ (1794–1870), pianist and composer. Born in Prague, he studied in Vienna, but settled in London in 1826 as a concert pianist. In 1846 Felix *Mendelssohn (to whom he had given piano lessons in 1824) invited him to become piano teacher at the Leipzig Conservatory. He taught there to the end of his life. Moscheles' playing was noted for its precision and brilliance, but in comparison with Chopin and Liszt was rather classicist in attitude. He wrote many compositions in a Mendelssohnian style, the best being the "Etudes" (Op. 70). He also prepared the piano-vocal score of Beethoven's *Fidelio* under the composer's supervision (1814), and translated A. Schindler's biography of Beethoven into English, with additions (1841).

BIBLIOGRAPHY: Baker, Biog Dict, s.v.; MGG, s.v.; Riemann-Gurlitt, s.v., incl. bibl.; J. Roche, in: *Musical Times* (March 1970), 264–6.

[Claude Abravanel]

MOSCOVITCH, MAURICE (1871–1940), actor-manager. Born in Odessa, Moscovitch won a reputation there on the Yiddish- and English-speaking stage. He acted in London with David *Kessler and reached New York with Jacob *Adler's company in 1890. Forming his own troupe, he toured the Americas and Europe in Jewish classics and Yiddish versions of Tolstoy, Turgenev, and Strindberg. He appeared in English in Manchester, England, in 1919, as Shylock, giving a controversial interpretation. Later he toured South Africa and Australia, and appeared in films, including Charles Chaplin's *The Great Dictator* (1940), just before his death.

MOSCOW (Rus. **Moskva**), capital of the Russian Federation, and, from the Middle Ages, the political, economic, and commercial center of *Russia. Up to the end of the 18th century, Jews were forbidden to reside in Moscow, although many Jewish merchants from Poland and Lithuania visited the city. In 1676 Jews who brought their wares to Moscow were expelled. Apostates and forced converts who maintained varying degrees of connection with Judaism and the Jews were to be found in Moscow during various periods. A few Jews among the prisoners brought to Moscow after the wars against Poland apostatized and settled there. A physician of Jewish origin, Daniel Gordon, was employed by the court in Moscow from 1657 to 1687; Peter Shafirov, one of the most important advisers of Czar Peter the Great, was also of Jewish origin.

With the Russian annexation of Belorussia (1772), the number of Jewish merchants living in Moscow for commercial reasons increased; they came in particular from *Shklov, then an important commercial center in Belorussia. One of these was the contractor and merchant Nathan Note *Notkin. In 1790 Moscow merchants requested that the presence and commercial activities of the Jews in the city be prohibited. A royal decree forbidding Jewish merchants to settle in the inner districts of Russia was issued in 1791. However, they were authorized to stay for temporary periods in Moscow to carry on their trade. Most of the Jews who came to Moscow lodged at the Glebovskoye podvorye, an inn which was situated in the center of the market quarter. Jewish merchants continued to play an important role in the trade between Moscow and the southern and western regions of Russia, as well as in the export of Moscow's goods, and in 1828 the turnover of this trade was estimated at 27,000,000 rubles. As a result, Russian industrialists in Moscow supported the rights of the Jews. In 1828 Jewish merchants who were members of the first and second guilds were authorized to remain in Moscow on business for a period of one month only. They were forbidden to open shops or to engage in trade within the city boundaries. To facilitate the execution of these regulations, the Jews were compelled to lodge solely in the Glebovskoye podvorye. The inn was a charitable trust which had been handed over to the Moscow city council to use its income for the maintenance of a municipal eye clinic. Exorbitant prices were soon extorted from Jewish merchants who had to stay at the inn. After a few years, third-class merchants were also authorized to enter the town under the same conditions and the period of their stay was prolonged to six months. About 250 people made use of this right every year. As a result of these restrictions, Jewish trade decreased to about 12,000,000 rubles annually during subsequent years. When Alexander II came to the throne (1855), Jewish merchants were permitted to reside temporarily in all the sections of the town.

The first Jews to settle permanently in Moscow, and the founders of the community, were *Cantonists who had finished military service, some of whom had married Jewish women from the *Pale of Settlement. In 1858 there were 340 Jewish men and 104 Jewish women in the whole of the district of Moscow. After Jewish merchants of the first guild, university graduates, and craftsmen were allowed to settle in the interior of Russia, the number of Jews increased rapidly. Some were extremely wealthy, such as Eliezer *Polyakov, one of the most important bankers in Russia and head of the community, and K.Z. *Wissotzki. From 1865 to 1884 Ḥayyim Berlin officiated as rabbi of Moscow, and in 1869 the community invited S.Z. *Minor, one of the outstanding students of the Vilna rabbinical seminary, to serve as the **kazyonny ravvin* (government-appointed rabbi). There was an estimated Jewish population of 8,000 in the city in 1871, which had grown to around 12,000 in 1882 and 35,000 (over 3% of the total population) in 1890, just before the expulsion. The governor of Moscow, Prince Dolgorukov, was known for his liberal attitude toward the Jews, and (after receiving bribes and gifts) the local administration overlooked their illegal presence (as in the case of fictive craftsmen). A considerable number of industrialists and merchants recognized the advantages deriving from Jewish presence in the city, and in a memorandum addressed to the minister of finance in 1882 they pointed out their great contribution to the city's prosperity. While anti-Jewish persecutions and decrees were gaining momentum throughout Russia after the accession of Alexander III, a period of relative ease, the legacy of the previous czar, continued in Moscow. This situation changed completely with the deposition of Prince Dolgorukov and the appointment of Grand Prince Sergei Alexandrovich as governor of the city. During the 14 years (1891–1905) of his term in office, his main aim was "to protect Moscow from Jewry."

The Expulsion

On March 28, 1891 (Passover Eve 5651), a law was issued abolishing the right of Jewish craftsmen to reside in Moscow and prohibiting their entry into the city in the future. The police immediately began to expel thousands of families, some of whom had lived in Moscow for several decades or were even born there. They were granted a period of from three months to a year to dispose of their property, and many were compelled to sell out to their neighbors at derisory prices. The poor and destitute were sent to the Pale of Settlement with criminal transports. On October 15 the right of descendants of the Cantonists to live in the town was abrogated, if they were not registered with the Moscow community. The expulsion reached its climax during the cold winter days of 1892. While the police made a concerted effort to search out the Jews and drive them out of the city, generous rewards were offered for the seizure of any still in hiding. The press was not permitted to report on the details of the expulsion. An appeal to the government made by merchants and industrialists in 1892 and their warning of the economic damage that would result from the expulsion were of no avail. Police sources estimated that about 30,000 persons were expelled. About 5,000 Jews remained – families of some Cantonists, wealthy merchants and their servants, and members of the liberal professions. The Moscow expulsion came as a deep shock to Russian Jewry. A considerable number of those expelled arrived in Warsaw and Lodz and transferred their economic activities there. Decrees regulating residence in Moscow became even more severe. In 1899 the authorities ordered that no more Jewish merchants were to be registered in the first guild unless authorized by the minister of finance. At the height of the expulsion period, the authorities closed down the new synagogue, as well as nine of the 14 prayer houses. Rabbi S.Z. Minor, who requested the reopening of the synagogue, was expelled from the city. The struggle for the use of the synagogue continued for many years and it was not until 1906 that permission was granted for its reopening. In 1897 there were 8,095 Jews and 216 Karaites in Moscow (0.8% of the total population). In 1902 there were 9,339 Jews there, and half of them declared Yiddish as their mother tongue; the overwhelming majority of the others declared it to be Russian. In 1893 J. *Mazeh was elected as rabbi of Moscow, remaining its spiritual leader until his death in 1923. A considerable number of the members of the small community were wealthy merchants and intellectuals. Assimilated Jews (some of whom apostatized) held an important place in the cultural life of the city. In 1911 there were around 700 Jewish students in the higher institutions of learning in Moscow.

After the outbreak of World War I, from 1915, a stream of Jewish refugees began to arrive in Moscow from the German-occupied regions. They took part in the development of war industries in the town and some of them amassed large fortunes. In a short time, Moscow became a Jewish center. Hebrew printing presses were set up, and in the town of Bogorodsk (near Moscow) a large yeshivah was established on the pattern of the Lithuanian yeshivot. The foundations of the Hebrew theater *Habimah were then laid. Among the new rich were Zionists and nationally conscious Jews who were ready to support every cultural activity. Most outstanding of these were H. *Zlatopolsky, his son-in-law Y. Persitz, and A.J. *Stybel. Authorization was given for the publication of a Hebrew weekly, *Ha-Am*. Cultural activity increased in scope with the outbreak of the February 1917 Revolution. It was symbolical that O. *Minor, the son of S.Z. Minor, a leader of the Social Revolutionary Party, was elected as chairman of the Moscow municipal council. *Ha-Am* became a daily newspaper and two large publishing houses, Ommanut (founded by Zlatopolsky and Persitz) and that of A.J. Stybel, were set up. The founding conference of the organization for Hebrew education and culture, *Tarbut, was held in Moscow in the spring of 1917. This activity also continued during the first year of the Bolshevik Revolution (three volumes of *Ha-Tekufah* were published in 1918, as well as others) but the new regime, with the assistance of its Jewish supporters, rapidly liquidated the institutions of Hebrew culture in Moscow. The Habimah theater was more fortunate; it presented An-Ski's *Dibbuk* (*Dybbuk*) in Moscow for the first time in January 1922 and continued to exist under the protection of several prominent members of the Russian artistic and literary world who defended it as a first class artistic institution, until it left the Soviet Union in 1926.

When Moscow became the capital of the Soviet Union, its Jewish population rapidly increased. In 1920 there were 28,000 Jews in the city, which had become severely depopulated as a result of the civil war. By 1923 the number had increased to 86,000 and by 1926 to 131,000 (6.5% of the total population). In 1939 the Jews there numbered 250,181 (6.05% of the total population). The headquarters of the *Yevsektsiya was situated in Moscow, and there its central newspaper. *Der Emes* (1920–38) was published, as well as many other Yiddish newspapers and books. The Jewish State Theater (known in Russian as GOSET from its initials), directed by S. *Mikhoels, was also situated in Moscow. For a number of years, small circles of organized Zionists continued to exist in the city, which was the central seat of the legal *He-Ḥalutz (which published its own newspaper from 1924 to 1926) and of the groups of the Left *Po'alei Zion. All these were liquidated by 1928. During World War II, the Jews shared the sufferings of the war with the city's other inhabitants. From 1943 Moscow was the seat of the Jewish *Anti-Fascist Committee which gathered together personalities of Jewish origin who were outstanding in Soviet public affairs. Founded to assist the Soviet Union in its war effort against Nazi Germany and to mobilize world Jewish opinion and aid for this purpose, it published a newspaper, *Eynikeyt*.

[Yehuda Slutsky]

After World War II

The Anti-Fascist Committee attempted to continue with its activities even after the war, until it was brutally liquidated in 1948–49, as a first step in the total liquidation of organized Jewish life in the "black years" of Stalin's regime. Most of its leading members were arrested and executed in 1952. Because Moscow is the capital and a "window" of the Soviet Union, it has been possible for world Jewry to follow the destinies of Moscow's Jews more than those in other cities, and the latter were more able to meet with Jews from outside the Soviet Union. When Golda *Meir, the first diplomatic representative of the State of Israel, arrived in Moscow in September 1948, a spontaneous mass demonstration of Jews in her honor took place on the High Holidays near and around the Great Synagogue. The mere presence of an Israeli diplomatic mission with an Israeli flag in the center of Moscow was a constant stimulus to Jewish and pro-Israel sentiments among the Jews of Moscow and Jewish visitors from other parts of the Soviet Union. The Israeli delegation to the Youth Festival, held in Moscow in 1957, was the first occasion of personal contacts between Jewish youth from Israel and the U.S.S.R. It is considered to have been a turning point in the revival of Jewish national feelings and their daring demonstration in public on the part of Soviet Jewish youth. Already in 1958, on *Simḥat Torah eve, more than 10,000 young Jews gathered around the Great Synagogue to dance and sing Yiddish and Hebrew songs. They refused to be intimidated by the militia and to disperse. Thus these mass gatherings of young Jews, which also take place on their Jewish holidays, became a traditional feature of Jewish life in Moscow.

In 1955 some elderly Jews were tried and sentenced to several years of imprisonment in labor camps for possessing and distributing Israeli newspapers and Hebrew literature and gathering in groups to read them. For similar "offenses" several Jews of the Great Synagogue congregation were punished in 1963.

In 1970 three synagogues were functioning in the city of Moscow. Apart from the Great Synagogue on Arkhipova Street, there were two small synagogues – in the suburbs of Maryina Roshcha and Cherkizovo, which were wooden buildings, more of the type of a *shtibl* than of a full-fledged synagogue. In addition to them, there was a synagogue in the nearby town of Malakhovka, practically also a suburb of Greater Moscow, which has had a sizable Jewish population from prerevolutionary times. The Great Synagogue and its rabbi (first S. *Schliefer and after his death J.L. *Levin) served the authorities often as unofficial representatives of Soviet Jewry to the outside world.

In the 1950s and 1960s the Great Synagogue was allowed to issue a Jewish calendar and to send it to other synagogues in the U.S.S.R. In 1956 Rabbi Schliefer was granted permission to print a prayer book, by photostat from old prayer books. He named it *Siddur ha-Shalom* ("peace prayer book") and deleted from it all references to wars and victories (as, e.g., in the Ḥanukkah benedictions). It was said to have been printed in 3,000 copies, but it was very rarely seen in other synagogues in the Soviet Union. (A second edition of it was printed, ostensibly in 10,000 copies, in 1968 by Rabbi Levin, but it also was not much in use in Soviet synagogues.) In 1957 Rabbi Schliefer received permission from the authorities to open a yeshivah on the premises of the Great Synagogue. He called it "Kol Ya'akov," and for several years a small number of young and middle-aged Jews (about 12 persons a year), mostly from Georgia, were trained there, almost all of them as **shoḥatim* (ritual slaughterers), whereas the number of ordained rabbis did not exceed one or two. In 1961 the yeshivah, though officially still in existence, almost ceased to function, mainly because of the refusal of the Soviet authorities to grant permission to yeshivah students, who went for the holiday to their homes outside Moscow, to come back and register again as temporary residents of the city for the purpose of study. By 1963, 37 students had passed through the yeshivah; 25 of them were trained as *shoḥatim*. In 1965 only one student was there, and in 1966 the number was six. The unrestricted baking of matzah in a rented bakery and its distribution in food stores was discontinued in Moscow, as in most areas of the Soviet Union, in 1962. However, it was partially permitted again in 1964 and definitely in 1965, but under a different system: it was done under the supervision of the synagogue board and was only for "believers" who brought their own flour and registered their names. The ritual slaughtering of poultry was allowed in the precincts of the Great Synagogue, whereas kosher beef was obtainable until 1964 twice a week at a special store on the outskirts of the city. From 1961 a barrier was erected in the Great Synagogue to separate foreign visitors, including Israeli diplomats, from the congregation, and the synagogue officers were responsible to the authorities for strictly enforcing the segregation.

In 1959, on Rosh Ha-Shanah eve, an anti-Jewish riot took place in Malakhovka, a suburb of Moscow. The synagogue was set afire, but quickly extinguished; the *shammash* of the Jewish cemetery was murdered by unknown persons and on the walls a typewritten antisemitic tract appeared, signed by "the B. Zh. S.R. Committee," the Russian initials of the prerevolutionary antisemitic slogan "Hit the Yids and save Russia." At first Soviet spokesmen denied the facts, but several months later admitted them to foreign visitors, assuring them that the hooligans were apprehended and severely punished. The Soviet press did not mention the incident at all. In 1960 a stir was created among Moscow Jewry when interment at the Jewish cemetery was almost discontinued and Jews were forced to bury their dead in a separate section of a general cemetery. This section was filled up in 1963 and subsequent Jewish burials had to take place alongside non-Jewish ones. Some Jews in various ways obtained the privilege of burying their dead in the remaining space of the old Jewish cemetery, others carried them to the Jewish cemetery of Malakhovka. In the same period several Jews in Moscow were accused, tried, and sentenced to the severest punishment, including execution, for "economic crimes," such as speculation, organizing illicit production and sale of consumer goods in collusion with high officials of the militia, directors of factories, etc. Their trials were accompanied by inflammatory feature articles (called "feuilletons") in the central Moscow press with pronounced antisemitic overtones. However, Moscow was also the center of other developments. In 1959 some Yiddish books, most of them selective works of the classics (*Shalom Aleichem, I.L. *Peretz, D. *Bergelson, etc.), were published there after a prolonged period of the complete obliteration of any printed Yiddish word. Yiddish folklore concerts took place relatively frequently in the city and drew large crowds. Even a semiprofessional theater troupe, headed by the elderly actor Benjamin Schwartzer, was established and mainly performed Shalom Aleichem plays in provincial cities. In 1961 the Yiddish journal **Sovetish Heymland*, edited by an officially appointed editor, the poet Aaron *Vergelis, began to appear as an "organ of the Soviet Writers' Union," first as a bimonthly, later as a monthly. It also served as a kind of Soviet-Jewish mouthpiece for foreign Jews, and visiting Jewish intellectuals were invited to its premises to meet members of its editorial staff. In 1963 and 1965 collections of Israeli Hebrew poetry and prose were published in Russian translation, as well as a Hebrew-Russian dictionary in 1965 (in 25,000 copies), which was sold out in a few weeks.

Contacts with Israel took manifold forms. The Israeli embassy invited to its receptions not only the rabbis and board members of the various synagogues, but also Jewish writers, artists, and other intellectuals. In various sport events, international scientific congresses, and international exhibitions Israel was almost always represented, and often not only Moscow Jews but also Jews from other parts of the Soviet Union, even from outlying regions, came especially to the capital "to see the Israelis." From time to time Israeli popular singers (e.g., Nechama Hendel, Geulah Gil, etc.) and other artists performed in Moscow and aroused great enthusiasm, particularly among young Jews.

The Six-Day War and the rupture of diplomatic relations between the Soviet Union and Israel (June 1967) put an end to these contacts. But, on the other hand, many Moscow Jews, especially the young, began more and more openly to demonstrate their pro-Israel feelings – by continuing increasingly their mass gatherings around the Great Synagogue, by signing collective protests against the refusal to grant them exit permits to Israel, by studying Hebrew in small groups, etc. Unlike other cities, like *Riga, *Leningrad, *Kishinev, and some towns in *Georgia, there were hardly any sanctions applied in Moscow in 1970 against pro-Israel Jews.

In the census of 1959, 239,246 Jews (4.7% of the total population) were registered in the municipal area of Moscow. Of these, 132,223 were women and 107,023 were men. 20,331 of them (about 8.5%) declared Yiddish to be their mother tongue. These numbers are thought to be a gross underestimate because many tens of thousands of Jews declared at the census their "nationality" to be Russian (some opinions evaluate the number of Moscow's Jews as high as 500,000).

Developments from the 1970s

The Six-Day War had a major impact on the life of Moscow Jews, as it had on the life of all Soviet Jewry. It also resulted in a considerable increase in the anti-Israel policy of the Soviet regime in international affairs and an increase in antisemitism domestically. The process of national rebirth which had already begun among many thousands of completely assimilated Jews took various forms. Tens of thousands of young Jews began to congregate in and around Moscow's Choral Synagogue during Jewish holidays, especially Simḥat Torah. With the beginning of mass *aliyah*, the Jews of Moscow played a significant role in the struggle for the right to emigrate. Demonstrations took place in Moscow which attracted Jews from various cities of the Soviet Union. On February 27, 1971, for example, 26 Jewish activists declared a hunger strike in the entrance to the presidium of the Supreme Soviet of the U.S.S.R., demanding permission to leave for Israel. Similar demonstrations followed.

Despite resistance from the authorities, the period from the 1960s to the early 1980s saw a process of revival in the cultural and religious life of Moscow's Jews. Dozens of teachers taught Hebrew in their apartments, there were seminars and groups studying Judaism and Jewish history and culture, and a Jewish kindergarten and Sunday schools were organized. In the 1970s and early 1980s a number of Jewish *samizdat* publications appeared in Moscow. These included *Evrei v S.S.R.* ("Jews in the U.S.S.R.," 1972–79, nos. 1–20); *Tarbut*, 1975–79, 1–13, *Nash ivrit* ("Our Hebrew," 1978–80, 1–4). Many *aliyah* activists were arrested during this time. One of the most severe sentences was meted out to Anatoly *Sharansky in 1978, and in 1982 Yosef Begun was imprisoned for the third time.

In 1972 the synagogue in the Cherkizov district was closed. Thereafter, until the early 1990s, only two synagogues were functioning in the city: the Choral Synagogue and the hasidic prayer house in the district of Marina Roshcha. Jacob Fischman served as rabbi of Moscow from 1972 to 1982, when he was succeeded by Adolf Shayevich.

While basically conducting an overtly antisemitic policy, the Soviet authorities occasionally resorted to gestures intended to persuade world public opinion that Jewish culture was flourishing in the country. Thus, in 1978 the so-called Birobidzhan Jewish Musical Chamber Theater was established; from 1981 this theater, despite its name, was based in Moscow. In 1986 the Moscow Jewish Dramatic Ensemble became the Jewish Drama Studio Shalom.

From 1987, during the evolution of glasnost and perestroika, Jewish public life in the Soviet Union flourished. Centers of a number of informal Jewish national organizations were established in Moscow including the Jewish Culture Association (EKA, headed by Mikhail Chlenov), the Zionist Federation of Soviet Jews (president Arye (Lev) Gorodetsky), and the Association for Friendship and Cultural Ties with Israel. A number of Moscow bodies began to function as well: the Moscow Jewish Cultural and Educational Association, the Jewish Information Center, and the cultural religious center Maḥanayim. As part of the an effort to maintain some control of this burgeoning cultural revival, the authorities established the Association of Activists and Friends of Soviet Jewish Culture, which, starting in April 1989, published the newspaper *Vestnik sovetso-evreiskoi kul'tury* ("Bulletin of Soviet Jewish Culture"). A number of Jewish libraries were founded. In late 1988, a yeshivah (headed by the Israeli scholar Rabbi Adin Steinsaltz) was established within the framework of the Academy of World Cultures. Also in 1988–89, branches of the international Jewish organizations Beta, WIZO, and B'nai B'rith were set up in Moscow.

After the failure of the August 19–21, 1991, coup in Moscow, the last barriers to free cultural and political activity in the country fell. Numerous Jewish bodies functioned in the city. Some of these had an All-Russian character, e.g., Va'ad Rosii (the Federation of Jewish Communities and Organizations of Russia (president: M. Chlenov), the Zionist Federation of Russia (chairman: A. Gorodetsky); Tkhiya, the International Center for Research and the Spreading of Jewish Culture (chairman: Leonid Roitman); the Orthodox All-Russian Jewish Religious Community (headed by the now chief rabbi of Russia, Adolf Shayevich). In 1991 a synagogue was opened on Malaya Bronnaya Street. Since that time three Orthodox synagogues have been operating (Rabbi Pinhas Goldschmidt now serves as chief rabbi of the city), as well as Reform and Conservative congregations.

Jewish cultural life exhibits new life. There are several Jewish high schools as well as evening and Sunday schools; a Jewish university, a Jewish Historical Society (chairman: Rashid Kaplanov), and a Jewish Scientific Center (chairman: Vladimir Shapiro). There has been a renewal of the publication of scientific works in Jewish studies: from 1992 *Vestnik evreskogo universiteta v Moskve* ("Bulletin of the Jewish University of Moscow") has appeared regularly, and in 1994 the Moscow-based *Rossiiskaya evreiskaya entsiklopedia* ("The Encyclopedia of Russian Jewry," editor-in-chief: Herman Branover) began publication. *Mazhdunarodnaya evreiskaya gazeta* ("International Jewish Newspaper," editor-in-chief: Tancred Galinpolsky) appears in Russia, while the Yiddish monthly *Idishe gas* ("Jewish Street," editor-in-chief: Aaron Vergelis, formerly the editor of the now defunct Yiddish journal *Sovetish Heymland*) began to appear in January 1993.

With the onset of political freedom, however, various, antisemitic groups also became active. In the late 1980s antisemitic slogans were heard with increasing frequency at public meetings of the "Pamyat" association. Antisemitic articles were printed in the journals *Nash sovremennik* ("Our Contemporary"), *Molodaya Gvardiya* ("Young Guard"), and

Moscow journals and 27 newspapers regularly publish antisemitic material. In April 1992 proto-fascist punks attacked the ḥasidic synagogue in Moscow with Molotov cocktails. In July 1993 the windows of the Choral Synagogue were broken and swastikas daubed on its walls. However, lacking broad support of the masses, the antisemites did not undertake more violent measures. Although the democratic-oriented public opposed antisemitic actions (articles against antisemitism appear regularly in a number of journals), and the Duma or parliament in November 1992 held hearings on antisemitism, where government and public figures condemned the phenomenon. Still, fear of antisemitism, along with the difficult economic situation and concern about the future of democracy in Russia, encouraged some Moscow Jews to emigrate. However, the rate of emigration for Moscow (and St. Petersburg) is much lower than that for the rest of the former U.S.S.R. The 1970 census recorded 251,000 Jews in the city. Estimates of the "core" (self-defined) Jewish population of Moscow based on subsequent census data give figures of 176,000 for 1989, 135,000 for 1994, and 88,000 for 2002, representing 35% of the Jews in the Russian Federation.

[Leonid Preisman (2nd ed.)]

BIBLIOGRAPHY: Ettinger, in: *Zion*, 18 (1953), 136–68; J. Mazeh, *Zikhronot*, 2 (1936); Dubnow, Divrei, 10 (1958), 94–97; Dubnow, Hist Russ, index; Marek, in: *Voskhod*, no. 2–3 (1893), 200–29; no. 6 (1893), 73–91; no. 9 (1895), 22–33; Goldovski, in: *Byloye*, 9 (1907); Katznelson, in: *Yevreyskaya Starina*, 1 (1909), 175–88; Hessen (Gessen), in: *Perezhitoye*, 1 (1908), 51–65; idem, in: *Yevreyskaya Starina*, 8 (1915), 1–19, 153–72; Eisenberg, *ibid.*, 13 (1930), 81–99. **ADD. BIBLIOGRAPHY:** M. Tolts, "The Post-Soviet Jewish Population in Russia and the World," in: *Jews in Russia and Eastern Europe*, no. 1 (2004), 37–63.

MOSENTHAL, South African family, who, in successive generations, played a major part in the 19th-century development of the country's commerce, banking, and, especially, agricultural export trade. The family came from Hesse-Cassel, Germany, and the first to immigrate was JOSEPH MOSENTHAL (1813–1871), who settled at the Cape in 1839. He was joined by his brothers ADOLPH (1812–1882) and JULIUS (1819–1880), and the three set up in business in Cape Town as Mosenthal Brothers. The firm continued to flourish under family control until well into the 20th century. From their main business centers in Cape Town, Port Elizabeth, and Graaff Reinet, the Mosenthals spread their activities throughout the Cape Colony, and later through the Transvaal. They established numerous trading posts in the interior and organized transport to and from the coast. Their first interest was the marketing of wool and hides, but they gradually expanded their activities to embrace gold and diamond mining, industrial enterprises, and banking. In the early years they issued their own banknotes, which were widely circulated but were withdrawn by the firm with the development of the colony's commercial banking system.

The Mosenthals made a special study of ostrich farming and opened up export markets for its products. They introduced merino sheep from France and Angora goats from Turkey; Adolph Mosenthal himself went to the Black Sea to arrange for the importation of the goats after earlier attempts had failed. This was the beginning of South Africa's staple mohair industry. In 1857 Julius Mosenthal was the first professing Jew to be elected to the Legislative Council of the Eastern (Cape) Province, and Joseph Mosenthal was elected to the same body in 1861. A fourth brother, Salomon Hermann *Mosenthal, became well known as a Viennese dramatist. Other leading members of the family were HARRY (1850–1915) and WILLIAM (1861–1933), both sons of Adolph.

In the 19th century, the Mosenthals helped a number of German-Jewish immigrants to settle in South Africa. Joseph Mosenthal, like his brothers, was a conforming Jew and was one of the founders of the Cape Town Hebrew Congregation in 1841. In later years the Mosenthals, like many of the other early Jewish families in South Africa, married out of the faith, and their descendants were no longer identified as Jews.

BIBLIOGRAPHY: L. Herrman, *History of the Jews in South Africa* (1935), index; G. Saron and H. Hotz, *The Jews in South Africa...* (1955), 349–52; I. Abrahams, *Birth of a Community* (1955), index.

[Lewis Sowden]

MOSENTHAL, SALOMON HERMANN (1821–1877), German playwright. Mosenthal, who was born in Cassel, was a member of the *Mosenthal family. While studying engineering in Karlsruhe, he published his first poems under the pseudonym "Friedrich Lehner," bringing him into contact with the Swabian Romantic circle. Though intellectual tendencies at that time were turning toward democracy and liberalism, Mosenthal neglected revolutionary impulses and turned toward conservatism. As a consequence, he moved to Vienna (where he worked as a private tutor) in 1842 – just as artistic life was fleeing the Austrian capital and its absolutistic, autocratic spirit. Soon he changed his aesthetic focus and embarked on a career as a playwright. Mosenthal's biggest success was the play *Deborah* (1850), which was adapted for the English stage as *Leah, the Forsaken*. After premiering in Hamburg, it was a success in New York and was performed more than 600 times in London. The play presents an 18th-century love story between Joseph, a minister's son, and Deborah, a passionate, gypsy-like Jewess, who ultimately renounces her love for the sake of Joseph's happiness. Though the highly emotionally charged scenes are soaked with social criticism, it nonetheless never targets contemporary political issues. On the contrary, it celebrates Joseph II as a founding figure of Jewish emancipation. Besides *Deborah* and a few other plays such as *Sonnenwendhof* (1857), Mosenthal wrote several opera libretti, some of them dealing explicitly with Jewish topics, including *Judith* (set to music by Albert Franz Doppler in 1870), *Moses*, and *Die Makkabäer* (set to music by Anton Rubinstein in 1892 and 1874, respectively). His most popular libretto in his lifetime was surely that for Otto Nikolai's *Die lustigen Weiber von Windsor* (*Merry Wives of Windsor*, 1849). In addition, Mosenthal published a volume of stories of characteristic Jewish life, *Bilder aus dem juedischen Familienleben* (1878). Obviously influenced by the genre of "Ghettoliteratur" and its most prominent representative Leopold Kompert, it portrays the problematic and chronically-endangered coexistence of Christians and Jews in Mosenthal's childhood homeland of Hessen. As a civil servant, Mosenthal had an impressive career. In 1849 the University of Marburg – where he had attained his doctorate six years before – awarded him an honorary doctorate. From 1850 onward, he worked in the Austrian ministry of education and was promoted to the rank of privy councilor in 1873. In 1871, he was knighted Ritter von Mosenthal. His collected works were published in six volumes in 1877/78.

BIBLIOGRAPHY: M. Martersteig, *Das deutsche Theater im 19. Jahrhundert* (1904), 402, 423. **ADD. BIBLIOGRAPHY:** K. Schug, *Salomon Hermann Mosenthals Leben und Werk in der Zeit* (1966).

[Samuel L. Sumberg / Philipp Theisohn (2nd ed.)]

MOSER, SIR CLAUDE, BARON (1922–), British statistician and academic. Born in Berlin, Moser immigrated to Britain in 1936. He taught at the London School of Economics from 1946 to 1970, where he was professor of social statistics, as well as serving as senior statistician to the British government and, from 1967 to 1978, as head of the Government Statistical Survey. An eminent statistician, he was elected to the British Academy in 1969. A distinguished academic, Moser served as warden (president) of Wadham College, Oxford, in 1984–93, as president of the British Association for the Advancement of Science, and as a trustee of the British Museum (1988–2002) and chairman of the British Museum Development Trust. He was chancellor of Keele University from 1986 to 2002 and received no fewer than 16 honorary degrees, as well as serving as chancellor of the Open University of Israel from 1994. He received a knighthood in 1973 and a life peerage in 2001.

[William D. Rubinstein (2nd ed.)]

MOSER, JACOB (1839–1922), early British Zionist and a sponsor of the Herzlia High School in Tel Aviv. Born in Kappeln, Schleswig, Moser moved to England in the 1860s and settled in Bradford, where he was a successful woollens merchant. He and his wife engaged in philanthropic activities there, especially the establishment of hospitals and schools for the poor. He joined the Zionist movement with the appearance of Theodor Herzl and was a member of the Zionist General Council, the board of the Jewish Colonial Trust, the Anglo-Palestine Corporation, the Jewish National Fund, and the presidium of a number of Zionist Congresses. At the Eighth Zionist Congress (1907), David *Wolffsohn announced Moser's contribution of 80,000 francs toward the establishment of the first Hebrew high school (in Jaffa) on the condition that the school bear Herzl's name. This was the largest contribution made by an individual to the Zionist Organization up to World War I. Moser visited Ereẓ Israel in 1908 and 1910 and followed the high school's early steps, adding large sums to his contribution, so that the building could be complete, supplies and equipment could be purchased, etc. He also supported other projects in Ereẓ Israel (e.g., Ben-Yehuda's Hebrew dictionary, the Bezalel School of Arts and Crafts, etc.). Moser continued his philanthropic activities until his last years. In 1909 he was chosen an honorary citizen of Bradford and served as its lord mayor in 1910–11.

BIBLIOGRAPHY: B. Ben-Yehuda (ed.), *Sippurah shel ha-Gimnazyah "Herẓliyyah"* (1970); Tidhar, 18 (n.d.), 5358 – 60 index.

[Getzel Kressel]

MOSER, MOSES (1796–1838), banker and a founder of the *Verein fuer Kultur und Wissenschaft des Judentums. An employee (and eventual partner) in the firm of Moses Friedlaender (son of David *Friedlaender), he attended philosophical lectures at Berlin University although he had no formal secondary education. There he met Eduard *Gans, Leopold *Zunz, and other young Jewish intellectuals, with whom he eventually founded the Verein (Nov. 7, 1819). Moser, who exerted a stabilizing and moderating influence within the Verein, was its treasurer (1821–22) and secretary (Nov. 1819; 1822–23). He also gave five lectures and contributed three articles. After the dissolution of the Verein, Moser, the one member esteemed by all, maintained his ties with L. Zunz, E. Wohlwill, and others. However, his most valued and most famous friend was Heinrich *Heine, who in his letters expressed his affection and esteem for Moser. Despite some setbacks the friendship endured. In 1819 Moser and some colleagues joined the patrician society, Gesellschaft der Freunde (founded in 1792 by I. Euchel and J. Mendelssohn), in the vain hope of subverting it from within. Moser eventually became its president (1836–38).

BIBLIOGRAPHY: H.G. Reissner, *Eduard Gans* (Ger., 1965), index; idem, in: YLBI, 2 (1957), 189–90; A. Friedlaender, *ibid.*, 11 (1966), 269–99; N.N. Glatzer (ed.), *L. Zunz* (Ger., 1964), index; *Briefe von H. Heine an seinen Freund M. Moser* (1862).

MOSES (Heb. מֹשֶׁה; LXX, *Mōusēs*; Vulg. *Moyses*), leader, prophet, and lawgiver (set in modern chronology in the first half of the 13th century B.C.E.). Commissioned to take the Israelites out of Egypt, Moses led them from his 80th year to his death at 120 during their wanderings in the wilderness until their arrival at the Plains of Moab.

This article is arranged according to the following outline:

BIBLICAL VIEW

The individual accounts of Moses combine to make him the most important biblical figure after God. As a prophet he is incomparable (Num. 12:6–8; Deut. 34:10). In the Bible, he is not only a national leader; it is he who fashions the nation of Israel, transforming a horde of slaves into a people potentially capable of becoming "a treasured possession" and "a kingdom of priests" (Ex. 19:5–6). He is portrayed as Israel's first religious teacher; he gave Israel the Torah – a law of justice, holiness, and loving-kindness. Nevertheless, Scripture portrays Moses as human (Ex. 33:21ff.) and mortal (Deut. 34:5). He had faults as well as virtues, and was punished by the very God whom he taught Israel to worship. Not till the advent of Hellenism was the lawgiver described as *theos aner* ("a divine man"). In the Bible he is only the "human rod" with which God performs wonders.

Biography

The primary sources for the story of Moses' life and works are contained in Exodus, Leviticus, Numbers, and Deuteronomy. Additional references are to be found in Joshua, Judges, I Samuel, I and II Kings, Isaiah, Hosea, Micah, Malachi, Psalms, Daniel, Ezra, Nehemiah, and I and II Chronicles. The salient references will be given in the course of the article. Because the stories of Moses originate from different times and places we cannot really reconstruct a biography of Moses. We cannot even be sure that Moses was a historical character. Even if he was, later writers wrote stories about Moses in which the ancient worthy represented their viewpoints. For example, the story in Numbers 12, in which all prophecy other than that of Moses is deemed unreliable, has the aim of elevating Scripture, the written Torah of Moses, at the expense of oral prophecy (Sperling).

EARLY LIFE. Moses' father and mother – Amram and Jochebed – were both of the tribe of Levi; he had an older sister, Miriam, and an older brother, Aaron (Ex. 2:1; 6:16–20; 7:7; Num. 26:59; I Chron. 23:12–14). The future redeemer of Israel was born at the height of the Egyptian persecution of the Israelites. The Pharaoh that "knew not Joseph" (Ex. 1:8) had set taskmasters over the Children of Israel to oppress them with forced labor (Ex. 1:11). In order to reduce their numbers he had also instructed the Hebrew midwives, Shiphrah and Puah, to kill the Israelite boys at birth, but owing to the piety of these women the plan failed (Ex. 1:15ff.). Thereupon Pharaoh charged all his people to throw every newborn Hebrew boy into the Nile (Ex. 1:22). Jochebed succeeded in concealing the infant Moses for three months (Ex. 2:2). Thereafter she made a wicker basket for him, caulked with bitumen and pitch, and placed it among the reeds of the river, while his unnamed sister watched from a distance. Pharaoh's daughter, spying the basket when she came down to bathe, ordered one of her maids to fetch it. The princess took pity on the crying babe and decided to adopt him. At the sister's suggestion Moses' own mother was given the task of nursing the child until he was old enough to be returned to Pharaoh's daughter. In this way Moses the Hebrew was, ironically, brought up as a prince in Pharaoh's own palace. The hand of providence is manifest in these events; Pharaoh's very plan of destruction became part of the divine design of redemption. The wondrous story is also intended to indicate the historic destiny awaiting the child. Possibly even his name *Moshe* is a pointer in this direction. The popular etymology (undoubtedly *Moshe* is an Egyptian name, probably meaning "son") "I drew him out of the water" (Ex. 2:10) should logically have required the form *mashui* ("one that has been drawn out"), not *moshe* ("one that draws out"). But the infant was one day to "draw out" his people from the Sea of Reeds and bondage. (See Isa. 63:11–12 and below.)

Although Moses was reared as an Egyptian, he remained conscious of his origin and sympathetic to his kindred. When he grew to manhood, he went out to his brethren and witnessed their tribulations. His early Egyptian upbringing seems to have been a necessary stage in the process of fitting him for his future role as Israel's liberator. His outlook was molded by a sense of freedom that his kinsfolk could not enjoy. Though "learned in all the wisdom of the Egyptians" (Acts 7:22), he was outraged by his first contact with the realities of the bondage. He saw an Egyptian beating a Hebrew slave and, overcome by an irresistible feeling of righteous indignation, he slew the Egyptian and hid him in the sand, thinking his deed would not be discovered. His second experience was even sadder: he found two Hebrews fighting. His intervention drew from the aggressor the retort: "Who made you chief and ruler over us? Do you mean to kill me as you killed the Egyptian?" To escape Pharaoh's wrath, Moses fled to Midian (Ex. 2:11–15).

FLIGHT TO MIDIAN AND THE MISSION. In Midian, Moses, always the foe of unrighteousness rose again in defense of the persecuted. He saved the daughters of the priest Reuel (also called Jethro, Jether, and Hobab), who had come to water their father's flocks, from the hands of the bullying local shepherds. As a result of the incident Moses stayed with the priest and married his daughter Zipporah, by whom he had two sons, Gershom and Eliezer (Ex. 2:15–22; 18:3–4; cf. Judg. 18:30; I Chron. 23:15–17). A turning point in his life came when he witnessed a theophany in the region of Horeb. He saw a bush aflame with a fire that did not consume it. On turning aside to investigate the marvelous sight, he heard the voice of a god, whose name he did not know, calling him. In the vision God bade Moses redeem Israel from Egypt, where a new king now reigned. Moses resisted the divine commission, with many new excuses. The dialogue veers in different directions. Four times Moses changes the course of his argument: he feels inadequate to the task; he inquires by what name God is to be announced to the Israelites; he doubts that the Children of Israel will listen to him; he protests that he is slow of speech. Patiently God answers each objection. He would be with Moses and the fact that the Israelites, when they left Egypt, would serve the Lord at this mountain would be a sign to him that God had sent him; he was to tell his people that "I am that I am" had spoken to him; and He who gives humans the power of speech would teach him what to say. Together with the elders he was to ask Pharaoh's permission for the Israelites to go on a three-day journey into the wilderness to sacrifice to the Lord, although the request would certainly be refused. To help him convince the Israelites, the Lord gave Moses three wondrous signs (the rod becomes a snake and is restored to its former state; his hand becomes afflicted with a skin disease (see *Leprosy) and is healed; the Nile water, poured out on the ground, turns to blood). But still, without further rational argument, Moses refuses. The Lord is angered, but promises to let Aaron be Moses' spokesman, and bids him take the rod with which to perform the signs (Ex. 3:1–4:17; 7:1).

The wonders wrought by Moses both in Egypt and in the wilderness have special quality. Moses' "signs and portents" served as evidence of God's will. Moses' "call" has no biblical parallel. Even Gideon (Judg. 6:11–24) and Jeremiah (1:4–10) in the end accepted the divine commission unconditionally.

THE RETURN TO EGYPT AND THE EXODUS. Moses' initial efforts were frustrating. At the very beginning of his homeward journey an obscure incident occurred that almost proved fatal to Moses; he was only saved by the timely action of Zipporah in circumcising their son (Ex. 4:24–26). Pharaoh responded to the request of Moses and Aaron by augmenting the people's burdens. Henceforth they were to provide their own straw for making the bricks. Understandably the Israelites lost confidence in their would-be redeemer, who was himself discouraged (Ex. 4:27–5:23).

Events now assume a new dynamic. In a second revelation God announced: "I am the Lord. I appeared to Abraham, Isaac, and Jacob as El Shaddai ["Almighty"], but I did not make Myself known to them by My name YHWH" (Ex. 6:2–3). The divine announcement means that according to the Priestly source, the Tetragrammaton (YHWH, the four-letter name of God) was first revealed to Moses. Names in the Bible are not merely labels but descriptive epithets. They are particularly significant when applied to God. YHWH, elaborated in the enigmatic "I am that I am," expressed the abiding providence that would sustain the people. (cf. Ex. 3:12).

Pharaoh's hardness of heart (for the statement "And the Lord hardened the heart of Pharaoh" see *God) called for sterner measures. By means of a series of ten devastating plagues (blood, frogs, gnats, swarm of flies, pest, boils, hail, locusts, darkness, death of the firstborn – humans and beasts), arranged schematically (see U. Cassuto, *Exodus* (1967), 92ff.), Pharaoh's resistance and tergiversations were gradually overcome. Before the incidence of the final and climactic plague, the Israelites were enjoined to offer up a sacrifice on the 14th of the first month (Abib = later, Nisan), and to daub the lintel and the two doorposts with its blood: "For when the Lord goes through to smite the Egyptians, He will see the blood… and will pass over (or: "protect") the door and not let the destroyer enter or smite your home" (Ex. 12:23). The last plague brought immediate surrender. The departure of the Israelites was now speeded by the panic-stricken Egyptians with the utmost impatience, so that the people had to take their dough before it was leavened and baked unleavened cakes (Ex.6:10–12:36).

The Israelites, accompanied by "a mixed multitude" Exodus, left Egypt on the 15th of what would later be called Nisan. Already in Egypt they had eaten the Passover/*Pesaḥ* sacrifice ("because He passed over/protected the houses of the Israelites"), instituted the Feast of Unleavened Bread ("for there was no time for the dough of our fathers to become leavened"), and promulgated the law of the consecration of the firstborn ("at the time that I smote every firstborn in the land of Egypt, I consecrated every firstborn in Israel, human and beast, to Myself").

CROSSING THE SEA OF REEDS. Pharaoh, however, soon repented his liberating act. The urgency with which the Israelites were expelled from Egypt was matched by the haste with which Pharaoh sought to recapture his slaves. The final scene was enacted by the Sea of Reeds. Hemmed in between the sea and the Egyptian cohorts, with only the pillar of cloud (of fire, by night) between the fugitives and their pursuers, the Israelites cried to the Lord, the only power that could now save them. The end came with dramatic swiftness. Moses sundered the waters with his rod; Israel crossed the seabed dry-shod, but their would-be captors were drowned by the returning waters (Ex. 14). The ode of triumph that Moses and the Children of Israel sang after their deliverance from the Egyptians (Ex. 15) is one of the most beautiful psalms in the Bible. Characteristically it contains no mention of Moses, just as the creedal recital in connection with the first fruits has no reference to the liberator (Deut. 26:5–9). The glory and the thanksgiving are accorded solely to the Lord.

COVENANT AT SINAI AND THE DESERT PERIOD. The ultimate goal lay ahead at Mount Horeb (Sinai), where in the third month after the Exodus the people were to witness the revelation of God, hear the Decalogue issuing forth from Sinai, and declare their eternal loyalty to the Divine Law in the words, "All that the Lord has spoken we will do and obey" (Ex. 19: 1ff.; 24:7). Israel entered into a covenant with the Lord (24:8), of which the Ten Words or *Decalogue, usually called the Ten Commandments, formed the preamble and the Torah precepts the conditions. The covenant with YHWH is depicted as the real purpose of the Exodus. Freedom was not just the negation of servitude. Even the plagues were intended not only to humble Pharaoh, but to establish divine sovereignty over Israel.

The Torah's narratives describe a descent; from the sublime heights of God's mountain Israel plunged into the abyss of the *Golden Calf. The narrative is not descriptive history but rather a polemic against the cult established by *Jeroboam I. According to the calf narrative, Moses had ascended the mountain of the Lord to receive the tablets of the Decalogue and spent 40 days and nights there. Disturbed by Moses' delay in returning to the camp, the Israelites persuaded Aaron to make them a god that would go before them, since they did not know what had happened to their leader. The bovine image that Aaron produced was to serve as a surrogate for Moses, and in Aaron's view probably only represented God's visible throne. It nevertheless constituted unforgivable religious treason, for the people regarded the calf as an actual deity ("These are your gods, O Israel"), and the lawgiver, conscious of the spiritual catastrophe that had befallen Israel, shattered the tablets of the Decalogue. For the Judahite author of this anti-Northern polemic, the covenant had been broken; the calf and the Ten Words could not exist in juxtaposition.

Moses ground the idol to dust and made the Israelites drink its powdered remains. With the help of the loyal tribe of Levi he slew 3,000 of the idolators. Then, in a heartrending supplication, he interceded with the Lord for his people: "But now, if Thou will forgive their sin – and if not, blot me, I pray Thee, out of Thy book which Thou has written." God forgave, in accordance with His attributes (cf. Ex. 34:7). Again Moses ascended the mountain and received a new copy of the Decalogue. He was also vouchsafed deeper insight into the divine glory and character (Ex. 34:6–7). Moses was also given credit for the establishment of – the *Mishkan* ("Dwelling Place"; usually called the Tabernacle). It was the sequel, as it were, of the theophany on Mount Sinai; it was the symbol of God's continuing presence. Although Moses performed certain sacerdotal functions on special occasions (Ex. 24:6; Lev. 8:6ff.), and is even called a priest in Psalm 99:6, he is never actually portrayed as such in the Torah. The Tent of Meeting, referred to in Exodus 33:7–11, is not to be identified with the Tabernacle. It was Moses' own tent, which served temporarily as a meeting place between him and God, until the time of "wrath was past." It was pitched outside the camp, which had been recently defiled by idolatry (see Rashi, Ibn Ezra, and Naḥmanides to Ex. 33:7; Cassuto, *Exodus* (1967), 429ff.).

The desert wanderings were, according to the Torah, a period of constant tension and crisis. The people lacked food and were not content with the manna; at times they demanded meat (Ex. 16:12ff.; Num. 11:4–6; 21:5). Often they were in need of drinking water (Ex. 15:23ff.; 17:2–7; Num. 20:1–13). On one occasion, when Moses struck the rock to produce water, instead of speaking to it, he was himself condemned for lack of faith (Num. 20:7–13). Repeatedly the people murmured and even threatened to leader to redirect themselves and return to Egypt (Ex. 5:21; 14:11–12; 15:24; 16:28; 17:2–7; Num. 11:4–6; 14:1–4; 20:2–5; 21:4–5). Of the 12 spies sent to investigate the nature of the Promised Land, ten brought back an unfavorable report: the land was exceedingly fertile (as evidence they showed a huge cluster of grapes), but unconquerable; moreover it devoured its inhabitants. Caleb and Joshua, who gave an encouraging account, failed to convince the people, and in consequence the entire generation (except Joshua and Caleb) were condemned to die in the wilderness and not enter the Land (Num. 13–14). The weary people were prey to all kinds of dangers. The Levite *Korah (Moses' cousin), aided by Dathan, Abiram, and On of the tribe of Reuben, accused Moses and Aaron of self-aggrandizement, and advanced a claim to the priesthood. The challenge and its implicit peril are reflected in the punishment meted out to the rebels: the earth swallowed them up and thousands of others died through plague (Num. 16–17). Even Miriam and Aaron criticized Moses on account of the Cushite woman (a black woman whose origin was Cush, modern day Sudan) whom he had married (Num. 12). Only after 40 years of wandering was Israel's goal in sight. Skirting Edom (Esau's territory), which would not permit them to pass through, and warned not to seize any Ammonite territory (Deut. 2:19), the wanderers were engaged in battle by Sihon the Amorite and Og, king of Bashan. The Israelites defeated both these kings and divided their lands among the tribes of Reuben, Gad, and the half-tribe of Manasseh (Num. 21:4–35; 32:1–42). While the period of the wilderness is depicted in the Pentateuch as a turbulent age, the prophets, in contrast, emphasize its positive aspects. In the desert the Children of Israel had evinced an unforgettable love of the Lord (Jer. 2:1–3).

Interestingly, though the Torah describes the priesthood as hereditary, Joshua, and not one of Moses' sons, was appointed by the lawgiver to be his successor. In regard to the judiciary, Moses accepts Jethro's advice in reorganizing the judicial system and selecting judges who can be taught the laws and expected to be honest (Ex. 18); in contrast to Numbers 11 in which judges are deemed to have prophetic vision. The numbering of the people (Num. 1:2ff.; 26:1ff.), the sending of emissaries to Edom (Num. 20:14) and to Sihon (21:21–22), and even the appointment of scouts to spy out the land (13:2ff.; 21:32; Deut. 1:22–23) are more secular than prophetic.

THE LAST DAYS. In the Plains of Moab Moses' life began to draw to its close. Miriam and Aaron had already died (Num. 20:1, 24–29); Moses, too, was denied entry by the Lord into the land that was the lodestar of his hopes. All his pleadings were in vain (Deut. 3:25). Instead Moses was bidden to appoint Joshua as his successor (Num. 27:16–23; Deut. 1:8; 31:3, 14, 23), and on the borders of the Promised Land the aged leader delivered three hortatory addresses (Deut. 1–4; 5–28; 29–30) in which he reviewed the history of the 40-years' wandering and gave a resume of the Torah Code. After admonishing and blessing his people and viewing the land from the top of Pisgah, he died at the age of 120 by the command of the Lord, and was buried by Him in an unknown grave (Deut. 34). The tomb of Moses was not to become a cultic site, a clear indication that such claims about the site were known to the writer (see below). The valedictory song (*Ha'azinu*) that Moses taught the Children of Israel (Deut. 32) and the testamentary benedictions (Deut. 33) form an epilogue to the biblical account of Moses. The tribute to Moses with which the Torah concludes (Deut. 34:10–12) underscores the uniqueness of Moses' character and achievements.

[Israel Abrahams]

Critical Assessment

(Note: Although there are certain overlaps between this section and that preceding, they have been retained so as not to impair the unity of either section (Ed.)).

No primary source of information on Moses exists outside the Bible. The Pentateuch is the main repository of the traditions regarding Moses' life and work. Some biblical allusions to Moses depend on the Pentateuch, while others are independent, e.g., Hosea 12:14, Micah 6:4 and Isaiah 63:11, and genealogical notices in Judges 1:16; 4:11; 18:30; I Chronicles 23:14–15. For critical treatment, the data are collected by topics in the following paragraphs: the pentateuchal data are followed by the extra-pentateuchal, and then assessed critically. The order of appearance in the narrative is followed in the main.

BIRTH STORY. Moses was born in Egypt to Levite parents – Amram son of Kohath son of Levi, and Jochebed daughter of Levi, Amram's aunt (Ex. 6:20; Num. 26:59; I Chron. 5:29; 23:13). He was their third child, after Aaron (older by three years, Ex. 7:7) and Miriam (older still, cf. 2:4). He was placed by his mother in the Nile to protect him from Pharaoh's decree against male infants of the Hebrews. Found by Pharaoh's daughter, he was returned to his mother for nursing, but later brought back to the princess who adopted him and named him *Moshe*, "explaining, 'I drew him out [*meshitihu*] of the water'" (Ex. 2:1–10).

The story contains generic elements that are discounted by historians. The infant castaway who grows up to be a hero is considered a legendary motif; it appears, for example, in the birth stories of Sargon of Akkad (Pritchard, Texts, 119) and Cyrus (Herodotus 1: 107 ff.); an Egyptian myth tells of the concealment of the infant god Horus by his mother among marsh reeds to protect him from Seth (Helck). Yet, the representation of Israel's savior as being of Egyptian provenance and rearing (though, to be sure, of Hebrew stock) is singularly unstereotypical, and is supported by the Egyptian names of other Levites – Phinehas, Merari, Hophni, and perhaps Aaron and Miriam as well (Albright). The name of Moses too is probably to be derived from the final, verbal element in such Egyptian names as Ptah-mose ("Ptah is born"), which occurs independently in names of the New Kingdom (Griffiths). Connection with Hebrew *mashah*, "draw out," like other such name interpretations, is based on assonance rather than etymology (e.g., the connection of Noah with the unrelated verb *nḥm*; Gen. 5:29); as a Hebrew name, *Moshe* is of very rare, if not unique, formation. (The derivation of the Greek form *Mōusēs* from Egyptian *môu*, "water," and *esês*, "saved," given by Josephus (Ant. 2:228; cf. Apion 1:286; Philo, I Mos. 17), has no bearing on the Hebrew (Černý in Griffiths, see bibl.)).

Moses' connection with the Levites figures in the *Golden Calf story (Ex. 32:26 ff.) and in Judges 18:30, where one of his Levite descendants (see below) is said to have founded the priestly line of the Danite sanctuary (cf. also the later Levitical status of Moses' descendants. I Chron. 23:14). His relationship to Aaron shares the obscurity surrounding the origins of the Aaronide priesthood. Friction between Moses and the Levites on the one hand and Aaron on the other appears in the Golden Calf story and suggests a background of rival ecclesiastical lines. But Aaron's impunity speaks for a high rank independent of Moses – in which respect he is Moses' "brother" and peer. Moses, Aaron, and Miriam are linked in Numbers 12:1–2 and with the Exodus in Micah 6:4; such a family of spiritual persons is unknown in later Israel, but has numerous extra-biblical analogues.

EARLY MANHOOD AND SOJOURN IN MIDIAN. Forced to flee Egypt because of his fatal intervention on behalf of a Hebrew slave, Moses rescues the shepherdess daughters of a Midianite priest from other shepherds who had driven them off. Invited to join the priest's family, he marries his daughter, Zipporah – who bears him two sons, Gershom and Eliezer – and tends his flocks (Ex. 2:10–22; 18:3–4). The episodes of Moses' early manhood foreshadow his career as a savior of the oppressed; they are poetically apt but historically unverifiable. His flight to Midian recalls the story of the Egyptian official Si-nuhe who, having fallen out of favor at the court, fled to Syria, where he settled and married among Semitic tribes (Pritchard, Texts, 18 ff.). The tradition of Moses' Midianite connection is unclear in details. His father-in-law is variously named Reuel (Ex. 2:18; cf. Num. 10:29), Hobab (Judg. 4:11; cf. Num. 10:29) and *Jethro-Jether (Ex. 3:1; 4:18; 18:1 ff.). A wife of Moses is called a Cushite (Num. 12:1) – considered by some to be of the tribe Cushan, a synonym of Midian in Habakkuk 3:7 (cf. W.F. Albright, in: BASOR, 83 (1941) 34, n. 8), and thus identical with Zipporah, though the absence of cross reference is remarkable. Yet the later alliance with Israel of the nomad Kenites, descendants of Hobab (Judg. 1:16; 4:11; I Sam. 15:6 ff.), coupled with the enmity between Midian and Israel that began in the pre-settlement age and continued for generations (Num. 22:4ff.; 31:1ff.; Judg. 6–7), supports the historicity of an early connection between Israel and a Midianite group – the Kenites, relatives of Moses.

THE COMMISSIONING AND THE EXODUS. Once while tending the flocks deep in the wilderness at the Mountain of God, Moses was surprised by a call out of a burning bush to become God's agent in the deliverance of Israel front bondage. God's name, YHWH, was revealed and interpreted to him, and identified with the God of the Patriarchs. Returning to Egypt with (Ex. 4:20) or without (18:2) his family, Moses was rebuffed by Pharaoh, re-commissioned by God, and armed with wonders to bring Pharaoh to his knees. A climactic series of plagues forced the king to release the Israelites. After executing the protective rite of the paschal sacrifice, which saved them from the final plague of the firstborn, the Israelites marched out of Egypt. Soon, however, the Egyptians set out to retake them. Overtaken at the Sea of Reeds, the Israelites escaped through the miraculously divided sea, while the pursuing Egyptians were drowned as the waters closed back on them. Thereupon the people "believed (i.e., attributed the quality of reliability to) in YHWH and in Moses, his servant" and sang a triumphal hymn to God (Ex. 3–15).

The present form of the burning bush story is a composite and elaborated account of the call of the first messenger of God to Israel. Its essence – the overpowering, unavoidable command to go on God's mission – reappears in all accounts of prophetic calls; there is little reason to doubt that it was the experience of the founder of the line (cf. the succession listed in I Sam. 12:8, 11). An allusion to this story seems to be contained in the divine epithet "Bush-Dweller" found in the (tenth-century?) Blessing of Moses (Deut. 33:16). The antiquity of the worship of YHWH and of his association with the "Mountain of God" variously named Horeb and Sinai is problematic. Pre-Mosaic worship of YHWH as a deity whose seat was in the wilderness south of Palestine is hinted at by 14th-century Egyptian references to "a land of the bedouin of YHWH" adjacent to Edom the (cf. provenance of YHWH in the old poems, Deut. 33:2; Judg. 5:4–5, and in Hab. 3:3), and the association of YHWH with Horeb-Sinai prior to Israel's coming there is suggested by Exodus 19:4 ("and brought you to me"). To be sure, Moses is depicted as ignorant of the sanctity of the place (as Jacob was of the sanctity of Beth-El, "the gate of heaven" (Gen. 18:16)) and his experience and conception of YHWH have no known antecedents, but some link with prior religious data cannot be ruled out (though the speculative association of *Kenites-*Midianites with YHWH worship has little to stand on).

The new significance of YHWH with the advent of Moses is indicated by the appearance of the first names bearing an element of the tetragrammaton in connection with Moses: Jochebed and Joshua; no such element occurs in theophoric names of the patriarchal age (on which fact light is shed by Ex. 6:3; modern criticism follows the acute suggestion of the Karaite Jeshua b. Judah (cited by Ibn Ezra, ad loc.) that occurrences of the tetragrammaton in divine communications with the Patriarchs is anachronistic, cf. *Pentateuch). The conception of the messenger or agent of YHWH, sent and equipped with wondrous signs to help Israel, has its first embodiment in Moses and is a distinctive and dominant feature of Israelite religion thereafter. That a new start was made with the God YHWH and his apostle Moses is the core of the burning bush story; the discontinuity that must be postulated at the beginning of Israel's history makes it credible. Moses plays a central role in the story of the *Plagues of Egypt and the Exodus, dramatically woven out of various strands of tradition (see *Exodus, Book of). The line of song ascribed to Miriam in Exodus 15:21 appears as the opening of a triumphal hymn to God in 15:1, which can hardly be detached from it (though verses 12–18 may be a later element), and must be allowed the same antiquity. Reflexes of these traditions, assigning a primary role to Moses, appear in Hosea 12:14 and Micah 6:4 datable to the eighth century; of indeterminate pre-Exilic date are the references in Joshua 24:5 and Psalms 105:26 to the role of Moses and Aaron in the plagues, and in I Samuel 12:6, 8 and Psalms 77:21 (where an echo of Ex. 15:13 occurs) to the brothers' part in the Exodus. Moses is linked with the parting of the sea in the post-Exilic Isaiah 63:11 (where, in the received Hebrew, a pun on Moses' name may appear (*mosheh ʿammo*, "who drew his people out [of the water]"); but the Septuagint lacks these words, and various manuscripts and the Syriac version read *mosheh ʿavdo*, "his servant Moses").

LEADER OF THE WANDERINGS THROUGH THE WILDERNESS. Moses conducted the people into the wilderness, aiming for "the Mountain of God" (cf. Ex. 3:12). On the way he had to organize them under the headship of his aide-de-camp, Joshua, into a fighting force to fend off marauding Amalekites (Ex. 17:8ff.). At Sinai, the first threat to his new faith appeared in the Golden Calf apostasy; Moses met it with harsh resolution, executing the offenders with the help of his Levite kinsmen (Ex. 32). At Sinai, too, Moses established the administrative organs of the people: advised by Jethro, he appointed a hierarchy of deputies to govern and judge them (Ex. 18:13ff.; Deut. 1:9ff.), whose military titles ("officers of thousands, hundreds, fifties, tens") accord with the disposition of the people, after their census, as an army (Num. 1–2). (For the revelation at Sinai, see below.) After celebrating the second Passover (Num. 9), Israel made ready to march on to the Promised Land. Moses requested his father-in-law's service as guide along the way (Num. 10:29ff.); then, with the Ark in the lead, Moses invoked YHWH's victory over all his enemies, and set off (Num. 10:35–36). The post-Sinai part of the wilderness wanderings was filled with challenges to Moses' authority (see next section). Numbers 11:11–12, 16ff. tells of the appointment of 70 elders, inspired by God with some of Moses' spirit to enable them to share the burden of leadership with Moses (but Ex. 24:9ff. seems to suppose their presence already at Sinai). The worst crises came with the demoralizing report of the spies sent from Kadesh to reconnoiter Canaan, and the failure of the subsequent rash attempt to invade directly, made in defiance of Moses' prohibition (Num. 13–14). Frustration induced by the prolonged, forced stay in the wilderness bred the revolt of *Korah and 250 chief men against the authority of Moses and Aaron (Num. 16), which ended with their miraculous destruction. Moses had to crush a second apostasy, incited by Moabite-Midianite women (on the advice of Balaam (Num. 22:16)), at Shittim, in Transjordan (Num. 25). Moses' martial achievements came at the close of his career. His request for peaceful passage through Amorite Transjordan having been denied, Moses led successful campaigns against the kings *Sihon and *Og and, after a preliminary reconnaissance, against the region of Jazer (Num. 21:21ff.; Deut. 2:24–3:11). He allocated the land to the tribes of Reuben, Gad, and half-Manasseh after their oath to participate in the conquest of Cisjordan (Num. 32; Deut. 3:12ff.; Josh. 13:15ff.), and reserved in it three cities of refuge (Deut. 4:41ff.; but cf. Josh. 20:8, which dates this act to the time of Joshua). His last campaign was a retributive war against Midian (Num. 31). In the last year of the wanderings, Moses appointed Eleazar to succeed his father, Aaron, in the priestly duties (Num. 20:23ff.), and his aide, Joshua, to succeed him in the leadership of the people (Num. 27:15ff.; Deut. 31).

The credibility of the wilderness narratives is impaired by their inconsistency (e.g., with respect to the 70 elders; and see the next section), chronological obscurities (e.g., the events in Num. 20–21 and their relation to Deut. 1–2), apparent doublets (e.g., Num. 21:1–3 and 14:45), and divergent itineraries (especially in Num. 33:17ff., which, e.g., has no trace of a southern movement from Kadesh, contrast 14:25, and in 14:41ff. which traces a route arriving at the Plains of Moab without circling the lands of Edom and Moab; contrast Num. 21:4; Deut. 2). Moreover, the presence of Moses is not consistent throughout this material (e.g., Num. 21:1–3), so that critics have assumed that data on tribal movements other than those led by Moses have been combined in these narratives (on the supposition that the migration of the Hebrews was not the single movement into which tradition has characteristically simplified it). Finally, the trek through the Sinai desert at the necessary time period is belied by the extensive archaeological studies of the Sinai following the 1967 Israeli victory.

INTERCESSOR. The stories of Israel's trials of God during their journey fall into two groups: the pre-Sinai trials, in which God's saving power is shown after Moses cries to God, or through a wonder announced by Moses (Ex. 14:15; 15:25; 16:1ff.; 17:4, 11), and the post-Sinai trials, in which the people, though answered, are punished for their faithlessness. Moses is still instrumental in supplying the people's needs, but he now must also intercede on their behalf to assuage God's anger. Moses' first intercession was his recrimination against God for allowing Israel's suffering to increase after his first audience with Pharaoh (Ex. 5:22–23). The longest is in the Golden Calf story – Moses' dramatic plea to God to rescind His decree of annihilation, then to agree to accompany Israel in their journey to the Promised Land. Banking on his favor with God, Moses cajoles Him to reveal to him His "ways," i.e., His merciful attributes (in effect a broader definition of His name; note the similarity of Ex. 33:13, 19 to 3:13–14), upon hearing which he presses God to forgive Israel (Ex. 32–34). Only less dramatic is Moses' other great confrontation with God, wrathful over Israel's disbelief in his capacity to give them victory over the Canaanites. Once again God threatens to destroy Israel, and once again Moses intercedes mightily on Israel's behalf, invoking God's revealed attribute of mercy, and calling upon him to manifest His strength through forbearance (Num. 14:11ff.). Further intercessions occur at Taberah (Num. 11), at the time of Miriam's leprosy (Num. 12), at the rebellion of Korah ("Will one man sin and you rage at the whole community?" Num. 16:22), and at the plague of serpents – to cure which Moses made a *copper serpent (Num. 21:4ff.). Tradition coupled Moses and Samuel as the archetypal intercessors on Israel's behalf (Jer. 15:1). A striking figure, taken from Ezekiel 22:30, is applied to Moses in the post-Exilic Psalm 106:23: "He would have destroyed them, had not Moses, His chosen one, stood in the breach in front of Him, to keep His wrath from destroying them." Psalm 103:7 alludes to Moses' eliciting God's attributes, and cites a few of them. The formulas of intercession in the two major narratives of Exodus 32–34 and Numbers 14 are doubtless part of a liturgical tradition (cf. Joel 2:13) whose attribution to Moses cannot be verified. The intercessory role of later prophets is firmly established; the depiction of Moses as a master of this role accords with his status as founder of Israel's prophetic line (see below), and may well be authentic. Singular authentication is given to Moses' copper serpent: down to the eighth century a copper serpent ascribed to Moses was lodged in the Jerusalem Temple; King Hezekiah ordered it cut down because the people were making burnt offerings to it (II Kings 18:4).

MEDIATOR OF THE COVENANT AND LAWGIVER. At Sinai, Moses negotiated Israel's acceptance of God's offer of a covenant, prepared the people for the covenant theophany, led them to God for the theophany, and strengthened them to sustain the experience (Ex. 19–20). The people heard the *Decalogue directly from God; Deuteronomy 5:5, however, insinuates Moses between the parties "to tell you what God spoke." Shattered by the experience, the people asked Moses to be their intermediary with God henceforth (Ex. 20:18–21 [15–18]; Deut. 5:20–28). Moses then received detailed stipulations of the covenant ("the *Book of the Covenant," Ex. 24:7) which he related to the people, and upon securing their assent to be bound by them, wrote down and ratified them in a solemn ceremony (Ex. 24:3–11). Later he received the written form of the Decalogue on stone tablets, which he deposited in the Ark of the Covenant (Ex. 24:12; 32:15–16; 34:1, 28–29; Deut. 9:9ff.; 10:1ff.). According to Deuteronomy, Moses recited all these stipulations to the generation about to enter Canaan during his last days, in the Plains of Moab. He concluded the recitation with warnings, blessings, and curses, then committed it to writing and deposited the document – "the Book of Torah" – in the Ark, alongside the tablets (Deut. 31:9, 24 ff.). In between the two covenant-makings, at the beginning and at the end of the journey through the wilderness, Moses received a host of ritual, religious, and moral injunctions, in the Tent of Meeting at Sinai and in the Plains of Moab (Lev. 1:1 ff.; 26:46; 27:34; Num. 36:13). In addition to these large and small collections of injunctions, issued at the initiative of God, Moses sought and received oracular decisions in difficult cases, as need arose. This role was reserved for him in the administrative organization of the camp suggested by Jethro (Ex. 18:19–20) and its performance is illustrated in the cases of the blasphemer (Lev. 24), the Sabbath breaker (Num. 15:32 ff.), and the daughters of Zelophehad (Num. 27; cf. Num. 36). The figure of Moses as the mediator of God's laws and admonitions to Israel appears in biblical literature influenced by Deuteronomy and in post-Exilic writings. Thus the deuteronomistically edited Book of Joshua is haunted by Moses, the lawgiver; indeed it reads as the record of fulfillment of Moses' admonitions (e.g., 1:1 ff.; 4:10 ff.; 8:31 ff.; 11:15 ff.; 14:6, 9; 17:4; 20:2). Material in the same spirit and style is found in Kings: I Kings 2:3; 8:53, 56; II Kings 14:6; 18:6; 21:8; 23:25. In writings of the Persian period, Moses appears exclusively as the author of the Torah and the founder of Israel's sacred institutions (Mal. 3:22; Ezra 3:2; Neh. 1:7 ff.; 8:1, 14; 9:14; 10:30; I Chron. 6:34; 21:29; II Chron. 8:13; 24:6; 35:6, 12). For a critical assessment of this representation of Moses, see the end of the next section.

CULT FOUNDER AND PRIEST. Moses not only proclaimed the proper name of God, by which He was henceforth to be invoked in worship ("This shall be My name forever/This My appellation [*zikhri*, lit. 'call-word'] for all time," Ex. 3:15), he instructed Israel in YHWH's sacred seasons-starting with Passover and *maẓẓot* (Ex. 12) and the Sabbath (Ex. 16) and proceeding to the whole cultic calendar and its related prescribed sacrifices (Ex. 23:14 ff.; 34:18 ff.; Lev. 23; Num. 28:29; Deut. 16). The non-festival sacrificial system, too, was ordained by him (Lev. 1–7). He received the blueprint of the Tabernacle and supervised its construction (Ex. 25–31; 35–40). He inaugurated it and consecrated its clergy (Lev. 8). Moses is described as exercising specific priestly functions (e.g., handling the blood of sacrifice) both in the ceremony of covenant ratification (Ex. 24:6, 8) and during the inauguration of the Tabernacle and priesthood (Lev. 8).

Only two allusions to Moses' priestly aspect occur in extra-pentateuchal writing: Psalm 99:6 counts Moses with Aaron as a priest of YHWH (traditional exegetes refer this to his role in Lev. 8), and the priesthood of the Danite sanctuary traced their line to a descendant of Moses (Judg. 18:30 – crediting the talmudic notice that the suspended *nun* of "Manasseh" is a deliberate device to obscure the derivation of this ignoble priesthood from Moses; BB 109b). According to the post-Exilic record, and in line with the Aaronide monopoly of the priesthood prescribed by the Torah, the descendants of Moses were counted as Levites, not priests (I Chron. 23:14). Criticism finds the ascription to Moses of the vast corpus of rules and admonitions in Exodus, Leviticus, Numbers, and Deuteronomy improbable. Its arguments – from inconsistency, variant repetitions, diversity in style and viewpoint, and divergent historical presuppositions – can be found in articles on the books in question and on the *Pentateuch as a whole. Yet the origin and motive of this ascription can be described, and its poetic justice defended. The constant, stable element in the history of Israel during the biblical period is the consciousness of being a religious community, bound together by a common link to YHWH. No political change or revolution broke the continuity of this element. Under tribal rule or united monarchy, in a divided kingdom or in exile, and no less under Persian rule, the idea of a primary allegiance to the will of YHWH, prior to all political forms, defined Israelite identity. From latest to earliest times this allegiance was expressed in zeal for YHWH's exclusive claim upon Israel (i.e., hostility toward foreign cults), in iconoclasm (persecution of idolatry), in peculiar religious institutions (e.g., the Sabbath), and in moral earnestness resulting from the communal responsibility to God for violations of morality (Judg. 20; II Sam. 4:11). Its symbol was the Ark of the Covenant (as early as the time of the Judges, I Sam. 4), and its exponents were agents and messengers of YHWH who admonished error and saved from distress (e.g., Jerubbaal, Judg. 6 ff.). These elements, constitutive of Israel's identity and singularity from the very beginning of its occupation of Canaan no doubt originated in Canaan proper through circumstances not fully understood and projected backward in time. The question of their author – is solved in Israelite tradition by assigning to Moses his role of covenant mediator and cult founder. The above-mentioned features of Israelite religion are ascribed to Moses, as well as their integrating framework, the idea of the covenant with YHWH. However rudimentary the terms of the Mosaic covenant may have been (some suppose no more than the Decalogue, others include parts of the Book of the Covenant; criteria for positive ascription are wanting), they were enough to serve as the constitution of the religio-political community of Israel; subsequent development of these terms, their ramifications, their adjustments to changing times, was regarded as part and parcel of the original. In theory, all regulations constitutive of the religious community of Israel were covenant regulations; all were issued by God and communicated to Israel by the mediator Moses. Something of the process may be glimpsed at in Nehemiah 10:30 ff. and II Chronicles 30:16; 35:12, where rites are ascribed to the Torah of Moses that are not in fact to be found there.

DEATH AND BURIAL. Although commissioned to bring Israel into the Promised Land (e.g., Ex. 33:1 ff.), Moses died in the Plains of Moab, outside its borders. Numbers 20:2–13 accounts for this by the offense of Moses and Aaron at Kadesh, in connection with procuring water for the grumbling people – "the waters of contention" *(me merivah)*. Wherein the brothers failed to "believe" God and "sanctify him in the sight of the Israelites" (Num. 20:12) is obscure. The interpretation in Psalms 106:32–33 is ambiguous: this much seems clear, however: that Moses is blamed for speaking rashly. In Deuteronomy, in contrast, Moses is denied entry into the Promised Land on account of the people: their display of faithlessness during the incident of the spies made God turn upon Moses as well. It was then He decreed that Moses (as well as his whole generation) would not enter the land (Deut. 1:37; 3:26; 4:21). When his time had come, Moses was commanded to ascend Mount Nebo, from which he could view the length and breadth of the Promised Land. There he died and was buried in the valley, "in the land of Moab, opposite Beth-Peor; and no man knows his burial place, to this day" (Deut. 34; cf. Num. 27:12ff.). The various theological explanations of Moses' death in Transjordan vouch for the existence of a grave tradition. Inasmuch as grave traditions were attached to such worthies as the patriarchs and matriarchs, the surprising obliteration of his burial-place savors of a deliberate aversion toward his apotheosis, which might have grown out of veneration of his grave as a shrine. Such an apotheosis was likely in view of the singular status accorded Moses in Israelite tradition (see Houtman).

UNIQUE STATUS. The wonders performed by Moses on behalf of Israel exceed those of any subsequent prophet (Deut. 34:11–12). He not only outdid Egypt's magicians (whose virtuosity, as displayed, e.g., in the Westcar Papyrus (A. Erman, *The Ancient Egyptians*, 36ff.), illuminates the issue of the first part of the plague narratives), he also prevailed over the mightiest forces of nature – splitting both the sea (Ex. 14) and the earth (Num. 16). That in so doing he no more than activated the power of God, and in God's own cause, is unfailingly noted; no room is left for regarding Moses as a magician, aggrandizing himself through native powers or occult arts. One superhuman trait, however, does pertain to him: the ability to endure, on more than one occasion, a fast of forty days (Ex. 24:18; 34:28; Deut. 9:9, 18; cf. Elijah's similar feat, I Kings 19:8). Miraculous features, part of the traditional image of the "man of God," are ascribed to Moses in the highest degree as befits his heroic role. No later figure is portrayed so close to God as Moses. God spoke with him "face to face" (Ex. 33:11), and allowed him such a prolonged intimacy that as a result (after Moses' intercession in the wake of the Golden Calf apostasy) Moses' face was fearsomely radiant, so that he had to wear a mask in ordinary intercourse with people (Ex. 34:19ff.). The covenant made after this apostasy, on the basis of Moses' favor with God, specifically names Moses as an equal party with the people (Ex. 34:27; cf. 34:10, and the corresponding usage in the intercession in Ex. 33:16 ("I and your people," twice)). The equation corresponds to God's substitution of Moses for all the rest of the people in Exodus 32:10 (cf. Num. 14:12) and Moses' readiness to lay down his life on their behalf (Ex. 32:32). That Moses cannot simply be subsumed under the rubric "prophet" (*navi*ʾ) is the lesson taught to Aaron and Miriam in Numbers 12:6ff.: prophetic revelation is in the form of dream or vision; Moses, however, has the freedom of YHWH's house (i.e., may obtain audiences at will), he speaks with God "mouth to mouth," and is granted sight of YHWH (not a necessary contradiction of Ex. 33:20ff., where Moses is denied sight of God's face, but not of His back). In fact, Moses is never called a "prophet" in the Pentateuch (he is alluded to as such only in Hosea 12:14), but rather YHWH's "servant" (*ʿeved*) – the usual epithet in extra-pentateuchal literature as well (Num. 12:7–8; Deut. 34:5; Josh. 1:1; once he is styled God's "chosen one" (*beḥir*, Ps. 106:23), a synonym of "servant" in Isa. 42:1, 45:4; Ps. 89:4). In Deuteronomy (33:1) and later literature (Josh. 14:6; Ps. 90:1; Ezra 3:2; I Chron. 23:14; II Chron. 30:16) Moses is occasionally called "the man of God," a prophetic epithet. His spirit inspires ecstasy (Num. 11:25), just as contact with the prophet Samuel does (I Sam. 19:20ff.). Moreover, he is compared to prophets in Numbers 12, Deuteronomy 18:18, and 34:10, and in the last passage he is represented as their unequaled archetype. But the catalog of gentile analogues to the Israelite prophet in Deuteronomy 18:10–11 suggests that the term *navi*ʾ was too restricted to oracular, divinatory, and magic-like functions to be applied to so comprehensive a figure as Moses (though, since he performed these functions, he might justly be considered a prophetic archetype). Just in those two narratives where Moses' relation to prophecy is manifest, a point is made of his meekness and forbearance. He does not share his servant's alarm at the apparently independent prophesying of *Eldad and Medad; on the contrary, he wishes the entire people were prophets (Num. 11:26ff.). Nor will he assert himself even against rival claims of his brother and sister, for he was "the meekest man on earth" (Num. 12:3). Perhaps here, too, a distinction between Moses' character and that of later prophets is intended (contrast II Kings 2:23–24).

FINAL CONSIDERATIONS. Moses is not consistently present in biblical literature. He dominates the Pentateuch and Joshua – the repository of traditions about the birth of the nation. He reappears in the revival and re-founding literature of late monarchic and post-Exilic times. But references to him in the prophetic and hymnal writings (e.g., Psalms) are negligible. Moses' slighting by prophets and psalmists is significant, but the implications of that omission are debated. All innovation in the later religion of Israel is attributable to individuals known by name: the monarchy to Samuel and David; the Temple to David and Solomon; reforms in the official religion to kings Asa, Jehu, Hezekiah, Josiah, the priests Jehoiada and Hilkiah, and the prophets Elisha, Elijah, and Huldah; new moral-historical and eschatological conceptions to Amos, Hosea, Isaiah, Jeremiah – and the list is not ended. Had no founder of the worship of YHWH and the covenant institutions that characterized Israel from its beginnings been recorded in tradition, analogy would have required postulating him; and that is probably what happened. The traditions of the Torah point unanimously to Moses as the founder of all the constitutional elements of the religious community of Israel (excepting the monarchy). No single figure in later Israel plays the many roles ascribed to Moses, itself an indication that whatever historical basis there might have been for the activity of Moses is beyond recovery.

[Moshe Greenberg / S. David Sperling (2nd ed.)]

IN HELLENISTIC LITERATURE

Inventor and Civilizer, Lawgiver and Philosopher

The Jewish-Hellenistic tendency to adopt the sages of ancient culture entailed a whole series of farfetched identifications (e.g., Isis-Eve; Serapis-Joseph; Atlas-Enoch; Bel Kronos-Nimrod; Orpheus-David; Musaeos-Moses; Zoroaster-Ezekiel) and culminated in the attribution of the most important contributions of civilization to Jewish cultural hero-figures. Thus, Moses became for Eupolemus (whose chronology placed him more than 500 years before the Trojan War) the first wise man, and the first to invent writing for the Jews (from whom it was taken over by the Phoenicians, and from the Phoenicians, by the Greeks; Eusebius, *Praeparatio Evangelica*, 9:26). According to Artapanos, Moses (who is identified with Musaeos and also with Hermes-Thot) was the teacher of Orpheus, discovered the art of writing, was the first philosopher, and invented a variety of machines for peace and war. He was also responsible for the political organization of Egypt (having divided the land into 36 nomes), and was the originator of the animal cults of the Egyptians, which were seen as the only practical means available to overcome the unstable character of the Egyptian masses (Eusebius, op. cit. 9:27). The earliest philosophical exegete of the Pentateuch, Aristobulus, claimed that Homer and Hesiod drew much of their material from the Books of Moses, which, according to him, had been translated long before the Septuagint (Eusebius, op. cit. 13:12). Philo maintains that Heraclitus snatched his theory of opposites from Moses "like a thief" (*Quaestiones et Solutiones in Genesin* 4:152). Similarly, he says that the Greek legislators "copied" various laws from the laws of Moses (Spec. 4:61). Philo even states that Moses anticipated Plato's doctrine of creation from preexistent matter, by teaching in Genesis that there was water, darkness, and chaos before the world came into being (*De Providentia*, ed. J.B. Aucher (1822), 111; cf. Justin Martyr, *Apologia*, 1:59). According to Josephus, Moses was the most ancient of all legislators in the records of the world. Indeed, he maintains that the very word "law" was unknown in ancient Greece (Jos., Apion 2:154). Moreover, "in two points in particular, Plato followed the example of our legislator [Moses]. He prescribed as the primary duty of the citizens a study of their laws, which they must all learn word for word by heart, and he took precautions to prevent foreigners from mixing with them at random" (*ibid.* 257). "Our earliest imitators," concludes Josephus, "were the Greek philosophers, who, though ostensibly observing the laws of their own countries, yet in their conduct and philosophy were Moses' disciples" (*ibid.* 281). The only analogue in the pagan world to these ascriptions of priority to Moses is the famous statement of Numenius of Apamea (second century C.E.), who introduced allegorical interpretation of the Hebrew Bible to the pagan world (fragments 19 and 32, L), that Plato was just a Moses who spoke Greek (fragment 10, L). Philo also asserts that Moses was "the best of all lawgivers in all countries," and that his laws are most excellent and truly come from God. This is proved by the fact that while other law codes have been upset for innumerable reasons, the laws of Moses have remained firm and immovable, and "we may hope that they will remain for all future ages… so long as the sun and moon and the whole heaven and universe exist" (II Mos. 12). Furthermore, not only Jews but almost every other people have attained enough holiness to value and honor these laws. In fact, says Philo, "it is only natural that when people are not flourishing, their belongings to some degree are under a cloud, but if a fresh start should be made to brighter prospects… each nation would… throw overboard its ancestral customs and turn to honoring our laws alone" (*ibid.* 44). In spite of the declining political fortunes of the Jews during the period of the Roman Empire, an occasional note of admiration for Moses is still found in writers like Pseudo-Longinus, who speaks glowingly of the great legislator's lofty genius (*On the Sublime* 9:9), but Numenius, Tacitus, Galen, Celsus, Porphyry, and Julian, on the other hand, are highly critical of, and even hostile to, Moses.

Antisemitic Attacks on Moses

The earliest Greek references to Moses were quite favorable. Hecataeus of Abdera presented Moses as the founder of the Jewish state, ascribing to him the conquest of Palestine and the building of Jerusalem and the Temple. He explained, in the Platonic manner, that Moses divided his people into 12 tribes, because 12 is a perfect number, corresponding to the number of months in the year (cf. Plato, *Laws*, 745b–d; *Republic*, 546b). He also discovered a solicitude for military training in Moses' endeavor to train the youth in moral restraint and heroic endurance (Diodorus 40:3; in: Th. Reinach, *Textes d'auteurs Grecs et Romains relatifs au Judaisme* (1895), 14ff.). More important, he emphasized that Moses instituted no images in the worship of God, so that God should not be conceived of anthropomorphically, since the all-encompassing heavens alone (i.e., the cosmos) are to be identified as God. Posidonius of Apamea similarly emphasized that Moses worshiped no idols, and identified God with nature (Strabo 16:35). Soon, however, a reaction set in, and Moses became the butt of a venomous antisemitic literature. Hecataeus had earlier observed that Moses had initiated a form of life encouraging seclusion from man and a hatred of aliens. According to the Egyptian priest Manetho (third century), Moses was a rebellious priest of Heliopolis, called Osarsiph (cf. Chaeremon and Jos., Apion 1:32), who commanded the Jews to slaughter the sacred animals of Egypt, and established, with the aid of the Hyksos, a 13-year reign of cruelty over the Egyptians, until he was finally expelled by Pharaoh Amenophis (Jos., Apion 1:228ff.; Reinach, *ibid.*, 11). Lysimachus wrote that he instructed the Jews to show goodwill to no man, to always offer the worst advice, and to overthrow any temples and altars of the gods which they found (Jos., Apion 1:309; Reinach, *ibid.*,

59). Apollonius Molon accused Moses of being a charlatan and impostor, who gave the Jews bad laws. Posidonius says that upon entering the Holy of Holies, Antiochus Epiphanes saw the statue of a bearded man riding on an ass (cf. Tacitus, *Histories*, 5:3) and holding a book. This was Moses, who gave the Jews laws of hatred toward all mankind (Diodorus 34:1, 3; Reinach, *ibid.* 57–58). Finally, Nicarchus (cf. Ptolemy Chennos of Alexandria, and Helladius) writes that Moses was called *Alpha* (an honorific title for members of the Museum at Alexandria, and possibly applied to Moses in Jewish-Hellenistic literature), because he had leprous spots (*alphous*) all over his body (Reinach, *ibid.*, 122, 361–62).

THE BIOGRAPHY OF MOSES. The sparse biographical details of the biblical narrative concerning Moses are considerably elaborated and expanded in the characteristic style of Jewish-Hellenistic literature. Demetrius (end of third century), in his "On the Kings in Judea," identified the Cushite woman whom Moses married (Num. 12:1) with Zipporah, by arguing that as far as one can infer from the names (the LXX lists among the sons of Dedan, Abraham's grandson from the family of Keturah, also Raguel, who, according to Demetrius, was Jethro's father), Zipporah was a sixth-generation descendant of Abraham's family. According to the Bible, Abraham sent the sons of Keturah away "eastward, to the land of the East" (Gen. 25:6), which Demetrius identified as the land of Cush. "It was on this account," concluded Demetrius, "that Aaron and Miriam declared that Moses took a Cushite woman" (Eusebius, op. cit. 9:29). The first elaborate account of Moses' life is to be found in Artapanus' "On the Jews." According to Artapanus, Pharaoh's daughter, Merris (Jos., Ant., 2:224 gives her name as Thermuthis), was barren, and therefore adopted a Jewish child whom she named Moshe. Merris' husband, Chenephres, king of Memphis, grew jealous of Moses, and tried to dispose of him by sending him into battle against the Ethiopians with inadequate forces. After a ten-year campaign, the Ethiopians so admired Moses that, under his influence, they adopted the rite of circumcision. Artapanus knew nothing, however, of Moses' romance with the Ethiopian king's daughter and her betrayal of the capital city to him (Jos., Ant., 2:252), and it must be assumed that, like Demetrius and Ezekiel the Poet, he identified the Cushite woman whom Moses married with Zipporah. Artapanus' version of the biblical story of Moses' slaying of the Egyptian emphasizes the latter's plotting against Moses' life. Indeed, it was in a last resort to defend his life, that Moses slew the Egyptian Chanethothes. Moses' efforts to free his people land him in jail, but the irons binding him miraculously fall off, and the jail doors open of themselves (cf. the experiences of the imprisoned god Dionysus in Euripides' *The Bacchanals*, 600ff.). Moses' rod, according to Artapanus, was found in every Egyptian temple and was similar to the *seistron* or "rattle" used in the worship of Isis. It was by means of the *seistron* that Isis raised the waters of the Nile, and thus she was called in the Isis hymns *Seistrophóros*. Artapanus mentions two traditions concerning the Red Sea, that of Memphis and that of Heliopolis. That of Heliopolis follows the Bible, while that of Memphis explains the event by saying that Moses knew the area well and waited for the ebb tide (cf. Jos., Ant. 2:341–49). Finally, the reason given for the Egyptians' pursuit of the Israelites was their desire to retrieve the property borrowed from them (cf. Philo, I Mos. 1:141). A similar explanation is given by Trogus Pompeius, who says, however, that the Jews stole the holy utensils of the Egyptians (Justin 36:2, 13). Artapanus' account closes with a description of Moses: "Moses, they say, was tall and ruddy, with long white hair, and dignified" (Eusebius, op. cit. 9:27). The 269 lines preserved from the tragedy of Ezekiel the Poet on Exodus include a long soliloquy by Moses recounting his career down to his flight to Midian; a dialogue which recounts a dream in which a royal personage enthrones Moses on a throne which reaches heavenward, whereupon Moses surveys the heavenly host who fall on their knees before him, and then pass by as he counts them; and a detailed description of a remarkable bird, apparently the phoenix, at Elim (cf. Herodotus 2:73; Pliny, *Natural History*, 10:3–5; Job. 29:18; Gen. R. 19:5; Sanh. 108b; II En. 6:6; 8:6; II Bar. 6–7; Eusebius, op. cit., 9:16–37). In his *De vita Mosis*, Philo depicts Moses in his fourfold role as king, legislator, priest, and prophet. Whereas the fame of Moses' law, writes Philo, has traveled throughout the civilized world, the man himself, as he really was, was known to few. Greek men of letters, perhaps through envy, have refused to treat him as worthy of memory. Although there is no attempt in this treatise to refute the antisemitic literature on Moses, Philo does refer in his *Hypothetica* (355) to the charge that Moses was "an impostor and prating mountebank." He also strangely explains the Exodus there as due partly to Jewish overpopulation in Egypt (cf. Tacitus, *Histories*, 5:4) and also to the revelations of God in dreams and visions bidding them to go forth. Moreover, he points out that the Israelites' admiration for the man who gave them their laws was so great, that anything which seemed good to him also seemed good to them. Therefore, whether what he told them came from his own reasoning or from some supernatural source, they referred it all to God (*ibid.*, 357). In the *De vita Mosis*, Philo explains how the child Moses happened to be found by Pharaoh's daughter. In a state of constant depression over not having a child who could succeed her father she finally broke down on one occasion, and, though she had hitherto always remained in her quarters, she set off with her maids to the river where Moses was exposed. Since he had been taken up from the waters, she called him Moses, *mou* being the Egyptian word for water. As he grew in beauty and nobility, she decided to claim him as her own son, having at an earlier time artificially enlarged the figure of her womb to make him pass as her real child. Teachers arrived from different parts of Egypt and even from Greece. In a short time, however, he advanced beyond their capacities. Moses thus acquired the best of both Greek and Egyptian education. In his desire to live for the soul alone and not for the body, he lived frugally, scorning all luxury. Moses' career as a shepherd served as good training and a preliminary exercise in kingship for one destined to command the herd of mankind. Since Moses abjured the accumulation of wealth, God rewarded him by placing the whole world in his hands. Therefore each element obeyed him as its master, and submitted to his command (cf. II Mos., 201; Wisd. 19:6). His partnership with God also entitled him to bear the same title: "For he was named god and the king of the whole nation, and entered into the darkness where God was, that is, into the unseen, invisible, incorporeal, and archetypal essence of existing things."

A few further details may be added from Josephus' account of Moses (Ant. 2: 201ff.). Pharaoh decreed that all male infants of the Hebrews be drowned on the advice of a sacred scribe who had divined the birth of one who, if allowed to live, would abase Egypt and exalt Israel. Moses' easy birth spared his mother violent pangs and discovery by the watchful Egyptian midwives. His size and beauty enchanted princess Thermuthis, who found him on the Nile. Because he refused to take the breast of any Egyptian wet nurse, his mother was engaged to suckle him. Moses' precocity was displayed in his very games. Moreover, when the princess laid the babe in her father's arms, and the latter, to please his daughter, placed his diadem upon the child's head, Moses tore it off, flung it to the ground, and trampled it underfoot. This was taken as an ill omen, and the sacred scribe who had foretold his birth rushed forward to kill him. Thermuthis, however, was too quick for him and snatched the child away. Carried away by his Hellenistic ambience, Josephus says that, after crossing the Red Sea, Moses composed a song to God in hexameter verse.

Some last points of interest may be gleaned from Pseudo-Philo's *Liber Antiquitatum Biblicarum* (first century C.E.). According to this work, Moses was born circumcised (cf. Sot. 12a, Ex. R. 1:20). Pharaoh's daughter comes down to bathe in the Nile at this particular time because she had had a dream. Before Moses smashes the tablets, he looks upon them and sees that there is no writing on them. The reason given for his not entering the Promised Land was that he should be spared the sight of the idols that were to mislead his people. Moses dies at the hands of God, who buries him personally (cf. Deut. R. 11:10), and on the day of his death the heavenly praise of God was omitted, something which never occurred before and was never to occur again.

MOSES IN THE APOCALYPTIC TRADITION. According to the *Assumption of Moses* (c. 7–30 C.E.), Moses was prepared from before the foundation of the world to be the mediator of God's covenant with his people (1:14; 3:12). No single place was worthy to mark the site of his burial, for his sepulcher was from the rising to the setting sun (11:8). Moses' relation to Israel did not cease with his death, for he was appointed by God to be their intercessor in the spiritual world. This work also includes the debate between Michael and Satan over the burial of Moses. Satan opposes Michael's commission to bury Moses, on the ground that he is the lord of matter. To this claim Michael rejoins: "The Lord rebuke thee, for it was God's spirit that created the world and all mankind." In other words, Satan grants God Moses' soul, but claims his body as belonging to his exclusive domain. The author, speaking through Michael, rejects this gnostic dualism by insisting that God is Lord of both spirit and flesh, since he is the creator of all (R.H. Charles, Apocrypha, 2 (1897), 105–7). It may be well to allude here to the apocalyptic tradition connected with the name of Moses and also with Ezra, the "second Moses." In the *Assumption of Moses*, Moses gives Joshua secret books which are to be preserved and hidden "until the day of repentance in the visitation wherewith the Lord shall visit thee in the consummation of the end of days" (1:18). In Jubilees, too, the account is given of a secret tradition revealed to Moses on Sinai in which he is shown all the events of history both past and future (1:26). With this may be compared II Esdras 14, where Ezra, the "second Moses," receives by divine revelation the 24 books of canonical Scripture which he has to publish openly and the 70 books representing the apocalyptic tradition which he has to keep secret.

MOSES AS MAGICIAN. In pagan literature, Moses was, naturally enough, sometimes represented as a great magician. Numenius of Apamea, for example, presents him as a magician greater than his rivals Iannes and Iambres because his prayers were more powerful than theirs (fragments 18 and 19, L; cf. Pliny, *Natural History*, 30:1, 11; Reinach, op. cit. 282; Trogus Pompeius = Justin *Epitome* 36:2; Reinach, op. cit., 253). Moreover, in some of the magic papyri, Moses appears as the possessor of mysteries given to him by God (K. Preisendanz, *Papyri Graecae Magicae*, 2, 87f.). Finally, it may be noted that in some of the Qumran fragments, secret astrological teachings were ascribed to Moses (J.T. Milik, in: RB, 63 (1956), 61).

[David Winston]

RABBINIC VIEW

A marked ambivalence is to be observed in the Jewish tradition with regard to the personality of Moses. On the one hand, Moses is the greatest of all the Jewish teachers, a powerfully numinous figure, the man with whom God speaks "face to face," the intermediary between God and man, the master of the prophets, and the recipient of God's law for mankind. On the other hand, the utmost care is taken to avoid the ascription of divine or semi-divine powers to Moses. Moses is a man, with human faults and failings. Strenuous attempts are made to reject any "personality cult," even when the personality in question is as towering as Moses. Judaism is not "Mosaism" but the religion of the Jewish people. God, not Moses, gives His Torah to His people Israel. There are to be found Jewish thinkers, evidently in response to the claims made for Jesus by Christianity and for Muhammad by Islam, who elevate the role of Moses so that the religion is made to center around him. However, the opposite tendency is equally notable. Precisely because Christianity and Islam center on a person, Jewish thinkers declared that Judaism, on the contrary, singles out no one person, not even a Moses, as belonging to the heart of the faith. The stresses in this matter vary in proportion to the particular strength of the challenge in the period during which the role of Moses is considered. The need is keenly felt to affirm the supremacy of Moses and yet, at the same time, to deny him any divine honors.

Rav and Samuel said that 50 gates of understanding were created in the world, and all but one were given to Moses, for it is said (Ps. 8:6): "For Thou hast made him [Moses] but a little lower than the angels" (Ned. 38a). All the prophets saw God as one looks into a dim glass, but Moses as one who looks through a clear glass (Yev. 49b). When Moses was born the whole house was filled with light (Sot. 12a). Moses was so kind, gentle, and considerate to his sheep when tending the flock of Jethro that God made him the shepherd of Israel (Ex. R. 2:2). For Moses such a great thing as the fear of God was very easy of attainment (Ber. 33b). R. Johanan said: "The Holy One, blessed be He, causes His Divine Presence to rest only upon him who is strong, wealthy, wise, and meek and Moses had all these qualifications" (Ned. 38a). According to one opinion, Moses did not really die but still stands and ministers to God as he did while on Mount Sinai (Sot. 13b). Moses was righteous from the beginning of his life to the end of it, as was Aaron (Meg. 11a). Here, and frequently in the rabbinic literature, the praise of Moses is coupled with that of Aaron. The humility of Moses and Aaron was greater than that of Abraham since Abraham spoke of himself as dust and ashes (Gen. 18:27) whereas Moses and Aaron declared that they were nothing at all (Ex. 16:8). The whole world exists only on account of the merit of Moses and Aaron (Ḥul. 89a). These and similar sayings are typical of the rabbinic determination to go to the utmost lengths in lauding Moses; yet sayings of a not too different nature are found lauding other biblical heroes, and in some of the passages Aaron is made to share Moses' glory.

For the rabbis generally Moses is *Moshe Rabbenu* ("Moses our master," i.e., teacher), the teacher of the Torah par excellence. Neumark (*Toledot ha-Ikkarim* (1919²), 85f.) has, however, conjectured that the absence of this title from the whole of the Mishnah is a conscious anti-Christian reaction in which the character of Moses is played down somewhat by avoiding the giving to him of a title given to Jesus (Acts. 2:36). It is also suggested in the Mishnah (RH 3:8) that the hands of Moses did not in themselves have any effect on the fortunes of Israel in the battle with Amalek. It was only when Israel lifted up their eyes to God in response to Moses' uplifted hands that God helped them. R. Eleazar, commenting on the verse "Go down" (Ex. 32:7), remarks: "The Holy One, blessed be He, said to Moses: 'Moses, descend from thy greatness. Have I given to thee greatness except for the sake of Israel? And now Israel have sinned; then why do I want thee?'" (Ber. 32a). R. Yose said that if Moses had not preceded him, Ezra would have been worthy of receiving the Torah for Israel (Sanh. 21b). Nor were the rabbis averse on occasion to criticizing Moses for his quick temper (Pes. 66b; Sot. 13b) and to stating that he erred, though ready to acknowledge his mistake (Zev. 101a).

In the rabbinic tradition Moses was not only given the Written Law but the Oral Law, including the "laws given to Moses at Sinai" (**Halakhah le-Moshe mi-Sinai*), and whatever new interpretation of the law is ever brought before his teacher by a keen student of the Torah was already given to Moses at Sinai (TJ, Pe'ah 2:6, 17a). The idea that new teachings were truly new and yet were implied in the Torah given to Moses is conveyed in the story of Moses being transported through time to the academy of Akiva and feeling disturbed at his inability to comprehend Akiva's teachings until he heard Akiva declare that he had received them as a tradition from Moses at Sinai (Men. 29b). The idea that the foremost Jewish teachers who produced innovations – Hillel, Johanan b. Zakkai, and Akiva – are to be identified with Moses, whose work they continued, is expressed in the statement that they, like Moses, also lived for 120 years, divided into three periods of 40 years (Sif. Deut. 327). According to one interpretation, widely accepted in the Middle Ages, the name "Moses" was, in fact, sometimes given to scholars as a title of honor (Beẓah 38b).

[Louis Jacobs]

In the Aggadah

Heaven and earth were only created for the sake of Moses (Lev. R. 36:4). The account of the creation of water on the second day does not close with the customary formula "and God saw that it was good" since Moses was destined to be punished through water (Gen. R. 4:6). Noah was only rescued from the Flood because Moses was destined to descend from him (Gen. R. 26:6). The ascending and descending angels seen by Jacob in his nocturnal vision (Gen. 28:12) were in reality Moses and Aaron (Gen. R. 68:12).

His parents' house was filled with light on the day of his birth. He was born circumcised (Sot. 12a) on Adar 7th (Meg. 13b). He spoke with his parents on the day of his birth, and prophesied at the age of three (Mid. Petirat Moshe, in: Jellinek, *Beit ha-Midrash*, 1:128). Pharaoh's daughter went down to bathe since she was afflicted with leprosy, but as soon as she touched the ark of Moses she was healed. She therefore took pity upon the child and saved him, despite the protests of her maidens. When she opened the ark she saw the *Shekhinah* next to Moses, and heard his cry, which sounded like that of a mature youngster (Ex. R. 1:23, 24). Pharaoh's astrologers had previously predicted that the savior of Israel would shortly be born and that he would be punished through water. After Moses was placed in the Nile, they told Pharaoh that the redeemer had already been cast into the water, whereupon Pharaoh rescinded his decree that the male children should be put to death (Ex. R. 1:24). Not only were all the future children saved, but even the 600,000 children cast into the Nile together with Moses were also rescued (Gen. R. 97:3). Moses refused to suck at the breast of Egyptian foster-mothers because the mouth which was destined to speak with the *Shekhinah* would not take unclean milk (Sot. 12b). His unique beauty captivated the royal household and he was adopted by Pharaoh's daughter, who constantly displayed her affection for him. Even Pharaoh played with the baby, who often took his crown and placed it upon his own head. The king's advisers were frightened by this behavior and they counseled Pharaoh to put him to death. However, Jethro, who was among the royal counselors, insisted on first testing the youngster. A gold vessel and a live coal were brought before Moses, and he was about to reach for the gold when the angel Gabriel came and deflected his hand to the hot coal. The baby placed a live coal into his mouth, burning his tongue, and as a result he acquired the impediment in his speech (Ex. R. 1:26).

Moses not only sympathized with the sufferings of his brethren, but he also aided them in their tasks by himself preparing the clay for the bricks. He also assigned them responsibilities in accordance with their abilities so that the strong carried greater burdens while the weak discharged lesser tasks (Ex. R. 1:27). He slew the cruel Egyptian taskmaster only after the angels decreed his death since he had previously defiled the wife of one of the Hebrew slaves in his charge and subsequently sought to slay the husband. Moses killed the Egyptian either by means of the Divine Name or by his own physical strength. After Dathan and Abiram informed on Moses to Pharaoh, he was condemned to death, but the executioner's sword had no effect on him, since his neck became like a pillar of ivory (Ex. R. 1: 28–31). Moses saved the daughters of Jethro after the shepherds had cast them into the well, and he also protected them from their immoral designs. Moses drew out only one bucketful and with this watered all the flock there assembled, since the water was blessed at his hands (Ex. R. 1:32). According to one tradition, Moses could marry Zipporah only after he agreed to Jethro's condition that one of their children be raised in Jethro's faith while the rest could be trained in the Hebraic tradition. Because of this agreement, Gershom was not circumcised, and on the way to Egypt Moses almost met his death because of this neglect (Ex. 4:24–26; Mekh., Amalek), but in the opinion of other sages (Mekh. *ibid.*; TJ, Ned. 3:14, 38b) Moses could not circumcise his second son Eliezer, because he had been born just prior to his departure for Egypt, and his only fault was that he did not do so immediately on reaching the resting place.

Before God confers greatness on a man he is first tested through small matters and then promoted to importance. Moses displayed his trustworthiness by leading the sheep into the wilderness in order to keep them from despoiling the fields of others. He then showed his mercy by carrying a young kid on his shoulders after it had exhausted itself by running to a pool of water (Ex. R. 2:2–3). God appeared to him in a burning bush to illustrate that the Jews were as indestructible as the bush which was not consumed by the flames (Ex. R. 2:5). Many reasons are given for Moses' initial hesitancy in accepting the mission of redeeming his brethren: he recoiled from the honor and prestige which would accrue to him for successfully completing the task (Tanḥ. va-Yikra, 3); he feared to trespass upon the domain of his elder brother whom he felt should be the redeemer (Ex. R. 3: 16); he desired the redeemer to be God Himself rather than a mortal so that the redemption would be eternal (Ex. R. 3:4); he was angry because God had already deserted the children of Israel for 210 years and permitted many pious individuals to be slain by their Egyptian taskmasters (Mekh. Sb-Y to 6:2).

The sages likewise were perplexed by Moses' seemingly disrespectful reply to God that since he had spoken to Pharaoh the lot of his people had not improved (Ex. 5:22–23). Various explanations are given for the tone of Moses' lament: the taunts of Dathan and Abiram regarding his lack of success provoked Moses' anger (Ex. R. 6:2); Moses mistakenly thought that the redemption would entirely come about through the attribute of mercy and would therefore be instantaneous (Ex. R. 6:3); he felt that his generation of Israelites did not deserve the severe punishment of bondage; and he did not doubt that God would ultimately redeem His people, but he was grieved for those children who were being daily immured in the new buildings and would not be redeemed. The attribute of justice sought to strike Moses, but God protected him since He knew that Moses only spoke out of his love for his brethren (Ex. R. 5:22). The elders started to accompany Moses and Aaron to Pharaoh's palace (Ex. 3:18) but gradually stole away furtively, singly or in pairs, so that by the time the palace was reached only Moses and Aaron were left (Ex. R. 5:14). Despite the harsh messages which Moses delivered to Pharaoh, he constantly accorded him the respect due to royalty (Ex. R. 5:15; Zev. 102a). Moses executed all the plagues except for those connected with water and dust, since he had been saved through water and the dust had concealed the body of the Egyptian he slew (Ex. 2:12; Ex. R. 9:10; 10:7). When Moses announced the final plague, he did not state the exact time of its incidence, saying only that "about midnight" (Ex. 11:4) because he feared that Pharaoh's astrologers might miscalculate and declare him a liar (Ber. 4a). During the Exodus, while the masses thought only of taking the gold and silver of the Egyptians, Moses went and retrieved the coffin of Joseph which subsequently accompanied the Israelites in the desert (Mekh. 2, Proem. Sot. 13a).

Moses went up to Mount Sinai, enveloped by a cloud which sanctified him for receiving the Torah (Yoma 4a). After he ascended on high, the ministering angels contested the right of "one born of woman to receive the treasures of the Torah." Encouraged by the Almighty, Moses demonstrated to the angels that only mortals were subject to the Torah's regulations and therefore it was rightfully theirs. The angels thereupon became friendly with Moses, and each one revealed its secret to him (Shab. 89a). In abstaining from food during the 40 days on Mt. Sinai Moses acted as do the angels (BM 86b). He received instruction from God by day and reviewed the teachings at night (Ex. R. 47:8). Not only were the Bible, Mishnah, Talmud, and *aggadah* taught to Moses, but all interpretations that were destined to be propounded by future students were also revealed to him (Ex. R. 47:1). Before Moses ascended the mountain, he promised to return by midday of the 41st day. On that day Satan confused the world so that to the Israelites it appeared to be afternoon when it was actually still morning. Satan told them that Moses had died and would never return, whereupon the people made the Golden Calf (Shab. 89a). Moses broke the tablets, and made it appear that the Torah had not been given, to prevent the sinners from being punished (ARN[2] 2:5–6). God approved of this action (Shab. 87a) and when Moses realized that Israel's fate depended upon him and his prayers, he began to defend them (Ber. 32a). He argued that God had not enjoined the prohibition against idolatry upon the children of Israel since the singular and not the plural is used in the command (Ex. 20:3–5), and it applied only to him (Ex. R. 47:9; for the additional justifications set forth by Moses see *Golden Calf). Moses refused God's offer to make him the ancestor of a great nation since he feared that he would be accused of seeking only his glory and not that of the people (Ber. 32a).

God would not grant Moses' wish to behold all His glory since Moses had refused to look at him through the burning bush (Ber. 7a). He was hidden in the same cave which was later occupied by Elijah (I Kings 19:9–14). If there had been an aperture even as minute as the point of a needle, Moses would have been consumed by the passing divine light (Meg. 19b). Moses received only the reflection of this light, and from its radiance his face subsequently shone (Ex. R. 47:6). During this revelation, Moses was granted profound insight into the problem of theodicy (Ber. 7a). Afterward he was known as the master of Torah, wisdom, and prophecy (Meg. 13a) since he possessed 49 of the 50 divisions of wisdom (RH 21b). He was the greatest prophet among the Israelites (Deut. 34:10) although, according to one view, Balaam was almost his equal so that the heathen nations could not attribute their wickedness to the lack of the prophetic spirit (Sif. Deut. 357; SER 26:141–2; but cf. TJ, Sot. 5:8, 20d; Lev. R. 1:12–14). Moses insisted on giving a complete account of the materials collected for the Tabernacle since he overheard scoffers claiming that he had embezzled a portion of the gold and silver (Ex. R. 51:6). During the seven days of the dedication of the sanctuary, Moses officiated as the high priest. He was also considered the king of Israel during the 40-year sojourn in the desert. When Moses requested these two offices for a permanent heritage, he was told that the priesthood was already assigned to Aaron, while royalty was designated for David (Ex. R. 2:6).

Moses insisted that his sin of striking the rock be recorded in the Torah (Num. 20:11) so that future generations would not mistakenly ascribe other transgressions or faults to him (Sif. Deut. 26; Num. R. 19:12). The impatience of the people and the jeers of the scoffers were the cause of his smiting the rock in anger (Num. R. 19:9). In reality, God had long before decreed that Moses should not enter the Promised Land and Moses' offense in Kadesh was only a pretext so that He might not appear unjust. God explained to Moses that if he were not buried in the desert with the generation that left Egypt, people would mistakenly declare that the generation of the wilderness had no share in the world to come (Num. R. 19:13). Moses immediately obeyed God's command to avenge the Israelite people on the Midianites (Num. 31:2), although he knew that after it was fulfilled he would die (Num. R. 22:22). Before his death, Moses pleaded for the appointment of a successor who would successfully cope with the dissimilar temperaments of the people (Num. R. 21:2). Moses also requested that his successor lead his people into war, and not remain behind the troops as was the customary practice of gentile kings (Sif. Num. 139). Moses pleaded that the decree against his entering the Holy Land be rescinded so that he could share in the joy of his people after experiencing their sorrow (Deut. R. 11:10). However, God refused his repeated requests since the leader of the generation should remain with his followers, and the generation of Moses was buried in the wilderness (Num. R. 19: 13); and because the time had come for Joshua to exercise his leadership (Deut. R., ed. S. Lieberman, pp. 48, 124).

Moses died at the kiss of God (Deut. R. 11:10; BB 17a) on the anniversary of his birth, Adar 7th (Tosef., Sof. 11:2). God himself buried Moses (Sot. 14a) in a grave which had been prepared for him since the eve of the Sabbath of creation (Pes. 54a). His tomb is opposite Beth-Peor to atone for the sin of the Israelites in worshiping the idol Peor (Num. 25:3). Nevertheless, his grave cannot be discovered, since to a person standing in the valley it looks as though it is on a mountain peak, whereas from the mountain peak it looks as though it is in the valley (Sot. 14a).

[Aaron Rothkoff]

IN MEDIEVAL JEWISH THOUGHT

All Jewish philosophers agree that the prophetic revelation of Moses was different from, and superior to, the prophecy (see *Prophets and Prophecy) of all other prophets. *Judah Halevi writes that Moses' prophecy came directly from God: He did not receive his prophecy while asleep or in a state between sleeping and waking, nor did he arrive at it through union with the active intellect (*Kuzari*, 1:87). The term "prophet" when applied to Moses and other prophets is, according to *Maimonides, amphibolous. In his discussion of prophecy in the *Guide of the Perplexed*, Maimonides states that he will allude to the prophecy of Moses only in order to contrast it with prophecy in general (*Guide*, 2:35). He spells out four distinctions between the prophecy of Moses and that of other prophets (Yad, Yesodei ha-Torah, 7:6; Comm. on Sanh, 10, 7th principle). The revelations of all the prophets, except for Moses, took place in dreams and visions (Num. 12:6); through the medium of an angel, and hence they prophesied in riddles and symbolic language (Num. 12:18); in a trancelike state (Gen. 15:12); and at intervals of varying duration according to God's choice. Moses, by contrast, received his prophetic message while fully awake; in nonsymbolic language; directly from God, rather than through the medium of an angel; and at the time of his own choosing (Num. 12:6–8; Ex. 33:11). It seems that these differences between the prophecy of Moses and that of other prophets can be reduced to one basic difference, namely, that imaginative faculty played no role in Moses' prophetic experience, while it played a major role in the case of the other prophets, prophecy being, according to Maimonides, "an overflow from God, through the intermediation of the active intellect, toward the rational faculty in the first place, and thereafter the imaginative faculty" (*Guide*, 2:36, see

Abrabanel's commentary on this passage). He writes that while other prophets "can hear only in a dream of prophecy that God has spoken to him… Moses… heard Him from above the ark cover, from between the two cherubim, without action on the part of the imaginative faculty" (*Guide*, 2:45). Moses' prophetic experience, then, seems to have been dependent on the superior development of his rational faculty, and it is probable that according to Maimonides – although he does not say so explicitly – Moses attained union with the active intellect (see S. Pines (tr.), *Guide of the Perplexed* (1963), translator's introduction, lxxvii–xcii). J. Guttmann has suggested that according to Maimonides, Moses' prophecy differed from that of the other prophets insofar as it transcended "the natural order and was wholly due to a supernatural action of God," while the prophecies of the other prophets resulted from the development of their rational and imaginative faculties. In this way, Guttmann maintains, Maimonides "safeguards the uniqueness of biblical religion which Moses transmitted against the danger inherent in a naturalistic interpretation of prophecy" (Guttmann, Philosophies, 172). S. Atlas, on the other hand, interprets Maimonides as asserting that while Moses' prophetic experience did not depend on his imaginative faculty, it did depend to a large extent on the superior development of his rational faculty, and was hence not totally dependent on the supernatural action of God. However, he too maintains that in Maimonides' view there was an important element in Moses' prophetic experience – an element not common to the experiences of the other prophets – which was the result of God's creative will, namely, the giving of laws (Atlas, in HUCA, 25 (1954), 369–400). Medieval philosophers considered Moses' qualities of courage, modesty, and justice to be prerequisites for prophetic experience (see for example *Guide*, 2:38–40).

[David Kadosh]

For Judah Loew b. Bazalel (the Maharal) of Prague (*Tiferet Yisrael* (1955), 64–67), Moses is a superhuman being occupying a midway position between the supernatural beings and humans. This is why he was able to be equally at home in heaven and on earth and this is hinted at in his name since the letter *mem* of *Moshe* is the middle letter of the alphabet. Samson Raphael Hirsch (Comm. to Ex. 24:1), on the other hand, denies any qualitative superiority to Moses. Very curious is the legend recorded by Israel Lipschuetz b. Gedaliah (*Tiferet Yisrael* to Kid. end, n. 77). A certain king, having heard of Moses' fame, sent a renowned painter to portray Moses' features. On the painter's return with the portrait the king showed it to his sages, who unanimously proclaimed that the features portrayed were those of a degenerate. The astonished king journeyed to the camp of Moses and observed for himself that the portrait did not lie. Moses admitted that the sages were right and that he had been given from birth many evil traits of character but that he had held them under control and succeeded in conquering them. This, the narrative concludes, was Moses' greatness, that, in spite of his tremendous handicaps, he managed to become the man of God. Various attempts have, in fact, been made by some rabbis to ban the further publication of this legend as a denigration of Moses' character.

The biblical commentators discuss why God arranged for Moses to be brought up by the daughter of Pharaoh. Abraham ibn Ezra (Comm. to Ex. 2:3) suggests that this was first to teach Moses courage and leadership, faculties he would not have been able to achieve if he had grown up among a slave people, and, secondly, so that Moses might have the respect of his people which he would not have had if he had grown up with them from infancy. Isaac Arama (*Akedat Yiẓḥak*, 43) understands the matter to belong to God's purpose that the tyrant king be defeated through a member of his own household. Naḥmanides (Comm. to Ex. 2:11) argues that Moses was brought up in Pharaoh's palace to accustom him to being in the royal presence, since it was his destiny to stand before Pharaoh to demand the release of the Israelites.

In the Kabbalah, too, there is great elevation of the character of Moses. On the verse: "And Moses went up to God" (Ex. 19:3), the Zohar (II, 79b) remarks: "See the difference between Moses and all other human beings. When other human beings ascend it is to wealth or honor or power, but when Moses ascends what does Scripture say? 'And Moses went up to God.' Happy is his portion." The section of the Zohar known as *Ra'aya Meheimna*, "Faithful Shepherd," is in the form of mystical discourses conveyed to Simeon b. Yaḥai by Moses in heaven. Moses and Aaron on earth are, for the Zohar, the counterparts of the **sefirot Neẓaḥ* and *Hod* (I, 21b–22a). The high mystical state of Moses is described in the Zohar as Moses having "intercourse" with the **Shekhinah*, whose "husband" he was. Moses was a reincarnation of Abel (*Sha'ar ha-Pesukim*, Exodus, beg.). Hence, like Abel, the first shepherd, he was a shepherd (*Avodat Yisrael* by Israel of Koznice, Exodus beg.). Godly men chose the occupation of shepherd because it kept them far from the cities where men are prone to sin and because it afforded them the opportunities of communing with God (Baḥya ibn Asher, Comm. to Ex. 3:1).

MODERN INTERPRETATIONS

*Aḥad Ha-Am begins his essay on Moses (*Al Parashat Derakhim*[3] 210–21) by stating that he remains unmoved by the speculations of scholars as to whether Moses really existed since the true hero is not the historical figure but the man who is portrayed in the Jewish tradition as the embodiment of the Jewish spirit. This Moses is neither a great military strategist nor an astute politician. Nor is his role primarily that of lawgiver in the accepted sense since the laws he gives are for the future ideal state still to be realized. Moses is rather the "master of the prophets," the highest example of the prophetic ideal as expressed in a human life. The prophet is ruthless in his pursuit of justice which is, for him, a categorical imperative brooking no opposition. Moses' vision is of the perfect society, of what ought to be rather than what is. Moses embarks on his prophetic career with a protest against injustice and oppression and devotes the rest of his life to his ideal. He hears the voice of God speaking to him in his heart urging him to become the deliverer of his downtrodden people. This God who speaks to him and to the people is not a tribal god but the God of all men, every one of whom is created in His image. Because his vision is unqualified Moses must die without entering the Promised Land. The prophet is too uncompromising to be the leader of the people in the stark realities of the actual human situation. The leadership must pass to another more capable of coming to terms with life as it is, even though this involves a diminution of the dream. Thus Moses is the symbol of Israel's divine discontent with the present. Like Moses, Israel learned to live only in the past and the future, its life a pilgrimage from past to future. For Israel as for Moses the present, as it falls short of the ideal, has no real existence.

Sigmund *Freud's *Moses and Monotheism* (1939) is an interpretation of Moses' work and character which has been widely discussed, though the majority of scholars reject Freud's anthropology and his views on biblical scholarship. According to Freud, Moses was not an Israelite but an Egyptian. The monotheism he taught was derived from a period of pure monotheism established during the reign of Ikhnaton. Following a hint thrown out by Sellin based on an obscure passage in the Book of Hosea, Freud believed that the Israelites, unable to accept Moses' new ideas, eventually murdered him. But Moses' monotheistic teachings lived on in the racial unconscious of the Israelites to reappear hundreds of years later in the monotheism of the prophets. The slaying of Moses repeated what, for Freud, was the sin of primitive man, the slaying of the primal father by his jealous sons. Because of this, monotheistic religion is haunted by guilt feelings and the need for atonement. Freud admits the speculative nature of his theory but feels that it is in accord with his ideas on how religion began and on man's needs for a father figure.

Martin *Buber in his book *Moses* accepts the basic historicity of Moses but makes a distinction between saga and history. The saga is not history but neither is it fiction. It follows in the footsteps of the historical events and describes the impact they had. Creative memory is at work in the saga. But the saga is not simply a matter of group psychology. We can get behind it to the actual historical events which made such an impact on the people that they could only explain these events as of divine power at work in them. It is not a case of "historization of myth" but of "mythization of history." At the same time, in the Moses saga, the "mythical" element is not a myth of the gods. The human figure is not transfigured, so that the element of sober historical recording is still present. Describing the God of Moses, Buber writes: "He is the One who brings His own out, He is their leader and advance guard; prince of the people, legislator and the sender of a great message. He acts on the level of history on the peoples and between the peoples. What He aims at and cares for is a people. He makes His demand that the people shall be entirely 'His' people, a 'holy' people; that means, a people whose entire life is hallowed by justice and loyalty, a people for God and for the world… That Moses experiences Him in this fashion and serves Him accordingly is what has set that man apart as a living and effective force at all times; and that is what places him thus apart in our own day, which possibly requires him more than any earlier day has ever done."

[Louis Jacobs]

IN CHRISTIAN TRADITION

Moses is mentioned more often than any other biblical figure in the New Testament, which emphasizes the parallel between the ministries of Moses and Jesus (Matt. 8:4; 17:1–8; Mark 7:10; 9:2–8; 10:2–9). As Israel's lawgiver and liberator, Moses – according to Christian tradition – prefigures the ministry of Jesus and prophesies the coming of the Savior and the mediator of the new covenant. Moses is an example of deep faith in God (Heb. 11:23–29), and like Jesus, he encounters the people's incomprehension and hostility (Acts 7:17–44). Jesus, however, surpasses Moses in all respects. Unlike the face of Moses, that of Jesus is unveiled and his superior glory is spiritual (II Cor. 3:6–18). Moses appears as God's faithful servant, but Jesus is God's son (Heb. 3:5–6). Moses seals the covenant with the blood of animals, but the Messiah's covenant, which for Christians definitely supersedes the Mosaic Law, is sealed by his own sacrifice (Heb. 9:11–22). In addition, the events of the Exodus appear to the Church Fathers as typological events of Jesus' life; the passage through the Red Sea is the type of Salvation through baptism; and the water gushing out of the rock that Moses struck is a symbol of the Eucharist.

IN ISLAM

The personality and deeds of Mūsā (Moses) occupy an important place in the Koran. The events of his life, from the moment of his birth, are related at length. Indeed Nūḥ (*Noah), Ibrāhīm (*Abraham), and Moses were the first believers, and it was Moses who prophesied the coming of Muhammad, whose faith was that of Moses (Sura 7:140, 156; 42:11). At the same time of the decree of Firʿawn (Pharaoh) and his counselors, Hāmām and Qārūn (Korah), Moses' life was endangered when he was placed in the ark. However, Āsiya (see *Pharaoh), the wife (!) of Firʿawn, pitied Moses, saved him, and brought him up in her house (26:17; 28:6–10). Muhammad adapts the biblical tale of Jacob's labor for Laban inserting its years as those of Moses' employment by Shuʿayb (Jethro) in order to gain the hand of his daughter (28:27). He also adds details from the *aggadah*: Moses refused to suckle at the breasts of Egyptian women (28:11); one of the believers at the court of Pharaoh attempted to save Moses (40:29); Allah hung the mountain over the people of Israel like a pail in order that they would accept the Torah (2:60, 87; 7:170); on the sending of the spies (see *Joshua b. Nun = Yūshaʿ); on Korah (Qārūn) and his treasures; and many similar details. The Koran also contains themes and figures which are unknown in the ancient literature, such as the tale of al-Sāmirī, who casts the Golden Calf, and the journey of Moses and his servant to the end of the world (18:59–81; see below). Some of the tales about Moses are also mentioned in the poetry of *Umayya ibn Abi al-Ṣalt, and are embellished by Muslim legend, and interwoven with new legends. The biblical ʿImrān (Amram), husband of Yukhābid (Jochebed) and father of Moses and Aaron, is only mentioned in post-koranic literature. ʿImrān (Amram) of the Koran is the husband of Hannah (her name is not mentioned in the Koran, but in later works) and the father of Miriam (Maryam), the mother of Jesus (Sura 3, "The House of ʿImrān"). ʿImrān, the father of Moses, was one of Pharaoh's bodyguards; after the decree against the male children was issued, he did not leave the palace and did not have marital relations with his wife. A great bird, however, brought his wife Yukhābid to him, to the bedroom of Pharaoh, without drawing the attention of the bodyguards; she became pregnant and gave birth to Moses (al-Kisāʾī, 201). The ark of Moses had marvelous healing powers from which Pharaoh's daughter benefited. The infant Moses was saved from the fiery furnace just as Abraham had been; Pharaoh examined the child by placing a plate of coals and a plate full of gold in front of him. Moses wished to touch the gold, but an angel diverted his hand and put a burning coal in his mouth, which caused him later to stammer. The sheep of Jethro gave birth to spotted and speckled lambs. The staff of Moses came from a tree which had grown in the Garden of Eden, and which he inherited from the prophets, from Adam via Jacob. The death of Moses is described as an event unparalleled in world history, particularly in the tales of ʿUmāra (Ms., fol. 23v). The number of pages devoted to Moses in the "Legends of the Prophets" emphasizes the many legends which have been circulated.

Moses' Journey

The tale of the journey of Moses and his servant (Sura 18:59–81) is a departure from the framework of the biblical tales and legends. Moses set out to find the confluence of the two seas. On the way the servant forgot the roasted fish which was to serve as their provisions. They encountered the prophet of Allah and Moses asked him for a sign which would teach him wisdom and lead him along the proper course. The prophet consented on the condition that he would not question the meaning of the events which would occur en route. They boarded a ship and the prophet drilled a hole in it. Moses wondered about this act, forgot his promise, and asked the prophet whether it was his intention to drown them. Continuing on their way, the prophet killed a youth; and when they reached a town whose inhabitants refused them hospitality, the prophet held up a fence which was about to collapse. The prophet then explained to Moses the meaning of his surprising actions. The ship, which was the property of poor men, was about to fall into the hands of a pirate king. The youth would have caused his upright parents to sin; in his place, an upright son was born. Under the fence there was a treasure, the property of orphans, which was discovered after a while.

Since this tale does not belong to the legends of Moses which were widespread in the Orient, some of the Muslim commentators attempted to explain that it did not refer to Moses son of ʿImrān, but to another Moses. Most of the commentators, however, uphold the traditional explanation; they also explain that the servant was Yūshaʿ b. Nūn. The name of the prophet whom Moses asked for guidance is al-Khaḍir (al-Khiḍr, "the Green One"). However, other names are also mentioned. Thaʿlabī (p. 188) reports in the name of *Wahb b. Munabbih that it was Irmiyā b. Ḥilfiyā (!). The principal outlines of the tale of the journey can be found in the epic Gilgamesh (see *Flood) and in the romance of Alexander the Great, as related in the Syrian sources. It closely corresponds to the Jewish legend about R. Joshua b. Levi who set out on a journey with the prophet Elijah. The Jewish tale is found in two almost identical versions, though with a change in the order of events. One was published by A. Jellinek (*Bet ha-Midrash*, 5 (1877)) and the other in *Ḥibbur Yafeh min ha-Yeshuʿah* by R. Nissim b. Jacob. The introduction to the Jewish tale is identical to that of the Koran, except that Moses is replaced by R. Joshua b. Levi and the prophet (al-Khaḍir) by the prophet Elijah. The details of the story also differ: Elijah kills the cow of poor men who had received him and his companion with hospitality. They later stay with a wealthy man who neither pays attention to them nor gives them anything to eat. Elijah, however, prayed and rebuilt the wall of his house, which was about to collapse. Elijah and R. Joshua again came to a place of wealthy men who were indifferent toward them. Nevertheless, Elijah blessed them that they all might become leaders. When, however, they came to a place of the poor who were hospitable to them, the blessing was that they should have one leader. Elijah explained that all his actions and words had been favorable to the poor. With the exception of the story of the wall which was about to collapse, the Jewish tale differs from the Muslim account in its details.

[Haïm Z'ew Hirschberg]

IN THE ARTS

Of all the major biblical figures, not excepting David, Jacob, Joseph, and Solomon, Moses has inspired the largest amount of creative endeavor in literature, art, and music. Treatment of this figure also involves several associated themes, such as the Ten Plagues, the Exodus, and the Revelation on Sinai. By far the earliest literary work on the subject was *Exagoge* ("The Exodus from Egypt"), a drama by the second-century B.C.E. Alexandrian writer *Ezekiel (Ezekielos) the Poet, preserved as a fragment by the Church Father *Eusebius of Caesarea (modern editions by E.H. Gifford, 1903; and by J. Bloch, 1929). The first play known to have been written by a Jew, this was also the first recorded biblical drama. The characters who appear in it include Moses, Zipporah, Jethro, and an invented Chum. The *Exagoge*, an interesting example of late classical Greek theater, anticipates the miracle and mystery plays of the Middle Ages. In medieval drama, Moses figures in the *Ordo Prophetarum*, the French *Mistère du Viel Testament*, and in some of the English cycles: the *Ludus Coventriae* of Lincoln (*Moses and the Two Tablets*), the Towneley plays (*Pharaoh*), and the York series (*The Departure of the Israelites from Egypt*). Interest in the theme thereafter waned for a time. In the 16th century there were only a few works of note, such as a play by Diego Sanchez (c. 1530), and the *Meistersinger* Hans Sach's *Die Kintheit Mosi* (1553). Although Moses was one of the Old Testament heroes that appealed to Protestant writers of the 17th century, most of the works about him were of Catholic inspiration: one of the English *Stonyhurst Pageants* (c. 1625); *Exodus*, a neo-Latin sacred tragedy by Balthasar Crusius (1605); *Moïse sauvé* (1653), a tedious epic by Marc-Antoine de Gérard Saint-Amant; and *Pascha, of tede verlossingte Israëls uit Egypten* (1612), a five-act play by Joost van den Vondel.

In the 18th century, treatment was at first light, but more serious attention was given by writers of the last decades, particularly with the rise of the oratorio and musical drama. *The Plagues of Egypt* (London, 1708), an anonymous English poem, was followed by Poisson's one-act comedy, *La Déroute de Pharaon* (1718), and by texts for many musical compositions; notably Joannes Theodorus' neo-Latin drama *Aaron a Moyse fratre sacerdos inauguratus* (1730); Charles Jennens' *Israel in Egypt* (c. 1738), which served as libretto for Handel's well-known oratorio; and Benjamin Stillingfleet's *Moses and Zipporah* (1765). Three works of greater significance, all written at about the same time, were Hannah More's *Moses in the Bulrushes*, one of her *Sacred Dramas* (1782); Friedrich *Schiller's youthful epic, *Die Sendung Mosis* (1783); and Naphtali (Hartwig) *Wessely's 18-canto Hebrew epic, *Shirei Tiferet* (1782–1829). Wessely's poem, an account of the Exodus culminating in the giving of the Law at Sinai, betrays the influence of F.G. Klopstock's *Der Messias* (1748–73) and, in the spirit of the *Haskalah, presents Moses as a devout philosopher battling against fanaticism and ignorance. *Shirei Tiferet* was later translated into German (*Die Moseide*, 1795) and part into French (1815).

A dramatic revival of literary interest in the theme took place from the first decade of the 19th century, possibly as a result of the political and social upheavals of the age. Among the earlier works were August Klingmann's five-act drama, *Moses* (1812); David Lyndsay's *The Plague of Darkness* and *The Last Plague* (in *Drama of the Ancient World*, 1822); and Antonio Maria Robiola's Italian verse epic, *Il Mosè* (1823). Moses was the hero of several poetic compositions by French writers, beginning with *Les bergères de Madian, ou La jeunesse de Moise* (1779–80) by Stéphanie Félicité Ducrest de Saint-Aubin, countess de Genlis, which was translated into Hebrew (1834). In Alfred de Vigny's "Moïse" (*Poèmes antiques et modernes*, 1826), the Lawgiver is a tragic, weary figure, pleading with God on Nebo for release from his consuming task. He is also the central character in three other French works: François René de Chateaubriand's verse tragedy, *Moïse* (1836); a 24-canto poem of the same title (1850) by Ambroise Anatole de Montesquiou-Fézensac; and Victor Hugo's brief poem, "Le Temple" (in *La Legende des Siecles*, 1859[1]), which is based on Exodus 31:1–6. Elsewhere, Imre Madách wrote the drama, *Mózes* (1860), where the Hebrew Exodus was reinterpreted in terms of the Hungarian struggle for liberation. During the 19th century, Jewish authors also found inspiration in the biblical and rabbinic accounts of the life of Moses. Solomon Ludwig *Steinheim wrote the story *Sinai* (1823); Isaac Candia published the Hebrew play, *Toledot Moshe* (1829); and Moritz Rappaport was the author of a German epic poem, *Mose* (1842). The U.S. dramatist Samuel B.H. *Judah wrote *The Maid of Midian*, a biblical tragedy that was never staged because of the writer's sacrilegious treatment of the slaying of the Midianite captives (Num. 31:2–18). Contrasting sharply with this approach was the reverence expressed by *Heine in his late *Gestaendnisse* ("Confessions," 1854) – "How small Sinai appears when Moses stands upon it!" According to Heine the Lawgiver was an artist on a colossal scale, who built "human pyramids and human obelisks" and fashioned "a great, holy, and eternal people" out of a poor shepherd clan that would serve as a model for all other nations.

Literary Works by 20th-Century Non-Jewish Writers

Verse inspired by the life and career of Moses includes S.D. Polevaya's Russian biblical poem *Iskhod* (1913), Rainer Maria Rilke's *Der Tod Moses*, and *Moysey* (1922; Eng. 1938), a poem in Ukrainian by Ivan Franko. The yield has been richer in fiction, especially from the years following World War I when a number of novels were written on the theme. During World War II Zora Neale Hurston published *The Man of the Mountain* (1941; U.S. ed., *Moses*) and the U.S. novelist William George Hardy produced *All the Trumpets Sounded* (1942). Among novels that appeared during the postwar era were Dorothy Clarke Wildon's *Prince of Egypt* (1949); the Polish Catholic Dobraczyński's *Pustynia* (1957; German ed. *Die Wueste*, 1957); and the Hungarian writer János Kodolányi's *Az égő csipkebokor* ("The Burning Bush," 1957). Moses was also the hero of a Danish trilogy by Poul Hoffmann: *Den braendende tornebusk* (1961; *The Burning Bush*, 1961); *Den evige ild* (1961; *The Eternal Fire*, 1962); and *Kobberslangen* (1958; *The Brazen Serpent*, 1963). There are several treatments of Moses in modern drama. Earlier plays of the 20th century include Henry R.C. Dobbs' *Korah* (1903); five-act dramas, both entitled *Moses*, by Karl Hauptmann (1906) and Viktor Hahn (1907); and Oskar Kokoschka's *Der brennende Dornbusch* (1911); the Czech author Stanislav Lom wrote the drama *Vüdce* (1916; *The Leader*, 1917). The Nietzschean idea of the superman which had inspired Isaac *Rosenberg's remarkable short drama *Moses* (1916) inspired first a play by Lawrence Langner (1924), who treated the story as a myth on which to develop modern theories, and later Christopher Fry's *The Firstborn* (1946), in which Moses is again divested of his biblical qualities. Fry transforms his central character into an Egyptian military hero torn between idealism and reality, who finds himself providing the impetus for the Hebrews' liberation movement.

20th-Century Jewish Writers

Some of the most powerful and significant literary treatments of Moses in the 20th century have, understandably, been written by Jews. Max Donkhim published the five-act Russian drama, *Moysey* (1901), and Israel *Zangwill's "Moses and Jesus" (in *Blind Children*, 1903) records the imaginary encounter and bitter dialogue of the protagonists. Angiolo

*Orvieto's dramatic poem *Mosè* (1905) was later set to music by his fellow-Italian G. Orefice; and Naomi Nunes Carvalho wrote three dialogues involving Moses (in *Vox Humana*, 1912). Other literary treatments include the Czech play *Mojzis* (1919), by Eduard *Leda, and Markus Gottfried's Hebrew epic, *Moshe*, published in the same year. After World War I, the subject was treated by a number of eminent Jewish authors in various genres. Midrashic legends were reworked by Rudolf *Kayser (*Moses Tod*, 1921) and Edmond *Fleg (*Moise reconté par les Sages*, 1925; Eng. *The Life of Moses*, 1928); and there were narrative works in Hebrew by David *Frischmann ("*Sinai*," in *Ba-Midbar*, 1923) and Ḥayyim *Hazaz – who showed a modern approach in *Ḥatan Damim* (1925; Eng. tr. by I.M. Lask, *Bridegroom of Blood*). Three other novels of the interwar years were Lina Eckenstein's *Tutankh-Aten; a Story of the Past* (1924), a fictionalized history; Louis *Untermeyer's *Moses* (1928); and *Fertzig Yohr in Midbor* (1934), a Yiddish work by Saul Saphire. The U.S. poet Robert Nathan's "Moses on Nebo" (in *A Winter Tide*, 1940) presented the sad vision of Israel's millennial wanderings; Károly *Pap's *Mózes* was staged by the Budapest Jewish Theater just before the author's deportation in 1944. Konrad Bercovici's *The Exodus* (1947) was probably the first postwar attempt to recreate the Bible story in U.S. fiction. It was followed by many new treatments, including *Moyshe* (1951; *Moses*, 1951), one of the best-known Yiddish novels of Sholem *Asch, and two Hebrew novels by Israel writers: Ben-Zion Firer's *Moshe* (1959) and Y. Shurun's *Ḥalom Leil Setav* ("Dream of an Autumn Night," 1960). Other works in the same genre have been written by Howard *Fast (*Moses, Prince of Egypt*, 1958) and the Dutch author Manuel van *Loggem (*Mozes, de wording van een volk*, 1947, 1960²).

In Art

Together with David, Jacob, and Samson, Moses is one of the most popular Old Testament figures in art. The medieval church considered him both a type of the Messiah and one of the prophets who foretold his coming. In early Christian art until the end of the Carolingian period, Moses was often represented as a beardless youth holding a rod. He was later conceived in the form in which he still lives in popular imagination: as a patriarchal figure with a flowing, double-pointed beard, clasping the Tablets of the Law. Two horns were shown protruding from his head, because the Latin (Vulgate) translation of the Bible used during the Middle Ages mistranslated the verb "sent forth beams" as "horns" (*karan*, קרן) in Exodus 34:35. There are medieval sculptures of Moses at Chartres and elsewhere, and a Renaissance figure by Donatello in the Campanile at Florence. The most striking examples are the horned figure by Claus Sluter (1406) for the Well of the Prophets (or Well of Moses) at Dijon, France, and the horned statue by Michelangelo at San Pietro in Vincoli, Rome. This work, the most famous portrayal of Moses in art, was originally intended for the mausoleum of Pope Julius II. Many art cycles relate the various episodes in the life of Moses. Among the earliest is a Jewish source, the third-century frescoes from the synagogue at *Dura-Europos. Fuller cycles appear in Italy after the fifth century, such as the mosaics at Santa Maria Maggiore, Rome. There is a portrayal of the early life of Moses carved in ivory relief (Lipsanotheca, Brescia). A modern cycle of paintings, "Moses" (1924), was executed by the artist Uriel *Birnbaum.

Scenes from the life of Moses figure in many famous manuscripts, such as the sixth-century Vienna Genesis, the seventh-century Ashburnham Pentateuch, the ninth-century Bible of Charles the Bald, the 12th-century *Hortus Deliciarum* and Admont Bible, the 13th-century St. Louis Psalter, and the 14th-century Queen Mary Psalter. They are also found in medieval Hebrew manuscripts. Illustrations of the Exodus played a major part in the adornment of Passover **Haggadot*. There are also illuminations in German *maḥzorim* and other manuscripts. The *Haggadot* also include illustrations to a number of midrashic legends, such as the tale of the infant Moses who took Pharaoh's crown from his head and placed it on his own (Ex. R. 1:26). An episode from the same legend is treated in paintings by Giorgione (Uffizi Gallery, Florence) and Nicolas Poussin (Paris, Louvre). Other legends depicted include the petrification of Moses' neck when he was sentenced to be executed for killing the Egyptian (Ex. R. 1:28–31) and Pharaoh bathing in the blood of Israelite children as a cure for leprosy (Ex. R. 1:34). Scenes from the life of Moses also appear in mosaics at St. Mark's, Venice. Two scenes from the Exodus appear on the wings to the triptych of the Last Supper by Dirk Bouts (St. Pierre, Louvain): the paschal feast eaten by the Israelites before their departure from Egypt (a prefiguration of the Last Supper), and the gathering of the manna. The life of Moses inspired many frescoes of the Italian Renaissance. Benozzo Gozzoli dealt with the subject in frescoes at the Campo Santo, Pisa, and there are frescoes in the Sistine Chapel of the Vatican by Botticelli, Pinturicio, and Signorelli. The Exodus was also treated in the Vatican frescoes of the school of Raphael. In the Brera Gallery, Milan, there is a series of paintings by Bernardino Luini that depict scenes from the Exodus, including the crossing of the Red Sea. In his murals for the School of San Rocco, Venice, Tintoretto painted "The Rain of Manna," "Moses Striking the Rock," and "The Raising of the Serpent in the Wilderness" with his usual boldness and employment of violent contrasts of light and darkness. More than any other painter, Nicolas Poussin was haunted by the figure of Moses. He painted a larger number of canvases, forming an almost complete cycle of the lawgiver's life. Among them are "Moses and the Burning Bush" (Copenhagen Museum), "The Rain of Manna," "Moses Striking the Rock" (a subject he treated seven times), "The Spies Carrying the Cluster of Grapes" (Louvre), and "The Dance Around the Golden Calf" (National Gallery, London). In the 20th century, the figure of Moses has interested *Chagall and Ben-Zion who have both painted scenes from his life.

Some individual episodes call for more detailed consideration. The finding of Moses, Moses and the burning bush, Moses striking the rock, and the giving of the Law are the subjects which have most interested artists. The finding of Moses

(Ex. 2:5–10) was painted with elegance by the Venetian artist Paolo Veronese (two versions in the Hermitage and Prado). There is also a painting of this subject by *Rembrandt (Johnson Collection, Philadelphia). Jochebed, the mother of Moses, and her infant son are the subject of a tender family group by the English artist Simeon *Solomon. Moses and the burning bush (Ex. 3:1–14) occasionally appeared in early Christian art, but this subject is particularly associated with the popularity of the Marial cult in the Middle Ages. The burning bush was held to symbolize virgin birth, in that the virgin was penetrated but not consumed by the flames of the Holy Spirit. In medieval art Mary is therefore represented as rising out of the bush which burns at her feet. An example of the Marial interpretation is a major work of the 15th-century Provençal school, "The Coronation of the Virgin" by Enguerrand Charenton (Hospice of Villeneuve-les-Avignon). There is a more traditional representation of the burning bush episode in an engraving by Hans Holbein the younger. The ten plagues of Egypt (Ex. 7–12) are sometimes represented by the last plague, the slaying of the firstborn. There is a treatment of this subject by the English landscape painter J.M.W. Turner in the National Gallery, London. In one of the many illustrations to the Bible executed by Paul Gustave Doré, Pharaoh, overwhelmed by the disaster, implores Moses to lead the Israelites out of Egypt. The crossing of the Red Sea (Ex. 12–15) often appears in Byzantine manuscripts. There is a painting of this subject by the German Renaissance artist Lucas Cranach (Pinakothek, Munich), who also depicted Miriam's dance of triumph (Ex. 15:20–21; Augsburg Gallery). Moses striking the rock (Ex. 17:1–7; Num. 10:1–3) was one of the most popular subjects in early Christian art, where it is found in the murals of the catacombs, on Roman sarcophagi, and on gilded glass. Another Holbein engraving shows the Israelites gathering the manna; while Moses is seen with his hands supported by Aaron and Hur in a painting of the battle with Amalek (Ex. 17:8–16) by the English artist Sir John Millais. The giving of the Law (Ex. 20:1–18) appears on early Christian sarcophagi and in medieval art. Apart from the above-mentioned statue by Michelangelo, the most famous treatment of this episode is the painting by Rembrandt (Berlin Museum) of Moses breaking the tablets (Ex. 32:19). The raising of the serpent in the wilderness (Num. 21:6–9) was a popular subject in the Middle Ages and Renaissance, being understood as a prefiguration of the raising of the cross. The subject also lent itself to the dramatic, convoluted compositions of baroque artists. There is a painting by Rubens in the National Gallery, London, and one by his pupil, Anthony Van Dyck in the Prado. The death of Moses (Deut. 34) is depicted in a watercolor by William *Blake in accordance with a legend that, when Moses died, Satan tried to snatch his soul but was warded off by St. Michael's lance.

The lawgiver's brother Aaron is shown clad in the long robes of a high priest, a stone-studded breastplate on his chest and a turban or tiara on his head. He carries his flowering rod or censer, signifying priesthood. The revolt of Korah against Moses and Aaron (Num. 16) and the tragic fate that overtakes the rebels form the subject of an illustration by Jean Fouquet to the *Jewish Antiquities* of Josephus (Bibliothèque Nationale, Paris). The medieval Church thought of the rebels as heretics; on the other hand, the papacy associated Aaron with itself and for this reason Botticelli was commissioned to include the episode in his frescoes for the Sistine Chapel in the Vatican.

In Music

The story of Moses, interwoven with that of the Israelites, has also inspired many musical compositions from the Renaissance era onward, as well as Jewish and other folk songs. The following survey lists selected settings of texts and episodes from the Pentateuch, including even the relatively few which do not mention Moses himself.

(1) Oratorios, Operas, Cantatas, and Choral Works: Jachet van Berchem, *Locutus est Dominus ad Moysen; Stetit Moyses coram Pharaone* (motets, printed 1538–59); Claudio Monteverdi, *Audi coelum* (motets, added to the *Vesperae* of 1610); Giovanni Paolo Colonna, *Mosé legato di Dio e liberatore del popolo ebreo* (oratorio, 1686); Giovanni Battista Bassani, *Mosé risorto dalle acque* (oratorio, 1694); Antonio Vivaldi, *Moyses Deus Pharaonis* (oratorio, 1714; libretto only preserved); Johann Adolf Hasse (1699–1783), *Serpentes in deserto* (oratorio; the authenticity of another oratorio, *Mosé*, is doubtful); Nicolo Porpora (1686–1768), *Israel ab Aegyptiis liberatus* (oratorio); Georg Friedrich Handel, *Israel in Egypt* (oratorio) – text compiled by Charles Jennens, first performed in London at the King's Theatre, April, 4, 1739. This is one of Handel's major compositions and ranks among the outstanding works in the genre. Built mainly on the expression of the chorus, symbolizing the people of Israel, it reaches its climax with its description of the crossing of the Red Sea and in the "Song of Triumph"; Carl Philipp Emanuel Bach, *Die Israeliten in der Wueste* (oratorio, text by Schiebeler, printed by the composer in Hamburg, 1775, and first performed in Breslau, 1798); François Giroust, *Le Mont-Sinai ou Le Décalogue* (oratorio, Latin text, 1785); Johann Christoph Friedrich Bach, *Mosis Mutter und ihre Tochter* (duodrama, 1788); Giovanni Paisello (1740–1816), *Mosé in Egitto* (cantata for three voices); Konradin Kreutzer, *Die Sendung Mosis* (oratorio, 1814); Gioacchino Rossini, *Mosé in Egitto* (opera, text by Léon Tottola, premiere in Italian at Naples, 1818) – The revised version in French, *Moïse*, first performed in Paris (1827), included the famous "Prayer of Moses" which was one of the favorite subjects for fantasias, variations, and arrangements throughout the 19th century. The plot is that of a typical grand opera, with an interwoven dramatic love story not found in the biblical text; Franz Schubert, *Miriams Siegesgesang* (for soprano solo, mixed choir, and piano, opus 136; text by Franz Grillparzer, 1828); Karl Loewe, *Die eherne Schlange* (cantata for men's choir a capella, 1834); Adolf Bernhard *Marx, *Moses* (oratorio, 1841); Félicien David, *Moïse au Sinai* ("ode symphonique," i.e., oratorio, 1846); Camille Saint-Saëns, *Moïse sauvé des eaux* (cantata, text by Victor Hugo, c. 1851); Anton *Berlijn, *Moses auf Nebo* (oratorio) Anton *Rubinstein, *Moses* (oratorio, 1892); Marcus *Hast, *The Death of Moses* (ora-

torio, 1897); Jules Massenet, *La terre promise* (oratorio, 1900); Bernard Rogers, *The Exodus* (cantata, 1932); Arnold *Schoenberg, *Moses und Aaron* (opera, text by the composer, two acts completed in 1932; composition resumed in 1951; unfinished) – *Moses und Aaron* was first performed, in concert form, as a radio broadcast from Hamburg (first two acts, 1954); and was first staged in Zurich (June 6, 1957). In this highly philosophical work, the composer expresses the conflict between the Lawgiver, who cannot communicate his vision to the people (Moses = Schoenberg himself?), the weak and wavering people, and the glib mediator (Aaron = the critics, conventional composers?). See K. Woerner, *Gotteswort und Magie: die Oper Moses und Aron* [sic] (1959); D. Newlin, *Yuval 1* (1968), 204–20; Darius Milhaud, *Opus Americanum 2*, op. 219 (orchestral suite, originally composed as a ballet, *The Man of Midian*, for the Ballet Theater (1940, not produced) and first performed as an orchestral suite, 1940); Wadi'a Sabrá (1876–1952), Lebanese Maronite composer, *Le chant de Moïse* (oratorio); Roger Vuataz, *Moïse* (oratorio for five reciters, soprano, choir, and orchestra, 1947); Jacob *Weinberg, *The Life of Moses* (oratorio, 1955); Josef Tal, *Exodus* (first version, for piano and drums, as "choreagraphic poem" for the dancer Deborah Bertonoff; second version ("Exodus I"), for baritone and orchestra (1945/46); third version ("Exodus II"), electronic composition, including processed human voices (1958/59); the first electronic work produced in Israel).

(2) Jewish Folk Tradition. Among the musical notations made by *Obadiah the (Norman) Proselyte (11th–12th centuries) there is a setting of a *piyyut* in honor of Moses, *Mi al Har Ḥorev ha-Amidi* (see illus. in col. 1307–8). Jewish folk-song tradition contains a large number of songs about Moses, such as *Yismaḥ Moshe*, found in almost all communities; the religious Ladino songs, e.g., *Cantar vos quiero un mahase* (on the birth of Moses) and *A catorce era del mes* (on the Exodus); and the epic Aramaic songs of the Jews of *Kurdistan about Moses and Pharaoh's daughter, the battle between Israel and Amalek, and the death of Moses. Many of these songs are sung on Shavuot or Simḥat Torah. Among modern Israel folk songs are Yedidyah *Admon's *U-Moshe Hikkah al Ẓur*, and two children's songs, *Benei Yisrael Po Kullanu* (Joel *Engel, after a Yemenite melody) and *Dumam Shatah Tevah Ketannah* (K.Y. Silman, after an East Ashkenazi melody). Yehuda *Sharett's setting of the *Haggadah* ("*Nusaḥ Yagur*") is both a functional "liturgy" for kibbutz use and an oratorio.

(3) Other Folk-Song Traditions. While a few songs about Moses and the Exodus exist in older Christian music, the most prominent examples can be found in the Afro-American spirituals – notably the powerful *Go Down Moses* ("When Israel was in Egypt land – let my people go!"), which has become an international favorite. The Palestinian Arab tradition of mass pilgrimage to the legendary tomb of Moses on the festival of Nebi Musa has given rise to its own repertory of mass chants. One of these, *Ya ḥalili ya ḥabibi, ya ḥawaja Musa*, has become an Israel *Hora*-song.

[Bathja Bayer]

BIBLIOGRAPHY: H. Gressmann, *Mose und seine Zeit* (1913); P. Volz, *Mose und seine Werk* (1932²); F. James, *Personalities of the Old Testament* (1939), 1–44; M. Buber, *Moses* (Eng., 1947); Kaufmann Y., Toledot, 2 (1947); Kaufmann Y., Religion, 212–44; J. Griffiths, in JNES, 12 (1953), 225ff.; G. van Rad, *Old Testament Theology*, 1 (1962), 289ff.; E. Osswald, *Das Bild des Mose* (1962); H.H. Rowley, *Men of God* (1963), 1ff.; W. Helck, in: VT, 15 (1965), 48; H. Schmid, *Mose, Überlieferung und Geschichte* (1968); S. Loewenstamm, in: EM, 5 (1968), 482–95; W.F. Albright, *Yahweh and the Gods of Canaan* (1968); A. Cody, *A History of the Old Testament Priesthood* (1969), 39ff. **ADDITIONAL BIBLIOGRAPHY:** J. van Seters, *The Life of Moses* (1994); W. Dever, in: ABD, 3:545–58; D. Beegle, in: ABD, 4:909–18 (with bibliography); C. Houtman, in: DDD: 593–98 (with bibliography); K. van der Toorn, *ibid.*, 910–19 (with bibliography); W. Propp, in: UF, 31 (1999), 537–75; S.D. Sperling, in: HUCA, 70–71 (1990–2000), 39–55. IN HELLENISTIC LITERATURE: J. Freudenthal, *Hellenistische Studien*, 1–2 (1878); F. Reinach, *Textes d'auteurs grecs et romains relatifs au judaïsme* (1895); I. Lévy, *La Légende de Pythagore de Grèce en Palestine* (1927), 137–53; K. Preisendanz (ed.), *Papyri Graecae Magicae*, 2 vols. (1928–31); E.R. Goodenough, *By Light, Light…* (1935), 181–234, 289–91; M. Braun, *History and Romance in Graeco-Oriental Literature* (1938); G. Vermés, *Moïse, L'Homme de l'Alliance* (1955); Alon, Meḥkarim, 1 (1957), 196–7; I. Guttman, *Ha-Sifrut ha-Yehudit ha-Hellenistit*, 2 vols. (1958–63); E.R. Dodds, in: *Entretiens sur l'Antiquité classique* (1966), 1–32; B.Z. Wacholder, *Nicolaus of Damascus* (1962), 57–58; R. Le Deaut, in: *Biblica*, 45 (1964), 198–219; M. Hengel, *Judentum und Hellenismus* (1969); J.G. Gayer, in: JTS, 20 (1969), 245–8; M. Stern, in: S. Safrai et al. (eds.), *Sefer… G. Alon* (1970), 169–91; R. Williamson, *Philo and the Epistle to the Hebrews* (1970). IN THE AGGADAH: R. Bloch, in: *Cahiers Sioniens*, 8 (1954), 211–85; S.E. Loewenstamm, in: *Tarbiz*, 27 (1958), 142–57; G. Vermes, *Scripture and Tradition in Judaism* (1961), 178–90. MEDIEVAL JEWISH THOUGHT: Y. Levinger, in: *Fourth World Congress of Jewish Studies, Papers*, 2 (1968), 335–9 (Heb.), 20 (Eng. summ.); A. Reines, in: HUCA, 33 (1962), 221–53; 34 (1963), 195–215. IN CHRISTIAN TRADITION: J. Daniélou, *Sacramentum futuri* (1950), 129–200; P. Demann, in: *Cahiers Sioniens*, 8 (1954), 189–244; DBI, Supplement, 5 (1957), 1335–37. IN ISLAM: Ṭabarī, *Ta'arīkh*, 1 (1357 A.H.), 270–312; ʿUmara, Ms. fol. 15v.–24v.; Thaʿlabī, *Qiṣaṣ* (1356 A.H.), 140–210; Kisāī, *Qiṣaṣ* (1356 A.H.), 194–240; H. Speyer, *Die biblischen Erzählungen im Qoran* (1961), 225–363; J.W. Hirschberg, *Jüdische und christliche Lehren im vor-und frühislamischen Arabien* (1939), 129–34; **ADD. BIBLIOGRAPHY:** "Mūsa," in: EIS², 7 (1993), 638–40 (includes bibliography). MOSES' JOURNEY: Ṭabarī, *Ta'arīkh*, 1 (1357 A.H.), 256–64; Ṭabarī, *Tafsīr*, 15 (1328 A.H.), 171–6, 16 (1328 A.H.), 2–7; ʿUmara Ms. fol. 3v–18v; Thaʿlabī, *Qiṣaṣ* (1356 A.H.), 183–94; Kisā'i, *Qiṣaṣ* (1356a. h.), 230–3; Zamakhsharī, 1 (1343 A.H.), 574–6; A. Jellinek (ed.), *Bet ha-Midrash*, 5 (1877), 133–5; J. Obermann, *Studies in Islam and Judaism* (1933), 10–13; H.Z. Hirschberg (ed. and tr.), *Ḥibbur Yafe me-ha-Yeshuʿah* (1969²), introd. 51, 61–62, tr. 6–8; EIS, S.V. *Khaḍir*. IN ARTS: M. Roston, *Biblical Drama in England* (1968), index; E. Becker, *Das Quellwunder des Moses in der altchristlichen Kunst* (1909); L. Réau, *Iconographie de l'Art chrétien*, 2 pt., 1 (1957), 175–216; R. Mellinkoff, *The Horned Moses in Medieval Art and Thought* (1971).

MOSES, ADOLPH (**Eliezer Adolph**; 1840–1902), rabbi. Moses was born in Kletchevo, Poland. His parents were Rabbi Israel Baruch Moses, a talmudic scholar, and Eva Graditz. An eldest child, Moses was born when his parents were living on stipend (*kest*) in the home of his mother's parents. In 1849, R. Israel Baruch took a rabbinic position in Santomishel, Posen. The young Adolph went back to Poland to study in yeshivot for three years, then returned for secular studies at Schrimm and Militsch. He moved on to Breslau, where he attended both the University of Breslau and Zechariah *Frankel's Rabbinical Seminary. Idealistic and devoted to his studies, Moses was especially interested in history, philosophy, and philology and like many young Jews of the time was strongly influenced by Western civilization. In 1859, carrying only a walking stick, he hiked to Italy where he fought under Garibaldi, attaining the rank of corporal. Returning to Breslau, he felt rejected by old friends who did not sympathize with some of his views. In 1863, Moses joined the Polish insurrection. Captured by the Russians, he later wrote a novel, *Luser Segermacher*, about his prison experiences. After his release, Moses went to Frankfurt on Main to study under Abraham *Geiger, a leading Reform scholar, and later spent two years at the University of Vienna, where he was close to Professor Adolph *Jellinek. In 1868, Moses took a teaching position in Steegnitz, Bavaria. Two years later he accepted a call to a pulpit in Montgomery, Alabama, and soon moved on to another in Mobile, where he served 1871–1881. He devoted himself to learning to deliver sermons in good English, rather than the German language prevalent in the American synagogues at the time, and he developed a life-long fascination with Shakespeare, even giving lectures on the Bard.

Moses leaned toward radical Reform, deprecating what he would term "physiological Judaism," by which he meant its ritual and nationalistic aspects. He preferred instead to see Judaism as a world monotheistic doctrine of truth and morality.

In 1885, he was the first to rise to advocate acceptance of the Platform at the famous meeting of Reform rabbis at Pittsburgh. He joined a group of rabbis in 1890 in rejecting the halakhic requirement of circumcision for male proselytes, although he criticized conversions for people who simply wanted to marry Jews. He opposed the budding Zionist movement, and like many Reform rabbis of that era moved his temple's main weekly service to Sundays, starting in 1892. He published many articles on Judaism, folklore, and anthropology and served as editor of *Zeitgeist*, a Jewish journal. A collection of his essays, along with a brief biography, was published in 1903 by Hyman G. Enelow.

He graduated from the medical school of the University of Louisville in 1893 and was particularly interested in working with the blind. From 1881, he served as rabbi of Temple Adath Israel in Louisville, Kentucky, where he remained until his death after a long illness.

[Matthew Schwartz (2nd ed.)]

MOSES, ASSUMPTION OF. Title of the incomplete text of an apocryphal writing, which consists, largely, of an address, in the form of a prophecy, by Moses to his successor, Joshua. The substance of the prophecy concerns the future fate of Israel and the End of Days. Only scant attention is paid to the epochs of the Judges and Kings, the onslaught of Nebuchadnezzar and the Babylonian Exile, and to the return of the exiles. However, with discussion of the Hasmonean period the story becomes considerably more detailed.

The defiling of the altar in the temple is described in detail, i.e., blemished offerings which were presented by slaves, the offspring of slaves, rather than by priests (5:4). It is unclear whether this is a specific reference to John Hyrcanus (cf. Jos., Ant. 13:288–92). Unmistakable, however, is the allusion to the Hasmoneans in the mention of the reunion of the kingdom with the priesthood (6:1). The subsequent cruel rule of "an insolent king… who will not be of the race of the priests" (6:2) is depicted in detail, and its length (34 years) is specified (6:6). The prophecy continues: "And he shall beget children (who) succeeding him shall rule for shorter periods" (6:7); cohorts will assault and a powerful king of the west will conquer the country (6:8). It is at this point that the prophecy of political events ends, and 7:1 reads: "And when this is done the times shall be ended…" The succeeding sequence describes: the hypocrisy of the ruling class; the chaos of the persecutions (in chap. 8, which contains traces of the era of Domitian, although this may be a later interpolation); the appearance of a Levite, Taxo, who with his seven sons prefers death to active resistance (9); and a poetic representation of the intervention of God and of the victory of Israel over "the eagle" (an obvious reference to Rome). The text ends, abruptly, with the reply of Joshua (11), and with the final answer of Moses.

The work was discovered as a palimpsest in the Ambrosiana library in Milan by M. Ceriani, the Italian orientalist, and first published in 1861. The present Latin version of the text has remained untouched by Christian annotators. It is based upon a Greek original, although whether the first version was in Hebrew or in Aramaic is unknown. The contents of chapter one strongly suggest that the work originated in the first century, although some details in the following chapters may indicate another date (c. 130). It is probable that "the insolent king" referred to is Herod the Great, the length of whose reign may have corresponded to the 34 years mentioned in the text (6:6). It is difficult to agree with opinions which maintain that the passage refers to Alexander Yannai and Pompey and that the reign of 34 years was inserted later. If the Herodian interpretation is correct, then the work was composed after the campaign of *Quintilus Varus in 4 B.C.E. (perhaps referred to in 6:8), i.e., during the rule of Herod's sons. Allusions in the text which refer to events after that period are obscure. A study by J. Licht (see bibl.) proposes a Hasmonean date for the basic elements of the work, together with a reworking and adaptation by a post-Herodian editor. The present title of the manuscript is based on a tradition of the Church Fathers that a work of this name existed in ancient times. Clement of Alexandria, Didymus, and Origen, for example, claimed that the mention of the struggle between the archangel Michael and Satan for the body of Moses, in Jude 5:9, is based upon a work entitled the *Assumptio* or *Ascensio Moysis (Mosis)*. However, although the lost sections of the work probably contained descriptions of the death of Moses and his ascent to heaven, this story is not mentioned in the portion of the text quoted by

Gelasius of Cyzicus in his "History of the Council of Nicaea" as being taken from the ᾿Ανάληψις Μωυσέως ("The Ascension of Moses"). Neither is any reference made to the ascent of Moses in the Ceriani fragment. Indeed a more appropriate title for the extant palimpsest would appear to be *The Testament of Moses* (which is also mentioned as a distinct work in ancient Church documents); especially in light of the fact that reference is made in the present text (1:10) to Deuteronomy 31:7–8. The words "*Liber Profetiae Moysis*" in the text itself (1:5) could, however, indicate that this may have been its original title. Whatever the case, the present version of the text is probably the result of an amalgamation between an original work, *Testamentum Moses* (or *Liber Profetiae Moysis*), and a later composition, the *Assumptio Moysis*.

BIBLIOGRAPHY: E. Kautzsch, *Apokryphen und Pseudepigraphen des Alten Testaments*, 2 (1900), 311–31; Kamenetzki, in: *Ha-Shiloʾah*, 15 (1905), 38–50; Beer, in: Herzog-Hauck, 16 (1905); O. Holtzmann, *Neutestamentliche Zeitgeschichte* (1906[2]), 301–3; Schuerer, Gesch, 3 (1909[4]), 294–305; Charles, Apocrypha, 2 (1913), 407–24; Licht, in: JJS, 12 (1961), 95–105.

[Werner Michaelis]

MOSES, BLESSING OF. Deuteronomy 33 is presented as Moses' blessing of the tribes of Israel shortly before his death, and it is traditionally considered a prophecy of future conditions. The critical view, however, is not that the poem is actually Mosaic, for it describes Israel after the conquest, when the tribes had settled in Canaan. It is of uncertain date. It has been dated on orthographic grounds to the 11th century B.C.E., although it may have been written down in the tenth century (Cross and Freedman). This dating also fits the political and social conditions described: Judah was oppressed by the Philistines, and Reuben, suffering from Ammonite encroachment, had practically disappeared; Simeon had vanished as an ethnic entity, and Dan had already moved north. Others date the poem later. Driver places it either shortly after the reign of Jeroboam I or in the middle of the reign of Jeroboam II. The poem is probably of northern origin, for Judah is portrayed as weak and separated from his brothers, while Joseph, who has the longest and most lavish blessing, is called *nezir ʾeḥaw* – the "prince" or "distinguished one" of his brothers. The poem is divided into two parts: the framework and the body. The framework consists of: (a) the exordium (verses 2–5) telling how God appeared from Sinai, gave Israel a law through Moses, and established himself as king in their midst (possibly verse 5 tells of the foundation of human kingship in Israel), and (b) the hymnic conclusion (verses 26–29) lauding God's glory and might, and celebrating Israel's happiness, prosperity, and security under God's protection.

The body (verses 6–25) consists of 11 eulogistic sayings characterizing the tribes or praying for their well-being (Simeon is not mentioned). The sayings themselves may be older than the song. Each blessing after the first is introduced by the narrator, e.g., "And of Levi he said …" (8). The ordering principle is a combination of the age of the eponyms and the importance of the tribes. In general the poem describes Israel in its ideal condition: a tribal league with God alone as king, settled in their land and flourishing (except for Judah and Reuben) under the protection of God and the theocratic guidance of Levi. The atmosphere is one of peace and security. The language of the poem is extremely difficult because of its antiquity and epigrammatic style, and the text apparently contains many corruptions, so that much of the interpretation is necessarily problematic.

BIBLIOGRAPHY: Commentaries on Deuteronomy; T.H. Gaster, in: JBL, 66 (1947), 53–62; F.M. Cross and D.N. Freedman, *ibid.*, 67 (1948), 191–210.

[Michael V. Fox]

MOSES, CHRONICLES OF (Heb. דִּבְרֵי הַיָּמִים לְמֹשֶׁה רַבֵּנוּ, *Divrei ha-Yamim le-Moshe Rabbenu*), a story on the life of Moses written in the early Middle Ages. The prophet's early life, before the Exodus from Egypt, forms the major part of the story, while his later life and death are described only very briefly. The author based himself on some of the midrashic interpretations of the life of Moses as told in the Book of Exodus, but the many adventures ascribed in the work to Moses are the product of the author's fertile imagination.

According to the story, *Balaam the Magician was adviser to the king of Egypt in Moses' time; *Jethro, also one of the king's advisers, was driven away from the royal court after he tried to help the Jews in Egypt. The author also describes a number of miracles (not mentioned in the Bible) that supposedly occurred in Moses' youth and which saved him from disaster. Completely new stories were also added to Moses' biography, e.g., a very detailed tale about his becoming king of Ethiopia, after he had driven away Balaam, who had seized the Ethiopian throne. In the story, Moses reigned for 40 years in the kingdom. A. Shinan published an edition of this book in 1977–78. There is a Spanish translation by L. Girón (1988). There is an East Slavic version of the "Life of Moses," preserved in manuscripts from the 15th century on, that agree in most details with the Hebrew text (Taube). "*Divrei ha-Yamim le-Moshe Rabbenu*" is similar to other early medieval tales in which a biblical story is adapted in the light of conventions, mores, and concepts of the Middle Ages. The narrative element is usually emphasized in these stories. Abraham and many other sages were also the subjects of such tales which were often erroneously considered to belong to midrashic literature. Later writers in adapting biblical stories also compiled and adapted these different versions, e.g., the author of *"*Sefer ha-Yashar*" (Venice, 1625; see *Fiction, Hebrew: The Hebrew Story in the Middle Ages). "*Midrash Petirat Moshe Rabbenu*" ("A Midrash on the Death of Moses") is another story about Moses written in the Middle Ages. The narrative aspect is not dominant, but rather the midrashic elements which are ethical in content and meant to convey a moral. Moses' death is described in a mythological setting involving a confrontation between God and Samael (Satan).

BIBLIOGRAPHY: A. Jellinek, *Beit ha-Midrash*, 1 (19382), xxif. (Ger.), 115–29 (Heb.); 2 (19382), vii–xi (Ger.), 1–11 (Heb.). **ADD. BIB-**

LIOGRAPHY: A. Shinan, in: *Scripta Hiersolymitana*, 27 (1978), 66–78; L. Girón, in: *Sefarad*, 48:2 (1988), 390–425; M. Taube, in: *Jews and Slavs*, 1 (1993), 84–119.

[Joseph Dan]

MOSES, ISAAC S. (1847–1926), U.S. Reform rabbi. Moses, who was born in Zaniemysl, Poznan, had not completed his education before he settled in the United States in the early 1870s. He was appointed to rabbinic positions in Quincy, Illinois (1876), Milwaukee (1879), and Chicago (1888). In 1901 he became rabbi of the Central Synagogue, New York, where he remained until his retirement in 1919.

In his early days in the United States, Moses was considered a radical Reformer, but later he took a more moderate position. In 1884 he introduced his own prayer book (*Tefillat Yisrael*). Moses was a founding member of the Central Conference of American Rabbis and a member of the Reform committee charged with compiling an official prayer book. The appearance of the *Union Prayer Book* in 1894 has been credited to his personal initiative in preparing and circulating a manuscript when the committee's work seemed to be leading nowhere. Moses also published a number of sermons and textbooks for children. His *Sabbath School Hymnal*, first issued in 1894, ran into 14 editions. While in Milwaukee, he edited the weekly *Der Zeitgeist* (1880–82).

BIBLIOGRAPHY: CCARY, 37 (1927), 250; L.J. Swichkow and L.P. Gartner, *The History of the Jews in Milwaukee* (1963), passim.

[Sefton D. Temkin]

MOSES, MARCUS (**Mordecai Hamburger**; d. 1735), Anglo-Indian pioneer. Son of Moses Libusch, a leader of Hamburg Jewry, he married a daughter of the famous *Glueckel von Hameln and settled in London. Here his criticism of a divorce issued by R. Aaron *Hart brought him into conflict with the established Ashkenazi community. He was excommunicated and, in consequence, in 1707 set up his own synagogue (later the Hambro synagogue). Becoming impoverished in 1712, he went to Fort St. George (*Madras) in India and was involved in the purchase for the governor of Madras, Thomas Pitt, of the famous Pitt diamond, later sold to the regent of France. In 1721 he returned to England a wealthy man and built his congregation a new synagogue. In 1731 he went back to India where he died. His eldest son, known as MOSES MARCUS (b. 1701), was converted to Christianity and published in 1724 an autobiographical tract (later translated into Dutch) justifying his action, as well as books on biblical study.

BIBLIOGRAPHY: C. Roth, *The Great Synagogue, London* (1950), 35–46, 114–9; Roth, Mag Bibl, 285, 351, 408; idem, *Anglo-Jewish Letters* (1938), 97–98; H.D. Love, *Vestige of Old Madras*, 4 vols. (1913); Hart, in: *Jewish Historical Society of England, Miscellanies*, 3 (1937), 57–76. **ADD. BIBLIOGRAPHY:** Katz, England, 206–15.

[Walter Joseph Fischel]

MOSES, MYER (1779–1833), U.S. merchant, soldier, and public official. Moses, who was born in Charleston, South Carolina, was active in the South Carolina Society for Promotion of Domestic Arts and Manufactories and was director of the Planters and Mechanics Bank. In 1809 Moses became a captain of volunteers and he later served in the War of 1812. He represented Charleston in the 1810 state legislature and served on the Charleston public school commission in 1811 and 1823. In 1825 Moses moved to New York City.

[Neil Ovadia]

MOSES, RAPHAEL J. (1812–1893), U.S. lawyer and state legislator. Born in Charleston, South Carolina, into a family of colonial American origin, Moses attended grade school but left school at the age of 13. After an apprenticeship in business, he set himself up in Charleston as a merchant. After the 1838 fire destroyed his business, he moved to St. Joseph, Florida, then to Apalachicola, Florida, where he studied law and opened his own practice. He then moved to Columbus, Georgia, where his practice flourished and he became a leader of the bar. He also ventured into fruit growing. Before the Civil War he was the first to ship Georgia peaches to Savannah and thence by steamer to New York City. An ardent secessionist, Moses, although over military age, quickly volunteered his services at the outbreak of the Civil War. He rose to the rank of major and served as Confederate Commissary for the State of Georgia until the war's end. Moses retained his deep feeling for the "Lost Cause" to the end of his life.

Returning to Columbus, Moses resumed his law practice and was elected to the first postwar Georgia state legislature, where he was made chairman of the Judiciary Committee. In 1878, while campaigning for the U.S. Congress, Moses heard that his opponent, W.O. Tuggle, had taunted him with being a Jew. In "An Open Letter to the Hon. W.O. Tuggle," first published in the Columbus *Daily Times* (Aug. 29, 1878) and reprinted many times, he eloquently answered: "… I feel it an honor to be one of a race whom persecution cannot crush… whom prejudice has in vain endeavored to subdue… who… after nearly nineteen centuries of persecution still survive as a nation and assert their manhood and intelligence… Would you honor me? Call me Jew. Would you place in unenviable prominence your unchristian prejudices and narrow bigotry? Call me Jew." Moses lost the election nevertheless.

BIBLIOGRAPHY: B.A. Elzas, *Jews of South Carolina* (1905), 199–202; C. Reznikoff and U.Z. Engelmann, *Jews of Charleston* (1950), 289–90 (reprint of letter to Tuggle).

[Thomas J. Tobias]

MOSES, ROBERT (1888–1981), U.S. parks and highways developer. Moses was born in New Haven, Connecticut, to well-to-do Spanish-Jewish parents. He denied his Jewish affiliation. He received his B.A. and M.A. degrees from Oxford University in 1911 and 1913, respectively. In 1914 he received a Ph.D. in political science from Columbia University, writing his dissertation on British colonial administration. It was published as *Civil Service of Great Britain* (1914). He later wrote *Theory and Practice in Politics* (1939), *Working for the People* (1956), *La Guardia: A Salute and a Memoir* (1957), *A*

Tribute to Governor Smith (1962), and *Public Works: A Dangerous Trade* (1970).

In 1919 Moses joined the staff of Governor Alfred E. Smith and served as chief of staff of a New York State commission on administrative reorganization. He then began his long career on state parks and highways agencies as president of the New York State Council of Parks (1924–63) and chairman of the Long Island State Parks Commission (1924–63). He also served as secretary of state for New York (1927–28). In 1934 Moses was the unsuccessful Republican candidate for governor of New York.

In 1934 Moses became Mayor Fiorello La Guardia's parks commissioner, a post he held under four mayors (to 1960). As commissioner, he inaugurated massive public works of the New Deal type. He was responsible, for example, for construction of the Triborough Bridge structures (dedicated 1936); Grand Central Parkway; Belt Parkway; West Side Highway and Henry Hudson Parkway, in Manhattan and the Bronx; East River (later called the Franklin D. Roosevelt) and Harlem River Drive, in Manhattan; Fire Island State Park; the Niagara power plant; and the Coliseum convention hall in Manhattan. His department developed 15 outdoor swimming pools, 84 miles of parkways, and 17 miles of beaches, including Jones Beach. The park acreage in New York City was increased from 14,000 acres to 34,673 acres. On the social level, he provided full entry for the city's working-class communities into a recreational world previously reserved for the middle and upper classes.

Moses also served as city construction coordinator (1946–60); as chairman of the Jones Beach State Parkway Authority (1933–63); as member (1934) and then chairman (1936–46) of the Triborough Bridge Authority and of the Consolidated Triborough Bridge and City Tunnel Authority (1946–68); as sole member (1938) of the New York City Parkway Authority; as chairman of the state committee on postwar employment (1948); and as chief consultant on public works to the federal Hoover Commission on Reorganization of the Executive Branch (1948). Among the city buildings he constructed were Shea Stadium, Lincoln Center, and the New York Aquarium in Coney Island.

Impatient for results, Moses was known as "the man who got things done." Outspoken and single-minded, he was frequently embroiled in controversies in which he displayed his acerbic wit and combative style. By the late 1950s, however, there was growing public resentment about his aggressive urban reconstruction programs. In 1960, Mayor Robert F. Wagner moved him out of his city positions to run the New York World's Fair of 1964. Under the administration of Governor Nelson Rockefeller, Moses lost his positions in New York State and thus left state government in 1968. Finally, in 1972, Mayor John Lindsay refused to reappoint him to the Triborough Authority, which essentially ended Moses' career.

Considered the single most powerful individual in the city and state of New York in the 20th century, Moses was the most influential nonfederal public official in the U.S. of his time without ever being elected to public office. Some of the landmarks named in his honor include the Robert Moses State Park in Long Island; Robert Moses State Park at Massena; the Robert Moses Causeway on Long Island; the Robert Moses Parkway at Niagara; and the dams at Niagara and Massena.

BIBLIOGRAPHY: C. Rodgers, *Robert Moses: Builder for Democracy* (1952). **ADD. BIBLIOGRAPHY:** J. Schwartz, *The New York Approach* (1993); B. Nicholson, *Hi Ho, Come to the Fair* (1990); E. Lewis, *Public Entrepreneurship* (1980); R. Caro, *The Power Broker: Robert Moses and the Fall of New York* (1975);

[Richard Skolnik / Ruth Beloff (2nd ed.)]

MOSES, SIEGFRIED (1887–1974), German Zionist leader and Israel public official. Born in Lautenburg, Germany, Moses practiced as a lawyer from 1912 to 1937. In 1917 he was appointed food controller of the city of Danzig and in 1919 he became deputy director of the Union of German Municipalities, a post he held until 1920. From 1923 to 1929 he was manager of the Schocken Department Store Co. in Zwickau. In his student days he was active in the union of Jewish student fraternities (see *Kartell Juedischer Verbindungen) and was the editor of *Der Juedische Student*. In 1920 he was appointed a member of the board of the Jewish Workers Aid Society in Berlin and was its executive chairman from 1921 to 1923. He was a delegate to several Zionist Congresses and was the president of the Zionist Organization of Germany during the period 1933–37. Moses was also active in Jewish communal affairs as vice chairman of the Reichsvertretung der Juden in Deutschland, 1933–37, and as a member of the Berlin Community Council. He settled in Palestine in 1937 and assumed the post of managing director of *Ha'avara (transfer of Jewish assets in Germany to Palestine). For a period of ten years (1939–49), he worked as a certified public accountant and income tax expert. He was a member of the *Jewish Agency Delegation to the United Nations in 1947 and in 1949 was appointed Israel's first State Comptroller, a post which he held until his retirement in 1961. In 1957 he was elected president of Irgun Olei Merkaz Europa ("Association of Settlers from Central Europe") and president of the Council of Jews from Germany and of the Leo Baeck Institute. He was the chairman of the Advisory Committee of the United Restitution Organization in Israel and a member of the board of Bank Leumi. Moses wrote *The Income Tax Ordinance of Palestine* (1942, 1946), *Jewish Post-War Claims* (1944), and articles on Jewish subjects and his professional work.

BIBLIOGRAPHY: D. Lazar, *Rashim be-Yisrael*, 2 (1955), 132–6.

[Kurt Loewenstein]

MOSES BEN ABRAHAM OF PONTOISE (12th century), French tosafist. Moses was a pupil of Jacob *Tam. The *Sefer ha-Yashar* of R. Tam discusses a number of problems, concerned mainly with the clarification of the plain meaning of various talmudic passages, which Moses put before his teacher (Responsa nos. 51, 52, 69–70). The theoretical nature of most of the questions, and the answers and their importance for an understanding of the relevant talmudic passages, led to their inclusion, in substance, in the standard *tosafot*, as well as in the works of such *rishonim* as *Mordecai b. Hillel, *Meir b. Baruch of Rothenburg, and others. The tosafists also mention Moses in connection with other subjects, and they cite his comments in the various collections of their biblical commentaries. A short verse of two lines by Moses, coming at the end of the list of positive precepts in the *Azharot of Elijah ha-Zaken, together with a commentary to it, has been preserved (*Kobez al Jad*, 1 (1936), 8).

BIBLIOGRAPHY: Urbach, Tosafot, 111–3.

[Israel Moses Ta-Shma]

MOSES BEN DANIEL OF ROHATYN (end of 17th century), Galician author. His name suggests that he was born in Rohatyn (Rogatin), but according to the preface of his works he lived in Zolkiew, where he published his *Sugyat ha-Talmud* (1693). The work, consisting of 40 paragraphs, is a methodology of the Talmud. It deals particularly with the commentaries of Rashi and *tosafot* and the manner in which they were studied at the time according to the two dialectical methods of Talmud study known as the "Nuremberger" and the "Regensburger" (see *Yeshivot). The work was translated into Latin by H.J. van Bashuysen and was published in the Latin translation of the *Halikhot Olam* of Joshua b. Joseph ha-Levi (Hanover, 1714 pp. 363ff.).

BIBLIOGRAPHY: S. Buber, *Kiryah Nisgavah* (1903), 58 no. 229.

MOSES BEN ELIJAH HA-LEVI (d. 1667), Karaite scholar from Feodosia (the Crimea), *ḥazzan* of the community and a teacher of Torah in the 17th century. In 1654–55 he went on a pilgrimage to Ereẓ Israel, which he described in his travel account (see Gurland; Ya'ari). Moses, with other members of the Karaite community, set out from Feodosia seaport. They traveled through Constantinople and Rhodes and spent Rosh Ha-Shanah and Yom Kippur on the ship. They visited Cairo and Alexandria, and he devoted part of his account to the depiction of Karaite communities of Egypt. From Egypt they moved to Gaza through the Sinai desert and then to Jerusalem. They also visited Hebron, Nablus, and Damascus. Moses copied Karaite books and was an author of the book *Darosh Darash Moshe* (JTS 3317, [JNUL, mic. 32002]), including 24 commentaries and sermons on different subjects. He composed several liturgical poems, which had been included in the Karaite *siddur*.

BIBLIOGRAPHY: A.B. Gottlober, *Bikkoret le-Toledot ha-Kara'im* (1865), 204; H.Y. Gurland, *Ginzei Yisrael*, 1 (1865); Mann, Texts, 2 (1935), 1363; 1427–28; A. Ya'ari, *Massa'ot Ereẓ Yisrael* (1976), 305–23.

[Golda Akhiezer (2nd ed.)]

MOSES BEN ELIJAH PASHA, Karaite scholar from Chufut-Qaleh, *ḥazzan* of the community and a teacher of Torah in the 16th century. In addition, he was mentioned in one manuscript as a corrector of prayer books. He corresponded with Karaite worthies of Constantinople, Moses Metsorodi and Eljah Maruli. He wrote a commentary on the liturgical poem by Aaron ben Joseph, *Hakdamat Aẓulah*, and composed several liturgical poems, some of which were included in the Karaite *siddur*.

BIBLIOGRAPHY: A.B. Gottlober, *Bikkoret le-Toledot ha-Kara'im* (1865), 204; Mann, Texts, 2 (1935), 446–47, 462ff., 1427.

[Golda Akhiever (2nd ed.)]

MOSES (ben Isaac) BEN HA-NESI'AH (late 13th century), Hebrew grammarian and lexicographer; lived in England. His mother was apparently Jewish and was known as "Countess" or "Contesse," in Hebrew *Ha-Nesi'ah*; hence his name: Ben ha-Nesi'ah. His only extant work, *Sefer ha-Shoham* ("The Onyx Book"), is the sole source for the scanty information available on him. In the introduction, he states that in his youth he wrote a grammar book, *Leshon Limmudim* ("Language of Learning"). This work is not extant and some scholars assume that extracts of it were included in *Sefer ha-Shoham*, written later. The author chose the name שֹׁהַם (Shoham), because it is an anagram of his name מֹשֶׁה (Moses). From the work, it can be learned that the author's teacher was R. *Moses b. Yom Tov ha-Nakdan ("the Punctuator") of London (c. 1268) and that he had a knowledge of Arabic. Moses b. ha-Nesi'ah was acquainted with many of the works of his predecessors.

Sefer ha-Shoham is divided into three parts. The first is a general introduction to the Hebrew language, a study of the origin of the letters, and on the formative letters and their role, etc. In the second part, the author reviews the verbs and divides them into seven groups. His system was possibly influenced by that of Judah b. David *Ḥayyuj. He then lists the nouns, classified into 162 metric groups, according to the method of David *Kimḥi. The third part deals with the particles, adverbs, numerals, vocalization, and accents. He added also a dictionary of the Aramaic words found in the Bible. Only the introduction to *Sefer ha-Shoham* and the section dealing with the verbs have been published (1947).

BIBLIOGRAPHY: Moses b. Isaac ha-Nesi'ah, *Sefer ha-Shoham*, ed. by B. Klar, 1 (1947), vii–viii (introd.), 5–16 (Eng. section) 16 n. 24 (additional bibliography).

[Nissan Netzer]

MOSES BEN ḤANOKH (d. c. 965), Spanish rabbi. The principal source for the biographic details of this famous scholar is the story of the *Four Captives told by Abraham *Ibn Daud in his *Sefer ha-Kabbalah* (*The Book of Tradition*, ed. by G.D. Cohen (1967), 63–69). This story tells how R. Moses' wife cast herself into the sea in order to escape from her captor, how he was sold as a slave at Cordoba and redeemed, and how his erudition resulted in his becoming recognized as rabbi of the community. But, according to sources which have since been discovered, this story seems to be unacceptable. It would indeed seem that R. Moses probably came from southern Italy. It is quite possible that he was indeed taken prisoner on a sea journey at the time he traveled to Spain, because a maritime war was then being waged between the Umayyad caliphate of Spain and the Fāṭimid kingdom of North Africa. In any case, it seems that R. Moses arrived in Spain during the 950s and became rabbi of Cordoba. He enjoyed the protection of the minister *Ḥisdai ibn Shaprut, who by coordinating the policies of Abd-al-Raḥmān III (912–961), the Umayyad caliph of Cordoba, sought to make the Jewish population of Spain independent of the Jewish center in Babylonia. R. Moses headed the yeshivah, which had many pupils, and also answered halakhic questions which were addressed to him from other towns. His responsa were regarded by his contemporaries as authoritative and no less valuable than the responsa of the Babylonian *geonim*. Many were included in the collections of geonic responsa, such as *Sha'arei Ẓedek* (Salonika, 1792), *Ge'onei Mizraḥ u-Ma'arav* (ed. by J. Miller, Berlin, 1888), and some were quoted by the *rishonim, particularly by the author of *"Ha-Ittur,"* R. *Isaac b. Abba Mari of Marseilles. His responsa in a German translation were collected by J. Miller. A responsum attributed to Moses, the *Gaon* of Sura, is in fact by Moses b. Ḥanokh. From the time of Moses b. Ḥanokh the practical dependence of Spanish scholars upon Babylonian scholars ceased in everything connected with *halakhah* and custom. In addition to his outstanding erudition, his great humility and exceptional modesty left a deep impression on his contemporaries. He was succeeded by his son *Ḥanokh.

BIBLIOGRAPHY: Ashtor, Korot, 1 (1966²), 155–9, 289–90; G.D. Cohen, in: PAAJR, 29 (1960/61), 55–131: M. Margolioth, *Hilkhot ha-Nagid* (1962), 6–8: S. Abramson, *R. Nissim Ga'on* (Heb., 1965), 307; J. Miller, *Siebenter Bericht ueber die Lehranstalt fuer die Wissenschaft des Judenthums in Berlin* (1889), 3–4, 8–10.

[Eliyahu Ashtor]

MOSES BEN ISAIAH KATZ (end of 17th and early 18th centuries), Polish rabbi and homilist. Katz was a pupil of Solomon *Luria and was rabbi successively of Medzibezh, Brody, and Przemysl. He is the author of *Penei Moshe* (Wilhermsdorf, 1716), a commentary on the aggadic passages of 18 treatises of the Babylonian and Jerusalem Talmuds. (This work should not be confused with *Penei Moshe*, the standard commentary on the Jerusalem Talmud by Moses *Margoliot.) He reveals a remarkable homiletic ingenuity in his work *Keren Or* (Zolkiew, 1721). As the title suggests, the work is a commentary on this phrase which occurs in Exodus 34:30, 35 ("the skin of his face shone"). He gives no less than 50 different explanations of the phrase. It has been suggested that Katz may be identical with Moses b. Isaiah Wengrow, the author of *Berit Matteh Moshe* (Berlin, 1701), a commentary on the Passover *Haggadah* with novellae on the tractate *Zevaḥim*.

BIBLIOGRAPHY: Fuerst, Bibliotheca, 3 (1863), 120; Halpern, Pinkas, 279–81, 501.

MOSES BEN JACOB OF COUCY (13th century), French scholar and tosafist. His father Jacob is mentioned a number of times in the printed *tosafot* (Kid. 43b; et al.). Moses was the maternal grandson of the tosafist *Ḥayyim ha-Kohen and brother-in-law of *Samson of Coucy. His principal teacher was *Judah ben Issac (Sir Leon).

Moses of Coucy is the first example among French Jews of an itinerant preacher, wandering from town to town and from country to country to rouse the masses to draw near to God by the active observance of His precepts. He began his preaching in Spain in 1236, being motivated to do so, according to his own words, by some mystical revelation which he experienced. The nature of this revelation is not clear, although it was possibly connected with the reckoning of the Redemption, a pursuit in which Judah Sir Leon, who designated 1236 for its beginning, also engaged. His sermons excited a massive response and, in his own words, brought about the repentance of "thousands and tens of thousands," especially in respect to observance of the precepts of *tefillin*, *mezuzah*, and *ẓiẓit*, which in that era (as other sources also testify) had grown very lax. He called also for the curbing of sexual relations with gentile women, widespread in Spain at that time, and taught in his sermons a method of repentance close in formula to the spirit of Ḥasidei Ashkenaz, though to a much less severe degree. He stressed the value of Torah study in a regular and orderly manner, and was one of the first to call for greater equity and propriety in economic dealings with the gentile community. Thus Moses checked, at least temporarily, the decline in the observance of the positive precepts of Judaism among the masses and the scholars in Spain, which had resulted from the tendency toward rationalization and to the extravagant allegorization of Scripture caused by the influence of Maimonides' philosophic writings. He later visited other countries (which, he does not specify) and in 1240 was in Paris, where he took part in the well-known disputation on the Talmud with Nicholas *Donin. These activities earned him the name of Moses ha-Darshan, in consequence of which he has sometimes been confused with *Moses ha-Darshan of Narbonne.

Moses of Coucy's reputation rests on his extensive and important work, the *Sefer Mitzvot Gadol* (*Se-Ma-G*; first published before 1480 (Rome?), and subsequently published three times by 1547, in Italy). The work is unique among the prolific rabbinic writing of the period. It includes, in effect, the essence of the Oral Law, arranged in the order of the precepts and divided into two parts: positive precepts and negative precepts. The work is based on Maimonides' *Mishneh Torah*, which is cited word by word on every page. He supplements Maimonides' words with an abundance of sources, from the Babylonian and Jerusalem Talmuds and the Midrashim, as well as from the works of French and German *rishonim*, which he possessed either in the original or in precis. Moses adapts the language of the Midrashim so closely to the style of Maimonides that one is often under the impression that he has before him an alternative reading of the halakhic Midrash. Although the book follows the arrangement of the precepts, their number and order differ from those of Maimonides, both because Moses did not know Maimonides' *Sefer ha-Mitzvot* but only the list of precepts in the introduction to the *Mishneh Torah*, and because at the end of the book he included rabbinic precepts, in keeping with the practical aim he had set himself in compiling it: to instruct the people in the way of the Lord. In pursuit of this aim, he also varied the arrangement of the precepts, separating those applicable in our time from those which are not. The *Se-Ma-G* marks the penetration of the works of Maimonides (which Moses probably "discovered" during his stay in Spain) into the halakhic world of France. Though Maimonides was known to Moses' teacher, Judah Sir Leon, as well as to *Samson of Sens, they merely quoted him a number of times, whereas Moses made him the basis of his whole project. He seems not to have been unaware of the great paradox in the possibility that it was precisely Maimonides who contributed to the undermining of practical *halakhah* in the countries under his influence, as a result of his use of allegory in general, and of his having posited reasons for the precepts in particular. Although the period of Moses' activity began only a few years after the first controversy in Europe around the works of Maimonides, he makes no reference whatsoever to it in his work, perhaps feeling that his special relationship to Maimonides disqualified him as an impartial judge in the matter. Among works of French and German scholars frequently used and cited by Moses, sometimes by name and sometimes not, are the *tosafot* of Samson of Sens, the *Sefer ha-Terumah* of *Baruch b. Isaac of Worms, and the *Sefer Yere'im* of *Eliezer b. Samuel of Metz. His practice, in general, is to begin with a scriptural verse touching on the subject, to cite the interpretations of the verse found in the Talmuds and the halakhic Midrashim, to give the relevant talmudic discussions, the words of the commentators and *posekim*, and a summary of the *halakhah* – all this with the degree of editing and adaptation of style necessary to give greater fluency to the language, every effort being made to avoid casuistry and prolixity. Moses weaves into his words an abundance of aggadic material, quotations from the sources, or the homiletic creations of his own spirit, all marked by their wholesomeness and simplicity, with love of God and of his fellow man.

The *Se-Ma-G* won great popularity among scholars and *posekim*. Many tens of manuscripts of the work have been preserved to the present time, an unusual phenomenon with a book of such great length. It was also one of the first Hebrew books to be printed. It has served as a standard guide to halakhic practice for scholars in all generations, notable among them being *Mordecai b. Hillel, *Meir ha-Kohen, a pupil of *Meir b. Baruch of Rothenburg, in his *Haggahot Maimuniyyot*, as well as all the pupils of *Perez of Corbeil. Quotations from it occur in the printed *tosafot*. Great scholars of all generations have written commentaries to it, among them Isaac *Stein, Joseph *Colon, Elijah *Mizrachi, Solomon *Luria, and Ḥayyim *Benveniste. Joshua *Boaz included the *SeMaG* with the Shulḥan Arukh and Maimonides' *Mishneh Torah* among the references given in his *Ein Mishpat*, an indication of the work's indispensability. The tremendous influence of the book is particularly evidenced by the fact that Isaac of Corbeil, who in his time bore the title "Head of the Yeshivot of France," found it necessary to compile the *Sefer Mitzvot Katan*, which is completely dependent upon the *SeMaG*, and to make it compulsory daily learning for every Jew. Perez, and his pupils after him, who wrote glosses and notes to the book of Isaac of Corbeil, all associated themselves in their rulings with the *SeMaG*, which they continually quoted. This estimate of the *Se-Ma-G* persisted, among both Ashkenazim and Sephardim, until the time of Joseph *Caro's Shulḥan Arukh; and Moses b. Jacob of Coucy is numbered among the great *posekim* of all generations.

The *tosafot* of Moses of Coucy to *Yoma*, first published with the title *Tosafot Yeshanim* in the Amsterdam (1714–17) edition of the Talmud, have come down to us. He also wrote a commentary on the Torah (known among *rishonim* as "*Peshatei ha-Ram mi-Coucy*"), which is much quoted in the *Minḥat Yehudah* (in *Da'at Zekenim*, Leghorn, 1783) of Judah b. Eliezer. In the *SeMaG* (positive precept no. 16) Moses tells of a special prayer he composed for the benefit of those wishing to repent. Two versions of such a prayer attributed to him have lately been published from manuscripts.

BIBLIOGRAPHY: E.E. Urbach, in: *Zion*, 12 (1946/47), 159; Urbach, Tosafot, 384–95 and index; Ch. Tchernowitz, *Toledot ha-Posekim*, 2 (1947), 87–92; Sonne, in: *Sefer ha-Yovel… A. Marx* (1950), 209–19; Gilat, in: *Tarbiz*, 28 (1958/59), 54–58.

[Israel Moses Ta-Shema]

MOSES BEN JACOB OF KIEV (also called **Moses ha-Goleh** and **Moses of Kiev** II; 1449–c. 1520), talmudic scholar and author. Moses was born, according to various scholars, in Seduva (Shadov), Lithuania (see A. Epstein, *Kitvei…* 1 (1950), 303–7). I. Zinberg, however, is of the opinion that he was born in Tarov, Kiev region (*Toledot Sifrut Yisrael*, 3 (1958), 161–6, 354). He died in Kaffa (Feodosiya), Crimea. At that time there were no important Torah institutions in Poland and Russia, and Moses traveled to Constantinople where he became friendly with both Rabbanites and Karaites. He also studied astronomy there under the Karaite Elijah ha-Shayazi, author of *Adderet Eliyahu*. He settled in Kiev and acquired a reputation in various branches of literature. He was a biblical exegete, talmudist, *paytan*, linguist, and kabbalist. From Kiev he wrote a polemical work against *Gan Eden*, the book of precepts of the Karaite scholar Abraham b. Elijah. In 1482 the Tatars attacked Kiev. Moses' possessions, including his library, were plundered. He himself escaped, but his children were taken captive to the Crimea, and Moses journeyed to various communities to collect money for their ransom. When passing through Karaite communities he disputed with their scholars. After ransoming his children, Moses returned to Kiev. He then wrote his works *Sefer ha-Dikduk*, a Hebrew grammar, and *Yesod ha-Ibbur*, on the calendar. In 1495 the Jews of Lithuania and the Ukraine were expelled, and Moses again was forced to wander. During these wanderings he wrote *Shushan Sodot* on automatic and cryptic writing, as well as *Oẓar ha-Shem* and *Sha'arei Ẓedek* on the upper *Sefirot*, which are no longer extant. In 1506, while he was staying in the Lithuanian (i.e., Belorussian) town of Lida, it was attacked by the Tatars and Moses was taken captive. He was carried off to the Crimea where he was ransomed by the Jews of the city of Salkhat. From there he removed to Kaffa in the Crimea where he settled. Here Moses filled an important cultural role as rabbi and head of the community. He succeeded in uniting the members of the community who had come from different countries, and also compiled a prayer book for them which became known as *Minhag Kaffa* and was adopted by all the communities of the Crimea. Moses also compiled special regulations for the community. There he succeeded in completing his *Oẓar Neḥmad*, a supercommentary to the Pentateuch commentary of Abraham ibn Ezra.

[Shlomo Eidelberg]

MOSES BEN JOAB (d. after 1530), Hebrew poet who lived in Florence. His *diwan* (Montefiore Collection, Ms. 366) contains a colorful variety of poems, ranging from elegy to satire, from love song to religious hymn, and from epigram to epithalamium. The collection consists of three groups: (1) satiric verses, in which the poet presents a series of persons characteristic of his time, such as Isaac of Correggio and Solomon of Poggibonsi; (2) love songs stylistically modeled on the Spanish poets and Immanuel of Rome; (3) religious poetry – artistically the most important of his work. While it contains all the flavor of the early hymnology, some well-known secular motives have also been included, without in any way detracting from the poetic form. The greater part of his religious verse is consecrated to the festivals. One of his poems describes the tragic conditions in Florence during the siege of 1529–30.

BIBLIOGRAPHY: U. Cassuto, *Gli ebrei a Firenze nell'età del Rinascimento* (1918), 340–54; idem, in: MGWJ, 77 (1933), 365–84; Davidson, Oẓar, 4 (1933), 36, no. 204; Schirmann, Italyah, 236–40.

[Yonah David]

MOSES BEN JOSEPH BEN MERWAN LEVI (12th century), one of the renowned scholars of Narbonne. Moses belonged to a distinguished family. His grandfather "was very pious, a man of substance and of good deeds, benefiting Israel with his wealth, and causing many evil decrees to be revoked." His uncle, under whom he studied, was Isaac b. Merwan Levi, rabbi of Narbonne. His father was also a scholar, and his brother Meir one of the scholars of Narbonne. Moses himself was head of a yeshivah and a member of the *bet din* of Narbonne headed by *Abraham b. Isaac. Most of the scholars of Narbonne were pupils of Moses, among them *Abraham b. David and *Zerahiah b. Isaac ha-Levi. A commentary which he wrote on most of the Talmud is no longer extant. The few quotations from it in the works of the scholars of Provence and Catalonia show it to have been written in the style of the early German and French scholars, with the aim of establishing the *halakhah*. It was intended (though not in the manner of a polemic) to defend the old Provençal traditions against the influence of the Spanish school in Lunel in the 12th century, the prime exponent of which was Abraham b. Isaac who follows in the steps of *Alfasi and *Judah b. Barzillai al-Bargeloni. In addition to his commentary, Moses' responsa and customs are also quoted in that literature. He exerted a great influence on the scholars of Provence and Catalonia, particularly on Zerahiah ha-Levi and *Naḥmanides, who quote him extensively.

BIBLIOGRAPHY: Benedikt, in: *Tarbiz*, 19 (1948), 19–34; 22 (1951), 85–109; I. Twersky, *Rabad of Posquières* (1962), index.

[Binyamin Zeev Benedikt]

MOSES BEN JOSEPH HA-LEVI (13th century), philosopher. Nothing is known about Moses' life; the suggestion that he was a member of the famous Abulafia family has not been proven. He was highly regarded by Joseph b. Abraham *Ibn Wakar, and is quoted by Crescas, Albo, and Isaac Abrabanel. His major work *Ma'amar Elohi* ("Metaphysical Treatise"), as well as fragments from two of his minor works (all written in Arabic), were discovered and incorporated in Ibn Wakar's *Treatise on the Harmony between Philosophy and the Revealed Law* (c. 1340). Two manuscripts of the Hebrew versions of the *Ma'amar* are extant (Bodleian and Leningrad), while a third, previously in the library of the cathedral of Pamplona, Spain, can no longer be traced. The *Ma'amar Elohi* seeks to establish the existence of the First Cause (God); to refute erroneous views concerning this subject and concerning the attributes of God; and to investigate the emanation of beings from the First Cause. Moses, disagreeing with Aristotle, Alexander of Aphrodisias, and Averroes, holds with Themistius, al-Fārābī, and Avicenna, that the "First Intellect," which emanated directly from God without an intermediary, is the Prime Mover of the celestial spheres. His doctrine of Divine attributes seeks to avoid plurality in God and therefore denies all attributes superadded to His essence. He admits, however, not only negative attributes but also attributes of essence, such as knowledge, will, and power, as well as attributes denoting action as "Creator." (Moses makes no reference whatever to Maimonides' thorough treatment of this theme.) Divine Providence, according to him, does not involve God's knowledge of individuals, but only the universal rule of God, employing the human intellect as an agent of the Active *Intellect. Of the two other fragments, one deals with the problem of Divine Providence and the other with al-Ghazālī's doctrine of the "Word" (*Kalima*). Approving of Ghazālī's doctrine, Moses establishes a metaphysical entity above the "First Intellect," the Prime Mover, and immediately below God, the First Cause.

[Alexander Altmann]

Moses also wrote, assuming that Steinschneider's identification is correct, a work on musical harmonies, a short section of which is quoted by Shemtov Shaprut b. Isaac of Tudela in his Hebrew commentary on Avicenna's *Canon* (Munich, Ms. Hebr. 8, fol. 330b). Moses describes the mathematical relations of musical intervals as well as some arithmetical operations carried out with them. The rather elementary contents of this text comply with Arabic musical theory. Its musical terminology is basically identical with that used in a Hebrew version of the musical chapter in Umayya ibn abī al-Ṣalt's encyclopedia (Paris, Cod. Hebr. 1037[1]); thus Moses' treatise may originally have been in Hebrew.

[Hanoch Avenary]

MOSES BEN JOSHUA (Ben Mar David) OF NARBONNE (Narboni, Lat., **Maestre Vidal Bellsom [Blasom?]**; d. 1362), French philosopher and physician. Moses was born in Perpignan at the end of the 13th, or beginning of the 14th, century, to a family originally from Narbonne. As a youth he studied with his father and private tutors and was introduced to the study of Maimonides at the age of 13. In addition to the Bible, rabbinic literature, and Jewish philosophy, he studied general philosophy and medicine. Moses began his literary career in Perpignan, where he remained until 1344, and continued in Spain, writing most of his works there. Although he lived in various Spanish cities – he mentions Cervera, Barcelona, Soria, Toledo, and Burgos – he never completely severed his ties with Perpignan. He expressed nostalgia for the intellectual circles there and intended to return. He probably spoke Provençal and Catalan, and it is likely that he knew Arabic and some Latin. He shows no familiarity, however, with Christian thinkers, the major philosophical influence on him being Islamic thought, particularly Averroes, whose works he read in Hebrew translation. Moses, who is known primarily for his commentary on Maimonides' *Guide of the Perplexed* and for his espousal of Averroes' teachings, is the author of some 20 works, an impressive number for the troubled period in which he lived. An early work, *Ma'amar ba-Sekhel ha-Hiyyulani* or *Ma'amar be-Efsharut ha-Devekut*, was written in Perpignan under conditions of siege and warfare; in Spain, as a physician, he undoubtedly had to cope with the bubonic plague of 1348–50 and, as a Jew, with the antisemitism that followed it. In 1349 he fled Cervera with the rest of the Jewish community, leaving his possessions and books behind. Before his work on Maimonides, Moses had written a number of commentaries and supercommentaries, most of them on Islamic philosophical texts. He composed major commentaries on al-*Ghāzalī's *Maqāṣid al-Falāsifa* ("Intentions of the Philosophers") and Ibn Ṭufayl's *Ḥayy ibn Yaqẓān*, and a number of supercommentaries to Averroes' commentaries on Aristotle's works on logic, physics, metaphysics, astronomy, and psychology. Moses' commentary on the *Guide* (ed. by I. Euchel, and printed together with text of the *Guide*, 1791; ed. J. Goldenthal, 1852; the latter reprinted with text, 1946, and in *Sheloshah Kadmonei Mefareshei ha-Moreh*, 1961), his last work, begun in Toledo in 1355 and finished in Soria in 1362, was based on his thorough knowledge of Islamic philosophy. He opposed Maimonides' neoplatonic interpretations of Aristotle's doctrines, which Maimonides had derived from al-Fārābī and Avicenna, with Averroes' more purely Aristotelian interpretations. He criticized, in particular, Maimonides' discussion of the proofs for the existence of God, his concept of God, and his doctrine of divine attributes. In the following, more conservative centuries, critics such as Isaac *Arama, Isaac *Abrabanel, and Joseph *Delmedigo opposed his Averroistic critique of Maimonides' *Guide* and his clarification of points that Maimonides had left discreetly implicit. They also disparaged his difficult style of writing and highly eclectic, often confusing use of sources.

In *Iggeret al Shi'ur Komah* (ed. and tr. into English as *Epistle on Shiur Qomah* by A. Altmann in his *Jewish Medieval and Renaissance Studies* (1967), 225–88), one of his early works, Moses attempted a reconciliation between philosophy and Kabbalah, reflecting the influence of Joseph *Ibn Waqar. He pursued a similar direction in his commentary on Ibn Ṭufayl's work (see G. Vajda, *Recherches sur la philosophie et la Kabbale* (1962), 396–403). Though more critical of kabbalistic concepts in his later years, Moses retained throughout his writings an affinity for the mystical phrase and symbol, a trait which has attracted recent scholarly attention (see Altmann's essay, *ibid.*). Averroes' doctrine of the conjunction of man's perfected intellect with the universal Agent Intellect that Moses accepted in his *Ma'amar bi-Shelemut ha-Nefesh* ("Treatise on the Perfection of the Soul," Paris, Bibliothèque Nationale, Ms. Heb., 988) resembles the mystic's experience of eternal being and loss of individuality in his relation to his creator. In his *Ma'amar bi-Shelemut ha-Nefesh*, Moses quoted almost the whole of Averroes' middle commentary on Aristotle's *De Anima*, as well as much of his "Treatise on the Possibility of Conjunction," to which he then added his own comments. Among Moses' other works are *Ha-Ma'amar bi-Veḥirah* ("Treatise on Free Will," ed. by E. Ashkenazi in *Sefer Divrei Ḥakhamim* (1849), 37–41), a polemical work written in answer to *Abner of Burgos' *Minḥat Kena'ot*, which expounds a theory of determinism; a number of medical treatises, in particular *Oraḥ Ḥayyim*, in which his reliance on classical and medieval sources is ostensibly tempered by an empirical approach; commentaries on Lamentations and Job; and four works which are no longer extant: a supercommentary on Abraham ibn Ezra's allegorical commentary on Genesis 2:2; *Pirkei Moshe*, a work containing philosophical aphorisms; a treatise on metaphysics; and a supercommentary on Averroes' commentary on Aristotle's *De Caelo et Mundo*.

BIBLIOGRAPHY: Husik, Philosophy, index, s.v. *Moses of Narbonne*; Guttmann, Philosophies, 206–8, 225; Munk, Mélanges, 502–6; Ivry, in: JQR, 57 (1966/67), 271–97; Steinschneider, Cat. Bod, 1967–77; Steinschneider, Uebersetzungen, index s.v. *Moses Narboni*; Renan, Ecrivains, 320–35; Ch. Touti, in: *Archives d'histoire doctrinale et littéraire du moyen âge*, 21 (1954), 193–205.

[Alfred L. Ivry]

MOSES BEN JUDAH, NOGA (14th century), philosopher. Nothing is known about Moses' life, but it has been proved that he is not identified with *Moses Nathan, as some of the Hebrew bibliographical works claim. It has been suggested that "Nogah" is not a part of his name but rather an abbreviation for "*nuḥo gan Hashem*" ("may he rest in divine paradise"), and that he was a disciple of one of *Nahmanides' students, probably of R. *Yom Tov ben Abraham Ishbili (the *Ritba*). Moses ben Judah is the author of the Hebrew encyclopedia

Ahavah ba-Ta'anugim ("Love in Delights"), which was written during the years 1353–56, and which has never been printed, although extant in four manuscripts. The title of the work, *Ahavah ba-Ta'anugim*, is taken from the biblical Song of Songs 7:7: "How fair and how pleasant art thou, O love in delights!" The "love" referred to in the encyclopedia's title is directed towards the philosophical pursuits, which are the true human delight. The object of the book is to defend philosophy and to demonstrate that Torah and philosophy are not in contradiction but rather complement one another in order to arouse in the educated reader a passion for such learning. According to this aim the book contains a comprehensive summary of the sciences popular among philosophically inclined Jews of the period: The first section is devoted to physics which Moses (like Maimonides) identifies with *ma'aseh bereshit*, and contains eight divisions on the following topics: (1) On Prime Matter; (2) On the Substance; (3) On the Four Elements; (4) On Motion, the Movers, and the Prime Mover; On Time, Infinity, and the Finite; (5) On Space and Vacuum; (6) On Human Nature; (7) On Astronomical Signs; and (8) On the Soul, Sleep, and Waking; On Dreams and the Human Soul. The second section is devoted to metaphysics which Moses (again like Maimonides) identifies with *ma'aseh merkavah*, and contains eight divisions on the following topics: (1) On Substance and Accident, Chance and Necessity; On the Nine [other] Categories; (2) On Existence; (3) On the Whole, Parts, and the One; (4) On the Substance of the Sphere; (5) On the Separate Movers; (6) On God's Names; (7) On Knowledge; and (8) On the Way the World is Related to God. The third section is a theological section and contains four chapters on the following topics: (1) On Magic; (2) On Prophecy and the Prophet's Acts; (3) On the Creation of the World; On Providence, Reward, and Punishment; On the Meaning of the Commandments; (4) On the Eternal Soul and the Resurrection of the Dead.

The first two parts present clearly and systematically the central topics of physics and metaphysics, the points of dispute among the philosophers on various issues, and it also resolves these disputes by questioning the fundamental arguments underlying the refuted views. After those discussions it demonstrates how the philosophical opinions are to be found in the Torah. Moses almost always adopts the views of *Averroes, whom he regards as second to Aristotle. On the other hand he sees *Avicenna and Al-*Ghazali as thinkers on a lower level, who attempted to produce a mixture of religion and philosophy. Moses is also an admirer of Maimonides, and sees him not only as the master of all philosophers but also as the master of all prophets, and he even calls the *Guide of the Perplexed* "the sacred book." Another Jewish philosopher whom Moses admires is Abraham *Ibn Ezra, and he draws extensively on his commentary on the Pentateuch. Moses' acceptance of Averroes' philosophical views alongside his unconditional admiration for Maimonides leads him to a unique interpretive reconstruction of Maimonides, in order to present his opinions in accordance with those of Averroes, or at least to blur the difference between them. Moses also presents Maimonides' views as identical with those of Ibn Ezra and as a consequence the gap between Ibn Ezra and Averroes is reconciled through Maimonides. Yet, for Moses, not only are the views of Maimonides, Ibn Ezra, and Averroes basically identical with each other, but also with the Kabbalah. Moses derives various terms and ideas from the Kabbalah. His interpretation of the Kabbalah, however, is distinctly philosophical, and eliminates much of its mythical and anti-philosophical language. In metaphysics Moses accepts Averroes' understanding of God as a form encompassing all the forms of the world and the prime mover of the sphere, and he rejects Avicenna's view identifying God with the necessary existent. He brings these views into unequivocal agreement with those of Maimonides in his *Guide* and interprets the kabbalistic theory of the 10 **sefirot* according to the Aristotelian doctrine of the 10 separated intellects. Moses accepts Avicenna's doctrine of *emanation, although according to Averroes matter has its own separate existence. According to Moses the entire world derives from God, and that is the meaning of creation *ex nihilo*. Moses accepted Averroes' view on the soul as presented in his Middle Commentary on the *De Anima*. According to this view, the individual's hylic intellect is none other than one of the aspects of the Active Intellect, and it has no separate and independent existence. Thus, in the state of the conjunction as it is *post mortem*, that is, the state of immortality and eternal bliss, there is no place for the individual intellect. As in the case of metaphysics, so too here with regard to psychology, Moses reads Maimonides' statements on the soul through the eyes of Averroes. He also explains the mystical notion of *gilgul* (transmigration of the soul) according to this theory: The Active Intellect enters the bodies of various human beings, and *post mortem* returns to its source and is united a second time with the Active Intellect, and so on ad infinitum. Moses also identifies the Averroean theory of the conjunction with prophecy. On the question of providence, Moses combines the Maimonidean view, explaining providence naturalistically, with astral elements. Regarding the reasons for the divine commandments Moses integrates the Maimonidean doctrines, the astrological notions of Ibn Ezra, and the symbolic kabbalistic ideas.

BIBLIOGRAPHY: E. Eisenmann, "Ahavah ba-Ta'anugim: A Fourteenth-Century Encyclopedia of Science and Theology," in: S. Harvey (ed.), *The Medieval Hebrew Encyclopedias of Science and Philosophy* (2000), 415–29; R. Glasner, "The Question of Celestial Matter in the Hebrew Encyclopedias," in: *ibid.*, 313–34.

[E. Eisenmann (2nd ed.)]

MOSES BEN LEVI (12th century), communal leader and poet in *Egypt. From fragments of the Cairo **Genizah*, it has become clear that Moses was in charge of the affairs of the Jewish community of Qalyub, north of *Cairo. In 1195 the heads of the Jewish community there addressed themselves to *Sar Shalom b. Moses ha-Levi, the *Gaon* of the Fostat yeshivah, with a request that he confirm the appointment of Moses b. Levi as officer in charge of communal affairs after his position had been challenged. In his reply, the *gaon* praises Moses, who also served in the offices of *ḥazzan*, *shoḥet*, and teacher of the community. An autobiographical *maqāma* by Moses is extant in the Kaufmann collection of the *Genizah*, which reveals details of his life before his arrival in Qalyub. At first he occupied himself with various matters, but after a time he immersed himself in Torah study alone. Two and a half years later he decided to leave his locality, the identity of which is unknown, after a quarrel with his parents. Reaching Qalyub, he was amazed at its beauty and wrote poems in its praise. He appears to be identical with Moses b. ha-Levi from whom there remains a blank verse poem (Ar. *muwashshaḥ*).

BIBLIOGRAPHY: Mann, Egypt, 1 (1920), 237; 2 (1922), 298; D.Z. Banet, in: *Sefer ha-Yovel… A. Marx* (1950), 77–79; J.H. Schirmann, *Shirim Ḥadashim min ha-Genizah* (1965), 377–84.

[Abraham David]

MOSES BEN MENAHEM GRAF (also known as **Moses Praeger**; 1650–1700/1710), kabbalist born in Prague. After the conflagration in the Prague ghetto (1689), Moses moved to Nikolsburg (Mikulov), where he studied under the kabbalist Eliezer Mendel b. Mordecai. He was given lodging and support by David *Oppenheim, who, like Samson *Wertheimer of Vienna, encouraged the publication of his writings. Leaving Nikolsburg, Moses attempted to settle in various European cities, reaching Fuerth in 1696 and Dessau in 1698. It is not certain whether he died there or whether he returned to Prague in his later years. Moses' published works include: *Zera Kodesh*, a kabbalistic work with an appendix describing the exorcism of a *dibbuk* in Nikolsburg (Fuerth, 1696); a second edition, without the *dibbuk* story, was published by Simeon b. David Abiob of Hebron, together with his *Bat Melekh* (Venice, 1712; reprinted Munkacz, 1893); and *Va-Yakhel Moshe*, a kabbalistic discussion of various portions of the Zohar and of the *Adam de-Aẓilut*, with a special commentary on the latter concept entitled *Masveh Moshe*, introduced and annotated by Samuel b. Solomon Kohen, cantor in Brody (Dessau, 1699). In this last work Moses often criticizes the teachings of Moses *Cordovero and his followers.

BIBLIOGRAPHY: J. Guenzig, *Die Wundermaenner im juedischen Volke* (1921), 102–6.

[Joseph Elijah Heller]

MOSES BEN MEVORAKH (12th century), leader of Egyptian Jewry. He was the *nagid* of Egyptian Jewry from c. 1110 to before 1141, having been appointed to the position after the death of his father, the *nagid* *Mevorakh. He was assisted by his two sons, Mevorakh and Judah, who acted as "vice *negidim*." In his time the Jews of Egypt were oppressed, and he intervened in their favor. A *kinah* on his mother's death, which appears to have been written by him, has been preserved in the Cairo *Genizah*. On her death, which made an impression on Egyptian Jewry, another *kinah* is known to have been written by Ẓedakah b. Judah. From the *kinah* of Moses, it appears that he was influenced by the poets of the Spanish school, an influence evident in Ẓedakah's *kinah* as well. A poem written in his honor by Abraham b. Shabbetai of Minyat Zifta, Egypt, which was found among the manuscripts of the *Genizah*, has also been published by J. Mann (see bibliography).

BIBLIOGRAPHY: Mann, Egypt, 1 (1920), 210, 213; 2 (1922), 255–59; J.H. Schirmann, *Shirim Ḥadashim min ha-Genizah* (1965), 97–102.

MOSES BEN SAMUEL OF DAMASCUS (14th century), Karaite poet. Moses, who was born in Safed, Ereẓ Israel, was employed in Damascus as clerk in charge of the emir's private estates. In 1354 the emir received an order requiring him to remove non-Muslims from government service. Moses was seized, charged with blasphemy against Islam, and given the choice of forfeiting his life or becoming a Muslim. He chose the latter. Some time later the emir went on a pilgrimage to Mecca, and Moses was compelled to accompany him. What he observed of the pilgrimage ritual led him to resolve to return to Judaism. The emir at first refused to release him but he fell ill and soon died. Moses then appears to have escaped to Egypt and entered the service of the royal vizier, apparently returning to his ancestral faith. His works, all in Hebrew verse, include a description of his tribulations and of his Mecca pilgrimage. His liturgical pieces display depth of feeling and an occasional lyrical inspiration.

BIBLIOGRAPHY: Mann, Texts, 2 (1935), 213–32; L. Nemoy, *Karaite Anthology* (1952), 147–69.

[Leon Nemoy]

MOSES BEN SHEM TOV DE LEON (c. 1240–1305), a leading kabbalist, author of the bulk of the *Zohar. (For later views on the authorship of the Zohar, see the addendum to *Zohar.) Moses was apparently born in Leon, near Castile – he also calls himself Moses "from the town of Leon," in his *Shekel ha-Kodesh*. Nothing is known of his teachers and early studies. Apart from religious study, he was also attracted to philosophy; *Maimonides' *Guide of the Perplexed* was copied for him in 1264 (Moscow, Ms. Guenzburg 771). Moses subsequently turned to *Kabbalah, and when wandering among the communities of Castile, he became friendly with the kabbalists there. He immersed himself in the lore of the Geronese school of kabbalists and in the traditions of the Gnostic circle of Moses of *Burgos and Todros *Abulafia and in the 1270s and 80s drew particularly close to Joseph *Gikatilla. Moved by an unusual enthusiasm, combined with the urge to counteract the influence of certain rationalistic trends, Moses composed various writings toward the close of the 1270s. Presented in the guise of pseudepigraphica, they were designed to propagate the doctrine of kabbalism in the pattern in which it had crystallized in his own mind. Completed before 1286, they form the *Midrash ha-Ne'elam* or "Mystical Midrash," and are the main substance of the Zohar. The later stratum in this composite work was written by another kabbalist. The major part of these writings is in Aramaic but Moses also composed Hebrew pseudepigraphica on ethics and the eschatology of the soul. The "Testament of R. Eliezer the Great," also called *Orḥot Ḥayyim*, is evidence of the author's hesitations in choosing between the *tannaim* Eliezer b. *Hyrcanus and Simeon b. *Yoḥai as the hero of his pseudepigraphical construction. He also intended to compose a new Book of Enoch, parts of which he embodies in his *Mishkan ha-Edut*.

For a number of years, during the composition of the Zohar, and at least until 1291, he resided in Guadalajara, circulating from his home the first parts of the Zohar, which included a partly different version of the *Midrash ha-Ne'elam* (G. Scholem, in *Sefer ha-Yovel... L. Ginzberg* (1946), 425–46, Heb. section). In Guadalajara he was associated with Isaac ibn *Sahulah, who is the first known to quote from the *Midrash ha-Ne'elam*. He dedicated some of his books to Joseph b. Todros Abulafia in Toledo. After 1292 Moses led a wandering life until, in later years, he settled in Ávila, and then probably devoted himself almost exclusively to the circulation of copies of the Zohar. Meeting Isaac b. Samuel of *Acre in Valladolid in 1305, he invited him to Ávila to see the ancient original manuscript of the Zohar in his home. However, on his return Moses fell ill and died in Arévalo (*Sefer Yuḥasin*, ed. H. Filipowski, 88). His widow denied the existence of such a manuscript. The Hebrew writings which bear his name are based on the same sources as those utilized in the Zohar and they frequently make veiled allusions to it without specifying it by name. These writings and the portions of the Zohar composed by Moses frequently serve to clarify one another; the former can be regarded as the authentic exegesis of the doctrine enshrined in the Zohar.

Numerous copies of several of these works were made in succeeding generations, and it seems that Moses himself circulated the texts in different versions. According to Abraham b. Solomon of Torrutiel (Neubauer, Chronicles, 1 (1887), 105), he was the author of 24 books. Those fully or partly extant are *Shoshan Edut* (1286), which Moses mentions as his first work (Cambridge, Add. Ms. 505, includes about half the work); *Sefer ha-Rimmon* (1287), an exposition of the kabbalistic reasons for the *mitzvot*, wholly constructed on Zohar homiletics (several Mss., e.g., Oxford, Bodleian, Ms. Opp. 344); *Or Zaru'a* (1288/89), on the act of *Creation (Oxford, Bodleian, Ms. Poc. 296, other parts in Ms. Vatican 428, 80–90): this was apparently extended by another kabbalist to cover the whole section *Bereshit*, Genesis 1–6 (Ms. Vatican 212); *Ha-Nefesh ha-Ḥakhamah*, written in 1290 for his pupil Jacob, whom Isaac of Acre met after Moses' death: a corrupt text was published in 1608 which contained numerous addenda from a work by a contemporary Spanish kabbalist; a lengthy titleless commentary on the ten *Sefirot* (see *Kabbalah) and penances (a large part in Munich Ms. 47); *Shekel ha-Kodesh* (1292, publ. 1912; an excellent text in Oxford, Bodleian Ms. Opp. 563); *Mishkan ha-Edut*, on the fate of the soul after death, with a commentary on the vision of Ezekiel appearing in numerous manuscripts (Berlin, Vatican, et al.) as an independent book: both here and in his introduction to *Or Zaru'a* Moses divulges the reasons for his literary activities; *Maskiyyot Kesef* (written after 1293), a commentary on the prayers, a sequel to the lost *Sefer Tappuḥei Zahav* (Ms. Adler, 1577); responsa on points of Kabbalah (ed. by Tishby, in: *Kobez al Jad*, vol. 5, 1951); a treatise on various mystical themes (Schocken Library, Ms. Kab. 14, 78–99; Ms. Vatican 428); another commentary on the ten *Sefirot, Sod Eser Sefirot Belimah*...(Madrid, Escorial, Ms. G III 14). Moses also wrote: *Sefer Pardes* ("Book of Paradise"); *Sha'arei Ẓedek*, on Ecclesiastes; *Mashal ha-Kadmoni* (after the title of his friend Isaac ibn Sahula's work); responsa on questions concerning Elijah; a commentary on Song of Songs; and a polemic directed against the Sadducees (or Karaites?), mentioned by Abner of *Burgos (REJ, 18 (1889), 62). The *Sefer ha-Shem* (publ. in *Heikhal ha-Shem*, Venice, 1605) on the designations of the *Sefirot*, ascribed to him from the 15th century onward, was written by another kabbalist named Moses in the middle of the 14th century.

BIBLIOGRAPHY: G. Scholem, Mysticism, ch. 5; idem, in: KS, 1 (1924), 45–52; idem, in: *Madda'ei ha-Yahadut*, 1 (1926), 16–29; idem, in: MGWJ, 71 (1927), 109–23; S.D. Luzzatto, *Iggerot Shadal* (1891), 259; Steinschneider, Cat Bod, 1847–56; idem, in: HB, 10 (1870), 156–61; A. Jellinek, *Moses ben Schem Tob de Leon und sein Verhaeltnis zum Sohar* (1851); I. Tishby, *Mishnat ha-Zohar*, 2 vols. (1949), general introd. and introds. to different *sidrot*; Y. Nadav, in: *Oẓar Yehudei Sefarad*, 2 (1959), 69–76; E. Gottlieb, in: *Tarbiz*, 33 (1964), 287–313; I. Ta-Shma, *ibid.*, 39 (1969), 184–94; 40 (1970), 105–6; S.Z. Havlin, *ibid.*, 107–9.

[Gershom Scholem]

MOSES BEN SOLOMON BEN SIMEON OF BURGOS

(1230/1235–c. 1300), kabbalist in Spain; he was rabbi in Burgos from about 1260. Moses – also known as Moses Cinfa, evidently after his mother – came from a distinguished family. The pupil and spiritual heir of the kabbalists *Isaac and *Jacob b. Jacob ha-Kohen (who were brothers), and a leading kabbalist in Castile, he began to impart a knowledge of Kabbalah as soon as he assumed office in Burgos; his pupils included Isaac b. Solomon ibn *Sahula and Todros *Abulafia. Isaac *Albalag regarded him as the foremost kabbalist of his generation. Abraham *Abulafia met him and his pupil Shem Tov (b. Maor; "Major") between 1271 and 1274 and endeavored to attract him to his doctrine of prophetic kabbalism. Toward the end of his life Moses met *Isaac b. Samuel of Acre, who recounts the event in his *Me'irat Einayim*. Isaac heard Moses utter the harsh epigram expressing the relationship of philosophy to Kabbalah: "The position attained by their heads reaches only the position of our feet" – a motto of a gnostic-type statement indicating that the kabbalist has access to realms where the philosopher is unable to tread. Moses was a strict traditionalist and the value of his kabbalistic writings lies not so much in their original thought, as in the service they render as a treasury and repository of many traditions rarely mentioned by his contemporaries, but those which were generally not absorbed into the *Zohar.

Moses' works consist of the following:

(1) a commentary on Song of Songs *in extenso*, no longer extant but available to Isaac ibn Sahula;

(2) a commentary on the ten "left" *sefirot* (*Eser ha-Sefirot ha-Semaliyyot*; i.e., the impure *Sefirot*), also called *Ammud ha-Semali* ("The Left Pillar"; published by G. Scholem);

(3) commentaries on the three *haftarot* – *Merkevet Yeshayahu* ("Throne and Chariot Vision of Isaiah"), *Merkevet Yeḥezkel* ("Throne and Chariot Vision of Ezekiel"), and *Mareh ha-Menorah shel Zekharyah* ("Zechariah's Vision of the Candelabrum"; fragments in Scholem);

(4) a commentary on the 42-lettered Divine Name, the bulk of which was published anonymously in the collection *Likkutim me-Rav Hai Gaon* (1798), the introduction and important concluding remarks are published by Scholem;

(5) an amplification of the treatise by his teacher Isaac ha-Kohen on "Emanation" (fragments published by Scholem);

(6) *Sod Shelosh Esreh Middot u-Ferushan* ("The Mystery of the 13 Divine Attributes and Their Interpretation"), which is, in fact, a kabbalistic explanation of the early tract **Shi'ur Komah* ("Measure of the Body"; published by Scholem);

(7) diverse mystical compositions on various subjects.

Moses had access to a variety of sources, including works affiliated to the circle centering on *Sefer ha-Iyyun*, as well as a number of pseudepigraphica. All the traditions upon which he relied in his *Ammud ha-Semali* are in this category. The crystallization of a definitely gnostic trend in kabbalism can be clearly traced in his writings. He also enlarges on kabbalistic traditions relating to the efficacy of pronouncing the Divine Names as incantations, but emphasizes that he never attempted to translate theory into practice.

BIBLIOGRAPHY: Scholem, in: *Tarbiz*, 3 (1931/32), 258–86; 4 (1932/33), 54–77, 207–25; 5 (1933/34), 50–60, 180–98,305–23.

[Gershom Scholem]

MOSES BEN YOM-TOV (d. 1268), London rabbi and grammarian, member of one of the most distinguished and wealthy families in England at that time. Moses himself was a businessman who did a great deal for the Jewish community of London. He was also known by the name of Magister Mosseus. His father, Yom-Tov, was the author of *Sefer ha-Tena'im*. Moses wrote a commentary to the Talmud and to the *halakhot* of Isaac *Alfasi, after the manner of the tosafists. Part of his commentaries were published by Urbach (see bibliography). In his commentary he quotes a great deal from the tosafist *Isaac b. Abraham. He was the first English talmudist who made much use of the rulings of Maimonides. Many of his contemporary scholars frequently mention and cite him in their writings. A responsum he wrote to his friend *Moses of Evreux is known. Among his pupils was the grammarian *Moses (b. Isaac) Ha-Nesi'ah, the author of the *Sefer ha-Shoham* (Jerusalem, 1947), who was mistakenly identified by A. Geiger with Moses ben Yom-Tov. Moses was the author of the *Darkhei ha-Nikkud ve-ha-Neginot*, principles of biblical punctuation and accentuation, first published by Jacob b. Ḥayyim ibn Adonijah in the margin of the masorah section at the end of the Daniel Bomberg edition of the Bible (Venice, 1524–25). From 1822 on this work was published separately several times. A scientific edition was published by D.S. Loewinger (see bibliography). Moses was also the author of a book on forbidden foods that was not published. He was the father of two sons, *Elijah Menahem b. Moses of London and *Benedict b. Moses of Lincoln.

BIBLIOGRAPHY: Steinschneider, Handbuch, 95 n. 1356; H.P. Stokes, *Studies in Anglo-Jewish History* (1913), 3ff.; D.S. Loewinger, in: HḤY, 3 (1929), 267–344; C. Roth, *The Jews of Medieval Oxford* (1951), 115f.; idem, in: JHSET, 15 (1939–45), 31; Urbach, Tosafot, 401–3; E.E. Urbach, in: *Tiferet Yisrael: Essays Presented to Chief Rabbi Israel Brodie* (1960), 10, 19–44 (Heb. pt.); I. Ta-Shema, in: *Sinai*, 65 (1969), 202f.

[Abraham David]

MOSES ESRIM VE-ARBA (late 15th century), rabbi and emissary of Jerusalem. His unusual name ("Moses twenty-four") derives from the fact that he was born in Vierundzwanzig Hoefe ("24 courts") in the Aberndorf region of the province of Wuerttemberg in Germany. In the opinion of Alfred *Freimann (disputed by others), who identifies this Moses with the Moses Ashkenazi mentioned in various documents included in the journal of Michael *Balbo, Moses was sent in 1474 as an emissary of the Jewish community of *Jerusalem to the island of Crete. There he became friendly with Michael Balbo, who frequently discussed with him philosophical and kabbalistic problems, such as the belief in metempsychosis, which Moses rejected. In 1475 he arrived in Constantinople, with the intention of collecting money to rebuild a synagogue in Jerusalem destroyed by the Muslims. Elijah *Capsali wrote to Joseph *Taitaẓak that when Moses was there he was the cause of a bitter dispute between Moses *Capsali, chief rabbi of Constantinople, and Joseph *Colon, one of the important rabbis of Italy in the 15th century. Moses Capsali refused to assist Moses in collecting contributions for fear of the Turkish government, which had forbidden the transfer of money from *Turkey to Ereẓ Israel, then under *Mamluk rule. Infuriated, Moses joined the opponents of Capsali who endeavored to undermine his reputation and spread allegations that he had given incorrect decisions in matrimonial matters, so causing many to enter unwittingly into prohibited relations. Moses took the accusations of Capsali's opponents to Joseph Colon who, without verifying the facts, excommunicated Capsali. Moses proceeded to Italy in continuation of his mission. According to S.Z. *Shazar (Rubashow), it was Moses who compiled or copied the classical work, *Dos *Shmuel Bukh* (Augsburg, 1544), an epic in Yiddish based on the Book of Samuel. From his signature on the colophon of the manuscript, it appears that he also compiled glosses to Abraham ibn Ezra's Pentateuch commentary.

BIBLIOGRAPHY: M. Lattes (ed.), *Likkutirn Shonim mi-Sefer de-Bei Eliyahu… Eliyahu Capsali* (1896), 13–15; Graetz-Rabbinowitz, 6 (1898), 305–8, 433–5; Rubashow, in: *Zukunft*, 32 (1927), 428f.; Rosanes, Togarmah, 1 (1930²), 44f.; Al. Freimann, in: *Zion*, 1 (1936), 188–202; Yaari, Sheluḥei, 214–7; Zinberg, Sifrut. 4 (1958), 60–66, 185f.; Gottlieb, in: *Sefunot*, 11(1967), 45.

[Abraham David]

MOSES HA-DARSHAN (11th century), scholar and aggadist of Narbonne. Moses was the teacher of *Nathan b. Jehiel of Rome, who quotes him in the *Arukh*, sometimes anonymously. Jacob *Tam in *Sefer ha-Yashar* (part of responsa ed. by F. Rosenthal (1898), 189f. no. 46:4) considers him, together with his brother Levi, and Joseph *Bonfils, among the early leaders of French Jewry. Moses is chiefly renowned for his contribution to midrashic literature. Rashi in his commentaries on Scripture, especially on the Pentateuch, frequently quotes from Moses ha-Darshan's *Yesod*, which was apparently a book of scriptural expositions, consisting chiefly of the exegesis of words and midrashic sayings. It is not known whether the work also embraced the rest of the Bible. For many years the *Genesis Rabbah* by Moses ha-Darshan, frequently quoted by Raymond *Martini in his polemic work *Pugio Fidei*, constituted a unique problem. No book of that name was known to scholars in previous centuries. Isaac *Abrabanel, for one, stated in his *Yeshu'ot Meshiḥo* that he did not know of such a book and suspected it to be a forgery. Only recently has it become evident that the early authorities did indeed know a midrashic anthology by Moses ha-Darshan, or at least one emanating from his school, and that this extensive anthology was the basis of the Midrash called *Genesis Rabbati, which was apparently adapted and abridged from the work of Moses. In this Midrash, Moses based himself entirely upon *Genesis Rabbah, but drew upon his vast store of knowledge and remarkable creative ability to develop and enlarge the central ideas of the source by comparing them with other verses and passages, and connecting them with homilies occurring elsewhere. Moses made abundant use of the Mishnah, the Talmud (chiefly the Babylonian), the *Midrashei Rabbah* and *Tanḥuma*, the *Pesikta*, *Pirkei de-Rabbi Eliezer*, and others.

There is ground for the suggestion that the portions *Ba-Midbar* and *Naso* in *Numbers Rabbah, as well as the midrashic anthology called *Midrash Aggadah* (ed. by S. Buber, 1894), largely emanate from the *bet-midrash* of Moses ha-Darshan. One unique characteristic of Moses' midrashic work is his use of the *aggadot* embedded in the *Apocrypha, such as Jubilees, Enoch, The Testament of the Twelve Patriarchs, and others, of which he possessed an improved Hebrew text. He also drew upon the collected Midrashim of his predecessors compiled from the Apocryphal literature, particularly from *Midrash Tadshe* (see Smaller *Midrashim) which, with its proem, was ascribed by Moses to the *tanna*, *Phinehas b. Jair. Some wish to ascribe to Moses several other extant minor Midrashim, on the basis of their similarity to his known work. In addition to citation in Rashi and Nathan b. Jehiel, the work was extensively quoted by Tobiah b. Eliezer in his midrashic collection, **Lekah Tov*; Menaḥem b. Solomon, in his anthology, *Sekhel Tov*; and, very much later by Abraham *Saba in his *Ẓeror ha-Mor*.

BIBLIOGRAPHY: A. Epstein, *Mi-Kadmoniyyot ha-Yehudim*, 1 (1887), i–xiv; idem, *Moshe ha-Darshan mi-Narbonah* (1891); *Kitvei R. Avraham Epstein*, 1 (1950), 215–44; S. Lieberman, *Sheki'in* (1939), 52ff.; Zunz-Albeck, *Derashot*, 144f.; S. Buber (ed.), *Midrash Aggadah*, 1 (1894), introd.; Ḥ. Albeck (ed.), *Bereshit Rabbati* (1940), introd. 1–36.

[Israel Moses Ta-Shma]

MOSES HA-KOHEN OF TORDESILLAS (second half of 14th century), rabbi born in Tordesillas, Spain. Moses experienced the terrible sufferings caused during the civil war in Castile, 1366–69. He moved to Avila and was evidently appointed rabbi of the congregation there. Moses represented the Jewish side in the religious *disputation ordered to be held in Avila in 1375. There were four sessions and Moses apparently emerged triumphant. After engaging successfully in an additional debate held with a pupil of *Abner of Burgos, he committed his arguments to writing in his still-unpublished work *Ezer ha-Emunah*.

BIBLIOGRAPHY: J. Loeb, in: REJ, 18 (1889), 226–30; Baer, Spain, 1 (1961), 374–5; J. Rosenthal, in: *Aresheth*, 2 (1960), 147 no. 61; D.S. Loewinger and B.D. Weinryb, *Catalogue of the Hebrew Manuscripts in the Library of the Juedisch-Theologisches Seminar in Breslau* (1965), 172.

MOSES ḤAYYIM EPHRAIM OF SUDYLKOW (c. 1740–1800?), ḥasidic preacher and *ẓaddik*, son of *Adel, the daughter of *Israel b. Eliezer Ba'al Shem Tov. He was the eldest brother of *Baruch b. Jehiel of Medzibezh. He is praised in the well-known letter of Israel Ba'al Shem Tov to his brother-in-law, *Abraham Gershon of Kutow. Although he knew that a *ẓaddik* was a highly influential figure, he did not gather many Ḥasidim round him, but lived in humility and poverty. He served as a preacher in Sudylkow and popularized Ḥasidism through his work, *Degel Maḥaneh Efrayim* (date and place of publication are unknown), a classic of Ḥasidism. The book is made up of sermons on the weekly portions from the Pentateuch. At the end of the book there is a collection of "dreams" (*ḥalomot*) from 1780 to 1785, describing mystical visions. The work, with the addition of stories and parables, is written in a pleasant and lucid manner. It contains important teachings and traditions of the Ba'al Shem Tov and his disciples, and shows also the influence of *Dov Baer of Mezhirech. It expresses social criticism of those scholars who boast of their Torah learning, in contrast with the Ḥasidim who are distinguished by their humility. He notes that in study for its own sake the letters of the Torah serve as a focus for meditation and concentration, and that the light of the **En Sof* (Infinite) shines through these letters to the student of the Torah. Because every generation interprets the Torah according to its needs, the *ẓaddik*, as the representative of the Torah, may be permitted to break a particular law when necessary. Moses Ḥayyim, however, warned Ḥasidim against superficial imitation of the *ẓaddikim*. The obligation, according to Lurianic Kabbalah, to "elevate the sparks" (*ha'ala'at ha-niẓozot*), is expanded by Moses Ḥayyim to everything including slaves and animals. Thus, he also advocates the elevation of undesirable thoughts (*ha'ala'at maḥashavot zarot*). Moses Ḥayyim held that man would enter the palace of truth and redemption of the soul only by constantly thinking of God. He emphasizes his admiration for his grandfather and states that redemption and the end of the Exile would occur when the teachings of the Ba'al Shem Tov were accepted. However, he states that, whereas in previous generations (i.e., during the time of Israel Ba'al Shem Tov) one might have hoped for the imminent advent of the messianic age, as a result of the spiritual decline in his time, this possibility had diminished.

BIBLIOGRAPHY: M. Gutman, *Geza Kodesh* (1951); Dubnow, Ḥasidut, 204–8; Y. Tishby, in: *Zion...* (1967), 33–34; J. Weiss, in: *I. Brodie Jubilee Volume* (1967), 167–8; R. Schatz-Uffenheimer, *Ha-Ḥasidut ke-Mistikah* (1968), 185, index.

[Moshe Hallamish]

MOSES ISAAC (**Darshan**; also known as the **Kelmer Maggid**; 1828–1899), the main preacher of the *Musar movement, Moses Isaac was born near Slonim. In his youth he already showed exceptional abilities as a preacher and delivered his first sermon in Slonim at the age of 15. Moses Isaac became a shopkeeper in a nearby town, but, failing to earn a livelihood, returned to Slonim to seek other means of subsistence. Reluctant to make a living from religious activity, he refused tempting offers to serve as a preacher, but at last accepted a position as preacher to a synagogue in Slonim, requesting the meager salary of half a ruble a week. Dissatisfied with his lack of influence, he accepted a similar position at Novaya Mysh, but there also he found no satisfaction. At the age of 21 he relinquished his position and proceeded to Kovno (Kaunas) in order to study under R. Israel *Lipkin, the founder of the Musar movement. He remained there until he had absorbed the teachings of that movement, and Lipkin, recognizing his outstanding abilities as a preacher and his potential influence, charged him with propagating its ideals. For over half a century Moses Isaac was the outstanding *Maggid* of the Musar movement. He accepted positions as preacher to various communities – Kelme (1850–53; whence his name, the Kelmer Maggid), Zagare (1853–58), Oshmyany (1858–60), and Minsk (1860–63) – but essentially he was an itinerant preacher, traveling from town to town.

In his sermons Moses Isaac departed entirely from the exegetical and expository method of preaching current in his time and applied himself solely to raising the moral and ethical standards of the communities. Wherever he went, he would first pay a visit to the local rabbi in order to acquaint himself with the social evils prevalent in the community and then fearlessly denounce them. The following extract from one of his published sermons (*Tokhaḥat Ḥayyim*, no. 7) is indicative of the content of his homilies: "If a man recites Psalms from morning to night but tells lies and is guilty of slander; if he prays with devotion and recites the Grace after Meals aloud, but has no compassion for his fellowman; if with the same enthusiasm as he fulfills every precept between man and God, he vindictively persecutes anyone who has done him a wrong... he can be called a wicked man." He inveighed particularly against commercial malpractices, exploitation of the poor, and dishonest practices toward non-Jews. His influence was unbounded. Contemporary newspapers report how on the morrow of his sermons he would visit the local market, and shopkeepers would destroy their false weights and measures. A dishonest shopkeeper is said to have lost his reason as a result of these denunciations, while another committed suicide. He did not hesitate to name flagrant transgressors, especially unworthy communal leaders, from the pulpit. As a result, on more than one occasion he was maligned, denounced to the government, and imprisoned, but, undeterred, he continued his reproofs.

Moses Isaac used to preach in a unique singsong, sometimes bursting into song, and although he was ridiculed for it, especially by the *maskilim* whom he vigorously attacked, the effect upon the masses was hypnotic. J.L. Gordon, the leader of the *maskilim*, complained (in *Allgemeine Zeitung des Judenthums*, 25 (1861), 168–70) of his "obscurantism" in establishing "Musar shtiebels" (conventicles for the study of Musar), and that he was so successful that he had established one in Mitau (Jelgava), Latvia, a center of the *maskilim*. Moses Isaac established scores of such "Musar shtiebels" throughout the country, synagogues for humble workers, arranging study courses for them, and philanthropic societies. In 1884 he visited London where the chief rabbi, Nathan Adler, and Samuel Montagu (the first Lord Swaythling), founder and head of the Federation of Synagogues, were greatly impressed by him and defrayed the expenses of his visit. In 1898 he moved to Lida, to settle with his son Ben Zion Darshan, and died in the following year. His only published work is the *Tokhaḥat Ḥayyim* (Vilna, 1897), ten of his sermons which he chose as examples of his teachings.

BIBLIOGRAPHY: D. Katz, *Tenu'at ha-Musar*, 2 (1954), 395–407.

[Louis Isaac Rabinowitz]

MOSES (**Mesharshia**) **KAHANA BEN JACOB**, *gaon* of Sura, 825–836. Moses, who succeeded Kimoi b. Rav Ashi, is identical with Mesharshia Kahana b. Mar Rav Jacob who is mentioned in the Spanish version of the "Letter of *Sherira Gaon" (ed. by B.M. Lewin (1921), 115). He is apparently not identical with Moses, *gaon* of Sura in the ninth century, who was a brother of Ẓadok Gaon, the father of *Nahshon Gaon. Many of his responsa have been preserved in the works of the *geonim* and the *rishonim*. Some touching on the liturgy are quoted in the *seder* of *Amram Gaon. In many responsa he is referred to simply as Moses Gaon. In one of his responsa Hai Gaon writes that Mesharshia occupied himself with amulets and charms, stating that faith in them was characteristic of the students of Sura (*Oẓar ha-Ge'onim*, B.M. Lewin, 4 (1931), Ḥagigah, 20).

BIBLIOGRAPHY: Rapoport, in: *Bikkurei ha-Ittim*, 10 (1829), 35 no. 25; J. Mueller, *Mafte'aḥ li-Teshuvot ha-Ge'onim* (1891), 75–79; Cowley, in: JQR, 18 (1905/06), 402; L. Ginzberg, *Geonica*, 2 (1909), index s.v. *Moshe Gaon*.

[Abraham David]

MOSES LEIB OF SASOV (1745–1807), ḥasidic rabbi. He was a pupil of Samuel Shmelke *Horowitz of Nikolsburg, *Dov Baer the Maggid of Mezhirech, and *Elimelech of Lyzhansk. He spent 13 years studying both Torah and Kabbalah under Samuel Shmelke who was then rabbi in Rychwal and Sieniawa.

Moses wrote novellae on several tractates of the Talmud, parts of which were published in the pamphlets *Likkutei ha-ReMaL* (1856), *Torat ha-ReMaL ha-Shalem* (1903), and *Ḥiddushei ha-ReMaL* (1921). For several years he lived in Opatov. When he moved to Sasov, he attracted many followers and the town became a great ḥasidic center. His disciples included Jacob Isaac of *Przysucha (Peshiskhah), Ẓevi Hirsch of *Zhidachov, Menahem Mendel of Kosov, and others. Moses was known for his abounding love for all Jews and for his charity, on account of which he was called "father of widows and orphans." He composed many ḥasidic melodies and dances. His successor was his only son, JEKUTHIEL SHMELKE, who was seven years old when his father died. Jekuthiel grew up in the homes of Abraham Ḥayyim of Zloczow, Menahem Mendel of Kosov, and Israel of *Ruzhin in Sadagora (Sadgora), and returned to Sasov in 1849.

BIBLIOGRAPHY: Y. Raphael, *Sefer ha-Ḥasidut* (1956); idem, *Sasov* (1946); M. Buber, *Tales of the Ḥasidim, The Later Masters* (1966), 81–95.

[Yitzchak Raphael]

MOSES (ben Nethanel) NATHAN (14th century), communal worker and poet. Moses, who lived in Tarrega, Catalonia, left a collection of moral parables in rhymed meter, entitled *Toẓe'ot Ḥayyim*, which was published in the *Shetei Yadot* (Venice, 1618, 142–50) of Menahem b. Judah de *Lonzano. It contains 58 sections with aphorisms on counsel, quickness, industry, humility, and other virtues. A short acrostic poem prefaces the proverbs, each word ending with a letter of his name. While the work contains no original ideas, it is composed in a clear and beautiful style. A manuscript of the book is extant in Paris (Bibliothèque Nationale, no. 1284). It is possible that its author is identical with the communal worker Moses Nathan who lived in the 14th century, known from Hebrew sources and also from Christian documents, where he is referred to as Moses Naçan (Nazan). In the *takkanot* issued in 1354 by the representatives of the communities of Aragon when they met in Barcelona, Moses Nathan was the first of the signatories. He may also be identical with the Mosse Açan (Azan), who wrote a poem on chess that has survived in a Castilian translation.

BIBLIOGRAPHY: Schirmann, Sefarad, 2 (1956), 541–3, 697; Davidson, Oẓar, 4 (1933), 449; Baer, Urkunden, 1 (1929), 306–7, 350–9.

[Abraham David]

MOSES OF EVREUX (Moses b. Schne'or), one of three brothers known as *Gedolei Evreux* ("the greatest [scholars] of Evreux") in the first half of the 13th century. Moses was the brother of *Isaac of Evreux and apparently a pupil of *Samson of Sens. Moses' individual teaching cannot always be identified since it is incorporated with that of his brothers, the whole being referred to by the *rishonim* as "the view of Evreux." He is mentioned by name, however, in the *Shitah Mekubbeẓet* to *Bava Kamma* and in late collections of *tosafot* to *Zevaḥim, Menaḥot*, and *Bekhorot*. His comments on the Pentateuch are known from the *Sefer ha-Gan* of Aaron b. Joseph ha-Kohen. The similarity of some of his ethical sayings quoted in the *Kol Bo* to Nahmanides' "Ethical Letter" to his son led some scholars to ascribe the latter work to Moses, but there are no solid grounds for doing so. Moses' son, Samuel, is referred to as the author of a prayer book. The work *Al ha-Kol* (published in *Ha-Goren*, 7 (1908)) containing rulings, *halakhot*, and customs, was compiled by one of his pupils.

BIBLIOGRAPHY: Weiss, in: *Ha-Goren*, 7 (1908), 76–111; Urbach, Tosafot, 395–9 and index s.v. *Moshe b. Senior me-Evreux*; Preschel, in: *Talpioth*, 8 (1961), 49–53; Y. Lipschitz (ed.), *Tosefot Evreux* (1969), 19–28.

[Israel Moses Ta-Shma]

MOSES OF KIEV (12th century), talmudist. No biographical details about him are known. He appears to have visited Western Europe and probably knew the tosafist Jacob *Tam personally. In Tam's *Sefer ha-Yashar* (1811 Vienna edition, no. 522) a halakhic saying occurs "that Moses of Kiev received from Rabbenu Tam." It is possible that he stayed for some time in the latter's yeshivah in Ramerupt. A. Epstein (in MGWJ, 39 (1895), 511) attempts to identify Moses of Kiev with Moses of Russia mentioned in the *Sefer ha-Shoham*. According to Epstein, Moses left Russia for France in 1124 following the expulsion of the Jews in that year from Kiev. Urbach (Tosafot, 193), however, disagrees, since in 1124 Rabbenu Tam was still very young. Moreover there is no information about an expulsion of the Jews from Kiev in 1124, though a great fire did break out there in that year. It appears that Moses arrived in France at a much later period.

Moses addressed queries to *Samuel b. Ali, head of the Babylonian academy: "Thus sent Samuel b. Ali head of the academy from Babylon to R. Moses of Kiev" (Responsa Meir of Rothenburg, ed. by R.N. Rabinowitz (1860), no. 443). The connection between Moses and Samuel b. Ali is also referred to in the *Sefer Yiḥusei Tanna'im ve-Amora'im* of Judah b. Kalonymus.

BIBLIOGRAPHY: A. Harkavy, *Ḥadashim Gam Yeshanim*, 1 no. 7 (1895–96), 44–45; F. Kupfer and T. Lewicki, *Żrodła hebrajskie do dziejów słowian* (1956).

[Shlomo Eidelberg]

MOSES OF PALERMO (c. 1275), Sicilian translator. Moses of Palermo was one of a group of Jewish translators from southern Italy who were active in Naples and Salerno at the request of Charles of Anjou (1226–85). Their work continued the tradition of Jewish translation that flourished during the reign of Frederick II and his natural son Manfred. Charles apparently paid Moses a regular stipend as an official translator. On the occasion of his journey from Salerno to Naples in 1270, Moses received payment of "an ounce of gold" at Charles' command. A document dated 1277 states that the king ordered Maestro Matteo Siciliaco to give Latin lessons to Moses of Palermo, thus enabling him to translate scientific texts from the Arabic. Moses' name is primarily linked with the translation of a "Treatise on the Healing of Horses" ascribed to Hippocrates

(*Liber de curationibus infirmitatum equorum quem translavit de lingua arabica in latinam Magister Moyses de Palermo*). This was translated into Italian, together with another article on the same subject, and published in 1865 as *Trattati di mascalcia attribuiti ad Ippocrate, tradotti dall'arabo in latino da Maestro Moise da Palermo, volgarizzati nel sec. XIII* (ed. P. Delprato). One of the earliest scientific texts written in Italian, this translation played an important part in the development of scientific terminology in the Italian language. It was widely circulated both in Italy and in other countries throughout the Middle Ages. Another version of the treatise, also in Italian, was entitled *Libro della natura dei cavalli*, and this was often reprinted during the Renaissance era.

There is, however, a possibility that there was another Moses of Palermo who flourished either at the court of the Norman kings, in the 12th century, or at the court of *Frederick II Hohenstaufen. A work attributed to Moses of Palermo, *Liber mariscaltie equorum et cura eorum*, is cited in the *De Medicina equorum* of Giordano Ruffo (c. 1200), thus indicating that the writer of this text lived in an earlier period. A list of the manuscripts attributed to Moses of Palermo was published by Stefano Arieti, "Mosè da Palermo e le traduzioni dei trattati di mascalcia di Ippocrate Indiano," in: *Gli ebrei in Sicilia*, ed. N. Bucaria (1998).

BIBLIOGRAPHY: M. Steinschneider, in: HB, 10 (1870), 8–11; Steinschneider, Uebersetzungen, 2 (1893), 985; U. Cassuto, in: *Vessillo Israelitico*, 59 (1911), 341; Roth, *Jews in the Renaissance* (1959), 69–70. **ADD. BIBLIOGRAPHY:** C. Sirat, "Les traducteurs juifs à la cour de Sicile et de Naples," in: *Traduction et traducteurs au Moyen Age, Actes du Colloque International du CNRS* (1989), 169–91; D. Trolli, "Le traduzioni di Mosè da Palermo," in: *Studi su antichi trattati di veterinaria* (1990), 43–57; R. Bonfil, "La cultura ebraica e Federico II, in: Federico II e le nuove culture," in: *Atti del XXXIo Convegno storico internazionale (del Centro Italiano di Studi sul Basso Medioevo – Accademia Tudertina & Centro di Studi sulla Spiritualità Medievale dell'Università degli Studi di Perugia)*, Todi, 9–12 ottobre 1994 (1995), 153–71; S. Arieti, "Mosè da Palermo e le traduzioni dei trattati di mascalcia di Ippocrate Indiano," in: N. Bucaria (ed.), *Gli ebrei in Sicilia* (1998), 55–61; M. Zonta, "La filosofia ebraica medievale in Sicilia," in: N. Bucaria et al. (eds.), *Ebrei e Sicilia* (2002), 163–68.

[Joseph Baruch Sermoneta / Nadia Zeldes (2nd ed.)]

MOSES OF PAVIA, medieval talmudist (dates unknown). Moses of Pavia is reported as being mentioned in the talmudic lexicon *Arukh* of *Nathan b. Jehiel, although his name nowhere appears in the printed editions. There are no certain details concerning the time and place of his labors. In the *Mikdash Me'at* of Moses de Rieti (15th cent.), it is noted that Moses of Pavia died a martyr's death in Lombardy, but there is no discernible historical basis for this statement. In the Parma manuscript (De'Rossi, 1360) the event is pinpointed as having taken place in 1096, i.e., at the time of the First Crusade. It is possible that Moses was one of the German scholars who migrated to Germany and were murdered there in 1096. Kaufmann's conjecture (*Schriften*, 3 (1915), 26) is that Moses of Pavia is to be identified with a tutor of the same name who, after having been banned, went to Capua and later to Pavia.

BIBLIOGRAPHY: Guedemann, Gesch Erz, 2 (1884), 14; Kohut, Arukh, 1 (1926²), xxxviii; S.J.L. Rapoport, *Toledot Rabbi Natan Ish Romi* (1913), 56 n. 41; Zunz, Gesch, 57; Zunz, Poesie, 19.

[Umberto (Moses David) Cassuto]

MOSES SHOHAM BEN DAN OF DOLINA (end of 18th century), ḥasidic author and preacher in Dolina in eastern Galicia. He was a disciple of *Israel b. Eliezer Ba'al Shem Tov and was related by marriage to *Jehiel Michael of Zloczow. He quotes traditions and teachings of both in his works: *Divrei Moshe* (Polonnoye, 1801), commentaries on the Torah; *Imrei Shoham* (1880), on the tractates *Ketubbot, Kiddushin* and *Bava Meẓia; Seraf Peri Eẓ Ḥayyim* (1866), on the *Peri Eẓ Ḥayyim* of Ḥayyim *Vital.

BIBLIOGRAPHY: S.Y. Agnon, *Ha-Esh ve-ha-Eẓim* (1962), 106–7; M. Kamelhar, *Ha-Ḥasidut ve-Ẓiyyon* (1963), 104–6.

MOSES ZE'EV (Wolf) BEN ELIEZER OF GRODNO (d. 1830), Lithuanian rabbi. Moses was born and grew up in Grodno. He was appointed *rosh yeshivah* there but left in 1813 to become the *av bet din* in Tiktin, where he stayed until 1824. He was then appointed *av bet din* in Bialystok, remaining there until his death. When Moses was first given this appointment, the people in Bialystok were concerned that he was so young, but he wittily replied that this was a fault which would improve with age. His best-known work, *Marot ha-Ẓove'ot* (Grodno, 1810) on the laws concerning *agunah*, is based upon the relevant chapter (17) of Shulḥan Arukh *Even ha-Ezer*. He also wrote *Ḥiddushei Moharmaz* (1858), on the commentary of R. Jonathan b. David Ha-Cohen of Lunel to Alfasi on tractate *Eruvin*, and three works all with the same title, *Aguddat Ezov*: (1) a collection of sermons (Bialystok, 1824) concluding with *Alon Bakhut*, nine funeral orations on great rabbis; (2) responsa (2 vols.; 1885–86); (3) novellae on the Shulḥan Arukh (1904). On the title page of the *Marot ha-Ẓove'ot* he gives his family tree in detail back to *Judah Loew b. Bezalel of Prague, stating where each of his forebears served as rabbi.

BIBLIOGRAPHY: Fuenn, Keneset, 301f.

[Anthony Lincoln Lavine]

MOSHAV (Heb. מוֹשָׁב) or **MOSHAV OVEDIM** (Heb. מוֹשָׁב עוֹבְדִים, "workers settlement"), cooperative smallholders' village in Ereẓ Israel combining some of the features of both cooperative and private farming. The idea was evolved during World War I in the quest for a form of settlement that would not only express national and social aspirations on the basis of collective principles like the kibbutz, but also provide scope for individual initiative and independent farm management. The idea was mooted in articles published in various periodicals and was given definite shape in a pamphlet *Yissud Moshevei Ovedim* ("The Establishment of Workers' Villages," 1919) by Eliezer *Joffe, who formulated the social and economic principles on which the moshav should be based:

nationally owned land, mutual aid, cooperative purchasing and marketing, and the family as the fundamental unit. These principles were further developed in the writings of Yiẓḥak Vilkanski (*Elazari-Volcani), the agronomist, who dealt with the economic structure desirable for the moshav and regarded it as the appropriate answer to the needs of mass settlement. This evaluation was fully vindicated after the establishment of the State of Israel, when tens of thousands of new immigrant families were settled on the land in hundreds of moshavim.

At first the moshav economy was based on mixed farming, which, it was expected, would supply most of the farmer's needs and give him greater stamina to withstand agricultural fluctuations and crises than the single-crop farm. It would also permit the work to be spread out evenly over the year, a point of particular importance since the settler and his family had to cultivate the farm by themselves without the aid of hired seasonal labor.

Milestones of Moshav Settlement

The first two moshavim were founded in 1921, *Nahalal in September in the northern Jezreel Valley and *Kefar Yeḥezkel in December in the eastern part. Most of the members had formerly lived in kibbutzim (Deganyah, Kinneret, Ḥuldah, and Merḥavyah). Within ten years another eight moshavim were founded, most of them in the Jezreel Valley. At the beginning of the 1930s, the movement was given a new impetus by widespread settlement in the Ḥefer Plain by the Hityashvut ha-Elef scheme, intended to settle 1,000 families on the land in the Sharon and Judea, and by the establishment of the first moshavim in the south. The landholdings were small compared with those of the first moshavim, as it was assumed that incomes would be supplemented and the farms consolidated by work outside the moshav in fruit groves and construction projects. During the Arab rebellion of 1936–39, more moshavim were established all over the country, especially in the valleys and in the south, as *Stockade and Watchtower settlements. At the end of World War II, a number of moshavim were established by demobilized soldiers from the *Jewish Brigade and other Jewish units in the British army. In 1948, when the State of Israel was established, there were 58 moshavim in the country.

Most of the new immigrants who arrived in large numbers immediately after the establishment of the state differed in many respects from the pioneers who had settled on the land after spending years in training and preparation. They consisted mainly of families with many children, elderly persons, even entire communities brought over en masse. The moshav ovedim, with its family structure, was felt to be the only medium of settling these immigrants on the land. Hundreds of veterans from the older moshavim came forward to recruit new immigrants for settlements, to set up moshavim, and particularly to instruct and guide the new settlers. In the period 1949–56, 250 new moshavim were established, with a population that approached 100,000 in 1970.

The Moshav Movement

The moshav movement (Tenu'at ha-Moshavim) was founded in the mid-1930s to cope with the problems of the existing moshavim, to mold and preserve their social structure, and to help establish more moshavim. The movement developed a series of economic, financial, and service institutions to advance these purposes. These include: Keren ha-Moshavim, a mutual assistance fund; the Ein Ḥai Bank; Tagmulim la-Moshavim, a savings and pension fund for members; Bittu'aḥ Hadadi, a mutual insurance company; Matam (Mishkei Tenu'at ha-Moshavim – Moshav Movement Farms), which provides low-priced, high-quality products; Bank le-Mashkanta'ot (Mortgage Bank), which provides loans for private and public building in the moshavim; and regional purchasing organizations, with some 30 to 50 moshavim in each, to organize marketing and supplies. The latter have set up enterprises, in cooperation with local councils, to lower the cost of services and supplies, and improve production facilities. Examples of these enterprises are citrus-canning plants, fodder plants, slaughterhouses, fruit-packing plants, egg-sorting warehouses, and cold storage plants. The movement has departments for education, culture, social activities, internal arbitration, advice and training in farming and organization, and absorption of new settlers. It also has a youth section with 15,000 teenagers and it publishes periodicals.

In 1970 there were 212 moshavim, with a total population of 75,000, affiliated to Tenu'at ha-Moshavim. Other moshav movements were: the Union of Religious Cooperative Movements of *Ha-Po'el ha-Mizrachi, with 56 moshavim and a membership of 24,000; the Farmers' Union (Ha-Iḥud ha-Ḥakla'i), with 32 villages and 10,000 people; and the cooperative Agricultural Center of the *Ḥerut Movement and *Betar, with eight moshavim and 1,500 people. There were also 13 moshavim with 4,000 people affiliated to *Ha-Oved ha-Ẓiyyoni; nine, with 2,500, to *Po'alei Agudat Israel and *Agudat Israel; six, with 1,600, to the *Farmers' Federation (Hitaḥdut ha-Ikkarim); two with 370 to *Mapam; and eight unaffiliated moshavim, with 3,400 people; making a total of 346 moshavim with a combined population of about 122,000–95,600 living in 269 moshavim founded after the establishment of the State of Israel in May 1948 and 26,500 living in 77 veteran moshavim. Since that time the moshav population has grown more slowly than the urban population, reaching around 230,000 in 2004, with 206,500 affiliated to the moshavim of Tenu'at ha-Moshavim.

Organization of the Moshav

Each moshav is organized as a cooperative society for agricultural settlement and constitutes a unit of local government administered by the management of the society. The moshav operates in accordance with the Cooperative Societies Ordinance, 1933, under the authority of the Registrar of Cooperative Societies; its accounts are audited by the audit unions for agricultural cooperation. Its activities are governed by a general set of regulations which serve as a pattern for those of the individual moshavim. At an annual assembly of members, each moshav elects its management, which comprises a managing committee, a control board, and committees for economic, social, educational, and cultural activities. Disputes between members or between a member and the management are submitted for arbitration and decision to the social committee or a judicial committee of the parent movement. The moshav helps its members to obtain credit, purchase seed, fertilizer, and fodder, and to market their produce. It maintains farming equipment and vehicles (sometimes together with neighboring moshavim), workshops, cooperative stores, etc. It provides members' children with primary and post-primary education in local or regional schools, and fosters cultural activities; members receive medical care in local clinics.

The society erects all the public buildings and installations including pumping installations, central irrigation network, supply stores, dairies, refrigeration and sorting plants, schools, clinics, and sports facilities. It finances its investments partly by direct taxation of members and partly by loans based on a general mutual guarantee by the members. The general assembly decides on the annual budget, composed of the local government budget (covered by direct taxes) and the administrative budget (covered partly by taxes and partly by levies on items of income and on various types of production outlays). In the 1960s the moshav set itself new goals: securing production rights in nationally planned branches of agriculture (dairy farming, poultry farming, orchards, etc.); the encouragement of new crops, notably for export purposes; and the protection of members' interests in taxation and social security. The expansion and social development of the moshavim at the time gave rise to the hope that they would continue to develop as an efficient and healthy unit of the national economy and society, and a measure of prosperity did indeed continue into the 1970s. However, with unmanageable debts piling up in the inflationary 1980s, many farms were liquidated, and with the younger generation leaving, some of the moshavim, especially those located near large population concentrations in central Israel, began to build new neighborhoods and absorb newcomers, mainly urbanites, in order to sustain the settlement. Moshavim also began renting land for commercial purposes and many farmers, especially in northern Israel, developed guest facilities and were occupied in tourism in addition to agriculture. Thus the moshav, like the kibbutz, found itself forced to adapt to changing realities and alter its economic and social base in the last decades of the 20th century.

The Moshav as an Example to Developing Countries

The moshav and its way of life attracted the interest of some leaders and many students from Asia, Africa, and Latin America. Thousands of them came Israel to study the methods of the moshav, which they regarded as a possible solution to the problems of organizing agriculture in their own countries. The moshav movement played host to students and organized study courses for them. It also provided Israel's technical assistance program (see State of Israel, Foreign *Policy) with many instructors to establish and advise settlements of the moshav type in these countries. Scores of such settlements were established in Africa, Asia, and Latin America, with moshav members from Israel as instructors. The moshav movement, together with the Israel Ministry of Foreign Affairs, also established a volunteer movement for foreign service, and many young men from moshavim served as volunteers in developing countries, living and working with the local population.

BIBLIOGRAPHY: H. Viteles, *A History of the Cooperative Movement in Israel*, 4 (1968), incl. bibl.; I.M. Klayman, *The Moshav in Israel* (1970); D. Weintraub, M. Lissak, and Y. Azmon, *Moshava, Kibbutz and Moshav* … (1969); R. Tamsma, *De Moshav Ovdiem* (Dutch, 1966), English summary; *ibid.*, 342–91, incl. bibl.; H. Darin-Drabkin, *Patterns of Cooperative Agriculture in Israel* (1962); S. Dayan, *Man and the Soil* (1965); E. Meyer, *Der Moshav 1948–1963* (1967); E. Joffe, *Ketavim*, 2 vols. (1947); idem, *Yissud Moshevei Ovedim* (1919); A. Assaf, *Moshevei ha-Ovedim be-Yisrael* (1954); Y. Uri, *Bi-Netivei Moshav ha-Ovedim* (1950); I. Korn, *Kibbutz ha-Galuyyot be-Hitnaḥaluto* (1964); R. Weitz, *Darkenu ba-Ḥakla'ut u-va-Hityashevut* (1959); Y. Shapira (ed.), *Nahalal* … (1947); *Kefar Yeḥezkel* (Heb. anthol., 1948); E. Labes, *Handbook of the Moshav* (1959); D. Weintraub, *Immigration and Social Change* (1971).

[Uzi Finerman / Shaked Gilboa (2nd ed.)]

MOSHAV SHITTUFI (Heb. מוֹשָׁב שִׁתּוּפִי, collective moshav), a form of settlement combining features of the *kibbutz and the *moshav. The originators of the idea wanted to combine the advantages of both forms of settlement, while avoiding what they regarded as overemphasis on collectivism in the kibbutz and on individual farming in the moshav. They therefore separated production from consumption, adopting the productive system of the kibbutz and the preservation of the family unit in the moshav. The village's lands and installations – sometimes including industrial plants – are collectively owned and operated, as in the kibbutz, but each family has its own home and is responsible for its own cooking, domestic economy, and the care of children, as in the moshav. Mothers generally work outside the home for two or three hours a day five times a week. From the proceeds of the moshav shittufi's farming and other enterprises, each family is allotted a sum to meet its own needs, while the village as a whole provides education for the children, medical services, cultural activities, and the like.

The first two moshavim shittufiyyim – *Kar Ḥittim in Lower Galilee and *Moledet in the Gilboa district – were founded in 1936–37, and after World War II many of the demobilized soldiers who settled on the land chose this form of settlement. In 1970 there were 22 moshavim shittufiyyim with a total population of 4,200. Eight belonged to Tenu'at ha-Moshavim, five to Ha-Oved ha-Ẓiyyoni, four to Ha-Po'el ha-Mizrachi, three to the Ḥerut movement, and one each to the Farmers' Union and Po'alei Agudat Israel. To coordinate their activities, the moshavim shittufiyyim maintained an inter-movement committee. In 2004 there were 27 moshavim shittufiyyim with a population of about 12,500.

For bibliography, see *Moshav.

[Uzi Finerman]

MOSHINSKY, ELIJAH (1946–), opera and theater producer-director. Moshinsky was educated at Melbourne University (B.A.) and St. Anthony's College, Oxford. He was appointed associate producer at the Royal Opera House in 1979 and became its principal producer. His most successful productions for Covent Garden included *Peter Grimes, Othello, Samson and Delilah*, and *Simon Boccanegra*. West End productions have included the prizewinning *Shadowlands* and *Cyrano de Bergerac*. He also produced five plays in the BBC Shakespeare cycle.

Moshinsky's preferences incline towards the classics, which include Chekhov and Ibsen, and he is considered a leading Verdi expert. However, the 20th century Ligeti's *Le Grand Macabre*, Berg's *Wozzeck*, and Sir Michael Tippett's *A Midsummer Marriage* are among his operatic productions.

Moshinsky described his favored method of working; he is first and foremost a respecter of the creative forces of composer and writer and is therefore not a believer in the current vogue of innovation for its own sake.

Moshinsky also staged operas for the New York Metropolitan, Australian Opera, Welsh National Opera, Chicago Lyric Opera, and the houses of Paris, Geneva, Amsterdam, and the Maggio Musicale in Florence. He also directed several films, including *The Midsummer Night's Dream* (1981) and *The Green Man* (1994), and has more recently been associated with the English National Opera in London. The Australian-born Moshinsky also headed several Adelaide Festivals and other cultural ventures in Australia.

[Sally Whyte / William D Rubinstein (2nd ed.)]

MOSKONI (Mashkoni), JUDAH LEON BEN MOSES (b. 1328), medieval philosopher and scholar from Ocrida in Bulgaria. As a result of disturbances caused by war Moskoni left his native town in 1360 and traveled extensively through many countries. While at Negropont he became a pupil of *Shemariah b. Elijah b. Jacob. During his travels he formed close ties with the great Jewish scholars of Egypt, Morocco, Italy, and southern France. Moskoni was well acquainted with the Hebrew and Arabic philosophic literature of his time and stressed the importance of studying grammar for an understanding of the Bible. His main work is a supercommentary to the commentaries of Abraham Ibn Ezra on the Pentateuch under the title *Even ha-Ezer*, which he wrote in 1362, but he also wrote other works in the fields of Hebrew grammar, biblical exegesis, and philosophy. The year of his death is not known. Some fragments of his commentary to Genesis (1:1–2) were published by N. Ben-Menahem; and to Exodus (some chapters) by A. Berliner and D. Hoffmann (see bibliography). Special importance is attached to Moskoni because of his edition of the Hebrew *Josippon. He had at his disposal a number of versions of the book but in the end selected the long adaptation of it, divided it into chapters, and added an interesting and detailed introduction. His edition has been preserved in two manuscripts and is the basis of the Constantinople edition of *Josippon*, where his introduction appears in an abbreviated and adapted form. All the standard editions of *Josippon* are merely reprints of this version. His introduction to *Josippon* was published by A. Berliner and D. Hoffmann.

BIBLIOGRAPHY: Vogelstein-Rieger, 1 (1896), 186, 450; HB, 9 (1869), 16; A. Berliner and D. Hoffmann (eds.), *Oẓar Tov*, 1 (1878), 1–10, 17–25, 41–42; N. Ben-Menahem, in: *Oẓar Yehudel Sefarad*, 2 (1959), 43–54; idem, in: *Aresheth*, 3 (1961), 74.

[David Flusser]

MOSKOVITZ, SHALOM (Shalom of Safed; 1887–1980), Israel primitive painter. Moskovitz worked in Safed as a watchmaker, stonemaker, and silversmith until at the age of 70, encouraged by the artist Yossl Bergner, he began painting, and gained international fame. Telling the story of the Bible in line and color, he laid out his visual narrations in strips, one above the other. These were characterized by a linear style and the use of repeated forms. In Moskovitz's work, kabbalistic and ḥasidic traditions blended anachronistically with features from his own surroundings.

MOSKOWITZ, HENRY (1879–1936), U.S. social worker and community leader. Moskowitz, who was born in Husse, Romania, went to the United States in his youth. He helped organize the Madison House Social Settlement. In 1907 he became active in the Ethical Culture Society and remained an associate leader of that group until 1913. From 1913 until 1917 Moskowitz served under the New York City reformist mayor, John P. Mitchell, as chairman of several city commissions. He was also an active leader of the Progressive Party under Theodore Roosevelt. In Jewish affairs Moskowitz served on the executive of the Joint Distribution Committee and as the executive chairman of American ORT and was elected in 1936 to the executive committee of its World Union. Moskowitz was closely associated with Governor Alfred E. Smith and, together with Norman Hapgood, wrote Smith's biography, *Up From City Streets* (1927). He also edited *Progressive Democracy: Speeches and State Papers of Alfred E. Smith* (1928) and wrote *Jewish Reconstruction in Russia, Poland, Romania; a report* (1925).

Moskowitz's wife BELLE LINDER ISRAELS MOSKOWITZ (1877–1933), who was born in New York City, worked on the professional staff of the Educational Alliance in New York City from 1900 to 1903 and married Henry Moskowitz in 1914. In 1908 she joined the staff of *The Survey*, remaining there for two years. She subsequently became increasingly involved in communal and political activity, and in public relations counseling. Belle Moskowitz later served on many of Governor Alfred E. Smith's state commissions and became his confidante and adviser. During the 1928 presidential campaign, when Smith was the Democratic nominee, Belle Moskowitz was the publicity chairman of the party. She also served as director of both the National Council of Jewish Women and the Women's City Club, and secretary to the Mayor's

Commission of Women on National Defense. She championed such causes as public health and housing. Following Smith's defeat in the 1928 presidential race, she became the president of Publicity Associates, where she remained until her death.

MOSLER, HENRY (1841–1920), U.S. painter and printmaker. Although in his lifetime Mosler claimed to have been born in America, he had immigrated from Germany at the age of eight with his parents, settling in New York. Two years later the family moved to Cincinnati. For years the Mosler family led a peripatetic life, living in several places, including Nashville, Tennessee, where Mosler received his first art instruction from a lithographer (1853) and again in Cincinnati (1859–1863), where he studied with a genre and portrait painter named James Henry Beard, whose subject matter and straightforward storytelling style on canvases comprised of small-scale figures influenced Mosler's early imagery. By 1860 Mosler had his own studio. During the Civil War, Mosler worked as an artist-correspondent for *Harper's Weekly*, which published 34 of his drawings. These images show battle as well as the daily life of soldiers. Later, three paintings explored war themes.

In 1863 Mosler began studying in Duesseldorf, Germany, a celebrated artistic center attractive to several American artists. Mosler's schooling in Germany strengthened his propensity for genre scenes and recording the intimate details of his subjects. Six months of study at the Ecole des Beaux Arts in Paris completed Mosler's extended training. The nomadic pattern of his youth brought Mosler back to Cincinnati from 1866 to 1874, where Reform Judaism began to gain prominence under the guidance of Isaac Mayer *Wise. Mosler painted *Plum Street Temple* (c. 1866, Skirball Museum, Hebrew Union College, Cincinnati), a canvas delineating the exterior of Wise's temple, Bene Yeshurun. A reproduction of the painting adorned the cover of the musical score "Progress March" a year later. Portraits commissioned by the Jewish community include a likeness of Wise's wife Therese Bloch Wise (c. 1867, Skirball Museum, Hebrew Union College, Cincinnati).

After eight years of living in cities in the United States, Mosler returned to Europe, continuing his studies at various times. He contributed entries to the French Salon from 1878 to 1897; his 1879 entry received honorable mention and was purchased for the Musée du Luxembourg, making the canvas the first by an American artist to be bought by the French government. Mosler began visiting Brittany in 1878, at which time he made paintings of Breton peasants, a subject that preoccupied his art until the 1890s. He meticulously recorded Breton dress, customs, and domestic interiors, and he painted wedding traditions on several occasions, including *The Wedding Feast* (c. 1892, collection unknown), shown at the 1892 Paris Salon. Returning permanently to the United States in 1894, Mosler lived in New York and painted scenes from American colonial history and genre works, employing a similar formula of attention to details and extensive research.

BIBLIOGRAPHY: B.C. Gilbert, *Henry Mosler Rediscovered: A Nineteenth-Century Jewish-American Artist* (1995); B.M. Foley, "Henry Mosler: Figure Drawings for Narrative Paintings," in: *American Art Review*, 8 (1996), 100–3.

[Samantha Baskind (2nd ed.)]

MOSS, CELIA (1819–1873) and **MARION** (1821–1907), Anglo-Jewish writers and educators. The Moss sisters were born in Portsmouth, England, two of the 12 children of Amelia and Joseph Moss. Avid readers, they began writing poetry in early childhood. Their first joint publication was a book of poems, *Early Efforts* (1839). This was followed by two collections of short stories, *The Romance of Jewish History* (1840) and its sequel, *Tales of Jewish History* (1843). Both collections, which were highly successful, were intended to convey a positive view of Jewish history, religion, and customs to a somewhat hostile Victorian society. As the Moss sisters remarked in their dedication to the writer Edward Bulwer Lytton, they blended "fiction with historical fact, to direct the attention of the reader to a branch of history too long neglected." Celia and Marion hoped their romantic tales would "call the attention of the reader to the records of our people – to awaken curiosity – not to satisfy it." Along with their compatriot Grace *Aguilar (1816–1847), the Moss sisters were the first Jewish women to publish narratives of this kind. They hoped their work would support the struggle for Jewish emancipation, and, more specifically, they wished to encourage improvement of female education and religious reform within the English Jewish community.

In 1840 the sisters moved to London to teach; in 1845 they opened their own day and boarding school for Jewish children. That same year Marion married the French Jewish scholar Alphonse Hartog. Five of their seven children survived to adulthood; each went on to a distinguished career in scholarship, science, or the arts. In 1857 Celia married L. Levetus, the ritual slaughterer of the New Synagogue in St. Helen's; it is not known if the couple had any children. Both sisters continued to write short stories while teaching and both contributed to Isaac Leeser's Jewish American periodical, *The Occident*. In 1854–55, Marion Moss Hartog established the first Jewish women's periodical, the *Jewish Sabbath Journal: A Penny and Moral Magazine for the Young*, intended to provide mothers with material with which to further their children's Jewish education. Initially, a great success, prompting submissions of all kinds from female authors and positively endorsed by the chief rabbi of the British Empire, the journal foundered after Hartog offended the editor of the powerful *Jewish Chronicle*, who proceeded to write a harsh review. Funding declined and publication ceased after five issues. Hartog, who was crushed, wrote next to nothing more for the remaining 52 years of her life. After moving to Birmingham with her husband, Celia wrote a collection of stories on her own, *The King's Physician and Other Tales* (1865).

BIBLIOGRAPHY: M. Galchinksy. *The Origin of the Modern Jewish Woman Writer* (1996).

[Traci M. Klass (2nd ed.)]

MOSS, JOHN (1771–1847), Philadelphia merchant, shipping magnate, and civic leader. Moss emigrated to the U.S. as a glass engraver from London in 1796. Opening a dry goods store in Philadelphia in 1807, he quickly became a major importer, ultimately owning a large number of ships. After he turned the active direction of his firm over to his brothers in 1823, Moss shifted his own concerns to banking and insurance, canal companies, and civic enterprises. In 1828 he was elected to the Common Council on the Jacksonian Democratic Party ticket, and in this role he participated in the establishment of the world-famous Wills Eye Hospital. Moss was one of the rich Philadelphia Jews who entered almost every phase of civic activity: he was a steward of the Society of Sons of St. George; a life subscriber to the Orphan Society; and a founding member of the Musical Fund Society. This status was not achieved at the sacrifice of Jewish identification; he was an active member of Mikveh Israel Congregation, a major contributor to its building fund of 1818, and, late in life, a supporter of Isaac Leeser's American Jewish Publication Society. As presiding officer at the Philadelphia *Damascus Affair protest meeting in 1840, Moss had become the representative of his community.

BIBLIOGRAPHY: Rosenbloom, Biogr Dict; L. Moss, in: AJHSP, 2 (1894), 171–4; E. Wolf and M. Whiteman, *History of the Jews of Philadelphia* (1957), index; S.A. Moss, *Genealogy of John Moss and his Wife, Rebecca…* (1937).

[Bertram Wallace Korn]

MOSSE, family originating from Graetz, a small town in the former Prussian province of Posen. Born in Friedland, Niederlausitz, MARKUS MOSSE (1808–1865), the family's founding father, moved to Graetz in 1835, where he became a committed physician, president of the local Jewish community in 1838, and deputy to the president of the town council. Unlike his coreligionists, he fought on the side of the Polish nationalists during the 1848 uprising and was wounded and taken prisoner. For the rest of his life, Mosse lived quietly in Graetz, engaged in the practice of his profession and the upbringing of his numerous descendants. Markus' wife, Ulrike (née Wolff; 1813–1888), was the aunt of Theodor *Wolff (1868–1943), one of the outstanding journalists of the early 20th century and from 1906 to 1933 chief editor of his cousin Rudolf Mosse's *Berliner Tageblatt*. Markus Mosse had eight sons and six daughters. His eldest son, Salomon (1837–1903), founded the Mosse linen house in Berlin and was joined by two other sons, Theodor (1842–1916) and Paul (1849–1920). Two other sons, ALBERT (see below) and Maximus (1857–1920), became lawyers, and RUDOLF (see below) was to be one of the three liberal press-czars of the Kaiserreich.

ALBERT MOSSE (1846–1925) specialized in administrative law, which he successfully taught to Japanese diplomats in Berlin. Thus, he became legal adviser to the Japanese government in Tokyo from 1886 to 1890. There he drafted the basic laws for the institutions of local self-government in provinces, districts, and communes. Moreover, he gave legal advice to several ministries and even prepared the Japanese constitution. Returning to Germany, he went to Koenigsberg, Prussia, where he became a state supreme court judge in 1890, the highest position hitherto attained by an unbaptized Jew in the Prussian judicial administration. Until his retirement, he was engaged in academic pursuits in his profession, and received a honorary doctorate and – in 1904 – even a honorary professorship at the University of Koenigsberg. Albert Mosse was active in Jewish affairs all of his life; he was married to Caroline Meyer (1859–1934), daughter of the former president of the Berlin Jewish community. After Mosse's return to Berlin in 1907, he became vice president of the Verband der Deutschen Juden and chairman of the board of the Hochschule fuer die Wissenschaft des Judentums. In recognition of his intensive work with its municipal administration, the City of Berlin made him its honorary citizen in 1917.

RUDOLF MOSSE (1843–1920), another son of Markus, founded in Berlin the Mosse publishing house, which acquired a worldwide reputation during the Empire and the Weimar republic. Born in Graetz, he learned the profession of bookselling in Posen and worked for several printing firms in Berlin and Leipzig, where, in 1864, he produced the advertising section for the widely read family magazine *Die Gartenlaube*. In 1867 he opened his own advertising agency in Berlin and was joined first by his brother-in-law Emil Cohn (1832–1905) and later on by his brother Emil Mosse (1854–1911). The firm expanded rapidly, established dozens of branch offices in Germany, Austria, Switzerland, and other European states ,and published the *Deutsches Reichs-Adreßbuch* every year from 1898. Only months after Germany had become an empire, Rudolf Mosse started to publish the *Berliner Tageblatt*, the mouthpiece of German left-wing liberalism. With the takeover of the *Allgemeine Zeitung des Judentums* (1890), the well-established *Berliner Volks-Zeitung* (1904), and the founding of the weekly *Berliner Morgen-Zeitung* (1889), the Mosse publishing house acquired nationwide prestige in the course of half a century. Even after World War I, the revolution, and the inflation, the House of Mosse remained a prominent, solidly financed, and highly regarded enterprise throughout Germany and Europe.

Beside his outstanding career as a businessman and a liberal-minded publisher, Rudolf Mosse was noted as a philanthropist. He established a hospital in Graetz and an educational institute in Wilhelmsdorf with an endowment of several million marks. He set up a fund for his employees and made large financial contributions to many literary, artistic, and, foremost, social institutions as well as academies, universities, and scientific pursuits. He was also active in the Jewish community in Berlin and was president of its Reform congregation from 1897 until 1910.

Rudolf's son-in-law Hans Lachmann-Mosse (1885–1944) was the last head of the Mosse publishing house. He worked in banking before entering the Mosse concern in 1910. Following the rise of Hitler, he resigned and the publishing house was seized by the Nazis. He moved to Paris in 1935 and in 1940 emigrated to the United States.

BIBLIOGRAPHY: R. Hamburger, *Zeitungsverlag und Annoncen-Expedition Rudolf Mosse* (1928); W.E. Mosse, in: YLBI, 4 (1959), 237–59; O. Neumann, in: *Juedische Familien-Forschung*, 11 (1935), 665ff., 685ff.; E. Kraus, *Die Familie Mosse* (1999).

[Elisabeth Kraus (2nd ed.)]

MOSSE, GEORGE L. (1918–1999), U.S. historian; grandson of Rudolph *Mosse. Born in Berlin into one of Germany's wealthiest publishing families, Mosse and his family fled to Britain in 1933; in 1936 Mosse moved to the United States. He received a B.S. from Haverford College in 1941 and a Ph.D. from Harvard University in 1946. In 1944 he joined the Army Specialized Training Program at the University of Iowa, where he lectured for soldiers who were scheduled to take part in the postwar U.S. occupation of Europe. In 1945 he became a member of the history faculty and was assigned to a newly established course on the history of Western civilization. He helped to develop the curriculum for the program as well as to implement it at other universities.

In 1955 Mosse became associate professor of European history at the University of Wisconsin-Madison, where he was recruited to build up the European history program. He served on the faculty until his retirement in 1988. He also taught at The Hebrew University of Jerusalem from 1969 to 1985 and held the Koebner Chair from 1978 to 1985. In 1994 he was the first Shapiro Senior Scholar in Residence at the Holocaust Memorial Museum in Washington, D.C.

Mosse was president of the American Society for Reformation Research (1961–62) and was a founding editor with Walter Lacquer of the *Journal of Contemporary History*.

Mosse's principal interests were in 16th-century history, cultural history, and modern Germany, with special reference to the Nazis and antisemitism. His books *The Reformation* (1963) and *Europe in the Sixteenth Century* (with H.G. Koenigsberger, 1968) were important contributions to early modern history, while a series of later works – *The Crisis of German Ideology* (ed., 1964), *Nazi Culture* (1966), and *Germans and Jews* (1968) – explored modern Germany, particularly the fate of German Jewry. To this latter subject he brought his expert knowledge of more than four centuries of German history and a close familiarity with the development of European culture, a subject on which he also wrote in *The Culture of Western Europe* (1961).

After the unification of Germany in 1990, Mosse succeeded in reclaiming much of the family fortune that had been confiscated by the Nazis and the Communists. He bequeathed a large part of his estate to the University of Wisconsin-Madison and The Hebrew University to sponsor history scholarships.

Other books by Mosse include *Toward the Final Solution* (1978), *International Fascism* (1979), *Masses and Man* (1980), *German Jews beyond Judaism* (1985), *Nationalism and Sexuality* (1985), *Confronting the Nation* (1993), and *The Image of Man: The Creation of Modern Masculinity* (1996). His autobiography, *Confronting History*, was published in 2000.

ADD. BIBLIOGRAPHY: S. Drescher, A. Sharlin, and D. Sabean (eds.), *Political Symbolism in Modern Europe: Essays in Honor of George L. Mosse* (1982).

[Theodore K. Rabb / Ruth Beloff (2nd ed.)]

MOSSERI, prominent family in *Egypt, said to have come there from Italy around 1750 (many of its members were Italian subjects). The family was active in the administration of the Jewish community in *Cairo as vice presidents and in its philanthropy towards the needy in the community.

NISSIM MOSSERI (1848–1897), his son and his brothers were at first moneylenders in Cairo, then founded the banking house of J.N. Mosseri et Fils Cie. (1876). JOSEPH (1869–1934), the eldest son of Nissim, was honored with the title of *bey* for his financial services to the Egyptian government. Joseph's three brothers, Eli, Jacques, and Maurice, founded a second bank in 1904, Banque Mosseri et Cie. ELI (1879–1940) headed many companies, one of which built the King David Hotel in *Jerusalem. JACQUES (1884–1934), Nissim's third son, studied languages at Cambridge and later secured permission for Solomon Schechter to investigate the Cairo **Genizah*. Jacques himself collected *genizah* fragments and wrote articles on the **genizah* and Cairo's synagogues. A delegate of Egyptian Jewry to the 11th Zionist Congress (1913), he founded the Zionist Organization in Egypt in 1917. VICTOR MOSSERI (1873–1930), brother-in-law and cousin of the Mosseri brothers, was an agricultural engineer. He did research for the improvement of several crops, publishing some 60 monographs, and developed an important new variety of cotton. ALBERT MOSSERI (1867–1933), also a cousin, was born in Cairo. He studied medicine in Paris, where he became acquainted with *Herzl and *Nordau. He began publishing a Zionist newspaper, *Kadimah*, there. Serving as a physician with the British army in World War I, he later left his profession and began in 1919 to publish the weekly *Israel* in Cairo, originally in Hebrew, then in Arabic, and French too. After his death, his wife, MAZAL MATHILDA (1894–1981), continued the publication until 1939. Their son MACCABEE (1914–1948) served as an officer in the Palmaḥ and was killed when bringing supplies to besieged Jerusalem. The effort to control the supply route (May 1948) was called "Operation Maccabee" after him.

ADD. BIBLIOGRAPHY: J. Mosseri, "The Synagogues of Egypt – Past and Present," in: *The Jewish Review*, 5 (1913–1914), 31–44; J.M. Landau, *Jews in Nineteenth-Century Egypt* (1969), index; idem (ed.), *Toledet Yehudei Miẓrayim ba-Tekufah ha-Otmanit* (1988), index; G. Krämer, *The Jews in Modern Egypt: 1914–1952* (1989), index; M.M. Laskier, *The Jews of Egypt 1920–1970* (1992), index.

[Hayyim J. Cohen / Jacob M. Landau (2nd ed.)]

MOSSINSOHN, YIGAL (1917–1994), Israeli author and playwright. Born in Ein-Gannim, Mossinsohn was a member of kibbutz Na'an from 1938 to 1950 and served in the Palmaḥ and the Israeli Defense Forces from 1943 to 1949. After six years in the United States (1959–65), he returned to Israel. Mossinsohn wrote stories, novels, plays, thrillers, and adventure books for children, and dealt with topical and historical themes. His first book, a collection of stories, *Aforim ka-Sak* ("Gray as a Sack"), was published in 1946. In 1948 the Habimah Theater staged his first play *Be-Arvot ha-Negev* ("In the Negev Desert"), which was a popular success. The theme of the play was the heroic stand of Kibbutz Negbah against the invading Egyptian army during the Israeli War of Independence. Mossinsohn also wrote several other topical plays. A great success was his series of thrillers for children and teenagers, *Ḥasambah*, starting in 1950, which found a host of imitators.

Additional works include (1) Stories and novels: *Mi Amar she-Hu Shaḥor* (1948); *Ha Derekh li-Yriḥo* (1950); *Derekh Gever* (1953); *Yehudah Ish Keriyyot* (1963, *Judas*, 1963); *Cherchez la femme* (stories, 1971); *Yeḥi ha-Hevdel ha-Katan* (1974); and *Taranella* (novel, 1979).

(2) Plays: *Tamar Eshet Er* (1947); *Im Yesh Ẓedek* (1951); *Cambyses* (Heb. 1955); *Casablan* (1958; later, the basis of a musical play); *Eldorado* (1963); *Shimshon* (1968); *Ha-Meragelim ba-Bordel shel Rahav ha-Zonah* (1980). For English translations, see Goell Bibl.

BIBLIOGRAPHY: A. Cohen, *Soferim Ivriyyim Benei Zemannenu* (1964), 73–77; Kressel, Leksikon, 2 (1967), 327. **ADD. BIBLIOGRAPHY:** M. Dekel, *"Darkhei ha-Siaḥ be-Maḥazotav shel Y. Mossinsohn,"* in: *Yerushalayim*, 9–10 (1975), 314–33; H. Shoham, *Etgar u-Meiut ba-Dramah ha-Yisraelit* (1975); G. Shaked, *Ha-Sipporet ha-Ivrit*, 4 (1993), 269–289; S. Levy, *"Elem, Alimut ve-Almenut: Sippur Tamar ke-Maḥazeh Feministi,"* in: *Ha-Kongres ha-Olami le-Mada'ei ha-Yahadut bi-Yrushalayim*, 11:3 (1994), 267–274; idem, in: L. Ben-Zvi (ed.), *Theatre in Israel* (1996), 312–13; Z. Hisner, *"Hamifgash,"* in: *Bishvil ha-Zikkaron*, 22 (1997), 15–18; T. Gidron, *"Idan ha-Parodiyah: Al Ḥasambah, al Ḥalaf im ha-Ru'aḥ ve-al Mah she-beinehem"* in: *Ha-Mishpat* 17 (2004), 2–19.

[Gitta (Aszkenazy) Avinor]

MOSSINSON, BENZION (1878–1942), Hebrew educator and Zionist leader. He was born in Andreyevka, in southern Russia. In 1904 he joined the opposition, headed by Menahem *Ussishkin, to Herzl's *Uganda Scheme and was sent as an emissary to Ereẓ Israel to try to eradicate the leanings to the Uganda idea among certain circles in the *yishuv*. He taught at the Herzlia high school from 1907 and served as its principal from 1912 to 1941. A teacher of Bible, he introduced "Bible criticism" into Ereẓ Israel high schools. Exiled by the Turkish authorities during World War I, Mossinson went to the United States. He was a delegate to Zionist Congresses, being elected to the General Zionist Council and its presidium, and went on missions to various countries on behalf of the Zionist Movement. Mossinson was a founder of the "A faction" of the *General Zionists (which later evolved into the Progressive Party). He edited the General Zionist weekly, *Ha-Ẓiyyoni ha-Kelali*. In 1941 he became director of the Education Department of the Va'ad Leumi. In addition to articles in Russian and Hebrew periodicals, Mossinson published *Ha-Ivrit be-Arẓenu* (1917), and *Ha-Nevi'im* (1919, 1944^2). The Youth Aliyah agricultural school at Magdi'el is named after him.

BIBLIOGRAPHY: Tidhar, 2 (1948), 645; D. Smilanski, *Im Benei Arẓi ve-Iri* (1958), 150–5.

[Abraham Aharoni]

MOSSNER, WALTHER VON (1846–1932), German general. Born in Berlin, Mossner, a superb cavalryman, was commissioned into the King's Hussars in 1865, a personal favor by King William I to Mossner's banker father, despite the hostility of the other officers, who regarded the commissioning of a Jew in a cavalry regiment as an unwelcome precedent. Mossner was eventually baptized and was decorated for distinguished services in the Austro-Prussian War of 1866. In 1872 he was appointed to the German general staff and later was ennobled. He was made William II's aide-de-camp in 1892 and from 1896 to 1898 commanded the third cavalry brigade. Mossner became governor of Strasbourg in 1903 and in the following year was given command of a cavalry division with the rank of major general. He retired in 1910 and was awarded the High Order of the Black Eagle, the last Prussian general to be so honored.

BIBLIOGRAPHY: B. Buelow, *Denkwuerdigkeiten*, 4 (1931). **ADD. BIBLIOGRAPHY:** F.H. Hansen, *Walther von Mossner* (1933) (eulogy).

MOST (Ger. **Bruex**), city in N.W. Bohemia, Czechoslovakia (town no longer exists). A Jewish moneylender is recorded in Most in 1393; there was a Jewish street situated near the monastery in the 14th century. When the Jews were expelled in 1453 most of them settled in *Litomerice. One Jew was allowed to settle in Most in 1839, and after 1848 some Jews from the surrounding villages moved to the city. There were 15 Jews in 1861, when a congregation was established; the synagogue was dedicated in 1872. Some of the rabbis of Most later became eminent: Alexander *Kisch (1874–77), Joseph Samuel *Bloch (1877–79), and Gotthard *Deutsch (1884–91). In 1930 there were 662 Jews in Most (2.4% of the total population). The community owed its importance and affluence to the development of lignite mining by the *Petschek and Weimann firms. During the Sudeten crisis the community dispersed, and the synagogue was destroyed on Nov. 10, 1938. The congregation was reestablished in 1945, mainly by Jews from *Subcarpathian Ruthenia, under the administration of the *Usti nad Labem community. In 1975 Most was evacuated to make way for open-cut mining and ceased to exist. The German-Jewish poet Yermiyahu Oskar Neumann (1894–1981), subsequently of Be'er Toviyyah, Israel, was born in Most.

BIBLIOGRAPHY: M. Halberstam, in: H. Gold (ed.), *Die Juden und Judengemeinden Boehmens* (1934), 70–77; J.C. Pick, in: *Jews of Czechoslovakia*, 1 (1968), 374–5; R. Iltis (ed.), *Die aussaeen unter Traenen…* (1959), 25; G. Deutsch, *Scrolls*, 2 (1917), 321–40; Bondy-Dworský nos. 180–1, 191, 194–5, 198, 200, 202–8, 214, 216–7, 229, 234, 236–8, 240, 246–7, 254, 266, 271, 277. **ADD. BIBLIOGRAPHY:** J. Fiedler, *Jewish Sights of Bohemia and Moravia* (1991), 194.

[Jan Herman]

MOSTEL, ZERO (**Samuel Joel Mostel**; 1915–1977), U.S. actor. Born in Brooklyn, N.Y., into an Orthodox Jewish family, Mostel graduated from City College in 1935, then taught painting and drawing and made extra money entertaining. Working as a comedian at a jazz club called Café Society, Mostel was nicknamed "Zero" by the club's press agent, who said, "Here's a guy who started from nothing." A successful career as a comedian followed in Hollywood and on Broadway, mostly in portrayals of corpulent villains. His leftist views, however, led to his blacklisting, and it was not until 1958, when the political climate had changed, that he resumed full-scale activity. He appeared as Leopold Bloom in an off-Broadway production, *Ulysses in Nighttown* (1958), which was followed by stage successes in such plays as Ionesco's *Rhinoceros* (1961), *A Funny Thing Happened on the Way to the Forum* (1962), *Fiddler on the Roof* (1964, and a revival in 1977). *Fiddler* won nine Tony Awards in 1965 and a special Tony in 1972 for the longest-running musical in Broadway history. Mostel won three Tony Awards: Best Actor in a Drama for *Rhinoceros* (1961) and Best Actor in a Musical for *A Funny Thing Happened on the Way to the Forum* (1963) and *Fiddler on the Roof* (1965). He was also nominated in 1974 as Best Actor in a Drama for a revival of *Ulysses in Nighttown*.

Mostel appeared in a number of movies, including *Panic in the Streets* (1950), *A Funny Thing Happened on the Way to the Forum* (1966), *The Producers* (1968), *The Angel Levine* (1970), *The Hot Rock* (1972), *Rhinoceros* (1974), *Journey into Fear* (1975), *Mastermind* (1976), and *The Front* (1976).

Mostel co-authored *Zero Mostel's Book of Villains* (with Alex Gotfryd and Israel Shenker, 1976) and *170 Years of Show Business* (1978). His son Josh Mostel is an actor.

[Raphael Rothstein and Jonathan Licht / Ruth Beloff (2nd ed.)]

MOSTISKA (Pol. **Mościska**), city in Lvov district, Ukraine; from 1772 to 1918 in eastern Galicia, under Austrian rule. Jews first settled there in the middle of the 16th century, but the community was destroyed during the Chmielnicki massacres. It was renewed in the 18th century. The community was under the jurisdiction of the Council of Red Russia (Reissen) province (see *Councils of the Lands). In 1880 there were 2,123 Jews in Mostiska (51% of the total population) and in 1900 they numbered 2,548 (55%). Jews dominated the towns' trade and artisanship. From 1919 to 1939 the city belonged to Poland. In 1921 the Jewish community numbered 2,328 (49%). The Jewish economy deteriorated because of competition and anti-Jewish boycotts. Before the outbreak of World War II there were about 2,500 Jews in Mostiska. The Germans occupied the town on June 27, 1941, and concentrated Jews from the environs there, numbering about 3,500 persons. During the first half of 1942 more than 500 were sent to labor camps. The Jewish community was liquidated on November 28 (or October 10) 1942, when 2,000 Jews were murdered or sent to Camp Janonska in Lvov. In December 1942 the remaining Jews were sent to the Jaworow ghetto and shared the fate of the local Jews.

BIBLIOGRAPHY: B. Wasiutyński, *Ludność żydowska w Polsce w XIX i XX wiekach* (1930), 96, 107, 116.

[Shmuel Spector (2nd ed.)]

MOSUL, city in N. *Iraq, on the Tigris river. Jews settled in Mosul, or rather in ancient *Nineveh (a suburb of which probably stood on the site of the present Mosul), on the left bank of the Tigris, when Shalmaneser, king of *Assyria (730–712 B.C.E.), conquered *Samaria.

In the middle of the seventh century C.E. there was a Jewish community in Mosul living in a special quarter called *Maḥallat al-Yahūd* ("the Jewish Quarter"; according to Ibn al-Faqīh, BGA V 129; Balādhuri, Futuḥ, 1907, 340). In the middle of the 10th century the Jewish philosopher Ibn Abi Saʿīd ibn Uthmān Saʿīd al-Mawṣilī lived in Mosul and through another Jew asked a contemporary Arab-Christian philosopher to settle several philosophical questions (S. Pines, in: PAAJR, 34 (1966), 103–36). During the first half of the 12th century the Jewish community of Mosul increased when a Muslim principality was established there. It was ruled by Atabeg Zangī (1127–46) and his sons who sought to unite all the small kingdoms in the vicinity of Mosul, to expand his domain up to *Syria, and later to make a joint attack on the Crusaders. Many Jews who had suffered from the Crusaders in Ereẓ Israel came to the town and placed themselves under the protection of the Muslim rulers, who did not harm them. The traveler *Benjamin of Tudela, who visited Mosul before 1170, found "approximately 7,000 Jews headed by R. Zakkai (b. Azariah b. Solomon), the *nasi* who claimed to be from the Davidic line, and R. Joseph, who is called Burhan al-Falak [Ar. "Globe"] who is the [astrologer] to the king Zein al-Dīn" (Benjamin, Travels, p. 94). R. *Pethahiah of Regensburg, who visited Mosul about ten years later, found more than 6,000 Jews and two *nesi'im*: David and Samuel, two cousins who were of the Davidic line. The *nesi'im* had the authority to imprison transgressors. Every Jew paid a tax, one *dīnār* per year, half of which was for the authorities and half for the *nesi'im*. They had fields and vineyards.

In 1289 the head of the flourishing community was the exilarch *David b. Daniel. He, together with 11 members of the local rabbinical college, signed a letter threatening Solomon Petit of Acre, the opponent of *Maimonides, with excommunication (Graetz, Gesch, 7 (c. 1900), 166).

After a brief period of prosperity at the beginning of the Il-Khan rule, at the time of the vizier *Saʿd al-Dawla in the second half of the 13th century, there followed a swift decline and harsh setbacks which impoverished the community. Tamerlane, who captured the city at the end of the 14th century, caused great harm to its inhabitants. Nevertheless, there was a great yeshivah in the city at the beginning of the 16th century, which sent one of its students to the Adoni family to serve as rabbi of the *Baghdad community (A. Ben-Yaacob, *Kehillot Yehudei Kurdistan* (1961), 34–36).

In 1848 the traveler Benjamin II found 450 Jewish families there (Benjamin II, *Masʿei Yisrael* (1859), 34). In the 20th century, there was no improvement in the situation of the Jews of Mosul. The figure of 3,000 Jews in the city remained more of less stable until the beginning of the 20th century. The decline of Mosul's economic standing seems to have contributed to the departure of the Jews for Baghdad. According to the census of 1947 there were in the city 5,688 Jews. The Jewish community of Mosul remained enclosed in its neighborhood, most of them poor and ignorant, a few of them merchants. Schools established by the *Alliance Israélite Universelle in 1906 (for boys) and in 1912 (for girls) were closed at the outbreak of World War I. In about 1930 schools for boys and girls were established by the philanthropist Eliezer *Kadoorie, but there was no Jewish high school. A few children attended government schools and a very small number attained a higher education.

Probably because of their lowly position, the Jews of Mosul did not arouse the envy of their neighbors and were not persecuted. Nevertheless, they lived in great fear throughout this entire period. The rabbis of the community were not highly regarded. During World War I the chief rabbi of the community was R. Elijah Barazani, and from the 1920s, his son R. Solomon Barazani (d. 1960), who remained in this position until he immigrated to Israel in 1951. In the years 1950–55 all the Jews of Mosul immigrated to Israel.

BIBLIOGRAPHY: D.S. Sassoon, *History of the Jews in Baghdad* (1949), index; A. Ben-Yaacob, *Yehudei Bavel* (1965), index; idem. *Kehillot Yehudei Kurdistan* (1961), index. **ADD. BIBLIOGRAPHY:** E. Laniado, *Yehudei Mosul mi-Galut Shomron ad Mivẓa Ezra ve-Nehemiah* (1981); *Enẓiklopedya shel Yehudei Kurdistan* (1993).

[Abraham Ben-Yaacob, Paul Borchardt, and Hayyim J. Cohen / Nissim Kazzaz (2nd ed.)]

MOSZKOWSKI, MORITZ (1854–1925), pianist and composer. Born in Breslau, Moszkowski taught at the Kullak Academy in Berlin until 1897 when he established his residence in Paris. He was renowned as a concert pianist, touring Europe and the United States, and also as a composer of tuneful piano pieces. Of these, *Spanish Dances* have retained a certain popularity, especially in the four-hand version. He also wrote some orchestral works and an opera *Boabdil, der letzte Maurenkoenig* (first performed in Berlin, 1892). His brother ALEXANDER MOSZKOWSKI (1851–1934), a literary critic, published two booklets of musical humor under the pseudonym Anton Notenquetscher, of which excerpts still appear in anthologies.

MOTA, NEHEMIA (d. 1615?), poet whose influence in *Kochi (Cochin) remains very tangible to this day. The Malabari Jews honor the anniversary of his death on the first day of Hannukah with a special banquet followed by singing his *hashkavah* (Sephardi memorial prayer). But his religious significance extends to the Paradesis as well, and his tomb in Jew Town functions as the focal point of many vows, a spot for consolation in times of distress, and as an object of pilgrimage for Christians, Muslims, and Hindus as well as Jews.

The earliest reference in scholarship devoted to Nehemia Mota is found in the 1907 edition of the *Jewish Encyclopedia*, where it is stated rather misleadingly that in 1615 a false messiah appeared among the Jews of Cochin in the person of Nehemia Mota. Most authorities accept that Mota was from the Yemen; others say he was an Italian Jew who came to Kochi via Yemen, and still others hold that he was Polish. He married a woman from the black Jewish community. The 1757 edition of the Shingli Maḥzor contains about 20 of Nehemia's songs which, for reasons unknown, were deleted from the 1769 edition. They have reappeared in recent Israeli editions of the Shingli rite.

Nehemia's tomb is located down an alley in a poor area just south of Jew Town. It resembles the "village deity" (*grammatadevata*) shrines of South India, except for the absence of any images or symbols of the saint. The presence of Nehemia inspires fear as well as blessings – such ambivalent feelings typify the cults of the village deities. Women, Jewish and Gentile, make vows and light candles at the tomb whenever they face a crisis of health, an employment opportunity, or a long journey.

The incorporation of a foreign saint into the Hindu pantheon is not uncommon, and this mechanism serves to acculturate the foreign community into Hindu society.

Nehemia's tomb bears the following Hebrew transcription:

Here rest the remains of
the famous kabbalist,
The influence of the light of whose learning
shines throughout the country,
The perfect sage, the hasid, and
God-fearing Nehemia, the son of
The dear rabbi and sage Abraham Mota.
Our Master departed this life on
Sunday, the 25th of Kislev, 5336.
May his soul rest in peace.

BIBLIOGRAPHY: N. Katz and E.S. Goldberg, *The Last Jews of Cochin: Jewish Identity in Hindu India* (1993); J.B Segal, *A History of the Jews of Cochin* (1993).

[Nathan Katz (2nd ed.)]

MOTAL, ABRAHAM BEN JACOB (1568–1658), rabbi and *dayyan* of Salonika. Motal was born in Salonika, where he studied under Samuel Ḥayyun and Solomon ha-Kohen, whose works he transcribed. He served first as head of the yeshivah of the Old Lisbon community of the city, and on the death of *Ḥayyim Shabbetai in 1647 succeeded him as Salonika's chief rabbi. Among his distinguished disciples were Aaron *Lapapa, Benjamin Melamad of Smyrna, Samuel Adarbi, Abraham ibn Naḥmias, Isaac Alkabeẓ of Constantinople, Abraham *Galanti, and Levi Passariel of Salonika. Of his many works, only *Torat Nazir*, on the tractate of that name, has been published (Salonika, 1821). Appended to it is his *Kunteres Shemot ha-Gittin*. Many of his halakhic discussions appear in the works of contemporary scholars, but most of his responsa have remained in manuscript.

BIBLIOGRAPHY: Conforte, Kore, index; I.S. Emmanuel, *Maẓẓevot Saloniki*, 1 (1963), 322f., no. 736.

[Abraham David]

MOTH (Heb. עָשׁ, *ash* and סָס, *sas*; AV, JPS – "worm"), insect said to eat and destroy clothes (Isa. 51:8; cf. 50:9; Job 13:28). The word *ash* is also used as a synonym for disintegration and destruction (Hos. 5:12; Ps. 39:12). These names refer to the clothes-moth *Tineola*, the larva of which feeds on wool. The metamorphosing larva (caterpillar) spins a cocoon, in which it develops into a chrysalis, to be transformed later into an imago. The tottering house of the wicked is compared to a cocoon (Job 27:18). Other species of moth that damage seeds, fruit, and trees are also to be found in Israel. The Talmud speaks of the *sasa* that infests trees (TJ, Ḥag. 2:3, 78a, according to the reading of Ha-Meiri; cf. Yoma 9b: the *sas-magor* which attacks cedars). The *noses* that destroys trees (Isa. 10:18) may be the *sas*, the reference here being to the moth which bores into trees, such as the larvae of the *Zeuzera pirina*, one of the worst arboreal pests in Israel.

BIBLIOGRAPHY: Lewysohn, Zool., 308; F.S. Bodenheimer, *Animal and Man in Bible Lands* (1960), 78, 114, 140; J. Feliks, *Animal World of the Bible* (1962), 126f.

[Jehuda Feliks]

MOTION PICTURES. Since the early years of motion pictures, Jews have played a major role in the development of the industry and have been prominent in all its branches. This is true not only of Hollywood, where the role played by Jews is generally known and acknowledged, but of the German film industry up to the Nazi era, Russian film production up to the time of the Stalinist purges of the 1930s, the British film industry up to the present, and contemporary underground motion pictures in the United States. The motion picture was created at a time when the Jews were seeking entry into the economic and cultural life of their host countries. Their involvement with motion pictures was due to a number of factors: the film business had not developed a tradition of its own and had no vested interests to defend; participation in it required no intimate knowledge of the vernacular; and films were not yet the realm of businessmen, entrepreneurs, or professional entertainers, but rather scientists, such as Edison and Lumière, who had no idea of the economic and industrial future of their inventions. In addition, the motion picture was initially regarded as a low-grade form of entertainment – suitable only for the immigrant or the uneducated masses – rather than a valid art form, and those connected with films were held in contempt. New immigrants, therefore, found it relatively easy to enter this field, and Jewish immigrants used the opportunity to transform the media from a marginal branch of entertainment into a multi-million dollar industry.

[Nahman Ingber]

In the United States

A century ago, motion pictures went from invention to entertainment to being an industry. First introduced in 1896, moving pictures were at first a novelty shown at the end of vaudeville shows or in penny arcades. Sigmund "Pop" Lubin (1851–1923), a Jewish immigrant from Germany built one of the first movie houses in 1899 (he charged ten cents, twice the customary rate). By 1907, more than 100 Nickelodeons – theaters seating fewer than 300 persons and charging a nickel per showing – had opened in New York, and more than a quarter of those were located in the densely populated Lower East Side – home of the great majority of Jewish immigrants.

Max Aronson (1882–1971), who changed his name to Gilbert Maxwell Anderson, was the first movie-star cowboy. He had played a role in Edwin S. Porter's *The Great Train Robbery* (1903), the first genuine American feature film. After working at Vitagraph as a production assistant Anderson moved to Chicago and then to California. In 1907, he cofounded the Essenay Co., where he worked as a writer, producer, and actor. In 1908 he launched the "Bronco Billy" western series, which was a great success, producing 375 films in a seven-year period.

On Christmas Eve 1908 Mayor McClellan of New York closed all the nickelodeon theaters calling them immoral. Leading the successful fight to have them reopened were former garment worked turned exhibitor William *Fox (1879–1952) and former newsboy Marcus Loew (1870–1927). Competition was so fierce among exhibitors and producers that in 1909 Thomas Edison signed an agreement with most of the large film companies that led to the founding of the Motion Picture Patents Co. The theater owners were forced to rent projectors and films only from the Motion Picture Patents Co. – in effect Edison was creating a monopoly to keep new independent producers out. Fox and German Jewish immigrant Carl *Laemmle (1867–1939), an exhibitor turned producer and distributor objected to such control; they sued and won in 1912. Laemmle relocated to Southern California with his Universal Film Manufacturing Company (later Universal Studios) leading the exodus of film producers to the West.

By 1909 the nickelodeon boom was over; by 1915 the age of movie palaces began. By 1915, movie production had effectively moved to California. The age of the movie moguls had begun.

The first large Hollywood company was Paramount, which was founded and managed by Adolph Zukor (1873–1976). Together with Daniel *Frohman, a theatrical agent, Zukor decided to import a prestigious European film, *Queen Elizabeth* (1912), starring Sarah *Bernhardt. The film was shown in legitimate theater halls and was reviewed in the regular press, enabling Zukor to claim that film was a legitimate art form. Under the slogan "Famous Players in Famous Plays," Zukor produced films based on literary and dramatic works, with casts of well-established, legitimate actors. He also initiated the practice of advertising the "star" actors in films; the first "star" he promoted was Mary Pickford.

Jesse *Lasky (1880–1958) owned a similar production company in Hollywood, and in 1917 he and Zukor founded a joint distribution company called Paramount; two years later their production companies also merged. Paramount produced, distributed, and exhibited films through its own worldwide theater chain. Lasky also brought two of his partners, Samuel *Goldwyn (Goldfish; 1882–1974) and Cecil B. De Mille, into the new company. As Paramount continued to grow, smaller producers were compelled either to disband or merge with one another in order to compete. Paramount's commercial power was based upon the block-booking system that forced local exhibitors to rent an outline group of Paramount's films, rather than choose only those they desired.

One producer who tried to fight Paramount was Carl Laemmle, who was developing Universal into one of the giants. William Fox, his former partner in the fight against the Patents Co., joined Twentieth Century and also made it into one of the large Hollywood companies.

Louis B. *Mayer, who owned a chain of movie theaters (mainly in New England), purchased the Metro Co. in Hollywood (which had its own studios) and founded the Metro-Mayer Co. Samuel Goldwyn left Paramount in 1919 and, together with the Selwyn brothers, founded the Goldwyn Co. In 1924 it merged with Metro-Mayer to form Metro-Goldwyn-Mayer (MGM), which was headed by Mayer; Goldwyn himself did not join MGM and instead established one of Hollywood's outstanding independent production companies.

Columbia, owned and dominated by Harry *Cohn from 1929 until his death in 1958, was built into a large company during the 1930s by producing a series of successful films by the clever use of stars and directors.

Warner Brothers was founded by Sam, Jack, Albert, and Harry *Warner, who started out with a small exhibition hall and later became the managers of the First National Theater chain, and eventually formed their own company. In 1923 they bought out the Vitagraph Company, owners of the Vitaphone, which was a sort of record that played simultaneously with the silent film. Seeking to improve their difficult financial situation, in 1926 they developed and presented the first film with its own musical score.

A year later Warner Brothers produced *The Jazz Singer*, starring Al *Jolson, containing both dialogue and singing parts. Written by Samson Raphaelson, based on his play, and starring Al Jolson as the son of a cantor torn between the observant and secular world, the film was a success and brought about the "sound revolution" in motion pictures and made Warner Brothers into one of the great Hollywood companies. Thus the majority of large Hollywood Studios were founded and controlled by Jews.

In addition, the first bank to finance the film industry was the Jewish-owned Kuhn, Loeb and Co., in 1919.

These founding fathers of the movie studio were part of a first generation who created "the dream factory," where Jewish immigrant movie moguls, eager to leave the Old World behind, became more American than the Americans (see N. Gabler, *An Empire of Their Own: How the Jews Created Hollywood*).

Other Jews who played a leading role in the large companies were Barney *Balaban, who joined Paramount and became its president in 1936; Nicholas and Joseph M. Schenk, who became presidents of MGM (while Mayer was in charge of its Hollywood operations); and Irving *Thalberg, who was production manager of MGM from the end of the 1920s until his death in 1936. Thalberg, who was responsible for production at the age of 23, was the wunderkind of the film industry and became the symbol of the successful Hollywood producer.

In the two years following Warner's *The Jazz Singer*, Hollywood frantically set about converting to sound. As the studios began importing New York talent, many Jews landed in Hollywood. Among the Jewish performers who made their way west were Jack *Benny, Ben Blue, Fanny *Brice, George *Burns, Harry Green, Ted Lewis, the *Marx Brothers, Sophie *Tucker, and Ed *Wynn. In addition, directors and writers shifted from theater to film, including men such as George *Cukor, Sidney Buchman, Norman *Krasna, Charles Lederer, Joseph *Mankiewicz, S.J. *Perelman, Robert Riskin, Morrie Ryskind, and Ben *Hecht.

In the 1920s and 1930s another wave of Jewish émigrés came to Hollywood. They were mainly directors and actors.

Ernst *Lubitsch, who came to the United States in 1923 after achieving fame in Germany, was best known for directing sophisticated comedies with a finesse that became known as the "Lubitsch touch." Among his films were *Ninotchka*, *To Be Or Not To Be*, and *Cluny Brown*. For several years Lubitsch served as president of production of Paramount, the first working director to also be head of a studio.

Erich van *Stroheim, an Austrian-born actor and director, became known in the 1920s for his realistic direction, especially in the film *Greed*. His acting captivated audiences for a period of 30 years.

Josef von *Sternberg directed several films in the United States in the 1920s; he directed *Blue Angel* in Germany in 1930 and became Marlene Dietrich's permanent director, famous for a grand style that made Dietrich into a screen goddess. William *Wyler, who was born in Germany, began his career as a director in 1928; his films were based mainly on adaptations of literary works, and he was particularly successful in the direction of female stars. Billy *Wilder also began his career in Germany, together with Fred Zinnemann and Robert Siodmak. Wilder's films were distinguished by their sharp humor and bitter irony.

Other Jewish actors and directors who arrived in Hollywood from Europe in the 1920s and 1930s leaving their past and sometimes their names behind, were Leslie *Howard, Peter *Lorre, and Michael *Curtiz.

Curtiz, a Hungarian, would go on to direct *Casablanca* – perhaps the greatest American movie – as well as other American classics, including *Captain Blood*, *Yankee Doodle Dandy*, *Robin Hood*, and *White Christmas*.

White Christmas is a great example of the ways in which Jews assimilated American culture, making it their own. "White Christmas" was first born as a song written by Irving *Berlin (né Izzy Baline in Siberia) for the 1942 film *Holiday Inn*. Wishing for an idealized world "I used to know" that is "merry and bright," the lyrics are, at the same time, wistful, hopeful, and all-inclusive. The song was so popular (it is one of the most popular songs of all time), it spawned a movie of its own.

The movie *White Christmas* as directed by Curtiz pairs Bing Crosby with the very versatile Danny Kaye (born David Kaminsky) in a romantic musical comedy, written by Norman

*Krasna, about two World War II veterans who achieve success in show business and then success in love. Its message is not religious, but universal.

Curtiz presents the world as it was and as it should be. Curtiz, like Berlin, was often critiqued for having no signature style. But for Curtiz and Berlin's generation of Jews, being able to work successfully in any number of styles was a virtue unto itself. Making a Christmas movie was not about assimilation, it was about versatility.

Curtiz had already assimilated back in Hungary when he first changed his name from Mano Kaminer to Mihaly Kertesz (a more Hungarian-sounding name). The jump from Kertesz to Curtiz was itself a testament to having an identity that was easily translated – that worked, literally and figuratively, in any culture. America was the land of freedom, and for Jewish directors and actors, it was a country where you could do anything, even make a Christmas movie.

In 1951, when Mayer was dismissed from his post at MGM, he was replaced by Dore *Schary, who had built a career as a writer. A similar position was held by William Goetz, who was head of 20th Century-Fox and, at a later stage, of Universal International Co.

Some of the most successful Jewish producers employed by the studios included Joe *Pasternak, Walter Wanger, Arthur *Freed, Jerry Wald, Pandro S. *Berman, among others. An even more important influence on the film industry – because of their greater control over the nature of the finished product – were the independent producers, such as Mike *Todd, producer of *Around the World in 80 Days*, who was connected with the Todd-AO method of cinematography; and David O. *Selznick, the son of Lewis J. Selznick, one of the industry's pioneers. Next to Samuel Goldwyn, David Selznick became the most famous and successful independent producer. He was responsible for the production of *Gone with the Wind* (1939), which was one of the most profitable films in Hollywood's history, having grossed $72,000,000 through 1970. Among his other films were *David Copperfield*, *King Kong*, *Spellbound*, and *Rebecca*.

Hal Roach, one of the most prolific producers of comedies, was responsible for a part of the Harold Lloyd series and for the Laurel and Hardy films during the 1920s and 1930s. Sam *Spiegel, who maintained a high artistic standard, using outstanding directors and choosing serious subjects, produced such films as *The African Queen*, *On the Waterfront*, *The Bridge on the River Kwai*, and *Lawrence of Arabia*. The *Mirisch Brothers, originally theater owners, established their own company in 1957. After the decline of the big studios, it became one of the most successful Hollywood enterprises, producing *West Side Story* and *The Great Escape*.

After 1945, Stanley *Kramer, an independent producer who was connected with Columbia, produced such films as *Home of the Brave*, *Champion*, *High Noon*, and *Death of a Salesman*. Later on he also directed *On the Beach*, *Judgment at Nuremberg*, and *Ship of Fools*. Kramer believed that audiences wanted films that dealt with contemporary life.

Joseph E. *Levine, who began as a theater owner and became an importer of cheap or erotic Italian films, then turned to the financing of outstanding European films (*8½*), and later produced such films as *Where Love Has Gone*, *The Carpetbaggers*, and *Harlow*.

Among Jewish directors who earned success at the box office or received great critical acclaim one must include Jules *Dassin, Garson *Kanin, Robert *Aldrich, James *Brooks, Fred *Zinnemann, Joseph L. *Mankiewicz, Sidney *Lumet, John *Frankenheimer, Alan Pakula, Martin *Ritt, Roman *Polanski, Michael Curtiz, Mervyn Le Roy, Otto *Preminger, Richard *Brooks, George *Cukor (d. 1983), Daniel *Mann (d. 1991), Delbert *Mann, and Robert *Rossen.

The number of successful Jewish scriptwriters is so vast that only a few can be mentioned here. Among the most famous were Ben *Hecht, Samson *Raphaelson; George *Axelrod; Carl *Forman; Herman *Mankiewicz; Aaron *Sorkin; William *Goldman; Nora *Ephron; Eric Roth; Norman Krasna; and Abby *Mann.

Among the prominent composers of musical scores are Irving *Berlin, Alfred Newman, Franz Waxman, Dmitri Tiomkin (d. 1979), Elmer *Bernstein, and Burt *Bacharach.

The first great sex symbol was Theda *Bara (1885–1955), born Theodisia Goodman, whose portrayal of a seductive vampire inspired the appellation "Vamp." Other Jewish actresses known as sex symbols included Mae *West, Mirna Loy, Sylvia Sydney, Hedy *Lamarr, Judy *Holliday, and more recently, Debra *Winger, Rachel Weisz, and Natalie Portman. There is also a long tradition of Jewish comediennes in which Mae West would also be included, but which begins with Fanny *Brice, and stretches to Barbra *Streisand and Bette *Midler.

A small sample of well-known Jewish actors and actresses includes the Marx Brothers, Danny *Kaye, Jerry *Lewis, Paul *Muni, Edward G. *Robinson, Eddie *Cantor, John *Garfield, Al Jolson, Peter Lorre, Zero *Mostel, Tony *Curtis, Alan *Arkin, Lee J. *Cobb, Kirk *Douglas, Melvyn *Douglas, Dustin *Hoffman, Elliot *Gould, Alla *Nazimova, Louise *Rainer, Paulette *Goddard, Shelley *Winters, Polly Bergen, Tovah *Feldshuh, and Lilli *Palmer. A number of film stars converted to Judaism including Sammy *Davis Junior, Marilyn *Monroe, and Elizabeth *Taylor.

By the mid-1930s ethnically distinct characters, especially Jews, were no longer considered desirable by studio heads. The degree to which Hollywood eliminated a Jewish presence can be assessed by comparing *The House of Rothschild* (1934) with *The Life of Emile Zola* (1937). In the former there is no question of Rothschild's identity. By contrast, *The Life of Emile Zola* treats the infamous *Dreyfus affair, yet oddly never reveals that Dreyfus was a Jew.

Despite Hitler's election as chancellor of the Third Reich in 1933, and the growing militarization, civilian restrictions, and legislated discrimination against Jews in Germany, Hollywood remained totally silent on the subject throughout the 1930s. The producers reflected the neutralist philosophy emanating from Washington. MGM's *Three Comrades* (1938) and the Warner Bros. film *Confessions of a Nazi Spy* (1939) merely intimated at the true horror.

Charlie Chaplin, a non-Jew (whom antisemites often labeled "Jewish"), broke ranks by producing *The Great Dictator* (1940), a comedy which lampooned Hitler and depicted contemporary conditions in his mythical Tomania.

With the onset of World War II, Hollywood set about dealing with Fascism, although it was less explicit about Jewish persecution. But it was not until Pearl Harbor that Hollywood went to war in full force. Increasingly the victims were identified as Jews rather than the previous nomenclature non-Aryans (ironically a Nazi classification). Titles include *The Pied Piper* (1942), *None Shall Escape* (1944), and *Address Unknown* (1944).

The war also saw the rise of the combat film, which depicted a fighting unit of ethnically and geographically diverse soldiers. Most typically Jews functioned as comic relief. More serious depictions of the Jewish participation in World War II can be found in *The Purple Heart* (1944) and *Pride of the Marines* (1945), where characters evidence intelligence, bravery, and patriotism.

Following the war and the full knowledge of the Nazi atrocities, it was natural to ask, "How could this happen?" "Could it happen here?" The response to these questions was *Crossfire* (1947), a murder thriller, and *Gentleman's Agreement* (1947), a drama which presented a journalist, played by Gregory Peck, posing as a Jew to gain firsthand experience of discrimination. Both films received critical and popular acclaim and, despite initial concern on the part of Jewish agencies, both works proved through testing to be effective tools in combating prejudice.

However, it is important to note that when Hollywood needed a handsome actor to play a role where the character was Jewish, such as King David, they preferred a non-Jew such as Gregory Peck to play him, as he did in *David and Batsheba* (1951), later reprised by Richard Gere in *King David* (1985).

The postwar period also produced an unexpected backlash against Jews, most particularly in Hollywood. Spurred on by anti-Communist fears, conservative individuals were able to effect their prejudices through the workings of the House Committee on Un-American Activities. Of the original "Hollywood Ten" who faced investigation and charges, seven were Jewish.

However, the films of the 1950s consistently promoted tolerance. In no decade are screen Jews so intelligent, patriotic, and unqualifiably likeable. At no other time is religious tolerance and good will so consistently foregrounded.

Beginning in 1951 with *The Magnificent Yankee*, which depicts Louis *Brandeis, to the screen adaptation of *Dark at the Top of the Stairs* (1960), the films all preach the same message – antisemitism is no longer acceptable; antisemitism is un-American.

In between these two works, several important films came to the screen. In 1952 Dore *Schary adapted *Ivanhoe*, with Elizabeth Taylor in the role of Rebecca. In 1953 the first remake of *The Jazz Singer*, directed by Michael Curtiz, appeared with Danny Thomas in the lead role. The once Orthodox family have now become assimilated Reform Jews. And in 1959 Paul Muni played the kindly old doctor in the film version of *The Last Angry Man* (1959). Antisemitism in the U.S. army became the subject of two films – *The Naked and the Dead* (1958) and *The Young Lions* (1958).

Other films of importance include *Majorie Morningstar* (1958), the first major film since the 1920s to focus on Jewish domestic life and a precursor of the self-critical approach of the 1960s; *Me and the Colonel* (1958), a bittersweet comedy about World War II starring Danny Kaye; *The Diary of Anne Frank* (1959), the first Hollywood film to focus exclusively on the plight of Jews caught in the Holocaust; *The Juggler* (1953), starring Kirk Douglas, in the first U.S. production shot entirely in Israel; and *Exodus* (1960), the film which fixed Israel in the American imagination for years to come.

Exodus with the handsome Paul *Newman, whose father was Jewish, and in which Newman appears bare-chested wearing a Jewish Star, paved the ground for a new sex symbol: the Jewish Man. The 1960s were a time when the anti-hero took center stage and such non-traditional leading men as Dustin Hoffman, Elliott Gould, and Richard *Dreyfus became stars.

Not since the silent era had so many Jewish characters appeared, especially in major roles. Beginning in 1967 with Dustin Hoffman in *The Graduate*, a series of comedies set a new direction and established Jewish humor as a major mainstream trend for the next two decades. Films such as *The Producers* (1968), *Funny Girl* (1968), *Take the Money and Run* (1969), and *Goodbye, Columbus* (1969) launched a new Jewish sensibility in America.

Although comedy dominated the decade in terms of Jewish film, the Holocaust was approached in two works with forceful impact. First, Abby Mann's *Judgment at Nuremburg* (1961) soberly approached the range of Nazi injustices. Then in 1965 *The Pawnbroker*, starring Rod Steiger in the role of a German survivor, was the first American fictional work to treat the camp experience with such harrowing reality. Closely related, *The Fixer* (1968) depicted Jewish victimization under the Czarist regime, and by implication called attention to current Soviet discrimination.

The decades closed with one of the most celebrated films about Jewish life ever to reach the screen – *Fiddler on the Roof* (1971). Based on *Sholem Aleichem, the film exposed millions around the world to Jewish family life, Jewish traditions, and the shtetl.

In the 1970s and 1980s, in such films as *Play It Again Sam* (1972), *Annie Hall* (1977), and *Manhattan* (1979), Woody *Allen became the embodiment of an urban Jewish humor-filled sensibility, and of a seeming nebbish who won the girl (who was often non-Jewish).

The other major comedies of this era focus once again on domestic life, some with a nostalgic look towards the past; others with a derisive look at the present. Films include *My*

Favorite Year (1982), *Down and Out in Beverly Hills* (1986), *Brighton Beach Memoirs* (1987), and *Radio Days* (1987).

Meanwhile Jewish women began to have their say in films such as *The Way We Were* (1973), starring Barbra Streisand; *Hester Street* (written and directed by Joan Micklin *Silver); and *Girlfriends* (1978, written and directed by Claudia Weill).

Jewish women came to the fore with great strength, in large measure due to women's participation in production. Beginning with *Private Benjamin* (1980), co-produced and starring Goldie *Hawn as the Jewish American Princess who finally grows into an autonomous woman, Jewish women are admirably depicted in *Tell Me a Riddle* (1980), *Baby, It's You* (1983), *Hanna K* (1983), *Yentl* (1983), *St. Elmo's Fire* (1985), *Sweet Lorraine* (1987), and *Dirty Dancing* (1987). Among the Jewish women active in film as directors, screenwriters, and producers were: Barbra Streisand, Susan Seidelman, Claudia Weill, Lee *Grant, Joan Micklin Silver, Gail Parent, and Sherry *Lansing (who would go on to be chairman of Paramount).

The 1970s also introduced many new types: the Jewish gambler (*The Gambler*, 1974), the Jewish madam (*For Pete's Sake*, 1974), blacklisted artists (*The Front*, 1976), the Jewish gumshoe (*The Big Fix*, 1976), the Jewish lesbian (*A Different Story*, 1978), a Yiddish cowboy (*The Frisco Kid*, 1979), a Jewish union organizer (*Norma Rae*, 1979), a Jewish murderess (*The Last Embrace*, 1979), and an elderly Jew pushed to violence (*Boardwalk*, 1979). *The Frisco Kid* deserves special mention. Despite its high comedy, the film is one of the few Hollywood works to treat Jewish values as a serious topic. Briefly stated, the film shows the confrontation between talmudic piety and American pragmatism, as personified by characters played by Gene *Wilder and Harrison *Ford, as the two influenced each other as Jew met Gentile in the New Land.

For the rest of the 20th Century Jews assumed a wide variety of roles. From the romantic, such as Billy *Crystal in *When Harry met Sally* to non-Jewish Ian McKellen as the evil Holocaust survivor Dr. Magneto in *X-Men* (2000), Jewish actors and Jews on screen took on a democratic smorgasbord of roles. Jewish leading men continue to be few and far between but a new crop of handsome young and versatile actors such as Ben *Stiller, Jason Schwartzman, Adam *Sandler, and David Duchovny continue to redefine Jewish actors on the screen.

In other areas, some things never change. Just as the non-Jewish Natalie Wood played Marjorie Morningstar, in the romantic comedy from Nancy Meyers, *Something's Got to Give* (2003), Diane Keaton is featured as playing a Jewish woman and Frances McDormand as her sister.

Regarding the Holocaust as a subject for Hollywood, prior to the 1980s, the Shoah was mainly used as a backdrop from which to create thrillers such as *The Odessa File* (1974), *Marathon Man* (1976), and *The Boys from Brazil* (1978). Only *The Man in the Glass Booth* (1975), based on a stage play, stands apart. However, after the successful 1978 TV broadcast of the mini-series *The Holocaust*, a proliferation of Holocaust-themed or related films were made, most notably *Schindler's List* (1993).

Finally, the beginning of the 21st century has been witness to a landmark event: the release of the first animated Chanukah feature-length movie, Adam Sandler's *Eight Crazy Nights*. Sandler's appeal is his endearing cretin-savant aesthetic: although his mind may be trapped in adolescence, his heart inevitably is in the right place.

In sum, 100 years after the start of the movie industry, the landscape is much changed. Born in America, the second, third, and fourth generation of Jews in Hollywood were raised during a time when institutional antisemitism had all but disappeared and where assimilation was not so much a goal as a norm. The melting pot has given way to the multicultural quilt – and religious choice is as varied as the combo plates on a Chinese menu. Jewish actors and directors continue to work in Hollywood making a diverse selection of studio and independent films. They no longer need to hide their religion or ethnicity but they are free to make movies on any subject, Christmas included.

Hollywood belongs to no religion – save a corporate one. The most marked change in the motion picture industry is one regarding ownership. The last several decades of the 20th century has seen tremendous change and consolidation in the motion picture industry. There are almost no truly independent studios, and the studios once owned by Jews are now part of international conglomerates and publicly traded companies. Warner Brothers was acquired by Time-Warner and in 2006 includes such former mini-major studios as New Line and Castle Rock; Disney is a public company that includes the Miramax independent film label and ABC television networks; Fox is owned by Rupert Murdoch's News Corp.; Columbia by the Japanese conglomerate Sony; Universal was sold to Matsushita, then to Edgar *Bronfman's Seagram, then to the French utility Vivendi, and then to General Electric which has also acquired the NBC television network. Paramount is owned by Viacom and, as of January 1, 2006, is part of a company that also includes MTV networks.

Stephen *Spielberg, Jeffrey Katzenberg and David Geffen launched their own studio in 1994, DREAMWORKS SKG. Although they produced such successful movies as *Shrek*, *Collateral*, *Seabiscuit*, and *Minority Report*, among others, they could not remain independent. They spun off Dreamworks Animation as a public company, and at the end of 2005 they concluded an agreement to sell Dreamworks' movie division to Paramount.

The first generation of Jewish movie moguls owned the studios. On the business side, adding to Hollywood's reputation as a Jewish industry was the fact that many of the talent agencies were founded and staffed by Jews – to mention a few: William Morris (founded by William Morris); MCA, led by Lew Wasserman and Jules Stein; International Creative Management (ICM), managed by Marvin Josephson, and in 2006 by Jeff Berg. One of the most powerful Hollywood agencies was founded by William Morris defectors Michael *Ovitz, Ron Meyer, and Bill Haber. CAA is led in 2006 by Richard Lovett. One of the newer agencies is Endeavor, whose founders include Ari Emmanuel.

At the beginning of the 21st century, by contrast, the studios are owned by corporations and controlled in great part by non-Jews. A great many Jewish people have continued to work in Hollywood as executives, agents, and attorneys. They are involved at every level in the creative decisions affecting the movies made in America and seen the world over. But increasingly, they are making those decisions with their eyes on a mass audience and for corporate masters concerned with the bottom line, profits and stock performance. So although there are many Jewish executives, they are merely employees, serving at the whim of the marketplace and their masters.

In this light, it is legitimate to wonder: can the movie industry still be considered Jewish?

[Tom Teicholz (2nd ed.)]

Yiddish films were made in the U.S. from the 1920s. These films, for all their bathos, were a uniquely authentic expression. Although provincial and stylized, they reflected and preserved a Jewish way of life, stressing the unity of the Jewish people, traditional values, belief in human goodness, the triumph of justice, respect for education, and the ideal of the happy family nucleus. The success of Yiddish shorts in Jewish neighborhoods in the late 1930s led to the production of full-length features. The stars of the Yiddish theater, such as Maurice Schwartz, Boris Thomashevsky, and Celia Alder, participated in these films, which were heavily melodramatic and sentimental. The films have a "happy ending" often with a family reconciliation. Religious ceremonies were often portrayed as part of the action. Some of the films were adapted from Yiddish stage classics, such as Hirschbein's *Green Fields* and Gordin's *Mirele Efros*.

Serious Yiddish film-making ended in the U.S. at the same time as it was being brought to an end in Poland. The decline of the Yiddish theater in the 1930s in the U.S. was paralleled by a similar trend in the Yiddish cinema. After 1940, the only Yiddish films being produced were made up of vaudeville acts taken from the "Borscht Belt," the chain of Jewish hotels in the Catskill Mountains hosting vaudeville acts. These, too, dried up within a few years. The end of the Yiddish cinema was inevitable with the disappearance of Yiddish as a spoken language in the younger generation. Moreover, even where the language was still spoken, the naiveté of the Yiddish films had no appeal to an acculturated and sophisticated public.

[Geoffrey Wigoder]

In Britain

Although the proportion of Jews involved in films was much smaller than in America, they made a significant contribution to the British film industry and were among its pioneers. For a long period, American competition made it impossible for the British motion picture to gain a foothold in the world market. It was a Hungarian Jew, Sir Alexander *Korda, who finally pulled the British industry out of the doldrums. Korda had been a pioneer of film making in Hungary and after World War I had worked in Austria, Germany, France, and Hollywood. In 1930 he moved to Britain and founded the London Films Company, for which he directed and produced some of the best films credited to Britain in the 1930s and the 1940s. His success was due to his fine artistic sense, his ability to build artists from different fields into a working team, and his belief that by employing great British actors and choosing the proper subjects, the British film could be adapted to suit the American market. His greatest success as a director was *The Private Life of Henry VIII* (1933), in which he punctured the formal rigidity associated with royalty; he had other successes in *The Private Life of Don Juan* and in *Rembrandt*. His greatest achievements were as the producer of such films as *The Scarlet Pimpernel, Catherine the Great, Elephant Boy, Lady Hamilton*, and *The Third Man*, which established Britain's reputation for fine films. His brother, Zoltan Korda, also worked for London Films as a successful director. Sir Michael *Balcon, who was initially in charge of Alfred Hitchcock's British films, earned his reputation after World War II managing the operations of Ealing Studios. This company created the series of comedies (known as the "Ealing Comedies") that depict the eccentric British character with subtle humor and irony (such films as *Kind Hearts and Coronets, Whisky Galore*, and *The Ladykillers*). Another outstanding producer was Harry Saltzman, a partner in the James Bond series; he later produced mainly war films and, from time to time, low-budget artistic films. Anatole de Grunwald also was a producer of note. A noted young director was John Schlesinger, who was responsible for such films as *Billy Liar, Darling*, and *Midnight Cowboy*. Among the outstanding British film actors were Leslie *Howard, Elizabeth *Bergner (who moved from Germany in the 1930s, as did Anton Walbrook), Claire *Bloom, Yvonne Mitchell, Laurence *Harvey, and Peter *Sellers.

[Nahman Ingber]

In France

What is a Jewish film? A film that is produced by a Jewish producer? A film that is made by a Jewish director? A film that has a Jewish theme? One may more specifically ask this question about France, for until the 1950s characters were not identified in French movies by religious or ethnic affiliation. However, after World War II it was impossible to ignore the Jewish presence in France, or the Holocaust.

In 1937, Jean Renoir directed *La grande illusion* ("The Great Illusion"), a pacifist film which depicts a group of French prisoners during World War I. One of them, Rosenthal, is a stereotyped *nouveau riche* Jew who, however, stands by his friends. At the end of the film, one of these friends, played by Jean Gabin, let's the cat out of the bag. "I never could stand Jews!" he says. This cutting remark and Rosenthal's ambivalent portrait brought accusations of antisemitism against Renoir. The controversy itself shows all the ambiguity of the Jews' situation in French society, for Rosenthal is generous and human. In his next film, La *règle du jeu* ("The Rules of the Game," 1938), the subtle and grand figure of the host goes under the name La Chesnay, but it is clearly said that he is of Jewish origin. It is significant that Marcel Dalio played both these parts. He was himself a Jew and had to leave France in

1940. The cliché about Jews who wish to believe they are accepted in French society is also the main theme of Julien Duvivier's *David Golder* (1931), from Irène Nemirovsky's book. After becoming wealthy, David Goldet is despised by his wife and daughter; he ends his days as a ruined and lonely old man. Unlike Renoir's films, *David Goldet* is undoubtedly antisemitic, echoing all the physical and psychological stereotypes spread by France's extreme right in the 1930s.

From the 1950s, documentaries – made from archives or from witness interviews – shed new light on the Jews' lot in French society during World War II. Thus in *Nuit et Brouillard* ("Night and Fog," 1955) by Alain Resnais, in *Le temps du ghetto* ("The Ghetto Time," 1968) by Frederic Rossif, *Le chagrin et la pitié* ("Distress and Compassion," 1971) by Marcel Ophuls, *Français si vous saviez* ("French Citizens, If Only You Knew," 1973) by André Harris and Alain de Sédouy, French eyes were opened to the realities of French society and the behavior of French politicians toward Jews under the German occupation. In other respects, at the same time Frederic Rossif and Claude Lanzmann made documentaries about Israel.

Some Jewish film makers were interested in making semi-autobiographical films on this period as well. These include Claude Berri (*Le vieil homme et l'enfant*, "The Old Man and the Boy," 1957), Henri Glaeser (*Une larme dans l'océan*, "A Tear in the Ocean," 1973), and Jacques Doillon (*Un sac de billes*, "A Bag of Marbles," 1976, from Joseph Joffo's book). Others produced stories in the context of collaboration: *Le dernier métro* ("The Last Subway," 1980) by François Truffaut tells the story of a Jewish director in Paris who hides in a cellar. Conversely, *Lacombe Lucien* (1974) by Louis Malle – from Patrick *Modiano's book – absolves the hero from responsibility (he becomes a militiaman by chance) and depicts Jews as passive victims. Some years later, Malle made *Au revoir les enfants* ("Good Bye, Children"), which expressed feelings of guilt about the persecution of Jewish children. In 2005, *La maison de Nina* ("Nina's House") by Richard Dembo told the story of young survivors of the Nazi camps.

Several documentaries have been made with survivors: *La mémoire est-elle soluble dans l'eau?* ("Is Memory Soluble in Water?" 1995) by Charles Najman and *La petite maison dans la forêt de bouleaux* ("The Little House in the Birch-Tree Forest," 2003) by Marceline Loridan. One must mention too Emmanuel Finkiel's work, especially *Voyages* (1999), dealing with the memory of the Holocaust, moving on, and Jewish identity in the Diaspora and Israel.

There have also been comedies with popular actors like Louis de Funès and Roger Hanin. Their humor and optimism as they show reconciliation among people made them successful films. Such films are *Les aventures de Rabbi Jacob* ("Rabbi Jacob's Adventures," 1973) by Gérard Oury, *Le coup de sirocco* ("Gust of Sirocco," 1979), *Le Grand Pardon* ("Yom Kippur," 1982), and *Le grand carnaval* ("The Great Carnival," 1985), the last three by Alexandre Arcady. *La vérité si je mens* ("Damn It If I'm Lying," 1996) by Thomas Gilou gives Jewish humor a different perspective with a Sephardi contribution dealing with North African Jews who settled in France from the 1960s. And Claude *Lelouch evokes men and women of all origins who are thrown into distress by History.

The most highly acclaimed of all these Jewish films was undoubtedly Claude *Lanzmann's masterpiece, *Shoah* (1985).

[Annie Goldmann (2nd ed.)]

In Germany

As in the United States, the impetus to produce films catering to popular taste in Germany came from Jewish owners of a chain of theaters. In 1913 Paul Davidson and Hermann Fellner, who had been exhibiting films since 1905, established their own production company and made films based on German folklore and legend, as well as comedies (it was for this company that Ernst Lubitsch made his early films). In 1919 Erich Pommer directed the Deutsches Eclair (Decla) film company, which some time later merged with UFA, a company that produced outstanding German films in the 1920s and the early 1930s. Pommer remained at the head of the company and determined the style and quality of the films in this period. He went in for daring artistic experiments and provided ample opportunity for talented film people to prove their mettle. As a result, the German film became the most advanced of its time; this was, in fact, the golden age of the German film industry. Lubitsch began his career with a series of comedies (some of them against a Jewish background) and then turned to the direction of light-hearted historical films. His overwhelming success resulted in his being invited to the United States. Another film produced by Pommer, *The Cabinet of Dr. Caligari*, which became a prestigious success for the German cinema, was written by Hans Janowitz and Carl Mayer. In general, Jews made a great contribution to the German cultural life in the 1920s and participated in the avant-garde artistic experimentation of this period. The painter Hans Richter produced experimental and abstract films and was a pioneer of this genre. The leading German-Jewish film director was Fritz *Lang, whose films are a marvelous portrayal of the social and cultural atmosphere prevailing in Germany at the time. They include *Der muede Tod* ("The Weary Death"), based on a medieval legend; two films based on the Nibelungen saga; two terror films; *Metropolis*, sharply critical of various aspects of industrial society; and *M*, the story of the Duesseldorf child murderer, which was Lang's last German film. When Hitler came to power, the Jews working for the German film industry were forced to flee the country. Most of them found their way to Hollywood, others to London, Paris, and Prague.

In Poland

Before the rise of the Jewish state, Poland was the only country that offered possibilities for the development of a Jewish film industry. Attempts to create a Jewish film tradition began before World War I, when film versions were made of the plays of Jacob *Gordin. Mark Tovbin, a pioneer in the field, filmed *Mirele Efros* with Esther Rachel *Kaminska in the title role and other members of her family in the cast. Nahum

Lipovski filmed Gordin's play *Hasa die Yesoeme* ("Hasa the Orphan") with Esther Lipovska as the orphan. It was not until the 1920s, however, that attempts at making films were resumed. In 1924 Leah Farber worked with Henrik Baum, as scenario writer, on producing films on Yiddish folk themes. Among them was *Tkies-Kaf* ("The Hand Contract"), based on a legend similar to that of *The Dybbuk*, directed by Zygmunt *Turkow, who also played the role of Elijah. Other roles were played by Esther Rachel Kaminska, her daughter Ida, and her granddaughter Ruth Turkow, then a child. In 1927 the same company filmed another legendary story, *Der Lamedvovnik* ("One of the Thirty-Six"), by H. Baum, starring Jonas *Turkow and directed by Henryk Shara (Shapira). In 1929 a company known as Forbert – after Leo Forbert, the first Jewish film producer after the war – filmed a version of Josef *Opatoshu's novel *In the Polish Woods*, with H. Baum as screenwriter, Jonas Turkow as director, and Dina Blumenfeld and Silver Rich in the leading roles.

The first Yiddish talking pictures were made in 1932, when Itzhak and Shaul Goskind formed a company known as Sektor and made documentaries of the Jewish communities in Warsaw, Lodz, Vilna, Lvov, Cracow, and Bialystok and then undertook popular productions with S. Dzigan and I. Szumacher. They produced *Al Khet*, with screenplay by the writer Israel Moshe Neiman, directed by A. Marten, with Rachel Holtzer and A. Morewski in the leading roles; *Un'a Heim* ("Without a Home," by A. Kacyzne), directed by Alexander Marten, with Ida Kaminska and the Dzigan-Szumacher partnership; and *Freylikhe Kabtsonim* ("The Merry Beggars"), a story by Moshe *Broderzon, with Zygmunt Turkow, Dzigan-Szumacher and Ruth Turkow in the cast. They also did a documentary called *Mir Kumen On* ("We're on the Way"), directed by Alexander Ford. Ford also did *Sabra* (1933).

Films of distinction were Josef Green's productions *Yidl mit'n Fidl*, lyrics by Itzik *Manger, starring Molly *Picon; *Mammele*, also starring Molly Picon; *Purim Shpiler*, with Z. Turkow, Anya Liton, L. Samberg, and Miriam Kressin (screenplays by Konrad Tam) and *A Brivele der Mammen*, written by M. Osherowitz (screenplay by A. Kacyzne) and directed by L. Tristan. This was the last Yiddish film made in Poland before the outbreak of World War II. Leo-Film did a talking version of *Tkies-Kaf* in 1937 with scenario by H. Baum, direction by Henrik Shara, and Z. Turkow as Elijah. *An-Sky's *Dybbuk* was also filmed in 1937, with a scenario by Katzisne, direction by Michal Vashiasky, and a cast including A. Morewski, Isaac Samberg, Moshe Lipman, Lili Liliana, and L. Leo Libgold. After World War II a cooperative, "Kinor," for Yiddish-speaking films was organized in Lodz by Shaul Goskind and Joseph Goldberg. From 1946 until 1950 two full-length films and about 12 shorts were produced including *Unzere Kinder*, which was made with Niusia Gold, Dzigan-Szumacher, and orphans from Alenuwek (Lodz). In 1951 "Kinor" was liquidated and the members left, mostly for Israel. The Polish State Film produced a work on the Warsaw Ghetto, *Ulica Graniczna* ("Border Street"), directed by A. Ford. Subsequently, several documentaries were made in Yiddish by American producers. Post-World War II films artists who did not specifically deal with Jewish themes were Alexander Ford (later in Israel) and Roman Polanski (who settled in the U.S. in the 1960s).

In the U.S.S.R.

Jews also took a large part in the motion picture industry in the U.S.S.R. Foremost among them was Sergei *Eisenstein, the great genius of the Soviet cinema, whose contribution to the progress made by motion pictures probably exceeds that of any other single film artist. His films, including *Battleship, Strike, Alexander, Old and New, October, Potemkin, Ivan the Terrible* (1 and 2), and *Alexander Nevski*, are still regarded as high achievements of the motion picture art and are studied by scholars and artists alike. His theories on the cinematic art, published in several volumes, remain an outstanding expression of motion picture aesthetics. The formalist experiments made by Eisentein in the 1920s provoked the ire of the Soviet authorities and caused him great hardship throughout the 1930s and 1940s; the controversy over *Ivan the Terrible* shortly preceded his death. Other Jews who entered the Soviet motion picture industry in the 1920s were Friedrich Ermler, Abraham Room, Mikhail Romm, Juli Raizman, Leonid Trauberg, Esther Schub, and L.O. Arnshtam. They sought formal solutions to the artistic problems encountered, and when socialist realism became the prescribed doctrine, they were forced to compromise with the new conditions. A noted Jewish director was Dziga Vertov, a native of Poland, whose real name was Denis Kaufman and whose brother, Boris Kaufman, was a well-known American cameraman. In 1924 Vertov propounded the theory of *Kino-Glas* ("Cinema-Eye"): *Kino-Glas* films were made outside the studio without actors, set, or a script. "They are written by the camera in the purest cine-language, and are completely visual." Vertov became the father of the documentary film, and his newsreels, "*kino pravda*," were the forerunners of *cinéma-verité*.

A number of Jewish directors were also active in the 1930s, including Yosif Heifitz and Alexander Zarkhy (who worked as a team for some time), Yosef Olshanski (also a scriptwriter), Samson Samsonov, and Yakov Segal. Yiddish motion pictures flourished in the Soviet Union in the 1930s, centering on the great Yiddish actor Shlomo *Mikhoels (who was later murdered during the Stalin purges), whose outstanding films were *King Lear* and *Menahem Mendel*.

Other European Countries

In other countries of Eastern Europe Jewish motion picture directors came to the fore after World War II, when film production first entered a serious phase of development. In Czechoslovakia Jan Kádar directed *Shop on Main Street*, and Milos Forman earned his reputation with such comedies as *Peter and Pavla, Firemen's Ball*, and *Loves of a Blonde*. A Swedish director named Mauritz Stiller became famous in the 1910s and 1920s for the style, humor, and aesthetic feeling of his films. His claim to fame now rests on his discovery of Greta

Garbo, whom he accompanied to the United States where he died soon after his arrival.

[Nahman Ingber]

For Israel, see *Israel, State of: Cultural Life (Film).

BIBLIOGRAPHY: T. Ramsaye, *A Million and One Nights, A History of the Motion Picture* (1964); E. Goodman, *The Fifty-Year Decline and Fall of Hollywood* (1961); R. Griffith and A. Mayer, *The Movies: The Sixty-Year Story of the World Hollywood and its Effects on America, from the pre-Nickelodeon Days to the Present* (1957); B.B. Hampton, *History of the Movies* (1930); Y. Harel, *Ha-Kolno'a me-Reshito ve-ad Ha-Yom* (1956), 216–40; N. Ingber, in: *Ha-Ummah*, 5 (1966), 246–61; *Omanut ha-Kolno'a*, 28 (1963), 5–15. **ADD. BIBLIOGRAPHY:** J. Hoberman and J. Shandler, *Entertaining America: Jews, Movies and Broadcasting* (2003); A. Insdorf, *Indelible Shadows: Film and the Holocaust* (20033); T. Teicholz, "Dreaming of a Blue and White Christmas," in: *Jewish Journal of Los Angeles* and www.tommywood.com (Dec 26, 2003).

MOTKE ḤABAD (c. 1820–c. 1885), Lithuanian jester (*badḥan). Motke (familiar form of Mordecai) was the most famous jester of Lithuania, the counterpart to Hershele *Ostropoler of Galicia. He eked out a poor living by acting as *badḥan* at weddings and other festive occasions, and his barbed wit, directed against the rich and the powerful, as well as his practical jokes, constituted a form of social protest, reflecting the condition of Jews in Russia generally and of the poor within the Jewish community. His subjects include government bureaucracy, autocratic powers exercised both by lay and religious authorities, the shrewish woman, and particularly the affluent and miserly. Collections of anecdotes and sayings ascribed to Motke, however, include many of apocryphal nature. Various suggestions have been made as to the name Ḥabad, which is identical with that of the Lithuanian *ḥasidic sect. One is that it is a distortion of his family name Hobat, another that he married into a Ḥabad family, and a third that it was a satirical anti-ḥasidic designation coined by Haskalah intellectuals, whereby Badḥan was changed to Ḥabad.

Whereas in Jewish folklore Hershele Ostropoler is the hero of the prankish deed, Motke is more the master of the biting witticism; but both were directed against those who hold the reins of wealth and power.

[Gershon Winer]

BIBLIOGRAPHY: (including collections of his anecdotes): M.J. Levitan, *Motke Ḥabad of Vilna* (1902); *Motke Ḥabad* (Heb. Publ. Co., N.Y., 1911); B.J. Bialostosky, *Jewish Humor and Jewish Jesters* (1953) (all in Yiddish).

MOTTELSON, BEN R. (1926–), U.S. and Danish physicist and Nobel laureate was born in Chicago and received his B.S. from Purdue University, Indiana (1947), and his Ph.D., supervised by Julian Schwinger, from Harvard University (1950). He worked at the Institute for Theoretical Physics (later the Niels Bohr Institute) in Copenhagen (1950–53), followed by a period working with the theoretical group of the European Organization for Nuclear Research (CERN). In 1957 he was appointed professor at the newly established Nordic Institute for Theoretical Atomic Physics in the same city (1957). With Aage Bohr, Mottelson investigated the structure of nuclei by theoretical and experimental means and established that a rotational spectrum and particle pairing account for the energy levels in nuclei. These observations had an important influence on subsequent particle physics and the elucidation of superconductivity. Mottelson and Bohr were awarded the 1975 Nobel Prize in physics, shared with James Rainwater. Mottelson subsequently made important contributions to understanding nuclear pairing and rotation and shell structure in metallic atom clusters. He married Nancy Jane Reno (1948) and they and their three children became Danish citizens in 1971.

[Michael Denman (2nd ed.)]

MOTTL, FELIX JOSEF (1856–1911), German conductor and composer. Born near Vienna, Mottl studied with Anton Bruckner and Joseph Hellmesberger. When he was 24, Liszt conducted his first composition, the opera *Agnes Bernauer*, at Weimar. From 1881 to 1903 he was court conductor and then *Generalmusikdirektor* at Karlsruhe, acquiring a brilliant reputation. For the next four years he was conductor of the opera at Munich, making the city a center of operatic life. Mottl devoted himself to the interpretation of the works of Berlioz, Peter Cornelius, and Wagner. In 1887 he appeared at the Wagner festival at Bayreuth and in 1890 presented the first full production of Berlioz' *Les Troyens* at Karlsruhe. He also conducted in London and New York. Mottl's compositions include three operas, lieder, and chamber music, but he is best remembered for his orchestral arrangement of works by Lully, Rameau, Mozart, and Gluck, and for his piano reductions of Wagner's operas.

BIBLIOGRAPHY: MGG; Grove, Dict; Riemann-Gurlitt.

[Judith Cohen]

MOTZKIN, LEO (**Aryeh Leib**; 1867–1933), Zionist leader and protagonist of the struggle for Jewish rights in the Diaspora. Born in Brovary, near Kiev, Motzkin received a traditional Jewish education and witnessed in his youth the Kiev pogrom in 1881. He studied in Berlin where he was among the founders of the Russian-Jewish Scientific Society (1887), whose members were Jewish students from Russia and Galicia who supported the *Ḥibbat Zion movement. They conducted heated debates with the majority of the Russian Jewish students, who were attracted to socialism and cosmopolitanism. When he completed his studies, Motzkin abandoned his opportunities for a scientific career and devoted himself to activities for the Jewish national cause. He was one of the strongest critics of the methods of Ḥovevei Zion and, with the appearance of Theodor *Herzl, Motzkin immediately joined the newly formed Zionist Organization at the First Zionist Congress and headed a group of delegates that demanded a clear and decisive wording of the *Basle Program. Before the Second Congress, Herzl sent him to Ereẓ Israel, and in his report to the Congress Motzkin criticized the settlement methods of Baron de *Rothschild and the Ḥovevei Zion and called for a political agreement with the Ottoman government. Despite his ideological closeness to Herzl, he joined the *Democratic Fraction, which he represented at the Fifth Zionist Congress (1901) and at the Conference of Russian Zionists in Minsk (1902). He kept aloof from the controversy over the *Uganda Scheme because of his deep attachment to Ereẓ Israel, on the one hand, and the urgent need to help the oppressed Jewish masses, on the other.

In 1905 Motzkin anonymously edited the revolutionary Russian *Russische Korrespondenz*, which was published in Berlin and provided West European newspapers with information on Russia in a radical spirit. He dedicated considerable space to the fate of the Jews and the anti-Jewish excesses. The Zionist Organization requested Motzkin to publish a book on the wave of pogroms in Russia; it was written for the most part by Motzkin himself (signed A. Linden) and was published in two parts in 1909–10 under the name *Die Judenpogrome in Russland*. The book contained thorough research into anti-Jewish violence in Russia from the beginning of the 19th century to its climax during the Russian Revolution of 1905–06, including descriptions of pogroms in various areas and towns and stressed the role of Jewish *self-defense. In 1912 Motzkin's pamphlet *The Legal Sufferings of the Jews in Russia* came out in an English translation by an anonymous author. It was also distributed in Russian among the Duma delegates in St. Petersburg. During the *Beilis trial (1911–13), Motzkin organized an information service in West European countries and Russia and spurred public figures to speak out against the blood libel. At the same time, he was a leading activist in the Hebrew language movement and among the first to speak Hebrew at conferences and meetings devoted to this subject. During World War I, he was head of the Copenhagen Office of the World Zionist Organization and the liaison between the various Zionist organizations in the warring countries. At the end of 1915 he left for the United States to mobilize support for the Jewish war victims on the East European front, and also for the struggle to ensure equal rights for the Jews of Russia. At the end of the war, Motzkin demanded that the Zionist Movement also concern itself with the civil rights of the Jews in the Diaspora. Thus, he took a leading part in the establishment of the *Comité des Délégations Juives at the Paris Peace Conference, to which various Jewish bodies were affiliated, including the World Zionist Organization, and which later became a standing institution at the League of Nations, serving as a world Jewish representative for all affairs other than those connected with Ereẓ Israel. In the following years as well, Motzkin continued to direct the committee, which concerned itself particularly with the struggle against antisemitism (inter alia with the legal defense of Shalom *Schwartzbard for the assassination of Simon *Petlyura, who was held responsible for the pogroms in the Ukraine) and with the defense of Jewish rights. For this purpose he was active in the movement supporting the League of Nations and in the international Congresses of National Minorities. He did not abandon his Zionist work, however, and served as permanent chairman of the Zionist General Council and of many Zionist Congresses.

When the Nazis came to power in Germany, Motzkin headed the anti-Nazi struggle of the Jewish people and brought the oppression of German Jewry before the League of Nations. When, under pressure from the German ethnic minorities in other countries, the Congress of National Minorities refused to deliberate on the situation of German Jews under the Nazis, Motzkin withdrew from the organization. He died in the midst of feverish activity to ensure political and financial aid to German Jewry. In 1939 *Sefer Motzkin*, including a selection of his writings and speeches, was published together with a monograph on him by the editor, A. Bein.

His son THEODORE SAMUEL (1908–1970) was a mathematician and educator. Born in Berlin, from 1936 to 1948 he taught at The Hebrew University, Jerusalem. He settled in the United States in 1948 and was a research fellow of Harvard University from 1948 to 1950, after which he was a professor and research mathematician at the University of California. He contributed to the subjects of inequalities, approximation, polynomials, and geometry. He wrote *Contributions to the Theory of Linear Inequalities*.

BIBLIOGRAPHY: S. Kling, in: *Herzl Year Book*, 2 (1959), 228–50; L. Lipsky, *A Gallery of Zionist Profiles* (1956), *Ha-Olam* (Nov. 16, 1933).

[Yehuda Slutsky]

MOUNTAIN JEWS, a Jewish ethnic and linguistic group living mainly in *Azerbaijan and Daghestan. The name "Mountain Jews" emerged in the first half of the 19th century when the Russian Empire annexed those territories. It is supposed that the name derives from "mountain of the Jews" (*Chufut* or *Dzuhud Dag* in the Tat language), an ancient name of Daghestan, indicating its large Jewish population.

The Mountain Jews call themselves *Juhur*. According to estimates based on the Soviet censuses of 1959 and 1970, they numbered between 50,000 and 70,000 in 1970. Of these, 17,109 registered as Tats in the 1970 census, so as to escape being registered as Jews and discriminated against by the authorities. About 22,000 did so in the 1979 census.

They speak several dialects (similar to each other) of the Tat language (see *Judeo-Tat), which belongs to the western branch of the Iranian languages group.

Their main centers of settlement are: in Azerbaijan, *Baku, capital of the republic, and the town of Kuba where the majority of Mountain Jews live in the suburb of Krasnaya Sloboda which has an all-Jewish population; in Daghestan, *Derbent, Makhachkalah, capital of the republic (which was called Petrovsk Port until 1922), and Buynaksk (Temir-Khan Shurah prior to 1922). Outside Azerbaijan and Daghestan, considerable numbers of Mountain Jews live in Nalchik, in the suburb of Yevreyskaya Kolonka, and also in the town of Grozny.

Linguistic and indirect historical evidence indicates that the community of Mountain Jews was formed as a result of constant emigration of Jews from northern Persia – and perhaps also from nearby regions of the Byzantine Empire – to the Transcaucasian Azerbaijan, where they settled in its eastern and north-eastern regions among a population speaking the Tat language which they also adopted in time. The Talmud mentions a Jewish community in the city of Derbent as early as the third century C.E., and the *amora* R. Simeon Safra taught there (TJ, Meg. 4, 5, 75b).

The immigration of the Jews evidently began when the Muslims invaded those regions in 639–643, and it continued for the whole period from the Arab to the 13th-century Mongol invasion. Apparently the main waves of migration ceased in the early 11th century under the impact of the mass invasion of a Turkic nomadic tribe. This intrusion might also have forced many of the Tat-speaking Jewish inhabitants of Transcaucasian Azerbaijan to move further north to Daghestan.

There they contacted remnants of the *Khazars who had adopted Judaism in the 8th century. Already in 1254 the monk Wilhelm Rubruquis, a Flemish traveler, noted the existence of "a great number of Jews" throughout eastern Caucasus, in both Daghestan and Azerbaijan.

The Mountain Jews had contacts with the Jewish communities of the Mediterranean region. Tagriberdi (1409–1470), the Muslim historiographer from Egypt, wrote of Jewish merchants from "Circassia" (i.e., from Caucasus) visiting Cairo. Through such contacts printed books reached the Mountain Jews. In the town of Kuba books were preserved until the beginning of the 20th century that had been printed in Venice in the late 16th and early 17th centuries.

From the 14th to the 16th centuries European travelers did not reach those regions, but rumors spread in Europe in the 16th and 17th centuries about "nine and a half Jewish tribes" driven by "Alexander the Great" behind the Caspian Mountains, i.e., into Daghestan. Those rumors might have originated with Jewish merchants from the eastern Caucasus appearing at the time in Italy. N. Vitsen, a Dutch traveler, who visited Daghestan in 1690 found many Jews there, especially in the village of Buynak, not far from the present Buynaksk, as well as in the Khanate of Qaraqaitagh where, according to him 15,000 Jews lived. The 17th and early 18th centuries can perhaps be considered for the Jews a period of relative peace and prosperity. A solid area of Jewish settlement existed in the north of present-day Azerbaidjan and in southern Daghestan, in the region between the towns of Kuba and Derbent. A valley near Derbent, called by the Muslim Juhud-Kata (Jewish Valley), was inhabited evidently mainly by Jews. Its largest settlement, named Aba-Sava, served as the spiritual center of the community. Several *piyyutim* (liturgical poems) written in Hebrew by Elisha ben Samuel, who lived in the region, have been preserved. Also in Aba-Sava there lived a scholar called Gershon Lalah ben Moses Naqdi who wrote a commentary on Maimonides' *Mishneh Torah*. Mattathias ben Samuel ha-Kohen from Shemakha to the south of Kuba wrote between 1806 and 1828 a kabbalistic work, *Kol Mevasser*, which is the last evidence of religious creativity in Hebrew in the community.

From the second half of the 18th century, the situation of the Mountain Jews severely deteriorated as the result of the struggle to conquer their region involving Russia, Persia, Turkey, and a number of local rulers. The Persian commander Nadir, who later became the Shah of Persia (1736–47), managed in the early 1730s to drive the Turks out of Azerbaijan and successfully to withstand Russian efforts to possess Daghestan. Several settlements of Mountain Jews were almost entirely destroyed by his troops; a number of others were partially demolished and plundered. The Jews saved from destruction settled in the town of Kuba under the protection of its ruler Khan Hussein. In 1797 or 1799 Surkhan-Khan (the Muslim ruler of *qazimuqs* or *laks*) attacked Aba-Sava and, after a bitter battle in which 157 defenders of the settlements perished, killed all the male prisoners, took the women and children prisoners, and destroyed the settlement. Thus the settlements of the Jewish valley came to an end. Those Jews who were so fortunate as to remain alive found refuge in Derbent under the protection of the local ruler, Fatkh-Ali-Khan, whose lands stretched to the town of Kuba.

In 1806 Russia annexed Derbent and the surrounding areas. In 1813 Transcaucasian Azerbaijan was annexed, the formal right to possession being finalized in 1828. Thus the majority of Mountain Jews who lived in these regions found themselves under Russian rule.

In 1830 a rebellion against Russia broke out in Daghestan, except for the coastal region including Derbent. The rebellion, headed by Shamil, continued with interruptions up to 1859. Its slogan was *Jihad* – holy war against non-believers, i.e., non-Muslims. Grave assaults on Mountain Jews occurred: the inhabitants of a number of *auls* (villages) were forced to convert to Islam, and in time they merged completely with the surrounding population. However, for several generations, the memory of their Jewish origin lingered. In 1840 the community heads of Mountain Jews in Derbent appealed to Czar Nicholas I in a petition (in Hebrew) beseeching the Russians to "gather the Jews dispersed in the mountains, the forests, and little villages, suffering under Tatars" (meaning the rebellious Muslims) "and settle them in towns and settlements" (meaning in areas controlled by the Russians).

The turning of the Mountain Jews to Russia for protection did not lead to immediate changes in their situation, occupations, or community structure.

Such changes emerged slowly only toward the end of the 19th century. In 1835, of 7,649 Mountain Jews under Russian rule 58.3% were involved in agriculture and 41.7% were urban dwellers. The town population, however, also engaged to a considerable extent in agriculture, mainly in viticulture and winemaking, especially in Kuba and Derbent; they also grew rubia, a plant from the roots of which red paint was extracted.

The rich families among the Mountain Jews were wine producers: the Ḥanukaevs, owners of a company for producing and selling wine, and the Dadashevs, who, besides wine production, founded the largest fishing company in Daghestan.

The raising of rubia was almost entirely dropped by the

early 20th century due to the development of aniline dye production; most Mountain Jews who had been involved in the business lost their property and became casual workers. This became their job mainly in Baku, where the number of Mountain Jews increased only toward the end of the 19th century, and to some extent also in Derbent, where the bankrupt Jews turned mostly to door to door trading or became seasonal fishing workers.

Almost all the Mountain Jews engaged in viticulture worked also in gardening. In some settlements of Azerbaijan they grew tobacco, and in Qaitagh and Tabasaran (Daghestan) they were engaged in land cultivation, an occupation which was also common in several villages of Azerbaijan.

In some of the villages their main employment was leather processing. This branch came to a standstill in the early 20th century when the Russian authorities forbade Mountain Jews to enter Central Asia where they used to buy the raw skins. A significant part of the leather processors became town laborers.

The number of Mountain Jews in petty trade, including peddling, was relatively small in the initial period of Russian power, but grew significantly from the late 19th century. The few affluent Jewish merchants lived mainly in Kuba and Derbent, and from the end of the 19th century they also began to settle in the towns of Baku and Temir-Khan-Shura, where they most notably dealt in textiles and carpet selling.

In his travel book *Sefer ha-Massa'ot be-Ereẓ Kavkaz* (1886), Joseph Judah *Chorny, who traveled in the Caucasus for eight years (1867–75), gives detailed information on the life and settlements (about 30 at the time) of the Mountain Jews. Another valuable source is the book of the Russian writer Nemirovich-Danchenko (*Voinstvuyushchii Izrail*; "Fighting Israel," 1886), in which he records his vivid impressions of his stay among the tribe. The Mountain Jews were then simple people, mostly illiterate, but proud, courageous, and freedom-loving. Farmers and hunters, they always carried a dagger or similar weapon in their typical Caucasian dress. The Tat Jews were prepared at any time to defend by their sword their family or their honor. Their dwellings were low mud huts, whose inside walls were hung with polished weapons. The synagogue, its exterior resembling a mosque, served as a *ḥeder* for the children. Sitting on the floor they learned the Torah by heart from the *ḥakham*. Of the Jewish festivals, Purim and Passover were especially celebrated. Their Passover **seder* had a special form differing from the traditional *seder*. During the night of *Hoshana Rabba the girls used to dance; according to Tat tradition, this is the night when a man's fate is decided. The marriage ceremony contained foreign influences, and the circumcision ceremony was generally held in the synagogue. Tat family names are mostly biblical names, to which the Russian suffix "ov" was added, e.g., Pinkhasov, Binyaminov, etc. The custom of the vendetta was practiced until recently.

The main social framework of the Mountain Jews up to the end of the 1920s was a large family unit encompassing three or four generations and reaching 70 or more people in number. As a rule, the extended family lived around a large single "yard" where each nuclear family, consisting of a father and mother with their children, occupied a separate house. The Mountain Jews practiced polygamy, and two or three wives at a time were common up to the Soviet period.

If a nuclear family consisted of a husband and two or three wives, then each wife with her children occupied a separate house. The father was head of the family, and after his death was succeeded by his eldest son. The head of the family took care of the property shared by all members of the family. He also fixed the work schedule for all the men in the family and his authority was beyond question.

The mother of the family, or in the polygamous families the first wife of the father, conducted the household and watched over the housework: cooking the food for all the family, cleaning the yard and the house, and so on.

Several large families originating from the same ancestor formed the broader and loosely connected community, *tukhum* (literally "seed"). Family links were of special importance in vendettas; if the murderer appeared Jewish and the relatives did not manage to avenge the blood of the victim within three days after the murder, then the families of the murderer and the victim reconciled and considered themselves tied by the bonds of blood kinship.

The population of the Jewish village consisted as a rule of three to five large families. The head of the rural community originated from the most respected or most numerous family of the settlement.

In the towns the Jews lived in special suburbs as in Kuba, or in a separate Jewish quarter as in Derbent. From the 1860s Mountain Jews began to live in towns where they had never lived before (Baku, Temir-Khan-Shura), and in towns founded by the Russians: Petrovsk Port, Nalchik, and Grozny. Such moves often resulted in the disintegration of the structure of the large family, for only part of it – one or two nuclear families – moved to a new settlement. Even in the towns where Mountain Jews had lived for a long time, such as Kuba and Derbent (but not in the villages), the process of the disintegration of large families began toward the end of the 19th century.

Precise data on the administrative structure of urbanized Mountain Jews is available only for Derbent, where the community was headed by three elected members. One of these took the post of head and the two others served as his deputies. They were responsible both for the relations with the authorities and for the internal affairs of the community.

The rabbinical hierarchy had two levels: "rabbi" and "*dayyan*." The rabbi served as *ḥazzan* and preacher in the *namaz* (synagogue) of his village or his quarter of the town, and also as a teacher in *talmid-khuna* (*ḥeder*) and as religious slaughterer (*shoḥet*). The *dayyan* was the chief rabbi of the town: he was elected by the leaders of the community and was the highest religious authority not only for his town, but also for the neighboring settlements; he chaired the religious court (**bet din*). He was also the *ḥazzan* and preacher in the main synagogue of the town and headed the yeshivah.

The level of halakhic knowledge among the yeshivah graduates was about that of a ritual slaughterer elsewhere, but they were reverently called "rabbi." From the middle of the 19th century a number of Mountain Jews studied in Ashkenazi yeshivot in Russia, mostly in Lithuania; there they were granted only the title of *shoḥet* but, on returning to the Caucasus, they served as rabbis. Very few of these Jews who studied in the yeshivot of Russia received the title of rabbi. From the mid-19th century, the Czarist authorities acknowledged the *dayyan* of Temir-Khan-Shra as the chief rabbi of northern Daghestan and northern Caucasus, and the *dayyan* of Derbent as chief rabbi of southern Daghestan and Azerbaijan. Besides their traditional duties, they acted as **kazyonny ravvin* (official rabbis in behalf of the authorities).

In the pre-Russian period, relations between the Mountain Jews and Muslims were determined by the so-called Covenant of *Omar, the special set of Islamic directives regarding **dhimmis* (non-Muslim protected citizens). However, the application of those laws in these regions was accompanied by special humiliation since the Mountain Jews depended to a great extent on the local ruler. According to the description of the German traveler I. Gerber, published in 1728, they had to pay a special ransom to the Muslim rulers for protection. Moreover, they had "to perform all kinds of difficult, dirty jobs which could not be enforced on a Muslim." The Jews had to give the ruler some of their yields free of charge: tobacco, rubia, tanned skins, and so on; they worked on his fields in harvest time, built and repaired his house, did gardening jobs, and were engaged in his vineyard. They also gave the ruler their horses on special occasions. Muslim soldiers who were feasting in the house of a Jew could demand money from their host "for causing them toothache."

Up to the end of the 1860s the Jews of certain mountain regions in Daghestan continued to pay ransom to the previous Muslim rulers of those regions, or to their descendants to whom the Czarist government has given rights equal to Russian noblemen, leaving the estates in their possession.

*Blood libels occurred in these regions only after they came under Russian rule. In 1814 disturbances occurred as the result of a blood libel in Baku; the Jews affected, mostly originating from Iran, fled to Kuba for protection. In 1878 on a similar allegation, dozens of Kuba Jews were arrested, and in 1911 the Jews of the settlement of Tarki suffered after being accused of kidnapping a Muslim girl.

The first contacts between the Mountain Jews and Ashkenazi Jews were established in the 1820s or 1830s. These links were reinforced and became more frequent only after regulations appeared which allowed those Russian Jews permitted to live outside the Pale of Settlement to move to areas where Mountain Jews were living.

In the 1870s the chief rabbi of Derbent. R. Jacob Itzhakovich-Yiẓhaki (1848–1917) contacted a number of Jewish scholars living in St. Petersburg. In 1884 R. Sharbat Nissim-Oghly, the chief rabbi of Temir-Khan-Shura, sent his son Elijah to the Higher Technical School in Moscow, and he became the first Mountain Jew to receive higher secular education. In the early 20th century Russian-language schools, where both religious and secular subjects were taught, were opened for Mountain Jews in Baku, Derbent, and Kuba.

Already in the 1840s or 1850s the yearning for the Holy Land led some Mountain Jews to Ereẓ Israel. In the 1870s and 1880s Jerusalem emissaries regularly visited Daghestan to collect **ḥalukkah* money. In the second half of the 1880s a Kolel Daghestan (Daghestan congregation) already existed in Jerusalem. R. Sharbat Nissim-Oghly settled in Jerusalem at the end of the 1880s or in the early 1890s. In 1894 he issued there a brochure, *Kadmoniyyot Yehudei he-Harim* ("The Ancient Traditions of the Mountain Jews"). In 1898 representatives of the Mountain Jews participated in the Second Zionist Congress in Basle. In 1907 R. Jacob Itzhakovich-Yizhaki moved to Ereẓ Israel and headed a group of 56 founders – mostly Mountain Jews – of the settlement Be'er Ya'akov near Ramleh, which is named for him.

Another group tried without success to settle in Maḥanaim in Upper Galilee in 1909–1911. Ezekiel Nisanov, who went to the country in 1908, became a pioneer of the *Ha-Shomer organization and was killed by the Arabs in 1911. His brothers Judah and Ẓevi also joined Ha-Shomer. Before World War I, the number of Mountain Jews in *Ereẓ Israel* reached several hundred, most of them living in the Beth Israel quarter of Jerusalem.

Asaf Pinhasov became an active advocate of Zionism among the Mountain Jews at the beginning of the 20th century. In Vilna he published in 1908 his Judeo-Tat translation from the Russian of Joseph Sapir's book *Zionism*, the first book published in the language of the Mountain Jews.

The varied Zionist activities in Baku during World War I attracted Mountain Jews. After the 1917 February Revolution, these activities gained some momentum. Four representatives of the Mountain Jews, one of them a woman, participated in the Conference of Caucasian Zionists, in August 1917.

In November 1917, the Bolsheviks seized power in Baku, but in September 1918 the independent Azerbaijan Republic was proclaimed. These changes left Zionist activity undisturbed up to the second Sovietization of Azerbaijan in 1921. The national Jewish Council of Azerbaijan, headed by Zionists, established the Jewish People's University in 1919 and Mountain Jews were among the students. In the same year the Regional Caucasian Zionist Committee started to issue in Baku a Judeo-Tat newspaper called *Tobushi sabaḥi* ("Twilight"). Among the Zionists, Gershon Muradoy and Asaf Pinhasov were outstanding.

The Mountain Jews in Daghestan viewed the struggle between Soviets and the local separatists as the continuation of the traditional fight between Russians and Muslims, and they therefore mostly sympathized with the Russians, i.e., with the Soviet rule. Seventy percent of the Red Guards of Daghestan were of the Mountain Jews. The Daghestan separatists and their Turkish supporters, for their part, destroyed Jewish settlements and massacred their population. Consequently the majority of Jews living in the mountains had to move to towns situated along the coast of the Caspian Sea, mainly to Derbent, Makhachkalah, and Buynaksk.

After Soviet power established itself in Daghestan, antisemitism did not disappear. In 1926 and 1929 the Jews faced blood libels, that of 1926 being accompanied by pogroms.

In the early 1920s, about 300 families of Mountain Jews from Azerbaijan and Daghestan managed to leave for Palestine. The majority of them settled in Tel Aviv where they established a Caucasian quarter. (One of the outstanding leaders of this immigration was Yehuda Adamovich, father of Yekutiel Adam, deputy chief of staff of the Israeli Defense Forces who was killed in the 1982 Lebanon War.)

In 1921–22 organized Zionist activities among the Mountain Jews were disrupted; immigration to Ereẓ Israel also subsided. In the period between the end of the Civil War in Russia and World War II, the main goal of the Soviet authorities for the Mountain Jews was their productivization and eradication of religious feeling. With the former objective, Jewish collective farms were established. Two Jewish collective farms were founded in the settlements of Bagdanovka and Ganshtakovka where about 320 families worked in 1929. The settlements were situated in the North-Caucasian Territory, presently Krasnodar Territory. In 1931 about 970 Mountain Jewish families were drawn into collective farms in Daghestan. In Azerbaijan collective farms were established in Jewish villages and in the Jewish suburb of the town of Kuba. In 1927 members of 250 Mountain Jewish families became collective farmers in the Republic.

However, toward the end of the 1930s the Mountain Jews began to abandon collective farming, although many Jewish collective farms were still in existence after World War II: in the beginning of the 1970s about 10 percent of the community members remained in collective farms.

As far as religion was concerned, the authorities preferred not to destroy it immediately, in accordance with their general policy in the eastern provinces of the U.S.S.R., but to undermine religious tradition gradually by secularizing the community. For this purpose a wide network of schools was established, and special attention given to indoctrinating youth and adults in the framework of clubs.

In 1922 the first Soviet newspaper in Judeo-Tat appeared in Baku called *Karsokh* ("Worker"). It was sponsored by the Caucasian Regional Committee of the Jewish Communist Party and its Youth Section. The Poalei Zion newspaper did not find support among the authorities and soon ceased to exist. In 1928 another Mountain Jewish newspaper appeared called *Zaḥmatkash* ("The Laborers") and it was issued in Derbent. From 1929 to 1930 Judeo-Tat was given in the Latin script instead of Hebrew, and from 1938 the Russian (Cyrillic) alphabet has been used. In 1934 the Tat Literary Circle was established in Derbent, and in 1936 a Tat Section was created in the Union of Soviet Writers of Daghestan. In 1926, the only census that registred Tats, they numbered 25,866, and probably reached 35,000 persons by 1941. Works by Mountain Jewish writers of the period evince strong Communist indoctrination, especially in drama which was considered by the authorities as the most effective propaganda weapon. As a result, amateur theatrical groups proliferated and later, in 1935, the professional Mountain Jewish theater opened in Derbent.

During World War II the Germans for a short time occupied the regions of the northern Caucasus populated by Mountain Jews. In those areas with mixed Ashkenazi and Mountain Jewish population – in Kislovodsk, Pyatigorsk, and so on – all the Jews were killed. The same fate struck the Mountain Jewish collective farms in Krasnodar Territory, and also the Crimean settlements of Mountain Jews founded in the 1920s. In the regions encompassing the towns of Nalchik and Grozny the Germans were awaiting instructions on how to deal with "the Jewish problem," but these did not arrive before they had to retreat from these areas.

After World War II the anti-religious campaign gained momentum. In the period 1948–53 teaching in Judeo-Tat ended, and all the Mountain Jews' schools were conducted in Russian. *Zakhmatash* no longer appeared and all literary activities in Judeo-Tat were ended.

In the latter part of the 1970s, the Mountain Jews became victims of assault in several towns, in particular Nalchik, because of their struggle to leave for Israel. Cultural and literary activities in Judeo-Tat, revived after Stalin's death remained rudimentary in nature. From the end of 1953 up to 1986, two books a year were published on the average.

The main – and at times the sole – language of the youth was now Russian. Even the middle generation used the language of their community only at home in the family circle; to discuss more sophisticated topics they had to turn to Russian. This development was most noticeable among the small urban population of Mountain Jews, as for example, in Baku, and also among persons of higher education.

Religious tradition suffered, but was still partly retained, especially in comparison with the Ashkenazi community of the Soviet Union. The majority of the Mountain Jews continued to observe customs connected with the Jewish life cycle. The dietary laws are observed in many homes. However, Sabbath observance has been mostly abandoned, and the same is true of the Jewish festivals, except Rosh ha-Shanah and Yom Kippur, the Passover seder and the eating of matzah. The knowledge of reading prayers and prayer rituals has been also largely lost.

Despite all this, the level of Jewish consciousness among the Mountain Jews has remained high and their Jewish identity is being preserved, even by those who formally register themselves as Tats. The mass immigration to Israel was resumed rather later than among other groups of Soviet Jewry; they began to leave not in 1971 but at the end of 1973 and early 1974 after the Yom Kippur War. About 12,000 Mountain Jews had arrived in Israel by the mid-1980s, and from 1989 through 1992 about another 5,000 reached Israel. In 2002, 3,394 were living in the Russian Federation.

Literature

The most important literary heritage of the Mountain Jews is the national epic in Judeo-Tat, *Shiraha* (the name probably derives from the Hebrew *shirah*, "poem"), which abounds in biblical associations and figures. One of the most beautiful poems is the "Song of the Mountain Jews," which expresses their yearning for the ancient homeland "so near, in front of your eyes, put out your hand and touch it." It also mentions the "maids of Deborah," the "brave horsemen of Samson," and the "heirs of Bar Kokhba." The epic was translated into Yiddish by the Soviet-Jewish writer M. Helmond. Mishi (Moshe) Bakhsheyev, poet, novelist, and playwright, born in Derbent in 1910, laid the foundations for the modern Tat literature, which began to develop in the 1930s. His publications include "Earth," a play dealing with life on a Jewish kolkhoz, a novel "Cluster of Grapes," and a collection of poetry. Other poets are Amrami Isakov, whose collection of children's songs has been translated into Russian, and Zion Izagayev, who has published three volumes of poems. A literary almanac, *Woton Sovetimag* ("Soviet Homeland"), the first of its kind in Judeo-Tat, edited by Hizigil (Ezekiel) Avshalomov and published in Makhachkala in 1963, assembled the works of 27 Tat writers, selecting mainly works which reflect the integration of the Mountain Jews in Soviet society. Visitors to the region reported a deep-felt longing for the State of Israel among the Mountain Jews, which became particularly strong after the 1967 Six-Day War, in spite of the official anti-Israel propaganda campaign (see also *Judeo-Tat).

BIBLIOGRAPHY: M. Altschuler, *The Jews of the Eastern Caucasus: The History of the Mountain Jews from the Beginning of the 19th Century* (1990); Z. Anisimov, in: *Ha-Shiloaḥ*, 18 (1908); D.G. Maggid, *Yevrei na Kavkaze* (1918); Yu. Larin, *Yevrei i Anti-semitizm v S.S.S.R.* (1929); M.M. Ikhilov, in: *Sovetskaya Etnologiya*, 1 (1950); A.L. Eliav, *Between Hammer and Sickle* (1969²), 166–71.

[Mordkhai Neishtat / Michael Zand / *The Shorter Jewish Encyclopaedia in Russian*]

MOUNT OF OLIVES (**Olivet**), mountain overlooking *Jerusalem from the east, beyond the *Kidron Brook. From the orographic point of view, the Mount of Olives is part of a spur projecting near Mount Scopus (Ra's al-Mushārif), from the country-long water divide which continues southward. The Mount of Olives ridge has three peaks. Upon the highest, 2,684 ft. (826 meters) above sea level, the original buildings of the *Hebrew University were constructed and opened in 1925. This area is commonly, although mistakenly, known as Mount Scopus. On the second peak, 2,645 ft. (814 meters) above the sea, is the site of Augusta Victoria Hospital. On the third, 2,652 ft. (816 meters) high, lies the Arab village of al-Tūr (*ha-har*, "the mountain"), an epithet whose source is in the Aramaic name of the Mount of Olives, Tura Zita. The Mount of Olives ends in this peak, though a spur of it continues to Ra's al-ʿAmūd (2,444 ft.; 752 meters), draining to the Kidron brook southward, to the village of *Shiloaḥ (Silwān). Even at its highest, the Mount of Olives is lower than the highest point in the Romemah district, which is the highest point of the water divide in Jerusalem (2,697 ft; 829 meters). However, since the Mount of Olives stands so very high (351 ft; 108 meters) in relation to the deep Kidron brook beneath it, it seems much higher than it actually is. From a geological point of view, the mountain is entirely within the Senonian region, while phytogeographically speaking, it is within the bounds of the Judean Desert.

In the Bible, the mountain is called the Ascent of the Olives (Heb. *Ma'aleh ha-Zeitim*; II Sam. 15:30), it being said of the top of the mountain (verse 32) "that this was where David was accustomed to worship God." This sanctity is apparently what prompted Solomon to build a *high place "in the mount that is before Jerusalem" (I Kings 11:7). However, according to II Kings 23:13, the high place which he built was "on the right hand [i.e., to the south] of the mount of corruption (i.e., the Mount of Olives)," that is, probably at Ra's al-ʿAmūd. Ezekiel 11:23 gives an important place to the Mount of Olives in his vision of the end of days: the glory of the Lord will arise and stand "upon the mountain which is on the east side of the city." The name Mount of Olives in its present form first appears in Zechariah 14:4: "His feet shall stand in that day upon the Mount of Olives, which is before Jerusalem on the east." Zechariah describes how in his vision the mountain is cleft in two. During the period of the Second Temple, the Mount of Olives was of great importance in Jerusalem: the *red heifer was burnt upon it; a bridge, or possibly two such bridges, connected its slopes with the Temple Mount. During the period of the Roman procurator Felix, thousands gathered upon it, there to be beguiled into believing the words of a false Egyptian prophet (Jos., Ant. 20:169; Wars 2:262). During the siege of Jerusalem, the Tenth Roman Legion encamped on it (Wars 5:70, where the location of the Mount of Olives is clearly established as being six *ris* (= 3,707 ft.; 1,110 meters) east of Jerusalem, across a deep valley called Kidron). During the period of the Second Temple, at the order of the Sanhedrin, beacons would be lit on the Mount of Olives (*har ha-meshiḥah*, "Mount of Anointing"), in order to announce the sanctification of the New Moon. These flares could be seen as far away as Sartaba (RH 2:4).

The Gospels frequently refer to the Mount of Olives (by its Greek name τὸ ὄρος Ἐλαων). Jesus and his followers encamped on one of its peaks on their way to Jerusalem. From its slopes, he wept for Jerusalem when he foresaw its coming destruction. At its foot is Gethsemane (Heb. Gat(h)-Shemanim), where he and his disciples spent the night before his arrest, and from it Jesus rose to heaven after being crucified and resurrected. For these reasons, Christianity, upon attaining supremacy, erected several churches and monasteries on the mountain. On its summit, the Church of the Ascension was erected and further down the Church of Eleona was built by the emperor Constantine. In Gethsemane a church was constructed during the Byzantine period and was refurbished by the Crusaders. According to Muslim tradition, the caliph Omar encamped on the Mount of Olives while receiving the surrender of Jerusalem (638).

Once the Jews were authorized to return to Jerusalem by the Arab conquerors, the pilgrimages to Jerusalem were also resumed. These pilgrimages generally took place during the month of Tishri. In these, the Mount of Olives held an important place, especially from the end of the eighth century, when the Jews were no longer allowed to enter the Temple Mount. On the festival of *Hoshana Rabba, they circled the Mount of Olives seven times, in song and prayer. On Hoshana Rabba, the Palestinian *rosh yeshivah* announced the "Proclamation of the Mount of Olives" concerning the new moons, the festivals, and the intercalation of years, a practice which was based on the ancient kindling of beacons on new moons on the Mount of Olives. On this same day, the *rosh yeshivah* appointed members to the "Great Sanhedrin" and accorded titles of honor to those who had worked in favor of the Palestinian academy. Bans on the unobservant and on those who rebelled against authority, especially against the Karaites, were not lacking on such occasions. The clashes with the Karaites resulted in the intervention of the authorities, and they even prohibited the *rashei yeshivah* from issuing bans.

The choice of the Mount of Olives as the site of pilgrimages and gatherings was based on midrashic tradition: "The Divine Presence traveled ten journeys, from the cover of the Ark to the Cherub ... and from the Town to the Mount of Olives" (RH 31a; Lam. R., Proem 25). In the letters of the *rashei yeshivah*, the Mount of Olives is referred to as "the site of the footstool of our God." A tenth-century guidebook found in the Cairo *Genizah* points out "the site of the footstool of our God" on "a stone whose length is ten cubits, its breadth two cubits, and its height two cubits." The armchair of the Palestinian *rosh yeshivah* was placed on this "stool" during the gatherings and the festive ceremonies which accompanied the pilgrimages. From this spot, the *rosh yeshivah* addressed the celebrants, and it was here that he received their contributions.

The site of the prayers and the gatherings was, according to the documents of the *Genizah*, above "Absalom's Monument," "opposite the Temple and the Gate of the Priest," which was situated along the southern third of the eastern wall of the Temple Mount. This corresponds to the open space above the slope of the Mount of Olives, which is today covered with Jewish graves, to the south of the Mount's summit. Here according to a medieval tradition, was the site "on which the priest who burnt the [Red] Heifer stood, sought out, and saw the Temple when he sprinkled the blood" (Mid. 2:6; Yoma 16a). The Arabs call this area "al-Qa'da" ("The Sitting Place"). This name might be an echo of the seat of the Palestinian *rosh yeshivah* during the pilgrimages to Jerusalem during the Arab period.

[Joseph Braslavi (Braslavski) and Michael Avi-Yonah]

At the foot of the mountain, in the area of Silwan Village, rock-hewn tombs are known from the time of the First Temple (Tomb of Pharaoh's Daughter) and Second Temple (so-called Tomb of Zechariah, Tomb of the Sons of Hezir, and Tomb of Absalom). Consequently, this spur of the Mount of Olives became, with the passage of time, especially from the Middle Ages, a burial place for the Jews of Jerusalem. Because the *Ma'aseh Daniel* (A. Jellinek, *Bet ha-Midrash*, vol. 5, 128) states that at the end of days the Messiah will ascend the Mount and it will be there that Ezekiel shall blow his trumpet for the resurrection of the dead (Ginzberg, *Legends of the Jews*, 6 (1959), 438), through the years the graves spread over the slopes and up to the top. At the end of the 19th century, the Russians erected the Church of Gethsemane at the foot of the mount, and on the al-Ṭūr summit, a monastery and tower. Kaiser William II of Germany, after visiting Jerusalem in 1898, erected a hospice for pilgrims known as Augusta Victoria on the second peak. The Englishman, Sir John Grey Hill, built a house on the third peak ("Mount Scopus"), which was later acquired by the Hebrew University for one of its buildings. During Israel's War of Independence, the university buildings remained in Israel hands even though they were surrounded by Arab held territory. This situation was frozen by the Armistice agreement, causing friction and many incidents. Israel was permitted to keep a number of policemen on the mount and these were changed every two weeks in a convoy which had to pass under UN auspices through Jordan-held territory. The Jewish cemeteries and monuments on the Mount of Olives, now outside Israeli territory, were vandalized by the Arabs. The entire Mount was captured by Israel troops in the Six-Day War (1967) and arrangements were subsequently made for the restoration of the Jewish cemeteries on its western flanks, and the Hebrew University returned to its earlier location on Mount Scopus.

BIBLIOGRAPHY: J. Braslavi, in: *Eretz-Israel*, 7 (1964), 69–80; idem, in: Israel Exploration Society, *Yerushalayim le-Doroteihah* (1968), 120–44 (Eng. summ. 63); H.Z. Hirschberg, in: BJPES, 13 (1947), 156–64; Mann, Egypt, index; Mann, Texts, index s.v. *Mount Olivet*; L.H. Vincent and F.M. Abel, *Jérusalem nouvelle*, 2 (1914), 3ff.; G.H. Dalman, *Jerusalem und sein Gelaende* (1930), 25–55; F.M. Abel, *Géographie de la Palestine*, 1 (1933), 372–4; S. Assaf and L. Meir (eds.), *Sefer ha-Yishuv*, 2 (1944), index s.v. *Har Ha-Zeitim*; Press, Ereẓ, 2 (1948), 207; M. Avi-Yonah (ed.), *Sefer Yerushalayim* (1956), illust. btwn. 16–17.

MOURNING (Heb. אֵבֶל), the expression of grief and sorrow over the death of a close relative, friend, national leader, or in response to a national calamity. The lamentation (Heb. קִינָה (*kinah, qinah*); נְהִי, *nehi*) is the specifically literary and musical expression of such grief. The rite of mourning most frequently attested in the narrative and poetic sections of the Bible is the rending of garments. Thus Reuben rends his garments on finding Joseph missing (Gen. 37:29). Jacob does so on seeing Joseph's bloodstained cloak (Gen. 37:34). Joshua responds in this way to the defeat at Ai (Josh. 7:6), Hezekiah, to the words of the Rab-Shakeh (II Kings 19:1 = Isa. 37:1), and Mordecai, to news of the decree of genocide (Esth. 4:1). Job rends his garments on hearing of the death of his children (Job 1:20), and his friends tear their clothing to commiserate with him (2:12). The rending of garments may be simply an outlet for pent-up emotions, or it may have developed as a symbolic substitute for the mutilation of the flesh. Almost as frequent as the rending of garments is the wearing of sackcloth (e.g.,

II Sam. 3:31; Ps. 30:12; Lam. 2:10). Ezekiel prophesies that Tyre will mourn by the removal of embroidered garments and the donning of special mourning robes (Ezek. 26:16; cf. 7:27). The woman of Tekoa whom Joab sent to King David was likewise dressed in mourning garments (II Sam. 14:2), which may be identical with the garments of widowhood worn by Tamar, the widow of Er (Gen. 38:14, 19). Micah suggests that it was not unusual for a mourner to appear naked (Micah 1:8). Other mourning practices which survived in later Judaism are the placing of dust on the head (Josh. 7:6; II Sam. 13:19; Jer. 6:26; 25:34; Ezek. 27:30; Lam. 2:10 etc.; cf. Ta'an. 15b), refraining from wearing ornaments (Ex. 33:4; cf. Sh. Ar., YD 389:3), abstaining from anointing and washing (II Sam. 12:20; cf. Ta'an. 1:6), and fasting (II Sam. 3:35; Esth. 4:3; Ezra 10:6; Neh. 1:4; cf. Ta'an. 1:4ff.). Isaiah describes mourners beating their breasts (Heb. *safad*, Isa. 32:12). The Hebrew term for beating the breast (*safad, misped*; Akk. *sipittu*) becomes a general term for "mourning" (e.g., Gen. 23:2), which takes on the sense of "wailing" (I Kings 13:30; Micah 1:8). Other rites of mourning related to the hair and beard. At the death of Nadab and Abihu, apparently, the Israelites uncovered or disheveled their hair as a sign of mourning. Aaron, Eleazar, and Ithamar, who as priests were forbidden to mourn, were thus prohibited from following this practice (Lev. 10:6). While it became obligatory in later Judaism for mourners to let their hair grow (MK 14b), the prophets (Isa. 22:12; Jer. 16:6; Ezek. 7:18; Amos 8:10) describe tonsure as a standard rite of mourning. Similarly Job shaves his head on hearing of the death of his children (Job 1:20). Deuteronomy 21:12 even prescribes the shaving of the head as a rite of mourning to be observed by the gentile maiden taken captive in war. According to Ezekiel 24:17 it was customary to remove one's turban as an expression of grief (cf. Isa. 61:10). The covering of the head may also be attested as a rite of mourning in II Samuel 15:30; Jeremiah 14:3–4 and Esther 6:12; 7:8, if the Hebrew *ḥafui* is derived from the Hebrew verb *ḥafah*, "to cover." If it is derived from the Arabic *ḥāfi*, "barefoot," which is also the root of Hebrew *yaḥef*, "barefoot," the latter references may corroborate the testimony of Ezekiel and Deutero-Isaiah. Alongside tonsure and the shaving of the beard, the prophets take for granted the practice of cutting gashes in the flesh of the hands or elsewhere (Jer. 16:6; 41:5). They seem unaware of any prohibition against these rites. Leviticus 21:5 prohibits only the priests from making incisions in the flesh, shaving the beard, and tonsure, as from all other rites of mourning, except on the occasion of the death of the priest's father, mother, son, daughter, brother, or unmarried sister. Leviticus 19:27–28 prohibits all Israel from shaving, cutting the hair, *tattooing, and making incisions as a rite of mourning. Deuteronomy 14:1 prohibits all Israel from making incisions in the flesh and from employing tonsure as a rite of mourning. In Leviticus 19 the prohibitions are motivated by the desire to avoid ritual impurity, while in Deuteronomy 14 they are motivated by the striving for holiness. Micah (3:7) and Ezekiel (24:17) mention the covering of the upper lip as an expression of grief. The same practice along with the uncovering (or disheveling) of the hair and the rending of garments is prescribed for lepers in Leviticus 13:45. In the Bible the typical posture for the mourner is sitting (Ezek. 26:16; Jonah 3:6; Job 2:13) or lying (II Sam. 13:31; Lam. 2:21) on the ground, as in later Judaism (Sh. Ar., YD 387:1). Placing the hands on the head (II Sam. 13:19; Jer. 2:37) and prostration (Jer. 4:28; 14:2; Ps. 35:14) are also attested. The Bible does not distinguish, as does later Judaism, between the mourning that precedes the funeral (Heb. *aninut*) and that which follows burial (cf. Ber. 17bff.). The practices which later Judaism associates with the former are therefore referred to simply as rites of mourning in the Bible. Thus Daniel (Dan. 10:23) mourned by abstaining from meat and wine. Although the Mishnah (Ket. 4:4) prescribes the playing of flutes at funerals, the Bible associates mourning with the cessation of both dancing and instrumental music (Isa. 24:8; Jer. 31:12; Ps. 30:12; Job 30:31; Lam. 5:15; Eccles. 3:4), as do later Jewish authorities (Sot. 48a). From the association of gift-giving with the cessation of mourning in Esther 9:22, one may surmise that the exchange of gifts was forbidden to mourners, as in later Judaism (Sh. Ar., YD 385:3). Later Judaism understood its various mourning rites both as an affirmation of the value of the deceased (Sem. 9) and as an appeal to God for mercy (Ta'an. 2:1). Each of these approaches has been advocated to the exclusion of the other by modern schools of anthropology. Most likely both lie behind many of the biblical practices. T.H. Gaster suggests that the mutilation of the body was originally intended to provide the ghost of the departed with blood to drink, while the cutting of the hair enabled the ghost to draw on the strength it embodied.

Lamentations

Lamentations are poetic compositions functionally equivalent to the modern eulogy. Composed by literary giants like David (II Sam. 1:17ff.; 3:33ff.) and Jeremiah (II Chron. 35:25), these tributes were, in accordance with the standard literary usage, chanted rather than declaimed. These eulogies were frequently composed in a special meter, which modern scholars have designated as the *qinah* meter (i.e., lamentation meter). It is characterized by the division of each verse into two unequal parts, in contrast to the usually parallel structure of biblical poetry. Jeremiah speaks of a professional class of women who composed and chanted lamentations (*mekonenot, meqonenot*, Jer. 9:16). Their art was regarded as a branch of wisdom, and thus they are called "skilled" (Heb. *ḥakhamot*). Men and women singers made lamentations and preserved them for future generations as part of the general education of the young (II Chron. 35:25). Another expression of grief was the exclamation *ho-ho* (Amos 5:16) or *hoi* (I Kings 13:30; Jer. 22:18; 34:5). A specified period of mourning is only prescribed by the Bible in connection with the captive gentile maiden (Deut. 21:13). She is required to mourn her parents for one month. The later Jewish custom of seven days of mourning is observed by Joseph on the death of Jacob (Gen. 50:10); the Egyptians mourned him for 70 (50:3)), the inhabitants of Jabesh-Gilead upon the burial of Saul and Jonathan (I Sam.

31:13 = I Chron. 10:12), and Job and his friends at the height of Job's suffering (Job 2:13). Daniel's observance of three weeks of mourning (Dan. 10:2) may reflect the author's awareness of the week as a standard period of mourning. Moses and Aaron were each mourned for 30 days (Num. 20:29; Deut. 34:8), while Jacob and Ephraim each mourned "many days" (Gen. 37:34; I Chron. 7:22) for their children. While Jeremiah (41:5) tells of contemporaries who expressed grief by bringing sacrifices to the Temple, Nehemiah (Neh. 8:9) suggests the incompatibility of religious festivities and mourning (cf. Ta'an. 2:8, 10). The comforting of mourners is accomplished by the tenderly spoken word (Isa. 40:1–2), by sitting with the mourner (Job. 2:13), by providing him with compensation for his loss (Gen. 24:67; Isa. 60:2–9), and by offering him bread and wine (II Sam. 3:35; Jer. 16:7). The bread is called "bread of agony" (*leḥem onashim*, Ezek. 24:17; cf. *leḥem 'onim* in Hos. 9:4), and the wine, "the cup of consolation" (Jer. 16:7). The serving of such a meal has been variously explained as an affirmation of the bonds between the survivors, a reaffirmation of life itself after a period of fasting from death to burial, and as an act of conviviality with the soul of the deceased.

[Mayer Irwin Gruber]

Talmudic and Medieval Periods

Although the laws and customs of mourning are largely based on the biblical references, many additional ones developed out of usage and custom and, as such, are of rabbinical rather than biblical authority. In general, there has been a consistency in mourning practices from the biblical era, but in particular between the talmudic period and modern times. With few exceptions, the rules of mourning described and laid down in the Talmud and the early sources are identical with those observed today. These laws were designed to provide both for the "dignity of the departed" and the "dignity of the living" (cf. Sanh. 46b–47a). The body, regarded as the creation of God and the dwelling place of the soul, was accorded every respect. Likewise, every attempt was made to ease the grief of the mourners and to share their sorrow. The pain of death was mitigated by viewing it as the moment of transition from the temporal world to the eternal world (Zohar No'ah, 66a). One of the rabbis interpreted the biblical verse "And, behold, it was very good" (Gen. 1:31) to refer to death (Gen. R. 9:5, 10; see *Life and Death).

It was customary "to pour out all drawn water" in the neighborhood of the house in which the person died (Sh. Ar., YD 339:5). Originally deriving from folk beliefs, this custom was subsequently explained as a method of announcing a death since Jews were always reluctant to be the bearers of evil tidings (*Siftei Kohen*, YD 339:5, n. 9). Others interpreted that this act indicated that the deceased was an important person, therefore the supply of water was lessened just as "there was no water for the congregation" (Num. 20:2) after the death of Miriam (*Be'er ha-Golah*, YD 339:5, n. 8). The dead body was not left alone, and watchers remained with the corpse until the funeral, either to honor the dead or to guard the corpse against possible damage. These watchers were exempted from the performance of other positive commandments while engaged in this meritorious deed (Bet. 3:1). Before the funeral the body was ritually purified (see *tohorah*). Professional women mourners, who clapped their hands in grief and sang dirges and lamentations, led the public display of grief at the funeral. Dirges were recited responsively while lamentations were sung in unison (MK 3:8, 9; see **Kinah*). The prevalent rabbinic opinion was that only the first day of the mourning period was of biblical authority (Asheri to MK 3:27; 34b; Maim. Yad, Avel, 1:1), while the seven-day mourning period was instituted by Moses (TJ, Ket. 1:1, 25a). The rabbis distinguished four stages in the mourning period: **aninut*, the period between death and burial; *avelut* or *shivah*, the seven days following burial; **sheloshim*, the time until the 30th day after burial; and the first year (TJ, MK 3:7, 83c).

ANINUT. During the *aninut* period, the mourner was called an *onen*. Although still obligated to abide by the negative precepts of the Torah, the *onen* was absolved from the performance of many positive religious duties such as the recital of the **Shema* and the donning of *tallit* and *tefillin* (MK 23b). He thus indicated his respect for the memory of the deceased since he was so distraught that he could not discharge his religious obligations (Sem. 10; Deut. R. 9:1). In addition, freedom from certain religious obligations enabled the *onen* to attend to the needs of the dead and his burial without distraction. The rule that "he who is engaged in a religious act is exempt from performing other religious duties" applied (Suk. 25a). It was also forbidden for the *onen* to eat meat or drink wine (Ber. 17b) or overindulge in eating (TJ, Ber. 3:1, 6a). If death occurred on the Sabbath, or if the Sabbath was part of the *aninut* period, the *onen* was obligated to discharge all his religious obligations (MK 23b), and he was even permitted to eat meat and drink wine on that day (Ber. 18a).

SHIVAH. Immediately after the funeral, the *shivah* ("seven") mourning period began. The bereaved family gathered in the house of the deceased and sat on overturned couches or beds and enrobed their heads. The mourners were obligated to rend their garments and to recite the *dayyan ha-emet* ("the true Judge") blessing (see **Keri'ah*). They were also not to leave the house (MK 23a), perform manual labor, conduct business transactions, bathe, anoint the body, cut the hair, cohabit, wear leather shoes, wash clothes, greet acquaintances, and study the Torah (MK 15a–b). They were, however, permitted to study sorrowful portions of the Bible and Talmud such as Job, Lamentations, parts of Jeremiah, and the laws of mourning. The mourner's first meal after the funeral was known as *Se'uddat Havra'ah* (Meal of Consolation). The meal was provided by friends and neighbors in accordance with the talmudic injunction that "a mourner is forbidden to eat of his own bread on the first day (of mourning" (MK 27b). It was also forbidden for the mourner to don *tefillin* on the first day of the *shivah* period (Ket. 6b; Sh. Ar., YD 388:1). The rabbis considered the first three days as the most intense, declaring, "Three days for weeping and seven for lamenting" (MK 27b).

SHELOSHIM. Modified mourning continued through the *sheloshim* period when the mourner was told "not to cut the hair and wear pressed clothes" (MK 27b). During the *sheloshim* it was also forbidden for the mourner to marry, to attend places of entertainment or festive events (even when primarily of religious significance), to embark on a business journey, or to participate in social gatherings (MK 22b–23a; Yad, Avel 6:2). When mourning for parents, some of the above prohibitions remained applicable during the entire 12 months following the day of death. The mourner was not permitted to trim his hair until his companions rebuked him. He was also enjoined from entering "a house of rejoicing" during this period (MK 22b).

RELATIONSHIPS REQUIRING MOURNING. The observance of these formal rules of mourning was required for the nearest of kin corresponding to those for whom a priest was to defile himself, i.e., a wife (husband), father, mother, son, daughter, brother, and sister (Lev. 21:1–3; MK 20b), but not an infant less than 30 days old (Yad, Avel 1:6). The Talmud also relates instances when aspects of mourning were observed upon the death of teachers and scholars. Thus when R. Johanan died, R. Ammi observed the seven and the 30 days of mourning (MK 25b). In mourning for a *ḥakham* one bared the arm and shoulder on the right for the *av bet din* on the left, and for a *nasi* on both sides (MK 22b; Sem. 9:2).

TERMINATION OF MOURNING. Although the Sabbath was included in the seven days of mourning, no outward signs of mourning were permitted on that day. Private observances such as the prohibition against washing remained in force on the Sabbath (MK 23b; Maim, Yad, Avel 10:1). If burial took place before a festival and the mourner observed the mourning rite for even a short period prior to the festival, the entire *shivah* period was annulled by the holiday. If the *shivah* had been completed, then the incoming festival canceled the entire *sheloshim* period. If, however, the funeral took place on *Ḥol ha-Mo'ed*, the *shivah* and *sheloshim* were observed after the termination of the festival. In the Diaspora, the last day of the festival counted as one of the days of the *shivah* and *sheloshim* (MK 3:5–7; Sh. Ar., YD 399, 13; 400).

Relatives and friends visited the mourner during the week of *shivah*. Discreet individuals expressed their condolences in sympathetic silence (cf. Job. 2:13). In general, visitors were advised not to speak until the mourner began the conversation (MK 28b). Upon leaving, it became customary for the visitor to approach the mourner and say: "May the Almighty comfort you among the other mourners for Zion and Jerusalem." Rabbinical literature explained the reasons for the choice of seven as the main period of mourning. Commenting on the verse "I will turn your feasts into mourning" (Amos 8:10), it was explained that, just as the days of the feasts (Passover and Sukkot) are seven, so the period of mourning is also for seven days (MK 20a). The Zohar gives a mystical reason: "For seven days the soul goes to and fro between the house and the grave, mourning for the body" (Zohar, *Va-Yeḥi*, 226a). The institution of *shivah* was considered even more ancient than the flood. The rabbis interpreted "And it came to pass after the seven days, that the waters of the flood were upon the earth" (Gen. 7:10) to mean that God postponed retribution until after the seven days of mourning for the righteous Methuselah (Gen. 5:27; Sanh. 108b). The rabbis discouraged excessive mourning. Jeremiah's charge, "Weep ye not for the dead, neither bemoan him" (Jer. 22:10) was interpreted to mean "weep not in excess, nor bemoan too much." Accordingly, intensive mourning ceased after the *sheloshim*. Thereafter, God declares to the one who continues to mourn "Ye are not more compassionate toward the departed than I." The rabbis stated that whoever indulged in excessive grief over his dead finally had to weep for another. It was related that a woman in the neighborhood of R. Huna ultimately lost all seven of her sons because she wept excessively for each one (MK 27b).

Modern Practice

Most of the observances described above are still practiced by traditional Jews all over the world. In most communities today there are burial societies or funeral chapels which arrange the details of the *tohorah* and the burial. The *onenim* still have the responsibility of contacting the burial society, as well as obtaining death and other certificates which may be required before the funeral can be held. They must also inform relatives and friends so that proper honor and respect can be paid to the deceased. In the house of *shivah* couches and beds are no longer overturned, the mourners sitting instead on low stools. With the exception that mourners no longer muffle their heads, all the other restrictions are observed. Slippers of cloth, felt, or rubber are worn instead of leather footwear. Women also abstain from using cosmetics during the *shivah* period. A candle burns continuously in the house of mourning for the entire seven days. It has also become customary to cover mirrors or turn them to the wall. Among the explanations offered for this practice is that prayer is forbidden in front of a mirror, since the reflection distracts the attention of the worshiper. Another interpretation is that mirrors, often associated with vanity, are out of place at such a time.

Prayers in the Home and Changes in the Liturgy

By the end of the Middle Ages, praying in the house of *shivah* was a well-established custom (cf. Shab. 152a–b). Nowadays a **minyan* gathers in the house of mourning for the daily *Shaḥarit* and *Minḥah-Ma'ariv* services. For the reading of the Law during these home services a Torah Scroll may be borrowed from the communal synagogue, provided that proper facilities for its care are available and that it will be read on three occasions. If it is not possible to obtain a *minyan* in the home, the mourner may attend the synagogue for services and the recitation of **Kaddish*. Generally the mourner attends the synagogue for Sabbath and festival service. In the house of mourning and in the mourner's personal prayers, the following changes in the normal order of the services are made:

(1) The talmudical passage *pittum ha-ketoret* (Ker. 6a; Hertz, Prayer, 546), describing the compounding of the in-

censes for daily offering in the Temple, is omitted by the mourner since he is forbidden to study Torah.

(2) Likewise the mourner omits the recitation of *eizehu mekoman*, the chapter of the Mishnah which describes the appointed places for the various animal sacrifices (Zev. 5:1–8; Hertz, Prayer, 38–40).

(3) The *Priestly Blessing (Num. 6:24–26; Hertz, Prayer, 154), which concludes with the greeting of peace, is omitted in the house of mourning because the mourner may not extend greetings. In Jerusalem, however, it is recited.

(4) **Taḥanun* (Hertz, Prayer, 168–86) is omitted because its theme, "I have sinned before thee," is deemed inappropriate for a mourner.

(5) Psalm 20 (Hertz, Prayer, 200) is also omitted because it will intensify the mourner's grief during his "day of trouble" (Ps. 20:2).

(6) The verse beginning, "And as for me, this is my covenant with them, saith the Lord" is omitted from the *u-Va le-Ẓiyyon* (Hertz, Prayer, 202) because the mourner does not desire a covenant which will perpetuate his unhappy situation.

(7) Psalm 49, which declares that the injustices and inequalities of human existence are corrected in the hereafter, is recited after the daily service in the house of mourning (Hertz, Prayer, 1088–90).

(8) The mourner omits the six Psalms (95–99; 29) recited before the *Ma'ariv* service on Friday night (Hertz, Prayer, 346–54). He remains in the anteroom until the conclusion of **lekhah dodi*. He then enters the synagogue and the congregation rises and greets him with the traditional greeting extended to mourners: "May the Almighty…" Hertz, Prayer, 358).

(9) **Hallel* (Hertz, Prayer, 756–72) is not recited in the house of *shivah* on *Rosh Ḥodesh because it contains such verses as "The dead praise not the Lord, neither any that go down into silence" (Ps. 115:17), and "This is the day which the Lord hath made, we will rejoice and be glad in it" (Ps. 118:24). In most rites, however, it is recited when the mourners leave the room. If Rosh Ḥodesh coincides with the Sabbath, Hallel should be recited even if the services are being held in the house of mourning since no public display of mourning is permissible on the Sabbath.

(10) The mourner is not called up to the reading of the Law during the week of *shivah* even if he is the only kohen or levite in the congregation.

There are indications that it was customary for mourners to wear black throughout the *sheloshim* (Yoma 39b; Shab. 114a; Sem. 2:8). Nowadays, however, Jews are not permitted to dress in black clothing or to wear black armbands as signs of mourning since these are considered non-Jewish customs (see *Ḥukkat ha-Goi). Similarly, the bringing of gifts to the house of *shivah* is considered an emulation of non-Jewish practice. During the *sheloshim* period it is customary for the mourner to change his synagogue seat for weekday services. When mourning for parents, a different seat is occupied during the entire 12-month period. The **Kaddish*, however, is recited by the person mourning a parent or child for 11 months. **Yahrzeit* is observed on the anniversary of the Jewish date of the person's death. There is an opinion that when three or more days elapse between death and burial, the first *Yahrzeit* is observed on the date of burial. Nevertheless, during subsequent years, *Yahrzeit* is observed on the anniversary of the date of death (*Taz, Shakh* and *Be'er Hetev*, YD 402:12). Reform Judaism has greatly modified the above laws and customs. The week of mourning is often shortened, and, frequently, only a period of three days is observed. Practices such as the rending of garments, sitting on low stools, not wearing leather shoes, and not attending places of entertainment during the period of the 30 days or first year are not generally observed by Reform Jews. Some have the religious services in the home only for the first three days, while others have them only after returning home from the funeral.

[Aaron Rothkoff]

BIBLIOGRAPHY: BIBLE: K. Budde, in: ZAW, 2 (1882), 1–52; B. Malinowski, *Magic, Science and Religion* (1925); E. Durkheim, *The Elementary Forms of the Religious Life* (1947); Kaufmann Y., Toledot, 2 (1960), 544–56; K.V.H. Ringgren, *Israelite Religion* (1963), 239–42; T.H. Gaster, *Myth, Legend and Custom in the Old Testament* (1969), 590–604. TALMUD AND MEDIEVAL PERIODS: Y.M. Tykocinski, *Sefer Gesher ha-Ḥayyim* (1947: 1960[2]); J.J.(L.) Greenwald (Grunwald), *Kol-Bo al Aveilut*, 3 vols. (1947–52); C.N. Denburg, *Code of Hebrew Law*, 1 (1954); B. Yashar, *Seder ha-Aveilut ve-ha-Niḥumim* (1956); S. Spero, *Journey into Light* (1959); H.M. Rabinowicz, *Guide to Life* (1964); D. Zlotnick (ed. and tr.), *The Tractate "Mourning" (Semaḥot)* (1966); M. Lamm, *Jewish Way in Death and Mourning* (1969). **ADD. BIBLIOGRAPHY:** S. Glick, *Light and Consolation: The Development of Jewish Consolation Practices* (2004).

MOUSE (Heb. עַכְבָּר, *akhbar*), small rodent enumerated in the Bible with the rat and five reptiles ("creeping things"). It is so classified because as a result of its short legs its belly touches the ground as it walks. Isaiah (66:17) vehemently assails those who "eat swine's flesh, detestable things, and the mouse" at idolatrous ceremonies. The *akhbar* includes both the house mouse, *Mus musculus*, and the field mouse, *Microtus guenthri*, the latter wreaking havoc with crops. Their depredations can amount to a plague destroying substantial parts of the harvest. It was such a plague which visited the Philistines who captured the Ark of the Covenant of the Lord (I Sam. 6:4–11). They not only "marred the land" but also caused a plague of "emerods." It has been suggested that the latter reference is to a pestilence caused by the microbe, *Pasteurella pestis*, transmitted to man by rodent fleas. The symptoms are a swelling of the lymphatic glands especially in the groins, which was thought to be a form of hemorrhoids. Both house and field mice are frequently mentioned in the Mishnah and Talmud. The ancient view of the possibility of spontaneous generation finds expression in the statement that the mouse was formed from the earth (Ḥul. 9:6). A mean person was called "a mouse lying in his money" (Sanh. 29b). One who eats food which has been nibbled by mice was said to forget his learning (Hor. 13a).

BIBLIOGRAPHY: Lewysohn, Zool, 105–7, 345; F.S. Bodenheimer, *Animal and Man in Bible Lands* (1960), 21–23, 46, 101, 110. **ADD. BIBLIOGRAPHY:** Feliks, Ha-Ẓome'aḥ, 261.

[Jehuda Feliks]

°MOWINCKEL, SIGMUND OLAF PLYTT (1884–1965), Norwegian biblical scholar. Mowinckel was educated at the University of Oslo (then Kristiania) and taught there from 1917 until his retirement in 1954. He also studied Assyriology in Germany. His doctoral thesis (1916) was a study of the Book of Nehemiah, and one of his last books was also devoted to Nehemiah (*Studien zu dem Buche Ezra-Nehemia*, 3 vols., 1964–65). Mowinckel was very much influenced by the form-critical and tradition-history approach of Hermann *Gunkel and Hugo Gressmann. His first book on the Psalms, *The Royal Psalms in the Bible*, was also issued in 1916, and his chief work, *Psalmenstudien* (vols. 1–6) was published between 1921 and 1924. In this work, he placed the psalms in their cultic context and interpreted them in the light of this background. These *Psalmenstudien* were republished in 1961, and in 1963 an English translation of his last work on the Psalms was issued (*The Psalms in Israel's Worship*, 2 vols, 1962; Norwegian version, *Offersang og Sangoffer*, 1951). In 1964 two works on the Pentateuch were published, *Erwägungen zur Pentateuchquellenfrage* ("Considerations of the Question of the Sources of the Pentateuch") and *Tetrateuch, Pentateuch, Hexateuch; Palestina for Israel* ("Palestine before Israel," 1965) and *Israels opphvog eldste historie* ("Israel's Origin and Oldest History," 1967) were published posthumously. Mowinckel's main ideas have been widely accepted by biblical scholars, and his influence in Europe, especially Scandinavia, has been considerable. H.L. *Ginsberg taught himself Norwegian so that he could speak it to Mowinckel.

ADD. BIBLIOGRAPHY: D. Rian, in: DBI, 2:166–68.

[Arvid S. Kapelrud / S. David Sperling (2nd ed.)]

MOWSHOWITZ, ISRAEL (1914–1991), U.S. rabbi, political intermediary. Mowshowitz was born in Poland and immigrated to the United States with his family in 1929. He attended Yeshiva University, where he earned a B.A., and was ordained at its Rabbi Yitzhak Elchanan Theological Seminary in 1937. He earned a Ph.D. in psychology from Duke University and Yeshiva University awarded him an honorary doctorate in 1966. Although trained as an Orthodox rabbi, the pulpits he held were at Conservative synagogues, first in Durham, N.C., and then at Omaha, Nebraska. In 1949, he was appointed rabbi of Hillcrest Jewish Center in Queens, N.Y., becoming rabbi emeritus in 1983.

Respected in both the Orthodox and Conservative movements, Mowshowitz rose to become arguably the most prominent Jewish communal leader in the city and state. He was a founder of the International Synagogue at Kennedy International Airport and served as its honorary president. He also served on the boards of numerous charitable, interfaith, and interracial organizations in New York.

In the 1960s Mowshowitz was the president of the New York Board of Rabbis, an organization of 1,000 rabbis representing all the major denominations; in that capacity, he became a nationally quoted spokesman, commenting on all political and social issues that impacted Jewish interests.

Mowshowitz forged close ties with New York Governor Mario M. Cuomo, a Roman Catholic who called Mowshowitz "my rabbi," and who lived nearby. He held the title of special assistant for community affairs in the governor's office, where he negotiated issues between the state and religious groups. According to Conference of Presidents of Major American Jewish Organizations head Israel *Miller, "He was the one all of us would call when we needed something done of a political nature."

Mowshowitz traveled throughout the world on behalf of Jewish causes. In 1956, he was a member of one of the first delegations of rabbis to visit the Soviet Union to investigate the conditions of Soviet Jewry. He also traveled to Poland, South Africa, Iran, Hungary, Poland, Romania, and other countries on similar missions, including a study trip to 13 countries with the National Conference of Christians and Jews.

The New York Board of Rabbis established the annual Rabbi Israel and Libby Mowshowitz Award, to honor both them and rabbis who excel in public service.

He wrote two books, *Fires to Warm Us* (1978) and *To Serve in Faithfulness* (1975), and co-authored with Debra Orenstein *From Generation to Generation* (1992).

[Bezalel Gordon (2nd ed.)]

MOYAL, ESTHER (1873–1948), Arabic journalist and feminist. Esther Moyal, a member of the Lazari (al-Azharī) family of *Beirut, began taking part in public affairs in 1893, while she was teaching for the Scottish Church mission. She took over the correspondence of the Lebanese Women's League and in the same year was sent to Chicago to represent *Lebanon at the International Women's Conference. She was active in various women's organizations such as Bākūrat Sūriya ("The Dawn of Syria") and Nahḍat al-Nisā' ("The Awakening Women"). In 1894 she married a medical student, Simon Moyal, in *Jaffa. After he qualified they settled in *Cairo, where in 1898 Esther founded the monthly *al-ʿĀ'ila* ("The Family"), which became a weekly in 1904. She also became a frequent contributor to the leading Cairo daily, *al-Ahrām* and the Egyptian literary periodical *al-Hilāl*. The Moyals moved to Jaffa in 1908 and the following year she helped establish an organization of Jewish women in the city. In 1913 she became joint editor with her husband of the Jaffa periodical, *Ṣawt al-ʿUthmāniyya* ("The Voice of Ottomanism"). Widowed in 1915, she went to live in Marseilles, returning to Jaffa in the mid-1940s. Her writings include a life of Emile Zola and Arabic translations of French books.

[Hayyim J. Cohen]

MOẒA or **(Ha)Moẓah** (Heb. הַמֹּצָה, מוֹצָא), town in Benjamin mentioned in the city list of Benjamin with Miẓpeh and

Chephirah (Josh. 18:26) and in the genealogy of Benjamin with Alemeth, Azmaveth, and Eleasah (1 Chron. 8:36). The name also occurs in the genealogy of Caleb (1 Chron. 2:46), but a connection between this Moẓa and the Benjamite Moẓa is doubtful, as another locality might be meant. According to one reading, the "*Mṣh*" seal stamps found on jar handles at Jericho and Tell ab-Naṣba and belonging to the Persian period attest the existence of an administrative center at Moza at that time. It is identified with Khirbat Beit Mizza to the west of Jerusalem and situated near a spring in a valley rich in olive groves and vineyards. It is probably identical with the Roman colony *Emmaus, established by Vespasian after the siege of Jerusalem at a distance of 30 stadia (c. 3½ mi.) from Jerusalem; he settled 800 veterans there (Jos., Wars, 7:217). A village below Jerusalem called Moẓa, where willow branches were cut for the rites at the Sukkot, is mentioned in the Mishnah (Suk. 4:5), i.e., in reference to the times before the destruction of the Second Temple. According to the Jerusalem Talmud (Suk. 4:3, 54b), the name of Moẓa was changed to Colonia and a "source of Colonia" is mentioned by Cyrillus Scythopolitanus (*Vita Sabae*, 67). The latter locality was probably at the site of the Arab village Qālūnya (see below). Remains of a Roman road station, a bath, Jewish and Roman tombs, and a Byzantine monastery were found in the area.

[Michael Avi-Yonah]

Modern Times

The land of Moẓa (moshavah), on the site of ancient Moza, was the first rural site in Ereẓ Israel acquired by Jews for farming purposes (by inhabitants of the old city of Jerusalem headed by Yehoshua *Yellin in 1859). A few families worked the land and terraced the hillsides, but did not live permanently at Moẓa. In 1894 the Jerusalem chapter of the *B'nai B'rith founded a small village on the site. One of the first industrial enterprises in the country was a tile and roof tile factory which used the local Moẓa marl as raw material. It was built by the Moẓa settlers at the beginning of the 20th century. In the 1929 Arab riots the village was largely destroyed and seven of its inhabitants were murdered, but the village was soon restored and in 1933 Moẓa Illit ("Upper Moẓa") was founded as an adjacent moshav. On the hilltop southwest of Moẓa, *Kuppat Ḥolim, the Histadrut Sick Fund, opened the Arza Convalescent Home in the 1930s, in the place where Theodor *Herzl on his 1898 visit to the country planted a cypress tree (at the time erroneously identified as the biblical cedar from which the name "Arza" was derived). The tree was felled in World War I by unknown persons. In the Israel *War of Independence (1948) Moẓa was in grave danger until the neighboring Arab village of Qālūnya fell to Jewish forces and was abandoned by its inhabitants. Although most of the inhabitants in Moẓa were employed in Jerusalem, some kept farms. From the late 1950s a garden suburb of Jerusalem developed there. In 2002 the population of Moẓa Illit was 796.

[Efraim Orni / Shaked Gilboa (2nd ed.)]

BIBLIOGRAPHY: EM, 4 (1962), 738; Avigad, in: IEJ, 8 (1958), 113–9.

MOZES, family of Israeli press magnates. The Mozes family played a major role in the Israeli press in the second half of the 20th century. From its flagship daily newspaper, *Yedioth Aharonoth*, through its subsidiary enterprises including a chain of local newspapers, women's and other special interest magazines, publishing and printing interests, and shares in Israel's Channel 2, the Mozes family had by the 1990s become the country's biggest media moguls.

In 1940, a small newspaper, *Yedioth Aharonoth*, founded the previous year as one of the country's few independent evening newspapers, had been acquired by ALEXANDER MOZES, a printer, from the newspaper's founder Nahum Komerov. While Alexander took charge of printing the paper, his father YEHUDAH MOZES (b. 1886), a textile entrepreneur and businessman, took charge of the newspaper's editorial operations, together with his son, NOAH (1912–1986), an agronomist. It consisted of some two pages each day, and had a circulation of 30,000. The paper failed financially in its early years, and in 1949 was forced to sell half of its shares to *Mapai. Its biggest crisis occurred in February 1948 when its editor, Dr. Azriel *Carlebach, together with most of its editorial staff as well as some of the printing and administrative workers, left the newspaper overnight – ostensibly upset over Yehudah Mozes' intervention in day-to-day editorial matters – and founded the rival *Maariv* newspaper. Rebuilding the paper, Yehudah Mozes appointed his cousin Dov *Yudkovsky as news editor and Dr. Herzl *Rosenblum as editor, whose responsibilities comprised the editorial column and the op-ed pages. Yudkovsky conceived the newspaper as "the people's newspaper": despite its popular tabloid appearance, it also carried editorial matter of interest to readers from the professional classes. With the death of Yehudah in 1955, Noah Mozes became the publisher. It took *Yedioth Aharonoth* until the late 1970s to overtake *Maariv* as Israel's biggest-selling newspaper. By 2005 42% of Israelis read the newspaper daily, and 54% its Friday weekend edition, according to a Teleseker survey. In the 1980s the newspaper entered the local newspaper market, developing local weekly newspapers (sold as supplements to the Friday paper) in key Israeli towns, exploiting the local advertising market.

The newspaper's corporate setup is characterized by a highly centralized structure in which company shares are divided between 100 basic shares and 1,400 regular shares. With only the family owning the basic shares, and an in-built clause that the company directors are determined only by the holders of the basic shares, it generated resentment among the regular shareholders, particular after Noah died in 1986 in a traffic accident and his son, ARNON ("Noni"; 1953–), an economics graduate from Tel Aviv University, replaced him as publisher.

Since the mid-1980s the newspaper's senior management was characterized by family in-fighting and court hearings as "Noni" Mozes sought to centralize control. In 1989 Yudkovsky was dismissed, and moved to *Maariv*, where he was appointed editor. While Ze'ev Mozes, the paper's co-director whose responsibilities included manpower, was initially allied with "Noni" Mozes – based on a 1986 agreement that the two men would share the two-man directorship of the newspaper for a 20-year period – he was subsequently eased out and sold his shares in 1997 to Eliezer Fishman and Haim Bar-On (the owners of the *Globes* financial newspaper). Ze'ev, who was Noah's nephew and Yehudah's grandson, was also responsible for moving the newspaper's printing press from the newspaper's editorial offices in Tel Aviv to a bigger site in Rishon le-Zion. Oded Mozes, son of Alexander, had been eased out years earlier when Noah Mozes set up a separate printing press, named after his son Gilad, killed in a traffic accident, to print the newspaper.

When Paula Mozes, Noah's widow, died in 1997, she bequeathed all her shares to her son, Noni, asking her two daughters, Judy Shalom-Mozes, wife of the Likud MK and former foreign minister Silvan *Shalom, and Tami-Mozes-Borowitz, to give their brother power of attorney to administer the newspaper. In building a coalition, Noni initially gave Tami management of Yediot Tikshoret, the sister company comprising the chain of local newspapers and magazines, as well as *Yedioth Aharonoth*'s share in the Channel 2 subsidiary, Reshet. But she sold her shares to Fishman and Bar-On in 1998. Noni Mozes received a setback in 1997 when the Israeli courts acceded to a petition to broaden the structure of the paper's directorship from two to five members.

After Yudkovky's departure from the paper in 1989, Moshe *Vardi, a managing editor, and Rozenblum's son, was appointed in his place. Vardi possessed an uncanny ability for identifying news stories and for news writing. This helped the paper maintain the lead which Yudkovsky had managed to bring about in the cirulation war with *Maariv*. In the mid-1990s the newspaper was embroiled in an affair involving mutual wiretapping among partners and editors of *Maariv* and *Yedioth Aharonoth*. *Yedioth Aharonoth*'s assignments editor, Ruth Ben-Ari, was charged with wiretapping *Maariv* boss Ofer Nimrodi, and its editor Dov Yudkovsky. Though subsequently cleared, Vardi, suspended himself from the editorship during the two year trial. During this period Alon Shalev, a news executive on Channel 2, was appointed editor. Vardi was subsequently reinstated, holding the post until his retirement in 2004. Rafi Ginat, an Israel television reporter who edited and presented the investigative *Kolbotek* consumer program, replaced him.

In 2000 the newspaper created its website, Y-Net, with its own separate reporting staff. In 2005 it had 3.3 million users monthly.

The *Yedioth Aharonoth* groups was valued in 1997 at around $450 million. In addition to the daily newspaper, the group's properties included 17 local newspapers, a woman's magazine and shares in another, a number of special interest magazines, a Russian-language daily newspaper, three publishing houses, shares in the Channel 2 subsidiary Reshet, two printing presses, and two modeling agencies. Noni Mozes' share alone was valued in 2004 at $200 million. Concerned at the power of *Yedioth Aharonoth*, and of other newspaper chains, with the perceived threat to freedom of the press, the Monopolies Commission allowed *Yedioth Aharonoth* to purchase no more than 24% of the shares of Reshet.

[Yoel Cohen (2nd ed.)]

MOZNAYIM (Heb. מֹאזְנַיִם), literary organ of the Hebrew Writers Association in Israel. *Moznayim* was founded in 1929, under the editorship of Y.D. *Berkowitz and F. Lachower, when the association ceased to endorse its previous organ, *Ketuvim*, edited by A. Steinman and A. *Shlonsky. Published first as a weekly in Tel Aviv, *Moznayim* became a monthly in 1933. It appeared regularly until the spring of 1947, when it ceased publication until the autumn of that year. *Moznayim* reappeared as a fortnightly only until the State of Israel was about to be established. *Moznayim*, in a new series, was published as a monthly from 1955.

The first volumes bear the stamp of *Bialik, a frequent contributor, and his contemporaries. Eventually, younger writers also left their influence upon this publication. All literary genres were encouraged: poetry, the story, the essay, criticism, the review, the scholarly study in the form of a popular lecture, publication of literary documents (e.g., letters), and translations from world literature. Hebrew writers from different generations and different parts of the world have participated. Until the Holocaust, the majority of East European Hebrew writers contributed and, later, Hebrew writers in the United States and other countries were published.

In honor of the U.S. Hebrew writer, Reuben *Wallenrod, *Moznayim* annually presents an award for the most distinguished poem, story, or essay published in the periodical. An index to the first hundred issues was issued in 1944.

[Getzel Kressel]

MOZYR, city in Polesie district, Belarus. After the second partition of Poland (1793), Mozyr was annexed by Russia and became a county town in the province (gubernia) of Minsk until the Russian Revolution. Jews are mentioned there in the 16th century. Many were wounded, killed, and robbed by the soldiers of *Chmielnicki in 1648. In 1766 there were 896 Jewish taxpayers in the community of Mozyr and the surrounding villages; these increased to 2,256 in 1847 and 5,631 (70% of the total population) in 1897. The Jews played an important role in the wood industry which developed in the town and its vicinity, owning several sawmills and match factories. Mozyr was one of the towns where the *Bund was active. A Russian language school operated from 1899, as did a yeshivah. During the Russian Civil War (1917–21) the Jews suffered at the hands of the "volunteer army" of Bulak-Balakhowich, who fought the Soviet regime. Many were wounded and 44 murdered, women were raped, and property looted. With the consolidation of the Soviet regime Jewish public institutions were liquidated. In 1926 there were 5,901 persons in the town (61.3% of the population), and 6,307 (36.1% of the total population) in 1939. Until 1938 there were two Yiddish elementary schools. Mozyr was occupied by the Germans on August 22,

1941. Some Jews succeeded in leaving town. In the fall a ghetto was established housing 1,500 persons. In the week of January 7, 1942, they were murdered, and another 700 Jews were drowned in the Pripet River.

BIBLIOGRAPHY: S. Agurski, *Revolyutsionnoye dvizheniye v Belorussii* (1928), 142; *Prestupleniya nemetsko – fashistskikn okkupantov v Belorussii* (1965), 310, 320.

[Yehuda Slutsky / Shmuel Spector (2nd ed.)]

MSTISLAVL (referred to by the Jews as **Amtchislav**), city in Mogilev district, Belarus; until 1772 in Poland-Lithuania; under czarist rule, part of Mogilev province. Jews are first mentioned as inhabitants of Mstislavl in 1590, although they had leased the taxes of the area from the mid-16th century. In 1639 there was a synagogue in Mstislavl. During the Northern War between Peter the Great and Charles XII of Sweden, Peter's troops entered Mstislavl (1708) and many Jews were injured. In 1765 there were 552 Jews registered as paying poll tax in the town and surrounding villages. As a result of their critical economic situation, 271 Jews left the town and district in 1808 for agricultural settlements in southern Russia. At the end of December 1843 a quarrel broke out between some Jews and a group of soldiers who had come to confiscate some smuggled merchandise in a Jewish shop. Magnifying the incident, the local authorities described it to the government as a Jewish rebellion against the authorities. When informed of the affair, Nicholas I ordered that every tenth Jew in the town be impressed into the army. It was only after numerous intercessions in the capital that investigators from St. Petersburg were sent to Mstislavl. The accusations of rebellion were refuted and the collective punishment revoked. Subsequently, the day the decree was rescinded (Kislev 3) was celebrated as the *Purim D'Amtchislav*. In 1847 there were 3,815 Jews registered in Mstislavl and in 1897 they numbered 5,076 (59.7% of the population). Because of the Jewish merchants, the town turned into an important commercial center. There were 194 Jewish artisans out of a total of 291. Most of them were *Mitnaggedim*, but there was also a considerable minority of *Ḥabad Ḥasidim. After World War I the Jewish population decreased, until in 1926 only 3,371 (42% of the total population) remained, and it dropped further to 2,067 (20% of the total) in 1939. A Yiddish school operated there from 1927, and two kolkhozes, with 110 families, were in the town in the 1930s. The Germans captured Mstislavl on July 14, 1941, and in early October killed 30 elderly Jews. On October 15, 1941, together with the local police, they murdered 850 (or perhaps 1,300) Jews in the marketplace. S. *Dubnow was a native of Mstislavl, as was Dr. Moshe Rachmilevich, one of the founders of the Hebrew University Medical School.

BIBLIOGRAPHY: Dubnow, in: *He-Avar*, 1 (1918), 63–75; 8 (1961), 149–52; Lifshits, *ibid.*, 8 (1961), 81–100; Smilak, in: *Reshumot*, 4 (1926), 287–94; Dubnow, in: *YIVO Bleter*, 1 (1931), 404–7; Dubnow, in: *Voskhod*, no. 1 (1889), 176–84; no. 8 (1893), 24–28; no. 9 (1899), 33–59; Gessen, in: *Perezhitoye*, 2 (1910), 54–77; Anski, *ibid.*, 248–57.

[Yehuda Slutsky / Shmuel Spector (2nd ed.)]

MUBARAK, MUHAMMAD HUSNI SAʿID (1928–), third president of *Egypt, following Abdul *Nasser and Anwar *Sadat. A successful career officer in the Egyptian air force and its commander (since 1972), he was appointed vice president of Egypt (1975) and vice chairman of the National Democratic Party (1978). Eight days after Sadat's assassination (on October 6, 1981), Mubarak was elected as chairman of the National Democratic Party and president of Egypt – confirmed by a countrywide referendum. He was re-elected by referenda in 1987, 1993, and 1999 and then by popular vote on September 7, 2005, for a fifth term, defeating (with more than 75% of the votes) nine other candidates for the presidency. This was a sign of democratic processes being gradually introduced into Egypt. Meanwhile, until this unusual development, President Mubarak, using the authoritarian system of government inherited from his predecessors, promised to cure some of the worst ills facing the country, but with moderate success only. Corruption continued to affect the bureaucracy. The economy improved in the early 1990s with the help of massive U.S. aid (rewarding Egypt for supporting the U.S. with 40,000 troops in the 1991 Gulf War), but 16% of its 77 million population (in 2005) lived below the poverty line and unemployment was still very high (reaching 25% of the labor force, according to unofficial data). Mubarak also contended with the specter of Islamic fundamentalism and limited its political activities in Egypt; for example, the Muslim Brethren were not allowed to set up a political party, while Mubarak's spokesmen accused them and their fellow-travelers of supporting terrorism, thus delegitimizing them.

Mubarak and his regime have not displayed enmity to the tiny Jewish community (about 200 souls in 2005, residing in *Cairo and *Alexandria), but they have not prevented or condemned the publication of books and articles or the propagation of films accusing the Jews in Egypt and elsewhere of blood-libels, plots, and intrigues. Similar accusations against the State of Israel abound in the press and are supported by the elites, chiefly the unions of writers, lawyers, and others. As for Mubarak's government, it insisted on maintaining a "cold peace" with Israel, calling back its ambassador from Tel Aviv and openly siding with the Palestinians in the Israeli-Palestinian conflict. However, there were signs, also, of a mild rapprochement in 2004–5, probably conditioned by Israel's disengagement from the *Gaza Strip and Mubarak's wish to score points with the U.S.: a bilateral gas deal (lucrative for Egypt) was signed with Israel and, in September 2005, 750 Egyptian border guards started patrolling, at Israel's request, the Philadelphi Road between Sinai (which is part of Egypt) and the Gaza Strip. Still, some thorny issues remained to be solved.

BIBLIOGRAPHY: L.C. Harris (ed.), *Egypt: Internal Challenges and Regional Stability* (1988); A. McDermot, *Egypt from Nasser to Mubarak: A Flawed Revolution* (1988); R. Springborg, *Mubarak's Egypt: Fragmentation of Political Order* (1989); Charles Tripp and Roger Owen (eds.), *Egypt under Mubarak* (1989); R.W. Baker, *Sadat and After* (1990); M.M. Ahmad, *Hiwār maʿa al-Raʾīs* (1991); A. al-

ʿAẓīm Ramadān, *al-Sirāʿ al-ijtimāʿi f ī ʿasr Mubārak* (1993); M.A. Hai, *Economic Reform in Egypt* (1993); N.A. Fattah, *Veiled Violence: Islamic Fundamentalism in Egyptian Politics in 1990s* (1994); M. Kharbouch (ed.), *al-Tatawwur al-siyāsī fī Misr 1982–1992* (1994); M. Khalifa, *Socioeconomic Aspects of the Economic Reform Policies in Egypt* (1996); M. Zaki, *Egyptian Business Elites* (1999); E. Kienle, *A Grand Delusion: Democracy and Economic Reform in Egypt* (2001); N. El-Mikawy and H. Handoussa (eds.), *Institutional Reforms and Economic Development in Egypt* (2002); H. al-Awadi, *In Pursuit of Legitimacy: The Muslim Brothers and Mubarak 1982–2000* (2004).

[Jacob M. Landau (2nd ed.)]

MUBASHSHIR BEN NISSI HA-LEVI (tenth century), Babylonian scholar who lived in *Baghdad; also known as Ibn Ussaba or ʿUnnāba. Mubashshir comments on the works of *Saadiah Gaon, contained in *Kitāb Istidrāk al-Sahw* ("Book of Correction of Errors"), fragments of which were found in the Cairo **Genizah* and printed. The purpose of his book is not quite clear; the introduction leads one to believe that he sought to point out Saadiah's errors rather than to correct them, and the contents of the book strengthen this impression to the extent that at times the author seems to agree with Saadiah Gaon's Karaite critics. The book had a large circulation, especially in Spain, and is mentioned by many Jewish scholars.

BIBLIOGRAPHY: A. Harkavy, *Zikkaron la-Rishonim ve-gam la-Aḥaronim*, 1, no. 4 (1891), 68–73, 182–5; Levin, Oẓar, 8 (1938), 86 (third section); Mevasser b. Nissi ha-Levi, *Hassagot Al Rav Saadyah Gaon*, ed. by M. Zucker (1955); Baron, Social, 5 (1957), 390 no. 21; 7 (1958), 15–16; S. Abramson, in: *Sinai*, 57 (1965), 15–17; M. Zucker, *ibid.*, 58 (1966), 95–98; S.M. Stern, in: REJ, 126 (1967), 113–7.

[Abraham David]

MUBASHSHIR BEN RAV KIMOI HA-KOHEN (d. 925), *Gaon* of the Pumbedita Academy from 917 to 925, a post to which he was appointed upon the death of R. Judah Gaon (the grandfather of R. *Sherira Gaon). Mubashshir belonged to the faction which opposed the appointment of *David b. Zakkai as exilarch, apparently because of his family relationship with Mar *Ukba, the deposed exilarch. In turn, when David b. Zakkai did become exilarch, he refused to recognize Mubashshir in his post and appointed R. *Kohen Ẓedek as head of the Pumbedita Academy; the members of the Academy were split into two factions, each supporting one of the two *geonim*. A prominent supporter of Mubashshir was *Ben Meir, the *gaon* of Ereẓ Israel, who conducted an active campaign against both David b. Zakkai and R. Kohen Ẓedek. Saadiah Gaon, on the other hand, when he came to Baghdad in 921, joined Mubashshir's opponents. Mubashshir appointed R. Aaron b. Joseph *Sarjado as *rosh kallah* Pumbedita, in spite of his not being the scion of a scholarly family. In 922 David b. Zakkai made peace with Mubashshir and most of the members of the Academy accepted the latter's leadership; R. Kohen Ẓedek, and the few members who remained loyal to him, left the Academy but continued to receive their share of its income. None of Mubashshir's teachings and responsa has been preserved. On Mubashshir's death in 925 his rival R. Kohen Ẓedek succeeded him as *gaon*.

BIBLIOGRAPHY: B.M. Lewin (ed.), *Iggeret Sherira Gaʾon* (1921), 119–20; Mann, in: *Tarbiz*, 5 (1933/34), 150–8; Abramson, Merkazim, 21–23.

[Abraham David]

°**MUCIANUS, CAIUS LICINIUS**, governor of Syria during the Roman War (66–70 C.E.) and a prominent supporter of Vespasian's successful attempt to assume the leadership of the Roman Empire. As governor of Syria, Mucianus is known to have supported certain privileges of the Jewish community at Antioch. In 69, together with other generals in the east, Mucianus urged Vespasian to become emperor, and subsequently was dispatched with a substantial force to Italy, to secure Rome from the supporters of Vitellius. He entered the city during the last days of 69, and prepared the way for Vespasian's triumphant arrival there in the summer of 70 C.E.

BIBLIOGRAPHY: Kappelmacher, in: Pauly-Wissowa, 25 (1926), 436–43 no. 116a; Schuerer, Hist, 263.

[Isaiah Gafni]

MUEHLHAUSEN, city in Germany. Though the exact date of the earliest Jewish settlement in Muehlhausen is unknown, there was certainly a Jewish settlement there c. 1300, and a synagogue is mentioned in 1311. The relationship between the town and the community ("*universitas Judaeorum*") was regulated by the municipal council in 1311. Jurisdiction over the Jews of Muehlhausen and the income from them was contested between the municipality and the landgraves of *Thuringia, who during the Black Death persecutions advised the burghers to massacre the Jews; this occurred on March 21, 1349. Among the martyrs was a scholar, R. Eliezer. Many of the exiles settled permanently in Erfurt and Frankfurt. The property of the deceased Jews was the object of bitter contention between Charles IV and the city. In 1374 Jews were again present in Muehlhausen, and the townspeople were released from all debts owed by them in 1391. In 1433 the Jews had to pay 200 florins as a coronation tax; throughout the 15th century they were taxed heavily by all governmental authorities. Regulations of 1472 ordered the Jews to stay out of the homes of Christians and to wear the yellow *badge; the women had to wear two blue stripes on their head coverings. In 1543 all Jews were expelled. Jews originating from Muehlhausen were living in Cracow, Poznan, and Lissa in the 17th century. The first *Schutzjuden returned to Muehlhausen in 1643, and in 1692 there were four Jewish households, rising to 14 families around 1781; 144 persons in 1843; 180 in 1907; and 170 in 1932. On the eve of the Nazi rise to power, the community possessed a synagogue, religious school, and three philanthropic organizations. Repressive measures resulting in emigration brought the number of Jews down to 70 in 1939. In 1942, only 19 Jews remained. The community was annihilated during World War II. After 1945 a small Jewish community was reestablished. It numbered 19 in 1946. Many members emigrated or moved to other places, and by the 1980s the community no longer existed. In 1985 a plaque was dedicated to the city's victims of the Holocaust. The synagogue, consecrated in 1841/42 and desecrated in 1938, was restored with public funding in 1998. It serves as a cultural and educational center and houses a small exhibition about the history of the Muehlhausen Jewish community.

BIBLIOGRAPHY: *Denkschrift zu dem Entwurf einer Verordnung die Verhaeltnisse der Juden betreffend* (1847), pt. 1 B, 26; P. Wertheim, *Kalendar und Jahrbuch* (1857); A. Jaraczewski, *Geschichte der Juden in Erfurt* (1868), 2 n. 2, 25 n. 2, 72; L. Lewin, in: JJLG, 5 (1907), 109–10; MGADJ, 3 (1912), 164; 4 (1913), 179; 5 (1914), 26, 114, 188; U. Weinberg, in: JJLG, 16 (1924), 275, 278, 280, 283, 287–8, 294–6; S. Neufeld, in: MGWJ, 69 (1925), 287, 291, 293; *Handbuch der juedischen Gemeindeverwaltung* (1907), 53; (1924), 45; S. Neufeld, *Die Juden im thueringen-saechsischen Gebiet waehrend des Mittelalters* (1927) passim; FJW, 118; Germ Jud, 2 (1968), 550–2. **ADD. BIBLIOGRAPHY:** *Germania Judaica* vol. 3, 1350–1514 (1987), 885–93; C. Liesenberg, *Zur Geschichte der Juden in Muehlhausen und Nordthueringen und die Muehlhaeuser Synagoge, Muehlhausen* (Muehlhaeuser Beitraege, vol. 11) (1998); S. Litt, *Juden in Thueringen in der fruehen Neuzeit* (1520–1650) (Veroeffentlichungen der Historischen Kommission Thueringen. Kleine Reihe, vol. 11) (2003), 77–82.

[Larissa Daemmig (2nd ed.)]

MUEHSAM, ERICH (1878–1934), German poet, playwright, and anarchist. Born in Berlin and raised in Luebeck, where he was expelled from school for "socialist activities," Muehsam, like his father, apprenticed as a pharmacist. Following his dream of becoming a writer, he left Luebeck for Berlin, establishing contact with Martin *Buber and Gustav *Landauer. The latter had an enormous influence on Muehsam's intellectual development and persuaded him to join the *Neue Gesellschaft*, a group of libertarian writers. Muehsam quickly became involved with the socialist-anarchist movement in Berlin, serving briefly, in 1902, as editor of the anarchist journal, *Der arme Teufel.* He advocated homosexual rights in his first publication, *Die Homosexualitaet*. In 1904 he left Berlin, traveling through Switzerland, Northern Italy, France, and Vienna before settling in Munich in 1909. While his years as a traveler brought forth poetic publications, among them his poem collections *Die Wueste* (1904) and *Krater* (1909), as well as the comedy *Die Hochstapler* (1906), Muehsam's time in Munich was characterized by increasing political activity. He founded the socialist circle *Die Tat* and the revolutionary journal *Kain: Zeitschrift fuer Menschlichkeit.* World War I put an end to the anti-militaristic journal. He tried to organize resistance to the war, seeking closer contact to the Spartacists and the independent social democrats around Kurt *Eisner. During the strike at the Krupp works in Munich in January, 1918, he called for revolution; one year later he was deeply involved in the founding of Eisner's Bavarian Soviet Republic. After a putsch brought down the republic, he was arrested and sentenced to 15 years for high treason. In prison, Muehsam again pursued his literary ambitions. Besides several publications on revolutionary issues, articles for *Die Aktion* and *Die Weltbühne,* and another poem collection titled *Brennende Erde* (1920), his drama *Judas*, staged in 1921 for 5,000 workers in Mannheim, should be singled out. In December 1924 he was reprieved. Back in Berlin, he immediately returned to supporting anarchist organizations within the Weimar Republic. From 1926 to 1931, he edited the anarchist monthly *Fanal.* His final publication was the manifesto *Die Befreiung der Gesellschaft vom Staat*, published only a few weeks before his arrest by the SA on February 28, 1933. After prolonged torture in various concentration camps, Muehsam was murdered by the Nazis in Oranienburg on July 9, 1934.

BIBLIOGRAPHY: K. Muehsam, *Der Leidensweg Erich Muehsams* (1935). **ADD. BIBLIOGRAPHY:** R. Kauffeldt, *Erich Mühsam: Literatur und Anarchie* (1983); C. Hirte, *Erich Mühsam: "Ihr seht mich nicht feige"* (1985); J.-W. Goette (ed.), *Erich Mühsam und das Judentum* (2002).

[Sol Liptzin /Philipp Theisohn (2nd ed.)]

MUELHAUSEN, YOM TOV LIPMANN (14th–15th centuries), scholar, polemist, philosopher, kabbalist, and one of the great rabbis of Bohemia in his time. His name indicates that he, or his family, probably originally came from Mulhouse in Alsace; all that is known with certainty, however, is that he was active chiefly in Prague, where he lived before 1389, that he was among those affected by the "Edict of Prague" which took place in that year, and that in 1407 he was appointed *Judex Judaeorum* ("judge of the Jews") there. Yom Tov was the pupil of the outstanding Austrian scholars, Meir b. Baruch *ha-Levi, Sar Shalom of Neustadt, Samson b. Eleazar, and particularly of the brothers, Menahem and Avigdor Kara, serving with the last two as *dayyan* in Prague. He journeyed a great deal in Bohemia, Austria and Poland with the aim of acquainting himself with shortcomings in the observance of *halakhah* and custom and rectifying them. There is information of his activities and his varied *takkanot in Cracow, Lindau (German Bavaria), and Erfurt, where he introduced permanent and amended rules for the writing of Scrolls of the Law, *tefillin*, and *mezuzot*, in the making of a *shofar* and the manner in which it should be sounded, the order of granting a bill of divorce, etc. These rules were adopted in many districts of Austria and Bohemia and named after him. He also had a ramified correspondence with great contemporary talmudists, including Jacob *Moellin and Jacob b. Judah *Weil. Between 1440 and 1450 he was one of the heads of the council of the Ashkenazi communities known as Va'ad Erfurt ("The Council at Erfurt"), but its exact date and activities are not known.

Yom Tov Lipmann's activity as a polemist gave him lasting renown even among non-Jews, who over many years produced a complete and ramified literature in refutation of him known by the general name of Anti-Lipmanniana. He began these activities early in his life when he conducted polemics with the bishop of Linda, on the initiative of the bishop, and in a spirit of mutual tolerance and non-provocation. Some of the other priests of Linda disputed with him also, and part of this series of polemics was later included in his *Nizzaḥon* (see below). According to a Christian source, Muelhausen went to listen to the sermons of their preachers, and it is possible that he actually initiated some of his polemics at those gatherings. His best-known disputation, which had the most serious consequences, was that with the apostate Pesaḥ (Peter). It was connected with the edict of apostasy issued against the Jews of Prague in 1389, as a result of which Peter came out with a series of public attacks upon the Jews who deny and despise Christianity. A proposal was made that the Jews hold a disputation with him to justify themselves, and Muelhausen was chosen for this purpose. No details are known either of the staging or the content of this disputation, but as a result of it 80 Jews were martyred, and the remainder, including Yom Tov Lipmann, were saved by a "miracle" of unknown nature.

Except for the *Sefer ha-Nizzaḥon*, Muelhausen's books were written after 1407, when he was *Judex Judaeorum* in Prague. He dealt chiefly with Kabbalah, *halakhah*, and philosophy, but all three topics were intertwined. His various works have become part of the contemporary Jewish heritage, as has the whole form of the *halakhah* laid down by him. They afford evidence of his great erudition in the sources of *halakhah* and *aggadah*, in the Bible and its exegesis, in Kabbalah, and particularly in philosophy – in which he attained the highest level reached until then among the Jews of that country. He is, in fact, the first known scholar of Bohemia who openly occupied himself with philosophy, having a sound knowledge of the subject. He based himself on Maimonides' *Guide of the Perplexed*, and it was he who first gave it wide publicity in Poland and the neighboring countries, just as he endeavored to establish his halakhic views in accordance with the opinion of Maimonides. Undoubtedly it was Muelhausen who influenced the great Polish rabbi, Moses *Isserles, to follow Maimonides in his study of philosophy and *halakhah*. Muelhausen was well acquainted with what was known of the teaching of Saadiah Gaon and also made frequent use of early works on Kabbalah, such as the Sefer *Yeẓirah, the *Heikhalot* literature (see Merkabah *mysticism), the *Sefer ha-Bahir, Sefer ha-Temurah, Ma'arekhet ha-Elohut*, etc. He also knew the works of Baḥya ibn *Paquda, Solomon ibn *Gabirol and Abraham ibn *Ezra. One contemporary scholar whose works he frequently used was Shemariah b. Elijah *ha-Ikriti of Negropont. Muelhausen occupied himself intensively with Kabbalah, and, in addition to the above-mentioned works the influence of Naḥmanides – whose esoteric remarks, like those of Ibn Ezra, he sought to explain – is evident. In his view, there is no contradiction between Kabbalah and philosophy; he maintained that Maimonides, too, was a kabbalist but that he merely gave a philosophical garb to his words. His writings on Kabbalah are also generally written in the accepted style of medieval Jewish philosophy, with the result that many scholars were led to the erroneous conclusion that as a philosopher, he was opposed to Kabbalah. However, the new texts published during recent decades have removed all doubts on this matter. The central problems which he discusses, namely the reasons for the precepts, the fundamentals of faith, free will, and omniscience, the suffering of the righteous, corporeality, etc. – all serve a threefold purpose: the refutation of heretics, the attainment of philosophical truth and the establishment of the foundations of kabbalistic mysticism. His chief kabbalistic work is the *Sefer ha-Eshkol* (ed. by J. Kaufman, 1927) written in 1413, which is wholly influenced by the Spanish kabbalists of the school of Azriel b. Menahem of *Gerona, and in his *Alfa Beta* the great influence upon him of the Ḥasidei Ashkenaz is recognizable.

Muelhausen's halakhic writings reveal his complete command of all rabbinic literature up to his own time. Some of his many polemics were assembled by him in the *Sefer ha-Nizzaḥon* which he intended to serve as a handbook for the ordinary Jew compelled at times to wrestle with complex theological problems beyond his ability. The work was written in 1390 and was much copied in manuscript. It was first published by the priest Theodore Hackspan (Altdorf, 1644). Hackspan strove to edit it with maximum faithfulness to the source, and with the aim of enabling Christian scholars to oppose it, but he did not succeed because neither he nor the workers in his press understood either the language of the sources or their subject matter. As a result this edition is full of errors; despite this, it has great value for correcting many mistakes in the subsequent editions. The first Jewish edition was published in Amsterdam in 1701. It was only rarely reprinted because of the papal decree against its publication and circulation, and there is a variety of bibliographical problems connected with the various editions of the book. Muelhausen's method was to expose the Christian lack of understanding of the Hebrew sources with their linguistic and contextual associations and to ridicule aspects of the Christian religion. His great superiority over other polemists was based on his knowledge of Latin and lay in his intimate knowledge of Christian literature – the New Testament, the Vulgate, and the leading Church Fathers, as well as the works of the late Christian scholars. Frequently his polemics are based on sound philology. His familiarity with Christian sources was, however, less than that of Isaac *Troki, and his arguments are more popular in character and not so "logical." He undoubtedly made use of early Jewish polemic material included in various collections, among them an earlier *Sefer Nizzaḥon* (probably by Joseph *Official) as well as of oral traditions. He selected and summarized the best of the answers, according to his understanding and according to the taste of his contemporaries, connecting them with topical questions. Among Christian scholars who applied themselves to refuting his arguments may be mentioned chiefly Bodker, Sebastian *Muenster, and J. *Buxtorf, and especially J.C. *Wagenseil, who also included short fragments both from the *Nizzaḥon* and from the *Nizzaḥon Yashan* in his book *Tela Ignea Satanae*.

Muelhausen's *Sefer Alfa Beta*, on the shape of the letters and their inner meaning, was written for the benefit of scribes of Scrolls of the Law, *tefillin*, and *mezuzot* and of those who wished to devote themselves to esoteric study. It was published in the second part of the *Barukh she-Amar* (Shklov, 1804) of Samson b. Eliezer and its identity was recognized only about a century ago (previously it had been regarded as part of the *Barukh she-Amar*). Muelhausen also wrote *haggahot to the *Barukh she-Amar* itself, but these were incorporated in the text so that they cannot be recognized. He also wrote *Tikkun Sefer Torah*, containing the order of open and closed sections of the Torah (see Sefer *Torah) as well as many essential scribal regulations. This work was issued by E. Kupfer and S. Loewinger (see bibl.). Other works are *Sefer ha-Eshkol* and *Sefer Kavvanot ha-Tefillah* (appended to *Sefer ha-Eshkol*, 1927), a commentary on the *Shir ha-Yiḥud* (see J. Kaufman, p. 80f.), and various prayers and *piyyutim* printed in different places. His *Sefer ha-Berit*, on the meaning of the 13 attributes, was published from a manuscript by E. Kupfer (see bibl.). Other works written by him have not been found. Muelhausen's works have important historical value, particularly regarding the status and the situation of the Jews at the time of the Hussite wars.

BIBLIOGRAPHY: J. Kaufmann, *R. Yom Tov Lipmann Muelhausen* (Heb., 1927); B. Mark and E. Kupfer, in: *Bleter far Geshikhte*, 6 no. 4 (1953), 79–83; E. Kupfer, in: *Sinai*, 56 (1965), 330–42; idem and S. Loewinger, *ibid.*, 60 (1967), 237–68; I. Sonne, in: *Studies in Bibliography and Booklore*, 1, no. 2 (1953), 60f., 68f.; I. Ta-Shema, in: KS, 45 (1969/70), 120–2; M.M. Meshi-Zahav, *Kovez Sifrei Setam* (1970).

[Israel Moses Ta-Shma]

MUELLER, DAVID HEINRICH (1846–1912), Orientalist. He was born in Buczacz (Galicia), which was also the hometown of his relative S.Y. *Agnon. In his youth Mueller was influenced by *Rappaport, *Zunz, *Krochmal, and *Smolenskin. He studied at the *Jewish Theological Seminary in Breslau, but his lack of talent as a preacher forced him to leave the seminary and to specialize in Semitic languages. From 1876 he taught Oriental languages at Vienna University and also lectured at the Vienna Jewish Theological Seminary from its foundation in 1893. In 1889 he was elected a member of the Austro-Hungarian Academy of Sciences. Shortly before his death he was ennobled under the title of Baron Mueller von Deham.

Mueller undertook in 1877 a journey to the Orient which produced a crop of publications on South-Arabian inscriptions, on castles and palaces in that region (2 parts, 1879–81), and a detailed report on this expedition (1878). He also edited S. Langer's journal on his travels in Syria and Arabia and the inscriptions he had discovered (1883); Hamadani's Arabian geography (2 parts, 1884–91); and Ṭabarī's annals (1888–89). Mueller also wrote comparative studies of Semitic languages (1884); on the cuneiform writings discovered at Ashrut Dargha (1886/87); and on the particular division of sibilants in the South-Arabian dialect (1888). His articles in the Vienna *Zeitschrift fuer die Kunde des Morgenlandes*, of which he was an editor, also dealt with early Semitic epigraphy. A second expedition to South Arabia led by Mueller resulted in several volumes of reports of which Mueller wrote three, dealing mainly with the linguistic and literary discoveries.

When the Code of *Hammurapi was discovered, Mueller wrote on its relationship to the laws of the Pentateuch (1903, translating the Code into biblical Hebrew), and to those of the Syrio-Roman Lawbook (1905). In biblical studies proper (*Biblische Studien*, 5 vols., 1895–98), Mueller advanced a novel theory on the structure and rhythm of biblical poetry. Mueller, in general, adopted a conservative attitude to the Bible text and was averse to emendations.

BIBLIOGRAPHY: G. Rosenmann, in: JJGL, 17 (1914), 145–57; Yeshayahu, in: S. Federbush (ed.), *Ḥokhmat Yisrael be-Eiropah* (1965), 401f.; *Epigraphische Denkmaeler aus Abessinien, nach Abklatschen von J. Theodore Bent, esq.* (1894); *Epigraphische Denkmaeler aus Arabien* (Wien, 1889); *Die Haggadah von Sarajevo* (1898); *Die Mehri-und Soqori-Sprache* (1902–07); *Das syrischroemische Rechtsbuch und ammurabi* (1905); G. Rosenmann, in: *Sefer ha-Zikkaron le-Beit ha-Midrash be-Vinah* (1946), 24–29.

[Naphtali Herz Tur-Sinai (Torczyner)]

MUELLER, ERNST (1880–1954), mathematician and writer on Kabbalah and philosophy. Born at Misslitz, Moravia, Mueller taught at the Kiryat Sefer agricultural school, Jaffa (1907–09). From 1911 he worked at the Jewish community library in Vienna, and after its closure by the Nazis immigrated to England. His *Der Sohar und seine Lehre* went through three editions (1920, 1923, 1959), and he translated selections of the Zohar into German (*Sohar, das heilige Buch der Kabbalah*, 1932). Mueller wrote a *History of Jewish Mysticism* (1946). He translated a selection of Bialik's poems (*Gedichte*, 1911) as well as Abraham ibn Ezra's *Sefer ha-Eḥad (Buch der Einheit*, 1920), with notes and an excursus on the author as mathematician. On the occasion of the tercentenary of Spinoza's birth he published a (supplementary) bibliography of Spinoza literature (1932). He prepared a German stage version of Plato's Symposium (1932).

°**MUELLER, HEINRICH** (1900–?), last chief of the *Gestapo. Mueller joined the Bavarian police after serving as a much decorated NCO pilot during World War I. He had a specific expertise in Leftist movements, communist and Marxist, which became ever more valuable as the Nazis came to power and targeted these groups. When the Nazis came to power, *Heydrich was appointed Bavarian police chief and retained him as an expert on communism in the Bavarian political police even though Mueller in this period was not a Nazi but a member of the Bavarian Volkspartei. Mueller in 1933 joined the *SS and the SD (secret police), but became a Nazi Party member only in 1939. When Heydrich took charge of the Gestapo in 1936, Mueller, who had become one of his top aides, went with him to Berlin. He soon became chief of the executive of the office (Main Branch II). When the Security Police (Sipo) was organized, he was appointed chief of its political police section and, in effect, head of the Gestapo. He earned his stripes with the "Night of the Long Knives," the attack on Ernst Rohm. He continued to impress his superiors with the suppression of all organized opposition to the Nazi regime, which was, among other factors, due to Mueller's efficiency and ruthlessness, which included the application of torture on his victims. Mueller was involved in the hoax whereby "Polish" attacks on Germany served as a pretext for the outbreak of World War II. On Sept. 27, 1939, Mueller was appointed chief of Office IV of the *RSHA (Reich Security Main Office). Besides being responsible for the murder of hundreds of thousands of Soviet prisoners of war and an untold number of political prisoners, Mueller was one of the key figures of the "Final Solution" (see *Holocaust, General Survey). *Eichmann's IVB 4 Section was part of his office and Eichmann his subordinate. Mueller participated in the *Wannsee Conference, representing the Gestapo, where the "Final Solution" was coordinated. In June 1942 he ordered that the evidence of the Einsatzgruppen murders be destroyed. As the war drew to a close, he opposed all efforts to spare Jews. He punished brutally those involved in the 1944 plot against Hitler, including personal friends such as Arthur Nebe. He made every effort to remain in the background throughout his career. Ruthless and efficient, he preferred to work in the shadows. Last seen in Hitler's bunker on April 29, 1945, he succeeded in quietly disappearing when the Third Reich collapsed. There were rumors that he was killed by the Russians or that he was in Brazil, rumors also that he was the enforcer among the Nazis who escaped. Clearly, he eluded capture.

BIBLIOGRAPHY: H. Hoehne, *Der Orden unter dem Totenkopf* (1967); Institut fuer Zeitgeschichte, *Gutachten des Instituts fuer Zeitgeschichte*, 1 (1958), 169, 219, 232, 297; G. Reitlinger, *Final Solution* (19682), index; IMT, *Trial of the Major War Criminals*, 24 (1949), index. R. Hilberg, *Destruction of the European Jews* (1961. 1985, 2003), index. J. Delarue, *The Gestapo* (1964). **ADD. BIBLIOGRAPHY:** S. Aronson, *Reinhard Heydrich und die Fruehgeschichte von Gestapo und SD*; idem, *Beginnings of the Gestapo System: The Bavarian Model in 1933* (1969); H.H. Wilhelm, "Heinrich Muller, in: I. Gutman (ed.), *Encyclopedia of the Holocaust* (1990).

[Yehuda Reshef]

MUELLER, JOEL (1827–1895), rabbinical scholar and authority on geonic texts. Born at Maehrisch Ostrau, Moravia, Mueller received his early talmudic education from his father, rabbi in Maehrisch Ostrau, whom he succeeded in 1853. After a period as rabbi in Leipa, Bohemia, and as a teacher of religion in Vienna, in 1884 he began teaching at the Berlin Hochschule fuer die Wissenschaft des Judentums.

Mueller published a series of rabbinic texts, chiefly responsa, of the geonic and immediate post-geonic period, which are models of scholarly editions. The most important are the post-talmudic tractate *Massekhet *Soferim* (1878), with an introduction and copious notes in German; a post-talmudic work on ritual differences between Ereẓ Israel and Babylon, *Hilluf Minhagim* (in *Ha-Shaar* 7 (1876), and 8 (1877); published separately, 1878); *Teshuvot akhmei arefat ve-Loter* ("Responsa of French and Lorraine Scholars," 1881, repr. 1959, 1967); *Teshuvot Ge'onei Mizraḥ u-Ma'arav* ("Responsa of Eastern and Western Geonim," in *Bet Talmud*, 4 (1885); and 5 (1886); published separately 1888; repr. 1959, 1966); *Mafte'a li-Teshuvot Ge'onim* ("Introduction to Geonic Responsa," 1891; repr. 1959); and *Halakhot Pesukot* ("Short Geonic Responsa," 1893). Mueller also edited Saadiah's "Book (on the law) of Inheritance," *Traité des Successions…*, for J. Derenbourg's edition of Saadiah's writings (*Oeuvres Complètes*; vol. 9, 1897). For the annual reports of the Lehranstalt he published studies on responsa in the pre-geonic period (in: 4, 1886); on those of tenth-century Spanish teachers (in: 7, 1889); on Yehudai Gaon (in: 8, 1890), and on the responsa of Meshullam b. Kalonymus (in: 11, 1893); see also his *Responsa of Kalonymos of Lucca* (*Teshuvot Rabbenu Kalonymos mi-Lucca*, 1891).

BIBLIOGRAPHY: M. Schreiner, *Gedaechtnisrede auf Joel Mueller* (1896); *Bericht ueber die Lehranstalt fuer die Wissenschaft des Judentums*, 15 (1897), 32ff.; S. Federbush, *Ḥokhmat Yisrael be-Eiropah* (1965), 402.

MUELLER-COHEN, ANITA (1890–1962), social worker. Born in Vienna, Anita Mueller-Cohen became a social worker while still in her youth. During World War I she did relief work in the war-stricken areas of Galicia and Bukovina. She devoted herself to establishing lying-in hospitals for mothers, day nurseries and medical services for children, and institutions for the care of the aged. After the war she led the effort to help returning soldiers to readjust themselves and established milk stations for undernourished children throughout Austria. She directed the placement of orphaned children in Jewish homes in a number of West European countries and in 1920 promoted the adoption in North and South America of child victims of persecution in Eastern Europe. In that year she became a member of the Vienna City Council. Anita Mueller-Cohen settled in Tel Aviv in 1936 and continued her child welfare and other social services.

ADD. BIBLIOGRAPHY: D.J. Hecht, *Anita Mueller Cohen (1890–1962) Sozialarbeiterin, Feministin, Politikerin, Zionistin und Journalistin. Ein Beitrag zur juedischen Frauengeschichte in Oesterreich 1914–1929* (2002).

MUENSTER, city in North Rhine Westphalia, Germany. Jews lived there from at least the middle of the 13th century, maintaining a synagogue, a cemetery (mentioned in 1301; a fragment of a tombstone dated 1324 has been preserved), and a *mikveh*. In the wake of the *Black Death persecutions (1349/50), the Jews were expelled or killed and their property confiscated or destroyed. Between 1350 and 1810, Jews were not allowed to reside in Muenster but were only allowed to pass through. They were, however, tolerated since the 16th century within the bishopric of Muenster. They received letters of protection from the bishop and founded several congregations. After 1650 these congregations were united in the *Landjudenschaft. The head of this corporation was the "*Judenvorgaenger*"; the first was (1657) Nini Levi, brother of Behrend *Levi. The seat of the rabbi of the *Landjudenschaft* (*Landrabbiner*) was in Warendorf (near Muenster), the largest Jewish community of the bishopric. The last *Landrabbiner* were the *Court Jew Michael Mayer Breslauer (1771–89) and his son David (1789–1815). When Muenster passed to the duchy of *Berg (1808–10) and to the French Empire (1810–13), the first

Jews settled in the city; their residence there was legalized by Prussia in 1819. They officially founded a new community in 1854. The first prayer house was situated in the Loerstrasse; the cemetery was established in 1811, and the synagogue was built in 1880.

From 1816 *Landrabbiner* Abraham *Sutro lived in Muenster, although he did not act as rabbi of the community, which in 1879 appointed Dr. J. Mansbach as preacher and cantor. He was succeeded by S. Kessler. The first rabbi, who took office in 1919, was Dr. Fritz Steinthal (who immigrated to South America in 1938). His successor, Dr. Julius Voos of Kamen, was deported to *Auschwitz in 1943. Among the most notable members of the community were Prof. Alexander Haindorf (1782–1862), co-founder of the Marks-Haindorf Foundation for the training of elementary school teachers and for the advancement of artisans and artists among the Jews, and the first Jewish professor at Muenster Academy (university); and the poet Eli Marcus (1854–1935), co-founder of the Zoological Evening Society, and author of poems and many plays in the Low German dialect of the Muensterland.

During the Nazi era, the community was reduced from 558 Jews (0.4% of the population) in 1933 to 308 (0.2%) in 1939. The synagogue was destroyed in November 1938 (see *Kristallnacht). The first deportation from Muenster city and district (to Riga) took place in December 1941 (403 persons); in 1942 the last large-scale transport went eastward, followed by individual deportations in 1943 and 1944. After World War II, a new congregation was founded which included, besides Muenster, the Jews of Ahaus, Beckum, Borken, Burgsteinfurt, and Coesfeld. This new community of Muenster numbered 142 members in 1970. The synagogue was built in 1961. The community numbered 101 in 1989 and 766 in 2005. The increase is explained by the immigration of Jews from the former Soviet Union after 1990.

BIBLIOGRAPHY: Complete bibliography by B. Brilling, in: H.C. Meyer, *Aus Geschichte und Leben der Juden in Westfalen* (1962), 251–3; idem, in: *Westfalen*, 44 (1966), 212–7; B. Brilling and H. Richtering (ed.), *Westfalia Judaica*, 1 (1967), index; idem (ed.), *Juden in Muenster 1933–1945* (1960); F. Lazarus, in: ZGJD, 7 (1937), 240–3; idem, in: MGWJ, 80 (1936), 106–17; 81 (1937), 444–5; J. Raphael, in: *Zeitschrift fuer die Geschichte der Juden*, 6 (1969), 74f.; H. Schnee, *Die Hoffinanz und der moderne Staat*, 3 (1955), 54–67; 6 (1967), 153–71; Leeser, in: AZJ, 73 (1909), 583ff.; Germ Jud, 1 (1963), 238–9; 2 (1968), 561–3. **ADD. BIBLIOGRAPHY:** U. Schnorbus, *Quellen zur Geschichte der Juden in Westfalen. Spezialinventar zu den Akten des Nordrhein-Westfaelischen Staatsarchivs Muenster* (1983); *Germania Judaica*, vol. 3, 1350–1514 (1987), 909; B. Ernst, *Die Marks-Haindorf-Stiftung. Ein juedisches Lehrerseminar in Muenster als Beispiel fuer die Assimilation der Juden in Westfalen im 19. Jahrhundert* (1989); A. Determann, (ed.), *Geschichte der Juden in Muenster* (1989); D. Aschoff, *Juden in Muenster* (*Westfalen im Bild. Westfaelische Kulturgeschichte*, vol. 9) (1993); D. Aschoff, *Quellen und Regesten zur Geschichte der Juden in der Stadt Muenster* (*Westfalica Judaica*, vol. 3, 1) (2000); G. Moellenhoff and R. Schlautmann-Overmeyer, *Juedische Familien in Muenster 1918 bis 1945*, vol. 1 and 2 (1995–2001).

[Bernhard Brilling / Larissa Daemmig (2nd ed.)]

°**MUENSTER, SEBASTIAN** (**Monsterus**; 1488–1552), German *Hebraist and reformer. Born in Ingelheim, Muenster entered the Franciscan order in 1505. Turning to the study of Hebrew, he became a pupil of Conrad *Pellicanus from about 1510, first in Rouffach, and then in Pforzheim and Basle. He converted to Protestantism in the 1520s, and was a professor of Hebrew at the University of Heidelberg from 1524 to 1528. During this time he found his true master in the Jewish Hebraist Elijah *Levita, whose major grammatical works he translated and edited beginning in 1525. In 1528, Muenster was appointed professor of Hebrew at the University of Basle, a position he held until his death from the plague. Muenster was a prolific author and translator. He contributed significantly to almost every aspect of Hebrew and Jewish studies, and next to Johann *Reuchlin, he was the outstanding Christian Hebraist of the 16th century. Muenster reissued Reuchlin's *De rudimentis Hebraicis* and published about 40 works, including *Epitome Hebraicae grammaticae* (1520); *Institutiones Grammaticae in Hebraeam Linguam* (Basle, 1524); *Chaldaica Grammatica* (Basle, 1527), the first Aramaic grammar by a Christian, based on the *Arukh* of *Nathan b. Jehiel of Rome; a list of the 613 Commandments (Basle, 1533) culled from the *Sefer Mitzvot Katan* of *Isaac b. Joseph of Corbeil; translations of *Josippon, and of works by David *Kimḥi and E. Levita; and a grammar of rabbinic Hebrew (Basle, 1542). His outstanding *Hebraica Biblia* (2 vols, Basle, 1534–35), which is provided with an original Latin text independent of the Vulgate, represents the first Protestant translation of the Old Testament from Hebrew into Latin. Like Paulus *Fagius, Muenster translated into Hebrew the Apocryphal Book of Tobit (Basle, 1542), which later reappeared in the London Polyglot Bible (1654–57).

He also published several missionary works directed toward the Jews, most notably *Vikuach* (1539), a dispute between a Christian and a Jew, and a Hebrew version (with annotations) of the Gospel of St. Matthew ("*Torat ha-Mashi'aḥ*," Basle, 1537). This work, dedicated to Henry VIII of England, was the first Hebrew translation of any portion of the New Testament. Muenster's use of Jewish polemical literature, as in the preparation of his Hebrew edition of Matthew, as well as his publications in the field of rabbinic thought, provoked many accusations of Judaization against him, by Martin *Luther, Guillaume *Postel, and others.

Muenster was also a mathematician, cosmographer, and cartographer. His *Cosmographia* (1544), the earliest German description of the world, appeared in many editions, and was translated into several European languages. He also annotated the Latin version of Abraham b. Ḥiyya's astronomical and geographical work, *Ẓurat ha-Areẓ* (Basle, 1546).

BIBLIOGRAPHY: J. Perles, *Beitraege zur Geschichte der hebraeischen und aramaeischen Studien*, (1884), 20–44, 154ff.; F. Secret, *Les Kabbalistes Chrétiens de la Renaissance* (1964), 141, 144f.; idem, in: *Bibliothèque d'Humanisme et Renaissance*, 22 (1960), 377–80; Baron, Social[2], 13 (1969), 233–4, 432; E.I.J. Rosenthal, in: I. Epstein (ed.), *Essays… J.H. Hertz* (1943), 350–69. **ADD. BIBLIOGRAPHY:** L. Geiger, *Das Studium der hebräischen Sprache in Deutschland* (1870), 74ff.;

K.H. Burmeister, *Sebastian Münster…* (1969); J. Friedman, in: *Archiv fuer Reformationsgeschichte*, 70 (1979), 238–59; J. Friedman, *The Most Ancient Testimony…* (1983).

[Godfrey Edmond Silverman / Aya Elyada (2nd ed.)]

MUENSTERBERG, HUGO (1863–1916), psychologist. Born in Danzig, baptized at the time of his appointment to the University of Freiburg, Muensterberg developed the first psychological laboratory there. His fields of research included such varied problems as auditory space perception, estimation of size, kinesthesis, memory, the time sense, attention, and the influence of drugs on mental work. These were published in the series *Beitraege zur experimentellen Psychologie* (1889–92). Muensterberg enjoyed a reputation as one of the most brilliant young psychologists. As the result of a quarrel in the field of work, he was prevented, on antisemitic grounds – in spite of his baptism – from receiving a Berlin University appointment. Other appointments were turned down on the basis of unfavorable comments on his work by his colleagues. On the other hand, his work had attracted the attention of America's preeminent psychologist, Harvard's William James. Muensterberg was given a trial period at Harvard (1892–95), which was followed by a permanent appointment. Muensterberg's contribution is not widely appreciated today, mainly because he left no disciples.

Many modern trends in psychology are traceable to Muensterberg. On the theoretical side, Muensterberg was a forerunner of the functionalist school of psychology. His principles were described in *Grundzuege der Psychologie* (1900), with a second edition published posthumously by Max *Dessoir in 1918. His English text, *Psychology, General and Applied* (1914), although not well received, shows the scope and originality of his thinking. In 1898 he served as president of the American Psychological Association and as president of the American Philosophical Association in 1908. He was undoubtedly responsible for the growth of applied psychology. He was a leading figure and pioneer in industrial psychology and became interested in film, publishing in 1916 his book *The Photoplay*, one of the first major books on film theory. His work inspired William *Stern, Otto Klemm, and Otto *Lipmann. He devised tests for the selection of motormen and developed other testing procedures. He had a hand in the invention of the so-called lie detector and he instituted some of the first attempts at psychotherapy. In his day he was the great popularizer of psychology. He also took an interest in psychic phenomena, exposing the medium Madame Eusapia Paladino and writing, in a negative vein, on thought transference.

Muensterberg's last years were marked by increasing political activity. Although originally a marginal German, he remained a superpatriotic German who never gave up his German citizenship. At the outbreak of World War I he tried by all possible means to prevent the entry of the U.S. into the war and to work for a negotiated peace. His correspondence with the German chancellor, von Bethmann-Hollweg, presenting his plans to have President Wilson act as mediator, was intercepted and aroused violent feelings. In the midst of this controversy, he died as he was lecturing to his class.

BIBLIOGRAPHY: F. Wunderlich, *Hugo Muensterberg's Bedeutung fuer die Nationaloekonomie* (1920); W. Stern, in: *Journal of Applied Psychology*, 1 (1917), 186–8; A.A. Roback, *History of American Psychology* (1964²), 212–39. **ADD. BIBLIOGRAPHY:** M. Hale, *Psychology and Social Order: An Intellectual Biography of Hugo Muensterberg* (1977); M. Hale, *Human Science and Social Order: Hugo Muensterberg and the Origins of Applied Psychology* (1980); A. Langdale, *Hugo Muensterberg on Film* (2002).

[Helmut E. Adler]

MUENZ, ELEAZAR (Lazar) BEN ARYEH LEIB (1837–1921), rabbi and preacher in Poland and Germany. Muenz was a grandson of Eleazar *Loew, the author of *Shemen Roke'aḥ*. He was appointed to the rabbinate of Oswiecim (Auschwitz) near Cracow before 1867. In 1875 he was appointed to the rabbinate of Kempen (Kepna) district of Posen, where he remained until after 1905. From there he moved to Wuerzburg and subsequently to Nuremberg. At the end of World War I he was living in Ansbach, where he died. He was the author of *Get Mesuddar* (1932), on the law of names in bills of divorce. Among his other works, written in German, are *Die modernen Anklagen gegen das Judentum als falsch nachgewiesen* (1882); *Religioese Zeitfragen* (1887, 1909²), a collection of his homilies; *Torat Nashim* (Ger., 1905), on the laws of family purity, frequently reprinted; and *Rabbi Eleasar, genannt Schemen Rokeach* (1895), a detailed biography of his grandfather.

BIBLIOGRAPHY: E. Muenz, *Get Mesuddar* (1932), introd.

MUENZ (Minz), MOSES BEN ISAAC HA-LEVI (c. 1750–1831), Hungarian rabbi. Muenz was born in Podolia or in Galicia. After serving as rabbi in Vishravitz and in Brody, he was appointed in 1789 rabbi of Alt-Ofen (Óbuda) where he remained for the rest of his life. As a result of his activity there and his great reputation, the community became renowned. He represented the community at all royal ceremonies, including the coronation of Francis I. The addresses he delivered on those occasions were published in Hebrew and German. In 1793 he was appointed by the government chief rabbi of the whole Pest region. By virtue of this appointment he was granted the right to serve as Jewish judge in all the judicial affairs of the communities in the area, and not only in religious matters. This right was limited in 1796, but it did not affect the prestige in which he was held. On his initiative, and as a result of his endeavor, a beautiful synagogue was built by the community in 1822. It is still standing and has been proclaimed by the Hungarian government as a protected historical site. The sermon he preached at its consecration, *Devir ha-Bayit*, was published that same year in Vienna. To the second edition (1931) a biography of the author was added by D.S. Loewinger.

During the period of Muenz's rabbinate, tendencies toward religious reform began to be manifested in Hungary. At the beginning Muenz was relatively tolerant toward these reforms and even maintained friendly ties with the leader of the reformers, Aaron *Chorin, but later he took a strong stand against their aspirations in general and against Chorin in particular. In 1803 Chorin's book *Emek ha-Shaveh* appeared with the commendation of Muenz, but by 1805 Muenz was presiding over the *bet din that summoned Chorin before it and rebuked him sharply, compelling him to rescind his progressive attitudes. Although the civil government revoked the ruling of rabbis headed by Muenz it was supported by the Orthodox community. His responsa were published by his son Joseph Isaac, under the title *Sefer Maharam Min* (Prague, 1827). He also published, with his annotations, *Peri Ya'akov* (Ofen, 1830) of Jacob ben Moses. Orthodox Jews of Budapest used to visit his grave in the cemetery of Alt-Ofen during the days of Elul and of *seliḥot*. In 1949 this cemetery was cleared by order of the government and Muenz's remains and the tombstones were transferred to another cemetery in Budapest and reinterred near the graves of those killed by the Nazis, where the custom of visiting his grave continues.

BIBLIOGRAPHY: S. Buechler, *A zsidók története Budapesten...* (1901), 299–320; *Magyar Zsidó Lexikon* (1929), 622; D.S. Loewinger, in: *Devir ha-Bayit* (1931), 1–6.

[Yehouda Marton]

MUGUR (Legrel), FLORIN (1934–1991), Romanian poet. He was deputy editor of *Argeș* and between 1953 and 1968 published seven verse collections, including *Visele de dimineață* ("Morning Dreams", 1962) and *Mituri* ("Myths", 1967). *Destinele intermediare* (1968) dealt with existentialist questions.

°**MUHAMMAD (Muhammad ibn ʿAbdallāh ibn ʿAbd al-Muṭṭalib ibn Hāshim ibn ʿAbd Manāf ibn Quṣayy**; c. 570–632), founder and prophet of *Islam. Muhammad was born in Mecca around 570 C.E. In his twenties he married Khadīja, in whose service he was trading; she was a few years older and bore him several children. According to the traditional account, he received his first revelation at the age of 40, following which he preached his religion with little success in his hometown Mecca for about a decade. The turning point was Muhammad's conclusion of an agreement with Arabs from *Medina who adopted the new religion and provided him with a new basis for continuing his mission. The *hijra* that followed the agreement marks the beginning of Muhammad's Medinan period, namely the decade that made Islam a world power. It is mainly with regard to the Medinan period that a student of Muhammad's biography finds himself on relatively firm ground.

The scholarly struggle with central issues of Muhammad's biography has not yet gone far beyond the starting point, because the accounts about specific events in Muhammad's life, their chronology, and their sequence are often incoherent or contradictory. In addition, they reveal legal and exegetical biases beside political and tribal ones. The famous biography of Muhammad by Ibn Hishām and several other early mainstream compilations were the mainstay of Western scholarship regarding the life of Muhammad. But in recent decades an increasingly critical attitude to these sources has been adopted by several scholars, which for the time being rules out the writing of a narrative biography along the lines of the medieval ones. The creators of the accounts that make up the medieval biographies were not unsophisticated and often had agendas of their own, beside their wish to tell the story of the Arabian Prophet. Students of these accounts cannot afford to be gullible or unsophisticated. Moreover, one has to bear in mind that many of the medieval scholars, on whom we sometimes pass judgment as if they were fellow historians, did not consider themselves as such, or in any case they were not historians in the modern sense of the term. The liberty with which these compilers treated the received texts, for example in creating "combined reports" by putting together fragments from the texts of their predecessors, is most revealing with regard to their concept of history. Besides, their compilations were products of their own time. Their foundations had been laid well before they came into being, and in the cultural context of early Islam that was marked by extreme conservatism, the compilers had little room for self-expression and creativity.

The sheer amount of evidence found in Muhammad's biography is misleading; for example, one looks in vain for the name of a fortress in which a certain tribe was besieged. To some extent the lack of concrete evidence in the biography can be remedied by resorting to other sources, since accounts about Muhammad's life are found everywhere in the vast Islamic literature. Even relatively late sources sometimes contain valuable evidence, because compilers who lived several centuries ago still included in their compilations extracts from much older works which have meanwhile been lost. In sum, one has to throw one's net beyond Muhammad's medieval biographies and employ relatively late sources, too.

Paradoxically, as more and more texts on the Prophet's life are being made available electronically or through the publication of texts hitherto unknown to science, Western scholars seem to be less and less interested in finding concrete evidence in this huge repository of source material. Such evidence does exist, mainly in the form of background information regarding the society of Arabia at the time of Muhammad. The thousands of persons mentioned in the sources, their families and property, in addition to the geographical and topographical data, provide a firm starting point for the study of events in Muhammad's life, their chronology, and their sequence. Between the naiveté of certain past scholars who were unaware of the complexity of Islamic accounts, and the total rejection of these accounts as historical sources, there are several interim positions. A rigorous scrutiny of the sources does point out problematic areas in the evidence, but enough playing cards remain in our hands to facilitate step-by-step progress in the study of Muhammad's life.

Many Jews are mentioned in the chapters of Muhammad's Medinan period. The amount of evidence about their relations with Muhammad is enormous and some of it goes back to Jewish converts or their descendants. It makes up a sizeable "Jewish chapter" in every medieval biography of Muhammad. Only a small number of Jews are treated positively in the biography and elsewhere in the Islamic literature. They include several Jews who adopted Islam and several others who helped Muhammad in one way or another. Other Jews who appear in the sources were hostile to him: this has major implications to this very day, far beyond the spheres of literature and culture.

Muhammad in Mecca

Arabia in general and Mecca in particular were not isolated from the rest of the world, mainly because of the rivalry between Byzantium and the Sassanian Empire. Being a significant Arabian cultic and trade center, Mecca and its vicinity must have attracted international traders of all religions. But because of lack of interest on the part of Muslim informants, and perhaps due to self-censorship and an apologetic attitude, concrete details about indigenous Meccans who abandoned idol worship and adhered to other religions, or about foreigners living in Mecca, is scarce; after all, Muhammad was accused by his Meccan adversaries of having had a human teacher rather than a heavenly one. There is evidence about a Jewish trader in Mecca who announced Muhammad's birth, lamenting the fact that prophecy had forsaken the Children of Israel. This may well have been a legendary person created in the context of the literary genre known as "the proofs of Muhammad's prophecy." But he represents the Jewish trader in Mecca and elsewhere in Arabia that must have been a well-known figure. A relatively more convincing account concerns a Jew from Najrān by the name of Udhayna who was a protégé of Muhammad's grandfather ʿAbd al-Muṭṭalib and was trading on the latter's behalf in the markets of Tihāma or the Arabian coast. When the Jew was murdered, ʿAbd al-Muṭṭalib saw to it that blood money be given to the Jew's cousin. Off the beaten track one also finds relatively reliable data of Jewish women who before Islam married prominent members of Muhammad's tribe, Quraysh. For example, two elder brothers of Muhammad's grandfather are said to have had a Jewish mother.

Since Muhammad himself was a trader, there can be no doubt that he had had some contacts with Jews before becoming a prophet. Also his family's links with Medina, which had a large and dominant Jewish population, point in the same direction. His great-grandfather Hāshim married a Medinan woman, Salmā, of the Arab tribe of Khazraj. Muhammad's grandfather ʿAbd al-Muṭṭalib was born in Medina and stayed there with his mother for several years. Other Qurashīs, too, had close links with Medina in which both trade interests and politics were involved. For example, when Abū Sufyān had married Hind, who in due course gave birth to the future caliph Muʿāwiya, the bride's father, ʿUtba ibn Rabīʿa, borrowed the jewelry of the Banū Abīl-Ḥuqayq, a leading family of the Jewish tribe *Naḍīr.

Muhammad at Medina

Negotiations between Muhammad and men from Medina of the Khazraj and Aws tribes (mainly of the former, which was stronger than the latter), referred to in Islam as *al-Anṣār* or "the helpers," preceded by several months the *hijra* that brought Muhammad from Mecca to Medina. The crucial agreement was concluded during the annual pilgrimage to Mecca at nearby al-ʿAqaba. Reportedly, the Jews of Medina told their Arab neighbors about the imminent appearance of a prophet. This sounds like yet another example of "the proofs of Muhammad's prophecy," but it may reflect historical fact. At the ʿAqaba meeting, twelve of the Medinan Arabs were designated as *nuqabāʿ* or tribal representatives, nine of the Khazraj and three of the Aws. Seven out of the twelve *nuqabāʿ* shared a common denominator: they were literate. Now since in pre-Islamic Medina literacy was acquired at the Jewish *bayt al-midrās*, this means that the literate *nuqabāʿ*, while they possibly did not convert to Judaism, were educated by the Jews, and hence were prepared to accept Muhammad as the messiah expected by the Jews. This conclusion, arrived at by comparing the list of *nuqabāʿ* with that of literate people, has a stronger claim to historicity than a direct statement found in a literary source.

Some have argued that the fate of the Jews of Medina was raised at the ʿAqaba meeting and that Muhammad had a predetermined plan to wipe them out. But this assumption is based on a corrupt text: the word *yahūd* or "Jews" in the story of the meeting on which this argument was based is wrong and should be replaced by *ʿuhūd* or "treaties" found in better versions of the same text. It is doubtful that Muhammad had such plans; in any case it is somewhat naive to expect to find Muhammad accused of insincerity in an Islamic source otherwise devoted to the protection of his image.

The Jewish Tribes

Several Jewish tribes in Medina are the subjects of separate chapters in Muhammad's biography because they were involved in bloody conflicts with him. In the traditional order of events these are the *Qaynuqāʿ, the Naḍīr, and the *Qurayẓa. A fourth tribe, the Thaʿlaba ibn al-Fiṭyawn, may have been on a similar level of significance, but it was expelled by Muhammad in 3/625 "without a fight," and hence only scanty details were preserved about it. The major Jewish tribes of Medina were the owners of weapons and fortresses *par excellence*. However, concerning the status of the Jews, modern students of Muhammad's life have been misled by a corrupt passage in Wāqidī's "Book of Battles" (*Kitāb al-maghāzī*) regarding the divisions in the population of Medina when Muhammad arrived there. The passage is from the introduction of the account about the assassination of Naḍīr's leader *Kaʿb ibn al-Ashraf. In its correct form, the passage reads as follows: "Ibn al-Ashraf was a poet. He would satirize the Prophet and his Companions and instigate against them in his poetry the infidels of Quraysh. When the Messenger of God came to Medina, its population was a mixture; among them there were the Muslims who were united by the call of Islam; the 'associators' who worshipped idols; and the Jews who were the owners of weapons and fortresses and allies of the two clans, the Aws and the Khazraj."

It can be shown that the Jewish tribes, Naḍīr and Qurayẓa, in addition to several Arab clans of the Aws, owned castles or special fortifications. Unlike the common tower-houses called in Arabic *uṭum*, pl. *āṭām* that were found everywhere in the Medina area, these castles were military buildings only used at times of war. In addition, the main Jewish tribes had huge arsenals of weapons of different kinds that are listed in the reports on the spoils taken from them. The above report also refers to alliances between the Jews and the Arab tribes of Medina. The Jewish tribes were part of the general system of alliances that was supposed to preserve a balance of power in Medina. In this system the Qaynuqāʿ and Naḍīr were allied with the Khazraj, while the Qurayẓa were allied with the Aws. In the Battle of Buʿāth several years before the *hijra*, the system was temporarily disturbed, when the Naḍīr fought against their former allies, the Khazraj, alongside the Qurayẓa and the Aws. But after the battle there was a reconciliation between the Naḍīr and the Khazraj following attempts by the Khazraj leader ʿAbdallāh ibn Ubayy, who had not been involved in the Battle of Buʿāth. He was the most prominent leader among the Khazraj, and probably in Medina at large, and was supported by the Jewish allies of the Khazraj, namely the Qaynuqāʿ and the Naḍīr.

The small group of *muhājirūn* including Qurashīs and clients who arrived at Medina, followed by Muhammad himself, did not cause an immediate upheaval in Medinan politics. Reconciliation between the Khazraj and the Aws was under way, although several wounds and blood with claims were still open. The tribal system was generally stable, with the exception of the occasional clan which had a dispute with its brother clans. Muhammad did not pose as a political reformer intent on destroying the existing equilibrium. It is true that his monotheistic message had immediate political implications, because the Arab tribal leadership of Medina was closely associated with idol worship. But as far as the Jewish tribes were concerned, there was nothing alarming about that: they could only rejoice at the sight of idols being destroyed.

The initial good intentions of Muhammad and the Jewish tribes vis-à-vis each other were expressed, not long after the *hijra*, by separate non-belligerency agreements with the three main tribes, Qaynuqāʿ, Naḍīr, and Qurayẓa. Besides having a time limit, these agreements basically included an assurance that the parties would not attack each other. Simply, the relationship between the newcomers and the native Jewish population had to be regulated by agreements so that trade and agriculture could continue without interruption.

Muhammad directed his attention to his community of disciples that included an increasing number of members from the Khazraj and Aws tribes. One of his first political actions, dating back to the very first period after the *hijra*, was the conclusion of the agreement known in Orientalist jargon by the misnomer, "The Constitution of Medina." The three main Jewish tribes were not a party to the agreement, which was far more binding than the basic non-belligerency agreements which they had concluded with Muhammad. The so-called "Constitution" was closely linked to Muhammad's creation of a territorial basis in the town of Zuhra in Lower Medina (the Sāfila): the only Jewish tribe that is listed in the agreement, the Thaʿlaba ibn al-Fiṭyawn, lived in Zuhra and hence was Muhammad's neighbor; as has been mentioned, the Thaʿlaba were expelled in 3/625. This precious document created a community defined by religion, while preserving the existing tribal system. Despite its religious framework, it had far-reaching political implications, since it separated the members of Muhammad's new community from their fellow tribesmen with regard to several key legal aspects. Thus it laid the foundations for Muhammad's victory over the Jews that was achieved despite his initial military inferiority. Muhammad introduced into the political system of Medina a new source of authority which destroyed it from within, namely Allah and His Messenger.

The first period after the *hijra* was marked by a stable relationship between Muhammad and the Jews that was possibly not free of polemics and friction. Muhammad sincerely expected the Jews to embrace Islam, but they were only prepared to recognize him as Allah's messenger to the Arabs. The small number of Jewish converts was for Muhammad a constant source of frustration; even declaring *Jerusalem as the Muslim *qibla* or direction of prayer did not help to attract the Jews to Muhammad's call. As long as Muhammad's relations with the main Jewish tribes were good, there was nothing menacing about the "Constitution" from their viewpoint. Problems began when conflicts of loyalties occurred among the Arab allies of the Jews. With the prominent exception of ʿAbdallāh ibn Ubayy, Islamic literature usually preserved the stories of former Arab allies who proved by their actions that they were no longer attached to the Jews. Hostilities broke out after Muhammad's major victory at Badr (2/624) at about the same time Jerusalem was replaced by Mecca as the Muslim direction of prayer. The first Jewish tribe to enter into a conflict with Muhammad was the Qaynuqāʿ. Muhammad's biography offers a variety of causes for this conflict, a phenomenon we meet time and again with regard to other Jewish tribes and to the assassination of the Naḍīr leader Kaʿb ibn al-Ashraf. Regarding the Qaynuqāʿ, the pride of place in the sources – and sometimes in scholarly writings as well – is given to the alleged events that followed the humiliation of an Arab woman by a Jewish goldsmith at the market of the Qaynuqāʿ. But this story is a suspicious *casus belli*, since a similar one exists regarding one of the pre-Islamic "Battles of the Arabs" (*ayyām al-ʿarab*). In fact, we have here a wandering literary motive unworthy of serious consideration.

Self-imposed censorship is not uncommon in Islamic literature, and Muhammad's biography is no exception. Therefore, straightforward answers to simple questions are in short supply. Even when this would have been appropriate, we are unlikely to come across a statement that "Muhammad attacked such-and-such an enemy, taking advantage of a propitious moment"; unrealistically, the Prophet is not supposed to have been driven by political or military considerations.

But Muhammad's brilliant achievement during the last decade of his life is proof enough that he knew how to choose a propitious moment in the interest of his new religion. To understand why the Qaynuqāʿ were the first Jewish tribe to find itself in conflict with Muhammad one has to consider two realities that can easily go unnoticed in the general tumult of the evidence. The Qaynuqāʿ lived in Lower Medina, not far from Muhammad's territorial basis – admittedly, this is also true of the Naḍīr, who lived in the nearby town of Zuhra; both Jewish tribes were allied with the Khazraj. More significantly, the Qaynuqāʿ lost most of their Arab allies. The Qaynuqāʿ were allied with the Khazraj, who were generally far more supportive of Muhammad than the Aws. However, their alliance was not with the Khazraj as a whole, but with a specific group within the Khazraj, namely the ʿAwf ibn al-Khazraj. The ʿAwf were divided into two subsections, the Ḥublā led by ʿAbdallāh ibn Ubayy and the Qawāqila led by ʿUbāda ibn al-Ṣāmit. The two leaders held equal shares of the alliance. Against the background of the conflict between Muhammad and the Qaynuqāʿ ʿUbāda repudiated his alliance with the Qaynuqāʿ. In practice this meant the collapse of their alliance with the ʿAwf ibn al-Khazraj, because it was inconceivable that one section of the ʿAwf, the Ḥublā, would fight against another section, the Qawāqila, in order to protect the Qaynuqāʿ.

This crucial account on the alliance – a rarity in Muhammad's biography that is otherwise poor in factual evidence – provides a matter-of-fact behind-the-scenes insight into the conflict with the Qaynuqāʿ. We owe it to ʿUbāda ibn al-Ṣāmit's offspring. They were naturally proud of ʿUbāda's repudiation of his alliance with the Qaynuqāʿ, which is emphasized against ʿAbdallāh ibn Ubayy's refusal "to move with the times." According to Arab values, the abandonment of one's allies was not a praiseworthy act; but there was a temporary abandonment of these values in the context of Muhammad's conflict with the Jews. The reversal of values is reflected by the expression "the hearts have changed" which is used as an excuse at least twice in connection with the alliances between the Jewish and Arab tribes of Medina. It is doubtful whether the dialogues which include this expression really took place; but obviously Islamic literature chose to refer in this manner to the changing circumstances when the former Arab allies of the Jews had to choose between their Jewish allies and Muhammad. By declaring their loyalty to Muhammad, they expunged the blemish of their former alliances.

The repudiation of former alliances with the Jews repeats itself in connection with the other main Jewish tribes. The assassination of the Naḍīr leader Kaʿb ibn al-Ashraf, the son of an Arab tribesman and an aristocratic woman of the Naḍīr, which was probably an introduction to the tribe's siege and expulsion, was carried out by his foster-brother, among others. The vivid account of how Kaʿb was lured out of his fortress and the precise details of his assassination belong to the "change of heart" theme.

As usual, one finds several alternative causes for the conflict with the Naḍīr where one good cause would have sufficed. Again a significant reality could easily have been overlooked. Some reports about the conflict with the Naḍīr have it that Muhammad ordered his men to attack the Naḍīr who were lamenting the death of their chief, Kaʿb ibn al-Ashraf, in their town of Zuhra. This suggests that the attack on the Naḍīr was a surprise one. As has already been mentioned, in addition to the common tower-houses which were also used for residence, the Naḍīr had a castle only used at times of war. But when Muhammad attacked them, they were in their town, not in their castle. Indeed accounts of their war with Muhammad speak of house-to-house fighting. The compilers of Muhammad's biography felt an understandable aversion to describing the attack on the Naḍīr as a surprise attack; the attachment of a proper *casus belli* to every act of war was for them a matter of high priority. The expelled Naḍīr probably went to places with which they had had former trading links: Edrei, Jericho, al-Ḥīra, and Khaybar. Two leading families of the Naḍīr, the Banū Abīl-Ḥuqayq and the family of Ḥuyayy ibn Akhṭab, went to Khaybar.

Like the other main Jewish tribes, the Qurayẓa concluded a non-belligerency agreement with Muhammad not long after his arrival at Medina. Agreements of this kind had a time limit. In any case, some sources mention a later agreement that neutralized the Qurayẓa and gave Muhammad a free hand to deal with the Naḍīr. It is reported that Muhammad laid siege to the Naḍīr, announcing that they would only be safe if they conclude an agreement (i.e. of non-belligerency) with him. They refused and he fought them for one day. In the following day he laid siege to the Qurayẓa, demanding that they conclude with him an agreement along the same lines. They consented and he returned to the Naḍīr and fought them until they surrendered and went into exile. This valuable fragment seems to have been marginalized in Islamic literature. Again, we realize that scholarly biographies of Muhammad which are solely based on his mainstream biographies lack crucial evidence.

The war against the Qurayẓa took place after the Battle of the Ditch (Khandaq) during which Medina was besieged by a coalition including Muhammad's own tribe, Quraysh, and several nomadic tribes. Unlike the war against the Naḍīr, in this case one may speak of a real siege: the Qurayẓa were probably in their castle in a state of alert ever since the Battle of the Ditch had started. The siege of the Qurayẓa was rather eventless, perhaps due to negotiations which were taking place between Muhammad and the leaders of the besieged tribe. The besiegers had only two casualties: a man who died of natural causes and another who was killed by a millstone thrown from the castle by a woman who was later executed.

The Qurayẓa are said to have violated their non-belligerency agreement with Muhammad, although evidence about hostile military actions on their part is meager. Reportedly, it was the angel Gabriel who told Muhammad after the Battle of the Ditch that the war was not over yet and that he had to march on the Qurayẓa. Obviously, the informant who brought Gabriel into the story did not give much thought to the question of *casus belli*. Typically, when the Qurayẓa surrendered without conditions, Muhammad yielded the power to decide their fate to a former ally of theirs from the Aws, who ordered that their fighting men (i.e. all those who had reached puberty) be killed and their wives and children be sold into slavery. Several accounts make it clear that while this person, Saʿd ibn Muʿādh, had undergone a full "change of heart," other members of the Aws were embittered by the fact that the Qaynuqāʿ, who had been allied with the Khazraj, had been allowed to leave Medina unharmed through the intercession of ʿAbdallāh ibn Ubayy, while their own allies were going to be slain. In itself, the execution of a whole tribe was not a new idea: after all, Muhammad had intended to execute the Qaynuqāʿ. The Qurayẓa could not rely on meaningful support from their allies, the Aws, for the simple reason that at the time of their execution most of the Aws were not yet Muslims. ʿAbdallāh ibn Ubayy, even after having lost some of his power among the Khazraj following Muhammad's arrival at Medina, commanded enough authority among the Khazraj to exert real pressure on Muhammad and spare the lives of the Qaynuqāʿ. It can be said that the execution of the Qurayẓa is yet another attestation of the collapse of the system of alliances that had safeguarded the security of the Jewish tribes.

The last major episode in Muhammad's conflict with the Jews of Arabia was the conquest of Khaybar. Here too we come across a little known chapter in Muhammad's diplomatic history, one that is completely absent from his biographies, probably due to self-imposed censorship. The expedition of Khaybar (7/628) was immediately preceded by that of Ḥudaybiyya (6/628) in which Muhammad led an enormous army to the fringes of the sacred area of Mecca. There he negotiated the terms of a non-belligerency treaty with his tribe, Quraysh. Muhammad's medieval biographies include lengthy accounts about the negotiations at Ḥudaybiyya, making no secret of the fact that Muhammad consented to far-reaching concessions to the Qurashī pagans. But there is no convincing explanation of why he was prepared to yield to such an extent. It is an 11th century doctor of law who has the answer. It is found in a discussion of whether it is legitimate for Muslims to accept humiliating demands if these are dictated by necessity. The case in question concerns the demands made by the inhabitants of a town which a Muslim troop needs to cross:

> Indeed the Messenger of God undertook in the non-belligerency agreement on the day of Ḥudaybiyya, commitments which were graver than this, since the people of Mecca imposed on him to undertake to return to them any of those who would come to him as a Muslim. He had fulfilled this undertaking until it was abrogated, because there was in it a benefit for the Muslims, owing to the conspiracy between the people of Mecca and the people of Khaybar. It prescribed that if the Messenger of God marched on one of the two parties, the other party would attack Medina. He concluded a non-belligerency agreement with the people of Mecca to secure his flank when he would march on Khaybar.

The Mecca-Khaybar "conspiracy" was adapted to the realities on the ground, since Medina is located between Khaybar in the north and Mecca in the south. Muhammad's rivals, the Jews of Khaybar and the Quraysh of Mecca, agreed that rather than coming to each other's rescue upon being attacked by Muhammad, the party that was not targeted would attack Muhammad's base in Medina. The sweet fruit of the Ḥudaybiyya non-belligerency agreement was the abolishment of the Mecca-Khaybar axis. The pagan Meccans gave Muhammad a free hand in Khaybar, the last major Jewish stronghold in northern Arabia. Khaybar was conquered shortly afterwards. The Jews of Khaybar and those of Fadak, Taymāʾ and Wādīl-Qurā were allowed to continue cultivating their lands in return for a certain share of the annual harvest.

Muhammad's phenomenal success in his war against the Jewish tribes of Medina gave him control over it. The accounts of the tragic events of this first encounter between Islam and Judaism remain with us. Regardless of their historicity, they became basic building blocks of Islamic culture and a source of edification, inspiration and entertainment for millions of Muslims.

BIBLIOGRAPHY: M. Gil, *Be-Malkhut Yismaʿel* (1997), 1, 3–46; H.Z. Hirschberg, *Yisraʾel be-Arav* (1946); J. Horovitz, *The Earliest Biographies of the Prophet and their Authors* (2002); M.J. Kister, "The Massacre of the Banū Qurayẓa: A Re-Examination of a Tradition," in: *Jerusalem Studies in Arabic and Islam*, 8 (1986), 61–96; idem, "The *Sīrah* Literature," in A.F.L. Beeston et al. (eds.), *Arabic Literature to the End of the Umayyad Period* (1983), 352–67; M. Lecker, *Jews and Arabs in Pre- and Early Islamic Arabia* (1998); H. Motzki (ed.), *The Biography of Muhammad: The Issue of the Sources* (2000); U. Rubin, "Muhammad," in: *Encyclopaedia of the Qurʾān*, 3, 440–58; M. Schoeller, *Exegetisches Denken und Prophetenbiographie* (1998); idem, "*Sīra* and *Tafsīr* Muhammad al-Kalbī and the Jews of Medina," in: H. Motzki (ed.), *The Biography of Muhammad: The Issue of the Sources* (2000), 18–48; R. Sellheim, "Prophet, Chaliph und Geschichte: Die Muhammad-Biographie des Ibn Isḥāq," in: *Oriens*, 18–19 (1965), 91–336; W.M. Watt, *Muhammad at Medina* (1956).

[Michael Lecker (2nd ed.)]

°**MUHAMMAD ALI** (1769–1849), ruler of *Egypt from 1805 to 1849. First coming to Egypt in 1799 with the Ottoman sultan's armies, Muhammad Ali quickly rose to power there and conquered the Sudan, *Palestine, and *Syria. He successfully subdued the *Mamluks, massacring them in 1811. By exploiting the weakness of the Ottomans and the disunity of the Great Powers, he consolidated his position by military campaigns outside Egypt and important reforms within the country. He also appointed French officers who had retired from their duties at the close of the Napoleonic Wars. Nevertheless he was unable to maintain his hold over Palestine and Syria, owing to the opposition of Britain and other European countries – with the exception of France – and finally came into conflict with the sultan in 1840. His only important achievement in his foreign policy was the commitment of the sultan to leave the governorship of Egypt in the hands of his family. His internal reforms were also largely motivated by personal interests, but they partially helped in developing and rebuilding Egypt. Despite his severity and his cruel punishments, the lot of his subjects improved. The public administration and the collection of taxes became more efficient, but the reforms essentially took place in the fields of irrigation, agriculture, industry, commerce, justice, health, and education. The relative security within Egypt encouraged commerce; the members of the religious minorities, such as Christians and Jews, also played an active role. Nevertheless, as a result of his personal retention of various monopolies during most of his rule, Muhammad Ali increased his income, but slowed down the development of commerce. His experiments in reforming the system of justice ran foul of a lengthy tradition of corruption among many qadis (religious judges); in order to circumvent them, he established two new courts of justice, in *Cairo and *Alexandria, to which he appointed Muslim and Christian merchants as judges (in Alexandria, there was also a Jewish judge); they were to deal with affairs of business and commerce, especially between members of different religions. Muhammad Ali's generation did not complete the modernization of Egypt and some of his reforms were neglected after his death; the seeds for the Arabization of the country had however been sown. In any event, the Jews of Egypt exchanged the arbitrariness of the many rulers of the land – namely the Mamluks – for the arbitrariness of a single ruler. Though they were still oppressed, the authority of the law protected their persons and their property. When taxes were levied, they were treated in the same way as the other non-Muslims in Egypt, i.e., without discrimination. Personal and material security resulted in an increase in the Jewish population in Egypt (Jews immigrated there from *Italy and *Greece), and by the close of Muhammad Ali's rule there were over 7,000 Jews, including about 1,200 Karaites. Most of the Jews lived in towns and were essentially occupied in commerce, crafts, and public services. Under the influence of Sir Moses *Montefiore, Muhammad Ali did not allow the *Damascus blood libel (1840) to spread to other places. The years of Muhammad Ali's rule of Palestine (1832–40) were a time of relief for the Jewish inhabitants of Ereẓ Israel and especially *Jerusalem, which had been troubled by the Fellaheen revolts.

BIBLIOGRAPHY: S. Ghorbal, *The Beginnings of the Egyptian Question and the Rise of Mehemet Ali* (1928); M. Sabry, *L'empire égyptien sous Mohamed-Ali et la question d' Orient (1811–1849)* (1930); H. Dodwell, *The Founder of Modern Egypt* (1931); M. Zeliger, *Mediniyyut Eiropit ba-Mizraḥ ha-Karov* (1941); H.A.B. Rivlin, *The Agricultural Policy of Muammad ʿAli in Egypt* (1961); J.M. Landau, *Jews in Nineteenth-century Egypt* (1969), index. **ADD. BIBLIOGRAPHY:** J.M. Landau (ed.), *Toledot Yehudei Miẓrayim be-Tekufah ha-Otmanit* (1988), index.

[Jacob M. Landau]

MUHLSTOCK, LOUIS (1904–2001), Canadian artist. Louis Muhlstock was born in Narajow, Galicia. In 1911 he resettled with his family in Montreal, Canada, where his father had immigrated a few years before. After early studies at the Conseil des arts et manufactures, he took evening classes at the Art Association of Montreal and the École des beaux-arts de Montréal while working during the day as an accountant for a fruit and vegetable merchant.

In 1928 Muhlstock made his way to Paris, where he studied at the Grande Chaumière and took part in several exhibitions. When his mother became ill in 1931 he returned to Canada and the difficult Depression era life of an artist. During this period, Muhlstock painted street scenes, abandoned slums, and some remarkable portraits of people marginalized by society – the poor, the sick, and the unemployed. With these works, he became one of the leading proponents of a new form of Canadian art that moved away from a nationalistic identification with the northern landscape to focus on the human condition and contemporary life. A founding member in 1939 of the Contemporary Arts Society, he was part of a dynamic group of artists from Montreal's Jewish community – which also included Jack Beder (1910–1987), Alexander Bercovitch (1891–1951), Sam Borenstein (1908–1969), and Ernst Neumann (1907–1956) – who gave a more decisively humanist, urban dimension to the art of their day. During World War II, Muhlstock made a number of pictures of war industry workers.

Over the following decades Muhlstock's work diversified, thematically and stylistically, but remained marked by an expressive sensibility evident in both the graphic quality of his drawings and the handling of his paintings. A regular exhibitor, he was a member of several associations, including the Canadian Society of Graphic Arts, the Canadian Group of Painters and the Federation of Canadian Artists. His works are represented in numerous public and private collections.

[Esther Trépanier (2nd ed.)]

MUHR, ABRAHAM (1781–1847), leader of Silesian Jewry. Muhr moved from his native city of Berlin to Plesse (Pszczyna; now in Poland), Prussian Silesia. In 1813 he published a pamphlet, *Jerubaal*, in opposition to David *Friedlaender's *Ein Wort zu seiner Zeit*, which demanded extreme reforms in the liturgy and education in response to the Prussian emancipatory edict of 1812. Although Muhr opposed the repudiation of tradition in favor of questionable changes, nevertheless he proposed that sermons in German and choir singing be allowed, and was prepared to sacrifice various customs in order to make the services more respected and meaningful. Subsequently he became an advocate of Reform and an admirer of Abraham *Geiger. He was instrumental in the building of a synagogue in Plesse (1835), where he carried out his 1813 proposals. In 1836 Muhr succeeded in having a cabinet order repealed which introduced the form of address "Jew" in official transactions. He also played a role in the partial repeal of the prohibition on the use of non-Jewish names. In 1840 he was one of the leaders in the organization of a regional body of Upper Silesian Jewry, the first modern union of Jewish communities in Germany. In 1844 he proposed establishing a Jewish agricultural colony, but in 1847 he died in Breslau (now in Poland). His brother Joseph (1772–1848) was leader of the Berlin community.

BIBLIOGRAPHY: M. Brann, *Abraham Muhr, ein Lebensbild* (1918); idem, in: *Festschrift Martin Philippson* (1916), 342–69; M. Antonov, in: BŻIH, no. 21 (1957), 118–24, 177; *Zur Judenfrage in Deutschland* (1844); B. Mevorach, in: *Zion*, 34 (1969), 194f.

[Henry Wasserman]

MUKACHEVO (Czech. **Mukačevo**; Hung. **Munkács**), city in Transcarpathian district, Ukraine. Until 1919 Mukachevo belonged to Hungary, then until 1938 to Czechoslovakia, and from 1938 to 1945 again to Hungary. From the end of World War II it formed part of the Soviet Union. The modest beginnings of the community are reflected in documents early in the 18th century. In Jewish sources, such as the place-formulas in divorce bills, the town is referred to as "Minkatchov, a town situated on the banks of the Latartza River and of springs." The Jewish population rapidly increased and it became one of the largest communities in Hungary, renowned on the one hand for its extreme conservatism and pronounced inclination toward ḥasidism, and on the other for its many undertakings in the fields of Hebrew education and Zionist activities. Many documents on the beginnings of the Jewish settlement in this town have been preserved and published. According to these, Jews settled there early in the second half of the 17th century. There is also evidence of isolated Jews living in the surrounding area prior to this period. In 1711 ownership of the town was transferred to the Schoenborn family of the nobility, who authorized the growth of the Jewish population on payment of taxes and levies. Local Jews were already engaged in commerce at that time and acted as brokers in trade between Galicia and Hungary. There were also Jewish farmers and craftsmen. The population was continuously augmented by arrivals from Galicia. In 1741 a Jewish community of 80 families was organized and a synagogue established; their numbers had doubled by 1815 (165), reached 202 in 1830, and 301 by 1842. In the 1848–49 Hungarian revolt against the Austrians, 247 Jews joined the local guard. From 1851, when there was already a large yeshivah in Mukachevo, the community maintained regular records of births, deaths, and marriages. A Hebrew press was founded in 1871 and many Hebrew books were published in Mukachevo (see *Kirjath Sepher, Index to Studies, Notes and Reviews* (1967), entries, 86, 192, 193, 473).

The most prominent rabbis of the community were Solomon Shapira (grandson of R. Zevi who had also occupied this rabbinical seat for a few years); Zevi Shapira, who succeeded his father in 1893; and Ḥayyim Eleazar Shapira, who led the community from 1913 and became known as the leading opponent of Zionism in the ḥasidic world. After his death in 1937 he was succeeded by his son-in-law, Baruch Rabinowitz, subsequently rabbi in Ḥolon, Israel (for ḥasidic dynasty, see *Shapira family). In 1891 the community numbered 5,049 (47.9% of the total population) and two additional synagogues were erected in 1895 and 1903. The Jewish population continued to grow and numbered 7,675 in 1910 (44%); 10,012 in 1921 (48%); and 11,241 (43%) in 1930, of whom 88% registered their nationality as Jewish.

Between the two world wars Jews participated actively in the administration of Mukachevo and its general political life. Despite opposition by the masses, the Zionist party of Czechoslovakia found many supporters in the town. Four Yiddish periodicals were published. Pupils of the town and its surroundings streamed to the first Hebrew elementary school, which was founded in 1920 by the Organization of Hebrew Schools in Subcarpathian Ruthenia. A Hebrew secondary school was established in 1925. This was headed from 1929 by Ḥayyim *Kugel, who became a member of the Czechoslovak parliament in 1935, and later by Eliahu Rubin. At the time of the Holocaust there were about 30 synagogues in Mukachevo. Many of these were ḥasidic *battei-midrash* and *kloyzen*.

When Mukachevo reverted to Hungarian rule in 1938, the Jews immediately suffered heavily.

Holocaust Period and After

In 1940–1941 many young Jews were drafted into work battalions and sent to the Russian front, where most of them died. In July and early August 1941 many Jewish families without Hungarian citizenship were expelled to Stanislavov (Galicia) and Kamenets-Podolski, and there most of them perished. After the German occupation of Hungary in March 1944, the Jews were herded together in a ghetto with about 15,000 others from the Berehovo district. The ghetto consisted of a few streets with extremely poor sanitary conditions and almost no food. The able-bodied were pressed into forced labor. In the second half of May 1944 transports started to leave for Auschwitz and by May 30 the city was pronounced **judenrein*. After the war some 2,500 returned to the city, but after it was annexed to the Soviet Union, many left for Czechoslovakia and Israel. Under Soviet rule the synagogues were confiscated; the last one was converted into a warehouse in 1959. Some Jews were imprisoned for practicing *sheḥitah*. Between 1,000 and 2,000 Jews were living in Mukachevo in the late 1960s. Most remaining Jews emigrated in the 1990s, leaving for Israel and the West.

BIBLIOGRAPHY: J.L. Ha-Kohen Weingarten, *Arim ve-Immahot be-Yisrael*, 1 (1946), 345–71, incl. bibl.; MHJ, 2 (1937); 3 (1937); 5 pt. 1 (1959); 5 pt. 2 (1960); 7 (1963); 8 (1965), index locorum s.v. *Munkács*; L.R. Braham, *Hungarian Jewish Studies* (1966), 223–33; A. Sas, in: *Juedisches Archiv*, 2 nos. 1–2 (1928), 1–6; 2 nos. 3–4 (1929), 33–39; 2 nos. 5–7 (1929), 33–44.

[Yehouda Marton]

MUKAMMIṢ (also **al-Mukammaṣ**, the spelling of the name is uncertain), **IBN MARWĀN AL-RĀQI** (from the city of Raqa, Iraq) **AL-SHIRAZI AL-** (also known as **David ha-Bavli**; c. 900), one of the first Jewish philosophers of the Islamic period. Al-*Kirkisani, the Karaite scholar, relates that he was a Jew who began to convert to Christianity when he was a student of Nonnus, a Christian philosopher and physician who lived at Nisibis. However, when he became better acquainted with the dogmas and teachings of Christianity, he composed two polemical works against this religion; nevertheless, from this fact it cannot be deduced with certainty that he returned to Judaism. Be that as it may, Jews and Muslims considered him a Jewish scholar. It is also not clear whether he was a Rabbanite or Karaite.

Al-Mukammiṣ translated Christian commentaries on Genesis and Ecclesiastes and wrote on different religions and sects. A manuscript which contains most of his theological-philosophical work entitled *ʿIshrūn Maqālāt* ("Twenty Treatises") is extant in the St. Petersburg library. Only a small portion of the Arabic original of the work has been published; this corresponds to one of the sections of a partial Hebrew translation of the work which forms part of Judah b. Barzillai al-Bargeloni's commentary on *Sefer Yeẓirah*. Al-Mukammiṣ' work deals with such topics as knowledge and truth, substance and accident, the existence of God, His unity and attributes, prophecy, and the Divine commandments. The portions of the work which are extant disclose that, like *Saadiah Gaon (*Emunot ve-De'ot*, 1:1), al-Mukammiṣ followed, generally speaking, the teachings of the Muslim Mu'tazilites (see *Kalām), though he also accepted some of the views of the Greek philosophers. Like the Mu'tazilites he argued that the attributes of God are not superadded to His essence, so that they would introduce multiplicity into God. God and His attributes are one, and only the shortcomings of human language require that men use a multiplicity of terms in describing His attributes. Attributes describing God must be understood negatively, that is to say, they must be interpreted as stating what God is not, rather than what He is (cf. *God, Attributes of). Al-Mukammiṣ holds further that a "negative theology" similar to his is already found in Aristotle. He rejects the Christian doctrine of the Trinity as false, since it is based on the notion that God possesses a multiplicity of attributes. He calls God the "uncaused cause." The soul, he holds, lives through itself, not through a force in something else. The reward of the righteous and the punishment of the wicked takes place throughout eternity in the World to Come. Describing the history of Christianity, he affirms that this religion has its root in two Jewish sects: the Sadducees and the Jewish pre-Christian sect of the Alkaraya. He points to the contradictions among the various Gospels and shows that these writings contain no laws. Laws were given to Christians only by the apostles Peter and Paul, though Christians see the source of these laws in a secret tradition stemming from Jesus. Since these apostolic laws were few and insufficient, Christians added new laws at the Council of Nicea, and still more laws were added later.

Al-Mukammiṣ wrote extensively about Jewish sects, and his discussion of this topic served, undoubtedly, as an important source for Jewish and Islamic authors.

BIBLIOGRAPHY: G. Vajda, in: A. Altmann (ed.), *Jewish Medieval and Renaissance Studies* (1967), 49–73 (Fr.); Steinschneider, Uebersetzungen, 259–62; Steinschneider, Arab Lit, 37; Baron, Social² (1958), 91–98, 297–8, 327; Husik, Philosophy, 17–22; Guttman, Philosophies, 74–75.

[Shlomo Pines]

MUKDONI, A. (pseudonym of **Alexander Kappel**; 1877–1958), Yiddish essayist, and theater critic. Born in Lyakhovichi, Belorussia, he began his literary career in Warsaw in 1906, specializing in theater criticism and publishing widely in Yiddish journals in Poland, Russia, and the U.S. Before earning a doctorate in labor law from the University of Bern, Switzerland, he studied in yeshivah and a Russian high school. After World War I, he edited the Kovno daily *Nayes*, before immigrating to the U.S in 1922. There he joined the daily *Morgn-Zhurnal* as literary and theater critic. He published *Ertseylungen un Skitsn* ("Stories and Sketches," 1911), and *Y.L. Perets un dos Yidishe Teater* ("I.L. Peretz and the Yiddish Theater," 1949) in addition to four volumes of memoirs: *Mayne Bagegenishn* ("My Encounters," 1949–55). He published his best critical essays in the volume *Teater* ("Theater," 1927), which includes keen observations on the Yiddish theater and Yiddish actors.

BIBLIOGRAPHY: Rejzen, Leksikon, 2 (1927), 360–4; LNYL, 5 (1963), 547–53; S. Bickel, *Shrayber fun mayn Dor* (1958), 215–21; *Mukdoni Yoyvl-Zamlbukh* (1927). **ADD. BIBLIOGRAPHY:** Z. Zilbercweig, *Leksikon fun Yidishn Teater*, 2 (1934), 1284–6.

[Shlomo Bickel / Anita Norich (2nd ed.)]

MUKẒEH (Heb. מֻקְצֶה; "set aside," "excluded"), rabbinical term for objects which it is forbidden to handle on the Sabbath or festivals. According to one authority in the Talmud, the law of *mukẓeh* is a biblical injunction derived from Exodus 16:15 (Beah 2b; Pes. 47b). Maimonides explains that the law is intended to emphasize the distinction between the Sabbath and festivals, and weekdays (Yad, Shabbat, 24:12).

The Talmud (Shab. 124a) enumerates several categories of *mukẓeh*, including: (1) objects, such as money and tools, whose nature renders them unfit for use on the Sabbath or festivals because of their connection with forbidden work (Sh. Ar., OḤ 308:1). Such objects may only be handled if they are needed for an act permitted on these days, such as a hammer for cracking nuts (308:3); (2) objects not normally used at all (e.g., broken property, pebbles), unless a specific use had been determined for them on the eve of the Sabbath or the festival (308:7); (3) objects which were not in existence (termed *nolad*), or were inaccessible at the commencement of the Sabbath or festival. This category includes newly laid eggs (322:1), fruit fallen from a tree on the same day (322:3), and milk obtained from an animal by a non-Jew (305:20); (4) objects which at the commencement of the holy day served as a base for others which are forbidden to be handled on that day, such as candlesticks or a candle tray (309:4).

An object which is *mukẓeh* can only be moved if its place is needed (311:8, 15a), and if it is moved in an unusual way, if it is kicked for instance, and not moved by hand (*Be'ur Halakhah* to 266:13). In all cases, objects which were *mukẓeh* at twilight on the eve of the holy day, remain *mukẓeh* throughout the holy day.

See general laws of *Sabbath.

BIBLIOGRAPHY: J.J. Neuwirth, *Shemirat Shabbat ke-Hilkhetah* (1965), 128–52.

MULBERRY (Heb. תות, *tut*). Two species of mulberry grow in Israel: the black, *Morus nigra*, and the white, *Morus alba*. The latter is a comparative newcomer to the region, the ancient sources referring only to the former. The mulberry seems to have originated in Persia, from where it was transferred to the Middle East. There is evidence that it was growing in Greece in the sixth century B.C.E. In Aramaic literature it is first mentioned in the Book of *Ahikar, which was discovered among *Elephantine papyri, where it says: "My son, be not in a hurry, like the almond tree whose blossom is the first to appear, but whose fruit is the last to be eaten; but be equal and sensible, like the mulberry tree whose blossom is the last to appear, but whose fruit is the first to be eaten" (Ahikar, Syriac Version A, 2:7). According to the Talmud the fruit of the mulberry ripens 52 days after the flowering (Bek. 8a). In I Maccabees 6:34 it is related that the elephants brought by the Syrians were incited to battle with the juice of grapes and mulberries. The staining of the hands by the juice is referred to by the rabbis in their parable of the dialogue between God and Cain, who pleaded "Am I my brother's keeper?" (Gen. 4:9): "This may be compared to one who stole mulberries and, on being caught by the owner, pleaded his innocence. The owner replied: 'But your hands are stained.' Thus said the Holy One, blessed be He, to Cain: 'Thy brother's blood crieth unto Me'" (Gen. R. 22: 9). The mulberry initially is white, then reddens and finally becomes black (see Ma'as. 1:2). It is a large, long-living tree. Until a generation ago, an old mulberry tree used to be shown in Jerusalem near the Pool of Siloam about which there was a legend (mentioned in a travel book of 1575) that Isaiah hid in the hollow of its trunk when pursued by Manasseh. Apparently the town Bertotha (Or. 1:4; et al.) takes its name from the mulberry. The white mulberry, the leaves of which are used for feeding silkworms, originated in China and was brought to Ereẓ Israel at a late date. Joseph *Nasi planted extensive orchards of them in Tiberias in 1565 with the intention of developing a silk industry. This venture, however, failed. Another effort was made in Petaḥ Tikvah by the Ḥovevei Zion, who in 1891 planted 576 dunams (144 acres) with mulberry trees, but this venture also failed. Nowadays the tree is grown in gardens for its beauty and for the shade it gives. There is no basis for the Authorized Version's rendering of *bekha'im* in II Samuel 5:23 and I Chronicles 14:14, as mulberry trees (see *Mastic).

BIBLIOGRAPHY: Joseph ha-Kohen, *Emek ha-Bakha* (1852), 129; Loew, Flora, 1 (1928), 266–74; H.N. and A.L. Moldenke, *Plants of the Bible* (1952), 140f.; M. Zohary, *Olam ha-Ẓemaḥim* (1954), 192f. **ADD. BIBLIOGRAPHY:** Feliks, Ha-Ẓome'aḥ, 169.

[Jehuda Feliks]

MULDER, SAMUEL ISRAEL (1792–1862), educator and Hebrew author, born in Amsterdam. He was a pupil of David *Friedrichsfeld and under his influence became one of the pillars of the Dutch Haskalah. As a youth he signed himself "Salomon" or "Schrijver," receiving the surname Mulder only in 1811. In 1818 he became an official court translator, and in 1826 was appointed principal of the Nederlands Israëlietisch Seminarium, the seminary for rabbis and teachers in Amsterdam. From 1835 he served as the superintendent of all Jewish religious schools in Holland, and from 1849 was secretary of the Amsterdam community.

Mulder's scholarly and literary work qualifies him as the Dutch equivalent of a late 18th-century Berlin *maskil*, his oeuvre showing many parallels with that of Joel *Loewe (Joel Brikl). Mulder made his name as a linguist, compiling, inter alia, an abridgement of Loewe's 1794 *Ammudei ha-Lashon* and a Hebrew-Dutch dictionary (1831; with M. *Lemans), and as a translator of the core texts of the Jewish liturgy. He translated large parts of the Bible (1827–38), the Passover *Haggadah* (1837), *Keter Malkhut* (1850), and *Sefer ha-Ḥayyim* (1851). He also published a Dutch Bible for Jewish youth in 17 parts (1850–55). In 1815 he had founded, together with Mozes Loonstein, the Hebrew literary society *Tongeleth*. Simultaneously, Mulder's work appears mildly influenced by the early German *Wissenschaft des Judentums*. He was the author of several historical overviews, ranging from ancient history to Dutch literature. As early as 1826 he published a (liberal) abridged translation of Zunz's groundbreaking study of Rashi (1822). Part of Mulder's Dutch compositions were collected in *Verspreide Lettervruchten* (1844).

BIBLIOGRAPHY: H.N. Shapira, *Toledot ha-Sifrut ha-Ivrit ha-Hadashah*, 1 (1940), 555–64; E.B. Asscher, *Levensschets van Samuel Israël Mulder* (1863); H. Boas, in: *Amstelodamum*, 52 (1965), 126–35; I. Maarsen, *Tongeleth* (1925). **ADD. BIBLIOGRAPHY:** F.J. Hoogewoud, in: *Studia Rosenthaliana* 14 (1980), 129–44.

[Yehuda Arye Klausner / Irene E. Zwiep (2nd ed.)]

MULE (Heb. פֶּרֶד), the offspring of a he-ass and a mare. Although a Jew is prohibited from producing such hybrids, their use is permitted (Tosef., Kil. 5:6 cites an individual view prohibiting it). Since there were different strains of horses and asses in Ereẓ Israel, the mules were also of different strains. The mule is a powerful, submissive animal, particularly suitable for riding and transporting goods in the mountainous regions of Ereẓ Israel, and hence was commonly used. Nor was riding on it regarded as inferior to riding on a horse; Solomon, on the occasion of his proclamation as king, was made to ride "upon King David's mule" (I Kings 1:38), while Absalom met his death while riding on a mule (II Sam. 18:9). Ezekiel (27:14) speaks in praise of the mules of Togarmah (Turkey?). The Talmud mentions white mules as being dangerous and some sages were indignant with Judah ha-Nasi for harboring them (ul. 7b). That the mule is sometimes dangerous, is sterile, and the female barren was regarded as proof that man is prohibited from interfering with the work of creation. Rabban Simeon b. Gamaliel maintained that the first to cross a horse with an ass in order to produce a mule, thereby committing an unworthy act, was "Anah who discovered the *yemim*" (Gen. 36: 24), which he explained as meaning mules. On the other hand, R. Yose held that on the termination of the first Sabbath after the Creation one of the two things which Adam did was "to cross two animals, and from them came forth the mule."

He contended that thereby Adam performed an action "of a kind similar to that of Heaven," that is, he created something new, to become, as it were, a partner with the Creator in the work of creation (Pes. 54a; cf. TJ, Ber. 8:6, 12b). Some also crossbred a stallion and a she-ass, and the Talmud gives the characteristics of the two types of mule: if its ears are short, it is the offspring of a mare and a he-ass, if large, of a she-ass and a stallion (TJ, Kil. 7:3, 31c).

BIBLIOGRAPHY: Lewysohn, Zool, 144–6, nos. 168, 169; S. Lieberman, *Tosefta ki-Feshutah*, 1 (1955), 99; F.S. Bodenheimer, *Animal and Man in Bible Lands* (1960), passim; J. Feliks, *Kilei Zera'im ve-Harkavah* (1967), 128–9. **ADD. BIBLIOGRAPHY:** Feliks, Ha-Ẓome'aḥ, 266.

[Jehuda Feliks]

MULHOUSE (Muelhausen), city in *Alsace, in the Haut-Rhin department, France. The earliest documentation of the presence of Jews in Mulhouse dates from 1290, when one Salman was victim of a persecution. The existence of a synagogue is confirmed from 1311. The Jews of Mulhouse suffered during the *Armleder riots in January 1338, and again during the outbreaks accompanying the Black *Death (1349). By 1385, however, there were once more Jews living in Mulhouse. At the beginning of the 15th century, several Jews who had arrived from other places in Alsace were granted the freedom of the city. The nine families who were there in 1418 owned houses, engaged in moneylending and traded in livestock. Although there was no expulsion, no Jews lived in the city between 1512 and 1655. At the beginning of the 18th century, when they were still insignificant in number, their trade flourished to the extent of arousing the jealousy of the Christian merchants, who demanded that their rights be restricted. In 1784 there were 23 Jewish families (94 persons) in the city. As it was free from the anti-Jewish riots which broke out throughout Alsace in 1789, Mulhouse became a refuge for many Jews from the surrounding district. The synagogue, built in 1822, soon proved to be too small and was replaced by a larger one in 1849. A cemetery was purchased in 1831, and the community established several other institutions, including a vocational school in 1842, and an almshouse-hospital in 1863. Two periodicals catering for all the Jews of Alsace and even beyond were published during the second half of the 19th century. From about 5,000 in 1900 the community declined to around 3,000 in 1921, remaining stable until just before World War II. Jacob *Kaplan, later chief rabbi of France, held office in Mulhouse in 1922.

[Bernhard Blumenkranz]

Holocaust and Contemporary Periods

Under German occupation in World War II, the Jews who had not managed to escape were expelled on July 16, 1940, along with the Jews in the rest of Alsace and Moselle. The synagogue, which had been partially damaged, was saved from total destruction when the edifice was requisitioned by the municipal theater. In 1970 Mulhouse had 1,800 Jewish inhabitants and a well-organized and active Jewish community.

[Georges Levitte]

BIBLIOGRAPHY: Germ Jud, 2 pt. 2 (1968), 554–5; E. Meininger, *Histoire de Mulhouse* (1923), 25–26 and passim; Z. Ginsburger, in: *Univers Israélite*, 54 (1898/99), 440–3; G. Wolf, in: ZGJD, 3 (1889), 182–4; S. Adler, *Geschichte der Juden in Muelhausen* (1914); M. Moeder, *Institutions de Mulhouse* (1951), 39; L.G. Werner, *Topographie historique* (1949), passim; Z. Szajkowski, *Analytical Franco-Jewish Gazetteer 1939–1945* (1966), 251.

MULISCH, HARRY (1927–), Dutch author. Born in Haarlem, Mulisch was of mixed descent, his father being a non-Jewish Czech banker and his mother a Jewess born in Antwerp. Widely recognized as one of Holland's most original modern writers, Mulisch published novels, short stories, and other prose works notable for their imaginative use of mythological, occult, and philosophical material to explore the existential problems of contemporary society. His earlier works include the novels *Archibald Strohalm* (1952), *De diamant* ("The Diamond," 1954), and *Het zwarte licht* ("The Black Light," 1956); also a play about the 12th-century heretic *Tanchelijn* (1960). Mulisch visited Israel in 1961 to cover the *Eichmann trial, which inspired *De zaak 40/61* ("Case 40/61," 1961). Two other works on Jewish themes are the novel *Het stenen bruidsbed* ("The Stone Bridal Bed," 1959) and the autobiographical *Voer voor psychologen* ("Food for Psychologists," 1961). In 1975 Mulisch published a novel on lesbian love, *Twee vrouwen* ("Two Women"). Another novel, *De aanslag* ("The Assault," 1982), deals with the problem-filled life of a man orphaned in the war due to a cruel coincidence. In *De ontdekking van de hemel* ("The Discovery of Heaven," 1992), World War II and its impact on private and public life take center stage once more. This vast novel, with its multi-layered narrative, counts as his masterpiece. The main story line has God renounce His trust in humanity and reclaim Moses' Stone Tablets with the Ten Commandments. The novel comes to an apocalyptic end in Jerusalem. Mulisch's work has been translated into many languages.

ADD. BIBLIOGRAPHY: F.C. de Rover, *De weg van het lachen: Over het oeuvre van Harry Mulisch* (1987); E.G.H.J. Kuipers, *De furie van het systeem. Over het literaire werk van Harry Mulisch in de jaren vijftig* (1988); M. Mathijsen, *Het voorbestemde toeval. Gesprekken met Harry Mulisch* (2002); H. Mulisch and O. Blom, *Mijn getijdenboek 1927–1951 & Zijn getijdenboek 1952–2002* (2002) (autobiography and biography).

[Gerda Alster-Thau / Maritha Mathijsen (2nd ed.)]

MULLER, BENJAMIN (1947–), *ḥazzan*. Muller was born in Geneva, Switzerland, where his grandfather, Samuel Sternberg, who was also his first teacher, was a ḥasidic *ḥazzan*. Muller attended Mir yeshivah in Jerusalem and studied voice development in Milan. He served as *ḥazzan* in Montreal and in Johannesburg, where he also studied *ḥazzanut* under both Shelomoh Mandel and Abraham Himmelstein. In 1975 he became the chief *ḥazzan* of the Shomre Hadass congregation in Antwerp. He recorded *ḥazzanut* and ḥasidic melodies and his rendering of *seliḥot* was broadcast annually on television from Belgium to all Western Europe. The wide range of his powerful tenor voice can be compared to the greatest opera singers. He is also a well-known exponent of the works of Yossele *Rosenblatt. Besides singing, Muller is also a composer and orchestrator of cantorial recitatives and other Jewish concert works.

[Akiva Zimmerman / Raymond Goldstein (2nd ed.)]

MULLER, HERMAN JOSEPH (1890–1967), U.S. geneticist and Nobel Prize winner. He was born in New York City, and after teaching at Columbia and the University of Texas went to Berlin (1932–33) on a Guggenheim Foundation fellowship. Having communist leanings, he moved to the Soviet Union (1933–37) where he served as senior geneticist at the U.S.S.R. Academy of Sciences. After breaking with communist philosophy, he spent three years at Edinburgh University and then returned to the United States in 1940 to teach at Amherst College. In 1945 he moved to Indiana University, becoming Distinguished Service Professor in 1953. The central theme of his work was the nature and significance of changes in the relatively stable gene material of the chromosome.

Muller is best known for his demonstration in 1926 that X-rays induce mutations, an achievement for which he received a Nobel Prize in physiology and medicine in 1946. His earlier contributions were concerned with the design of techniques for quantitatively determining the frequencies of gene mutations, and he was among the first to recognize that these mutations constitute the basis for evolutionary change in populations. His collaborative efforts with others in Thomas Hunt Morgan's laboratory at Columbia established the association between chromosome duplication and genetic defect. He speculated on the course of human evolution based upon the genetic principles which he helped to establish, with his classical work on the fruit fly, and long championed the establishment of a human sperm bank. He also called attention to the extreme danger to genetic material inherent in atomic activity.

Muller was the recipient of many honors. He published many works and was coauthor of *The Mechanism of Mendelian Heredity* (1915) and *Genetics, Medicine and Man* (1947). He also wrote *Out of the Night, a Biologist's View of the Future* (1935) and *Studies in Genetics* (1962).

BIBLIOGRAPHY: Carlson, in: *Canadian Journal of Genetics and Cytology*, 9 (1967), 437–48, includes bibliography; T.N. Levitan, *Laureates: Jewish Winners of the Nobel Prize* (1960), 156–60; L.G. Grenfell, *Nobel Prize Winners in Medicine and Physiology, 1901–1950* (1953), 238–43.

[George H. Fried]

MULLER, ROBERT (1925–1998), German-born novelist. Muller came to Britain in 1938. The Nazi era plays a prominent role in *The Shores of Night* (1961) and *The Lost Diaries of Albert Smith* (1965), a study of the psychology of a fascist and a fantasy of fascism in modern Britain. Another of his novels, *The World That Summer* (1959), portrays the Germany of 1936, as seen by a Jewish adolescent. Muller also wrote prolifically for British television, particularly science fiction and dramas of the supernatural, and, after the 1960s, wrote works in German for German television.

MULT ÉS JÖVŐ (Hung. "Past and Future"), a literary and artistic monthly journal in the Hungarian language which appeared from 1911 to 1944. Its founder was the writer József *Patai, who edited it until 1939 and made it one of the foremost Jewish illustrated periodicals. It maintained a high standard in both its literary and pictorial content and attracted contributions by Jewish scholars from many parts of the world. It stimulated the Jewish revivalist movement in Hungary and established links between Hungarian and other Jewries. The journal was banned in 1944 at the time of the German invasion.

[Baruch Yaron]

MULŪK AL-ṬAWĀ'IF (Ar. "kings of parties," petty kings; Sp. **reyes de taifas**), term referring to the petty kingdoms that arose on the ruins of the *Umayyad caliphate in al-Andalus, Islamic *Spain, in the early 11th century, some of them surviving until the end of that century. The dynasties were of varying origins – *Berber, Arab, so-called "Slav" (generally European slaves) – and states little more than cities with their surroundings, larger in thinly populated areas and dependent on agriculture, smaller in the port cities of the eastern coast. The *taifa* states sought to replicate the political might and cultural wealth of the Umayyads; their large number and their small size encouraged greater reliance on Jews as servants of the ruler. Jews might be more loyal than others, having little potential or temptation for political plotting. In consequence Jewish viziers are found in several of these states. The most famous are *Samuel ha-Nagid (d. 1056) and his son Jehoseph (murdered in a pogrom in 1066) in *Granada, but Jews with the title of vizier are found in Seville, Saragossa, Almeria, and elsewhere. Samuel ha-Nagid stands out as not only a political figure but also a military commander, almost unique in Jewish history between the second century C.E. and the modern period.

The period of the *mulūk al-ṭawā'if* was one of great cultural flowering for Iberian Muslims. It offered the Jews greatly increased opportunity, too. Political participation gave Jewish viziers means and reason to offer patronage to Jewish poets and others, who not only sang the praises of their successful co-religionists but also became immensely productive across the whole range of cultural activity. We find many works by Jews in al-Andalus from this period not only in poetry, religious and secular, but also in Hebrew grammar, philosophy, theology, and the sciences.

The period encouraged social and cultural closeness between Jews and their neighbors. Jews wrote not only in Hebrew but also in Judeo-Arabic (the problems of the *kharja*, a peculiarly Iberian addition to Arabic poetic genres, were resolved by S.M. Stern thanks in part to material written by Jews), and in Arabic, and took part in cultural and educational activities alongside Muslims. Nonetheless, this central period of what is known as the Golden Age of Jewish life in Spain went unnoticed by Muslims. The invasions of the *Almoravids at the end of the 11th century destroyed the *taifa* system, and Iberian Jewish life began to enter into a decline.

BIBLIOGRAPHY: Ibn Daud, *The Book of Tradition, Sefer ha-Qabbalah*, ed. G.D. Cohen (1967), 71–90. Moses Ibn Ezra, *Kitāb al-Muḥādara wa'l-Mudhākara*, ed. and trans. (Hebrew) A.S. Halkin, 1975; D. Wasserstein, *The Rise and Fall of the Party-Kings, Politics and Society in Islamic Spain, 1002–1086* (1985), 190–223; idem, "Samuel Ibn Naghrila ha-Nagid and Islamic Historiography in al-Andalus," in: *al-Qantara*, 14 (1993), 109–25; idem, "The Muslims and the Golden Age of the Jews in al-Andalus," in: *Israel Oriental Studies*, 17 (1997), 179–96; R. Brann, *Power in the Portrayal. Representations of Jews and Muslims in Eleventh- and Twelfth-Century Islamic Spain* (2002).

[David J. Wasserstein (2nd ed.)]

MUNI, PAUL (**Muni Weisenfreund**; 1895–1967), U.S. actor. He started acting at the age of 12 in Chicago. Maurice *Schwartz recognized his talent and persuaded him to join his new Yiddish-speaking Jewish Art Theater in 1918. Muni got his first real opportunity in an English role on Broadway in *We Americans* in 1926 and his success was immediate. He had a rich voice, good command of mime and facial expression, and a capacity for varied characterization. He played his first gangster in *Four Walls*, went to Hollywood and was acknowledged a star for his work in *The Valiants* (1929). *Scarface* established his reputation and *I am a Fugitive from a Chain Gang* seemed to confirm him as a player of "tough" roles. However, he resisted typecasting and starred in *The Story of Louis Pasteur* (1935), which won him a Motion Picture Academy award, *The Good Earth* (1936), *The Life of Emile Zola* (1937), and *Juarez* (1939). These roles expressed his true stature as an interpreter of heroism in spirit rather than in violence. Muni continued to appear in Broadway plays, including Elmer Rice's *Counselor-at-Law* (1931–33), Maxwell Anderson's *Key Largo* (1939), and in *Inherit the Wind* (1955). He also acted in the London run of *Death of a Salesman* and played his last film role in *The Last Angry Man*.

MUNICH (Heb. עיר הכמרים), capital of *Bavaria, central Germany. In 1229 a Jew called Abraham, from Munich, appeared as a witness at a Regensburg trial. In the second half of the 13th century Munich appears to have had a sizable Jewish community; the Jews lived in their own quarter and possessed a synagogue, a ritual bath, and a hospital. On Oct. 12, 1285, in the wake of a *blood libel, 180 Jews who had sought refuge in the synagogue were burnt to death; the names of 68 of the victims are listed in the Nuremberg **Memorbuch*, which dates from 1296. The Jews obtained permission to rebuild the synagogue in 1287, but for several centuries they remained few in number and suffered from various restrictions, which from time to time were further exacerbated (e.g., in 1315 and 1347). During the *Black Death (1348/49) the community was again annihilated. However, by 1369 there were Jews in the city once more, and in 1375 Duke Frederick of Bavaria granted them (and the other Jews resident in Upper Bavaria) the privilege of paying customs duties at the same rate as non-Jews. Some years later the Jews planned the construction of a synagogue and a **hekdesh*, but their plans do not seem to have been realized. The remission of debts owed to Jews ordained by Emperor Wenceslaus (1378–1400) resulted in Munich Jews losing all their assets. They also suffered severely in 1413, when they were accused of desecration of the *Host. In 1416 the small community was granted some privileges, including permission to acquire a lot for a cemetery; in 1432, when Duke Albert III sought to impose a special tax on Munich Jews, the results were disappointing. The clergy succeeded in having all the Jews of Upper Bavaria expelled in 1442, and eight years later they were also driven out of Lower Bavaria, where they had taken temporary refuge. Duke Albert gave the Munich synagogue (in the modern Gruftgasse) to Johann Hartlieb, a physician, and it was subsequently converted into a church. For almost three centuries Jews were excluded from Munich and Bavaria (although there may have been some periods when their residence was permitted, as may be deduced from a renewal of the ban announced in a 1553 police ordinance).

During the Austrian occupation, Jews were readmitted to Bavaria and some of them presumably found their way to Munich. At any rate, a new decree issued on March 22, 1715, again ordered them to leave the country. Some ten years later, a few Jews who had business dealings with the Bavarian count began to settle in Munich, and by 1728 several Jews resided in the city. In 1729 (or 1734) the Court Jew, Wolf *Wertheimer, took up residence there and was joined by his family in 1742; in 1750 all Court Jews and Jews in possession of passes granting them freedom of movement were excepted from the general ban on Jewish entry into the city. A community was formed by Jews who maintained connections with the court. Of the 20 of them in 1750, there was only one woman and a single child, which attests to the temporary and migratory nature of the settlement. Except for these **Schutzjuden*, the only Jews permitted to reside in the city were those who had been commissioned as purveyors or who had made loans to the state; all others were permitted to stay in the city for a short while only and had to pay a substantial body tax (**Leibzoll*). This situation continued for most of the 18th century, and it was not until 1794 and 1798 that the number of women and children in the city was commensurate with the number of heads of families. In 1794 there were 153 Jews, including 27 heads of families, 28 women, and 70 children; in 1798 the respective figures were 35, 33, and 98. Up to the end of the 18th century, Jewish women had to go to Kriegshaber to give birth to their children, and it was not until 1816 that Jews were permitted to bury their dead in Munich rather than transport them to Kriegshaber for burial. At this time Munich Jews earned their livelihood as *contractors for the army and the royal mint (see *mintmasters), merchants dealing in luxury wares and *livestock, moneylenders, and *peddlers. Since there was no legal basis for their residence in Munich, they did not have the right to practice their religion, and every year they had to pay a special tax to enable them to observe Sukkot. In 1805 a "Regulation for Munich Jewry" was issued (it formed the basis for the

Bavarian *Judenmatrikel* of 1813); among other privileges, the Jews were permitted to inherit the right of domicile, to conduct services, and to reside in all parts of the city.

During the Napoleonic Wars, the number of Jews was augmented by immigrants, and by 1814 there were 451 Jews in the city. Two years later, the Jewish community was formally organized. In the same year the community was given permission to establish a cemetery, and in 1824 a permit was issued for the construction of a synagogue (dedicated in 1827). The first Jewish religious school was founded in 1815 and a private one in 1817. The community played a leading part in Bavarian Jewry's struggle for civil rights, which lasted up to the founding of the German Reich (1871); delegates of the Bavarian communities frequently met in Munich (1819, 1821) to make common representations to the government. In the second half of the century the community grew further (from 842 in 1848 to 4,144 in 1880, and 8,739 in 1900) as a result of increased immigration from the smaller communities (especially in the last few decades of the 19th century). By 1910, some 20% of Bavarian Jews lived in the capital (11,000). There was also a steady immigration of Jews from Eastern Europe, mainly from Galicia, which lasted up to World War I.

Jews were prominent in the cultural life of Munich, a center of German arts, in the late 19th and 20th centuries, as well as being more equally represented in Bavarian political affairs than in other German states. After World War I a revolutionary government on the Soviet model was formed, in which Kurt *Eisner, Eugene *Levine, and Gustav *Landauer were prominent. It was routed by counterrevolutionary forces, and a "White Terror" against Communists, Socialists, and Jews was instigated. In the postwar years of economic and political upheaval, Munich was a hotbed of antisemitic activity and the cradle of the Nazi *party; many Jews from Eastern Europe were forced to leave Munich. Sporadic antisemitic outbursts characterized the years until the Nazi seizure of power in 1933, when Reinhold *Heydrich and Heinrich *Himmler took control of the police; the first concentration camp, *Dachau, was erected near Munich. At the time, the community numbered 10,000 persons, including an independent Orthodox community and many cultural, social, and charitable organizations. Munich Jewry was subjected to particularly vicious and continuous acts of desecration, discrimination, terror, and *boycotts but responded with a Jewish cultural and religious revival. Between 1933 and May 15, 1938, some 3,574 Jews left Munich. On July 8, 1938, the main synagogue was torn down on Hitler's express orders. During the *Kristallnacht*, two synagogues were burnt down, 1,000 male Jews were arrested and interned in Dachau, and one was murdered. The communal center was completely ransacked. During the war a total of 4,500 Jews were deported from Munich (3,000 of them to *Theresienstadt); only about 300 returned; 160 managed to outlive the war in Munich. A new community was founded in 1945 by former concentration camp inmates, refugees, displaced persons, and local Jews. In the following five years, about 120,000 Jews, refugees, and displaced persons passed through Munich on their way to Israel. In 1946 there were 2,800. The community increased from 1,800 persons in 1952 to 3,522 in January 1970 (70% of Bavarian Jewry). In 1966 a Jewish elementary school was opened, the second in Gemany, but the postwar community was repeatedly troubled by acts of desecration and vandalism (against synagogue and cemetery). In March 1970 the Jewish home for the aged was burned down and seven people lost their lives. The Munich library contains a particularly valuable collection of Hebrew manuscripts.

During the Olympic games, which took place in Munich in 1972, Palestinian terrorists took eleven Israeli sportsmen as hostages. All of them died. In 1982 the first Jewish bookshop in Germany was opened in Munich. It has branches in Berlin and Vienna. In 1995 Hagalil was established in Munich, which is the largest Internet site on Jewish life in Europe.

The Jewish community numbered 4,050 in 1989, 5,000 in 1995, and 9,097 in 2004, making it the second largest Jewish community in Germany. The increase is explained by the immigration of Jews from the former Soviet Union. In 2003 the cornerstone was laid for the new Jewish center. The complex was to have a new community center (with kindergarten, elementary school, youth center, library, offices, etc.), a main synagogue, and a Jewish museum. Partially financed by the Jewish community, the city of Munich, the Federal State of Bavaria, and private donors, the center was slated to open in 2006.

In 1995 the liberal Jewish community Beth Shalom was founded. It is a member of the Union of Progressive Jews in Germany and of the World Union of Progressive Judaism. Since 2003 the community has had its own community center. It had about 275 members in 2005. Munich is the seat of the Association of Jewish Communities in Bavaria.

BIBLIOGRAPHY: L. Baerwald, in: *Festgabe 50 Jahre Hauptsynagoge Muenchen* (1937), 11–16; H. Lamm (ed.), *Von Juden in Muenchen* (1958); idem, in: ZGJD, 8 (1938), 99–103; Germ Jud, 1 (1963), 237f.; 2 (1968), 556–8; P. Hauke, *Zur Geschichte der Juden in Muenchen zwischen 1933 und 1945* (1968); W.J. Cahnmann, in: JSOS, 3 (1941), 283–300; idem, in: ZGJD, 7 (1937), 180–8; idem, in: HJ, 3 (1941), 7–23; A. Cohen, in: *Zeitschrift fuer Demographie und Statistik der Juden*, 15 (1919), 8–12, 121–30; idem, in: ZGJD, 2 (1931), 262–83; J. Segall, *Die Entwicklung der juedischen Bevoelkerung in Muenchen 1875–1905* (1910); P. Weiner-Odenheimer, in: *Zeitschrift fuer Demographie und Statistik der Juden*, 11 (1915), 85–96; 12 (1916), 34–43; H. Schnee, *Die Hoffinanz und der moderne Staat*, 4 (1963), 187ff.; L. Prijs, in: BLBI, 6 (1963), 67–80; *Germania Judaica*, vol. 3, 1350–1514 (1987) 900 – 06. **ADD. BIBLIOGRAPHY:** Y. Gleibs, *Juden im kulturellen und wissenschaftlichen Leben Muenchens in der zweiten Haelfte des 19. Jahrhunderts* (Miscellanea Bavarica Monacensia, vol. 76. Neue Schriftenreihe des Stadtarchivs Muenchen, vol. 96) (1981); W. Selig (ed.), *Synagogen und juedische Friedhoefe in Muenchen* (1988); D. Bokovoy (ed.), *Versagte Heimat. Juedisches Leben in Muenchens Isarvorstadt 1914–1945* (1994); A. Heusler and T. Weger, *Kristallnacht. Gewalt gegen Muenchner Juden im November 1938* (1998); E. Angermair et al., *Beth ha-Knesseth – Ort der Zusammenkunft. Zur Geschichte der Muenchner Synagogen, ihrer Rabbiner und Kantoren* (1999); S. Wimmer, *Vergangene Tage. Juedisches Leben in Munich* (1999); P. Landau and H. Nehlsen (eds.), *Grosse juedische Gelehrte an der Muenchener*

Juristischen Fakultaet (Abhandlungen zur rechtswissenschaftlichen Grundlagenforschung, vol. 84) (2001); A. Heusler, et al., *Biographisches Gedenkbuch der Muenchner Juden. 1933 – 1945* (2003); I. Petersdorf, *Lebenswelten. Juedische buergerliche Familien im Muenchen der Prinzregentenzeit* (Studien zur Zeitgeschichte, vol. 32) (2003); W. Selig, *Arisierung in Muenchen. Die Vernichtung juedischer Existenz 1937–1939* (2004); A. Baumann and A. Heusler (eds.), *Muenschen arisiert. Entrechtung und Enteignung der Juden in der NS-Zeit* (2004). **WEBSITES:** www.ikg-muenchen.de.

[Larissa Daemmig (2nd ed.)]

MUÑIZ-HUBERMAN, ANGELINA (1936–), Mexican poet, novelist, and esssayist. Muñiz-Huberman was born in Hyères, France, to parents who were refugees of the Spanish Civil War. In addition to her career as a writer, she is also a professor of comparative literature at the Universidad Nacional Autónoma de México. When she was still a young girl her mother revealed to her that she had Sephardi roots. Following the discovery of her ancestral origins, she undertook the study of Judaism and eventually underwent a formal conversion. In her brief autobiographical text, *El juego de escribir* (1991), she narrates this experience along with other significant moments that have shaped her life and her literature. Her work has been recognized with numerous honors and some of the most prestigious literary awards from Mexico and Spain.

Her first novel, *Morada interior* (1972), draws on the life of Santa Teresa de Jesús. It explores the converso Jewish identity of the Spanish mystic poet by presenting a spiritual crisis, but the main character is a thinly veiled representation of the author herself struggling with issues of identity, exile, nationality, and religion. In her second novel, *Tierra adentro* (1977), Muñiz-Huberman again recalls the Sephardi heritage of Spain by telling the story of a young Jew during the time of the Expulsion. The monumental novel *El mercader de Tudela* (1998) is closely modeled after the real-life travels of Benjamin of Tudela and is based on Tudela's own 12th-century travelogue. Muñiz-Huberman also demonstrates her interest in Sephardi culture in her two books *La lengua florida: antología sefardí* (1989) and *Las raíces y las ramas: fuentes y derivaciones de la Cábala hispanohebrea* (1993). The first is an anthology of traditional Sephardi texts accompanied by her own essays on the subject. The second is an in-depth study of the kabbalistic tradition in Jewish Iberia. In addition to her prolific narrative, Muñiz-Huberman is an accomplished poet. Her poetry, as one would expect, expresses issues of identity, exile, gender, and death, which serve as a starting point for exploring human nature and the experience of life.

[Darrell Lockhart (2nd ed.)]

MUNK, family of rabbis. Ezra (1867–1940), an Orthodox rabbi in Germany, was the son of Elias Munk, *dayyan* at Altona. He studied at the Berlin Rabbinical Seminary under his uncle Azriel (Israel) *Hildesheimer and at the Universities of Berlin and Koenigsberg. In 1897, when he was rabbi at Koenigsberg (an office he held from 1893 to 1900), his congregation seceded from the general community. In 1900 he succeeded Hildesheimer as rabbi of the Adass Yisroel congregation in Berlin. Munk acted as Orthodox adviser to the Prussian Ministry of Education and Religious Affairs, where he enjoyed great confidence. He expanded the office for *sheḥitah affairs, founded by Hirsch *Hildesheimer in 1907, making it the international center for the defense of *sheḥitah*. Cofounder of the BJA (Bund Juedischer Akademiker), the association of Orthodox students in German universities, and of the Union of Orthodox Congregations (the so-called Halberstaedter Verband), he was also chairman of the "Association of Traditional Torah-True Rabbis" and a member of the rabbinical council of the German *Agudat Israel. Among his publications are *Gefaelschte Talmudzitate* (1924) and *Entwicklung der Verhaeltnisse der preussischen Synagogengemeinden…* (1931). Some of his responsa (*Kahana Messayye'a Kahana*) were published by S.Z. Klein (1938). In 1938 Munk left Germany for Jerusalem, where he died. Among his sons were ELI (1899–1978), rabbi of the Golders Green Beth Hamidrash, London, and MICHAEL (1905–1984), educator in the U.S., author of *Ezra ha-Sofer* (1933) and coauthor (with I. Lewin and J. Berman) of *Religious Freedom: the Right to Practice Sheḥitah* (1946). He also published with I. Lewin *Shechita: A Religious, Historical and Scientific Background* (1976).

LEO (1851–1917), Ezra's brother, was district rabbi at Marburg (Hesse) from 1876. He took an active part in the work of the *Deutsch-Israelitischer Gemeindebund, the *Hilfsverein der deutschen Juden, and the rabbinical associations, both general and Orthodox. Among his publications was a scholarly edition of *Targum Sheni* on Esther (1876). ELIE (b. 1900–1981), Ezra's nephew, a rabbi and writer, was district rabbi of Ansbach (Bavaria) from 1926, and from 1937 was rabbi of the Communauté Israélite de la Stricte Observance in Paris. His published works include *Die Welt der Gebete* (2 vols. (1938); Eng., *The World of Prayer*, 2 vols., 1954–63), a commentary on the *siddur; Das Licht der Ewigkeit* (1935); *La justice sociale en Israel* (1947); *Rachel* (on the duties of Jewish women; 1951[5]); and a translation into French of Rashi's Pentateuch commentary (1957).

BIBLIOGRAPHY: H. Seidman, in: L. Jung (ed.), *Guardians of our Heritage* (1958), 551ff.; A. Hildesheimer, in: M. Sinasohn (ed.), *Adass Jisroel Berlin* (1966), 72–83; J. Rothschild (ed.), *Leo Munk Gedenkbuch* (1918).

MUNK, HERMANN (1839–1912), German physiologist; a pioneer in the field of cerebral physiology. Munk was a director of the physiological laboratory of the Veterinary School in Berlin and a member of the German Academy of Science. He studied the localization centers in the brain and his name is associated with the so-called visual sphere of the cerebrum. He also did research on the function of the thyroid gland and studied the mechanism of motion. His younger brother IMMANUEL MUNK (1852–1900), was also a physiologist. He was his brother's assistant and then taught at the Physiological Institute of Berlin University (professor from 1899).

Munk and Nathan Zuntz did research in the field of metabolism and nutrition, with particular emphasis on the function of the kidneys. He wrote *Physiologie des Menschen und der Saeugetiere* (1881) and co-edited *Zentralblatt fuer die Medizinischen Wissenschaften*.

BIBLIOGRAPHY: S.R. Kagan, *Jewish Medicine* (1952), 163f., 168f.; *Biographisches Lexikon der hervorragenden Aerzte*, 2 (1933).

[Suessmann Muntner]

°**MUNK, KAJ** (pseudonym of **Harald Leininger**; 1898–1944), Danish pastor and playwright. He showed an unusual interest in Jewish themes and his anti-Nazi writings and sermons had an incalculable effect on the Danish resistance movement during World War II. Perhaps the most influential, and certainly the most controversial, Danish playwright of his time, Munk lived – and died – for his ideals. At first he showed some sympathy for ultranationalism, betraying a certain preoccupation with the "strong men" of history. *En idealist* ("An Idealist," 1928) was a study of Herod the Great; *De udvalgte* ("The Chosen One," 1933) dealt with King David; and *Sejren* ("The Victory," 1936) was based on Mussolini's invasion of Ethiopia. Munk was, however, outraged by what he saw during a visit to Berlin in 1938, and his drama *Han sidder ved smedltediglen* (*He sits at the Melting Pot*, 1938) attacked Hitler's persecution of the Jews. Two other works by Munk which appeared in the 1930s were *Vedersø Jerusalem retur* (1934), an account of the author's journey to the Holy Land among other places; and *Os boerer den himmelske gloede* ("Heavenly Joy Bears Us," 1934), a collection of verse containing impressions of Palestine. After Denmark was overrun by the Germans, Kaj Munk came to be regarded, by Danes and Germans alike, as one of the leading spokesmen of the Danish resistance. His play *Niels Ebbesen* (1942), which deals with the Nazi occupation, was suppressed but nevertheless enjoyed a clandestine circulation. He was murdered by the Nazis.

BIBLIOGRAPHY: R.P. Keigwin, *Kaj Munk, Playwright, Priest and Patriot* (1944); P.M. Mitchell, *History of Danish Literature* (1957), 258–62.

MUNK, SOLOMON (1803–1867), French Orientalist. Born in Glogau, Silesia, Munk studied at the universities of Bonn and Berlin. Realizing that as a Jew he had no academic future in Germany, he left for Paris in 1828. Here he first worked as a tutor in the Rothschild family, but was soon engaged by the *Bibliothèque Nationale* and put in charge of Semitic manuscripts. His assiduous work with them led to his becoming totally blind by 1850, but it did not prevent 17 more years of fruitful scholarly activity. Before then (1840) he joined the Montefiore-Crémieux delegation to *Egypt – as the latter's secretary and interpreter – which was to intervene in the *Damascus affair. When the Egyptian khedive *Muhammad Ali at last agreed to issue an order to *Damascus to set the falsely accused free, Munk – though some say it was L. Loewe, Montefiore's secretary – detected in the Arabic draft the word "mercy" to be granted, which at the insistence of Crémieux was changed into "freedom and peace." Crémieux and Munk used the opportunity of their visit to persuade Egyptian Jewry to modernize their school system and to bring about a rapprochement between Rabbanites and Karaites. Munk also acquired valuable manuscripts, particularly Karaitica, for the Bibliothèque Nationale. Back in Paris, Munk joined the *Consistoire Central* and was elected a member of the *Académie des Inscriptions et des Belles Lettres*. In 1864 he succeeded E. *Renan as professor of Hebrew and Syriac literature at the Collège de France.

Munk devoted himself to the study of the Hebrew and Arabic literature of the Golden Age of *Spain. It was Munk who discovered that the author of the philosophical work *Fons Vitae*, which had been preserved only in a Latin translation from the Arabic original, and whose author, called Avicebron, was believed to have been either a Muslim or an Arab Christian, was none other than the 11th-century Hebrew poet Solomon ibn *Gabirol. He discovered a manuscript of Shem Tov ibn *Falaquera's Hebrew translation of excerpts from Gabirol's original and identified this with passages in the Latin version (in his *Mélanges de philosophie juive et arabe* (1857–59; text, translation with an extensive essay on Gabirol, his writings, and philosophy). The crowning work of Munk's life was his three-volume edition of the original Arabic text (in Hebrew characters) of Maimonides' *Guide of the Perplexed* from Paris, Oxford, and Leyden manuscripts with a French translation (*Guide des Egarés*) and extensive notes (1856–66; Arabic text re-edited by B.J. Joel, 1960). All subsequent translations are based on this classic edition.

BIBLIOGRAPHY: G.A. Kohut, *Solomon Munk* (Eng., 1902); M. Schwab, *Salomon Munk* (1900); A. Jellinek, *Salomon Munk* (Ger., 1865); H.S. Morais, *Eminent Israelites* (1880), 247–52; P. Immanuel, in: S. Federbush (ed.), *Ḥokhmat Yisrael be-Eiropah* (1965), 239–41; M. Brann, in: JJGL, 2 (1899), 148–203 (44 letters of Munk).

MUNKÁCSI, BERNÁT (**Bernhard**; 1860–1937), Hungarian philologist and ethnographer. Born in Nagyvárad (now Oradea, Romania) into a family of rabbis, as a student in Budapest he came under the influence of several distinguished specialists in Hungarian studies (including Arminius *Vámbéry) and decided to dedicate himself to Hungarian linguistics and ethnography. He and a fellow student undertook a journey, collecting linguistic and other data on the Sereth (Siret) and Moldavo areas. Additional scientific trips were made from 1885 to study the language of the Votyak and Chuvash in the Kama and Middle Volga regions. With grants from the Hungarian Academy of Sciences and the Russian government, he made ethnographic tours of the northern parts of the Urals. After 1893 he served as editor of *Ethnographia*, and in 1900 he was cofounder of a philological journal *Keleti Szemle, Revue orientale des études oural-altaïques* (1900–32), to which he contributed numerous studies on Magyar culture, linguistics, and history. During World War I he carried out linguistic research in Ossetic by interrogating Russian prisoners of war who spoke this Iranian language of the Caucasus.

From 1890 to 1930 he served as an inspector of religious instruction in the Jewish schools of Budapest. As a professional teacher, he helped raise the level of existing schools, specifically the Jewish ones in Pest which he had helped to found. He prepared a program of studies for teachers, evolved a series of tests, and edited textbooks published by the Jewish community. Munkácsi's *Volksbraeuche und Volksdichtungen der Wotjaken* was edited by D.R. Fuchs and posthumously published in 1952.

BIBLIOGRAPHY: N. Munkácsi, *Egy nagy magyar nyelvész* (1943); D. Fokos, in: *Munkácsi Bernát…* (1930), 140–6 (incl. bibl.); UJE, 8 (1942), 39–40; *Magyar Zsidó Lexikon* (1929), 620–1.

[Ellen Friedman]

MUNKÁCSI, ERNÖ (1896–1950), Hungarian jurist and art writer. Born in Páncélcseh, then Hungary, the son of Bernát *Munkácsi, he entered public service in Budapest in 1921 and was the secretary of the Neolog community. In 1923 he became legal adviser and served as chief secretary from 1942 until he went underground. During the period of the Holocaust, he proposed the idea of contacting the Hungarian anti-Nazi underground movement, and he was one of the editors of the underground manifesto which revealed to the non-Jewish community the horrors of deportation. After the war he published documents and lists from the period of the Holocaust *Hogyan történt?* ("How Did It Happen?" 1947). As a jurist, Munkácsi devoted himself to the interpretation of the laws relating to the legal standing of the Jews. He strove for complete autonomy of the Jews in Hungary, within the framework of the laws of emancipation (1867) and repatriation (1895). He wished within this framework to educate toward a historical Jewish consciousness, and to eradicate the widespread ignorance of Jewish matters. He published many articles in Jewish journals, in particular the periodical *Mult és Jövö* ("Past and Future"), and *Libanon*, where he served as one of its editors. He later collected these articles in a volume entitled *Könyvek és kövek* ("Books and Stones," 1944). In his short book *Római napló* ("Diary from Rome," 1931), he described the relics of the Jewish past in Rome. In his comprehensive *Miniatürmüvészet Itália könyvtáraiban; héber kódexek* ("The Art of the Miniature in the Libraries of Italy. Hebrew Codices," 1937), he traced most of the miniature material found in the leading libraries of Italy. His German book *Der Jude von Neapel* (1939) dealt with the remants of Jewish art in southern Italy, and his English article "Ancient and Medieval Synagogues in Representations of the Fine Arts" (*Jubilee Volume Bernhard Heller*, 1941, 241–51 ed. by Munkácsi) was devoted to the representations of art in synagogues.

BIBLIOGRAPHY: *Egyenlöség* (Nov. 1, 1930), 16; B. Munkácsi (ed.), *A nyitrai, nagyváradi és budapesti Munk család … genealógiája* (1939), 17.

[Baruch Yaron]

MUNTNER, ALEXANDER SUESSMAN (1897–1973), medical historian. Muntner was born in Kolomyya, Poland, and received his medical education in Berlin, at the same time pursuing Jewish studies. He graduated in 1928 and in 1933 immigrated to Ereẓ Israel where, apart from his military service during the War of Liberation and as medical officer in the South of France in charge of North African immigrants to Israel, he engaged in private practice. In 1959, he was appointed visiting professor in the history of medicine at The Hebrew University. Muntner devoted his life to the history of Jewish medicine in the Middle Ages, and particularly to *Asaph ha-Rofe, Shabbetai *Donnolo, and *Maimonides. He undertook the publication of the medieval Hebrew translation of Maimonides' medical treatises, both from manuscripts and previous versions.

In 1949, he published a fully annotated book on Donnolo, which included his extant works, and in 1957 he published his *Mavo le-Sefer Asaph Ha-Rofe*, and later an edition of the full Hebrew text. He was the *Encyclopaedia Judaica* first-edition departmental editor for medicine.

A bibliographical list of his works appears in *Korot* (see Bibliography).

BIBLIOGRAPHY: *Korot*, 6, nos. 3–4 (February 1973). This volume is dedicated to the memory of Muntner.

MUQADDIM (Ar. مُقَدَّم, "leader," also *muqaddam*, literally "the one in front"), Arabic word, one meaning of which designates a chief heading an army, a ship, or a community. In North African countries, this term was employed to designate a *parnas* of the Jewish community, while in the Hebrew documents of Castile, Aragon, and Navarre it was employed as a synonym for **adelantados*.

BIBLIOGRAPHY: Baer, Spain, index; Neuman, Spain, index; Hirschberg, Afrikah, index.

MURABBAʿAT SCROLLS, manuscripts found in 1951 and 1952 in caves in Wadi Murabbaʿat, which runs down to the Dead Sea from the west about 18 km. (11 mi.) south of Wadi Qumrān and some 25 km. (15 mi.) southeast of *Jerusalem. The presence of inscribed material in this area was first suspected in October 1951 when Taʿāmra Bedouin offered some fragments of skin with Hebrew and Greek writing to the Palestine Archeological Museum, Jerusalem. The site was visited early in 1952 by a team led by G.L. Harding and Père R. de Vaux, and they explored four caves, which yielded a considerable quantity of manuscript material. In March 1955 another cave was entered by local shepherds, who found a scroll of the *Twelve Minor Prophets*, containing substantial portions of the Hebrew text of nine of the 12 books.

General

The Murabbaʿat caves contained traces of human occupation at six distinct periods in antiquity – the Chalcolithic Age (4th millennium B.C.E.), the Middle Bronze Age (c. 2000–1500 B.C.E.), the Iron Age (more specifically the 8th and 7th centuries B.C.E.), the Hellenistic period, the Roman period, and the Arab period. From the third, fourth, fifth, and sixth of these periods written documents were discovered. From the third period, the era of the later kings of Judah, came a papyrus palimpsest inscribed in Phoenician (paleo-Hebrew) characters. The earlier writing seems to have been a letter; part of it runs: "... yahu says to you, 'I send greetings to your family. And now, do not believe every word that... tells you...'" The original writing was washed out and replaced by four lines of script, each containing a personal name followed by numbers (perhaps listing quantities of produce to be delivered by peasants to the royal exchequer). From the Hellenistic period come two inscribed potsherds (2nd century B.C.E.). From the Arab period come some paper documents in Arabic and one or two Greek papyri. But the most numerous and by far the most interesting manuscripts come from the Roman period. These last are specially interesting because their presence at Murabbaʿat is due to the use made of the caves as outposts of guerrilla fighters during the Bar Kokhba Revolt (132–5 C.E.). There are fragments of Genesis, Exodus, Deuteronomy, and Isaiah on skin, a few *tefillin* fragments, and a piece of a *mezuzah*. The biblical texts are uniformly of protomasoretic type. The *tefillin* are of the type which became standard from the beginning of the second century C.E. onward, unlike those found at Qumrān, which belong to an earlier type and include the Ten Commandments. There is a fragment of a liturgical document in Hebrew and fragments of some literary works in Greek. There are quite a number of contracts and deeds of sale in Hebrew, Aramaic, and Greek; of those which are intelligibly dated, the majority belong to the period preceding and during the Bar Kokhba Revolt. There are several lists of deliveries of grain and vegetables, one or two in Aramaic and/or Hebrew but mostly in Greek. Some papyrus fragments and one potsherd contain Latin writing.

The Ben Kosebah Letters

Chief interest attaches to some correspondence between Joshua b. Galgula, apparently leader of the Murabbaʿat guerrillas, and other insurgents. One letter comes to him from the administrators of Bet Mashiko (a village in southern Judea, it appears) informing him that a certain cow has changed ownership. Another letter comes from the defenders of En-Gedi, yet another from someone at Meẓad Ḥasidin, "the fortress of the saints," perhaps meaning Khirbat Qumrān – which is shown by archaeological excavation to have been occupied by insurgents during the Bar Kokhba Revolt. Two letters come to Joshua from the leader of the revolt in person, whose name is shown to have been Simeon b. Kosebah. (It was formerly known that the name Bar Kokhba, "son of the star," had been given him by R. Akiva and other supporters on the basis of Numbers 24:17, and the name Bar Koziba, "son of falsehood," given him by his opponents. His official designation "Simeon prince of Israel" is also found on coins of the Second Revolt.) One of the letters runs: "From Simeon b. Kosebah to Joshua b. Galgula and the people of Ha-Baruk (?), greeting! I call heaven to witness against me that if any of the Galileans who are with you is ill-treated, I will put fetters on your feet as I did to Beni Aflul. Simeon b. Kosebah in [his own person]." It is not known who the luckless Beni Aflul was, or what he had done; neither is there any information that would throw light on the Galileans mentioned (there is no reason to suppose that they were Christians). The second letter (which, like the other, is in Hebrew) runs: "From Simeon to Joshua b. Galgula, greeting! Take cognizance of the fact that you must arrange for five *kors* of wheat to be sent by the [members of] my household. So prepare for each of them his lodging place. Let them stay with you over the Sabbath. See to it that the heart of each is satisfied. Be brave and keep up the courage of the people of the place. Peace! I have ordered whosoever delivers his wheat to you to bring it the day after the Sabbath." Plainly Simeon b. Kosebah was a man of peremptory temperament, a quality no doubt desirable in the leader of a revolt. With this requisition of wheat it is possible to correlate the lists of grain and vegetables discovered in the same caves. The Murabbaʿat caves seem to have been the last redoubt of Joshua and his men and their families. The Romans pursued them there and wiped them out, as they did to their comrades in Naḥal Ḥever. Some of the manuscripts bear signs of having been violently torn up by the invaders.

Linguistic Importance

The Murabbaʿat scrolls provide evidence that the inhabitants of Judea were trilingual at the time of the Second Revolt as they had been in the Herodian period: Hebrew, Aramaic, and Greek were used by Jews with equal facility. One Aramaic manuscript of earlier date than most (55–56 C.E.) contains the name of the Emperor Nero spelt in such a way as to yield the total 666 (NRWN QSR) – a pointer to the "number of the beast" in Revelation 13:18.

BIBLIOGRAPHY: Benoit et al., *Discoveries in the Judaean Desert*, 2 (1961); Yaron, in: JJS, 11 (1960), 157–77.

[Frederick Fyvie Bruce]

MURASHU'S SONS, prominent banking and commercial family in the Babylonian city of Nippur, active during the reigns of Artaxerxes I and Darius II. In 1893 an expedition from the University of Pennsylvania uncovered 730 clay tablets from the family archive dating from 455 to 403 B.C.E. The texts deal with diverse undertakings such as payment of taxes on behalf of others, land management, and the granting of loans to be repaid at a high rate of interest. Some 50 of the 730 tablets contain names which were thought to be Jewish, and this led some to deduce that the Murashu family itself was Jewish. However, the conclusion is unfounded. Apart from the purely indigenous name of the firm (*muraššû* – means "wildcat" in Akkadian), caution must be exercised in deciding which of the names of the clients or witnesses are characteristically Jewish and which are merely of West Semitic origin. The fact that names like Ḫanana (חנן, Hanan), Minaḫḫimmu (מנחם, Menahem), Miniamini (מנימין, Minyamin), or names compounded with *ilī* (אֵל, El) are attested elsewhere in Jewish contexts does not necessarily mean that their bearers at Nippur were Jews. They may have been Arameans or members of some other West Semitic group living in Babylonia. Undisputed evidence for the presence of Jews is furnished by such names as Aḫiyama (אחיה, Ahijah, Aiyyah), Yaḫulakim (יהולכם, Yeholakhem), Yaḫulunu (יהולינו, Yeholanu), and Yaḫunatanu (יהונתן, Jonathan, Yehonatan), which are compounded with the Tetragrammaton or some combining form of it and by such names as Shabbetai son of Haggai. The picture of the Jewish exiles in Mesopotamia which emerges after an examination of these names is one of a people engaged in a wide range of activities: they act as witnesses in documents dealing with taxes, as tenants cultivating the land of others, and as landowners on whose behalf taxes are paid. Some seem to be highly placed royal officials.

BIBLIOGRAPHY: G. Cardascia, *Les archives des Murašû* (1951), incl. bibl.

[David B. Weisberg]

MURCIA, capital of the former kingdom of Murcia, S.E. Spain. The kingdom was first taken from the Muslims (1243) during the reign of Ferdinand III of Castile. After the revolt of the Muslims, it was reconquered by James I, king of Aragon, who handed it over to Castile in 1265. Among those who assisted the king in his conquest of the region were Judad de la *Cavallería, who lent money for outfitting the navy in the war against the Muslims, and Astruc (or Astrug) Bonsenyor (d. 1280), father of Judah *Bonsenyor, who conducted the negotiations with the Muslims for their capitulation, and who was also translator of Arabic documents in the kingdom. Jewish officials of the kingdom of Aragon met with Jewish officials of the kingdom of Castile in the town, and in 1292, Moses ibn Turiel of Castile held important administrative positions there. *Alfonso X of Castile (1252–84), son-in-law of James I, allocated a special quarter for the Jewish community, explicitly ordering that Jews were not to live among the Christians. However, at the time of their settlement various Jews received properties in the Jewish quarter and beyond it, in the town itself. A site was also allocated for the Jewish cemetery. Once the regulations of the settlement had been stipulated, an annual tax of 30 dinars was imposed on every Jew. Jews were also compelled to hand over tithes and the first fruits of all their possessions and herds to the cathedral, as was customary in Seville. In 1307 jurisdiction over the Muslims of the kingdom of Murcia was entrusted to Don Isaac ibn Yaish, the last Jew to hold such a function.

Toward the close of the 14th century, several Jewish tax farmers were active in the kingdom and in the town, among them Solomon ibn Lop, who settled in Majorca after 1378 and who was granted the special protection of the king of Aragon. During this period, the Jews of Murcia were noted for their generosity in the redemption of prisoners and for their participation in maritime trade; this was in addition to their usual occupations in commerce, crafts and agriculture. Although there are no details available on how the Jews of the town fared during the persecutions of 1391, the community continued to exist after that time. Some 2,000 Jews earned their livelihood in a great variety of activities. Close mutual relations were maintained with the Christian population, and two of the community elders attended the meetings of the municipal council. Throughout the 15th century, Jews of Murcia were often tax farmers, both in the kingdom of Murcia and in other towns near and distant. In 1488 Samuel Abulafia was taken under the protection of the Catholic monarchs for two years in appreciation of his services to the crown during the war against Granada. Solomon b. Maimon Zalmati printed Hebrew books in Murcia in 1490.

Details on the departure of the Jews from Murcia at the time of the expulsion are unknown but it may be assumed that they left from the port of Cartagena. After the expulsion, debts owed by Christians to the Jews were transferred to Fernando Nuñez Coronel (formerly Abraham *Seneor) and Luis de Alcaláfor collection. Murcia also had Conversos, some of whom remained faithful to Judaism. Conversos even used to come there in order to return to Judaism; one such case is mentioned in the La Guardia trial (1490). At an early date, an Inquisition tribunal was established at Murcia.

BIBLIOGRAPHY: Baer, Spain, index; Baer, Urkunden, 1 (1929), index; H.C. Lea, *A History of the Inquisition of Spain*, 1 (1906), 550; L. Piles Ros, in: *Sefarad*, 7 (1947), 357; J. Torres Fontes, *Repartimiento de Murcia* (1960), passim; idem, *Los judíos murcianos en el siglo XIII* (1962); idem, *Los judíos murcianos en el reinado de Juan II* (1965); idem, *La incorporación a la caballería de los judíos murcianos en el siglo XV* (1966); Suárez Fernández, Documentos, index; J. Valdeón Baruque, *Los judíos de Castilla y la revolución Trastamara* (1968), 57, 69, 70, and passim.

[Haim Beinart]

MURMELSTEIN, BENJAMIN (1905–1989), rabbi, scholar, and public figure of the Holocaust period. Born in Galicia, Murmelstein studied at the Juedisch-Theologische Lehranstalt, Vienna, where he became a lecturer in 1930. From 1923 he served as rabbi of the Vienna Jewish community. He was associated with S. Krauss in preparing the supplementary volume, published in 1936, to *A. Kohut's famous talmudic dictionary, *Arukh ha-Shalem*, and Murmelstein published a popular *Geschichte der Juden* and annotated selections from Josephus (both in 1938). When the Nazis occupied Austria in 1938, Murmelstein became a member of the *Judenrat appointed by them. In this capacity he wielded power, which he was accused of having used arbitrarily. Later he was deported to *Theresienstadt concentration camp; he was made deputy *Judenaeltester* (head of the Jewish council) in January 1943 and succeeded P. Epstein as chief *Judenaeltester* in December 1943, after Epstein was murdered by the Nazis. As *Judenaeltester* – an officer whose exact and tragic powers and responsibilities are difficult to assess – Murmelstein was both hated and feared; he was described as a complex character, gifted, ambitious, cynical, and calculating. When the camp was liberated in May 1945, Murmelstein remained and held himself at the disposal of the Czech authorities. He was arrested in June and remained in custody until December 1946, when the public prosecutor withdrew the indictment because "he had been able to disprove all accusations." Murmelstein settled in Rome, where he worked first at the Papal Biblical Institute and later as a commercial agent, taking no part in Jewish communal life. He published an account of events in *Terezin-Ghetto Modello di Eichmann* (1961) and in several newspaper articles (in *Neue Zuercher Zeitung* (Dec. 17, 1963), 3; Hamburg *Die Welt* (Jan. 14, 1964)).

BIBLIOGRAPHY: H.G. Adler, *Theresienstadt* (Ger., 1960²), introd. and index; Z. Lederer, *Ghetto Theresienstadt* (Eng., 1953), 166–7.

MURRAY, ARTHUR (**Moses Teichman**, 1895–1991), America's most famous ballroom dance instructor; businessman. He was born in New York and trained with Irene and Vernon Cast. After winning a waltz contest at the age of 17, he started selling dance lessons via mail, by sending out footprint diagrams designed to teach students the steps of the popular social dances. Shortly after 1923 Murray opened a highly structured dance studio in New York occupying six floors and employing dozens of teachers, which was followed by the establishment of an extensive network of other studios which provided dance instruction in the U.S. and Europe.

In the 1950s, Murray and his wife, Kathryn Kohnfelder, who became his dance and business partner, presented a long-running television series, which helped to popularize ballroom dancing. Murray is credited with creating many of the standard steps still used today in the foxtrot and the rumba.

In 1964, Murray resigned as president of the Arthur Murray Dance Studios but remained as a consultant.

[Amnon Shiloah (2nd ed.)]

MURVIEDRO (in Catalan, **Morvedre**; now **Sagunto**), city in Valencia, E. Spain, near the Mediterranean coast, built on the ruins of the Roman city Saguntum. According to a legend, a tombstone was found there bearing the inscription in Hebrew "Adoniram, treasurer of King Solomon, who came to collect the tax tribute and died." Another spurious inscription mentioned King Amaziah's military commander as having also met his death in Murviedro. Jews lived in Murviedro during Muslim rule. On capture of the city by King James I of Aragon, the Vives family was given a bakery in the city, as a reward for services rendered during the siege. Several Jews served as royal bailiffs there including Solomon Baye, Solomon b. Lavi de la *Cavallería (1273), and Joseph ibn Shaprut (1279–80). At the time the community numbered 50 taxpayers. The Jewish quarter was on the west side of the Roman theater, the present Calle Segovia and Calle Ramos being the main streets. In 1321 James II authorized the Jews to fortify their quarter. A large portion of the community's revenue was derived from taxes on the sale of meat and wine. Silversmiths and cobblers are specifically mentioned among the artisans obliged to pay taxes; artisans who earned less than six *denarii* a day were exempt from taxes. R. *Isaac b. Sheshet permitted indigent artisans in Murviedro to work during the intermediate days of the Jewish festivals. In 1328 the community acquired grounds for a new cemetery, tombstones from which are still preserved.

During the 1391 persecutions, the Jews of Murviedro found refuge in the fortress which was near the Jewish quarter. Hence after the massacres, Murviedro, the only surviving community in the Kingdom of Valencia, became one of the most important communities of the Crown of Aragon. In the 15th century, the Jewish quarter had 120 houses and probably more than 600 residents. In 1394 the king ordered that the Jews of Murviedro should not be investigated in respect of their activities to counteract conversion or for bringing back Conversos to Judaism and assisting them to leave the country. In 1402 Queen Doña María authorized the Murviedro community to establish several societies for catering to communal needs: the *Bikkur Ḥolim society, to care for the sick; a burial society; and a *Talmud Torah* society. Various problems arose with the increased number of conversions. In 1416 Alfonso V dealt with the division of property of deceased Jews between the heirs who had remained Jews and those who had been converted. The Jewish silversmiths of Murviedro were celebrated for their craft; especially notable was Vidal Astori, who in 1467–69 worked for the future King Ferdinand the Catholic. In 1474 the *muqaddimūn* (*adelantados*) complained to the bailiff-general about some nobles who had forbidden their vassals to trade with the Jews of Murviedro. The bailiff decided in favor of the community and proclaimed freedom of trade in the area.

The Jews of Murviedro did much to encourage their Converso brethren to return to Judaism. After the decree of expulsion was issued in March 1492, Gerica, one of the local Jews, reached an agreement with Valencia merchants to transfer 300 Jews from Murviedro to Oran, in North Africa. Other agreements dating from the end of July relate to the conveyance of Jews from Murviedro to Naples. A total of 500 Jews left the city, and the synagogue in the present Calle de la Sangre Vieja was turned into a church named Sangre de Cristo ("Blood of Jesus").

The Jewish quarter of Murviedro is one of the best preserved in Spain, probably because it did not suffer any attack in 1391. The Jewish quarter is in the upper part of the city. Entrance to the quarter is through an arch which was called *Portal de la juheria.* It is situated near the Roman theater and includes within its boundaries the streets Antigones, Segovia, Pelayo, Ramos and Sang Vella. The Portal is at the beginning of Sang Vella Street when one enters from Castillo Street. The synagogue was probably at the corner of Sang Vella and Segovia streets.

BIBLIOGRAPHY: Baer, Spain, index; A. Chabret, *Sagunto [Murviedro], su historia y sus monumentos*, 1 (1880), 324f.; 2 (1880), 329–51, 408f., 463f.; Vendrell Gallostra, in: *Sefarad*, 3 (1943), 119, Cantera, *ibid.*, 5 (1945), 250; Piles Ros, *ibid.*, 8 (1948), 81ff., 358; 12 (1952), 119, 121; 15 (1955), 99ff.; 17 (1957), 352–73; 20 (1960), 368; F. Cantera, *Sinagogas españolas* (1955), 268–71; Cantera-Millás, Inscripciones, 293ff.; Jiménez Jiménez, in: *Actas y communiciones de IV congreso de historia de la Corona de Aragón*, 1 (1961), 251–62; Beinart, in: *Estudios*, 3 (1962), 15ff. **ADD. BIBLIOGRAPHY:** M.D. Meyerson, in: T. Burman, M.D. Meyerson, L. Shopkow (eds.), *Religion, Text, and Society in Medieval Spain and Northern Europe* (2002), 70–102; idem,

Jews in an Iberian Frontier Kingdom, Society, Economy, and Politics in Morvedre, 1248–1391 (2004); idem, *A Jewish Renaissance in Fifteenth-Century Spain* (2004).

[Haim Beinart / Yom Tov Assis (2nd ed.)]

MUSAF (Heb. מוּסָף), the additional sacrifice or prayer instituted on the Sabbath and the festivals. In addition to the daily morning and afternoon sacrifices offered in the Temple, the Bible prescribed additional offerings to be brought on Sabbaths, the three *Pilgrim festivals, Rosh Ha-Shanah, the Day of Atonement, and the New Moon (Num. 28–29; see *Sacrifice). These were offered after the regular morning sacrifices (Yoma 33a). An additional prayer was already recited on these days by some worshipers even when the sacrificial cult still existed (Tosef., Ber. 3:3; Suk. 53a). After the abolition of sacrifice with the destruction of the Temple, the additional prayer was formalized and took the place of these sacrifices (Ber. 26b; see *Prayer, *Liturgy). There were some *tannaim* who regarded the *Musaf* prayer service as exclusively communal, and they held that it could only be recited when one worshiped with a quorum (*minyan; Ber. 4:7 and Ber. 30a–b). The rabbis, however, made the additional service obligatory upon every individual, both when praying alone or with a quorum, and they endowed it with the same importance as the regular morning service (Ber. 30b; Sh. Ar., OḤ 286:2).

It is customary to recite the *Musaf* service immediately after the reading of the weekly Torah and *haftarah* portions which follow the morning prayers on Sabbaths and festivals. It is, however, permissible to recite it at any time during the day. Nevertheless, one who negligently postpones its recitation until after the seventh hour of the day is considered a "transgressor" (Ber. 4:1 and Ber. 26b, 28a).

The *Musaf* is introduced by the reader's recitation of the Half *Kaddish. This is followed by the *Musaf *Amidah* which, except on Rosh Ha-Shanah, consists of seven benedictions. The first three benedictions of praise and the last three benedictions of thanks are identical with those of the daily *Amidah*. The benediction *Kedushat ha-Yom* ("Sanctity of the Day") is inserted between these blessings. It consists of an introductory paragraph, followed by a prayer for the restoration of the Temple service, and concludes with the appropriate selection from the Torah detailing the additional sacrifice for the day. In the *Musaf* for Rosh Ha-Shanah three blessings are added in the middle: the **malkhuyyot* (*malkhiyyot*), **zikhronot*, and **shofarot*. In communal prayer, the *Musaf Amidah* is generally repeated in full by the *ḥazzan* (*Rema* to Sh. Ar., OḤ 286:2). In some congregations, however, particularly among the Sephardi Jews, the *ḥazzan* chants the first three blessings aloud with the congregation. This, however, is not done on the High Holy Days, when the entire *Amidah* is always repeated by the *ḥazzan*.

The Sabbath *Musaf Amidah*, after the initial three regular blessings, consists of a composition in which the initial letters of the first 22 words follow the inverted order of the Hebrew alphabet. This prayer concludes with the description of the Sabbath *Musaf* offering from Numbers 28:9–10. A short prayer for those who observe the Sabbath follows, and the "Sanctity of the Day" concludes with the prayer beginning with the invocation "Our God and God of our fathers," common to all the *Amidot* of the Sabbath (Hertz, Prayer, 530–4).

On New Moons, the *Musaf* consists of a prayer expressing sorrow over the abolition of the sacrificial ritual and hope for its restoration. Numbers 28:11, describing the New Moon sacrifice, is quoted, and it concludes with a prayer for a blessed and happy month (*ibid.*, 778–82). When the New Moon falls on a Sabbath, the first prayer is greatly altered and is very similar to the corresponding formula for the festivals. It concludes with the quotations from Numbers for both Sabbaths and New Moon offerings (*ibid.*, 542–4).

The *Musaf Amidah* for the three festivals begins with the prayer "But on account of our sins we were exiled from our land." God is asked to gather the scattered remnant of Israel to the Holy Land and to build the Temple. The appropriate passage detailing the *Musaf* offering is then inserted, and the regular prayer for the blessings of the festival concludes this section (*ibid.*, 820–8).

The *Musaf* service for the New Year is the longest in the liturgy. It opens with the same format as the other *Amidot* of that day, followed by the prayer "But on account of our sins," and concludes with the selection from Numbers 29:1–2 describing the *Musaf* sacrifice. After this, *Aleinu* is recited, followed by the above mentioned three additional benedictions.

The *Musaf Amidah* for the Day of Atonement begins in the same way as that of the New Year. After the biblical selection in which the additional sacrifices for the day are detailed (Num. 29:7–8), a prayer for the forgiveness of sins is recited. The *Confession (see **Al Ḥet*; **Ashamnu*) forms an integral portion of this *Musaf* service, just as it does in the other *Amidot* of the Day of Atonement.

It was customary to interlace the *ḥazzan's* repetition of the *Musaf Amidah* on festivals and special Sabbaths with various *piyyutim*. Except for Rosh Ha-Shanah and the Day of Atonement, this is hardly done nowadays. Even on those two holidays most modern congregations recite only selections from the huge volume of *piyyutim* composed throughout the generations.

The *Musaf* services of the first day of Passover and of Shemini Aẓeret are known by special names: the former as *Tal* ("dew"), because prayers for abundant dew are recited during the repetition of the first two blessings by the cantor; the latter as *Geshem* ("rain"), because prayers for rain are recited by the cantor at the same juncture. (In Israel, the custom is to recite these two prayers before *Musaf*.)

In Reform congregations in the 19th century the *Musaf* service was either entirely abolished or modified, since Reform Judaism no longer anticipated the restoration of the sacrificial cult. In the course of time, the tendency was to omit it entirely. Some Conservative congregations have rephrased references to the sacrifices so that they indicate solely past events without implying any hope for a future restoration of sacrifice.

BIBLIOGRAPHY: Elbogen, *Gottesdienst*, 115–7 and index; Idelsohn, Liturgy, 142–4, 284; E. Levy, *Yesodot ha-Tefillah* (1952²), 45–47; J. Heinemann, *Ha-Tefillah bi-Tekufat ha-Tanna'im ve-ha-Amora'im* (1966²), 34, 172; J.J. Petuchowski, *Prayerbook Reform in Europe* (1968), 240–64, index (for Reform usage).

[Aaron Rothkoff]

MUSAR HASKEL (Heb. מוּסַר הַשְּׂכֵל; also known as **Shirei Musar Haskel** or **Sha'arei Musar Haskel**), the name of a frequently printed ethical poem of the 11th century, usually attributed to *Hai ben Sherira Gaon (939–1038). The poem as printed consists of 180 verses, but there is a possibility that it was not printed in full and that in some manuscripts there is more material belonging to it. It was first printed in Fano, probably in 1505, and has appeared many times since then, mostly together with the *Ka'arat Kesef* of Jehoseph b. Hanan b. Nathan *Ezobi and occasionally also with S.J. Rapoport's essay on Hai Gaon. Although there is not sufficient proof to support the traditional attribution of the work to Hai Gaon, neither is there any evidence that the attribution is impossible. The poem is written in the literary style of the Book of Proverbs and of the Wisdom of Ben Sira. It deals with many aspects of human life, religious and social; it shows in short, rhymed epigrams the ethical way of life. Among other subjects it deals with prayer, the love of God, the love of knowledge, fear of the divine judgment, the treatment of women, and the correct way to conduct business. Every couplet of the poem usually stands alone as an epigram, and only rarely is a topic dealt with in more than two lines. The work was translated into Latin by Jacob Ebert (Frankfurt, 1597).

BIBLIOGRAPHY: Benjacob, Oẓar, 307. **ADD. BIBLIOGRAPHY:** *Musarei Haskel bi-Meliẓah Na'ah le-Rabbenu Hai Ga'on* (n.p., 19th cent.).

[Joseph Dan]

MUSAR MOVEMENT, movement for the education of the individual toward strict ethical behavior in the spirit of *halakhah*; it arose in the 19th century, continuing into the 20th, in the Jewish culture of the *mitnaggedim* in Lithuania, in particular becoming a trend in its yeshivot. Originally inspired by the teachings and example of the life of Joseph Sundel b. Benjamin Benish *Salanter, it began as a movement for influencing members within the community. Circumstances, however, caused a radical change in its character at an early stage and turned it from the ideal of creating a pattern for leading and exemplary members of the community to forming the personality of the young students in the yeshivot.

Israel *Lipkin (Salanter) had primarily intended to establish the movement for members of the community through their activities. About the middle of the 19th century, the mitnaggedic Jewish culture was facing a severe crisis as a result of its vulnerability to the corroding influence of Haskalah ideology. The growing poverty and congestion in the *shtetl* in the *Pale of Settlement were causing severe tension and bitterness within Jewish society. The world of the leading circles of Lithuanian Jewry was breaking up. The pupil and co-worker of Israel Lipkin, Isaac *Blaser, complained in the second half of the 19th century about the moral degeneration: "The fear of God has terribly deteriorated … sins are proliferating whereas formerly Torah and the fear of God went together among Jews … now, because of our many sins, this unity has broken up; the bonds have gone and the connection joining them has been severed. In the end, without the fear of God, the knowledge of Torah will disappear too, God forbid" (his introduction to Lipkin's *Or Yisrael* (1900)). This expressed a typical complaint of the *Mitnaggedim* of the period. Blaser was alarmed by the new phenomenon presented by the graduates of the yeshivah, who, though learned, were no longer devoted to the rigorous pattern of *halakhah*. Confronted by ḥasidism on the one hand, and on the other by the trends in German Jewry of *Haskalah, *Reform, and *Neo-Orthodoxy, mitnaggedic Jewry was faced with the problem of how to sustain a rigorous traditional Jewish life, based mainly on learning and intellectuality. Israel Salanter at first intended to tackle the problem directly in the communities. In his first letter to the Vilna community in 1849, proposing the creation of a *musar shtibl* ("a room for moral deliberation") he wrote: "The busy man does evil wherever he turns. His business doing badly, his mind and strength become confounded and subject to the fetters of care and confusion. Therefore appoint a time on the Holy Sabbath to gather together at a fixed hour … the notables of the city, whom many will follow, for the study of morals. Speak quietly and deliberately without joking or irony, estimate the good traits of man and his faults, how he should be castigated to turn away from the latter and strengthen the former. Do not decide matters at a single glance, divide the good work among you – not taking up much time, not putting on too heavy a burden. Little by little, much will be gathered … In the quiet of reflection, in reasonable deliberation, each will strengthen his fellow and cure the foolishness of his heart and eliminate his lazy habits." His program, meant to meet the needs of busy traders, proposed their meeting for moral reflection and self-improvement on the day of rest. In his third letter to the Vilna community he proposed that women join in this concern with the study of morals. In his *Iggeret ha-Musar*, Salanter particularly stressed the sin of financial fraud.

However, the movement failed to attract the settled members of the community; their "laziness of habit" was too deeply ingrained. Blaser, and not Salanter, had estimated correctly: the trouble lay not so much in the area of individual morality as in the dichotomy between Torah learning and the fear of God. It may be surmised that Israel Salanter's personality – which was both admired and criticized by Orthodox and Haskalah circles – was also one of the reasons for the failure of the movement among the upper circles of mitnaggedic society.

In the later years of Israel Salanter, through the energetic drive of his devoted pupils Isaac Blaser and Simah Zissel *Broida, the supporters of the Musar movement turned to the education of the young, and in particular to influencing the students of the yeshivot to form early in life the alertness of moral habit which had proved so difficult to instill at a later age. Blaser founded a *kolel* at Lubcz (Lyutcha). In 1872 Simah Zissel founded a *musar shtibl* at Kelme. He also founded a school for youngsters at Grobina, Courland, obtaining some financial support from Orthodox circles in Germany. As the Musar movement began to penetrate the yeshivot, both through the indirect influence of its own institutions and through the direct introduction of *musar* study and methods (see below) into the yeshivot, sharp opposition arose from the traditional yeshivah leadership. Rabbis and leaders, such as Aryeh Leib *Shapiro and Isaac Elhanan *Spektor of Kovno, openly opposed the new educational system, but without success. Subsequently some of its opponents explicitly renounced their objection, while others ceased to speak openly against it. By the beginning of the 20th century, *musar* had become the prevailing trend in the Lithuanian yeshivot.

Methods and Goals

After its adoption by the yeshivot, and the earlier establishment of *musar shtibl* and educational institutions, the Musar movement developed an individual institutional and educational pattern. The reading of ethical works, of isolated sayings from the Midrash and Talmud, and of verses from the Bible served as vehicles for creating a certain mood and for implanting certain feelings. The principal activity was to recite passages from these works, or a saying or verse, to a melody – taken from the repertoire of the **maggidim* – suitable for evoking a pensive atmosphere of isolation and mood of emotional receptivity toward God and His commandments, preferably in twilight or subdued lighting (from a certain aspect this resembles the "spiritual exercises" recommended by Ignatius of Loyola for the Jesuits). The reading of the intellectual matter in the text served to stimulate an emotional response, which was intended to help the student both in forming moral personality and in devotion to Talmud study.

Formally, the Musar movement was based on the study of *ethical literature, although its conception of this was highly eclectic, and its libraries included works by authors as diverse as *Jonah b. Abraham Gerondi, Moses b. Jacob *Cordovero, Moses Ḥayyim *Luzzatto (who had been excommunicated in his time), and Naphtali Herz *Wessely (one of the leaders of Enlightenment). However, several generations of study of this variegated literature by many brilliant young men did not produce for the movement, as far as is known, a single systematic commentary, either on the literature as a whole or on an individual work.

In the "minimalistic" *musar* yeshivot, students devoted at least half an hour daily to studying one of these texts in unison, intoning them in the same plaintive melody. Unity was demanded only in the melody used, each student being allowed to read the book of his own choice. In these yeshivot, the **mashgi'aḥ* ("supervisor") became a second spiritual mentor of the students, equal to the *rosh yeshivah*; in the case of some personalities, such as Jeroham Lebovitch at the *Mir yeshivah, he was even superior. The *mashgi'aḥ* held a *shmues* ("talk") with all the yeshivah students at least weekly, on either a general moral topic – a kind of a special yeshivah sermon – or some specific incident that had occurred in yeshivah life. Devout *musar* students often combined into a *va'ad*, several youngsters gathering together for a period to chant some *musar* saying and achieve the proper *musar* mood. Larger groups would create a *musar berzhe*, in which they would act collectively and enter collectively through a more protracted way into the same mood. In these yeshivot, commonly called "Slobodka-style" yeshivot (see also *Kovno), the student's mind was molded through this activity, through his comradeship in emotivity with fellow students, and through the influence of the *mashgi'aḥ*. In this highly charged emotional life intellectual Talmud study became encapsulated by the atmosphere created by *musar*.

The crisis in the yeshivot brought about by secularizing influences, such as the *Bund, general socialist revolutionary trends, Zionism, and Haskalah, was counteracted to a large extent by the influence of the Musar movement. Israel Salanter's original aim was also largely achieved, though indirectly, as the "*muserniks*" who entered the life of the upper circles of the *shtetl* were now imbued with the new proud and rigoristic spirit engendered by *musar* and the collective sense of identity.

There also developed a second, "maximalist," trend of *musar* yeshivot, in the so-called "Nowardok style." Its proponent, Joseph Josel, the "old man of Nowardok" (Novogrudok), applied a deeper psychological approach. This not only included many hours devoted to the study of the *musar* texts, employing if possible a more plaintive melody, with less light, but the student would also be taught to discipline himself by a series of *peules af* ... ("actions to ..."). Such actions were calculated to subdue his natural instincts of vanity, economic calculation, or love of material goods. A student, for example, might be ordered to go to a drug store and ask for something inappropriate, such as nails, to mingle with well-dressed people in rags, or to enter a train without a coin in his purse. By the Nowardok method, a man not only trained himself to subdue his animal and social nature, but also to check if he did so in complete emotional depth. Ḥayyim *Grade described it:

"When you ask the *Nawardoker*, 'How do you do?' the meaning is 'How is Jewishness with you? Have you advanced in spirituality?' ... He who has studied *musar* will never enjoy his life further, Ḥayyim, you will remain a cripple your whole life. You write heresy... but is there any one of you really so strong that he does not desire public approval for himself? Which one of you is prepared to publish his book anonymously? ... Our spiritual calm you have exchanged for passions which you will never attain, for doubts which, even after much self-torture, you will not be able to explain away. Your writing will not improve a single person, and it will make you worse" (from his "My Quarrel with Hersh Rasseyner," in: I. Howe and E. Greenberg (eds.), *Treasury of Yiddish Stories* (1954), 579–606).

Even after many years the *musarnik* remembered this naked prolonged cry, "O voices of ecstasy, O hoary voices, I follow you – I follow the echo of my Elul nights seven years ago" (idem, *Mussernikes* (1969), 9).

The Musar movement is thus a civic trend which, deflected from its original aim, gradually developed an entire educational system, based on, and aiming toward, integration and subjection of the youthful emotions to a deeply instilled emotional defense system of a rigoristic Jewish life according to *halakhah*. It promoted unity through pride in this fraternity of feelings and intentions and thus served as a social bond among those who emerged from the *musar* hothouse in the yeshivot. The Slobodka and Nawardok approaches differed in their degree of extremism and the emphasis on spiritual exercise, but were based on the same principle. By 1970 the main yeshivot of the Lithuanian type were *musar* oriented, the majority of Slobodka style, and a small minority Nawardok style. Despite the system, or to some extent because of it, many left the *musar* yeshivot for more secular trends of education.

BIBLIOGRAPHY: Ba'al Mashoves, in: *He-Avar*, 1 (1918), 107–16; E. Carlebach, *Mussar; Geschichte einer Bewegung* (1932; repr. from JJLG, 22 (1931/32), 293–393); D. Katz, *Tenu'at ha-Musar – Toledoteha, Ishehah ve-Shitoteha*, 5 vols. (1948–633); H.H. Ben-Sasson, in: *Divrei ha-Kinnus ha-Olami le-Madda'ei ha-Yahadut*, 1 (1952), 446–9; Z.F. Ury, *Musar Movement* (1970); J.J. Weinberg, in: L. Jung (ed.), *Men of the Spirit* (1964), 213–83.

[Haim Hillel Ben-Sasson]

MUSÉE D'ART ET D'HISTOIRE DU JUDAÏSME (MAHJ). Open to the public since December 1998, the MAHJ is located in the area of le Marais, the historical heart of Paris and, since the 19th century, one of the main Jewish residential areas in the city. The MAHJ is located in a renovated 17th-century mansion, property of the city of Paris and assigned to the housing of a museum of Jewish civilization by Jacques Chirac, then mayor of Paris, already in 1986. All the costs for the construction and functioning of the museum were and are covered in equal terms by the municipality of Paris and the Ministry of Culture. The very rich collections of the MAHJ originated in the collections of the Musée d'Art Juif, a former Jewish museum created in 1948 which discontinued its activities, and in the Jewish collection of the National Museum for the Middle Ages. Among several donors and depositors, one can mention the Paris Consistory, which entrusted to the MAHJ its important collection of ritual objects. Apart from the permanent exhibition, the MAHJ organizes temporary exhibitions, hosts cultural events in its auditorium, receives the public in its library and documentation center, and puts very special emphasis on workshops for youth. The founder-president of MAHJ was Claude-Gérard Marcus, who was succeeded by Théo *Klein. In 2006 the director was Laurence Sigal.

MUSELMANN (German for Muslim), death camp slang word for prisoners on the edge of death who have surrendered to their fate, i.e., showing the symptoms of the last stages of hunger, disease, mental indifference and physical exhaustion. This term was mostly used at Auschwitz. It seems to have originated from the typical deportment of the sufferers, e.g., to squat with their legs tucked in an "Oriental" fashion, their faces masklike in stiffness. Often the muselmann was the target of anger from fellow prisoners, who avoided them lest they too be overcome by despair at the conditions they faced.

Primo *Levi has argued that had the *lagers* lasted a little longer they would have developed a language of their own. His chilling description of the muselmann indicates the depth of their despair: "The musselmaner, the drowned, form the backbone of the camp, an anonymous mass, continually renewed and always identical, of non-men who march to labor in silence, the divine spark dead within them, already too empty to suffer. One hesitates to call them living; one hesitates to call their death death, in the face of which they have no fear, they are too tired to understand.... If I could enclose all the evil of our time in one image, I would choose this image, which is familiar to me: an emaciated man with head dropped and shoulders curved, on which face and in whose eyes not a trace of thought is to be seen."

BIBLIOGRAPHY: Kowalczykowa, in: *Przegląd Lekarski*, 18 (Eng., 1962), 28–31 (incl. refs. to British medical publications). **ADD. BIBLIOGRAPHY:** P. Levi, *Survival in Auschwitz* (1960).

[Yehuda Reshef / Michael Berenbaum (2nd ed.)]

MUSEUM OF JEWISH HERITAGE: A LIVING MEMORIAL TO THE HOLOCAUST (MJH: ALMTTH). The opening of MJH: ALMTTH, in September 1997, marked the culmination of a long and difficult process to create a Holocaust Memorial in New York City. Beginning with the dedication of the site for a Holocaust Memorial, in Manhattan's Riverside Park, on October 19, 1947, and until the Museum opened its doors to the public 50 years later, the aspirations and plans to establish an appropriate commemoration of the Holocaust were loaded with frustrations and repeated dismissal.

Over the years, numerous plans for a N.Y. Holocaust Memorial were submitted but were either rejected by the City's planning authorities or failed to raise the necessary funding. The artists chosen by the various planners to submit designs for the planned monument included some of the most renowned architects and sculptors. These included Eric Mendelsohn (1951), two designs by Nathan Rapoport (1962 and 1964), and Louis Kahn (1968). Rapport's 1964 rejected submission was ultimately installed in the Jerusalem Hills and titled *Scrolls of Fire.*

A heightened awareness of the significance of the Holocaust for contemporary society from the late 1970s onwards, resulted in increased endeavors to commemorate the Holocaust and address both Jews and non-Jews alike. This included major TV productions, educational curriculums, and ultimately the establishment of Holocaust memorial centers and museums. Especially significant was the 1979 decision to create the *United States Holocaust Memorial Museum in Washington, D.C.

In July 1981, New York's Mayor, Edward *Koch established a Holocaust Memorial Task Force, which evolved in September 1982 to the New York City Holocaust Commission, co-chaired by philanthropist and real estate developer George Klein and Manhattan district attorney, Robert M. Morgenthau. The stated goal was the creation of "a living memorial," meaning a museum rather than only a monument. Koch's declared rationale was clear: " New York City is regarded by all as the cultural and spiritual nucleus of American Jewry and is home to the largest number of Holocaust survivors… It is tragic that the city… still does not have a fitting memorial to the six million martyrs lost in the Second World War."

In February 1986, Governor Mario Cuomo was added to Mayor Koch as founding chairman of the now State Commission. This new development allowed for greater leverage in obtaining State-controlled properties on the tip of Manhattan in Battery Park. Other than allocation of land by the State, the project was to be funded by private financing. Yet, despite support by the local authorities, the project was unable to raise the required funds, resulting in repeated delays and causing it to be nearly forsaken.

Finally in October 1994, ground-breaking ceremonies unveiled Kevin Roche's design for a substantially reduced 30,000 sq. ft. building in Battery Park, symbolically situated opposite two major icons of American Jewish life, the Statue of Liberty and Ellis Island.

Having weathered the ups and downs of creating the new memorial since 1986, Museum director David Altshuler enthusiastically moved ahead in 1995 to create the team that would develop the Core Exhibit. Patrick Gallagher was hired as exhibit designer, Yitzchak Mais, the former director of Yad Vashem's Historical Museum, was appointed chief curator and together with filmmaker Max Lewkowicz combined to create a novel approach to Holocaust commemoration.

The three floors of the Museum portray Jewish life in the 20th century, before, during and after the Holocaust, thus providing an essential but all too often overlooked context for this tragic period in Jewish history. The exhibit's integration of artifacts, photos, text and videos, depict the human drama and highlight the personal narrative of individuals who actually experienced the historical events. This allows the visitors to develop an intimacy with the historical "participants," and results in a powerful emotional experience that will be remembered long after many of the facts, figures, and maps have faded.

The exhibit's narrative, while emphasizing the particular Jewish tragedy, permits its diverse audiences the opportunity to also focus on themselves – their own backgrounds, traditions and history – as they encounter the values, customs, and heritage of the Jewish people. The more universal a story is in its appeal, the more it can bridge cultural differences. Any group's life experiences are unique, but there are characteristics that are common to all people – hope, desire, frustration, fear, courage, and the instinct for survival. The museum's innovative approach of highlighting Human history, with a capital "H," tells the particular Jewish story with universal relevance for all audiences.

This approach is especially evident in the museum's second floor, "The War Against the Jews." In contrast to most other Holocaust exhibitions in North America which depict the Jews under Nazi domination as mere objects in a reign of ongoing terror, MJH:ALMTTH highlights how the Jews perceived and responded to the evolving persecution. Hence, based on the changing Nazi policies and the Jews' understanding of its implications, the Jews are not perceived by the visitors as passive victims, but rather as active agents who exhibited resourcefulness and vitality within the limitations imposed by the tragedy and calamity the Jews experienced during the Holocaust.

The review of the Core Exhibition in *The Wall Street Journal,* highlighted this innovative approach:

> Although the Museum of Jewish Heritage documents with unflinching detail Hitler's war against the Jews, it never permits its visitors to view Jews as faceless extras in the drama of Nazi butchery.

Appointed Museum director in 2000, David Marwell guided MJH: ALMTTH, to its role as a major educational and cultural institution. The realization of the original plans, which were scaled down for lack of budget, were finally accomplished with the dedication of the Robert M. Morgenthau wing in 2003 which provided auditoria, classrooms, a conference center as well as temporary exhibition space.

BIBLIOGRAPHY: R.G. Saidel, *Never Too Late To Remember: The Politics Behind New York City's Holocaust Museum* (1996); T.L. Freudenheim, "Exhibition Reviews: Museum of Jewish Heritage – A Living Memorial to the Holocaust," in: *Curator,* 40:4 (Dec. 1997), 296–300.

[Yitzchak Mais (2nd ed.)]

MUSEUMS. In her entry on museums for the 1948 *Universal Jewish Encyclopedia* the eminent historian of Jewish art Rachel Bernstein Wischnitzer (1885–1989), founding curator of the Jewish Museum in Berlin, cited the origin of collecting and exhibiting of objects of Jewish art and archaeology as dating to 1863 when Félicien de Saulcy brought sarcophagi discovered in Jerusalem to the Louvre. In this way, she wrote, "Since the excavations in Palestine and other sites of [Jewish] archaeological interest were conducted by expeditions from many countries, Jewish excavation finds found their way into various museums all over the world …" Many finds were not related to the Jewish cultural heritage, but the significance of excavating in the Land of Israel was the study of the Bible. Similarly, interest in the Bible and other texts of the "people of the Book" led to the acquisition of important manuscripts and printed texts as some ceremonial objects for libraries and museums throughout Europe. The earliest group of Jewish ritual artifacts was acquired by the Victoria and Albert Museum, then called the South Kensington Museum, in London in 1855, just four years after the museum was established.

It is only in the modern age that there has been a concerted effort to develop museums of the Jewish cultural heritage with far-ranging collections to reflect the 4,000 year history of the Jewish people and Jewish life as it evolved in many lands among many different peoples. Beginning in the 1890s, the formation of Jewish museums in Europe, the United States, and in Ereẓ Israel reflected the phenomenon in Europe of the creation of public museums that began a century earlier and specifically the establishment of ethnographic collections in the mid-19th century. Prior to that time, collecting was the provenance of the nobility and the wealthy. While private wealth did enable some individuals to form collections of Jewish art, in the period before World War I, with increasing secularization, demographic changes, and the rise of nationalism, there was a growing trend to mobilize community preservation efforts and to raise public awareness of the importance of sustaining cultural heritage. Jewish art activities in Europe continued to thrive in Europe even after the Russian Revolution and World War I and heroically persisted even as the Nazis came to power.

In the decades following the Holocaust, there was some limited activity in Europe, but the major mantle of scholarship in the field of Jewish art became the responsibility of Jewish communities in the United States and in Israel. After the Six-Day War in 1967, there was a tremendous upsurge in interest in Jewish life and culture. In America, this occurrence paralleled a focus on ethnicity which significantly impacted American life. Since the late 1970s the most profound aspect of the emphasis on history as memory has been the building of hundreds of Holocaust museums and memorials worldwide. The effort to preserve local Jewish history has been a major impetus to establish Jewish museums in communities across the globe by restoring historic synagogues, in many cases where few Jews remain. Perhaps most astonishing is the revival of Jewish museums in Europe even where the Jewish community was largely destroyed during the Holocaust. By the 1950s Jewish museums had been established or reopened in the Netherlands, Germany, Austria, Greece, Italy, Spain, England, Ireland, Scandinavia, France, and Belgium.

With the collapse of communism in the late 1980s, Jewish museums, many in restored synagogues and other former Jewish communal buildings, have been created in the former East Germany, Hungary, Poland, the Czech Republic, Slovakia, Belarus, Bosnia-Herzegovina, Bulgaria, Croatia, Latvia, Lithuania, Romania, Serbia, and Ukraine. Several collections thought to have been plundered during World War II have been brought to light. An ironic consequence of the loss of cultural artifacts during the Holocaust, is the development of contemporary *genizah* projects, the search for once discarded and hidden Judaica in Europe. The efforts of the Hidden Legacy Foundation in London and the Jewish Museum in Prague for example, have led to the discovery in *genizot* buried artifacts of a number of communities in Germany and Czechoslovakia. While these documents, sacred texts, and ritual objects were buried because they were outworn or no longer usable, their conservation has now become necessary because of the dire fate of the locations in which they were placed for safekeeping and the destruction of the communities that cared for them.

Over 20 countries with representation of several dozen museums are members of the Association of European Jewish Museums (AEFM), an important forum for new plans and developments. The association was established to promote the study of European Jewish history and seeks to protect and preserve Jewish sites and the Jewish cultural heritage in Europe. The Association of European Jewish Museums, the Council of American Jewish Museums (CAJM), which represents over 80 institutional and associate members, along with representatives of the vast network of museums in Israel, and colleagues worldwide – from Australia to South Africa, from Chile to China – seek more and more ways to work in partnership to preserve and interpret the Jewish cultural heritage.

Western Europe and the Mediterranean Rim

Isaac Strauss (1806–1888), conductor of the orchestra at the Paris Opera and for Napoleon III, was an avid art collector and purchased Judaica during his extensive travels. The first public display of Jewish ceremonial art was an exhibition of his collection at the Exposition Universelle at the Palais de Trocadéro in Paris in 1878. The Strauss Collection was purchased in 1890 by Baronne Charlotte, wife of Nathaniel de Rothschild, given to the State, and housed at the Musée de Cluny. The Strauss collection was fortuitously spared during World War II. The Strauss Collection was given a new home in 1999 when the *Musée d'art et d'histoire du Judaïsme opened in Paris in the magnificent restored 17th-century Hôtel de Saint-Aignan in the Marais quarter. The new museum is a successor to the Musée d'Art Juif which was founded in 1948 and acquired its collections. The grandchildren of Captain Alfred *Dreyfus (1859–1935) gifted the museum with the archives, numbering over 3,000 items, that chronicle the "Dreyfus Affair" – the accusation of treason, his court-martial, conviction, imprisonment, and finally exoneration in 1904 – which revealed the persistence of antisemitism in France and became an international issue. The museum also has a long-term loan of ceremonial objects from the Consistory of Paris, never before seen by the general public.

Paris was also the home of the oldest Jewish national historical society, the Société des Études Juives, founded in 1880. On the eve of the French Revolution, Alsace was home to more than half of French Jewry. When the decree of emancipation in 1791 gave Jews full citizenship and the right to practice any trade, many Jews left the rural communities. In 1905, the Société d'Histoire des Israélites d'Alsace et de Lorraine was established to preserve traditional folkways. Headed by Rabbi Moise Ginsburger and Charlés Levy, the society collected objects and recorded oral traditions. These were deposited in the Musée Alsacien in Strasbourg specifically created to preserve the distinctive regional folk culture. In recent years, there has been an upsurge in documentation of Jewish life in Alsace. Over 200 sites are on record, a number of which have already been restored and now are home to Jewish museums including in Bischheim, Bouxwiller, Colmar, and Marmoutier. Two 18th-century synagogues in Carpentras and Cavaillon in Comtat Venaissan, formerly an area where Jews were given protection by the popes of Avignon, have also been preserved.

The first attempt to create a Jewish museum in Belgium dates to 1932, but it was not successful. The 1981 exhibition, "150 years of Belgium Jewish Life," held at the Brussels town hall was the impetus for establishing the Pro Museo Judaico. The Jewish Museum in Brussels opened in 1990 and in 2004 moved to a building donated by the Belgian government.

The Anglo-Jewish Historical Exhibition presented at the Royal Albert Hall in London in 1887 was the first major exposition organized to further interest in the historic preservation of Judaic art and artifacts. Plans for the exhibition grew out of the attempt to establish an Anglo-Jewish historical society and motivated by the threatened demolition of the Bevis Marks Synagogue, a landmark since its dedication in 1701. The exhibition was spearheaded by Lucien Wolf (1857–1930), a historian and publicist, and Alfred A. Newman (1851–1887), a collector of Anglo-Jewish books, pamphlets, and portraits, and guided by Sir Isidore Spielmann (1854–1925), an organizer of art exhibitions. Some 2,500 items were displayed, including ceremonial objects, antiquities, paintings, prints, documents and books on loan from some 345 lenders, both individuals and institutions and included the Strauss collection from Paris. Another important collection was that of Reuben D. Sassoon (1835–1905), largely purchased from Philip Salomons (1796–1867), the brother of Sir David *Salomons, the first Jew to serve as lord mayor of London.

A diverse, ecumenical general committee participated in the planning of the exhibition and related public programs. This inclusion reflects a political agenda that factored in the rescue and preservation of the cultural artifacts of the Jewish people. In England, as elsewhere in Europe and in the United States, an underlying aim was to dispel age-old prejudices and stereotypes and to increase awareness of the contributions made by Jews and the Jewish community to society at large. The Anglo-Jewish Historical Society was formed in 1893. The London Jewish Museum was established in 1932, an effort spearheaded by historian Cecil *Roth (1899–1970) and Wilfred *Samuel (1886–1958). The Jewish Museum is considered the National Collection of Judaica. Important early collections include objects from the Arthur Howitt collection purchased in 1932, the Kahn Collection of 18th-century textiles, and the Franklin Collection of ceremonial silver. For many years, the collection was housed in the Library of the Jews' college at Woburn House in Tavistock Square, along with the main institutions of the Jewish community. Since 1995, the museum has been located in the Raymond Burton House in Camden, a restored 1844 building. Today, the London Jewish Museum also encompasses the London Museum of Jewish Life founded in 1983 to focus on the more recent history of Jewish life in Britain from the late 19th century to the present. The Ben-Uri Society was established in 1915. The founders, many of whom were Yiddish-speaking immigrants, aspired to develop a collection of fine arts that would demonstrate the significant contribution of Jewish artists. Today its collections represent the work of some 350 artists and is one of the most important of its type in Europe. In Manchester the Jewish Museum opened in 1984 in the former Spanish and Portuguese Synagogue built in 1874.

The Irish Jewish Museum, dedicated in 1985, is housed in the now restored Walworth Road Synagogue, in the heart of what was once a Jewish neighborhood of Dublin. The collections represent Jewish communities in Belfast, Cork, Derry, Dublin, Limerick, and Waterford.

The Jewish community in Italy was the very first in Western Europe, and only in Italy has there been continuous settlement since Jews first arrived during the era of the Roman Empire. Today few, if any, Jewish residents remain in many of the once thriving communities. A number of synagogues have been restored and often ceremonial objects, along with a history of the particular locale, are displayed.

Rome is home to the largest Jewish community in Italy. The Jewish Museum in Rome is located in the Tempio Israelitico, built in 1904 in the area of the old demolished ghetto. The Jewish Museum in Florence is located in the historic 1882 Moorish revival style synagogue. Also in Tuscany, there is a Jewish museum in Livorno, and the Sienna synagogue has been restored. In Venice, all of the five synagogues in the area that was the ghetto have been preserved. Each represents one aspect of the community's diverse background, the richly appointed interiors epitomizing the greatness of Italian Jewish art. In nearby Padua, the museum is at the site of the last surviving synagogue, which dates back to 1548 and which was actually closed from 1893 until after World War II. The Jewish Museum in Bologna, located in the area of the former ghetto, and along with the synagogue of Modena and the Jewish museums of Soragna and Ferrara promote an awareness of the long, rich history of Jewish culture in the Emilia-Romagna region. In Piedmont, Jewish museums are found in the restored synagogues in Asti, Casale Monferrato, and Turin. There is also a Jewish Museum in Trieste.

Jewish settlement in Spain also dates to the first centuries of the Roman Empire. The expulsion of the Jews from Spain in 1492 was a major turning point in the history of the Jewish people, and it was not until the second half of the 19th century that Jews returned. The Museo Sefardi in Toledo, Spain established in 1964 which is now located in the restored El Tránsito Synagogue, built between 1336 and 1357 by Samuel ha-Levi, who held several important posts in the court of King Pedro I of Castilla. Fortunately, in 1877, the building, which had been used as a hospital and later a church, was declared a National Monument. Preservation was begun by the government and completed under the auspices of the Museo Sefardi. A museum has also been formed in Girona in conjunction with the Naḥmanides Institute for Jewish Studies. Following the expulsion from Spain some 150,000 Jews fled to Portugal. But it was not to be a safe haven and in 1497 Jews were forced to leave. The oldest existing synagogue in Portugal was built in 1438 in Tomar. Classified as a national monument in 1921, it was donated to the state in 1939 for use as a museum. Today it houses the Abraham Zacuto Luso Jewish Museum.

The Joodsch Historisch Museum (Jewish Historical Museum) in Amsterdam, founded in 1931 was re-opened in its original home in the medieval Waagebouw (Weigh-House) in 1955. Eighty percent of its collection was lost during the war; the rest was recovered in Germany. In 1974, the Amsterdam City Council, which then held title to the buildings, voted that the abandoned Ashkenazi Synagogue complex should become the new home of the Jewish Historical Museum. Four historic synagogues, two of which were built in the 17th century and two in the 18th, were restored and physically linked to form the museum. The buildings had been badly damaged in the war, and the replacement elements are all of contemporary design, symbolically serving as a reminder of what has been lost.

The effort to establish a Jewish museum in Denmark was launched in 1985. The museum opened in 2003, in what was the Royal Boat House, built by King Christian IV at the turn of the 17th century. The choice of this site is significant because it was at the invitation of King Christian that Jews were fist invited to settle in Scandinavia. Noted architect Daniel *Libeskind transformed the historic space for use as the Jewish museum using the concept of *mitzvah* for the overall matrix of his plan.

The Jewish Museum in Basle exhibits objects and documents related to the history of the Jewish community in Switzerland. Basle was the site of the First Zionist Congress in 1897 and documents and mementos from the Congress are on display. A group of tombstones from the 13th century are installed in the courtyard.

The Jewish Museum in Stockholm, was founded in 1987. In 1999, it was accorded the status of a national museum by the Swedish government. In Norway, the Jewish Museum in Trondheim opened in 1997 in the main building of the former railway station, built in 1864, which was converted for use as a synagogue in 1925 and rededicated after World War II.

The Jewish Museum of Greece in Athens was founded in 1977 by Nikos Stavroulakis, who was also the founding director of the Jewish Museum in Thessaloniki in 2000. In addition to collecting archives and artifacts of the two-millennia-old Jewish heritage in Greece, both museums have undertaken the recording and photographing of Jewish monuments, synagogues, and cemeteries endangered because nearly 90 percent of the Jewish population perished during the Holocaust. The Jewish Museum of Rhodes was founded in 1997 and is located adjacent to the Kahal Shalom Synagogue built in 1577. The Jewish community in Turkey also traces its roots to antiquity. The Jewish Museum in Istanbul, housed in the historic Zülfaris Synagogue, was founded in 2001 by the Quincentennial Foundation, which commemorates the 500th anniversary of the 1492 expulsion of the Jews from Spain and the welcome to the Ottoman Empire. The Jewish Museum is the first to be established in a predominantly Muslim country. The vast majority of Moroccan Jews left for Israel, France, and the United States after 1948. The Jewish Museum in Casablanca, Morocco, preserves and records the long history of Jewish life in Morocco and has been involved in the restoration of synagogues.

Central and Eastern Europe

Beginning with a study group in Vienna established in 1895, there was a proliferation of societies in Europe dedicated to the furtherance of Jewish art, which was a consequence of the growing awareness of issues of Jewish identity in the face of modern life. The Gesellschaft fuer Sammlung und Konservierung von Kunst und historischen Denkmälern des Judentums (Society for the Collection and Conservation of Jewish Art and Historic Monuments) also established the first Jewish museum. About 20,000 objects and 30,000 books were recovered in 1945 and returned to the Jewish community. In the 1960s there was a short-lived effort at re-opening the museum. In 1990, the city of Vienna founded a new Jewish Museum, which opened in 1993. The Museum Judenplatz Vienna was inaugurated in 2000 along with a Holocaust memorial designed by Rachel Whiteread. The museum, entered through a 500-year-old Jewish community building still active today, preserves the remains of a newly discovered 13th-century synagogue.

The home of Samson *Wertheimer (1658–1724), court Jew to Emperor Leopold I, in Eisenstadt today houses the Austrian Jewish Museum that opened in 1982. An earlier Jewish museum that was founded by Sándor Wolf (1871–1946) in the 1930s was plundered during World War II. Samson Wertheimer, who was also a rabbi, had a private synagogue in his home. His *schul*, one of the few Jewish places of worship not destroyed during the Holocaust, was rededicated in 1979. A Jewish museum in Hohenems is located in the historic Heimann-Rosenthal villa which dates to 1864 and focuses on Salomon *Sulzer (1804–1890), renowned composer of Jewish music.

Alexander David (1687–1765), a Court Jew from Braunschweig, formed the earliest known collection of Judaica originating with the ceremonial objects used in his private synagogue. In 1747, the private synagogue became a community house of prayer and was maintained as such until 1875. Today, David's collection forms the core of the Judaica department of the Braunschweig Landesmuseum in Germany.

In Frankfurt-am-Main, a Catholic art historian and director of the Duesseldorf Kunstgewerbemuseum (Museum of Applied Art), Heinrich Frauberger (1845–1920), formed the Gesellschaft zur Erforschung Juedischer Kunstdenkmaeler (Society for the Research of Jewish Art Objects) in 1901. The Frankfurt Jewish Museum, established in 1922, was destroyed on **Kristallnacht*, the Night of the Broken Glass, Nov. 9, 1938, and was reopened in 1988 in the former Rothschild Palais on the 50th anniversary of the infamous pogrom that began the massive destruction by the Nazis of Jewish homes, businesses, and cultural and religious institutions. Frauberger also formed a collection of Jewish art. In 1908, he curated the first exhibition in Germany of Jewish ceremonial objects at the Duesseldorf Kunstgewerbemuseum. Frauberger later sold his collection to Salli Kirschstein (1869–1935), a successful Berlin businessman. In addition to the influence of Frauberger and the Frankfurt group, Salli Kirschstein's collection also reflects the work of Max *Grunwald (1871–1953), who had issued a call in Hamburg in 1896 to establish a Museum fuer juedische Volkskunde, which aimed to study Jewish folklore studies as a means for Jews to represent what they shared in common with other peoples. A Jewish museum was subsequently established in Hamburg prior to World War I. Today, the Hamburg Historical Museum maintains Judaica department.

Salli *Kirschstein established a private museum in his Berlin home to educate Jews and non-Jews alike through the material evidence of Jewish culture. In particular this was his response to the absence of any representation of Jewish life in the Arts and Crafts and Ethnology Museum in Berlin. Kirschstein's encyclopedic approach to collecting including ceremonial objects, fine arts, manuscripts and rare books as well as historic documents would later serve as a paradigm for other Jewish museums.

There were other initiatives to bring Jewish art to Berlin. The first exhibition of the work of Jewish artists sponsored by the Verein zur Foederung juedischer Kunst (Society for the Furthering of Jewish Art) was held in Berlin in 1908. Another effort at establishing a Jewish Museum in Berlin was based on the art collection of Albert Wolf (1841–1907). In 1917, the collection was displayed in the community administration building adjacent to the historic Neue Synagog on Oranienburgerstrasse. Lack of funding, and a theft in 1923, left the community collection in compromised straits. A new society to support a Jewish Museum in Berlin was established in 1924, with Salli Kirschstein as a participant. However, his collection never became the nucleus of the expanded effort. In 1926, Kirschstein sold his collection numbering over 6,000 items to the Hebrew Union College in Cincinnati, Ohio, in the United States. A second group of objects he collected was sold at auction in 1932. Fifteen of them became part of the collection of the Jewish Museum in Berlin which was, at long last, dedicated on January 24, 1933, just six days before the Nazis came to power. The Nazis closed the museum in 1938 and Allied bombing heavily damaged the Oranienburgerstrasse Synagogue. When the city became divided, the synagogue was in the eastern sector. A change in government policy precipitated by the declining fortunes of communism led to the decision in 1988 to create the Stiftung Centrum Judaicum-Neue Synagoge, which established a memorial and cultural center in the synagogue. In West Berlin, a Jewish Department of the Berlin City Museum, which was located in the Kollegienhaus, a former Baroque Prussian courthouse, was established in the early 1970s. In 1989, Daniel Libeskind's design won a competition for what was officially the "Expansion of the Berlin Museum with a Jewish-Museum Section." The striking post-modern building became a destination in its own right and was visited by a quarter of a million people during a year and a half period after the building was completed in 1999 before closing to install the exhibitions. The Jewish Museum Berlin opened officially on September 8, 2001. Among its creators were two men exiled from Berlin by the Nazis: Michael Blumenthal and Jeshajahu Weinberg,

In the interwar period, Jewish museums were also established in Kassel, Munich, and Mainz. Theodor Harbinger conducted a survey for the Center for Collecting Jewish Art in Bavaria in Munich under the auspices of the Verband Bayerishcher Israelitischer Gemeinden. Plans are in the works for a new Jewish museum to be built in Munich in a complex that will also include a synagogue and community center. In Mainz the museum was formed by the Verein zur Pflege Juedischer Altertuemer in Mainz where in 1931 there was a landmark convention of Jewish art historians, collectors, and curators who met to discuss collaborating on developing a unified methodology of cataloging, photographing and exhibiting collections of Jewish art.

From the mid-1980s and especially since the reunification of Germany, numerous Jewish museums have been established and nearly 100 synagogues have been restored, many of them with exhibitions. The Jewish Museum of Franconia has three sites: in Fuerth, in the former home of the Court Jew family Fromm, built in 1702; in Schnaittach, in a synagogue built in 1570; and in Schwabach, where a painted *sukkah* was found in a house on Synagogengasse. The Jewish Museum in Augsburg is in a restored synagogue – originally dedicated in 1917, it was badly damaged in 1938 and restored in 1985. In 1982, the former wedding hall of the Jewish quarter of Worms located next to the destroyed Romanesque synagogue became the home of Rashi House, a Jewish museum and archive named in honor of the leading commentator of the Bible Rabbi Solomon ben Isaac (*Rashi; 1040–1105). Others are to be found in Baisingen, Essen, Groebzig, Halberstadt, Ichenhausen, Rendsburg, and Veitshoechheim. The site of Jewish Museum Creglingen was a Jewish property from 1618 which was restored to Jewish ownership in 1998 by a descendant of the original owner.

In Prague, Salomon Hugo *Lieben (1881–1942), a historian, galvanized efforts to collect Judaica when urban renewal threatened the demolition of several historic synagogues. He founded the Verein zur Gruendung und Erhaltung eines juedisches Museums in Prag (Organization for the founding and Maintenance of a Jewish Museum in Prague). Lieben's efforts to preserve the Jewish cultural heritage of Bohemia and Moravia extended to rural villages as well. In 1926, the growing collection was moved into the former Ceremonial Hall of the Prague Ḥevra Kaddisha, the burial society, which is still used as an exhibit space for the museum. Lieben headed the museum until 1938. During World War II the Prague synagogues and the museum were used as storehouses for confiscated Jewish property from Bohemia and Moravia. Ironically, a plan for preservation of the property in order to care for and promote the unique heritage of Jewish culture suggested by Dr. Karel Stein (1906–1961) led to the establishment of a Central Jewish Museum in Prague. The plan was accepted by the Nazis for a very different reason – they wanted to create a perfect storehouse – a resource for the study of the Jewish people from which future exhibitions could be developed. They presumed that the Jewish "race," as they termed it, would be extinct.

At the end of the war, the collection which numbered 1,000 objects in 1939, had over 100,000 catalog cards recording information about the over 200,000 objects, books, and archives handled by the museum staff. The museum, under the aegis of the Prague Jewish Community Council, renewed its work focusing on efforts to return property to individuals and to any re-established Jewish communities. However, by 1949, the council determined it could no longer maintain the historic buildings in Prague's Jewish Quarter or the museum collections. In April 1950 the Prague Jewish Museum was taken over by the state and placed under the control of the Ministry of Education. Finally, in October 1994, five years after the fall of the Communist government, the museum was returned to the Federation of Jewish communities of the Czech Republic. In addition to the former ceremonial hall of the Prague burial society, the exhibits are housed in five historic synagogues. Across Bohemia and Moravia, with the leadership of the Jewish Museum in Prague, sites are being researched, reclaimed, and preserved. A number of restored synagogues, some of which serve other functions such as concert halls, also have museums including in Boskovice, Decín, Holešov, Kolin, Mikulov-Nikolsburg, Plzeň, Polná, Rakovnik, Rychnov, Slavkov-Austerlitz, and Třebíč.

In the Slovak Republic the Museum of Jewish Culture in Slovakia was established in 1991 Bratislava as part of the Slovak National Museum. The Jewish Museum Prešov housed in the restored 1898 synagogue is seen as the successor to the museum organized in 1928 by Rabbi Theodore Austerlitz and Eugen Bárkány. That collection was among those sent to Prague during the war and when returned became part of the Bratislava collection.

The Jewish museum in Budapest was founded in 1910 and officially opened in 1916. In 1932, under the direction of Erno Naményi (d. 1958), the museum, which had fallen on hard times, reopened in a building attached to the famed Dohány Synagogue. During the war, the most important of the museum's objects were crated and hidden in the basement of the Hungarian National Museum, fortunately these were returned in good order. After the war, Naményi and others worked to restore the museum. The museum was reopened in 1947, but the next years would be difficult. Ilona Benoschofsky, director for two decades from 1963, with the expertise of renowned manuscript scholar Alexander Scheiber catalogued the collection. The museum underwent a major renovation in the 1990s.

The Jewish Historical Museum in Belgrade, Serbia, was established in 1948 and since 1969 has been housed in the Federation of Jewish Communities building. The collection includes many objects saved during World War II and later returned to Jewish hands and the archives document many destroyed Jewish communities. Marking the 400th anniversary of Sephardi settlement in Bosnia-Herzegovina, a museum of the history of the Jews was opened in Sarajevo in 1965 in the synagogue built in 1580. Closed during the Bosnian War, the museum has not reopened. The famed Sarajevo *Haggadah* was put on display in the National Museum in 2002. The Jewish Museum in Sofia, Bulgaria is located adjacent to the Sofia Central Synagogue. In Dubrovnik, Croatia a museum was established in the 17th-century Kahal Adat Yisrael Synagogue which was restored and rededicated in 1997. In Bucharest, the Museum of the Jewish Community in Romania opened in the former Great Synagogue in 1992.

The demographics of the Jewish world rapidly shifted with the onset of a wave of pogroms in Eastern Europe beginning in 1881 following the assassination of Czar Alexander II. No longer willing to endure the poverty and degradation, over two million Jews left Eastern Europe and moved westward, with the United States, and the promise of economic opportunity and religious and political freedom, the chosen destination of the majority of them. Even as many were leaving there were already profound changes taking place within Jewish society, as many Jews had begun to abandon traditional Judaism as they sought a more modern way of life. Simon Dubnow (1860–1941) issued what was the earliest appeal to recognize the importance of the historical documents and other cultural artifacts of the Jews of Eastern Europe. The rapid changes in Jewish life also motivated the well-known author S. *An-Ski (Solomon Zainwil Rapoport, 1863–1920) to organize an expedition to collect documents, ceremonial objects, and ethnographic artifacts and to gather folktales and songs. An-Ski's motivation was the idealistic belief that the materials collected would provide a source for a Jewish cultural renaissance. The collecting efforts went on from 1912 to 1914 throughout the Ukraine, Podolia, and Volhynia. Even during the war, An-Ski, dressed as a Russian officer and working with the Red Cross, continued to salvage what he could from destroyed Jewish villages on the Galician front. The An-Ski collection was deposited in the State Ethnographic Museum in St. Petersburg. There is now also a Jewish Museum in St. Petersburg which sees its work as being in the tradition of An-Ski and of the first Jewish museum which closed in 1929.

An-Ski escaped from Russia in 1918 and made his way to Vilna. Though in poor health, he re-established the museum founded by the Society of Lovers of Jewish Antiquity in 1913, its collection having been destroyed during the war. *YIVO, the Yidisher Visenshaftlikher Institute (Institute for Jewish Research) founded in Berlin in 1925, with Vilna selected to be the central site of the new organization, became the most important center for research on Eastern European Jewish art and ethnography. In 1939 Max *Weinreich (1894–1969), co-founder and guiding light of YIVO, was on a lecture tour in Finland when the Germans invaded Poland. He made his way to New York and immediately began to work to keep YIVO active. Fortunately, a large portion of the collection of books, manuscripts, and archival items looted by the Germans was recovered after the war and transferred to YIVO's new home in New York.

During the war, Herman Kruk (1897–1944) led a heroic effort of cultural resistance by maintaining a library in the ghetto and collecting ceremonial objects, artwork, and other cultural artifacts belonging to deported Jews and in abandoned Jewish institutions. Aware that the Nazis were on to their plan Kruk and a few assistants known as the "Paper Brigade" attempted to hide rare books and documents. Two survivors of the Paper brigade, Abraham Sutzkever and Smerke Kaczerginski, returned to Vilna in July 1944 with the Soviet army liberating the city. Little remained, but they determined to reopen the Jewish museum. Beset with difficulties from the authorities, the museum staff shipped out what they could from Soviet Vilnius. The museum was shut down in 1948. After the breakup of the former Soviet Union, YIVO documents were discovered in Vilnius in a church used by the Lithuanian national library for storage. Though not returned to YIVO, a compromise was reached and the documents were sent to New York to be microfilmed then sent back to Vilnius. In 1989, a new Jewish museum was established in Vilnius as the Vilna Gaon State Jewish Museum. On October 3, 2000, the Lithuanian Parliament voted to return 300 scrolls from the holdings of the National Library to the Jewish people. In January 2002, a delegation from Israel led by then Ashkenazi chief rabbi Israel Meir *Lau, himself a survivor, traveled to Vilnius to bring the scrolls to Israel. YIVO now a partner in the Center for Jewish History which opened in New York in the spring of 2000 expanded its scope of work after the move to New York, with the scholarly mission adding a focus on the influence of East European Jewish culture as it has developed in the Americas.

Another group of objects rediscovered in the aftermath of the collapse of the Soviet Union were artifacts from the private collection of Maksymilian Goldstein (1880–1942) and which, along with the contents of the Lvov (Lviv) Jewish Community Museum, were feared to have been destroyed or lost during World War II. Today the collection is housed in the Ukrainian Museum of Ethnography and Artistic Crafts. Goldstein had placed his collection with the museum after the German occupation 1942. Though the movement to form a collection in Lvov had been spearheaded by Goldstein, there was interest in the general community to form such a collection. The nationalist impulse was a major factor, and indeed, Jewish objects had already been displayed at the Municipal Museum as early as 1894 as part of a regional exhibition.

A Jewish museum established by the Jewish Cultural League in Kiev in 1920 existed for about a decade and another in Odessa, also closed in the 1930s. Plundered by the Nazis, the Odessa collection was removed to Germany and was discovered in Bavaria by British forces after the war. The Museum of the History of Odessa's Jews opened in 2002 during an international conference. Other Jewish Museums in the Ukraine are located in Nikolaev, Simferopol, and Sevastopol.

In Belarus, the Marc Chagall Museum, opened in the artist's boyhood home in Vitebsk in 1992. In Riga, the Museum of the Jews in Latvia is housed in the Jewish Community Center and highlights many important Jewish personalities from Latvia, including R. Abraham *Kook, the first Ashkenazi chief rabbi of Palestine during the period of the British Mandate. With the political change in Russia, there even are now plans to develop a major Jewish museum in Moscow to be located in a former bus depot donated by the government.

In Poland, Matthias Bersohn (1823–1908) spearheaded the effort to establish a Jewish museum in Warsaw. Bersohn also contributed to ethnographic and folklore studies with his photographic survey of wooden synagogues in Poland. The museum in Warsaw which opened in 1910 was founded with his bequest. The museum was destroyed during the bombardment of Warsaw in 1939. The Museum of the Jewish Historical Institute in Warsaw began its activities in 1948, the first museum to collect artifacts of the Jewish cultural heritage in the postwar period. In the early 21st century building plans were underway for a new museum.

Bersohn's survey was expanded through the efforts of Majer Balaban (1877–1942), a Lvov native and historian of Polish Jewry who photographed Jewish landmarks, life, and artifacts. In Krakow in 1935, Balaban encouraged the creation of a Jewish museum to preserve the many treasures of the large synagogues, the Stara Synagoga, the Rema Synagogue, and the Hoyche Schul. During the war the collection was plundered and the Stara Synagoga was used as a warehouse by the Nazis. Restored after the war, since 1958 the synagogue has housed a Museum of Jewish History and Culture as a branch of the Krakow History Museum. A Jewish museum was established in Breslau (now Wroclaw) in 1929, also by a Society of friends, the Verein Juedisches Museum Breslau.

In Danzig (Gdansk, Poland, since 1945) a museum was founded in the Great Synagogue in 1904 when Lesser Gieldzinski (1830–1910) presented his private collection of Judaica to the synagogue to commemorate his 75th birthday. In 1939, the Gieldzinski Collection, along with the ceremonial objects of the Great Synagogue of Danzig, was sent to the Jewish Museum in New York. An agreement stipulated that if after 15 years there were no safe and free Jews in Danzig the objects were to remain in America for the education and inspiration of the rest of the world.

[Grace Cohen Grossman (2nd ed.)]

Ereẓ Israel

The history of Jewish museums in Ereẓ Israel began with the efforts of Boris *Schatz, who founded the *Bezalel School for Arts and Crafts in Jerusalem. The Lithuanian-born Schatz (1866–1932) trained in Paris and in 1895 became court sculptor to Prince Ferdinand of Bulgaria. In a meeting with Theodor Herzl in 1903 Schatz proposed his vision for an art school that meshed with Zionist ideology. He chose the name of the biblical artist Bezalel as a symbol of the continuity of art in Jewish life. Schatz expressed that his mission was for a Jewish art to come into being which would weave together the cultural threads that had been pulled apart and damaged during the 2,000 years of the Diaspora experience. His idealism was tempered with reality for he planned for the students to learn crafts, which could be sold to help support the school. In the wake of Herzl's untimely death at age 44 in 1904, Schatz sought the backing of various Zionist institutions. His proposal was officially accepted at the 1905 Zionist Congress and the school was launched a year later. The Bezalel Museum was founded soon thereafter. By 1910, Bezalel had 32 different departments, over 500 students and a ready market for its works in Jewish communities in Europe and the United States. The school was closed during World War I and again after Schatz passed away in 1932. The museum was incorporated into the *Israel Museum when it opened in 1964 as the national museum (see below). The Bezalel Academy of Art and Design remains as a premier art school today.

From its beginnings in the mid-19th century archaeologists have actively explored the land of Israel seeking evidence of the rich heritage of cultures and civilizations of the peoples who have played a part in shaping its history. Some 15,000 archaeological sites are currently known and new ones are discovered all the time. Though of course many date well before the period of the Israelites and span in time to much later settlers, the sense of being enveloped by history is all-encompassing. Numerous excavation sites have become archaeological parks.

It is perhaps emblematic of how deeply museums are entwined with history that David Ben-Gurion announced the establishment of the State of Israel in the Tel Aviv Museum of Art. Independence Hall is located in what was originally the home of Meir *Dizengoff, first mayor of Tel Aviv. Dizengoff gave it to the city for the creation of an art museum. With its rich collections of modern paintings, sculpture, and graphic art, and its many visiting exhibits, the museum was housed in a new building in 1971. Founded in 1932, it expanded with the addition of the Helena Rubinstein Pavilion in 1958.

The complex Ha-Areẓ ("Homeland") Museum started with nine separate pavilions: museums for glass, ceramics, numismatics, ethnography and folklore, science and technology (including a planetarium), antiquities of Jaffa and Tel Aviv, the history of Tel Aviv, the alphabet, and Tel Qasile excavations. There are also ten other museums in Tel Aviv, including a Museum of Man and his Work, the Haganah, and the Jabotinsky Museum.

The Israel Museum, situated in the heart of modern Jerusalem, houses a collection of Jewish and world art, the archaeology of the Holy Land, and the Dead Sea Scrolls. The museum was founded to collect, preserve, study, and display the cultural and artistic treasures of the Jewish people throughout its long history as well as the art, ethnology, and archeology of the Land of Israel and its neighboring countries. It also aims at encouraging original Israeli art. The exhibition area totaled 17,000 sq. m. (about 20,500 sq. yd.) with an additional 19,000 sq. m. (about 23,000 sq. yd.) for storage, laboratories, workshops, a library, and offices, including those of the Israel government Department of Antiquities. The museum includes the Billy Rose Art Garden and the Shrine of the Book.

The Haifa municipality administers museums of ancient and modern art, a maritime museum, and the "Dagon," a grain museum showing the cultivation and storage of grain through the ages.

No section of the country is without its regional and local museums, most of them created and maintained to satisfy the intense interest of the people in their past. In the north, *Beth-Shean, the ancient fortress city guarding the road from the east, displays a collection of archaeological finds and mosaics from the town and its environs; at the nearby kibbutz *Nir David is a museum of Mediterranean archaeology. The Mishkan le-Ommanut, the art museum at kibbutz *En-Harod, the first rural museum in the country, started in 1933. The object of this museum is to collect Jewish art, and it has already a rich collection of Jewish painting, sculpture, and Jewish folk art from all over the world. Beit Sturman at En-Harod exhibits the history and archaeology of the region. Wilfred Israel House, at kibbutz *Ha-Zore'a, exhibits artistic objects from the Far East and archaeological finds from the village fields; Bet Ussishkin, in kibbutz *Dan, is both a natural history museum for the Ḥuleh region and the site museum for the excavations at nearby Tel Dan. There are museums at *Ḥanitah and *Sasa in Upper Galilee, Tiberias and Nazareth in Lower Galilee, *Ayyelet ha-Shaḥar by ancient *Ḥazor, *Bet She'arim, close to the Jewish necropolis of the talmudic period, and *Megiddo with its imposing mound.

The coastal region is represented by municipal museums in *Acre, site museums in *Sedot Yam showing the antiquities of *Caesarea, and *Ma'agan Mikha'el showing objects found in the sea; the regional museum at Midreshet Ruppin in Ḥefer Plain exemplifies the local flora and fauna, as well as the history of the area's modern villages and their ancient sites. In the Negev, Beersheba has an archaeological museum; the kibbutzim Gevulot, Kissufim, Mishmar ha-Negev, and Nirim have their own collections; the site museums of Masadah, En-Gedi, Arad, and Avedat exhibit representative collections of the finds; *Eilat has a museum of modern art, as well as a maritime museum.

Since 1948, museums have flourished throughout Israel and today number over 150. Among them are numerous museums devoted to topics of Jewish and Israeli history, Jewish art, ceremonial art, ethnography and folklore. Important collections have been developed reflecting the ingathering to Israel of refugees from Europe and Arab Lands. An important development in recent years has been the focus on the vibrant legacies of communities like Afghanistan, Kurdistan, Iraq, Morocco, Yemen and of Jews who lived under Ottoman rule.

[Avraham Biran / Grace Cohen Grossman (2nd ed.)]

The Americas

UNITED STATES. The oldest collection of Judaica in the United States was established in 1887 as part of a department of comparative religion at the Smithsonian Institution. The collection was acquired under the direction of Cyrus *Adler (1863–1940), a young curator who had just completed his Ph.D. at Johns Hopkins University, the first to be awarded in the field of Semitics in the United States. Like his compatriots in England who organized the Anglo-Jewish Historical Exhibition, Adler intended that the collection of Jewish ceremonial objects be used in educational exhibitions in order to counteract ignorance of Judaism and prejudice against Jews.

Adler was also a central figure in the founding of the *American Jewish Historical Society in 1892. The AJHS, which has the distinction of being the first ethnic historical organization in the United States, pioneered the collection of archives, books, and artifacts of American Jewry.

In 1904, Judge Mayer *Sulzberger (1843–1923) presented the Jewish Theological Seminary Library in New York with a gift of 26 ceremonial objects to serve as the nucleus for a Jewish museum. Judge Sulzberger was a cousin of Cyrus Adler's, who by this time had become president of JTS in addition to his responsibilities at the Smithsonian. In 1925, Adler was responsible for the acquisition of the collection of Hadji Ephraim Benguiat (d. 1918), an antique dealer who amassed the earliest collection of Sephardic Jewish objects, which he brought to the United States in 1888 and which was displayed at the 1893 World's Fair and subsequently at the Smithsonian Institution. The ominous storm clouds gathering in Europe in the late 1930s brought two additional collections to the museum. The first, through the American Jewish *Joint Distribution Committee, was the Danzig Collection. The second was the collection of Benjamin and Rose Mintz which they brought to the United States from Poland in 1939. The Mintz Collection was purchased by the museum in 1947.

In 1947, the *Jewish Museum moved to its own quarters in the former Warburg Mansion on Fifth Avenue. Stephen Kayser (1900–1988) and Guido Schoenberger (1891–1974), both distinguished art historians and émigrés from Nazi Germany, set a standard of leadership in exhibitions and collections development for nearly two decades. The collection would grow even more with the gift of 10,000 objects from museum supporter Harry G. Friedman (d. 1965), who began acquiring Judaica during the war years. The Jewish Cultural Reconstruction (JCR) was based at the Jewish Museum through 1952. In the aftermath of World War II, the JCR was the organization given the authority by the U.S. State Department to identify and redistribute Nazi looted Jewish ceremonial objects, archives, and books for which no heirs could be found that were located in the American Occupied Sector of Germany. Salo W. *Baron (1895–1989), pre-eminent Jewish historian, spearheaded the campaign to form the JCR, which included representatives of all the major Jewish national and international organizations and served as its president. Hannah *Arendt (1906–1979), political philosopher and author, was the executive secretary for day-to-day operations.

A pioneering initiative was the establishment in 1956 of the Tobe Pascher Workshop for contemporary ceremonial art, whose founding director was Ludwig Wolpert (1900–1981), a German-trained silversmith who came from his home in Jerusalem to direct the workshop. Another was the annual commission by collectors of contemporary art, Albert and Vera List, to commission prominent American artists to make an original graphic for the museum for the Jewish New Year.

From 1970, when Joy Ungerleider-Mayerson (1920–1994), archaeologist and philanthropist, became director, and during the tenure of her successor Joan Rosenbaum beginning in 1980, the museum has continued to actively develop its collections and to present a wide-ranging series of exhibitions and programs. In recent years, The Jewish Museum has focused on presenting a series of major art exhibitions. The JTS Library has maintained a large and important collection of illustrated manuscripts, illuminated ceremonial texts, and prints.

A second Jewish Museum was founded at the Hebrew Union College Library in Cincinnati in 1913 through the impetus of the National Federation of Temple Sisterhoods, whose members recognized the merit of saving family heirlooms. The HUC Librarian Adolph Oko (1883–1944) undertook to develop the museum by acquiring important collections in Europe. His crowning achievement was the purchase of the Salli Kirschstein collection in 1926. Unfortunately, the collections remained in storage for many years until the museum was officially reestablished in 1948 by then president Dr. Nelson *Glueck (1900–1971), a pioneering biblical archaeologist who contributed to the museums growth by depositing artifacts from his excavation in Israel. Franz Landsberger (1883–1964), former director of the Berlin Jewish Museum, rescued through the displaced European Jewish Scholars program, became director of the museum and he was succeeded by Joseph *Gutmann (1923–2004), who became one of the preeminent scholars in the field of Jewish art. In 1947, Jacob Rader *Marcus (1896–1995) established the American Jewish Archives at HUC, which now bears his name. The Union Museum was renamed the Skirball Museum when the collection was moved to Los Angeles in 1972. During a 30-year tenure as director, Nancy Berman fostered the growth of the collection with a focus on contemporary Judaica. In 1996, the museum opened in greatly expanded quarters in the new *Skirball Cultural Center. Exhibitions and related programs reflect the mission of the cultural center to explore the connections between 4,000 years of Jewish history and American democratic values. A branch of the Skirball Museum is in Cincinnati and the HUC Klau Library in Cincinnati maintains an important collection of visual arts. Established in 1983, Hebrew Union College-Jewish Institute of Religion Museum in New York presents exhibitions illuminating Jewish history, culture, and contemporary creativity. The Skirball Museum of Biblical Archaeology in Jerusalem exhibits archaeological artifacts discovered during the HUC-JIR excavations from 1963 to the present.

Fortuitously some major synagogues saved historic commemorative artifacts as well as important ceremonial objects that later formed the basis of museum collections in those congregations. Congregation Emanu-El of the City of New York established a collection in 1928 with the gift of the private collection of Henry Toch, a trustee, and dedicated the Herbert and Eileen Bernard Museum decades later in 1997. In the post-World War II era, new Jewish museums slowly began to be founded in the United States. While it took another generation before the American Jewish community focused efforts on creating Holocaust memorials and museums, in the aftermath of the destruction of the European Jewish community, there was a new sense of the importance for Jews in the United States and in the new state of Israel to preserve Jewish culture. The first formally established synagogue museum, at Temple-Tifereth Israel in Cleveland, was dedicated in 1950 by the eminent Rabbi Abba Hillel *Silver (1893–1963) in 1950 on the occasion of the centennial anniversary of the congregation.

The Leo Baeck Institute, dedicated to the history of German-speaking Jewry, was founded in New York in 1955. The B'nai B'rith Klutznick National Museum in Washington, DC, was founded in 1957. The core of its collection was the gift of Joseph B. and Olyn Horwitz of Cleveland. The Judah L. Magnes Museum is in Berkeley, California in 1962. The prime mover behind the founding of the museum and its director for more than 30 years was Seymour Fromer, who built the collection as a community-based endeavor, without the resources of a parent institution. The Spertus Museum of Judaica was created in Chicago in 1968 in large measure with the private collection of Maurice Spertus. Two additional Jewish museums were founded in the 1970s. The Yeshiva University Museum in New York was officially opened in 1973, but the university did maintain some collections of Jewish art in its library prior to that time. Sylvia Herskowitz was the director of the museum from its opening. The *National Museum of American Jewish History in Philadelphia opened in 1976 in honor of the Bicentennial of the United States. The museum is located across Independence Mall from the Liberty Bell and Independence Hall. It shares its site with Congregation Mikveh Israel, one of the oldest synagogues in America.

In 1977, at a meeting of the Association of Jewish Studies, Dov Noy, professor of Jewish folklore of the Hebrew University, proposed that the U.S. Jewish museums form an organization to further the efforts of the museums to "collect, preserve, and interpret Jewish art and artifacts." The Council of American Jewish Museums (CAJM), affiliated since 1980 with the National Foundation for Jewish Culture, has now grown to represent over 80 institutional and associate members.

In the late 1970s planning began for the *United States Holocaust Memorial Museum in Washington, D.C. which opened in 1993. The USHMM serves as America's national institution for the documentation, study, and interpretation of Holocaust history, and as the memorial of the United States to the millions of victims. Through its multifaceted programs, the museum's mission is "to advance and disseminate knowledge about this unprecedented tragedy; to preserve the memory of those who suffered; and to encourage its visitors to reflect upon the moral and spiritual questions raised by the events of the Holocaust as well as their own responsibilities as citizens of a democracy." The USHMM is a Federal institution. There are Holocaust memorials in communities throughout the United States and many Holocaust museums. The *Simon Wiesenthal Center, Museum of Tolerance in Los Angeles, which opened in 1993 is named in honor of the survivor and well-known Nazi hunter Simon *Wiesenthal and is dedicated to the cause of human rights. The *Museum of Jewish Heritage: A Living Memorial to the Holocaust in New York opened in 1997. It is sited in view of the Statue of Liberty and Ellis Island and just five blocks form the former site of the World Trade Center. The museum was "created as a living memorial to the Holocaust" to honor the lives and legacy of the victims of the Holocaust even as it recounts the tragedy of their deaths.

The tremendous growth in interest in preserving Jewish cultural heritage has reached communities large and small throughout the United States. An important aspect of the work of many of these museums is the focus on local and regional history. The Gomez Hill House, built in Marlboro, New York in 1714 by Luis Moses Gomez, a Sephardi immigrant, is the oldest surviving homestead in the country and a foundation to preserve it was established in 1979. Museums have been formed in a number of historically important synagogues. The Touro Synagogue in Newport, Rhode Island, built in 1763, was the first prominent synagogue to be built in America, and is the only one to survive from the colonial era. The beginnings of Kahal Kadosh Beth Elohim in Charleston, South Carolina can be traced to 1775. The temple and a museum are housed in an 1841 Greek Revival building that is the second oldest synagogue in the United States and the oldest in continuous use. The Jewish Historical Society of Greater Washington is housed in the Adas Israel Synagogue dedicated in 1876. The Beth Ahabah Museum and Archives in Richmond, Virginia, maintains materials dating back to the 18th century. The Jewish Museum of Maryland in Baltimore is unique in that it saved and restored two historic structures – the Lloyd Street Synagogue of the Baltimore Hebrew Congregation built in 1845 and the original house of worship of the Chizuk Amuno Congregation which dates to 1876 – and incorporated them into a museum complex. The Eldridge Street Synagogue, completed in 1887, was the first designed and built in America by immigrants from Eastern Europe. The Vilna Shul, built in 1919, is now the Boston Center for Jewish Heritage.

The Museum of the Southern Jewish Experience, now incorporated as part of the Goldring/Woldenberg Institute of the Southern Jewish Experience, was founded in 1986, through the initiative of Macy Hart to represent Jewish culture in the states of Mississippi, Louisiana, Alabama, Arkansas, and Tennessee and is now endeavoring to cover all 12 states of the South. With changing demographics especially in rural communities and small towns, the Jewish population in them has dwindled or no longer exists. The collection in many ways serves as a rescue mission. In addition to collecting artifacts and archives, the museum provides planning assistance for congregations, works to save historic properties, and to care for untended cemeteries. The museum is also a genealogical center. The Jewish Museum of Florida in Miami Beach restored Congregation Beth Jacob, an art deco building dating from 1936. The museum originated as MOSAIC, a project organized by Marcia Kerstein Zerivitz, as a statewide grassroots preservation effort on the history of Jewish life in Florida. The Oregon Jewish Museum was founded in 1986 and in 1996 merged with the Jewish Historical Society of Oregon, acquiring its archives of 150 years of Jewish experience in Oregon and the Pacific Northwest.

Numerous other Jewish museums have been established in synagogues and in Jewish community centers including: the Sylvia Plotkin Museum at Temple Beth Israel in Scottsdale, Arizona; the Elizabeth S. and Alvin I. Fine Museum of Congregation Emanu-El in San Francisco; the San Francisco Jewish Museum originated in 1982 at the Jewish Federation and is developing a major new site designed by Daniel Libeskind; the Gotthelf Gallery at the San Diego Center for Jewish Culture; the Mizel Center for Arts and Culture in Denver; the Chase/Freedman Gallery of the Greater Hartford Jewish Community Center; the Harold and Vivian Beck Museum of Judaica at the Beth David Congregation in Miami, Florida; the William Breman Jewish Heritage Museum in Atlanta, Georgia; the Rabbi Frank F. Rosenthal Memorial Museum at Temple Anshe Sholom in Olympia Fields, Illinois; the Kansas City Jewish Museum; the Goldsmith Museum at Chizuk Amuno Congregation in Baltimore, Maryland; the Janice Charach Epstein Gallery at the Jewish Community Center of Metropolitan Detroit, Michigan; the Temple Israel Judaic Archival Museum in West Bloomfield, Michigan; the Benjamin and Dr. Edgar R. Cofeld Judaica Museum of Temple Beth Zion; the Judaica Museum of the Hebrew Home for the Aged in Riverdale; the Judaica Museum of Temple Beth Sholom in Roslyn, New York; Judaica Museum of Central Synagogue in New York City; Kehila Kedosha Janina Synagogue and Museum in New York City; the Rosenzweig Museum and the Jewish Heritage Foundation of North Carolina in Durham; the Sherwin Miller Museum at the Tulsa Jewish Community Center in Oklahoma; the American Jewish Museum of the Jewish Community Center of Greater Pittsburgh; Philadelphia Museum of Jewish Art of Congregation Rodeph Shalom in Philadelphia; Temple Judea Museum of Reform Congregation Keneseth Israel in Elkins Park, Pennsylvania; Mollie and Louis Kaplan Judaica Museum at Congregation Beth Yeshurun in Houston, Texas; Rabbi Joseph Baron Museum in Milwaukee, Wisconsin.

A unique initiative was the creation of the *National Yiddish Book Center founded in 1980 to rescue Yiddish books. The center's headquarters in Amherst, Massachusetts, is described as a lively "cultural shtetl." The newest and most ambitious Jewish cultural entity to be established in the United States is the Center for Jewish History located in New York City which opened in 2000. The center houses the combined holdings of the American Jewish Historical Society, the American Sephardi Federation, the Leo Baeck Institute, the Yeshiva University Museum, and the YIVO Institute for Jewish Research. The Center for Jewish History is the largest repository of Jewish artifacts, archives, and historical materials in the United States. Undoubtedly the brightest note in the Jewish museum world in the United States is the focus on special installations for children and the creation of independent Jewish children's museums including the Zimmer Children's Museum in Los Angeles, the Jewish Children's Museum in Brooklyn and the Jewish Children's Learning Lab in New York City.

CANADA. In Canada, the Beth Tzedec Reuben & Helene Dennis Museum in Toronto was established in 1965 with the purchase of Cecil Roth's collection. Roth, a pre-eminent scholar of Jewish history and founder of the London Jewish Museum, formed his collection over a 50-year period. Also in Toronto is the Silverman Heritage Museum, located at the Baycrest Centre for Geriatric Care. The Royal Ontario Museum maintains a gallery of Jewish ceremonial objects. Jewish historical societies document life in several cities across Canada in Alberta; Vancouver, British Columbia; Winnepeg, Manitoba; St. John, New Brunswick; and in Montreal, Quebec.

LATIN AMERICA. Several Jewish Museums are active in Latin America. In Argentina, the Museo Judio de Buenos Aires established in 1967 and re-opened in 2000 is located in the Congregación Israelite. It is dedicated to the Jewish historical contribution to the Argentine Republic. A museum dedicated to Jewish immigration is located in Moiséville. A museum is being planned in Cochambamba, Bolivia. The Jewish Museum in Rio de Janeiro was established in 1977. In Chile, there is the Sephardic Historical Museum in Santiago and in Valparaiso there is a Jewish museum and the Israelite Society of Education "Max Nordau." The Museo Historico Judio "Tuvie Maizel" is located in the Ashkenazi community headquarters in Mexico City. The Jewish Museum of Paraguay, established in 1990, is located in Asunción. In Venezuela, the Separdi Museum of Caracus "Morris E. Curiel" was founded in 1998.

THE CARIBBEAN. Mikvé Israel Emanuel Synagogue in Curaçao, Netherlands Antilles, was founded in 1651 and its current building, which dates to 1732 is the oldest continuously functioning congregation in the western hemisphere. The museum opened in 1970. The Hebrew Congregation of St. Thomas was established in 1796. The present building dates to 1833. The community celebrated its bicentennial in 1995 and the Weibel Museum was created to commemorate the history of the Jews in the community. Plans are underway to develop a Jewish museum in Kingston, Jamaica.

Australia

In Melbourne, Australia Rabbi Ronald Lubofsky, London born and raised, initiated plans for a Jewish museum which was established in 1982. An important focus of the museum has been the acquisition of archives, art, and artifacts reflecting the 200 years of Jewish experience in Australia which "helps strengthen and define our identity as Jewish Australians." Originally housed at the Melbourne Hebrew Congregation, the museum moved to new quarters opposite the stately 1927 St. Kilda Synagogue in 1995. The Sydney Jewish Museum established in 1992 is dedicated to the documenting and teaching about the Holocaust.

South Africa

In Capetown, South Africa a new cultural and heritage center opened in 2000 and located on a site which over a century ago had served a growing immigrant population from Europe. Vivienne Anstey, who directed the effort to develop the new museum, wrote of the South African Jewish community that it has "grappled with the responsibility of upholding moral and religious values aimed to serve the needs of its own community and the needs of South Africans in general. It has walked the tightrope in its integration in the South African context, at the same time dedicating itself to Jewish continuity." Adjacent to the new South Africa Jewish Museum is the Cape Town Holocaust Centre. There are also Jewish museums in Calvinia, in Malmesbury in the former synagogue, the C.P. Nel Museum in Oudtshoorn, the Jewish Pioneers' Museum in Port Elizabeth, and in Pretoria there is the Sammy Marks Museum, a historic house of this South African Jewish pioneer who immigrated from Lithuania in the mid-nineteenth century.

India

The Paradesi Synagogue in Cochin, India was built in 1568 by descendants of Spanish, Dutch, and other European Jews. Though the synagogue is still functioning, the Cochin Jewish community intends to deed the synagogue to the Indian government as a historic monument when the last Jews have left Cochin. Restoration work on the synagogue was made possible by the Yad Hanadiv Foundation under the leadership of Jacob Lord Rothschild. There are several historic synagogues in Mumbai (Bombay) that are preserved including the Gate of Mercy Synagogue (Shaar Harachmim) built in 1796, Keneseth Eliyahoo Synagogue, and the Tifereth Israel Synagogue.

China

The Ohel Rachel Synagogue in Shanghai, China, built in 1920 by Sir Victor Sassoon is currently being renovated, although it is not yet in use again for worship services. Once a center of Jewish life for the 30,000 Jews who found refuge in Shanghai, first when fleeing the 1905 pogroms of Russia, and then from Nazi persecution, the synagogue was last used for services in 1952. The building was then confiscated by the Communist government. Attention was given to the preservation efforts when the synagogue was visited by then First Lady Hilary Rodham Clinton in 1998. Ohel Rachel was added to the World Monuments Fund Watch List of 100 Most Endangered Sites in 2002. The Ohel Moishe Synagogue, the Jewish Refugee Memorial Hall of Shanghai, was the center of religious life for Jewish refugees during World War II. The museum was established in 2002.

Ongoing Endeavors

The search for art and artifacts of the 4,000-year long Jewish experience continues and new finds are regularly being discovered. The most ambitious effort to document the visual culture of the Jewish people is the Index of Jewish Art of the Centre for Jewish Art established in 1980 at the Hebrew University. Founded by Bezalel *Narkiss, the centre has ongoing research projects in Europe and in Israel, presents symposia on a wide-range of projects, maintains an active publications program, including the annual journal *Jewish Art* and organizes tours to Jewish sites. A center for the study of Jewish art has been created at Bar-Ilan University and has published its first journal. The International Survey of Jewish Monuments, spearheaded by Samuel Gruber in the United States, has been actively involved not only in identifying and studying historic Jewish sites in over 35 countries that are in need of preservation, but in spearheading efforts to undertake the needed work. The Ronald S. Lauder Foundation supports vital educational programs and community projects in Central and Eastern Europe with a special focus on developing schools and camps. The commitment on the part of the Lauder Foundation to "pick up the pieces of a history shattered by Nazism and stifled by Communism" includes preservation efforts as well. Ronald Lauder has also long chaired the Jewish Heritage Program of the World Monuments Fund. Centropa is a project of the Central Europe Center for Research and Documentation, with headquarters in Vienna. The vision of its director, photographer and filmmaker Edward Serotta, an international team works to explore both the history of the Jewish communities and what is currently happening to Jews in Central and Eastern Europe the former Soviet Union, and Turkey & the Balkans, to convey that information to the public through a variety of technologies.

Holocaust Memorials and Museums

The importance of memory is central to all of the efforts in developing Jewish museums, but it is even more so in the dedication of Holocaust memorials and museums. It is a remarkable phenomenon that so many Holocaust memorials and museums have been established in recent years. In 1969, the American Jewish Congress published *In Everlasting Remembrance: A Guide to Memorials and Monuments Honoring the Six Million*. The slim booklet, only 48 pages in length, was compiled so that American Jews visiting Europe could visit the sites "where European Jewry suffered its catastrophe," the rationale being so that the American Jew could "remember as a witness, to recall the particulars of the Holocaust by [his] presence at the actual sites." At the time, there were but 20 listings. Of the 17 in Europe, most were at sites of ghettos and concentration camps, the Anne Frank House was listed for Amsterdam. Memorials in Brussels and London were only in the planning stages. In Israel, a documentation center and museum had opened in 1951 at kibbutz *Loḥamei ha-Getta'ot, at Ghetto Fighters House. *Yad Vashem, the Martyrs and Heroes Remembrance Authority, was created by an Act of the Israeli Knesset (Parliament) in 1953. In the United States, plans had just been developed for a memorial in New York City, designed by architect Louis Kahn, and sponsored by a coalition of more than 30 national and local Jewish organizations. The original Kahn design was never realized.

Three decades later, the publication of the Association of Holocaust Organizations includes hundreds of listings. The mission of the Association is "to serve as a network of organizations and individuals for the advancement of Holocaust programming, awareness, education, and research." Today, around the world, millions of people visit Holocaust memorials and museums annually. The places of memory differ widely. As James Young wrote in his 1994 book *The Art of Memory*, "the reasons for Holocaust memorials and the kind of memory they generate vary as widely as the sites themselves.

Some are built in response to traditional Jewish injunctions to remember, others according to a government's need to explain a nation's past to itself." In 1993, the United States Holocaust Memorial Museum opened in Washington, D.C., adjacent to the national mall and within view of monuments to U.S. Presidents Washington, Lincoln and Jefferson. During the 1990s with the collapse of the Soviet Union and the reunification of Germany many more Holocaust memorials and museums have been created or are in the planning stages. Perhaps most symbolic among them, a Holocaust Memorial in Berlin is situated close by the restored Reichstag (parliament) under a law passed on the Tenth Anniversary of the Treaty of German Unity, the so- called "Foundation for Remembrance, Responsibility and Future." (See also *Holocaust: Museums.)

[Grace Cohen Grossman (2nd ed.)]

BIBLIOGRAPHY: G.C. Grossman, *Jewish Museums of the World* (2003); N. Folberg, *And I Shall Dwell Among Them: Historic Synagogues of the World* (1995); B.G. Frank, *A Travel Guide to Jewish Europe* (1996); R.E. Gruber, *Jewish Heritage Travel Guide: A Guide to East-Central Europe* (1999); S. Offe, *Juedische Museen in Deutschland und Oesterreich* (2000); N. Rosovsky and J. Ungerleider-Mayerson, *Jewish Museums of Israel* (1989); A. Sacerdoti (series ed.), *Itinerari Ebraici* (1992–); J.E. Young, *The Texture of Memory: Holocaust Memorials and Meaning* (1993); M. Zaidner (ed.), *Jewish Travel Guide* (2003).

MUSHER, SIDNEY (1905–1990), U.S. food and pharmaceutical chemist, born in New Jersey. His career was in industrial chemical development and he was vice president of Cooper Tinsley Laboratories Inc. from 1963. He took an active interest in the economic development of the State of Israel, being treasurer of the Pan-American-Israel Economic Corporation, president of the American Committee for Palestine Inc., and a board member of Palestine Endowment Funds Inc., as well as being member of the Jewish Reconstruction Foundation and the American Jewish Historical Society, etc.

MUSHROOMS, fungus. Israel is rich in various species of mushroom which grow chiefly in the winter. A large number of them are poisonous. The poisonous ones are mainly of the genus *Amanita*. Easily recognizable among edible mushrooms are those of the genus *Boletus*, called in modern Hebrew *orniyyot* because they grow on the roots of the pine (mod. Heb. *oren*), of which most of the forests planted in Israel consist. The mushroom is not mentioned in the Bible, though some exegetes (Rashi, D. Kimi) identify it with the poisonous *pakku'ot* of II Kings 4:39–40. The *pakku'ot*, however, are the colocynth. In rabbinic literature the combination *kemehim u-fitriyyot* ("truffles and mushrooms") is usually found. They have in common that, although they "grow in the soil," one does not recite over them the blessing for vegetables but the blessing "by whose word everything was created." The Talmud gives as the reason that, unlike ordinary plants, "they do not draw their nourishment from the ground but from the air" (Ber. 40b). In this way they explained the fact that they possess no true roots, being fed by other plants, and absorbing moisture from the air. Mushrooms and truffles are also exempt from tithes (see: *Ma'aser), "because they do not grow by being sown, or, because the earth extrudes them" (TJ, Ma'as. 1:1, 48d). The latter reason refers to their quick growth, which makes it seem as if the earth is expelling them. The extensive sprouting of mushrooms after rain is reflected in the *aggadah* about *Honi ha-Ma'agel who prayed for rain after drought. After rain had fallen in abundance and the heavens were free from clouds "the people went into the fields and brought home mushrooms and truffles" (Ta'an. 23a). Truffles are found chiefly in the light soils of the Judean wilderness and in the sands of the Negev. In contrast to mushrooms, they grow under the surface. In addition to *kemehim*, truffles are called *shemarka'im* (Uk. 3:2) in the Mishnah.

BIBLIOGRAPHY: Loew, Flora, 1 (1928), 26–44.

[Jehuda Feliks]

MUSIC. This article is arranged according to the following outline:

INTRODUCTION

The most workable definition of Jewish music would seem to be the functional one proposed by Curt *Sachs: "Jewish music is that music which is made by Jews, for Jews, as Jews" (in his opening lecture, to the First International Congress of Jewish Music, in Paris 1957). This defines the scope of inquiry without prejudicing its results, leaving it free to undertake the tasks of description, analysis and whatever conclusions may be drawn.

As in all other national and ethnic cultures, the musical dimension of Jewish culture is both determined by its origins and modified by its history in proportions peculiarly its own. Through their dispersion, the Jews came into contact with a multiplicity of regional musical styles, practices, and ideas, some of which were more closely related to their own patrimony (as in the Near East and around the Mediterranean) and others intrinsically different (as in Europe north of the Alps and the Pyrénées).

These factors shaped the character of the mainstream of Jewish music. They have also determined the nature and location of the sources, which the musicologist must explore in order to obtain his facts. The problem can be most easily understood by a comparison with the source situation of European historical musicology. There the sources of information can be ranked as follows: compositions by individuals, created and preserved by musical notation; theoretical treatises; historical documents; instrumental relics; evidence from the visual arts (iconography); and complementary evidence from the fields of religion, the verbal arts, philosophy, political history; and other complementary evidence exploited at the discretion of each scholar. Among the latter, the most important source is the folk music of the area, which survives both in tone and word by a purely oral tradition, except for a few accidental notations made in the past by curious savants, and is in itself the subject of a parallel discipline – ethnomusicology.

The source situation of Jewish music is completely different. All the factors listed above are present, but in entirely different proportions – both absolutely and for each Diaspora area and period. A particularly complicated case is that of musical notation. On the one hand, no tone script, in the European sense of the term (one sound = one symbol) was evolved in Jewish musical culture. Even European Jewry adopted the tone script of the surrounding culture only in a few communities during certain periods and only for certain sections of its total musical activity. On the other hand, the masoretic accents serve as universal indicators of certain melodic motives for the cantillation of some of the biblical books (according to principles basically common to all Jewish communities), and their syntactical and grammatical function is supported by a written tradition of doctrine and discussion. Nevertheless the melodic content of this cantillation differs in each Diaspora area and is transmitted by a purely oral tradition (cf. *Masoretic Accents, Musical Rendition).

Although this oral tradition cannot convey information of its own past, some motives (of both the Ashkenazi and the Sephardi tradition) have been preserved in notation from the beginning of the 16th century onward. Thus even for this single category of Jewish music, the "art" and "folk" components, the historical and ahistorical, musical and extra-musical, and the local and universal are woven together so tightly that no single strand can serve as the base for any generalization.

As in all other parts of the mainstream tradition of music in Jewish culture, the notated document is not the point of departure, but a fortunate find which may occur on the way but more often is absent. The same holds for autonomous treatises on the "art of music," whether technical or philosophical. Literary sources of all kinds are the main storehouse of historical fact, and very often the only source, since it is here that Jewish life has always documented itself most fully, including its musical actions and thoughts. Yet another important source are the relics of actual musical instruments (especially for the biblical period) and the depictions of instruments and music making ranging from the dawn of history through *illuminated manuscripts to the photographs of *klezmer* ensembles in Eastern Europe before the Holocaust. The living oral traditions preserved and studied through sound recording, followed by sophisticated techniques of acoustical analysis and musical transcription, are equal in importance to the written, notated, and visual relic, and the application of the historical evidence can very often give them a great measure of historical dimension. Finally, there are the external sources. Judicious comparisons with the musical heritage of those cultures, with which the Jewish people came into contact, taking and – especially in the case of the formation of Christianity – also giving, can yield valuable insights. In addition, through still wider comparisons, even with historically unrelated cultures, Jewish music can be put into the overall perspective of the music of mankind.

The following survey of the sources is intended to give a general picture of the situation.

WRITTEN SOURCES OF DIRECT AND CIRCUMSTANTIAL EVIDENCE

Most of these do not appear as independent literary units but as parts of larger works. Potentially, the field includes the entire written heritage of Jewish culture. Some source categories have proved to be particularly fruitful in information, such as rabbinic Responsa, community registers and regulations, the literature of philosophy and the sciences, the early Midrash, travelers' accounts and various kinds of traditional exegesis. In many cases, textual criticism must be applied before the source can be utilized. Manuscripts of medieval and later poetry very often contain indications that the poem is to be sung "to the tune of..." (*be-laḥan, be-noʿam, be-niggun*); even if the tunes themselves cannot be recovered, the existence of the repertoire itself is thus documented. When the tunes are taken from a gentile environment, which uses notation – as in the German-speaking areas – even the tunes themselves can often be recovered from contemporary manuscripts or printed music. A further stage is reached by the libretti of the cantata-like works, which were written mainly in Italy from the 16th century onward. The music for some of these has also survived or still waits to be recovered from the archives; but even if only the texts remain, they often contain indications such as *aria*, *solo*, and *duetto*. Finally, there are also a certain number of theoretical and practical treatises on music, as independent works or more often as chapters in larger treatises. Except for the "cantors' books" (such as Solomon Lipschitz' *Teʿudat Shelomo*, Offenbach, 1718), the material naturally reflects the theories and practices of the surrounding culture, in the Islamic regions of Spain and the Near East or in Italy and France. Direct biographical and social evidence can be gleaned from inscriptions (including tombstones), community registers, the **Memorbuch* sources, and other archival material. A special contribution is made by extra-Jewish sources. Both non-Jewish writers and apostates from Judaism often give very detailed descriptions of musical practices in Jewish society, in works written for enlightenment or polemic, and echoes of the musical life of a Jewish community are also bound to appear in official documents of the local and state authorities. They range from a tax collector's list from Ptolemaic Egypt, mentioning "Jacob the son of Jacob, an aulos-player," to the petitions of gentile musicians to the municipality of Prague against their Jewish competitors in the 17th century.

THE MATERIAL RELICS AND ICONOGRAPHY

For the biblical and Second Temple periods, the written sources are complemented by literally hundreds of archaeological finds from Palestine itself. The soil conditions of Palestine are generally not favorable to the survival of instruments made of organic material, such as drums or string instruments. The archaeological finds, including metal cymbals, bells, pottery rattles, bone and ivory clappers, however, are effectively supplemented by figurines, frescoes, mosaics, pottery decorations, graffiti, images on coins, etc. External sources, such as the Phoenician ivories and bowls which reached the neighboring countries by way of commerce or booty, the decorations of synagogues in the early Diaspora (particularly important for the history of the form of the *shofar*), or the trumpets depicted in relief on the Arch of *Titus, further add to the evidence. It is, therefore, no longer necessary to "illustrate" the story of music in ancient Israel by archaeological finds from the Egyptian or Mesopotamian cultures. Such material may still be used for purposes of comparison, but only if corroborated by a local find.

The correlation of these material relics with the textual ones, above all the Bible, is a task as difficult as it is important. In later periods, the wide choice of instruments in other cultures is limited, for Jewish society, to the *shofar* and simple noisemakers, such as decorative bells on the *rimmonim* of the synagogal scrolls or the various forms of rattling and banging devices for *Purim. The iconographical evidence, however, is to be found in many sources: illuminated manuscripts and marriage contracts, printed books (especially those written by gentiles on "Jewish customs"), synagogue decorations, embellished ritual objects, and, in later periods, even portraits.

NOTATED SOURCES

As indicated above, one cannot expect the notated sources of Jewish music to be plentiful. For the entire period before the 19th century, these notations come only from the settlements of the Ashkenazi, Italian and European Sephardi communities (except for the earliest specimen so far discovered, the 12th-century notations of *Obadiah the Norman Proselyte, which was found in the Cairo *Genizah*). These documents are most conveniently divided into two categories: notations reflecting oral tradition, liturgical, religious, and secular; and manuscript or printed compositions in the style of contemporary art music.

Several German humanists of the 16th century included specimens of masoretic cantillation in their works on the Hebrew language, *masorah*, etc. The best known of these is the notation in Johannes *Reuchlin's *De accentibus et orthographia linguae hebraicae* (Haguenau, 1518). Some 15 other gentile writers up to the end of the 18th century feature such notations of masoretic cantillation in works on Judaist subjects and later on also in chapters on the "Music of the Hebrews" in histories of music. As a rule, they copied and recopied the specimens from their predecessors, so that the total stock of notated documentation rises very slowly. The most prominent additions are those by Athanasius Kircher (*Musurgia Universalis*, Rome, 1650), who features the German-Italian cantillation which he heard in a Roman synagogue; by Daniel Jablonski, in his edition of the Hebrew Bible (Berlin, 1699), where a specimen of notated cantillation of the Pentateuch according to the tradition of the Amsterdam Sephardi community was supplied by David de Pinna (cf. *Masoretic Accents, Musical Rendition); and the 12 specimens of Ashkenazi and Sephardi cantillation, psalm intonation, and hymn tunes collected by the composer Benedetto Marcello in Venice in order to base his collection of Psalm compositions, *Estro poetico-armonico* (1724–27, and subsequent editions), on "authentic Jewish tunes." They are featured in his own notation at the head of the respective settings. The musical scholar Giovanni Battista Martini gathered all the notations of his predecessors in the first volume of his *Storia della Musica* (Bologna, 1757–81, repr. facsim. 1967), whence they were taken over (with one omission) by Johann Nikolaus Forkel in his *Allgemeine Geschichte der Musik* (Leipzig, 1788–1801, repr. facsim., 1967).

A few notations of other kinds of traditional music are found from the beginning of the 17th century onward, such as the "learning tune" of the Talmud, some of the songs of the Passover *seder*, the *Priestly Blessing, and the 13 religious folk song tunes printed by Elhanan Kirchhan (Kirchhain) in his *Simḥat ha-Nefesh*, part 2 (Fuerth, 1726/27). The earliest cantorial manual found to date is that of Judah Elias of Hanover, dated 1740, and it is followed by many others, especially toward the end of the 18th century (cf. Aaron *Beer; Isaac *Offenbach). Whether the "Jew parodies" found in the works of several Renaissance and baroque composers actually reproduce what was heard in a synagogue or played by a Jewish musician still remains to be ascertained in each case.

Art music composed in the Western European style is documented by a certain number of scores and parts of scores from Italy, southern France and the "Portuguese" community of Amsterdam. The earliest work of this kind is Salamon de *Rossi's *Ha-Shirim Asher li-Shelomo* (Venice, 1622/23); for a more extended description of these sources see *Cantatas, Hebrew.

ORAL TRADITION

The chief treasure house of Jewish music is the living oral tradition – the many thousands of melodies and variants still current in the synagogues, schools, and homes in all Jewish communities, which adhere, or at least have kept in some measure, to the ways of the past. Their systematic collection, now being made by sound recording, is an awesome and theoretically endless task. A fairly representative selection of several regional traditions was collected by A.Z. *Idelsohn in Jerusalem at the beginning of the 20th century and published in his *Thesaurus of Hebrew-Oriental Melodies* (10 vols. 1914–32): Yemen, Iraq, Persia (with some material from Bukhara and Dagestan), the "Jerusalem Sephardic" tradition, Morocco and Eastern Europe. Earlier and contemporary collections of synagogal music (see bibliography), mainly of the Ashkenazi and European Sephardi areas, also contain varying amounts of truly traditional melodies, even if these are sometimes distorted by inadequate notation or attempts at "modernization." Much essential material still remains to be recorded.

[Bathja Bayer]

ARCHIVES AND IMPORTANT COLLECTIONS OF JEWISH MUSIC COLLECTIONS

Since most of the traditional Jewish music was transmitted orally from generation to generation, there was a need to create a sound archive to document the music and promote its study. This need was fulfilled by the establishment of the National Sound Archives in Jerusalem (NSA) in 1965 as a section of the Music Department of the Jewish National and University Library (JNUL). The musicologist Israel *Adler founded the archive incorporating the field recordings of Jewish music (and recordings of other people living in the area) that were made since the 1920s. The NSA also holds a large collection of commercial recordings of Jewish and Israeli music as well as music and other sound documents produced by Kol Israel (Israel Broadcast Authority).

The first great scholars who recorded Jewish music were Abraham Zvi *Idelsohn and Robert *Lachmann. Idelsohn's recordings are at the Austrian Phonogramm Archive in Vienna; those of Lachmann are mainly at the Berlin Phonogramm-Archiv but some copies as well as unique records are at the NSA.

Important collections at the NSA are known by the names of their creators such as: The Robert Lachmann collection (300 wax cylinders, which are copies of the originals of Berlin), 960 unique ethnographic records, most of which are made of tin, and 167 early commercial records of Oriental music. Robert Lachmann (1892–1939) recorded in North Africa and in Palestine. His interest was Oriental music. His recordings were made during the 1930s. His lectures and the musical demonstrations survived and are preserved at the NSA and at the Music Department (Mus. 26). Other collections are that of Johanna *Spector, who recorded in the late 1940s and early 1950s, including about 60 hours of music performed by Jewish immigrants just arriving in the new State of Israel from Yemen, Tunisia, Morocco, Pakistan, and Iraq as well as the

Samaritans of Israel; the collection of Leo *Levi made during the late 1950s and the 1960s, including about 70 hours of Jewish musical traditions of the Italian Jews, Greek Jews, and Jews from Holland, Ethiopia (in Israel), Georgia, Czechoslovakia, and other locations; and the collection of Edith *Gerson-Kiwi, who was a student of Lachmann, including 700 records and 240 reel-to-reel tapes of new immigrant Oriental traditions made between the 1950s and 1970s.

A historical collection of commercial records and broadcasting material is included in the Jacob Michael Collection, collected in New York during the 1950s and 1960s. The Jacob Michael collection contains 3,000 records and 480 tapes, mostly of Yiddish radio material.

Since 1965 the NSA has continuously expanded its collections by promoting new recordings both through fieldwork and recordings at the NSA studio. Most of the Jewish liturgical recordings are made in the studio or other locations, but not during actual prayer services, since it is forbidden to use any electrical equipment on the Sabbath and holidays. The NSA also benefits from donations from scholars who deposit their recordings at the NSA; to mention just a few of them: Amnon *Shiloah, Shoshana Weich-Shahak, Mark Kligman, Yaakov Mazor, Simha *Arom.

Since 2000, the Depository Law for books and prints in Israel has been expanded to include all non-book material. Thus a copy of all CDs and videotapes produced in Israel must be deposited at the NSA. Also, recordings made by Kol Israel during the 1950s and the 1970s were deposited at the NSA. These include mainly Israeli songs, Israeli art music, and some traditional music. The NSA catalogue is available online on the JNUL website. It is open to the public (at the JNUL) and serves mainly scholars and educators. The NSA continues to collect, preserve and publish its collections.

Other collections in Israel are at The Institute for Religious Jewish Music – *Renanot*, which has its own archive as well as copies at the NSA. It contains recordings of experts in Jewish musical performance, especially *ḥazzanim* of different traditions and their liturgical repertoire. The Beit Hatefutsot Music Center has a good collection of commercial recordings, which are available on site. All the departments of music and musicology in Israel have collections of recorded sound; however, their focus is not on Jewish music.

In America, universities, libraries, museums and Jewish institutions also have collections of recorded sound. Some of the important collections of Jewish music are: The Robert and Molly Freedman Jewish Music Archive, which was donated to the University of Pennsylvania's Rare Book and Manuscript Library. The Freedman Jewish Music Archive comprises over 1,800 recordings, primarily in Yiddish and Hebrew. The Harvard University Judaic Library has a large collection of Israeli popular music. The YIVO Institute in New York holds a good collection of commercial and broadcasting material of Yiddish music. The Library of Congress Folklife Center and the Sound Archives also have Jewish recordings, both field recordings and commercial records.

Some institutions and private music lovers and collectors provide Jewish music databases and music online for research and teaching, for example Hazzanut Online and Virtual Cantor.

[Gila Flam (2nd ed.)]

HISTORY

BIBLICAL PERIOD

The Bible is the foremost and richest source for knowledge of the musical life of ancient Israel until some time after the return from the Babylonian Exile. It is complemented by several external sources: archaeological relics of musical instruments and depictions of musical scenes; comparative material from the neighboring cultures; and post-biblical sources, such as the writings of *Philo and *Josephus, the *Apocrypha, and the *Mishnah. A truly chronological ordering of the biblical evidence on music is hardly possible, since it frequently happens that a relatively late source attributes certain occurrences to an early period, in which they could not have existed. A case in point is the chronicler's reports about the ordering of the Temple music by King David. Many details – above all the prominent status of the Levitical singers, which almost overshadows that of the priests – are probably a projection back from the chronicler's own time. Some of the reports may even be nothing more than an attempt to furnish the Levitical singers with a Davidic authorization in order to strengthen their position. It is therefore more prudent to draw a synthetic picture in which most of the facts can be assumed to have existed for at least a considerable part of the time.

The mythical dimension of music is represented in biblical tradition only by the story of Jubal, who was "the ancestor of all who play the *kinnor* and *uggav*" (Gen. 4:21; for names of instruments see below). Another relic of the same kind may well be found in the allusion, in God's speech to Job, to the day on which the creation was finished, whereupon, "the morning stars sang together and the Sons of the God[s?] Raised a shout of acclamation" (Job 38:7). Most of the evidence concerns the place of music in the cult. Music is conspicuously absent in the stories of the Tabernacle in the desert wanderings. The bells (perhaps only rattling platelets, see below) on the tunic of the high priest had no musical function but an apotropaic one. The trumpets served mainly to direct the movements of the camping multitude, and their function for arousing God's "remembrance" is common to their use in the sacrifice and in war (Num 10:1–10). In the transport of the Ark to Jerusalem by David, which is accompanied by the playing of lyres, drums, rattles, and cymbals (II Sam. 6:5; I Chron. 13:8), the context is that of a popular fête, not an established cult ritual. Even the description of the inauguration of Solomon's Temple in the first chapters of I Kings lacks an explicit reference to music. Only the trumpets are mentioned in the reconstitution of the Temple services in the time of Joash (II Kings 12:14).

In Chronicles, the musical element suddenly appears as the most prominent part of the service, with detailed and repeated "duty rosters" (and genealogies) of the levitic singers and instrumentalists, as planned by David and established by Solomon. Since the lists of the returned exiles from Babylon, in Ezra and Nehemiah, include a certain number of families of Temple singers, it can be assumed that, at least toward the end of the First Temple, there was already some kind of organized cult music in Jerusalem. On the other hand, there are grounds to believe that the role of music in the First Temple was minimal. In the sanctuaries outside Jerusalem, it was probably much more prominent: witness the "prophets' orchestra" at the high place of Gibeah (I Sam. 10:5) and Amos' fulminations against the external pomp in one of the cult centers of the northern tribes, perhaps in Shechem, "take away from me the roaring of thy songs and the playing of thy lyres will I not hear" (Amos 5:23).

After the return from Babylon, music as a sacred art and an artistic sacred act was gradually given its place in the organization of the Temple services. It seems that this did not pass without opposition. Some scholars have even tried to adduce a power struggle between the levites and the priests. Although the evidence does not mention music as a subject for quarrel, the striving of the levitic singers for prestige is implicit in the chronicler's descriptions, and may even be the reason for the insertion of the poem, or set of poems "By the waters of Babylon," in the collection of Psalms (Ps. 137). The weepers by the waters of Exile were not an abstract personification; they were the levitic singers, whom their captors would have join the other exotic court orchestras that the Assyrian and Babylonian kings kept for entertainment and took care to replenish by their expeditions of conquest. The court and temple orchestras of Mesopotamia in this period are the prototype for the Temple music established in Jerusalem after the return: a large body of stringed instruments of one or two types only (in Jerusalem *kinnor* and *nevel*); a small number, or a single pair, of cymbals; and a large choir. The trumpets of the priests constituted a separate body in every respect, with a ritual but not really musical function. In the earlier stages of religious organization, centered on inspirational ecstatic prophecy, the role of music was understandably important (cf. I Sam. 10:5 and the story of Elisha's musically-induced prophetic seizure in II Kings 3:15). David's playing and singing before Saul belongs to a related psychological aspect.

At coronations, the trumpets were blown as part of the formal proclamation (II Kings 11:14), and the spontaneous and organized rejoicings after victory in war were accompanied by women who sang, drummed and danced; (a practice still current among the Bedouin), cf. The Song of the *Sea, and the women's welcome of David and Saul in I Sam. 18:6–7. Music at popular feasts is described in Judges 21:19ff. Finally, the musical accompaniment at the feasts of the rich and, of course, at the king's court is also described several times, often with a note of reproach (II Sam. 19:36; Isa. 5:12; Amos 6:5; Eccles. 2:8). The musical expression of mourning is implicit in the verses of David's lament for Saul and Jonathan and explicit in the mention of the male and female mourners who repeated specially composed dirges (II Chron. 35:25). True folk music is mentioned only rarely, such as the songs and rhythmic shouts of the workers in the vineyards (probably the grape treaders) alluded to by the prophets.

The number of identifiable terms for musical instruments in the Bible comes to about 19. Some other terms, notably those appearing in the headings of the Psalms, have also been taken to represent instruments but probably mean some kind of indication of the melody. For many of the terms, a precise archaeological equivalent can already be proposed. Others still await the yield of future excavations. In the following section, the instruments will be listed and described briefly.

(1) *Asor* (עָשׂוֹר), see below, under *nevel*.

(2) *Ḥalil* (חָלִיל), double-pipe wind instrument, with the mouthpieces probably of the single-reed ("clarinet") type and probably made up of one melody pipe and one drone pipe. A folk and popular instrument, it was used for rejoicing and also in mourning ceremonies.

(3) *Ḥaẓoẓerah* (חֲצוֹצְרָה), trumpet, made of precious metal, generally silvers. Blown by the priests, it was used in the sacrificial ceremony, in war, and in royal coronations.

(4) *Kaitros/Katros*, see below, under "Daniel instruments."

(5) *Keren* (קֶרֶן), Aram. *karna* (קַרְנָא), see below, under *shofar*.

(6) *Kinnor* (כִּנּוֹר). A stringed instrument of the lyre family, constituted by a body, two arms, and a yoke. The Canaanite type of the instrument, which was certainly the same as used by the Israelites, is asymmetric, with one arm shorter than the other, and its body is box shaped. The instrument was probably of an average height of 20–23 in. (50–60 cm.) and sounded in the alto range, as evinced by surviving specimens from Egypt (which took over the form and even kept the name of the instrument from the neighboring Semites). The *kinnor* is the noble string instrument of Semitic civilization, and became the chief instrument of the orchestra of the Second Temple. It was played by David and was therefore held in particular honor by the Levites. According to Josephus, it had ten strings and was sounded with a plectrum (Ant., 7:306), and according to the Mishnah, its strings were made of the small intestines of sheep (Kin. 3:6).

(7) *Mashrokita* (מַשְׁרוֹקִיתָא), cf. below, under "Daniel instruments."

(8) *Mena*ʿ*ane*ʿ*im* (מְנַעַנְעִים), mentioned only in II Samuel 6:5 among the instruments played during David's transport of the Ark to Jerusalem. The parallel narrative in I Chronicles 13:8 substitutes *meẓiltayim* (cymbals). The numerous finds of pottery rattles make it highly probable, by etymological analogy (נענע "shaking"), that the term can be applied to them. After about the seventh century B.C.E., these rattles disappeared and were replaced by the newly-invented metal bell (see below, under *pa'amon*).

(9) *Meẓiltayim, Ẓilẓalim, Meẓillot* (צִלְצְלִים, מְצִילוֹת, מְצִלְתַּיִם), the first two forms probably standing for cymbals. The cymbals found in excavations were made of bronze, in the form of plates with a central hollow boss and with a metal

thumb-loop. The average diameter of the finds is about 4.5 in. (12 cm.). They were played by the Levites in the Temple. The *mezillot* of the horses, mentioned in Zechariah 14:20, are probably the same metal ball-jingles as those depicted on Assyrian reliefs.

(10) *Minnim* (מִנִּים), an unclear term (Ps. 150:5 and perhaps also Ps. 45:9), presumably a stringed instrument, and perhaps the lute, which was never an integral part of the Canaanite and Israelite instrumentarium.

(11) *Nevel* (נֶבֶל), a type of lyre, perhaps originating in Asia Minor, constructed differently from the *kinnor*-lyre – larger, and therefore of deeper tone. The coins of Bar Kokhba show it in a schematized form. According to Josephus, it had 12 strings and was played by plucking with the fingers (Ant., 7:306). Extra-biblical sources, which describe it under the name of *nabla* mention its "breathy" or "rumbling" tone. It was the second main instrument in the Temple orchestra. According to the Mishnah (Kin. 3:6), its strings were made of the large intestines of sheep. The *nevel asor* (נֵבֶל עָשׂוֹר), or, in its brief form, *asor* (Ps. 33:2; 92:4; 144:9), was perhaps a slightly smaller *nevel* with ten strings only.

(12) *Pa'amon* (פַּעֲמוֹן), mentioned only in Exodus 28:33–34 and 39:25–26 (and later by Josephus), as attached to the tunic of the High Priest alternating with the ornament called *rimmon* (pomegranate) and made of gold. The usual meaning of the term is a bell. Bells came into use in the Near East only in the seventh century B.C.E., so that the noise-making attachments to the high priest's garment in the desert Tabernacle could not have been bells proper. If the description in Exodus is not a pure projection back from the period of the First or Second Temple, the original *pa'amonim* must have been metal platelets. Later on, real bells substituted these. Most bells found in Palestine are small, made of bronze and have an iron clapper.

(13–14) *Pesanterin* פְּסַנְתְּרִין and *sabbekha* (סַבְּכָא/שַׂבְּכָא), see below, under "Daniel instruments."

(15) *Shalishim* (שָׁלִישִׁים), mentioned only in I Samuel 18:6–7, as played by women. By analogy with Ugaritic *tlt*-metal (and not *tlt* and *shlsh* as meaning "three"), these may be cymbals or struck metal bowls.

(16) *Shofar* (שׁוֹפָר), the horn of the ram or a wild ovine, and the only instrument to have survived in Jewish usage, probably identical with the *keren* (קֶרֶן) and *keren ha-yovel* (קֶרֶן הַיּוֹבֵל). In the Bible, its function is that of a signaling instrument especially in war; its famous appearance at the siege of Jericho must be understood in this sense and not as a magical noisemaker. The *shofar*-like sound at the receiving of the Ten Commandments is also a transfer from the same domain. Only after the *shofar* was taken into the service in the Second Temple did it regain its primitive magical connotation.

(17) *Sumponyah* (סוּמְפּוֹנְיָה), cf. below, under "Daniel instruments."

(18) *Tof* (תּוֹף), a shallow round frame drum, frequently played by women (cf. *Miriam), and associated with the dance.

(19) *Uggav* (עוּגָב), still unclear, but very probably not the wind instrument which medieval exegesis would have it to be. Perhaps the harp, which, like the lute (*minnim*?) was never an integral part of the Canaanite and Israelite instrumentarium.

(20) "Daniel Instruments." Daniel 3:5 describes, in Aramaic, an orchestra at the court of the Babylonian king, which includes the *karna, mashrokita, kaitros, sabbekha, pesanterin sumponyah*, "and all kinds of instruments." *Karna* is the horn, and *kaitros, sabbekha*, and *pesanterin* are but Aramaized versions of the Greek *kithara, sambyke*, and *psalterion*. *Mashrokita* is a whistling or piping instrument; *sumponyah* parallels the Greek *symphoneia*, which, in itself, means only "the sounding together." It is highly probable that the term does not stand for an instrument at all, but means the concerted sound of those mentioned before. The closing of the sentence, "and all kinds of instruments," would thus be nothing but an explanatory gloss.

The forms of music can only be surmised from the forms of those parts of biblical poetry, which are clearly meant to be sung. The most important of these are the Psalms, or at least a great part of the 150 poems gathered into the canon of the Psalter. Many of these, open with an "invitation to music" ("Let us go and sing," "Sing to the Lord a new song"). Before the body of the Psalm itself, a shorter or longer heading formula often appears, in which at least some of the elements have a presumably musical meaning. *Mizmor* and *shir*, also combined as *mizmor-shir* and *shir-mizmor*, are clearly of this kind, but their musical difference has so far remained obscure. The term *lamenazze'aḥ* has often been thought to mean "to the choirmaster." Most tantalizing of all are the phrases prefixed by *al* ("upon"?) such as "*al-ayyelet ha-shaḥar*" (Ps. 22, literally "upon the hind [?] of the dawn"), or "*al ha-sheminit*" (Ps. 6, literally "upon the eighth"), and others which are untranslatable even literally. The most reasonable hypothesis is that these designate certain melodic types. Whether the term *selah* which appears at the end of certain verses in many psalms (and often creates a tripartite division of the psalm) has a musical meaning still remains to be proved.

The sounds themselves are lost. Although comparative studies of living Jewish and other Near Eastern traditions may be able to point to certain melodic and formal elements as "very old," their attribution to the biblical or early post-biblical period can never be confirmed by objective proof.

SECOND TEMPLE PERIOD

Only the last part of this period is documented by contemporary literature (chiefly Philo, Josephus, and in the writings of the sectarians of Qumran). Much of the mishnaic narrative concerning music in the Temple service is based on eyewitness memories. The information is often very precise, such as the description of the daily morning sacrifice in Mishnah *Tamid* and the numbers of instruments in the Temple orchestra in Mishnah *Arakhin*. The figure of the Temple musician himself appears much more clearly. Thus there is Hogras ben

Levi, who was prefect of the singers and would not teach his own technique of virtuoso voice production to others (Shek. 5:1; Yoma 3:11). Of the instruments mentioned in the Bible, only the Temple instruments proper appear again: *kinnor, nevel, tziltzal* and *metziltayim, ḥaẓoẓerah*, and the newly accepted *shofar.* The *ḥalil* is also mentioned as a popular instrument, which was played in the Temple only on 12 days of the year (Ar. 2:3). The term *abbuv* (pipe) is used for the separate pipes of the *ḥalil.*

Other terms proposed as musical instruments by later commentaries, from the *Gemara* onward, are very probably not instruments at all, such as *niktimon, batnun, markof, iros.* Neither is the *magrefah*, a rake, which was noisily thrown on the floor after the cleaning of the altar to signal to the singers in their chambers to proceed to their stations, which talmudic exegesis later turned into the equivalent of the Byzantine organ.

A separate body of musical practice and doctrine was evolved by the dissident sectarians of the period. The choral singing of the *Therapeutae in Egypt is described by Philo and Josephus and seems to be the musical base of some of the hymns found in the Dead Sea Scrolls. The sectarians seem to have eschewed the use of musical instruments, holding "the fruit of the mouth," i.e., singing, as the more pure expression of devotion. Some passages in their writings and in Ben Sira may indicate the existence of ideas, which approach very closely to the sphere of musical, or rather musical-poetical theory. The catastrophe in 70 C.E. put an end to the Temple-centered music of the Jewish people and opened a new period, in which the *synagogue became the focal point of creativity in word and tone.

[Bathja Bayer]

THE EMERGENCE OF SYNAGOGUE SONG

Late Hellenistic civilization made music an all-penetrating cultural activity. The Eastern scene was dotted with theaters, arenas, and circuses where singers and virtuosos flocked together at musical contests (organized even by Herod; Jos., Ant., 15:269ff.; 16:137). Amateur philosophers at social gatherings of every kind discussed music. Jingling, banging, and rattling accompanied heathen cults, and the frenzying shawms of a dozen ecstatic rites intoxicated the masses. Amid this euphoric farewell feast of a dying civilization, the voices of nonconformists were emerging from places of Jewish and early Christian worship; *Philo of Alexandria had already emphasized the ethical qualities of music, spurning the "effeminate" art of his gentile surroundings. In the same spirit, early synagogue song intentionally foregoes artistic perfection, renounces the playing of instruments, and attaches itself entirely to "the word" – the text of the Bible.

The new style of Jewish music made its appearance at a specific and fateful moment. When the destruction of the Temple in 70 C.E. demanded a complete rearrangement in the religious, liturgical, and spiritual fields, music became involved in several ways. The abolition of Temple worship also put an end to the refined instrumental art of the levites. The use of instruments in the synagogue service was prohibited (and remained so, with certain exceptions), leaving music a strictly vocal art. Needless to say, this limitation left its imprint on musical style and form. Moreover, the musical skill of the Levitic singers and their tradition, accumulated over generations, were not utilized in synagogue song, and their professional teaching and rules had not survived in writing. Synagogue song was thus a new beginning in every respect – especially with regard to its spiritual basis.

In the new era, prayer was to take the place of sacrifice in providing atonement and grace (RH 17b). Levitical music had been an integral part of the order of sacrifices (Er. 13:2; Ar. 11a; TJ, Pes. 4:1, 30c). Its nature probably was to be as pure and flawless as the offering itself, for it was directed at the heavens and not at a human audience. It must have striven for objective and transcendental beauty and have been "art music." The task of synagogue song was a different one. The individual and the congregation both appeal to God by means of the spoken word. Prayer, regarded as "service of the heart" (*'avodah she-ba-lev*), had to express a broad scale of human feelings: joy, thanksgiving, and praise, but also supplication, consciousness of guilt, and contrition. All these emotions urge subjective expression in song and human warmth, rather than abstract beauty. The strong human element in synagogue music made itself acutely felt as soon as the professional solo singer began to appear. Before this, however, any member of a congregation could be called up to lead in prayer as a "delegate of the community" (*sheli'aḥ ẓibbur*). The gift of a fine voice obliged a member of the community to accept the function of lay precentor (PR 25: PdRK 97a).

Among the different singing styles in which the early nonprofessional *sheliḥei ẓibbur* may have performed, are elementary ones that can be ascribed with certainty to the early synagogue. They are suited to a gathering of people assembled for singing prayer and praise and for the majority of whom artistically contrived song and complicated tunes were normally out of range. Such congregations had to be cemented together by a kind of music that was easily grasped and performed. The musical forms of psalmody, chanted Bible reading, and prayer tunes bases on a simple melodic patternfullfil these conditions. These are the archetypes of synagogue song and have been preserved by the whole range of Jewish communities over the ages.

THE ROOTS OF SYNAGOGUE SONG IN THE NEAR EASTERN COMMUNITIES (C. 70–950 C.E.)

The Formation of the Basic Pattern (c. 70–500 C.E.)
A strong similarity of style can be detected in the recitation of the Psalms or chapters from other biblical books by different Jewish communities. Exactly the same recitation style is to be found in the most ancient traditions of the Catholic, Orthodox, and Syrian churches. Since there was a close contact between the faiths only at an early period, the musical structure or styles of singing must have been accepted by Christianity

together with the Holy Scriptures themselves. Many of its different forms, which are still employed by Jewish communities in many different parts of the world, were also described in ancient literature. The findings point to a common source of Bible song in the early synagogue.

PSALMODY. The singing of Psalms occupies an important place in Jewish and in Christian worship. Both creeds share a musical pattern, traditionally and also in musicological parlance known as psalmody (Greek-Christian *psalmodia*). Its outlines and internal organization follow closely those of the poetic form. Each psalm may consist of a smaller or greater number of verses, without being organized in symmetrical stanzas. Accordingly, the melody of one verse may become a musical unit, which is repeated, as many times as there are verses in the psalm. Most of the verses are subdivided into two equal parts (hemistichs) by a caesura; similarly, the psalmodic melody is given a bipartite structure. The biblical verse is formed and characterized solely by the number of its stressed syllables, disregarding completely how many weak syllables there are between the stresses. The verse of a psalm may consequently vary widely in length, since the overall number of syllables is not constant. The tune has to be adaptable to these floating conditions; a "recitation note," which may be repeated according to the particular situation, provides for the required elasticity.

In practice, the singer of a psalm verse reaches the "recitation note" through a short initial motion of the voice, dwells on the former for the main part of the text, and concludes the first hemistich with a medial cadence. The second hemistich is performed in the same manner, but concludes with a final cadence. Thus the basic psalmodic formula consists of:

Initial motion/recitation note/medial cadence//
initial motion/recitation note/final cadence (see Mus. ex. 1).

The simple melodic material of this basic formula can be grasped and reproduced by an average audience after listening to a verse or two. In this respect, psalmody is a truly collective genre of music. Its aesthetic and psychological effect is governed by the recurrent repetition of the same melodic phrase – an element of stability coupled and contrasting with the constantly changing text. The tune, after a few repetitions, loses all its interest: the attention automatically turns to the words, which continually offer something new. The accompanying vocal inflections merge and form an acoustical background which infiltrates the subconscious and creates a distinct mood, which eventually becomes associated with a certain feast or time of prayer or with grief and other emotions. The unchanging repetition of the formula throughout a psalm, which is the rule in Gregorian chant, is, in fact, seldom practiced in Jewish song. Apparently, even an unsophisticated congregation wanted to avoid dullness and to enliven the sound of the Davidic hymns (Song R. 4:4).

One line of development in psalmody led to the distribution of the performance between groups of singers. Responsorial psalmody was described as early as the Mishnah (Suk. 3:11; Sot. 5:4) and both Talmuds (Sot. 30b; Suk. 38b; TJ, Suk. 3:12, 53d). Precentor and congregation alternated in singing full verses or hemistichs; the precentor may intone the beginning and the choir takes over; or the choir may sing the concluding words. Moreover, a verse or part thereof may serve as refrain, "like an adult reading the *Hallel*, and they respond to him with the initial verse [as, e.g., in the Song of the Sea]: Moses said, 'I will sing unto the Lord,' and they say, 'I will sing unto the Lord'; Moses said, 'for he hath triumphed gloriously,' and they say, 'I will sing unto the Lord'…" This *baraita*, transmitted in the name of R. Akiva (d. 136 C.E.) and some of his contemporaries, treats the various forms of responsorial psalmody as

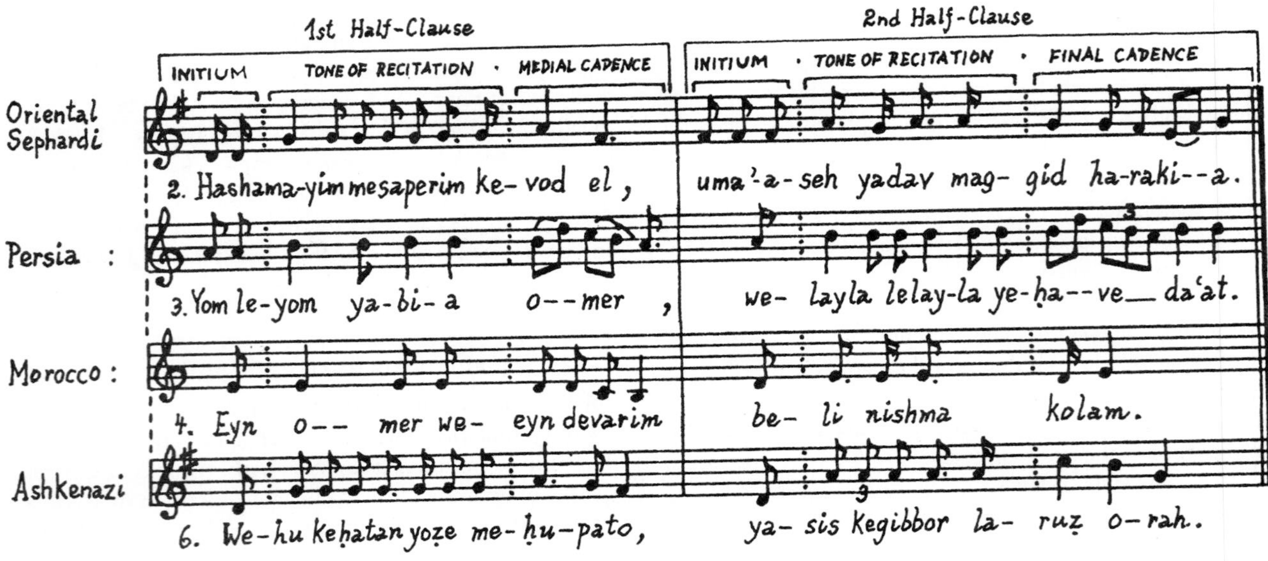

Example 1. The basic formula of psalmody. Verses of Psalm 19, as chanted in various communities. After Idelsohn, Melodien, *vol. 4, no. 25 (Oriental Sephardi):* ibid., *vol. 3, no. 51 (Persia);* ibid., *vol. 3, no. 171 (Morocco): I. Lachmann,* Awaudas Yisroeil, *vol. 1, 1897, no. 154 (Western Ashkenazi).*

old and well established. It demonstrates the transformation of the first hemistich into an actual refrain. The exclamation "Hallelujah" may be given this role when it is inserted at discretion between verses. This practice was described by Rava (c. 300 C.E.; Suk. 38b), and is found in the Christian tradition as *Psalmus alleluiatus*, and is still perpetuated by the Yemenite Jews (see mus. ex. 2a)

Additions alien to the biblical text are very rare in Jewish tradition (mus. ex. 2b) but have become the rule in the antiphonal psalmody of the churches. The Greek term *antiphonos* originally meant alternate singing in different pitches (e.g., by men and women or men and boys); Philo heard this performed by the sect of Therapeutae. However, worship in the synagogue, which was a congregation exclusively of men and lacked a separate clergy, was unfavorable to the formation of permanent choirs, and the embellishment of a psalm was contrary to the obligation of faithfulness to the holy text. There was no limitation, however, on the strictly musical development of psalmody, with the basic formula serving as a mere skeleton for more complex forms. The musical evolution is achieved mainly by means of variation – just as the poetic language of the Psalms draws largely upon variation within the framework of *Parallelismus membrorum*. Once again, musical composition enhances the poetry.

Jewish psalmody prefers to have hemistichs recited on different tone levels, which is very exceptional in Plain song. Moreover, the recitation note need not remain rigid but may hover around its axis, raising stressed syllables here, marking a subdivision there, or simply adorning the tune. The initial phrases may be redoubled as well as omitted. Finally, several psalmodic formulas may be joined within the same psalm. The device of variation is capable of producing true artistic effects by a gradual escalation of its resources as, for instance, in Psalm 29 for Sabbath eve as sung in Iran (Idelsohn, *Melodien*, III (1922), no. 3): here the melody gradually gains momentum and increasingly dense texture in accord with the intensification of the poetic images. Psalmodic music may change its features to a certain extent according to its multiple uses as well as the contents of the text, nevertheless, it must be content to strengthen, but never outdo, the effect of the words. The ancient pattern of psalmody is still extensively used in Jewish communities all over the world. It is worth noting that the detailed accents later added to the psalm text by the Masoretes were disregarded: the traditional manner of intoning psalms was already too deeply rooted (see also *Psalms, Musical Rendition).

BIBLE READING BY CHANT. Chapters from the Pentateuch and the Prophets are regularly read in the synagogue service, the other books of the Bible being reserved for certain feasts. It is characteristic of the synagogue that the Bible is never read like speech or declamation; it is always chanted to mu-

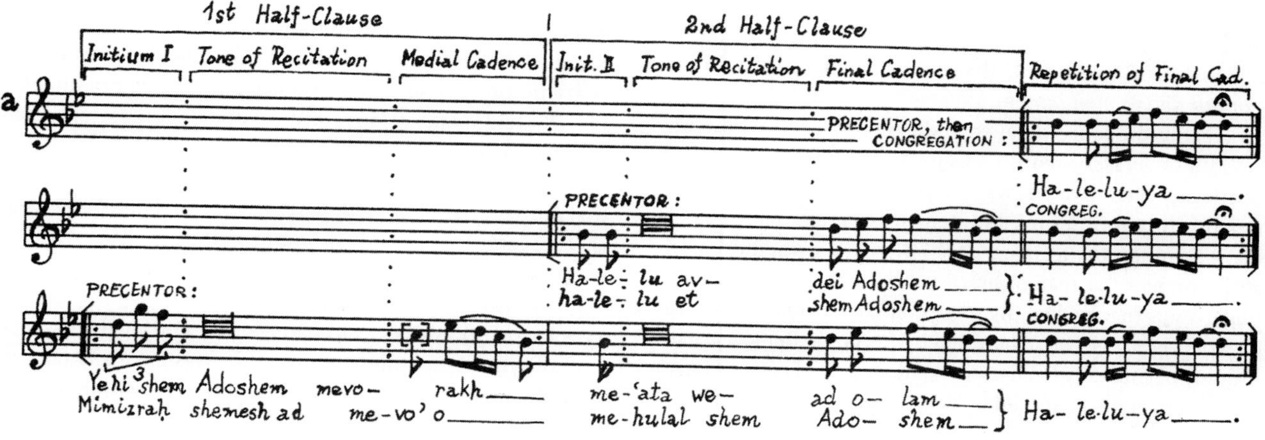

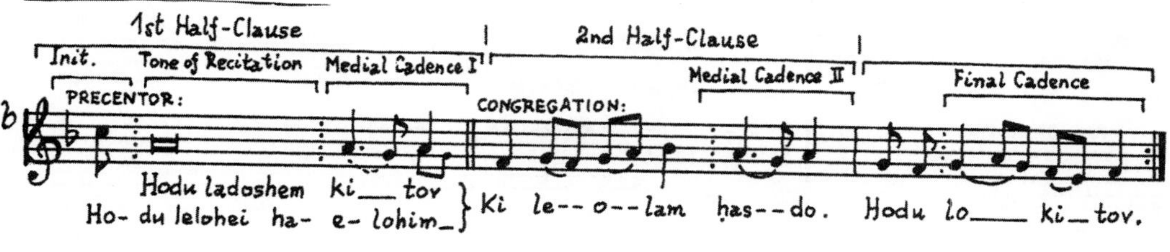

Example 2. Responsial psalmody. (a) Hallel *Psalm 113, as chanted in Yemen, with a Hallelujah response by the congregation after each verse, similar to the Gregorian* Psalmus alleluiatus. *After Idelsohn,* Melodien, *vol. 1 no. 32; (b)* Hallel *Psalm 136, as chanted in Iraq, with the unwritten response,* Hodu Lo ki tov *(Praise Him for [He] is good), by the congregation after each verse. After Idelsohn,* Melodien, *vol. 2, no. 23.*

sical pitches and punctuated by melodic cadences attached to clauses and periods. The reading of the Bible at home or at school is performed in the same way (see also *Masoretic Accents, Musical Rendition). This custom is strange to European habits. The ancient Greeks already knew well how to distinguish between the rising and falling of the voice in rhetorical speech or stage declamation on the one hand, and true musical intervals, on the other. When the Church took over biblical chanting from the synagogue, its Roman branch retained the chant in a simple form and did not develop it any further. Eastern Christianity, however, embarked on its own development and elaboration of scriptural chanting, which took a course parallel to the developments within Judaism.

There is ample evidence of Bible chant in Jewish sources as early as the second century C.E., by which time it was an old and well-established custom. In the third century, Rav interpreted the verse "And they read in the book, in the Law of God… and caused them to understand the reading" (Neh. 8:8) as a reference to the *piskei teʿamim*, i.e., punctuation by means of melodic cadences (Meg. 3a). Still earlier, Rabbi Akiva expressed his demand for daily study – also executed in chant – by the words "Sing it every day, sing it every day" (Sanh. 99a). Finally, Johanan, head of the Tiberias Academy (d. 279), formulated the central idea of chant in this categorical manner: "Whoever reads [the Torah] without melody and the studies [Mishnah] without song, to him may be applied the verse (Ezek. 20:25): Wherefore I gave them also statutes that were not good, and ordinances whereby they should not live" (Meg. 32a). As an external witness, Jerome (c. 400 C.E., in Bethlehem) testifies that the Jews "chant off" the Torah (*decantant divina mandata*: PL 24. 561).

Talmudic sources state that the biblical verse was subdivided into clauses according to its meaning and the rhythm of speech. This division was called *pissuk teʿamim* and was strictly an oral tradition, the transmission of which was incumbent upon the teachers of children. Their method of instruction was the ancient practice of chironomy – hand and finger signs that evoked the medial, final, and other cadences of Bible chant (Ned. 37b; attested by R. Akiva, Ber. 62a). Chironomy had already been used by the singers of ancient Egypt and was later also adopted by the Byzantines. Jews practiced it in the time of the masoretes, of Rashi (comm. on Ber. 62a) and, until recently, in Italy and Yemen. On the other hand, their absence in the sources indicates that there were no written "accents" (*teʿamim*) during the Talmudic period. These were gradually developed and introduced – together with vocalization – by the masoretes in the second half of the first millennium ("Although the cadential division of the verses and the reading tune were given at Mount Sinai, they were uttered according to oral tradition and not to accent marks in the book" *Maḥzor Vitry*, par. 424; 11th century). The nature of this primitive, unwritten Bible chant can be inferred from the present custom of some communities, notably the Yemenites and Bukharans, which still disregard the written accents and read the Bible in a much simpler manner, using only the well-known cadences of psalmody plus an intermediate stop (see Mus. ex. 3).

The antiquity of this modest kind of chanting is proven by its existence in the Roman Church. Like psalmody, it appears to have been accepted there as a body foreign to Western musical concepts and remained, therefore, in its primitive state.

Psalmody and melodic reading are common traits of all the "peoples of the Bible." Repeated attempts to find an archetype of it in pagan antiquity have not succeeded. Melodic enunciation has been connected with Bible recitation from the very beginning and has accompanied the Holy Scriptures through their translation into every tongue. In contrast to sensualist tendencies in art, which take the Bible text as a mere opportunity for writing a beautiful piece of music, Bible chant is the genuine expression of a spiritual concept and, as such, is opposed to the general trend of the Hellenistic period. Its restriction to a small range of notes and limited ornamentation is intentional, not "primitive," with the purpose of ensuring that the melody will never interfere with the perception of the words and the apprehension of their meaning and spiritual message. As defined by Curt *Sachs, such music making is "logogenic" – proceeding from the word and serving the word (see *Masoretic Accents, Musical Rendition).

THE EARLY STYLE OF PRAYER CHANT. During the first period of synagogue song, the precentor was normally chosen from the ranks of the congregation, and his devotion did not

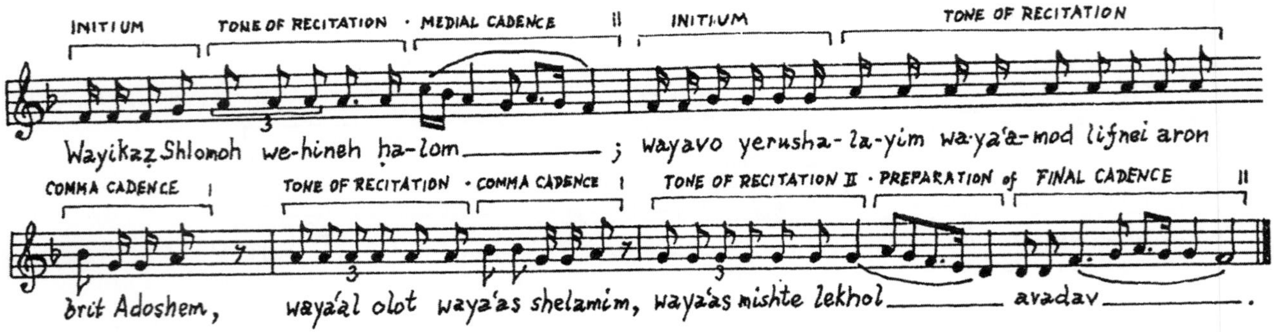

Example 3. Simple form of biblical cantillation. I Kings 3:15, as chanted in Bukhara to a psalmodic pattern. After Idelsohn, Melodien, *vol. 3, no. 138.*

always have to be balanced by musical gifts and skills. Prayer tunes thus had to be simple and, simultaneously, of a plastic and variable nature in order to be fitted to longer or shorter phrases of the prose texts without difficulty. These demands are met by the "prayer modes" (*nusaḥim*) traditional and common in the Eastern and Western synagogues of today. Although it is impossible to ascribe individual tunes heard today to the early synagogue with any degree of certainty, it is legitimate to speak of the principle of chanting according to a *nusaḥ*.

Jewish prayer chant is essentially an evolution of traditional melodic patterns classifiable as "*Tefillah*-mode," "*Yotzer*-mode," and so on. The melodic pattern of a certain *nusaḥ* consists of several motives, which are not in any fixed rhythm or meter, but are rather a melodic formula, which is apt to be expanded or shortened according to the text. The motives may be repeated or omitted, they may change places and, above all, they may be subjected to variation by the singer. Melodic patterns of this kind are used in Sephardi, Ashkenazi, and Oriental communities alike. Their nature may best be recognized from their adaptation to metrical prayer texts (see mus. ex. 4a), as well as to free recitation (mus. ex. 4b).

The musical effect of an Ashkenazi prayer mode rests on its "varied unity"; it establishes a common stock of motives for a whole group of prayers without imposing a rigid, unchanging framework upon it. The melodic development is stimulated by improvised variation – which has always been an important element in Jewish music (see **Nusaḥ*; **Shtayger*).

THE POPULAR BACKGROUND. Psalmody, melodic reading of Bible texts, and prayer chant were made to fulfill a function in collective Jewish worship; they grew organically from a popular treasure of forms, under the guidance of basic religious ideas. The latter excluded from worship the use of the multitude of instruments which were, in fact, in the hands of Jews in Palestine and Babylonia: the frame drum tabla (Ar. *duff*;) accompanied non-synagogal song and dance and pleased the women especially ("The sexagenarian as much as the six-year-old runs after the drum": MK 9b); the reed-pipe abbuv was blown; the long-necked lute tanbura (Ar. *ṭunbūr*) plucked. Workmen used to sing to lighten monotonous toil such as plowing, boat towing, or weaving (Sot. 48a). Song was heard in the tavern (Sanh. 101a), and every kind of musical entertainment at the fair (Ta'an. 22a; BK 86a see Rashi) and social gatherings (Sot. 48a).

Radical religious authorities of the Babylonian Jews opposed popular music making as unsuitable for a nation in distress (relying upon Sot. 9:11 and 14). Their negative attitude ("Song in the house – destruction at the threshold," Sot. 48a) became even more entrenched when the feudal aristocracy of Sassanian Persia made music part of their hedonistic enjoyment of life, and even the exilarch Mar *Ukba I, who was, according to the chronicle of the scribe R. Nathan ha-Bavli (written in the 10th century), a poet-musician himself and throughout the year composed and performed his own paeans of praise to the king, who allowed himself to be attended with music at his ceremonial levee (TJ, Meg. 3:2, 74a; Git. 7a). At this time Rav *Huna issued his famous prohibition of music, which, however, had undesirable side effects and was dropped by his successor *Ḥisda (Sot. 48a). Palestine was apparently spared this unrealizable prohibition. There was never any intention to interfere with the music making at wedding festivities (hillula); on the contrary, this was regarded as a religious duty (*mitzvah*).

Several legends tell of the rabbis' eagerness "to gladden the groom and bride" (Ber. 6b; TJ, Pe'ah 1:1, 15d, etc.). On these occasions, genuine responsorial singing was performed (Ber. 31a): an honored guest had to improvise a verse suitable for the company to answer with one of the current refrains (such as Ket. 16b–17a). Responsorial psalmody may have been influenced by such common customs. Antiphony, in its original meaning of alternating choirs of different pitch, was also employed at the popular level (Sot. 48a). Instrumental playing at the wedding hillula was officially encouraged, and this favorable attitude of the Talmud teachers became a guideline for later legal decisions.

It is not known when and why playing the flute before the bridal pair (rooted in ancient life and fertility symbolism) was abandoned; it was once a familiar and absolutely legal custom (BM 6:1). The same question arises with regard to flute playing at funerals, where this instrument symbolized life and resurrection; it was customary at the time of Josephus (Wars 3:437) and the Gospels (Matt. 9:23), and its legal aspects were still given consideration by the tannaim (Shab. 23:4; Ket. 4:4), but it, too, disappeared without any trace. Lamentation of the dead by wailing women could assume the form of a dirge (**kinah*, hesped) in responsorial patterns (MK 3:8; Meg. 3b; 6a); but it often remained a short acclamation (MK 28b), probably repeated to current melodic phrases. A funeral song of the Diaspora Jews is attested in Canon 9 of the Council of Narbonne in 589 (Juster, Juifs, 1 (1914), 368, n. 3).

A relationship between synagogal and domestic singing patterns has already been noted. Since responsorial and antiphonal song is found as a frequent practice among many peoples, it may be surmised that the related forms of psalmody also derived from popular usages. As far as can be judged from the necessarily one-sided talmudic sources, Jewish folk music remained relatively immune to the omnipresent Hellenistic influences. Near Eastern Jewry belonged to the Aramaic-speaking peoples (as evinced, for example, by the nomenclature of their musical instruments) and may have kept away from Greek theaters and circuses at the behest of their teachers (Av. Zar. 1:7; TJ, ibid., 1:7, 40a; Av. Zar. 18b, etc.). In the Diaspora, however, the Jews of Miletus, Antioch, and Carthage liked the stage and the arena (Juster, Juifs, 2 (1914), 239–41). Jewish (Purim?) plays were restricted by the Codex Theodosianus of 425 (ibid., 1 (1914), 360 n. 2). At any rate, the lasting influence of Hellenistic musical activities in the Jewish sphere cannot be proven.

Example 4. Structures of prayer modes (nusah),
(a) Sephardi: Musaf *of the High Holy Days;* Aleinu le Shabbe'ah. *Oriental Sephardi, After Idelsohn,* Melodien, *vol. 4 no. 249.* Ata Nigleta, *ibid., no. 254;* Adonai Sefatai Tiftah, *ibid., no. 233: European Sephardi (Leghorn), after F. Consolo,* Sefer Shirei Yisrael – Libro dei Canti d'Israele, *1892, no. 335.*
(b) Western Ashkenazi: prayers on feast days and the New Moon, blessing for Passover, after S. Naumbourg, Zemirot Yisrael, *vol. II. 1847, no. 141.*

IDEAS ABOUT MUSIC. The influence of religious law (*halakhah*) on the structure of synagogue music, such as the discontinuation of instrument playing and the entire Levitical tradition, has been noted above. To this should be added the rejection of the female voice from the service and other public performances, exemplified by Rav's harsh statement: "The voice of a woman is indecency" (Ber. 24a, etc.). The rabbi's indifference or hostility to the sound of music changes, however, in the aggadic parts of the Talmud, where many instances of true musical feeling and appreciation of the charm of sounds are recorded. The rabbis dwelled on King David's allegoric lyre, which was sounded by the midnight wind like an Aeolian harp (Ber. 4a, etc.), they perceived the "song of the ears of grain" in the field (RH 8a), and let trees burst into song (TJ, Ḥag. 2:1, 77a). They fostered ideas that became universal sources of artistic inspiration: the parallel singing of celestial music of the angels and the righteous (Ḥag. 12b; 14a; Av. Zar. 3b; Er. 21a; Sanh. 91b; Meg. 10b, etc.; Tosef. Sot. 6:2); and the "trump of doom" (later Midrashim: *Otiyyot de-Rabbi Akiva*, letter T; Midrash Daniel, etc.). In other Midrashim (of more or less disputed date), the eternal link between mystical and musical conceptions, already extant in some of the above-quoted Talmud passages, reveals its full strength in certain peculiar hymns aimed at inducing a visionary trance. These hymns were assembled in the treatise *Heikhalot Rabbati* ("All these songs Rabbi Akiva heard when approaching the *Merkabah and understood and learned before the heavenly throne what its servants sang unto it"). They are composed in a language rich in "word-music" and vocal harmony; and one can imagine them being sung to the repetition of short melodic phrases characteristic of suggestion-inducing and spell-casting songs all over the world.

The same *Heikhalot* treatise reveals a guiding idea of sacred song in legendary form: "R. Ishmael said: Blessed is Israel – how much dearer are they to the Holy One than the servant-angels! Since as soon as the servant-angels wish to proceed with their song in the heights, rivers of fire and hills of flames encircle the throne of glory, and the Holy One says: Let every angel, cherub, and seraph that I created be silenced before Me, until I have heard and listened to the voice of song and praise of Israel, my children!" Human song of praise is given preference over the pure and flawless beauty heard from the heavenly hosts, and the standards of sacred song are set by the warmth of devotion resounding from earthly voices, imperfect and human as they may be.

This concept differs from the basic idea of ecclesiastical song as laid down by Dionysius the Areopagite and repeated throughout the Middle Ages. This notion propounds that the perfect beauty of angelic song descends to the lower ranks in heaven and reaches earth as a faint echo. Church music endeavored by imitation to approach the heavenly model; it had to strive increasingly for superhuman, transcendental beauty, thus creating a perfect but cold product of art. This fundamental difference between the Jewish and Christian view of sacred music indicates what to look for in the evaluation of synagogue song. It must be judged by the perseverance of its original intention, which is to be an expression of human feelings, disregarding beauty for its own sake. Whenever, during its development, appreciation of the pleasant sound as such became prominent, this attitude was most often initiated by foreign influences. As a rule, however, the basic patterns set during its first period have survived as a permanent background of Jewish music.

Evolution of the Basic Pattern and Creation of New Forms (c. 500–950)

After the completion of the Talmud, c. 500 C.E., new developments began in the liturgical and musical fields. The Near Eastern communities maintained their leadership, and the innovations created there became an integral part of Jewish tradition in the entire Diaspora. During this time, as far as can be judged, Jewish music was spared serious conflict with foreign influences.

THE "LEARNED ART" OF BIBLE CHANT. According to the early, oral tradition of reading the Bible by chant, only a few main sections of a verse were distinguished by means of melodic cadences (see Mus. ex. 3 above). Although the text of the Hebrew Bible was fixed long since, every sequence of words could become meaningful only by the correct grouping of the words and a clear interrelation of clauses and sub-clauses. The division of a verse could become a matter of interpretation, or even ideology, and raise debates with dissenting sects or a foreign creed. It was no wonder that in epochs of insecurity a need was felt to mark the accepted infrastructure of biblical verses in an indisputable way – in writing. This was achieved by the masoretic accents which have accompanied the text ever since.

Written reading accents are a feature unknown in the Talmud (that is to say, until c. 500 C.E.). They appear to have developed from the sixth century onward. During the same period, the Syrian and Byzantine churches also introduced written reading signs. Even small groups like the Samaritans invented such signs, although the period of their origin is uncertain. No priority can be ascertained today, but the former hypothesis of a Hellenistic prototype has been finally abandoned, as has the idea of interdependence between the different accent systems. It was a general but variously realized tendency of this era to make a new attempt at a musical script – the first one since the ancient Greeks, and completely different from their method. Greek musicians had expressed single pitches by means of graphic signs, as is done in modern European notation. This method is based on analytical thought. Writing music with accents, however, rests upon the conception of complete melodic figures or motives, which are retained in the singer's memory. Their specific application in singing may be brought about by gestures of the hand (chironomy), as documented already in the talmudic era. The motive may be given a suggestive name (*etnaḥta* "sign of rest"; *zakef* "upright," etc.); the first letter of its name may be written above the text, as was done by the Babylonian masoretes.

Finally, freely invented signs could also be used, as was done by the masoretes of Tiberias.

The development of biblical accents (*taʿamei mikra*) was a prolonged process which was completed definitely only between 900 and 930 by Aaron b. Moses *Ben-Asher of Tiberias. This final and authoritative system was imposed upon the whole of Jewry. The earlier Palestinian and Babylonian accentuations fell into disuse and have only recently been recovered from rare manuscripts. The general trend of development was from simplicity to complexity. The masoretes "in good faith furnished the 24 biblical books with accents of correct judgment, with a clear manner of speech, with a sweetly enunciating palate, with beautiful oration… Whoever reads shall hear, whoever hears shall understand, and whoever sees shall grasp" (Moses Ben-Asher, autograph colophon of the Cairo Codex of the Prophets, dated 895 C.E.). They proceeded from the subdivision of a sentence by accent pairs (Babylonian system) to a total accentuation of one sign, and occasionally two, on every word. Having begun with the simple indication of the traditional places of the cadences, they ultimately arrived at a "learned art" of Bible chant, prescribing how the reader was to organize his recitation.

In evaluating the musical consequences of the Tiberian "total accentuation," one basic fact should be borne in mind: an accent can seldom be regarded as a detached, self-contained unit. Not only is a disjunctive accent ("king") most often accompanied by a conjunctive one ("servant"), but also several of these pairs are frequently combined to form typical groups. In music, motive groups or melodic phrases match these accent groups: a chanted Bible verse is made into a continuous chain of musical motives (see Mus. ex. 5) and is clearly distinguished from the old-fashioned, psalmody-like style (see Mus. ex. 3 above).

Since the single motives are often linked by a short bridge of linear recitation (see ex. 5), this kind of chant may also be likened to a string of beads. An entire chapter read in this manner resembles a mosaic in which the same pieces are assembled in constantly varying combinations.

The translation of the masoretes' intentions into music was not accomplished smoothly. First of all, the Tiberian system of accentuation is too detailed and complex to be followed perfectly by even the most scrupulous reader. Moreover, there were Jewish communities with closer ties to the Babylonian than to the Tiberian school; they accepted the Tiberian system as a matter of book learning, but interpreted in song only part of it (the king accents) or disregarded it altogether. Writers of the 14th and 16th centuries (Simeon b. Ẓemaḥ *Duran, Elijah *Levita) explicitly attest that the Sephardim who used to obtain books and teachers from Babylonia neglected all the servant accents and some of the kings as well, and they still do so today. In Iran and Yemen there arose hybrid styles of melodic reading in which the three or four cadences of the old style are permutated arbitrarily in order to comply with the Tiberian rulings. Some remote communities, such as that of Bukhara, continue to recite simply in the old, psalmody-like style (Mus. ex. 3 above). In this way, Jewish reading practices of today form a living museum of chanting styles as they were at different stages of their development.

THE LITURGICAL HYMN (PIYYUT). Although the composition of religious poetry most certainly did not break off with the destruction of the Second Temple, the introduction of hymns as an integral part of synagogue liturgy is ascribed to the sixth century. An old tradition (first recorded by *Yehudai Gaon c. 760) connects the admission of hymns into the synagogue with an interdiction against studying the law and reciting the *Shema Yisrael*, generally linked with the hostile edict of Emperor Justinian I promulgated in 553 (Juster, Juifs, 1 (1914), 369–77). This, however, is not sufficient to explain the continuing production of hymns over the centuries, the immense creative power invested in them, the mystical touch present since the very beginning, nor the musical elaboration which they brought about. Hymn writing and singing must be regarded rather as an elementary religious force, effective in Jewry as in every other faith, and one of the main promoting forces of musical evolution.

Example 5. Ashkenazi biblical chant according to the masoretic accents. I Kings 3:15, following the rendition of Joshua 1:1 in Idelsohn, Melodien, *vol. 2, 50 no. 11.*

The early designation of the genre, **ma'amad*, was soon replaced by the borrowed Greek word *piyyut*. The choice of a foreign term probably indicates the introduction of innovations, such as consequent rhyming and the division of a poem into stanzas of identical structure. In time, the stanza form became highly important to musical form: it offered the opportunity of changing the unarticulated cumulation of verses into a divisive organization of the song. This possibility, however, is hardly exploited in tunes of the older style. In present-day synagogue song, *piyyut* melodies continue the traditional usage of repeating the first line throughout the entire song. The cause is certainly the poetic rhythm, which remained as it was in biblical poetry: an equal number of stresses in the verses, occurring at unequal intervals because of the changing number of unaccentuated syllables in between. Thus, a well-known hymn of Eleazar *Kallir (early seventh century?) reads:

> Ṭal ya'asis ẓuf harim = 3 accents, 6 syllables
> ṭa'em bi-meodkha muvḥarim = 3 accents, 8 syllables
> ḥannunekha ḥaleẓ mi-masgerim = 3 accents, 10 syllables

A tune appropriate to such poems in "free rhythm" must be capable of extension or contraction according to the length of the text. In addition to psalmody and the principle of prayer chant, another solution to this problem was found by singing according to modal patterns, still practiced today by the Sephardim and the Eastern communities. The basic musical idea or modal pattern consists of not more than one or two tetrachords (four-tone rows); this framework is filled, in actual singing, with melodic curves, step patterns, and ornaments of every kind. A particular musical realization of the scale model will seldom be repeated, but every verse of the stanza offers a new variation of the preconceived pattern (Mus. ex. 6b).

This method of "endless variation" is characteristic of the Oriental style of Jewish song. Its Ashkenazi counterpart is more closely related to the *nusaḥ* structure of prayer chant (see above), being a plastic sequence of variable and interchangeable motives (Mus. ex. 6a). The Ashkenazi style is distinguished by the clear-cut outline of its motives and the retention of the recitation tone technique related to psalmody.

It should be understood that there is no other means of evaluating the historical forms of *piyyut* singing than by inference from present-day traditions. Tunes, which show archaic features and conform neatly to the poetical form, may be regarded, as a working hypothesis, as representative of the original style. The texts of the *piyyutim* contain a considerable admixture of mystical elements recognizable, inter alia, by the exuberant accumulation of divine attributes (found as early as in the hymns of the Qumran sect and later explicitly condemned by the *tanna'im*, Ber. 33b; Meg. 18a). The exact musical consequences of these tendencies are not known, but they caused the later *geonim* (Yehudai, Nahshon) to urge the general removal of hymns from the liturgy. However, hymnal song had captivated the hearts of the people to such a degree that this proved impossible. The rabbis, therefore, looked with a certain suspicion upon the principal exponents of *piyyut* singing, the precentors who by then had already become professional ministers.

THE ḤAZZAN AND THE SYNAGOGAL SOLO STYLE. *Piyyut* as sung art-poetry demanded the expertness of a gifted soloist,

Example 6a. Hymn-tune constructed as a chain of variated motifs. Ashkenazi melody for the kerovah *hymns for the High Holy Days: (a) for* Ne'ilah *of the Day of Atonement, Bavarian version c. 1800–40 (Loew Saenger, 1781–1843), after Idelsohn,* Melodien, *vol. 7 part 3, no. 211; (b) for* Shaḥarit *of the New Year, Frankfurt version c. 1883 after F. Ogutsch (1845–1922),* Der Frankfurter Kantor, *1930, no. 179; (c) for* Musaf *of the New Year, Ukrainian version, c. 1860–80, after J. Bachmann,* Schirath Jacob, *1884 no. 90; (d) for* Musaf *of the New Year, Jerusalem version of the Lithuanian tradition as noted in 1963, after J.L. Neeman,* Nusaḥ la-Ḥazzan, *vol. 1, 1963, part 2. no. 17; (e) Psalm 65:3, chanted at* Kol Nidrei *to motives A and B of the kerovah melody, "Polish" version, 19th century, after A. Baer,* Baal T'fillah, *1883^3, no. 1307.*

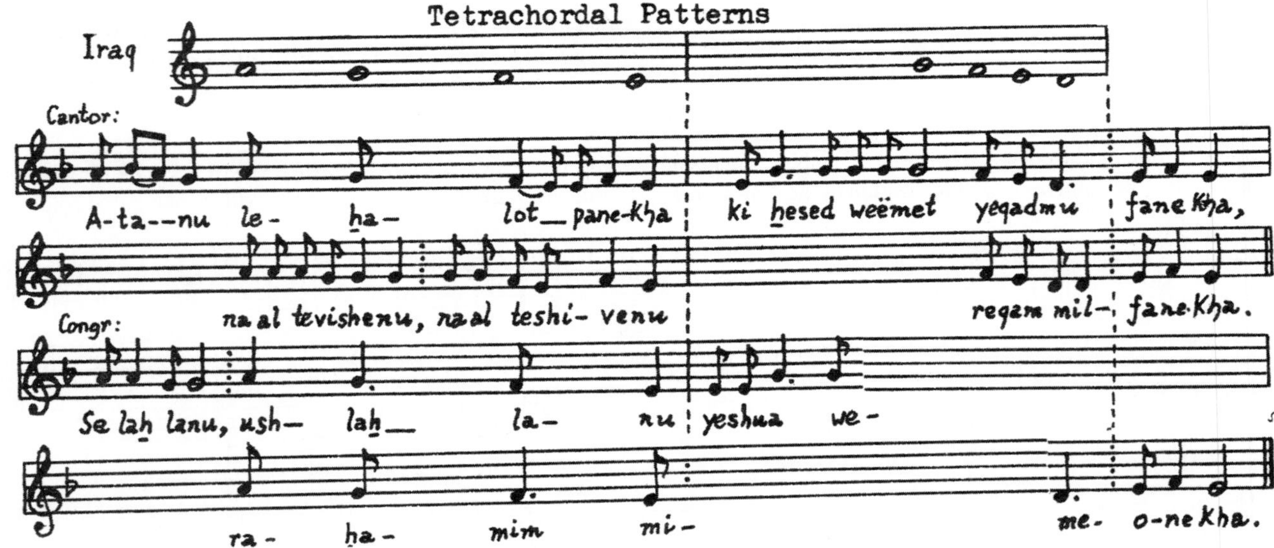

Example 6b. Hymn-tunes constructed of variations on a modal pattern. The penitential hymn, Atanu leḥalot. *Oriental Sephardi, after Idelsohn,* Melodien, *vol. 4, no. 95 and Iraq,* ibid., *vol. 2, no 45. For the same as sung in Persia to a pattern comprising one tetrachord only, cf.* ibid., *vol. 3, no. 40.*

especially when the singer himself was expected to compose both text and tune. A lay precentor could hardly continue to fulfill such a task. It is surmised that the early *paytanim* performed their creations themselves, having also composed or adapted the melody. It was at this period, in the last quarter of the first millennium, that the new function of the professional solo singer came into existence – presently the well-known figure of the **ḥazzan*. The title *ḥazzan* was not new. It had formerly designated an assistant of the *archisynagogus. In addition to several secular tasks, this functionary had to arrange and supervise the ceremonies in public worship. It was an honored post: the Code of Theodosius exempted its holders from taxes in 438 and Pope Gregory the Great endorsed it c. 600. It was reasonable enough also to require musical ability of applicants for the post of this synagogue master of ceremonies. The term *ḥazzanut*, derived from the title *ḥazzan* designates, either the official post or, more often, the specific melodies and musical style of the solo singer.

For the chronological determination of the *ḥazzan's* specialization in music, a *terminus ante quem* is to be found in

*Nahshon's decision of about 875–880: "A *ḥazzan* who knows *piyyut* shall not be admitted to the synagogue" (B.M. Lewin, *Oẓar ha-Ge'onim*, 1 (1928), 70). The assumption of the title *ḥazzan* by the singer probably took place during the ninth century. Since the function of *ḥazzanut* soon came to be passed on from father to son, this vocation became almost a closed social class, where it was the custom for a *ḥazzan* to marry the daughter of his master or of a colleague. The ties of certain families to a musical profession are important for the growth and early training of talents and, in the long run, for the preservation of a musical tradition. There is mention, for instance, of a family of *ḥazzanim* flourishing in Baghdad in the 10th and 11th centuries: Joseph *Albaradani, the "Great *Ḥazzan*" (d. 1006), left sons and grandsons who became successive incumbents of his position, and all of them also wrote *piyyutim*.

The close connection between *ḥazzanut* and *piyyut* is demonstrated by some letters preserved in the Cairo **Genizah* (S.D. Goitein, *Sidrei Ḥinnukh* (1962), 97–102; idem, in: *Tarbitz*, 29 (1960), 357f.). The congregations in medieval Egypt were always eager to hear new hymns, and the *ḥazzanim* were compelled to exchange *piyyutim* among themselves, write them down secretly from the singing of a colleague, and engaged in correspondence as far afield as Marseilles.

It is difficult to imagine the musical character of early *ḥazzanut*. One can, however, attempt to demonstrate the common features of Oriental and European *ḥazzanim* of today with comparable gentile melodies taken as a control group. In addition, the tunes noted down by Obadiah the Norman Proselyte in the first half of the 12th century is available for comparison. With due precaution, it may be said that *ḥazzanut* implies the free evolution of a melodic line (without reference to any system of harmony). The tune therefore proceeds by seconds and other small steps, while leaping intervals are avoided. The melodic texture is dense: there are no empty intervals, no extended notes that are enlivened by dissolution into small steps (Mus. ex. 7).

The *ḥazzan* must command a good measure of musical creativeness. He does not simple reproduce a preconceived piece of music, but must give final shape to the general outlines of a theme by an improvisation of his own. In this way, the stanza of a *piyyut* may develop in a series of variations on the traditional theme (Mus. ex. 8a)

This feature is already found in the tunes notated by Obadiah the Norman Proselyte (Mus. ex. 8b) in the 12th century. The expressive element so characteristic of *ḥazzanut* can also be discovered in Obadiah's notations. The music of a *piyyut* fragment exhibits the repetition of words, the expressive motives, and the lively "pulsation" around a single note that have remained the pride of the *ḥazzan* until today.

To sum up, musical tradition in *ḥazzanut* means a melodic pattern to be followed, the choice of a specific tetrachord or other scale, which is representative of a certain mood, or a stock of motives to be arranged and rearranged in changing melodic structures. The most ancient heritage of synagogue music cannot be confined to bar lines or enclosed in a framework of symmetric phrases. Its rhythm is as free as that of the Hebrew poetry of the time. It is worth noting that melodies in free rhythm have been preserved even in European communities, as a body separate from Western music.

MUSIC OF THE MEDIEVAL DIASPORA (C. 950–1500)

The close connection between musical development and changes in thought and national or social conditions is demonstrated perfectly by the changes which occurred in Jewish music as a result of the Islamic conquests, which introduced strong secular and cosmopolitan traits into the cultural life of the Near East, North Africa, and Spain. The Jewish mind does not favor revolutions in sacred music, but new and powerful elements were added to the ancient stock and gave rise to mutual reactions and interactions. In the field of secular music, however, there was a strong trend towards integration, often impeded by forced separation from the gentiles, but thrusting forward as soon as conditions allowed. This general picture is colored by the existence and interplay of different spiritual factors within Jewry itself, each of which contributed to the shaping of musical ideas and forms.

The beginning of a new period in Jewish music may be placed about the middle of the tenth century. By then, the accent systems of Bible chant had been completed; music was made a subject of philosophical reasoning; and sung poetry took on a new look by the introduction of meter and the aesthetic values connected with it. These developments in the spiritual and artistic fields went hand in hand with most important events and changes in the Near East. The conquest and unification of the Near Eastern countries by Islam brought the local Jewries into a larger world of relative liberty and openmindedness. Art and science were no longer restricted to the service of certain religious dogmas, and Jews were free to integrate themselves into the material and spiritual realms of the general culture, but the price was paid by giving up the administrative autonomy of the Jewish population, and the

Example 7. Ornamentation of single notes in Eastern Ashkenazi ḥazzanut.

Example 8a. Improvisatory variation of a theme. Oriental Sephardi, after Idelsohn, Melodien, *vol. 4, no. 255.*

Example 8b. Variative development. Two of the melodies notated in the 12th century by Obadiah, the Norman proselyte. Transcription by H. Avenary (cf. JJS 16, 1966, 87ff.).

rapid decline of the academies and geonic authority. As a result, the hegemony of Eastern Jewry – which, until then, had supplied the Diaspora with legal decisions, books, *piyyutim*, *masorah*, rabbis, teachers, and *ḥazzanim* – came to an end. The dispersed Jewish communities were compelled to take matters into their own hands.

Integration in the Realm of Secular Music

THE SCIENCE OF MUSIC. The term *musica* did not exist in the Hebrew vocabulary until the tenth century, when it made its first appearance in the Arabized form, *mūsīqī*. It served to express the concept of the science of music (Ar. *'ilm al-mūsīqī*), as *ḥokhmat ha-musikah*, later also *ḥokhmat ha-niggun*. This branch of science is reckoned as the fourth in the classical quadrivium, "the most excellent and last of the propaedeutic disciplines" (*Dunash ibn Tamim). Muslim scholars followed the ancient Greeks when analyzing acoustic and musical phenomena in the spirit of an abstract science – an idea that attracted Jewish thinkers. In the early tenth century, Isaac *Israeli and his disciple Dunash ibn Tamim held that a full command of philosophical reasoning was indispensable for religious exegesis; they actually employed musical science for their commentary on the *Sefer *Yeẓirah* (ed. by M. Grossberg (1902), 16, 40, 48). Their great contemporary *Saadiah Gaon, who took it upon himself to bridge the widening gap between philosophy and religious tradition, is the author of the oldest known text on music written by a Jew. This is a paragraph at the end of the 10th treatise of his *Kitāb al-amānāt wa'l I'tiaqādāt* (*Book of Beliefs and Opinions*) written in 933. Its subject is the eight rhythmic modes known at the time and their influence on the human soul. Its approach largely expresses the prevailing doctrine of the ethos, which emphasizes the importance of harmony in its broad sense as an equilibrating force. Saadiah's 10th treatise as a whole is entitled "Concerning

How It Is Most Proper for Man to Conduct Himself in This World." It should be noted that the then prevailing ancient doctrine of the ethical influence of music formulated by the Greek philosophers, had been expressed earlier in the biblical stories of David playing before the melancholy King Saul and of prophetic ecstasy aroused by hearing musical instruments (I Sam. 10:6, 16:16, 23; II Kings 3:15).

It is quite likely that Saadiah's major source was the Arabic "Treatise Imparting Concise Information on Music" of the great Arab philosopher al-*Kindī (d. after 870). However, a close comparison of the respective passages shows that Saadiah's contains significant differences and deviations from al-Kindī's.

The historical significance of Saadiah's short chapter far exceeds that of its musical content. It demonstrates the integration of musical theory into Jewish learning. It had now become a challenge for erudite Jews in the Islamic countries to comprehend this art intellectually. Fragments of several books on music discovered in the Cairo *Genizah* were written during the 11th to 13th centuries in the Arabic language, but in Hebrew letters. Among them are extracts from the famous treatise on music of the secret 10th century Arab confraternity Ikhwān al-Ṣafā', and a fragment on the elements of lute playing. Contemporary book lists also provide an indication of what could be found on music in private libraries and on bookstalls, and one can imagine how much must have been lost in Cairo and in cities like Baghdad, Damascus, Kairouan, or Cordova.

The scientific approach also makes itself felt in the fields of grammar and *masorah*, thus transferring the treatment of biblical accentuation to a higher level. The system of accents itself had been completed and summed up in somewhat naïve rhymes designed to aid memorization (*Dikdukei ha-Teʿamim*, ascribed to Aaron Ben-Asher himself). This old-fashioned method of teaching continued only by the Ashkenazim (versified teachings of Rabbenu Jacob *Tam in the 12th century and of *Joseph b. Kalonymus in the 13th century). A completely different spirit governs the dry but scientific classification given to the accents by Judah *Ḥayyuj (late tenth century), *Ibn Balaʿam or *Ibn Janaḥ (11th century). It is difficult to gauge the extent to which these works influenced musical performance proper, but they are witnesses to a new trend in the theoretical foundations of synagogue chant.

The classes of literature mentioned so far were addressed to a small stratum of society and never exerted as broad an influence as the books of biblical exegesis, whose study was everyone's moral duty. Thus the exegetes and their works achieved great power in the spiritual life of the nation and inevitably played a part in forming a body of common ideas about music. It was Saadiah Gaon who won the title "head of the speakers and first of the exegetes" in the post-midrashic era. His Arabic translation of and commentary on the Book of Psalms adheres scrupulously to the principle that all instrumental music be prohibited until the Temple is rebuilt, and he even claims that instrumental music was restricted to the Temple in ancient times. Saadiah was very particular about explaining obscure musical passages in the Bible out of the biblical text alone, but, on the other hand, he rather unconcernedly translated the Hebrew words *nevel* and *kinnor* by the Arabic names of contemporary string instruments. His practice was continued by Abraham *Ibn Ezra and innumerable others.

An example of an exegesis drawing on current philosophical opinions is *Baḥya b. Asher's comments on Ex. 32:19 and 15:20 (*Be'ur*, written 1291 in Spain). Relying upon the view of "the masters of musical science" that the nine musical instruments of Psalm 150 allude to the nine heavenly spheres and that seven of them derive their power from the seven planets, he explains why the *maḥol* (= Mars = evil) was the instrument played before the golden calf, while the *tof* (= Jupiter (*ẓedek*) = Justice) was beaten by Miriam, sister of the just priest Aaron. The *maḥol*, he points out, was the symbol of a sinful woman. In the course of time the opinion took shape that *maḥol* and other terms from the headings of the psalms, such as *ayyelet ha-shaḥar* and *alamot*, were musical instruments or names of musical "modes." This view recurs in literature until quite recent times. In general, the exegetical books spread an understanding and a high esteem of music; they endowed it with an image of strong spiritual power – not very different from that developed by philosophy – rather than of a self-sufficient art or a despised entertainment.

THE CHALLENGE OF NEW FORMS OF ARTS. The philosophy and theory of music were conceived by scholars and, as an abstract science, were detached from musical composition and performance. This did not prevent leaders like Saadiah Gaon from writing hymns in the free rhythms of Kallir's school. The following generation (about 940–950), with Saadiah's disciple *Dunash b. Labrat as its leader, introduced contemporary Arab metrics into Hebrew poetry. This was a revolutionary act of immense influence on poetry and music. Arabic poets had accepted the ancient Greek metrics based upon measured syllable durations as early as the eighth century: "Since the ancient Arabs by nature measured [their language], its very nature accorded with tonal proportions and musical composition" (*Ibn Danan, *Perek be-Ḥerez*, 15th century). The differentiation of long and short syllables is foreign to the Hebrew language; it was, rather, the intensity of enunciation that provided the poetic "weight" (*mishkal*). It may be seen, for instance, from *Yose b. Yose's *Darkekha Eloheinu le-Ha'arikh Appekha* that the singer had to utter one, two, or three syllables, as the case may be, between the accents; this precluded a regular beat and meter, and the tune had to be either psalmodic or in free rhythm. It can be said that this poetry did not include the dimension of time as an object of artistic configuration.

This old Semitic heritage was challenged by the Greco-Arab meters, which give a precise order and division to the continuum of time. The heavy pace of the old *piyyutim* was regarded as "bothersome to the public," which now preferred smoothly flowing rhythms flattering to the ear. The formal element had become autonomous, so to speak; its former dependence upon an idea (expressed in a natural flow of speech) had weakened. This process was justified by the slogan "that the beauty of Japheth should dwell in the tents of Shem." Aesthetic appreciation was clearly a new aspect in Hebrew poetry and song. Of course, it had to overcome stiff opposition, but its victory was almost complete and lasted more than half a millennium. "A pleasant musical sound" was henceforth demanded when offering a prayer (Joseph *Albo, *Ikkarim*, 4:23, 8).

In the musical field, too, a new type of melody made its appearance. Its novelty in Jewish musical tradition is signaled by the fact that there was no term to designate it, and the Arabic word *laḥn* had to be adopted for the purpose. This type of melody demanded metrical texts, and an early Muslim theoretician, Ibn Rashik, held that meter was also the foundation of melody. This idea was repeated and developed by several Jewish writers down to the 17th century (e.g., Samuel *Archevolti). Both Moses and Abraham ibn Ezra (*Ẓaḥut* (Venice, 1546), 142a, written in 1145) advocated that a poem intended to be sung should be written in equal metrical units throughout. It is understandable that mixed meters would have led to alternating double and triple time within the melodic phrase and this seems to have been regarded as unbalanced.

Since neither Islamic nor Jewish culture record their music in writing, it is only by inference that the *laḥan* can be regarded as a "melody" according to European notions, i.e., a musical structure built of equal or corresponding sections and shaped according to a rhythmic scheme (meter). This design differs from the traditional tunes of free rhythm, as metrical poetry differs from biblical verse, and has the same advantages and drawbacks, as *Judah Halevi demonstrated (*Kuzari* 2:69).

In modern Jewish singing practice, a *laḥan* may be very closely to the cyclic structure of the stanzas and can be notated with bars according to the meter of the text (Mus. Ex. 9).

It is evident from the example that a "metrical" tune need not be syllabic; a series of short notes may appear on a long syllable. To judge from present practice, however, the absolute identity of poetic and musical rhythm is relatively rare. More often the tune is given its own rhythm, but even then it will be symmetrical or cyclic.

With the emergence of metrical poetry, the formal idea of the stanza became predominant; it constituted a major cycle, which comprised the minor elements of metrical units and rhythms of light character. Its introduction into serious songs was apt to broaden their public appeal. In the Jewish sphere, this implied the explicit invasion of musical tradition by environmental elements. This development was heralded by the extensive use of the Arabic strophic forms established in Spain: the *shir ezor* ("girdle song," *muwaššaḥ* in Arabic and the more popular genre the *zajal*, which were probably the ancestors of both the Spanish *villancico* and the French *virelai*). This form is characterized by a certain order of rhymes and by an unchanging refrain (*pizmon*) to be performed in chorus by the audience (*Tanḥum ha-Yerushalmi*, s.v. *pazzem*; see Y. Ratzhaby in: *Taẓlil*, 8 (1968), 16). The melody of a *shir ezor* could be either original or taken from an earlier composition ("With the Greeks, the song was composed together with its tune; with the Arabs, every song has a tune, but not every tune has a song [exclusively associated with it]," Moses ibn Ezra, c. 1100 (Heb. transl. B.Z. Halper, *Shirat Yisrael*, 1924, 110)). The transfer of melodies from one song to another is also a common feature of Hebrew hymns from the 11th century onward ("The scribes of Spain… would write the tune of a well-known *piyyut* above the column of the *piyyut*," Abraham ibn Ezra, commentary on Ps. 7:1). In a sample of about 80 hymns from the Cairo *Genizah*, published by J.H. *Schirmann in 1966 (*Piyyutim Ḥadashim min ha-Genizah*), the superscriptions of 32 refer the reader to the tunes of other Hebrew poems. Seventeen others, however, were written to Arabic melodies assumingly well known in their day. This shows clearly that the acceptance of a foreign form was often accompanied by the adoption of foreign music – either by the transfer of actual melodies or as an imitation of style. Simeon Duran writes (c. 1400) of "the tunes for songs and elegies:.. some were composed in the lands of Spain and taken by the poets from the songs of Ishmael [i.e., of the Arabs] which are very attractive: others were taken from the popular songs of the French countries and are driven to extreme melodic height and extension" (*Magen Avot*, ed. Leghorn 1785, 55b). Sometimes approved, but more often attacked, the custom of using foreign tunes remained a permanent feature in Jewish music. Later it even became an issue of mystical ideology and, in music itself, a source of hybrid forms.

Example 9. Melodies shaped according to the meter of the poetry. (a) Oriental Sephardi, after Idelsohn, Melodien, *vol. 4, no. 218; (b) basic Western Ashkenazi melody; cf. A. Baer,* Baal T'fillah, *1883[3], no. 225.*

The new development in poetry and music may be reduced to one common formula: both arts are given a periodic ordering, an artificial structuring of the dimension of time acquired from Greco-Arabic precedents. The mere sound of speech and song thereby becomes an experience of its own. The listener may give himself up to rhythms and sounds more harmonious and relaxed than those found in harsh reality; the words may pass before him without posing a special challenge or demand. This phenomenon was alien to the older forms of Hebrew poetry in which the "weight" of accents, like pounding hammers, drove the words into the consciousness. It is difficult to imagine that one could listen to the "beautiful flow of speech" of Isaiah or Job without being moved by its message. The impact of a sensual and aesthetic appreciation of art was a new element in Jewish music, and the first tangible sign of its progressive integration with the cultural environment.

MUSIC AT THE SOCIAL AND POPULAR LEVELS. As a result of the relative freedom in daily life that the Jews were granted, musical elements that had no connection whatsoever with either religion or secular learning came to the fore. At the popular level, song and play had certainly never ceased to enliven festival and ordinary activities, exactly as is related of the Talmudic era (see above). An uninterrupted stream of reports and notices from the Middle Ages tell about Jewish minstrels and jugglers roaming the countries and performing before Jews and gentiles. The wandering artist had a very low status in medieval society; he was almost an outcast in Christian civilization and was regarded with the same suspicion, as sometimes were the Jews. Nevertheless, minstrelsy was a very old vocation, which had spread over the continent in the path of the Roman legions. When the Jews were expelled from their country, many joined the universally open class of *ludarii* (M. Jastrow, REJ, 17, 308–10), *ministrerii*, and *ioculatores*. The movement of Jews into this way of life continued during the Middle Ages and later on. Most of the Jewish communities could not offer a livelihood to all who possessed an artistic gift and felt an urge to practice it. These artists used to master not only singing and instrumental play but also the recitation of long epics and the composition of various kinds of poetry, as well as dancing, rope walking, knife throwing, etc.

This kind of "art" was acceptable not only in the villages or market places; men of high standing were also fond of hearing and seeing the minstrel and juggler, and those they liked best they would attach to their retinue. Since the roaming artist was an outsider in any case, his Jewish extraction was of no consequence in making him the court musician of a caliph or emir or of a Christian king, bishop, or knight. Some examples of the Jewish minstrels' appearance before high-class audiences may shed some light on this continuously recurring phenomenon. From Jewish tribes who settled in seventh-century Hijaz and went to war with shawm and drum came the famous singer *al-Gharid al-Yahudi of Medina, said to have pleased Muhammad himself by his song. In Andalusia, *al-Mansur al-Yahudi was appointed court musician by al-Hakam I, the caliph of Cordoba, early in the ninth century and sent to Kairouan to escort the famous musician Ziryab to Cordoba; others are known to have served the nobles of the Ibn Shaprut family, such as a certain Isaac b. Simeon (c. 1100). The Christian kings of Spain also held Jewish musicians in high esteem. Their court accounts of the 14th–16th centuries repeatedly mention Jewish *juglares* (mostly vihuela players) who received considerable remuneration and were granted pompous titles (*ministrerii de stroments de corda de casa de la señora reyna*). Wandering singer-poets of Jewish descent were welcome with kings and aristocrats since they added a popular flavor to the sophisticated, but sometimes dull, court atmosphere. "El Ropero," the son of a Jewish tailor, was maliciously called *malvado cohen, judio, zafío, logrero* by his rivals, but nevertheless allowed to address Isabella the Catholic with a protest song against the persecution of the Marranos in 1473. One of his contemporaries Juan (Poeta) of Valladolid, pleased the Spanish court of Naples.

The activities of Jewish singers immediately before the expulsion of the Jews from Spain, testifies again that they were regarded as outsiders in every respect. They also appear in the company of Provençal troubadours, French trouvères, or, like *Suesskind of Trimberg (c. 1220), at the seat of the bishop of Wuerzburg. The poetries of these Jewish singers, even the songs on biblical subjects and those obviously written for a Jewish audience, were in the vernacular. They mastered the international repertoire to no less a degree than their gentile colleagues and added to it subjects from Bible and Midrash. One of the unexpected discoveries in the Cairo *Genizah* was the notebook of a Jewish minstrel of 1382, writing German in Hebrew letters. It contains a lengthy German epic, as well as songs on Moses, Abraham, Joseph, and a parable from the Midrash. The authors, "Eizik and Abraham the Scribes," rarely use Hebrew words (but "church" is pejoratively called *tifleh*).

The wandering singers were a class between the nations and, in general, rather estranged to their origin. They spread the works and motifs of literature over the countries and continents (e.g., Samson Pine, who interpreted the French epic of Parzival to German scribes in 1335). The tales of King Arthur were introduced to the Jewish public as well when they were transferred to the Jewish idiom or imitated, as in the **Shmuel Bukh* (15th century), the *Akedat Yiẓḥak* poem, and similar compositions. Reliable sources show that such Jewish epics were sung to a fixed melodic phrase throughout the whole work like the *Chanson de Geste* and similar poems the world over. Regrettably, such tunes as the *Niggun Shmuel Bukh* were never recorded in music, but their counterparts have been preserved in the biblical ballads of the Sephardim, which show that the recurrent standard phrase was varied with every repetition (Mus. ex. 10).

Minstrelsy in general holds an important share in the formation of common European melody types. Its Jewish repre-

Example 10. Standard phrase of epic song. In this example, the phrase is varied by alternating open and closed cadences. Ladino ballad on the sacrifice of Isaac, Morocco, after A. Larrea Palacin, Cancionero Judio del Norte de Marrucos, *vol. 1,* Romances de Tetuan, *1952, 123.*

sentatives served as intermediaries between the ghettoes and their environment. They were also the bearers of an instrumental tradition, especially in the field of dance music. When conducting the elaborate musical rites of wedding ceremonies and other occasions, they transferred part of the international repertoire to the Jewish quarter (Mus. ex. 11).

It is no wonder that common European formulas of dance melodies invaded the more popular part of religious and even synagogue song (Mus. ex. 12). Although these processes belong to the popular level, their importance can hardly be overrated. It was the broad masses of the people who sang certain hymns and regulated the musical taste by giving or denying their emotional approval to the precentor. Periods when an educated musical understanding decided the forms of liturgical song remained rather isolated phenomena. One can hardly discover any influence of that art music which was so highly esteemed during the Golden Age of Andalusian Jewry, when *Moses ibn Ezra gained relief from melancholy by listening to a lute player ("The sinew of my heart becomes one of his strings… skillful hands that feel their way and jump on a fret in just time, spread joy over the breathing souls… the dark doors closed, and the seat of the Most-High lies open to the initiated eyes…," *Shirei Ḥol*, ed. Brody, no. 72), or *Al-Ḥarizi who gave his thankful greetings to a certain Isaiah, master on the Arabic lute (he "stirs up the lute strings to sing… like a child in mother's lap who smiles and emits exultant shouts, not weeping… His playing over a dead body would awaken it, and the spirit of life would dwell upon it again…," *Taḥkemoni*, ed. Kahana, 463). Those beautiful and poetic words bear witness of the deep emotions felt on listening to elaborate art music. However, the conditions of the Jewish exile did not allow for a continued delight in the refined art; time and again the Jews were thrown back to the level of poor people and to the kind of music enjoyed by the same.

THE FORMATION OF CONCEPTS OF JEWISH MUSIC (12TH–14TH CENTURIES)

Since the dawn of the second millennium the impact of the musical idioms of the host cultures was felt more and more in Jewish life, religious and secular. In the face of powerful external influences, the traditional attitude to music was also revised and, eventually, rearranged. By the 13th century, three main concepts had developed that circumscribed the role of music in Jewish life in such a fundamental way as to retain their power through the ages down to the present.

The Rabbinic Attitude to Music

Wherever the Torah is applied to life in its entirety, the ethical potential of music is esteemed above its aesthetic values. Beauty of sound and formal perfection fade and are ranked as a mere means of reaching a higher goal, beyond the realm of art. Rabbis did not appreciate any kind of music that was merely pleasing to hear but had no edifying objective. It goes without saying that they condemned music that was likely to stir up excessive human passion. From the time of *Hai Gaon (c. 1000) the most important Talmud commentaries and legal decisions constantly uttered warnings against listening to Arab love songs (*shiʿir al-ghazal*, *Alfasi) or the popular "girdle songs" (*muwaššaḥ*, *Maimonides). The latter called the occupation with songbooks (*sifrei niggun*) a "waste of time in vanity" (Comm. to Sanh. 10:1). On the condition that the singer refrains from losing himself in sensual pleasure and evoking primitive instincts, however, most rabbis held music in high esteem. Song is regarded as a very desirable accompaniment to prayer. Musical performance at

Example 11. International dance tunes in the Jewish klezmer repertoire. (a) Italian dance tune, "Lamento di Tristano," *late 14th century, after A. T. Davison and W. Apel (eds.),* Historical Anthology of Music, *vol. 1, 1950, no. 59; (b)* klezmer *tune, after Elhanan Kirchhan,* Simḥat ha-Nefesh, *part II, Fuerth, 1727, fol. 4r.*

public worship was naturally subject to certain prohibitions, e.g., the prohibition on playing instruments and listening to them during the Sabbath, imitating rites of foreign worship, or listening to female singing voices. Regulations of this kind impeded the introduction of the organ or the formation of mixed choirs in synagogues, for example. Another rabbinical doctrine demands that everyone in full, including the participants in responsorial chant, should enunciate the psalms. This gave rise to the strange "concatenated" alternation of hemistichs still practiced in several Eastern communities:

> *Solo*: The heavens declare the glory of God,
> *Choir*: and the firmament sheweth his handiwork. Day unto day uttereth speech,
> *Solo*: and the firmament sheweth his handiwork. Day unto day uttereth speech,
> *Choir*: and night unto night sheweth knowledge. There is neither speech nor language,
> *Solo*: and night unto night sheweth knowledge. There is neither speech nor language (Psalm 19).

Rabbi Isaiah *Horowitz, who settled in Jerusalem in the early 17th century, recommended this custom also to the West (*Kiẓẓur Shelah* (ed. 1715), fol. 66a).

The competence of the *ḥazzan* was judged by his personal respectability and good repute rather than by musical standards. This frequently expressed view was codified later in the Shulḥan Arukh (OḤ 53:4). Time and again, rabbis were inclined to reject *ḥazzanim* of a prominently artistic or virtuoso disposition, since they were suspect of aiming at public applause alone. Nevertheless, rabbis very often had to compromise or even resign themselves to the demands of the public (Solomon Luria, *Yam shel Shelomo*; Ḥul. 1:49). The guardians of law however, did not cease calling singers to order by their warnings not to disturb the balance of word and tone or sever the bond between related words by extended coloraturas: indeed, a style of singing came into existence in which vocalized coloraturas occurred only as a sort of interlude between integral word groups, instead of being sung to the syllable or a word. In the later centuries, *ḥazzanim* were often blamed by their rabbis for a "theatrical" or "operatic" mode of performance or (in unconscious conformity with Plato) for their "imitation of nature," such as when they pictured vocally the "sound of great waters" in Ps. 93:4 (Judah Leib Zelichower, *Shirei Yehudah*, 1696, fol. 27b).

The innermost meaning of music was defined by Maimonides with reference to the perfect music of the Levites in the Temple as cognate to the faculty of discerning the pure idea (*Guide of the Perplexed*, 3, 46), with pleasantness of sound a precondition of its effect on the soul (*ibid.*, 3, 45). About three centuries later an exile from Spain, Isaac ben Ḥayyim Cohen wrote in his *Eẓ Ḥayyim* that the singing of the Levites is intended to prepare their minds for contemplation, as befits those fulfilling sacred tasks. These statements demonstrate how a well-established tradition may be corroborated by philosophical argumentation.

Philosophy and Secular Education

Music was included in the ardent debates about this problem, since it formed part of the curriculum of sciences. It remained for Maimonides' followers to establish its rightful place within Jewish education and learning. Joseph ibn *Aknin was the first to undertake this task in his book *Cure of the Souls* (*Tibb al-Nufus*, ch. 27). In Ibn Aknin's opinion the Bible itself obliges the Jewish people to learn the art of music, not only because of its association with the holy sacrifices and its high esteem in the ancient times, but because the spiritual power of music had been a source of prophecy, "guiding the mind to clear sight, to keen distinction, to the faculty of meditation." Music now penetrated education as a medium of shaping the character and developing emotional abilities. "Understanding music" (as a goal apart from practical execution) was accepted as an educational factor by the Jews of Moorish Andalusia and of Christian southern Europe, from about 1230–40. Transfer of the language of musical literature from Arabic to Hebrew marked the turning point. Already a century earlier *Abraham b. Ḥiyya wrote in Hebrew a comprehensive encyclopedia of the sciences of which the section on music, "On *Ḥokhmat ha-Niggun* called *musika* in Greek" is in manuscript in the Vatican library. Shemtov *Falaquera gave music its appropriate place in his educational work of 1236 *Ha-Mevakkesh* ("The Searcher" – after wisdom and happiness) and in his *Reshit Ḥokhmah* ("Beginnings of Wisdom," also translated into Latin); he also advocated Hebrew as the preferred language of studies. The latter idea guided the Jews of Provence when they appointed Andalusian authors to translate science books into Hebrew. Judah ibn *Tibbon had already supplied a version of Saadiah's philosophical work together with its musical appendix (see above). Judah Al-Ḥarizi translated the Ḥunayn ibn Isḥāq's *Sayings of the Philosophers* (ch. 18–20 about music). Anonymous translators contributed the extensive music treatise from the encyclopedia of *Ibn Abi al-Ṣalt. Fragments of a musical treatise by *Moses b. Joseph ha-Levi have been preserved as a quotation.

The activities of these promoters of music education coincided – certainly not by chance – with the endeavors made in Christian Castile, Provençe, and Sicily to create a European spiritual culture independent of ecclesiastical dogma but following classical antiquity. A cosmopolitan and humanistic spirit governed the circles that fostered this movement, and the above-mentioned Abraham b. Ḥiyya served them as a translator, as did many Jews and Moors. This breath of fresh air awoke hopes for a normalization of exile conditions by transferring ingredients of secular culture into Hebrew. During these heydays of medieval civilization, Jews ornamented their books with excellent miniatures, sang the love songs of the troubadours ("a very bad custom, taken over from the surrounding peoples," Jacob *Anatoli, c. 1230) or romances (*Sefer *Ḥasidim* 142; cf. 3; 238, c. 1200) and listened to popular tales and epics. Hebrew poets of Provence appreciated the art of famous troubadours (Abraham *Bedersi, late 13th century) but wrote exclusively in their own tongue, albeit for a limited au-

Example 12. Common European idioms in Western Ashkenazi melodies. (a) Psalm 144, Ashkenazi, as sung on Sabbath eve, notated by H. Avenary; (b) German dance song, 1556, after W. Salmen, MGG, vol. 7, 1957, col, 227; (c) Bulgarian dance melody, ibid., *(d)* Bergamasca, *a north Italian melody widely known since the 16th century; here in a version by Salamon de' Rossi, after P. Nettl,* Altjuedische Spielleute und Musiker, *1923, 21; (e) Ashkenaz Passover hymn, after G. Ephros,* Cantorial Anthology, *vol. 3, 1948, 85; (f)* klezmer *tune, 1727, after E. Kirchhan,* Simḥat ha-Nefesh, *part 11. fol. 2v.; (g)* klezmer *tune* ibid., *fol. 5v; (h) European dance-music formula, descending the major scale, after W. Wiora in* Report, Sixth Congress of the International Musicological Society, *Bamberg, 1953, 1954, 170.*

dience ("My lyre, awaking melodies in this generation, what is it more than a forlorn song?" Abraham Bedersi).

Such tendencies received fresh impulse from the movement of the Proto-Renaissance and from new trends in French and Italian music early in the 14th century. The poet and thinker *Immanuel of Rome ("O science of music, who will understand any more the art of thy flutes and drums?" *Maḥbarot*, 21) complained: "It is a well-known fact that the science of music – a wonderful and esoteric science and art – was once thoroughly understood by our nation… but nowadays, none of us knows anything of it, and it is entirely in Christian hands" (Comm. Prov. 23:13). Such ideas, of whom Immanuel was only one exponent, now gave rise to a new wave of Hebrew musical literature drawn from Latin and Italian sources. The connection of its compilers with the Proto-Renaissance movement is obvious. *Kalonymus b. Kalonymus, who served King Robert II of Anjou as a science translator, also wrote a Hebrew version of Al-*Farabi's *Classification of the Sciences* (3:5 on music), in 1314. *Levi b. Gershom, collaborating with Johannes de Muris in mathematics and astronomy, was commissioned by Philippe de Vitry to write a treatise *De numeris harmonicis* in 1343 and was thus in close touch with two outstanding figures of the *Ars Nova* in France, as was probably also that unknown music student whose Hebrew notebook refers to teachings of Jean Vaillant (c. 1400). Italian Trecento music is reflected by the notebook of another anonymous Jew who translated into Hebrew a brief compilation of musical theory attributed to the famous Marchettus of Padua from Italian. A more comprehensive treatise of musical theory was translated from Latin by a certain *Judah b. Isaac. In his preface, the translator brings forward the favorite idea of that epoch: that Jewish occupation with musical science actually means the recovery of one's own property, lost in the turmoil of exile. 14th-century Spain contributed some discussions on the role of music in medicine; they are only marginal phenomena, when compared to the strong tendency of Provençal and Italian Jewry to make the science of music a building stone of a secular culture of their own.

The endeavors of medieval Jewry to attach themselves to contemporary musical conceptions were buried under an avalanche of severe catastrophes that threatened the very existence of the Jews. These prompted the question whether the devotion to art and worldly goods was at all appropriate to a people in exile. Solomon *Ibn Verga (late 15th century) expressed such opinions in a fictional discussion between King Alfonso VIII and three Jewish leaders (*Shevet Yehudah*, par. 8): "Why should you teach your children music" asks the king, "whereas you are obliged to tears and mourning all your life since the God of Heavens called you a wretched people and dispersed you for it, which he did to no other nation." The Jewish respondents cannot proffer a real answer and demonstrate a disheartened retreat from their former aims and hopes. Pushed back by the turn taken by medieval civilization, Jews had to abandon their tentative contacts with art music and musical learning. This problem was to repeat itself several times later on.

According to a pattern that became standard, rejection led to a return to traditional standards and ideas. In music, this meant a move back to the use of musical language for predominantly religious expression. By the 15th century, however, the latter had already lost its original sober purity by the adoption of metric tunes for hymnal song and by the practice of florid melodies fostered by a strong mystical movement.

Mystical Ideas and Forms

Tradition on the lines of pure *halakhah* hardly considered the innate dynamics of musical expression, but judged it by external (albeit exalted) standards. Direct and constant relations between religious experience and music are rather found in the mystical approach to faith, which needed music for communicating ideas that cannot be expressed by words and as a means of imparting visions and secret revelations. Such tendencies are already evident in the Midrashim of earlier Jewish mysticism. During the 13th century, the mystical trend gained in impetus and exerted an unprecedented power over both the contemplative and the active modes of life.

When the Kabbalah attempts to reveal the secrets of creation or of the heavens, it often has recourse to musical symbols, metaphors, and allegories. The reciprocal relation between the lower and the upper world, for exampe, is made comprehensible by analogy with musical resonance; divine love and grace are pictured by various allegories of song and dance. The Zohar gathers almost every musical allusion to mystical ideas found in the Talmud and Midrash, without adding anything really new; but it renovates and strengthens the impact of such visions as the angelical choirs (*Va-Yetze*, ed. Mantua, fol. 158b–159b) and their counterpart, Israel's song of praise ("so that the Holy One may be exalted from above and from below in harmony," *Shemot*, 164b; cf. *Va-Yeḥi*, 231a–b). Images of this kind had earlier been drawn in the *Heikhalot* literature (see above). Especially significant is the demand for cheerfulness in prayer, concretely expressed in song and melody: "… we know that the **Shekhinah* does not dwell in sad surroundings, but only amid cheerfulness. For this reason Elisha said (II Kings 3:15): 'But now bring me a minstrel; and it came to pass, when the minstrel played, that the hand of God came upon him'" (*Va-Yeshev*, 180b; cf. *Va-Yeḥi*, 216b; 249b). Contemporary and later kabbalists connect their allegories with a rather precise, almost scientific, description of musical phenomena (e.g., Abraham *Abulafia; Isaac *Arama). Mystical meditation, however, by its very nature, had to remain a privilege of the selected few. Its massive influence on music was made effective by books or commentaries in the prayer book and, more directly, by the personal example of individual mystics acting as cantors and rabbis.

Among the *Ḥasidei Ashkenaz, mystical ideas penetrated the particular mode of devout life taught by Judah he-Ḥasid and his followers. Their aim was to demonstrate the love of God and the joy in his commandments every day, and this strongly emotional element shaped a musical idiom of its own. Prayer and praise are the center of life, but they can be conducted in true perfection only by inseparable union with a tune. Singing is the natural expression of joy, and a frequent change of melodies prevents daily prayer from becoming mere routine. Absorption in song releases the abandonment of the self and the innermost concentration on the words uttered. Moreover, mystical prayer also has an active end in sight: **kavvanah*, the "intention" or concentration on the mystical union of world and creator, is to be brought about by contemplating the hidden sense behind the plain meaning of the words. These unspoken matters must be deliberated during the utterance of certain key words of the prayers. In this context, the tune has several tasks: to eliminate the diversion of mind by the surroundings, to make room for a chain of thoughts around a word, and to remind the congregation of a specific "intention." The technical term for this application of melody was *le-ha'arikh be-niggun, li-meshokh niggunim* (extending the tune), *be-orekh u-vemeshekh niggun*, or *niggunim arukhim* (long tunes). All these terms point to the long melismas, mostly wordless coloraturas, before or within the prayer that became a distinguishing mark of mystical prayer song.

A rather simple example of melodically expressed *kavvanah* may be found in the recitation of the Book of Esther, which does not contain any explicit mention of God. When reaching chapter 6, verse 1, "On that night the king could not sleep," the same long melisma which ornaments the word "the King" during High Holiday morning prayers is intoned, symbolizing that it actually was the King of the World who intervened at this point. Other examples are the legendary association of the **Aleinu* prayer with Joshua and the walls of Jericho, which is evoked by inserted trumpet-like flourishes, or the extended tune of *Barekhu* on Sabbath night which was believed to give the souls suffering in hell an additional moment of relief. Undoubtedly a certain poetical element dwells in the "long melodies" and, at the same time, provides a challenge for the performing cantor. The latter always took pride in giving musical shape to these sometimes phantasmagorical ideas.

Along with this outlet of dynamic music making, medieval mysticism also opened the door to the intrusion of definitely popular musical elements. Just as everyone was obliged to say daily prayers, no one would be dispensed from doing so in song:

> You should never say: My voice is not agreeable… Speaking this way, you complain against him who did not make your voice beautiful. There is nothing that induces man to love his Creator and to enjoy his love more than the voice raised in an extended tune… If you are unable to add something [of your own to the prescribed text], pick out a tune that is beautiful and sweet to your ears. Offer up your prayer in such tunes, and it will be full of *kavvanah*, and your heart will be enchanted by the utterings of your mouth… (*Sefer Ḥasidim*, 11; 13th century).

This trend necessarily led away from every artistic or elaborate kind of music. Although the *Sefer Ḥasidim* clearly rejected "music from the tavern," the door was thrown open to a new invasion of foreign melodies, at least at the popular level of Jewish mysticism. A time was even to come when the "redemption" of a beautiful gentile tune, by its adaptation to a sacred text, was to be regarded as a great merit. The concepts of music developed by the Ḥasidei Ashkenaz deeply penetrated the communities and lasted for a long time in Central Europe. Made popular by the writings of *Eleazar b. Judah (Ha-Roke'aḥ) of Worms and numerous prayer books with commentaries of his inspiration, the musical expression of *kavvanot* became an essential task of *ḥazzanut*. It remained so as late as the 18th century, when it was replaced by the influence of East European Ḥasidism.

THE CONSOLIDATION OF REGIONAL STYLES

The spiritual developments which shaped the various concepts of sacred song were largely concluded by 1300. It fell to the 15th century to shape music itself according to the chosen ideal and to direct the accepted patterns into the channels of a continuous tradition. Differences of ideology and taste gave rise to separate musical traditions – not only of the larger groups (*Minhag Ashkenaz, Sefarad, Italyah, Romanyah*), but even on the community level. Important but limited groups, such as the Jews of Avignon (*Carpentras), Mainz, and Prague, developed a characteristic musical custom (*minhag*) of their own.

Musical Minhag

Scattered references related to the music of certain prayer or hymn texts can already be found in the earlier compendia of liturgical practice, such as *Abraham b. Nathan ha-Yarḥi's *Ha-Manhig* (c. 1205). Moreover, their disciples passed down the practices of venerable rabbis and *ḥazzanim* through oral tradition. Some of the musical *minhagim* go back to the talmudic period, such as extending the melodies of "*eḥad*" in *Shema Yisrael* (Ber. 13b; 61b), (Mus. ex. 13a), of the *Amen (Ber. 47a), and of the *Priestly Blessing (Kid. 71c), see Mus. ex. 13c. The halakhic sayings that *shofar* and *megillah* are to be treated alike (Ber. 30a; Meg. 4b, etc.) are evoked by the use of an identical tune for the benedictions of both of them (Mus. ex. 13b).

The efforts to consolidate an Ashkenazi tradition of sacred song were concentrated in the school of Jacob b. Moses *Moellin, commonly called the Maharil. Although a rabbi by rank and authority, he liked to function as a *ḥazzan* (*Sefer Maharil*, ed. Lemberg, 1860, fol. 55a–b; 49b). The musical usage taught by him was, on the one hand, a continuation of existing traditions accepted from former *Ḥazzanim* (*ibid.*, 28a; 82b), but on the other, his personal choice and example became normative. As a rule, the Maharil used to acknowledge the right of local custom:

> Maharil said: Local custom should not be altered at any price, even not by unfamiliar melodies. And he told us an event in his life. Once he was *ḥazzan* during the High Holidays at the Regensburg community and sang all the prayers according to the custom of the land of Austria, which is followed there. It was difficult for him, however, so that he said the *haftorah* in the tune customary in the settlements near the Rhine.

It is remarkable how elaborate and thoughtful the musical performance of the Maharil was. His disciple, Zalman of St. Goar, recorded many details with great care and transmitted to posterity a "score without music," so to speak, of the most important parts of the liturgy. In the service for the Ninth of Av, for instance (fol. 49b–50b), not only is the distribution of texts between congregation and cantor defined, but also what the latter had to sing in a loud, medium, and low voice, what in a mournful intonation, and where a cry of pain was to be sent up. The pauses at the end of the verses and chapters are not forgotten, nor are the extension of melodies and other discriminate implements of expression. The music of the Day of Atonement is treated in a similar way (fol. 63a; 65a).

The Maharil used to stress the importance of hymns (*Krovez*, 83b), but he wished to exclude those in the German vernacular (117a), which apparently existed then, as do such in *Ladino with the Sephardim to the present. Often the Ma-

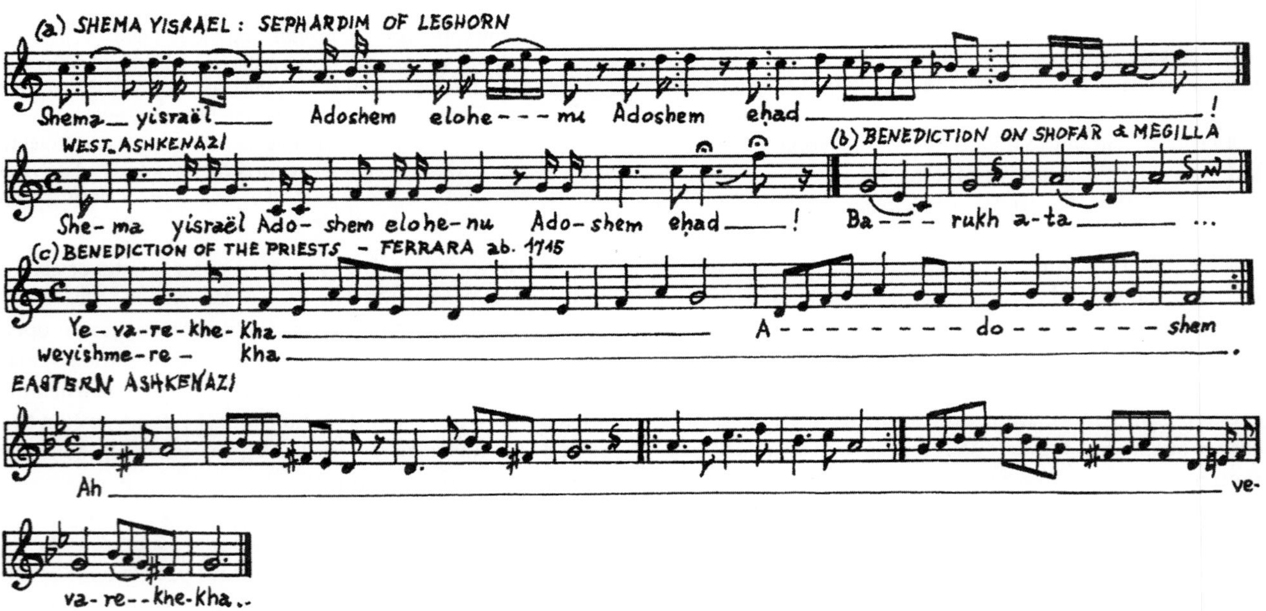

Example 13. Old tradition of melodic extension. (a) Italian Sephardi, after F. Consolo, op. cit., Ex. 4, no. 12; Western Ashkenazi, after I. Lachmann (see Mus. ex. 1) no 8: (b) Western Ashkenazi, notated by H. Avenary: (c) Italian, after Mordecai Tzahalon, Metzitz u-Melitz, *Venice, 1715; Eastern Ashkenazi, after H. Wasserzug,* Schirei Mikdosch, *I, 1878, no. 65.*

haril points to the identity between certain hymn tunes (28b; 74b). Unlike many other rabbis, he regarded melody as an essential element of liturgical traditon.

The "musical *minhag*" of the Maharil is also full of mystical "intentions" (*kavvanot* 40b; 55b; 56a; 66a). There are striking examples of their influence on melodical configuration: "He used to extend [the tune at] the word 'Thou' very much, obviously concentrating his mind on the faculty of 'Thou' known to all the adepts of mystics" (56a). Such musical suggestions of a hidden sense of the words were indicated by remarks in the prayer books. The *Maḥzor Hadrat Kodesh* (Venice, 1512), for instance, advises the *ḥazzan* to sing a certain chapter "to a melody" or "in a long and beautiful tune" and assigns to the prayer *Nishmat Kol Ḥai* "a beautiful melody, since all the people of Israel are given *Neshama yetera* on the Sabbath." Other books attest the use of veritable leitmotifs in the recitation of the Book of Esther when, for instance, the drinking vessels of Ahasuerus are mentioned to the tune of the Lamentations (for they supposedly formed part of the booty from the Temple of Jerusalem). It was also an old custom to prolong the tune of *Barukh she-Amar* in the Morning Prayer (mentioned in *Ha-Manhig*, c. 1205 and in 1689 by the convert Anton *Margarita); the author *Samson b. Eliezer (14th century) relates that he used to sing it as an orphan in Prague with such a sweet voice that he was given the name *Shimshon Barukh she-Amar* (*Sefer Barukh she-Amar*, preface). Although directions for musical execution are found in the works of many authors, the Maharil was made the legendary patron of Ashkenazi *ḥazzanut* and the invention of traditional melodies was ascribed to him. In particular, the so-called **Mi-Sinai* melodies – a common heritage of Ashkenazi synagogues in both Western and Eastern Europe – were believed to go back to the authority of the Maharil (sometimes confused, by uneducated cantors, with *Judah Loew b. Bezalel, Maharal of Prague). As a matter of fact, these melodies, ascribed to an oral tradition stemming "from Mount Sinai," i.e., revealed to Moses, are common to Ashkenazi congregations all over the world. They kept their identity in Jewish settlements as distant from each other as eastern Russia and northern France, south of the Carpathians, and in Scandinavia or Britain. There is no doubt that they antedate the great migrations from Central to Eastern Europe in the 15th century or even earlier. The structural principle of the *Mi-Sinai* melodies is basically Oriental, inasmuch as a cycle of certain themes or motifs is used in manifold combinations and variants according to a traditional master plan. Of course, manifestations of local taste and of "acculturation" are most often present (see **Aleinu le-Shabbe'aḥ*; **Avodah*); however, the essential identity of all the variants is undeniable. They may well have been inherited by the Ashkenazim from a still unspecified epoch in the Middle Ages.

Modal Scales in Synagogue Song

The term "modal" in music is often used (although not with scientific precision) for those tone sequences which are different from the familiar major and minor scales, an example being the Church modes. When applying the term "modal" to Jewish music, several precautions should be borne in mind. Firstly, a modal scale need not be an octave, but may be composed of more or less than eight notes. Furthermore, it must not necessarily repeat the same intervals over the whole gamut; on the contrary, an E natural, for instance, may appear in the lower octave and an E-flat in the upper one. Finally, the interval of the augmented second sometimes joins the tone and semitone as a note proper to the key. Of course, scales of vocal music will not necessarily be in the equal temperament of the piano, but may retain a certain flexibility (sharpened leading notes, neutral thirds). In Oriental Jewish song, micro-intervals in the style of the region are common.

The peculiarity of Jewish modes can be recognized and evaluated best in the Ashkenazi and European-Sephardi song, since their special character stands out against the background of the music of the gentile environment. The structural framework of West and North European song consists of chains of thirds bridged by whole tones, but repressing or avoiding semitones (as does Scotch and Irish folksong still today). Oriental song, on the other hand, is built on the **maqam* modal scale system, which is basically conceived as a combination of several small groups of notes, whether of the same intervallic structure or not, called "genera," a skeleton of consecutive notes, including a semitone or even micro-intervals as may be seen from examples 4a and 6b.

As to the Jewish settlements in Europe, tunes determined by a tetrachordal skeleton are found among the Sephardim, including the communities of Carpentras (Avignon and Com\tat Venaissin), Bayonne, Rome, and the rest of Italy (the Balkans belonging to the realm of Eastern music). In Ashkenazi song, however, tetrachordal patterns have almost entirely vanished. This has preserved, instead, some features of the earliest Western, semitoneless melodics (Mus. Ex 14)

In spite of this environmental influence on Ashkenazi song, a particular "Jewish" character does prevail there in certain scale structures, which are strange in the context of Western music. These are called **shtayger* (a Yiddish term equivalent to mode, manner). Actually there are more *shtaygers* than the "four synagogue modes" proposed by earlier research, but two of them outweigh the others by far: the *Ahavah Rabbah* and the *Adonai Malakh*. Their special features may be recognized from the melody-excerpts given in example 15 and accompanying analyses of their scales (Mus. ex. 15).

As the present Ashkenazi liturgy is an accumulation of hymns and prayers successively added in the course of time, its music also exhibits many characteristics of medieval monody. Among them are the Re- and Mi-modes (similar to the Dorian and Phrygian of plainsong), and several peculiar final clauses. A Jewish origin has often been claimed for them but can hardly be proved. An Oriental or Mediterranean character is evident, however, in most of the genuine *shtaygers*, especially the *Ahavah Rabbah* and kindred scales. Its nearest par-

Example 14. Old European scales in Ashkenazi melodies. Blessing formula, after Idelsohn, Melodien, *vol. 7, part I, no. 10: motifs of masoretic cantillation, after J. Reuchlin,* De accentibus, *Hagenau, 1518; Sabbath song after A. Nadel,* Die haeuslichen Sabbatgesaenge.

Example 15. Scales and examples of two Ashkenazi shtayger. *(a) after A.B. Birnbaum,* Ommanut ha-Ḥazzanut *2, 1912(?), no. 35; (b) after M. Deutsch,* Vorbeterschule, *1871, no. 409.*

allel is the second mode of the Greek Orthodox tradition; it may also be compared with the Persian-Arab *ḥijāz* scale, but it has no parallel in Western art or folk music.

The Sephardi communities that settled in Italy, France, Amsterdam, and London after their expulsion from Spain also preserve European elements in their melodies. The most remarkable of these is a strange chromaticism which imparts a certain soft and floating tonality to some of their tunes (Mus. ex. 16); it might possibly be defined as a superimposition of two different modes, or as a bi-modality, which is very remote from Western concepts of functional harmony. This kind of chromaticism is found most characteristically in examples of biblical chant notated in 1693 (Rome) and 1699 (Amsterdam), as well as during the 19th and 20th centuries. Similar "floating" phrases are found in prayers and hymns; they are a characteristic of the "sweet singing of Sepharad," whose Oriental roots may at present be postulated only speculatively but cannot as yet be proved by scientific deduction.

Performance and Practice of Synagogue Song

The collaboration of a soloist (*sheli'aḥ ẓibbur* or *ḥazzan*) and the choir formed by the whole congregation represents the main feature of synagogue music. These two bodies alternate or answer each other according to a traditional division of the liturgical texts. Especially the Sephardi communities have preserved very old practices of responsorial performance. As indicated in the Talmud (Sot. 30b) and also adopted by the Roman Church, the cantor may intone the first words of a chapter, whereupon the choir takes over, or they may alternate and respond one to the other. Among the Sephardim the congregation is also accustomed to take up the keywords of the more important prayers from the mouth of the cantor. The division of tasks between solo and choir sometimes affects the melodical configuration. If a particular prayer is sung to a *nusaḥ* (see above), its original free rhythm may change into measured time when taken over by the congregation, and the *ḥazzan* may execute the simple pattern in elaborate coloraturas (Mus.ex. 17).

Many non-Ashkenazi communities provide the cantor with two assistants (*mezammerim, somekhim, maftirim*) who flank him at the prayer desk and take over at certain points of the liturgy. This custom is rooted in certain ideas about the community's representation before the Most High; here the participation of three singers does not influence the shape and manner of their music making. However, a special development in this field took place in the Ashkenazi synagogues. Their cantors also attached to themselves two assistant singers, but they did so with a view to the enrichment and beauty of their singing. According to a fixed rule, one of these assistants (*meshorerim*) had to be a boy-descant, called *singer*, and the other an adult, called *bass*. It is not known, when and why this custom was introduced; a picture in the so-called *Leipzig Maḥzor* of the 14th century may be regarded as the earliest representation of such a trio. The heyday of *ḥazzanut* with accompanying *meshorerim* was the 17th and 18th centuries, and it is only from the sources of this late period that its nature can be inferred. According to it, the assistants improvised an accompaniment of hummed chords, drones, or short figures; the *singer* also intoned thirds and sixths parallel to the cantilena of the *ḥazzan*. In addition, both *singer* and *bass* had their solo parts – most often extended coloraturas to be performed while the cantor paused. Famous cantors traveled, with the *meshorerim* as a part of their household, from one large center to another as guest ministers, while the less famed undertook such wanderings in search for a hoped-for permanent post. In the late baroque period, if not earlier, the traditional number of two assistants was supplemented by performers of distinctive tasks, such as the *fistel singer* (falsetto) and specialists in the imitation of musical instruments (*Sayt-bass, fagott-bass, fleyt-singer,* for strings, bassoon, and flute, respectively).

The use of musical instruments proper is attested in medieval Baghdad by the traveler *Pethaḥiah of Regensburg, between 1175 and 1190. However, this was a rare exception and restricted to the half-holidays, since the ban on instrumental music remained in force. It was only by the influence of later mystical movements that the play of instruments was employed in some 17th century Ashkenazi synagogues before the entry of the Sabbath as a token of the joy of the day of rest. Vocal performances nevertheless remained the basic characteristic of synagogue music. An incessant struggle took place in this field between older singing styles and the musical expression of spiritual tendencies that arose during the Middle Ages. This interplay of forces kept Jewish liturgical music from the petrifaction typical of many other traditions of religious chant.

Example 16. *Typical Western Sephardi chromaticism. Amsterdam, 1699, as notated by David de Pinna in D. E. Jablonski,* Biblica Hebraica, *Berlin, 1699; Rome, 1955(?), after E.Gerson-Kiwi, Bat Kol, I, 1955, 15; Rome, 1966, after E. Piattelli,* Canti Liturgici di rito Italiano, *1967, 15; Leghorn, 1892, after F. Consolo, op. cit., Ex. 4, no. 335; Florence, 1956, after L. Levi,* Scritti in memoria di Sally Mayer, *1956, 174.*

Example 17. Mutations of a nusaḥ *pattern, Italian Sephardi, after F. Consolo, op.cit., nos. 335–6.*

MIGRATION AND BLENDING OF MUSIC STYLES (C. 1500–1750/1800)

The era of the Middle Ages is generally regarded as completed at about 1500. The Jews, however, were not yet relieved of the pressure that had built up during medieval times. For them the period between 1500 and about 1800 was a time of forced migrations, of many a spiritual crisis, of ethno-geographical regrouping, and the formation of new centers. The uprooting of large communities and their confrontation with new environments inevitably left its imprint on their music. The most conspicuous event was the migration of these exiled from Spain to the Ottoman Empire, Italy, and other countries, followed by a steadily trickling rearguard of *Marranos; the persecutions in Central Europe also directed a Jewish mass movement to the (then very spacious) Polish kingdom. The eastbound migrations of both Sephardi and Ashkenazi Jews share the fact that the emigrants preserved their original vernacular and their liturgical customs, as well as part of their music, and even imposed these on the local communities. In the long run, however, the musical atmosphere of the new lands permeated the intonation and scale structure of their song, while its melodic structure was affected to a lesser degree. The developments were not left to mere chance. New ideologies came into being and also became guiding stars for the forms and contents of musical expression.

[Hanoch Avenary]

The Mystical Movement of Safed

MUSIC AS CONCEPT AND PRACTICE. An ideological approach to music and its role in worship took root particularly within the mystical movement. In the mystic's world, prayer and the singing associated with it were perceived as elevating the soul to celestial realms where it could bask in the supreme glory. The mystic hears singing everywhere, in his imagination the entire universe incessantly sings the praise of the Lord, as is written in Psalm 150: "Let everything that have breath praise the Lord." Leaders of this movement claimed that music is shared by angels and the Children of Israel and is part of the music of the cosmos destined to sing the Glory of the Creator; as such it helps to establish harmony between the micro- and the macrocosmos. The role assigned to music as leading to knowledge and the constant repetition of music's revelation through mystical intention indicates, according to the Kabbalists, that music was God's creation. He created it on the third day, making angels out of his own breath to sing his glory day and night. This special attitude deriving from the cosmic meaning inherent in the kabbalist's approach to song also encouraged the use of song as an enhancement to ritual.

THE LURIANIC KABBALAH. Theories dealing with the meaning, power and function of song were, in particular, developed and given important practical application in the kabbalistic doctrine that flourished in Safed in the 16th century; this kabbalistic school had its wellsprings in the teachings of Isaac Luria, reverently called *ha-Ari ha-Kadosh* (the saintly Ari). These kabbalists, among whom were talented poets and musicians, believed in fostering poetic and musical creativity, since they could raise the individual and help him overcome the drabness and mundane tribulations of life in this world. They believed that the heavenly gates opened to receive one who intoned a Psalm and conscientiously sang hymns and supplications. He thus became a part, so to speak, of the universal singing of the celestial angels, and of the wind that stirs the trees in paradise. The systematic thinker of this kabbalistic circle, Moses Jacob Cordovero (d. 1570) wrote: "The peoples on earth are birds of varied plumage, each with its own type of music and its own song, and no sooner does the boundless power of God descend to the lower spheres than the song of the birds is heard drawing Him through all the rooms to hear the sweet music. Their singing symbolizes the fulfillment of the Divine command, and therefore great skill is required for the birds to sing the song as it should be sung; since it is part of the sage's wisdom, this skill cannot be gained unless the sage himself teaches it to the birds" (*Shi'ur Komah*, Warsaw, 1883, par. 20–44).

MAJOR THEMES CHARACTERIZING THEIR APPROACH. It should be noted at the outset that concepts relating to the importance and virtues of music that developed in the mystical doctrine and contributed to the enrichment of the musical repertoire are so interwoven with the symbols and concepts comprising the word of the Kabbalah that it is often difficult to treat them separately.

Some of the major themes that expanded considerably and influenced the development and practice of song are the following:

(1) The sanctity of the Sabbath considered as a kind of small-scale paradise and personified as a heavenly queen imprisoned in the sky, which descends to earth once a week to dispense her holiness. This idea gave birth to a fundamental rite associated with the day, *Kabbalat Shabbat*, receiving the Sabbath with the singing of appropriate hymns, as well as the introduction of the concept, *oneg shabbat* (Sabbath enjoyment), which consists of honoring the Sabbath through engaging in pleasurable activities. This includes the three obligatory meals which are times of supreme joy and exaltation expressed by communal singing while eating, etc.

(2) The idea of rising at the midnight hour to sing became very popular. This led to the establishment of choral groups of early risers and Watchmen of the Morning to perform a sophisticated sequence of special hymns called **bakkashot* (supplications). The custom has been perpetuated up to our own days and continues to be held in great esteem.

(3) The analogy between man and the universe and the sought-after resonance and harmony between them are frequent themes in mystical speculation. It is said in this regard that everything done by the individual or the community in the mundane sphere is magically reflected in the upper region. The sublime nature of Israel's singing is related to the theme of the parallel singing of the angels, the power of this singing achieves its highest expression only when both choirs simultaneously intone the praise of God. This acquires particular

importance in the performance of the *Kedushah* – the Trisagion. This parallelism extends not only to the *Kedushah*, but implies full concordance between the singing of those on high and those below. Hence the singing of hymns on earth contributes to the establishment of perfect tuning and harmony between man and the macrocosm.

(4) Evil forces constantly obstruct the way leading to this perfect harmony meaning salvation; sacred music and prayer directed by mystical intention are the most formidable weapons in the combat for salvation.

(5) This combat is partly related to the magical power of the *shofar* and the symbolical roles it fulfills. Indeed many passages of the Zohar deal with its shape, the material it is made of, and the sounds it emits. Among the salient roles assigned to it are the dissipating of harsh divine judgment and to change its nature from punishment to clemency; important historical events in the life of the nation are associated with the sound of its blowing (the Exodus, the revelation of Sinai) as are events of the future – that is to say the redemption.

Some of the many symbols developed in Jewish mystical theories and practice, made their mark on and were bound up with daily activities of the past several hundreds years.

[Amnon Shiloah (2nd ed.)]

The democratic tendencies in the ideology of religious song gave rise to a new wave of popular and profane tunes that infiltrated Hebrew hymnody. The Sephardim had always been very fond of singing and did not lose this predilection during the bitter days of the expulsion. This is proven by the respectable production of Hebrew hymns for extra-synagogal use, written in the popular style and connected with tunes borrowed from songs in the vernacular. An early print of **bakkashot* (Constantinople, c. 1525) attests the popularity of 13 Spanish songs with the exiles from the peninsula; six of the hymns by Solomon b. Mazal Tov (printed in 1545) were to be sung to the tune of Spanish songs, 30 to Turkish, and 29 to older Jewish ones. Solomon Mevorakh's song book of 1555 refers to only ten Turkish melodies (since it was written in Greece), and 14 taken from Jewish songs, but it quotes no less than 30 Spanish tunes that obviously were familiar to his contemporaries. Among the latter are "evergreens" of the Iberian repertoire and many pieces that have since fallen into oblivion. The natural inclination of the people to sing, both in Hebrew and in vernacular tongues, received backing from a mystical idea which, suggested that every melody, even those drawn from popular or gentile sources, may become a vehicle of elated feelings.

Menahem di Lonzano preferred to compose hymns to Turkish melodies because of their ascending "to the tenth over the note *duga*" (the note D in the Persian-Arabic scale); he held that this "utmost range of the human voice," not reached by Greek, Romaniote, or Arabic tunes, was the real meaning of the Psalm verse "On the *Asor* and on the *Nevel*" (*Shetei Yadot*, fol. 141b–142a). Thus, a rabbi and mystic used his well-founded musical knowledge for imparting high flight to his hymnal song. Religious hymns designed both for the prayer house and outside (*pizmonim*; *bakkashot*) propagated the pious mood of Safed in the Jewish world. Among the most prominent songs of this kind are: *Asadder bi-Shevaḥin* (ascribed to Isaac Luria himself), **Lekhah Dodi* by Solomon *Alkabeẓ, *Yedid Nefesh* by Azikri, and *Yah Ribbon Olam* by Israel *Najara. The last was a very productive and inspired poet-musician gifted with a sense for musical nuances. Many of his hymns (printed between 1587 and 1600) were written to the tunes of well-known secular songs in the Spanish or Turkish vernacular, less often in Greek and Arabic.

Najara continued an older custom of providing for a phonetic correspondence of the foreign and the Hebrew text. In this manner, the singer of a gentile song was reminded of the preferred religious alternative. The manuscript of Solomon Mevorakh (Greece, 1555), for instance, shows the replacement of the Spanish song "*Alma me llaman a mi alma*" by the very similar sounding Hebrew "'*Al mah ke-alman ammi, al mah*." Najara substituted for the Arabic "*Ana al-samra wa-sammuni sumayra*" the words "*Anna El shomera nafshi mi-levayim*." He strengthened the associative bridge still further by giving the plot of the gentile song a religious meaning. Thus the famous romance on the knight-errant Amadis becomes a tour de force of phonetic sound imitation and, at the same time, a fine allegory of Israel and God's errant glory:

(Spanish-Jewish romance)
Arbo*leda*, arbo*leda*,
Arboleda tan gen*til*,
La rais tiene d'*oro*
Y la rama de mar*fil*.
(Najara)
Ḥil yo*ledah* bi so*ledah*
Ḥil yo*ledah* bi so*ledah*
Keshurah al lev bi-fe*til*
Al dod meni histir *oro*
U-me'oni me-az he'e*fil*
(Mevorakh)
Ashorerah li-fe'*erah*
Azam*erah* na be-*shir*

Najara fostered music in the broadest meaning by acknowledging the union of word and tone – not as an artistic game (as did later imitators), but for the pious inspiration of the common people by ways of a musical language that was their own.

Humanism and the Renaissance

Contemporary with the era of Safed mysticism, another encounter of East and West in the field of Jewish music was initiated by the Renaissance and Humanist movements in Italy and other parts of Europe. This was an interlude in history acted out in the circles of learned scholars and before an erudite and refined audience of art music.

THE HUMANISTIC APPROACH TO LETTERS AND MUSIC. In the world of science, a direct dialogue with the authors of antiquity replaced the traditional definitions and views of the

Middle Ages. This trend extended to the Bible and later Hebrew works. Several Christian scholars studied Hebrew language and grammar, including the rules of *masorah* and its accentuation. After a short time, the students themselves wrote books on Hebrew grammar, which contained chapters on the *teʿamim*, sometimes adding the music of biblical chants. Among these were Johannes Reuchlin (*De accentibus et orthographia linguae Hebraicae*; Hagenau, 1518), Sebastian *Muenster (*Institutiones grammaticae in Hebraeam linguam*; Basel, 1524), and Johann *Boeschenstein (Munich Cod. Hebr. 401). Many later writers, such as Johannes Vallensis (*Opus de prosodia Hebraeorum*; Paris, 1545) and Ercole Bottrigari (*Il Trimerone*, Ms. dated 1599) took over their notated examples. The Ashkenazi Pentateuch tunes, notated independently by several of the authors, are of very similar outlines and are based upon that same semitoneless scale which is still recognizable in the Bible chant of modern times. The renewed interest in grammar and *masorah* seized Jewish circles as well. Early in the 16th century, several Hebrew authors undertook the description of contemporary practices of biblical chant. The features of the Sephardi version were described by Calo Kalonymus (Appendix to Abraham de *Balmes, *Mikneh Avram*, 1523), and compared with Ashkenazi practice by Elijah Levita (*Tuv Taʿam*, 1538).

In the field of art proper, the open-mindedness of the Renaissance period favored the reconciliation of a progressive Jewish public with art music, especially in the small town-states of upper Italy and Tuscany. A very dry historical source – the book lists delivered to the papal censor by the Jewish families of Mantua in 1559 – speaks eloquently when stating that a certain Samuel Ariano had Zarlino's voluminous *Instituzioni harmoniche* in his library and that Isaac *Norzi possesed madrigal books of Cipriano de Rore, Donato, Stabile, and others. Two influential leaders of the Mantua community discussed the integration of art music in Jewish life. Judah *Moscato, rabbi of that town in 1587–94, preached a long sermon titled *Higgayon be-Khinnor* ("Meditations on the Lyre"), published in *Nefuẓot Yehudah* (Venice, 1589). He examined the subject "man and music" under the aspects of Jewish tradition from the Talmud and Midrash down to the contemporary kabbalists, as well as with reference to the Greek and Arabic philosophers. The rabbi stressed the interrelation of the harmony found in music and the harmony imagined in the soul and character of man, striving to show the legitimacy of musical art in Judaism.

His contemporary, the physician and rabbi Abraham *Portaleone II of Mantua, wrote the book *Shiltei ha-Gibborim* ("Shields of the Heroes"; posthumously printed Venice, 1612) which may be viewed as an early attempt at biblical archaeology based on the interpretation of literary sources, in the spirit of Renaissance scholarship. The author dwells at length on Levitic song and the form and nature of its musical instruments. Outstanding Christian writers soon regarded these chapters as a "source" of Hebrew music, especially after Blasio Ugolino had translated them into Latin in 1767. Disregarding its dubious informative value, this book is symptomatic of the mood governing Renaissance Jewry. Even before 1480, *Judah b. Jehiel Messer Leon of Mantua had become enthusiastic about the concordance between the Bible and ancient Greek rhetoric and other literary genres; Azariah de *Rossi took up these views, and Abraham Portaleone finally applied them to the field of music. At the time, R. Portaleone's book was likely to strengthen the consciousness of the Hebrew share in the culture of antiquity and the importance of its musical achievements.

ART MUSIC. With the partial release of external and internal pressure, a generation of gifted Jewish musicians and composers cropped up during the 16th century. They straightway were absorbed into the fervent development of Italian music, and several Jewish composers saw their works appear in the famous printing establishments of Venice between 1575 and 1628. Outstanding talents had already begun to run the social blockade early in the Cinquecento. The convert Giovan Maria, a lute player, won great fame even beyond the Alps. He successively served the courts of Urbino (1510), Mantua (tutor of the princes, 1513–15), and finally Pope Leo X (chamber musician, 1515–21) and Clement VII (1525–26). At the Gonzaga court of Mantua the harp players Abramo (Abraham Levi) dall' *Arpa and his family were appointed before 1550. They are mentioned as high-ranking musicians by the art theoretician G.P. Lomazzo (1584; 1587); Daniel Levi dall'Arpa was sent to the imperial court of Vienna between 1550 and 1560. The social situation of such Jewish musicians is understood from the fact that Abramo dall' Arpa also held a license for the ritual slaughterhouse and for moneylending in his native town; his son Daniel was granted a special passport to move freely about the country.

The first Jewish composer to see his works appear in print was David *Sacerdote (Cohen) of Rovere. His first book of six-part madrigals was dedicated to the Marchese del Vasto and printed in 1575 (until now only the *Quinto* part book has been rediscovered). For the first time the designation *Hebreo* was added to the composer's name; this became the rule with all those who came after him, most probably by decree of the censor.

The most conspicuous developments took place in the duchy or Mantua, whose court harbored composers of worldwide fame such as Monteverdi. Ensembles of Jewish actors and musicians contributed to the fervent musical life of that town, including several members of the de Rossi family ("Min-ha-Adumim"). A female singer of this family participated in the performance of one of the precursors of the opera (1608), and an Anselmo Rossi had a motet based on psalm texts printed in a collective work (1618). In 1651, Giuseppe de Rossi served the duke of Savoy at Turin. The most important musician of the family was composer Salamone de *Rossi, whose life is documented between 1586 and 1628 (see below). His works were much favored by his contemporaries, as attested by several reprints and their admission to collected editions published in

Copenhagen (1605) and Antwerp (1613; 1616). He also secured a firm place in the general history of music, especially by his progressive instrumental compositions and the early application of the thorough bass. Other Jewish composers whose works have been preserved in print were Davit *Civita (1616; 1622; 1625) and Allegro Porto (1619).

Outside Italy Jewish folk musicians were very active but were not given an opportunity to gain a footing in the ranks of art music. The relative freedom prevailing in Renaissance Italy came to a sudden end with one of the usual crises of Jewish existence. When the House of Gonzaga died out and troubles seized the duchy of Mantua, the Jewish musicians had to emigrate (most went to Venice). The prosperity of that city and its large Jewish population encouraged them to found a Jewish *accademia musicale* (concert society) called "accademia degli Impediti" and later on "Compagnia dei musici." The music-loving R. Leone *Modena promoted their activities. Attempts were made to introduce instrumental play into the synagogue at the feast of *Simḥat Torah*; but the initiators had to yield to rabbinical objections, since the organ used by them was too reminiscent of "the foreign cult." Finally it was again a catastrophe – the plague of 1630 – that cut off the manifestations of Jewish integration in art music. Severe rabbis about the middle of the century quenched the last flickering of such intentions, but not before the first works of synagogal art music had come into existence.

EFFORTS TO ESTABLISH ART MUSIC IN THE SYNAGOGUE. From the eloquent recommendation of Judah Moscato and the delight in art music fostered in wide circles of Renaissance Judaism, it was not a far cry to welcome art music in the synagogue as well. The enthusiasm for the ancient Temple music (Abraham Portaleone, see above) suggested its reinstitution in the house of prayer. The power of conservatism and exile – conditioned humility and pessimism, however, proved hard to overcome. The power behind these progressive tendencies was Leone Modena, who, although ordained as a rabbi, was actually rather one of the errant literati and jack-of-all-trades like many a learned humanist or his younger contemporary Joseph *Delmedigo. While music was for Delmedigo a matter of science (*Sefer Elim*, Amsterdam, 1629), it was one of the 26 crafts in which Leone Modena claimed to have been engaged.

As a rabbi in his native Ferrara about 1605, he saw to the installation of a synagogue choir and to the systematical instruction of its six to eight singers in music. They performed hymns such as **Adon Olam*, **Yigdal*, **Ein ke-Eloheinu*, and *Aleinu le-Shabbe'aḥ* on the occasion of feasts and special Sabbaths, "in honor of God according to the order and right proportion of the voices in the art [of music]." This innovation met with the stiff resistance of a local rabbi who held that music was prohibited in exile; but Leone Modena secured a decision of four other rabbis in favor of polyphonic synagogue singing. This document was to become the main weapon for many later attempts in this direction. It was reprinted by the progressive cantor Solomon Lipschitz in 1718, as well as by Adolf *Jellinek of Vienna in 1861 (Ben Chananja 4, no. 27 suppl. as "topical for the still pending question of introducing choir singing in the sacred service of the Hungarian communities"). The most prominent place in which this decision was printed, and, at the same time, the recompense of Leone Modena's efforts, was the edition in print of Salamone de Rossi's collected synagogue compositions *Ha-Shirim Asher li-Shelomo* (Venice, 1622/23). The preface of the editor (de Modena) states that de Rossi, after his success in secular music, "dedicated his talents to God… and wrote down psalms, prayers and praises. As soon as one started singing [them], all the listeners were taken away by their ear-flattering beauty." The wealthy Moses Sullam and other notabilities of Jewish Venice (including the editor himself) worked hard in persuading the composer to have these liturgical works published in print.

If the flowery language of this preface can be taken at face value, de Rossi's choral works for the synagogue had already been performed from the manuscript at Mantua (possibly also at Ferrara where a Benjamin Saul Min-ha-Adumim was *ḥazzan* before 1612). The three-to eight-voiced compositions of the *Ha-Shirim Asher li-Shelomo* are not only a "first" and a solitary phenomenon in early synagogue music, they have also a particular standing within the musical work of Salamone de Rossi himself. Considering his way from the youthful freshness of the *Canzonette* (1589) down to the ripe and dramatized lyricism in his *Madrigaletti* (1628), the restraint and objectivity of his religious works becomes obvious. Rossi had no Jewish tradition of choral polyphony to start from; he could not use the idiom of church music, nor did he wish to employ his command of madrigalesque expressivity. Thus he turned to a sort of objective choral psalmody, on the one hand, and to the representative chordal columns of Gabrieli, on the other, interspersed with fine specimens of polyphonic voice weaving and a diversity of nonfunctional chords. The expressive values and musical declamation are austere, however, as compared with Rossi's secular works. They comply with Pietro Cerone's rules for psalm composition (*El Melopeo*, 1613) rather than evoking the customary conceptions of synagogue style. It should be emphasized that Rossi's compositions were intended only for particular occasions, such as "special Sabbaths and feasts," and were not designed to replace the traditional synagogue chants.

At the Crossroads of the East and West

In the course of the 16th century, a rearrangement of the Jewish population in the lands of the Diaspora had taken place. The most important moves were the influx of exiles from Spain and Portugal into the Ottoman-ruled East and the immigration of Ashkenazim into Poland and the rest of Eastern Europe. These mainstreams of migration led to the formation of an Oriental-Sephardi and an East-Ashkenazi branch of Jewish music each developing a special character that had not previously existed.

CONSOLIDATION OF THE ORIENTAL STYLE OF JEWISH MUSIC. The obstinacy shown by the Sephardim in their cling-

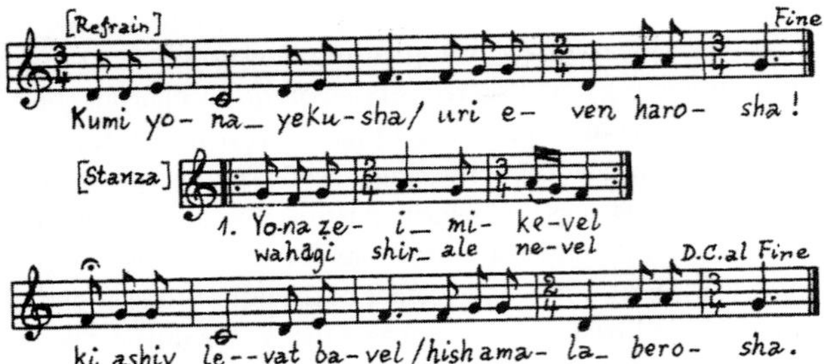

Example 18. Hymn in Spanish villancico form. Poem by Israel Najara, from his Zemirot Yisrael, *Safed, 1587; melody as sung in Iraq, beginning of 20th century, after Idelsohn,* Melodien, *vol. 2, no. 120.*

ing to the Castilian vernacular and folk song did not prevent them from yielding to the powerful influence of Oriental, especially Turkish, music. This is indicated, for instance, by the increasing use of Turkish melodies for Hebrew hymns. Musical assimilation became more spectacular when the system of **maqām* was adopted in Jewish song. Israel Najjara, late in the 16th century, appears to have been the first to assign every poem to a cetain *maqām*, even when he demands a Spanish folk tune for it. His *Kumi Yonah Yekushah*, for instance, is accompanied by the instruction "Tune: *Linda era y fermosa*" but, at the same time, is classified as belonging to the *maqām Ḥusaynī* (today it is sung to the *maqām Nawā;* see Mus. ex. 18) According to the Eastern custom, Najjara arranged his hymns for publication in a *diwān* of 12 *maqāmāt*. The framework of *maqāmāt*, each of which also represents a certain mood or "ethos," was imposed on synagogue song in general and extended even beyond hymnody proper. The majestic *Siga* became the mode for reading the Torah and all texts referring to it; the gay *Ajam-Nawruz* was used on *Shabbat Shirah*, *Simḥat Torah*, and for weddings; the mournful *Ḥijāz* expressed the mood of the Ninth of Av, funerals, and pericopes mentioning death. *Ṣabā* ("chaste love, filial affection") was reserved for texts connected with circumcisions. The most systematic adherence to the mood conventions of the *maqāmāt* was by the Aleppo community.

Poetry books dating from the 17th century onward open the section of every *maqām* with an introductory verse or independent verses called (*petiḥah*) – an improvised vocal piece rhythmically free and highly ornamented underlining the characteristics of the *maqām* as well as the art skillfulness of the performer. The Jews of North Africa (Maghreb) adhere to the Andalusian modal system called *ṭubuʿ* ("natures," *maqāmāt*), which include sequences of rhythmical pieces introduced and interspersed with improvised free rhythmical short pieces similar to the *petiḥah*, which are called *Bitain* and *mawwāl* and constitute part of the prestigious compound form, the *Nuba* (see *North African Musical Tradition).

All musical characteristics quoted up to now demonstrate the progressive Orientalization of the Jews who came from the Iberian Peninsula and intermingled with the veteran settlers. However, while the melodic configuration itself came to follow the ways of the East, some formal traits of European origin were retained such as the syllable-counting verse known from the Romance literature.

After Najara's time, the Orientalization of Eastern Sephardi music went on both at the popular and the artistic levels. In major centers of the Muslim world Jewish musicians became powerful agents in the exchange of tunes and styles; they were also fully accepted by the gentiles and their rulers. Jewish ensembles and entertainers were active in the major cities of Morocco. The most famous of them was Samuel ben Radan's group in Marakesh. Sultan ʿAbd al-Aziz, who ruled from 1894 to 1908, was particularly fond of Jewish musicians. In Iraq there were ensembles that excelled in the art of the prestigious *Iraki maqam* genre. In Tunisia, Iran, Central Asia, and elsewhere, Jewish musicians formed famous bands. The Turkish traveler Evliya Tchelebi describes the parade of the guilds before Sultan Murad IV in 1638: 300 Jewish musicians were led by their chief, Patakoglu, together with the famous Yaco and the *tunbur*-player Karakash; later on marched the Jewish dancers, jugglers, and buffoons. The reliability of the recorded numbers is proven by Ludwig August *Frankl, who found 500 Jewish musicians of Turkish nationality in Constantinople of 1856 forming 5.6% of all the craftsmen registered by the Jewish community.

The ranks of respected Turkish musician-composers were joined by Aaron Hamon (Yahudi Harun) late in the 17th century. Some of his *peshref*-suites were preserved in the so-called Harpasun notation. After him, Moses Faro ("Musi," d. 1776) and Isaac Fresco Romano ("Tanburi Issak") won great fame in the late 18th century. Turkish art music left its unmistakable imprint on the *ḥazzanut* of that country (Mus. ex. 19), as it did also in the case of the *maftirim* choirs (see above) that sometimes claim dependence on the fine melodies of the dervish orders.

As to the Sephardim settling in Italy, Amsterdam, and other parts of Christian Europe, the situation was quite different. Certainly they preserved modes and tunes of an old standing, which they held in common with their Oriental brothers; there was also a steady immigration from the Eastern communities. On the other hand, Marranos escaping from the peninsula permanently reinforced the European Sephardi congregations; they were most often highly-educated people with a flair for contemporary music. The writer Daniel Levi de *Barrios (born in Spain, from 1674 in Amsterdam) mentions several newcomers to the "Portuguese community" who excelled in playing the harp and *vihuela* (guitar) or flute, as well as in singing. As these returning converts were setting the fashion in cultural life, it is not surprising that the preserved music exhibits the character of contemporary art. It was in this style that Purim plays and comedies with music were performed and cantatas were composed for *Simḥat Torah* and other festive occasions. One of the better-known composers of this style of music was Abraham *Caceres in Amsterdam early in the 18th century. De Barrios also refers to the cantors of the Amsterdam Portuguese community, some of whom re-

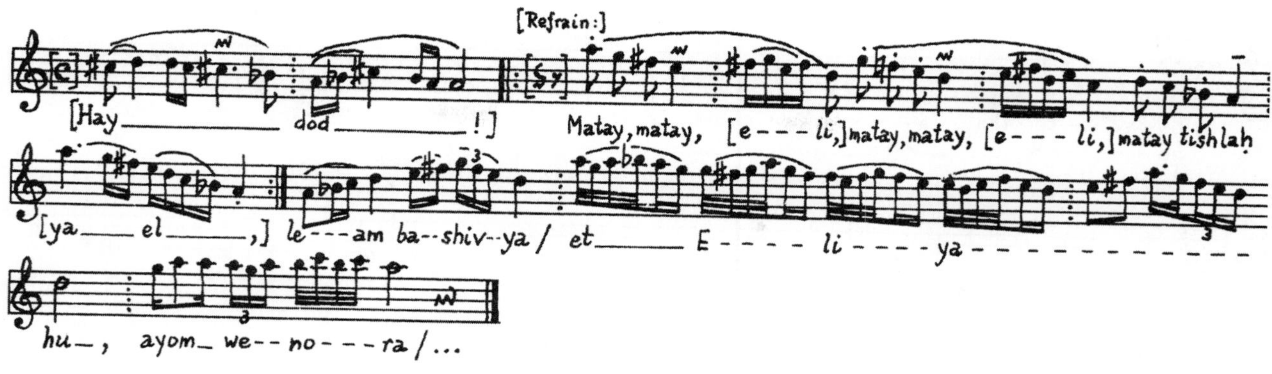

Example 19. Turkish style of ḥazzanut. *Refrain of a* pizmon *by Israel Najara. The addition by the singer of words and interjections such as those shown in brackets is typical of this style of art music. Notated in Istanbul in 1936 and published by Th. Fuchs in* Ommanut, *Zagreb, 1, 1936–37, music supplement, 2.*

ceived commissions from the London, Hamburg, and other Sephardi synagogues. A musical manuscript of the *ḥazzan* Joseph de Isaac Sarfati (mid-18th century) contains liturgical solo pieces composed in the taste of his time or directly taken over from contemporary secular works Mus. ex. 20). It must be born in mind, however, that the *ḥazzanim* of that period used to write down only "composed" music of their own production or that of their contemporaries; there was no need to notate traditional melodies and recitations that every cantor knew by heart.

Traditional Amsterdam-Sephardi song as it is intoned or recorded today makes a deep but somewhat strange impression on the listener. One is tempted to say that this Oriental music is misunderstood both by singers and notators and nevertheless performed in naïve faithfulness. Further research may perhaps disclose that it was brought to the Netherlands by *ḥazzanim* recruited from Tunis or other Eastern areas in order to fill the vacuum of traditional song felt by the Marranos. The sound of Hebrew prayers was like a revelation to them and was faithfully preserved in spite of its displaced Oriental character. But the transplantation of Eastern music to the north inevitably ended in degeneration. That this was a slow process is indicated by a tune of a *kinah* (lament) for the Ninth of Av notated in 1775 (Mus. ex. 21): the modality, the articulation of the profuse coloraturas, and especially the attack of every new phrase after a caesura still bears the unmistakable mark of Eastern origin.

The biased character of Amsterdam Portuguese music is found in the other Sephardi communities of Europe in varying degrees. London proved more "progressive" in the direction of Westernization, while the Bayonne and other Carpentras communities preserved more of the Mediterranean character (see **Avi Avi*). Leghorn and Rome retained many a non-European feature in their synagogue songs, such as tetrachord scales, free rhythm, and the variative development of modal patterns. Side by side with this conservative attitude, the Italian congregations liked to celebrate certain holidays, weddings, circumcisions, and special events (like the dedication of a new prayerhouse) by Hebrew *cantatas written in the contemporary style. Their music was of a strictly utilitarian character and significant only for the very average taste of their respective times.

THE EASTERN BRANCH OF ASHKENAZI SONG. An uninterrupted flow of Ashkenazi emigrants poured forth to the East European countries beginning in the Middle Ages and accumulated to form the most powerful Jewish community until the 20th century. The Eastern Ashkenazim preserved their old German-Jewish idiom but developed a rich religious and secular culture of their own. The special flavor of their melodies and singing habits can be distinguished from that of the Western Ashkenazim even when the tunes are identical. The material roots of this musical evolution are uncertain. The proposed influence of the *Khazars or of Byzantine Jews is only hypothetical and cannot be proven. What remains credible is the effect of country and surroundings, just as these factors imparted a Slavic tint to the song of the German settlers in the Volga region. Such influence has been proven to alter intonation and rhythm and promote the favoring of certain modal shades, as well as supply a predominantly sentimental disposition of the singer. The Eastern Ashkenazi way of singing was first discerned at its appearance in Western Europe after the renewed migration in about 1650 caused by the *Chmielnicki persecutions. A small but steady flow of rabbis, teachers, and cantors continued infiltrating the West during the 17th and 18th centuries. Thus, in 1660, Ḥayyim Selig from Lemberg was appointed *ḥazzan* at *Fuerth: Judah Leib served in several synagogues of western Germany and published a critical essay entitled *Shirei Yehudah* (Amsterdam, 1696); Jehiel Michael from Lublin established, in about 1700, *ḥazzanut* with assistant singers in the Amsterdam Ashkenazi synagogue; a traveling *ḥazzan* of great fame during the years 1715–25 was Jokele of Rzeszow; and Leib b. Elyakum from Gorokhov-Volhynia was made the first cantor of the new Ashkenazi prayerhouse of Amsterdam (1730). Through the activities of cantors from Poland in the most prominent places, Western Jewry

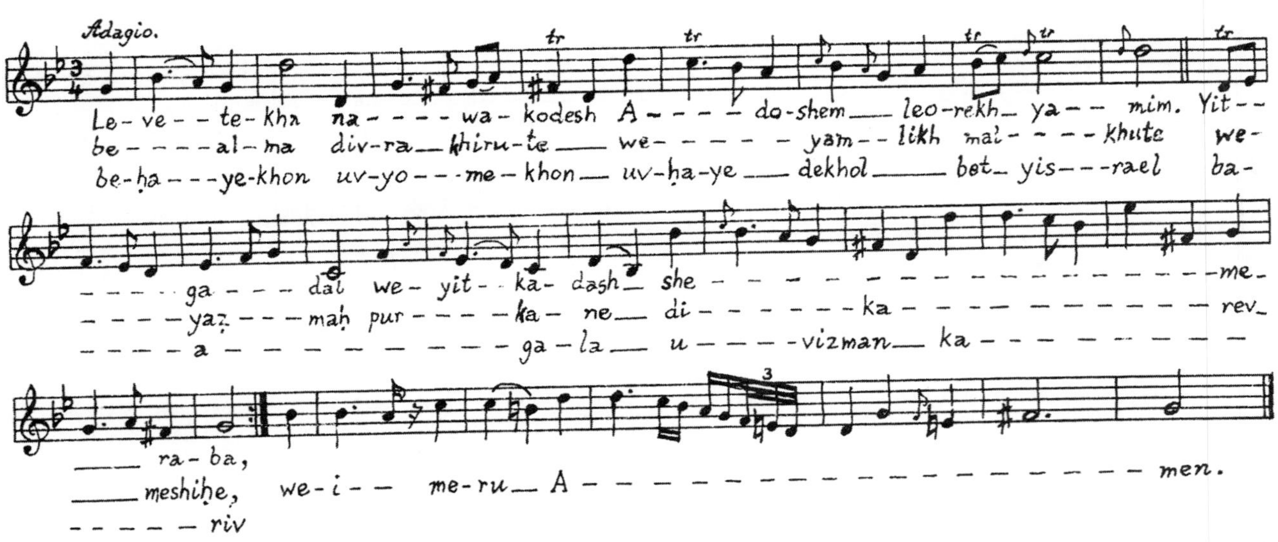

Example 20. Kaddish *for Sabbath eve, from the notebook of the ḥazzan Joseph Sarfati, Amsterdam, middle of 18th century. The melody is adapted from the composition* Ha-Mesi'aḥ Illemim *by Abraham Caceres (fl. 1720). Jerusalem,* J.N.U.L., *ms. 8° Mus 2, fol. [21]v.*

*Example 21. Oriental singing style in the Amsterdam synagogue, 18th century. Lamentation (*kinah*) for the Ninth of Av, after H. Krieg,* Spanish Liturgical Melodies of the Portuguese Israelitisch Community, Amsterdam, *vol. 2, 1954, 2.*

was confronted with the Eastern Ashkenazi style of singing and came to like it.

Among the special features of the East Ashkenazi *ḥazzanut* was its emotional power, which was stressed in particular by the early writers. The chronicle of martyrdom *Yeven Metzulah* (by Nathan *Hannover) tells of the surrender of four communities to the Tatars in 1648. When the *ḥazzan* Hirsh of Zywotow chanted the memorial prayer *El Malei Raḥamim*, the whole congregation burst forth in tears, and even the compassion of the rough captors was stirred, until they released the Jews. A similar story was told much later of the *ḥazzan* Razumny; his *El Malei Raḥamim*, said after the *Kishinev pogrom of 1913, has been taken over by many cantors (Mus. Ex. 22).

Common to the Russian and other East European peoples is the tendency to attribute to music a decisive power over human behavior and mode of action; the same is true of the Jews living among them. A highly significant characterization of East Ashkenazi *ḥazzanut* was given by Rabbi Selig Margolis in 1715 (*Ḥibburei Likkutim*, 4b–5a): a *ḥazzan* who delivers his prayers devotedly and with beautiful melodies, he holds, may stir up hearts more than any preacher. Margolis gives as an example the fact that the *ḥazzan* Baruch of Kalish moved the congregation to tears by his expressive rendition of "Perhaps the feeble and miserable people may vanish" or even by the recitation of the "Thirteen Attributes of God." In particular, during the penitential days, when he chanted the prayers that had always been the domain of individual cantorial creation (*Zokhrenu le-Ḥayyim; Mekhalkel Ḥayyim*; *Seder ha-Avodah*), "there was nobody in the synagogue whose heart was not struck and moved to repentance… all of them pouring out their hearts like water – the like of which does not occur in other countries that have neither melody (*niggun*) nor emotion (*hitorerut*); the *ḥazzanim* of our country, however, know well how to arouse penitence by their voices." This self-assertion stresses the emotional attitude, which already distinguished Eastern Ashkenazi *ḥazzanut* in the pre-ḥasidic period. Since the late 18th century, the Jews of the West have called it "the Polish style." This designation implied, *inter alia*, a certain profile of rhythm shaped by syncopes and dance-like configurations. Western cantors wrote down some early examples around 1800. It is possible that some of them reflect the practices of ḥasidic singing, such as the dance tune to the words "He redeemeth from death and releaseth from perdition" (Mus. ex. 23a); dancing is suggested here by the four-bar strains repeated with open and closed cadenzas and, especially, by the "bridge bars" between the phrases, which are also known from the *oberek* and other Slavic dances.

A minor tune of the same type (Mus. ex. 23b) embodies the full pattern of what is called "a Jewish dance." Since it is very remote from the music written by Western cantors of the 18th century, this may also be regarded as an echo of the East Ashkenazi style.

The vigor of musical life in Eastern Europe is reflected by several historical sources. It is proved by the very restrictions that the Council of the Four Lands imposed on it. As early as 1623 this board of congregations limited the creative impulse of its cantors to three or four extended works on Sabbath day; the victims of the 1650 and 1655 pogroms were mourned by reducing the instrumental music of the wedding celebration to those ceremonies where it was regarded as essential ("covering" the bride and during the night after the wedding). The council also protected the *sheli'aḥ ẓibbur* and the beadle from arbitrary dismissal (1670). It controlled the livelihood of popular singers and entertainers (*marshalek, *badḥan*) by obliging them to apply for a special license (*ketav badḥanut*).

Incipient Westernization of Ashkenazi Song

It was for good reasons that the music of the Jews from Eastern Europe was appreciated in the West as a genuine and heartwarming manifestation of the true Jewish spirit in song. Whether its special character resulted from the intense "Jewishness" of life in the Eastern countries or was the outcome of a happy merger with the melos and rhythms of Slavic music, Western European Jewry has welcomed it with a sort of nostalgic feeling down to the 20th century. Apparently it was felt to be a counterpoise to the Westernization that progressively displaced national music.

This process of Westernization started and developed first at the bordering strata of Jewish society, one of which was the substratum of folk musicians (*klezmerim*) who had ever been "wanderers between two worlds" and agents of musical exchange between peoples. Their instrumental performance

Example 22. El Malei Raḥamim, *as sung by Shlomo Razummi, 1903. After A. Nadel, EJ, vol. 6, 1930, cols. 381–2.*

Example 23. Dance-like melodies from cantorial manuals of the late 18th century. (a) After Idelsohn, Melodien, *vol, 6, part 2, no. 20; (b)* ibid., *vol 10, no. 245; cf. sections C and D with sections A and B of the first melody.*

was accorded a definite social function, since wedding music was regarded as a sort of religious obligation, and *klezmerim* were regularly employed at the feast of Simḥat Torah and Purim, the transfer of the Torah scrolls to a new synagogue, and numerous other occasions. Even the rabbinical authorities were willing to make special legal arrangements in order to secure instrumental performance wherever it was desired.

The folk musicians of Ashkenaz used to play the lute or form small ensembles of bowed strings, preferably two violins and a gamba. They were mostly true professionals and sometimes formed trade unions or guilds (Prague, 17th century). The more important communities put their musical capacity to full display at festival processions in honor of their sovereigns (Prague in 1678, 1716, 1741; Frankfurt in 1716). At the Prague festival of 1678 (described in a special Yiddish booklet) five of the usual string trios, cembalo with two fiddlers, a harpsichord with two fiddlers, a portable organ, two choirs with organ accompaniment, and a choir of *ḥazzanim* with their *meshorerim* (who "carried a sheet of music in their hands and pointed with the finger") marched in procession. The many trumpeters and drummers were probably hired from the outside, but Jewish dilettante musicians played the organs and the keyboard instruments..

Splendid performances of this kind did not take place every day; as a matter of fact, professional musicians seldom found a base for a decent living in their community alone. The rule was that Jewish musicians also served their Christian neighbors, and the *klezmerim* met stiff opposition from their Christian colleagues and their guilds. In 1651 the *arme Prager Juden Musicanten und Spielleuthe* had to appeal to the authorities to retain the privilege of 1640 granting them the right to play "when we are demanded by various people of rank and Christians to make music at Sundays and holidays" lest "we are bound to die miserably and to perish together with our folks" since "we poor people have to make a living of the art acquired by ourselves." Serving a broad and diversified audience called for a repertoire that pleased wide circles. The Jews in their closed quarters thus obtained their share of popular songs and fashionable dance music, besides their traditional Jewish dances and tunes.

The musical features of *klezmer* music are largely unknown today, but there is some circumstancial evidence that the Jewish minstrels played in a kind of "hot style" of unusual scales and lively rhythms. This becomes obvious from Hans Newsidler's parody of a "Jews' dance" (Mus. ex. 24a) and from the scornful description by their gentile competitors (Prague, 1651) that "they keep neither time nor beat, and mockingly deprive noble and sweet music of its dignity." It appears that people nevertheless liked the exotic spices of *klezmer* music, which may perhaps be compared with the fascination exerted by gypsy tunes.

Several old *klezmer* tunes were notated by Elhanan Kirchhan of Fuerth in 1727 (*Simḥat ha-Nefesh* 2; facs. repr. New York, 1926). Mus. ex. 24b shows a Purim song obviously composed in a humorous mood. These specimens of 1727 indicate that the general trend was already directed toward adoption of the European baroque style. A Purim *niggun* notated by cantor Judah Elias in 1744 (Mus. ex. 24c) exemplifies the inorganic linking of a traditional Jewish tune (I, G minor) through dance-like "bridge bars" (II), with a continuation in the contemporary taste (III, D minor; IV, B-flat major, modulation and *da capo*); some strains of the melody are echoed in the 1794 Purim tunes of Aaron Beer (Idelsohn, *Melodien*, 6, nos. 117–8) suggesting a common popular source. Songs in the vernacular followed the same direction as instrumental music. Although their foreign melodies were balanced by original invention, their constant use advanced the Westernization of music at the popular level.

Since the 17th century, the affluent classes had become accustomed to have their children, especially daughters, instructed in singing and instruments (cf. Jos. Kosman, *Noheg ka-Ẓon Yosef*, 1718, 18a; Jos. Hahn, *Yosif Omeẓ*, 1723, 890). *Glueckel of Hameln relates that her stepsister knew how to play the harpsichord well (c. 1650). During the Prague festival of 1678, the granddaughter of the community chairman played the cembalo, and Isaac Mahler's daughter the harpsichord. The tendency toward integration in music grew stronger among the upper classes during the late 18th century, when Rachel (Levin) *Varnhagen could report: "My musical instruction consisted of nothing but the music of Sebastian (Bach) and the entire school [of the period]." Heinrich *Heine's mother, Peierche van Geldern (b. 1771), had to conceal her flute ("my truly harmonious friend both in joy and grief") from her strict father. Sara Levi, daughter of the Berlin financier Daniel *Itzig, was the last and most faithful disciple of Wilhelm Friedemann Bach (d. 1784) and preserved many of his autograph works for posterity. These developments in the upper class prepared the way for the emergence of composers like Giacomo *Meyerbeer and Felix *Mendelssohn.

The trend of integration in European music finally came to affect the broad masses of the people, and the *ḥazzan*, their speaker and representative, was too dependent upon the goodwill of the public not to gratify its taste. Whereas early in the 17th century only the use of foreign melodies had been protested (by Isaiah *Horowitz and Joseph *Hahn), about 1700 and thereafter the entire style of cantorial performance was challenged by practices adopted from secular music. Violent discussions about the unstable state and reputation of cantorial art are reflected in several pamphlets. The deeper reasons for this crisis were exposed by Judah Leib Zelichover (*Shirei Yehudah*, Amsterdam, 1696). The author still clings to the medieval idea that *ḥazzanut* should be the musical expression of mystical intentions (*kavvanot*) by means of extended vocalises; he begrudges the cantors applauded by his genera-

Example 24. Characteristics of early klezmer *music. (a) parody,* "Der Juden Tantz," *lute piece by Hans Newsidler, 1554, after P. Nettl,* Alte juedische Spielleute und Musiker, *64–65; (b) Purim song, after E. Kirchhan,* Simḥat ha-Nefesh, *part II, fol. 7r.; (c)* "Purim Niggun" *from the manual of Judah Elias of Hanover, 1744, no. 224, after A. Nadel, unidentified facsimile publication, Jerusalem, J.N.U.L., Jakob Michael Collection of Jewish Music, JMA 3997.*

tion for neglecting the traditional mode of singing ("saying: It's outdated and does not satisfy us") and replacing it by their own inventions or borrowings from the opera, dance bands, of street singers.

Considering the isolation of Judaism in those days and its divorce from secular art, these declarations could hardly be called overstatement. A remedy was suggested about one generation later by the cantor Solomon *Lipschitz (*Teʿudat Shelomo*, Offenbach 1718, no. 30). He also censures the ambitious individualism of his colleagues ("everybody builds a stage for himself"), which mostly turned out to be imitations of the simplest forms of music, since the cantors lacked any formal musical education. Lipschitz wishes to replace the old form of Jewish singing leaning on the lower strata of the music of the gentile environment, by more accomplished forms of art: "Making music without knowing the rules of *musica* is like a prayer without true intention [*kavvanah*]!"

The results of such ideas soon became manifest. Close to the middle of the 18th century, cantors began to use musical notation and thus began the "literary period" of Ashkenazi *ḥazzanut*. It was not the old and venerable traditions of synagogue song, however, which were put on paper, but rather the new compositions of the individual *ḥazzanim*. The earliest known document of this kind is a manuscript from 1744 written by the *Herr Musicus und Vor Saenger Juda Elias in Hannover*. After this work come the manuscripts of the most eminent cantor of his age, Aaron *Beer (1738–1821); famous as *der Bamberger Ḥazzan*; from December 1764 in Berlin). His collection contains both his own versions or new creations of synagogue melodies and those of a dozen contemporaries (published in Idelsohn, *Melodien*, 6). Other important manuscripts go back to *meshorerim* who also served their cantors as "musical secretaries" (Idelsohn, op. cit.).

The character of these cantorial works is defined, first of all, by its strict homophony, tailored to the needs of a virtuoso singer wishing to display his coloraturas (*lenaggen*), while the text is given a subordinate role. The structure of these compositions remains in the line of traditional *ḥazzanut* by developing a theme by means of variative improvisation. The resources of the basic melodies, however, are borrowed from the post-baroque music of about 1700 to 1760, often recalling the fashionable composers of that period (Monn, Wagenseil, Zach). There is little left of the strong pathos and dramatics of the true baroque, although the artistic evolution of the opening theme statement and the extensive use of sequences were imitated, as was the instrument-like treatment of the voice (Mus. ex. 25a); later in the century, some influence of the early classicists can be observed (Mus. Ex 25b).

The "new trend" of cantorial art catered to the musical taste of about 1720, but the merger of traditional and modern style was far from complete. The customary Jewish freedom of rhythm and the roving melodical line could not easily be harnessed; attempts to do so resulted in asymmetrical phrases, awkward modulation, and other flaws in conventional workmanship. Most of these cantorial compositions shared only the platitudes and the most insipid musical idioms of the period. They were the product of a superficial connection between incompatible styles – the first sign of that dualism in the West Ashkenazi musical practice that was to become the hallmark of the 19th century.

MODERN TIMES

The Nineteenth Century

By the 18th century, conditions of life had become almost unbearable in the ghettos and crowded Jewish settlements of the continent. The protracted persecutions aimed at economic, moral, and physical ruins nearly accomplished their purpose and were balanced only by the firm belief in final redemption, unbroken self-confidence, and vital energy. The growing pressure put European Jewry on two different paths of self-deliverance, as divergent from each other as the leaders Moses *Mendelssohn and *Israel b. Eliezer Baʿal Shem Tov. Assimilation, aiming at civil emancipation, was the external way toward joining the society of an enlightened Europe; *Ḥasidism, on the other hand, was entirely directed toward intrinsic values and was coupled with a certain abrogation of bitter reality. Both tendencies penetrated all aspects of life and had strong repercussions on music. A specific kind of music could demonstrate a certain ideology (e.g., use of the organ in synagogue service) or be made an essential means of spiritual exaltation (the ḥasidic *niggun*); music became a vehicle of both social integration and spiritual escapism.

THE ḤASIDIC NIGGUN. East European Jewry, suffering from increasing pauperization and the incessant menace of extermination for centuries, underwent a critical disillusionment with the failure of *Shabbetai Ẓevi and its aftereffects. At this doleful juncture, between 1730 and 1750, arose the ḥasidic movement, with its message of delivery of the soul from its detention in the body and the troubled earthly life by its ascent to spiritual, true values, thus partaking of a higher existence. As a continuation of the mystical tenets of Safed (see above), "a joyful heart and a devoted soul learning for our Father in Heaven" were made the cornerstone of prayer, and singing became a focal point of religious experience. For the first time, music of Jewish mysticism itself becomes known and may still be heard today. Ḥasidic singing spans the entire gamut from grief and deep concern to extreme joy, from a meditative mood to ecstatic exaltation, from purposeful melodic construction to open forms or shallow banality (see *Ḥasidism: Musical Tradition).

THE ABSORPTION OF THE EUROPEAN ART STYLE. While the Jews of Eastern Europe decided to overcome their miseries by a spiritual divorce from the environment, those of the West witnessed Lessing declare the equivalence of religions and the French Revolution proclaim freedom and equality for all men. This atmosphere encouraged their striving for integration in a future society of enlightened Europeans and tendencies of assimilation that ranged from slight external changes to total surrender. Music was regarded as an essential part of future

Example 25. Cantorial compositions in 18th-century style. (a) Hodu *for* Ḥanukkah *from the manual of Judah Elias of Hanover, 1744, after A. Nadel,* Der Orden Bne Briss 9–10, 95; *(b) from Hodu for* Ḥanukkah *by Moses Pan (before 1791), after Idelsohn,* Melodien, *vol. 6, no. 55. Both compositions use the traditional melody of* Ma'oz Ẓur *as a point of departure.*

integration. Therefore, both tradition and acquired practices (which could barely be kept apart) were put to a test against the taste, rules, and forms of contemporary music. The prolonged prelude of this process has already been mentioned; by the 19th century, it gained sway and momentum of decisive power. As soon as the obstacles of personal advancement were removed, musicians of Jewish birth broke away from their faith, either formally or tacitly. The Jewish community suffered from a heavy drain of talent of higher and medium caliber. This incessant process principally affected synagogue music until, in the second half of the century; it became partly dependent upon immigration of cantors from Eastern Europe – not to speak of the lack of high-ranking composers.

The extent and nature of this exodus can be gauged by the numerous Jewish-born musicians who entered the fields of European art and were famous enough to merit entries in general encyclopedias. Among those born between 1790 and 1850, the most prominent categories were instrumentalists, especially virtuosos (28), and composers (21); next came singers and the scholars and pedagogues (11). Allegedly "typical Jewish" occupations are as yet clearly in the minority: conductors (6), publishers (2), impressarios (1), critics (0). A peak (60%) is formed by those born in the decade 1830 to 1839 who chose their profession about 1848, hopeful of being granted full civil rights. These forces were practically lost for the cultivation and development of the Jewish musical heritage. As to synagogue music, the impetus for immediate and drastic innovations came from a sudden turn at the political level. Napoleon wished to promote the social integration of his Jewish subjects by granting the superintendents of all communities with over 2,000 members an official status. Consequently, organized and binding changes in liturgy and its music could be enforced against the will of any opposition.

The Reform Movement. Napoleon also conferred his synagogue constitution upon some annexed countries, such as the

Kingdom of Westphalia; among them, the Koeniglich Wuerttembergische israelitische Oberkirchenbehoerde even survived his rule. These authorities gave the official and legal framework to the already existing tendencies of correcting and amending the synagogue service. The disregard of external form, dignity, and beauty was regarded by many as an abasing stigma of exile conditions. The mystical ideas and symbols that provided so much content to *ḥazzanut* and its coloraturas were no longer understood; the congregations had changed into an audience that expected music to evoke feelings they could not find within themselves. A small but energetic circle of extremists used the communal constitution given to Westphalian Jewry to materialize its vision of a liturgy modeled after European ideas and aesthetics. Perspicaciously, they started working with the young generation, on the initiative of Israel *Jacobsohn, court factor of Jerome Bonaparte and fervent champion of synagogue reform. The pupils of the Jewish mechanics school at Seesen were given formal instruction in music from 1804; they formed the choir and sang to the *organ installed in the prayer hall of their institution (1807). The music consisted of chorale-like melodies composed by their Christian music teacher to Hebrew and German texts. Soon afterward, Jacobsohn opened another Reform synagogue with organ and part-singing in the Westphalian capital of Kassel. Both his institutions were forced to close, however, with the end of the kingdom in 1814. The reformer and his musical assistant went to Berlin and opened a private synagogue with an organ and a boys' choir from the free school (1815). Two years later (1817), they moved to the private synagogue established in the house of Meyerbeer's father, the banker Jacob Herz Beer, where an organ with two manuals and pedal was put at their disposition. The bold innovations of liturgy and liturgical singing aroused disputes and quarrels with the conservatives, whereupon the government ordered the synagogue to be closed (1818).

Meanwhile, the Reform movement has spread to other communities. The Hungarian rabbi Aaron *Chorin published a book in defense of the synagogue organ (*Nogah ha-Ẓedek*, Dessau, 1818). Reform congregations had been founded at Frankfurt (Philanthropin orphanage, 1816), Hamburg (1817), and during the Leipzig Fair (a synagogue opened in 1820 with tunes composed by Meyerbeer). The Hamburg synagogue was joined by many of the local Sephardim and their cantors, was very active, and existed until 1938. Its members regarded the melodic recitation of prayers and Bible reading as opposed to the spirit of the age and replaced them by plain declamation. On the other hand, some Sephardi tunes (of the "civilized" kind favored by the Marranos) were adopted. Above all, Reform congregations created German-language hymnals on the pattern of the Protestant *Gesangbuch* (first: Jos. Joelson's *Shirei Yeshurun*, Frankfurt (1816)). The Hamburg hymnal (1819, many editions) contained some melodies composed by well-known musicians like A.G. Methfessel and, later, the Jewish-born Ferdinand *Hiller.

Reform congregations, however, were generally unable to recruit composers with both stature and real involvement with the task. The original tunes of their hymnals, mostly the products of music teachers, match the feebleness and absence of inspiration found in the texts. Furthermore, there existed an ideological impulse to integrate prayers with the Christian environment by adopting the tunes of well-known Protestant chorales. Banal new texts were connected with the melodies of Christological songs (*Sefer Zemirot Yisrael*, Stuttgart, 1836). After all the effort, a few jewels also took root outside Reform synagogues (*Seele, was betruebst du dich*, music by J.H.G. Stoewing; *Hoert, die Posaune toent mit Macht*, poetry by Abraham *Geiger). More important are two achievements of a general nature. First, the instruction of the youth in part singing – no longer in the old, improvised manner, but of music written according to the rules of harmony – through the schools, orphanages, and seminaries spread the understanding of European music to the less-privileged classes as well. Another innovation of lasting effect was playing the organ during the service. An object of raging and never-settled debates, the use of the organ in synagogues was made a cornerstone and symbol of later liberalism against strict observance in religious matters.

The "Improved Service" and Its Music. Attempts at radical reformation of the liturgy and its music did not go beyond a certain sector of the larger communities; in the provinces, they failed almost completely. This does not imply indifference or sluggishness on the part of the majority. In fact, a more decided and massive move toward musical "acculturation" has seldom been observed. Even where the liturgical tradition was handled with caution or left untouched, the conditions prevailing in prayer performance caused much indignation. Western Jewry strove for an improvement – for a *geordneter Gottesdienst* – and this concept included the entire field of sacred song ("orderly music of the divine service"; Sulzer).

First came the renunciation of the brilliant coloratura in the cantorial solo, once regarded as an asset in its own right. By 1800 *ḥazzanut* was hopelessly pervaded with foreign elements (mostly baroque) and had developed as a sort of half-breed that, unfortunately, demonstrated the weak spots of both its ancestors. Independent attempts at modernization were initiated by provincial cantors (Mus. ex. 26) whose abilities and taste were not up to their exaggerated aspirations. Therefore, these experimental works were discarded by the more urbanized taste.

The changed attitude toward musical performance also wished to dispose of the usual trio consisting of the cantor and two assistant singers (*meshorerim*). The improvised accompaniment executed by the latter was to be replaced by harmonies of academic regular structure, and their solo coloraturas were to be clipped as eccentricities of an outmoded taste. Likewise, the boisterous chorus of the entire congregation lost its value as a moving acoustical experience with ancient roots and was to be silenced and substituted by well-rehearsed part singing. Such ideas and tendencies materialized during the period between the Congress of Vienna (1814–15;

disappointing the hope for emancipation) and the revolutions of 1848 that led to the admission to citizenship. In the meantime, synagogue music was remodeled according to the ideas of the "Jewish European." Fortunately, a cadre of real talents remained after the great exodus of musicians to devote itself entirely to this task. All of them were proficient in synagogue song and were backed by family tradition in this vocation. Most of them were gifted with extraordinary voices, and some had already excelled as child prodigies; rich patronage had paved their way to studies of musical theory and instrumental playing. They were given the chance to realize their ideas on a large scale when they were between 19 and 30 years of age: the ardent idealism of youth contributed much to the breakthrough of the new trend.

Two forerunners had already set the first standards. Israel *Lovy, a cantor and concert singer with a phenomenal voice, established a four-part choir in the new Paris synagogue in 1822. The music he composed for this body indiscriminately combined the old *meshorerim* tradition and the choral style of the *opéra comique*. The other precursor of things to come, Maier (Meir) *Kohn of Munich, did not demonstrate Lovy's creativeness when he was commissioned to establish a choir of boys and men in 1832. He had to resort to local non-Jewish musicians for choral compositions or, at least, the harmonization of melodies arranged or composed by himself and others. Kohn's compilations, (*Vollstaendiger Jahrgang von Terzett-und Chorgesaengen der Synagoge in Muenchen…*) known as the *Muenchner Terzettgesaenge* (1839), became, for some decades, a vademecum for small to medium-sized communities. The compositions offered by the early proponents of the "improved service" extended to selected chapters of the liturgy and touched upon only a small part of the highly important role of the *ḥazzan*. Thoroughgoing changes of the whole extent of the musical liturgy were finally put into effect by Solomon *Sulzer in Vienna (from 1826), Hirsch *Weintraub at Koenigsberg (1838), Louis *Lewandowski in Berlin (1840), and Samuel *Naumbourg in Paris (1845). The principles guiding the various renovators of synagogue music have much in common:

> We might find out the original noble forms to which we should anchor ourselves, developing them in an artistic style… Jewish liturgy must satisfy the musical demands while remaining Jewish; and it should not be necessary to sacrifice the Jewish characteristics to artistic forms… The old tunes and singing modes, which became national should be improved, selected, and adjusted to the rules of art. But new musical creations should also not be avoided (Sulzer, *Denkschrift*, 1876).

The point of departure had to be a survey of the entire body of tunes and recitatives transmitted by oral tradition. For the first time in history, the complete cycle of obligatory or commonly accepted melodies was recorded in musical notation (until then, only the extraordinary, individual compositions and arrangements had been written down). In examining these invaluable documents, one should disregard the enclosure in bars of recitative and free-rhythmic tunes by which the notators paid tribute to contemporary usage; the obligation to fill the bars regularly resulted in shortening and lengthening of notes, and most of the ornamental passages do not disclose their deliberate *rubato* tempo.

The tendencies of "improvement, selection, and adjustment to artistic forms" (Sulzer) enter the picture at this point. They were justified for their time, however painful to the adherents of modern historicism and folklore conservation. However, personal liberty in the aural interpretation of traditional melody patterns or "ideas" had been the characteristic procedure of Jewish music at all times; it was also the duty of the 19th-century cantor, as it had been of his predecessors. Therefore it was not a fault but their right when can-

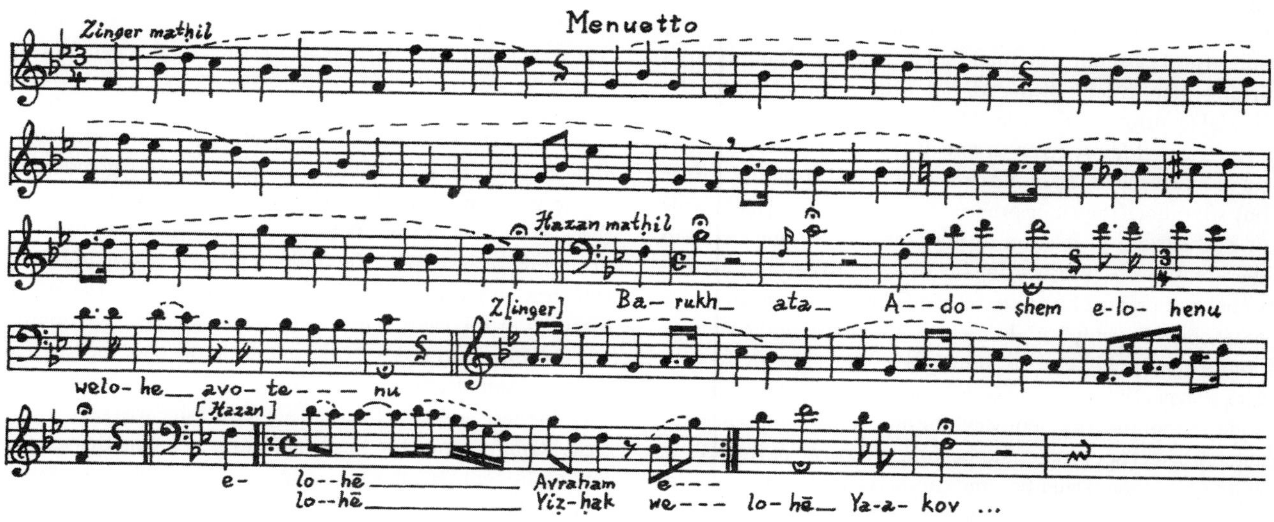

Example 26. German provincial setting of the Amidah *prayer for* ḥazzan *and "singer." The indications are: singer begins,* ḥazzan *begins. From an anonymous Ms., possibly Bavarian, probably early 19th century. Jerusalem,* J.N.U.L., *Jakob Michael Collection of Jewish Music, Ms.* JMA *4249 (1), fol. 15v.*

Example 27. A traditional melody and its 19th-century adaptation. (a) A. Baer, Baal T'fillah, *1883³, no. 1158; (b) Ch. Vinaver,* Anthology of Jewish Music, *1955, no. 23; (c) S. Naumbourg,* Zemirot Yisrael, *vol. 2, 1847, no. 228; (d) L. Lewandowski,* Todah W'Simrah, *part 2, 1882, no. 179.*

tors now followed the earlier trend toward classicism with a new trend oriented toward the early romantic style in music. Consequently, their arrangements of traditional material tend toward melodies of clean-cut outlines and logical, if possible symmetric, structures. The old modes were preferably transformed to major or minor; if the specific *shtayger* scales are preserved, they are sometimes disturbed by leading notes and other dressings of modern tonality (Mus. ex. 27). The recitatives were toned down to a rational declamation, in which melismatic figures are admitted only for scoring meaningful words or marking the clauses of the sentence.

The intended "improvement" of the cantor's part demanded a gentle touch guided by sensitivity for genuine and authentic values. A bolder approach was suited to the passages assigned to the choir. Precedents of choral performance were the *meshorerim* accompaniment of the cantor and the largely turbulent responses of the entire congregation. The traditional singing of *meshorerim* contained elements that could be rearranged to form a choral style of genuine flavor. Naumbourg, Sulzer, and Lewandowski made attempts at this. Naumbourg's arrangement of one of the *Mi-Sinai* tunes demonstrates the special features of this style (Mus. ex. 28).

The melody is given to one of the inner parts, the cantor's tenor, embedded in the chords of male voices and tender boy sopranos. The latter proceed very often in parallel thirds or sixths (both in relation to the cantor's tune and between themselves) and produce an effect similar to certain mixture stops of an organ. The basses refrain from a steady accompaniment, entering only with hummed chords at melodic vantage points or acting like a community that joins in with the cantor's prayer. There are also solo sections provided for the bass and the soprano, frequently exhibiting an instrumental character; a sweet soprano could become a favorite of the public, and many of them later became famous cantors. The resources of this original style were tapped but not developed to any importance in Western Ashkenaz, but they became preeminent in East Ashkenazi synagogue music, as shall be seen later.

The free composition of choral works in the contemporary style was challenged by still another factor–the need to give shape to the songs and responses of the congregation itself. Sulzer and Lewandowski were gifted with the inventiveness and skill for creating choir pieces of high quality. The religious element in Sulzer's music exhibits delicate feeling with a sentimental timbre, clad in simple but sweet harmonies, while Lewandowski expresses himself in a more forceful manner and avoids that common intelligibility which is apt to turn into triviality in a short while.

The first synagogue choirs were quite an experience to the congregations who had been annoyed by singing habits perpetuated by inertia alone or by barren experimentation. Sulzer's choir in the Vienna Seitenstettengassen Synagoge, was also praised by Christian visitors such as Liszt, the Abbé Mainzer, and others as both a human and musical experience. The impact of Sulzer's achievements was felt very soon by the brisk demand for his scores. Synagogue choirs were founded in Prague, Copenhagen (before 1838), Breslau, Berlin, Dresden (1840), and London (1841). Sulzer's disciples or choir singers transmitted the music of the "improved service" to the United States as well (G.M. Cohen, New York 1845; A. Kaiser, Baltimore 1866; M. Goldstein, Cincinnati 1881; E.J. Stark); their appearance antedated that of East Ashkenazi synagogue song in the Western hemisphere (New York, 1852). Cantors from the East European communities came to Vienna in order to perfect themselves with the "father of the new song in Israel" (Pinchas *Minkowski). The more important of Sulzer's Eastern disciples or followers were Osias *Abrass, Jacob *Bachmann, Nissan *Blumenthal, Wolf *Shestapol, Spitzburg ("the Russian Sulzer"), and others.

In these ways and by these men, the stage was set for musical life in the Western houses of prayer. During the second half of the century, after 1848, the liberal wing of conservative (non-Reform) synagogues added organ playing to the service order. A progressive cadre of communal leaders had decreed its admissability during the second Assembly of Rabbis held at Frankfurt in 1845. It was, however, a partial vote that did not oblige or convince any sworn opponent. For instance, five years before the Berlin New Synagogue was finally furnished with an organ (1866), seven rabbis were consulted; Rabbi Michael Sachs was among the opponents, Abraham *Geiger was with the advocates. In the end 74 German-Jewish communities came to have organs played at their service, according to a count made in 1933. In Russia, the first synagogue organ was installed not before 1901 (Union Temple, Odessa). Very few of the composers writing for this instrument understood its technique and spirit. Lewandowski, a pupil of E.A. Grell, was the first to produce real organ music for the synagogue.

The absorption of European standards in the musical service was paid for later in the 19th century with the weakened understanding and cultivation of the old tradition, especially of the cantor's role. The impending loss of acknowledged values was noticed in time and was averted by collecting and publishing what remained of oral tradition. Some of the related publications exhibit a remarkable sense of authenticity: outstanding is Abraham *Baer's voluminous, almost single-handed, collection, *Baal T'fillah* (1877); relatively reliable is F. *Consolo's *Libro dei canti d'Israele* (Leghorn-Sephardi tradition, 1892). Other authors who intended to create handbooks for the cantor's training imparted a little polish to the original tunes, but may still serve well for critical research (Moritz *Deutsch, *Vorbeterschule*, 1871; Meier Wodak, *Ha-Menaẓẓe'aḥ*, 1898; etc.). The Sephardi rite of Carpentras was noted by J.S. & M. Crémieu (1887), that of Paris by E. Jonas (1854), and a selection of London Portuguese melodies by the piano virtuoso E. *Aguilar and D.A. de *Sola (1857, unfortunately in a harmonized and metricized arrangement).

Parallel with the activities in collecting and editing, inquisitive minds strove to answer the question of the distinctive elements in Jewish music. The particular nature of the *shtayger* scales or modes, already noted by Weintraub (1854) and Naumbourg (1874), was demonstrated by the Viennese cantor and disciple of Sulzer, Josef *Singer in an attempt at systematization (1886). Outstanding in this first generation of researchers was Eduard *Birnbaum, Weintraub's successor at Koenigsberg from 1879. A sound Jewish education enabled him to place musical questions in the context of history and literature and achieve an unusually high level. His inconspicuous article (later a booklet) *Juedische Musiker am Hofe von Mantua* (1893) has become a classic in its field. An asset of lasting value is Birnbaum's collection of cantorial manuscripts and other source material (at present in the Hebrew Union College Library, Cincinnati); partly exploited by Idelsohn, it holds research tasks for generations to come.

The 19th century also witnessed the professional organization of West European cantors and the edition of periodicals in which the publication of source material and research had a place (*Der Juedische Cantor*, ed. A. Blaustein, 1879–98; *Oesterreichisch-Ungarische Cantorenzeitung*, founded by Jacob *Bauer, 1881–1902). In spite of all the activity and alertness in matters of synagogue song, the West European communities were drained more and more of its musical talents, including cantorial candidates. The gap was filled by immigrants from Eastern Europe, especially after the Russian persecutions of 1882. The Western synagogues could maintain their musical standard by recruiting the often-brilliant singers originating, on a nearly equal scale, in Russia, the Baltic states, Poland, Hungary, and the neo-Prussian provinces. Finally, they outnumbered their local colleagues in the ratio of three to two. The newcomers, mostly ambitious and studious youths, learned the melodies of the Western rite with great zeal; as prescribed by Jacob Moellin (Maharil), there was no intermingling of regional traditions before 1900. Exceptions were Joseph Goldstein's enclave of Eastern virtuoso song in Vienna (1858–99), and Ḥayyim Wasserzug (Lomser), who went to London (1875) as a famous *ḥazzan*.

THE EVOLUTION OF EAST ASHKENAZI ḤAZZANUT. The breakdown of inherited musical forms in the West was the work of a few decades and generally affected synagogue and Jewish communal life, albeit to varying degrees. East European Jewry remained completely immune from the advance of the times and kept its ears shut before art music, which had now become available to the middle classes throughout Europe. The developments there, however, occurred by way of a gradual and organic evolution.

The reasons for this development in Eastern Europe must be sought both in social and intellectual conditions. The Jewish population of Eastern Europe was massed in its assigned *Pale of Settlement and bound by almost medieval restrictions. Even outstanding musical talents could find an outlet only in synagogue song or, alternatively, in popular music making and entertaining. They had to contribute their sometimes- considerable gifts compulsorily, to the musical life of their community, which was deeply concerned with all matters of music. Within that responsive musical microcosm, synagogue song represented the highest level of art; the interest and knowledgeability of the public was focused on the solo performance of the *ḥazzan* and subjected it to both relentless criticism and unconditional adulation. P. Minkowski, for example, commented:

> The Odessa community was not an ordinary one, but was split in two factions, accusers and defenders… When I had sung ancient melodies known to every listener, a dispute arose on the spot… as to whether my song was in the style of Abrass [Pitche] or of Bachman, and people of venerable age also conjured Zalel [Shulsinger] up from his grave in Ereẓ Israel in order to pitch my singing against Tzalel's… (Recollections).

Ashkenazi *ḥazzanut* represented an original and self-sufficient kind of music, comparable only with certain Oriental styles of song. Its most conspicuous attribute is its expressivity, the prayer of the community subsiding, as soon as the *ḥazzan's* voice is heard, and the mind completely identifies itself with the voice. Unlike the self-imposed restraint of the Western cantor, the aim is to produce an upsurge of religious feelings (*hitorerut*) and a strong and immediate response. The

Cantor
ad libitum
Yit-ga-dal w'yitkadash shemē — ra — — — — — ba: A- men. Be-alma — div-ra — khi-ru-te
Ten.
Basso
we-yam — — — likh malkhu — — — — — te be-ḥayekhon uv-yo — — — me-khon uve-ḥa — — — — —
yē dekhol bet yisra — — — — — — — — — — el baa-ga-la uvizman kariv weïm-ru: A — — — — — — men.
Solo Soprani
pp
in tempo
Yit-ba — — — rakh — weyish-ta-baḥ weyit-pa--ar weyit-ro-mam we-yit-nas--se — weyithadar weyit a-
Sopr.
(tacet 17 bars)
leh weyit-ha — — — lal — shemē de-Kudesha — : Brikh hu. Leela ul-e — — — — — —
— — — — — — — — — — — la — min kol birkha-ta we-shi-ra- ta tush — — — be-ha —
— — — — — — — — — — — — ta — we-ne — ḥe-ma — — ta daa-mi — — — — — —

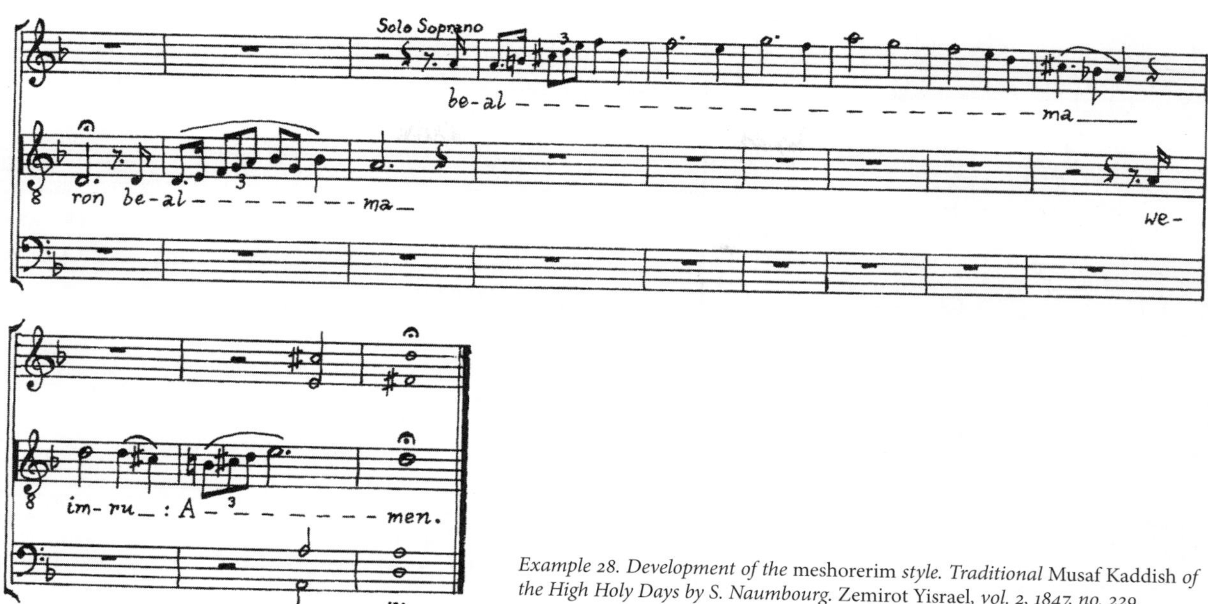

Example 28. Development of the meshorerim *style. Traditional* Musaf Kaddish *of the High Holy Days by S. Naumbourg.* Zemirot Yisrael, *vol. 2, 1847, no. 229.*

impressive capacities of this particular kind of song are not easily described in precise technical terms. The cantorial melody develops as a strictly monodic line, with structural points of support quite different from those of European harmony. It proceeds by many small movements, creating melodic cells, which build up the body of the tune (Mus. ex. 29 and 30) Phrases composed of long-drawn single notes are nonexistent: they appear to be dissolved into flickering. Rhythm is not confined to bars and stringent symmetry, but is as free as in the music of the Oriental ancestors and relations of this style. Melodies are often shaped to *shtayger* scales; modulations are rather frequent and a proof of mastery, like the Oriental singers' shifting from *maqām* to *maqām*. Another archaic element is still in full vigor: the principle of variation

Example 29. Eastern Ashkenazi ḥazzanut, c. 1800. Introductory prayer to the confession of sins on the Day of Atonement, by Solomon Weintraub (Kashtan), as notated from oral translation by D. Roitman, after G. Ephros (ed.), Cantorial Anthology, *vol. 2, 1940, 135.*

Example 30. Eastern Ashkenazi ḥazzanut *with "singer" soli, c. 1990.* Retzeh, *by Aryeh Lev Schlossberg (1841–1925), after G. Ephros (ed.),* Cantorial Anthology, *vol. 4, 1953, 368–9.*

governs both the melodic cells at every instance of recurrence and the whole structure of a piece. Often a cantorial composition contains a "double course" of the same section – first as an original statement and then as a variation of the same (Mus. ex. 29). At times, the work is composed of melodic cells arranged without any apparent order (Mus. ex. 30) exactly as the ancient *nusaḥ* style demands (see above).

One of the rules of *ḥazzanut*, however, is that there is no rule of adhering to one plan or the other: expression is the element, which counts. The expressive intention is overwhelming: it dissolves the form of the underlying poetic text past recognition; single words may be repeated over and over (Mus. ex. 30), in spite of halakhic prohibition; emotional exclamations intermingle and long coloraturas expand certain syllables, in particular towering above the penultima at the end of compositions. These traits may appear exaggerated to a taste accustomed to classicist restraint, but they are capable of the most suggestive presentation of sentiments, mostly in the pitiful and lachrymose mood (the expression of joy being channeled mostly through imitations of foreign song). The *ḥazzan*'s voice plays on a variety of sound colors, complemented by a high falsetto (in the old contralto manner) and prefers techniques such as the gliding passage from tone to tone, slowly entering trills, and other characteristics of an advanced vocal culture.

The development of East Ashkenazi *ḥazzanut* is known only since its early 19th-century protagonists, whose exploits and compositions had been preserved in the memory of their congregations and disciples. Besides, regional schools and stylistic subdivisions, such as the Jewish-Lithuanian, Ukrainian, etc., a parting line is recognized between an older, "classical" *ḥazzanut* and a younger style influenced by Western art music.

The "classical" stage is represented in the communities of the Ukraine and Volhynia by the impressive personalities of Bezalel *Shulsinger ("Tzalel Odesser"), Yeruḥam *Blindman ("Yeruḥam ha-Koton"), Yeḥezkel of Zhitomir, and Solomon *Weintraub (Kashtan). The old style was perpetuated by Israel Shkuder (1804–46) and Nissan *Spivak ("Nissi Belzer"). To judge from the small part of their music preserved, the early cantors did not indulge in the excessive coloraturas and superficial tricks preferred by the later synagogue singers. In Lithuania and Poland, the old style was upheld by Sender *Polachek of Minsk, who excelled in particular melodic formations (Sender's *shtayger*), and his disciple Baruch *Karliner, a master of spontaneous improvisation "when the spirit dwelled upon him." Galicia and Hungary had David'l

Strelisker ("Dovidl *Brod"), who assumed the airs of a noble dilettante and would not give in to the modernistic tendencies of the Budapest *chor shul* of 1830.

The first waves of Sulzer's musical reform reached Eastern Europe promptly and impressed both singers and ambitious community leaders. Cantor Nissan *Blumenthal of Odessa was the first to adopt Western ways by cultivating a smooth bel canto style. Some went or were sent to Sulzer himself in Vienna (see above). Others acquired their formal education in Eastern Europe, such as Joel David Strashunsky (the "Vilner Balabess'l") with Moniuszko in Poland, and Jacob *Bachmann with Anton Rubinstein in Russia. The "Westernizing" *ḥazzanim* limited the influence of art music to choral composition, while the solo parts of their own were left almost untouched. In general, choral composition kept to the *meshorerim* style, touched up with more regular harmonic sequences; but those who were tempted to introduce fugues or other musical devices of advanced academic training also inserted showpieces of artful elaboration indiscriminately. In addition, their works frequently reflect the fascination exerted by Rossini and other idols of the day. The so-called choral synagogues soon brought forth specialists in choral leadership and composition, such as A. Dunajewski, Eliezer *Gerovich, and David *Nowakowski. Their creations do not lack touching moments, but are "conductors' music," incompatible with the strong and style-conscious works of their older contemporary Nissan *Spivak ("Nissi Belzer").

Research in traditional Jewish music was taken up by cantor Pinchas *Minkowski, one of the prominent *ḥazzanim* who left for the West. Immediately before the mass emigration of star cantors, the splendor of Ukrainian *ḥazzanut* flashed once again with Solomon *Razumny.

The Twentieth Century

At the beginning of the 20th century, the specific kind of music inherited by European Jewry had no good expectations. The spiritual and social landslides in the West had buried the characteristic features under the quicksand of fashionable tastes, leaving the original outlines barely recognizable. The traditional solo style, still fostered in the East, drifted toward brilliant but shallow display and mingled with the first attempts in formal artistry. The musical situation reflected the general conditions of European Jewry during the period. A major part of the Jewish musicians seemed to have been integrated into the gentile environment as composers and performers; nevertheless, they were looked upon as outsiders by society.

Even the most liberal individuals referred disparagingly to these Jewish musicians. *Moscheles was referred to by Schuppanzigh in a letter to Beethoven in 1823 as "this Jewish boy"; H.A. Marschner in a letter to his wife referred to the "Jews' music fabrication" while *Tausig is referred to as "the little Jew" (Esser to the publisher Schott, 1861). They vary from the single reference to descent (with certain overtones) to the blunt identification of Jewish musicianship with the negative elements in art (a point driven home in Richard Wagner's pamphlet *Das Judentum in der Musik* (1850) and accepted by certain composers from Pfitzner's standing downward). The keen observer Heinrich *Heine held (1842) that Jewish-born artists, *Mendelssohn among them, were characterized by "the complete lack of naiveté; but is there, in art, any ingenious originality without naiveté?" He obviously intended to ascribe a certain degree of mannerism to their works of art. The general validity of this sweeping statement is not easily proven; but the greatest Jewish talents did go to the extreme boundaries of stylistic means or sentiment, as if they were looking for an indefinable something that would bestow ultimate perfection upon their creations. Arnold *Schoenberg has demonstrated (*Style and Idea*, 82–84) how Gustav Mahler probed into the subconscious and unknown in his last major work of 1911 (Mus. ex. 31), "An extraordinary case, even among contemporary composers, is the melody from *Abschied*, the last movement of Mahler's *Das Lied von der Erde*. All the units vary greatly in shape, size, and content, as if they were not motivic parts of a melodic unit, but words, each of which has a purpose of its own in the sentence."

The free rhythm of this truly "talking" passage; its construction by means of addition, instead of subordination of elements; and even certain melodic idiomatics have a familiar ring to an ear trained in Jewish singing and belonging to a sphere of sound forms which includes Jewish music. A similar structural affinity is also found with the "principle of permanent variation" that governs the formation of Schoenberg's serial compositions from the early 1920s onward. It was, how-

Example 31. Gustav Mahler, Das Lied von der Erde, *opening melody of the last movement, "Abschied" ("Parting"), singled out by Arnold Schoenberg for its unique melodic character (see A. Schoenberg,* Style and Idea, *1950, 85–86). Music, courtesy Universal Edition Vienna.*

ever, a far cry from the visionary and subconscious achievements of the great masters in the open field of pure music and the practical solutions demanded for applied music, such as synagogue song, which had to cope with tradition and habitude. But its composers also felt the need to express Jewish identity much more strongly than in the past century. The first obstacle to be overcome was their estrangement from the genuine sources of inspiration; moreover, these sources lay buried under much debris.

THE COLLECTION AND EXAMINATIONS OF THE INHERITANCE. Gathering and transcribing the oral tradition of synagogue song had begun in the Western countries during the 19th century and was almost completed by the end of that era. This labor and the incipient research had been the work of cantors personally involved in maintaining the vocal traditions. It became the task of the present century to approach the material under broader aspects and, above all, to extend its scope to the Oriental Jewish communities. The decisive step was taken by Abraham Zvi *Idelsohn (1882–1938), a disciple of Eduard Birnbaum – who imbued him with the inquisitive and historical approach to tradition – educated at German conservatories and in the principles of the Leipzig school of musicology.

The impact of Idelsohn's publications made itself immediately felt in general musicology, especially in Plainchant research (Peter Wagner, *Einfuehrung in die Gregorianischen Melodien* 3, 1921; frequently borrowed and repeated in later research). The reaction of specialized Jewish research came with the confrontation of European and Oriental music in Israel. A wave of re-recording and extensive or intensive surveying swept over the fields of folklore, now widened beyond expectation by the "ingathering of the exiles" (from 1948). These activities form a base for present research, in addition to historical and liturgical studies by modern methods. The integration of Jewish music in the general history of music (especially its comparative branch, foreshadowed in Curt *Sachs' writings) is close to being accomplished.

Parallel to the research in Jewish Oriental song went the collection of musical folklore in the European communities. The collection and transcription of these treasures began about 1900. It was not necessarily in the wake of Herder's ideas on folk song and national character that the Warsaw watchmaker Judah Leib *Cahan began his famous collection of folk song texts and music in 1896 (published from 1912); rather he felt the waning of his Jewish world so lovingly described in I.L. *Peretz's and *Shalom Aleichem's novels. The menace came from secularization (*Haskalah) and the attraction of the Russian big cities but it was the progressive and assimilated circles themselves that approached Jewish folk music with the methods of ethnomusicology. In 1898, the writers Saul *Ginsburg and Pesaḥ *Marek initiated a collecting campaign of folk song texts (published 1901), and the critic and composer Joel *Engel began noting down Jewish folk tunes. Their motivation sprang from the conscious acceptance of the national trend in music, already realized by the Czechs, Spaniards, and the Russians themselves. Texts alone were still published by Noah Prilutzki (1911–13); but music was the foremost issue in the phonograph recordings of "expeditions" sent to the countryside by the *Petrograd Society for Jewish Folk Music and Baron *Guenzburg in 1912–14 (under the direction of S. *An-Ski). The output of Edison cylinders found its way into Soviet archives in Kiev, and the recordings were transcribed and published in part by M. *Beregovski.

After World War I, An-Ski's Jewish Historical-Ethnographical Society took over (1925–39) and published the first volume of its *Muzikalisher Pinkas* (1927, ed. A.M. *Bernstein). Only a fraction of its members as well as some of their collections reached the United States and set up the YIVO Society, New York, among others. Yiddish folk song found warm and intelligent attention there (such as the collecting activity of Ruth *Rubin). Several smaller anthologies, like those of Menahem *Kipnis (Warsaw, from 1930) and Fritz Mordecai Kaufmann (Berlin, 1920) were instrumental in deepening the appreciation of Ashkenazi folkways in song.

The development was quite different as regards the Judeo-Spanish folk song of the Sephardim. The first texts, published by A. Danon in 1896/97 (REJ, 32–33), aroused the interest of historians of Spanish literature (see Romancero Musical Tradition).

THE REVIVAL OF NATIONAL VALUES IN MUSIC. The idea of imprinting a "national style" on art music of nonreligious description came late to the Jewish composers. It sprang up in Russia, but not from those composers who were linked to traditional or folk music (M. Dulitzki, D. Kabunowski, A.M. *Bernstein) and had set to music the Hebrew lyrics of the Haskalah and *Ḥibbat Zion authors. It cropped up, rather, within the thin layer of gifted students paying their precious admittance to metropolitan conservatories by complete assimilation. They were either unaware of their people's special singing style or ashamed of it and did not follow the model of the national trend in Russian music, from Glinka to Mussorgsky. The impulse had to come from the outside. In St. Petersburg in about 1902, Rimsky-Korsakov used to refer all his non-Russian students to their folk music. He also urged the Jews among them to cultivate their "wonderful music, which still awaits its Glinka" (according to *Saminsky). In a similar way, the young critic Yuli Dmitrevich (Joel) *Engel of Moscow was aroused to think of his cultural identity after having been asked point-blank by the mentor of the Russian national school, Vladimir Stassov: "Where is your national pride in being a Jew?" (according to Jacob *Weinberg). Many of these Jewish musicians, born between the 1870s and 1890s (the generation of Scriabin and Stravinsky), had little inner relation with living folk and traditional music (except for the few who had been disciples of cantors, such as E. Shkliar, M. *Gnesin, S. *Rosowsky). Saminsky, *Milner, *Zhitomirsky, *Achron, Lvov, and *Engel became enthusiasts of folk song collecting and arranging.

The rediscovered treasures were quickly brought before the public in unsophisticated arrangements for concert performance. Engel presented his folk song arrangements at concerts of the Moscow Ethnographical Society as early as 1901–02. The Petrograd Society for Jewish Folk Music (1908–18) had a statistically splendid record of concert performances. Its publishing house, Juwal, produced 58 works of 16 composers up to 1914, in addition to Engel's numerous songs and a collective songbook for schools. The results were sound craft-productions but not creative art. In consequence, the works of the National School did not gain ground beyond a certain sector of the Jewish audience. Talents like Joseph Achron struggled tragically for the fusion of Eastern-rooted Jewish and Western art music. The important problem of connecting self-sufficient melodic lines and modal (anti-harmonic) structures with harmonies was not solved; experiments went on in the tracks of Balakirev and Mussorgsky and later with the application of sound shading à la Debussy.

A short Russian spring after the October Revolution promised a new efflorescence of national aspirations in art. Hebrew and Yiddish *theaters (after having been banned since 1883) were founded (*Habimah, 1917; Vilna Troupe), and gave a fresh stimulus to Jewish composers. In fact, the latter's performances were at their best with incidental music such as Engel's *Dybbuk Suite* (op. 35), or A. *Krein's music to I.L. Peretz' *Night in the Old Market Place*. But very soon Jewish national art was dispersed for political reasons and its exponents went westward. After a short rallying in Berlin (about 1920–22), they made their way to the United States or Palestine. Others rode the tide and became useful members of the Soviet musical establishment (M. Gnesin, A. Krein, A. *Veprik).

Those who remained in Central Europe continued the national trend. The Juwal publications of music were transferred to Vienna and carried over to the new Jibneh series (closed in 1938). This group of composers did much to foster the conscience of Jewish identity in the Western communities (J. *Stutschewsky, A. *Nadel, J.S. Roskin, and singers like cantor L. Gollanin); they also became closely associated with the Zionist movement.

The earlier delegates of the National School who went to Palestine left only a superficial and transitory imprint on local art development because of their inflexible views and frozen stylistic traits; but a few representatives of the old guard, such as J. Engel and J. Stutschewsky (from 1938) played important roles in musical life.

The massive immigration of Jewish composers and musicians to America was quickly absorbed in the well established communities of East Ashkenazi extraction with their own music theaters, choral societies, and virtuoso star cantors. Members of the National School such as Lazare Saminsky, Joseph *Yasser, and others became important organizers of both sacred and secular music. They remained indebted to East Ashkenazi folk song or the styles based upon it, as can be seen, for instance, from the proceedings of the Jewish Music Forum (New York, from 1939) and similar institutions. The hope of deriving a universal Jewish style from that particular sector, with a directness bordering on imitation, is still nurtured by composers who have not experienced the pluralism of forms brought together in Israel – especially the Oriental components.

The production of Jewish music in America was well appreciated within its own small province of well-disposed listeners, but it did not conquer the general and international audience of the concert halls. This was accomplished by those few Jewish composers who were gifted enough to assimilate tradition and folkways to their own language and make them part of a profound expression of musicality. They are represented by Ernest *Bloch, Darius *Milhaud, Arnold Schoenberg, and Leonard *Bernstein – each in his own, highly individual way. A new leaf in national music was turned by the generation of composers who witnessed the reestablishment of the Jewish state in Israel (for the artistic problems to be overcome and the ideas and tracks followed by them, see *Israel, State of: Cultural Life).

NEW WAYS IN SACRED MUSIC. The trend in art-music of Jewish orientation was from the display of an upgraded Ashkenazi idiom to a more universally understood language. This language was the common musical vernacular; it also encroached upon liturgical music, but did not altogether supersede the traditional style. The contribution of the 20th century to synagogue song must therefore be evaluated in the light of the development of East Ashkenazi *ḥazzanut* in the West. It is true that the image of this original art has been marred by virtuosity for its own sake, the search for external effects, flattering the tastes of an undiscriminating public, and by the inroads of the record industry. The field is too wide and variegated for generalizations, however, and any judgment should Orient itself to the outstanding accomplishments. The development of East Ashkenazi *ḥazzanut* in the United States was initiated and furthered by immigrants from about 1880 until the end of World War II. Earlier arrivals, such as *Minkowsky and Samuel *Morogowski ("Seidel Rovner"), were followed by Joseph *Rosenblatt, David *Roitman, Moses (Moshe) *Koussevitzky, and many others, who continued the traditional personal union of performer-composer. From the ranks of this generation, Zevulun (Zavel) *Kwartin (immigrated 1920) created and published works that can be taken as models of progressive *ḥazzanut* (Mus. ex. 32)

The most evident mark of this purely single-voice composition is the coloratura. Although it includes some recurrent patterns, these appear in no way as merely decorative adornment and avoid the brilliance for the sake of brilliance displayed by J. *Rosenblatt and others. The ornament often underlines the sense and expressive contents of the text, sometimes recalling the old cantors' musical *kavvanot* (mystical "intentions"). Coloraturas are affixed to points of internal or external tension, concentrating on the essential, while the intervening, preparatory words may be passed by with a certain indifference. Kwartin claimed that he absorbed "genuine

Example 32. Eastern Ashkenazi style ḥazzanut *from the United States. Two compositions by Zawel Kwartin. After Z. Kwartin,* Zmiroth Zebulon, *vol. 1, 1928, nos. 35 and 18.*

Oriental formulations" during his stay in Palestine (1926–27), and took them as a model for his compositions (*Zmiroth Zebulon* 1, preface, 1928). He succeeded in combining the two related musical styles and paved the way for a revival of the venerable, but outworn, art of *ḥazzanut*.

This sphere of music, well circumscribed by tradition, barely raised the problem of harmonic accompaniment or choral harmonies; the latter was left to the usual semi-improvisatory *meshorerim* style, with the spontaneous congregational responses. However, where the service followed the Western trend of part singing and eventually came to include the organ accompaniment of choir and cantor, the problem of harmony became acute. Out of dissatisfaction with the solutions propounded during the 19th century, three specific questions – old and new – came to the fore: how to harmonize melodies of an unharmonic conception, by what means to replace romanticism in synagogue composition, and how to write choral tunes inviting the participation of the congregants. Since there was no ready-made solution, the demands of the various communities had to be met by trial and error. From the 1920s, American synagogues did much to encourage the search for solutions of this problem, by sponsoring the composition of complete services or sections, often according a great measure of freedom to the composer.

The initiative in composing new synagogue music was taken by immigrant adherents of the National School, such as Lazare Saminsky (in the U.S. from 1921) and Joseph Achron (from 1925). Previously, these had dealt with the folkloristic manifestations of sacred song, or, occasionally, with single pieces of concert appeal; now they had to adopt a modern musical language appropriate to the Jewish service or, at least, had to modernize the traditional idiom (a venture quite legitimate in the flexible ideological framework of Jewish music). They understood that they should abandon the well-trodden ways of romanticism as well as the feeble "edifying" style and obtrusive sentimentality ("to vitriol away the 'cello sentimentality' of Messrs. Bruch, etc."; A. Schoenberg on his *Kol Nidrei* version, letter to Paul *Dessau, 1914). Saminsky, for instance, consciously renounced the plaintive *shtayger* scales in favour of what he called "the beautiful and majestic major and Aeolian minor of Hebrew melodies" (*Sabbath Evening Service*, preface, 1926). He drew much inspiration from the motive stock of Ashkenazi biblical chant and its basically pentatonic structure (*ibid.*, ch. 36). He has the Sabbath Psalm 93 sung to a tune derived from the motive-chains of Bible reading (Mus. ex. 33). The effect is an unusual relaxed expression of joy, Jewish in substance, but completely divorced from the perpetual tension of *ḥazzanut*. The composer evaded the problem of harmony by prescribing the unison of choir and organ.

Lazar *Weiner, too, relied upon pentatonics (Mus. ex. 34a), but in a more schematic way and took some of his inspiration from the earlier Israel song composers (Daniel *Sambursky, Marc *Lavry). Russian-born Isadore *Freed, educated in America and in France with Vincent d'Indy, approached the problem of harmony by employing the subtle, somewhat pallid, chords of late French romanticism (Mus. ex. 34b).

The harder line of the "expanded tonality" featured by Ernst *Toch or Hindemith, with its tonal flexibility and harsh harmonies, had a refreshing influence on modern synagogue composition: here was an antithesis to romanticism, and a certain affinity to the antiharmonic elements and heterophonic performing habits of the earlier synagogue. Heinrich *Schalit applied some of these topical principles to his *Sabbath Eve Liturgy* (Munich, 1933; revised ed. New York, 1951), using several original Oriental-Sephardi tunes (e.g., the radiant ecstasy of the *Kedushah* in Idelsohn's *Melodien* 4, no. 41). A remarkable, but isolated, progress toward a synagogue choral style was made by American-born Frederick *Jacobi in one of his later works. The harmonies brought forth by the four-part choir have been severed from functionalism; the doubling of the

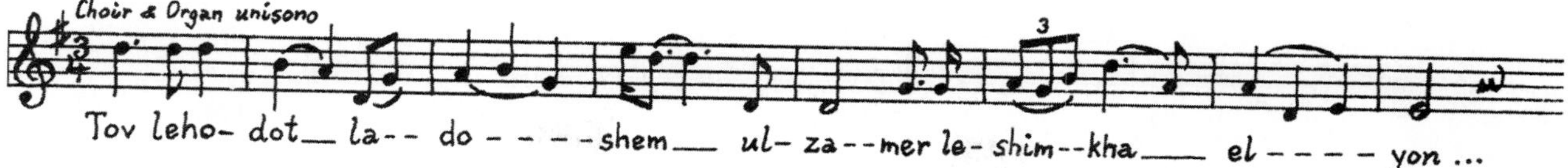

Example 33. Choir tune developed from motifs of biblical cantillation. From L Saminsky, Sabbath Evening Service, *op. 26, 1930.*

voices serves rather for the acoustical strengthening and coloration as known, in principle, from *meshorerim* practice. The voices go in unison at one time and move apart at another, as in the natural heterophony of a praying congregation; there are also reminiscences of choral psalmody.

Perhaps the most prolific innovator was Hugo Chaim *Adler, cantor and disciple of Toch. When still in Germany, in Mannheim, he recoined the concept of Brecht-Hindemith's ethical cantata to the ideas of Buber's *Juedisches Lehrhaus*. After escaping to the United States in 1939, he gave a new shape to the musical service and community life of his Worcester, Massachusetts, congregation (synagogue compositions 1934–52; cantatas 1934–48). Drawing upon the same techniques as Schalit and Jacobi, Adler was more consistent in stressing the specific Jewish elements. Traditional features such as *shtayger* modality, and restraint to the musical essentials endow his works with character and stature.

The specimens quoted so far may demonstrate some important trends and achievements in adapting contemporary musical language to the synagogue. Among the considerable number of commissioned works are the liturgies of L. Saminsky (1926), J. Achron (1932), Darius *Milhaud (op. 279; 1947), and L. *Algazi (1952). In a different category are the para-synagogal cantatas and prayer arrangements with obligatory orchestra accompaniment that are suited to concerts or meetings of religious or national celebration; this class is represented by the important works of Ernest *Bloch (*Avodat ha-Kodesh*, 1930), which was commissioned for a Reform synagogue and which entered the concert repertoire, and Arnold Schoenberg (*Kol Nidrei*, 1938). Selected prayers were set to music, on the commission of prominent communities, by Leonard Bernstein (1946), Mario *Castelnuovo-Tedesco (op. 90; 1936), Lukas *Foss, Morton *Gould (op. 164; 1943). Alexander *Tansmann (1946), Kurt *Weill, and others. The composers' names suggest the wide range of schools and individual styles employed but do not guarantee a degree of personal involvement and familiarity with the actual demands of the service. At any rate, the publication of new synagogue compositions, both on the traditional and the decidedly contemporary line, is growing in number, the output of the 1960s exceeding by far that of the 1950s. The impact of modern tendencies on synagogue music as a whole is checked, however, by the differences of approach to liturgy and service which form part of more comprehensive principles and ideological controversies. A new factor has been added to the question of conservativism or progress in sacred music by the meeting and clash of widely differing ritual and singing cultures in Israel. The most ancient fundamentals of Jewish song form the only common ground left for any synthesis that may be in the offing.

[Hanoch Avenary]

FOLK MUSIC

It is today acknowledged that differences between folk music and art music, and what is called "popular music," are not clearly defined. However, major features are usually noted as characteristic of folk music. It is transmitted orally from mouth to ear and learned through listening rather than through written notated documents. This suggests that the music can change when passed from one individual to another depending on the memory and creative power of the performer and the measure of acceptance in the performer's community. Gifted individuals who gave of the fruits of their poetical and musical talents frequently borrowed familiar pre-existing melodies and made new songs out of them. In many cases the names of the composers were forgotten and the compositions became anonymous. Folk song, primarily rural in origin, is functional, meaning that it is associated with other activities; yet it also exists in cultures in which there is a technically more sophisticated urban musical tradition and where this cultivated music is essentially the art of a small social elite.

As a whole, these and other characteristics are hardly applicable to the complex web of Jewish musical traditions, which have been rooted in many and diverse cultures through the long years of dispersion where alien traditions impinged on Jews wherever they resided. Viewed as a unit they represent a multiplicity of idioms, simple and more sophisticated musical styles in which the sacred and secular overlap. Considered separately, each tradition has numerous forms of expression, being partly folkloristic in character and partly drawing upon the sophisticated art of the surrounding environment. Thus, for instance, non-Jewish art music from the surrounding culture insinuates itself into the Oriental synagogues and other forms through the the art music spread through the areas under Islamic control, which in itself, despite its considerable sophistication, is based on oral transmission.

Another characteristic that sets Jewish musical traditions apart from other musical traditions is the use of Hebrew as a common language and the recourse to the same corpus of sacred classical texts for reading from biblical books and the liturgy. This has created a special blend of highly varied musical lore transmitted orally from generation to generation and written textual lore that operates as a unifying and stabilizing factor.

Example 34. Modern compositions for the synagogue. (a) Lazar Weiner, 1932, in G. Ephros (ed.), Cantorial Anthology, *vol. 5, 1957, 64; (b) Isadore Freed, 1955, in G. Ephros,* ibid.,*66; (c) Frederick Jacobi, 1946, in D. Puttermand (ed.),* Synagogue Music by Contemporary Composers, *New York, 1951, 180–2.*

Example 35. Modern psalmody for cantor and choir. Hugo Chaim Adler, Nachlat Israel – Sabbath Eve Service, *1952, 28–29. The organ accompaniment has been omitted here.*

Although Hebrew is dominant and shared by all Jews in the religious hymns enhancing events marking the cycle of life and the Jewish year, extra-synagogal music displays a complex and diversified idiomatic picture in both language and music.

Celebrations of circumcision, the bar mitzvah, and weddings usually consist of two musical parts: the distinctly paraliturgical, which is almost indistinguishable from synagogue music, and what may include an almost unlimited use of secular music from the surrounding society, including instrumental accompaniment, despite the fact that musical instruments continue to be banned inside the synagogue. The accompaniment is often no more sophisticated than simple rhythm instruments but professional singing and playing is often included. One famous example out of many instrumental entertainers is that of the *klezmerim*. This represents a purely oral tradition, with its practitioners true professionals who, although of relatively low social status, are often given an important place in social life and public events.

The musical manifestations found in the various Jewish communities that have exclusively or predominantly folk elements are associated with the aforementioned events; at other times it focuses on the private life of the individual. There are times when the singing has a defined function, but it may also be entirely dissociated from any specific happening. Individuals may express themselves in lyrical song even if there is no apparent relation between the song and whatever evoked the urge to sing. The themes and contents of the songs are as extensive as the range of occasions that inspire them. Generally speaking they encompass events associated with (1) the Jewish calendar such as Sabbath songs (*zemirot*), the Purim plays, the Passover *Seder* and the like; (2) general festive gatherings such as the songs of *hillulot* or pilgrimage to the tombs of saints. Among those whose holiness has been recognized by the entire nation the outstanding figure is certainly Simeon bar Yoḥai, whose grave at Meron attracts great masses from all Jewish groups. One can add to this category the celebrations of the *Maimuna by the Moroccans and the *Seherane* by the Kurds; (3) The third category and undoubtedly the richest concerns the life cycle. A person's lifetime, from birth to death, is filled with a succession of outstanding occasions, many of which are celebrated in song and dance. A new element enters the scene here, one that is totally nonexistent in synagogue singing: women take part and even create texts that are performed in suitable circumstances and on occasions have unique reference to their world, some being considered their exclusive province, such as cradle songs and dirges (see below).

WOMEN'S FOLK MUSIC

The phenomenon of women singing for other women on various occasions was undoubtedly a way of circumventing restrictions engendered by religious and social bias that limited their public musical activities and their participation in synagogue rituals. Women are also circumscribed by the talmudic injunction to the effect that "hearing a woman's voice is an abomination," which was interpreted as a prohibition against their singing in public. In his extensive response to the Jews of *Aleppo concerning the lawfulness of music, Maimonides, the prominent religious authority, included among the major prohibitions "Listening to the singing and playing of a woman."

All this seems to have encouraged the emergence and crystallization of songs with unique values and characteristics, as women singing for other women became a way of getting around these prohibitions. In their songs women can express their world of experiences and the Jewish and human values they uphold. The songs seem to have been a form of release through which they could express – even if only to themselves – those experiences and aspects of their lives that were special. They also often included Jewish ethical instructions, reaction to public and political events, as well as various communal happenings.

The song's texts have a broad thematic scope: comments on important historical and current events; songs of religious character, which are in the form of translations or paraphrases of biblical stories; the life cycle from birth to death with special emphasis on the wedding and its colorful attendant ceremonies; lyrical songs that accompany a woman when she is alone, when doing housework, when remembering the bitter experiences in her life, her troubles, complaints, and dreams, whether in a lullaby or a song of love or jealousy. There are also humorous and satiric songs like the songs of curses ostensibly meant to entertain women by introducing a light atmosphere.

With few exceptions, women's songs are in the language and Jewish idiom spoken locally. Their singing falls within the realm of oral tradition and consequently their songs are usually not fixed in permanent form so that gifted women can exhibit their creative ability by adding verses of their own or by rearranging the material they include in their repertoires.

The songs are sung in public on occasions of a folk nature either by a group of women or by one individual with a good voice. There are also professional performances by female musicians who are specialists in specific genres; particularly notable is the performance of funeral laments and dirges, which are considered the province of women who excel as keeners. Professional performances, much like of those of men, are given by one or two specialists – the main singer and her "assistant." They are usually performed in responsorial form and the women accompany themselves on the most characteristically feminine instrument, the frame drum. This phenomenon goes back to ancient times; one finds such instances in biblical stories like that of Miriam the prophetess in the Book of Exodus.

There are also female ensembles that enhanced women festivities such as the professional singers called *tañaderas* (drummers). This is a group of three women who sing and drum and are well versed not only in the musical repertoire but in all the customs. Another, larger all-female ensembles is the *daqqaqat* (drummers) in Baghdad, which at one time was a Jewish ensemble comprising four to five women beating various drums (frame drum, kettle drums, two-headed drum). The leader of the band was noted for her fine voice and, being a talented performer, she was the soloist.

From a musical standpoint, are the women's songs different from those of the men? Reflecting on the sexual aspect in the development of music, the prominent musicologist C. *Sachs wrote in *The Rise of Music in the Ancient World:* "If singing is indeed an activity of all our being, sex, the strongest difference between human-beings must have a decisive influence on musical style … woman's influence was particularly strong in shaping the structure of melody" (1943). Another great figure, composer Bela Bartok, who studied the folk songs of Hungary, Romania, and elsewhere, noted in his "Essay on the Collecting of Folk Music" (1976) the uniqueness and archaic nature of women's singing. He was of the opinion that an ancient stratum of song was reproduced therein because in the traditional societies they had little contact with the external world.

In recent decades, great interest in the subject has arisen, particularly in the United States and Canada, with deepening focus on gender as an analytical category in music research. In the realm of Jewish music, one should note in this respect Ellen Koskoff's article: "The Sound of a Woman's Voice: Gender and Music in a New York Ḥasidic Community," which has been included in the collection essays of which she is the editor: *Women and Music in Cross-Cultural Perspective* (1989).

In this context, it would be interesting to briefly draw attention to the phenomenon of the emergence of a professional class of talented Jewish women musicians by the beginning of the 20th century. These artists gained prominence and recognition as outstanding vocalists and creative artists in Muslim societies in a broad cultural region extending from Central Asia to the major centers of North Africa.

[Amnon Shiloah (2nd ed)]

ART MUSIC IN MODERN ISRAEL

Musical life in the *Yishuv* and in Israel has always been dominated by dialectical contrasts. In the broader spheres of musical activity, each Jewish ethnic group conducted intensive daily musical activity within its traditional community life, ruled by the yearly and life cycle. Such activity was inherently compartmentalized and intended only for members of the specific group (as may still be observed in the older, Orthodox neighborhoods of Jerusalem). By contrast, the national ideology – first carried forward by the Zionist movement and then as an official policy of the State of Israel – activated a drive for national unification around common values, most importantly the revival of the Hebrew language. In the case of music the national ideology was expressed in the endeavor to create a new and inherently national style of folk, popular, and art music, which acted as a powerful unifying social agent, including social gatherings in contexts of music making and concert activity. At the same time, the immigrants from Europe were reluctant to discard their rich cultural heritage. The immigrants from Europe were thus dominated by the dialectical conflict between the Vision of the East and the Heritage of the West.

Within the narrower sphere of art (concert) music and concert life, the maintenance and practice of European music – whether as active music making at home or in passive attendance of concerts – played a paramount role in softening the trauma of immigration and resettlement. By contrast, composers, strongly guided by the Vision of the East, endeavored to create a new, intrinsically national Israeli musical style. Reaching beyond a blurred vision to actual musical parameters proved a nearly insurmountable obstacle, which composers have been struggling with to the present day.

THE YISHUV PERIOD

Music was second only to the revived Hebrew language as a powerful agent in the creation of a unified, national culture in the *Yishuv* and in Israel. As the most sociable art, it had the power to bring people together, mostly for singing folk songs at work and in leisure time, but also for group performance and for passive listening.

Transplantation of Music Institutions

The Jewish immigrants from Europe took the momentous step of transplanting the European institutional model to the social setting of the *yishuv*. In 1895 a community orchestra was founded in the early settlement of Rishon le-Zion. It was a well-organized amateur wind band with a paid conductor, which took part in all festive and social functions of the settlement (including playing at the historical visit by Herzl in 1897). The model was soon adapted by all other settlements, such as Petaḥ Tikvah, as well as in the Jewish community of Jaffa. All of the orchestras were grouped under the rubric "Kinnor Zion" (the Violin of Zion).

The German-born singer Shulamit Ruppin founded in Jaffa in 1910 the first music school (named after her upon her untimely death in 1912). The Shulamit School maintained a pure German curriculum, with individual instrumental instruction of violin, piano, and voice, theory classes, and a student chorus and orchestra. The first director was the versatile violinist, conductor, and concert manager Moshe Hopenko, who also owned a music store and imported pianos to Palestine. The school stimulated lively interest with an unexpectedly large enrollment. Shulamit Ruppin founded a branch in Jerusalem, which soon became an independent school. The Shulamit School served as model for additional music schools such as Bet Leviim (Levite House) in Tel Aviv and Conservatoire Dunya Weizmann in Haifa.

The horrendous hardships of World War I dealt a heavy blow to all musical activities of the *Yishuv*, yet recovery after the institution of the British Mandate in Palestine was strikingly quick, especially due to the renewal of Jewish immigration. In 1923, conductor Mark Golinkin made the daring step of founding the Palestine Opera, which lasted against all economic odds for four seasons. Golinkin presented mostly mainstream operas such as *La Traviata*, *Otello*, *Faust*, and *The Barber of Seville*. Yet he placed special emphasis on operas by Jewish composers, with Meyerbeer's *Les Huguenots*, Halevy's *La Juive*, and Anton Rubinstein's *The Maccabeans*. The performers were fine singers, mostly from Russia, and the productions enjoyed full houses. Yet the lack of funds, which did not allow a proper orchestra and chorus, and the bad physical conditions of performances in badly equipped movie houses plunged the opera into deep financial crisis and it collapsed in 1927. Between 1941 and 1947 composer and conductor Marc *Lavri established the Folk Opera, which presented operettas, occasionally accompanied by two pianos. Yet the Folk Opera also pioneered the first production of a local opera, Lavri's *Dan ha-Shomer* ("Dan the Watchman").

There were several short-lived attempts in the 1920s to form symphony orchestras, such as conductor Max Lampel's extremely popular outdoor concert series in Tel Aviv. The performances of these groups attracted large audiences, which showed that they answered a deep need among the immigrants to maintain their connection to European art music. But these were ad hoc ensembles that recruited musicians at their miserable venues in cafes and silent movie houses, and no regular orchestra could emerge from such initiatives.

A European quality prevailed in the unique Chamber Music Association founded in Jerusalem by cellist Thelma *Bentwich-Yellin and her sister, violinist Marjorie, in 1921. They performed full seasons with their fine string quartet, including an all-Beethoven series, as well as concerts by piano trios, piano recitals, and baroque ensembles.

The most significant developments occurred in the 1930s with the Fifth Aliyah, which was called the German Aliyah. While most immigrants in the 1930s came from Poland, the Fifth Aliyah effected a major cultural change in general and in music in particular in the *Yishuv*, due to the high musical standards of the Jews who came from Central Europe (Germany, Austria, and countries strongly affected by German culture such as Hungary and Czechoslovakia). The so-called German immigration brought to Palestine not only well-trained composers, performers, and music teachers but also a discerning audience.

The Palestine Orchestra

The momentous act which violinist Bronislaw *Huberman undertook in founding the Palestine Orchestra (later the

Israel Philhamronic Orchestra) in 1936 was of paramount importance in placing musical activity in Palestine on a high international level. Huberman's original vision was to turn the Jewish community of Palestine into an international center replacing what he considered "the declining West." The rapid deterioration of conditions in Europe made him take the emergency step of establishing a first-class philharmonic orchestra. He obtained the consent of the British Mandate authorities to grant entry certificates to the musicians he auditioned in Europe from among the fine Jewish instrumentalists who had been fired from their orchestras by the Nazi and Fascist managements. In this way he saved scores of musicians and their families from the Holocaust. The Palestine Orchestra was inaugurated in December 1936 with a concert, which served as a national celebration, conducted by the legendary Arturo Toscanini, who turned it into a powerful, internationally publicized anti-Nazi demonstration. The best international conductors and soloists followed Toscanini and performed with the orchestra, most of them gratis, and in this way it maintained the strict professional standards, which Toscanini had demanded. The core of the repertoire was the mainstream Classic-Romantic symphonic repertoire, but the orchestra also performed almost every new orchestral composition composed in Palestine. The members of the orchestra also founded fine chamber music ensembles and provided high-level instrumental instruction to children.

The Palestine Conservatoire

In 1933 violinist Emil *Hauser founded the Palestine Conservatoire in Jerusalem, with a large faculty of over 30 teachers and a comprehensive curriculum for most instruments as well as classes in composition, history, and theory in addition to instruction in the Arabic *'ūd* given by Ezra *Aharon and courses in non-Western music given by Edith *Gerson-Kiwi. The conservatoire also initiated advanced professional studies. Hauser received 70 certificates from the Mandate authorities and in this way saved the most brilliant young Jewish music students from the Nazis. The conservatoire gave rise in the mid-1940s to the Academies of Music in Jerusalem and Tel Aviv, which have continued to be the leading professional music schools in the country

The Palestine Broadcast Service

In March 1936, the British founded the Palestine Broadcast Service, which alternated broadcasts in Arabic, English, and Hebrew. The Music Department included a large chamber ensemble, which soon became the radio orchestra, later the Jerusalem Symphony. The Music Department also initiated an ensemble of Arabic instrumentalists and singers headed by Ezra Aharon.

Bridging East and West

Pioneer individuals made the first attempts. The great researcher Abraham Zvi *Idelsohn (1882–1938) settled in Jerusalem in 1907 with the original vision of rediscovering the original chant of the ancient Hebrew Temple through thorough fieldwork which would reveal elements common to all Eastern ethnic groups, Arabic music, and Plainchant. Idelsohn's hypothesis was that the groups of Jews in the Middle East, such as in Yemen and Babylon (Iraq) were barely influenced by the neighboring Arabs, unlike the European Jews whose liturgical chant and music were strongly imbued with Western influences. Idelsohn selected Jerusalem as the center of his activity since it presented to him a unique concentration of all Jewish ethnic groups in one location. Idelsohn's ambitious project could not be realized, yet he did extensive and unprecedented fieldwork, using the newly-invented Edison phonograph. The first volume of his monumental and influential *Thesaurus of Jewish Melodies*, the one including the Yemenite chants, was published in 1914. The travails of World War I and the lack of public support made his life in Jerusalem unbearable and in 1921 he left Palestine and settled in the United States, where he continued his monumental Thesaurus.

In 1924 the researcher and collector Yoel *Engel moved the center of activities of the Society of Jewish Folk Music, founded in St. Petersburg (1908) and briefly domiciled in Berlin (1922), to Tel Aviv. His main project was the publication of hundreds of Jewish folk songs, which he and his colleagues had assembled, as cheap sheet music, easily available. His project was curtailed by his untimely death in 1927.

Proceeding from the East westwards, singer Bracha *Zefira (1910–1990) started a unique project. Born to a Yemenite family, she was orphaned in childhood and raised by foster families of different ethnic origins, registering in her superb memory scores of traditional songs. After studies in Jerusalem and Berlin, she initiated in 1931 public concerts of songs of diverse ethnic Jewish and Arabic groups with improvising pianist Nahum *Nardi, which revealed the wealth of Eastern traditions to Western-educated concertgoers. From 1939 she commissioned arrangements from most local composers, deliberately using piano and Western chamber ensembles, as well as performing with the Palestine Orchestra. The Yemenite composer, singer, and choreographer Sara *Levi-Tanay made a lasting contribution to Israeli folk song, with her *Kol Dodi* and *Ali Be'er*. In 1948 she founded the *Inbal Yemenite Dance Company. The Yemenite singer Shoshana *Damari was one of the most important performers of the newly-invented Israeli folk song, having frequently performed with composer Moshe *Wilensky at the piano.

The Yemenite artists effected a major change in the self-image of Yemenite women in Palestine and Israel and were pioneers in the liberation of the Yemenite woman from her traditional boundaries.

Composition, First Generation

About 30 composers immigrated from Europe between 1931 and 1938. Most of them were of German origin and had finished their studies also in Germany. A smaller group originated from Eastern Europe, most of whom did their advanced studies in Paris. Having never met before, they did not coalesce into any "school." The often mentioned concept of a so-called "Mediterranean School" is misleading. Each composer responded to the powerful internal and external ideological pressure in an individual way. Moreover, most composers found ways to compose in different idioms and techniques at the same time, thus maintaining their Western heritage on the one hand and trying to find links with the East – whether ethnic or imaginary – at the same time. Such was Stefan *Wolpe (1902–1972), who remained dedicated to the powerful expressionism and dodecaphonic technique of *Schoenberg in his orchestral and piano works (1935–38) while composing at the same time simple settings of modern Hebrew poetry for voice and piano and arrangements of folk songs for kibbutz choirs. Wolpe's avant-garde approach was not accepted in Jerusalem and in 1939 he emigrated to the U.S. All other major immigrant composers overcame the immigration trauma and initiated intensive activity in creation and instruction in Tel Aviv and Jerusalem.

The only person who produced a clearly defined ideology was Alexander U. *Boskovitch (1907–1964), who demanded that the Israeli composer acts as a *shali'aḥ ẓibbur* representing the collective and responding to the local "static and dynamic landscape," i.e., both the visual and acoustical scenery of the country, especially the sound of biblical and modern Hebrew as well as Arabic. Boskovitch created the regional concept of "Mediterranean Music," according to which Jewish music from Europe had nothing to do with the future Israeli national style. Boskovitch turned to the sonorities and the melos of Arabic music, but stressed the difference between "the Jewish and the Arabic shepherds." Boskovitch systematically realized his ideology in his early works, the Oboe Concerto (1943), Semitic *Suite* (1946), and *Adonai Roʿi* ("The Lord is my Shepherd," 1943).

The other composers never subscribed to his ideology, and the term itself was quoted only once, by Menahem *Avidom, in his *Mediterranean Sinfonietta*. Still, all composers responded to the ideological call of the Vision of the East. Most characteristic was the substitution of modes (in the romantic sense of scales with no leading tone) for the Western major-minor tonal system. Erich Walter *Sternberg (1891–1974) rejected all external ideological pressures and in his introduction to his large-scale *Twelve Tribes of Israel* (1938) he proclaimed his commitment to the inner call of a composer to respond to new surroundings in his own individual way. His language was deeply ingrained with late Romanticism, especially under the influence of Brahms, Bruckner, Reger, and *Mahler. Joseph *Tal (1910) repeatedly declared that the very fact of his being a composer creating in the social and cultural environment of Israel would shape his music in a new way. Tal insisted on staying abreast of new developments in Western music. A concise illustration of Tal's attitude is found in the second movement of his Piano sonata (1952) in which an ostinato quote of simple, modal melody by his friend Yehudah *Sharett serves as the basis for a series of extremely chromatic and dissonant variations. The prolific Paul *Ben-Haim found his own manner of proceeding in simultaneous tracks. He produced over 30 arrangements for Bracha Zefira, whose melodies he later quoted and interpreted in his large scale works, such as the Clarinet Quintet and his two symphonies. In his early piano works he resorted to naïve, romantic depiction of imaginary Eastern pastorals, whereas his First Symphony (1940) is a powerful artistic response to the horrendous first months of World War II, with strong Mahlerian influences. Ben Haim also initiated the genre of the Hebrew Lied, setting great poetry by Bialik, Rachel, Sh. Shalom, and Leah Goldberg. In his *Sabbath Cantata* (1940) Mordechai *Seter made a strongly personal synthesis of melodic quotes of Baylonian Jews from Idelsohn's Thesaurus, cast in a combination of contrapuntal Palestrina style and 20th century modal-dissonant harmony. Marc *Lavri (1903–1967) departed from the ideology of creating an easily accessible, tuneful, and popular style, which would obliterate the dividing line between folk and art music, as in his extremely popular Emek (Jezreel Valley) song which he developed into a folk-like symphonic poem. Lavri was the first to incorporate the Hora dance into chamber and symphonic music (the Palestinian Hora has nothing to do with the Romanian Hora Lungha; it is a dance cast in regular, brief phrases in common time, with constant syncopations, and it came out of ḥasidic dance).

During the last two decades of the British Mandate period the immigrant composers created a large repertoire of symphonic, chamber, and especially piano music, as well as songs, which was the basis of Israeli art music.

AFTER THE FOUNDATION OF THE STATE OF ISRAEL

Institutional Expansion

By the time the State of Israel was proclaimed in 1948 the institutional and ideological musical infrastructure had been established. The Palestine Orchestra was renamed the Israel Philharmonic Orchestra, which continued to be the leading representative ensemble of Israel, attracting large subscription audiences. Concert life evolved in the direction of expansion and diversification. Orchestras were formed in Haifa and Beersheba. In 1972 the small radio orchestra was expanded and became the Jerusalem Symphony.

Soprano Edis *de Philippe founded and directed the Israeli Opera from 1948, but financial difficulties and abrasive personal relations hindered its progress for more than 30 years. New municipal orchestras emerged such as in Haifa and Beersheba. The first wave of immigration from the Soviet Union in the early 1970s made possible a significant expansion of the radio orchestra, which as mentioned became the Jerusalem Symphony. Direct initiatives of the government, other than providing for limited financial subsidies through the Public Council for Culture and the Arts, were realized in a few large-scale ventures, most importantly the establishment of the annual Israel Festival in 1960, which from the start introduced some of the foremost international artists such as Pablo Casals and Igor Stravinsky to the Israeli audience. Once every few years the State of Israel has granted the prestigious Israel Prize to composers and performers.

Following the demise of the Israeli Opera following de Philippe's death, a new opera company was founded in 1985 with a new house erected in Tel Aviv. The New Israeli Opera (later named The Israeli Opera) soon reached high professional standards and brought about a significant change on the Israeli musical scene, collaborating with major opera houses in productions of operatic masterpieces. It started a project of commissioning new operas from Israeli composers, the first of which was Tal's *Joseph*.

The large wave of immigration from the former Soviet Union after 1990 effected an unprecedented expansion of the community of professional musicians, leading to the founding of several new orchestras, foremost among them the Rishon le-Zion Symphony (which is also the opera orchestra) and the Ra'anannah Orchestra.

Musicological Research

The immigration of the ethnomusicologists Robert *Lachmann and Edith (Gerson) Kiwi in 1935 initiated a highly productive period of field research, now preserved and digitalized at the Sound Archives of the Hebrew University. The Music Department of the National and University Library and the Center for Jewish Music Research, founded by Israel *Adler, initiated studies and publications and became the world repository of archives of Jewish and Israeli music. The first Department of Musicology was founded at the Hebrew University in 1965, with scholars doing high-standard historical and ethnomusicological research, including extensive field work and recording in the ethnically extremely diverse Jewish and Arab society in Israel, among them ethnomusicologists and historians Amnon *Shiloah, Ruth *Katz, Dalia Cohen, and Don *Harran. This was followed by musicology departments at Tel Aviv University (1966) whose faculty included Edith Gerson-Kiwi, Herzl *Shmueli, and Judith Cohen, and Bar-Ilan University (1969) with Bathia *Churgin, Uri Sharvit, and Judith Frygesi on the faculty.

Composition, Second and Third Generations

The founders of Israeli music persisted in their individual ways of coping with the expectations of critics, fellow musicians, and the composers themselves for a new Israeli style to emerge as a fusion of east and west. After the long period of isolation during wartime, the country was reopened to the west and composers renewed direct contacts with new music, such as when Haim *Alexander (1915) participated in the Darmstadt workshops, interpreting the serial techniques in his personal way (*Sound Patterns* for piano) while retaining folk-like modal tuneful writing such as in *Nature Songs*. Mordekhai *Seter developed an extremely individual synthesis of Eastern chant and primeval dissonant harmony, combined with direct quotes of traditional Yemenite tunes in his monumental *Midnight Vigil*. Paul *Ben Haim persisted in simultaneous tracks, ranging from the daring adoption of Arabic melos and sonorities in his *Sonata a tré* for mandolin, guitar, and harpsichord, to the dense contrapuntal texture of his Metamorphoses on a Bach Chorale, written a year apart (1967–68). Joseph Tal composed dramatic, innovative symphonies, and founded the first studio of electronic music in Israel, his work there culminating in the opera *Metzada* for singers and magnetic tape, and the large-scale vocal work *Death Came to the Wooden Horse Michael* to a poem by Nathan Zach.

The second and third generations of composers included Ben-Zion *Orgad, Zvi *Avni, Yehezkel *Braun, Ami *Maayani, Noam *Sheriff, and others. They all received their initial training under the founders of Israeli music, but then went abroad for advanced studies. Their styles branched in new directions of increased pluralism. Yehezkel Braun always maintained flowing tuneful melodies, even in his dodecaphonic works, Orgad found his inspiration in the rhythms and sound qualities of the Hebrew language, whether biblical or modern. Avni established his own individual synthesis of Eastern declamation and rich Western atonal harmony, such as in his powerful *Meditations on a Drama*, and Maayani likewise turned to syntheses of Arabic maqams with Western counterpoint, such as in his tense and dramatic String Quartet.

New waves of immigrations, such as from the Soviet Union in the early 1970s, further diversified Israeli music. Mark *Kopytman (1929) found his own strongly personal heterophonic technique with strong influences of Eastern music, such as in *Memory*, which is a complex orchestral interpretation of a traditional Yemenite song which opens and closes the composition, and of traditional Jewish prayer chant of Eastern Europe such as in *Beyond*.

The younger generations of composers further diversified the extreme pluralism of Israeli music, in response to the increasing diversification of Western music since the 1970s. Haim Permont (1950) turned in his powerful opera *Dear Son of Mine* to a direct commentary and critique of painful issures in contemporary Israeli society. The endeavor to achieve a synthesis of Jewish traditions continued and reached its peak with Betti *Olivero (1954–), whose rich repertoire presents a strongly personal interpretation of Jewish Eastern, ḥasidic, and Sephardi traditions within advanced Western harmonic techniques.

Since the 1980s several composers have achieved new breakthroughs in Arab music, strongly influenced by the contemporary emergence of "World Music." Ensembles combining Arab and Western instruments such as Bustan Avraham with the *'ūd* and violin virtuoso Taisir Elias were founded, and the Music Academy in Jerusalem opened a department for applied study of Arab music. Composer Tzipi *Fleischer (1946–) undertook full academic studies of Arab music and culture and composed vocal works to classical and modern Arabic poetry, culminating in her Hexaptichon – six versions of the same composition moving from a powerful Arab rendition to a purely Western version for two pianos. Michael Wolpe (1960) combined the *'ūd* and Arab drum with a string trio and the voice of a Persian-born singer in his poignant *Songs of Memory*. Wolpe also turned to nostalgic evocation and commentary in the style of early instrumental and folk music, such as in his Piano Trio no. 3 "On Israeli Songs."

The musical scene was further expanded with the large-scale immigration from the former Soviet Union in the 1990s, especially with a group of composers coming from the Central Asian republics, such as Joseph *Bardanashvili and Benjamin Yosupov (see below).

Interest in the performance of contemporary music was stimulated through the regular performances of three fine ensembles: Musica Nova, The Ensemble of the Twenty-First-Century, and Caprizma.

(See also "Israel, State of: Culture Life – Music and Dance.)

[Jehoash Hirshberg (2nd ed.)]

Immigrant Artists

The wave of over one million immigrants from the former Soviet Union since 1989 brought to Israel a great number of musicians. To the 1,500 active professional musicians in Israel, another 5,500 arrived from the U.S.S.R. Some of them went back to their countries of origin; some moved on to other countries, and some even changed their professions. Those who continued their careers in Israel changed the musical life of the country. They were employed in existing orchestras, chamber ensembles, and ballet troops, founded new orchestras (the Israel Symphony Orchestra of Rishon Le-Zion, Camerata Jerusalem, the Hed Big Band of Tel Aviv and others). They have also filled pedagogical positions at academies and conservatories. New concert halls were built for some of these orchestras, like those in Rishon le-Zion and in Kefar Shmaryahu. Concert life has also been enriched by the performances of new soloists. The most noted among them are the singers Susanna Poretsky, Felix Lipshitz, and Yuri Shapovalov; pianists Raimonda Sheinfeld, Irena Berkovich, Dinna Yoffe, Gabriela Talrose, and Evgeny Shenderovich; jazz-pianists Viacheslav Ganelin and Leonid Ptashka; violinists Maxim Vengerov and Sergey Ostrovski; cellists Mikhail Homitzer and Oleg Stolpner; clarinetist Evgeny Ehudin; bassoonist Alexander Fain; harpist Julia Sverdlova, and others. Many of the new artists appear as guests in concerts.

As many as 50 new composers from the former Soviet Union have joined the existing 150 members of the Israel Composers' League. The musicians imported a variety of styles, from followers of "socialist realism" to followers of Gubaidulina, Kancheli and other representatives of the Russian post-modernism. Among the post-modernists, the highest achievements were attained by Josef *Bardanashvili, who in a few years won the most prestigious Israeli awards and became one of the leading composers (especially in the fields of theater and film scores). His piano composition was selected as the compulsory piece at the 2005 International Rubinstein piano competition. Even though he spent only his last years in Israel (from 1994), Valentin Bibik (1942–2003) had significant achievements and produced important new works. The composers who came from the Asian republics of the former Soviet Union also had interesting achievements combining the elements of modernism and post-modernism along with a variety of local musical elements from their regions. In Israel, Jewish elements were added (Yusupov, Pigovat, Davydov, Fel, Perez, Freidlin, Heifets). Most of the composers from this group display a growing interest in Jewish themes. Many new compositions have been written in the "Jewish style." In most cases it is only a simple rearrangement of popular Jewish melodies. However, some composers have created remarkable works (Bardanashvili, *The Children of God*; Yusupov, Sonata for Two Pianos).

Among the winners of the Klon Prize for the best young Israeli composer are also some newcomers: Benjamin Yusupov, Karel Volnianski, and Uri Brener.

In the field of electro-acoustic music, the most noted newcomer artists are Marcel Goldmann (from France) and Simon Lazar (from Bulgaria). Among the musicologists, Marina Ritzareva and Yulia Kreinina achieved the best works.

[Dushan Mihalek (2nd ed.)]

MUSIC AND THE HOLOCAUST

Life during the Holocaust, the suffering of the Jews under the Nazi regime, has been reflected in music and musical life. Musical performance created venues to express humanity under inhuman conditions, it was a way to escape from reality, a way to find comfort and hopes and express freedom.

Shortly after the Nazi rise to power in 1933, the regime established a central office to control all musical activity in Germany. The composer Richard Strauss was appointed its president, and the conductor Wilhelm Furtwangler his deputy. All Jewish professional musicians in Germany were dismissed from their posts and works of Jewish composers were banned. Many of them immigrated to Palestine and the U.S. and resumed their careers there.

In July 1933, Jewish performers set up the Kulturbund Deutscher Juden (Cultural Society of German Jews) for promoting music and the arts among German Jews. In its eight years of existence the Kulturbund organized over 500 concerts of opera, operettas, symphonic and chamber music, Jewish cantorial music, and other genres. When the Kulturbund could no longer function, some of the musicians left Germany while others were sent to ghettos and concentration camps and continued to perform there, like those at the Theresienstadt (Terezin).

During the war, there were public musical activities in some ghettos as well as performances for private occasions where people sang, played, and even danced. Street performances were known in some ghettos, such as Lodz, Warsaw, and Cracow, where several singers performed songs, some of them composed ad hoc, on ghetto life while others were set to pre-composed melodies. One of the popular street performers in the Lodz ghetto was Yankele Hershkowitz (1910–1970).

Professional musical performance was censored and controlled by the authorities; however, the freedom to sing and compose music could not be controlled or censored totally. Thus music became a symbol of freedom. In Warsaw, Adam Furmanski (1883–1943) organized small orchestras in cafés and in soup kitchens. In the Warsaw ghetto a symphonic orchestra played until April 1942, when the German authorities put an end to the orchestra, punishing it for having performed works by German composers. In Lodz, the Jewish Council chairman, Mordechai Chaim Rumkowski, centrally directed musical activities. The community center organized musical and theatrical performances, a symphony orchestra, the Zamir choral society, and a revue theater appeared on its stage. In the Cracow ghetto, chamber music recitals and concerts of liturgical music were performed. The Vilna ghetto had an extensive program of musical activities, with a symphony orchestra and several choirs. A revue theater presented many popular songs composed in the ghetto on ghetto life. A conservatory with 100 students was established in the Vilna ghetto.

Many songs were heard in the ghettos – some old, perhaps with new words, and some new. One of the first anthologies of songs was published in 1948, under the title *Di Lider fun Getos un Lagern* ("Songs of Ghettos and Camps"), which was collected and edited by the poet, teacher, and partisan from Vilna Shmerke Kaczerginski (1908–1954). The anthology contains 236 songs (lyrics) and 100 melodies. However, many songs were lost forever.

Among the best-known songs composed and performed during the Holocaust are songs of the Vilna Ghetto *"Zog nit Keymol"* ("Never Say"), also known by its postwar title "Song of the Partisans," written by Hirsh Glik (1922–1944) to a melody of Russian composer Dimitry Pokrass; *"Shtiler, Shtiler"* ("Quiet, Quiet") with words by S. Kaczerginski and music by the 11-year-old Alexander Volkoviski (*Tamir; 1931–); *"Friling"* ("Spring"), words by S. Kaczerginski, music by Abraham Brudno (1910(?)–1943), and *"Yisrolik,"* words by Leyb Rozental and music by Mischa Veksler (1907–1943). Songs of the Vilna ghetto inspired the writer Yehoshua *Sobol in his play *Ghetto*, which made the songs popular in many languages around the world. Many of the Vilna ghetto theater songs became songs of remembrance and are still performed in commemoration ceremonies, mainly in translation, especially in Hebrew and English. The songwriter Mordecai *Gebirtig (1877–1942) from Cracow wrote another song *"Es Brent"* ("It Burns") that became popular during the Holocaust and afterward. The song was written in 1938 under the impact of the pogrom in Przytyk and became a prophecy of the Holocaust. It became after the war a symbol for the fate of the Jews in Eastern Europe.

Those who became partisans composed songs in a variety of languages, which were performed mostly in group singing. Some of the partisan groups also used an instrument for accompaniment. The best-know partisans' songs from Vilna gained fame thanks to the collection work of Kaczerginski.

Many songs performed and composed in the camps were popular prewar songs in a variety of languages and were not transmitted from one ghetto to another. However, after the war, at the DP camps, songs were also transmitted and were shared by Holocaust survivors.

In the Theresienstadt ghetto, where professional composers as well as classical and jazz musicians were interned, many compositions were created and many musical pieces were performed. Viktor Ullman (1898–1944) composed there three of his piano sonatas (No. 5, Op. 45, 1943; No. 6,Op. 49, 1943; No. 7, 1944), String Quartet (No. 3, Op. 46, 1943), three songs for baritone and piano, and arrangements of songs for choir. His last piece, the opera *The Emperor of Atlantis*, was never performed, and Ullman was sent to the gas chambers in Auschwitz in August 1944. In the same transport, his colleagues Pavel Haas (1899–1944), Hans Krasa (1899–1944), and Gideon Klein (1919–1945) were also sent to Auschwitz. Gideon Klein composed in Theresienstadt a Piano Sonata (1943), Fantasie and Fugue for string quartet (1942–43), Trio for violin and cello (1944), Two Madrigals (1942–43), and arrangements of folk songs. One of the more memorable performances was of the children's opera *Brundibar* by Hans Krasa (1899–1944) (in Czech), which was composed in 1935 and performed in the ghetto with a children's choir, soloists, and piano. Hans Krasa also composed a Theme and Variations, based on Brundibar's song for string quartet (1942), Songs (1943) for baritone, clarinet, viola and cello, Dance (1943) for trio, Passacaglia and Fugue for trio, and more. Other composers interned in Theresienstadt who composed there were Zigmund Schul (1916–1944), Erwin Schulhoff (1894–1942), and Carlo S. Taube (1897–1944), who was also a singer and conductor.

In most of the big concentration and extermination camps, the Germans formed orchestras from among the prisoners and forced them to play when Jews arrived at the camps, on their way to the gas chambers, when they marched to work, and also for the pleasures of the SS men.

The Auschwitz camp had six orchestras at one point. The biggest one, in Auschwitz I (the main camp), consisted of 50 musicians. A women's orchestra in Auschwitz-Birkenau consisted of 36 members and eight women who wrote musical notes under the musical direction of the singer Fania Fenelon. All four of the extermination camps – Treblinka, Majdanek, Belzec and Sobibor – had orchestras as well as Mauthausen and Buchenwald camps. Dachau had four orchestras and a string quartet.

The written documentation published after the Holocaust includes the earliest anthologies of ghetto and camp songs compiled by Yehuda Eisman (Bucharest 1945); that of Zami Feder (Bergen-Belsen, 1946), and that of Kaczerginski (New York, 1948). Kaczerginski also made recordings among survivors in Displaced Persons camps in 1946, some of which survived at Yad Vashem archives. Composers and poets who immigrated to Israel, the U.S., and other countries composed new songs about the Holocaust, such as Henek Kon in the anthology *Kdoishim-Martyrs* (New York, 1947). Later even popular musicians such as the Israeli Yehudah *Poliker composed songs to lyrics of Yaakov Gilad, like *"Efer ve-Avak"* ("Ashes and Dust," 1988). Both of them are sons of Holocaust survivors.

Several organizations of people from the same home city or ghetto, the State of Israel, other countries around the world, etc. organized commemoration gatherings for Holocaust survivors. In these ceremonies the song *"Zog Nit Keynmol"* of the partisans of Vilna became the Holocaust hymn. Other ghetto and camp songs were never performed again while new songs about the Holocaust or related themes such as survival, uprising, belief, and hope were added to the ceremonies.

New compositions have been composed since the Holocaust, including Arnold Schonberg's *Survivor from Warsaw* (1947), *Dies Irae* of the Polish composer Krzystof Penderecki, the *Thirteenth Symphony Babi Yar* by the Russian composer Dimitry Shostakovich, *I Never Saw Another Butterfly* by Charles Davidson, and more.

With the growth of research on music of the Holocaust and the revival of Jewish Yiddish music since the 1980s more songs were recorded, especially by American musicians, and performed to mixed audiences around the world. (See also: *Israel, State of – Cultural Life, Music and Dance; *Hasidism; Dance.)

[Gila Flam (2nd ed.)]

BIBLIOGRAPHY: GENERAL: Idelsohn, Music; idem, *Toledot ha-Neginah ha-Ivrit, Mahutah, Yesodoteha ve-Hitpatteḥutah*, 1 (1924); E. Werner, in: Grove, Dict, 4 (1954[5]), 615–36; idem, *From Generation to Generation; Studies in Jewish Musical Tradition* (1968); P. Gradenwitz, *The Music of Israel; its Rise and Growth Through 5000 Years* (1949); A. Nadel, in: *Der Jude*, 7 (1923), 227–36; H. Avenary, in: MGG, 7 (1958), 226–61; E. Gerson-Kiwi, *ibid.*, 261–80; idem, in: *Madda*, 4 (1960), 26–33; idem, *The Legacy of Jewish Music Through the Ages* (1963); idem, in: *Yuval* (1968), 169–93, mus. ex. 16–25; A.M. Rothmueller, *The Music of the Jews* (1967); A. Ackermann, in: AZJ, 63 (1899), 379–82, 392–4, 414–5; A. Friedmann, *Der synagogale Gesang* (1908); idem (ed.), *Dem Andenken Eduard Birnbaums* (1922); A.Z. Idelsohn, *Phonographierte Gesaenge und Aussprache-Proben des Hebraeischen der jemenitischen, persischen und syrischen Juden* (1917); D. Milhaud, in: *Musica Hebraica*, 1–2 (1938), 18–20; M. Wohlberg, in: UJE, 8 (1942), 48–55; H. Harris, *Toledot ha-Neginah ve-ha-Ḥazzanut be-Yisrael* (1950); I. Rabinovitch, *Of Jewish Music, Ancient and Modern* (1952); E. Werner, in: *New Oxford History of Music*, 1 (1957), 313–35; A. Rechtman, *Yidishe Etnografye un Folklor* (1958); I. Adler, in: *Encyclopédie de la Musique Fasquelle*, 2 (1959), 640–54; idem, in: J. Porte (ed.), *Encyclopédie des musiques sacrées*, 1 (1968), 469–93; L. Algazi, *ibid.*, 494–9; E. Gerson-Kiwi, *ibid.*, 512–4; H. Avenary, in: R. Patai (ed.), *Studies in Biblical and Jewish Folklore* (1960), 185–98; J. Walbe, *Der Gesang Israels und seine Quellen* (1964); I. Heskes (ed.), *The Cantorial Art* (1966); Levy, Antologia; E. Piattelli, *Canti liturgici ebraici di rito italiano* (1967); C. Vinaver, *Anthology of Jewish Music* (1953); A. Herzog, *Renanot – Dappim le-Shirah u-le-Musikah Datit*, 1–10 (1958–63). THE BIBLICAL PERIOD (to c. 200 B.C.E.): Sendrey, Music, nos. 10,005–10,682; Finesinger, in: HUCA, 8–9 (1931/32), 193–228; O.R. Sellers, in: *Biblical Archaeologist*, 4 (1941), 33–47; A. Buechler, in: ZAWB, 19 (1899), 93–133, 329–44; 20 (1900), 97–135; C. Sachs, *The Rise of Music in the Ancient World – East and West* (1943); E. Werner, in: *Musical Quarterly*, 43 (1957), 21–37; idem, in: Grove, Dict, 4 (1954), 615–21; idem, in: MGG, 10 (1962), 1668–76; H. Avenary, *ibid.*, 7 (1958), 238ff. (incl. bibl.); Kraeling-Mowry, in: *New Oxford Dictionary of Music*, 1 (1957), 238ff. G. Rinaldi, in: *Biblica*, 40 (1959), 267–89; E. Gerson-Kiwi, in: *Enciclopedia de la Biblia*, 5 (1963), 364–79; O. Eissfeldt, *An Introduction to the Old Testament* (1965), 88–127, 444–54, 483–91; B. Bayer, in: EM, 5 (1967), 755–82 (incl. bibl.); idem, in: *Yuval*, 1 (1968), 89–131; idem, *The Material Relics of Music in Ancient Palestine and its Environs* (1963); S. Hoffman, *Mikra'ei Musikah* (1966); D. Wohlenberg, *Kultmusik in Israel – eine forschungsgeschichtliche Untersuchung* (1967); A. Sendrey, *Music in Ancient Israel* (1969). THE SECOND TEMPLE PERIOD (to c. 70 C.E.): H. Avenary, in: *Revue de Quamrân*, 13 (1963), 15–21; E. Werner, *The Sacred Bridge* (1959), FIRST PERIOD (c. 70 to 950 C.E.): A. Buechler, *Untersuchungen zur Entstehung und Entwicklung der hebraeischen Accente* (1891); J. Adams, *Hebrew Accentuation* (1906); S. Krauss, Tal Arch, 3 (1912), 76–99; P. Kahle, *Masoreten des Ostens* (1913); idem, *Masoreten des Westens*, 2 vols. (1927–30); A.Z. Idelsohn, in: A.M. Luncz (ed.), *Yerushalayim*, 11–12 (1916), 335–73; idem, in: *Zeitschrift fuer Musikwissenschaft*, 4 (1922), 515–24; H. Loewenstein (Avenary), *ibid.*, 12 (1930), 513–20; idem, in: *The Jewish Music Forum*, 7–8 (1946–47), 27–33; idem, in: JJS, 16 (1965), 87–104; S. Rosowsky, in: *Proceedings of the Musical Association* (1934), session 60; E. Werner, in: *Review of Religion*, 7 (1942/43), 339–52; idem, in: HUCA, 20 (1947), 407–70; 23 (1950–51), 397–432; 25 (1954), 327–45); idem, in: *Actes du Congrès de Musique Sacrée, Rome 1950* (1952), 134–48; idem, in: MGG, 10 (1962), 1668–76; A. Scheiber, in: *Sinai*, 29 (1951), 80–89; J. Kafih, *ibid.*, 29 (1951), 261–6; idem, in: *Tarbiz*, 31 (1961/62), 371–6; B. Szabolcsi, in: *Ignace Goldziher Memorial Volume*, 1 (1948); A. Shlesinger, in: *Ereẓ Yisrael… le-Zikhro shel M.D. Cassuto* (1954); M. Gonzalo, in: *Miscelanea de Estudios Arabes y Hebraicos*, 4 (1955), 129–41; J.L. Ne'eman, *Ẓelilei ha-Mikra* (1955); L. Levi, in: *Estratto da Scritti in Memoria di Sally Mayer* (1956), 139–93; A.W. Binder, *Biblical Chant* (1959); E. Gerson-Kiwi, in: *Festschrift Heinrich Besseler* (1962), 43–49; idem, in: *Festschrift Brunno Staeblein* (1967), 64–73; D. Weisberg, in: JQR, 56 (1965/66), 315–36; G. Engberg, in: E. Wellesz, ed., *Studies in Eastern Chant*, 1 (1966), 37–49; Y. Walbe, in: *Ethnomusicology*, 11 (1967), 54–70; A. Herzog and A. Hajdu, in: *Yuval* (1968), 194–203, mus. ex. 1–15. SECOND PERIOD, THE MUSIC OF THE MEDIEVAL DIASPORA (c. 950–1500): Y. Singer, *Die Entwicklung des synagogalen Gesanges* (1882); idem, *Die Tonarten des traditionellen Synagogengesanges (Steiger); ihr Verhaeltnis zu den Kirchentonarten und den Tonarten der Vorchristlichen Musikperiode* (1886); M. Steinschneider, in: *Beit Oẓar ha-Sifrut*, 1 (1887), 29–37; E. Kirschner, *Ueber Mittelalterliche hebraeische Poesien und ihre Singweisen* (1914); S. Krauss, *Synagogale Altertuemer* (1922), paragraphs 16.2, 16.3, 44.6; J. Schoenberg, *Die traditionellen Gesaenge des israelitischen Gottesdienstes in Deutschland* (1926); A.Z. Idelsohn, in: *Zeitschrift fuer Musikwissenschaft*, 8 (1926), 449–72; idem, in: *Reshummot*, 5 (1927), 351–61; 6 (1930), 411–22; idem, in: *Acta Musicologica*, 5 (1933), 162–8; idem, in: HUCA, 8–9 (1931–32), 495–503; 14 (1939), 559–74; H.G. Farmer, *Maimonides on Listening to Music* (1941); idem, in: *The Music Review*, 3 (1942); M.S. Geshuri, in: *Sinai*, 13 (1943–44), 317–49; 39 (1956), 298–316; B. Szabolcsi, in: *Semitic Studies in Memory of Immanuel Loew* (1947), 131–3; B.J. Cohon, in: *Journal of American Musicological Society*, 3 (1950), 17–32; H. Avenary, in: *Musica Disciplina*, 4 (1950), 51–57; 6 (1952), 27–32; idem, in: HUCA, 39 (1968), 145–62; E. Werner, in: G. Reese and R. Brandel (eds.), *The Commonwealth of Music; in Honour of Curt Sachs* (1965), 71–96; H. Wagenaar-Nolthenius, in: *Mélanges offerts à René Crozet* (1966), 881–5; Y. Ratzaby, in: *Taẓlil*, 6 (1966), 8–13; A. Shiloah, *ibid.*, 5–8; idem, in: *Fourth World Congress of Jewish Studies, Papers*, 2 (1968); idem, in: *Yuval*, 1 (1968), 221–50; I. Adler, *ibid.*, 1–47; N. Alloni, *ibid.*, 12–35; Angles, *ibid.*, 48–64; A. Heshel, in: J. Porte (ed.), *Encyclopédie des musiques sacrées*, 1 (1968), 515–20; B. Cohen, *Law and Tradition in Judaism* (1969). THIRD PERIOD, THE MIGRATION AND BLENDING OF MUSICAL STYLES (c. 1500–1800): E. Birnbaum, *Juedische Musiker am Hofe von Mantua von 1542–1628* (1893); D. Kaufmann, in: MGWJ, 39 (1895), 350–7; A.Z. Idelsohn, *ibid.*, 57 (1913), 314–25; idem, in: HUCA, 11 (1936), 569–91; P. Nettl, *Alte juedische Spielleute und Musiker* (1923); idem, in: *Musical Quarterly*, 17 (1931), 40–46; R.L. Henriques and H.M.J. Loewe, *Medieval Hebrew Minstrelsy* (1926); C. Roth, in: *Rassegna Mensile di Israel*, 3 (1927–28), 152–62; E. Werner, in: MGWJ, 45 (1937) 92–416; idem, in: *Studies in Bibliography and Booklore*, 5 (1961), 110–21; A. Nadel, in: *Musica He-*

braica, 2 (1938), 28–31; M. Vital, *Di Khazonim Velt*, 3 (1939), 2–4; E. Lifschutz, in: YIVO *Annual of Jewish Social Science*, 7 (1952), 48–83; H. Shmueli, *Higgajon Bechinnor (Betrachtung zum Leierspiel) des Jehudah... Moscato* (1953); J. Stutschevsky, *Ha-Klezmerim: Toledoteihem, Oraḥ-Ḥayyeihem vi-Yẓiroteihem* (1959); A. Hemsi, in: *Sefarad*, 20 (1960), 148 ff.; I. Adler, *La Pratique musicale savante dans quelques communautés juives en Europe aux* XVII*e et* XVIII*e siècles*, 2 vols. (1966); idem, in: A. Altmann (ed.), *Jewish Medieval and Renaissance Studies* (1967), 321–64; S. Simonsohn, in: *Proceedings of the American Academy for Jewish Research*, 34 (1966), 99–110; H. Avenary, in: *Yuval* (1968), 65–85, mus. ex. 26–34; R.D. Barnett, in: JHSET, 22 (1968), 1–38; R. Katz, in: *Acta Musicologica*, 40 (1968), 65–85; M. Gorali, in: *Tatzlil*, 10 (1970), 9–28. FOURTH PERIOD, MODERN TIMES: D. Deutsch, *Die Orgel in der Synagoge* (1863); S. Sulzer, *Denkschrift an die hochgeehrte Wiener israelitische Cultus-Gemeinde, zum 50 jaehr. Jubilaeum des alten Bethauses am 1. Nissan 5636* (1876); A. Berliner, *Zur Lehr' und zur Wehr; ueber und gegen die Kirchliche Orgel im juedischen Gottesdienste* (1904); J. Lebermann, *Aus dem Kunstleben der Hessischen Residenz am Anfang des vorigen Jahrhunderts* (1904), 22–31; A Friedmann, *Lebensbilder beruehmter Kantoren*, 3 vols, (1918–28); S. Krauss, *Zur Orgelfrage* (1919); M. Brod, in: *Musikblaetter des Anbruch*, 2 (1920); H. Berl, *Das Judentum in der Musik* (1926); A. Einstein, in: *Der Morgen*, 2 (1926), 290–602; L.L. Ssabanejew, *Die nationale juedische Schule in der Musik* (1927); M. Joseph and L. Seligman, in: JL, 4 (1930), 601–4; L. Kornitzer, in: *Juedisch-liberale Zeitung*, 11, nos. 31–33 (1931); O. Guttmann, in: *Der juedische Kantor* (1934), nos. 1–4, 6; J. Stuschevsky, *Mein Weg zur juedischen Musik* (1936); M.S. Geshuri, *La-Ḥasidim Mizmor* (1936); idem, *Neginah va-Ḥasidut be-Veit Kuzmir u-Venoteha* (1952); idem, *Ha-Niggun ve-ha-Rikkud ba-Ḥasidut*, 3 vols. (1955–59); idem, in: *Sefer ha-Besht* (1960); M. Ravina, *Mikhtavim al Musikah Yehudit me'et Yo'el Engel, M.M. Warshavsky, Shalom Aleichem* (1942); E. Werner, in: *Contemporary Jewish Record*, 6 (1943), 607–15; A. Berliner, *Ketavim Nivḥarim*, 1 (1945); R. Glanz, in: YIVO *Bleter*, 28 (1946), 394–97; M. Lewison, in: *Di Tsukunft*, 52 no. 4 (1947); W.Z. Rabinowitsch, *Ha-Ḥasidut ha-Lita'it* (1951), music appendix; H.D. Weisgal, in: *Judaism*, 3 (1954), 427–36; A. Weisser, *The Modern Renaissance of Jewish Music, Events and Figures; Eastern Europe and America* (1954); A.W. Binder, in: *The Jewish Forum*, 38 (1955), 19–21, 44–46; I. Freed, *Harmonizing the Jewish Modes* (1958); A.L. Holde, *Jews in Music* (1959); O.D. Kulka, in: BLBI, 4 (1961), 281–300; G. Krause, in: *Mitteilungen aus dem Arbeitskreis fuer Jiddistik* (1961), 36–39; A.W. Binder, *The Jewish Music Movement in America* (1963); N. Stolnitz, in: *Canadian Jewish Reference Book and Directory* (1963), 101–4; A. Tarshish, in: AJHSQ, 54 (1964), 411–49; P. Nettl, in: *Music and Letters*, 45 (1964), 337–44; D.S. Lifson, *The Yiddish Theatre in America* (1965); E. Werner, in: *Central Conference of American Rabbis Journal*, 13 (1965/66), 35–40; A. Soltes, in: I. Heskes and A. Wolfson (eds.), *The Historic Contribution of Russian Jewry to Jewish Music* (1967); A.L. Ringer, in: *Studia Musicologica*, 11 (1969), 355–70; P.E. Gradenwitz, in: *Fourth World Congress of Jewish Studies, Papers*, 2 (1968), 147–51. FOLK MUSIC; C. Seeger, "Oral Traditions in Music," in: *Funk and Wagnall's Standard Dictionary of Folklore, Mythology and Legend*, 2 (1950); G. Herzog, "Song, Folk-Song and Music of Folk-Song," in: *ibid.*; Sendrey, Music; (1951), see table of contents; Waterman, in: *Music Library Association Notes* (1950/51); *Répertoire International de Littérature Musicale (RILM)* (1967–); *The Music Index*, 1–13 (1949–); Shunami, Bibl; I. Joel, *Reshimat Ma'amarim be-Madda'ei ha-Yahadut*, 1 (1964), 49–51, 87–90; 2 (1967), 61 f., 121 f., 124 f.; 3 (1968), 56–58, 114 f., 117 f.; D. Noy, in: *Meḥkerei ha-Merkaz le-Ḥeker ha-Folklor*, 1 (1970), 389–423; *Tazlil*, 10 (1970), 82–91 (index to vols. 1–10). GENERAL ARTICLES: E. Gerson-Kiwi, in: MGG, 7 (1958), 261–80 (incl. bibl.); idem, in: Grove, Dict, 3 (1954), 304–13. RECENT PARTICULAR STUDIES AND SOURCE-PUBLICATIONS: A. EUROPE, GENERAL: D. Sadan, in: *Bamah*, 9–10 (1961), 27–33; J. Stutschewsky, *Folklor Musikali shel Yehudei Mizraḥ Eiropah* (1958); W. Heiske, in: *Jahrbuch fuer Volksliedforschung*, 9 (1964), 31–44; M. Gorali et al. (eds.), *Di Goldene Pave* (1970); E. Sekuletz, *Shirei Am Yehudiyyim mi-Romanyah* (1970[2]); S. Prizament, *Di Broder Zinger* (1960); A. Rechtman, *Yidishe Etnografye un Folklor, Zikhroynes vegn der Etnografisher Ekspeditsye Angefirt fun S. An-Ski* (1958); E. Mayer, in: YLBI, 3 (1958), 202–10. B. KLEZMORIM AND BADḤANIM: J. Stutschewsky, *Ha-Kleizmerim* (1959); I. Riwkind, in: *Hadoar*, 9 (1960), 412 f., 463 f., 483 f., 504–30, 533 f., 574 f.; idem, in: *Minḥahli-Yhudaḥ* (1950), 235–57; E. Lifschutz, in: YIVOA, 7 (1952), 43–83; H. Liberman, in: *Yidishe Sprakh*, 13 (1953), 149–53; A. Yaari, in: KS, 35 (1960), 109–26; 36 (1961), 264–72. C. ASIA AND AFRICA: A. Shiloah, in: *Meḥkerei ha-Merkaz le-Ḥeker ha-Folklor*, 1 (1970), 349–68; Levi, Antologia, 5 vols. (1965–69); idem, *Chants judéo-espagnols*, 3 vols. (1959–71); A. Larrea Palacin, *Cancionero judío del Norte de Marruecos*, 2 vols. (1952–54); See also articles on musical traditions of various communities and areas, and bibliographies in articles on E. *Gerson-Kiwi, R. *Rubin, and M.S. *Geshuri. MUSIC IN MODERN ISRAEL: P.E. Gradenwitz, *The Music of Israel* (1949); idem, *Music and Musicians in Israel* (1959[2]); E. Gerson-Kiwi, in: *Acta Musicologica*, 30 (1958), 17–26; M. Smoira-Roll (Zmora), *Folk Song in Israel: An Analysis Attempted* (1963); idem (ed.), *Yesodot Mizraḥiyyim u-Ma'araviyyim ba-Musikah be-Yisrael* (1968); A.L. Ringer, in: *Musical Quarterly*, 50 (1965); idem, in: P.H. Lang and N. Broder (eds.), *Contemporary Music in Europe* (1965), 282–98; A. Shaḥar and B. Bayer, *Ha-Jazz* (1966), 149–56; B. Bayer, in: *Dukhan*, 7 (1966), 11–30, 89–98; Y. Boehm, *The Making of Music* (19664); D. Harran, in: *Current Musicology*, 7 (1968), 120–7; *Tazlil*, 10 (1970), 82–91 (index to vols. 1–10); I. Miron-Michrowsky, *A Profile of Israeli Music Today* (1964); B. Bar-Am (ed.), *Twenty Years of Israeli Music* (1968). BIBLIOGRAPHICAL WORKS: J.N. Forkel, *Allgemeine Litteratur der Music* (1792), 33–44; A.Z. Idelsohn, in: *Studies in Jewish Bibliography and Related Subjects in Memory of A.S. Freidus* (1929), 388–403; O. Kinkeldey, *ibid.*, 329–72; R. Rubin, *Jewish Book Annual*, 6 (1947), 64–70; Sendrey, Music; W. Sparger, in: *The American Hebrew* (1892), 197–9, 229, 265–6; A. Weisser, *Bibliography of Publications and Other Sources of Jewish Music* (1969); E. Werner, in: HUCA, 18 (1943/44), 397–428; idem, in: *Historia Judaica*, 6 (1944), 175–88. **ADD. BIBLIOGRAPHY:** *Journal of Synagogue Music* (1967–); *Musica Judaica* (1975–); *Journal of Jewish Music and Liturgy* (1976–); E. Werner, *A Voice Still Heard: The Sacred Songs of the Ashkenazic Jews* (1976); A. Shiloah, *The Musical Subjects in the Zohar* (1978), with the assistance of R. Tene (Yuval Monograph Series V); H. Avenary, *Encounters of East and West in Music* (1979); E. Gerson-Kiwi, *Migrations and Mutations of the Music in East and West: Selected Writings* (1980); B. Bayer, "The Titles of the Psalms – A Renewed Investigation of an Old Problem," in: *Yuval* 4 (1982), 29–123; M. Slobin (ed.), *Old Jewish Folk Music, The Collections and Writings of Moshe Beregovski* (1982); E. Werner, *The Sacred Bridge: The Interdependence of Liturgy and Music in Synagogue and Church during the First Millennium*, vol. 2 (1984); M. Nulman, *Concepts of Jewish and Prayer* (1985); H. Avenary, *Kantor Salomon Sulzer und seine Zeit: eine Dokumentation*, with an Introduction by Israel Adler (1985); K.K. Shelemay, *Music, Ritual, and Falasha History* (1986); M.I. Beregovski, *Evreiskaya narodnaya instrumentalnaya muzyka* (ed. M. Goldin) (1987); R. Flender, *Der biblische Sprechgesang und seine muendliche Ueberlieferung in Synagoge und griechische Kirche* (Quellen zu Musikgeschichte, 20) (1988); I. Adler, *Hebrew Notated Manuscript Sources up to circa 1840 – with a Checklist of Printed sources...* with assistance of Lea Shalem, 2 vols. (RISM BIX1) (1989); P.V. Bohlman, *The Land Where Two Streams Flow, Music in the German-Jewish Community of Israel* (1989); A. Tischler, *A Descriptive Bibliography of Art*

Music by Israeli Composers (1989); M. Slobin, *Chosen Voices, The Story of the American Cantorate* (1989); F. Alvarez-Pereyre, *La transmission orale de la misnah: une méthode d'analyse appliquée à la tradition d'Alep* (Yuval Monograph Series 8) (1990); J. Hirschberg, *Paul ben Haim, His Life and Works* (1990); S. Hofman, *Music in the Talmud* (1990); Y.W. Cohen, *The Heirs of the Psalmist: Israel's New Music* (1990); P. Dorn, *Change and Ideology: The Ethnomusicology of Turkish Jewry*, UMI Dissertation Services (2001); W. Salmen, *Juedische Musikanten und Taenzer vom 13. bis 20 Jahrhundert* (1991); P.V. Bohlman, *The World Centre for Jewish Music in Palestine 1936–1940* (1992); G. Flam, *Singing for Survival: Songs of the Lodz Ghetto* (1992); L.A. Hoffman and J.R. Walton (eds.), *Sacred Sound and Social Change: Liturgical Music in Jewish and Christian Experience* (1992); R. Flender, *Hebrew Psalmody; A Structural Investigation* (Yuval Monograph Series IX) (1992); I. Heskes, *Yiddish American Popular Songs 1895–1950*, a catalog based on the Lawrence Marwick Roster of Copyright Entries, Washington, Library of Congress (1992); A. Shiloah, *Jewish Musical Traditions* (1992); M. Slobin, *Tenement Songs, The Popular Music of the Jewish Immigrants* (1992); A. Shiloah, *The Dimension of Music in Islamic and Jewish Cultures* (1993); M. Gorali, *The Old Testament in Music* (1993); A. Hemsi, *Cancionero Sefardi*, ed. and intro. by E. Seroussi in collaboration with P. Diaz-Mas, J.M. Pedrosa, and E. Romero (Yuval Music Series, IV) (1985); J. Hirshberg, *Music in the Jewish Community of Palestine 1880–1948* (1995); A. Tietze and J. Yahalom. *Ottoman Melodies, Hebrew Hymns: A 16th Century Cross-Cultural Adventure* (Bibliotrca Orientalis Hungarica, vol. 43) (1995); D.M. Weil, *The Masoretic Chant of the Bible* (1995); I. Adler, *The Study of Jewish Music*: A Bibliographical Guide (Yuval Monograph Series X) (1995); P. Gradenwitz, *The Music of Israel: From the Biblical Era to Modern Times* (1996); K.K. Shelemay, *Let Jasmine Rain Down: Song and Remembrance among Syrian Jews* (1996); R. Fleisher, *Twenty Israeli Composers Voices of a Culture* (1997); A. Shiloah (ed.), *The Performance of Jewish and Arab Music in Israel Today*, 2 vols. (1997); H. Sapoznik, *Klezmer Jewish Music from Old World to Our World* (1999); D. Harran, *Salamone Rossi: Jewish Musician in Late Renaissance Mantua* (1999); J. Braun, *Die Musikkultur Altisraels/Palaestinas: Studien zu archaeologischen, shriftischen un vergleichenden Quellen* (1999) (translated from the German by D.W. Stott, 2002); H. Rotten, *Les Traditions musicales Judéo-portuguaise en France* (2000); J. Levine, *A Synagogue Song in America* (2000); Y. Mazor, *The Klezmer Tradition in the Land of Israel* (2000); K.K. Shelemay (ed.), *Studies in Jewish Musical Traditions: Insights from the Harvard Collection of Judaica Sound Recordings* (2001); E. Koskoff, *Music in Lubavitcher Life* (2001); F.C. Lemaire, *Le Destin Juif et la musique* (2001); M. Slobin (ed.), *American Klezmer – Its Roots and Offshoots* (2002); A.L. Ringer, *Arnold Schoenberg das Leben im Werk, Mit einem nachwort von Thomas Emmering* (2002); Y. Strom, *The Book of Klezmer: the History, the Music, the Folklore* (2002); S. Kalib, *The Musical Tradition of the Eastern European Synagogue* (2002); I. Heskes, *Passport to Jewish Music: Its History, Traditions and Culture* (paperback ed., 2002); R. Katz, *The Lachmann Problem* (Yuval Monograph Series XII) (2003); M. Regev, and E. Seroussi, *Popular Music and National Culture in Israel* (2004). HOLOCAUST: F. Fenelon, *Playing for Time*. trans. J. Landry (1979); J. Karas, *Music in Terezin, 1941–1945* (1985).

°**MUSIL, ALOIS** (1868–1944), Czech Orientalist, born in Rychtarov in Bohemia. He studied at the theological faculty of Olomouc and was ordained a priest in 1891; in 1895 he went to Jerusalem to join the Dominican Ecole Biblique. His field exploration began with a trip to *Egypt in 1896 and to Petra in 1897, when he traveled from *Gaza to *Damascus by way of the Negev and Transjordan. In 1898 the Vienna Academy sent him on a mission to Arabia Petrea, which he explored until 1902, discovering the desert palaces at Quṣayr ʿAmra, Ṭūba, al-Bāyir, and al-Muwaqqar. He was one of the first explorers of the ancient cities of the Negev. In addition to archaeology, he was greatly interested in mapping and in the manners and customs of the Bedouin. From 1902 to 1909 he taught at Olomouc and from 1909 to 1918 at Vienna. He explored the Syrian Desert in 1908–09, the northern *Hejaz in 1910, and the Palmyrene and northern *Arabia to the Hejaz in 1912–15; the last mission was semipolitical. In 1920 he began to teach at Prague University. Musil published *Ḳuṣejr ʿAmra und andere Schloesser…* (2 vols., 1902); *Arabia Petraea* (Ger., 4 vols., 1907–08), which contains the first good map of the Negev; and a four-volume series of topographical itineraries through northern Arabia, including maps of the region (1926–28). He was an exact observer, although his archaeological training was insufficient.

BIBLIOGRAPHY: Rypka, in: *Archiv Orientálni*, 10 (1938), 1ff.

[Michael Avi-Yonah]

°**MUSOLINO, BENEDETTO** (1809–1885), Italian statesman who foretold the return of the Jews to Ereẓ Israel. Born in Pizzo (Calabria), Musolino was an exile in his youth and later joined Garibaldi's army. From 1861 he served as member of the Italian parliament and later as a senator in united Italy. He published seven books on philosophy, law, and social justice. Musolino visited Ereẓ Israel four times and wrote *Gerusalemme ed il Popolo Ebreo* (1851, first published in 1951). Based upon an analysis of the situation of the Jews in the Diaspora and their yearning to return to Ereẓ Israel, the book suggests that Britain support the establishment of a Jewish principality in Ereẓ Israel under the Turkish Crown. Musolino even formulated a complete constitution, which stipulates a prince at the head of the principality and a bicameral parliament. The official religion of the principality is Judaism and the language is Hebrew. The right to vote and to be elected would be granted only to those who read and write Hebrew. All the public offices, including jurisdiction, would be determined by the elections for one-year terms. Citizenship would automatically be granted to Jews settling there and to non-Jews who request it. Other laws include freedom of speech and assembly, the prohibition of polygamy, and compulsory education between the ages of four and sixteen. Immigration and absorption would be under the control of a domestic settlement company, and the principality would guarantee the right to work.

BIBLIOGRAPHY: M. Ishai, in: *Scritti in Memoria di Sally Mayer* (1956), 145–66 (Heb. sect.). **ADD. BIBLIOGRAPHY:** B. Musolino, *Gerusalemme e il Popolo Ebraico*, in: RMI (1951); P. Alatri, "Benedetto Musolino, Biografia di un Rivoluzionario Europeo," in: *Benedetto Musolino. Il Mezzogiorno nel Risorgimento tra Rivoluzione e Utopia* (1988), 34; D. Carpi, "Benjamin Disraeli, la Questione Orientale e un suo Presunto Progetto di Costituire uno Stato Ebraico in Palestina," in: *Gli Ebrei a Cento e a Pieve di Cento, tra Medioevo ed Età Moderna* (1994), 88–90; J.M. Landau, "A Project for Reforms in the Ottoman

Empire, 1883," in J.M. Landau, *Exploring Ottoman and Turkish History* (2004), 89–93.

[Moshe Ishai]

MUSSAFIA, ADOLFO (1834–1905), Italian philologist. Born in Split (Spalato), Croatia, Mussafia specialized in Romance studies and taught for almost 50 years at the University of Vienna, first (from 1855) as an Italian professor, then (from 1860 to 1903) as a professor of Romance philology, to which he added the role of curator of the manuscripts at the Imperial Library. In 1901 he was appointed a member of the Austrian House of Lords. Having tried in vain to have an Italian center for higher studies established in Trieste, he eventually moved to Florence, where he spent the last years of his life. Though the son of the rabbi of Split John Amadeus, Mussafia was estranged from Judaism and converted to Catholicism in 1860. A philologist of wide interests, he was one of the pioneers who took up the study of the Italian and Romance dialects, founding Romance philology in Vienna, and devoting his valuable and painstaking attention to early texts in Italian and the Italian dialects (*Monumenti antichi dei dialetti italiani*, 1864, and *Darstellung der romagnolischen Mundart*, 1871). Mussafia also did research in comparative literature, investigating the origins of many medieval legends about Christian saints (*Zur Katharinen-Legende*, 1874, and *Sulla leggenda del segno della Croce*, 1870), elucidating many texts, and writing critical reviews. His other major publications include *Italienische Sprachlere in Regeln und Beispielen* (1860; reprinted until recent years under the title *Der neues Mussafia*); *Sul testo della "Divina Commedia"* (1865); *Sul testo del "Tesoro" di Brunetto Latini* (1870); *La difesa d'un illustre* (G. Boccaccio, 1861); and the *I codici Vaticani Latini 3195 e 3196 delle "Rime" del Petrarca* (1899).

BIBLIOGRAPHY: E. Richter, in: *Zeitschrift fuer franzoesische Sprache und Literatur*, 55 (1932), 168–93; V. Crescini, *Romanica fragmenta* (1932), 148–53; *Bausteine zur romanischen Philologie, Festgabe… A. Mussafia* (1905). **ADD. BIBLIOGRAPHY:** "Il carteggio di Adolfo Mustafia con Elise e Helene Richter," in: *Atti dell'Istituto Veneto. Classe di scienze morali* … (1963–64), 511ff.; L. Renzi, in: *Letteratura italiana. I critici*, vol. 1 (1983), 323–41; L. Curti (ed.), *D'Ancona-Mussafia* (1978); A. Daniele, in: *Adolfo Mustafia, Scritti di filologia e linguistica* (1983), xxvii–lxxvi.

[Louisa Cuomo / Alessandro Guetta (2nd ed.)]

MUSSAFIA, BENJAMIN BEN IMMANUEL (1606–1675), rabbi, philologist, physician, and author. A descendant of Spanish Marranos, he was probably born in Spain; little is known of his early years. He received a broad philosophical education, and, apart from his great talmudic scholarship, had a sound knowledge of Latin, Greek, and Arabic. He lived in Hamburg where he distinguished himself as a physician and gained fame in the medical profession with the publication of his books on medicine. Consequently, he was invited to act as personal physician to King Christian IV of Denmark, to whom he dedicated the scientific work *Mei ha-Yam* (Amsterdam, 1642). When the king died in 1648, Mussafia moved to Amsterdam where he became a member of the well-known *bet ha-midrash* "Keter Torah." In his old age, he acted as one of the scholars of Amsterdam, and his signature was first on the eulogy and letter of recognition of Shabbetai Ẓevi, the false messiah, which was signed by Portuguese and *bet ha-midrash* "Keter Torah" scholars. In consequence, Jacob Sasportas, a zealous fighter against the Shabbateans, attacked him in his *Oholei Ya'akov*.

Mussafia's most important work is *Musaf he-Arukh* (Amsterdam, 1655), a supplement of linguistic entries to the *Arukh* of *Nathan b. Jehiel of Rome, in which he also gave new explanations to Latin and Greek words in that work. In his research he based himself largely on *Buxtorf's lexicon. The book gave him a world reputation as a scholar, and it was published in more than 20 editions. *Zekher Rav* (Hamburg, 1638) is his first published work (subsequently in about 16 editions and many translations); written in verse, it relates the marvels of the creation. His commentary on the Jerusalem Talmud has not been published. His scientific works, written under the Latin pseudonym, Dionysius, include *Mei Zahav* (Hamburg, 1638), on the healing properties of gold; and *Mei ha-Yam* (Amsterdam, 1642), on the tidal flow.

BIBLIOGRAPHY: Fuenn, Keneset, 169; Michael, Or, 284–5.

[Itzhak Alfassi]

MUSSAFIA, ḤAYYIM ISAAC (1754–1831), rabbi. Mussafia was born in Jerusalem. In 1796, while serving as an emissary of Jerusalem to the Balkan states, he was appointed *av bet din* of Spalato in Dalmatia. His only published work is *Ḥayyim va-Ḥesed* (pt. 1, Leghorn, 1844), responsa, appended to which are the laws of blessings by Yom Tov b. Abraham *Ishbili and talmudic novellae by early Jerusalem rabbis. Isaac Badhab affirmed that part two was in his possession. Mussafia also wrote *Derekh ha-Ḥayyim ve-Tokhaḥat Musar*, and *Maskil le-Eitan*, a supercommentary on the Pentateuch commentary of Rashi and Elijah Mizraḥi (see introd. to the responsa). He was succeeded at Spalato by his son, ABRAHAM ḤAI, who was also born in Jerusalem and served as a rabbi there. Abraham founded a yeshivah in Jerusalem called Shevet Aḥim (acronym of **A**vraham **H**ai **I**saac **M**ussafia), which was in existence until shortly before World War I. He composed poems and was a contributor to *Ha-Maggid*.

BIBLIOGRAPHY: Frumkin-Rivlin, 3 (1929), 214; M.D. Gaon, *Yehudei ha-Mizraḥ be-Ereẓ Yisrael*, 1 (1928), 145; 2 (1938), 387f.; Yaari, Sheluḥei, 691.

[Simon Marcus]

°MUSSERT, ANTON ADRIAAN (1894–1946), National Socialist leader in Holland. Originally an engineer in government service, he became active in politics in 1925. He founded the National-Socialist movement (1931), which at the peak of its popularity in the 1935 election received 8% of the votes. When Holland was occupied by Nazi Germany in May 1940, he tried to conduct a national policy and resisted annexation to Germany, but eventually he became a mere tool in the hands of the Germans. After the war he was condemned to death for collaboration with the enemy. Initially Mussert did not follow an anti-Jewish policy, and even accepted Jews as members of his party. From 1935, however, Jews could not hold office in the party, and in 1940 it was decided under German pressure to expel them altogether. Mussert unsuccessfully warned against the introduction of the yellow badge. For this reason, and because he tried to save some of his Jewish comrades, the Germans regarded him as a "Jew-servant."

BIBLIOGRAPHY: Netherlands. Rijksinstituut voor oorlogsdocumentatie, *Processen*, no. 3, "Het proces Mussert" (1948); L. de Jong, *Het Koninkrijk der Nederlanden in de Tweede Wereldoorlog*, 1 (1969), 278–385.

[Jozeph Michman (Melkman)]

°**MUSSOLINI, BENITO** (1883–1945), Italian dictator, founder of Fascism. Mussolini's policy toward the Jews was opportunistic, while his personal view of them, although unsystematic, was not unbiased. As early as 1908, in his essay "*La filosofia della forza*," Mussolini the socialist adopted *Nietzsche's view that Christianity, as a "reevaluation of all values," was the spiritual revenge by which the Jews in Ereẓ Israel overcame their secular enemies, the Romans. In June 1919, reflecting the line of the extreme right-wing "fasci" he had created shortly before, Mussolini attacked world Jewry in his organ *Popolo d'Italia*, defining it as "the accomplices, the soul of both Bolshevism and of capitalism." However, he reversed this stand in October 1924, saying that "Bolshevism is not, as is believed, a Jewish phenomenon," and further claiming that "Italy does not know antisemitism and we believe that it will never know it." At the same time he excluded Zionism, declaring that "the new Zion *[nuova Sionne]* of the Italian Jews is found here, in our beloved land, that many of them heroically defended with their blood." By its very nature, Mussolini's opportunistic maneuvering delayed a systematic anti-Jewish policy, to a greater extent than did the presence of Jews in the ranks of Fascism from its earliest phases. From 1922, when he acceded to power, to 1938, when he branded them as racially impure, Mussolini endeavored to use the Jews as an instrument of policy, especially on the international level, in conformity with his distorted view of Judaism as an "international, occult body." At the same time, he permitted a parallel undercurrent of antisemitism (see *Preziosi, *Farinacci) which he repudiated or encouraged in turn, whenever he saw a chance of blackmailing the Western democracies. As a rule, antisemitism was deemed counterproductive as a propaganda tool, as well as on the official level. In November 1923, Mussolini declared to Angelo *Sacerdoti, chief rabbi of Rome, that "the Italian government and Italian Fascism have never intended to follow nor are following an antisemitic policy." Concerning mixed marriage, however, Mussolini's views were strictly Catholic. In 1929, the year of the Concordat with the Vatican, he forbade his daughter Edda's projected marriage with a Jew as "a real and proper scandal."

His attitude to Zionism was similarly ambivalent. To Chaim *Weizmann he said, shortly after his accession, "You know, we could build your state *en toute pièce*." In February 1928, he personally approved and encouraged the creation of the Italy-Palestine Committee, but rebuked the Italian Zionists in November of the same year (probably in deference to the Vatican, with whom he was about to sign the concordat) charging them with disloyalty to Italy: "We therefore ask the Italian Jews: are you a religion or a nation?" (*Popolo di Roma*, Nov. 29, 1928). Subsequently he resumed his pro-Zionist policy, purely from expansionist motives, and maintained it until after the conquest of Ethiopia. As long as Mussolini kept an open window on the Western world, he was eager to present an image of Italian Fascism as "Latin" and unprejudiced, in contrast with "savage and barbarous" National Socialism. Antisemitism remained a "German vice" and Hitler "a fanatical idiot." Racialism was "the Aryan fallacy" (*Popolo d'Italia*, Aug. 4, 1934).

Mussolini soon reversed his position. From 1936, to all intents and purposes, he dissociated himself from the Western world and drew near to his derided disciple and future master. He blamed "international Jewry" for the sanctions which castigated Italy for its Ethiopian adventure and marked the end of his rapprochement with the Western democracies. As a result, the Italian Jews had become expendable and could finally be treated in conformity with Fascist latent intolerance toward "alien groups." Undoubtedly, Mussolini also sought to please his new German ally, but the Italian Jews were not sacrificed merely for the sake of Hitler's "brutal friendship." In search of a formula which would bind his own irresolute hands, create an unbridgeable gap between non-Jews and Jews in Italy, and enable him to be rid of all the latter in one stroke, Mussolini resorted to racialism which he now saw as politically profitable. The *Dichiarazione della Razza* of July 1938, introducing racial measures in Italy, was largely compiled and edited by himself and due entirely to his initiative; there is no evidence whatsoever that he was subjected at any moment to pressure by Hitler. His acceptance of the racial vice, deliberate and cynical, was rejected by the Italian people in their great numbers. The extent to which he was personally willing to cooperate in the physical destruction of Jews is shown by events occurring during World War II. In August 1942 the Germans asked the Italians to hand over to the German-Croatian authorities the Jews who had gone into hiding in Dalmatia, in the Italian occupation zone, and a memorandum on the subject, indicating the terrible fate in store for the Jews, was submitted to Mussolini. He scrawled in the margin: "nulla osta" ("no objection").

BIBLIOGRAPHY: R. de Felice, *Storia degli ebrei italiani sotto il fascismo* (1961), passim; L. Salvatorelli and G. Mira, *Storia d'Italia nel periodo fascista* (1956), index; G. Bedarida, *Ebrei d'Italia* (1950), index; L. Poliakov and J. Sabille, *Jews under the Italian Occupation* (1955), 137ff.; L. Fermi, *Ebrei d'Italia* (1950), index; Ch. Weizmann, *Trial and Error* (1966), index; N. Goldmann, *Sixty Years of Jewish Life* (1970), index; E. Ludwig, *Talks with Mussolini* (1933), 69ff.; M. Michaelis, in: *Yad Vashem Studies*, 4 (1960), 7–41; Carpi, in: *Rivista di studi politici internazionali*, 28, no. 1 (1961), 35–56; idem, in: *Moreshet*, 10 (1969), 79–88. **ADD. BIBLIOGRAPHY:** A. Freud, "Wohin mit den Juden? Roosevelt und Mussolini zur Wanderfrage; das State Department und Palästina," in: *Zeitschrift fuer die Geschichte der Juden* 4 (1967), 113–18; M. Salomon, "Mussolini et les juifs; un étrange dialogue," in: *Les Nouveaux Cahiers*, 34 (1973), 30–33; S. I Minerbi, "Gli ultimi due incontri Weizmann-Mussolini (1933–1934)," in: *Storia Contemporanea* 5 (1974), 431–477; M. Michaelis, "The 'Duce' and the Jews: An Assessment of the Literature on Italian Jewry under Fascism 1922–1945," in: YVS, 11 (1976), 7–32; A.M. Canepa, "Half-Hearted Cynicism; Mussolini's Racial Politics," in: *PaP* 13, 6 (1979), 18–27; A. Maillet, *Hitler et Mussolini dans la Bible: la vérité terrible et merveilleuse* (1980); M. Michaelis, *Mussolini e la questione ebraica, Milano: Edizioni di Comunità* (1982); E. Robertson, "Race as a Factor in Mussolini's Policy in Africa and Europe," in: *Journal of Contemporary History*, 23, 1 (1988), 37–58; "1938 – le leggi contro gli ebrei," in: *Rassegna Mensile di Israel*, 54, 1–2 (1988); P. Blasina, "Documenti e problemi. Mussolini, mons. Santin e il problema razziale (settembre 1938)," in: QS, 2–3 (1990), 189–96; L. Passerini, *Mussolini Immaginario* (1991); A. Spinosa, *Mussolini razzista riluttante* (1994); M. Sarfatti, *Mussolini contro gli ebrei: cronaca dell'elaborazione delle leggi del 1938* (1994); A. Gillette, "The Origins of the 'Manifesto of Racial Scientists'," in: *Journal of Modern Italian Studies*, 6, 3 (2001), 305–23; L. Nemeth, "The First Anti-Semitic Campaign of the Fascist Regime," in: *The Most Ancient of Minorities* (2002), 247–58; I. Nidam Orvieto, "Lettere a Mussolini; gli ebrei italiani e le leggi antiebraiche," in: *Rassegna Mensile di Israel*, 69, 1 (2003), 321–46; M. Michaelis, "L'influenza di Hitler sulla svolta razzista adottata da Mussolini," in: *Rassegna Mensile di Israel*, 69, 1 (2003), 257–66; G. Fabre, "Mussolini e gli ebrei alla salita al potere di Hitler," in: *Rassegna Mensile di Israel*, 69, 1 (2003), 187–236; V. Pinto, "Between 'Imago' and 'Res': The Revisionist-Zionist Movement's Relationship with Fascist Italy, 1922–1938," in: *Israel Affairs*, 10, 3 (2004), 90–109; S. Luconi, "Recent Trends in the Study of Italian Antisemitism under the Fascist Regime," in: *Patterns of Prejudice*, 38, 1 (2004), 1–17; T. Schlemmer, "Der italienische Faschismus und die Juden 1922 bis 1945," in: *Vierteljahrshefte fuer Zeitgeschichte*, 53, 2 (2005), 165–201; F.H. Adler, "Why Mussolini Turned on the Jews," in: *Patterns of Prejudice*, 39, 3 (2005), 285–300.

[Emmanuel Beeri]

MUSTAʿRAB, MUSTAʿRABS, name of the Arab-speaking, old, established Jewish communities and residents in the Middle East. The term is borrowed from the Arabic. According to Arab genealogists, the "ʿArab al-Mustaʿriba" were not of native Arab stock; they were naturalized, "Arabized," Arabs. In Muslim Spain the Christians who adopted Arabic and Arab customs were called "Mozarabs." The term Mustaʿrab (better: Mustaʿrib) for Arabized Jews seems a late one; it occurs from the 15th century onward and seems to have been first used by immigrants from Christian Europe for the old, established Jews in Egypt, Palestine, and Syria. The terms al-Mashāriqa ("Easterners") and Moriscos are sometimes used in the same sense.

BIBLIOGRAPHY: Neubauer, Chronicles, 1 (1887), 146, 150; A. Yaari, *Iggerot Ereẓ Yisrael* (1943), 169; I. Ben-Zvi, *Meḥkarim u-Mekorot* (1966), 15–20.

[Haïm Z'ew Hirschberg]

MUSTARD (Heb. חַרְדָּל, *ḥardal*), the name applied to two species, the common mustard (*Sinapis alba*), known in rabbinical literature as "Egyptian mustard," and the kind called simply "mustard." The latter was extracted from the seeds of a different botanical genus, *Brassica nigra*, the mustard prepared from it being darker and more pungent than the former. This species, like white mustard, grows wild in Ereẓ Israel but was also cultivated. Given favorable conditions, the plant reaches a height of more than six feet. The *aggadah* relates that a man having sown "a single seed of mustard… would climb it as he would a fig tree" (TJ, Pe'ah 7:4, 206). The seed of this species is very small (1–1.6 mm.) and was used to indicate the smallest measure of size (Ber. 31a). The contrast between the size of the plant and the seed is used in a parable in the New Testament (Matt. 13:31). Although these two species of mustard belong to different botanical genera they are very similar in appearance (except that the white mustard plant is smaller and its seed larger). Hence the rule that mustard and Egyptian mustard do not constitute *mixed species (*kilayim*; Kil. 1:2). Both have conspicuous yellow flowers (cf. Kil. 2:8–9). In Israel there are many species belonging to the family of Cruciferae which have yellow flowers and seeds with a pungent flavor. Among these the species *Sinapis arvensis* is very widespread. This is called in the Mishnah *lafsan* ("charlock") and it was laid down that "mustard and charlock, although resembling one another, do constitute *kilayim*" (Kil. 1:5).

BIBLIOGRAPHY: Loew, Flora, 1 (1928), 516–27; H.N. and A.L. Moldenke, *Plants of the Bible* (1952), 316 (index), s.v.; J. Feliks, *Kilei Zera'im ve-Harkavah (1967), 65–67, 256–69, 284–6; idem, Ẓimḥiyyat ha-Mishnah*, in: *Marot ha-Mishnah, Seder Zera'im* (1967), 55f. **ADD. BIBLIOGRAPHY:** Feliks, Ha-Ẓome'aḥ, 69, 70, 97.

[Jehuda Feliks]

MUSZKAT, MARION (**Marian, Maks**; 1915–1995), jurist. Born in Suwalki, Muszkat served in the Polish army during World War II, rising to the rank of colonel. In 1944 he was appointed a military judge and in the following year headed the Polish military delegation at the Nuremberg war-crimes trials. In 1949 Muszkat became lecturer at the Polish Academy of Political Science and later professor of international law at the University of Warsaw. He emigrated to Israel in 1957 and lectured in international law at the Tel Aviv extension of The Hebrew University, being appointed professor when the institution became Tel Aviv University. Muszkat's works include *Interwencja – zbrodńiczej-polityki Stanów Zjednoczonych* ("Intervention – Criminal Weapon of U.S. Policy," 1953), *Kavei-Yesod ha-Mishpat ha-Bein-Le'umi* (2 vols., 1959–61), and *Hitpatteḥuyyot Ḥadishot be-Mishpat u-ve-Irgunim Bein-Le'ummiyyim* (1967); and he edited *Zarys prawa międzynarodowego publicznego* ("Outlines of Public International Law," 2 vols., 1955–56) and the quarterly *Be'ayot Bein-Le'ummiyyot*.

BIBLIOGRAPHY: Tidhar, 18 (n.d.), 5430 – 31. **ADD. BIBLIOGRAPHY:** M. Muszkat, *Studium o wspolczesnych aspektach ekstradycji* (1950); idem, *Mishpat Nirenberg, Pesak ha-Din shel Beit ha-Din ha-Ẓeva'i ha-Beinle'ummi* (1961).

[Israel (Ignacy) Isserles]

MUTER, MELA (1873–1967), French painter. She was born in Warsaw and as a young woman left Poland to study in France. There she abbreviated her family name, Mutermilch, using

"Muter" as her professional name. In 1937 she received a gold medal at the Paris World's Fair, and two years later she was represented in the World's Fair of New York. When the Nazis invaded France, Mela Muter was in her late sixties. Her son was killed in the war, but she managed to elude the Germans in Avignon, in southern France. There she continued to live for many years, in great poverty, until in 1965 she was rediscovered by a gallery in Cologne. Two years later, a few months before her death, her work was exhibited in New York. Crippled and no longer able to paint, she enjoyed her new fame; she used most of her earnings to aid sick children. Her "psychological portraits" were much admired. In addition to portraits, she painted mother and child groups, landscapes and still lifes, either in vigorous oils or in tender aquarelles.

BIBLIOGRAPHY: Hahn, in: *Das Zelt*, 1 (1924), 180–2.

[Alfred Werner]

MUTNIK (Mutnikovich), ABRAHAM (pseud. **Gleb**; 1868–1930), cofounder of the *Bund. Mutnik was born in Vilkomir (Ukmerge), Russian Lithuania. In Kovno he belonged to a revolutionary circle of Narodnaya Volya (the People's Will movement) which functioned among the pupils of his school, and he was subsequently expelled from the school. In the 1880s he studied in Berlin and became acquainted with the German workers' movement. He was expelled from Germany and on returning to Russia lived in Ponevez, Lithuania, gave private lessons, and disseminated illegal revolutionary propaganda which led to his arrest. From 1894 he was a central figure among the *Jewish Social Democrats in Vilna. On its behalf he wrote a detailed report for the Congress of the Socialist International in London (1896). At the founding convention of the Bund he was elected, with V. *Kossovski and A. *Kremer, to its central committee. Mutnik drew up the first proclamation of the Bund (May 1, 1898) and represented it at the first conference of the Russian Social Democratic Workers' Party (March 1898). He was arrested in Lodz, but in 1900 he escaped abroad. In the years 1902–06 he was secretary of the Bund "committee abroad" in London and Geneva and a member of the editorial board of its organ, *Der Yidisher Arbeter*. He published an important article on the history of the Bund and its activity (in *Zhizn*, no. 2, May 1902 signed G. Ya.); he returned to Russia in 1906 and took charge of the Bund press. He then withdrew from party activities and after World War I lived in Germany. His autobiographical memoirs were published in *Zukunft* (38 (1933), 509–13, 595–6, 664–6, 718–20).

BIBLIOGRAPHY: J.S. Hertz (ed.), *Doyres Bundistn*, 1 (1956), 122–30; J. Hertz et al. (eds.), *Geshikhte fun Bund*, 1–2 (1960–62), indexes.

[Moshe Mishkinsky]

MUYAL (Moyal), AVRAHAM (1847–1885), representative of Ḥovevei Zion in Ereẓ Israel. Born in Rabat, Morocco, Muyal went to Ereẓ Israel with his parents in 1860, becoming a wealthy merchant and banker. As a French national, he had close ties with the French consul in Jaffa. He also had considerable influence in Turkish government circles and was treated with respect by the Arab population, with whose customs and way of life he was well acquainted. Muyal did much to help Jewish settlement and obtained a permit to build houses at Ekron. He was also entrusted with financial dealings by Baron Edmond de *Rothschild concerning the settlements of Ekron and Rishon le-Zion. In 1885 Muyal was appointed as the Ḥovevei Zion representative. He built houses and established farms in Petaḥ Tikvah and put the settlement on a sounder basis. In the *Bilu settlement Gederah, where it was forbidden to build houses, he secured shelter for the settlers by rapidly erecting a structure of wooden boards and covering it with a roof. Under Turkish law, destruction was thereupon illegal.

BIBLIOGRAPHY: I. Klausner, *Mi-Katoviẓ ad Basel*, 1 (1965), 84–89, 150–62, index; A. Druyanow, *Ketavim le-Toledot Ḥibbat Ẓiyyon ve-Yishuv Ereẓ Yisrael*, 1 (1925[2]), 546–9, index; S.P. Rabinowitz (ed.), *Keneset Yisrael*, 1 (1886), 934–9.

[Israel Klausner]

MYER, MORRIS (**Mayer**; 1876–1944), Romanian-born Yiddish editor and Zionist worker, settled in London in 1902 and became active in Yiddish journalism and the Labor movement. A member of the Po'alei Zion, he became prominent in the British Zionist Federation and was a delegate to Zionist Congresses. From 1919 he sat on the Board of Deputies of British Jews and its joint foreign committee. Through the popular Yiddish daily, *Die Tsayt*, which he founded in 1913 and which existed until 1950, he was a prime molder of opinion among Yiddish readers in England when Whitechapel was a hub of Jewish life. He founded the Federation of Jewish Relief Organizations and was a Yiddish theater enthusiast and perceptive drama critic, as seen in his lively *Yidish Teater in London 1902–1942* ("Yiddish Theater in London, 1902–1942," 1943). His Yiddish writings include *Der Sveting System, Vi Vert Men fun ihr Poter* ("The Sweating System, How to Abolish It?" 1907), *A Yidishe Utopye* ("A Jewish Utopia," 1918), *Dzhordzh Elyot, di Englishe Nevie fun der Renesans fun Idishen Folk* ("George Eliot, English Prophetess of the Jewish People's Renaissance," 1920), and *Dos Organizirte Yidntum in England* ("Organized Jewry in England," 1943).

BIBLIOGRAPHY: Rejzen, Leksikon, 2 (1930), 388–94; LNYL, 5 (1963), 602–4 (incl. bibl.). **ADD. BIBLIOGRAPHY:** L. Prager, *Yiddish Culture in Britain: A Guide* (1990), 443–4.

[Joseph Leftwich / Leonard Prager (2nd ed.)]

MYER, SIDNEY (Simcha) BAEVSKI (1878–1934), Australian retailer and philanthropist. Myer was born in Poland and in 1897 he migrated to Australia. After working briefly at odd jobs in Melbourne, he opened a shop in Bendigo in partnership with his brother, Elkan B. Myer. This venture failed, but later Myer bought another shop in Bendigo, and this time his business expanded rapidly. In 1911 Myer purchased a store in Melbourne which he called the Myer Emporium and which became the largest business of its kind in Australia. He had also obtained control of Marshall's of Adelaide, another large department store. In the early 1930s Myer had 5,300 employees working for him in his enterprises. He provided rest houses for his workers at the seaside and in the country. The Myer Emporium is still one of the largest and most successful retailers in Australia, and its flagship store in central Melbourne is probably the leading department store on the continent.

In 1920 Myer divorced his Jewish wife and married an 18-year-old girl, Marjorie Merlyn Baillieu, the daughter of a prominent gentile financier in Melbourne. The marriage caused a scandal, and Myer and his wife were forced to live in America for nine years. To placate his wife's family, Myer converted to Anglicanism and distanced himself from the Jewish community. Ironically, two of his sons were allegedly blackballed from membership in the exclusive Melbourne Club on antisemitic grounds.

Sidney Myer was one of Australia's richest men when he died. In addition to his many contributions to Jewish and general charities, Myer donated large sums for unemployment relief during the depression of the 1930s. He left sizable endowments for the promotion of free orchestral concerts and the Melbourne Symphony Orchestra and an additional large sum for the general purposes of the University of Melbourne.

ADD. BIBLIOGRAPHY: J. Browning and L. Critchley, *Dynasties* (2002), 131–67; A. Pratt, *Sidney Myer: A Biography* (1993); H.L. Rubinstein, *Jews in Australia, II*, 321–22, index.

MYERHOFF, BARBARA GAY SIEGEL (1935–1985), U.S. anthropologist. Myerhoff was born in Cleveland, Ohio, and was raised there and in Los Angeles by her mother Florence Siegel and her stepfather Norman Siegel. She received a B.A. in sociology (1958) and an M.A. in human development (1963) from the University of Chicago, and a Ph.D. in anthropology from UCLA in 1968. Myerhoff served on the Anthropology faculty at the University of Southern California for her entire academic career, developing a program in visual anthropology and chairing the department. She was part of a group of scholars in the 1970s who introduced the importance of understanding storytelling, who pioneered the study of one's own community, and who investigated the relationships among age, ethnic identity, and gender.

Myerhoff's initial scholarship was devoted to the developing field of ritual and symbolic studies. Her dissertation and subsequent book, *Peyote Hunt: the Sacred Journey of the Huichol Indians* (1974), was highly regarded for its treatment of pilgrimage and the religious life of a Mexican Indian group. She explored those same themes in *Number Our Days* (1979), her innovative ethnographic study of elderly Jews who met at a senior center in Los Angeles, demonstrating the ways in which rituals, both traditional and invented, gave the aged the visibility they had been denied by family and society. Performances of all types, including storytelling, rituals, and quarrels, provided a certainty of their place in social interaction that was both reassuring and tenuous. From these observations Myerhoff wrote about the ways in which culture offers and withholds visibility. One of her most important contributions to the study of women and religion was the concept of "domestic Judaism" that she developed in *Number Our Days*. Myerhoff effectively challenged the notion that religion can best be understood from an elite, usually male perspective linked to formal practices. Rather, her work demonstrated that a well-articulated religious system for women ran parallel to men's sacred worlds.

Prior to the publication of *Number Our Days*, Myerhoff collaborated with Lyn Littman on a documentary film with the same title that was awarded an Oscar and two Emmys.

BIBLIOGRAPHY: B. Myerhoff. "Bobbes and Zeydes: Old and New Roles for Elderly Jews," in: J. Hoch-Smith and A. Spring (eds.), *Women in Ritual and Symbolic Roles* (1978); B. Kirshenblatt-Gimblett, "Forward," in: M. Kaminsky (ed.), *Remembered Lives: The Work of Ritual and Story Telling, and Growing Older* (1992); R.E. Prell, "The Double Frame of Life History in the Work of Barbara Myerhoff," in: Personal Narratives Group (ed.), *Interpreting Women's Lives* (1980).

[Riv-Ellen Prell (2nd ed.)]

MYERS, SIR ARTHUR MELZINER (1867–1926), New Zealand businessman and politician. Myers came from a family of German immigrants who opened a brewery in New Zealand. His father, who became a jewelry salesman, drowned in 1870 and Myers was raised by an uncle in Wellington, where he eventually became head of the family brewery. Myers became managing director of a large business concern in his native city, Auckland, and from 1905 to 1909 was mayor of Auckland. He entered the New Zealand parliament in 1910 and in 1912 became a member of the cabinet as minister of finance, defense, and railways. In the National Government from 1915 to 1919, he was minister of customs, munitions, and supplies, in which capacity he laid the foundations for compulsory military service. He retired from parliament in 1921. Myers was noted for his benefactions to the city of Auckland, including the Myers Park in which he built a kindergarten and a school for backward children. He lived in England from 1923 and was a member of the Royal Commission on Local Government. He was knighted in 1924.

ADD. BIBLIOGRAPHY: R.C.J. Stone, "Sir Arthur Myers," in: *The New Zealand Dictionary of Biography*; A. Gluckman (ed.), *Identity and Involvement: The Jewish Community in Auckland, 1840–1990* (1990).

MYERS, ASHER ISAAC (1848–1902), British journalist. Born in London, Myers started in the clothing trade and then became publisher of the *Jewish Record*. In 1869 he joined the *Jewish Chronicle*, later becoming general manager. After the death of the editor, Abraham *Benisch, in 1878, he achieved editorial control and part-ownership, and conducted the paper successfully until 1902, broadening its contents to include more cultural material. He also engaged widely in Jewish communal service. In 1874 he published *The Jewish Directory*, the first British compilation of its kind.

ADD. BIBLIOGRAPHY: D. Cesarani, *The Jewish Chronicle and Anglo-Jewry, 1841–1991* (1994).

MYERS, CHARLES SAMUEL (1873–1946), British psychologist. Born in London, Myers was educated at the City of London School and Cambridge. He became a physician and, on taking his degree, immediately left on an anthropological expedition to Torres Strait and Borneo with W.H.R. Rivers, the founder and first director of the Cambridge Psychological Laboratory. The successful expedition returned the following year with data on hearing, smell, taste, reaction time, rhythms, and music of the local population. In 1900 he spent some time in Egypt, studying hieroglyphics, excavating, and taking anthropometric measurements in Cairo and Khartoum. On returning to Cambridge he was appointed to the psychological laboratory where, after considerable opposition, he succeeded Rivers. He published his *Textbook of Experimental Psychology* in 1909 (1925[3]). It was the first text to have laboratory exercises and to treat statistics for psychology students. There was also a briefer *Introduction to Experimental Psychology*, which he published in 1911 (1925[3]). Myers held the posts of professor in experimental psychology at King's College, London (1906–09), and also held a variety of positions at Cambridge, where, in 1921–22, he was reader in experimental psychology.

During his stay in Cambridge, Myers conducted research on primitive music, synesthesia, auditory localization, and individual differences among listeners to music. He helped to found the *British Journal of Psychology* in 1904 and edited it from 1911 to 1924. The new psychological laboratory at Cambridge, established in 1912, was made possible by a grant which he made anonymously. He was elected secretary and, in 1920, president of the British Psychological Society.

Myers' interest in applied psychology was initiated in World War I, when he was the first to recognize shell shock as an essentially psychological condition and to treat it by psychotherapy. He had secured a commission in the Royal Army Medical Corps. In 1922 he resigned his post at Cambridge and went to London to establish the National Institute of Industrial Psychology, where work was conducted on tests of mechanical ability, manual dexterity, performance measures of general intelligence, problems of attention, and industrial fatigue. Myers became the driving force in British applied psychology and helped to gain official recognition for psychological practitioners. He was widely honored for his work. Although his desire to occupy the first chair in psychology at Cambridge was not fulfilled, he exerted considerable influence on the next generation of British psychologists through his students and his textbooks. He also wrote: *Psychology* (1910), *Mind and Work* (1920, 1921[2]), *Industrial Psychology* (1926), *Ten Years of Industrial Psychology: An Account of the First Decade of the National Institute of Industrial Psychology* (1932).

BIBLIOGRAPHY: T.H. Pear, in: *American Journal of Psychology*, 60 (1947), 289–96. **ADD. BIBLIOGRAPHY:** ODNB online.

[Helmut E. Adler]

MYERS, GUSTAVUS (1872–1942), U.S. political reformer and historian. Myers was born in Trenton, New Jersey. As a reporter for several newspapers, he belonged to the muckraking movement, attacking big business and political abuses. Myers' first exposé, *History of Public Franchises in New York City* (1900), was followed by *History of Tammany Hall* (1901, 1917[2]), and his best-known work, the *History of Great American Fortunes* (1910, 1936[3]). Among Myers' other works are: *Beyond the Borderline of Life* (1910), *History of the Supreme Court of the United States* (1912), *The History of American Idealism* (1925), *The Ending of Hereditary American Fortunes* (1939), and *History of Bigotry in the United States* (1943), in which he attacked all forms of prejudice, including antisemitism. Myers' reputation rests principally on his painstaking research. Highly critical of the conditions that had made abuses possible, he became convinced in later years that modern innovations were contributing toward the elimination of some economic inequalities.

BIBLIOGRAPHY: S.J. Kunitz and H. Haycroft, *Twentieth Century Authors* (1942); J. Chamberlain, *Farewell to Reform* (1932), index; L. Filler, *Crusaders for American Liberalism* (1939), index.

[Hans L. Trefousse]

MYERS, LAWRENCE E. (**Lon**; 1858–1899), U.S. track athlete. Born in Richmond, Virginia, Myers began his career as a runner in 1878 and a year later became the first man to better 50 seconds for 440 yards. Between 1879 and 1884, Myers won 15 U.S., ten Canadian, and three British national titles at distances from 100 to 880 yards. He visited Great Britain in 1881, 1884, and 1885, and set the then world marks for 440 yards (48.6 seconds) and 880 yards (1:55.4). In 1881 he became the first foreign runner to win a British national title.

Myers faced his most formidable opponent, Britain's Walter George, for the first time in 1882. George won two of three races at the Polo Grounds in New York City. Racing three years later as a professional, Myers won all three races at New York's Madison Square Garden. After repeating his victory over George in Australia in 1887, Myers retired from track the following year.

BIBLIOGRAPHY: B. Postal et al. (eds.), *Encyclopedia of Jews in Sports* (1965), 475–8.

[Jesse Harold Silver]

MYERS, SIR MICHAEL (1873–1950), lawyer; chief justice of New Zealand. Born in the small township of Motueka, Myers was educated in Wellington and joined the largest law firm there, acting in crown cases that were both criminal and civil. In 1922 he was appointed king's counsel and began his own practice. Six cases in which he was involved went to the Privy Council and in all of them he was successful. From 1929 to 1946, Myers was chief justice of New Zealand, and his wide practical experience and keen sense of justice earned him a high reputation. In 1936 he served as justice on the Privy Council and in 1946 he represented New Zealand on the United Nations committee of jurists. Myers took an active interest in all Jewish affairs and was president of the Wellington synagogue from 1912 to 1921, a post previously held by both his father and elder brother. Myers was intensely interested in Jewish history and was patron of the Australian Jewish Historical Society. On several occasions he acted for the governor-general during the latter's absences from New Zealand.

ADD. BIBLIOGRAPHY: P. Spiller, "Sir Michael Myers," in: *The Dictionary of New Zealand Biography.*

[Maurice S. Pitt]

MYERS, MORDECAI (1776–1871), U.S. merchant, army officer, and politician. Myers was born in Newport, R.I. He lived in New York State most of his life, while intermittently maintaining residence in Charleston, S.C. A member of New York City's Shearith Israel Congregation after 1792, he served as a trustee from 1800 to 1805 and donated a generous sum toward the construction of a new synagogue in Greenwich Village. Subsequently he joined the army and was commissioned captain in the Third Regiment of the First Brigade Infantry (1811). He served with the Thirteenth Infantry in the War of 1812, was wounded in the battle of Chrysler's Field, and was later promoted to major. In 1814 Myers married a non-Jewish woman, and thereafter ceased to play a role in the Jewish community. He was a ranking Mason from 1823 to 1834 and was offered the office of grand master for New York State, which, however, he declined. In 1828 and from 1831 to 1834 Myers served as a Democratic assemblyman in the state legislature from New York County. Subsequently he moved to Schenectady, where he was elected mayor in 1851 and 1854. In 1860, at the age of 84, he ran unsuccessfully for a seat in the U.S. Congress.

[Leo Hershkowitz]

MYERS, MOSES (1752–1835), U.S. merchant and civic leader. Moses Myers, the son of Haym and Rachel Louzada Myers, was born in New York City. For a time he was a junior partner in Isaac Moses & Co., a New York import-export firm, but the bankruptcy of Isaac *Moses in 1786 led Moses Myers to seek a new enterprise. With his friend Samuel *Myers, also a junior partner in the bankrupted firm, he opened a store in Norfolk, Virginia, 1787. After Samuel moved to Petersburg, Virginia (1789), Moses expanded his operations into importing and exporting. By 1812 he was the leading merchant south of the Potomac. During his early years in Norfolk, he functioned also as agent for the Philadelphia financier Stephen Girard, as superintendent of the Norfolk branch of the Bank of Richmond, and as consular agent for France and the Batavian Republic. He was elected to the city's Common Council for 1795–97 and, because he polled the largest vote, served as council president. The Embargo Acts of 1807–15 and a second bankruptcy of Isaac Moses, with whom he had investments, led Moses Myers and his eldest son, John, into bankruptcy. Myers never totally recovered from this setback, despite the testimonials of 277 Norfolk and Portsmouth merchants. President John Quincy Adams later named him collector of customs, superintendent of lights, and agent for the Marine Hospital, declaring him "the first honest man in the post"; he served from 1827 to 1830.

In 1787, he married Eliza Judah of Montreal, widow of Detroit pioneer Chapman Abraham. Myers' handsome home, erected in 1792, remains a Norfolk landmark.

BIBLIOGRAPHY: Stern, in: *Southern Jewish Historical Society Journal*, 1 (1958), 5–13; Rosenbloom, Biogr Dict.

[Simon Vega]

MYERS, MYER (1723–1795), U.S. silversmith. Myers was born in New York, where his parents had emigrated from Holland. He learned his trade early and at 23 set up shop on Lower Wall Street, where he not only engaged successfully in his craft but also sold tea, coffee, spices, and tobacco. By 1755 he had expanded his trade to Philadelphia. Myers was active in the general community, in Freemasonry, and in the synagogue, serving as president of Congregation Shearith Israel in New York in 1759 and again in 1770. During the American Revolution he was a patriotic stalwart, and he and his family moved from the city during the British occupation, going first to Norwalk, Connecticut, and later to Philadelphia. There he used his skill to smelt down metal household goods and turn them into bullets. Myers returned to New York in 1783 and was a signatory of the address to Governor George Clinton from the "congregation of Israelites lately returned from exile." Myers was a highly skillful and versatile master craftsman, who created the first American examples of Jewish ceremonial objects and was also distinguished for his general ornamental and functional pieces. There are many examples of his work in places of worship, museums, and private collections. For the synagogues of New York, Newport, and Philadelphia he made silver Torah bells (*rimmonim*) which are still in use. His versatility is revealed in his alms basins and baptismal bowls. His mark "myers" was most frequently stamped on his work in script in a shaped cartouche though sometimes he merely used his initials, MM. In 1786 he was elected chairman of the Gold and Silversmiths' Society of New York. He was buried in the cemetery that still exists off Chatham Square in Lower Manhattan.

The U.S. Post Office issued an 8-cent stamp on American Independence Day 1972 to commemorate Colonial American craftsmen. The first day cover reproduces the Torah Scroll ornaments which Myers created for Congregation Shearith Israel in New York City. The single largest collection of Myers' silver is on display in the Klutznik Exhibit Hall of the B'nai B'rith Building in Washington.

BIBLIOGRAPHY: J.W. Rosenbaum, *Myer Myers, Goldsmith* (1954), includes bibliography; G. Schoenberger, in: AJHSP, 43 (1953), 1–9.

[Alfred Werner]

MYERS, SAMUEL (1755–1836), U.S. merchant. Samuel Myers was the second child of New York silversmith Myer *Myers and his first wife, Elkaleh Myers-Cohen. As a child he worked in his father's silver shop, but soon joined his friend Moses *Myers as a junior partner in Isaac *Moses' import-export firm. A year after the firm's bankruptcy in 1786, Samuel and Moses opened a store in Norfolk, Virginia, but two years later they separated. Samuel moved to Petersburg, Virginia, the first known Jewish resident of the town. His half-brothers MOSES MEARS MYERS and SAMPSON MEARS MYERS joined him there, all three becoming tobacco dealers. By 1798, Samuel was active in Richmond, contributing to Congregation Beth Shalome. He settled there permanently by 1803 and played an active role in business and social life as a leading Jewish citizen. Samuel's first wife, Sarah, daughter of Samuel *Judah of New York, died a year after their marriage. In 1796 Samuel and his brother Moses married daughters of the Boston merchant Moses Michael Hays. His second son, GUSTAVUS ADOLPHUS MYERS (1801–1869), became Richmond's leading Jew, serving for nearly three decades on the City Council and for 12 years as its president.

BIBLIOGRAPHY: Rosenbloom, Biogr Dict; J.W. Rosenbaum, *Myer Myers, Goldsmith* (1954); H.T. Ezekiel and G. Lichtenstein, *History of the Jews of Richmond* (1917), index.

[Saul Viener]

MYERSON, BESS (1924–), Miss America and philanthropist. Born to Louis and Bella Myerson in the Bronx, New York City, Myerson grew up in the Sholom Aleichem Cooperative. She attended the High School of Music and Art and graduated from Hunter College in 1945. In 1945, the 5-foot-10 Myerson won the Miss New York City pageant after her sister Sylvia entered her in the contest, and on a lark she entered the Miss America contest with the hope of winning a $5,000 scholarship to continue with her music studies and buy a piano. A pageant official suggested she change her name to the less Jewish-sounding Beth Merrick, but she refused. After her win, Myerson encountered blatant antisemitism among sponsors and during her tour of the United States over the next year. Inspired by the bigotry she encountered, she spoke out on behalf of the Anti-Defamation League. Myerson went on to study music at Juilliard School and Columbia University, and appeared as a guest soloist for the New York Philharmonic in 1946. In October 1946, she married Allan Wayne. The couple had a daughter together, but divorced in 1957. Myerson became a hostess and game show panelist on a variety of television programs from 1947 to 1968. In 1962, she married Arnold Grant, who adopted her daughter. Mayor John Lindsay appointed Myerson as New York City's commissioner of consumer affairs in 1969. During her four-year term, she helped pass the city's Consumer Protection Act and hosted the consumer affairs television show, *What Every Woman Wants to Know*. She went on two publish two books, *The Complete Consumer Book* and the *I Love New York Diet*. Myerson enjoyed presidential appointments to a variety of commissions in the 1970s, but the decade also brought another divorce and a fight with ovarian cancer. In 1980, she lost a Democratic Senate bid and suffered a stroke. From 1983 to 1987 she served as New York's commissioner of cultural affairs, but her reputation was tarnished by bribery and conspiracy charges. Myerson was acquitted, but not before pleading guilty to separate shoplifting charges in South Williamsport, Pa. In 1987, she released her autobiography, *Miss America, 1945: Bess Myerson's Own Story*. A founder of the Museum of Jewish Heritage in New York, she continued to champion social causes and Israel.

[Adam Wills (2nd ed.)]

MYNONA (**Salomo Friedlaender**; 1871–1946), German philosopher and author. Born in Gollantsch in Posen, Mynona studied medicine, philosophy, German literature, archaeology, and art history in Munich, Berlin, and Jena between 1894 and 1902. In Jena he wrote his dissertation on Schopenhauer and Kant (1902), seeing from then on in Kantian philosophy not only the solution of the central problems of 20th century in general, as did his contemporary teacher, the neo-Kantian Ernst Marcus, but also an expression of modern Judaism. Also in his later, main philosophical work *Die schoepferische Indifferenz* (1918), Mynona relied on Kant to overcome the classical dualism of subject and object in a purified, absolute self. In 1906, Mynona went to Berlin, starting to write under the literary name "Mynona," an anagram of "anonym" (i.e., anonymous), poetry, which he published in books like *Durch blaue Schleier* (1908) and expressionist publications like *Der Sturm* and *Die Aktion*, being intimate with the Berlin expressionist circle of Herwarth *Walden, Else *Lasker-Schueler, and Samuel *Lublinski. At the same time he wrote satirical and grotesque prose works (*Rosa, die schoene Schutzmannsfrau*, 1913; *Mein Papa und die Jungfrau von Orleans*, 1921; *Das Eisenbahunglueck oder der Anti-Freud*, 1925; *Mein hundertster Geburtstag und andere Grimassen*, 1928); in these philosophical satires Mynona exposed the other side of Kantian rationalism. In 1933, he fled to Paris, where he wrote his last published literary work, the grotesque *Der lachende Hiob* (1935), confronting the will to annihilation of the Nazis with his idea of the purified self by answering torture with laughter. Other works, like *Vernunftgewitter* and *Das Experiment Mensch*, remained unpublished. The autobiographical work *Ich* was published in 2003. Mynona died in Paris. In 1980, H. Geerken published two volumes of Mynona's prose.

BIBLIOGRAPHY: *Salomo Friedlaender/Mynona. Ausstellungskatalog der Akademie der Kuenste* (1972); P. Cardorff, *Salomo Friedlaender (Mynona)* (1988).

[Andreas Kilcher (2nd ed.)]

MYRRH (Heb. מוֹר, *mor*), one of the most important perfumes of ancient times. It is referred to 11 times in the Bible, more than any other perfume. The Hebrew, *mor*, refers to its bitter taste (*mar*, "bitter"); the root is common to the various Semitic languages, from where it was transferred to Greek Μύῤῥα and Latin *myrrha*. It is first mentioned along with the ingredients from which the holy anointing oil in the Tabernacle was prepared (Ex. 30:23–25), where it is called *mor deror*, i.e., myrrh congealed to form granules (*deror* from *dar*, "pearl") and then dissolved in olive oil. The king's garments were perfumed with myrrh (Ps. 45:9), and the faithless wife perfumed her couch with it when she wanted to seduce men (Prov. 7:17). The maidens were treated with it for six months before being presented to Ahasuerus (Esth. 2:12). In the Song of Songs myrrh is mentioned no less than seven times. It grew in the imaginary spice garden to which the charms of the beloved one are compared (Song 4:14; 5:1). It is upon "the mountain of myrrh" that the beloved dreams he will meet his heart's desire (4:6). The queen arrives for a meeting with the king "from the wilderness… perfumed with myrrh and frankincense" (3:6). The beloved one watched for her lover with her fingers dripping "flowing myrrh" (5:5), i.e., oil of myrrh, and his lips too were "dripping with flowing myrrh" (5:13). The man lying in the arms of his beloved is likened to the crystallized myrrh which the women used to wear as "a bag of myrrh" (1:13).

Myrrh is extracted from certain trees or shrubs growing in Africa or in the Arabian peninsula: *Commiphora abyssinica* and *Commiphora schimperi*. These plants contain a fragrant sap under the bark like the sap of the *acacia, from which gum arabic is prepared (Gr. κόμι; mishnaic Heb. קומוס, *kumos*). The sages warned against those who adulterated myrrh with this *kumos* (Sifra 1:12). Myrrh is variously interpreted homiletically by the rabbis as referring to Moses and Aaron or to Abraham: myrrh, the prince of spices, is Abraham who offered his son Isaac on Mt. Moriah (connecting "*mor*" with "Moriah"; Song R. 3:6, no. 2). They also connected it with Mordecai whose name was explained to mean *mor-dakhya*: "pure myrrh" (Ḥul. 139b). The *mor over,* "flowering myrrh," of the Song of Songs alludes to Israel's troubles which will pass: "Read not *mor over* but *mar over*: "passing bitterness" (cf. Shab. 30b). Saadiah Gaon, followed by Maimonides, identified "a bag of *mor*" with musk, the perfume extracted from the aromatic gland of the musk deer (see *Incense and Perfumes) but there is no basis for this.

BIBLIOGRAPHY: Loew, Flora, 1 (1928), 249, 305–11; H.N. and A.L. Moldenke, *Plants of the Bible* (1952), 316 (index), s.v.; J. Feliks, *Olam ha-Ẓome'aḥ ha-Mikra'i* (1968[2]), 252–4.

[Jehuda Feliks]

MYRTLE (Heb. הֲדַס; *Hadas*), *Myrtus communis*, a shrub, and occasionally a tree, possessing fragrant and glossy leaves. It grows wild on Mount Carmel and in Upper Galilee, and its use as a decorative shrub is widespread. The leaves usually grow in series of two and opposite each other. Some have leaves arranged in groups of three. Burning the shrubs produces a higher proportion of the latter form. The plant flowers during the summer months and later bears black berries. There are other varieties whose ripe fruit is white and whose small leaves are arranged in groups of four or more. The plant is called *asu* in Akkadian and *asa* in Aramaic. The *eẓ avot*, twice mentioned in Scripture, refers, according to rabbinical tradition, to the myrtle. It is one of the *Four Species (Lev. 23:40). The Book of Nehemiah, however, refers to both *hadas* and *eẓ avot*, in connection with the observance of the Feast of Tabernacles (Neh. 8:15). In consequence some scholars think that the name *eẓ avot* applies to any tree whose branches are closely braided together (*avotim*, "compact"). The rabbis explain that *hadas* refers to the wild myrtle branches gathered for covering the *sukkah*, while *eẓ avot* refers to the twigs of three-leaved myrtles which were "with the *lulav*" (Suk. 12a). They explained that *eẓ avot* means a tree "whose branches cover its trunk… is shaped like a plait and resembles a chain" (Suk. 32b). The leaves of the *oleander are of similar form but were declared invalid on the grounds that it is poisonous (*ibid.*). To satisfy the regulation concerning Tabernacles "a myrtle producing groups of three leaves from a single node" is necessary; there was a dispute concerning the validity of those varieties of myrtle, like the Egyptian myrtle, which produce many leaves from a single node (Suk. 32b–33a).

The myrtle is an evergreen (Targ. Sheni, Esth. 2:7), and the rabbis thus compared it with the good qualities of Esther whose Hebrew name was Hadassah ("myrtle"). Its aromatic branches were used for preparing the bride-groom's wreaths (Tosef., Sot. 15:8). They were used in festivities and betrothal celebrations, and some of the sages would juggle with myrtle branches, throwing them up and catching them (Ket. 17a). The leaves of the myrtle have the shape of the eye (Lev. R. 30: 14). Its fruits, called *benot Hadas* ("myrtle products"), were occasionally eaten, but are tasteless (TJ, Or. 1:1, 60c–d; Suk. 32b). Some recommended myrtle leaves as a remedy for blood pressure in the head (Git. 68b). The custom still obtains in some places of pronouncing the blessings for spices at the *Havdalah on the termination of the Sabbath over myrtle leaves. According to *Bet Hillel the benediction over the myrtle takes precedence over the benediction over aromatic oil (Ber. 43b).

BIBLIOGRAPHY: Loew, Flora, 2 (1924), 257–74; H.N. and A.L. Moldenke, *Plants of the Bible* (1952), 316 (index), s.v.; J. Feliks, *Olam ha-Ẓome'aḥ ha-Mikra'i* (1968[2]), 99–101. **ADD. BIBLIOGRAPHY:** Feliks, Ha-Ẓome'aḥ, 51.

[Jehuda Feliks]

MYSH, MICHAEL (1846–?), Russian lawyer and writer; born in Korets, Volhynia. Of a poor family, Mysh attended the government Jewish school of his town. He completed his studies at the law faculty of the University of Kiev and contributed to the Russian Jewish press, devoting himself to the study of anti-Jewish legislation in Russia. He wrote commentaries, surveys, and guides on the restrictive laws against the Jews. The most important of them was *Rukovodstvo po russkim zakonam o Yevreyakh* ("Guide to the Russian Laws Concerning the Jews," 1892), which ran into four editions. He also wrote essays and books on general legal problems. His son, VLADIMIR (1873–1947), was a professor of medicine and a member of the Soviet Academy.

BIBLIOGRAPHY: J. Frumkin (ed.), *Russian Jewry 1860–1917* (1966), 475.

[Yehuda Slutsky]

MYTH, MYTHOLOGY (Gr. μῦθος; "word," "word content," "narrative"). A myth is a story about the universe that is considered sacred. Such a story deals with the great moments of man's life: birth, initiation, and death, referring them to events that took place in "mythical time." The myth is often recited during a dramatic representation of the event it narrates (e.g., the *Enūma eliš* was recited at the Babylonian New Year festival). Through the ritual, man becomes contemporary with the mythical event and participates in the gods' creative actions. Thus man can create, maintain, or renew fecundity, life, etc. Myths can be classified according to their subjects, as: theogonic, cosmogonic, anthropogonic, soteriological, and eschatological, myths of paradise, myths of flood, hero myths, etc.

In the Bible

The word "myth" was first applied to biblical narratives in the 18th century, when the question of the historicity of the first chapters of Genesis arose. For J.G. Eichhorn, for instance, the biblical narratives contain philosophical truth (e.g., the Garden of Eden narrative) or are based on a kernel of historical truth (the narratives concerning the Patriarchs). In the mid-19th century the term myth acquired a more precise meaning in biblical research. Biblical scholars who held that myth and polytheism were inseparable (e.g., Y. Kaufmann and H. Frankfort) denied any possibility of finding myths in the Bible, though they do not deny the existence of residues of myths or "demythologized myths" in the Bible. A number of apparent myths and mythical subjects which found their way into the Bible, have been collected and compared with extra-biblical parallels. In the prophetic and poetic books, references are made to the Lord's struggle with the primeval dragon, variously named *Tannin* ("Dragon," Isa. 27:1, 51:9; Ps. 74:13; Job 7:12), *Yam* ("Sea," Isa. 51:10; Hab. 3:8; Ps. 74:13; Job 7:12), *Nahar* ("River," Hab. 3:8; Ps. 93?), Leviathan (Isa. 27:1; Ps. 74:14), and *Rahab* (Isa. 30:7; 51:9; Ps. 89:11; Job 9:13; 26:12–13). A special parallel to this theme is found in the Ugaritic myth of Baal and his struggle against *Yam*, in which mention is made of Leviathan (*ltn*; C.H. Gordon, *Ugaritic Textbook* (1965), 67, 1:1) and *Tannin* (*tnn*; *nt, ibid.*, 3:37) as well as of *Nahar* (*nhr*). In this myth the dragon is called, as in Isaiah 27:1, *bari'aḥ* ("fleeing serpent") and *'aqallaton* ("twisting serpent"; cf. Gordon, *ibid.*, 67, 1:2–3). The same theme is found in the Babylonian creation epic *Enūma eliš* (Marduk's fight with Tiamat, "Sea") and in the Hittite myth of the storm-god and the dragon Illuyankas (Pritchard, Texts, 125–6), and with variations in Sumerian, Egyptian, Phoenician, and other literatures.

The idea that man was made out of clay (Gen. 2:7; Job 33:6) is common to the Bible and other extra-biblical literatures, especially the myth of Atraḥasis (W.G. Lambert and A.R. Millard, *Atra-Ḫasīs* (1969), 56 ff.; cf. also *Enūma eliš*, 6:1–38 and the creation of Enkidu, *Gilgamesh* 1:30–40, in Pritchard, Texts, 68, 74). In Genesis 2:7, the Lord breathed into man's nostrils the breath of life; in Atraḥasis, man is the product of the mixture of clay and the flesh and blood of a slaughtered god. In the latter source, man is created to do the work the inferior gods refused to do (cf. Gen. 2:15).

The biblical story which has the most striking Mesopotamian parallel is the flood story (Gen. 6–8; *Gilgamesh*, tablet 11 – in Pritchard, Texts, 93–97, cf. also Atraḥasis). In both accounts a man and his household escape the deluge thanks to divine providence; the flood hero is told to build a ship (ark); after the flood, the ship comes to rest upon a mountain (Ararat or Niṣir); birds are sent out in exploration; a much appreciated sacrifice is offered by the survivor; God (or the gods) repents of His bringing about the flood. As in other myths, the main difference between the biblical and extra-biblical version of the flood story resides in the fact that the biblical one is monotheistic. Other differences can be pointed out. For example, the fact that Noah takes with him only his family, while Utnapishtim (the Babylonian flood hero) makes a point of taking craftsmen with him, may well point to different types of society.

Residues of hero myths can be found in Genesis 5:24; 6:1–4; 10:8–9; and II Samuel 23:8 ff., for example. The stories about Samson, Jephthah, Gideon, and so on have much in common with the hero myth genre.

In biblical poetry there are echoes of myths: the wind has wings (I Sam. 22:11: Hos. 4:19); thunder is the Lord's voice (II Sam. 22:14; et al.); the Lord rides the clouds (Ps. 68:5), etc. Although mythical patterns can be found in the Bible, the biblical authors are not especially interested in "extra-temporal events," but rather deal with God's intervention in history. The Bible is less interested in the cosmos than in man.

BIBLIOGRAPHY: T.J. Meek, in: JBL, 42 (1924), 245–52; E. Norden, *Die Geburt des Kindes* (1924); Th. H. Gaster, *Thespis* (1950), idem, in: *Numen*, 1 (1964), 184 ff.; Y. Kaufmann, in: JBL, 70 (1951), 179–97; H. Frankfort et al., *Before Philosophy* (1952); M. Eliade, *The Myth of the Eternal Return* (1954); idem, *Patterns in Comparative Religion* (1958); S.H. Hooke (ed.), *Myth, Ritual and Kingship* (1958); E.O. James, *Myth and Ritual in the Ancient Near East* (1958); J. Barr, in: VT, 9 (1959), 1–10; J.L. Mc-Kenzie, in: CBQ, 21 (1959), 265–82; B.S. Childs, *Myth and Reality in the Old Testament* (1960).

M'ZAB, region containing six towns, one of the major groups of oases of the Sahara in central *Algeria. It was founded in the 11th century by M'zabite *Berbers belonging to the Ibadiyya sect who formerly dominated *Tripoli (part of modern *Libya today). Although the French had occupied Algeria in 1830 and removed it from Ottoman domination, the M'zab was annexed to France only in 1882 and reverted to Algerian indigenous rule in summer 1962 upon its national independence. Ghardaia is the main town and capital of the M'zab, while el-Ateuf is the oldest settlement in the region. Beni Isguene is the most sacred Berber Islamic town. It prohibits all non-M'zabites from various sections of this town and all foreigners from spending the night within its walls. Melika is populated by black Africans and contains spacious cemeteries, while Guerrera and Berriane have been part of the M'zab since the 17th century. The total population of the M'zab in the early 21st century exceeded 70,000.

M'zab Jewry are apparently the descendants of Jews from Tahert, an ancient metropolis destroyed in 902 C.E., but also from Sedrata and Ouargla in the important region of Ifriqiyya – which in ancient and medieval times contained the territories of present-day Libya and *Tunisia. Ouargla was a center of *Karaite Jews. Until 1300 the Jewish community of the M'zab was reinforced demographically by Jews from the island of *Djerba (southern Tunisia) and Jebel Nafusa (the region of Tripolitania in modern Libya). Overwhelmingly residing in Ghardaia, the Jews were mainly employed as goldsmiths as well as being suppliers of ostrich feathers whose exports to Europe were monopolized by their coreligionists in parts of the Mediterranean.

The Jews of Ghardaia dwelled in their own special quarter, were forced to wear black clothes, and were not allowed to engage in farming or to purchase rural land. Unlike the Jews of the major urban centers of the regions of *Algiers, *Oran, and *Constantine, M'zab Jewry were not beneficiaries of the October 1870 Crémieux Decree which granted French citizenship to Algeria's Jews. This is attributed to the fact that the French could only grant this privilege to Jews in their sphere of influence. The M'zab was not under French control until over a decade later. It was only in the early 1960s that the Crémieux Decree was extended to include M'zabite Jews. By then, however, it was too late, for in 1962 the French granted Algerian Muslims independence. On the eve of Algerian independence, after numerous M'zabites Jews (out of 6,000) relocated to France (many resettled in Strasbourg), as many as 3,000 still remained behind.

In June 1962, as the Jewish Agency Israeli immigration emissaries were about to leave Algerian soil, a cable arrived at the Immigration Office in Algiers from Jerusalem. It instructed them to remain there for the time being because, based on reliable information, Algerian Muslim rebels in the south intended to harm the 3,000 remaining Jews of the Saharan community of Ghardaia. On June 12, 1962, the Jewish Agency requested Ben-Zion Cohen, one of the emissaries in Algiers, to fly to Ghardaia and warn that community about the potential dangers. The State of Israel also contacted the French authorities in the south to inform them of Cohen's arrival. Upon his arrival Cohen met with Jacob Blocca, Ghardaia's community president. Blocca then convened an emergency meeting of the community council members in which Cohen prodded them to permit the Jewish Agency to evacuate the Jews before it was too late. The community leadership gave its approval.

Already in mid-June Cohen began to register the families at the local *talmud torah* building. Of the 3,000 Jews in Ghardaia, 2,700 agreed to leave immediately. Meanwhile, the Jewish Agency in Europe received from Cohen precise data on the size of the immigration and the number of planes needed for the operation. The Grande Arenas transit camp in Marseilles was prepared to accommodate the transients. However, the Algerian rebels found out about the operation and were determined to prevent the departures. Not wanting to risk lives, Cohen telephoned the French governor, who himself was about to leave Algeria. The latter sent a military vehicle with several armed paratroopers to guard Cohen and accompany him to the local military base for his own protection. Toward the end of June the French planes chartered by the Jewish Agency reached Ghardaia's military airport. The immigrants could now take the 12-kilometer ride to the airport on buses, guarded by military jeeps and a helicopter. Algeria was a sovereign nation when the evacuation process ended successfully in July 1962.

BIBLIOGRAPHY: A. Chouraqui, *Between East and West: A History of the Jews of North Africa* (1968); H.Z. Hirschberg, *A History of the Jews in North Africa*² (English trans., 1974); M.M. Laskier, *North African Jewry in the 20th Century* (1994); N.A. Stillman, The *Jews of Arab Lands in Modern Times* (1991).

[Michael M. Laskier (2nd ed.)]

*The letter "N," a part of the illuminated word In (*diebus Assueri*) at the beginning of the Book of Esther in a 12*[th]*-century Latin Bible. On the right of King Ahasuerus, Haman is being hanged. The "I" frames the figure of Esther. Rheims. Bibliothèque Municipale, Ms. 159, fol. 5v.*

NAAMAH (Heb. נַעֲמָה; "pleasantness"), two biblical figures.

(1) Daughter of Lamech and Zillah and sister of Tubal-Cain (Gen. 4:22).

(2) Ammonite wife of Solomon, mother of Rehoboam (I Kings 14:21; II Chron. 12:13).

BIBLIOGRAPHY: EM, 5 (1968), 891–2 (incl. bibl.).

NAAMAN (Heb. נַעֲמָן, "pleasant"; the name occurs in Ugaritic and is an epithet of heroes in Ugaritic epics), Syrian commander, healed of leprosy by the prophet *Elisha. According to II Kings 5, Naaman, a valorous man, held by his king in great esteem but afflicted with leprosy, had a female slave from the land of Israel. From her, his wife learned that "the prophet that is in Samaria" could cure Naaman of his leprosy. Naaman departed for the land of Israel taking with him a letter from the king of Aram to the king of Israel, as well as lavish presents. The king of Israel thought that the letter asking him to cure Naaman was nothing but a trick "to seek an occasion against him." Elisha, however, asked that Naaman be brought to him. When Naaman and his escort arrived at Elisha's house, he was told by a messenger to wash seven times in the Jordan River. Offended by the prophet's brusqueness and aloofness, Naaman decided to leave the land of Israel, but on the way his servants convinced him to do what the prophet prescribed. He washed in the Jordan and was cured. Naaman then went back to Elisha convinced that "there was no God in all the earth but in Israel." In vain he entreated the prophet to accept his presents. He then asked for "two mules' burden of earth, for thy servant will henceforth offer neither burnt offering nor sacrifices unto other gods, but unto the Lord." The fact that Naaman felt it was necessary to take earth from the land of Israel to build an altar for the Lord hints at the belief that sacrifices to YHWH could only be offered on Israelite soil (cf. Josh. 22:10ff.; II Sam. 26:19). Naaman also asked forgiveness for the fact that because of his office at the court he would be obliged to perform acts that could be interpreted as idolatry. Soon after Naaman's departure, Gehazi, Elisha's servant, ran after Naaman and through deceit received from him two talents of silver and two changes of clothing. As a punishment he was cursed with Naaman's disease. That neither Naaman nor Gehazi was isolated from society (II Kings 8:4; cf. Lev. 13–14) suggests that Naaman's disease was not what is now known as *leprosy.

In the Aggadah

Naaman was the archer who drew his bow at a venture and mortally wounded Ahab, King of Israel (I Kings 22:34) and thus it was that through him "the Lord had given deliverance unto Syria" (II Kings 5:1). It would therefore follow that his master, referred to in 5:18, was Ben Hadad (Mid. Ps. 90). Two reasons are given for his leprosy, one that it was a punishment for his haughtiness (Num. R. 7:5; cf. Rashi to Lev. 14:4) and the other that it was for taking an Israelite girl as maidservant to his wife (Tanḥ. Tazri'a, end). According to the *Mekhilta* (Yitro, Amalek 1), Naaman was an example of the righteous proselyte, ranking even higher than Jethro; according to the Talmud, however (Git. 57a), he became merely a *ger toshav*, a "resident alien" who accepted only the seven Noachide laws but not all the commandments.

NA'AN (Heb. נַעַן), kibbutz in central Israel, E. of Reḥovot, affiliated with Ha-Kibbutz ha-Me'uḥad. It was founded in 1930 as the first village of *Ha-No'ar ha-Oved youth. The founders were later joined by immigrants from many countries. During the 1936–39 disturbances Na'an maintained friendly ties with Arab villages in the vicinity and was not attacked, but it came under siege by the British army on "Black Saturday," June 29, 1946, when 23 settlers were wounded. In 1969 Na'an had 870 inhabitants; in 2002, 1,140. Its economy was based on highly intensive farming (citrus groves, avocado plantations, field crops, and dairy cattle) and it ran a metal plant producing irrigation and other equipment. The settlement's name is adapted from the Arabic name of the site, Naʿana, which in turn may be the original town of Naamah of the tribe of Judah (Josh. 15:41).

[Efram Orni / Shaked Gilboa (2nd ed.)]

NAAR, DAVID (1800–1880), U.S. politician, journalist, and public servant. Naar, who was born in St. Thomas, Danish West Indies (now Virgin Islands), was sent to Manhattanville, New York, at the age of 15 to be educated. He spent about five years there. Because of Black insurrections in the Caribbean and the decline of trade, his family moved to New York City in 1834 and continued their tobacco importing and exporting business. In 1838 Naar purchased a farm near Elizabeth, New Jersey, became active in politics as a Democrat, and was rewarded politically with an appointment as lay judge of the Court of Common Pleas. He was appointed mayor of Elizabeth in 1849. In 1844 he was a delegate to the state constitutional convention where he vigorously and successfully advocated giving Roman Catholics the right to vote and hold office. President James K. Polk appointed him as commercial agent of the United States to St. Thomas (1845–48). Naar moved to Trenton in 1853 and bought the *Daily True American* which he edited until 1870. His nephew and son then edited the paper until 1905. The newspaper, which became a very influential factor in the Democratic Party, espoused the cause of the South, favored (at first) secession and states' rights, and was pro-slavery. Naar was attacked by his Republican opponents as "a West Indian Jew" and other epithets. Naar served as treasurer of New Jersey and a member of the Trenton Common Council. He favored free public school education, free public libraries, and was one of the founders of the Normal School for Teachers (now the College of New Jersey).

BIBLIOGRAPHY: Kohn, in: AJHSQ, 53 (1964), 372–95.

[S. Joshua Kohn]

NAARAH (Heb. נַעֲרָה), town in the Jordan Valley on the boundary between the territories of Ephraim and Benjamin (Josh. 16:7; 1 Chron. 7:28 – Naaran). It is called Neara by Josephus, who relates that Herod's son *Archelaus diverted the waters of the village to irrigate groves of palm trees (Ant., 17:340). Eusebius refers to it as Noorath and describes it as a Jewish village five miles from Jericho (Onom. 136:24). A Midrash mentions that hostile relations existed between Naarah and Jericho (Lam. R., 1:17, no. 52). The Jews living there are mentioned in late Christian sources (Simeon Metaphrastes, *Life of St. Chariton* (Gr.) 7:578; Palladius, *Historia Lausiaca*, 48). Naarah is now identified with ʿAyn al-Dūk, 4½ mi. (7 km.) north of Jericho. In 1918 a mosaic pavement was accidentally uncovered there by Australian troops when a shell exploded, and some fragments were removed and transported to Sydney. The site was subsequently excavated by L.H. Vincent and B. Carrière in 1919 and 1921, and published by P. Benoit in 1961. The pavement was found to be part of a synagogue which consisted of a court with a pool, an L-shaped narthex, and a hall, 72 × 49 ft. (22 × 15 m.), paved with mosaics. On the pavement are depicted two gazelles at the entrance and geometric designs in the aisles. The nave is decorated with images of birds within interlocking rhombuses and circles; a zodiac with the sun in the center and the symbols of the seasons in the corners; Daniel flanked by two lions; two candelabra and ritual objects. Another candelabrum was depicted in front of the main entrance to the hall. Inscriptions in the pavement commemorate the donors: Phinehas the priest, his wife Rebekah, a certain Samuel, Benjamin the *parnas*, Marutah, Ḥalifu, etc. The images of living beings had suffered from iconoclasm at a later date. The synagogue dates to the sixth century. The pavement (and some additional details, previously unknown) was rediscovered in 1970.

ADD. BIBLIOGRAPHY: S.J. Saller, *Second Revised Catalogue of the Ancient Synagogues of the Holy Land* (1972), 15–17; Z. Ilan, *Ancient Synagogues in Israel* (1991), 149–50; Y. Tsafrir, L. Di Segni, and J. Green, *Tabula Imperii Romani. Iudaea – Palaestina. Maps and Gazetteer.* (1994), 197; A. Ariotti, "A Missing Piece Found: Tracing the History of a Mosaic Fragment at the Church of St James from Jericho to Sydney and Back Again," in: *Bulletin of the Anglo-Israel Archaeological Society*, 22 (2004), 9–22.

[Michael Avi-Yonah / Shimon Gibson (2nd ed.)]

NABAL (Heb. נָבָל; connected with the Ar. *nabīl*, "noble"), man of the town of Maon who owned much livestock near the neighboring town of Carmel, southeast of Hebron on the edge of the desert of Judah; a Calebite (1 Sam. 25:3; *keri* and versions). David extended his protection to Nabal's flocks when he was camping with his men in the desert of Judah (25:14–16). Nabal refused to give him a "gift" out of his produce at the time of the sheep-shearing (25:10–11). *Abigail, Nabal's beautiful wife, appeased David and dissuaded him from taking revenge (25:18ff.). Her husband, she said, punning on his name, "as his name is, so is he; Nabal [נָבָל] is his name and outrage [נְבָלָה] is with him" (25:25). After Nabal's death by a stroke, she became

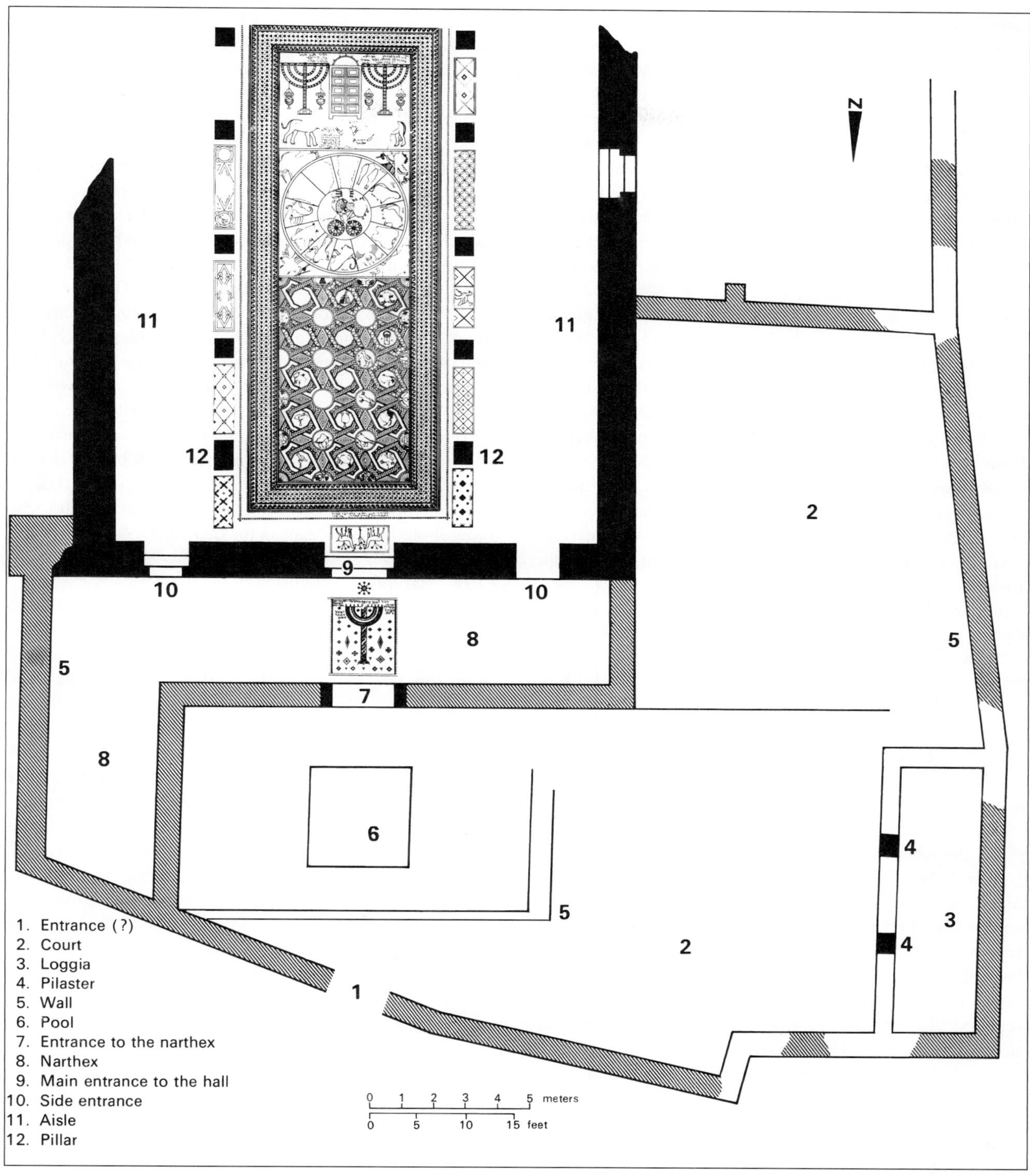

Plan of the synagogue at Naarah, sixth century C.E., *with drawing of the mosaic floors in the nave and in the narthex. Based on* Encyclopaedia of Archaeological Excavation in the Holy Land, *Jerusalem, 1970.*

David's wife (I Sam. 25:42). This tale is one of the finest narratives in the Bible and is a faithful description of the life of the prosperous cattlemen on the border of the desert of Judah.

[Yohanan Aharoni]

In the Aggadah

In the Aggadah Nabal is referred to as a descendant of Caleb in order to compare his own illustrious ancestry to that of David who was descended from Ruth the Moabitess (TJ, Sanh. 2:3,

20b). He denied God, had idolatrous thoughts and was guilty of unchastity. Like *Laban, the letters of whose name are identical with those of Nabal, he was a scoundrel (Mid. Ps. 53:1). Ten days intervened between his illness and his death (I Sam. 25:38) because he had given food to each of David's ten men (I Sam. 25:5; RH 18a); or because these were the Ten Days of Penitence, when God hoped that Nabal would repent (TJ, Bik. 2:1, 64d). According to another opinion, however, Nabal was smitten more than a week after Samuel died, his death being delayed in order to avoid any confusion between the mourning for a righteous man and a wicked one (Mid. Ps. 26:7).

NABATEANS, ancient people in the Middle East. Originally a pastoral, nomadic people, the Nabateans became merchants in the trade of oils, aromatics and spices, frankincense and myrrh from southern Arabia. By the second century B.C.E., they controlled the Red Sea coastal cities and were considered unwelcome competition by Ptolemaic shipping interests (Diodorus 3, 43:5). Soon thereafter the expansionist Nabateans established settlements on the lucrative trade route, dominating the passage from the Hejaz through Petra to Damascus, and from Petra through the Negev to the Mediterranean port city of Gaza. Nabatean remains are found at over 1,000 sites in this area. At their height they controlled and colonized parts of modern-day Syria, Jordan, the Israeli Negev, Sinai, parts of eastern Egypt, and a northwestern section of Saudi Arabia. Nabatea's apogee is from the first century B.C.E. to the second century C.E. Nabatean material culture reaches its zenith in the second half of the first century B.C.E., before the Romans established control in 106 C.E.

The Nabateans (Gk. *Nabataioi*) are identified as people from the Arab kingdom of Nabatea. They refer to themselves as *Nabatu* on their Aramaic inscriptions. Their origins are controversial, but according to Graf the Nabateans arose within the Aramaic-speaking world of the so-called "Fertile Crescent" (Hieronymous of Cardia, *apud* Diodorus Siculus 19:95), and they may have been a sub-tribe from Qedar or the Persian Gulf. Philip C. Hammond places their origins in the Arabian Hejaz. However, the fact is that we do not know where they come from; thus, their origins are unknown. Whatever their origins, we do know that by 312 B.C.E. the Nabateans were already living in Petra, where they defended themselves successfully from an attack by Antigonus the "One-Eyed," a veteran commander from Alexander the Great's eastern campaigns.

The Nabatean Kingdom was strategically located. It was interlaced with east-west routes traversing the desert of the region now designated as the Israeli Negev (south of Beersheba) to the ports of Gaza, Ascalon, and Raphia (Rafa) in the Sinai, the latter a border town between Gaza and Egypt on the Mediterranean Coast. It also included the vast desert of the Sinai. From Petra, which served as the nexus for the redistribution of goods for the caravan traffic, the most important route to the west crossed the Negev to the Sinai. Here the Nabateans established settlements in the Negev that served as their intermediary links either to the Mediterranean or to Jerusalem and Phoenicia in the north. The best known of these towns include: Nessana (Auja al-Hafir in Arabic, Nitzana in Hebrew), and in the Negev, Sbeita or Sobata (Isbeita in Arabic, Shivta in Hebrew), Elusa (Khalasa in Arabic, Halutza in Hebrew), Oboda (Abda in Arabic, Avdat in Hebrew), Rehovot-in-the-Negev (Ruheibeh in Arabic), and Mampsis (Kurnub in Arabic, Mamshit in Hebrew). From Mediterranean ports ships sailed westward to the North African coast to Egypt and Alexandria, and northwards to Palestinian and Phoenician ports, primarily Caesarea and Tyre, and to Anatolian ports, such as Miletus. Goods were then transported further afield to Europe.

What little is known of Nabatean history is through Greek, Latin, Hebrew, and Nabatean sources which have been extensively researched by the Abbé J. Starcky (1966), P.C. Hammond (1973), R. Wenning (1987), and G.W. Bowersock (1983). Writing in the Augustan period, two writers are particularly important for our understanding of the Nabateans. One is the first century B.C.E. Sicilian-born Greek historian, Diodorus Siculus, whose *Bibliotheca historica* (19:94–100) is based on Hieronymos of Cardia. The second historian is Strabo, who wrote about the Nabateans in his *Geography*.

Petra – Capital of Nabatea

Located in a north-south deep canyon, approximately 50 miles (80 km.) south of the Dead Sea, via the Desert Highway some 160 miles (260 km.) south of Amman, Petra is enclosed by the towering majesty of the scarp which forms the Dead Sea Rift System. It can be said that the city of Petra (*Raqmu* in Nabatean) is symbolic of the religious, social, and political order of the Nabateans, and we have little physical evidence that is more central to their study. This complex, remarkable capital of the Nabatean kingdom is unique in its setting and architecture, including not only opulent temples and 800 tombs but also all the trappings of an active major urban center with a theater, baths, and administrative buildings.

The chronologies of Nabatean monarchs for these periods are provided by Abbé J. Starcky 1966, Z.T. Fiema and R.N. Jones 1990, and R. Wenning 1993 (see chart of Nabatean kings below). Although the early rulers are shrouded in mystery, the list begins with a reference to the Nabateans in the war with the Seleucid king Antigonus of Syria. The Nabatean King Aretas I (ca. 170–160 B.C.E.) is referred to as the "tyrant of the Arabs" and the "King of the Nabatu," or King of the Nabateans. It is also Aretas I who is cited in II Maccabees 5:8 as the protector of the High Priest Jason, who asks for asylum in Petra. He also rules when cordial hospitality is offered to the Maccabean leaders Judas and Jonathan. There is scholarly debate (see Bowersock 1983) as to whether Aretas I is or is not succeeded by a king known as Rabbel I.

Although the known rulers are male, there is clear evidence for the high status accorded queens, for the coinage demonstrates that both the king and the queen occupied prominent positions. And in some cases they probably serve as joint rulers.

Nabatean Language and Writing

The Nabateans were apparently multilingual. Their native language was Arabic, many of their personal names were in Arabic, and they spoke Arabic, but they adopted the *lingua franca*, Aramaic, which they wrote in their own script for formal inscriptions. After the Romans occupied and established a strong military presence in the area, Petra continued to retain its native language but used Greek for business. After 106 C.E. the Nabateans incorporated Roman institutions and employed Latin for government and business.

Nabatean Religion

The main deities of the Nabateans were Dushara, and Al-'Uzza (on the various deities see Sourdel, 1952). Dushara – Dusares in Greek, Dus-sara (pronounced Dushara, or "Lord of the Shara") – was the tutelary deity of Petra, the supreme deity of the Nabateans and of Petra. He is associated with vegetation and fertility, and is also the everlasting, deathless god. At Petra Dushara has been recognized by a black obelisk and huge rectangular blocks of stone that carried his spirit (Glueck 1965). The tradition handed down by Arab folklore is that the djinn blocks and tower tombs are representations of Dushara and embody his spirit. The djinn are considered to be malevolent spirits that inhabit some 26 of these blocks of stone found at Petra. Dushara was also worshipped in carved quadrangular niches with *betyls* in them.

In the Hellenistic period, Dushara became equated with Dionysos, and was syncretized with the Egyptian gods Serapis and Osiris. Later he may be identified with the Hellenistic Zeus and Ares.

Al-'Uzza (sometimes associated with the Syrian Atargatis, meaning "the mighty One") is the Nabatean mother goddess, the Arabian Aphrodite sometimes referred to as Al-'Uzza-Aphrodite. She symbolizes fertility and vegetation, and is also the paramount queen, the sky-mother, and the patroness of travelers. Most important of all, she is the creator and sustainer of life.

Nabatean Material Culture

Among the most remarkable of Nabatean technological achievements are the hydraulic engineering systems they developed for water conservation. Utilizing their ingenuity, they constructed dams, terraces, and aqueducts to divert and harness the rush of swollen winter waters. As brilliant engineers they diverted flash flood conduits to funnel the precious resource throughout Petra.

Nabatean architecture exhibits an eclecticism achieved by a combination of styles, with Hellenistic Greek, Seleucid, Ptolemaic, Egyptian, and to a lesser extent Parthian architectural concepts. These are combined with a Nabatean sense of Orientalism. A strong native style asserts itself in both architecture and sculpture. Most of their monuments were constructed within a 200-year period. The artisans were probably imported, perhaps from Alexandria. With time the stylistic development of sculptural decoration became simplified, so that by the Roman period, most of the recovered sculpture is more bold and crude in character with less warmth, and a metamorphosis takes place resulting in a style that has all but lost its individuality.

Nabatean construction primarily employed sandstone ashlar blocks – either bonded together with mortar or dry-laid. Their walls are set with timber stringcourses that provide tensile reinforcement against earthquakes. The diagonally chiseled surfaces are designed to hold colorful stucco commonly used for decoration. Ornamented plaster, and sometimes marble imported for use as revetments, also decorated many of the buildings.

Nabatean Coinage

Minted for 170 years, the earliest Nabatean coins were struck during the period of 62–60 B.C.E. These coins are important sources of information about Nabatean political standing.

Nabatean Pottery

Nabatean pottery is unique. It is what archaeologists refer to as a "horizon-marker" or an "index fossil," because it is different from any other wares produced at this time. Not only is it recovered in prodigious numbers at Petra and known Nabatean sites in Jordan, but large quantities also are found in Saudi Arabia, the Negev, and the Sinai. The origins of Nabatean pottery are obscure, but it makes its earliest appearance at Petra during the reign of Aretas II, or between 100 and 92 B.C.E.

In conclusion, Nabatean research proves the existence of a highly original culture that flourished from the second century B.C.E. to the second century C.E. Nabatea has not yet, however, yielded all the secrets concealed in its soil.

(The names of sites and monuments in Petra and Jordan are based on the official transliteration system used by the Royal Jordanian Geographic Center (RJGC).)

The Chronology of Nabatean Kings
(based on Z.T. Fiema and R.N. Jones (1990)

Aretas I	ca. 170–160 B.C.E.
(?) Rabbel I	
Aretas II	ca. 100–96/92 B.C.E.
Obedas I	93–85 B.C.E.
Aretas III Philhellenos	85–62 B.C.E.
Obedas II	62/61–59 B.C.E.
Malichus I	59/58–30 B.C.E.
Obedas III	30–9/8 B.C.E.
Aretas IV "Lover of his People"	9 B.C.E.–40 C.E.
Malichus II	40–70 C.E.
Rabbel II	70–106 C.E.

BIBLIOGRAPHY: W. Bachmann, T. Watzinger, and T. Wiegand, *Petra, Wissenschaftliche Veröffentlichungen des Deutsch-Tuerkischen Denkmalschutz-Kommandos* (1921); J.R. Bartlett, "From Edomites to Nabateans: A Study of Continuity," in: *Palestine Exploration Quarterly*, 111 (1979), 53–66; C.M. Bennett, "The Nabateans in Petra," in: *Archaeology*, 15 (1962), 233–43; P. Bienkowski (ed.), *Early Edom and Moab: The Beginning of the Iron Age in Southern Jordan*, Sheffield Archaeological Monographs 7 (1992); G.W. Bowersock, *Roman Arabia.* (1983), 71–73; idem, "The Cult and Representation of Dusares in Roman Arabia," in: F. Zayadine (ed.), *Petra and the Caravan Cities* (1990), 31–36; I. Browning, *Petra* (1982); R.E. Brünnow and A. von

Domaszewski, *Die Provincia Arabia*, 3 vols. (1904–1909); G. Crawford, *Petra and the Nabateans: A Bibliography*, ATLA Bibliography Series (2003); Z.T. Fiema and R.N. Jones, "The Nabatean King-List Revised: Further Observations on the Second Nabatean Inscription from Tell Esh-Shuqafiya, Egypt," in: *Annual of the Department of Antiquities of Jordan*, 34 (1990), 239–48; P.C. Hammond, *The Nabateans: Their History Culture and Archaeology* (1973), 11; J.F. Healey, "Were the Nabateans Arabs?" First International Conference, The Nabateans. Oxford, September 26–29, 1989, in: *Aram*, 1 (1989), 38–44; N. Glueck, *Deities and Dolphins: The Story of the Nabateans* (1965): Pl. 215a; J.S. McKenzie, *The Architecture of Petra*, British Academy Monographs in Archaeology (1990); Y. Meshorer, *Nabatean Coins*, Monographs of the Institute of Archaeology of the Hebrew University of Jerusalem, *Qedem* 3 (1975); F. Millar, *The Roman Near East, 31 BC–AD 337* (1993); A. Negev, *Nabatean Archaeology Today* (1986); P.J. Parr, "Sixty Years of Excavation in Petra: A Critical Assessment," First International Conference, The Nabateans. Oxford, September 26–29, 1989, in: *Aram* 2 (1990), 1 and 2:7–23; J. Patrich, *The Formation of Nabatean Art: Prohibition of a Graven Image Among the Nabateans: The Evidence and Its Significance*, First International Conference, The Nabateans, Oxford, September 26–29, 1989, in: *Aram* 2 (1990), 185–96; R. Rosenthal-Heginbottom (ed.), *The Nabateans in the Negev* (2003); S.G. Schmid, *Die Feinkeramik der Nabatäer im Spiegel ihrer kulturhistorischen Kontakte, Hellenistische und kaiserzeitliche Keramik des oestlichen Mittelmeergebietes*, Kolloquium, Frankfurt, April 24–25, 1995 (1996), 127–45; Diodorus Siculus, trans. C.H. Oldfather et al. (1933–67); J. Starcky, "Pétra et la nabatène," in: *Dictionnaire de la Bible*, Supp. 7 (1966), 886–1017; Tacitus, *Histories* and *Annals*, C.H. Moore and J. Jackson (eds.), Loeb Classical Library; J. Taylor, *Petra and the Lost Kingdom of the Nabateans* (2001); F. Villeneuve, "Pétra et le royaume nabatèen," in: *L'historie*, 11 (1979), 50–58; R. Wenning, "Die Nabatäer – Denkmäler und Geschichte, Eine Bestandesaufnahme des archäologischen," in: Befundes, *Novum Testamentum et Orbis Antiquus*, 3 (1987); idem, "Eine neuerstellte Liste der nabaaeische Dynastie," in: BOREAS, Munstersche Beitraege zur Archaeologie, vol. 16 (1993), 25–38; F. Zayadine, (ed.), *Petra and the Caravan Cities*, Proceedings of the Symposium organized at Petra in September 1985 (1990).

[Martha Sharp Joukowsky (2nd ed.)]

NABLUS, city in Ereẓ Israel (in later times called *Shechem in Hebrew). Nablus was founded by Vespasian in 72/73 C.E. as Flavia Neapolis on the site of the Samaritan village Mabartha ("the passage") situated between Mts. Ebal and Gerizim near biblical Shechem (Jos., Wars 4:449). Biblical Shechem is identified with Tel Balatah, which has remains from protohistoric times down to the late Persian period. Because of its favorable geographic position and abundance of water the Roman city prospered; it was endowed with an extensive territory including the former Judean toparchy of Acraba. Neapolis was hostile to Septimius Severus, who therefore temporarily deprived it of municipal status. In 244 Philip the Arab turned it into a Roman colony called Julia Neapolis; its coinage continued until the time of Trebonianus Gallus (251–3). Its temples included an Artemision and the city also had an agora, colonnaded streets, a stepped nymphaeum, a theater and hippodrome, etc. In recent years important remains of Roman Neapolis have been unearthed by Y. Magen. Christianity took root early in Neapolis; it was the birthplace of *Justin Martyr (c. 100) and had a bishop as early as the Council of Ancyra in 314. In Byzantine times it was depicted on the Madaba Map as a walled town, Neapolis was also an important center for the *Samaritans who twice revolted and set up a "king." The city was conquered in 636 by the Arabs, who retained its name in the form Nablus. It is mentioned several times in talmudic literature as Nipolis (TJ, Av. Zar. 5:4, 44d); the rabbis, as well as some early Christian authors, confused it with Shechem, and even with Samaria. Under Muslim rule Nablus contained a mixed population of Muslims, Persians, Samaritans, and Jews. The synagogue built in 362 by the high priest Akbon was turned into a mosque (al-Khaḍra'). From 1099 to 1187 the city was held by the crusaders, who called it Naples. It was the second capital of the royal domain and contained a palace and a citadel; the city itself was unwalled at that time. In 1522 a Jewish community is mentioned in Nablus; its fortunes varied throughout the 18th and 19th centuries until it completely abandoned the city shortly after 1900. Nablus remained a center of the Samaritans, some of whom still live there.

[Michael Avi-Yonah / Shimon Gibson (2nd ed.)]

Modern Period

After World War I Jews again tried to live there, but Nablus was a center of Muslim fanaticism, and the 1929 Arab riots ended these attempts. The town suffered severe damage in the 1927 earthquake and was largely destroyed. The Mandatory Government aided its reconstruction along modern lines but sought to preserve its Oriental character. The Samaritan quarter lies at the foot of Mt. Gerizim; wealthier inhabitants have built their homes, mostly in the last decades, on the slopes of Mt. Ebal and Mt. Gerizim. Under the Jordanian regime (1948–67), the economy of Nablus, then the center of the largest district of the West Bank, was based mainly on administrative services and farming. In addition to its traditional industry of soapmaking (its raw material coming from the extensive olive groves of the vicinity), the first modern manufacturing enterprises made their appearance, most of them in the Sokher Valley to the east. In the *Six-Day War, on June 7, 1967, Nablus was taken by an Israeli column coming from the east. In the census held by Israel in the fall of 1967, Nablus had 44,000 inhabitants (as against 23,300 in 1943), of whom all were Muslim, except for 370 Christians and about 250 Samaritans. When, however, the populations of villages and refugee camps next to the town were added, the total number amounted to about 70,000, making Nablus the largest urban center of Samaria.

By the early 21st century the population of the city had reached 100,000, while the Nablus district had a population of 200,000. Nablus was one of the West Bank towns from which Israeli troops withdrew in the wake of the 1995 Oslo II agreement signed at Taba. With the outbreak of the second intifada in 2000 it became part of the terrorist infrastructure and a jump-off point for terrorists making their way to Israel. In 2002 it was targeted by Israeli forces in Operation Defensive Shield and since then has been subjected to roadblocks, searches, and security actions by Israel.

[Efraim Orni]

BIBLIOGRAPHY: Schuerer, Gesch, 2 (1907[2]), 41ff.; Abel, Geog, 2 (1938), 396–7; idem, in: RB, 32 (1923), 120ff. **ADD. BIBLIOGRAPHY:** B. Bagatti, *Ancient Christian Villages of Samaria* (2002), 61–69; Y. Tsafrir, L. Di Segni, and J. Green, *Tabula Imperii Romani. Iudaea – Palaestina. Maps and Gazetteer.* (1994), 194–95; G.S.P. Grenville, R.L. Chapman, and J.E. Taylor, *Palestine in the Fourth Century. The Onomasticon by Eusebius of Caesarea* (2003), 147–48; Y. Magen, *Flavia Neapolis* (Judea and Samaria Publications Series, 2005).

NABONIDUS (Nabû-na'id), last king of Babylon (556–539 B.C.E.), son of a governor, Nabû-balaṭsu-iqbi, and a votaress of Sin. A native of *Haran, Nabonidus was a military commander in his sixties when he ascended the throne of Babylon.

The principal cuneiform sources concerning his reign are: the Nabonidus Chronicle (Pritchard, Texts, 305–7); a basalt stela, which relates his rise to power (*ibid.*, 308–11); a memorial inscription from Haran, which tells the story of his mother (*ibid.*, 311–2); the so-called "Verse Account of Nabonidus," a libel which accuses Nabonidus of mendacity, madness, and of impiety (*ibid.*, 312–5); and foundation documents relating the rebuilding of sanctuaries.

The same period is recorded also by Herodotus, Xenophon, and Josephus. His religious activities were multiple. He restored the ziggurat of Ur and its various temples, e.g., Esagila – the great temple of Marduk in Babylon. One of his dreams was to reconstruct the temple of Sin in Haran. This important city commanding the highways from northern Mesopotamia to Syria and Asia Minor had been in the hands of the Medes since 610. To expel the Medes, Nabonidus sought the help of the young Persian king *Cyrus. In the battle that followed, Cyrus captured the Median king Astyages – his grandfather – and annexed the Median kingdom, thus initiating the building of a great empire which was to include Babylonia as well. In the third year of his reign, Nabonidus went to Syria to raise troops for his campaign in Arabia. He took Hamath, rebuilt the temple of Sin in Haran, stayed during a brief illness in the Anti-Lebanon, and started for Arabia. He took Adummu (al-Jauf) and destroyed *Tema, which he rebuilt and made his residence for several years. His son Bêl-šar-uṣur (*Belshazzar, cf. Dan. 5) stayed in Babylon as regent during Nabonidus' long absence. His stay in Tema still puzzles historians, and various explanations have been put forward, the most accepted being that his major aim was the resurrection of the ancient moon religion of Sin.

In the fall of 539 Cyrus, with the approval and perhaps even on the initiative of the priesthoods of Babylon and the other cities of southern Mesopotamia, invaded the Babylonian empire. By that time Nabonidus was back in the capital. During Cyrus' siege of Opis on the Tigris, the inhabitants revolted against Nabonidus, who massacred them. On the 15th of Tashritu (September–October), Sippar surrendered to Cyrus without battle. Nabonidus fled. The next day Babylon – whose priests, especially the priest of Marduk, opposed him – opened its gates to Cyrus and his allies (the Gutians). Nabonidus was later arrested upon his return to Babylon. On the third day of the following month Cyrus made his triumphal entrance into Babylon. "Great twigs were spread before him. The state of 'peace' was imposed on the city." Nabonidus' end is obscure; according to Josephus, however, he was treated humanely by the conqueror, who assigned Carmania (Central Iran) for his residence (Jos., Apion 1:153). Aramaic fragments from Qumran in which Nabonidus (*Nbny*) relates that while in Teman (so!) he was afflicted with an inflammation of the skin (*sheḥin*) for seven years until an unnamed Jewish soothsayer (*gazar*, a word which also appears in the Aramaic of *Daniel) advised him to pray to the God of Heaven instead of to the idols, show what sort of speculations the king's prolonged residence in remote Tema gave rise to. This suggests that the story about the seven years' lycanthropy of Nebuchadnezzar in Daniel 4 goes back ultimately to such malicious speculations about Nabonidus on the part of disaffected Babylonians.

BIBLIOGRAPHY: S. Smith, *Babylonian Historical Texts Relating to the Capture and Downfall of Babylon* (1924) 27ff., 98ff.; R.P. Dougherty, *Nabonidus and Belshazzar* (1929); J. Lewy, in: HUCA, 19 (1946), 405–89; J.T. Milik, in: RB, 62 (1956), 407ff.; J. Roux, *Ancient Iraq* (1966), 346ff.; Pritchard, Texts, 305–15; E. Bickerman, *Four Strange Books of the Bible* (1967), 74–7.

[Laurentino Jose Afonso]

NABOTH (Heb. נָבוֹת), owner of a vineyard close to the palace of *Ahab king of Israel (I Kings 21:2). Naboth came from the town of Jezreel. Ahab coveted Naboth's vineyard, but Naboth refused to sell or exchange it, basing his refusal on the tradition that inherited family property cannot be taken out of the family's hands: "The Lord forbid it me, that I should give the inheritance of my fathers unto thee" (21:3). In order to obtain the vineyard, Ahab's wife *Jezebel fabricated an accusation against Naboth that he blasphemed God and the king (21:10). According to the custom in the Ancient East, the property of a rebel against the monarchy was confiscated and taken into the royal treasury. Evidence of this custom has also been preserved in one of the *Alalakh documents (No. 17). As a result of a staged trial Naboth's property was confiscated and he himself was stoned. Another biblical tradition states that his children were also killed. Elijah the prophet raised his voice against Ahab because of Naboth's execution, and Elijah's scornful words branded Ahab a murderer and robber and foretold the doom of the royal house (I Kings 21:17–24). The story of Naboth serves as an example and symbol of the Israelite's close attachment to his inheritance and his family-tribe tradition. Furthermore, this story points to the limits of royal authority in Israel, which cannot deal arbitrarily with the lands belonging to the people. For this reason Jezebel had to represent Naboth as a rebel against the king and as blaspheming God.

[Hanoch Reviv]

In the Aggadah

Naboth was Ahab's cousin, with the result that the king, by killing Naboth's sons (II Kings 9:26), could claim his vineyard by right of inheritance (Sanh. 48b). He used to make regular pilgrimages to Jerusalem, and as a great singer, many followed him. It was because he once failed to make his customary journey that his false conviction took place (PR 25, 127a). Naboth's opportunity for revenge, however, came when God asked: "Who shall entice Ahab that he may go up and fall at Ramoth-Gilead?" (I Kings 22:20–21). It was the "spirit" of Naboth which volunteered for the task (Shab. 149b).

BIBLIOGRAPHY: Ginzberg, Legends, 4 (1913), 187–8; 6 (1928), 311–2; I. Ḥasida, *Ishei ha-Tanakh* (1964), 329.

NACHÉZ, TIVADAR (**Theodor Naschitz**; 1859–1930), violinist and composer. Born in Pest, Hungary, Nachéz as a boy played with Liszt and studied under *Joachim in Berlin. In 1889, after settling in London, he embarked on his career as an internationally renowned violin virtuoso. His compositions include *Danses Tsiganes*, a violin concerto, and a string quartet. He also edited Vivaldi's violin concertos in A minor and G minor.

NACHMANN, WERNER (1925–1988), industrialist and German-Jewish communal leader. Born in Karlsruhe (Baden), he fled with his family to France in 1938 and returned as an officer in the French army to his native city in 1945. He was the chairman of the Karlsruhe Jewish community (1961–88), of the Association of Jewish Communities (Oberrat) in Baden, and of the Central Council of Jews in Germany between 1969 and his death in 1988. He received numerous awards, such as the Theodor Heuss Prize, for his efforts regarding the improvement of Jewish-Christian relations. He was, however, also criticized during his long tenure as top official of Germany's Jewish communities as being too lenient toward former Nazis. Thus, his defense of the minister president of Baden-Wuerttemberg, Hans Filbinger, who faced accusations over his role as a judge during World War II, caused considerable protest within and beyond the Jewish community. Immediately after Nachmann's death it was discovered that he had embezzled about DM 33 million of restitution money. Although his successor, Heinz Galinski, made this affair public and tried to discover where the money had gone, it was never resolved conclusively.

BIBLIOGRAPHY: Y.M. Bodemann, *Gedaechtnistheater* (1996).

[Michael Brenner (2nd ed.)]

NACHMANOVICH (Pol. **Nachmanowicz**), wealthy family in *Lvov, Poland; its members were among the leaders of the community within the walled city of Lvov during the late 16th and early 17th centuries.

The first-known member of the family, ISAAC BEN NAḤMAN (d. 1595), is mentioned in 1565 as *dayyan* of the community, and for many years was among its leaders. As chief of the representatives of the communities of the "Land of Russia" (*Senior generalis ziem ruskich*) he participated in meetings of the Council of the Four Lands. In 1589 he was *parnas* of the Council and in 1590 he and his son Mordecai paid the first installment of a tax in its behalf. Isaac attained his high position in the community through his diversified activities as a spice merchant and tax farmer. Among other undertakings he leased an important customs station in Sniatyń, in the Lvov region, and held the rights to the lease of the state revenues in the city of Lvov and the sub-district (*starostwo*). He was also engaged in large-scale moneylending against pledges of real estate and valuables. Through his wealth and prestige he was able to appear in the Polish law courts without having to take the Jewish *oath (*more judaico*). Isaac also had access to the Polish kings Sigismund II Augustus and Stephen Báthory. In 1581, he was authorized to acquire a plot of municipal land where he built a magnificent synagogue in Gothic style at his own expense after the plans of an Italian architect. It became known as the "Turei Zahav" synagogue.

Isaac's elder son, NAḤMAN ISAAKOVICH (Naḥman ben Isaac; d. 1616), took over his father's affairs, including his tax farming and moneylending undertakings, and acquired the lease of the market imposts and other revenues of Lvov. He served as head of the community a number of times, and was admitted to the citizenship of Lvov, being known among Christians by the honorific "Generosus." He was also a scholar. Naḥman, who was stringent in collecting the taxes, had frequent conflicts with the local inhabitants who accused him of overcharging the customs dues, but the city council, which was dependent on his loans, rejected their complaints. From 1603 Naḥman headed a struggle to preserve the synagogue erected by his father which the Jesuits in Lvov wished to convert into a church and seminary. In 1609 a compromise was reached which left the synagogue in the ownership of the Nachmanovich family, while the Jewish community undertook to procure a suitable site for the needs of the Jesuits in the suburbs of Lvov for a sum of 20,600 zlotys. Immediately afterward, Naḥman and his brother Mordecai completed the construction of the synagogue, adding a women's gallery and magnificent religious requisites. In honor of its opening R. Isaac ha-Levi composed a "Song of Redemption" which was sung by the Jews of Lvov for many generations. The deliverance of the synagogue was preserved in the memory of the local community and gave rise to a number of legends. It was connected in folklore with Naḥman's wife Rojse ("Di gildene Rojse," as she was called by the Jews) who was renowned for her beauty and wisdom. After the death of her husband, Rojse took charge of his business affairs until her death in 1637. Her tombstone, which was preserved until the Nazi occupation, was inscribed with a Renaissance-style epitaph extolling her deeds.

The younger son of Isaac, MORDECAI (MARCUS) BEN ISAAC (d. 1635?), ranked among the elders (*seniores*) of the Lvov community, and also engaged in tax farming. In 1627 the merchants of Lvov accused him of overcharging the customs duties. He became court purveyor in 1634 to King Ladislaus IV, furnishing supplies to the Polish army in the war with Russia.

The son of Naḥman Isaakovich and Rojse, ISAAC NACHMANOVICH (Junior; b. 1595), after years of apprenticeship under the tutelage of his mother and uncle, resumed the business in his own right and on occasion acted as court banker. In 1626 he lent considerable sums of money to the royal treasury during the war with Sweden. In 1634 Isaac was given the status **servus camerae* by King Ladislaus IV, and exempted from paying all customs duties and imposts, whether levied by the crown or privately. He also expanded his commercial activities, especially the trade in textiles and supply of oxen to the army, and in partnership with others, leased the state revenues in the districts of Lvov and *Drogobych. However, by 1637 he was on the verge of bankruptcy, and in 1646 was arrested for debt. He succeeded in escaping from prison and disappeared.

BIBLIOGRAPHY: Halpern, Pinkas, index; M. Balaban, *Żydzi lwowscy na przelomie 16 i 17 wieku* (1906), 41–88; W. Lozinski, *Patrycjat i mieszczanstwo lwowskie w 16 i 17 wieku* (1892); J. Caro, *Geschichte der Juden in Lemberg* (1894), 34–43.

[Arthur Cygielman]

NACHOD (Czech **Náchod**), town in N.E. Bohemia, Czech Republic. Its Jewish community was one of the four oldest in *Bohemia and is first mentioned in the city records of 1455. The Jewish street dates from the end of the 15th century. Jews were expelled from Nachod in 1542 and robbed on their way to Poland. They returned in 1544 and founded a school which is mentioned in 1547. The cemetery dates from 1550 and a *mikveh* from 1592. Eleven families were recorded in the town in 1570. In 1663, the Jews were accused of having caused a conflagration in which their quarter and a large part of the town was destroyed. One member of the community was executed; the whole community was attacked, and its members fled. Some founded a community in Ceska Skalice which was expelled in 1705. Soon reestablished, the Nachod community had 60 families in 1724. The synagogue was rebuilt in 1777. Jews were active in making Nachod a center of the textile industry; in 1848 Isaac Mautner founded the famous Mautner textile company. At the end of the century they were beset by antisemitic riots and plunder in connection with the *Hilsner case (1899). There were 150 Jewish families in Nachod in 1852; 630 persons in 1893; 463 in 1921; and 293 in 1930 (2.1% of the total population). In 1902 there were 100 Jews in 22 surrounding localities, among them formerly important communities such as Hronov, Cerveny Kostelec (Ger. Rothkosteletz), and Police nad Metuji, who were affiliated to the Nachod community. In 1934 the *Moller family transferred their textile factory to Palestine, founding the Ata company at *Kiryat Ata. Among the rabbis of Nachod were Heinrich (Ḥayyim) *Brody, who officiated from 1898 to 1905, and Gustav *Sicher. Under Nazi occupation in June 1939, the synagogue was desecrated, and in July the Gestapo raided Jewish homes. The cemetery – its oldest monument dating from 1648 – was also destroyed. In December 1942 the Jews were deported to Theresienstadt, and from there to the death camps of Poland. After World War II a small congregation affiliated with the *Liberec community was established, primarily by veteran soldiers from *Subcarpathian Ruthenia. Nachod was one of the important transit stations for *Beriḥah (1945–46). A monument was erected there for the victims of the Holocaust in 1958. The synagogue building was demolished in the 1960s.

BIBLIOGRAPHY: H. Gold, *Die Juden und Judengemeinden Boehmens* (1934), 412–3; Jakobovitz, in JGGJČ, 9 (1938), 271–305; PK.

[Jan Herman]

NACHOD, JACOB (1814–1882), merchant and second president of the *Deutsch-Israelitischer Gemeindebund. An orphan, he studied at the Wolfenbuettel Samsonschule and went to Leipzig in 1830. There he founded in 1844 the Gesellschaft der Freunde, the forerunner of the Leipzig communal organization established in 1868. He cooperated with M. Kohner in the founding of the Deutsch-Israelitischer Gemeindebund (1869) and succeeded him as its president on Kohner's death in 1877. Nachod's main contributions were in the field of education and welfare.

BIBLIOGRAPHY: *Gedenkblaetter an J. Nachod* (1882).

NACHOD, OSKAR (1859–1933), German historian and bibliographer. Born in Leipzig, Nachod began to write a definitive history of Japan. He abandoned the immense task after completing two volumes. These volumes, *Die Urzeit* (1906) and *Die Uebernahme der chinesichen Kultur* (1930), have remained classics. Nachod's magnum opus was the seven-volume *Bibliographie von Japan* (1928–44), the last parts of which were completed by other scholars. It is a catalog of books and periodical articles dealing with Japan published in European languages between 1906 and 1943.

NADAB (Heb. נָדָב; "[God] has been generous"), eldest son of *Aaron and Elisheba daughter of Amminadab (Ex. 6:23; Num. 3:2, et al.). For details see *Abihu. (The two are always mentioned together and what applies to Abihu is also true of Nadab.) Nadab too left no sons (Num. 3:4; I Chron. 24:2).

[Morris M. Schnitzer]

Nadab and Abihu in the Aggadah

Apart from the one sin which brought about their mysterious deaths, Nadab and Abihu were righteous men. As to the nature of the sin – the "strange fire" which they offered up – there are various interpretations. The most obvious explanation bases itself on the injunction against the priests' partaking of wine and strong drink before entering the sanctuary (Lev. 10:9), which immediately follows this episode. It is therefore suggested that Nadab and Abihu were in a state of intoxication when they offered up the "strange fire." A number of interpretations suggest that they neglected the various ritual requirements connected with the offerings (Lev. R. 20:8–9).

It is also suggested that their overbearing haughtiness was responsible for their deaths. They did not marry because they considered no woman good enough for themselves, saying, "Our father's brother [Moses] is a king, our mother's brother [Nahshon] is a prince, our father [Aaron] is a high priest, and we are both deputy high priests – what woman is worthy of us?" (Lev. R. 20:10). They even went so far as to wish for the death of Moses and Aaron so that they could assume the mantle of leadership (Sanh. 52a; Lev. R. 20:10). Even in the performance of the sacrifice they displayed their haughtiness by refraining from consulting with one another and by neglecting to ask Moses and Aaron whether they might offer such a sacrifice, depending instead upon their own judgment. The sages deduce from this episode that it is forbidden for a disciple to render a legal decision in the presence of his master (Lev. R. 20:7). It is, however, also suggested that their death was a vicarious punishment for their father's sin with regard to the golden calf. Moses relates: "Moreover the Lord was very angry with Aaron to have destroyed him" (Deut. 9:20), and "destruction" means extinction of offspring (Lev. R. 10:5). Moses attempted to comfort his brother by assuring him that his two remaining sons were greater than Nadab and Abihu. At Sinai, Moses was told that he would sanctify the Tabernacle through the death of a great man. He thought that the reference was to himself or Aaron, but now he realized that Nadab and Abihu were nearer to God (Lev. R. 12:2).

Their deaths were caused by "two streams of fire,… branched off into four, and two entered into each of the nostrils of Nadab and Abihu." Their souls were burnt, although no external injury was visible (Sanh. 52a). The whole House of Israel was bidden to bewail the death of Nadab and Abihu (Lev. R. 20:12) for "the death of a pious man is a greater misfortune to Israel than the destruction of the Temple" (Sif. Deut. 31).

[Aaron Rothkoff]

BIBLIOGRAPHY: H. Gressmann, *Mose und seine Zeit* (1913), 257–9; Noth, Personennamen, 193, 251; T.J. Meek, in: AJSLL, 45 (1929), 157; K. Moehlenbrink, in: ZAW, 52 (1934), 214–5; G. Ryckmans, *Les noms propres sud-sémitiques*, 1 (1934), 136; F. Dornseiff, in: ZAW, 53 (1935), 164; Kaufmann, Y., Toledot, 2 (1938), 264, 276; S. Feigin, *Mysteries of the Past* (1953), 430; L.A. Snijders, in: OTS, 10 (1954), 116–23; M. Haran, in: *Tarbiz*, 26 (1956/57), 116 idem, in: VT, 10 (1960), 115, 127; J. Liver, in: *Scripta Hierosolymitana*, 8 (1961), 207, 216; R. Gradwohl, in: ZAW, 75 (1963), 288ff.; U. Cassuto, *A Commentary on the Book of Exodus* (1967), 310–5. IN THE AGGADAH: Ginzberg, Legends, index.

NADAB (Heb. נָדָב), son of Jeroboam whom he succeeded on the throne of Israel (907–906 B.C.E.). Nadab is said to have ruled for two years (1 kings 14:20; 15:25). Since it is also related that he came to the throne in the second year of Asa's reign in Judah and that he was assassinated and succeeded by *Baasha in the third year of Asa's reign (15:28), the actual period of his rule must have been less than two years. During his short reign he fought against the Philistines and laid siege to *Gibbethon. Baasha, who presumably was one of his officers, revolted against him. The usurper assassinated all the descendants of Jeroboam as predicted by Ahijah the Shilonite (15:29).

BIBLIOGRAPHY: J.A. Montgomery, *The Book of Kings* (ICC, 1951), 279; Bright, Hist, 218–219.

[Josef Segal]

NADAV, ZEVI (1891–1959), Second Aliyah and Ha-Shomer activist, editor, and author. Born in Ein Zeitim near Safed, he was brought up in Bobruisk, Belorussia, and returned to Ereẓ Israel in 1906. Nadav was one of the founders and outstanding members of *Ha-Shomer ("Watchmen's Organization") and among the first settlers at Umm Jūnī (*Deganyah) and *Merḥavyah. In 1917, when the Nili intelligence network was uncovered, he was sentenced to forced labor in Turkey, but escaped to Russia and returned to Palestine in 1919. He was a member of *Gedud ha-Avodah ("The Labor Legion") and was active in the organization of Jewish defense in Jerusalem in 1920, in Jaffa in 1921, and in Haifa in 1929. He studied engineering and was the editor of the journal *Tekhnikah u-Madda* ("Mechanics and Science"). His memoirs, which appeared in *Koveẓ ha-Shomer* ("Ha-Shomer Anthology," 1937), and his books, *Mi-Ymei Shemirah ve-Haganah* ("The Days of Vigilance and Defense," 1954), and *Kakh Hitḥalnu* ("Thus We Began," 1958), are a source for the history of the period.

BIBLIOGRAPHY: J. Slutzky (ed.), *Sefer Bobruisk* (1967), 572–3; Tidhar, 10 (1959), 3547–49; E. Livneh (ed.), *Nili* (Heb., 1961), index.

[Yehuda Slutsky]

NADDAF, ABRAHAM ḤAYYIM (1866–1940). Born in *San'a, Yemen, to a family of rabbis and communal leaders, he settled in Jerusalem in 1891 with R. Shalom *Alsheikh, his close friend and partner for many years in the leadership of the Yemenite community in Jerusalem. From his arrival he acted to disengage the Yemenite community from the Sephardi *kolel* (communal organization) in order to promote the economic and cultural life of his community, which was included in the Sephardi *kolel* and was discriminated against in the distribution of financial resources. With R. Alsheikh he took decisive steps to separate his community from the Sephardi *kolel*, against the policy of the older recognized leadership. As a young person he was the first in the communal leadership to understand and use modern political and communal standards. For that end he established independent community institutions such as schools, yeshivot, and a hostel for newcomers from Yemen, and what was crucial for their independent existence, namely, a network of fundraising to finance these institutions. He traveled several times as an emissary of both the Sephardi and the Yemenite communities to *Syria, *Lebanon, and Yemen. Following complaints by the Sephardi *kolel,* he and many other Yemenite separationist leaders were arrested in 1907 by the Ottoman government in Jerusalem, but he was successful in escaping from prison dressed as a woman and went to Constantinople, where he could obtain a *firman* from the Sublime Port for establishing an independent Yemenite *kolel.* In 1908 he carried out a comprehensive and detailed census of the Yemenite community in Jerusalem which constitutes a very helpful source for our knowledge of that community. To preserve the Yemenite tradition he worked for the publication of the essential liturgical religious books: *tāj* (Pentateuch, including the *tafsīr,* Arabic translation of *Sa'adia Gaon) and a *tiklāl* (*siddur*). In 1903, he represented the Yemenites of Jerusalem at the first assembly of Ereẓ-Israeli Jews in Zikhron Ya'akov's *kolel*. He was the first Yemenite rabbi in Ereẓ Israel to investigate Yemenite traditions and published several books and articles on the subject, such as the first bibliography of the works of Yemenite scholars, *Seridei Teiman* ("Remnants of Yemen," 1928), *Anaf Ḥayyim* (notes on *tiklāl Eẓ Ḥayyim* by R. Yiḥye Ṣaliḥ). In consequence of a disagreement with younger leaders in the community he retired and moved to Tel Aviv, devoting his last years to research. His rich literary legacy, preserved by his descendants, was used by Prof. Y. Ratzaby for his research on Yemenite Jews, including his memoir *Zekhor le-Avraham*.

BIBLIOGRAPHY: Y. Ratzaby, "The Diary of Rabbi Avraham Alnadaf," in: *Peraqim be-Toldot ha-Yishuv ha-Yehudi Bi-Yerushalayim*, 2 (1976), 144–91; Y. Tobi, *The Yemenite Community of Jerusalem 1881–1921* (Hebr., 1994).

[Yosef Tobi (2nd ed.)]

NADEL, ARNO (1878–1943), German poet and liturgical musicologist. Born in Vilna, Lithuania, Nadel studied liturgical music under Eduard *Birnbaum in Koenigsberg. In 1895, he entered the Jewish Teachers' Institute in Berlin and spent the rest of his life in Berlin. His first book, a volume of aphorisms and verse entitled *Aus vorletzten und letzten Gruenden* (1909), betrayed the influence of Nietzschean philosophy. His later works dealt mainly with biblical and Jewish themes. They include the play *Adam*, staged in Karlsruhe in 1917; *Das Jahr des Juden* (1920), a collection of 12 poems; *Rot und gluehend ist das Auge des Juden* (1920); *Der Suendenfall* (1920); and *Juedische Volkslieder* (1923). His most important verse collection, *Der Ton* (1921, enlarged 1926), constitutes his Jewish reply to the nihilism of his time. He also published a German translation of *An-Ski's drama, *Der Dybbuk* (1921). *Der weissagende Dionysos* (1934), a collection of his later poetry, was republished after World War II.

In 1916 Nadel was appointed conductor of the choir at the synagogue in the Pestalozzistrasse, and later became musical supervisor of the Berlin synagogues. He devoted much effort to the collection and study of synagogal music and East European Jewish folk song, searching for manuscripts and noting oral traditions. Many of these he published and discussed in the music supplements of the *Berlin Gemeindeblatt* and *Ost und West*, and in his articles on Jewish music in the *Juedisches Lexicon* and the German *Encyclopaedia Judaica*. Some of the Yiddish folk songs were also published separately, as in his *Jonteff Lieder* (1919) and *Juedische Liebeslieder* (1923). Drawing on his researches, Nadel restored old traditions and raised the standards of the synagogue choirs. His manuscript collection included several unique cantors' manuals, such as that of Judah Elias of Hanover (1744). All of this he planned to incorporate in a multivolume compendium of synagogal music entitled *Hallelujah*, which was to have been published under the auspices of the Berlin community. The preparation of the earlier volumes was apparently well under way before Nadel was transported to Auschwitz, where he was murdered. His papers were reported to have been hidden in time, but most have not been recovered.

Nadel was himself a composer, and wrote the incidental music for Stefan *Zweig's *Jeremias* (1918). A man of many talents, he also excelled as a graphic artist and as a painter of landscapes and portraits.

BIBLIOGRAPHY: Stoessinger, in: *Israelitisches Wochenblatt fuer die Schweiz* (Aug. 9, 1946); A. Nadel, *Der weissagende Dionysos*, ed. by F. Kemp ([1934] 1959), contains a critical biography; Sendrey, Music, indexes; Baker, Biog Dict.

[Sol Liptzin and Bathja Bayer]

NADEL, SIEGFRED FERDINAND STEPHAN (Frederick; 1903–1956), British anthropologist. Born in Austria, Nadel studied with Moritz Schlick and Karl Buehler, and developed a command of contemporary philosophical and psychological theory. In 1932 he began the serious study of anthropology at the London School of Economics under B. Malinowski and C.G. Seligman. He studied the music of primitive peoples, and African linguistics with D. Westermann. He did field work in the Anglo-Egyptian Sudan and with the Nuba, from 1938 to 1940. During World War II he served with the British armed forces and later as a lieutenant colonel with the British Military Administration, 1945–46. He successfully applied his anthropological knowledge to the administration of peoples of various origins and traditions. When a department of anthropology was established at the University of Durham in 1948 he was appointed to the chair, and in 1950 took the new chair of anthropology and sociology at the Australian National University, and was dean of the Research School of Pacific Studies. His ethnographic work was shown in *A Black Byzantium* (1942). In his research he investigated the deeper bases of cultures and employed new psychological techniques of investigation such as intelligence tests. Nadel's primary accomplishment, however, is in theory, which he developed in two major works, *The Foundations of Social Anthropology* (1951) and the *Theory of Social Structure* (1957). His great concern was how to unify the conceptual systems of social anthropology and sociology with a psychological framework. His *Theory of Social Structure* has been described as "one of the great theoretical teatises of twentieth century anthropology… which will have a lasting place in the fundamental literature of our subject" (Meyer Fortes). Nadel died unexpectedly of a heart attack at the age of only 52.

BIBLIOGRAPHY: R. Firth, in: *American Anthropologist*, 59 (1957), 117–24, incl. bibl.; M. Fortes, in: S.F. Nadel, *The Theory of Social Structure* (1957), ix–xvi; M. Janowitz, in: *Current Anthropology*, 4:2 (1963), 139, 149–54; IESS, index. **ADD. BIBLIOGRAPHY:** ODNB online; J. Salat, *Reasoning as Enterprise: The Anthropology of S.F. Nadel* (1983).

[Ephraim Fischoff]

NADELMAN, ELIE (1882–1946), U.S. sculptor. Nadelman, who was born in Warsaw, studied art there and in Cracow. He lived in extreme poverty in Paris for some years, but his first one-man show in 1909 was a triumph. His work at this time was mainly influenced by classical Greek art, but certain drawings and pieces of sculpture hinted at a search for a new direction. Andre Gide wrote in his *Journal* (1909): "Nadelman draws with a compass and sculpts by assembling rhombs. He has discovered that each curve of the human body is accompanied by a reciprocal curve opposite it and corresponding to it." Nadelman, who regarded himself as the father of cubism, resented his not being recognized as such. He made his way to the U.S. early in World War I, and had his first American one-man show in New York at the end of 1915. Over the years Nadelman became very successful with his fashionable, witty portrait busts. Nadelman and his wealthy wife assembled one of the finest collections of American folk art. The depression of the 1930s, however, brought a change in his fortunes and after 1932 he was virtually forgotten. He spent his last years doing voluntary occupational therapy at the Bronx Veterans' Hospital and making sentimental little plaster figures for mass reproduction. Nadelman was rediscovered when in 1948, two years after his death, the New York Museum of Modern Art, in collaboration with the Boston Institute of Contemporary Art and the Baltimore Museum of Art, mounted a memorial exhibition of his work. This revealed him as an important sculptor, remarkable for the supple languor of his marble heads, his translations of folk art, and his comments on human foibles.

BIBLIOGRAPHY: L. Kirstein, *Sculpture of Elie Nadelman* (1948), includes bibliography; idem, *Elie Nadelman, Drawings* (1949).

[Alfred Werner]

NĀDER SHAH, Persian king of the Turkish-speaking tribe of Afshār, originating from the northeastern region of Iran, who according to reliable sources acted as the head of a band of highway robbers and later became the king of Iran (1736–47). Nāder was a Sunni and thus aimed at diminishing the influence of the Shiʿite religious authority which became predominant in Iran during the Safavid period (1501–1736). This trend of thought to some extent brought relative relief to the Jews, who suffered extreme persecution and conversions under the Safavids. He may have entertained the idea of uniting all the monotheistic religions, at least in Iran, but he never acted seriously to implement his idea except for ordering the heads of the Jews, Christians, and Muslims to translate their holy books into Persian. The translation of the Jewish Holy Scriptures was made by Rabbi Bābāi ben Nuriel of *Isfahan. The translation was made into *Judeo-Persian (Persian language in Hebrew letters). It was later transliterated into Persian script by a Muslim. The manuscripts of these Bible translations are preserved in the Vatican Library, the Bibliothèque Nationale in Paris, and the *Ben-Zvi Institute in Jerusalem.

In addition, Nāder entered Jewish history for being involved in two other events: (1) According to the Chronicle of *Bābāi ben Farhād (written around 1730), during his wars to expel the invading Afghans from Iran (1722–30), Nāder, who in the Chronicle is called by his pre-royal name, Tahmasb Nader-Quli, extracted a large amount of money from the Jews of *Kashan and Isfahan and treated them badly. (2) Nāder, who made *Meshed the capital city of Iran, was responsible for the transfer of many Jews from *Kazvin and *Gilān provinces to the east and northeast of Iran which eventually resulted in the settlement of a group of Jews in Meshed around 1746. Nāder's mistreatment of the Jews in the Eastern Caucasus is described by Altshuler.

BIBLIOGRAPHY: M. Altshuler, *Yehudei Mizraḥ Kavkaz* (1990), index; W.J. Fischel, "Bible in Persian Translation," in: *Harvard Theological Review* (1952), 3–45; A. Levi, "Eduyot u-Te'udot le-Toledot Yehudei Mashhad," in: *Pe'amim* 6 (1980), 57–73; L. Lockhart, *Nadir Shah: A Critical Study Based Mainly upon Contemporary Sources* (1938); V.B. Moreen, *Iranian Jewry During the Afghan Invasion* (1990); A. Netzer, "*Korot Anusei Mashhad le-fi Ya'akov Dilmanian*," in: *Pe'amim* 42 (1990), 127–56; idem, *Oẓar Kitvei ha-Yad shel Yehudei Paras be-Makhon Ben-Zvi* (1985), 14, 17, 74, 87, 115, 143.

[Amnon Netzer (2nd ed.)]

NADICH, JUDAH (1912–), Conservative rabbi and postwar special advisor for Jewish affairs to General Dwight David Eisenhower. Nadich received his Bachelor of Arts degree with Phi Beta Kappa honors from the City College of New York and his Master of Arts degree from Columbia University. He was ordained by the Jewish Theological Seminary of America, which also awarded him the degrees of Master of Hebrew Literature, Doctor of Hebrew Literature, and Doctor of Divinity (*honoris causa*).

Upon ordination he served as rabbi of Temple Beth David in Buffalo from 1936 to 1940 and of Anshe Emet Synagogue in Chicago from 1940 to 1942. He then enlisted and served as an army chaplain for four years, spending 3½ years in the European Theater of Operations as senior Jewish chaplain with the U.S. armed forces and deputy to the theater chaplain. After the first German concentration camps were liberated, General Eisenhower appointed him his advisor on Jewish affairs, in which capacity he was instrumental in creating livable conditions for Jews who had survived the Holocaust, working with Displaced Persons and with other Jewish chaplians to urgently alleviate their desperate conditions. He received several American decorations, the French Croix de Guerre, and the Order of the British Empire. He retired from active duty in 1946 with the rank of lieutenant-colonel. The government of Israel decorated him with the Ittur Loḥamei ha-Medinah for his service during wartime. The Jewish Welfare Board honored him with the Frank L. Weil Award for distinguished service in the Armed Forces. Following his retirement from the Army, Nadich spent a year and a half on an extended speaking tour, addressing Jewish communities in 40 states on behalf of the *United Jewish Appeal. On behalf of the *Joint Distribution Committee, he addressed Jewish communities throughout South Africa, Zimbabwe, and Zambia as the guest of the South African Jewish War Appeal.

He then went on to serve in the pulpits of two major Conservative congregations, very different in kind and in constituency. He was rabbi of Kehillath Israel (KI) in Brookline, Massachusetts, from 1947 to 1957; and in 1957 he came to Park Avenue Synagogue in Manhattan after the death of Milton *Steinberg, where he remained for three decades as rabbi and, after 1987, as rabbi emeritus. KI was located in a middle class suburb of Boston and its congregants were arch traditionalists; a four-day a week Hebrew School was the norm, followed by high school supplemental education at Boston Hebrew College. The congregation produced dozens of rabbis and Judaic scholars from its student body. Park Avenue Synagogue is located on the prestigious upper East Side. Its congregants were leaders of business and industry, Wall Street and the worlds of banking and finance. Nadich served both communities well.

Active in national as well as local affairs, Nadich was president of the Rabbinical Assembly; the Association of Jewish Chaplains of the Armed Forces; and the Jewish Book Council of America; vice president of *Hadoar*, the American Hebrew weekly magazine and an honorary vice president of the Jewish Braille Institute and a member of its board of directors from 1957. He was chairman of the Commission on Jewish Chaplaincy of the Jewish Welfare Board. At the invitation of the Department of Defense and the Armed Forces Chaplains Board during November 1971, he conducted Torah Convocations in South Vietnam and Japan and visited Jewish chaplains and servicemen in those countries and in Thailand, with the brevet rank of major-general; similarly, in Germany in November 1974. In July 1990, he officiated at the first bat mitzvah in China. In 1992 the secretary of the Army appointed him to the commitee of the Department of Defense commemorating the 50th anniversary of World War II.

He wrote *Rabbi Akiba and His Contemporaries, The Legends of the Rabbis* (2 vols.; 1994), *The Jewish Legends of the Second Commonwealth* (1983), and *Eisenhower and the Jews* (1953); he was the editor and translator of *The Flowering of Modern Hebrew Literature* (1959) by his late father-in-law, Menachem Ribalow; the editor of *Al Halakhah ve-Aggadah* (1960), a volume of Hebrew essays by Louis Ginzberg. His brochure on Yom Kippur, written for Jews in the armed forces of the United States, has a distribution in the hundreds of thousands.

[Michael Berenbaum (2nd ed.)]

NAḌĪR, BANŪ I-, one of the three major Jewish tribes in *Medina (pre-Islamic Yathrib) that became famous in Islamic historiography through their conflict with *Muhammad. Following their defeat, the Naḍīr left their fortifications and orchards and went into exile. The Naḍīr and their brother-clan, the *Qurayẓa, probably considered themselves descendants of Aaron ben Amram, and hence their nickname *al-kāhināni*, "the two priests," or "the two priestly tribes." Several years before Muhammad's arrival at Medina (the *hijra*), the two tribes cooperated with the Arab tribe of Aws in the battle of Buʿāth, although the Naḍīr had been beforehand, and were afterwards, allied with the Arab tribe of Khazraj; the Qurayẓa were constantly allied with the Aws. But with regard to tribal status the two tribes were unequal: the Naḍīr were more prestigious than the Qurayẓa and were entitled to a higher rate of blood money. Against this background there was tension between the tribes of which Muhammad presumably took advantage.

Roughly up to the middle of the sixth century Medina was controlled by a Sassanian military governor whose seat was in al-Zāra on the coast of the Persian Gulf; the Naḍīr and Qurayẓa were then "kings" and exacted tribute from the Aws and Khazraj on behalf of the Sassanians. In the last quarter of the sixth century the king of al-Ḥīra made an Arab of the Khazraj the king of Medina, which indicates that the Jews were no longer "kings" and tribute collectors. However, they later regained their power, and in the above-mentioned battle of Buʿāth they, together with the Aws, defeated the stronger Khazraj. After Muhammad's arrival the Jews were still the owners of fortresses and weapons par excellence. Muhammad concluded non-belligerency agreements with the Naḍīr as he did with the other main Jewish tribes; these agreements were not related to the so-called "Constitution of Medina" in which the main Jewish tribes did not participate.

The town of Zuhra in the Medina area that was close to al-Quff, the town of the *Qaynuqāʿ, was "the town of the Naḍīr," although it was also inhabited by others. In Zuhra there were reportedly 300 goldsmiths, but it is not clear whether all or part of them belonged to the Naḍīr. The town was located near the eastern Ḥarra (stony tract) of Medina that was named after it, Ḥarrat Zuhra.

Beside agriculture, the Naḍīr were involved in commerce: one of them, Abu Rafi, is referred to as "the biggest merchant among the people of Hijaz." They traded in textiles, wine, and weapons. In addition to the common tower-houses (*uṭum*, pl. *āṭām*) which were also used for residence, the Naḍīr had a castle capable of sheltering the whole tribe in times of war. But the accounts of Muhammad's war against them speak of house-to-house fighting, which may indicate that they were taken by surprise.

BIBLIOGRAPHY: V. Vacca, "Naḍīr," in: EIS², 7, 852b–853a; M.J. Kister, "Notes on the Papyrus Text about Muhammad's Campaign against the Banu al-Naḍīr," in: *Archív Orientální*, 32 (1964), 233–36; M. Lecker, *Muslims, Jews and Pagans: Studies on Early Islamic Medina* (1995).

[Michael Lecker (2nd ed.)]

NADIR, MOYSHE (pseudonym of **Isaac Reis**; 1885–1943), Yiddish poet and humorist. Born in eastern Galicia, Nadir emigrated to New York at the age of 13 and at 16 began to write lyrics in which he emphasized the hardships of the immigrant generation. His later lyrics were more skeptical and often bitingly satirical. In addition to poetry, Nadir published feuilletons, essays, short stories, plays, and criticism in dozens of different Yiddish periodicals and anthologies, as well as dozens of his own books. He tried to mask his sentimentalism in biting irony, which increased as he found life increasingly meaningless, and sought escape from nihilistic moodiness in jesting. He said: "When God had nothing to do, He created a world. When I have nothing to do, I destroy it." He coedited the humorous biweekly *Der Yidisher Gazlen* and was a frequent contributor to *Der Groyser Kundes*, the most widely read Yiddish humorous periodical of his time. He participated in the literary projects of Di *Yunge and aroused interest with his volume of erotic lyrics *Vilde Royzn* ("Wild Roses," 1915). His popular poem "Rivington Strit" ("Rivington Street," 1936), published with the illustrations of Yosl Cutler and William Gropper, was transformed into a performance piece. Delighting readers with his paradoxes and wit, his writings served, at the same time, as a means through which he vented his anger at the world. His plays, poems, and essays were intended to shock respectable society. The fantastic is a thread often running through his stories. His major contribution to Yiddish literature, however, was his imaginative use of the language, demonstrating through his puns and coinages the plasticity of Yiddish. Active in communist circles, he was hailed by adoring Jewish crowds during a 1926 visit to the Soviet Union, and in his articles in the communist Jewish daily, *Frayhayt* (1922–39), he attacked opponents of the Communist Party line. However, severe disillusionment came with the Stalin-Hitler pact of 1939, and his collection of poetry *Moyde Ani* ("I Confess"), written in 1941 and published posthumously in 1944, includes an autobiographical section in which he repudiated his former beliefs (English transl. in I. Howe and E. Greenberg, *A Treasury of Yiddish Stories*, 1953).

BIBLIOGRAPHY: I.C. Biletzky, *Essays on Yiddish Poetry and Prose Writers* (1969), 129–36; Rejzen, *Leksikon*, 2 (1927), 500–13; LNYL, 6 (1965), 126–33; S. Leshchinsky, *Literarishe Eseyen* (1955), 126–36; S.D. Singer, *Dikhter un Prozaiker* (1959), 57–66; I. Manger, *Noente Geshtaltn* (1961), 448–55; A. Tabachnik, *Dikhter un Dikhtung* (1965), 268–374; S. Liptzin, *Maturing of Yiddish Literature* (1970), 34–6.

[Sol Liptzin / Edward Portnoy (2nd ed.)]

NADLER, JERROLD LEWIS (1947–), U.S. congressman, lawyer, and activist. Born in Brooklyn, N.Y., to Emanuel and Miriam, Nadler was raised as an Orthodox Jew. He attended the Crown Heights Yeshiva and then Stuyvesant High School. He holds an A.B. from Columbia College, where he was a Pulitzer scholar and co-founded a youth activist group called "West Side Kids" that sought better housing and education for Manhattan's West Side, supported liberal political candidates, and opposed the Vietnam War. He also holds a J.D. from Fordham University. Nadler's varied positions within Congress have included committees and subcommittees on transportation, the environment, and law. He is widely regarded as one of the most liberal members of Congress, representing one of the most liberal districts in the United States.

After serving in the New York State Assembly for 16 years, Nadler was elected to the House of Representatives in 1992, filling the seat of Ted Weiss who had died in office. He was elected to his seventh term in 2004. Nadler is best known as a defender of civil rights and civil liberties, efficient transportation options, affordable health care and housing, support for the arts, and defense of the Social Security system. Nadler has been an outspoken supporter of some of politics' most sensitive issues, including reproductive rights and sexual orientation discrimination. An expert in transportation issues, Nadler has worked with New York City officials to relieve congestion of major arteries, enhance bus and ferry routes, and improve subway access.

Nadler's commitment is tied to his constituents, those residents of the 8th Congressional District of New York, which is considered one of the most diverse districts in the nation; the district is also known as having one of the largest Jewish communities in any congressional district. Nadler has been a constant supporter of the Jewish community, authoring the bill granting federal tax exemptions on settlements received by Holocaust survivors, working to improve African American–Jewish relations, and backing federal hate crimes legislation. He also represents the largest gay community in the United States and took forceful issue with President Bill Clinton's "don't ask, don't tell" policy, adding that it also meant "don't get caught." He argued that it sanctioned bigotry in the United States, only changing the means by which it will be enforced.

Nadler acted as a staunch and vocal advocate of efforts to clean up the contaminants left behind in the wake of the World Trade Center terrorist attacks and the subsequent buildings' collapse. Nadler's immediate reaction to the attacks in 2001 was to help coordinate aid and supplies to residents and to help secure funds for victims; following that he worked for funding for community development and small businesses. He then focused on air quality, and called attention to what he felt was negligence by the Environmental Protection Agency (EPA) in allowing residents to return to their homes near the collapse site, citing unsafe levels of environmental contaminants.

[Lisa DeShantz-Cook (2nd ed.)]

NADLER, MARCUS (1895–1965), U.S. economist. Born in Austria, he joined the Austrian army in 1912. During World War I he became a Russian prisoner of war and was sent to Siberia. From there he worked his way through Manchuria to the United States, where he enrolled as a night student at Columbia University and completed his studies at George Washington University. For several years he worked for the Federal Reserve Board, and in 1927 joined the faculty of New York University as professor of finance. He also served as a consulting economist for several New York banks and research director of the Devine Institute of Finance at New York University. His publications include *The Banking Situation in New York State* (1956), *The Money Market and its Institutions* (1955), and *International Money Markets* (1935) with J.T. Madden.

[Joachim O. Ronall]

NADSON, SEMYON YAKOVLEVICH (1862–1887), poet. He was grandson of an apostate Jew. After the death of his parents, his uncle, despite his opposition, sent him to army high school and to officers' school, from which he was discharged only because he became ill with tuberculosis. Owing to his illnesses during childhood, he suffered from antisemitic persecution from members of his mother's noble family. The sensitive and optimistic lyrics of his *Stikhotvoreniya* ("Poems," 1885) reflect an orphan's childhood and tragically brief career. Often republished in the U.S.S.R., Nadson's verse appealed especially to younger readers. Despite his Christian upbringing, he dedicated one poem to the Jews – "Ya ros tebe chuzhim, otverzhenny narod" ("I Grew Up Strange to You, Parish People") – which appeared in *Pomoshch* (1901), an anthology published to raise funds to aid devastated Jewish communities.

NADVORNAYA (Pol. **Nadwórna**), city in Ivano-Frankovsk (Stanislavov) district, Ukraine. An organized Jewish community existed from the beginning of the 18th century. According to the 1765 census, 937 Jews paid the poll tax in Nadvornaya and the surrounding villages. During the second half of the 18th century the ḥasidic movement made its influence felt among the local Jews. Nadvornaya Jews engaged largely in agricultural trade and owned oil wells, refineries, and saw mills. In 1880 the community numbered 4,182 (64% of the total population); by 1900 the number had decreased to 3,644 (48%); and in 1921 only 2,042 Jews (34%) remained, because of the pogroms perpetrated by Cossacks, Ukrainians, and Petlyura soldiers during World War I. Between the two world wars many Jews earned their livelihood from the lumber industry.

Holocaust Period

In 1941 there were about 5,000 Jews in Nadvornaya. Under Soviet rule (1939–41), community institutions and all Jewish parties ceased to function. With the outbreak of war between Germany and the U.S.S.R. (June 22, 1941), the city was occupied by the Hungarians, who were allies of the Germans. Some 2,000 Jews were expelled to there from the Transcarpathian province. The Ukrainians attacked the Jews, murdering many of them and looting their property. In September the Germans entered the town. On Nov. 6, 1941, an *Aktion* took place in which about 2,500 Jews were killed, among them 1,000 expellees. In the winter of 1941–42 a number of Jews were taken to concentration camps. A ghetto was established on June 20, 1942, and in another *Aktion* in the summer of 1942, hundreds were sent to the *Belzec death camp. In September and October 1942 groups of Jews were transported to the ghetto at Stanislav and murdered there. Although at the end of 1942 the ghetto at Nadvornaya was destroyed, a few Jews succeeded in escaping and hiding in the surrounding forest; some crossed the border into Hungary. Jewish life was not reconstituted in Nadvornaya after the war.

BIBLIOGRAPHY: R. Mahler, *Yidn in Amolikn Poyln in Likht fun Tsifern* (1958), index; B. Wasiutyński, *Ludność żydowska w Polsce w wiekach XIX i XX* (1930), 101, 123, 154, 157.

[Aharon Weiss]

NAEH, BARUKH BEN MENAHEM (1880–1943), Turkish translator and legal writer. Active in Adrianople (Edirne) public affairs, he was a Turkish infantry officer during World War I and immigrated to Palestine in 1923. Naeh's translations include works by Yehuda Burla, A.S. Friedberg, and Sholem Asch, as well as part of the Ottoman *Majalla* legal code. He also compiled a volume of guarantees and laws governing loans and debts (1937).

NAFTALI, PERETZ (**Fritz;** 1888–1961), Israeli economist and politician, member of the First to Third Knessets. Born in Berlin, he studied at a Realschule in Berlin and at the Higher School for Trade (ZIA). In 1909–12 he worked for an export company in Berlin and Brussels. Naftali joined the German Social Democratic Party in 1911. In 1911–12 he served in the German army and in 1917–18 fought in World War I. In 1921–26 he was the economic editor of the German daily *Frankfurter Allgemeine Zeitung*, and in 1926 became the director of the economic research institute of the Deutscher Gewerkschaftsbund (German Trade Union Federation). Naftali was viewed as a pioneer in the field of "economic democracy" and published a book under that title which earned him considerable fame in the international labor movement. Naftali joined the Zionist Organization in 1925, was chairman of the League for Labor Palestine, and a member of the Zionist Executive in Germany. In 1931 he took part in the Zionist Congress. In 1933, when the Nazis came to power in Germany, Naftali settled in Palestine. In 1933–36 he was a lecturer in economics at the Haifa Technion, and in 1936–37 at the Tel Aviv School of Economics and Law. In 1938–49 he served as the director general of Bank Hapoalim. He was a member of Asefat ha-Nivḥarim in 1941–48 on behalf of Mapai and a member of the Tel Aviv Municipal Council and the *Histadrut Executive. Naftali was elected to the first three Knessets on the Mapai list and served as minister without portfolio in 1951–52 and again in 1958–59, minister of agriculture in the years 1952–55, minister of commerce and industry in 1955, and minister of social welfare in 1959. In the First and Second Knessets, when he did not serve as a minister, Naftali was a member of the Knesset Finance Committee.

Among his writings are *Kalkalat Yisrael: Halakhah u-Ma'aseh* ("Israel's Economy: Theory and Practice," 1[illegible]64); *Demokratya Kalkalit: Mivḥar Ketavim* ("Democratic E[illegible]mics: A Selection of Writings," 1965).

BIBLIOGRAPHY: Y. Rimmer, *Pereẓ Naftali: Soẓi'al Demokrat ba-Ẓiyyonut u-be-Ereẓ Yisrael* (1983).

[Susan Hattis Rolef (2nd ed.)]

NAGARI (Na'ari), MOSES BEN JUDAH (14th century), philosopher. Nagari probably lived in Rome around 1300. He is the author of *Ma'amar ba-Ma'arekhet*, an index to Maimonides' *Guide of the Perplexed*, which also contains explanations of philosophical terms. This work was printed together with questions on the *Guide* addressed to Isaac *Abrabanel by Saul Cohen (Venice, 1574; reprinted in *Abrabanel, Ketavim al-Maḥashevet Yisrael*, vol. 3, 1967). Steinschneider suggested that Nagari's name should be read Na'ari and that he was a member of the Ne'arim (Adolescentoli) family. He also corrected certain mistaken notions about Nagari (Cat Bod, 1834).

BIBLIOGRAPHY: Benjacob, Oẓar, 282 (no. 204), 355 (no. 33).

NAGASAKI, port in S. Japan. With the opening of Japan to international relations in the mid-19th century, Nagasaki gradually grew into a center of foreign trade. In the 1860s a small number of Jews, mainly from Eastern Europe, settled in the city. In the following years they organized religious and communal activities, built a synagogue, and maintained a burial ground. In the late 19th century (when the community numbered around 100) many of them earned a livelihood by catering to the needs of Russian sailors whose ships called regularly at the port. When this business ceased with the outbreak of the Russo-Japanese War in 1904, many of the Jews moved elsewhere, and the organized Jewish community came to an end.

[Hyman Kublin]

NAGEL, ERNEST (1901–1985), U.S. philosopher. Nagel, who was born in Nove Mesto (Moravia), emigrated to America at an early age. He received a B.S. from the City College of New York in 1923 and an M.A. (1925) and a Ph.D. (1930) from Columbia University. He was appointed to Columbia's faculty in 1930. He became John Dewey Professor of Philosophy in 1955 and university professor in 1967. Upon his retirement, he was professor emeritus at Columbia.

Though he was best known for his incisive and learned essays in the philosophy of science, Nagel's interests as a philosopher were broad. Many of his writings deal with social and political questions and with questions of religion. In these latter domains, influenced by his interest in the philosophy of science, his work emerges as a type of philosophical naturalism. According to Nagel, the types of explanation of the world that produce human knowledge are essentially those based on the model of explanation in the physical sciences. He argued, however, that such types of explanation must not be interpreted narrowly, as a kind of rigid scientism, but rather broadly; e.g., explanations of mental phenomena are not to be reduced to descriptions of the movement of material particles as in the physical sciences. He thus distinguished between naturalistic explanations and materialistic ones, where "materialism" is taken to mean that philosophical view which denies the existence of mind or mental qualities. In a similar vein, Nagel argued that "determinism" in physical theory is not such as to entail the denial of human freedom with regard to moral and political decisions. His analysis of morality and of human history accordingly allowed for the attribution of responsibility to human agents for their actions. Thus he maintained that naturalism, although committed to giving a correct account of scientific knowledge, includes within its scope a place for imagination, liberal values, and human wisdom. Nagel's main contribution to the philosophy of science is to be found in *The Structure of Science* (1961). He served as president of the Association of Symbolic Logic (1947–49), and as president of the Philosophy of Science Association (1960–62).

Among Nagel's other important writings are *An Introduction to Logic and Scientific Method*, with Morris Raphael Cohen (1934); *Principles of the Theory of Probability* (1939); *Sovereign Reason* (1954); *Logic without Metaphysics* (1956); *Gödel's Proof*, with James R. Newman (1958); *Observation and Theory in Science* (1971); and *Teleology Revisited and Other Essays in the Philosophy and History of Science* (1979).

ADD. BIBLIOGRAPHY: S. Morgenbesser (ed.), *Philosophy, Science, and Method; Essays in Honor of Ernest Nagel* (1969); E. Madden, *Philosophical Problems of Psychology* (1962).

[Avrum Stroll / Ruth Beloff (2nd ed.)]

NAG HAMMADI CODICES, a collection of Coptic papyrus manuscripts discovered in 1945 in the Egyptian desert near the base of the Gebel et-Tarif in the vicinity of Nag Hammadi. The manuscripts, 13 in all, date from the fourth century and comprise a "library" of 52 tractates (not all of which are fully preserved). Presumably all of these writings are translations from Greek originals. Most, but not all, of the documents are gnostic in character, and therefore shed considerable light on the history and character of the gnostic religion of late antiquity, since before the discovery of this library of original texts, most of our knowledge of Gnosticism was dependent upon the writings of opponents, especially the Church Fathers.

These documents contain massive evidence concerning the Jewish elements in the development of Gnosticism, and refute once and for all the old opinion that Gnosticism originated as a Christian heresy. What follows is but a small sampling of this literature.

The Apocalypse of Adam (Codex v, tractate 5) is especially important, since it appears to be devoid of Christian influences, and it, or perhaps rather its *Grundschrift*, may even be a pre-Christian work. The *incipit* indicates at once the literary genre of the work: "The relevation which Adam taught his son Seth in the seven-hundredth year, saying …" The document is in direct continuity with the pseudepigraphic Adam literature of the Second Temple period (e.g., the Book of the Life of *Adam and Eve) and with well-known legends concerning Adam and Seth (cf., Jos., Ant. 1:67–71). In form it is an example of the "testament" literature (cf. e.g., the Testaments of the Twelve *Patriarchs and Gen. 49), Adam in this document giving his dying speech to his son Seth. (The "seven-hundredth year" is reckoned from Seth's birth, and according to the chronology of Gen. 5:3, the Septuagint, Pseudo-Philo, *Liber Anti-quitatum Biblicarum* 1:2, and Jos., Ant. 1:68, is the year of Adam's death.) Adam's speech deals with the experience of himself and Eve after creation, alluding to the Genesis accounts and to well-known Jewish *aggadot* (e.g., the "glory" of Adam before his fall). But the thrust is typically gnostic. The Creator, called "Saclas" (Aramaic for "fool"), holds Adamic man in fear and bondage. A revelation from the higher realm is necessary to effect salvation for gnostic man, the "Sethians." Adam recounts to Seth and his seed a revelation he has received from three angelic figures (cf. Gen. 18:2) prophesying the coming destruction by flood, by fire (cf. Sodom and Gomorrah), and the end of the world. The coming of a savior-figure, the "Illuminator," is also prophesied, in terms reminiscent of Iranian traditions, but also of Jewish messianic traditions. The Jewish elements in the *Apocalypse of Adam* are central, yet mutated in a heretical direction.

This is the case, too, with very many of the other Nag Hammadi documents. An "Ophite" version of the Paradise story is recounted in *On the Origin of the World* (II, 5), *The Hypostasis of the Archons* (II, 4), and, probably in its earliest form, in a Midrash imbedded in *The Testimony of Truth* (IX, 3), wherein the serpent and Eve are the revealers of knowledge, and the Creator is an envious villain. In addition to the Genesis story itself, aggadic traditions known from the Jewish Midrashim, including Aramaic word-plays ("serpent" חויא / "Eve" חוה / "instruct" חוא, cf. Gen. R. 20:27) are utilized in the text, but are, of course, retold in a gnostic, heretical direction.

The Apocryphon of John (II, 1; III, 1; IV, 1) is a document which is attributed, in an obviously secondary redactional framework, to *Jesus as a revelation to his disciple John. However, the basic revelation consists of a cosmogonic myth, with a Midrash on the first six chapters of Genesis, in which the figure of Jesus is altogether extraneous. At least a part of this myth was known also to Irenaeus (Adversus haereses 1:29). The myth contains speculations concerning the Highest God and the divine world (*ma'aseh merkabah*) and on the creation of the cosmos (*ma'aseh bereshit*). Speculation in, and study of, both these subjects was severely limited if not actually condemned by the rabbis of the tannaitic period (cf. Hag. 2:1 and see *Merkabah Mysticism). In accordance with a trend in post-biblical Jewish theology (cf. Jos., Apion, 2.167: "uncreated … immutable … unknowable"), the Highest God is described in negative terms which stress his utter transcendence. From him emanate other divine beings, including four angelic "light-bearers" that serve as attendants (cf. the four *ḥayyot* of Ezek. 1:5). However, what marks this document as heretical is that the Transcendent God is not also the Creator. Creation results from the "fall" of Sophia ("Wisdom," cf. the role of *ḥokhmah* in Prov. 8:22ff.; and sophia in Wisd. 7:22ff.), whose product is Ialdabaoth (also called "Saklas" and "Samael"). "Ialdabaoth" is the biblical Creator, and he, together with his fellow "archons," creates the world and the corporeal part of man. In his "ignorance" he claims to be the only God (he quotes Ex. 20:5 and Isa. 45:5). This myth is found not only in the Apocryphon of John, but in numerous other gnostic writings as well.

The creation of man in the *Apocryphon of John* is not only a retelling of the Genesis story, but is based on Jewish traditions of interpretation of key biblical texts. For example, the account of the fashioning of man's lower nature by Ialdabaoth and his fellow-archons is based on the Alexandrian-Jewish interpretation of Genesis 1:26f. and 2:7, that God relegated the creation of man's mortal nature to the angels (cf. Fug. 68–70: Justin, *Dialogue with Trypho the Jew*, 62). The duality of man's soul, i.e., a lower *psyche* and a higher *pneuma* ("spirit"), is based on the Hellenistic Jewish (probably Alexandrian) interpretation of the Septuagint of Genesis 2:7 (cf. Spec. 4.123; Det. 84). The detail that Adam was inert and lifeless until he received the heavenly "inbreathing" is developed from the Palestinian interpretation of Genesis 2:7 that depicts Adam as a *golem (cf. Gen. R. 8:1; 14:8; Sanh. 38b).

An interesting example of continuity between the *Dead Sea Scrolls and the Nag Hammadi documents is the tractate *Melchizedek* (IX, 1), wherein the figure of *Melchizedek is presented as a redeemer-holy-war figure, just as in the fragmentary scroll discovered in cave 11 at Qumran (11 Q Melch.). Other features of Melchizedek's role as presented in the Nag Hammadi tractate are reminiscent of Jewish traditions found in the Enoch literature, esp. 2 (Slavonic) Enoch.

Study of the Nag Hammadi documents provides a clearer picture of some of the gnostic groups described by the Church Fathers, especially the Valentinians and the so-called "Sethians." The following Nag Hammadi tractates are related to the Sethian form of Gnosticism: *The Apocryphon of John* (II, 1; III, 1; IV, 1), *The Hypostasis of the Archons* (II, 4), *The Gospel of the Egyptians* (III, 2; IV, 2), *The Apocalypse of Adam* (V, 5), The *Three Steles of Seth* (VII, 5), *Zostrianos* (VIII, 1), *Melchizedek* (IX, 1), *The Thought of Norea* (IX, 2), *Marsanes* (X, 1), *Allogenes* (XI, 3), and *The Trimorphic Protennoia* (XIII, 1). While some of these documents (but not all) are Christian in their present form, it is now clear that Sethian Gnosticism, in its earliest stages, developed independently of, and possibly even prior to, Christianity. The Jewish components of Sethian Gnosticism are central and constitutive.

In short, a wide variety of Jewish traditions may be found in the Nag Hammadi documents, biblical and extra-biblical, "main-line" and "sectarian," from Palestine and from the Diaspora, to the extent that the Jewish element in Gnosticism must be seen as primary and not secondary. Paradoxically, the hermeneutical thrust in the use of these materials is outspokenly heretical, even "anti-Jewish." These documents, therefore, present an exceedingly interesting area of study for scholars working in the fields of religious history, sociology, and psychology.

BIBLIOGRAPHY: J.M. Robinson et al. (ed.), *The Facsimile Edition of the Nag Hammadi Codices* (11 vols., 1972–79); idem (ed.), *The Nag Hammadi Library in English* (1977); idem (ed.), The Coptic Gnostic Library (Coptic-English critical edition of the Nag Hammadi Codices, 11 vols., 1974–); J.É. Ménard (Éditeur-en-chef), Bibliothèque copte de Nag Hammadi, Section "Textes" (Coptic-French critical edition of the Nag Hammadi Codices, 1977–); K. Rudolph, *Die Gnosis: Wesen und Geschichte einer spätantiken Religion* (1977); B. Pearson, "Jewish Haggadic Traditions in *The Testimony of Truth* from Nag Hammadi (CG IX, 3)," in: J. Bergman et al. (ed.), *Ex Orbe Religionum: Studia Geo Widengren* (1972), 457–470; *ibid.*, "Biblical Exegesis in Gnostic Literature," in: M. Stone (ed.), *Armenian and Biblical Studies* (1976), 70–80; *ibid.*, "The Figure of Seth in Gnostic Literature," in: B. Layton (ed.), *The Rediscovery of Gnosticism* (1979); H.-M. Schenke, "Das Sethianische System nach Nag Hammadi-Handschriften," in: P. Nagel (ed.), *Studia Coptica* (1974), 165–172; D. Scholer, *Nag Hammadi Bibliography 1948–1969* (1971), supplemented annually in *Novum Testamentum*: E. Pagels, *The Gnostic Gospels* (1979).

[Birger A. Pearson]

NAGID (Heb. נָגִיד, pl. נְגִידִים; Ar. *ra'īs al-yahūd*), the head of the Jewish community in Islamic countries (except under

*Abbasid rule where Jewry was led by the *exilarchs). In the Middle Ages, beginning with the tenth century, there were *negidim* in *Spain, *Kairouan, *Egypt, and *Yemen; in *Morocco, *Algeria, and *Tunisia there were *negidim* from the 16th to the 19th centuries.

History of the Institution of the Nagid

When the Abbasid caliphate was split up and independent kingdoms came into being, the new rulers found it necessary to appoint a leader for each non-Muslim community. ʿAbd al-Raḥmān I (751–788), founder of the *Umayyad emirate in Spain, appointed a Visigoth prince to head the Christian community, and subsequent leaders of the Christians were appointed from among Christian courtiers or candidates proposed by the community. The duties of the head of the Christian community consisted of representing the community before the authorities, ensuring the payment of taxes, supervising community life, and administering the judiciary, which applied Visigoth law. In a similar manner, the heads of the Jewish community were appointed from among persons holding high rank at the court of the caliph or sultan, such as vizier, secretary, or treasurer; most, however, were physicians. Their task was to see to it that the Jewish community fulfilled the duties imposed on it (such as observing the Covenant of *Omar); they also appointed *dayyanim* and other community officials. Thus, the office of *nagid* came into being to serve the purposes of the Muslim state, but its existence was also in the interests of the Jews, for these *nesi'im* (the term *nagid* was first applied in the beginning of the 11th century) would intervene in their behalf to obtain better conditions or to bring about the cancellation of anti-Jewish decrees. The archetype of the institution of *nagid* was the Babylonian exilarch, with certain differences. The *negidim* did not claim Davidic descent, their appointment being based on their own achievements and their standing with the authorities, rather than their blood line, and they did not, as a rule, derive their income from taxes imposed on the community, as did the exilarchs. The similarity of the duties of the two institutions seems to account for the legend mentioned by *David b. Solomon ibn Abi Zimra (Responsa no. 944) and Joseph b. Isaac Sambari (Neubauer, Chronicles, 1 (1887), 115–6), according to which the office of *nagid* in Egypt was created by a member of the Babylonian exilarch's family who had been invited to Egypt by the Abbasid wife of the Egyptian ruler; D. Ayalon (Neustadt, see bibliography) has shown that there is no historical truth to this legend, for there is no record of any daughter of an Abbasid caliph marrying a Fatimid caliph, and, as stated, the *negidim* did not claim Davidic descent.

Spain

Among those known to have held the office of *nagid* in Spain are Ḥisdai ibn *Shaprut, physician and statesman at the courts of ʿAbd al-Raḥmān III (ruled 912–61) and his son al-Ḥakam II (961–76). Ibn Shaprut did a great deal for the Jews in his own country, as well as for Jewish communities in other parts of the world; Dunash b. *Labrat refers to him as "judge." Jacob ibn *Jau, who succeeded Ibn Shaprut, was, according to Abraham ibn *Daud, appointed head of the Jewish community by Manṣur ibn Abi ʿAmir, the guardian of Hisham II (976–1013); the latter "issued him a document placing him in charge of all the Jewish communities from Sijilmassa to the river Duero… [The decree stated] that he was to adjudicate all their litigations, and that he was empowered to appoint over them whomsoever he wished and to exact from them any tax or payment to which they might be subject… he placed at his disposal… the carriage of a vicegerent. Then all the members of the community of Córdoba assembled and signed an agreement [certifying] his position as *nasi*, which stated: 'Rule thou over us, both thou, and thy son, and thy son's son also" (Abraham ibn Daud's *The Book of Tradition*, ed. by G.D. Cohen (1967), 69). Ibn Jau was in office for only one year, and was removed by the vizier al-Manṣur. The source quoted above illustrates the duties of the office, the manner in which the appointee was chosen by the authorities, and the appointee's acceptance by the community. Both Ibn Shaprut and Ibn Jau fulfilled the duties of *nagid*, but neither bore the title. Two Spanish *negidim* who did hold the title were Samuel ibn Nagrela (Samuel *ha-Nagid; 993–1056) and his son Jehoseph *ha-Nagid. Samuel was the treasurer and secretary of King Ḥabbus of Granada; S.D. Goitein (see bibliography) assumes that the title *nagid* was awarded to him by *Hai Gaon. His son, who also served as the king's secretary, was killed in 1066; according to Goitein, he was awarded his title by Daniel b. *Azariah, *nasi* and *Gaon* of Palestine from 1051 to 1062. Both *negidim* received their titles in recognition of the aid they extended to the *yeshivot*, both in Palestine and in Iraq (Babylonia).

Kairouan

During the same period, there was a separate Jewish leadership in Kairouan, Tunisia. The first official *nagid* who was appointed by the Zirid emir was ʿAbu Isḥaq Ibrahim ibn ʿAta (Natan), who served as court physician to the emir Badis (966–1016) and his son al-Muʿizz (1016–62), the rulers of the eastern Maghreb (Tunisia and Algeria). The appointment apparently was made during the period of the Fatimid al-Ḥākim bi-Amri'llah (1010–1221), at which time the opportunity was grasped to free themselves from Fatimid rule. It may be assumed that even before this there was local Jewish government in Kairouan, but without formal independent status. Ibrahim, like the Spanish *negidim*, extended aid to the Babylonian *yeshivot*, in addition to attending to the needs of his own community, and earned the praise of Hai Gaon, who in 1015 awarded him the honorary title of *negid ha-Golah* ("*nagid* of the Diaspora"). He died in about 1020 and was succeeded by Jacob b. Amram, who was referred to by such titles as *negid ha-Golah, sar ha-Segullah* ("the chosen prince"), and *pe'er ha-'edah* ("pride of the community"). There is no record of his early activities and the last report about him dates from 1041. He helped the Kairouan community in times of need, sent contributions to the *yeshivot* in Palestine and Babylonia,

List of Negidim in Egypt

1. **Judah b. Saadiah** 1067(?)–1079(?)
2. **Mevorakh b. Saadiah** 1079(?)–1110(?)
3. **Moses b. Mevorakh** before 1115–after 1124
4. **Samuel b. Hananiah** 1141–1159
5. **Zuta** intermittently for some years after 1159
6. **Moses b. Maimon (Maimonides)**? after Zuta
7. **Abraham b. Moses Maimuni** before 1213–1237
8. **David b. Abraham Maimuni** 1237–1300
9. **Abraham b. David Maimuni** before 1291–after 1313
10. **Moses b. Abraham Maimuni**? after his father
11. **Joshua b. Abraham Maimuni** d. 1355
12. **David b. Joshua Maimuni** 1355–1374
13. **Amram** 1374– after 1384
14. **Simeon** before 1422
15. **Joseph b. Obadiah**? after 1430
16. **Abd al-Latif b. Ibrahim b. Sams** before 1442
17. **Joseph b. Khalifah** before 1458–after 1465
18. **Solomon b. Joseph** d. 1482
19. **Nathan (Jonathan) b. Saadiah ha-Kohen Sholal** before 1484–1502
20. **Isaac ha-Kohen Sholal** 1502–1517
21. **Abraham de Castro** 1520(?)–after 1524
22. **Tajid**? second half of 16th century
23. **Jacob b. Ḥayyim Talmid**? second half of 16th century

1. Ashtor, Toledot, 1 (1944), 41; S.D. Goitein, in: HUCA, 34 (1963), 180.
2. S.D. Goitein, *Sidrei Ḥinnukh* (1962), 37, 128.
3–4. idem, in JQR, 53 (1962/63), 95–96.
5. E. Ashtor, in: HUCA, 27 (1956), 313–5.
6. D. Neustadt, in: *Zion*, 11 (1945/46), 147–8.
7. Goitein, in JQR, 53 (1962/63), 96, 104.
8. *Ibid.*, 104; idem, *Sidrei Ḥinnukh*, 114.
9. idem., *Sidrei Ḥinnukh*,114; idem, in: *Tarbiz*, 34 (1965), 249–50. He served as *nagid* for several years with his father.
10. idem, in: Tarbiz, 34 (1965), 255.
11. Ashtor, Toledot, 1 (1944), 298 ff.
12. Ibid., 3002–2; 3 (1970), 88; A.H. Freimann, in: *Minḥah li-Yhudah*, dedicated to J.L. Zlotnik (1950), 175–8.
13–17. Ashtor, Toledot, 2 (1951), 22–26, 84, 86–87.
18. *Ibid.*, 3 (1970), 154.
19. *Ibid.*, 2 (1951), 450–3.
20. *Ibid.*, 505 ff.; A. Shoḥet, in: *Zion*, 13–14 (1948/49), 43.
21. A.N. Pollack, *ibid.*, 1 (1936), 24, 28–31.
22–23. Rosanes, Togarmah, 3 (1937/38)^2, 220–1.

and earned the praise of the exilarch Hezekiah b. *David. He was also in contact with the Jewish community in Sicily. It is probable that there was one more *nagid* in Kairouan before the community ended in the 1160s.

Egypt

In Egypt the office of *nagid* remained in existence for over 500 years; there are extant documents which contain a wealth of details on the *negidim* and their authority and acts. Some scholars accept the view that the first *nagid* of Egyptian Jewry was *Paltiel, an Italian Jew who was brought to Egypt by al-Muʿizz, the Fatimid conqueror of Egypt (969), and was part of the ruler's officialdom. The sole source for this information is the *Ahimaaz Scroll; there is an assumption that the Shiʿite Fatimids, who decreed themselves Imams (caliphs), did not wish to depend in any way upon the Sunnite Abbasid caliphs, preferring to appoint a separate head for the Jews under their ruler rather than have them acknowledge the authority of the Babylonian exilarch, an official who was part of the Abbasid hierarchy. There are various theories concerning the true identity of Paltiel, the most recent being the one expressed by M. Gil (see bibliography), according to which he was Fadl ben Salih, a chief commander of the Fatimid army. Another theory is B. Lewis's (see bibliography), according to which he was Musa b. Eleazar, al-Muʿizz's physician. Mann (Egypt, 1920, see bibliography) was the first to suggest this theory of Paltiel's being the first *nagid* on the Fatimids initiative.

The *Genizah* documents contain no proof of the existence of the office of *nagid* in the first half of the 11th century. On this basis some scholars, such as Goitein (1971, see bibliography), Cohen (1980, see bibliography), and Gil (1992, see bibliography), wrote against Mann's theory. Today there are certain scholars, such as Sela (1995, 1998, see bibliography) and Bareket (1998, 1999, see bibliography) who are re-adapting the old Mann theory. The first *negidim* for whom details are found in the *Genizah* are Judah b. Saadiah, who was a court physician, held the post of *nagid* in the 1060s and the 1070s, and was referred to as "*nagid* of the People of God," and his brother *Mevorakh, who was *nagid* from about 1079 (with temporary interruptions) to 1110. Mevorakh was the physician and adviser of al-Malik al-Afdal, the acting ruler of Egypt, and was awarded no less than 14 honorary titles, some of which were typical of those used by the *yeshivot* in Babylonia and Palestine. For a while, Mevorakh was removed from office, a result of the machinations of David b. *Daniel, a member of the house of the Babylonian exilarch who had succeeded in gaining the governor's support for his claim to the leadership of Egyptian Jewry. Such competition for the office occurred on several occasions, up to the 13th century. As a rule the challenge came from members of the Babylonian exilarch's house or the Palestinian yeshivah.

THE INSTITUTION OF NAGID. The *nagid* was appointed by the authorities after receiving the agreement of prominent members of the community. The choice, however, was not made in a democratic manner. Rather than the official representatives, it was the influential members of the community who recommended the candidate. Sometimes the vizier was bribed to recommend a particular person; this happened, for example, in the middle of the 12th century, in the case of

*Zuta. The appointment of the *nagid* did not depend upon the consent of the exilarch or the heads of the *yeshivot*, and the mention of such consent in the existing documents must be regarded as a mere formality. At times it was the son of the deceased *nagid* who was appointed in his father's place, while on some occasions preference was given to a person who had achieved a prominent position at the ruler's court. Beginning with Abraham b. Moses b. *Maimon, the son of *Maimonides, the office became hereditary, and four of his descendants served as *negidim*, the last being David b. Joshua *Maimuni. From the end of the Ayyubid dynasty and throughout the Mamluk period, the office of *nagid*, or *ra'īs al-yahūd*, had the character of a permanent institution, whose functions were defined by the authorities. Several letters of appointment from the Mamluk period are extant which contain the provision that the *ra'īs* always be a Rabbanite and that he also be in charge of the *Karaites and *Samaritans. It was his duty to appoint a prominent Karaite as leader of that community, although the head of the Samaritans received his own letter of appointment from the government. According to Qalqashandi (d. 1418), the status of *nagid* was parallel in nature to that of the Christian patriarch, and like any person of official rank wore official dress, the *khal'a*. The Arab chronicler Ibn Faḍl Allah al-'Omarī, whose work was written in 1340, tells about a *nagid's* letter of appointment in which his authority and functions were described as follows: consolidation of the community; administration of justice to the members of the community on the basis of its religious law; responsibility for matters of personal status – betrothals, marriages, and divorces; the right of excommunication; supervision of the observance of the commandments, according to the Law of Moses and the decisions of the rabbis; the duty to ensure compliance with the Covenant of Omar, especially the prohibition of constructing new synagogues, and the order concerning the wearing of garb different from that of the Muslims; supervision of synagogues and prayer services; grading the status of the members of the community (this apparently applies to tax assessment, for there were three different rates for the poll tax, depending upon a person's economic situation); and general responsibility for the maintenance of law and order by the community. Jewish sources, primarily *Genizah* documents dating from the Fatimid period and after, give further information on the wide range of the *nagid's* duties and activities. He protected his community from oppression by government officials and interceded with the authorities for the cancellation of unjust and severe decrees. He served as arbitrator in cases of injustice, discrimination, and unfair economic competition; attended to the needs of the weak and the suffering; and tried to retrieve lost goods, rescue Jews from prison and captivity, and raise the ransoms required for such purposes. It was he who authorized the payment of tuition fees from the communal trust fund for the education of orphans and children of the poor (five such payment orders by a single *nagid*, Abraham b. Moses b. Maimon, were found in the *Genizah*). The *nagid* was not responsible for collecting the poll tax, but it was he who ensured the payment of the tax on behalf of the poor, when the authorities did not exempt them. He had his own officials through whom he supervised *kashrut*, ritual slaughter, and marriages. Decisions made by the various communities required his confirmation, and in general he supervised the community operations by means of the *muqaddam*, his personal representative to the local community. Although he was the supreme legal authority for the community, he did not actually function as a judge, but appointed *dayyanim* who sat on his *bet din* and handled legal conflicts; the court was known as the Great *Bet Din* and it was headed by the *dayyan al-yahud*. Legal documents such as marriage writs, divorce writs, and wills were issued "by the authority" of the *nagid*. According to Meshullam of *Volterra, who visited Egypt in 1481, the *nagid's* penal powers included the right to impose capital punishment (*Massa Meshullam mi-Volterah*, ed. by A. Yaari, 1948, 57), but it is doubtful whether the authorities did in fact grant him such power. Obadiah *Bertinoro, writing in 1487–88, states that the *nagid* was empowered by the caliph "to punish, imprison, and flog" anyone who opposed his will; this seems to be a more realistic description of the *nagid's* authority. He could also use excommunication and imprisonment in those cases where the prestige of his office was not sufficient to achieve compliance with his decisions. In the Fatimid and Ayyubid periods the *negidim* did not impose taxes for the maintenance of their office; usually they were wealthy court physicians and property owners, and also received gifts from members of the community. In the Mamluk period a change seems to have taken place, and according to the testimony of David b. Solomon ibn Abi Zimra marriage and divorce proceedings became subject to a fee, out of which the *nagid* would pay the scribe, while the rest would go into his own treasury. The honors accorded to the Egyptian *nagid* were similar to those of the exilarch. Thus, the reading of the weekly portion of the Torah would be preceded by an introductory recital in honor of the *nagid*, in which he was mentioned by name. Special *Yizkor* (i.e., memorial) *piyyutim* were composed to commemorate departed *negidim*. The conquest of Palestine by Saladin (1187) created the need for the appointment of a separate leadership for Jewish communities of Palestine and Syria, and the office of *nagid* of "Ereẓ Israel and Judah" was created. The names of two such *negidim* are known, both of whom served in the 13th century; Obadiah b. 'Ulah and Hillel b. Moses. Under Mamluk rule, Palestine had a deputy *nagid*, who was under the authority of the *nagid* of Egypt. As a rule the Egyptian *negidim* were chosen from local Jewish leaders. The last two *negidim* appointed under Mamluk rule, however, were from a family of Maghreb *ḥakhamim*: Nathan (or Jonathan) *Sholal, *nagid* from 1484 to 1502, who went from Algeria to Palestine but then moved to Egypt, and his nephew Isaac *Sholal, who was director of the Egyptian mint. Isaac founded a yeshiva in Jerusalem and attended to the needs of the city's scholars. In 1509 he and his *bet din* enacted an ordinance exempting religious scholars from all taxes, except for the poll tax. He was deposed from his office in 1517, when Egypt was taken over by the Ottomans, and died in 1524. Under Ottoman rule, two more *negidim* were appointed in Egypt: Abraham *Castro, who was also the director of the Egyptian mint, and Jacob b. Ḥayyim *Talmid, who was sent from *Istanbul to Egypt in order to take up the post. According to a report by Joseph *Sambari (Neubauer, Chronicles, 1 (1887), 116–7), Jacob Talmid became involved in a controversy with Bezalel *Ashkenazi, whereupon the Egyptian governor decided to abolish the office of *nagid* in Egypt. Henceforth, it was the *ḥakham* (chief rabbi) who acted as the representative of Egyptian Jewry before the authorities.

Yemen

The existence of the office of *nagid* in Yemen may be deduced from fragmentary information contained in letters found in the *Genizah* and from inscriptions on Yemenite tombstones, both sources dating from the end of the 11th up to the beginning of the 14th centuries. The first *nagid* of whom there is knowledge was Japheth (Hasan) b. Bendar, apparently of Persian origin, who in a document dating from 1097 is referred to as a "prince of the communities." He and his descendants were residents of *Aden, were clerks for merchants, and dealt in the trade with India; they exercised some measure of control over the trade routes and the price of the transit goods which passed through Yemen on their way to Egypt. Japheth's son, Maḍmun, mentioned in letters from the period 1132–51, was granted the title of "*nagid* of the Land of Yemen" by the exilarch; he also maintained contact with the gaon Maẓliaḥ *ha-Kohen from Egypt and received an honorary title from him (in addition to six other titles of honor that he bore). In an official report of the *bet din* he is described as "appointed by the exilarchs and heads of the *yeshivot* over all of Israel and acknowledged by the respective rulers in the lands of the sea and of the desert"; the latter passage seems to imply that Maḍmun had agreements with the pirate chiefs who controlled the sea routes. His son Ḥalfon inherited the title of *nagid* and served from 1152 to 1172. During his lifetime there were two other *negidim*, R. Nethanel *al-Fayyumi (d. after 1164) and his son Jacob b. Nethanel *al-Fayyumi, who was in charge of the communities in central Yemen; the latter received Maimonides' famous *Iggeret Teiman*. There are reports of another *nagid* by the name of Maḍmun (he may be identical with Shemariah b. David), who served from 1202 to 1218. Three *negidim* are known from the first half of the 13th century: Maḍmun (apparently a descendant of the first Maḍmun mentioned above) and his sons, Ḥalfon and Joshua. The title of *nagid* was also held by David b. Amram *Adani, author of *Ha-Midrash ha-Gadol*, who lived at the end of the 13th and the beginning of the 14th centuries, and may have been a descendant of the Maḍmun family.

North Africa

In the Jewish communities of the Maghreb from the 16th to the 19th centuries the office of *nagid* was held either by prominent Jewish merchants or Jews who had close contacts at the ruler's court and served as interpreters and diplomatic agents. In rabbinic literature of the time, they are referred to as *nagid me'ulleh* ("most excellent *nagid*") or *nasi*. They differed from the medieval *negidim* in that they served only a single community, rather than a whole country, and were really *rashei kahal*. Some of them, however, extended their influence beyond the confines of their own community. They were elected by the prominent members of the community and in some cases also received an appointment from the Muslim ruler. They participated in the drafting of community statutes, and were authorized to impose corporal punishment and fines and report to the Muslim authorities any person violating community regulations. The *negidim* are frequently mentioned in the "Statutes of Fez" (*Kerem Ḥemed*, 2, 1871). In the 18th century their official title in Algeria was *muqaddam*, while in Tunisia and Tripolitania it was *qā'id*.

BIBLIOGRAPHY: SPAIN: Dinur, Golah, 3 (1961²), 128–68; H. Schirmann, in: *Zion*, 1 (1936), 261–83, 357–76; idem, in: JSS, 13 (1951), 99–126; Ashtor, Korot, 1 (1966²), 103–51; 2 (1966), 26–117. KAIROUAN: J. Mann, in: JQR, 11 (1920–21), 429–32; Hirschberg, in: *Zion*, 23–24 (1958–59), 116–73; 25 (1960), 62; Hirschberg, Afrikah, 1 (1965), 152–61; S.D. Goitein, in: *Zion*, 27 (1962), 11–13, 156–65; idem, in: *Tarbiz*, 34 (1965), 162–82. EGYPT: A. Neubauer, in: JQR, 8 (1896), 551–5; E.N. Adler, *ibid.*, 9 (1897), 712–20; D. Kaufman, *ibid.*, 10 (1898), 162–4; R.J.H. Gottheil, *ibid.*, 19 (1907), 500f., 528–32; Mann, Egypt, index; J. Mann, in: HUCA, 3 (1926), 303–5; A.N. Pollack, in: *Zion*, 1 (1936), 24–36; S. Assaf, *ibid.*, 256–7; idem, *Mekorot u-Meḥkarim* (1946), 186–99; D. Neustadt, in: *Zion*, 4 (1939), 126–49; 11 (1946), 147–8; D.Z. Baneth, in: *Sefer ha-Yovel li-Khevod… A. Marx* (1950), 75–87; Ashtor, Toledot, 2 (1951), 28–30, 237–58, 448–54; E. Ashtor, in: *Zion*, 30 (1965), 139–47; S.D. Goitein, *Sidrei Ḥinnukh* (1962), index; idem, in: JQR, 53 (1962–63), 93–119; idem, in: *Tarbiz*, 34 (1965), 232–56; B. Lewis, in: *Bulletin of the School of Oriental and African Studies*, 30 (1967), 177–81. YEMEN: J. Mann, in: HUCA, 3 (1926), 301–3; E. Strauss (Ashtor), in: *Zion*, 4 (1939), 217–37; Maimonides, *Iggeret Teiman*, ed. by A.S. Halkin (1952), Heb. introd., viii; Goitein, in: *Sinai*, 33 (1953), 225–37; idem, in: *Bo'i Teiman*, ed. by Y. Ratzaby (1967), 15–25. NORTH AFRICA: J.M. Toledano, *Ner ha-Ma'arav* (1911), 80, no. 25; G. Vajda, *Un recueil de textes historiques judéo-marocains* (1951), index s.v. *Nagid*; Hirschberg, Afrikah, index, s.v. *Muqaddam, Negidim, Kaid*. **ADD. BIBLIOGRAPHY:** KAIROUAN: M. Ben-Sasson, *The Emergence of the Local Jewish Community in the Muslim World* (1996), 347–77 (Hebrew). EGYPT: S.D. Goitein, *A Mediterranean Society*, vol. II (1971), 23–40; M.R. Cohen, *Jewish Self-Government in Medieval Egypt* (1980); M. Gil, *A History of Palestine, 634–1099* (1992), pars. 809–11; S. Sela, "*Rashut ha-Yehudim*," in: *Mas'at Moshe* (1998), 256–81; idem, "The Head of the Rabbanite, Karaite and Samaritan Jews," in: BSOAS, 57 (1995), 255–67; E. Bareket, *Fustat on the Nile; The Jewish Elite in Medieval Egypt* (1999), 23–25; E. Bareket, "*Rosh ha-Yehudim taḥat Shilton ha-Fatimim*," in: *Zemanim*, 64 (1998), 34–44.

[Eliezer Bashan (Sternberg) / Elinoar Bareket (2nd ed.)]

NAGIN, HARRY S. (1890–), U.S. civil engineer. Born in Romny, Russia, Nagin went to the U.S. in 1906. From 1924 he was executive vice president of a large steel products company in Pennsylvania. He took out over a hundred patents on steel structures, bridge floors, gratings, concrete, and plastics.

NAGLER, ISADORE (1895–1959), U.S. labor leader. Born in Austria, Nagler went to the United States in 1909 and worked as a cutter, joining Local 10 of the Cutters' Union. In 1920 he was made an official of the International Ladies Garment Workers Union (ILGWU) and was a prominent anti-communist. He became vice president of the ILGWU in 1929 and worked closely with the union president, Benjamin *Schlesinger and his successor David *Dubinsky. Nagler was general manager of the Joint Board of the Cloakmakers Union from 1928 to 1939 and was one of the founders of the American Labor Party (ALP). In 1944 he left the Labor Party with Dubinsky in protest against its pro-communist line and helped found the Liberal Party in which he was a prominent figure. He was prominent in the New York Jewish Education Committee, the Federation of Jewish Philanthropic Societies, and *ORT.

BIBLIOGRAPHY: H. Haskel, *A Leader of the Garment Workers* (1950), incl. bibl.

[Melvyn Dubofsky]

NAGY, ENDRE (1877–1938), Hungarian author and stage manager. Some of Nagy's early stories had Jewish themes, but he later converted to Christianity. He was founder and manager of Hungary's first political cabaret, to which he contributed topical commentaries. Two of his more important works were *A kaberé regénye* ("The Story of the Cabaret," 1935) and *Várad-Pest-Párizs* (1958).

°NAGYBACZONI-NAGY, VILMOS (1884–1976), Hungarian general and minister of defense. In 1942 Nagybaczoni-Nagy was appointed minister of defense. At that time Jews were excluded from the Hungarian army and were drafted into the labor service. Their situation was at times intolerable, particularly at the Russian front. When Nagybaczoni-Nagy assumed office, he reviewed the labor battalions at the front and immediately ordered an improvement in their conditions. Claiming that labor service was the same as military service, he abolished the discriminations against Jewish draftees and their families, then in force through anti-Jewish legislation. He ordered officers and commanders "when dealing with Jews to refrain from showing their personal feelings, and not to increase work norms and discipline by unlawful means." Nagybaczoni-Nagy expressly forbade attacking or humiliating Jews in public. He was concerned with the release of the sick and invalids, with healthy and sufficient food, a daily eight-hour rest, and with the personal cleanliness of the members of the labor battalions. In addition, he gave his attention to the religious needs of the draftees, e.g., the keeping of the Jewish festivals, as well as allotting sufficient time for donning the phylacteries. Nagybaczoni-Nagy did not hesitate to put on trial officers and commanders who behaved with cruelty.

Following repeated pressure by the Arrow Cross opposition in the Hungarian parliament, Nagybaczoni-Nagy was forced to resign. After the German occupation of Hungary (March 19, 1944) Nagybaczoni-Nagy was arrested and deported to Germany. His memoirs for the years 1939–44 were published in 1946 under the title *Végzetes esztendők* ("Crucial Years"). In 1967 Nagybaczoni-Nagy was recognized by *Yad Vashem as one of the *Righteous of the Nations.

BIBLIOGRAPHY: E. Karsai (ed.), *Fegyvertelen álltak az aknamezőkön*, 2 vols. (1962).

[Baruch Yaron]

NAGYKANIZSA, city in S. Hungary. It is almost certain that Jews were living in Nagykanizsa in 1710, and by 1745 the community owned a synagogue. The first inscription in the register of the *ḥevra kaddisha* dates from 1782. The community was officially established in 1786 and the new *bet midrash* was erected in 1805. The community of Nagykanizsa was among the first to join the *Reform movement, although only after bitter disputes. In 1829 it adopted the ritual of the famous composer S. *Sulzer (which was identical with the traditional ritual) and introduced an ensemble of ten violinists to accompany the choir during all services except those of the New Year and the Day of Atonement. In 1845 an organ was also introduced, the first case of its kind in the service of a Hungarian Jewish community. Noteworthy Orthodox rabbis of the community were H. Torai (1776–92) and Meir Szántó (until 1831). The first rabbi belonging to the Reform movement was L. *Loew (1841–46). He was succeeded by H.B. Fassel (1851–83) and E. Neumann (1883–1918). The latter was the only Hungarian rabbi to incorporate some of the ritual reforms suggested by A. *Geiger. The last rabbi of the community, E. Winkler (1919–44), who reintroduced the traditional ritual, accompanied his community to Auschwitz. He died in Melk (1945).

In the first Jewish school (1786–1809), opened following the reforms of Joseph II, the language of instruction was German. In 1832 Jewish education was offered in the Hungarian language. A pre-secondary school was opened in 1867, which offered courses in natural sciences as well as religious matters. In 1891–92 it was converted into a secondary commercial school (the only Jewish school of its kind in Hungary) which functioned until 1933. In addition, a general pre-secondary school was opened in 1890. The Jews of Nagykanizsa played an important role in the industrial and commercial development of the town during the first years of the 20th century. The golden era of the community lasted from 1863 to 1902 under the community presidents of the Guttman family who received the title Baron. The leading charitable institutions were the *ḥevra kaddisha* (founded in 1782), whose beautiful *pinkas* has been preserved in the Jewish Museum of Budapest, the Jewish Hospital (founded in 1832), and the women's organization (1843). The population rose from 500 in 1782 to 1,000 in 1830, 2,875 in 1880, 3,378 in 1910, and 3,663 in 1920. After the German occupation (March 19, 1944), Jewish males between the ages of 16 and 60 became the first Jews of Hungary to be deported to Auschwitz, on April 29. The rest were sent to Auschwitz on June 3–4. Only 300 returned in 1945. In 1970, 100 Jews were living in Nagykanizsa.

BIBLIOGRAPHY: H. Villányi, in: L. Barbarits, *Nagykanizsa* (1929), 251–62; E. László, in: R.L. Braham (ed.), *Hungarian Jewish Studies*, 1 (1966), 61–136, incl. bibl. and notes.

[Jeno Zsoldos]

NAḤAL (Heb. נח"ל, *Noar Ḥalutzi Loḥem*; Fighting Pioneer Youth), in its classic form a regular unit of the Israel Defense Forces whose soldiers were organized in *garinim* ("groups") of pioneering youth movements in Israel and Zionist youth movements in the Diaspora that educated their members toward cooperative settlement in Israel. During their term of military service, these soldiers simultaneously participated in intensive training and social and ideological preparation toward their future as members of cooperative agricultural settlements. Naḥal had two aims: to produce first-class soldiers and to prepare *garinim* for establishing new settlements or joining existing ones. All members of such a potential group were mobilized together, form a single army unit, and together underwent training. Training consisted of initial military training (at a Naḥal army camp) which was combined with ideological and social activities. There was then a period of combined agricultural and military training in a kibbutz or at a Naḥal outpost. Advanced military training in paratroop, tank, artillery, engineering, or other units followed for the men, while the girls went to live in their destined settlement where they were later joined by the men. The group then served for a period of *shalat* (*sherut le-lo tashlum*, "unpaid service").

The Naḥal outpost was a typical army camp with military ranks and discipline, but at the same time preparations were made for a civilian agricultural settlement. During the first 20 years of its existence, Naḥal founded 36 outposts, of which 22 became permanent settlements. Another 18 settlements were founded or refounded by soldiers who once served in Naḥal; in a further 70 settlements, Naḥal soldiers constituted half the membership, while in hundreds of other kibbutzim and moshavim there were smaller groups of ex-Naḥal soldiers. It has been found that four years after mobilization (i.e., a year after completing Naḥal), about a third of the soldiers remained on the land and, of these, about half (that is 15% of those who were originally members of the group), stayed in their settlements after 15 and 20 years.

Naḥal was sometimes employed on special projects. For example, in 1949 it built a road to En-Gedi along the west bank of the Dead Sea. In the early 1950s it organized large-scale vegetable production. In the 1960s it employed its soldiers to teach reading and writing to both young and adult illiterates in development towns. Other countries showed interest in Naḥal methods, and courses for Naḥal instructors were organized in Israel for countries in Asia, Africa, and South America. Many Israelis were employed as instructors in training similar groups in developing countries.

In the 1980s, Naḥal changed its character. The name Naḥal is now used for two different army units: the Naḥal Command working under the Education Corps and responsible for the *garin* activity; and the Naḥal brigade, which is a regular infantry brigade and part of the Central Command. It includes the Naḥal *haredi* battalion for ultra-Orthodox soldiers. The Naḥal *garinim* focus on educational activity in civilian communities.

BIBLIOGRAPHY: G. Levitas, *Naḥal – Israel's Pioneer Fighting Youth* (1967); Ministry of Defense, Israel, *Naḥal* (1970).

[Yehuda Schuster / Shaked Gilboa (2nd ed.)]

NAHALAL or **NAHALOL** (Heb. נַהֲלָל, נַהֲלֹל).

(1) Town in the territory of the tribe of Zebulun, along with Shimron and Beth-Lehem (Josh. 19:15, 21:35). The Israelites were apparently unable to dispossess the Canaanites from Nahalol (Judg. 1:30). Later, probably in the days of David, it became a levitical city belonging to the family of Merari (Josh. 21:35). In the Talmud (TJ, Meg. 1:1, 70a), it is identified with Mahalol, which corresponds to the present-day Arab village of Maʿlūl southwest of Nazareth; the remains that can be found there are of the Roman period only and include a mausoleum (Qaṣr al-Deir). The site of Nahalal proper is still in dispute.

[Michael Avi Yonah]

(2) The first moshav ovedim in Ereẓ Israel. It was founded in 1921 in the western Jezreel Valley by veteran pioneers of the Second *Aliyah, some of whom had been members of the first kevuẓah, *Deganyah. The 80 settling families each received 25 acres (100 dunams) of land, and they drained the malarial swamps. (Malaria had prevented two previous attempts at settlement, one by Arabs and one by Germans.) In the 1920s, the first farm branches – field crops, cattle, and poultry – were developed and concrete stables built, while the settlers lived in wooden huts for 15 years. The village layout, devised by the architect Richard *Kauffmann, became the pattern for many of the moshavim established before 1948; it is based on concentric circles, with the public buildings (school, administrative, and cultural buildings, cooperative shops, and warehouses) at the center, the homesteads in the innermost circle, the farm buildings in the next, and beyond it ever wider circles of gardens and fields. In 1929 a Girls' Agricultural Training Farm was established at Nahalal by *WIZO; it was headed by Hannah Maisel-Shoḥat, wife of Eliezer *Shoḥat. In the 1940s it became a coeducational farming school of *Youth Aliyah. Nahalal is one of the principal centers of the Tenu'at ha-Moshavim. More water became available in the 1930s from the *Mekorot regional network and deep wells were drilled in the vicinity. Farming then became more intensive, fruit orchards were added, and existing branches expanded. In 1969 Nahalal, including the agricultural school, had 1,020 inhabitants. By the mid-1990s its population had grown to 1,240, but in 2002 it was down to 925, with 350 resident farmers, 165 permanent non-farming residents, 100 school employees, and the rest temporary residents. The main farming branches were dairy cattle, poultry, fruit orchards, flowers, and field crops.

[Efraim Orni / Shaked Gilboa (2nd ed.)]

BIBLIOGRAPHY: Albright, in: AASOR, 2/3 (1923), 26; Aharoni, Land, index; EM, s.v. (incl. bibl.). **WEBSITE:** www.nahalal.org.il.

NAḤALAT YEHUDAH (Heb. נַחֲלַת יְהוּדָה), urban community with municipal council status, on the Coastal Plain of Israel near Rishon le-Zion, founded in 1914 as a moshavah by members of the Ḥibbat Zion movement of Russia. Naḥalat Yehudah was characterized by auxiliary farmsteads whose owners were employed in Rishon le-Zion or in Jaffa and Tel Aviv. After 1948 an immigrant camp (*ma'barah*) was established in Naḥalat Yehudah's municipal area, increasing its population to over 5,000. The new immigrants were later given permanent housing in other localities, so that the population decreased to 2,350 (1969). Although a number of industrial enterprises existed in Naḥalat Yehudah, many inhabitants were employed in other communities in the Tel Aviv conurbation. Subsequently Naḥalat Yehudah became part of Rishon le-Zion and its name was given to a *WIZO youth village accommodating approximately 300 students. The youth village had originally been founded in 1922 as a workers farm training women in various farm branches. After the establishment of the State of Israel it became an agriculture high school with a dormitory. The name Naḥalat Yehudah commemorates Judah Leib *Pinsker.

WEBSITE: www.nachlat.org.il.

[Efraim Orni / Shaked Gilboa (2nd ed.)]

NAḤAL OZ (Heb. נַחַל עֹז), kibbutz in southern Israel, established in 1951 as a border settlement by a *Naḥal group near the Gaza Strip, affiliated with Iḥud ha-Kevuẓot ve-ha-Kibbutzim. Later, pioneers from South America and other countries joined the kibbutz. Before the *Sinai Campaign (1956), and in the days before the *Six-Day War (1967), Naḥal Oz was frequently a target for attacks and shelling from beyond the Gaza Strip border. After June 1967, a point near the kibbutz became an entrance gate to the Strip. The kibbutz economy was based on intensive farming (field crops, dairy cattle, and poultry) and a hi-tech enterprise in the field of video communications. In 1997–98 the kibbutz began going over to a private wage economy. This was accompanied by a great crisis causing many residents to leave the kibbutz and the population to drop from 495 in the mid-1990s to 288 in 2002. The name Naḥal Oz points both to the original Naḥal outpost, and to nearby Gaza (whose Hebrew name, Azzah, is derived from the same root as *oz*, meaning "strength").

WEBSITE: www.sng.org.il/meida/yeshuvim/nahal-oz.htm.

[Efraim Orni / Shaked Gilboa (2nd ed.)]

NAHARIN, OHAD (1952–), Israeli dancer and choreographer. He was born in Israel on kibbutz Mizra, and grew up in the town of Tivon, near Haifa; he is the son of artistic parents who were involved in music and theater.

Naharin started professional dance training after he finished his army service. After a year of training with the *Batsheva Dance Company, he performed in *The Dream* (1974) and was asked to stay on with the troupe for another year. He then studied for a year at Juilliard in its Professional Studies Program. He danced for a year with Maurice Béjart's Ballet of the 20th Century and moved to New York. He married Mari Kajiwara, the Japanese-American dancer who danced in the Alvin Ailey Company. His dance creations are performed by the top dance companies of the world. Naharin's first work as choreographer was *Haru No Umi* (1980). In New York he founded the Ohad Naharin Dance Company, which toured worldwide. In 1990, he was appointed the artistic director of the Batsheva Dance Company. His choreography challenges visually and excites the senses. "If you could hold one of Ohad Naharin's dances in your hand, it would feel smooth. Think of a polished stone, it looks like a piece of secret sculpture, but hurl it and it becomes a weapon" (Deborah Jowitt, *Village Voice*, New York). His works include: *Black Milk* (1986), *Tabula Rasa* (1987), *Sinking of the Titanic* (1990), *Kyr* (1990), *King of Wara* (1990), *Anaphase* (1993), and *Mamootot* (2003). In his work *Playback* (2004), performed in Eilat, he appeared as dancer, singer, and instrumentalist. Naharin won the Israel Prize for dance of 2005.

[Ruth Eshel (2nd ed.)]

NAHARIYYAH (Heb. נַהֲרִיָּה), city in N. Israel, 6 mi. (10 km.) N. of Acre. Nahariyyah was founded in 1934 as a village (moshavah) by a group of middle-class immigrants from Germany. Their company, headed by the engineer Yosef Levi, bought the land, and thus gained the first Jewish foothold in the Acre Plain and Western Galilee. The settlers encountered difficulties in changing over to farming from their previous occupations in commerce and the professions. They also found themselves in an endangered and isolated position when the 1936–39 Arab riots broke out. By then beginnings were made to turn Nahariyyah into a seaside resort, in addition to developing agriculture. The population, with about 1,000 in 1941, increased to 1,400 in 1945 when manufacturing, particularly in the food branch, first began. In the years just prior to statehood, Nahariyyah served as a landing place for "illegal" immigrant ships. In the War of Independence (1948), Nahariyyah, together with ten other Jewish settlements in Western Galilee founded in the preceding decade, was completely cut off by Arab Acre, and only intermittently were communications with Haifa maintained by means of small motor boats going to Haifa. With the capture of Acre by Israel forces, Nahariyyah was able to resume contact with the rest of the country and was included in the State of Israel. Numerous immigrants from various countries, mainly from Romania, North Africa, and Iraq settled there. The population grew from 9,200 in 1953 to 20,700 in 1968, 37,100 in the mid-1990s, and 47,400 in 2002, occupying a municipal area of about 4 sq. mi. (10 sq. km.). The city's economy was based on tourism and recreation, industry, farming, trade, and services. In 1968 the city had over 30 hotels and pensions with a total capacity for 1,400 tourists. On the bathing beach a breakwater was built creating two bays, for swimming and for sailboats. There were also swimming pools. Farming was mostly for specialized export crops (strawberries, avocados, flowers). Local industry included textiles, asbestos cement, metal instruments, electrical appliances, fine mechanics, paper products, agricultural machinery, etc. A new industrial zone for large enterprises was added in the north to supplement the older industrial zone near the railroad station. The commercial center was laid out along the central avenue on both sides of the Ga'aton Stream. The hotel zone stretched mainly along the beach and the city had 21 public parks and ornamental gardens. At the turn of the 20th century, residents earned their living in industry (45%), services (40%), tourism (11%), and agriculture (4%). The city's name is derived from *nahar* ("stream"), referring to the Ga'aton Stream which passes through part of the city.

WEBSITE: www.nahariya.muni.il.

[Efraim Orni / Shaked Gilboa (2nd ed.)]

NAHASH (Heb. נָחָשׁ; "snake"), king of the Ammonites, who enjoyed a long reign from the beginning of Saul's reign over Israel (I Sam. 11:1ff.) until some years after David was established at Jerusalem (II Sam. 10:1). Nahash is first mentioned when he encamped against Jabesh-Gilead and sought to subjugate it on most humiliating terms. The Jabeshites appealed for help to their fellow Israelites, and the crisis called forth Saul's latent capacity for leadership. He issued a call to the tribes to rally behind him and march to the relief of Jabesh-Gilead; and the force that responded inflicted a stunning defeat on the Ammonites (I Sam. 11:1ff.). Nothing more is related about Nahash until the notice of his death, where the Bible states that he had shown kindness to David (II Sam. 10:2). It is likely that he was friendly toward David because David was also an opponent of Saul. David attacked Nahash's son and successor Hanun and reduced the Ammonites to dependency. Shobi, another son of Nahash, who was one of those who befriended David at Mahanaim during Absalom's rebellion, may later have been reigning over the Ammonites as David's vassal. Nahash, according to II Samuel 17:25, was the father of David's sister Abigail. Since David's father was Jesse, this would imply that David and his sister had only one parent in common – their mother, the tracing of their relationship through their mother being a characteristic of a beena marriage. The Nahash referred to in this verse might be Nahash king of the Ammonites, which would be an additional reason for the latter's friendliness toward David. It has been suggested, however, that there is a corruption in the text, and Nahash intruded into this verse from verse 27. According to this, "daughter of Nahash" is to be emended to read, with the Septuagint, "daughter of Jesse."

BIBLIOGRAPHY: Noth, Personennamen 230; J. Morgenstern, in: ZAW, 47 (1929), 91–110; 49 (1931), 46–58.

NAH'ĀWENDĪ (Nahāwandī), BENJAMIN BEN MOSES AL- (mid-ninth century), *Karaite scholar, surnamed after the city of *Nehāvand (Nahavand, Nihavand), in Persia. He probably lived in Persia or Iraq, since Karaite settlement in Palestine, particularly in Jerusalem, did not begin until after Nah'āwendī's death. In the official Karaite memorial prayer he is ranked next to *Anan's son Saul, and in medieval Arabic accounts the Karaites as a group are sometimes referred to as "the followers of Anan and Benjamin." Al-*Kirkisānī, who lived a century later and whose information is usually highly reliable, states that Nah'āwendī was "learned in the lore of the Rabbanites and strong in Scripture, and served for many years as a judge." Karaite tradition regards Nah'āwendī as the person who established early Karaite teaching on a firm footing by purging it of Anan's supposedly excessive leaning toward Rabbanite doctrines. It is true that Nah'āwendī disagreed with Anan on many points of law, but at the same time he appears to have been rather tolerant; he not only had no objection to adopting Rabbanite legal ordinances, including some which have no direct support in Scripture, but is even said to have declared that every person may be guided in legal matters by his own judgment and is not obliged to submit to the decisions of commonly acknowledged authorities. On the other hand, later Karaites rejected some of Nah'āwendī's views, particularly his theory that the world was not created immediately by God, but that God created an angel who, in turn, created the world. Further, he was of the opinion that the Law was revealed by an angel, not by God, and the prophets received their prophecy from an angel. The purpose of this theory was to refer all the anthropomorphic passages in Scripture, or those which might be contrary to pure monotheism, to this angel-creator, and not to God Himself. This theory presumably represents an adaptation of a Gnostic idea, subsequently modified into the Philonic-Christian doctrine of the *logos (creative word). Nah'āwendī's borrowings from Rabbanite law seem to testify to his realization that the cry "Back to the Bible!" raised by Anan and earlier pre-Karaite schismatics, while tactically useful for their purpose of basing their laws solely on the Bible, was impractical, since biblical legislation alone could not efficiently govern the Karaites' social and economic life a thousand years later, in the vastly different conditions prevailing in the Muhammadan empire. Hence he was forced to provide guidance for his coreligionists (probably out of his own experience as a practicing judge) in such matters as identification of witnesses, loans, agency, conjugal property rights, revokable gifts, and inheritance and wills, for which Scripture supplies only vague guide rules or none at all. Unlike Anan, who wrote (so far as is known) only in Aramaic, and unlike his own successors who wrote in Arabic, Nah'āwendī wrote (again, so far as is known) in clear and fluent Hebrew, sharply distinct from the stilted Hebrew of later Karaite scholars and translators in the Byzantine Empire. His legal works comprise *Sefer Mitzvot* ("Book of Precepts") and *Sefer Dinim* ("Book of Rules"), both presumably parts of a comprehensive code of Karaite law. The *Sefer Dinim*, dealing with civil and criminal law, was published by A. Firkovich under the title *Masat Binyamin* (1835); extracts in English translation are found in L. Nemoy, *Karaite Anthology* (1952). Fragments, presumably of the *Sefer Mitzvot*, were published by A. Harkavy (*Studien und Mittheilungen*, 8 (1903), 175–84).

Nah'āwendī also wrote commentaries on some of the books of the Bible (the Pentateuch, Isaiah, Song of Songs, Ecclesiastes, Daniel), which were highly regarded even by an authority like Abraham ibn Ezra. The colophon of the *Sefer Dinim* contains the earliest-known occurrence of the term "Karaites."

BIBLIOGRAPHY: Baron, Social², 5 (1957), 223–6; H. Wolfson, in: JQR, 51 (1960–61), 89–106; Guttmann, Philosophies, 58–59.

[Leon Nemoy]

NAḤMAN BAR RAV HUNA (first half of the fifth century C.E.), Babylonian *amora*. According to the letter of Sherira Gaon (ed. by B.M. Lewin (1921), 94f.), during 452–55 Naḥman was head of the academy in Mata Meḥasya which had been revived by Ashi, succeeding Idi b. Avin, Ashi's successor. According to Halevy, the *amora* Naḥman mentioned in the Babylonian Talmud as a contemporary of Ravina and Ashi (Er. 27a; Ket. 7a; Kid. 6b; et al.) is the same person. Halevy suggests that he was the brother of the younger Ravina who was considered by some scholars to have completed the editing of the Babylonian Talmud, since, according to Sherira, the father of Ravina was also Huna, but this is refuted by S. and Ḥ. Albeck (see bibl.).

BIBLIOGRAPHY: Hyman, Toledot, 940f.; Halevy, Dorot, 3 (1923), 91–93; S. Albeck, in: *Sinai – Sefer Yovel* (1958), 70f.; Ḥ. Albeck, *Mavo la-Talmudim* (1969), 434.

[David Joseph Bornstein]

NAḤMAN BEN ISAAC (d. c. 356), Babylonian *amora*. His mother was the sister of Aḥa b. Joseph (Shab. 140a). Naḥman studied under his uncle Aḥa, who because of his age leaned upon Naḥman's shoulder and was led by him (Shab. 140a). He is referred to as having waited upon a Mar Samuel (Beẓah 25b). According to R.N. Rabbinovicz, however (*Dikdukei Soferim*, ad loc.), the reference is to Simeon b. Abba and the great *amora* Samuel of a previous generation. He was the head of the **kallah* in the academy of Rava where he was friendly with Adda b. Abba, with whom he attended Rava's discourses (BB 22a). He also taught in Drukeret (Shab. 94b), where he went at the invitation of Naḥman b. Ḥisda (Ta'an. 21b) and assisted him in his teaching (BB 8a), defending him several times against the criticism of Rava (Ket. 63b; Shevu. 12b; Ḥul. 88b). It is probable that he was active in Drukeret before his appointment with Rava. After Rava's death in 352 Naḥman joined the academy of Pumbedita which, since the death of Abbaye in 338, had been combined with Rava's school in Maḥoza, and held this post for the last four years of his life.

Naḥman b. Isaac is frequently quoted in the Babylonian Talmud (the occurrence of his name in the Jerusalem Talmud – BK 9:1; BB 3:3; et al. – is a mistake for Naḥman b. Jacob). Naḥman continually stressed the need for assembling and arranging the material taught, as in Pes. 105a–b, where he calls himself *sadrana*, an arranger of tradition (cf. Epstein, *Introduction*, 432; E.S. Rosenthal, *Pesaḥ Rishon*, 254). As a result he paid careful attention to the correct name of the transmitters of teachings (Pes. 107a; Kid. 44a) and also made frequent use of mnemonic formulae (Shab. 60b; Ta'an. 10a; et al.). He devoted himself to biblical study and was well versed in the *masorah* (Shab. 28b, 55b; Yoma 75b; et al.), often using it to arrive at the correct text of the Mishnah (Shab. 77a; Beẓah 35b; BK 60a).

The Talmud relates that his mother was told by astrologers when she was pregnant that her son would be a thief, so she watched over him from his childhood, taking care he should always go about with his head covered in order to make him conscious of the fear of Heaven. One day he was sitting and studying under a palm tree when temptation overcame him, and climbing up he bit off some of the dates. He then realized why his mother insisted on his keeping his head covered. This is one of the talmudic sources for keeping the head covered (*ibid.*; see *Head, Covering of the). It is also told that since Naḥman's father was not a scholar, Naḥman showed greater honor to his friend Naḥman, son of the leading *amora* Ḥisda, than he would permit his namesake to show him (Ta'an. 21b). Among his colleagues were Mar son of Ravina (Shab. 61a, 108a), Papa, and Ḥuna son of Joshua (BB 22a). He died in Pumbedita.

BIBLIOGRAPHY: Halevy, Dorot, 2 (1923), 499–502; S. Albeck, *Mishpeḥot Soferim* (1903), 181ff.; Hyman, Toledot, 941–5; Ḥ. Albeck, *Mavo la-Talmudim* (1969), 371f. **ADD. BIBLIOGRAPHY:** E.S. Rosenthal, "The Redaction of Pesaḥ Rishon" (Ph.D. diss., 1959), 222–96.

[David Joseph Bornstein / Stephen G. Wald (2nd ed.)]

NAḤMAN BEN JACOB (usually referred to without patronymic; d. c. 320 C.E.), Babylonian *amora* and a leading personality of his time. Born in Nehardea, where his father was a scribe of Samuel's *bet din* (BM 16b), Naḥman sometimes quotes his father's teachings (Beẓah 26a; Zev. 56a). Naḥman may have studied under Samuel, since he transmits teachings in his name (Ber. 27b; Shab. 57b) and refers to him as *rabbenu* ("our master"; Ber. 38b, Er. 16b); but if so he must have then been very young, since Samuel died in 254. Naḥman also transmits sayings in the names of Rav (Er. 72b; Pes. 13a), Adda b. Ahavah (BK 24a), Shila (Ber. 49b), and Isaac (Shab. 131b), with whom he was on close terms (Ta'an. 5a–6a). His main teacher, however, was Rabbah b. Avuha (Yev. 80b; Git. 72a) in whose name he frequently transmits statements (Ber. 36b; Shab. 17a). Rabbah b. Avuha wanted to give him his daughter in marriage (Yev. 80b), although it is not clear whether this occurred. It is known that Naḥman ultimately married into the family of the exilarch (Ḥul. 124a) and in consequence was held in high esteem (Kid. 70a), and that his wife, *Yalta, had influence in the house of the exilarch (Rashi to Git. 67b). When Nehardea was destroyed in 259 by Odenathus, Naḥman went to Shekanzib, but returned to Nehardea when it was rebuilt, teaching and serving as *dayyan* there (Er. 34b; Kid. 70a–b; BB 153a). There are many statements by him on both *halakhah* and *aggadah* in the Talmud, and his name is one of those most frequently mentioned in the Babylonian Talmud and also appears quite frequently in the Jerusalem Talmud. Huna held him equal to

Samuel as a judge in civil law (BK 96b), and Naḥman regarded himself as of sufficient standing to judge cases on his own (Sanh. 5a). In later generations it was laid down that in any dispute between Naḥman and a colleague, the former's opinion was to prevail (Ket. 13a; Kid. 59b). He often visited Sura (Suk. 14b; Ket. 94a) and frequently transmitted teachings in the name of Huna, who taught there (Pes. 40a), and with whom Naḥman frequently disputed (Er. 42a), referring to him as "our colleague Huna" (Git. 52b). An important contemporary was *Judah b. Ezekiel, the founder of the academy of Pumbedita; Naḥman often differed with him (BK 27b) but held him in high esteem (BM 66a). On one occasion he summoned Judah to court. Judah was advised by Huna to overlook the discourtesy, and he appeared. It was only then that Naḥman realized who the respondent was. Judah, however, plainly showed his irritation, whereupon Yalta advised her husband to settle the case quickly lest Judah make him appear an ignoramus (Kid. 70a–b). Other of his colleagues were Ammi (Ber. 47b) and Assi (Er. 32b), as well as Ḥiyya b. Abba *(ibid).* and R. Isaac of Palestine. Once, when parting from Naḥman, Isaac compared him to a rich shady fruit tree growing by the side of a stream, not lacking wealth, reputation, or honor, and said that he could only pray that each shoot taken from the parent tree should be the equal of the sire (Ta'an. 5b–6a). Among his pupils were Zera (RH 20b), Rabbah (Pes. 40a), Joseph (Yev. 66b) and Rava (Ber. 23b). Some of his aggadic sayings are: "When a woman is talking she is spinning" (a web to capture the male; Meg. 14b); "Haughtiness does not become a woman" (*ibid.*). There is definite mention of a number of his sons, Rabbah (Shab. 119a), Hon (Yev. 34b), Mar Zutra (BB 7a), and Ḥiyya (BB 46a). Naḥman is said to have had two daughters who were taken captive. R. Elesh, taken captive with them, wanted to take them with him when he was about to escape, but did not do so, on discovering that they practiced witchcraft (Git. 45a). On his deathbed Naḥman requested Rava, who was sitting by the bed, to pray to the angel of death to spare him a painful death. He later appeared to Rava in a dream and said that though his death was not painful, he would prefer not to face the fear of it again (MK 28a).

BIBLIOGRAPHY: Hyman, Toledot, 928–39; Frankel, Mevo, 116b; Halevy, Dorot, 2 (1923), 417–21; Bacher, Bab. Amor., 79–83; Ḥ. Albeck, *Mavo la-Talmudim* (1969), 298–301; Neusner, Babylonia, 3 (1968), index.

[David Joseph Bornstein]

NAḤMANIDES (**Moses b. Naḥman**, also known as **Naḥamani** and **RaMBaN** – an acronym of **R**abbi **M**oses **B**en **N**aḥman; 1194–1270), Spanish rabbi and scholar and one of the leading authors of talmudic literature in the Middle Ages; philosopher, kabbalist, biblical exegete, poet, and physician. Naḥmanides was born in Gerona, Catalonia, and it was after his native town that he was also referred to as Rabbenu Moses Gerondi or Yerondi. His Spanish name was Bonastrug da Porta. Naḥmanides was a descendant of Isaac b. Reuben, a contemporary of Isaac b. Jacob *Alfasi. His mother was the sister of Abraham, father of Jonah b. Abraham Gerondi. His teachers included *Judah b. Yakar, a disciple of *Isaac b. Abraham of Dampierre, who established his yeshivah in Barcelona, and *Meir b. Isaac of Trinquetaille. From the first, he received the tradition of the tosafists of northern France, while from the second he learned the methods of study employed in the yeshivot of Provence. He maintained close contact with Meir b. Todros ha-Levi Abulafia of Toledo who replied to his queries, and even more so with his cousin, Jonah b. Abraham of Gerona. His colleagues also included Samuel b. Isaac *Sardi, to whom he sent the largest number of his responsa, as well as *Isaac b. Abraham of Narbonne. The responsa of Solomon b. Abraham *Adret (part 1, 120, 167) relate that Naḥmanides earned his livelihood as a physician. Even though there is no information available on Naḥmanides' yeshivah in Gerona, there is no doubt that it existed. His disciples included the leading halakhists of the following generation, such as Solomon b. Abraham Adret, *Aaron b. Joseph ha-Levi, David Bonafed, Jonah b. Joseph, Naḥmanides' cousin, and many others. There is reason to believe that after the death of Jonah b. Abraham Gerondi in 1264, Naḥmanides acted as chief rabbi of Catalonia until his emigration to Ereẓ Israel. The Spanish rabbis of subsequent generations regarded him as their great teacher and referred to him as *ha-rav ha-ne'eman* ("the trustworthy rabbi"). In his *Nomologia*, Immanuel *Aboab states that throughout Spain it was the custom to refer to him simply as "the rabbi" or "the teacher."

When the *Maimonidean controversy broke out in *Montpellier in 1232, Naḥmanides attempted to find a compromise between the opposing camps, although he agreed with *Solomon b. Abraham of Montpellier and his followers in condemning the detrimental use which had been made of the works of Maimonides by the "philosophizers" to whom the study of secular sciences was a principal object. On the one hand, in the letters which he sent to the community leaders of Aragon, Navarre, and Castile, he sought to prevent them from taking measures against the extremists of Montpellier, while on the other hand, in his famous letter "Before I raise my voice, I err," he requested the rabbis of France that they annul the *ḥerem* which they had proclaimed against the writings of Maimonides. He argued that these were not intended for French Jewry, which was faithful to Jewish tradition, but for the Jews of the south (Provence and Spain), among whom philosophic culture had struck roots, with the objective of bringing them back to the path of the faithful. In order to avert a schism between the opposed communities and camps, he proposed a detailed program which would suit the varying conditions prevailing in France and Spain and would regulate the study of the various sciences according to the age of the students and the locality. Naḥmanides' program failed because the extremists in both camps gained the upper hand and he was isolated.

He exercised extensive influence over Jewish public life in Catalonia; even King James I (1213–1276) consulted him and in 1232, on the strength of Naḥmanides' opinion, rejected the claims of the *Alconstantini family to the position of *dayyan* over all the Jews of the kingdom. In 1263 King James coerced him into a public disputation in Barcelona with the apostate Pablo *Christiani. The disputation, which was held in July in the presence of the king and the leaders of the *Dominicans and the *Franciscans, was a victory for Naḥmanides, the king even presenting him with 300 dinars in appreciation of the manner in which he had stated his arguments. (For further details see *Barcelona, Disputation of.) At the request of the bishop of Gerona, Naḥmanides summarized his views in a book, apparently the *Sefer ha-Vikku'aḥ*, which is still extant. The Dominicans, who had initiated the disputation, did not remain inactive, and in April 1265 they called Naḥmanides to trial for his supposed abuses against Christianity. Before the tribunal Naḥmanides stated that his words had been spoken during the disputation after the king had promised him freedom of speech, and that he had written his work at the request of the bishop. The king thereupon succeeded in extricating Naḥmanides from the complications of the trial, which was postponed for an indefinite period. Dissatisfied, the Dominicans sought the aid of Pope *Clement IV, who sent a letter to the king of Aragon requesting him to penalize Naḥmanides for writing the above work. Naḥmanides barely succeeded in escaping from Spain and during the same year emigrated to Ereẓ Israel.

A prayer in the spirit of the Psalms, which Naḥmanides composed at sea while on his way to Ereẓ Israel, has been preserved. He arrived in *Acre during the summer of 1267 and on Elul 9 of that year he went to Jerusalem. In a letter to his son Naḥman, he described the ruined state of the city seven years after the invasion of the Tatar hordes. He found few Jews, "only two brothers, dyers who bought their dye from the governor and were joined by up to ten Jews in their home on Sabbaths for prayers." On his arrival in the town he organized the remnants of the Jewish community and erected a synagogue in a derelict house; it appears that he also founded a yeshivah. Reports of his activities circulated rapidly; many Jews streamed into Jerusalem. In 1268 Naḥmanides moved to Acre, where he became the spiritual leader of the Jewish community, in succession to *Jehiel b. Joseph of Paris. From this period a sermon which he delivered in the synagogue on Rosh Ha-Shanah in 1269 has been preserved. The site of his tomb has not been ascertained; some believe that he was buried at the foot of Mount Carmel; others that he was buried in Haifa, beside the tomb of Jehiel b. Joseph of Paris; while others say that he was interred in Acre. There is also a tradition that he was buried in Jerusalem, under the slope of the mountain near the village of Silwan, and another that his tomb is in Hebron.

Naḥmanides had three sons: Naḥman, to whom he sent the above-mentioned letter from Jerusalem; Solomon, who married the daughter of Jonah b. Abraham Gerondi; and Joseph, who was a favorite at the court of the king of Castile and owned an estate in *Valladolid. One of Naḥmanides' daughters married *Gershom b. Solomon, and their son was *Levi b. Gershom.

Works

About 50 of Naḥmanides' works have been preserved, in addition to many works which are doubtfully attributed to him. The majority of his works are novellae on the Talmud and *halakhah*. He also wrote books and letters connected with his public activities, including the *Sefer ha-Vikku'aḥ* already mentioned. He devoted a special work to the nature of the belief in Redemption, the *Sefer ha-Ge'ullah*, written in about 1263. He was also a gifted *paytan*, writing a number of poems and prayers, including a prayer which he composed on his entry into Jerusalem. Four of his sermons have been preserved: *Ha-Derashah la-Ḥatunnah*, dating from his youth; *Torat ha-Shem Temimah*, which he apparently delivered after the disputation of Barcelona; one on the Book of Ecclesiastes, which he delivered before his departure for Ereẓ Israel; and the sermon mentioned above, delivered in Acre on Rosh Ha-Shanah. All his works bear the imprint of his original personality, a synthesis of the culture of Spain and the piety of Germany, a talmudic education together with the teachings of Kabbalah, as well as a broad knowledge of sciences and Christian theological works. An edition of his works has been published by Ch. D. Chavel (see bibliography).

[Joseph Kaplan]

As Biblical Commentator

Naḥmanides wrote his commentary on the Torah in his old age. He composed the main part in Spain, but added to it after his arrival in Ereẓ Israel. In the introduction he states the purpose of his commentary: "To appease the minds of the students, weary through exile and trouble, when they read the portion on Sabbaths and festivals." It is an extensive commentary, both on the narrative and legislative part of the Bible. Unlike his most noted predecessors, *Rashi and Abraham *Ibn Ezra, who devoted themselves chiefly to the elucidation of individual words and verses, Naḥmanides, though he followed strict philological procedure when he deemed it necessary to establish the exact meaning of a word, concerns himself mainly with the sequence of the biblical passages and with the deeper meaning of the Bible's laws and narrative. He makes frequent use of the aggadic and halakhic interpretations of the talmudic and midrashic sages, but whereas Rashi quotes these without expressing his own opinions, Naḥmanides dwells on them at length, analyzes them critically, develops their ideas, and probes their compatibility with the biblical text.

The commentary of Naḥmanides is more than a mere commentary. It reflects his views on God, the Torah, Israel, and the world. The Torah is the word of God and is the source of all knowledge. The narratives of the Bible are not simple records of the past, but are portents of the future. The account of the six days of creation contains prophecies regarding the most important events of the succeeding 6,000 years, while the Sabbath foreshadows the seventh millennium which will be the Day of the Lord, and the accounts told about the patriarchs foreshadow the history of the Jewish people as a whole. Naḥmanides does not hesitate to criticize the patriarchs when their actions seem to him unjustifiable. According to him

(Gen. 12:11), Abraham "unintentionally committed a great sin," when, on coming to Egypt, he said out of fear for his life that his wife Sarah was his sister, for in this way he exposed her to moral corruption; rather, he should have had faith that God would save both him and his wife. Naḥmanides demonstrates great psychological insight when describing the behavior of biblical personalities. In the story of Joseph the Bible relates that "he fell on his neck and wept on his neck for a while" (Gen. 46:29). The question arises: Who wept? Jacob or Joseph? It is obvious who is more likely to weep at such a time, Naḥmanides says, the old father who finds his son alive after he had mourned for him as lost, not the son who has risen to become a king. Naḥmanides explains the laws in the light of halakhic tradition. He maintains that there is a reason for every commandment. The commandments are all for the good of man, either to keep from him something that is hurtful, to remove from him evil beliefs and habits, to teach him mercy and goodness, or to make him remember the miracles of the Lord and to know him. He explains some of the dietary laws in terms of health regulations; others he interprets as seeking to keep us from eating foods that dull the mind and harden the heart.

Naḥmanides very often quotes Rashi and Abraham ibn Ezra. Despite his great reverence for Rashi, he polemicizes with him. At times he praises Ibn Ezra, but attacks him sharply for those of his views which run counter to tradition. He holds Maimonides in high esteem, but rejects some of the reasons given in the *Guide of the Perplexed* for the commandments. He regards (Gen. 18:1) Maimonides' view that the visit of the angels to Abraham was a mere vision to contradict the Bible. Naḥmanides was the first commentator to introduce Kabbalah into his commentary.

The commentary, written in a lucid style, contains many a word of encouragement and solace to the Jewish people. At the end of the Song of *Ha'azinu* (Deut. 32), Naḥmanides writes: "And behold there is nothing conditional in this song. It is a charter testifying that we shall have to suffer heavily for our sins, but that, nevertheless, God will not destroy us, being reconciled to us (though we shall have no merits) and forgiving our sins for His name's sake alone.... And so our rabbis said: 'Great is the song, embracing as it does the present, the past (of Israel) and the future, this world and the world to come....' And if this song were the composition of a mere astrologer we should be constrained to believe in it, considering that all its words were fulfilled. How much more have we to hope with all our hearts and to trust to the word of God, through the mouth of his prophet Moses, the faithful in all his house, like unto whom there was none, whether before him or after him." Naḥmanides' commentary became very popular and has been widely drawn upon by later commentators. Supercommentaries have been written upon it and kabbalistic treatises have been composed on its kabbalistic allusions (see below). Baḥya b. Asher and Jacob b. Asher incorporated large parts of it into their commentaries. The commentary was printed for the first time in Rome prior to 1480. A scholarly edition based on manuscripts and early printings, prepared by Ch. D. Chavel, was published in Jerusalem in 1959–60.

The commentary on Job, too, was probably written by Naḥmanides in his old age. Naḥmanides regards Job as a historical figure. He intimates that the answer to the problem of the suffering of the righteous and the prosperity of the wicked – the central theme of the book – is to be found in the belief in the transmigration of souls. The righteous are punished and the wicked rewarded for their deeds in an earlier life. Comments on other books of the Bible are found dispersed throughout Naḥmanides' writings. His *Book of Redemption* (*Sefer ha-Ge'ullah*) contains comments on various passages of the Book of Daniel. He also wrote a commentary on Isaiah 52:13–53:12.

[Tovia Preschel]

As Halakhist

Naḥmanides' halakhic works rank among the masterpieces of rabbinic literature, and some of them have become classics. They may be divided into four categories: novellae on the Talmud, halakhic monographs, **hassagot* ("criticisms"), and responsa.

Naḥmanides' novellae, which originally covered the entire orders of *Mo'ed, Nashim*, and *Nezikin* – from early times the parts of the Talmud customarily studied in Spain – and which are for the most part extant, mark the summit of the halakhic and religious literary creativity of Spanish Jewry. They also opened a new chapter in the cultural history of that cultural community. In his novellae Naḥmanides based himself on the best of the earlier Spanish tradition and constantly availed himself of the writings of *Samuel ha-Nagid, most of which are no longer extant, of *Hananel b. Ḥushi'el, Isaac *Alfasi, Isaac *Ibn Ghayyat, *Judah al-Bargeloni, Joseph *Ibn Migash, and their contemporaries. Nevertheless, he mainly adopted the mode of learning characteristic of the French *tosafists, whose teachings were previously little known in Spain and whose method was not followed there. In this way Naḥmanides created a new synthesis in the method of study in Spain which was henceforward concerned with a comprehension of the talmudic argumentation for its own sake after the manner of the French scholars and not merely with elucidating *halakhah* for practical purposes, as had until then been customary among the Spanish scholars. Accordingly Naḥmanides emphasizes in his work the theoretical meaning and academic significance of the pronouncements and decisions of the leading earlier Spanish codifiers. Thus he inaugurated a new school in the method of studying the Oral Law which laid the stress on an apprehension, for its own sake, of the talmudic *sugyah* ("theme") as a whole, in point both of its inner tenor and of its relation to other relevant *sugyot* dispersed throughout the Talmud, without, however, becoming entangled in lengthy, sterile discussion. Yet there was no complete dissociation from the practical halakhic aspect. While these two trends are to be found side by side also in the *tosafot*, Naḥmanides was undoubtedly the first fully to achieve this synthesis, which pervades his novellae.

A further local "Spanish" factor which he synthesized with the French system was his constant search for ancient, critically examined, and established texts of the Talmud so as not to become involved in needless discussions to solve questions arising from corrupt readings. The tosafists, too, were aware of this problem, but not having access to enough ancient texts, they were compelled to take such versions from secondary sources, such as Hananel's glosses or the works of the *geonim*, available to them largely at second or third hand, or they made conjectural emendations of the talmudic text which led to a grave and protracted controversy among the tosafists. In this respect, Naḥmanides enjoyed an obvious advantage. Living in Spain, he had at his disposal the best talmudic texts that had been sent to that country direct from the academies of the Babylonian *geonim* 200–300 years earlier. Another factor, chiefly Spanish and conspicuous in Naḥmanides, is his extensive use of the geonic writings and the Jerusalem Talmud. This system of Naḥmanides completely superseded the earlier Spanish tradition. The greatest of his pupils, as also their pupils, having continued, developed, and improved this system, established it as the method for future generations among ever broadening circles of students of the Oral Law.

In addition to the teachings of the French scholars, of whom he speaks with profound esteem, Naḥmanides' works also contain the teachings of Provence, which he incorporated into his system of study as an inseparable part of it. The teachings of *Abraham b. Isaac of Narbonne, *Abraham b. David of Posquières, *Isaac b. Abba Mari, and many others, form an integral part of his works, the last mentioned to a large extent anonymously. Although not very apparent from a superficial reading, his associations with the teachings of Provence are even closer than with those of Spain. Besides the earlier Provençal scholars, he mentions many others from Provence, contemporaries of his, whose statements he discusses. This threefold Spanish, French, and Provençal trend is undoubtedly connected with two of his principal teachers, *Judah b. Yakar and *Nathan b. Meir of Trinquetaille, both of whom were pupils of *Isaac b. Abraham of Dampierre, the well-known tosafist. Naḥmanides' contemporary and relation, Jonah Gerondi, who likewise studied under the tosafists, also based his teachings on a similar method of study.

Naḥmanides' novellae are notable for their wealth of sources and mode of presentation, their clear, lucid style and logical structure. In his desire to arrive at the authentic literal meaning, he did not hesitate to disagree even with the *geonim* and the most illustrious of the earlier authorities, such as *Hai Gaon, Isaac *Alfasi, and others. He was among the first of those who in their writings developed the theoretical method, at once logical and profound, that aimed at comprehending the pivotal argument on which the *sugyah* as a whole depends. Often his novellae range far beyond the limits of the *sugyah* under discussion to a fundamental investigation of various subjects central to the *halakhah*. He also devotes much space to methodological discussions, to be found dispersed in his glosses, on the principles of the Talmud. The novellae on the Talmud were not published simultaneously, the first to appear having been those on *Bava Batra* (Venice, 1523) and the last those on *Bava Meẓia* (Jerusalem, 1929) and, in a complete edition, on *Ḥullin* (New York, ed. by S.Z. Reichmann, 1955). Most of his novellae – those on *Berakhot*, on *Mo'ed, Nashim, Nezikin*, and on *Ḥullin* and *Niddah* – were published between 1740 and 1840. His novellae to *Ketubbot* go to this day under the name of Solomon b. Adret. Nearly all these were known throughout the intervening years from many manuscripts, and leading scholars, particularly among the Sephardim, quoted them in their works. His novellae were published in their entirety for the first time in 1928 in Jerusalem in two volumes. Some of his novellae on a few tractates are extant in the form of short extracts on several pages of a tractate only. He presumably composed them in this manner and was unable to complete the entire work.

Until the expulsion from Spain, Naḥmanides' novellae occupied, alongside Rashi's commentary, the place that the *tosafot* do among students of the Talmud. To such an extent were his words minutely examined and debated that methodological rules were laid down for them. In this respect, Isaac *Campanton was especially notable, declaring that Naḥmanides' statements are to be so closely studied that not a single word should appear superfluous. He even established many minute rules for extracting Naḥmanides' underlying meaning from every single passage. From the time his novellae first appeared in print their influence has become increasingly pronounced also among Ashkenazi students and yeshivot. To this day their study occupies in yeshivot of Polish-Lithuanian origin a principal place together with Rashi, the *tosafot*, and Maimonides.

The second class of Naḥmanides' halakhic literary works comprises his halakhic monographs, of which there are seven:

(1) *Dinei de-Garme* deals with a clarification of the laws regarding inconvenience to a neighbor, injury to his property, and their relation to the law of torts. Since the subject is treated in the second chapter of *Bava Batra*, this short excellent monograph was appended to his novellae on that tractate from its first appearance in print. In it Naḥmanides summarizes the principal views of the earlier authorities on the various aspects of the laws of the *assailant and his victim in general, including damage to a neighbor. In presenting the various opinions Naḥmanides treats of each with great profundity. On this subject he was, he says, forestalled by monographs of French scholars, whose names, however, he does not mention. In recent years there was published (in *Hadorom*, 23 (1966), 31–53), from a manuscript *Gerama ve-Garme* by one of the tosafists, apparently *Ephraim b. Isaac of Regensburg, and Naḥmanides may be referring to this or to a similar work. This small work of Naḥmanides was highly praised by scholars, several of whom wrote commentaries on it. A comparison between his work and that of the scholar previously mentioned clearly reveals Naḥmanides' superiority as a writer of glosses and systematizer.

(2) *Mishpetei ha-Ḥerem* deals with the ways in which a ban is imposed and release obtained from it. It also treats at length of **Kol Nidrei*, said on the eve of the Day of Atonement. Although casting some doubt on its value, he nevertheless states that those accustomed to say it should not be prevented from doing so, since they rely on a custom instituted by the earlier authorities.

(3–5) *Hilkhot Bekhorot* and *Hilkhot Ḥallah* written by Naḥmanides as a supplement to *Hilkhot ha-Rif* of Alfasi, from which these laws were omitted. Here Naḥmanides adopts, with great fidelity, the Aramaic used by Alfasi, as well as his particular style and mode of writing. Naḥmanides also wrote *Hilkhot Nedarim* to fill a gap in Alfasi (those printed on tractate *Nedarim* are not Alfasi's). In this work Naḥmanides included, to a much larger extent than is to be found in the writings of Alfasi, novellae and argumentations in the style characteristic of his glosses on the Talmud.

(6) *Torat ha-Adam* is a comprehensive and unique monograph on all the laws concerning death, starting with what is prohibited and permitted and what is a *mitzvah* as regards the sick and dying, and concluding with the laws of mourning. In point of fact this work is also in the nature of a "supplement" to *Hilkhot ha-Rif*, but in it Naḥmanides, expatiating on the subject, included many scores of talmudic and tannaitic sources as also of Sephardi and Ashkenazi views, which he compared and discussed at length in the light of the sources. Very great importance was attached to the work by the leading codifiers, *Jacob b. Asher incorporated it, in its actual order and form and with corresponding sections, in his *Tur*, as did Joseph *Caro later in his Shulḥan Arukh. Commentators on the Talmud set great store by it when dealing with the interpretation of the relevant *sugyot* in the Talmud. Of special interest on its own account is *Sha'ar ha-Gemul*, the 30th chapter of the work which, published separately some 30 years before the whole (Naples, 1490), deals with reward and punishment after death.

(7) *Hilkhot Niddah* was printed in *Todat Shelamim* (Venice, 1741) of Isaiah *Bassani.

The third category of Naḥmanides' halakhic writings, and the first to appear in print, comprises his works of criticism, of which there are three:

(a) *Hassagot* ("criticisms") of *Maimonides' *Sefer ha-Mitzvot* (Constantinople, 1510);

(b) *Milḥamot Adonai* (in *Rif*, Venice, 1552) attacking *Zerahiah ha-Levi of Lunel's criticisms of *Hilkhot ha-Rif* as well as criticizing Zerahiah's *Sefer ha-Ẓava*; and

(c) *Sefer ha-Zekhut*, (in *Shivah Einayim*, Leghorn, 1745) attacking Abraham b. David's criticisms of Alfasi.

These three share a common feature, namely Naḥmanides' desire to vindicate the earlier authorities against the criticism of later scholars, and hence their contents do not everywhere reflect Naḥmanides' own view; thus, Maimonides having written his *Sefer ha-Mitzvot* mainly against the enumeration of the 613 commandments by the author of the *Halakhot Gedolot*, Naḥmanides took upon himself the task of defending the earlier authority against this criticism. The most important of them is *Milḥamot Adonai* which also has great intrinsic value for the comprehension of a *sugyah*, Naḥmanides devoting himself with his signal profundity and unique talents to an accurate reconstruction of the earlier views that appear to conflict with the *sugyah*. The style of the work is terse, vigorous, and not always easy to understand, calling for much concentration by the reader. In general Naḥmanides, in keeping with the basic purpose of the work, limited himself to the criticisms directed against Alfasi, but in its earlier parts the author went beyond these self-imposed limits to include in them arguments against Zerahiah ha-Levi even where the subject matter did not touch directly on Alfasi.

Naḥmanides' halakhic writings had a decisive influence on the entire history of subsequent rabbinic literature. Solomon b. Abraham Adret's glosses on the Talmud are founded on those of Naḥmanides, and Adret literally copied extracts from his work. Based principally on Naḥmanides' writings are *Sefer *Ha-Ḥinnukh* (which is also based on Maimonides) and Samuel b. Meshullam *Gerondi's *Ohel Mo'ed*. A complete series of works on *Hilkhot ha-Rif* by an anonymous author, mistakenly identified as Nissim *Gerondi, are by a "pupil of Naḥmanides" and based on his teachings. Menahem b. Solomon *ha-Me'iri devoted an entire work, *Magen Avot*, to a controversy with Naḥmanides' pupils who had brought with them to Provence their teacher's customs, which were diametrically opposed to those of Provence. The very great authority enjoyed by Naḥmanides is apparent from the fact that ha-Me'iri found himself compelled to defend the views of the leading earlier authorities of Provence against those of Naḥmanides. Of his responsa only a small number are extant; a large number of them being written in reply to the questions of Samuel b. Isaac ha-*Sardi, who incorporated them in their entirety in his *Sefer ha-Terumot*. A few other responsa by him appeared in *She'elot u-Teshuvot ha-Ramban*, the vast majority of which, despite the title of the work, are by Solomon b. Abraham Adret.

It is difficult to fix the chronological order of Naḥmanides' halakhic works. It is known that he composed *Hilkhot Nedarim* in his youth, and it is clear that he wrote *Milḥamot Adonai* before most of his novellae on the Talmud. Since he composed his novellae over many years, it is impossible to determine their order.

[Israel Moses Ta-Shma]

In Kabbalah

There is evidence that in an earlier version of his Commentary on the Pentateuch (Rome, 1480) Naḥmanides intended to discuss kabbalistic matters more explicitly, but he fell ill and was informed in a dream that he should desist. An extant fragment from an earlier version seems to indicate such a tendency. However, immediate doubts about the authenticity of the fragment were raised by Naḥmanides' students. Hints of kabbalistic references sprinkle his prolific writings, especially his commentary on the Pentateuch (Naples, 1490), commentary on the Book of Job, and the sermons. Kabbalistic concepts are woven into the eschatological discussion in the last section of his halakhic work, *Torat ha-Adam*; this section has often been printed as a separate work titled *Sha'ar ha-Gemul*. Kabbalistic elements are readily recognizable in his liturgical poems, e.g., in *Shir ha-Neshamah*, and in the prayer on the death of R. Abraham Ḥazzan, one of the kabbalists of Gerona. Naḥmanides' single work dealing exclusively with the Kabbalah is his commentary on the first chapter of *Sefer Yeẓirah*.

Despite the paucity of his kabbalistic writings, he came to be known in his later years as an expert on the subject. Kabbalists in the late 13th and early 14th centuries made considerable literary attempts to try and solve the secrets of Naḥmanides' commentary on the Pentateuch. The most important commentaries in this vein are *Keter Shem Tov* by R. Shem Tov *Ibn Gaon and *Me'irat Einayim* by R. Isaac b. Samuel of Acre. Even as late as the beginning of the 14th century, Naḥmanides' kabbalistic writings were studied and relied upon to a far greater degree than the *Zohar itself; a definite preference for the Zohar became apparent only in about 1325.

In the course of time Naḥmanides came to be regarded as such an authority that other authors' works were wrongly attributed to him, e.g., *Ha-Emunah ve-ha-Bittaḥon* (Korets, 1485), which has been proven to be the work of R. Jacob b. Sheshet *Gerondi. G. Scholem has made intensive surveys of Naḥmanides' method in Kabbalah in his *Ursprung und Anfaenge der Kabbala* (1962) and in his series of lectures, *Ha-Kabbalah be-Geronah*, ed. by I. Ben Shlomo (1964).

[Efraim Gottlieb]

Naḥmanides' Mysticism in Light of Late 20th Century Research

Researchers throughout the 20th century attempted to decipher Naḥmanides' mystical teachings in the context of their general and Jewish cultural contexts, and there were several efforts to present his mysticism and theology systematically, both by academic and Orthodox authors. In the 1980s a collection was published in which various articles explored diverse aspects of Naḥmanides and his thought: his Andalusian background, his conservative transmission of kabbalistic traditions, and the blatant contrast between Naḥmanides and *Azriel of Gerona regarding Adam's sin and other physical and spiritual subjects. In the 1990s scholarly interest grew regarding Naḥmanides' exegetical writings and their social implications, and major advances were made in focusing on Naḥmanides' hermeneutics in their Jewish and general context.

MYSTICISM IN NAḤMANIDES' BIBLE COMMENTARIES. Bible commentaries formed the literary and spiritual context in which Naḥmanides functioned as a kabbalist. His kabbalistic creativity cannot be separated from its appearance in his Bible commentary, and this exegetical work forms the essential context for understanding his kabbalistic teaching. Naḥmanides functioned in a context in which the literary genre of Bible exegesis – especially exegesis of the *peshat* (plain meaning of the text) – had already been developed by its classical exponents: Abraham Ibn Ezra in Spain, and Rashi and his school in France. In contrast with the *peshat* exegesis, which was thus already an established and structured literary genre, there was not yet any tradition of kabbalistic exegesis, especially in the specific sense of attempting to explicate the secrets of the Kabbalah in an exegesis following the *peshat*-exegetical paradigm. Accordingly, Naḥmanides had to shape a new strategy of writing, and made a highly significant choice to distinguish between two different paths in the text: the path of *peshat* and the path of truth. This choice created a problematical exacerbation of the gap between prior bodies of knowledge and the mysticism evolving in this period.

Whole sections of the Bible had, perhaps, not previously been dealt with from a mystical perspective, and certain parts of Scripture had no specific traditions of esoteric interpretation, just as other parts had rich traditions of interpretation. The question of attitude toward the Torah was especially sharp.

Naḥmanides sought to compose a consistent and continuous mystical commentary to the Torah, relying only on existing mystical material or on established tradition. He thereby encountered two complementary problems: (a) the Torah contains passages lacking any mystical exegetical tradition; (b) there are mystical doctrines which lack any clear and direct relation to the text of the Torah. This does not mean that Nahmanides faced discontinuity in the mystical tradition; there is an essential and profound difference between what seem to the reader to be "interpretative gaps" and what is lost material. These two phenomena should not be confused. Even if the exegete's self-conception is related to lost knowledge, the processes leading to this phenomenon are frequently related to the gap resulting from a change in the focus of the exegesis. Another complementary problem exists, namely that the rules of preserving the mysteries, which were at the heart of ancient mysticism, and which were also involved in oral transmission, often led to their being lost.

CONSERVATISM AND INNOVATION. A lively controversy has surrounded the question of Naḥmanides' innovation or conservatism in the Kabbalah. We can state, however, that both factors are active in his Kabbalah, and we need to explicate the relations between them. On the one hand, Naḥmanides transmitted bodies of knowledge which were transmitted in whispers, carefully preserving their character; on the other hand, he transmits them in a reorganized and different manner, in the form of Bible exegesis. One facet of innovation was his attempt to interpret the Bible mystically, an attempt motivated by the notion, characteristic of his time, that "everything is learned from the Torah." Presenting the mystical meaning while following the linear continuity of the text was also related to his time, since prior mystical traditions were not shaped in direct relation to the text of the Torah. To what, and by means of what exegesis, and on the basis of which texts, could the mystical traditions be connected? This was the urgent and immediate question faced by the early kabbalists, a question closely connected to the process of historical and social uncovering of the Kabbalah and its becoming written down.

Rabbi Ezra and Rabbi Azriel, in contrast with Naḥmanides, chose to interpret the talmudic *aggadot*. Their choice was simpler: they could review and write Kabbalistic commentaries on *aggadot* which had a mystical background or tendency. In this respect they remained closely and obviously related to rabbinic materials arranged in a midrashic manner. At the same time, the connection between what they chose to interpret is related to specific points in the Talmud, just as Naḥmanides did in his commentary to the Torah, which reflects the fact that we are referring to a process of uncovering existing knowledge, and not merely an exegetical decision.

CONCEPTIONS OF HISTORY AND TIME: CHRISTIANITY AND ISLAM. Attitudes toward Christianity and Islam alike provide additional contexts for Naḥmanides' writings. His attitude toward the Christianity of 13th century Europe becomes blatant in his concept of history and his historiosophy. His attitude toward Islam also finds occasional expression, but less in historical references than in more substantive phenomenological parallels to contemporary mystical doctrines known from the Ismaili Islam.

Naḥmanides' method regarding "the actions of the ancestors are a sign for their children" and "pictures of things," implemented on the level of *peshat*, confirms the relationship between his conception and Christian conceptions of history, whereas his overall conception of time (of which the conception of history is a part), such as his theory of *shemitot* (sabbatical years of release) based on his theory of the **Sefirot*, is implemented on the mystical level, and is related to Ismaili concepts of cyclical cosmic time.

NAḤMANIDES' THEOLOGY: THE RELATION BETWEEN CONCEPT AND SYMBOL. Naḥmanides' thought, which can be called kabbalistic thought or a "religious system," connects basic symbols of the mystical tradition and fundamental concepts in Jewish religion. Naḥmanides was a creative theologian, whose new system of thought includes such theological and philosophical concepts as miracle, nature, providence, exile, redemption, time, will, commandment, Torah, faith, image and story. In turn, his thought influenced a broad spectrum of Jewish thinkers, kabbalists and non-kabbalists alike, including thinkers of an opposite point of view from his, such as Crescas, Judah Loew ben Bezalel (Maharal), Isaac Luria, Cordovero, Abraham Cardozo, Elijah ben Solomon Zalman (Vilna Gaon), Moses Sofer (Ḥatam Sofer), Krochmal, Rabbi Kook, the Satmar *rebbe*, and others. Basic ideas of his theology are also subtly connected to a body of symbolic knowledge and render Naḥmanides' Kabbalah uniquely profound, and resulted in its influencing a broader circle outside of Kabbalah alone.

THE STRUGGLE BETWEEN TWO MYSTICAL THEORIES: NAḤMANIDES AND THE ZOHAR. The conservative and normative aspect of Naḥmanides' mystical theory reflects his communal and halakhic leadership as well as his being a kabbalist. However this conservatism was expressed more in the oral manner of his transmitting his theory than in its content. Recent research has increasingly explored the social aspect of two different conceptions of mysticism, related to two strategies of transmission and writing.

The controversy between Naḥmanides' school and the school of the Zohar surrounds a core issue: a differing view of God and man, which in turn is reflected in a differing view of reality and history. Naḥmanides' conception of God contains a dimension of transcendence, absolutely beyond human comprehension, expression, revelation or theurgy, and is experienced by God's remoteness from language. By the language of the *Sefirot*, Naḥmanides was able to express a hierarchy between two levels of divinity: the known and the unknown, reminiscent of Pseudo-Dionysius.

The school of the Zohar, by contrast, provides a different conception of God and man: the transcendent is open to revelation, theurgic contact and even ecstasy (what can be called theurgic ecstasy). The transcendent is experienced by its absolute proximity to language. The concept of God and man is thus "realized" in the concept of history as a gate open to infinite fields. The acosmic vector of this concept applies to history's beginning or pre-history, and not to its end. By giving up on the concept of cyclical *shemitot*, it cuts any link to an apocalyptic world-view, and thus the center of gravity shifts from the cosmos seeking its end, to a cosmos moved by its beginning, and the shift from a cosmic process to a historical process.

There is a close correlation between determining an unequivocal and sharp end to the cosmos and history, and the concept of a defined reservoir of souls, just as there is between the infinity of history, especially in the transition to messianic times, and the continual renewal of souls and the perpetual self-perfection of God.

In recent research there have been diverse claims regarding the pseudepigraphical authorship of the Zohar in relation to the school of Naḥmanides, which faithfully preserved his oral teachings in the generation after his death, and served as guardians of canonical kabbalistic writing. The texts of the school of the Zohar, on the other hand, did not exist as a formed corpus in the 13th century, and only at the end of the 13th and beginning of the 14th century did the idea of "the Book of the Zohar" take shape, in response to the canonization of Naḥmanides' commentary to the Torah and to the rise of a genre of mystical exegesis.

COMMENTATORS ON NAḤMANIDES. Some of the commentators on Naḥmanides are known by name; others are anonymous. The supercommentaries of R. Joshua *Ibn Shuaib and R. Shem Tov *Ibn Gaon are regarded as the most authoritative for the transmission of the teachings of Naḥmanides and his students Solomon ben *Adret and *Isaac Todros, and are important to understanding Naḥmanides. Although *Isaac of Acre's commentary *Me'irat Einayim* also follows the order of the biblical text, it is a topical key to Naḥmanides' thought. Other commentaries of an interpretative and homilectical character are R. Joshua ibn Shuaib's *Derashot* on the Torah and Bahya ben Asher's Torah commentary. R. Menahem Recanati's commentary to the Torah also contains commentary on Naḥmanides and citations from the Zohar.

The works which present Naḥmanides' teachings in a systematic manner are anonymous, and differ in strategy from super-commentaries: they uncover a system, rather than follow step by step. These include *Ma'arekhet ha-Elohut*, and two works referred to in scholarly literature as the unknown commentary of Naḥmanides' mysteries, and an anonymous commentary from the circle of Solomon ben Adret, as well as a commentary to the *Sefer ha-Bahir.*

Following these anonymous works written in Spain, the literature of the circle of the *Sefer ha-*Temunah* in Byzantium also needs to be mentioned. These writings discuss the meaning of the shapes of the letters of the Hebrew alphabet together with the theory of Sabbatical cycles. A similar combination may also be found in the thought of Naḥmanides' grandson, R. David ben Judah he-Ḥasid, whose contacts with the circle of the Zohar were complex. He combined knowledge of the Zohar with knowledge of Naḥmanides' teachings, and was a primary conduit for the transmission of Naḥmanides' Kabbalah to the circle of *Sefer ha-Temunah.*

In the first and second generations after Naḥmanides, there were thus students who received his teachings and transmitted them, sometimes by personal word of mouth. Some of them, however, combined his teachings with other kabbalistic systems. In terms of content, many of the anonymous works focus on the mysteries of time and the nature and character of its historical or cosmic cycles. In this regard, they resemble ancient apocalyptic literature. In terms of form, the anonymous works break out of the limits of oral transmission.

Later developments, which follow in the path of *Sefer ha-Temunah* and, like it, rely on Naḥmanides' teachings, are *Sefer ha-*Kaneh* and *Sefer ha-Peli'ah*, which reinforce its apocalyptic paradigm, in which the *shemitot* cycles are also used to explain the commandments, in terms of the cycle of human religious life. The mystical transmission is no longer only oral and within the family, but now includes revelation and written transmission, personal revelations and revelations of Elijah.

Such transmission by anonymous revelation is dialectically related to Naḥmanides' own conceptions. It is not necessarily opposed to his strict rules of oral transmission. Rather, the rich power and agitation already existing in the oral circles branched out in writing and revelation. Naḥmanides himself had been described, shortly after his life, as someone capable of restraining his horses while galloping at full speed.

NAḤMANIDES BETWEEN CATALONIA AND CASTILLE. The great difference between the behavior of Naḥmanides' students and that of kabbalists in the area of Castille leads to the conclusion that the earlier kabbalists of Naḥmanides' circle, who tended to preserve traditions and to obey strict rules of transmission, were careful in the way they committed these teachings to writing, at the same time that the Zohar was being distributed and thereafter. This does not, however, provide evidence of influence of Castille on Catalonia. To the contrary: earlier material was uncovered later on, in diverse dialogical relations with the kabbalists of Castille. Parallels between the kabbalists of Catalonia and Castille do not necessarily mean that the Catalonians internalized teachings from Castille, but just the opposite: it is possible that the kabbalists in Castille broke earlier restrictions and were the first to commit to writing theories they learned from people close to the circle of Solomon ben Adret, without accepting their strict rules of secrecy, whereas Naḥmanides' students were reticent to take this step. We know about some of these people from the testimony of R. Shem Tov Ibn Gaon, and one of them was likely R. David ha-Kohen.

Such violation of the rules of transmission made possible a much broader explication of mystical teachings than had been previously known through oral transmission, whether direct or indirect. Naḥmanides' students, as well as those of Solomon ben Adret and Isaac Todros, had committed themselves to the strict restrictions of oral transmission. We have the testimony of R. Shem Tov ibn Gaon, one of Adret's students, that his teachers made the condition that he only transmit the kabbalistic teachings to a wise and humble student, over the age of 40. His testimony also indicates that these strict restrictions sometimes failed; the teachers occasionally misjudged a person who had already learned Naḥmanides' teachings.

The difference regarding innovation and knowledge is not what divided the circle of Naḥmanides from the kabbalists in Castille. It is merely an external symptom of a more extreme struggle over the content of completely differing conceptions of reality and God, and the dynamics of the controversy cannot be separated from the essential content.

MOSES DE LEON'S CONTROVERSY WITH NAḤMANIDES. *Moses de Leon's attitude toward Naḥmanides was quite complex. Their ideological and religious controversy was conducted on several levels: the concept of transcendence; the concept of God as binary (i.e., the dichotomy of good and evil, being vs. destruction) or unitary; later on "positive" destruction at the end of time (i.e., rest, identified with the good) or "negative" destruction in the beginning (i.e., motion, identified with evil); theurgy directed at part of the divine vs. a theurgic connection to all of divinity; dimensions of divinity closed to experiential knowledge vs. all levels of divinity being open to contact in ecstatic revelation; the destiny of the sinful soul after death: purification and immersion in water (according to Naḥmanides' circle) vs. purification by fire (according to Moses de Leon); cosmic cycles of time vs. cycles of the year, festivals and Sabbaths. A correct understanding of Naḥmanides' theories thus provides a criterion which may permit a break-through in understanding how Moses de Leon's circle accepted and rejected Naḥmanides.

The awareness of the *peshat* was critical for the development for Naḥmanides' awareness of *sod* (mystical meaning) as a defined exegetical layer of the text. Such refinement of the concept of *sod*, not only in the content but also in the literary expressions and forms of the text and its transmission led to mystical exegesis, but also to a reaction against Naḥmanides in the Zohar, which rejected the distinction between the two layers.

Naḥmanides conceived of the transcendent as entailing a level closed to human attainment. This accords with the concept of the infinite as a dimension lacking any representation in the stories of the Torah, the concept of the three highest *Sefirot* which the Torah's commandments can only hint at but not aim at them or affect them. In other words, theurgic contact with them is absolutely precluded. Similarly, these *sefirot* cannot be imagined in anthropomorphic terms of any human bodily organ. There is a fundamental connection between the concept of the divine image and the concept of the cycles of *shemitot*, in other words between the anthropomorphic conception of God in terms of only some of the *Sefirot* and the limitations of religious language, and the conception of the cosmos as limiting history. This conception of two dimensions of God – the revealed and the hidden – may be congruent to mystical doctrines known from Hasidei Ashkenaz and from ancient mysticism; but in Naḥmanides' teachings they find additional expression.

The Zohar, on the other hand, in most places, offers a different view: it mentions the *Ein Sof* (infinite), and it relates to all the *Sefirot*, even to the highest ones, in anthropomorphic terms, and provides a theurgic and ecstatic connection with all of them.

THE CONTROVERSY OVER ESCHATOLOGY AND THE THEORY OF SHEMITOT. The controversy described above, regarding conceptions of God and the world, also involves completely differing conceptions of exile, the present and the messianic era. At this critical stage in the history of the Kabbalah and its transition from esoteric to exoteric teaching, the apparently temporary collapse of the theory cosmic cycles, namely the ancient doctrine concerning the passage of time, is related to a completely different conception of the present, an immeasurably long exile, which the circle of the Zohar regarded as the building blocks of the immeasurably long messianic future, to be effected by the knowledge of God and influencing Him.

This early kabbalistic interest in eschatology is congruent in some respects to general culture. On the level of the fate of the individual soul there is prominent interest in locating and characterizing the stages of the trial of the soul after death. Such interest may already be found in Sa'adiah Gaon's *Book of Beliefs and Doctrines* and in Eleazar of Worms' book *Wisdom of the Soul*, and it is particularly prominent in Naḥmanides' *Sha'ar ha-Gemul* as well as in the thought of his bitter opponent, Moses de Leon. Naḥmanides' work describes a continuity from the time of illness to the time of dying and death, to the fate of the soul after death, and also describes allusions to a collective eschatology. Similar questions occupied other kabbalistic trends of thought: where are paradise and hell located – on heaven or on earth, or in both? What is the essence of the judgment fortifying the soul for the life of the world to come – burning in fire (according to Moses de Leon) or immersion in water (according to Naḥmanides' circle)? Is there an intermediate state, a liminal area in which there is no right to be judged, or (in the Zohar's terms) a naked state? Can the *ẓaddik* effect an improvement of the sinful souls of the dead? The kabbalists disagreed over these questions and over their answers. In some cases they accommodated their views to ideas they heard in contemporary Christianity, but generally they related to a broad range of options found in rabbinic sources.

Questions of esoterics vs. exoterics, of closed vs. open knowledge, were only the tip of the iceberg in a much deeper struggle over a wide spectrum of religious issues (theology and praxis) grounded in differing world-views. Naḥmanides' conservative theory of *shemitot* preserved a more ancient worldview, which apparently no longer was relevant to the contemporary experience of reality of some 13th century kabbalists. A different conception of time bursts out of the writings of the kabbalists in Castille, who rejected the theory of *shemitot*. Instead, they regarded the present day as the time for creative messianic activity, a view related to general processes taking place in Christian European society, such as the rise of the city and mercantile economy, with their concepts of time. These new concepts of time were internalized in the religious life of these kabbalists, and not merely in the way they supported themselves financially. These differences split the world of 13th century Kabbalah, but we would not be witness to these changes of seasons in the conception of time were it not for the conservative component in Naḥmanides' teaching.

[Haviva Pedaya (2nd ed.)]

BIBLIOGRAPHY: GENERAL: A. Yeruham, *Ohel Raḥel* (1942); Y. Unna, R. *Moses ben Naḥman* (Heb., 1954); Hurwitz, in: *Hadorom*, 24 (1967), 39–48; I. Ta-Shma, in: KS, 43 (1968), 569–74; H. Chone, *Nachmanides* (Ger., 1930); F. Rosenthal, in: J. Guttmann (ed.), *Moses Maimonides* (vol. 1, 1908). IN THE KABBALAH: G. Scholem, in: KS, 6 (1930), 385–419; 21 (1044/45), 179–86; idem, *Ursprung und Anfaenge der Kabbala* (1962); idem, *Ha-Kabbalah be-Geronah*, I. Ben Shlomo (ed., 1964); Ch.D. Chavel, *Kitvei ha-Ramban* (1963); E. Gottlieb, in: J. ben Sheshet, *Meshiv Devarim Nekhoḥim*, G. Vajda (ed., 1968), 18–20; idem, in: KS, 40 (1964/65), 1–9; idem, in: *Tarbiz*, 39 (1970), 87–89; M.Z. Eisenstadt, in: *Talpiot* 4 (1950), 606–21; T. Preschel, in: *Sinai* 57 (1961), 161–2; idem, in: *Talpiot* 8 (1961), 44–53; D. Chavel, *Rabbenu Moses ben Nahman* (1967); Y. Hasida, in: *Sinai* 61 (1967); 240–8; D. Margalit, in: *Korot*, 4 (1967); K. Cahana, in: *Ha-Meayyan* 9 (1969), 25–48; S. Abramson, in: *Sinai* 66 (1970), 185–94; idem, *ibid.*, 68 (1971), 105–37; 235–69; E. Kupfer, in: *Tarbiz* 40 (1971), 64–83; J. Perles, in: MGWJ 7 (1858), 81–97; 117–36; Z. Frankel, *ibid.*, 17 (1868), 449–58; A. Marmorstein, *ibid.*, 71 (1927), 39–48; L.M. Epstein, in: *Students' Annual* 1 (1914), 95–123; M. Grajwer, *Die kabbalistischen Lehren des Moses Nachmanides in seinem Kommentare zum Pentateuch* (1933). **ADD. BIBLIOGRAPHY:** I. Twersky (ed.), *Rabbi Moses Nachmanides (Ramban): Explorations on his Religious and Literary Virtuosity* (1983),

107–28; M. Idel, "Some Concepts of Time and History in Kabbalah," in: E. Carlebach, Y. Efron, D. Myers (eds.), *Jewish History and Jewish Memory, Essays in Honor of Yosef Haim Yerushalmi* (1998), 153–88; idem, "The Jubilee in Jewish Mysticism," in: E.I. Rambaldi (ed), *Millenarismi nelle cultura contemporanea – Con un'appendice su* yovel *abraico e giubileo cristiono* (2000), 209–32; idem, *Messianic Mystics* (1998); idem, *"Kabbalah, Halakhah u-Manhigut Ruḥanit,"* in: *Tarbiz*, 64 (1995), 535–80; D. Novak, *The Theology of Naḥmanides Systematically Presented* (1992); idem, "Naḥmanides Commentary on the Torah," *The Solomon Goldman Lectures*, 5 (1990), 87–104; E. Gottlieb, *Ha-Kabbalah be-Khitvei Rabbenu Baḥya ben Asher* (1970); M. Meira, *Ha-Ramban be-Ḥug Gerona* (1980); H. Pedaya, *Ha-Mareh ve-ha-Dibbur: Iyyun be-Teva ha-Ḥavayah ha-Datit ba-Mistorin ha-Yehudi* (2002); idem, *Ha-Ramban: Hitalut Zeman Maḥzori ve-Tekst Kadosh* (2003); idem, *Ha-Shem ve-ha-Mikdash be-Mishnat Rabbi Yiẓḥak Sagi Nahor: Iyyun Mashveh be-Khitvei Rishonei ha-Mekubbalim* (2001); I. Ta-Shma, *Ha-Niglah she-ba-Nistar: Le-Ḥeker Sheki'ei ha-Halakhah be-Sefer ha-Zohar* (1995); D. Abrams, "Orality in the Kabbalistic School of Naḥmanides: Preserving and Interpreting Esoteric Traditions and Texts," in: *Jewish Studies Quarterly*, 2 (1995), 85–102; R. Chazan, *Barcelona and Beyond* (1992); J. Dan, "Naḥmanides and the Development of the Concept of Evil in the Kabbalah," in: *Moses Ben Nahman i el seu temps* (1994), 159–82; idem, "The Vicissitudes of Kabbalah in Catalonia," in: M. Lazar (ed.), *The Jews of Spain and the Expulsion of 1492* (1997), 25–40; E. Kanarfogel, "On the Assessment of R. Moses Ben Nahman and His Literary Oeuvre," in: *Jewish Book Annual*, 51 (1993), 158–72; Y.T. Langerman, "Acceptance and Devaluation; Naḥmanides Attitude to Science," in: *Journal of Jewish Thought and Philosophy*, 1 (1992), 223–45; M. Saperstein, "Jewish Typological Exegesis after Naḥmanides," in: *Jewish Studies Quarterly*, 1 (1993–1994), 158–70; B. Septimus, *Hispano Jewish Culture in Transition* (1982); E. Wolfson, "By Way of Truth – Aspects of Naḥmanides Kabbalistic Hermeneutic," in: AJS *Review*, 14 (1989), 103–78; M. Halberthal, *"Ha-Minhag ve-ha-Historiyah shel ha-Halakhah be-Torato shel ha-Ramban,"* in: *Zion*, 67 (1992), 25–26; idem, *"Mavet, Ḥok u-Ge'ulah be-Mishnat ha-Ramban,"* in: *Tarbiz*, 71 (1992) 133–62; idem, *"Torat ha-Nistar: Revadeha shel Sharsheret ha-Ḥavayah be-Torat ha-Ramban,"* in: *Kabbalah*, 7 (2002); A. Funkenstein, *"Parshanuto ha-Tipologit shel ha-Ramban,"* in: *Zion*, 45a (1980), 35–59; S. Pines, *"Divrei ha-Ramban al Adam ha-Rishon be-Gan Eden,"* in: *Galut Aḥar Galut: Meḥkarim be-Toledot Am Yisrael ha-Mugashim le-Prof. Ḥayyim Beinart* (1988), 159–64.

NAḤMAN OF BRATSLAV (1772–1810), ḥasidic *admor* ("master, rabbi, and teacher") and fertile thinker in the fields of philosophy and literature. His personality and his work resonate to this day far beyond the boundaries of the ḥasidic stream he founded.

On his mother's side, Naḥman was the great-grandchild of the Ba'al Shem Tov, Rabbi *Israel ben Eliezer, considered to be the founder of ḥasidic Judaism. His mother, Feiga, was the daughter of Adil, daughter of the Ba'al Shem Tov. On the side of his father, Rabbi Simḥah, Naḥman was the grandson of *Naḥman of Horodenka (Gorodenka), a disciple of the Ba'al Shem Tov and part of the first group of Ḥasidim headed by the Ba'al Shem Tov.

Naḥman was born in Medzhibezh, in the Ukraine, the town where the Ba'al Shem Tov worked and was buried, and where Naḥman's uncle and the grandson of the Ba'al Shem Tov, Rabbi Baruch of Medzhibezh, continued to work. Naḥman therefore grew up in the heart of the ḥasidic world, and from a young age already saw his destiny as being a ḥasidic rabbi. He was betrothed as soon as he reached bar mitzvah age, and married a year later, at the age of 14. At his wedding he met Rabbi Simeon, who became a student and loyal friend and accompanied him throughout his life. After his wedding, as was the custom at that time, he went to live in the home of his father-in-law, Rabbi Ephraim of Ossatin, in the Kiev district of Podolia. The rural nature of this place attracted Naḥman, and he often wandered among the fields and went off by himself to the caves and forests, to commune with God. He used to go out rowing by himself on the river, although he was not a very good oarsman. His life during this period had a considerable influence on the life he encouraged his disciples to live. Seclusion, walks in the countryside, and conversations with the Maker as if conversing with a friend, are the salient features of Bratslav Ḥasidism to this day.

After Rabbi Ephraim became widowed and remarried, Naḥman did not get on with his father-in-law's new wife and moved to the town of Medvedevka, in the Kiev district. There he began to gather his first disciples around him, and embarked on the path of a ḥasidic leader.

In 1798 Naḥman set out on a journey to Ereẓ Israel. He traveled anonymously, and only his friend Simeon accompanied him and knew his identity. On his way to Ereẓ Israel he acted childishly, playing soldiers with youngsters and unnecessarily provoking other Ḥasidim traveling with him on the boat. These actions can be interpreted in various different ways. In Ereẓ Israel he met the local ḥasidic leadership, who received him with great honor and respect, as befitting the great grandson of the Ba'al Shem Tov. He visited Acre, Safed, and Tiberias, as well as other places, but after a few months, when Napoleon's army began to arrive in the country, he fled back home. His return journey was also accompanied by various adventures, since he mistakenly boarded a Turkish warship and was only released after payment of a large ransom.

After his journey to Ereẓ Israel he returned to Medvedevka and to leadership of his ḥasidic community. During this period, the first disputes also began to take place with other ḥasidic leaders in the same area. At the same time, Naḥman began to develop his view of disputation as a source of growth and development and as something with positive aspects, arising in places where new paths are broken in the worship of God.

In Elul 5560 (1800) Naḥman moved to Zlatopol, in the Kiev district, not far from the town of Shpola, home of Reb *Aryeh Leib, known as the Shpola Zeide ("the Grand Old Man of Shpola"), who was the oldest of the ḥasidic *admorim* in the region and whose authority also extended to Zlatopol. Shortly after Naḥman arrived in the town, a serious disagreement broke out with the Shpola Zeide, who apparently saw Naḥman's arrival in town – which had not been coordinated with him as was customary – as an encroachment and an affront. In due course Baruch of Medzibezh and other *admorim* in the Ukraine joined the dispute against Naḥman.

From a series of meetings that he had with ḥasidic rabbis in the area on his return from Ereẓ Israel, it appears that Naḥman did not conceal his criticism of the *admorim*, most of whom were many years older than he. Naḥman told them bluntly that the revelations of which they were so proud were false, and frequently attacked the "erroneously famous" rabbis who did not know how to lead themselves, but wanted to lead others.

Naḥman saw himself as the greatest **ẓaddik* of his generation, and as a true saintly man. He considered his rank to be incomparably higher than that of the other rabbis of his generation, and also of *ẓaddikim* of previous generations, including the Ba'al Shem Tov, the founder of Ḥasidism. Naḥman even hinted that he was higher in rank, at least in some respects, than all the outstanding Jewish figures throughout the generations, from the creation of the world and the first man and right up to the days of the Messiah. This is the message that comes across from the conversations, sermons, and stories of Naḥman, and more explicitly from the esoteric material discovered and published only at the beginning of the 21st century, in particular from those parts that were censored and omitted in the printed version of the book *Ḥayyei Moharan* ("The Life of our Teacher Rabbi Naḥman"), but preserved in the manuscript version.

These bold pretensions naturally aroused opposition, which came as no surprise to Naḥman; he even said: "How could there not be disputes around me, since I am taking a new path that no one has ever taken before, not even the Ba'al Shem Tov, nor any being since the Torah was received, even though it is a very ancient path and even though it is completely new" (*Ḥayyei Moharan*, Jerusalem 5760, p. 338). Naḥman even saw himself as a potential messiah, and as the trailblazer for the coming of the Messiah, who would lead the world with the help of the tools and the advice that Naḥman had prepared and renewed, and the whole world would become Bratslav Ḥasidim.

As a result of the dispute, Naḥman was forced to move to Bratslav (1802). At this stage he was joined by Rabbi Nathan Steinhartz (1780–1845), who soon became Naḥman's scribe and the disseminator of his doctrine. Naḥman stayed in Bratslav for some eight years, until the last year of his life, and there he established and expanded his work as a ḥasidic rabbi and teacher. Even then, the disputes did not abate, accompanying Naḥman until his final days. The most notable of the ḥasidic rabbis who supported Naḥman during these difficult times was Rabbi *Levi Isaac of Berdichev, who stood by him until his own death, about a year before Naḥman's.

In 1805 Naḥman's son Solomon Ephraim was born. Naḥman had messianic hopes for the infant, which increased in fervor during 1806. In the summer of 1806 the "Holy Child" died, and with him the hopes of coming redemption. Shortly afterwards Naḥman first revealed the *Megillat Setarim*, an esoteric discourse describing the "order of the coming of the righteous redeemer." This scroll, to which Naḥman returned in 1809, was encompassed by walls of stringent secrecy, and Bratslav tradition claims that only one person in each generation should know it. The scroll was set out in writing but only in brief hints and acronyms. In the book *Yemei Moharanat*, which is Reb Nosen's autobiography, it was claimed by the publisher that the scroll was lost. However it emerged that contrary to what was declared, the scroll is still in existence and is preserved by the Bratslav Ḥasidim. Recently, the scroll has also been exposed to research.

Naḥman regularly traveled between the towns where his supporters lived. One important journey that left an impression on him was his journey to Lemberg (Lvov). At the time, there were important doctors staying in Lemberg and Naḥman went to see them because he was suffering from tuberculosis, the disease from which he would eventually die. However, apart from the medical aspect, the encounter with the doctors in Lemberg, which continued for some eight months, was significant for Naḥman in that, for the first time, he came into lengthy and intensive contact with educated Jews. Naḥman also made other journeys, some of them incognito, whose purpose and meaning he did not explain.

Some six months before his death, in the spring of 1810, when he was already well aware that his days were numbered, Naḥman moved to the town of Uman. There were a number of reasons for the move. Naḥman, who had prayed for a long time for the privilege of dying a martyr's death, apparently wanted to be buried in the cemetery in *Uman, where many Jews martyred in the 1788 Gonta massacre were buried, and in this context declared that he had come to engage in *tikkun neshamot*, the perfection of souls. Naḥman was also interested in meeting with the Uman intellectuals. To the amazement of his disciples, he preferred to live in a house previously occupied by one of the important intellectuals of the town, Naḥman Nathan Rapaport, and not in the home of one of his followers. Naḥman even used to meet with prominent members of the circle of Uman intellectuals, and had a special connection with Hirsch Be'er Horowitz, who some time later immigrated to England, changed his name to Herman Bernard, and became a professor of Oriental languages at Cambridge University. It is not clear what they talked about at these meetings, but we know that the meetings were social in nature and that they played chess together. Naḥman saw them as an important mission and found them very interesting, even though they prompted surprise among his disciples. Bratslav tradition tells that these intellectuals "almost" returned to their religious roots, and had Naḥman not died an untimely death they would certainly have fully returned to the fold.

Bratslav Ḥasidism was never a large sect, and after the move to Uman it became even smaller, with only a few hundred loyal Ḥasidim remaining and not put off by the disputes and persecution, or by the strange actions of the rabbi.

The tuberculosis from which Naḥman was suffering for a third year become worse, and any conversation or speech cost him great effort and severe pain. Nonetheless, to his last days Naḥman continued his homiletic and literary activities, and even expounded doctrine to his congregation of disciples, and some of his most complex and interesting teachings were given during this difficult period. During *Ḥol ha-Mo'ed* Sukkot of 1810 Naḥman died and was buried in Uman.

Naḥman of Bratslav's Spiritual Work and Character

Naḥman of Bratslav is one of the most original creative minds of ḥasidic contemplation and oration and the most notable writer in the field of ḥasidic literature. His book *Likkutei Moharan* (1808) contains theoretical homilies which were, for the most part, written down by his disciple Reb Nosen, with a few written by Naḥman himself. In terms of genre, the book clearly belongs to ḥasidic homiletic literature, containing Naḥman's teachings presented in a manner that is full of imagination and vision. The innovation and imagination can be seen both in the content and the penetrating way in which the theological and existential problems are presented, and at the level of the literary qualities of the homilies, such as the surprising linking of characters and the unexpected way in which Naḥman quotes sources in order to build his sermon. Although on first reading the homilies appear to document Naḥman's disorganized flow of associations, at the end and on second reading it becomes clear that Naḥman has woven a colorful and changing tapestry into a tale whose end lies in its beginning, and which has both structure and a point to make.

The book *Sippurei Ma'asiyyot* (1815) presents 13 stories told by Naḥman during the last three years of his life, written down by his disciple Rabbi Nathan of Nemirov (Reb Nosen). The stories were published, on Naḥman's instructions, in a bilingual edition – Hebrew and Yiddish, with the Hebrew version above and the Yiddish version below. These stories represent an independent division in ḥasidic literature, and there is nothing else like them in the field. Unlike most ḥasidic stories, these were told by the rabbi and not by the disciples. However, a more important characteristic lies not in the identity of the author but in the character and content of the stories. Unlike other ḥasidic literature, which is entirely hagiographic, the tales of Naḥman are not paeans of praise dealing with an exemplary figure, and only one of the 13 deals with the ḥasidic world, while most of them make no mention at all of the Jewish world. The stories in *Sippurei Ma'asiyyot* are told about the daughter of a king captured by the Evil One, about a gang of pirates, about dust that makes anyone who steps on it mad, about the heart of the world and its pining, and about the love of birds, lovers' yearnings and their song. In addition to the tales collected in *Sippurei Ma'asiyyot*, there are dozens more short stories by Naḥman published in Bratslav literature down the generations. A group of stories was written down by Reb Nosen and disseminated in his various writings (mainly in *Ḥayyei Moharan*), while the other stories are scattered through later Bratslav literature. These stories are not all the same in character; they include parables and tales of praise, dreams and visions.

Other than the sermons and stories, Reb Nosen also collected conversations and short sayings of Naḥman which, although they are not as complex and well developed as his homiletic and literary work, contain a clarity of thought and a directness that are not to be found in the work that is clad in literary and homiletic dress.

Naḥman attributed great importance to the rituals he established with the aim of amending man's sins and defects. He instituted a *Tikkun le-Mikra Laila* (nocturnal pollution), which mainly involved reciting ten psalms; the *Tikkun Kelali* (General Remedy), which does not deal with a specific sin but is intended to amend entire areas where man is defective, such as the subject of speech, money, and particularly eroticism; and a third *tikkun* which is visiting his grave after his death, and which also allows general amendment of all man's sins, and to which we will relate below.

The figure of the *ẓaddik* is very important in Naḥman's work, and he emphasized rank and virtue and the importance of believing in the *ẓaddik*. And yet, Naḥman's teachings and conversations were spoken and written in a personal and confessional tone, including the reader not only in the *ẓaddik's* moments of elation but also in his moments of crisis. Naḥman often refers in his conversations to his struggle with evil inclinations and his times of weakness, bordering on despair and depression. Even questions of belief and denial are presented in all their seriousness, and the feelings of helplessness that even a *ẓaddik* feels when faced with the skepticism which has no answer are brought up openly. Despite the noticeable presence of the threat of skepticism, weakness, and despair, it would not be correct to say that the Bratslav climate is pessimistic. Naḥman declared war against sadness and despair in a unique way. He called upon his disciples not to ignore and escape sorrow and anguish but to draw them too into a joyous dance and turn pain and suffering into a source for the awakening of life, elation, and happiness. In Naḥman's work there is a rare combination of a pessimistic sense of reality and a positive and optimistic response to the question of what a man can accomplish in life and whether it is given to a man to achieve joy in his life. These extremes are also expressed in Naḥman's theological world and in his sermons, which place side by side the strong feeling of distance and absence of God on the one hand, and at the same time the ability to sense the divine in everything. The role of the *ẓaddik*, according to Naḥman, is to know the *ḥasid* standing before him and to adapt his words accordingly. With a spiritually arrogant *ḥasid*, the feeling of distance and the question "Where is God's place?" should be emphasized, whereas with a *ḥasid* who is feeling distant from God, it is the divine presence that should be stressed, and the saying that "The earth is filled with the Lord."

Naḥman is one of the greatest of the mystics of the Jewish people who have left written records of their mystical experiences. He gave voice to his mystic world in his sermons, in stories, and in direct documentation of the revelations he experienced, both while awake and when dreaming. One of these intense experiences, which undoubtedly had considerable weight in shaping Naḥman's self-awareness, was documented in the secret tale called "*Ma'aseh me-ha-Leḥem*." In this tale, Naḥman describes a mystic experience in which he received a new Torah, with a re-statement of the ten commandments and the Torah as a whole. This story was kept secret for over 200 years, and only in recent years has it been published. In the published Bratslav literature there are also reports by Naḥman of various revelations he experienced and teachings he developed as a result. Naḥman's self-confidence in this respect was so great that he even dared to attack other *ẓaddikim*, even those who were many years older than he, who claimed to have seen revelations and angels, saying to them: "This is not how Metatron appears … many have anticipated expounding on the Chariot, but have never actually seen it" (*Ḥayyei Moharan*, 113, p. 148).

When Naḥman's disciples raised doubts as to the ability of *ẓaddikim* to experience revelations such as Ezekiel's chariot, Naḥman replied: "Why are you so surprised? Ezekiel was only human" (*Ḥayyei Moharan*, 553, p. 437). In his sermons and conversations, Naḥman often related to devotion to God and to the states of awareness that are derived from this. He dedicated long sermons in clarification of the issue of devotion, the Holy Spirit, and prophetic visions. Belief and prophecy, for Naḥman, are part of a single spiritual scale whose basis is man's simple faith and whose highest point is the prophetic experience. Both belief and prophecy, each at its own level, require man to be willing to cast aside his intellect in order to reach a state of awareness without knowledge, in which the power of imagination, which is an active and vital part of belief and prophecy, is the central and dominant power at work in his consciousness. Naḥman considered mystic devotion to be a main aim, and all Bratslav work and customs are directed towards helping man to achieve it. Seclusion and conversing with the Creator, shouting and clapping hands, paying attention to the song of the wild grass and searching for hints – all of these modes lead to devotion to God.

Bratslav Ḥasidism after the Death of Naḥman

Naḥman's view of himself as the *Ẓaddik le-Dorot*, the likes of whom would not be seen again until the coming of the Messiah, left no room for the appointment of a successor after his death, and the Bratslav Ḥasidim remained a ḥasidic community without a living rabbi. This phenomenon, which had not been seen before in Ḥasidism, provoked astonishment and mockery, manifested in the nickname that adhered to the community: the *Toete Ḥasidim* – the Dead Ḥasidim. It was Rabbi Nathan of Nemirov (Reb Nosen), Naḥman's disciple and scribe, who took it upon himself to lead the community and ensure its continuity. At first the older Ḥasidim objected, but Reb Nosen's leadership gradually took shape. Although Reb Nosen did not try to take the place of Naḥman, he played a central role in shaping Bratslav literature and customs for the following generations. Apart from the fact that all the Bratslav literature about Naḥman was written by Reb Nosen, he also continued his own creative momentum, following in the spirit and footsteps of Naḥman, especially in his greatest work, *Likkutei Halakhot*. Reb Nosen set up an independent printing press and ensured that the writings of his rabbi would be published and distributed, while completely neglecting his own affairs. Reb Nosen wandered among the disciples and encouraged them to continue adhering to the path of their rabbi even after his death, and even succeeded in attracting new disciples and infusing a new spirit into the community, which had been in deep crisis after Naḥman death. Reb Nosen initiated the construction of a new *bet midrash* for the Bratslav Ḥasidim in Uman, and also established the Rosh Ha-Shanah gathering at Naḥman's grave. During this period the dispute over Bratslav Ḥasidism was rekindled, with Reb Nosen at the center of the disputes and persecution this time, the persecutor being Rabbi Moses Ẓevi of Savran. At the height of the dispute, many left the path of their master and did not return even after the dispute died down. After the death of Reb Nosen, the unofficial leadership passed to Rabbi Naḥman of Tulchin (1814–1884), who acquired this status as Reb Nosen's student and right-hand man. In the next generation, the outstanding figure accepted as having authority and continuing the Bratslav tradition was his son, Rabbi Abraham Ḥazan (1849–1917), who was a prolific writer. In addition to expositions on the work of Naḥman, he and his students wrote up many Bratslav traditions which until then had been preserved only orally. After his death, Rabbi Levi Isaac Bender (1897–1989) achieved prominence and was considered by many as the main channel for passing on the Bratslav tradition to the next generation, and as the most devoted student of Abraham Ḥazan. From the beginning of the 20th century and until World War I, there was an improvement in the standing of Bratslav Ḥasidism, and Bratslav centers also sprang up in Poland alongside those in the Ukraine. However, the instability in Eastern Europe, World War I, the Holocaust, and then Soviet rule all had a serious effect on this small ḥasidic community and the only center that survived was a small group of Ḥasidim in Israel.

Since the 1970s there has been a surprising renaissance in the strength and scale of Bratslav Ḥasidism and the status of Naḥman in Israeli culture. Thousands of new disciples joined the community, and wider circles of students and admirers of Naḥman also developed who are not counted as his disciples. Bratslav Ḥasidism split up into a number of factions, some of which have a very tense relationship with each other. During this period, from being a small and persecuted group Bratslav Ḥasidism became a large and influential community. Most of the outstanding figures of this generation were students of Rabbi Levi Isaac Bender.

The following are the different factions of Bratslav Ḥasidism at the turn of the 20th century:

The main faction, also known as Bratslav Me'ah She'arim, comprises veteran Bratslav families, a small minority of them the descendents of Naḥman and Reb Nosen and the majority the descendants of families which joined Bratslav Ḥasidism in later generations. This sect does not have a single leader, and has a number of influential rabbis, including Rabbi Ya'akov Meir Schechter, Rabbi Shemuel Moshe Kramer, Rabbi Nathan Libermunsh, and others. The head of the World Bratslav Ḥasidism Committee, which constitutes the official leadership of this sect, is the elderly ḥasidic rabbi Mikhal Derfman, head of the Bratslav yeshivah Or ha-Ne'elam in the Me'ah She'arim neighborhood of Jerusalem.

Unlike this sect, the majority of members of the other Bratslav factions are new Ḥasidim with no previous family connection to Bratslav Ḥasidism. The vast majority are *ba'alei teshuvah* from secular families, and a minority are from an ultra-Orthodox or religious Zionist background. A large number of them are from Oriental communities.

The largest faction is led by Rabbi Eliezer Berland, the head of the Shuvu Banim Yeshivah, and his student Rabbi Shalom Arush, head of the Ḥut shel Ḥesed institutions. The center of this sect is in Jerusalem, on the outskirts of the Me'ah She'arim neighborhood, and its communities are scattered throughout Israel.

Another sect is led by Rabbi Eliezer Schik (Moharash), who travels between the two main centers of his followers in the town of Yavniel in Galilee and in New York City. Rabbi Schik's literary activity is extensive and includes free distribution of his booklets. It is worth noting his correspondence, which includes over 40 volumes of letters to his disciples. In his writings there are hints that indicate that he sees himself as a kind of incarnation of Naḥman and as continuing not only his path but also his personality.

A faction that is small in number but has a large public presence in Israel are the followers of Rabbi Yisroel Ber Odesser, known as the "*Na Naḥim*." Odesser (1888–1994) claimed to have found a note personally sent to him by Naḥman of Bratslav. Among other things, the note contained the expression "*Na Naḥ Naḥm Naḥman mi-Uman*," which became the mantra and charm of Reb Yisroel's disciples. These Ḥasidim believe that repeated chanting and dissemination of this phrase play a key role in speeding up redemption, which is why they spread it by means of stickers and graffiti and in any other way they can. White knitted yarmulkes with this phrase embroidered on them have become the dress code of this faction. After the death of Reb Yisroel "*Ba'al ha-Petek*," his followers split up and have no agreed leadership, and their main occupation is spreading word of the note and Bratslav literature.

One of the main characteristics of these factions, as opposed to the mainstream, is the considerable status accorded to their living *ẓaddik* leader. For the first time in Bratslav tradition since the death of Naḥman, the respect and honor given to the leader is not significantly different from that given by other ḥasidic communities to their living rabbi. However, it is still the case among these factions that the figure of Naḥman is the unequivocal center of the ḥasidic experience.

The great expansion of Bratslav Ḥasidism is part of broader processes that took place in the second half of the 20th century, one of which is the increasing resonance of the figure of Naḥman in Israeli culture outside Bratslav ḥasidic circles. Both in secular circles and in national religious and traditional circles there is increasing interest in the works of Naḥman, manifested among other things in study of his writings in the national religious yeshivah framework and in informal secular frameworks, and in the ever-increasing presence of his personality and writings in Israeli literature and culture. This phenomenon in itself is part of the wider phenomenon of the rise of mysticism in Israeli and Western cultures as part of the "New Age" phenomenon. Yet even against the background of the New Age, the Bratslav renaissance provokes astonishment in its scale and power, and it seems today (2006) that we are still in the midst of the process and that it is too early to summarize it and predict its future.

The main and most significant event in Bratslav Ḥasidism, bringing together all the different factions, is the Rosh Ha-Shanah pilgrimage to Naḥman's grave in Uman. Naḥman felt a special connection with this holiday and instructed all his disciples to gather together every Rosh Ha-Shanah, even if this involved great effort and devotion. Not directly connected to this matter, Naḥman also expressed his wish that his followers come to visit him even after his death, and in preparation for this he laid down a special ritual for the pilgrims visiting his grave, offering great benefits in return: Naḥman promised anyone who comes to his grave, no matter who he is and what his sins are, providing he undertakes not to repeat his sins, gives charity for the elevation of Naḥman's soul, and says 10 particular verses of Psalms, that he will intercede on his behalf and will drag him up from the depths of Hell by his sidelocks. After his death, his followers put these two dictates together and, under the leadership of Reb Nosen, made Rosh Ha-Shanah the holiday when all the Bratslav Ḥasidim gather in Uman at their rabbi's graveside. And indeed, throughout the generations the Bratslav Ḥasidim made great efforts to maintain this tradition. When they were not able to reach Naḥman's grave in Uman, the Ḥasidim gathered in Lublin, Jerusalem, or Meron.

In the 1990s, after the fall of the Soviet Union, the gathering in Uman was reestablished and the number of participants gradually increased. In 2004–05 over 20,000 people arrived in Uman for Rosh ha-Shanah. The vast majority came from Israel, by air, on the eve of the holiday, and a minority came from the United States, Canada, and France. A new synagogue was built. On the top floor and in the surrounding courtyard over 4,000 people pray in the traditional Bratslav manner, and on the ground floor some 2,000 people pray in Mizrachi style. The other worshipers pray in smaller *minyanim* nearby. On Rosh Ha-Shanah it is not only Naḥman's Ḥasidim who come to Uman but also people who clearly belong to other streams of Judaism, both religious and secular, and yet take an interest in this gathering. Only men are allowed in Uman on Rosh ha-Shanah. Not all Bratslav ḥasidism are able to join the gathering on Rosh ha-Shanah and various Bratslav gatherings are held in parallel in Israel and other parts of the world. Due to the fast-changing dynamics of the movement, it is difficult to estimate the number of Bratslav Ḥasidim in the different factions. It is harder still to estimate the scope of the widening circles of people who see Naḥman as a figure of authority and inspiration with a significant influence on their lives but who do not belong to any particular Bratslav community. The processes of change in Bratslav Ḥasidism are still in formation and it is too early to speculate on the future of this lively branch of Ḥasidism.

BIBLIOGRAPHY: In David Assaf's *Bratslav – Bibliografyah Mu'eret* (2000) there are more than 1,100 titles on the subject of Bratslav Ḥasidism, original and research literature, accompanied by keys and commentary helping the reader find what he is looking for and know what the item before him contains. We are therefore presenting here only a basic research bibliography. Y. Elstein, *Pa'amei Bat Melekh* (1984); D. Assaf, "*'Adayin Lo Nishkat ha-Riv Ḥinam': ha-Ma'avak Neged Ḥasidut Breslav bi-Shenot ha-Shishim shel ha-Me'ah ha-Tesha-Esreh*," in: *Zion*, 59 (1994), 465–506; A.Y. Green, *Ba'al Historyah – Parashat Ḥayyav shel Reb Naḥman mi-Breslav* (1981); J. Dan, *Ha-Sippur ha-Ḥasidi* (1975), 34–39, 132–88; Y. Weiss, *Meḥkarim be-Ḥasidut Breslav*, ed. and reprinted by M. Peikage (1975); O. Wiskind-Elper, *Tradition and Fantasy in the Tales of Reb Nahman of Bratslav* (1998); Y. Leibes, *Ha-Tikkun ha-Kelali shel Reb Naḥman mi-Breslav ve-Yaḥaso le-Shabta'ut* (1995), 238–61, 429–49; idem, "*Ha-Ḥiddush shel Reb Naḥman mi-Breslav*," in: *Da'at*, 45 (Summer 2000), 91–103; idem, "*Megamot be-Ḥeker Ḥasidut Breslav – le-Bikorto shel Y. Mondshein al Ma'amarei ha-Tikkun ha-Kelali shel Reb Naḥman mi-Breslav ve-Yaḥaso Le-Shabta'ut*," in: *Zion*, 47 (1982), 224–31; C. Leiberman, "*Reb Naḥman mi-Breslav u-Maskilei Uman*," in: *Ohel Raḥel*, 3 (1984), 10–338; S. Magid (ed.), *God's Voice from the Void: Old and New Studies in Bratslav Hasidism* (2002); idem, "Through the Void: The Absence of God in R. Nahman Bratzlav's Likkutei Moharan," in: *Harvard Theological Review*, 88 (1995), 495–519; Y. Mondshein, "*Al ha-Tikkun ha-Kelali shel Reb Naḥman mi-Breslav ve-Yaḥaso le-Shabta'ut*," in: *Zion*, 47 (1982), 201–45; R. Margolin, "*Ha-Emunah ve-ha-Kefirah be-Ḥasidut Breslav al pi ha-Sefer Likkutei Halakhot le-Reb Nathan Steinhartz*" (graduate thesis, Haifa University 1991); T. Mark, *Mistikah ve-Shiga'on bi-Yẓirat Reb Naḥman mi-Breslav* (2004); idem, "*Hama'aseh me-ha-Leḥem – mi-Ginzei ha-Ẓenzurah ha-Breslavi*," in: *Tarbiz*, 72:3 (2003), 415–52; idem, "*Lamah Radaf Moshe Ẓevi mi-Sauran et Reb Natan mi-Nemirov ve-Ḥasidei Breslav*," in: *Zion*, 89:4 (2004), 487–500; idem, "*Hama'aseh me-ha-Shirion ve-ha-Tikkun le-Mikra Layla – mi-Ginzei Ha-Ẓenzura ha-Breslavit*," in: *Zion*, 70:2 (2004), 191–216; idem, "*Tahalikh Hitgabbeshutam shel ha-Tikkun ha-Kelali, ha-Tikkun le-Mikre Layla ve-ha-Aliyah le-Kivro shel Reb Naḥman mi-Breslav ve-Zikkatam la-Metaḥ ha-Meshiḥi*," in: *Da'at*, 56 (2005), 101–33; M. Peikage, *Ḥasidut Breslav: Perakim be-Ḥayyei Meḥolela u-bi-Khetaveha* (expanded ed., 1996); M. Pachter, "*Le-Sugyat ha-Emunah ve-ha-Kefirah be-Mishnat Reb Naḥman mi-Breslav*," in: *Da'at*, 45 (2000), 105–34; H. Zeitlin, "*Reb Nachman mi-Breslav: Ẓa'ar ha-Olam ve-Kissufei Mashiaḥ; Shtei Masot me'et Hillel Zeitlin*," intro. and annotations Y. Meir, in: G. Efrat, E. Reiner, I. Ta-Shma (eds.), *Yeriot*, 5 (2006); A. Rapoport, "*Shnei Mekorot le-Te'ur Nesi'ato shel Reb Naḥman mi-Breslav le-Ereẓ Yisrael*," in: *Kiryat Sefer*, 46 (5731), 147–53; A. Rapoport-Albert, "*'Ketannot,' 'Peshitot' ve-'Eini Yode'a' shel Reb Naḥman mi-Breslav*," in: *Studies in Jewish Religious and Intellectual History, Presented to A. Altmann* (1979), Heb. section, 7–33; idem, "Confession in the Circle of Rabbi Nahman of Bratslav," in: *Bulletin for the Institute of Jewish Studies*, 1 (1973), 65–96.

[Zvi Mark (2nd ed.)]

NAḤMAN OF HORODENKA (Gorodenka; d. 1780), disciple of *Israel b. Eliezer Ba'al Shem Tov; his son married Feige, the granddaughter of the Ba'al Shem Tov, and their son was *Naḥman of Bratslav. Little information is available on the personality of Naḥman of Horodenka and his teachings. From the scattered quotations in the early ḥasidic literature attributed to him, it appears that he occupied himself essentially with practical questions on the method of divine worship. His encounter with the Ba'al Shem Tov became the turning point of his life, as he himself confirms: "When I was a great pietist I immersed myself every day in a *mikveh*, so cold that nobody else could bear. When I came to my house and found the place so warm that the walls were almost burning, I did not feel the warmth for almost an hour. Even so, I could not rid myself from impure thoughts until I was compelled to seek the wisdom of the Besht [Ba'al Shem Tov]" (*Shivḥei ha-Besht* (1961), 112). This change of attitude expresses the complete reversal of his world outlook from ascetic to non-ascetic Ḥasidism. In 1764 Naḥman emigrated to Ereẓ Israel with *Menahem Mendel of Peremyshlany at the head of a group of Ḥasidim and settled in Tiberias.

His journey was described by Simḥah b. Joshua of Zalozhtsy in *Ahavat Ẓiyyon* (Gorodnya, 1790; published a second time under the title *Doresh Ẓiyyon*, Jerusalem, 1887). Some teachings are recorded in his name by his father-in-law *Moses Ḥayyim Ephraim of Sudylkow in *Degel Maḥaneh Efrayim*, as well as in the *Toledot Ya'akov Yosef* by *Jacob Joseph of Polonnoye.

BIBLIOGRAPHY: A. Rubinstein, in: *Tarbiz*, 35 (1965/66) 174–91; Horodezky, Ḥasidut, index; *Shivḥei ha-Besht* (1961), 112, 117–8, 126; Dubnow, Ḥasidut, 102–3, 291.

[Esther (Zweig) Liebes]

NAḤMAN OF KOSOV (d. 1746), kabbalist and one of the early Ḥasidim. A wealthy land contractor and grain dealer, he lived for a time in Ludomir (Vladimir *Volynsky) where he built a *bet midrash* with adjoining bathhouse; Naḥman was associated with a group of Ḥasidim in Kutow (Kuty) which was active even before the appearance of *Israel b. Eliezer Ba'al Shem Tov and possibly remained independent of him even later. At first Naḥman was opposed to the Ba'al Shem Tov, refusing to accept him as a religious leader. Even after recognizing the latter's authority Naḥman preserved his spiritual independence, and his connections with the Ba'al Shem Tov were apparently weak. It is known that among the Kutow group "there was a condition that none of them should prophesy" (*Shivḥei ha-Besht*) but Naḥman did not always observe this condition. He was considered a "man of the spirit," possessing contemplative power and known for his ecstatic manner of praying; he was one of the first to introduce into public prayer the *Nosaḥ ha-Ari* (prayer rite of Isaac *Luria).

Naḥman was among the foremost teachers of devotion (**devekut*), emphasizing constant contemplation of God; *devekut*, according to him, does not contradict the requirements of social life and is not confined to moments of spiritual concentration or a propitious occasion. It is carried out by a visual technique, the letters of the Tetragrammaton and the other names of God appearing before the eyes of the person meditating (the visual method of seeing letters). Naḥman recognized the importance of the dialectical fabric of a society composed of "men of matter" (the masses) and "men of form" (i.e., of the spirit), holding that man's spiritual elevation from his lowliness will take place by his association with the great and pious. Everyone should aim at progress toward perfection day by day and a gradual ascent through completeness and unity of will and intention (*kavvanah*). Naḥman admitted the struggle in man's soul between the powers which are his good and evil inclinations. Life is like a "running and returning" (Ezek. 1:14), with ascents and descents; sometimes what seems to be an ascent is actually a descent, but the descents are prerequisites of the ascents and are not absolutely evil, for "intellect proceeds from instinct and spiritual desire from physical desire" (*Ẓafenat Pa'ne'aḥ*, 38a).

Naḥman was suspected of Shabbateanism and since he supported Jonathan *Eybeschuetz, Jacob *Emden publicly censured him as "Naḥman Kosover, the ignoramus of the Shabbatean sect" (Emden, *Petaḥ Einayim*, 14b; *Sefer Hitabbekut* (1862), 20b). However there is no real proof that Naḥman was a Shabbatean. His teachings are cited in *Toledot Ya'akov Yosef* by Jacob Joseph of Polonnoye, in *Shivḥei ha-Besht* (Horodezky ed. (1922), 56–57), etc.

BIBLIOGRAPHY: A.J. Heschel, in: *H.A. Wolfson Jubilee Volume* (Heb., 1965), 113–41; J.G. Weiss, in: JJS, 8 (1957), 199–213; G. Scholem, in: *Tarbiz*, 20 (1949), 234, 239.

[Esther (Zweig) Liebes]

NAḤMIAS, IBN (15th–16 centuries), family of Hebrew printers from Spain. DAVID IBN NAḤMIAS, his brother SAMUEL, and David's son SAMUEL left Spain in 1492 and made their way to *Constantinople. There they published *Jacob b. Asher's *Turim* in 1493 (5254). The correctness of this date, written out in words in the colophon, has been doubted by scholars such as M. *Steinschneider (*Juedische Typographie*, 1938, 17), who assume an error of ten years. More recently, the case for the 1493 date has been strongly defended by A.K. Offenberg (see bibliography). After an interval of over ten years, the Ibn Naḥmias brothers printed a Pentateuch with Rashi, including *haftarot* with David Kimḥi's commentary and the Five Scrolls with that of Abraham ibn Ezra (1505–06). Several other books followed, among them Alfasi's *Halakhot* and Maimonides' *Code* (both 1509), and three works by Abrabanel, the only ones printed in the author's lifetime. Samuel Sr. died in 1509 or 1510, and David ibn Naḥmias about a year later. David's son Samuel carried on, alone or with a partner, to 1518, when the press was leased to others. The first two works printed (*Turim* and Pentateuch) have as *printer's mark a *Magen David* surrounded by leaves and flowers.

BIBLIOGRAPHY: A.K. Offenberg, in: *Studia Rosenthaliana*, 2 (1969), 96–112 (incl. illus. and bibl.); A. Yaari, *Ha-Defus ha-Ivri be-Kushta* (1967), 17–18, 59ff.; idem, *Diglei ha-Madpisim ha-Ivriyyim* (1944), 3, 123; A. Freimann, *Thesaurus typographiae hebraicae saeculi XV* (1924), CI, 4; Rosanes, Togarmah, 1 (1930²), 316–8.

NAḤMIAS, JOSEPH BEN JOSEPH (first half of 14th century), biblical commentator in Toledo. Naḥmias belonged to an ancient and distinguished Spanish family. Apart from the fact that he studied under *Asher b. Jehiel, little is known of his life. His reputation rests upon his biblical commentary which apparently originally encompassed most of the Bible.

The following parts have been published with introductions by M.A. Bamberger: Esther (1891), Proverbs (1912), and Jeremiah (1913). Bamberger also published Naḥmias' commentaries to *Avot* (1907) and to the *piyyut Attah Konanta* (in: JJLG, 6 (1909)), on the order of the Temple service for the Day of Atonement. His commentary to the tractate *Nedarim* has been preserved in manuscript. Naḥmias is also known to have translated many parts of Maimonides' *Guide of the Perplexed*.

BIBLIOGRAPHY: Bamberger's introd. to his edition of the commentary to Jeremiah, Proverbs, Esther (all in German); Neubauer, in: JQR, 5 (1892/93), 709–13; Poznański, in ZHB, 1 (1896/97), 118–21.

[Israel Moses Ta-Shma]

NAHMIJAS, DANILO (1926–), novelist. Born in Bosnia and raised in Sarajevo, Nahmijas joined the partisans at the age of 17 and after the war became a writer and journalist. He published short stories about his war experiences and three novels dealing with the Holocaust, the Nazi occupation, and Jewish resistance: *Nema mjesta pod suncem* ("No Place under the Sun," 1959), *Razvejano seme* ("Seeds Scattered by the Wind," 1960), and *Oganj* ("Conflagration," 1963).

NAHON, family of rabbis and community leaders of Portuguese origin, in various cities of *Morocco. R. ISAAC BEN JOSEPH NAHON (mid-16th century) was a rabbi of the community of Spanish exiles (Heb. *megorashim*) in *Fez and a signatory of its *takkanot* in 1545. Apparently either BENJAMIN (Joseph's father or brother) or JOSEPH was the author of *Sefer ha-Derashot* (Neubauer, Cat Bod 998). In the 17th and 18th centuries, the Nahons were international merchants in *Algiers; the family originating in *Tetuán. ISAAC (d. 1730) was rabbi in Tetuán. During the 18th and 19th centuries the family was prominent in *Marrakesh, *Mogador, and particularly *Tangier, where they built the Great Synagogue. They greeted Sir Moses *Montefiore on his trip to Morocco in 1864. JONAS BENASULI (b. 1888) was an architect in Tangier. MOSES (Moïse; b. 1870), a distinguished educator, Francophile, and the inspector of the Alliance Israélite Universelle schools throughout Morocco, was active in several philanthropic societies, as were the Nahon women. Other members lived in London, Gibraltar, and Leghorn, Italy.

BIBLIOGRAPHY: J.M. Toledano, *Ner ha-Ma'arav* (1911), 61ff., 101–2; I. Laredo, *Memorias de un viejo tangerino* (1935), 120–2, 267–72; Hirschberg, Afrikah, 2 (1965), 310.

NAHON, GERARD (1931–), Jewish scholar and historian. Nahon was born in Paris to a family that came from Algeria in the 1920s and took refuge in Pau during the war. He studied philosophy, history, and Hebrew at the Sorbonne, the Institut national des langues et civilisations orientales (INALCO), and the Ecole Pratique des Hautes Etudes (EPHE). After working as an educator for the Oeuvre de Secours aux Enfants, and as a high school history teacher, he was appointed in 1965 to the Centre National de la Recherche Scientifique, where he developed a research unit devoted to French Jewish history, "Nouvelle Gallia Judaica," which he directed until 1992. In 1977 he becomes directeur d'études at the Ecole Pratique des Hautes Etudes, section des Sciences religieuses, where he held the chair of medieval and modern Jewish history until 2000. He also taught Jewish history at the Séminaire israélite de France, at the INALCO, and at the University of Brussels. A former curator of the Archives of the Consistoire de Paris and president of the Société des études juives, he served from 1980 to 1996 as editor of the *Revue des études juives*. A student of Georges *Vajda and I.S. *Revah, and an indefatigable archive researcher, he devoted a large part of his studies to the scholarly edition of sources and documents and trained numerous students in this rigorous craft.

Chronologically, his research and publications cover extensive ground with a clear focus on two distinct areas, French medieval Jewry and early modern Sephardi history, and revolve around a few recurrent themes. He did research on the history of rabbinical literature, institutions, and personae. Through the study and publication of wills and epitaphs Nahon contributed to the historiographical emergence of the issue of death in Jewish studies. The bulk of his work focuses on the Sephardi Diaspora, particularly on the Portuguese nations of southwestern France, Bayonne, Bordeaux as well as the lesser communities. Through works on the relations between the Portuguese nations of Western Europe and their links to the Holy Land, he promoted the investigation of intercommunal links within the early modern Jewish world. Finally, he devoted several studies to the history of the Jews in Ereẓ Israel and translated Joshua Prawer's works.

As well as numerous articles in the aforementioned areas, his works and publications include: "Communautés judéo-portugaises du Sud-Ouest de la France (Bayonne et sa région) (1684–1791)," unpubl. diss., 1969; Menasseh ben Israël, *The Hope of Israel*, with Henry Mechoulan, (1987); *Les "Nations" juives portugaises du Sud-Ouest de la France (1684–1791) Documents* (1981); *Inscriptions hébraïques et juives de France médiévale* (1986); *Métropoles et périphéries sefarades d'Occident. Kairouan, Amsterdam, Bayonne, Bordeaux, Jérusalem* (1993); *La Terre sainte au temps des Kabbalistes 1492–1592*, (1997); *Juifs et judaïsme à Bordeaux* (2003).

[Evelyne Oliel-Grausz (2nd ed.)]

NAHOR (Heb. נָחוֹר; cf. Assyrian personal names Naḫaru, Naḫiri, Ur III, Naḫarum).

(1) The son of Serug, the father of Terah, and the grandfather of Abraham. Of those enumerated in the genealogy of the descendants of Shem, he had the shortest life – 148 years (Gen. 11:22–25; I Chron. 1:26).

(2) The son of Terah, the brother of Abraham and Haran, and the grandson of Nahor (1). His wife was Milcah, the daughter of his brother Haran (Gen. 11:26–29).

This was a consanguineous marriage such as is common in the narratives of the Patriarchs (for example, that of Jacob with Rachel and Leah). According to E.A. Speiser, such marriages are to be seen in the light of a custom known from Horite law, whereby a girl was adopted as a daughter with the intention that the adoptive father or his son would marry her. Apparently Bethuel, the son of Nahor and Milcah, died while still young, and his children came under the protection of their grandfather Nahor. Hence Laban is called "the son of Nahor" (Gen. 29:5). However, "the son of Nahor" may constitute a clan name, as is sometimes the case in the Bible.

Abraham and Nahor are described as the progenitors of two clans which intermarried. In the ceremony marking the covenant between Jacob and Laban, the latter declared (31:53): "'May the God of Abraham and the god of Nahor' – their ancestral deities – 'judge between us'"; the patriarchal god of each family would judge in any dispute between them, this being customary also in treaties in the ancient Near East, in which each party cited his gods as witnesses to the pact.

The genealogy of Nahor states that his wife Milcah bore him eight sons and his concubine Reumah four. This represents a schematic genealogical outlook whereby 12 sons are ascribed to a progenitor, analogous to the 12 sons of Ishmael or of Jacob. B. Mazar holds that the genealogy of the sons of Nahor reflects an ancient historical reality which tallies with the expansion of the West Semitic tribes in the first half of the second millennium B.C.E. Support for this assumption is to be found in the reference to Aram as the grandson of Nahor, which indicates that the Aramean tribes were still a young and insignificant element. However, in the Table of the Nations, Aram is represented as descended from Shem himself, and Uz, the firstborn of Nahor, is represented as the firstborn of Aram (Gen. 10:22ff.). This genealogy points to a later period, when the Arameans had attained the pinnacle of their power in the Fertile Crescent. Thus the "Aramaization" of Bethuel and Laban (cf. Gen. 31:47) – and indirectly of Nahor himself, which contradicts the genealogical scheme of Nahor's sons – is to be apprehended as a later anachronism engendered after the rise and expansion of the Arameans in the region of Nahor and of Aram-Naharaim at the end of the 12th and in the 11th centuries B.C.E. The ascription of Nahor's sons to a wife and a concubine expresses a geographical and population distribution – the sons of the wife symbolizing tribes, clans, and geographical limits in the region of Aram-Naharaim and the middle Euphrates and on the borders of the Syrian desert, and the sons of the concubine, areas, tribes, and cities in the south of Syria and northern Transjordan.

(3) The city of Nahor (Assyrian Naḫur, Til Naḫiri). In Genesis 24:10 it is related that the servant of Abraham went to "Aram-Naharaim, to the city of Nahor." Whether this was a place named Nahor or a city in which Nahor's family lived cannot be determined. Those holding the latter view identify the place, on the basis of Genesis 27:43 and 29:4, with *Haran. Nahor is also mentioned in Akkadian sources dating from the beginning of the second millennium to the middle of the seventh century B.C.E., as the name of a city in the Balikh valley. Nahor is first mentioned in Assyrian documents from Kanish of the 20th–19th centuries B.C.E. as an important station

in the Assyrian trade with Asia Minor. Much information on the city during this period is contained in the *Mari archives, from which it is clear that Nahor was a regional capital subject to Mari and a location of its agents. From Nahor supervision was exercised over the Balikh area and the upper stretch of the Habor river; in Nahor intelligence was collected from all parts of Aram-Naharaim. Nahor was also a center for nomadic tribes which, defying all authority, endangered the caravan trade. Accordingly, the rulers of Mari were from time to time constrained to employ military means to suppress their depredations.

In the Middle Assyrian period, Nahor belonged to the kingdom of Hanigalbat, whose rulers erected a palace there. In the 13th century it was captured by the Assyrian kings Adad-Nirari I and Shalmaneser I. During this period it was the seat of a governor, as attested by Assyrian documents, from which it appears that Nahor was included in a district whose capital was Haran, near which it was apparently situated. Although the sources, as well as the archaeological survey conducted in the region of Haran, do not help to fix the exact site of Nahor, it is to be located at an important junction on the caravan route.

BIBLIOGRAPHY: On Nahor and the Sons of Nahor: G. May, in: JBL, 60 (1941), 123–6; B. Meisler (Mazar), in: *Zion*, 11 (1946), 1–16; R. de Vaux, in: RB, 55 (1948), 323–4; 72 (1965), 10; N. Schneider, in: *Biblica*, 33 (1952), 519–22; J.P. Hyatt, in: VT, 5 (1955), 130–6; A. Malamat, in: BIES, 20 (1956), 71–72; idem, in: *Sefer Y.F. Baer* (1961), 1–7; idem, in: *Compte rendu, XVe Rencontre assyrienne internationale* (1966), 129ff.; idem, in: EM, 5 (1968), 805–7; K.T. Andersen, in: *Studia Theologica*, 16 (1962), 170ff.; E.A. Speiser, in: A. Altmann (ed.), *Biblical and Other Studies* (1963) 15–28; U. Cassuto, *Commentary on the Book of Exodus* (1964), 252. On the City of Nahor: W.F. Albright, in: BASOR, 67 (1937), 27; 78 (1940), 29–30; J. Lewy, in: *Orientalia*, 21 (1952), 272ff., 280ff.; A. Goetze, in: JCS, 7 (1953), 67; J. Bottéro and A. Finet, *Archives royales de Mari*, 5 (1954), 130, s.v. *Naḫur*; E. Weidner, in: AFO, 17 (1955–56), 45–46; M. Falkner, *ibid.*, 18 (1957), 20; F.J. Kupper, *Les nomades en Mésopotamie…* (1957), s.v. *Naḫur*; F.M. Tocci, *La Siria nell'età di Mari* (1960), s.v. *Naḫur*; M. Birot, in: *Archives royales de Mari*, 9 (1960), 91; G. Dossin, et al., *ibid.*, 13 (1964), 81–82, 149; A. Finet, in: *Revue d'assyriologie et d'archéologie orientale*, 60 (1966), 17ff.; A. Malamat, in: EM, 5 (1968), 807–8.

NAHOUM, ḤAIM (1872–1960), chief rabbi of *Istanbul and *Cairo. Born in Manisa, Turkey, Nahoum moved to *Tiberias with his family and received his elementary education there. He then went to Smyrna, Turkey, where he was graduated from government high school, and then to Istanbul, where he studied law. Between 1893 and 1897 he studied at the rabbinical seminary in Paris, where he was ordained, and at the Higher Seminary for Semitic Languages of the Collège de France. When he returned to Istanbul, Nahoum was appointed secretary-general of the community committee and deputy director of the rabbinical seminary founded in 1898 by his father-in-law, R. Abraham *Danon. At the same time, he received a government appointment as history teacher in the Turkish Military Academy. At that time, he became acquainted with the "Young Turks" who were exiled in Paris, and when they seized power in the *Ottoman Empire in 1908 they appointed him chief rabbi of the Empire. In this position, Nahoum successfully intervened in favor of Jews in various localities of the Empire, especially in assuring government protection for them during World War I (it seems that it was due to him that the project of expelling the Jews from Jerusalem was averted). After the defeat of the Ottoman Empire and the removal of the "Young Turks" from power, Nahoum left Istanbul for Paris in 1920. In 1925 he was elected chief rabbi of Cairo, a post he held until his death. In June 1931 the king of Egypt appointed Nahoum a member of the Egyptian senate, and in 1933 he was appointed a member of the Arabic Language Academy in Cairo. He was also awarded many honors by the governments of Turkey, Egypt, France, Austria-Hungary, and Ethiopia. Proficient in many languages, he engaged in research on the history of Egyptian Jewry. He also published – with a French translation, notes, and a glossary of Turkish terms – a collection of 1,064 firmans (decrees by the sultan) that had been sent to the rulers of Egypt between 1597 and 1904. This work is entitled *Recueil de firmans impériaux* (1934).

BIBLIOGRAPHY: *The Muslim World* (Hartford, Conn.), 51 (1961), 233–4; M. Fargeon, *Les Juifs en Egypte* (1938), 202–3; M.D. Gaon, *Yehudei ha-Mizraḥ be-Ereẓ Yisrael*, 2 (1938), 461, 736; H. Rabbi Abraham, in: *Haaretz* (Dec. 16, 1960), 12; Nathan, in: JJSO, 6:2 (1964), 172, 187; A. Galanté, *Histoire des Juifs d'Anatolie*, 2 (1939), 98. **ADD. BIBLIOGRAPHY:** E. Benbassa, *Un Grand Rabbin Sépharade en politique, 1892–1923* (1990).

[Haim J. Cohen]

NAHRAI BEN NISSIM (11th century), community leader of the Iraqi Jews in Cairo. Nahrai, who was originally from *Kairouan, settled in Egypt where he became a wealthy merchant. He maintained commercial ties with several countries and specialized in the export of such precious goods as spices, pearls, and indigo to Tunisia and Sicily. However, he was also a scholar with halakhic experience and religious and legal questions were addressed to him. He was referred to as "The eminent Rabbi, the greatest of the yeshivah." He is mentioned in documents dated between 1048–95. Nearly 200 letters addressed to him were found in the *genizah* of Fostat; these are certainly only a part of his original archives.

BIBLIOGRAPHY: Mann, Egypt, index; Starr, in: *Zion*, 1 (1935/36), 436–53; Strauss, *ibid.*, 7 (1941/42), 151–5; M. Michael, "The Archives of Nahrai b. Nissim" (1965, thesis, Hebrew University); S.D. Goitein, *Studies in Islamic History and Institutions* (1966), 287, 295, 321; idem, *A Mediterranean Society* (1967), index; idem, in: *Tarbiz*, 36 (1966/67), 59ff.

[Eliyahu Ashtor]

NAHRAWĀN, town in Iraq, E. of *Baghdad. Nahrawān was a flourishing town during the time of the *Abbasid caliphs (8th and 9th centuries) because the main highway to Persia passed through the town, crossing the Nahrawān canal at this point. At this time it had a large Jewish community, some of whose members were said to have come there from *Egypt. The Nahrawān community belonged to the "domain" of the exilarch. To judge by the large income that the exilarch derived from the Nahrawān community (and from Jews living in its vicinity), according to Nathan ha-Bavli the community must have been of considerable size. In the first half of the tenth century a blind scholar from Nahrawān, R. *Nissi (Nissim) al-Nahrawāni was *resh kallah* at one of the academies. He brought about a reconciliation between the exilarch David b. Zakkai and the head of the Pumbedita academy. R. Nissi subsequently became one of the exilarch's advisers. In the late Middle Ages the caravans to Persia changed their route and as a result Nahrawān fell into decay.

BIBLIOGRAPHY: Neubauer, Chronicles, 2 (1893), 79–80, 85; A.E. Harkavy, *Zikkaron la-Rishonim ve-gam la-Aḥaronim*, 1 (1887), 141, no. 285; G. Le Strange, *The Lands of the Eastern Caliphate* (1930), 61; Mann, in: *Tarbiz*, 5 (1934), 154–5.

[Eliyahu Ashtor]

NAHSHON (Heb. נַחְשׁוֹן; "little (?) serpent"), son of Amminadab (Ex. 6:23; Num. 2:3, et al.). Nahshon was chieftain of the tribe of Judah (Num. 2:3) which consisted of 74,600 men (Num. 2:3–4; 10:14). He assisted Moses in taking a census of the community (Num. 1:7). He was the first to present his offering at the dedication of the Tabernacle (Num. 7:12–17) and the first to proceed in the desert marches (Num. 10:14). Elisheba, his sister, married Aaron (Ex. 6:23). He was the descendant of *Perez, the son of Judah and Tamar, and his son Salmah (Ruth 4:20; Salmon, 4:21; Salma, I Chron. 2:11) was the father of Boaz. King David was thus one of his descendants.

In the Aggadah

According to a well-known *aggadah*, Nahshon was the only one among the Israelites on reaching the Red Sea to obey the command of Moses to descend into the waters and courageously enter the waves, trusting that the promised miracle would occur and the sea be parted. The members of the tribe of Judah followed their leader's example (Mekh., Be-Shallaḥ 5; Sot. 37a). This version of the story is attributed to Tarfon (early second century).

According to an opposing version, all the tribes were eager to obey the command and competed among themselves, who was to be the first; eventually, the tribe of Benjamin jumped first into the water, but the tribe of Judah, infuriated by Benjamin's success, attacked them with stones (Mekh. loc. cit.; Sot. 36b). Benjamin's reward for being the first to descend into the sea was that the first king of Israel – Saul – was chosen from their tribe (Targum Ps. 68:28 and I Sam. 15:17), or else that the *Shekhinah* (Divine Presence) dwelt in their territory (the Temple was built in the territory of Benjamin; Mekh. and Sot., loc. cit.). According to the version which ascribes the outstanding feat of courage to Nahshon, the reward to the tribe of Judah was that kingship in Israel was accorded to them permanently. Tarfon's version was probably meant to encourage acts of rebellion – in the period of unrest preceding the Bar Kokhba Revolt – as the one and only means to reattain kingship for Judah, that is to say, to regain political independence. Various attempts to explain this *aggadah* against the background of other events remain unconvincing.

BIBLIOGRAPHY: Ginzberg, Legends, 3 (1947^3), 195, 220–1; 6 (1946^3), 75–76.

[Joseph Heinemann]

NAHSHON BAR ZADOK, *gaon* of Sura from 871–79, succeeding *Amram Gaon (who mentions him several times in his *Seder*). Nahshon's father, Zadok, had previously been *gaon* of Sura for more than 50 years, and Nahshon's son, Hai, held the office from 889–96.

Nahshon is the author of numerous responsa, in reply to queries addressed to him from various countries. Various works have been attributed to him, among them *Sefer Re'umah* (in J. Onkeneira, *Ẓafenat Pa'ne'aḥ*, Constantinople, 1566), on ritual slaughter, and he is thought by some to have been the author of *Seder Tanna'im ve-Amora'im*. Nahshon made a special study of the Jewish calendar, and is best known for his discovery that the Jewish calendar repeats itself exactly every 247 years. His writing on this phenomenon, known as the *Iggul de-R. Naḥshon*, was published under that name in the *She'erit Yosef* of *Joseph b. Shem Tov (Salonika, 1521). It is possible that it was this calendrical research which led him to take up the study of Karaite literature, since he had to familiarize himself with the works of the founder of the Karaite sect for this purpose (L. Ginzberg, *Gaonica*. 1, (1909), 158), and his interpretations of words in the Bible and Talmud may well be related to his polemics with the Karaites. Nahshon's conservative outlook led him to discourage the innovation of reciting *piyyutim* in prayer, and he disapproved of the recitation of *Kol Nidrei* on the eve of the Day of Atonement, as did his son Hai. Most of Nahshon's responsa are written in terse and difficult Aramaic, but those ascribed to him in D. Cassel's *Teshuvot Ge'onim Kadmoniyyim* (1848; see German introduction, 45) are written in a simple and fluent Hebrew. Some of his decisions conflict with the Talmud and his talmudic-aggadic interpretations do not always agree with those of former aggadists.

BIBLIOGRAPHY: B.Z. Kahana (ed.), *Seder Tanna'im ve-Amora'im* (1935), introd. xff.; Baron, Social², 5 (1957), 22; 6 (1958), 124–5, 425; 7 (1958), 101; D. Cassel, *Teshuvot Ge'onim Kadmoniyyim* (1848), 9a/b; Abramson, Merkazim, 12; L. Ginzberg, *Geonica*, 1 (1909), 154–9.

[Meir Havazelet]

NAHUM (Heb. נַחוּם; a *qattūl* hypocoristic of a name like נְחֶמְיָה, "YHWH has comforted," like שַׁלּוּם for שֶׁלֶמְיָה, שַׁמּוּעַ for שְׁמַעְיָה etc.), one of the Twelve Minor Prophets. Nothing is known of the man himself other than the statement in the book's title that he was an "Elkoshite." A place called al-Qūsh, containing a grave said to be that of Nahum, is located in the neighborhood of Mosul near ancient *Nineveh, whose ruin Nahum depicts in chapters 2 and 3; this tradition connecting al-Qūsh with the prophet cannot, however, be traced beyond the 16th century. Jerome, in the prologue to his commentary on Nahum, records that the prophet was a native of a village in Galilee, which in Jerome's time was called Elcesi and is identified with el-Qauze, west of Tibnin. Some older modern scholars, such as A.W. Knobel and F. Hitzig, have suggested locating Elkosh at Capernaum ("Village of Nahum"). More credible seems to be the tradition recorded by Pseudo-Epiphanius (*De Vitis Prophetarum*), which mentions a Judean Elkesi, "yonder," i.e., south of Eleutheropolis or Bet Guvrin, but the name Elkesi may represent Lachish, since the town of this name was situated directly south of Bet Guvrin. No definite identification of the locality denoted by the designation "Elkoshite" can therefore be made.

Nahum's literary activity took place after the capture of the Egyptian Thebes (biblical No-Amon) by Ashurbanipal in 663 B.C.E., an event which is alluded to in Nahum 3:8–10. It is not certain, however, whether he wrote before the fall of Nineveh in August 612, when the Assyrian capital was captured and razed by the Babylonians and Medes, or shortly after its fall, when the joyful news of the oppressor's defeat was conveyed to Judah. The perfect tenses employed in chapters 2 and 3, where the event is depicted with poetic vividness and force, suggest that Nineveh had already fallen. But several passages (such as 3:11, 14–15) seem to indicate that the resistance was not yet completely crushed. It may therefore be inferred that the Book of Nahum was composed in the very year 612, shortly before Nineveh's final downfall.

The Book of Nahum

The original title of the book as a whole is probably contained in the second part of the superscription: "The book of the vision of Nahum the Elkoshite." The first part – "Oracle concerning Nineveh" – was perhaps the title of the oracle proper on Nineveh's fall; in any case, it correctly describes the main contents of the book. Chapter 1 is generally thought to form an acrostic hymn of theophany. In the opinion of several scholars the entire alphabet was represented in the original poem. The text of Nahum 1 and 2:1, 3 has accordingly been rearranged and reconstructed, mainly by G. Bickell and H. Gunkel, to form a complete alphabetic psalm of an eschatological character which they regarded as a later addition to the book. The restoration of a complete acrostic, however, is impossible; in fact, the poem seems to follow the alphabet only down to the letter *samekh* (1:2a, 3b–8, 9c–10a, 9ab, 2b, 10bc), with verses 9ab and 2b having been transferred to their present position by the book's last editor. One can only conjecture whether the acrostic was composed by Nahum; it is more probable that this text, like other similar ones in the Psalter, was a part of the Jerusalem liturgy. The theophany proper, employing the ancient themes of God's rule over the primordial forces of nature, is contained in verses 3b–6. It serves here as an introductory motif to a national psalm of confidence (1:7–8, 9c–10a, 9ab, 2b, 10bc), followed by an oracle addressed to Judah (1:12–13; 2:1). This liturgy actually forms the exordium to the poem on the fall of Nineveh.

The oracle addressed to the Assyrian capital was perhaps headed by the words "Oracle concerning Nineveh" (1:1). It opens with the introduction 1:11, 14, and is followed by 2:2, 4ff. and 3. The descriptions in Nahum's masterful poetry are singularly picturesque and vivid (especially 2:4–6, 11; 3:2–3, 17–19). The absence of distinctly religious motifs is remarkable, and yet P. Humbert (followed to a certain extent by E. Sellin, A. Lods, H. Lamparter, and S.J. de Vries) tried to prove that the whole Book of Nahum was a liturgy for the enthronement festival of the Lord after the fall of Nineveh in 612. Although other scholars have rejected this view, A. Bentzen (*Introduction to the Old Testament*, 2 (1958^4), 151) considered that the book might be an "imitated" liturgy, consisting of the introductory hymn (chapter 1), the invitation to a festival (2:1), and the curse against Nineveh (chapters 2–3). A. Haldar, on the other hand, has ascribed the Book of Nahum to a cultic prophet who, in c. 614 B.C.E., foretold the approaching destruction of Nineveh by the Lord and employed the images and expressions normally used in depicting the cultic-mythical struggle of God against his foes. As these motifs are paralleled in Sumero-Akkadian and Ugaritic texts, the Book of Nahum would accordingly derive from cultic circles (see below). S. Mowinckel early considered Nahum one of the nationalistic temple prophets of the kind attacked by Jeremiah (*Jesaja-disiplene, Profetien fra Jesaja til Jeremia* (1926), 56). Following A. Kuenen (*De Boeken des Ouden Verbonds*, 2 (1889^2), 384), he suggested that the immediate occasion of the oracle may have been the Median attack upon Nineveh in 623 B.C.E. which, though it was aborted and cost King Phraortes his life, may have turned the prophet's thoughts toward the city and its future destiny. Several other commentators (such as Th. H. Robinson, K. Elliger, and M. Delcor) also consider the book an actual prophecy of doom against Nineveh uttered before its fall in 612. Nahum, however, in his extant writings, was more a nationalist poet than a prophet predicting the future. He expressed his joy over the imminent downfall of Nineveh in the forceful and vivid language of poetry, depicting the assault upon the city, the entrance effected by her foes, the scene of carnage and tumult in the streets, the flight of her inhabitants, the treasures plundered by the captors (chapter 2), and in 3:2–3 he again visualized the chariots and horsemen of the victor forcing a path through the streets. Since the Lord is against Nineveh (3:5–6), she will be as unable to avert her doom as was Thebes in Upper Egypt (3:8–11). Nineveh's fortresses have given way; her men have become as women (3:12–13); in vain she tries to endure the siege (3:14); and amid the rejoicings of all who have suffered at her hands, the proud empire of Nineveh passes away forever (3:18–19). The Book of Nahum thus indirectly depicts God's moral government of the world; He is the Avenger of wrongdoers and the sole source of security to those who trust in Him. Though some of the text is very difficult (1:10, 12; 2:4, 11), the book makes use of vivid images in rapid succession (e.g. 1:3–6). Christensen posits musical influence on the book, which he traces to the prophet's participation in the temple cult of Jerusalem. The book was known to the Qumran sectarians who composed a **pesher* to the book, an exegetical commentary based on the premise that ancient prophecies found their fulfillment in the life and times of the sect. The graphic imagery of the exposure of a harlot (3:4–5) finds its parallel in Jeremiah 13:26–27; Hosea 2:4–5; Ezekiel 16:37–38; and in the eighth century Aramaic treaty from Sefire (Avishur; see COS II, 214; 11, 35b–42).

BIBLIOGRAPHY: H. Gunkel, in: ZAW 13 (1893), 223–44; W.R. Arnold, *ibid.*, 21 (1901), 225–65; S.R. Driver, *The Minor Prophets...* (1906, The Century Bible); P. Haupt, in: JBL, 26 (1907), 1–53; J.M.P. Smith, *Micah, Zephaniah, Nahum, Habakkuk, Obadiah, and Joel* (ICC, 1911); W. Nowack, *Die kleinen Propheten* (1922[2]); G. Hirshler, in: Kahana (ed.), *Terei Asar* (1930), 51–71; Th. H. Gaster, in: JBL, 63 (1944), 51–52; A. Haldar, *Studies in the Book of Nahum* (1947); Th. Laetsch, *The Minor Prophets* (1956); Kaufmann Y., Toledot; A. George, in: DBI, s.v.; S.J. de Vries, in: VT, 16 (1966), 476–81; E.G. Kraeling, *Commentary on the Prophets* (1966); Y. Licht, in: EM, 5 (1968), s.v. **ADD. BIBLIOGRAPHY:** J. Roberts, *Nahum, Habakkuk and Zephaniah* (1991); M. Floyd, in: JBL, 113 (1994), 421–37; K. Cathcart, in: ABD, 4, 998–1000; Y. Avishur, in: Z. Weisman (ed.), *Sefer Terei Asar Bet* (*Enziklopediyah Olam ha-Tanakh* 15b, 1994), 66–85; D. Christensen, in DBI, 2, 199–201; K. Spronk, *Nahum* (1997).

[Edward Lipinski / S. David Sperling (2nd ed.)]

NAHUM, AARON SASSON BEN ELIJAH (c. 1872–1962), educator and communal worker in *Iraq. From 1920 he was chairman of the Zionist Organization in Iraq; his Zionist work was done underground because of Iraqi persecution of the Zionist movement. In 1920 he helped found a Hebrew Literary Society in *Baghdad. He was the founder and, from 1924 to 1935, director of Pardes Yeladim, a school which fostered the use of Hebrew. In 1935 he settled in Palestine, where he continued to work as an educator. In 1920 he founded a Hebrew-Arab weekly in Baghdad, *Yeshurun*, of which only five numbers appeared. Under the pseudonym of "Ha-Moreh," he published a book of poems, *Sefer Shirei ha-Teḥiyyah*, containing translations and original works (2 parts, 1925; part 3 in 1931). His poems express his longing for Zion. In Palestine he also published a number of booklets, in which he appealed for religious observance.

BIBLIOGRAPHY: H. Ben-Yoseph, in: *Ba-Ma'arakhah*, 2 (March 1963), 15; H.J. Cohen, *Ha-Pe'ilut ha-Ẓiyyonit be-Iraq* (1969), passim.

[Abraham Ben-Yaacob]

NAHUM, ELIEZER BEN JACOB (c. 1653–c. 1746), rabbi in *Turkey and Ereẓ Israel. He served as rabbi in Adrianople, where his pupils included Solomon Shalem, later rabbi of the Sephardi community in *Amsterdam. He later settled in Jerusalem and was elected *rishon le-Zion* (chief rabbi), a position he held for ten years. Among his colleagues in the *bet din* were Meyuḥas b. Samuel, Isaac *Azulai (father of Ḥ.J.D. Azulai), and Judah *Diwan. He wrote a number of works, including a commentary on the mishnaic orders *Kodashim* and *Tohorot*, entitled *Ḥazon Naḥum* (Constantinople, 1705). The commentary on the order *Zera'im* is still in manuscript form.

BIBLIOGRAPHY: Frumkin-Rivlin, 2 (1928), 161–3.

[Samuel Abba Horodezky]

NAHUM THE MEDE (fl. second half of the first century C.E.), *tanna*. Nahum lived in Jerusalem during the period of the destruction of the Temple (Naz. 5:4). According to the *tanna* *Nathan, he was one of the judges of civil law, known as *dayyanei gezerot* (Ket. 105a; Tosef., BB 9:1). Three of Nahum's teachings have been preserved in the Mishnah (Shab. 2:1; Naz. 5:4; BB 5:2), and several more in *beraitot* (Av. Zar. 7b; Tosef., BB 9:1).

BIBLIOGRAPHY: Bacher, Tann, 1; Hyman, Toledot, s.v.

[David Joseph Bornstein]

NAHUM OF GIMZO (late first and early second century C.E.), *tanna*, mentioned once only in tannaitic sources (Tosef. Shav. 1:6) as the man from whom R. Akiva derived his famous hermeneutical method of expounding the particles "*akh*" (but) and "*rak*" (only) as exclusionary, on the one hand, and "*et*" and "*gam*" (also) as inclusory, on the other (see **Midrashei Halakhah*, Distinct Exegetical Methods). Though in all our talmudic sources his name is written "*gam zo*" (two words), it has been suggested his name is derived from *Gimzo (II Chron. 28:18) in the center of Ereẓ Israel. Despite the importance of his contribution to the history of rabbinic exegetical methodology, no additional information about him or his teachings has been preserved from the early tannaitic period. In three places, Gen. R. (1, 22, and 53) ascribes to R. Ishmael the statement that R. Akiva studied under Nahum for "22 years." This, however, is almost certainly a late aggadic embellishment of the tradition in Tosefta *Shavuot*, based on the notion that Akiva was willing to expound not only particles like "*et*" and "*gam*," but also individual Hebrew letters – hence 22 years, one for each letter of the Hebrew alphabet.

Like many tannaitic figures about whom we possess only the most meager information, the talmudic *aggadah* transmits a number of fascinating legends concerning Nahum. The designation Gimzo (גמזו) was regarded as meaning "this too" (גם זו, *gam zo*), in reference to his custom of asserting of every happening, however inauspicious it seemed, "this too is for the best" (*gam zo le-tovah*), a habit elsewhere attributed to Akiva (Ber. 60b). Thus when on one occasion he was carrying a casket full of jewels as a gift to the Roman emperor and they were stolen from him at an inn and replaced by earth, he declared "this too is for the best." When he arrived at his destination and the emperor desired to put him to death for mocking him, the prophet Elijah appeared in the guise of a senator and suggested that this was possibly the legendary earth which, if thrown at the enemy in battle, is converted into deadly arrows. On being put to the test, it did indeed prove to be that earth (Ta'an. 21a). Nahum's piety is described in a story concerning a journey on which a poor man accosted him and asked for food. The *tanna* asked the man to wait until he had unloaded his ass, but meanwhile the hungry man died. Nahum reproached himself for not being quicker in providing help and prayed that, as a punishment, he should lose his hands, feet, and sight, and his whole body be covered with sores. Thereafter he lay in that condition in a dilapidated house on a bed with its legs immersed in water to keep away the ants, with his disciples tending him (*ibid.*, cf. TJ Peah 8:8, 21b, Shek. 5:4, 49b).

BIBLIOGRAPHY: Bacher, Tann, s.v.; Hyman, Toledot, 920–1.

[David Joseph Bornstein / Stephen G. Wald (2nd ed.)]

NAIDITSCH, ISAAC ASHER (1868–1949), philanthropist and Zionist. Born in Pinsk, Naiditsch joined the Ḥibbat Zion movement in his youth. Later, he settled in Moscow and became one of Russia's greatest alcohol industrialists. He was sent by the Russian government on commercial missions several times. He carried on his Zionist work, wrote about literary subjects in Hebrew periodicals, and generously supported Hebrew writers. At the beginning of World War I he was one of the founders and directors of the Central Committee for the Relief of Jewish War Sufferers (YEKOPO). After the Russian Revolution (1917), he donated large sums of money for the purpose of promoting Hebrew culture. When the Soviet regime became established, he emigrated to France. Together with Hillel *Zlatopolsky, he suggested the idea of the *Keren Hayesod and was one of its first directors. When the Nazis occupied France, he fled to the United States, but returned to Paris in 1946. He was a close friend and adviser of Chaim *Weizmann from their youth.

Naiditsch wrote articles on Zionism and current events. Some of them were in the book *Ba-Ḥalom u-va-Ma'aseh* ("In Dream and in Practice," 1956), which also contains a collection of appreciations of his personality. He also wrote a book entitled *Edmond de Rothschild* (1945), based upon his conversations with the baron.

BIBLIOGRAPHY: I. Gruenbaum, *Penei ha-Dor* (1958), 333–5.

[Yehuda Slutsky]

NAIDUS, LEIB (**Leo Najdus**; 1890–1918), Yiddish poet. Born in Grodno, Belorussia, Naidus began writing poems in Yiddish, Hebrew, and Russian while attending gymnasium in Vilna. His first book of Yiddish poems, *Lirik* ("Lyrics," 1915) revealed virtuosity in versification and was a manifestation of modern literary aestheticism. From 1916 to 1918 Naydus composed large poetry cycles and epic poems, where he expressed vitalism as his poetic philosophy. After his premature death, his works were published in six volumes (1923–28), including two volumes of translations of Russian, German, French, and English romantic and symbolist poetry.

BIBLIOGRAPHY: Rejzen, Leksikon, 2 (1927), 552–61; LNYL, 6 (1965), 213–8; Sh. Rozhansky, in: L. Naydus, *Oysgeklibene Verk* (1958), introd.; J. Glatstein, *In Tokh Genumen* (1963), 147–54; A. Zak, *In Kinigraykh fun Yidish Vort* (1966), 28–51; E.H. Jeshurin, *Leyb Naydus Bibliografye* (1962). **ADD. BIBLIOGRAPHY:** A. Zak, in: L. Naydus, *Ale verk. Litvishe Arabeskn* (1924), v–xix.

[Melech Ravitch / Mindaugas Kvietkauskas (2nd ed.)]

NAIN, village in the Jezreel Valley, 2 mi. south of Mount Tabor, where according to the New Testament Jesus revived a dead man (Luke 7:11). It was situated on the slopes of the hill of Moreh. In the Midrash, it is located in the territory of Issachar (Gen. R. 98:12). For many centuries, it was one of the villages of the district of Sepphoris. It was a large village, for it had a gate and presumably a wall (if one accepts the testimony of Luke). In the fourth century, Nain was made independent, remaining a separate district within Palaestina Secunda until the Arab conquest. The area of the village included the valley of Iksalo (Exaloth). In 1101 Naym appeared in a list of villages in the possession of the abbey of Mount Tabor. The present-day village (Kafr Na'im) has retained the same name and is built on a slope, 5 mi. (8 km.) south-southwest of Nazareth. A spring in the village irrigates plantations of olives and figs. Rock-cut graves were found in the crags along the road leading from the village to the southwest. In the area of the village are remains of a church or chapel, later transformed into a mosque (maqam Sayidna), ruined buildings, and a mosaic pavement.

BIBLIOGRAPHY: Alt, in: PJB, 22 (1926), 60; idem, in: ZDPV, 68 (1951), 61; see also: ZDPV, 73 (1957), 141–2. **ADD. BIBLIOGRAPHY:** B. Bagatti, *Ancient Christian Villages of Galilee* (2001), 218–24; Y. Tsafrir, L. Di Segni, and J. Green, *Tabula Imperii Romani. Iudaea – Palaestina. Maps and Gazetteer.* (1994), 192; D. Pringle, *The Churches of the Crusader Kingdom of Jerusalem. A Corpus.* Vol. 2: L–Z *(excluding Tyre)* (1998) 115–16.

[Michael Avi-Yonah / Shimon Gibson (2nd ed.)]

NAJAR (**Nadjar**), prominent rabbinical family of Spanish refugees in *Algeria and *Tunis. R. MAIMON NAJAR (14th and early 15th century) left Majorca for Algeria in 1395. He settled in *Constantine, serving as *dayyan*. Author of *Kunteres ha-Minhagot* on local practices, he corresponded with Simeon b. Ẓemaḥ *Duran on religious matters. His brother MORDECAI went to Tunis in 1391 because of persecutions in *Spain; Mordecai later spent some time in Bougie, but returned to Majorca where, under duress, he had accepted Christianity. He finally settled in Algiers in 1435. NATHAN BEN MAIMON (15th century) was rabbi in Constantine and corresponded with Solomon b. Simeon Duran. JUDAH BEN JACOB (d. 1830), talmudist, author, and *dayyan* in Tunis, wrote the following works: *Limmudei ha-Shem* (Leghorn, 1787), on hermeneutics in the Talmud; *Alfei Yehudah* (Leghorn, 1794), a commentary on *Shevuot; Shevet Yehudah* (Leghorn, 1801), a commentary on the *Mekhilta; Simḥat Yehudah* (Pisa, 1816), on *Keritot, Soferim*, and *Semaḥot; Ḥayyei Yehudah* (Pisa, 1816), on *Gerim, Avadim*, and *Kuttim*; and *Oholei Yehudah* (Leghorn, 1823), on the *Sifrei*. DAVID (early 19th century) was a rabbi in Tunis and wrote *Ẓemaḥ David*, which was published posthumously with Judah Cohen *Tanuji's *Admat Yehudah* (Leghorn, 1828) and contains novellae on tractates of the Talmud and on parts of Maimonides' *Yad ha-Ḥazakah*.

BIBLIOGRAPHY: D. Cazès, Notes Bibliographiques… (1893), s.v.; I. Epstein, *'Responsa' of… Rabbi Simon b. Ẓemaḥ Duran…* (1930, 1968²), 94–96; A.M. Hershman, *Rabbi Isaac ben Sheshet Perfet and his Times* (1943), 53, 185.

NAJARA, family of rabbis and kabbalists in Ereẓ Israel and *Syria, originating from the town of Nájera in *Spain. Apparently, the head of the family, LEVI NAJARA, settled in Constantinople after the expulsion from Spain (1492). His son MOSES (1) (1508?–1581), rabbi and kabbalist, lived in *Damascus and in *Safed. Apparently before 1546, he served as a rabbi in Damascus and corresponded with Moses di *Trani. He remained in Damascus until after 1555. He spent some time in Safed as a student of Isaac *Luria and wrote a commentary on the Torah, *Lekaḥ Tov* (Constantinople, 1571). *Sha'ar ha-Kelalim*, published in the beginning of *Eẓ Ḥayyim* of Ḥayyim *Vital, is attributed to Najara in several manuscripts. Different discourses on Lurianic Kabbalah are found in his name in manuscripts and in published works of Ḥayyim Vital. According to Shabbatean tradition, Baruchia (Russo), the head of the *Shabbateans in *Salonika, is reputed to have been a reincarnation of Maharam Nayar, i.e., Moses Najara. In his last years he continued to serve as rabbi in Damascus, where he died. His son was the distinguished poet Israel *Najara. The son of Israel, MOSES (2), succeeded his father as the head of the Jewish community in *Gaza, according to David Conforte (*Kore ha-Dorot*, 49b), who passed through Gaza in 1645 and studied Torah with Najara. Kabbalistic sermons preserved in manuscript were attributed to him but it is possible that they were written by his grandfather, Moses Najara (1). JACOB, his son, who succeeded Moses (2), is known to have been a fervent believer in Shabbetai *Ẓevi. When Shabbetai Ẓevi reached Gaza in 1665, he stayed with Najara, whom he appointed "High Priest," although Najara was not of a priestly family (*Kohen*). In 1666 Jacob Najara sent propagandistic letters abroad supporting the messianism of Shabbetai Ẓevi and the prophecy of *Nathan of Gaza. Even after Shabbetai Ẓevi's apostasy, Najara believed in him and visited him in Adrianople in 1671 (*Sefunot*, 5 (1961), 254–61). MOSES (3), apparently a member of this family, may have been a rabbinic emissary. Between 1760 and 1790 he was one of the rabbis in Debdou, in eastern Morocco. JUDAH NAJARA, a rabbi in Constantinople, may also have been a member of this family.

BIBLIOGRAPHY: Neubauer, Chronicles, 1 (1887), 151, 153; Rosanes, Togarmah, 3 (1938), 218–9; 4 (1935), 357; G. Scholem, *Kitvei Yad ba-Kabbalah* (1930), 127; idem, in: *Zion*, 6 (1940/41), 129; Scholem, Shabbetai Ẓevi, 1 (1967), index; J.M. Toledano, *Sarid u-Falit* (1945), 73–74; I. Ben-Zvi, *She'ar Yashuv* (1966), 378.

[Abraham David]

NAJARA, ISRAEL BEN MOSES (1555?–1625?), Hebrew poet. Born apparently in *Damascus, Israel served as secretary of that community, in which his father, Moses *Najara, was rabbi. While acknowledging Israel's poetic ability, some of the rabbis of Damascus, e.g. Menahem *Lonzano and Ḥayyim *Vital, spoke disparagingly of his unconventional conduct and of his imitation of foreign poetic styles and melodies, acquired, it seems, in Arab taverns. His conduct may also account for his many wanderings. In 1587 Israel published his books *Zemirot Yisrael* and *Mesaḥeket ba-Tevel* in *Safed. One of his responsa is preserved in manuscript (Oxford, Mich. Add. 66). Subsequently, he served as rabbi in *Gaza, where, upon his death, his son Moses succeeded him as rabbi. Though during his youth Israel also wrote secular and love poems, his chief compositions are sacred. These are distinguished by their deep religiosity, by their references to Jewish suffering, and by his yearning for redemption. He learned much from the great Jewish poets of the Spanish-Arabic period, but nevertheless frequently employed original forms and contents. His poems, numbering hundreds – the greater part still in manuscript – are outstanding in both their wealth of language and in their polished style. His poems and *piyyutim* achieved wide circulation among the various Oriental communities and countries and are sung in those synagogues. The Ashkenazi communities also adopted his Sabbath song, written in Aramaic, **Yah Ribbon Olam ve-Alemayya* ("God of the World, Eternity's Sole Lord"). Well known, too, is his *Ketubbah le-Ḥag ha-Shavu'ot* ("Marriage Contract for Shavuot"), a poetic parody describing the wedding conditions made between Israel and God, read in many Oriental communities on Shavuot. The Shabbateans and Frankists highly respected him, mistakenly regarding him as a kabbalist. They were so fond of one of his poems that they made it a hymn.

Israel's works include *Zemirot Yisrael* (Safed, 1587), 109 poems; second edition (Salonika, 1594); third edition enlarged (Venice, 1599–1600), 346 poems (a scientific edition printed by A. Avrunin and edited by I. Pris-Ḥorev, 1946); *Mesaḥeket ba-Tevel* (Safed, 1587), moral instruction in a rhetorical style similar to that of the *Beḥinat Olam* of *Jedaiah ha-Penini Bedersi; *Meimei Yisrael*, rhetorical letters with secular and love poems, composed during his youth and appended to the third edition of his *Zemirot Yisrael; Keli Maḥazik Berakhah* (Venice, 1620), laws of grace after meals; *Shoḥatei ha-Yeladim* (Amsterdam, 1718), laws of slaughtering in an easy language comprehensible even to children; *Pizmonim* (1858), 120 poems; *She'erit Yisrael* (in ms.), a large collection of poems, many of which have been published by various scholars; *Piẓei Ohev* (Constantinople? 1597?) a commentary on the Book of Job. Some other of his works are known but not extant: *Ma'arekhot Yisrael*, a commentary to the Torah; *Mikveh Yisrael*, homilies.

BIBLIOGRAPHY: Davidson, *Oẓar*, 4 (1933), 426–9; idem, *Parody in Jewish Literature* (1907), 34–36; idem, in: *Sefer ha-Yovel… S. Krauss* (1937), 193–270; idem, in: *Sefer ha-Shanah li-Yehudei Amerikah*, 4 (1939), 282–94; A. Ben-Yisrael, *Shirat ha-Ḥen* (1918), 23–58; M.D. Gaon, in: *Mizraḥ u-Ma'arav*, 5 (1930–32), 145–63; D. Yellin, in: *Jewish Studies… G.A. Kohut* (1935), 59–88 (Heb. pt.); I. Mendelson, in: *Horeb*, 9 (1946), 50–58; A. Mirsky, in: *Sefer Ish ha-Torah ve-ha-Ma'aseh… M. Ostrowsky* (1946), 125–32; idem, in: KS, 25 (1948/49), 39–47; idem, in: *Sefunot*, 5 (1961), 207–34; 6 (1962), 259–302; G. Scholem, in: *I. Goldziher Memorial Volume*, 1 (1948), 41–44 (Heb. pt.); idem, in: *Beḥinot*, 8 (1955), 85–86; Zinberg, Sifrut, 3 (1958), 84–100, 373–80; Waxman, Literature, 2 (1960), 93–97; H. Avenary, in: *Divrei ha-Congress ha-Olami ha-Revi'i le-Madda'ei ha-Yahadut*, 2 (1968), 383–4.

[Abraham David]

NAJDORF, MIGUEL (1910–1997), Polish-Argentinean chess grandmaster. Born in Warsaw, Poland, as Mieczysław Najdorf, at age 20 he was an International Chess Master. In 1939, at the outbreak of the World War II he was in Buenos Aires, where he participated in the 8th Chess Olympiad representing Poland. He decided to stay in Argentina and became separated from his family. There he adopted Argentine nationality and developed his chess prowess, although for many years he worked in insurance. Between 1943 and 1965 he won many international tournaments. In 1950 Najdorf became an International Grandmaster. He played well in Candidates' tournaments, in 1950 (finishing in fifth place) and 1953 (finishing sixth). He won important contests in Mar del Plata (1961) and Havana (1962 and 1964). In the Chess Olympiads in Helsinki he obtained second place. Najdorf was noted for some extraordinary feats of simultaneous play. At São Paulo in 1950 he played 250 boards, winning 226 and drawing 15. His blindfold exhibitions were also impressive. At one time he held the record of 40 such games played simultaneously.

[Gerald Abrahams / Efraim Zadoff (2nd ed.)]

NÁJERA (**Najara, Nagara, Naiera**), city in Castile, N. Spain. It had an old and important community which maintained relations with the Babylonian *geonim*. Letters from the community have been found in the Cairo **Genizah*. As early as the beginning of the 11th century, the community enjoyed a *fuero* ("municipal charter"), which later served as a model for similar grants of privileges to other localities. The blood price for a Jew as specified in the charter was equal to that paid for killing a knight or a member of the clergy. The charter was ratified in 1136 by Alfonso VII, and in the 13th century was included in the *fuero* of Castile. The Jewish quarter of Nájera was located near the city wall and the marketplace in the southern part of the city, and remains of the synagogue have been discovered there. The Jews of Nájera owned land and vineyards in the vicinity of the city. The importance of the community toward the end of the 13th century is shown by the tax levied upon it, which amounted in 1290 to 30,318 (according to another source 24,106) maravedis. In 1360, during the civil war between Peter the Cruel and Henry of Trastamara, Henry's supporters attacked the Jews in Nájera and many were killed. The community suffered once more at the time of Peter's victory over Henry in 1367 near Nájera. During the 15th century the position of the community in Nájera, as well as of the others in the kingdom, deteriorated, although at the beginning of the century some Jews still owned land and real estate in the old city. During the war against Granada a special levy of 18½ gold castellanos was imposed on the Jews of Nájera, San Millán de la Cogolla, and Cañas. No details are known about the fate of the community at the time of the expulsion of the Jews from Spain in 1492.

BIBLIOGRAPHY: Baer, Spain, 1 (1961), 43, 53, 366; Baer, Urkunden, index; F. Cantera, *Sinagogas españolas* (1955), 252–3; idem, in: *Sefarad*, 2 (1942), 326; 22 (1962), 89; L. Serrano, *Cartulario de San Millán de Cogolla* (1930), 219; J. González, *El Reino de Castilla en la época de Alfonso VIII* (1960), 132; F. Cantera Orive, *Un cartulario de Santa María la Real de Nájera del año 1209* (1960); Suárez Fernández, Documentos, 69, 76, 101; Ashtor, Korot, 2 (1966), 20; Ashtor, in: *Sefarad*, 24 (1964), 44ff.

[Haim Beinart]

NAJĪB AL-DAWLA (d. c. 1315), court physician and administrator at the court of the Il-Khāns in Persia at the end of the 13th century and beginning of the 14th century. Najīb al-Dawla was closely associated with the Jewish vizier, *Sa'd al-Dawla, and with the court physician, vizier, and historian, Rashīd al-Dīn (of Jewish origin, according to some sources). He seems also to have been for some time governor of the city of Nubandagan, near Shiraz in Persia.

BIBLIOGRAPHY: Fischel, Islam, 105; B. Spuler, *Mongolen in Iran* (1968^3), index.

[Walter Joseph Fischel]

NAJMAN, JULIJA (1905–1989), author and translator. Born in Slavonia, Najman studied in Vienna and Lausanne. In some works, such as the short story collection *Pri ča o Ani* ("The Story of Anna," 1968) and the drama *Žuti kavez* ("Yellow Cage"), she chose Jewish themes. Her fiction dealt mainly with World War II or contemporary life, showing a keen insight into female psychology and employing a simple, compelling style. Her best-known work is *Lica, nameštanja, lica* ("Appearance, Simulacrum, Appearance"), which contains psychological insights into the behavior of Jewish refugees in troubled times. She also translated French works and published interviews with famous literary personalities.

NAJNUDEL, LEÓN DAVID (1941–1998), Argentinean basketball player and coach. Born in Villa Crespo, one of the traditional Jewish neighborhoods of Buenos Aires, Najnudel started his career as a basketball coach in 1963. After many years in the U.S. and Europe, where he learned more about basketball, he was one of the creators of the Liga Nacional de Básquet en Argentina (Argentinean National Basketball League) in 1982. Najnudel was the manager of the Sport Club and Ferrocarril Oeste teams, and led the latter in winning many championships. He was considered a teacher and pioneer of basketball in Argentina.

[Alejandro Dubesarsky (2nd ed.)]

NAJRĀN, chain of fertile oases and a town in north *Yemen; in 1936 the area became part of *Saudi Arabia, after the war between the two states. A Jewish community made up of both merchants and farmers existed in Najrān long before the influx in the fifth century of Christians, who were mostly Monophysites from al-*Hira. Najrān became the center of Christian propaganda in southern *Arabia. The persecution of the Christians of Najrān by the Jewish proselyte king of *Himyar, Yosef Dhū Nuwās, in about 523, is recorded in Greek, Syriac, and Ethiopic Christian literature. The Ethiopians, aided by Justinian to some extent, wrested control of the town from Dhū Nuwās and the Himyaris. Nonetheless, Jews continued to live in Najrān, maintaining their former status. Muhammad guaranteed the Christians rights in Najrān, as they quickly made an agreement with him which was confirmed by his successors *Abu Bakr and *Omar. Jewish communities continued to exist in Najrān until their emigration to Israel in 1949.

Contemporary Period

According to Yemenite Jewish tradition, the Jews of Najrān trace their origin to the Ten Tribes. They lived in the region of Najrān in Saudi Arabia and were the only group of Yemenite Jews who lived outside Yemen under the rule of another kingdom. On the strength of the laws of the desert and tribal protection, they were not subjected to persecution as were the Jews of Yemen. They enjoyed the same equality of rights as the Arabs of Saudi Arabia, were not taxed, and did not pay the **jizya* (the poll tax imposed on non-Muslims in the Muslim countries "in exchange for the protection" granted them by the government). The Bedouin of Saudi Arabia, who belonged to the Sunni Islam sect, practiced religious tolerance toward them and ate meat slaughtered under their laws of *sheḥitah*. The Jews of Najrān carried weapons in self-defense, as did the other inhabitants, and were renowned for their courage and strength. There was no other place in the Arabian Peninsula where Jews lived in such dignity and freedom as in Najrān. By profession they were craftsmen: they worked essentially in goldsmithing and repairing arms. They earned a good livelihood and their material conditions surpassed those of Yemenite Jews. Their settlements were scattered throughout Najrān in small units of two to forty families. They lived in clay houses or in huts. Their clothes, of both men and women, were slightly different from that of Saudi Arabians and Yemenite Jews. The strict barrier between men and women, which was customary in social life throughout Yemen, was nonexistent among them. At festivities and celebrations men and women sat together and women danced to the sound of the men's singing. After 1936, their relations with Yemenite Jews were not very close, because the two groups were under the rule of different kingdoms which occasionally were at war with each other. The life of the Jews of Najrān, dispersed as they were in small settlements, did not encourage the development of Torah studies among them or the fostering of an independent spiritual culture. In matters of religion and *halakhah* they were dependent on the community of nearby Saʿdah (one day away from them), and when necessary, on the *bet din* of *Sanʿa. The Jews of Saʿdah served as their spiritual guardians in times of need: they provided them with religious books and guided them in their religious practices. Therefore, their prayers, customs, and system of study were very closely related. In Israel they are concentrated in Kiryat Ekron, which is inhabited by the Jews of Saʿdah. When the Jews of Najrān immigrated to Israel in 1949, they numbered about 250.

BIBLIOGRAPHY: H.Z. Hirschberg, *Israel Ba-'Arav* (1947). **ADD. BIBLIOGRAPHY:** Newby, *The History of the Jews in Arabia*; Y. Tobi, *Jews of Yemen* (1999).

[Yehuda Ratzaby]

NAKAR, MEIR (1926–1947), Jew executed by the British in Palestine. Nakar was born in Jerusalem and joined Betar at the early age of 13. In 1943 he joined the British army and served for four years in Egypt, Cyprus, and Greece. On his release from the army in 1946, he joined IẒL and five months later was captured during the break into the Acre prison together with Avshalom Ḥaviv and Yaacov Weiss, was sentenced to death and hanged with them.

BIBLIOGRAPHY: Y. Nedava, *Olei-ha-Gardom* (1966); Y. Gurion, *Ha-Nizzaḥon Olei Gardom* (1971).

NAKDIMON BEN GURYON (first century C.E.), mentioned in one version of a tannaitic story (Sifre Deut. 305; cf. Mekh. Baḥodesh 1) concerning *Johanan b. Zakkai, as the aristocratic and wealthy father of a young woman reduced to abject poverty and humiliation in the aftermath of the destruction of Jerusalem. Like many figures mentioned in passing in the early tannaitic sources, the later talmudic and post-talmudic *aggadah* transmits many elaborate legends concerning his life and the dramatic events in which he reportedly took part. According to the Talmud (Git. 56a) he was one of three celebrated wealthy men of Jerusalem during the last years of the Second Temple. Like his affluent associates *Ben Ẓiẓit ha-Kassat and *Ben Kalba Savu'a, Nakdimon studied under the rabbis and was highly regarded by *Johanan b. Zakkai (cf. PdRE 2). Legendary accounts are given of his wealth and philanthropy. On his daily journey to the house of study (the texts of that period often confuse the house of study with the Temple), he had the whole way covered with woolen carpets which he left lying there for the poor to take (Ket. 66b). Other accounts speak of his daughter's excessive use of cosmetics (*ibid.*) and his daughter-in-law's expenditure on her kitchen (Ket. 65a). He was also regarded as a wonder-worker. During a water shortage he borrowed 12 cisterns filled with water from a wealthy Roman official on condition that by a certain day he would either return the cisterns full of water or pay 12 silver talents. On the evening of the last day of the appointed time, in answer to his prayers, rain fell and filled the cisterns. When the Roman objected that the sun had already set and the appointed time had passed, Nakdimon caused the sun to shine by means of his prayer (Ta'an. 19b). During the siege of Jerusalem, he and his two associates promised to supply the city for 21 years with all necessary provisions. The Zealots, however, burned all the provisions so that need would induce the people to fight against the Romans (Git. 56a). With the fall of Jerusalem, Nakdimon lost all his wealth, and Johanan b. Zakkai met his daughter (Miriam; Lam. R. 1:16, no. 48, cf. Sifre Deut. 305) picking out barley corns from cattle dung (Ket. 66b; Lam. R. *ibid.*). According to a talmudic tradition his proper name was not Nakdimon but Boni (Ta'an. 20a).

BIBLIOGRAPHY: Hyman, Toledot, 948–9; J. Neusner, *Development of a Legend: Studies on the Traditions Concerning Yohanan Ben Zakkai* (*Studia Post-Biblica*, vol. 16) (1970), 21–22, 235–38.

[David Joseph Bornstein / Stephen G. Wald (2nd ed.)]

NAME, CHANGE OF. The Bible records changing of names as symbolic of a new status or destiny, e.g., Abraham (Gen. 17:5), Sarah (*ibid.* 15), Jacob (*ibid.* 32:38), and Joshua (Num. 13:16). Basing itself upon this precedent, the Talmud declares that among the "four things that cancel the doom of man" is change of name (RH 16b). From this there developed in the Middle Ages the custom of changing, or more accurately giving an additional name to, the name of a person who was dangerously ill, or suffered some other misfortune, in the belief that the Angel of Death would be confused as a result of the new name. This new name was sometimes chosen by opening a Bible at random and selecting a name which occurred there, except for such names of ill repute as Esau or Korah. The most widespread custom, however, which persists to the present day, was to choose auspicious names such as Ḥayyim or, among the Sephardim, Ḥai (Life), Raphael (may God heal), Hezekiah (may God give strength) for males, and Ḥayyah for females. (The name Alter (old) was frequently given to a boy if several children in the family had died during infancy, this name being regarded as a good omen that he should reach old age.) In the Ashkenazi rite the change of name is effected by pronouncing a special *Mi she-Berakh* prayer which contains the following passage: "Just as his [her] name has been changed, so may the evil decree passed on him [her] be changed from justice to mercy, from death to life, from illness to a complete cure." The Sephardi rite has a different formula.

The new name given to a person is henceforth used in addition to his former name (e.g., Ḥayyim Abraham) for all religious purposes (e.g., to be called up to the Torah, in a bill of divorce, on the tombstone, etc.).

BIBLIOGRAPHY: L. Zunz, *Namen der Juden* (1837), 51; H.E. Goldin, *Ha-Madrikh: The Rabbi's Guide* (1939), 103ff.; J. Trachtenberg, *Jewish Magic and Superstition* (1961[2]), 204–6.

NAMÉNYI, ERNEST (**Ernö**; 1888–1957), Hungarian art historian, economist, and writer. Born in Nagykanizsa, Naményi was the son of Rabbi Ede Neumann. He studied in Budapest and in Brussels, and after he received his doctorate in law was appointed a research associate in the Institut de Sociologie Solvay from 1911 to 1914. He specialized in banking with his uncle, the noted banker P. *Philipson. With the outbreak of World War I he returned to Hungary, and from 1916 to 1949 served as the secretary and later the director of Országos Iparegyesület ("National Industrial Association"). He published economic and sociological articles in Hungarian and French. He also did research in Jewish art, which he felt was an educational means of striving for aesthetics and ethics in Judaism. This outlook led him to found the Jewish Liberal program movement known as "Ézsajás Vallásos Társaság" ("Isaiah Religious Society"). He was among the leaders of the Jewish Museum, and from 1942 served as its director and from 1947 as chairman, succeeding in collecting for it the best works of Jewish artists in and out of Hungary. He also worked for the central Jewish library, which included the remnants of both public and private Jewish libraries, and these collections were housed in the Rabbinical Seminary in Budapest. When the journal *Libanon* was transferred to the Jewish Museum, Naményi participated in its editing until 1944. Together with P. Gruenwald, he wrote the history of the synagogues in Budapest, *Budapesti zsinagógak* ("Synagogues of Budapest," 1949). In 1949 he emigrated to Paris, where he devoted himself to literary work exclusively in the field of Jewish art. He also published two essays on Jewish art in: C. Roth, ed., *Jewish Art* (1961), 423–54, 575–638. His last book was *L'Esprit de l'Art Juif* (1957; *The Essence of Jewish Art*, 1960).

BIBLIOGRAPHY: *Libanon*, 8 (1943), 107–11 (Hung.).

[Baruch Yaron]

NAMES.

In the Bible

Biblical proper names, together with proper names in Old South Arabic, Canaanite (East-or Proto-Canaanite, Ugaritic, and Phoenician), Old Aramaic, Akkadian, and – with some reservations – Old Egyptian, comprise one division of the Semitic onomasticon. Within this division, the Hebrew names have particularly archaic traits. In this respect they are connected with Old South Arabic, East-or Proto-Canaanite, and Ugaritic proper names, and are distinguished from the Akkadian and Old Egyptian names, whose development led them away from the early Semitic type of naming (cf. Stamm, in *Fourth World Congress*..., 141–7).

The most important source for Hebrew proper names is the Bible. In addition to individual proper names found throughout the Bible, biblical genealogies from early and late times also offer numerous examples. Other sources of Hebrew names are Palestinian inscriptions (ostraca and seals), the Elephantine Papyri, and Babylonian clay tablets from the Persian period.

In Hebrew, as in old Semitic generally, two forms of proper names are to be distinguished: propositional names and epithetic names. Propositional names can be classified as either verbal or nominal sentences. A separate group is constituted by the very numerous short names, which cannot be taken into consideration here (see Noth, in bibl., p. 36ff.).

In addition to these formal criteria, another distinction, relating more to content, is that between theophoric and secular proper names.

The predicate of the (theophoric) verbal propositional names is generally in the perfect or imperfect tense. In contrast to the Akkadian, the use of the imperative mood, directed either to the divinity or to the environment, is rare. Late names such as עֲשִׂיאֵל (Asiel, "Do it, O God!") and חֲזִיאֵל (Haziel, "Look, O God!") may be considered as belonging to the former, and רְאוּבֵן (Reuben, "See, a son!"; cf. also Noth, in bibl., p. 32, and Stamm, op. cit., p. 142), as belonging to the latter.

In the perfect-tense names the "predicate-subject" type (e.g., נְתַנְאֵל, Nethanel) is, according to Hebrew syntax, on the whole more frequent than the inverse, i.e., "subject-predicate" (e.g., אֶלְנָתָן, Elnathan; cf. Noth, in bibl., pp. 20–21). The meaning of these names is expressed by the use of the past tense: they signify thanksgiving for an act of charity bestowed by the divine (e.g., "God has given").

In names formed with the imperfect tense, the "subject-predicate" type is hardly represented. This type appears only in the later monarchical and the post-Exilic periods (יְהוֹיָכִין, Jehoiachin; cf. Noth, in bibl., p. 28). On the other hand, the "predicate-subject" type is much more frequent (יְכוֹנְיָה, Jechoniah). Certain of the oldest proper names are of this type, some appearing as abridged forms not containing the word אֵל of the complete form. Examples of these are יִצְחָק (Isaac), יַעֲקֹב (Jacob), יִשְׂרָאֵל (Israel), יוֹסֵף (Joseph), and יְרַחְמְאֵל (Jerahmeel). This type occurs more often in the periods of Moses and the Judges. It becomes scarcer during the Davidic period, almost disappearing, but regaining favor shortly before the Exile and in post-Exilic times (cf. Noth, loc. cit.).

As the Hebrew imperfect tense is both preterit and jussive in character, its meaning in proper names is disputed. Noth, probably because he believed that the perfect expresses the past tense unequivocally, preferred the jussive interpretation for the imperfect, as expressing a wish. Several proper names, which certainly contain such wishes, e.g., יְחִיאֵל ,יְחִיָּה (Jehiel, Jehiah, "may he live, O God/YHWH!"), יוֹסֵף (Joseph, "may he [God] add!"), and יַחְדִּיאֵל ,יֶחְדְּיָהוּ (Jahdiel, Jehdeiah, "may he rejoice, O God/YHWH!"), can be quoted in support of this theory. In opposition to it, however, there are to be found names which are vocalized not as jussive forms but as statements, such as אֶלְיָקִים (Eliakim, "God had made [the deceased] stand up again"), אֶלְיָשִׁיב (Eliashib, "God has brought back [the deceased]"), and יָעִיר (Jair, "He has protected"; for the translation of this name on the basis of the Ugaritic and Hebrew (Deut. 32:11a; Job 8:6b; root *ʿyr/ʿwr*), see Stamm, in: *Studies ... B. Landsberger...*, p. 421a). It should, therefore, be taken into account that the imperfect tense should be rendered in proper names, as in general usage, sometimes as a statement, sometimes as a wish. It is not always easy to decide which of these it is, and the subject warrants further investigation. It appears that the past tense is to be preferred for the oldest names, whereas in the case of the later names the jussive is also to be considered (cf. Stamm, *ibid.*, pp. 414–5; Stamm, in: *Fourth World Congress...*, p. 142).

The content of theophoric propositional names is that the divinity: (1) has given, created/made, or added the child named; (2) has granted, helped, saved, and had mercy, spared, restored justice, and cured, or that it may do so. Whereas in Akkadian the content of groups 1 and 2 both refer to the child named, insofar as it is not only the object of divine gift and creation but also of mercy and salvation (cf. J.J. Stamm, *Die akkadische Namesgebung* (1939), 23 ff.), this is not the case in Hebrew. Here, naturally, the content of group 1 also refers to the child; however, the content of group 2 refers to the parents. They are the ones whose prayer was granted or to whom justice was done. This is explained in the interpretation of names in the Bible (Gen. 29:31–30:24; Ex. 2:10, 22; 1 Sam. 1:27–28). This may well have been the case originally, while the situation in Akkadian (and in Egyptian) may represent a modernization which might have taken place under the influence of liturgical literature.

Such a modernization can also be seen in the fact that in Akkadian and Egyptian there exist propositional names with a suffix indicating the child named. Thus there are in Akkadian (for Egyptian, see J.J. Stamm, in: *Die Welt des Orients* (1955), 111–9), besides Išme-^{d}Adad ("Adad has hearkened"), the forms Ili-išmeanni ("My God has hearkened to me") and Ištar-išmēšu ("Ishtar has hearkened to him"; cf. also Stamm, in: *Fourth World Congress...*, 145). Hebrew, on the other hand, has nothing but נְתַנְאֵל ,נְתַנְיָה(וּ) (Nethanel, Nethaniah(u), "God/YHWH has given") and יִשְׁמָעֵאל ,שְׁמַעְיָה(וּ) (Ishmael, Shemaiah(u), "God/YHWH has granted"). This concise, coined form dominates also in corresponding names in Old South Arabic, and with a few exceptions, also in Ugaritic-Canaanite (cf. Stamm, in: *Fourth World Congress...*, pp. 143–4).

In (theophoric) nominal propositional names, the first remarkable trait is that, unlike the Akkadian, those names containing a participle are scarce and of rather late origin. The only biblical examples are: מְשֵׁיזַבְאֵל (Meshezabel), מְהֵיטַבְאֵל (Mehetabel), מַהֲלַלְאֵל (Mahalalel),

((מְשֶׁלֶמְיָה(וּ (Meshelemiah(u)). Very common, on the contrary, are the so-called names of reliance, consisting of a theophoric element and an appellative, such as אֵלִיָּה(וּ) (Elijah(u), "YHWH is my God") and עֻזִּיאֵל ,עֻזִּיָּה(וּ) (Uzziel, Uzziah(u), "God is my strength"). In these, the possessive "my" can refer both to the giver of the name and to its bearer. It expresses a personal utterance which the father or mother pronounces at first for the child, until the child is able to make it his own. Besides the forms containing the suffix of the first person singular there are also forms which are suffixless and, therefore, do not contain any reference to the speaker. Examples of the latter are יוֹאָב (Joab), יוֹאָח (Joah), יוֹאֵל (Joel), יוֹעֶזֶר (Joezer) ("YHWH is father/ brother/God/help"). Again, in contrast to Akkadian and Egyptian, there are no forms with a suffix of the third person singular ("YHWH is his/her father"). The suffix of the first person plural occurs only in the cry for salvation, which later became a name, עִמָּנוּאֵל (Immanuel), and in the messianic name, ה׳ צִדְקֵנוּ (Jer. 23:6).

Theophoric epithetic names are not particularly common in Hebrew, a fact which is related to the absence of the following type, common in Akkadian and Egyptian: "son/daughter of divinity X." The most popular names in this category are those constructed with עֶבֶד (*ʿeved*, "slave"), e.g., עַבְדִּיאֵל (Abdiel, "God's slave") and עֹבַדְיָה(וּ) (Obadiah(u), "[small] slave of YHWH"; cf. further Noth, in bibl., pp. 135–9).

In the above-mentioned name groups, the most frequently occurring theophoric elements are אֵל (*ʾel*) and the tetragrammaton, the latter always used in abridged form, namely, יְהוֹ (*yeho*) and יוֹ (*yo*) at the beginning, יָהוּ (*yahu*) and יָה (*yah*) at the end, of the word. The first personal name that was definitely constructed with the tetragrammaton is יְהוֹשֻׁעַ (Joshua). The name of Moses' mother, יוֹכֶבֶד (Jochebed), is more ancient, but it is extremely questionable if it really contains the biblical divine name; as for יְהוּדָה (Judah), it is certain that it does not contain the divine name. From the period of the Judges, five personal names belonging to this group, יוֹאָשׁ

(Joash), יוֹתָם (Jotham), מִיכָיָה(וּ) (Micaiah(u), יְהוֹנָתָן (Jonathan), and יוֹאֵל (Joel) should be mentioned. During the monarchical period, names of this group became frequent and dominant and even retained their lasting predominance – together with those containing the theophoric אֵל (*ʾel*) – afterward. אֵל (*ʾel*) is common in personal names up to the beginning of the monarchical period, during which time it fell into almost complete disuse, reappearing again and becoming more frequent from the seventh century onward, and remaining common after the Exile (see Gray, in bibl., pp. 166ff.; Noth, in bibl., pp. 82ff.).

With other old Semitic personal names, especially South Arabic and Proto-or East-Canaanite, Hebrew names have in common the particularity that terms of kinship can take the place of the theophoric element. These are terms like אָב (*ʾav*, "father"), אָח (*ʾaḥ*, "brother"), and עַם (*ʿam*, "paternal uncle"), thus, for instance, אֲבִירָם (Abiram), אֲחִיטוּב (Ahitub), and עַמְרָם (Amram; for other examples, see Noth, in bibl., pp. 66ff.; Stamm, in: *Studies … B. Landsberger…*, pp. 416ff.). These names have their origin in the early Semitic and nomadic conceptions of tribal and clan structure, according to which deceased relatives enjoyed the divine privilege of being worshiped. In Israel, after the Conquest, this belief became extinct. If corresponding names continued to be used, this was undoubtedly based on the supposition that terms denoting kinship could be assimilated to YHWH. However, not all of these originally had a theophoric meaning. There exist those in which אָב (*ʾav*), אָח (*ʾaḥ*), and עַם (*ʿam*) designate the (deceased) father, brother, or uncle of the one named. These are the so-called substitute names (see below). (On the problem of distinguishing these secular names from the theophoric, see Stamm, in: *Studies … B. Landsberger…*, p. 418.)

Other words, some of which are very ancient, which can be used in a theophoric sense in names are צוּר (*ẓur*, "Rock"), שַׁדַּי (*shaddai*, "the Almighty"), אָדוֹן (*ʾadon*, "Lord"), בַּעַל (*baʿal*, "Possessor/Lord"), and מֶלֶךְ (*melekh*, "king"; cf. Noth, in bibl., pp. 114ff.).

Secular epithetic names have in Hebrew, as in related languages – particularly Akkadian and Egyptian, the most diverse and disparate contents. These retain the day of birth (חַגַּי, Haggai, "he who was born on the festival"), or the origin (יְהוּדִי, Jehudi, "the Judean"), or the position within the family (בְּכוֹרַת, Becorath, "firstborn"). Other proper names give expression either to the relationship between the child and his parents, or to their joy, such as יְדִידָה (Jedidah, "the loved one") and שִׁמְשׁוֹן (Samson, "little sun"). Also frequent are names given on the basis of particularly distinctive physical traits or flaws, e.g., לָבָן/לִבְנִי (Laban/Libni, "white," probably after the color of the skin, particularly of the face), גָּדוֹל ("tall"; a proper name from Elephantine), הַקָּטָן/צוּעַר (Hakkatan/Ẓuar, "[the] small one"), בַּרְזִלַּי (Barzillai, "as hard as iron"), and קֹרַח/קָרֵחַ (Kareah/Korah, "the bald headed"; for other examples see Noth, in bibl., pp. 221ff.). In addition, names of animals and plants are not infrequent as proper names.

Two other groups of names which should be mentioned specially are substitute names, names in which expression is given, in some manner, to the view that the bearer of the name reincarnates a deceased relative, or that the latter has returned to life in, or through, the former, and women's names. This is an ancient idea which has its roots in the conception of tribal and clan structure and which does not presuppose the belief in the transmigration of souls. Parallel forms to this category of proper names can be found in many peoples; among the Semitic peoples they are particularly numerous with the Babylonians and the Egyptians.

Most groups which occur in other proper names can be found also among the substitute names. Only a few examples of each will be given here (for further illustration of the subject see Stamm, in: *Studies … B. Landsberger…*, 213–24): verbal proposition (secular): יָשָׁבְעָם (Jashobeam, "the uncle has come back"), יָשׁוּב (Jashub, "he [the deceased] has returned"); verbal proposition (theophoric): אֶלְיָקִים (Eliakim), אֶלְיָשִׁיב (Eliashib), and יָעִיר (Jair, see above); nominal proposition: אֲבִירָם (Abiram), עַמְרָם (Amram; "the father/uncle is great"), and אֲבִיהוּד (Abihud), אֲחִיהוּד (Ahihud), עַמִּיהוּד (Ammihud; "my father/brother/uncle is splendor"). In these proper names the praise of the deceased simultaneously keeps his memory alive.

A form which cannot be found outside this category of substitute names is represented by those uttering, in the sense of a complaint, the quest after the deceased, thus אִיכָבוֹד (Ichabod) and אֵהוּד (Ehud; "where is the glory?"), also אִיזֶבֶל (Jezebel; "where is nobility?"), and אִיעֶזֶר (Iezer; "where is help?"). The interrogative particle *ai/e/i*, used in all these names, may also be discerned in אִיּוֹב (Job; "where is the father?").

In the epithetic names, the child either simply bears the epithet of the relative whom he replaces, thus אַחְאָב (Ahab; "father's brother"), or is named after the function which devolves to him as substitute, מְשֻׁלָּם (Meshullam, "the replaced"), מְנַחֵם (Menahem, "one that consoles"), and מְנַשֶּׁה (Manasseh, "he who makes forget").

As for women's names, the theophoric ones are relatively scarce. Much more frequent are the secular ones, i.e., designations based on the time of birth, or the origin of the bearer (of the name), on a characteristic physical or spiritual quality, or the relationship with the parents. Names of jewels, plants, and animals are also used as women's names (for details, see Stamm, in: VTS, 16, where the question as to the reasons for the relative scarceness of theophoric women's names also is raised).

[Johann Jakob Stamm]

Hypocoristica, or shortened names, were common, and were formed in various ways (see Noth, Personennamen, 36–41). Very common, especially in later times, was the formation *qattūl*, as in זַכּוּר (Zakkur) for זְכַרְיָה (Zechariah), חשוב for חֲשַׁבְיָה, נַחוּם for נְחֶמְיָה, etc. At Elephantine we even find הצול, Haẓẓūl, for הצליה and יחמול, Yaḥmūl, for יחמליה, so that the Elephantine name גדול, which was interpreted above as the adjective *gadol*, "large," is more probably to be read Gaddūl as a hypocoristicon of גְּדַלְיָה, Gedaliah.

[Harold Louis Ginsberg]

In the Talmud

Insofar as names are concerned the talmudic literature covers a period of some 700 years, from the time of Simeon the Just (c. 200 B.C.E.) to 500 C.E. A distinction must be made between fact and homiletical propaganda. Thus, the often repeated statement giving one of the causes of the deliverance of the Children of Israel from bondage as "they did not change their names" (e.g., Lev. R. 32:5) is certainly to be viewed as a homily appealing for the retention or giving of Hebrew names, in view of the prevalent tendency of adopting foreign names. It is in this light that the interesting equivalents, Rofe (Rufus?) for Judah, Luliani (Julianus?) for Reuben, Lestim (Justus?) for Joseph, and Aleksandri for Benjamin, quoted there are to be regarded. Zunz, somewhat casuistically, suggests that these passages are to be understood as referring specifically to the change from a Hebrew name already given to a gentile name, a custom which was disapproved of as a sign of deliberate assimilation, but not to the initial granting of non-Jewish names. To be regarded in a similar light is the Targum to Amos 6:1 which renders *nekuvei reshit ha-goyim*, "they give their children the same names as do gentiles." The Talmud states only that "the majority of Jews in the Diaspora have the same names as the gentiles" (Git. 11b; in Babylonia only names of idols were avoided – Git. 11a; the name Tammuza (Judah b. Tammuza; TJ, Meg. 4:5, 75b) is not evidence of the adoption of the name of the god Tammuz (= Adonis), since Tammuz had already become Hebraized as the name of the Hebrew month, cf. Dosa b. Tevet, Song R. 7:8). However, the evidence of the widespread use of non-Jewish names also in Ereẓ Israel is too obvious to be overlooked.

All the characteristics and permutations of names which are found in later generations are found among the names of the rabbis. Examples of almost every type of nomenclature can be found in the short list of the **zugot* (including their fathers) as they appear in the first chapter of *Avot*. They include purely traditional biblical names, such as Simeon (see later), Joshua, and Judah; Hebrew names which are not those of biblical worthies, though they occur there, such as Hillel, Gamliel, Johanan, and Joezer; purely Greek names such as Antigonus (in the generation immediately after Alexander the Great; cogent evidence of the rapidity of the social assimilation in nomenclature) and Avtalyon; and Aramaized forms of Hebrew names, such as Yose (twice) for Joseph, Tabbai (probably for Tobiah), and what appears to be a purely Aramaic name, Nittai. Of special interest are purely Hebrew names which do not occur in the Bible, such as Peraḥyah and (probably) Shetaḥ.

With few exceptions, all other names fall into those categories. The only forms missing are Greek names which are an obvious Grecization of Hebrew names, such as Dositheus for Nethanel or Jonathan, and purely Roman names, such as Julianus (Lulianus). There are fathers with non-Hebrew names whose sons have Hebrew names, such as Eliezer b. Hyrcanus, as there is the reverse, such as Dostai (Dositheus) b. Judah. Of interest are the names of the five sons of R. Yose b. Ḥalafta, given as Ishmael, Eleazar, Ḥalafta, Abtilus, and Menahem (Shab. 118b). Three (Ishmael, Eleazar, and Menahem; for Ishmael see below) have purely biblical names; Ḥalafta has an Aramaic name, like his grandfather (cf. Gen. R. 37:7, where R. Yose explicitly refers to the custom of giving a child the name of "our fathers," and the eight other examples in the Talmud, of which the best known are the dynasty of Hillel, the son of Eliezer b. Hyrcanus (Men. 35a), and R. Ishmael; this custom is thought to have been derived from the Greeks – L. Loew, *Beitraege zur jued. Alterskunde*, 2, 9b); and the fifth Abtilus, has a Greek name (probably a corruption of Εὐπολεηος). Another passage (TJ, Yev. 1:1) gives the names as Ishmael, Eleazar (Lazar), Menahem, Ḥalafta, and Avdimos (Eudymos) and asks about another son of Yose called Vardimon; the Talmud explains that Vardimon is identical with Menahem, but he was so called because "his face was like [*domeh*] a rose [*vered*]." This is a homiletical interpretation similar to that which makes of Tiberias *Tovah Re'iyyatah* ("of goodly appearance"; Meg. 6a). These names raise the interesting question whether it was not the custom to have two names, one Semitic (Hebrew or Aramaic) and one Greek, as was the case with Hasmonean rulers such as John (Johanan) Hyrcanus and Salome Alexandra, and whether that is not the simple explanation of the names of the five sons of Mattathias: "Johanan called Gaddis, Simeon called Thassi, Judas called Maccabeus, Eleazar called Avarah, and Jonathan called Apphus" (I Macc. 2:2).

It is equally natural that there were names which were avoided because of their unhappy associations, and this is explicitly stated. The Talmud interprets the verse "and the name of the wicked shall rot" (Prov. 10:7) to the effect that "none name their children after them" and points to the grim example of a child being given the name of *Doeg, whose mother would every day give the increase in his weight in gold to the Temple, yet "when the enemy prevailed she slaughtered and ate him" and, because of the unfortunate choice of the name of a wicked person, "see what happened to him" (Yoma 38b). Similarly the Midrash states, "Have you ever heard that a man should call his son Pharaoh, or Sisera or Sennacherib? But (one does give the name) Abraham, Isaac, Jacob, Reuben, Simeon, Levi or Judah" (Gen. R. 49:1), and in general it is stated that the name of a person determines his destiny (Ber. 7b).

In respect to this, the repeated name of Ishmael raises a difficulty. R. Yose (Gen. R. 71:3) divides names into four categories according to their beauty or ugliness as well as according to their bearers' deeds and gives Ishmael as an example of one whose "name was beautiful but his actions ugly." How then is this name so frequently found? The *tosafot* (loc. cit.) explain that it was only because, according to rabbinic tradition, he repented; and because of the bad association of the names they alter the name of Absalom, the father of Hanan the Judge (Ket. 13:1), to Avishalom (because Absalom "has no portion in the world to come" (Sanh. 103b)) and Shebna to Shechna (Tos. Yoma 38b; Ket. 104b).

By the same token, there are homilies as to the efficacy and desirability of giving names after those of biblical worthies. To the above quoted passage that fathers call their children Abraham, Isaac, Jacob, Reuben, Simeon, Levi, Judah, there is the positive injunction "One should ever examine names, to give his son a name worthy for him to become a righteous man, for sometimes the name is a contributory factor for good as for evil" (Tanḥ. Ha'azinu 7). Ephraim is praised that "the best of my sons shall be called after thee" (Lev. R. 3:2). On the contemporary plane there are quoted cases of a woman in gratitude calling her child after Nathan ha-Bavli because he had saved its life (Shab. 134a) and children called Eleazar after Eleazar b. Simeon because of a similar boon (BM 84b).

Despite that fact, however, there is one puzzling phenomenon, namely, the complete absence of names which one would expect. Not a single rabbi is known by the name of Moses (the name occurs only once in the whole talmudic literature as borne by the father-in-law of a certain scholar Huna – BB 174b, Ar. 23a), Abraham, Israel, David, or Solomon. Aaron is borne by only two *amoraim*. Of the sons of Jacob, a decided preference is given to Simeon and Judah, and among the *amoraim* to Levi and Joseph (there are no *tannaim* called Joseph and only two called Levi though, as stated, the Aramaized form Yose is common). Dan, Gad, and Asher do not occur at all, the others only rarely. (Steinschneider draws attention to a similar phenomenon among the Jews in Arabic-speaking countries.) A similar position exists with regard to the names of the prophets. Of the 15 prophets, Jeremiah, the name of one *tanna*, appears to have become popular in the amoraic period, and only one *amora* is known by the name of Ezekiel. Nahum and Jonah are of greater frequency, but the former seems to be in a class by itself, since the frequent occurrence of other names of the same root, Naḥman, Tanḥum, Tanḥuma, suggests that it was the root meaning "comfort" which decided its choice. Similarly Jonah, which occurs only among the *amoraim*, may have been influenced by the many amoraic *aggadot* (cf. Gen. R. 33:6) which identified the dove (Jonah) with Israel. Zechariah is the only name which occurs with any frequency (three *tannaim* and two *amoraim*) and Haggai (and Ḥagga). Isaiah, Hosea, Joel, Amos, Obadiah, Micah, Habakkuk, Zephaniah, and Malachi are not found at all.

It is specifically mentioned (ARN 12) that humans were not given the names of angels, and in fact such names as Raphael and Gabriel are not found.

Lastly, attention should be drawn to a passage in *Pesaḥim* 113b to the effect that Joseph of Huẓal is identical, inter alia, with Issi, the son of Gur Aryeh, who is also named Issi b. Judah. The alternatives Judah and Gur Aryeh seem to be the only example known of the custom widely prevalent in later ages to give double or alternative names on the basis of Genesis 49 and Deuteronomy 33: "Judah Aryeh." "Naphtali Zevi," "Benjamin Ze'ev," and "Joseph Bekhor Shor."

On the other hand, there is clear evidence of the use of different names. In *Gittin* 34b there is a case mentioned of a woman in Babylonia known in one place as Miriam and in another as Sarah, and of a query sent from the Diaspora to Rabban Gamliel as to the procedure to be adopted with regard to the name to be inserted on a bill of divorce in the case of a man who came from Palestine where he was known as Joseph but in Babylonia (probably) as Johanan. The fact that the vice versa is mentioned suggests that this case is also one of "anonymous names."

[Louis Isaac Rabinowitz]

Medieval Period and Establishment of Surnames

Variations in onomastic styles – generally a useful index of cultural diversity and change – are especially prominent in Jewish history. As the Jews moved from area to area, through many linguistic milieus, they were affected, in varying degrees, by the patterns of nomenclature in the societies around them. The tendency toward adoption of names in vogue with the non-Jewish majority – discernible throughout the Middle Ages – accelerated during the late 18th and 19th centuries with intensification of the process of emancipation. As modern Jews reaped the benefits of this emancipation, they increasingly imitated the mores of their neighbors, appellations included. Governments in some instances furthered this tendency by rewarding or even legislating the adoption of European forenames and family names. The 20th century – witness to both a deepening of the thrust toward integration of the Jews into Western society as well as repudiation of such integration – has seen rapid changes in Jewish name styles. While the Jews of the Americas and Western Europe have continued to pursue onomastic assimilation, their brethren in Israel have revived the old Hebrew nomenclature and created a new one.

Middle Ages

During the Middle Ages, Jews retained a preference for Hebrew forenames. In most cases these names were readily adaptable to the language of the surrounding society. Thus, in the Arab world, Abraham became Ibrahīm and David, Dāwud. In the Greek milieu, Joseph became Iosiph (Ἰωσηΐφ) and Shemariah, Samargia, while in the Latin West, Moses (Moshe) became Moyses and Ḥayyim, Hagin. Often Jews bore Hebrew names along with related, but not identical, non-Hebrew appellations, e.g., Eleazar-Manṣūr, Yefet-Ḥasan, Eliakim-Anastasios, Mattathia-Dieudonné, Jehiel-Vivant, Ḥayyim-Vital. Some designations popular in non-Jewish circles were taken over by Jews with no regard for Hebrew equivalence. In general, there was a greater likelihood of a non-Hebrew given name among the female members of the community. The range of non-Hebrew names adopted was broader and the percentage of women bearing such designations was higher than among the male Jewish population. Popular female forenames included Masʿūda and Sulṭāna (Arabic); Anastassu, Cali, and Zoe (Greek); Angélique, Fleurette, and Précieuse (French); Esperanza and Gracia (Spanish). Conversion into and out of the Jewish community was almost always accompanied by a symbolic change of name. The most common names for those entering the Jewish faith were Abraham and Sarah. Jews leaving their heritage took new names as well. In the Christian world, for example, designations such as Paul, Christian, and Mary were widespread, as was adoption of the names of prominent ecclesiastical or secular sponsors.

Designations appended to the given name, to identify more clearly the individual, developed already during antiquity. This tendency grew more marked throughout the Middle Ages. The most traditional of these surnames was the patronym, readily adapted from the Hebrew "ben" to the Arabic "ibn" and the French "fils." A special Arabic usage was the identification of the father by his firstborn son, the "abū" designation. In most areas a favored style of byname was that which derived from locale, in some cases the bearer's birthplace and others his adult residence. In the Arab world prominent examples are R. Isaac Alfasi and R. Saadiah al-Fayyumi. The great 13th-century leader of French Jewry was known both by the Hebrew R. Jehiel of Paris and by the French Vivant of Meaux, the latter his birthplace and the former the locus of his adult activities. Surnames derived from locale became particularly widespread in the wake of the periodic expulsions suffered by medieval Jewry. Both for ease of identification and out of nostalgia, Jews chose names that recalled their earlier homes. Thus, for example, in Turkish Jewry subsequent to 1492 surnames such as De Leon, D'Alvo, Zamora, and Toledano abounded. Another source of bynames was occupation. Medicine, printing, masonry, tailoring, dyeing, minting – all left their mark on Jewish onomastics. Physical and spiritual characteristics, such as size, age, complexion, honesty, and piety, also gave rise to series of widely used surnames. With the passage of time, in Jewish society as in general, these surnames tended to crystallize into family names, passed on from generation to generation.

There are two special types of designation, popular during the Middle Ages and early modern period, which deserve special mention. The first is the acronym. The components drawn upon for the acronym might include a title (rabbi, morenu ha-rav, ha-gaon), the given name, or the surname. Well-known examples include RASHI (Rabbi Solomon Yiẓḥaki), RAMBAM (Rabbi Moses b. Maimon), HA-GRA (Ha-Gaon Rabbi Elijah). The second style of designation stems from an author's *magnum opus*. In many instances, e.g., the Roke'aḥ (R. Eleazar b. Judah) and the Tur (R. Jacob b. Asher), given names and surnames were almost totally obscured by such literary appellations.

Modern Times

With the onset of emancipation there was growing imitation of forenames current in general society. Study of Berlin Jewish forenames at the beginning of the 20th century has shown a marked tendency toward appropriation of popular German designations, although some names remained peculiarly Jewish. In the U.S., the transition from immigrant-generation to first-, second-, and third-generation status has been accompanied by constantly changing given name styles. Certain names extremely popular with an earlier generation have subsequently been totally rejected, usually out of a sense that such names were excessively identified with immigrant status and with Jewishness.

Concern over the process of emancipation occasionally led governments to restrict the range of choices for Jewish given names. Such was the force, e.g., of the Austrian edict of 1787, limiting the Jews to biblical first names. The total repudiation of emancipation espoused by the Nazis expressed itself clearly in the sphere of nomenclature. On Aug. 17, 1938, a governmental decree specified 185 forenames for men and 91 for women – many with derogatory connotations – which were henceforth to be used by German Jews. Jews already bearing names other than those specified were to assume, by Jan. 1, 1939, the additional name of Israel for a male and Sarah for a female. These new appellations were to be duly registered and faithfully used in all business and legal transactions.

Along with Zionism and the revival of the Hebrew language came a new interest in Hebrew forenames. This interest was expressed in the establishment of a Commission for Hebrew Nomenclature (Va'ad Shemon Ivri) and in the compilation of a multivolume *Shemon Ivri*, containing both rules for Hebraization of non-Hebrew names and a wealth of information on specific Hebrew designations. Within the Jewish community of Palestine and subsequently the State of Israel there have been numerous forename styles, reflecting differences of origin and of generation. Each of the various elements that have been woven together into Israeli society has retained its own traditional nomenclature. Successive generations of native-born Israelis have tended to reject older patterns and create their own – sometimes utilizing obscure biblical names, sometimes reviving prebiblical Canaanite designations, sometimes fashioning wholly new appellations. This dignified return to Hebrew forenames has been carried over, in limited measure, into the Western Jewish communities. While the predominant tendency remains Westernized, a steady growth in the utilization of Hebrew names popular in Israel can be discerned in the United States and Western Europe.

As the Jews passed increasingly into the mainstream of European life, the adoption of a fixed surname became ever more important. The modes of establishing these surnames, already noted, included patronyms (Abramson, Abramowitz, Jacobson, Jacobowitz, Mendelssohn), names based on localities (Berliner, Bresslau, Poznanski, Moscowitz), vocational designations (Drucker, Schneider, Wechsler), and appellations drawn from characteristics (Alt, Klein, Schwartz). The process of altering names to suit increasingly Western tastes has been inevitable. This tendency has been obvious in the U.S. Jewish community, where the family names brought from Eastern Europe generally branded their bearers as immigrants. Cumbersome Slavic endings were dropped to form short and American-sounding names. In the earlier stages of emancipation, government edicts often had to be enacted in order to institute among the Jews the regular use of surnames. Such a step was included in the Austrian legislation of 1787. Jewish surnames were to be registered by a government commission, and where the Jews refused to select a name, this same commission was empowered to make the choice. In France, Napoleon decreed the fixing of family names for the

Jews in 1808, and in Prussia in 1812 emancipation of the Jews was made contingent upon the adoption within six months of acceptable surnames. In the United States the practical necessity of registration of immigrants coupled with ignorance of English resulted in the creation of a host of new surnames for bewildered newcomers. The Zionist experience has often been associated with the Hebraization of family names. The major political figures of the first few decades of the State of Israel reflect this phenomenon: Ben-Zvi (formerly Shimshelevitz), Shazar (Rubashov), Ben-Gurion (Gruen), Sharett (Shertok), Eshkol (Shkolnik), Meir (Myerson). The most common methods of fashioning new Hebrew surnames have been the use of patronyms, the translation of the non-Hebrew name into a Hebrew equivalent, and the adoption of a Hebrew designation phonetically similar to the non-Hebrew.

The demographic upheavals and the ideological conflicts of the 19th and 20th centuries have thoroughly shattered the onomastic unity of many Jewish families. Brothers and cousins spread across the Diaspora and Israel often bear totally different family appellations – a curious testimony to the unparalleled disruptions of the past century of Jewish life.

[Robert Chazan]

BIBLIOGRAPHY: IN THE BIBLE: G.B. Gray, *Studies in Hebrew Proper Names* (1896); Noth, Personennamen; J.J. Stamm, in: VTS, 7 (1960), 165–83; 16 (1967), 301–39; idem, in: *Theologische Zeitschrift*, 16 (1960), 285–97; idem, in: *Studies in Honor of D. Landsberger* (= *Assyriological Studies*, 16 (1965)), 413–24; idem, in: *Fourth World Congress of Jewish Studies*, Papers, 1 (1967), 141–7 301. IN THE TALMUD: The two major studies of Jewish onomastics are L. Zunz, *Namen der Juden* (1837), and H. Loewe, *Geschichte der juedischen Namen* (1929). MEDIEVAL PERIOD AND ESTABLISHMENT OF SURNAMES: Useful source material can often be found in onomastic excursuses or detailed indexes in descriptions of particular Jewish communities, e.g., S. Rosanes, Togarmah, 1 (1930^2), and U. Cassuto, *Gli Ebrei a Firenze* (1918). Valuable information is also preserved in tax records, e.g., Loeb, in: REJ, 1 (1880), and Levy, *ibid.*, 19 (1889), and in funerary inscriptions, e.g., Schwab, in: *Nouvelles archives des missions scientifiques et littéraires*, 12 (1904); Kober, in: PAAJR, 14–15 (1944–45); Avneri, *ibid.*, 33 (1965); Ankori, *ibid.*, 38 (1970); A. Beider, *A Dictionary of Jewish Surnames from the Russian Empire* (1993). Specialized studies of general interest include Steinschneider, in: JQR, 9–13 (1897–1901); Kober, in: HJ, 5 (1943); G. Kessler, *Die Familiennamen der Juden in Deutschland* (1935); Glanz, in: JSOS, 23 (1961); Friedman, in: HJ, 7 (1945). **ADD. BIBLIOGRAPHY:** A. Laredo, *Les Noms des Juifs du Maroc, Essai d'onomastique Judeo-Marocaine* (1978); H.W. Guggenheimer and E.H. Guggenheimer, *Jewish Family Names and Their Origins* (1992); A. Ariel, *The Book of Names – The 200 Most Popular Surnames in Israel* (Heb., 1997); and the series *These Are the Names: Studies in Jewish Onomastics* (ed. by A. Demsky et al., 1997–).

NAMIAS, JEROME (1910–1997), U.S. meteorologist. Born in Bridgeport, Conn., Namias worked during the 1930s at the Blue Hill Observatory affiliated with Harvard University. In 1941 he set up the extended forecast division of the U.S. Weather Bureau in Washington, D.C., and during the years of World War II prepared the weather forecasts for the convoys crossing the Atlantic and for military maneuvers. After the war Namias was appointed assistant director of the National Meteorological Center at Suitland, Maryland. Here he developed methods for the study of weather phenomena in three dimensions.

[Dov Ashbel]

NAMIER (Bernstein-Namierowski), SIR LEWIS (1888–1960), English historian and Zionist, pioneer of the trend in historical scholarship known as "Namierism." Born in eastern Galicia, where his parents were landowners, Namier became aware of his Jewish origin at the age of nine, upon overhearing antisemitic sneers at his parents' efforts to work their way into the Polish gentry. This traumatic experience turned him into a dedicated Zionist. After a spell at Vienna and Lausanne, he arrived in England in 1908. He graduated from Balliol College, Oxford, where he mixed with young men who were later to become famous, such as T.E. Lawrence and the historian Arnold J. Toynbee. Among his Jewish contemporaries were Leonard Stein and Leonard Montefiore. In 1914 Namier volunteered for the British army. He served for a time in the Foreign Office Intelligence Service and was taken to the Versailles Peace Conference to advise on problems concerning the old Hapsburg Empire, Poland, and Eastern Europe. After the war he did not turn at once to an academic career but tried his luck – unsuccessfully – in business. He needed the help of friends to complete the research for his first book and masterpiece, *The Structure of Politics at the Accession of George III* (1929). After publication of *England in the Age of the American Revolution* (1930) he was appointed professor of modern history at Manchester University (1931), holding the chair until 1953. Namier was one of the most influential British historians of the 20th century. His method, of deeply researched collective biography, widely known as "namierization," influenced several generations of historians. He was also seen as an influential conservative thinker, whose respect for the virtues of the British constitution was heavily influenced by its contrast with the catastrophic experience of the continental nations.

After his war service Namier devoted himself to the Zionist cause, although he was viewed with distrust by leaders of the Zionist movement, especially from Eastern Europe, as an outsider. Namier's Zionist creed, stemming from the outsider's need for roots and the wanderer's yearning for an anchor, found expression in 1930 in a powerful cry (in *England in the Age of the American Revolution*):

> To every man the native land is his life-giving Mother and the State raised upon the land is his law-giving Father, and the days cannot be long of a nation which fails to honor either. Only one nation has survived for two thousand years, though an orphan – my own people, the Jews. But then in the God-given Law we have enshrined the authority of a state, in the God-promised Land the idea of a Mother-Country; through the centuries from Mount Sinai we have faced Eretz Israel, our Land. Take away either, and we cease to be a nation; let both live again, and we shall be ourselves once more.

From 1929 to 1931 Namier served as political secretary to the Zionist Executive, and it was as the chief draftsman of the

*Jewish Agency, with Blanche Dugdale, that Namier, with his pedantic insistence on the niceties of formulation and protocol, made his chief contribution to the Zionist cause. He played a considerable role as an intermediary in obtaining the Ramsay MacDonald Letter, which in fact canceled the Passfield *White Paper of 1930. Thanks to his friendship with Reginald Coupland, the author of the 1937 report of the Peel Commission (the first British document to bring up the idea of a Jewish state in a partitioned Palestine), Namier was able to exercise a direct impact on matters of great political importance. He served for a time as deputy to Chaim Weizmann on the Anglo-Jewish Committee for Refugees from Germany, taking up a determined stand against the "barons" of Anglo-Jewry. At the time of the St. James' Conference on Palestine, which resulted in the anti-Zionist White Paper of May 1939, Namier insisted on a forceful Zionist policy toward the British government, occasionally criticizing the line taken by Weizmann. On the outbreak of World War II he was on loan full time from Manchester University to the Jewish Agency, for which he worked until 1945. Namier kept aloof from the ideological struggles among the Zionist factions. He disliked the religious parties and had close friends in the Labor leadership. His Zionism was a romantic nationalism in the tradition of Mazzini and Pilsudski – the vision of a historic breakthrough conceived in messianic terms – but it lacked any Jewish cultural sustenance.

Namier's historical research may be classified under four headings: the social-political structure of England in the 18th century; the 1848 revolutions; the twilight of the Hapsburg monarchy; and the international crisis leading up to World War II. All four inquiries may be said to be variations on one theme: cohesion versus disintegration. His chief work, *The Structure of Politics…*, is a microscopic examination of the composition of the successive Houses of Commons under George III. His concern was with how politics are made by members of a governing elite, to the neglect of intellectual trends and social forces. Namier's biographical method was applied to the great collective *History of Parliament* (initiated by Whitehall and Westminister), of which he was coeditor. In recognition of his achievement as an historian, Namier was elected a member of the British Academy in 1944, was knighted in 1952, and was invited to give the prestigious Romanes Lecture at Oxford. These honors went some way to assuage his feelings of disappointment at having been bypassed for the Regius Professorship of Modern History at Oxford University. The rather eccentric and intensely self-centered outsider with strong and forcefully expressed likes and dislikes scared off many contemporaries. There has long been speculation as to whether his academic disappointments, beginning with his failure to be elected to a fellowship at All Souls College, Oxford, in 1912, was chiefly due to his foreign Jewish background or to his unpleasant and gauche personality. While capable of deep emotions, he lacked flexibility and was very vulnerable. After an unhappy first marriage, Namier married in church the former Julia de Beausobre, a daughter of the Russian gentry who was deeply committed to the Greek Orthodox Church and had suffered in Soviet prisons and concentration camps (described in her book *The Woman Who Could Not Die*, 1938). She played a great role in Namier's life.

Namier paid many visits to Palestine. His only visit to the State of Israel took place in 1959 in connection with the scheme for the publication of the Weizmann papers, in which he took great interest. On that occasion he gave a memorable address to the modern history seminar at the Hebrew University. It contained a kind of confession and testament and was preceded by the Hebrew incantation "If I forget thee, O Jerusalem" tearfully.

Namier's publications include *Skyscrapers* (1931); *Additions and Corrections to Sir John Fortescue's Edition of the Correspondence of King George III* (1957); *In the Margin of History* (1939); *Conflicts* (1942); *1848: The Revolution of the Intellectuals* (1946); *Facing East* (1947); *Diplomatic Prelude* (1938–39, 1948); *Europe in Decay* (1936–40, 1950); *Avenues of History* (1952); *In the Nazi Era* (1952); *Personalities and Powers* (1958); and *Vanished Supremacies* (1958).

BIBLIOGRAPHY: L Sutherland, in: *Proceedings of the British Academy*, 48 (1962), 371–85; J.L. Talmon, in: *Commentary*, 33 (1962), 237–46; J. Namier, *Lewis Namier* (1971). **ADD. BIBLIOGRAPHY:** ODNB online; L. Colley, *Namier* (1994); J. Namier, *Lewis Namier: A Biography* (1971).

[Jacob L. Talmon]

NAMIR (Nemirovsky), MORDECHAI (1897–1975), Israeli labor leader and politician, mayor of Tel Aviv-Jaffa, member of the Second to Sixth Knessets. Born in Bratolinbovka in the Ukraine, Namir studied in a traditional *ḥeder*, a reformed *ḥeder*, and a secular high school. After the Bolshevik Revolution Namir studied economics and law at the University of Odessa but was arrested for underground activities within the framework of the *Zionist Socialist Party, and expelled from the university. He also studied music. Namir settled in Ereẓ Israel in 1924, working at first as a laborer but soon joining the management of the Histadrut's daily *Davar*. In 1926–30 he served as the secretary of Aḥdut ha-Avodah in Tel Aviv. He was the director of the statistical section of the Histadrut in 1929–35. In 1935 he was elected to the Tel Aviv City Council and in 1936–43 he was secretary of the Tel Aviv Workers' Council. Namir joined the Haganah Command in Tel Aviv in 1933. In 1940 he was arrested by the Mandatory authorities for organizing demonstrations against the White Paper policy. In World War II he served as head of the bureaus for Jewish enlistment to the British army. After the establishment of the state, Namir was sent on diplomatic missions to Bulgaria, Czechoslovakia, and Romania. In 1948–49 he served as first advisor in the Israeli consulate in Moscow, and in 1940–50 served as consul in Moscow. Namir was elected to the Second Knesset in 1951 on the Mapai list, simultaneously being elected to the position of secretary-general of the Histadrut, in which capacity he served until 1955. He served as minister of labor in 1956, holding the post until he was elected mayor of Tel Aviv-Jaffa in 1959. As mayor, Namir was responsible for extensive modernization and development schemes. Namir remained mayor and a Knesset member until 1969.

Among his writings are a book about Aḥdut ha-Avodah, *Aḥdut ha-Avodah: Ma'asef Mifleget Po'alei Ereẓ Yisrael* (1946) and one about his years as consul in Moscow, *Sheliḥut be-Moskva: Yeraḥ Devash u-Shenot Za'am* (1972).

BIBLIOGRAPHY: S. Honigman, *Be-Shem ha-Ir u-be-Sherutah: Eser Shenot Kehunat Mordekhai Namir ke-Rosh Iriyyat Tel Aviv* (1973).

[Susan Hattis Rolef (2nd ed.)]

NAMIR (née **Toib**), **ORA** (1930–), Israeli politician, member of the Eighth to Thirteenth Knessets. Namir was born in Ḥaderah, and grew up in Moshav Ḥoglah. In the War of Independence she served as an officer in Upper Galilee. During the Second Knesset she served as the secretary of the Mapai parliamentary group, and secretary of the coalition administration. In Israel she studied at the Lewinsky Seminary and the Givat ha-Sheloshah Seminary. In 1954–57 she studied English literature at Hunter College in New York, and served as a secretary with the Israeli delegation to the United Nations, in the years when Abba *Eban was ambassador. When she returned to Israel she went back to her job in the Knesset, and for a while worked as the secretary of the architects' office that was designing the new Knesset building, under Tel Aviv architect Shimon Powsner. In 1959, she married Mordechai *Namir, who was elected as Mapai's first mayor of Tel Aviv in that year, and started to work in the field of social work. In 1967–79 she was secretary of Na'amat (the Histadrut women's section) in Tel Aviv, serving also on the secretariat of national Na'amat (1970–74).

Namir was first elected on the Labor Alignment list to the Knesset in 1973. In 1975, after her husband had passed away, she was appointed by Prime Minister Yitzhak *Rabin as chairperson of a committee of inquiry concerning the status of women in Israel. The committee completed its work after the 1977 political upheaval, and Namir presented its report to Prime Minister Menaḥem *Begin in 1978. After the publication of this report, which pointed to widespread discrimination against women in Israel, the official approach to the subject started to change.

In the Ninth and Tenth Knessets, Namir served as chairperson of the Knesset Education and Culture Committee, and in the Eleventh and Twelfth as chairperson of the Labor and Welfare Committee, earning for herself the reputation of a hard-working and highly demanding MK. Her hope to be appointed minister in the National Unity government formed in 1988 was not fulfilled. The following year she considered running for secretary-general of the Labor Party opposite Micha Harish, but withdrew her candidacy claiming that the competition was not fair. In the primaries to the Labor Party leadership in February 1992 she contended opposite Yitzhak *Rabin, Shimon *Peres, and Israel *Kessar, but received less than five percent of the vote. In the government formed by Rabin after the elections to the Thirteenth Knesset she was at first appointed minister of the environment, and in December 1992, minister of labor and welfare. Namir ran in the Labor primaries for the elections to the Fourteenth Knesset, but even though she received a realistic place in the list, she was offended by the fact that among the women Dalia *Itzik came before her. She then resigned from the Thirteenth Knesset shortly before the elections, after being appointed ambassador to Beijing – a position she held from 1996 to 2000.

[Susan Hattis Rolef (2nd ed.)]

NANCY, capital of Meurthe-et-Moselle department, northeastern France; former capital of the Duchy of *Lorraine. In 1286 the Jews acquired a cemetery at nearby Laxou. In 1341, and later in 1455, several Jews settled in Nancy itself but were expelled from the Duchy in 1477. The Jews temporarily reappeared in Nancy in 1595. Maggino Gabrieli, known as the "consul-general of the Hebrew and Levantine nation," attempted to establish two banks and a pawnshop in 1637–1643. In 1707 and 1712 Duke Leopold authorized three Jewish bankers from *Metz to settle in Nancy, one of whom, Samuel *Lévy, became the duke's chief tax collector in 1715. After Lévy fell into disgrace, there was a hostile reaction toward the Jews. Nevertheless, in 1721 an edict authorized 70 Jewish families to remain in Lorraine, eight of them in Nancy and its surroundings. The 90 Jewish families in Nancy in 1789 (50 of whom were without authorization) included such wealthy merchants and manufacturers as the *Alcan, Goudchaux, and Berr families from whom the trustees of the Duchy's Jewish community were chosen. Herz *Cerfberr became squire of Tomblaine, and *Berr Isaac Berr became the leader of the Ashkenazi Jews in 1789. There was a house of prayer in 1745, but it was not until 1788 that a synagogue was officially built, eight years after the chief rabbi of Lorraine established himself in Nancy. (The synagogue was renovated in 1842 and again in 1935.) Notable among the chief rabbis of the consistory formed in 1808 were Marchand Ennery and Solomon *Ullmann. With the influx of refugees from Alsace and Moselle after 1870, the number of Jews in Nancy increased to some 4,000 by the end of the century. Nancy made important contributions to French Jewish cultural life. The prayer room of the Polish Jews was decorated by the artist *Mané-Katz. Nancy was the birthplace of the writer André *Spire and Nobel Prize winner F. *Jacob.

[Gilbert Cahen]

Holocaust Period

Many of Nancy's prewar Jewish population (about 3,800 in 1939) fled the city under the German occupation. Those who stayed were brutally persecuted. In three *Aktionen* in 1942–43, 130 Jews of foreign origin were arrested and deported, while over 400 others who had fled to the "free" zone in the south were arrested and deported after it was overrun by the Germans in 1942. Only 22 survivors returned. Among the old French Jewish families, 250 victims were deported, of whom only two survived. The majority were arrested on March 2, 1944, along with 72-year-old Chief Rabbi Haguenauer, who despite his being forewarned, refused to desert the members of his community. A street in postwar Nancy bears his name. The synagogue, as well as other buildings belonging to the Jews, were plundered by the Nazis. The synagogue interior was destroyed, while the holy books were sold to a rag collector. Several of the art works and books in the local Musée Historique Lorrain and departmental archives were saved. After the war the community of Nancy rapidly recovered, and by 1969 it had about 3,000 members with a full range of Jewish communal institutions. A chair for Hebrew studies was set up at the university. In 1987, the community was said to number 4,000.

[Georges Levitte]

BIBLIOGRAPHY: Gross, Gal Jud, 400: C. Pfister, *Histoire de Nancy*, 1 (1902), 678–81; 3 (1908), 310–38; A. Gain et. al., in: *Revue juive de Lorraine*, 2–3 (1926–27); 9–11 (1933–35), passim; J. Godchot, in: REJ, 86 (1928), 1–35. **ADD. BIBLIOGRAPHY:** *Guide de judaïsme français* (1987), 39; *Jewish Travel Guide* (2002), 73.

NANTES, city in Brittany, capital of the department of Loire-Atlantique, western France. The first mention of Jews there dates from 1234. In 1236 the Jews of Nantes, as well as those in the rest of *Brittany and other provinces of western France, were victims of a riot that broke out during the Sixth Crusade. The attack was followed by their expulsion in 1240. The importance of the community is shown by the cemetery for which evidence exists from 1231. The Rue des Juifs which the community occupied still retains its name.

From the second half of the 16th century many Portuguese of *Marrano origin settled in Nantes. The Vaz, Mendez, Rodriguez, and other families found here generally became loyal Christians, whose members frequently chose an ecclesiastical career. Some Marranos whose sympathies remained with Judaism occasionally passed through Nantes but did not settle there. Thus, toward the end of the 16th century, Abraham d'Espinoza, the grandfather of Baruch *Spinoza, stayed in Nantes with a few members of his family before establishing himself in Holland. In 1636, however, several Portuguese Jews of *Bayonne, expelled from this frontier town at the time of the Franco-Spanish War, settled in Nantes. At the end of the 18th century local merchants, led largely by the old clothes dealers, leveled legal charges against several Jewish merchants who were newly established in the town. Public opinion sympathized with the Jews, however, as evidenced in articles in the *Journal de la Correspondence de Nantes* of 1789 to 1791, and in the Feuille Nantaise of 1795. There were 25 Jewish families in Nantes in 1808–09. In 1834 they established an organized community with a membership of 18 families. A synagogue was built in 1870, and by 1898 there were about 50 families.

According to the census of 1942 carried out by the Vichy government, there were 531 Jews in Nantes. By the beginning of September 1943, the number had been reduced to 53 as a result of arrests and deportations. At first, some Jews were arrested and imprisoned in the Caserne Richemont of Nantes, but in January 1944 they were deported. After World War II, few Jewish families settled in Nantes and in 1960 there were said to be only about 25. The growth of the city, and especially the arrival of Jews from North Africa, led to an increase in the Jewish population. By 1969 Nantes had over 500 Jewish inhabitants. There was a combined synagogue and community center, religious instruction classes, and youth activities.

BIBLIOGRAPHY: H. de Berranger, *Evocation du vieux Nantes* (1966), 15, 25; Brunschvicg, in: REJ, 14 (1887), 80ff.; 17 (1888), 123ff.; 19 (1889), 294ff.; 49 (1904), 110, 112: Z. Szajkowski, *Analytical Franco-Jewish Gazetteer 1939–1945* (1966), 213.

[Bernhard Blumenkranz / David Weinberg (2nd ed.)]

NAOMI (Heb. נָעֳמִי; probably from *nuʿmay* (Ugaritic, *nʿmy*), "pleasantness"), the wife of *Elimelech the Ephrathite from Beth-Lehem in Judah who, because of famine, immigrated to Moab with his wife and his sons Mahlon and *Chilion (Ruth 1:1–2). Her husband and her two sons, who had married Moabite women, died in Moab. When she heard that the famine in Judah had ended, Naomi returned there. Her daughters-in-law wanted to accompany her, but she tried to dissuade them from binding their destiny to hers. Chilion's widow, *Orpah, was persuaded, but Mahlon's widow, *Ruth, clung to her mother-in-law (4:10). Naomi, in return, looked after the interests of her faithful daughter-in-law so that Ruth was taken in marriage by *Boaz, a relative of the family. Naomi adopted and nursed the son born to Ruth and Boaz and so achieved a measure of consolation in her old age.

[Isaac Avishur]

In the Aggadah

Naomi was of outstanding beauty. She and Elimelech were cousins, their fathers being the sons of Nahshon son of Amminadab. From this the rabbis taught, "even the merit of one's ancestor is of no avail when one emigrates from Ereẓ Israel" (BB 91a). Naomi was so anxious to return to Ereẓ Israel that she set out on her journey barefoot and in rags. She did not even stop to rest on the Sabbath (Ruth R. 2: 12). On the way she taught Ruth the laws concerning proselytes (*ibid.*). She arrived in Beth-Lehem on the day of the funeral of Boaz's wife (BB 91a). In her youth Naomi had been a nurse to Boaz as she later became a nurse to Ruth's son, Obed (*Lekaḥ Tov* on Ruth 4:16). Proverbs 31:19 is interpreted to refer to Naomi who brought Ruth under the wings of the *Shekhinah* (Mid. Hag., Gen. 23:1). She is thus included in the 22 women of valor enumerated by the rabbis (*ibid.*).

BIBLIOGRAPHY: Ginzberg, Legends, 4 (1913), 31–32; 6 (1928), 189–92.

NAPHTALI (Heb. נַפְתָּלִי), the sixth son of Jacob and second son of Bilhah, Rachel's maid (Gen. 30:7). The name is said to derive from Rachel's words, "A fateful contest (*naftule*) I waged (*niftalti*) with my sister; yes, and I have prevailed" (Gen. 30:8). Its exact origin is uncertain. Nothing is related about Naphtali in the biblical sources except that he had four sons. He gave his name to one of the tribes of Israel.

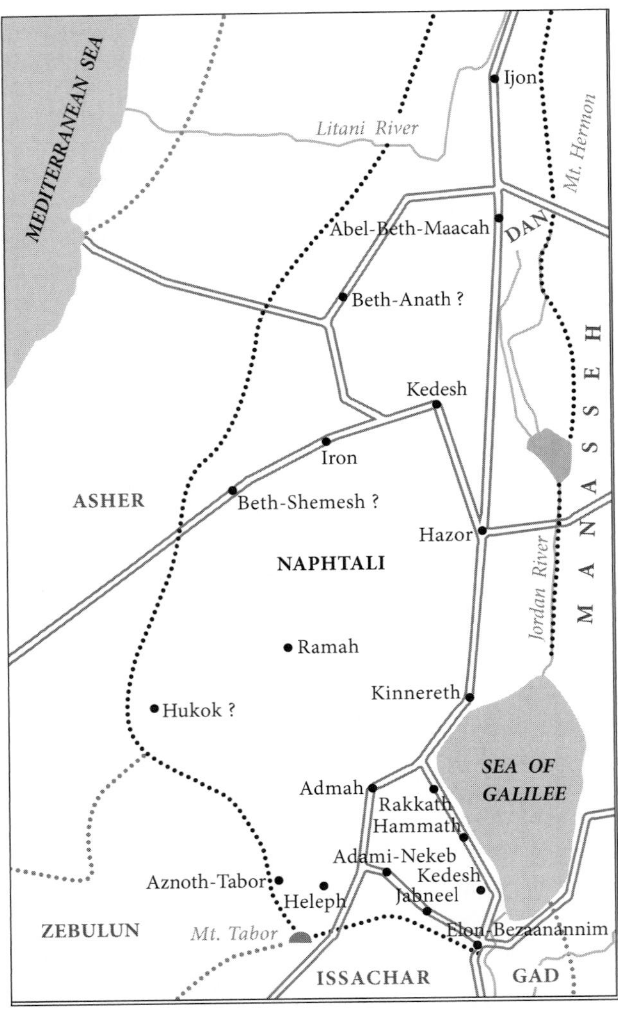

Territory of the tribe of Naphtali. After Y. Aharoni, Lexicon Biblicum, *Dvir Co. Ltd, Tel Aviv, 1965.*

The Tribe and its Territory

The affiliation of Naphtali to Bilhah testifies to an inferior status, at some period, among the tribes of Israel, as does its position in the listings of the sons of Jacob where it appears in the ninth (Deut. 33:23; Gen. 49:21), tenth (Gen. 35:23ff.; I Chron. 2:1), eleventh (Num. 1:15, 42), and occasionally even in last place (Gen. 46:24; Deut. 27:13). The four clans of the tribe of Naphtali are Jahzeel, Guni, Jezer, and Shillem (Gen. 46:24; Num. 26:48–50; and with some slight variants, I Chron. 7:13). These names do not seem to have any connection with settlements, a fact which testifies to their tribal, rather than territorial, origins. This would contradict the view of the German school about the formation of the Israelite tribes. (Guni may be an exception as a place name, possibly to be identified with Umm Jūnī on the east bank of the Jordan.) However, the matter is complicated because of a Gadite family with the same name (I Chron. 5:15). Naphtali's territory was the sixth to be decided by lots at Shiloh in the tribal division of the land. The description in Joshua comprises border points and a list of cities (Josh. 19:32–39). The description of the boundary begins with the south, and proceeds from west to east, from the Tabor to the Jordan, with five designated border points: Heleph (apparently Khirbat ʿArbītā north of the Tabor), the Elon-Bezaanannim (apparently a geographic designation; cf. Judg. 4:11), Adami-Nekeb (apparently Khirbat Dāmiya), Jabneel (either Tell Anʿam or Khirbat Yamma), and Lakkum (apparently Khirbat el-Manṣūra close to the Jordan). The western and eastern boundaries are only alluded to by reference to the boundary of Zebulun at the south and Asher on the west. In the south, the text designates only Hukok, the point of intersection of the three tribes Naphtali, Zebulun, and Asher (Hukok is apparently the ruins of Khirbat Jumayjima to the east of Cabul). The description of the northern boundary is missing, but by reference to the northern boundary of Asher which extended to Sidon (Josh. 19:28), and relying on the fact that the northern border of David's kingdom at the time of David's census was "to Dan and from Dan they went around to Sidon" (II Sam. 24:6), it may be assumed that it followed the line Dan-Ijon-Sidon. The northern boundary of Naphtali's territory can thus be envisioned to have been to the east of this line. The list of cities is probably not complete since, according to its title, it includes only "fortified cities" (Josh. 19:35), which testifies to the character and origin of the list. Furthermore, an archaeological survey has shown that there were many populated areas in the territory of Naphtali during the period of settlement. The total number of 19 cities given at the end of the list (19:38) does not refer to the given list, and perhaps it includes also the settlements described in the list as border points.

The History of the Tribe

Information is sparse and is based only on inference. The importance of Naphtali's territory from an agricultural (Deut. 33:23) and military standpoint (Josh. 19:35, "fortified cities") and the designation of the whole of Galilee as "the land of Naphtali" (II Kings 15:29) testify to the prominent and central role of this tribe among the northern tribes during the historical period, in contrast to the nomadic. At the beginning of the period of the Judges, the members of the tribe of Naphtali appear to have constituted a minority living among the Canaanites and to have been subject to them (Judg. 1:33). Only after the decisive battle between the Canaanites and the Israelite tribes during the time of Deborah did they overcome those Canaanites living within their territory. In this war, the tribe played an outstanding role. The rebellion was led by Barak the son of Abinoam from Kedesh-Naphtali (Judg. 4:6) and the men of his tribe risked their lives on the heights of the field (5:18). High praise is given to Naphtali and its territory both in the blessings of Jacob and Moses which refer to the period of the Judges. In the united kingdom of David and Solomon, Naphtali became a royal administrative district which seems to have also included the territory of Dan. (Apparently, the families of Dan were absorbed by Naphtali; cf. I Kings 7:13–14 with II Sam. 24:6; I Kings 15:20; II Chron. 2:13; 16:4.) The importance of the tribe and the districts is perhaps expressed in the appointment of the king's son-in-law as his officer there (I Kings 4: 15). Apparently deriving from the same period is the list of three levitical cities in Naphtali – Kedesh, Hammoth-Dor, and Kartan (Josh. 21:32, with minor variants in I Chron. 6:61), which were religious and administrative centers set up by the central government. One of the important fortresses established in the days of Solomon was the city of Hazor in the territory of Naphtali (I Kings 9:15). Information about the tribe and its territory after the division of the kingdom is exceedingly scanty. From the little available it is clear that the tribe suffered from the protracted conflict between the kingdoms of Israel and Aram. In the reign of Baasha, Ben-Hadad, the king of Aram, invaded "and conquered Ijon, Dan, Abel-Beth-Maacah and all Chinneroth, with all the land of Naphtali" (I Kings 15:20), and he may possibly have annexed them to his kingdom. However, in the time of Omri and Ahab the tribe was certainly liberated. In 732 B.C.E., Tiglath-Pileser III conquered, among other places, "all the land of Naphtali and he carried the people captive to Assyria" (II Kings 15:29). It is reasonable to assume that he exiled only a section of the population, and that the territory, along with those remaining, was annexed as an Assyrian province with its center at Megiddo. In the days of Josiah, an attempt was made to reunite the northern tribes with the kingdom of the house of David, and apparently Naphtali was among them (II Chron. 34:6). However, it proved unsuccessful owing to the death of Josiah at Megiddo and the subsequent subjugation of the land.

BIBLIOGRAPHY: A. Saarisalt, *Boundary Between Issachar and Naphtali* (1927); Abel, Georg, 2 (1938), 63–65; J. Lewy, in: HUCA, 18 (1943–44), 452, n. 122; Alt, Kl Schr, index; Y. Aharoni, *Hitnaḥalut Shivtei Yisrael ba-Galil ha-Elyon* (1957); idem, Land; Z. Kalai, *Naḥalot Shivtei Yisrael* (1967), 56–57, 191ff., 259–60, 367ff., 401ff.; *Kol Ereẓ Naphtali* (1968).

[Isaac Avishur]

NAPHTALI, TESTAMENT OF. A Hebrew fragment of a Testament of Naphtali was identified among the *Dead Sea Scrolls. It seems that this work was one of the sources of the Jewish Greek Pseudepigrapha, the Testament of the Twelve *Patriarchs. The Hebrew fragment deals with the genealogy of Bilhah and is longer than the parallel passage in the Greek text. A Testament of Naphtali in medieval Hebrew is preserved in two versions, the second, published by Wertheimer, being a secondary elaboration of the first one. The medieval Hebrew Testament, which is not identical with the text discovered in Qumran – it does not contain a genealogy of Bilhah – nor with the Greek Testament of Naphtali in the Testament of the Patriarchs, is a translation from a non-Hebrew source, probably Greek. This source was composed in the same trend as the Testament of the Patriarchs and shows clear affinities with the extant Greek Testament of Naphtali.

The ethical teaching of the medieval Hebrew Testament is based on fear of God and the golden rule (in the negative form). The stress on the importance of Levi and Judah is common to this text, the Greek Testament of the Patriarchs, and the Book of Jubilees; behind this idea lies, apparently, the Qumran concept of the two Messiahs, Messiah b. David, the anointed of Judah, and Messiah, the anointed of Aaron. In the text a dream of Naphtali is narrated which is similar to that in the Greek text (Naphtali 5:1–3). In both versions of the dream, Levi is identified with the sun and Judah with the moon. This passage, as indeed the whole work, shows a polemical tendency against Joseph and his descendants, in sharp opposition to the very positive appreciation of Joseph in the Testament of the Patriarchs. The second dream also has a parallel in chapter 6 of the Greek Testament of Naphtali, and it also shows the same polemical attitude toward Joseph. It is an interesting fact that the text praises the Hebrew language, which is in accordance with the ideology of the whole major religious trend exemplified in the Testament of the Patriarchs and the Dead Sea Scrolls. The treatise ends with the blessing of the man "who does not defile the Holy Spirit of God which hath been put and breathed into him," a theologoumenon which has its exact parallel in the *Damascus Document.

BIBLIOGRAPHY: T. Gaster, *Studies and Texts*, 1 (1925–28), 69–91; 3 (1925–28), 22–30; R.H. Charles, *The Greek Version of the Testament of the Twelve Patriarchs* (1908); idem, *The Testament of the Twelve Patriarchs* (1908), lxvi–lxviii, 221–7; A.J. Wertheimer, *Battei Midrashot*, 1 (1950), 193–203; Milik, *Dix ans découvertes dans le Désert de Juda* (1957), 320.

[David Flusser]

NAPLES, city and former kingdom in Campania, S. Italy. The first Jewish settlement there probably dates to the beginning of the first century C.E., if not before. Josephus (Antiquities, XVII, 23–25, and Wars, II, 101–05) reports that during Augustus' rule there was already a Jewish community at Puteoli (Dicaearchia), near Napoli. Puteoli was the most important mercantile harbor of Roman Italy in that period. Some sepulchral inscriptions in Latin dated to a later period indeed attest a Jewish presence in the area. By the fourth century C.E. the community of Naples was of considerable size and economically important. A Jewish burial ground was excavated in 1908 in Corso Malta. The tombs date from the end of the fourth century to the middle of the fifth century C.E. Three of the inscriptions are in Latin, one in Greek. It is interesting that one of the inscriptions in Latin is followed by an inscription in Hebrew. All the inscriptions are decorated with the *menorah*. The *etrog* as well as the Holy Ark decorate two of the inscriptions. In 536, according to the Byzantine historian Procopius (War V, 8:41, 10:24–25), the Jewish population helped the Goths, although unsuccessfully, to defend the city when it was besieged by the Byzantines.

Eleventh- and twelfth-century documents show that the Naples community had a synagogue and a school. Jews enjoyed the right to own real estate and to dispose of it as they wished. *Benjamin of Tudela, who visited the town in c. 1159, found 500 Jews living there. From 1288, under Charles II, anti-

Jewish disorders incited by Dominican preachers occurred; they reached their height in 1290 when serious outrages were committed and a synagogue was converted into a church. However, in 1330, Robert of Anjou invited Jews from the Balearic Islands to settle in Naples and in the rest of his kingdom, promising them protection against annoyance and the same taxation rights as those enjoyed by Christians. From 1442, under the rule of Aragon, conditions for the Jews in Naples and its surroundings were favorable, and attracted Jews from various parts of Europe.

At the end of 1492 and the beginning of 1493, a large influx of refugees from Sicily, Sardinia, and Spain found temporary asylum in Naples. The Spanish refugees, undernourished and sick, probably introduced the pestilence in 1492 that struck down 20,000 persons in Naples alone. Among the Spanish refugees who landed in Naples in 1492 was Don Isaac *Abrabanel, who became fiscal adviser to King Ferdinand I and Alfonso II. In 1495 the Kingdom of Naples was conquered by the Spanish and in 1496 a decree for the expulsion of the Jews was issued, although it was not implemented. The expulsion of the Jews was definitively ordered in 1510 and finally carried out: exception was made for 200 wealthy Jewish families who undertook to pay an annual tax of 300 ducats to the crown. In 1515 the *New Christians were also expelled from the kingdom. The 200 wealthy families, who had been joined by others in 1520, had increased to 600 within the following decade. Although a new decree of expulsion was issued in 1533, permission was granted to the Jews in November 1535 to reside in Naples for a further ten years against the payment of 10,000 ducats. However, the agreement was not respected by Emperor Charles V, and in 1541 he ordered the total expulsion of the Jews; this coincided with the establishment of a Christian loan bank (*Monte di Pietá) in Naples.

It was not until 1735, when the kingdom passed to the Bourbons, that Jews were readmitted into Naples and the vicinity by an edict signed by Charles IV on Feb. 3, 1740. However, following pressure by Jesuits and the Church, the few Jews who had accepted the invitation were again expelled (Sept. 18, 1746). In 1822, under the suggestion of Metternich, the Austrian premier, Solomon de Rothschild had his brother, Karl Mayer von *Rothschild of Frankfurt on the Main, settled in Naples as court banker of the Bourbons. There Rothschild did much to help the ruling dynasty economically, and he pushed for a liberalization of the government. Rothschild resided in Villa Acton-Pignatelli in Via Chiaia. Rothschild's task came to an end in 1860, when Garibaldi conquered Naples. By then a small Jewish community had developed around Rothschild. Religious services began to be held in Naples in 1831, but a synagogue was not opened until June 1864. The synagogue located in the Palazzo Sessa was inaugurated in 1864 thanks to the influence of Baron Rothschild. In the entrance there are two marble statues; one in honor of the community president Dario Ascarelli who bought the premises for the synagogue in 1910 and the other which commemorates the deportation of Neapolitan Jews during World War II. Restoration was carried out in 1992.

[Ariel Toaff / Samuele Rocca (2nd ed.)

In 1931 there were 998 Jews in the community of Naples, whose authority extended to all southern Italy. Persecutions during World War II had minor consequences as the Allied landing led to a speedy liberation of southern Italy. Nevertheless, 11 Jews were taken to extermination camps from Naples and others were killed elsewhere. From 1943 to 1945 Naples was the biggest harbor that served the Allies in the Mediterranean. Thus various Jewish units from Palestine served in the area as well as Jewish chaplains from the U.S. Army. Both assisted the local Jewish community. After the war, the U.S. Navy held regular services for American Jewish sailors in Naples. At the war's end 534 Jews remained in the community. In 1969 there were 450 Jews in Naples. In the early 21st century the community numbered a handful of families.

[Sergio DellaPergola / Samuele Rocca (2nd ed.)]

Hebrew Printing

A Hebrew press was established in Naples not later than 1485, and in the decade which followed nearly 20 books were published, making the city one of the most important cradles of Hebrew *incunabula. Naples was then a center of general book printing and the book trade, and wealthy members of the Jewish community including immigrants from Spain and Portugal, financed the publishing of Hebrew books. The first Jewish printer there was the German Joseph b. Jacob *Gunzenhausen, who was followed in 1490 by Joshua Solomon *Soncino. A third printer was Isaac b. Judah ibn Katorzo (of Calatayud in Spain). The first book published (in 1487) was Psalms with David Kimḥi's commentary, followed by Proverbs with a commentary by Immanuel of Rome (n.d.), and the rest of the Hagiographa in 1488. A Pentateuch (with Rashi), the Five Scrolls, and the Antiochus *Scroll appeared in 1491. The first printed edition of Abraham ibn Ezra's Pentateuch commentary came out in 1488; Naḥmanides' Pentateuch commentary was printed in 1490 by Katorzo; and that of Baḥya b. Asher in 1492. The magnificent first edition of the entire Mishnah (with Maimonides' commentary) was published in 1492. Halakhic works included Jacob Landau's *Agur* (n.d.), the first Hebrew work with approbations (*Haskamot) and the second printed in the lifetime of the author (who was one of Gunzenhausen's typesetters); the first edition of the *Kol Bo* (n.d.); and Kimḥi's *Sefer ha-Shorashim* was published by Gunzenhausen in 1490, and by Soncino (and Katorzo?) in 1491. Baḥya b. Joseph ibn Paquda's "Duties of the Heart" (*Ḥovot ha-Levavot*) appeared in 1489, and Naḥmanides' *Sha'ar ha-Gemul* in 1490. Of particular interest are Pereẓ Trabot's *Makre Dardekei* (1488), a 14th-century Hebrew glossary with Italian, Arabic, and also French, Provençal, and German translations; Kalonymus b. Kalonymus' satirical *Even Boḥan* (1489); a Hebrew grammar, *Petaḥ Devarai* (1492); a five-volume Hebrew translation of Avicenna's medical canon *Ha-Kanon ha-Gadol* printed for the first and only time. The fourth edition of Dante's *Divina*

Commedia was published by an anonymous Jewish printer in Naples in 1477.

BIBLIOGRAPHY: Roth, Italy, passim; Milano, Italia, passim; E. Munkacsi, *Der Jude von Neapel* (Zurich, 1939); N. Ferorelli, *Ebrei nell'Italia meridionale…* (1915), passim; idem, in: *Vessillo Israelitico*, 54 (1906), 397–401, 466–74; 63 (1915), 146–7; Sacerdote, in: RMI, 31 (1965), 90–96; L. Poliakov, *Banquiers juifs et le Saint-Siege…* (1965), 191–5. PRINTING: J. Bloch, *Hebrew Printing in Naples* (1942) (= New York Public Library Bulletin, June 1942); D.W. Amram, *Makers of Hebrew Books in Italy…* (1909), 63ff.; H.D. Friedberg, *Toledot ha-Defus ha-Ivri be-Italyah* (1956), 49–50; Roth, Renaissance, 170–2, 176; A.M. Habermann, *Ha-Madpisim Benei Soncino* (1933), 25–30, 35–36. **ADD. BIBLIOGRAPHY:** D., Abulafia, "Il Mezzogiorno peninsulare dai Bizantini all'espulsione (1541)," in: C. Vivanti (ed.), *Gli ebrei in Italia I, Storia d'Italia, Annali*, 11 (1996) 5–46; C. Giordano and I. Kahn, *Gli Ebrei in Pompeii, in Ercolano e nelle citta della campania Felix* (1965), 20–23, 35–40; V. Giura, "Gli ebrei nel regno di Napoli tra Aragona e Spagna," in: *Ebrei e Venezia* (1987), 771–80; E. Serao, "Nuove iscrizioni da un sepolcro giudaico di Napoli," in: *Puteoli*, 12–13 (1988–89), 103–17; A. Silvestri, "Gli ebrei nel Regno di Napoli durante la dominazione aragonese," in: *Campania sacra*, 18 (1987), 21–77.

NAPLES AND COLLIER COUNTY, county in Florida, U.S. At the beginning of the 21st century, Naples and Collier County hosted perhaps the newest and fastest-growing Jewish community in Florida. This area on the southwest coast of Florida did not welcome Jews and there are none recorded there until the late 1950s. When Joseph and Helen Weinfeld drove into Naples, interested in purchasing real estate, they were told, "If you are Jewish, just keep going." Through persistence, by 1956, Joe Weinfeld was selling lots in Naples. The earliest known families to settle were the Freschels, Gilmans, Dinaburgs, and Luffs. These families with young children ventured to Naples and established businesses. The Freschels and Gilmans opened the Anchor Bar; the Dinaburgs made cement blocks; and Gabriel Luff was the first Jewish real estate person in town. There were no streetlights and no doctors and mosquitoes were a major challenge. A few years later the developer of Golden Gate and Golden Gate Estates employed some Jewish salesmen who added to the tiny community and there were enough Jews to have High Holiday services. In 1962 the Jewish Community Center of Collier County was founded with Garson Dinaburg as the lay leader and Leo Spiegel as the volunteer cantor. Three years later a board of directors was established. Services were held in various venues around town and the family of builder Sam Chudnow donated a Torah in 1965 when he had to say *kaddish*. In 1966 the State of Florida issued a charter, signed by president Garson Dinaburg, secretary Gabriel Luff and vice president/treasurer William Freschel. By 1970 retirees helped increase their numbers along with younger professionals and retailers with families. Judy Dinaburg married Charles Wallowitz in the first Jewish wedding and their daughter, Jennifer Relkin, was the community's first baby naming. Joseph Weinfeld started a religious school in 1972 with eight children. By 1973 there was a bar mitzvah and congregation president Joseph Weinfeld and lay leader Garson Dinaburg led efforts to secure from Collier Development Corporation about two acres of land on Pine Ridge Road for $15,000. Led by Rabbi Simon Friedman of Cape Coral, 57 member families participated in the dedication of the new synagogue on April 31, 1975. The first paid rabbi was Abraham Shusterman of Baltimore, who came in 1977. An educational and social wing was added in 1980 and the name of the reform congregation was changed to Temple Shalom that year. Rabbis Mark Golub, Alan Tuffs, and Seth Philips each served the congregation for three years. Recognizing the need for expanded space in 1988, young congregation members purchased another piece of property on Pine Ridge Road, close to State Road 951. A new synagogue was dedicated in 1991 with a membership of 375 families. In 2005 there were 713 member families of this pioneer congregation. Rabbi James Perman became spiritual leader in 1993 and Rabbi Daniel Sherman joined him as assistant in 1999.

As of 2005 the Jewish population of about 6,000 (not including snowbirds), mostly from the Midwest and lately also from the New England area, was distributed all over the county from Marco Island north through Naples and into Bonita Springs and Estero. With an annual growth rate of about 15%, there are many young families, a gap in the 50-somethings and then early retirees. A high percentage of the Jews are affiliated; about 50% belong to a congregation. There are three Reform congregations (Temple Shalom of Naples, Jewish Congregation of Marco Island, and Naples Jewish Center), a Conservative (Ma'ayan Congregation), and a Chabad with their various havurot, Sisterhoods, and Men's Clubs. Jewish organizations are vibrant and diverse: Jewish Family Services, Naples Friends of ARMDI (Magen David Adom); Hadassah, National Council of Jewish Women; Brandeis; ORT, Israel Bonds, Jewish War Veterans, Southern Florida Holocaust Museum, and even a Yiddish Club. Monies have been raised for the United Jewish Appeal since about 1980.The Jewish Federation of Collier County raised $660,000 in 2004. The Federation, which counts 30% of the households as contributors, publishes *Federation Star* monthly with community news.

[Marcia Jo Zerivitz (2nd ed.)]

°**NAPOLEON BONAPARTE** (1769–1821), emperor of the French. He proclaimed the *emancipation of the Jews in the Italian states which he had established, and the majority of the Jews in Italy hailed Napoleon as a liberator and political savior, calling him "Ḥelek Tov" (lit. "Good Part"; cf. Bona-Parte). Even by this time, however, problems had arisen from the contradictions posed by Jewish laws and communal autonomy on the one hand and the political and civic obligations of the Jews on the other. In May 1799, during Napoleon's campaign in Palestine (see below), the government newspaper *Moniteur* published the information that Napoleon had issued a manifesto in Palestine which promised the Jews their return to their country. Many European newspapers reproduced this information, although today it is questioned whether Napoleon really issued such a declaration. The news concerning the manifesto and Napoleon's Palestine campaign made little impression on the Jews in Europe. On the other hand, the campaign gave rise to millenarian hopes among certain nonconformist circles in England; for the first time, their expectation of the return of Israel to Palestine and hence to the Church was linked with realistic political projects.

The principal influence exercised by Napoleon as emperor on Jewish history was in the years 1806 to 1808 when he convened the Assembly of Jewish *Notables and the (French) *Sanhedrin, and established the *Consistories. The programmatic documents formulated during this period and the institutions which then came into being embody the first practical expression of the demands made by a centralized modern state on the Jews who had become its citizens – "the separation of the political from the religious elements in Judaism." The news of the activities of the Jewish assemblies stirred both Jewish and gentile sectors of society in Central and Western Europe. The Austrian authorities were apprehensive that the Jews would regard Napoleon in the light of a messiah. In England, theological hopes and political projects for the "Return of Israel" intensified. On March 17, 1808, however, Napoleon issued an order restricting the economic activity and the freedom of movement of the Jews in the eastern provinces of the empire for a period of ten years, an order which became known among Jews as the "Infamous Decree."

Napoleon's victorious armies brought civic emancipation to the Jews in all the countries of Central and Western Europe where governments dependent on him were formed. The central Jewish Consistory established in the Kingdom of Westphalia was the first Jewish institution in Europe to introduce reforms into the Jewish religion. The Jews of Eastern Europe were only ephemerally influenced by Napoleon's conquests. Discussions were held among Ḥasidim as to whether support should be given to Napoleon or the Russian Czar Alexander I in order to hasten the coming of the messiah.

[Baruch Mevorah]

The Palestine Campaign (Feb. 8–June 1, 1799)

After the conquest of Egypt in August 1798 by Napoleon's army, the defeated survivors fled to Palestine, where the pasha of *Acre, Ahmad al-Jazzār, and the Turks attempted to organize resistance. At the beginning of February, Napoleon moved into Palestine at the head of a 13,000-man army. He took El Arish on Feb. 20 and reached Gaza on Feb. 24; the small Jewish community there fled to Hebron. On March 1 Napoleon reached Ramleh and on March 7 Jaffa surrendered after a four-day siege. The French army continued northward, crossed the southern Carmel on March 16 and 17, and reached al-Ḥāvithiyya (west of Sha'ar ha-Amakim). Haifa was captured on March 18. On March 19 the French army reached the walls of Acre; however, supported by British warships, the city withstood a protracted siege and several assaults by the French. A Jew, Ḥ.S. *Farḥi, Ahmad al-Jazzār's chief aide, played an important role in its defense. By June 1799, Napoleon's army, now plague-ridden and decimated, had moved back into Egypt.

From a political point of view, Napoleon's campaign in Palestine marked the beginning of a renewed interest of the Western Powers in Palestine as occupying an important international position. From a social-cultural point of view, the importance of the campaign was much more limited. However, this was the first substantial contact made between the inhabitants of Palestine and Westerners since the destruction of Crusader Acre.

[Abraham J. Brawer]

Impact on Jewish History

The forces unleashed by Napoleon brought in their wake contradictory effects on the course of modern Jewish history. The breakup of old European feudal patterns of societal organization was eventually to open up a range of new economic and political options for the Jew. The closed societies that restricted but sheltered him were never again to be the same. On the other hand, the immediate effect of these forces was to provoke an almost total reversal in the process of civic emancipation brought about in the course of Napoleonic conquests. Nonetheless, Jewish Emancipation was to come eventually, even if its triumph was to be delayed till later in the century. Well in advance of that time the Napoleonic uprooting of the established order forced the Jewish community to contend with the many challenges posed by that process to their traditions and their lives. Already before Napoleon there were individual Jews seeking an accommodation with the world outside the ghetto. The events that surrounded the Napoleonic adventure extended the concern of the few to the preoccupation of the people as a whole. Moreover, Napoleon's insistence on a price to be paid by the Jew for his entrance into the modern world was to set the tone for much of the debate within the Jewish community during the Emancipation era. How to remain loyal to the traditions of his people and at home in the modern world was a problem with which the Jew wrestled throughout the period of his modern history; it is a problem first posed practically and seriously by the threat of Napoleonic successes.

[Alexander Shapiro]

BIBLIOGRAPHY: R. Anchel, *Napoléon et les Juifs* (1928); E.A. Halphen (ed.), *Recueil des lois, décrets et ordonnances concernant les Israélites* (1851); Sagnac, in: *Revue de l'histoire moderne et contemporaine*, 2–3 (1901–02); P. Guedalla, *Napoleon and Palestine* (1925); Gelber, in: REJ, 83 (1927), 1–21, 113–45; F. Kobler, *The Vision Was There* (1956), 42–47; F. Pietri, *Napoléon et les Israélites* (1965); B. Mevorakh, *Napoleon u-Tekufato* (1968).

NAQUET, ALFRED JOSEPH (1834–1916), French chemist and republican politician. Born at Carpentras, Vaucluse, Naquet became professor of chemistry at the Polytechnic Institute at Palermo in 1863 and later professor of medicine in Paris. He participated in the 1867 Peace Conference at Geneva, where he spoke out against the French Empire and was imprisoned for 15 months. Naquet was again imprisoned following the publication of *Réligion, Propriété, Famille* in 1869, in which he opposed religious marriage, and was also deprived of his civic rights. Following his release he went to Spain but returned to France in 1870, working for the republican government in Tours. In 1871 he was elected deputy for

Vaucluse, and from 1882 was a member of the senate. Naquet represented the left wing of the Assembly and the Senate and repeatedly pressed for legislation on divorce, the laws of 1884 being known as the "loi Naquet." His support for General Boulanger in 1888 did considerable harm to his career, and following allegations of complicity in the Panama scandal, he fled to England. Although subsequently vindicated, Naquet did not take any further part in French politics. His writings include *Principes de chimie fondés sur les théories modernes* (1865); *Le Divorce* (1877); *L'Humanité et la patrie* (1901); *La République radicale* (1873); and *Socialisme collectiviste et socialisme libéral* (1890).

[Samuel Aaron Miller]

NARA (also **ONR: Obóz Narodowo-Radykalny:** "National-Radical Camp"), a nationalistic, antisemitic organization in Poland, formed on April 14, 1934. The group was organized by youth who seceded from the *Endecja (ND) Party, which was also antisemitic. Whereas ND was anti-German, NARA, inspired and supported by the Nazis, wanted to serve as a bridge between the antisemitic ideologies of both Germany and Poland. The program of NARA envisaged a fascist regime modeled on the Nazi plan. It called for the assimilation of the Slavic minorities in Poland (Ukrainians, Belorussians), and the expulsion of Jews by means of economic boycott, by seizing their sources of living, confiscating their assets, and denying them all civil rights. With such forceful economic measures against Jews, NARA aimed to win the sympathy of the masses during a critical economic period and, at the same time, form a strong movement in oppositon to *Pilsudski's regime. The membership of NARA embraced mainly city youth and university students. After widespread terrorist activities against Jews, particularly Jewish students, NARA was dissolved by the government (July 10, 1934) and its newspaper *Sztafeta*, prohibited. The group continued its illegal activities, supported and increased by various rightist groups, until it met with complete defeat in the municipal elections of December 1938.

BIBLIOGRAPHY: R.L. Buell, *Poland: Key to Europe* (1939); 108, 117, 187; I. Greenbaum, in: EG, 1 (1953), 113–6; *Wielka Encyklopedia Powszechna*, 8 (1966), 89–90. **ADD. BIBLIOGRAPHY:** S. Rudnicki, *Oboz Narodowo Radykalny geneza i dzialalnosc* (1985), 83.

NARBATA, Jewish district E. of Caesarea, which perhaps inherited the name of Arubboth in the third district of Solomon (I Kings 4:10); it appears in the Book of Maccabees (I Macc. 5:23) as Arbatta, a city from which Simeon evacuated Jews at the beginning of the Hasmonean revolt. In 66 C.E., the Jews of Caesarea moved to the toparchy of Narbata because of persecution (Jos., Wars. 2:291). It is mentioned (in a different form) in the Jerusalem Talmud as the site of an inn (Ber. 6:1, 10b). The district of Narbata was inhabited by a mixture of Jews, Samaritans, and pagans. It is identified with Khirbat Baydūs, where there are remains of a town of the Roman period.

BIBLIOGRAPHY: Avi-Yonah, Geog, 127 (incl. bibl.).

[Michael Avi-Yonah]

NARBONI, family of French origin which established itself in Algeria toward the close of the 14th century. ALLAL BEN SIDUN BEN JOSHUA (15th century) was a wonder-working rabbi in Tlemcen. He composed a large number of *piyyutim*, some of which were included in the *maḥzor* of Tlemcen. Until recently, frequent pilgrimages were made to his grave. SHALOM (d. 1691), a financier in Algiers, was appointed **muqaddim* of the Jews of that town and played a political role in the relations with the Christian countries. MORDECAI (d. 1794) edited the work *Kol Yehudah* by Judah *Ayash of Algiers. Accused of having blasphemed Islam, he was given the alternative of conversion or death; he was beheaded in Algiers. ELIE and GEORGES, both heroes in World War I, were respectively president of the Jewish Consistory in Constantine and an army medical officer. ANDRÉ (1912–1979), lawyer and a leader of Algerian Jewry, participated in the defense of his coreligionists, particularly during the antisemitic Vichy government. A fervent Zionist, he was one of the founders of the Algerian Zionist movement. When Algeria achieved independence (1962), he settled in Israel, where he became a member of the executive of the Jewish Agency. From 1972, he headed the department for Sephardi communities.

BIBLIOGRAPHY: A. Cahen, *Les Juifs de l'Afrique Septentrionale* (1867), 100; M. Eisenbeth, *Le Judaïsme Nord-Africain* (1931), 273; Hirschberg, Afrikah, 2 (1965), 53, 90.

[David Corcos]

NARBONNE, town in S. France, 5 mi. (8 km.) from the Mediterranean. The capital of medieval Septimania, Narbonne was ruled successively by the Visigoths (413?), the Saracens (719), and the Franks (759). About 900 it became the possession of the local viscount. In 1508 Louis XII of France annexed it to his domains. The earliest written evidence of a Jewish presence in France, from about 471, comes from Narbonne. Sidonius Apollinaris, bishop of *Clermont, entrusted a Jew by the name of Gozolas and a customer of Magnus Felix of Narbonne, with a letter for the latter. Jews are not mentioned again in Narbonne until a *Church council was held there in 589, which forbade Jews, under penalty of a heavy fine, to recite prayers aloud, even in Jewish funeral processions (canon 9, in Mansi, Collectio, IX, 1016). Soon after (597) Pope *Gregory I ordered an inquiry into a report that four captive Christian brothers had been bought by Jews of Narbonne who held them in their service. The earliest known inscription relating to the Jews of France also comes from Narbonne. It is an epitaph in Latin, including the phrase "Peace to Israel" in Hebrew, to three siblings who died either at the same time or within a short period of one another, probably victims of a plague recorded in Septimania at about the same period.

While there is no information about the Jews of Narbonne during the period of Muslim occupation, a legendary tradition of the 12th and 13th centuries tells of the election of "Jewish kings" there when the town was taken by Pépin the Short in 759. According to some sources (Philomena, *Gesta Caroli Magni ad Carcassonam; Milḥemet Mitzvah* of *Meir

Simeon ha-Me'ili), Jews helped to drive out the Muslims and as a sure means of appreciation, were granted the right to be governed by a "Jewish king." Another source (the addition to the *Sefer ha-Kabbalah* of Abraham *Ibn Daud) states that Charlemagne invited a certain Machir to become the founder of the dynasty of "Jewish kings." Although this princely dynasty is confirmed authentically only from the 11th or 12th centuries, the Jews held freehold properties by 768. Pope Stephen III in a letter addressed to Aribert, archbishop of Narbonne, was critical of the fact that Jews, by virtue of the privileges granted by the kings of France, not only owned alodial properties in both the towns and their surroundings, but also employed Christians to work in their vineyards and fields. At the close of the ninth century King Charles III the Simple (898–923) tried to dispossess the Jews of Narbonne of their estates, at first those that had been recently acquired from Christians, and later all others. These measures did not remain in force for long, and a short while later Jews again owned property, including mills which they also worked.

The partition of jurisdiction over the town between the viscount and the archbishop resulted in the emergence of two distinct groups of Jews, from the point of view of their civic administration (among themselves the Jews formed a single community). In the 11th century Archbishop Pons d'Arce nominated two Jews as toll gatherers. Between 1134 and 1143 clashes which broke out as a result of differences between Ermengarde, viscountess of Narbonne, and Alphonse Jourdain, count of Toulouse, worsened the situation of Narbonne's Jews, and many of them then emigrated to *Anjou, *Poitou, and to the kingdom of France. According to the addition to the *Sefer ha-Kabbalah*, the Jews of Narbonne numbered 2,000 around 1143; in 1161 Benjamin of Tudela mentions 300 Jews there (but since this figure probably refers to heads of families there was probably a Jewish population of some 1,500). In 1163 Jews were the objects of attacks by the Spanish crusaders but were protected by both Viscount Bérenger and Archbishop Guiffrey.

The Jewish quarter of the viscounty (known as *Grande Juiverie, Jouzaigas Majours*, etc.), which was of considerable size, situated to the north of the present Place de l'Hotel de Ville and Cours de la République, did not constitute a "closed" quarter and non-Jews and Jews lived side by side. From 1217 the Jews benefited from a very advantageous charter granted by the viscount, in which they were represented by ten arbitrators. Although the Jewish quarter under the archbishop's jurisdiction, situated in the Belvèze quarter, did not obtain such an advantageous charter until 1284, the two Jewish sections shared all community resources. In the viscounty there were at least two synagogues, a hospital, baths, and workrooms, and in the archbishopric there was a cemetery, known as Mont judaïque (or Montjuzaic), some of whose epitaphs were found and preserved in the museum.

In 1236 a petty brawl between a Jew and a fisherman that ended in an accidental homicide set off an anti-Jewish riot which was rapidly suppressed by Viscount Aimeri IV, who ordered the restitution of all objects stolen during the pillage. The Jewish community celebrated its good fortune by a local Purim. At the end of 1246 Viscount Amauri I demonstrated his sympathy toward the Jews by attending a protest meeting against the anti-Jewish policies of King *Louis IX. It was, therefore, not surprising that the Jewish quarter of the viscounty attracted Jews from the rest of the province as well as from the archbishop's part of the town. After disputes between the two overlords of the town over the judicial status of certain Jews, both joined forces to defend themselves against the claims of the monarchy, which sought to deprive them (from the close of the 13th century) of the jurisdiction over "their" Jews. When the expulsion order was issued, however, there was no evidence of protest by either the archbishop or the viscount, and it was only with the liquidation of Jewish property that both intervened to claim their share of the profits. (Only the viscount made a satisfactory settlement with the king.) In 1306, on the eve of the expulsion, the town register indicated 165 Jewish households, or about 825 persons (less than 5% of the total population). The exiled Jews moved mainly to *Roussillon or to the Catalonian regions. A few returned in 1315 and later, in 1359, more returned. Tradition has it that three events caused the decline of the town of Narbonne: the silting of the Aude River; the expulsion of the Jews in 1306; and the *Black Death plague of 1348.

The Jews of Narbonne were engaged in both agriculture and the production of wine. With the transfer of ownership of cultivable areas Jews, nevertheless, often retained part of the harvest for themselves. Jews were also involved with salt mines and water mills. Serving as public functionaries, Narbonne's Jews also collected fees for the archbishop and acted as brokers as well as traders. A Jewish notary served to draw up contracts between Jews. There were a number of Jewish physicians in Narbonne and also some goldsmiths. Many Jews practiced moneylending, particularly from the beginning of the 13th century. (Loans were generally given against pledges, personal property, or real estate.)

In his *Sefer ha-Kabbalah*, Abraham ibn Daud mentions only two French communities which were outstanding for their learning and one of them was Narbonne. Important scholars were R. *Moses b. Joseph b. Merwan ha-Levi, R. *Abraham b. Isaac of Narbonne, and R. Meir b. Joseph (toward the middle of the 13th century), who "caused the Torah to shine forth before their disciples by the study of the Pentateuch, the Bible, the Mishnah, the Babylonian Talmud, and the Jerusalem Talmud." Benjamin of Tudela praised the town "which already has an ancient reputation for erudition. And from there, the Torah has spread throughout all countries. Scholars and men of great authority live there." Among Narbonne's most famous scholars were *Moses ha-Darshan, exegete and head of the yeshivah (toward the middle of the 11th century); Abraham b. Isaac of Narbonne, referred to as *av bet din*, the father-in-law of *Abraham b. David of Posquières and author of ritual works and talmudic commentaries (second half of the 12th century); Joseph *Kimḥi (*Maistre Petit*) and his two sons Moses *Kimḥi and David *Kimḥi (second half of the 12th and early 13th centuries); *Isaac b. Meir of Narbonne, liturgic poet (first half of the 13th century); Moses b. Joseph b. Merwan ha-Levi, teacher of (among others) Abraham b. David; Meir b. Simeon ha-Me'ili, author of *Milḥemet Mitzvah* (middle of the 13th century); and Maestro David de Caslari, physician and poet famous for his commentary on *Maimonides' *Guide*; and *Moses b. Joshua b. Har David Narboni (late 13th century). There were others who stayed for a time in Narbonne or who were born there but whose activities were restricted to other places. Numerous personalities later bore the surname *Narboni. The 13th-century Jewish troubadour, Bofilh, also came from Narbonne.

From the beginning of the 18th century, Jewish merchants from Avignon were authorized to visit Narbonne four times a year in order to trade there for a period of one month each time. From the close of the 18th century Jews settled in the town as permanent residents. On the eve of World War II there were hardly any Jews in Narbonne, as was still the situation in subsequent decades.

BIBLIOGRAPHY: Gross, Gal Jud, 401ff.; G. Saige, *Les Juifs du Languedoc* (1881), index; J. Regne, *Etude sur la condition des Juifs à Narbonne* (1912); B. Blumenkranz, *Juifs et chrétiens…* (1960), index; I. Levi, in: REJ, 48 (1904), 197ff.; 49 (1904), 147ff.; Frey, Corpus, no. 670; R.W. Emery, *Heresy and Inquisition in Narbonne…* (1941), 22; Z. Szajkowski, *Franco-Judaica* (1962), no. 309; idem, *Analytical Franco-Jewish Gazetteer* (1966), 164; Ibn Daud, Tradition, index.

[Bernhard Blumenkranz]

NARDI (Narodietzky), NAHUM (1901–1977), composer. Born in Kiev, Nardi studied the piano and composition at the Kiev, Warsaw, and Vienna conservatories and went to Palestine in 1923. There he began to give piano recitals but soon turned to composing, inspired by Arab Bedouin and peasant songs and the Sephardi and Yemenite melos. Many of his songs for children and adults became folk songs for which he developed an original style of piano accompaniment. Many of them were first performed at his joint recitals with the Yemenite singer, Brachah *Zefira, his first wife. For these recitals he developed an original style of piano accompaniment. In later years Nardi also promoted the careers of several other singers of Yemenite origin. Among other associations which contributed to his production and style were those with Ḥayyim Naḥman *Bialik, the poet and educator Levin *Kipnis, and the poet and composer Yiẓḥak Navon.

Nardi's songs, which have achieved folk song status, include: *Shir ha-Avodah ve-ha-Melakhah, Bein Nehar Perat, Yesh Li Gan* (Bialik), *Mi Yivneh Bayit be-Tel Aviv, Shanah Halkhah, Ani Purim* (L. Kipnis, the latter also metamorphosed by an unknown kindergarten poet into the ubiquitous *Ha-Shafan ha-Katan); Kakhol Yam ha-Mayim* (N. Alterman); *Udi Ḥamudi* (M. Dafna); *Alei Givah* (Broides, the tune beginning DGFED as distinct from M. *Ravina's setting); *Pattish Masmer Nikkakh Maher* (E. Harussi); *Shetu ha-Adarim* (A. Penn); *Sisi Admat ha-Sharon* (Y. Fichmann); *Mi Yitteneni Of* (D. Shimoni), *Im Yesh Ei Sham* (Y. Karni) – both transformations of Oriental Jewish folk melodies.

[Bathja Bayer]

NARESH, town situated on the bank of the Euphrates, south of the old city of Babylon and of *Sura. A canal went from near Naresh to Nippur. The town was situated in a hilly district and extended over a very wide area (Er. 56a). As a result it was not surrounded by a wall and this constituted a danger to the safety of its inhabitants at night (Ḥul. 127a). This particularly affected the women of the city who were obliged to undergo their ritual bathing (Nid. 67b). Naresh became renowned in the talmudic era because of Rav Papa, a native of Naresh, who lived and was active there in the middle of the fourth century C.E. Rav Papa studied at *Maḥoza under Rava, and after Rava's death some of his pupils left for Naresh, where Papa served as head of the academy and Huna b. Joshua as head of the *Kallah*. The Jews of Naresh engaged in agriculture (BM 68a), and among the products made by its inhabitants, thick blankets were famous (Yoma 69a). The inhabitants had a bad reputation and were known as extortioners and thieves; it was said: "If a native of Naresh kisses you, count your teeth" (Ḥul. 127a).

BIBLIOGRAPHY: Neubauer, Geog. 365; A. Berliner, in: *Jahresbericht des Rabbiner-Seminars zu Berlin pro 5643 (1882–1883)*, 54; J. Obermeyer, *Die Landschaft Babylonien im Zeualter des Talmuds und des Gaonates* (1929), 306–12. **ADD. BIBLIOGRAPHY:** B. Eshel, *Jewish Settlements in Babylonia during Talmudic Times* (1979), 191–93.

[Moshe Beer]

NARKISS, BEZALEL (1926–), Jewish art historian. Narkiss was born in Jerusalem, the son of Mordechai *Narkiss, director of the Bezalel Art Museum. He studied at the Hebrew University of Jerusalem and then taught history for five years at a secondary school in Haifa. It was only after his father's death, while examining and arranging his papers, that Narkiss found his vocation; to establish Jewish art as a specialized academic discipline. Consequently, he retrained, studying at the Courtauld Institute of Art and the Warburg Institute at the University of London. Specializing in the history of medieval art, where his interests were divided between iconographic and stylistic studies, he was particularly influenced in his approach to art by Hugo Buchthal and Francis Wormald, his supervisors in London, and Yitzḥak *Baer, professor of medieval Jewish history in Jerusalem. After his return to Israel in 1963, Narkiss taught in the department of art history at the Hebrew University, serving as chairman from 1974 to 1976. His positions included serving as art editor of Masada Press (1963–73) and foreign editor of *Gesta* International Center of Medieval Art (1973–80). He was the editor-in-chief of the *Journal of Jewish Art* (1974–86) and director of the Catalogue of Hebrew Illustrated Manuscripts of the British Isles. He was illustrations consultant and art editor of the first edition of the *Encyclopaedia Judaica* (1970). He was also the art adviser to the Diaspora Museum (Beth Hatefutsoth), and sat on the boards of the Israel Museum and the Wolf Foundation.

Narkiss' unique contribution was as the founder of the Index of Jewish Art in 1974, thus undertaking the task of indexing all works of Jewish art worldwide. Through Narkiss' seminal work, the study of Jewish art has been transformed into a specialized academic discipline. He stressed the relationship of the style to that of the general art of the region, while pointing to specific Jewish elements and iconography. The Center for Jewish Art at the Hebrew University, founded and initially led by him (1979–91), established the *Journal of Jewish Art* (now *Jewish Art*) and he served as its editor in 1974–86. He worked towards the computerization of the Index, while concomitantly encouraging the continuing documentation of Jewish art around the world. He also encouraged documentation and preservation activities in areas of Eastern Europe and the former Soviet Union that had been less accessible before 1989. As a result of his activity, a school of students and researchers has evolved since the mid-1980s and the study of Jewish art as a discipline has spread from Israel to Europe and the United States. For this significant work he was awarded the Israel Prize in 1999. From 1999 he was a visiting scholar at Princeton and the National Gallery of Art in Washington, DC. Narkiss published widely on the subject of illuminated Hebrew Manuscripts, and his major work on the subject, *Hebrew Illuminated Manuscripts*, has appeared in several editions.

BIBLIOGRAPHY: "Bezalel Narkiss, List of Publications," in: *Jewish Art*, 23/24 (1997–98), xv–xviii; G. Sed-Rajna, "From Bezalel to Bezalel," in: *Jewish Art*, 23/24 (1997–98), xi–xiv; Y. Zirlin, "The Publications of Bezalel Narkiss," in: *Jewish Art* 12/13 (1986–87), 349–50.

[Susan Nashman Fraiman (2nd ed.)]

NARKISS, MORDECHAI (1898–1957), Israel curator and art historian. Narkiss was born in Skala, Poland. In 1920 he settled in Ereẓ Israel, where he continued his studies at the *Bezalel School, Jerusalem, and became assistant to the director, Boris *Schatz. Narkiss began to devote himself to amassing a collection of Jewish art and antiquities, and in 1932 became director of the *Bezalel Museum. The museum had closed down with the school after Schatz's death, but Narkiss founded the Society of Friends of the Bezalel National Museum and reopened it under the auspices of the executive of the Zionist Organization.

Narkiss wrote on many aspects of Jewish art. Among his publications were *Matbe'ot Ereẓ Yisrael* ("Coins of Ereẓ Israel," two parts, 1936 and 1938), *The Channuka Lamp* (1939), *The Artcraft of the Yemenite Jews* (1941), and *Niello Work as a Jewish Craft* (1942). He also wrote many articles, translated books on art, and was art editor of the *Encyclopaedia Hebraica*. The sixth volume of *Eretz Israel* (1960), one of the publications of the Israel Exploration Society, was dedicated to his memory. It included a complete bibliography of his works.

NAROL, small town in the region of Lubaczow, southeastern Poland. Founded in 1585 as the settlement of Floryjanowa, the town later received the name of Narol. Jews who settled there were active as merchants and lessees. They developed an economically flourishing community which existed until 1648–49, when the entire settlement of some 12,000 was destroyed in the *Chmielnicki pogroms. About 40,000 refugees from neighboring settlements fled to Narol in 1648 in fear of the Cossacks. When the town was captured (1649) all of them were slaughtered. Nathan Nata *Hannover, in his *Yeven Meẓulah*, described the massacre in these words: "Many were drowned in the water, many hundreds shut themselves up in the synagogue, but they broke down the doors and first slew the Jews inside it and then burnt the synagogue with the slain. There was no such slaughter in the whole of Poland …" Documents on the history of the Jews in the town were also destroyed during the massacre. Although much wealth was lost in the Cossack plunder, a large part of it hidden under the ruins of the houses was discovered in the 19th century. Moses Kohen, rabbi of Narol, who was saved from the slaughter and later appointed rabbi of Metz in France, composed a **seliḥah* in which he lamented the destruction of Narol – the death of its scholars and the loss of the Torah centers in the town. The settlement never returned to its prior glory. When the *Council of Four Lands was disbanded, the town still owed sums of money on taxes and other payments to the Council. Narol was incorporated into the territory of Austria following the partition of Poland in 1772. After World War I, Narol became part of independent Poland, and in 1921 the number of Jews totaled 734 (out of 1,817). The majority of its Jews were Zionists who took an active part in the affairs of the Zionist Federation. In 1933 misfortune again overtook the town when a fire completely destroyed the houses of 23 families. In 1939 the Germans expelled the Jews to the Soviet sector.

[Shimshon Leib Kirshenboim]

NAROT, JOSEPH (1913–1980), U.S. Reform rabbi and communal leader. Narot, who was born in Vilna, immigrated with his family to Ohio where he grew up and was educated. He was ordained by Hebrew Union College in 1940. He served first as assistant rabbi (1940–41), then as rabbi (1941–50) of Temple Beth Israel in Atlantic City, New Jersey. In 1950 he became rabbi of Temple Israel, Miami, that city's oldest Reform synagogue. In Atlantic City, Narot was active in UJA drives and was founder and president of the Atlantic City Forum, composed of 60 civic organizations. He continued to divide his time between Jewish and civic concerns in Miami where he was member and chairman of the Dade County Community Board (1964–68). He was also president of the Dade County Welfare Planning Council (1961–63) and a founder of the Interfaith Agency for Social Justice.

[Gladys Rosen]

NARROWE, MORTON (1932–), rabbi. Born in Philadelphia in the U.S., Narrowe came to Sweden in 1965 as rabbi for the Stockholm Jewish congregation, becoming chief rabbi in 1975 and emeritus in 1998. He was a member of the Swedish Bible Commission from 1974 to 2000 and in 1975 cofounded the Joint Jewish-Christian Interfaith Council. In 1977 he published a book entitled *Handledning för sörjande* ("Guidelines for the Bereaved") and in 1990 he received his doctorate at the Jewish Theological Seminary of America. His thesis, "Zionism in Sweden: From Its Beginning until the End of World War I," provides unique insight into early Zionist history in Sweden. Rabbi Narrowe also wrote numerous newspaper and magazine articles about Jews and Judaism, and participated in many radio and TV programs.

BIBLIOGRAPHY: *Svensk-judisk litteratur 1775–1994 – en litteraturhistorisk översikt* (1995).

[Ilya Meyer (2nd ed.)]

NASATIR, ABRAHAM PHINEAS (1904–1991), U.S. historian. Born in Santa Ana, California, Nasatir taught at the University of Iowa and then moved to San Diego State College. He was a fellow of the Social Science Research Council and president of the Pacific Coast Branch of the American Historical Association.

Nasatir specialized in the history of the United States West and Southwest, and published *Before Lewis and Clark* (2 vols., 1952). He edited Etienne Derbec's *A French Journalist in the California Gold Rush* (1964). Later his interest in the southwest expanded beyond the U.S. frontier to include Hispanic America and led to a history of that area, together with Helen M. Baily, *Latin America* (1960, 1968[2]). He was active in Jewish affairs.

In 1965 he received the Outstanding Professor Award from the California State University Foundation. The Nasatir Professorship of Modern Jewish History was established in his honor at San Diego State University, where Nasatir taught history for 46 years and was active in the community as an advocate of Jewish education.

His writings include *French Activities in California* (1945); with G.E. Monell, *French Consuls in the United States* (1967); with N.M. Loomis, *Pedro Vial and the Roads to Santa Fe* (1967); *Spanish War Vessels on the Mississippi, 1792–1796* (1968); *Borderland in Retreat* (1976); and *The Imperial Osages* (with G. Din, 1983).

BIBLIOGRAPHY: *Contemporary Authors*, 11–12 (1965), 287.

[Stanley J. Stein / Ruth Beloff (2nd ed.)]

NASAUD (Rom. **Năsăud**; Hung. **Naszód**), town in Bistrita-Năsăud county (Transylvania), Romania. Until 1918 and between 1940 and 1945, Nasaud was part of Hungary. While still under Hungarian rule, it was a center of the Romanian nationalist movement. Jews settled in Nasaud after the law prohibiting their settlement was abrogated in 1848 while residence in the town itself was still barred. Jews lived in the nearby village of Jidovitza (Entredam), today named *Rebreanu. The community was Orthodox and strongly influenced by *Ḥasidism. In 1885 the government designated the community as the administrative center for the Jews of all the villages in the district. At the beginning of their residence in Nasaud the Jews belonged to two different communities: the "Hungarian" and the "Polish." This situation lasted until the 1880s, when they decided to unite the congregations. The community possessed a large synagogue, a *bet midrash*, and a *ḥeder*. Jewish children attended elementary and secondary school in which the language of instruction was Romanian. The Jewish population in Nasaud itself declined from 859 in 1866 to 425 (12% of the total) in 1930, and 415 (12.9%) in 1940. Between the two world wars there was an important Zionist movement in the town. There were 1,198 Jews living in the surrounding villages in 1930. Some 400 Jews were deported to Auschwitz in the summer of 1944. In 1941 the Hungarian Horthiite authorities deported the "foreign" Jews to Kamenets-Podolski, in the Ukraine, where they were soon murdered by the Nazis. In 1944 the remaining local Jews were sent to a ghetto in Bistrita, the district capital, and from there deported to Auschwitz. After World War II, about 110 Jews returned to Nasaud, including former residents who had survived the camps and some who had previously lived in the surrounding district. As a result of immigration to Israel and elsewhere, the Jewish population dwindled and by 1971 only two families were left in the town.

[Yehouda Marton / Paul Schveiger (2nd ed.)]

NASHIM (Heb. נָשִׁים; "Women"), third order of the Mishnah, according to the accepted order mentioned in the homily of *Simeon b. Lakish (Shab. 31a; according to the order given by Tanḥuma (Num. R. 13:15), it is the first). *Nashim* deals essentially with matrimonial law and with the laws governing the relations between husband and wife. It also includes the tractates **Nedarim* ("vows") and **Nazir* ("the Nazirite"), respectively, since according to the Bible (Num. 30:4ff.), the vow of a wife or a girl during her minority can be annulled by the husband or father (cf. Sot. 2a). The tractates included in *Nashim* are **Yevamot*, 16 chapters; **Ketubbot*, 13; *Nedarim*, 11; *Nazir*, 9; **Sotah*, 9; **Gittin*, 9; and **Kiddushin*, 4. As is customary, the tractates are arranged in descending order according to the number of chapters (see *Mishnah). The *mishnayot* of *Nashim* also contain incidental aggadic passages, but at the end of *Sotah* and *Kiddushin* there are more continuous aggadic passages. In the Tosefta, *Yevamot* has 14 chapters; *Ketubbot*, 12 (or 13); *Nedarim*, 7; *Nazir*, 6; *Sotah*, 15; *Gittin*, 7 (or 9); and *Kiddushin*, 5. The aggadic section is richer than that of the Mishnah, particularly in *Sotah*. Because of their practical importance for matrimonial law and sexual morality, the tractates of the order *Nashim* are stressed in rabbinic study, and the more practically relevant parts have received extensive treatment by both the medieval commentators and the later rabbinical authorities, including all the responsa literature.

[David Joseph Bornstein]

NASH PAPYRUS, a second-century (c. 150) B.C.E. papyrus fragment written in square Hebrew script, containing the *Decalogue and the *Shema. The Nash Papyrus was the oldest biblical text known before the discovery of the *Dead Sea Scrolls. A single sheet, not from a scroll, was purchased from an Egyptian dealer by W.L. Nash, secretary of the Society of Biblical Archaeology in England, and published by S.A. Cooke in 1903. The papyrus is of unknown provenance, although allegedly from Fayyum. The text of the Decalogue accords closely with the Septuagint of Exodus (20:2ff.), and must resemble the Hebrew that underlay the Septuagint translation (see table of variants in article *Decalogue). The *Shema* follows (Deut. 6:4–5), including the Septuagint's preliminary to verse 4: "And these are the statutes and the judgments that Moses (so Nash; LXX, "the Lord") commanded [the Israelites] in the wilderness when they left the land of Egypt." The papyrus breaks off after the second letter of verse 5. The combination of the Decalogue and the *Shema* indicates that the text of the papyrus represents the Torah readings included in the daily morning liturgy of Second Temple times (cf. Tam. 5:1: "they recited the Decalogue, the *Shema*, etc.").

BIBLIOGRAPHY: S.A. Cooke, in: PSBA, 25 (1903), 34–56; F.C. Burkitt, in: JQR, 15 (1903), 392–408; J. Mann, in: HUCA, 2 (1925), 283; W.F. Albright, in: JBL, 56 (1937), 145–76; idem, in: BASOR, 115 (1949), 10–19; M.Z.(H.) Segal, in: *Leshonenu*, 15 (1947), 27–36; Birnbaum, in: BASOR, 115 (1949), 20–22; F.M. Cross, in: JBL, 74 (1955), 148 n. 3.

[Moshe Greenberg]

NASHVILLE, city in central Tennessee, U.S. Although there had been individual Jewish families in Nashville almost since it was founded in 1780, it was not until 1851 that the Hebrew Benevolent Burial Society purchased land for a cemetery. This piece of land is still a part of The Temple Cemetery, which was listed on the National Register of Historic Places in 2004. The first congregation, K.K. Mogen David, chartered in 1854, was made up of the mostly German members of the Hebrew Benevolent Burial Society. A second congregation, Ohava Emes, was chartered in 1860. In 1867 the two congregations reunited under the name of Ohava Sholom. A short-lived Reform congregation, B'nai Yeshurun, had begun in 1864. Ohava Sholom adopted the Reform ritual and took the name "Vine Street Temple" when it completed a new sanctuary in 1876. It later relocated and took the name The Temple, Congregation Ohabai Sholom. Also in 1876 the Conservative congregation Adas Israel was chartered. It later became the present West End Synagogue. The Hungarian Benevolent Society, chartered in 1871, evolved into the Orthodox congregation Sherith Israel. In 1992 a second Reform congregation, Congregation Micah was started. The Chabad Congregation Beit Tefilah began in 2001.

Nashville's very active Jewish community belies its population of barely 8,000. The Gordon Jewish Community Center was established in 1902 as the YMHA. Because of Jewish involvement in the civil rights movement, the Jewish Community Center was dynamited in 1958. The Jewish Federation, founded in 1936 as the Jewish Community Council, helps Jews everywhere sustain communal life. The Nashville Section of the National Council of Jewish Women was founded in 1901. Jewish Family Service celebrated its first hundred and fifty years in 2003. It has assisted in the settlement in Nashville of Holocaust refugees and survivors and Jews from the former Soviet Union. B'nai B'rith and Hadassah are active in Nashville.

Nashville's Vanderbilt University has an active Ben Schulman Center for Jewish Life and offers undergraduate and graduate degrees in Jewish studies.

BIBLIOGRAPHY: F.S. Frank, *Five Families and Eight Young Men* (1962); idem, *Beginnings on Market Street* (1976); J. Roseman, *From Y to J, the Hundred-Year History of Nashville's Jewish Community Center* (2004).

[Annette Ratkin (2nd ed.)]

NASI. In biblical usage, *nasi* signifies an important person, ranging from a king to a tribal chief or the head of a large family. The *nesi'im* are the leaders of the people in the wilderness (Ex. 16:22, 34:31) and are counted by name (Num. 1:5–16); they are sent to spy out the land and are charged with its apportionment (Num. 13:1–15, 34:16ff.); they bring special gifts and sacrifices to the tabernacle (Ex. 35:27; Num. 7: 10ff.). The institution reflects the tribal covenant and declines with the conquest of Canaan; it is revived by Ezekiel, who denotes by it the future ruler of the people. This prophet so names the rulers of other small nations as well, but his avoidance of the term *melekh* ("king") for the future ruler of Israel may signify disapproval of monarchical absolutism. Jewish rulers during the period of the Second Temple used the title *nasi*, thus asserting their authority while avoiding the assumption of kingship. I Maccabees 14:41 tells that Simeon the Hasmonean was declared ethnarch ("ruler of the people") by the people in 141 B.C.E., the Hebrew original of that title probably being *nasi*. Coins minted by *Bar Kokhba during the abortive revolt against Rome bear the inscription *Shimon Nesi Yisrael*, demonstrating that the rebel leader considered himself *nasi* of the people; the title is similarly found in letters credited to Bar Kokhba.

While the rabbis understood certain biblical instances of the term to mean "king" (see Hor. 3:3), they applied the title in a more limited sense to the president of the Sanhedrin, and perhaps to the heads of other bodies and orders too. The secular head of the sect described in the *Dead Sea Scrolls also bore the title (War Scroll, ed. Yadin, p. 184; in the English edition, p. 279). Rabbinic sources call one of the "pairs" (*zugot*), going back to Yose b. Joezer (c. 165 B.C.E), the *nasi* (Ḥag. 2:2), and continue to use the term for the head of the court through amoraic times. Historians have long been divided on the reliability of these early sources: some claim the title is used anachronistically, its actual usage commencing only with *Judah ha-Nasi (fl. 190 C.E.); others believe it first came into use after 70 C.E., or in 30 B.C.E. at the time of Hillel the Elder; yet others accept the mishnaic testimony (the head of a Phoenician *synodos* is called *nasi* in 96 B.C.E.) and even claim that the office is pre-Maccabean. The office was held by scions of the Hillelite family, though unusual circumstances may have allowed others to hold the office for relatively short periods, and it may have been unfilled when conditions were most disturbed (such as during the Hadrianic persecutions). The last Hillelite *nasi* was Rabban Gamaliel (VI), who died in 425.

With the destruction of the Temple in 70 C.E., the office of the *nasi* becomes more significant. Onkelos performed the mourning ritual for Rabban Gamaliel II as though he were a king (see Sem. 8), and there is a strong implication that Rome extended him its recognition (see Eduy. 7:7). The Hillelite *nasi* was recognized as political head ("Patriarch") of the people by the Roman government (Cod. Theod. xvi. 8), an arrangement that allowed for more effective control and administration of its Jewish subjects. From the Jewish point of view, the Patriarchate provided the people with a Roman official sympathetic to their needs, and it placed significant power in rabbinic hands. The rabbis, for their part, relaxed certain religious laws so as to allow the patriarch greater ease in Roman society. Internally, the *nasi* presided over the Sanhedrin, fixed the calendar together with the court by proclaiming the new month and intercalating the year, led public prayers for rain, and ordained scholars (the content and scope of this ordination being somewhat unclear). He kept in touch with the Jewish communities of the Diaspora, dispatching apostles to preach, teach, set up courts, and raise funds. His court possessed legislative powers, and so most *takkanot* ("enactments") were attributed to the presiding *nasi*.

[Gerald Y. Blidstein]

Post-Geonic Period

The title *nasi* persisted for many centuries and in different lands throughout the Middle Ages, sometimes as the title of a defined head of a Jewish institution, sometimes as an honorific title only, given to important personages and to sons of illustrious families. The *nasi* as the leader of the community (see *Autonomy) is found in Jerusalem; in Fostat, Egypt; in Baghdad, Damascus, and Mosul, Syria; and in Spain under Muslim rule. Some had considerable power, similar to that of the exilarch, especially the *nesi'im* of Ereẓ Israel, Syria, and Egypt. The earliest person known in the post-geonic period to bear this title is Ẓemaḥ in Egypt or Syria, with the latest Sar Shalom b. Phinehas, who is mentioned in 1341 in Egypt and Baghdad. Most of the other twenty-odd names are from the 11th century, among them *Daniel b. Azariah, *David b. *Daniel, and Jedidiah b. Zakkai. One, Shem Tov, a most respected *nasi* of Jerusalem, could not prove Davidic descent and was exiled. Some *nesi'im* in Muslim Spain were appointed by the court and repesented the Jews at court, collected taxes, and acted as chief justices. The *Karaites also called their heads *nasi*, from their founder *Anan b. David through the 18th century. From early modern times the title *nasi* was also given to the heads of the **kolel* institutions of the **Ḥalukkah*. In later modern times the title "president," especially of democratic political and social bodies, was translated into Hebrew as *nasi*; as such it has been carried over into the political nomenclature of the State of Israel, being used to designate the president of the State.

[Isaac Levitats]

BIBLIOGRAPHY: R. de Vaux, Anc Isr, 8; H. Mantel, *Studies in the History of the Sanhedrin* (1961), 1–53, 175–253; idem, in: HTR, 60 (1967), 90; Alon, Meḥkarim, 2 (1958), 15–57; S. Zeitlin, *Religious and Secular Leadership* (1943), 7–15; Baron, Social², 2 (1952), 191–209; 5 (1957), 38–46, 314; E.A. Speiser, *Oriental and Biblical Studies* (1967), 113–26; S. Abramsky, *Bar Kokhva, Nesi Yisrael* (1961). POST-GEONIC: S. Poznański, *Babylonische Geonim im nachgaonaeischen Zeitalter* (1914); Mann, Egypt, index; Ashtor. Korot.

NASI, GRACIA (c. 1510–1569), Marrano stateswoman and patroness. A member of the first generation of Portuguese Marranos (probably of Spanish descent), her original name as a Christian in Portugal, where she was born, was Beatrice de Luna. In 1528 she married Francisco Mendes, also a Marrano, who with his brother Diogo *Mendes built up out of a business in precious stones an important banking establishment, with a branch in Antwerp (directed by Diogo) which soon outdid the main establishment in importance. In 1537, after her husband's death, the widow left Portugal with her family (including her nephew, João Micas (Miques, Miguez), later Joseph *Nasi) and went via England to the Low Countries, where she joined her brother-in-law. There she became known in aristocratic society, and assisted her brother-in-law in his efforts to aid the flight of the Marranos and to stop the activity of the Inquisition in Portugal. After Diogo's death in 1543 she fled from Flanders (1545), leaving much of her property behind, and settled in Venice. There she was denounced to the authorities as a Judaizer by her own sister Reyna, Diogo's widow. João Miques, however, secured Turkish diplomatic intervention on her behalf and she was released. She and her family then settled in Ferrara. About this time she threw off the disguise of Christianity and became known by her Jewish name of Gracia Nasi.

In Ferrara she continued her remarkable work for organizing the flight of fugitive Marranos from Portugal; this is described in Samuel *Usque's *Consolaçam as Tribulaçoens de Israel*, which (together with the Ferrara Spanish Bible of 1553) is dedicated to her in admiring terms. In 1553 Gracia Nasi settled in Constantinople, where she continued similar activity; she also patronized scholars and established academies and synagogues in Constantinople and Salonika, and perhaps elsewhere. In 1556–57, she attempted to organize a punitive boycott of the port of *Ancona in Italy, in retaliation for the burning there of 26 Marranos as renegades from the Christian faith; she secured the intervention of the sultan for some of the accused who were Turkish subjects, including her business agents. In 1554 she was joined in Constantinople by her nephew (henceforth Joseph Nasi), who married her only child Reyna and was now associated closely with all her enterprises, both political and commercial. In 1558 or 1559 she secured from the sultan, in return for an annual payment of 1,000 ducats, a grant of the ruined city of *Tiberias in Ereẓ Israel, where she set up a yeshivah; this grant was subsequently renewed, with a political motivation by Joseph Nasi.

Doña Gracia was certainly the outstanding Jewess of her day, and perhaps of the entire period between the fall of the Jewish state and the present. She was known as *La Senora*, or *Ha-Geveret*, and the synagogue known by this name long continued to exist in Constantinople. She was, however, inactive, perhaps because of ill health, for some years before her death, possibly in Ereẓ Israel, in 1569.

BIBLIOGRAPHY: C. Roth, *The House of Nasi: Dona Gracia* (1947); idem, in: *The Seventy-Fifth Anniversary Volume of the Jewish Quarterly Review* (1967), 460–72; A. Fernand-Halphen, *Une grande* *dame juive de la Renaissance: Gracia Mendesia Nasi* (1929); P. Grunebaum-Ballin, *Joseph Naci duc de Naxos* (1968), passim; Ginsberger, in: REJ, 83 (1930), 179–92.

[Cecil Roth]

NASI, JOSEPH (c. 1524–1579), statesman. Nasi was born as a Marrano in Portugal, perhaps descended from the ancient Spanish Jewish family of Nasi. (See Chart: Nasi Family). He was the son of the Portuguese royal physician Agostinho (formerly Samuel) Micas (d. 1525), who taught medicine at the University of Lisbon. Joseph, known originally as a Christian by the name of João Micas (Miques, Míguez), accompanied his paternal aunt, Beatrice de Luna (Gracia *Nasi), when she went from Lisbon to Antwerp in 1537. After studying at the University of Louvain, he entered the banking establishment of *Mendes and was responsible for settling the family's affairs when Gracia left in 1545 for Italy. He was then in contact with Emperor *Charles V and the queen regent of the Netherlands, and is said to have been the jousting partner of their nephew, the future emperor Maximilian. Despite the dexterity of his negotiations, he was unable to save the family property from confiscation, and fled after them in about 1547. The following years he spent in France, where he became known to King Francis I, and later in Italy. He is alleged to have sought the Venetian government's concession of one of their islands as a refuge for fugitive *Marranos. Early in 1554 he joined his aunt, Gracia Nasi, in Constantinople, where he was circumcised and assumed the name of Joseph Nasi. In August he married her daughter Reyna. Henceforth, he was closely associated with his aunt in her commercial and political activities. In 1556 he joined her in organizing the blockade of the port of *Ancona to avenge the persecution of the Marranos there.

In the struggle for the succession to Sultan *Suleiman I between his sons Selim and Bajazet he supported the former, with the result that he received many favors from him, including the rank and emoluments of *muterferik* ("gentleman of the imperial retinue"). Due to his intimate knowledge of European affairs and statesmen, and his chain of agents throughout the Western world, he exercised great influence on the foreign policy of tile Sublime Porte, helping Alexander Lapuseanu, the former voivode of Moldavia, to recover his throne and taking a prominent part in the peace negotiations between Poland and Turkey in 1562. In 1569 he encouraged the Netherlands' revolt against Spain and a letter of his, promising Turkish support, was read out at a meeting of the Calvinist consistory of Amsterdam. By then his influence at Constantinople had grown, due to the accession to the throne (1566) of his friend Sultan *Selim II, who esteemed him as his favorite. Immediately after this, he was granted a monopoly on the import of wines through the Bosporus, said to have brought him a net income of 15,000 ducats annually. In addition, he obtained important trading privileges in Poland. In order to satisfy certain claims against the king of France (who had sequestered the family property left in that country, on the pretext that Jews were not tolerated there), he obtained the sultan's firman (1568) ordering the confiscation of one-third of the merchandise on French ships docking at Alexandria. This firman was revoked in August 1569, the sultan stating that he had been misled. At this period, Nasi's influence at court seemed to wane and the French envoy, Grandchamp, launched an elaborate plot with Nasi's former physician, Daoud, in the hope of disgracing him. The plot failed and Daoud was excommunicated by the principal Jewish communities of the Turkish Empire.

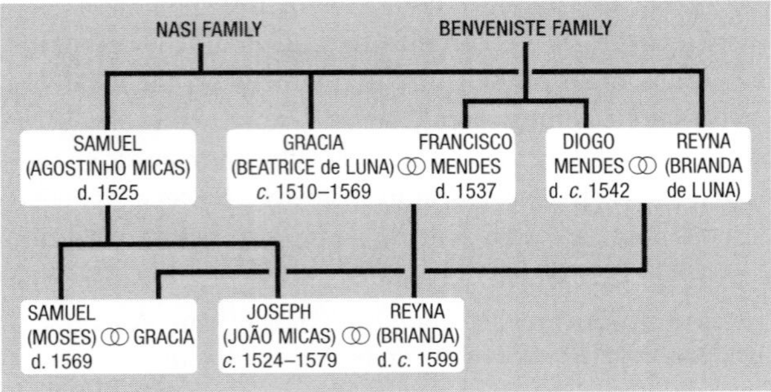

Soon after Selim's accession, he appointed Nasi duke of the island of Naxos and the adjacent archipelago, whose Christian duke had recently been deposed, and eventually he also became count of Andros. He administered his duchy mainly from his palace at Belvedere near Constantinople, his local representative being Francisco Coronel or Coronello, a descendant of Abraham *Seneor, the last chief rabbi of Castile. During the War of Lepanto (1570–71) Nasi's dominions were reconquered by the Venetians for the former duke, but Nasi's authority was soon reinstated. In compensation for his loss, he is supposed to have been appointed voivode of Walachia in 1571, but the facts concerning this are obscure.

As early as 1558 or 1559, Doña Gracia obtained from the sultan various concessions in *Tiberias, then in ruins, probably with the intention of founding a yeshivah there. In 1561 Joseph obtained confirmation and extension of this grant, giving him plenary authority in Tiberias and seven nearby villages in consideration of an annual payment. In the winter of 1564–65 the rebuilding of the ruined walls of Tiberias was completed, ensuring a certain degree of physical security. This was the only practical attempt to establish some sort of Jewish political center in Palestine between the fourth and 19th centuries. It is not clear, however, whether Nasi thought of it primarily as a political, a charitable, or even an economic enterprise; it is certain in any case that he never visited his domain. He attempted to develop it commercially, fostering the wool and silk industries. He also sent a circular letter to the Jewish communities of Italy inviting them to settle there, and the community of Cori in the Campania made preparations (not perhaps fulfilled) to accept his invitation *en masse*. The intrigues of the native Arabs and Christians and the jealousy of Nasi's rivals in Constantinople led him to concentrate his interest elsewhere. Nevertheless, he remained titular lord of Tiberias until his death, the concession being afterward renewed for Solomon *Abenaes.

Nasi encouraged Jewish scholarship by his patronage of various scholars, such as Moses *Almosnino who composed his "Treatise on Dreams" at Nasi's request; the physician *Amatus Lusitanus, who dedicated his fifth *Centuria* to Nasi; Isaac *Akrish, whom he supported when he was impoverished by the Constantinople fire of 1569; and Isaac Onkeneira, his translator and director of the yeshivah and synagogue that he maintained at Belvedere. A fine library from which some manuscripts still survive adjoined these institutions. Joseph's only independent literary production, edited by the same Isaac Onkeneira, was his *Ben Porat Yosef* (Constantinople, 1577) – a polemic against astrology, which records a dispute he had with certain Christian dignitaries.

In 1569 Nasi threw his powerful influence on the side of the war party in Constantinople, and was considered to be mainly responsible for the Turkish war against Venice over Cyprus. It was reported that the sultan had promised to make him king of this island, though it would remain a Turkish fief. Some suggest that Nasi thus planned to provide a political solution to the Jewish problem of the day. Although the Turks conquered Cyprus in 1571 they suffered a naval disaster at Lepanto, in consequence of which the peace party led by Grand Vizier Mehemet Sokolli gained the ascendant. Nasi's influence henceforth waned, though he remained in possession of his dignities and privileges until his death. The balance of his achievement was disappointing, due to his inconstancy of purpose. It is difficult to decide what credence can be placed in the Spanish report that he repented of his action in abandoning Christianity and desired to return to Western Europe.

Joseph was survived by his widow, REYNA, duchess of Naxos (d. c. 1599), who maintained his library and allowed scholars access to it. In 1592 she set up a printing press in her palace at Belvedere. It was directed by Joseph b. Isaac Ashkeloni, and operated until 1594; it operated again from 1597 to 1599. Some 12 works, commemorating Reyna's generosity on the title page, were issued from the press.

BIBLIOGRAPHY: C. Roth, *House of Nasi: The Duke of Naxos* (1948); P. Grunebaum-Ballin, *Joseph Naci, duc de Naxos* (1968); J. Reznik, *Le Duc Joseph de Naxos* (1936); A. Galanté, *Don Joseph Nasi, Duc de Naxos, d'aprés de nouveaux documents* (1913); idem, in: REJ, 64 (1912), 236–43; M.A. Levy, *Don Joseph Nasi, Herzog von Naxos, seine Familie, und zwei juedische Diplomaten seiner Zeit* (1859); P. Wittek, in: *Bulletin of the School of Oriental and African Studies*, 14 (1952), 381–3; Arce, in: *Sefarad*, 13 (1953), 257–86; Kaufmann, in: JQR, 2 (1889/90), 291–7; 4 (1891/92), 509–12; 13 (1900/01), 520–32; Besohn, in: MGWJ, 18 (1869), 422–4; Rahn, *ibid.*, 28 (1879), 113–21.

[Cecil Roth]

NASIELSK (Rus. **Nasyelsk**), town in Warszawa province, E. central Poland. It received its first municipal privileges in 1386. The date of the first Jewish settlement is unknown, but a wooden synagogue was erected in 1650. The community listed 1,410 Jews in 1808, 4,741 in 1910 (76% of the total population), and 2,691 in 1921. Jews were not integrated into the economic life of the town and many of them emigrated after World War I. During the period of Polish independence, there was a significant number of unemployed and poor among the Jews, a situation which deteriorated even further as a result of a boycott by Polish antisemites. Tension between Jews and Christians came to the fore in 1923, when the latter accused the Jews of a ritual murder. Dominant in the community was the *Agudat Israel, which in 1920, 1924, and 1931 won half of the seats of the community council. Among the educational institutions, there were the Beth Jacob schools of the Agudat Israel, the *Tarbut of the Zionists, and a Yiddish school, as well as such cultural institutions as a library and various drama circles. The wooden synagogue was rebuilt in 1880. Renowned *ẓaddikim*, such as R. Jacob Landa (d. 1886) and Ezekiel ha-Levi b. Meir Jehiel (d. during the Holocaust) settled in the town.

[Shimshon Leib Kirshenboim]

Holocaust Period

During the Nazi occupation, Nasielsk belonged to Bezirk Zichenau, established and incorporated into East Prussia by Hitler's decree of Oct. 26, 1939. Before World War II Nasielsk had about 3,000 Jews. During the bombardment of the town, a considerable number of Jews fled eastward. After the Germans entered, the Jewish community there existed for only three months. Existing data leave doubt whether the Jews were deported in one mass *Aktion* (deportation) on Dec. 3, 1939, or in two deportations, beginning in September or October. Some of the victims were shut up for a day or more in the local synagogue, beaten, and herded to the station. They were loaded onto trains and dispatched to Lukow, Mezhirech, and Biala Podlaska railroad stations. There they were driven out of the train and dispersed among various towns in the Lublin region of the General Government. Some of them reached the Warsaw Ghetto, where many Jews from Nasielsk, refugees from the first days of the war, already lived. After the deportation from Nasielsk, the local Germans and soldiers seized all Jewish property. Only about 80 Jews from Nasielsk survived the Holocaust.

[Danuta Dombrowska]

BIBLIOGRAPHY: *Sefer ha-Ẓeva'ot*, 1 (1945), 145.

NASNA (generally referred to in Hungarian Jewish historiography as **Náznánfalva**), village near Tîrgu-Mureş in Transylvania, Romania, within Hungary to 1918 and from 1940 to 1945. With the exception of *Alba-Iulia, Nasna had the oldest Jewish community within the borders of historic Transylvania. The first reliable information about the Jews there dates from 1601. Several were members of the Turkish Sephardi community and had family or communal connections with Jews in Alba-Iulia. The curious wooden synagogue of Nasna, of which only the eastern wall was constructed of brick, was apparently built in 1747 (or according to some opinions in 1757 or 1785). The exterior resembled a granary or warehouse and the walls, ceiling, pillars, and platform were painted and ornamented in the style of the contemporary church decoration of the local Unitarians. Quotations from the Psalms and prayers were inscribed on the walls and ceiling. The synagogue was completely demolished in 1940. Some of the decorated boards which were salvaged were transferred to the Jewish Museum in Budapest. Members of the Nasna community were among the first Jews to settle in Tîrgu-Mureş from which Jews had been excluded until 1848. After the prohibition was abolished the Jewish population of Nasna dwindled. During the Holocaust the last two Jewish residents were deported to the ghetto in Tîrgu-Mures (and from there to their deaths). After World War II the Jewish community of Nasna was not revived.

BIBLIOGRAPHY: M. Avi-Shaul, in: *Reshumot*, 4 (1926), 387–90; F. Lőwy, in: *Magyar Zsidó Almanach* (1911), 144–7; G. Balázs, in: *Libanon* (Hung., 1941).

[Yehouda Marton]

NASSAU, former duchy in Germany. In the Middle Ages Jews were to be found in Limburg on the Lahn, Diez, Montabaur, and other towns in the duchy. Limburg was the most important community before the *Black Death persecutions (1348), when all the Jews were annihilated. The settlement was reestablished, but there is evidence that they were again severely persecuted and expelled. After the Thirty-Years War (1618–48) *Wiesbaden emerged as the leading community. When the duchy of Nassau split up into minor principalities, Jews settled in the villages, where they engaged in peddling and livestock trading. In 1798 the French army abolished the **Leibzoll* ("body tax") in Nassau-Usingen, but it was reapplied in 1801 and only finally abolished in 1808 through the intervention of Wolf *Breidenbach, the *Court Jew of Brunswick. The authorities compensated themselves by raising the *Schutzgeld* ("protection money"; see **Schutzjuden*). Nassau-Usingen, which had 104 Jewish families, increased its territory and included about 530 Jewish families in 1805; after 1815–16, a single duchy was created. In 1836 there were 1,238 Jewish families (6,147 persons) distributed in 229 localities and conducting services in 95 *Judenschulen*. Only 11 communities in the various localities had more than 100 persons; the largest, Heddernheim, had 327, but almost all of the men were peddlers who were generally absent on their business. The capital, Wiesbaden, had 234 persons, and its rabbi, Abraham *Geiger, who served from 1832 to 1838, appealed unsuccessfully to the government to be appointed **Landrabbiner*. The Orthodox communities opposed his efforts, and Geiger left in frustration. In 1842 Reform services modeled on those of Wuerttemberg were introduced and four district rabbinates created. In 1848 full civic equality was temporarily granted, and in 1861 the Jewish *oath was abolished. In 1865, a year before it was annexed to *Prussia, as part of the province of Hesse-Nassau, there were in Nassau 7,000 Jews (1.5% of the population). Through emigration from the rural communities to the cities, in particular to Wiesbaden, their numbers subsequently decreased.

BIBLIOGRAPHY: M. Silberstein, in: ZGJD, 5 (1892), 126–45, 335–47; A. Kober, in: *Festschrift S. Dubnow* (1930), 215–25; idem, in: *Festschrift M. Philippson* (1916), 275–301; idem, in: *Nassauische Annalen*, 66 (1955), 220–50; J.L. Frank, *Loschen Hakodesch* (1961); H. Wiener, *Abraham Geiger and Liberal Judaism* (1962), 9–17.

NASSAUER, RUDOLF (1924–1996), German-born poet and novelist. From a wealthy family of German Jews, Rudolf Nassauer was, by profession, a wine merchant as well as a writer. He wrote *Poems* (1947), and an ambitious novel, *The Hooligan* (1960), a powerful, imaginary picture of concentration-camp life. The victim's search for power over the aggressor is also the theme of *The Cuckoo* (1962). In 1947 he married the well-known British novelist Berenice *Rubens. They were divorced in 1967.

[William D. Rubinstein (2nd ed.)]

°NASSER, GAMAL ABDUL (1918–1970), president of the United Arab Republic (Egypt) and spokesman of the Pan-Arab movement. As a leading member of the revolutionary group of "free officers," in 1952 Nasser participated in overthrowing the Egyptian monarchy and establishing a republican regime. Quickly becoming the political leader of the "new" Egypt, he tried, with considerable success, not only to introduce economic and social reforms into his own country (including an agrarian reform and efforts at industrialization), but also to place Egypt and himself in the forefront of the nonaligned nations, the so-called Third World, together with Nehru's India and Tito's Yugoslavia. During this process, his extremely belligerent attitude toward Israel, as well as his interventions in the internal affairs of other Arab states, served as the main instruments of his policy. His anti-Israel policy included the organization of an economic boycott, armed infiltration and sabotage, closing of the Suez Canal to Israel shipping, and open belligerency.

Nasser participated as an officer in Egypt's invasion of the newly established State of Israel in 1948 and was a commander of the regiment besieged at the Faluja pocket. Upon his return to Egypt, he was decisively instrumental in the bloodless military coup, led by General Mohammad Naguib, which overthrew King Farouk. By 1954 he had succeeded in ousting Naguib, assuming full power, and overcoming the opposition of the Muslim Brotherhood and remnants of the previous ruling Wafd Party and the Communists. To reinforce his leadership, he created a political framework that became the only legal party in Egypt. At that time he wrote his book *The Philosophy of the Revolution* (1955). In the first years of his rule Nasser decisively changed the political course of events in Egypt and the Middle East by several drastic steps. His arms deal with the Soviet Union (ostensibly with Czechoslovakia) overturned the delicate balance of forces between Israel and her Arab neighbors, maintained by the Western powers, and inaugurated the Israel-Egyptian arms race, which from then on dominated the Middle Eastern scene and almost evolved into a confrontation of the super powers in the late 1960s and the beginning of the 1970s. By evicting the last remnant of British forces from the Suez Canal zone and nationalizing the Suez Canal Company (1956), thus removing a barrier between Egypt and Israel, and by his deliberate policy of actively supporting the murderous *fedayeen* raids deep into Israel territory, from the *Gaza Strip and from Sinai, Nasser exacerbated the situation until it exploded in the *Sinai Campaign. In spite of Egypt's total military defeat, Nasser, mainly with Soviet support, succeeded in converting it, at least in the eyes of his devoted followers, into a political victory that enhanced his prestige.

In 1956 and 1965 Nasser was the only candidate for presidential election. In the course of his reforms, Nasser nationalized the Egyptian press and removed his enemies and critics from influential positions. Over the years his anti-imperialist policy became more and more pro-Soviet, until Egypt became so dependent on the U.S.S.R. in military and economic spheres (heavy armament deliveries, military advisers, the construction of the Aswan Dam and of individual industrial plants, etc.) that in May 1967 Moscow was able to lead Nasser into the adventurous steps that provoked the *Six-Day War. After the defeat, Nasser resigned (on June 9) for a few hours, but reassumed power in response to mass demonstrations in the streets of Cairo demanding the continuation of his leadership. He tried to place the blame for the defeat on the senior military echelons, including his vice president, Marshal Abdel Ḥakīm ʿAmer, who committed suicide. Other military leaders were convicted in show trials, and Nasser held a new election to the Arab Socialist Union.

After 1967 Nasser visited the U.S.S.R. several times. In his public pronouncements about Israel, he was careful to formulate the aim of Israel's destruction in non-explicit terms, though from time to time, particularly just before the Six-Day War, he left no doubt that this was the real aim of his policy. This again became clear at the Arab Summit Conference in Khartoum (Aug. 29–Sept. 2, 1967), when he initiated the policy of pledging the Arabs not to recognize Israel, not to negotiate with her, and not to conclude peace agreements with her. Nasser maintained that Egypt's acceptance of the Nov. 22, 1967 Security Council resolution was compatible with the "three noes" of Khartoum, but he interpreted the resolution as demanding an Israeli withdrawal from all occupied territories without negotiations and a peace treaty. When his policy failed to achieve any effective pressure on Israel, he renewed military attacks along the Suez Canal zone. When this failed to achieve its aim and ultimately turned into military setbacks for Egypt, in August 1970 Nasser accepted a U.S. initiative for a limited cease-fire period and indirect negotiations with Israel, under the Security Council resolution, in exchange for an Israeli acceptance of the principle of withdrawal from occupied territories. Nasser died suddenly in September 1970 before the new stage of his policy bore any fruit.

Nasser was adept at adjusting his personal image and tone to whomever he addressed, so that while in Arab eyes he was the incarnation of the fight against Israel and for Arab glory, many Western circles and media were impressed by his reasonableness and moderation. This diversity became particularly evident when, on the one hand, he gave an Indian newspaper editor a copy of the Protocols of the *Elders of Zion as an explanation of the Jewish "world conspiracy," while on the other, with Western people, he continuously stressed that he clearly distinguished between Jewry and Zionism. These declarations notwithstanding, Egypt's Jews suffered persecution and humiliation during his rule, chiefly after Egypt's defeat in 1967.

BIBLIOGRAPHY: P. Mansfield, *Nasser* (Eng., 1969), incl. bibl.: M.H. Kerr, *Egypt under Nasser* (1968), incl. bibl.; R. St. John, *The Boss* (1960); J. Joesten, *Nasser: The Rise to Power* (1960); W. Wynn, *Nasser of Egypt* (1959); K. Wheelock, *Nasser's New Egypt* (1960), incl. bibl.; E. Beʾeri, *Army Officers in Arab Politics and Society* (1969).

NASSY, DAVID DE ISAAC COHEN (late 18th century), Caribbean physician, Jewish community leader, and publicist. Nassy, born in Surinam into its leading Sephardi family, was a descendant of David Nassy, who had founded the Jewish community there in 1664. The younger David first appears in 1785 as a signatory to a petition for a college of letters in Surinam. Shortly thereafter he became president of the *Regenten* (board) of the local Jewish community, and in this capacity was the first signatory of a communication to the German Christian advocate of Jewish rights, Christian Wilhelm von *Dohm. At the latter's request, Nassy played a leading role in compiling *Essai historique sur la Colonie de Surinam* (2 vols., Paramaribo, 1788), a record of the Jewish role in the history of the colony. Restrictions on Jewish freedom led him to St. Thomas for a time and subsequently to Philadelphia (1792), where he was the first Jewish physician to practice in that city. An outbreak of yellow fever the following year brought him into conflict with his foremost colleague, Dr. Benjamin Rush, over diagnosis and treatment. Nassy published his findings in *Observations on the Cause, Nature, and Treatment of the Epidemic Disorder Prevalent in Philadelphia* (1793), in which he pointed out his success in losing only 19 patients (11 of whom had already received Rush's treatment) out of 117 afflicted. Nassy's scientific work earned him election to the American Philosophical Society. In 1795 he returned to Surinam, where he went into business. Three years later he published *Lettre Politico-Theologico-Morale sur les Juifs* (1798?) with a Dutch translation, supporting the emancipation of Dutch Jewry.

BIBLIOGRAPHY: Rosenbloom, Biogr Dict; J.L. Blau and S.W. Baron (eds.), *Jews of the United States*, 2 (1963), 459–64; AJHSP, 22 (1914), 25–38; H. Bloch, in: *Journal of American Medical Association* (Feb. 10, 1969).

[Malcolm H. Stern]

NASZ PRZEGLĄD ("Our Review"), Jewish Polish-language newspaper. *Nasz Przegląd* was published in Warsaw from 1923 to 1939 and served as an informative political organ with a Zionist-nationalist orientation. It had been preceded by *Nasz Kurjer*, which first appeared in 1917 at the incentive of the journalist Jacob Appenszlak, aided financially by Joseph *Dawidsohn and Samuel Jacob *Jatzkan, editor of **Haynt*. In 1920 *Nasz Kurjer* was reorganized on a cooperative basis, and in 1923 appeared under its new name *Nasz Przegląd* as a nonparty nationalist organ. Nathan Szwalbe, Saul Wagman, Jacob Appenszlak, and Samuel Wołkowicz all served as associate editors. Its permanent contributors included noted Jewish writers and publicists, such as Samuel *Hirschhorn, Florian Sokolow, Fishel *Rotenstreich, Janusz *Korczak, the political writer Bernard Singer (who wrote under the pseudonym "Regnis"), and the historians Majer *Balaban and Emanuel *Ringelblum. Several prominent progressive Polish intellectuals worked within the framework of the newspaper, including the philologist Baudouin de Courtenay and the journalist W. Rzymowski. It had many Polish non-Jews among its readers.

Nasz Przegląd was not a campaigning newspaper and did not take a fixed ideological stand, developing a tendency to adapt to the changing political situation. The members of its staff differed in their outlooks, although the pro-Zionist trend was marked. While *Nasz Przegląd* supported the Polonization of Jewish culture, many of the Jewish intelligentsia became influenced by it toward the Zionist cause. It published installments of important works of Yiddish and modern Hebrew literature in Polish translation, including those of Joseph *Opatoshu and Singer, and J. *Klausner's *Jesus of Nazareth. Nasz Przegląd* 's daily circulation reached 40,000 and its staff comprised some 50 writers. The newspaper owned a modern printing-house which published a children's supplement, *Mały Przegląd*, edited by Janusz Korczak, as well as a women's weekly, *Eva*, edited by Paulina Appenszlak.

BIBLIOGRAPHY: EG, Warsaw, 1 (1953), 512–4; A. Levinson, *Toledot Yehudei Varshah* (1953), 305–6. **ADD. BIBLIOGRAPHY:** M. Fuks, *Prasa zydowska w Warszawie* (1979), 259–74; J. Gothelf (ed.), *Ha-Ittonut ha-Yehudit she-Hayeta* (1973), 207–13.

[Moshe Landau]

ABBREVIATIONS

GENERAL ABBREVIATIONS

This list contains abbreviations used in the Encyclopaedia (apart from the standard ones, such as geographical abbreviations, points of compass, etc.). For names of organizations, institutions, etc., in abbreviation, see Index. For bibliographical abbreviations of books and authors in Rabbinical literature, see following lists.

*	Cross reference; i.e., an article is to be found under the word(s) immediately following the asterisk (*).
°	Before the title of an entry, indicates a non-Jew (post-biblical times).
‡	Indicates reconstructed forms.
>	The word following this sign is derived from the preceding one.
<	The word preceding this sign is derived from the following one.

ad loc.	*ad locum*, "at the place"; used in quotations of commentaries.
A.H.	*Anno Hegirae*, "in the year of Hegira," i.e., according to the Muslim calendar.
Akk.	Addadian.
A.M.	*anno mundi*, "in the year (from the creation) of the world."
anon.	anonymous.
Ar.	Arabic.
Aram.	Aramaic.
Ass.	Assyrian.
b.	born; *ben, bar.*
Bab.	Babylonian.
B.C.E.	Before Common Era (= B.C.).
bibl.	bibliography.
Bul.	Bulgarian.
c., ca.	Circa.
C.E.	Common Era (= A.D.).
cf.	*confer*, "compare."
ch., chs.	chapter, chapters.
comp.	compiler, compiled by.
Cz.	Czech.
D	according to the documentary theory, the Deuteronomy document.
d.	died.
Dan.	Danish.
diss., dissert,	dissertation, thesis.
Du.	Dutch.
E.	according to the documentary theory, the Elohist document (i.e., using Elohim as the name of God) of the first five (or six) books of the Bible.
ed.	editor, edited, edition.
eds.	editors.
e.g.	*exempli gratia*, "for example."
Eng.	English.
et al.	*et alibi*, "and elsewhere"; or *et alii*, "and others"; "others."
f., ff.	and following page(s).
fig.	figure.
fl.	flourished.
fol., fols	folio(s).
Fr.	French.
Ger.	German.
Gr.	Greek.
Heb.	Hebrew.
Hg., Hung	Hungarian.
ibid	*Ibidem*, "in the same place."
incl. bibl.	includes bibliography.
introd.	introduction.
It.	Italian.
J	according to the documentary theory, the Jahwist document (i.e., using YHWH as the name of God) of the first five (or six) books of the Bible.
Lat.	Latin.
lit.	literally.
Lith.	Lithuanian.
loc. cit.	*loco citato*, "in the [already] cited place."
Ms., Mss.	Manuscript(s).
n.	note.
n.d.	no date (of publication).
no., nos	number(s).
Nov.	Novellae (Heb. *Ḥiddushim*).
n.p.	place of publication unknown.
op. cit.	*opere citato*, "in the previously mentioned work."
P.	according to the documentary theory, the Priestly document of the first five (or six) books of the Bible.
p., pp.	page(s).
Pers.	Persian.
pl., pls.	plate(s).
Pol.	Polish.
Port.	Potuguese.
pt., pts.	part(s).
publ.	published.
R.	Rabbi or Rav (before names); in Midrash (after an abbreviation) – *Rabbah.*
r.	recto, the first side of a manuscript page.
Resp.	Responsa (Latin "answers," Hebrew *She'elot u-Teshuvot* or *Teshuvot),* collections of rabbinic decisions.
rev.	revised.

Rom. Romanian.
Rus(s). Russian.
Slov. Slovak.
Sp. Spanish.
s.v. *sub verbo, sub voce*, "under the (key) word."
Sum Sumerian.
summ. Summary.
suppl. supplement.
Swed. Swedish.
tr., trans(l). translator, translated, translation.
Turk. Turkish.
Ukr. Ukrainian.
v., vv. *verso*. The second side of a manuscript page; also verse(s).
Yid. Yiddish.

ABBREVIATIONS USED IN RABBINICAL LITERATURE

Adderet Eliyahu, Karaite treatise by Elijah b. Moses *Bashyazi.
Admat Kodesh, Resp. by Nissim Ḥayyim Moses b. Joseph |Mizraḥi.
Aguddah, Sefer ha-, Nov. by *Alexander Suslin ha-Kohen.
Ahavat Ḥesed, compilation by *Israel Meir ha-Kohen.
Aliyyot de-Rabbenu Yonah, Nov. by *Jonah b. Avraham Gerondi.
Arukh ha-Shulḥan, codification by Jehiel Michel *Epstein.
Asayin (= positive precepts), subdivision of: (1) *Maimonides, *Sefer ha-Mitzvot;* (2) *Moses b. Jacob of Coucy, *Semag.*
Asefat Dinim, subdivision of *Sedei Ḥemed* by Ḥayyim Hezekiah *Medini, an encyclopaedia of precepts and responsa.
Asheri = *Asher b. Jehiel.
Aeret Ḥakhamim, by Baruch *Frankel-Teomim; pt, 1: Resp. to Sh. Ar.; pt2: Nov. to Talmud.
Ateret Zahav, subdivision of the *Levush*, a codification by Mordecai b. Abraham (Levush) *Jaffe; *Ateret Zahav* parallels Tur. YD.
Ateret Ẓevi, Comm. To Sh. Ar. by Ẓevi Hirsch b. Azriel.
Avir Ya'akov, Resp. by Jacob Avigdor.
Avkat Rokhel, Resp. by Joseph b. Ephraim *Caro.
Avnei Millu'im, Comm. to Sh. Ar., EH, by *Aryeh Loeb b. Joseph ha-Kohen.
Avnei Nezer, Resp. on Sh. Ar. by Abraham b. Ze'ev Nahum Bornstein of *Sochaczew.
Avodat Massa, Compilation of Tax Law by Yoasha Abraham Judah.
Azei ha-Levanon, Resp. by Judah Leib *Zirelson.

Ba'al ha-Tanya – *Shneur Zalman of Lyady.
Ba'ei Ḥayyei, Resp. by Ḥayyim b. Israel *Benveniste.
Ba'er Heitev, Comm. To Sh. Ar. The parts on OḤ and EH are by Judah b. Simeon *Ashkenazi, the parts on YD AND ḤM by *Zechariah Mendel b. Aryeh Leib. Printed in most editions of Sh. Ar.
Baḥ = Joel *Sirkes.
Baḥ, usual abbreviation for *Bayit Ḥadash*, a commentary on Tur by Joel *Sirkes; printed in most editions of Tur.
Bayit Ḥadash, see *Baḥ*.
Berab = Jacob Berab, also called Ri Berav.
Bedek ha-Bayit, by Joseph b. Ephraim *Caro, additions to his *Beit Yosef* (a comm. to Tur). Printed sometimes inside *Beit Yosef*, in smaller type. Appears in most editions of Tur.
Be'er ha-Golah, Commentary to Sh. Ar. By Moses b. Naphtali Hirsch *Rivkes; printed in most editions of Sh. Ar.
Be'er Mayim, Resp. by Raphael b. Abraham Manasseh Jacob.
Be'er Mayim Ḥayyim, Resp. by Samuel b. Ḥayyim *Vital.
Be'er Yiẓḥak, Resp. by Isaac Elhanan *Spector.
Beit ha-Beḥirah, Comm. to Talmud by Menahem b. Solomon *Meiri.
Beit Me'ir, Nov. on Sh. Ar. by Meir b. Judah Leib Posner.
Beit Shelomo, Resp. by Solomon b. Aaron Ḥason (the younger).
Beit Shemu'el, Comm. to Sh. Ar., EH, by *Samuel b. Uri Shraga Phoebus.
Beit Ya'akov, by Jacob b. Jacob Moses *Lorberbaum; pt.1: Nov. to Ket.; pt.2: Comm. to EH.
Beit Yisrael, collective name for the commentaries *Derishah*, *Perishah*, and *Be'urim* by Joshua b. Alexander ha-Kohen *Falk. See under the names of the commentaries.
Beit Yiẓḥak, Resp. by Isaac *Schmelkes.
Beit Yosef: (1) Comm. on Tur by Joseph b. Ephraim *Caro; printed in most editions of Tur; (2) Resp. by the same.
Ben Yehudah, Resp. by Abraham b. Judah Litsch (ליטש) Rosenbaum.
Bertinoro, Standard commentary to Mishnah by Obadiah *Bertinoro. Printed in most editions of the Mishnah.
[Be'urei] Ha-Gra, Comm. to Bible, Talmud, and Sh. Ar. By *Elijah b. Solomon Zalmon (Gaon of Vilna); printed in major editions of the mentioned works.
Be'urim, Glosses to Isserles *Darkhei Moshe* (a comm. on Tur) by Joshua b. Alexander ha-Kohen *Falk; printed in many editions of Tur.
Binyamin Ze'ev, Resp. by *Benjamin Ze'ev b. Mattathias of Arta.
Birkei Yosef, Nov. by Ḥayyim Joseph David *Azulai.
Ha-Buẓ ve-ha-Argaman, subdivision of the *Levush* (a codification by Mordecai b. Abraham (Levush) *Jaffe); *Ha-Buẓ ve-ha-Argaman* parallels Tur, EH.

Comm. = Commentary

Da'at Kohen, Resp. by Abraham Isaac ha-Kohen. *Kook.
Darkhei Moshe, Comm. on Tur Moses b. Israel *Isserles; printed in most editions of Tur.
Darkhei No'am, Resp. by *Mordecai b. Judah ha-Levi.
Darkhei Teshuvah, Nov. by Ẓevi *Shapiro; printed in the major editions of Sh. Ar.
De'ah ve-Haskel, Resp. by Obadiah Hadaya (see *Yaskil Avdi).*

Derashot Ran, Sermons by *Nissim b. Reuben Gerondi.
Derekh Ḥayyim, Comm. to *Avot* by *Judah Loew (Lob., Liwa) b. Bezalel (Maharal) of Prague.
Derishah, by Joshua b. Alexander ha-Kohen *Falk; additions to his *Perishah* (comm. on Tur); printed in many editions of Tur.
Derushei ha-Ẓelaḥ, Sermons, by Ezekiel b. Judah Halevi *Landau.
Devar Avraham, Resp. by Abraham *Shapira.
Devar Shemu'el, Resp. by Samuel *Aboab.
Devar Yehoshu'a, Resp. by Joshua Menahem b. Isaac Aryeh Ehrenberg.
Dikdukei Soferim, variae lections of the talmudic text by Raphael Nathan*Rabbinowicz.
Divrei Emet, Resp. by Isaac Bekhor David.
Divrei Ge'onim, Digest of responsa by Ḥayyim Aryeh b. Jeḥiel Ẓevi *Kahana.
Divrei Ḥamudot, Comm. on *Piskei ha-Rosh* by Yom Tov Lipmann b. Nathan ha-Levi *Heller; printed in major editions of the Talmud.
Divrei Ḥayyim several works by Ḥayyim *Halberstamm; if quoted alone refers to his Responsa.
Divrei Malkhi'el, Resp. by Malchiel Tenebaum.
Divrei Rivot, Resp. by Isaac b. Samuel *Adarbi.
Divrei Shemu'el, Resp. by Samuel Raphael Arditi.

Edut be-Ya'akov, Resp. by Jacob b. Abraham *Boton.
Edut bi-Yhosef, Resp. by Joseph b. Isaac *Almosnino.
Ein Ya'akov, Digest of talmudic *aggadot* by Jacob (Ibn) *Habib.
Ein Yiẓḥak, Resp. by Isaac Elhanan *Spector.
Ephraim of Lentshitz = Solomon *Luntschitz.
Erekh Leḥem, Nov. and glosses to Sh. Ar. by Jacob b. Abraham *Castro.
Eshkol, Sefer ha-, Digest of *halakhot* by *Abraham b. Isaac of Narbonne.
Et Sofer, Treatise on Law Court documents by Abraham b. Mordecai *Ankawa, in the 2nd vol. of his Resp. *Kerem Ḥamar.*
Etan ha-Ezraḥi, Resp. by Abraham b. Israel Jehiel (Shrenzl) *Rapaport.
Even ha-Ezel, Nov. to Maimonides' *Yad Ḥazakah* by Isser Zalman *Meltzer.
Even ha-Ezer, also called *Raban* of *Ẓafenat Pa'ne'aḥ,* rabbinical work with varied contents by *Eliezer b. Nathan of Mainz; not identical with the subdivision of Tur, Shulḥan Arukh, etc.
Ezrat Yehudah, Resp. by *Isaar Judah b. Nechemiah of Brisk.

Gan Eden, Karaite treatise by *Aaron b. Elijah of Nicomedia.
Gersonides = *Levi b. Gershom, also called Leo Hebraecus, or Ralbag.
Ginnat Veradim, Resp. by *Abraham b. Mordecai ha-Levi.

Haggahot, another name for *Rema.*
Haggahot Asheri, glosses to *Piskei ha-Rosh* by *Israel of Krems; printed in most Talmud editions.
Haggahot Maimuniyyot, Comm,. to Maimonides' Yad Ḥazakah by *Meir ha-Kohen; printed in most eds. of Yad.
Haggahot Mordekhai, glosses to *Mordekhai* by Samuel *Schlettstadt; printed in most editions of the Talmud after *Mordekhai.*
Haggahot ha-Rashash on Tosafot, annotations of Samuel *Strashun on the Tosafot (printed in major editions of the Talmud).
Ha-Gra = *Elijah b. Solomon Zalman (Gaon of Vilna).
Ha-Gra, Commentaries on Bible, Talmud, and Sh. Ar. respectively, by *Elijah b. Solomon Zalman (Gaon of Vilna); printed in major editions of the mentioned works.
Hai Gaon, Comm. = his comm. on Mishnah.
Ḥakham Ẓevi, Resp. by Ẓevi Hirsch b. Jacob *Ashkenazi.
Halakhot = Rif, *Halakhot.* Compilation and abstract of the Talmud by Isaac b. Jacob ha-Kohen *Alfasi; printed in most editions of the Talmud.
Halakhot Gedolot, compilation of *halakhot* from the Geonic period, arranged acc. to the Talmud. Here cited acc. to ed. Warsaw (1874). Author probably *Simeon Kayyara of Basra.
Halakhot Pesukot le-Rav Yehudai Ga'on compilation of *halakhot.*
Halakhot Pesukot min ha-Ge'onim, compilation of *halakhot* from the geonic period by different authors.
Ḥananel, Comm. to Talmud by *Hananel b. Ḥushi'el; printed in some editions of the Talmud.
Harei Besamim, Resp. by Aryeh Leib b. Isaac *Horowitz.
Ḥassidim, Sefer, Ethical maxims by *Judah b. Samuel he-Ḥasid.
Hassagot Rabad on Rif, Glosses on Rif, *Halakhot,* by *Abraham b. David of Posquières.
Hassagot Rabad [on Yad], Glosses on Maimonides, *Yad Ḥazakah,* by *Abraham b. David of Posquières.
Hassagot Ramban, Glosses by Naḥmanides on Maimonides' *Sefer ha-Mitzvot;* usually printed together with *Sefer ha-Mitzvot.*
Ḥatam Sofer = Moses *Sofer.
Ḥavvot Ya'ir, Resp. and varia by Jair Ḥayyim *Bacharach
Ḥayyim Or Zaru'a = *Ḥayyim (Eliezer) b. Isaac.
Ḥazon Ish = Abraham Isaiah *Karelitz.
Ḥazon Ish, Nov. by Abraham Isaiah *Karelitz
Ḥedvat Ya'akov, Resp. by Aryeh Judah Jacob b. David Dov Meisels (article under his father's name).
Heikhal Yiẓḥak, Resp. by Isaac ha-Levi *Herzog.
Ḥelkat Meḥokek, Comm. to Sh. Ar., by Moses b. Isaac Judah *Lima.
Ḥelkat Ya'akov, Resp. by Mordecai Jacob Breisch.
Ḥemdah Genuzah, , Resp. from the geonic period by different authors.
Ḥemdat Shelomo, Resp. by Solomon Zalman *Lipschitz.
Ḥida = Ḥayyim Joseph David *Azulai.
Ḥiddushei Halakhot ve-Aggadot, Nov. by Samuel Eliezer b. Judah ha-Levi *Edels.
Ḥikekei Lev, Resp. by Ḥayyim *Palaggi.
Ḥikrei Lev, Nov. to Sh. Ar. by Joseph Raphael b. Ḥayyim Joseph Ḥazzan (see article *Ḥazzan Family).
Hil. = Hilkhot … (e.g. *Hilkhot Shabbat).*
Ḥinnukh, Sefer ha-, List and explanation of precepts attributed (probably erroneously) to Aaron ha-Levi of Barcelona (see article **Ha-Ḥinnukh).*
Ḥok Ya'akov, Comm. to Hil. Pesaḥ in Sh. Ar., OḤ, by Jacob b. Joseph *Reicher.
Ḥokhmat Sehlomo (1), Glosses to Talmud, *Rashi* and Tosafot by Solomon b. Jehiel "Maharshal") *Luria; printed in many editions of the Talmud.
Ḥokhmat Sehlomo (2), Glosses and Nov. to Sh. Ar. by Solomon b. Judah Aaron *Kluger printed in many editions of Sh. Ar.
Ḥur, subdivision of the *Levush,* a codification by Mordecai b. Abraham (Levush) *Jaffe; *Hur* (or *Levush ha-Hur)* parallels Tur, OḤ, 242–697.
Ḥut ha-Meshullash, fourth part of the *Tashbeẓ* (Resp.), by Simeon b. Zemaḥ *Duran.

Ibn Ezra, Comm. to the Bible by Abraham *Ibn Ezra; printed in the major editions of the Bible *("Mikra'ot Gedolot").*
Imrei Yosher, Resp. by Meir b. Aaron Judah *Arik.
Ir Shushan, Subdivision of the *Levush,* a codification by Mordecai b. Abraham (Levush) *Jaffe; *Ir Shushan* parallels Tur, ḤM.
Israel of Bruna = Israel b. Ḥayyim *Bruna.
Ittur. Treatise on precepts by *Isaac b. Abba Mari of Marseilles.

Jacob Be Rab = *Be Rab.
Jacob b. Jacob Moses of Lissa = Jacob b. Jacob Moses *Lorberbaum.
Judah B. Simeon = Judah b. Simeon *Ashkenazi.
Judah Minz = Judah b. Eliezer ha-Levi *Minz.

Kappei Aharon, Resp. by Aaron Azriel.
Kehillat Ya'akov, Talmudic methodology, definitions etc. by Israel Jacob b. Yom Tov *Algazi.
Kelei Ḥemdah, Nov. and *pilpulim* by Meir Dan *Plotzki of Ostrova, arranged acc. to the Torah.
Keli Yakar, Annotations to the Torah by Solomon *Luntschitz.
Keneh Ḥokhmah, Sermons by Judah Loeb *Pochwitzer.
Keneset ha-Gedolah, Digest of *halakhot* by Ḥayyim b. Israel *Benveniste; subdivided into annotations to *Beit Yosef* and annotations to Tur.
Keneset Yisrael, Resp. by Ezekiel b. Abraham Katzenellenbogen (see article *Katzenellenbogen Family).
Kerem Ḥamar, Resp. and varia by Abraham b. Mordecai *Ankawa.
Kerem Shelmo. Resp. by Solomon b. Joseph *Amarillo.
Keritut, [Sefer], Methodology of the Talmud by *Samson b. Isaac of Chinon.
Kesef ha-Kedoshim, Comm. to Sh. Ar., ḤM, by Abraham *Wahrmann; printed in major editions of Sh. Ar.
Kesef Mishneh, Comm. to Maimonides, *Yad Ḥazakah,* by Joseph b. Ephraim *Caro; printed in most editions of *Yad Ḥazakah.*
Keẓot ha-Ḥoshen, Comm. to Sh. Ar., ḤM, by *Aryeh Loeb b. Joseph ha-Kohen; printed in major editions of Sh. Ar.
Kol Bo [Sefer], Anonymous collection of ritual rules; also called *Sefer ha-Likkutim.*
Kol Mevasser, Resp. by Meshullam *Rath.
Korban Aharon, Comm. to *Sifra* by Aaron b. Abraham *Ibn Ḥayyim; pt. 1 is called: *Middot Aharon.*
Korban Edah, Comm. to Jer. Talmud by David *Fraenkel; with additions: *Shiyyurei Korban;* printed in most editions of Jer. Talmud.
Kunteres ha-Kelalim, subdivision of *Sedei Ḥemed,* an encyclopaedia of precepts and responsa by Ḥayyim Hezekiah *Medini.
Kunteres ha-Semikhah, a treatise by *Levi b. Ḥabib; printed at the end of his responsa.
Kunteres Tikkun Olam, part of *Mispat Shalom* (Nov. by Shalom Mordecai b. Moses *Schwadron).

Lavin (negative precepts), subdivision of: (1) *Maimonides, *Sefer ha-Mitzvot;* (2) *Moses b. Jacob of Coucy, *Semag.*
Leḥem Mishneh, Comm. to Maimonides, *Yad Ḥazakah,* by Abraham [Ḥiyya] b. Moses *Boton; printed in most editions of *Yad Ḥazakah.*
Leḥem Rav, Resp. by Abraham [Ḥiyya] b. Moses *Boton.
Leket Yosher, Resp and varia by Israel b. Pethahiah *Isserlein, collected by *Joseph (Joselein) b. Moses.
Leo Hebraeus = *Levi b. Gershom, also called Ralbag or Gersonides.
Levush = Mordecai b. Abraham *Jaffe.
Levush [Malkhut], Codification by Mordecai b. Abraham (Levush) *Jaffe, with subdivisions: *[Levush ha-] Tekhelet* (parallels Tur OḤ 1–241); *[Levush ha-] Ḥur* (parallels Tur OḤ 242–697); *[Levush] Ateret Zahav* (parallels Tur YD); *[Levush ha-Buẓ ve-ha-Argaman* (parallels Tur EH); *[Levush] Ir Shushan* (parallels Tur ḤM); under the name *Levush* the author wrote also other works.
Li-Leshonot ha-Rambam, fifth part (nos. 1374–1700) of Resp. by *David b. Solomon ibn Abi Zimra (Radbaz).
Likkutim, Sefer ha-, another name for *[Sefer] Kol Bo.*

Ma'adanei Yom Tov, Comm. on *Piskei ha-Rosh* by Yom Tov Lipmann b. Nathan ha-Levi *Heller; printed in many editions of the Talmud.
Mabit = Moses b. Joseph *Trani.
Magen Avot, Comm. to *Avot* by Simeon b. Ẓemaḥ *Duran.
Magen Avraham, Comm. to Sh. Ar., OḤ, by Abraham Abele b. Ḥayyim ha-Levi *Gombiner; printed in many editions of Sh. Ar., OḤ.
Maggid Mishneh, Comm. to Maimonides, *Yad Ḥazakah,* by *Vidal Yom Tov of Tolosa; printed in most editions of the *Yad Ḥazakah.*
Maḥaneh Efrayim, Resp. and Nov., arranged acc. to Maimonides' *Yad Ḥazakah* , by Ephraim b. Aaron *Navon.
Maharai = Israel b. Pethahiah *Isserlein.
Maharal of Prague = *Judah Loew (Lob, Liwa), b. Bezalel.
Maharalbaḥ = *Levi b. Ḥabib.
Maharam Alashkar = Moses b. Isaac *Alashkar.
Maharam Alshekh = Moses b. Ḥayyim *Alashekh.
Maharam Mintz = Moses *Mintz.
Maharam of Lublin = *Meir b. Gedaliah of Lublin.
Maharam of Padua = Meir *Katzenellenbogen.
Maharam of Rothenburg = *Meir b. Baruch of Rothenburg.
Maharam Shik = Moses b. Joseph Schick.
Maharash Engel = Samuel b. Ze'ev Wolf Engel.
Maharashdam = Samuel b. Moses *Medina.
Maharḥash = Ḥayyim (ben) Shabbetai.
Mahari Basan = Jehiel b. Ḥayyim Basan.
Mahari b. Lev = Joseph ibn Lev.
Mahari'az = Jekuthiel Asher Zalman Ensil Zusmir.
Maharibal = *Joseph ibn Lev.
Mahariḥ = Jacob (Israel) *Ḥagiz.
Maharik = Joseph b. Solomon *Colon.
Maharikash = Jacob b. Abraham *Castro.
Maharil = Jacob b. Moses *Moellin.
Maharimat = Joseph b. Moses di Trani (not identical with the Maharit).
Maharit = Joseph b. Moses *Trani.
Maharitaẓ = Yom Tov b. Akiva Ẓahalon. (See article *Ẓahalon Family).
Maharsha = Samuel Eliezer b. Judah ha-Levi *Edels.
Maharshag = Simeon b. Judah Gruenfeld.
Maharshak = Samson b. Isaac of Chinon.
Maharshakh = *Solomon b. Abraham.
Maharshal = Solomon b. Jeḥiel *Luria.
Mahasham = Shalom Mordecai b. Moses *Sschwadron.
Maharyu = Jacob b. Judah *Weil.
Maḥazeh Avraham, Resp. by Abraham Nebagen v. Meir ha-Levi Steinberg.
Maḥazik Berakhah, Nov. by Ḥayyim Joseph David *Azulai.

*Maimonides = Moses b. Maimon, or Rambam.
*Malbim = Meir Loeb b. Jehiel Michael.
Malbim = Malbim's comm. to the Bible; printed in the major editions.
Malbushei Yom Tov, Nov. on *Levush,* OḤ, by Yom Tov Lipmann b. Nathan ha-Levi *Heller.
Mappah, another name for *Rema.*
Mareh ha-Panim, Comm. to Jer. Talmud by Moses b. Simeon *Margolies; printed in most editions of Jer. Talmud.
Margaliyyot ha-Yam, Nov. by Reuben *Margoliot.
Masat Binyamin, Resp. by Benjamin Aaron b. Abraham *Slonik
Mashbir, Ha- = *Joseph Samuel b. Isaac Rodi.
Massa Ḥayyim, Tax *halakhot* by Ḥayyim *Palaggi, with the subdivisions *Missim ve-Arnomiyyot* and *Torat ha-Minhagot.*
Massa Melekh, Compilation of Tax Law by Joseph b. Isaac *Ibn Ezra with concluding part *Ne'ilat She'arim.*
Matteh Asher, Resp. by Asher b. Emanuel Shalem.
Matteh Shimon, Digest of Resp. and Nov. to Tur and *Beit Yosef,* ḤM, by Mordecai Simeon b. Solomon.
Matteh Yosef, Resp. by Joseph b. Moses ha-Levi Nazir (see article under his father's name).
Mayim Amukkim, Resp. by Elijah b. Abraham *Mizraḥi.
Mayim Ḥayyim, Resp. by Ḥayyim b. Dov Beresh Rapaport.
Mayim Rabbim, , Resp. by Raphael *Meldola.
Me-Emek ha-Bakha, , Resp. by Simeon b. Jekuthiel Ephrati.
Me'irat Einayim, usual abbreviation: *Sma* (from: *Sefer Me'irat Einayim*); comm. to Sh. Ar. By Joshua b. Alexander ha-Kohen *Falk; printed in most editions of the Sh. Ar.
Melammed le-Ho'il, Resp. by David Ẓevi *Hoffmann.
Meisharim, [*Sefer*], Rabbinical treatise by *Jeroham b. Meshullam.
Meshiv Davar, Resp. by Naphtali Ẓevi Judah *Berlin.
Mi-Gei ha-Haregah, Resp. by Simeon b. Jekuthiel Ephrati.
Mi-Ma'amakim, Resp. by Ephraim Oshry.
Middot Aharon, first part of *Korban Aharon,* a comm. to *Sifra* by Aaron b. Abraham *Ibn Ḥayyim.
Migdal Oz, Comm. to Maimonides, *Yad Ḥazakah,* by *Ibn Gaon Shem Tov b. Abraham; printed in most editions of the *Yad Ḥazakah.*
Mikhtam le-David, Resp. by David Samuel b. Jacob *Pardo.
Mikkaḥ ve-ha-Mimkar, Sefer ha-, Rabbinical treatise by *Hai Gaon.
Milḥamot ha-Shem, Glosses to Rif, *Halakhot,* by *Naḥmanides.
Minḥat Ḥinnukh, Comm. to *Sefer ha-Ḥinnukh,* by Joseph b. Moses *Babad.
Minḥat Yizḥak, Resp. by Isaac Jacob b. Joseph Judah Weiss.
Misgeret ha-Shulḥan, Comm. to Sh. Ar., ḤM, by Benjamin Ze'ev Wolf b. Shabbetai; printed in most editions of Sh. Ar.
Mishkenot ha-Ro'im, Halakhot in alphabetical order by Uzziel Alshekh.
Mishnah Berurah, Comm. to Sh. Ar., OḤ, by *Israel Meir ha-Kohen.
Mishneh le-Melekh, Comm. to Maimonides, *Yad Ḥazakah,* by Judah *Rosanes; printed in most editions of *Yad Ḥazakah.*
Mishpat ha-Kohanim, Nov. to Sh. Ar., ḤM, by Jacob Moses *Lorberbaum, part of his *Netivot ha-Mishpat;* printed in major editions of Sh. Ar.
Mishpat Kohen, Resp. by Abraham Isaac ha-Kohen *Kook.
Mishpat Shalom, Nov. by Shalom Mordecai b. Moses *Schwadron; contains: *Kunteres Tikkun Olam.*
Mishpat u-Ẓedakah be-Ya'akov, Resp. by Jacob b. Reuben *Ibn Ẓur.
Mishpat ha-Urim, Comm. to Sh. Ar., ḤM by Jacob b. Jacob Moses *Lorberbaum, part of his *Netivot ha-Mishpat;* printed in major editons of Sh. Ar.
Mishpat Ẓedek, Resp. by *Melammed Meir b. Shem Tov.
Mishpatim Yesharim, Resp. by Raphael b. Mordecai *Berdugo.
Mishpetei Shemu'el, Resp. by Samuel b. Moses *Kalai (Kal'i).
Mishpetei ha-Tanna'im, Kunteres, Nov on *Levush,* OḤ by Yom Tov Lipmann b. Nathan ha-Levi *Heller.
Mishpetei Uzzi'el (Uziel), Resp. by Ben-Zion Meir Hai *Ouziel.
Missim ve-Arnoniyyot, Tax *halakhot* by Ḥayyim *Palaggi, a subdivision of his work *Massa Ḥayyim* on the same subject.
Mitzvot, Sefer ha-, Elucidation of precepts by *Maimonides; subdivided into *Lavin* (negative precepts) and *Asayin* (positive precepts).
Mitzvot Gadol, Sefer, Elucidation of precepts by *Moses b. Jacob of Coucy, subdivided into *Lavin* (negative precepts) and *Asayin* (positive precepts); the usual abbreviation is *Semag.*
Mitzvot Katan, Sefer, Elucidation of precepts by *Isaac b. Joseph of Corbeil; the usual, abbreviation is *Semak.*
Mo'adim u-Zemannim, Rabbinical treatises by Moses Sternbuch.
Modigliano, Joseph Samuel = *Joseph Samuel b. Isaac, Rodi (Ha-Mashbir).
Mordekhai (Mordecai), halakhic compilation by *Mordecai b. Hillel; printed in most editions of the Talmud after the texts.
Moses b. Maimon = *Maimonides, also called Rambam.
Moses b. Naḥman = Naḥmanides, also called Ramban.
Muram = Isaiah Menahem b. Isaac (from: Morenu R. Mendel).

Naḥal Yizḥak, Comm. on Sh. Ar., ḤM, by Isaac Elhanan *Spector.
Naḥalah li-Yhoshu'a, Resp. by Joshua Ẓunẓin.
Naḥalat Shivah, collection of legal forms by *Samuel b. David Moses ha-Levi.
*Naḥmanides = Moses b. Naḥman, also called Ramban.
Naẓiv = Naphtali Ẓevi Judah *Berlin.
Ne'eman Shemu'el, Resp. by Samuel Isaac *Modigilano.
Ne'ilat She'arim, concluding part of *Massa Melekh* (a work on Tax Law) by Joseph b. Isaac *Ibn Ezra, containing an exposition of customary law and subdivided into *Minhagei Issur* and *Minhagei Mamon.*
Ner Ma'aravi, Resp. by Jacob b. Malka.
Netivot ha-Mishpat, by Jacob b. Jacob Moses *Lorberbaum; subdivided into *Mishpat ha-Kohanim,* Nov. to Sh. Ar., ḤM, and *Mishpat ha-Urim,* a comm. on the same; printed in major editions of Sh. Ar.
Netivot Olam, Saying of the Sages by *Judah Loew (Lob, Liwa) b. Bezalel.
Nimmukei Menaḥem of Merseburg, Tax *halakhot* by the same, printed at the end of Resp. Maharyu.
Nimmukei Yosef, Comm. to Rif. *Halakhot,* by Joseph *Ḥabib (Ḥabiba); printed in many editions of the Talmud.
Noda bi-Yhudah, Resp. by Ezekiel b. Judah ha-Levi *Landau; there is a first collection *(Mahadura Kamma)* and a second collection *(Mahadura Tinyana).*
Nov. = Novellae, Ḥiddushim.

Ohel Moshe (1), Notes to Talmud, *Midrash Rabbah,* Yad, *Sifrei* and to several Resp., by Eleazar *Horowitz.

Ohel Moshe (2), Resp. by Moses Jonah Zweig.
Oholei Tam. Resp. by *Tam ibn Yaḥya Jacob b. David; printed in the rabbinical collection *Tummat Yesharim.*
Oholei Ya'akov, Resp. by Jacob de *Castro.
Or ha-Me'ir Resp by Judah Meir b. Jacob Samson Shapiro.
Or Same'aḥ, Comm. to Maimonides, *Yad Ḥazakah,* by *Meir Simḥah ha-Kohen of Dvinsk; printed in many editions of the *Yad Ḥazakah.*
Or Zaru'a [the father] = *Isaac b. Moses of Vienna.
Or Zaru'a [the son] = *Ḥayyim (Eliezer) b. Isaac.
Or Zaru'a, Nov. by *Isaac b. Moses of Vienna.
Orah, Sefer ha-, Compilation of ritual precepts by *Rashi.
Oraḥ la-Ẓaddik, Resp. by Abraham Ḥayyim Rodrigues.
Oẓar ha-Posekim, Digest of Responsa.

Paḥad Yiẓḥak, Rabbinical encyclopaedia by Isaac *Lampronti.
Panim Me'irot, Resp. by Meir b. Isaac *Eisenstadt.
Parashat Mordekhai, Resp. by Mordecai b. Abraham Naphtali *Banet.
Pe'at ha-Sadeh la-Dinim and Pe'at ha-Sadeh la-Kelalim, subdivisions of the *Sedei Ḥemed,* an encyclopaedia of precepts and responsa, by Ḥayyim Hezekaih *Medini.
Penei Moshe (1), Resp. by Moses *Benveniste.
Penei Moshe (2), Comm. to Jer. Talmud by Moses b. Simeon *Margolies; printed in most editions of the Jer. Talmud.
Penei Moshe (3), Comm. on the aggadic passages of 18 treatises of the Bab. and Jer. Talmud, by Moses b. Isaiah Katz.
Penei Yehoshu'a, Nov. by Jacob Joshua b. Ẓevi Hirsch *Falk.
Peri Ḥadash, Comm. on Sh. Ar. By Hezekiah da *Silva.
Perishah, Comm. on Tur by Joshua b. Alexander ha-Kohen *Falk; printed in major edition of Tur; forms together with *Derishah* and *Be'urim* (by the same author) the *Beit Yisrael.*
Pesakim u-Khetavim, 2nd part of the *Terumat ha-Deshen* by Israel b. Pethahiah *Isserlein' also called *Piskei Maharai.*
Pilpula Ḥarifta, Comm. to *Piskei ha-Rosh, Seder Nezikin,* by Yom Tov Lipmann b. Nathan ha-Levi *Heller; printed in major editions of the Talmud.
Piskei Maharai, see *Terumat ha-Deshen,* 2nd part; also called *Pesakim u-Khetavim.*
Piskei ha-Rosh, a compilation of *halakhot,* arranged on the Talmud, by *Asher b. Jehiel (Rosh); printed in major Talmud editions.
Pitḥei Teshuvah, Comm. to Sh. Ar. by Abraham Hirsch b. Jacob *Eisenstadt; printed in major editions of the Sh. Ar.

Rabad = *Abraham b. David of Posquières (Rabad III.).
Raban = *Eliezer b. Nathan of Mainz.
Raban, also called *Ẓafenat Pa'ne'aḥ* or *Even ha-Ezer,* see under the last name.
Rabi Abad = *Abraham b. Isaac of Narbonne.
Radad = David Dov. b. Aryeh Judah Jacob *Meisels.
Radam = Dov Berush b. Isaac Meisels.
Radbaz = *David b Solomon ibn Abi Ziumra.
Radbaz, Comm. to Maimonides, *Yad Ḥazakah,* by *David b. Solomon ibn Abi Zimra.
Ralbag = *Levi b. Gershom, also called Gersonides, or Leo Hebraeus.
Ralbag, Bible comm. by *Levi b. Gershon.
Rama [da Fano] = Menaḥem Azariah *Fano.
Ramah = Meir b. Todros [ha-Levi] *Abulafia.
Ramam = *Menaham of Merseburg.
Rambam = *Maimonides; real name: Moses b. Maimon.
Ramban = *Naḥmanides; real name Moses b. Naḥman.
Ramban, Comm. to Torah by *Naḥmanides; printed in major editions. ("Mikra'ot Gedolot").
Ran = *Nissim b. Reuben Gerondi.
Ran of Rif, Comm. on Rif, *Halakhot,* by Nissim b. Reuben Gerondi.
Ranaḥ = *Elijah b. Ḥayyim.
Rash = *Samson b. Abraham of Sens.
Rash, Comm. to Mishnah, by *Samson b. Abraham of Sens; printed in major Talmud editions.
Rashash = Samuel *Strashun.
Rashba = Solomon b. Abraham *Adret.
Rashba, Resp., see also; *Sefer Teshuvot ha-Rashba ha-Meyuḥasot le-ha-Ramban,* by Solomon b. Abraham *Adret.
Rashbad = Samuel b. David.
Rashbam = *Samuel b. Meir.
Rashbam = Comm. on Bible and Talmud by *Samuel b. Meir; printed in major editions of Bible and most editions of Talmud.
Rashbash = Solomon b. Simeon *Duran.
*Rashi = Solomon b. Isaac of Troyes.
Rashi, Comm. on Bible and Talmud by *Rashi; printed in almost all Bible and Talmud editions.
Raviah = Eliezer b. Joel ha-Levi.
Redak = David *Kimḥi.
Redak, Comm. to Bible by David *Kimḥi.
Redakh = *David b. Ḥayyim ha-Kohen of Corfu.
Re'em = Elijah b. Abraham *Mizraḥi.
Rema = Moses b. Israel *Isserles.
Rema, Glosses to Sh. Ar. by Moses b. Israel *Isserles; printed in almost all editions of the Sh. Ar. inside the text in Rashi type; also called *Mappah* or *Haggahot.*
Remek = Moses Kimḥi.
Remakh = Moses ha-Kohen mi-Lunel.
Reshakh = *Solomon b. Abraham; also called Maharshakh.
Resp. = Responsa, *She'elot u-Teshuvot.*
Ri Berav = *Berab.
Ri Escapa = Joseph b. Saul *Escapa.
Ri Migash = Joseph b. Meir ha-Levi *Ibn Migash.
Riba = Isaac b. Asher ha-Levi; Riba II (Riba ha-Baḥur) = his grandson with the same name.
Ribam = Isaac b. Mordecai (or: Isaac b. Meir).
Ribash = *Isaac b. Sheshet Perfet (or: Barfat).
Rid= *Isaiah b. Mali di Trani the Elder.
Ridbaz = Jacob David b. Ze'ev *Willowski.
Rif = Isaac b. Jacob ha-Kohen *Alfasi.
Rif, *Halakhot,* Compilation and abstract of the Talmud by Isaac b. Jacob ha-Kohen *Alfasi.
Ritba = Yom Tov b. Abraham *Ishbili.
Riẓbam = Isaac b. Mordecai.
Rosh = *Asher b. Jehiel, also called Asheri.
Rosh Mashbir, Resp. by *Joseph Samuel b. Isaac, Rodi.

Sedei Ḥemed, Encyclopaedia of precepts and responsa by Ḥayyim Ḥezekiah *Medini; subdivisions: *Asefat Dinim, Kunteres ha-Kelalim, Pe'at ha-Sadeh la-Dinim, Pe'at ha-Sadeh la-Kelalim.*
Semag, Usual abbreviation of *Sefer Mitzvot Gadol,* elucidation of precepts by *Moses b. Jacob of Coucy; subdivided into *Lavin* (negative precepts) *Asayin* (positive precepts).
Semak, Usual abbreviation of *Sefer Mitzvot Katan,* elucidation of precepts by *Isaac b. Joseph of Corbeil.

Sh. Ar. = *Shulḥan Arukh,* code by Joseph b. Ephraim *Caro.

Sha'ar Mishpat, Comm. to Sh. Ar., ḤM. By Israel Isser b. Ze'ev Wolf.

Sha'arei Shevu'ot, Treatise on the law of oaths by *David b. Saadiah; usually printed together with Rif, *Halakhot;* also called: *She'arim of R. Alfasi.*

Sha'arei Teshuvah, Collection of resp. from Geonic period, by different authors.

Sha'arei Uzzi'el, Rabbinical treatise by Ben-Zion Meir Ha *Ouziel.

Sha'arei Ẓedek, Collection of resp. from Geonic period, by different authors.

Shadal [or Shedal] = Samuel David *Luzzatto.

Shai la-Moreh, Resp. by Shabbetai Jonah.

Shakh, Usual abbreviation of *Siftei Kohen,* a comm. to Sh. Ar., YD and ḤM by *Shabbetai b. Meir ha-Kohen; printed in most editions of Sh. Ar.

Sha'ot-de-Rabbanan, Resp. by *Solomon b. Judah ha-Kohen.

She'arim of R. Alfasi see *Sha'arei Shevu'ot.*

Shedal, see Shadal.

She'elot u-Teshuvot ha-Ge'onim, Collection of resp. by different authors.

She'erit Yisrael, Resp. by Israel Ze'ev Mintzberg.

She'erit Yosef, Resp. by *Joseph b. Mordecai Gershon ha-Kohen.

She'ilat Yaveẓ, Resp. by Jacob *Emden (Yaveẓ).

She'iltot, Compilation arranged acc. to the Torah by *Aḥa (Aḥai) of Shabḥa.

Shem Aryeh, Resp. by Aryeh Leib *Lipschutz.

Shemesh Ẓedakah, Resp. by Samson *Morpurgo.

Shenei ha-Me'orot ha-Gedolim, Resp. by Elijah *Covo.

Shetarot, Sefer ha-, Collection of legal forms by *Judah b. Barzillai al-Bargeloni.

Shevut Ya'akov, Resp. by Jacob b. Joseph Reicher.

Shibbolei ha-Leket Compilation on ritual by Zedekiah b. Avraham *Anav.

Shiltei Gibborim, Comm. to Rif, *Halakhot,* by *Joshua Boaz b. Simeon; printed in major editions of the Talmud.

Shittah Mekubbeẓet, Compilation of talmudical commentaries by Bezalel *Ashkenazi.

Shivat Ẓiyyon, Resp. by Samuel b. Ezekiel *Landau.

Shiyyurei Korban, by David *Fraenkel; additions to his comm. to Jer. Talmud *Korban Edah;* both printed in most editions of Jer. Talmud.

Sho'el u-Meshiv, Resp. by Joseph Saul ha-Levi *Nathanson.

Sh[ulḥan] Ar[ukh] [of Ba'al ha-Tanyal], Code by *Shneur Zalman of Lyady; not identical with the code by Joseph Caro.

Siftei Kohen, Comm. to Sh. Ar., YD and ḤM by *Shabbetai b. Meir ha-Kohen; printed in most editions of Sh. Ar.; usual abbreviation: *Shakh.*

Simḥat Yom Tov, Resp. by Tom Tov b. Jacob *Algazi.

Simlah Ḥadashah, Treatise on *Sheḥitah* by Alexander Sender b. Ephraim Zalman *Schor; see also *Tevu'ot Shor.*

Simeon b. Ẓemaḥ = Simeon b. Ẓemaḥ *Duran.

Sma, Comm. to Sh. Ar. by Joshua b. Alexander ha-Kohen *Falk; the full title is: *Sefer Me'irat Einayim;* printed in most editions of Sh. Ar.

Solomon b. Isaac ha-Levi = Solomon b. Isaac *Levy.

Solomon b. Isaac of Troyes = *Rashi.

Tal Orot, Rabbinical work with various contents, by Joseph ibn Gioia.

Tam, Rabbenu = *Tam Jacob b. Meir.

Tashbaẓ = Samson b. Zadok.

Tashbeẓ = Simeon b. Zemaḥ *Duran, sometimes also abbreviation for Samson b. Zadok, usually known as Tashbaẓ.

Tashbeẓ [Sefer ha-], Resp. by Simeon b. Ẓemaḥ *Duran; the fourth part of this work is called: *Ḥut ha-Meshullash.*

Taz, Usual abbreviation of *Turei Zahav,* comm., to Sh. Ar. by *David b. Samnuel ha-Levi; printed in most editions of Sh. Ar.

(Ha)-Tekhelet, subdivision of the *Levush* (a codification by Mordecai b. Abraham (Levush) *Jaffe); *Ha-Tekhelet* parallels Tur, OḤ 1-241.

Terumat ha-Deshen, by Israel b. Pethahiah *Isserlein; subdivided into a part containing responsa, and a second part called *Pesakim u-Khetavim* or *Piskei Maharai.*

Terumot, Sefer ha-, Compilation of *halakhot* by Samuel b. Isaac *Sardi.

Teshuvot Ba'alei ha-Tosafot, Collection of responsa by the Tosafists.

Teshjvot Ge'onei Mizraḥ u-Ma'aav, Collection of responsa.

Teshuvot ha-Geonim, Collection of responsa from Geonic period.

Teshuvot Ḥakhmei Provinẓyah, Collection of responsa by different Provencal authors.

Teshuvot Ḥakhmei Ẓarefat ve-Loter, Collection of responsa by different French authors.

Teshuvot Maimuniyyot, Resp. pertaining to Maimonides' *Yad Ḥazakah;* printed in major editions of this work after the text; authorship uncertain.

Tevu'ot Shor, by Alexander Sender b. Ephraim Zalman *Schor, a comm. to his *Simlah Ḥadashah,* a work on *Sheḥitah.*

Tiferet Ẓevi, Resp. by Ẓevi Hirsch of the "AHW" Communities (Altona, Hamburg, Wandsbeck).

Tiktin, Judah b. Simeon = Judah b. Simeon *Ashkenazi.

Toledot Adam ve-Ḥavvah, Codification by *Jeroham b. Meshullam.

Torat Emet, Resp. by Aaron b. Joseph *Sasson.

Torat Ḥayyim, , Resp. by Ḥayyim (ben) Shabbetai.

Torat ha-Minhagot, subdivision of the *Massa Ḥayyim* (a work on tax law) by Ḥayyim *Palaggi, containing an exposition of customary law.

Tosafot Rid, Explanations to the Talmud and decisions by *Isaiah b. Mali di Trani the Elder.

Tosefot Yom Tov, comm. to Mishnah by Yom Tov Lipmann b. Nathan ha-Levi *Heller; printed in most editions of the Mishnah.

Tummim, subdivision of the comm. to Sh. Ar., ḤM, *Urim ve-Tummim* by Jonathan *Eybeschuetz; printed in the major editions of Sh. Ar.

Tur, usual abbreviation for the *Arba'ah Turim* of *Jacob b. Asher.

Turei Zahav, Comm. to Sh. Ar. by *David b. Samuel ha-Levi; printed in most editions of Sh. Ar.; usual abbreviation: *Taz.*

Urim, subdivision of the following.

Urim ve-Tummim, Comm. to Sh. Ar., ḤM, by Jonathan *Eybeschuetz; printed in the major editions of Sh. Ar.; subdivided in places into *Urim* and *Tummim.*

Vikku'aḥ Mayim Ḥayyim, Polemics against Isserles and Caro by Ḥayyim b. Bezalel.

Yad Malakhi, Methodological treatise by *Malachi b. Jacob ha-Kohen.

Yad Ramah, Nov. by Meir b. Todros [ha-Levi] *Abulafia.
Yakhin u-Vo'az, Resp. by Ẓemaḥ b. Solomon *Duran.
Yam ha-Gadol, Resp. by Jacob Moses *Toledano.
Yam shel Shelomo, Compilation arranged acc. to Talmud by Solomon b. Jehiel (Maharshal) *Luria.
Yashar, Sefer ha-, by *Tam, Jacob b. Meir (Rabbenu Tam); 1st pt.: Resp.; 2nd pt.: Nov.
Yaskil Avdi, Resp. by Obadiah Hadaya (printed together with his Resp. *De'ah ve-Haskel).*
Yaveẓ = Jacob *Emden.
Yehudah Ya'aleh, Resp. by Judah b. Israel *Aszod.
Yekar Tiferet, Comm. to Maimonides' *Yad Ḥazakah,*by David b. Solomon ibn Zimra, printed in most editions of *Yad Ḥazakah.*
Yere'im [*ha-Shalem*], [*Sefer*], Treatise on precepts by *Eliezer b. Samuel of Metz.
Yeshu'ot Ya'akov, Resp. by Jacob Meshullam b. Mordecai Ze'ev *Ornstein.
Yiẓhak Rei'aḥ, Resp. by Isaac b. Samuel Abendanan (see article *Abendanam Family).
Ẓafenat Pa'ne'aḥ (1), also called *Raban* or *Even ha-Ezer,* see under the last name.
Ẓafenat Pa'ne'aḥ (2), Resp. by Joseph *Rozin.
Zayit Ra'anan, Resp. by Moses Judah Leib b. Benjamin Auerbach.
Ẓeidah la-Derekh, Codification by *Menahem b. Aaron ibn Zerah.
Ẓedakah u-Mishpat, Resp. by Ẓedakah b. Saadiah Huẓin.
Zekan Aharon, Resp. by Elijah b. Benjamin ha-Levi.
Zekher Ẓaddik, Sermons by Eliezer *Katzenellenbogen.
Ẓemaḥ Ẓedek (1) Resp. by Menaham Mendel Shneersohn (see under *Shneersohn Family).
Zera Avraham, Resp. by Abraham b. David *Yiẓhaki.
Zera Emet Resp. by *Ishmael b. Abaham Isaac ha-Kohen.
Ẓevi la-Ẓaddik, Resp. by Ẓevi Elimelech b. David Shapira.
Zikhron Yehudah, Resp. by *Judah b. Asher
Zikhron Yosef, Resp. by Joseph b. Menahem *Steinhardt.
Zikhronot, Sefer ha-, Sermons on several precepts by Samuel *Aboab.
Zikkaron la-Rishonim . . ., by Albert (Abraham Elijah) *Harkavy; contains in vol. 1 pt. 4 (1887) a collection of Geonic responsa.
Ẓiẓ Eliezer, Resp. by Eliezer Judah b. Jacob Gedaliah Waldenberg.

BIBLIOGRAPHICAL ABBREVIATIONS

Bibliographies in English and other languages have been extensively updated, with English translations cited where available. In order to help the reader, the language of books or articles is given where not obvious from titles of books or names of periodicals. Titles of books and periodicals in languages with alphabets other than Latin, are given in transliteration, even where there is a title page in English. Titles of articles in periodicals are not given. Names of Hebrew and Yiddish periodicals well known in English-speaking countries or in Israel under their masthead in Latin characters are given in this form, even when contrary to transliteration rules. Names of authors writing in languages with non-Latin alphabets are given in their Latin alphabet form wherever known; otherwise the names are transliterated. Initials are generally not given for authors of articles in periodicals, except to avoid confusion. Non-abbreviated book titles and names of periodicals are printed in *italics*. Abbreviations are given in the list below.

AASOR	*Annual of the American School of Oriental Research* (1919ff.).
AB	*Analecta Biblica* (1952ff.).
Abel, Géog	F.-M. Abel, *Géographie de la Palestine,* 2 vols. (1933-38).
ABR	*Australian Biblical Review* (1951ff.).
Abr.	Philo, *De Abrahamo.*
Abrahams, Companion	I. Abrahams, *Companion to the Authorised Daily Prayer Book* (rev. ed. 1922).
Abramson, Merkazim	S. Abramson, *Ba-Merkazim u-va-Tefuẓot bi-Tekufat ha-Ge'onim* (1965).
Acts	Acts of the Apostles (New Testament).
ACUM	*Who is who in ACUM* [*Aguddat Kompozitorim u-Meḥabbrim*].
ADAJ	*Annual of the Department of Antiquities, Jordan* (1951ff.).
Adam	Adam and Eve (Pseudepigrapha).
ADB	*Allgemeine Deutsche Biographie,* 56 vols. (1875–1912).
Add. Esth.	The Addition to Esther (Apocrypha).
Adler, Prat Mus	1. Adler, *La pratique musicale savante dans quelques communautés juives en Europe au XVIIe et XVIIIe siècles,* 2 vols. (1966).
Adler-Davis	H.M. Adler and A. Davis (ed. and tr.), *Service of the Synagogue, a New Edition of the Festival Prayers with an English Translation in Prose and Verse,* 6 vols. (1905–06).
Aet.	Philo, *De Aeternitate Mundi.*
AFO	*Archiv fuer Orientforschung* (first two volumes under the name *Archiv fuer Keilschriftforschung)* (1923ff.).
Ag. Ber	*Aggadat Bereshit* (ed. Buber, 1902*).*
Agr.	Philo, *De Agricultura.*
Ag. Sam.	*Aggadat Samuel.*
Ag. Song	*Aggadat Shir ha-Shirim* (Schechter ed., 1896).
Aharoni, Ereẓ	Y. Aharoni, *Ereẓ Yisrael bi-Tekufat ha-Mikra: Geografyah Historit* (1962).
Aharoni, Land	Y. Aharoni, *Land of the Bible* (1966).

Ahikar	Ahikar (Pseudepigrapha).
AI	*Archives Israélites de France* (1840–1936).
AJA	*American Jewish Archives* (1948ff.).
AJHSP	*American Jewish Historical Society – Publications* (after vol. 50 = AJHSQ).
AJHSQ	*American Jewish Historical (Society) Quarterly* (before vol. 50 =AJHSP).
AJSLL	*American Journal of Semitic Languages and Literature* (1884–95 under the title *Hebraica*, since 1942 JNES).
AJYB	*American Jewish Year Book* (1899ff.).
AKM	Abhandlungen fuer die Kunde des Morgenlandes (series).
Albright, Arch	W.F. Albright, *Archaeology of Palestine* (rev. ed. 1960).
Albright, Arch Bib	W.F. Albright, *Archaeology of Palestine and the Bible* (1935[3]).
Albright, Arch Rel	W.F. Albright, *Archaeology and the Religion of Israel* (1953[3]).
Albright, Stone	W.F. Albright, *From the Stone Age to Christianity* (1957[2]).
Alon, Meḥkarim	G. Alon, *Meḥkarim be-Toledot Yisrael bi-Ymei Bayit Sheni u-vi-Tekufat ha-Mishnah ve-ha Talmud,* 2 vols. (1957–58).
Alon, Toledot	G. Alon, *Toledot ha-Yehudim be-Ereẓ Yisrael bi-Tekufat ha-Mishnah ve-ha-Talmud,* I (1958[3]), (1961[2]).
ALOR	Alter Orient (series).
Alt, Kl Schr	A. Alt, *Kleine Schriften zur Geschichte des Volkes Israel,* 3 vols. (1953–59).
Alt, Landnahme	A. Alt, *Landnahme der Israeliten in Palaestina* (1925); also in Alt, Kl Schr, 1 (1953), 89–125.
Ant.	Josephus, *Jewish Antiquities* (Loeb Classics ed.).
AO	*Acta Orientalia* (1922ff.).
AOR	*Analecta Orientalia* (1931ff.).
AOS	American Oriental Series.
Apion	Josephus, *Against Apion* (Loeb Classics ed.).
Aq.	Aquila's Greek translation of the Bible.
Ar.	*Arakhin* (talmudic tractate).
Artist.	Letter of Aristeas (Pseudepigrapha).
ARN[1]	*Avot de-Rabbi Nathan,* version (1) ed. Schechter, 1887.
ARN[2]	*Avot de-Rabbi Nathan,* version (2) ed. Schechter, 1945[2].
Aronius, Regesten	I. Aronius, *Regesten zur Geschichte der Juden im fraenkischen und deutschen Reiche bis zum Jahre 1273* (1902).
ARW	*Archiv fuer Religionswissenschaft* (1898–1941/42).
AS	*Assyrological Studies* (1931ff.).
Ashtor, Korot	E. Ashtor (Strauss), *Korot ha-Yehudim bi-Sefarad ha-Muslemit,* 1(1966[2]), 2(1966).
Ashtor, Toledot	E. Ashtor (Strauss), *Toledot ha-Yehudim be-Miẓrayim ve-Suryah Taḥat Shilton ha-Mamlukim,* 3 vols. (1944–70).
Assaf, Ge'onim	S. Assaf, *Tekufat ha-Ge'onim ve-Sifrutah* (1955).
Assaf, Mekorot	S. Assaf, *Mekorot le-Toledot ha-Ḥinnukh be-Yisrael,* 4 vols. (1925–43).
Ass. Mos.	Assumption of Moses (Pseudepigrapha).
ATA	Alttestamentliche Abhandlungen (series).
ATANT	Abhandlungen zur Theologie des Alten und Neuen Testaments (series).
AUJW	*Allgemeine unabhaengige juedische Wochenzeitung* (till 1966 = AWJD).
AV	Authorized Version of the Bible.
Avad.	*Avadim* (post-talmudic tractate).
Avi-Yonah, Geog	M. Avi-Yonah, *Geografyah Historit shel Ereẓ Yisrael* (1962[3]).
Avi-Yonah, Land	M. Avi-Yonah, *The Holy Land from the Persian to the Arab conquest (536 B.C. to A.D. 640)* (1960).
Avot	*Avot* (talmudic tractate).
Av. Zar.	*Avodah Zarah* (talmudic tractate).
AWJD	*Allgemeine Wochenzeitung der Juden in Deutschland* (since 1967 = AUJW).
AZDJ	*Allgemeine Zeitung des Judentums.*
Azulai	Ḥ.Y.D. Azulai, *Shem ha-Gedolim,* ed. by I.E. Benjacob, 2 pts. (1852) (and other editions).
BA	*Biblical Archaeologist* (1938ff.).
Bacher, Bab Amor	W. Bacher, *Agada der babylonischen Amoraeer* (1913[2]).
Bacher, Pal Amor	W. Bacher, *Agada der palaestinensischen Amoraeer* (Heb. ed. *Aggadat Amora'ei Ereẓ Yisrael),* 2 vols. (1892–99).
Bacher, Tann	W. Bacher, *Agada der Tannaiten* (Heb. ed. *Aggadot ha-Tanna'im,* vol. 1, pt. 1 and 2 (1903); vol. 2 (1890).
Bacher, Trad	W. Bacher, *Tradition und Tradenten in den Schulen Palaestinas und Babyloniens* (1914).
Baer, Spain	Yitzhak (Fritz) Baer, *History of the Jews in Christian Spain,* 2 vols. (1961–66).
Baer, Studien	Yitzhak (Fritz) Baer, *Studien zur Geschichte der Juden im Koenigreich Aragonien waehrend des 13. und 14. Jahrhunderts* (1913).
Baer, Toledot	Yitzhak (Fritz) Baer, *Toledot ha-Yehudim bi-Sefarad ha-Noẓerit mi-Teḥillatan shel ha-Kehillot ad ha-Gerush,* 2 vols. (1959[2]).
Baer, Urkunden	Yitzhak (Fritz) Baer, *Die Juden im christlichen Spanien,* 2 vols. (1929–36).
Baer S., Seder	S.I. Baer, *Seder Avodat Yisrael* (1868 and reprints).
BAIU	*Bulletin de l'Alliance Israélite Universelle* (1861–1913).
Baker, Biog Dict	*Baker's Biographical Dictionary of Musicians,* revised by N. Slonimsky (1958[5]; with Supplement 1965).
I Bar.	I Baruch (Apocrypha).
II Bar.	II Baruch (Pseudepigrapha).
III Bar.	III Baruch (Pseudepigrapha).
BAR	*Biblical Archaeology Review.*
Baron, Community	S.W. Baron, *The Jewish Community, its History and Structure to the American Revolution,* 3 vols. (1942).

Baron, Social — S.W. Baron, *Social and Religious History of the Jews*, 3 vols. (1937); enlarged, 1-2(1952^{2}), 3-14 (1957–69).

Barthélemy-Milik — D. Barthélemy and J.T. Milik, *Dead Sea Scrolls: Discoveries in the Judean Desert*, vol. 1 *Qumram Cave* I (1955).

BASOR — *Bulletin of the American School of Oriental Research*.

Bauer-Leander — H. Bauer and P. Leander, *Grammatik des Biblisch-Aramaeischen* (1927; repr. 1962).

BB — (1) *Bava Batra* (talmudic tractate). (2) *Biblische Beitraege* (1943ff.).

BBB — Bonner biblische Beitraege (series).

BBLA — *Beitraege zur biblischen Landes- und Altertumskunde* (until 1949–ZDPV).

BBSAJ — *Bulletin*, British School of Archaeology, Jerusalem (1922–25; after 1927 included in PEFQS).

BDASI — *Alon* (since 1948) or *Hadashot Arkhe'ologiyyot* (since 1961), bulletin of the Department of Antiquities of the State of Israel.

Begrich, Chronologie — J. Begrich, *Chronologie der Koenige von Israel und Juda* (1929).

Bek. — *Bekhorot* (talmudic tractate).

Bel — Bel and the Dragon (Apocrypha).

Benjacob, Oẓar — I.E. Benjacob, *Oẓar ha-Sefarim* (1880; repr. 1956).

Ben Sira — see Ecclus.

Ben-Yehuda, Millon — E. Ben-Yedhuda, *Millon ha-Lashon ha-Ivrit*, 16 vols (1908–59; repr. in 8 vols., 1959).

Benzinger, Archaeologie — I. Benzinger, *Hebraeische Archaeologie* (1927^{3}).

Ben Zvi, Eretz Israel — I. Ben-Zvi, *Eretz Israel under Ottoman Rule* (1960; offprint from L. Finkelstein (ed.), *The Jews, their History, Culture and Religion* (vol. 1).

Ben Zvi, Ereẓ Israel — I. Ben-Zvi, *Ereẓ Israel bi-Ymei ha-Shilton ha-Ottomani (1955).*

Ber. — *Berakhot* (talmudic tractate).

Beẓah — *Beẓah* (talmudic tractate).

BIES — Bulletin of the Israel Exploration Society, see below BJPES.

Bik. — *Bikkurim* (talmudic tractate).

BJCE — Bibliography of Jewish Communities in Europe, catalog at General Archives for the History of the Jewish People, Jerusalem.

BJPES — Bulletin of the Jewish Palestine Exploration Society – English name of the Hebrew periodical known as:
1. *Yedi'ot ha-Ḥevrah ha-Ivrit la-Ḥakirat Ereẓ Yisrael va-Attikoteha* (1933–1954);
2. *Yedi'ot ha-Ḥevrah la-Ḥakirat Ereẓ Yisrael va-Attikoteha* (1954–1962);
3. *Yedi'ot ba-Ḥakirat Ereẓ Yisrael va-Attikoteha* (1962ff.).

BJRL — *Bulletin of the John Rylands Library* (1914ff.).

BK — *Bava Kamma* (talmudic tractate).

BLBI — *Bulletin of the Leo Baeck Institute* (1957ff.).

BM — (1) *Bava Meẓia* (talmudic tractate). (2) *Beit Mikra* (1955/56ff.). (3) British Museum.

BO — *Bibbia e Oriente* (1959ff.).

Bondy-Dworský — G. Bondy and F. Dworský, *Regesten zur Geschichte der Juden in Boehmen, Maehren und Schlesien von 906 bis 1620*, 2 vols. (1906).

BOR — *Bibliotheca Orientalis* (1943ff.).

Borée, Ortsnamen — W. Borée *Die alten Ortsnamen Palaestinas* (1930).

Bousset, Religion — W. Bousset, *Die Religion des Judentums im neutestamentlichen Zeitalter* (1906^{2}).

Bousset-Gressmann — W. Bousset, *Die Religion des Judentums im spaethellenistischen Zeitalter* (1966^{3}).

BR — *Biblical Review* (1916–25).

BRCI — *Bulletin of the Research Council of Israel* (1951/52–1954/55; then divided).

BRE — *Biblical Research* (1956ff.).

BRF — *Bulletin of the Rabinowitz Fund for the Exploration of Ancient Synagogues* (1949ff.).

Briggs, Psalms — Ch. A. and E.G. Briggs, *Critical and Exegetical Commentary on the Book of Psalms*, 2 vols. (ICC, 1906–07).

Bright, Hist — J. Bright, *A History of Israel* (1959).

Brockelmann, Arab Lit — K. Brockelmann, *Geschichte der arabischen Literatur*, 2 vols. 1898–1902), supplement, 3 vols. (1937–42).

Bruell, Jahrbuecher — *Jahrbuecher fuer juedische Geschichte und Litteratur*, ed. by N. Bruell, Frankfurt (1874–90).

Brugmans-Frank — H. Brugmans and A. Frank (eds.), *Geschiedenis der Joden in Nederland* (1940).

BTS — *Bible et Terre Sainte* (1958ff.).

Bull, Index — S. Bull, *Index to Biographies of Contemporary Composers* (1964).

BW — *Biblical World* (1882–1920).

BWANT — *Beitraege zur Wissenschaft vom Alten und Neuen Testament* (1926ff.).

BZ — *Biblische Zeitschrift* (1903ff.).

BZAW — *Beihefte zur Zeitschrift fuer die alttestamentliche Wissenschaft*, supplement to ZAW (1896ff.).

BŻIH — *Biuletyn Zydowskiego Instytutu Historycznego* (1950ff.).

CAB — *Cahiers d'archéologie biblique* (1953ff.).

CAD — *The* [*Chicago*] *Assyrian Dictionary* (1956ff.).

CAH — *Cambridge Ancient History*, 12 vols. (1923–39)

CAH^{2} — *Cambridge Ancient History*, second edition, 14 vols. (1962–2005).

Calwer, Lexikon — *Calwer, Bibellexikon.*

Cant. — Canticles, usually given as Song (= Song of Songs).

Cantera-Millás, Inscripciones	F. Cantera and J.M. Millás, *Las Inscripciones Hebraicas de España* (1956).
CBQ	*Catholic Biblical Quarterly* (1939ff.).
CCARY	Central Conference of American Rabbis, *Yearbook* (1890/91ff.).
CD	*Damascus Document* from the Cairo *Genizah* (published by S. Schechter, *Fragments of a Zadokite Work*, 1910).
Charles, Apocrypha	R.H. Charles, *Apocrypha and Pseudepigrapha . . .*, 2 vols. (1913; repr. 1963–66).
Cher.	Philo, *De Cherubim.*
I (or II) Chron.	Chronicles, book I and II (Bible).
CIG	*Corpus Inscriptionum Graecarum.*
CIJ	*Corpus Inscriptionum Judaicarum,* 2 vols. (1936–52).
CIL	*Corpus Inscriptionum Latinarum.*
CIS	*Corpus Inscriptionum Semiticarum* (1881ff.).
C.J.	Codex Justinianus.
Clermont-Ganneau, Arch	Ch. Clermont-Ganneau, *Archaeological Researches in Palestine*, 2 vols. (1896–99).
CNFI	*Christian News from Israel* (1949ff.).
Cod. Just.	Codex Justinianus.
Cod. Theod.	Codex Theodosinanus.
Col.	Epistle to the Colosssians (New Testament).
Conder, Survey	Palestine Exploration Fund, *Survey of Eastern Palestine*, vol. 1, pt. I (1889) = C.R. Conder, *Memoirs of the . . . Survey.*
Conder-Kitchener	Palestine Exploration Fund, *Survey of Western Palestine*, vol. 1, pts. 1-3 (1881–83) = C.R. Conder and H.H. Kitchener, *Memoirs.*
Conf.	Philo, *De Confusione Linguarum.*
Conforte, Kore	D. Conforte, *Kore ha-Dorot* (1842²).
Cong.	Philo, *De Congressu Quaerendae Eruditionis Gratia.*
Cont.	Philo, *De Vita Contemplativa.*
I (or II) Cor.	Epistles to the Corinthians (New Testament).
Cowley, Aramic	A. Cowley, *Aramaic Papyri of the Fifth Century B.C.* (1923).
Colwey, Cat	A.E. Cowley, *A Concise Catalogue of the Hebrew Printed Books in the Bodleian Library* (1929).
CRB	*Cahiers de la Revue Biblique* (1964ff.).
Crowfoot-Kenyon	J.W. Crowfoot, K.M. Kenyon and E.L. Sukenik, *Buildings of Samaria* (1942).
C.T.	Codex Theodosianus.
DAB	*Dictionary of American Biography* (1928–58).
Daiches, Jews	S. Daiches, *Jews in Babylonia* (1910).
Dalman, Arbeit	G. Dalman, *Arbeit und Sitte in Palaestina,* 7 vols.in 8 (1928–42 repr. 1964).
Dan	Daniel (Bible).
Davidson, Oẓar	I. Davidson, *Oẓar ha-Shirah ve-ha-Piyyut,* 4 vols. (1924–33); Supplement in: HUCA, 12–13 (1937/38), 715–823.
DB	J. Hastings, *Dictionary of the Bible,* 4 vols. (1963²).
DBI	F.G. Vigoureaux et al. (eds.), *Dictionnaire de la Bible,* 5 vols. in 10 (1912); Supplement, 8 vols. (1928–66)
Decal.	Philo, *De Decalogo.*
Dem.	*Demai* (talmudic tractate).
DER	*Derekh Ereẓ Rabbah* (post-talmudic tractate).
Derenbourg, Hist	J. Derenbourg *Essai sur l'histoire et la géographie de la Palestine* (1867).
Det.	Philo, *Quod deterius potiori insidiari solet.*
Deus	Philo, *Quod Deus immutabilis sit.*
Deut.	Deuteronomy (Bible).
Deut. R.	*Deuteronomy Rabbah.*
DEZ	*Derekh Ereẓ Zuta* (post-talmudic tractate).
DHGE	*Dictionnaire d'histoire et de géographie ecclésiastiques,* ed. by A. Baudrillart et al., 17 vols (1912–68).
Dik. Sof	*Dikdukei Soferim,* variae lections of the talmudic text by Raphael Nathan Rabbinovitz (16 vols., 1867–97).
Dinur, Golah	B. Dinur (Dinaburg), *Yisrael ba-Golah,* 2 vols. in 7 (1959–68) = vols. 5 and 6 of his *Toledot Yisrael,* second series.
Dinur, Haganah	B. Dinur (ed.), *Sefer Toledot ha-Haganah* (1954ff.).
Diringer, Iscr	D. Diringer, *Iscrizioni antico-ebraiche palestinesi* (1934).
Discoveries	*Discoveries in the Judean Desert* (1955ff.).
DNB	*Dictionary of National Biography,* 66 vols. (1921–222) with Supplements.
Dubnow, Divrei	S. Dubnow, *Divrei Yemei Am Olam,* 11 vols (1923–38 and further editions).
Dubnow, Ḥasidut	S. Dubnow, *Toledot ha-Ḥasidut* (1960²).
Dubnow, Hist	S. Dubnow, *History of the Jews* (1967).
Dubnow, Hist Russ	S. Dubnow, *History of the Jews in Russia and Poland,* 3 vols. (1916 20).
Dubnow, Outline	S. Dubnow, *An Outline of Jewish History,* 3 vols. (1925–29).
Dubnow, Weltgesch	S. Dubnow, *Weltgeschichte des juedischen Volkes* 10 vols. (1925–29).
Dukes, Poesie	L. Dukes, *Zur Kenntnis der neuhebraeischen religioesen Poesie* (1842).
Dunlop, Khazars	D. H. Dunlop, *History of the Jewish Khazars* (1954).
EA	El Amarna Letters (edited by J.A. Knudtzon), *Die El-Amarna Tafel,* 2 vols. (1907 14).
EB	*Encyclopaedia Britannica.*
EBI	*Estudios biblicos* (1941ff.).
EBIB	T.K. Cheyne and J.S. Black, *Encyclopaedia Biblica,* 4 vols. (1899–1903).
Ebr.	Philo, *De Ebrietate.*
Eccles.	Ecclesiastes (Bible).
Eccles. R.	*Ecclesiastes Rabbah.*
Ecclus.	Ecclesiasticus or Wisdom of Ben Sira (or Sirach; Apocrypha).
Eduy.	*Eduyyot* (mishanic tractate).

EG	*Enziklopedyah shel Galuyyot* (1953ff.).
EH	*Even ha-Ezer.*
EHA	*Enziklopedyah la-Ḥafirot Arkheologiyyot be-Ereẓ Yisrael,* 2 vols. (1970).
EI	*Enzyklopaedie des Islams,* 4 vols. (1905–14). Supplement vol. (1938).
EIS	*Encyclopaedia of Islam,* 4 vols. (1913–36; repr. 1954–68).
EIS²	*Encyclopaedia of Islam, second edition (1960–2000).*
Eisenstein, Dinim	J.D. Eisenstein, *Oẓar Dinim u-Minhagim* (1917; several reprints).
Eisenstein, Yisrael	J.D. Eisenstein, *Oẓar Yisrael* (10 vols, 1907–13; repr. with several additions 1951).
EIV	*Enziklopedyah Ivrit* (1949ff.).
EJ	*Encyclopaedia Judaica* (German, A-L only), 10 vols. (1928–34).
EJC	*Enciclopedia Judaica Castellana,* 10 vols. (1948–51).
Elbogen, Century	I Elbogen, *A Century of Jewish Life* (1960²).
Elbogen, Gottesdienst	I Elbogen, *Der juedische Gottesdienst ...* (1931³, repr. 1962).
Elon, Mafte'aḥ	M. Elon (ed.), *Mafte'aḥ ha-She'elot ve-ha-Teshuvot ha-Rosh* (1965).
EM	*Enziklopedyah Mikra'it* (1950ff.).
I (or II) En.	I and II Enoch (Pseudepigrapha).
EncRel	*Encyclopedia of Religion,* 15 vols. (1987, 2005²).
Eph.	Epistle to the Ephesians (New Testament).
Ephros, Cant	G. Ephros, *Cantorial Anthology,* 5 vols. (1929–57).
Ep. Jer.	Epistle of Jeremy (Apocrypha).
Epstein, Amora'im	J N. Epstein, *Mevo'ot le-Sifrut ha-Amora'im* (1962).
Epstein, Marriage	L M. Epstein, *Marriage Laws in the Bible and the Talmud* (1942).
Epstein, Mishnah	J. N. Epstein, *Mavo le-Nusaḥ ha-Mishnah,* 2 vols. (1964²).
Epstein, Tanna'im	J. N. Epstein, *Mavo le-Sifruth ha-Tanna'im.* (1947).
ER	*Ecumenical Review.*
Er.	*Eruvin* (talmudic tractate).
ERE	*Encyclopaedia of Religion and Ethics,* 13 vols. (1908–26); reprinted.
ErIsr	*Eretz-Israel,* Israel Exploration Society.
I Esd.	I Esdras (Apocrypha) (= III Ezra).
II Esd.	II Esdras (Apocrypha) (= IV Ezra).
ESE	*Ephemeris fuer semitische Epigraphik,* ed. by M. Lidzbarski.
ESN	*Encyclopaedia Sefaradica Neerlandica,* 2 pts. (1949).
ESS	*Encyclopaedia of the Social Sciences,* 15 vols. (1930–35); reprinted in 8 vols. (1948–49).
Esth.	Esther (Bible).
Est. R.	*Esther Rabbah.*
ET	*Enziklopedyah Talmudit* (1947ff.).
Eusebius, Onom.	E. Klostermann (ed.), *Das Onomastikon* (1904), Greek with Hieronymus' Latin translation.
Ex.	Exodus (Bible).
Ex. R.	*Exodus Rabbah.*
Exs	Philo, *De Exsecrationibus.*
EẒD	*Enziklopeday shel ha-Ẓiyyonut ha-Datit* (1951ff.).
Ezek.	Ezekiel (Bible).
Ezra	Ezra (Bible).
III Ezra	III Ezra (Pseudepigrapha).
IV Ezra	IV Ezra (Pseudepigrapha).
Feliks, Ha-Ẓome'aḥ	*J. Feliks, Ha-Ẓome'aḥ ve-ha-Ḥai ba-Mishnah* (1983).
Finkelstein, Middle Ages	L. Finkelstein, *Jewish Self-Government in the Middle Ages* (1924).
Fischel, Islam	W.J. Fischel, *Jews in the Economic and Political Life of Mediaeval Islam* (1937; reprint with introduction "The Court Jew in the Islamic World," 1969).
FJW	*Fuehrer durch die juedische Gemeindeverwaltung und Wohlfahrtspflege in Deutschland* (1927/28).
Frankel, Mevo	Z. Frankel, *Mevo ha-Yerushalmi* (1870; reprint 1967).
Frankel, Mishnah	Z. Frankel, *Darkhei ha-Mishnah* (1959²; reprint 1959²).
Frazer, Folk-Lore	J.G. Frazer, *Folk-Lore in the Old Testament,* 3 vols. (1918–19).
Frey, Corpus	J.-B. Frey, *Corpus Inscriptionum Iudaicarum,* 2 vols. (1936–52).
Friedmann, Lebensbilder	A. Friedmann, *Lebensbilder beruehmter Kantoren,* 3 vols. (1918–27).
FRLT	*Forschungen zur Religion und Literatur des Alten und Neuen Testaments* (series) (1950ff.).
Frumkin-Rivlin	A.L. Frumkin and E. Rivlin, *Toledot Ḥakhmei Yerushalayim,* 3 vols. (1928–30), Supplement vol. (1930).
Fuenn, Keneset	S.J. Fuenn, *Keneset Yisrael,* 4 vols. (1887–90).
Fuerst, Bibliotheca	J. Fuerst, *Bibliotheca Judaica,* 2 vols. (1863; repr. 1960).
Fuerst, Karaeertum	J. Fuerst, *Geschichte des Karaeertums,* 3 vols. (1862–69).
Fug.	Philo, *De Fuga et Inventione.*
Gal.	Epistle to the Galatians (New Testament).
Galling, Reallexikon	K. Galling, *Biblisches Reallexikon* (1937).
Gardiner, Onomastica	A.H. Gardiner, *Ancient Egyptian Onomastica,* 3 vols. (1947).
Geiger, Mikra	A. Geiger, *Ha-Mikra ve-Targumav,* tr. by J.L. Baruch (1949).
Geiger, Urschrift	A. Geiger, *Urschrift und Uebersetzungen der Bibel* 1928²).
Gen.	Genesis (Bible).
Gen. R.	*Genesis Rabbah.*
Ger.	*Gerim* (post-talmudic tractate).
Germ Jud	M. Brann, I. Elbogen, A. Freimann, and H. Tykocinski (eds.), *Germania Judaica,* vol. 1 (1917; repr. 1934 and 1963); vol. 2, in 2 pts. (1917–68), ed. by Z. Avneri.

GHAT	*Goettinger Handkommentar zum Alten Testament* (1917–22).
Ghirondi-Neppi	M.S. Ghirondi and G.H. Neppi, *Toledot Gedolei Yisrael u-Ge'onei Italyah ... u-Ve'urim al Sefer Zekher Ẓaddikim li-Verakhah . . .*(1853), index in ZHB, 17 (1914), 171–83.
Gig.	Philo, *De Gigantibus*.
Ginzberg, Legends	L. Ginzberg, *Legends of the Jews*, 7 vols. (1909–38; and many reprints).
Git.	*Gittin* (talmudic tractate).
Glueck, Explorations	N. Glueck, *Explorations in Eastern Palestine*, 2 vols. (1951).
Goell, Bibliography	Y. Goell, *Bibliography of Modern Hebrew Literature in English Translation* (1968).
Goodenough, Symbols	E.R. Goodenough, *Jewish Symbols in the Greco-Roman Period*, 13 vols. (1953–68).
Gordon, Textbook	C.H. Gordon, *Ugaritic Textbook* (1965; repr. 1967).
Graetz, Gesch	H. Graetz, *Geschichte der Juden* (last edition 1874–1908).
Graetz, Hist	H. Graetz, *History of the Jews*, 6 vols. (1891–1902).
Graetz, Psalmen	H. Graetz, *Kritischer Commentar zu den Psalmen*, 2 vols. in 1 (1882–83).
Graetz, Rabbinowitz	H. Graetz, *Divrei Yemei Yisrael*, tr. by S.P. Rabbinowitz. (1928 1929[2]).
Gray, Names	G.B. Gray, *Studies in Hebrew Proper Names* (1896).
Gressmann, Bilder	H. Gressmann, *Altorientalische Bilder zum Alten Testament* (1927[2]).
Gressmann, Texte	H. Gressmann, *Altorientalische Texte zum Alten Testament* (1926[2]).
Gross, Gal Jud	H. Gross, *Gallia Judaica* (1897; repr. with add. 1969).
Grove, Dict	*Grove's Dictionary of Music and Musicians*, ed. by E. Blum 9 vols. (1954[5]) and suppl. (1961[5]).
Guedemann, Gesch Erz	M. Guedemann, *Geschichte des Erziehungswesens und der Cultur der abendlaendischen Juden*, 3 vols. (1880–88).
Guedemann, Quellenschr	M. Guedemann, *Quellenschriften zur Geschichte des Unterrichts und der Erziehung bei den deutschen Juden* (1873, 1891).
Guide	Maimonides, *Guide of the Perplexed*.
Gulak, Oẓar	A. Gulak, *Oẓar ha-Shetarot ha-Nehugim be-Yisrael* (1926).
Gulak, Yesodei	A. Gulak, *Yesodei ha-Mishpat ha-Ivri, Seder Dinei Mamonot be-Yisrael, al pi Mekorot ha-Talmud ve-ha-Posekim*, 4 vols. (1922; repr. 1967).
Guttmann, Mafte'aḥ	M. Guttmann, *Mafte'aḥ ha-Talmud*, 3 vols. (1906–30).
Guttmann, Philosophies	J. Guttmann, *Philosophies of Judaism* (1964).
Hab.	*Habakkuk* (Bible).
Ḥag.	*Ḥagigah* (talmudic tractate).
Haggai	*Haggai* (Bible).
Ḥal.	*Ḥallah* (talmudic tractate).
Halevy, Dorot	I. Halevy, *Dorot ha-Rishonim*, 6 vols. (1897–1939).
Halpern, Pinkas	I. Halpern (Halperin), *Pinkas Va'ad Arba Araẓot* (1945).
Hananel-Eškenazi	A. Hananel and Eškenazi (eds.), *Fontes Hebraici ad res oeconomicas socialesque terrarum balcanicarum saeculo XVI pertinentes*, 2 vols, (1958–60; in Bulgarian).
HB	*Hebraeische Bibliographie* (1858–82).
Heb.	Epistle to the Hebrews (New Testament).
Heilprin, Dorot	J. Heilprin (Heilperin), *Seder ha-Dorot*, 3 vols. (1882; repr. 1956).
Her.	Philo, *Quis Rerum Divinarum Heres*.
Hertz, Prayer	J.H. Hertz (ed.), *Authorised Daily Prayer Book* (rev. ed. 1948; repr. 1963).
Herzog, Instit	I. Herzog, *The Main Institutions of Jewish Law*, 2 vols. (1936–39; repr. 1967).
Herzog-Hauck	J.J. Herzog and A. Hauch (eds.), *Real-encyklopaedie fuer protestantische Theologie* (1896–1913[3]).
HḤY	*Ha-Ẓofeh le-Ḥokhmat Yisrael* (first four volumes under the title *Ha-Ẓofeh me-Ereẓ Hagar)* (1910/11–13).
Hirschberg, Afrikah	H.Z. Hirschberg, *Toledot ha-Yehudim be-Afrikah ha-Zofonit*, 2 vols. (1965).
HJ	*Historia Judaica* (1938–61).
HL	*Das Heilige Land* (1857ff.)
ḤM	*Ḥoshen Mishpat*.
Hommel, Ueberliefer.	F. Hommel, *Die altisraelitische Ueberlieferung in inschriftlicher Beleuchtung* (1897).
Hor.	*Horayot* (talmudic tractate).
Horodezky, Ḥasidut	S.A. Horodezky, *Ha-Ḥasidut ve-ha-Ḥasidim*, 4 vols. (1923).
Horowitz, Ereẓ Yis	I.W. Horowitz, *Ereẓ Yisrael u-Shekhenoteha* (1923).
Hos.	Hosea (Bible).
HTR	*Harvard Theological Review* (1908ff.).
HUCA	*Hebrew Union College Annual* (1904; 1924ff.)
Ḥul.	*Ḥullin* (talmudic tractate).
Husik, Philosophy	I. Husik, *History of Medieval Jewish Philosophy* (1932[2]).
Hyman, Toledot	A. Hyman, *Toledot Tanna'im ve-Amora'im* (1910; repr. 1964).
Ibn Daud, Tradition	Abraham Ibn Daud, *Sefer ha-Qabbalah – The Book of Tradition*, ed. and tr. By G.D. Cohen (1967).
ICC	International Critical Commentary on the Holy Scriptures of the Old and New Testaments (series, 1908ff.).
IDB	*Interpreter's Dictionary of the Bible*, 4 vols. (1962).
Idelsohn, Litugy	A. Z. Idelsohn, *Jewish Liturgy and its Development* (1932; paperback repr. 1967)
Idelsohn, Melodien	A. Z. Idelsohn, *Hebraeisch-orientalischer Melodienschatz*, 10 vols. (1914 32).
Idelsohn, Music	A. Z. Idelsohn, *Jewish Music in its Historical Development* (1929; paperback repr. 1967).

IEJ	*Israel Exploration Journal* (1950ff.).
IESS	*International Encyclopedia of the Social Sciences* (various eds.).
IG	*Inscriptiones Graecae,* ed. by the Prussian Academy.
IGYB	*Israel Government Year Book* (1949/50ff.).
ILR	*Israel Law Review* (1966ff.).
IMIT	*Izraelita Magyar Irodalmi Társulat Évkönyv* (1895 1948).
IMT	International Military Tribunal.
INB	*Israel Numismatic Bulletin* (1962–63).
INJ	*Israel Numismatic Journal* (1963ff.).
Ios	Philo, *De Iosepho.*
Isa.	Isaiah (Bible).
ITHL	Institute for the Translation of Hebrew Literature.
IZBG	*Internationale Zeitschriftenschau fuer Bibelwissenschaft und Grenzgebiete* (1951ff.).
JA	*Journal asiatique* (1822ff.).
James	Epistle of James (New Testament).
JAOS	*Journal of the American Oriental Society* (c. 1850ff.)
Jastrow, Dict	M. Jastrow, *Dictionary of the Targumim, the Talmud Babli and Yerushalmi, and the Midrashic literature,* 2 vols. (1886 1902 and reprints).
JBA	*Jewish Book Annual* (19242ff.).
JBL	*Journal of Biblical Literature* (1881ff.).
JBR	*Journal of Bible and Religion* (1933ff.).
JC	*Jewish Chronicle* (1841ff.).
JCS	*Journal of Cuneiform Studies* (1947ff.).
JE	*Jewish Encyclopedia,* 12 vols. (1901–05 several reprints).
Jer.	Jeremiah (Bible).
Jeremias, Alte Test	A. Jeremias, *Das Alte Testament im Lichte des alten Orients* 1930^4).
JGGJČ	*Jahrbuch der Gesellschaft fuer Geschichte der Juden in der Čechoslovakischen Republik* (1929–38).
JHSEM	Jewish Historical Society of England, *Miscellanies* (1925ff.).
JHSET	Jewish Historical Society of England, *Transactions* (1893ff.).
JJGL	*Jahrbuch fuer juedische Geschichte und Literatur* (Berlin) (1898–1938).
JJLG	*Jahrbuch der juedische-literarischen Gesellschaft* (Frankfurt) (1903–32).
JJS	*Journal of Jewish Studies* (1948ff.).
JJSO	*Jewish Journal of Sociology* (1959ff.).
JJV	*Jahrbuch fuer juedische Volkskunde* (1898–1924).
JL	*Juedisches Lexikon,* 5 vols. (1927–30).
JMES	*Journal of the Middle East Society* (1947ff.).
JNES	*Journal of Near Eastern Studies* (continuation of AJSLL) (1942ff.).
J.N.U.L.	Jewish National and University Library.
Job	Job (Bible).
Joel	Joel (Bible).
John	Gospel according to John (New Testament).
I, II and III John	Epistles of John (New Testament).
Jos., Ant	Josephus, *Jewish Antiquities* (Loeb Classics ed.).
Jos. Apion	Josephus, *Against Apion* (Loeb Classics ed.).
Jos., index	*Josephus Works,* Loeb Classics ed., index of names.
Jos., Life	Josephus, *Life* (ed. Loeb Classics).
Jos, Wars	Josephus, *The Jewish Wars* (Loeb Classics ed.).
Josh.	Joshua (Bible).
JPESB	Jewish Palestine Exploration Society Bulletin, see BJPES.
JPESJ	Jewish Palestine Exploration Society Journal – Eng. Title of the Hebrew periodical *Kovez̄ ha-Ḥevrah ha-Ivrit la-Ḥakirat Erez̄ Yisrael va-Attikoteha.*
JPOS	*Journal of the Palestine Oriental Society* (1920–48).
JPS	Jewish Publication Society of America, *The Torah* (1962, 1967^2); *The Holy Scriptures* (1917).
JQR	*Jewish Quarterly Review* (1889ff.).
JR	*Journal of Religion* (1921ff.).
JRAS	*Journal of the Royal Asiatic Society* (1838ff.).
JHR	*Journal of Religious History* (1960/61ff.).
JSOS	*Jewish Social Studies* (1939ff.).
JSS	*Journal of Semitic Studies* (1956ff.).
JTS	*Journal of Theological Studies* (1900ff.).
JTSA	Jewish Theological Seminary of America (also abbreviated as JTS).
Jub.	Jubilees (Pseudepigrapha).
Judg.	Judges (Bible).
Judith	Book of Judith (Apocrypha).
Juster, Juifs	J. Juster, *Les Juifs dans l'Empire Romain,* 2 vols. (1914).
JYB	*Jewish Year Book* (1896ff.).
JZWL	*Juedische Zeitschift fuer Wissenschaft und Leben* (1862–75).
Kal.	*Kallah* (post-talmudic tractate).
Kal. R.	*Kallah Rabbati* (post-talmudic tractate).
Katz, England	*The Jews in the History of England, 1485-1850 (1994).*
Kaufmann, Schriften	D. Kaufmann, *Gesammelte Schriften,* 3 vols. (1908 15).
Kaufmann Y., Religion	Y. Kaufmann, *The Religion of Israel* (1960), abridged tr. of his *Toledot.*
Kaufmann Y., Toledot	Y. Kaufmann, *Toledot ha-Emunah ha-Yisre'elit,* 4 vols. (1937 57).
KAWJ	*Korrespondenzblatt des Vereins zur Gruendung und Erhaltung der Akademie fuer die Wissenschaft des Judentums* (1920 30).
Kayserling, Bibl	M. Kayserling, *Biblioteca Española-Portugueza-Judaica* (1880; repr. 1961).
Kelim	*Kelim* (mishnaic tractate).
Ker.	*Keritot* (talmudic tractate).
Ket.	*Ketubbot* (talmudic tractate).

Kid.	*Kiddushim* (talmudic tractate).
Kil.	*Kilayim* (talmudic tractate).
Kin.	*Kinnim* (mishnaic tractate).
Kisch, Germany	G. Kisch, *Jews in Medieval Germany* (1949).
Kittel, Gesch	R. Kittel, *Geschichte des Volkes Israel,* 3 vols. (1922–28).
Klausner, Bayit Sheni	J. Klausner, *Historyah shel ha-Bayit ha-Sheni,* 5 vols. (1950/512).
Klausner, Sifrut	J. Klausner, *Historyah shel haSifrut ha-Ivrit ha-Ḥadashah,* 6 vols. (1952–582).
Klein, corpus	S. Klein (ed.), *Juedisch-palaestinisches Corpus Inscriptionum* (1920).
Koehler-Baumgartner	L. Koehler and W. Baumgartner, *Lexicon in Veteris Testamenti libros* (1953).
Kohut, Arukh	H.J.A. Kohut (ed.), *Sefer he-Arukh ha-Shalem,* by Nathan b. Jehiel of Rome, 8 vols. (1876–92; Supplement by S. Krauss et al., 1936; repr. 1955).
Krauss, Tal Arch	S. Krauss, *Talmudische Archaeologie,* 3 vols. (1910–12; repr. 1966).
Kressel, Leksikon	G. Kressel, *Leksikon ha-Sifrut ha-Ivrit ba-Dorot ha-Aḥaronim,* 2 vols. (1965–67).
KS	*Kirjath Sepher* (1923/4ff.).
Kut.	*Kuttim* (post-talmudic tractate).
LA	Studium Biblicum Franciscanum, *Liber Annuus* (1951ff.).
L.A.	Philo, *Legum allegoriae.*
Lachower, Sifrut	F. Lachower, *Toledot ha-Sifrut ha-Ivrit ha-Ḥadashah,* 4 vols. (1947–48; several reprints).
Lam.	Lamentations (Bible).
Lam. R.	*Lamentations Rabbah.*
Landshuth, Ammudei	L. Landshuth, *Ammudei ha-Avodah* (1857–62; repr. with index, 1965).
Legat.	Philo, *De Legatione ad Caium.*
Lehmann, Nova Bibl	R.P. Lehmann, *Nova Bibliotheca Anglo-Judaica* (1961).
Lev.	Leviticus (Bible).
Lev. R.	*Leviticus Rabbah.*
Levy, Antologia	I. Levy, *Antologia de liturgia judeo-española* (1965ff.).
Levy J., Chald Targ	J. Levy, *Chaldaeisches Woerterbuch ueber die Targumim,* 2 vols. (1967–68; repr. 1959).
Levy J., Nuehebr Tal	J. Levy, *Neuhebraeisches und chaldaeisches Woerterbuch ueber die Talmudim . . .,* 4 vols. (1875–89; repr. 1963).
Lewin, Oẓar	Lewin, *Oẓar ha-Ge'onim,* 12 vols. (1928–43).
Lewysohn, Zool	L. Lewysohn, *Zoologie des Talmuds* (1858).
Lidzbarski, Handbuch	M. Lidzbarski, *Handbuch der nordsemitischen Epigraphik,* 2 vols (1898).
Life	Josephus, *Life* (Loeb Classis ed.).
LNYL	*Leksikon fun der Nayer Yidisher Literatur* (1956ff.).
Loew, Flora	I. Loew, *Die Flora der Juden,* 4 vols. (1924 34; repr. 1967).
LSI	*Laws of the State of Israel* (1948ff.).
Luckenbill, Records	D.D. Luckenbill, *Ancient Records of Assyria and Babylonia,* 2 vols. (1926).
Luke	Gospel according to Luke (New Testament)
LXX	Septuagint (Greek translation of the Bible).
Ma'as.	*Ma'aserot* (talmudic tractate).
Ma'as. Sh.	*Ma'ase Sheni* (talmudic tractate).
I, II, III, and IVMacc.	Maccabees, I, II, III (Apocrypha), IV (Pseudepigrapha).
Maimonides, Guide	Maimonides, *Guide of the Perplexed.*
Maim., Yad	Maimonides, *Mishneh Torah (Yad Ḥazakah).*
Maisler, Untersuchungen	B. Maisler (Mazar), *Untersuchungen zur alten Geschichte und Ethnographie Syriens und Palaestinas,* 1 (1930).
Mak.	*Makkot* (talmudic tractate).
Makhsh.	*Makhshrin* (mishnaic tractate).
Mal.	Malachi (Bible).
Mann, Egypt	J. Mann, *Jews in Egypt in Palestine under the Fatimid Caliphs,* 2 vols. (1920–22).
Mann, Texts	J. Mann, *Texts and Studies,* 2 vols (1931–35).
Mansi	G.D. Mansi, *Sacrorum Conciliorum nova et amplissima collectio,* 53 vols. in 60 (1901–27; repr. 1960).
Margalioth, Gedolei	M. Margalioth, *Enẓiklopedyah le-Toledot Gedolei Yisrael,* 4 vols. (1946–50).
Margalioth, Ḥakhmei	M. Margalioth, *Enẓiklopedyah le-Ḥakhmei ha-Talmud ve-ha-Ge'onim,* 2 vols. (1945).
Margalioth, Cat	G. Margalioth, *Catalogue of the Hebrew and Samaritan Manuscripts in the British Museum,* 4 vols. (1899–1935).
Mark	Gospel according to Mark (New Testament).
Mart. Isa.	Martyrdom of Isaiah (Pseudepigrapha).
Mas.	Masorah.
Matt.	Gospel according to Matthew (New Testament).
Mayer, Art	L.A. Mayer, *Bibliography of Jewish Art* (1967).
MB	*Wochenzeitung* (formerly *Mitteilungsblatt*) *des Irgun Olej Merkas Europa* (1933ff.).
MEAH	*Miscelánea de estudios drabes y hebraicos* (1952ff.).
Meg.	Megillah (talmudic tractate).
Meg. Ta'an.	*Megillat Ta'anit* (in HUCA, 8 9 (1931–32), 318–51).
Me'il	*Me'ilah* (mishnaic tractate).
MEJ	*Middle East Journal* (1947ff.).
Mehk.	*Mekhilta de-R. Ishmael.*
Mekh. SbY	*Mekhilta de-R. Simeon bar Yoḥai.*
Men.	*Menaḥot* (talmudic tractate).
MER	*Middle East Record* (1960ff.).
Meyer, Gesch	E. Meyer, *Geschichte des Alterums,* 5 vols. in 9 (1925–58).
Meyer, Ursp	E. Meyer, *Urspring und Anfaenge des Christentums* (1921).
Mez.	*Mezuzah* (post-talmudic tractate).
MGADJ	*Mitteilungen des Gesamtarchivs der deutschen Juden* (1909–12).
MGG	*Die Musik in Geschichte und Gegenwart,* 14 vols. (1949–68).

MGG[2]	*Die Musik in Geschichte und Gegenwart, 2nd edition (1994)*
MGH	*Monumenta Germaniae Historica* (1826ff.).
MGJV	*Mitteilungen der Gesellschaft fuer juedische Volkskunde* (1898–1929); title varies, see also JJV.
MGWJ	*Monatsschrift fuer Geschichte und Wissenschaft des Judentums* (1851–1939).
MHJ	*Monumenta Hungariae Judaica,* 11 vols. (1903–67).
Michael, Or	H.Ḥ. Michael, *Or ha-Ḥayyim: Ḥakhmei Yisrael ve-Sifreihem,* ed. by S.Z. Ḥ. Halberstam and N. Ben-Menahem (1965²).
Mid.	*Middot* (mishnaic tractate).
Mid. Ag.	*Midrash Aggadah.*
Mid. Hag.	*Midrash ha-Gadol.*
Mid. Job.	*Midrash Job.*
Mid. Jonah	*Midrash Jonah.*
Mid. Lek. Tov	*Midrash Lekaḥ Tov.*
Mid. Prov.	*Midrash Proverbs.*
Mid. Ps.	*Midrash Tehillim* (Eng tr. *The Midrash on Psalms* (JPS, 1959).
Mid. Sam.	*Midrash Samuel.*
Mid. Song	*Midrash Shir ha-Shirim.*
Mid. Tan.	*Midrash Tanna'im* on Deuteronomy.
Miége, Maroc	J.L. Miège, *Le Maroc et l'Europe,* 3 vols. (1961 62).
Mig.	Philo, *De Migratione Abrahami.*
Mik.	*Mikva'ot* (mishnaic tractate).
Milano, Bibliotheca	A. Milano, *Bibliotheca Historica Italo-Judaica* (1954); supplement for 1954–63 (1964); supplement for 1964–66 in RMI, 32 (1966).
Milano, Italia	A. Milano, *Storia degli Ebrei in Italia* (1963).
MIO	*Mitteilungen des Instituts fuer Orientforschung* 1953ff.).
Mish.	Mishnah.
MJ	*Le Monde Juif* (1946ff.).
MJC	see Neubauer, Chronicles.
MK	*Mo'ed Katan* (talmudic tractate).
MNDPV	*Mitteilungen und Nachrichten des deutschen Palaestinavereins* (1895–1912).
Mortara, Indice	M. Mortara, *Indice Alfabetico dei Rabbini e Scrittori Israeliti ... in Italia ...* (1886).
Mos	Philo, *De Vita Mosis.*
Moscati, Epig	S, Moscati, *Epigrafia ebraica antica* 1935–1950 (1951).
MT	Masoretic Text of the Bible.
Mueller, Musiker	[E.H. Mueller], *Deutisches Musiker-Lexikon* (1929)
Munk, Mélanges	S. Munk, *Mélanges de philosophie juive et arabe* (1859; repr. 1955).
Mut.	Philo, *De Mutatione Nominum.*
MWJ	*Magazin fuer die Wissenshaft des Judentums* (18745 93).
Nah.	Nahum (Bible).
Naz.	*Nazir* (talmudic tractate).
NDB	*Neue Deutsche Biographie* (1953ff.).
Ned.	*Nedarim* (talmudic tractate).
Neg.	*Nega'im* (mishnaic tractate).
Neh.	Nehemiah (Bible).
NG[2]	*New Grove Dictionary of Music and Musicians* (2001).
Nuebauer, Cat	A. Neubauer, *Catalogue of the Hebrew Manuscripts in the Bodleian Library ...,* 2 vols. (1886–1906).
Neubauer, Chronicles	A. Neubauer, *Mediaeval Jewish Chronicles,* 2 vols. (Heb., 1887–95; repr. 1965), Eng. title of *Seder ha-Ḥakhamim ve-Korot ha-Yamim.*
Neubauer, Géogr	A. Neubauer, *La géographie du Talmud* (1868).
Neuman, Spain	A.A. Neuman, *The Jews in Spain, their Social, Political, and Cultural Life During the Middle Ages,* 2 vols. (1942).
Neusner, Babylonia	J. Neusner, *History of the Jews in Babylonia,* 5 vols. 1965–70), 2nd revised printing 1969ff.).
Nid.	*Niddah* (talmudic tractate).
Noah	Fragment of Book of Noah (Pseudepigrapha).
Noth, Hist Isr	M. Noth, *History of Israel* (1958).
Noth, Personennamen	M. Noth, *Die israelitischen Personennamen. ...* (1928).
Noth, Ueberlief	M. Noth, *Ueberlieferungsgeschichte des Pentateuchs* (1949).
Noth, Welt	M. Noth, *Die Welt des Alten Testaments* (1957³).
Nowack, Lehrbuch	W. Nowack, *Lehrbuch der hebraeischen Archaeologie,* 2 vols (1894).
NT	New Testament.
Num.	Numbers (Bible).
Num R.	*Numbers Rabbah.*
Obad.	Obadiah (Bible).
ODNB online	*Oxford Dictionary of National Biography.*
OḤ	*Oraḥ Ḥayyim.*
Oho.	*Oholot* (mishnaic tractate).
Olmstead	H.T. Olmstead, *History of Palestine and Syria* (1931; repr. 1965).
OLZ	*Orientalistische Literaturzeitung* (1898ff.)
Onom.	Eusebius, *Onomasticon.*
Op.	Philo, *De Opificio Mundi.*
OPD	*Osef Piskei Din shel ha-Rabbanut ha-Rashit le-Ereẓ Yisrael, Bet ha-Din ha-Gadol le-Irurim* (1950).
Or.	*Orlah* (talmudic tractate).
Or. Sibyll.	Sibylline Oracles (Pseudepigrapha).
OS	*L'Orient Syrien* (1956ff.)
OTS	*Oudtestamentische Studien* (1942ff.).
PAAJR	*Proceedings of the American Academy for Jewish Research* (1930ff.)
Pap 4QS[e]	A papyrus exemplar of IQS.
Par.	*Parah* (mishnaic tractate).
Pauly-Wissowa	A.F. Pauly, *Realencyklopaedie der klassichen Alertumswissenschaft,* ed. by G. Wissowa et al. (1864ff.)

PD	*Piskei Din shel Bet ha-Mishpat ha-Elyon le-Yisrael* (1948ff.)
PDR	*Piskei Din shel Battei ha-Din ha-Rabbaniyyim be-Yisrael.*
PdRE	*Pirkei de-R. Eliezer* (Eng. tr. 1916. (1965^2).
PdRK	*Pesikta de-Rav Kahana.*
Pe'ah	*Pe'ah* (talmudic tractate).
Peake, Commentary	A.J. Peake (ed.), *Commentary on the Bible* (1919; rev. 1962).
Pedersen, Israel	J. Pedersen, *Israel, Its Life and Culture,* 4 vols. in 2 (1926–40).
PEFQS	*Palestine Exploration Fund Quarterly Statement* (1869–1937; since 1938–PEQ).
PEQ	*Palestine Exploration Quarterly* (until 1937 PEFQS; after 1927 includes BBSAJ).
Perles, Beitaege	J. Perles, *Beitraege zur rabbinischen Sprach- und Alterthumskunde* (1893).
Pes.	*Pesaḥim* (talmudic tractate).
Pesh.	Peshitta (Syriac translation of the Bible).
Pesher Hab.	Commentary to Habakkuk from Qumran; see 1Qp Hab.
I and II Pet.	Epistles of Peter (New Testament).
Pfeiffer, Introd	R.H. Pfeiffer, *Introduction to the Old Testament* (1948).
PG	J.P. Migne (ed.), *Patrologia Graeca,* 161 vols. (1866–86).
Phil.	Epistle to the Philippians (New Testament).
Philem.	Epistle to the Philemon (New Testament).
PIASH	*Proceedings of the Israel Academy of Sciences and Humanities* (1963/7ff.).
PJB	*Palaestinajahrbuch des deutschen evangelischen Institutes fuer Altertumswissenschaft,* Jerusalem (1905–1933).
PK	*Pinkas ha-Kehillot,* encyclopedia of Jewish communities, published in over 30 volumes by Yad Vashem from 1970 and arranged by countries, regions and localities. For 3-vol. English edition see Spector, *Jewish Life.*
PL	J.P. Migne (ed.), *Patrologia Latina* 221 vols. (1844–64).
Plant	Philo, *De Plantatione.*
PO	R. Graffin and F. Nau (eds.), *Patrologia Orientalis* (1903ff.)
Pool, Prayer	D. de Sola Pool, *Traditional Prayer Book for Sabbath and Festivals* (1960).
Post	Philo, *De Posteritate Caini.*
PR	*Pesikta Rabbati.*
Praem.	Philo, *De Praemiis et Poenis.*
Prawer, Ẓalbanim	J. Prawer, *Toledot Mamlekhet ha-Ẓalbanim be-Ereẓ Yisrael,* 2 vols. (1963).
Press, Ereẓ	I. Press, *Ereẓ-Yisrael, Enẓiklopedyah Topografit-Historit,* 4 vols. (1951–55).
Pritchard, Pictures	J.B. Pritchard (ed.), *Ancient Near East in Pictures* (1954, 1970).
Pritchard, Texts	J.B. Pritchard (ed.), *Ancient Near East Texts* ... (1970^3).
Pr. Man.	Prayer of Manasses (Apocrypha).
Prob.	Philo, *Quod Omnis Probus Liber Sit.*
Prov.	Proverbs (Bible).
PS	*Palestinsky Sbornik* (Russ. (1881 1916, 1954ff).
Ps.	Psalms (Bible).
PSBA	*Proceedings of the Society of Biblical Archaeology* (1878–1918).
Ps. of Sol	Psalms of Solomon (Pseudepigrapha).
IQ Apoc	The *Genesis Apocryphon* from Qumran, cave one, ed. by N. Avigad and Y. Yadin (1956).
6QD	*Damascus Document* or *Sefer Berit Dammesk* from Qumran, cave six, ed. by M. Baillet, in RB, 63 (1956), 513–23 (see also CD).
QDAP	*Quarterly of the Department of Antiquities in Palestine* (1932ff.).
4QDeut. 32	Manuscript of Deuteronomy 32 from Qumran, cave four (ed. by P.W. Skehan, in BASOR, 136 (1954), 12–15).
4QEx^a	Exodus manuscript in Jewish script from Qumran, cave four.
4QEx$^\alpha$	Exodus manuscript in Paleo-Hebrew script from Qumran, cave four (partially ed. by P.W. Skehan, in JBL, 74 (1955), 182–7).
4QFlor	*Florilegium,* a miscellany from Qumran, cave four (ed. by J.M. Allegro, in JBL, 75 (1956), 176–77 and 77 (1958), 350–54).).
QGJD	*Quellen zur Geschichte der Juden in Deutschland* 1888–98).
IQH	*Thanksgiving Psalms* of *Hodayot* from Qumran, cave one (ed. by E.L. Sukenik and N. Avigad, *Oẓar ha-Megillot ha-Genuzot* (1954).
IQIs^a	Scroll of Isaiah from Qumran, cave one (ed. by N. Burrows et al., *Dead Sea Scrolls* ..., 1 (1950).
IQIs^b	Scroll of Isaiah from Qumran, cave one (ed. E.L. Sukenik and N. Avigad, *Oẓar ha-Megillot ha-Genuzot* (1954).
IQM	The *War Scroll* or *Serekh ha-Milḥamah* (ed. by E.L. Sukenik and N. Avigad, *Oẓar ha-Megillot ha-Genuzot* (1954).
4QpNah	Commentary on Nahum from Qumran, cave four (partially ed. by J.M. Allegro, in JBL, 75 (1956), 89–95).
IQphyl	Phylacteries *(tefillin)* from Qumran, cave one (ed. by Y. Yadin, in *Eretz Israel,* 9 (1969), 60–85).
4Q Prayer of Nabonidus	A document from Qumran, cave four, belonging to a lost Daniel literature (ed. by J.T. Milik, in RB, 63 (1956), 407–15).
IQS	*Manual of Discipline* or *Serekh ha-Yaḥad* from Qumran, cave one (ed. by M. Burrows et al., *Dead Sea Scrolls* ..., 2, pt. 2 (1951).

IQS[a] — The *Rule of the Congregation or Serekh ha-Edah* from Qumran, cave one (ed. by Burrows et al., *Dead Sea Scrolls* ..., 1 (1950), under the abbreviation IQ28a).
IQS[b] — *Blessings* or *Divrei Berakhot* from Qumran, cave one (ed. by Burrows et al., *Dead Sea Scrolls* ..., 1 (1950), under the abbreviation IQ28b).
4QSam[a] — Manuscript of I and II Samuel from Qumran, cave four (partially ed. by F.M. Cross, in BASOR, 132 (1953), 15–26).
4QSam[b] — Manuscript of I and II Samuel from Qumran, cave four (partially ed. by F.M. Cross, in JBL, 74 (1955), 147–72).
4QTestimonia — Sheet of Testimony from Qumran, cave four (ed. by J.M. Allegro, in JBL, 75 (1956), 174–87).).
4QT.Levi — *Testament of Levi* from Qumran, cave four (partially ed. by J.T. Milik, in RB, 62 (1955), 398–406).

Rabinovitz, Dik Sof — See Dik Sof.
RB — *Revue biblique* (1892ff.)
RBI — *Recherches bibliques* (1954ff.)
RCB — *Revista de cultura biblica* (São Paulo) (1957ff.)
Régné, Cat — J. Régné, *Catalogue des actes . . . des rois d'Aragon, concernant les Juifs* (1213–1327), in: REJ, vols. 60 70, 73, 75–78 (1910–24).
Reinach, Textes — T. Reinach, *Textes d'auteurs Grecs et Romains relatifs au Judaïsme* (1895; repr. 1963).
REJ — *Revue des études juives* (1880ff.).
Rejzen, Leksikon — Z. Rejzen, *Leksikon fun der Yidisher Literature,* 4 vols. (1927–29).
Renan, Ecrivains — A. Neubauer and E. Renan, *Les écrivains juifs français* ... (1893).
Renan, Rabbins — A. Neubauer and E. Renan, *Les rabbins français* (1877).
RES — *Revue des étude sémitiques et Babyloniaca* (1934–45).
Rev. — Revelation (New Testament).
RGG[3] — *Die Religion in Geschichte und Gegenwart,* 7 vols. (1957–65[3]).
RH — *Rosh Ha-Shanah* (talmudic tractate).
RHJE — *Revue de l'histoire juive en Egypte* (1947ff.).
RHMH — *Revue d'histoire de la médecine hébraïque* (1948ff.).
RHPR — *Revue d'histoire et de philosophie religieuses* (1921ff.).
RHR — *Revue d'histoire des religions* (1880ff.).
RI — *Rivista Israelitica* (1904–12).
Riemann-Einstein — *Hugo Riemanns Musiklexikon,* ed. by A. Einstein (1929[11]).
Riemann-Gurlitt — *Hugo Riemanns Musiklexikon,* ed. by W. Gurlitt (1959–67[12]), Personenteil.
Rigg-Jenkinson, Exchequer — J.M. Rigg, H. Jenkinson and H.G. Richardson (eds.), *Calendar of the Pleas Rolls of the Exchequer of the Jews,* 4 vols. (1905–1970); cf. in each instance also J.M. Rigg (ed.), *Select Pleas* ... (1902).
RMI — *Rassegna Mensile di Israel* (1925ff.).
Rom. — Epistle to the Romans (New Testament).
Rosanes, Togarmah — S.A. Rosanes, *Divrei Yemei Yisrael be-Togarmah,* 6 vols. (1907–45), and in 3 vols. (1930–38[2]).
Rosenbloom, Biogr Dict — J.R. Rosenbloom, *Biographical Dictionary of Early American Jews* (1960).
Roth, Art — C. Roth, *Jewish Art* (1961).
Roth, Dark Ages — C. Roth (ed.), *World History of the Jewish People,* second series, vol. 2, *Dark Ages* (1966).
Roth, England — C. Roth, *History of the Jews in England* (1964[3]).
Roth, Italy — C. Roth, *History of the Jews in Italy* (1946).
Roth, Mag Bibl — C. Roth, *Magna Bibliotheca Anglo-Judaica* (1937).
Roth, Marranos — C. Roth, *History of the Marranos* (2nd rev. ed 1959; reprint 1966).
Rowley, Old Test — H.H. Rowley, *Old Testament and Modern Study* (1951; repr. 1961).
RS — *Revue sémitiques d'épigraphie et d'histoire ancienne* (1893/94ff.).
RSO — *Rivista degli studi orientali* (1907ff.).
RSV — Revised Standard Version of the Bible.
Rubinstein, Australia I — *H.L. Rubinstein, The Jews in Australia, A Thematic History, Vol. I (1991).*
Rubinstein, Australia II — *W.D. Rubinstein, The Jews in Australia, A Thematic History, Vol. II (1991).*
Ruth — Ruth (Bible).
Ruth R. — *Ruth Rabbah.*
RV — Revised Version of the Bible.

Sac. — Philo, *De Sacrificiis Abelis et Caini.*
Salfeld, Martyrol — S. Salfeld, *Martyrologium des Nuernberger Memorbuches* (1898).
I and II Sam. — Samuel, book I and II (Bible).
Sanh. — *Sanhedrin* (talmudic tractate).
SBA — Society of Biblical Archaeology.
SBB — *Studies in Bibliography and Booklore* (1953ff.).
SBE — *Semana Biblica Española.*
SBT — *Studies in Biblical Theology* (1951ff.).
SBU — *Svenkst Bibliskt Uppslogsvesk,* 2 vols. (1962–63[2]).
Schirmann, Italyah — J.Ḥ. Schirmann, *Ha-Shirah ha-Ivrit be-Italyah* (1934).
Schirmann, Sefarad — J.Ḥ. Schirmann, *Ha-Shirah ha-Ivrit bi-Sefarad u-vi-Provence,* 2 vols. (1954–56).
Scholem, Mysticism — G. Scholem, *Major Trends in Jewish Mysticism* (rev. ed. 1946; paperback ed. with additional bibliography 1961).
Scholem, Shabbetai Ẓevi — G. Scholem, *Shabbetai Ẓevi ve-ha-Tenu'ah ha-Shabbeta'it bi-Ymei Ḥayyav,* 2 vols. (1967).
Schrader, Keilinschr — E. Schrader, *Keilinschriften und das Alte Testament* (1903[3]).
Schuerer, Gesch — E. Schuerer, *Geschichte des juedischen Volkes im Zeitalter Jesu Christi,* 3 vols. and index-vol. (1901–11[4]).

Schuerer, Hist	E. Schuerer, *History of the Jewish People in the Time of Jesus,* ed. by N.N. Glatzer, abridged paperback edition (1961).
Set. T.	*Sefer Torah* (post-talmudic tractate).
Sem.	*Semahot* (post-talmudic tractate).
Sendrey, Music	A. Sendrey, *Bibliography of Jewish Music* (1951).
SER	*Seder Eliyahu Rabbah.*
SEZ	*Seder Eliyahu Zuta.*
Shab	*Shabbat* (talmudic tractate).
Sh. Ar.	J. Caro Shulḥan Arukh. OḤ – *Oraḥ Ḥayyim* YD – *Yoreh De'ah* EH – *Even ha-Ezer* ḤM – *Ḥoshen Mishpat.*
Shek.	*Shekalim* (talmudic tractate).
Shev.	*Shevi'it* (talmudic tractate).
Shevu.	*Shevu'ot* (talmudic tractate).
Shunami, Bibl	S. Shunami, *Bibliography of Jewish Bibliographies* (1965[2]).
Sif.	*Sifrei Deuteronomy.*
Sif. Num.	*Sifrei Numbers.*
Sifra	*Sifra* on Leviticus.
Sif. Zut.	*Sifrei Zuta.*
SIHM	Sources inédites de l'histoire du Maroc (series).
Silverman, Prayer	M. Silverman (ed.), *Sabbath and Festival Prayer Book* (1946).
Singer, Prayer	S. Singer *Authorised Daily Prayer Book* (1943[17]).
Sob.	Philo, *De Sobrietate.*
Sof.	*Soferim* (post-talmudic tractate).
Som.	Philo, *De Somniis.*
Song	Song of Songs (Bible).
Song. Ch.	Song of the Three Children (Apocrypha).
Song R.	*Song of Songs Rabbah.*
SOR	*Seder Olam Rabbah.*
Sot.	*Sotah* (talmudic tractate).
SOZ	*Seder Olam Zuta.*
Spec.	Philo, *De Specialibus Legibus.*
Spector, Jewish Life	*S. Spector (ed.), Encyclopedia of Jewish Life Before and After the Holocaust (2001).*
Steinschneider, Arab lit	M. Steinschneider, *Die arabische Literatur der Juden* (1902).
Steinschneider, Cat Bod	M. Steinschneider, *Catalogus Librorum Hebraeorum in Bibliotheca Bodleiana,* 3 vols. (1852–60; reprints 1931 and 1964).
Steinschneider, Hanbuch	M. Steinschneider, *Bibliographisches Handbuch ueber die . . . Literatur fuer hebraeische Sprachkunde* (1859; repr. with additions 1937).
Steinschneider, Uebersetzungen	M. Steinschneider, *Die hebraeischen Uebersetzungen des Mittelalters* (1893).
Stern, Americans	M.H. Stern, *Americans of Jewish Descent* (1960).
van Straalen, Cat	S. van Straalen, *Catalogue of Hebrew Books in the British Museum Acquired During the Years 1868–1892* (1894).
Suárez Fernández, Docmentos	L. Suárez Fernández, *Documentos acerca de la expulsion de los Judios de España* (1964).
Suk.	*Sukkah* (talmudic tractate).
Sus.	Susanna (Apocrypha).
SY	*Sefer Yeẓirah.*
Sym.	Symmachus' Greek translation of the Bible.
SZNG	*Studien zur neueren Geschichte.*
Ta'an.	*Ta'anit* (talmudic tractate).
Tam.	*Tamid* (mishnaic tractate).
Tanḥ.	*Tanḥuma.*
Tanḥ. B.	*Tanḥuma.* Buber ed (1885).
Targ. Jon	Targum Jonathan (Aramaic version of the Prophets).
Targ. Onk.	Targum Onkelos (Aramaic version of the Pentateuch).
Targ. Yer.	Targum Yerushalmi.
TB	Babylonian Talmud or Talmud Bavli.
Tcherikover, Corpus	V. Tcherikover, A. Fuks, and M. Stern, *Corpus Papyrorum Judaicorum,* 3 vols. (1957–60).
Tef.	*Tefillin* (post-talmudic tractate).
Tem.	*Temurah* (mishnaic tractate).
Ter.	*Terumah* (talmudic tractate).
Test. Patr.	Testament of the Twelve Patriarchs (Pseudepigrapha). Ash. – Asher Ben. – Benjamin Dan – Dan Gad – Gad Iss. – Issachar Joseph – Joseph Judah – Judah Levi – Levi Naph. – Naphtali Reu. – Reuben Sim. – Simeon Zeb. – Zebulun.
I and II	Epistle to the Thessalonians (New Testament).
Thieme-Becker	U. Thieme and F. Becker (eds.), *Allgemeines Lexikon der bildenden Kuenstler von der Antike bis zur Gegenwart,* 37 vols. (1907–50).
Tidhar	D. Tidhar (ed.), *Enẓiklopedyah la-Ḥalutzei ha-Yishuv u-Vonav* (1947ff.).
I and II Timothy	Epistles to Timothy (New Testament).
Tit.	Epistle to Titus (New Testament).
TJ	Jerusalem Talmud or Talmud Yerushalmi.
Tob.	Tobit (Apocrypha).
Toh.	*Tohorot* (mishnaic tractate).
Torczyner, Bundeslade	H. Torczyner, *Die Bundeslade und die Anfaenge der Religion Israels* (1930[3]).
Tos.	*Tosafot.*
Tosef.	Tosefta.
Tristram, Nat Hist	H.B. Tristram, *Natural History of the Bible* (1877[5]).
Tristram, Survey	Palestine Exploration Fund, *Survey of Western Palestine,* vol. 4 (1884) = *Fauna and Flora* by H.B. Tristram.
TS	*Terra Santa* (1943ff.).

TSBA	*Transactions of the Society of Biblical Archaeology* (1872–93).
TY	*Tevul Yom* (mishnaic tractate).
UBSB	United Bible Society, *Bulletin*.
UJE	*Universal Jewish Encyclopedia*, 10 vols. (1939–43).
Uk.	*Ukẓin* (mishnaic tractate).
Urbach, Tosafot	E.E. Urbach, *Ba'alei ha-Tosafot* (1957^2).
de Vaux, Anc Isr	R. de Vaux, *Ancient Israel: its Life and Institutions* (1961; paperback 1965).
de Vaux, Instit	R. de Vaux, *Institutions de l'Ancien Testament*, 2 vols. (1958 60).
Virt.	Philo, *De Virtutibus*.
Vogelstein, Chronology	M. Volgelstein, *Biblical Chronology (1944).*
Vogelstein-Rieger	H. Vogelstein and P. Rieger, *Geschichte der Juden in Rom*, 2 vols. (1895–96).
VT	*Vetus Testamentum* (1951ff.).
VTS	*Vetus Testamentum* Supplements (1953ff.).
Vulg.	Vulgate (Latin translation of the Bible).
Wars	Josephus, *The Jewish Wars*.
Watzinger, Denkmaeler	K. Watzinger, *Denkmaeler Palaestinas*, 2 vols. (1933–35).
Waxman, Literature	M. Waxman, *History of Jewish Literature*, 5 vols. (1960^2).
Weiss, Dor	I.H. Weiss, *Dor, Dor ve-Doreshav*, 5 vols. (1904^4).
Wellhausen, Proleg	J. Wellhausen, *Prolegomena zur Geschichte Israels* (1927^6).
WI	*Die Welt des Islams* (1913ff.).
Winniger, Biog	S. Wininger, *Grosse juedische National-Biographie ...*, 7 vols. (1925–36).
Wisd.	Wisdom of Solomon (Apocrypha)
WLB	*Wiener Library Bulletin* (1958ff.).
Wolf, Bibliotheca	J.C. Wolf, *Bibliotheca Hebraea*, 4 vols. (1715–33).
Wright, Bible	G.E. Wright, *Westminster Historical Atlas to the Bible* (1945).
Wright, Atlas	G.E. Wright, *The Bible and the Ancient Near East* (1961).
WWWJ	*Who's Who in the World Jewry* (New York, 1955, 1965^2).
WZJT	*Wissenschaftliche Zeitschrift fuer juedische Theologie* (1835–37).
WZKM	*Wiener Zeitschrift fuer die Kunde des Morgenlandes* (1887ff.).
Yaari, Sheluḥei	A. Yaari, *Sheluḥei Ereẓ Yisrael* (1951).
Yad	Maimonides, *Mishneh Torah (Yad Ḥazakah).*
Yad	*Yadayim* (mishnaic tractate).
Yal.	*Yalkut Shimoni.*
Yal. Mak.	*Yalkut Makhiri.*
Yal. Reub.	*Yalkut Reubeni.*
YD	*Yoreh De'ah.*
YE	*Yevreyskaya Entsiklopediya*, 14 vols. (c. 1910).
Yev.	*Yevamot* (talmudic tractate).
YIVOA	*YIVO Annual of Jewish Social Studies* (1946ff.).
YLBI	*Year Book of the Leo Baeck Institute* (1956ff.).
YMḤEY	See BJPES.
YMḤSI	*Yedi'ot ha-Makhon le-Ḥeker ha-Shirah ha-Ivrit* (1935/36ff.).
YMMY	*Yedi'ot ha-Makhon le-Madda'ei ha-Yahadut* (1924/25ff.).
Yoma	*Yoma* (talmudic tractate).
ZA	*Zeitschrift fuer Assyriologie* (1886/87ff.).
Zav.	*Zavim* (mishnaic tractate).
ZAW	*Zeitschrift fuer die alttestamentliche Wissenschaft und die Kunde des nachbiblishchen Judentums* (1881ff.).
ZAWB	*Beihefte* (supplements) to ZAW.
ZDMG	*Zeitschrift der Deutschen Morgenlaendischen Gesellschaft* (1846ff.).
ZDPV	*Zeitschrift des Deutschen Palaestina-Vereins* (1878–1949; from 1949 = BBLA).
Zech.	Zechariah (Bible).
Zedner, Cat	J. Zedner, *Catalogue of Hebrew Books in the Library of the British Museum* (1867; repr. 1964).
Zeitlin, Bibliotheca	W. Zeitlin, *Bibliotheca Hebraica Post-Mendelssohniana* (1891–95).
Zeph.	Zephaniah (Bible).
Zev.	*Zevaḥim* (talmudic tractate).
ZGGJT	*Zeitschrift der Gesellschaft fuer die Geschichte der Juden in der Tschechoslowakei* (1930–38).
ZGJD	*Zeitschrift fuer die Geschichte der Juden in Deutschland* (1887–92).
ZHB	*Zeitschrift fuer hebraeische Bibliographie* (1896–1920).
Zinberg, Sifrut	I. Zinberg, *Toledot Sifrut Yisrael*, 6 vols. (1955–60).
Ẓiẓ.	*Ẓiẓit* (post-talmudic tractate).
ZNW	*Zeitschrift fuer die neutestamentliche Wissenschaft* (1901ff.).
ZS	*Zeitschrift fuer Semitistik und verwandte Gebiete* (1922ff.).
Zunz, Gesch	L. Zunz, *Zur Geschichte und Literatur* (1845).
Zunz, Gesch	L. Zunz, *Literaturgeschichte der synagogalen Poesie* (1865; Supplement, 1867; repr. 1966).
Zunz, Poesie	L. Zunz, *Synogogale Posie des Mittelalters*, ed. by Freimann (1920^2; repr. 1967).
Zunz, Ritus	L. Zunz, *Ritus des synagogalen Gottesdienstes* (1859; repr. 1967).
Zunz, Schr	L. Zunz, *Gesammelte Schriften*, 3 vols. (1875–76).
Zunz, Vortraege	L. Zunz, *Gottesdienstliche vortraege der Juden ...* 1892^2; repr. 1966).
Zunz-Albeck, Derashot	L. Zunz, *Ha-Derashot be-Yisrael*, Heb. Tr. of Zunz Vortraege by H. Albeck (1954^2).

TRANSLITERATION RULES

HEBREW AND SEMITIC LANGUAGES:

	General	*Scientific*
א	not transliterated[1]	ʾ
בּ	b	b
ב	v	v, b̲
גּ	g	g
ג		ḡ
דּ	d	d
ד		d̲
ה	h	h
ו	v – when not a vowel	w
ז	z	z
ח	ḥ	ḥ
ט	t	ṭ, t
י	y – when vowel and at end of words – i	y
כּ	k	k
כ, ך	kh	kh, k̲
ל	l	l̲
מ, ם	m	m
נ, ן	n	n
ס	s	s
ע	not transliterated[1]	ʿ
פּ	p	p
פ, ף	f	p, f, ph
צ, ץ	ẓ	ṣ, ẓ
ק	k	q, k
ר	r	r
שׁ	sh[2]	š
שׂ	s	ś, s
תּ	t	t
ת		ṯ
ג׳	dzh, J	ǧ
ז׳	zh, J	ž
צ׳	ch	č
—ָ		å, o, o̊ (short) â, ā (long)
—ַ	a	a
—ֲ		a, ^{a}
—ֵ		e, ẹ, ē
—ֶ	e	æ, ä, ȩ
—ֱ		œ, ĕ, ^{e}
—ְ	only *sheva na* is transliterated	ə, ĕ, e; only *sheva na* transliterated
—ִ, —ִי	i	i
—ֹ, וֹ	o	o, o, o
—ֻ, וּ	u	u, ŭ û, ū
—ֵי	ei; biblical e	
‡		reconstructed forms of words

1. The letters א and ע are not transliterated.
An apostrophe (ʾ) between vowels indicates that they do not form a diphthong and are to be pronounced separately.
2. *Dagesh ḥazak* (forte) is indicated by doubling of the letter, except for the letter שׁ.
3. Names. Biblical names and biblical place names are rendered according to the Bible translation of the Jewish Publication Society of America. Post-biblical Hebrew names are transliterated; contemporary names are transliterated or rendered as used by the person. Place names are transliterated or rendered by the accepted spelling. Names and some words with an accepted English form are usually not transliterated.

YIDDISH

א	not transliterated
אַ	a
אָ	o
בּ	b
בֿ	v
ג	g
ד	d
ה	h
ו, וּ	u
וו	v
וי	oy
ז	z
זש	zh
ח	kh
ט	t
טש	tsh, ch
י	(consonant) y (vowel) i
יִ	i
יי	ey
ײַ	ay
כּ	k
כ, ך	kh
ל	l
מ, ם	m
נ, ן	n
ס	s
ע	e
פּ	p
פֿ, ף	f
צ, ץ	ts
ק	k
ר	r
שׁ	sh
שׂ	s
תּ	t
ת	s

1. Yiddish transliteration rendered according to U. Weinreich's Modern *English-Yiddish Yiddish-English* Dictionary.
2. Hebrew words in Yiddish are usually transliterated according to standard Yiddish pronunciation, e.g., חזנות = *khazones*.

LADINO

Ladino and Judeo-Spanish words written in Hebrew characters are transliterated phonetically, following the General Rules of Hebrew transliteration (see above) whenever the accepted spelling in Latin characters could not be ascertained.

ARABIC

ا ء	a[1]	ض	ḍ
ب	b	ط	ṭ
ت	t	ظ	ẓ
ث	th	ع	c
ج	j	غ	gh
ح	ḥ	ف	f
خ	kh	ق	q
د	d	ك	k
ذ	dh	ل	l
ر	r	م	m
ز	z	ن	n
س	s	ه	h
ش	sh	و	w
ص	ṣ	ي	y
ـَ	a	ـَا ى	ā
ـِ	i	ـِي	ī
ـُ	u	ـُو	ū
ـَو	aw	ـِيّ	iyy[2]
ـَي	ay	ـُوّ	uww[2]

1. not indicated when initial
2. see note (f)

a) The EJ follows the *Columbia Lippincott Gazetteer* and the *Times Atlas* in transliteration of Arabic place names. Sites that appear in neither are transliterated according to the table above, and subject to the following notes.

b) The EJ follows the *Columbia Encyclopedia* in transliteration of Arabic names. Personal names that do not therein appear are transliterated according to the table above and subject to the following notes (e.g., Ali rather than ʿAlī, Suleiman rather than Sulayman).

c) The EJ follows the *Webster's Third International Dictionary, Unabridged* in transliteration of Arabic terms that have been integrated into the English language.

d) The term "Abu" will thus appear, usually in disregard of inflection.

e) Nunnation (end vowels, *tanwīn*) are dropped in transliteration.

f) Gemination (*tashdīd*) is indicated by the doubling of the geminated letter, unless an end letter, in which case the gemination is dropped.

g) The definitive article *al-* will always be thus transliterated, unless subject to one of the modifying notes (e.g., El-Arish rather than al-ʿArīsh; modification according to note (a)).

h) The Arabic transliteration disregards the Sun Letters (the antero-palatals (*al-Ḥurūf al-Shamsiyya*).

i) The *tā-marbūṭa* (o) is omitted in transliteration, unless in construct-stage (e.g., *Khirba* but *Khirbat Mishmish*).

These modifying notes may lead to various inconsistencies in the Arabic transliteration, but this policy has deliberately been adopted to gain smoother reading of Arabic terms and names.

GREEK

Ancient Greek	*Modern Greek*	*Greek Letters*
a	a	*Α; α; ᾳ*
b	v	*Β; β*
g	gh; g	*Γ; γ*
d	dh	*Δ; δ*
e	e	*Ε; ε*
z	z	*Ζ; ζ*
e; e	i	*Η; η; ῃ*
th	th	*Θ; θ*
i	i	*Ι; ι*
k	k; ky	*Κ; κ*
l	l	*Λ; λ*
m	m	*Μ; μ*
n	n	*Ν; ν*
x	x	*Ξ; ξ*
o	o	*Ο; ο*
p	p	*Π; π*
r; rh	r	*Ρ; ρ; ῥ*
s	s	*Σ; σ; ς*
t	t	*Τ; τ*
u; y	i	*Υ; υ*
ph	f	*Φ; φ*
ch	kh	*Χ; χ*
ps	ps	*Ψ; ψ*
o; ō	o	*Ω; ω; ῳ*
ai	e	*αι*
ei	i	*ει*
oi	i	*οι*
ui	i	*υι*
ou	ou	*ου*
eu	ev	*ευ*
eu; ēu	iv	*ηυ*
–	j	*τζ*
nt	d; nd	*ντ*
mp	b; mb	*μπ*
ngk	g	*γκ*
ng	ng	*νγ*
h	–	ʻ
–	–	ʼ
w	–	*Ϝ*

RUSSIAN

А	A
Б	B
В	V
Г	G
Д	D
Е	E, Ye[1]
Ё	Yo, O[2]
Ж	Zh
З	Z
И	I
Й	Y[3]
К	K
Л	L
М	M
Н	N
О	O
П	P
Р	R
С	S
Т	T
У	U
Ф	F
Х	Kh
Ц	Ts
Ч	Ch
Ш	Sh
Щ	Shch
Ъ	omitted; see note [1]
Ы	Y
Ь	omitted; see note [1]
Э	E
Ю	Yu
Я	Ya

1. Ye at the beginning of a word; after all vowels except ***Ы***; and after ***Ъ*** and ***Ь***.
2. O after ***Ч***, ***Ш*** and ***Щ***.
3. Omitted after ***Ы***, and in names of people after ***И***.

A. Many first names have an accepted English or quasi-English form which has been preferred to transliteration.
B. Place names have been given according to the *Columbia Lippincott Gazeteer*.
C. Pre-revolutionary spelling has been ignored.
D. Other languages using the Cyrillic alphabet (e.g., Bulgarian, Ukrainian), inasmuch as they appear, have been phonetically transliterated in conformity with the principles of this table.

GLOSSARY

Asterisked terms have separate entries in the Encyclopaedia.

Actions Committee, early name of the Zionist General Council, the supreme institution of the World Zionist Organization in the interim between Congresses. The Zionist Executive's name was then the "Small Actions Committee."

***Adar**, twelfth month of the Jewish religious year, sixth of the civil, approximating to February–March.

***Aggadah**, name given to those sections of Talmud and Midrash containing homiletic expositions of the Bible, stories, legends, folklore, anecdotes, or maxims. In contradistinction to **halakhah.*

***Agunah**, woman unable to remarry according to Jewish law, because of desertion by her husband or inability to accept presumption of death.

***Aharonim**, later rabbinic authorities. In contradistinction to **rishonim* ("early ones").

Ahavah, liturgical poem inserted in the second benediction of the morning prayer *(*Ahavah Rabbah)* of the festivals and/or special Sabbaths.

Aktion (Ger.), operation involving the mass assembly, deportation, and murder of Jews by the Nazis during the *Holocaust.

***Aliyah**, (1) being called to Reading of the Law in synagogue; (2) immigration to Ereẓ Israel; (3) one of the waves of immigration to Ereẓ Israel from the early 1880s.

***Amidah**, main prayer recited at all services; also known as *Shemoneh Esreh* and *Tefillah.*

***Amora** (pl. **amoraim**), title given to the Jewish scholars in Ereẓ Israel and Babylonia in the third to sixth centuries who were responsible for the **Gemara.*

Aravah, the *willow; one of the *Four Species used on *Sukkot ("festival of Tabernacles") together with the **etrog, hadas*, and **lulav.*

***Arvit**, evening prayer.

Asarah be-Tevet, fast on the 10th of Tevet commemorating the commencement of the siege of Jerusalem by Nebuchadnezzar.

Asefat ha-Nivḥarim, representative assembly elected by Jews in Palestine during the period of the British Mandate (1920–48).

***Ashkenaz**, name applied generally in medieval rabbinical literature to Germany.

***Ashkenazi** (pl. **Ashkenazim**), German or West-, Central-, or East-European Jew(s), as contrasted with *Sephardi(m).

***Av**, fifth month of the Jewish religious year, eleventh of the civil, approximating to July–August.

***Av bet din**, vice president of the supreme court (*bet din ha-gadol*) in Jerusalem during the Second Temple period; later, title given to communal rabbis as heads of the religious courts (see **bet din*).

***Badḥan**, jester, particularly at traditional Jewish weddings in Eastern Europe.

***Bakkashah** (Heb. "supplication"), type of petitionary prayer, mainly recited in the Sephardi rite on Rosh Ha-Shanah and the Day of Atonement.

Bar, "son of . . . "; frequently appearing in personal names.

***Baraita** (pl. **beraitot**), statement of **tanna* not found in *Mishnah.

***Bar mitzvah**, ceremony marking the initiation of a boy at the age of 13 into the Jewish religious community.

Ben, "son of . . . ", frequently appearing in personal names.

Berakhah (pl. **berakhot**), *benediction, blessing; formula of praise and thanksgiving.

***Bet din** (pl. **battei din**), rabbinic court of law.

***Bet ha-midrash**, school for higher rabbinic learning; often attached to or serving as a synagogue.

***Bilu**, first modern movement for pioneering and agricultural settlement in Ereẓ Israel, founded in 1882 at Kharkov, Russia.

***Bund**, Jewish socialist party founded in Vilna in 1897, supporting Jewish national rights; Yiddishist, and anti-Zionist.

Cohen (pl. **Cohanim**), see Kohen.

***Conservative Judaism**, trend in Judaism developed in the United States in the 20th century which, while opposing extreme changes in traditional observances, permits certain modifications of *halakhah* in response to the changing needs of the Jewish people.

***Consistory** (Fr. *consistoire*), governing body of a Jewish communal district in France and certain other countries.

***Converso(s)**, term applied in Spain and Portugal to converted Jew(s), and sometimes more loosely to their descendants.

***Crypto-Jew**, term applied to a person who although observing outwardly Christianity (or some other religion) was at heart a Jew and maintained Jewish observances as far as possible (see Converso; Marrano; Neofiti; New Christian; Jadīd al-Islām).

***Dayyan**, member of rabbinic court.

Decisor, equivalent to the Hebrew *posek* (pl. **posekim*), the rabbi who gives the decision (*halakhah*) in Jewish law or practice.

***Devekut**, "devotion"; attachment or adhesion to God; communion with God.

***Diaspora**, Jews living in the "dispersion" outside Ereẓ Israel; area of Jewish settlement outside Ereẓ Israel.

Din, a law (both secular and religious), legal decision, or lawsuit.

Divan, diwan, collection of poems, especially in Hebrew, Arabic, or Persian.

Dunam, unit of land area (1,000 sq. m., c. ¼ acre), used in Israel.

Einsatzgruppen, mobile units of Nazi S.S. and S.D.; in U.S.S.R. and Serbia, mobile killing units.

***Ein-Sof**, "without end"; "the infinite"; hidden, impersonal aspect of God; also used as a Divine Name.

***Elul**, sixth month of the Jewish religious calendar, 12th of the civil, precedes the High Holiday season in the fall.

Endloesung, see *Final Solution.

***Ereẓ Israel**, Land of Israel; Palestine.

***Eruv**, technical term for rabbinical provision permitting the alleviation of certain restrictions.

***Etrog**, citron; one of the *Four Species used on *Sukkot together with the **lulav, hadas*, and *aravah.*

Even ha-Ezer, see Shulḥan Arukh.

***Exilarch**, lay head of Jewish community in Babylonia (see also *resh galuta*), and elsewhere.

***Final Solution** (Ger. *Endloesung*), in Nazi terminology, the Nazi-planned mass murder and total annihilation of the Jews.

***Gabbai**, official of a Jewish congregation; originally a charity collector.

***Galut**, "exile"; the condition of the Jewish people in dispersion.

*__Gaon__ (pl. **geonim**), head of academy in post-talmudic period, especially in Babylonia.

Gaonate, office of *gaon.

*__Gemara__, traditions, discussions, and rulings of the **amoraim*, commenting on and supplementing the *Mishnah, and forming part of the Babylonian and Palestinian Talmuds (see Talmud).

*__Gematria__, interpretation of Hebrew word according to the numerical value of its letters.

General Government, territory in Poland administered by a German civilian governor-general with headquarters in Cracow after the German occupation in World War II.

*__Genizah__, depository for sacred books. The best known was discovered in the synagogue of Fostat (old Cairo).

Get, bill of *divorce.

*__Ge'ullah__, hymn inserted after the **Shema* into the benediction of the morning prayer of the festivals and special Sabbaths.

*__Gilgul__, metempsychosis; transmigration of souls.

*__Golem__, automaton, especially in human form, created by magical means and endowed with life.

*__Ḥabad__, initials of *ḥokhmah, binah, da'at*: "wisdom, understanding, knowledge"; ḥasidic movement founded in Belorussia by *Shneur Zalman of Lyady.

Hadas, *myrtle; one of the *Four Species used on Sukkot together with the **etrog, *lulav*, and *aravah*.

*__Haftarah__ (pl. **haftarot**), designation of the portion from the prophetical books of the Bible recited after the synagogue reading from the Pentateuch on Sabbaths and holidays.

*__Haganah__, clandestine Jewish organization for armed self-defense in Ereẓ Israel under the British Mandate, which eventually evolved into a people's militia and became the basis for the Israel army.

*__Haggadah__, ritual recited in the home on *Passover eve at seder table.

Haham, title of chief rabbi of the Spanish and Portuguese congregations in London, England.

*__Hakham__, title of rabbi of *Sephardi congregation.

*__Hakham bashi__, title in the 15th century and modern times of the chief rabbi in the Ottoman Empire, residing in Constantinople (Istanbul), also applied to principal rabbis in provincial towns.

Hakhsharah ("preparation"), organized training in the Diaspora of pioneers for agricultural settlement in Ereẓ Israel.

*__Halakhah__ (pl. **halakhot**), an accepted decision in rabbinic law. Also refers to those parts of the *Talmud concerned with legal matters. In contradistinction to **aggadah*.

Ḥaliẓah, biblically prescribed ceremony (Deut. 25:9–10) performed when a man refuses to marry his brother's childless widow, enabling her to remarry.

*__Hallel__, term referring to Psalms 113-18 in liturgical use.

*__Ḥalukkah__, system of financing the maintenance of Jewish communities in the holy cities of Ereẓ Israel by collections made abroad, mainly in the pre-Zionist era (see *kolel*).

Ḥalutz (pl. **ḥalutzim**), pioneer, especially in agriculture, in Ereẓ Israel.

Ḥalutziyyut, pioneering.

*__Ḥanukkah__, eight-day celebration commemorating the victory of *Judah Maccabee over the Syrian king *Antiochus Epiphanes and the subsequent rededication of the Temple.

Ḥasid, adherent of *Ḥasidism.

*__Ḥasidei Ashkenaz__, medieval pietist movement among the Jews of Germany.

*__Ḥasidism__, (1) religious revivalist movement of popular mysticism among Jews of Germany in the Middle Ages; (2) religious movement founded by *Israel ben Eliezer Ba'al Shem Tov in the first half of the 18th century.

*__Haskalah__, "enlightenment"; movement for spreading modern European culture among Jews c. 1750–1880. See *maskil*.

*__Havdalah__, ceremony marking the end of Sabbath or festival.

*__Ḥazzan__, precentor who intones the liturgy and leads the prayers in synagogue; in earlier times a synagogue official.

*__Ḥeder__ (lit. "room"), school for teaching children Jewish religious observance.

Heikhalot, "palaces"; tradition in Jewish mysticism centering on mystical journeys through the heavenly spheres and palaces to the Divine Chariot (see Merkabah).

*__Ḥerem__, excommunication, imposed by rabbinical authorities for purposes of religious and/or communal discipline; originally, in biblical times, that which is separated from common use either because it was an abomination or because it was consecrated to God.

Ḥeshvan, see Marḥeshvan.

*__Ḥevra kaddisha__, title applied to charitable confraternity (**ḥevrah*), now generally limited to associations for burial of the dead.

*__Ḥibbat Zion__, see Ḥovevei Zion.

*__Histadrut__ (abbr. For Heb. **Ha-Histadrut ha-Kelalit shel ha-Ovedim ha-Ivriyyim be-Ereẓ Israel**). Ereẓ Israel Jewish Labor Federation, founded in 1920; subsequently renamed Histadrut ha-Ovedim be-Ereẓ Israel.

*__Holocaust__, the organized mass persecution and annihilation of European Jewry by the Nazis (1933–1945).

*__Hoshana Rabba__, the seventh day of *Sukkot on which special observances are held.

Ḥoshen Mishpat, see Shulḥan Arukh.

Ḥovevei Zion, federation of *Ḥibbat Zion, early (pre-*Herzl) Zionist movement in Russia.

Illui, outstanding scholar or genius, especially a young prodigy in talmudic learning.

*__Iyyar__, second month of the Jewish religious year, eighth of the civil, approximating to April-May.

I.Ẓ.L. (initials of Heb. *__Irgun Ẓeva'i Le'ummi__; "National Military Organization"), underground Jewish organization in Ereẓ Israel founded in 1931, which engaged from 1937 in retaliatory acts against Arab attacks and later against the British mandatory authorities.

*__Jadīd al-Islām__ (Ar.), a person practicing the Jewish religion in secret although outwardly observing Islām.

*__Jewish Legion__, Jewish units in British army during World War I.

*__Jihād__ (Ar.), in Muslim religious law, holy war waged against infidels.

*__Judenrat__ (Ger. "Jewish council"), council set up in Jewish communities and ghettos under the Nazis to execute their instructions.

*__Judenrein__ (Ger. "clean of Jews"), in Nazi terminology the condition of a locality from which all Jews had been eliminated.

*__Kabbalah__, the Jewish mystical tradition:
Kabbala iyyunit, speculative Kabbalah;
Kabbala ma'asit, practical Kabbalah;
Kabbala nevu'it, prophetic Kabbalah.

Kabbalist, student of Kabbalah.

*__Kaddish__, liturgical doxology.

Kahal, Jewish congregation; among Ashkenazim, *kehillah*.

*Kalām (Ar.), science of Muslim theology; adherents of the Kalām are called *mutakallimūn*.

***Karaite**, member of a Jewish sect originating in the eighth century which rejected rabbinic (*Rabbanite) Judaism and claimed to accept only Scripture as authoritative.

***Kasher**, ritually permissible food.

Kashrut, Jewish *dietary laws.

***Kavvanah**, "intention"; term denoting the spiritual concentration accompanying prayer and the performance of ritual or of a commandment.

***Kedushah**, main addition to the third blessing in the reader's repetition of the *Amidah* in which the public responds to the precentor's introduction.

Kefar, village; first part of name of many settlements in Israel.

Kehillah, congregation; see *kahal*.

Kelippah (pl. **kelippot**), "husk(s)"; mystical term denoting force(s) of evil.

***Keneset Yisrael**, comprehensive communal organization of the Jews in Palestine during the British Mandate.

Keri, variants in the masoretic (*masorah) text of the Bible between the spelling (*ketiv*) and its pronunciation (*keri*).

***Kerovah** (collective plural (corrupted) from **kerovez̦**), poem(s) incorporated into the **Amidah*.

Ketiv, see *keri*.

***Ketubbah**, marriage contract, stipulating husband's obligations to wife.

Kevuz̦ah, small commune of pioneers constituting an agricultural settlement in Erez̦ Israel (evolved later into *kibbutz).

***Kibbutz** (pl. **kibbutzim**), larger-size commune constituting a settlement in Erez̦ Israel based mainly on agriculture but engaging also in industry.

***Kiddush**, prayer of sanctification, recited over wine or bread on eve of Sabbaths and festivals.

***Kiddush ha-Shem**, term connoting martyrdom or act of strict integrity in support of Judaic principles.

***Kinah** (pl. **kinot**), lamentation dirge(s) for the Ninth of Av and other fast days.

***Kislev**, ninth month of the Jewish religious year, third of the civil, approximating to November-December.

Klaus, name given in Central and Eastern Europe to an institution, usually with synagogue attached, where *Talmud was studied perpetually by adults; applied by Ḥasidim to their synagogue ("*kloyz*").

***Knesset**, parliament of the State of Israel.

K(c)ohen (pl. **K(c)ohanim**), Jew(s) of priestly (Aaronide) descent.

***Kolel**, (1) community in Erez̦ Israel of persons from a particular country or locality, often supported by their fellow countrymen in the Diaspora; (2) institution for higher Torah study.

Kosher, see *kasher*.

***Kristallnacht** (Ger. "crystal night," meaning "night of broken glass"), organized destruction of synagogues, Jewish houses, and shops, accompanied by mass arrests of Jews, which took place in Germany and Austria under the Nazis on the night of Nov. 9–10, 1938.

***Lag ba-Omer**, 33rd (Heb. **lag**) day of the **Omer* period falling on the 18th of *Iyyar; a semi-holiday.

Leḥi (abbr. For Heb. ***Loḥamei Ḥerut Israel**, "Fighters for the Freedom of Israel"), radically anti-British armed underground organization in Palestine, founded in 1940 by dissidents from *I.Z.L.

Levir, husband's brother.

***Levirate marriage** (Heb. *yibbum*), marriage of childless widow (*yevamah*) by brother (*yavam*) of the deceased husband (in accordance with Deut. 25:5); release from such an obligation is effected through *ḥaliz̦ah*.

LHY, see Leḥi.

***Lulav**, palm branch; one of the *Four Species used on *Sukkot together with the **etrog*, *hadas*, and *aravah*.

***Ma'aravot**, hymns inserted into the evening prayer of the three festivals, Passover, Shavuot, and Sukkot.

Ma'ariv, evening prayer; also called **arvit*.

***Ma'barah**, transition camp; temporary settlement for newcomers in Israel during the period of mass immigration following 1948.

***Maftir**, reader of the concluding portion of the Pentateuchal section on Sabbaths and holidays in synagogue; reader of the portion of the prophetical books of the Bible (**haftarah*).

***Maggid**, popular preacher.

***Maḥzor** (pl. **maḥzorim**), festival prayer book.

***Mamzer**, bastard; according to Jewish law, the offspring of an incestuous relationship.

***Mandate, Palestine**, responsibility for the administration of Palestine conferred on Britain by the League of Nations in 1922; mandatory government: the British administration of Palestine.

***Maqāma** (Ar. pl. **maqamāt**), poetic form (rhymed prose) which, in its classical arrangement, has rigid rules of form and content.

***Marḥeshvan**, popularly called Ḥeshvan; eighth month of the Jewish religious year, second of the civil, approximating to October–November.

***Marrano(s)**, descendant(s) of Jew(s) in Spain and Portugal whose ancestors had been converted to Christianity under pressure but who secretly observed Jewish rituals.

Maskil (pl. **maskilim**), adherent of *Haskalah ("Enlightenment") movement.

***Masorah**, body of traditions regarding the correct spelling, writing, and reading of the Hebrew Bible.

Masorete, scholar of the masoretic tradition.

Masoretic, in accordance with the masorah.

Meliz̦ah, in Middle Ages, elegant style; modern usage, florid style using biblical or talmudic phraseology.

Mellah, *Jewish quarter in North African towns.

***Menorah**, candelabrum; seven-branched oil lamp used in the Tabernacle and Temple; also eight-branched candelabrum used on *Ḥanukkah.

Me'orah, hymn inserted into the first benediction of the morning prayer (*Yoz̦er ha-Me'orot*).

***Merkabah**, *merkavah*, "chariot"; mystical discipline associated with Ezekiel's vision of the Divine Throne-Chariot (Ezek. 1).

Meshullaḥ, emissary sent to conduct propaganda or raise funds for rabbinical academies or charitable institutions.

***Mezuzah** (pl. **mezuzot**), parchment scroll with selected Torah verses placed in container and affixed to gates and doorposts of houses occupied by Jews.

***Midrash**, method of interpreting Scripture to elucidate legal points (*Midrash Halakhah*) or to bring out lessons by stories or homiletics (*Midrash Aggadah*). Also the name for a collection of such rabbinic interpretations.

***Mikveh**, ritual bath.

***Minhag** (pl. **minhagim**), ritual custom(s); synagogal rite(s); especially of a specific sector of Jewry.

***Minḥah**, afternoon prayer; originally meal offering in Temple.

*****Minyan**, group of ten male adult Jews, the minimum required for communal prayer.

*****Mishnah**, earliest codification of Jewish Oral Law.

Mishnah (pl. **mishnayot**), subdivision of tractates of the Mishnah.

Mitnagged (pl. ***Mitnaggedim**), originally, opponents of *Ḥasidism in Eastern Europe.

*****Mitzvah**, biblical or rabbinic injunction; applied also to good or charitable deeds.

Mohel, official performing circumcisions.

*****Moshav**, smallholders' cooperative agricultural settlement in Israel, see moshav ovedim.

Moshavah, earliest type of Jewish village in modern Ereẓ Israel in which farming is conducted on individual farms mostly on privately owned land.

Moshav ovedim ("workers' moshav"), agricultural village in Israel whose inhabitants possess individual homes and holdings but cooperate in the purchase of equipment, sale of produce, mutual aid, etc.

*****Moshav shittufi** ("collective moshav"), agricultural village in Israel whose members possess individual homesteads but where the agriculture and economy are conducted as a collective unit.

Mostegab (Ar.), poem with biblical verse at beginning of each stanza.

*****Muqaddam** (Ar., pl. **muqaddamūn**), "leader," "head of the community."

*****Musaf**, additional service on Sabbath and festivals; originally the additional sacrifice offered in the Temple.

Musar, traditional ethical literature.

*****Musar movement**, ethical movement developing in the latter part of the 19th century among Orthodox Jewish groups in Lithuania; founded by R. Israel *Lipkin (Salanter).

*****Nagid** (pl. **negidim**), title applied in Muslim (and some Christian) countries in the Middle Ages to a leader recognized by the state as head of the Jewish community.

Nakdan (pl. **nakdanim**), "punctuator"; scholar of the 9th to 14th centuries who provided biblical manuscripts with masoretic apparatus, vowels, and accents.

*****Nasi** (pl. **nesi'im**), talmudic term for president of the Sanhedrin, who was also the spiritual head and later, political representative of the Jewish people; from second century a descendant of Hillel recognized by the Roman authorities as patriarch of the Jews. Now applied to the president of the State of Israel.

*****Negev**, the southern, mostly arid, area of Israel.

*****Ne'ilah**, concluding service on the *Day of Atonement.

Neofiti, term applied in southern Italy to converts to Christianity from Judaism and their descendants who were suspected of maintaining secret allegiance to Judaism.

*****Neology; Neolog; Neologism**, trend of *Reform Judaism in Hungary forming separate congregations after 1868.

*****Nevelah** (lit. "carcass"), meat forbidden by the *dietary laws on account of the absence of, or defect in, the act of **sheḥitah* (ritual slaughter).

*****New Christians**, term applied especially in Spain and Portugal to converts from Judaism (and from Islam) and their descendants; "Half New Christian" designated a person one of whose parents was of full Jewish blood.

*****Niddah** ("menstruous woman"), woman during the period of menstruation.

*****Nisan**, first month of the Jewish religious year, seventh of the civil, approximating to March-April.

Niẓoẓot, "sparks"; mystical term for sparks of the holy light imprisoned in all matter.

Nosaḥ (**nusaḥ**) "version"; (1) textual variant; (2) term applied to distinguish the various prayer rites, e.g., *nosaḥ Ashkenaz*; (3) the accepted tradition of synagogue melody.

*****Notarikon**, method of abbreviating Hebrew works or phrases by acronym.

Novella(e) (Heb. **ḥiddush (im)*), commentary on talmudic and later rabbinic subjects that derives new facts or principles from the implications of the text.

*****Nuremberg Laws**, Nazi laws excluding Jews from German citizenship, and imposing other restrictions.

Ofan, hymns inserted into a passage of the morning prayer.

*****Omer**, first sheaf cut during the barley harvest, offered in the Temple on the second day of Passover.

Omer, Counting of (Heb. *Sefirat ha-Omer*), 49 days counted from the day on which the *omer* was first offered in the Temple (according to the rabbis the 16th of Nisan, i.e., the second day of Passover) until the festival of Shavuot; now a period of semi-mourning.

Oraḥ Ḥayyim, see Shulḥan Arukh.

*****Orthodoxy** (Orthodox Judaism), modern term for the strictly traditional sector of Jewry.

*****Pale of Settlement**, 25 provinces of czarist Russia where Jews were permitted permanent residence.

*****Palmaḥ** (abbr. for Heb. *peluggot maḥaẓ*; "shock companies"), striking arm of the *Haganah.

*****Pardes**, medieval biblical exegesis giving the literal, allegorical, homiletical, and esoteric interpretations.

*****Parnas**, chief synagogue functionary, originally vested with both religious and administrative functions; subsequently an elected lay leader.

Partition plan(s), proposals for dividing Ereẓ Israel into autonomous areas.

Paytan, composer of **piyyut* (liturgical poetry).

*****Peel Commission**, British Royal Commission appointed by the British government in 1936 to inquire into the Palestine problem and make recommendations for its solution.

Pesaḥ, *Passover.

*****Pilpul**, in talmudic and rabbinic literature, a sharp dialectic used particularly by talmudists in Poland from the 16th century.

*****Pinkas**, community register or minute-book.

*****Piyyut**, (pl. **piyyutim**), Hebrew liturgical poetry.

*****Pizmon**, poem with refrain.

Posek (pl. ***posekim**), decisor; codifier or rabbinic scholar who pronounces decisions in disputes and on questions of Jewish law.

*****Prosbul**, legal method of overcoming the cancelation of debts with the advent of the *sabbatical year.

*****Purim**, festival held on Adar 14 or 15 in commemoration of the delivery of the Jews of Persia in the time of *Esther.

Rabban, honorific title higher than that of rabbi, applied to heads of the *Sanhedrin in mishnaic times.

*****Rabbanite**, adherent of rabbinic Judaism. In contradistinction to *Karaite.

Reb, rebbe, Yiddish form for rabbi, applied generally to a teacher or ḥasidic rabbi.

*****Reconstructionism**, trend in Jewish thought originating in the United States.

*****Reform Judaism**, trend in Judaism advocating modification of *Orthodoxy in conformity with the exigencies of contemporary life and thought.

Resh galuta, lay head of Babylonian Jewry (see exilarch).

Responsum (pl. ***responsa**), written opinion (*teshuvah*) given to question (*she'elah*) on aspects of Jewish law by qualified authorities; pl. collection of such queries and opinions in book form (*she'elot u-teshuvot*).

***Rishonim**, older rabbinical authorities. Distinguished from later authorities (**aḥaronim*).

***Rishon le-Zion**, title given to Sephardi chief rabbi of Ereẓ Israel.

***Rosh Ha-Shanah**, two-day holiday (one day in biblical and early mishnaic times) at the beginning of the month of *Tishri (September–October), traditionally the New Year.

Rosh Hodesh, *New Moon, marking the beginning of the Hebrew month.

Rosh Yeshivah, see *Yeshivah.

***R.S.H.A.** (initials of Ger. *Reichssicherheitshauptamt*: "Reich Security Main Office"), the central security department of the German Reich, formed in 1939, and combining the security police (Gestapo and Kripo) and the S.D.

***Sanhedrin**, the assembly of ordained scholars which functioned both as a supreme court and as a legislature before 70 C.E. In modern times the name was given to the body of representative Jews convoked by Napoleon in 1807.

***Savora** (pl. **savoraim**), name given to the Babylonian scholars of the period between the **amoraim* and the **geonim*, approximately 500–700 C.E.

S.D. (initials of Ger. *Sicherheitsdienst*: "security service"), security service of the *S.S. formed in 1932 as the sole intelligence organization of the Nazi party.

Seder, ceremony observed in the Jewish home on the first night of Passover (outside Ereẓ Israel first two nights), when the *Haggadah is recited.

***Sefer Torah**, manuscript scroll of the Pentateuch for public reading in synagogue.

***Sefirot, the ten**, the ten "Numbers"; mystical term denoting the ten spheres or emanations through which the Divine manifests itself; elements of the world; dimensions, primordial numbers.

Selektion (Ger.), (1) in ghettos and other Jewish settlements, the drawing up by Nazis of lists of deportees; (2) separation of incoming victims to concentration camps into two categories – those destined for immediate killing and those to be sent for forced labor.

Seliḥah (pl. ***seliḥot**), penitential prayer.

***Semikhah**, ordination conferring the title "rabbi" and permission to give decisions in matters of ritual and law.

Sephardi (pl. ***Sephardim**), Jew(s) of Spain and Portugal and their descendants, wherever resident, as contrasted with *Ashkenazi(m).

Shabbatean, adherent of the pseudo-messiah *Shabbetai Ẓevi (17th century).

Shaddai, name of God found frequently in the Bible and commonly translated "Almighty."

***Shaḥarit**, morning service.

Shali'aḥ (pl. **sheliḥim**), in Jewish law, messenger, agent; in modern times, an emissary from Ereẓ Israel to Jewish communities or organizations abroad for the purpose of fund-raising, organizing pioneer immigrants, education, etc.

Shalmonit, poetic meter introduced by the liturgical poet *Solomon ha-Bavli.

***Shammash**, synagogue beadle.

***Shavuot**, Pentecost; Festival of Weeks; second of the three annual pilgrim festivals, commemorating the receiving of the Torah at Mt. Sinai.

***Sheḥitah**, ritual slaughtering of animals.

***Shekhinah**, Divine Presence.

Shelishit, poem with three-line stanzas.

***Sheluḥei Ereẓ Israel** (or **shadarim**), emissaries from Ereẓ Israel.

***Shema** ([Yisrael]; "hear… [O Israel]," Deut. 6:4), Judaism's confession of faith, proclaiming the absolute unity of God.

Shemini Aẓeret, final festal day (in the Diaspora, final two days) at the conclusion of *Sukkot.

Shemittah, *Sabbatical year.

Sheniyyah, poem with two-line stanzas.

***Shephelah**, southern part of the coastal plain of Ereẓ Israel.

***Shevat**, eleventh month of the Jewish religious year, fifth of the civil, approximating to January–February.

***Shi'ur Komah**, Hebrew mystical work (c. eighth century) containing a physical description of God's dimensions; term denoting enormous spacial measurement used in speculations concerning the body of the **Shekhinah*.

Shivah, the "seven days" of *mourning following burial of a relative.

***Shofar**, horn of the ram (or any other ritually clean animal excepting the cow) sounded for the memorial blowing on *Rosh Ha-Shanah, and other occasions.

Shoḥet, person qualified to perform **sheḥitah*.

Shomer, *Ha-Shomer, organization of Jewish workers in Ereẓ Israel founded in 1909 to defend Jewish settlements.

***Shtadlan**, Jewish representative or negotiator with access to dignitaries of state, active at royal courts, etc.

***Shtetl**, Jewish small-town community in Eastern Europe.

***Shulḥan Arukh**, Joseph *Caro's code of Jewish law in four parts:
Oraḥ Ḥayyim, laws relating to prayers, Sabbath, festivals, and fasts;
Yoreh De'ah, dietary laws, etc;
Even ha-Ezer, laws dealing with women, marriage, etc;
Ḥoshen Mishpat, civil, criminal law, court procedure, etc.

Siddur, among Ashkenazim, the volume containing the daily prayers (in distinction to the **maḥzor* containing those for the festivals).

***Simḥat Torah**, holiday marking the completion in the synagogue of the annual cycle of reading the Pentateuch; in Ereẓ Israel observed on Shemini Aẓeret (outside Ereẓ Israel on the following day).

***Sinai Campaign**, brief campaign in October–November 1956 when Israel army reacted to Egyptian terrorist attacks and blockade by occupying the Sinai peninsula.

Sitra aḥra, "the other side" (of God); left side; the demoniac and satanic powers.

***Sivan**, third month of the Jewish religious year, ninth of the civil, approximating to May–June.

***Six-Day War**, rapid war in June 1967 when Israel reacted to Arab threats and blockade by defeating the Egyptian, Jordanian, and Syrian armies.

***S.S.** (initials of Ger. *Schutzstaffel*: "protection detachment"), Nazi formation established in 1925 which later became the "elite" organization of the Nazi Party and carried out central tasks in the "Final Solution."

***Status quo ante** community, community in Hungary retaining the status it had held before the convention of the General Jewish Congress there in 1868 and the resultant split in Hungarian Jewry.

***Sukkah**, booth or tabernacle erected for *Sukkot when, for seven days, religious Jews "dwell" or at least eat in the *sukkah* (Lev. 23:42).

***Sukkot**, festival of Tabernacles; last of the three pilgrim festivals, beginning on the 15th of Tishri.

Sūra (Ar.), chapter of the Koran.

Ta'anit Esther (Fast of *Esther), fast on the 13th of Adar, the day preceding Purim.

Takkanah (pl. ***takkanot**), regulation supplementing the law of the Torah; regulations governing the internal life of communities and congregations.

***Tallit (gadol)**, four-cornered prayer shawl with fringes (*ẓiẓit*) at each corner.

***Tallit katan**, garment with fringes (*ẓiẓit*) appended, worn by observant male Jews under their outer garments.

***Talmud**, "teaching"; compendium of discussion on the Mishnah by generations of scholars and jurists in many academies over a period of several centuries. The Jerusalem (or Palestinian) Talmud mainly contains the discussions of the Palestinian sages. The Babylonian Talmud incorporates the parallel discussion in the Babylonian academies.

Talmud torah, term generally applied to Jewish religious (and ultimately to talmudic) study; also to traditional Jewish religious public schools.

***Tammuz**, fourth month of the Jewish religious year, tenth of the civil, approximating to June-July.

Tanna (pl. ***tannaim**), rabbinic teacher of mishnaic period.

***Targum**, Aramaic translation of the Bible.

***Tefillin**, phylacteries, small leather cases containing passages from Scripture and affixed on the forehead and arm by male Jews during the recital of morning prayers.

Tell (Ar. "mound," "hillock"), ancient mound in the Middle East composed of remains of successive settlements.

***Terefah**, food that is not **kasher*, owing to a defect on the animal.

***Territorialism**, 20th century movement supporting the creation of an autonomous territory for Jewish mass-settlement outside Ereẓ Israel.

***Tevet**, tenth month of the Jewish religious year, fourth of the civil, approximating to December–January.

Tikkun ("restitution," "reintegration"), (1) order of service for certain occasions, mostly recited at night; (2) mystical term denoting restoration of the right order and true unity after the spiritual "catastrophe" which occurred in the cosmos.

Tishah be-Av, Ninth of *Av, fast day commemorating the destruction of the First and Second Temples.

***Tishri**, seventh month of the Jewish religious year, first of the civil, approximating to September–October.

Tokheḥah, reproof sections of the Pentateuch (Lev. 26 and Deut. 28); poem of reproof.

***Torah**, Pentateuch or the Pentateuchal scroll for reading in synagogue; entire body of traditional Jewish teaching and literature.

Tosafist, talmudic glossator, mainly French (12–14th centuries), bringing additions to the commentary by *Rashi.

***Tosafot**, glosses supplied by tosafist.

***Tosefta**, a collection of teachings and traditions of the *tannaim*, closely related to the Mishnah.

Tradent, person who hands down a talmudic statement on the name of his teacher or other earlier authority.

***Tu bi-Shevat**, the 15th day of Shevat, the New Year for Trees; date marking a dividing line for fruit tithing; in modern Israel celebrated as arbor day.

***Uganda Scheme**, plan suggested by the British government in 1903 to establish an autonomous Jewish settlement area in East Africa.

***Va'ad Le'ummi**, national council of the Jewish community in Ereẓ Israel during the period of the British *Mandate.

***Wannsee Conference**, Nazi conference held on Jan. 20, 1942, at which the planned annihilation of European Jewry was endorsed.

Waqf (Ar.), (1) a Muslim charitable pious foundation; (2) state lands and other property passed to the Muslim community for public welfare.

***War of Independence**, war of 1947–49 when the Jews of Israel fought off Arab invading armies and ensured the establishment of the new State.

***White Paper(s)**, report(s) issued by British government, frequently statements of policy, as issued in connection with Palestine during the *Mandate period.

***Wissenschaft des Judentums** (Ger. "Science of Judaism"), movement in Europe beginning in the 19th century for scientific study of Jewish history, religion, and literature.

***Yad Vashem**, Israel official authority for commemorating the *Holocaust in the Nazi era and Jewish resistance and heroism at that time.

Yeshivah (pl. ***yeshivot**), Jewish traditional academy devoted primarily to study of rabbinic literature; *rosh yeshivah*, head of the yeshivah.

YHWH, the letters of the holy name of God, the Tetragrammaton.

Yibbum, see levirate marriage.

Yiḥud, "union"; mystical term for intention which causes the union of God with the **Shekhinah*.

Yishuv, settlement; more specifically, the Jewish community of Ereẓ Israel in the pre-State period. The pre-Zionist community is generally designated the "old yishuv" and the community evolving from 1880, the "new yishuv."

Yom Kippur, Yom ha-Kippurim, *Day of Atonement, solemn fast day observed on the 10th of Tishri.

Yoreh De'ah, see Shulḥan Arukh.

Yoẓer, hymns inserted in the first benediction (*Yoẓer Or*) of the morning **Shema*.

***Ẓaddik**, person outstanding for his faith and piety; especially a ḥasidic rabbi or leader.

Ẓimẓum, "contraction"; mystical term denoting the process whereby God withdraws or contracts within Himself so leaving a primordial vacuum in which creation can take place; primordial exile or self-limitation of God.

***Zionist Commission (1918)**, commission appointed in 1918 by the British government to advise the British military authorities in Palestine on the implementation of the *Balfour Declaration.

Ẓyyonei Zion, the organized opposition to Herzl in connection with the *Uganda Scheme.

***Ẓiẓit**, fringes attached to the **tallit* and **tallit katan*.

***Zohar**, mystical commentary on the Pentateuch; main textbook of *Kabbalah.

Zulat, hymn inserted after the **Shema* in the morning service.